Churches and Church Membership in the United States 1990

An Enumeration by Region, State and County
Based on Data Reported for 133 Church Groupings

Martin B. Bradley · Norman M. Green, Jr. · Dale E. Jones
Mac Lynn · Lou McNeil

GLENMARY RESEARCH CENTER / ATLANTA, GEORGIA

GRC A-86/P-450
International Standard Book Number: 0-914422-22-7
Library of Congress Catalog Card Number: 92-070469
Printed in the United States of America

Cover design by Charles Haver.

Printed on recycled paper.

Published by the Glenmary Research Center, 750 Piedmont Ave., NE, Atlanta, Georgia 30308.
Book includes fold-out map, *Major Denominational Families, by Counties of the United States: 1990*. Map is also available separately.

TEXAS

Table 4. Churches and Church Membership by County and Denomination: 1990

County and Denomination	Number of churches	Communicant, confirmed, full members	Total adherents Number	Percent of total population	Percent of total adherents
GRAY	**44**	**14,876**	**20,824***	**86.9**	**100.0**
001 ADVENT CHR CH	1	0	0*	-	-
053 ASSEMB OF GOD	4	263	429	1.8	2.1
081 CATHOLIC	1	NA	1,288	5.4	6.2
081d LATIN	1	NA	1,288	5.4	6.2
093 CHR CH (DISC)	1	421	568	2.4	2.7
097 CHR CHS&CHS CR	1	165	209*	.9	1.0
127 CH GOD (CLEVE)	1	159	201*	.8	1.0
145 CH GOD PROPHCY	1	19	24*	.1	.1
151 L-D SAINTS	1	NA	245	1.0	1.2
157 CH OF BRETHREN	1	60	76*	.3	.4
165 CH OF NAZARENE	1	87	115	.5	.6
167 CHS OF CHRIST	8	1,036	1,323	5.5	6.4
193 EPISCOPAL	1	255	366	1.5	1.8
223 FREE WILL BAPT	1	37	47*	.2	.2
283 LUTH—MO SYNOD	1	151	190	.8	.9
349 PENT HOLINESS	3	127	161*	.7	.8
355 PRESB CH (USA)	1	371	469*	2.0	2.3
403 SALVATION ARMY	1	55	55	.2	.3
413 S.D.A.	1	23	29*	.1	.1
419 SO BAPT CONV	9	9,450	11,951*	49.9	57.4
449 UN METHODIST	4	1,963	2,482*	10.4	11.9
497 BLACK BAPT EST[2]	NA	234	296*	1.2	1.4
499 INDEP.NON-CHAR[3]	1	NA	300	1.3	1.4

County and Denomination	Number of churches	Communicant, confirmed, full members	Total adherents Number	Percent of total population	Percent of total adherents
GRAYSON	**171**	**50,090**	**68,659***	**72.3**	**100.0**
053 ASSEMB OF GOD	12	2,400	2,716	2.9	4.0
059 BAPT MISS ASSN	1	85	106*	.1	.2
081 CATHOLIC	4	NA	4,350	4.6	6.3
081d LATIN	4	NA	4,350	4.6	6.3
093 CHR CH (DISC)	5	670	1,014	1.1	1.5
097 CHR CHS&CHS CR	1	25	31*	-	-
111 CH CR,SCIENTST	1	NR	NR	-	-
127 CH GOD (CLEVE)	2	294	367*	.4	.5
151 L-D SAINTS	1	NA	546	.6	.8
165 CH OF NAZARENE	3	486	709	.7	1.0
167 CHS OF CHRIST	34	4,127	5,264	5.5	7.7
185 CUMBER PRESB	2	83	86	.1	.1
193 EPISCOPAL	3	806	837	.9	1.2
207 E.L.C.A.	1	134	183	.2	.3
223 FREE WILL BAPT	1	65	81*	.1	.1
283 LUTH—MO SYNOD	1	223	302	.3	.4
339 PENT CH OF GOD	3	124	192	.2	.3
349 PENT HOLINESS	1	36	45*	-	.1
355 PRESB CH (USA)	8	1,629	2,033*	2.1	3.0
356 PRESB CH AMER	1	69	69	.1	.1
361 PRIM BAPT ASCS	2	39	49*	.1	.1
403 SALVATION ARMY	1	97	98	.1	.1
413 S.D.A.	1	108	135*	.1	.2
419 SO BAPT CONV	53	30,748	38,382*	40.4	55.9
449 UN METHODIST	25	5,687	7,099*	7.5	10.3
496 JEWISH EST[1]	1	NA	125	.1	.2
497 BLACK BAPT EST[2]	NA	2,155	2,690*	2.8	3.9
499 INDEP.NON-CHAR[3]	3	NA	1,150	1.2	1.7

METROPOLITAN SUMMARY

Table 5. Churches and Church Membership by Metropolitan Status and Denomination: 1990

Denomination	Total Adherents	Percent Adherents in Metro Size of: 1,000,000 or More	250,000 to 999,999	100,000 to 249,999	Less Than 100,000	Percent Adherents Outside Metro Area	Percent Churches Outside Metro Area
167 CHS OF CHRIST	1,681,013	26.2	23.2	11.9	1.3	37.5	53.9

NA—Not applicable   NR—Not reported   *Total adherents estimated from known number of communicant, confirmed, full members.   - Represents a percent less than 0.1.   Percentages may not total due to rounding.
[1]See Appendix E   [2]See Appendix F   [3]See Appendix G   Lines in italic represent a breakdown of Catholic rites or Friends affiliations. They are included in their respective denominational total.

Acknowledgments

The authors gratefully acknowledge the generous grant from
LILLY ENDOWMENT, INC., of Indianapolis, Indiana.

Additionally, the following denominations contributed varying
amounts to enable this study to be made: American Baptist
Churches, Baptist General Conference, Christian Church
(Disciples), Church of God (Anderson, Ind.), Evangelical
Lutheran Church in America, Free Methodist Church, Latvian
Evangelical Lutheran Church in America, Lutheran Church—
Missouri Synod, Mennonite Church, Missionary Church,
Pentecostal Holiness Church, Presbyterian Church (USA),
Seventh Day Adventists, the Southern Baptist Convention's
Sunday School and Home Mission boards, United Church of
Christ, United Methodist Church, and the Wesleyan Church.
Financial assistance was also provided by Glenmary Research
Center. The generosity of these groups has made this study and
its publication possible.

Special thanks are due to the Church of the Nazarene International
Headquarters in Kansas City, Missouri. Their offices distributed
the survey instruments, collected the data, and prepared the
information for publication. The availability of their office and
staff encouraged us to undertake this task, and their continued
support has been invaluable.

Contents

Preface

This report contains statistics for 133 Judaeo-Christian church bodies or groupings, providing information on the number of their churches and members for regions, states, and counties of the United States.

The study on which this report is based was sponsored by the Association of Statisticians of American Religious Bodies (ASARB). The permanent members of the Church Membership Study Operations Committee and the Secretary-Treasurer of ASARB served as editors of this book. Martin Bradley, Sunday School Board of the Southern Baptist Convention, served as Chairman of the Operations Committee; Norman M. Green, Jr., American Baptist Churches, U.S.A., has served as Secretary-Treasurer of ASARB during the length of this study; Dale Jones, Church of the Nazarene, served as Vice Chairman of the Operations Committee and Liaison for Data Collection; Lou McNeil, Glenmary Research Center, served as Secretary of the Operations Committee; and Mac Lynn, David Lipscomb University, served as Treasurer of the Operations Committee.

A generous grant from Lilly Endowment, Inc. covered major costs for the study. Additional funds came from proceeds of the sale of books and tapes from the 1980 church membership study. Nineteen denominations together contributed another significant sum to make the study possible.

The authors wish to thank the members of the study's advisory committee: Win Arn, Erik W. Austin, Jackson Carroll, Ken Crow, Winston Elliott, Edwin S. Gaustad, H.A. Gleason, Kirk Hadaway, Peter L. Halvorson, Dean Hoge, Constant Jacquet, Douglas Johnson, Phil Jones, Sheila M. Kelly, James Lowry, Monty L. Lynn, William McCready, Orrin Morris, William Newman, Paul Picard, Bernard Quinn, Wade Clark Roof, James Shortridge, C. Peter Wagner, Wilbur Zelinski.

Special thanks are also due to those who served as denominational contact persons for furnishing the data: David L. Alderfer, José Amorós, Calvin Babcock, Ilene Bargerstock, Joel R. Beeke, James C. Blaylock, John W. Bowers, Ronald Brannon, Barbara Kelleher Bunten, Titus K. Burkholder, Calvin Burrell, Sylvia Callahan, Harvey Callies, Clifford R. Christensen, Gloria Conrad, Sherri Doty Coussens, William Czekaluk, Becky Durfee, Milton B. Efthimiou, Dale Eisenmann, Wm. Larry Elkington, Charlene Ezinga, Carl Fetterhoff, Ronnie Fieker, Rogene Foster, Robert L. Frey, Eugene R. Galat, Vazken Ghougassian, Paul R. Gilchrist, Doris Gillespie, Perry Gillum, Marcos Gilmore, Hugh W. Good, Cliff Grammich, Norman M. Green, Jr., Richard Gregory, Tom G. Grinder, Henry C. Heagy, Frank R. Helme, Gerald Hinz, Ed Hogan, Kenneth Hood, James E. Horsch, Bill Hull, Joe Iaquinta, Kenneth Ives, W. Robert Johnson, Alice Jones, Ilia Katre, Larry Keene, Sheila M. Kelly, James Kilgore, Charles H. Klutz, Wayne Knipmeyer, Dale Koehn, Sviatoslaw Kous, David Krogh, Paul Kucynda, Greta Lauria, Curt Lehman, James A. Lowry, David Luthy, Mac Lynn, Harvey Mehlhaff,

Alf Merseth, C. Ray Miller, Frank P. Miloro, Ronald R. Minor, Paul Mundey, Jacob Nelson, Daniel A. Nielsen, John P. O'Hara, Robert Overgaard, Vernon Perkins, Udo Petersoo, Vern Preheim, Karl Pruter, Robert L. Ransom, Roland Reimer, William H. Reist, J. Fred Rennebohm, Robert Ricker, Graham H. Rights, William Riikonen, Janis Robins, Julian B. Robinson, Diane Rodocker, Athanasius Y. Samuel, David W. Schreuder, Stephen Scott, R. Donald Shafer, Kenneth D. Slough Jr., Richard Snipstead, Gordon L. Sommers, Roger F. Spence, Jack Stone, Nathan A. Talbot, Richard Taylor, Reginald H. Thomas, Susan Tranquilla, John N. Vaughan, Evelyn Walpole, Albert Wardin, Ronald W. Waters, Deborah Weiner, Delores Winegar, David Worgull, Steven Work, Anne Worthington, Steve Yoder, F. Donald Yost.

Several people contributed to special studies included for the first time in this report: Barry Kosmin, Peter Halvorson, and Bill Newman made the Jewish data available for this study; Albert Wardin of Belmont University, Nashville, Tenn., Orrin Morris, Richie Stanley, Lorna Clark, and other staff from the Southern Baptist Home Mission Board provided the basis for the Black Baptists estimates in the study; John Vaughan put together a team to provide data on independent churches throughout the country for this report; and Cliff Grammich contacted many people with knowledge concerning Baptist groups located primarily in Appalachia. Especially helpful to him were Howard Dorgan, Allan Gleason, and Chester Young.

Richard Taylor, First Congregational Church, Benton Harbor, Michigan, was instrumental in reviewing data from several groups. Beth Becker of CenSRCH, Concordia University, River Forest, Illinois, was instrumental in providing the population figures necessary for the report.

Martha Garcia of the Glenmary Research Center did the mapping and graphics.

Rich Houseal, Program Manager for the Church Growth Research Center, Church of the Nazarene, served as manager of the data collection, checking, and entry process. Other persons who worked on the data at Nazarene Headquarters were Mabel Adamson, Arlene Elkins, Mark Mann, Ellen Sowder, and three students who served as summer interns, contributing their time to check and enter data: Timothy Askew, Joel Beiler, and Cathy Darulla.

Statistics contained in this study are also available on computer tape. Inquiries regarding the tape may be addressed to the Roper Center, Office of User Services, Box U-164R, University of Connecticut, Storrs, Connecticut 06268.

It is hoped that this report, despite its limitations, will stimulate ecumenical awareness at the judicatory and county level, aid in denominational planning, and contribute to the study of long-range religious trends in America.

Introduction

SCOPE OF THE STUDY

This publication presents data reported by the 133 church bodies (128 denominations, associations, or communions, and 5 arbitrarily defined groups) which participated in a study sponsored by the Association of Statisticians of American Religious Bodies.

The sponsors invited all church bodies that could be identified as Judaeo-Christian to participate. The 133 groups that furnished data reported 255,173 churches with 137,064,509 adherents.[1]

The present study is related to three previous studies.[2] The first reported 1952 statistics and was sponsored and published by the National Council of the Churches of Christ in the U.S.A. in 1956. The second reported 1971 statistics and was sponsored by the Office of Research, Evaluation and Planning of the National Council of the Churches of Christ in the U.S.A., the Department of Research and Statistics of the Lutheran Church—Missouri Synod, and the Glenmary Research Center. It was published in 1974 by the Glenmary Research Center. The third reported 1979 statistics and was sponsored by the Department of Records and Research of the African Methodist Episcopal Zion Church, the Research Services Department of the Sunday School Board of the Southern Baptist Convention, the Office of Research, Evaluation and Planning of the National Council of the Churches of Christ in the U.S.A., the Lutheran Council in the U.S.A., and the Glenmary Research Center (a Catholic agency).

PARTICIPATING CHURCH BODIES

The 15 denominations with adherents of a million or more account for 81.6 percent of the reported adherents. The 22 groups with adherents of 100,000 to 999,999 account for an additional 4.9 percent. The 80 other groups reporting adherents account for 1.2 percent. 11 groups report only church locations in this report, but are unable to estimate adherents. Finally, 5 groups (Black Baptists; Congregational Christian Churches [not part of any national CCC body]; Independent, Charismatic Churches; Independent, Non-Charismatic Churches; and Jewish adherents)

1: For purposes of this study, adherents were defined as "all members, including full members, their children and the estimated number of other regular participants who are not considered as communicant, confirmed or full members, for example, the 'baptized,' 'those not confirmed,' 'those not eligible for communion,' and the like." See "Defining Membership," below.

2: Lauris B. Whitman and Glen W. Trimble, *Churches and Church Membership in the United States: An Enumeration and Analysis by Counties, States, and Regions* (New York: National Council of the Churches of Christ in the U.S.A., 1956-1958), 80 bulletins; Douglas Johnson, Paul R. Picard and Bernard Quinn, *Churches and Church Membership in the United States 1971: An Enumeration by Region, State, and County* (Washington, D.C.: Glenmary Research Center, 1974); Bernard Quinn, Herman Anderson, Martin Bradley, Paul Goetting and Peggy Shriver, *Churches and Church Membership in the United States 1980: An Enumeration by Region, State, and County Based on Data Reported by 111 Church Bodies* (Atlanta, Georgia: Glenmary Research Center, 1982).

are not denominations or fellowships, but account for 12.2 percent of the adherents in the United States.

The following groups are included in the 1990 study. The number of counties in which the groups report churches or adherents will provide a general idea of their geographic extension. (At the time of the study, there were 3,105 counties or county-equivalents in the United States.)

Communions with Adherents of 1,000,000 or More	Counties with a Presence
African Methodist Episcopal Zion Church	448
American Baptist Churches in the U.S.A.	1,103
Assemblies of God	2,575
Catholic Church	2,965
Christian Church (Disciples of Christ)	1,380
Christian Churches and Churches of Christ	1,564
Church of Jesus Christ of Latter-day Saints	1,671
Churches of Christ	2,417
Episcopal Church	2,088
Evangelical Lutheran Church in America	1,712
Lutheran Church - Missouri Synod	1,787
Presbyterian Church (USA)	2,384
Southern Baptist Convention	2,514
United Church of Christ	1,270
United Methodist Church	2,965

Communions with Adherents of 100,000 to 999,999	Counties with a Presence
Baptist General Conference	354
Baptist Missionary Association of America	362
Christian and Missionary Alliance	739
Christian Reformed Church	241
Church of the Brethren	427
Church of the Nazarene	1,889
Church of God (Anderson, Indiana)	1,038
Church of God (Cleveland, Tennessee)	1,508
Evangelical Free Church of America	579
Free Will Baptist, National Association of, Inc.	678
Friends	666
International Church of the Foursquare Gospel	588
Mennonite Church	445
Old Order Amish Church	166
Pentecostal Holiness Church, Inc.	515
Presbyterian Church in America	559
Reformed Church in America	232
Salvation Army	778
Seventh-Day Adventists	1,802

Introduction

	Counties
Groupingss for Which Special Counts or	*with a*
Estimates Have Been Made	*Presence*
Black Baptists Estimate	1,493
Congregational Christian Churches (not part of any national CCC body)	144
Independent, Charismatic Churches.	304
Independent, Non-Charismatic Churches	528
Jewish Estimate	862

PARTICIPATION IN 1980 AND 1990 COMPARED

There are 79 denominations that participated in both studies, 54 groups that participated in 1990 but not 1980, and 32 that participated in 1980 but not in 1990.

79 Participants in Both Studies

Advent Christian Church
African Methodist Episcopal Zion Church
American Baptist Churches U.S.A.
Apostolic Christian Church (Nazarene)
Apostolic Lutheran Church of America
Armenian Apostolic Church of America, Eastern Prelacy
Assemblies of God
Associate Reformed Presbyterian Church
Baptist General Conference
Baptist Missionary Association of America
Beachy Amish Mennonite Churches
Berean Fundamental Church Fellowship
Bible Church of Christ, Inc.
Brethren Church, Inc. (Ashland, Ohio)
Brethren in Christ Church
Catholic Church
Christ Catholic Church
Christian and Missionay Alliance
Christian Church (Disciples of Christ)
Christian Churches/Churches of Christ
Christian (Plymouth) Brethren
Christian Reformed Church in North America
Church of God (Anderson, Ind.)
Church of God (Cleveland, Tenn.)
Church of God (Seventh Day)
Church of God in Christ (Mennonite)
Church of God General Conference (Oregon, Ill.)
Church of Jesus Christ of Latter-day Saints
Church of the Brethren
Church of the Lutheran Brethren of America

Church of the Lutheran Confession
Church of the Nazarene
Churches of Christ
Congregational Christian Churches, National Association of
Conservative Baptist Association of America
Conservative Congregational Christian Conference
Cumberland Presbyterian Church
Episcopal Church
Estonian Evangelical Lutheran Church
Evangelical Bible Churches, Fellowship of
    (formerly Evangelical Mennonite Brethren)
Evangelical Congregational Church
Evangelical Free Church of America
Evangelical Lutheran Synod
Evangelical Mennonite Church, Inc.
Evangelical Methodist Church
Fire Baptized Holiness Church (Wesleyan)
Free Lutheran Congregations, Association of
Free Methodist Church of North America
Friends
General Conference of Mennonite Brethren Churches
International Church of the Foursquare Gospel
Latvian Evangelical Lutheran Church in America
Lutheran Church—Missouri Synod
Mennonite Church
Mennonite Church, General Conference
Missionary Church
Moravian Church in America (Unitas Fratrum),
    Northern Province
Moravian Church in America (Unitas Fratrum),
    Southern Province
North American Baptist Conference
Old Order Amish Church
Open Bible Standard Churches, Inc.
Pentecostal Holiness Church, Inc.
Presbyterian Church in America
Primitive Advent Christian Church
Primitive Methodist Church in the U.S.A.
Protes'tant Conference (Lutheran), Inc.
Reformed Church in America
Reformed Episcopal Church
Salvation Army
Seventh-day Adventist Church
Seventh Day Baptist General Conference
Southern Baptist Convention
Syrian Orthodox Church of Antioch
Ukrainian Orthodox Church of America
    (Ecumenical Patriarchate)
Unitarian Universalist Association
United Christian Church
United Church of Christ
United Methodist Church
Wisconsin Evangelical Lutheran Synod

Introduction

In 1980, the Fellowship of Evangelical Bible Churches was listed as Evangelical Mennonite Brethren; the Christian (Plymouth) Brethren were listed as the Christian Brethren; and the Protes'tant Conference (Lutheran), Inc. was listed as the Protes'tant Conference of the Wisconsin Synod.

54 New Participants in 1990

Albanian Orthodox Archdiocese in America
Albanian Orthodox Diocese of America
Allegheny Wesleyan Methodist Connection
American Carpatho-Russian Orthodox Greek Catholic Diocese
Apostolic Christian Churches of America
Barren River Missionary Baptists Association
Byelorussian Council of Orthodox Churches in North America
Central Baptists
Church of Christ, Scientist
Church of God of the Mountain Assembly, Inc.
Church of God of Prophecy
Churches of God, General Conference
Duck River (and Kindred) Associations of Baptists
Eastern Pennsylvania Mennonite Church
Enterprise Baptists Association
Evangelical Lutheran Church in America
Evangelical Presbyterian Church
Fundamental Methodist Church, Inc.
General Six Principle Baptists
Greek Orthodox Archdiocese of North and South America
Holy Apostolic Catholic Assyrian Church of the East,
    Diocese Eastern USA
Hutterian Brethren
Independent Fundamental Churches of America
International Pentecostal Church of Christ
Interstate & Foreign Landmark Missionary Baptists Association
Jasper & Pleasant Valley Baptists Associations
Lutheran Churches, The American Association of
Midwest Congregational Christian Fellowship
Moravian Church in America, Alaska Province
National Association of Free Will Baptists, Inc.
Netherlands Reformed Congregations
New Hope Baptists Association
"Old" Missionary Baptists Associations
Old Order River Brethren
Old Regular Baptist
Orthodox Church in America
Pentecostal Church of God
Presbyterian Church (U.S.A.)
Primitive Baptists Associations
Reformed Church in the United States
Regular Baptists
Romanian Orthodox Episcopate of America
Schwenkfelder Church
Truevine Baptists Association
Two-Seed-in-the-Spirit Predestinarian Baptists
United Baptists
United Brethren in Christ
Wayne Trail Missionary Baptist Association
Wesleyan Church
    Groupings with Special Counts or Estimates
Congregational Christian Churches
    (not part of any national CCC body)
Black Baptists (Estimate)
Independent, Charismatic
Independent, Non-Charismatic
Jewish (Estimate)

In 1980, the Moravian Church in America (Unitas Fratrum), Northern Province, included statistics for Alaska, which was technically separate from the Northern Province. In 1990, the Alaska Province data is reported separately.

The Evangelical Lutheran Church in America is reported for the first time in 1990, though three denominations that merged to create the church participated in 1980 (see below).

The Presbyterian Church (U.S.A.) is reported for the first time in 1990, though two denominations that merged to create the church participated in 1980 (see below).

Five groups that are not denominations are included in this report. They were not included in 1980, so are in fact new to this study: Congregational Christian Churches (not part of any national CCC body); Black Baptists Estimate (see below); Independent, Charismatic Churches (see below); Independent, Non-Charismatic Churches (see below); Jewish Estimate (see below).

The 54 bodies participating in 1990 but not in 1980 represent a total of 25.0 million adherents. The largest among the new participants are the estimates for the Black Baptists, with 8.7 million adherents; Jewish estimates, with 6.0 million; the Evangelical Lutheran Church in America, with 5.2 million; the Presbyterian Church (USA), with 3.6 million; Independent, Non-charismatic Churches with 1.2 million; Independent, Charismatic Churches with 0.8 million; the National Association of Free Will Baptists, with 0.3 million; and the Wesleyan Church, with 0.3 million adherents.

32 Denominations Participating in 1980 but not 1990

Amana Church Society
American Baptist Association
American Lutheran Church
Bethel Ministerial Association
Christian Catholic Church
Christian Methodist Episcopal Church
Christian Union
Church of Jesus Christ (Bickertonites)
Congregational Holiness Church
Evangelical Church of North America
Evangelical Covenant Church of America
Evangelical Lutheran Churches, Association of

General Church of the New Jerusalem
General Convention of The Swedenborgian Church
Grace Brethren Churches, Fellowship of
Holiness Church of God, Inc.
Lutheran Church in America
Metropolitan Community Churches, Universal Fellowship of
Orthodox Presbyterian Church
Pentecostal Free Will Baptist Church, Inc.
Presbyterian Church in the United States
Protestant Reformed Churches in America
Reformed Presbyterian Church, Evangelical Synod
Reformed Presbyterian Church of North America
Romanian Orthodox Church in America
Separate Baptists in Christ
Social Brethren
Southern Methodist Church
Union of American Hebrew Congregations (Reform Judaism)
United Presbyterian Church in the U.S.A.
United Synagogue of America (Conservative Judaism)
United Zion Church

The American Lutheran Church, the Lutheran Church in America, and the Association of Evangelical Lutheran Churches merged to become the Evangelical Lutheran Church in America, which is included in the 1990 study.

Likewise, the Presbyterian Church in the United States and the United Presbyterian Church in the U.S.A. merged to become the Presbyterian Church (U.S.A.), which is included in the 1990 study.

The Reformed Presbyterian Church, Evangelical Synod, joined the Presbyterian Church in America, a 1990 participant. The Evangelical Church of North America joined the Evangelical Church, which did not participate in 1990.

Reports from the United Synagogue of America and the Union of American Hebrew Congregations were not listed separately this time, since an estimate for the total Jewish community was provided from other sources.

INCLUSIVENESS OF THE STUDY

The study identified by county 137.1 million adherents in 133 groups. It is not known what percent of total Judaeo-Christian adherents this actually represents. The difficulty is in obtaining an agreed-upon basis for determining the total Judaeo-Christian adherents for the whole United States.

The *Yearbook of American and Canadian Churches: 1990*[3] lists 45.1 million "full, communicant or confirmed members" reported officially by U.S. church bodies. The present study reports 55.4 million full, communicant, or confirmed members. From this perspective, the present study includes 22.9 percent more communicant membership than currently reported to the *Yearbook of American and Canadian Churches*.

Independent Bodies. It is well known that there are independent and community churches, as well as religious movements and associations that might be considered churches, whose membership is not reported to the *Yearbook*. Because the total membership of these groups is unknown, there is no way of determining the percent of church membership this study would represent if these groups were included in the total.

Adherent figures for large (300 or more in attendance) independent churches in major cities (20,000 or more people) were obtained directly from 2,192 such churches throughout the United States by John Vaughan of the International Mega-Church Center. These churches and adherents were identified by county, and are included in the study under two headings: Independent, Charismatic Churches and Independent, Non-Charismatic Churches (see Appendix G for methodology).

Jewish Bodies. William Newman and Peter Halvorson provided county estimates of the Jewish population for this study, based upon the *American Jewish Year Book*.[4]

Generally, a county was included in the study only if it or its metropolitan area contained at least 100 adherents.

Barry Kosmin provided a list of synagogues throughout the United States. These have been located by county and are included in the study.

Together, the reports indicate nearly 6 million adherents in 3,975 synagogues. Due to the differing reporting procedures (see Appendix E), some counties report adherents with no synagogues, and others report synagogues but no adherents.

Black Church Members. Three predominantly Black denominations, accounting for 1.2 million adherents, participated in the study.[5] There is no way of telling how many Blacks are adherents of the other denominations appearing in the study.

Major efforts to enlist the participation of other Black denominations were made. Generally, membership records are not kept nationally, at least not in a form conducive to participation in a study such as this.

However, an exhaustive study by the City University of New York was able to identify denominational preferences by race within the United States. Special surveys were commissioned by the book's editors to obtain estimates for the Black Baptist population for counties throughout the nation (see Appendix F for methodology). Albert Wardin conducted the survey in Tennessee and the Portland, Oregon, area and Orrin Morris and Lorna Clark oversaw the survey in Georgia.

Orthodox Bodies. 4 Orthodox bodies, accounting for combined adherents of 152,556, participated in the study. 7 other

---

3: Constant H. Jacquet, Jr., ed., *Yearbook of American and Canadian Churches: 1990* (Nashville: Abingdon Press, 1990), pp. 248-255.

4: David Singer & Ruth R. Seldin, eds., *American Jewish Year Book* (Philadelphia: Jewish Publication Society, 1990).

5: The African Methodist Episcopal Zion Church, the Bible Church of Christ, Inc., and the Fire Baptized Holiness Church (Wesleyan).

Introduction

groups were able to provide lists of churches that were identified by county only.

Other Groups. There are 21 non-participating church bodies (including some mentioned above) that reported more than 100,000 members to the *Yearbook of American and Canadian Churches:* African Methodist Episcopal Church; American Baptist Association; Antiochan Orthodox Christian Archdiocese of North America; Baptist Bible Fellowship International; Christian Congregation, Inc.; Christian Methodist Episcopal Church; Church of God in Christ; Church of God in Christ, International; Community Churches, International Council; Coptic Orthodox Church; Diocese of the Armenian Church of America; General Association of Regular Baptist Churches; Jehovah's Witnesses; Liberty Baptist Fellowship; National Baptist Convention of America; National Baptist Convention, U.S.A., Inc.; National Primitive Baptist Convention, Inc.; Polish National Catholic Church of America; Progressive National Baptist Convention, Inc.; Reorganized Church of Jesus Christ of Latter Day Saints; United Pentecostal Church International. These 21 groups reported a combined membership of 20.8 million in the *Yearbook.*

In addition to groups mentioned above as previous participants or large denominations, the following groups were also invited to participate, but for various reasons, were unable to do so: American Evangelical Christian Churches; American Rescue Workers; Anglican Orthodox Church; Apostolic Catholic Assyrian Church of the Western United States; Apostolic Faith Mission of Portland, Oregon; Apostolic Faith Mission Church of God; Apostolic Overcoming Holy Church of God, Inc.; Assemblies of God International Fellowship; Bible Way Church of Our Lord Christ World Wide, Inc.; Bulgarian Eastern Orthodox Church; Christadelphians; Christian Church of North America, General Council; Christian Nation Church U.S.A.; Church of the Living God; Church of Christ; Church of Daniel's Band; Church of God; Church of God (Which He Purchased with His Own Blood); Church of God by Faith, Inc.; Church of Illumination; Church of Our Lord Jesus Christ of the Apostolic Faith, Inc.; Churches of Christ in Christian Union; Ethical Culture Movement; Evangelical Church; Fellowship of Fundamental Bible Churches; Free Christian Zion Church of Christ; Full Gospel Assemblies International; Full Gospel Fellowship of Churches and Ministers International; General Baptist (General Association of); General Conference of the Evangelical Baptist Church, Inc.; General Six Principle Baptists Pennsylvania Association; General Six Principle Baptists Rhode Island Conference; Grace Gospel Fellowship; Holy Ukrainian Autocephalic Orthodox Church in Exile; House of God, Which is the Church of the Living God, the Pillar and Ground of the Truth, Inc.; Hungarian Reformed Church in America; Israelite House of David; Kodesh Church of Immanuel; Korean Presbyterian Church in America; Liberal Catholic Church-Province of the United States of America; Metropolitan Church Association, Inc.; National Spiritualist Association of Churches; New Apostolic Church of North America; North American Old

Roman Catholic Church; North American Old Roman Catholic Church (Archdiocese of New York); Old German Baptist Brethren; Old Order (Wisler) Mennonite Church; Pentecostal Assemblies of the World, Inc.; Pentecostal Fire-Baptized Holiness Church; Pillar of Fire; Reconstructionist Rabbinical Association; Reformed Mennonite Church; Reformed Methodist Union Episcopal Church; Reformed Zion Union Apostolic Church; Russian Orthodox Church in the U.S.A., Patriarchal Parishes; Russian Orthodox Church Outside of Russia; Second Cumberland Presbyterian Church in U.S.; Serbian Orthodox Church in the U.S.A. and Canada; Sovereign Grace Baptists; The (Original) Church of God, Inc.; Triumph the Church and Kingdom of God in Christ; True Orthodox Church of Greece, American Exarchate; Ukrainian Orthodox Church of the U.S.A.; Union of Orthodox Jewish Congregations of America; United Holy Church of America, Inc.; Unity of the Brethren; Vineyard Fellowship of Churches; Volunteers of America; Wesleyan Holiness Association of Churches; World Confessional Lutheran Association

PROBLEMS

Defining Membership. The most critical methodological problem was that of defining church membership. Since there is no generally acceptable statistical definition of church membership, it was felt that the designation of members rested finally with the denominations themselves.

In an effort to achieve comparability of data, however, two major categories were established:

> COMMUNICANT, CONFIRMED, FULL MEMBERS; regular members with full membership status; and

> TOTAL ADHERENTS; all members, including full members, their children and the estimated number of other regular participants who are not considered as communicant, confirmed or full members, for example, the "baptized," "those not confirmed," "those not eligible for communion," and the like.

Of the 133 participating groups, 57 reported communicants and adherents; 8 reported adherents only; 57 reported communicants only; and 11 reported only church locations. For purposes of this report, the church membership study staff estimated the total adherents for the 57 groups that reported communicants only, according to a formula discussed below.

Estimating Total Adherents. Since it was planned to use total adherents in computing percent of church membership to total population, for those 57 groups that reported only communicant members, total adherents were estimated according to the following procedure: The total county population was divided by the total county population less children 13 years and under, and the resulting figure was multiplied by the communicant members. The 1990 U.S. Census was used to determine for each county the population 13 years and under. An asterisk after a figure in the tables indicates that total adherents were estimated through use

of this procedure, rather than reported directly by denominations.

The 57 groups whose total adherents were estimated in this way were asked to comment on the procedure. Of the 34 which responded, 31 approved the formula, 3 had reservations. The comments submitted are reproduced in Appendix B.

Locating Members by County. Membership statistics are generally reported for the county in which the church itself is located, rather than for the county in which the member resides. It is assumed the county of residence will correspond to the county where the church is located in a majority of cases, although modern mobility patterns suggest caution in accepting this assumption in every case.

County Listings. The church membership study employed the same counties or county-equivalents as the 1990 U.S. Census. Since the 1980 church memberhsip study was published two new counties have been created: La Paz County, Arizona (from part of Yuma County), and Cibola County, New Mexico (from part of Valencia County). These changes have been incorporated into the 1990 Church membership study.

In Virginia there are independent cities that are legally separate from the counties of that state. Since most denominations record location of churches within the counties from which these cities have been separated, it was decided to combine most of these cities with contiguous counties. A list of combinations and exceptions will be found in Appendix J.

Because Alaska has no counties, the 1990 census areas and boroughs that serve as county-equivalents for statistical reporting purposes were employed in this study. These 1990 county-equivalents differ from those used in the 1980 church membership study. Appendix I provides a comparative listing of the two. The change in geographic boundaries may be observed by comparing the fold-out maps of the 1980 and 1990 church membership studies.

Reporting Date. The study was designed to gather statistics as close as possible to the April 1, 1990 U.S Census date. Accordingly, the request to the denominations stated: "We are asking that statistics be reported to us by the month of June, 1991. We hope to receive data for your statistical year that ends during 1990; report earlier data only if that is all that is available by June 1991."

Accuracy of Reporting Procedures. Most large denominations maintain national offices that receive statistical reports from their individual congregations; these reports were combined to provide the membership data for this study. On the other hand, many smaller denominations, as well as those in which local churches have a great deal of autonomy, only request and do not require such reports. This means that data for a few denominations will not be as complete and current as might be desired.

During the course of the study, the denominational offices furnishing data were asked to comment on the accuracy of their own reporting procedures and to furnish copies of the forms they used to collect the data. Forms were received from 31 denominations, and these are available for study at the offices of the Church Growth Research Center, Church of the Nazarene Headquarters. Comments were received from 75 denominations; these comments will be found in Appendix C.

Dual Affiliation. In the 1990 church membership study some attempt was made to assess the extent of the practice whereby a local congregation affiliates with more than one denomination. The denominations were asked: "Do any local congregations of your denomination maintain affiliation with another denomination as well?" Of the 89 groups that replied, 67 responded No. The comments of the 22 denominations which responded Yes are contained in Appendix D. In many cases the comments will also reveal how dual membership statistics were handled for purposes of reporting to this study.

Membership Greater Than Population. There are 64 counties in this study reporting more adherents than total population: ALABAMA: Butler, Macon, Marengo; GEORGIA: Baker, Clay, Dooly; IOWA: Mitchell; KANSAS: Comanche; KENTUCKY: Caldwell, Fulton, Washington; LOUISIANA: Saint James; MINNESOTA: Big Stone, Faribault, Lac Qui Parle, Swift, Traverse; NEBRASKA: Cuming, Greeley, Thayer; NEW MEXICO: De Baca, Harding, Mora; NORTH CAROLINA: Anson; NORTH DAKOTA: Benson, Burke, Hettinger, La Moure, McIntosh, Rolette, Steele; OKLAHOMA: Grant, Harmon, Tillman; SOUTH DAKOTA: Aurora, Douglas, Potter; TENNESSEE: Hancock; TEXAS: Baylor, Castro, Cochran, Colorado, Cottle, Culberson, Dallam, Dawson, Dickens, Floyd, Foard, Gray, Hall, Haskell, Jeff Davis, Knox, La Salle, Potter, Reeves, Refugio, Roberts, Throckmorton, Upton, Ward, Willacy, Winkler.

Reasons for the discrepancy will no doubt differ from county to county, but among the explanations the following might be suggested: U.S. Census undercount, church membership overcount, or county of residence differing from county of membership.

DATA PRESENTATION

This report consists of five tables and a fold-out map. The information is also available on computer tape[6].

In all the tables, denominational names are abbreviated. A list of abbreviations will be found on the pages immediately preceding Table 1.

Table 1. The first table, "Churches and Church Membership by Denomination, for the United States: 1990," presents for each

---

6: Inquiries regarding the computer tape may be addressed to the Roper Center, Office of User Services, Box U-164R, University of Connecticut, Storrs, Connecticut 06268 (telephone 203-486-4440).

Introduction

denomination the number of churches: the number of communicant, confirmed or full members; and the total adherents for the entire United States. It also indicates, for each denomination, what percent of the U.S. population and what percent of the total reported church adherents it comprises. Population figures are from the 1990 U.S. Census.

Table 2. The second table, "Churches and Church Membership by Region and Denomination: 1990," presents, for each of the nine census regions of the United States, the total of churches and members for each participating denomination. Both communicant, confirmed or full members and total adherents are given, as well as the percent of regional population and of total adherents that each denomination represents.

A map displaying the nine census regions will be found on the page immediately preceding Table 2.

Table 3. The third table, "Churches and Church Membership by State and Denomination: 1990," presents for each state the total of churches and members for each participating denomination. Both communicant, confirmed or full members and total adherents are given, as well as the percent of state population and of total adherents that each denomination represents. States are arranged alphabetically within the table.

Table 4. The fourth table, "Churches and Church Membership by County and Denomination: 1990," provides the detailed data on which the totals in Tables 1-3 and 5 are based.

For each county of the United States, there is given the grand total of churches and members reported. Both communicant, confirmed or full members and total adherents are shown, as well as the percent of the county population that the combined total church adherents represent.

In addition, for each county there is a breakdown of data by

denomination, showing for each communion the number of churches; the number of communicant, confirmed or full members; the number of total adherents; and the percent of county population and of total adherents its adherents comprise.

Table 5. The fifth table, "Churches and Church Membership by Metropolitan Status and Denomination: 1990," presents for each denomination or group the proportion of adherents in different-sized metropolitan areas. Also shown is the proportion of churches within each denomination located outside metropolitan areas. For comparison, the proportion of the total U.S. population in each metropolitan category is shown on the first line of the table; and the proportion of total adherents within each category is shown on the second line.

Sizes are based on the four standard categories of the U.S. Census Bureau, with a fifth category of "Non-Metropolitan" areas included for comparison. The Metropolitan Statistical Area definitions used are those of the Office of Management and the Budget as of June, 1991, with population figures from the 1990 census. All PMSA's were included in the largest size category, inasmuch as each is part of a consolidated area of at least one million people. For New England, the New England County Metropolitan Areas were used, with the Bridgeport-Stamford-Norwalk-Danbury, CT NECMA included in the New York-Northern New Jersey-Long Island, NY-NJ-CT CMSA.

Fold-out Map. Accompanying this report is a color map, 28" x 41", entitled Major Denominational Families by Counties of the United States: 1990. By means of a color code, this map indicates, for each county of the United States, the participating group that predominates. Based primarily upon family groupings found in the *Yearbook*, the various Adventist, Baptist, Brethren, Christian, Churches of God, Lutheran, Mennonite, Methodist, Moravian, Pentecostal, Presbyterian, Reformed and United Brethren church bodies were grouped into families.[7] Catholics, Congregational

---

7: The family groups are as follows: ADVENTIST: Advent Christian Church; Church of God General Conference (Abrahamic Faith), Oregon, Ill.; Primitive Advent Christian Church; Seventh-day Adventists; BAPTIST American Baptist Churches in the U.S.A.; Baptist General Conference; Baptist Missionary Association of America; Barren River Missionary Baptists; Central Baptists; Conservative Baptist Association of America; Duck River and Kindred Baptists Associations; Enterprise Baptist; Free Will Baptist, National Association of, Inc.; General Six Principle Baptists; Interstate & Foreign Landmark Missionary Baptists; Jasper and Pleasant Valley Baptists; New Hope Baptist Association; North American Baptist Conference; "Old" Missionary Baptists Association; Old Regular Baptists; Primitive Baptists Associations; Regular Baptists; Seventh Day Baptist General Conference; Southern Baptist Convention; Two-Seed-in-the-Spirit Predestinarian Baptists; Truevine Baptists Association; United Baptists; Wayne Trail Missionary Baptists Association; also included is the estimate for Black Baptists; BRETHREN: Brethren Church (Ashland, Ohio); Church of the Brethren; CHURCHES OF GOD: Church of God (Anderson, Indiana); Church of God (Seventh Day), Denver, Colorado; Churches of God, General Conference; CHRISTIAN: Christian Church (Disciples of Christ); Christian Churches and Churches of Christ; Churches of Christ; also included are the Congregational Christian Churches not affiliated with any national group; EASTERN: Albanian Orthodox Archdiocese in America; Albanian Orthodox Diocese of America; American Carpatho-Russian Orthodox Greek Catholic Diocese of the U.S.A.; Armenian Apostolic Church of America, Eastern Prelacy; Byelorussian Council of Orthodox Churches in North America; Greek Orthodox Archdiocese of North and South America; Holy Apostolic Catholic Assyrian Church of the East; Orthodox Church in America; Romanian Orthodox Episcopate of America; Syrian Orthodox Church of Antioch (Archdiocese of the U.S.A. and Canada); Ukrainian Orthodox Church of America (Ecumenical Patriarchate); LUTHERAN: Apostolic Lutheran Church of America; Church

of the Lutheran Brethren of America; Church of the Lutheran Confession; Estonian Evangelical Lutheran Church; Evangelical Lutheran Church in America; Evangelical Lutheran Synod; Free Lutheran Congregations, Association of; Latvian Evangelical Lutheran Church in America; Lutheran Church - Missouri Synod; Lutheran Churches, American Association of; The Protes'tant Conference (Lutheran); Wisconsin Evangelical Lutheran Synod; MENNONITE: Beachy Amish Mennonite Churches; Church of God in Christ (Mennonite); Evangelical Mennonite Brethren Conference; Evangelical Mennonite Church Inc.; General Conference of Mennonite Brethren Churches; Hutterian Brethren; Mennonite Church; Eastern Pennsylvania Mennonite Church; Mennonite Church, General Conference; Old Order Amish Church; Old Order River Brethren; METHODIST: African Methodist Episcopal Zion Church; Allegheny Wesleyan Methodist Connection; Evangelical Methodist Church; Free Methodist Church of North America; Fundamental Methodist Church, Inc.; Primitive Methodist Church, U.S.A.; United Methodist Church; The Wesleyan Church; MORAVIAN: Moravian Church in America (Unitas Fratrum), Alaska Province; Moravian Church in America (Unitas Fratrum), Northern Province; Moravian Church in America (Unitas Fratrum), Southern Province; PENTECOSTAL: Assemblies of God; Bible Church of Christ, Inc.; Church of God (Cleveland, Tennessee); Church of God of Prophecy; Church of God of the Mountain Assembly, Inc.; International Church of the Foursquare Gospel; International Pentecostal Church of Christ; Open Bible Standard Churches, Inc.; Pentecostal Church of God; Pentecostal Holiness Church, Inc.; also included are Independent, Charismatic Churches; PRESBYTERIAN: Associate Reformed Presbyterian Church (Gen Synod); Cumberland Presbyterian Church; Evangelical Presbyterian Church; Presbyterian Church (U.S.A.); Presbyterian Church in America; REFORMED: Christian Reformed Church; Netherlands Reformed Congregations; Reformed Church in America; Reformed Church In The United States; UNITED BRETHREN: United Brethren in Christ; United Christian Church.

Christians, Episcopalians, Friends, Jewish adherents, Latter-day Saints and members of the United Church of Christ were not grouped into families but were treated as separate units.

The number of counties in which the above mentioned families or units predominate is as follows:

Baptist	1,322
Catholic	959
Lutheran	266
Methodist	249
Latter-day Saints	83
Christian	54
Reformed	8
Mennonite	7
United Church of Christ	6
Pentecostal	5
Presbyterian	5
Brethren	2
Jewish	2
Moravian	2
Adventist	1
Episcopal	1
Friends	1

A solid color on the map indicates that a group has 50 percent or more of the adherents in that county, as reported in the present study. When no group has 50 percent, a striped shading indicates the largest group with 25-49 percent of adherents in a county. The 132 counties where no group has 25 percent are left blank.

The percentages on which the map is based are taken from Table 4, Column 5 of this report.

METHODOLOGY

The actual data collection was carried out in the offices of the Church Growth Research Center at the Church of the Nazarene Headquarters, Kansas City, Missouri. The data collection was managed by Rich Houseal, Program Manager for the Research Center, under the supervision of Dale Jones, who served as committee liaison for that purpose. Rich Houseal also assisted in enlisting denominational participation and in a variety of other administrative and editorial tasks.

In October, 1989 an invitation to participate in the study was sent to all the Judaeo-Christian church bodies listed in the *Yearbook of American and Canadian Churches*. The initial written invitation was followed by two additional general mailings and by special letters, personal visits and phone calls. As a result of these efforts, which extended over a two year period, 246 groups were invited, 133 actually participated, 18 expressed the intention to participate but were prevented from doing so, 15 declined to participate, and 80 did not respond.

Denominations agreeing to participate were asked to appoint a contact person. Two forms were then sent to the contact person: instructions for reporting data; and a transmittal sheet to be signed and sent with the data collected. A state-county form for listing the statistics themselves was made available by request. The contact persons were given the option of submitting the data via their own computer print-out, of sending the data on diskette, or of using the state-county listing provided by the study.

This process put the major burden of work on the denominational offices, since they were asked to compile data by county for all their congregations. In some cases, however, denominations were able to furnish information only in the form of yearbooks or other sources. Transferring yearbook information into county data then became the responsibility of the Research Center staff. In a few cases the denominations instructed the Research Center staff to estimate congregational membership according to some formula, and approved the result. In all instances, however, the denominational contact person reviewed the statistics.

The Research Center staff employed the following procedures for checking the data submitted. The state and national totals were first checked against the county data and discrepancies adjusted. A print-out was then made of all data. To insure the accuracy of data entry into the computer, the state and national totals were then compared to the original documents, as checked and adjusted. If the denomination participated in 1980 and the difference in a given county's membership for 1990 was unusual, this was noted on the print-out. The print-out was then sent back to the denominational contact person, along with the staff's comments and questions. Only after all problems raised by both the staff and the denominational contact person were solved were the statistics considered ready for publication.

When the 1990 U.S. county figures for persons 13 years of age or under were received, the total adherents for groups reporting only communicants were estimated, according to the formula described earlier (see Estimating Total Adherents in the Problems section of the Introduction). The final step was to run a series of computer edit tests to check for errors and to produce the print-out of tables for this report.

Abbreviations

001	ADVENT CHR CH	ADVENT CHRISTIAN CHURCH
005	AME ZION	AFRICAN METHODIST EPISCOPAL ZION CHURCH
007	ALBAN ORTH ARC	ALBANIAN ORTHODOX ARCHDIOCESE IN AMERICA
009	ALBAN ORTH DIO	ALBANIAN ORTHODOX DIOCESE OF AMERICA
011	A.W.M.C.	ALLEGHENY WESLEYAN METHODIST CONNECTION
019	AMER BAPT USA	AMERICAN BAPTIST CHURCHES IN THE U.S.A.
022	EASTERN ORTH	AMERICAN CARPATHO-RUSSIAN ORTHODOX GREEK CATHOLIC DIOCESE OF THE U.S.A.
039	AP CHR CH(NAZ)	APOSTOLIC CHRISTIAN CHURCH (NAZARENE)
040	AP CHR CH-AMER	APOSTOLIC CHRISTIAN CHURCHES OF AMERICA
045	APOSTOLIC LUTH	APOSTOLIC LUTHERAN CHURCH OF AMERICA
049	ARMEN AP CH AM	ARMENIAN APOSTOLIC CHURCH OF AMER, EASTERN PRELACY
053	ASSEMB OF GOD	ASSEMBLIES OF GOD
055	AS REF PRES CH	ASSOCIATE REFORMED PRESBYTERIAN CHURCH (GENERAL SYNOD)
057	BAPT GEN CONF	BAPTIST GENERAL CONFERENCE
059	BAPT MISS ASSN	BAPTIST MISSIONARY ASSOCIATION OF AMERICA
060	BRN RVR MB ASC	BARREN RIVER MISSIONARY BAPTISTS ASSOCIATION
061	BEACHY AMISH	BEACHY AMISH MENNONITE CHURCHES
063	BEREAN FUND CH	BEREAN FUNDAMENTAL CHURCH
066	BIBLE CH OF CR	BIBLE CHURCH OF CHRIST, INC., THE
071	BRETHREN (ASH)	BRETHREN CHURCH (ASHLAND, OHIO)
075	BRETHREN IN CR	BRETHREN IN CHRIST CHURCH
080	BYELORSSN ORTH	BYELORUSSIAN COUNCIL OF ORTHODOX CHURCHES IN NORTH AMERICA
081	CATHOLIC	CATHOLIC CHURCH
081a	*ARMENIAN*	*ARMENIAN RITE*
081b	*BYZAN RUTH*	*BYZANTINE RUTHENIAN RITE*
081c	*CHALDEAN*	*CHALDEAN RITE*
081d	*LATIN*	*LATIN RITE*
081e	*MARONITE*	*MARONITE RITE*
081f	*MELKITE-GK*	*MELKITE-GREEK RITE*
081g	*ROMANIAN*	*ROMANIAN BYZANTINE RITE*
081h	*UKRAINIAN*	*UKRANIAN BYZANTINE RITE*
082	CENTRAL BAPT	CENTRAL BAPTISTS
083	CHRIST CATH CH	CHRIST CATHOLIC CHURCH
089	CHR & MISS AL	CHRISTIAN AND MISSIONARY ALLIANCE, THE
093	CHR CH (DISC)	CHRISTIAN CHURCH (DISCIPLES OF CHRIST)
097	CHR CHS&CHS CR	CHRISTIAN CHURCHES AND CHURCHES OF CHRIST
105	CHRISTIAN REF	CHRISTIAN REFORMED CHURCH
111	CH CR,SCIENTST	CHURCH OF CHRIST, SCIENTIST
121	CH GOD (ABR)	CHURCH OF GOD GENERAL CONFERENCE (ABRAHAMIC FAITH)
123	CH GOD (ANDER)	CHURCH OF GOD (ANDERSON, INDIANA)
127	CH GOD (CLEVE)	CHURCH OF GOD (CLEVELAND, TENNESSEE)
133	CH GOD(7TH)DEN	CHURCH OF GOD (SEVENTH DAY), DENVER, COLORADO, THE
143	CG IN CR(MENN)	CHURCH OF GOD IN CHRIST (MENNONITE)
145	CH GOD PROPHCY	CHURCH OF GOD OF PROPHECY
146	CH GOD MTN ASM	CHURCH OF GOD OF THE MOUNTAIN ASSEMBLY, INC.
151	L-D SAINTS	CHURCH OF JESUS CHRIST OF LATTER-DAY SAINTS, THE
157	CH OF BRETHREN	CHURCH OF THE BRETHREN
163	CH OF LUTH BR	CHURCH OF THE LUTHERAN BRETHREN OF AMERICA
164	CH LUTH CONF	CHURCH OF THE LUTHERAN CONFESSION

Lines in *italic* represent a breakdown of Catholic rites or Friends affiliations. They are included in their respective denominational total.

165	CH OF NAZARENE	CHURCH OF THE NAZARENE
167	CHS OF CHRIST	CHURCHES OF CHRIST
171	CH GOD-GEN CON	CHURCHES OF GOD, GENERAL CONFERENCE
175	CONGR CHR CHS	CONGREGATIONAL CHRISTIAN CHURCHES, NATIONAL ASSOCIATION OF
176	CCC, NOT NAT'L	CONGREGATIONAL CHRISTIAN CHURCHES (NOT PART OF ANY NATIONAL CCC BODY)
179	CONSRV BAPT	CONSERVATIVE BAPTIST ASSOCIATION OF AMERICA
181	CONSRV CONGR	CONSERVATIVE CONGREGATIONAL CHRISTIAN CONFERENCE
185	CUMBER PRESB	CUMBERLAND PRESBYTERIAN CHURCH
189	DUCK RIVR BAPT	DUCK RIVER (AND KINDRED) ASSOCIATIONS OF BAPTISTS
191	ENTRPR BPT ASC	ENTERPRISE BAPTISTS ASSOCIATION
193	EPISCOPAL	EPISCOPAL CHURCH, THE
195	ESTONIAN ELC	ESTONIAN EVANGELICAL LUTHERAN CHURCH
199	EVAN CONGR CH	EVANGELICAL CONGREGATIONAL CHURCH
203	EVAN FREE CH	EVANGELICAL FREE CHURCH OF AMERICA, THE
207	E.L.C.A.	EVANGELICAL LUTHERAN CHURCH IN AMERICA
209	EVAN LUTH SYN	EVANGELICAL LUTHERAN SYNOD
211	FEL EVG BIB CH	EVANGELICAL BIBLE CHURCHES, FELLOWSHIP OF (FORMERLY EVANGELICAL MENNONITE BRETHREN)
213	EVAN MENN INC	EVANGELICAL MENNONITE CHURCH INC.
215	EVAN METH CH	EVANGELICAL METHODIST CHURCH
216	EVAN PRESBY CH	EVANGELICAL PRESBYTERIAN CHURCH
217	FIRE BAPTIZED	FIRE BAPTIZED HOLINESS CHURCH, (WESLEYAN), THE
220	FREE LUTHERAN	FREE LUTHERAN CONGREGATIONS, THE ASSOCIATION OF
221	FREE METHODIST	FREE METHODIST CHURCH OF NORTH AMERICA
223	FREE WILL BAPT	FREE WILL BAPTIST, NATIONAL ASSOCIATION OF, INC.
226	FRIENDS-USA	FRIENDS
226a	*CONSERV*	*CONSERVATIVE (WILBURITE) FRIENDS*
226b	*EFI*	*EVANGELICAL FRIENDS INTERNATIONAL (FORMERLY EVANGELICAL FRIENDS ALLIANCE)*
226c	*FGC*	*FRIENDS GENERAL CONFERENCE*
226d	*FGC & FUM*	*FRIENDS GENERAL CONFERENCE & FRIENDS UNITED MEETING (DUALLY AFFILIATED)*
226e	*FUM*	*FRIENDS UNITED MEETING*
226f	*INDEPENDNT*	*FRIENDS INDEPENDENT*
226g	*INDEP EVAN*	*FRIENDS INDEPENDENT EVANGELICAL*
230	FUND METHODIST	FUNDAMENTAL METHODIST CHURCH, INC.
237	GC MENN BR CHS	GENERAL CONFERENCE OF MENNONITE BRETHREN CHURCHES
241	GEN SIX PR BPT	GENERAL SIX PRINCIPLE BAPTISTS
246	GREEK ORTHODOX	GREEK ORTHODOX ARCHDIOCESE OF NORTH AND SOUTH AMERICA
249	AP CATH ASSYR	HOLY APOSTOLIC CATHOLIC ASSYRIAN CHURCH OF THE EAST
257	HUTTERIAN BR	HUTTERIAN BRETHREN
259	IFCA	INDEPENDENT FUNDAMENTAL CHURCHES OF AMERICA
263	INT FOURSQ GOS	INTERNATIONAL CHURCH OF THE FOURSQUARE GOSPEL
265	INT PENT C CHR	INTERNATIONAL PENTECOSTAL CHURCH OF CHRIST
266	INTRSTAT & ASC	INTERSTATE & FOREIGN LANDMARK MISSIONARY BAPTISTS ASSOCIATION
269	JASPER&PVB ASC	JASPER AND PLEASANT VALLEY BAPTISTS ASSOCIATIONS
274	LAT EVAN LUTH	LATVIAN EVANGELICAL LUTHERAN CHURCH IN AMERICA, THE
283	LUTH—MO SYNOD	LUTHERAN CHURCH - MISSOURI SYNOD, THE
284	LUTH CH-AM ASC	LUTHERAN CHURCHES, THE AMERICAN ASSOCIATION OF
285	MENNONITE CH	MENNONITE CHURCH
286	E.PA MENNONITE	EASTERN PENNSYLVANIA MENNONITE CHURCH
287	MENN GEN CONF	MENNONITE CHURCH, THE GENERAL CONFERENCE

Lines in *italic* represent a breakdown of Catholic rites or Friends affiliations. They are included in their respective denominational total.

Abbreviations

289	NEW HOPE B ASC	NEW HOPE BAPTIST ASSOCIATION
291	MISSIONARY CH	MISSIONARY CHURCH, THE
292	MORAV CH-AK	MORAVIAN CHURCH IN AMERICA (UNITAS FRATRUM), ALASKA PROVINCE
293	MORAV CH-NORTH	MORAVIAN CHURCH IN AMERICA (UNITAS FRATRUM), NORTHERN PROVINCE
295	MORAV CH-SOUTH	MORAVIAN CHURCH IN AMERICA (UNITAS FRATRUM), SOUTHERN PROVINCE
296	MIDW CONGR FEL	MIDWEST CONGREGATIONAL CHRISTIAN FELLOWSHIP
307	NETH REF CONGR	NETHERLANDS REFORMED CONGREGATIONS
313	N AM BAPT CONF	NORTH AMERICAN BAPTIST CONFERENCE
320	"OLD" MB ASCS	"OLD" MISSIONARY BAPTISTS ASSOCIATIONS
323	OLD ORD AMISH	OLD ORDER AMISH CHURCH
324	OLD ORD RVR BR	OLD ORDER RIVER BRETHREN
325	OLD REG BAPT	OLD REGULAR BAPTISTS
329	OPEN BIBLE STD	OPEN BIBLE STANDARD CHURCHES, INC.
331	ORTH CH IN AM	ORTHODOX CHURCH IN AMERICA
339	PENT CH OF GOD	PENTECOSTAL CHURCH OF GOD
349	PENT HOLINESS	PENTECOSTAL HOLINESS CHURCH, INC.
353	CHR BRETHREN	CHRISTIAN (PLYMOUTH) BRETHREN
355	PRESB CH (USA)	PRESBYTERIAN CHURCH (USA)
356	PRESB CH AMER	PRESBYTERIAN CHURCH IN AMERICA
359	PRIM AD CHR CH	PRIMITIVE ADVENT CHRISTIAN CHURCH
361	PRIM BAPT ASCS	PRIMITIVE BAPTISTS ASSOCIATIONS
363	PRIMITIVE METH	PRIMITIVE METHODIST CHURCH, U.S.A.
367	PROT CONF (LU)	THE PROTES'TANT CONFERENCE (LUTHERAN)
371	REF CH IN AM	REFORMED CHURCH IN AMERICA
373	REF CH IN U.S.	REFORMED CHURCH IN THE UNITED STATES
375	REF EPISCOPAL	REFORMED EPISCOPAL CHURCH
386	REGULAR BAPT	REGULAR BAPTISTS
397	ROMANIAN ORTH	ROMANIAN ORTHODOX EPISCOPATE OF AMERICA
403	SALVATION ARMY	SALVATION ARMY, THE
405	SCHWENKFELDER	SCHWENKFELDER CHURCH, THE
413	S.D.A.	SEVENTH-DAY ADVENTISTS
415	S-D BAPTIST GC	SEVENTH DAY BAPTIST GENERAL CONFERENCE
419	SO BAPT CONV	SOUTHERN BAPTIST CONVENTION
423	SYRIAN ANTIOCH	SYRIAN ORTHODOX CHURCH OF ANTIOCH (ARCHDIOCESE OF THE U.S.A. AND CANADA)
426	2SEED-SPRT BPT	TWO-SEED-IN-THE-SPIRIT PREDESTINARIAN BAPTISTS
430	TRUEVINE B ASC	TRUEVINE BAPTISTS ASSOCIATION
431	UKRANIAN AMER	UKRAINIAN ORTHODOX CHURCH OF AMER (ECUMENICAL PATRIARCHATE)
435	UNITARIAN-UNIV	UNITARIAN UNIVERSALIST ASSOCIATION
436	UNITED BAPT	UNITED BAPTISTS
438	UN BRETH IN CR	UNITED BRETHREN IN CHRIST
441	UN CHRISTIAN	UNITED CHRISTIAN CHURCH
443	UN C OF CHRIST	UNITED CHURCH OF CHRIST
449	UN METHODIST	UNITED METHODIST CHURCH, THE
466	WAYN TR MB ASC	WAYNE TRAIL MISSIONARY BAPTISTS ASSOCIATION
467	WESLEYAN	THE WESLEYAN CHURCH
469	WELS	WISCONSIN EVANGELICAL LUTHERAN SYNOD
496	JEWISH EST[1]	JEWISH ESTIMATE
497	BLACK BAPT EST[2]	BLACK BAPTISTS ESTIMATE
498	INDEP.CHARIS.[3]	INDEPENDENT, CHARISMATIC CHURCHES
499	INDEP.NON-CHAR[3]	INDEPENDENT, NON-CHARISMATIC CHURCHES

[1]See Appendix E   [2]See Appendix F   [3]See Appendix G

Table 1. Churches and Church Membership by Denomination, for the U.S.: 1990

Denomination		Number of churches	Communicant, confirmed, full members	Total adherents		
				Number	Percent of total population	Percent of total adherents
THE NATION		**255,173**	**55,433,052**	**137,064,509** *	**55.1**	**100.0**
001	ADVENT CHR CH	329	19,099	23,794 *	-	-
005	AME ZION	1,962	942,857	1,142,016	.5	.8
007	ALBAN ORTH ARC	13	NR	NR	-	-
009	ALBAN ORTH DIO	2	NR	NR	-	-
011	A.W.M.C.	120	2,037	2,526 *	-	-
019	AMER BAPT USA	5,801	1,504,573	1,873,731 *	.8	1.4
022	EASTERN ORTH	69	14,610	14,610	-	-
039	AP CHR CH(NAZ)	48	2,821	3,516 *	-	-
040	AP CHR CH-AMER	79	11,189	19,809	-	-
045	APOSTOLIC LUTH	53	3,005	7,812	-	-
049	ARMEN AP CH AM	22	13,125	73,300	-	.1
053	ASSEMB OF GOD	11,149	1,280,760	2,161,610	.9	1.6
055	AS REF PRES CH	187	32,787	37,988	-	-
057	BAPT GEN CONF	786	132,994	167,874 *	.1	.1
059	BAPT MISS ASSN	1,374	228,287	289,969 *	.1	.2
060	BRN RVR MB ASC	11	1,139	1,408 *	-	-
061	BEACHY AMISH	91	6,525	8,243 *	-	-
063	BEREAN FUND CH	47	2,726	5,457	-	-
066	BIBLE CH OF CR	6	6,500	8,156 *	-	-
071	BRETHREN (ASH)	124	13,060	16,331 *	-	-
075	BRETHREN IN CR	188	17,277	19,769	-	-
080	BYELORSSN ORTH	4	NR	NR	-	-
081	CATHOLIC	22,441	NA	53,385,998	21.5	38.9
081a	*ARMENIAN*	*7*	*NA*	*26,520*	-	-
081b	*BYZAN RUTH*	*246*	*NA*	*215,753*	*.1*	*.2*
081c	*CHALDEAN*	*14*	*NA*	*49,800*	-	-
081d	*LATIN*	*21,863*	*NA*	*52,900,126*	*21.3*	*38.6*
081e	*MARONITE*	*55*	*NA*	*53,795*	-	-
081f	*MELKITE-GK*	*41*	*NA*	*27,613*	-	-
081g	*ROMANIAN*	*16*	*NA*	*5,152*	-	-
081h	*UKRAINIAN*	*199*	*NA*	*107,239*	-	*.1*
082	CENTRAL BAPT	35	3,297	4,031 *	-	-
083	CHRIST CATH CH	12	169	235	-	-
089	CHR & MISS AL	1,797	132,112	271,865	.1	.2
093	CHR CH (DISC)	4,035	677,223	1,037,757	.4	.8
097	CHR CHS&CHS CR	5,238	966,976	1,213,188 *	.5	.9
105	CHRISTIAN REF	716	146,402	226,163	.1	.2
111	CH CR,SCIENTST	1,862	NR	NR	-	-
121	CH GOD (ABR)	88	4,263	5,370 *	-	-
123	CH GOD (ANDER)	2,336	182,419	232,876	.1	.2
127	CH GOD (CLEVE)	4,996	555,828	695,074 *	.3	.5
133	CH GOD(7TH)DEN	153	5,491	7,511	-	-
143	CG IN CR(MENN)	75	9,665	12,535 *	-	-
145	CH GOD PROPHCY	2,101	73,244	91,861 *	-	.1
146	CH GOD MTN ASM	103	4,938	6,231 *	-	-
151	L-D SAINTS	9,208	NA	3,540,820	1.4	2.6
157	CH OF BRETHREN	1,121	149,951	186,588 *	.1	.1
163	CH OF LUTH BR	109	7,487	17,793	-	-
164	CH LUTH CONF	69	6,397	8,753	-	-
165	CH OF NAZARENE	5,167	563,728	888,123	.4	.6
167	CHS OF CHRIST	13,097	1,280,838	1,681,013	.7	1.2

NA–Not applicable   NR–Not reported   *Total adherents estimated from known number of communicant, confirmed, full members.   - Represents a percent less than 0.1.   Percentages may not total due to rounding.
[1]See Appendix E   [2]See Appendix F   [3]See Appendix G   Lines in *italic* represent a breakdown of Catholic rites or Friends affiliations. They are included in their respective denominational total.

Table 1. Churches and Church Membership by Denomination, for the U.S.: 1990

Denomination		Number of churches	Communicant, confirmed, full members	Total adherents		
				Number	Percent of total population	Percent of total adherents
171	CH GOD-GEN CON	352	33,335	41,499 *	-	-
175	CONGR CHR CHS	399	79,255	99,110 *	-	.1
176	CCC, NOT NAT'L	232	29,390	36,679 *	-	-
179	CONSRV BAPT	1,121	NR	NR	-	-
181	CONSRV CONGR	177	28,355	35,600 *	-	-
185	CUMBER PRESB	737	85,027	91,040	-	.1
189	DUCK RIVR BAPT	102	10,672	13,215 *	-	-
191	ENTRPR BPT ASC	70	4,766	6,001 *	-	-
193	EPISCOPAL	7,333	1,695,878	2,445,286	1.0	1.8
195	ESTONIAN ELC	25	4,057	4,942 *	-	-
199	EVAN CONGR CH	159	24,619	33,166	-	-
203	EVAN FREE CH	1,046	106,523	181,692	.1	.1
207	E.L.C.A.	10,912	3,889,462	5,226,798	2.1	3.8
209	EVAN LUTH SYN	126	16,173	21,523	-	-
211	FEL EVG BIB CH	16	1,510	2,089	-	-
213	EVAN MENN INC	26	4,014	5,122 *	-	-
215	EVAN METH CH	128	8,860	11,105 *	-	-
216	EVAN PRESBY CH	138	43,960	45,464	-	-
217	FIRE BAPTIZED	49	700	889 *	-	-
220	FREE LUTHERAN	203	20,818	27,316	-	-
221	FREE METHODIST	1,038	57,696	82,766	-	.1
223	FREE WILL BAPT	2,461	234,588	293,448 *	.1	.2
226	FRIENDS	1,296	99,301	130,484 *	.1	.1
226a	CONSERV	25	1,396	1,873 *	-	-
226b	EFI	245	21,435	29,701 *	-	-
226c	FGC	280	17,442	23,573 *	-	-
226d	FGC & FUM	240	13,460	17,053 *	-	-
226e	FUM	337	40,252	49,844 *	-	-
226f	INDEPENDNT	144	3,264	5,345 *	-	-
226g	INDEP EVAN	25	2,052	3,095 *	-	-
230	FUND METHODIST	13	707	1,037	-	-
237	GC MENN BR CHS	134	17,075	22,097 *	-	-
241	GEN SIX PR BPT	2	140	172 *	-	-
246	GREEK ORTHODOX	515	NR	NR	-	-
249	AP CATH ASSYR	17	8,141	34,646	-	-
257	HUTTERIAN BR	111	NA	11,037	-	-
259	IFCA	698	NR	NR	-	-
263	INT FOURSQ GOS	1,445	201,806	255,092 *	.1	.2
265	INT PENT C CHR	78	2,612	4,102	-	-
266	INTRSTAT & ASC	129	14,128	18,293 *	-	-
269	JASPER&PVB ASC	40	7,312	9,209 *	-	-
274	LAT EVAN LUTH	56	13,004	14,299	-	-
283	LUTH—MO SYNOD	6,020	1,954,883	2,603,725	1.0	1.9
284	LUTH CH-AM ASC	79	10,865	14,545	-	-
285	MENNONITE CH	1,242	108,760	154,259	.1	.1
286	E.PA MENNONITE	47	3,111	3,881 *	-	-
287	MENN GEN CONF	257	32,472	40,951	-	-
289	NEW HOPE B ASC	22	2,459	3,150 *	-	-
291	MISSIONARY CH	303	26,910	39,948	-	-
292	MORAV CH-AK	22	2,698	5,338	-	-
293	MORAV CH-NORTH	98	23,680	31,250	-	-
295	MORAV CH-SOUTH	55	17,146	21,269	-	-

NA–Not applicable   NR–Not reported   *Total adherents estimated from known number of communicant, confirmed, full members.   - Represents a percent less than 0.1.   Percentages may not total due to rounding.
[1]See Appendix E   [2]See Appendix F   [3]See Appendix G   Lines in *italic* represent a breakdown of Catholic rites or Friends affiliations. They are included in their respective denominational total.

Table 1. Churches and Church Membership by Denomination, for the U.S.: 1990

Denomination		Number of churches	Communicant, confirmed, full members	Total adherents		
				Number	Percent of total population	Percent of total adherents
296	MIDW CONGR FEL	30	1,500	1,880 *	-	-
307	NETH REF CONGR	15	2,769	5,169	-	-
313	N AM BAPT CONF	267	42,689	54,010 *	-	-
320	"OLD" MB ASCS	73	13,093	16,289 *	-	-
323	OLD ORD AMISH	830	NA	121,750	-	.1
324	OLD ORD RVR BR	7	319	514	-	-
325	OLD REG BAPT	326	15,218	19,257 *	-	-
329	OPEN BIBLE STD	337	NR	NR	-	-
331	ORTH CH IN AM	426	NR	NR	-	-
339	PENT CH OF GOD	1,171	39,673	91,072	-	.1
349	PENT HOLINESS	1,490	125,940	157,728 *	.1	.1
353	CHR BRETHREN	820	52,740	85,600	-	.1
355	PRESB CH (USA)	11,433	2,847,329	3,553,335 *	1.4	2.6
356	PRESB CH AMER	1,161	183,090	221,392	.1	.2
359	PRIM AD CHR CH	9	350	427 *	-	-
361	PRIM BAPT ASCS	1,159	39,354	49,294 *	-	-
363	PRIMITIVE METH	81	5,626	7,937	-	-
367	PROT CONF (LU)	7	870	1,095	-	-
371	REF CH IN AM	917	196,953	362,932	.1	.3
373	REF CH IN U.S.	35	2,881	3,722	-	-
375	REF EPISCOPAL	80	5,889	6,559	-	-
386	REGULAR BAPT	41	3,938	4,722 *	-	-
397	ROMANIAN ORTH	43	NR	NR	-	-
403	SALVATION ARMY	1,167	115,320	127,577	.1	.1
405	SCHWENKFELDER	5	2,488	3,031 *	-	-
413	S.D.A.	4,214	717,443	903,062 *	.4	.7
415	S-D BAPTIST GC	83	5,145	6,439 *	-	-
419	SO BAPT CONV	37,922	15,032,798	18,940,682 *	7.6	13.8
423	SYRIAN ANTIOCH	29	NA	30,000	-	-
426	2SEED-SPRT BPT	3	70	87 *	-	-
430	TRUEVINE B ASC	3	458	561 *	-	-
431	UKRANIAN AMER	23	NR	NR	-	-
435	UNITARIAN-UNIV	965	141,330	190,193	.1	.1
436	UNITED BAPT	436	54,248	68,187 *	-	-
438	UN BRETH IN CR	240	24,014	25,749	-	-
441	UN CHRISTIAN	11	380	770	-	-
443	UN C OF CHRIST	6,260	1,599,539	1,993,459 *	.8	1.5
449	UN METHODIST	37,238	8,849,803	11,091,032 *	4.5	8.1
466	WAYN TR MB ASC	11	1,934	2,467 *	-	-
467	WESLEYAN	1,657	102,726	259,740	.1	.2
469	WELS	1,228	316,745	419,928	.2	.3
496	JEWISH EST[1]	3,975	NA	5,982,529	2.4	4.4
497	BLACK BAPT EST[2]	NA	6,955,723	8,737,667 *	3.5	6.4
498	INDEP.CHARIS.[3]	829	NA	794,254	.3	.6
499	INDEP.NON-CHAR[3]	1,363	NA	1,207,173	.5	.9

NA–Not applicable   NR–Not reported   *Total adherents estimated from known number of communicant, confirmed, full members.   - Represents a percent less than 0.1.   Percentages may not total due to rounding.
[1]See Appendix E   [2]See Appendix F   [3]See Appendix G   Lines in *italic* represent a breakdown of Catholic rites or Friends affiliations. They are included in their respective denominational total.

CENSUS REGIONS OF THE UNITED STATES

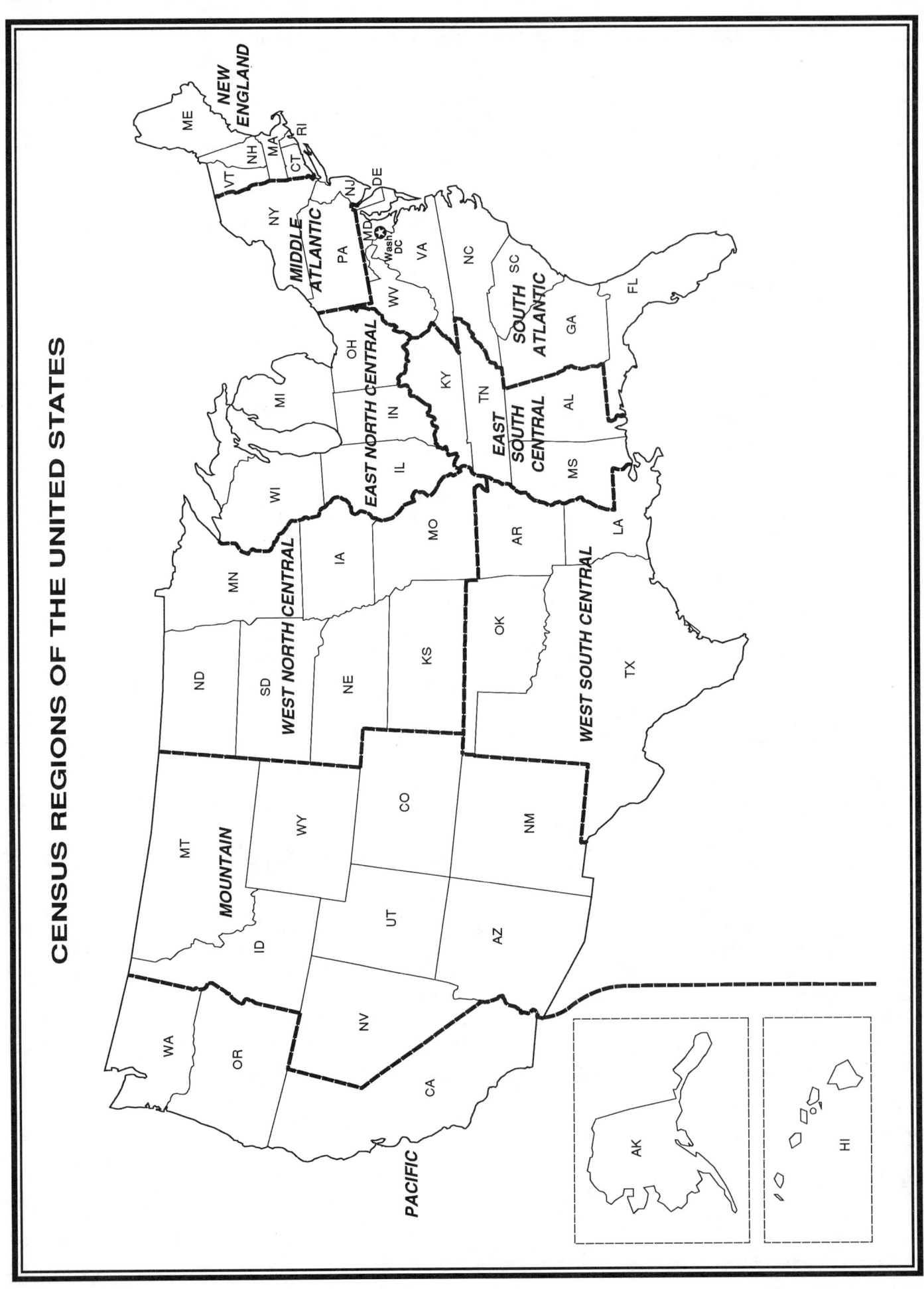

Table 2. Churches and Church Membership by Region and Denomination: 1990

Region and Denomination	Number of churches	Communicant, confirmed, full members	Total adherents Number	Total adherents Percent of total population	Total adherents Percent of total adherents
NEW ENGLAND	**8,876**	**1,277,333**	**7,881,895***	**59.7**	**100.0**
001 ADVENT CHR CH	77	4,481	5,566*	-	.1
005 AME ZION	56	27,697	33,701	.3	.4
007 ALBAN ORTH ARC	6	NR	NR	-	-
009 ALBAN ORTH DIO	1	NR	NR	-	-
011 A.W.M.C.	1	0	0*	-	-
019 AMER BAPT USA	786	159,684	196,065*	1.5	2.5
022 EASTERN ORTH	4	1,333	1,333	-	-
039 AP CHR CH(NAZ)	1	18	22*	-	-
040 AP CHR CH-AMER	1	335	595	-	-
045 APOSTOLIC LUTH	2	80	1,430	-	-
049 ARMEN AP CH AM	7	4,975	27,250	.2	.3
053 ASSEMB OF GOD	299	30,662	51,216	.4	.6
057 BAPT GEN CONF	45	5,861	7,178*	.1	.1
059 BAPT MISS ASSN	1	24	30*	-	-
081 CATHOLIC	1,922	NA	5,674,976	43.0	72.0
081a ARMENIAN	*1*	*NA*	*3,100*		
081b BYZAN RUTH	*6*	*NA*	*2,120*	-	-
081d LATIN	*1,880*	*NA*	*5,647,081*	*42.8*	*71.6*
081e MARONITE	*13*	*NA*	*14,181*	*.1*	*.2*
081f MELKITE-GK	*7*	*NA*	*5,338*	-	*.1*
081h UKRANIAN	*15*	*NA*	*3,156*	-	-
083 CHRIST CATH CH	4	82	92	-	-
089 CHR & MISS AL	76	4,116	8,805	.1	.1
093 CHR CH (DISC)	9	646	952	-	-
097 CHR CHS&CHS CR	24	1,267	1,561*	-	-
105 CHRISTIAN REF	7	1,345	2,050	-	-
111 CH CR,SCIENTST	156	NR	NR	-	-
123 CH GOD (ANDER)	10	1,518	1,673	-	-
127 CH GOD (CLEVE)	95	7,575	9,279*	.1	.1
145 CH GOD PROPHCY	33	922	1,130*	-	-
151 L-D SAINTS	113	NA	34,052	.3	.4
157 CH OF BRETHREN	2	68	85*	-	-
163 CH OF LUTH BR	3	169	260	-	-
165 CH OF NAZARENE	136	11,486	19,081	.1	.2
167 CHS OF CHRIST	112	8,880	12,446	.1	.2
175 CONGR CHR CHS	100	15,964	19,534*	.1	.2
176 CCC, NOT NAT'L	87	12,327	15,221*	.1	.2
179 CONSRV BAPT	128	NR	NR	-	-
181 CONSRV CONGR	42	5,614	6,839*	.1	.1
193 EPISCOPAL	677	166,973	275,163	2.1	3.5
195 ESTONIAN ELC	1	567	690*	-	-
203 EVAN FREE CH	37	2,895	4,572	-	.1
207 E.L.C.A.	195	58,980	78,188	.6	1.0
209 EVAN LUTH SYN	2	176	215	-	-
220 FREE LUTHERAN	1	17	24	-	-
221 FREE METHODIST	13	451	880	-	-
223 FREE WILL BAPT	3	219	272*	-	-
226 FRIENDS-USA	100	4,550	5,774*	-	.1
226b EFI	*2*	*127*	*223*	-	-
226d FGC & FUM	*97*	*4,422*	*5,547**	-	*.1*
226f INDEPENDNT	*1*	*1*	*4*	-	-
241 GEN SIX PR BPT	1	120	147*	-	-
246 GREEK ORTHODOX	75	NR	NR	-	-
249 AP CATH ASSYR	1	134	515	-	-
257 HUTTERIAN BR	1	NA	225	-	-
259 IFCA	9	NR	NR	-	-
263 INT FOURSQ GOS	33	1,456	1,815*	-	-
274 LAT EVAN LUTH	4	1,044	1,111	-	-
283 LUTH—MO SYNOD	73	20,151	26,566	.2	.3
285 MENNONITE CH	12	533	853	-	-
286 E.PA MENNONITE	1	12	15*	-	-
287 MENN GEN CONF	1	20	25	-	-
313 N AM BAPT CONF	1	30	37*	-	-
329 OPEN BIBLE STD	1	NR	NR	-	-
331 ORTH CH IN AM	26	NR	NR	-	-
339 PENT CH OF GOD	2	49	135	-	-
349 PENT HOLINESS	4	87	107*	-	-
353 CHR BRETHREN	44	2,858	4,421	-	.1
355 PRESB CH (USA)	91	18,505	22,641*	.2	.3
356 PRESB CH AMER	11	535	739	-	-
363 PRIMITIVE METH	12	713	1,033	-	-
371 REF CH IN AM	1	79	166	-	-
397 ROMANIAN ORTH	2	NR	NR	-	-
403 SALVATION ARMY	71	5,689	6,310	-	.1
413 S.D.A.	157	19,235	23,610*	.2	.3
415 S-D BAPTIST GC	5	429	525*	-	-
419 SO BAPT CONV	111	21,189	25,943*	.2	.3
423 SYRIAN ANTIOCH	3	NA	2,100	-	-
431 UKRANIAN AMER	1	NR	NR	-	-
435 UNITARIAN-UNIV	256	38,307	52,012	.4	.7
443 UN C OF CHRIST	1,197	305,792	375,411*	2.8	4.8
449 UN METHODIST	843	176,923	217,725*	1.6	2.8
467 WESLEYAN	17	742	2,063	-	-
469 WELS	7	605	875	-	-
496 JEWISH EST[1]	364	NA	434,721	3.3	5.5
497 BLACK BAPT EST[2]	NA	120,139	145,670*	1.1	1.8
498 INDEP.CHARIS.[3]	21	NA	13,765	.1	.2
499 INDEP.NON-CHAR[3]	42	NA	22,414	.2	.3
MIDDLE ATLANTIC	**28,345**	**5,259,558**	**23,838,924***	**63.4**	**100.0**
001 ADVENT CHR CH	3	103	129*	-	-
005 AME ZION	222	196,024	242,924	.6	1.0
007 ALBAN ORTH ARC	5	NR	NR	-	-
011 A.W.M.C.	58	1,217	1,499*	-	-
019 AMER BAPT USA	1,275	345,873	425,857*	1.1	1.8
022 EASTERN ORTH	49	11,701	11,701	-	-
039 AP CHR CH(NAZ)	7	311	379*	-	-
040 AP CHR CH-AMER	2	84	149	-	-
049 ARMEN AP CH AM	7	4,850	31,150	.1	.1
053 ASSEMB OF GOD	950	116,505	209,862	.6	.9
055 AS REF PRES CH	3	392	520	-	-
057 BAPT GEN CONF	28	4,300	5,301*	-	-
059 BAPT MISS ASSN	6	211	262*	-	-
061 BEACHY AMISH	17	1,598	2,001*	-	-
066 BIBLE CH OF CR	4	6,030	7,573*	-	-
071 BRETHREN (ASH)	19	1,749	2,138*	-	-
075 BRETHREN IN CR	98	11,664	13,265	-	.1
080 BYELORSSN ORTH	3	NR	NR	-	-
081 CATHOLIC	4,504	NA	14,145,053	37.6	59.3
081a ARMENIAN	*4*	*NA*	*8,120*	-	-
081b BYZAN RUTH	*144*	*NA*	*159,937*	*.4*	*.7*
081d LATIN	*4,205*	*NA*	*13,879,150*	*36.9*	*58.2*
081e MARONITE	*15*	*NA*	*13,839*	-	*.1*
081f MELKITE-GK	*8*	*NA*	*6,576*	-	-
081g ROMANIAN	*5*	*NA*	*1,610*	-	-
081h UKRANIAN	*123*	*NA*	*75,821*	*.2*	*.3*
089 CHR & MISS AL	455	30,020	64,959	.2	.3
093 CHR CH (DISC)	142	21,714	31,976	.1	.1
097 CHR CHS&CHS CR	206	26,294	32,109*	.1	.1
105 CHRISTIAN REF	37	6,440	9,493	-	-
111 CH CR,SCIENTST	211	NR	NR	-	-
123 CH GOD (ANDER)	153	13,876	16,821	-	.1
127 CH GOD (CLEVE)	262	24,903	30,772*	.1	.1
133 CH GOD(7TH)DEN	7	224	310	-	-
143 CG IN CR(MENN)	4	305	374*	-	-
145 CH GOD PROPHCY	99	4,093	5,055*	-	-
151 L-D SAINTS	215	NA	66,291	.2	.3
157 CH OF BRETHREN	250	46,708	57,732*	.2	.2
163 CH OF LUTH BR	13	1,290	3,148	-	-
164 CH LUTH CONF	1	49	60	-	-
165 CH OF NAZARENE	323	30,723	47,811	.1	.2
167 CHS OF CHRIST	275	20,155	26,769	.1	.1
171 CH GOD-GEN CON	154	17,599	21,642*	.1	.1
175 CONGR CHR CHS	32	4,142	5,099*	-	-
176 CCC, NOT NAT'L	25	2,176	2,701*	-	-
179 CONSRV BAPT	186	NR	NR	-	-
181 CONSRV CONGR	26	3,013	3,735*	-	-
193 EPISCOPAL	1,400	323,693	475,449	1.3	2.0
195 ESTONIAN ELC	10	1,876	2,248*	-	-
199 EVAN CONGR CH	133	22,390	29,847	.1	.1
203 EVAN FREE CH	95	9,525	15,877	-	.1
207 E.L.C.A.	2,036	704,257	956,487	2.5	4.0
215 EVAN METH CH	3	232	285*	-	-
216 EVAN PRESBY CH	4	1,288	1,323	-	-
217 FIRE BAPTIZED	1	2	3*	-	-
220 FREE LUTHERAN	1	83	95	-	-
221 FREE METHODIST	211	9,321	14,072	-	.1
223 FREE WILL BAPT	6	424	529*	-	-
226 FRIENDS-USA	189	16,569	20,485*	.1	.1
226a CONSERV	*2*	*14*	*16**	-	-
226b EFI	*2*	*130*	*177*	-	-
226c FGC	*110*	*11,964*	*14,810**	-	*.1*
226d FGC & FUM	*73*	*4,423*	*5,423**	-	-
226e FUM	*1*	*33*	*41**	-	-
226f INDEPENDNT	*1*	*5*	*18*	-	-
241 GEN SIX PR BPT	1	20	25*	-	-
246 GREEK ORTHODOX	123	NR	NR	-	-

NA–Not applicable NR–Not reported *Total adherents estimated from known number of communicant, confirmed, full members. - Represents a percent less than 0.1. Percentages may not total due to rounding.
[1]See Appendix E [2]See Appendix F [3]See Appendix G Lines in *italic* represent a breakdown of Catholic rites or Friends affiliations. They are included in their respective denominational total.

Table 2. Churches and Church Membership by Region and Denomination: 1990

Region and Denomination	Number of churches	Communicant, confirmed, full members	Total adherents		
			Number	Percent of total population	Percent of total adherents
249 AP CATH ASSYR	1	763	11	-	-
257 HUTTERIAN BR	5	NA	1,125	-	-
259 IFCA	110	NR	NR	-	-
263 INT FOURSQ GOS	46	3,371	4,155*	-	-
265 INT PENT C CHR	2	67	81	-	-
274 LAT EVAN LUTH	11	3,328	3,610	-	-
283 LUTH—MO SYNOD	362	100,926	140,074	.4	.6
284 LUTH CH-AM ASC	5	206	248	-	-
285 MENNONITE CH	399	38,374	54,653	.1	.2
286 E.PA MENNONITE	35	2,653	3,305*	-	-
287 MENN GEN CONF	30	4,483	5,587	-	-
291 MISSIONARY CH	13	589	692	-	-
293 MORAV CH-NORTH	42	12,802	17,212	-	.1
307 NETH REF CONGR	2	538	964	-	-
313 N AM BAPT CONF	26	3,244	3,983*	-	-
323 OLD ORD AMISH	231	NA	34,400	.1	.1
324 OLD ORD RVR BR	5	276	442	-	-
329 OPEN BIBLE STD	17	NR	NR	-	-
331 ORTH CH IN AM	143	NR	NR	-	-
339 PENT CH OF GOD	6	210	372	-	-
349 PENT HOLINESS	15	1,052	1,278*	-	-
353 CHR BRETHREN	141	9,802	15,142	-	.1
355 PRESB CH (USA)	2,242	592,780	727,056*	1.9	3.0
356 PRESB CH AMER	119	15,592	19,887	.1	.1
361 PRIM BAPT ASCS	1	6	7*	-	-
363 PRIMITIVE METH	48	4,018	5,741	-	-
371 REF CH IN AM	402	61,909	125,248	.3	.5
373 REF CH IN U.S.	1	15	21	-	-
375 REF EPISCOPAL	25	1,562	1,939	-	-
386 REGULAR BAPT	2	95	118*	-	-
397 ROMANIAN ORTH	8	NR	NR	-	-
403 SALVATION ARMY	182	15,052	16,982	-	.1
405 SCHWENKFELDER	5	2,488	3,031*	-	-
413 S.D.A.	444	75,196	92,690*	.2	.4
415 S-D BAPT GC	18	1,311	1,632*	-	-
419 SO BAPT CONV	325	47,626	58,580*	.2	.2
423 SYRIAN ANTIOCH	6	NA	9,800	-	-
431 UKRANIAN AMER	9	NR	NR	-	-
435 UNITARIAN-UNIV	119	18,802	24,997	.1	.1
438 UN BRETH IN CR	41	7,792	8,025	-	-
441 UN CHRISTIAN	11	380	770	-	-
443 UN C OF CHRIST	1,155	306,304	376,033*	1.0	1.6
449 UN METHODIST	4,629	1,100,138	1,355,959*	3.6	5.7
467 WESLEYAN	211	12,494	34,347	.1	.1
469 WELS	14	1,098	1,520	-	-
496 JEWISH EST[1]	2,007	NA	2,602,776	6.9	10.9
497 BLACK BAPT EST[2]	NA	766,200	940,793*	2.5	3.9
498 INDEP.CHARIS.[3]	53	NA	56,690	.2	.2
499 INDEP.NON-CHAR[3]	72	NA	43,603	.1	.2
EAST NORTH CENTRAL	**40,271**	**8,496,871**	**22,767,644***	**54.2**	**100.0**
001 ADVENT CHR CH	27	1,613	2,059*	-	-
005 AME ZION	88	101,130	124,000	.3	.5
007 ALBAN ORTH ARC	2	NR	NR	-	-
009 ALBAN ORTH DIO	1	NR	NR	-	-
011 A.W.M.C.	28	462	580*	-	-
019 AMER BAPT USA	1,290	354,132	443,947*	1.1	1.9
022 EASTERN ORTH	9	1,187	1,187	-	-
039 AP CHR CH(NAZ)	19	1,513	1,888*	-	-
040 AP CHR CH-AMER	40	8,381	14,831	-	.1
045 APOSTOLIC LUTH	19	1,133	2,154	-	-
049 ARMEN AP CH AM	6	2,100	10,400	-	-
053 ASSEMB OF GOD	1,224	156,261	304,843	.7	1.3
057 BAPT GEN CONF	214	30,372	38,292*	.1	.2
059 BAPT MISS ASSN	31	3,823	4,856*	-	-
061 BEACHY AMISH	31	2,097	2,717*	-	-
071 BRETHREN (ASH)	64	8,390	10,602*	-	-
075 BRETHREN IN CR	28	1,429	1,693	-	-
080 BYELORSSN ORTH	1	NR	NR	-	-
081 CATHOLIC	4,505	NA	10,344,884	24.6	45.4
081a *ARMENIAN*	*1*	*NA*	*600*	-	-
081b *BYZAN RUTH*	*50*	*NA*	*42,044*	*.1*	*.2*
081c *CHALDEAN*	*7*	*NA*	*35,000*	*.1*	*.2*
081d *LATIN*	*4,388*	*NA*	*10,226,291*	*24.3*	*44.9*
081e *MARONITE*	*9*	*NA*	*10,583*	-	-
081f *MELKITE-GK*	*11*	*NA*	*6,053*	-	-
081g *ROMANIAN*	*11*	*NA*	*3,542*	-	-
081h *UKRAINIAN*	*28*	*NA*	*20,771*	-	*.1*
082 CENTRAL BAPT	3	226	291*	-	-

Region and Denomination	Number of churches	Communicant, confirmed, full members	Total adherents		
			Number	Percent of total population	Percent of total adherents
083 CHRIST CATH CH	3	24	24	-	-
089 CHR & MISS AL	279	24,869	49,667	.1	.2
093 CHR CH (DISC)	672	142,134	231,749	.6	1.0
097 CHR CHS&CHS CR	1,609	351,522	441,758*	1.1	1.9
105 CHRISTIAN REF	327	84,955	130,877	.3	.6
111 CH CR,SCIENTST	363	NR	NR	-	-
121 CH GOD (ABR)	37	1,936	2,432*	-	-
123 CH GOD (ANDER)	639	61,700	78,271	.2	.3
127 CH GOD (CLEVE)	546	66,158	83,204*	.2	.4
133 CH GOD(7TH)DEN	19	636	850	-	-
143 CG IN CR(MENN)	6	923	1,180*	-	-
145 CH GOD PROPHCY	173	6,032	7,600*	-	-
146 CH GOD MTN ASM	50	2,499	3,171*	-	-
151 L-D SAINTS	369	NA	117,237	.3	.5
157 CH OF BRETHREN	287	36,959	46,837*	.1	.2
163 CH OF LUTH BR	10	670	1,804	-	-
164 CH LUTH CONF	16	1,955	2,700	-	-
165 CH OF NAZARENE	1,265	137,085	240,217	.6	1.1
167 CHS OF CHRIST	1,342	117,807	156,522	.4	.7
171 CH GOD-GEN CON	94	10,085	12,778*	-	.1
175 CONGR CHR CHS	146	32,601	41,035*	.1	.2
176 CCC, NOT NAT'L	27	5,044	6,376*	-	-
179 CONSRV BAPT	92	NR	NR	-	-
181 CONSRV CONGR	51	7,082	8,988*	-	-
185 CUMBER PRESB	54	4,710	4,934	-	-
191 ENTRPR BPT ASC	35	1,920	2,411*	-	-
193 EPISCOPAL	835	167,973	244,443	.6	1.1
195 ESTONIAN ELC	5	528	667*	-	-
199 EVAN CONGR CH	22	2,016	2,880	-	-
203 EVAN FREE CH	212	23,563	39,527	.1	.2
207 E.L.C.A.	2,541	988,568	1,323,482	3.2	5.8
209 EVAN LUTH SYN	36	6,661	9,089	-	-
211 FEL EVG BIB CH	1	12	20	-	-
213 EVAN MENN INC	24	3,705	4,731*	-	-
215 EVAN METH CH	12	580	734*	-	-
216 EVAN PRESBY CH	25	10,683	11,059	-	-
217 FIRE BAPTIZED	1	17	21*	-	-
220 FREE LUTHERAN	32	3,674	4,937	-	-
221 FREE METHODIST	316	21,934	30,366	.1	.1
223 FREE WILL BAPT	251	21,432	26,890*	.1	.1
226 FRIENDS-USA	305	26,167	34,235*	.1	.2
226a *CONSERV*	*7*	*582*	*722**	-	-
226b *EFI*	*58*	*6,634*	*9,175*	-	-
226c *FGC*	*63*	*1,904*	*2,969**	-	-
226d *FGC & FUM*	*8*	*741*	*882*	-	-
226e *FUM*	*157*	*16,034*	*20,130**	-	*.1*
226f *INDEPENDNT*	*3*	*14*	*33*	-	-
226g *INDEP EVAN*	*9*	*258*	*324**	-	-
237 GC MENN BR CHS	1	20	25*	-	-
246 GREEK ORTHODOX	92	NR	NR	-	-
249 AP CATH ASSYR	6	5,842	28,191	.1	.1
257 HUTTERIAN BR	1	NA	100	-	-
259 IFCA	250	NR	NR	-	-
263 INT FOURSQ GOS	139	18,892	23,640*	.1	.1
265 INT PENT C CHR	33	1,125	1,818	-	-
274 LAT EVAN LUTH	18	4,616	5,098	-	-
283 LUTH—MO SYNOD	1,756	743,372	988,068	2.4	4.3
284 LUTH CH-AM ASC	15	2,550	3,310	-	-
285 MENNONITE CH	345	36,103	50,828	.1	.2
286 E.PA MENNONITE	3	110	135*	-	-
287 MENN GEN CONF	57	6,743	8,769	-	-
291 MISSIONARY CH	190	17,355	26,771	.1	.1
293 MORAV CH-NORTH	36	7,985	10,193	-	-
296 MIDW CONGR FEL	30	1,500	1,880*	-	-
307 NETH REF CONGR	6	1,174	2,107	-	-
313 N AM BAPT CONF	57	11,607	14,574*	-	.1
320 "OLD" MB ASCS	3	257	317*	-	-
323 OLD ORD AMISH	489	NA	71,750	.2	.3
324 OLD ORD RVR BR	1	5	8	-	-
325 OLD REG BAPT	52	1,635	2,068*	-	-
329 OPEN BIBLE STD	66	NR	NR	-	-
331 ORTH CH IN AM	59	NR	NR	-	-
339 PENT CH OF GOD	154	4,940	12,492	-	.1
349 PENT HOLINESS	27	1,618	2,039*	-	-
353 CHR BRETHREN	143	8,512	14,199	-	.1
355 PRESB CH (USA)	1,812	496,924	624,611*	1.5	2.7
356 PRESB CH AMER	59	8,912	10,466	-	-
361 PRIM BAPT ASCS	61	1,518	1,906*	-	-
363 PRIMITIVE METH	15	772	1,019	-	-

NA—Not applicable   NR—Not reported   *Total adherents estimated from known number of communicant, confirmed, full members.   - Represents a percent less than 0.1.   Percentages may not total due to rounding.
[1]See Appendix E   [2]See Appendix F   [3]See Appendix G   Lines in *italic* represent a breakdown of Catholic rites or Friends affiliations. They are included in their respective denominational total.

Table 2. Churches and Church Membership by Region and Denomination: 1990

Region and Denomination	Number of churches	Communicant, confirmed, full members	Total adherents Number	Percent of total population	Percent of total adherents
367 PROT CONF (LU)	6	820	1,020	-	-
371 REF CH IN AM	262	76,952	126,994	.3	.6
373 REF CH IN U.S.	2	407	536	-	-
375 REF EPISCOPAL	4	308	344	-	-
397 ROMANIAN ORTH	18	NR	NR	-	-
403 SALVATION ARMY	237	25,469	28,634	.1	.1
413 S.D.A.	604	85,139	107,293 *	.3	.5
415 S-D BAPTIST GC	11	912	1,157 *	-	-
419 SO BAPT CONV	2,028	533,650	669,158 *	1.6	2.9
423 SYRIAN ANTIOCH	5	NA	3,600	-	-
426 2SEED-SPRT BPT	1	20	24 *	-	-
431 UKRANIAN AMER	8	NR	NR	-	-
435 UNITARIAN-UNIV	139	19,291	26,368	.1	.1
436 UNITED BAPT	72	6,271	7,859 *	-	-
438 UN BRETH IN CR	147	13,231	14,532	-	.1
443 UN C OF CHRIST	1,520	483,471	609,992 *	1.5	2.7
449 UN METHODIST	6,488	1,465,329	1,845,273 *	4.4	8.1
466 WAYN TR MB ASC	11	1,934	2,467 *	-	-
467 WESLEYAN	565	33,512	96,620	.2	.4
469 WELS	615	218,319	286,507	.7	1.3
496 JEWISH EST[1]	461	NA	556,055	1.3	2.4
497 BLACK BAPT EST[2]	NA	1,096,779	1,377,738 *	3.3	6.1
498 INDEP.CHARIS.[3]	92	NA	86,970	.2	.4
499 INDEP.NON-CHAR[3]	240	NA	297,194	.7	1.3
WEST NORTH CENTRAL	**27,197**	**5,254,205**	**10,783,237 ***	**61.1**	**100.0**
001 ADVENT CHR CH	5	240	299 *	-	-
005 AME ZION	17	6,611	7,845	-	.1
011 A.W.M.C.	2	17	21 *	-	-
019 AMER BAPT USA	548	124,195	157,326 *	.9	1.5
039 AP CHR CH(NAZ)	2	33	41 *	-	-
040 AP CHR CH-AMER	21	1,814	3,219	-	-
045 APOSTOLIC LUTH	19	1,240	2,995	-	-
053 ASSEMB OF GOD	1,191	106,830	205,419	1.2	1.9
055 AS REF PRES CH	2	137	157	-	-
057 BAPT GEN CONF	240	36,475	46,312 *	.3	.4
059 BAPT MISS ASSN	106	9,901	12,605 *	.1	.1
061 BEACHY AMISH	11	788	984 *	-	-
063 BEREAN FUND CH	37	2,110	4,219	-	-
071 BRETHREN (ASH)	5	397	504 *	-	-
075 BRETHREN IN CR	5	341	352	-	-
081 CATHOLIC	3,240	NA	3,454,297	19.6	32.0
081b BYZAN RUTH	3	NA	355	-	-
081d LATIN	3,224	NA	3,450,696	19.5	32.0
081e MARONITE	3	NA	2,173	-	-
081h UKRAINIAN	10	NA	1,073	-	-
083 CHRIST CATH CH	1	23	62	-	-
089 CHR & MISS AL	162	12,600	29,964	.2	.3
093 CHR CH (DISC)	791	141,358	228,272	1.3	2.1
097 CHR CHS&CHS CR	790	126,455	159,695 *	.9	1.5
105 CHRISTIAN REF	116	22,327	34,467	.2	.3
111 CH CR,SCIENTST	139	NR	NR	-	-
121 CH GOD (ABR)	22	633	805 *	-	-
123 CH GOD (ANDER)	194	15,681	19,463	.1	.2
127 CH GOD (CLEVE)	145	10,677	13,562 *	.1	.1
133 CH GOD(7TH)DEN	18	526	685	-	-
143 CG IN CR(MENN)	28	3,928	5,051 *	-	-
145 CH GOD PROPHCY	95	2,462	3,127 *	-	-
151 L-D SAINTS	307	NA	87,846	.5	.8
157 CH OF BRETHREN	94	8,138	10,305 *	.1	.1
163 CH OF LUTH BR	49	3,505	8,483	-	.1
164 CH LUTH CONF	30	2,832	3,819	-	-
165 CH OF NAZARENE	502	50,987	83,542	.5	.8
167 CHS OF CHRIST	879	60,625	79,652	.5	.7
171 CH GOD-GEN CON	27	1,862	2,340 *	-	-
175 CONGR CHR CHS	32	11,843	14,865 *	.1	.1
176 CCC, NOT NAT'L	15	855	1,100 *	-	-
179 CONSRV BAPT	64	NR	NR	-	-
181 CONSRV CONGR	27	3,221	4,089 *	-	-
185 CUMBER PRESB	33	2,223	2,326	-	-
193 EPISCOPAL	569	86,138	122,497	.7	1.1
195 ESTONIAN ELC	1	100	123 *	-	-
203 EVAN FREE CH	289	26,016	46,745	.3	.4
207 E.L.C.A.	2,983	1,180,491	1,585,959	9.0	14.7
209 EVAN LUTH SYN	53	6,501	8,472	-	.1
211 FEL EVG BIB CH	9	921	1,403	-	-
213 EVAN MENN INC	2	309	391 *	-	-
215 EVAN METH CH	6	276	353 *	-	-
216 EVAN PRESBY CH	11	3,723	3,845	-	-

Region and Denomination	Number of churches	Communicant, confirmed, full members	Total adherents Number	Percent of total population	Percent of total adherents
217 FIRE BAPTIZED	28	525	670 *	-	-
220 FREE LUTHERAN	145	15,129	19,743	.1	.2
221 FREE METHODIST	89	3,442	5,025	-	-
223 FREE WILL BAPT	187	16,349	20,528 *	.1	.2
226 FRIENDS-USA	133	10,821	14,196 *	.1	.1
226a CONSERV	9	581	729 *	-	-
226b EFI	52	4,534	5,767 *	-	.1
226c FGC	23	470	1,056 *	-	-
226d FGC & FUM	1	18	23 *	-	-
226e FUM	42	5,194	6,540 *	-	.1
226f INDEPENDNT	6	24	81	-	-
230 FUND METHODIST	13	707	1,037	-	-
237 GC MENN BR CHS	43	5,613	7,142 *	-	.1
246 GREEK ORTHODOX	21	NR	NR	-	-
257 HUTTERIAN BR	59	NA	5,900	-	.1
259 IFCA	65	NR	NR	-	-
263 INT FOURSQ GOS	96	8,857	11,181 *	.1	.1
274 LAT EVAN LUTH	8	1,313	1,418	-	-
283 LUTH--MO SYNOD	1,711	547,962	722,074	4.1	6.7
284 LUTH CH-AM ASC	37	5,847	7,871	-	.1
285 MENNONITE CH	97	9,240	12,235	.1	.1
286 E.PA MENNONITE	1	33	40 *	-	-
287 MENN GEN CONF	93	16,877	21,127	.1	.2
291 MISSIONARY CH	22	960	1,413	-	-
293 MORAV CH-NORTH	11	1,582	2,028	-	-
307 NETH REF CONGR	4	905	1,781	-	-
313 N AM BAPT CONF	101	13,432	17,052 *	.1	.2
323 OLD ORD AMISH	66	NA	9,550	.1	.1
324 OLD ORD RVR BR	1	38	64	-	-
329 OPEN BIBLE STD	77	NR	NR	-	-
331 ORTH CH IN AM	12	NR	NR	-	-
339 PENT CH OF GOD	91	2,714	6,776	-	-
349 PENT HOLINESS	36	2,609	3,321 *	-	.1
353 CHR BRETHREN	99	4,948	8,279	-	.1
355 PRESB CH (USA)	1,346	293,682	371,183 *	2.1	3.4
356 PRESB CH AMER	46	5,774	7,041	-	.1
361 PRIM BAPT ASCS	20	533	663 *	-	-
363 PRIMITIVE METH	2	16	24	-	-
371 REF CH IN AM	142	33,153	53,679	.3	.5
373 REF CH IN U.S.	20	1,884	2,346	-	-
375 REF EPISCOPAL	1	34	35	-	-
397 ROMANIAN ORTH	2	NR	NR	-	-
403 SALVATION ARMY	110	12,590	13,875	.1	.1
413 S.D.A.	389	37,679	47,644 *	.3	.4
415 S-D BAPTIST GC	8	532	680 *	-	-
419 SO BAPT CONV	2,256	737,534	928,830 *	5.3	8.6
431 UKRANIAN AMER	1	NR	NR	-	-
435 UNITARIAN-UNIV	59	8,804	12,365	.1	.1
436 UNITED BAPT	30	2,514	3,146 *	-	-
438 UN BRETH IN CR	14	515	571	-	-
443 UN C OF CHRIST	915	202,382	255,913 *	1.4	2.4
449 UN METHODIST	3,816	886,722	1,120,319 *	6.3	10.4
467 WESLEYAN	173	9,507	24,228	.1	.2
469 WELS	288	61,926	81,180	.5	.8
496 JEWISH EST[1]	104	NA	110,073	.6	1.0
497 BLACK BAPT EST[2]	NA	210,156	264,460 *	1.5	2.5
498 INDEP.CHARIS.[3]	69	NA	54,170	.3	.5
499 INDEP.NON-CHAR[3]	106	NA	70,458	.4	.7
SOUTH ATLANTIC	**50,035**	**13,571,220**	**22,239,483 ***	**51.0**	**100.0**
001 ADVENT CHR CH	172	10,383	12,872 *	-	.1
005 AME ZION	1,009	402,481	483,785	1.1	2.2
011 A.W.M.C.	21	215	266 *	-	-
019 AMER BAPT USA	826	251,161	308,574 *	.7	1.4
022 EASTERN ORTH	7	389	389	-	-
039 AP CHR CH(NAZ)	5	129	155 *	-	-
040 AP CHR CH-AMER	4	137	237	-	-
045 APOSTOLIC LUTH	1	78	154	-	-
049 ARMEN AP CH AM	2	1,200	4,500	-	-
053 ASSEMB OF GOD	1,519	182,844	293,822	.7	1.3
055 AS REF PRES CH	148	29,112	33,831	.1	.2
057 BAPT GEN CONF	24	2,680	3,279 *	-	-
059 BAPT MISS ASSN	14	1,432	1,805 *	-	-
061 BEACHY AMISH	17	1,224	1,522 *	-	-
066 BIBLE CH OF CR	2	470	583 *	-	-
071 BRETHREN (ASH)	25	1,981	2,390 *	-	-
075 BRETHREN IN CR	22	863	1,053	-	-
081 CATHOLIC	1,729	NA	3,556,368	8.2	16.0
081b BYZAN RUTH	15	NA	5,062	-	-

NA–Not applicable   NR–Not reported   *Total adherents estimated from known number of communicant, confirmed, full members.   - Represents a percent less than 0.1.   Percentages may not total due to rounding.
[1]See Appendix E   [2]See Appendix F   [3]See Appendix G   Lines in *italic* represent a breakdown of Catholic rites or Friends affiliations. They are included in their respective denominational total.

Table 2. Churches and Church Membership by Region and Denomination: 1990

Region and Denomination	Number of churches	Communicant, confirmed, full members	Total adherents Number	Percent of total population	Percent of total adherents
081d LATIN	*1,689*	*NA*	*3,538,702*	*8.1*	*15.9*
081e MARONITE	*7*	*NA*	*4,916*	*-*	*-*
081f MELKITE-GK	*4*	*NA*	*2,286*	*-*	*-*
081h UKRAINIAN	*14*	*NA*	*5,402*	*-*	*-*
082 CENTRAL BAPT	16	821	997*	-	-
089 CHR & MISS AL	281	18,896	36,025	.1	.2
093 CHR CH (DISC)	832	104,676	158,290	.4	.7
097 CHR CHS&CHS CR	848	140,724	173,596*	.4	.8
105 CHRISTIAN REF	25	2,659	3,885	-	-
111 CH CR,SCIENTST	229	NR	NR	-	-
121 CH GOD (ABR)	9	588	724*	-	-
123 CH GOD (ANDER)	435	28,680	36,234	.1	.2
127 CH GOD (CLEVE)	2,102	268,524	333,645*	.8	1.5
133 CH GOD(7TH)DEN	13	291	401	-	-
143 CG IN CR(MENN)	3	457	584*	-	-
145 CH GOD PROPHCY	818	29,026	36,063*	.1	.2
146 CH GOD MTN ASM	9	468	573*	-	-
151 L-D SAINTS	628	NA	217,208	.5	1.0
157 CH OF BRETHREN	369	47,464	58,118*	.1	.3
163 CH OF LUTH BR	2	106	222	-	-
164 CH LUTH CONF	6	415	558	-	-
165 CH OF NAZARENE	698	77,779	121,302	.3	.5
167 CHS OF CHRIST	1,705	152,678	203,098	.5	.9
171 CH GOD-GEN CON	31	2,154	2,670*	-	-
175 CONGR CHR CHS	18	1,915	2,300*	-	-
176 CCC, NOT NAT'L	37	4,735	5,825*	-	-
179 CONSRV BAPT	28	NR	NR	-	-
181 CONSRV CONGR	4	338	416*	-	-
185 CUMBER PRESB	11	1,320	1,432	-	-
189 DUCK RIVR BAPT	2	121	151*	-	-
193 EPISCOPAL	1,611	426,932	598,942	1.4	2.7
195 ESTONIAN ELC	4	388	474*	-	-
199 EVAN CONGR CH	3	180	366	-	-
203 EVAN FREE CH	41	3,740	5,910	-	-
207 E.L.C.A.	1,173	358,698	470,986	1.1	2.1
209 EVAN LUTH SYN	8	753	952	-	-
215 EVAN METH CH	51	4,297	5,312*	-	-
216 EVAN PRESBY CH	46	12,199	12,535	-	.1
220 FREE LUTHERAN	1	15	29	-	-
221 FREE METHODIST	85	3,750	5,224	-	-
223 FREE WILL BAPT	826	81,471	101,665*	.2	.5
226 FRIENDS-USA	219	19,162	24,954*	.1	.1
226a CONSERV	*6*	*158*	*343*	*-*	*-*
226b EFI	*28*	*1,695*	*2,546*	*-*	*-*
226c FGC	*40*	*2,056*	*2,943*	*-*	*-*
226d FGC & FUM	*61*	*3,856*	*5,178*	*-*	*-*
226e FUM	*82*	*11,370*	*13,895*	*-*	*.1*
226f INDEPENDNT	*1*	*6*	*23*	*-*	*-*
226g INDEP EVAN	*1*	*21*	*26*	*-*	*-*
237 GC MENN BR CHS	6	198	236*	-	-
246 GREEK ORTHODOX	85	NR	NR	-	-
249 AP CATH ASSYR	0	16	48	-	-
259 IFCA	36	NR	NR	-	-
263 INT FOURSQ GOS	119	10,844	13,389*	-	.1
265 INT PENT C CHR	32	959	1,537	-	-
266 INTRSTAT & ASC	1	89	111*	-	-
269 JASPER&PVB ASC	40	7,312	9,209*	-	-
274 LAT EVAN LUTH	4	837	937	-	-
283 LUTH—MO SYNOD	389	115,678	151,705	.3	.7
284 LUTH CH-AM ASC	3	292	402	-	-
285 MENNONITE CH	205	14,837	20,941	-	.1
286 E.PA MENNONITE	6	273	347*	-	-
287 MENN GEN CONF	4	89	129	-	-
289 NEW HOPE B ASC	21	2,332	2,995*	-	-
291 MISSIONARY CH	11	508	690	-	-
293 MORAV CH-NORTH	4	768	1,049	-	-
295 MORAV CH-SOUTH	55	17,146	21,269	-	.1
313 N AM BAPT CONF	3	129	155*	-	-
320 "OLD" MB ASCS	2	33	41*	-	-
323 OLD ORD AMISH	18	NA	2,500	-	-
325 OLD REG BAPT	89	3,919	4,927*	-	-
329 OPEN BIBLE STD	43	NR	NR	-	-
331 ORTH CH IN AM	40	NR	NR	-	-
339 PENT CH OF GOD	80	2,642	5,450	-	-
349 PENT HOLINESS	907	84,077	104,489*	.2	.5
353 CHR BRETHREN	169	11,109	18,647	-	.1
355 PRESB CH (USA)	2,656	660,599	813,321*	1.9	3.7
356 PRESB CH AMER	468	90,763	108,975	.3	.5
359 PRIM AD CHR CH	9	350	427*	-	-

Region and Denomination	Number of churches	Communicant, confirmed, full members	Total adherents Number	Percent of total population	Percent of total adherents
361 PRIM BAPT ASCS	661	20,014	25,015*	.1	.1
363 PRIMITIVE METH	4	107	120	-	-
371 REF CH IN AM	20	2,982	5,225	-	-
375 REF EPISCOPAL	43	3,788	3,973	-	-
386 REGULAR BAPT	39	3,843	4,604*	-	-
397 ROMANIAN ORTH	3	NR	NR	-	-
403 SALVATION ARMY	175	19,636	21,049	-	.1
413 S.D.A.	719	132,812	163,658*	.4	.7
415 S-D BAPTIST GC	13	790	966*	-	-
419 SO BAPT CONV	12,087	4,850,979	6,032,005*	13.8	27.1
423 SYRIAN ANTIOCH	5	NA	2,500	-	-
430 TRUEVINE B ASC	3	458	561*	-	-
431 UKRANIAN AMER	2	NR	NR	-	-
435 UNITARIAN-UNIV	132	20,865	28,065	.1	.1
436 UNITED BAPT	20	2,441	3,066*	-	-
438 UN BRETH IN CR	19	1,681	1,781	-	-
443 UN C OF CHRIST	590	128,187	156,727*	.4	.7
449 UN METHODIST	9,832	2,397,714	2,969,467*	6.8	13.4
467 WESLEYAN	444	31,822	62,487	.1	.3
469 WELS	60	6,208	8,604	-	-
496 JEWISH EST[1]	456	NA	991,730	2.3	4.5
497 BLACK BAPT EST[2]	NA	2,237,895	2,786,986*	6.4	12.5
498 INDEP.CHARIS.[3]	126	NA	117,892	.3	.5
499 INDEP.NON-CHAR[3]	303	NA	241,825	.6	1.1
EAST SOUTH CENTRAL	**30,381**	**7,058,399**	**9,886,172***	**65.1**	**100.0**
001 ADVENT CHR CH	13	372	467*	-	-
005 AME ZION	466	179,845	213,597	1.4	2.2
011 A.W.M.C.	4	25	31*	-	-
019 AMER BAPT USA	18	7,709	9,708*	.1	.1
040 AP CHR CH-AMER	2	57	102	-	-
053 ASSEMB OF GOD	874	96,676	133,036	.9	1.3
055 AS REF PRES CH	28	2,737	3,028	-	-
057 BAPT GEN CONF	1	46	59*	-	-
059 BAPT MISS ASSN	217	34,035	43,465*	.3	.4
060 BRN RVR MB ASC	11	1,139	1,408*	-	-
061 BEACHY AMISH	11	675	840*	-	-
071 BRETHREN (ASH)	3	29	37*	-	-
075 BRETHREN IN CR	9	381	464	-	-
081 CATHOLIC	817	NA	735,255	4.8	7.4
081d LATIN	*815*	*NA*	*733,169*	*4.8*	*7.4*
081e MARONITE	*1*	*NA*	*1,366*	*-*	*-*
081f MELKITE-GK	*1*	*NA*	*720*	*-*	*-*
082 CENTRAL BAPT	16	2,250	2,743*	-	-
089 CHR & MISS AL	59	2,996	4,897	-	-
093 CHR CH (DISC)	438	68,321	101,814	.7	1.0
097 CHR CHS&CHS CR	577	105,015	130,258*	.9	1.3
105 CHRISTIAN REF	1	75	123	-	-
111 CH CR,SCIENTST	51	NR	NR	-	-
121 CH GOD (ABR)	1	10	12*	-	-
123 CH GOD (ANDER)	326	18,203	25,750	.2	.3
127 CH GOD (CLEVE)	1,069	111,161	138,814*	.9	1.4
133 CH GOD(7TH)DEN	10	162	216	-	-
143 CG IN CR(MENN)	11	1,128	1,502*	-	-
145 CH GOD PROPHCY	430	17,652	22,108*	.1	.2
146 CH GOD MTN ASM	44	1,971	2,487*	-	-
151 L-D SAINTS	208	NA	56,894	.4	.6
157 CH OF BRETHREN	29	1,719	2,120*	-	-
165 CH OF NAZARENE	481	45,495	65,704	.4	.7
167 CHS OF CHRIST	3,364	335,572	437,865	2.9	4.4
171 CH GOD-GEN CON	5	297	371*	-	-
175 CONGR CHR CHS	5	324	402*	-	-
176 CCC, NOT NAT'L	11	723	904*	-	-
179 CONSRV BAPT	1	NR	NR	-	-
185 CUMBER PRESB	487	57,190	60,905	.4	.6
189 DUCK RIVR BAPT	100	10,551	13,064*	.1	.1
191 ENTRPR BPT ASC	35	2,846	3,590*	-	-
193 EPISCOPAL	401	91,232	118,817	.8	1.2
199 EVAN CONGR CH	1	33	73	-	-
203 EVAN FREE CH	14	469	954	-	-
207 E.L.C.A.	129	26,220	34,168	.2	.3
215 EVAN METH CH	9	625	785*	-	-
216 EVAN PRESBY CH	18	5,917	6,086	-	.1
220 FREE LUTHERAN	1	13	17	-	-
221 FREE METHODIST	29	935	1,562	-	-
223 FREE WILL BAPT	575	62,425	77,421*	.5	.8
226 FRIENDS-USA	23	786	1,112	-	-
226a CONSERV	*1*	*61*	*63*	*-*	*-*
226c FGC	*15*	*334*	*572*	*-*	*-*

NA–Not applicable   NR–Not reported   *Total adherents estimated from known number of communicant, confirmed, full members.   - Represents a percent less than 0.1.   Percentages may not total due to rounding.
[1]See Appendix E   [2]See Appendix F   [3]See Appendix G   Lines in *italic* represent a breakdown of Catholic rites or Friends affiliations. They are included in their respective denominational total.

Table 2. Churches and Church Membership by Region and Denomination: 1990

Region and Denomination	Number of churches	Communicant, confirmed, full members	Total adherents Number	Percent of total population	Percent of total adherents
226e *FUM*	7	391	477*	-	-
246 GREEK ORTHODOX	13	NR	NR	-	-
249 AP CATH ASSYR	0	17	72	-	-
259 IFCA	11	NR	NR	-	-
263 INT FOURSQ GOS	26	2,047	2,548*	-	-
265 INT PENT C CHR	10	436	641	-	-
266 INTRSTAT & ASC	97	10,797	13,981*	.1	.1
274 LAT EVAN LUTH	1	18	21	-	-
283 LUTH—MO SYNOD	168	27,973	37,038	.2	.4
285 MENNONITE CH	45	1,399	2,262	-	-
287 MENN GEN CONF	1	6	12	-	-
289 NEW HOPE B ASC	1	127	155*	-	-
291 MISSIONARY CH	3	102	122	-	-
320 "OLD" MB ASCS	67	12,785	15,909*	.1	.2
323 OLD ORD AMISH	19	NA	2,550	-	-
325 OLD REG BAPT	182	9,581	12,159*	.1	.1
329 OPEN BIBLE STD	4	NR	NR	-	-
331 ORTH CH IN AM	4	NR	NR	-	-
339 PENT CH OF GOD	47	1,846	3,807	-	-
349 PENT HOLINESS	88	6,024	7,584*	-	.1
353 CHR BRETHREN	20	833	1,282	-	-
355 PRESB CH (USA)	845	139,048	173,289*	1.1	1.8
356 PRESB CH AMER	293	45,699	54,318	.4	.5
361 PRIM BAPT ASCS	292	12,993	16,240*	.1	.2
371 REF CH IN AM	4	218	462	-	-
403 SALVATION ARMY	62	5,976	6,450	-	.1
413 S.D.A.	318	47,577	59,563*	.4	.6
415 S-D BAPTIST GC	5	124	155*	-	-
419 SO BAPT CONV	10,109	3,582,284	4,490,106*	29.6	45.4
426 2SEED-SPRT BPT	1	8	10*	-	-
435 UNITARIAN-UNIV	32	3,348	4,432	-	-
436 UNITED BAPT	292	41,792	52,577*	.3	.5
438 UN BRETH IN CR	2	51	61	-	-
443 UN C OF CHRIST	86	14,678	18,311*	.1	.2
449 UN METHODIST	5,477	954,439	1,196,359*	7.9	12.1
467 WESLEYAN	84	3,330	6,524	-	.1
469 WELS	10	676	965	-	-
496 JEWISH EST[1]	68	NA	43,100	.3	.4
497 BLACK BAPT EST[2]	NA	836,125	1,063,494*	7.0	10.8
498 INDEP.CHARIS.[3]	60	NA	35,710	.2	.4
499 INDEP.NON-CHAR[3]	101	NA	108,868	.7	1.1
WEST SOUTH CENTRAL	**31,902**	**8,983,099**	**17,399,292***	**65.2**	**100.0**
001 ADVENT CHR CH	9	305	387*	-	-
005 AME ZION	64	16,217	19,823	.1	.1
019 AMER BAPT USA	44	14,348	18,397*	.1	.1
040 AP CHR CH-AMER	1	8	13	-	-
053 ASSEMB OF GOD	2,441	268,572	393,065	1.5	2.3
055 AS REF PRES CH	6	409	452	-	-
057 BAPT GEN CONF	5	475	594*	-	-
059 BAPT MISS ASSN	956	176,600	224,029*	.8	1.3
061 BEACHY AMISH	4	143	179*	-	-
075 BRETHREN IN CR	5	291	313	-	-
081 CATHOLIC	2,252	NA	5,160,474	19.3	29.7
081b *BYZAN RUTH*	3	*NA*	718	-	-
081d *LATIN*	2,245	*NA*	5,157,881	19.3	29.6
081e *MARONITE*	2	*NA*	1,282	-	-
081f *MELKITE-GK*	1	*NA*	522	-	-
081h *UKRAINIAN*	1	*NA*	71	-	-
083 CHRIST CATH CH	1	3	3	-	-
089 CHR & MISS AL	62	2,033	4,044	-	-
093 CHR CH (DISC)	728	127,038	181,242	.7	1.0
097 CHR CHS&CHS CR	439	69,995	89,299*	.3	.5
105 CHRISTIAN REF	10	540	888	-	-
111 CH CR,SCIENTST	158	NR	NR	-	-
121 CH GOD (ABR)	12	424	545*	-	-
123 CH GOD (ANDER)	258	13,560	18,421	.1	.1
127 CH GOD (CLEVE)	401	37,270	47,752*	.2	.3
133 CH GOD(7TH)DEN	46	1,754	2,419	-	-
143 CG IN CR(MENN)	13	1,314	1,686*	-	-
145 CH GOD PROPHCY	208	5,903	7,574*	-	-
151 L-D SAINTS	493	NA	156,011	.6	.9
157 CH OF BRETHREN	12	798	1,010*	-	-
163 CH OF LUTH BR	1	36	71	-	-
164 CH LUTH CONF	3	107	144	-	-
165 CH OF NAZARENE	731	71,297	100,432	.4	.6
167 CHS OF CHRIST	3,816	445,220	578,895	2.2	3.3
171 CH GOD-GEN CON	28	1,043	1,304*	-	-
175 CONGR CHR CHS	5	916	1,176*	-	-

Region and Denomination	Number of churches	Communicant, confirmed, full members	Total adherents Number	Percent of total population	Percent of total adherents
176 CCC, NOT NAT'L	6	313	414*	-	-
179 CONSRV BAPT	1	NR	NR	-	-
181 CONSRV CONGR	2	189	241*	-	-
185 CUMBER PRESB	143	16,210	17,938	.1	.1
193 EPISCOPAL	660	177,743	235,288	.9	1.4
203 EVAN FREE CH	48	3,491	6,644	-	-
207 E.L.C.A.	480	136,673	177,287	.7	1.0
209 EVAN LUTH SYN	2	119	146	-	-
211 FEL EVG BIB CH	3	133	169	-	-
215 EVAN METH CH	20	1,457	1,868*	-	-
216 EVAN PRESBY CH	12	762	786	-	-
217 FIRE BAPTIZED	7	84	105*	-	-
220 FREE LUTHERAN	4	308	379	-	-
221 FREE METHODIST	52	1,587	2,027	-	-
223 FREE WILL BAPT	502	44,524	56,008*	.2	.3
226 FRIENDS-USA	51	3,052	4,126*	-	-
226b *EFI*	22	*2,263*	2,863*	-	-
226c *FGC*	25	*654*	*1,093*	-	-
226e *FUM*	2	*107*	134*	-	-
226f *INDEPENDNT*	1	*15*	20*	-	-
226g *INDEP EVAN*	1	*13*	16*	-	-
237 GC MENN BR CHS	24	3,154	4,029*	-	-
246 GREEK ORTHODOX	24	NR	NR	-	-
249 AP CATH ASSYR	1	80	334	-	-
257 HUTTERIAN BR	1	NA	100	-	-
259 IFCA	31	NR	NR	-	-
263 INT FOURSQ GOS	103	4,627	5,962*	-	-
266 INTRSTAT & ASC	31	3,242	4,201*	-	-
283 LUTH—MO SYNOD	549	143,853	191,839	.7	1.1
285 MENNONITE CH	35	1,563	2,231	-	-
286 E.PA MENNONITE	1	30	39*	-	-
287 MENN GEN CONF	25	1,410	1,722	-	-
313 N AM BAPT CONF	20	1,676	2,160*	-	-
323 OLD ORD AMISH	6	NA	850	-	-
329 OPEN BIBLE STD	3	NR	NR	-	-
331 ORTH CH IN AM	14	NR	NR	-	-
339 PENT CH OF GOD	371	13,389	27,736	.1	.2
349 PENT HOLINESS	248	19,093	24,376*	.1	.1
353 CHR BRETHREN	51	4,854	7,945	-	-
355 PRESB CH (USA)	1,003	233,195	298,636*	1.1	1.7
356 PRESB CH AMER	73	7,903	10,000	-	.1
361 PRIM BAPT ASCS	113	3,992	5,083*	-	-
371 REF CH IN AM	6	1,527	3,037	-	-
375 REF EPISCOPAL	1	71	115	-	-
397 ROMANIAN ORTH	1	NR	NR	-	-
403 SALVATION ARMY	88	9,199	9,932	-	.1
413 S.D.A.	447	52,133	67,077*	.3	.4
415 S-D BAPTIST GC	11	403	514*	-	-
419 SO BAPT CONV	8,414	4,374,539	5,599,173*	21.0	32.2
423 SYRIAN ANTIOCH	5	NA	2,200	-	-
426 2SEED-SPRT BPT	1	42	53*	-	-
431 UKRANIAN AMER	1	NR	NR	-	-
435 UNITARIAN-UNIV	62	7,745	10,421	-	.1
436 UNITED BAPT	20	1,210	1,514*	-	-
443 UN C OF CHRIST	112	21,605	27,698*	.1	.2
449 UN METHODIST	4,231	1,329,816	1,700,690*	6.4	9.8
467 WESLEYAN	36	1,967	5,684	-	-
469 WELS	50	4,070	5,816	-	-
496 JEWISH EST[1]	115	NA	130,974	.5	.8
497 BLACK BAPT EST[2]	NA	1,093,447	1,406,994*	5.3	8.1
498 INDEP.CHARIS.[3]	139	NA	164,327	.6	.9
499 INDEP.NON-CHAR[3]	230	NA	161,762	.6	.9
MOUNTAIN	**15,167**	**1,635,559**	**6,586,558***	**48.2**	**100.0**
001 ADVENT CHR CH	3	223	293*	-	-
005 AME ZION	3	358	423	-	-
011 A.W.M.C.	5	80	102*	-	-
019 AMER BAPT USA	247	57,436	73,184*	.5	1.1
039 AP CHR CH(NAZ)	4	272	342*	-	-
040 AP CHR CH-AMER	3	247	437	-	-
045 APOSTOLIC LUTH	2	16	40	-	-
053 ASSEMB OF GOD	807	84,689	153,704	1.1	2.3
057 BAPT GEN CONF	44	7,326	9,297*	.1	.1
059 BAPT MISS ASSN	16	604	791*	-	-
063 BEREAN FUND CH	5	267	548	-	-
071 BRETHREN (ASH)	3	217	274*	-	-
075 BRETHREN IN CR	5	210	351	-	-
081 CATHOLIC	1,481	NA	2,088,445	15.3	31.7
081b *BYZAN RUTH*	9	*NA*	2,351	-	-

NA–Not applicable   NR–Not reported   *Total adherents estimated from known number of communicant, confirmed, full members.   - Represents a percent less than 0.1.   Percentages may not total due to rounding.
[1]See Appendix E   [2]See Appendix F   [3]See Appendix G   Lines in *italic* represent a breakdown of Catholic rites or Friends affiliations. They are included in their respective denominational total.

Table 2. Churches and Church Membership by Region and Denomination: 1990

Region and Denomination	Number of churches	Communicant, confirmed, full members	Total adherents		
			Number	Percent of total population	Percent of total adherents
081c CHALDEAN	1	NA	300	-	-
081d LATIN	1,465	NA	2,084,164	15.3	31.6
081e MARONITE	1	NA	266	-	-
081f MELKITE-GK	2	NA	1,045	-	-
081h UKRAINIAN	3	NA	319	-	-
083 CHRIST CATH CH	3	37	54	-	-
089 CHR & MISS AL	118	4,506	11,679	.1	.2
093 CHR CH (DISC)	129	24,081	34,812	.3	.5
097 CHR CHS&CHS CR	260	49,099	62,894*	.5	1.0
105 CHRISTIAN REF	63	6,653	10,731	.1	.2
111 CH CR,SCIENTST	128	NR	NR	-	-
121 CH GOD (ABR)	2	398	504*	-	-
123 CH GOD (ANDER)	87	6,504	7,665	.1	.1
127 CH GOD (CLEVE)	133	8,587	11,080*	.1	.2
133 CH GOD(7TH)DEN	10	302	437	-	-
143 CG IN CR(MENN)	5	578	757*	-	-
145 CH GOD PROPHCY	78	1,790	2,308*	-	-
151 L-D SAINTS	4,786	NA	1,977,251	14.5	30.0
157 CH OF BRETHREN	23	2,032	2,613*	-	-
163 CH OF LUTH BR	12	506	1,269	-	-
164 CH LUTH CONF	6	307	460	-	-
165 CH OF NAZARENE	340	42,751	60,229	.4	.9
167 CHS OF CHRIST	623	47,492	63,901	.5	1.0
171 CH GOD-GEN CON	3	39	57*	-	-
175 CONGR CHR CHS	11	2,170	2,800*	-	-
176 CCC, NOT NAT'L	1	838	1,061*	-	-
179 CONSRV BAPT	192	NR	NR	-	-
181 CONSRV CONGR	7	1,410	1,856*	-	-
185 CUMBER PRESB	2	2,310	2,347	-	-
193 EPISCOPAL	415	73,197	107,426	.8	1.6
203 EVAN FREE CH	98	7,985	14,382	.1	.2
207 E.L.C.A.	460	152,842	211,732	1.6	3.2
209 EVAN LUTH SYN	4	244	297	-	-
211 FEL EVG BIB CH	1	85	115	-	-
215 EVAN METH CH	7	294	377*	-	-
216 EVAN PRESBY CH	13	8,461	8,875	.1	.1
217 FIRE BAPTIZED	3	13	16*	-	-
220 FREE LUTHERAN	4	157	205	-	-
221 FREE METHODIST	58	2,671	3,912	-	.1
223 FREE WILL BAPT	32	1,555	2,021*	-	-
226 FRIENDS-USA	90	3,828	5,428*	-	.1
226b EFI	36	2,455	3,537*	-	.1
226e FUM	4	252	307*	-	-
226f INDEPENDNT	50	1,121	1,584*	-	-
237 GC MENN BR CHS	6	448	568*	-	-
246 GREEK ORTHODOX	32	NR	NR	-	-
249 AP CATH ASSYR	0	60	72	-	-
257 HUTTERIAN BR	40	NA	3,307	-	.1
259 IFCA	50	NR	NR	-	-
263 INT FOURSQ GOS	177	18,489	23,594*	.2	.4
265 INT PENT C CHR	1	25	25	-	-
274 LAT EVAN LUTH	2	167	188	-	-
283 LUTH—MO SYNOD	393	93,928	129,043	.9	2.0
284 LUTH CH-AM ASC	5	449	640	-	-
285 MENNONITE CH	53	3,095	4,523	-	.1
287 MENN GEN CONF	23	970	1,189	-	-
291 MISSIONARY CH	5	1,037	1,216	-	-
293 MORAV CH-NORTH	1	80	121	-	-
313 N AM BAPT CONF	9	1,045	1,380*	-	-
320 "OLD" MB ASCS	1	18	22*	-	-
323 OLD ORD AMISH	1	NA	150	-	-
325 OLD REG BAPT	1	9	11*	-	-
329 OPEN BIBLE STD	33	NR	NR	-	-
331 ORTH CH IN AM	10	NR	NR	-	-
339 PENT CH OF GOD	98	3,158	7,133	.1	.1
349 PENT HOLINESS	37	1,572	2,005*	-	-
353 CHR BRETHREN	44	2,763	4,717	-	.1
355 PRESB CH (USA)	466	113,390	145,314*	1.1	2.2
356 PRESB CH AMER	27	2,818	3,486	-	.1
371 REF CH IN AM	22	3,627	7,337	.1	.1
373 REF CH IN U.S.	5	105	154	-	-
375 REF EPISCOPAL	1	11	12	-	-
397 ROMANIAN ORTH	1	NR	NR	-	-
403 SALVATION ARMY	62	4,688	5,227	-	.1
413 S.D.A.	317	40,668	51,986*	.4	.8
415 S-D BAPTIST GC	2	342	430*	-	-
419 SO BAPT CONV	1,055	380,411	491,755*	3.6	7.5
431 UKRAINIAN AMER	1	NR	NR	-	-
435 UNITARIAN-UNIV	46	6,015	8,069	.1	.1

Region and Denomination	Number of churches	Communicant, confirmed, full members	Total adherents		
			Number	Percent of total population	Percent of total adherents
436 UNITED BAPT	2	20	25*	-	-
438 UN BRETH IN CR	9	380	405	-	-
443 UN C OF CHRIST	191	45,811	58,588*	.4	.9
449 UN METHODIST	701	213,687	273,922*	2.0	4.2
467 WESLEYAN	59	2,264	11,083	.1	.2
469 WELS	97	12,488	18,423	.1	.3
496 JEWISH EST[1]	71	NA	149,785	1.1	2.3
497 BLACK BAPT EST[2]	NA	75,854	95,852*	.7	1.5
498 INDEP.CHARIS.[3]	74	NA	61,300	.4	.9
499 INDEP.NON-CHAR[3]	101	NA	83,719	.6	1.3
PACIFIC	**22,999**	**3,896,808**	**15,681,304***	**40.1**	**100.0**
001 ADVENT CHR CH	20	1,379	1,722*	-	-
005 AME ZION	37	12,494	15,918	-	.1
011 A.W.M.C.	1	21	27*	-	-
019 AMER BAPT USA	767	190,035	240,673*	.6	1.5
039 AP CHR CH(NAZ)	10	545	689*	-	-
040 AP CHR CH-AMER	5	126	226	-	-
045 APOSTOLIC LUTH	10	458	1,039	-	-
053 ASSEMB OF GOD	1,844	237,721	416,643	1.1	2.7
057 BAPT GEN CONF	185	45,459	57,562*	.1	.4
059 BAPT MISS ASSN	27	1,657	2,126*	-	-
063 BEREAN FUND CH	5	349	690	-	-
071 BRETHREN (ASH)	5	297	386*	-	-
075 BRETHREN IN CR	16	2,098	2,278	-	-
081 CATHOLIC	1,991	NA	8,226,246	21.0	52.5
081a ARMENIAN	1	NA	14,700	-	.1
081b BYZAN RUTH	16	NA	3,166	-	-
081c CHALDEAN	6	NA	14,500	-	.1
081d LATIN	1,952	NA	8,182,992	20.9	52.2
081e MARONITE	4	NA	5,189	-	-
081f MELKITE-GK	7	NA	5,073	-	-
081h UKRAINIAN	5	NA	626	-	-
089 CHR & MISS AL	305	32,076	61,825	.2	.4
093 CHR CH (DISC)	294	47,255	68,650	.2	.4
097 CHR CHS&CHS CR	485	96,605	122,018*	.3	.8
105 CHRISTIAN REF	130	21,408	33,649	.1	.2
111 CH CR,SCIENTST	427	NR	NR	-	-
121 CH GOD (ABR)	5	274	348*	-	-
123 CH GOD (ANDER)	234	22,697	28,578	.1	.2
127 CH GOD (CLEVE)	243	20,973	26,966*	.1	.2
133 CH GOD(7TH)DEN	30	1,596	2,193	-	-
143 CG IN CR(MENN)	5	1,032	1,401*	-	-
145 CH GOD PROPHCY	167	5,364	6,896*	-	-
151 L-D SAINTS	2,089	NA	828,030	2.1	5.3
157 CH OF BRETHREN	55	6,065	7,768*	-	-
163 CH OF LUTH BR	19	1,205	2,536	-	-
164 CH LUTH CONF	7	732	1,012	-	-
165 CH OF NAZARENE	691	96,125	149,805	.4	1.0
167 CHS OF CHRIST	981	92,409	121,865	.3	.8
171 CH GOD-GEN CON	10	256	337*	-	-
175 CONGR CHR CHS	50	9,380	11,899*	-	.1
176 CCC, NOT NAT'L	23	2,379	3,077*	-	-
179 CONSRV BAPT	429	NR	NR	-	-
181 CONSRV CONGR	18	7,488	9,436*	-	.1
185 CUMBER PRESB	7	1,064	1,158	-	-
193 EPISCOPAL	765	181,997	267,261	.7	1.7
195 ESTONIAN ELC	4	598	740*	-	-
203 EVAN FREE CH	212	28,839	47,081	.1	.3
207 E.L.C.A.	915	282,733	388,509	1.0	2.5
209 EVAN LUTH SYN	21	1,719	2,352	-	-
211 FEL EVG BIB CH	2	359	382	-	-
215 EVAN METH CH	20	1,099	1,391*	-	-
216 EVAN PRESBY CH	9	927	955	-	-
217 FIRE BAPTIZED	9	59	74*	-	-
220 FREE LUTHERAN	14	1,422	1,887	-	-
221 FREE METHODIST	185	13,605	19,698	.1	.1
223 FREE WILL BAPT	79	6,189	8,114*	-	.1
226 FRIENDS-USA	186	14,366	20,174*	.1	.1
226b EFI	45	3,597	5,413	-	-
226c FGC	4	60	130*	-	-
226e FUM	42	6,871	8,320*	-	.1
226f INDEPENDNT	81	2,078	3,582*	-	-
226g INDEP EVAN	14	1,760	2,729*	-	-
237 GC MENN BR CHS	54	7,642	10,097*	-	.1
246 GREEK ORTHODOX	50	NR	NR	-	-
249 AP CATH ASSYR	8	1,229	5,403	-	-
257 HUTTERIAN BR	4	NA	280	-	-
259 IFCA	136	NR	NR	-	-

NA–Not applicable   NR–Not reported   *Total adherents estimated from known number of communicant, confirmed, full members.   - Represents a percent less than 0.1.   Percentages may not total due to rounding.
[1]See Appendix E   [2]See Appendix F   [3]See Appendix G   Lines in *italic* represent a breakdown of Catholic rites or Friends affiliations. They are included in their respective denominational total.

Table 2. Churches and Church Membership by Region and Denomination: 1990

Region and Denomination	Number of churches	Communicant, confirmed, full members	Total adherents		
			Number	Percent of total population	Percent of total adherents
263 INT FOURSQ GOS	706	133,223	168,808*	.4	1.1
274 LAT EVAN LUTH	8	1,681	1,916	-	-
283 LUTH—MO SYNOD	619	161,138	217,318	.6	1.4
284 LUTH CH-AM ASC	14	1,521	2,074	-	-
285 MENNONITE CH	51	3,616	5,733	-	-
287 MENN GEN CONF	23	1,874	2,391	-	-
291 MISSIONARY CH	59	6,359	9,044	-	.1
292 MORAV CH-AK	22	2,698	5,338	-	-
293 MORAV CH-NORTH	4	463	647	-	-
307 NETH REF CONGR	3	152	317	-	-
313 N AM BAPT CONF	50	11,526	14,669*	-	.1
325 OLD REG BAPT	2	74	92*	-	-
329 OPEN BIBLE STD	93	NR	NR	-	-
331 ORTH CH IN AM	118	NR	NR	-	-
339 PENT CH OF GOD	322	10,725	27,171	.1	.2
349 PENT HOLINESS	128	9,808	12,529*	-	.1
353 CHR BRETHREN	109	7,061	10,968	-	.1
355 PRESB CH (USA)	972	299,206	377,284*	1.0	2.4
356 PRESB CH AMER	65	5,094	6,480	-	-
361 PRIM BAPT ASCS	11	298	380*	-	-
367 PROT CONF (LU)	1	50	75	-	-
371 REF CH IN AM	58	16,506	40,784	.1	.3
373 REF CH IN U.S.	7	470	665	-	-
375 REF EPISCOPAL	5	115	141	-	-
397 ROMANIAN ORTH	8	NR	NR	-	-
403 SALVATION ARMY	180	17,021	19,118	-	.1
413 S.D.A.	819	227,004	289,541*	.7	1.8
415 S-D BAPTIST GC	10	302	380*	-	-
419 SO BAPT CONV	1,537	504,586	645,132*	1.6	4.1
423 SYRIAN ANTIOCH	5	NA	9,800	-	.1
435 UNITARIAN-UNIV	120	18,153	23,464	.1	.1
438 UN BRETH IN CR	8	364	374	-	-
443 UN C OF CHRIST	494	91,309	114,786*	.3	.7
449 UN METHODIST	1,221	325,035	411,318*	1.1	2.6
467 WESLEYAN	68	7,088	16,704	-	.1
469 WELS	87	11,355	16,038	-	.1
496 JEWISH EST[1]	329	NA	963,315	2.5	6.1
497 BLACK BAPT EST[2]	NA	519,128	655,680*	1.7	4.2
498 INDEP.CHARIS.[3]	195	NA	203,430	.5	1.3
499 INDEP.NON-CHAR[3]	168	NA	177,330	.5	1.1

Region and Denomination	Number of churches	Communicant, confirmed, full members	Total adherents		
			Number	Percent of total population	Percent of total adherents

NA–Not applicable   NR–Not reported   *Total adherents estimated from known number of communicant, confirmed, full members.   - Represents a percent less than 0.1.   Percentages may not total due to rounding.
[1]See Appendix E   [2]See Appendix F   [3]See Appendix G   Lines in *italic* represent a breakdown of Catholic rites or Friends affiliations. They are included in their respective denominational total.

Table 3. Churches and Church Membership by State and Denomination: 1990

State and Denomination	Number of churches	Communicant, confirmed, full members	Total adherents Number	Percent of total population	Percent of total adherents
ALABAMA	**8,447**	**2,119,898**	**2,867,460***	**71.0**	**100.0**
001 ADVENT CHR CH	6	183	225*	-	-
005 AME ZION	308	134,305	160,167	4.0	5.6
019 AMER BAPT USA	3	2,025	2,568*	.1	.1
040 AP CHR CH-AMER	1	50	90	-	-
053 ASSEMB OF GOD	372	38,442	53,228	1.3	1.9
055 AS REF PRES CH	7	316	363	-	-
059 BAPT MISS ASSN	20	1,769	2,239*	.1	.1
061 BEACHY AMISH	1	39	51*	-	-
081 CATHOLIC	172	NA	137,834	3.4	4.8
081d *LATIN*	170	*NA*	*135,748*	*3.4*	*4.7*
081e *MARONITE*	1	*NA*	*1,366*	-	-
081f *MELKITE-GK*	1	*NA*	*720*	-	-
089 CHR & MISS AL	30	1,483	2,175	.1	.1
093 CHR CH (DISC)	64	5,937	8,496	.2	.3
097 CHR CHS&CHS CR	31	2,772	3,500*	.1	.1
111 CH CR,SCIENTST	12	NR	NR	-	-
123 CH GOD (ANDER)	76	3,661	4,515	.1	.2
127 CH GOD (CLEVE)	382	40,950	51,201*	1.3	1.8
133 CH GOD(7TH)DEN	4	80	108	-	-
143 CG IN CR(MENN)	2	213	278*	-	-
145 CH GOD PROPHCY	119	4,172	5,212*	.1	.2
151 L-D SAINTS	64	NA	17,256	.4	.6
157 CH OF BRETHREN	4	216	275*	-	-
165 CH OF NAZARENE	116	9,677	14,288	.4	.5
167 CHS OF CHRIST	890	91,660	118,561	2.9	4.1
171 CH GOD-GEN CON	1	4	5*	-	-
175 CONGR CHR CHS	4	234	293*	-	-
176 CCC, NOT NAT'L	11	723	904*	-	-
185 CUMBER PRESB	60	7,573	8,183	.2	.3
189 DUCK RIVR BAPT	29	3,516	4,353*	.1	.2
193 EPISCOPAL	117	29,271	38,257	.9	1.3
203 EVAN FREE CH	3	82	145	-	-
207 E.L.C.A.	22	4,120	5,436	.1	.2
215 EVAN METH CH	2	122	156*	-	-
216 EVAN PRESBY CH	2	147	153	-	-
220 FREE LUTHERAN	1	13	17	-	-
221 FREE METHODIST	6	173	204	-	-
223 FREE WILL BAPT	168	19,170	23,911*	.6	.8
226 FRIENDS-USA	3	79	112	-	-
226a *CONSERV*	1	*61*	*63*	-	-
226c *FGC*	2	*18*	*49*	-	-
246 GREEK ORTHODOX	5	NR	NR	-	-
259 IFCA	2	NR	NR	-	-
263 INT FOURSQ GOS	8	514	640*	-	-
266 INTRSTAT & ASC	12	1,499	1,926*	-	.1
283 LUTH—MO SYNOD	60	9,909	13,237	.3	.5
285 MENNONITE CH	13	364	617	-	-
289 NEW HOPE B ASC	1	127	155*	-	-
331 ORTH CH IN AM	2	NR	NR	-	-
339 PENT CH OF GOD	8	204	479	-	-
349 PENT HOLINESS	45	3,171	3,976*	.1	.1
353 CHR BRETHREN	8	223	350	-	-
355 PRESB CH (USA)	171	30,578	38,278*	.9	1.3
356 PRESB CH AMER	103	16,065	19,194	.5	.7
361 PRIM BAPT ASCS	112	3,199	3,986*	.1	.1
371 REF CH IN AM	1	45	95	-	-
403 SALVATION ARMY	16	1,290	1,370	-	-
413 S.D.A.	87	14,550	18,247*	.5	.6
415 S-D BAPTIST GC	2	53	66*	-	-
419 SO BAPT CONV	3,065	1,049,441	1,313,907*	32.5	45.8
435 UNITARIAN-UNIV	10	610	806	-	-
443 UN C OF CHRIST	33	3,230	4,020*	.1	.1
449 UN METHODIST	1,472	264,968	332,029*	8.2	11.6
467 WESLEYAN	17	1,123	2,205	.1	.1
469 WELS	3	227	340	-	-
496 JEWISH EST[1]	19	NA	8,350	.2	.3
497 BLACK BAPT EST[2]	NA	315,331	398,793*	9.9	13.9
498 INDEP.CHARIS.[3]	30	NA	18,335	.5	.6
499 INDEP.NON-CHAR[3]	29	NA	21,300	.5	.7
ALASKA	**814**	**72,399**	**177,337***	**32.2**	**100.0**
005 AME ZION	3	316	366	.1	.2
019 AMER BAPT USA	10	1,463	1,942*	.4	1.1
053 ASSEMB OF GOD	85	4,904	8,779	1.6	5.0
057 BAPT GEN CONF	5	293	384*	.1	.2
059 BAPT MISS ASSN	1	38	50*	-	-
081 CATHOLIC	93	NA	45,203	8.2	25.5
081b *BYZAN RUTH*	1	*NA*	*225*	-	*.1*
081d *LATIN*	92	*NA*	*44,978*	*8.2*	*25.4*
089 CHR & MISS AL	9	459	1,096	.2	.6
093 CHR CH (DISC)	1	167	247	-	.1
097 CHR CHS&CHS CR	11	1,083	1,456*	.3	.8
105 CHRISTIAN REF	1	138	239	-	.1
111 CH CR,SCIENTST	6	NR	NR	-	-
123 CH GOD (ANDER)	11	674	826	.2	.5
127 CH GOD (CLEVE)	14	1,438	1,933*	.4	1.1
145 CH GOD PROPHCY	6	116	159*	-	.1
151 L-D SAINTS	58	NA	15,751	2.9	8.9
164 CH LUTH CONF	1	30	47	-	-
165 CH OF NAZARENE	24	1,849	3,935	.7	2.2
167 CHS OF CHRIST	28	1,654	2,226	.4	1.3
175 CONGR CHR CHS	3	448	598*	.1	.3
179 CONSRV BAPT	5	NR	NR	-	-
193 EPISCOPAL	43	4,244	7,540	1.4	4.3
203 EVAN FREE CH	1	60	110	-	.1
207 E.L.C.A.	28	6,275	9,690	1.8	5.5
221 FREE METHODIST	3	76	219	-	.1
226 FRIENDS-USA	17	1,793	2,814*	.5	1.6
226c *FGC*	3	*33*	*85*	-	-
226g *INDEP EVAN*	14	*1,760*	*2,729***	*.5*	*1.5*
246 GREEK ORTHODOX	1	NR	NR	-	-
259 IFCA	1	NR	NR	-	-
263 INT FOURSQ GOS	2	88	116*	-	.1
283 LUTH—MO SYNOD	10	2,163	3,404	.6	1.9
285 MENNONITE CH	1	2	2	-	-
292 MORAV CH-AK	22	2,698	5,338	1.0	3.0
331 ORTH CH IN AM	86	NR	NR	-	-
339 PENT CH OF GOD	7	239	539	.1	.3
349 PENT HOLINESS	9	257	366*	.1	.2
353 CHR BRETHREN	6	281	434	.1	.2
355 PRESB CH (USA)	37	4,617	6,307*	1.1	3.6
403 SALVATION ARMY	32	2,073	2,487	.5	1.4
413 S.D.A.	25	2,187	2,961*	.5	1.7
419 SO BAPT CONV	59	21,477	28,718*	5.2	16.2
435 UNITARIAN-UNIV	4	222	271	-	.2
449 UN METHODIST	26	3,712	4,956*	.9	2.8
467 WESLEYAN	2	68	461	.1	.3
469 WELS	7	622	1,012	.2	.6
496 JEWISH EST[1]	1	NA	0	-	-
497 BLACK BAPT EST[2]	NA	4,175	5,530*	1.0	3.1
498 INDEP.CHARIS.[3]	3	NA	2,500	.5	1.4
499 INDEP.NON-CHAR[3]	6	NA	6,325	1.1	3.6
ARIZONA	**2,766**	**446,650**	**1,577,427***	**43.0**	**100.0**
005 AME ZION	1	68	87	-	-
011 A.W.M.C.	2	25	32*	-	-
019 AMER BAPT USA	42	9,526	12,076*	.3	.8
039 AP CHR CH(NAZ)	2	187	237*	-	-
040 AP CHR CH-AMER	2	210	370	-	-
045 APOSTOLIC LUTH	1	10	30	-	-
053 ASSEMB OF GOD	218	30,468	49,962	1.4	3.2
057 BAPT GEN CONF	8	715	904*	-	.1
059 BAPT MISS ASSN	5	96	124*	-	-
071 BRETHREN (ASH)	2	144	180*	-	-
081 CATHOLIC	243	NA	655,664	17.9	41.6
081b *BYZAN RUTH*	3	*NA*	*1,530*	-	*.1*
081c *CHALDEAN*	1	*NA*	*300*	-	-
081d *LATIN*	236	*NA*	*653,145*	*17.8*	*41.4*
081f *MELKITE-GK*	1	*NA*	*523*	-	-
081h *UKRAINIAN*	2	*NA*	*166*	-	-
089 CHR & MISS AL	22	655	1,698	-	.1
093 CHR CH (DISC)	25	4,060	4,925	.1	.3
097 CHR CHS&CHS CR	71	16,818	21,379*	.6	1.4
105 CHRISTIAN REF	11	1,075	1,673	-	.1
111 CH CR,SCIENTST	30	NR	NR	-	-
121 CH GOD (ABR)	2	398	504*	-	-
123 CH GOD (ANDER)	19	2,264	2,465	.1	.2
127 CH GOD (CLEVE)	38	2,928	3,719*	.1	.2
133 CH GOD(7TH)DEN	2	30	53	-	-
143 CG IN CR(MENN)	2	134	171*	-	-
145 CH GOD PROPHCY	8	269	341*	-	-
151 L-D SAINTS	469	NA	199,761	5.5	12.7
157 CH OF BRETHREN	4	356	450*	-	-
163 CH OF LUTH BR	3	135	343	-	-
164 CH LUTH CONF	1	88	142	-	-
165 CH OF NAZARENE	88	10,622	14,991	.4	1.0
167 CHS OF CHRIST	136	11,585	15,334	.4	1.0

NA–Not applicable   NR–Not reported   *Total adherents estimated from known number of communicant, confirmed, full members.   - Represents a percent less than 0.1.   Percentages may not total due to rounding.
[1]See Appendix E   [2]See Appendix F   [3]See Appendix G   Lines in *italic* represent a breakdown of Catholic rites or Friends affiliations. They are included in their respective denominational total.

Table 3. Churches and Church Membership by State and Denomination: 1990

State and Denomination	Number of churches	Communicant, confirmed, full members	Total adherents Number	Total adherents Percent of total population	Total adherents Percent of total adherents
171 CH GOD-GEN CON	1	0	0*	-	-
175 CONGR CHR CHS	2	446	565*	-	-
179 CONSRV BAPT	91	NR	NR	-	-
185 CUMBER PRESB	1	86	123	-	-
193 EPISCOPAL	71	20,033	26,780	.7	1.7
203 EVAN FREE CH	17	1,401	2,644	.1	.2
207 E.L.C.A.	88	40,751	54,473	1.5	3.5
209 EVAN LUTH SYN	3	201	242	-	-
215 EVAN METH CH	7	294	377*	-	-
216 EVAN PRESBY CH	2	40	40	-	-
217 FIRE BAPTIZED	3	13	16*	-	-
220 FREE LUTHERAN	2	90	130	-	-
221 FREE METHODIST	17	821	1,117	-	.1
223 FREE WILL BAPT	13	773	979*	-	.1
226 FRIENDS-USA	14	493	629*	-	-
226b EFI	4	50	74*	-	-
226e FUM	3	223	270	-	-
226f INDEPENDNT	7	220	285*	-	-
237 GC MENN BR CHS	1	43	54*	-	-
246 GREEK ORTHODOX	5	NR	NR	-	-
249 AP CATH ASSYR	0	48	0	-	-
259 IFCA	9	NR	NR	-	-
263 INT FOURSQ GOS	34	3,191	4,019*	.1	.3
283 LUTH—MO SYNOD	60	17,501	23,708	.6	1.5
284 LUTH CH-AM ASC	1	7	10	-	-
285 MENNONITE CH	15	1,093	1,587	-	.1
287 MENN GEN CONF	9	176	221	-	-
291 MISSIONARY CH	4	981	1,154	-	.1
293 MORAV CH-NORTH	1	80	121	-	-
325 OLD REG BAPT	1	9	11*	-	-
329 OPEN BIBLE STD	1	NR	NR	-	-
331 ORTH CH IN AM	1	NR	NR	-	-
339 PENT CH OF GOD	40	1,374	3,073	.1	.2
349 PENT HOLINESS	13	330	429*	-	-
353 CHR BRETHREN	9	639	1,141	-	.1
355 PRESB CH (USA)	95	28,447	36,129*	1.0	2.3
356 PRESB CH AMER	10	510	654	-	-
371 REF CH IN AM	9	1,398	2,666	.1	.2
375 REF EPISCOPAL	1	11	12	-	-
397 ROMANIAN ORTH	1	NR	NR	-	-
403 SALVATION ARMY	17	1,814	1,945	.1	.1
413 S.D.A.	58	9,238	11,777*	.3	.7
419 SO BAPT CONV	268	127,818	162,887*	4.4	10.3
435 UNITARIAN-UNIV	10	1,526	1,998	.1	.1
436 UNITED BAPT	1	15	19*	-	-
438 UN BRETH IN CR	6	274	288	-	-
443 UN C OF CHRIST	31	13,445	17,010*	.5	1.1
449 UN METHODIST	113	47,008	59,504*	1.6	3.8
467 WESLEYAN	15	485	2,147	.1	.1
469 WELS	50	8,116	12,152	.3	.8
496 JEWISH EST[1]	26	NA	70,850	1.9	4.5
497 BLACK BAPT EST[2]	NA	22,765	28,851*	.8	1.8
498 INDEP.CHARIS.[3]	30	NA	23,580	.6	1.5
499 INDEP.NON-CHAR[3]	32	NA	33,700	.9	2.1
ARKANSAS	**5,209**	**1,033,124**	**1,425,192***	**60.6**	**100.0**
005 AME ZION	27	4,132	5,092	.2	.4
019 AMER BAPT USA	1	46	57*	-	-
053 ASSEMB OF GOD	434	32,156	55,438	2.4	3.9
055 AS REF PRES CH	6	409	452	-	-
057 BAPT GEN CONF	1	257	316*	-	-
059 BAPT MISS ASSN	365	61,979	78,121*	3.3	5.5
061 BEACHY AMISH	2	42	52*	-	-
081 CATHOLIC	134	NA	72,952	3.1	5.1
081d LATIN	134	NA	72,952	3.1	5.1
089 CHR & MISS AL	8	189	458	-	-
093 CHR CH (DISC)	68	8,208	10,773	.5	.8
097 CHR CHS&CHS CR	61	6,820	8,499*	.4	.6
111 CH CR,SCIENTST	18	NR	NR	-	-
121 CH GOD (ABR)	5	165	205*	-	-
123 CH GOD (ANDER)	30	1,313	1,773	.1	.1
127 CH GOD (CLEVE)	83	5,810	7,408*	.3	.5
133 CH GOD(7TH)DEN	4	134	176	-	-
143 CG IN CR(MENN)	2	111	140*	-	-
145 CH GOD PROPHCY	42	1,160	1,469*	.1	.1
151 L-D SAINTS	43	NA	10,446	.4	.7
157 CH OF BRETHREN	1	56	73*	-	-
165 CH OF NAZARENE	117	11,194	15,394	.7	1.1
167 CHS OF CHRIST	760	66,736	86,502	3.7	6.1

State and Denomination	Number of churches	Communicant, confirmed, full members	Total adherents Number	Total adherents Percent of total population	Total adherents Percent of total adherents
171 CH GOD-GEN CON	11	329	402*	-	-
185 CUMBER PRESB	66	4,822	5,082	.2	.4
193 EPISCOPAL	57	10,339	13,845	.6	1.0
203 EVAN FREE CH	7	233	385	-	-
207 E.L.C.A.	18	4,334	5,178	.2	.4
215 EVAN METH CH	2	209	265*	-	-
216 EVAN PRESBY CH	1	19	19	-	-
217 FIRE BAPTIZED	1	18	22*	-	-
220 FREE LUTHERAN	1	44	55	-	-
221 FREE METHODIST	3	25	49	-	-
223 FREE WILL BAPT	201	20,167	25,237*	1.1	1.8
226 FRIENDS-USA	4	53	94*	-	-
226c FGC	3	40	78	-	-
226g INDEP EVAN	1	13	16*	-	-
237 GC MENN BR CHS	2	79	97*	-	-
246 GREEK ORTHODOX	3	NR	NR	-	-
259 IFCA	9	NR	NR	-	-
263 INT FOURSQ GOS	10	403	504*	-	-
283 LUTH—MO SYNOD	60	11,244	14,154	.6	1.0
285 MENNONITE CH	10	274	361	-	-
331 ORTH CH IN AM	1	NR	NR	-	-
339 PENT CH OF GOD	116	4,091	8,865	.4	.6
349 PENT HOLINESS	13	403	508*	-	-
353 CHR BRETHREN	2	45	90	-	-
355 PRESB CH (USA)	136	23,068	28,947*	1.2	2.0
356 PRESB CH AMER	10	721	944	-	.1
361 PRIM BAPT ASCS	30	924	1,147*	-	.1
403 SALVATION ARMY	12	950	1,041	-	.1
413 S.D.A.	57	5,118	6,393*	.3	.4
415 S-D BAPTIST GC	4	183	234*	-	-
419 SO BAPT CONV	1,290	490,106	617,524*	26.3	43.3
435 UNITARIAN-UNIV	6	463	582	-	-
436 UNITED BAPT	20	1,210	1,514*	.1	.1
443 UN C OF CHRIST	3	186	240*	-	-
449 UN METHODIST	788	156,962	197,402*	8.4	13.9
467 WESLEYAN	4	130	273	-	-
469 WELS	5	248	332	-	-
496 JEWISH EST[1]	12	NA	2,389	.1	.2
497 BLACK BAPT EST[2]	NA	94,807	121,542*	5.2	8.5
498 INDEP.CHARIS.[3]	5	NA	2,065	.1	.1
499 INDEP.NON-CHAR[3]	17	NA	11,615	.5	.8
CALIFORNIA	**14,427**	**2,752,215**	**12,585,339***	**42.3**	**100.0**
001 ADVENT CHR CH	12	774	968*	-	-
005 AME ZION	28	11,031	14,264	-	.1
011 A.W.M.C.	1	21	27*	-	-
019 AMER BAPT USA	555	145,509	184,723*	.6	1.5
039 AP CHR CH(NAZ)	8	392	498*	-	-
040 AP CHR CH-AMER	3	70	125	-	-
045 APOSTOLIC LUTH	2	58	89	-	-
053 ASSEMB OF GOD	1,123	157,872	263,059	.9	2.1
057 BAPT GEN CONF	125	34,442	43,661*	.1	.3
059 BAPT MISS ASSN	18	1,233	1,584*	-	-
063 BEREAN FUND CH	4	319	660	-	-
071 BRETHREN (ASH)	5	297	386*	-	-
075 BRETHREN IN CR	14	1,886	2,066	-	-
081 CATHOLIC	1,280	NA	7,142,067	24.0	56.7
081a ARMENIAN	1	NA	14,700	-	.1
081b BYZAN RUTH	11	NA	2,366	-	-
081c CHALDEAN	6	NA	14,500	-	.1
081d LATIN	1,248	NA	7,100,070	23.9	56.4
081e MARONITE	3	NA	4,748	-	-
081f MELKITE-GK	7	NA	5,073	-	-
081h UKRAINIAN	4	NA	610	-	-
089 CHR & MISS AL	189	22,610	38,525	.1	.3
093 CHR CH (DISC)	171	27,159	39,654	.1	.3
097 CHR CHS&CHS CR	230	50,365	63,930*	.2	.5
105 CHRISTIAN REF	84	14,363	22,172	.1	.2
111 CH CR,SCIENTST	295	NR	NR	-	-
121 CH GOD (ABR)	2	69	87*	-	-
123 CH GOD (ANDER)	130	15,081	16,586	.1	.1
127 CH GOD (CLEVE)	160	13,586	17,457*	.1	.1
133 CH GOD(7TH)DEN	22	1,082	1,520	-	-
143 CG IN CR(MENN)	3	889	1,215*	-	-
145 CH GOD PROPHCY	113	3,976	5,119*	-	-
151 L-D SAINTS	1,323	NA	533,741	1.8	4.2
157 CH OF BRETHREN	36	4,213	5,435*	-	-
163 CH OF LUTH BR	3	165	429	-	-
164 CH LUTH CONF	2	143	196	-	-

NA–Not applicable   NR–Not reported   *Total adherents estimated from known number of communicant, confirmed, full members.   - Represents a percent less than 0.1.   Percentages may not total due to rounding.
[1]See Appendix E   [2]See Appendix F   [3]See Appendix G   Lines in *italic* represent a breakdown of Catholic rites or Friends affiliations. They are included in their respective denominational total.

Table 3. Churches and Church Membership by State and Denomination: 1990

State and Denomination	Number of churches	Communicant, confirmed, full members	Total adherents Number	Percent of total population	Percent of total adherents
165 CH OF NAZARENE	397	56,862	92,273	.3	.7
167 CHS OF CHRIST	694	70,457	92,154	.3	.7
171 CH GOD-GEN CON	10	256	337*	-	-
175 CONGR CHR CHS	39	7,704	9,742*	-	.1
176 CCC, NOT NAT'L	4	1,182	1,539*	-	-
179 CONSRV BAPT	176	NR	NR	-	-
181 CONSRV CONGR	13	7,339	9,253*	-	.1
185 CUMBER PRESB	7	1,064	1,158	-	-
193 EPISCOPAL	450	122,124	178,263	.6	1.4
195 ESTONIAN ELC	2	421	523*	-	-
203 EVAN FREE CH	158	24,787	39,874	.1	.3
207 E.L.C.A.	477	141,854	193,389	.6	1.5
209 EVAN LUTH SYN	9	427	550	-	-
215 EVAN METH CH	9	577	734*	-	-
216 EVAN PRESBY CH	6	302	315	-	-
217 FIRE BAPTIZED	5	40	51*	-	-
220 FREE LUTHERAN	4	473	630	-	-
221 FREE METHODIST	88	5,844	7,976	-	.1
223 FREE WILL BAPT	70	5,529	7,276*	-	.1
226 FRIENDS-USA	88	8,262	10,916*	-	.1
226c FGC	*1*	*27*	*45**	-	-
226e FUM	*42*	*6,871*	*8,320**	-	.1
226f INDEPENDNT	*45*	*1,364*	*2,551*	-	-
237 GC MENN BR CHS	46	6,917	9,186*	-	.1
246 GREEK ORTHODOX	40	NR	NR	-	-
249 AP CATH ASSYR	7	1,144	5,208	-	-
259 IFCA	93	NR	NR	-	-
263 INT FOURSQ GOS	497	87,987	111,850*	.4	.9
274 LAT EVAN LUTH	4	915	1,021	-	-
283 LUTH—MO SYNOD	395	107,246	143,987	.5	1.1
284 LUTH CH-AM ASC	9	902	1,173	-	-
285 MENNONITE CH	18	774	1,346	-	-
287 MENN GEN CONF	13	941	1,162	-	-
291 MISSIONARY CH	36	5,266	6,989	-	.1
293 MORAV CH-NORTH	4	463	647	-	-
307 NETH REF CONGR	1	18	27	-	-
313 N AM BAPT CONF	25	7,846	10,053*	-	.1
329 OPEN BIBLE STD	40	NR	NR	-	-
331 ORTH CH IN AM	28	NR	NR	-	-
339 PENT CH OF GOD	240	8,195	21,225	.1	.2
349 PENT HOLINESS	90	7,880	10,030*	-	.1
353 CHR BRETHREN	59	3,782	6,107	-	-
355 PRESB CH (USA)	576	205,382	258,854*	.9	2.1
356 PRESB CH AMER	51	3,655	4,534	-	-
361 PRIM BAPT ASCS	9	265	339*	-	-
367 PROT CONF (LU)	1	50	75	-	-
371 REF CH IN AM	48	14,400	37,092	.1	.3
373 REF CH IN U.S.	7	470	665	-	-
375 REF EPISCOPAL	3	77	95	-	-
397 ROMANIAN ORTH	7	NR	NR	-	-
403 SALVATION ARMY	96	9,941	11,047	-	.1
413 S.D.A.	500	161,384	206,514*	.7	1.6
415 S-D BAPTIST GC	6	198	251*	-	-
419 SO BAPT CONV	1,114	394,600	504,516*	1.7	4.0
423 SYRIAN ANTIOCH	4	NA	9,400	-	.1
435 UNITARIAN-UNIV	74	12,026	14,740	-	.1
438 UN BRETH IN CR	5	200	200	-	-
443 UN C OF CHRIST	254	51,493	64,855*	.2	.5
449 UN METHODIST	735	210,395	266,306*	.9	2.1
467 WESLEYAN	44	6,370	14,542	-	.1
469 WELS	44	7,049	9,812	-	.1
496 JEWISH EST[1]	293	NA	918,935	3.1	7.3
497 BLACK BAPT EST[2]	NA	470,875	595,070*	2.0	4.7
498 INDEP.CHARIS.[3]	141	NA	148,115	.5	1.2
499 INDEP.NON-CHAR[3]	123	NA	142,175	.5	1.1
COLORADO	**2,813**	**483,532**	**1,294,376***	**39.3**	**100.0**
005 AME ZION	2	290	336	-	-
019 AMER BAPT USA	84	22,620	28,333*	.9	2.2
039 AP CHR CH(NAZ)	1	81	99*	-	-
040 AP CHR CH-AMER	1	37	67	-	-
053 ASSEMB OF GOD	165	18,574	34,138	1.0	2.6
057 BAPT GEN CONF	24	4,825	6,123*	.2	.5
059 BAPT MISS ASSN	2	72	96*	-	-
063 BEREAN FUND CH	3	129	233	-	-
075 BRETHREN IN CR	3	112	253	-	-
081 CATHOLIC	286	NA	482,892	14.7	37.3
081b BYZAN RUTH	*2*	*NA*	*259*	-	-
081d LATIN	*283*	*NA*	*482,480*	*14.6*	*37.3*

State and Denomination	Number of churches	Communicant, confirmed, full members	Total adherents Number	Percent of total population	Percent of total adherents
081h UKRAINIAN	*1*	*NA*	*153*	-	-
089 CHR & MISS AL	21	1,036	2,037	.1	.2
093 CHR CH (DISC)	41	9,696	14,911	.5	1.2
097 CHR CHS&CHS CR	77	14,332	18,265*	.6	1.4
105 CHRISTIAN REF	18	2,952	4,516	.1	.3
111 CH CR,SCIENTST	37	NR	NR	-	-
123 CH GOD (ANDER)	29	1,711	2,141	.1	.2
127 CH GOD (CLEVE)	21	2,407	3,044*	.1	.2
133 CH GOD(7TH)DEN	2	152	228	-	-
145 CH GOD PROPHCY	19	418	529*	-	-
151 L-D SAINTS	193	NA	70,313	2.1	5.4
157 CH OF BRETHREN	9	885	1,121*	-	.1
163 CH OF LUTH BR	4	137	331	-	-
164 CH LUTH CONF	2	112	167	-	-
165 CH OF NAZARENE	88	13,224	17,455	.5	1.3
167 CHS OF CHRIST	150	12,866	17,312	.5	1.3
175 CONGR CHR CHS	3	263	329*	-	-
176 CCC, NOT NAT'L	1	838	1,061*	-	.1
179 CONSRV BAPT	48	NR	NR	-	-
181 CONSRV CONGR	4	869	1,128*	-	.1
193 EPISCOPAL	104	23,355	36,119	1.1	2.8
203 EVAN FREE CH	43	4,435	7,732	.2	.6
207 E.L.C.A.	119	44,537	61,668	1.9	4.8
209 EVAN LUTH SYN	1	43	55	-	-
216 EVAN PRESBY CH	11	8,421	8,835	.3	.7
221 FREE METHODIST	14	886	1,288	-	.1
223 FREE WILL BAPT	6	191	244*	-	-
226 FRIENDS-USA	27	1,488	1,862*	.1	.1
226b EFI	*17*	*1,009*	*1,247**	-	.1
226e FUM	*1*	*29*	*37**	-	-
226f INDEPENDNT	*9*	*450*	*578**	-	-
237 GC MENN BR CHS	3	252	316*	-	-
246 GREEK ORTHODOX	7	NR	NR	-	-
259 IFCA	19	NR	NR	-	-
263 INT FOURSQ GOS	47	6,443	8,172*	.2	.6
274 LAT EVAN LUTH	2	167	188	-	-
283 LUTH—MO SYNOD	114	34,818	47,262	1.4	3.7
284 LUTH CH-AM ASC	1	169	242	-	-
285 MENNONITE CH	18	1,252	1,849	.1	.1
287 MENN GEN CONF	6	218	293	-	-
313 N AM BAPT CONF	4	315	408*	-	-
320 "OLD" MB ASCS	1	18	22*	-	-
329 OPEN BIBLE STD	16	NR	NR	-	-
331 ORTH CH IN AM	6	NR	NR	-	-
339 PENT CH OF GOD	10	290	759	-	.1
349 PENT HOLINESS	16	919	1,152*	-	.1
353 CHR BRETHREN	20	1,510	2,463	.1	.2
355 PRESB CH (USA)	129	40,236	50,831*	1.5	3.9
356 PRESB CH AMER	10	1,779	2,228	.1	.2
371 REF CH IN AM	8	1,547	3,099	.1	.2
373 REF CH IN U.S.	4	85	119	-	-
403 SALVATION ARMY	11	500	628	-	-
413 S.D.A.	75	13,458	16,892*	.5	1.3
415 S-D BAPTIST GC	2	342	430*	-	-
419 SO BAPT CONV	192	64,265	81,627*	2.5	6.3
431 UKRANIAN AMER	1	NR	NR	-	-
435 UNITARIAN-UNIV	12	2,113	2,921	.1	.2
443 UN C OF CHRIST	73	17,818	22,622*	.7	1.7
449 UN METHODIST	222	72,042	91,310*	2.8	7.1
467 WESLEYAN	18	877	2,080	.1	.2
469 WELS	21	2,253	3,260	.1	.3
496 JEWISH EST[1]	26	NA	48,550	1.5	3.8
497 BLACK BAPT EST[2]	NA	27,852	34,887*	1.1	2.7
498 INDEP.CHARIS.[3]	23	NA	26,450	.8	2.0
499 INDEP.NON-CHAR[3]	33	NA	18,055	.5	1.4
CONNECTICUT	**1,944**	**413,414**	**2,047,646***	**62.3**	**100.0**
001 ADVENT CHR CH	9	524	640*	-	-
005 AME ZION	31	18,427	22,155	.7	1.1
007 ALBAN ORTH ARC	1	NR	NR	-	-
019 AMER BAPT USA	127	39,470	48,204*	1.5	2.4
022 EASTERN ORTH	4	1,333	1,333	-	.1
039 AP CHR CH(NAZ)	1	18	22*	-	-
040 AP CHR CH-AMER	1	335	595	-	-
049 ARMEN AP CH AM	1	500	1,600	-	.1
053 ASSEMB OF GOD	76	8,437	14,060	.4	.7
057 BAPT GEN CONF	13	1,981	2,412*	.1	.1
081 CATHOLIC	416	NA	1,374,747	41.8	67.1
081b BYZAN RUTH	*5*	*NA*	*1,970*	*.1*	*.1*

NA–Not applicable   NR–Not reported   *Total adherents estimated from known number of communicant, confirmed, full members.   - Represents a percent less than 0.1.   Percentages may not total due to rounding.
[1]See Appendix E   [2]See Appendix F   [3]See Appendix G   Lines in *italic* represent a breakdown of Catholic rites or Friends affiliations. They are included in their respective denominational total.

14

Table 3. Churches and Church Membership by State and Denomination: 1990

State and Denomination	Number of churches	Communicant, confirmed, full members	Total adherents Number	Total adherents Percent of total population	Total adherents Percent of total adherents
081d LATIN	398	NA	1,365,943	41.6	66.7
081e MARONITE	3	NA	3,427	.1	.2
081f MELKITE-GK	2	NA	1,153	-	.1
081h UKRAINIAN	8	NA	2,254	.1	.1
083 CHRIST CATH CH	1	4	4	-	-
089 CHR & MISS AL	12	610	1,363	-	.1
093 CHR CH (DISC)	5	424	683	-	-
097 CHR CHS&CHS CR	8	435	530*	-	-
105 CHRISTIAN REF	1	167	263	-	-
111 CH CR,SCIENTST	26	NR	NR	-	-
123 CH GOD (ANDER)	2	245	310	-	-
127 CH GOD (CLEVE)	30	2,928	3,569*	.1	.2
145 CH GOD PROPHCY	10	280	342*	-	-
151 L-D SAINTS	24	NA	8,075	.2	.4
163 CH OF LUTH BR	2	121	164	-	-
165 CH OF NAZARENE	19	1,115	2,453	.1	.1
167 CHS OF CHRIST	31	1,629	2,438	.1	.1
175 CONGR CHR CHS	26	3,664	4,491*	.1	.2
176 CCC, NOT NAT'L	12	3,473	4,240*	.1	.2
179 CONSRV BAPT	14	NR	NR	-	-
181 CONSRV CONGR	4	224	280*	-	-
193 EPISCOPAL	186	48,042	78,804	2.4	3.8
195 ESTONIAN ELC	1	567	690*	-	-
203 EVAN FREE CH	16	1,736	2,519	.1	.1
207 E.L.C.A.	76	27,432	35,537	1.1	1.7
221 FREE METHODIST	1	97	199	-	-
226 FRIENDS-USA	10	636	791*	-	-
226d FGC & FUM	10	636	791*	-	-
246 GREEK ORTHODOX	16	NR	NR	-	-
249 AP CATH ASSYR	1	125	488	-	-
257 HUTTERIAN BR	1	NA	225	-	-
259 IFCA	3	NR	NR	-	-
263 INT FOURSQ GOS	5	124	152*	-	-
274 LAT EVAN LUTH	2	224	228	-	-
283 LUTH—MO SYNOD	36	11,937	15,206	.5	.7
285 MENNONITE CH	3	130	195	-	-
313 N AM BAPT CONF	1	30	37*	-	-
329 OPEN BIBLE STD	1	NR	NR	-	-
331 ORTH CH IN AM	12	NR	NR	-	-
339 PENT CH OF GOD	1	30	85	-	-
349 PENT HOLINESS	1	32	39*	-	-
353 CHR BRETHREN	15	1,386	2,178	.1	.1
355 PRESB CH (USA)	20	8,372	10,191*	.3	.5
356 PRESB CH AMER	3	146	190	-	-
397 ROMANIAN ORTH	1	NR	NR	-	-
403 SALVATION ARMY	18	1,357	1,461	-	.1
413 S.D.A.	28	3,962	4,837*	.1	.2
415 S-D BAPTIST GC	2	73	89*	-	-
419 SO BAPT CONV	28	7,278	8,925*	.3	.4
431 UKRANIAN AMER	1	NR	NR	-	-
435 UNITARIAN-UNIV	20	3,067	4,167	.1	.2
443 UN C OF CHRIST	260	110,800	135,231*	4.1	6.6
449 UN METHODIST	134	46,214	56,372*	1.7	2.8
467 WESLEYAN	1	70	165	-	-
469 WELS	2	196	244	-	-
496 JEWISH EST[1]	106	NA	115,460	3.5	5.6
497 BLACK BAPT EST[2]	NA	53,007	64,609*	2.0	3.2
498 INDEP.CHARIS.[3]	16	NA	9,815	.3	.5
499 INDEP.NON-CHAR[3]	9	NA	3,540	.1	.2
DELAWARE	**523**	**134,904**	**306,364***	**46.0**	**100.0**
005 AME ZION	4	461	535	.1	.2
019 AMER BAPT USA	10	3,379	4,217*	.6	1.4
040 AP CHR CH-AMER	1	21	36	-	-
053 ASSEMB OF GOD	12	1,116	2,457	.4	.8
057 BAPT GEN CONF	2	762	944*	.1	.3
066 BIBLE CH OF CR	1	290	358*	.1	.1
071 BRETHREN (ASH)	1	33	41*	-	-
081 CATHOLIC	45	NA	116,341	17.5	38.0
081d LATIN	44	NA	115,696	17.4	37.8
081h UKRAINIAN	1	NA	645	.1	.2
089 CHR & MISS AL	7	345	661	.1	.2
093 CHR CH (DISC)	1	91	141	-	-
097 CHR CHS&CHS CR	9	850	1,059*	.2	.3
111 CH CR,SCIENTST	5	NR	NR	-	-
123 CH GOD (ANDER)	5	239	303	-	.1
127 CH GOD (CLEVE)	13	1,659	2,053*	.3	.7
145 CH GOD PROPHCY	9	245	305*	-	.1
151 L-D SAINTS	8	NA	2,786	.4	.9
157 CH OF BRETHREN	2	208	261*	-	.1
165 CH OF NAZARENE	10	1,117	1,691	.3	.6
167 CHS OF CHRIST	9	865	1,168	.2	.4
179 CONSRV BAPT	1	NR	NR	-	-
193 EPISCOPAL	38	9,239	13,307	2.0	4.3
203 EVAN FREE CH	1	601	601	.1	.2
207 E.L.C.A.	11	5,061	6,780	1.0	2.2
223 FREE WILL BAPT	4	496	614*	.1	.2
226 FRIENDS-USA	8	623	774*	.1	.3
226c FGC	8	623	774*	.1	.3
246 GREEK ORTHODOX	1	NR	NR	-	-
259 IFCA	1	NR	NR	-	-
263 INT FOURSQ GOS	1	0	0*	-	-
265 INT PENT C CHR	1	6	12	-	-
274 LAT EVAN LUTH	1	100	117	-	-
283 LUTH—MO SYNOD	7	1,657	2,172	.3	.7
285 MENNONITE CH	7	668	915	.1	.3
286 E.PA MENNONITE	2	93	118*	-	-
323 OLD ORD AMISH	8	NA	1,200	.2	.4
331 ORTH CH IN AM	1	NR	NR	-	-
353 CHR BRETHREN	2	80	115	-	-
355 PRESB CH (USA)	37	12,422	15,401*	2.3	5.0
356 PRESB CH AMER	8	1,935	2,539	.4	.8
375 REF EPISCOPAL	1	14	14	-	-
403 SALVATION ARMY	2	161	239	-	.1
413 S.D.A.	12	1,633	2,044*	.3	.7
419 SO BAPT CONV	13	4,621	5,772*	.9	1.9
435 UNITARIAN-UNIV	3	1,126	1,453	.2	.5
443 UN C OF CHRIST	3	529	671*	.1	.2
449 UN METHODIST	169	49,118	61,091*	9.2	19.9
467 WESLEYAN	17	1,149	2,703	.4	.9
469 WELS	1	128	191	-	.1
496 JEWISH EST[1]	4	NA	9,500	1.4	3.1
497 BLACK BAPT EST[2]	NA	31,763	39,514*	5.9	12.9
499 INDEP.NON-CHAR[3]	4	NA	3,150	.5	1.0
DISTRICT OF COLUMBIA	**343**	**219,241**	**374,160***	**61.7**	**100.0**
005 AME ZION	15	33,400	39,500	6.5	10.6
019 AMER BAPT USA	39	28,560	33,744*	5.6	9.0
022 EASTERN ORTH	1	10	10	-	-
053 ASSEMB OF GOD	5	726	771	.1	.2
055 AS REF PRES CH	1	22	28	-	-
061 BEACHY AMISH	1	29	34*	-	-
071 BRETHREN (ASH)	1	32	38*	-	-
081 CATHOLIC	41	NA	77,532	12.8	20.7
081d LATIN	38	NA	75,000	12.4	20.0
081e MARONITE	1	NA	444	.1	.1
081h UKRAINIAN	2	NA	2,088	.3	.6
089 CHR & MISS AL	2	141	169	-	-
093 CHR CH (DISC)	5	1,136	1,358	.2	.4
097 CHR CHS&CHS CR	10	0	0*	-	-
105 CHRISTIAN REF	1	141	179	-	-
111 CH CR,SCIENTST	6	NR	NR	-	-
123 CH GOD (ANDER)	6	483	666	.1	.2
127 CH GOD (CLEVE)	3	232	274*	-	.1
145 CH GOD PROPHCY	2	61	72*	-	-
151 L-D SAINTS	1	NA	336	.1	.1
157 CH OF BRETHREN	1	219	259*	-	.1
165 CH OF NAZARENE	2	595	788	.1	.2
167 CHS OF CHRIST	5	660	972	.2	.3
179 CONSRV BAPT	1	NR	NR	-	-
193 EPISCOPAL	34	11,767	16,273	2.7	4.3
207 E.L.C.A.	13	3,482	4,353	.7	1.2
226 FRIENDS-USA	4	540	638*	.1	.2
226d FGC & FUM	4	540	638*	.1	.2
246 GREEK ORTHODOX	2	NR	NR	-	-
249 AP CATH ASSYR	0	1	1	-	-
263 INT FOURSQ GOS	1	0	0*	-	-
283 LUTH—MO SYNOD	4	760	1,156	.2	.3
285 MENNONITE CH	5	264	466	.1	.1
293 MORAV CH-NORTH	1	114	160	-	-
331 ORTH CH IN AM	1	NR	NR	-	-
353 CHR BRETHREN	5	179	283	-	.1
355 PRESB CH (USA)	17	8,150	9,629*	1.6	2.6
403 SALVATION ARMY	3	432	445	.1	.1
413 S.D.A.	10	4,702	5,556*	.9	1.5
415 S-D BAPTIST GC	1	80	95*	-	-
419 SO BAPT CONV	29	14,893	17,597*	2.9	4.7
423 SYRIAN ANTIOCH	1	NA	500	.1	.1

NA–Not applicable   NR–Not reported   *Total adherents estimated from known number of communicant, confirmed, full members.   - Represents a percent less than 0.1.   Percentages may not total due to rounding.
[1]See Appendix E   [2]See Appendix F   [3]See Appendix G   Lines in *italic* represent a breakdown of Catholic rites or Friends affiliations. They are included in their respective denominational total.

15

Table 3. Churches and Church Membership by State and Denomination: 1990

State and Denomination	Number of churches	Communicant, confirmed, full members	Total adherents		
			Number	Percent of total population	Percent of total adherents
435 UNITARIAN-UNIV	3	651	765	.1	.2
443 UN C OF CHRIST	8	4,185	4,945*	.8	1.3
449 UN METHODIST	35	15,506	18,321*	3.0	4.9
496 JEWISH EST[1]	13	NA	25,400	4.2	6.8
497 BLACK BAPT EST[2]	NA	87,088	102,897*	17.0	27.5
498 INDEP.CHARIS.[3]	3	NA	5,950	1.0	1.6
499 INDEP.NON-CHAR[3]	1	NA	2,000	.3	.5
FLORIDA	**8,577**	**2,651,825**	**5,672,756***	**43.8**	**100.0**
001 ADVENT CHR CH	35	1,839	2,285*	-	-
005 AME ZION	32	6,304	7,983	.1	.1
011 A.W.M.C.	1	0	0*	-	-
019 AMER BAPT USA	33	7,805	9,449*	.1	.2
022 EASTERN ORTH	2	116	116	-	-
039 AP CHR CH(NAZ)	3	72	85*	-	-
040 AP CHR CH-AMER	3	116	201	-	-
045 APOSTOLIC LUTH	1	78	154	-	-
049 ARMEN AP CH AM	1	200	500	-	-
053 ASSEMB OF GOD	576	84,077	134,297	1.0	2.4
055 AS REF PRES CH	13	3,074	3,607	-	.1
057 BAPT GEN CONF	20	1,819	2,212*	-	-
059 BAPT MISS ASSN	11	1,129	1,420*	-	-
061 BEACHY AMISH	1	145	165*	-	-
071 BRETHREN (ASH)	6	395	457*	-	-
075 BRETHREN IN CR	9	301	377	-	-
081 CATHOLIC	479	NA	1,598,457	12.4	28.2
081b *BYZAN RUTH*	8	*NA*	*1,747*	-	-
081d *LATIN*	464	*NA*	*1,593,771*	*12.3*	*28.1*
081e *MARONITE*	1	*NA*	*1,326*	-	-
081f *MELKITE-GK*	1	*NA*	*750*	-	-
081h *UKRAINIAN*	5	*NA*	*863*	-	-
089 CHR & MISS AL	119	8,083	15,133	.1	.3
093 CHR CH (DISC)	87	16,996	23,725	.2	.4
097 CHR CHS&CHS CR	179	35,695	43,070*	.3	.8
105 CHRISTIAN REF	16	1,885	2,713	-	-
111 CH CR,SCIENTST	94	NR	NR	-	-
123 CH GOD (ANDER)	105	10,326	12,440	.1	.2
127 CH GOD (CLEVE)	479	57,587	70,108*	.5	1.2
133 CH GOD(7TH)DEN	4	45	86	-	-
143 CG IN CR(MENN)	1	188	235*	-	-
145 CH GOD PROPHCY	125	4,301	5,276*	-	.1
146 CH GOD MTN ASM	5	213	258*	-	-
151 L-D SAINTS	160	NA	59,845	.5	1.1
157 CH OF BRETHREN	16	1,891	2,276*	-	-
163 CH OF LUTH BR	2	106	222	-	-
164 CH LUTH CONF	3	109	167	-	-
165 CH OF NAZARENE	227	26,323	39,413	.3	.7
167 CHS OF CHRIST	514	55,123	73,462	.6	1.3
175 CONGR CHR CHS	10	1,468	1,746*	-	-
176 CCC, NOT NAT'L	2	110	139*	-	-
179 CONSRV BAPT	15	NR	NR	-	-
181 CONSRV CONGR	1	18	22*	-	-
185 CUMBER PRESB	7	937	994	-	-
193 EPISCOPAL	334	114,236	158,595	1.2	2.8
195 ESTONIAN ELC	3	164	194*	-	-
199 EVAN CONGR CH	1	57	88	-	-
203 EVAN FREE CH	21	1,835	3,331	-	.1
207 E.L.C.A.	209	73,121	92,732	.7	1.6
209 EVAN LUTH SYN	6	675	858	-	-
215 EVAN METH CH	2	150	186*	-	-
216 EVAN PRESBY CH	8	2,140	2,271	-	-
221 FREE METHODIST	39	1,940	2,978	-	.1
223 FREE WILL BAPT	77	6,103	7,527*	.1	.1
226 FRIENDS-USA	25	800	1,460*	-	-
226b *EFI*	4	*285*	*567*	-	-
226d *FGC & FUM*	20	*457*	*821*	-	-
226e *FUM*	1	*58*	*72**	-	-
246 GREEK ORTHODOX	33	NR	NR	-	-
249 AP CATH ASSYR	0	15	47	-	-
259 IFCA	11	NR	NR	-	-
263 INT FOURSQ GOS	30	1,843	2,240*	-	-
266 INTRSTAT & ASC	1	89	111*	-	-
269 JASPER&PVB ASC	1	50	58*	-	-
274 LAT EVAN LUTH	2	295	303	-	-
283 LUTH—MO SYNOD	152	52,966	67,645	.5	1.2
284 LUTH CH-AM ASC	1	120	142	-	-
285 MENNONITE CH	31	2,918	4,435	-	.1
286 E.PA MENNONITE	1	39	49*	-	-
291 MISSIONARY CH	10	493	665	-	-

State and Denomination	Number of churches	Communicant, confirmed, full members	Total adherents		
			Number	Percent of total population	Percent of total adherents
295 MORAV CH-SOUTH	2	596	857	-	-
313 N AM BAPT CONF	2	85	101*	-	-
323 OLD ORD AMISH	1	NA	150	-	-
325 OLD REG BAPT	6	198	244*	-	-
329 OPEN BIBLE STD	29	NR	NR	-	-
331 ORTH CH IN AM	19	NR	NR	-	-
339 PENT CH OF GOD	25	938	1,705	-	-
349 PENT HOLINESS	87	9,609	11,815*	.1	.2
353 CHR BRETHREN	47	2,918	4,988	-	.1
355 PRESB CH (USA)	358	136,910	165,255*	1.3	2.9
356 PRESB CH AMER	94	31,031	35,998	.3	.6
361 PRIM BAPT ASCS	66	1,406	1,755*	-	-
363 PRIMITIVE METH	4	107	120	-	-
371 REF CH IN AM	16	2,454	4,350	-	.1
375 REF EPISCOPAL	2	23	23	-	-
397 ROMANIAN ORTH	1	NR	NR	-	-
403 SALVATION ARMY	37	4,516	4,880	-	.1
413 S.D.A.	229	46,968	57,336*	.4	1.0
415 S-D BAPTIST GC	5	233	278*	-	-
419 SO BAPT CONV	1,741	951,040	1,167,850*	9.0	20.6
423 SYRIAN ANTIOCH	2	NA	1,000	-	-
431 UKRANIAN AMER	1	NR	NR	-	-
435 UNITARIAN-UNIV	35	4,587	5,506	-	.1
436 UNITED BAPT	1	15	18*	-	-
438 UN BRETH IN CR	5	298	371	-	-
443 UN C OF CHRIST	112	36,621	43,854*	.3	.8
449 UN METHODIST	849	380,963	462,174*	3.6	8.1
467 WESLEYAN	41	2,498	7,014	.1	.1
469 WELS	36	3,924	5,317	-	.1
496 JEWISH EST[1]	183	NA	566,945	4.4	10.0
497 BLACK BAPT EST[2]	NA	444,964	544,592*	4.2	9.6
498 INDEP.CHARIS.[3]	38	NA	35,202	.3	.6
499 INDEP.NON-CHAR[3]	108	NA	84,048	.6	1.5
GEORGIA	**8,300**	**2,627,409**	**3,730,757***	**57.6**	**100.0**
001 ADVENT CHR CH	16	802	1,018*	-	-
005 AME ZION	32	5,651	6,748	.1	.2
019 AMER BAPT USA	16	9,114	11,389*	.2	.3
053 ASSEMB OF GOD	222	22,293	31,973	.5	.9
055 AS REF PRES CH	15	1,879	2,146	-	.1
059 BAPT MISS ASSN	1	153	197*	-	-
061 BEACHY AMISH	2	263	346*	-	-
075 BRETHREN IN CR	1	26	52	-	-
081 CATHOLIC	168	NA	210,210	3.2	5.6
081d *LATIN*	165	*NA*	*208,888*	*3.2*	*5.6*
081e *MARONITE*	1	*NA*	*276*	-	-
081f *MELKITE-GK*	2	*NA*	*1,046*	-	-
089 CHR & MISS AL	36	2,830	5,227	.1	.1
093 CHR CH (DISC)	70	9,620	14,083	.2	.4
097 CHR CHS&CHS CR	126	30,763	38,725*	.6	1.0
105 CHRISTIAN REF	3	120	207	-	-
111 CH CR,SCIENTST	23	NR	NR	-	-
123 CH GOD (ANDER)	52	2,165	2,828	-	.1
127 CH GOD (CLEVE)	466	76,097	96,173*	1.5	2.6
133 CH GOD(7TH)DEN	1	0	0	-	-
143 CG IN CR(MENN)	1	244	318*	-	-
145 CH GOD PROPHCY	153	5,646	7,170*	.1	.2
146 CH GOD MTN ASM	2	120	150*	-	-
151 L-D SAINTS	95	NA	32,593	.5	.9
157 CH OF BRETHREN	1	32	40*	-	-
165 CH OF NAZARENE	92	8,804	12,675	.2	.3
167 CHS OF CHRIST	402	34,799	46,832	.7	1.3
175 CONGR CHR CHS	2	133	170*	-	-
176 CCC, NOT NAT'L	1	100	129*	-	-
179 CONSRV BAPT	1	NR	NR	-	-
185 CUMBER PRESB	4	383	438	-	-
189 DUCK RIVR BAPT	2	121	151*	-	-
193 EPISCOPAL	155	46,550	62,738	1.0	1.7
203 EVAN FREE CH	3	223	400	-	-
207 E.L.C.A.	80	24,618	32,447	.5	.9
209 EVAN LUTH SYN	2	78	94	-	-
215 EVAN METH CH	10	1,170	1,478*	-	-
216 EVAN PRESBY CH	5	1,558	1,600	-	-
221 FREE METHODIST	5	131	150	-	-
223 FREE WILL BAPT	118	9,534	12,193*	.2	.3
226 FRIENDS-USA	11	144	380*	-	-
226b *EFI*	1	*45*	*69*	-	-
226c *FGC*	7	*72*	*243*	-	-
226d *FGC & FUM*	3	*27*	*68**	-	-

Table 3. Churches and Church Membership by State and Denomination: 1990

State and Denomination	Number of churches	Communicant, confirmed, full members	Total adherents Number	Percent of total population	Percent of total adherents
246 GREEK ORTHODOX	8	NR	NR	-	-
259 IFCA	1	NR	NR	-	-
263 INT FOURSQ GOS	9	974	1,240*	-	-
265 INT PENT C CHR	3	122	126	-	-
269 JASPER&PVB ASC	39	7,262	9,151*	.1	.2
283 LUTH—MO SYNOD	32	6,718	8,997	.1	.2
285 MENNONITE CH	7	245	387	-	-
286 E.PA MENNONITE	1	68	87*	-	-
287 MENN GEN CONF	1	0	0	-	-
289 NEW HOPE B ASC	21	2,332	2,995*	-	.1
295 MORAV CH-SOUTH	1	136	192	-	-
323 OLD ORD AMISH	1	NA	50	-	-
329 OPEN BIBLE STD	3	NR	NR	-	-
331 ORTH CH IN AM	3	NR	NR	-	-
339 PENT CH OF GOD	11	290	791	-	-
349 PENT HOLINESS	57	4,134	5,180*	.1	.1
353 CHR BRETHREN	16	1,150	1,920	-	.1
355 PRESB CH (USA)	305	80,776	101,274*	1.6	2.7
356 PRESB CH AMER	76	12,164	14,823	.2	.4
361 PRIM BAPT ASCS	273	10,697	13,559*	.2	.4
371 REF CH IN AM	1	167	249	-	-
403 SALVATION ARMY	27	2,872	3,074	-	.1
413 S.D.A.	112	22,400	28,162*	.4	.8
415 S-D BAPTIST GC	1	35	46*	-	-
419 SO BAPT CONV	3,041	1,249,723	1,582,520*	24.4	42.4
423 SYRIAN ANTIOCH	1	NA	500	-	-
430 TRUEVINE B ASC	3	458	561*	-	-
431 UKRANIAN AMER	1	NR	NR	-	-
435 UNITARIAN-UNIV	16	1,943	2,770	-	.1
443 UN C OF CHRIST	23	2,836	3,574*	.1	.1
449 UN METHODIST	1,659	418,835	530,076*	8.2	14.2
467 WESLEYAN	27	1,028	1,895	-	.1
469 WELS	5	635	954	-	-
496 JEWISH EST[1]	38	NA	72,747	1.1	1.9
497 BLACK BAPT EST[2]	NA	503,245	639,303*	9.9	17.1
498 INDEP.CHARIS.[3]	32	NA	33,265	.5	.9
499 INDEP.NON-CHAR[3]	50	NA	36,821	.6	1.0
HAWAII	**758**	**87,579**	**390,827***	**35.3**	**100.0**
019 AMER BAPT USA	4	697	866*	.1	.2
053 ASSEMB OF GOD	69	8,475	13,005	1.2	3.3
057 BAPT GEN CONF	3	152	190*	-	-
081 CATHOLIC	102	NA	232,780	21.0	59.6
081d *LATIN*	*102*	*NA*	*232,780*	*21.0*	*59.6*
089 CHR & MISS AL	9	848	1,485	.1	.4
093 CHR CH (DISC)	3	230	305	-	.1
097 CHR CHS&CHS CR	11	1,136	1,413*	.1	.4
105 CHRISTIAN REF	1	53	72	-	-
111 CH CR,SCIENTST	6	NR	NR	-	-
123 CH GOD (ANDER)	1	31	34	-	-
127 CH GOD (CLEVE)	12	1,255	1,578*	.1	.4
145 CH GOD PROPHCY	5	121	153*	-	-
151 L-D SAINTS	109	NA	38,303	3.5	9.8
165 CH OF NAZARENE	20	1,842	2,556	.2	.7
167 CHS OF CHRIST	13	811	1,076	.1	.3
175 CONGR CHR CHS	2	43	55*	-	-
176 CCC, NOT NAT'L	17	943	1,212*	.1	.3
179 CONSRV BAPT	3	NR	NR	-	-
181 CONSRV CONGR	1	20	26*	-	-
193 EPISCOPAL	40	6,990	10,396	.9	2.7
203 EVAN FREE CH	2	35	40	-	-
207 E.L.C.A.	12	2,879	3,944	.4	1.0
221 FREE METHODIST	1	0	15	-	-
223 FREE WILL BAPT	1	50	62*	-	-
226 FRIENDS-USA	7	91	137	-	-
226f *INDEPENDNT*	*7*	*91*	*137*	*-*	*-*
246 GREEK ORTHODOX	1	NR	NR	-	-
249 AP CATH ASSYR	0	3	11	-	-
263 INT FOURSQ GOS	21	3,727	4,726*	.4	1.2
283 LUTH—MO SYNOD	11	1,323	1,852	.2	.5
291 MISSIONARY CH	10	618	1,368	.1	.4
339 PENT CH OF GOD	1	32	46	-	-
349 PENT HOLINESS	7	744	931*	.1	.2
353 CHR BRETHREN	3	125	200	-	.1
355 PRESB CH (USA)	6	1,365	1,764*	.2	.5
356 PRESB CH AMER	1	71	97	-	-
403 SALVATION ARMY	11	1,155	1,267	.1	.3
413 S.D.A.	21	4,722	5,931*	.5	1.5
419 SO BAPT CONV	56	16,245	20,331*	1.8	5.2

State and Denomination	Number of churches	Communicant, confirmed, full members	Total adherents Number	Percent of total population	Percent of total adherents
435 UNITARIAN-UNIV	1	176	204	-	.1
443 UN C OF CHRIST	110	18,202	22,852*	2.1	5.8
449 UN METHODIST	31	6,677	8,348*	.8	2.1
469 WELS	1	66	96	-	-
496 JEWISH EST[1]	6	NA	0	-	-
497 BLACK BAPT EST[2]	NA	5,626	7,000*	.6	1.8
498 INDEP.CHARIS.[3]	5	NA	3,600	.3	.9
499 INDEP.NON-CHAR[3]	1	NA	500	-	.1
IDAHO	**1,600**	**114,833**	**507,426***	**50.4**	**100.0**
001 ADVENT CHR CH	2	44	55*	-	-
019 AMER BAPT USA	39	7,729	10,146*	1.0	2.0
053 ASSEMB OF GOD	78	6,814	13,781	1.4	2.7
057 BAPT GEN CONF	1	691	879*	.1	.2
081 CATHOLIC	115	NA	73,897	7.3	14.6
081d *LATIN*	*115*	*NA*	*73,897*	*7.3*	*14.6*
089 CHR & MISS AL	10	399	1,427	.1	.3
093 CHR CH (DISC)	18	2,841	4,328	.4	.9
097 CHR CHS&CHS CR	24	5,858	7,566*	.8	1.5
105 CHRISTIAN REF	2	178	302	-	.1
111 CH CR,SCIENTST	12	NR	NR	-	-
123 CH GOD (ANDER)	10	585	685	.1	.1
127 CH GOD (CLEVE)	13	551	718*	.1	.1
133 CH GOD(7TH)DEN	1	46	58	-	-
143 CG IN CR(MENN)	3	444	586*	.1	.1
145 CH GOD PROPHCY	10	250	328*	-	.1
151 L-D SAINTS	662	NA	268,060	26.6	52.8
157 CH OF BRETHREN	7	661	865*	.1	.2
163 CH OF LUTH BR	1	65	157	-	-
164 CH LUTH CONF	1	26	31	-	-
165 CH OF NAZARENE	54	9,878	13,560	1.3	2.7
167 CHS OF CHRIST	41	2,337	3,309	.3	.7
175 CONGR CHR CHS	1	80	103*	-	-
179 CONSRV BAPT	15	NR	NR	-	-
181 CONSRV CONGR	2	406	549*	.1	.1
193 EPISCOPAL	38	4,268	6,338	.6	1.2
203 EVAN FREE CH	5	215	430	-	.1
207 E.L.C.A.	40	9,017	12,711	1.3	2.5
221 FREE METHODIST	9	576	913	.1	.2
223 FREE WILL BAPT	4	335	465*	-	.1
226 FRIENDS-USA	17	1,388	2,233*	.2	.4
226b *EFI*	*14*	*1,362*	*2,174*	*.2*	*.4*
226f *INDEPENDNT*	*3*	*26*	*59***	*-*	*-*
246 GREEK ORTHODOX	2	NR	NR	-	-
259 IFCA	4	NR	NR	-	-
263 INT FOURSQ GOS	24	1,245	1,643*	.2	.3
283 LUTH—MO SYNOD	43	9,553	13,303	1.3	2.6
285 MENNONITE CH	7	263	414	-	.1
287 MENN GEN CONF	1	281	335	-	.1
291 MISSIONARY CH	1	56	62	-	-
313 N AM BAPT CONF	2	316	436*	-	.1
329 OPEN BIBLE STD	3	NR	NR	-	-
339 PENT CH OF GOD	13	370	792	.1	.2
353 CHR BRETHREN	2	140	188	-	-
355 PRESB CH (USA)	51	8,475	11,121*	1.1	2.2
371 REF CH IN AM	2	449	877	.1	.2
403 SALVATION ARMY	7	546	622	.1	.1
413 S.D.A.	46	6,314	8,172*	.8	1.6
419 SO BAPT CONV	54	12,017	15,802*	1.6	3.1
435 UNITARIAN-UNIV	5	364	563	.1	.1
436 UNITED BAPT	1	5	6*	-	-
438 UN BRETH IN CR	3	106	117	-	-
443 UN C OF CHRIST	15	2,080	2,726*	.3	.5
449 UN METHODIST	66	16,008	20,979*	2.1	4.1
467 WESLEYAN	3	99	455	-	.1
469 WELS	1	128	170	-	-
496 JEWISH EST[1]	2	NA	320	-	.1
497 BLACK BAPT EST[2]	NA	336	442*	-	.1
498 INDEP.CHARIS.[3]	4	NA	1,965	.2	.4
499 INDEP.NON-CHAR[3]	3	NA	1,436	.1	.3
ILLINOIS	**9,799**	**2,175,908**	**6,848,422***	**59.9**	**100.0**
001 ADVENT CHR CH	9	787	1,019*	-	-
005 AME ZION	14	14,423	18,426	.2	.3
009 ALBAN ORTH DIO	1	NR	NR	-	-
011 A.W.M.C.	1	15	19*	-	-
019 AMER BAPT USA	296	77,140	96,440*	.8	1.4
022 EASTERN ORTH	2	355	355	-	-
039 AP CHR CH(NAZ)	4	232	293*	-	-

NA–Not applicable   NR–Not reported   *Total adherents estimated from known number of communicant, confirmed, full members.   - Represents a percent less than 0.1.   Percentages may not total due to rounding.
[1] See Appendix E   [2] See Appendix F   [3] See Appendix G   Lines in *italic* represent a breakdown of Catholic rites or Friends affiliations. They are included in their respective denominational total.

17

Table 3. Churches and Church Membership by State and Denomination: 1990

State and Denomination	Number of churches	Communicant, confirmed, full members	Total adherents — Number	Total adherents — Percent of total population	Total adherents — Percent of total adherents
040 AP CHR CH-AMER	18	4,763	8,428	.1	.1
049 ARMEN AP CH AM	3	700	4,050	-	.1
053 ASSEMB OF GOD	339	43,151	80,656	.7	1.2
057 BAPT GEN CONF	79	13,252	16,649*	.1	.2
059 BAPT MISS ASSN	12	1,746	2,226*	-	-
061 BEACHY AMISH	2	169	215*	-	-
071 BRETHREN (ASH)	4	541	671*	-	-
075 BRETHREN IN CR	2	41	71	-	-
080 BYELORSSN ORTH	1	NR	NR	-	-
081 CATHOLIC	1,089	NA	3,611,033	31.6	52.7
081b BYZAN RUTH	2	NA	1,016	-	-
081c CHALDEAN	2	NA	4,000	-	.1
081d LATIN	1,073	NA	3,593,896	31.4	52.5
081e MARONITE	2	NA	1,673	-	-
081f MELKITE-GK	1	NA	351	-	-
081g ROMANIAN	2	NA	644	-	-
081h UKRAINIAN	7	NA	9,453	.1	.1
083 CHRIST CATH CH	2	17	17	-	-
089 CHR & MISS AL	60	3,797	6,147	.1	.1
093 CHR CH (DISC)	202	37,759	65,546	.6	1.0
097 CHR CHS&CHS CR	498	95,396	119,161*	1.0	1.7
105 CHRISTIAN REF	51	11,208	17,390	.2	.3
111 CH CR,SCIENTST	104	NR	NR	-	-
121 CH GOD (ABR)	12	674	837*	-	-
123 CH GOD (ANDER)	115	7,445	9,932	.1	.1
127 CH GOD (CLEVE)	124	12,139	15,169*	.1	.2
133 CH GOD(7TH)DEN	4	222	325	-	-
145 CH GOD PROPHCY	28	1,075	1,355*	-	-
151 L-D SAINTS	85	NA	30,352	.3	.4
157 CH OF BRETHREN	44	5,325	6,719*	.1	.1
163 CH OF LUTH BR	1	72	97	-	-
164 CH LUTH CONF	1	46	65	-	-
165 CH OF NAZARENE	268	23,900	42,056	.4	.6
167 CHS OF CHRIST	298	24,963	33,334	.3	.5
171 CH GOD-GEN CON	29	3,526	4,380*	-	.1
175 CONGR CHR CHS	33	4,138	5,175*	-	.1
176 CCC, NOT NAT'L	3	1,117	1,395*	-	-
179 CONSRV BAPT	35	NR	NR	-	-
181 CONSRV CONGR	7	1,572	2,017*	-	-
185 CUMBER PRESB	43	3,087	3,195	-	-
193 EPISCOPAL	184	39,017	54,751	.5	.8
195 ESTONIAN ELC	2	310	397*	-	-
199 EVAN CONGR CH	10	935	1,085	-	-
203 EVAN FREE CH	89	13,085	19,601	.2	.3
207 E.L.C.A.	568	222,907	296,968	2.6	4.3
209 EVAN LUTH SYN	3	284	402	-	-
213 EVAN MENN INC	8	1,069	1,343*	-	-
215 EVAN METH CH	3	133	171*	-	-
216 EVAN PRESBY CH	3	373	377	-	-
217 FIRE BAPTIZED	1	17	21*	-	-
220 FREE LUTHERAN	10	1,915	2,579	-	-
221 FREE METHODIST	78	4,581	5,576	-	.1
223 FREE WILL BAPT	41	4,229	5,309*	-	.1
226 FRIENDS-USA	27	1,644	2,012*	-	-
226c FGC	16	486	613*	-	-
226d FGC & FUM	3	382	428	-	-
226e FUM	8	776	971*	-	-
237 GC MENN BR CHS	1	20	25*	-	-
246 GREEK ORTHODOX	33	NR	NR	-	-
249 AP CATH ASSYR	3	5,658	27,182	.2	.4
259 IFCA	68	NR	NR	-	-
263 INT FOURSQ GOS	41	9,022	11,315*	.1	.2
274 LAT EVAN LUTH	4	1,167	1,320	-	-
283 LUTH—MO SYNOD	519	222,985	295,820	2.6	4.3
284 LUTH CH-AM ASC	5	1,096	1,433	-	-
285 MENNONITE CH	52	4,991	7,424	.1	.1
286 E.PA MENNONITE	3	110	135*	-	-
287 MENN GEN CONF	23	1,776	2,204	-	-
291 MISSIONARY CH	17	1,858	2,490	-	-
293 MORAV CH-NORTH	1	321	447	-	-
307 NETH REF CONGR	1	10	16	-	-
313 N AM BAPT CONF	14	1,876	2,370*	-	-
323 OLD ORD AMISH	19	NA	2,800	-	-
325 OLD REG BAPT	2	54	69*	-	-
329 OPEN BIBLE STD	18	NR	NR	-	-
331 ORTH CH IN AM	13	NR	NR	-	-
339 PENT CH OF GOD	20	722	1,561	-	-
349 PENT HOLINESS	6	291	367*	-	-
353 CHR BRETHREN	45	3,201	5,452	-	.1

State and Denomination	Number of churches	Communicant, confirmed, full members	Total adherents — Number	Total adherents — Percent of total population	Total adherents — Percent of total adherents
355 PRESB CH (USA)	474	126,123	158,320*	1.4	2.3
356 PRESB CH AMER	27	5,003	5,493	-	.1
361 PRIM BAPT ASCS	12	260	323*	-	-
363 PRIMITIVE METH	1	90	142	-	-
371 REF CH IN AM	56	12,520	20,196	.2	.3
375 REF EPISCOPAL	2	245	281	-	-
397 ROMANIAN ORTH	2	NR	NR	-	-
403 SALVATION ARMY	57	6,611	7,209	.1	.1
413 S.D.A.	129	19,471	24,442*	.2	.4
415 S-D BAPTIST GC	1	55	67*	-	-
419 SO BAPT CONV	917	234,224	292,644*	2.6	4.3
423 SYRIAN ANTIOCH	3	NA	1,900	-	-
431 UKRANIAN AMER	2	NR	NR	-	-
435 UNITARIAN-UNIV	40	6,120	8,194	.1	.1
436 UNITED BAPT	1	29	37*	-	-
438 UN BRETH IN CR	9	271	293	-	-
443 UN C OF CHRIST	411	146,907	185,558*	1.6	2.7
449 UN METHODIST	1,480	351,260	440,681*	3.9	6.4
467 WESLEYAN	35	1,385	4,204	-	.1
469 WELS	36	7,864	10,689	.1	.2
496 JEWISH EST[1]	184	NA	269,188	2.4	3.9
497 BLACK BAPT EST[2]	NA	317,020	397,339*	3.5	5.8
498 INDEP.CHARIS.[3]	22	NA	14,930	.1	.2
499 INDEP.NON-CHAR[3]	40	NA	48,055	.4	.7
INDIANA	**7,134**	**1,306,718**	**2,634,841***	**47.5**	**100.0**
001 ADVENT CHR CH	2	176	220*	-	-
005 AME ZION	17	17,757	22,661	.4	.9
011 A.W.M.C.	1	15	19*	-	-
019 AMER BAPT USA	397	106,106	132,970*	2.4	5.0
022 EASTERN ORTH	2	286	286	-	-
040 AP CHR CH-AMER	11	2,132	3,777	.1	.1
053 ASSEMB OF GOD	218	27,419	51,907	.9	2.0
057 BAPT GEN CONF	7	647	824*	-	-
059 BAPT MISS ASSN	3	264	322*	-	-
061 BEACHY AMISH	10	729	946*	-	-
071 BRETHREN (ASH)	36	4,168	5,307*	.1	.2
075 BRETHREN IN CR	4	233	267	-	-
081 CATHOLIC	476	NA	699,188	12.6	26.5
081b BYZAN RUTH	5	NA	1,726	-	.1
081d LATIN	466	NA	696,249	12.6	26.4
081f MELKITE-GK	2	NA	774	-	-
081g ROMANIAN	1	NA	322	-	-
081h UKRAINIAN	2	NA	117	-	-
082 CENTRAL BAPT	3	226	291*	-	-
083 CHRIST CATH CH	1	7	7	-	-
089 CHR & MISS AL	29	1,507	3,085	.1	.1
093 CHR CH (DISC)	221	55,244	89,932	1.6	3.4
097 CHR CHS&CHS CR	482	127,317	160,099*	2.9	6.1
105 CHRISTIAN REF	14	3,070	5,343	.1	.2
111 CH CR,SCIENTST	48	NR	NR	-	-
121 CH GOD (ABR)	7	308	390*	-	-
123 CH GOD (ANDER)	159	18,331	22,569	.4	.9
127 CH GOD (CLEVE)	85	8,117	10,212*	.2	.4
133 CH GOD(7TH)DEN	1	15	20	-	-
145 CH GOD PROPHCY	42	1,403	1,764*	-	.1
146 CH GOD MTN ASM	12	517	646*	-	-
151 L-D SAINTS	70	NA	20,901	.4	.8
157 CH OF BRETHREN	105	13,625	17,388	.3	.7
165 CH OF NAZARENE	331	36,562	68,131	1.2	2.6
167 CHS OF CHRIST	345	30,366	39,953	.7	1.5
171 CH GOD-GEN CON	22	2,963	3,796*	.1	.1
175 CONGR CHR CHS	10	1,215	1,524*	-	.1
176 CCC, NOT NAT'L	13	1,062	1,328*	-	.1
179 CONSRV BAPT	5	NR	NR	-	-
181 CONSRV CONGR	2	509	644*	-	-
185 CUMBER PRESB	8	1,391	1,494	-	.1
191 ENTRPR BPT ASC	1	56	71*	-	-
193 EPISCOPAL	81	14,431	21,102	.4	.8
195 ESTONIAN ELC	1	26	33*	-	-
199 EVAN CONGR CH	1	31	113	-	-
203 EVAN FREE CH	12	1,984	3,510	.1	.1
207 E.L.C.A.	210	59,222	78,727	1.4	3.0
209 EVAN LUTH SYN	1	46	69	-	-
213 EVAN MENN INC	9	1,109	1,417*	-	.1
215 EVAN METH CH	6	402	506*	-	-
216 EVAN PRESBY CH	1	200	207	-	-
220 FREE LUTHERAN	1	158	206	-	-
221 FREE METHODIST	44	4,496	5,450	.1	.2

NA–Not applicable   NR–Not reported   *Total adherents estimated from known number of communicant, confirmed, full members.   - Represents a percent less than 0.1.   Percentages may not total due to rounding.
[1]See Appendix E   [2]See Appendix F   [3]See Appendix G   Lines in *italic* represent a breakdown of Catholic rites or Friends affiliations. They are included in their respective denominational total.

Table 3. Churches and Church Membership by State and Denomination: 1990

State and Denomination	Number of churches	Communicant, confirmed, full members	Total adherents Number	Percent of total population	Percent of total adherents
223 FREE WILL BAPT	27	1,869	2,352*	-	.1
226 FRIENDS-USA	128	12,915	16,167*	.3	.6
226c FGC	5	116	144*	-	-
226d FGC & FUM	1	166	203	-	-
226e FUM	112	12,380	15,489*	.3	.6
226f INDEPENDNT	2	10	27	-	-
226g INDEP EVAN	8	243	304*	-	-
246 GREEK ORTHODOX	7	NR	NR	-	-
249 AP CATH ASSYR	1	53	329	-	-
259 IFCA	28	NR	NR	-	-
263 INT FOURSQ GOS	20	3,150	3,890*	.1	.1
265 INT PENT C CHR	1	59	59	-	-
274 LAT EVAN LUTH	1	373	409	-	-
283 LUTH—MO SYNOD	219	82,577	109,895	2.0	4.2
284 LUTH CH-AM ASC	1	263	351	-	-
285 MENNONITE CH	97	12,478	17,976	.3	.7
287 MENN GEN CONF	16	2,526	3,084	.1	.1
291 MISSIONARY CH	69	9,223	14,009	.3	.5
293 MORAV CH-NORTH	4	553	693	-	-
296 MIDW CONGR FEL	20	976	1,206*	-	-
313 N AM BAPT CONF	1	66	83*	-	-
323 OLD ORD AMISH	149	NA	22,300	.4	.8
325 OLD REG BAPT	17	384	484*	-	-
329 OPEN BIBLE STD	2	NR	NR	-	-
331 ORTH CH IN AM	3	NR	NR	-	-
339 PENT CH OF GOD	33	895	2,321	-	.1
349 PENT HOLINESS	2	47	61*	-	-
353 CHR BRETHREN	10	307	479	-	-
355 PRESB CH (USA)	277	68,559	86,194*	1.6	3.3
356 PRESB CH AMER	12	1,564	2,001	-	.1
361 PRIM BAPT ASCS	20	381	478*	-	-
363 PRIMITIVE METH	1	39	69	-	-
371 REF CH IN AM	9	2,094	3,418	.1	.1
397 ROMANIAN ORTH	3	NR	NR	-	-
403 SALVATION ARMY	41	4,043	4,500	.1	.2
413 S.D.A.	87	9,114	11,459*	.2	.4
419 SO BAPT CONV	306	92,174	115,560*	2.1	4.4
426 2SEED-SPRT BPT	1	20	24*	-	-
431 UKRANIAN AMER	1	NR	NR	-	-
435 UNITARIAN-UNIV	17	2,340	3,038	.1	.1
436 UNITED BAPT	20	2,435	3,017*	.1	.1
438 UN BRETH IN CR	30	3,257	3,433	.1	.1
443 UN C OF CHRIST	173	48,253	60,773*	1.1	2.3
449 UN METHODIST	1,373	272,999	343,930*	6.2	13.1
467 WESLEYAN	238	12,483	34,025	.6	1.3
469 WELS	8	1,190	1,660	-	.1
496 JEWISH EST[1]	31	NA	20,314	.4	.8
497 BLACK BAPT EST[2]	NA	111,191	140,166*	2.5	5.3
498 INDEP.CHARIS.[3]	15	NA	19,855	.4	.8
499 INDEP.NON-CHAR[3]	48	NA	105,157	1.9	4.0
IOWA	**4,560**	**845,107**	**1,681,062***	**60.5**	**100.0**
001 ADVENT CHR CH	2	91	113*	-	-
005 AME ZION	1	254	269	-	-
019 AMER BAPT USA	124	25,619	32,175*	1.2	1.9
040 AP CHR CH-AMER	8	813	1,443	.1	.1
053 ASSEMB OF GOD	131	11,001	21,650	.8	1.3
057 BAPT GEN CONF	34	4,768	6,005*	.2	.4
061 BEACHY AMISH	2	202	243*	-	-
071 BRETHREN (ASH)	1	178	223*	-	-
075 BRETHREN IN CR	2	57	68	-	-
081 CATHOLIC	564	NA	520,322	18.7	31.0
081d LATIN	564	NA	520,322	18.7	31.0
089 CHR & MISS AL	28	1,565	3,871	.1	.2
093 CHR CH (DISC)	167	30,657	50,771	1.8	3.0
097 CHR CHS&CHS CR	123	19,220	24,137*	.9	1.4
105 CHRISTIAN REF	62	13,543	21,129	.8	1.3
111 CH CR,SCIENTST	24	NR	NR	-	-
121 CH GOD (ABR)	4	80	102*	-	-
123 CH GOD (ANDER)	11	397	670	-	-
127 CH GOD (CLEVE)	16	1,059	1,335*	-	.1
133 CH GOD(7TH)DEN	1	59	73	-	-
145 CH GOD PROPHCY	12	264	328*	-	-
151 L-D SAINTS	37	NA	10,383	.4	.6
157 CH OF BRETHREN	31	2,865	3,599*	.1	.2
163 CH OF LUTH BR	6	300	483	-	-
165 CH OF NAZARENE	72	6,487	12,934	.5	.8
167 CHS OF CHRIST	73	3,055	4,006	.1	.2
171 CH GOD-GEN CON	10	523	658*	-	-

State and Denomination	Number of churches	Communicant, confirmed, full members	Total adherents Number	Percent of total population	Percent of total adherents
175 CONGR CHR CHS	12	1,964	2,473*	.1	.1
176 CCC, NOT NAT'L	8	417	530*	-	-
179 CONSRV BAPT	17	NR	NR	-	-
181 CONSRV CONGR	2	436	547*	-	-
185 CUMBER PRESB	1	111	124	-	-
193 EPISCOPAL	67	9,890	14,198	.5	.8
203 EVAN FREE CH	51	4,678	8,056	.3	.5
207 E.L.C.A.	519	201,010	265,423	9.6	15.8
209 EVAN LUTH SYN	19	1,459	1,795	.1	.1
215 EVAN METH CH	1	8	10*	-	-
216 EVAN PRESBY CH	1	209	209	-	-
220 FREE LUTHERAN	4	451	559	-	-
221 FREE METHODIST	21	827	1,073	-	.1
223 FREE WILL BAPT	1	79	102*	-	-
226 FRIENDS-USA	51	4,933	6,235*	.2	.4
226a CONSERV	7	494	621*	-	-
226c FGC	1	2	15	-	-
226e FUM	40	4,421	5,544*	.2	.3
226f INDEPENDNT	3	16	55	-	-
246 GREEK ORTHODOX	6	NR	NR	-	-
259 IFCA	17	NR	NR	-	-
263 INT FOURSQ GOS	28	2,597	3,262*	.1	.2
274 LAT EVAN LUTH	1	74	75	-	-
283 LUTH—MO SYNOD	293	94,069	124,021	4.5	7.4
284 LUTH CH-AM ASC	9	1,343	1,810	.1	.1
285 MENNONITE CH	27	3,515	4,691	.2	.3
287 MENN GEN CONF	6	505	613	-	-
291 MISSIONARY CH	7	202	376	-	-
307 NETH REF CONGR	2	787	1,525	.1	.1
313 N AM BAPT CONF	14	2,205	2,782*	.1	.2
323 OLD ORD AMISH	23	NA	3,450	.1	.2
324 OLD ORD RVR BR	1	38	64	-	-
329 OPEN BIBLE STD	47	NR	NR	-	-
339 PENT CH OF GOD	6	247	478	-	-
353 CHR BRETHREN	37	1,759	2,968	.1	.2
355 PRESB CH (USA)	311	67,665	85,186*	3.1	5.1
356 PRESB CH AMER	6	604	768	-	-
363 PRIMITIVE METH	2	16	24	-	-
371 REF CH IN AM	74	21,297	33,337	1.2	2.0
373 REF CH IN U.S.	1	151	196	-	-
403 SALVATION ARMY	21	2,486	2,794	.1	.2
413 S.D.A.	55	4,325	5,426*	.2	.3
419 SO BAPT CONV	60	11,158	13,960*	.5	.8
435 UNITARIAN-UNIV	11	1,546	2,157	.1	.1
438 UN BRETH IN CR	4	66	82	-	-
443 UN C OF CHRIST	209	47,277	59,450*	2.1	3.5
449 UN METHODIST	887	216,489	272,098*	9.8	16.2
467 WESLEYAN	25	2,712	5,615	.2	.3
469 WELS	11	1,151	1,596	.1	.1
496 JEWISH EST[1]	20	NA	6,701	.2	.4
497 BLACK BAPT EST[2]	NA	11,294	14,188*	.5	.8
498 INDEP.CHARIS.[3]	4	NA	5,520	.2	.3
499 INDEP.NON-CHAR[3]	14	NA	7,525	.3	.4
KANSAS	**3,958**	**704,542**	**1,354,657***	**54.7**	**100.0**
005 AME ZION	4	281	367	-	-
011 A.W.M.C.	2	17	21*	-	-
019 AMER BAPT USA	249	58,385	74,440*	3.0	5.5
040 AP CHR CH-AMER	7	479	849	-	.1
053 ASSEMB OF GOD	159	13,847	25,922	1.0	1.9
057 BAPT GEN CONF	1	24	29*	-	-
059 BAPT MISS ASSN	11	1,339	1,686*	.1	.1
061 BEACHY AMISH	2	283	355*	-	-
063 BEREAN FUND CH	4	140	350	-	-
071 BRETHREN (ASH)	3	175	226*	-	-
075 BRETHREN IN CR	3	284	284	-	-
081 CATHOLIC	397	NA	369,241	14.9	27.3
081d LATIN	396	NA	369,181	14.9	27.3
081h UKRAINIAN	1	NA	60	-	-
089 CHR & MISS AL	4	498	565	-	-
093 CHR CH (DISC)	172	36,896	58,314	2.4	4.3
097 CHR CHS&CHS CR	187	37,167	47,310*	1.9	3.5
105 CHRISTIAN REF	2	312	431	-	-
111 CH CR,SCIENTST	24	NR	NR	-	-
121 CH GOD (ABR)	1	11	14*	-	-
123 CH GOD (ANDER)	52	7,699	8,518	.3	.6
127 CH GOD (CLEVE)	28	1,772	2,262*	.1	.2
133 CH GOD(7TH)DEN	3	48	60	-	-
143 CG IN CR(MENN)	20	3,309	4,269*	.2	.3

NA–Not applicable   NR–Not reported   *Total adherents estimated from known number of communicant, confirmed, full members.   - Represents a percent less than 0.1.   Percentages may not total due to rounding.
[1]See Appendix E   [2]See Appendix F   [3]See Appendix G   Lines in *italic* represent a breakdown of Catholic rites or Friends affiliations. They are included in their respective denominational total.

Table 3. Churches and Church Membership by State and Denomination: 1990

State and Denomination	Number of churches	Communicant, confirmed, full members	Total adherents Number	Percent of total population	Percent of total adherents
145 CH GOD PROPHCY	16	527	672*	-	-
151 L-D SAINTS	54	NA	16,941	.7	1.3
157 CH OF BRETHREN	30	3,411	4,369*	.2	.3
165 CH OF NAZARENE	134	19,177	29,741	1.2	2.2
167 CHS OF CHRIST	188	14,973	19,305	.8	1.4
171 CH GOD-GEN CON	2	147	182*	-	-
175 CONGR CHR CHS	7	2,208	2,841*	.1	.2
176 CCC, NOT NAT'L	2	99	127*	-	-
181 CONSRV CONGR	2	86	111*	-	-
193 EPISCOPAL	82	14,155	19,366	.8	1.4
203 EVAN FREE CH	14	1,311	2,758	.1	.2
207 E.L.C.A.	139	34,447	45,138	1.8	3.3
211 FEL EVG BIB CH	1	86	86	-	-
213 EVAN MENN INC	2	309	391*	-	-
215 EVAN METH CH	3	120	155*	-	-
216 EVAN PRESBY CH	4	511	573	-	-
217 FIRE BAPTIZED	15	296	373*	-	-
221 FREE METHODIST	24	1,493	2,185	.1	.2
223 FREE WILL BAPT	9	501	645*	-	-
226 FRIENDS-USA	48	4,789	6,111*	.2	.5
226b *EFI*	*43*	*4,074*	*5,170**	*.2*	*.4*
226c *FGC*	*3*	*33*	*61*	-	-
226d *FGC & FUM*	*1*	*18*	*23**	-	-
226e *FUM*	*1*	*664*	*857**	-	*.1*
237 GC MENN BR CHS	18	3,564	4,534*	.2	.3
246 GREEK ORTHODOX	2	NR	NR	-	-
259 IFCA	17	NR	NR	-	-
263 INT FOURSQ GOS	18	2,292	2,909*	.1	.2
283 LUTH—MO SYNOD	171	47,526	63,145	2.5	4.7
284 LUTH CH-AM ASC	1	19	28	-	-
285 MENNONITE CH	23	2,543	3,173	.1	.2
287 MENN GEN CONF	50	10,559	13,326	.5	1.0
291 MISSIONARY CH	6	304	400	-	-
313 N AM BAPT CONF	14	1,436	1,808*	.1	.1
323 OLD ORD AMISH	5	NA	750	-	.1
329 OPEN BIBLE STD	3	NR	NR	-	-
331 ORTH CH IN AM	2	NR	NR	-	-
339 PENT CH OF GOD	6	197	455	-	-
349 PENT HOLINESS	16	1,394	1,775*	.1	.1
353 CHR BRETHREN	14	694	1,249	.1	.1
355 PRESB CH (USA)	207	50,102	63,658*	2.6	4.7
356 PRESB CH AMER	3	386	509	-	-
371 REF CH IN AM	2	314	612	-	-
403 SALVATION ARMY	20	1,936	2,128	.1	.2
413 S.D.A.	64	6,643	8,486*	.3	.6
415 S-D BAPTIST GC	2	133	172*	-	-
419 SO BAPT CONV	218	75,511	96,524*	3.9	7.1
435 UNITARIAN-UNIV	6	628	860	-	.1
438 UN BRETH IN CR	8	372	409	-	-
443 UN C OF CHRIST	83	13,914	17,622*	.7	1.3
449 UN METHODIST	757	187,473	238,029*	9.6	17.6
467 WESLEYAN	52	2,573	6,806	.3	.5
469 WELS	9	748	987	-	.1
496 JEWISH EST[1]	7	NA	9,151	.4	.7
497 BLACK BAPT EST[2]	NA	31,669	40,566*	1.6	3.0
498 INDEP.CHARIS.[3]	12	NA	8,735	.4	.6
499 INDEP.NON-CHAR[3]	31	NA	18,268	.7	1.3
KENTUCKY	**7,255**	**1,439,334**	**2,227,747***	**60.4**	**100.0**
001 ADVENT CHR CH	2	43	54*	-	-
005 AME ZION	44	16,910	18,551	.5	.8
011 A.W.M.C.	1	25	31*	-	-
019 AMER BAPT USA	4	742	918*	-	-
040 AP CHR CH-AMER	1	7	12	-	-
053 ASSEMB OF GOD	146	21,646	27,989	.8	1.3
055 AS REF PRES CH	1	128	133	-	-
057 BAPT GEN CONF	1	46	59*	-	-
059 BAPT MISS ASSN	1	33	41*	-	-
060 BRN RVR MB ASC	11	1,139	1,408*	-	.1
061 BEACHY AMISH	5	273	342*	-	-
071 BRETHREN (ASH)	3	29	37*	-	-
075 BRETHREN IN CR	6	200	271	-	-
081 CATHOLIC	347	NA	365,270	9.9	16.4
081d *LATIN*	*347*	*NA*	*365,270*	*9.9*	*16.4*
082 CENTRAL BAPT	4	372	475*	-	-
089 CHR & MISS AL	20	975	1,804	-	.1
093 CHR CH (DISC)	254	42,879	66,798	1.8	3.0
097 CHR CHS&CHS CR	355	72,585	90,520*	2.5	4.1
111 CH CR,SCIENTST	12	NR	NR	-	-
123 CH GOD (ANDER)	120	7,559	11,747	.3	.5
127 CH GOD (CLEVE)	214	19,227	24,134*	.7	1.1
143 CG IN CR(MENN)	1	46	57*	-	-
145 CH GOD PROPHCY	93	3,996	5,027*	.1	.2
146 CH GOD MTN ASM	23	1,256	1,606*	-	.1
151 L-D SAINTS	49	NA	13,586	.4	.6
157 CH OF BRETHREN	5	328	427*	-	-
165 CH OF NAZARENE	149	14,422	22,118	.6	1.0
167 CHS OF CHRIST	624	45,139	58,775	1.6	2.6
171 CH GOD-GEN CON	1	223	276*	-	-
179 CONSRV BAPT	1	NR	NR	-	-
185 CUMBER PRESB	119	11,811	12,378	.3	.6
191 ENTRPR BPT ASC	35	2,846	3,590*	.1	.2
193 EPISCOPAL	76	14,649	19,655	.5	.9
199 EVAN CONGR CH	1	33	73	-	-
203 EVAN FREE CH	7	223	360	-	-
207 E.L.C.A.	39	7,939	10,383	.3	.5
215 EVAN METH CH	3	207	257*	-	-
216 EVAN PRESBY CH	3	73	73	-	-
221 FREE METHODIST	12	477	846	-	-
223 FREE WILL BAPT	129	13,089	16,470*	.4	.7
226 FRIENDS-USA	3	137	168*	-	-
226c *FGC*	*3*	*137*	*168**	-	-
246 GREEK ORTHODOX	2	NR	NR	-	-
259 IFCA	1	NR	NR	-	-
263 INT FOURSQ GOS	4	131	167*	-	-
265 INT PENT C CHR	10	436	641	-	-
283 LUTH—MO SYNOD	28	4,346	5,637	.2	.3
285 MENNONITE CH	15	355	705	-	-
287 MENN GEN CONF	1	6	12	-	-
291 MISSIONARY CH	3	102	122	-	-
320 "OLD" MB ASCS	16	3,030	3,770*	.1	.2
323 OLD ORD AMISH	13	NA	1,650	-	.1
325 OLD REG BAPT	181	9,562	12,136*	.3	.5
329 OPEN BIBLE STD	3	NR	NR	-	-
339 PENT CH OF GOD	17	886	1,617	-	.1
349 PENT HOLINESS	1	87	107*	-	-
353 CHR BRETHREN	3	75	110	-	-
355 PRESB CH (USA)	209	35,382	44,016*	1.2	2.0
356 PRESB CH AMER	6	439	554	-	-
361 PRIM BAPT ASCS	44	2,636	3,328*	.1	.1
371 REF CH IN AM	3	173	367	-	-
403 SALVATION ARMY	18	1,759	1,915	.1	.1
413 S.D.A.	51	5,129	6,396*	.2	.3
419 SO BAPT CONV	2,266	770,425	962,945*	26.1	43.2
435 UNITARIAN-UNIV	8	729	971	-	-
436 UNITED BAPT	250	35,945	45,164*	1.2	2.0
438 UN BRETH IN CR	2	51	61	-	-
443 UN C OF CHRIST	35	9,575	11,984*	.3	.5
449 UN METHODIST	1,060	182,302	227,143*	6.2	10.2
467 WESLEYAN	46	1,609	2,946	.1	.1
469 WELS	2	100	124	-	-
496 JEWISH EST[1]	10	NA	14,810	.4	.7
497 BLACK BAPT EST[2]	NA	72,352	89,939*	2.4	4.0
498 INDEP.CHARIS.[3]	5	NA	2,300	.1	.1
499 INDEP.NON-CHAR[3]	17	NA	9,391	.3	.4
LOUISIANA	**4,025**	**1,193,779**	**2,975,409***	**70.5**	**100.0**
001 ADVENT CHR CH	1	12	16*	-	-
005 AME ZION	23	8,738	10,719	.3	.4
019 AMER BAPT USA	6	2,359	3,019*	.1	.1
053 ASSEMB OF GOD	243	31,655	46,765	1.1	1.6
059 BAPT MISS ASSN	41	8,309	10,735*	.3	.4
081 CATHOLIC	627	NA	1,369,154	32.4	46.0
081d *LATIN*	*627*	*NA*	*1,369,154*	*32.4*	*46.0*
089 CHR & MISS AL	2	39	103	-	-
093 CHR CH (DISC)	23	4,092	6,073	.1	.2
097 CHR CHS&CHS CR	31	2,687	3,513*	.1	.1
111 CH CR,SCIENTST	16	NR	NR	-	-
121 CH GOD (ABR)	4	188	247*	-	-
123 CH GOD (ANDER)	60	3,081	4,123	.1	.1
127 CH GOD (CLEVE)	51	5,323	6,919*	.2	.2
143 CG IN CR(MENN)	2	292	384*	-	-
145 CH GOD PROPHCY	30	761	995*	-	-
151 L-D SAINTS	56	NA	15,182	.4	.5
157 CH OF BRETHREN	1	74	98*	-	-
165 CH OF NAZARENE	60	3,514	4,716	.1	.2
167 CHS OF CHRIST	231	19,665	26,252	.6	.9
171 CH GOD-GEN CON	1	62	81*	-	-

NA–Not applicable   NR–Not reported   *Total adherents estimated from known number of communicant, confirmed, full members.   - Represents a percent less than 0.1.   Percentages may not total due to rounding.
[1] See Appendix E   [2] See Appendix F   [3] See Appendix G   Lines in *italic* represent a breakdown of Catholic rites or Friends affiliations. They are included in their respective denominational total.

Table 3. Churches and Church Membership by State and Denomination: 1990

State and Denomination	Number of churches	Communicant, confirmed, full members	Total adherents Number	Percent of total population	Percent of total adherents
176 CCC, NOT NAT'L	5	295	391*	-	-
185 CUMBER PRESB	5	658	707	-	-
193 EPISCOPAL	100	25,434	33,423	.8	1.1
203 EVAN FREE CH	1	0	170	-	-
207 E.L.C.A.	20	4,106	5,647	.1	.2
215 EVAN METH CH	2	59	77*	-	-
216 EVAN PRESBY CH	3	241	248	-	-
217 FIRE BAPTIZED	1	2	3*	-	-
221 FREE METHODIST	12	436	462	-	-
223 FREE WILL BAPT	5	345	459*	-	-
226 FRIENDS-USA	4	50	91	-	-
226c *FGC*	4	*50*	*91*	-	-
246 GREEK ORTHODOX	4	NR	NR	-	-
249 AP CATH ASSYR	0	10	52	-	-
259 IFCA	7	NR	NR	-	-
263 INT FOURSQ GOS	3	123	159*	-	-
266 INTRSTAT & ASC	30	3,183	4,125*	.1	.1
283 LUTH—MO SYNOD	64	14,535	19,102	.5	.6
285 MENNONITE CH	3	252	394	-	-
313 N AM BAPT CONF	1	67	90*	-	-
331 ORTH CH IN AM	2	NR	NR	-	-
339 PENT CH OF GOD	4	138	307	-	-
349 PENT HOLINESS	3	1,221	1,597*	-	.1
353 CHR BRETHREN	9	386	694	-	-
355 PRESB CH (USA)	126	21,010	27,105*	.6	.9
356 PRESB CH AMER	18	2,161	2,567	.1	.1
361 PRIM BAPT ASCS	20	553	713*	-	-
403 SALVATION ARMY	8	921	952	-	-
413 S.D.A.	49	8,158	10,516*	.2	.4
419 SO BAPT CONV	1,349	583,124	757,639*	18.0	25.5
435 UNITARIAN-UNIV	8	911	1,201	-	-
443 UN C OF CHRIST	20	3,171	4,060*	.1	.1
449 UN METHODIST	576	133,256	172,676*	4.1	5.8
467 WESLEYAN	7	322	885	-	-
469 WELS	4	267	391	-	-
496 JEWISH EST[1]	24	NA	15,625	.4	.5
497 BLACK BAPT EST[2]	NA	297,533	386,062*	9.1	13.0
498 INDEP.CHARIS.[3]	8	NA	12,000	.3	.4
499 INDEP.NON-CHAR[3]	11	NA	5,725	.1	.2
MAINE	**1,336**	**123,672**	**447,053***	**36.4**	**100.0**
001 ADVENT CHR CH	28	1,803	2,249*	.2	.5
005 AME ZION	1	209	254	-	.1
011 A.W.M.C.	1	0	0*	-	-
019 AMER BAPT USA	165	26,094	32,549*	2.7	7.3
053 ASSEMB OF GOD	52	3,891	6,453	.5	1.4
057 BAPT GEN CONF	2	163	203*	-	-
059 BAPT MISS ASSN	1	24	30*	-	-
081 CATHOLIC	200	NA	264,443	21.5	59.2
081d *LATIN*	199	*NA*	*263,327*	*21.4*	*58.9*
081e *MARONITE*	1	*NA*	*1,116*	*.1*	*.2*
083 CHRIST CATH CH	1	29	35	-	-
089 CHR & MISS AL	11	336	691	.1	.2
093 CHR CH (DISC)	1	94	115	-	-
097 CHR CHS&CHS CR	6	131	162*	-	-
111 CH CR,SCIENTST	24	NR	NR	-	-
127 CH GOD (CLEVE)	21	1,382	1,718*	.1	.4
145 CH GOD PROPHCY	2	56	69*	-	-
151 L-D SAINTS	23	NA	5,956	.5	1.3
157 CH OF BRETHREN	2	68	85*	-	-
165 CH OF NAZARENE	54	3,791	7,207	.6	1.6
167 CHS OF CHRIST	21	682	1,009	.1	.2
175 CONGR CHR CHS	22	2,429	3,027*	.2	.7
176 CCC, NOT NAT'L	24	1,798	2,236*	.2	.5
179 CONSRV BAPT	32	NR	NR	-	-
181 CONSRV CONGR	5	183	230*	-	.1
193 EPISCOPAL	68	10,069	16,375	1.3	3.7
203 EVAN FREE CH	7	314	645	.1	.1
207 E.L.C.A.	16	2,900	4,149	.3	.9
221 FREE METHODIST	2	73	92	-	-
223 FREE WILL BAPT	1	87	109*	-	-
226 FRIENDS-USA	23	757	944*	.1	.2
226d *FGC & FUM*	23	*757*	*944**	*.1*	*.2*
246 GREEK ORTHODOX	4	NR	NR	-	-
259 IFCA	1	NR	NR	-	-
263 INT FOURSQ GOS	5	340	426*	-	.1
283 LUTH—MO SYNOD	2	298	490	-	.1
285 MENNONITE CH	2	68	126	-	-
331 ORTH CH IN AM	1	NR	NR	-	-

State and Denomination	Number of churches	Communicant, confirmed, full members	Total adherents Number	Percent of total population	Percent of total adherents
349 PENT HOLINESS	1	10	12*	-	-
353 CHR BRETHREN	3	80	168	-	-
355 PRESB CH (USA)	10	650	819*	.1	.2
403 SALVATION ARMY	10	924	1,037	.1	.2
413 S.D.A.	30	2,524	3,147*	.3	.7
419 SO BAPT CONV	10	1,413	1,754*	.1	.4
435 UNITARIAN-UNIV	33	2,954	4,152	.3	.9
443 UN C OF CHRIST	183	26,764	33,265*	2.7	7.4
449 UN METHODIST	193	29,043	36,164*	2.9	8.1
467 WESLEYAN	11	541	1,562	.1	.3
469 WELS	1	60	84	-	-
496 JEWISH EST[1]	12	NA	8,160	.7	1.8
497 BLACK BAPT EST[2]	NA	640	792*	.1	.2
498 INDEP.CHARIS.[3]	2	NA	1,250	.1	.3
499 INDEP.NON-CHAR[3]	6	NA	2,610	.2	.6
MARYLAND	**3,519**	**938,574**	**2,311,614***	**48.3**	**100.0**
001 ADVENT CHR CH	2	57	72*	-	-
005 AME ZION	19	15,331	17,601	.4	.8
011 A.W.M.C.	1	0	0*	-	-
019 AMER BAPT USA	67	30,039	37,317*	.8	1.6
022 EASTERN ORTH	1	135	135	-	-
039 AP CHR CH(NAZ)	1	36	45*	-	-
049 ARMEN AP CH AM	1	1,000	4,000	.1	.2
053 ASSEMB OF GOD	107	12,763	22,932	.5	1.0
055 AS REF PRES CH	5	906	1,163	-	.1
057 BAPT GEN CONF	1	27	34*	-	-
061 BEACHY AMISH	3	87	104*	-	-
071 BRETHREN (ASH)	4	672	824*	-	-
075 BRETHREN IN CR	5	215	275	-	-
081 CATHOLIC	296	NA	832,763	17.4	36.0
081b *BYZAN RUTH*	2	*NA*	*506*	-	-
081d *LATIN*	291	*NA*	*831,152*	*17.4*	*36.0*
081h *UKRAINIAN*	3	*NA*	*1,105*	-	-
089 CHR & MISS AL	23	1,333	3,134	.1	.1
093 CHR CH (DISC)	34	4,962	7,176	.2	.3
097 CHR CHS&CHS CR	31	4,734	5,903*	.1	.3
105 CHRISTIAN REF	1	128	178	-	-
111 CH CR,SCIENTST	25	NR	NR	-	-
123 CH GOD (ANDER)	22	2,125	2,336	-	.1
127 CH GOD (CLEVE)	84	17,213	21,359*	.4	.9
133 CH GOD(7TH)DEN	2	103	135	-	-
145 CH GOD PROPHCY	28	853	1,060*	-	-
151 L-D SAINTS	52	NA	21,505	.4	.9
157 CH OF BRETHREN	63	9,449	11,781*	.2	.5
165 CH OF NAZARENE	42	5,041	7,579	.2	.3
167 CHS OF CHRIST	42	5,731	7,207	.2	.3
171 CH GOD-GEN CON	19	1,410	1,759*	-	.1
175 CONGR CHR CHS	2	154	189*	-	-
179 CONSRV BAPT	3	NR	NR	-	-
181 CONSRV CONGR	1	43	54*	-	-
193 EPISCOPAL	221	52,949	82,714	1.7	3.6
195 ESTONIAN ELC	1	224	280*	-	-
199 EVAN CONGR CH	2	123	278	-	-
203 EVAN FREE CH	5	313	495	-	-
207 E.L.C.A.	214	75,166	106,188	2.2	4.6
215 EVAN METH CH	1	23	28*	-	-
216 EVAN PRESBY CH	2	2,448	2,492	.1	.1
220 FREE LUTHERAN	1	15	29	-	-
221 FREE METHODIST	12	624	695	-	-
223 FREE WILL BAPT	3	402	494*	-	-
226 FRIENDS-USA	21	2,166	2,710*	.1	.1
226c *FGC*	8	*762*	*972**	-	-
226d *FGC & FUM*	13	*1,404*	*1,738**	-	*.1*
246 GREEK ORTHODOX	7	NR	NR	-	-
259 IFCA	11	NR	NR	-	-
263 INT FOURSQ GOS	11	920	1,146*	-	-
265 INT PENT C CHR	2	73	73	-	-
274 LAT EVAN LUTH	1	442	517	-	-
283 LUTH—MO SYNOD	69	22,595	31,393	.7	1.4
284 LUTH CH-AM ASC	1	47	65	-	-
285 MENNONITE CH	45	2,932	3,722	.1	.2
286 E.PA MENNONITE	2	73	93*	-	-
287 MENN GEN CONF	1	58	75	-	-
291 MISSIONARY CH	1	15	25	-	-
293 MORAV CH-NORTH	3	654	889	-	-
313 N AM BAPT CONF	1	44	54*	-	-
323 OLD ORD AMISH	6	NA	900	-	-
325 OLD REG BAPT	1	48	61*	-	-

NA–Not applicable   NR–Not reported   *Total adherents estimated from known number of communicant, confirmed, full members.   - Represents a percent less than 0.1.   Percentages may not total due to rounding.
[1]See Appendix E   [2]See Appendix F   [3]See Appendix G   Lines in *italic* represent a breakdown of Catholic rites or Friends affiliations. They are included in their respective denominational total.

Table 3. Churches and Church Membership by State and Denomination: 1990

State and Denomination	Number of churches	Communicant, confirmed, full members	Total adherents		
			Number	Percent of total population	Percent of total adherents
329 OPEN BIBLE STD	2	NR	NR	-	-
331 ORTH CH IN AM	4	NR	NR	-	-
339 PENT CH OF GOD	4	303	600	-	-
349 PENT HOLINESS	6	656	798*	-	-
353 CHR BRETHREN	21	1,710	2,711	.1	.1
355 PRESB CH (USA)	142	37,270	46,360*	1.0	2.0
356 PRESB CH AMER	43	8,305	10,136	.2	.4
375 REF EPISCOPAL	5	847	1,008	-	-
386 REGULAR BAPT	2	251	319*	-	-
403 SALVATION ARMY	11	1,097	1,150	-	-
413 S.D.A.	77	19,848	24,619*	.5	1.1
415 S-D BAPTIST GC	1	31	39*	-	-
419 SO BAPT CONV	305	105,869	131,627*	2.8	5.7
423 SYRIAN ANTIOCH	1	NA	500	-	-
435 UNITARIAN-UNIV	20	4,482	6,255	.1	.3
438 UN BRETH IN CR	6	460	460	-	-
443 UN C OF CHRIST	80	18,848	23,417*	.5	1.0
449 UN METHODIST	979	250,056	310,008*	6.5	13.4
467 WESLEYAN	34	1,575	5,682	.1	.2
469 WELS	2	320	468	-	-
496 JEWISH EST[1]	99	NA	210,965	4.4	9.1
497 BLACK BAPT EST[2]	NA	209,745	260,695*	5.5	11.3
498 INDEP.CHARIS.[3]	17	NA	11,725	.2	.5
499 INDEP.NON-CHAR[3]	26	NA	18,036	.4	.8
MASSACHUSETTS	**3,382**	**500,580**	**3,942,101***	**65.5**	**100.0**
001 ADVENT CHR CH	12	709	877*	-	-
005 AME ZION	21	8,681	10,710	.2	.3
007 ALBAN ORTH ARC	5	NR	NR	-	-
009 ALBAN ORTH DIO	1	NR	NR	-	-
019 AMER BAPT USA	261	54,417	66,156*	1.1	1.7
045 APOSTOLIC LUTH	1	80	400	-	-
049 ARMEN AP CH AM	5	3,075	16,650	.3	.4
053 ASSEMB OF GOD	100	12,164	20,160	.3	.5
057 BAPT GEN CONF	26	3,597	4,416*	.1	.1
081 CATHOLIC	832	NA	2,961,359	49.2	75.1
081a ARMENIAN	*1*	*NA*	*3,100*	*.1*	*.1*
081b BYZAN RUTH	*1*	*NA*	*150*	-	-
081d LATIN	*815*	*NA*	*2,946,137*	*49.0*	*74.7*
081e MARONITE	*7*	*NA*	*8,475*	*.1*	*.2*
081f MELKITE-GK	*3*	*NA*	*2,828*	-	*.1*
081h UKRAINIAN	*5*	*NA*	*669*	-	-
083 CHRIST CATH CH	1	6	6	-	-
089 CHR & MISS AL	31	1,761	3,649	.1	.1
093 CHR CH (DISC)	3	128	154	-	-
097 CHR CHS&CHS CR	4	278	335*	-	-
105 CHRISTIAN REF	4	946	1,372	-	-
111 CH CR,SCIENTST	69	NR	NR	-	-
123 CH GOD (ANDER)	4	978	1,047	-	-
127 CH GOD (CLEVE)	30	2,227	2,709*	-	.1
145 CH GOD PROPHCY	13	364	444*	-	-
151 L-D SAINTS	33	NA	11,093	.2	.3
165 CH OF NAZARENE	41	5,036	7,048	.1	.2
167 CHS OF CHRIST	29	4,863	6,621	.1	.2
175 CONGR CHR CHS	33	8,206	9,931*	.2	.3
176 CCC, NOT NAT'L	17	3,263	3,996*	.1	.1
179 CONSRV BAPT	45	NR	NR	-	-
181 CONSRV CONGR	26	4,409	5,332*	.1	.1
193 EPISCOPAL	257	72,205	122,190	2.0	3.1
203 EVAN FREE CH	6	402	681	-	-
207 E.L.C.A.	71	21,308	28,269	.5	.7
209 EVAN LUTH SYN	2	176	215	-	-
220 FREE LUTHERAN	1	17	24	-	-
221 FREE METHODIST	8	237	504	-	-
226 FRIENDS-USA	36	1,961	2,398*	-	.1
226d FGC & FUM	*35*	*1,960*	*2,394**	-	*.1*
226f INDEPENDNT	*1*	*1*	*4*	-	-
246 GREEK ORTHODOX	38	NR	NR	-	-
263 INT FOURSQ GOS	15	830	1,036*	-	-
274 LAT EVAN LUTH	2	820	883	-	-
283 LUTH—MO SYNOD	21	5,175	7,053	.1	.2
285 MENNONITE CH	4	162	252	-	-
287 MENN GEN CONF	1	20	25	-	-
331 ORTH CH IN AM	9	NR	NR	-	-
339 PENT CH OF GOD	1	19	50	-	-
353 CHR BRETHREN	16	835	1,275	-	-
355 PRESB CH (USA)	33	4,623	5,608*	.1	.1
356 PRESB CH AMER	3	135	189	-	-
363 PRIMITIVE METH	8	464	650	-	-
371 REF CH IN AM	1	79	166	-	-
403 SALVATION ARMY	29	2,322	2,609	-	.1
413 S.D.A.	65	10,524	12,862*	.2	.3
419 SO BAPT CONV	46	8,261	9,978*	.2	.3
423 SYRIAN ANTIOCH	2	NA	1,400	-	-
435 UNITARIAN-UNIV	153	26,525	35,787	.6	.9
443 UN C OF CHRIST	437	111,366	135,983*	2.3	3.4
449 UN METHODIST	246	58,929	71,858*	1.2	1.8
467 WESLEYAN	2	76	232	-	-
469 WELS	1	94	128	-	-
496 JEWISH EST[1]	204	NA	283,920	4.7	7.2
497 BLACK BAPT EST[2]	NA	57,827	69,672*	1.2	1.8
499 INDEP.NON-CHAR[3]	17	NA	11,739	.2	.3
MICHIGAN	**7,229**	**1,583,261**	**4,686,550***	**50.4**	**100.0**
001 ADVENT CHR CH	3	111	135*	-	-
005 AME ZION	18	39,774	47,183	.5	1.0
007 ALBAN ORTH ARC	1	NR	NR	-	-
011 A.W.M.C.	2	0	0*	-	-
019 AMER BAPT USA	176	53,812	67,895*	.7	1.4
039 AP CHR CH(NAZ)	2	84	105*	-	-
040 AP CHR CH-AMER	3	328	583	-	-
045 APOSTOLIC LUTH	19	1,133	2,154	-	-
049 ARMEN AP CH AM	1	1,000	5,000	.1	.1
053 ASSEMB OF GOD	268	34,307	67,404	.7	1.4
057 BAPT GEN CONF	53	7,528	9,544*	.1	.2
059 BAPT MISS ASSN	15	1,663	2,118*	-	-
061 BEACHY AMISH	1	44	57*	-	-
071 BRETHREN (ASH)	1	10	13*	-	-
075 BRETHREN IN CR	7	216	340	-	-
081 CATHOLIC	915	NA	2,338,608	25.2	49.9
081a ARMENIAN	*1*	*NA*	*600*	-	-
081b BYZAN RUTH	*7*	*NA*	*2,447*	-	*.1*
081c CHALDEAN	*5*	*NA*	*31,000*	*.3*	*.7*
081d LATIN	*888*	*NA*	*2,292,593*	*24.7*	*48.9*
081e MARONITE	*2*	*NA*	*3,457*	-	*.1*
081f MELKITE-GK	*3*	*NA*	*2,274*	-	-
081g ROMANIAN	*2*	*NA*	*644*	-	-
081h UKRAINIAN	*7*	*NA*	*5,593*	*.1*	*.1*
089 CHR & MISS AL	32	2,312	4,313	-	.1
093 CHR CH (DISC)	39	6,326	9,170	.1	.2
097 CHR CHS&CHS CR	114	16,521	20,930*	.2	.4
105 CHRISTIAN REF	235	65,792	100,680	1.1	2.1
111 CH CR,SCIENTST	79	NR	NR	-	-
121 CH GOD (ABR)	7	428	544*	-	-
123 CH GOD (ANDER)	131	12,553	14,901	.2	.3
127 CH GOD (CLEVE)	110	15,865	20,024*	.2	.4
133 CH GOD(7TH)DEN	11	341	431	-	-
143 CG IN CR(MENN)	2	355	453*	-	-
145 CH GOD PROPHCY	29	1,025	1,297*	-	-
146 CH GOD MTN ASM	8	410	522*	-	-
151 L-D SAINTS	77	NA	23,475	.3	.5
157 CH OF BRETHREN	26	1,428	1,794*	-	-
164 CH LUTH CONF	6	711	943	-	-
165 CH OF NAZARENE	197	20,242	34,214	.4	.7
167 CHS OF CHRIST	198	23,075	30,591	.3	.7
171 CH GOD-GEN CON	8	200	253*	-	-
175 CONGR CHR CHS	52	13,924	17,571*	.2	.4
176 CCC, NOT NAT'L	6	2,322	2,967*	-	.1
179 CONSRV BAPT	28	NR	NR	-	-
181 CONSRV CONGR	21	2,182	2,768*	-	.1
185 CUMBER PRESB	3	232	245	-	-
193 EPISCOPAL	246	47,929	71,727	.8	1.5
195 ESTONIAN ELC	1	90	111*	-	-
203 EVAN FREE CH	26	1,976	3,791	-	.1
207 E.L.C.A.	362	123,952	167,598	1.8	3.6
209 EVAN LUTH SYN	9	1,109	1,549	-	-
211 FEL EVG BIB CH	1	12	20	-	-
213 EVAN MENN INC	3	257	331*	-	-
215 EVAN METH CH	1	4	5*	-	-
216 EVAN PRESBY CH	17	9,360	9,711	.1	.2
220 FREE LUTHERAN	7	534	712	-	-
221 FREE METHODIST	137	9,369	14,465	.2	.3
223 FREE WILL BAPT	33	3,998	5,007*	.1	.1
226 FRIENDS-USA	21	1,142	1,497*	-	-
226b EFI	*8*	*653*	*845*	-	-
226c FGC	*9*	*343*	*446**	-	-
226e FUM	*4*	*146*	*206**	-	-
246 GREEK ORTHODOX	22	NR	NR	-	-

NA–Not applicable NR–Not reported *Total adherents estimated from known number of communicant, confirmed, full members. - Represents a percent less than 0.1. Percentages may not total due to rounding.
[1]See Appendix E [2]See Appendix F [3]See Appendix G Lines in *italic* represent a breakdown of Catholic rites or Friends affiliations. They are included in their respective denominational total.

Table 3. Churches and Church Membership by State and Denomination: 1990

State and Denomination	Number of churches	Communicant, confirmed, full members	Total adherents		
			Number	Percent of total population	Percent of total adherents
249 AP CATH ASSYR	2	131	680	-	-
259 IFCA	109	NR	NR	-	-
263 INT FOURSQ GOS	10	659	825*	-	-
265 INT PENT C CHR	8	215	308	-	-
274 LAT EVAN LUTH	6	1,492	1,640	-	-
283 LUTH—MO SYNOD	404	185,240	250,141	2.7	5.3
284 LUTH CH–AM ASC	2	61	86	-	-
285 MENNONITE CH	56	3,246	5,230	.1	.1
287 MENN GEN CONF	5	142	207	-	-
291 MISSIONARY CH	69	4,015	7,192	.1	.2
293 MORAV CH–NORTH	4	633	798	-	-
307 NETH REF CONGR	3	1,025	1,817	-	-
313 N AM BAPT CONF	22	5,353	6,692*	.1	.1
320 "OLD" MB ASCS	1	121	149*	-	-
323 OLD ORD AMISH	38	NA	5,250	.1	.1
325 OLD REG BAPT	11	412	517*	-	-
329 OPEN BIBLE STD	3	NR	NR	-	-
331 ORTH CH IN AM	9	NR	NR	-	-
339 PENT CH OF GOD	53	1,813	4,729	.1	.1
349 PENT HOLINESS	6	136	173*	-	-
353 CHR BRETHREN	50	3,322	5,424	.1	.1
355 PRESB CH (USA)	275	100,122	126,324*	1.4	2.7
356 PRESB CH AMER	5	908	1,116	-	-
361 PRIM BAPT ASCS	4	138	176*	-	-
367 PROT CONF (LU)	1	50	65	-	-
371 REF CH IN AM	162	53,029	88,399	1.0	1.9
397 ROMANIAN ORTH	6	NR	NR	-	-
403 SALVATION ARMY	56	6,873	7,896	.1	.2
413 S.D.A.	185	29,905	37,949*	.4	.8
415 S-D BAPTIST GC	2	217	277*	-	-
419 SO BAPT CONV	236	49,133	61,953*	.7	1.3
423 SYRIAN ANTIOCH	2	NA	1,700	-	-
431 UKRANIAN AMER	2	NR	NR	-	-
435 UNITARIAN-UNIV	21	3,075	4,266	-	.1
436 UNITED BAPT	1	26	31*	-	-
438 UN BRETH IN CR	48	3,935	4,803	.1	.1
443 UN C OF CHRIST	200	58,740	74,302*	.8	1.6
449 UN METHODIST	938	199,321	252,129*	2.7	5.4
467 WESLEYAN	142	12,026	39,404	.4	.8
469 WELS	138	36,051	47,357	.5	1.0
496 JEWISH EST[1]	73	NA	107,116	1.2	2.3
497 BLACK BAPT EST[2]	NA	295,710	374,325*	4.0	8.0
498 INDEP.CHARIS.[3]	21	NA	20,830	.2	.4
499 INDEP.NON-CHAR[3]	50	NA	38,525	.4	.8
MINNESOTA	**4,981**	**1,222,359**	**2,837,418***	**64.9**	**100.0**
001 ADVENT CHR CH	1	49	60*	-	-
019 AMER BAPT USA	39	10,136	12,649*	.3	.4
039 AP CHR CH(NAZ)	1	7	9*	-	-
040 AP CHR CH-AMER	3	342	607	-	-
045 APOSTOLIC LUTH	15	1,115	2,755	.1	.1
053 ASSEMB OF GOD	194	19,782	39,877	.9	1.4
057 BAPT GEN CONF	142	25,153	31,946*	.7	1.1
061 BEACHY AMISH	2	66	86*	-	-
063 BEREAN FUND CH	1	59	151	-	-
081 CATHOLIC	768	NA	1,110,071	25.4	39.1
081b BYZAN RUTH	1	NA	250	-	-
081d LATIN	763	NA	1,108,658	25.3	39.1
081e MARONITE	2	NA	707	-	-
081h UKRAINIAN	2	NA	456	-	-
089 CHR & MISS AL	85	7,475	17,644	.4	.6
093 CHR CH (DISC)	11	1,594	2,282	.1	.1
097 CHR CHS&CHS CR	52	5,380	6,890*	.2	.2
105 CHRISTIAN REF	30	5,452	8,313	.2	.3
111 CH CR,SCIENTST	27	NR	NR	-	-
121 CH GOD (ABR)	5	227	291*	-	-
123 CH GOD (ANDER)	8	450	525	-	-
127 CH GOD (CLEVE)	10	752	970*	-	-
133 CH GOD(7TH)DEN	1	67	96	-	-
143 CG IN CR(MENN)	2	27	34*	-	-
145 CH GOD PROPHCY	8	193	245*	-	-
151 L-D SAINTS	48	NA	14,576	.3	.5
157 CH OF BRETHREN	3	338	427*	-	-
163 CH OF LUTH BR	25	1,976	4,380	.1	.2
164 CH LUTH CONF	14	1,937	2,603	.1	.1
165 CH OF NAZARENE	42	2,558	4,781	.1	.2
167 CHS OF CHRIST	43	2,174	3,255	.1	.1
175 CONGR CHR CHS	6	6,654	8,260*	.2	.3
176 CCC, NOT NAT'L	1	245	318*	-	-

State and Denomination	Number of churches	Communicant, confirmed, full members	Total adherents		
			Number	Percent of total population	Percent of total adherents
179 CONSRV BAPT	43	NR	NR	-	-
181 CONSRV CONGR	10	1,036	1,313*	-	-
193 EPISCOPAL	126	21,305	31,980	.7	1.1
195 ESTONIAN ELC	1	100	123*	-	-
203 EVAN FREE CH	118	12,007	20,627	.5	.7
207 E.L.C.A.	1,207	604,902	823,372	18.8	29.0
209 EVAN LUTH SYN	29	4,627	6,158	.1	.2
211 FEL EVG BIB CH	2	209	209	-	-
220 FREE LUTHERAN	85	9,386	12,420	.3	.4
221 FREE METHODIST	13	366	593	-	-
226 FRIENDS-USA	13	224	680	-	-
226c FGC	12	221	670	-	-
226f INDEPENDNT	1	3	10	-	-
237 GC MENN BR CHS	3	307	382*	-	-
246 GREEK ORTHODOX	4	NR	NR	-	-
257 HUTTERIAN BR	4	NA	400	-	-
259 IFCA	6	NR	NR	-	-
263 INT FOURSQ GOS	10	203	252*	-	-
274 LAT EVAN LUTH	2	862	949	-	-
283 LUTH—MO SYNOD	452	164,745	215,564	4.9	7.6
284 LUTH CH–AM ASC	17	1,842	2,451	.1	.1
285 MENNONITE CH	13	454	703	-	-
287 MENN GEN CONF	10	1,330	1,547	-	.1
293 MORAV CH–NORTH	7	1,118	1,465	-	.1
313 N AM BAPT CONF	10	1,456	1,862*	-	.1
323 OLD ORD AMISH	8	NA	1,200	-	-
329 OPEN BIBLE STD	1	NR	NR	-	-
331 ORTH CH IN AM	6	NR	NR	-	-
339 PENT CH OF GOD	9	308	691	-	-
353 CHR BRETHREN	11	583	935	-	-
355 PRESB CH (USA)	201	52,806	66,715*	1.5	2.4
356 PRESB CH AMER	4	294	417	-	-
371 REF CH IN AM	26	5,474	8,910	.2	.3
397 ROMANIAN ORTH	1	NR	NR	-	-
403 SALVATION ARMY	21	2,670	2,923	.1	.1
413 S.D.A.	65	5,428	6,874*	.2	.2
415 S-D BAPTIST GC	1	97	130*	-	-
419 SO BAPT CONV	32	4,125	5,218*	.1	.2
435 UNITARIAN-UNIV	24	3,907	5,669	.1	.2
443 UN C OF CHRIST	158	43,863	55,497*	1.3	2.0
449 UN METHODIST	426	112,200	142,771*	3.3	5.0
467 WESLEYAN	14	700	1,542	-	.1
469 WELS	149	45,163	58,908	1.3	2.1
496 JEWISH EST[1]	26	NA	33,779	.8	1.2
497 BLACK BAPT EST[2]	NA	24,054	29,943*	.7	1.1
498 INDEP.CHARIS.[3]	15	NA	9,325	.2	.3
499 INDEP.NON-CHAR[3]	11	NA	8,820	.2	.3
MISSISSIPPI	**5,433**	**1,307,928**	**1,806,049***	**70.2**	**100.0**
001 ADVENT CHR CH	3	73	96*	-	-
005 AME ZION	50	10,253	12,531	.5	.7
019 AMER BAPT USA	2	350	471*	-	-
053 ASSEMB OF GOD	174	14,291	20,189	.8	1.1
055 AS REF PRES CH	6	600	666	-	-
059 BAPT MISS ASSN	185	30,726	39,295*	1.5	2.2
081 CATHOLIC	156	NA	94,948	3.7	5.3
081d LATIN	156	NA	94,948	3.7	5.3
089 CHR & MISS AL	1	33	58	-	-
093 CHR CH (DISC)	53	4,078	5,534	.2	.3
097 CHR CHS&CHS CR	30	3,340	4,259*	.2	.2
111 CH CR,SCIENTST	10	NR	NR	-	-
123 CH GOD (ANDER)	57	2,511	3,300	.1	.2
127 CH GOD (CLEVE)	127	11,400	14,758*	.6	.8
143 CG IN CR(MENN)	6	815	1,102*	-	.1
145 CH GOD PROPHCY	72	2,405	3,113*	.1	.2
151 L-D SAINTS	42	NA	10,417	.4	.6
165 CH OF NAZARENE	51	4,112	5,906	.2	.3
167 CHS OF CHRIST	378	29,840	40,533	1.6	2.2
171 CH GOD-GEN CON	3	70	90*	-	-
185 CUMBER PRESB	19	1,573	1,660	.1	.1
193 EPISCOPAL	86	16,382	20,554	.8	1.1
207 E.L.C.A.	17	1,713	2,264	.1	.1
215 EVAN METH CH	1	70	90*	-	-
216 EVAN PRESBY CH	6	1,076	1,106	-	.1
223 FREE WILL BAPT	59	4,919	6,214*	.2	.3
246 GREEK ORTHODOX	2	NR	NR	-	-
249 AP CATH ASSYR	0	17	72	-	-
263 INT FOURSQ GOS	4	317	409*	-	-
266 INTRSTAT & ASC	85	9,298	12,055*	.5	.7

NA–Not applicable NR–Not reported *Total adherents estimated from known number of communicant, confirmed, full members. - Represents a percent less than 0.1. Percentages may not total due to rounding.
[1]See Appendix E [2]See Appendix F [3]See Appendix G Lines in *italic* represent a breakdown of Catholic rites or Friends affiliations. They are included in their respective denominational total.

Table 3. Churches and Church Membership by State and Denomination: 1990

State and Denomination	Number of churches	Communicant, confirmed, full members	Total adherents Number	Percent of total population	Percent of total adherents
283 LUTH—MO SYNOD	29	3,169	4,183	.2	.2
285 MENNONITE CH	13	558	729	-	-
331 ORTH CH IN AM	1	NR	NR	-	-
339 PENT CH OF GOD	13	489	1,072	-	.1
349 PENT HOLINESS	17	1,165	1,499*	.1	.1
353 CHR BRETHREN	3	175	224	-	-
355 PRESB CH (USA)	138	15,449	19,866*	.8	1.1
356 PRESB CH AMER	127	15,981	18,659	.7	1.0
361 PRIM BAPT ASCS	43	2,094	2,686*	.1	.1
403 SALVATION ARMY	14	1,298	1,378	.1	.1
413 S.D.A.	59	5,998	7,801*	.3	.4
415 S-D BAPTIST GC	1	31	40*	-	-
419 SO BAPT CONV	1,977	675,738	869,942*	33.8	48.2
435 UNITARIAN-UNIV	4	102	128	-	-
443 UN C OF CHRIST	1	36	47*	-	-
449 UN METHODIST	1,270	186,445	240,325*	9.3	13.3
467 WESLEYAN	3	160	295	-	-
469 WELS	1	34	47	-	-
496 JEWISH EST[1]	18	NA	2,466	.1	.1
497 BLACK BAPT EST[2]	NA	248,744	324,272*	12.6	18.0
498 INDEP.CHARIS.[3]	4	NA	2,150	.1	.1
499 INDEP.NON-CHAR[3]	12	NA	6,550	.3	.4
MISSOURI	**7,666**	**1,542,347**	**2,944,890***	**57.6**	**100.0**
001 ADVENT CHR CH	2	100	126*		
005 AME ZION	11	5,876	6,941	.1	.2
019 AMER BAPT USA	21	9,369	11,693*	.2	.4
039 AP CHR CH(NAZ)	1	26	32*	-	-
040 AP CHR CH-AMER	3	180	320	-	-
053 ASSEMB OF GOD	501	45,092	84,193	1.6	2.9
055 AS REF PRES CH	2	137	157	-	-
057 BAPT GEN CONF	5	396	494*	-	-
059 BAPT MISS ASSN	95	8,562	10,919*	.2	.4
061 BEACHY AMISH	5	237	300*	-	-
081 CATHOLIC	578	NA	802,083	15.7	27.2
081b *BYZAN RUTH*	2	*NA*	105	-	-
081d *LATIN*	573	*NA*	800,345	15.6	27.2
081e *MARONITE*	1	*NA*	1,466	-	-
081h *UKRAINIAN*	2	*NA*	167	-	-
083 CHRIST CATH CH	1	23	62	-	-
089 CHR & MISS AL	8	277	523	-	-
093 CHR CH (DISC)	385	63,923	101,756	2.0	3.5
097 CHR CHS&CHS CR	323	51,907	65,035*	1.3	2.2
105 CHRISTIAN REF	3	231	387	-	-
111 CH CR,SCIENTST	40	NR	NR	-	-
121 CH GOD (ABR)	10	203	257*	-	-
123 CH GOD (ANDER)	93	5,845	7,887	.2	.3
127 CH GOD (CLEVE)	60	5,266	6,646*	.1	.2
133 CH GOD(7TH)DEN	6	252	331	-	-
143 CG IN CR(MENN)	3	327	408*	-	-
145 CH GOD PROPHCY	44	1,094	1,377*	-	-
151 L-D SAINTS	89	NA	27,877	.5	.9
157 CH OF BRETHREN	23	966	1,206*	-	-
164 CH LUTH CONF	1	46	70	-	-
165 CH OF NAZARENE	170	17,944	26,507	.5	.9
167 CHS OF CHRIST	489	36,143	46,936	.9	1.6
171 CH GOD-GEN CON	15	1,192	1,500*	-	.1
175 CONGR CHR CHS	3	455	571*	-	-
181 CONSRV CONGR	1	73	92*	-	-
185 CUMBER PRESB	32	2,112	2,202	-	.1
193 EPISCOPAL	104	22,363	29,066	.6	1.0
203 EVAN FREE CH	15	1,414	2,498	-	.1
207 E.L.C.A.	82	22,307	28,958	.6	1.0
209 EVAN LUTH SYN	3	233	298	-	-
215 EVAN METH CH	2	148	188*	-	-
216 EVAN PRESBY CH	6	3,003	3,063	.1	.1
217 FIRE BAPTIZED	13	229	297*	-	-
220 FREE LUTHERAN	1	54	69	-	-
221 FREE METHODIST	17	453	642	-	-
223 FREE WILL BAPT	174	15,686	19,676*	.4	.7
226 FRIENDS-USA	8	398	517*	-	-
226a *CONSERV*	1	53	66*	-	-
226b *EFI*	3	139	174*	-	-
226c *FGC*	4	206	277*	-	-
230 FUND METHODIST	13	707	1,037	-	-
246 GREEK ORTHODOX	3	NR	NR	-	-
259 IFCA	22	NR	NR	-	-
263 INT FOURSQ GOS	17	1,804	2,257*	-	.1
274 LAT EVAN LUTH	1	21	21	-	-
283 LUTH—MO SYNOD	314	110,383	145,741	2.8	4.9
285 MENNONITE CH	16	1,111	1,595	-	.1
286 E.PA MENNONITE	1	33	40*	-	-
287 MENN GEN CONF	2	234	335	-	-
313 N AM BAPT CONF	1	51	63*	-	-
323 OLD ORD AMISH	30	NA	4,150	.1	.1
329 OPEN BIBLE STD	3	NR	NR	-	-
331 ORTH CH IN AM	3	NR	NR	-	-
339 PENT CH OF GOD	66	1,824	4,845	.1	.2
349 PENT HOLINESS	20	1,215	1,546*	-	.1
353 CHR BRETHREN	27	1,613	2,607	.1	.1
355 PRESB CH (USA)	314	63,638	79,600*	1.6	2.7
356 PRESB CH AMER	23	3,213	3,742	.1	.1
361 PRIM BAPT ASCS	20	533	663*	-	-
371 REF CH IN AM	1	85	150	-	-
373 REF CH IN U.S.	1	41	47	-	-
375 REF EPISCOPAL	1	34	35	-	-
397 ROMANIAN ORTH	1	NR	NR	-	-
403 SALVATION ARMY	24	2,892	3,147	.1	.1
413 S.D.A.	83	10,147	12,705*	.2	.4
415 S-D BAPTIST GC	3	83	103*	-	-
419 SO BAPT CONV	1,848	628,341	789,183*	15.4	26.8
435 UNITARIAN-UNIV	8	1,753	2,427	-	.1
436 UNITED BAPT	30	2,514	3,146*	.1	.1
438 UN BRETH IN CR	1	56	56	-	-
443 UN C OF CHRIST	181	52,985	66,776*	1.3	2.3
449 UN METHODIST	1,004	203,787	255,111*	5.0	8.7
467 WESLEYAN	16	802	2,402	-	.1
469 WELS	10	782	1,099	-	-
496 JEWISH EST[1]	35	NA	53,092	1.0	1.8
497 BLACK BAPT EST[2]	NA	127,123	159,266*	3.1	5.4
498 INDEP.CHARIS.[3]	33	NA	25,940	.5	.9
499 INDEP.NON-CHAR[3]	42	NA	27,803	.5	.9
MONTANA	**1,415**	**125,160**	**341,247***	**42.7**	**100.0**
011 A.W.M.C.	2	46	58*	-	-
019 AMER BAPT USA	26	3,321	4,294*	.5	1.3
045 APOSTOLIC LUTH	1	6	10	-	-
053 ASSEMB OF GOD	77	7,285	16,235	2.0	4.8
057 BAPT GEN CONF	5	366	456*	.1	.1
081 CATHOLIC	233	NA	125,799	15.7	36.9
081d *LATIN*	233	*NA*	125,799	15.7	36.9
089 CHR & MISS AL	41	1,639	4,358	.5	1.3
093 CHR CH (DISC)	18	2,125	3,222	.4	.9
097 CHR CHS&CHS CR	23	2,172	2,812*	.4	.8
105 CHRISTIAN REF	6	1,111	1,893	.2	.6
111 CH CR,SCIENTST	12	NR	NR	-	-
123 CH GOD (ANDER)	11	436	601	.1	.2
127 CH GOD (CLEVE)	11	463	587*	.1	.2
145 CH GOD PROPHCY	6	107	136*	-	-
151 L-D SAINTS	106	NA	28,620	3.6	8.4
157 CH OF BRETHREN	1	47	66*	-	-
163 CH OF LUTH BR	4	169	438	.1	.1
165 CH OF NAZARENE	22	1,618	2,942	.4	.9
167 CHS OF CHRIST	52	2,071	2,909	.4	.9
175 CONGR CHR CHS	2	161	205*	-	.1
179 CONSRV BAPT	8	NR	NR	-	-
181 CONSRV CONGR	1	135	179*	-	.1
193 EPISCOPAL	47	4,543	6,644	.8	1.9
203 EVAN FREE CH	11	613	1,127	.1	.3
207 E.L.C.A.	147	34,988	49,106	6.1	14.4
211 FEL EVG BIB CH	1	85	115	-	-
220 FREE LUTHERAN	2	67	75	-	-
221 FREE METHODIST	1	11	33	-	-
223 FREE WILL BAPT	2	43	55*	-	-
226 FRIENDS-USA	7	41	77*	-	-
226f *INDEPENDNT*	7	*41*	77*	-	-
237 GC MENN BR CHS	2	153	198*	-	.1
246 GREEK ORTHODOX	3	NR	NR	-	-
257 HUTTERIAN BR	40	NA	3,307	.4	1.0
259 IFCA	4	NR	NR	-	-
263 INT FOURSQ GOS	22	3,325	4,254*	.5	1.2
283 LUTH—MO SYNOD	64	11,612	16,172	2.0	4.7
284 LUTH CH-AM ASC	2	238	353	-	.1
285 MENNONITE CH	7	231	286	-	-
287 MENN GEN CONF	6	278	313	-	.1
313 N AM BAPT CONF	2	343	436*	.1	.1
323 OLD ORD AMISH	1	NA	150	-	-
329 OPEN BIBLE STD	5	NR	NR	-	-

NA–Not applicable   NR–Not reported   *Total adherents estimated from known number of communicant, confirmed, full members.   - Represents a percent less than 0.1.   Percentages may not total due to rounding.

[1]See Appendix E   [2]See Appendix F   [3]See Appendix G   Lines in *italic* represent a breakdown of Catholic rites or Friends affiliations. They are included in their respective denominational total.

Table 3. Churches and Church Membership by State and Denomination: 1990

State and Denomination	Number of churches	Communicant, confirmed, full members	Total adherents Number	Percent of total population	Percent of total adherents
339 PENT CH OF GOD	10	316	735	.1	.2
349 PENT HOLINESS	2	43	54*	-	-
353 CHR BRETHREN	6	155	290	-	.1
355 PRESB CH (USA)	54	8,885	11,455*	1.4	3.4
371 REF CH IN AM	1	58	120	-	-
403 SALVATION ARMY	8	505	551	.1	.2
413 S.D.A.	41	3,246	4,140*	.5	1.2
419 SO BAPT CONV	77	9,138	11,776*	1.5	3.5
435 UNITARIAN-UNIV	6	190	218	-	.1
443 UN C OF CHRIST	38	6,154	7,915*	1.0	2.3
449 UN METHODIST	95	15,186	19,461*	2.4	5.7
467 WESLEYAN	13	325	1,099	.1	.3
469 WELS	12	775	1,067	.1	.3
496 JEWISH EST[1]	2	NA	310	-	.1
497 BLACK BAPT EST[2]	NA	335	430*	.1	.1
498 INDEP.CHARIS.[3]	2	NA	980	.1	.3
499 INDEP.NON-CHAR[3]	4	NA	2,125	.3	.6
NEBRASKA	**2,629**	**477,349**	**1,006,572***	**63.8**	**100.0**
005 AME ZION	1	200	268	-	-
019 AMER BAPT USA	62	12,207	15,513*	1.0	1.5
053 ASSEMB OF GOD	91	8,776	17,579	1.1	1.7
057 BAPT GEN CONF	33	2,906	3,702*	.2	.4
063 BEREAN FUND CH	30	1,841	3,567	.2	.4
071 BRETHREN (ASH)	1	44	55*	-	-
081 CATHOLIC	381	NA	335,372	21.2	33.3
081d LATIN	379	NA	335,263	21.2	33.3
081h UKRAINIAN	2	NA	109	-	-
089 CHR & MISS AL	18	2,180	5,916	.4	.6
093 CHR CH (DISC)	54	7,910	14,605	.9	1.5
097 CHR CHS&CHS CR	87	11,366	14,488*	.9	1.4
105 CHRISTIAN REF	1	100	170	-	-
111 CH CR,SCIENTST	14	NR	NR	-	-
121 CH GOD (ABR)	2	112	141*	-	-
123 CH GOD (ANDER)	22	649	1,117	.1	.1
127 CH GOD (CLEVE)	9	715	912*	.1	.1
133 CH GOD(7TH)DEN	2	18	18	-	-
143 CG IN CR(MENN)	1	90	117*	-	-
145 CH GOD PROPHCY	6	141	179*	-	-
151 L-D SAINTS	34	NA	10,556	.7	1.0
157 CH OF BRETHREN	4	372	461*	-	-
164 CH LUTH CONF	1	86	128	-	-
165 CH OF NAZARENE	38	2,557	4,815	.3	.5
167 CHS OF CHRIST	50	3,124	4,475	.3	.4
175 CONGR CHR CHS	4	562	720*	-	.1
179 CONSRV BAPT	2	NR	NR	-	-
181 CONSRV CONGR	5	1,111	1,420*	.1	.1
193 EPISCOPAL	68	9,108	12,575	.8	1.2
203 EVAN FREE CH	56	4,349	8,424	.5	.8
207 E.L.C.A.	275	97,181	128,667	8.2	12.8
211 FEL EVG BIB CH	5	556	1,028	.1	.1
220 FREE LUTHERAN	2	272	330	-	-
221 FREE METHODIST	7	175	302	-	-
223 FREE WILL BAPT	2	58	73*	-	-
226 FRIENDS-USA	8	447	574*	-	.1
226a CONSERV	1	34	42*	-	-
226b EFI	5	300	386*	-	-
226e FUM	1	109	139*	-	-
226f INDEPENDNT	1	4	7	-	-
237 GC MENN BR CHS	5	376	483*	-	-
246 GREEK ORTHODOX	4	NR	NR	-	-
259 IFCA	2	NR	NR	-	-
263 INT FOURSQ GOS	15	1,311	1,665*	.1	.2
274 LAT EVAN LUTH	3	332	349	-	-
283 LUTH—MO SYNOD	271	86,525	114,944	7.3	11.4
284 LUTH CH-AM ASC	1	442	572	-	.1
285 MENNONITE CH	12	1,332	1,763	.1	.2
287 MENN GEN CONF	5	1,553	2,063	.1	.2
291 MISSIONARY CH	6	337	514	-	.1
313 N AM BAPT CONF	5	219	283*	-	-
329 OPEN BIBLE STD	12	NR	NR	-	-
353 CHR BRETHREN	5	205	360	-	-
355 PRESB CH (USA)	153	38,141	48,591*	3.1	4.8
356 PRESB CH AMER	4	318	427	-	-
371 REF CH IN AM	7	1,137	2,088	.1	.2
373 REF CH IN U.S.	4	498	651	-	.1
403 SALVATION ARMY	12	1,529	1,708	.1	.2
413 S.D.A.	55	6,635	8,383*	.5	.8
415 S-D BAPTIST GC	1	189	236*	-	-

State and Denomination	Number of churches	Communicant, confirmed, full members	Total adherents Number	Percent of total population	Percent of total adherents
419 SO BAPT CONV	35	9,412	12,175*	.8	1.2
431 UKRANIAN AMER	1	NR	NR	-	-
435 UNITARIAN-UNIV	4	793	1,019	.1	.1
443 UN C OF CHRIST	116	22,342	28,342*	1.8	2.8
449 UN METHODIST	428	114,289	145,248*	9.2	14.4
467 WESLEYAN	29	679	1,790	.1	.2
469 WELS	38	4,859	6,457	.4	.6
496 JEWISH EST[1]	7	NA	6,732	.4	.7
497 BLACK BAPT EST[2]	NA	14,683	18,770*	1.2	1.9
498 INDEP.CHARIS.[3]	5	NA	4,650	.3	.5
499 INDEP.NON-CHAR[3]	8	NA	8,042	.5	.8
NEVADA	**664**	**86,694**	**386,312***	**32.1**	**100.0**
019 AMER BAPT USA	21	5,374	6,698*	.6	1.7
053 ASSEMB OF GOD	36	3,920	7,085	.6	1.8
059 BAPT MISS ASSN	1	81	101*	-	-
081 CATHOLIC	53	NA	156,956	13.1	40.6
081b BYZAN RUTH	1	NA	256	-	.1
081d LATIN	52	NA	156,700	13.0	40.6
089 CHR & MISS AL	2	25	67	-	-
093 CHR CH (DISC)	3	578	651	.1	.2
097 CHR CHS&CHS CR	9	2,295	2,846*	.2	.7
105 CHRISTIAN REF	1	40	55	-	-
111 CH CR,SCIENTST	5	NR	NR	-	-
123 CH GOD (ANDER)	4	238	277	-	.1
127 CH GOD (CLEVE)	8	335	417*	-	.1
133 CH GOD(7TH)DEN	1	29	44	-	-
145 CH GOD PROPHCY	3	96	120*	-	-
151 L-D SAINTS	198	NA	89,033	7.4	23.0
165 CH OF NAZARENE	15	1,114	1,843	.2	.5
167 CHS OF CHRIST	26	1,707	2,186	.2	.6
179 CONSRV BAPT	4	NR	NR	-	-
193 EPISCOPAL	33	3,605	5,524	.5	1.4
203 EVAN FREE CH	4	281	523	-	.1
207 E.L.C.A.	13	5,829	8,197	.7	2.1
221 FREE METHODIST	2	23	80	-	-
226 FRIENDS-USA	1	20	49	-	-
226f INDEPENDNT	1	20	49	-	-
246 GREEK ORTHODOX	4	NR	NR	-	-
249 AP CATH ASSYR	0	12	72	-	-
259 IFCA	7	NR	NR	-	-
263 INT FOURSQ GOS	17	2,257	2,817*	.2	.7
283 LUTH—MO SYNOD	19	4,486	6,219	.5	1.6
331 ORTH CH IN AM	1	NR	NR	-	-
339 PENT CH OF GOD	6	189	430	-	.1
349 PENT HOLINESS	1	100	134*	-	-
355 PRESB CH (USA)	18	4,507	5,641*	.5	1.5
356 PRESB CH AMER	1	0	0	-	-
403 SALVATION ARMY	4	470	505	-	.1
413 S.D.A.	15	2,278	2,843*	.2	.7
419 SO BAPT CONV	74	22,218	27,889*	2.3	7.2
435 UNITARIAN-UNIV	2	179	211	-	.1
443 UN C OF CHRIST	4	567	703*	.1	.2
449 UN METHODIST	29	6,835	8,529*	.7	2.2
467 WESLEYAN	1	45	168	-	-
469 WELS	4	538	745	.1	.2
496 JEWISH EST[1]	6	NA	20,400	1.7	5.3
497 BLACK BAPT EST[2]	NA	16,423	20,454*	1.7	5.3
498 INDEP.CHARIS.[3]	3	NA	2,300	.2	.6
499 INDEP.NON-CHAR[3]	5	NA	3,500	.3	.9
NEW HAMPSHIRE	**896**	**94,202**	**438,374***	**39.5**	**100.0**
001 ADVENT CHR CH	19	971	1,210*	.1	.3
005 AME ZION	1	50	87	-	-
019 AMER BAPT USA	93	14,892	18,663*	1.7	4.3
045 APOSTOLIC LUTH	1	0	1,030	.1	.2
053 ASSEMB OF GOD	35	2,784	4,698	.4	1.1
057 BAPT GEN CONF	2	26	33*	-	-
081 CATHOLIC	170	NA	297,062	26.8	67.8
081d LATIN	167	NA	296,513	26.7	67.6
081e MARONITE	1	NA	251	-	.1
081f MELKITE-GK	1	NA	207	-	-
081h UKRAINIAN	1	NA	91	-	-
089 CHR & MISS AL	8	248	594	.1	.1
097 CHR CHS&CHS CR	3	313	396*	-	.1
105 CHRISTIAN REF	1	29	46	-	-
111 CH CR,SCIENTST	18	NR	NR	-	-
123 CH GOD (ANDER)	1	40	55	-	-
127 CH GOD (CLEVE)	4	360	454*	-	.1

NA–Not applicable   NR–Not reported   *Total adherents estimated from known number of communicant, confirmed, full members.   - Represents a percent less than 0.1.   Percentages may not total due to rounding.
[1]See Appendix E   [2]See Appendix F   [3]See Appendix G   Lines in *italic* represent a breakdown of Catholic rites or Friends affiliations. They are included in their respective denominational total.

Table 3. Churches and Church Membership by State and Denomination: 1990

State and Denomination	Number of churches	Communicant, confirmed, full members	Total adherents Number	Percent of total population	Percent of total adherents
145 CH GOD PROPHCY	3	84	105*	-	-
151 L-D SAINTS	16	NA	4,635	.4	1.1
165 CH OF NAZARENE	9	770	974	.1	.2
167 CHS OF CHRIST	14	796	1,120	.1	.3
175 CONGR CHR CHS	15	1,424	1,788*	.2	.4
176 CCC, NOT NAT'L	17	2,048	2,579*	.2	.6
179 CONSRV BAPT	28	NR	NR	-	-
181 CONSRV CONGR	4	501	630*	.1	.1
193 EPISCOPAL	50	9,154	16,301	1.5	3.7
203 EVAN FREE CH	3	200	340	-	.1
207 E.L.C.A.	13	2,180	3,211*	.3	.7
223 FREE WILL BAPT	1	98	121*	-	-
226 FRIENDS-USA	10	437	586*	.1	.1
226d *FGC & FUM*	*10*	*437*	*586**	*.1*	*.1*
246 GREEK ORTHODOX	12	NR	NR	-	-
249 AP CATH ASSYR	0	9	27	-	-
259 IFCA	1	NR	NR	-	-
263 INT FOURSQ GOS	2	41	51*	-	-
283 LUTH—MO SYNOD	8	1,328	1,908	.2	.4
331 ORTH CH IN AM	2	NR	NR	-	-
349 PENT HOLINESS	1	40	50*	-	-
353 CHR BRETHREN	5	328	420	-	.1
355 PRESB CH (USA)	9	1,711	2,157*	.2	.5
356 PRESB CH AMER	3	137	175	-	-
403 SALVATION ARMY	8	679	763	.1	.2
413 S.D.A.	15	1,000	1,247*	.1	.3
419 SO BAPT CONV	10	2,208	2,785*	.3	.6
435 UNITARIAN-UNIV	23	3,029	4,189	.4	1.0
443 UN C OF CHRIST	139	29,579	36,989*	3.3	8.4
449 UN METHODIST	101	15,469	19,328*	1.7	4.4
467 WESLEYAN	1	3	30	-	-
469 WELS	1	94	144	-	-
496 JEWISH EST[1]	11	NA	6,680	.6	1.5
497 BLACK BAPT EST[2]	NA	1,142	1,438*	.1	.3
498 INDEP.CHARIS.[3]	1	NA	1,600	.1	.4
499 INDEP.NON-CHAR[3]	4	NA	1,675	.2	.4
NEW JERSEY	**4,183**	**813,759**	**4,734,822***	**61.3**	**100.0**
005 AME ZION	45	34,283	40,872	.5	.9
019 AMER BAPT USA	254	67,409	82,795*	1.1	1.7
022 EASTERN ORTH	7	1,637	1,637	-	-
039 AP CHR CH(NAZ)	2	88	105*	-	-
040 AP CHR CH-AMER	1	11	21	-	-
049 ARMEN AP CH AM	1	1,500	9,000	.1	.2
053 ASSEMB OF GOD	180	22,286	39,374	.5	.8
057 BAPT GEN CONF	1	159	196*	-	-
059 BAPT MISS ASSN	2	50	62*	-	-
071 BRETHREN (ASH)	2	40	49*	-	-
080 BYELORSSN ORTH	1	NR	NR	-	-
081 CATHOLIC	776	NA	3,189,315	41.3	67.4
081a *ARMENIAN*	*1*	*NA*	*1,500*	-	-
081b *BYZAN RUTH*	*23*	*NA*	*17,634*	*.2*	*.4*
081d *LATIN*	*727*	*NA*	*3,148,377*	*40.7*	*66.5*
081e *MARONITE*	*1*	*NA*	*716*	-	-
081f *MELKITE-GK*	*2*	*NA*	*3,122*	-	*.1*
081g *ROMANIAN*	*2*	*NA*	*644*	-	-
081h *UKRAINIAN*	*20*	*NA*	*17,322*	*.2*	*.4*
089 CHR & MISS AL	46	3,313	7,689	.1	.2
093 CHR CH (DISC)	8	1,503	1,968	-	-
097 CHR CHS&CHS CR	7	982	1,210*	-	-
105 CHRISTIAN REF	21	4,565	6,543	.1	.1
111 CH CR,SCIENTST	39	NR	NR	-	-
123 CH GOD (ANDER)	21	1,049	1,272	-	-
127 CH GOD (CLEVE)	47	3,702	4,565*	.1	.1
145 CH GOD PROPHCY	16	438	541*	-	-
151 L-D SAINTS	35	NA	11,806	.2	.2
157 CH OF BRETHREN	1	126	156*	-	-
163 CH OF LUTH BR	5	557	1,570	-	-
165 CH OF NAZARENE	42	4,157	5,348	.1	.1
167 CHS OF CHRIST	39	3,440	4,149	.1	.1
175 CONGR CHR CHS	4	665	825*	-	-
179 CONSRV BAPT	46	NR	NR	-	-
193 EPISCOPAL	294	70,624	105,607	1.4	2.2
195 ESTONIAN ELC	4	672	828*	-	-
199 EVAN CONGR CH	1	266	266	-	-
203 EVAN FREE CH	23	2,549	3,640	-	.1
207 E.L.C.A.	205	60,529	86,825	1.1	1.8
216 EVAN PRESBY CH	1	409	420	-	-
221 FREE METHODIST	9	254	543	-	-

State and Denomination	Number of churches	Communicant, confirmed, full members	Total adherents Number	Percent of total population	Percent of total adherents
223 FREE WILL BAPT	2	78	99*	-	-
226 FRIENDS-USA	37	3,275	4,058*	.1	.1
226c *FGC*	*28*	*2,519*	*3,139**	-	*.1*
226d *FGC & FUM*	*9*	*756*	*919**	-	-
246 GREEK ORTHODOX	23	NR	NR	-	-
249 AP CATH ASSYR	0	3	11	-	-
259 IFCA	24	NR	NR	-	-
263 INT FOURSQ GOS	4	248	310*	-	-
265 INT PENT C CHR	1	57	57	-	-
274 LAT EVAN LUTH	2	410	441	-	-
283 LUTH—MO SYNOD	69	18,446	25,387	.3	.5
285 MENNONITE CH	11	531	859	-	-
286 E.PA MENNONITE	1	37	46*	-	-
293 MORAV CH-NORTH	5	973	1,223	-	-
307 NETH REF CONGR	2	538	964	-	-
313 N AM BAPT CONF	4	252	307*	-	-
331 ORTH CH IN AM	21	NR	NR	-	-
339 PENT CH OF GOD	1	35	55	-	-
349 PENT HOLINESS	2	156	187*	-	-
353 CHR BRETHREN	41	2,769	4,203	.1	.1
355 PRESB CH (USA)	373	113,296	138,763*	1.8	2.9
356 PRESB CH AMER	24	1,516	2,003	-	-
371 REF CH IN AM	140	21,436	41,392	.5	.9
375 REF EPISCOPAL	7	399	529	-	-
403 SALVATION ARMY	24	1,883	2,108	-	-
413 S.D.A.	97	12,515	15,371*	.2	.3
415 S-D BAPTIST GC	4	474	589*	-	-
419 SO BAPT CONV	48	8,893	10,881*	.1	.2
423 SYRIAN ANTIOCH	2	NA	7,700	.1	.2
431 UKRANIAN AMER	1	NR	NR	-	-
435 UNITARIAN-UNIV	20	3,602	4,894	.1	.1
443 UN C OF CHRIST	59	15,113	18,405*	.2	.4
449 UN METHODIST	583	134,996	166,502*	2.2	3.5
467 WESLEYAN	16	753	2,147	-	-
469 WELS	2	195	264	-	-
496 JEWISH EST[1]	326	NA	429,885	5.6	9.1
497 BLACK BAPT EST[2]	NA	183,617	225,445*	2.9	4.8
498 INDEP.CHARIS.[3]	5	NA	10,600	.1	.2
499 INDEP.NON-CHAR[3]	16	NA	9,940	.1	.2
NEW MEXICO	**1,824**	**259,196**	**889,298***	**58.7**	**100.0**
001 ADVENT CHR CH	1	179	238*	-	-
011 A.W.M.C.	1	9	12*	-	-
019 AMER BAPT USA	4	1,502	1,885*	.1	.2
053 ASSEMB OF GOD	152	11,919	20,841	1.4	2.3
059 BAPT MISS ASSN	8	355	470*	-	.1
075 BRETHREN IN CR	2	98	98	-	-
081 CATHOLIC	403	NA	467,356	30.8	52.6
081b *BYZAN RUTH*	*2*	*NA*	*256*	-	-
081d *LATIN*	*400*	*NA*	*466,578*	*30.8*	*52.5*
081f *MELKITE-GK*	*1*	*NA*	*522*	-	*.1*
083 CHRIST CATH CH	2	17	26	-	-
089 CHR & MISS AL	3	59	215	-	-
093 CHR CH (DISC)	16	2,787	4,224	.3	.5
097 CHR CHS&CHS CR	34	5,036	6,572*	.4	.7
105 CHRISTIAN REF	19	940	1,690	.1	.2
111 CH CR,SCIENTST	16	NR	NR	-	-
123 CH GOD (ANDER)	8	494	536	-	.1
127 CH GOD (CLEVE)	37	1,640	2,240*	.1	.3
133 CH GOD(7TH)DEN	4	45	54	-	-
145 CH GOD PROPHCY	14	310	406*	-	-
151 L-D SAINTS	106	NA	39,429	2.6	4.4
157 CH OF BRETHREN	2	83	111*	-	-
164 CH LUTH CONF	1	8	15	-	-
165 CH OF NAZARENE	48	4,954	6,571	.4	.7
167 CHS OF CHRIST	169	14,745	19,780	1.3	2.2
171 CH GOD-GEN CON	2	39	57*	-	-
179 CONSRV BAPT	6	NR	NR	-	-
185 CUMBER PRESB	1	2,224	2,224	.1	.3
193 EPISCOPAL	47	7,764	10,691	.7	1.2
203 EVAN FREE CH	7	425	830	.1	.1
207 E.L.C.A.	22	7,947	11,378	.8	1.3
221 FREE METHODIST	10	350	355	-	-
223 FREE WILL BAPT	5	146	192*	-	-
226 FRIENDS-USA	13	292	396*	-	-
226b *EFI*	*1*	*34*	*42*	-	-
226f *INDEPENDNT*	*12*	*258*	*354**	-	-
246 GREEK ORTHODOX	2	NR	NR	-	-
259 IFCA	3	NR	NR	-	-

NA–Not applicable   NR–Not reported   *Total adherents estimated from known number of communicant, confirmed, full members.   - Represents a percent less than 0.1.   Percentages may not total due to rounding.
[1]See Appendix E   [2]See Appendix F   [3]See Appendix G   Lines in *italic* represent a breakdown of Catholic rites or Friends affiliations. They are included in their respective denominational total.

Table 3. Churches and Church Membership by State and Denomination: 1990

State and Denomination	Number of churches	Communicant, confirmed, full members	Total adherents Number	Percent of total population	Percent of total adherents
263 INT FOURSQ GOS	13	862	1,114*	.1	.1
265 INT PENT C CHR	1	25	25	-	-
283 LUTH—MO SYNOD	32	4,948	6,604	.4	.7
284 LUTH CH-AM ASC	1	35	35	-	-
285 MENNONITE CH	6	256	387	-	-
329 OPEN BIBLE STD	1	NR	NR	-	-
331 ORTH CH IN AM	2	NR	NR	-	-
339 PENT CH OF GOD	14	447	960	.1	.1
349 PENT HOLINESS	5	180	236*	-	-
353 CHR BRETHREN	6	294	610	-	.1
355 PRESB CH (USA)	67	11,354	14,730*	1.0	1.7
356 PRESB CH AMER	5	465	527	-	.1
371 REF CH IN AM	2	175	575	-	.1
403 SALVATION ARMY	8	711	796	.1	.1
413 S.D.A.	46	3,447	4,523*	.3	.5
419 SO BAPT CONV	271	120,807	158,873*	10.5	17.9
435 UNITARIAN-UNIV	6	1,052	1,301	.1	.1
443 UN C OF CHRIST	9	2,006	2,556*	.2	.3
449 UN METHODIST	121	41,920	54,664*	3.6	6.1
467 WESLEYAN	1	19	75	-	-
469 WELS	5	388	541	-	.1
496 JEWISH EST[1]	6	NA	6,075	.4	.7
497 BLACK BAPT EST[2]	NA	5,438	7,046*	.5	.8
498 INDEP.CHARIS.[3]	9	NA	5,075	.3	.6
499 INDEP.NON-CHAR[3]	19	NA	23,078	1.5	2.6
NEW YORK	**10,878**	**1,974,175**	**11,813,403***	**65.7**	**100.0**
001 ADVENT CHR CH	3	103	129*	-	-
005 AME ZION	123	140,044	174,011	1.0	1.5
007 ALBAN ORTH ARC	3	NR	NR	-	-
011 A.W.M.C.	2	32	40*	-	-
019 AMER BAPT USA	584	186,307	230,037*	1.3	1.9
022 EASTERN ORTH	8	2,611	2,611	-	-
039 AP CHR CH(NAZ)	3	166	204*	-	-
040 AP CHR CH-AMER	1	73	128	-	-
049 ARMEN AP CH AM	5	1,850	14,650	.1	.1
053 ASSEMB OF GOD	418	54,801	95,872	.5	.8
055 AS REF PRES CH	2	184	255	-	-
057 BAPT GEN CONF	11	1,549	1,917*	-	-
059 BAPT MISS ASSN	4	161	200*	-	-
061 BEACHY AMISH	2	67	86*	-	-
066 BIBLE CH OF CR	4	6,030	7,573*	-	.1
075 BRETHREN IN CR	4	280	283	-	-
080 BYELORSSN ORTH	2	NR	NR	-	-
081 CATHOLIC	1,874	NA	7,280,488	40.5	61.6
081a *ARMENIAN*	2	NA	6,370	-	.1
081b *BYZAN RUTH*	13	NA	5,078	-	-
081d *LATIN*	1,813	NA	7,244,766	40.3	61.3
081e *MARONITE*	5	NA	5,953	-	.1
081f *MELKITE-GK*	5	NA	3,204	-	-
081g *ROMANIAN*	1	NA	322	-	-
081h *UKRAINIAN*	35	NA	14,795	.1	.1
089 CHR & MISS AL	150	9,860	20,264	.1	.2
093 CHR CH (DISC)	65	9,625	12,389	.1	.1
097 CHR CHS&CHS CR	66	3,718	4,592*	-	-
105 CHRISTIAN REF	14	1,748	2,779	-	-
111 CH CR,SCIENTST	108	NR	NR	-	-
123 CH GOD (ANDER)	37	2,500	2,855	-	-
127 CH GOD (CLEVE)	123	11,505	14,270*	.1	.1
133 CH GOD(7TH)DEN	5	198	264	-	-
145 CH GOD PROPHCY	37	2,023	2,503*	-	-
151 L-D SAINTS	97	NA	29,997	.2	.3
157 CH OF BRETHREN	1	165	208*	-	-
163 CH OF LUTH BR	7	655	1,323	-	-
164 CH LUTH CONF	1	49	60	-	-
165 CH OF NAZARENE	125	10,237	15,837	.1	.1
167 CHS OF CHRIST	95	8,621	11,866	.1	.1
175 CONGR CHR CHS	10	1,691	2,102*	-	-
176 CCC, NOT NAT'L	18	1,299	1,625*	-	-
179 CONSRV BAPT	87	NR	NR	-	-
181 CONSRV CONGR	20	2,529	3,143*	-	-
193 EPISCOPAL	703	155,561	231,690	1.3	2.0
195 ESTONIAN ELC	5	1,128	1,326*	-	-
203 EVAN FREE CH	23	1,805	2,671	-	-
207 E.L.C.A.	441	132,726	187,551	1.0	1.6
215 EVAN METH CH	1	19	24*	-	-
216 EVAN PRESBY CH	1	98	112	-	-
217 FIRE BAPTIZED	1	2	3*	-	-
220 FREE LUTHERAN	1	83	95	-	-

State and Denomination	Number of churches	Communicant, confirmed, full members	Total adherents Number	Percent of total population	Percent of total adherents
221 FREE METHODIST	82	4,658	7,132	-	.1
226 FRIENDS-USA	62	3,540	4,346*	-	-
226d *FGC & FUM*	62	3,540	4,346*	-	-
246 GREEK ORTHODOX	65	NR	NR	-	-
249 AP CATH ASSYR	1	760	0	-	-
257 HUTTERIAN BR	3	NA	675	-	-
259 IFCA	12	NR	NR	-	-
263 INT FOURSQ GOS	11	450	563*	-	-
274 LAT EVAN LUTH	6	2,359	2,581	-	-
283 LUTH—MO SYNOD	201	64,166	90,837	.5	.8
284 LUTH CH-AM ASC	2	87	97	-	-
285 MENNONITE CH	41	2,588	3,785	-	-
286 E.PA MENNONITE	2	107	138*	-	-
287 MENN GEN CONF	1	0	0	-	-
291 MISSIONARY CH	2	114	121	-	-
293 MORAV CH-NORTH	11	2,628	4,265	-	-
313 N AM BAPT CONF	12	1,530	1,880*	-	-
323 OLD ORD AMISH	26	NA	3,850	-	-
329 OPEN BIBLE STD	8	NR	NR	-	-
331 ORTH CH IN AM	37	NR	NR	-	-
339 PENT CH OF GOD	2	93	175	-	-
349 PENT HOLINESS	1	60	75*	-	-
353 CHR BRETHREN	54	3,756	5,784	-	-
355 PRESB CH (USA)	747	161,602	199,519*	1.1	1.7
356 PRESB CH AMER	13	1,699	2,042	-	-
363 PRIMITIVE METH	2	294	474	-	-
371 REF CH IN AM	253	38,407	79,865	.4	.7
375 REF EPISCOPAL	2	92	120	-	-
397 ROMANIAN ORTH	4	NR	NR	-	-
403 SALVATION ARMY	77	5,893	6,711	-	.1
413 S.D.A.	220	47,599	58,740*	.3	.5
415 S-D BAPTIST GC	11	708	882*	-	-
419 SO BAPT CONV	157	18,605	22,917*	.1	.2
423 SYRIAN ANTIOCH	3	NA	1,600	-	-
431 UKRANIAN AMER	5	NR	NR	-	-
435 UNITARIAN-UNIV	64	10,474	13,648	.1	.1
438 UN BRETH IN CR	2	60	71	-	-
443 UN C OF CHRIST	300	59,555	73,353*	.4	.6
449 UN METHODIST	1,478	376,410	466,586*	2.6	3.9
467 WESLEYAN	121	6,253	19,704	.1	.2
469 WELS	6	365	498	-	-
496 JEWISH EST[1]	1,424	NA	1,843,240	10.2	15.6
497 BLACK BAPT EST[2]	NA	407,160	500,028*	2.8	4.2
498 INDEP.CHARIS.[3]	32	NA	25,590	.1	.2
499 INDEP.NON-CHAR[3]	20	NA	13,478	.1	.1
NORTH CAROLINA	**11,331**	**3,004,855**	**3,977,923***	**60.0**	**100.0**
001 ADVENT CHR CH	57	4,925	6,064*	.1	.2
005 AME ZION	651	256,267	312,693	4.7	7.9
019 AMER BAPT USA	37	22,212	27,361*	.4	.7
053 ASSEMB OF GOD	199	21,645	33,101	.5	.8
055 AS REF PRES CH	39	8,580	9,934	.1	.2
059 BAPT MISS ASSN	1	0	0*	-	-
066 BIBLE CH OF CR	1	180	225*	-	-
081 CATHOLIC	175	NA	149,483	2.3	3.8
081d *LATIN*	174	NA	149,117	2.2	3.7
081e *MARONITE*	1	NA	366	-	-
089 CHR & MISS AL	48	3,712	6,347	.1	.2
093 CHR CH (DISC)	293	33,949	50,460	.8	1.3
097 CHR CHS&CHS CR	161	21,949	27,158*	.4	.7
105 CHRISTIAN REF	1	159	279	-	-
111 CH CR,SCIENTST	28	NR	NR	-	-
121 CH GOD (ABR)	2	106	128*	-	-
123 CH GOD (ANDER)	56	3,092	3,556	.1	.1
127 CH GOD (CLEVE)	417	44,221	54,828*	.8	1.4
133 CH GOD(7TH)DEN	3	70	88	-	-
143 CG IN CR(MENN)	1	25	31*	-	-
145 CH GOD PROPHCY	190	6,779	8,373*	.1	.2
146 CH GOD MTN ASM	1	109	133*	-	-
151 L-D SAINTS	112	NA	33,079	.5	.8
157 CH OF BRETHREN	16	1,516	1,830*	-	-
164 CH LUTH CONF	1	29	35	-	-
165 CH OF NAZARENE	69	6,291	8,902	.1	.2
167 CHS OF CHRIST	179	14,676	20,158	.3	.5
175 CONGR CHR CHS	3	125	152*	-	-
176 CCC, NOT NAT'L	29	3,295	4,048*	.1	.1
179 CONSRV BAPT	1	NR	NR	-	-
181 CONSRV CONGR	1	175	211*	-	-
193 EPISCOPAL	252	55,591	73,664	1.1	1.9

NA–Not applicable   NR–Not reported   *Total adherents estimated from known number of communicant, confirmed, full members.   - Represents a percent less than 0.1.   Percentages may not total due to rounding.
[1]See Appendix E   [2]See Appendix F   [3]See Appendix G   Lines in *italic* represent a breakdown of Catholic rites or Friends affiliations. They are included in their respective denominational total.

Table 3. Churches and Church Membership by State and Denomination: 1990

State and Denomination	Number of churches	Communicant, confirmed, full members	Total adherents Number	Percent of total population	Percent of total adherents
203 EVAN FREE CH	4	411	520	-	2.2
207 E.L.C.A.	231	69,463	87,815	1.3	2.2
215 EVAN METH CH	25	1,721	2,118*	-	.1
216 EVAN PRESBY CH	18	3,777	3,824	.1	.1
221 FREE METHODIST	2	42	45	-	-
223 FREE WILL BAPT	230	29,373	36,346*	.5	.9
226 FRIENDS-USA	106	12,605	15,723*	.2	.4
226a *CONSERV*	4	*108*	*168*	-	-
226b *EFI*	8	*445*	*620*	-	-
226c *FGC*	13	*460*	*771*	-	-
226d *FGC & FUM*	4	*522*	*646*	-	-
226e *FUM*	76	*11,049*	*13,492*	.2	.3
226g *INDEP EVAN*	1	*21*	*26*	-	-
237 GC MENN BR CHS	6	198	236*	-	-
246 GREEK ORTHODOX	10	NR	NR	-	-
259 IFCA	2	NR	NR	-	-
263 INT FOURSQ GOS	44	5,205	6,424*	.1	.2
265 INT PENT C CHR	8	247	401	-	-
283 LUTH—MO SYNOD	61	15,181	19,275	.3	.5
285 MENNONITE CH	11	438	697	-	-
287 MENN GEN CONF	2	31	54	-	-
295 MORAV CH-SOUTH	48	16,140	19,864	.3	.5
323 OLD ORD AMISH	1	NA	150	-	-
325 OLD REG BAPT	2	20	25*	-	-
331 ORTH CH IN AM	2	NR	NR	-	-
339 PENT CH OF GOD	5	180	327	-	-
349 PENT HOLINESS	303	31,376	39,125*	.6	1.0
353 CHR BRETHREN	32	2,873	4,877	.1	.1
355 PRESB CH (USA)	743	166,707	205,548*	3.1	5.2
356 PRESB CH AMER	72	9,764	11,922	.2	.3
361 PRIM BAPT ASCS	151	2,854	3,508*	.1	.1
371 REF CH IN AM	3	361	626	-	-
386 REGULAR BAPT	34	3,321	3,961*	.1	.1
403 SALVATION ARMY	35	3,685	3,924	.1	.1
413 S.D.A.	99	15,954	19,522*	.3	.5
419 SO BAPT CONV	3,527	1,176,617	1,446,228*	21.8	36.4
435 UNITARIAN-UNIV	19	2,747	3,717	.1	.1
443 UN C OF CHRIST	243	43,550	53,322*	.8	1.3
449 UN METHODIST	1,983	491,742	605,362*	9.1	15.2
467 WESLEYAN	157	15,417	22,866	.3	.6
469 WELS	5	338	480	-	-
496 JEWISH EST[1]	37	NA	28,870	.4	.7
497 BLACK BAPT EST[2]	NA	372,859	462,785*	7.0	11.6
498 INDEP.CHARIS.[3]	12	NA	7,225	.1	.2
499 INDEP.NON-CHAR[3]	34	NA	27,890	.4	.7
NORTH DAKOTA	**1,622**	**228,131**	**484,628***	**75.9**	**100.0**
019 AMER BAPT USA	19	1,856	2,359*	.4	.5
045 APOSTOLIC LUTH	1	0	30	-	-
053 ASSEMB OF GOD	63	4,823	9,444	1.5	1.9
057 BAPT GEN CONF	6	357	452*	.1	.1
081 CATHOLIC	281	NA	173,432	27.1	35.8
081d *LATIN*	278	*NA*	*173,151*	27.1	35.7
081h *UKRAINIAN*	3	*NA*	*281*	-	.1
089 CHR & MISS AL	5	116	301	-	.1
097 CHR CHS&SCIENTS CR	3	170	218*	-	-
105 CHRISTIAN REF	1	86	126	-	-
111 CH CR,SCIENTST	5	NR	NR	-	-
123 CH GOD (ANDER)	2	85	106	-	-
127 CH GOD(CLEVE)	11	639	829*	.1	.2
133 CH GOD(7TH)DEN	3	54	70	-	-
143 CG IN CR(MENN)	1	78	100*	-	-
145 CH GOD PROPHCY	6	122	159*	-	-
151 L-D SAINTS	12	NA	2,358	.4	.5
157 CH OF BRETHREN	3	186	243*	-	.1
163 CH OF LUTH BR	15	1,115	3,389	.5	.7
164 CH LUTH CONF	2	148	197	-	-
165 CH OF NAZARENE	29	1,439	3,138	.5	.6
167 CHS OF CHRIST	12	299	500	.1	.1
176 CCC, NOT NAT'L	2	50	64*	-	-
179 CONSRV BAPT	2	NR	NR	-	-
181 CONSRV CONGR	7	479	606*	.1	.1
193 EPISCOPAL	24	2,144	3,372	.5	.7
203 EVAN FREE CH	23	1,536	2,916	.5	.6
207 E.L.C.A.	488	135,310	179,711	28.1	37.1
209 EVAN LUTH SYN	1	110	136	-	-
220 FREE LUTHERAN	35	3,553	4,530	.7	.9
221 FREE METHODIST	2	42	64	-	-
226 FRIENDS-USA	3	8	33	-	-
226c *FGC*	3	*8*	*33*	-	-
237 GC MENN BR CHS	6	349	440*	.1	.1
246 GREEK ORTHODOX	1	NR	NR	-	-
257 HUTTERIAN BR	5	NA	500	.1	.1
263 INT FOURSQ GOS	4	289	370*	.1	.1
283 LUTH—MO SYNOD	96	19,608	25,691	4.0	5.3
284 LUTH CH-AM ASC	7	1,832	2,540	.4	.5
285 MENNONITE CH	5	254	276	-	.1
287 MENN GEN CONF	5	270	311	-	.1
293 MORAV CH-NORTH	4	464	563	.1	.1
313 N AM BAPT CONF	34	4,663	5,903*	.9	1.2
331 ORTH CH IN AM	1	NR	NR	-	-
353 CHR BRETHREN	5	94	160	-	-
355 PRESB CH (USA)	69	9,369	11,960*	1.9	2.5
356 PRESB CH AMER	2	84	104	-	-
371 REF CH IN AM	6	580	1,116	.2	.2
373 REF CH IN U.S.	4	172	202	-	-
403 SALVATION ARMY	6	425	443	.1	.1
413 S.D.A.	43	2,692	3,427*	.5	.7
419 SO BAPT CONV	18	3,444	4,470*	.7	.9
435 UNITARIAN-UNIV	2	98	135	-	-
443 UN C OF CHRIST	70	7,535	9,619*	1.5	2.0
449 UN METHODIST	139	18,781	23,850*	3.7	4.9
467 WESLEYAN	6	233	530	.1	.1
469 WELS	12	1,406	1,775	.3	.4
496 JEWISH EST[1]	5	NA	483	.1	.1
497 BLACK BAPT EST[2]	NA	684	877*	.1	.2
OHIO	**11,086**	**2,278,892**	**5,437,630***	**50.1**	**100.0**
001 ADVENT CHR CH	7	186	235*	-	-
005 AME ZION	37	28,947	35,427	.3	.7
007 ALBAN ORTH ARC	1	NR	NR	-	-
011 A.W.M.C.	24	432	542*	-	-
019 AMER BAPT USA	337	101,688	127,219*	1.2	2.3
022 EASTERN ORTH	5	546	546	-	-
039 AP CHR CH(NAZ)	13	1,197	1,490*	-	-
040 AP CHR CH-AMER	8	1,158	2,043	-	-
049 ARMEN AP CH AM	1	150	350	-	-
053 ASSEMB OF GOD	249	34,082	69,349	.6	1.3
057 BAPT GEN CONF	17	2,811	3,504*	-	.1
059 BAPT MISS ASSN	1	150	190*	-	-
061 BEACHY AMISH	18	1,155	1,499*	-	-
071 BRETHREN (ASH)	23	3,671	4,611*	-	.1
075 BRETHREN IN CR	14	905	978	-	-
081 CATHOLIC	1,057	NA	2,141,777	19.7	39.4
081b *BYZAN RUTH*	35	*NA*	*36,775*	.3	.7
081d *LATIN*	996	*NA*	*2,089,938*	19.3	38.4
081e *MARONITE*	5	*NA*	*5,453*	.1	.1
081f *MELKITE-GK*	4	*NA*	*2,254*	-	-
081g *ROMANIAN*	6	*NA*	*1,932*	-	-
081h *UKRAINIAN*	11	*NA*	*5,425*	.1	.1
089 CHR & MISS AL	106	11,439	25,334	.2	.5
093 CHR CH (DISC)	207	42,489	66,665	.6	1.2
097 CHR CHS&CHS CR	480	107,772	135,830*	1.3	2.5
105 CHRISTIAN REF	8	939	1,418	-	-
111 CH CR,SCIENTST	77	NR	NR	-	-
121 CH GOD (ABR)	11	526	661*	-	-
123 CH GOD (ANDER)	220	22,470	29,931	.3	.6
127 CH GOD (CLEVE)	208	29,082	36,587*	.3	.7
133 CH GOD(7TH)DEN	2	50	61	-	-
143 CG IN CR(MENN)	2	222	283*	-	-
145 CH GOD PROPHCY	63	2,260	2,844*	-	.1
146 CH GOD MTN ASM	30	1,572	2,003*	-	-
151 L-D SAINTS	95	NA	30,979	.3	.6
157 CH OF BRETHREN	109	16,448	20,765*	.2	.4
163 CH OF LUTH BR	2	72	189	-	-
165 CH OF NAZARENE	419	53,793	90,659	.8	1.7
167 CHS OF CHRIST	432	36,109	47,949	.4	.9
171 CH GOD-GEN CON	35	3,396	4,349*	-	.1
175 CONGR CHR CHS	20	5,483	6,858*	.1	.1
176 CCC, NOT NAT'L	3	117	149*	-	-
179 CONSRV BAPT	12	NR	NR	-	-
181 CONSRV CONGR	10	1,250	1,564*	-	-
191 ENTRPR BPT ASC	34	1,864	2,340*	-	-
193 EPISCOPAL	194	47,141	69,302	.6	1.3
195 ESTONIAN ELC	1	102	126*	-	-
199 EVAN CONGR CH	11	1,050	1,682	-	-
203 EVAN FREE CH	13	875	1,959	-	-
207 E.L.C.A.	658	237,108	320,021	3.0	5.9

NA–Not applicable   NR–Not reported   *Total adherents estimated from known number of communicant, confirmed, full members.   - Represents a percent less than 0.1.   Percentages may not total due to rounding.
[1]See Appendix E   [2]See Appendix F   [3]See Appendix G   Lines in *italic* represent a breakdown of Catholic rites or Friends affiliations. They are included in their respective denominational total.

Table 3. Churches and Church Membership by State and Denomination: 1990

State and Denomination	Number of churches	Communicant, confirmed, full members	Total adherents Number	Percent of total population	Percent of total adherents
209 EVAN LUTH SYN	2	618	932	-	-
213 EVAN MENN INC	4	1,270	1,640*	-	-
215 EVAN METH CH	2	41	52*	-	-
216 EVAN PRESBY CH	4	750	764	-	-
221 FREE METHODIST	45	2,792	3,921	-	.1
223 FREE WILL BAPT	150	11,336	14,222*	.1	.3
226 FRIENDS-USA	112	9,991	13,436*	.1	.2
226a *CONSERV*	*7*	*582*	*722**	-	-
226b *EFI*	*50*	*5,981*	*8,330*	*.1*	*.2*
226c *FGC*	*18*	*639*	*840**	-	-
226d *FGC & FUM*	*4*	*193*	*251*	-	-
226e *FUM*	*31*	*2,577*	*3,267**	-	*.1*
226f *INDEPENDNT*	*1*	*4*	*6*	-	-
226g *INDEP EVAN*	*1*	*15*	*20**	-	-
246 GREEK ORTHODOX	23	NR	NR	-	-
257 HUTTERIAN BR	1	NA	100	-	-
259 IFCA	9	NR	NR	-	-
263 INT FOURSQ GOS	55	4,944	6,204*	.1	.1
265 INT PENT C CHR	24	851	1,451	-	-
274 LAT EVAN LUTH	5	919	1,011	-	-
283 LUTH—MO SYNOD	186	62,571	83,336	.8	1.5
285 MENNONITE CH	123	14,744	19,352	.2	.4
287 MENN GEN CONF	12	2,264	3,228	-	.1
291 MISSIONARY CH	35	2,259	3,080	-	.1
293 MORAV CH-NORTH	7	1,884	2,409	-	-
296 MIDW CONGR FEL	10	524	674*	-	-
313 N AM BAPT CONF	7	1,755	2,180*	-	-
320 "OLD" MB ASCS	2	136	168*	-	-
323 OLD ORD AMISH	238	NA	35,200	.3	.6
324 OLD ORD RVR BR	1	5	8	-	-
325 OLD REG BAPT	22	785	998*	-	-
329 OPEN BIBLE STD	40	NR	NR	-	-
331 ORTH CH IN AM	27	NR	NR	-	-
339 PENT CH OF GOD	38	1,187	3,166	-	.1
349 PENT HOLINESS	11	1,099	1,379*	-	-
353 CHR BRETHREN	22	1,063	1,782	-	-
355 PRESB CH (USA)	615	164,045	205,721*	1.9	3.8
356 PRESB CH AMER	12	1,246	1,580	-	-
361 PRIM BAPT ASCS	25	739	929*	-	-
363 PRIMITIVE METH	3	245	293	-	-
371 REF CH IN AM	8	1,125	2,110	-	-
373 REF CH IN U.S.	1	110	141	-	-
375 REF EPISCOPAL	2	63	63	-	-
397 ROMANIAN ORTH	7	NR	NR	-	-
403 SALVATION ARMY	63	5,644	6,455	.1	.1
413 S.D.A.	120	19,575	24,508*	.2	.5
415 S-D BAPTIST GC	1	26	32*	-	-
419 SO BAPT CONV	511	149,589	188,219*	1.7	3.5
431 UKRANIAN AMER	3	NR	NR	-	-
435 UNITARIAN-UNIV	38	4,823	6,531	.1	.1
436 UNITED BAPT	49	3,772	4,763*	-	.1
438 UN BRETH IN CR	60	5,768	6,003	.1	.1
443 UN C OF CHRIST	483	155,331	195,349*	1.8	3.6
449 UN METHODIST	2,181	521,445	656,107*	6.0	12.1
466 WAYN TR MB ASC	11	1,934	2,467*	-	-
467 WESLEYAN	121	5,757	13,549	.1	.2
469 WELS	24	3,397	4,650	-	.1
496 JEWISH EST[1]	138	NA	124,832	1.2	2.3
497 BLACK BAPT EST[2]	NA	309,763	386,280*	3.6	7.1
498 INDEP.CHARIS.[3]	27	NA	22,755	.2	.4
499 INDEP.NON-CHAR[3]	92	NA	93,332	.9	1.7
OKLAHOMA	**5,707**	**1,473,855**	**2,102,290***	**66.8**	**100.0**
001 ADVENT CHR CH	3	121	150*	-	-
005 AME ZION	5	1,505	1,821	.1	.1
019 AMER BAPT USA	13	1,897	2,416*	.1	.1
053 ASSEMB OF GOD	490	58,073	88,780	2.8	4.2
059 BAPT MISS ASSN	52	7,803	9,850*	.3	.5
061 BEACHY AMISH	1	45	57*	-	-
075 BRETHREN IN CR	3	238	240	-	-
081 CATHOLIC	201	NA	143,640	4.6	6.8
081d *LATIN*	*201*	*NA*	*143,640*	*4.6*	*6.8*
089 CHR & MISS AL	7	200	401	-	-
093 CHR CH (DISC)	209	40,640	58,901	1.9	2.8
097 CHR CHS&CHS CR	200	34,476	43,521*	1.4	2.1
105 CHRISTIAN REF	1	12	22	-	-
111 CH CR,SCIENTST	31	NR	NR	-	-
123 CH GOD (ANDER)	74	4,948	6,671	.2	.3
127 CH GOD (CLEVE)	61	4,409	5,597*	.2	.3
133 CH GOD(7TH)DEN	10	377	500	-	-
143 CG IN CR(MENN)	4	505	640*	-	-
145 CH GOD PROPHCY	53	1,731	2,192*	.1	.1
151 L-D SAINTS	65	NA	19,107	.6	.9
157 CH OF BRETHREN	6	433	537*	-	-
165 CH OF NAZARENE	229	25,426	35,225	1.1	1.7
167 CHS OF CHRIST	610	66,234	85,193	2.7	4.1
171 CH GOD-GEN CON	16	652	821*	-	-
175 CONGR CHR CHS	2	360	455*	-	-
181 CONSRV CONGR	1	108	137*	-	-
185 CUMBER PRESB	22	1,553	1,776	.1	.1
193 EPISCOPAL	79	14,655	18,908	.6	.9
203 EVAN FREE CH	7	486	626	-	-
207 E.L.C.A.	41	8,229	11,186	.4	.5
211 FEL EVG BIB CH	2	115	149	-	-
215 EVAN METH CH	1	35	44*	-	-
216 EVAN PRESBY CH	1	29	29	-	-
217 FIRE BAPTIZED	5	64	80*	-	-
220 FREE LUTHERAN	1	149	180	-	-
221 FREE METHODIST	15	577	630	-	-
223 FREE WILL BAPT	241	20,129	25,376*	.8	1.2
226 FRIENDS-USA	18	1,096	1,393*	-	.1
226b *EFI*	*12*	*894*	*1,105**	-	*.1*
226c *FGC*	*4*	*95*	*154*	-	-
226e *FUM*	*2*	*107*	*134**	-	-
237 GC MENN BR CHS	14	2,839	3,603*	.1	.2
246 GREEK ORTHODOX	2	NR	NR	-	-
257 HUTTERIAN BR	1	NA	100	-	-
259 IFCA	11	NR	NR	-	-
263 INT FOURSQ GOS	16	815	1,021*	-	-
283 LUTH—MO SYNOD	80	18,100	24,303	.8	1.2
285 MENNONITE CH	3	364	464	-	-
287 MENN GEN CONF	17	1,238	1,506	-	.1
313 N AM BAPT CONF	5	347	436*	-	-
323 OLD ORD AMISH	3	NA	450	-	-
329 OPEN BIBLE STD	1	NR	NR	-	-
331 ORTH CH IN AM	2	NR	NR	-	-
339 PENT CH OF GOD	88	2,683	6,268	.2	.3
349 PENT HOLINESS	142	13,248	16,754*	.5	.8
353 CHR BRETHREN	5	198	395	-	-
355 PRESB CH (USA)	162	32,952	41,615*	1.3	2.0
356 PRESB CH AMER	5	800	1,044	-	-
361 PRIM BAPT ASCS	10	538	679*	-	-
371 REF CH IN AM	3	767	1,445	-	-
403 SALVATION ARMY	18	2,071	2,263	.1	.1
413 S.D.A.	83	6,872	8,698*	.3	.4
415 S-D BAPTIST GC	1	30	38*	-	-
419 SO BAPT CONV	1,490	763,064	964,615*	30.7	45.9
423 SYRIAN ANTIOCH	1	NA	400	-	-
431 UKRANIAN AMER	1	NR	NR	-	-
435 UNITARIAN-UNIV	8	1,931	2,795	.1	.1
443 UN C OF CHRIST	15	1,927	2,448*	.1	.1
449 UN METHODIST	681	258,209	326,294*	10.4	15.5
467 WESLEYAN	14	1,186	3,634	.1	.2
469 WELS	5	438	630	-	-
496 JEWISH EST[1]	7	NA	4,980	.2	.2
497 BLACK BAPT EST[2]	NA	65,928	83,619*	2.7	4.0
498 INDEP.CHARIS.[3]	13	NA	22,412	.7	1.1
499 INDEP.NON-CHAR[3]	20	NA	12,130	.4	.6
OREGON	**2,908**	**365,034**	**915,285***	**32.2**	**100.0**
001 ADVENT CHR CH	3	85	107*	-	-
005 AME ZION	3	470	518	-	.1
019 AMER BAPT USA	61	13,529	16,912*	.6	1.8
039 AP CHR CH(NAZ)	1	120	148*	-	-
040 AP CHR CH-AMER	2	56	101	-	-
045 APOSTOLIC LUTH	3	121	197	-	-
053 ASSEMB OF GOD	216	23,788	47,035	1.7	5.1
057 BAPT GEN CONF	11	1,493	1,860*	.1	.2
059 BAPT MISS ASSN	4	159	201*	-	-
063 BEREAN FUND CH	1	30	30	-	-
075 BRETHREN IN CR	2	212	212	-	-
081 CATHOLIC	199	NA	279,650	9.8	30.6
081b *BYZAN RUTH*	*1*	*NA*	*40*	-	-
081d *LATIN*	*196*	*NA*	*279,153*	*9.8*	*30.5*
081e *MARONITE*	*1*	*NA*	*441*	-	-
081h *UKRAINIAN*	*1*	*NA*	*16*	-	-
089 CHR & MISS AL	34	2,320	7,272	.3	.8
093 CHR CH (DISC)	47	9,725	13,657	.5	1.5

NA–Not applicable NR–Not reported *Total adherents estimated from known number of communicant, confirmed, full members. - Represents a percent less than 0.1. Percentages may not total due to rounding.
[1]See Appendix E [2]See Appendix F [3]See Appendix G Lines in *italic* represent a breakdown of Catholic rites or Friends affiliations. They are included in their respective denominational total.

Table 3. Churches and Church Membership by State and Denomination: 1990

State and Denomination	Number of churches	Communicant, confirmed, full members	Total adherents Number	Percent of total population	Percent of total adherents
097 CHR CHS&CHS CR	167	29,177	36,650 *	1.3	4.0
105 CHRISTIAN REF	7	661	1,056	-	.1
111 CH CR,SCIENTST	47	NR	NR	-	-
123 CH GOD (ANDER)	46	4,390	5,148	.2	.6
127 CH GOD (CLEVE)	23	1,538	1,925 *	.1	.2
133 CH GOD(7TH)DEN	5	369	470	-	.1
143 CG IN CR(MENN)	1	99	125 *	-	-
145 CH GOD PROPHCY	16	432	544 *	-	.1
151 L-D SAINTS	228	NA	89,601	3.2	9.8
157 CH OF BRETHREN	6	338	424 *	-	-
163 CH OF LUTH BR	3	126	270	-	-
165 CH OF NAZARENE	115	16,449	22,877	.8	2.5
167 CHS OF CHRIST	117	8,495	11,549	.4	1.3
175 CONGR CHR CHS	1	66	83 *	-	-
176 CCC, NOT NAT'L	2	254	326 *	-	-
179 CONSRV BAPT	178	NR	NR	-	-
181 CONSRV CONGR	2	57	70 *	-	-
193 EPISCOPAL	99	18,584	26,816	.9	2.9
195 ESTONIAN ELC	1	106	130 *	-	-
203 EVAN FREE CH	10	1,020	1,795	.1	.2
207 E.L.C.A.	118	36,116	48,958	1.7	5.3
209 EVAN LUTH SYN	7	382	514	-	.1
211 FEL EVG BIB CH	2	359	382	-	-
215 EVAN METH CH	6	274	342 *	-	-
217 FIRE BAPTIZED	3	9	11 *	-	-
220 FREE LUTHERAN	2	211	243	-	-
221 FREE METHODIST	34	2,435	3,494	.1	.4
223 FREE WILL BAPT	2	213	266 *	-	-
226 FRIENDS-USA	41	2,886	4,396 *	.2	.5
226b EFI	30	2,602	4,015	.1	.4
226f INDEPENDNT	11	284	381 *	-	-
237 GC MENN BR CHS	4	414	522 *	-	.1
246 GREEK ORTHODOX	2	NR	NR	-	-
259 IFCA	12	NR	NR	-	-
263 INT FOURSQ GOS	90	23,732	29,763 *	1.0	3.3
274 LAT EVAN LUTH	1	149	166	-	-
283 LUTH—MO SYNOD	88	19,837	26,159	.9	2.9
284 LUTH CH-AM ASC	4	619	833	-	.1
285 MENNONITE CH	30	2,633	4,119	.1	.5
287 MENN GEN CONF	5	578	739	-	.1
291 MISSIONARY CH	5	240	373	-	-
313 N AM BAPT CONF	10	1,626	2,018 *	.1	.2
329 OPEN BIBLE STD	27	NR	NR	-	-
331 ORTH CH IN AM	1	NR	NR	-	-
339 PENT CH OF GOD	38	1,043	2,656	.1	.3
349 PENT HOLINESS	5	240	300 *	-	-
353 CHR BRETHREN	13	1,015	1,474	.1	.2
355 PRESB CH (USA)	135	30,511	38,086 *	1.3	4.2
356 PRESB CH AMER	1	42	42	-	-
361 PRIM BAPT ASCS	1	17	21 *	-	-
371 REF CH IN AM	1	16	29	-	-
375 REF EPISCOPAL	1	14	15	-	-
397 ROMANIAN ORTH	1	NR	NR	-	-
403 SALVATION ARMY	19	1,333	1,619	.1	.2
413 S.D.A.	123	27,439	34,468 *	1.2	3.8
415 S-D BAPTIST GC	1	25	31 *	-	-
419 SO BAPT CONV	120	24,890	31,260 *	1.1	3.4
423 SYRIAN ANTIOCH	1	NA	400	-	-
435 UNITARIAN-UNIV	16	2,161	3,252	.1	.4
438 UN BRETH IN CR	1	106	106	-	-
443 UN C OF CHRIST	38	7,100	8,898 *	.3	1.0
449 UN METHODIST	177	33,607	42,209 *	1.5	4.6
467 WESLEYAN	12	420	1,030	-	.1
469 WELS	9	881	1,247	-	.1
496 JEWISH EST[1]	10	NA	10,691	.4	1.2
497 BLACK BAPT EST[2]	NA	7,192	8,894 *	.3	1.0
498 INDEP.CHARIS.[3]	11	NA	20,900	.7	2.3
499 INDEP.NON-CHAR[3]	19	NA	16,600	.6	1.8
PENNSYLVANIA	**13,284**	**2,471,624**	**7,290,699** *	**61.4**	**100.0**
005 AME ZION	54	21,697	28,041	.2	.4
007 ALBAN ORTH ARC	2	NR	NR	-	-
011 A.W.M.C.	56	1,185	1,459 *	-	-
019 AMER BAPT USA	437	92,157	113,025 *	1.0	1.6
022 EASTERN ORTH	34	7,453	7,453	.1	.1
039 AP CHR CH(NAZ)	2	57	70 *	-	-
049 ARMEN AP CH AM	1	1,500	7,500	.1	.1
053 ASSEMB OF GOD	352	39,418	74,616	.6	1.0
055 AS REF PRES CH	1	208	265	-	-

State and Denomination	Number of churches	Communicant, confirmed, full members	Total adherents Number	Percent of total population	Percent of total adherents
057 BAPT GEN CONF	16	2,592	3,188 *	-	-
061 BEACHY AMISH	15	1,531	1,915 *	-	-
071 BRETHREN (ASH)	17	1,709	2,089 *	-	-
075 BRETHREN IN CR	94	11,384	12,982	.1	.2
081 CATHOLIC	1,854	NA	3,675,250	30.9	50.4
081a ARMENIAN	1	NA	250	-	-
081b BYZAN RUTH	108	NA	137,225	1.2	1.9
081d LATIN	1,665	NA	3,486,007	29.3	47.8
081e MARONITE	9	NA	7,170	.1	.1
081f MELKITE-GK	1	NA	250	-	-
081g ROMANIAN	2	NA	644	-	-
081h UKRAINIAN	68	NA	43,704	.4	.6
089 CHR & MISS AL	259	16,847	37,006	.3	.5
093 CHR CH (DISC)	69	10,586	17,619	.1	.2
097 CHR CHS&CHS CR	133	21,594	26,307 *	.2	.4
105 CHRISTIAN REF	2	127	171	-	-
111 CH CR,SCIENTST	64	NR	NR	-	-
123 CH GOD (ANDER)	95	10,327	12,694	.1	.2
127 CH GOD (CLEVE)	92	9,696	11,937 *	.1	.2
133 CH GOD(7TH)DEN	2	26	46	-	-
143 CG IN CR(MENN)	4	305	374 *	-	-
145 CH GOD PROPHCY	46	1,632	2,011 *	-	-
151 L-D SAINTS	83	NA	24,488	.2	.3
157 CH OF BRETHREN	248	46,417	57,368 *	.5	.8
163 CH OF LUTH BR	1	78	255	-	-
165 CH OF NAZARENE	156	16,329	26,626	.2	.4
167 CHS OF CHRIST	141	8,094	10,754	.1	.1
171 CH GOD-GEN CON	154	17,599	21,642 *	.2	.3
175 CONGR CHR CHS	18	1,786	2,172 *	-	-
176 CCC, NOT NAT'L	7	877	1,076 *	-	-
179 CONSRV BAPT	53	NR	NR	-	-
181 CONSRV CONGR	6	484	592 *	-	-
193 EPISCOPAL	403	97,508	138,152	1.2	1.9
195 ESTONIAN ELC	1	76	94 *	-	-
199 EVAN CONGR CH	132	22,124	29,581	.2	.4
203 EVAN FREE CH	49	5,171	9,566	.1	.1
207 E.L.C.A.	1,390	511,002	682,111	5.7	9.4
215 EVAN METH CH	2	213	261 *	-	-
216 EVAN PRESBY CH	2	781	791	-	-
221 FREE METHODIST	120	4,409	6,397	.1	.1
223 FREE WILL BAPT	4	346	430 *	-	-
226 FRIENDS-USA	90	9,754	12,081 *	.1	.2
226a CONSERV	2	14	16 *	-	-
226b EFI	2	130	177	-	-
226c FGC	82	9,445	11,671 *	.1	.2
226d FGC & FUM	2	127	158 *	-	-
226e FUM	1	33	41 *	-	-
226f INDEPENDNT	1	5	18	-	-
241 GEN SIX PR BPT	1	20	25 *	-	-
246 GREEK ORTHODOX	35	NR	NR	-	-
257 HUTTERIAN BR	2	NA	450	-	-
259 IFCA	74	NR	NR	-	-
263 INT FOURSQ GOS	31	2,673	3,282 *	-	-
265 INT PENT C CHR	1	10	24	-	-
274 LAT EVAN LUTH	3	559	588	-	-
283 LUTH—MO SYNOD	92	18,314	23,850	.2	.3
284 LUTH CH-AM ASC	3	119	151	-	-
285 MENNONITE CH	347	35,255	50,009	.4	.7
286 E.PA MENNONITE	32	2,509	3,121 *	-	-
287 MENN GEN CONF	29	4,483	5,587	-	.1
291 MISSIONARY CH	11	475	571	-	-
293 MORAV CH-NORTH	26	9,201	11,724	.1	.2
313 N AM BAPT CONF	10	1,462	1,796 *	-	-
323 OLD ORD AMISH	205	NA	30,550	.3	.4
324 OLD ORD RVR BR	5	276	442	-	-
329 OPEN BIBLE STD	9	NR	NR	-	-
331 ORTH CH IN AM	85	NR	NR	-	-
339 PENT CH OF GOD	3	82	142	-	-
349 PENT HOLINESS	12	836	1,016 *	-	-
353 CHR BRETHREN	46	3,277	5,155	-	.1
355 PRESB CH (USA)	1,122	317,882	388,774 *	3.3	5.3
356 PRESB CH AMER	82	12,377	15,842	.1	.2
361 PRIM BAPT ASCS	1	6	7 *	-	-
363 PRIMITIVE METH	46	3,724	5,267	-	.1
371 REF CH IN AM	9	2,066	3,991	-	.1
373 REF CH IN U.S.	1	15	21	-	-
375 REF EPISCOPAL	16	1,071	1,290	-	-
386 REGULAR BAPT	2	95	118 *	-	-
397 ROMANIAN ORTH	4	NR	NR	-	-

NA–Not applicable   NR–Not reported   *Total adherents estimated from known number of communicant, confirmed, full members.   - Represents a percent less than 0.1.   Percentages may not total due to rounding.
[1]See Appendix E   [2]See Appendix F   [3]See Appendix G   Lines in *italic* represent a breakdown of Catholic rites or Friends affiliations. They are included in their respective denominational total.

Table 3. Churches and Church Membership by State and Denomination: 1990

State and Denomination	Number of churches	Communicant, confirmed, full members	Total adherents Number	Percent of total population	Percent of total adherents
403 SALVATION ARMY	81	7,276	8,163	.1	.1
405 SCHWENKFELDER	5	2,488	3,031*	-	-
413 S.D.A.	127	15,082	18,579*	.2	.3
415 S-D BAPTIST GC	3	129	161*	-	-
419 SO BAPT CONV	120	20,128	24,782*	.2	.3
423 SYRIAN ANTIOCH	1	NA	500	-	-
431 UKRANIAN AMER	3	NR	NR	-	-
435 UNITARIAN-UNIV	35	4,726	6,455	.1	.1
438 UN BRETH IN CR	39	7,732	7,954	.1	.1
441 UN CHRISTIAN	11	380	770	-	-
443 UN C OF CHRIST	796	231,636	284,275*	2.4	3.9
449 UN METHODIST	2,568	588,732	722,871*	6.1	9.9
467 WESLEYAN	74	5,488	12,496	.1	.2
469 WELS	6	538	758	-	-
496 JEWISH EST[1]	257	NA	329,651	2.8	4.5
497 BLACK BAPT EST[2]	NA	175,423	215,320*	1.8	3.0
498 INDEP.CHARIS.[3]	16	NA	20,500	.2	.3
499 INDEP.NON-CHAR[3]	36	NA	20,185	.2	.3
RHODE ISLAND	**554**	**81,604**	**769,964***	**76.7**	**100.0**
001 ADVENT CHR CH	4	157	191*	-	-
005 AME ZION	2	330	495	-	.1
019 AMER BAPT USA	77	17,824	21,703*	2.2	2.8
049 ARMEN AP CH AM	1	1,400	9,000	.9	1.2
053 ASSEMB OF GOD	18	1,922	3,203	.3	.4
057 BAPT GEN CONF	2	94	114*	-	-
081 CATHOLIC	165	NA	633,427	63.1	82.3
081d LATIN	162	NA	631,223	62.9	82.0
081e MARONITE	1	NA	912	.1	.1
081f MELKITE-GK	1	NA	1,150	.1	.1
081h UKRAINIAN	1	NA	142	-	-
083 CHRIST CATH CH	1	43	47	-	-
089 CHR & MISS AL	4	475	802	.1	.1
111 CH CR,SCIENTST	6	NR	NR	-	-
123 CH GOD (ANDER)	2	240	240	-	-
127 CH GOD (CLEVE)	8	594	723*	.1	.1
145 CH GOD PROPHCY	3	84	102*	-	-
151 L-D SAINTS	5	NA	1,438	.1	.2
163 CH OF LUTH BR	1	48	96	-	-
165 CH OF NAZARENE	4	237	434	-	.1
167 CHS OF CHRIST	6	449	605	.1	.1
175 CONGR CHR CHS	2	141	172*	-	-
176 CCC, NOT NAT'L	2	592	721*	.1	.1
179 CONSRV BAPT	6	NR	NR	-	-
181 CONSRV CONGR	2	173	211*	-	-
193 EPISCOPAL	66	21,476	31,865	3.2	4.1
207 E.L.C.A.	12	3,998	5,500	.5	.7
221 FREE METHODIST	1	27	40	-	-
223 FREE WILL BAPT	1	34	42*	-	-
226 FRIENDS-USA	9	449	617*	.1	.1
226b EFI	2	127	223	-	-
226d FGC & FUM	7	322	394*	-	.1
241 GEN SIX PR BPT	1	120	147*	-	-
246 GREEK ORTHODOX	3	NR	NR	-	-
263 INT FOURSQ GOS	3	48	58*	-	-
283 LUTH—MO SYNOD	4	1,082	1,415	.1	.2
331 ORTH CH IN AM	1	NR	NR	-	-
353 CHR BRETHREN	3	179	280	-	-
355 PRESB CH (USA)	9	2,331	2,835*	.3	.4
356 PRESB CH AMER	1	44	68	-	-
363 PRIMITIVE METH	4	249	383	-	-
397 ROMANIAN ORTH	1	NR	NR	-	-
403 SALVATION ARMY	3	277	297	-	-
413 S.D.A.	6	571	695*	.1	.1
415 S-D BAPTIST GC	3	356	436*	-	.1
419 SO BAPT CONV	5	1,346	1,641*	.2	.2
423 SYRIAN ANTIOCH	1	NA	700	.1	.1
435 UNITARIAN-UNIV	8	1,226	1,661	.2	.2
443 UN C OF CHRIST	30	7,791	9,482*	.9	1.2
449 UN METHODIST	26	7,748	9,425*	.9	1.2
469 WELS	1	85	139	-	-
496 JEWISH EST[1]	24	NA	16,101	1.6	2.1
497 BLACK BAPT EST[2]	NA	7,364	8,963*	.9	1.2
498 INDEP.CHARIS.[3]	1	NA	600	.1	.1
499 INDEP.NON-CHAR[3]	6	NA	2,850	.3	.4
SOUTH CAROLINA	**5,509**	**1,612,322**	**2,157,828***	**61.9**	**100.0**
001 ADVENT CHR CH	11	812	1,042*	-	-
005 AME ZION	167	57,093	65,122	1.9	3.0

State and Denomination	Number of churches	Communicant, confirmed, full members	Total adherents Number	Percent of total population	Percent of total adherents
019 AMER BAPT USA	3	1,294	1,591*	-	.1
053 ASSEMB OF GOD	115	9,575	16,045	.5	.7
055 AS REF PRES CH	64	12,597	14,624	.4	.7
061 BEACHY AMISH	2	163	206*	-	-
081 CATHOLIC	120	NA	78,768	2.3	3.7
081d LATIN	120	NA	78,768	2.3	3.7
082 CENTRAL BAPT	2	200	248*	-	-
089 CHR & MISS AL	11	498	921	-	-
093 CHR CH (DISC)	52	3,954	5,958	.2	.3
097 CHR CHS&CHS CR	29	3,031	3,910*	.1	.2
111 CH CR,SCIENTST	11	NR	NR	-	-
121 CH GOD (ABR)	3	340	420*	-	-
123 CH GOD (ANDER)	42	2,291	3,070	.1	.1
127 CH GOD (CLEVE)	267	35,447	44,422*	1.3	2.1
133 CH GOD(7TH)DEN	1	24	37	-	-
145 CH GOD PROPHCY	150	4,906	6,179*	.2	.3
151 L-D SAINTS	49	NA	16,896	.5	.8
157 CH OF BRETHREN	1	48	60*	-	-
164 CH LUTH CONF	1	258	334	-	-
165 CH OF NAZARENE	57	7,369	12,203	.3	.6
167 CHS OF CHRIST	111	9,563	12,861	.4	.6
179 CONSRV BAPT	2	NR	NR	-	-
193 EPISCOPAL	135	37,516	48,655	1.4	2.3
207 E.L.C.A.	164	48,330	61,489	1.8	2.8
215 EVAN METH CH	2	142	176*	-	-
216 EVAN PRESBY CH	4	623	650	-	-
223 FREE WILL BAPT	117	14,122	17,789*	.5	.8
226 FRIENDS-USA	3	52	89*	-	-
226c FGC	1	15	30	-	-
226d FGC & FUM	1	37	50*	-	-
226f INDEPENDNT	1	0	9	-	-
246 GREEK ORTHODOX	6	NR	NR	-	-
259 IFCA	3	NR	NR	-	-
263 INT FOURSQ GOS	9	597	754*	-	-
283 LUTH—MO SYNOD	15	2,232	3,026	.1	.1
285 MENNONITE CH	7	393	542	-	-
331 ORTH CH IN AM	1	NR	NR	-	-
349 PENT HOLINESS	242	19,881	25,112*	.7	1.2
353 CHR BRETHREN	19	820	1,394	-	.1
355 PRESB CH (USA)	330	74,665	93,714*	2.7	4.3
356 PRESB CH AMER	95	16,548	19,987	.6	.9
361 PRIM BAPT ASCS	4	96	124*	-	-
375 REF EPISCOPAL	32	2,848	2,848	.1	.1
403 SALVATION ARMY	16	1,544	1,626	-	.1
413 S.D.A.	51	6,517	8,195*	.2	.4
415 S-D BAPTIST GC	2	77	97*	-	-
419 SO BAPT CONV	1,781	713,099	894,390*	25.7	41.4
435 UNITARIAN-UNIV	8	921	1,229	-	.1
443 UN C OF CHRIST	2	187	235*	-	-
449 UN METHODIST	1,074	244,591	308,915*	8.9	14.3
467 WESLEYAN	68	4,135	7,676	.2	.4
469 WELS	3	164	233	-	-
496 JEWISH EST[1]	20	NA	8,558	.2	.4
497 BLACK BAPT EST[2]	NA	272,759	345,858*	9.9	16.0
498 INDEP.CHARIS.[3]	5	NA	3,900	.1	.2
499 INDEP.NON-CHAR[3]	20	NA	15,650	.4	.7
SOUTH DAKOTA	**1,781**	**234,370**	**474,010***	**68.1**	**100.0**
019 AMER BAPT USA	34	6,623	8,497*	1.2	1.8
045 APOSTOLIC LUTH	3	125	210	-	-
053 ASSEMB OF GOD	52	3,509	6,754	1.0	1.4
057 BAPT GEN CONF	19	2,871	3,684*	.5	.8
063 BEREAN FUND CH	2	70	151	-	-
081 CATHOLIC	271	NA	143,776	20.7	30.3
081d LATIN	271	NA	143,776	20.7	30.3
089 CHR & MISS AL	14	489	1,144	.2	.2
093 CHR CH (DISC)	2	378	544	.1	.1
097 CHR CHS&CHS CR	15	1,245	1,617*	.2	.3
105 CHRISTIAN REF	17	2,603	3,911	.6	.8
111 CH CR,SCIENTST	5	NR	NR	-	-
123 CH GOD (ANDER)	6	556	640	.1	.1
127 CH GOD (CLEVE)	11	474	608*	.1	.1
133 CH GOD(7TH)DEN	2	28	37	-	-
143 CG IN CR(MENN)	1	97	123*	-	-
145 CH GOD PROPHCY	3	121	167*	-	-
151 L-D SAINTS	33	NA	5,155	.7	1.1
163 CH OF LUTH BR	3	114	231	-	-
164 CH LUTH CONF	12	615	821	.1	.2
165 CH OF NAZARENE	17	825	1,626	.2	.3

NA–Not applicable NR–Not reported *Total adherents estimated from known number of communicant, confirmed, full members. - Represents a percent less than 0.1. Percentages may not total due to rounding.
[1]See Appendix E [2]See Appendix F [3]See Appendix G Lines in *italic* represent a breakdown of Catholic rites or Friends affiliations. They are included in their respective denominational total.

Table 3. Churches and Church Membership by State and Denomination: 1990

State and Denomination	Number of churches	Communicant, confirmed, full members	Total adherents Number	Percent of total population	Percent of total adherents
167 CHS OF CHRIST	24	857	1,175	.2	.2
176 CCC, NOT NAT'L	2	44	61*	-	-
193 EPISCOPAL	98	7,173	11,940	1.7	2.5
203 EVAN FREE CH	12	721	1,466	.2	.3
207 E.L.C.A.	273	85,334	114,690	16.5	24.2
209 EVAN LUTH SYN	1	72	85	-	-
211 FEL EVG BIB CH	1	70	80	-	-
220 FREE LUTHERAN	18	1,413	1,835	.3	.4
221 FREE METHODIST	5	86	166	-	-
223 FREE WILL BAPT	1	25	32*	-	-
226 FRIENDS-USA	2	22	46*	-	-
226b EFI	1	21	37*	-	-
226f INDEPENDNT	1	1	9	-	-
237 GC MENN BR CHS	11	1,017	1,303*	.2	.3
246 GREEK ORTHODOX	1	NR	NR	-	-
257 HUTTERIAN BR	50	NA	5,000	.7	1.1
259 IFCA	1	NR	NR	-	-
263 INT FOURSQ GOS	4	361	466*	.1	.1
274 LAT EVAN LUTH	1	24	24	-	-
283 LUTH—MO SYNOD	114	25,106	32,968	4.7	7.0
284 LUTH CH-AM ASC	2	369	470	.1	.1
285 MENNONITE CH	1	31	34	-	-
287 MENN GEN CONF	15	2,426	2,932	.4	.6
291 MISSIONARY CH	3	117	123	-	-
307 NETH REF CONGR	2	118	256	-	.1
313 N AM BAPT CONF	23	3,402	4,351*	.6	.9
329 OPEN BIBLE STD	11	NR	NR	-	-
339 PENT CH OF GOD	4	138	307	-	.1
355 PRESB CH (USA)	91	11,961	15,473*	2.2	3.3
356 PRESB CH AMER	4	875	1,074	.2	.2
371 REF CH IN AM	26	4,266	7,466	1.1	1.6
373 REF CH IN U.S.	10	1,022	1,250	.2	.3
403 SALVATION ARMY	6	652	732	.1	.2
413 S.D.A.	24	1,809	2,343*	.3	.5
415 S-D BAPTIST GC	1	30	39*	-	-
419 SO BAPT CONV	45	5,543	7,300*	1.0	1.5
435 UNITARIAN-UNIV	4	79	98	-	-
438 UN BRETH IN CR	1	21	24	-	-
443 UN C OF CHRIST	98	14,466	18,607*	2.7	3.9
449 UN METHODIST	175	33,703	43,212*	6.2	9.1
467 WESLEYAN	31	1,808	5,543	.8	1.2
469 WELS	59	7,817	10,358	1.5	2.2
496 JEWISH EST[1]	4	NA	135	-	-
497 BLACK BAPT EST[2]	NA	649	850*	.1	.2
TENNESSEE	**9,246**	**2,191,239**	**2,984,916***	**61.2**	**100.0**
001 ADVENT CHR CH	2	73	92*	-	-
005 AME ZION	64	18,377	22,348	.5	.7
011 A.W.M.C.	3	0	0*	-	-
019 AMER BAPT USA	9	4,592	5,751*	.1	.2
053 ASSEMB OF GOD	182	22,297	31,630	.6	1.1
055 AS REF PRES CH	14	1,693	1,866	-	.1
059 BAPT MISS ASSN	11	1,507	1,890*	-	.1
061 BEACHY AMISH	5	363	447*	-	-
075 BRETHREN IN CR	3	181	193	-	-
081 CATHOLIC	142	NA	137,203	2.8	4.6
081d LATIN	142	NA	137,203	2.8	4.6
082 CENTRAL BAPT	12	1,878	2,268*	-	.1
089 CHR & MISS AL	8	505	860	-	-
093 CHR CH (DISC)	67	15,427	20,986	.4	.7
097 CHR CHS&CHS CR	161	26,318	31,979*	.7	1.1
105 CHRISTIAN REF	1	75	123	-	-
111 CH CR,SCIENTST	17	NR	NR	-	-
121 CH GOD (ABR)	1	10	12*	-	-
123 CH GOD (ANDER)	73	4,472	6,188	.1	.2
127 CH GOD (CLEVE)	346	39,584	48,721*	1.0	1.6
133 CH GOD(7TH)DEN	6	82	108	-	-
143 CG IN CR(MENN)	2	54	65*	-	-
145 CH GOD PROPHCY	146	7,079	8,756*	.2	.3
146 CH GOD MTN ASM	21	715	881*	-	-
151 L-D SAINTS	53	NA	15,635	.3	.5
157 CH OF BRETHREN	20	1,175	1,418*	-	-
165 CH OF NAZARENE	165	17,284	23,392	.5	.8
167 CHS OF CHRIST	1,472	168,933	219,996	4.5	7.4
175 CONGR CHR CHS	1	90	109*	-	-
185 CUMBER PRESB	289	36,233	38,684	.8	1.3
189 DUCK RIVR BAPT	71	7,035	8,711*	.2	.3
193 EPISCOPAL	122	30,930	40,351	.8	1.4
203 EVAN FREE CH	4	164	449	-	-

State and Denomination	Number of churches	Communicant, confirmed, full members	Total adherents Number	Percent of total population	Percent of total adherents
207 E.L.C.A.	51	12,448	16,085	.3	.5
215 EVAN METH CH	3	226	282*	-	-
216 EVAN PRESBY CH	7	4,621	4,754	.1	.2
221 FREE METHODIST	11	285	512	-	-
223 FREE WILL BAPT	219	25,247	30,826*	.6	1.0
226 FRIENDS-USA	17	570	832*	-	-
226c FGC	10	179	355	-	-
226e FUM	7	391	477*	-	-
246 GREEK ORTHODOX	4	NR	NR	-	-
259 IFCA	8	NR	NR	-	-
263 INT FOURSQ GOS	10	1,085	1,332*	-	-
274 LAT EVAN LUTH	1	18	21	-	-
283 LUTH—MO SYNOD	51	10,549	13,981	.3	.5
285 MENNONITE CH	4	122	211	-	-
320 "OLD" MB ASCS	51	9,755	12,139*	.2	.4
323 OLD ORD AMISH	6	NA	900	-	-
325 OLD REG BAPT	1	19	23*	-	-
329 OPEN BIBLE STD	1	NR	NR	-	-
331 ORTH CH IN AM	1	NR	NR	-	-
339 PENT CH OF GOD	9	267	639	-	-
349 PENT HOLINESS	25	1,601	2,002*	-	.1
353 CHR BRETHREN	6	360	598	-	-
355 PRESB CH (USA)	327	57,639	71,129*	1.5	2.4
356 PRESB CH AMER	57	13,214	15,911	.3	.5
361 PRIM BAPT ASCS	93	5,064	6,240*	.1	.2
403 SALVATION ARMY	14	1,629	1,787	-	.1
413 S.D.A.	121	21,900	27,119*	.6	.9
415 S-D BAPTIST GC	2	40	49*	-	-
419 SO BAPT CONV	2,801	1,086,680	1,343,312*	27.5	45.0
426 2SEED-SPRT BPT	1	8	10*	-	-
435 UNITARIAN-UNIV	10	1,907	2,527	.1	.1
436 UNITED BAPT	42	5,847	7,413*	.2	.2
443 UN C OF CHRIST	17	1,837	2,260*	-	.1
449 UN METHODIST	1,675	320,724	396,862*	8.1	13.3
467 WESLEYAN	18	438	1,078	-	-
469 WELS	4	315	454	-	-
496 JEWISH EST[1]	21	NA	17,474	.4	.6
497 BLACK BAPT EST[2]	NA	199,698	250,490*	5.1	8.4
498 INDEP.CHARIS.[3]	21	NA	12,925	.3	.4
499 INDEP.NON-CHAR[3]	43	NA	71,627	1.5	2.4
TEXAS	**16,961**	**5,282,341**	**10,896,401***	**64.1**	**100.0**
001 ADVENT CHR CH	5	172	221*	-	-
005 AME ZION	9	1,842	2,191	-	-
019 AMER BAPT USA	24	10,046	12,905*	.1	.1
040 AP CHR CH-AMER	1	8	13	-	-
053 ASSEMB OF GOD	1,274	146,688	202,082	1.2	1.9
057 BAPT GEN CONF	4	218	278*	-	-
059 BAPT MISS ASSN	498	98,509	125,323*	.7	1.2
061 BEACHY AMISH	1	56	70*	-	-
075 BRETHREN IN CR	2	53	73	-	-
081 CATHOLIC	1,290	NA	3,574,728	21.0	32.8
081b BYZAN RUTH	3	NA	718	-	-
081d LATIN	1,283	NA	3,572,135	21.0	32.8
081e MARONITE	2	NA	1,282	-	-
081f MELKITE-GK	1	NA	522	-	-
081h UKRAINIAN	1	NA	71	-	-
083 CHRIST CATH CH	1	3	3	-	-
089 CHR & MISS AL	45	1,605	3,082	-	-
093 CHR CH (DISC)	428	74,098	105,495	.6	1.0
097 CHR CHS&CHS CR	147	26,012	33,766*	.2	.3
105 CHRISTIAN REF	9	528	866	-	-
111 CH CR,SCIENTST	93	NR	NR	-	-
121 CH GOD (ABR)	3	71	93*	-	-
123 CH GOD (ANDER)	94	4,218	5,854	-	.1
127 CH GOD (CLEVE)	206	21,728	27,828*	.2	.3
133 CH GOD(7TH)DEN	32	1,243	1,743	-	-
143 CG IN CR(MENN)	5	406	522*	-	-
145 CH GOD PROPHCY	83	2,251	2,918*	-	-
151 L-D SAINTS	329	NA	111,276	.7	1.0
157 CH OF BRETHREN	4	235	302*	-	-
163 CH OF LUTH BR	1	36	71	-	-
164 CH LUTH CONF	3	107	144	-	-
165 CH OF NAZARENE	325	31,163	45,097	.3	.4
167 CHS OF CHRIST	2,215	292,585	380,948	2.2	3.5
175 CONGR CHR CHS	3	556	721*	-	-
176 CCC, NOT NAT'L	1	18	23*	-	-
179 CONSRV BAPT	1	NR	NR	-	-
181 CONSRV CONGR	1	81	104*	-	-

NA–Not applicable   NR–Not reported   *Total adherents estimated from known number of communicant, confirmed, full members.   - Represents a percent less than 0.1.   Percentages may not total due to rounding.
[1]See Appendix E   [2]See Appendix F   [3]See Appendix G   Lines in *italic* represent a breakdown of Catholic rites or Friends affiliations. They are included in their respective denominational total.

Table 3. Churches and Church Membership by State and Denomination: 1990

State and Denomination	Number of churches	Communicant, confirmed, full members	Total adherents Number	Percent of total population	Percent of total adherents
185 CUMBER PRESB	50	9,177	10,373	.1	.1
193 EPISCOPAL	424	127,315	169,112	1.0	1.6
203 EVAN FREE CH	33	2,772	5,463	-	.1
207 E.L.C.A.	401	120,004	155,276	.9	1.4
209 EVAN LUTH SYN	2	119	146	-	-
211 FEL EVG BIB CH	1	18	20	-	-
215 EVAN METH CH	15	1,154	1,482*	-	-
216 EVAN PRESBY CH	7	473	490	-	-
220 FREE LUTHERAN	2	115	144	-	-
221 FREE METHODIST	22	549	886	-	-
223 FREE WILL BAPT	55	3,883	4,936*	-	-
226 FRIENDS-USA	25	1,853	2,548*	-	-
226b EFI	10	1,369	1,758*	-	-
226c FGC	14	469	770	-	-
226f INDEPENDNT	1	15	20*	-	-
237 GC MENN BR CHS	8	236	329*	-	-
246 GREEK ORTHODOX	15	NR	NR	-	-
249 AP CATH ASSYR	1	70	282	-	-
259 IFCA	4	NR	NR	-	-
263 INT FOURSQ GOS	74	3,286	4,278*	-	-
266 INTRSTAT & ASC	1	59	76*	-	-
283 LUTH—MO SYNOD	345	99,974	134,280	.8	1.2
285 MENNONITE CH	19	673	1,012	-	-
286 E.PA MENNONITE	1	30	39*	-	-
287 MENN GEN CONF	8	172	216	-	-
313 N AM BAPT CONF	14	1,262	1,634*	-	-
323 OLD ORD AMISH	3	NA	400	-	-
329 OPEN BIBLE STD	2	NR	NR	-	-
331 ORTH CH IN AM	9	NR	NR	-	-
339 PENT CH OF GOD	163	6,477	12,296	.1	.1
349 PENT HOLINESS	90	4,221	5,517*	-	.1
353 CHR BRETHREN	35	4,225	6,766	-	.1
355 PRESB CH (USA)	579	156,165	200,969*	1.2	1.8
356 PRESB CH AMER	40	4,221	5,445	-	-
361 PRIM BAPT ASCS	53	1,977	2,544*	-	-
371 REF CH IN AM	3	760	1,592	-	-
375 REF EPISCOPAL	1	71	115	-	-
397 ROMANIAN ORTH	1	NR	NR	-	-
403 SALVATION ARMY	50	5,257	5,676	-	.1
413 S.D.A.	258	31,985	41,470*	.2	.4
415 S-D BAPTIST GC	6	190	242*	-	-
419 SO BAPT CONV	4,285	2,538,245	3,259,395*	19.2	29.9
423 SYRIAN ANTIOCH	4	NA	1,800	-	-
426 2SEED-SPRT BPT	1	42	53*	-	-
435 UNITARIAN-UNIV	40	4,440	5,843	-	.1
443 UN C OF CHRIST	74	16,321	20,950*	.1	.2
449 UN METHODIST	2,186	781,389	1,004,318*	5.9	9.2
467 WESLEYAN	11	329	892	-	-
469 WELS	36	3,117	4,463	-	-
496 JEWISH EST[1]	72	NA	107,980	.6	1.0
497 BLACK BAPT EST[2]	NA	635,179	815,771*	4.8	7.5
498 INDEP.CHARIS.[3]	113	NA	127,850	.8	1.2
499 INDEP.NON-CHAR[3]	182	NA	132,292	.8	1.2
UTAH	**3,319**	**45,080**	**1,374,097***	**79.8**	**100.0**
019 AMER BAPT USA	10	1,971	2,775*	.2	.2
039 AP CHR CH(NAZ)	1	4	6*	-	-
053 ASSEMB OF GOD	29	2,919	6,450	.4	.5
081 CATHOLIC	74	NA	66,316	3.8	4.8
081b BYZAN RUTH	1	NA	50	-	-
081d LATIN	72	NA	66,000	3.8	4.8
081e MARONITE	1	NA	266	-	-
083 CHRIST CATH CH	1	20	28	-	-
089 CHR & MISS AL	4	243	441	-	-
093 CHR CH (DISC)	4	426	644	-	-
097 CHR CHS&CHS CR	5	678	949*	.1	.1
105 CHRISTIAN REF	6	357	602	-	-
111 CH CR,SCIENTST	7	NR	NR	-	-
127 CH GOD (CLEVE)	3	194	265*	-	-
145 CH GOD PROPHCY	6	132	181*	-	-
151 L-D SAINTS	2,924	NA	1,236,242	71.8	90.0
165 CH OF NAZARENE	6	266	583	-	-
167 CHS OF CHRIST	17	606	912	.1	.1
175 CONGR CHR CHS	1	290	403*	-	-
179 CONSRV BAPT	9	NR	NR	-	-
193 EPISCOPAL	25	4,312	5,436	.3	.4
203 EVAN FREE CH	5	315	600	-	-
207 E.L.C.A.	11	3,516	5,111	.3	.4
221 FREE METHODIST	2	0	65	-	-

State and Denomination	Number of churches	Communicant, confirmed, full members	Total adherents Number	Percent of total population	Percent of total adherents
226 FRIENDS-USA	4	81	120*	-	-
226f INDEPENDNT	4	81	120*	-	-
246 GREEK ORTHODOX	4	NR	NR	-	-
259 IFCA	4	NR	NR	-	-
263 INT FOURSQ GOS	8	530	739*	-	.1
283 LUTH—MO SYNOD	17	3,028	4,547	.3	.3
339 PENT CH OF GOD	5	172	384	-	-
355 PRESB CH (USA)	23	4,754	6,658*	.4	.5
403 SALVATION ARMY	3	38	71	-	-
413 S.D.A.	14	1,287	1,818*	.1	.1
419 SO BAPT CONV	52	10,012	14,227*	.8	1.0
435 UNITARIAN-UNIV	2	477	718	-	.1
443 UN C OF CHRIST	9	1,552	2,211*	.1	.2
449 UN METHODIST	16	4,598	6,376*	.4	.5
469 WELS	1	70	135	-	-
496 JEWISH EST[1]	1	NA	2,950	.2	.2
497 BLACK BAPT EST[2]	NA	2,232	3,134*	.2	.2
498 INDEP.CHARIS.[3]	3	NA	950	.1	.1
499 INDEP.NON-CHAR[3]	3	NA	1,050	.1	.1
VERMONT	**764**	**63,861**	**236,757***	**42.1**	**100.0**
001 ADVENT CHR CH	5	317	399*	.1	.2
019 AMER BAPT USA	63	6,987	8,786*	1.6	3.7
053 ASSEMB OF GOD	18	1,464	2,642	.5	1.1
081 CATHOLIC	139	NA	143,938	25.6	60.8
081d LATIN	139	NA	143,938	25.6	60.8
089 CHR & MISS AL	10	686	1,706	.3	.7
097 CHR CHS&CHS CR	3	110	138*	-	.1
105 CHRISTIAN REF	1	203	369	.1	.2
111 CH CR,SCIENTST	13	NR	NR	-	-
123 CH GOD (ANDER)	1	15	21	-	-
127 CH GOD (CLEVE)	2	84	106*	-	-
145 CH GOD PROPHCY	2	54	68*	-	-
151 L-D SAINTS	12	NA	2,855	.5	1.2
165 CH OF NAZARENE	9	537	965	.2	.4
167 CHS OF CHRIST	11	461	653	.1	.3
175 CONGR CHR CHS	2	100	125*	-	.1
176 CCC, NOT NAT'L	15	1,153	1,449*	.3	.6
179 CONSRV BAPT	3	NR	NR	-	-
181 CONSRV CONGR	1	124	156*	-	.1
193 EPISCOPAL	50	6,027	9,628	1.7	4.1
203 EVAN FREE CH	5	243	387	.1	.2
207 E.L.C.A.	7	1,162	1,522	.3	.6
221 FREE METHODIST	1	17	45	-	-
226 FRIENDS-USA	12	310	438*	.1	.2
226d FGC & FUM	12	310	438*	.1	.2
246 GREEK ORTHODOX	2	NR	NR	-	-
259 IFCA	4	NR	NR	-	-
263 INT FOURSQ GOS	3	73	92*	-	-
283 LUTH—MO SYNOD	2	331	494	.1	.2
285 MENNONITE CH	3	173	280	-	.1
286 E.PA MENNONITE	1	12	15*	-	-
331 ORTH CH IN AM	1	NR	NR	-	-
349 PENT HOLINESS	1	5	6*	-	-
353 CHR BRETHREN	2	50	100	-	-
355 PRESB CH (USA)	10	818	1,031*	.2	.4
356 PRESB CH AMER	1	73	117	-	-
403 SALVATION ARMY	3	130	143	-	.1
413 S.D.A.	13	654	822*	.1	.3
419 SO BAPT CONV	12	683	860*	.2	.4
435 UNITARIAN-UNIV	19	1,506	2,056	.4	.9
443 UN C OF CHRIST	148	19,492	24,461*	4.3	10.3
449 UN METHODIST	143	19,520	24,578*	4.4	10.4
467 WESLEYAN	2	52	74	-	-
469 WELS	1	76	136	-	.1
496 JEWISH EST[1]	7	NA	4,400	.8	1.9
497 BLACK BAPT EST[2]	NA	159	196*	-	.1
498 INDEP.CHARIS.[3]	1	NA	500	.1	.2
VIRGINIA	**7,490**	**1,899,605**	**2,966,083***	**47.9**	**100.0**
001 ADVENT CHR CH	15	847	1,030*	-	-
005 AME ZION	80	26,698	32,114	.5	1.1
011 A.W.M.C.	4	27	33*	-	-
019 AMER BAPT USA	88	41,399	51,181*	.8	1.7
039 AP CHR CH(NAZ)	1	21	25*	-	-
053 ASSEMB OF GOD	178	23,600	38,044	.6	1.3
055 AS REF PRES CH	9	1,805	2,063	-	.1
057 BAPT GEN CONF	1	72	89*	-	-
059 BAPT MISS ASSN	1	150	188*	-	-

NA–Not applicable   NR–Not reported   *Total adherents estimated from known number of communicant, confirmed, full members.   - Represents a percent less than 0.1.   Percentages may not total due to rounding.
[1]See Appendix E   [2]See Appendix F   [3]See Appendix G   Lines in *italic* represent a breakdown of Catholic rites or Friends affiliations. They are included in their respective denominational total.

Table 3. Churches and Church Membership by State and Denomination: 1990

State and Denomination	Number of churches	Communicant, confirmed, full members	Total adherents			State and Denomination	Number of churches	Communicant, confirmed, full members	Total adherents		
			Number	Percent of total population	Percent of total adherents				Number	Percent of total population	Percent of total adherents
061 BEACHY AMISH	7	506	629*	-	-	019 AMER BAPT USA	137	28,837	36,230*	.7	2.2
071 BRETHREN (ASH)	7	638	772*	-	-	039 AP CHR CH(NAZ)	1	33	43*	-	-
075 BRETHREN IN CR	7	321	349	-	-	045 APOSTOLIC LUTH	5	279	753	-	-
081 CATHOLIC	228	NA	384,285	6.2	13.0	053 ASSEMB OF GOD	351	42,682	84,765	1.7	5.3
081b BYZAN RUTH	2	NA	800	-	-	057 BAPT GEN CONF	41	9,079	11,467*	.2	.7
081d LATIN	221	NA	380,962	6.2	12.8	059 BAPT MISS ASSN	4	227	291*	-	-
081e MARONITE	2	NA	1,588	-	.1	081 CATHOLIC	317	NA	526,546	10.8	32.7
081f MELKITE-GK	1	NA	490	-	-	081b BYZAN RUTH	3	NA	535	-	-
081h UKRAINIAN	2	NA	445	-	-	081d LATIN	314	NA	526,011	10.8	32.6
082 CENTRAL BAPT	14	621	749*	-	-	089 CHR & MISS AL	64	5,839	13,447	.3	.8
089 CHR & MISS AL	25	1,231	3,358	.1	.1	093 CHR CH (DISC)	72	9,974	14,787	.3	.9
093 CHR CH (DISC)	224	25,803	42,038	.7	1.4	097 CHR CHS&CHS CR	66	14,844	18,569*	.4	1.2
097 CHR CHS&CHS CR	210	32,450	39,949*	.6	1.3	105 CHRISTIAN REF	37	6,193	10,110	.2	.6
105 CHRISTIAN REF	3	226	329	-	-	111 CH CR,SCIENTST	73	NR	NR	-	-
111 CH CR,SCIENTST	28	NR	NR	-	-	121 CH GOD (ABR)	3	205	261*	-	-
121 CH GOD (ABR)	4	142	176*	-	-	123 CH GOD (ANDER)	46	2,521	5,984	.1	.4
123 CH GOD (ANDER)	56	3,222	4,000	.1	.1	127 CH GOD (CLEVE)	34	3,156	4,073*	.1	.3
127 CH GOD (CLEVE)	177	20,079	24,614*	.4	.8	133 CH GOD(7TH)DEN	3	145	203	-	-
145 CH GOD PROPHCY	126	5,214	6,373*	.1	.2	143 CG IN CR(MENN)	1	44	61*	-	-
146 CH GOD MTN ASM	1	26	32*	-	-	145 CH GOD PROPHCY	27	719	921*	-	.1
151 L-D SAINTS	120	NA	42,073	.7	1.4	151 L-D SAINTS	371	NA	150,634	3.1	9.3
157 CH OF BRETHREN	181	26,503	32,228*	.5	1.1	157 CH OF BRETHREN	13	1,514	1,909*	-	.1
164 CH LUTH CONF	1	19	22	-	-	163 CH OF LUTH BR	13	914	1,837	-	.1
165 CH OF NAZARENE	75	8,124	12,240	.2	.4	164 CH LUTH CONF	4	559	769	-	-
167 CHS OF CHRIST	153	11,752	15,304	.2	.5	165 CH OF NAZARENE	135	19,123	28,164	.6	1.7
176 CCC, NOT NAT'L	5	1,230	1,509*	-	.1	167 CHS OF CHRIST	129	10,992	14,860	.3	.9
179 CONSRV BAPT	2	NR	NR	-	-	175 CONGR CHR CHS	5	1,119	1,421*	-	.1
181 CONSRV CONGR	1	102	129*	-	-	179 CONSRV BAPT	67	NR	NR	-	-
193 EPISCOPAL	360	89,027	129,070	2.1	4.4	181 CONSRV CONGR	2	72	87*	-	-
203 EVAN FREE CH	6	322	503	-	-	193 EPISCOPAL	133	30,055	44,246	.9	2.7
207 E.L.C.A.	193	48,380	64,337	1.0	2.2	195 ESTONIAN ELC	1	71	87*	-	-
215 EVAN METH CH	5	550	671*	-	-	203 EVAN FREE CH	41	2,937	5,262	.1	.3
216 EVAN PRESBY CH	8	1,653	1,698	-	.1	207 E.L.C.A.	280	95,609	132,528	2.7	8.2
221 FREE METHODIST	6	267	337	-	-	209 EVAN LUTH SYN	5	910	1,288	-	.1
223 FREE WILL BAPT	98	9,688	12,086*	.2	.4	215 EVAN METH CH	5	248	315*	-	-
226 FRIENDS-USA	39	2,192	3,116*	.1	.1	216 EVAN PRESBY CH	3	625	640	-	-
226a CONSERV	2	50	175*	-	-	217 FIRE BAPTIZED	1	10	12*	-	-
226b EFI	15	920	1,290	-	-	220 FREE LUTHERAN	8	738	1,014	-	.1
226c FGC	1	90	103*	-	-	221 FREE METHODIST	59	5,250	7,994	.2	.5
226d FGC & FUM	16	869	1,217*	-	-	223 FREE WILL BAPT	6	397	510*	-	-
226e FUM	5	263	331*	-	-	226 FRIENDS-USA	33	1,334	1,911*	-	.1
246 GREEK ORTHODOX	12	NR	NR	-	-	226b EFI	15	995	1,398	-	.1
259 IFCA	5	NR	NR	-	-	226f INDEPENDNT	18	339	513*	-	-
263 INT FOURSQ GOS	12	1,183	1,434*	-	-	237 GC MENN BR CHS	4	311	389*	-	-
265 INT PENT C CHR	9	265	473	-	-	246 GREEK ORTHODOX	6	NR	NR	-	-
283 LUTH—MO SYNOD	45	13,114	17,413	.3	.6	249 AP CATH ASSYR	1	82	184	-	-
284 LUTH CH-AM ASC	1	125	195	-	-	257 HUTTERIAN BR	4	NA	280	-	-
285 MENNONITE CH	79	6,496	9,176	.1	.3	259 IFCA	30	NR	NR	-	-
295 MORAV CH-SOUTH	4	274	356	-	-	263 INT FOURSQ GOS	96	17,689	22,353*	.5	1.4
323 OLD ORD AMISH	1	NA	50	-	-	274 LAT EVAN LUTH	3	617	729	-	-
325 OLD REG BAPT	46	1,903	2,378*	-	.1	283 LUTH—MO SYNOD	115	30,569	41,916	.9	2.6
329 OPEN BIBLE STD	1	NR	NR	-	-	284 LUTH CH-AM ASC	1	0	68	-	-
331 ORTH CH IN AM	7	NR	NR	-	-	285 MENNONITE CH	2	207	266	-	-
339 PENT CH OF GOD	11	288	695	-	-	287 MENN GEN CONF	5	355	490	-	-
349 PENT HOLINESS	171	15,647	19,041*	.3	.6	291 MISSIONARY CH	8	235	314	-	-
353 CHR BRETHREN	21	1,157	1,849	-	.1	307 NETH REF CONGR	2	134	290	-	-
355 PRESB CH (USA)	512	112,937	138,554*	2.2	4.7	313 N AM BAPT CONF	15	2,054	2,598*	.1	.2
356 PRESB CH AMER	69	10,119	12,548	.2	.4	325 OLD REG BAPT	2	74	92*	-	-
361 PRIM BAPT ASCS	146	4,561	5,582*	.1	.2	329 OPEN BIBLE STD	26	NR	NR	-	-
375 REF EPISCOPAL	3	56	80	-	-	331 ORTH CH IN AM	3	NR	NR	-	-
386 REGULAR BAPT	3	271	324*	-	-	339 PENT CH OF GOD	36	1,216	2,705	.1	.2
397 ROMANIAN ORTH	2	NR	NR	-	-	349 PENT HOLINESS	17	687	902*	-	.1
403 SALVATION ARMY	26	3,894	4,175	.1	.1	353 CHR BRETHREN	28	1,858	2,753	.1	.2
413 S.D.A.	91	12,034	14,828*	.2	.5	355 PRESB CH (USA)	218	57,331	72,273*	1.5	4.5
419 SO BAPT CONV	1,515	599,996	742,860*	12.0	25.0	356 PRESB CH AMER	12	1,326	1,807	-	.1
435 UNITARIAN-UNIV	22	4,214	6,119	.1	.2	361 PRIM BAPT ASCS	1	16	20*	-	-
438 UN BRETH IN CR	5	676	676	-	-	371 REF CH IN AM	9	2,090	3,663	.1	.2
443 UN C OF CHRIST	112	20,263	25,269*	.4	.9	375 REF EPISCOPAL	1	24	31	-	-
449 UN METHODIST	1,626	398,191	490,789*	7.9	16.5	403 SALVATION ARMY	22	2,519	2,698	.1	.2
467 WESLEYAN	66	5,236	12,476	.2	.4	413 S.D.A.	150	31,272	39,667*	.8	2.5
469 WELS	7	674	925	-	-	415 S-D BAPTIST GC	3	79	98*	-	-
496 JEWISH EST[1]	45	NA	66,564	1.1	2.2	419 SO BAPT CONV	188	47,374	60,307*	1.2	3.7
497 BLACK BAPT EST[2]	NA	301,124	373,756*	6.0	12.6	435 UNITARIAN-UNIV	25	3,568	4,997	.1	.3
498 INDEP.CHARIS.[3]	17	NA	19,725	.3	.7	438 UN BRETH IN CR	2	58	68	-	-
499 INDEP.NON-CHAR[3]	51	NA	50,030	.8	1.7	443 UN C OF CHRIST	92	14,514	18,181*	.4	1.1
WASHINGTON	**4,092**	**619,581**	**1,612,516***	**33.1**	**100.0**	449 UN METHODIST	252	70,644	89,499*	1.8	5.6
001 ADVENT CHR CH	5	520	647*	-	-	467 WESLEYAN	10	230	671	-	-
005 AME ZION	3	677	770	-	-	469 WELS	26	2,737	3,871	.1	.2
						496 JEWISH EST[1]	19	NA	33,689	.7	2.1

NA–Not applicable NR–Not reported *Total adherents estimated from known number of communicant, confirmed, full members. - Represents a percent less than 0.1. Percentages may not total due to rounding.
[1] See Appendix E [2] See Appendix F [3] See Appendix G Lines in *italic* represent a breakdown of Catholic rites or Friends affiliations. They are included in their respective denominational total.

Table 3. Churches and Church Membership by State and Denomination: 1990

Left table:

State and Denomination	Number of churches	Communicant, confirmed, full members	Total adherents Number	Percent of total population	Percent of total adherents
497 BLACK BAPT EST[2]	NA	31,260	39,186*	.8	2.4
498 INDEP.CHARIS.[3]	35	NA	28,315	.6	1.8
499 INDEP.NON-CHAR[3]	19	NA	11,730	.2	.7
WEST VIRGINIA	**4,443**	**482,485**	**741,998***	**41.4**	**100.0**
001 ADVENT CHR CH	36	1,101	1,361*	.1	.2
005 AME ZION	9	1,276	1,489	.1	.2
011 A.W.M.C.	15	188	233*	-	-
019 AMER BAPT USA	533	107,359	132,325*	7.4	17.8
022 EASTERN ORTH	3	128	128	-	-
053 ASSEMB OF GOD	105	7,049	14,202	.8	1.9
055 AS REF PRES CH	2	249	266	-	-
061 BEACHY AMISH	1	31	38*	-	-
071 BRETHREN (ASH)	6	211	258*	-	-
081 CATHOLIC	177	NA	108,529	6.1	14.6
081b BYZAN RUTH	*3*	*NA*	*2,009*	*.1*	*.3*
081d LATIN	*172*	*NA*	*105,348*	*5.9*	*14.2*
081e MARONITE	*1*	*NA*	*916*	*.1*	*.1*
081h UKRAINIAN	*1*	*NA*	*256*	*-*	*-*
089 CHR & MISS AL	10	723	1,075	.1	.1
093 CHR CH (DISC)	66	8,165	13,351	.7	1.8
097 CHR CHS&CHS CR	93	11,272	13,822*	.8	1.9
111 CH CR,SCIENTST	9	NR	NR	-	-
123 CH GOD (ANDER)	91	4,737	7,035	.4	.9
127 CH GOD (CLEVE)	196	15,989	19,814*	1.1	2.7
133 CH GOD(7TH)DEN	2	49	55	-	-
145 CH GOD PROPHCY	35	1,021	1,255*	.1	.2
151 L-D SAINTS	31	NA	8,095	.5	1.1
157 CH OF BRETHREN	88	7,598	9,383*	.5	1.3
165 CH OF NAZARENE	124	14,115	25,811	1.4	3.5
167 CHS OF CHRIST	290	19,509	25,134	1.4	3.4
171 CH GOD-GEN CON	12	744	911*	.1	.1
175 CONGR CHR CHS	1	35	43*	-	-
179 CONSRV BAPT	2	NR	NR	-	-
193 EPISCOPAL	82	10,057	13,926	.8	1.9
203 EVAN FREE CH	1	35	60	-	-
207 E.L.C.A.	58	11,077	14,845	.8	2.0
215 EVAN METH CH	6	541	655*	-	.1
216 EVAN PRESBY CH	1	0	0	-	-
221 FREE METHODIST	21	746	1,019	.1	.1
223 FREE WILL BAPT	179	11,753	14,616*	.8	2.0
226 FRIENDS-USA	2	40	64*	-	-
226c FGC	*2*	*34*	*50*	*-*	*-*
226f INDEPENDNT	*0*	*6*	*14*	*-*	*-*
246 GREEK ORTHODOX	6	NR	NR	-	-
259 IFCA	2	NR	NR	-	-
263 INT FOURSQ GOS	2	122	151*	-	-
265 INT PENT C CHR	9	246	452	-	.1
283 LUTH—MO SYNOD	4	455	628	-	.1
285 MENNONITE CH	13	483	601	-	.1
320 "OLD" MB ASCS	2	33	41*	-	-
325 OLD REG BAPT	34	1,750	2,219*	.1	.3
329 OPEN BIBLE STD	8	NR	NR	-	-
331 ORTH CH IN AM	2	NR	NR	-	-
339 PENT CH OF GOD	24	643	1,332	.1	.2
349 PENT HOLINESS	41	2,774	3,418*	.2	.5
353 CHR BRETHREN	6	222	510	-	.1
355 PRESB CH (USA)	212	30,762	37,586*	2.1	5.1
356 PRESB CH AMER	11	897	1,022	.1	.1
359 PRIM AD CHR CH	9	350	427*	-	.1
361 PRIM BAPT ASCS	21	400	487*	-	.1
403 SALVATION ARMY	18	1,435	1,536	.1	.2
413 S.D.A.	38	2,756	3,396*	.2	.5
415 S-D BAPTIST GC	3	334	411*	-	.1
419 SO BAPT CONV	135	35,121	43,161*	2.4	5.8
435 UNITARIAN-UNIV	6	194	251	-	-
436 UNITED BAPT	19	2,426	3,048*	.2	.4
438 UN BRETH IN CR	3	247	274	-	-
443 UN C OF CHRIST	7	1,168	1,440*	.1	.2
449 UN METHODIST	1,458	148,712	182,731*	10.2	24.6
467 WESLEYAN	34	784	2,175	.1	.3
469 WELS	1	25	36	-	-
496 JEWISH EST[1]	17	NA	2,181	.1	.3
497 BLACK BAPT EST[2]	NA	14,348	17,586*	1.0	2.4
498 INDEP.CHARIS.[3]	2	NA	900	.1	.1
499 INDEP.NON-CHAR[3]	9	NA	4,200	.2	.6
WISCONSIN	**5,023**	**1,152,092**	**3,160,201***	**64.6**	**100.0**
001 ADVENT CHR CH	6	353	450*	-	-

Right table:

State and Denomination	Number of churches	Communicant, confirmed, full members	Total adherents Number	Percent of total population	Percent of total adherents
005 AME ZION	2	229	303	-	-
019 AMER BAPT USA	84	15,386	19,423*	.4	.6
049 ARMEN AP CH AM	1	250	1,000	-	-
053 ASSEMB OF GOD	150	17,302	35,527	.7	1.1
057 BAPT GEN CONF	58	6,134	7,771*	.2	.2
075 BRETHREN IN CR	1	34	37	-	-
081 CATHOLIC	968	NA	1,554,278	31.8	49.2
081b BYZAN RUTH	*1*	*NA*	*80*	*-*	*-*
081d LATIN	*965*	*NA*	*1,553,615*	*31.8*	*49.2*
081f MELKITE-GK	*1*	*NA*	*400*	*-*	*-*
081h UKRAINIAN	*1*	*NA*	*183*	*-*	*-*
089 CHR & MISS AL	52	5,814	10,788	.2	.3
093 CHR CH (DISC)	3	316	436	-	-
097 CHR CHS&CHS CR	35	4,516	5,738*	.1	.2
105 CHRISTIAN REF	19	3,946	6,046	.1	.2
111 CH CR,SCIENTST	55	NR	NR	-	-
123 CH GOD (ANDER)	14	901	938	-	-
127 CH GOD (CLEVE)	19	955	1,212*	-	-
133 CH GOD(7TH)DEN	1	8	13	-	-
143 CG IN CR(MENN)	2	346	444*	-	-
145 CH GOD PROPHCY	11	269	340*	-	-
151 L-D SAINTS	42	NA	11,530	.2	.4
157 CH OF BRETHREN	3	133	171*	-	-
163 CH OF LUTH BR	7	526	1,518	-	-
164 CH LUTH CONF	9	1,198	1,692	-	.1
165 CH OF NAZARENE	50	2,588	5,157	.1	.2
167 CHS OF CHRIST	69	3,294	4,695	.1	.1
175 CONGR CHR CHS	31	7,841	9,907*	.2	.3
176 CCC, NOT NAT'L	2	426	537*	-	-
179 CONSRV BAPT	12	NR	NR	-	-
181 CONSRV CONGR	11	1,569	1,995*	-	.1
193 EPISCOPAL	130	19,455	27,561	.6	.9
203 EVAN FREE CH	72	5,643	10,666	.2	.3
207 E.L.C.A.	743	345,379	460,168	9.4	14.6
209 EVAN LUTH SYN	21	4,604	6,137	.1	.2
220 FREE LUTHERAN	14	1,067	1,440	-	-
221 FREE METHODIST	12	696	954	-	-
226 FRIENDS-USA	17	475	1,123*	-	-
226c FGC	*15*	*320*	*926*	*-*	*-*
226e FUM	*2*	*155*	*197*	*-*	*-*
246 GREEK ORTHODOX	7	NR	NR	-	-
259 IFCA	36	NR	NR	-	-
263 INT FOURSQ GOS	13	1,117	1,406*	-	-
274 LAT EVAN LUTH	2	665	718	-	-
283 LUTH—MO SYNOD	428	189,901	248,876	5.1	7.9
284 LUTH CH-AM ASC	7	1,130	1,440	-	-
285 MENNONITE CH	17	644	846	-	-
287 MENN GEN CONF	1	35	46	-	-
293 MORAV CH-NORTH	20	4,594	5,846	.1	.2
307 NETH REF CONGR	2	139	274	-	-
313 N AM BAPT CONF	13	2,557	3,249*	.1	.1
323 OLD ORD AMISH	45	NA	6,200	.1	.2
329 OPEN BIBLE STD	3	NR	NR	-	-
331 ORTH CH IN AM	7	NR	NR	-	-
339 PENT CH OF GOD	10	323	715	-	-
349 PENT HOLINESS	2	45	59*	-	-
353 CHR BRETHREN	16	619	1,062	-	-
355 PRESB CH (USA)	171	38,055	48,052*	1.0	1.5
356 PRESB CH AMER	3	191	276	-	-
363 PRIMITIVE METH	10	398	515	-	-
367 PROT CONF (LU)	5	770	955	-	-
371 REF CH IN AM	27	8,184	12,871	.3	.4
373 REF CH IN U.S.	1	297	395	-	-
403 SALVATION ARMY	20	2,298	2,574	.1	.1
413 S.D.A.	83	7,074	8,935*	.2	.3
415 S-D BAPTIST GC	7	614	781*	-	-
419 SO BAPT CONV	58	8,530	10,782*	.2	.3
435 UNITARIAN-UNIV	23	2,933	4,339	.1	.1
436 UNITED BAPT	1	9	11*	-	-
443 UN C OF CHRIST	253	74,240	94,010*	1.9	3.0
449 UN METHODIST	516	120,304	152,426*	3.1	4.8
467 WESLEYAN	29	1,861	5,438	.1	.2
469 WELS	409	169,817	222,151	4.5	7.0
496 JEWISH EST[1]	35	NA	34,605	.7	1.1
497 BLACK BAPT EST[2]	NA	63,095	79,628*	1.6	2.5
498 INDEP.CHARIS.[3]	7	NA	8,600	.2	.3
499 INDEP.NON-CHAR[3]	10	NA	12,125	.2	.4

NA–Not applicable   NR–Not reported   *Total adherents estimated from known number of communicant, confirmed, full members.   - Represents a percent less than 0.1.   Percentages may not total due to rounding.
[1]See Appendix E   [2]See Appendix F   [3]See Appendix G   Lines in *italic* represent a breakdown of Catholic rites or Friends affiliations. They are included in their respective denominational total.

Table 3. Churches and Church Membership by State and Denomination: 1990

State and Denomination	Number of churches	Communicant, confirmed, full members	Total adherents			State and Denomination	Number of churches	Communicant, confirmed, full members	Total adherents		
---	---	---	Number	Percent of total population	Percent of total adherents	---	---	---	Number	Percent of total population	Percent of total adherents
WYOMING	**766**	**74,414**	**216,375 ***	**47.7**	**100.0**						
019 AMER BAPT USA	21	5,393	6,977 *	1.5	3.2						
053 ASSEMB OF GOD	52	2,790	5,212	1.1	2.4						
057 BAPT GEN CONF	6	729	935 *	.2	.4						
063 BEREAN FUND CH	2	138	315	.1	.1						
071 BRETHREN (ASH)	1	73	94 *	-	-						
081 CATHOLIC	74	NA	59,565	13.1	27.5						
081d LATIN	*74*	*NA*	*59,565*	*13.1*	*27.5*						
089 CHR & MISS AL	15	450	1,436	.3	.7						
093 CHR CH (DISC)	4	1,568	1,907	.4	.9						
097 CHR CHS&CHS CR	17	1,910	2,505 *	.6	1.2						
111 CH CR,SCIENTST	9	NR	NR	-	-						
123 CH GOD (ANDER)	6	776	960	.2	.4						
127 CH GOD (CLEVE)	2	69	90 *	-	-						
145 CH GOD PROPHCY	12	208	267 *	.1	.1						
151 L-D SAINTS	128	NA	45,793	10.1	21.2						
164 CH LUTH CONF	1	73	105	-	-						
165 CH OF NAZARENE	19	1,075	2,284	.5	1.1						
167 CHS OF CHRIST	32	1,575	2,159	.5	1.0						
175 CONGR CHR CHS	2	930	1,195 *	.3	.6						
179 CONSRV BAPT	11	NR	NR	-	-						
193 EPISCOPAL	50	5,317	9,894	2.2	4.6						
203 EVAN FREE CH	6	300	496	.1	.2						
207 E.L.C.A.	20	6,257	9,088	2.0	4.2						
221 FREE METHODIST	3	4	61	-	-						
223 FREE WILL BAPT	2	67	86 *	-	-						
226 FRIENDS-USA	7	25	62 *	-	-						
226f INDEPENDNT	*7*	*25*	*62 **	*-*	*-*						
246 GREEK ORTHODOX	5	NR	NR	-	-						
263 INT FOURSQ GOS	12	636	836 *	.2	.4						
283 LUTH—MO SYNOD	44	7,982	11,228	2.5	5.2						
287 MENN GEN CONF	1	17	27	-	-						
313 N AM BAPT CONF	1	71	100 *	-	-						
329 OPEN BIBLE STD	7	NR	NR	-	-						
353 CHR BRETHREN	1	25	25	-	-						
355 PRESB CH (USA)	29	6,732	8,749 *	1.9	4.0						
356 PRESB CH AMER	1	64	77	-	-						
373 REF CH IN U.S.	1	20	35	-	-						
403 SALVATION ARMY	4	104	109	-	.1						
413 S.D.A.	22	1,400	1,821 *	.4	.8						
419 SO BAPT CONV	67	14,136	18,674 *	4.1	8.6						
435 UNITARIAN-UNIV	3	114	139	-	.1						
443 UN C OF CHRIST	12	2,189	2,845 *	.6	1.3						
449 UN METHODIST	39	10,090	13,099 *	2.9	6.1						
467 WESLEYAN	8	414	5,059	1.1	2.3						
469 WELS	3	220	353	.1	.2						
496 JEWISH EST[1]	2	NA	330	.1	.2						
497 BLACK BAPT EST[2]	NA	473	608 *	.1	.3						
499 INDEP.NON-CHAR[3]	2	NA	775	.2	.4						

NA–Not applicable   NR–Not reported   *Total adherents estimated from known number of communicant, confirmed, full members.   - Represents a percent less than 0.1.   Percentages may not total due to rounding.
[1]See Appendix E   [2]See Appendix F   [3]See Appendix G   Lines in *italic* represent a breakdown of Catholic rites or Friends affiliations. They are included in their respective denominational total.

Table 4. Churches and Church Membership by County and Denomination: 1990

County and Denomination	Number of churches	Communicant, confirmed, full members	Total adherents Number	Percent of total population	Percent of total adherents
ALABAMA					
THE STATE.....	8,447	2,119,898	2,867,460*	71.0	100.0
AUTAUGA	**70**	**17,308**	**23,543***	**68.8**	**100.0**
005 AME ZION	7	1,537	1,904	5.6	8.1
053 ASSEMB OF GOD	1	95	105	.3	.4
081 CATHOLIC	1	NA	1,025	3.0	4.4
081d LATIN	1	NA	1,025	3.0	4.4
089 CHR & MISS AL	1	120	136	.4	.6
093 CHR CH (DISC)	1	38	53	.2	.2
097 CHR CHS&CHS CR	1	119	154*	.5	.7
123 CH GOD (ANDER)	1	25	25	.1	.1
127 CH GOD (CLEVE)	4	365	472*	1.4	2.0
151 L-D SAINTS	1	NA	323	.9	1.4
167 CHS OF CHRIST	6	361	433	1.3	1.8
193 EPISCOPAL	1	211	296	.9	1.3
283 LUTH—MO SYNOD	1	85	139	.4	.6
353 CHR BRETHREN	1	25	50	.1	.2
355 PRESB CH (USA)	1	6	8*	-	-
356 PRESB CH AMER	1	395	395	1.2	1.7
413 S.D.A.	3	102	132*	.4	.6
419 SO BAPT CONV	26	8,797	11,374*	33.2	48.3
449 UN METHODIST	11	2,466	3,188*	9.3	13.5
467 WESLEYAN	1	74	115	.3	.5
497 BLACK BAPT EST[2]	NA	2,487	3,216*	9.4	13.7
BALDWIN	**181**	**40,347**	**59,109***	**60.1**	**100.0**
005 AME ZION	8	1,465	2,059	2.1	3.5
053 ASSEMB OF GOD	14	811	1,244	1.3	2.1
081 CATHOLIC	11	NA	6,509	6.6	11.0
081d LATIN	11	NA	6,509	6.6	11.0
089 CHR & MISS AL	3	198	340	.3	.6
093 CHR CH (DISC)	3	322	418	.4	.7
097 CHR CHS&CHS CR	1	80	100*	.1	.2
111 CH CR,SCIENTST	2	NR	NR	-	-
123 CH GOD (ANDER)	1	66	78	.1	.1
127 CH GOD (CLEVE)	10	1,008	1,261*	1.3	2.1
145 CH GOD PROPHCY	3	105	131*	.1	.2
151 L-D SAINTS	1	NA	412	.4	.7
165 CH OF NAZARENE	1	40	94	.1	.2
167 CHS OF CHRIST	9	989	1,259	1.3	2.1
193 EPISCOPAL	8	1,565	2,233	2.3	3.8
207 E.L.C.A.	1	49	65	.1	.1
221 FREE METHODIST	1	20	28	-	-
226 FRIENDS-USA	1	61	63	.1	.1
226a CONSERV	1	61	63	.1	.1
246 GREEK ORTHODOX	1	NR	NR	-	-
283 LUTH—MO SYNOD	8	1,328	1,669	1.7	2.8
349 PENT HOLINESS	4	315	394*	.4	.7
355 PRESB CH (USA)	8	1,896	2,372*	2.4	4.0
356 PRESB CH AMER	5	190	251	.3	.4
413 S.D.A.	2	72	90*	.1	.2
419 SO BAPT CONV	49	19,817	24,790*	25.2	41.9
435 UNITARIAN-UNIV	1	34	34	-	.1
449 UN METHODIST	23	5,208	6,515*	6.6	11.0
467 WESLEYAN	1	115	427	.4	.7
496 JEWISH EST[1]	0	NA	227	.2	.4
497 BLACK BAPT EST[2]	NA	4,593	5,746*	5.8	9.7
498 INDEP.CHARIS.[3]	1	NA	300	.3	.5
BARBOUR	**67**	**12,562**	**16,801***	**66.1**	**100.0**
053 ASSEMB OF GOD	9	497	691	2.7	4.1
081 CATHOLIC	1	NA	288	1.1	1.7
081d LATIN	1	NA	288	1.1	1.7
127 CH GOD (CLEVE)	2	61	79*	.3	.5
145 CH GOD PROPHCY	1	35	45*	.2	.3
151 L-D SAINTS	1	NA	261	1.0	1.6
167 CHS OF CHRIST	1	87	122	.5	.7
193 EPISCOPAL	1	127	174	.7	1.0
223 FREE WILL BAPT	3	347	449*	1.8	2.7
355 PRESB CH (USA)	1	250	323*	1.3	1.9
356 PRESB CH AMER	4	250	267	1.1	1.6
419 SO BAPT CONV	26	5,874	7,594*	29.9	45.2
443 UN C OF CHRIST	1	43	56*	.2	.3
449 UN METHODIST	16	1,695	2,191*	8.6	13.0
497 BLACK BAPT EST[2]	NA	3,296	4,261*	16.8	25.4
BIBB	**65**	**8,596**	**10,941***	**66.0**	**100.0**
005 AME ZION	4	703	810	4.9	7.4
053 ASSEMB OF GOD	1	24	30	.2	.3
081 CATHOLIC	0	NA	51	.3	.5
081d LATIN	0	NA	51	.3	.5
127 CH GOD (CLEVE)	2	76	97*	.6	.9
145 CH GOD PROPHCY	3	105	134*	.8	1.2
165 CH OF NAZARENE	2	87	150	.9	1.4
167 CHS OF CHRIST	3	73	108	.7	1.0
223 FREE WILL BAPT	1	74	95*	.6	.9
259 IFCA	1	NR	NR	-	-
355 PRESB CH (USA)	1	9	11*	.1	.1
356 PRESB CH AMER	2	218	223	1.3	2.0
361 PRIM BAPT ASCS	1	45	57*	.3	.5
413 S.D.A.	1	12	15*	.1	.1
419 SO BAPT CONV	37	5,821	7,437*	44.9	68.0
449 UN METHODIST	6	346	442*	2.7	4.0
497 BLACK BAPT EST[2]	NA	1,003	1,281*	7.7	11.7
BLOUNT	**138**	**20,979**	**26,428***	**67.3**	**100.0**
001 ADVENT CHR CH	1	15	19*	-	.1
053 ASSEMB OF GOD	2	327	348	.9	1.3
081 CATHOLIC	1	NA	100	.3	.4
081d LATIN	1	NA	100	.3	.4
089 CHR & MISS AL	1	46	53	.1	.2
127 CH GOD (CLEVE)	11	770	955*	2.4	3.6
145 CH GOD PROPHCY	2	70	87*	.2	.3
151 L-D SAINTS	1	NA	110	.3	.4
157 CH OF BRETHREN	1	66	82*	.2	.3
165 CH OF NAZARENE	3	170	266	.7	1.0
167 CHS OF CHRIST	8	369	483	1.2	1.8
185 CUMBER PRESB	4	254	263	.7	1.0
223 FREE WILL BAPT	1	23	29*	.1	.1
285 MENNONITE CH	1	51	63	.2	.2
361 PRIM BAPT ASCS	3	54	67*	.2	.3
419 SO BAPT CONV	70	15,332	19,023*	48.5	72.0
449 UN METHODIST	28	3,243	4,024*	10.3	15.2
496 JEWISH EST[1]	0	NA	221	.6	.8
497 BLACK BAPT EST[2]	NA	189	235*	.6	.9
BULLOCK	**29**	**7,296**	**9,309***	**84.3**	**100.0**
005 AME ZION	6	1,850	2,100	19.0	22.6
053 ASSEMB OF GOD	2	49	57	.5	.6
081 CATHOLIC	1	NA	48	.4	.5
081d LATIN	1	NA	48	.4	.5
167 CHS OF CHRIST	1	30	60	.5	.6
193 EPISCOPAL	1	7	10	.1	.1
355 PRESB CH (USA)	1	66	87*	.8	.9
356 PRESB CH AMER	1	19	19	.2	.2
413 S.D.A.	1	16	21*	.2	.2
419 SO BAPT CONV	8	1,602	2,104*	19.1	22.6
449 UN METHODIST	7	374	491*	4.4	5.3
497 BLACK BAPT EST[2]	NA	3,283	4,312*	39.1	46.3
BUTLER	**110**	**19,659**	**24,806***	**113.3**	**100.0**
005 AME ZION	22	7,263	8,500	38.8	34.3
053 ASSEMB OF GOD	2	151	201	.9	.8
081 CATHOLIC	1	NA	143	.7	.6
081d LATIN	1	NA	143	.7	.6
093 CHR CH (DISC)	2	67	140	.6	.6
097 CHR CHS&CHS CR	1	50	65*	.3	.3
127 CH GOD (CLEVE)	3	107	139*	.6	.6
165 CH OF NAZARENE	1	13	0	-	-
167 CHS OF CHRIST	13	684	853	3.9	3.4
193 EPISCOPAL	1	114	169	.8	.7
349 PENT HOLINESS	5	179	233*	1.1	.9
356 PRESB CH AMER	1	136	161	.7	.6
361 PRIM BAPT ASCS	2	50	65*	.3	.3
413 S.D.A.	1	7	9*	-	-
419 SO BAPT CONV	32	5,913	7,708*	35.2	31.1
449 UN METHODIST	23	1,309	1,706*	7.8	6.9
497 BLACK BAPT EST[2]	NA	3,616	4,714*	21.5	19.0
CALHOUN	**202**	**64,202**	**83,494***	**72.0**	**100.0**
005 AME ZION	5	1,996	2,351	2.0	2.8
053 ASSEMB OF GOD	5	558	745	.6	.9
081 CATHOLIC	4	NA	2,192	1.9	2.6
081d LATIN	4	NA	2,192	1.9	2.6
089 CHR & MISS AL	1	0	32	-	-
093 CHR CH (DISC)	1	138	271	.2	.3
097 CHR CHS&CHS CR	4	297	367*	.3	.4
123 CH GOD (ANDER)	2	27	40	-	-
127 CH GOD (CLEVE)	13	1,623	2,007*	1.7	2.4
145 CH GOD PROPHCY	4	140	173*	.1	.2
151 L-D SAINTS	1	NA	636	.5	.8
165 CH OF NAZARENE	2	132	119	.1	.1
167 CHS OF CHRIST	17	2,186	2,884	2.5	3.5
185 CUMBER PRESB	1	156	174	.1	.2
193 EPISCOPAL	3	727	942	.8	1.1
207 E.L.C.A.	3	201	315	.3	.4
263 INT FOURSQ GOS	1	219	271*	.2	.3
349 PENT HOLINESS	1	57	70*	.1	.1
355 PRESB CH (USA)	8	1,151	1,423*	1.2	1.7

NA–Not applicable   NR–Not reported   *Total adherents estimated from known number of communicant, confirmed, full members.   - Represents a percent less than 0.1.   Percentages may not total due to rounding.
[1]See Appendix E   [2]See Appendix F   [3]See Appendix G   Lines in *italic* represent a breakdown of Catholic rites or Friends affiliations. They are included in their respective denominational total.

Table 4. Churches and Church Membership by County and Denomination: 1990

County and Denomination	Number of churches	Communicant, confirmed, full members	Total adherents		
			Number	Percent of total population	Percent of total adherents
356 PRESB CH AMER	1	134	181	.2	.2
403 SALVATION ARMY	1	149	156	.1	.2
413 S.D.A.	2	125	155*	.1	.2
415 S-D BAPTIST GC	1	30	37*	-	-
419 SO BAPT CONV	89	39,870	49,297*	42.5	59.0
449 UN METHODIST	28	6,403	7,917*	6.8	9.5
467 WESLEYAN	1	43	45	-	.1
496 JEWISH EST[1]	1	NA	0		
497 BLACK BAPT EST[2]	NA	7,840	9,694*	8.4	11.6
498 INDEP.CHARIS.[3]	1	NA	300	.3	.4
499 INDEP.NON-CHAR[3]	1	NA	700	.6	.8
CHAMBERS	**104**	**20,833**	**26,390***	**71.6**	**100.0**
053 ASSEMB OF GOD	4	291	420	1.1	1.6
081 CATHOLIC	1	NA	365	1.0	1.4
081d LATIN	*1*	*NA*	*365*	*1.0*	*1.4*
093 CHR CH (DISC)	5	407	633	1.7	2.4
097 CHR CHS&CHS CR	1	162	202*	.5	.8
123 CH GOD (ANDER)	3	220	227	.6	.9
127 CH GOD (CLEVE)	2	119	148*	.4	.6
165 CH OF NAZARENE	5	686	804	2.2	3.0
167 CHS OF CHRIST	4	261	335	.9	1.3
176 CCC, NOT NAT'L	1	93	116*	.3	.4
339 PENT CH OF GOD	1	44	63	.2	.2
355 PRESB CH (USA)	1	12	15*	-	.1
356 PRESB CH AMER	1	7	7	-	-
361 PRIM BAPT ASCS	2	15	19*	.1	.1
419 SO BAPT CONV	38	9,856	12,262*	33.3	46.5
443 UN C OF CHRIST	6	756	941*	2.6	3.6
449 UN METHODIST	29	4,011	4,990*	13.5	18.9
497 BLACK BAPT EST[2]	NA	3,893	4,843*	13.1	18.4
CHEROKEE	**89**	**10,488**	**12,784***	**65.4**	**100.0**
001 ADVENT CHR CH	1	63	77*	.4	.6
127 CH GOD (CLEVE)	2	91	111*	.6	.9
145 CH GOD PROPHCY	1	35	43*	.2	.3
167 CHS OF CHRIST	4	170	216	1.1	1.7
289 NEW HOPE B ASC	1	127	155*	.8	1.2
355 PRESB CH (USA)	1	31	38*	.2	.3
419 SO BAPT CONV	54	7,644	9,310*	47.6	72.8
449 UN METHODIST	25	1,955	2,381*	12.2	18.6
497 BLACK BAPT EST[2]	NA	372	453*	2.3	3.5
CHILTON	**103**	**18,578**	**23,613***	**72.7**	**100.0**
053 ASSEMB OF GOD	9	550	793	2.4	3.4
081 CATHOLIC	1	NA	73	.2	.3
081d LATIN	*1*	*NA*	*73*	*.2*	*.3*
089 CHR & MISS AL	1	7	9	-	-
123 CH GOD (ANDER)	1	34	45	.1	.2
127 CH GOD (CLEVE)	6	682	857*	2.6	3.6
145 CH GOD PROPHCY	1	35	44*	.1	.2
151 L-D SAINTS	1	NA	93	.3	.4
165 CH OF NAZARENE	1	16	17	.1	.1
167 CHS OF CHRIST	8	296	393	1.2	1.7
175 CONGR CHR CHS	1	117	147*	.5	.6
356 PRESB CH AMER	1	37	38	.1	.2
361 PRIM BAPT ASCS	2	75	94*	.3	.4
413 S.D.A.	1	165	207*	.6	.9
419 SO BAPT CONV	55	14,365	18,041*	55.6	76.4
449 UN METHODIST	14	1,118	1,404*	4.3	5.9
497 BLACK BAPT EST[2]	NA	1,081	1,358*	4.2	5.8
CHOCTAW	**77**	**9,914**	**13,414***	**83.7**	**100.0**
005 AME ZION	4	1,209	1,700	10.6	12.7
053 ASSEMB OF GOD	10	449	873	5.5	6.5
081 CATHOLIC	1	NA	160	1.0	1.2
081d LATIN	*1*	*NA*	*160*	*1.0*	*1.2*
123 CH GOD (ANDER)	1	15	15	.1	.1
127 CH GOD (CLEVE)	2	137	175*	1.1	1.3
151 L-D SAINTS	1	NA	115	.7	.9
167 CHS OF CHRIST	2	110	145	.9	1.1
283 LUTH—MO SYNOD	1	24	28	.2	.2
349 PENT HOLINESS	1	30	38*	.2	.3
353 CHR BRETHREN	1	28	50	.3	.4
355 PRESB CH (USA)	1	19	24*	.1	.2
413 S.D.A.	1	43	55*	.3	.4
419 SO BAPT CONV	30	3,922	5,014*	31.3	37.4
449 UN METHODIST	21	1,019	1,303*	8.1	9.7
497 BLACK BAPT EST[2]	NA	2,909	3,719*	23.2	27.7
CLARKE	**93**	**17,105**	**22,446***	**82.4**	**100.0**
005 AME ZION	5	1,576	1,891	6.9	8.4
053 ASSEMB OF GOD	4	480	576	2.1	2.6
081 CATHOLIC	3	NA	324	1.2	1.4
081d LATIN	*3*	*NA*	*324*	*1.2*	*1.4*
123 CH GOD (ANDER)	1	15	21	.1	.1
127 CH GOD (CLEVE)	2	106	137*	.5	.6
145 CH GOD PROPHCY	1	35	45*	.2	.2
151 L-D SAINTS	2	NA	186	.7	.8
165 CH OF NAZARENE	1	27	25	.1	.1
167 CHS OF CHRIST	8	274	369	1.4	1.6
193 EPISCOPAL	1	40	54	.2	.2
283 LUTH—MO SYNOD	1	17	37	.1	.2
355 PRESB CH (USA)	1	122	158*	.6	.7
361 PRIM BAPT ASCS	1	7	9*	-	-
413 S.D.A.	2	70	90*	.3	.4
419 SO BAPT CONV	43	9,112	11,774*	43.2	52.5
449 UN METHODIST	17	1,801	2,327*	8.5	10.4
497 BLACK BAPT EST[2]	NA	3,423	4,423*	16.2	19.7
CLAY	**80**	**9,054**	**11,175***	**84.3**	**100.0**
053 ASSEMB OF GOD	2	53	80	.6	.7
127 CH GOD (CLEVE)	3	89	110*	.8	1.0
167 CHS OF CHRIST	7	238	303	2.3	2.7
176 CCC, NOT NAT'L	1	2	2*	-	-
349 PENT HOLINESS	1	28	34*	.3	.3
361 PRIM BAPT ASCS	2	31	38*	.3	.3
419 SO BAPT CONV	44	6,519	8,029*	60.6	71.8
449 UN METHODIST	20	1,470	1,810*	13.7	16.2
497 BLACK BAPT EST[2]	NA	624	769*	5.8	6.9
CLEBURNE	**55**	**7,728**	**9,661***	**75.9**	**100.0**
127 CH GOD (CLEVE)	4	386	482*	3.8	5.0
167 CHS OF CHRIST	2	112	146	1.1	1.5
193 EPISCOPAL	1	70	95	.7	1.0
361 PRIM BAPT ASCS	1	3	4*	-	-
419 SO BAPT CONV	32	6,259	7,813*	61.4	80.9
449 UN METHODIST	15	729	910*	7.1	9.4
497 BLACK BAPT EST[2]	NA	169	211*	1.7	2.2
COFFEE	**101**	**23,233**	**30,555***	**75.9**	**100.0**
053 ASSEMB OF GOD	18	1,234	1,932	4.8	6.3
081 CATHOLIC	1	NA	900	2.2	2.9
081d LATIN	*1*	*NA*	*900*	*2.2*	*2.9*
111 CH CR,SCIENTST	1	NR	NR	-	-
127 CH GOD (CLEVE)	4	360	446*	1.1	1.5
145 CH GOD PROPHCY	1	35	43*	.1	.1
151 L-D SAINTS	1	NA	330	.8	1.1
167 CHS OF CHRIST	7	798	1,063	2.6	3.5
193 EPISCOPAL	1	76	117	.3	.4
223 FREE WILL BAPT	1	65	81*	.2	.3
283 LUTH—MO SYNOD	1	158	214	.5	.7
349 PENT HOLINESS	1	35	43*	.1	.1
355 PRESB CH (USA)	1	128	159*	.4	.5
356 PRESB CH AMER	2	63	102	.3	.3
419 SO BAPT CONV	47	15,485	19,184*	47.7	62.8
449 UN METHODIST	14	2,760	3,419*	8.5	11.2
497 BLACK BAPT EST[2]	NA	2,036	2,522*	6.3	8.3
COLBERT	**119**	**29,835**	**38,186***	**73.9**	**100.0**
053 ASSEMB OF GOD	2	195	281	.5	.7
055 AS REF PRES CH	1	23	29	.1	.1
081 CATHOLIC	1	NA	1,023	2.0	2.7
081d LATIN	*1*	*NA*	*1,023*	*2.0*	*2.7*
123 CH GOD (ANDER)	1	48	54	.1	.1
127 CH GOD (CLEVE)	5	364	449*	.9	1.2
145 CH GOD PROPHCY	1	35	43*	.1	.1
151 L-D SAINTS	1	NA	123	.2	.3
165 CH OF NAZARENE	3	353	438	.8	1.1
167 CHS OF CHRIST	35	4,019	5,295	10.2	13.9
185 CUMBER PRESB	6	460	469	.9	1.2
193 EPISCOPAL	1	178	213	.4	.6
223 FREE WILL BAPT	2	272	335*	.6	.9
283 LUTH—MO SYNOD	1	111	135	.3	.4
355 PRESB CH (USA)	3	293	361*	.7	.9
356 PRESB CH AMER	1	282	335	.6	.9
419 SO BAPT CONV	38	16,644	20,518*	39.7	53.7
449 UN METHODIST	17	3,445	4,247*	8.2	11.1
497 BLACK BAPT EST[2]	NA	3,113	3,838*	7.4	10.1
CONECUH	**66**	**9,988**	**12,663***	**90.1**	**100.0**
005 AME ZION	0	2,416	2,901	20.6	22.9
053 ASSEMB OF GOD	4	183	336	2.4	2.7
059 BAPT MISS ASSN	1	16	20*	.1	.2
081 CATHOLIC	1	NA	8	.1	.1
081d LATIN	*1*	*NA*	*8*	*.1*	*.1*
127 CH GOD (CLEVE)	1	35	45*	.3	.4
167 CHS OF CHRIST	5	235	319	2.3	2.5
223 FREE WILL BAPT	2	69	88*	.6	.7
349 PENT HOLINESS	2	31	39*	.3	.3

NA–Not applicable   NR–Not reported   *Total adherents estimated from known number of communicant, confirmed, full members.   - Represents a percent less than 0.1.   Percentages may not total due to rounding.

[1]See Appendix E   [2]See Appendix F   [3]See Appendix G   Lines in *italic* represent a breakdown of Catholic rites or Friends affiliations. They are included in their respective denominational total.

Table 4. Churches and Church Membership by County and Denomination: 1990

County and Denomination	Number of churches	Communicant, confirmed, full members	Total adherents Number	Percent of total population	Percent of total adherents
355 PRESB CH (USA)	1	44	56*	.4	.4
361 PRIM BAPT ASCS	3	36	46*	.3	.4
419 SO BAPT CONV	25	3,156	4,014*	28.6	31.7
449 UN METHODIST	21	1,332	1,694*	12.1	13.4
497 BLACK BAPT EST[2]	NA	2,435	3,097*	22.0	24.5
COOSA	**46**	**5,679**	**7,151***	**64.6**	**100.0**
059 BAPT MISS ASSN	1	26	33*	.3	.5
123 CH GOD (ANDER)	1	13	46	.4	.6
127 CH GOD (CLEVE)	2	92	115*	1.0	1.6
145 CH GOD PROPHCY	1	35	44*	.4	.6
167 CHS OF CHRIST	1	30	38	.3	.5
355 PRESB CH (USA)	4	169	212*	1.9	3.0
361 PRIM BAPT ASCS	4	63	79*	.7	1.1
419 SO BAPT CONV	19	2,617	3,281*	29.7	45.9
449 UN METHODIST	13	1,079	1,353*	12.2	18.9
497 BLACK BAPT EST[2]	NA	1,555	1,950*	17.6	27.3
COVINGTON	**122**	**22,193**	**28,417***	**77.9**	**100.0**
053 ASSEMB OF GOD	12	638	1,228	3.4	4.3
055 AS REF PRES CH	1	73	85	.2	.3
081 CATHOLIC	1	NA	172	.5	.6
081d LATIN	*1*	*NA*	*172*	*.5*	*.6*
127 CH GOD (CLEVE)	5	301	374*	1.0	1.3
151 L-D SAINTS	1	NA	196	.5	.7
165 CH OF NAZARENE	2	72	111	.3	.4
167 CHS OF CHRIST	12	853	1,103	3.0	3.9
193 EPISCOPAL	1	37	40	.1	.1
223 FREE WILL BAPT	2	73	91*	.2	.3
266 INTRSTAT & ASC	1	29	36*	.1	.1
283 LUTH—MO SYNOD	1	3	34	.1	.1
349 PENT HOLINESS	2	100	124*	.3	.4
355 PRESB CH (USA)	1	218	271*	.7	1.0
356 PRESB CH AMER	2	84	91	.2	.3
361 PRIM BAPT ASCS	4	81	101*	.3	.4
413 S.D.A.	1	46	57*	.2	.2
419 SO BAPT CONV	58	16,230	20,140*	55.2	70.9
443 UN C OF CHRIST	2	89	110*	.3	.4
449 UN METHODIST	13	1,860	2,308*	6.3	8.1
497 BLACK BAPT EST[2]	NA	1,406	1,745*	4.8	6.1
CRENSHAW	**78**	**9,561**	**12,385***	**90.8**	**100.0**
005 AME ZION	7	1,713	2,284	16.8	18.4
053 ASSEMB OF GOD	7	224	262	1.9	2.1
081 CATHOLIC	1	NA	43	.3	.3
081d LATIN	*1*	*NA*	*43*	*.3*	*.3*
127 CH GOD (CLEVE)	1	134	168*	1.2	1.4
145 CH GOD PROPHCY	1	35	44*	.3	.4
151 L-D SAINTS	1	NA	201	1.5	1.6
167 CHS OF CHRIST	12	603	796	5.8	6.4
361 PRIM BAPT ASCS	1	14	18*	.1	.1
419 SO BAPT CONV	30	4,282	5,366*	39.4	43.3
443 UN C OF CHRIST	2	40	50*	.4	.4
449 UN METHODIST	15	1,059	1,327*	9.7	10.7
497 BLACK BAPT EST[2]	NA	1,457	1,826*	13.4	14.7
CULLMAN	**208**	**40,208**	**52,724***	**78.0**	**100.0**
053 ASSEMB OF GOD	5	316	547	.8	1.0
081 CATHOLIC	2	NA	2,696	4.0	5.1
081d LATIN	*2*	*NA*	*2,696*	*4.0*	*5.1*
093 CHR CH (DISC)	1	50	60	.1	.1
097 CHR CHS&CHS CR	1	45	56*	.1	.1
123 CH GOD (ANDER)	1	122	148	.2	.3
127 CH GOD (CLEVE)	9	779	965*	1.4	1.8
145 CH GOD PROPHCY	1	35	43*	.1	.1
165 CH OF NAZARENE	5	427	530	.8	1.0
167 CHS OF CHRIST	30	2,326	3,046	4.5	5.8
185 CUMBER PRESB	6	582	602	.9	1.1
193 EPISCOPAL	1	191	213	.3	.4
223 FREE WILL BAPT	3	414	513*	.8	1.0
283 LUTH—MO SYNOD	2	1,053	1,334	2.0	2.5
355 PRESB CH (USA)	1	124	154*	.2	.3
361 PRIM BAPT ASCS	3	148	183*	.3	.3
413 S.D.A.	1	63	78*	.1	.1
419 SO BAPT CONV	107	28,755	35,635*	52.7	67.6
443 UN C OF CHRIST	3	1,135	1,407*	2.1	2.7
449 UN METHODIST	26	3,478	4,310*	6.4	8.2
497 BLACK BAPT EST[2]	NA	165	204*	.3	.4
DALE	**99**	**20,863**	**28,784***	**58.0**	**100.0**
005 AME ZION	2	160	220	.4	.8
053 ASSEMB OF GOD	11	981	1,381	2.8	4.8
081 CATHOLIC	1	NA	820	1.7	2.8
081d LATIN	*1*	*NA*	*820*	*1.7*	*2.8*
127 CH GOD (CLEVE)	3	177	228*	.5	.8
151 L-D SAINTS	2	NA	976	2.0	3.4
165 CH OF NAZARENE	1	69	121	.2	.4
167 CHS OF CHRIST	4	320	412	.8	1.4
193 EPISCOPAL	1	55	74	.1	.3
223 FREE WILL BAPT	6	483	621*	1.3	2.2
283 LUTH—MO SYNOD	1	80	126	.3	.4
355 PRESB CH (USA)	1	8	10*	-	-
356 PRESB CH AMER	1	107	122	.2	.4
361 PRIM BAPT ASCS	3	91	117*	.2	.4
403 SALVATION ARMY	1	78	82	.2	.3
413 S.D.A.	2	221	284*	.6	1.0
419 SO BAPT CONV	35	11,381	14,636*	29.5	50.8
449 UN METHODIST	24	3,438	4,421*	8.9	15.4
497 BLACK BAPT EST[2]	NA	3,214	4,133*	8.3	14.4
DALLAS	**85**	**24,339**	**32,727***	**68.0**	**100.0**
005 AME ZION	5	698	851	1.8	2.6
053 ASSEMB OF GOD	1	129	230	.5	.7
055 AS REF PRES CH	1	39	39	.1	.1
061 BEACHY AMISH	1	39	51*	.1	.2
081 CATHOLIC	1	NA	570	1.2	1.7
081d LATIN	*1*	*NA*	*570*	*1.2*	*1.7*
093 CHR CH (DISC)	2	113	168	.3	.5
097 CHR CHS&CHS CR	2	180	237*	.5	.7
123 CH GOD (ANDER)	1	25	35	.1	.1
127 CH GOD (CLEVE)	5	374	493*	1.0	1.5
145 CH GOD PROPHCY	1	35	46*	.1	.1
151 L-D SAINTS	1	NA	190	.4	.6
165 CH OF NAZARENE	1	172	183	.4	.6
167 CHS OF CHRIST	9	598	787	1.6	2.4
193 EPISCOPAL	2	586	661	1.4	2.0
220 FREE LUTHERAN	1	13	17	-	.1
223 FREE WILL BAPT	1	165	218*	.5	.7
283 LUTH—MO SYNOD	2	248	304	.6	.9
355 PRESB CH (USA)	8	733	966*	2.0	3.0
356 PRESB CH AMER	2	242	266	.6	.8
403 SALVATION ARMY	1	92	95	.2	.3
413 S.D.A.	2	199	262*	.5	.8
419 SO BAPT CONV	21	9,567	12,613*	26.2	38.5
449 UN METHODIST	11	1,864	2,457*	5.1	7.5
467 WESLEYAN	2	34	86	.2	.3
496 JEWISH EST[1]	1	NA	100	.2	.3
497 BLACK BAPT EST[2]	NA	8,194	10,802*	22.4	33.0
DE KALB	**192**	**28,987**	**36,231***	**66.3**	**100.0**
005 AME ZION	1	55	66	.1	.2
053 ASSEMB OF GOD	2	46	60	.1	.2
081 CATHOLIC	1	NA	146	.3	.4
081d LATIN	*1*	*NA*	*146*	*.3*	*.4*
089 CHR & MISS AL	1	3	30	.1	.1
097 CHR CHS&CHS CR	2	101	125*	.2	.3
127 CH GOD (CLEVE)	17	1,260	1,560*	2.9	4.3
133 CH GOD(7TH)DEN	1	20	27	-	.1
145 CH GOD PROPHCY	5	175	217*	.4	.6
151 L-D SAINTS	1	NA	79	.1	.2
165 CH OF NAZARENE	1	49	50	.1	.1
167 CHS OF CHRIST	10	524	669	1.2	1.8
189 DUCK RIVR BAPT	22	2,811	3,481*	6.4	9.6
193 EPISCOPAL	2	168	231	.4	.6
355 PRESB CH (USA)	3	141	175*	.3	.5
356 PRESB CH AMER	1	45	86	.2	.2
361 PRIM BAPT ASCS	4	244	302*	.6	.8
413 S.D.A.	1	37	46*	.1	.1
419 SO BAPT CONV	77	19,379	23,998*	43.9	66.2
449 UN METHODIST	38	3,559	4,407*	8.1	12.2
467 WESLEYAN	2	67	101	.2	.3
497 BLACK BAPT EST[2]	NA	303	375*	.7	1.0
ELMORE	**118**	**25,971**	**34,311***	**69.7**	**100.0**
005 AME ZION	9	2,703	3,604	7.3	10.5
053 ASSEMB OF GOD	5	253	384	.8	1.1
059 BAPT MISS ASSN	1	142	177*	.4	.5
081 CATHOLIC	3	NA	240	.5	.7
081d LATIN	*3*	*NA*	*240*	*.5*	*.7*
093 CHR CH (DISC)	1	70	100	.2	.3
123 CH GOD (ANDER)	1	25	25	.1	.1
127 CH GOD (CLEVE)	3	372	464*	.9	1.4
151 L-D SAINTS	1	NA	211	.4	.6
165 CH OF NAZARENE	1	64	153	.3	.4
167 CHS OF CHRIST	11	806	1,042	2.1	3.0
175 CONGR CHR CHS	3	117	146*	.3	.4
193 EPISCOPAL	2	194	239	.5	.7
207 E.L.C.A.	1	202	285	.6	.8
355 PRESB CH (USA)	1	104	130*	.3	.4
356 PRESB CH AMER	1	183	183	.4	.5
361 PRIM BAPT ASCS	4	213	266*	.5	.8

NA–Not applicable   NR–Not reported   *Total adherents estimated from known number of communicant, confirmed, full members.   - Represents a percent less than 0.1.   Percentages may not total due to rounding.

[1]See Appendix E   [2]See Appendix F   [3]See Appendix G   Lines in *italic* represent a breakdown of Catholic rites or Friends affiliations. They are included in their respective denominational total.

Table 4. Churches and Church Membership by County and Denomination: 1990

County and Denomination	Number of churches	Communicant, confirmed, full members	Total adherents Number	Percent of total population	Percent of total adherents
413 S.D.A.	1	31	39*	.1	.1
419 SO BAPT CONV	41	13,199	16,472*	33.5	48.0
443 UN C OF CHRIST	1	40	50*	.1	.1
449 UN METHODIST	24	3,242	4,046*	8.2	11.8
497 BLACK BAPT EST[2]	NA	4,011	5,005*	10.2	14.6
498 INDEP.CHARIS.[3]	1	NA	350	.7	1.0
499 INDEP.NON-CHAR[3]	2	NA	700	1.4	2.0
ESCAMBIA	**116**	**18,617**	**24,395***	**68.7**	**100.0**
005 AME ZION	4	256	384	1.1	1.6
053 ASSEMB OF GOD	10	832	1,294	3.6	5.3
081 CATHOLIC	2	NA	400	1.1	1.6
081d LATIN	*2*	*NA*	*400*	*1.1*	*1.6*
127 CH GOD (CLEVE)	3	198	247*	.7	1.0
145 CH GOD PROPHCY	2	70	87*	.2	.4
151 L-D SAINTS	1	NA	200	.6	.8
165 CH OF NAZARENE	2	125	200	.6	.8
167 CHS OF CHRIST	9	391	512	1.4	2.1
193 EPISCOPAL	3	229	341	1.0	1.4
216 EVAN PRESBY CH	1	83	84	.2	.3
223 FREE WILL BAPT	3	166	207*	.6	.8
266 INTRSTAT & ASC	1	86	107*	.3	.4
283 LUTH—MO SYNOD	1	88	181	.5	.7
285 MENNONITE CH	6	203	310	.9	1.3
349 PENT HOLINESS	12	810	1,012*	2.8	4.1
355 PRESB CH (USA)	1	224	280*	.8	1.1
356 PRESB CH AMER	1	204	241	.7	1.0
361 PRIM BAPT ASCS	5	130	162*	.5	.7
413 S.D.A.	1	55	69*	.2	.3
419 SO BAPT CONV	33	9,528	11,906*	33.5	48.8
449 UN METHODIST	15	1,981	2,475*	7.0	10.1
497 BLACK BAPT EST[2]	NA	2,958	3,696*	10.4	15.2
ETOWAH	**218**	**62,151**	**81,580***	**81.7**	**100.0**
001 ADVENT CHR CH	2	60	74*	.1	.1
053 ASSEMB OF GOD	4	352	622	.6	.8
081 CATHOLIC	2	NA	2,404	2.4	2.9
081d LATIN	*2*	*NA*	*2,404*	*2.4*	*2.9*
089 CHR & MISS AL	1	54	70	.1	.1
093 CHR CH (DISC)	1	53	80	.1	.1
111 CH CR,SCIENTST	1	NR	NR	-	-
123 CH GOD (ANDER)	1	60	60	.1	.1
127 CH GOD (CLEVE)	21	2,503	3,069*	3.1	3.8
133 CH GOD(7TH)DEN	1	20	27	-	-
145 CH GOD PROPHCY	2	70	86*	.1	.1
151 L-D SAINTS	1	NA	467	.5	.6
165 CH OF NAZARENE	2	162	253	.3	.3
167 CHS OF CHRIST	16	1,670	2,139	2.1	2.6
185 CUMBER PRESB	4	424	441	.4	.5
189 DUCK RIVR BAPT	1	130	159*	.2	.2
193 EPISCOPAL	2	463	543	.5	.7
283 LUTH—MO SYNOD	3	243	325	.3	.4
355 PRESB CH (USA)	1	101	124*	.1	.2
356 PRESB CH AMER	3	666	769	.8	.9
361 PRIM BAPT ASCS	2	81	99*	.1	.1
403 SALVATION ARMY	1	100	104	.1	.1
413 S.D.A.	2	161	197*	.2	.2
419 SO BAPT CONV	100	41,332	50,681*	50.8	62.1
449 UN METHODIST	40	8,432	10,339*	10.4	12.7
496 JEWISH EST[1]	1	NA	0	-	-
497 BLACK BAPT EST[2]	NA	5,014	6,148*	6.2	7.5
498 INDEP.CHARIS.[3]	2	NA	1,950	2.0	2.4
499 INDEP.NON-CHAR[3]	1	NA	350	.4	.4
FAYETTE	**92**	**10,476**	**13,170***	**73.3**	**100.0**
005 AME ZION	3	546	591	3.3	4.5
053 ASSEMB OF GOD	1	76	91	.5	.7
059 BAPT MISS ASSN	1	74	92*	.5	.7
081 CATHOLIC	1	NA	66	.4	.5
081d LATIN	*1*	*NA*	*66*	*.4*	*.5*
127 CH GOD (CLEVE)	5	350	434*	2.4	3.3
145 CH GOD PROPHCY	1	35	43*	.2	.3
165 CH OF NAZARENE	4	153	312	1.7	2.4
167 CHS OF CHRIST	21	1,368	1,768	9.8	13.4
193 EPISCOPAL	1	58	91	.5	.7
223 FREE WILL BAPT	4	614	761*	4.2	5.8
419 SO BAPT CONV	36	5,418	6,711*	37.4	51.0
449 UN METHODIST	14	1,153	1,428*	8.0	10.8
497 BLACK BAPT EST[2]	NA	631	782*	4.4	5.9
FRANKLIN	**88**	**12,585**	**15,847***	**57.0**	**100.0**
053 ASSEMB OF GOD	1	21	41	.1	.3
081 CATHOLIC	1	NA	150	.5	.9
081d LATIN	*1*	*NA*	*150*	*.5*	*.9*
127 CH GOD (CLEVE)	3	338	418*	1.5	2.6
133 CH GOD(7TH)DEN	1	20	27	.1	.2

County and Denomination	Number of churches	Communicant, confirmed, full members	Total adherents Number	Percent of total population	Percent of total adherents
145 CH GOD PROPHCY	4	140	173*	.6	1.1
165 CH OF NAZARENE	1	69	104	.4	.7
167 CHS OF CHRIST	26	1,775	2,287	8.2	14.4
185 CUMBER PRESB	1	22	22	.1	.1
223 FREE WILL BAPT	5	635	785*	2.8	5.0
339 PENT CH OF GOD	1	15	35	.1	.2
355 PRESB CH (USA)	1	16	20*	.1	.1
356 PRESB CH AMER	1	52	63	.2	.4
413 S.D.A.	1	9	11*	-	.1
419 SO BAPT CONV	31	7,897	9,763*	35.1	61.6
449 UN METHODIST	10	1,208	1,493*	5.4	9.4
497 BLACK BAPT EST[2]	NA	368	455*	1.6	2.9
GENEVA	**100**	**14,048**	**17,781***	**75.2**	**100.0**
053 ASSEMB OF GOD	23	1,005	1,666	7.0	9.4
081 CATHOLIC	1	NA	16	.1	.1
081d LATIN	*1*	*NA*	*16*	*.1*	*.1*
127 CH GOD (CLEVE)	2	113	139*	.6	.8
145 CH GOD PROPHCY	1	35	43*	.2	.2
167 CHS OF CHRIST	10	451	586	2.5	3.3
223 FREE WILL BAPT	1	119	147*	.6	.8
349 PENT HOLINESS	1	65	80*	.3	.4
355 PRESB CH (USA)	1	19	23*	.1	.1
361 PRIM BAPT ASCS	1	17	21*	.1	.1
419 SO BAPT CONV	38	9,133	11,252*	47.6	63.3
449 UN METHODIST	21	2,277	2,805*	11.9	15.8
497 BLACK BAPT EST[2]	NA	814	1,003*	4.2	5.6
GREENE	**34**	**6,555**	**8,701***	**85.7**	**100.0**
005 AME ZION	7	1,100	1,320	13.0	15.2
081 CATHOLIC	1	NA	58	.6	.7
081d LATIN	*1*	*NA*	*58*	*.6*	*.7*
093 CHR CH (DISC)	2	95	147	1.4	1.7
185 CUMBER PRESB	1	75	75	.7	.9
193 EPISCOPAL	3	77	111	1.1	1.3
356 PRESB CH AMER	3	130	177	1.7	2.0
413 S.D.A.	1	28	38*	.4	.4
419 SO BAPT CONV	6	954	1,280*	12.6	14.7
449 UN METHODIST	10	733	983*	9.7	11.3
497 BLACK BAPT EST[2]	NA	3,363	4,512*	44.4	51.9
HALE	**54**	**9,086**	**12,113***	**78.2**	**100.0**
005 AME ZION	7	937	1,173	7.6	9.7
081 CATHOLIC	1	NA	51	.3	.4
081d LATIN	*1*	*NA*	*51*	*.3*	*.4*
123 CH GOD (ANDER)	4	28	44	.3	.4
151 L-D SAINTS	2	NA	108	.7	.9
165 CH OF NAZARENE	2	89	150	1.0	1.2
167 CHS OF CHRIST	2	87	106	.7	.9
193 EPISCOPAL	1	82	98	.6	.8
353 CHR BRETHREN	1	30	50	.3	.4
355 PRESB CH (USA)	1	10	13*	.1	.1
356 PRESB CH AMER	3	119	140	.9	1.2
419 SO BAPT CONV	15	2,607	3,443*	22.2	28.4
449 UN METHODIST	14	1,307	1,726*	11.1	14.2
467 WESLEYAN	1	3	10	.1	.1
497 BLACK BAPT EST[2]	NA	3,787	5,001*	32.3	41.3
HENRY	**45**	**9,362**	**12,131***	**78.9**	**100.0**
053 ASSEMB OF GOD	5	110	217	1.4	1.8
081 CATHOLIC	0	NA	35	.2	.3
081d LATIN	*0*	*NA*	*35*	*.2*	*.3*
127 CH GOD (CLEVE)	1	4	5*	-	-
167 CHS OF CHRIST	2	60	78	.5	.6
176 CCC, NOT NAT'L	1	118	148*	1.0	1.2
223 FREE WILL BAPT	7	614	768*	5.0	6.3
419 SO BAPT CONV	22	5,242	6,559*	42.7	54.1
449 UN METHODIST	6	996	1,246*	8.1	10.3
497 BLACK BAPT EST[2]	NA	2,218	2,775*	18.0	22.9
499 INDEP.NON-CHAR[3]	1	NA	300	2.0	2.5
HOUSTON	**135**	**46,041**	**62,021***	**76.3**	**100.0**
053 ASSEMB OF GOD	16	1,513	2,436	3.0	3.9
081 CATHOLIC	2	NA	2,547	3.1	4.1
081d LATIN	*2*	*NA*	*2,547*	*3.1*	*4.1*
089 CHR & MISS AL	1	0	21	-	-
093 CHR CH (DISC)	1	110	150	.2	.2
097 CHR CHS&CHS CR	1	31	39*	-	.1
111 CH CR,SCIENTST	1	NR	NR	-	-
127 CH GOD (CLEVE)	1	82	104*	.1	.2
145 CH GOD PROPHCY	2	70	89*	.1	.1
165 CH OF NAZARENE	2	169	222	.3	.4
167 CHS OF CHRIST	7	805	1,028	1.3	1.7
193 EPISCOPAL	1	583	695	.9	1.1
207 E.L.C.A.	1	111	154	.2	.2

NA–Not applicable   NR–Not reported   *Total adherents estimated from known number of communicant, confirmed, full members.   - Represents a percent less than 0.1.   Percentages may not total due to rounding.
[1]See Appendix E   [2]See Appendix F   [3]See Appendix G   Lines in *italic* represent a breakdown of Catholic rites or Friends affiliations. They are included in their respective denominational total.

Table 4. Churches and Church Membership by County and Denomination: 1990

County and Denomination	Number of churches	Communicant, confirmed, full members	Total adherents Number	Percent of total population	Percent of total adherents
223 FREE WILL BAPT	11	1,862	2,367*	2.9	3.8
259 IFCA	1	NR	NR	-	-
263 INT FOURSQ GOS	1	96	122*	.2	.2
283 LUTH—MO SYNOD	1	125	172	.2	.3
355 PRESB CH (USA)	2	263	334*	.4	.5
356 PRESB CH AMER	3	883	1,037	1.3	1.7
413 S.D.A.	1	166	211*	.3	.3
419 SO BAPT CONV	53	26,677	33,909*	41.7	54.7
435 UNITARIAN-UNIV	1	14	19	-	-
449 UN METHODIST	23	5,594	7,111*	8.7	11.5
496 JEWISH EST[1]	1	NA	150	.2	.2
497 BLACK BAPT EST[2]	NA	6,887	8,754*	10.8	14.1
498 INDEP.CHARIS.[3]	1	NA	350	.4	.6
JACKSON	**153**	**20,922**	**26,964***	**56.4**	**100.0**
001 ADVENT CHR CH	1	27	33*	.1	.1
053 ASSEMB OF GOD	1	60	80	.2	.3
081 CATHOLIC	1	NA	825	1.7	3.1
081d LATIN	*1*	*NA*	*825*	*1.7*	*3.1*
127 CH GOD (CLEVE)	15	1,265	1,568*	3.3	5.8
145 CH GOD PROPHCY	2	70	87*	.2	.3
151 L-D SAINTS	1	NA	177	.4	.7
165 CH OF NAZARENE	1	28	99	.2	.4
167 CHS OF CHRIST	20	1,188	1,540	3.2	5.7
176 CCC, NOT NAT'L	1	17	21*	-	.1
185 CUMBER PRESB	5	644	697	1.5	2.6
189 DUCK RIVR BAPT	6	575	713*	1.5	2.6
193 EPISCOPAL	1	146	173	.4	.6
283 LUTH—MO SYNOD	1	40	51	.1	.2
355 PRESB CH (USA)	1	7	9*	-	-
361 PRIM BAPT ASCS	4	158	196*	.4	.7
413 S.D.A.	4	362	449*	.9	1.7
415 S-D BAPTIST GC	1	23	29*	.1	.1
419 SO BAPT CONV	61	13,495	16,725*	35.0	62.0
449 UN METHODIST	26	2,238	2,774*	5.8	10.3
497 BLACK BAPT EST[2]	NA	579	718*	1.5	2.7
JEFFERSON	**829**	**352,979**	**502,310***	**77.1**	**100.0**
001 ADVENT CHR CH	1	18	22*	-	-
005 AME ZION	25	17,540	21,048	3.2	4.2
053 ASSEMB OF GOD	23	8,671	9,807	1.5	2.0
055 AS REF PRES CH	1	18	18	-	-
059 BAPT MISS ASSN	3	321	399*	.1	.1
081 CATHOLIC	31	NA	40,830	6.3	8.1
081d LATIN	*29*	*NA*	*38,744*	*5.9*	*7.7*
081e MARONITE	*1*	*NA*	*1,366*	*.2*	*.3*
081f MELKITE-GK	*1*	*NA*	*720*	*.1*	*.1*
089 CHR & MISS AL	12	824	1,083	.2	.2
093 CHR CH (DISC)	7	1,246	1,704	.3	.3
097 CHR CHS&CHS CR	2	207	257*	-	.1
111 CH CR,SCIENTST	1	NR	NR	-	-
123 CH GOD (ANDER)	18	975	1,203	.2	.2
127 CH GOD (CLEVE)	52	7,505	9,335*	1.4	1.9
133 CH GOD(7TH)DEN	1	20	27	-	-
145 CH GOD PROPHCY	17	601	748*	.1	.1
151 L-D SAINTS	7	NA	2,506	.4	.5
157 CH OF BRETHREN	1	15	19*	-	-
165 CH OF NAZARENE	15	1,723	2,836	.4	.6
167 CHS OF CHRIST	74	9,928	12,538	1.9	2.5
185 CUMBER PRESB	6	1,217	1,314	.2	.3
193 EPISCOPAL	18	8,618	11,072	1.7	2.2
207 E.L.C.A.	4	1,006	1,273	.2	.3
221 FREE METHODIST	2	87	88	-	-
223 FREE WILL BAPT	11	1,117	1,389*	.2	.3
226 FRIENDS-USA	1	10	18	-	-
226c FGC	*1*	*10*	*18*	*-*	*-*
246 GREEK ORTHODOX	1	NR	NR	-	-
283 LUTH—MO SYNOD	11	1,665	2,274*	.3	.5
285 MENNONITE CH	4	63	157	-	-
331 ORTH CH IN AM	1	NR	NR	-	-
339 PENT CH OF GOD	1	35	76	-	-
349 PENT HOLINESS	6	513	638*	.1	.1
353 CHR BRETHREN	3	100	125	-	-
355 PRESB CH (USA)	33	9,270	11,530*	1.8	2.3
356 PRESB CH AMER	10	5,373	6,832	1.0	1.4
361 PRIM BAPT ASCS	7	279	347*	.1	.1
403 SALVATION ARMY	4	201	226	-	-
413 S.D.A.	12	3,177	3,952*	.6	.8
419 SO BAPT CONV	253	161,252	200,570*	30.8	39.9
435 UNITARIAN-UNIV	1	137	167	-	-
443 UN C OF CHRIST	2	256	318*	-	.1
449 UN METHODIST	122	49,058	61,020*	9.4	12.1
467 WESLEYAN	2	99	257	-	.1
469 WELS	1	53	70	-	-
496 JEWISH EST[1]	3	NA	3,660	.6	.7
497 BLACK BAPT EST[2]	NA	59,781	74,357*	11.4	14.8
498 INDEP.CHARIS.[3]	9	NA	7,200	1.1	1.4

County and Denomination	Number of churches	Communicant, confirmed, full members	Total adherents Number	Percent of total population	Percent of total adherents
499 INDEP.NON-CHAR[3]	10	NA	9,000	1.4	1.8
LAMAR	**95**	**9,791**	**12,239***	**77.9**	**100.0**
053 ASSEMB OF GOD	3	146	215	1.4	1.8
059 BAPT MISS ASSN	1	93	115*	.7	.9
127 CH GOD (CLEVE)	8	388	480*	3.1	3.9
165 CH OF NAZARENE	2	120	152	1.0	1.2
167 CHS OF CHRIST	14	1,105	1,456	9.3	11.9
223 FREE WILL BAPT	16	1,954	2,417*	15.4	19.7
361 PRIM BAPT ASCS	6	36	45*	.3	.4
419 SO BAPT CONV	26	3,847	4,759*	30.3	38.9
449 UN METHODIST	19	1,565	1,936*	12.3	15.8
497 BLACK BAPT EST[2]	NA	537	664*	4.2	5.4
LAUDERDALE	**163**	**37,965**	**53,759***	**67.5**	**100.0**
053 ASSEMB OF GOD	1	120	181	.2	.3
081 CATHOLIC	2	NA	2,777	3.5	5.2
081d LATIN	*2*	*NA*	*2,777*	*3.5*	*5.2*
093 CHR CH (DISC)	1	345	351	.4	.7
123 CH GOD (ANDER)	2	65	83	.1	.2
127 CH GOD (CLEVE)	3	113	139*	.2	.3
145 CH GOD PROPHCY	1	35	43*	.1	.1
151 L-D SAINTS	1	NA	480	.6	.9
165 CH OF NAZARENE	2	273	424	.5	.8
167 CHS OF CHRIST	60	9,979	12,884	16.2	24.0
185 CUMBER PRESB	6	1,086	1,118	1.4	2.1
193 EPISCOPAL	2	450	613	.8	1.1
207 E.L.C.A.	1	76	95	.1	.2
223 FREE WILL BAPT	2	64	79*	.1	.1
283 LUTH—MO SYNOD	1	123	149	.2	.3
355 PRESB CH (USA)	3	656	805*	1.0	1.5
361 PRIM BAPT ASCS	4	195	239*	.3	.4
403 SALVATION ARMY	1	94	96	.1	.2
413 S.D.A.	2	135	166*	.2	.3
419 SO BAPT CONV	32	14,303	17,550*	22.0	32.6
435 UNITARIAN-UNIV	1	20	22	-	-
449 UN METHODIST	30	7,037	8,634*	10.8	16.1
496 JEWISH EST[1]	1	NA	150	.2	.3
497 BLACK BAPT EST[2]	NA	2,796	3,431*	4.3	6.4
498 INDEP.CHARIS.[3]	2	NA	1,400	1.8	2.6
499 INDEP.NON-CHAR[3]	2	NA	1,850	2.3	3.4
LAWRENCE	**71**	**14,568**	**18,443***	**58.5**	**100.0**
053 ASSEMB OF GOD	1	63	75	.2	.4
127 CH GOD (CLEVE)	1	202	255*	.8	1.4
145 CH GOD PROPHCY	1	35	44*	.1	.2
167 CHS OF CHRIST	18	1,370	1,781	5.7	9.7
185 CUMBER PRESB	1	20	20	.1	.1
223 FREE WILL BAPT	1	60	76*	.2	.4
355 PRESB CH (USA)	1	57	72*	.2	.4
356 PRESB CH AMER	1	50	53	.2	.3
413 S.D.A.	1	20	25*	.1	.1
419 SO BAPT CONV	29	9,465	11,964*	38.0	64.9
449 UN METHODIST	16	1,483	1,875*	5.9	10.2
497 BLACK BAPT EST[2]	NA	1,743	2,203*	7.0	11.9
LEE	**106**	**44,482**	**56,111***	**64.4**	**100.0**
005 AME ZION	12	13,305	15,966	18.3	28.5
053 ASSEMB OF GOD	8	787	1,068	1.2	1.9
081 CATHOLIC	2	NA	1,736	2.0	3.1
081d LATIN	*2*	*NA*	*1,736*	*2.0*	*3.1*
089 CHR & MISS AL	1	22	34	-	.1
093 CHR CH (DISC)	2	106	118	.1	.2
097 CHR CHS&CHS CR	1	0	0*	-	-
111 CH CR,SCIENTST	1	NR	NR	-	-
123 CH GOD (ANDER)	2	44	55	.1	.1
127 CH GOD (CLEVE)	2	162	195*	.2	.3
145 CH GOD PROPHCY	1	35	42*	-	.1
151 L-D SAINTS	2	NA	345	.4	.6
165 CH OF NAZARENE	1	49	75	.1	.1
167 CHS OF CHRIST	8	1,021	1,386	1.6	2.5
193 EPISCOPAL	2	512	766	.9	1.4
223 FREE WILL BAPT	1	30	36*	-	.1
283 LUTH—MO SYNOD	1	238	317	.4	.6
355 PRESB CH (USA)	2	759	915*	1.0	1.6
356 PRESB CH AMER	2	297	355	.4	.6
413 S.D.A.	3	159	192*	.2	.3
419 SO BAPT CONV	29	15,328	18,477*	21.2	32.9
435 UNITARIAN-UNIV	1	66	96	.1	.2
449 UN METHODIST	22	5,555	6,696*	7.7	11.9
497 BLACK BAPT EST[2]	NA	6,007	7,241*	8.3	12.9
LIMESTONE	**126**	**23,525**	**30,938***	**57.1**	**100.0**
040 AP CHR CH-AMER	1	50	90	.2	.3
053 ASSEMB OF GOD	2	95	194	.4	.6
081 CATHOLIC	1	NA	1,023	1.9	3.3

NA–Not applicable   NR–Not reported   *Total adherents estimated from known number of communicant, confirmed, full members.   - Represents a percent less than 0.1.   Percentages may not total due to rounding.
[1]See Appendix E   [2]See Appendix F   [3]See Appendix G   Lines in *italic* represent a breakdown of Catholic rites or Friends affiliations. They are included in their respective denominational total.

Table 4. Churches and Church Membership by County and Denomination: 1990

County and Denomination	Number of churches	Communicant, confirmed, full members	Total adherents Number	Percent of total population	Percent of total adherents
081d LATIN	1	NA	1,023	1.9	3.3
093 CHR CH (DISC)	1	166	244	.5	.8
123 CH GOD (ANDER)	1	54	66	.1	.2
127 CH GOD (CLEVE)	2	79	98*	.2	.3
145 CH GOD PROPHCY	1	35	43*	.1	.1
151 L-D SAINTS	1	NA	230	.4	.7
167 CHS OF CHRIST	51	6,020	7,826	14.5	25.3
185 CUMBER PRESB	1	48	55	.1	.2
193 EPISCOPAL	1	126	154	.3	.5
203 EVAN FREE CH	1	0	0	-	-
355 PRESB CH (USA)	4	383	475*	.9	1.5
361 PRIM BAPT ASCS	1	26	32*	.1	.1
413 S.D.A.	2	112	139*	.3	.4
419 SO BAPT CONV	33	11,698	14,519*	26.8	46.9
443 UN C OF CHRIST	1	33	41*	.1	.1
449 UN METHODIST	21	2,502	3,105*	5.7	10.0
497 BLACK BAPT EST[2]	NA	2,098	2,604*	4.8	8.4
LOWNDES	**46**	**7,680**	**10,363***	**81.9**	**100.0**
005 AME ZION	6	1,536	1,904	15.0	18.4
081 CATHOLIC	0	NA	7	.1	.1
081d LATIN	0	NA	7	.1	.1
093 CHR CH (DISC)	11	453	738	5.8	7.1
167 CHS OF CHRIST	6	223	298	2.4	2.9
193 EPISCOPAL	1	47	55	.4	.5
356 PRESB CH AMER	4	169	185	1.5	1.8
419 SO BAPT CONV	9	835	1,141*	9.0	11.0
449 UN METHODIST	9	530	724*	5.7	7.0
497 BLACK BAPT EST[2]	NA	3,887	5,311*	42.0	51.2
MACON	**57**	**30,621**	**36,409***	**146.1**	**100.0**
005 AME ZION	21	18,630	21,023	84.3	57.7
053 ASSEMB OF GOD	2	42	63	.3	.2
081 CATHOLIC	1	NA	278	1.1	.8
081d LATIN	1	NA	278	1.1	.8
093 CHR CH (DISC)	2	203	344	1.4	.9
127 CH GOD (CLEVE)	1	41	51*	.2	.1
167 CHS OF CHRIST	3	199	259	1.0	.7
193 EPISCOPAL	1	131	150	.6	.4
207 E.L.C.A.	1	47	100	.4	.3
355 PRESB CH (USA)	3	168	210*	.8	.6
356 PRESB CH AMER	2	59	59	.2	.2
413 S.D.A.	1	194	242*	1.0	.7
419 SO BAPT CONV	7	1,188	1,485*	6.0	4.1
449 UN METHODIST	12	947	1,183*	4.7	3.2
497 BLACK BAPT EST[2]	NA	8,772	10,962*	44.0	30.1
MADISON	**269**	**102,356**	**144,406***	**60.4**	**100.0**
019 AMER BAPT USA	1	850	1,056*	.4	.7
053 ASSEMB OF GOD	7	577	913	.4	.6
055 AS REF PRES CH	1	26	32	-	-
081 CATHOLIC	6	NA	11,692	4.9	8.1
081d LATIN	6	NA	11,692	4.9	8.1
089 CHR & MISS AL	1	28	61	-	-
093 CHR CH (DISC)	2	596	724	.3	.5
097 CHR CHS&CHS CR	2	300	373*	.2	.3
111 CH CR,SCIENTST	1	NR	NR	-	-
123 CH GOD (ANDER)	3	269	273	.1	.2
127 CH GOD (CLEVE)	7	1,200	1,492*	.6	1.0
145 CH GOD PROPHCY	5	175	218*	.1	.2
151 L-D SAINTS	5	NA	2,016	.8	1.4
165 CH OF NAZARENE	6	697	1,312	.5	.9
167 CHS OF CHRIST	38	8,250	10,650	4.5	7.4
185 CUMBER PRESB	8	1,123	1,246	.5	.9
193 EPISCOPAL	4	1,885	2,567	1.1	1.8
203 EVAN FREE CH	1	52	110	-	.1
207 E.L.C.A.	5	1,237	1,549	.6	1.1
221 FREE METHODIST	1	25	25	-	-
223 FREE WILL BAPT	2	275	342*	.1	.2
226 FRIENDS-USA	1	8	31	-	-
226c FGC	1	8	31	-	-
246 GREEK ORTHODOX	1	NR	NR	-	-
263 INT FOURSQ GOS	1	61	76*	-	.1
283 LUTH—MO SYNOD	2	1,060	1,472	.6	1.0
349 PENT HOLINESS	2	565	702*	.3	.5
353 CHR BRETHREN	1	20	40	-	-
355 PRESB CH (USA)	12	3,671	4,563*	1.9	3.2
356 PRESB CH AMER	4	574	729	.3	.5
361 PRIM BAPT ASCS	5	167	208*	.1	.1
403 SALVATION ARMY	1	88	97	-	.1
413 S.D.A.	7	4,158	5,168*	2.2	3.6
419 SO BAPT CONV	78	42,243	52,505*	22.0	36.4
435 UNITARIAN-UNIV	1	151	219	.1	.2
443 UN C OF CHRIST	1	167	208*	.1	.1
449 UN METHODIST	39	14,299	17,773*	7.4	12.3
469 WELS	1	77	110	-	.1

County and Denomination	Number of churches	Communicant, confirmed, full members	Total adherents Number	Percent of total population	Percent of total adherents
496 JEWISH EST[1]	2	NA	150	.1	.1
497 BLACK BAPT EST[2]	NA	17,482	21,729*	9.1	15.0
498 INDEP.CHARIS.[3]	2	NA	950	.4	.7
499 INDEP.NON-CHAR[3]	2	NA	1,025	.4	.7
MARENGO	**78**	**17,782**	**23,118***	**100.1**	**100.0**
005 AME ZION	12	3,275	3,930	17.0	17.0
053 ASSEMB OF GOD	2	158	236	1.0	1.0
081 CATHOLIC	2	NA	292	1.3	1.3
081d LATIN	2	NA	292	1.3	1.3
097 CHR CHS&CHS CR	1	120	156*	.7	.7
127 CH GOD (CLEVE)	2	71	92*	.4	.4
143 CG IN CR(MENN)	1	115	150*	.6	.6
165 CH OF NAZARENE	1	20	21	.1	.1
167 CHS OF CHRIST	3	177	232	1.0	1.0
193 EPISCOPAL	2	243	305	1.3	1.3
356 PRESB CH AMER	5	278	358	1.6	1.5
419 SO BAPT CONV	32	6,760	8,800*	38.1	38.1
449 UN METHODIST	14	1,737	2,261*	9.8	9.8
496 JEWISH EST[1]	1	NA	0	-	-
497 BLACK BAPT EST[2]	NA	4,828	6,285*	27.2	27.2
MARION	**112**	**15,088**	**19,322***	**64.8**	**100.0**
053 ASSEMB OF GOD	2	82	181	.6	.9
059 BAPT MISS ASSN	1	66	81*	.3	.4
081 CATHOLIC	1	NA	365	1.2	1.9
081d LATIN	1	NA	365	1.2	1.9
089 CHR & MISS AL	1	52	112	.4	.6
127 CH GOD (CLEVE)	6	301	370*	1.2	1.9
145 CH GOD PROPHCY	5	175	215*	.7	1.1
151 L-D SAINTS	1	NA	97	.3	.5
167 CHS OF CHRIST	27	2,136	2,794	9.4	14.5
223 FREE WILL BAPT	24	3,705	4,549*	15.2	23.5
339 PENT CH OF GOD	1	34	77	.3	.4
361 PRIM BAPT ASCS	2	67	82*	.3	.4
419 SO BAPT CONV	27	6,287	7,719*	25.9	39.9
449 UN METHODIST	14	1,898	2,330*	7.8	12.1
497 BLACK BAPT EST[2]	NA	285	350*	1.2	1.8
MARSHALL	**177**	**35,985**	**45,527***	**64.3**	**100.0**
053 ASSEMB OF GOD	5	440	519	.7	1.1
081 CATHOLIC	1	NA	730	1.0	1.6
081d LATIN	1	NA	730	1.0	1.6
123 CH GOD (ANDER)	2	88	88	.1	.2
127 CH GOD (CLEVE)	7	768	946*	1.3	2.1
145 CH GOD PROPHCY	4	140	172*	.2	.4
151 L-D SAINTS	1	NA	328	.5	.7
165 CH OF NAZARENE	2	118	420	.6	.9
167 CHS OF CHRIST	22	1,992	2,278	3.2	5.0
193 EPISCOPAL	2	365	518	.7	1.1
221 FREE METHODIST	1	3	13	-	-
283 LUTH—MO SYNOD	1	65	76	.1	.2
355 PRESB CH (USA)	2	291	358*	.5	.8
356 PRESB CH AMER	1	43	66	.1	.1
361 PRIM BAPT ASCS	8	297	366*	.5	.8
413 S.D.A.	1	52	64*	.1	.1
419 SO BAPT CONV	85	25,746	31,715*	44.8	69.7
449 UN METHODIST	32	5,257	6,476*	9.1	14.2
497 BLACK BAPT EST[2]	NA	320	394*	.6	.9
MOBILE	**388**	**169,119**	**263,315***	**69.5**	**100.0**
005 AME ZION	20	12,245	14,694	3.9	5.6
019 AMER BAPT USA	2	1,175	1,512*	.4	.6
053 ASSEMB OF GOD	34	3,822	5,881	1.6	2.2
059 BAPT MISS ASSN	8	662	852*	.2	.3
081 CATHOLIC	36	NA	37,801	10.0	14.4
081d LATIN	36	NA	37,801	10.0	14.4
089 CHR & MISS AL	1	15	18	-	-
093 CHR CH (DISC)	3	208	326	.1	.1
097 CHR CHS&CHS CR	3	435	560*	.1	.2
111 CH CR,SCIENTST	1	NR	NR	-	-
123 CH GOD (ANDER)	4	84	149	-	.1
127 CH GOD (CLEVE)	23	5,512	7,093*	1.9	2.7
145 CH GOD PROPHCY	6	210	270*	.1	.1
151 L-D SAINTS	4	NA	1,431	.4	.5
157 CH OF BRETHREN	1	81	104*	-	-
165 CH OF NAZARENE	5	411	611	.2	.2
167 CHS OF CHRIST	19	2,361	2,926	.8	1.1
171 CH GOD-GEN CON	1	4	5*	-	-
193 EPISCOPAL	15	4,684	5,978	1.6	2.3
207 E.L.C.A.	2	481	652	.2	.2
215 EVAN METH CH	1	85	109*	-	-
216 EVAN PRESBY CH	1	64	69	-	-
221 FREE METHODIST	1	38	50	-	-
223 FREE WILL BAPT	1	34	44*	-	-

NA–Not applicable NR–Not reported *Total adherents estimated from known number of communicant, confirmed, full members. - Represents a percent less than 0.1. Percentages may not total due to rounding.
[1]See Appendix E [2]See Appendix F [3]See Appendix G Lines in *italic* represent a breakdown of Catholic rites or Friends affiliations. They are included in their respective denominational total.

Table 4. Churches and Church Membership by County and Denomination: 1990

County and Denomination	Number of churches	Communicant, confirmed, full members	Total adherents Number	Percent of total population	Percent of total adherents
246 GREEK ORTHODOX	1	NR	NR	-	-
266 INTRSTAT & ASC	7	1,225	1,576*	.4	.6
283 LUTH—MO SYNOD	6	1,479	2,124	.6	.8
285 MENNONITE CH	1	18	40	-	-
349 PENT HOLINESS	5	379	488*	.1	.2
355 PRESB CH (USA)	13	3,142	4,043*	1.1	1.5
356 PRESB CH AMER	1	119	190	.1	.1
361 PRIM BAPT ASCS	1	25	32*	-	-
371 REF CH IN AM	1	45	95	-	-
403 SALVATION ARMY	2	189	194	.1	.1
413 S.D.A.	4	1,578	2,031*	.5	.8
419 SO BAPT CONV	93	78,279	100,733*	26.6	38.3
435 UNITARIAN-UNIV	1	60	75	-	-
449 UN METHODIST	46	18,962	24,401*	6.4	9.3
467 WESLEYAN	1	92	120	-	-
469 WELS	1	97	160	-	.1
496 JEWISH EST[1]	2	NA	873	.2	.3
497 BLACK BAPT EST[2]	NA	30,835	39,680*	10.5	15.1
498 INDEP.CHARIS.[3]	5	NA	2,600	.7	1.0
499 INDEP.NON-CHAR[3]	5	NA	2,725	.7	1.0
MONROE	**69**	**14,277**	**19,178***	**80.0**	**100.0**
005 AME ZION	3	556	669	2.8	3.5
053 ASSEMB OF GOD	8	432	803	3.4	4.2
081 CATHOLIC	2	NA	238	1.0	1.2
081d LATIN	*2*	*NA*	*238*	*1.0*	*1.2*
151 L-D SAINTS	1	NA	232	1.0	1.2
165 CH OF NAZARENE	2	182	228	1.0	1.2
167 CHS OF CHRIST	1	140	170	.7	.9
193 EPISCOPAL	1	129	162	.7	.8
223 FREE WILL BAPT	1	42	55*	.2	.3
283 LUTH—MO SYNOD	1	54	54	.2	.3
355 PRESB CH (USA)	1	36	47*	.2	.2
356 PRESB CH AMER	1	177	198	.8	1.0
361 PRIM BAPT ASCS	3	31	40*	.2	.2
419 SO BAPT CONV	29	7,398	9,638*	40.2	50.3
449 UN METHODIST	15	1,248	1,626*	6.8	8.5
497 BLACK BAPT EST[2]	NA	3,852	5,018*	20.9	26.2
MONTGOMERY	**234**	**114,747**	**157,371***	**75.3**	**100.0**
005 AME ZION	33	18,060	21,672	10.4	13.8
053 ASSEMB OF GOD	7	4,450	3,529	1.7	2.2
059 BAPT MISS ASSN	3	369	470*	.2	.3
081 CATHOLIC	8	NA	6,975	3.3	4.4
081d LATIN	*8*	*NA*	*6,975*	*3.3*	*4.4*
089 CHR & MISS AL	1	14	15	-	-
093 CHR CH (DISC)	5	306	421	.2	.3
097 CHR CHS&CHS CR	1	85	108*	.1	.1
111 CH CR,SCIENTST	1	NR	NR	-	-
123 CH GOD (ANDER)	2	145	177	.1	.1
127 CH GOD (CLEVE)	2	467	595*	.3	.4
145 CH GOD PROPHCY	1	35	45*	-	-
151 L-D SAINTS	4	NA	1,320	.6	.8
165 CH OF NAZARENE	2	85	159	.1	.1
167 CHS OF CHRIST	40	7,313	9,662	4.6	6.1
193 EPISCOPAL	7	2,708	3,603	1.7	2.3
207 E.L.C.A.	2	375	484	.2	.3
215 EVAN METH CH	1	37	47*	-	-
223 FREE WILL BAPT	1	29	37*	-	-
246 GREEK ORTHODOX	1	NR	NR	-	-
263 INT FOURSQ GOS	2	15	19*	-	-
283 LUTH—MO SYNOD	4	433	517	.2	.3
353 CHR BRETHREN	1	20	35	-	-
355 PRESB CH (USA)	3	1,256	1,600*	.8	1.0
356 PRESB CH AMER	8	2,796	3,022	1.4	1.9
361 PRIM BAPT ASCS	2	95	121*	.1	.1
403 SALVATION ARMY	2	110	123	.1	.1
413 S.D.A.	4	1,566	1,995*	1.0	1.3
419 SO BAPT CONV	46	34,922	44,491*	21.3	28.3
435 UNITARIAN-UNIV	1	56	67	-	-
443 UN C OF CHRIST	1	89	113*	.1	.1
449 UN METHODIST	27	16,070	20,474*	9.8	13.0
467 WESLEYAN	1	0	140	.1	.1
496 JEWISH EST[1]	4	NA	1,300	.6	.8
497 BLACK BAPT EST[2]	NA	22,841	29,100*	13.9	18.5
498 INDEP.CHARIS.[3]	4	NA	2,135	1.0	1.4
499 INDEP.NON-CHAR[3]	2	NA	2,800	1.3	1.8
MORGAN	**197**	**52,895**	**71,182***	**71.2**	**100.0**
005 AME ZION	2	270	307	.3	.4
053 ASSEMB OF GOD	3	740	1,719	1.7	2.4
081 CATHOLIC	2	NA	2,411	2.4	3.4
081d LATIN	*2*	*NA*	*2,411*	*2.4*	*3.4*
093 CHR CH (DISC)	4	412	574	.6	.8
097 CHR CHS&CHS CR	3	297	372*	.4	.5
111 CH CR,SCIENTST	1	NR	NR	-	-

County and Denomination	Number of churches	Communicant, confirmed, full members	Total adherents Number	Percent of total population	Percent of total adherents
123 CH GOD (ANDER)	6	641	667	.7	.9
127 CH GOD (CLEVE)	7	739	927*	.9	1.3
145 CH GOD PROPHCY	3	105	132*	.1	.2
151 L-D SAINTS	2	NA	567	.6	.8
165 CH OF NAZARENE	4	396	457	.5	.6
167 CHS OF CHRIST	22	3,065	4,028	4.0	5.7
193 EPISCOPAL	2	684	776	.8	1.1
203 EVAN FREE CH	1	30	35	-	-
223 FREE WILL BAPT	3	477	598*	.6	.8
283 LUTH—MO SYNOD	1	554	666	.7	.9
355 PRESB CH (USA)	5	1,198	1,502*	1.5	2.1
356 PRESB CH AMER	2	111	128	.1	.2
361 PRIM BAPT ASCS	3	133	167*	.2	.2
403 SALVATION ARMY	1	113	120	.1	.2
413 S.D.A.	3	249	312*	.3	.4
419 SO BAPT CONV	74	30,230	37,905*	37.9	53.3
449 UN METHODIST	41	8,788	11,019*	11.0	15.5
497 BLACK BAPT EST[2]	NA	3,663	4,593*	4.6	6.5
498 INDEP.CHARIS.[3]	1	NA	500	.5	.7
499 INDEP.NON-CHAR[3]	1	NA	700	.7	1.0
PERRY	**41**	**8,606**	**10,988***	**86.1**	**100.0**
005 AME ZION	1	1,350	1,458	11.4	13.3
053 ASSEMB OF GOD	1	41	80	.6	.7
081 CATHOLIC	1	NA	50	.4	.5
081d LATIN	*1*	*NA*	*50*	*.4*	*.5*
127 CH GOD (CLEVE)	3	107	140*	1.1	1.3
167 CHS OF CHRIST	1	42	55	.4	.5
193 EPISCOPAL	1	45	53	.4	.5
223 FREE WILL BAPT	1	87	114*	.9	1.0
356 PRESB CH AMER	2	132	146	1.1	1.3
361 PRIM BAPT ASCS	1	17	22*	.2	.2
419 SO BAPT CONV	16	2,343	3,063*	24.0	27.9
443 UN C OF CHRIST	1	9	12*	.1	.1
449 UN METHODIST	12	1,055	1,379*	10.8	12.6
497 BLACK BAPT EST[2]	NA	3,378	4,416*	34.6	40.2
PICKENS	**91**	**12,739**	**16,452***	**79.5**	**100.0**
053 ASSEMB OF GOD	3	105	155	.7	.9
081 CATHOLIC	1	NA	75	.4	.5
081d LATIN	*1*	*NA*	*75*	*.4*	*.5*
127 CH GOD (CLEVE)	3	115	147*	.7	.9
145 CH GOD PROPHCY	4	140	179*	.9	1.1
167 CHS OF CHRIST	3	129	164	.8	1.0
185 CUMBER PRESB	1	33	34	.2	.2
223 FREE WILL BAPT	9	757	970*	4.7	5.9
339 PENT CH OF GOD	2	37	135	.7	.8
355 PRESB CH (USA)	3	57	73*	.4	.4
356 PRESB CH AMER	2	256	277	1.3	1.7
361 PRIM BAPT ASCS	2	14	18*	.1	.1
419 SO BAPT CONV	35	5,827	7,470*	36.1	45.4
449 UN METHODIST	23	1,716	2,200*	10.6	13.4
497 BLACK BAPT EST[2]	NA	3,553	4,555*	22.0	27.7
PIKE	**74**	**14,323**	**18,501***	**67.0**	**100.0**
005 AME ZION	2	170	255	.9	1.4
053 ASSEMB OF GOD	4	356	613	2.2	3.3
081 CATHOLIC	1	NA	382	1.4	2.1
081d LATIN	*1*	*NA*	*382*	*1.4*	*2.1*
127 CH GOD (CLEVE)	2	41	51*	.2	.3
151 L-D SAINTS	1	NA	142	.5	.8
167 CHS OF CHRIST	8	553	746	2.7	4.0
193 EPISCOPAL	1	133	186	.7	1.0
355 PRESB CH (USA)	2	56	69*	.3	.4
356 PRESB CH AMER	1	224	262	.9	1.4
361 PRIM BAPT ASCS	1	7	9*	-	-
413 S.D.A.	2	99	122*	.4	.7
419 SO BAPT CONV	33	8,174	10,094*	36.6	54.6
449 UN METHODIST	16	1,698	2,097*	7.6	11.3
497 BLACK BAPT EST[2]	NA	2,812	3,473*	12.6	18.8
RANDOLPH	**108**	**10,823**	**13,643***	**68.6**	**100.0**
053 ASSEMB OF GOD	1	19	19	.1	.1
081 CATHOLIC	1	NA	44	.2	.3
081d LATIN	*1*	*NA*	*44*	*.2*	*.3*
093 CHR CH (DISC)	2	92	129	.6	.9
097 CHR CHS&CHS CR	2	156	194*	1.0	1.4
123 CH GOD (ANDER)	1	50	79	.4	.6
127 CH GOD (CLEVE)	7	416	518*	2.6	3.8
165 CH OF NAZARENE	2	96	182	.9	1.3
167 CHS OF CHRIST	11	554	703	3.5	5.2
176 CCC, NOT NAT'L	6	309	385*	1.9	2.8
193 EPISCOPAL	1	33	51	.3	.4
361 PRIM BAPT ASCS	1	11	14*	.1	.1
419 SO BAPT CONV	33	4,665	5,814*	29.2	42.6
443 UN C OF CHRIST	6	362	451*	2.3	3.3

NA–Not applicable   NR–Not reported   *Total adherents estimated from known number of communicant, confirmed, full members.   - Represents a percent less than 0.1.   Percentages may not total due to rounding.
[1]See Appendix E   [2]See Appendix F   [3]See Appendix G   Lines in *italic* represent a breakdown of Catholic rites or Friends affiliations. They are included in their respective denominational total.

Table 4. Churches and Church Membership by County and Denomination: 1990

County and Denomination	Number of churches	Communicant, confirmed, full members	Total adherents: Number	Total adherents: Percent of total population	Total adherents: Percent of total adherents
449 UN METHODIST	34	2,709	3,376*	17.0	24.7
497 BLACK BAPT EST[2]	NA	1,351	1,684*	8.5	12.3
RUSSELL	**96**	**24,308**	**31,857***	**68.0**	**100.0**
005 AME ZION	10	2,525	2,790	6.0	8.8
053 ASSEMB OF GOD	10	800	1,448	3.1	4.5
081 CATHOLIC	3	NA	855	1.8	2.7
081d LATIN	*3*	*NA*	*855*	*1.8*	*2.7*
093 CHR CH (DISC)	1	50	95	.2	.3
097 CHR CHS&CHS CR	1	95	120*	.3	.4
123 CH GOD (ANDER)	1	30	30	.1	.1
127 CH GOD (CLEVE)	2	159	200*	.4	.6
145 CH GOD PROPHCY	1	35	44*	.1	.1
151 L-D SAINTS	1	NA	262	.6	.8
165 CH OF NAZARENE	1	101	131	.3	.4
167 CHS OF CHRIST	6	465	603	1.3	1.9
176 CCC, NOT NAT'L	1	184	232*	.5	.7
193 EPISCOPAL	2	87	127	.3	.4
223 FREE WILL BAPT	4	315	397*	.8	1.2
355 PRESB CH (USA)	1	55	69*	.1	.2
361 PRIM BAPT ASCS	2	48	60*	.1	.2
413 S.D.A.	3	238	300*	.6	.9
419 SO BAPT CONV	31	12,326	15,532*	33.1	48.8
443 UN C OF CHRIST	1	47	59*	.1	.2
449 UN METHODIST	14	2,016	2,540*	5.4	8.0
497 BLACK BAPT EST[2]	NA	4,732	5,963*	12.7	18.7
SAINT CLAIR	**130**	**23,154**	**30,273***	**60.5**	**100.0**
053 ASSEMB OF GOD	3	119	127	.3	.4
081 CATHOLIC	2	NA	658	1.3	2.2
081d LATIN	*2*	*NA*	*658*	*1.3*	*2.2*
127 CH GOD (CLEVE)	8	549	690*	1.4	2.3
145 CH GOD PROPHCY	4	140	176*	.4	.6
151 L-D SAINTS	1	NA	192	.4	.6
165 CH OF NAZARENE	1	46	45	.1	.1
167 CHS OF CHRIST	7	344	448	.9	1.5
185 CUMBER PRESB	3	205	213	.4	.7
193 EPISCOPAL	1	297	429	.9	1.4
223 FREE WILL BAPT	10	920	1,156*	2.3	3.8
285 MENNONITE CH	1	29	47	.1	.2
355 PRESB CH (USA)	2	51	64*	.1	.2
356 PRESB CH AMER	1	223	320	.6	1.1
413 S.D.A.	2	130	163*	.3	.5
419 SO BAPT CONV	65	15,816	19,878*	39.7	65.7
449 UN METHODIST	18	2,628	3,303*	6.6	10.9
467 WESLEYAN	1	0	0	-	-
496 JEWISH EST[1]	0	NA	281	.6	.9
497 BLACK BAPT EST[2]	NA	1,657	2,083*	4.2	6.9
SHELBY	**144**	**34,358**	**45,892***	**46.2**	**100.0**
005 AME ZION	1	96	103	.1	.2
053 ASSEMB OF GOD	13	1,415	2,313	2.3	5.0
081 CATHOLIC	1	NA	365	.4	.8
081d LATIN	*1*	*NA*	*365*	*.4*	*.8*
123 CH GOD (ANDER)	2	201	245	.2	.5
127 CH GOD (CLEVE)	9	650	832*	.8	1.8
145 CH GOD PROPHCY	5	175	224*	.2	.5
151 L-D SAINTS	1	NA	109	.1	.2
165 CH OF NAZARENE	2	188	243	.2	.5
167 CHS OF CHRIST	12	1,026	1,341	1.3	2.9
185 CUMBER PRESB	4	956	1,172	1.2	2.6
193 EPISCOPAL	2	344	531	.5	1.2
207 E.L.C.A.	1	335	464	.5	1.0
223 FREE WILL BAPT	5	336	430*	.4	.9
339 PENT CH OF GOD	1	5	16	-	-
349 PENT HOLINESS	1	16	20*	-	-
355 PRESB CH (USA)	2	134	172*	.2	.4
356 PRESB CH AMER	2	120	136	.1	.3
413 S.D.A.	2	40	51*	.1	.1
419 SO BAPT CONV	52	19,403	24,847*	25.0	54.1
449 UN METHODIST	25	6,114	7,829*	7.9	17.1
496 JEWISH EST[1]	0	NA	558	.6	1.2
497 BLACK BAPT EST[2]	NA	2,804	3,591*	3.6	7.8
499 INDEP.NON-CHAR[3]	1	NA	300	.3	.7
SUMTER	**64**	**9,330**	**12,134***	**75.0**	**100.0**
005 AME ZION	17	1,550	1,860	11.5	15.3
081 CATHOLIC	1	NA	146	.9	1.2
081d LATIN	*1*	*NA*	*146*	*.9*	*1.2*
123 CH GOD (ANDER)	2	29	41	.3	.3
127 CH GOD (CLEVE)	1	28	37*	.2	.3
143 CG IN CR(MENN)	1	98	128*	.8	1.1
167 CHS OF CHRIST	3	160	210	1.3	1.7
193 EPISCOPAL	2	61	77	.5	.6
355 PRESB CH (USA)	4	211	275*	1.7	2.3
356 PRESB CH AMER	7	123	133	.8	1.1

County and Denomination	Number of churches	Communicant, confirmed, full members	Total adherents: Number	Total adherents: Percent of total population	Total adherents: Percent of total adherents
419 SO BAPT CONV	13	1,655	2,160*	13.4	17.8
449 UN METHODIST	13	742	968*	6.0	8.0
497 BLACK BAPT EST[2]	NA	4,673	6,099*	37.7	50.3
TALLADEGA	**165**	**40,472**	**52,060***	**70.2**	**100.0**
005 AME ZION	4	1,620	1,836	2.5	3.5
053 ASSEMB OF GOD	7	438	789	1.1	1.5
081 CATHOLIC	3	NA	438	.6	.8
081d LATIN	*3*	*NA*	*438*	*.6*	*.8*
089 CHR & MISS AL	1	67	97	.1	.2
123 CH GOD (ANDER)	2	103	153	.2	.3
127 CH GOD (CLEVE)	9	779	984*	1.3	1.9
145 CH GOD PROPHCY	5	175	221*	.3	.4
151 L-D SAINTS	2	NA	237	.3	.5
165 CH OF NAZARENE	3	243	224	.3	.4
167 CHS OF CHRIST	10	1,031	1,346	1.8	2.6
193 EPISCOPAL	4	216	359	.5	.7
223 FREE WILL BAPT	3	392	495*	.7	1.0
263 INT FOURSQ GOS	1	14	18*	-	-
349 PENT HOLINESS	1	48	61*	.1	.1
355 PRESB CH (USA)	4	601	759*	1.0	1.5
356 PRESB CH AMER	2	120	150	.2	.3
361 PRIM BAPT ASCS	1	20	25*	-	-
413 S.D.A.	3	242	306*	.4	.6
419 SO BAPT CONV	69	22,453	28,373*	38.3	54.5
443 UN C OF CHRIST	2	44	56*	.1	.1
449 UN METHODIST	27	5,096	6,440*	8.7	12.4
467 WESLEYAN	2	64	219	.3	.4
497 BLACK BAPT EST[2]	NA	6,706	8,474*	11.4	16.3
TALLAPOOSA	**121**	**23,220**	**28,935***	**74.5**	**100.0**
005 AME ZION	6	2,430	2,754	7.1	9.5
053 ASSEMB OF GOD	3	201	258	.7	.9
081 CATHOLIC	1	NA	146	.4	.5
081d LATIN	*1*	*NA*	*146*	*.4*	*.5*
123 CH GOD (ANDER)	2	21	27	.1	.1
127 CH GOD (CLEVE)	2	176	218*	.6	.8
145 CH GOD PROPHCY	1	35	43*	.1	.1
151 L-D SAINTS	1	NA	64	.2	.2
165 CH OF NAZARENE	1	23	22	.1	.1
167 CHS OF CHRIST	7	627	720	1.9	2.5
193 EPISCOPAL	1	158	204	.5	.7
263 INT FOURSQ GOS	1	61	75*	.2	.3
355 PRESB CH (USA)	5	466	576*	1.5	2.0
361 PRIM BAPT ASCS	5	92	114*	.3	.4
419 SO BAPT CONV	52	11,962	14,797*	38.1	51.1
435 UNITARIAN-UNIV	1	8	8	-	-
443 UN C OF CHRIST	3	120	148*	.4	.5
449 UN METHODIST	28	3,833	4,741*	12.2	16.4
497 BLACK BAPT EST[2]	NA	3,007	3,720*	9.6	12.9
498 INDEP.CHARIS.[3]	1	NA	300	.8	1.0
TUSCALOOSA	**231**	**74,194**	**95,709***	**63.6**	**100.0**
005 AME ZION	16	8,810	10,572	7.0	11.0
053 ASSEMB OF GOD	6	585	868	.6	.9
081 CATHOLIC	4	NA	2,190	1.5	2.3
081d LATIN	*4*	*NA*	*2,190*	*1.5*	*2.3*
089 CHR & MISS AL	1	21	44	-	-
093 CHR CH (DISC)	2	251	422	.3	.4
111 CH CR,SCIENTST	1	NR	NR	-	-
123 CH GOD (ANDER)	4	67	224	.1	.2
127 CH GOD (CLEVE)	7	1,657	2,029*	1.3	2.1
145 CH GOD PROPHCY	2	70	86*	.1	.1
151 L-D SAINTS	2	NA	843	.6	.9
165 CH OF NAZARENE	8	749	1,034	.7	1.1
167 CHS OF CHRIST	12	1,699	2,361	1.6	2.5
185 CUMBER PRESB	2	268	268	.2	.3
193 EPISCOPAL	3	1,272	1,604	1.1	1.7
223 FREE WILL BAPT	12	1,577	1,931*	1.3	2.0
263 INT FOURSQ GOS	1	48	59*	-	.1
283 LUTH—MO SYNOD	3	345	453	.3	.5
331 ORTH CH IN AM	1	NR	NR	-	-
355 PRESB CH (USA)	6	1,653	2,025*	1.3	2.1
356 PRESB CH AMER	1	134	159	.1	.2
361 PRIM BAPT ASCS	3	33	40*	-	-
403 SALVATION ARMY	1	76	77	.1	.1
413 S.D.A.	2	358	438*	.3	.5
419 SO BAPT CONV	87	35,343	43,288*	28.8	45.2
435 UNITARIAN-UNIV	1	64	99	.1	.1
449 UN METHODIST	39	8,281	10,143*	6.7	10.6
467 WESLEYAN	2	532	685	.5	.7
496 JEWISH EST[1]	1	NA	300	.2	.3
497 BLACK BAPT EST[2]	NA	10,301	12,617*	8.4	13.2
499 INDEP.NON-CHAR[3]	1	NA	850	.6	.9
WALKER	**231**	**35,226**	**45,254***	**66.9**	**100.0**

NA–Not applicable NR–Not reported *Total adherents estimated from known number of communicant, confirmed, full members. - Represents a percent less than 0.1. Percentages may not total due to rounding.
[1]See Appendix E [2]See Appendix F [3]See Appendix G Lines in *italic* represent a breakdown of Catholic rites or Friends affiliations. They are included in their respective denominational total.

Table 4. Churches and Church Membership by County and Denomination: 1990

County and Denomination	Number of churches	Communicant, confirmed, full members	Total adherents Number	Percent of total population	Percent of total adherents
005 AME ZION	2	150	196	.3	.4
053 ASSEMB OF GOD	7	352	559	.8	1.2
081 CATHOLIC	2	NA	585	.9	1.3
081d *LATIN*	*2*	*NA*	*585*	*.9*	*1.3*
089 CHR & MISS AL	1	12	20	-	-
093 CHR CH (DISC)	1	40	86	.1	.2
097 CHR CHS&CHS CR	1	12	15*	-	-
123 CH GOD (ANDER)	2	72	92	.1	.2
127 CH GOD (CLEVE)	23	3,086	3,814*	5.6	8.4
145 CH GOD PROPHCY	10	351	434*	.6	1.0
151 L-D SAINTS	1	NA	288	.4	.6
165 CH OF NAZARENE	9	889	1,176	1.7	2.6
167 CHS OF CHRIST	48	3,553	4,592	6.8	10.1
193 EPISCOPAL	1	75	104	.2	.2
223 FREE WILL BAPT	8	1,004	1,241*	1.8	2.7
355 PRESB CH (USA)	1	70	87*	.1	.2
356 PRESB CH AMER	1	96	114	.2	.3
361 PRIM BAPT ASCS	2	50	62*	.1	.1
413 S.D.A.	1	53	66*	.1	.1
419 SO BAPT CONV	82	20,760	25,657*	37.9	56.7
449 UN METHODIST	27	3,001	3,709*	5.5	8.2
496 JEWISH EST[1]	1	NA	380	.6	.8
497 BLACK BAPT EST[2]	NA	1,600	1,977*	2.9	4.4
WASHINGTON	**84**	**10,831**	**14,048***	**84.1**	**100.0**
005 AME ZION	7	1,670	2,004	12.0	14.3
053 ASSEMB OF GOD	11	484	644	3.9	4.6
081 CATHOLIC	2	NA	83	.5	.6
081d *LATIN*	*2*	*NA*	*83*	*.5*	*.6*
127 CH GOD (CLEVE)	4	237	309*	1.9	2.2
157 CH OF BRETHREN	1	54	70*	.4	.5
165 CH OF NAZARENE	2	74	100	.6	.7
167 CHS OF CHRIST	1	9	12	.1	.1
266 INTRSTAT & ASC	3	159	207*	1.2	1.5
419 SO BAPT CONV	34	4,806	6,267*	37.5	44.6
449 UN METHODIST	19	1,438	1,875*	11.2	13.3
497 BLACK BAPT EST[2]	NA	1,900	2,477*	14.8	17.6
WILCOX	**44**	**7,363**	**9,957***	**73.4**	**100.0**
005 AME ZION	2	334	417	3.1	4.2
055 AS REF PRES CH	2	137	160	1.2	1.6
081 CATHOLIC	2	NA	68	.5	.7
081d *LATIN*	*2*	*NA*	*68*	*.5*	*.7*
127 CH GOD (CLEVE)	1	52	70*	.5	.7
151 L-D SAINTS	1	NA	88	.6	.9
167 CHS OF CHRIST	4	141	181	1.3	1.8
283 LUTH—MO SYNOD	3	290	386	2.8	3.9
355 PRESB CH (USA)	3	173	233*	1.7	2.3
356 PRESB CH AMER	2	145	168	1.2	1.7
419 SO BAPT CONV	13	1,758	2,363*	17.4	23.7
449 UN METHODIST	11	489	657*	4.8	6.6
497 BLACK BAPT EST[2]	NA	3,844	5,166*	38.1	51.9
WINSTON	**74**	**11,742**	**15,015***	**68.1**	**100.0**
053 ASSEMB OF GOD	2	399	720	3.3	4.8
081 CATHOLIC	1	NA	146	.7	1.0
081d *LATIN*	*1*	*NA*	*146*	*.7*	*1.0*
127 CH GOD (CLEVE)	6	629	773*	3.5	5.1
145 CH GOD PROPHCY	1	35	43*	.2	.3
151 L-D SAINTS	1	NA	85	.4	.6
165 CH OF NAZARENE	1	22	35	.2	.2
167 CHS OF CHRIST	9	901	1,188	5.4	7.9
283 LUTH—MO SYNOD	1	0	0	-	-
339 PENT CH OF GOD	1	34	77	.3	.5
419 SO BAPT CONV	42	8,688	10,677*	48.4	71.1
449 UN METHODIST	9	1,034	1,271*	5.8	8.5

ALASKA

County and Denomination	Number of churches	Communicant, confirmed, full members	Total adherents Number	Percent of total population	Percent of total adherents
THE STATE.....	814	72,399	177,337*	32.2	100.0
ALEUTIANS EAST	**11**	**380**	**605***	**24.6**	**100.0**
053 ASSEMB OF GOD	2	84	107	4.3	17.7
057 BAPT GEN CONF	1	27	33*	1.3	5.5
151 L-D SAINTS	1	NA	58	2.4	9.6
331 ORTH CH IN AM	5	NR	NR	-	-
469 WELS	2	269	407	16.5	67.3
ALEUTIANS WEST	**8**	**364**	**502***	**5.3**	**100.0**
005 AME ZION	1	242	280	3.0	55.8

County and Denomination	Number of churches	Communicant, confirmed, full members	Total adherents Number	Percent of total population	Percent of total adherents
151 L-D SAINTS	1	NA	72	.8	14.3
167 CHS OF CHRIST	1	10	14	.1	2.8
331 ORTH CH IN AM	5	NR	NR	-	-
497 BLACK BAPT EST[2]	NA	112	136*	1.4	27.1
ANCHORAGE	**169**	**32,944**	**75,837***	**33.5**	**100.0**
019 AMER BAPT USA	3	993	1,310*	.6	1.7
053 ASSEMB OF GOD	21	1,986	3,585	1.6	4.7
057 BAPT GEN CONF	4	266	351*	.2	.5
059 BAPT MISS ASSN	1	38	50*	-	.1
081 CATHOLIC	9	NA	16,518	7.3	21.8
081b *BYZAN RUTH*	*1*	*NA*	*225*	*.1*	*.3*
081d *LATIN*	*8*	*NA*	*16,293*	*7.2*	*21.5*
089 CHR & MISS AL	3	87	226	.1	.3
093 CHR CH (DISC)	1	167	247	.1	.3
097 CHR CHS&CHS CR	3	465	613*	.3	.8
105 CHRISTIAN REF	1	138	239	.1	.3
111 CH CR,SCIENTST	1	NR	NR	-	-
123 CH GOD (ANDER)	5	188	338	.1	.4
127 CH GOD (CLEVE)	5	720	950*	.4	1.3
145 CH GOD PROPHCY	2	40	53*	-	.1
151 L-D SAINTS	13	NA	5,611	2.5	7.4
165 CH OF NAZARENE	6	637	918	.4	1.2
167 CHS OF CHRIST	6	753	980	.4	1.3
175 CONGR CHR CHS	2	303	400*	.2	.5
179 CONSRV BAPT	1	NR	NR	-	-
193 EPISCOPAL	5	1,130	1,759	.8	2.3
203 EVAN FREE CH	1	60	110	-	.1
207 E.L.C.A.	7	2,589	3,917	1.7	5.2
221 FREE METHODIST	2	76	168	.1	.2
226 FRIENDS-USA	2	100	143*	.1	.2
226c *FGC*	*1*	*15*	*31*	-	-
226g *INDEP EVAN*	*1*	*85*	*112**	-	*.1*
246 GREEK ORTHODOX	1	NR	NR	-	-
259 IFCA	1	NR	NR	-	-
263 INT FOURSQ GOS	1	67	88*	-	.1
283 LUTH—MO SYNOD	4	1,169	1,876	.8	2.5
285 MENNONITE CH	1	2	2	-	-
292 MORAV CH-AK	0	25	137	.1	.2
331 ORTH CH IN AM	2	NR	NR	-	-
349 PENT HOLINESS	1	10	13*	-	-
353 CHR BRETHREN	3	134	240	.1	.3
355 PRESB CH (USA)	6	1,275	1,682*	.7	2.2
403 SALVATION ARMY	2	165	195	.1	.3
413 S.D.A.	5	831	1,096*	.5	1.4
419 SO BAPT CONV	19	13,260	17,492*	7.7	23.1
435 UNITARIAN-UNIV	1	151	166	.1	.2
449 UN METHODIST	9	1,883	2,484*	1.1	3.3
467 WESLEYAN	1	16	76	-	.1
469 WELS	1	117	186	.1	.2
496 JEWISH EST[1]	1	NA	0	-	-
497 BLACK BAPT EST[2]	NA	3,103	4,093*	1.8	5.4
498 INDEP.CHARIS.[3]	3	NA	2,500	1.1	3.3
499 INDEP.NON-CHAR[3]	3	NA	5,025	2.2	6.6
BETHEL	**52**	**2,386**	**7,237***	**53.0**	**100.0**
053 ASSEMB OF GOD	2	49	71	.5	1.0
081 CATHOLIC	10	NA	2,805	20.5	38.8
081d *LATIN*	*10*	*NA*	*2,805*	*20.5*	*38.8*
123 CH GOD (ANDER)	1	0	0	-	-
145 CH GOD PROPHCY	1	19	28*	.2	.4
151 L-D SAINTS	1	NA	79	.6	1.1
292 MORAV CH-AK	17	2,211	4,096	30.0	56.6
331 ORTH CH IN AM	17	NR	NR	-	-
349 PENT HOLINESS	2	90	133*	1.0	1.8
413 S.D.A.	1	17	25*	.2	.3
BRISTOL BAY	**6**	**66**	**124***	**8.8**	**100.0**
151 L-D SAINTS	1	NA	39	2.8	31.5
331 ORTH CH IN AM	4	NR	NR	-	-
413 S.D.A.	1	66	85*	6.0	68.5
DILLINGHAM	**29**	**592**	**1,445***	**36.0**	**100.0**
081 CATHOLIC	2	NA	90	2.2	6.2
081d *LATIN*	*2*	*NA*	*90*	*2.2*	*6.2*
151 L-D SAINTS	1	NA	44	1.1	3.0
207 E.L.C.A.	1	42	77	1.9	5.3
292 MORAV CH-AK	5	462	1,105	27.5	76.5
331 ORTH CH IN AM	19	NR	NR	-	-
413 S.D.A.	1	88	129*	3.2	8.9
FAIRBANKS NORTH STAR	**81**	**9,646**	**22,677***	**29.2**	**100.0**
005 AME ZION	1	54	54	.1	.2
019 AMER BAPT USA	3	181	245*	.3	1.1
053 ASSEMB OF GOD	8	739	1,159	1.5	5.1

NA–Not applicable NR–Not reported *Total adherents estimated from known number of communicant, confirmed, full members. - Represents a percent less than 0.1. Percentages may not total due to rounding.
[1]See Appendix E [2]See Appendix F [3]See Appendix G Lines in *italic* represent a breakdown of Catholic rites or Friends affiliations. They are included in their respective denominational total.

ALASKA

Table 4. Churches and Church Membership by County and Denomination: 1990

County and Denomination	Number of churches	Communicant, confirmed, full members	Total adherents Number	Percent of total population	Percent of total adherents
081 CATHOLIC	6	NA	5,117	6.6	22.6
081d LATIN	*6*	*NA*	*5,117*	*6.6*	*22.6*
089 CHR & MISS AL	1	32	40	.1	.2
097 CHR CHS&CHS CR	1	100	135*	.2	.6
111 CH CR,SCIENTST	1	NR	NR	-	-
123 CH GOD (ANDER)	1	150	150	.2	.7
127 CH GOD (CLEVE)	2	131	177*	.2	.8
145 CH GOD PROPHCY	1	19	26*	-	.1
151 L-D SAINTS	9	NA	2,599	3.3	11.5
165 CH OF NAZARENE	4	355	1,009	1.3	4.4
167 CHS OF CHRIST	3	232	326	.4	1.4
179 CONSRV BAPT	2	NR	NR	-	-
193 EPISCOPAL	2	510	1,133	1.5	5.0
207 E.L.C.A.	3	801	1,276	1.6	5.6
226 FRIENDS-USA	2	27	48*	.1	.2
226c FGC	*1*	*15*	*32*	-	*.1*
226g INDEP EVAN	*1*	*12*	*16**	-	*.1*
283 LUTH—MO SYNOD	1	280	431	.6	1.9
331 ORTH CH IN AM	1	NR	NR	-	-
339 PENT CH OF GOD	2	69	154	.2	.7
353 CHR BRETHREN	2	137	174	.2	.8
355 PRESB CH (USA)	5	582	789*	1.0	3.5
403 SALVATION ARMY	1	48	63	.1	.3
413 S.D.A.	2	216	293*	.4	1.3
419 SO BAPT CONV	11	3,401	4,608*	5.9	20.3
435 UNITARIAN-UNIV	1	35	58	.1	.3
449 UN METHODIST	3	513	695*	.9	3.1
469 WELS	1	74	117	.2	.5
497 BLACK BAPT EST[2]	NA	960	1,301*	1.7	5.7
499 INDEP.NON-CHAR[3]	1	NA	500	.6	2.2
HAINES	**8**	**120**	**393***	**18.6**	**100.0**
053 ASSEMB OF GOD	1	20	58	2.7	14.8
081 CATHOLIC	1	NA	105	5.0	26.7
081d LATIN	*1*	*NA*	*105*	*5.0*	*26.7*
151 L-D SAINTS	3	NA	98	4.6	24.9
167 CHS OF CHRIST	1	10	13	.6	3.3
355 PRESB CH (USA)	1	85	109*	5.1	27.7
403 SALVATION ARMY	1	5	10	.5	2.5
JUNEAU	**34**	**3,667**	**8,405***	**31.4**	**100.0**
053 ASSEMB OF GOD	7	363	650	2.4	7.7
081 CATHOLIC	2	NA	2,376	8.9	28.3
081d LATIN	*2*	*NA*	*2,376*	*8.9*	*28.3*
111 CH CR,SCIENTST	1	NR	NR	-	-
123 CH GOD (ANDER)	1	150	150	.6	1.8
127 CH GOD (CLEVE)	1	72	95*	.4	1.1
151 L-D SAINTS	2	NA	857	3.2	10.2
165 CH OF NAZARENE	1	132	320	1.2	3.8
167 CHS OF CHRIST	1	141	180	.7	2.1
193 EPISCOPAL	2	212	305	1.1	3.6
207 E.L.C.A.	2	414	586	2.2	7.0
226 FRIENDS-USA	1	3	22	.1	.3
226c FGC	*1*	*3*	*22*	*.1*	*.3*
283 LUTH—MO SYNOD	1	119	170	.6	2.0
331 ORTH CH IN AM	1	NR	NR	-	-
355 PRESB CH (USA)	2	616	812*	3.0	9.7
403 SALVATION ARMY	1	143	168	.6	2.0
413 S.D.A.	1	143	189*	.7	2.2
419 SO BAPT CONV	3	784	1,034*	3.9	12.3
435 UNITARIAN-UNIV	1	10	10	-	.1
449 UN METHODIST	3	365	481*	1.8	5.7
KENAI PENINSULA	**69**	**3,921**	**10,835***	**26.6**	**100.0**
053 ASSEMB OF GOD	4	207	424	1.0	3.9
081 CATHOLIC	7	NA	2,642	6.5	24.4
081d LATIN	*7*	*NA*	*2,642*	*6.5*	*24.4*
097 CHR CHS&CHS CR	3	425	577*	1.4	5.3
127 CH GOD (CLEVE)	2	84	114*	.3	1.1
151 L-D SAINTS	5	NA	1,627	4.0	15.0
165 CH OF NAZARENE	5	317	584	1.4	5.4
167 CHS OF CHRIST	8	220	317	.8	2.9
179 CONSRV BAPT	1	NR	NR	-	-
193 EPISCOPAL	3	115	147	.4	1.4
207 E.L.C.A.	2	297	445	1.1	4.1
283 LUTH—MO SYNOD	3	246	458	1.1	4.2
331 ORTH CH IN AM	6	NR	NR	-	-
339 PENT CH OF GOD	1	34	77	.2	.7
403 SALVATION ARMY	1	24	34	.1	.3
413 S.D.A.	1	97	132*	.3	1.2
419 SO BAPT CONV	7	1,319	1,790*	4.4	16.5
449 UN METHODIST	7	436	592*	1.5	5.5
467 WESLEYAN	1	52	385	.9	3.6
469 WELS	1	48	90	.2	.8
499 INDEP.NON-CHAR[3]	1	NA	400	1.0	3.7

County and Denomination	Number of churches	Communicant, confirmed, full members	Total adherents Number	Percent of total population	Percent of total adherents
KETCHIKAN GATEWAY	**30**	**1,939**	**4,682***	**33.9**	**100.0**
053 ASSEMB OF GOD	4	225	430	3.1	9.2
081 CATHOLIC	2	NA	1,200	8.7	25.6
081d LATIN	*2*	*NA*	*1,200*	*8.7*	*25.6*
089 CHR & MISS AL	2	232	410	3.0	8.8
111 CH CR,SCIENTST	1	NR	NR	-	-
127 CH GOD (CLEVE)	1	194	256*	1.9	5.5
151 L-D SAINTS	3	NA	573	4.1	12.2
164 CH LUTH CONF	1	30	47	.3	1.0
165 CH OF NAZARENE	1	74	113	.8	2.4
167 CHS OF CHRIST	1	75	97	.7	2.1
193 EPISCOPAL	1	112	181	1.3	3.9
207 E.L.C.A.	1	239	335	2.4	7.2
263 INT FOURSQ GOS	1	21	28*	.2	.6
331 ORTH CH IN AM	1	NR	NR	-	-
339 PENT CH OF GOD	1	34	77	.6	1.6
355 PRESB CH (USA)	1	78	103*	.7	2.2
403 SALVATION ARMY	3	164	224	1.6	4.8
413 S.D.A.	2	123	162*	1.2	3.5
419 SO BAPT CONV	2	147	194*	1.4	4.1
449 UN METHODIST	1	191	252*	1.8	5.4
KODIAK ISLAND	**21**	**783**	**2,454***	**18.4**	**100.0**
019 AMER BAPT USA	1	120	162*	1.2	6.6
053 ASSEMB OF GOD	1	65	100	.8	4.1
081 CATHOLIC	1	NA	600	4.5	24.4
081d LATIN	*1*	*NA*	*600*	*4.5*	*24.4*
089 CHR & MISS AL	1	108	365	2.7	14.9
111 CH CR,SCIENTST	1	NR	NR	-	-
151 L-D SAINTS	1	NA	273	2.1	11.1
165 CH OF NAZARENE	1	78	212	1.6	8.6
167 CHS OF CHRIST	1	25	30	.2	1.2
193 EPISCOPAL	1	62	234	1.8	9.5
207 E.L.C.A.	1	192	295	2.2	12.0
331 ORTH CH IN AM	8	NR	NR	-	-
403 SALVATION ARMY	1	5	10	.1	.4
413 S.D.A.	1	69	93*	.7	3.8
419 SO BAPT CONV	1	59	80*	.6	3.3
LAKE AND PENINSULA	**1**	**0**	**50***	**3.0**	**100.0**
081 CATHOLIC	1	NA	50	3.0	100.0
081d LATIN	*1*	*NA*	*50*	*3.0*	*100.0*
MATANUSKA-SUSITNA	**57**	**3,742**	**11,994***	**30.2**	**100.0**
005 AME ZION	1	20	32	.1	.3
019 AMER BAPT USA	1	33	46*	.1	.4
053 ASSEMB OF GOD	2	206	350	.9	2.9
081 CATHOLIC	6	NA	3,200	8.1	26.7
081d LATIN	*6*	*NA*	*3,200*	*8.1*	*26.7*
089 CHR & MISS AL	2	0	55	.1	.5
097 CHR CHS&CHS CR	4	93	131*	.3	1.1
111 CH CR,SCIENTST	1	NR	NR	-	-
123 CH GOD (ANDER)	2	126	128	.3	1.1
127 CH GOD (CLEVE)	1	104	146*	.4	1.2
145 CH GOD PROPHCY	1	19	27*	.1	.2
151 L-D SAINTS	7	NA	2,589	6.5	21.6
165 CH OF NAZARENE	2	130	266	.7	2.2
167 CHS OF CHRIST	1	97	149	.4	1.2
193 EPISCOPAL	3	134	298	.8	2.5
207 E.L.C.A.	2	379	670	1.7	5.6
221 FREE METHODIST	1	0	51	.1	.4
283 LUTH—MO SYNOD	1	349	469	1.2	3.9
331 ORTH CH IN AM	1	NR	NR	-	-
339 PENT CH OF GOD	2	68	154	.4	1.3
355 PRESB CH (USA)	2	499	702*	1.8	5.9
403 SALVATION ARMY	1	34	44	.1	.4
413 S.D.A.	2	253	356*	.9	3.0
419 SO BAPT CONV	7	1,045	1,470*	3.7	12.3
449 UN METHODIST	1	91	128*	.3	1.1
469 WELS	1	62	133	.3	1.1
499 INDEP.NON-CHAR[3]	1	NA	400	1.0	3.3
NOME	**25**	**1,230**	**3,290***	**39.7**	**100.0**
053 ASSEMB OF GOD	3	70	134	1.6	4.1
081 CATHOLIC	7	NA	1,139	13.7	34.6
081d LATIN	*7*	*NA*	*1,139*	*13.7*	*34.6*
151 L-D SAINTS	1	NA	47	.6	1.4
165 CH OF NAZARENE	1	31	113	1.4	3.4
207 E.L.C.A.	5	734	1,275	15.4	38.8
226 FRIENDS-USA	1	10	15*	.2	.5
226g INDEP EVAN	*1*	*10*	*15**	*.2*	*.5*
331 ORTH CH IN AM	1	NR	NR	-	-
353 CHR BRETHREN	1	10	20	.2	.6
355 PRESB CH (USA)	3	242	353*	4.3	10.7
413 S.D.A.	1	30	44*	.5	1.3

NA–Not applicable NR–Not reported *Total adherents estimated from known number of communicant, confirmed, full members. - Represents a percent less than 0.1. Percentages may not total due to rounding.
[1]See Appendix E [2]See Appendix F [3]See Appendix G Lines in *italic* represent a breakdown of Catholic rites or Friends affiliations. They are included in their respective denominational total.

Table 4. Churches and Church Membership by County and Denomination: 1990

County and Denomination	Number of churches	Communicant, confirmed, full members	Total adherents Number	Percent of total population	Percent of total adherents
449 UN METHODIST	1	103	150*	1.8	4.6
NORTH SLOPE	**14**	**1,208**	**2,193***	**36.7**	**100.0**
053 ASSEMB OF GOD	5	130	455	7.6	20.7
081 CATHOLIC	1	NA	51	.9	2.3
081d *LATIN*	*1*	*NA*	*51*	*.9*	*2.3*
151 L-D SAINTS	1	NA	81	1.4	3.7
193 EPISCOPAL	2	442	668	11.2	30.5
355 PRESB CH (USA)	5	636	938*	15.7	42.8
NORTHWEST ARCTIC	**21**	**2,078**	**3,680***	**60.2**	**100.0**
053 ASSEMB OF GOD	1	10	19	.3	.5
081 CATHOLIC	1	NA	306	5.0	8.3
081d *LATIN*	*1*	*NA*	*306*	*5.0*	*8.3*
127 CH GOD (CLEVE)	1	67	105*	1.7	2.9
167 CHS OF CHRIST	1	6	8	.1	.2
193 EPISCOPAL	2	111	296	4.8	8.0
226 FRIENDS-USA	11	1,653	2,586*	42.3	70.3
226g *INDEP EVAN*	*11*	*1,653*	*2,586***	*42.3*	*70.3*
413 S.D.A.	2	70	110*	1.8	3.0
419 SO BAPT CONV	1	109	171*	2.8	4.6
469 WELS	1	52	79	1.3	2.1
PR OF WALES-OUT KETCHIKAN	**16**	**580**	**962***	**15.3**	**100.0**
081 CATHOLIC	2	NA	245	3.9	25.5
081d *LATIN*	*2*	*NA*	*245*	*3.9*	*25.5*
127 CH GOD (CLEVE)	1	66	90*	1.4	9.4
175 CONGR CHR CHS	1	145	198*	3.2	20.6
355 PRESB CH (USA)	3	138	188*	3.0	19.5
403 SALVATION ARMY	9	231	241	3.8	25.1
SITKA	**17**	**1,253**	**2,684***	**31.3**	**100.0**
053 ASSEMB OF GOD	1	134	292	3.4	10.9
081 CATHOLIC	1	NA	453	5.3	16.9
081d *LATIN*	*1*	*NA*	*453*	*5.3*	*16.9*
151 L-D SAINTS	2	NA	249	2.9	9.3
165 CH OF NAZARENE	1	52	209	2.4	7.8
167 CHS OF CHRIST	1	65	78	.9	2.9
179 CONSRV BAPT	1	NR	NR	-	-
193 EPISCOPAL	1	115	240	2.8	8.9
207 E.L.C.A.	1	244	309	3.6	11.5
331 ORTH CH IN AM	2	NR	NR	-	-
355 PRESB CH (USA)	1	161	215*	2.5	8.0
403 SALVATION ARMY	1	59	71	.8	2.6
413 S.D.A.	1	69	92*	1.1	3.4
419 SO BAPT CONV	1	198	265*	3.1	9.9
435 UNITARIAN-UNIV	1	26	37	.4	1.4
449 UN METHODIST	1	130	174*	2.0	6.5
SKAGWAY-YAKUTAT-ANGOON	**13**	**276**	**641***	**14.6**	**100.0**
053 ASSEMB OF GOD	3	110	237	5.4	37.0
081 CATHOLIC	3	NA	188	4.3	29.3
081d *LATIN*	*3*	*NA*	*188*	*4.3*	*29.3*
331 ORTH CH IN AM	2	NR	NR	-	-
355 PRESB CH (USA)	4	112	152*	3.5	23.7
403 SALVATION ARMY	1	54	64	1.5	10.0
SOUTHEAST FAIRBANKS	**9**	**1,124**	**2,159***	**36.5**	**100.0**
053 ASSEMB OF GOD	2	53	90	1.5	4.2
081 CATHOLIC	2	NA	510	8.6	23.6
081d *LATIN*	*2*	*NA*	*510*	*8.6*	*23.6*
193 EPISCOPAL	1	58	93	1.6	4.3
339 PENT CH OF GOD	1	34	77	1.3	3.6
355 PRESB CH (USA)	1	76	108*	1.8	5.0
413 S.D.A.	1	28	40*	.7	1.9
419 SO BAPT CONV	1	875	1,241*	21.0	57.5
VALDEZ-CORDOVA	**23**	**495**	**1,360***	**13.7**	**100.0**
019 AMER BAPT USA	1	136	179*	1.8	13.2
081 CATHOLIC	4	NA	200	2.0	14.7
081d *LATIN*	*4*	*NA*	*200*	*2.0*	*14.7*
145 CH GOD PROPHCY	1	19	25*	.3	1.8
151 L-D SAINTS	3	NA	316	3.2	23.2
165 CH OF NAZARENE	2	43	191	1.9	14.0
167 CHS OF CHRIST	2	15	24	.2	1.8
193 EPISCOPAL	1	20	39	.4	2.9
207 E.L.C.A.	1	51	109	1.1	8.0
331 ORTH CH IN AM	4	NR	NR	-	-
413 S.D.A.	1	44	58*	.6	4.3
419 SO BAPT CONV	3	167	219*	2.2	16.1
WADE HAMPTON	**20**	**79**	**4,692***	**81.0**	**100.0**
053 ASSEMB OF GOD	3	79	85	1.5	1.8
081 CATHOLIC	12	NA	4,607	79.6	98.2
081d *LATIN*	*12*	*NA*	*4,607*	*79.6*	*98.2*
331 ORTH CH IN AM	5	NR	NR	-	-
WRANGELL-PETERSBURG	**20**	**872**	**1,693***	**24.0**	**100.0**
053 ASSEMB OF GOD	3	129	177	2.5	10.5
081 CATHOLIC	2	NA	370	5.3	21.9
081d *LATIN*	*2*	*NA*	*370*	*5.3*	*21.9*
123 CH GOD (ANDER)	1	60	60	.9	3.5
151 L-D SAINTS	2	NA	182	2.6	10.8
193 EPISCOPAL	2	75	102	1.4	6.0
207 E.L.C.A.	2	293	396	5.6	23.4
355 PRESB CH (USA)	3	117	156*	2.2	9.2
403 SALVATION ARMY	2	88	103	1.5	6.1
413 S.D.A.	2	43	57*	.8	3.4
419 SO BAPT CONV	1	67	90*	1.3	5.3
YUKON-KOYUKUK	**60**	**2,654**	**6,743***	**79.5**	**100.0**
053 ASSEMB OF GOD	12	245	356	4.2	5.3
081 CATHOLIC	11	NA	2,431	28.7	36.1
081d *LATIN*	*11*	*NA*	*2,431*	*28.7*	*36.1*
151 L-D SAINTS	1	NA	357	4.2	5.3
167 CHS OF CHRIST	1	5	10	.1	.1
193 EPISCOPAL	17	1,148	2,045	24.1	30.3
331 ORTH CH IN AM	2	NR	NR	-	-
349 PENT HOLINESS	6	157	220*	2.6	3.3
403 SALVATION ARMY	8	1,053	1,260	14.9	18.7
419 SO BAPT CONV	2	46	64*	.8	.9

ARIZONA

County and Denomination	Number of churches	Communicant, confirmed, full members	Total adherents Number	Percent of total population	Percent of total adherents
THE STATE.....	2,766	446,650	1,577,427*	43.0	100.0
APACHE	**98**	**3,812**	**20,593***	**33.4**	**100.0**
053 ASSEMB OF GOD	10	639	924	1.5	4.5
081 CATHOLIC	19	NA	6,097	9.9	29.6
081d *LATIN*	*19*	*NA*	*6,097*	*9.9*	*29.6*
105 CHRISTIAN REF	4	172	352	.6	1.7
123 CH GOD (ANDER)	1	70	70	.1	.3
127 CH GOD (CLEVE)	1	25	38*	.1	.2
151 L-D SAINTS	20	NA	8,486	13.8	41.2
165 CH OF NAZARENE	3	61	128	.2	.6
167 CHS OF CHRIST	4	110	179	.3	.9
171 CH GOD-GEN CON	1	0	0*	-	-
193 EPISCOPAL	8	383	710	1.2	3.4
207 E.L.C.A.	1	90	180	.3	.9
221 FREE METHODIST	1	0	15	-	.1
226 FRIENDS-USA	2	25	38*	.1	.2
226b *EFI*	*2*	*25*	*38***	*.1*	*.2*
259 IFCA	1	NR	NR	-	-
285 MENNONITE CH	2	25	40	.1	.2
349 PENT HOLINESS	1	31	47*	.1	.2
355 PRESB CH (USA)	4	537	808*	1.3	3.9
413 S.D.A.	2	73	110*	.2	.5
419 SO BAPT CONV	11	1,503	2,261*	3.7	11.0
449 UN METHODIST	1	32	48*	.1	.2
469 WELS	1	36	62	.1	.3
COCHISE	**132**	**11,082**	**48,094***	**49.3**	**100.0**
019 AMER BAPT USA	1	139	178*	.2	.4
053 ASSEMB OF GOD	17	1,144	1,589	1.6	3.3
081 CATHOLIC	13	NA	28,290	29.0	58.8
081d *LATIN*	*13*	*NA*	*28,290*	*29.0*	*58.8*
093 CHR CH (DISC)	2	60	100	.1	.2
097 CHR CHS&CHS CR	1	172	220*	.2	.5
111 CH CR,SCIENTST	2	NR	NR	-	-
127 CH GOD (CLEVE)	2	116	148*	.2	.3
133 CH GOD(7TH)DEN	1	15	26	-	.1
143 CG IN CR(MENN)	1	27	35*	-	.1
151 L-D SAINTS	14	NA	4,773	4.9	9.9
165 CH OF NAZARENE	5	333	497	.5	1.0
167 CHS OF CHRIST	9	431	620	.6	1.3
179 CONSRV BAPT	5	NR	NR	-	-
193 EPISCOPAL	6	338	404	.4	.8
203 EVAN FREE CH	1	13	50	.1	.1
207 E.L.C.A.	2	540	636	.7	1.3
226 FRIENDS-USA	1	7	9*	-	-
226f *INDEPENDNT*	*1*	*7*	*9***	-	-
283 LUTH—MO SYNOD	3	228	279	.3	.6
339 PENT CH OF GOD	1	34	77	.1	.2
349 PENT HOLINESS	1	12	15*	-	-
355 PRESB CH (USA)	4	500	639*	.7	1.3

NA–Not applicable   NR–Not reported   *Total adherents estimated from known number of communicant, confirmed, full members.   - Represents a percent less than 0.1.   Percentages may not total due to rounding.
[1]See Appendix E   [2]See Appendix F   [3]See Appendix G   Lines in *italic* represent a breakdown of Catholic rites or Friends affiliations. They are included in their respective denominational total.

Table 4. Churches and Church Membership by County and Denomination: 1990

County and Denomination	Number of churches	Communicant, confirmed, full members	Total adherents Number	Percent of total population	Percent of total adherents
403 SALVATION ARMY	1	23	25	-	.1
413 S.D.A.	4	230	294*	.3	.6
419 SO BAPT CONV	16	4,052	5,181*	5.3	10.8
443 UN C OF CHRIST	3	403	515*	.5	1.1
449 UN METHODIST	10	1,191	1,523*	1.6	3.2
469 WELS	4	196	248	.3	.5
496 JEWISH EST[1]	1	NA	250	.3	.5
497 BLACK BAPT EST[2]	NA	878	1,123*	1.2	2.3
498 INDEP.CHARIS.[3]	1	NA	350	.4	.7
COCONINO	**121**	**8,634**	**30,398***	**31.5**	**100.0**
019 AMER BAPT USA	1	47	62*	.1	.2
053 ASSEMB OF GOD	11	766	1,232	1.3	4.1
081 CATHOLIC	8	NA	6,784	7.0	22.3
081d LATIN	8	NA	6,784	7.0	22.3
089 CHR & MISS AL	2	52	58	.1	.2
093 CHR CH (DISC)	2	36	45	-	.1
097 CHR CHS&CHS CR	4	375	498*	.5	1.6
105 CHRISTIAN REF	1	37	46	-	.2
111 CH CR,SCIENTST	3	NR	NR	-	-
127 CH GOD (CLEVE)	1	31	41*	-	.1
151 L-D SAINTS	23	NA	10,902	11.3	35.9
165 CH OF NAZARENE	9	552	788	.8	2.6
167 CHS OF CHRIST	6	199	285	.3	.9
179 CONSRV BAPT	5	NR	NR	-	-
193 EPISCOPAL	3	255	506	.5	1.7
203 EVAN FREE CH	1	30	68	.1	.2
207 E.L.C.A.	3	741	998	1.0	3.3
223 FREE WILL BAPT	1	15	20*	-	.1
226 FRIENDS-USA	1	15	20*	-	.1
226f INDEPENDNT	1	15	20*	-	.1
259 IFCA	1	NR	NR	-	-
263 INT FOURSQ GOS	1	50	66*	.1	.2
283 LUTH—MO SYNOD	2	223	339	.4	1.1
287 MENN GEN CONF	1	12	17	-	.1
339 PENT CH OF GOD	4	138	308	.3	1.0
353 CHR BRETHREN	1	12	23	-	.1
355 PRESB CH (USA)	3	288	382*	.4	1.3
403 SALVATION ARMY	1	65	67	.1	.2
413 S.D.A.	1	91	121*	.1	.4
419 SO BAPT CONV	9	2,227	2,955*	3.1	9.7
435 UNITARIAN-UNIV	1	30	37	-	.1
443 UN C OF CHRIST	2	688	913*	.9	3.0
449 UN METHODIST	5	1,205	1,599*	1.7	5.3
467 WESLEYAN	1	28	48	-	.2
469 WELS	1	181	245	.3	.8
496 JEWISH EST[1]	0	NA	250	.3	.8
497 BLACK BAPT EST[2]	NA	245	325*	.3	1.1
498 INDEP.CHARIS.[3]	1	NA	350	.4	1.2
GILA	**77**	**6,540**	**28,687***	**71.3**	**100.0**
019 AMER BAPT USA	1	23	29*	.1	.1
053 ASSEMB OF GOD	9	678	1,169	2.9	4.1
081 CATHOLIC	8	NA	16,179	40.2	56.4
081d LATIN	8	NA	16,179	40.2	56.4
093 CHR CH (DISC)	1	76	90	.2	.3
097 CHR CHS&CHS CR	2	215	271*	.7	.9
111 CH CR,SCIENTST	2	NR	NR	-	-
151 L-D SAINTS	9	NA	3,022	7.5	10.5
165 CH OF NAZARENE	2	113	191	.5	.7
167 CHS OF CHRIST	5	188	244	.6	.9
179 CONSRV BAPT	4	NR	NR	-	-
193 EPISCOPAL	2	190	211	.5	.7
203 EVAN FREE CH	1	55	170	.4	.6
207 E.L.C.A.	2	511	611	1.5	2.1
263 INT FOURSQ GOS	1	25	32*	.1	.1
283 LUTH—MO SYNOD	2	85	107	.3	.4
339 PENT CH OF GOD	1	35	76	.2	.3
355 PRESB CH (USA)	3	404	509*	1.3	1.8
403 SALVATION ARMY	1	47	51	.1	.2
413 S.D.A.	2	140	176*	.4	.6
419 SO BAPT CONV	9	2,748	3,463*	8.6	12.1
449 UN METHODIST	4	504	635*	1.6	2.2
469 WELS	5	503	1,091	2.7	3.8
498 INDEP.CHARIS.[3]	1	NA	360	.9	1.3
GRAHAM	**43**	**1,911**	**17,075***	**64.3**	**100.0**
053 ASSEMB OF GOD	3	136	190	.7	1.1
059 BAPT MISS ASSN	1	27	37*	.1	.2
081 CATHOLIC	2	NA	6,500	24.5	38.1
081d LATIN	2	NA	6,500	24.5	38.1
097 CHR CHS&CHS CR	1	40	54*	.2	.3
151 L-D SAINTS	20	NA	7,717	29.1	45.2
165 CH OF NAZARENE	1	21	52	.2	.3
167 CHS OF CHRIST	1	48	72	.3	.4
179 CONSRV BAPT	1	NR	NR	-	-

County and Denomination	Number of churches	Communicant, confirmed, full members	Total adherents Number	Percent of total population	Percent of total adherents
193 EPISCOPAL	1	39	42	.2	.2
203 EVAN FREE CH	1	26	35	.1	.2
207 E.L.C.A.	2	184	213	.8	1.2
355 PRESB CH (USA)	1	76	103*	.4	.6
413 S.D.A.	1	96	130*	.5	.8
419 SO BAPT CONV	2	459	623*	2.3	3.6
438 UN BRETH IN CR	1	33	33	.1	.2
449 UN METHODIST	1	345	468*	1.8	2.7
467 WESLEYAN	1	15	61	.2	.4
469 WELS	2	279	627	2.4	3.7
497 BLACK BAPT EST[2]	NA	87	118*	.4	.7
GREENLEE	**18**	**1,171**	**5,116***	**63.9**	**100.0**
019 AMER BAPT USA	1	15	20*	.2	.4
053 ASSEMB OF GOD	1	86	175	2.2	3.4
081 CATHOLIC	3	NA	2,500	31.2	48.9
081d LATIN	3	NA	2,500	31.2	48.9
151 L-D SAINTS	2	NA	969	12.1	18.9
167 CHS OF CHRIST	2	114	153	1.9	3.0
179 CONSRV BAPT	2	NR	NR	-	-
193 EPISCOPAL	1	22	32	.4	.6
355 PRESB CH (USA)	1	106	144*	1.8	2.8
419 SO BAPT CONV	3	762	1,033*	12.9	20.2
449 UN METHODIST	1	53	72*	.9	1.4
469 WELS	1	13	18	.2	.4
LA PAZ	**22**	**490**	**6,848***	**49.5**	**100.0**
053 ASSEMB OF GOD	2	139	270	2.0	3.9
081 CATHOLIC	4	NA	5,000	36.1	73.0
081d LATIN	4	NA	5,000	36.1	73.0
089 CHR & MISS AL	1	44	94	.7	1.4
151 L-D SAINTS	4	NA	963	7.0	14.1
165 CH OF NAZARENE	2	74	151	1.1	2.2
167 CHS OF CHRIST	1	28	40	.3	.6
179 CONSRV BAPT	3	NR	NR	-	-
259 IFCA	1	NR	NR	-	-
283 LUTH—MO SYNOD	1	82	109	.8	1.6
339 PENT CH OF GOD	2	70	154	1.1	2.2
413 S.D.A.	1	53	67*	.5	1.0
MARICOPA	**1,266**	**276,033**	**896,620***	**42.3**	**100.0**
005 AME ZION	1	68	87	-	-
011 A.W.M.C.	1	25	32*	-	-
019 AMER BAPT USA	27	8,158	10,331*	.5	1.2
039 AP CHR CH(NAZ)	2	187	237*	-	-
040 AP CHR CH-AMER	1	175	310	-	-
045 APOSTOLIC LUTH	1	10	30	-	-
053 ASSEMB OF GOD	78	19,688	30,347	1.4	3.4
057 BAPT GEN CONF	7	607	769*	-	.1
059 BAPT MISS ASSN	2	26	33*	-	-
081 CATHOLIC	88	NA	325,438	15.3	36.3
081b BYZAN RUTH	2	NA	1,355	.1	.2
081c CHALDEAN	1	NA	300	-	-
081d LATIN	83	NA	323,177	15.2	36.0
081f MELKITE-GK	1	NA	523	-	.1
081h UKRAINIAN	1	NA	83	-	-
089 CHR & MISS AL	7	230	446	-	-
093 CHR CH (DISC)	10	2,362	2,989	.1	.3
097 CHR CHS&CHS CR	38	11,156	14,128*	.7	1.6
105 CHRISTIAN REF	4	685	1,012	-	.1
111 CH CR,SCIENTST	11	NR	NR	-	-
121 CH GOD (ABR)	2	398	504*	-	.1
123 CH GOD (ANDER)	9	1,712	1,837	.1	.2
127 CH GOD (CLEVE)	20	1,709	2,164*	.1	.2
133 CH GOD(7TH)DEN	1	15	27	-	-
143 CG IN CR(MENN)	1	107	136*	-	-
145 CH GOD PROPHCY	5	167	211*	-	-
151 L-D SAINTS	260	NA	115,080	5.4	12.8
157 CH OF BRETHREN	3	276	350*	-	-
163 CH OF LUTH BR	2	70	147	-	-
164 CH LUTH CONF	1	88	142	-	-
165 CH OF NAZARENE	30	5,986	8,484	.4	.9
167 CHS OF CHRIST	47	6,538	8,581	.4	1.0
175 CONGR CHR CHS	2	446	565*	-	.1
179 CONSRV BAPT	34	NR	NR	-	-
193 EPISCOPAL	26	11,216	15,191	.7	1.7
203 EVAN FREE CH	7	549	1,108	.1	.1
207 E.L.C.A.	52	28,892	38,723	1.8	4.3
209 EVAN LUTH SYN	1	31	43	-	-
215 EVAN METH CH	3	176	223*	-	-
216 EVAN PRESBY CH	1	40	40	-	-
217 FIRE BAPTIZED	3	13	16*	-	-
221 FREE METHODIST	12	581	801	-	.1
223 FREE WILL BAPT	10	677	857*	-	.1
226 FRIENDS-USA	5	281	337*	-	-
226e FUM	2	159	183	-	-

NA–Not applicable   NR–Not reported   *Total adherents estimated from known number of communicant, confirmed, full members.   - Represents a percent less than 0.1.   Percentages may not total due to rounding.

[1]See Appendix E   [2]See Appendix F   [3]See Appendix G   Lines in *italic* represent a breakdown of Catholic rites or Friends affiliations. They are included in their respective denominational total.

48

Table 4. Churches and Church Membership by County and Denomination: 1990

County and Denomination	Number of churches	Communicant, confirmed, full members	Total adherents Number	Percent of total population	Percent of total adherents
226f *INDEPENDNT*	3	122	154*	-	-
237 GC MENN BR CHS	1	43	54*	-	-
246 GREEK ORTHODOX	4	NR	NR	-	-
249 AP CATH ASSYR	0	48	0	-	-
259 IFCA	3	NR	NR	-	-
263 INT FOURSQ GOS	15	2,291	2,901*	.1	.3
283 LUTH—MO SYNOD	29	11,488	15,071	.7	1.7
284 LUTH-CH-AM ASC	1	7	10	-	-
285 MENNONITE CH	11	991	1,401	.1	.2
287 MENN GEN CONF	3	136	163	-	-
291 MISSIONARY CH	4	981	1,154	.1	.1
293 MORAV CH-NORTH	1	80	121	-	-
325 OLD REG BAPT	1	9	11*	-	-
329 OPEN BIBLE STD	1	NR	NR	-	-
331 ORTH CH IN AM	1	NR	NR	-	-
339 PENT CH OF GOD	18	618	1,382	.1	.2
349 PENT HOLINESS	7	188	238*	-	-
353 CHR BRETHREN	4	452	718	-	.1
355 PRESB CH (USA)	41	15,491	19,617*	.9	2.2
356 PRESB CH AMER	7	387	488	-	.1
371 REF CH IN AM	6	1,090	2,066	.1	.2
375 REF EPISCOPAL	1	11	12	-	-
397 ROMANIAN ORTH	1	NR	NR	-	-
403 SALVATION ARMY	7	1,126	1,205	.1	.1
413 S.D.A.	23	4,840	6,129*	.3	.7
419 SO BAPT CONV	102	71,762	90,877*	4.3	10.1
435 UNITARIAN-UNIV	5	970	1,282	.1	.1
436 UNITED BAPT	1	15	19*	-	-
438 UN BRETH IN CR	3	165	165	-	-
443 UN C OF CHRIST	17	9,817	12,432*	.6	1.4
449 UN METHODIST	50	29,642	37,538*	1.8	4.2
467 WESLEYAN	6	191	738	-	.1
469 WELS	15	4,009	5,368	.3	.6
496 JEWISH EST[1]	17	NA	50,000	2.4	5.6
497 BLACK BAPT EST[2]	NA	15,840	20,059*	.9	2.2
498 INDEP.CHARIS.[3]	18	NA	16,495	.8	1.8
499 INDEP.NON-CHAR[3]	27	NA	27,150	1.3	3.0
MOHAVE	**74**	**8,950**	**24,048***	**25.7**	**100.0**
053 ASSEMB OF GOD	6	350	598	.6	2.5
081 CATHOLIC	4	NA	8,947	9.6	37.2
081d *LATIN*	4	*NA*	*8,947*	*9.6*	*37.2*
089 CHR & MISS AL	2	69	213	.2	.9
097 CHR CHS&CHS CR	5	430	524*	.6	2.2
111 CH CR,SCIENTST	2	NR	NR	-	-
151 L-D SAINTS	9	NA	3,482	3.7	14.5
165 CH OF NAZARENE	2	200	338	.4	1.4
167 CHS OF CHRIST	4	310	401	.4	1.7
179 CONSRV BAPT	2	NR	NR	-	-
193 EPISCOPAL	3	247	313	.3	1.3
207 E.L.C.A.	3	1,036	1,340	1.4	5.6
209 EVAN LUTH SYN	2	170	199	.2	.8
221 FREE METHODIST	1	40	58	.1	.2
259 IFCA	1	NR	NR	-	-
263 INT FOURSQ GOS	4	125	152*	.2	.6
283 LUTH—MO SYNOD	2	283	363	.4	1.5
339 PENT CH OF GOD	1	34	77	.1	.3
355 PRESB CH (USA)	2	479	584*	.6	2.4
403 SALVATION ARMY	1	20	20	-	.1
413 S.D.A.	3	281	343*	.4	1.4
419 SO BAPT CONV	10	3,594	4,384*	4.7	18.2
438 UN BRETH IN CR	1	58	72	.1	.3
449 UN METHODIST	3	1,104	1,347*	1.4	5.6
469 WELS	1	120	193	.2	.8
496 JEWISH EST[1]	0	NA	100	.1	.4
NAVAJO	**144**	**8,556**	**36,332***	**46.8**	**100.0**
019 AMER BAPT USA	4	177	255*	.3	.7
053 ASSEMB OF GOD	13	657	1,024	1.3	2.8
081 CATHOLIC	12	NA	5,311	6.8	14.6
081d *LATIN*	12	*NA*	*5,311*	*6.8*	*14.6*
089 CHR & MISS AL	2	17	55	.1	.2
097 CHR CHS&CHS CR	2	295	425*	.5	1.2
111 CH CR,SCIENTST	1	NR	NR	-	-
127 CH GOD (CLEVE)	2	48	69*	.1	.2
151 L-D SAINTS	37	NA	17,525	22.6	48.2
165 CH OF NAZARENE	9	384	476	.6	1.3
167 CHS OF CHRIST	8	307	404	.5	1.1
179 CONSRV BAPT	2	NR	NR	-	-
193 EPISCOPAL	3	262	349	.4	1.0
207 E.L.C.A.	2	324	508	.7	1.4
226 FRIENDS-USA	2	25	36*	-	.1
226b *EFI*	2	*25*	*36**	-	*.1*
283 LUTH—MO SYNOD	1	34	86	.1	.2
287 MENN GEN CONF	3	0	0	-	-
339 PENT CH OF GOD	6	205	460	.6	1.3
353 CHR BRETHREN	2	65	125	.2	.3

County and Denomination	Number of churches	Communicant, confirmed, full members	Total adherents Number	Percent of total population	Percent of total adherents
355 PRESB CH (USA)	4	266	384*	.5	1.1
413 S.D.A.	2	432	623*	.8	1.7
419 SO BAPT CONV	14	3,619	5,220*	6.7	14.4
438 UN BRETH IN CR	1	18	18	-	-
449 UN METHODIST	3	453	653*	.8	1.8
467 WESLEYAN	2	26	350	.5	1.0
469 WELS	7	821	1,801	2.3	5.0
497 BLACK BAPT EST[2]	NA	121	175*	.2	.5
PIMA	**367**	**77,902**	**325,335***	**48.8**	**100.0**
019 AMER BAPT USA	3	687	858*	.1	.3
040 AP CHR CH-AMER	1	35	60	-	-
053 ASSEMB OF GOD	21	2,785	5,580	.8	1.7
057 BAPT GEN CONF	1	108	135*	-	-
059 BAPT MISS ASSN	2	43	54*	-	-
071 BRETHREN (ASH)	2	144	180*	-	.1
081 CATHOLIC	39	NA	178,448	26.8	54.9
081b *BYZAN RUTH*	1	*NA*	*175*		*.1*
081d *LATIN*	37	*NA*	*178,190*	*26.7*	*54.8*
081h *UKRAINIAN*	1	*NA*	*83*		
089 CHR & MISS AL	5	118	467	.1	.1
093 CHR CH (DISC)	7	1,290	1,436	.2	.4
097 CHR CHS&CHS CR	8	1,578	1,971*	.3	.6
105 CHRISTIAN REF	2	181	263	-	.1
111 CH CR,SCIENTST	5	NR	NR	-	-
123 CH GOD (ANDER)	4	294	319	-	.1
127 CH GOD (CLEVE)	7	764	954*	.1	.3
145 CH GOD PROPHCY	1	34	42*	-	-
151 L-D SAINTS	35	NA	14,064	2.1	4.3
157 CH OF BRETHREN	1	80	100*	-	-
165 CH OF NAZARENE	13	1,569	1,975	.3	.6
167 CHS OF CHRIST	19	1,759	2,326	.3	.7
179 CONSRV BAPT	15	NR	NR	-	-
185 CUMBER PRESB	1	86	123	-	-
193 EPISCOPAL	10	5,480	6,872	1.0	2.1
203 EVAN FREE CH	4	594	1,043	.2	.3
207 E.L.C.A.	16	6,831	9,216	1.4	2.8
216 EVAN PRESBY CH	1	0	0	-	-
220 FREE LUTHERAN	1	30	36	-	-
221 FREE METHODIST	2	80	123	-	-
223 FREE WILL BAPT	1	72	90*	-	-
226 FRIENDS-USA	2	136	177*	-	.1
226e *FUM*	1	*64*	*87*		
226f *INDEPENDNT*	1	*72*	*90**		
246 GREEK ORTHODOX	1	NR	NR	-	-
259 IFCA	1	NR	NR	-	-
263 INT FOURSQ GOS	8	550	687*	.1	.2
283 LUTH—MO SYNOD	9	3,304	4,885	.7	1.5
285 MENNONITE CH	1	60	114	-	-
287 MENN GEN CONF	1	17	28	-	-
339 PENT CH OF GOD	2	68	154	-	-
353 CHR BRETHREN	2	110	275	-	.1
355 PRESB CH (USA)	14	7,661	9,568*	1.4	2.9
356 PRESB CH AMER	1	52	87	-	-
371 REF CH IN AM	2	165	385	.1	.1
403 SALVATION ARMY	3	273	293	-	.1
413 S.D.A.	5	1,563	1,952*	.3	.6
419 SO BAPT CONV	40	21,961	27,428*	4.1	8.4
435 UNITARIAN-UNIV	2	425	554	.1	.2
443 UN C OF CHRIST	4	1,778	2,221*	.3	.7
449 UN METHODIST	15	9,159	11,439*	1.7	3.5
467 WESLEYAN	3	154	556	.1	.2
469 WELS	5	1,388	1,732	.3	.5
496 JEWISH EST[1]	8	NA	20,000	3.0	6.1
497 BLACK BAPT EST[2]	NA	4,436	5,540*	.8	1.7
498 INDEP.CHARIS.[3]	7	NA	4,975	.7	1.5
499 INDEP.NON-CHAR[3]	4	NA	5,550	.8	1.7
PINAL	**148**	**15,686**	**54,536***	**46.9**	**100.0**
053 ASSEMB OF GOD	20	1,228	2,326	2.0	4.3
081 CATHOLIC	12	NA	26,950	23.2	49.4
081d *LATIN*	12	*NA*	*26,950*	*23.2*	*49.4*
089 CHR & MISS AL	1	8	17	-	-
093 CHR CH (DISC)	2	70	86	.1	.2
097 CHR CHS&CHS CR	4	652	850*	.7	1.6
111 CH CR,SCIENTST	2	NR	NR	-	-
123 CH GOD (ANDER)	1	23	29	-	.1
127 CH GOD (CLEVE)	3	121	158*	.1	.3
145 CH GOD PROPHCY	1	34	44*	-	.1
151 L-D SAINTS	13	NA	5,041	4.3	9.2
165 CH OF NAZARENE	2	344	527	.5	1.0
167 CHS OF CHRIST	10	551	711	.6	1.3
179 CONSRV BAPT	6	NR	NR	-	-
193 EPISCOPAL	3	313	399	.3	.7
207 E.L.C.A.	3	606	763	.7	1.4
215 EVAN METH CH	3	118	154*	.1	.3
223 FREE WILL BAPT	1	9	12*	-	-

NA–Not applicable NR–Not reported *Total adherents estimated from known number of communicant, confirmed, full members. - Represents a percent less than 0.1. Percentages may not total due to rounding.
[1]See Appendix E [2]See Appendix F [3]See Appendix G Lines in *italic* represent a breakdown of Catholic rites or Friends affiliations. They are included in their respective denominational total.

Table 4. Churches and Church Membership by County and Denomination: 1990

County and Denomination	Number of churches	Communicant, confirmed, full members	Total adherents		
			Number	Percent of total population	Percent of total adherents
283 LUTH—MO SYNOD	3	592	740	.6	1.4
339 PENT CH OF GOD	2	68	154	.1	.3
349 PENT HOLINESS	4	99	129*	.1	.2
355 PRESB CH (USA)	9	1,507	1,965*	1.7	3.6
403 SALVATION ARMY	1	49	52	-	.1
413 S.D.A.	4	250	326*	.3	.6
419 SO BAPT CONV	27	7,456	9,720*	8.4	17.8
449 UN METHODIST	6	777	1,013*	.9	1.9
467 WESLEYAN	2	71	394	.3	.7
469 WELS	2	110	155	.1	.3
497 BLACK BAPT EST[2]	NA	630	821*	.7	1.5
499 INDEP.NON-CHAR[3]	1	NA	1,000	.9	1.8
SANTA CRUZ	**24**	**901**	**14,258***	**48.0**	**100.0**
053 ASSEMB OF GOD	3	208	431	1.5	3.0
081 CATHOLIC	9	NA	12,850	43.3	90.1
081d LATIN	*9*	*NA*	*12,850*	*43.3*	*90.1*
167 CHS OF CHRIST	1	26	34	.1	.2
179 CONSRV BAPT	1	NR	NR	-	-
193 EPISCOPAL	1	120	180	.6	1.3
220 FREE LUTHERAN	1	60	94	.3	.7
283 LUTH—MO SYNOD	1	19	30	.1	.2
413 S.D.A.	3	199	272*	.9	1.9
419 SO BAPT CONV	1	66	90*	.3	.6
443 UN C OF CHRIST	1	100	136*	.5	1.0
449 UN METHODIST	2	103	141*	.5	1.0
YAVAPAI	**148**	**12,604**	**30,060***	**27.9**	**100.0**
011 A.W.M.C.	1	0	0*	-	-
019 AMER BAPT USA	3	220	265*	.2	.9
053 ASSEMB OF GOD	13	1,219	2,085	1.9	6.9
081 CATHOLIC	16	NA	8,420	7.8	28.0
081d LATIN	*16*	*NA*	*8,420*	*7.8*	*28.0*
089 CHR & MISS AL	1	117	327	.3	1.1
093 CHR CH (DISC)	1	166	179	.2	.6
097 CHR CHS&CHS CR	4	485	584*	.5	1.9
111 CH CR,SCIENTST	1	NR	NR	-	-
123 CH GOD (ANDER)	2	110	110	.1	.4
127 CH GOD (CLEVE)	1	15	18*	-	.1
151 L-D SAINTS	14	NA	4,644	4.3	15.4
165 CH OF NAZARENE	4	454	676	.6	2.2
167 CHS OF CHRIST	12	526	680	.6	2.3
179 CONSRV BAPT	7	NR	NR	-	-
193 EPISCOPAL	3	659	766	.7	2.5
203 EVAN FREE CH	2	134	170	.2	.6
207 E.L.C.A.	1	743	946	.9	3.1
215 EVAN METH CH	1	0	0*	-	-
221 FREE METHODIST	1	120	120	.1	.4
226 FRIENDS-USA	1	4	12	-	-
226f INDEPENDNT	*1*	*4*	*12*	*-*	*-*
259 IFCA	1	NR	NR	-	-
263 INT FOURSQ GOS	3	150	181*	.2	.6
283 LUTH—MO SYNOD	5	610	751	.7	2.5
285 MENNONITE CH	1	17	32	-	.1
287 MENN GEN CONF	1	11	13	-	-
339 PENT CH OF GOD	2	70	154	.1	.5
355 PRESB CH (USA)	4	512	616*	.6	2.0
356 PRESB CH AMER	1	54	61	.1	.2
371 REF CH IN AM	1	143	215	.2	.7
403 SALVATION ARMY	1	73	87	.1	.3
413 S.D.A.	5	572	688*	.6	2.3
419 SO BAPT CONV	16	2,778	3,343*	3.1	11.1
435 UNITARIAN-UNIV	1	77	97	.1	.3
443 UN C OF CHRIST	4	659	793*	.7	2.6
449 UN METHODIST	7	1,544	1,858*	1.7	6.2
469 WELS	5	362	469	.4	1.6
496 JEWISH EST[1]	0	NA	150	.1	.5
498 INDEP.CHARIS.[3]	1	NA	550	.5	1.8
YUMA	**84**	**12,378**	**39,427***	**36.9**	**100.0**
019 AMER BAPT USA	1	60	78*	.1	.2
053 ASSEMB OF GOD	11	745	2,022	1.9	5.1
081 CATHOLIC	6	NA	17,950	16.8	45.5
081d LATIN	*6*	*NA*	*17,950*	*16.8*	*45.5*
089 CHR & MISS AL	1	0	21	-	.1
097 CHR CHS&CHS CR	2	1,420	1,854*	1.7	4.7
111 CH CR,SCIENTST	1	NR	NR	-	-
123 CH GOD (ANDER)	2	55	100	.1	.3
127 CH GOD (CLEVE)	1	99	129*	.1	.3
145 CH GOD PROPHCY	1	34	44*	-	.1
151 L-D SAINTS	9	NA	3,093	2.9	7.8
163 CH OF LUTH BR	1	65	196	.2	.5
165 CH OF NAZARENE	6	531	708	.7	1.8
167 CHS OF CHRIST	7	450	604	.6	1.5
179 CONSRV BAPT	4	NR	NR	-	-
193 EPISCOPAL	1	509	805	.8	2.0

County and Denomination	Number of churches	Communicant, confirmed, full members	Total adherents		
			Number	Percent of total population	Percent of total adherents
207 E.L.C.A.	1	253	339	.3	.9
263 INT FOURSQ GOS	1	0	0*	-	-
283 LUTH—MO SYNOD	2	553	948	.9	2.4
339 PENT CH OF GOD	1	34	77	.1	.2
355 PRESB CH (USA)	5	620	810*	.8	2.1
356 PRESB CH AMER	1	17	18	-	-
403 SALVATION ARMY	1	138	145	.1	.4
413 S.D.A.	2	418	546*	.5	1.4
419 SO BAPT CONV	8	4,831	6,309*	5.9	16.0
435 UNITARIAN-UNIV	1	24	28	-	.1
449 UN METHODIST	5	896	1,170*	1.1	3.0
469 WELS	1	98	143	.1	.4
496 JEWISH EST[1]	0	NA	100	.1	.3
497 BLACK BAPT EST[2]	NA	528	690*	.6	1.8
498 INDEP.CHARIS.[3]	1	NA	500	.5	1.3

ARKANSAS

County and Denomination	Number of churches	Communicant, confirmed, full members	Total adherents		
			Number	Percent of total population	Percent of total adherents
THE STATE.....	5,209	1,033,124	1,425,192*	60.6	100.0
ARKANSAS	**57**	**11,136**	**14,992***	**69.2**	**100.0**
053 ASSEMB OF GOD	4	349	431	2.0	2.9
059 BAPT MISS ASSN	8	767	972*	4.5	6.5
081 CATHOLIC	2	NA	630	2.9	4.2
081d LATIN	*2*	*NA*	*630*	*2.9*	*4.2*
093 CHR CH (DISC)	1	147	314	1.5	2.1
097 CHR CHS&CHS CR	2	218	276*	1.3	1.8
165 CH OF NAZARENE	2	69	104	.5	.7
167 CHS OF CHRIST	3	208	270	1.2	1.8
193 EPISCOPAL	1	47	103	.5	.7
207 E.L.C.A.	1	175	224	1.0	1.5
215 EVAN METH CH	1	189	240*	1.1	1.6
226 FRIENDS-USA	1	13	16*	.1	.1
226g INDEP EVAN	*1*	*13*	*16**	*.1*	*.1*
283 LUTH—MO SYNOD	3	832	1,054	4.9	7.0
339 PENT CH OF GOD	2	69	153	.7	1.0
355 PRESB CH (USA)	1	151	191*	.9	1.3
419 SO BAPT CONV	11	3,900	4,942*	22.8	33.0
449 UN METHODIST	14	2,864	3,630*	16.8	24.2
497 BLACK BAPT EST[2]	NA	1,138	1,442*	6.7	9.6
ASHLEY	**75**	**15,754**	**21,108***	**86.8**	**100.0**
005 AME ZION	8	969	1,282	5.3	6.1
053 ASSEMB OF GOD	5	291	513	2.1	2.4
059 BAPT MISS ASSN	2	317	404*	1.7	1.9
081 CATHOLIC	2	NA	300	1.2	1.4
081d LATIN	*2*	*NA*	*300*	*1.2*	*1.4*
123 CH GOD (ANDER)	1	110	158	.6	.7
127 CH GOD (CLEVE)	1	48	61*	.3	.3
151 L-D SAINTS	1	NA	100	.4	.5
165 CH OF NAZARENE	1	0	0	-	-
167 CHS OF CHRIST	6	530	661	2.7	3.1
193 EPISCOPAL	1	43	74	.3	.4
223 FREE WILL BAPT	3	698	890*	3.7	4.2
283 LUTH—MO SYNOD	1	23	34	.1	.2
339 PENT CH OF GOD	2	69	152	.6	.7
355 PRESB CH (USA)	1	112	143*	.6	.7
419 SO BAPT CONV	29	8,925	11,374*	46.8	53.9
449 UN METHODIST	10	1,353	1,724*	7.1	8.2
497 BLACK BAPT EST[2]	NA	2,266	2,888*	11.9	13.7
498 INDEP.CHARIS.[3]	1	NA	350	1.4	1.7
BAXTER	**64**	**10,166**	**16,541***	**53.0**	**100.0**
053 ASSEMB OF GOD	5	370	1,013	3.2	6.1
059 BAPT MISS ASSN	1	38	45*	.1	.3
081 CATHOLIC	1	NA	3,000	9.6	18.1
081d LATIN	*1*	*NA*	*3,000*	*9.6*	*18.1*
093 CHR CH (DISC)	1	215	269	.9	1.6
097 CHR CHS&CHS CR	1	250	294*	.9	1.8
111 CH CR,SCIENTST	1	NR	NR	-	-
127 CH GOD (CLEVE)	1	31	36*	.1	.2
151 L-D SAINTS	1	NA	265	.8	1.6
165 CH OF NAZARENE	1	104	186	.6	1.1
167 CHS OF CHRIST	18	1,044	1,356	4.3	8.2
185 CUMBER PRESB	2	301	318	1.0	1.9
193 EPISCOPAL	1	86	97	.3	.6
207 E.L.C.A.	1	125	134	.4	.8
220 FREE LUTHERAN	1	44	55	.2	.3
223 FREE WILL BAPT	1	54	63*	.2	.4
259 IFCA	1	NR	NR	-	-
283 LUTH—MO SYNOD	1	1,145	1,275	4.1	7.7
285 MENNONITE CH	1	12	28	.1	.2

NA–Not applicable NR–Not reported *Total adherents estimated from known number of communicant, confirmed, full members. - Represents a percent less than 0.1. Percentages may not total due to rounding.
[1]See Appendix E [2]See Appendix F [3]See Appendix G Lines in *italic* represent a breakdown of Catholic rites or Friends affiliations. They are included in their respective denominational total.

Table 4. Churches and Church Membership by County and Denomination: 1990

County and Denomination	Number of churches	Communicant, confirmed, full members	Total adherents Number	Percent of total population	Percent of total adherents
355 PRESB CH (USA)	3	337	396*	1.3	2.4
413 S.D.A.	1	92	108*	.3	.7
419 SO BAPT CONV	14	4,365	5,130*	16.4	31.0
435 UNITARIAN-UNIV	1	37	37	.1	.2
449 UN METHODIST	3	1,476	1,735*	5.6	10.5
469 WELS	1	40	51	.2	.3
499 INDEP.NON-CHAR[3]	1	NA	650	2.1	3.9
BENTON	**180**	**39,088**	**56,532***	**58.0**	**100.0**
019 AMER BAPT USA	1	46	57*	.1	.1
053 ASSEMB OF GOD	13	1,199	2,204	2.3	3.9
059 BAPT MISS ASSN	18	2,035	2,532*	2.6	4.5
081 CATHOLIC	4	NA	3,744	3.8	6.6
081d LATIN	*4*	*NA*	*3,744*	*3.8*	*6.6*
093 CHR CH (DISC)	5	911	1,073	1.1	1.9
097 CHR CHS&CHS CR	8	1,210	1,505*	1.5	2.7
111 CH CR,SCIENTST	2	NR	NR	-	-
127 CH GOD (CLEVE)	1	114	142*	.1	.3
143 CG IN CR(MENN)	1	93	116*	.1	.2
145 CH GOD PROPHCY	1	28	35*	-	.1
151 L-D SAINTS	2	NA	681	.7	1.2
165 CH OF NAZARENE	6	799	1,419	1.5	2.5
167 CHS OF CHRIST	16	1,990	2,605	2.7	4.6
193 EPISCOPAL	3	562	682	.7	1.2
203 EVAN FREE CH	2	41	83	.1	.1
207 E.L.C.A.	2	1,333	1,518	1.6	2.7
217 FIRE BAPTIZED	1	18	22*	-	-
221 FREE METHODIST	1	18	25	-	-
223 FREE WILL BAPT	7	507	631*	.6	1.1
237 GC MENN BR CHS	1	42	52*	.1	.1
259 IFCA	4	NR	NR	-	-
263 INT FOURSQ GOS	1	35	44*	-	.1
283 LUTH—MO SYNOD	4	656	797	.8	1.4
285 MENNONITE CH	1	0	14	-	-
331 ORTH CH IN AM	1	NR	NR	-	-
339 PENT CH OF GOD	3	77	197	.2	.3
349 PENT HOLINESS	4	137	170*	.2	.3
355 PRESB CH (USA)	7	1,368	1,702*	1.7	3.0
361 PRIM BAPT ASCS	1	35	44*	-	.1
403 SALVATION ARMY	1	27	27	-	-
413 S.D.A.	6	1,355	1,686*	1.7	3.0
419 SO BAPT CONV	29	19,060	23,714*	24.3	41.9
449 UN METHODIST	18	5,306	6,602*	6.8	11.7
467 WESLEYAN	2	86	119	.1	.2
499 INDEP.NON-CHAR[3]	3	NA	2,290	2.3	4.1
BOONE	**81**	**11,616**	**16,040***	**56.7**	**100.0**
053 ASSEMB OF GOD	8	760	1,516	5.4	9.5
059 BAPT MISS ASSN	1	56	69*	.2	.4
061 BEACHY AMISH	1	15	19*	.1	.1
081 CATHOLIC	1	NA	700	2.5	4.4
081d LATIN	*1*	*NA*	*700*	*2.5*	*4.4*
089 CHR & MISS AL	1	33	78	.3	.5
093 CHR CH (DISC)	3	516	630	2.2	3.9
097 CHR CHS&CHS CR	1	35	43*	.2	.3
123 CH GOD (ANDER)	1	82	82	.3	.5
127 CH GOD (CLEVE)	1	71	88*	.3	.5
151 L-D SAINTS	1	NA	234	.8	1.5
165 CH OF NAZARENE	1	40	68	.2	.4
167 CHS OF CHRIST	14	907	1,182	4.2	7.4
185 CUMBER PRESB	1	71	74	.3	.5
193 EPISCOPAL	1	166	248	.9	1.5
207 E.L.C.A.	1	54	62	.2	.4
223 FREE WILL BAPT	2	81	100*	.4	.6
283 LUTH—MO SYNOD	1	216	263	.9	1.6
339 PENT CH OF GOD	1	34	77	.3	.5
353 CHR BRETHREN	1	25	50	.2	.3
355 PRESB CH (USA)	2	535	662*	2.3	4.1
413 S.D.A.	1	142	176*	.6	1.1
419 SO BAPT CONV	25	6,452	7,980*	28.2	49.8
436 UNITED BAPT	1	47	58*	.2	.4
449 UN METHODIST	10	1,278	1,581*	5.6	9.9
BRADLEY	**49**	**8,199**	**10,401***	**88.2**	**100.0**
005 AME ZION	1	100	114	1.0	1.1
053 ASSEMB OF GOD	1	154	300	2.5	2.9
055 AS REF PRES CH	1	33	33	.3	.3
059 BAPT MISS ASSN	7	1,022	1,274*	10.8	12.2
081 CATHOLIC	1	NA	20	.2	.2
081d LATIN	*1*	*NA*	*20*	*.2*	*.2*
127 CH GOD (CLEVE)	1	46	57*	.5	.5
167 CHS OF CHRIST	3	125	160	1.4	1.5
223 FREE WILL BAPT	6	640	798*	6.8	7.7
339 PENT CH OF GOD	2	68	153	1.3	1.5
355 PRESB CH (USA)	3	206	257*	2.2	2.5
361 PRIM BAPT ASCS	1	6	7*	.1	.1

County and Denomination	Number of churches	Communicant, confirmed, full members	Total adherents Number	Percent of total population	Percent of total adherents
419 SO BAPT CONV	14	3,572	4,452*	37.8	42.8
449 UN METHODIST	8	978	1,219*	10.3	11.7
497 BLACK BAPT EST[2]	NA	1,249	1,557*	13.2	15.0
CALHOUN	**28**	**2,989**	**3,783***	**64.9**	**100.0**
053 ASSEMB OF GOD	3	164	215	3.7	5.7
059 BAPT MISS ASSN	10	663	841*	14.4	22.2
167 CHS OF CHRIST	2	186	242	4.2	6.4
185 CUMBER PRESB	1	207	240	4.1	6.3
361 PRIM BAPT ASCS	2	79	100*	1.7	2.6
419 SO BAPT CONV	5	1,003	1,273*	21.9	33.7
449 UN METHODIST	5	339	430*	7.4	11.4
497 BLACK BAPT EST[2]	NA	348	442*	7.6	11.7
CARROLL	**62**	**7,242**	**10,114***	**54.2**	**100.0**
053 ASSEMB OF GOD	5	563	1,135	6.1	11.2
057 BAPT GEN CONF	1	257	316*	1.7	3.1
059 BAPT MISS ASSN	1	19	23*	.1	.2
081 CATHOLIC	2	NA	220	1.2	2.2
081d LATIN	*2*	*NA*	*220*	*1.2*	*2.2*
093 CHR CH (DISC)	1	158	206	1.1	2.0
097 CHR CHS&CHS CR	2	206	253*	1.4	2.5
111 CH CR,SCIENTST	1	NR	NR	-	-
151 L-D SAINTS	1	NA	99	.5	1.0
165 CH OF NAZARENE	2	53	157	.8	1.6
167 CHS OF CHRIST	5	249	324	1.7	3.2
193 EPISCOPAL	1	73	80	.4	.8
223 FREE WILL BAPT	6	410	504*	2.7	5.0
259 IFCA	1	NR	NR	-	-
283 LUTH—MO SYNOD	1	124	164	.9	1.6
285 MENNONITE CH	2	44	51	.3	.5
353 CHR BRETHREN	1	20	40	.2	.4
355 PRESB CH (USA)	2	149	183*	1.0	1.8
413 S.D.A.	1	18	22*	.1	.2
419 SO BAPT CONV	11	3,404	4,188*	22.5	41.4
435 UNITARIAN-UNIV	1	23	38	.2	.4
436 UNITED BAPT	9	528	650*	3.5	6.4
449 UN METHODIST	4	944	1,161*	6.2	11.5
498 INDEP.CHARIS.[3]	1	NA	300	1.6	3.0
CHICOT	**34**	**7,698**	**10,730***	**68.3**	**100.0**
005 AME ZION	2	200	212	1.3	2.0
053 ASSEMB OF GOD	3	106	201	1.3	1.9
081 CATHOLIC	2	NA	500	3.2	4.7
081d LATIN	*2*	*NA*	*500*	*3.2*	*4.7*
167 CHS OF CHRIST	3	93	121	.8	1.1
193 EPISCOPAL	1	51	68	.4	.6
223 FREE WILL BAPT	3	203	270*	1.7	2.5
355 PRESB CH (USA)	3	127	169*	1.1	1.6
419 SO BAPT CONV	13	3,321	4,411*	28.1	41.1
449 UN METHODIST	4	563	748*	4.8	7.0
497 BLACK BAPT EST[2]	NA	3,034	4,030*	25.6	37.6
CLARK	**73**	**12,574**	**15,673***	**73.1**	**100.0**
053 ASSEMB OF GOD	5	207	388	1.8	2.5
059 BAPT MISS ASSN	5	817	987*	4.6	6.3
081 CATHOLIC	2	NA	180	.8	1.1
081d LATIN	*2*	*NA*	*180*	*.8*	*1.1*
093 CHR CH (DISC)	3	64	82	.4	.5
111 CH CR,SCIENTST	1	NR	NR	-	-
123 CH GOD (ANDER)	2	68	78	.4	.5
151 L-D SAINTS	1	NA	139	.6	.9
165 CH OF NAZARENE	1	36	27	.1	.2
167 CHS OF CHRIST	4	281	331	1.5	2.1
193 EPISCOPAL	1	32	44	.2	.3
223 FREE WILL BAPT	1	73	88*	.4	.6
339 PENT CH OF GOD	2	50	107	.5	.7
355 PRESB CH (USA)	4	308	372*	1.7	2.4
361 PRIM BAPT ASCS	1	13	16*	.1	.1
413 S.D.A.	1	28	34*	.2	.2
419 SO BAPT CONV	29	7,404	8,943*	41.7	57.1
449 UN METHODIST	10	2,013	2,432*	11.3	15.5
497 BLACK BAPT EST[2]	NA	1,180	1,425*	6.6	9.1
CLAY	**67**	**7,699**	**9,644***	**53.3**	**100.0**
053 ASSEMB OF GOD	3	121	198	1.1	2.1
059 BAPT MISS ASSN	5	520	629*	3.5	6.5
081 CATHOLIC	2	NA	200	1.1	2.1
081d LATIN	*2*	*NA*	*200*	*1.1*	*2.1*
097 CHR CHS&CHS CR	2	200	242*	1.3	2.5
123 CH GOD (ANDER)	1	44	64	.4	.7
165 CH OF NAZARENE	1	16	16	.1	.2
167 CHS OF CHRIST	15	1,254	1,557	8.6	16.1
223 FREE WILL BAPT	3	97	117*	.6	1.2
283 LUTH—MO SYNOD	1	95	109	.6	1.1

NA–Not applicable   NR–Not reported   *Total adherents estimated from known number of communicant, confirmed, full members.   - Represents a percent less than 0.1.   Percentages may not total due to rounding.
[1]See Appendix E   [2]See Appendix F   [3]See Appendix G   Lines in *italic* represent a breakdown of Catholic rites or Friends affiliations. They are included in their respective denominational total.

Table 4. Churches and Church Membership by County and Denomination: 1990

County and Denomination	Number of churches	Communicant, confirmed, full members	Total adherents Number	Total adherents Percent of total population	Total adherents Percent of total adherents
339 PENT CH OF GOD	1	34	77	.4	.8
355 PRESB CH (USA)	1	39	47*	.3	.5
361 PRIM BAPT ASCS	1	14	17*	.1	.2
419 SO BAPT CONV	18	3,954	4,785*	26.4	49.6
449 UN METHODIST	13	1,311	1,586*	8.8	16.4
CLEBURNE	**47**	**6,452**	**8,299***	**42.8**	**100.0**
053 ASSEMB OF GOD	2	226	526	2.7	6.3
059 BAPT MISS ASSN	4	496	594*	3.1	7.2
081 CATHOLIC	2	NA	320	1.6	3.9
081d LATIN	2	NA	320	1.6	3.9
097 CHR CHS&CHS CR	1	38	45*	.2	.5
111 CH CR,SCIENTST	1	NR	NR	-	-
127 CH GOD (CLEVE)	2	105	126*	.6	1.5
165 CH OF NAZARENE	2	50	67	.3	.8
167 CHS OF CHRIST	6	375	465	2.4	5.6
193 EPISCOPAL	1	98	115	.6	1.4
207 E.L.C.A.	1	217	245	1.3	3.0
223 FREE WILL BAPT	3	166	199*	1.0	2.4
283 LUTH—MO SYNOD	1	41	43	.2	.5
355 PRESB CH (USA)	1	176	211*	1.1	2.5
419 SO BAPT CONV	15	3,285	3,932*	20.3	47.4
449 UN METHODIST	5	1,179	1,411*	7.3	17.0
CLEVELAND	**30**	**3,028**	**3,848***	**49.5**	**100.0**
053 ASSEMB OF GOD	2	160	202	2.6	5.2
055 AS REF PRES CH	1	12	18	.2	.5
059 BAPT MISS ASSN	9	943	1,176*	15.1	30.6
123 CH GOD (ANDER)	1	65	93	1.2	2.4
151 L-D SAINTS	1	NA	62	.8	1.6
167 CHS OF CHRIST	2	64	73	.9	1.9
223 FREE WILL BAPT	3	519	647*	8.3	16.8
419 SO BAPT CONV	2	402	501*	6.4	13.0
449 UN METHODIST	9	609	759*	9.8	19.7
497 BLACK BAPT EST[2]	NA	254	317*	4.1	8.2
COLUMBIA	**69**	**14,715**	**19,007***	**74.0**	**100.0**
053 ASSEMB OF GOD	3	91	222	.9	1.2
059 BAPT MISS ASSN	23	4,700	5,920*	23.0	31.1
081 CATHOLIC	1	NA	180	.7	.9
081d LATIN	1	NA	180	.7	.9
123 CH GOD (ANDER)	1	15	20	.1	.1
151 L-D SAINTS	1	NA	152	.6	.8
165 CH OF NAZARENE	1	0	0	-	-
167 CHS OF CHRIST	8	829	1,089	4.2	5.7
185 CUMBER PRESB	2	71	71	.3	.4
193 EPISCOPAL	1	47	71	.3	.4
283 LUTH—MO SYNOD	1	38	42	.2	.2
355 PRESB CH (USA)	1	199	251*	1.0	1.3
413 S.D.A.	1	19	24*	.1	.1
419 SO BAPT CONV	6	3,561	4,485*	17.5	23.6
449 UN METHODIST	19	2,939	3,702*	14.4	19.5
497 BLACK BAPT EST[2]	NA	2,206	2,778*	10.8	14.6
CONWAY	**62**	**6,764**	**10,727***	**56.0**	**100.0**
053 ASSEMB OF GOD	4	261	488	2.5	4.5
059 BAPT MISS ASSN	10	1,792	2,266*	11.8	21.1
081 CATHOLIC	5	NA	1,770	9.2	16.5
081d LATIN	5	NA	1,770	9.2	16.5
121 CH GOD (ABR)	1	14	18*	.1	.2
145 CH GOD PROPHCY	1	28	35*	.2	.3
151 L-D SAINTS	1	NA	158	.8	1.5
165 CH OF NAZARENE	1	127	266	1.4	2.5
167 CHS OF CHRIST	16	1,283	1,564	8.2	14.6
185 CUMBER PRESB	1	96	96	.5	.9
223 FREE WILL BAPT	3	190	240*	1.3	2.2
283 LUTH—MO SYNOD	1	11	13	.1	.1
339 PENT CH OF GOD	2	68	153	.8	1.4
355 PRESB CH (USA)	2	227	287*	1.5	2.7
419 SO BAPT CONV	5	1,212	1,533*	8.0	14.3
449 UN METHODIST	9	764	966*	5.0	9.0
497 BLACK BAPT EST[2]	NA	691	874*	4.6	8.1
CRAIGHEAD	**145**	**35,422**	**47,159***	**68.4**	**100.0**
053 ASSEMB OF GOD	11	721	1,261	1.8	2.7
059 BAPT MISS ASSN	26	4,732	5,866*	8.5	12.4
081 CATHOLIC	1	NA	1,575	2.3	3.3
081d LATIN	1	NA	1,575	2.3	3.3
093 CHR CH (DISC)	2	268	367	.5	.8
097 CHR CHS&CHS CR	4	567	703*	1.0	1.5
111 CH CR,SCIENTST	1	NR	NR	-	-
127 CH GOD (CLEVE)	2	147	182*	.3	.4
133 CH GOD(7TH)DEN	1	33	43	.1	.1
145 CH GOD PROPHCY	2	55	68*	.1	.1
151 L-D SAINTS	1	NA	271	.4	.6

County and Denomination	Number of churches	Communicant, confirmed, full members	Total adherents Number	Total adherents Percent of total population	Total adherents Percent of total adherents
165 CH OF NAZARENE	4	457	704	1.0	1.5
167 CHS OF CHRIST	19	3,219	4,116	6.0	8.7
193 EPISCOPAL	1	332	463	.7	1.0
207 E.L.C.A.	1	44	55	.1	.1
223 FREE WILL BAPT	3	282	350*	.5	.7
283 LUTH—MO SYNOD	1	68	99	.1	.2
339 PENT CH OF GOD	2	68	154	.2	.3
355 PRESB CH (USA)	1	411	509*	.7	1.1
403 SALVATION ARMY	1	122	130	.2	.3
413 S.D.A.	1	58	72*	.1	.2
419 SO BAPT CONV	34	18,239	22,609*	32.8	47.9
435 UNITARIAN-UNIV	1	16	16	-	-
449 UN METHODIST	22	4,642	5,754*	8.3	12.2
467 WESLEYAN	1	15	44	.1	.1
496 JEWISH EST[1]	1	NA	0	-	-
497 BLACK BAPT EST[2]	NA	926	1,148*	1.7	2.4
498 INDEP.CHARIS.[3]	1	NA	600	.9	1.3
CRAWFORD	**94**	**15,337**	**22,623***	**53.2**	**100.0**
053 ASSEMB OF GOD	16	1,777	3,893	9.2	17.2
059 BAPT MISS ASSN	2	101	130*	.3	.6
081 CATHOLIC	1	NA	520	1.2	2.3
081d LATIN	1	NA	520	1.2	2.3
089 CHR & MISS AL	1	28	51	.1	.2
093 CHR CH (DISC)	3	192	269	.6	1.2
123 CH GOD (ANDER)	1	56	67	.2	.3
151 L-D SAINTS	1	NA	365	.9	1.6
165 CH OF NAZARENE	2	297	413	1.0	1.8
167 CHS OF CHRIST	10	614	820	1.9	3.6
171 CH GOD-GEN CON	1	22	28*	.1	.1
193 EPISCOPAL	1	110	169	.4	.7
223 FREE WILL BAPT	15	1,285	1,660*	3.9	7.3
283 LUTH—MO SYNOD	1	43	59	.1	.3
339 PENT CH OF GOD	7	247	480	1.1	2.1
349 PENT HOLINESS	1	30	39*	.1	.2
355 PRESB CH (USA)	3	447	578*	1.4	2.6
419 SO BAPT CONV	18	8,568	11,070*	26.1	48.9
449 UN METHODIST	10	1,520	1,964*	4.6	8.7
496 JEWISH EST[1]	0	NA	48	.1	.2
CRITTENDEN	**58**	**19,560**	**28,071***	**56.2**	**100.0**
053 ASSEMB OF GOD	5	391	663	1.3	2.4
059 BAPT MISS ASSN	1	311	415*	.8	1.5
081 CATHOLIC	3	NA	1,200	2.4	4.3
081d LATIN	3	NA	1,200	2.4	4.3
093 CHR CH (DISC)	1	34	53	.1	.2
097 CHR CHS&CHS CR	1	0	0*	-	-
127 CH GOD (CLEVE)	4	264	353*	.7	1.3
145 CH GOD PROPHCY	1	28	37*	.1	.1
151 L-D SAINTS	1	NA	207	.4	.7
165 CH OF NAZARENE	2	142	182	.4	.6
167 CHS OF CHRIST	7	1,280	1,593	3.2	5.7
193 EPISCOPAL	1	161	184	.4	.7
283 LUTH—MO SYNOD	1	83	90	.2	.3
339 PENT CH OF GOD	3	89	176	.4	.6
355 PRESB CH (USA)	3	343	458*	.9	1.6
413 S.D.A.	2	51	68*	.1	.2
419 SO BAPT CONV	16	9,669	12,915*	25.9	46.0
449 UN METHODIST	6	2,050	2,738*	5.5	9.8
496 JEWISH EST[1]	0	NA	509	1.0	1.8
497 BLACK BAPT EST[2]	NA	4,664	6,230*	12.5	22.2
CROSS	**51**	**9,936**	**13,785***	**71.7**	**100.0**
053 ASSEMB OF GOD	10	710	1,072	5.6	7.8
059 BAPT MISS ASSN	3	379	491*	2.6	3.6
081 CATHOLIC	1	NA	720	3.7	5.2
081d LATIN	1	NA	720	3.7	5.2
127 CH GOD (CLEVE)	4	374	485*	2.5	3.5
145 CH GOD PROPHCY	1	28	36*	.2	.3
157 CH OF BRETHREN	1	56	73*	.4	.5
165 CH OF NAZARENE	1	0	0	-	-
167 CHS OF CHRIST	4	372	507	2.6	3.7
193 EPISCOPAL	1	6	15	.1	.1
223 FREE WILL BAPT	1	43	56*	.3	.4
355 PRESB CH (USA)	1	207	268*	1.4	1.9
419 SO BAPT CONV	14	5,182	6,718*	34.9	48.7
449 UN METHODIST	9	1,430	1,854*	9.6	13.4
497 BLACK BAPT EST[2]	NA	1,149	1,490*	7.8	10.8
DALLAS	**42**	**5,422**	**7,007***	**72.9**	**100.0**
053 ASSEMB OF GOD	4	241	392	4.1	5.6
059 BAPT MISS ASSN	3	673	843*	8.8	12.0
081 CATHOLIC	1	NA	45	.5	.6
081d LATIN	1	NA	45	.5	.6
151 L-D SAINTS	1	NA	79	.8	1.1
167 CHS OF CHRIST	3	84	107	1.1	1.5

NA–Not applicable   NR–Not reported   *Total adherents estimated from known number of communicant, confirmed, full members.   - Represents a percent less than 0.1.   Percentages may not total due to rounding.
[1]See Appendix E   [2]See Appendix F   [3]See Appendix G   Lines in *italic* represent a breakdown of Catholic rites or Friends affiliations. They are included in their respective denominational total.

Table 4. Churches and Church Membership by County and Denomination: 1990

County and Denomination	Number of churches	Communicant, confirmed, full members	Total adherents Number	Percent of total population	Percent of total adherents
355 PRESB CH (USA)	3	106	133*	1.4	1.9
361 PRIM BAPT ASCS	2	50	63*	.7	.9
419 SO BAPT CONV	10	2,170	2,718*	28.3	38.8
449 UN METHODIST	15	832	1,042*	10.8	14.9
497 BLACK BAPT EST[2]	NA	1,266	1,585*	16.5	22.6
DESHA	**48**	**9,604**	**13,257***	**78.9**	**100.0**
005 AME ZION	2	210	245	1.5	1.8
053 ASSEMB OF GOD	6	324	528	3.1	4.0
059 BAPT MISS ASSN	2	330	439*	2.6	3.3
081 CATHOLIC	2	NA	290	1.7	2.2
081d LATIN	2	NA	290	1.7	2.2
097 CHR CHS&CHS CR	1	115	153*	.9	1.2
143 CG IN CR(MENN)	1	18	24*	.1	.2
165 CH OF NAZARENE	1	71	156	.9	1.2
167 CHS OF CHRIST	2	166	216	1.3	1.6
171 CH GOD-GEN CON	1	9	12*	.1	.1
193 EPISCOPAL	2	26	28	.2	.2
223 FREE WILL BAPT	1	50	67*	.4	.5
283 LUTH—MO SYNOD	1	2	10	.1	.1
339 PENT CH OF GOD	2	55	142	.8	1.1
355 PRESB CH (USA)	1	130	173*	1.0	1.3
419 SO BAPT CONV	16	4,324	5,753*	34.2	43.4
449 UN METHODIST	6	1,329	1,768*	10.5	13.3
496 JEWISH EST[1]	1	NA	0	-	-
497 BLACK BAPT EST[2]	NA	2,445	3,253*	19.4	24.5
DREW	**47**	**8,764**	**11,189***	**64.4**	**100.0**
005 AME ZION	1	366	386	2.2	3.4
053 ASSEMB OF GOD	3	177	249	1.4	2.2
055 AS REF PRES CH	1	45	61	.4	.5
059 BAPT MISS ASSN	1	223	284*	1.6	2.5
081 CATHOLIC	1	NA	100	.6	.9
081d LATIN	1	NA	100	.6	.9
097 CHR CHS&CHS CR	1	50	64*	.4	.6
127 CH GOD (CLEVE)	1	34	43*	.2	.4
167 CHS OF CHRIST	1	155	170	1.0	1.5
185 CUMBER PRESB	1	154	165	.9	1.5
193 EPISCOPAL	1	16	20	.1	.2
223 FREE WILL BAPT	4	350	446*	2.6	4.0
339 PENT CH OF GOD	1	34	77	.4	.7
355 PRESB CH (USA)	2	291	371*	2.1	3.3
413 S.D.A.	1	49	62*	.4	.6
419 SO BAPT CONV	15	4,101	5,226*	30.1	46.7
449 UN METHODIST	12	1,091	1,390*	8.0	12.4
497 BLACK BAPT EST[2]	NA	1,628	2,075*	11.9	18.5
FAULKNER	**115**	**24,841**	**37,385***	**62.3**	**100.0**
005 AME ZION	1	100	105	.2	.3
053 ASSEMB OF GOD	4	479	805	1.3	2.2
059 BAPT MISS ASSN	18	4,449	5,565*	9.3	14.9
081 CATHOLIC	1	NA	4,000	6.7	10.7
081d LATIN	1	NA	4,000	6.7	10.7
093 CHR CH (DISC)	1	61	72	.1	.2
121 CH GOD (ABR)	1	75	94*	.2	.3
127 CH GOD (CLEVE)	1	44	55*	.1	.1
151 L-D SAINTS	1	NA	606	1.0	1.6
165 CH OF NAZARENE	6	899	1,130	1.9	3.0
167 CHS OF CHRIST	19	1,948	2,505*	4.2	6.7
193 EPISCOPAL	1	121	171	.3	.5
207 E.L.C.A.	1	90	132	.2	.4
223 FREE WILL BAPT	7	699	874*	1.5	2.3
263 INT FOURSQ GOS	1	14	18*	-	-
283 LUTH—MO SYNOD	1	179	202	.3	.5
339 PENT CH OF GOD	2	19	43	.1	.1
355 PRESB CH (USA)	1	325	407*	.7	1.1
413 S.D.A.	1	36	45*	.1	.1
419 SO BAPT CONV	30	10,504	13,140*	21.9	35.1
449 UN METHODIST	15	3,353	4,194*	7.0	11.2
496 JEWISH EST[1]	0	NA	13	-	-
497 BLACK BAPT EST[2]	NA	1,446	1,809*	3.0	4.8
499 INDEP.NON-CHAR[3]	2	NA	1,400	2.3	3.7
FRANKLIN	**45**	**4,788**	**7,416***	**49.8**	**100.0**
053 ASSEMB OF GOD	7	296	551	3.7	7.4
081 CATHOLIC	2	NA	945	6.3	12.7
081d LATIN	2	NA	945	6.3	12.7
093 CHR CH (DISC)	2	75	141	.9	1.9
151 L-D SAINTS	1	NA	166	1.1	2.2
165 CH OF NAZARENE	2	122	151	1.0	2.0
167 CHS OF CHRIST	5	249	340	2.3	4.6
185 CUMBER PRESB	1	18	18	.1	.2
221 FREE METHODIST	1	7	11	.1	.1
223 FREE WILL BAPT	3	185	230*	1.5	3.1
339 PENT CH OF GOD	2	57	160	1.1	2.2
355 PRESB CH (USA)	1	77	96*	.6	1.3

County and Denomination	Number of churches	Communicant, confirmed, full members	Total adherents Number	Percent of total population	Percent of total adherents
356 PRESB CH AMER	1	5	5	-	.1
413 S.D.A.	1	28	35*	.2	.5
419 SO BAPT CONV	7	2,713	3,377*	22.7	45.5
449 UN METHODIST	9	956	1,190*	8.0	16.0
FULTON	**47**	**3,676**	**4,629***	**46.1**	**100.0**
053 ASSEMB OF GOD	3	158	262	2.6	5.7
059 BAPT MISS ASSN	1	38	46*	.5	1.0
093 CHR CH (DISC)	1	40	85	.8	1.8
127 CH GOD (CLEVE)	2	49	60*	.6	1.3
165 CH OF NAZARENE	1	0	0	-	-
167 CHS OF CHRIST	18	885	1,105	11.0	23.9
185 CUMBER PRESB	3	79	79	.8	1.7
339 PENT CH OF GOD	1	20	61	.6	1.3
355 PRESB CH (USA)	1	17	21*	.2	.5
413 S.D.A.	1	31	38*	.4	.8
419 SO BAPT CONV	12	1,997	2,431*	24.2	52.5
449 UN METHODIST	3	362	441*	4.4	9.5
GARLAND	**106**	**30,784**	**41,368***	**56.4**	**100.0**
005 AME ZION	1	98	113	.2	.3
053 ASSEMB OF GOD	7	906	1,382	1.9	3.3
059 BAPT MISS ASSN	1	230	276*	.4	.7
081 CATHOLIC	3	NA	3,327	4.5	8.0
081d LATIN	3	NA	3,327	4.5	8.0
093 CHR CH (DISC)	2	542	613	.8	1.5
097 CHR CHS&CHS CR	1	110	132*	.2	.3
111 CH CR,SCIENTST	1	NR	NR	-	-
121 CH GOD (ABR)	1	44	53*	.1	.1
123 CH GOD (ANDER)	3	247	260	.4	.6
127 CH GOD (CLEVE)	1	69	83*	.1	.2
145 CH GOD PROPHCY	1	28	34*	-	.1
151 L-D SAINTS	1	NA	442	.6	1.1
165 CH OF NAZARENE	3	552	538	.7	1.3
167 CHS OF CHRIST	10	1,006	1,283	1.7	3.1
171 CH GOD-GEN CON	1	31	37*	.1	.1
193 EPISCOPAL	2	449	561	.8	1.4
203 EVAN FREE CH	1	110	150	.2	.4
207 E.L.C.A.	2	772	842	1.1	2.0
223 FREE WILL BAPT	1	201	241*	.3	.6
246 GREEK ORTHODOX	1	NR	NR	-	-
283 LUTH—MO SYNOD	2	408	455	.6	1.1
339 PENT CH OF GOD	1	35	77	.1	.2
355 PRESB CH (USA)	4	1,667	1,997*	2.7	4.8
361 PRIM BAPT ASCS	3	122	146*	.2	.4
403 SALVATION ARMY	1	117	126	.2	.3
413 S.D.A.	2	288	345*	.5	.8
419 SO BAPT CONV	30	16,019	19,193*	26.1	46.4
435 UNITARIAN-UNIV	1	18	22	-	.1
449 UN METHODIST	14	5,315	6,368*	8.7	15.4
469 WELS	1	26	26	-	.1
496 JEWISH EST[1]	2	NA	0	-	-
497 BLACK BAPT EST[2]	NA	1,374	1,646*	2.2	4.0
499 INDEP.NON-CHAR[3]	1	NA	600	.8	1.5
GRANT	**27**	**3,728**	**4,818***	**34.5**	**100.0**
053 ASSEMB OF GOD	4	319	439	3.1	9.1
059 BAPT MISS ASSN	1	418	525*	3.8	10.9
081 CATHOLIC	1	NA	70	.5	1.5
081d LATIN	1	NA	70	.5	1.5
093 CHR CH (DISC)	1	16	20	.1	.4
127 CH GOD (CLEVE)	1	73	92*	.7	1.9
167 CHS OF CHRIST	2	102	133	1.0	2.8
185 CUMBER PRESB	1	86	91	.7	1.9
223 FREE WILL BAPT	1	25	31*	.2	.6
339 PENT CH OF GOD	2	69	126	.9	2.6
419 SO BAPT CONV	5	1,783	2,240*	16.1	46.5
449 UN METHODIST	8	837	1,051*	7.5	21.8
GREENE	**99**	**16,703**	**21,603***	**67.9**	**100.0**
053 ASSEMB OF GOD	3	115	254	.8	1.2
059 BAPT MISS ASSN	4	325	403*	1.3	1.9
081 CATHOLIC	1	NA	550	1.7	2.5
081d LATIN	1	NA	550	1.7	2.5
097 CHR CHS&CHS CR	1	100	124*	.4	.6
123 CH GOD (ANDER)	1	69	69	.2	.3
127 CH GOD (CLEVE)	1	100	124*	.4	.6
133 CH GOD(7TH)DEN	1	33	43	.1	.2
145 CH GOD PROPHCY	1	28	35*	.1	.2
165 CH OF NAZARENE	3	122	150	.5	.7
167 CHS OF CHRIST	23	2,621	3,351	10.5	15.5
193 EPISCOPAL	1	35	49	.2	.2
223 FREE WILL BAPT	3	135	167*	.5	.8
283 LUTH—MO SYNOD	2	255	367	1.2	1.7
339 PENT CH OF GOD	2	55	151	.5	.7
355 PRESB CH (USA)	1	66	82*	.3	.4

NA–Not applicable   NR–Not reported   *Total adherents estimated from known number of communicant, confirmed, full members.   - Represents a percent less than 0.1.   Percentages may not total due to rounding.
[1]See Appendix E   [2]See Appendix F   [3]See Appendix G   Lines in *italic* represent a breakdown of Catholic rites or Friends affiliations. They are included in their respective denominational total.

Table 4. Churches and Church Membership by County and Denomination: 1990

County and Denomination	Number of churches	Communicant, confirmed, full members	Total adherents Number	Total adherents Percent of total population	Total adherents Percent of total adherents
419 SO BAPT CONV	34	9,991	12,393*	39.0	57.4
449 UN METHODIST	17	2,653	3,291*	10.3	15.2
HEMPSTEAD	**67**	**11,343**	**14,883***	**68.8**	**100.0**
053 ASSEMB OF GOD	3	185	330	1.5	2.2
059 BAPT MISS ASSN	16	3,208	4,096*	18.9	27.5
081 CATHOLIC	1	NA	227	1.0	1.5
081d *LATIN*	1	*NA*	*227*	*1.0*	*1.5*
093 CHR CH (DISC)	1	92	118	.5	.8
123 CH GOD (ANDER)	1	40	40	.2	.3
145 CH GOD PROPHCY	1	28	36*	.2	.2
151 L-D SAINTS	1	NA	90	.4	.6
165 CH OF NAZARENE	2	90	117	.5	.8
167 CHS OF CHRIST	9	511	630	2.9	4.2
193 EPISCOPAL	1	69	72	.3	.5
226 FRIENDS-USA	1	3	6	-	-
226c *FGC*	1	*3*	*6*	-	-
339 PENT CH OF GOD	1	34	77	.4	.5
355 PRESB CH (USA)	2	148	189*	.9	1.3
413 S.D.A.	1	38	49*	.2	.3
419 SO BAPT CONV	11	2,866	3,659*	16.9	24.6
449 UN METHODIST	15	1,817	2,320*	10.7	15.6
497 BLACK BAPT EST[2]	NA	2,214	2,827*	13.1	19.0
HOT SPRINGS	**52**	**6,766**	**9,156***	**35.1**	**100.0**
005 AME ZION	1	102	119	.5	1.3
053 ASSEMB OF GOD	10	710	1,164	4.5	12.7
059 BAPT MISS ASSN	2	272	339*	1.3	3.7
081 CATHOLIC	1	NA	180	.7	2.0
081d *LATIN*	1	*NA*	*180*	*.7*	*2.0*
127 CH GOD (CLEVE)	1	64	80*	.3	.9
145 CH GOD PROPHCY	1	28	35*	.1	.4
165 CH OF NAZARENE	1	41	89	.3	1.0
167 CHS OF CHRIST	4	189	232	.9	2.5
223 FREE WILL BAPT	1	28	35*	.1	.4
283 LUTH—MO SYNOD	1	77	103	.4	1.1
339 PENT CH OF GOD	1	35	77	.3	.8
355 PRESB CH (USA)	1	126	157*	.6	1.7
361 PRIM BAPT ASCS	2	163	203*	.8	2.2
413 S.D.A.	2	207	258*	1.0	2.8
419 SO BAPT CONV	9	2,358	2,937*	11.2	32.1
449 UN METHODIST	14	1,663	2,072*	7.9	22.6
496 JEWISH EST[1]	0	NA	200	.8	2.2
497 BLACK BAPT EST[2]	NA	703	876*	3.4	9.6
HOWARD	**50**	**7,196**	**9,050***	**66.7**	**100.0**
053 ASSEMB OF GOD	2	152	280	2.1	3.1
059 BAPT MISS ASSN	12	1,504	1,914*	14.1	21.1
081 CATHOLIC	1	NA	135	1.0	1.5
081d *LATIN*	1	*NA*	*135*	*1.0*	*1.5*
097 CHR CHS&CHS CR	1	25	32*	.2	.4
123 CH GOD (ANDER)	2	63	77	.6	.9
167 CHS OF CHRIST	15	1,495	1,603	11.8	17.7
285 MENNONITE CH	1	96	96	.7	1.1
413 S.D.A.	1	17	22*	.2	.2
419 SO BAPT CONV	5	2,283	2,905*	21.4	32.1
449 UN METHODIST	10	860	1,094*	8.1	12.1
497 BLACK BAPT EST[2]	NA	701	892*	6.6	9.9
INDEPENDENCE	**95**	**14,619**	**19,152***	**61.4**	**100.0**
053 ASSEMB OF GOD	7	425	809	2.6	4.2
059 BAPT MISS ASSN	7	981	1,230*	3.9	6.4
081 CATHOLIC	1	NA	370	1.2	1.9
081d *LATIN*	1	*NA*	*370*	*1.2*	*1.9*
097 CHR CHS&CHS CR	1	75	94*	.3	.5
111 CH CR,SCIENTST	1	NR	NR	-	-
127 CH GOD (CLEVE)	3	132	165*	.5	.9
145 CH GOD PROPHCY	1	28	35*	.1	.2
151 L-D SAINTS	1	NA	136	.4	.7
165 CH OF NAZARENE	1	155	305	1.0	1.6
167 CHS OF CHRIST	16	1,399	1,733	5.6	9.0
185 CUMBER PRESB	2	131	145	.5	.8
193 EPISCOPAL	1	219	249	.8	1.3
223 FREE WILL BAPT	6	742	930*	3.0	4.9
283 LUTH—MO SYNOD	1	102	129	.4	.7
355 PRESB CH (USA)	1	323	405*	1.3	2.1
413 S.D.A.	1	81	102*	.3	.5
419 SO BAPT CONV	24	6,992	8,763*	28.1	45.8
449 UN METHODIST	20	2,688	3,369*	10.8	17.6
497 BLACK BAPT EST[2]	NA	146	183*	.6	1.0
IZARD	**55**	**5,055**	**6,507***	**57.3**	**100.0**
053 ASSEMB OF GOD	4	162	270	2.4	4.1
059 BAPT MISS ASSN	1	69	82*	.7	1.3
081 CATHOLIC	1	NA	430	3.8	6.6
081d *LATIN*	1	*NA*	*430*	*3.8*	*6.6*
145 CH GOD PROPHCY	1	28	33*	.3	.5
165 CH OF NAZARENE	1	52	65	.6	1.0
167 CHS OF CHRIST	9	306	426	3.7	6.5
185 CUMBER PRESB	6	439	459	4.0	7.1
193 EPISCOPAL	1	33	36	.3	.6
223 FREE WILL BAPT	2	120	143*	1.3	2.2
283 LUTH—MO SYNOD	1	179	182	1.6	2.8
285 MENNONITE CH	1	39	44	.4	.7
355 PRESB CH (USA)	2	173	207*	1.8	3.2
419 SO BAPT CONV	17	2,720	3,251*	28.6	50.0
449 UN METHODIST	8	735	879*	7.7	13.5
JACKSON	**66**	**8,917**	**11,440***	**60.4**	**100.0**
053 ASSEMB OF GOD	5	221	343	1.8	3.0
059 BAPT MISS ASSN	3	451	559*	3.0	4.9
081 CATHOLIC	1	NA	110	.6	1.0
081d *LATIN*	1	*NA*	*110*	*.6*	*1.0*
093 CHR CH (DISC)	1	106	138	.7	1.2
123 CH GOD (ANDER)	1	4	4	-	-
127 CH GOD (CLEVE)	1	30	37*	.2	.3
165 CH OF NAZARENE	1	38	37	.2	.3
167 CHS OF CHRIST	24	1,618	2,107	11.1	18.4
193 EPISCOPAL	1	122	164	.9	1.4
223 FREE WILL BAPT	5	565	700*	3.7	6.1
339 PENT CH OF GOD	2	62	182	1.0	1.6
355 PRESB CH (USA)	1	134	166*	.9	1.5
419 SO BAPT CONV	13	3,663	4,536*	23.9	39.7
449 UN METHODIST	7	1,240	1,536*	8.1	13.4
497 BLACK BAPT EST[2]	NA	663	821*	4.3	7.2
JEFFERSON	**102**	**36,373**	**49,402***	**57.8**	**100.0**
005 AME ZION	1	192	267	.3	.5
053 ASSEMB OF GOD	5	888	1,287	1.5	2.6
059 BAPT MISS ASSN	8	1,194	1,527*	1.8	3.1
081 CATHOLIC	4	NA	1,684	2.0	3.4
081d *LATIN*	4	*NA*	*1,684*	*2.0*	*3.4*
093 CHR CH (DISC)	2	287	505	.6	1.0
097 CHR CHS&CHS CR	1	50	64*	.1	.1
111 CH CR,SCIENTST	1	NR	NR		
123 CH GOD (ANDER)	1	14	14	-	-
127 CH GOD (CLEVE)	2	116	148*	.2	.3
145 CH GOD PROPHCY	1	28	36*	-	.1
151 L-D SAINTS	1	NA	326	.4	.7
165 CH OF NAZARENE	1	148	128	.1	.3
167 CHS OF CHRIST	9	858	1,144	1.3	2.3
185 CUMBER PRESB	2	248	257	.3	.5
193 EPISCOPAL	2	590	861	1.0	1.7
223 FREE WILL BAPT	1	344	440*	.5	.9
283 LUTH—MO SYNOD	1	320	408	.5	.8
339 PENT CH OF GOD	4	164	269	.3	.5
355 PRESB CH (USA)	5	1,341	1,715*	2.0	3.5
403 SALVATION ARMY	1	79	89	.1	.2
413 S.D.A.	3	257	329*	.4	.7
419 SO BAPT CONV	29	15,509	19,829*	23.2	40.1
449 UN METHODIST	15	5,709	7,299*	8.5	14.8
496 JEWISH EST[1]	1	NA	100	.1	.2
497 BLACK BAPT EST[2]	NA	8,037	10,276*	12.0	20.8
499 INDEP.NON-CHAR[3]	1	NA	400	.5	.8
JOHNSON	**48**	**5,720**	**7,825***	**42.9**	**100.0**
053 ASSEMB OF GOD	10	565	989	5.4	12.6
081 CATHOLIC	2	NA	346	1.9	4.4
081d *LATIN*	2	*NA*	*346*	*1.9*	*4.4*
097 CHR CHS&CHS CR	1	23	28*	.2	.4
165 CH OF NAZARENE	1	47	156	.9	2.0
167 CHS OF CHRIST	6	611	693	3.8	8.9
223 FREE WILL BAPT	2	122	151*	.8	1.9
283 LUTH—MO SYNOD	1	108	139	.8	1.8
339 PENT CH OF GOD	1	67	160	.9	2.0
355 PRESB CH (USA)	3	417	515*	2.8	6.6
413 S.D.A.	0	17	21*	.1	.3
419 SO BAPT CONV	14	2,580	3,189*	17.5	40.8
449 UN METHODIST	7	1,163	1,438*	7.9	18.4
LAFAYETTE	**34**	**5,001**	**6,365***	**66.0**	**100.0**
053 ASSEMB OF GOD	2	46	82	.9	1.3
059 BAPT MISS ASSN	8	1,028	1,300*	13.5	20.4
081 CATHOLIC	2	NA	10	.1	.2
081d *LATIN*	2	*NA*	*10*	*.1*	*.2*
165 CH OF NAZARENE	1	51	52	.5	.8
167 CHS OF CHRIST	6	273	360	3.7	5.7
355 PRESB CH (USA)	1	11	14*	.1	.2
356 PRESB CH AMER	1	15	22	.2	.3
419 SO BAPT CONV	6	1,586	2,006*	20.8	31.5
449 UN METHODIST	7	720	911*	9.4	14.3

NA–Not applicable   NR–Not reported   *Total adherents estimated from known number of communicant, confirmed, full members.   - Represents a percent less than 0.1.   Percentages may not total due to rounding.
[1]See Appendix E   [2]See Appendix F   [3]See Appendix G   Lines in *italic* represent a breakdown of Catholic rites or Friends affiliations. They are included in their respective denominational total.

Table 4. Churches and Church Membership by County and Denomination: 1990

County and Denomination	Number of churches	Communicant, confirmed, full members	Total adherents		
			Number	Percent of total population	Percent of total adherents
497 BLACK BAPT EST[2]	NA	1,271	1,608*	16.7	25.3
LAWRENCE	**64**	**6,964**	**9,128***	**52.3**	**100.0**
053 ASSEMB OF GOD	7	250	384	2.2	4.2
059 BAPT MISS ASSN	2	484	596*	3.4	6.5
081 CATHOLIC	1	NA	115	.7	1.3
081d *LATIN*	*1*	*NA*	*115*	*.7*	*1.3*
145 CH GOD PROPHCY	1	28	34*	.2	.4
165 CH OF NAZARENE	1	8	23	.1	.3
167 CHS OF CHRIST	16	879	1,393	8.0	15.3
223 FREE WILL BAPT	6	542	668*	3.8	7.3
339 PENT CH OF GOD	1	34	76	.4	.8
355 PRESB CH (USA)	1	65	80*	.5	.9
419 SO BAPT CONV	14	3,381	4,166*	23.9	45.6
449 UN METHODIST	14	1,293	1,593*	9.1	17.5
LEE	**22**	**5,348**	**7,313***	**56.0**	**100.0**
053 ASSEMB OF GOD	1	51	88	.7	1.2
059 BAPT MISS ASSN	2	181	242*	1.9	3.3
081 CATHOLIC	1	NA	150	1.1	2.1
081d *LATIN*	*1*	*NA*	*150*	*1.1*	*2.1*
097 CHR CHS&CHS CR	1	200	268*	2.1	3.7
127 CH GOD (CLEVE)	1	55	74*	.6	1.0
145 CH GOD PROPHCY	1	28	37*	.3	.5
167 CHS OF CHRIST	5	198	260	2.0	3.6
193 EPISCOPAL	1	67	80	.6	1.1
355 PRESB CH (USA)	1	60	80*	.6	1.1
419 SO BAPT CONV	4	1,442	1,930*	14.8	26.4
449 UN METHODIST	4	502	672*	5.1	9.2
497 BLACK BAPT EST[2]	NA	2,564	3,432*	26.3	46.9
LINCOLN	**30**	**4,891**	**6,156***	**45.0**	**100.0**
005 AME ZION	1	102	127	.9	2.1
053 ASSEMB OF GOD	2	104	189	1.4	3.1
059 BAPT MISS ASSN	1	0	0*	-	-
081 CATHOLIC	2	NA	70	.5	1.1
081d *LATIN*	*2*	*NA*	*70*	*.5*	*1.1*
097 CHR CHS&CHS CR	1	79	96*	.7	1.6
167 CHS OF CHRIST	3	80	164	1.2	2.7
185 CUMBER PRESB	1	20	23	.2	.4
223 FREE WILL BAPT	3	462	563*	4.1	9.1
355 PRESB CH (USA)	2	15	18*	.1	.3
419 SO BAPT CONV	8	1,902	2,316*	16.9	37.6
449 UN METHODIST	6	437	532*	3.9	8.6
497 BLACK BAPT EST[2]	NA	1,690	2,058*	15.0	33.4
LITTLE RIVER	**36**	**5,846**	**7,964***	**57.0**	**100.0**
053 ASSEMB OF GOD	2	132	191	1.4	2.4
059 BAPT MISS ASSN	2	568	721*	5.2	9.1
081 CATHOLIC	2	NA	30	.2	.4
081d *LATIN*	*2*	*NA*	*30*	*.2*	*.4*
093 CHR CH (DISC)	1	16	20	.1	.3
097 CHR CHS&CHS CR	1	28	36*	.3	.5
151 L-D SAINTS	1	NA	375	2.7	4.7
165 CH OF NAZARENE	1	60	108	.8	1.4
167 CHS OF CHRIST	4	410	586	4.2	7.4
185 CUMBER PRESB	2	105	105	.8	1.3
193 EPISCOPAL	1	57	82	.6	1.0
339 PENT CH OF GOD	1	34	77	.6	1.0
355 PRESB CH (USA)	1	60	76*	.5	1.0
419 SO BAPT CONV	10	2,739	3,478*	24.9	43.7
449 UN METHODIST	7	933	1,185*	8.5	14.9
497 BLACK BAPT EST[2]	NA	704	894*	6.4	11.2
LOGAN	**77**	**8,610**	**13,548***	**65.9**	**100.0**
053 ASSEMB OF GOD	14	684	1,277	6.2	9.4
059 BAPT MISS ASSN	1	81	102*	.5	.8
081 CATHOLIC	8	NA	2,156	10.5	15.9
081d *LATIN*	*8*	*NA*	*2,156*	*10.5*	*15.9*
093 CHR CH (DISC)	1	120	160	.8	1.2
121 CH GOD (ABR)	1	10	13*	.1	.1
127 CH GOD (CLEVE)	1	54	68*	.3	.5
167 CHS OF CHRIST	6	384	583	2.8	4.3
171 CH GOD-GEN CON	1	14	18*	.1	.1
185 CUMBER PRESB	7	426	429	2.1	3.2
207 E.L.C.A.	1	116	138	.7	1.0
223 FREE WILL BAPT	4	163	205*	1.0	1.5
339 PENT CH OF GOD	3	327	577	2.8	4.3
349 PENT HOLINESS	1	17	21*	.1	.2
355 PRESB CH (USA)	1	29	36*	.2	.3
413 S.D.A.	1	15	19*	.1	.1
419 SO BAPT CONV	17	5,024	6,307*	30.7	46.6
449 UN METHODIST	9	1,146	1,439*	7.0	10.6

County and Denomination	Number of churches	Communicant, confirmed, full members	Total adherents		
			Number	Percent of total population	Percent of total adherents
LONOKE	**83**	**17,946**	**24,750***	**63.0**	**100.0**
005 AME ZION	1	80	98	.2	.4
053 ASSEMB OF GOD	5	364	681	1.7	2.8
059 BAPT MISS ASSN	8	1,599	2,066*	5.3	8.3
081 CATHOLIC	1	NA	410	1.0	1.7
081d *LATIN*	*1*	*NA*	*410*	*1.0*	*1.7*
093 CHR CH (DISC)	1	8	10	-	-
145 CH GOD PROPHCY	1	28	36*	.1	.1
151 L-D SAINTS	1	NA	571	1.5	2.3
165 CH OF NAZARENE	2	100	154	.4	.6
167 CHS OF CHRIST	8	881	1,184	3.0	4.8
339 PENT CH OF GOD	6	206	465	1.2	1.9
355 PRESB CH (USA)	3	357	461*	1.2	1.9
419 SO BAPT CONV	26	10,522	13,592*	34.6	54.9
449 UN METHODIST	20	2,731	3,528*	9.0	14.3
496 JEWISH EST[1]	0	NA	112	.3	.5
497 BLACK BAPT EST[2]	NA	1,070	1,382*	3.5	5.6
MADISON	**39**	**3,232**	**4,309***	**37.1**	**100.0**
053 ASSEMB OF GOD	3	134	229	2.0	5.3
059 BAPT MISS ASSN	1	102	129*	1.1	3.0
081 CATHOLIC	1	NA	33	.3	.8
081d *LATIN*	*1*	*NA*	*33*	*.3*	*.8*
151 L-D SAINTS	1	NA	129	1.1	3.0
167 CHS OF CHRIST	17	780	994	8.6	23.1
223 FREE WILL BAPT	5	430	543*	4.7	12.6
355 PRESB CH (USA)	1	105	132*	1.1	3.1
413 S.D.A.	1	62	78*	.7	1.8
419 SO BAPT CONV	5	1,258	1,587*	13.7	36.8
436 UNITED BAPT	2	166	209*	1.8	4.9
449 UN METHODIST	2	195	246*	2.1	5.7
MARION	**37**	**4,018**	**5,090***	**42.4**	**100.0**
053 ASSEMB OF GOD	3	136	175	1.5	3.4
081 CATHOLIC	1	NA	190	1.6	3.7
081d *LATIN*	*1*	*NA*	*190*	*1.6*	*3.7*
089 CHR & MISS AL	1	0	55	.5	1.1
093 CHR CH (DISC)	1	80	104	.9	2.0
097 CHR CHS&CHS CR	2	280	337*	2.8	6.6
127 CH GOD (CLEVE)	1	66	79*	.7	1.6
167 CHS OF CHRIST	9	443	543	4.5	10.7
207 E.L.C.A.	1	103	109	.9	2.1
355 PRESB CH (USA)	2	212	255*	2.1	5.0
413 S.D.A.	1	26	31*	.3	.6
419 SO BAPT CONV	11	2,002	2,407*	20.1	47.3
449 UN METHODIST	4	670	805*	6.7	15.8
MILLER	**75**	**19,664**	**26,797***	**69.7**	**100.0**
053 ASSEMB OF GOD	6	467	734	1.9	2.7
059 BAPT MISS ASSN	2	508	654*	1.7	2.4
081 CATHOLIC	1	NA	1,265	3.3	4.7
081d *LATIN*	*1*	*NA*	*1,265*	*3.3*	*4.7*
093 CHR CH (DISC)	1	335	410	1.1	1.5
111 CH CR,SCIENTST	1	NR	NR	-	-
123 CH GOD (ANDER)	1	26	26	.1	.1
145 CH GOD PROPHCY	1	28	36*	.1	.1
165 CH OF NAZARENE	1	224	361	.9	1.3
167 CHS OF CHRIST	14	893	1,099	2.9	4.1
185 CUMBER PRESB	1	12	14	-	.1
339 PENT CH OF GOD	3	102	231	.6	.9
355 PRESB CH (USA)	1	389	501*	1.3	1.9
413 S.D.A.	1	167	215*	.6	.8
415 S-D BAPTIST GC	2	121	156*	.4	.6
419 SO BAPT CONV	27	10,839	13,949*	36.3	52.1
449 UN METHODIST	12	2,942	3,786*	9.8	14.1
497 BLACK BAPT EST[2]	NA	2,611	3,360*	8.7	12.5
MISSISSIPPI	**126**	**29,854**	**40,366***	**70.2**	**100.0**
053 ASSEMB OF GOD	8	390	616	1.1	1.5
059 BAPT MISS ASSN	7	1,397	1,854*	3.2	4.6
081 CATHOLIC	2	NA	670	1.2	1.7
081d *LATIN*	*2*	*NA*	*670*	*1.2*	*1.7*
093 CHR CH (DISC)	2	222	278	.5	.7
111 CH CR,SCIENTST	1	NR	NR	-	-
127 CH GOD (CLEVE)	10	822	1,091*	1.9	2.7
145 CH GOD PROPHCY	2	55	73*	.1	.2
165 CH OF NAZARENE	2	153	230	.4	.6
167 CHS OF CHRIST	18	1,126	1,271	2.2	3.1
193 EPISCOPAL	2	136	178	.3	.4
223 FREE WILL BAPT	1	46	61*	.1	.2
283 LUTH—MO SYNOD	1	182	253	.4	.6
339 PENT CH OF GOD	6	173	415	.7	1.0
349 PENT HOLINESS	1	58	77*	.1	.2
355 PRESB CH (USA)	1	325	431*	.7	1.1
356 PRESB CH AMER	2	141	185	.3	.5

NA–Not applicable   NR–Not reported   *Total adherents estimated from known number of communicant, confirmed, full members.   - Represents a percent less than 0.1.   Percentages may not total due to rounding.
[1]See Appendix E   [2]See Appendix F   [3]See Appendix G   Lines in *italic* represent a breakdown of Catholic rites or Friends affiliations. They are included in their respective denominational total.

Table 4. Churches and Church Membership by County and Denomination: 1990

County and Denomination	Number of churches	Communicant, confirmed, full members	Total adherents Number	Percent of total population	Percent of total adherents
413 S.D.A.	0	19	25*	-	.1
419 SO BAPT CONV	45	17,528	23,261*	40.4	57.6
449 UN METHODIST	14	3,154	4,186*	7.3	10.4
496 JEWISH EST[1]	1	NA	0	-	-
497 BLACK BAPT EST[2]	NA	3,927	5,211*	9.1	12.9
MONROE	**30**	**5,437**	**7,130***	**62.9**	**100.0**
053 ASSEMB OF GOD	2	74	101	.9	1.4
059 BAPT MISS ASSN	3	213	276*	2.4	3.9
081 CATHOLIC	1	NA	90	.8	1.3
081d LATIN	1	NA	90	.8	1.3
127 CH GOD (CLEVE)	1	22	28*	.2	.4
145 CH GOD PROPHCY	1	28	36*	.3	.5
167 CHS OF CHRIST	4	247	332	2.9	4.7
193 EPISCOPAL	1	27	32	.3	.4
283 LUTH—MO SYNOD	1	130	174	1.5	2.4
355 PRESB CH (USA)	2	133	172*	1.5	2.4
356 PRESB CH AMER	1	90	102	.9	1.4
413 S.D.A.	1	15	19*	.2	.3
419 SO BAPT CONV	6	2,216	2,867*	25.3	40.2
449 UN METHODIST	6	728	942*	8.3	13.2
497 BLACK BAPT EST[2]	NA	1,514	1,959*	17.3	27.5
MONTGOMERY	**36**	**3,050**	**3,823***	**48.8**	**100.0**
053 ASSEMB OF GOD	2	80	114	1.5	3.0
081 CATHOLIC	1	NA	67	.9	1.8
081d LATIN	1	NA	67	.9	1.8
165 CH OF NAZARENE	2	134	206	2.6	5.4
167 CHS OF CHRIST	2	100	125	1.6	3.3
171 CH GOD-GEN CON	6	243	294*	3.7	7.7
355 PRESB CH (USA)	2	65	79*	1.0	2.1
361 PRIM BAPT ASCS	2	33	40*	.5	1.0
419 SO BAPT CONV	17	2,043	2,472*	31.5	64.7
449 UN METHODIST	2	352	426*	5.4	11.1
NEVADA	**42**	**5,705**	**7,044***	**69.7**	**100.0**
053 ASSEMB OF GOD	1	90	133	1.3	1.9
059 BAPT MISS ASSN	15	2,277	2,868*	28.4	40.7
093 CHR CH (DISC)	1	32	41	.4	.6
123 CH GOD (ANDER)	1	40	40	.4	.6
165 CH OF NAZARENE	3	167	110	1.1	1.6
167 CHS OF CHRIST	6	442	509	5.0	7.2
185 CUMBER PRESB	1	12	12	.1	.2
355 PRESB CH (USA)	1	46	58*	.6	.8
419 SO BAPT CONV	5	826	1,040*	10.3	14.8
449 UN METHODIST	8	679	855*	8.5	12.1
497 BLACK BAPT EST[2]	NA	1,094	1,378*	13.6	19.6
NEWTON	**27**	**1,557**	**2,112***	**27.6**	**100.0**
053 ASSEMB OF GOD	3	168	322	4.2	15.2
089 CHR & MISS AL	1	18	23	.3	1.1
133 CH GOD(7TH)DEN	1	34	45	.6	2.1
167 CHS OF CHRIST	6	190	259	3.4	12.3
223 FREE WILL BAPT	2	112	143*	1.9	6.8
259 IFCA	1	NR	NR	-	-
419 SO BAPT CONV	7	613	782*	10.2	37.0
436 UNITED BAPT	5	326	416*	5.4	19.7
449 UN METHODIST	1	96	122*	1.6	5.8
OUACHITA	**78**	**16,579**	**22,161***	**72.5**	**100.0**
053 ASSEMB OF GOD	11	972	1,639	5.4	7.4
059 BAPT MISS ASSN	6	1,140	1,445*	4.7	6.5
081 CATHOLIC	1	NA	310	1.0	1.4
081d LATIN	1	NA	310	1.0	1.4
093 CHR CH (DISC)	1	58	63	.2	.3
123 CH GOD (ANDER)	1	12	12	-	.1
151 L-D SAINTS	1	NA	61	.2	.3
165 CH OF NAZARENE	1	78	106	.3	.5
167 CHS OF CHRIST	8	550	721	2.4	3.3
185 CUMBER PRESB	5	288	300	1.0	1.4
193 EPISCOPAL	1	54	75	.2	.3
283 LUTH—MO SYNOD	1	25	30	.1	.1
355 PRESB CH (USA)	2	341	432*	1.4	1.9
413 S.D.A.	1	22	28*	.1	.1
419 SO BAPT CONV	20	7,724	9,788*	32.0	44.2
449 UN METHODIST	17	2,681	3,398*	11.1	15.3
497 BLACK BAPT EST[2]	NA	2,634	3,338*	10.9	15.1
498 INDEP.CHARIS.[3]	1	NA	415	1.4	1.9
PERRY	**29**	**3,113**	**4,083***	**51.2**	**100.0**
053 ASSEMB OF GOD	4	149	207	2.6	5.1
081 CATHOLIC	1	NA	200	2.5	4.9
081d LATIN	1	NA	200	2.5	4.9
165 CH OF NAZARENE	1	35	58	.7	1.4
167 CHS OF CHRIST	5	196	247	3.1	6.0
223 FREE WILL BAPT	1	156	192*	2.4	4.7
419 SO BAPT CONV	12	2,312	2,852*	35.8	69.9
449 UN METHODIST	5	265	327*	4.1	8.0
PHILLIPS	**44**	**13,848**	**19,279***	**66.9**	**100.0**
053 ASSEMB OF GOD	2	103	235	.8	1.2
059 BAPT MISS ASSN	5	1,116	1,518*	5.3	7.9
081 CATHOLIC	1	NA	436	1.5	2.3
081d LATIN	1	NA	436	1.5	2.3
097 CHR CHS&CHS CR	1	60	82*	.3	.4
123 CH GOD (ANDER)	1	11	16	.1	.1
127 CH GOD (CLEVE)	2	193	262*	.9	1.4
145 CH GOD PROPHCY	2	55	75*	.3	.4
151 L-D SAINTS	1	NA	66	.2	.3
165 CH OF NAZARENE	1	74	82	.3	.4
167 CHS OF CHRIST	5	603	810	2.8	4.2
193 EPISCOPAL	1	317	312	1.1	1.6
283 LUTH—MO SYNOD	1	12	12	-	.1
355 PRESB CH (USA)	2	235	320*	1.1	1.7
413 S.D.A.	1	18	24*	.1	.1
419 SO BAPT CONV	11	5,715	7,772*	27.0	40.3
443 UN C OF CHRIST	1	58	79*	.3	.4
449 UN METHODIST	5	1,413	1,922*	6.7	10.0
496 JEWISH EST[1]	1	NA	0	-	-
497 BLACK BAPT EST[2]	NA	3,865	5,256*	18.2	27.3
PIKE	**49**	**3,781**	**5,001***	**49.6**	**100.0**
053 ASSEMB OF GOD	6	249	402	4.0	8.0
059 BAPT MISS ASSN	1	48	60*	.6	1.2
093 CHR CH (DISC)	1	26	34	.3	.7
097 CHR CHS&CHS CR	2	337	420*	4.2	8.4
151 L-D SAINTS	1	NA	81	.8	1.6
167 CHS OF CHRIST	13	826	1,072	10.6	21.4
223 FREE WILL BAPT	6	452	563*	5.6	11.3
361 PRIM BAPT ASCS	2	25	31*	.3	.6
419 SO BAPT CONV	5	1,189	1,481*	14.7	29.6
449 UN METHODIST	11	600	747*	7.4	14.9
467 WESLEYAN	1	29	110	1.1	2.2
POINSETT	**82**	**13,911**	**17,962***	**72.8**	**100.0**
053 ASSEMB OF GOD	6	277	461	1.9	2.6
059 BAPT MISS ASSN	3	479	604*	2.4	3.4
081 CATHOLIC	2	NA	188	.8	1.0
081d LATIN	2	NA	188	.8	1.0
093 CHR CH (DISC)	2	155	205	.8	1.1
097 CHR CHS&CHS CR	1	140	177*	.7	1.0
127 CH GOD (CLEVE)	4	371	468*	1.9	2.6
145 CH GOD PROPHCY	4	102	129*	.5	.7
167 CHS OF CHRIST	12	867	1,161	4.7	6.5
283 LUTH—MO SYNOD	1	139	177	.7	1.0
339 PENT CH OF GOD	1	35	77	.3	.4
419 SO BAPT CONV	35	9,434	11,903*	48.3	66.3
449 UN METHODIST	11	1,486	1,875*	7.6	10.4
497 BLACK BAPT EST[2]	NA	426	537*	2.2	3.0
POLK	**62**	**8,239**	**10,844***	**62.5**	**100.0**
053 ASSEMB OF GOD	3	216	339	2.0	3.1
059 BAPT MISS ASSN	2	303	378*	2.2	3.5
081 CATHOLIC	1	NA	320	1.8	3.0
081d LATIN	1	NA	320	1.8	3.0
097 CHR CHS&CHS CR	6	829	1,033*	6.0	9.5
127 CH GOD (CLEVE)	1	102	127*	.7	1.2
145 CH GOD PROPHCY	1	28	35*	.2	.3
151 L-D SAINTS	1	NA	130	.7	1.2
165 CH OF NAZARENE	3	355	407	2.3	3.8
167 CHS OF CHRIST	8	333	439	2.5	4.0
193 EPISCOPAL	1	31	33	.2	.3
223 FREE WILL BAPT	1	78	97*	.6	.9
283 LUTH—MO SYNOD	1	83	87	.5	.8
285 MENNONITE CH	1	21	47	.3	.4
339 PENT CH OF GOD	3	180	294	1.7	2.7
355 PRESB CH (USA)	1	206	257*	1.5	2.4
361 PRIM BAPT ASCS	1	31	39*	.2	.4
413 S.D.A.	2	114	142*	.8	1.3
419 SO BAPT CONV	20	4,418	5,505*	31.7	50.8
449 UN METHODIST	5	911	1,135*	6.5	10.5
POPE	**113**	**15,711**	**22,159***	**48.3**	**100.0**
053 ASSEMB OF GOD	23	1,926	3,079	6.7	13.9
055 AS REF PRES CH	1	161	173	.4	.8
059 BAPT MISS ASSN	1	241	303*	.7	1.4
081 CATHOLIC	2	NA	1,347	2.9	6.1
081d LATIN	2	NA	1,347	2.9	6.1
089 CHR & MISS AL	1	67	137	.3	.6
093 CHR CH (DISC)	2	115	139	.3	.6

NA–Not applicable   NR–Not reported   *Total adherents estimated from known number of communicant, confirmed, full members.   - Represents a percent less than 0.1.   Percentages may not total due to rounding.
[1]See Appendix E   [2]See Appendix F   [3]See Appendix G   Lines in *italic* represent a breakdown of Catholic rites or Friends affiliations. They are included in their respective denominational total.

Table 4. Churches and Church Membership by County and Denomination: 1990

County and Denomination	Number of churches	Communicant, confirmed, full members	Total adherents Number	Percent of total population	Percent of total adherents
097 CHR CHS&CHS CR	1	130	164*	.4	.7
127 CH GOD (CLEVE)	2	125	157*	.3	.7
145 CH GOD PROPHCY	2	55	69*	.2	.3
151 L-D SAINTS	1	NA	386	.8	1.7
165 CH OF NAZARENE	1	71	155	.3	.7
167 CHS OF CHRIST	14	1,162	1,412	3.1	6.4
185 CUMBER PRESB	7	688	743	1.6	3.4
193 EPISCOPAL	1	264	288	.6	1.3
215 EVAN METH CH	1	20	25*	.1	.1
223 FREE WILL BAPT	16	1,653	2,079*	4.5	9.4
263 INT FOURSQ GOS	1	25	31*	.1	.1
283 LUTH—MO SYNOD	2	408	514	1.1	2.3
339 PENT CH OF GOD	4	135	305	.7	1.4
355 PRESB CH (USA)	2	524	659*	1.4	3.0
361 PRIM BAPT ASCS	1	47	59*	.1	.3
403 SALVATION ARMY	1	10	13	-	.1
419 SO BAPT CONV	16	5,332	6,707*	14.6	30.3
449 UN METHODIST	9	2,222	2,795*	6.1	12.6
469 WELS	1	53	72	.2	.3
497 BLACK BAPT EST[2]	NA	277	348*	.8	1.6
PRAIRIE	**27**	**3,231**	**4,406***	**46.3**	**100.0**
053 ASSEMB OF GOD	3	106	183	1.9	4.2
059 BAPT MISS ASSN	1	23	29*	.3	.7
081 CATHOLIC	2	NA	200	2.1	4.5
081d LATIN	*2*	*NA*	*200*	*2.1*	*4.5*
145 CH GOD PROPHCY	1	28	35*	.4	.8
165 CH OF NAZARENE	1	27	20	.2	.5
167 CHS OF CHRIST	4	205	267	2.8	6.1
193 EPISCOPAL	1	46	153	1.6	3.5
283 LUTH—MO SYNOD	1	244	301	3.2	6.8
339 PENT CH OF GOD	1	16	54	.6	1.2
355 PRESB CH (USA)	1	28	35*	.4	.8
419 SO BAPT CONV	5	1,490	1,859*	19.5	42.2
449 UN METHODIST	6	707	882*	9.3	20.0
497 BLACK BAPT EST[2]	NA	311	388*	4.1	8.8
PULASKI	**346**	**153,700**	**223,094***	**63.8**	**100.0**
005 AME ZION	7	1,613	2,024	.6	.9
053 ASSEMB OF GOD	28	3,471	5,254	1.5	2.4
055 AS REF PRES CH	1	128	137	-	.1
059 BAPT MISS ASSN	17	5,243	6,607*	1.9	3.0
081 CATHOLIC	16	NA	20,175	5.8	9.0
081d LATIN	*16*	*NA*	*20,175*	*5.8*	*9.0*
089 CHR & MISS AL	1	43	92	-	-
093 CHR CH (DISC)	11	1,536	2,045	.6	.9
097 CHR CHS&CHS CR	4	360	454*	.1	.2
111 CH CR,SCIENTST	2	NR	NR	-	-
123 CH GOD (ANDER)	2	15	225	.1	.1
127 CH GOD (CLEVE)	3	322	406*	.1	.2
145 CH GOD PROPHCY	3	83	105*	-	-
151 L-D SAINTS	5	NA	1,616	.5	.7
165 CH OF NAZARENE	15	2,762	2,835	.8	1.3
167 CHS OF CHRIST	29	7,218	9,592	2.7	4.3
185 CUMBER PRESB	2	350	383	.1	.2
193 EPISCOPAL	7	3,674	4,792	1.4	2.1
203 EVAN FREE CH	1	13	35	-	-
207 E.L.C.A.	2	346	468	.1	.2
221 FREE METHODIST	1	0	13	-	-
223 FREE WILL BAPT	5	559	704*	.2	.3
226 FRIENDS-USA	1	34	57	-	-
226c FGC	*1*	*34*	*57*	-	-
246 GREEK ORTHODOX	1	NR	NR	-	-
259 IFCA	1	NR	NR	-	-
263 INT FOURSQ GOS	2	79	100*	-	-
283 LUTH—MO SYNOD	8	2,276	3,007	.9	1.3
339 PENT CH OF GOD	6	184	423	.1	.2
355 PRESB CH (USA)	12	3,959	4,989*	1.4	2.2
356 PRESB CH AMER	2	329	450	.1	.2
361 PRIM BAPT ASCS	1	94	118*	-	.1
403 SALVATION ARMY	3	252	301	.1	.1
413 S.D.A.	3	659	830*	.2	.4
415 S-D BAPTIST GC	2	62	78*	-	-
419 SO BAPT CONV	85	68,062	85,767*	24.5	38.4
435 UNITARIAN-UNIV	1	265	365	.1	.2
443 UN C OF CHRIST	2	128	161*	-	.1
449 UN METHODIST	45	29,447	37,107*	10.6	16.6
469 WELS	1	40	65	-	-
496 JEWISH EST[1]	2	NA	993	.3	.4
497 BLACK BAPT EST[2]	NA	20,094	25,321*	7.2	11.3
499 INDEP.NON-CHAR[3]	6	NA	5,000	1.4	2.2
RANDOLPH	**50**	**7,031**	**10,355***	**62.5**	**100.0**
053 ASSEMB OF GOD	1	150	260	1.6	2.5
059 BAPT MISS ASSN	1	124	154*	.9	1.5
081 CATHOLIC	2	NA	1,300	7.9	12.6
081d LATIN	*2*	*NA*	*1,300*	*7.9*	*12.6*
121 CH GOD (ABR)	1	22	27*	.2	.3
145 CH GOD PROPHCY	1	28	35*	.2	.3
151 L-D SAINTS	1	NA	116	.7	1.1
167 CHS OF CHRIST	21	1,355	1,772	10.7	17.1
203 EVAN FREE CH	1	0	6	-	.1
223 FREE WILL BAPT	2	1,335	1,659*	10.0	16.0
339 PENT CH OF GOD	1	34	77	.5	.7
349 PENT HOLINESS	1	15	19*	.1	.2
355 PRESB CH (USA)	1	52	65*	.4	.6
413 S.D.A.	1	30	37*	.2	.4
419 SO BAPT CONV	9	3,252	4,040*	24.4	39.0
449 UN METHODIST	6	634	788*	4.8	7.6
SAINT FRANCIS	**52**	**12,989**	**17,632***	**61.9**	**100.0**
053 ASSEMB OF GOD	2	153	174	.6	1.0
059 BAPT MISS ASSN	3	615	826*	2.9	4.7
081 CATHOLIC	1	NA	277	1.0	1.6
081d LATIN	*1*	*NA*	*277*	*1.0*	*1.6*
093 CHR CH (DISC)	1	69	72	.3	.4
127 CH GOD (CLEVE)	3	363	487*	1.7	2.8
165 CH OF NAZARENE	1	22	50	.2	.3
167 CHS OF CHRIST	6	348	444	1.6	2.5
185 CUMBER PRESB	1	148	157	.6	.9
193 EPISCOPAL	2	139	213	.7	1.2
283 LUTH—MO SYNOD	1	53	62	.2	.4
355 PRESB CH (USA)	1	247	332*	1.2	1.9
356 PRESB CH AMER	1	20	20	.1	.1
413 S.D.A.	1	22	30*	.1	.2
419 SO BAPT CONV	17	5,809	7,800*	27.4	44.2
449 UN METHODIST	11	1,664	2,234*	7.8	12.7
497 BLACK BAPT EST[2]	NA	3,317	4,454*	15.6	25.3
SALINE	**71**	**18,467**	**24,623***	**38.4**	**100.0**
053 ASSEMB OF GOD	7	537	777	1.2	3.2
059 BAPT MISS ASSN	2	605	765*	1.2	3.1
081 CATHOLIC	1	NA	900	1.4	3.7
081d LATIN	*1*	*NA*	*900*	*1.4*	*3.7*
093 CHR CH (DISC)	1	82	124	.2	.5
123 CH GOD (ANDER)	2	105	114	.2	.5
127 CH GOD (CLEVE)	3	202	255*	.4	1.0
165 CH OF NAZARENE	4	388	452	.7	1.8
167 CHS OF CHRIST	12	1,168	1,482	2.3	6.0
193 EPISCOPAL	1	70	91	.1	.4
223 FREE WILL BAPT	2	91	115*	.2	.5
263 INT FOURSQ GOS	1	171	216*	.3	.9
283 LUTH—MO SYNOD	2	338	486	.8	2.0
339 PENT CH OF GOD	2	68	154	.2	.6
355 PRESB CH (USA)	1	195	247*	.4	1.0
413 S.D.A.	1	94	119*	.2	.5
419 SO BAPT CONV	21	10,510	13,286*	20.7	54.0
449 UN METHODIST	8	3,435	4,342*	6.8	17.6
496 JEWISH EST[1]	0	NA	182	.3	.7
497 BLACK BAPT EST[2]	NA	408	516*	.8	2.1
SCOTT	**56**	**4,355**	**5,942***	**58.2**	**100.0**
053 ASSEMB OF GOD	5	206	315	3.1	5.3
081 CATHOLIC	1	NA	80	.8	1.3
081d LATIN	*1*	*NA*	*80*	*.8*	*1.3*
089 CHR & MISS AL	1	0	5	-	.1
165 CH OF NAZARENE	1	149	386	3.8	6.5
167 CHS OF CHRIST	4	255	325	3.2	5.5
185 CUMBER PRESB	2	121	124	1.2	2.1
223 FREE WILL BAPT	7	326	407*	4.0	6.8
339 PENT CH OF GOD	6	188	420	4.1	7.1
361 PRIM BAPT ASCS	1	15	19*	.2	.3
419 SO BAPT CONV	22	2,725	3,399*	33.3	57.2
449 UN METHODIST	6	370	462*	4.5	7.8
SEARCY	**24**	**2,086**	**2,698***	**34.4**	**100.0**
053 ASSEMB OF GOD	4	125	237	3.0	8.8
097 CHR CHS&CHS CR	1	86	106*	1.4	3.9
127 CH GOD (CLEVE)	1	9	11*	.1	.4
165 CH OF NAZARENE	1	16	34	.4	1.3
167 CHS OF CHRIST	5	233	325	4.1	12.0
223 FREE WILL BAPT	1	40	49*	.6	1.8
237 GC MENN BR CHS	1	37	45*	.6	1.7
419 SO BAPT CONV	7	1,340	1,645*	21.0	61.0
449 UN METHODIST	3	200	246*	3.1	9.1
SEBASTIAN	**172**	**52,246**	**75,979***	**76.3**	**100.0**
053 ASSEMB OF GOD	17	1,555	3,294	3.3	4.3
059 BAPT MISS ASSN	2	269	338*	.3	.4
081 CATHOLIC	6	NA	6,566	6.6	8.6
081d LATIN	*6*	*NA*	*6,566*	*6.6*	*8.6*

NA–Not applicable NR–Not reported *Total adherents estimated from known number of communicant, confirmed, full members. - Represents a percent less than 0.1. Percentages may not total due to rounding.
[1]See Appendix E [2]See Appendix F [3]See Appendix G Lines in *italic* represent a breakdown of Catholic rites or Friends affiliations. They are included in their respective denominational total.

Table 4. Churches and Church Membership by County and Denomination: 1990

County and Denomination	Number of churches	Communicant, confirmed, full members	Total adherents Number	Percent of total population	Percent of total adherents
093 CHR CH (DISC)	1	498	599	.6	.8
097 CHR CHS&CHS CR	3	447	562*	.6	.7
111 CH CR,SCIENTST	1	NR	NR	-	-
123 CH GOD (ANDER)	1	0	68	.1	.1
127 CH GOD (CLEVE)	1	78	98*	.1	.1
133 CH GOD(7TH)DEN	1	34	45	-	.1
145 CH GOD PROPHCY	1	28	35*	-	-
151 L-D SAINTS	3	NA	827	.8	1.1
165 CH OF NAZARENE	5	506	828	.8	1.1
167 CHS OF CHRIST	22	2,542	3,346	3.4	4.4
171 CH GOD-GEN CON	1	10	13*	-	-
185 CUMBER PRESB	1	186	196	.2	.3
193 EPISCOPAL	3	724	976	1.0	1.3
207 E.L.C.A.	1	366	514	.5	.7
223 FREE WILL BAPT	10	1,869	2,349*	2.4	3.1
246 GREEK ORTHODOX	1	NR	NR	-	-
283 LUTH—MO SYNOD	3	1,077	1,414	1.4	1.9
339 PENT CH OF GOD	7	247	509	.5	.7
349 PENT HOLINESS	2	53	67*	.1	.1
355 PRESB CH (USA)	5	1,848	2,323*	2.3	3.1
356 PRESB CH AMER	1	43	54	.1	.1
361 PRIM BAPT ASCS	2	62	78*	.1	.1
403 SALVATION ARMY	1	154	154	.2	.2
413 S.D.A.	2	210	264*	.3	.3
419 SO BAPT CONV	45	29,913	37,600*	37.8	49.5
449 UN METHODIST	20	7,812	9,819*	9.9	12.9
496 JEWISH EST[1]	1	NA	112	.1	.1
497 BLACK BAPT EST[2]	NA	1,715	2,156*	2.2	2.8
498 INDEP.CHARIS.[3]	1	NA	400	.4	.5
499 INDEP.NON-CHAR[3]	1	NA	375	.4	.5
SEVIER	**48**	**6,572**	**8,742***	**64.1**	**100.0**
053 ASSEMB OF GOD	3	297	395	2.9	4.5
059 BAPT MISS ASSN	3	429	539*	4.0	6.2
081 CATHOLIC	1	NA	412	3.0	4.7
081d LATIN	1	NA	412	3.0	4.7
093 CHR CH (DISC)	1	48	62	.5	.7
097 CHR CHS&CHS CR	1	135	170*	1.2	1.9
145 CH GOD PROPHCY	1	28	35*	.3	.4
165 CH OF NAZARENE	2	65	69	.5	.8
167 CHS OF CHRIST	5	434	578	4.2	6.6
185 CUMBER PRESB	4	114	123	.9	1.4
207 E.L.C.A.	1	97	131	1.0	1.5
339 PENT CH OF GOD	1	34	77	.6	.9
355 PRESB CH (USA)	1	61	77*	.6	.9
413 S.D.A.	1	198	249*	1.8	2.8
419 SO BAPT CONV	10	3,302	4,152*	30.4	47.5
449 UN METHODIST	13	1,141	1,435*	10.5	16.4
497 BLACK BAPT EST[2]	NA	189	238*	1.7	2.7
SHARP	**58**	**5,552**	**7,421***	**52.6**	**100.0**
053 ASSEMB OF GOD	3	120	233	1.7	3.1
059 BAPT MISS ASSN	4	332	395*	2.8	5.3
081 CATHOLIC	1	NA	650	4.6	8.8
081d LATIN	1	NA	650	4.6	8.8
093 CHR CH (DISC)	1	32	32	.2	.4
111 CH CR,SCIENTST	1	NR	NR	-	-
127 CH GOD (CLEVE)	3	144	171*	1.2	2.3
165 CH OF NAZARENE	1	6	12	.1	.2
167 CHS OF CHRIST	15	782	1,063	7.5	14.3
185 CUMBER PRESB	2	57	57	.4	.8
193 EPISCOPAL	1	63	63	.4	.8
203 EVAN FREE CH	1	24	36	.3	.5
207 E.L.C.A.	1	69	69	.5	.9
223 FREE WILL BAPT	2	50	59*	.4	.8
283 LUTH—MO SYNOD	1	347	387	2.7	5.2
355 PRESB CH (USA)	1	267	318*	2.3	4.3
413 S.D.A.	1	17	20*	.1	.3
419 SO BAPT CONV	10	2,181	2,594*	18.4	35.0
449 UN METHODIST	9	1,061	1,262*	8.9	17.0
STONE	**26**	**2,411**	**3,305***	**33.8**	**100.0**
053 ASSEMB OF GOD	3	115	223	2.3	6.7
061 BEACHY AMISH	1	27	33*	.3	1.0
081 CATHOLIC	1	NA	60	.6	1.8
081d LATIN	1	NA	60	.6	1.8
097 CHR CHS&CHS CR	1	45	55*	.6	1.7
145 CH GOD PROPHCY	1	28	34*	.3	1.0
151 L-D SAINTS	1	NA	115	1.2	3.5
165 CH OF NAZARENE	1	19	88	.9	2.7
167 CHS OF CHRIST	6	496	642	6.6	19.4
285 MENNONITE CH	2	32	32	.3	1.0
413 S.D.A.	1	45	55*	.6	1.7
419 SO BAPT CONV	6	1,230	1,509*	15.4	45.7
449 UN METHODIST	2	374	459*	4.7	13.9

County and Denomination	Number of churches	Communicant, confirmed, full members	Total adherents Number	Percent of total population	Percent of total adherents
UNION	**120**	**27,319**	**36,301***	**77.7**	**100.0**
053 ASSEMB OF GOD	10	740	1,019	2.2	2.8
059 BAPT MISS ASSN	12	2,187	2,781*	6.0	7.7
081 CATHOLIC	1	NA	800	1.7	2.2
081d LATIN	1	NA	800	1.7	2.2
093 CHR CH (DISC)	1	140	210	.4	.6
123 CH GOD (ANDER)	2	185	193	.4	.5
127 CH GOD (CLEVE)	1	71	90*	.2	.2
145 CH GOD PROPHCY	1	28	36*	.1	.1
151 L-D SAINTS	1	NA	193	.4	.5
165 CH OF NAZARENE	1	116	152	.3	.4
167 CHS OF CHRIST	14	991	1,237	2.6	3.4
185 CUMBER PRESB	1	63	63	.1	.2
193 EPISCOPAL	1	323	422	.9	1.2
283 LUTH—MO SYNOD	1	104	138	.3	.4
285 MENNONITE CH	1	30	49	.1	.1
339 PENT CH OF GOD	2	68	153	.3	.4
355 PRESB CH (USA)	5	672	854*	1.8	2.4
361 PRIM BAPT ASCS	4	32	41*	.1	.1
403 SALVATION ARMY	1	45	52	.1	.1
413 S.D.A.	1	69	88*	.2	.2
419 SO BAPT CONV	35	14,096	17,923*	38.4	49.4
436 UNITED BAPT	2	94	120*	.3	.3
449 UN METHODIST	20	3,816	4,852*	10.4	13.4
496 JEWISH EST[1]	1	NA	0	-	-
497 BLACK BAPT EST[2]	NA	3,449	4,385*	9.4	12.1
499 INDEP.NON-CHAR[3]	1	NA	450	1.0	1.2
VAN BUREN	**54**	**6,291**	**8,354***	**59.6**	**100.0**
053 ASSEMB OF GOD	3	165	269	1.9	3.2
059 BAPT MISS ASSN	3	620	746*	5.3	8.9
081 CATHOLIC	2	NA	661	4.7	7.9
081d LATIN	2	NA	661	4.7	7.9
165 CH OF NAZARENE	1	17	39	.3	.5
167 CHS OF CHRIST	11	585	756	5.4	9.0
263 INT FOURSQ GOS	3	61	73*	.5	.9
283 LUTH—MO SYNOD	1	111	118	.8	1.4
355 PRESB CH (USA)	1	142	171*	1.2	2.0
361 PRIM BAPT ASCS	2	72	87*	.6	1.0
413 S.D.A.	1	64	77*	.5	.9
419 SO BAPT CONV	18	3,234	3,890*	27.8	46.6
449 UN METHODIST	8	1,220	1,467*	10.5	17.6
WASHINGTON	**193**	**42,058**	**58,967***	**52.0**	**100.0**
053 ASSEMB OF GOD	13	929	1,399	1.2	2.4
059 BAPT MISS ASSN	13	2,332	2,899*	2.6	4.9
081 CATHOLIC	5	NA	3,846	3.4	6.5
081d LATIN	5	NA	3,846	3.4	6.5
093 CHR CH (DISC)	3	715	959	.8	1.6
097 CHR CHS&CHS CR	4	355	441*	.4	.7
111 CH CR,SCIENTST	2	NR	NR	-	-
127 CH GOD (CLEVE)	5	328	408*	.4	.7
145 CH GOD PROPHCY	1	28	35*	-	.1
151 L-D SAINTS	3	NA	853	.8	1.4
165 CH OF NAZARENE	5	576	846	.7	1.4
167 CHS OF CHRIST	27	3,001	4,101	3.6	7.0
185 CUMBER PRESB	2	148	155	.1	.3
193 EPISCOPAL	2	738	1,263	1.1	2.1
203 EVAN FREE CH	1	45	75	.1	.1
207 E.L.C.A.	1	427	537	.5	.9
216 EVAN PRESBY CH	1	19	19	-	-
223 FREE WILL BAPT	14	1,582	1,966*	1.7	3.3
226 FRIENDS-USA	1	3	15	-	-
226c FGC	1	3	15	-	-
259 IFCA	1	NR	NR	-	-
283 LUTH—MO SYNOD	4	510	690	.6	1.2
339 PENT CH OF GOD	7	241	538	.5	.9
349 PENT HOLINESS	2	63	78*	.1	.1
355 PRESB CH (USA)	9	1,476	1,835*	1.6	3.1
356 PRESB CH AMER	1	78	106	.1	.2
403 SALVATION ARMY	2	144	149	.1	.3
413 S.D.A.	4	315	392*	.3	.7
419 SO BAPT CONV	34	19,883	24,714*	21.8	41.9
435 UNITARIAN-UNIV	1	104	104	.1	.2
436 UNITED BAPT	1	49	61*	.1	.1
449 UN METHODIST	21	7,373	9,165*	8.1	15.5
469 WELS	1	89	118	.1	.2
496 JEWISH EST[1]	1	NA	120	.1	.2
497 BLACK BAPT EST[2]	NA	507	630*	.6	1.1
499 INDEP.NON-CHAR[3]	1	NA	450	.4	.8
WHITE	**156**	**25,108**	**33,481***	**61.2**	**100.0**
053 ASSEMB OF GOD	11	1,073	2,297	4.2	6.9
059 BAPT MISS ASSN	16	3,211	3,976*	7.3	11.9
081 CATHOLIC	2	NA	146	.3	.4
081d LATIN	2	NA	146	.3	.4

NA–Not applicable NR–Not reported *Total adherents estimated from known number of communicant, confirmed, full members. - Represents a percent less than 0.1. Percentages may not total due to rounding.

[1]See Appendix E [2]See Appendix F [3]See Appendix G Lines in *italic* represent a breakdown of Catholic rites or Friends affiliations. They are included in their respective denominational total.

Table 4. Churches and Church Membership by County and Denomination: 1990

County and Denomination	Number of churches	Communicant, confirmed, full members	Total adherents Number	Percent of total population	Percent of total adherents
093 CHR CH (DISC)	3	197	251	.5	.7
097 CHR CHS&CHS CR	1	37	46*	.1	.1
123 CH GOD (ANDER)	1	12	23	-	.1
127 CH GOD (CLEVE)	7	515	638*	1.2	1.9
145 CH GOD PROPHCY	2	55	68*	.1	.2
151 L-D SAINTS	1	NA	349	.6	1.0
165 CH OF NAZARENE	4	358	650	1.2	1.9
167 CHS OF CHRIST	37	5,164	6,945	12.7	20.7
185 CUMBER PRESB	3	116	118	.2	.4
193 EPISCOPAL	1	115	168	.3	.5
223 FREE WILL BAPT	5	517	640*	1.2	1.9
263 INT FOURSQ GOS	1	18	22*	-	.1
283 LUTH—MO SYNOD	1	200	267	.5	.8
339 PENT CH OF GOD	4	137	308	.6	.9
349 PENT HOLINESS	1	30	37*	.1	.1
355 PRESB CH (USA)	2	123	152*	.3	.5
413 S.D.A.	1	18	22*	-	.1
419 SO BAPT CONV	28	9,315	11,533*	21.1	34.4
449 UN METHODIST	24	3,479	4,307*	7.9	12.9
497 BLACK BAPT EST[2]	NA	418	518*	.9	1.5
WOODRUFF	**31**	**5,243**	**6,843***	**71.9**	**100.0**
053 ASSEMB OF GOD	3	65	87	.9	1.3
081 CATHOLIC	1	NA	78	.8	1.1
081d LATIN	*1*	*NA*	*78*	*.8*	*1.1*
127 CH GOD (CLEVE)	2	57	73*	.8	1.1
145 CH GOD PROPHCY	1	28	36*	.4	.5
165 CH OF NAZARENE	1	110	220	2.3	3.2
167 CHS OF CHRIST	4	389	468	4.9	6.8
419 SO BAPT CONV	10	2,702	3,459*	36.3	50.5
449 UN METHODIST	9	868	1,111*	11.7	16.2
497 BLACK BAPT EST[2]	NA	1,024	1,311*	13.8	19.2
YELL	**73**	**6,486**	**8,501***	**47.9**	**100.0**
053 ASSEMB OF GOD	7	343	569	3.2	6.7
055 AS REF PRES CH	1	30	30	.2	.4
059 BAPT MISS ASSN	2	151	188*	1.1	2.2
081 CATHOLIC	2	NA	156	.9	1.8
081d LATIN	*2*	*NA*	*156*	*.9*	*1.8*
089 CHR & MISS AL	1	0	17	.1	.2
123 CH GOD (ANDER)	1	30	30	.2	.4
165 CH OF NAZARENE	1	20	30	.2	.4
167 CHS OF CHRIST	13	601	821	4.6	9.7
185 CUMBER PRESB	1	67	67	.4	.8
223 FREE WILL BAPT	11	890	1,107*	6.2	13.0
339 PENT CH OF GOD	2	69	154	.9	1.8
355 PRESB CH (USA)	1	137	170*	1.0	2.0
361 PRIM BAPT ASCS	1	31	39*	.2	.5
413 S.D.A.	2	107	133*	.7	1.6
419 SO BAPT CONV	12	2,966	3,691*	20.8	43.4
449 UN METHODIST	15	1,044	1,299*	7.3	15.3

CALIFORNIA

County and Denomination	Number of churches	Communicant, confirmed, full members	Total adherents Number	Percent of total population	Percent of total adherents
THE STATE.....	14,427	2,752,215	12,585,339*	42.3	100.0
ALAMEDA	**590**	**144,121**	**568,125***	**44.4**	**100.0**
001 ADVENT CHR CH	1	28	35*	-	-
005 AME ZION	2	599	899	.1	.2
019 AMER BAPT USA	27	9,760	12,071*	.9	2.1
045 APOSTOLIC LUTH	1	47	59	-	-
053 ASSEMB OF GOD	33	4,946	10,567	.8	1.9
057 BAPT GEN CONF	7	343	424*	-	.1
059 BAPT MISS ASSN	2	228	282*	-	-
081 CATHOLIC	56	NA	320,523	25.1	56.4
081d LATIN	*55*	*NA*	*320,000*	*25.0*	*56.3*
081f MELKITE-GK	*1*	*NA*	*523*	*-*	*.1*
089 CHR & MISS AL	14	2,849	5,490	.4	1.0
093 CHR CH (DISC)	9	764	1,010	.1	.2
097 CHR CHS&CHS CR	7	640	792*	.1	.1
105 CHRISTIAN REF	3	389	608	-	.1
111 CH CR,SCIENTST	12	NR	NR	-	-
123 CH GOD (ANDER)	8	245	349	-	.1
127 CH GOD (CLEVE)	6	346	428*	-	.1
133 CH GOD(7TH)DEN	1	49	69	-	-
145 CH GOD PROPHCY	2	62	77*	-	-
151 L-D SAINTS	47	NA	19,420	1.5	3.4
157 CH OF BRETHREN	1	48	59*	-	-
164 CH LUTH CONF	1	54	72	-	-
165 CH OF NAZARENE	12	1,519	2,312	.2	.4
167 CHS OF CHRIST	23	2,261	2,975	.2	.5
175 CONGR CHR CHS	1	120	148*	-	-

County and Denomination	Number of churches	Communicant, confirmed, full members	Total adherents Number	Percent of total population	Percent of total adherents
179 CONSRV BAPT	11	NR	NR	-	-
185 CUMBER PRESB	1	22	22	-	-
193 EPISCOPAL	21	4,860	6,563	.5	1.2
203 EVAN FREE CH	4	594	1,085	.1	.2
207 E.L.C.A.	25	6,484	8,890	.7	1.6
215 EVAN METH CH	1	65	80*	-	-
221 FREE METHODIST	1	22	27	-	-
223 FREE WILL BAPT	2	30	37*	-	-
226 FRIENDS-USA	4	266	491*	-	.1
226e FUM	*1*	*85*	*105**	*-*	*-*
226f INDEPENDNT	*3*	*181*	*386*	*-*	*.1*
237 GC MENN BR CHS	1	39	48*	-	-
246 GREEK ORTHODOX	2	NR	NR	-	-
249 AP CATH ASSYR	0	13	72	-	-
259 IFCA	2	NR	NR	-	-
263 INT FOURSQ GOS	7	538	665*	.1	.1
274 LAT EVAN LUTH	1	88	104	-	-
283 LUTH—MO SYNOD	17	4,091	5,374	.4	.9
329 OPEN BIBLE STD	1	NR	NR	-	-
331 ORTH CH IN AM	1	NR	NR	-	-
339 PENT CH OF GOD	2	76	177	-	-
349 PENT HOLINESS	3	215	266*	-	-
353 CHR BRETHREN	8	645	1,035	.1	.2
355 PRESB CH (USA)	28	9,744	12,052*	.9	2.1
356 PRESB CH AMER	2	120	120	-	-
361 PRIM BAPT ASCS	1	95	117*	-	-
371 REF CH IN AM	2	214	389	-	.1
397 ROMANIAN ORTH	1	NR	NR	-	-
403 SALVATION ARMY	5	582	658	.1	.1
413 S.D.A.	12	3,952	4,888*	.4	.9
419 SO BAPT CONV	65	24,063	29,762*	2.3	5.2
435 UNITARIAN-UNIV	5	1,173	1,368	.1	.2
443 UN C OF CHRIST	21	3,134	3,876*	.3	.7
449 UN METHODIST	31	8,469	10,475*	.8	1.8
469 WELS	2	205	280	-	-
496 JEWISH EST[1]	12	NA	30,500	2.4	5.4
497 BLACK BAPT EST[2]	NA	49,025	60,635*	4.7	10.7
498 INDEP.CHARIS.[3]	8	NA	5,800	.5	1.0
499 INDEP.NON-CHAR[3]	4	NA	3,600	.3	.6
ALPINE	**1**	**35**	**45***	**4.0**	**100.0**
097 CHR CHS&CHS CR	1	35	45*	4.0	100.0
AMADOR	**35**	**2,565**	**7,148***	**23.8**	**100.0**
053 ASSEMB OF GOD	4	210	344	1.1	4.8
057 BAPT GEN CONF	1	26	31*	.1	.4
081 CATHOLIC	7	NA	3,055	10.2	42.7
081d LATIN	*7*	*NA*	*3,055*	*10.2*	*42.7*
111 CH CR,SCIENTST	1	NR	NR	-	-
151 L-D SAINTS	2	NA	891	3.0	12.5
165 CH OF NAZARENE	1	51	145	.5	2.0
167 CHS OF CHRIST	2	28	33	.1	.5
179 CONSRV BAPT	2	NR	NR	-	-
193 EPISCOPAL	1	140	170	.6	2.4
203 EVAN FREE CH	1	231	231	.8	3.2
207 E.L.C.A.	1	241	325	1.1	4.5
221 FREE METHODIST	1	25	25	.1	.3
226 FRIENDS-USA	1	7	11	-	.2
226f INDEPENDNT	*1*	*7*	*11*	*-*	*.2*
413 S.D.A.	1	149	175*	.6	2.4
419 SO BAPT CONV	6	612	719*	2.4	10.1
449 UN METHODIST	3	554	651*	2.2	9.1
497 BLACK BAPT EST[2]	NA	291	342*	1.1	4.8
BUTTE	**137**	**18,999**	**50,082***	**27.5**	**100.0**
019 AMER BAPT USA	3	611	755*	.4	1.5
053 ASSEMB OF GOD	13	1,381	2,453	1.3	4.9
081 CATHOLIC	8	NA	15,382	8.4	30.7
081d LATIN	*8*	*NA*	*15,382*	*8.4*	*30.7*
089 CHR & MISS AL	6	1,665	3,789	2.1	7.6
093 CHR CH (DISC)	2	594	735	.4	1.5
097 CHR CHS&CHS CR	3	328	405*	.2	.8
111 CH CR,SCIENTST	4	NR	NR	-	-
123 CH GOD (ANDER)	3	81	91	-	.2
127 CH GOD (CLEVE)	3	243	300*	.2	.6
145 CH GOD PROPHCY	1	31	38*	-	.1
151 L-D SAINTS	19	NA	7,066	3.9	14.1
157 CH OF BRETHREN	1	52	64*	-	.1
165 CH OF NAZARENE	4	609	943	.5	1.9
167 CHS OF CHRIST	8	494	569	.3	1.1
175 CONGR CHR CHS	1	340	420*	.2	.8
193 EPISCOPAL	4	692	1,266	.7	2.5
203 EVAN FREE CH	4	763	1,242	.7	2.5
207 E.L.C.A.	2	776	1,004	.6	2.0
209 EVAN LUTH SYN	1	4	4	-	-
217 FIRE BAPTIZED	1	14	17*	-	-

NA–Not applicable NR–Not reported *Total adherents estimated from known number of communicant, confirmed, full members. - Represents a percent less than 0.1. Percentages may not total due to rounding.
[1]See Appendix E [2]See Appendix F [3]See Appendix G Lines in *italic* represent a breakdown of Catholic rites or Friends affiliations. They are included in their respective denominational total.

Table 4. Churches and Church Membership by County and Denomination: 1990

County and Denomination	Number of churches	Communicant, confirmed, full members	Total adherents		
			Number	Percent of total population	Percent of total adherents
221 FREE METHODIST	1	99	150	.1	.3
226 FRIENDS-USA	1	15	46	-	.1
226f INDEPENDNT	1	15	46	-	.1
263 INT FOURSQ GOS	3	486	601*	.3	1.2
283 LUTH—MO SYNOD	4	1,087	1,439	.8	2.9
339 PENT CH OF GOD	4	171	354	.2	.7
353 CHR BRETHREN	1	12	24	-	-
355 PRESB CH (USA)	3	1,068	1,320*	.7	2.6
356 PRESB CH AMER	1	17	17	-	-
403 SALVATION ARMY	2	132	147	.1	.3
413 S.D.A.	6	2,768	3,421*	1.9	6.8
419 SO BAPT CONV	9	1,948	2,407*	1.3	4.8
435 UNITARIAN-UNIV	1	46	58	-	.1
443 UN C OF CHRIST	2	254	314*	.2	.6
449 UN METHODIST	7	1,713	2,117*	1.2	4.2
496 JEWISH EST[1]	1	NA	500	.3	1.0
497 BLACK BAPT EST[2]	NA	505	624*	.3	1.2
CALAVERAS	**36**	**1,453**	**9,767***	**30.5**	**100.0**
019 AMER BAPT USA	1	50	62*	.2	.6
053 ASSEMB OF GOD	3	138	231	.7	2.4
081 CATHOLIC	7	NA	7,005	21.9	71.7
081d LATIN	7	NA	7,005	21.9	71.7
089 CHR & MISS AL	1	0	50	.2	.5
111 CH CR,SCIENTST	1	NR	NR	-	-
123 CH GOD (ANDER)	1	15	21	.1	.2
151 L-D SAINTS	1	NA	774	2.4	7.9
165 CH OF NAZARENE	1	29	42	.1	.4
167 CHS OF CHRIST	3	70	90	.3	.9
193 EPISCOPAL	2	211	256	.8	2.6
207 E.L.C.A.	1	95	121	.4	1.2
283 LUTH—MO SYNOD	1	75	99	.3	1.0
291 MISSIONARY CH	1	0	25	.1	.3
339 PENT CH OF GOD	1	34	77	.2	.8
413 S.D.A.	3	165	205*	.6	2.1
419 SO BAPT CONV	5	347	431*	1.3	4.4
443 UN C OF CHRIST	2	224	278*	.9	2.8
COLUSA	**27**	**1,676**	**5,792***	**35.6**	**100.0**
019 AMER BAPT USA	2	228	302*	1.9	5.2
053 ASSEMB OF GOD	5	165	392	2.4	6.8
081 CATHOLIC	6	NA	2,929	18.0	50.6
081d LATIN	6	NA	2,929	18.0	50.6
089 CHR & MISS AL	1	52	161	1.0	2.8
093 CHR CH (DISC)	1	50	65	.4	1.1
151 L-D SAINTS	1	NA	275	1.7	4.7
193 EPISCOPAL	1	59	129	.8	2.2
283 LUTH—MO SYNOD	1	57	75	.5	1.3
339 PENT CH OF GOD	1	33	100	.6	1.7
349 PENT HOLINESS	1	35	46*	.3	.8
355 PRESB CH (USA)	1	143	189*	1.2	3.3
413 S.D.A.	0	32	42*	.3	.7
419 SO BAPT CONV	2	416	550*	3.4	9.5
449 UN METHODIST	4	406	537*	3.3	9.3
CONTRA COSTA	**378**	**78,259**	**324,874***	**40.4**	**100.0**
019 AMER BAPT USA	18	3,995	5,004*	.6	1.5
053 ASSEMB OF GOD	19	2,778	4,905	.6	1.5
057 BAPT GEN CONF	3	1,007	1,261*	.2	.4
081 CATHOLIC	34	NA	180,000	22.4	55.4
081d LATIN	34	NA	180,000	22.4	55.4
089 CHR & MISS AL	5	463	1,070	.1	.3
093 CHR CH (DISC)	4	685	911	.1	.3
097 CHR CHS&CHS CR	3	415	520*	.1	.2
105 CHRISTIAN REF	1	209	320	-	.1
111 CH CR,SCIENTST	9	NR	NR	-	-
123 CH GOD (ANDER)	2	57	64	-	-
127 CH GOD (CLEVE)	3	341	427*	.1	.1
145 CH GOD PROPHCY	2	62	78*	-	-
151 L-D SAINTS	46	NA	19,636	2.4	6.0
165 CH OF NAZARENE	6	1,053	2,215	.3	.7
167 CHS OF CHRIST	21	2,267	2,861	.4	.9
175 CONGR CHR CHS	1	42	53*	-	-
179 CONSRV BAPT	4	NR	NR	-	-
193 EPISCOPAL	17	4,159	6,236	.8	1.9
203 EVAN FREE CH	6	1,162	1,476	.2	.5
207 E.L.C.A.	16	5,107	6,826	.8	2.1
221 FREE METHODIST	3	262	262	-	.1
223 FREE WILL BAPT	5	480	601*	.1	.2
226 FRIENDS-USA	1	62	72	-	-
226e FUM	1	62	72	-	-
246 GREEK ORTHODOX	2	NR	NR	-	-
249 AP CATH ASSYR	0	11	47	-	-
263 INT FOURSQ GOS	7	1,698	2,127*	.3	.7
283 LUTH—MO SYNOD	14	3,328	4,535	.6	1.4
329 OPEN BIBLE STD	7	NR	NR	-	-

County and Denomination	Number of churches	Communicant, confirmed, full members	Total adherents		
			Number	Percent of total population	Percent of total adherents
331 ORTH CH IN AM	1	NR	NR	-	-
339 PENT CH OF GOD	7	315	958	.1	.3
349 PENT HOLINESS	4	243	304*	-	.1
353 CHR BRETHREN	4	340	655	.1	.2
355 PRESB CH (USA)	15	10,362	12,979*	1.6	4.0
356 PRESB CH AMER	2	51	72	-	-
361 PRIM BAPT ASCS	1	7	9*	-	-
403 SALVATION ARMY	3	139	149	-	-
413 S.D.A.	7	2,319	2,905*	.4	.9
415 S-D BAPTIST GC	1	51	64*	-	-
419 SO BAPT CONV	35	9,579	11,998*	1.5	3.7
435 UNITARIAN-UNIV	1	334	444	.1	.1
443 UN C OF CHRIST	9	2,309	2,892*	.4	.9
449 UN METHODIST	21	6,530	8,179*	1.0	2.5
467 WESLEYAN	1	47	127	-	-
469 WELS	1	42	56	-	-
496 JEWISH EST[1]	4	NA	21,000	2.6	6.5
497 BLACK BAPT EST[2]	NA	15,948	19,976*	2.5	6.1
499 INDEP.NON-CHAR[3]	2	NA	600	.1	.2
DEL NORTE	**25**	**2,954**	**7,986***	**34.0**	**100.0**
053 ASSEMB OF GOD	2	177	325	1.4	4.1
081 CATHOLIC	2	NA	3,212	13.7	40.2
081d LATIN	2	NA	3,212	13.7	40.2
097 CHR CHS&CHS CR	1	40	51*	.2	.6
111 CH CR,SCIENTST	1	NR	NR	-	-
145 CH GOD PROPHCY	1	31	40*	.2	.5
151 L-D SAINTS	2	NA	651	2.8	8.2
165 CH OF NAZARENE	1	97	232	1.0	2.9
167 CHS OF CHRIST	1	12	14	.1	.2
193 EPISCOPAL	1	66	96	.4	1.2
203 EVAN FREE CH	1	19	75	.3	.9
259 IFCA	1	NR	NR	-	-
263 INT FOURSQ GOS	2	378	485*	2.1	6.1
283 LUTH—MO SYNOD	1	289	405	1.7	5.1
339 PENT CH OF GOD	1	34	77	.3	1.0
413 S.D.A.	1	286	367*	1.6	4.6
419 SO BAPT CONV	3	911	1,169*	5.0	14.6
449 UN METHODIST	1	468	600*	2.6	7.5
497 BLACK BAPT EST[2]	NA	146	187*	.8	2.3
EL DORADO	**64**	**7,205**	**25,828***	**20.5**	**100.0**
019 AMER BAPT USA	1	198	252*	.2	1.0
053 ASSEMB OF GOD	4	475	695	.6	2.7
081 CATHOLIC	5	NA	11,615	9.2	45.0
081d LATIN	5	NA	11,615	9.2	45.0
089 CHR & MISS AL	1	0	126	.1	.5
097 CHR CHS&CHS CR	1	136	173*	.1	.7
111 CH CR,SCIENTST	2	NR	NR	-	-
145 CH GOD PROPHCY	1	31	39*	-	.2
151 L-D SAINTS	7	NA	3,422	2.7	13.2
165 CH OF NAZARENE	1	158	253	.2	1.0
167 CHS OF CHRIST	3	196	267	.2	1.0
179 CONSRV BAPT	2	NR	NR	-	-
193 EPISCOPAL	1	353	439	.3	1.7
203 EVAN FREE CH	2	120	265	.2	1.0
207 E.L.C.A.	2	418	593	.5	2.3
237 GC MENN BR CHS	1	60	76*	.1	.3
259 IFCA	1	NR	NR	-	-
263 INT FOURSQ GOS	3	159	202*	.2	.8
283 LUTH—MO SYNOD	1	568	767	.6	3.0
313 N AM BAPT CONF	1	139	177*	.1	.7
329 OPEN BIBLE STD	1	NR	NR	-	-
339 PENT CH OF GOD	2	117	222	.2	.9
355 PRESB CH (USA)	2	691	878*	.7	3.4
413 S.D.A.	5	1,051	1,336*	1.1	5.2
419 SO BAPT CONV	7	1,148	1,459*	1.2	5.6
443 UN C OF CHRIST	2	99	126*	.1	.5
449 UN METHODIST	3	958	1,218*	1.0	4.7
496 JEWISH EST[1]	0	NA	1,063	.8	4.1
497 BLACK BAPT EST[2]	NA	130	165*	.1	.6
FRESNO	**469**	**79,946**	**267,048***	**40.0**	**100.0**
005 AME ZION	1	13	27	-	-
019 AMER BAPT USA	20	4,534	6,076*	.9	2.3
039 AP CHR CH(NAZ)	1	34	46*	-	-
053 ASSEMB OF GOD	45	8,948	14,200	2.1	5.3
057 BAPT GEN CONF	6	1,634	2,190*	.3	.8
059 BAPT MISS ASSN	1	137	184*	-	.1
081 CATHOLIC	37	NA	130,050	19.5	48.7
081b BYZAN RUTH	1	NA	50	-	-
081d LATIN	36	NA	130,000	19.5	48.7
089 CHR & MISS AL	4	1,910	2,177	.3	.8
093 CHR CH (DISC)	3	315	417	.1	.2
097 CHR CHS&CHS CR	6	1,573	2,108*	.3	.8
105 CHRISTIAN REF	1	193	318	-	.1

NA–Not applicable   NR–Not reported   *Total adherents estimated from known number of communicant, confirmed, full members.   - Represents a percent less than 0.1.   Percentages may not total due to rounding.
[1]See Appendix E   [2]See Appendix F   [3]See Appendix G   Lines in *italic* represent a breakdown of Catholic rites or Friends affiliations. They are included in their respective denominational total.

Table 4. Churches and Church Membership by County and Denomination: 1990

County and Denomination	Number of churches	Communicant, confirmed, full members	Total adherents		
			Number	Percent of total population	Percent of total adherents
111 CH CR,SCIENTST	3	NR	NR	-	-
123 CH GOD (ANDER)	6	501	583	.1	.2
127 CH GOD (CLEVE)	11	1,045	1,400*	.2	.5
145 CH GOD PROPHCY	8	270	362*	.1	.1
151 L-D SAINTS	46	NA	16,561	2.5	6.2
157 CH OF BRETHREN	3	580	777*	.1	.3
165 CH OF NAZARENE	15	1,611	2,428	.4	.9
167 CHS OF CHRIST	32	3,090	4,185	.6	1.6
175 CONGR CHR CHS	2	495	663*	.1	.2
179 CONSRV BAPT	2	NR	NR	-	-
185 CUMBER PRESB	1	64	79	-	-
193 EPISCOPAL	10	1,614	2,328	.3	.9
203 EVAN FREE CH	5	1,575	2,270	.3	.9
207 E.L.C.A.	18	4,780	6,678	1.0	2.5
221 FREE METHODIST	2	54	93	-	-
223 FREE WILL BAPT	8	1,327	1,778*	.3	.7
226 FRIENDS-USA	2	425	591*	.1	.2
226e FUM	*1*	*399*	*535**	*.1*	*.2*
226f INDEPENDNT	*1*	*26*	*56*	*-*	*-*
237 GC MENN BR CHS	13	3,061	4,102*	.6	1.5
246 GREEK ORTHODOX	2	NR	NR	-	-
263 INT FOURSQ GOS	8	2,133	2,858*	.4	1.1
283 LUTH—MO SYNOD	4	1,068	1,325	.2	.5
285 MENNONITE CH	1	92	153	-	.1
287 MENN GEN CONF	3	462	577	.1	.2
329 OPEN BIBLE STD	1	NR	NR	-	-
339 PENT CH OF GOD	15	544	1,615	.2	.6
349 PENT HOLINESS	9	472	632*	.1	.2
353 CHR BRETHREN	1	17	50	-	-
355 PRESB CH (USA)	14	4,356	5,837*	.9	2.2
356 PRESB CH AMER	1	60	60	-	-
361 PRIM BAPT ASCS	1	45	60*	-	-
403 SALVATION ARMY	1	158	194	-	.1
413 S.D.A.	15	4,116	5,515*	.8	2.1
419 SO BAPT CONV	39	12,397	16,612*	2.5	6.2
435 UNITARIAN-UNIV	1	188	268	-	.1
443 UN C OF CHRIST	6	1,974	2,645*	.4	1.0
449 UN METHODIST	24	4,790	6,419*	1.0	2.4
469 WELS	2	143	204	-	.1
496 JEWISH EST[1]	2	NA	2,000	.3	.7
497 BLACK BAPT EST[2]	NA	7,148	9,578*	1.4	3.6
498 INDEP.CHARIS.[3]	4	NA	1,725	.3	.6
499 INDEP.NON-CHAR[3]	3	NA	6,050	.9	2.3
GLENN	**37**	**3,069**	**9,962***	**40.2**	**100.0**
019 AMER BAPT USA	3	459	606*	2.4	6.1
053 ASSEMB OF GOD	3	151	316	1.3	3.2
081 CATHOLIC	3	NA	4,878	19.7	49.0
081d LATIN	*3*	*NA*	*4,878*	*19.7*	*49.0*
089 CHR & MISS AL	1	0	60	.2	.6
097 CHR CHS&CHS CR	2	210	277*	1.1	2.8
143 CG IN CR(MENN)	1	215	284*	1.1	2.9
151 L-D SAINTS	2	NA	663	2.7	6.7
165 CH OF NAZARENE	1	50	106	.4	1.1
167 CHS OF CHRIST	2	38	52	.2	.5
193 EPISCOPAL	2	163	258	1.0	2.6
203 EVAN FREE CH	2	172	275	1.1	2.8
207 E.L.C.A.	1	200	241	1.0	2.4
226 FRIENDS-USA	1	44	55	.2	.6
226e FUM	*1*	*44*	*55*	*.2*	*.6*
237 GC MENN BR CHS	1	40	53*	.2	.5
263 INT FOURSQ GOS	1	38	50*	.2	.5
283 LUTH—MO SYNOD	2	135	198	.8	2.0
339 PENT CH OF GOD	1	22	90	.4	.9
355 PRESB CH (USA)	1	63	83*	.3	.8
373 REF CH IN U.S.	1	31	46	.2	.5
413 S.D.A.	2	113	149*	.6	1.5
419 SO BAPT CONV	2	516	682*	2.8	6.8
449 UN METHODIST	2	409	540*	2.2	5.4
HUMBOLDT	**144**	**14,748**	**35,186***	**29.5**	**100.0**
019 AMER BAPT USA	3	626	790*	.7	2.2
053 ASSEMB OF GOD	16	1,276	2,173	1.8	6.2
081 CATHOLIC	17	NA	10,706	9.0	30.4
081d LATIN	*17*	*NA*	*10,706*	*9.0*	*30.4*
093 CHR CH (DISC)	1	85	150	.1	.4
097 CHR CHS&CHS CR	4	564	712*	.6	2.0
111 CH CR,SCIENTST	3	NR	NR	-	-
127 CH GOD (CLEVE)	3	161	203*	.2	.6
145 CH GOD PROPHCY	2	62	78*	.1	.2
151 L-D SAINTS	8	NA	2,593	2.2	7.4
165 CH OF NAZARENE	7	614	1,253	1.1	3.6
167 CHS OF CHRIST	4	243	275	.2	.8
193 EPISCOPAL	5	795	1,467	1.2	4.2
203 EVAN FREE CH	2	173	245	.2	.7
207 E.L.C.A.	7	961	1,297	1.1	3.7
226 FRIENDS-USA	2	8	32	-	.1

County and Denomination	Number of churches	Communicant, confirmed, full members	Total adherents		
			Number	Percent of total population	Percent of total adherents
226f INDEPENDNT	*2*	*8*	*32*	*-*	*.1*
259 IFCA	1	NR	NR	-	-
263 INT FOURSQ GOS	5	478	603*	.5	1.7
283 LUTH—MO SYNOD	4	401	526	.4	1.5
339 PENT CH OF GOD	4	136	303	.3	.9
349 PENT HOLINESS	1	5	6*	-	-
355 PRESB CH (USA)	15	2,745	3,466*	2.9	9.9
403 SALVATION ARMY	1	86	98	.1	.3
413 S.D.A.	6	1,251	1,579*	1.3	4.5
419 SO BAPT CONV	14	2,749	3,471*	2.9	9.9
435 UNITARIAN-UNIV	1	120	156	.1	.4
443 UN C OF CHRIST	1	109	138*	.1	.4
449 UN METHODIST	3	896	1,131*	.9	3.2
467 WESLEYAN	1	38	75	.1	.2
496 JEWISH EST[1]	1	NA	500	.4	1.4
497 BLACK BAPT EST[2]	NA	166	210*	.2	.6
498 INDEP.CHARIS.[3]	2	NA	950	.8	2.7
IMPERIAL	**96**	**9,284**	**60,919***	**55.7**	**100.0**
019 AMER BAPT USA	4	630	859*	.8	1.4
053 ASSEMB OF GOD	15	1,372	2,665	2.4	4.4
081 CATHOLIC	13	NA	44,620	40.8	73.2
081d LATIN	*13*	*NA*	*44,620*	*40.8*	*73.2*
093 CHR CH (DISC)	1	75	112	.1	.2
097 CHR CHS&CHS CR	4	839	1,144*	1.0	1.9
111 CH CR,SCIENTST	2	NR	NR	-	-
145 CH GOD PROPHCY	2	73	100*	.1	.2
151 L-D SAINTS	4	NA	1,859	1.7	3.1
165 CH OF NAZARENE	5	259	1,058	1.0	1.7
167 CHS OF CHRIST	9	266	371	.3	.6
193 EPISCOPAL	2	219	314	.3	.5
203 EVAN FREE CH	1	30	30	-	-
226 FRIENDS-USA	2	52	108	.1	.2
226e FUM	*2*	*52*	*108*	*.1*	*.2*
259 IFCA	2	NR	NR	-	-
263 INT FOURSQ GOS	3	150	205*	.2	.3
283 LUTH—MO SYNOD	4	473	730	.7	1.2
339 PENT CH OF GOD	1	21	35	-	.1
355 PRESB CH (USA)	3	368	502*	.5	.8
361 PRIM BAPT ASCS	1	0	0*	-	-
403 SALVATION ARMY	1	53	77	.1	.1
413 S.D.A.	4	946	1,290*	1.2	2.1
419 SO BAPT CONV	9	2,401	3,274*	3.0	5.4
449 UN METHODIST	4	603	822*	.8	1.3
496 JEWISH EST[1]	0	NA	125	.1	.2
497 BLACK BAPT EST[2]	NA	454	619*	.6	1.0
INYO	**30**	**1,952**	**5,222***	**28.6**	**100.0**
053 ASSEMB OF GOD	2	131	290	1.6	5.6
081 CATHOLIC	5	NA	2,000	10.9	38.3
081d LATIN	*5*	*NA*	*2,000*	*10.9*	*38.3*
111 CH CR,SCIENTST	1	NR	NR	-	-
151 L-D SAINTS	2	NA	569	3.1	10.9
165 CH OF NAZARENE	2	160	239	1.3	4.6
167 CHS OF CHRIST	1	37	48	.3	.9
179 CONSRV BAPT	1	NR	NR	-	-
193 EPISCOPAL	2	161	229	1.3	4.4
209 EVAN LUTH SYN	1	41	45	.2	.9
263 INT FOURSQ GOS	2	255	317*	1.7	6.1
283 LUTH—MO SYNOD	1	160	234	1.3	4.5
355 PRESB CH (USA)	2	246	306*	1.7	5.9
413 S.D.A.	2	136	169*	.9	3.2
419 SO BAPT CONV	3	224	278*	1.5	5.3
449 UN METHODIST	3	401	498*	2.7	9.5
KERN	**433**	**67,227**	**190,667***	**35.1**	**100.0**
019 AMER BAPT USA	16	4,554	6,125*	1.1	3.2
053 ASSEMB OF GOD	43	5,678	10,734	2.0	5.6
057 BAPT GEN CONF	1	151	203*	-	.1
059 BAPT MISS ASSN	2	83	112*	-	.1
081 CATHOLIC	29	NA	75,000	13.8	39.3
081d LATIN	*29*	*NA*	*75,000*	*13.8*	*39.3*
089 CHR & MISS AL	3	213	586	.1	.3
093 CHR CH (DISC)	2	408	461	.1	.2
097 CHR CHS&CHS CR	7	1,000	1,345*	.2	.7
105 CHRISTIAN REF	1	50	78	-	-
111 CH CR,SCIENTST	6	NR	NR	-	-
123 CH GOD (ANDER)	1	190	190	-	.1
127 CH GOD (CLEVE)	10	874	1,176*	.2	.6
133 CH GOD(7TH)DEN	1	49	69	-	-
145 CH GOD PROPHCY	7	262	352*	.1	.2
151 L-D SAINTS	28	NA	11,630	2.1	6.1
157 CH OF BRETHREN	3	306	412*	.1	.2
165 CH OF NAZARENE	16	2,455	3,329	.6	1.7
167 CHS OF CHRIST	36	3,328	4,338	.8	2.3
171 CH GOD-GEN CON	2	87	117*	-	.1

NA–Not applicable   NR–Not reported   *Total adherents estimated from known number of communicant, confirmed, full members.   - Represents a percent less than 0.1.   Percentages may not total due to rounding.
[1]See Appendix E   [2]See Appendix F   [3]See Appendix G   Lines in *italic* represent a breakdown of Catholic rites or Friends affiliations. They are included in their respective denominational total.

Table 4. Churches and Church Membership by County and Denomination: 1990

County and Denomination	Number of churches	Communicant, confirmed, full members	Total adherents Number	Percent of total population	Percent of total adherents
179 CONSRV BAPT	4	NR	NR	-	-
193 EPISCOPAL	9	1,482	2,133	.4	1.1
203 EVAN FREE CH	5	130	225	-	.1
207 E.L.C.A.	6	1,622	2,170	.4	1.1
223 FREE WILL BAPT	7	542	729*	.1	.4
226 FRIENDS-USA	2	127	174*	-	.1
226e FUM	*1*	*127*	*171**	*-*	*.1*
226f INDEPENDNT	*1*	*0*	*3*		
237 GC MENN BR CHS	6	1,318	1,773*	.3	.9
246 GREEK ORTHODOX	1	NR	NR	-	-
259 IFCA	1	NR	NR	-	-
263 INT FOURSQ GOS	8	1,772	2,383*	.4	1.2
283 LUTH—MO SYNOD	12	2,826	4,294	.8	2.3
339 PENT CH OF GOD	23	931	2,540	.5	1.3
349 PENT HOLINESS	9	331	445*	.1	.2
355 PRESB CH (USA)	6	2,090	2,811*	.5	1.5
356 PRESB CH AMER	1	20	30	-	-
373 REF CH IN U.S.	2	223	269	-	.1
403 SALVATION ARMY	2	214	237	-	.1
413 S.D.A.	16	3,381	4,547*	.8	2.4
419 SO BAPT CONV	58	18,904	25,425*	4.7	13.3
435 UNITARIAN-UNIV	2	72	85	-	-
443 UN C OF CHRIST	7	889	1,196*	.2	.6
449 UN METHODIST	19	4,192	5,638*	1.0	3.0
467 WESLEYAN	1	18	50	-	-
469 WELS	1	11	14	-	-
496 JEWISH EST[1]	3	NA	1,400	.3	.7
497 BLACK BAPT EST[2]	NA	6,444	8,667*	1.6	4.5
498 INDEP.CHARIS.[3]	7	NA	4,175	.8	2.2
499 INDEP.NON-CHAR[3]	1	NA	3,000	.6	1.6
KINGS	**87**	**9,772**	**30,918***	**30.5**	**100.0**
019 AMER BAPT USA	4	986	1,310*	1.3	4.2
053 ASSEMB OF GOD	11	1,082	1,959	1.9	6.3
057 BAPT GEN CONF	1	52	69*	.1	.2
081 CATHOLIC	8	NA	15,000	14.8	48.5
081d LATIN	*8*	*NA*	*15,000*	*14.8*	*48.5*
093 CHR CH (DISC)	1	244	286	.3	.9
105 CHRISTIAN REF	1	447	684	.7	2.2
123 CH GOD (ANDER)	2	27	115	.1	.4
127 CH GOD (CLEVE)	1	92	122*	.1	.4
151 L-D SAINTS	3	NA	1,308	1.3	4.2
165 CH OF NAZARENE	4	208	306	.3	1.0
167 CHS OF CHRIST	9	497	721	.7	2.3
179 CONSRV BAPT	2	NR	NR	-	-
193 EPISCOPAL	3	196	293	.3	.9
203 EVAN FREE CH	1	51	105	.1	.3
207 E.L.C.A.	1	143	280	.3	.9
223 FREE WILL BAPT	2	101	134*	.1	.4
259 IFCA	1	NR	NR	-	-
263 INT FOURSQ GOS	1	47	62*	.1	.2
283 LUTH—MO SYNOD	2	209	315	.3	1.0
339 PENT CH OF GOD	5	86	277	.3	.9
349 PENT HOLINESS	1	20	27*	-	.1
355 PRESB CH (USA)	4	642	853*	.8	2.8
403 SALVATION ARMY	1	89	93	.1	.3
413 S.D.A.	5	897	1,192*	1.2	3.9
419 SO BAPT CONV	7	1,458	1,937*	1.9	6.3
449 UN METHODIST	5	770	1,023*	1.0	3.3
496 JEWISH EST[1]	0	NA	125	.1	.4
497 BLACK BAPT EST[2]	NA	1,428	1,897*	1.9	6.1
498 INDEP.CHARIS.[3]	1	NA	425	.4	1.4
LAKE	**54**	**4,065**	**10,881***	**21.5**	**100.0**
019 AMER BAPT USA	1	115	143*	.3	1.3
053 ASSEMB OF GOD	4	412	535	1.1	4.9
081 CATHOLIC	8	NA	4,283	8.5	39.4
081d LATIN	*8*	*NA*	*4,283*	*8.5*	*39.4*
093 CHR CH (DISC)	1	67	100	.2	.9
097 CHR CHS&CHS CR	1	25	31*	.1	.3
111 CH CR,SCIENTST	1	NR	NR	-	-
127 CH GOD (CLEVE)	1	38	47*	.1	.4
151 L-D SAINTS	2	NA	1,305	2.6	12.0
165 CH OF NAZARENE	1	78	117	.2	1.1
167 CHS OF CHRIST	2	111	138	.3	1.3
193 EPISCOPAL	1	66	155	.3	1.4
203 EVAN FREE CH	2	134	245	.5	2.3
207 E.L.C.A.	1	114	164	.3	1.5
226 FRIENDS-USA	1	0	8	-	.1
226f INDEPENDNT	*1*	*0*	*8*	*-*	*.1*
259 IFCA	1	NR	NR	-	-
263 INT FOURSQ GOS	1	26	32*	.1	.3
283 LUTH—MO SYNOD	2	168	184	.4	1.7
329 OPEN BIBLE STD	1	NR	NR	-	-
339 PENT CH OF GOD	1	35	77	.2	.7
349 PENT HOLINESS	1	66	82*	.2	.8
355 PRESB CH (USA)	2	283	351*	.7	3.2

County and Denomination	Number of churches	Communicant, confirmed, full members	Total adherents Number	Percent of total population	Percent of total adherents
413 S.D.A.	4	465	576*	1.1	5.3
419 SO BAPT CONV	7	1,022	1,267*	2.5	11.6
449 UN METHODIST	7	678	840*	1.7	7.7
497 BLACK BAPT EST[2]	NA	162	201*	.4	1.8
LASSEN	**28**	**2,170**	**6,898***	**25.0**	**100.0**
019 AMER BAPT USA	1	100	124*	.4	1.8
053 ASSEMB OF GOD	4	313	662	2.4	9.6
081 CATHOLIC	4	NA	2,525	9.1	36.6
081d LATIN	*4*	*NA*	*2,525*	*9.1*	*36.6*
151 L-D SAINTS	5	NA	1,207	4.4	17.5
165 CH OF NAZARENE	1	44	131	.5	1.9
167 CHS OF CHRIST	1	45	50	.2	.7
193 EPISCOPAL	1	68	113	.4	1.6
259 IFCA	1	NR	NR	-	-
263 INT FOURSQ GOS	1	57	71*	.3	1.0
283 LUTH—MO SYNOD	1	164	217	.8	3.1
339 PENT CH OF GOD	2	75	176	.6	2.6
413 S.D.A.	1	177	220*	.8	3.2
419 SO BAPT CONV	4	618	769*	2.8	11.1
449 UN METHODIST	1	211	262*	.9	3.8
497 BLACK BAPT EST[2]	NA	298	371*	1.3	5.4
LOS ANGELES	**3,536**	**855,804**	**4,879,355***	**55.1**	**100.0**
001 ADVENT CHR CH	6	350	443*	-	-
005 AME ZION	7	6,200	7,458	.1	.2
019 AMER BAPT USA	202	60,091	76,010*	.9	1.6
039 AP CHR CH(NAZ)	2	203	257*	-	-
040 AP CHR CH-AMER	2	48	88	-	-
045 APOSTOLIC LUTH	1	11	30	-	-
053 ASSEMB OF GOD	231	38,188	55,107	.6	1.1
057 BAPT GEN CONF	29	13,046	16,502*	.2	.3
059 BAPT MISS ASSN	3	392	496*	-	-
071 BRETHREN (ASH)	2	81	102*	-	-
075 BRETHREN IN CR	3	113	179	-	-
081 CATHOLIC	272	NA	3,077,114	34.7	63.1
081a ARMENIAN	*1*	*NA*	*14,700*	*.2*	*.3*
081b BYZAN RUTH	*1*	*NA*	*544*	*-*	*-*
081c CHALDEAN	*1*	*NA*	*2,500*	*-*	*.1*
081d LATIN	*265*	*NA*	*3,052,629*	*34.4*	*62.6*
081e MARONITE	*1*	*NA*	*3,416*	*-*	*.1*
081f MELKITE-GK	*2*	*NA*	*3,000*	*-*	*.1*
081h UKRAINIAN	*1*	*NA*	*325*	*-*	*-*
089 CHR & MISS AL	47	4,487	6,214	.1	.1
093 CHR CH (DISC)	64	10,539	15,767	.2	.3
097 CHR CHS&CHS CR	62	11,762	14,878*	.2	.3
105 CHRISTIAN REF	23	4,524	6,693	.1	.1
111 CH CR,SCIENTST	75	NR	NR	-	-
121 CH GOD (ABR)	1	46	58*	-	-
123 CH GOD (ANDER)	31	6,856	7,038	.1	.1
127 CH GOD (CLEVE)	30	2,689	3,401*	-	.1
133 CH GOD(7TH)DEN	6	296	416	-	-
145 CH GOD PROPHCY	20	769	973*	-	-
151 L-D SAINTS	271	NA	103,286	1.2	2.1
157 CH OF BRETHREN	16	2,047	2,589*	-	.1
163 CH OF LUTH BR	1	50	85	-	-
165 CH OF NAZARENE	102	15,575	29,917	.3	.6
167 CHS OF CHRIST	114	18,623	24,257	.3	.5
175 CONGR CHR CHS	18	4,420	5,591*	.1	.1
176 CCC, NOT NAT'L	2	269	340*	-	-
179 CONSRV BAPT	39	NR	NR	-	-
181 CONSRV CONGR	7	5,349	6,766*	.1	.1
193 EPISCOPAL	85	32,803	50,674	.6	1.0
195 ESTONIAN ELC	1	341	431*	-	-
203 EVAN FREE CH	30	3,397	5,357	.1	.1
207 E.L.C.A.	132	32,124	43,542	.5	.9
209 EVAN LUTH SYN	1	46	65	-	-
215 EVAN METH CH	4	233	295*	-	-
216 EVAN PRESBY CH	3	189	198	-	-
217 FIRE BAPTIZED	2	14	18*	-	-
220 FREE LUTHERAN	1	44	63	-	-
221 FREE METHODIST	29	1,841	2,060	-	-
223 FREE WILL BAPT	7	320	405*	-	-
226 FRIENDS-USA	25	2,872	3,414	-	.1
226e FUM	*17*	*2,599*	*3,002*	*-*	*.1*
226f INDEPENDNT	*8*	*273*	*412*		
237 GC MENN BR CHS	5	240	304*	-	-
246 GREEK ORTHODOX	8	NR	NR	-	-
249 AP CATH ASSYR	1	90	387	-	-
259 IFCA	21	NR	NR	-	-
263 INT FOURSQ GOS	231	51,608	65,280*	.7	1.3
274 LAT EVAN LUTH	1	457	495	-	-
283 LUTH—MO SYNOD	93	23,312	30,684	.3	.6
284 LUTH CH-AM ASC	3	491	621	-	-
285 MENNONITE CH	11	569	927	-	-
287 MENN GEN CONF	2	114	154	-	-
291 MISSIONARY CH	14	2,625	3,584	-	.1

NA—Not applicable   NR–Not reported   *Total adherents estimated from known number of communicant, confirmed, full members.   - Represents a percent less than 0.1.   Percentages may not total due to rounding.
[1]See Appendix E   [2]See Appendix F   [3]See Appendix G   Lines in *italic* represent a breakdown of Catholic rites or Friends affiliations. They are included in their respective denominational total.

Table 4. Churches and Church Membership by County and Denomination: 1990

County and Denomination	Number of churches	Communicant, confirmed, full members	Total adherents Number	Percent of total population	Percent of total adherents
293 MORAV CH-NORTH	2	273	388	-	-
307 NETH REF CONGR	1	18	27	-	-
313 N AM BAPT CONF	2	68	86*	-	-
329 OPEN BIBLE STD	11	NR	NR	-	-
331 ORTH CH IN AM	4	NR	NR	-	-
339 PENT CH OF GOD	20	672	1,432	-	-
349 PENT HOLINESS	12	2,488	3,147*	-	.1
353 CHR BRETHREN	17	916	1,464	-	-
355 PRESB CH (USA)	170	50,729	64,168*	.7	1.3
356 PRESB CH AMER	17	1,705	2,125	-	-
371 REF CH IN AM	13	4,031	7,936	.1	.2
373 REF CH IN U.S.	1	19	28	-	-
375 REF EPISCOPAL	2	33	40	-	-
397 ROMANIAN ORTH	3	NR	NR	-	-
403 SALVATION ARMY	24	3,034	3,332	-	.1
413 S.D.A.	123	43,097	54,514*	.6	1.1
415 S-D BAPTIST GC	1	52	66*	-	-
419 SO BAPT CONV	226	101,900	128,895*	1.5	2.6
423 SYRIAN ANTIOCH	3	NA	9,000	.1	.2
435 UNITARIAN-UNIV	15	2,631	3,127	-	.1
438 UN BRETH IN CR	3	107	107	-	-
443 UN C OF CHRIST	58	12,324	15,589*	.2	.3
449 UN METHODIST	186	55,806	70,590*	.8	1.4
467 WESLEYAN	17	1,483	2,691	-	.1
469 WELS	9	1,315	1,750	-	-
496 JEWISH EST[1]	145	NA	501,700	5.7	10.3
497 BLACK BAPT EST[2]	NA	212,349	268,605*	3.0	5.5
498 INDEP.CHARIS.[3]	30	NA	34,565	.4	.7
499 INDEP.NON-CHAR[3]	22	NA	32,970	.4	.7
MADERA	**82**	**8,091**	**25,239***	**28.7**	**100.0**
005 AME ZION	1	100	135	.2	.5
019 AMER BAPT USA	3	321	425*	.5	1.7
053 ASSEMB OF GOD	11	1,242	1,833	2.1	7.3
057 BAPT GEN CONF	3	225	298*	.3	1.2
081 CATHOLIC	5	NA	12,000	13.6	47.5
081d LATIN	*5*	*NA*	*12,000*	*13.6*	*47.5*
097 CHR CHS&CHS CR	1	225	298*	.3	1.2
111 CH CR,SCIENTST	3	NR	NR	-	-
123 CH GOD (ANDER)	3	420	420	.5	1.7
127 CH GOD (CLEVE)	2	148	196*	.2	.8
145 CH GOD PROPHCY	2	72	95*	.1	.4
151 L-D SAINTS	5	NA	1,933	2.2	7.7
165 CH OF NAZARENE	3	169	286*	.3	1.1
167 CHS OF CHRIST	4	483	552	.6	2.2
175 CONGR CHR CHS	1	150	199*	.2	.8
193 EPISCOPAL	2	188	274	.3	1.1
203 EVAN FREE CH	2	111	244	.3	1.0
207 E.L.C.A.	3	398	559	.6	2.2
223 FREE WILL BAPT	1	27	36*	-	.1
237 GC MENN BR CHS	2	118	156*	.2	.6
263 INT FOURSQ GOS	1	91	121*	.1	.5
339 PENT CH OF GOD	2	79	207	.2	.8
349 PENT HOLINESS	1	45	60*	.1	.2
355 PRESB CH (USA)	3	340	451*	.5	1.8
361 PRIM BAPT ASCS	1	27	36*	-	.1
413 S.D.A.	5	1,168	1,548*	1.8	6.1
419 SO BAPT CONV	8	1,042	1,381*	1.6	5.5
443 UN C OF CHRIST	1	65	86*	.1	.3
449 UN METHODIST	2	405	537*	.6	2.1
497 BLACK BAPT EST[2]	NA	432	573*	.7	2.3
499 INDEP.NON-CHAR[3]	1	NA	300	.3	1.2
MARIN	**121**	**15,899**	**74,014***	**32.2**	**100.0**
019 AMER BAPT USA	6	783	924*	.4	1.2
053 ASSEMB OF GOD	8	752	1,612	.7	2.2
081 CATHOLIC	19	NA	34,700	15.1	46.9
081d LATIN	*19*	*NA*	*34,700*	*15.1*	*46.9*
097 CHR CHS&CHS CR	3	100	118*	.1	.2
111 CH CR,SCIENTST	6	NR	NR	-	-
123 CH GOD (ANDER)	1	0	0	-	-
151 L-D SAINTS	3	NA	1,783	.8	2.4
165 CH OF NAZARENE	2	87	112	-	.2
167 CHS OF CHRIST	3	111	149	.1	.2
179 CONSRV BAPT	1	NR	NR	-	-
193 EPISCOPAL	11	2,749	3,618	1.6	4.9
207 E.L.C.A.	6	1,285	1,756	.8	2.4
226 FRIENDS-USA	1	20	26	-	-
226f INDEPENDNT	*1*	*20*	*26*	-	-
246 GREEK ORTHODOX	1	NR	NR	-	-
249 AP CATH ASSYR	0	20	53	-	.1
263 INT FOURSQ GOS	1	2	2*	-	-
283 LUTH—MO SYNOD	4	824	1,053	.5	1.4
331 ORTH CH IN AM	2	NR	NR	-	-
355 PRESB CH (USA)	16	3,272	3,859*	1.7	5.2
403 SALVATION ARMY	1	33	42	-	.1
413 S.D.A.	2	178	210*	.1	.3

County and Denomination	Number of churches	Communicant, confirmed, full members	Total adherents Number	Percent of total population	Percent of total adherents
419 SO BAPT CONV	8	1,894	2,234*	1.0	3.0
435 UNITARIAN-UNIV	2	232	267	.1	.4
443 UN C OF CHRIST	4	912	1,076*	.5	1.5
449 UN METHODIST	4	897	1,058*	.5	1.4
496 JEWISH EST[1]	5	NA	17,000	7.4	23.0
497 BLACK BAPT EST[2]	NA	1,748	2,062*	.9	2.8
498 INDEP.CHARIS.[3]	1	NA	300	.1	.4
MARIPOSA	**19**	**915**	**2,638***	**18.4**	**100.0**
053 ASSEMB OF GOD	1	51	90	.6	3.4
081 CATHOLIC	3	NA	1,100	7.7	41.7
081d LATIN	*3*	*NA*	*1,100*	*7.7*	*41.7*
111 CH CR,SCIENTST	1	NR	NR	-	-
151 L-D SAINTS	3	NA	340	2.4	12.9
167 CHS OF CHRIST	3	164	212	1.5	8.0
193 EPISCOPAL	1	20	28	.2	1.1
207 E.L.C.A.	1	198	277	1.9	10.5
263 INT FOURSQ GOS	1	0	0*	-	-
413 S.D.A.	2	142	174*	1.2	6.6
419 SO BAPT CONV	1	63	77*	.5	2.9
449 UN METHODIST	2	277	340*	2.4	12.9
MENDOCINO	**88**	**7,542**	**19,531***	**24.3**	**100.0**
019 AMER BAPT USA	3	669	855*	1.1	4.4
053 ASSEMB OF GOD	8	602	958	1.2	4.9
081 CATHOLIC	9	NA	7,494	9.3	38.4
081d LATIN	*9*	*NA*	*7,494*	*9.3*	*38.4*
093 CHR CH (DISC)	1	68	79	.1	.4
111 CH CR,SCIENTST	4	NR	NR	-	-
145 CH GOD PROPHCY	1	31	40*	-	.2
151 L-D SAINTS	7	NA	1,932	2.4	9.9
165 CH OF NAZARENE	3	93	203	.3	1.0
167 CHS OF CHRIST	4	105	134	.2	.7
179 CONSRV BAPT	4	NR	NR	-	-
193 EPISCOPAL	3	370	573	.7	2.9
203 EVAN FREE CH	1	235	255	.3	1.3
207 E.L.C.A.	2	442	607	.8	3.1
226 FRIENDS-USA	1	3	12	-	.1
226f INDEPENDNT	*1*	*3*	*12*	-	.1
259 IFCA	2	NR	NR	-	-
263 INT FOURSQ GOS	2	185	236*	.3	1.2
283 LUTH—MO SYNOD	3	206	266	.3	1.4
339 PENT CH OF GOD	3	103	231	.3	1.2
355 PRESB CH (USA)	5	812	1,037*	1.3	5.3
413 S.D.A.	4	1,185	1,514*	1.9	7.8
419 SO BAPT CONV	9	1,541	1,969*	2.5	10.1
435 UNITARIAN-UNIV	1	13	13	-	.1
449 UN METHODIST	8	791	1,011*	1.3	5.2
497 BLACK BAPT EST[2]	NA	88	112*	.1	.6
MERCED	**134**	**18,249**	**60,694***	**34.0**	**100.0**
001 ADVENT CHR CH	1	10	14*	-	-
005 AME ZION	1	120	135	.1	.2
019 AMER BAPT USA	6	1,289	1,781*	1.0	2.9
053 ASSEMB OF GOD	19	1,522	2,535	1.4	4.2
081 CATHOLIC	15	NA	30,000	16.8	49.4
081d LATIN	*15*	*NA*	*30,000*	*16.8*	*49.4*
089 CHR & MISS AL	1	546	546	.3	.9
093 CHR CH (DISC)	2	133	187	.1	.3
097 CHR CHS&CHS CR	1	75	104*	.1	.2
105 CHRISTIAN REF	1	72	126	.1	.2
111 CH CR,SCIENTST	1	NR	NR	-	-
123 CH GOD (ANDER)	2	293	373	.2	.6
127 CH GOD (CLEVE)	1	77	106*	.1	.2
143 CG IN CR(MENN)	2	674	931*	.5	1.5
145 CH GOD PROPHCY	1	31	43*	-	.1
151 L-D SAINTS	9	NA	3,655	2.0	6.0
165 CH OF NAZARENE	3	413	573	.3	.9
167 CHS OF CHRIST	10	682	858	.5	1.4
179 CONSRV BAPT	2	NR	NR	-	-
193 EPISCOPAL	3	344	559	.3	.9
203 EVAN FREE CH	1	94	190	.1	.3
207 E.L.C.A.	4	678	905	.5	1.5
223 FREE WILL BAPT	1	37	51*	-	.1
259 IFCA	1	NR	NR	-	-
263 INT FOURSQ GOS	2	123	170*	.1	.3
283 LUTH—MO SYNOD	2	548	757	.4	1.2
331 ORTH CH IN AM	1	NR	NR	-	-
339 PENT CH OF GOD	7	350	1,014	.6	1.7
349 PENT HOLINESS	1	20	28*	-	-
355 PRESB CH (USA)	4	845	1,167*	.7	1.9
403 SALVATION ARMY	1	86	86	-	.1
413 S.D.A.	3	566	782*	.4	1.3
419 SO BAPT CONV	15	5,112	7,062*	4.0	11.6
438 UN BRETH IN CR	1	29	29	-	-
449 UN METHODIST	6	1,657	2,289*	1.3	3.8

NA–Not applicable   NR–Not reported   *Total adherents estimated from known number of communicant, confirmed, full members.   - Represents a percent less than 0.1.   Percentages may not total due to rounding.
[1]See Appendix E   [2]See Appendix F   [3]See Appendix G   Lines in *italic* represent a breakdown of Catholic rites or Friends affiliations. They are included in their respective denominational total.

Table 4. Churches and Church Membership by County and Denomination: 1990

County and Denomination	Number of churches	Communicant, confirmed, full members	Total adherents Number	Percent of total population	Percent of total adherents
496 JEWISH EST¹	1	NA	170	.1	.3
497 BLACK BAPT EST²	NA	1,823	2,518*	1.4	4.1
498 INDEP.CHARIS.³	1	NA	400	.2	.7
499 INDEP.NON-CHAR³	1	NA	550	.3	.9
MODOC	**24**	**756**	**2,241***	**23.2**	**100.0**
053 ASSEMB OF GOD	3	145	283	2.9	12.6
081 CATHOLIC	2	NA	660	6.8	29.5
081d *LATIN*	*2*	*NA*	*660*	*6.8*	*29.5*
151 L-D SAINTS	3	NA	405	4.2	18.1
165 CH OF NAZARENE	1	18	123	1.3	5.5
167 CHS OF CHRIST	2	58	93	1.0	4.1
179 CONSRV BAPT	3	NR	NR	-	-
193 EPISCOPAL	1	49	60	.6	2.7
413 S.D.A.	2	65	83*	.9	3.7
419 SO BAPT CONV	2	149	189*	2.0	8.4
443 UN C OF CHRIST	5	272	345*	3.6	15.4
MONO	**12**	**520**	**2,573***	**25.8**	**100.0**
081 CATHOLIC	3	NA	1,788	18.0	69.5
081d *LATIN*	*3*	*NA*	*1,788*	*18.0*	*69.5*
151 L-D SAINTS	1	NA	58	.6	2.3
193 EPISCOPAL	1	44	49	.5	1.9
283 LUTH—MO SYNOD	1	63	159	1.6	6.2
349 PENT HOLINESS	1	250	314*	3.2	12.2
355 PRESB CH (USA)	2	42	53*	.5	2.1
419 SO BAPT CONV	2	114	143*	1.4	5.6
449 UN METHODIST	1	7	9*	.1	.3
MONTEREY	**186**	**29,192**	**127,351***	**35.8**	**100.0**
019 AMER BAPT USA	3	476	613*	.2	.5
053 ASSEMB OF GOD	20	1,750	2,935	.8	2.3
081 CATHOLIC	21	NA	80,442	22.6	63.2
081d *LATIN*	*21*	*NA*	*80,442*	*22.6*	*63.2*
093 CHR CH (DISC)	1	119	141	-	.1
111 CH CR,SCIENTST	4	NR	NR	-	-
123 CH GOD (ANDER)	1	35	40	-	-
127 CH GOD (CLEVE)	2	112	144*	-	.1
133 CH GOD(7TH)DEN	1	49	68	-	.1
145 CH GOD PROPHCY	3	103	133*	-	.1
151 L-D SAINTS	9	NA	3,931	1.1	3.1
165 CH OF NAZARENE	2	284	561	.2	.4
167 CHS OF CHRIST	10	519	754	.2	.6
175 CONGR CHR CHS	1	52	67*	-	.1
179 CONSRV BAPT	8	NR	NR	-	-
193 EPISCOPAL	16	4,065	5,624	1.6	4.4
207 E.L.C.A.	7	1,754	2,390	.7	1.9
223 FREE WILL BAPT	3	95	122*	-	.1
226 FRIENDS-USA	1	24	33	-	-
226f *INDEPENDNT*	*1*	*24*	*33*	-	-
263 INT FOURSQ GOS	6	326	420*	.1	.3
283 LUTH—MO SYNOD	4	518	819	.2	.6
339 PENT CH OF GOD	9	349	714	.2	.6
349 PENT HOLINESS	1	43	55*	-	-
355 PRESB CH (USA)	9	3,465	4,465*	1.3	3.5
356 PRESB CH AMER	1	33	54	-	-
403 SALVATION ARMY	2	268	275	.1	.2
413 S.D.A.	5	713	919*	.3	.7
419 SO BAPT CONV	17	6,568	8,463*	2.4	6.6
435 UNITARIAN-UNIV	2	277	348	.1	.3
443 UN C OF CHRIST	2	74	95*	-	.1
449 UN METHODIST	10	2,235	2,880*	.8	2.3
496 JEWISH EST¹	2	NA	2,000	.6	1.6
497 BLACK BAPT EST²	NA	4,886	6,296*	1.8	4.9
498 INDEP.CHARIS.³	2	NA	1,050	.3	.8
499 INDEP.NON-CHAR³	1	NA	500	.1	.4
NAPA	**67**	**13,311**	**37,581***	**33.9**	**100.0**
019 AMER BAPT USA	3	538	660*	.6	1.8
053 ASSEMB OF GOD	2	259	345	.3	.9
057 BAPT GEN CONF	1	391	480*	.4	1.3
081 CATHOLIC	7	NA	18,272	16.5	48.6
081d *LATIN*	*7*	*NA*	*18,272*	*16.5*	*48.6*
089 CHR & MISS AL	3	73	195	.2	.5
097 CHR CHS&CHS CR	2	775	951*	.9	2.5
105 CHRISTIAN REF	1	31	52	-	.1
111 CH CR,SCIENTST	2	NR	NR	-	-
123 CH GOD (ANDER)	1	40	40	-	.1
145 CH GOD PROPHCY	1	31	38*	-	.1
151 L-D SAINTS	5	NA	1,830	1.7	4.9
165 CH OF NAZARENE	1	178	398	.4	1.1
167 CHS OF CHRIST	2	65	84	.1	.2
193 EPISCOPAL	3	737	1,005	.9	2.7
203 EVAN FREE CH	1	114	190	.2	.5
207 E.L.C.A.	2	333	443	.4	1.2
226 FRIENDS-USA	1	1	15	-	-
226f *INDEPENDNT*	*1*	*1*	*15*	-	-
249 AP CATH ASSYR	0	10	42	-	.1
263 INT FOURSQ GOS	1	68	83*	.1	.2
283 LUTH—MO SYNOD	2	701	939	.8	2.5
331 ORTH CH IN AM	1	NR	NR	NR	
339 PENT CH OF GOD	1	28	90	.1	.2
353 CHR BRETHREN	1	47	80	.1	.2
355 PRESB CH (USA)	4	1,273	1,562*	1.4	4.2
361 PRIM BAPT ASCS	1	23	28*	-	.1
403 SALVATION ARMY	1	78	83	.1	.2
413 S.D.A.	9	5,348	6,564*	5.9	17.5
419 SO BAPT CONV	5	1,209	1,484*	1.3	3.9
449 UN METHODIST	2	703	863*	.8	2.3
496 JEWISH EST¹	1	NA	450	.4	1.2
497 BLACK BAPT EST²	NA	257	315*	.3	.8
NEVADA	**46**	**5,809**	**15,323***	**19.5**	**100.0**
019 AMER BAPT USA	1	82	102*	.1	.7
053 ASSEMB OF GOD	3	310	573	.7	3.7
081 CATHOLIC	4	NA	5,031	6.4	32.8
081d *LATIN*	*4*	*NA*	*5,031*	*6.4*	*32.8*
089 CHR & MISS AL	1	140	335	.4	2.2
097 CHR CHS&CHS CR	1	54	67*	.1	.4
111 CH CR,SCIENTST	2	NR	NR	-	-
123 CH GOD (ANDER)	1	0	84	-	.5
151 L-D SAINTS	5	NA	2,103	2.7	13.7
165 CH OF NAZARENE	1	69	110	.1	.7
167 CHS OF CHRIST	5	171	189	.2	1.2
179 CONSRV BAPT	1	NR	NR	-	-
193 EPISCOPAL	2	387	584	.7	3.8
207 E.L.C.A.	1	412	498	.6	3.3
226 FRIENDS-USA	1	50	114	.1	.7
226f *INDEPENDNT*	*1*	*50*	*114*	*.1*	*.7*
263 INT FOURSQ GOS	1	104	129*	.2	.8
283 LUTH—MO SYNOD	1	238	270	.3	1.8
339 PENT CH OF GOD	1	34	76	.1	.5
355 PRESB CH (USA)	1	558	692*	.9	4.5
403 SALVATION ARMY	1	26	26	-	.2
413 S.D.A.	3	704	873*	1.1	5.7
419 SO BAPT CONV	3	1,731	2,147*	2.7	14.0
449 UN METHODIST	4	697	865*	1.1	5.6
467 WESLEYAN	1	42	55	.1	.4
499 INDEP.NON-CHAR³	1	NA	400	.5	2.6
ORANGE	**859**	**186,468**	**968,040***	**40.2**	**100.0**
001 ADVENT CHR CH	1	123	153*	-	-
019 AMER BAPT USA	28	8,195	10,165*	.4	1.1
053 ASSEMB OF GOD	53	8,590	15,426	.6	1.6
057 BAPT GEN CONF	10	1,166	1,446*	.1	.1
059 BAPT MISS ASSN	2	75	93*	-	-
075 BRETHREN IN CR	1	59	71	-	-
081 CATHOLIC	60	NA	503,628	20.9	52.0
081b *BYZAN RUTH*	*1*	*NA*	*635*	-	*.1*
081c *CHALDEAN*	*1*	*NA*	*1,000*	-	*.1*
081d *LATIN*	*56*	*NA*	*501,375*	*20.8*	*51.8*
081e *MARONITE*	*1*	*NA*	*366*	-	-
081f *MELKITE-GK*	*1*	*NA*	*252*	-	-
089 CHR & MISS AL	18	1,039	2,548	.1	.3
093 CHR CH (DISC)	11	2,501	3,799	.2	.4
097 CHR CHS&CHS CR	16	11,131	13,807*	.6	1.4
105 CHRISTIAN REF	13	1,547	2,336	.1	.2
111 CH CR,SCIENTST	20	NR	NR	-	-
123 CH GOD (ANDER)	6	388	508	-	.1
127 CH GOD (CLEVE)	9	1,631	2,023*	.1	.2
133 CH GOD(7TH)DEN	1	49	69	-	-
145 CH GOD PROPHCY	4	148	184*	-	-
151 L-D SAINTS	115	NA	49,608	2.1	5.1
157 CH OF BRETHREN	2	46	57*	-	-
163 CH OF LUTH BR	1	84	129	-	-
165 CH OF NAZARENE	18	3,471	4,100	.2	.4
167 CHS OF CHRIST	38	4,167	5,357	.2	.6
175 CONGR CHR CHS	4	720	893*	-	.1
176 CCC, NOT NAT'L	1	237	294*	-	-
179 CONSRV BAPT	9	NR	NR	-	-
193 EPISCOPAL	22	8,783	13,078	.5	1.4
203 EVAN FREE CH	16	6,261	10,174	.4	1.1
207 E.L.C.A.	38	17,006	23,091	1.0	2.4
209 EVAN LUTH SYN	1	58	68	-	-
217 FIRE BAPTIZED	1	4	5*	-	-
221 FREE METHODIST	9	814	1,051	-	.1
223 FREE WILL BAPT	1	47	58*	-	-
226 FRIENDS-USA	10	2,420	2,895	.1	.3
226e *FUM*	*8*	*2,369*	*2,812*	*.1*	*.3*
226f *INDEPENDNT*	*2*	*51*	*83*	-	-
246 GREEK ORTHODOX	2	NR	NR	-	-
249 AP CATH ASSYR	1	80	325	-	-

NA–Not applicable   NR–Not reported   *Total adherents estimated from known number of communicant, confirmed, full members.   - Represents a percent less than 0.1.   Percentages may not total due to rounding.
¹See Appendix E   ²See Appendix F   ³See Appendix G   Lines in *italic* represent a breakdown of Catholic rites or Friends affiliations. They are included in their respective denominational total.

Table 4. Churches and Church Membership by County and Denomination: 1990

County and Denomination	Number of churches	Communicant, confirmed, full members	Total adherents Number	Percent of total population	Percent of total adherents
259 IFCA	8	NR	NR	-	-
263 INT FOURSQ GOS	17	3,500	4,341*	.2	.4
283 LUTH—MO SYNOD	30	14,079	19,374	.8	2.0
284 LUTH CH-AM ASC	3	191	261	-	-
287 MENN GEN CONF	1	0	0	-	-
293 MORAV CH-NORTH	1	109	131	-	-
313 N AM BAPT CONF	7	1,538	1,908*	.1	.2
329 OPEN BIBLE STD	1	NR	NR	-	-
331 ORTH CH IN AM	1	NR	NR	-	-
339 PENT CH OF GOD	3	113	264	-	-
349 PENT HOLINESS	1	30	37*	-	-
353 CHR BRETHREN	2	195	303	-	-
355 PRESB CH (USA)	36	21,423	26,573*	1.1	2.7
356 PRESB CH AMER	4	313	363	-	-
371 REF CH IN AM	7	4,157	16,850	.7	1.7
375 REF EPISCOPAL	1	44	55	-	-
397 ROMANIAN ORTH	1	NR	NR	-	-
403 SALVATION ARMY	4	789	948	-	.1
413 S.D.A.	16	6,753	8,376*	.3	.9
419 SO BAPT CONV	46	21,732	26,956*	1.1	2.8
435 UNITARIAN-UNIV	7	489	580	-	.1
443 UN C OF CHRIST	13	2,299	2,852*	.1	.3
449 UN METHODIST	45	17,930	22,240*	.9	2.3
467 WESLEYAN	2	90	375	-	-
469 WELS	3	727	988	-	.1
496 JEWISH EST[1]	22	NA	95,000	3.9	9.8
497 BLACK BAPT EST[2]	NA	9,127	11,321*	.5	1.2
498 INDEP.CHARIS.[3]	15	NA	33,950	1.4	3.5
499 INDEP.NON-CHAR[3]	20	NA	26,555	1.1	2.7
PLACER	**128**	**15,124**	**50,895***	**29.5**	**100.0**
019 AMER BAPT USA	2	318	402*	.2	.8
053 ASSEM OF GOD	9	1,327	2,375	1.4	4.7
057 BAPT GEN CONF	1	12	15*	-	-
081 CATHOLIC	11	NA	20,767	12.0	40.8
081d LATIN	11	NA	20,767	12.0	40.8
089 CHR & MISS AL	1	46	76	-	.1
093 CHR CH (DISC)	2	61	87	.1	.2
111 CH CR,SCIENTST	2	NR	NR	-	-
123 CH GOD (ANDER)	1	50	50	-	.1
133 CH GOD(7TH)DEN	1	49	69	-	.1
145 CH GOD PROPHECY	1	31	39*	-	.1
151 L-D SAINTS	16	NA	7,377	4.3	14.5
165 CH OF NAZARENE	5	590	993	.6	2.0
167 CHS OF CHRIST	4	367	517	.3	1.0
171 CH GOD-GEN CON	1	40	51*	-	.1
179 CONSRV BAPT	2	NR	NR	-	-
193 EPISCOPAL	4	803	1,072	.6	2.1
203 EVAN FREE CH	1	272	300	.2	.6
207 E.L.C.A.	5	1,659	2,188	1.3	4.3
237 GC MENN BR CHS	1	10	13*	-	-
259 IFCA	2	NR	NR	-	-
263 INT FOURSQ GOS	5	356	451*	.3	.9
283 LUTH—MO SYNOD	2	282	356	.2	.7
313 N AM BAPT CONF	1	166	210*	.1	.4
339 PENT CH OF GOD	5	109	238	.1	.5
349 PENT HOLINESS	2	34	43*	-	.1
355 PRESB CH (USA)	2	951	1,203*	.7	2.4
356 PRESB CH AMER	1	44	74	-	.1
371 REF CH IN AM	1	50	100	.1	.2
403 SALVATION ARMY	2	61	65	-	.1
413 S.D.A.	6	1,433	1,813*	1.0	3.6
419 SO BAPT CONV	13	3,024	3,827*	2.2	7.5
435 UNITARIAN-UNIV	1	56	71	-	.1
443 UN C OF CHRIST	2	922	1,167*	.7	2.3
449 UN METHODIST	9	1,548	1,959*	1.1	3.8
467 WESLEYAN	1	76	175	.1	.3
469 WELS	1	156	214	.1	.4
496 JEWISH EST[1]	0	NA	1,458	.8	2.9
497 BLACK BAPT EST[2]	NA	221	280*	.2	.6
498 INDEP.CHARIS.[3]	1	NA	450	.3	.9
499 INDEP.NON-CHAR[3]	1	NA	350	.2	.7
PLUMAS	**35**	**2,138**	**4,963***	**25.1**	**100.0**
053 ASSEM OF GOD	4	280	524	2.7	10.6
081 CATHOLIC	4	NA	1,391	7.0	28.0
081d LATIN	4	NA	1,391	7.0	28.0
111 CH CR,SCIENTST	1	NR	NR	-	-
151 L-D SAINTS	3	NA	581	2.9	11.7
165 CH OF NAZARENE	2	56	156	.8	3.1
167 CHS OF CHRIST	2	155	200	1.0	4.0
193 EPISCOPAL	2	92	133	.7	2.7
207 E.L.C.A.	1	67	78	.4	1.6
263 INT FOURSQ GOS	1	0	0*	-	-
283 LUTH—MO SYNOD	3	141	171	.9	3.4
413 S.D.A.	2	62	78*	.4	1.6
419 SO BAPT CONV	4	611	766*	3.9	15.4

County and Denomination	Number of churches	Communicant, confirmed, full members	Total adherents Number	Percent of total population	Percent of total adherents
449 UN METHODIST	5	642	805*	4.1	16.2
467 WESLEYAN	1	32	80	.4	1.6
RIVERSIDE	**587**	**98,329**	**385,068***	**32.9**	**100.0**
019 AMER BAPT USA	16	3,483	4,540*	.4	1.2
053 ASSEM OF GOD	50	5,366	8,065	.7	2.1
057 BAPT GEN CONF	9	1,586	2,067*	.2	.5
059 BAPT MISS ASSN	1	0	0*	-	-
075 BRETHREN IN CR	2	110	201	-	.1
081 CATHOLIC	44	NA	202,048	17.3	52.5
081b *BYZAN RUTH*	*1*	*NA*	*53*	-	-
081d *LATIN*	*43*	*NA*	*201,995*	*17.3*	*52.5*
089 CHR & MISS AL	4	210	322	-	.1
093 CHR CH (DISC)	5	924	1,448	.1	.4
097 CHR CHS&CHS CR	11	2,822	3,678*	.3	1.0
105 CHRISTIAN REF	1	89	156	-	-
111 CH CR,SCIENTST	9	NR	NR	-	-
123 CH GOD (ANDER)	6	339	494	-	.1
127 CH GOD (CLEVE)	9	563	734*	.1	.2
133 CH GOD(7TH)DEN	1	49	69	-	-
145 CH GOD PROPHCY	3	106	138*	-	-
151 L-D SAINTS	67	NA	28,987	2.5	7.5
157 CH OF BRETHREN	1	0	0*	-	-
165 CH OF NAZARENE	15	2,147	3,476	.3	.9
167 CHS OF CHRIST	33	2,616	3,485	.3	.9
179 CONSRV BAPT	7	NR	NR	-	-
181 CONSRV CONGR	1	112	146*	-	-
193 EPISCOPAL	16	3,236	4,504	.4	1.2
203 EVAN FREE CH	7	1,014	2,106	.2	.5
207 E.L.C.A.	15	4,681	6,395	.5	1.7
215 EVAN METH CH	1	76	99*	-	-
216 EVAN PRESBY CH	1	0	0	-	-
220 FREE LUTHERAN	1	56	73	-	-
221 FREE METHODIST	5	217	738	.1	.2
223 FREE WILL BAPT	1	10	13*	-	-
226 FRIENDS-USA	4	205	305*	-	.1
226e *FUM*	*2*	*173*	*226*	-	*.1*
226f *INDEPENDNT*	*2*	*32*	*79*	-	-
246 GREEK ORTHODOX	1	NR	NR	-	-
249 AP CATH ASSYR	0	7	36	-	-
259 IFCA	8	NR	NR	-	-
263 INT FOURSQ GOS	26	3,950	5,149*	.4	1.3
283 LUTH—MO SYNOD	17	5,914	7,750	.7	2.0
285 MENNONITE CH	1	0	20	-	-
291 MISSIONARY CH	6	585	571	-	.1
293 MORAV CH-NORTH	1	81	128	-	-
313 N AM BAPT CONF	1	52	68*	-	-
329 OPEN BIBLE STD	2	NR	NR	-	-
339 PENT CH OF GOD	11	379	936	.1	.2
349 PENT HOLINESS	6	347	452*	-	.1
353 CHR BRETHREN	2	143	200	-	.1
355 PRESB CH (USA)	12	5,029	6,555*	.6	1.7
356 PRESB CH AMER	2	51	72	-	-
371 REF CH IN AM	6	1,801	4,581	.4	1.2
397 ROMANIAN ORTH	1	NR	NR	-	-
403 SALVATION ARMY	1	161	167	-	-
413 S.D.A.	26	11,907	15,521*	1.3	4.0
415 S-D BAPTIST GC	2	48	63*	-	-
419 SO BAPT CONV	51	15,426	20,108*	1.7	5.2
435 UNITARIAN-UNIV	3	163	173	-	-
443 UN C OF CHRIST	8	1,611	2,100*	.2	.5
449 UN METHODIST	21	6,414	8,361*	.7	2.2
467 WESLEYAN	2	457	522	-	.1
469 WELS	1	187	267	-	.1
496 JEWISH EST[1]	8	NA	11,720	1.0	3.0
497 BLACK BAPT EST[2]	NA	13,599	17,726*	1.5	4.6
498 INDEP.CHARIS.[3]	8	NA	3,860	.3	1.0
499 INDEP.NON-CHAR[3]	7	NA	3,675	.3	1.0
SACRAMENTO	**481**	**111,088**	**359,231***	**34.5**	**100.0**
005 AME ZION	1	520	720	.1	.2
011 A.W.M.C.	1	21	27*	-	-
019 AMER BAPT USA	19	5,680	7,230*	.7	2.0
053 ASSEM OF GOD	34	10,430	21,022	2.0	5.9
057 BAPT GEN CONF	3	138	176*	-	-
081 CATHOLIC	38	NA	147,882	14.2	41.2
081b *BYZAN RUTH*	*1*	*NA*	*223*	-	*.1*
081d *LATIN*	*36*	*NA*	*147,407*	*14.2*	*41.0*
081f *MELKITE-GK*	*1*	*NA*	*252*	-	*.1*
089 CHR & MISS AL	6	760	971	.1	.3
093 CHR CH (DISC)	5	840	930	.1	.3
097 CHR CHS&CHS CR	5	875	1,114*	.1	.3
105 CHRISTIAN REF	2	166	258	-	.1
111 CH CR,SCIENTST	5	NR	NR	-	-
123 CH GOD (ANDER)	6	925	955	.1	.3
127 CH GOD (CLEVE)	4	472	601*	.1	.2
133 CH GOD(7TH)DEN	2	98	138	-	-

NA–Not applicable NR–Not reported *Total adherents estimated from known number of communicant, confirmed, full members. - Represents a percent less than 0.1. Percentages may not total due to rounding.
[1] See Appendix E [2] See Appendix F [3] See Appendix G Lines in *italic* represent a breakdown of Catholic rites or Friends affiliations. They are included in their respective denominational total.

CALIFORNIA

Table 4. Churches and Church Membership by County and Denomination: 1990

County and Denomination	Number of churches	Communicant, confirmed, full members	Total adherents Number	Percent of total population	Percent of total adherents
145 CH GOD PROPHCY	3	93	118*	-	-
151 L-D SAINTS	67	NA	30,320	2.9	8.4
157 CH OF BRETHREN	1	92	117*	-	-
165 CH OF NAZARENE	14	2,572	3,670	.4	1.0
167 CHS OF CHRIST	23	2,391	3,192	.3	.9
179 CONSRV BAPT	6	NR	NR	-	-
193 EPISCOPAL	12	3,275	4,464	.4	1.2
203 EVAN FREE CH	3	571	863	.1	.2
207 E.L.C.A.	19	7,309	10,374	1.0	2.9
221 FREE METHODIST	2	244	244	-	.1
223 FREE WILL BAPT	2	316	402*	-	.1
226 FRIENDS-USA	4	320	418*	-	.1
226c FGC	1	27	45*	-	-
226e FUM	3	293	373*	-	.1
237 GC MENN BR CHS	1	95	121*	-	-
246 GREEK ORTHODOX	2	NR	NR	-	-
249 AP CATH ASSYR	1	50	127	-	-
259 IFCA	7	NR	NR	-	-
263 INT FOURSQ GOS	6	626	797*	.1	.2
283 LUTH—MO SYNOD	13	3,258	4,327	.4	1.2
313 N AM BAPT CONF	6	2,943	3,746*	.4	1.0
329 OPEN BIBLE STD	3	NR	NR	-	-
331 ORTH CH IN AM	1	NR	NR	-	-
339 PENT CH OF GOD	8	231	516	-	.1
349 PENT HOLINESS	2	52	66*	-	-
353 CHR BRETHREN	2	70	150	-	-
355 PRESB CH (USA)	16	9,128	11,619*	1.1	3.2
371 REF CH IN AM	5	1,234	2,252	.2	.6
373 REF CH IN U.S.	1	95	169	-	-
403 SALVATION ARMY	2	288	304	-	.1
413 S.D.A.	16	5,169	6,580*	.6	1.8
419 SO BAPT CONV	44	19,776	25,172*	2.4	7.0
435 UNITARIAN-UNIV	2	450	510	-	.1
443 UN C OF CHRIST	5	965	1,228*	.1	.3
449 UN METHODIST	27	6,430	8,185*	.8	2.3
467 WESLEYAN	3	522	1,120	.1	.3
469 WELS	2	827	1,159	.1	.3
496 JEWISH EST[1]	4	NA	8,788	.8	2.4
497 BLACK BAPT EST[2]	NA	20,771	26,439*	2.5	7.4
498 INDEP.CHARIS.[3]	11	NA	17,950	1.7	5.0
499 INDEP.NON-CHAR[3]	4	NA	1,700	.2	.5
SAN BENITO	**21**	**1,348**	**10,174***	**27.7**	**100.0**
053 ASSEMB OF GOD	2	199	260	.7	2.6
081 CATHOLIC	3	NA	7,521	20.5	73.9
081d LATIN	3	NA	7,521	20.5	73.9
127 CH GOD (CLEVE)	1	15	20*	.1	.2
145 CH GOD PROPHCY	1	41	55*	.1	.5
151 L-D SAINTS	2	NA	808	2.2	7.9
167 CHS OF CHRIST	2	34	45	.1	.4
179 CONSRV BAPT	1	NR	NR	-	-
207 E.L.C.A.	1	134	203	.6	2.0
263 INT FOURSQ GOS	1	37	49*	.1	.5
339 PENT CH OF GOD	1	35	76	.2	.7
355 PRESB CH (USA)	1	181	242*	.7	2.4
403 SALVATION ARMY	1	5	5	-	-
413 S.D.A.	1	211	282*	.8	2.8
419 SO BAPT CONV	2	237	316*	.9	3.1
449 UN METHODIST	1	219	292*	.8	2.9
SAN BERNARDINO	**752**	**151,455**	**471,354***	**33.2**	**100.0**
019 AMER BAPT USA	29	6,180	8,273*	.6	1.8
053 ASSEMB OF GOD	64	7,192	11,519	.8	2.4
057 BAPT GEN CONF	6	1,217	1,629*	.1	.3
059 BAPT MISS ASSN	3	149	199*	-	-
075 BRETHREN IN CR	7	1,524	1,535	.1	.3
081 CATHOLIC	59	NA	211,519	14.9	44.9
081b BYZAN RUTH	1	NA	201	-	-
081d LATIN	57	NA	210,795	14.9	44.7
081f MELKITE-GK	1	NA	523	-	.1
089 CHR & MISS AL	12	567	1,478	.1	.3
093 CHR CH (DISC)	7	1,025	1,908	.1	.4
097 CHR CHS&CHS CR	13	2,504	3,352*	.2	.7
105 CHRISTIAN REF	8	2,124	3,462	.2	.7
111 CH CR,SCIENTST	11	NR	NR	-	-
123 CH GOD (ANDER)	7	664	758	.1	.2
127 CH GOD (CLEVE)	10	817	1,094*	.1	.2
133 CH GOD(7TH)DEN	2	99	139	-	-
145 CH GOD PROPHCY	5	189	253*	-	.1
151 L-D SAINTS	95	NA	38,532	2.7	8.2
163 CH OF LUTH BR	1	31	215	-	-
165 CH OF NAZARENE	25	4,413	5,725	.4	1.2
167 CHS OF CHRIST	38	3,010	3,917	.3	.8
175 CONGR CHR CHS	1	107	143*	-	-
176 CCC, NOT NAT'L	1	676	905*	.1	.2
179 CONSRV BAPT	12	NR	NR	-	-
185 CUMBER PRESB	1	108	111	-	-

County and Denomination	Number of churches	Communicant, confirmed, full members	Total adherents Number	Percent of total population	Percent of total adherents
193 EPISCOPAL	19	3,258	4,350	.3	.9
203 EVAN FREE CH	13	1,578	2,637	.2	.6
207 E.L.C.A.	17	4,793	6,752	.5	1.4
217 FIRE BAPTIZED	1	8	11*	-	-
221 FREE METHODIST	11	867	1,190	.1	.3
223 FREE WILL BAPT	3	94	126*	-	-
226 FRIENDS-USA	2	93	132*	-	-
226e FUM	1	90	120*	-	-
226f INDEPENDNT	1	3	12	-	-
237 GC MENN BR CHS	1	32	43*	-	-
246 GREEK ORTHODOX	3	NR	NR	-	-
249 AP CATH ASSYR	0	15	57	-	-
259 IFCA	14	NR	NR	-	-
263 INT FOURSQ GOS	27	3,598	4,816*	.3	1.0
283 LUTH—MO SYNOD	22	5,227	7,437	.5	1.6
285 MENNONITE CH	2	50	105	-	-
287 MENN GEN CONF	2	91	107	-	-
291 MISSIONARY CH	3	76	208	-	-
329 OPEN BIBLE STD	1	NR	NR	-	-
331 ORTH CH IN AM	1	NR	NR	-	-
339 PENT CH OF GOD	10	281	819	.1	.2
349 PENT HOLINESS	4	377	505*	-	.1
353 CHR BRETHREN	3	176	245	-	.1
355 PRESB CH (USA)	18	6,752	9,038*	.6	1.9
356 PRESB CH AMER	3	70	77	-	-
371 REF CH IN AM	3	853	1,446	.1	.3
403 SALVATION ARMY	4	490	563	-	.1
413 S.D.A.	36	21,404	28,652*	2.0	6.1
419 SO BAPT CONV	50	33,672	45,075*	3.2	9.6
435 UNITARIAN-UNIV	1	160	187	-	-
443 UN C OF CHRIST	13	2,270	3,039*	.2	.6
449 UN METHODIST	27	7,631	10,215*	.7	2.2
467 WESLEYAN	2	48	218	-	-
469 WELS	2	316	436	-	.1
496 JEWISH EST[1]	4	NA	6,175	.4	1.3
497 BLACK BAPT EST[2]	NA	24,579	32,902*	2.3	7.0
498 INDEP.CHARIS.[3]	7	NA	3,175	.2	.7
499 INDEP.NON-CHAR[3]	6	NA	3,950	.3	.8
SAN DIEGO	**1,013**	**218,185**	**858,051***	**34.3**	**100.0**
001 ADVENT CHR CH	1	159	198*	-	-
005 AME ZION	3	1,098	1,598	.1	.2
019 AMER BAPT USA	25	3,957	4,934*	.2	.6
039 AP CHR CH(NAZ)	3	88	110*	-	-
040 AP CHR CH-AMER	1	22	37	-	-
053 ASSEMB OF GOD	59	10,208	15,982	.6	1.9
057 BAPT GEN CONF	17	6,168	7,691*	.3	.9
081 CATHOLIC	105	NA	413,025	16.5	48.1
081b BYZAN RUTH	1	NA	351	-	-
081c CHALDEAN	1	NA	6,000	.2	.7
081d LATIN	102	NA	406,591	16.3	47.4
081h UKRAINIAN	1	NA	83	-	-
089 CHR & MISS AL	17	1,268	2,064	.1	.2
093 CHR CH (DISC)	12	2,928	4,516	.2	.5
097 CHR CHS&CHS CR	14	4,517	5,632*	.2	.7
105 CHRISTIAN REF	9	1,068	1,724	.1	.2
111 CH CR,SCIENTST	23	NR	NR	-	-
123 CH GOD (ANDER)	9	905	1,035	-	.1
127 CH GOD (CLEVE)	6	638	795*	-	.1
133 CH GOD(7TH)DEN	1	49	68	-	-
145 CH GOD PROPHCY	7	254	317*	-	-
151 L-D SAINTS	112	NA	46,863	1.9	5.5
157 CH OF BRETHREN	2	194	242*	-	-
165 CH OF NAZARENE	20	3,706	5,227	.2	.6
167 CHS OF CHRIST	48	6,642	9,254	.4	1.1
171 CH GOD-GEN CON	2	55	69*	-	-
175 CONGR CHR CHS	5	810	1,010*	-	.1
179 CONSRV BAPT	11	NR	NR	-	-
181 CONSRV CONGR	3	1,690	2,107*	.1	.2
193 EPISCOPAL	39	13,399	17,742	.7	2.1
203 EVAN FREE CH	11	1,306	2,549	.1	.3
207 E.L.C.A.	37	13,817	18,687	.7	2.2
209 EVAN LUTH SYN	1	120	175	-	-
215 EVAN METH CH	1	58	72*	-	-
216 EVAN PRESBY CH	1	27	31	-	-
220 FREE LUTHERAN	1	45	56	-	-
221 FREE METHODIST	5	292	617	-	.1
223 FREE WILL BAPT	2	49	61*	-	-
226 FRIENDS-USA	4	367	565*	-	.1
226e FUM	2	261	325*	-	-
226f INDEPENDNT	2	106	240	-	-
237 GC MENN BR CHS	1	10	12*	-	-
246 GREEK ORTHODOX	2	NR	NR	-	-
259 IFCA	5	NR	NR	-	-
263 INT FOURSQ GOS	26	6,610	8,242*	.3	1.0
274 LAT EVAN LUTH	1	34	34	-	-
283 LUTH—MO SYNOD	36	11,288	14,789	.6	1.7

NA–Not applicable   NR–Not reported   *Total adherents estimated from known number of communicant, confirmed, full members.   - Represents a percent less than 0.1.   Percentages may not total due to rounding.
[1]See Appendix E   [2]See Appendix F   [3]See Appendix G   Lines in *italic* represent a breakdown of Catholic rites or Friends affiliations. They are included in their respective denominational total.

Table 4. Churches and Church Membership by County and Denomination: 1990

County and Denomination	Number of churches	Communicant, confirmed, full members	Total adherents Number	Percent of total population	Percent of total adherents
285 MENNONITE CH	2	30	75	-	-
287 MENN GEN CONF	1	5	8	-	-
291 MISSIONARY CH	3	197	172	-	-
331 ORTH CH IN AM	2	NR	NR	-	-
339 PENT CH OF GOD	6	165	374	-	-
349 PENT HOLINESS	5	279	348*	-	-
353 CHR BRETHREN	9	589	803	-	.1
355 PRESB CH (USA)	31	20,210	25,199*	1.0	2.9
356 PRESB CH AMER	8	882	1,057	-	.1
361 PRIM BAPT ASCS	1	19	24*	-	-
367 PROT CONF (LU)	1	50	75	-	-
371 REF CH IN AM	2	297	596	-	.1
403 SALVATION ARMY	5	715	821	-	.1
413 S.D.A.	31	10,303	12,846*	.5	1.5
415 S-D BAPTIST GC	1	28	35*	-	-
419 SO BAPT CONV	73	24,304	30,304*	1.2	3.5
435 UNITARIAN-UNIV	6	1,486	1,913	.1	.2
443 UN C OF CHRIST	26	6,725	8,385*	.3	1.0
449 UN METHODIST	46	19,406	24,197*	1.0	2.8
467 WESLEYAN	11	3,466	8,924	.4	1.0
469 WELS	8	1,115	1,652	.1	.2
496 JEWISH EST[1]	17	NA	70,000	2.8	8.2
497 BLACK BAPT EST[2]	NA	34,068	42,478*	1.7	5.0
498 INDEP.CHARIS.[3]	13	NA	13,005	.5	1.5
499 INDEP.NON-CHAR[3]	17	NA	26,630	1.1	3.1
SAN FRANCISCO	**302**	**56,953**	**315,599***	**43.6**	**100.0**
001 ADVENT CHR CH	1	39	45*	-	-
005 AME ZION	2	773	900	.1	.3
019 AMER BAPT USA	15	5,865	6,714*	.9	2.1
053 ASSEMB OF GOD	16	2,518	3,491	.5	1.1
081 CATHOLIC	58	NA	195,160	27.0	61.8
081b BYZAN RUTH	*1*	*NA*	*35*	-	-
081d LATIN	*56*	*NA*	*195,000*	*26.9*	*61.8*
081h UKRAINIAN	*1*	*NA*	*125*	-	-
089 CHR & MISS AL	4	485	629	.1	.2
093 CHR CH (DISC)	2	213	268	-	.1
097 CHR CHS&CHS CR	1	30	34*	-	-
111 CH CR,SCIENTST	8	NR	NR	-	-
123 CH GOD (ANDER)	2	63	73	-	-
127 CH GOD (CLEVE)	3	201	230*	-	.1
145 CH GOD PROPHCY	1	31	35*	-	-
151 L-D SAINTS	5	NA	1,937	.3	.6
157 CH OF BRETHREN	1	50	57*	-	-
165 CH OF NAZARENE	5	354	517	.1	.2
167 CHS OF CHRIST	8	1,809	2,287	.3	.7
185 CUMBER PRESB	2	729	764	.1	.2
193 EPISCOPAL	19	4,625	6,456	.9	2.0
195 ESTONIAN ELC	1	80	92*	-	-
203 EVAN FREE CH	1	200	350	-	.1
207 E.L.C.A.	12	1,949	2,702	.4	.9
221 FREE METHODIST	1	90	90	-	-
226 FRIENDS-USA	1	62	128	-	-
226f INDEPENDNT	*1*	*62*	*128*	-	-
249 AP CATH ASSYR	1	42	193	-	.1
263 INT FOURSQ GOS	1	130	149*	-	-
274 LAT EVAN LUTH	1	336	388	.1	.1
283 LUTH—MO SYNOD	7	1,586	1,923	.3	.6
285 MENNONITE CH	1	33	66	-	-
287 MENN GEN CONF	2	72	94	-	-
329 OPEN BIBLE STD	1	NR	NR	-	-
331 ORTH CH IN AM	3	NR	NR	-	-
349 PENT HOLINESS	1	7	8*	-	-
353 CHR BRETHREN	1	60	75	-	-
355 PRESB CH (USA)	18	4,057	4,644*	.6	1.5
371 REF CH IN AM	2	150	225	-	.1
403 SALVATION ARMY	7	742	822	.1	.3
413 S.D.A.	8	1,382	1,582*	.2	.5
419 SO BAPT CONV	22	3,930	4,499*	.6	1.4
435 UNITARIAN-UNIV	1	586	696	.1	.2
443 UN C OF CHRIST	8	1,215	1,391*	.2	.4
449 UN METHODIST	18	5,556	6,360*	.9	2.0
496 JEWISH EST[1]	22	NA	45,500	6.3	14.4
497 BLACK BAPT EST[2]	NA	16,903	19,350*	2.7	6.1
498 INDEP.CHARIS.[3]	5	NA	3,225	.4	1.0
499 INDEP.NON-CHAR[3]	3	NA	1,450	.2	.5
SAN JOAQUIN	**270**	**49,060**	**176,314***	**36.7**	**100.0**
005 AME ZION	1	95	110	-	.1
019 AMER BAPT USA	5	1,340	1,761*	.4	1.0
053 ASSEMB OF GOD	23	3,381	6,673	1.4	3.8
057 BAPT GEN CONF	1	227	298*	.1	.2
059 BAPT MISS ASSN	1	86	113*	-	.1
071 BRETHREN (ASH)	3	216	284*	.1	.2
081 CATHOLIC	20	NA	96,735	20.1	54.9
081b BYZAN RUTH	*1*	*NA*	*40*	-	-
081d LATIN	*19*	*NA*	*96,695*	*20.1*	*54.8*

County and Denomination	Number of churches	Communicant, confirmed, full members	Total adherents Number	Percent of total population	Percent of total adherents
089 CHR & MISS AL	4	1,539	1,594	.3	.9
093 CHR CH (DISC)	3	749	810	.2	.5
097 CHR CHS&CHS CR	4	283	372*	.1	.2
105 CHRISTIAN REF	5	1,585	2,463	.5	1.4
111 CH CR,SCIENTST	3	NR	NR	-	-
123 CH GOD (ANDER)	3	310	310	.1	.2
127 CH GOD (CLEVE)	4	172	226*	-	.1
133 CH GOD(7TH)DEN	2	99	139	-	.1
145 CH GOD PROPHCY	3	103	135*	-	.1
151 L-D SAINTS	24	NA	9,615	2.0	5.5
165 CH OF NAZARENE	8	993	1,620	.3	.9
167 CHS OF CHRIST	21	1,566	2,155	.4	1.2
171 CH GOD-GEN CON	1	0	0*	-	-
179 CONSRV BAPT	3	NR	NR	-	-
181 CONSRV CONGR	1	39	51*	-	-
193 EPISCOPAL	7	844	1,453	.3	.8
203 EVAN FREE CH	3	99	190	-	.1
207 E.L.C.A.	6	2,819	3,717	.8	2.1
215 EVAN METH CH	1	97	127*	-	.1
221 FREE METHODIST	2	93	115	-	.1
223 FREE WILL BAPT	3	375	493*	.1	.3
226 FRIENDS-USA	1	11	17	-	-
226f INDEPENDNT	*1*	*11*	*17*	-	-
237 GC MENN BR CHS	1	290	381*	.1	.2
246 GREEK ORTHODOX	1	NR	NR	-	-
249 AP CATH ASSYR	0	27	112	-	.1
259 IFCA	3	NR	NR	-	-
263 INT FOURSQ GOS	7	978	1,285*	.3	.7
283 LUTH—MO SYNOD	6	2,549	3,624	.8	2.1
313 N AM BAPT CONF	5	2,851	3,746*	.8	2.1
329 OPEN BIBLE STD	2	NR	NR	-	-
339 PENT CH OF GOD	14	550	1,334	.3	.8
349 PENT HOLINESS	2	99	130*	-	.1
355 PRESB CH (USA)	8	2,008	2,638*	.5	1.5
371 REF CH IN AM	1	682	1,188	.2	.7
403 SALVATION ARMY	2	155	165	-	.1
413 S.D.A.	11	3,807	5,002*	1.0	2.8
419 SO BAPT CONV	20	6,727	8,839*	1.8	5.0
435 UNITARIAN-UNIV	1	273	333	.1	.2
443 UN C OF CHRIST	3	810	1,064*	.2	.6
449 UN METHODIST	14	4,174	5,485*	1.1	3.1
469 WELS	1	165	199	-	.1
496 JEWISH EST[1]	2	NA	1,600	.3	.9
497 BLACK BAPT EST[2]	NA	5,794	7,613*	1.6	4.3
SAN LUIS OBISPO	**162**	**18,592**	**68,269***	**31.4**	**100.0**
019 AMER BAPT USA	3	448	544*	.3	.8
053 ASSEMB OF GOD	15	1,138	1,611	.7	2.4
057 BAPT GEN CONF	3	505	613*	.3	.9
081 CATHOLIC	17	NA	35,577	16.4	52.1
081b BYZAN RUTH	*1*	*NA*	*98*	-	*.1*
081d LATIN	*16*	*NA*	*35,479*	*16.3*	*52.0*
093 CHR CH (DISC)	3	175	232	.1	.3
097 CHR CHS&CHS CR	5	497	604*	.3	.9
105 CHRISTIAN REF	1	83	113	.1	.2
111 CH CR,SCIENTST	6	NR	NR	-	-
123 CH GOD (ANDER)	1	0	20	-	-
127 CH GOD (CLEVE)	1	63	77*	-	.1
133 CH GOD(7TH)DEN	1	49	69	-	.1
145 CH GOD PROPHCY	3	97	118*	.1	.2
151 L-D SAINTS	11	NA	3,948	1.8	5.8
165 CH OF NAZARENE	5	1,666	2,763	1.3	4.0
167 CHS OF CHRIST	10	613	828	.4	1.2
193 EPISCOPAL	7	1,310	1,738	.8	2.5
203 EVAN FREE CH	3	628	1,000	.5	1.5
207 E.L.C.A.	4	1,056	1,409	.6	2.1
226 FRIENDS-USA	1	10	12	-	-
226f INDEPENDNT	*1*	*10*	*12*	-	-
246 GREEK ORTHODOX	1	NR	NR	-	-
259 IFCA	1	NR	NR	-	-
263 INT FOURSQ GOS	8	406	493*	.2	.7
283 LUTH—MO SYNOD	4	1,374	1,688	.8	2.5
284 LUTH CH-AM ASC	1	24	39	-	.1
287 MENN GEN CONF	1	147	147	.1	.2
339 PENT CH OF GOD	2	48	79	-	.1
353 CHR BRETHREN	1	90	300	.1	.4
355 PRESB CH (USA)	6	1,269	1,541*	.7	2.3
356 PRESB CH AMER	2	127	162	.1	.2
403 SALVATION ARMY	1	43	45	-	.1
413 S.D.A.	4	810	984*	.5	1.4
419 SO BAPT CONV	10	1,956	2,376*	1.1	3.5
435 UNITARIAN-UNIV	1	168	183	.1	.3
443 UN C OF CHRIST	3	814	989*	.5	1.4
449 UN METHODIST	9	1,986	2,412*	1.1	3.5
496 JEWISH EST[1]	1	NA	1,500	.7	2.2
497 BLACK BAPT EST[2]	NA	992	1,205*	.6	1.8
498 INDEP.CHARIS.[3]	2	NA	1,100	.5	1.6

NA–Not applicable   NR–Not reported   *Total adherents estimated from known number of communicant, confirmed, full members.   - Represents a percent less than 0.1.   Percentages may not total due to rounding.
[1]See Appendix E   [2]See Appendix F   [3]See Appendix G   Lines in *italic* represent a breakdown of Catholic rites or Friends affiliations. They are included in their respective denominational total.

Table 4. Churches and Church Membership by County and Denomination: 1990

County and Denomination	Number of churches	Communicant, confirmed, full members	Total adherents Number	Percent of total population	Percent of total adherents
499 INDEP.NON-CHAR[3]	4	NA	1,750	.8	2.6
SAN MATEO	**264**	**43,680**	**277,206***	**42.7**	**100.0**
005 AME ZION	5	673	1,158	.2	.4
019 AMER BAPT USA	13	2,795	3,392*	.5	1.2
053 ASSEMB OF GOD	23	2,197	3,525	.5	1.3
057 BAPT GEN CONF	4	188	228*	-	.1
081 CATHOLIC	39	NA	165,966	25.5	59.9
081d *LATIN*	*38*	*NA*	*165,000*	*25.4*	*59.5*
081e *MARONITE*	*1*	*NA*	*966*	*.1*	*.3*
089 CHR & MISS AL	3	122	210	-	.1
093 CHR CH (DISC)	1	120	150	-	.1
097 CHR CHS&CHS CR	2	284	345*	.1	.1
105 CHRISTIAN REF	1	233	298	-	.1
111 CH CR,SCIENTST	8	NR	NR	-	-
123 CH GOD (ANDER)	3	167	167	-	.1
127 CH GOD (CLEVE)	2	67	81*	-	-
145 CH GOD PROPHCY	1	31	38*	-	-
151 L-D SAINTS	22	NA	9,642	1.5	3.5
165 CH OF NAZARENE	6	379	457	.1	.2
167 CHS OF CHRIST	9	887	1,090	.2	.4
179 CONSRV BAPT	3	NR	NR	-	-
193 EPISCOPAL	15	4,095	6,683	1.0	2.4
203 EVAN FREE CH	1	17	20	-	-
207 E.L.C.A.	10	2,757	3,676	.6	1.3
221 FREE METHODIST	3	109	147	-	.1
246 GREEK ORTHODOX	3	NR	NR	-	-
263 INT FOURSQ GOS	3	168	204*	-	.1
283 LUTH—MO SYNOD	8	2,361	2,907	.4	1.0
291 MISSIONARY CH	1	32	65	-	-
329 OPEN BIBLE STD	1	NR	NR	-	-
331 ORTH CH IN AM	1	NR	NR	-	-
353 CHR BRETHREN	1	45	60	-	-
355 PRESB CH (USA)	11	8,409	10,205*	1.6	3.7
356 PRESB CH AMER	1	0	0	-	-
371 REF CH IN AM	1	84	161	-	.1
403 SALVATION ARMY	1	88	94	-	-
413 S.D.A.	8	1,064	1,291*	.2	.5
419 SO BAPT CONV	15	2,291	2,780*	.4	1.0
435 UNITARIAN-UNIV	2	321	423	.1	.2
443 UN C OF CHRIST	12	2,869	3,482*	.5	1.3
449 UN METHODIST	14	3,183	3,863*	.6	1.4
469 WELS	1	99	142	-	.1
496 JEWISH EST[1]	5	NA	41,500	6.4	15.0
497 BLACK BAPT EST[2]	NA	7,545	9,156*	1.4	3.3
498 INDEP.CHARIS.[3]	1	NA	3,600	.6	1.3
SANTA BARBARA	**192**	**31,120**	**154,080***	**41.7**	**100.0**
019 AMER BAPT USA	7	705	868*	.2	.6
053 ASSEMB OF GOD	10	1,231	2,138	.6	1.4
057 BAPT GEN CONF	4	2,483	3,058*	.8	2.0
081 CATHOLIC	15	NA	101,754	27.5	66.0
081d *LATIN*	*15*	*NA*	*101,754*	*27.5*	*66.0*
089 CHR & MISS AL	3	373	591	.2	.4
093 CHR CH (DISC)	2	294	441	.1	.3
097 CHR CHS&CHS CR	1	74	91*	-	.1
111 CH CR,SCIENTST	6	NR	NR	-	-
123 CH GOD (ANDER)	1	120	120	-	.1
127 CH GOD (CLEVE)	3	288	355*	.1	.2
145 CH GOD PROPHCY	5	189	233*	.1	.2
151 L-D SAINTS	17	NA	6,321	1.7	4.1
165 CH OF NAZARENE	5	1,078	1,579	.4	1.0
167 CHS OF CHRIST	9	797	1,009	.3	.7
179 CONSRV BAPT	2	NR	NR	-	-
181 CONSRV CONGR	1	149	183*	-	.1
193 EPISCOPAL	7	2,627	3,500	.9	2.3
203 EVAN FREE CH	3	133	225	.1	.1
207 E.L.C.A.	8	2,325	2,858	.8	1.9
216 EVAN PRESBY CH	1	86	86	-	.1
221 FREE METHODIST	2	206	229	.1	.1
223 FREE WILL BAPT	1	10	12*	-	-
226 FRIENDS-USA	1	50	76	-	-
226f *INDEPENDNT*	*1*	*50*	*76*	*-*	*-*
246 GREEK ORTHODOX	1	NR	NR	-	-
263 INT FOURSQ GOS	9	1,502	1,850*	.5	1.2
283 LUTH—MO SYNOD	7	2,044	2,547	.7	1.7
291 MISSIONARY CH	3	222	328	.1	.2
329 OPEN BIBLE STD	1	NR	NR	-	-
331 ORTH CH IN AM	2	NR	NR	-	-
339 PENT CH OF GOD	1	34	77	-	-
355 PRESB CH (USA)	11	3,966	4,884*	1.3	3.2
371 REF CH IN AM	1	85	165	-	.1
403 SALVATION ARMY	2	151	199	.1	.1
413 S.D.A.	4	1,008	1,241*	.3	.8
415 S-D BAPTIST GC	1	19	23*	-	-
419 SO BAPT CONV	13	2,732	3,364*	.9	2.2
435 UNITARIAN-UNIV	2	647	795	.2	.5

County and Denomination	Number of churches	Communicant, confirmed, full members	Total adherents Number	Percent of total population	Percent of total adherents
443 UN C OF CHRIST	3	675	831*	.2	.5
449 UN METHODIST	8	2,376	2,926*	.8	1.9
469 WELS	2	217	284	.1	.2
496 JEWISH EST[1]	4	NA	4,100	1.1	2.7
497 BLACK BAPT EST[2]	NA	2,224	2,739*	.7	1.8
498 INDEP.CHARIS.[3]	2	NA	1,200	.3	.8
499 INDEP.NON-CHAR[3]	1	NA	800	.2	.5
SANTA CLARA	**552**	**105,394**	**579,833***	**38.7**	**100.0**
005 AME ZION	1	234	309	-	.1
019 AMER BAPT USA	11	2,353	2,910*	.2	.5
053 ASSEMB OF GOD	48	7,077	10,532	.7	1.8
057 BAPT GEN CONF	5	798	987*	.1	.2
059 BAPT MISS ASSN	1	44	54*	-	-
081 CATHOLIC	52	NA	368,611	24.6	63.6
081b *BYZAN RUTH*	*1*	*NA*	*136*		
081c *CHALDEAN*	*1*	*NA*	*2,000*	*.1*	*.3*
081d *LATIN*	*48*	*NA*	*365,875*	*24.4*	*63.1*
081f *MELKITE-GK*	*1*	*NA*	*523*		*.1*
081h *UKRAINIAN*	*1*	*NA*	*77*	*-*	*-*
089 CHR & MISS AL	5	1,010	1,383	.1	.2
093 CHR CH (DISC)	3	406	606	-	.1
097 CHR CHS&CHS CR	13	2,165	2,678*	.2	.5
105 CHRISTIAN REF	4	422	657	-	-
111 CH CR,SCIENTST	12	NR	NR	-	-
123 CH GOD (ANDER)	3	133	267	-	-
127 CH GOD (CLEVE)	7	363	449*	-	.1
133 CH GOD(7TH)DEN	1	49	69	-	-
145 CH GOD PROPHCY	2	72	89*	-	-
151 L-D SAINTS	57	NA	23,595	1.6	4.1
165 CH OF NAZARENE	14	1,742	2,269	.2	.4
167 CHS OF CHRIST	15	1,736	2,267	.2	.4
175 CONGR CHR CHS	1	52	64*	-	-
179 CONSRV BAPT	12	NR	NR	-	-
185 CUMBER PRESB	2	141	182	-	-
193 EPISCOPAL	19	7,038	9,593	.6	1.7
203 EVAN FREE CH	4	619	795	.1	.1
207 E.L.C.A.	26	8,717	11,866	.8	2.0
221 FREE METHODIST	5	202	343	-	.1
223 FREE WILL BAPT	1	87	108*	-	-
226 FRIENDS-USA	2	181	271	-	-
226f *INDEPENDNT*	*2*	*181*	*271*	*-*	*-*
237 GC MENN BR CHS	6	574	710*	-	.1
246 GREEK ORTHODOX	2	NR	NR	-	-
259 IFCA	1	NR	NR	-	-
263 INT FOURSQ GOS	7	599	741*	-	.1
283 LUTH—MO SYNOD	12	3,965	5,184	.3	.9
287 MENN GEN CONF	1	50	75	-	-
313 N AM BAPT CONF	1	64	79*	-	-
329 OPEN BIBLE STD	3	NR	NR	-	-
331 ORTH CH IN AM	1	NR	NR	-	-
339 PENT CH OF GOD	7	214	566	-	.1
349 PENT HOLINESS	5	1,677	2,074*	.1	.4
353 CHR BRETHREN	2	290	425	-	.1
355 PRESB CH (USA)	26	9,078	11,228*	.7	1.9
356 PRESB CH AMER	5	162	251	-	-
361 PRIM BAPT ASCS	1	8	10*	-	-
371 REF CH IN AM	1	337	422	-	.1
397 ROMANIAN ORTH	1	NR	NR	-	-
403 SALVATION ARMY	4	320	340	-	.1
413 S.D.A.	18	4,754	5,880*	.4	1.0
419 SO BAPT CONV	45	17,103	21,153*	1.4	3.6
423 SYRIAN ANTIOCH	1	NA	400	-	.1
435 UNITARIAN-UNIV	4	865	1,154	.1	.2
443 UN C OF CHRIST	12	3,393	4,197*	.3	.7
449 UN METHODIST	32	13,462	16,651*	1.1	2.9
469 WELS	3	816	1,161	.1	.2
496 JEWISH EST[1]	13	NA	32,000	2.1	5.5
497 BLACK BAPT EST[2]	NA	12,021	14,868*	1.0	2.6
498 INDEP.CHARIS.[3]	5	NA	9,760	.7	1.7
499 INDEP.NON-CHAR[3]	7	NA	9,550	.6	1.6
SANTA CRUZ	**121**	**15,568**	**65,022***	**28.3**	**100.0**
001 ADVENT CHR CH	1	65	80*	-	.1
019 AMER BAPT USA	2	236	292*	.1	.4
053 ASSEMB OF GOD	16	1,765	2,712	1.2	4.2
081 CATHOLIC	12	NA	40,058	17.4	61.6
081d *LATIN*	*12*	*NA*	*40,058*	*17.4*	*61.6*
089 CHR & MISS AL	1	65	127	.1	.2
093 CHR CH (DISC)	2	227	481	.2	.7
097 CHR CHS&CHS CR	1	1,100	1,360*	.6	2.1
111 CH CR,SCIENTST	5	NR	NR	-	-
123 CH GOD (ANDER)	1	256	256	.1	.4
127 CH GOD (CLEVE)	1	56	69*	-	.1
151 L-D SAINTS	6	NA	2,614	1.1	4.0
164 CH LUTH CONF	1	89	124	.1	.2
165 CH OF NAZARENE	3	464	651	.3	1.0

NA–Not applicable   NR–Not reported   *Total adherents estimated from known number of communicant, confirmed, full members.   - Represents a percent less than 0.1.   Percentages may not total due to rounding.
[1]See Appendix E   [2]See Appendix F   [3]See Appendix G   Lines in *italic* represent a breakdown of Catholic rites or Friends affiliations. They are included in their respective denominational total.

Table 4. Churches and Church Membership by County and Denomination: 1990

County and Denomination	Number of churches	Communicant, confirmed, full members	Total adherents Number	Percent of total population	Percent of total adherents
167 CHS OF CHRIST	2	168	201	.1	.3
175 CONGR CHR CHS	1	329	407*	.2	.6
179 CONSRV BAPT	5	NR	NR	-	-
193 EPISCOPAL	5	1,208	2,005	.9	3.1
203 EVAN FREE CH	2	348	390	.2	.6
207 E.L.C.A.	4	1,026	1,439	.6	2.2
221 FREE METHODIST	1	122	182	.1	.3
226 FRIENDS-USA	2	66	151	.1	.2
226f *INDEPENDNT*	2	66	151	.1	.2
237 GC MENN BR CHS	1	64	79*	-	.1
246 GREEK ORTHODOX	2	NR	NR	-	-
249 AP CATH ASSYR	1	105	326	.1	.5
263 INT FOURSQ GOS	5	882	1,090*	.5	1.7
283 LUTH—MO SYNOD	3	660	869	.4	1.3
339 PENT CH OF GOD	3	46	189	.1	.3
349 PENT HOLINESS	2	193	239*	.1	.4
355 PRESB CH (USA)	7	1,367	1,690*	.7	2.6
403 SALVATION ARMY	2	125	130	.1	.2
413 S.D.A.	5	1,219	1,507*	.7	2.3
419 SO BAPT CONV	5	1,070	1,323*	.6	2.0
435 UNITARIAN-UNIV	1	152	192	.1	.3
443 UN C OF CHRIST	2	455	562*	.2	.9
449 UN METHODIST	7	1,077	1,331*	.6	2.0
496 JEWISH EST[1]	1	NA	1,200	.5	1.8
497 BLACK BAPT EST[2]	NA	563	696*	.3	1.1
SHASTA	**110**	**11,634**	**36,958***	**25.1**	**100.0**
019 AMER BAPT USA	2	280	358*	.2	1.0
053 ASSEMB OF GOD	9	1,849	3,244	2.2	8.8
057 BAPT GEN CONF	1	33	42*	-	.1
081 CATHOLIC	9	NA	12,498	8.5	33.8
081d *LATIN*	9	NA	12,498	8.5	33.8
089 CHR & MISS AL	3	378	2,042	1.4	5.5
093 CHR CH (DISC)	1	49	57	-	.2
097 CHR CHS&CHS CR	2	155	198*	.1	.5
105 CHRISTIAN REF	1	45	70	-	.2
111 CH CR,SCIENTST	2	NR	NR	-	-
123 CH GOD (ANDER)	1	0	60	-	.2
127 CH GOD (CLEVE)	1	41	52*	-	.1
145 CH GOD PROPHCY	1	31	40*	-	.1
151 L-D SAINTS	10	NA	4,674	3.2	12.6
165 CH OF NAZARENE	4	585	908	.6	2.5
167 CHS OF CHRIST	8	539	700	.5	1.9
179 CONSRV BAPT	3	NR	NR	-	-
193 EPISCOPAL	2	441	575	.4	1.6
203 EVAN FREE CH	1	85	100	.1	.3
207 E.L.C.A.	1	477	593	.4	1.6
221 FREE METHODIST	1	0	33	-	.1
223 FREE WILL BAPT	1	48	61*	-	.2
226 FRIENDS-USA	1	7	32	-	.1
226f *INDEPENDNT*	1	7	32	-	.1
246 GREEK ORTHODOX	1	NR	NR	-	-
259 IFCA	3	NR	NR	-	-
263 INT FOURSQ GOS	5	176	225*	.2	.6
283 LUTH—MO SYNOD	2	474	580	.4	1.6
329 OPEN BIBLE STD	1	NR	NR	-	-
339 PENT CH OF GOD	5	183	628	.4	1.7
349 PENT HOLINESS	1	75	96*	.1	.3
355 PRESB CH (USA)	2	390	499*	.3	1.4
373 REF CH IN U.S.	1	76	99	.1	.3
403 SALVATION ARMY	1	87	92	.1	.2
413 S.D.A.	4	1,125	1,439*	1.0	3.9
419 SO BAPT CONV	7	2,155	2,757*	1.9	7.5
435 UNITARIAN-UNIV	1	33	33	-	.1
443 UN C OF CHRIST	1	289	370*	.3	1.0
449 UN METHODIST	4	949	1,214*	.8	3.3
469 WELS	2	348	498	.3	1.3
496 JEWISH EST[1]	1	NA	145	.1	.4
497 BLACK BAPT EST[2]	NA	231	296*	.2	.8
498 INDEP.CHARIS.[3]	1	NA	450	.3	1.2
499 INDEP.NON-CHAR[3]	2	NA	1,200	.8	3.2
SIERRA	**11**	**261**	**1,339***	**40.4**	**100.0**
019 AMER BAPT USA	1	106	135*	4.1	10.1
053 ASSEMB OF GOD	2	98	141	4.2	10.5
081 CATHOLIC	3	NA	800	24.1	59.7
081d *LATIN*	3	NA	800	24.1	59.7
151 L-D SAINTS	2	NA	191	5.8	14.3
259 IFCA	1	NR	NR	-	-
449 UN METHODIST	2	57	72*	2.2	5.4
SISKIYOU	**74**	**4,887**	**12,897***	**29.6**	**100.0**
019 AMER BAPT USA	3	147	187*	.4	1.4
053 ASSEMB OF GOD	8	386	772	1.8	6.0
063 BEREAN FUND CH	4	319	660	1.5	5.1
081 CATHOLIC	12	NA	4,734	10.9	36.7

County and Denomination	Number of churches	Communicant, confirmed, full members	Total adherents Number	Percent of total population	Percent of total adherents
081d *LATIN*	12	NA	4,734	10.9	36.7
089 CHR & MISS AL	1	42	82	.2	.6
097 CHR CHS&CHS CR	3	331	420*	1.0	3.3
105 CHRISTIAN REF	1	0	0	-	-
111 CH CR,SCIENTST	1	NR	NR	-	-
151 L-D SAINTS	4	NA	1,097	2.5	8.5
165 CH OF NAZARENE	3	128	414	1.0	3.2
167 CHS OF CHRIST	4	106	133	.3	1.0
179 CONSRV BAPT	1	NR	NR	-	-
193 EPISCOPAL	2	233	227	.5	1.8
203 EVAN FREE CH	1	86	150	.3	1.2
207 E.L.C.A.	2	198	295	.7	2.3
215 EVAN METH CH	1	48	61*	.1	.5
263 INT FOURSQ GOS	1	35	44*	.1	.3
283 LUTH—MO SYNOD	1	0	0	-	-
339 PENT CH OF GOD	1	35	77	.2	.6
355 PRESB CH (USA)	3	304	386*	.9	3.0
413 S.D.A.	3	288	365*	.8	2.8
419 SO BAPT CONV	7	1,300	1,650*	3.8	12.8
449 UN METHODIST	7	781	991*	2.3	7.7
497 BLACK BAPT EST[2]	NA	120	152*	.3	1.2
SOLANO	**155**	**36,712**	**119,508***	**35.1**	**100.0**
005 AME ZION	1	350	475	.1	.4
019 AMER BAPT USA	10	4,511	5,888*	1.7	4.9
053 ASSEMB OF GOD	11	1,766	4,092	1.2	3.4
057 BAPT GEN CONF	1	370	483*	.1	.4
059 BAPT MISS ASSN	1	39	51*	-	-
081 CATHOLIC	11	NA	56,833	16.7	47.6
081d *LATIN*	11	NA	56,833	16.7	47.6
089 CHR & MISS AL	2	110	245	.1	.2
093 CHR CH (DISC)	2	220	273	.1	.2
097 CHR CHS&CHS CR	3	226	295*	.1	.2
105 CHRISTIAN REF	1	67	101	-	.1
111 CH CR,SCIENTST	3	NR	NR	-	-
123 CH GOD (ANDER)	2	121	121	-	.1
127 CH GOD (CLEVE)	2	295	385*	.1	.3
145 CH GOD PROPHCY	2	62	81*	-	.1
151 L-D SAINTS	16	NA	8,924	2.6	7.5
165 CH OF NAZARENE	5	633	840	.2	.7
167 CHS OF CHRIST	7	981	1,207	.4	1.0
171 CH GOD-GEN CON	1	19	25*	-	-
179 CONSRV BAPT	2	NR	NR	-	-
193 EPISCOPAL	4	1,121	1,837	.5	1.5
203 EVAN FREE CH	1	249	551	.2	.5
207 E.L.C.A.	4	1,435	2,172	.6	1.8
223 FREE WILL BAPT	1	97	127*	-	.1
246 GREEK ORTHODOX	1	NR	NR	-	-
259 IFCA	2	NR	NR	-	-
263 INT FOURSQ GOS	5	169	221*	.1	.2
283 LUTH—MO SYNOD	4	1,224	1,903	.6	1.6
329 OPEN BIBLE STD	1	NR	NR	-	-
339 PENT CH OF GOD	2	104	330	.1	.3
349 PENT HOLINESS	2	92	120*	-	.1
355 PRESB CH (USA)	6	2,112	2,757*	.8	2.3
403 SALVATION ARMY	2	99	109	-	.1
413 S.D.A.	5	959	1,252*	.4	1.0
419 SO BAPT CONV	16	7,080	9,241*	2.7	7.7
435 UNITARIAN-UNIV	1	41	47	-	-
443 UN C OF CHRIST	4	345	450*	.1	.4
449 UN METHODIST	6	2,012	2,626*	.8	2.2
496 JEWISH EST[1]	1	NA	1,200	.4	1.0
497 BLACK BAPT EST[2]	NA	9,803	12,796*	3.8	10.7
498 INDEP.CHARIS.[3]	1	NA	300	.1	.3
499 INDEP.NON-CHAR[3]	3	NA	1,150	.3	1.0
SONOMA	**211**	**26,300**	**115,902***	**29.9**	**100.0**
019 AMER BAPT USA	1	470	588*	.2	.5
039 AP CHR CH(NAZ)	1	52	65*	-	.1
053 ASSEMB OF GOD	16	1,637	2,494	.6	2.2
057 BAPT GEN CONF	1	379	474*	.1	.4
081 CATHOLIC	22	NA	63,097	16.3	54.4
081d *LATIN*	22	NA	63,097	16.3	54.4
089 CHR & MISS AL	7	810	1,227	.3	1.1
093 CHR CH (DISC)	2	82	107	-	.1
097 CHR CHS&CHS CR	5	881	1,101*	.3	.9
105 CHRISTIAN REF	1	29	43	-	-
111 CH CR,SCIENTST	5	NR	NR	-	-
123 CH GOD (ANDER)	2	124	124	-	.1
127 CH GOD (CLEVE)	1	62	78*	-	.1
145 CH GOD PROPHCY	3	93	116*	-	.1
151 L-D SAINTS	20	NA	7,591	2.0	6.5
165 CH OF NAZARENE	3	488	1,121	.3	1.0
167 CHS OF CHRIST	12	783	967	.2	.8
175 CONGR CHR CHS	2	67	84*	-	.1
179 CONSRV BAPT	4	NR	NR	-	-
193 EPISCOPAL	9	1,765	2,671	.7	2.3

NA–Not applicable   NR–Not reported   *Total adherents estimated from known number of communicant, confirmed, full members.   - Represents a percent less than 0.1.   Percentages may not total due to rounding.
[1] See Appendix E   [2] See Appendix F   [3] See Appendix G   Lines in *italic* represent a breakdown of Catholic rites or Friends affiliations. They are included in their respective denominational total.

CALIFORNIA

Table 4. Churches and Church Membership by County and Denomination: 1990

County and Denomination	Number of churches	Communicant, confirmed, full members	Total adherents Number	Percent of total population	Percent of total adherents
203 EVAN FREE CH	3	173	378	.1	.3
207 E.L.C.A.	4	1,935	3,016	.8	2.6
209 EVAN LUTH SYN	1	44	53	-	-
223 FREE WILL BAPT	1	130	163*	-	.1
226 FRIENDS-USA	1	93	136	-	.1
226f INDEPENDNT	1	93	136	-	.1
249 AP CATH ASSYR	0	76	130	-	.1
259 IFCA	1	NR	NR	-	-
263 INT FOURSQ GOS	7	322	403*	.1	.3
283 LUTH—MO SYNOD	8	1,887	2,685	.7	2.3
329 OPEN BIBLE STD	1	NR	NR	-	-
331 ORTH CH IN AM	3	NR	NR	-	-
339 PENT CH OF GOD	3	97	234	.1	.2
353 CHR BRETHREN	1	70	140	-	.1
355 PRESB CH (USA)	9	2,626	3,283*	.8	2.8
371 REF CH IN AM	1	44	80	-	.1
403 SALVATION ARMY	2	200	221	.1	.2
413 S.D.A.	8	1,872	2,340*	.6	2.0
419 SO BAPT CONV	14	3,803	4,754*	1.2	4.1
435 UNITARIAN-UNIV	1	333	443	.1	.4
443 UN C OF CHRIST	8	1,183	1,479*	.4	1.3
449 UN METHODIST	10	2,431	3,039*	.8	2.6
469 WELS	1	73	94	-	.1
496 JEWISH EST[1]	4	NA	8,500	2.2	7.3
497 BLACK BAPT EST[2]	NA	1,186	1,483*	.4	1.3
498 INDEP.CHARIS.[3]	1	NA	300	.1	.3
499 INDEP.NON-CHAR[3]	1	NA	600	.2	.5
STANISLAUS	**250**	**37,116**	**139,238***	**37.6**	**100.0**
005 AME ZION	1	150	200	.1	.1
019 AMER BAPT USA	6	742	987*	.3	.7
053 ASSEMB OF GOD	35	5,509	8,988	2.4	6.5
057 BAPT GEN CONF	1	220	293*	.1	.2
059 BAPT MISS ASSN	1	0	0*	-	-
081 CATHOLIC	15	NA	66,083	17.8	47.5
081c CHALDEAN	2	NA	3,000	.8	2.2
081d LATIN	13	NA	63,083	17.0	45.3
089 CHR & MISS AL	3	0	357	.1	.3
093 CHR CH (DISC)	4	563	856	.2	.6
097 CHR CHS&CHS CR	3	730	971*	.3	.7
105 CHRISTIAN REF	2	514	829	.2	.6
111 CH CR,SCIENTST	3	NR	NR	-	-
123 CH GOD (ANDER)	2	105	153	-	.1
127 CH GOD (CLEVE)	4	359	478*	.1	.3
145 CH GOD PROPHCY	2	62	82*	-	.1
151 L-D SAINTS	23	NA	9,350	2.5	6.7
157 CH OF BRETHREN	3	612	814*	.2	.6
165 CH OF NAZARENE	6	982	1,360	.4	1.0
167 CHS OF CHRIST	18	1,933	2,505	.7	1.8
179 CONSRV BAPT	2	NR	NR	-	-
193 EPISCOPAL	5	1,293	2,176	.6	1.6
203 EVAN FREE CH	3	821	1,008	.3	.7
207 E.L.C.A.	3	1,090	1,436	.4	1.0
221 FREE METHODIST	3	260	347	.1	.2
223 FREE WILL BAPT	4	336	447*	.1	.3
226 FRIENDS-USA	2	208	280*	.1	.2
226e FUM	1	206	274*	.1	.2
226f INDEPENDNT	1	2	6	-	-
246 GREEK ORTHODOX	1	NR	NR	-	-
249 AP CATH ASSYR	2	576	3,201	.9	2.3
259 IFCA	1	NR	NR	-	-
263 INT FOURSQ GOS	3	713	949*	.3	.7
283 LUTH—MO SYNOD	5	1,387	1,911	.5	1.4
284 LUTH CH-AM ASC	1	94	126	-	.1
291 MISSIONARY CH	1	64	100	-	.1
313 N AM BAPT CONF	1	25	33*	-	-
339 PENT CH OF GOD	13	496	1,267	.3	.9
349 PENT HOLINESS	3	74	98*	-	.1
353 CHR BRETHREN	1	11	22	-	-
355 PRESB CH (USA)	9	1,897	2,524*	.7	1.8
361 PRIM BAPT ASCS	1	41	55*	-	-
371 REF CH IN AM	1	177	316	.1	.2
373 REF CH IN U.S.	1	26	54	-	-
403 SALVATION ARMY	2	191	200	.1	.1
413 S.D.A.	7	2,793	3,716*	1.0	2.7
419 SO BAPT CONV	24	6,314	8,400*	2.3	6.0
435 UNITARIAN-UNIV	1	128	152	-	.1
443 UN C OF CHRIST	2	440	585*	.2	.4
449 UN METHODIST	10	3,710	4,936*	1.3	3.5
469 WELS	1	91	133	-	.1
496 JEWISH EST[1]	1	NA	450	.1	.3
497 BLACK BAPT EST[2]	NA	1,379	1,835*	.5	1.3
498 INDEP.CHARIS.[3]	1	NA	450	.1	.3
499 INDEP.NON-CHAR[3]	3	NA	7,725	2.1	5.5
SUTTER	**44**	**6,502**	**20,555***	**31.9**	**100.0**
053 ASSEMB OF GOD	6	1,083	3,591	5.6	17.5

County and Denomination	Number of churches	Communicant, confirmed, full members	Total adherents Number	Percent of total population	Percent of total adherents
081 CATHOLIC	1	NA	7,600	11.8	37.0
081d LATIN	1	NA	7,600	11.8	37.0
093 CHR CH (DISC)	1	106	144	.2	.7
097 CHR CHS&CHS CR	2	95	123*	.2	.6
111 CH CR,SCIENTST	1	NR	NR	-	-
123 CH GOD (ANDER)	1	100	100	.2	.5
151 L-D SAINTS	4	NA	1,750	2.7	8.5
157 CH OF BRETHREN	1	94	122*	.2	.6
165 CH OF NAZARENE	3	369	582	.9	2.8
167 CHS OF CHRIST	3	286	361	.6	1.8
193 EPISCOPAL	1	30	54	.1	.3
203 EVAN FREE CH	1	188	300	.5	1.5
263 INT FOURSQ GOS	2	14	18*	-	.1
283 LUTH—MO SYNOD	1	496	656	1.0	3.2
284 LUTH CH-AM ASC	1	102	126	.2	.6
339 PENT CH OF GOD	1	37	167	.3	.8
349 PENT HOLINESS	1	38	49*	.1	.2
355 PRESB CH (USA)	1	380	492*	.8	2.4
413 S.D.A.	1	413	535*	.8	2.6
419 SO BAPT CONV	5	1,483	1,921*	3.0	9.3
449 UN METHODIST	4	965	1,250*	1.9	6.1
497 BLACK BAPT EST[2]	NA	223	289*	.4	1.4
498 INDEP.CHARIS.[3]	2	NA	325	.5	1.6
TEHAMA	**44**	**3,930**	**9,860***	**19.9**	**100.0**
019 AMER BAPT USA	2	195	249*	.5	2.5
053 ASSEMB OF GOD	4	498	810	1.6	8.2
081 CATHOLIC	3	NA	3,012	6.1	30.5
081d LATIN	3	NA	3,012	6.1	30.5
093 CHR CH (DISC)	2	125	194	.4	2.0
111 CH CR,SCIENTST	1	NR	NR	-	-
123 CH GOD (ANDER)	1	375	375	.8	3.8
151 L-D SAINTS	3	NA	1,420	2.9	14.4
165 CH OF NAZARENE	2	205	459	.9	4.7
167 CHS OF CHRIST	4	237	262	.5	2.7
179 CONSRV BAPT	1	NR	NR	-	-
193 EPISCOPAL	2	189	254	.5	2.6
263 INT FOURSQ GOS	2	106	135*	.3	1.4
283 LUTH—MO SYNOD	2	231	287	.6	2.9
339 PENT CH OF GOD	2	41	197	.4	2.0
349 PENT HOLINESS	1	8	10*	-	.1
355 PRESB CH (USA)	2	307	392*	.8	4.0
403 SALVATION ARMY	1	2	2	-	-
413 S.D.A.	2	340	434*	.9	4.4
419 SO BAPT CONV	2	501	640*	1.3	6.5
449 UN METHODIST	5	570	728*	1.5	7.4
TRINITY	**19**	**744**	**1,980***	**15.2**	**100.0**
053 ASSEMB OF GOD	3	234	383	2.9	19.3
081 CATHOLIC	3	NA	505	3.9	25.5
081d LATIN	3	NA	505	3.9	25.5
111 CH CR,SCIENTST	1	NR	NR	-	-
151 L-D SAINTS	2	NA	309	2.4	15.6
165 CH OF NAZARENE	1	96	260	2.0	13.1
167 CHS OF CHRIST	2	60	76	.6	3.8
263 INT FOURSQ GOS	1	6	8*	.1	.4
331 ORTH CH IN AM	1	NR	NR	-	-
413 S.D.A.	3	176	222*	1.7	11.2
419 SO BAPT CONV	1	74	93*	.7	4.7
443 UN C OF CHRIST	1	98	124*	.9	6.3
TULARE	**301**	**39,603**	**104,787***	**33.6**	**100.0**
005 AME ZION	1	106	140	-	.1
019 AMER BAPT USA	8	3,254	4,430*	1.4	4.2
039 AP CHR CH(NAZ)	1	15	20*	-	-
053 ASSEMB OF GOD	36	3,495	5,278	1.7	5.0
057 BAPT GEN CONF	3	585	796*	.3	.8
075 BRETHREN IN CR	1	80	80	-	.1
081 CATHOLIC	19	NA	40,000	12.8	38.2
081d LATIN	19	NA	40,000	12.8	38.2
089 CHR & MISS AL	2	334	646	.2	.6
093 CHR CH (DISC)	3	904	1,125	.4	1.1
097 CHR CHS&CHS CR	6	753	1,025*	.3	1.0
105 CHRISTIAN REF	2	476	783	.3	.7
111 CH CR,SCIENTST	3	NR	NR	-	-
123 CH GOD (ANDER)	5	800	856	.3	.8
127 CH GOD (CLEVE)	12	903	1,229*	.4	1.2
133 CH GOD(7TH)DEN	1	49	69	-	.1
145 CH GOD PROPHCY	7	254	346*	.1	.3
151 L-D SAINTS	17	NA	5,042	1.6	4.8
157 CH OF BRETHREN	1	92	125*	-	.1
165 CH OF NAZARENE	13	2,310	2,963	.9	2.8
167 CHS OF CHRIST	24	1,896	2,504	.8	2.4
171 CH GOD-GEN CON	2	47	64*	-	.1
193 EPISCOPAL	5	1,107	1,565	.5	1.5
203 EVAN FREE CH	1	125	270	.1	.3

NA–Not applicable   NR–Not reported   *Total adherents estimated from known number of communicant, confirmed, full members.   - Represents a percent less than 0.1.   Percentages may not total due to rounding.

[1]See Appendix E   [2]See Appendix F   [3]See Appendix G   Lines in *italic* represent a breakdown of Catholic rites or Friends affiliations. They are included in their respective denominational total.

Table 4. Churches and Church Membership by County and Denomination: 1990

County and Denomination	Number of churches	Communicant, confirmed, full members	Total adherents Number	Percent of total population	Percent of total adherents
207 E.L.C.A.	3	855	1,221	.4	1.2
223 FREE WILL BAPT	9	807	1,099*	.4	1.0
226 FRIENDS-USA	1	28	40	-	-
226f INDEPENDNT	1	28	40	-	-
237 GC MENN BR CHS	5	966	1,315*	.4	1.3
263 INT FOURSQ GOS	7	662	901*	.3	.9
283 LUTH—MO SYNOD	6	1,331	1,776	.6	1.7
339 PENT CH OF GOD	18	406	1,259	.4	1.2
349 PENT HOLINESS	3	80	109*	-	.1
353 CHR BRETHREN	1	6	16	-	-
355 PRESB CH (USA)	12	2,400	3,267*	1.0	3.1
371 REF CH IN AM	1	204	385	.1	.4
403 SALVATION ARMY	1	30	30	-	-
413 S.D.A.	12	2,435	3,315*	1.1	3.2
419 SO BAPT CONV	23	7,042	9,587*	3.1	9.1
435 UNITARIAN-UNIV	2	42	52	-	-
438 UN BRETH IN CR	1	64	64	-	.1
443 UN C OF CHRIST	2	389	530*	.2	.5
449 UN METHODIST	14	3,283	4,470*	1.4	4.3
496 JEWISH EST[1]	1	NA	375	.1	.4
497 BLACK BAPT EST[2]	NA	988	1,345*	.4	1.3
498 INDEP.CHARIS.[3]	3	NA	1,300	.4	1.2
499 INDEP.NON-CHAR[3]	3	NA	2,975	1.0	2.8
TUOLUMNE	**40**	**4,014**	**15,657***	**32.3**	**100.0**
019 AMER BAPT USA	1	153	186*	.4	1.2
053 ASSEMB OF GOD	5	395	1,077	2.2	6.9
081 CATHOLIC	7	NA	8,075	16.7	51.6
081d LATIN	7	NA	8,075	16.7	51.6
111 CH CR,SCIENTST	1	NR	NR	-	-
123 CH GOD (ANDER)	1	250	250	.5	1.6
151 L-D SAINTS	2	NA	859	1.8	5.5
165 CH OF NAZARENE	1	69	84	.2	.5
167 CHS OF CHRIST	3	154	200	.4	1.3
193 EPISCOPAL	3	229	336	.7	2.1
203 EVAN FREE CH	2	186	275	.6	1.8
207 E.L.C.A.	1	200	291	.6	1.9
249 AP CATH ASSYR	0	22	100	.2	.6
263 INT FOURSQ GOS	1	58	71*	.1	.5
283 LUTH—MO SYNOD	1	231	264	.5	1.7
339 PENT CH OF GOD	2	68	154	.3	1.0
355 PRESB CH (USA)	1	225	274*	.6	1.8
413 S.D.A.	1	664	809*	1.7	5.2
419 SO BAPT CONV	2	457	556*	1.1	3.6
449 UN METHODIST	4	384	468*	1.0	3.0
497 BLACK BAPT EST[2]	NA	269	328*	.7	2.1
498 INDEP.CHARIS.[3]	1	NA	1,000	2.1	6.4
VENTURA	**313**	**54,313**	**341,360***	**51.0**	**100.0**
019 AMER BAPT USA	13	2,880	3,681*	.6	1.1
053 ASSEMB OF GOD	18	2,183	4,026	.6	1.2
057 BAPT GEN CONF	3	1,492	1,907*	.3	.6
081 CATHOLIC	17	NA	237,426	35.5	69.6
081d LATIN	17	NA	237,426	35.5	69.6
089 CHR & MISS AL	3	67	97	-	-
093 CHR CH (DISC)	1	294	354	.1	.1
097 CHR CHS&CHS CR	9	2,016	2,576*	.4	.8
111 CH CR,SCIENTST	8	NR	NR	-	-
121 CH GOD (ABR)	1	23	29*	-	-
123 CH GOD (ANDER)	2	62	62	-	-
127 CH GOD (CLEVE)	5	335	428*	.1	.1
145 CH GOD PROPHCY	3	106	135*	-	-
151 L-D SAINTS	42	NA	16,294	2.4	4.8
165 CH OF NAZARENE	9	969	1,364	.2	.4
167 CHS OF CHRIST	23	1,946	2,436	.4	.7
179 CONSRV BAPT	2	NR	NR	-	-
193 EPISCOPAL	9	3,080	5,054	.8	1.5
203 EVAN FREE CH	5	665	1,175	.2	.3
207 E.L.C.A.	12	5,813	7,871	1.2	2.3
209 EVAN LUTH SYN	1	77	82	-	-
220 FREE LUTHERAN	1	328	438	.1	.1
221 FREE METHODIST	1	25	33	-	-
223 FREE WILL BAPT	2	92	118*	-	-
226 FRIENDS-USA	3	116	169*	-	-
226e FUM	1	111	142*	-	-
226f INDEPENDNT	2	5	27	-	-
246 GREEK ORTHODOX	1	NR	NR	-	-
259 IFCA	1	NR	NR	-	-
263 INT FOURSQ GOS	13	1,451	1,854*	.3	.5
283 LUTH—MO SYNOD	11	3,141	4,519	.7	1.3
291 MISSIONARY CH	4	1,465	1,936	.3	.6
331 ORTH CH IN AM	1	NR	NR	-	-
339 PENT CH OF GOD	2	63	128	-	-
349 PENT HOLINESS	3	124	158*	-	-
353 CHR BRETHREN	1	60	60	-	-
355 PRESB CH (USA)	12	4,868	6,221*	.9	1.8
403 SALVATION ARMY	2	136	143		

County and Denomination	Number of churches	Communicant, confirmed, full members	Total adherents Number	Percent of total population	Percent of total adherents
413 S.D.A.	10	3,057	3,907*	.6	1.1
419 SO BAPT CONV	18	6,347	8,111*	1.2	2.4
435 UNITARIAN-UNIV	4	262	314	-	.1
443 UN C OF CHRIST	4	639	817*	.1	.2
449 UN METHODIST	16	6,542	8,360*	1.2	2.4
467 WESLEYAN	1	51	130	-	-
469 WELS	1	196	281	-	.1
496 JEWISH EST[1]	5	NA	8,000	1.2	2.3
497 BLACK BAPT EST[2]	NA	3,342	4,271*	.6	1.3
498 INDEP.CHARIS.[3]	4	NA	2,950	.4	.9
499 INDEP.NON-CHAR[3]	4	NA	3,445	.5	1.0
YOLO	**80**	**9,170**	**40,283***	**28.6**	**100.0**
019 AMER BAPT USA	1	40	50*	-	.1
053 ASSEMB OF GOD	6	584	1,175	.8	2.9
081 CATHOLIC	11	NA	23,530	16.7	58.4
081d LATIN	11	NA	23,530	16.7	58.4
089 CHR & MISS AL	1	0	50	-	.1
093 CHR CH (DISC)	1	141	360	.3	.9
111 CH CR,SCIENTST	2	NR	NR	-	-
123 CH GOD (ANDER)	1	64	64	-	.2
127 CH GOD (CLEVE)	1	30	37*	-	.1
145 CH GOD PROPHCY	1	31	39*	-	.1
151 L-D SAINTS	8	NA	2,773	2.0	6.9
165 CH OF NAZARENE	3	305	489	.3	1.2
167 CHS OF CHRIST	4	239	305	.2	.8
179 CONSRV BAPT	2	NR	NR	-	-
193 EPISCOPAL	2	542	682	.5	1.7
203 EVAN FREE CH	1	58	63	-	.2
207 E.L.C.A.	4	1,004	1,269	.9	3.2
223 FREE WILL BAPT	1	28	35*	-	.1
226 FRIENDS-USA	1	49	87	.1	.2
226f INDEPENDNT	1	49	87	.1	.2
263 INT FOURSQ GOS	3	211	262*	.2	.7
283 LUTH—MO SYNOD	2	571	762	.5	1.9
331 ORTH CH IN AM	1	NR	NR	-	-
339 PENT CH OF GOD	3	164	332	.2	.8
349 PENT HOLINESS	1	61	76*	.1	.2
355 PRESB CH (USA)	5	1,488	1,850*	1.3	4.6
413 S.D.A.	1	292	363*	.3	.9
419 SO BAPT CONV	5	1,102	1,370*	1.0	3.4
435 UNITARIAN-UNIV	1	285	355	.3	.9
443 UN C OF CHRIST	2	448	557*	.4	1.4
449 UN METHODIST	4	755	939*	.7	2.3
496 JEWISH EST[1]	0	NA	1,191	.8	3.0
497 BLACK BAPT EST[2]	NA	678	843*	.6	2.1
498 INDEP.CHARIS.[3]	1	NA	375	.3	.9
YUBA	**50**	**6,939**	**17,028***	**29.2**	**100.0**
019 AMER BAPT USA	1	81	110*	.2	.6
053 ASSEMB OF GOD	6	802	1,416	2.4	8.3
081 CATHOLIC	1	NA	4,848	8.3	28.5
081d LATIN	1	NA	4,848	8.3	28.5
089 CHR & MISS AL	1	987	987	1.7	5.8
093 CHR CH (DISC)	1	66	87	.1	.5
097 CHR CHS&CHS CR	1	100	135*	.2	.8
111 CH CR,SCIENTST	1	NR	NR	-	-
127 CH GOD (CLEVE)	1	49	66*	.1	.4
145 CH GOD PROPHCY	1	31	42*	.1	.2
151 L-D SAINTS	4	NA	1,633	2.8	9.6
165 CH OF NAZARENE	3	211	834	1.4	4.9
167 CHS OF CHRIST	6	375	425	.7	2.5
171 CH GOD-GEN CON	1	8	11*	-	.1
193 EPISCOPAL	2	441	568	1.0	3.3
207 E.L.C.A.	1	167	224	.4	1.3
209 EVAN LUTH SYN	2	37	58	.1	.3
223 FREE WILL BAPT	1	44	60*	.1	.4
283 LUTH—MO SYNOD	1	36	34	.1	.2
339 PENT CH OF GOD	2	51	142	.2	.8
355 PRESB CH (USA)	1	420	569*	1.0	3.3
403 SALVATION ARMY	1	85	85	.1	.5
413 S.D.A.	3	314	425*	.7	2.5
419 SO BAPT CONV	6	1,715	2,324*	4.0	13.6
449 UN METHODIST	1	398	539*	.9	3.2
497 BLACK BAPT EST[2]	NA	521	706*	1.2	4.1
499 INDEP.NON-CHAR[3]	1	NA	700	1.2	4.1

NA–Not applicable   NR–Not reported   *Total adherents estimated from known number of communicant, confirmed, full members.   - Represents a percent less than 0.1.   Percentages may not total due to rounding.
[1]See Appendix E   [2]See Appendix F   [3]See Appendix G   Lines in *italic* represent a breakdown of Catholic rites or Friends affiliations. They are included in their respective denominational total.

COLORADO

Table 4. Churches and Church Membership by County and Denomination: 1990

County and Denomination	Number of churches	Communicant, confirmed, full members	Total adherents Number	Percent of total population	Percent of total adherents
COLORADO					
THE STATE.....	2,813	483,532	1,294,376*	39.3	100.0
ADAMS	**128**	**25,110**	**80,102***	**30.2**	**100.0**
019 AMER BAPT USA	2	880	1,149*	.4	1.4
053 ASSEMB OF GOD	6	1,503	1,809	.7	2.3
057 BAPT GEN CONF	2	435	568*	.2	.7
081 CATHOLIC	8	NA	32,308	12.2	40.3
081d LATIN	8	NA	32,308	12.2	40.3
089 CHR & MISS AL	3	86	405	.2	.5
093 CHR CH (DISC)	1	120	192	.1	.2
097 CHR CHS&CHS CR	6	1,773	2,316*	.9	2.9
111 CH CR,SCIENTST	3	NR	NR	-	-
123 CH GOD (ANDER)	1	45	45	-	.1
127 CH GOD (CLEVE)	1	224	293*	.1	.4
151 L-D SAINTS	10	NA	4,074	1.5	5.1
165 CH OF NAZARENE	5	894	1,240	.5	1.5
167 CHS OF CHRIST	4	242	330	.1	.4
179 CONSRV BAPT	2	NR	NR	-	-
181 CONSRV CONGR	1	96	125*	-	.2
193 EPISCOPAL	3	274	469	.2	.6
203 EVAN FREE CH	1	90	175	.1	.2
207 E.L.C.A.	9	3,026	4,936	1.9	6.2
221 FREE METHODIST	1	25	50	-	.1
223 FREE WILL BAPT	1	56	73*	-	.1
259 IFCA	1	NR	NR	-	-
263 INT FOURSQ GOS	6	221	289*	.1	.4
283 LUTH—MO SYNOD	7	2,568	3,798	1.4	4.7
284 LUTH CH-AM ASC	1	169	242	.1	.3
313 N AM BAPT CONF	1	88	115*	-	.1
349 PENT HOLINESS	1	164	214*	.1	.3
355 PRESB CH (USA)	10	2,298	3,002*	1.1	3.7
403 SALVATION ARMY	1	49	50	-	.1
413 S.D.A.	2	670	875*	.3	1.1
419 SO BAPT CONV	10	3,215	4,199*	1.6	5.2
443 UN C OF CHRIST	3	347	453*	.2	.6
449 UN METHODIST	8	3,502	4,574*	1.7	5.7
467 WESLEYAN	2	75	299	.1	.4
469 WELS	1	91	146	.1	.2
496 JEWISH EST[1]	0	NA	6,453	2.4	8.1
497 BLACK BAPT EST[2]	NA	1,884	2,461*	.9	3.1
498 INDEP.CHARIS.[3]	1	NA	675	.3	.8
499 INDEP.NON-CHAR[3]	3	NA	1,700	.6	2.1
ALAMOSA	**22**	**2,427**	**8,695***	**63.9**	**100.0**
019 AMER BAPT USA	1	75	98*	.7	1.1
053 ASSEMB OF GOD	2	221	560	4.1	6.4
057 BAPT GEN CONF	1	39	51*	.4	.6
081 CATHOLIC	1	NA	4,300	31.6	49.5
081d LATIN	1	NA	4,300	31.6	49.5
093 CHR CH (DISC)	1	139	203	1.5	2.3
097 CHR CHS&CHS CR	1	40	52*	.4	.6
105 CHRISTIAN REF	2	272	505	3.7	5.8
111 CH CR,SCIENTST	1	NR	NR	-	-
151 L-D SAINTS	2	NA	682	5.0	7.8
167 CHS OF CHRIST	1	63	90	.7	1.0
179 CONSRV BAPT	1	NR	NR	-	-
193 EPISCOPAL	1	65	99	.7	1.1
283 LUTH—MO SYNOD	1	174	236	1.7	2.7
353 CHR BRETHREN	1	100	200	1.5	2.3
355 PRESB CH (USA)	1	242	316*	2.3	3.6
413 S.D.A.	1	140	183*	1.3	2.1
419 SO BAPT CONV	1	537	702*	5.2	8.1
449 UN METHODIST	2	320	418*	3.1	4.8
ARAPAHOE	**180**	**58,252**	**150,738***	**38.5**	**100.0**
019 AMER BAPT USA	7	795	1,015*	.3	.7
040 AP CHR CH-AMER	1	37	67	-	-
053 ASSEMB OF GOD	8	2,909	4,642	1.2	3.1
057 BAPT GEN CONF	1	891	1,137*	.3	.8
081 CATHOLIC	8	NA	49,887	12.7	33.1
081d LATIN	8	NA	49,887	12.7	33.1
089 CHR & MISS AL	1	29	78	-	.1
093 CHR CH (DISC)	1	608	840	.2	.6
097 CHR CHS&CHS CR	3	677	864*	.2	.6
111 CH CR,SCIENTST	2	NR	NR	-	-
123 CH GOD (ANDER)	2	120	148	-	.1
127 CH GOD (CLEVE)	2	180	230*	.1	.2
145 CH GOD PROPHCY	1	22	28*	-	-
151 L-D SAINTS	22	NA	9,387	2.4	6.2
163 CH OF LUTH BR	1	7	48	-	-
165 CH OF NAZARENE	4	2,586	3,274	.8	2.2
167 CHS OF CHRIST	8	1,283	1,858	.5	1.2
179 CONSRV BAPT	5	NR	NR	-	-
193 EPISCOPAL	6	1,573	2,516	.6	1.7

County and Denomination	Number of churches	Communicant, confirmed, full members	Total adherents Number	Percent of total population	Percent of total adherents
203 EVAN FREE CH	6	717	1,337	.3	.9
207 E.L.C.A.	11	6,222	8,395	2.1	5.6
216 EVAN PRESBY CH	6	7,269	7,659	2.0	5.1
221 FREE METHODIST	2	180	307	.1	.2
226 FRIENDS-USA	1	29	37*	-	-
226e FUM	1	29	37*	-	.1
237 GC MENN BR CHS	1	140	179*	-	.1
246 GREEK ORTHODOX	1	NR	NR	-	-
259 IFCA	1	NR	NR	-	-
263 INT FOURSQ GOS	3	845	1,078*	.3	.7
283 LUTH—MO SYNOD	7	4,644	6,478	1.7	4.3
285 MENNONITE CH	1	57	82	-	.1
329 OPEN BIBLE STD	2	NR	NR	-	-
331 ORTH CH IN AM	1	NR	NR	-	-
339 PENT CH OF GOD	1	34	77	-	.1
349 PENT HOLINESS	2	117	149*	-	.1
353 CHR BRETHREN	2	396	642	.2	.4
355 PRESB CH (USA)	8	3,347	4,272*	1.1	2.8
356 PRESB CH AMER	1	47	57	-	-
403 SALVATION ARMY	2	86	102	-	.1
413 S.D.A.	3	857	1,094*	.3	.7
419 SO BAPT CONV	12	7,081	9,037*	2.3	6.0
443 UN C OF CHRIST	6	2,937	3,748*	1.0	2.5
449 UN METHODIST	8	6,363	8,121*	2.1	5.4
467 WESLEYAN	1	43	46	-	-
469 WELS	1	158	227	.1	.2
496 JEWISH EST[1]	1	NA	9,532	2.4	6.3
497 BLACK BAPT EST[2]	NA	4,966	6,338*	1.6	4.2
498 INDEP.CHARIS.[3]	3	NA	3,250	.8	2.2
499 INDEP.NON-CHAR[3]	3	NA	2,475	.6	1.6
ARCHULETA	**14**	**1,151**	**2,293***	**42.9**	**100.0**
053 ASSEMB OF GOD	1	63	145	2.7	6.3
081 CATHOLIC	4	NA	500	9.4	21.8
081d LATIN	4	NA	500	9.4	21.8
151 L-D SAINTS	1	NA	186	3.5	8.1
167 CHS OF CHRIST	2	42	63	1.2	2.7
193 EPISCOPAL	1	50	83	1.6	3.6
283 LUTH—MO SYNOD	1	91	130	2.4	5.7
413 S.D.A.	1	10	13*	.2	.6
419 SO BAPT CONV	2	631	827*	15.5	36.1
449 UN METHODIST	1	264	346*	6.5	15.1
BACA	**23**	**982**	**1,670***	**36.7**	**100.0**
053 ASSEMB OF GOD	2	75	111	2.4	6.6
081 CATHOLIC	2	NA	400	8.8	24.0
081d LATIN	2	NA	400	8.8	24.0
123 CH GOD (ANDER)	2	60	71	1.6	4.3
167 CHS OF CHRIST	4	102	133	2.9	8.0
226 FRIENDS-USA	3	97	100	2.2	6.0
226b EFI	3	97	100	2.2	6.0
349 PENT HOLINESS	2	26	32*	.7	1.9
413 S.D.A.	1	17	21*	.5	1.3
419 SO BAPT CONV	1	253	316*	6.9	18.9
449 UN METHODIST	4	319	398*	8.7	23.8
467 WESLEYAN	2	33	88	1.9	5.3
BENT	**14**	**797**	**2,138***	**42.4**	**100.0**
053 ASSEMB OF GOD	1	14	16	.3	.7
081 CATHOLIC	1	NA	1,050	20.8	49.1
081d LATIN	1	NA	1,050	20.8	49.1
093 CHR CH (DISC)	1	81	127	2.5	5.9
165 CH OF NAZARENE	1	29	86	1.7	4.0
167 CHS OF CHRIST	2	34	52	1.0	2.4
226 FRIENDS-USA	2	33	43	.9	2.0
226b EFI	2	33	43	.9	2.0
355 PRESB CH (USA)	1	111	139*	2.8	6.5
413 S.D.A.	1	17	21*	.4	1.0
419 SO BAPT CONV	1	108	135*	2.7	6.3
449 UN METHODIST	2	342	428*	8.5	20.0
469 WELS	1	28	41	.8	1.9
BOULDER	**152**	**33,182**	**83,838***	**37.2**	**100.0**
019 AMER BAPT USA	3	1,071	1,315*	.6	1.6
053 ASSEMB OF GOD	4	263	339	.2	.4
057 BAPT GEN CONF	1	209	257*	.1	.3
081 CATHOLIC	10	NA	27,336	12.1	32.6
081d LATIN	10	NA	27,336	12.1	32.6
089 CHR & MISS AL	2	135	182	.1	.2
093 CHR CH (DISC)	1	269	399	.2	.5
097 CHR CHS&CHS CR	6	2,570	3,156*	1.4	3.8
105 CHRISTIAN REF	2	161	239	.1	.3
111 CH CR,SCIENTST	2	NR	NR	-	-
123 CH GOD (ANDER)	1	36	48	-	.1
127 CH GOD (CLEVE)	1	33	41*	-	-
151 L-D SAINTS	11	NA	4,711	2.1	5.6

NA–Not applicable NR–Not reported *Total adherents estimated from known number of communicant, confirmed, full members. - Represents a percent less than 0.1. Percentages may not total due to rounding.

[1]See Appendix E [2]See Appendix F [3]See Appendix G Lines in *italic* represent a breakdown of Catholic rites or Friends affiliations. They are included in their respective denominational total.

Table 4. Churches and Church Membership by County and Denomination: 1990

County and Denomination		Number of churches	Communicant, confirmed, full members	Total adherents		
				Number	Percent of total population	Percent of total adherents
157	CH OF BRETHREN	1	0	0*	-	-
165	CH OF NAZARENE	4	459	780	.3	.9
167	CHS OF CHRIST	5	696	918	.4	1.1
175	CONGR CHR CHS	1	90	111*	-	.1
179	CONSRV BAPT	4	NR	NR	-	-
193	EPISCOPAL	7	2,049	3,593	1.6	4.3
203	EVAN FREE CH	3	720	893	.4	1.1
207	E.L.C.A.	10	4,936	6,778	3.0	8.1
221	FREE METHODIST	1	38	53	-	.1
226	FRIENDS-USA	1	164	201*	.1	.2
226f	INDEPENDNT	1	164	201*	.1	.2
246	GREEK ORTHODOX	1	NR	NR	-	-
263	INT FOURSQ GOS	4	477	586*	.3	.7
283	LUTH—MO SYNOD	8	2,348	3,209	1.4	3.8
287	MENN GEN CONF	1	54	74	-	.1
349	PENT HOLINESS	2	303	372*	.2	.4
353	CHR BRETHREN	3	151	226	.1	.3
355	PRESB CH (USA)	10	4,474	5,495*	2.4	6.6
356	PRESB CH AMER	1	45	78	-	.1
403	SALVATION ARMY	1	16	21	-	-
413	S.D.A.	3	983	1,207*	.5	1.4
415	S-D BAPTIST GC	1	75	92*	-	.1
419	SO BAPT CONV	8	2,050	2,518*	1.1	3.0
435	UNITARIAN-UNIV	2	303	381	.2	.5
443	UN C OF CHRIST	5	2,008	2,466*	1.1	2.9
449	UN METHODIST	12	5,322	6,536*	2.9	7.8
467	WESLEYAN	1	0	0	-	-
469	WELS	2	256	353	.2	.4
496	JEWISH EST[1]	2	NA	5,486	2.4	6.5
497	BLACK BAPT EST[2]	NA	418	513*	.2	.6
498	INDEP.CHARIS.[3]	2	NA	1,975	.9	2.4
499	INDEP.NON-CHAR[3]	2	NA	900	.4	1.1
CHAFFEE		**29**	**2,446**	**6,272***	**49.4**	**100.0**
053	ASSEMB OF GOD	2	76	148	1.2	2.4
081	CATHOLIC	3	NA	2,860	22.5	45.6
081d	LATIN	3	NA	2,860	22.5	45.6
093	CHR CH (DISC)	1	166	194	1.5	3.1
097	CHR CHS&CHS CR	1	65	79*	.6	1.3
111	CH CR,SCIENTST	1	NR	NR	-	-
127	CH GOD (CLEVE)	1	66	80*	.6	1.3
145	CH GOD PROPHCY	1	22	27*	.2	.4
151	L-D SAINTS	1	NA	281	2.2	4.5
165	CH OF NAZARENE	1	14	0	-	-
167	CHS OF CHRIST	4	120	199	1.6	3.2
179	CONSRV BAPT	2	NR	NR	-	-
193	EPISCOPAL	2	141	196	1.5	3.1
263	INT FOURSQ GOS	1	27	33*	.3	.5
283	LUTH—MO SYNOD	2	182	273	2.2	4.4
355	PRESB CH (USA)	1	149	181*	1.4	2.9
413	S.D.A.	1	13	16*	.1	.3
419	SO BAPT CONV	2	1,009	1,225*	9.7	19.5
443	UN C OF CHRIST	1	226	274*	2.2	4.4
449	UN METHODIST	1	170	206*	1.6	3.3
CHEYENNE		**11**	**495**	**1,416***	**59.1**	**100.0**
081	CATHOLIC	2	NA	755	31.5	53.3
081d	LATIN	2	NA	755	31.5	53.3
097	CHR CHS&CHS CR	1	110	147*	6.1	10.4
167	CHS OF CHRIST	2	26	31	1.3	2.2
207	E.L.C.A.	1	14	14	.6	1.0
283	LUTH—MO SYNOD	2	132	184	7.7	13.0
419	SO BAPT CONV	1	18	24*	1.0	1.7
449	UN METHODIST	2	195	261*	10.9	18.4
CLEAR CREEK		**10**	**324**	**992***	**13.0**	**100.0**
057	BAPT GEN CONF	1	31	39*	.5	3.9
081	CATHOLIC	2	NA	540	7.1	54.4
081d	LATIN	2	NA	540	7.1	54.4
167	CHS OF CHRIST	1	10	20	.3	2.0
193	EPISCOPAL	1	8	9	.1	.9
207	E.L.C.A.	1	84	142	1.9	14.3
355	PRESB CH (USA)	2	128	162*	2.1	16.3
413	S.D.A.	1	14	18*	.2	1.8
449	UN METHODIST	1	49	62*	.8	6.2
CONEJOS		**19**	**154**	**3,617***	**48.5**	**100.0**
053	ASSEMB OF GOD	2	43	86	1.2	2.4
081	CATHOLIC	6	NA	1,200	16.1	33.2
081d	LATIN	6	NA	1,200	16.1	33.2
151	L-D SAINTS	8	NA	2,182	29.3	60.3
285	MENNONITE CH	1	23	28	.4	.8
355	PRESB CH (USA)	2	88	121*	1.6	3.3

County and Denomination		Number of churches	Communicant, confirmed, full members	Total adherents		
				Number	Percent of total population	Percent of total adherents
COSTILLA		**2**	**9**	**2,443***	**76.6**	**100.0**
081	CATHOLIC	0	NA	2,090	65.5	85.6
081d	LATIN	0	NA	2,090	65.5	85.6
151	L-D SAINTS	1	NA	341	10.7	14.0
355	PRESB CH (USA)	1	9	12*	.4	.5
CROWLEY		**8**	**454**	**920***	**23.3**	**100.0**
053	ASSEMB OF GOD	1	49	74	1.9	8.0
081	CATHOLIC	1	NA	340	8.6	37.0
081d	LATIN	1	NA	340	8.6	37.0
093	CHR CH (DISC)	1	100	150	3.8	16.3
207	E.L.C.A.	1	31	31	.8	3.4
283	LUTH—MO SYNOD	1	30	30	.8	3.3
449	UN METHODIST	2	229	276*	7.0	30.0
469	WELS	1	15	19	.5	2.1
CUSTER		**6**	**306**	**542***	**28.1**	**100.0**
081	CATHOLIC	1	NA	163	8.5	30.1
081d	LATIN	1	NA	163	8.5	30.1
167	CHS OF CHRIST	1	10	12	.6	2.2
193	EPISCOPAL	1	33	34	1.8	6.3
283	LUTH—MO SYNOD	1	101	129	6.7	23.8
419	SO BAPT CONV	1	39	49*	2.5	9.0
449	UN METHODIST	1	123	155*	8.0	28.6
DELTA		**52**	**4,045**	**9,406***	**44.8**	**100.0**
019	AMER BAPT USA	3	465	573*	2.7	6.1
053	ASSEMB OF GOD	4	401	725	3.5	7.7
081	CATHOLIC	4	NA	3,207	15.3	34.1
081d	LATIN	4	NA	3,207	15.3	34.1
097	CHR CHS&CHS CR	2	326	402*	1.9	4.3
111	CH CR,SCIENTST	1	NR	NR	-	-
123	CH GOD (ANDER)	2	94	102	.5	1.1
151	L-D SAINTS	3	NA	910	4.3	9.7
165	CH OF NAZARENE	3	114	198	.9	2.1
167	CHS OF CHRIST	6	196	257	1.2	2.7
193	EPISCOPAL	2	95	125	.6	1.3
207	E.L.C.A.	1	58	67	.3	.7
226	FRIENDS-USA	1	128	165	.8	1.8
226b	EFI	1	128	165	.8	1.8
259	IFCA	2	NR	NR	-	-
283	LUTH—MO SYNOD	2	223	276	1.3	2.9
331	ORTH CH IN AM	1	NR	NR	-	-
349	PENT HOLINESS	1	8	10*	-	.1
355	PRESB CH (USA)	2	273	337*	1.6	3.6
413	S.D.A.	3	248	306*	1.5	3.3
419	SO BAPT CONV	4	669	825*	3.9	8.8
449	UN METHODIST	5	747	921*	4.4	9.8
DENVER		**323**	**83,631**	**216,428***	**46.3**	**100.0**
005	AME ZION	2	290	336	.1	.2
019	AMER BAPT USA	17	8,978	10,951*	2.3	5.1
039	AP CHR CH(NAZ)	1	81	99*	-	-
053	ASSEMB OF GOD	16	2,932	5,129	1.1	2.4
057	BAPT GEN CONF	5	826	1,007*	.2	.5
081	CATHOLIC	39	NA	83,614	17.9	38.6
081b	BYZAN RUTH	1	NA	203	-	.1
081d	LATIN	37	NA	83,258	17.8	38.5
081h	UKRAINIAN	1	NA	153	-	.1
089	CHR & MISS AL	2	60	155	-	.1
093	CHR CH (DISC)	11	2,289	3,139	.7	1.5
097	CHR CHS&CHS CR	4	350	427*	.1	.2
105	CHRISTIAN REF	9	1,911	2,773	.6	1.3
111	CH CR,SCIENTST	5	NR	NR	-	-
123	CH GOD (ANDER)	4	358	373	.1	.2
127	CH GOD (CLEVE)	3	583	711*	.2	.3
133	CH GOD(7TH)DEN	2	152	228	-	.1
145	CH GOD PROPHCY	2	44	54*	-	-
151	L-D SAINTS	11	NA	5,002	1.1	2.3
157	CH OF BRETHREN	1	191	233*	.1	.1
165	CH OF NAZARENE	5	345	536	.1	.2
167	CHS OF CHRIST	10	2,371	3,301	.7	1.5
179	CONSRV BAPT	7	NR	NR	-	-
193	EPISCOPAL	16	7,848	12,782	2.7	5.9
203	EVAN FREE CH	3	613	1,086	.2	.5
207	E.L.C.A.	12	4,926	6,433	1.4	3.0
216	EVAN PRESBY CH	2	689	704	.2	.3
226	FRIENDS-USA	2	458	559*	.1	.3
226b	EFI	1	246	300*	.1	.1
226f	INDEPENDNT	1	212	259*	.1	.1
237	GC MENN BR CHS	2	112	137*	-	.1
246	GREEK ORTHODOX	1	NR	NR	-	-
259	IFCA	3	NR	NR	-	-
263	INT FOURSQ GOS	3	414	505*	.1	.2
283	LUTH—MO SYNOD	10	3,947	5,015	1.1	2.3

NA–Not applicable   NR–Not reported   *Total adherents estimated from known number of communicant, confirmed, full members.   - Represents a percent less than 0.1.   Percentages may not total due to rounding.
[1]See Appendix E   [2]See Appendix F   [3]See Appendix G   Lines in *italic* represent a breakdown of Catholic rites or Friends affiliations. They are included in their respective denominational total.

73

COLORADO

Table 4. Churches and Church Membership by County and Denomination: 1990

County and Denomination	Number of churches	Communicant, confirmed, full members	Total adherents Number	Percent of total population	Percent of total adherents
285 MENNONITE CH	1	241	397	.1	.2
287 MENN GEN CONF	1	34	51	-	-
320 "OLD" MB ASCS	1	18	22*	-	-
331 ORTH CH IN AM	1	NR	NR	-	-
339 PENT CH OF GOD	3	84	178	-	.1
349 PENT HOLINESS	1	32	39*	-	-
355 PRESB CH (USA)	16	5,936	7,240*	1.5	3.3
371 REF CH IN AM	6	1,141	1,898	.4	.9
403 SALVATION ARMY	2	115	144	-	.1
413 S.D.A.	9	4,032	4,918*	1.1	2.3
419 SO BAPT CONV	9	6,734	8,214*	1.8	3.8
431 UKRANIAN AMER	1	NR	NR	-	-
435 UNITARIAN-UNIV	2	700	911	.2	.4
443 UN C OF CHRIST	11	1,640	2,000*	.4	.9
449 UN METHODIST	24	8,796	10,729*	2.3	5.0
467 WESLEYAN	2	107	170	-	.1
469 WELS	1	444	569	.1	.3
496 JEWISH EST[1]	16	NA	11,385	2.4	5.3
497 BLACK BAPT EST[2]	NA	12,809	15,624*	3.3	7.2
498 INDEP.CHARIS.[3]	4	NA	5,750	1.2	2.7
499 INDEP.NON-CHAR[3]	2	NA	900	.2	.4
DOLORES	**7**	**378**	**578***	**38.4**	**100.0**
053 ASSEMB OF GOD	1	25	64	4.3	11.1
081 CATHOLIC	1	NA	60	4.0	10.4
081d *LATIN*	1	NA	60	4.0	10.4
167 CHS OF CHRIST	1	7	13	.9	2.2
413 S.D.A.	1	44	56*	3.7	9.7
419 SO BAPT CONV	2	250	319*	21.2	55.2
449 UN METHODIST	1	52	66*	4.4	11.4
DOUGLAS	**42**	**5,784**	**16,736***	**27.7**	**100.0**
053 ASSEMB OF GOD	1	15	20	-	.1
057 BAPT GEN CONF	1	328	439*	.7	2.6
075 BRETHREN IN CR	1	0	115	.2	.7
081 CATHOLIC	2	NA	5,383	8.9	32.2
081d *LATIN*	2	NA	5,383	8.9	32.2
097 CHR CHS&CHS CR	3	166	222*	.4	1.3
151 L-D SAINTS	3	NA	1,503	2.5	9.0
163 CH OF LUTH BR	1	43	89	.1	.5
165 CH OF NAZARENE	1	38	65	.1	.4
167 CHS OF CHRIST	2	112	159	.3	1.0
179 CONSRV BAPT	1	NR	NR	-	-
193 EPISCOPAL	3	449	615	1.0	3.7
203 EVAN FREE CH	1	15	90	.1	.5
207 E.L.C.A.	3	1,306	2,094	3.5	12.5
216 EVAN PRESBY CH	1	115	119	.2	.7
263 INT FOURSQ GOS	1	0	0*	-	-
283 LUTH—MO SYNOD	3	512	717	1.2	4.3
329 OPEN BIBLE STD	2	NR	NR	-	-
353 CHR BRETHREN	1	118	200	.3	1.2
355 PRESB CH (USA)	1	218	292*	.5	1.7
356 PRESB CH AMER	1	0	0	-	-
413 S.D.A.	1	63	84*	.1	.5
419 SO BAPT CONV	3	591	791*	1.3	4.7
443 UN C OF CHRIST	1	97	130*	.2	.8
449 UN METHODIST	3	1,500	2,007*	3.3	12.0
469 WELS	1	98	132	.2	.8
496 JEWISH EST[1]	0	NA	1,470	2.4	8.8
EAGLE	**25**	**1,179**	**5,262***	**24.0**	**100.0**
053 ASSEMB OF GOD	2	44	110	.5	2.1
081 CATHOLIC	7	NA	2,845	13.0	54.1
081d *LATIN*	7	NA	2,845	13.0	54.1
151 L-D SAINTS	3	NA	406	1.9	7.7
167 CHS OF CHRIST	1	22	40	.2	.8
193 EPISCOPAL	1	64	136	.6	2.6
203 EVAN FREE CH	1	42	180	.8	3.4
207 E.L.C.A.	2	216	401	1.8	7.6
283 LUTH—MO SYNOD	1	145	220	1.0	4.2
355 PRESB CH (USA)	1	80	102*	.5	1.9
419 SO BAPT CONV	3	235	300*	1.4	5.7
449 UN METHODIST	3	331	422*	1.9	8.0
496 JEWISH EST[1]	0	NA	100	.5	1.9
ELBERT	**11**	**880**	**1,362***	**14.1**	**100.0**
019 AMER BAPT USA	2	216	285*	3.0	20.9
053 ASSEMB OF GOD	1	16	21	.2	1.5
097 CHR CHS&CHS CR	1	83	110*	1.1	8.1
151 L-D SAINTS	1	NA	179	1.9	13.1
165 CH OF NAZARENE	1	15	35	.4	2.6
179 CONSRV BAPT	1	NR	NR	-	-
283 LUTH—MO SYNOD	1	15	25	.3	1.8
355 PRESB CH (USA)	1	380	502*	5.2	36.9
419 SO BAPT CONV	1	61	81*	.8	5.9
449 UN METHODIST	1	94	124*	1.3	9.1

County and Denomination	Number of churches	Communicant, confirmed, full members	Total adherents Number	Percent of total population	Percent of total adherents
EL PASO	**259**	**68,222**	**154,624***	**38.9**	**100.0**
019 AMER BAPT USA	6	1,439	1,849*	.5	1.2
053 ASSEMB OF GOD	12	1,928	3,150	.8	2.0
057 BAPT GEN CONF	2	170	218*	.1	.1
063 BEREAN FUND CH	1	46	88	-	.1
075 BRETHREN IN CR	2	112	138	-	.1
081 CATHOLIC	19	NA	48,052	12.1	31.1
081b *BYZAN RUTH*	1	*NA*	*56*	-	-
081d *LATIN*	18	*NA*	*47,996*	*12.1*	*31.0*
089 CHR & MISS AL	6	288	552	.1	.4
093 CHR CH (DISC)	2	911	1,220	.3	.8
097 CHR CHS&CHS CR	7	1,853	2,382*	.6	1.5
105 CHRISTIAN REF	2	301	466	.1	.3
111 CH CR,SCIENTST	1	NR	NR	-	-
123 CH GOD (ANDER)	3	74	267	.1	.2
127 CH GOD (CLEVE)	2	204	262*	.1	.2
145 CH GOD PROPHCY	1	22	28*	-	-
151 L-D SAINTS	21	NA	8,188	2.1	5.3
157 CH OF BRETHREN	1	34	44*	-	-
165 CH OF NAZARENE	17	3,315	3,995	1.0	2.6
167 CHS OF CHRIST	9	1,521	1,966	.5	1.3
179 CONSRV BAPT	3	NR	NR	-	-
193 EPISCOPAL	8	2,396	3,450	.9	2.2
203 EVAN FREE CH	3	337	511	.1	.3
207 E.L.C.A.	13	5,236	7,084	1.8	4.6
209 EVAN LUTH SYN	1	43	55	-	-
221 FREE METHODIST	3	63	140	-	.1
223 FREE WILL BAPT	1	33	42*	-	-
226 FRIENDS-USA	2	159	204*	.1	.1
226b *EFI*	1	*148*	*190***	-	*.1*
226f *INDEPENDNT*	1	*11*	*14***	-	-
259 IFCA	2	NR	NR	-	-
263 INT FOURSQ GOS	3	780	1,002*	.3	.6
274 LAT EVAN LUTH	1	40	48	-	-
283 LUTH—MO SYNOD	6	3,409	4,561	1.1	2.9
285 MENNONITE CH	3	261	381	.1	.2
287 MENN GEN CONF	1	27	42	-	-
329 OPEN BIBLE STD	7	NR	NR	-	-
331 ORTH CH IN AM	2	NR	NR	-	-
339 PENT CH OF GOD	1	51	195	-	.1
353 CHR BRETHREN	3	185	380	.1	.2
355 PRESB CH (USA)	8	6,456	8,297*	2.1	5.4
356 PRESB CH AMER	3	1,545	1,897	.5	1.2
371 REF CH IN AM	1	168	522	.1	.3
373 REF CH IN U.S.	1	11	17	-	-
403 SALVATION ARMY	1	36	53	-	-
413 S.D.A.	4	865	1,112*	.3	.7
419 SO BAPT CONV	19	15,194	19,528*	4.9	12.6
435 UNITARIAN-UNIV	1	224	297	.1	.2
443 UN C OF CHRIST	9	3,122	4,012*	1.0	2.6
449 UN METHODIST	17	8,839	11,360*	2.9	7.3
467 WESLEYAN	4	204	386	.1	.2
469 WELS	2	221	344	.1	.2
496 JEWISH EST[1]	2	NA	1,500	.4	1.0
497 BLACK BAPT EST[2]	NA	6,099	7,839*	2.0	5.1
498 INDEP.CHARIS.[3]	5	NA	3,900	1.0	2.5
499 INDEP.NON-CHAR[3]	5	NA	2,600	.7	1.7
FREMONT	**46**	**6,488**	**10,105***	**31.3**	**100.0**
019 AMER BAPT USA	2	514	623*	1.9	6.2
053 ASSEMB OF GOD	2	161	175	.5	1.7
081 CATHOLIC	4	NA	1,297	4.0	12.8
081d *LATIN*	4	*NA*	*1,297*	*4.0*	*12.8*
089 CHR & MISS AL	1	52	127	.4	1.3
093 CHR CH (DISC)	1	219	275	.9	2.7
097 CHR CHS&CHS CR	2	360	436*	1.4	4.3
111 CH CR,SCIENTST	1	NR	NR	-	-
123 CH GOD (ANDER)	1	54	54	.2	.5
127 CH GOD (CLEVE)	1	54	65*	.2	.6
145 CH GOD PROPHCY	1	22	27*	.1	.3
151 L-D SAINTS	2	NA	624	1.9	6.2
165 CH OF NAZARENE	3	234	421	1.3	4.2
167 CHS OF CHRIST	2	210	280	.9	2.8
193 EPISCOPAL	1	343	460	1.4	4.6
203 EVAN FREE CH	1	125	256	.8	2.5
207 E.L.C.A.	1	0	0	-	-
221 FREE METHODIST	1	52	52	.2	.5
226 FRIENDS-USA	1	43	55	.2	.5
226b *EFI*	1	*43*	*55*	*.2*	*.5*
263 INT FOURSQ GOS	2	389	471*	1.5	4.7
283 LUTH—MO SYNOD	1	150	201	.6	2.0
329 OPEN BIBLE STD	1	NR	NR	-	-
349 PENT HOLINESS	2	72	87*	.3	.9
355 PRESB CH (USA)	3	566	686*	2.1	6.8
413 S.D.A.	1	292	354*	1.1	3.5
419 SO BAPT CONV	5	1,841	2,230*	6.9	22.1
449 UN METHODIST	2	501	607*	1.9	6.0

NA–Not applicable   NR–Not reported   *Total adherents estimated from known number of communicant, confirmed, full members.   - Represents a percent less than 0.1.   Percentages may not total due to rounding.
[1]See Appendix E   [2]See Appendix F   [3]See Appendix G   Lines in *italic* represent a breakdown of Catholic rites or Friends affiliations. They are included in their respective denominational total.

Table 4. Churches and Church Membership by County and Denomination: 1990

County and Denomination	Number of churches	Communicant, confirmed, full members	Total adherents Number	Percent of total population	Percent of total adherents
467 WESLEYAN	1	87	64	.2	.6
497 BLACK BAPT EST[2]	NA	147	178*	.6	1.8
GARFIELD	**43**	**3,473**	**8,397***	**28.0**	**100.0**
019 AMER BAPT USA	2	112	145*	.5	1.7
053 ASSEMB OF GOD	4	301	773	2.6	9.2
057 BAPT GEN CONF	1	204	264*	.9	3.1
081 CATHOLIC	3	NA	2,331	7.8	27.8
081d LATIN	*3*	*NA*	*2,331*	*7.8*	*27.8*
097 CHR CHS&CHS CR	2	170	220*	.7	2.6
111 CH CR,SCIENTST	1	NR	NR	-	-
145 CH GOD PROPHCY	1	22	28*	.1	.3
151 L-D SAINTS	3	NA	1,077	3.6	12.8
165 CH OF NAZARENE	1	80	78	.3	.9
167 CHS OF CHRIST	4	189	248	.8	3.0
193 EPISCOPAL	3	152	271	.9	3.2
207 E.L.C.A.	1	195	275	.9	3.3
263 INT FOURSQ GOS	2	131	170*	.6	2.0
283 LUTH—MO SYNOD	2	294	414	1.4	4.9
285 MENNONITE CH	1	43	58	.2	.7
355 PRESB CH (USA)	1	198	256*	.9	3.0
413 S.D.A.	2	135	175*	.6	2.1
419 SO BAPT CONV	4	436	564*	1.9	6.7
443 UN C OF CHRIST	2	89	115*	.4	1.4
449 UN METHODIST	3	722	935*	3.1	11.1
GILPIN	**3**	**185**	**297***	**9.7**	**100.0**
081 CATHOLIC	1	NA	77	2.5	25.9
081d LATIN	*1*	*NA*	*77*	*2.5*	*25.9*
193 EPISCOPAL	1	31	31	1.0	10.4
449 UN METHODIST	1	154	189*	6.2	63.6
GRAND	**20**	**620**	**1,734***	**21.8**	**100.0**
053 ASSEMB OF GOD	1	51	120	1.5	6.9
081 CATHOLIC	5	NA	718	9.0	41.4
081d LATIN	*5*	*NA*	*718*	*9.0*	*41.4*
151 L-D SAINTS	1	NA	115	1.4	6.6
167 CHS OF CHRIST	1	6	14	.2	.8
193 EPISCOPAL	2	91	140	1.8	8.1
207 E.L.C.A.	1	64	106	1.3	6.1
226 FRIENDS-USA	1	5	17	.2	1.0
226f INDEPENDNT	*1*	*5*	*17*	*.2*	*1.0*
246 GREEK ORTHODOX	1	NR	NR	-	-
259 IFCA	1	NR	NR	-	-
355 PRESB CH (USA)	2	216	270*	3.4	15.6
413 S.D.A.	1	20	25*	.3	1.4
419 SO BAPT CONV	3	167	209*	2.6	12.1
GUNNISON	**12**	**800**	**2,191***	**21.3**	**100.0**
053 ASSEMB OF GOD	1	52	95	.9	4.3
057 BAPT GEN CONF	1	57	69*	.7	3.1
081 CATHOLIC	3	NA	1,025	10.0	46.8
081d LATIN	*3*	*NA*	*1,025*	*10.0*	*46.8*
151 L-D SAINTS	1	NA	86	.8	3.9
167 CHS OF CHRIST	1	30	45	.4	2.1
193 EPISCOPAL	1	99	174	1.7	7.9
283 LUTH—MO SYNOD	1	111	153	1.5	7.0
419 SO BAPT CONV	2	386	466*	4.5	21.3
443 UN C OF CHRIST	1	65	78*	.8	3.6
HINSDALE	**4**	**91**	**179***	**38.3**	**100.0**
081 CATHOLIC	1	NA	75	16.1	41.9
081d LATIN	*1*	*NA*	*75*	*16.1*	*41.9*
193 EPISCOPAL	1	14	14	3.0	7.8
355 PRESB CH (USA)	1	58	68*	14.6	38.0
419 SO BAPT CONV	1	19	22*	4.7	12.3
HUERFANO	**16**	**735**	**4,162***	**69.3**	**100.0**
019 AMER BAPT USA	2	95	118*	2.0	2.8
053 ASSEMB OF GOD	1	45	120	2.0	2.9
081 CATHOLIC	4	NA	3,188	53.1	76.6
081d LATIN	*4*	*NA*	*3,188*	*53.1*	*76.6*
145 CH GOD PROPHCY	1	22	27*	.4	.6
167 CHS OF CHRIST	1	35	46	.8	1.1
285 MENNONITE CH	1	24	24	.4	.6
413 S.D.A.	1	25	31*	.5	.7
419 SO BAPT CONV	2	271	337*	5.6	8.1
449 UN METHODIST	3	218	271*	4.5	6.5
JACKSON	**3**	**71**	**261***	**16.3**	**100.0**
081 CATHOLIC	1	NA	69	4.3	26.4
081d LATIN	*1*	*NA*	*69*	*4.3*	*26.4*
167 CHS OF CHRIST	1	20	28	1.7	10.7
449 UN METHODIST	1	51	64*	4.0	24.5

County and Denomination	Number of churches	Communicant, confirmed, full members	Total adherents Number	Percent of total population	Percent of total adherents
496 JEWISH EST[1]	0	NA	100	6.2	38.3
JEFFERSON	**213**	**43,287**	**162,011***	**37.0**	**100.0**
019 AMER BAPT USA	3	334	423*	.1	.3
053 ASSEMB OF GOD	6	844	2,037	.5	1.3
057 BAPT GEN CONF	4	699	885*	.2	.5
063 BEREAN FUND CH	1	30	30	-	-
081 CATHOLIC	16	NA	70,000	16.0	43.2
081d LATIN	*16*	*NA*	*70,000*	*16.0*	*43.2*
089 CHR & MISS AL	2	386	406	.1	.3
093 CHR CH (DISC)	1	113	113	-	.1
097 CHR CHS&CHS CR	3	390	494*	.1	.3
111 CH CR,SCIENTST	4	NR	NR	-	-
123 CH GOD (ANDER)	2	201	204	-	.1
127 CH GOD (CLEVE)	3	431	546*	.1	.3
145 CH GOD PROPHCY	1	22	28*	-	-
151 L-D SAINTS	27	NA	10,942	2.5	6.8
163 CH OF LUTH BR	1	43	115	-	.1
165 CH OF NAZARENE	6	1,560	1,580	.4	1.0
167 CHS OF CHRIST	9	1,352	1,810	.4	1.1
176 CCC, NOT NAT'L	1	838	1,061*	.2	.7
179 CONSRV BAPT	9	NR	NR	-	-
193 EPISCOPAL	11	2,730	3,732	.9	2.3
203 EVAN FREE CH	6	395	750	.2	.5
207 E.L.C.A.	16	6,625	9,101	2.1	5.6
221 FREE METHODIST	2	290	290	.1	.2
223 FREE WILL BAPT	1	39	49*	-	-
226 FRIENDS-USA	1	60	76*	-	-
226b EFI	*1*	*60*	*76*￼*	*-*	*-*
259 IFCA	2	NR	NR	-	-
263 INT FOURSQ GOS	1	15	19*	-	-
274 LAT EVAN LUTH	1	127	140	-	.1
283 LUTH—MO SYNOD	9	5,055	6,987	1.6	4.3
285 MENNONITE CH	1	114	182	-	.1
287 MENN GEN CONF	1	67	81	-	-
353 CHR BRETHREN	4	280	425	.1	.3
355 PRESB CH (USA)	8	3,530	4,471*	1.0	2.8
356 PRESB CH AMER	2	54	89	-	.1
371 REF CH IN AM	1	238	679	.2	.4
373 REF CH IN U.S.	1	24	32	-	-
413 S.D.A.	3	505	640*	.1	.4
415 S-D BAPTIST GC	1	267	338*	.1	.2
419 SO BAPT CONV	9	5,496	6,962*	1.6	4.3
435 UNITARIAN-UNIV	1	378	538	.1	.3
443 UN C OF CHRIST	6	1,248	1,581*	.4	1.0
449 UN METHODIST	13	7,564	9,581*	2.2	5.9
469 WELS	1	254	397	.1	.2
496 JEWISH EST[1]	0	NA	10,674	2.4	6.6
497 BLACK BAPT EST[2]	NA	689	873*	.2	.5
498 INDEP.CHARIS.[3]	4	NA	7,500	1.7	4.6
499 INDEP.NON-CHAR[3]	8	NA	5,150	1.2	3.2
KIOWA	**6**	**444**	**572***	**33.9**	**100.0**
053 ASSEMB OF GOD	1	13	19	1.1	3.3
097 CHR CHS&CHS CR	1	55	71*	4.2	12.4
226 FRIENDS-USA	1	20	22	1.3	3.8
226b EFI	*1*	*20*	*22*	*1.3*	*3.8*
419 SO BAPT CONV	1	222	287*	17.0	50.2
449 UN METHODIST	2	134	173*	10.2	30.2
KIT CARSON	**27**	**2,756**	**5,353***	**75.0**	**100.0**
019 AMER BAPT USA	1	242	315*	4.4	5.9
053 ASSEMB OF GOD	1	169	320	4.5	6.0
081 CATHOLIC	2	NA	1,484	20.8	27.7
081d LATIN	*2*	*NA*	*1,484*	*20.8*	*27.7*
093 CHR CH (DISC)	1	240	311	4.4	5.8
097 CHR CHS&CHS CR	2	159	207*	2.9	3.9
123 CH GOD (ANDER)	1	61	93	1.3	1.7
151 L-D SAINTS	1	NA	117	1.6	2.2
165 CH OF NAZARENE	1	16	30	.4	.6
167 CHS OF CHRIST	2	72	96	1.3	1.8
179 CONSRV BAPT	1	NR	NR	-	-
181 CONSRV CONGR	1	82	107*	1.5	2.0
203 EVAN FREE CH	1	28	28	.4	.5
207 E.L.C.A.	2	342	455	6.4	8.5
283 LUTH—MO SYNOD	2	329	475	6.7	8.9
287 MENN GEN CONF	1	16	16	.2	.3
353 CHR BRETHREN	1	40	50	.7	.9
413 S.D.A.	1	11	14*	.2	.3
419 SO BAPT CONV	1	214	278*	3.9	5.2
443 UN C OF CHRIST	1	102	133*	1.9	2.5
449 UN METHODIST	3	633	824*	11.5	15.4
LAKE	**11**	**444**	**4,149***	**69.1**	**100.0**
053 ASSEMB OF GOD	2	66	107	1.8	2.6

NA–Not applicable   NR–Not reported   *Total adherents estimated from known number of communicant, confirmed, full members.   - Represents a percent less than 0.1.   Percentages may not total due to rounding.
[1]See Appendix E   [2]See Appendix F   [3]See Appendix G   Lines in *italic* represent a breakdown of Catholic rites or Friends affiliations. They are included in their respective denominational total.

75

COLORADO

Table 4. Churches and Church Membership by County and Denomination: 1990

County and Denomination	Number of churches	Communicant, confirmed, full members	Total adherents Number	Percent of total population	Percent of total adherents
081 CATHOLIC	2	NA	3,564	59.3	85.9
081d *LATIN*	*2*	*NA*	*3,564*	*59.3*	*85.9*
167 CHS OF CHRIST	1	20	22	.4	.5
193 EPISCOPAL	1	10	12	.2	.3
203 EVAN FREE CH	1	0	0	-	-
283 LUTH—MO SYNOD	1	97	119	2.0	2.9
355 PRESB CH (USA)	1	112	145*	2.4	3.5
413 S.D.A.	1	43	56*	.9	1.3
419 SO BAPT CONV	1	96	124*	2.1	3.0
LA PLATA	**46**	**4,225**	**11,439***	**35.4**	**100.0**
053 ASSEMB OF GOD	3	138	338	1.0	3.0
081 CATHOLIC	5	NA	4,000	12.4	35.0
081d *LATIN*	*5*	*NA*	*4,000*	*12.4*	*35.0*
097 CHR CHS&CHS CR	2	35	44*	.1	.4
111 CH CR,SCIENTST	1	NR	NR	-	-
151 L-D SAINTS	4	NA	1,319	4.1	11.5
165 CH OF NAZARENE	1	55	141	.4	1.2
167 CHS OF CHRIST	6	334	399	1.2	3.5
179 CONSRV BAPT	1	NR	NR	-	-
193 EPISCOPAL	1	224	379	1.2	3.3
203 EVAN FREE CH	1	86	200	.6	1.7
207 E.L.C.A.	1	198	286	.9	2.5
221 FREE METHODIST	1	19	41	.1	.4
226 FRIENDS-USA	1	26	33*	.1	.3
226f *INDEPENDNT*	*1*	*26*	*33**	*.1*	*.3*
263 INT FOURSQ GOS	1	649	817*	2.5	7.1
283 LUTH—MO SYNOD	1	150	210	.7	1.8
355 PRESB CH (USA)	5	629	792*	2.5	6.9
413 S.D.A.	1	202	254*	.8	2.2
419 SO BAPT CONV	6	855	1,076*	3.3	9.4
435 UNITARIAN-UNIV	1	18	21	.1	.2
449 UN METHODIST	2	607	764*	2.4	6.7
499 INDEP.NON-CHAR3	1	NA	325	1.0	2.8
LARIMER	**136**	**28,260**	**69,667***	**37.4**	**100.0**
019 AMER BAPT USA	2	466	585*	.3	.8
053 ASSEMB OF GOD	8	797	1,347	.7	1.9
057 BAPT GEN CONF	2	520	653*	.4	.9
081 CATHOLIC	7	NA	24,218	13.0	34.8
081d *LATIN*	*7*	*NA*	*24,218*	*13.0*	*34.8*
089 CHR & MISS AL	1	0	32	-	-
093 CHR CH (DISC)	2	1,678	3,299	1.8	4.7
097 CHR CHS&CHS CR	3	145	182*	.1	.3
105 CHRISTIAN REF	2	216	377	.2	.5
111 CH CR,SCIENTST	3	NR	NR	-	-
123 CH GOD (ANDER)	1	210	210	.1	.3
127 CH GOD (CLEVE)	1	34	43*	-	.1
145 CH GOD PROPHCY	1	22	28*	-	-
151 L-D SAINTS	10	NA	3,807	2.0	5.5
163 CH OF LUTH BR	1	44	79	-	.1
164 CH LUTH CONF	1	48	76	-	.1
165 CH OF NAZARENE	4	441	604	.3	.9
167 CHS OF CHRIST	7	873	1,187	.6	1.7
179 CONSRV BAPT	2	NR	NR	-	-
193 EPISCOPAL	4	1,655	2,234	1.2	3.2
203 EVAN FREE CH	3	505	970	.5	1.4
207 E.L.C.A.	7	4,350	5,912	3.2	8.5
216 EVAN PRESBY CH	2	348	353	.2	.5
221 FREE METHODIST	1	179	280	.2	.4
223 FREE WILL BAPT	1	35	44*	-	.1
226 FRIENDS-USA	2	59	81*	-	.1
226b *EFI*	*1*	*37*	*46**	*-*	*.1*
226f *INDEPENDNT*	*1*	*22*	*35*	*-*	*.1*
259 IFCA	1	NR	NR	-	-
263 INT FOURSQ GOS	4	220	276*	.1	.4
283 LUTH—MO SYNOD	7	2,582	3,281	1.8	4.7
285 MENNONITE CH	1	43	59	-	.1
287 MENN GEN CONF	1	20	29	-	-
329 OPEN BIBLE STD	1	NR	NR	-	-
339 PENT CH OF GOD	1	34	77	-	.1
353 CHR BRETHREN	1	100	150	.1	.2
355 PRESB CH (USA)	10	3,394	4,261*	2.3	6.1
356 PRESB CH AMER	1	42	61	-	.1
373 REF CH IN U.S.	1	26	31	-	-
403 SALVATION ARMY	1	40	51	-	.1
413 S.D.A.	5	1,188	1,491*	.8	2.1
419 SO BAPT CONV	9	1,651	2,073*	1.1	3.0
435 UNITARIAN-UNIV	1	384	634	.3	.9
443 UN C OF CHRIST	2	999	1,254*	.7	1.8
449 UN METHODIST	6	4,462	5,601*	3.0	8.0
467 WESLEYAN	1	30	275	.1	.4
469 WELS	1	182	279	.1	.4
496 JEWISH EST1	NA	NA	584	.3	.8
497 BLACK BAPT EST2	NA	238	299*	.2	.4
498 INDEP.CHARIS.3	1	NA	2,000	1.1	2.9
499 INDEP.NON-CHAR3	1	NA	300	.2	.4

County and Denomination	Number of churches	Communicant, confirmed, full members	Total adherents Number	Percent of total population	Percent of total adherents
LAS ANIMAS	**35**	**1,177**	**4,315***	**31.3**	**100.0**
019 AMER BAPT USA	1	60	75*	.5	1.7
053 ASSEMB OF GOD	2	17	21	.2	.5
081 CATHOLIC	15	NA	2,515	18.3	58.3
081d *LATIN*	*15*	*NA*	*2,515*	*18.3*	*58.3*
093 CHR CH (DISC)	1	68	147	1.1	3.4
145 CH GOD PROPHCY	1	22	27*	.2	.6
151 L-D SAINTS	1	NA	233	1.7	5.4
165 CH OF NAZARENE	1	27	49	.4	1.1
167 CHS OF CHRIST	2	56	77	.6	1.8
193 EPISCOPAL	1	66	89	.6	2.1
207 E.L.C.A.	1	91	120	.9	2.8
226 FRIENDS-USA	1	3	8	.1	.2
226f *INDEPENDNT*	*1*	*3*	*8*	*.1*	*.2*
263 INT FOURSQ GOS	1	46	57*	.4	1.3
355 PRESB CH (USA)	2	64	80*	.6	1.9
413 S.D.A.	1	60	75*	.5	1.7
419 SO BAPT CONV	2	445	553*	4.0	12.8
449 UN METHODIST	1	152	189*	1.4	4.4
496 JEWISH EST1	1	NA	0	-	-
LINCOLN	**23**	**1,322**	**2,644***	**58.4**	**100.0**
019 AMER BAPT USA	1	180	228*	5.0	8.6
081 CATHOLIC	2	NA	917	20.2	34.7
081d *LATIN*	*2*	*NA*	*917*	*20.2*	*34.7*
157 CH OF BRETHREN	1	46	58*	1.3	2.2
165 CH OF NAZARENE	1	24	66	1.5	2.5
167 CHS OF CHRIST	1	56	73	1.6	2.8
193 EPISCOPAL	1	15	21	.5	.8
207 E.L.C.A.	2	126	151	3.3	5.7
283 LUTH—MO SYNOD	3	111	134	3.0	5.1
285 MENNONITE CH	1	21	27	.6	1.0
353 CHR BRETHREN	1	25	50	1.1	1.9
373 REF CH IN U.S.	1	24	39	.9	1.5
413 S.D.A.	1	11	14*	.3	.5
419 SO BAPT CONV	2	94	119*	2.6	4.5
443 UN C OF CHRIST	1	56	71*	1.6	2.7
449 UN METHODIST	4	533	676*	14.9	25.6
LOGAN	**36**	**4,689**	**12,034***	**68.5**	**100.0**
019 AMER BAPT USA	2	413	523*	3.0	4.3
053 ASSEMB OF GOD	3	125	239	1.4	2.0
081 CATHOLIC	3	NA	5,809	33.1	48.3
081d *LATIN*	*3*	*NA*	*5,809*	*33.1*	*48.3*
093 CHR CH (DISC)	1	190	306	1.7	2.5
097 CHR CHS&CHS CR	1	25	32*	.2	.3
111 CH CR,SCIENTST	1	NR	NR	-	-
123 CH GOD (ANDER)	1	55	55	.3	.5
145 CH GOD PROPHCY	1	22	28*	.2	.2
165 CH OF NAZARENE	1	115	175	1.0	1.5
167 CHS OF CHRIST	1	47	61	.3	.5
193 EPISCOPAL	1	119	246	1.4	2.0
203 EVAN FREE CH	2	66	71	.4	.6
207 E.L.C.A.	1	306	412	2.3	3.4
263 INT FOURSQ GOS	1	134	170*	1.0	1.4
283 LUTH—MO SYNOD	3	663	856	4.9	7.1
355 PRESB CH (USA)	1	680	861*	4.9	7.2
413 S.D.A.	1	53	67*	.4	.6
419 SO BAPT CONV	3	274	347*	2.0	2.9
443 UN C OF CHRIST	1	111	141*	.8	1.2
449 UN METHODIST	7	1,291	1,635*	9.3	13.6
MESA	**102**	**14,847**	**35,758***	**38.4**	**100.0**
019 AMER BAPT USA	4	1,094	1,389*	1.5	3.9
053 ASSEMB OF GOD	8	1,436	3,352	3.6	9.4
081 CATHOLIC	4	NA	8,068	8.7	22.6
081d *LATIN*	*4*	*NA*	*8,068*	*8.7*	*22.6*
093 CHR CH (DISC)	1	292	386	.4	1.1
097 CHR CHS&CHS CR	6	1,246	1,582*	1.7	4.4
111 CH CR,SCIENTST	1	NR	NR	-	-
123 CH GOD (ANDER)	1	69	69	.1	.2
127 CH GOD (CLEVE)	1	234	297*	.3	.8
145 CH GOD PROPHCY	1	22	28*	-	.1
151 L-D SAINTS	13	NA	4,755	5.1	13.3
157 CH OF BRETHREN	1	227	288*	.3	.8
165 CH OF NAZARENE	2	373	611	.7	1.7
167 CHS OF CHRIST	2	400	520	.6	1.5
179 CONSRV BAPT	2	NR	NR	-	-
193 EPISCOPAL	2	586	753	.8	2.1
203 EVAN FREE CH	2	105	145	.2	.4
207 E.L.C.A.	2	698	920	1.0	2.6
223 FREE WILL BAPT	1	12	15*	-	-
226 FRIENDS-USA	1	67	85*	.1	.2
226b *EFI*	*1*	*67*	*85**	*.1*	*.2*
246 GREEK ORTHODOX	1	NR	NR	-	-
259 IFCA	1	NR	NR	-	-

NA–Not applicable   NR–Not reported   *Total adherents estimated from known number of communicant, confirmed, full members.   - Represents a percent less than 0.1.   Percentages may not total due to rounding.

[1]See Appendix E   [2]See Appendix F   [3]See Appendix G   Lines in *italic* represent a breakdown of Catholic rites or Friends affiliations. They are included in their respective denominational total.

Table 4. Churches and Church Membership by County and Denomination: 1990

County and Denomination	Number of churches	Communicant, confirmed, full members	Total adherents Number	Total adherents Percent of total population	Total adherents Percent of total adherents
263 INT FOURSQ GOS	2	329	418*	.4	1.2
283 LUTH—MO SYNOD	2	805	1,074	1.2	3.0
285 MENNONITE CH	1	28	28	-	.1
329 OPEN BIBLE STD	1	NR	NR	-	-
339 PENT CH OF GOD	2	69	154	.2	.4
349 PENT HOLINESS	4	157	199*	.2	.6
353 CHR BRETHREN	1	65	90	.1	.3
355 PRESB CH (USA)	2	683	867*	.9	2.4
403 SALVATION ARMY	1	56	74	.1	.2
413 S.D.A.	3	611	776*	.8	2.2
419 SO BAPT CONV	6	2,228	2,828*	3.0	7.9
435 UNITARIAN-UNIV	1	18	20	-	.1
443 UN C OF CHRIST	2	433	550*	.6	1.5
449 UN METHODIST	7	2,422	3,074*	3.3	8.6
467 WESLEYAN	1	20	65	.1	.2
469 WELS	1	62	98	.1	.3
496 JEWISH EST[1]	1	NA	250	.3	.7
498 INDEP.CHARIS.[3]	1	NA	600	.6	1.7
499 INDEP.NON-CHAR[3]	3	NA	1,330	1.4	3.7
MINERAL	**4**	**134**	**179***	**32.1**	**100.0**
167 CHS OF CHRIST	1	12	28	5.0	15.6
193 EPISCOPAL	1	13	16	2.9	8.9
419 SO BAPT CONV	1	79	98*	17.6	54.7
443 UN C OF CHRIST	1	30	37*	6.6	20.7
MOFFAT	**19**	**2,046**	**5,592***	**49.2**	**100.0**
053 ASSEMB OF GOD	1	34	48	.4	.9
081 CATHOLIC	1	NA	1,544	13.6	27.6
081d LATIN	1	NA	1,544	13.6	27.6
097 CHR CHS&CHS CR	1	250	339*	3.0	6.1
127 CH GOD (CLEVE)	1	164	222*	2.0	4.0
151 L-D SAINTS	3	NA	1,273	11.2	22.8
165 CH OF NAZARENE	1	37	0	-	-
167 CHS OF CHRIST	2	107	138	1.2	2.5
193 EPISCOPAL	1	39	77	.7	1.4
246 GREEK ORTHODOX	1	NR	NR	-	-
283 LUTH—MO SYNOD	1	239	357	3.1	6.4
413 S.D.A.	1	45	61*	.5	1.1
419 SO BAPT CONV	2	845	1,146*	10.1	20.5
443 UN C OF CHRIST	2	229	310*	2.7	5.5
449 UN METHODIST	1	57	77*	.7	1.4
MONTEZUMA	**38**	**3,092**	**6,735***	**36.1**	**100.0**
019 AMER BAPT USA	2	252	335*	1.8	5.0
053 ASSEMB OF GOD	4	275	397	2.1	5.9
059 BAPT MISS ASSN	2	72	96*	.5	1.4
081 CATHOLIC	4	NA	640	3.4	9.5
081d LATIN	4	NA	640	3.4	9.5
097 CHR CHS&CHS CR	1	125	166*	.9	2.5
111 CH CR,SCIENTST	1	NR	NR	-	-
145 CH GOD PROPHCY	1	22	29*	.2	.4
151 L-D SAINTS	4	NA	1,548	8.3	23.0
165 CH OF NAZARENE	1	80	90	.5	1.3
167 CHS OF CHRIST	5	283	342	1.8	5.1
193 EPISCOPAL	1	163	294	1.6	4.4
226 FRIENDS-USA	1	6	10	.1	.1
226f INDEPENDNT	1	6	10	.1	.1
259 IFCA	1	NR	NR	-	-
283 LUTH—MO SYNOD	1	214	311	1.7	4.6
355 PRESB CH (USA)	2	248	330*	1.8	4.9
413 S.D.A.	1	215	286*	1.5	4.2
419 SO BAPT CONV	2	612	813*	4.4	12.1
449 UN METHODIST	3	525	698*	3.7	10.4
499 INDEP.NON-CHAR[3]	1	NA	350	1.9	5.2
MONTROSE	**41**	**4,890**	**10,779***	**44.1**	**100.0**
019 AMER BAPT USA	2	465	595*	2.4	5.5
053 ASSEMB OF GOD	4	292	526	2.2	4.9
081 CATHOLIC	2	NA	3,230	13.2	30.0
081d LATIN	2	NA	3,230	13.2	30.0
097 CHR CHS&CHS CR	2	1,180	1,509*	6.2	14.0
111 CH CR,SCIENTST	1	NR	NR	-	-
127 CH GOD (CLEVE)	1	7	9*	-	.1
145 CH GOD PROPHCY	1	22	28*	.1	.3
151 L-D SAINTS	4	NA	1,099	4.5	10.2
165 CH OF NAZARENE	1	137	144	.6	1.3
167 CHS OF CHRIST	2	136	189	.8	1.8
179 CONSRV BAPT	1	NR	NR	-	-
193 EPISCOPAL	1	93	112	.5	1.0
207 E.L.C.A.	1	304	385	1.6	3.6
263 INT FOURSQ GOS	1	81	104*	.4	1.0
283 LUTH—MO SYNOD	1	110	138	.6	1.3
339 PENT CH OF GOD	2	18	78	.3	.7
355 PRESB CH (USA)	1	318	407*	1.7	3.8
356 PRESB CH AMER	1	46	46	.2	.4

County and Denomination	Number of churches	Communicant, confirmed, full members	Total adherents Number	Total adherents Percent of total population	Total adherents Percent of total adherents
413 S.D.A.	2	266	340*	1.4	3.2
419 SO BAPT CONV	3	709	907*	3.7	8.4
443 UN C OF CHRIST	4	175	224*	.9	2.1
449 UN METHODIST	2	478	611*	2.5	5.7
469 WELS	1	53	98	.4	.9
MORGAN	**41**	**6,934**	**12,304***	**56.1**	**100.0**
019 AMER BAPT USA	1	356	467*	2.1	3.8
053 ASSEMB OF GOD	3	241	385	1.8	3.1
081 CATHOLIC	4	NA	2,663	12.1	21.6
081d LATIN	4	NA	2,663	12.1	21.6
093 CHR CH (DISC)	1	274	378	1.7	3.1
145 CH GOD PROPHCY	1	22	29*	.1	.2
151 L-D SAINTS	1	NA	244	1.1	2.0
165 CH OF NAZARENE	3	281	517	2.4	4.2
167 CHS OF CHRIST	2	135	175	.8	1.4
179 CONSRV BAPT	1	NR	NR	-	-
181 CONSRV CONGR	1	202	265*	1.2	2.2
193 EPISCOPAL	1	80	126	.6	1.0
207 E.L.C.A.	3	773	998	4.5	8.1
263 INT FOURSQ GOS	1	120	157*	.7	1.3
283 LUTH—MO SYNOD	1	556	808	3.7	6.6
355 PRESB CH (USA)	3	693	908*	4.1	7.4
413 S.D.A.	1	82	107*	.5	.9
419 SO BAPT CONV	3	913	1,197*	5.5	9.7
443 UN C OF CHRIST	3	937	1,228*	5.6	10.0
449 UN METHODIST	5	1,149	1,506*	6.9	12.2
469 WELS	2	120	146	.7	1.2
OTERO	**52**	**4,988**	**11,483***	**56.9**	**100.0**
019 AMER BAPT USA	3	590	760*	3.8	6.6
053 ASSEMB OF GOD	4	203	298	1.5	2.6
081 CATHOLIC	4	NA	4,240	21.0	36.9
081d LATIN	4	NA	4,240	21.0	36.9
093 CHR CH (DISC)	4	391	710	3.5	6.2
097 CHR CHS&CHS CR	1	60	77*	.4	.7
111 CH CR,SCIENTST	1	NR	NR	-	-
123 CH GOD (ANDER)	2	30	100	.5	.9
127 CH GOD (CLEVE)	1	55	71*	.4	.6
151 L-D SAINTS	1	NA	291	1.4	2.5
157 CH OF BRETHREN	1	73	94*	.5	.8
165 CH OF NAZARENE	4	234	472	2.3	4.1
167 CHS OF CHRIST	3	179	230	1.1	2.0
193 EPISCOPAL	1	87	106	.5	.9
207 E.L.C.A.	2	244	309	1.5	2.7
226 FRIENDS-USA	2	22	30	.1	.3
226b EFI	2	22	30	.1	.3
283 LUTH—MO SYNOD	2	138	208	1.0	1.8
285 MENNONITE CH	3	238	339	1.7	3.0
329 OPEN BIBLE STD	1	NR	NR	-	-
355 PRESB CH (USA)	2	448	577*	2.9	5.0
413 S.D.A.	1	104	134*	.7	1.2
419 SO BAPT CONV	3	582	750*	3.7	6.5
449 UN METHODIST	6	1,310	1,687*	8.4	14.7
OURAY	**6**	**293**	**508***	**22.1**	**100.0**
053 ASSEMB OF GOD	1	11	15	.7	3.0
081 CATHOLIC	2	NA	125	5.4	24.6
081d LATIN	2	NA	125	5.4	24.6
193 EPISCOPAL	1	65	97	4.2	19.1
355 PRESB CH (USA)	1	141	176*	7.7	34.6
419 SO BAPT CONV	1	76	95*	4.1	18.7
PARK	**7**	**462**	**629***	**8.8**	**100.0**
057 BAPT GEN CONF	1	57	73*	1.0	11.6
097 CHR CHS&CHS CR	1	45	58*	.8	9.2
283 LUTH—MO SYNOD	1	135	210	2.9	33.4
355 PRESB CH (USA)	1	41	53*	.7	8.4
413 S.D.A.	1	8	10*	.1	1.6
419 SO BAPT CONV	2	176	225*	3.1	35.8
PHILLIPS	**16**	**1,884**	**3,087***	**73.7**	**100.0**
053 ASSEMB OF GOD	1	51	90	2.1	2.9
063 BEREAN FUND CH	1	53	115	2.7	3.7
081 CATHOLIC	2	NA	606	14.5	19.6
081d LATIN	2	NA	606	14.5	19.6
097 CHR CHS&CHS CR	1	225	282*	6.7	9.1
157 CH OF BRETHREN	1	150	188*	4.5	6.1
165 CH OF NAZARENE	1	54	63	1.5	2.0
167 CHS OF CHRIST	2	72	99	2.4	3.2
179 CONSRV BAPT	1	NR	NR	-	-
283 LUTH—MO SYNOD	3	590	781	18.6	25.3
413 S.D.A.	1	26	33*	.8	1.1
449 UN METHODIST	2	663	830*	19.8	26.9

NA–Not applicable   NR–Not reported   *Total adherents estimated from known number of communicant, confirmed, full members.   - Represents a percent less than 0.1.   Percentages may not total due to rounding.
[1]See Appendix E   [2]See Appendix F   [3]See Appendix G   Lines in *italic* represent a breakdown of Catholic rites or Friends affiliations. They are included in their respective denominational total.

COLORADO

Table 4. Churches and Church Membership by County and Denomination: 1990

County and Denomination	Number of churches	Communicant, confirmed, full members	Total adherents Number	Percent of total population	Percent of total adherents
PITKIN	8	370	2,194*	17.3	100.0
081 CATHOLIC	1	NA	1,467	11.6	66.9
081d *LATIN*	*1*	*NA*	*1,467*	*11.6*	*66.9*
111 CH CR,SCIENTST	1	NR	NR	-	-
179 CONSRV BAPT	1	NR	NR	-	-
193 EPISCOPAL	1	159	217	1.7	9.9
283 LUTH—MO SYNOD	1	75	104	.8	4.7
435 UNITARIAN-UNIV	1	10	10	.1	.5
449 UN METHODIST	2	126	146*	1.2	6.7
496 JEWISH EST[1]	0	NA	250	2.0	11.4
PROWERS	38	4,086	7,758*	58.1	100.0
019 AMER BAPT USA	2	511	681*	5.1	8.8
053 ASSEMB OF GOD	2	88	145	1.1	1.9
081 CATHOLIC	3	NA	1,952	14.6	25.2
081d *LATIN*	*3*	*NA*	*1,952*	*14.6*	*25.2*
097 CHR CHS&CHS CR	2	840	1,119*	8.4	14.4
111 CH CR,SCIENTST	1	NR	NR	-	-
123 CH GOD (ANDER)	2	48	96	.7	1.2
151 L-D SAINTS	2	NA	192	1.4	2.5
157 CH OF BRETHREN	1	112	149*	1.1	1.9
164 CH LUTH CONF	1	64	91	.7	1.2
165 CH OF NAZARENE	3	123	231	1.7	3.0
167 CHS OF CHRIST	5	182	236	1.8	3.0
193 EPISCOPAL	1	60	94	.7	1.2
226 FRIENDS-USA	1	21	25	.2	.3
226b *EFI*	*1*	*21*	*25*	*.2*	*.3*
263 INT FOURSQ GOS	1	255	340*	2.5	4.4
283 LUTH—MO SYNOD	1	138	213	1.6	2.7
355 PRESB CH (USA)	2	203	270*	2.0	3.5
413 S.D.A.	1	66	88*	.7	1.1
419 SO BAPT CONV	1	384	512*	3.8	6.6
449 UN METHODIST	5	978	1,303*	9.8	16.8
467 WESLEYAN	1	13	21	.2	.3
PUEBLO	121	16,603	61,190*	49.7	100.0
019 AMER BAPT USA	6	2,116	2,664*	2.2	4.4
053 ASSEMB OF GOD	7	1,167	3,250	2.6	5.3
081 CATHOLIC	27	NA	34,446	28.0	56.3
081d *LATIN*	*27*	*NA*	*34,446*	*28.0*	*56.3*
089 CHR & MISS AL	1	0	56	-	.1
093 CHR CH (DISC)	3	881	1,217	1.0	2.0
097 CHR CHS&CHS CR	2	120	151*	.1	.2
111 CH CR,SCIENTST	1	NR	NR	-	-
123 CH GOD (ANDER)	1	56	66	.1	.1
127 CH GOD (CLEVE)	2	138	174*	.1	.3
145 CH GOD PROPHCY	1	22	28*	-	-
151 L-D SAINTS	5	NA	1,800	1.5	2.9
165 CH OF NAZARENE	4	665	692	.6	1.1
167 CHS OF CHRIST	4	577	674	.5	1.1
179 CONSRV BAPT	1	NR	NR	-	-
193 EPISCOPAL	2	537	735	.6	1.2
203 EVAN FREE CH	1	0	70	.1	.1
207 E.L.C.A.	2	842	1,216	1.0	2.0
221 FREE METHODIST	1	26	42	-	.1
226 FRIENDS-USA	1	87	110*	.1	.2
226b *EFI*	*1*	*87*	*110*	*.1*	*.2*
246 GREEK ORTHODOX	1	NR	NR	-	-
259 IFCA	1	NR	NR	-	-
263 INT FOURSQ GOS	1	228	287*	.2	.5
283 LUTH—MO SYNOD	3	597	771	.6	1.3
285 MENNONITE CH	1	35	50	-	.1
329 OPEN BIBLE STD	1	NR	NR	-	-
331 ORTH CH IN AM	1	NR	NR	-	-
349 PENT HOLINESS	1	40	50*	-	.1
353 CHR BRETHREN	1	30	30	-	-
355 PRESB CH (USA)	3	1,381	1,739*	1.4	2.8
403 SALVATION ARMY	1	18	22	-	-
413 S.D.A.	2	578	728*	.6	1.2
419 SO BAPT CONV	11	2,632	3,313*	2.7	5.4
435 UNITARIAN-UNIV	1	22	28	-	-
443 UN C OF CHRIST	2	227	286*	.2	.5
449 UN METHODIST	11	2,964	3,731*	3.0	6.1
467 WESLEYAN	1	32	66	.1	.1
469 WELS	1	104	167	.1	.3
496 JEWISH EST[1]	2	NA	250	.2	.4
497 BLACK BAPT EST[2]	NA	481	606*	.5	1.0
499 INDEP.NON-CHAR[3]	3	NA	1,675	1.4	2.7
RIO BLANCO	17	895	2,161*	36.2	100.0
019 AMER BAPT USA	1	168	219*	3.7	10.1
053 ASSEMB OF GOD	2	42	71	1.2	3.3
081 CATHOLIC	2	NA	501	8.4	23.2
081d *LATIN*	*2*	*NA*	*501*	*8.4*	*23.2*
097 CHR CHS&CHS CR	2	165	215*	3.6	9.9
151 L-D SAINTS	1	NA	434	7.3	20.1

County and Denomination	Number of churches	Communicant, confirmed, full members	Total adherents Number	Percent of total population	Percent of total adherents
167 CHS OF CHRIST	2	62	79	1.3	3.7
193 EPISCOPAL	2	99	172	2.9	8.0
259 IFCA	1	NR	NR	-	-
283 LUTH—MO SYNOD	1	35	47	.8	2.2
419 SO BAPT CONV	2	121	158*	2.6	7.3
449 UN METHODIST	1	203	265*	4.4	12.3
RIO GRANDE	28	2,200	6,478*	60.1	100.0
019 AMER BAPT USA	1	77	101*	.9	1.6
053 ASSEMB OF GOD	2	102	215	2.0	3.3
081 CATHOLIC	5	NA	3,000	27.9	46.3
081d *LATIN*	*5*	*NA*	*3,000*	*27.9*	*46.3*
093 CHR CH (DISC)	1	80	83	.8	1.3
151 L-D SAINTS	3	NA	430	4.0	6.6
165 CH OF NAZARENE	1	144	274	2.5	4.2
167 CHS OF CHRIST	2	121	167	1.6	2.6
193 EPISCOPAL	1	47	72	.7	1.1
283 LUTH—MO SYNOD	1	185	232	2.2	3.6
313 N AM BAPT CONF	1	46	60*	.6	.9
355 PRESB CH (USA)	2	270	354*	3.3	5.5
413 S.D.A.	1	54	71*	.7	1.1
419 SO BAPT CONV	3	528	693*	6.4	10.7
449 UN METHODIST	3	532	698*	6.5	10.8
469 WELS	1	14	28	.3	.4
ROUTT	19	1,268	3,533*	25.1	100.0
053 ASSEMB OF GOD	1	34	55	.4	1.6
081 CATHOLIC	2	NA	1,641	11.6	46.4
081d *LATIN*	*2*	*NA*	*1,641*	*11.6*	*46.4*
111 CH CR,SCIENTST	1	NR	NR	-	-
151 L-D SAINTS	1	NA	174	1.2	4.9
167 CHS OF CHRIST	1	24	33	.2	.9
193 EPISCOPAL	1	101	202	1.4	5.7
203 EVAN FREE CH	1	0	0	-	-
226 FRIENDS-USA	1	1	1*	-	-
226f *INDEPENDNT*	*1*	*1*	*1*	*-*	*-*
259 IFCA	1	NR	NR	-	-
283 LUTH—MO SYNOD	1	208	291	2.1	8.2
413 S.D.A.	1	20	25*	.2	.7
419 SO BAPT CONV	3	378	476*	3.4	13.5
443 UN C OF CHRIST	1	118	149*	1.1	4.2
449 UN METHODIST	2	362	456*	3.2	12.9
469 WELS	1	22	30	.2	.8
SAGUACHE	11	637	2,145*	46.4	100.0
019 AMER BAPT USA	1	109	146*	3.2	6.8
053 ASSEMB OF GOD	1	35	55	1.2	2.6
081 CATHOLIC	2	NA	1,300	28.1	60.6
081d *LATIN*	*2*	*NA*	*1,300*	*28.1*	*60.6*
123 CH GOD (ANDER)	1	35	35	.8	1.6
167 CHS OF CHRIST	2	28	33	.7	1.5
419 SO BAPT CONV	2	132	177*	3.8	8.3
449 UN METHODIST	2	298	399*	8.6	18.6
SAN JUAN	4	42	310*	41.6	100.0
081 CATHOLIC	1	NA	200	26.8	64.5
081d *LATIN*	*1*	*NA*	*200*	*26.8*	*64.5*
151 L-D SAINTS	1	NA	55	7.4	17.7
167 CHS OF CHRIST	1	10	13	1.7	4.2
443 UN C OF CHRIST	1	32	42*	5.6	13.5
SAN MIGUEL	6	300	770*	21.1	100.0
081 CATHOLIC	2	NA	300	8.2	39.0
081d *LATIN*	*2*	*NA*	*300*	*8.2*	*39.0*
097 CHR CHS&CHS CR	1	35	43*	1.2	5.6
175 CONGR CHR CHS	1	93	115*	3.1	14.9
355 PRESB CH (USA)	1	85	105*	2.9	13.6
419 SO BAPT CONV	1	87	107*	2.9	13.9
496 JEWISH EST[1]	0	NA	100	2.7	13.0
SEDGWICK	11	1,009	1,944*	72.3	100.0
053 ASSEMB OF GOD	2	42	97	3.6	5.0
081 CATHOLIC	2	NA	660	24.5	34.0
081d *LATIN*	*2*	*NA*	*660*	*24.5*	*34.0*
097 CHR CHS&CHS CR	1	150	184*	6.8	9.5
283 LUTH—MO SYNOD	1	245	302	11.2	15.5
285 MENNONITE CH	1	65	79	2.9	4.1
355 PRESB CH (USA)	1	43	53*	2.0	2.7
413 S.D.A.	1	40	49*	1.8	2.5
449 UN METHODIST	2	424	520*	19.3	26.7
SUMMIT	11	900	2,706*	21.0	100.0
053 ASSEMB OF GOD	1	36	49	.4	1.8
081 CATHOLIC	2	NA	1,285	10.0	47.5

NA–Not applicable NR–Not reported *Total adherents estimated from known number of communicant, confirmed, full members. - Represents a percent less than 0.1. Percentages may not total due to rounding.
[1]See Appendix E [2]See Appendix F [3]See Appendix G Lines in *italic* represent a breakdown of Catholic rites or Friends affiliations. They are included in their respective denominational total.

Table 4. Churches and Church Membership by County and Denomination: 1990

County and Denomination	Number of churches	Communicant, confirmed, full members	Total adherents Number	Percent of total population	Percent of total adherents
081d　*LATIN*	*2*	*NA*	*1,285*	*10.0*	*47.5*
111　CH CR,SCIENTST	1	NR	NR	-	-
151　L-D SAINTS	1	NA	176	1.4	6.5
167　CHS OF CHRIST	1	15	20	.2	.7
193　EPISCOPAL	1	104	143	1.1	5.3
207　E.L.C.A.	1	410	628	4.9	23.2
259　IFCA	1	NR	NR	-	-
419　SO BAPT CONV	1	134	162*	1.3	6.0
449　UN METHODIST	1	201	243*	1.9	9.0
TELLER	**13**	**1,227**	**2,461***	**19.7**	**100.0**
019　AMER BAPT USA	1	78	101*	.8	4.1
053　ASSEMB OF GOD	1	40	61	.5	2.5
081　CATHOLIC	1	NA	823	6.6	33.4
081d　*LATIN*	*1*	*NA*	*823*	*6.6*	*33.4*
097　CHR CHS&CHS CR	1	102	133*	1.1	5.4
165　CH OF NAZARENE	1	80	56	.4	2.3
167　CHS OF CHRIST	1	40	66	.5	2.7
193　EPISCOPAL	2	39	120	1.0	4.9
283　LUTH—MO SYNOD	1	306	397	3.2	16.1
413　S.D.A.	1	26	34*	.3	1.4
419　SO BAPT CONV	2	191	248*	2.0	10.1
449　UN METHODIST	1	325	422*	3.4	17.1
WASHINGTON	**17**	**1,380**	**2,383***	**49.5**	**100.0**
053　ASSEMB OF GOD	2	44	77	1.6	3.2
081　CATHOLIC	1	NA	328	6.8	13.8
081d　*LATIN*	*1*	*NA*	*328*	*6.8*	*13.8*
151　L-D SAINTS	1	NA	242	5.0	10.2
167　CHS OF CHRIST	2	53	65	1.4	2.7
207　E.L.C.A.	3	300	420	8.7	17.6
263　INT FOURSQ GOS	1	153	195*	4.1	8.2
283　LUTH—MO SYNOD	1	57	73	1.5	3.1
355　PRESB CH (USA)	2	313	398*	8.3	16.7
413　S.D.A.	1	21	27*	.6	1.1
419　SO BAPT CONV	1	53	67*	1.4	2.8
449　UN METHODIST	2	386	491*	10.2	20.6
WELD	**139**	**21,105**	**56,890***	**43.2**	**100.0**
019　AMER BAPT USA	3	469	605*	.5	1.1
053　ASSEMB OF GOD	15	989	1,991	1.5	3.5
057　BAPT GEN CONF	1	359	463*	.4	.8
081　CATHOLIC	15	NA	24,955	18.9	43.9
081d　*LATIN*	*15*	*NA*	*24,955*	*18.9*	*43.9*
089　CHR & MISS AL	2	0	44	-	.1
093　CHR CH (DISC)	3	492	771	.6	1.4
097　CHR CHS&CHS CR	3	382	493*	.4	.9
105　CHRISTIAN REF	1	91	156	.1	.3
111　CH CR,SCIENTST	1	NR	NR	-	-
123　CH GOD (ANDER)	1	105	105	.1	.2
145　CH GOD PROPHCY	2	44	57*	-	.1
151　L-D SAINTS	4	NA	1,248	.9	2.2
157　CH OF BRETHREN	1	52	67*	.1	.1
165　CH OF NAZARENE	2	442	479	.4	.8
167　CHS OF CHRIST	3	222	306	.2	.5
175　CONGR CHR CHS	1	80	103*	.1	.2
179　CONSRV BAPT	2	NR	NR	-	-
181　CONSRV CONGR	1	489	631*	.5	1.1
193　EPISCOPAL	3	489	873	.7	1.5
203　EVAN FREE CH	6	591	970	.7	1.7
207　E.L.C.A.	7	2,549	3,501	2.7	6.2
221　FREE METHODIST	1	14	33	-	.1
223　FREE WILL BAPT	1	16	21*	-	-
263　INT FOURSQ GOS	6	901	1,162*	.9	2.0
283　LUTH—MO SYNOD	6	1,574	2,059	1.6	3.6
285　MENNONITE CH	1	59	115	.1	.2
313　N AM BAPT CONF	2	181	233*	.2	.4
353　CHR BRETHREN	1	20	20	-	-
355　PRESB CH (USA)	5	1,352	1,744*	1.3	3.1
403　SALVATION ARMY	1	84	111	.1	.2
413　S.D.A.	3	714	921*	.7	1.6
419　SO BAPT CONV	9	2,053	2,648*	2.0	4.7
435　UNITARIAN-UNIV	1	56	81	.1	.1
443　UN C OF CHRIST	6	2,511	3,238*	2.5	5.7
449　UN METHODIST	13	3,240	4,178*	3.2	7.3
467　WESLEYAN	1	233	600	.5	1.1
469　WELS	2	131	186	.1	.3
496　JEWISH EST[1]	0	NA	416	.3	.7
497　BLACK BAPT EST[2]	NA	121	156*	.1	.3
498　INDEP.CHARIS.[3]	2	NA	800	.6	1.4
499　INDEP.NON-CHAR[3]	1	NA	350	.3	.6
YUMA	**27**	**2,665**	**4,817***	**53.8**	**100.0**
053　ASSEMB OF GOD	2	56	101	1.1	2.1
081　CATHOLIC	2	NA	741	8.3	15.4
081d　*LATIN*	*2*	*NA*	*741*	*8.3*	*15.4*

County and Denomination	Number of churches	Communicant, confirmed, full members	Total adherents Number	Percent of total population	Percent of total adherents
093　CHR CH (DISC)	1	95	451	5.0	9.4
097　CHR CHS&CHS CR	1	55	71*	.8	1.5
165　CH OF NAZARENE	3	213	473	5.3	9.8
167　CHS OF CHRIST	2	51	71	.8	1.5
207　E.L.C.A.	1	65	98	1.1	2.0
263　INT FOURSQ GOS	1	28	36*	.4	.7
283　LUTH—MO SYNOD	2	548	775	8.7	16.1
355　PRESB CH (USA)	2	381	490*	5.5	10.2
413　S.D.A.	2	64	82*	.9	1.7
419　SO BAPT CONV	2	210	270*	3.0	5.6
443　UN C OF CHRIST	1	79	102*	1.1	2.1
449　UN METHODIST	5	820	1,056*	11.8	21.9

CONNECTICUT

County and Denomination	Number of churches	Communicant, confirmed, full members	Total adherents Number	Percent of total population	Percent of total adherents
THE STATE.....	1,944	413,414	2,047,646*	62.3	100.0
FAIRFIELD	**452**	**112,006**	**545,988***	**66.0**	**100.0**
001　ADVENT CHR CH	3	109	133*	-	-
005　AME ZION	6	1,057	2,012	.2	.4
007　ALBAN ORTH ARC	1	NR	NR	-	-
019　AMER BAPT USA	27	10,407	12,656*	1.5	2.3
022　EASTERN ORTH	4	1,333	1,333	.2	.2
053　ASSEMB OF GOD	19	2,847	5,287	.6	1.0
057　BAPT GEN CONF	1	459	558*	.1	.1
081　CATHOLIC	99	NA	347,526	42.0	63.7
081b　*BYZAN RUTH*	*3*	*NA*	*1,540*	*.2*	*.3*
081d　*LATIN*	*92*	*NA*	*343,139*	*41.5*	*62.8*
081e　*MARONITE*	*1*	*NA*	*1,445*	*.2*	*.3*
081f　*MELKITE-GK*	*1*	*NA*	*890*	*.1*	*.2*
081h　*UKRAINIAN*	*2*	*NA*	*512*	*.1*	*.1*
089　CHR & MISS AL	3	179	244	-	-
093　CHR CH (DISC)	3	234	437	.1	.1
097　CHR CHS&CHS CR	1	56	68*	-	-
111　CH CR,SCIENTST	10	NR	NR	-	-
127　CH GOD (CLEVE)	14	1,073	1,305*	.2	.2
145　CH GOD PROPHCY	4	112	136*	-	-
151　L-D SAINTS	6	NA	1,833	.2	.3
165　CH OF NAZARENE	5	188	895	.1	.2
167　CHS OF CHRIST	5	412	594	.1	.1
175　CONGR CHR CHS	1	51	62*	-	-
176　CCC, NOT NAT'L	2	1,257	1,529*	.2	.3
179　CONSRV BAPT	3	NR	NR	-	-
181　CONSRV CONGR	1	51	62*	-	-
193　EPISCOPAL	46	16,660	27,705	3.3	5.1
203　EVAN FREE CH	6	769	977	.1	.2
207　E.L.C.A.	17	6,215	7,733	.9	1.4
221　FREE METHODIST	1	97	199	-	-
226　FRIENDS-USA	2	165	201*	-	-
226d　*FGC & FUM*	*2*	*165*	*201**	*-*	*-*
246　GREEK ORTHODOX	5	NR	NR	-	-
283　LUTH—MO SYNOD	10	4,240	5,429	.7	1.0
285　MENNONITE CH	1	33	58	-	-
331　ORTH CH IN AM	3	NR	NR	-	-
353　CHR BRETHREN	1	80	100	-	-
355　PRESB CH (USA)	9	6,270	7,625*	.9	1.4
397　ROMANIAN ORTH	1	NR	NR	-	-
403　SALVATION ARMY	4	284	295	-	.1
413　S.D.A.	5	737	896*	.1	.2
419　SO BAPT CONV	7	1,807	2,198*	.3	.4
431　UKRAINIAN AMER	1	NR	NR	-	-
435　UNITARIAN-UNIV	5	925	1,228	.1	.2
443　UN C OF CHRIST	45	22,864	27,805*	3.4	5.1
449　UN METHODIST	33	15,156	18,431*	2.2	3.4
469　WELS	1	94	117	-	-
496　JEWISH EST[1]	27	NA	45,800	5.5	8.4
497　BLACK BAPT EST[2]	NA	15,785	19,196*	2.3	3.5
498　INDEP.CHARIS.[3]	3	NA	2,925	.4	.5
499　INDEP.NON-CHAR[3]	1	NA	400	-	.1
HARTFORD	**472**	**121,195**	**569,902***	**66.9**	**100.0**
001　ADVENT CHR CH	3	161	196*	-	-
005　AME ZION	9	6,103	7,064	.8	1.2
019　AMER BAPT USA	32	12,227	14,885*	1.7	2.6
049　ARMEN AP CH AM	1	500	1,600	.2	.3
053　ASSEMB OF GOD	15	1,611	2,954	.3	.5
057　BAPT GEN CONF	7	1,083	1,318*	.2	.2
081　CATHOLIC	99	NA	382,719	44.9	67.2
081b　*BYZAN RUTH*	*1*	*NA*	*300*	*-*	*.1*
081d　*LATIN*	*95*	*NA*	*381,267*	*44.8*	*66.9*
081h　*UKRAINIAN*	*3*	*NA*	*1,152*	*.1*	*.2*
083　CHRIST CATH CH	1	4	4	-	-

CONNECTICUT

Table 4. Churches and Church Membership by County and Denomination: 1990

County and Denomination	Number of churches	Communicant, confirmed, full members	Total adherents Number	Percent of total population	Percent of total adherents
089 CHR & MISS AL	2	76	146	-	-
097 CHR CHS&CHS CR	2	200	243*	-	-
105 CHRISTIAN REF	1	167	263	-	-
111 CH CR,SCIENTST	5	NR	NR	-	-
123 CH GOD (ANDER)	1	40	70	-	-
127 CH GOD (CLEVE)	8	1,146	1,395*	.2	.2
145 CH GOD PROPHCY	2	56	68*	-	-
151 L-D SAINTS	4	NA	1,465	.2	.3
163 CH OF LUTH BR	2	121	164	-	-
165 CH OF NAZARENE	7	560	953	.1	.2
167 CHS OF CHRIST	9	450	707	.1	.1
175 CONGR CHR CHS	2	1,594	1,941*	.2	.3
176 CCC, NOT NAT'L	1	165	201*	-	-
179 CONSRV BAPT	2	NR	NR	-	-
193 EPISCOPAL	38	11,247	17,628	2.1	3.1
195 ESTONIAN ELC	1	567	690*	.1	.1
203 EVAN FREE CH	3	367	540	.1	.1
207 E.L.C.A.	24	10,381	13,523	1.6	2.4
226 FRIENDS-USA	1	203	247*	-	-
226d *FGC & FUM*	*1*	*203*	*247**	-	-
246 GREEK ORTHODOX	4	NR	NR	-	-
249 AP CATH ASSYR	1	110	379	-	.1
259 IFCA	1	NR	NR	-	-
263 INT FOURSQ GOS	1	13	16*	-	-
274 LAT EVAN LUTH	1	194	198	-	-
283 LUTH—MO SYNOD	8	3,642	4,644	.5	.8
285 MENNONITE CH	1	17	57	-	-
329 OPEN BIBLE STD	1	NR	NR	-	-
331 ORTH CH IN AM	2	NR	NR	-	-
339 PENT CH OF GOD	1	30	85	-	-
353 CHR BRETHREN	6	307	435	.1	.1
355 PRESB CH (USA)	5	1,221	1,486*	.2	.3
356 PRESB CH AMER	1	52	80	-	-
403 SALVATION ARMY	5	535	561	.1	.1
413 S.D.A.	7	1,683	2,049*	.2	.4
419 SO BAPT CONV	8	1,577	1,920*	.2	.3
435 UNITARIAN-UNIV	5	1,165	1,678	.2	.3
443 UN C OF CHRIST	58	32,530	39,603*	4.6	6.9
449 UN METHODIST	32	12,092	14,721*	1.7	2.6
469 WELS	1	102	127	-	-
496 JEWISH EST[1]	32	NA	26,200	3.1	4.6
497 BLACK BAPT EST[2]	NA	16,896	20,569*	2.4	3.6
498 INDEP.CHARIS.[3]	6	NA	3,090	.4	.5
499 INDEP.NON-CHAR[3]	3	NA	1,020	.1	.2
LITCHFIELD	**144**	**24,085**	**97,881***	**56.2**	**100.0**
001 ADVENT CHR CH	1	108	133*	.1	.1
005 AME ZION	2	123	197	.1	.2
019 AMER BAPT USA	4	637	782*	.4	.8
053 ASSEMB OF GOD	3	315	614	.4	.6
081 CATHOLIC	29	NA	64,593	37.1	66.0
081d *LATIN*	*27*	*NA*	*63,048*	*36.2*	*64.4*
081e *MARONITE*	*1*	*NA*	*1,266*	*.7*	*1.3*
081h *UKRAINIAN*	*1*	*NA*	*279*	*.2*	*.3*
111 CH CR,SCIENTST	1	NR	NR	-	-
151 L-D SAINTS	2	NA	706	.4	.7
167 CHS OF CHRIST	1	47	67	-	.1
175 CONGR CHR CHS	4	165	203*	.1	.2
176 CCC, NOT NAT'L	2	141	173*	.1	.2
193 EPISCOPAL	22	3,928	6,209	3.6	6.3
207 E.L.C.A.	6	2,308	2,862	1.6	2.9
226 FRIENDS-USA	2	60	74*	-	.1
226d *FGC & FUM*	*2*	*60*	*74**	-	*.1*
257 HUTTERIAN BR	1	NA	225	.1	.2
263 INT FOURSQ GOS	1	27	33*	-	-
283 LUTH—MO SYNOD	3	645	908	.5	.9
331 ORTH CH IN AM	1	NR	NR	-	-
353 CHR BRETHREN	2	80	125	.1	.1
403 SALVATION ARMY	1	30	31	-	-
413 S.D.A.	1	52	64*	-	.1
419 SO BAPT CONV	2	281	345*	.2	.4
435 UNITARIAN-UNIV	2	107	122	.1	.1
443 UN C OF CHRIST	35	10,743	13,190*	7.6	13.5
449 UN METHODIST	14	4,032	4,951*	2.8	5.1
496 JEWISH EST[1]	2	NA	960	.6	1.0
497 BLACK BAPT EST[2]	NA	256	314*	.2	.3
MIDDLESEX	**94**	**17,801**	**78,610***	**54.9**	**100.0**
005 AME ZION	3	1,395	2,037	1.4	2.6
019 AMER BAPT USA	5	782	945*	.7	1.2
053 ASSEMB OF GOD	3	165	205	.1	.3
081 CATHOLIC	18	NA	51,948	36.3	66.1
081d *LATIN*	*18*	*NA*	*51,948*	*36.3*	*66.1*
111 CH CR,SCIENTST	2	NR	NR	-	-
127 CH GOD (CLEVE)	1	21	25*	-	-
167 CHS OF CHRIST	1	35	50	-	.1
175 CONGR CHR CHS	2	315	381*	.3	.5
176 CCC, NOT NAT'L	1	892	1,078*	.8	1.4
193 EPISCOPAL	12	1,936	3,795	2.7	4.8
203 EVAN FREE CH	1	160	214	.1	.3
207 E.L.C.A.	6	1,524	2,030	1.4	2.6
226 FRIENDS-USA	1	26	31*	-	-
226d *FGC & FUM*	*1*	*26*	*31**	-	-
259 IFCA	2	NR	NR	-	-
283 LUTH—MO SYNOD	1	248	332	.2	.4
403 SALVATION ARMY	1	41	45	-	.1
413 S.D.A.	1	25	30*	-	-
415 S-D BAPTIST GC	1	30	36*	-	-
419 SO BAPT CONV	2	144	174*	.1	.2
443 UN C OF CHRIST	18	6,740	8,145*	5.7	10.4
449 UN METHODIST	8	2,160	2,610*	1.8	3.3
496 JEWISH EST[1]	3	NA	2,775	1.9	3.5
497 BLACK BAPT EST[2]	NA	1,162	1,404*	1.0	1.8
499 INDEP.NON-CHAR[3]	1	NA	320	.2	.4
NEW HAVEN	**422**	**85,636**	**518,416***	**64.5**	**100.0**
001 ADVENT CHR CH	2	146	178*	-	-
005 AME ZION	8	6,831	7,705	1.0	1.5
019 AMER BAPT USA	23	8,820	10,770*	1.3	2.1
039 AP CHR CH(NAZ)	1	18	22*	-	-
053 ASSEMB OF GOD	22	2,277	3,077	.4	.6
057 BAPT GEN CONF	5	439	536*	.1	.1
081 CATHOLIC	106	NA	368,313	45.8	71.0
081b *BYZAN RUTH*	*1*	*NA*	*130*	-	-
081d *LATIN*	*104*	*NA*	*367,467*	*45.7*	*70.9*
081e *MARONITE*	*1*	*NA*	*716*	*.1*	*.1*
089 CHR & MISS AL	5	211	624	.1	.1
093 CHR CH (DISC)	2	190	246	-	-
097 CHR CHS&CHS CR	4	149	182*	-	-
111 CH CR,SCIENTST	5	NR	NR	-	-
123 CH GOD (ANDER)	1	205	240	-	-
127 CH GOD (CLEVE)	4	364	444*	.1	.1
145 CH GOD PROPHCY	3	84	103*	-	-
151 L-D SAINTS	6	NA	1,749	.2	.3
165 CH OF NAZARENE	1	53	100	-	-
167 CHS OF CHRIST	8	509	758	.1	.1
175 CONGR CHR CHS	2	189	231*	-	-
179 CONSRV BAPT	1	NR	NR	-	-
193 EPISCOPAL	45	9,191	15,036	1.9	2.9
203 EVAN FREE CH	4	354	640	.1	.1
207 E.L.C.A.	14	4,659	6,090	.8	1.2
226 FRIENDS-USA	1	79	96*	-	-
226d *FGC & FUM*	*1*	*79*	*96**	-	-
246 GREEK ORTHODOX	4	NR	NR	-	-
249 AP CATH ASSYR	0	15	109	-	-
263 INT FOURSQ GOS	1	44	54*	-	-
274 LAT EVAN LUTH	1	30	30	-	-
283 LUTH—MO SYNOD	7	2,054	2,412	.3	.5
285 MENNONITE CH	1	80	80	-	-
313 N AM BAPT CONF	1	30	37*	-	-
331 ORTH CH IN AM	4	NR	NR	-	-
353 CHR BRETHREN	4	472	782	.1	.2
355 PRESB CH (USA)	4	561	685*	.1	.1
403 SALVATION ARMY	4	266	303	-	.1
413 S.D.A.	8	930	1,136*	.1	.2
419 SO BAPT CONV	2	423	517*	.1	.1
435 UNITARIAN-UNIV	4	603	791	.1	.2
443 UN C OF CHRIST	48	21,319	26,033*	3.2	5.0
449 UN METHODIST	22	8,161	9,966*	1.2	1.9
496 JEWISH EST[1]	25	NA	34,250	4.3	6.6
497 BLACK BAPT EST[2]	NA	15,880	19,391*	2.4	3.7
498 INDEP.CHARIS.[3]	6	NA	3,200	.4	.6
499 INDEP.NON-CHAR[3]	3	NA	1,500	.2	.3
NEW LONDON	**183**	**30,081**	**124,289***	**48.7**	**100.0**
005 AME ZION	2	2,851	3,013	1.2	2.4
019 AMER BAPT USA	21	4,832	5,965*	2.3	4.8
053 ASSEMB OF GOD	9	610	886	.3	.7
081 CATHOLIC	33	NA	78,979	31.0	63.5
081d *LATIN*	*31*	*NA*	*78,618*	*30.8*	*63.3*
081f *MELKITE-GK*	*1*	*NA*	*263*	*.1*	*.2*
081h *UKRAINIAN*	*1*	*NA*	*98*	-	*.1*
089 CHR & MISS AL	1	117	309	.1	.2
097 CHR CHS&CHS CR	1	30	37*	-	-
111 CH CR,SCIENTST	2	NR	NR	-	-
127 CH GOD (CLEVE)	2	308	380*	.1	.3
145 CH GOD PROPHCY	1	28	35*	-	-
151 L-D SAINTS	3	NA	1,172	.5	.9
165 CH OF NAZARENE	3	150	256	.1	.2
167 CHS OF CHRIST	3	83	121	-	.1
175 CONGR CHR CHS	11	1,071	1,322*	.5	1.1
176 CCC, NOT NAT'L	3	914	1,128*	.4	.9
179 CONSRV BAPT	5	NR	NR	-	-
193 EPISCOPAL	11	2,969	4,884	1.9	3.9

NA–Not applicable   NR–Not reported   *Total adherents estimated from known number of communicant, confirmed, full members.   - Represents a percent less than 0.1.   Percentages may not total due to rounding.
[1] See Appendix E   [2] See Appendix F   [3] See Appendix G   Lines in *italic* represent a breakdown of Catholic rites or Friends affiliations. They are included in their respective denominational total.

Table 4. Churches and Church Membership by County and Denomination: 1990

County and Denomination	Number of churches	Communicant, confirmed, full members	Total adherents		
			Number	Percent of total population	Percent of total adherents
203 EVAN FREE CH	1	12	28	-	-
207 E.L.C.A.	2	960	1,375	.5	1.1
226 FRIENDS–USA	1	27	33*	-	-
226d FGC & FUM	1	27	33*	-	-
246 GREEK ORTHODOX	2	NR	NR	-	-
263 INT FOURSQ GOS	1	40	49*	-	-
283 LUTH—MO SYNOD	4	796	1,041	.4	.8
331 ORTH CH IN AM	1	NR	NR	-	-
353 CHR BRETHREN	1	430	700	.3	.6
355 PRESB CH (USA)	2	320	395*	.2	.3
356 PRESB CH AMER	1	0	0	-	-
403 SALVATION ARMY	2	145	158	.1	.1
413 S.D.A.	3	320	395*	.2	.3
415 S-D BAPTIST GC	1	43	53*	-	-
419 SO BAPT CONV	4	2,201	2,717*	1.1	2.2
435 UNITARIAN-UNIV	2	200	266	.1	.2
443 UN C OF CHRIST	20	5,869	7,246*	2.8	5.8
449 UN METHODIST	12	2,408	2,973*	1.2	2.4
496 JEWISH EST[1]	10	NA	4,575	1.8	3.7
497 BLACK BAPT EST[2]	NA	2,347	2,898*	1.1	2.3
498 INDEP.CHARIS.[3]	1	NA	600	.2	.5
499 INDEP.NON-CHAR[3]	1	NA	300	.1	.2
TOLLAND	**77**	**13,386**	**48,358***	**37.6**	**100.0**
019 AMER BAPT USA	3	422	514*	.4	1.1
040 AP CHR CH-AMER	1	335	595	.5	1.2
053 ASSEMB OF GOD	2	111	222	.2	.5
081 CATHOLIC	13	NA	29,986	23.3	62.0
081d LATIN	13	NA	29,986	23.3	62.0
151 L-D SAINTS	1	NA	510	.4	1.1
165 CH OF NAZARENE	1	25	57	-	.1
167 CHS OF CHRIST	3	68	101	.1	.2
179 CONSRV BAPT	2	NR	NR	-	-
193 EPISCOPAL	5	1,104	1,944	1.5	4.0
207 E.L.C.A.	4	919	1,267	1.0	2.6
226 FRIENDS–USA	1	73	89*	.1	.2
226d FGC & FUM	1	73	89*	.1	.2
263 INT FOURSQ GOS	1	0	0*	-	-
283 LUTH—MO SYNOD	3	312	440	.3	.9
349 PENT HOLINESS	1	32	39*	-	.1
356 PRESB CH AMER	1	94	110	.1	.2
403 SALVATION ARMY	1	56	68	.1	.1
413 S.D.A.	1	87	106*	.1	.2
419 SO BAPT CONV	1	243	296*	.2	.6
435 UNITARIAN-UNIV	1	45	60	-	.1
443 UN C OF CHRIST	21	7,528	9,171*	7.1	19.0
449 UN METHODIST	6	1,354	1,649*	1.3	3.4
467 WESLEYAN	1	70	165	.1	.3
496 JEWISH EST[1]	3	NA	350	.3	.7
497 BLACK BAPT EST[2]	NA	508	619*	.5	1.3
WINDHAM	**100**	**9,224**	**64,202***	**62.6**	**100.0**
005 AME ZION	1	67	127	.1	.2
019 AMER BAPT USA	12	1,343	1,691*	1.6	2.6
053 ASSEMB OF GOD	3	501	815	.8	1.3
081 CATHOLIC	19	NA	50,683	49.4	78.9
081d LATIN	18	NA	50,470	49.2	78.6
081h UKRAINIAN	1	NA	213	.2	.3
089 CHR & MISS AL	1	27	40	-	.1
111 CH CR,SCIENTST	1	NR	NR	-	-
127 CH GOD (CLEVE)	1	16	20*	-	-
151 L-D SAINTS	2	NA	640	.6	1.0
165 CH OF NAZARENE	2	139	192	.2	.3
167 CHS OF CHRIST	1	25	40	-	.1
175 CONGR CHR CHS	4	279	351*	.3	.5
176 CCC, NOT NAT'L	3	104	131*	.1	.2
179 CONSRV BAPT	1	NR	NR	-	-
181 CONSRV CONGR	3	173	218*	.2	.3
193 EPISCOPAL	7	1,007	1,603	1.6	2.5
203 EVAN FREE CH	1	74	120	.1	.2
207 E.L.C.A.	3	466	657	.6	1.0
226 FRIENDS–USA	1	3	20*	-	-
226d FGC & FUM	1	3	20*	-	-
246 GREEK ORTHODOX	1	NR	NR	-	-
331 ORTH CH IN AM	1	NR	NR	-	-
353 CHR BRETHREN	1	17	36	-	.1
413 S.D.A.	2	128	161*	.2	.3
419 SO BAPT CONV	2	602	758*	.7	1.2
435 UNITARIAN-UNIV	1	22	22	-	-
443 UN C OF CHRIST	15	3,207	4,038*	3.9	6.3
449 UN METHODIST	7	851	1,071*	1.0	1.7
496 JEWISH EST[1]	4	NA	550	.5	.9
497 BLACK BAPT EST[2]	NA	173	218*	.2	.3

County and Denomination	Number of churches	Communicant, confirmed, full members	Total adherents		
			Number	Percent of total population	Percent of total adherents
DELAWARE					
THE STATE.....	523	134,904	306,364*	46.0	100.0
KENT	**98**	**21,163**	**38,582***	**34.8**	**100.0**
019 AMER BAPT USA	2	812	1,038*	.9	2.7
053 ASSEMB OF GOD	1	389	1,247	1.1	3.2
081 CATHOLIC	4	NA	6,861	6.2	17.8
081d LATIN	4	NA	6,861	6.2	17.8
089 CHR & MISS AL	1	33	73	.1	.2
097 CHR CHS&CHS CR	2	215	275*	.2	.7
111 CH CR,SCIENTST	1	NR	NR	-	-
123 CH GOD (ANDER)	2	40	82	.1	.2
127 CH GOD (CLEVE)	2	93	119*	.1	.3
145 CH GOD PROPHCY	2	55	70*	.1	.2
151 L-D SAINTS	2	NA	732	.7	1.9
157 CH OF BRETHREN	1	91	116*	.1	.3
165 CH OF NAZARENE	4	414	642	.6	1.7
167 CHS OF CHRIST	1	70	100	.1	.3
193 EPISCOPAL	5	1,122	1,899	1.7	4.9
207 E.L.C.A.	1	422	556	.5	1.4
226 FRIENDS–USA	1	45	58*	.1	.2
226c FGC	1	45	58*	.1	.2
263 INT FOURSQ GOS	1	0	0*	-	-
283 LUTH—MO SYNOD	2	421	524	.5	1.4
285 MENNONITE CH	1	97	166	.1	.4
286 E.PA MENNONITE	1	57	73*	.1	.2
323 OLD ORD AMISH	8	NA	1,200	1.1	3.1
353 CHR BRETHREN	1	35	60	.1	.2
355 PRESB CH (USA)	2	581	743*	.7	1.9
356 PRESB CH AMER	1	111	111	.1	.3
403 SALVATION ARMY	1	45	50	-	.1
413 S.D.A.	5	538	688*	.6	1.8
419 SO BAPT CONV	4	1,283	1,640*	1.5	4.3
443 UN C OF CHRIST	1	388	496*	.4	1.3
449 UN METHODIST	32	8,301	10,610*	9.6	27.5
467 WESLEYAN	4	446	937	.8	2.4
496 JEWISH EST[1]	1	NA	650	.6	1.7
497 BLACK BAPT EST[2]	NA	5,059	6,466*	5.8	16.8
499 INDEP.NON-CHAR[3]	1	NA	300	.3	.8
NEW CASTLE	**252**	**84,230**	**225,316***	**51.0**	**100.0**
005 AME ZION	2	326	387	.1	.2
019 AMER BAPT USA	8	2,567	3,179*	.7	1.4
040 AP CHR CH-AMER	1	21	36	-	-
053 ASSEMB OF GOD	7	461	703	.2	.3
057 BAPT GEN CONF	2	762	944*	.2	.4
081 CATHOLIC	35	NA	105,069	23.8	46.6
081d LATIN	34	NA	104,424	23.6	46.3
081h UKRAINIAN	1	NA	645	.1	.3
089 CHR & MISS AL	3	131	237	.1	.1
093 CHR CH (DISC)	1	91	141	-	.1
097 CHR CHS&CHS CR	1	20	25*	-	-
111 CH CR,SCIENTST	2	NR	NR	-	-
123 CH GOD (ANDER)	3	199	221	.1	.1
127 CH GOD (CLEVE)	2	253	313*	.1	.1
145 CH GOD PROPHCY	4	108	134*	-	.1
151 L-D SAINTS	5	NA	1,850	.4	.8
157 CH OF BRETHREN	1	117	145*	-	.1
165 CH OF NAZARENE	4	482	459	.1	.2
167 CHS OF CHRIST	5	650	883	.2	.4
179 CONSRV BAPT	1	NR	NR	-	-
193 EPISCOPAL	21	6,360	9,216	2.1	4.1
203 EVAN FREE CH	1	601	601	.1	.3
207 E.L.C.A.	9	4,335	5,816	1.3	2.6
223 FREE WILL BAPT	4	496	614*	.1	.3
226 FRIENDS–USA	7	578	716*	.2	.3
226c FGC	7	578	716*	.2	.3
246 GREEK ORTHODOX	1	NR	NR	-	-
283 LUTH—MO SYNOD	3	866	1,178	.3	.5
285 MENNONITE CH	1	24	31	-	-
286 E.PA MENNONITE	1	36	45*	-	-
331 ORTH CH IN AM	1	NR	NR	-	-
353 CHR BRETHREN	1	45	55	-	-
355 PRESB CH (USA)	26	10,559	13,075*	3.0	5.8
356 PRESB CH AMER	6	1,763	2,355	.5	1.0
375 REF EPISCOPAL	1	14	14	-	-
403 SALVATION ARMY	1	116	189	-	.1
413 S.D.A.	4	951	1,178*	.3	.5
419 SO BAPT CONV	7	2,952	3,655*	.8	1.6
435 UNITARIAN-UNIV	3	1,126	1,453	.3	.6
443 UN C OF CHRIST	1	138	171*	-	.1
449 UN METHODIST	56	24,785	30,690*	6.9	13.6
467 WESLEYAN	3	123	349	.1	.2
469 WELS	1	128	191	-	.1
496 JEWISH EST[1]	3	NA	8,850	2.0	3.9

NA–Not applicable   NR–Not reported   *Total adherents estimated from known number of communicant, confirmed, full members.   - Represents a percent less than 0.1.   Percentages may not total due to rounding.
[1]See Appendix E   [2]See Appendix F   [3]See Appendix G   Lines in *italic* represent a breakdown of Catholic rites or Friends affiliations. They are included in their respective denominational total.

Table 4. Churches and Church Membership by County and Denomination: 1990

County and Denomination	Number of churches	Communicant, confirmed, full members	Total adherents Number	Percent of total population	Percent of total adherents
497 BLACK BAPT EST[2]	NA	22,046	27,298*	6.2	12.1
499 INDEP.NON-CHAR[3]	3	NA	2,850	.6	1.3
SUSSEX	**173**	**29,511**	**42,466***	**37.5**	**100.0**
005 AME ZION	2	135	148	.1	.3
053 ASSEMB OF GOD	4	266	507	.4	1.2
066 BIBLE CH OF CR	1	290	358*	.3	.8
071 BRETHREN (ASH)	1	33	41*	-	.1
081 CATHOLIC	6	NA	4,411	3.9	10.4
081d LATIN	*6*	*NA*	*4,411*	*3.9*	*10.4*
089 CHR & MISS AL	3	181	351	.3	.8
097 CHR CHS&CHS CR	6	615	759*	.7	1.8
111 CH CR,SCIENTST	2	NR	NR	-	-
127 CH GOD (CLEVE)	9	1,313	1,621*	1.4	3.8
145 CH GOD PROPHCY	3	82	101*	.1	.2
151 L-D SAINTS	1	NA	204	.2	.5
165 CH OF NAZARENE	2	221	590	.5	1.4
167 CHS OF CHRIST	3	145	185	.2	.4
193 EPISCOPAL	12	1,757	2,192	1.9	5.2
207 E.L.C.A.	1	304	408	.4	1.0
259 IFCA	1	NR	NR	-	-
265 INT PENT C CHR	1	6	12	-	-
274 LAT EVAN LUTH	1	100	117	.1	.3
283 LUTH—MO SYNOD	2	370	470	.4	1.1
285 MENNONITE CH	5	547	718	.6	1.7
355 PRESB CH (USA)	9	1,282	1,583*	1.4	3.7
356 PRESB CH AMER	1	61	73	.1	.2
413 S.D.A.	3	144	178*	.2	.4
419 SO BAPT CONV	2	386	477*	.4	1.1
443 UN C OF CHRIST	1	3	4*	-	-
449 UN METHODIST	81	16,032	19,791*	17.5	46.6
467 WESLEYAN	10	580	1,417	1.3	3.3
497 BLACK BAPT EST[2]	NA	4,658	5,750*	5.1	13.5

DISTRICT OF COLUMBIA

County and Denomination	Number of churches	Communicant, confirmed, full members	Total adherents Number	Percent of total population	Percent of total adherents
THE DISTRICT.....	343	219,241	374,160*	61.7	100.0
DISTRICT OF COLUMBIA	**343**	**219,241**	**374,160***	**61.7**	**100.0**
005 AME ZION	15	33,400	39,500	6.5	10.6
019 AMER BAPT USA	39	28,560	33,744*	5.6	9.0
022 EASTERN ORTH	1	10	10	-	-
053 ASSEMB OF GOD	5	726	771	.1	.2
055 AS REF PRES CH	1	22	28	-	-
061 BEACHY AMISH	1	29	34*	-	-
071 BRETHREN (ASH)	1	32	38*	-	-
081 CATHOLIC	41	NA	77,532	12.8	20.7
081d LATIN	*38*	*NA*	*75,000*	*12.4*	*20.0*
081e MARONITE	*1*	*NA*	*444*	*.1*	*.1*
081h UKRAINIAN	*2*	*NA*	*2,088*	*.3*	*.6*
089 CHR & MISS AL	2	141	169	-	-
093 CHR CH (DISC)	5	1,136	1,358	.2	.4
097 CHR CHS&CHS CR	10	0	0*	-	-
105 CHRISTIAN REF	1	141	179	-	-
111 CH CR,SCIENTST	6	NR	NR	-	-
123 CH GOD (ANDER)	6	483	666	.1	.2
127 CH GOD (CLEVE)	3	232	274*	-	.1
145 CH GOD PROPHCY	2	61	72*	-	-
151 L-D SAINTS	1	NA	336	.1	.1
157 CH OF BRETHREN	1	219	259*	-	.1
165 CH OF NAZARENE	2	595	788	.1	.2
167 CHS OF CHRIST	5	660	972	.2	.3
179 CONSRV BAPT	1	NR	NR	-	-
193 EPISCOPAL	34	11,767	16,273	2.7	4.3
207 E.L.C.A.	13	3,482	4,353	.7	1.2
226 FRIENDS-USA	4	540	638*	.1	.2
226d FGC & FUM	*4*	*540*	*638***	*.1*	*.2*
246 GREEK ORTHODOX	2	NR	NR	-	-
249 AP CATH ASSYR	0	1	1	-	-
263 INT FOURSQ GOS	1	0	0*	-	-
283 LUTH—MO SYNOD	4	760	1,156	.2	.3
285 MENNONITE CH	5	264	466	.1	.1
293 MORAV CH-NORTH	1	114	160	-	-
331 ORTH CH IN AM	1	NR	NR	-	-
353 CHR BRETHREN	5	179	283	-	.1
355 PRESB CH (USA)	17	8,150	9,629*	1.6	2.6
403 SALVATION ARMY	3	432	445	.1	.1
413 S.D.A.	10	4,702	5,556*	.9	1.5
415 S-D BAPTIST GC	1	80	95*	-	-
419 SO BAPT CONV	29	14,893	17,597*	2.9	4.7

County and Denomination	Number of churches	Communicant, confirmed, full members	Total adherents Number	Percent of total population	Percent of total adherents
423 SYRIAN ANTIOCH	1	NA	500	.1	.1
435 UNITARIAN-UNIV	3	651	765	.1	.2
443 UN C OF CHRIST	8	4,185	4,945*	.8	1.3
449 UN METHODIST	35	15,506	18,321*	3.0	4.9
496 JEWISH EST[1]	13	NA	25,400	4.2	6.8
497 BLACK BAPT EST[2]	NA	87,088	102,897*	17.0	27.5
498 INDEP.CHARIS.[3]	3	NA	5,950	1.0	1.6
499 INDEP.NON-CHAR[3]	1	NA	2,000	.3	.5

FLORIDA

County and Denomination	Number of churches	Communicant, confirmed, full members	Total adherents Number	Percent of total population	Percent of total adherents
THE STATE.....	8,577	2,651,825	5,672,756*	43.8	100.0
ALACHUA	**176**	**49,210**	**78,394***	**43.2**	**100.0**
001 ADVENT CHR CH	1	21	25*	-	-
005 AME ZION	1	160	160	.1	.2
053 ASSEMB OF GOD	6	461	798	.4	1.0
057 BAPT GEN CONF	1	79	96*	.1	.1
081 CATHOLIC	6	NA	15,603	8.6	19.9
081d LATIN	*6*	*NA*	*15,603*	*8.6*	*19.9*
089 CHR & MISS AL	2	54	111	.1	.1
093 CHR CH (DISC)	1	116	140	.1	.2
097 CHR CHS&CHS CR	1	125	152*	.1	.2
111 CH CR,SCIENTST	1	NR	NR	-	-
123 CH GOD (ANDER)	2	89	93	.1	.1
127 CH GOD (CLEVE)	5	500	606*	.3	.8
145 CH GOD PROPHCY	1	34	41*	-	.1
151 L-D SAINTS	3	NA	1,168	.6	1.5
165 CH OF NAZARENE	4	492	603	.3	.8
167 CHS OF CHRIST	13	1,674	2,121	1.2	2.7
179 CONSRV BAPT	1	NR	NR	-	-
193 EPISCOPAL	7	1,487	2,088	1.1	2.7
203 EVAN FREE CH	1	282	437	.2	.6
207 E.L.C.A.	2	618	875	.5	1.1
223 FREE WILL BAPT	1	16	19*	-	-
226 FRIENDS-USA	1	90	99	.1	.1
226d FGC & FUM	*1*	*90*	*99*	*.1*	*.1*
246 GREEK ORTHODOX	1	NR	NR	-	-
283 LUTH—MO SYNOD	1	669	857	.5	1.1
285 MENNONITE CH	1	24	45	-	.1
331 ORTH CH IN AM	1	NR	NR	-	-
349 PENT HOLINESS	3	184	223*	.1	.3
353 CHR BRETHREN	1	30	45	-	.1
355 PRESB CH (USA)	9	2,542	3,081*	1.7	3.9
356 PRESB CH AMER	1	189	246	.1	.3
361 PRIM BAPT ASCS	1	17	21*	-	-
403 SALVATION ARMY	1	63	63	-	.1
413 S.D.A.	3	623	755*	.4	1.0
419 SO BAPT CONV	49	20,245	24,538*	13.5	31.3
435 UNITARIAN-UNIV	1	224	269	.1	.3
443 UN C OF CHRIST	1	399	484*	.3	.6
449 UN METHODIST	39	8,747	10,602*	5.8	13.5
469 WELS	1	110	140	.1	.2
496 JEWISH EST[1]	1	NA	1,068	.6	1.4
497 BLACK BAPT EST[2]	NA	8,846	10,722*	5.9	13.7
BAKER	**22**	**3,857**	**5,963***	**32.3**	**100.0**
001 ADVENT CHR CH	1	15	20*	.1	.3
053 ASSEMB OF GOD	1	88	134	.7	2.2
081 CATHOLIC	1	NA	358	1.9	6.0
081d LATIN	*1*	*NA*	*358*	*1.9*	*6.0*
127 CH GOD (CLEVE)	3	352	461*	2.5	7.7
151 L-D SAINTS	1	NA	453	2.5	7.6
165 CH OF NAZARENE	1	58	114	.6	1.9
167 CHS OF CHRIST	2	115	201	1.1	3.4
193 EPISCOPAL	1	47	53	.3	.9
361 PRIM BAPT ASCS	5	71	93*	.5	1.6
419 SO BAPT CONV	4	2,169	2,842*	15.4	47.7
449 UN METHODIST	2	378	495*	2.7	8.3
497 BLACK BAPT EST[2]	NA	564	739*	4.0	12.4
BAY	**125**	**40,938**	**59,014***	**46.5**	**100.0**
001 ADVENT CHR CH	2	184	230*	.2	.4
053 ASSEMB OF GOD	19	1,787	3,155	2.5	5.3
081 CATHOLIC	7	NA	3,363	2.6	5.7
081d LATIN	*7*	*NA*	*3,363*	*2.6*	*5.7*
089 CHR & MISS AL	1	83	101	.1	.2
097 CHR CHS&CHS CR	2	185	231*	.2	.4
111 CH CR,SCIENTST	1	NR	NR	-	-
123 CH GOD (ANDER)	2	52	95	.1	.2
127 CH GOD (CLEVE)	4	303	379*	.3	.6
145 CH GOD PROPHCY	2	69	86*	.1	.1

NA–Not applicable NR–Not reported *Total adherents estimated from known number of communicant, confirmed, full members. - Represents a percent less than 0.1. Percentages may not total due to rounding.
[1]See Appendix E [2]See Appendix F [3]See Appendix G Lines in *italic* represent a breakdown of Catholic rites or Friends affiliations. They are included in their respective denominational total.

Table 4. Churches and Church Membership by County and Denomination: 1990

County and Denomination		Number of churches	Communicant, confirmed, full members	Total adherents		
				Number	Percent of total population	Percent of total adherents
151	L-D SAINTS	3	NA	1,278	1.0	2.2
165	CH OF NAZARENE	2	190	240	.2	.4
167	CHS OF CHRIST	9	1,163	1,567	1.2	2.7
193	EPISCOPAL	4	841	1,102	.9	1.9
207	E.L.C.A.	1	264	363	.3	.6
223	FREE WILL BAPT	1	33	41*		.1
246	GREEK ORTHODOX	1	NR	NR	-	-
283	LUTH—MO SYNOD	4	804	1,058	.8	1.8
339	PENT CH OF GOD	1	35	76	.1	.1
355	PRESB CH (USA)	5	1,171	1,464*	1.2	2.5
356	PRESB CH AMER	3	860	915	.7	1.6
403	SALVATION ARMY	1	96	97	.1	.2
413	S.D.A.	2	355	444*	.3	.8
419	SO BAPT CONV	28	21,296	26,618*	21.0	45.1
435	UNITARIAN-UNIV	1	28	28	-	-
449	UN METHODIST	14	7,559	9,448*	7.4	16.0
467	WESLEYAN	1	4	6	-	-
469	WELS	1	53	76	.1	.1
497	BLACK BAPT EST[2]	NA	3,523	4,403*	3.5	7.5
498	INDEP.CHARIS.[3]	1	NA	350	.3	.6
499	INDEP.NON-CHAR[3]	2	NA	1,800	1.4	3.1
BRADFORD		**41**	**8,546**	**11,277***	**50.1**	**100.0**
053	ASSEMB OF GOD	1	37	55	.2	.5
081	CATHOLIC	1	NA	345	1.5	3.1
081d	*LATIN*	*1*	*NA*	*345*	*1.5*	*3.1*
097	CHR CHS&CHS CR	2	210	258*	1.1	2.3
127	CH GOD (CLEVE)	3	259	319*	1.4	2.8
145	CH GOD PROPHCY	2	69	85*	.4	.8
151	L-D SAINTS	1	NA	260	1.2	2.3
167	CHS OF CHRIST	3	108	142	.6	1.3
193	EPISCOPAL	1	89	109	.5	1.0
355	PRESB CH (USA)	2	381	469*	2.1	4.2
361	PRIM BAPT ASCS	2	69	85*	.4	.8
413	S.D.A.	1	51	63*	.3	.6
419	SO BAPT CONV	15	5,102	6,278*	27.9	55.7
449	UN METHODIST	6	934	1,149*	5.1	10.2
469	WELS	1	67	88	.4	.8
496	JEWISH EST[1]	0	NA	132	.6	1.2
497	BLACK BAPT EST[2]	NA	1,170	1,440*	6.4	12.8
BREVARD		**244**	**77,865**	**154,836***	**38.8**	**100.0**
001	ADVENT CHR CH	1	31	38*	-	-
005	AME ZION	1	263	263	.1	.2
019	AMER BAPT USA	1	50	61*	-	-
053	ASSEMB OF GOD	10	1,119	1,607	.4	1.0
055	AS REF PRES CH	2	302	401	.1	.3
081	CATHOLIC	13	NA	43,252	10.8	27.9
081d	*LATIN*	*13*	*NA*	*43,252*	*10.8*	*27.9*
089	CHR & MISS AL	3	118	205	.1	.1
093	CHR CH (DISC)	2	445	488	.1	.3
097	CHR CHS&CHS CR	8	1,627	1,973*	.5	1.3
105	CHRISTIAN REF	1	87	128	-	.1
111	CH CR,SCIENTST	4	NR	NR	-	-
123	CH GOD (ANDER)	2	139	176	-	.1
127	CH GOD (CLEVE)	15	1,659	2,012*	.5	1.3
145	CH GOD PROPHCY	3	103	125*	-	.1
146	CH GOD MTN ASM	1	153	186*	-	.1
151	L-D SAINTS	6	NA	2,622	.7	1.7
165	CH OF NAZARENE	14	1,175	1,861	.5	1.2
167	CHS OF CHRIST	13	1,820	2,345	.6	1.5
179	CONSRV BAPT	1	NR	NR	-	-
193	EPISCOPAL	11	3,677	5,315	1.3	3.4
203	EVAN FREE CH	1	53	107	-	.1
207	E.L.C.A.	13	3,397	4,432	1.1	2.9
223	FREE WILL BAPT	5	463	561*	.1	.4
226	FRIENDS-USA	1	15	28	-	-
226d	*FGC & FUM*	*1*	*15*	*28*	-	-
246	GREEK ORTHODOX	1	NR	NR	-	-
283	LUTH—MO SYNOD	6	2,214	2,813	.7	1.8
331	ORTH CH IN AM	1	NR	NR	-	-
349	PENT HOLINESS	1	137	166*	-	.1
353	CHR BRETHREN	3	148	210	.1	.1
355	PRESB CH (USA)	12	5,002	6,065*	1.5	3.9
356	PRESB CH AMER	2	443	559	.1	.4
361	PRIM BAPT ASCS	1	10	12*	-	-
403	SALVATION ARMY	3	219	226	.1	.1
413	S.D.A.	6	772	936*	.2	.6
419	SO BAPT CONV	35	27,637	33,512*	8.4	21.6
435	UNITARIAN-UNIV	2	176	222	.1	.1
443	UN C OF CHRIST	4	857	1,039*	.3	.7
449	UN METHODIST	21	15,316	18,572*	4.7	12.0
467	WESLEYAN	2	52	111	-	.1
469	WELS	2	114	144	-	.1
496	JEWISH EST[1]	3	NA	3,000	.8	1.9
497	BLACK BAPT EST[2]	NA	8,072	9,788*	2.5	6.3
498	INDEP.CHARIS.[3]	3	NA	2,950		1.9

County and Denomination		Number of churches	Communicant, confirmed, full members	Total adherents		
				Number	Percent of total population	Percent of total adherents
499	INDEP.NON-CHAR[3]	4	NA	6,325	1.6	4.1
BROWARD		**422**	**161,719**	**615,880***	**49.1**	**100.0**
001	ADVENT CHR CH	1	16	19*	-	-
005	AME ZION	3	515	665	.1	.1
019	AMER BAPT USA	2	870	1,039*	.1	.2
022	EASTERN ORTH	1	54	54	-	-
039	AP CHR CH(NAZ)	2	64	76*	-	-
040	AP CHR CH-AMER	1	42	72	-	-
053	ASSEMB OF GOD	21	2,529	3,644	.3	.6
081	CATHOLIC	44	NA	230,079	18.3	37.4
081b	*BYZAN RUTH*	*1*	*NA*	*200*		
081d	*LATIN*	*43*	*NA*	*229,879*	*18.3*	*37.3*
089	CHR & MISS AL	6	140	363	-	.1
093	CHR CH (DISC)	8	2,614	3,573	.3	.6
097	CHR CHS&CHS CR	8	834	996*	.1	.2
105	CHRISTIAN REF	1	171	261	-	-
111	CH CR,SCIENTST	7	NR	NR	-	-
123	CH GOD (ANDER)	8	584	926	.1	.2
127	CH GOD (CLEVE)	28	3,374	4,031*	.3	.7
145	CH GOD PROPHCY	7	241	288*	-	-
151	L-D SAINTS	8	NA	3,048	.2	.5
165	CH OF NAZARENE	7	1,202	1,900	.2	.3
167	CHS OF CHRIST	19	5,486	7,170	.6	1.2
175	CONGR CHR CHS	1	360	430*	-	.1
193	EPISCOPAL	18	5,966	8,591	.7	1.4
195	ESTONIAN ELC	2	118	141*	-	-
203	EVAN FREE CH	1	143	275	-	-
207	E.L.C.A.	14	5,193	6,956	.6	1.1
216	EVAN PRESBY CH	1	1,116	1,227	.1	.2
221	FREE METHODIST	4	158	180	-	-
223	FREE WILL BAPT	2	351	419*	-	.1
226	FRIENDS-USA	1	0	7	-	-
226d	*FGC & FUM*	*1*	*0*	*7*	-	-
246	GREEK ORTHODOX	2	NR	NR	-	-
259	IFCA	3	NR	NR	-	-
263	INT FOURSQ GOS	1	0	0*	-	-
283	LUTH—MO SYNOD	13	3,986	5,324	.4	.9
313	N AM BAPT CONF	1	NR	0*	-	-
329	OPEN BIBLE STD	1	NR	NR	-	-
331	ORTH CH IN AM	3	NR	NR	-	-
349	PENT HOLINESS	2	127	152*	-	-
353	CHR BRETHREN	4	460	750	.1	.1
355	PRESB CH (USA)	17	6,960	8,315*	.7	1.4
356	PRESB CH AMER	7	10,151	10,856	.9	1.8
371	REF CH IN AM	3	417	744	.1	.1
397	ROMANIAN ORTH	1	NR	NR	-	-
403	SALVATION ARMY	1	182	205	-	-
413	S.D.A.	13	3,445	4,116*	.3	.7
419	SO BAPT CONV	41	34,088	40,725*	3.2	6.6
435	UNITARIAN-UNIV	2	274	332	-	.1
443	UN C OF CHRIST	4	951	1,136*	.1	.2
449	UN METHODIST	29	18,475	22,072*	1.8	3.6
467	WESLEYAN	3	76	254	-	-
469	WELS	2	282	367	-	.1
496	JEWISH EST[1]	34	NA	176,000	14.0	28.6
497	BLACK BAPT EST[2]	NA	49,704	59,382*	4.7	9.6
498	INDEP.CHARIS.[3]	3	NA	2,720	.2	.4
499	INDEP.NON-CHAR[3]	6	NA	6,000	.5	1.0
CALHOUN		**31**	**3,829**	**5,282***	**48.0**	**100.0**
001	ADVENT CHR CH	2	26	33*	.3	.6
053	ASSEMB OF GOD	3	132	188	1.7	3.6
081	CATHOLIC	1	NA	61	.6	1.2
081d	*LATIN*	*1*	*NA*	*61*	*.6*	*1.2*
127	CH GOD (CLEVE)	3	84	105*	1.0	2.0
151	L-D SAINTS	1	NA	309	2.8	5.9
165	CH OF NAZARENE	1	50	97	.9	1.8
223	FREE WILL BAPT	2	310	389*	3.5	7.4
285	MENNONITE CH	2	175	271	2.5	5.1
349	PENT HOLINESS	4	472	592*	5.4	11.2
355	PRESB CH (USA)	1	12	15*	.1	.3
419	SO BAPT CONV	8	1,724	2,163*	19.6	41.0
449	UN METHODIST	3	506	635*	5.8	12.0
497	BLACK BAPT EST[2]	NA	338	424*	3.9	8.0
CHARLOTTE		**62**	**16,164**	**33,349***	**30.1**	**100.0**
053	ASSEMB OF GOD	3	735	1,705	1.5	5.1
081	CATHOLIC	4	NA	11,937	10.8	35.8
081d	*LATIN*	*4*	*NA*	*11,937*	*10.8*	*35.8*
089	CHR & MISS AL	3	336	804	.7	2.4
097	CHR CHS&CHS CR	3	874	995*	.9	3.0
111	CH CR,SCIENTST	1	NR	NR	-	-
123	CH GOD (ANDER)	1	25	30	-	.1
127	CH GOD (CLEVE)	4	246	280*	.3	.8
145	CH GOD PROPHCY	1	34	39*	-	.1

NA–Not applicable   NR–Not reported   *Total adherents estimated from known number of communicant, confirmed, full members.   - Represents a percent less than 0.1.   Percentages may not total due to rounding.
[1]See Appendix E   [2]See Appendix F   [3]See Appendix G   Lines in *italic* represent a breakdown of Catholic rites or Friends affiliations. They are included in their respective denominational total.

Table 4. Churches and Church Membership by County and Denomination: 1990

County and Denomination	Number of churches	Communicant, confirmed, full members	Total adherents Number	Percent of total population	Percent of total adherents
146 CH GOD MTN ASM	1	4	5*	-	-
151 L-D SAINTS	1	NA	421	.4	1.3
165 CH OF NAZARENE	2	147	425	.4	1.3
167 CHS OF CHRIST	3	138	182	.2	.5
193 EPISCOPAL	2	839	1,216	1.1	3.6
207 E.L.C.A.	5	1,381	1,627	1.5	4.9
246 GREEK ORTHODOX	1	NR	NR	-	-
283 LUTH—MO SYNOD	3	629	675	.6	2.0
355 PRESB CH (USA)	3	1,973	2,246*	2.0	6.7
356 PRESB CH AMER	1	31	31	-	.1
403 SALVATION ARMY	1	47	50	-	.1
413 S.D.A.	2	561	639*	.6	1.9
419 SO BAPT CONV	6	3,155	3,592*	3.2	10.8
435 UNITARIAN-UNIV	1	72	79	.1	.2
443 UN C OF CHRIST	2	704	802*	.7	2.4
449 UN METHODIST	7	3,350	3,814*	3.4	11.4
496 JEWISH EST[1]	0	NA	400	.4	1.2
497 BLACK BAPT EST[2]	NA	883	1,005*	.9	3.0
499 INDEP.NON-CHAR[3]	1	NA	350	.3	1.0
CITRUS	**75**	**16,754**	**37,554***	**40.2**	**100.0**
053 ASSEMB OF GOD	4	687	1,488	1.6	4.0
057 BAPT GEN CONF	1	57	66*	.1	.2
081 CATHOLIC	6	NA	16,277	17.4	43.3
081d LATIN	6	NA	16,277	17.4	43.3
097 CHR CHS&CHS CR	4	495	574*	.6	1.5
111 CH CR,SCIENTST	1	NR	NR	-	-
123 CH GOD (ANDER)	2	140	148	.2	.4
127 CH GOD (CLEVE)	5	954	1,106*	1.2	2.9
146 CH GOD MTN ASM	1	20	23*	-	.1
151 L-D SAINTS	2	NA	742	.8	2.0
165 CH OF NAZARENE	1	221	388	.4	1.0
167 CHS OF CHRIST	9	405	528	.6	1.4
175 CONGR CHR CHS	1	150	174*	.2	.5
193 EPISCOPAL	2	837	958	1.0	2.6
207 E.L.C.A.	3	1,027	1,158	1.2	3.1
246 GREEK ORTHODOX	1	NR	NR	-	-
263 INT FOURSQ GOS	2	8	9*	-	-
283 LUTH—MO SYNOD	1	334	463	.5	1.2
355 PRESB CH (USA)	2	871	1,010*	1.1	2.7
356 PRESB CH AMER	1	377	563	.6	1.5
413 S.D.A.	3	319	370*	.4	1.0
419 SO BAPT CONV	16	6,132	7,107*	7.6	18.9
449 UN METHODIST	6	3,124	3,621*	3.9	9.6
469 WELS	1	137	149	.2	.4
496 JEWISH EST[1]	0	NA	100	.1	.3
497 BLACK BAPT EST[2]	NA	459	532*	.6	1.4
CLAY	**85**	**28,551**	**51,556***	**48.6**	**100.0**
053 ASSEMB OF GOD	5	765	1,570	1.5	3.0
057 BAPT GEN CONF	1	39	50*	-	.1
081 CATHOLIC	4	NA	11,661	11.0	22.6
081d LATIN	4	NA	11,661	11.0	22.6
089 CHR & MISS AL	2	209	367	.3	.7
097 CHR CHS&CHS CR	3	340	437*	.4	.8
123 CH GOD (ANDER)	1	99	113	.1	.2
127 CH GOD (CLEVE)	6	289	372*	.4	.7
151 L-D SAINTS	2	NA	1,159	1.1	2.2
157 CH OF BRETHREN	1	86	111*	.1	.2
165 CH OF NAZARENE	1	77	107	.1	.2
167 CHS OF CHRIST	6	618	822	.8	1.6
193 EPISCOPAL	5	1,019	1,512	1.4	2.9
203 EVAN FREE CH	1	35	125	.1	.2
207 E.L.C.A.	1	799	1,187	1.1	2.3
223 FREE WILL BAPT	1	32	41*	-	.1
283 LUTH—MO SYNOD	1	173	214	.2	.4
325 OLD REG BAPT	1	40	51*	-	.1
349 PENT HOLINESS	1	62	80*	.1	.2
353 CHR BRETHREN	1	178	230	.2	.4
355 PRESB CH (USA)	4	1,166	1,499*	1.4	2.9
356 PRESB CH AMER	1	271	384	.4	.7
419 SO BAPT CONV	27	16,795	21,597*	20.4	41.9
435 UNITARIAN-UNIV	1	20	20	-	-
443 UN C OF CHRIST	2	153	197*	.2	.4
449 UN METHODIST	6	3,869	4,975*	4.7	9.6
496 JEWISH EST[1]	0	NA	853	.8	1.7
497 BLACK BAPT EST[2]	NA	1,417	1,822*	1.7	3.5
COLLIER	**83**	**22,869**	**57,296***	**37.7**	**100.0**
053 ASSEMB OF GOD	6	507	1,068	.7	1.9
081 CATHOLIC	9	NA	26,737	17.6	46.7
081d LATIN	9	NA	26,737	17.6	46.7
089 CHR & MISS AL	1	26	67	-	.1
093 CHR CH (DISC)	1	170	214	.1	.4
097 CHR CHS&CHS CR	2	245	292*	.2	.5
111 CH CR,SCIENTST	1	NR	NR		

County and Denomination	Number of churches	Communicant, confirmed, full members	Total adherents Number	Percent of total population	Percent of total adherents
127 CH GOD (CLEVE)	6	743	884*	.6	1.5
151 L-D SAINTS	2	NA	498	.3	.9
165 CH OF NAZARENE	3	232	405	.3	.7
167 CHS OF CHRIST	3	258	329	.2	.6
193 EPISCOPAL	5	1,934	2,738	1.8	4.8
207 E.L.C.A.	3	1,019	1,306	.9	2.3
209 EVAN LUTH SYN	1	136	169	.1	.3
221 FREE METHODIST	1	69	130	.1	.2
246 GREEK ORTHODOX	1	NR	NR	-	-
283 LUTH—MO SYNOD	4	755	916	.6	1.6
285 MENNONITE CH	1	22	41	-	.1
331 ORTH CH IN AM	1	NR	NR	-	-
339 PENT CH OF GOD	1	34	77	.1	.1
355 PRESB CH (USA)	5	3,869	4,604*	3.0	8.0
356 PRESB CH AMER	2	476	629	.4	1.1
403 SALVATION ARMY	1	66	68	-	.1
413 S.D.A.	2	250	297*	.2	.5
419 SO BAPT CONV	9	4,790	5,700*	3.7	9.9
435 UNITARIAN-UNIV	1	100	106	.1	.2
443 UN C OF CHRIST	3	1,299	1,546*	1.0	2.7
449 UN METHODIST	6	4,004	4,765*	3.1	8.3
467 WESLEYAN	1	70	274	.2	.5
496 JEWISH EST[1]	0	NA	750	.5	1.3
497 BLACK BAPT EST[2]	NA	1,795	2,136*	1.4	3.7
499 INDEP.NON-CHAR[3]	1	NA	550	.4	1.0
COLUMBIA	**71**	**13,953**	**20,227***	**47.5**	**100.0**
001 ADVENT CHR CH	5	207	265*	.6	1.3
053 ASSEMB OF GOD	4	150	209	.5	1.0
081 CATHOLIC	1	NA	1,135	2.7	5.6
081d LATIN	1	NA	1,135	2.7	5.6
097 CHR CHS&CHS CR	1	150	192*	.5	.9
111 CH CR,SCIENTST	1	NR	NR	-	-
127 CH GOD (CLEVE)	5	562	719*	1.7	3.6
145 CH GOD PROPHCY	1	34	44*	.1	.2
151 L-D SAINTS	2	NA	977	2.3	4.8
165 CH OF NAZARENE	2	184	378	.9	1.9
167 CHS OF CHRIST	5	341	448	1.1	2.2
193 EPISCOPAL	1	133	205	.5	1.0
207 E.L.C.A.	2	109	141	.3	.7
283 LUTH—MO SYNOD	1	175	231	.5	1.1
339 PENT CH OF GOD	3	71	137	.3	.7
349 PENT HOLINESS	1	37	47*	.1	.2
355 PRESB CH (USA)	2	641	820*	1.9	4.1
361 PRIM BAPT ASCS	1	24	31*	.1	.2
413 S.D.A.	2	112	143*	.3	.7
419 SO BAPT CONV	20	7,466	9,553*	22.4	47.2
449 UN METHODIST	11	1,959	2,507*	5.9	12.4
497 BLACK BAPT EST[2]	NA	1,598	2,045*	4.8	10.1
DADE	**766**	**251,704**	**900,133***	**46.5**	**100.0**
001 ADVENT CHR CH	1	83	102*	-	-
005 AME ZION	5	547	946	-	.1
019 AMER BAPT USA	8	2,442	3,015*	.2	.3
049 ARMEN AP CH AM	1	200	500	-	.1
053 ASSEMB OF GOD	44	5,836	8,606	.4	1.0
057 BAPT GEN CONF	3	174	215*	-	-
075 BRETHREN IN CR	4	161	216	-	-
081 CATHOLIC	65	NA	364,257	18.8	40.5
081b BYZAN RUTH	1	NA	262	-	-
081d LATIN	61	NA	361,674	18.7	40.2
081e MARONITE	1	NA	1,326	.1	.1
081f MELKITE-GK	1	NA	750	-	-
081h UKRAINIAN	1	NA	245	-	-
089 CHR & MISS AL	15	798	1,468	.1	.2
093 CHR CH (DISC)	7	913	1,404	.1	.2
097 CHR CHS&CHS CR	4	319	394*	-	-
105 CHRISTIAN REF	3	293	452	-	.1
111 CH CR,SCIENTST	10	NR	NR	-	-
123 CH GOD (ANDER)	6	661	765	-	.1
127 CH GOD (CLEVE)	34	3,486	4,303*	.2	.5
145 CH GOD PROPHCY	18	628	775*	-	.1
151 L-D SAINTS	14	NA	4,802	.2	.5
157 CH OF BRETHREN	2	124	153*	-	-
165 CH OF NAZARENE	22	3,685	5,011	.3	.6
167 CHS OF CHRIST	25	3,149	4,189	.2	.5
179 CONSRV BAPT	2	NR	NR	-	-
193 EPISCOPAL	29	11,915	16,741	.9	1.9
207 E.L.C.A.	24	6,423	8,586	.4	1.0
216 EVAN PRESBY CH	1	206	206	-	-
221 FREE METHODIST	11	329	592	-	.1
223 FREE WILL BAPT	4	466	575*	-	.1
226 FRIENDS-USA	2	181	233*	-	-
226d FGC & FUM	1	123	161	-	-
226e FUM	1	58	72*	-	-
246 GREEK ORTHODOX	4	NR	NR	-	-
249 AP CATH ASSYR	0	15	47	-	-

NA–Not applicable   NR–Not reported   *Total adherents estimated from known number of communicant, confirmed, full members.   - Represents a percent less than 0.1.   Percentages may not total due to rounding.
[1]See Appendix E   [2]See Appendix F   [3]See Appendix G   Lines in *italic* represent a breakdown of Catholic rites or Friends affiliations. They are included in their respective denominational total.

Table 4. Churches and Church Membership by County and Denomination: 1990

County and Denomination	Number of churches	Communicant, confirmed, full members	Total adherents Number	Percent of total population	Percent of total adherents
259 IFCA	4	NR	NR	-	-
263 INT FOURSQ GOS	9	269	332*	-	-
274 LAT EVAN LUTH	1	92	94	-	-
283 LUTH—MO SYNOD	10	1,846	2,558	.1	.3
285 MENNONITE CH	5	128	229	-	-
295 MORAV CH-SOUTH	1	283	492	-	.1
329 OPEN BIBLE STD	5	NR	NR	-	-
331 ORTH CH IN AM	2	NR	NR	-	-
349 PENT HOLINESS	6	703	868*	-	.1
353 CHR BRETHREN	7	532	1,010	.1	.1
355 PRESB CH (USA)	24	5,410	6,678*	.3	.7
356 PRESB CH AMER	13	5,889	6,615	.3	.7
371 REF CH IN AM	1	69	117	-	-
403 SALVATION ARMY	3	478	501	-	.1
413 S.D.A.	38	11,128	13,737*	.7	1.5
415 S-D BAPTIST GC	1	31	38*	-	-
419 SO BAPT CONV	92	53,127	65,582*	3.4	7.3
435 UNITARIAN-UNIV	2	289	374	-	-
443 UN C OF CHRIST	16	6,387	7,884*	.4	.9
449 UN METHODIST	54	19,589	24,182*	1.2	2.7
467 WESLEYAN	1	62	90	-	-
469 WELS	2	97	132	-	-
496 JEWISH EST[1]	84	NA	201,800	10.4	22.4
497 BLACK BAPT EST[2]	NA	102,261	126,236*	6.5	14.0
498 INDEP.CHARIS.[3]	10	NA	8,146	.4	.9
499 INDEP.NON-CHAR[3]	7	NA	3,885	.2	.4
DE SOTO	**36**	**7,277**	**10,228***	**42.9**	**100.0**
053 ASSEMB OF GOD	2	216	385	1.6	3.8
081 CATHOLIC	1	NA	995	4.2	9.7
081d LATIN	*1*	*NA*	*995*	*4.2*	*9.7*
097 CHR CHS&CHS CR	1	125	153*	.6	1.5
127 CH GOD (CLEVE)	5	314	384*	1.6	3.8
145 CH GOD PROPHCY	1	34	42*	.2	.4
151 L-D SAINTS	1	NA	120	.5	1.2
157 CH OF BRETHREN	1	59	72*	.3	.7
165 CH OF NAZARENE	1	143	238	1.0	2.3
167 CHS OF CHRIST	3	167	216	.9	2.1
193 EPISCOPAL	1	91	121	.5	1.2
283 LUTH—MO SYNOD	1	74	79	.3	.8
285 MENNONITE CH	1	20	38	.2	.4
355 PRESB CH (USA)	1	339	415*	1.7	4.1
413 S.D.A.	1	82	100*	.4	1.0
419 SO BAPT CONV	10	3,688	4,514*	18.9	44.1
449 UN METHODIST	5	1,165	1,426*	6.0	13.9
497 BLACK BAPT EST[2]	NA	760	930*	3.9	9.1
DIXIE	**30**	**3,927**	**5,079***	**48.0**	**100.0**
053 ASSEMB OF GOD	2	67	92	.9	1.8
081 CATHOLIC	1	NA	148	1.4	2.9
081d LATIN	*1*	*NA*	*148*	*1.4*	*2.9*
127 CH GOD (CLEVE)	3	176	219*	2.1	4.3
167 CHS OF CHRIST	2	107	139	1.3	2.7
339 PENT CH OF GOD	1	30	70	.7	1.4
349 PENT HOLINESS	3	161	200*	1.9	3.9
413 S.D.A.	1	58	72*	.7	1.4
419 SO BAPT CONV	14	2,854	3,549*	33.5	69.9
449 UN METHODIST	3	286	356*	3.4	7.0
497 BLACK BAPT EST[2]	NA	188	234*	2.2	4.6
DUVAL	**486**	**221,816**	**352,315***	**52.4**	**100.0**
001 ADVENT CHR CH	5	280	354*	.1	.1
005 AME ZION	3	248	248	-	.1
019 AMER BAPT USA	2	800	1,011*	.2	.3
053 ASSEMB OF GOD	30	5,865	7,347	1.1	2.1
059 BAPT MISS ASSN	2	363	459*	.1	.1
081 CATHOLIC	22	NA	44,875	6.7	12.7
081d LATIN	*22*	*NA*	*44,875*	*6.7*	*12.7*
089 CHR & MISS AL	4	161	307	-	.1
093 CHR CH (DISC)	11	2,126	2,845	.4	.8
097 CHR CHS&CHS CR	9	2,274	2,875*	.4	.8
105 CHRISTIAN REF	2	106	154	-	-
111 CH CR,SCIENTST	4	NR	NR	-	-
123 CH GOD (ANDER)	8	959	1,142	.2	.3
127 CH GOD (CLEVE)	33	3,908	4,940*	.7	1.4
145 CH GOD PROPHCY	13	447	565*	.1	.2
151 L-D SAINTS	11	NA	5,151	.8	1.5
157 CH OF BRETHREN	1	59	75*	-	-
165 CH OF NAZARENE	11	1,559	2,022	.3	.6
167 CHS OF CHRIST	31	5,066	6,467	1.0	1.8
193 EPISCOPAL	22	9,110	14,340	2.1	4.1
203 EVAN FREE CH	1	125	230	-	.1
207 E.L.C.A.	10	3,453	4,584	.7	1.3
223 FREE WILL BAPT	5	175	221*	-	.1
226 FRIENDS-USA	1	11	25	-	-
226d FGC & FUM	*1*	*11*	*25*	-	-

County and Denomination	Number of churches	Communicant, confirmed, full members	Total adherents Number	Percent of total population	Percent of total adherents
246 GREEK ORTHODOX	1	NR	NR	-	-
263 INT FOURSQ GOS	1	311	393*	.1	.1
283 LUTH—MO SYNOD	5	1,557	2,023	.3	.6
329 OPEN BIBLE STD	2	NR	NR	-	-
331 ORTH CH IN AM	1	NR	NR	-	-
339 PENT CH OF GOD	1	0	27	-	-
349 PENT HOLINESS	5	920	1,163*	.2	.3
353 CHR BRETHREN	2	80	110	-	-
355 PRESB CH (USA)	24	9,567	12,094*	1.8	3.4
356 PRESB CH AMER	4	443	594	.1	.2
361 PRIM BAPT ASCS	6	150	190*	-	.1
403 SALVATION ARMY	2	215	257	-	.1
413 S.D.A.	6	1,621	2,049*	.3	.6
419 SO BAPT CONV	115	103,301	130,584*	19.4	37.1
435 UNITARIAN-UNIV	1	216	253	-	.1
443 UN C OF CHRIST	1	557	704*	.1	.2
449 UN METHODIST	48	23,307	29,463*	4.4	8.4
467 WESLEYAN	1	35	210	-	.1
469 WELS	2	268	440	.1	.1
496 JEWISH EST[1]	5	NA	5,418	.8	1.5
497 BLACK BAPT EST[2]	NA	42,113	53,236*	7.9	15.1
498 INDEP.CHARIS.[3]	2	NA	1,900	.3	.5
499 INDEP.NON-CHAR[3]	10	NA	10,970	1.6	3.1
ESCAMBIA	**230**	**90,175**	**136,386***	**51.9**	**100.0**
005 AME ZION	11	2,990	3,990	1.5	2.9
019 AMER BAPT USA	1	37	46*	-	-
053 ASSEMB OF GOD	19	2,666	3,996	1.5	2.9
059 BAPT MISS ASSN	5	286	358*	.1	.3
081 CATHOLIC	18	NA	18,832	7.2	13.8
081d LATIN	*18*	*NA*	*18,832*	*7.2*	*13.8*
089 CHR & MISS AL	3	123	203	.1	.1
093 CHR CH (DISC)	3	394	509	.2	.4
097 CHR CHS&CHS CR	3	223	279*	.1	.2
111 CH CR,SCIENTST	1	NR	NR	-	-
123 CH GOD (ANDER)	1	14	40	-	-
127 CH GOD (CLEVE)	5	641	801*	.3	.6
143 CG IN CR(MENN)	1	188	235*	.1	.2
145 CH GOD PROPHCY	1	34	43*	-	-
151 L-D SAINTS	3	NA	1,308	.5	1.0
165 CH OF NAZARENE	2	501	752	.3	.6
167 CHS OF CHRIST	16	2,710	3,490	1.3	2.6
193 EPISCOPAL	7	3,876	4,514	1.7	3.3
207 E.L.C.A.	1	570	724	.3	.5
223 FREE WILL BAPT	5	637	796*	.3	.6
246 GREEK ORTHODOX	1	NR	NR	-	-
266 INTRSTAT & ASC	1	89	111*	-	.1
283 LUTH—MO SYNOD	7	1,990	2,675	1.0	2.0
285 MENNONITE CH	1	13	23	-	-
286 E.PA MENNONITE	1	39	49*	-	-
329 OPEN BIBLE STD	2	NR	NR	-	-
355 PRESB CH (USA)	3	2,225	2,781*	1.1	2.0
356 PRESB CH AMER	4	1,197	1,300	.5	1.0
361 PRIM BAPT ASCS	4	144	180*	.1	.1
403 SALVATION ARMY	1	114	123	-	.1
413 S.D.A.	1	127	159*	.1	.1
419 SO BAPT CONV	62	43,348	54,189*	20.6	39.7
435 UNITARIAN-UNIV	1	93	118	-	.1
443 UN C OF CHRIST	1	249	311*	.1	.2
449 UN METHODIST	27	11,097	13,872*	5.3	10.2
467 WESLEYAN	2	40	247	.1	.2
496 JEWISH EST[1]	2	NA	581	.2	.4
497 BLACK BAPT EST[2]	NA	13,520	16,901*	6.4	12.4
499 INDEP.NON-CHAR[3]	3	NA	1,850	.7	1.4
FLAGLER	**21**	**4,452**	**11,969***	**41.7**	**100.0**
053 ASSEMB OF GOD	1	260	450	1.6	3.8
081 CATHOLIC	4	NA	6,045	21.1	50.5
081d LATIN	*4*	*NA*	*6,045*	*21.1*	*50.5*
089 CHR & MISS AL	1	0	55	.2	.5
127 CH GOD (CLEVE)	2	127	149*	.5	1.2
151 L-D SAINTS	1	NA	161	.6	1.3
165 CH OF NAZARENE	1	13	19	.1	.2
193 EPISCOPAL	1	263	663	2.3	5.5
207 E.L.C.A.	1	470	520	1.8	4.3
283 LUTH—MO SYNOD	1	77	95	.3	.8
413 S.D.A.	0	47	55*	.2	.5
419 SO BAPT CONV	5	1,591	1,871*	6.5	15.6
449 UN METHODIST	3	1,111	1,306*	4.6	10.9
497 BLACK BAPT EST[2]	NA	493	580*	2.0	4.8
FRANKLIN	**21**	**2,406**	**3,662***	**40.8**	**100.0**
053 ASSEMB OF GOD	3	142	426	4.8	11.6
081 CATHOLIC	2	NA	465	5.2	12.7
081d LATIN	*2*	*NA*	*465*	*5.2*	*12.7*
127 CH GOD (CLEVE)	3	180	220*	2.5	6.0

NA–Not applicable   NR–Not reported   *Total adherents estimated from known number of communicant, confirmed, full members.   - Represents a percent less than 0.1.   Percentages may not total due to rounding.
[1]See Appendix E   [2]See Appendix F   [3]See Appendix G   Lines in *italic* represent a breakdown of Catholic rites or Friends affiliations. They are included in their respective denominational total.

Table 4. Churches and Church Membership by County and Denomination: 1990

County and Denomination	Number of churches	Communicant, confirmed, full members	Total adherents Number	Percent of total population	Percent of total adherents
193 EPISCOPAL	2	125	146	1.6	4.0
349 PENT HOLINESS	2	158	193*	2.2	5.3
419 SO BAPT CONV	5	934	1,144*	12.8	31.2
449 UN METHODIST	3	625	765*	8.5	20.9
467 WESLEYAN	1	15	25	.3	.7
497 BLACK BAPT EST[2]	NA	227	278*	3.1	7.6
GADSDEN	**56**	**13,478**	**18,531***	**45.1**	**100.0**
053 ASSEMB OF GOD	7	266	357	.9	1.9
081 CATHOLIC	2	NA	553	1.3	3.0
081d *LATIN*	*2*	*NA*	*553*	*1.3*	*3.0*
145 CH GOD PROPHCY	3	103	134*	.3	.7
151 L-D SAINTS	1	NA	205	.5	1.1
167 CHS OF CHRIST	3	89	119	.3	.6
193 EPISCOPAL	2	133	192	.5	1.0
223 FREE WILL BAPT	1	20	26*	.1	.1
329 OPEN BIBLE STD	1	NR	NR	-	-
349 PENT HOLINESS	3	245	318*	.8	1.7
355 PRESB CH (USA)	4	601	781*	1.9	4.2
356 PRESB CH AMER	2	143	154	.4	.8
413 S.D.A.	1	34	44*	.1	.2
419 SO BAPT CONV	18	5,813	7,551*	18.4	40.7
449 UN METHODIST	8	1,647	2,139*	5.2	11.5
496 JEWISH EST[1]	0	NA	264	.6	1.4
497 BLACK BAPT EST[2]	NA	4,384	5,694*	13.9	30.7
GILCHRIST	**19**	**3,329**	**4,202***	**43.5**	**100.0**
001 ADVENT CHR CH	1	25	31*	.3	.7
127 CH GOD (CLEVE)	2	108	133*	1.4	3.2
165 CH OF NAZARENE	1	25	73	.8	1.7
167 CHS OF CHRIST	5	245	350	3.6	8.3
361 PRIM BAPT ASCS	1	16	20*	.2	.5
419 SO BAPT CONV	8	2,583	3,191*	33.0	75.9
449 UN METHODIST	1	159	196*	2.0	4.7
497 BLACK BAPT EST[2]	NA	168	208*	2.2	5.0
GLADES	**9**	**1,329**	**1,912***	**25.2**	**100.0**
081 CATHOLIC	1	NA	272	3.6	14.2
081d *LATIN*	*1*	*NA*	*272*	*3.6*	*14.2*
097 CHR CHS&CHS CR	1	60	74*	1.0	3.9
127 CH GOD (CLEVE)	1	34	42*	.6	2.2
145 CH GOD PROPHCY	1	34	42*	.6	2.2
419 SO BAPT CONV	4	851	1,050*	13.8	54.9
449 UN METHODIST	1	162	200*	2.6	10.5
497 BLACK BAPT EST[2]	NA	188	232*	3.1	12.1
GULF	**30**	**4,580**	**5,975***	**51.9**	**100.0**
053 ASSEMB OF GOD	3	294	399	3.5	6.7
081 CATHOLIC	2	NA	226	2.0	3.8
081d *LATIN*	*2*	*NA*	*226*	*2.0*	*3.8*
093 CHR CH (DISC)	1	80	111	1.0	1.9
127 CH GOD (CLEVE)	2	52	64*	.6	1.1
165 CH OF NAZARENE	1	18	27	.2	.5
167 CHS OF CHRIST	2	68	95	.8	1.6
193 EPISCOPAL	2	141	228	2.0	3.8
259 IFCA	1	NR	NR	-	-
349 PENT HOLINESS	1	114	140*	1.2	2.3
355 PRESB CH (USA)	2	57	70*	.6	1.2
419 SO BAPT CONV	9	2,575	3,164*	27.5	53.0
449 UN METHODIST	4	740	909*	7.9	15.2
497 BLACK BAPT EST[2]	NA	441	542*	4.7	9.1
HAMILTON	**32**	**4,210**	**5,806***	**53.1**	**100.0**
001 ADVENT CHR CH	1	26	33*	.3	.6
053 ASSEMB OF GOD	2	49	74	.7	1.3
081 CATHOLIC	1	NA	70	.6	1.2
081d *LATIN*	*1*	*NA*	*70*	*.6*	*1.2*
093 CHR CH (DISC)	1	120	190	1.7	3.3
127 CH GOD (CLEVE)	5	260	332*	3.0	5.7
165 CH OF NAZARENE	1	38	46	.4	.8
167 CHS OF CHRIST	2	83	117	1.1	2.0
355 PRESB CH (USA)	2	120	153*	1.4	2.6
361 PRIM BAPT ASCS	4	58	74*	.7	1.3
419 SO BAPT CONV	9	1,799	2,299*	21.0	39.6
449 UN METHODIST	3	420	537*	4.9	9.2
497 BLACK BAPT EST[2]	NA	1,237	1,581*	14.5	27.2
498 INDEP.CHARIS.[3]	1	NA	300	2.7	5.2
HARDEE	**47**	**8,905**	**12,203***	**62.6**	**100.0**
053 ASSEMB OF GOD	3	381	759	3.9	6.2
081 CATHOLIC	3	NA	205	1.1	1.7
081d *LATIN*	*3*	*NA*	*205*	*1.1*	*1.7*
097 CHR CHS&CHS CR	2	317	411*	2.1	3.4
127 CH GOD (CLEVE)	5	349	452*	2.3	3.7
151 L-D SAINTS	1	NA	125	.6	1.0

County and Denomination	Number of churches	Communicant, confirmed, full members	Total adherents Number	Percent of total population	Percent of total adherents
165 CH OF NAZARENE	1	26	45	.2	.4
167 CHS OF CHRIST	2	67	91	.5	.7
193 EPISCOPAL	1	48	73	.4	.6
283 LUTH—MO SYNOD	1	70	106	.5	.9
291 MISSIONARY CH	1	17	61	.3	.5
356 PRESB CH AMER	1	142	174	.9	1.4
361 PRIM BAPT ASCS	1	29	38*	.2	.3
363 PRIMITIVE METH	1	20	25	.1	.2
413 S.D.A.	2	164	212*	1.1	1.7
419 SO BAPT CONV	18	6,246	8,093*	41.5	66.3
449 UN METHODIST	4	818	1,060*	5.4	8.7
497 BLACK BAPT EST[2]	NA	211	273*	1.4	2.2
HENDRY	**35**	**5,705**	**9,333***	**36.2**	**100.0**
053 ASSEMB OF GOD	4	282	575	2.2	6.2
081 CATHOLIC	2	NA	1,471	5.7	15.8
081d *LATIN*	*2*	*NA*	*1,471*	*5.7*	*15.8*
093 CHR CH (DISC)	1	175	295	1.1	3.2
097 CHR CHS&CHS CR	1	70	93*	.4	1.0
123 CH GOD (ANDER)	1	56	65	.3	.7
127 CH GOD (CLEVE)	5	447	594*	2.3	6.4
167 CHS OF CHRIST	3	90	100	.4	1.1
193 EPISCOPAL	2	212	316	1.2	3.4
283 LUTH—MO SYNOD	1	49	60	.2	.6
339 PENT CH OF GOD	1	100	150	.6	1.6
349 PENT HOLINESS	1	21	28*	.1	.3
355 PRESB CH (USA)	1	95	126*	.5	1.4
413 S.D.A.	1	24	32*	.1	.3
419 SO BAPT CONV	9	2,451	3,258*	12.6	34.9
449 UN METHODIST	2	736	978*	3.8	10.5
497 BLACK BAPT EST[2]	NA	897	1,192*	4.6	12.8
HERNANDO	**77**	**16,814**	**38,286***	**37.9**	**100.0**
022 EASTERN ORTH	1	62	62	.1	.2
053 ASSEMB OF GOD	5	1,017	1,529	1.5	4.0
081 CATHOLIC	5	NA	16,258	16.1	42.5
081d *LATIN*	*5*	*NA*	*16,258*	*16.1*	*42.5*
089 CHR & MISS AL	1	28	68	.1	.2
097 CHR CHS&CHS CR	1	361	421*	.4	1.1
111 CH CR,SCIENTST	1	NR	NR	-	-
123 CH GOD (ANDER)	2	39	57	.1	.1
127 CH GOD (CLEVE)	4	159	186*	.2	.5
145 CH GOD PROPHCY	1	34	40*	-	.1
165 CH OF NAZARENE	3	360	674	.7	1.8
167 CHS OF CHRIST	5	269	336	.3	.9
193 EPISCOPAL	2	674	809	.8	2.1
203 EVAN FREE CH	1	47	88	.1	.2
207 E.L.C.A.	3	1,253	1,423	1.4	3.7
216 EVAN PRESBY CH	1	215	215	.2	.6
283 LUTH—MO SYNOD	3	797	933	.9	2.4
339 PENT CH OF GOD	1	127	163	.2	.4
349 PENT HOLINESS	1	13	15*	-	-
353 CHR BRETHREN	1	31	60	.1	.2
355 PRESB CH (USA)	2	1,278	1,491*	1.5	3.9
356 PRESB CH AMER	1	73	78	.1	.2
403 SALVATION ARMY	1	54	54	.1	.1
413 S.D.A.	2	193	225*	.2	.6
419 SO BAPT CONV	14	4,578	5,341*	5.3	14.0
435 UNITARIAN-UNIV	1	34	34	-	.1
443 UN C OF CHRIST	2	387	452*	.4	1.2
449 UN METHODIST	6	3,369	3,931*	3.9	10.3
467 WESLEYAN	3	283	700	.7	1.8
469 WELS	1	78	85	.1	.2
496 JEWISH EST[1]	0	NA	1,390	1.4	3.6
497 BLACK BAPT EST[2]	NA	1,001	1,168*	1.2	3.1
HIGHLANDS	**78**	**19,821**	**27,803***	**40.6**	**100.0**
053 ASSEMB OF GOD	5	377	768	1.1	2.8
055 AS REF PRES CH	3	1,075	1,154	1.7	4.2
081 CATHOLIC	4	NA	3,652	5.3	13.1
081d *LATIN*	*4*	*NA*	*3,652*	*5.3*	*13.1*
089 CHR & MISS AL	1	34	50	.1	.2
093 CHR CH (DISC)	1	258	351	.5	1.3
097 CHR CHS&CHS CR	3	620	727*	1.1	2.6
111 CH CR,SCIENTST	1	NR	NR	-	-
123 CH GOD (ANDER)	2	144	150	.2	.5
127 CH GOD (CLEVE)	4	309	362*	.5	1.3
145 CH GOD PROPHCY	1	34	40*	.1	.1
151 L-D SAINTS	1	NA	215	.3	.8
157 CH OF BRETHREN	2	434	509*	.7	1.8
165 CH OF NAZARENE	3	376	822	1.2	3.0
167 CHS OF CHRIST	5	407	511	.7	1.8
193 EPISCOPAL	2	542	691	1.0	2.5
207 E.L.C.A.	2	364	390	.6	1.4
226 FRIENDS-USA	1	0	3	-	-
226d *FGC & FUM*	*1*	*0*	*3*	*-*	*-*

Table 4. Churches and Church Membership by County and Denomination: 1990

County and Denomination	Number of churches	Communicant, confirmed, full members	Total adherents Number	Percent of total population	Percent of total adherents
283 LUTH—MO SYNOD	2	615	700	1.0	2.5
291 MISSIONARY CH	3	88	127	.2	.5
355 PRESB CH (USA)	1	197	231*	.3	.8
356 PRESB CH AMER	1	109	122	.2	.4
403 SALVATION ARMY	1	46	50	.1	.2
413 S.D.A.	4	1,106	1,297*	1.9	4.7
419 SO BAPT CONV	15	7,320	8,586*	12.5	30.9
443 UN C OF CHRIST	2	601	705*	1.0	2.5
449 UN METHODIST	7	3,339	3,917*	5.7	14.1
497 BLACK BAPT EST[2]	NA	1,426	1,673*	2.4	6.0
HILLSBOROUGH	**585**	**188,278**	**385,303***	**46.2**	**100.0**
001 ADVENT CHR CH	3	232	287*	-	.1
005 AME ZION	3	595	676	.1	.2
019 AMER BAPT USA	2	63	78*	-	-
053 ASSEMB OF GOD	44	6,563	9,285	1.1	2.4
055 AS REF PRES CH	1	171	205	-	.1
057 BAPT GEN CONF	4	261	323*	-	.1
071 BRETHREN (ASH)	2	42	52*	-	-
081 CATHOLIC	25	NA	120,722	14.5	31.3
081d LATIN	25	NA	120,722	14.5	31.3
089 CHR & MISS AL	9	378	718	.1	.2
093 CHR CH (DISC)	6	1,104	1,744	.2	.5
097 CHR CHS&CHS CR	12	2,178	2,697*	.3	.7
111 CH CR,SCIENTST	3	NR	NR	-	-
123 CH GOD (ANDER)	11	1,009	1,261	.2	.3
127 CH GOD (CLEVE)	33	6,105	7,561*	.9	2.0
145 CH GOD PROPHCY	8	275	341*	-	.1
151 L-D SAINTS	10	NA	3,358	.4	.9
157 CH OF BRETHREN	1	46	57*	-	-
165 CH OF NAZARENE	20	1,269	1,960	.2	.5
167 CHS OF CHRIST	53	5,766	7,459	.9	1.9
179 CONSRV BAPT	1	NR	NR	-	-
185 CUMBER PRESB	7	937	994	.1	.3
193 EPISCOPAL	15	5,580	8,242	1.0	2.1
203 EVAN FREE CH	1	65	140	-	-
207 E.L.C.A.	12	4,478	5,727	.7	1.5
216 EVAN PRESBY CH	1	110	112	-	-
221 FREE METHODIST	4	265	365	-	.1
223 FREE WILL BAPT	4	1,062	1,315*	.2	.3
226 FRIENDS-USA	1	19	31	-	-
226d FGC & FUM	1	19	31	-	-
246 GREEK ORTHODOX	1	NR	NR	-	-
259 IFCA	1	NR	NR	-	-
263 INT FOURSQ GOS	4	257	318*	-	.1
283 LUTH—MO SYNOD	8	2,839	3,839	.5	1.0
285 MENNONITE CH	2	113	178	-	-
329 OPEN BIBLE STD	2	NR	NR	-	-
339 PENT CH OF GOD	6	216	429	.1	.1
349 PENT HOLINESS	7	415	514*	.1	.1
353 CHR BRETHREN	5	195	330	-	.1
355 PRESB CH (USA)	20	8,743	10,828*	1.3	2.8
356 PRESB CH AMER	5	930	1,083	.1	.3
361 PRIM BAPT ASCS	4	164	203*	-	.1
363 PRIMITIVE METH	1	24	26	-	-
371 REF CH IN AM	1	129	216	-	.1
403 SALVATION ARMY	1	380	399	-	.1
413 S.D.A.	15	3,105	3,845*	.5	1.0
419 SO BAPT CONV	117	74,733	92,554*	11.1	24.0
423 SYRIAN ANTIOCH	2	NA	1,000	.1	.3
435 UNITARIAN-UNIV	1	147	203	-	.1
443 UN C OF CHRIST	4	1,990	2,465*	.3	.6
449 UN METHODIST	50	26,874	33,282*	4.0	8.6
467 WESLEYAN	1	32	105	-	-
469 WELS	1	83	98	-	-
496 JEWISH EST[1]	9	NA	11,110	1.3	2.9
497 BLACK BAPT EST[2]	NA	28,336	35,093*	4.2	9.1
498 INDEP.CHARIS.[3]	5	NA	3,300	.4	.9
499 INDEP.NON-CHAR[3]	16	NA	8,175	1.0	2.1
HOLMES	**71**	**7,851**	**10,195***	**64.6**	**100.0**
053 ASSEMB OF GOD	14	846	1,326	8.4	13.0
081 CATHOLIC	1	NA	150	1.0	1.5
081d LATIN	1	NA	150	1.0	1.5
127 CH GOD (CLEVE)	2	142	175*	1.1	1.7
145 CH GOD PROPHCY	3	103	127*	.8	1.2
151 L-D SAINTS	1	NA	124	.8	1.2
165 CH OF NAZARENE	1	45	31	.2	.3
167 CHS OF CHRIST	4	150	194*	1.2	1.9
223 FREE WILL BAPT	1	40	49*	.3	.5
283 LUTH—MO SYNOD	1	21	25	.2	.2
355 PRESB CH (USA)	1	11	14*	.1	.1
413 S.D.A.	1	28	34*	.2	.3
419 SO BAPT CONV	30	5,572	6,849*	43.4	67.2
443 UN C OF CHRIST	1	10	12*	.1	.1
449 UN METHODIST	10	724	890*	5.6	8.7
497 BLACK BAPT EST[2]	NA	159	195*	1.2	1.9

County and Denomination	Number of churches	Communicant, confirmed, full members	Total adherents Number	Percent of total population	Percent of total adherents
INDIAN RIVER	**72**	**19,684**	**36,552***	**40.5**	**100.0**
053 ASSEMB OF GOD	4	782	1,202	1.3	3.3
081 CATHOLIC	3	NA	11,315	12.5	31.0
081d LATIN	3	NA	11,315	12.5	31.0
089 CHR & MISS AL	1	31	125	.1	.3
093 CHR CH (DISC)	1	73	111	.1	.3
097 CHR CHS&CHS CR	2	370	437*	.5	1.2
111 CH CR,SCIENTST	1	NR	NR	-	-
123 CH GOD (ANDER)	1	800	921	1.0	2.5
127 CH GOD (CLEVE)	7	663	783*	.9	2.1
151 L-D SAINTS	1	NA	370	.4	1.0
165 CH OF NAZARENE	4	255	307	.3	.8
167 CHS OF CHRIST	3	305	385	.4	1.1
179 CONSRV BAPT	1	NR	NR	-	-
193 EPISCOPAL	3	1,748	2,546	2.8	7.0
207 E.L.C.A.	3	746	928	1.0	2.5
209 EVAN LUTH SYN	2	347	438	.5	1.2
223 FREE WILL BAPT	1	32	38*	-	.1
283 LUTH—MO SYNOD	1	187	214	.2	.6
339 PENT CH OF GOD	1	34	77	.1	.2
355 PRESB CH (USA)	3	1,461	1,725*	1.9	4.7
356 PRESB CH AMER	1	61	76	.1	.2
361 PRIM BAPT ASCS	3	17	20*	-	.1
413 S.D.A.	1	89	105*	.1	.3
419 SO BAPT CONV	11	4,787	5,653*	6.3	15.5
435 UNITARIAN-UNIV	1	103	112	.1	.3
443 UN C OF CHRIST	2	1,621	1,914*	2.1	5.2
449 UN METHODIST	7	3,565	4,210*	4.7	11.5
467 WESLEYAN	1	12	57	.1	.2
496 JEWISH EST[1]	1	NA	300	.3	.8
497 BLACK BAPT EST[2]	NA	1,595	1,883*	2.1	5.2
499 INDEP.NON-CHAR[3]	1	NA	300	.3	.8
JACKSON	**112**	**18,747**	**23,910***	**57.8**	**100.0**
001 ADVENT CHR CH	1	8	10*	-	-
053 ASSEMB OF GOD	16	1,183	1,624	3.9	6.8
081 CATHOLIC	1	NA	200	.5	.8
081d LATIN	1	NA	200	.5	.8
089 CHR & MISS AL	1	35	72	.2	.3
127 CH GOD (CLEVE)	5	280	343*	.8	1.4
145 CH GOD PROPHCY	1	34	42*	.1	.2
151 L-D SAINTS	1	NA	490	1.2	2.0
165 CH OF NAZARENE	1	27	50	.1	.2
167 CHS OF CHRIST	2	140	181	.4	.8
193 EPISCOPAL	1	169	207	.5	.9
223 FREE WILL BAPT	14	859	1,053*	2.5	4.4
283 LUTH—MO SYNOD	1	63	79	.2	.3
339 PENT CH OF GOD	1	18	38	.1	.2
349 PENT HOLINESS	5	312	382*	.9	1.6
355 PRESB CH (USA)	1	327	401*	1.0	1.7
413 S.D.A.	2	92	113*	.3	.5
419 SO BAPT CONV	40	10,584	12,973*	31.4	54.3
435 UNITARIAN-UNIV	1	27	27	.1	.1
449 UN METHODIST	17	2,331	2,857*	6.9	11.9
497 BLACK BAPT EST[2]	NA	2,258	2,768*	6.7	11.6
JEFFERSON	**27**	**4,602**	**6,257***	**55.4**	**100.0**
053 ASSEMB OF GOD	1	9	14	.1	.2
081 CATHOLIC	1	NA	273	2.4	4.4
081d LATIN	1	NA	273	2.4	4.4
127 CH GOD (CLEVE)	1	27	35*	.3	.6
145 CH GOD PROPHCY	1	34	44*	.4	.7
165 CH OF NAZARENE	1	93	107	.9	1.7
167 CHS OF CHRIST	2	56	72	.6	1.2
193 EPISCOPAL	1	122	202	1.8	3.2
223 FREE WILL BAPT	1	25	32*	.3	.5
349 PENT HOLINESS	2	250	323*	2.9	5.2
355 PRESB CH (USA)	1	133	172*	1.5	2.7
361 PRIM BAPT ASCS	1	5	6*	.1	.1
419 SO BAPT CONV	7	1,833	2,371*	21.0	37.9
449 UN METHODIST	7	592	766*	6.8	12.2
497 BLACK BAPT EST[2]	NA	1,423	1,840*	16.3	29.4
LAFAYETTE	**18**	**2,592**	**3,231***	**57.9**	**100.0**
053 ASSEMB OF GOD	1	112	175	3.1	5.4
127 CH GOD (CLEVE)	1	107	131*	2.3	4.1
167 CHS OF CHRIST	2	50	75	1.3	2.3
419 SO BAPT CONV	12	1,951	2,394*	42.9	74.1
449 UN METHODIST	2	212	260*	4.7	8.0
497 BLACK BAPT EST[2]	NA	160	196*	3.5	6.1
LAKE	**159**	**42,178**	**64,111***	**42.1**	**100.0**
011 A.W.M.C.	1	0	0*	-	-
053 ASSEMB OF GOD	8	885	1,488	1.0	2.3
081 CATHOLIC	5	NA	9,349	6.1	14.6

NA–Not applicable   NR–Not reported   *Total adherents estimated from known number of communicant, confirmed, full members.   - Represents a percent less than 0.1.   Percentages may not total due to rounding.
[1]See Appendix E   [2]See Appendix F   [3]See Appendix G   Lines in *italic* represent a breakdown of Catholic rites or Friends affiliations. They are included in their respective denominational total.

Table 4. Churches and Church Membership by County and Denomination: 1990

County and Denomination		Number of churches	Communicant, confirmed, full members	Total adherents		
				Number	Percent of total population	Percent of total adherents
081d	LATIN	5	NA	9,349	6.1	14.6
089	CHR & MISS AL	3	171	353	.2	.6
093	CHR CH (DISC)	1	76	108	.1	.2
097	CHR CHS&CHS CR	5	1,162	1,377*	.9	2.1
111	CH CR,SCIENTST	3	NR	NR	-	-
123	CH GOD (ANDER)	4	106	304	.2	.5
127	CH GOD (CLEVE)	19	1,284	1,521*	1.0	2.4
145	CH GOD PROPHCY	3	103	122*	.1	.2
151	L-D SAINTS	3	NA	888	.6	1.4
165	CH OF NAZARENE	4	385	794	.5	1.2
167	CHS OF CHRIST	13	1,149	1,630	1.1	2.5
175	CONGR CHR CHS	2	377	447*	.3	.7
193	EPISCOPAL	5	1,836	2,478	1.6	3.9
203	EVAN FREE CH	2	293	510	.3	.8
207	E.L.C.A.	4	945	1,069	.7	1.7
221	FREE METHODIST	1	0	21	-	-
283	LUTH—MO SYNOD	3	1,023	1,225	.8	1.9
285	MENNONITE CH	1	31	48	-	.1
349	PENT HOLINESS	2	110	130*	.1	.2
355	PRESB CH (USA)	9	3,167	3,752*	2.5	5.9
356	PRESB CH AMER	1	71	87	.1	.1
413	S.D.A.	4	600	711*	.5	1.1
419	SO BAPT CONV	29	17,052	20,202*	13.3	31.5
443	UN C OF CHRIST	2	391	463*	.3	.7
449	UN METHODIST	16	7,897	9,356*	6.2	14.6
467	WESLEYAN	2	50	102	.1	.2
469	WELS	1	60	76	-	.1
496	JEWISH EST[1]	0	NA	800	.5	1.2
497	BLACK BAPT EST[2]	NA	2,954	3,500*	2.3	5.5
499	INDEP.NON-CHAR[3]	3	NA	1,200	.8	1.9
LEE		**212**	**63,495**	**113,928***	**34.0**	**100.0**
040	AP CHR CH-AMER	1	13	23	-	-
053	ASSEMB OF GOD	14	2,394	4,496	1.3	3.9
057	BAPT GEN CONF	1	131	155*	-	.1
075	BRETHREN IN CR	1	6	12	-	-
081	CATHOLIC	14	NA	29,298	8.7	25.7
081b	BYZAN RUTH	1	NA	200	.1	.2
081d	LATIN	13	NA	29,098	8.7	25.5
089	CHR & MISS AL	6	920	1,576	.5	1.4
093	CHR CH (DISC)	3	465	630	.2	.6
097	CHR CHS&CHS CR	6	1,598	1,894*	.6	1.7
105	CHRISTIAN REF	1	80	90	-	.1
111	CH CR,SCIENTST	4	NR	NR	-	-
123	CH GOD (ANDER)	3	162	168	.1	.1
127	CH GOD (CLEVE)	9	1,240	1,470*	.4	1.3
133	CH GOD(7TH)DEN	1	11	21	-	-
145	CH GOD PROPHCY	4	138	164*	-	.1
146	CH GOD MTN ASM	1	12	14*	-	-
151	L-D SAINTS	3	NA	984	.3	.9
157	CH OF BRETHREN	2	195	231*	.1	.2
163	CH OF LUTH BR	1	35	101	-	.1
165	CH OF NAZARENE	4	573	953	.3	.8
167	CHS OF CHRIST	10	867	1,097	.3	1.0
175	CONGR CHR CHS	2	293	347*	.1	.3
179	CONSRV BAPT	2	NR	NR	-	-
193	EPISCOPAL	11	3,498	4,738	1.4	4.2
203	EVAN FREE CH	1	61	90	-	.1
207	E.L.C.A.	7	3,303	4,125	1.2	3.6
221	FREE METHODIST	1	62	151	-	.1
226	FRIENDS-USA	2	40	54	-	-
226b	EFI	1	40	40	-	-
226d	FGC & FUM	1	0	14	-	-
246	GREEK ORTHODOX	1	NR	NR	-	-
283	LUTH—MO SYNOD	6	2,376	2,927	.9	2.6
285	MENNONITE CH	2	103	272	.1	.2
329	OPEN BIBLE STD	1	NR	NR	-	-
331	ORTH CH IN AM	1	NR	NR	-	-
353	CHR BRETHREN	1	25	50	-	-
355	PRESB CH (USA)	10	5,361	6,355*	1.9	5.6
356	PRESB CH AMER	2	427	547	.2	.5
361	PRIM BAPT ASCS	1	0	0*	-	-
371	REF CH IN AM	1	57	93	-	.1
403	SALVATION ARMY	1	131	146	-	.1
413	S.D.A.	5	700	830*	.2	.7
419	SO BAPT CONV	30	17,718	21,004*	6.3	18.4
435	UNITARIAN-UNIV	1	360	413	.1	.4
438	UN BRETH IN CR	1	30	38	-	-
443	UN C OF CHRIST	6	2,515	2,981*	.9	2.6
449	UN METHODIST	19	11,303	13,399*	4.0	11.8
467	WESLEYAN	3	199	670	.2	.6
469	WELS	4	393	564	.2	.5
496	JEWISH EST[1]	1	NA	4,000	1.2	3.5
497	BLACK BAPT EST[2]	NA	5,700	6,757*	2.0	5.9
LEON		**130**	**54,852**	**84,580***	**43.9**	**100.0**
001	ADVENT CHR CH	1	19	23*	-	-

County and Denomination		Number of churches	Communicant, confirmed, full members	Total adherents		
				Number	Percent of total population	Percent of total adherents
053	ASSEMB OF GOD	8	1,191	1,705	.9	2.0
081	CATHOLIC	5	NA	9,841	5.1	11.6
081d	LATIN	5	NA	9,841	5.1	11.6
089	CHR & MISS AL	1	99	159	.1	.2
093	CHR CH (DISC)	1	20	20	-	-
097	CHR CHS&CHS CR	3	315	383*	.2	.5
111	CH CR,SCIENTST	1	NR	NR	-	-
123	CH GOD (ANDER)	1	12	12	-	-
127	CH GOD (CLEVE)	4	431	524*	.3	.6
145	CH GOD PROPHCY	2	69	84*	-	.1
151	L-D SAINTS	6	NA	1,702	.9	2.0
165	CH OF NAZARENE	2	164	298	.2	.4
167	CHS OF CHRIST	6	988	1,495	.8	1.8
193	EPISCOPAL	7	3,145	4,123	2.1	4.9
207	E.L.C.A.	2	589	785	.4	.9
223	FREE WILL BAPT	2	110	134*	.1	.2
226	FRIENDS-USA	1	16	38	-	-
226d	FGC & FUM	1	16	38	-	-
246	GREEK ORTHODOX	1	NR	NR	-	-
263	INT FOURSQ GOS	1	58	71*	-	.1
283	LUTH—MO SYNOD	1	476	647	.3	.8
285	MENNONITE CH	1	41	41	-	-
329	OPEN BIBLE STD	1	NR	NR	-	-
349	PENT HOLINESS	7	2,103	2,559*	1.3	3.0
355	PRESB CH (USA)	8	3,305	4,021*	2.1	4.8
356	PRESB CH AMER	3	405	453	.2	.5
361	PRIM BAPT ASCS	1	14	17*	-	-
403	SALVATION ARMY	1	64	66	-	.1
413	S.D.A.	2	474	577*	.3	.7
419	SO BAPT CONV	28	20,743	25,237*	13.1	29.8
435	UNITARIAN-UNIV	1	118	140	.1	.2
443	UN C OF CHRIST	1	100	122*	.1	.1
449	UN METHODIST	14	7,779	9,464*	4.9	11.2
469	WELS	1	49	83	-	.1
496	JEWISH EST[1]	1	NA	1,236	.6	1.5
497	BLACK BAPT EST[2]	NA	11,955	14,545*	7.6	17.2
499	INDEP.NON-CHAR[3]	4	NA	3,975	2.1	4.7
LEVY		**51**	**8,487**	**12,177***	**47.0**	**100.0**
053	ASSEMB OF GOD	2	206	332	1.3	2.7
081	CATHOLIC	3	NA	1,021	3.9	8.4
081d	LATIN	3	NA	1,021	3.9	8.4
097	CHR CHS&CHS CR	1	11	14*	.1	.1
127	CH GOD (CLEVE)	6	332	409*	1.6	3.4
151	L-D SAINTS	1	NA	474	1.8	3.9
167	CHS OF CHRIST	9	394	565	2.2	4.6
193	EPISCOPAL	3	173	238	.9	2.0
203	EVAN FREE CH	1	20	50	.2	.4
283	LUTH—MO SYNOD	1	89	123	.5	1.0
355	PRESB CH (USA)	2	166	205*	.8	1.7
361	PRIM BAPT ASCS	1	18	22*	.1	.2
413	S.D.A.	1	35	43*	.2	.4
419	SO BAPT CONV	12	5,124	6,316*	24.4	51.9
449	UN METHODIST	8	1,251	1,542*	5.9	12.7
497	BLACK BAPT EST[2]	NA	668	823*	3.2	6.8
LIBERTY		**18**	**1,876**	**2,734***	**49.1**	**100.0**
053	ASSEMB OF GOD	4	122	149	2.7	5.4
097	CHR CHS&CHS CR	1	90	110*	2.0	4.0
127	CH GOD (CLEVE)	1	112	137*	2.5	5.0
145	CH GOD PROPHCY	1	34	42*	.8	1.5
151	L-D SAINTS	2	NA	440	7.9	16.1
349	PENT HOLINESS	1	106	130*	2.3	4.8
419	SO BAPT CONV	5	1,116	1,368*	24.6	50.0
449	UN METHODIST	2	92	113*	2.0	4.1
467	WESLEYAN	1	4	0	-	-
497	BLACK BAPT EST[2]	NA	200	245*	4.4	9.0
MADISON		**47**	**7,767**	**10,355***	**62.5**	**100.0**
053	ASSEMB OF GOD	1	15	31	.2	.3
081	CATHOLIC	1	NA	207	1.2	2.0
081d	LATIN	1	NA	207	1.2	2.0
127	CH GOD (CLEVE)	3	115	146*	.9	1.4
145	CH GOD PROPHCY	1	34	43*	.3	.4
151	L-D SAINTS	2	NA	248	1.5	2.4
165	CH OF NAZARENE	2	37	66	.4	.6
167	CHS OF CHRIST	2	45	60	.4	.6
193	EPISCOPAL	1	67	101	.6	1.0
355	PRESB CH (USA)	1	25	32*	.2	.3
356	PRESB CH AMER	1	115	135	.8	1.3
361	PRIM BAPT ASCS	2	43	55*	.3	.5
413	S.D.A.	1	33	42*	.3	.4
419	SO BAPT CONV	21	4,080	5,180*	31.3	50.0
449	UN METHODIST	8	1,148	1,457*	8.8	14.1
497	BLACK BAPT EST[2]	NA	2,010	2,552*	15.4	24.6

NA–Not applicable   NR–Not reported   *Total adherents estimated from known number of communicant, confirmed, full members.   - Represents a percent less than 0.1.   Percentages may not total due to rounding.
[1]See Appendix E   [2]See Appendix F   [3]See Appendix G   Lines in *italic* represent a breakdown of Catholic rites or Friends affiliations. They are included in their respective denominational total.

Table 4. Churches and Church Membership by County and Denomination: 1990

County and Denomination	Number of churches	Communicant, confirmed, full members	Total adherents Number	Percent of total population	Percent of total adherents
MANATEE	**137**	**42,238**	**70,798***	**33.4**	**100.0**
019 AMER BAPT USA	2	149	176*	.1	.2
053 ASSEMB OF GOD	8	555	793	.4	1.1
057 BAPT GEN CONF	2	458	541*	.3	.8
071 BRETHREN (ASH)	1	52	61*	-	.1
081 CATHOLIC	7	NA	16,452	7.8	23.2
081d *LATIN*	*7*	*NA*	*16,452*	*7.8*	*23.2*
089 CHR & MISS AL	2	136	227	.1	.3
093 CHR CH (DISC)	1	206	243	.1	.3
097 CHR CHS&CHS CR	3	709	838*	.4	1.2
105 CHRISTIAN REF	1	488	648	.3	.9
111 CH CR,SCIENTST	2	NR	NR	-	-
123 CH GOD (ANDER)	1	400	411	.2	.6
127 CH GOD (CLEVE)	7	574	678*	.3	1.0
145 CH GOD PROPHCY	1	34	40*	-	.1
151 L-D SAINTS	2	NA	792	.4	1.1
157 CH OF BRETHREN	1	310	366*	.2	.5
165 CH OF NAZARENE	3	935	876	.4	1.2
167 CHS OF CHRIST	10	702	924	.4	1.3
179 CONSRV BAPT	1	NR	NR	-	-
193 EPISCOPAL	4	2,224	2,556	1.2	3.6
203 EVAN FREE CH	1	53	105	-	.1
207 E.L.C.A.	4	1,313	1,515	.7	2.1
221 FREE METHODIST	1	27	51	-	.1
283 LUTH—MO SYNOD	2	1,020	1,316	.6	1.9
329 OPEN BIBLE STD	1	NR	NR	-	-
331 ORTH CH IN AM	1	NR	NR	-	-
339 PENT CH OF GOD	1	20	40	-	.1
349 PENT HOLINESS	1	25	30*	-	-
355 PRESB CH (USA)	5	3,119	3,685*	1.7	5.2
356 PRESB CH AMER	1	68	89	-	.1
361 PRIM BAPT ASCS	1	19	22*	-	-
371 REF CH IN AM	1	259	676	.3	1.0
403 SALVATION ARMY	1	163	168	.1	.2
413 S.D.A.	3	365	431*	.2	.6
415 S-D BAPTIST GC	1	30	35*	-	-
419 SO BAPT CONV	25	14,295	16,891*	8.0	23.9
435 UNITARIAN-UNIV	1	131	156	.1	.2
438 UN BRETH IN CR	1	41	70	-	.1
443 UN C OF CHRIST	2	723	854*	.4	1.2
449 UN METHODIST	16	8,208	9,699*	4.6	13.7
467 WESLEYAN	1	40	122	.1	.2
469 WELS	1	173	232	.1	.3
496 JEWISH EST¹	1	NA	0	-	-
497 BLACK BAPT EST²	NA	4,214	4,979*	2.4	7.0
498 INDEP.CHARIS.³	2	NA	1,400	.7	2.0
499 INDEP.NON-CHAR³	3	NA	1,610	.8	2.3
MARION	**181**	**49,354**	**79,970***	**41.0**	**100.0**
053 ASSEMB OF GOD	10	1,393	4,339	2.2	5.4
057 BAPT GEN CONF	1	52	63*	-	.1
081 CATHOLIC	8	NA	15,209	7.8	19.0
081d *LATIN*	*8*	*NA*	*15,209*	*7.8*	*19.0*
089 CHR & MISS AL	2	147	289	.1	.4
093 CHR CH (DISC)	4	687	760	.4	1.0
097 CHR CHS&CHS CR	5	2,105	2,550*	1.3	3.2
111 CH CR,SCIENTST	1	NR	NR	-	-
123 CH GOD (ANDER)	1	200	201	.1	.3
127 CH GOD (CLEVE)	8	1,254	1,519*	.8	1.9
145 CH GOD PROPHCY	2	69	84*	-	.1
151 L-D SAINTS	2	NA	857	.4	1.1
165 CH OF NAZARENE	2	313	553	.3	.7
167 CHS OF CHRIST	12	992	1,322	.7	1.7
193 EPISCOPAL	5	1,623	1,745	.9	2.2
207 E.L.C.A.	6	1,483	1,667	.9	2.1
221 FREE METHODIST	1	92	215	.1	.3
223 FREE WILL BAPT	2	61	74*	-	.1
226 FRIENDS-USA	1	0	15	-	-
226d *FGC & FUM*	*1*	*0*	*15*	*-*	*-*
263 INT FOURSQ GOS	2	113	137*	.1	.2
283 LUTH—MO SYNOD	4	1,230	1,475	.8	1.8
291 MISSIONARY CH	1	28	43	-	.1
325 OLD REG BAPT	1	57	69*	-	.1
349 PENT HOLINESS	2	371	449*	.2	.6
353 CHR BRETHREN	1	40	70	-	.1
355 PRESB CH (USA)	10	3,306	4,005*	2.1	5.0
356 PRESB CH AMER	1	422	639	.3	.8
403 SALVATION ARMY	1	72	77	-	.1
413 S.D.A.	5	805	975*	.5	1.2
419 SO BAPT CONV	43	18,010	21,820*	11.2	27.3
435 UNITARIAN-UNIV	1	38	38	-	-
436 UNITED BAPT	1	15	18*	-	-
443 UN C OF CHRIST	2	257	311*	.2	.4
449 UN METHODIST	29	7,680	9,305*	4.8	11.6
467 WESLEYAN	1	8	40	-	.1
469 WELS	1	48	104	.1	.1
496 JEWISH EST¹	0	NA	100	.1	.1
497 BLACK BAPT EST²	NA	6,383	7,733*	4.0	9.7
499 INDEP.NON-CHAR³	2	NA	1,100	.6	1.4
MARTIN	**65**	**17,769**	**36,396***	**36.1**	**100.0**
053 ASSEMB OF GOD	2	123	165	.2	.5
081 CATHOLIC	4	NA	13,623	13.5	37.4
081d *LATIN*	*4*	*NA*	*13,623*	*13.5*	*37.4*
089 CHR & MISS AL	1	66	109	.1	.3
097 CHR CHS&CHS CR	3	425	494*	.5	1.4
111 CH CR,SCIENTST	1	NR	NR	-	-
127 CH GOD (CLEVE)	8	496	576*	.6	1.6
145 CH GOD PROPHCY	1	34	39*	-	.1
151 L-D SAINTS	1	NA	459	.5	1.3
165 CH OF NAZARENE	2	246	396	.4	1.1
167 CHS OF CHRIST	5	319	428	.4	1.2
193 EPISCOPAL	6	1,748	2,273	2.3	6.2
207 E.L.C.A.	2	559	667	.7	1.8
209 EVAN LUTH SYN	1	26	32	-	.1
226 FRIENDS-USA	2	25	59	.1	.2
226b *EFI*	*1*	*25*	*47*	*-*	*.1*
226d *FGC & FUM*	*1*	*0*	*12*	*-*	*-*
283 LUTH—MO SYNOD	2	1,322	1,713	1.7	4.7
355 PRESB CH (USA)	4	1,343	1,560*	1.5	4.3
356 PRESB CH AMER	1	154	214	.2	.6
413 S.D.A.	1	78	91*	.1	.3
419 SO BAPT CONV	8	4,516	5,244*	5.2	14.4
443 UN C OF CHRIST	3	861	1,000*	1.0	2.7
449 UN METHODIST	5	3,875	4,500*	4.5	12.4
497 BLACK BAPT EST²	NA	1,553	1,804*	1.8	5.0
499 INDEP.NON-CHAR³	2	NA	950	.9	2.6
MONROE	**60**	**7,893**	**27,220***	**34.9**	**100.0**
053 ASSEMB OF GOD	3	300	317	.4	1.2
081 CATHOLIC	5	NA	17,217	22.1	63.3
081d *LATIN*	*5*	*NA*	*17,217*	*22.1*	*63.3*
127 CH GOD (CLEVE)	3	178	208*	.3	.8
145 CH GOD PROPHCY	1	34	40*	.1	.1
151 L-D SAINTS	2	NA	286	.4	1.1
165 CH OF NAZARENE	1	33	57	.1	.2
167 CHS OF CHRIST	3	72	110	.1	.4
193 EPISCOPAL	6	650	1,005	1.3	3.7
207 E.L.C.A.	2	162	209	.3	.8
226 FRIENDS-USA	1	0	3	-	-
226d *FGC & FUM*	*1*	*0*	*3*	*-*	*-*
283 LUTH—MO SYNOD	3	380	497	.6	1.8
353 CHR BRETHREN	1	25	40	.1	.1
355 PRESB CH (USA)	3	325	379*	.5	1.4
403 SALVATION ARMY	1	33	40	.1	.1
413 S.D.A.	4	100	117*	.1	.4
419 SO BAPT CONV	8	2,799	3,263*	4.2	12.0
435 UNITARIAN-UNIV	1	41	44	.1	.2
443 UN C OF CHRIST	2	195	227*	.3	.8
449 UN METHODIST	10	1,691	1,971*	2.5	7.2
496 JEWISH EST¹	0	NA	170	.2	.6
497 BLACK BAPT EST²	NA	875	1,020*	1.3	3.7
NASSAU	**55**	**15,561**	**22,691***	**51.6**	**100.0**
053 ASSEMB OF GOD	4	426	718	1.6	3.2
081 CATHOLIC	2	NA	1,563	3.6	6.9
081d *LATIN*	*2*	*NA*	*1,563*	*3.6*	*6.9*
089 CHR & MISS AL	2	62	77	.2	.3
127 CH GOD (CLEVE)	8	613	775*	1.8	3.4
145 CH GOD PROPHCY	1	34	43*	.1	.2
151 L-D SAINTS	1	NA	340	.8	1.5
167 CHS OF CHRIST	2	105	118	.3	.5
193 EPISCOPAL	2	419	739	1.7	3.3
207 E.L.C.A.	1	221	278	.6	1.2
221 FREE METHODIST	1	21	21	-	.1
349 PENT HOLINESS	2	81	102*	.2	.4
355 PRESB CH (USA)	1	406	513*	1.2	2.3
361 PRIM BAPT ASCS	2	33	42*	.1	.2
419 SO BAPT CONV	19	10,548	13,332*	30.3	58.8
449 UN METHODIST	6	1,430	1,807*	4.1	8.0
496 JEWISH EST¹	0	NA	354	.8	1.6
497 BLACK BAPT EST²	NA	1,162	1,469*	3.3	6.5
499 INDEP.NON-CHAR³	1	NA	400	.9	1.8
OKALOOSA	**150**	**43,532**	**67,088***	**46.7**	**100.0**
053 ASSEMB OF GOD	24	1,847	2,846	2.0	4.2
059 BAPT MISS ASSN	1	351	443*	.3	.7
081 CATHOLIC	6	NA	8,740	6.1	13.0
081d *LATIN*	*6*	*NA*	*8,740*	*6.1*	*13.0*
093 CHR CH (DISC)	1	126	171	.1	.3
097 CHR CHS&CHS CR	2	18	23*	-	-
111 CH CR,SCIENTST	1	NR	NR	-	-

NA–Not applicable   NR–Not reported   *Total adherents estimated from known number of communicant, confirmed, full members.   - Represents a percent less than 0.1.   Percentages may not total due to rounding.
¹See Appendix E   ²See Appendix F   ³See Appendix G   Lines in *italic* represent a breakdown of Catholic rites or Friends affiliations. They are included in their respective denominational total.

Table 4. Churches and Church Membership by County and Denomination: 1990

County and Denomination	Number of churches	Communicant, confirmed, full members	Total adherents Number	Percent of total population	Percent of total adherents
123 CH GOD (ANDER)	1	50	65	-	.1
127 CH GOD (CLEVE)	3	281	354*	.2	.5
145 CH GOD PROPHCY	2	69	87*	.1	.1
151 L-D SAINTS	3	NA	1,288	.9	1.9
165 CH OF NAZARENE	2	136	159	.1	.2
167 CHS OF CHRIST	14	1,127	1,598	1.1	2.4
176 CCC, NOT NAT'L	2	110	139*	.1	.2
193 EPISCOPAL	4	1,637	2,478	1.7	3.7
207 E.L.C.A.	2	716	1,022	.7	1.5
216 EVAN PRESBY CH	1	185	195	.1	.3
223 FREE WILL BAPT	2	27	34*	-	.1
246 GREEK ORTHODOX	2	NR	NR	-	-
283 LUTH—MO SYNOD	3	619	829	.6	1.2
285 MENNONITE CH	1	10	40	-	.1
329 OPEN BIBLE STD	1	NR	NR	-	-
339 PENT CH OF GOD	1	30	30	-	-
349 PENT HOLINESS	1	16	20*	-	-
353 CHR BRETHREN	1	12	25	-	-
355 PRESB CH (USA)	5	696	877*	.6	1.3
356 PRESB CH AMER	3	337	414	.3	.6
361 PRIM BAPT ASCS	1	22	28*	-	-
403 SALVATION ARMY	1	72	80	.1	.1
413 S.D.A.	2	149	188*	.1	.3
419 SO BAPT CONV	43	24,161	30,460*	21.2	45.4
435 UNITARIAN-UNIV	1	63	74	.1	.1
449 UN METHODIST	10	7,296	9,198*	6.4	13.7
469 WELS	1	27	40	-	.1
497 BLACK BAPT EST[2]	NA	3,342	4,213*	2.9	6.3
498 INDEP.CHARIS.[3]	1	NA	330	.2	.5
499 INDEP.NON-CHAR[3]	1	NA	600	.4	.9
OKEECHOBEE	**30**	**6,463**	**10,586***	**35.7**	**100.0**
053 ASSEMB OF GOD	3	263	476	1.6	4.5
081 CATHOLIC	1	NA	1,870	6.3	17.7
081d LATIN	*1*	*NA*	*1,870*	*6.3*	*17.7*
097 CHR CHS&CHS CR	1	174	220*	.7	2.1
111 CH CR,SCIENTST	1	NR	NR	-	-
127 CH GOD (CLEVE)	3	395	500*	1.7	4.7
145 CH GOD PROPHCY	1	34	43*	.1	.4
151 L-D SAINTS	1	NA	201	.7	1.9
165 CH OF NAZARENE	1	75	127	.4	1.2
167 CHS OF CHRIST	2	58	70	.2	.7
193 EPISCOPAL	1	164	297	1.0	2.8
223 FREE WILL BAPT	1	35	44*	.1	.4
283 LUTH—MO SYNOD	1	188	277	.9	2.6
325 OLD REG BAPT	1	27	34*	.1	.3
339 PENT CH OF GOD	1	34	77	.3	.7
355 PRESB CH (USA)	1	143	181*	.6	1.7
361 PRIM BAPT ASCS	1	35	44*	.1	.4
413 S.D.A.	1	107	135*	.5	1.3
419 SO BAPT CONV	7	3,720	4,710*	15.9	44.5
449 UN METHODIST	1	616	780*	2.6	7.4
497 BLACK BAPT EST[2]	NA	395	500*	1.7	4.7
ORANGE	**386**	**166,904**	**297,547***	**43.9**	**100.0**
019 AMER BAPT USA	4	743	919*	.1	.3
053 ASSEMB OF GOD	23	8,909	12,737	1.9	4.3
057 BAPT GEN CONF	4	407	503*	.1	.2
075 BRETHREN IN CR	1	52	52	-	-
081 CATHOLIC	14	NA	49,690	7.3	16.7
081b BYZAN RUTH	*1*	*NA*	*210*	*-*	*.1*
081d LATIN	*12*	*NA*	*49,410*	*7.3*	*16.6*
081h UKRAINIAN	*1*	*NA*	*70*	*-*	*-*
089 CHR & MISS AL	10	889	1,356	.2	.5
093 CHR CH (DISC)	4	762	1,492	.2	.5
097 CHR CHS&CHS CR	15	2,662	3,291*	.5	1.1
105 CHRISTIAN REF	1	125	197	-	.1
111 CH CR,SCIENTST	2	NR	NR	-	-
123 CH GOD (ANDER)	5	465	517	.1	.2
127 CH GOD (CLEVE)	19	3,264	4,035*	.6	1.4
133 CH GOD(7TH)DEN	1	11	21	-	-
145 CH GOD PROPHCY	7	241	298*	-	.1
146 CH GOD MTN ASM	1	24	30*	-	-
151 L-D SAINTS	6	NA	3,494	.5	1.2
157 CH OF BRETHREN	3	406	502*	.1	.2
165 CH OF NAZARENE	19	2,516	3,335	.5	1.1
167 CHS OF CHRIST	20	3,393	4,661	.7	1.6
179 CONSRV BAPT	1	NR	NR	-	-
181 CONSRV CONGR	1	18	22*	-	-
193 EPISCOPAL	14	6,209	8,417	1.2	2.8
207 E.L.C.A.	9	4,221	5,790	.9	1.9
215 EVAN METH CH	1	40	49*	-	-
221 FREE METHODIST	2	48	56	-	-
223 FREE WILL BAPT	4	198	245*	-	.1
226 FRIENDS-USA	2	63	103	-	-
226d FGC & FUM	*2*	*63*	*103*	*-*	*-*
246 GREEK ORTHODOX	1	NR	NR	-	-

County and Denomination	Number of churches	Communicant, confirmed, full members	Total adherents Number	Percent of total population	Percent of total adherents
263 INT FOURSQ GOS	3	217	268*	-	.1
283 LUTH—MO SYNOD	8	3,732	5,024	.7	1.7
285 MENNONITE CH	1	77	141	-	-
329 OPEN BIBLE STD	1	NR	NR	-	-
349 PENT HOLINESS	2	455	562*	.1	.2
353 CHR BRETHREN	4	228	383	.1	.1
355 PRESB CH (USA)	19	11,604	14,346*	2.1	4.8
356 PRESB CH AMER	3	1,290	1,761	.3	.6
371 REF CH IN AM	2	412	695	.1	.2
375 REF EPISCOPAL	1	17	17	-	-
403 SALVATION ARMY	1	342	378	.1	.1
413 S.D.A.	18	5,279	6,526*	1.0	2.2
419 SO BAPT CONV	64	56,425	69,756*	10.3	23.4
435 UNITARIAN-UNIV	1	340	440	.1	.1
443 UN C OF CHRIST	5	1,608	1,988*	.3	.7
449 UN METHODIST	33	22,285	27,550*	4.1	9.3
467 WESLEYAN	1	68	150	-	.1
469 WELS	2	370	521	.1	.2
496 JEWISH EST[1]	6	NA	11,305	1.7	3.8
497 BLACK BAPT EST[2]	NA	26,489	32,747*	4.8	11.0
498 INDEP.CHARIS.[3]	7	NA	9,456	1.4	3.2
499 INDEP.NON-CHAR[3]	10	NA	11,721	1.7	3.9
OSCEOLA	**63**	**16,320**	**34,438***	**32.0**	**100.0**
005 AME ZION	1	424	473	.4	1.4
053 ASSEMB OF GOD	6	628	922	.9	2.7
055 AS REF PRES CH	1	0	0	-	-
081 CATHOLIC	2	NA	10,589	9.8	30.7
081d LATIN	*2*	*NA*	*10,589*	*9.8*	*30.7*
089 CHR & MISS AL	2	185	283	.3	.8
097 CHR CHS&CHS CR	4	2,350	2,936*	2.7	8.5
111 CH CR,SCIENTST	2	NR	NR	-	-
123 CH GOD (ANDER)	1	59	62	.1	.2
127 CH GOD (CLEVE)	5	319	398*	.4	1.2
151 L-D SAINTS	3	NA	1,144	1.1	3.3
165 CH OF NAZARENE	4	349	625	.6	1.8
167 CHS OF CHRIST	2	226	300	.3	.9
179 CONSRV BAPT	1	NR	NR	-	-
193 EPISCOPAL	2	614	805	.7	2.3
207 E.L.C.A.	1	693	939	.9	2.7
215 EVAN METH CH	1	110	137*	.1	.4
221 FREE METHODIST	1	42	100	.1	.3
259 IFCA	1	NR	NR	-	-
283 LUTH—MO SYNOD	1	186	228	.2	.7
355 PRESB CH (USA)	2	625	781*	.7	2.3
413 S.D.A.	4	318	397*	.4	1.2
419 SO BAPT CONV	10	4,989	6,232*	5.8	18.1
443 UN C OF CHRIST	1	91	114*	.1	.3
449 UN METHODIST	3	2,575	3,217*	3.0	9.3
467 WESLEYAN	1	21	37	-	.1
496 JEWISH EST[1]	1	NA	1,825	1.7	5.3
497 BLACK BAPT EST[2]	NA	1,516	1,894*	1.8	5.5
PALM BEACH	**347**	**121,856**	**379,678***	**44.0**	**100.0**
019 AMER BAPT USA	1	150	178*	-	-
045 APOSTOLIC LUTH	1	78	154	-	-
053 ASSEMB OF GOD	14	2,726	4,540	.5	1.2
081 CATHOLIC	32	NA	108,913	12.6	28.7
081b BYZAN RUTH	*1*	*NA*	*150*	*-*	*-*
081d LATIN	*30*	*NA*	*108,743*	*12.6*	*28.6*
081h UKRAINIAN	*1*	*NA*	*20*	*-*	*-*
089 CHR & MISS AL	8	529	943	.1	.2
093 CHR CH (DISC)	4	633	993	.1	.3
097 CHR CHS&CHS CR	6	792	940*	.1	.2
105 CHRISTIAN REF	3	424	631	.1	.2
111 CH CR,SCIENTST	7	NR	NR	-	-
123 CH GOD (ANDER)	5	602	675	.1	.2
127 CH GOD (CLEVE)	22	3,860	4,583*	.5	1.2
133 CH GOD(7TH)DEN	1	12	23	-	-
145 CH GOD PROPHCY	8	275	326*	-	.1
151 L-D SAINTS	8	NA	2,477	.3	.7
165 CH OF NAZARENE	12	1,341	1,965	.2	.5
167 CHS OF CHRIST	14	1,507	2,070	.2	.5
179 CONSRV BAPT	1	NR	NR	-	-
193 EPISCOPAL	22	7,951	11,915	1.4	3.1
203 EVAN FREE CH	1	110	200	-	.1
207 E.L.C.A.	12	4,902	6,546	.8	1.7
221 FREE METHODIST	4	118	193	-	.1
223 FREE WILL BAPT	1	44	52*	-	-
226 FRIENDS-USA	1	32	62	-	-
226d FGC & FUM	*1*	*32*	*62*	*-*	*-*
246 GREEK ORTHODOX	2	NR	NR	-	-
263 INT FOURSQ GOS	2	15	18*	-	-
283 LUTH—MO SYNOD	8	3,791	4,933	.6	1.3
313 N AM BAPT CONF	1	85	101*	-	-
329 OPEN BIBLE STD	1	NR	NR	-	-
331 ORTH CH IN AM	1	NR	NR	-	-

NA–Not applicable NR–Not reported *Total adherents estimated from known number of communicant, confirmed, full members. - Represents a percent less than 0.1. Percentages may not total due to rounding.
[1]See Appendix E [2]See Appendix F [3]See Appendix G Lines in *italic* represent a breakdown of Catholic rites or Friends affiliations. They are included in their respective denominational total.

Table 4. Churches and Church Membership by County and Denomination: 1990

County and Denomination	Number of churches	Communicant, confirmed, full members	Total adherents Number	Percent of total population	Percent of total adherents
349 PENT HOLINESS	2	291	345*	-	.1
353 CHR BRETHREN	4	459	870	.1	.2
355 PRESB CH (USA)	15	6,237	7,405*	.9	2.0
356 PRESB CH AMER	8	2,915	3,409	.4	.9
371 REF CH IN AM	1	151	213	-	.1
403 SALVATION ARMY	2	228	237	-	.1
413 S.D.A.	12	2,394	2,842*	.3	.7
419 SO BAPT CONV	39	30,885	36,667*	4.2	9.7
435 UNITARIAN-UNIV	2	383	508	.1	.1
443 UN C OF CHRIST	7	3,119	3,703*	.4	1.0
449 UN METHODIST	24	17,018	20,204*	2.3	5.3
467 WESLEYAN	1	26	70	-	-
469 WELS	2	99	169	-	-
496 JEWISH EST[1]	18	NA	112,000	13.0	29.5
497 BLACK BAPT EST[2]	NA	27,674	32,855*	3.8	8.7
499 INDEP.NON-CHAR[3]	7	NA	4,750	.6	1.3
PASCO	**161**	**38,225**	**97,372***	**34.6**	**100.0**
053 ASSEMB OF GOD	10	1,414	1,990	.7	2.0
081 CATHOLIC	13	NA	48,462	17.2	49.8
081b *BYZAN RUTH*	1	*NA*	*200*	.1	.2
081d *LATIN*	11	*NA*	*47,984*	17.1	49.3
081h *UKRAINIAN*	1	*NA*	*278*	.1	.3
089 CHR & MISS AL	3	164	317	.1	.3
093 CHR CH (DISC)	1	207	328	.1	.3
097 CHR CHS&CHS CR	5	1,121	1,305*	.5	1.3
111 CH CR,SCIENTST	3	NR	NR	-	-
123 CH GOD (ANDER)	3	138	290	.1	.3
127 CH GOD (CLEVE)	8	1,580	1,839*	.7	1.9
145 CH GOD PROPHCY	1	34	40*	-	-
151 L-D SAINTS	2	NA	810	.3	.8
163 CH OF LUTH BR	1	71	121	-	.1
165 CH OF NAZARENE	6	569	1,056	.4	1.1
167 CHS OF CHRIST	7	512	632	.2	.6
179 CONSRV BAPT	1	NR	NR	-	-
193 EPISCOPAL	5	1,389	2,016	.7	2.1
203 EVAN FREE CH	1	138	296	.1	.3
207 E.L.C.A.	8	2,263	2,620	.9	2.7
221 FREE METHODIST	2	210	310	.1	.3
246 GREEK ORTHODOX	1	NR	NR	-	-
263 INT FOURSQ GOS	1	45	52*	-	.1
283 LUTH—MO SYNOD	4	1,555	1,756	.6	1.8
325 OLD REG BAPT	1	29	34*	-	-
331 ORTH CH IN AM	1	NR	NR	-	-
339 PENT CH OF GOD	1	34	77	-	.1
353 CHR BRETHREN	2	120	155	.1	.2
355 PRESB CH (USA)	6	2,240	2,607*	.9	2.7
356 PRESB CH AMER	1	84	141	.1	.1
361 PRIM BAPT ASCS	1	25	29*	-	-
363 PRIMITIVE METH	1	25	25	-	-
371 REF CH IN AM	2	548	888	.3	.9
403 SALVATION ARMY	1	112	113	-	.1
413 S.D.A.	3	639	744*	.3	.8
419 SO BAPT CONV	33	13,010	15,144*	5.4	15.6
443 UN C OF CHRIST	3	886	1,031*	.4	1.1
449 UN METHODIST	13	7,230	8,416*	3.0	8.6
467 WESLEYAN	3	111	373	.1	.4
469 WELS	2	320	393	.1	.4
496 JEWISH EST[1]	0	NA	1,000	.4	1.0
497 BLACK BAPT EST[2]	NA	1,402	1,632*	.6	1.7
499 INDEP.NON-CHAR[3]	1	NA	330	.1	.3
PINELLAS	**396**	**161,893**	**350,396***	**41.1**	**100.0**
001 ADVENT CHR CH	2	210	244*	-	.1
019 AMER BAPT USA	6	1,774	2,062*	.2	.6
053 ASSEMB OF GOD	16	4,270	8,614	1.0	2.5
057 BAPT GEN CONF	1	12	14*	-	-
071 BRETHREN (ASH)	1	10	12*	-	-
075 BRETHREN IN CR	1	6	17	-	-
081 CATHOLIC	28	NA	131,099	15.4	37.4
081b *BYZAN RUTH*	1	*NA*	*325*	-	.1
081d *LATIN*	26	*NA*	*130,524*	15.3	37.3
081h *UKRAINIAN*	1	*NA*	*250*	-	.1
089 CHR & MISS AL	4	312	717	.1	.2
093 CHR CH (DISC)	6	1,490	2,011	.2	.6
097 CHR CHS&CHS CR	8	5,305	6,166*	.7	1.8
105 CHRISTIAN REF	2	92	117	-	-
111 CH CR,SCIENTST	9	NR	NR	-	-
123 CH GOD (ANDER)	4	490	502	.1	.1
127 CH GOD (CLEVE)	13	4,183	4,862*	.6	1.4
145 CH GOD PROPHCY	2	69	80*	-	-
151 L-D SAINTS	7	NA	2,932	.3	.8
157 CH OF BRETHREN	1	159	185*	-	.1
165 CH OF NAZARENE	11	1,308	2,414	.3	.7
167 CHS OF CHRIST	23	2,823	4,219	.5	1.2
179 CONSRV BAPT	1	NR	NR	-	-
193 EPISCOPAL	21	10,393	13,150	1.5	3.8
195 ESTONIAN ELC	1	46	53*	-	-
203 EVAN FREE CH	2	115	147	-	-
207 E.L.C.A.	18	9,824	11,929	1.4	3.4
221 FREE METHODIST	2	365	365	-	.1
226 FRIENDS-USA	2	58	146	-	-
226d *FGC & FUM*	2	*58*	*146*	-	-
246 GREEK ORTHODOX	4	NR	NR	-	-
263 INT FOURSQ GOS	2	444	516*	.1	.1
269 JASPER&PVB ASC	1	50	58*	-	-
274 LAT EVAN LUTH	1	203	209	-	.1
283 LUTH—MO SYNOD	8	5,479	6,715	.8	1.9
285 MENNONITE CH	1	22	37	-	-
291 MISSIONARY CH	4	314	349	-	.1
329 OPEN BIBLE STD	7	NR	NR	-	-
331 ORTH CH IN AM	1	NR	NR	-	-
349 PENT HOLINESS	3	93	108*	-	.1
353 CHR BRETHREN	1	101	202	-	.1
355 PRESB CH (USA)	32	12,830	14,912*	1.8	4.3
356 PRESB CH AMER	3	160	243	-	.1
361 PRIM BAPT ASCS	1	49	57*	-	-
371 REF CH IN AM	2	269	398	-	.1
375 REF EPISCOPAL	1	6	6	-	-
403 SALVATION ARMY	3	610	674	.1	.2
413 S.D.A.	7	1,490	1,732*	.2	.5
415 S-D BAPTIST GC	1	30	35*	-	-
419 SO BAPT CONV	35	35,385	41,126*	4.8	11.7
431 UKRANIAN AMER	1	NR	NR	-	-
435 UNITARIAN-UNIV	4	588	707	.1	.2
443 UN C OF CHRIST	10	3,804	4,421*	.5	1.3
449 UN METHODIST	43	38,024	44,193*	5.2	12.6
467 WESLEYAN	4	1,060	2,669	.3	.8
469 WELS	3	644	795	.1	.2
496 JEWISH EST[1]	8	NA	9,500	1.1	2.7
497 BLACK BAPT EST[2]	NA	16,924	19,670*	2.3	5.6
498 INDEP.CHARIS.[3]	1	NA	1,600	.2	.5
499 INDEP.NON-CHAR[3]	12	NA	7,407	.9	2.1
POLK	**383**	**126,107**	**191,721***	**47.3**	**100.0**
001 ADVENT CHR CH	1	29	36*	-	-
019 AMER BAPT USA	1	67	83*	-	-
053 ASSEMB OF GOD	43	8,568	13,197	3.3	6.9
055 AS REF PRES CH	4	1,427	1,719	.4	.9
059 BAPT MISS ASSN	1	61	75*	-	-
081 CATHOLIC	9	NA	25,292	6.2	13.2
081d *LATIN*	9	*NA*	*25,292*	6.2	13.2
089 CHR & MISS AL	4	306	532	.1	.3
093 CHR CH (DISC)	5	1,015	1,289	.3	.7
097 CHR CHS&CHS CR	8	1,243	1,534*	.4	.8
111 CH CR,SCIENTST	4	NR	NR	-	-
123 CH GOD (ANDER)	9	1,105	1,171	.3	.6
127 CH GOD (CLEVE)	30	4,861	5,997*	1.5	3.1
133 CH GOD(7TH)DEN	1	11	21	-	-
145 CH GOD PROPHCY	3	103	127*	-	.1
151 L-D SAINTS	5	NA	2,064	.5	1.1
164 CH LUTH CONF	1	72	101	-	.1
165 CH OF NAZARENE	15	2,488	2,986	.7	1.6
167 CHS OF CHRIST	28	2,878	4,020	1.0	2.1
193 EPISCOPAL	12	2,971	4,494	1.1	2.3
203 EVAN FREE CH	1	80	135	-	.1
207 E.L.C.A.	5	1,157	1,359	.3	.7
209 EVAN LUTH SYN	1	92	126	-	.1
221 FREE METHODIST	2	129	204	.1	.1
223 FREE WILL BAPT	6	574	708*	.2	.4
226 FRIENDS-USA	1	0	12	-	-
226d *FGC & FUM*	1	*0*	*12*	-	-
246 GREEK ORTHODOX	1	NR	NR	-	-
283 LUTH—MO SYNOD	5	3,680	4,667	1.2	2.4
291 MISSIONARY CH	1	46	85	-	-
331 ORTH CH IN AM	1	NR	NR	-	-
339 PENT CH OF GOD	2	70	82	-	-
349 PENT HOLINESS	1	12	15*	-	-
353 CHR BRETHREN	1	25	50	-	-
355 PRESB CH (USA)	14	5,432	6,702*	1.7	3.5
356 PRESB CH AMER	2	871	1,035	.3	.5
361 PRIM BAPT ASCS	6	135	167*	-	.1
363 PRIMITIVE METH	1	38	44	-	-
403 SALVATION ARMY	2	250	275	.1	.1
413 S.D.A.	6	756	933*	.2	.5
419 SO BAPT CONV	98	54,441	67,167*	16.6	35.0
435 UNITARIAN-UNIV	1	89	94	-	-
443 UN C OF CHRIST	1	166	205*	.1	.1
449 UN METHODIST	33	16,825	20,758*	5.1	10.8
467 WESLEYAN	1	60	220	.1	.1
496 JEWISH EST[1]	1	NA	0	-	-
497 BLACK BAPT EST[2]	NA	13,974	17,240*	4.3	9.0
498 INDEP.CHARIS.[3]	2	NA	2,750	.7	1.4
499 INDEP.NON-CHAR[3]	3	NA	1,950	.5	1.0

NA–Not applicable   NR–Not reported   *Total adherents estimated from known number of communicant, confirmed, full members.   - Represents a percent less than 0.1.   Percentages may not total due to rounding.

[1] See Appendix E   [2] See Appendix F   [3] See Appendix G   Lines in *italic* represent a breakdown of Catholic rites or Friends affiliations. They are included in their respective denominational total.

Table 4. Churches and Church Membership by County and Denomination: 1990

County and Denomination	Number of churches	Communicant, confirmed, full members	Total adherents		
			Number	Percent of total population	Percent of total adherents
PUTNAM	**85**	**19,881**	**27,859***	**42.8**	**100.0**
005 AME ZION	1	100	100	.2	.4
053 ASSEMB OF GOD	2	369	700	1.1	2.5
059 BAPT MISS ASSN	1	23	29*	-	.1
081 CATHOLIC	3	NA	1,910	2.9	6.9
081d LATIN	3	NA	1,910	2.9	6.9
089 CHR & MISS AL	1	33	43	.1	.2
097 CHR CHS&CHS CR	1	50	62*	.1	.2
111 CH CR,SCIENTST	1	NR	NR	-	-
123 CH GOD (ANDER)	2	117	188	.3	.7
127 CH GOD (CLEVE)	3	233	291*	.4	1.0
145 CH GOD PROPHCY	2	69	86*	.1	.3
151 L-D SAINTS	2	NA	800	1.2	2.9
165 CH OF NAZARENE	1	40	67	.1	.2
167 CHS OF CHRIST	5	330	421	.6	1.5
175 CONGR CHR CHS	1	80	100*	.2	.4
193 EPISCOPAL	6	596	783	1.2	2.8
207 E.L.C.A.	1	116	145	.2	.5
325 OLD REG BAPT	2	45	56*	.1	.2
349 PENT HOLINESS	1	175	219*	.3	.8
355 PRESB CH (USA)	3	510	637*	1.0	2.3
361 PRIM BAPT ASCS	1	19	24*	-	.1
413 S.D.A.	3	341	426*	.7	1.5
415 S-D BAPTIST GC	1	30	37*	.1	.1
419 SO BAPT CONV	30	11,702	14,613*	22.5	52.5
443 UN C OF CHRIST	1	136	170*	.3	.6
449 UN METHODIST	10	2,281	2,848*	4.4	10.2
497 BLACK BAPT EST[2]	NA	2,486	3,104*	4.8	11.1
SAINT JOHNS	**59**	**15,057**	**30,544***	**36.4**	**100.0**
053 ASSEMB OF GOD	1	59	85	.1	.3
081 CATHOLIC	8	NA	10,734	12.8	35.1
081d LATIN	8	NA	10,734	12.8	35.1
097 CHR CHS&CHS CR	1	75	91*	.1	.3
111 CH CR,SCIENTST	1	NR	NR	-	-
123 CH GOD (ANDER)	2	32	85	.1	.3
127 CH GOD (CLEVE)	1	33	40*	-	.1
151 L-D SAINTS	1	NA	465	.6	1.5
165 CH OF NAZARENE	1	117	186	.2	.6
167 CHS OF CHRIST	2	185	234	.3	.8
193 EPISCOPAL	5	2,123	2,800	3.3	9.2
207 E.L.C.A.	2	365	447	.5	1.5
246 GREEK ORTHODOX	2	NR	NR	-	-
283 LUTH—MO SYNOD	1	8	90	.1	.3
349 PENT HOLINESS	3	796	965*	1.2	3.2
355 PRESB CH (USA)	2	781	947*	1.1	3.1
356 PRESB CH AMER	2	0	0	-	-
413 S.D.A.	2	226	274*	.3	.9
419 SO BAPT CONV	13	6,377	7,733*	9.2	25.3
435 UNITARIAN-UNIV	1	56	56	.1	.2
443 UN C OF CHRIST	1	52	63*	.1	.2
449 UN METHODIST	7	1,889	2,291*	2.7	7.5
496 JEWISH EST[1]	0	NA	675	.8	2.2
497 BLACK BAPT EST[2]	NA	1,883	2,283*	2.7	7.5
SAINT LUCIE	**80**	**25,011**	**53,248***	**35.5**	**100.0**
053 ASSEMB OF GOD	2	1,016	1,650	1.1	3.1
081 CATHOLIC	4	NA	17,485	11.6	32.8
081d LATIN	4	NA	17,485	11.6	32.8
089 CHR & MISS AL	2	59	115	.1	.2
093 CHR CH (DISC)	1	64	102	.1	.2
097 CHR CHS&CHS CR	3	200	246*	.2	.5
105 CHRISTIAN REF	1	19	35	-	.1
111 CH CR,SCIENTST	1	NR	NR	-	-
123 CH GOD (ANDER)	1	25	34	-	.1
127 CH GOD (CLEVE)	5	706	867*	.6	1.6
151 L-D SAINTS	1	NA	333	.2	.6
165 CH OF NAZARENE	4	540	809	.5	1.5
167 CHS OF CHRIST	5	368	471	.3	.9
193 EPISCOPAL	3	1,187	1,419	.9	2.7
207 E.L.C.A.	3	902	1,109	.7	2.1
209 EVAN LUTH SYN	1	74	93	.1	.2
216 EVAN PRESBY CH	1	106	113	.1	.2
226 FRIENDS-USA	1	196	450	.3	.8
226b EFI	1	196	450	.3	.8
246 GREEK ORTHODOX	1	NR	NR	-	-
283 LUTH—MO SYNOD	1	335	416	.3	.8
331 ORTH CH IN AM	1	NR	NR	-	-
339 PENT CH OF GOD	1	35	77	.1	.1
353 CHR BRETHREN	3	42	49	-	.1
355 PRESB CH (USA)	4	1,375	1,688*	1.1	3.2
361 PRIM BAPT ASCS	1	26	32*	-	.1
403 SALVATION ARMY	1	98	102	.1	.2
413 S.D.A.	3	583	716*	.5	1.3
419 SO BAPT CONV	14	6,776	8,318*	5.5	15.6
443 UN C OF CHRIST	3	765	939*	.6	1.8

County and Denomination	Number of churches	Communicant, confirmed, full members	Total adherents		
			Number	Percent of total population	Percent of total adherents
449 UN METHODIST	6	3,176	3,899*	2.6	7.3
496 JEWISH EST[1]	1	NA	3,500	2.3	6.6
497 BLACK BAPT EST[2]	NA	6,338	7,781*	5.2	14.6
499 INDEP.NON-CHAR[3]	1	NA	400	.3	.8
SANTA ROSA	**110**	**24,813**	**39,127***	**47.9**	**100.0**
005 AME ZION	2	242	242	.3	.6
053 ASSEMB OF GOD	20	3,239	7,000	8.6	17.9
081 CATHOLIC	3	NA	3,757	4.6	9.6
081d LATIN	3	NA	3,757	4.6	9.6
123 CH GOD (ANDER)	1	11	21	-	.1
127 CH GOD (CLEVE)	1	46	59*	.1	.2
145 CH GOD PROPHCY	1	34	43*	.1	.1
151 L-D SAINTS	3	NA	731	.9	1.9
165 CH OF NAZARENE	1	70	101	.1	.3
167 CHS OF CHRIST	9	723	952	1.2	2.4
193 EPISCOPAL	3	515	727	.9	1.9
283 LUTH—MO SYNOD	2	288	326	.4	.8
285 MENNONITE CH	1	24	34	-	.1
349 PENT HOLINESS	2	37	47*	.1	.1
355 PRESB CH (USA)	2	363	462*	.6	1.2
356 PRESB CH AMER	2	242	261	.3	.7
361 PRIM BAPT ASCS	2	38	48*	.1	.1
413 S.D.A.	2	473	602*	.7	1.5
419 SO BAPT CONV	38	13,280	16,913*	20.7	43.2
449 UN METHODIST	15	4,347	5,536*	6.8	14.1
496 JEWISH EST[1]	0	NA	194	.2	.5
497 BLACK BAPT EST[2]	NA	841	1,071*	1.3	2.7
SARASOTA	**175**	**53,943**	**109,446***	**39.4**	**100.0**
039 AP CHR CH(NAZ)	1	8	9*	-	-
040 AP CHR CH-AMER	1	61	106	-	.1
053 ASSEMB OF GOD	8	762	1,263	.5	1.2
061 BEACHY AMISH	1	145	165*	.1	.2
071 BRETHREN (ASH)	2	291	332*	.1	.3
075 BRETHREN IN CR	2	76	80	-	.1
081 CATHOLIC	9	NA	30,641	11.0	28.0
081d LATIN	9	NA	30,641	11.0	28.0
089 CHR & MISS AL	2	65	212	.1	.2
093 CHR CH (DISC)	3	911	1,353	.5	1.2
097 CHR CHS&CHS CR	3	318	363*	.1	.3
111 CH CR,SCIENTST	5	NR	NR	-	-
123 CH GOD (ANDER)	3	353	474	.2	.4
127 CH GOD (CLEVE)	6	609	695*	.3	.6
151 L-D SAINTS	1	NA	610	.2	.6
157 CH OF BRETHREN	1	13	15*	-	-
164 CH LUTH CONF	1	10	12	-	-
165 CH OF NAZARENE	4	527	731	.3	.7
167 CHS OF CHRIST	9	721	924	.3	.8
175 CONGR CHR CHS	1	60	68*	-	.1
179 CONSRV BAPT	1	NR	NR	-	-
193 EPISCOPAL	11	4,978	5,881	2.1	5.4
203 EVAN FREE CH	2	155	271	.1	.2
207 E.L.C.A.	8	3,934	4,682	1.7	4.3
226 FRIENDS-USA	2	54	85	-	.1
226b EFI	1	24	30	-	-
226d FGC & FUM	1	30	55	-	.1
246 GREEK ORTHODOX	1	NR	NR	-	-
263 INT FOURSQ GOS	1	0	0*	-	-
283 LUTH—MO SYNOD	4	1,393	1,629	.6	1.5
285 MENNONITE CH	10	2,115	2,997	1.1	2.7
323 OLD ORD AMISH	1	NA	150	.1	.1
331 ORTH CH IN AM	1	NR	NR	-	-
353 CHR BRETHREN	2	65	105	-	.1
355 PRESB CH (USA)	12	8,821	10,062*	3.6	9.2
356 PRESB CH AMER	4	711	828	.3	.8
371 REF CH IN AM	2	143	310	.1	.3
403 SALVATION ARMY	2	211	241	.1	.2
413 S.D.A.	4	493	562*	.2	.5
419 SO BAPT CONV	17	9,538	10,879*	3.9	9.9
435 UNITARIAN-UNIV	1	345	405	.1	.4
443 UN C OF CHRIST	4	2,016	2,300*	.8	2.1
449 UN METHODIST	13	10,591	12,081*	4.3	11.0
467 WESLEYAN	1	38	115	-	.1
469 WELS	2	310	422	.2	.4
496 JEWISH EST[1]	3	NA	9,750	3.5	8.9
497 BLACK BAPT EST[2]	NA	3,102	3,538*	1.3	3.2
499 INDEP.NON-CHAR[3]	3	NA	4,100	1.5	3.7
SEMINOLE	**144**	**48,657**	**113,136***	**39.3**	**100.0**
053 ASSEMB OF GOD	8	1,148	1,813	.6	1.6
055 AS REF PRES CH	2	99	128	-	.1
057 BAPT GEN CONF	1	149	186*	.1	.2
081 CATHOLIC	8	NA	40,679	14.1	36.0
081d LATIN	8	NA	40,679	14.1	36.0
089 CHR & MISS AL	5	414	946	.3	.8

NA–Not applicable   NR–Not reported   *Total adherents estimated from known number of communicant, confirmed, full members.   - Represents a percent less than 0.1.   Percentages may not total due to rounding.
[1]See Appendix E   [2]See Appendix F   [3]See Appendix G   Lines in *italic* represent a breakdown of Catholic rites or Friends affiliations. They are included in their respective denominational total.

Table 4. Churches and Church Membership by County and Denomination: 1990

County and Denomination	Number of churches	Communicant, confirmed, full members	Total adherents Number	Percent of total population	Percent of total adherents
093 CHR CH (DISC)	2	301	322	.1	.3
097 CHR CHS&CHS CR	6	452	563*	.2	.5
111 CH CR,SCIENTST	1	NR	NR	-	-
123 CH GOD (ANDER)	1	0	0	-	-
127 CH GOD (CLEVE)	4	822	1,024*	.4	.9
145 CH GOD PROPHCY	3	103	128*	-	.1
151 L-D SAINTS	5	NA	2,177	.8	1.9
165 CH OF NAZARENE	6	475	953	.3	.8
167 CHS OF CHRIST	8	780	1,122	.4	1.0
175 CONGR CHR CHS	1	83	103*	-	.1
193 EPISCOPAL	6	2,063	3,747	1.3	3.3
199 EVAN CONGR CH	1	57	88	-	.1
203 EVAN FREE CH	1	0	0	-	-
207 E.L.C.A.	4	1,486	1,990	.7	1.8
216 EVAN PRESBY CH	1	20	21	-	-
283 LUTH—MO SYNOD	4	2,456	3,166	1.1	2.8
284 LUTH CH-AM ASC	1	120	142	-	.1
295 MORAV CH-SOUTH	1	313	365	.1	.3
331 ORTH CH IN AM	1	NR	NR	-	-
355 PRESB CH (USA)	9	3,121	3,889*	1.4	3.4
356 PRESB CH AMER	1	252	425	.1	.4
361 PRIM BAPT ASCS	1	15	19*	-	-
403 SALVATION ARMY	1	88	106	-	.1
413 S.D.A.	14	4,946	6,163*	2.1	5.4
419 SO BAPT CONV	20	14,887	18,549*	6.5	16.4
438 UN BRETH IN CR	1	67	83	-	.1
443 UN C OF CHRIST	3	482	601*	.2	.5
449 UN METHODIST	10	7,194	8,964*	3.1	7.9
467 WESLEYAN	1	17	70	-	.1
496 JEWISH EST[1]	0	NA	4,870	1.7	4.3
497 BLACK BAPT EST[2]	NA	6,247	7,784*	2.7	6.9
499 INDEP.NON-CHAR[3]	2	NA	1,950	.7	1.7
SUMTER	**50**	**9,886**	**13,030***	**41.3**	**100.0**
005 AME ZION	1	220	220	.7	1.7
053 ASSEMB OF GOD	6	452	743	2.4	5.7
081 CATHOLIC	1	NA	872	2.8	6.7
081d LATIN	1	NA	872	2.8	6.7
127 CH GOD (CLEVE)	7	549	664*	2.1	5.1
167 CHS OF CHRIST	5	256	344	1.1	2.6
193 EPISCOPAL	1	82	113	.4	.9
355 PRESB CH (USA)	3	176	213*	.7	1.6
361 PRIM BAPT ASCS	1	9	11*	-	.1
413 S.D.A.	1	56	68*	.2	.5
419 SO BAPT CONV	14	5,815	7,034*	22.3	54.0
449 UN METHODIST	10	1,209	1,463*	4.6	11.2
497 BLACK BAPT EST[2]	NA	1,062	1,285*	4.1	9.9
SUWANNEE	**77**	**13,460**	**17,948***	**67.0**	**100.0**
001 ADVENT CHR CH	5	401	502*	1.9	2.8
053 ASSEMB OF GOD	3	141	290	1.1	1.6
059 BAPT MISS ASSN	1	45	56*	.2	.3
081 CATHOLIC	2	NA	601	2.2	3.3
081d LATIN	2	NA	601	2.2	3.3
097 CHR CHS&CHS CR	3	195	244*	.9	1.4
111 CH CR,SCIENTST	1	NR	NR	-	-
123 CH GOD (ANDER)	2	34	61	.2	.3
127 CH GOD (CLEVE)	4	458	573*	2.1	3.2
151 L-D SAINTS	1	NA	368	1.4	2.1
164 CH LUTH CONF	1	27	54	.2	.3
165 CH OF NAZARENE	1	77	96	.4	.5
167 CHS OF CHRIST	5	347	451	1.7	2.5
193 EPISCOPAL	1	235	271	1.0	1.5
223 FREE WILL BAPT	1	25	31*	.1	.2
355 PRESB CH (USA)	2	126	158*	.6	.9
356 PRESB CH AMER	1	272	329	1.2	1.8
361 PRIM BAPT ASCS	4	36	45*	.2	.3
413 S.D.A.	1	39	49*	.2	.3
419 SO BAPT CONV	33	9,286	11,621*	43.4	64.7
449 UN METHODIST	5	894	1,119*	4.2	6.2
497 BLACK BAPT EST[2]	NA	822	1,029*	3.8	5.7
TAYLOR	**43**	**7,774**	**10,475***	**61.2**	**100.0**
053 ASSEMB OF GOD	1	108	250	1.5	2.4
081 CATHOLIC	1	NA	216	1.3	2.1
081d LATIN	1	NA	216	1.3	2.1
123 CH GOD (ANDER)	1	50	75	.4	.7
127 CH GOD (CLEVE)	2	206	263*	1.5	2.5
145 CH GOD PROPHCY	2	69	88*	.5	.8
165 CH OF NAZARENE	1	42	165	1.0	1.6
167 CHS OF CHRIST	4	277	337	2.0	3.2
193 EPISCOPAL	1	94	119	.7	1.1
223 FREE WILL BAPT	1	36	46*	.3	.4
349 PENT HOLINESS	1	39	50*	.3	.5
355 PRESB CH (USA)	1	207	265*	1.5	2.5
361 PRIM BAPT ASCS	1	29	37*	.2	.4

County and Denomination	Number of churches	Communicant, confirmed, full members	Total adherents Number	Percent of total population	Percent of total adherents
413 S.D.A.	1	56	72*	.4	.7
419 SO BAPT CONV	17	5,097	6,513*	38.1	62.2
449 UN METHODIST	6	754	963*	5.6	9.2
467 WESLEYAN	2	81	212	1.2	2.0
497 BLACK BAPT EST[2]	NA	629	804*	4.7	7.7
UNION	**20**	**3,152**	**4,315***	**42.1**	**100.0**
001 ADVENT CHR CH	1	26	33*	.3	.8
053 ASSEMB OF GOD	1	12	11	.1	.3
097 CHR CHS&CHS CR	1	175	220*	2.1	5.1
127 CH GOD (CLEVE)	2	61	77*	.8	1.8
151 L-D SAINTS	1	NA	351	3.4	8.1
167 CHS OF CHRIST	2	151	199	1.9	4.6
223 FREE WILL BAPT	2	201	252*	2.5	5.8
361 PRIM BAPT ASCS	2	54	68*	.7	1.6
419 SO BAPT CONV	6	1,827	2,294*	22.4	53.2
449 UN METHODIST	2	160	201*	2.0	4.7
497 BLACK BAPT EST[2]	NA	485	609*	5.9	14.1
VOLUSIA	**257**	**72,272**	**133,672***	**36.1**	**100.0**
019 AMER BAPT USA	3	660	781*	.2	.6
053 ASSEMB OF GOD	9	2,928	3,759	1.0	2.8
081 CATHOLIC	13	NA	40,168	10.8	30.0
081b BYZAN RUTH	1	NA	200	.1	.1
081d LATIN	12	NA	39,968	10.8	29.9
089 CHR & MISS AL	7	972	1,795	.5	1.3
093 CHR CH (DISC)	6	1,445	1,928	.5	1.4
097 CHR CHS&CHS CR	9	2,113	2,502*	.7	1.9
111 CH CR,SCIENTST	5	NR	NR	-	-
123 CH GOD (ANDER)	4	1,105	1,142	.3	.9
127 CH GOD (CLEVE)	11	1,051	1,244*	.3	.9
145 CH GOD PROPHCY	6	206	244*	.1	.2
151 L-D SAINTS	4	NA	1,632	.4	1.2
165 CH OF NAZARENE	6	506	943	.3	.7
167 CHS OF CHRIST	12	1,308	1,737	.5	1.3
175 CONGR CHR CHS	1	65	77*	-	.1
193 EPISCOPAL	11	3,840	5,060	1.4	3.8
203 EVAN FREE CH	1	60	125	-	.1
207 E.L.C.A.	8	2,403	2,912	.8	2.2
216 EVAN PRESBY CH	1	182	182	-	.1
221 FREE METHODIST	1	5	24	-	-
223 FREE WILL BAPT	2	58	69*	-	.1
226 FRIENDS-USA	1	0	7	-	-
226d FGC & FUM	1	0	7	-	-
246 GREEK ORTHODOX	1	NR	NR	-	-
259 IFCA	1	NR	NR	-	-
263 INT FOURSQ GOS	1	106	126*	-	.1
283 LUTH—MO SYNOD	3	1,359	1,638	.4	1.2
329 OPEN BIBLE STD	3	NR	NR	-	-
331 ORTH CH IN AM	1	NR	NR	-	-
339 PENT CH OF GOD	1	50	78	-	.1
349 PENT HOLINESS	6	467	553*	.1	.4
353 CHR BRETHREN	2	122	244	.1	.2
355 PRESB CH (USA)	14	5,350	6,334*	1.7	4.7
356 PRESB CH AMER	4	450	609	.2	.5
361 PRIM BAPT ASCS	1	13	15*	-	-
403 SALVATION ARMY	1	82	84	-	.1
413 S.D.A.	7	933	1,105*	.3	.8
415 S-D BAPTIST GC	1	112	133*	-	.1
419 SO BAPT CONV	42	22,335	26,445*	7.1	19.8
435 UNITARIAN-UNIV	2	232	254	.1	.2
438 UN BRETH IN CR	2	160	180	-	.1
443 UN C OF CHRIST	10	2,289	2,710*	.7	2.0
449 UN METHODIST	25	10,533	12,471*	3.4	9.3
467 WESLEYAN	1	34	85	-	.1
469 WELS	2	142	199	.1	.1
496 JEWISH EST[1]	3	NA	2,500	.7	1.9
497 BLACK BAPT EST[2]	NA	8,596	10,178*	2.7	7.6
499 INDEP.NON-CHAR[3]	2	NA	1,400	.4	1.0
WAKULLA	**25**	**3,764**	**4,983***	**35.1**	**100.0**
053 ASSEMB OF GOD	2	188	245	1.7	4.9
081 CATHOLIC	1	NA	150	1.1	3.0
081d LATIN	1	NA	150	1.1	3.0
167 CHS OF CHRIST	3	77	91	.6	1.8
193 EPISCOPAL	1	21	41	.3	.8
283 LUTH—MO SYNOD	1	57	91	.6	1.8
349 PENT HOLINESS	1	70	89*	.6	1.8
413 S.D.A.	1	64	82*	.6	1.6
419 SO BAPT CONV	10	2,283	2,913*	20.5	58.5
449 UN METHODIST	5	629	803*	5.7	16.1
497 BLACK BAPT EST[2]	NA	375	478*	3.4	9.6
WALTON	**79**	**8,954**	**12,384***	**44.6**	**100.0**
053 ASSEMB OF GOD	10	416	618	2.2	5.0
081 CATHOLIC	4	NA	661	2.4	5.3

NA–Not applicable   NR–Not reported   *Total adherents estimated from known number of communicant, confirmed, full members.   - Represents a percent less than 0.1.   Percentages may not total due to rounding.
[1]See Appendix E   [2]See Appendix F   [3]See Appendix G   Lines in *italic* represent a breakdown of Catholic rites or Friends affiliations. They are included in their respective denominational total.

Table 4. Churches and Church Membership by County and Denomination: 1990

County and Denomination	Number of churches	Communicant, confirmed, full members	Total adherents Number	Percent of total population	Percent of total adherents
081d LATIN	4	NA	661	2.4	5.3
097 CHR CHS&CHS CR	1	35	43*	.2	.3
127 CH GOD (CLEVE)	3	161	197*	.7	1.6
151 L-D SAINTS	2	NA	611	2.2	4.9
167 CHS OF CHRIST	6	241	314	1.1	2.5
193 EPISCOPAL	2	80	106	.4	.9
355 PRESB CH (USA)	6	474	581*	2.1	4.7
413 S.D.A.	1	50	61*	.2	.5
419 SO BAPT CONV	32	5,826	7,143*	25.7	57.7
449 UN METHODIST	12	1,279	1,568*	5.6	12.7
497 BLACK BAPT EST2	NA	392	481*	1.7	3.9
WASHINGTON	**47**	**6,494**	**8,904***	**52.6**	**100.0**
053 ASSEMB OF GOD	7	794	1,005	5.9	11.3
081 CATHOLIC	2	NA	356	2.1	4.0
081d LATIN	2	NA	356	2.1	4.0
127 CH GOD (CLEVE)	2	81	100*	.6	1.1
145 CH GOD PROPHCY	1	34	42*	.2	.5
151 L-D SAINTS	1	NA	523	3.1	5.9
167 CHS OF CHRIST	2	92	105	.6	1.2
193 EPISCOPAL	1	33	42	.2	.5
223 FREE WILL BAPT	5	213	263*	1.6	3.0
349 PENT HOLINESS	1	31	38*	.2	.4
355 PRESB CH (USA)	1	124	153*	.9	1.7
419 SO BAPT CONV	16	3,876	4,778*	28.2	53.7
449 UN METHODIST	8	715	881*	5.2	9.9
497 BLACK BAPT EST2	NA	501	618*	3.7	6.9

GEORGIA

County and Denomination	Number of churches	Communicant, confirmed, full members	Total adherents Number	Percent of total population	Percent of total adherents
THE STATE.....	8,300	2,627,409	3,730,757*	57.6	100.0
APPLING	**50**	**10,434**	**13,387***	**85.0**	**100.0**
001 ADVENT CHR CH	1	18	23*	.1	.2
081 CATHOLIC	1	NA	30	.2	.2
081d LATIN	1	NA	30	.2	.2
127 CH GOD (CLEVE)	5	1,069	1,367*	8.7	10.2
145 CH GOD PROPHCY	2	74	95*	.6	.7
167 CHS OF CHRIST	1	14	18	.1	.1
193 EPISCOPAL	1	31	56	.4	.4
223 FREE WILL BAPT	5	546	698*	4.4	5.2
361 PRIM BAPT ASCS	1	87	111*	.7	.8
413 S.D.A.	1	92	118*	.7	.9
419 SO BAPT CONV	21	5,659	7,235*	46.0	54.0
449 UN METHODIST	11	1,609	2,057*	13.1	15.4
497 BLACK BAPT EST2	NA	1,235	1,579*	10.0	11.8
ATKINSON	**22**	**2,640**	**3,878***	**62.4**	**100.0**
053 ASSEMB OF GOD	1	66	84	1.4	2.2
081 CATHOLIC	1	NA	100	1.6	2.6
081d LATIN	1	NA	100	1.6	2.6
127 CH GOD (CLEVE)	1	34	44*	.7	1.1
145 CH GOD PROPHCY	3	110	143*	2.3	3.7
151 L-D SAINTS	1	NA	350	5.6	9.0
167 CHS OF CHRIST	1	20	26	.4	.7
223 FREE WILL BAPT	2	175	227*	3.7	5.9
361 PRIM BAPT ASCS	1	11	14*	.2	.4
419 SO BAPT CONV	5	989	1,285*	20.7	33.1
449 UN METHODIST	6	464	603*	9.7	15.5
497 BLACK BAPT EST2	NA	771	1,002*	16.1	25.8
BACON	**26**	**4,267**	**5,557***	**58.1**	**100.0**
081 CATHOLIC	1	NA	30	.3	.5
081d LATIN	1	NA	30	.3	.5
127 CH GOD (CLEVE)	4	630	815*	8.5	14.7
145 CH GOD PROPHCY	1	37	48*	.5	.9
167 CHS OF CHRIST	1	14	18	.2	.3
223 FREE WILL BAPT	3	307	397*	4.2	7.1
413 S.D.A.	1	23	30*	.3	.5
419 SO BAPT CONV	10	2,299	2,975*	31.1	53.5
449 UN METHODIST	4	540	699*	7.3	12.6
467 WESLEYAN	1	17	27	.3	.5
497 BLACK BAPT EST2	NA	400	518*	5.4	9.3
BAKER	**17**	**2,794**	**3,648***	**100.9**	**100.0**
053 ASSEMB OF GOD	1	26	39	1.1	1.1
167 CHS OF CHRIST	1	5	6	.2	.2
223 FREE WILL BAPT	2	140	182*	5.0	5.0
339 PENT CH OF GOD	1	15	32	.9	.9
355 PRESB CH (USA)	1	25	32*	.9	.9
419 SO BAPT CONV	8	748	972*	26.9	26.6
449 UN METHODIST	3	120	156*	4.3	4.3
497 BLACK BAPT EST2	NA	1,715	2,229*	61.7	61.1
BALDWIN	**40**	**14,270**	**18,613***	**47.1**	**100.0**
053 ASSEMB OF GOD	1	40	38	.1	.2
081 CATHOLIC	1	NA	900	2.3	4.8
081d LATIN	1	NA	900	2.3	4.8
097 CHR CHS&CHS CR	1	175	212*	.5	1.1
127 CH GOD (CLEVE)	3	152	185*	.5	1.0
145 CH GOD PROPHCY	2	74	90*	.2	.5
151 L-D SAINTS	1	NA	346	.9	1.9
167 CHS OF CHRIST	2	80	88	.2	.5
193 EPISCOPAL	1	354	466	1.2	2.5
263 INT FOURSQ GOS	1	26	32*	.1	.2
283 LUTH—MO SYNOD	1	45	63	.2	.3
355 PRESB CH (USA)	1	354	430*	1.1	2.3
356 PRESB CH AMER	1	56	82	.2	.4
361 PRIM BAPT ASCS	2	61	74*	.2	.4
403 SALVATION ARMY	1	21	25	.1	.1
413 S.D.A.	1	165	200*	.5	1.1
419 SO BAPT CONV	14	5,922	7,191*	18.2	38.6
449 UN METHODIST	6	1,683	2,044*	5.2	11.0
497 BLACK BAPT EST2	NA	5,062	6,147*	15.6	33.0
BANKS	**30**	**5,068**	**6,366***	**61.8**	**100.0**
089 CHR & MISS AL	1	0	28	.3	.4
097 CHR CHS&CHS CR	3	205	256*	2.5	4.0
127 CH GOD (CLEVE)	2	228	285*	2.8	4.5
167 CHS OF CHRIST	1	20	25	.2	.4
355 PRESB CH (USA)	1	51	64*	.6	1.0
419 SO BAPT CONV	16	4,244	5,308*	51.5	83.4
449 UN METHODIST	6	320	400*	3.9	6.3
BARROW	**44**	**9,782**	**13,635***	**45.9**	**100.0**
005 AME ZION	1	188	218	.7	1.6
053 ASSEMB OF GOD	1	49	65	.2	.5
081 CATHOLIC	1	NA	248	.8	1.8
081d LATIN	1	NA	248	.8	1.8
093 CHR CH (DISC)	4	453	699	2.4	5.1
127 CH GOD (CLEVE)	1	74	95*	.3	.7
145 CH GOD PROPHCY	1	37	48*	.2	.4
167 CHS OF CHRIST	1	45	78	.3	.6
193 EPISCOPAL	1	80	132	.4	1.0
355 PRESB CH (USA)	2	192	247*	.8	1.8
356 PRESB CH AMER	1	55	63	.2	.5
361 PRIM BAPT ASCS	1	1	1*	-	.1
419 SO BAPT CONV	14	5,027	6,470*	21.8	47.5
435 UNITARIAN-UNIV	1	10	10	-	.1
449 UN METHODIST	12	2,314	2,978*	10.0	21.8
467 WESLEYAN	2	169	201	.7	1.5
496 JEWISH EST1	0	NA	682	2.3	5.0
497 BLACK BAPT EST2	NA	1,088	1,400*	4.7	10.3
BARTOW	**77**	**19,445**	**26,043***	**46.6**	**100.0**
053 ASSEMB OF GOD	1	28	70	.1	.3
081 CATHOLIC	1	NA	680	1.2	2.6
081d LATIN	1	NA	680	1.2	2.6
097 CHR CHS&CHS CR	2	250	319*	.6	1.2
127 CH GOD (CLEVE)	5	2,045	2,613*	4.7	10.0
145 CH GOD PROPHCY	2	74	95*	.2	.4
151 L-D SAINTS	1	NA	267	.5	1.0
165 CH OF NAZARENE	1	35	158	.3	.6
167 CHS OF CHRIST	4	285	381	.7	1.5
185 CUMBER PRESB	1	116	133	.2	.5
193 EPISCOPAL	1	179	313	.6	1.2
215 EVAN METH CH	1	67	86*	.2	.3
269 JASPER&PVB ASC	3	138	176*	.3	.7
283 LUTH—MO SYNOD	1	49	81	.1	.3
355 PRESB CH (USA)	2	477	609*	1.1	2.3
361 PRIM BAPT ASCS	1	61	78*	.1	.3
413 S.D.A.	1	36	46*	.1	.2
419 SO BAPT CONV	32	11,139	14,232*	25.5	54.6
449 UN METHODIST	17	3,126	3,994*	7.1	15.3
497 BLACK BAPT EST2	NA	1,340	1,712*	3.1	6.6
BEN HILL	**34**	**11,289**	**14,982***	**92.2**	**100.0**
053 ASSEMB OF GOD	1	85	90	.6	.6
081 CATHOLIC	1	NA	125	.8	.8
081d LATIN	1	NA	125	.8	.8
093 CHR CH (DISC)	1	0	0	-	-
127 CH GOD (CLEVE)	1	220	289*	1.8	1.9
145 CH GOD PROPHCY	1	37	49*	.3	.3
165 CH OF NAZARENE	1	271	284	1.7	1.9
167 CHS OF CHRIST	3	209	287	1.8	1.9

NA–Not applicable   NR–Not reported   *Total adherents estimated from known number of communicant, confirmed, full members.   - Represents a percent less than 0.1.   Percentages may not total due to rounding.
[1]See Appendix E   [2]See Appendix F   [3]See Appendix G   Lines in italic represent a breakdown of Catholic rites or Friends affiliations. They are included in their respective denominational total.

Table 4. Churches and Church Membership by County and Denomination: 1990

County and Denomination		Number of churches	Communicant, confirmed, full members	Total adherents		
				Number	Percent of total population	Percent of total adherents
193	EPISCOPAL	1	47	53	.3	.4
355	PRESB CH (USA)	1	101	133*	.8	.9
361	PRIM BAPT ASCS	3	105	138*	.8	.9
413	S.D.A.	2	88	116*	.7	.8
419	SO BAPT CONV	14	6,529	8,571*	52.8	57.2
449	UN METHODIST	3	1,232	1,617*	10.0	10.8
496	JEWISH EST[1]	1	NA	125	.8	.8
497	BLACK BAPT EST[2]	NA	2,365	3,105*	19.1	20.7
BERRIEN		**21**	**4,490**	**5,860***	**41.4**	**100.0**
081	CATHOLIC	2	NA	88	.6	1.5
081d	*LATIN*	*2*	*NA*	*88*	*.6*	*1.5*
127	CH GOD (CLEVE)	3	135	172*	1.2	2.9
165	CH OF NAZARENE	1	39	101	.7	1.7
167	CHS OF CHRIST	1	14	21	.1	.4
361	PRIM BAPT ASCS	1	35	45*	.3	.8
419	SO BAPT CONV	6	2,742	3,491*	24.7	59.6
449	UN METHODIST	7	1,046	1,332*	9.4	22.7
497	BLACK BAPT EST[2]	NA	479	610*	4.3	10.4
BIBB		**151**	**70,518**	**99,745***	**66.5**	**100.0**
053	ASSEMB OF GOD	5	612	931	.6	.9
081	CATHOLIC	3	NA	5,916	3.9	5.9
081d	*LATIN*	*3*	*NA*	*5,916*	*3.9*	*5.9*
089	CHR & MISS AL	1	18	36	-	-
093	CHR CH (DISC)	3	431	649	.4	.7
097	CHR CHS&CHS CR	2	218	275*	.2	.3
111	CH CR,SCIENTST	1	NR	NR	-	-
123	CH GOD (ANDER)	1	238	238	.2	.2
127	CH GOD (CLEVE)	6	1,038	1,310*	.9	1.3
145	CH GOD PROPHCY	2	74	93*	.1	.1
151	L-D SAINTS	2	NA	816	.5	.8
165	CH OF NAZARENE	2	201	310	.2	.3
167	CHS OF CHRIST	9	662	841	.6	.8
193	EPISCOPAL	4	1,462	1,724	1.1	1.7
207	E.L.C.A.	1	535	685	.5	.7
215	EVAN METH CH	1	307	387*	.3	.4
221	FREE METHODIST	1	42	42	-	-
223	FREE WILL BAPT	1	135	170*	.1	.2
226	FRIENDS-USA	1	0	3	-	-
226c	*FGC*	*1*	*0*	*3*	*-*	*-*
246	GREEK ORTHODOX	1	NR	NR	-	-
263	INT FOURSQ GOS	1	49	62*	-	.1
283	LUTH—MO SYNOD	1	110	140	.1	.1
349	PENT HOLINESS	2	302	381*	.3	.4
353	CHR BRETHREN	2	107	160	.1	.2
355	PRESB CH (USA)	6	826	1,042*	.7	1.0
356	PRESB CH AMER	3	1,526	1,875	1.3	1.9
361	PRIM BAPT ASCS	5	160	202*	.1	.2
403	SALVATION ARMY	1	159	178	.1	.2
413	S.D.A.	2	884	1,116*	.7	1.1
419	SO BAPT CONV	41	32,686	41,246*	27.5	41.4
435	UNITARIAN-UNIV	1	121	161	.1	.2
443	UN C OF CHRIST	1	21	26*	-	-
449	UN METHODIST	28	12,962	16,357*	10.9	16.4
467	WESLEYAN	1	24	26	-	-
496	JEWISH EST[1]	2	NA	477	.3	.5
497	BLACK BAPT EST[2]	NA	14,608	18,434*	12.3	18.5
498	INDEP.CHARIS.[3]	3	NA	1,570	1.0	1.6
499	INDEP.NON-CHAR[3]	4	NA	1,866	1.2	1.9
BLECKLEY		**28**	**5,916**	**7,786***	**74.7**	**100.0**
053	ASSEMB OF GOD	1	35	60	.6	.8
081	CATHOLIC	1	NA	45	.4	.6
081d	*LATIN*	*1*	*NA*	*45*	*.4*	*.6*
127	CH GOD (CLEVE)	1	110	138*	1.3	1.8
145	CH GOD PROPHCY	1	37	46*	.4	.6
151	L-D SAINTS	1	NA	306	2.9	3.9
165	CH OF NAZARENE	1	57	62	.6	.8
167	CHS OF CHRIST	1	25	35	.3	.4
193	EPISCOPAL	1	75	100	1.0	1.3
223	FREE WILL BAPT	2	175	219*	2.1	2.8
361	PRIM BAPT ASCS	3	132	166*	1.6	2.1
419	SO BAPT CONV	13	4,013	5,033*	48.3	64.6
449	UN METHODIST	2	579	726*	7.0	9.3
497	BLACK BAPT EST[2]	NA	678	850*	8.1	10.9
BRANTLEY		**29**	**4,734**	**6,206***	**56.0**	**100.0**
001	ADVENT CHR CH	1	19	25*	.2	.4
127	CH GOD (CLEVE)	3	182	237*	2.1	3.8
145	CH GOD PROPHCY	3	110	144*	1.3	2.3
361	PRIM BAPT ASCS	3	34	44*	.4	.7
419	SO BAPT CONV	14	3,912	5,104*	46.1	82.2
449	UN METHODIST	3	168	219*	2.0	3.5
467	WESLEYAN	2	84	139	1.3	2.2
497	BLACK BAPT EST[2]	NA	225	294*	2.7	4.7

County and Denomination		Number of churches	Communicant, confirmed, full members	Total adherents		
				Number	Percent of total population	Percent of total adherents
BROOKS		**51**	**8,743**	**11,588***	**75.3**	**100.0**
053	ASSEMB OF GOD	1	56	80	.5	.7
081	CATHOLIC	1	NA	16	.1	.1
081d	*LATIN*	*1*	*NA*	*16*	*.1*	*.1*
093	CHR CH (DISC)	1	96	151	1.0	1.3
127	CH GOD (CLEVE)	2	57	75*	.5	.6
151	L-D SAINTS	1	NA	84	.5	.7
165	CH OF NAZARENE	1	38	55	.4	.5
167	CHS OF CHRIST	5	365	498	3.2	4.3
193	EPISCOPAL	1	26	35	.2	.3
355	PRESB CH (USA)	1	85	111*	.7	1.0
361	PRIM BAPT ASCS	5	101	132*	.9	1.1
413	S.D.A.	2	88	115*	.7	1.0
419	SO BAPT CONV	20	3,775	4,934*	32.0	42.6
449	UN METHODIST	10	1,086	1,420*	9.2	12.3
497	BLACK BAPT EST[2]	NA	2,970	3,882*	25.2	33.5
BRYAN		**26**	**5,283**	**8,036***	**52.1**	**100.0**
001	ADVENT CHR CH	1	7	9*	.1	.1
081	CATHOLIC	1	NA	427	2.8	5.3
081d	*LATIN*	*1*	*NA*	*427*	*2.8*	*5.3*
093	CHR CH (DISC)	1	110	175	1.1	2.2
097	CHR CHS&CHS CR	1	35	47*	.3	.6
127	CH GOD (CLEVE)	2	119	160*	1.0	2.0
151	L-D SAINTS	1	NA	491	3.2	6.1
167	CHS OF CHRIST	1	40	47	.3	.6
193	EPISCOPAL	1	62	85	.6	1.1
209	EVAN LUTH SYN	1	40	46	.3	.6
349	PENT HOLINESS	1	12	16*	.1	.2
355	PRESB CH (USA)	1	48	65*	.4	.8
361	PRIM BAPT ASCS	1	81	109*	.7	1.4
419	SO BAPT CONV	10	2,944	3,959*	25.6	49.3
449	UN METHODIST	3	1,100	1,479*	9.6	18.4
497	BLACK BAPT EST[2]	NA	685	921*	6.0	11.5
BULLOCH		**74**	**15,228**	**19,923***	**46.2**	**100.0**
053	ASSEMB OF GOD	1	45	62	.1	.3
081	CATHOLIC	1	NA	745	1.7	3.7
081d	*LATIN*	*1*	*NA*	*745*	*1.7*	*3.7*
097	CHR CHS&CHS CR	1	50	61*	.1	.3
105	CHRISTIAN REF	1	45	86	.2	.4
123	CH GOD (ANDER)	4	127	241	.6	1.2
127	CH GOD (CLEVE)	2	339	413*	1.0	2.1
145	CH GOD PROPHCY	1	37	45*	.1	.2
165	CH OF NAZARENE	1	31	43	.1	.2
167	CHS OF CHRIST	2	135	167	.4	.8
193	EPISCOPAL	1	104	142	.3	.7
223	FREE WILL BAPT	1	32	39*	.1	.2
226	FRIENDS-USA	1	9	39*	.1	.2
226d	*FGC & FUM*	*1*	*9*	*39**	*.1*	*.2*
283	LUTH—MO SYNOD	1	121	151	.4	.8
349	PENT HOLINESS	1	10	12*	-	.1
355	PRESB CH (USA)	1	352	429*	1.0	2.2
356	PRESB CH AMER	1	78	146	.3	.7
361	PRIM BAPT ASCS	16	1,455	1,772*	4.1	8.9
413	S.D.A.	1	110	134*	.3	.7
419	SO BAPT CONV	23	6,848	8,340*	19.3	41.9
435	UNITARIAN-UNIV	1	20	25	.1	.1
449	UN METHODIST	11	3,235	3,940*	9.1	19.8
497	BLACK BAPT EST[2]	NA	2,045	2,491*	5.8	12.5
499	INDEP.NON-CHAR[3]	1	NA	400	.9	2.0
BURKE		**44**	**11,216**	**15,448***	**75.1**	**100.0**
005	AME ZION	3	414	519	2.5	3.4
055	AS REF PRES CH	1	86	90	.4	.6
081	CATHOLIC	1	NA	300	1.5	1.9
081d	*LATIN*	*1*	*NA*	*300*	*1.5*	*1.9*
089	CHR & MISS AL	1	24	34	.2	.2
093	CHR CH (DISC)	1	36	98	.5	.6
123	CH GOD (ANDER)	1	69	85	.4	.6
127	CH GOD (CLEVE)	2	156	211*	1.0	1.4
145	CH GOD PROPHCY	1	37	50*	.2	.3
167	CHS OF CHRIST	1	36	64	.3	.4
193	EPISCOPAL	1	130	170	.8	1.1
285	MENNONITE CH	1	37	39	.2	.3
353	CHR BRETHREN	1	65	100	.5	.6
355	PRESB CH (USA)	2	78	106*	.5	.7
356	PRESB CH AMER	1	119	139	.7	.9
419	SO BAPT CONV	12	3,288	4,452*	21.6	28.8
449	UN METHODIST	14	1,642	2,223*	10.8	14.4
497	BLACK BAPT EST[2]	NA	4,999	6,768*	32.9	43.8
BUTTS		**27**	**5,948**	**8,425***	**55.0**	**100.0**
053	ASSEMB OF GOD	1	58	95	.6	1.1
081	CATHOLIC	1	NA	139	.9	1.6

NA–Not applicable NR–Not reported *Total adherents estimated from known number of communicant, confirmed, full members. - Represents a percent less than 0.1. Percentages may not total due to rounding.
[1]See Appendix E [2]See Appendix F [3]See Appendix G Lines in *italic* represent a breakdown of Catholic rites or Friends affiliations. They are included in their respective denominational total.

Table 4. Churches and Church Membership by County and Denomination: 1990

County and Denomination	Number of churches	Communicant, confirmed, full members	Total adherents Number	Percent of total population	Percent of total adherents
081d LATIN	1	NA	139	.9	1.6
097 CHR CHS&CHS CR	1	100	125*	.8	1.5
145 CH GOD PROPHCY	1	37	46*	.3	.5
151 L-D SAINTS	1	NA	490	3.2	5.8
165 CH OF NAZARENE	1	111	98	.6	1.2
167 CHS OF CHRIST	1	23	30	.2	.4
355 PRESB CH (USA)	2	111	139*	.9	1.6
361 PRIM BAPT ASCS	2	18	23*	.2	.3
419 SO BAPT CONV	11	3,429	4,302*	28.1	51.1
449 UN METHODIST	5	790	991*	6.5	11.8
496 JEWISH EST[1]	0	NA	352	2.3	4.2
497 BLACK BAPT EST[2]	NA	1,271	1,595*	10.4	18.9
CALHOUN	**15**	**3,322**	**4,269***	**85.2**	**100.0**
127 CH GOD (CLEVE)	1	1	1*	-	-
167 CHS OF CHRIST	1	13	30	.6	.7
223 FREE WILL BAPT	1	107	137*	2.7	3.2
355 PRESB CH (USA)	1	9	12*	.2	.3
419 SO BAPT CONV	6	1,396	1,788*	35.7	41.9
449 UN METHODIST	5	423	542*	10.8	12.7
497 BLACK BAPT EST[2]	NA	1,373	1,759*	35.1	41.2
CAMDEN	**42**	**7,788**	**11,284***	**37.4**	**100.0**
053 ASSEM OF GOD	2	120	185	.6	1.6
081 CATHOLIC	1	NA	300	1.0	2.7
081d LATIN	1	NA	300	1.0	2.7
097 CHR CHS&CHS CR	1	18	24*	.1	.2
127 CH GOD (CLEVE)	6	584	780*	2.6	6.9
145 CH GOD PROPHCY	1	37	49*	.2	.4
151 L-D SAINTS	1	NA	427	1.4	3.8
165 CH OF NAZARENE	1	22	42	.1	.4
167 CHS OF CHRIST	3	153	193	.6	1.7
193 EPISCOPAL	2	159	320	1.1	2.8
283 LUTH—MO SYNOD	1	76	127	.4	1.1
355 PRESB CH (USA)	1	179	239*	.8	2.1
356 PRESB CH AMER	1	48	60	.2	.5
419 SO BAPT CONV	8	3,569	4,767*	15.8	42.2
449 UN METHODIST	13	2,058	2,749*	9.1	24.4
497 BLACK BAPT EST[2]	NA	765	1,022*	3.4	9.1
CANDLER	**23**	**4,233**	**5,367***	**69.3**	**100.0**
053 ASSEM OF GOD	1	10	15	.2	.3
081 CATHOLIC	1	NA	47	.6	.9
081d LATIN	1	NA	47	.6	.9
127 CH GOD (CLEVE)	1	146	183*	2.4	3.4
145 CH GOD PROPHCY	1	37	46*	.6	.9
167 CHS OF CHRIST	2	30	40	.5	.7
223 FREE WILL BAPT	1	133	167*	2.2	3.1
355 PRESB CH (USA)	1	67	84*	1.1	1.6
361 PRIM BAPT ASCS	5	464	583*	7.5	10.9
419 SO BAPT CONV	8	1,774	2,228*	28.8	41.5
449 UN METHODIST	2	454	570*	7.4	10.6
497 BLACK BAPT EST[2]	NA	1,118	1,404*	18.1	26.2
CARROLL	**111**	**28,019**	**37,628***	**52.7**	**100.0**
053 ASSEM OF GOD	1	41	60	.1	.2
081 CATHOLIC	1	NA	1,670	2.3	4.4
081d LATIN	1	NA	1,670	2.3	4.4
097 CHR CHS&CHS CR	5	735	928*	1.3	2.5
127 CH GOD (CLEVE)	9	764	965*	1.4	2.6
145 CH GOD PROPHCY	2	74	93*	.1	.2
151 L-D SAINTS	1	NA	234	.3	.6
167 CHS OF CHRIST	7	424	546	.8	1.5
193 EPISCOPAL	1	436	506	.7	1.3
207 E.L.C.A.	1	149	216	.3	.6
226 FRIENDS-USA	1	0	5	-	-
226c FGC	1	0	5	-	-
289 NEW HOPE B ASC	2	60	76*	.1	.2
349 PENT HOLINESS	1	59	75*	.1	.2
355 PRESB CH (USA)	3	325	410*	.6	1.1
356 PRESB CH AMER	1	67	67	.1	.2
361 PRIM BAPT ASCS	2	3	4*	-	-
413 S.D.A.	1	70	88*	.1	.2
419 SO BAPT CONV	43	16,611	20,978*	29.4	55.8
449 UN METHODIST	28	4,636	5,855*	8.2	15.6
497 BLACK BAPT EST[2]	NA	3,565	4,502*	6.3	12.0
498 INDEP.CHARIS.[3]	1	NA	350	.5	.9
CATOOSA	**50**	**13,305**	**18,550***	**43.7**	**100.0**
081 CATHOLIC	1	NA	1,932	4.5	10.4
081d LATIN	1	NA	1,932	4.5	10.4
127 CH GOD (CLEVE)	4	408	508*	1.2	2.7
145 CH GOD PROPHCY	1	37	46*	.1	.2
165 CH OF NAZARENE	2	235	330	.8	1.8
167 CHS OF CHRIST	2	286	367	.9	2.0
189 DUCK RIVR BAPT	1	85	106*	.2	.6
193 EPISCOPAL	1	144	151	.4	.8
349 PENT HOLINESS	1	9	11*	-	.1
355 PRESB CH (USA)	2	87	108*	.3	.6
356 PRESB CH AMER	1	78	106	.2	.6
361 PRIM BAPT ASCS	2	63	79*	.2	.4
413 S.D.A.	1	156	194*	.5	1.0
419 SO BAPT CONV	23	9,486	11,822*	27.8	63.7
449 UN METHODIST	7	2,216	2,762*	6.5	14.9
467 WESLEYAN	1	15	28	.1	.2
CHARLTON	**24**	**5,490**	**7,416***	**87.3**	**100.0**
053 ASSEM OF GOD	1	28	35	.4	.5
081 CATHOLIC	1	NA	50	.6	.7
081d LATIN	1	NA	50	.6	.7
127 CH GOD (CLEVE)	3	213	282*	3.3	3.8
145 CH GOD PROPHCY	1	37	49*	.6	.7
151 L-D SAINTS	1	NA	173	2.0	2.3
167 CHS OF CHRIST	1	18	28	.3	.4
207 E.L.C.A.	1	1,284	1,448	17.0	19.5
223 FREE WILL BAPT	1	116	154*	1.8	2.1
419 SO BAPT CONV	8	2,451	3,251*	38.3	43.8
449 UN METHODIST	6	598	793*	9.3	10.7
496 JEWISH EST[1]	0	NA	165	1.9	2.2
497 BLACK BAPT EST[2]	NA	745	988*	11.6	13.3
CHATHAM	**193**	**91,537**	**139,525***	**64.3**	**100.0**
001 ADVENT CHR CH	1	10	13*	-	-
053 ASSEM OF GOD	9	659	1,054	.5	.8
081 CATHOLIC	11	NA	18,098	8.3	13.0
081d LATIN	11	NA	18,098	8.3	13.0
089 CHR & MISS AL	5	366	587	.3	.4
093 CHR CH (DISC)	2	263	467	.2	.3
097 CHR CHS&CHS CR	5	1,340	1,699*	.8	1.2
111 CH CR,SCIENTST	1	NR	NR	-	-
123 CH GOD (ANDER)	2	108	150	.1	.1
127 CH GOD (CLEVE)	7	2,662	3,376*	1.6	2.4
145 CH GOD PROPHCY	1	37	47*	-	-
151 L-D SAINTS	3	NA	1,070	.5	.8
165 CH OF NAZARENE	3	237	225	.1	.2
167 CHS OF CHRIST	7	1,121	1,368	.6	1.0
193 EPISCOPAL	12	3,761	4,659	2.1	3.3
207 E.L.C.A.	8	2,849	3,714	1.7	2.7
221 FREE METHODIST	2	13	29	-	-
223 FREE WILL BAPT	1	160	203*	.1	.1
246 GREEK ORTHODOX	1	NR	NR	-	-
263 INT FOURSQ GOS	1	531	673*	.3	.5
283 LUTH—MO SYNOD	1	340	468	.2	.3
331 ORTH CH IN AM	1	NR	NR	-	-
349 PENT HOLINESS	2	62	79*	-	.1
353 CHR BRETHREN	2	118	185	.1	.1
355 PRESB CH (USA)	7	2,674	3,391*	1.6	2.4
356 PRESB CH AMER	3	335	405	.2	.3
361 PRIM BAPT ASCS	5	648	822*	.4	.6
403 SALVATION ARMY	1	137	142	.1	.1
413 S.D.A.	3	2,141	2,715*	1.3	1.9
419 SO BAPT CONV	49	29,964	37,998*	17.5	27.2
431 UKRANIAN AMER	1	NR	NR	-	-
435 UNITARIAN-UNIV	1	99	127	.1	.1
443 UN C OF CHRIST	1	102	129*	.1	.1
449 UN METHODIST	29	13,823	17,529*	8.1	12.6
467 WESLEYAN	1	15	30	-	-
496 JEWISH EST[1]	3	NA	2,447	1.1	1.8
497 BLACK BAPT EST[2]	NA	26,962	34,191*	15.8	24.5
499 INDEP.NON-CHAR[3]	1	NA	1,435	.7	1.0
CHATTAHOOCHEE	**5**	**1,818**	**2,459***	**14.5**	**100.0**
167 CHS OF CHRIST	1	25	32	.2	1.3
419 SO BAPT CONV	1	381	497*	2.9	20.2
449 UN METHODIST	3	189	247*	1.5	10.0
496 JEWISH EST[1]	0	NA	87	.5	3.5
497 BLACK BAPT EST[2]	NA	1,223	1,596*	9.4	64.9
CHATTOOGA	**80**	**11,535**	**14,421***	**64.8**	**100.0**
005 AME ZION	5	564	699	3.1	4.8
081 CATHOLIC	0	NA	39	.2	.3
081d LATIN	0	NA	39	.2	.3
089 CHR & MISS AL	1	81	116	.5	.8
127 CH GOD (CLEVE)	3	477	593*	2.7	4.1
145 CH GOD PROPHCY	2	74	92*	.4	.6
165 CH OF NAZARENE	1	28	20	.1	.1
167 CHS OF CHRIST	13	787	1,038	4.7	7.2
193 EPISCOPAL	1	37	38	.2	.3
355 PRESB CH (USA)	5	299	372*	1.7	2.6
356 PRESB CH AMER	1	88	106	.5	.7
413 S.D.A.	2	86	107*	.5	.7

NA–Not applicable   NR–Not reported   *Total adherents estimated from known number of communicant, confirmed, full members.   - Represents a percent less than 0.1.   Percentages may not total due to rounding.
[1]See Appendix E   [2]See Appendix F   [3]See Appendix G   Lines in *italic* represent a breakdown of Catholic rites or Friends affiliations. They are included in their respective denominational total.

Table 4. Churches and Church Membership by County and Denomination: 1990

County and Denomination	Number of churches	Communicant, confirmed, full members	Total adherents Number	Percent of total population	Percent of total adherents
419 SO BAPT CONV	36	7,821	9,719*	43.7	67.4
449 UN METHODIST	10	953	1,184*	5.3	8.2
497 BLACK BAPT EST2	NA	240	298*	1.3	2.1
CHEROKEE	**95**	**23,169**	**32,815***	**36.4**	**100.0**
053 ASSEMB OF GOD	3	188	260	.3	.8
081 CATHOLIC	1	NA	525	.6	1.6
081d LATIN	*1*	*NA*	*525*	*.6*	*1.6*
097 CHR CHS&CHS CR	1	340	441*	.5	1.3
127 CH GOD (CLEVE)	9	1,226	1,589*	1.8	4.8
145 CH GOD PROPHCY	3	110	143*	.2	.4
167 CHS OF CHRIST	4	486	642	.7	2.0
193 EPISCOPAL	1	70	101	.1	.3
207 E.L.C.A.	1	150	227	.3	.7
269 JASPER&PVB ASC	14	2,272	2,945*	3.3	9.0
283 LUTH—MO SYNOD	1	256	428	.5	1.3
355 PRESB CH (USA)	4	373	483*	.5	1.5
356 PRESB CH AMER	1	128	187	.2	.6
361 PRIM BAPT ASCS	2	50	65*	.1	.2
413 S.D.A.	1	37	48*	.1	.1
419 SO BAPT CONV	29	13,917	18,039*	20.0	55.0
449 UN METHODIST	20	3,017	3,911*	4.3	11.9
496 JEWISH EST1	0	NA	2,069	2.3	6.3
497 BLACK BAPT EST2	NA	549	712*	.8	2.2
CLARKE	**58**	**29,808**	**37,756***	**43.1**	**100.0**
005 AME ZION	1	50	65	.1	.2
053 ASSEMB OF GOD	1	146	229	.3	.6
081 CATHOLIC	1	NA	1,087	1.2	2.9
081d LATIN	*1*	*NA*	*1,087*	*1.2*	*2.9*
093 CHR CH (DISC)	2	270	427	.5	1.1
097 CHR CHS&CHS CR	1	200	238*	.3	.6
111 CH CR,SCIENTST	1	NR	NR	-	-
127 CH GOD (CLEVE)	2	499	594*	.7	1.6
151 L-D SAINTS	1	NA	385	.4	1.0
165 CH OF NAZARENE	1	51	60	.1	.2
167 CHS OF CHRIST	3	375	525	.6	1.4
193 EPISCOPAL	3	1,046	1,460	1.7	3.9
207 E.L.C.A.	1	362	448	.5	1.2
215 EVAN METH CH	1	19	23*	-	.1
226 FRIENDS-USA	1	0	25	-	.1
226c FGC	*1*	*0*	*25*	*-*	*.1*
246 GREEK ORTHODOX	1	NR	NR	-	-
283 LUTH—MO SYNOD	1	267	301	.3	.8
349 PENT HOLINESS	1	275	327*	.4	.9
355 PRESB CH (USA)	3	2,251	2,678*	3.1	7.1
356 PRESB CH AMER	1	88	107	.1	.3
361 PRIM BAPT ASCS	1	15	18*	-	-
403 SALVATION ARMY	1	97	111	.1	.3
413 S.D.A.	2	233	277*	.3	.7
419 SO BAPT CONV	15	12,462	14,828*	16.9	39.3
435 UNITARIAN-UNIV	1	194	264	.3	.7
449 UN METHODIST	11	5,550	6,604*	7.5	17.5
496 JEWISH EST1	0	NA	300	.3	.8
497 BLACK BAPT EST2	NA	5,358	6,375*	7.3	16.9
CLAY	**21**	**2,982**	**3,929***	**116.8**	**100.0**
167 CHS OF CHRIST	8	867	1,177	35.0	30.0
355 PRESB CH (USA)	1	26	34*	1.0	.9
419 SO BAPT CONV	7	821	1,068*	31.7	27.2
449 UN METHODIST	5	381	496*	14.7	12.6
497 BLACK BAPT EST2	NA	887	1,154*	34.3	29.4
CLAYTON	**92**	**60,071**	**92,051***	**50.6**	**100.0**
053 ASSEMB OF GOD	3	341	517	.3	.6
081 CATHOLIC	1	NA	4,579	2.5	5.0
081d LATIN	*1*	*NA*	*4,579*	*2.5*	*5.0*
093 CHR CH (DISC)	2	110	153	.1	.2
097 CHR CHS&CHS CR	4	1,476	1,893*	1.0	2.1
127 CH GOD (CLEVE)	5	1,567	2,009*	1.1	2.2
145 CH GOD PROPHCY	1	37	47*	-	.1
151 L-D SAINTS	2	NA	1,390	.8	1.5
165 CH OF NAZARENE	2	279	527	.3	.6
193 EPISCOPAL	1	155	288	.2	.3
207 E.L.C.A.	3	1,040	1,353	.7	1.5
265 INT PENT C CHR	1	63	66	-	.1
283 LUTH—MO SYNOD	2	519	756	.4	.8
339 PENT CH OF GOD	1	41	200	.1	.2
355 PRESB CH (USA)	6	1,186	1,521*	.8	1.7
356 PRESB CH AMER	1	141	164	.1	.2
361 PRIM BAPT ASCS	1	48	62*	-	.1
413 S.D.A.	2	382	490*	.3	.5
419 SO BAPT CONV	31	32,139	41,212*	22.6	44.8
443 UN C OF CHRIST	1	205	263*	.1	.3
449 UN METHODIST	13	6,258	8,025*	4.4	8.7
496 JEWISH EST1	1	NA	4,176	2.3	4.5
497 BLACK BAPT EST2	NA	14,084	18,060*	9.9	19.6
498 INDEP.CHARIS.3	1	NA	600	.3	.7
499 INDEP.NON-CHAR3	7	NA	3,700	2.0	4.0
CLINCH	**15**	**2,504**	**3,234***	**52.5**	**100.0**
053 ASSEMB OF GOD	1	12	22	.4	.7
127 CH GOD (CLEVE)	3	418	539*	8.8	16.7
145 CH GOD PROPHCY	2	74	95*	1.5	2.9
167 CHS OF CHRIST	1	18	22	.4	.7
223 FREE WILL BAPT	1	100	129*	2.1	4.0
419 SO BAPT CONV	3	780	1,006*	16.3	31.1
449 UN METHODIST	4	320	413*	6.7	12.8
497 BLACK BAPT EST2	NA	782	1,008*	16.4	31.2
COBB	**275**	**142,192**	**226,097***	**50.5**	**100.0**
053 ASSEMB OF GOD	9	916	1,021	.2	.5
055 AS REF PRES CH	1	108	154	-	.1
081 CATHOLIC	7	NA	28,647	6.4	12.7
081d LATIN	*7*	*NA*	*28,647*	*6.4*	*12.7*
089 CHR & MISS AL	1	170	386	.1	.2
093 CHR CH (DISC)	2	291	383	.1	.2
097 CHR CHS&CHS CR	9	980	1,227*	.3	.5
111 CH CR,SCIENTST	1	NR	NR	-	-
123 CH GOD (ANDER)	3	120	143	-	.1
127 CH GOD (CLEVE)	15	3,030	3,794*	.8	1.7
145 CH GOD PROPHCY	5	184	230*	.1	.1
151 L-D SAINTS	8	NA	3,770	.8	1.7
165 CH OF NAZARENE	3	574	676	.2	.3
167 CHS OF CHRIST	13	1,876	2,387	.5	1.1
189 DUCK RIVR BAPT	1	36	45*	-	-
193 EPISCOPAL	7	3,168	4,919	1.1	2.2
203 EVAN FREE CH	1	68	120	-	.1
207 E.L.C.A.	7	3,087	4,198	.9	1.9
209 EVAN LUTH SYN	1	38	48	-	-
215 EVAN METH CH	1	59	74*	-	-
216 EVAN PRESBY CH	1	282	290	.1	.1
223 FREE WILL BAPT	1	47	59*	-	-
226 FRIENDS-USA	1	45	69	-	-
226b EFI	*1*	*45*	*69*	*-*	*-*
246 GREEK ORTHODOX	1	NR	NR	-	-
263 INT FOURSQ GOS	1	0	0*	-	-
269 JASPER&PVB ASC	2	471	590*	.1	.3
283 LUTH—MO SYNOD	1	774	1,000	.2	.4
289 NEW HOPE B ASC	1	113	141*	-	.1
349 PENT HOLINESS	1	76	95*	-	-
353 CHR BRETHREN	1	30	30	-	-
355 PRESB CH (USA)	13	5,634	7,054*	1.6	3.1
356 PRESB CH AMER	5	1,290	1,453	.3	.6
361 PRIM BAPT ASCS	3	58	73*	-	-
403 SALVATION ARMY	1	58	60	-	-
413 S.D.A.	0	2	3*	-	-
419 SO BAPT CONV	99	78,684	98,517*	22.0	43.6
435 UNITARIAN-UNIV	1	79	124	-	.1
443 UN C OF CHRIST	1	252	316*	.1	.1
449 UN METHODIST	36	25,060	31,377*	7.0	13.9
469 WELS	2	204	284	.1	.1
496 JEWISH EST1	2	NA	10,271	2.3	4.5
497 BLACK BAPT EST2	NA	14,328	17,939*	4.0	7.9
498 INDEP.CHARIS.3	1	NA	1,000	.2	.4
499 INDEP.NON-CHAR3	5	NA	3,130	.7	1.4
COFFEE	**59**	**12,449**	**17,347***	**58.6**	**100.0**
053 ASSEMB OF GOD	2	235	339	1.1	2.0
081 CATHOLIC	1	NA	540	1.8	3.1
081d LATIN	*1*	*NA*	*540*	*1.8*	*3.1*
127 CH GOD (CLEVE)	9	1,247	1,627*	5.5	9.4
145 CH GOD PROPHCY	4	147	192*	.6	1.1
151 L-D SAINTS	1	NA	633	2.1	3.6
165 CH OF NAZARENE	1	20	0	-	-
167 CHS OF CHRIST	2	67	93	.3	.5
193 EPISCOPAL	1	189	167	.6	1.0
223 FREE WILL BAPT	1	10	13*	-	.1
355 PRESB CH (USA)	1	109	142*	.5	.8
361 PRIM BAPT ASCS	3	171	223*	.8	1.3
419 SO BAPT CONV	23	6,498	8,478*	28.6	48.9
443 UN C OF CHRIST	1	30	39*	.1	.2
449 UN METHODIST	9	1,452	1,894*	6.4	10.9
497 BLACK BAPT EST2	NA	2,274	2,967*	10.0	17.1
COLQUITT	**81**	**22,390**	**29,468***	**80.4**	**100.0**
053 ASSEMB OF GOD	4	358	565	1.5	1.9
081 CATHOLIC	1	NA	350	1.0	1.2
081d LATIN	*1*	*NA*	*350*	*1.0*	*1.2*
089 CHR & MISS AL	1	62	147	.4	.5
127 CH GOD (CLEVE)	5	309	396*	1.1	1.3

NA–Not applicable   NR–Not reported   *Total adherents estimated from known number of communicant, confirmed, full members.   - Represents a percent less than 0.1.   Percentages may not total due to rounding.
[1] See Appendix E   [2] See Appendix F   [3] See Appendix G   Lines in *italic* represent a breakdown of Catholic rites or Friends affiliations. They are included in their respective denominational total.

Table 4. Churches and Church Membership by County and Denomination: 1990

County and Denomination	Number of churches	Communicant, confirmed, full members	Total adherents Number	Percent of total population	Percent of total adherents
145 CH GOD PROPHCY	1	37	47*	.1	.2
151 L-D SAINTS	1	NA	204	.6	.7
165 CH OF NAZARENE	1	207	274	.7	.9
167 CHS OF CHRIST	1	98	130	.4	.4
193 EPISCOPAL	1	103	140	.4	.5
223 FREE WILL BAPT	5	466	598*	1.6	2.0
355 PRESB CH (USA)	1	444	570*	1.6	1.9
361 PRIM BAPT ASCS	3	70	90*	.2	.3
413 S.D.A.	1	88	113*	.3	.4
419 SO BAPT CONV	43	15,227	19,532*	53.3	66.3
449 UN METHODIST	12	1,992	2,555*	7.0	8.7
497 BLACK BAPT EST[2]	NA	2,929	3,757*	10.3	12.7
COLUMBIA	**43**	**13,597**	**19,068***	**28.9**	**100.0**
053 ASSEMB OF GOD	1	57	75	.1	.4
097 CHR CHS&CHS CR	3	362	477*	.7	2.5
127 CH GOD (CLEVE)	1	71	94*	.1	.5
145 CH GOD PROPHCY	1	37	49*	.1	.3
151 L-D SAINTS	1	NA	427	.6	2.2
165 CH OF NAZARENE	1	74	81	.1	.4
167 CHS OF CHRIST	3	113	149	.2	.8
193 EPISCOPAL	2	260	450	.7	2.4
223 FREE WILL BAPT	1	25	33*	-	.2
355 PRESB CH (USA)	1	42	55*	.1	.3
356 PRESB CH AMER	1	197	197	.3	1.0
419 SO BAPT CONV	17	7,676	10,111*	15.3	53.0
449 UN METHODIST	8	2,207	2,907*	4.4	15.2
469 WELS	1	113	190	.3	1.0
496 JEWISH EST[1]	0	NA	336	.5	1.8
497 BLACK BAPT EST[2]	NA	2,363	3,112*	4.7	16.3
499 INDEP.NON-CHAR[3]	1	NA	325	.5	1.7
COOK	**26**	**7,038**	**9,634***	**71.6**	**100.0**
053 ASSEMB OF GOD	1	91	142	1.1	1.5
081 CATHOLIC	1	NA	26	.2	.3
081d LATIN	*1*	*NA*	*26*	*.2*	*.3*
127 CH GOD (CLEVE)	1	74	95*	.7	1.0
151 L-D SAINTS	1	NA	558	4.1	5.8
165 CH OF NAZARENE	1	36	32	.2	.3
167 CHS OF CHRIST	2	186	248	1.8	2.6
223 FREE WILL BAPT	1	25	32*	.2	.3
355 PRESB CH (USA)	1	38	49*	.4	.5
419 SO BAPT CONV	13	3,705	4,753*	35.3	49.3
449 UN METHODIST	4	1,009	1,295*	9.6	13.4
497 BLACK BAPT EST[2]	NA	1,874	2,404*	17.9	25.0
COWETA	**75**	**21,296**	**29,456***	**54.7**	**100.0**
053 ASSEMB OF GOD	1	40	90	.2	.3
055 AS REF PRES CH	1	235	272	.5	.9
081 CATHOLIC	1	NA	365	.7	1.2
081d LATIN	*1*	*NA*	*365*	*.7*	*1.2*
093 CHR CH (DISC)	1	20	30	.1	.1
097 CHR CHS&CHS CR	3	311	401*	.7	1.4
127 CH GOD (CLEVE)	2	86	111*	.2	.4
145 CH GOD PROPHCY	2	74	95*	.2	.3
151 L-D SAINTS	1	NA	282	.5	1.0
167 CHS OF CHRIST	4	489	613	1.1	2.1
193 EPISCOPAL	1	178	274	.5	.9
207 E.L.C.A.	1	51	57	.1	.2
283 LUTH—MO SYNOD	1	124	176	.3	.6
339 PENT CH OF GOD	1	34	77	.1	.3
349 PENT HOLINESS	1	163	210*	.4	.7
355 PRESB CH (USA)	2	447	577*	1.1	2.0
413 S.D.A.	2	269	347*	.6	1.2
419 SO BAPT CONV	27	10,599	13,671*	25.4	46.4
449 UN METHODIST	22	4,194	5,410*	10.0	18.4
467 WESLEYAN	1	25	59	.1	.2
496 JEWISH EST[1]	0	NA	1,235	2.3	4.2
497 BLACK BAPT EST[2]	NA	3,957	5,104*	9.5	17.3
CRAWFORD	**14**	**2,503**	**3,196***	**35.5**	**100.0**
145 CH GOD PROPHCY	1	37	47*	.5	1.5
175 CONGR CHR CHS	1	40	51*	.6	1.6
361 PRIM BAPT ASCS	2	47	60*	.7	1.9
419 SO BAPT CONV	4	658	840*	9.3	26.3
449 UN METHODIST	6	440	562*	6.3	17.6
497 BLACK BAPT EST[2]	NA	1,281	1,636*	18.2	51.2
CRISP	**44**	**9,618**	**12,622***	**63.1**	**100.0**
053 ASSEMB OF GOD	1	29	38	.2	.3
081 CATHOLIC	1	NA	150	.7	1.2
081d LATIN	*1*	*NA*	*150*	*.7*	*1.2*
127 CH GOD (CLEVE)	1	118	153*	.8	1.2
145 CH GOD PROPHCY	2	74	96*	.5	.8
167 CHS OF CHRIST	3	128	150	.7	1.2

County and Denomination	Number of churches	Communicant, confirmed, full members	Total adherents Number	Percent of total population	Percent of total adherents
193 EPISCOPAL	1	69	75	.4	.6
223 FREE WILL BAPT	1	83	108*	.5	.9
355 PRESB CH (USA)	2	77	100*	.5	.8
361 PRIM BAPT ASCS	4	89	116*	.6	.9
419 SO BAPT CONV	21	5,418	7,043*	35.2	55.8
449 UN METHODIST	7	1,593	2,071*	10.3	16.4
497 BLACK BAPT EST[2]	NA	1,940	2,522*	12.6	20.0
DADE	**30**	**3,116**	**3,943***	**30.0**	**100.0**
081 CATHOLIC	0	NA	4	-	.1
081d LATIN	*0*	*NA*	*4*	*-*	*.1*
127 CH GOD (CLEVE)	5	216	269*	2.0	6.8
145 CH GOD PROPHCY	1	37	46*	.3	1.2
167 CHS OF CHRIST	4	208	313	2.4	7.9
413 S.D.A.	2	190	237*	1.8	6.0
419 SO BAPT CONV	9	1,592	1,985*	15.1	50.3
449 UN METHODIST	9	873	1,089*	8.3	27.6
DAWSON	**24**	**4,689**	**6,077***	**64.5**	**100.0**
081 CATHOLIC	1	NA	49	.5	.8
081d LATIN	*1*	*NA*	*49*	*.5*	*.8*
127 CH GOD (CLEVE)	1	172	219*	2.3	3.6
145 CH GOD PROPHCY	1	37	47*	.5	.8
167 CHS OF CHRIST	1	37	48	.5	.8
413 S.D.A.	4	1,297	1,652*	17.5	27.2
419 SO BAPT CONV	12	2,808	3,577*	37.9	58.9
449 UN METHODIST	4	338	431*	4.6	7.1
496 JEWISH EST[1]	0	NA	54	.6	.9
DECATUR	**53**	**11,525**	**15,590***	**61.1**	**100.0**
053 ASSEMB OF GOD	3	109	189	.7	1.2
081 CATHOLIC	1	NA	130	.5	.8
081d LATIN	*1*	*NA*	*130*	*.5*	*.8*
097 CHR CHS&CHS CR	1	200	259*	1.0	1.7
123 CH GOD (ANDER)	1	24	24	.1	.2
127 CH GOD (CLEVE)	3	481	622*	2.4	4.0
145 CH GOD PROPHCY	1	37	48*	.2	.3
165 CH OF NAZARENE	1	72	87	.3	.6
167 CHS OF CHRIST	3	140	180	.7	1.2
193 EPISCOPAL	1	83	121	.5	.8
223 FREE WILL BAPT	3	116	150*	.6	1.0
355 PRESB CH (USA)	1	357	462*	1.8	3.0
361 PRIM BAPT ASCS	2	70	91*	.4	.6
419 SO BAPT CONV	20	5,212	6,744*	26.4	43.3
449 UN METHODIST	10	1,573	2,035*	8.0	13.1
496 JEWISH EST[1]	1	NA	0	-	-
497 BLACK BAPT EST[2]	NA	3,051	3,948*	15.5	25.3
499 INDEP.NON-CHAR[3]	1	NA	500	2.0	3.2
DE KALB	**296**	**166,753**	**287,862***	**52.7**	**100.0**
001 ADVENT CHR CH	1	78	96*	-	-
019 AMER BAPT USA	2	2,310	2,841*	.5	1.0
053 ASSEMB OF GOD	10	2,113	2,114	.4	.7
055 AS REF PRES CH	4	904	1,035	.2	.4
081 CATHOLIC	10	NA	36,923	6.8	12.8
081d LATIN	*9*	*NA*	*36,400*	*6.7*	*12.6*
081f MELKITE-GK	*1*	*NA*	*523*	*.1*	*.2*
089 CHR & MISS AL	7	749	850	.2	.3
093 CHR CH (DISC)	4	1,258	1,764	.3	.6
097 CHR CHS&CHS CR	6	5,347	6,575*	1.2	2.3
105 CHRISTIAN REF	1	75	121	-	-
111 CH CR,SCIENTST	1	NR	NR	-	-
123 CH GOD (ANDER)	5	342	377	.1	.1
127 CH GOD (CLEVE)	11	3,073	3,779*	.7	1.3
145 CH GOD PROPHCY	5	184	226*	-	.1
151 L-D SAINTS	10	NA	2,723	.5	.9
165 CH OF NAZARENE	3	746	790	.1	.3
167 CHS OF CHRIST	14	3,178	4,258	.8	1.5
193 EPISCOPAL	9	5,513	7,634	1.4	2.7
203 EVAN FREE CH	1	85	210	-	.1
207 E.L.C.A.	9	2,420	3,010	.6	1.0
216 EVAN PRESBY CH	2	150	161	-	.1
223 FREE WILL BAPT	2	26	32*	-	-
226 FRIENDS-USA	1	69	190	-	.1
226c FGC	*1*	*69*	*190*	*-*	*.1*
283 LUTH—MO SYNOD	2	506	631	.1	.2
285 MENNONITE CH	1	64	117	-	-
349 PENT HOLINESS	1	208	256*	-	.1
353 CHR BRETHREN	2	285	360	.1	.1
355 PRESB CH (USA)	26	11,310	13,908*	2.5	4.8
356 PRESB CH AMER	6	961	1,002	.2	.3
361 PRIM BAPT ASCS	3	334	411*	.1	.1
403 SALVATION ARMY	1	90	90	-	-
413 S.D.A.	3	571	702*	.1	.2
419 SO BAPT CONV	61	66,582	81,877*	15.0	28.4
435 UNITARIAN-UNIV	2	911	1,281	.2	.4

NA–Not applicable   NR–Not reported   *Total adherents estimated from known number of communicant, confirmed, full members.   - Represents a percent less than 0.1.   Percentages may not total due to rounding.
[1]See Appendix E   [2]See Appendix F   [3]See Appendix G   Lines in *italic* represent a breakdown of Catholic rites or Friends affiliations. They are included in their respective denominational total.

98

Table 4. Churches and Church Membership by County and Denomination: 1990

County and Denomination		Number of churches	Communicant, confirmed, full members	Total adherents		
				Number	Percent of total population	Percent of total adherents
443	UN C OF CHRIST	1	592	728*	.1	.3
449	UN METHODIST	47	32,837	40,380*	7.4	14.0
467	WESLEYAN	3	289	645	.1	.2
469	WELS	1	105	159	-	.1
496	JEWISH EST[1]	7	NA	12,512	2.3	4.3
497	BLACK BAPT EST[2]	NA	22,488	27,654*	5.1	9.6
498	INDEP.CHARIS.[3]	6	NA	18,900	3.5	6.6
499	INDEP.NON-CHAR[3]	5	NA	10,540	1.9	3.7
DODGE		**68**	**11,863**	**14,845***	**84.3**	**100.0**
081	CATHOLIC	1	NA	10	.1	.1
081d	LATIN	1	NA	10	.1	.1
093	CHR CH (DISC)	2	43	66	.4	.4
127	CH GOD (CLEVE)	3	169	210*	1.2	1.4
145	CH GOD PROPHCY	1	37	46*	.3	.3
165	CH OF NAZARENE	1	59	120	.7	.8
167	CHS OF CHRIST	1	45	58	.3	.4
223	FREE WILL BAPT	5	361	450*	2.6	3.0
349	PENT HOLINESS	1	60	75*	.4	.5
355	PRESB CH (USA)	2	119	148*	.8	1.0
361	PRIM BAPT ASCS	2	38	47*	.3	.3
419	SO BAPT CONV	41	7,765	9,671*	54.9	65.1
449	UN METHODIST	8	906	1,128*	6.4	7.6
497	BLACK BAPT EST[2]	NA	2,261	2,816*	16.0	19.0
DOOLY		**33**	**8,423**	**11,301***	**114.1**	**100.0**
145	CH GOD PROPHCY	1	37	48*	.5	.4
151	L-D SAINTS	1	NA	268	2.7	2.4
167	CHS OF CHRIST	1	3	4	-	-
223	FREE WILL BAPT	2	264	346*	3.5	3.1
361	PRIM BAPT ASCS	1	12	16*	.2	.1
419	SO BAPT CONV	19	3,037	3,978*	40.2	35.2
449	UN METHODIST	8	975	1,277*	12.9	11.3
497	BLACK BAPT EST[2]	NA	4,095	5,364*	54.2	47.5
DOUGHERTY		**79**	**42,157**	**60,276***	**62.6**	**100.0**
019	AMER BAPT USA	1	424	555*	.6	.9
053	ASSEMB OF GOD	2	590	950	1.0	1.6
081	CATHOLIC	1	NA	3,456	3.6	5.7
081d	LATIN	1	NA	3,456	3.6	5.7
093	CHR CH (DISC)	1	91	229	.2	.4
097	CHR CHS&CHS CR	3	571	747*	.8	1.2
111	CH CR,SCIENTST	1	NR	NR	-	-
123	CH GOD (ANDER)	1	24	24	-	-
127	CH GOD (CLEVE)	4	852	1,115*	1.2	1.8
145	CH GOD PROPHCY	1	37	48*	-	.1
165	CH OF NAZARENE	2	181	234	.2	.4
167	CHS OF CHRIST	7	1,184	1,497	1.6	2.5
193	EPISCOPAL	4	839	1,125	1.2	1.9
207	E.L.C.A.	1	228	285	.3	.5
223	FREE WILL BAPT	2	347	454*	.5	.8
246	GREEK ORTHODOX	1	NR	NR	-	-
283	LUTH—MO SYNOD	1	126	181	.2	.3
349	PENT HOLINESS	1	43	56*	.1	.1
353	CHR BRETHREN	1	100	250	.3	.4
355	PRESB CH (USA)	4	818	1,070*	1.1	1.8
356	PRESB CH AMER	1	87	121	.1	.2
361	PRIM BAPT ASCS	2	40	52*	.1	.1
403	SALVATION ARMY	1	174	178	.2	.3
413	S.D.A.	2	318	416*	.4	.7
419	SO BAPT CONV	20	16,236	21,246*	22.1	35.2
449	UN METHODIST	9	7,542	9,869*	10.2	16.4
467	WESLEYAN	1	0	0	-	-
496	JEWISH EST[1]	2	NA	400	.4	.7
497	BLACK BAPT EST[2]	NA	11,305	14,793*	15.4	24.5
498	INDEP.CHARIS.[3]	2	NA	925	1.0	1.5
DOUGLAS		**50**	**22,287**	**33,050***	**46.5**	**100.0**
053	ASSEMB OF GOD	2	309	454	.6	1.4
081	CATHOLIC	2	NA	1,511	2.1	4.6
081d	LATIN	2	NA	1,511	2.1	4.6
097	CHR CHS&CHS CR	2	440	566*	.8	1.7
127	CH GOD (CLEVE)	5	804	1,033*	1.5	3.1
145	CH GOD PROPHCY	1	37	48*	.1	.1
151	L-D SAINTS	2	NA	645	.9	2.0
165	CH OF NAZARENE	1	68	124	.2	.4
167	CHS OF CHRIST	4	311	411	.6	1.2
193	EPISCOPAL	2	267	427	.6	1.3
215	EVAN METH CH	1	189	243*	.3	.7
283	LUTH—MO SYNOD	1	134	221	.3	.7
355	PRESB CH (USA)	1	642	825*	1.2	2.5
356	PRESB CH AMER	1	94	129	.2	.4
419	SO BAPT CONV	18	13,776	17,707*	24.9	53.6
449	UN METHODIST	6	3,126	4,018*	5.6	12.2
496	JEWISH EST[1]	0	NA	1,632	2.3	4.9
497	BLACK BAPT EST[2]	NA	2,090	2,686*	3.8	8.1

County and Denomination		Number of churches	Communicant, confirmed, full members	Total adherents		
				Number	Percent of total population	Percent of total adherents
498	INDEP.CHARIS.[3]	1	NA	370	.5	1.1
EARLY		**33**	**6,690**	**8,789***	**74.1**	**100.0**
053	ASSEMB OF GOD	2	78	141	1.2	1.6
081	CATHOLIC	1	NA	40	.3	.5
081d	LATIN	1	NA	40	.3	.5
123	CH GOD (ANDER)	2	10	10	.1	.1
127	CH GOD (CLEVE)	1	67	87*	.7	1.0
167	CHS OF CHRIST	3	133	174	1.5	2.0
193	EPISCOPAL	1	19	29	.2	.3
223	FREE WILL BAPT	5	213	277*	2.3	3.2
355	PRESB CH (USA)	1	73	95*	.8	1.1
413	S.D.A.	1	89	116*	1.0	1.3
419	SO BAPT CONV	10	2,686	3,496*	29.5	39.8
449	UN METHODIST	6	893	1,162*	9.8	13.2
497	BLACK BAPT EST[2]	NA	2,429	3,162*	26.7	36.0
ECHOLS		**8**	**697**	**910***	**39.0**	**100.0**
127	CH GOD (CLEVE)	1	86	111*	4.8	12.2
145	CH GOD PROPHCY	1	37	48*	2.1	5.3
167	CHS OF CHRIST	1	50	72	3.1	7.9
361	PRIM BAPT ASCS	1	11	14*	.6	1.5
419	SO BAPT CONV	2	384	498*	21.3	54.7
449	UN METHODIST	2	129	167*	7.2	18.4
EFFINGHAM		**45**	**9,155**	**12,963***	**50.5**	**100.0**
053	ASSEMB OF GOD	1	123	209	.8	1.6
081	CATHOLIC	1	NA	140	.5	1.1
081d	LATIN	1	NA	140	.5	1.1
089	CHR & MISS AL	1	30	30	.1	.2
093	CHR CH (DISC)	1	95	168	.7	1.3
097	CHR CHS&CHS CR	3	350	462*	1.8	3.6
123	CH GOD (ANDER)	1	14	30	.1	.2
127	CH GOD (CLEVE)	1	183	242*	.9	1.9
145	CH GOD PROPHCY	1	37	49*	.2	.4
167	CHS OF CHRIST	2	73	97	.4	.7
193	EPISCOPAL	1	25	33	.1	.3
207	E.L.C.A.	6	868	1,079	4.2	8.3
413	S.D.A.	1	91	120*	.5	.9
419	SO BAPT CONV	13	4,077	5,387*	21.0	41.6
449	UN METHODIST	11	2,014	2,661*	10.4	20.5
496	JEWISH EST[1]	0	NA	303	1.2	2.3
497	BLACK BAPT EST[2]	NA	1,175	1,553*	6.0	12.0
499	INDEP.NON-CHAR[3]	1	NA	400	1.6	3.1
ELBERT		**54**	**12,364**	**15,903***	**83.9**	**100.0**
053	ASSEMB OF GOD	1	44	60	.3	.4
081	CATHOLIC	1	NA	85	.4	.5
081d	LATIN	1	NA	85	.4	.5
097	CHR CHS&CHS CR	1	200	254*	1.3	1.6
127	CH GOD (CLEVE)	3	402	510*	2.7	3.2
145	CH GOD PROPHCY	1	37	47*	.2	.3
151	L-D SAINTS	1	NA	118	.6	.7
165	CH OF NAZARENE	0	0	14	.1	.1
167	CHS OF CHRIST	2	60	63	.3	.4
193	EPISCOPAL	1	43	58	.3	.4
207	E.L.C.A.	1	139	176	.9	1.1
349	PENT HOLINESS	4	436	553*	2.9	3.5
355	PRESB CH (USA)	3	257	326*	1.7	2.0
356	PRESB CH AMER	1	22	27	.1	.2
419	SO BAPT CONV	20	5,944	7,545*	39.8	47.4
443	UN C OF CHRIST	1	45	57*	.3	.4
449	UN METHODIST	13	2,077	2,636*	13.9	16.6
497	BLACK BAPT EST[2]	NA	2,658	3,374*	17.8	21.2
EMANUEL		**71**	**10,880**	**14,607***	**71.1**	**100.0**
001	ADVENT CHR CH	1	23	30*	.1	.2
053	ASSEMB OF GOD	1	71	114	.6	.8
081	CATHOLIC	1	NA	190	.9	1.3
081d	LATIN	1	NA	190	.9	1.3
123	CH GOD (ANDER)	2	10	17	.1	.1
127	CH GOD (CLEVE)	5	332	434*	2.1	3.0
151	L-D SAINTS	1	NA	76	.4	.5
165	CH OF NAZARENE	2	65	168	.8	1.2
167	CHS OF CHRIST	1	10	13	.1	.1
223	FREE WILL BAPT	3	211	276*	1.3	1.9
349	PENT HOLINESS	2	51	67*	.3	.5
355	PRESB CH (USA)	1	23	30*	.1	.2
361	PRIM BAPT ASCS	16	781	1,022*	5.0	7.0
419	SO BAPT CONV	20	4,397	5,752*	28.0	39.4
449	UN METHODIST	15	1,801	2,356*	11.5	16.1
497	BLACK BAPT EST[2]	NA	3,105	4,062*	19.8	27.8

NA–Not applicable   NR–Not reported   *Total adherents estimated from known number of communicant, confirmed, full members.   - Represents a percent less than 0.1.   Percentages may not total due to rounding.
[1]See Appendix E   [2]See Appendix F   [3]See Appendix G   Lines in *italic* represent a breakdown of Catholic rites or Friends affiliations. They are included in their respective denominational total.

Table 4. Churches and Church Membership by County and Denomination: 1990

County and Denomination	Number of churches	Communicant, confirmed, full members	Total adherents Number	Percent of total population	Percent of total adherents
EVANS	**22**	**4,575**	**6,049***	**69.3**	**100.0**
081 CATHOLIC	1	NA	150	1.7	2.5
081d *LATIN*	*1*	*NA*	*150*	*1.7*	*2.5*
127 CH GOD (CLEVE)	1	57	73*	.8	1.2
145 CH GOD PROPHCY	1	37	48*	.6	.8
165 CH OF NAZARENE	1	50	74	.8	1.2
167 CHS OF CHRIST	1	30	36	.4	.6
223 FREE WILL BAPT	1	66	85*	1.0	1.4
361 PRIM BAPT ASCS	3	139	179*	2.1	3.0
419 SO BAPT CONV	6	1,472	1,896*	21.7	31.3
449 UN METHODIST	7	1,347	1,735*	19.9	28.7
497 BLACK BAPT EST[2]	NA	1,377	1,773*	20.3	29.3
FANNIN	**54**	**10,276**	**12,618***	**78.9**	**100.0**
081 CATHOLIC	1	NA	107	.7	.8
081d *LATIN*	*1*	*NA*	*107*	*.7*	*.8*
127 CH GOD (CLEVE)	2	307	373*	2.3	3.0
145 CH GOD PROPHCY	1	37	45*	.3	.4
167 CHS OF CHRIST	4	349	454	2.8	3.6
207 E.L.C.A.	1	81	85	.5	.7
361 PRIM BAPT ASCS	1	14	17*	.1	.1
419 SO BAPT CONV	38	8,709	10,590*	66.2	83.9
449 UN METHODIST	6	779	947*	5.9	7.5
FAYETTE	**61**	**27,733**	**40,974***	**65.6**	**100.0**
053 ASSEMB OF GOD	3	1,095	895	1.4	2.2
081 CATHOLIC	2	NA	3,613	5.8	8.8
081d *LATIN*	*2*	*NA*	*3,613*	*5.8*	*8.8*
093 CHR CH (DISC)	1	64	76	.1	.2
097 CHR CHS&CHS CR	5	1,300	1,678*	2.7	4.1
111 CH CR,SCIENTST	1	NR	NR	-	-
127 CH GOD (CLEVE)	2	200	258*	.4	.6
145 CH GOD PROPHCY	1	37	48*	.1	.1
151 L-D SAINTS	1	NA	531	.9	1.3
167 CHS OF CHRIST	2	435	566	.9	1.4
193 EPISCOPAL	1	293	412	.7	1.0
207 E.L.C.A.	2	1,138	1,537	2.5	3.8
221 FREE METHODIST	1	24	27	-	.1
223 FREE WILL BAPT	1	40	52*	.1	.1
355 PRESB CH (USA)	2	1,148	1,482*	2.4	3.6
356 PRESB CH AMER	2	217	298	.5	.7
361 PRIM BAPT ASCS	1	2	3*	-	-
413 S.D.A.	2	191	247*	.4	.6
419 SO BAPT CONV	19	15,397	19,877*	31.8	48.5
449 UN METHODIST	12	5,055	6,526*	10.5	15.9
496 JEWISH EST[1]	0	NA	1,432	2.3	3.5
497 BLACK BAPT EST[2]	NA	1,097	1,416*	2.3	3.5
FLOYD	**140**	**46,060**	**57,799***	**71.1**	**100.0**
005 AME ZION	2	144	159	.2	.3
053 ASSEMB OF GOD	2	213	285	.4	.5
081 CATHOLIC	1	NA	883	1.1	1.5
081d *LATIN*	*1*	*NA*	*883*	*1.1*	*1.5*
089 CHR & MISS AL	1	30	49	.1	.1
093 CHR CH (DISC)	1	80	106	.1	.2
097 CHR CHS&CHS CR	2	520	637*	.8	1.1
111 CH CR,SCIENTST	1	NR	NR	-	-
127 CH GOD (CLEVE)	8	1,522	1,865*	2.3	3.2
145 CH GOD PROPHCY	4	147	180*	.2	.3
151 L-D SAINTS	1	NA	353	.4	.6
165 CH OF NAZARENE	1	57	108	.1	.2
167 CHS OF CHRIST	5	628	869	1.1	1.5
193 EPISCOPAL	2	706	1,040	1.3	1.8
216 EVAN PRESBY CH	1	1,040	1,057	1.3	1.8
283 LUTH—MO SYNOD	1	113	145	.2	.3
289 NEW HOPE B ASC	1	46	56*	.1	.1
355 PRESB CH (USA)	2	519	636*	.8	1.1
361 PRIM BAPT ASCS	2	15	18*	-	-
403 SALVATION ARMY	1	80	86	.1	.1
413 S.D.A.	2	94	115*	.1	.2
419 SO BAPT CONV	66	30,337	37,182*	45.8	64.3
430 TRUEVINE B ASC	3	458	561*	.7	1.0
435 UNITARIAN-UNIV	1	14	14	-	-
449 UN METHODIST	28	5,658	6,935*	8.5	12.0
496 JEWISH EST[1]	1	NA	0	-	-
497 BLACK BAPT EST[2]	NA	3,639	4,460*	5.5	7.7
FORSYTH	**58**	**19,287**	**26,075***	**59.1**	**100.0**
053 ASSEMB OF GOD	1	33	56	.1	.2
081 CATHOLIC	1	NA	786	1.8	3.0
081d *LATIN*	*1*	*NA*	*786*	*1.8*	*3.0*
097 CHR CHS&CHS CR	1	600	752*	1.7	2.9
127 CH GOD (CLEVE)	2	326	409*	.9	1.6
145 CH GOD PROPHCY	1	37	46*	.1	.2
167 CHS OF CHRIST	1	26	34	.1	.1
193 EPISCOPAL	1	217	319	.7	1.2
207 E.L.C.A.	1	127	184	.4	.7
226 FRIENDS-USA	1	1	4	-	-
226c *FGC*	*1*	*1*	*4*	*-*	*-*
355 PRESB CH (USA)	2	336	421*	1.0	1.6
419 SO BAPT CONV	37	15,657	19,636*	44.5	75.3
449 UN METHODIST	9	1,927	2,417*	5.5	9.3
496 JEWISH EST[1]	0	NA	1,011	2.3	3.9
FRANKLIN	**54**	**10,760**	**13,204***	**79.3**	**100.0**
081 CATHOLIC	0	NA	73	.4	.6
081d *LATIN*	*0*	*NA*	*73*	*.4*	*.6*
097 CHR CHS&CHS CR	1	200	244*	1.5	1.8
127 CH GOD (CLEVE)	7	945	1,154*	6.9	8.7
167 CHS OF CHRIST	1	17	22	.1	.2
216 EVAN PRESBY CH	1	86	92	.6	.7
349 PENT HOLINESS	5	586	716*	4.3	5.4
355 PRESB CH (USA)	4	98	120*	.7	.9
419 SO BAPT CONV	25	6,922	8,455*	50.8	64.0
449 UN METHODIST	10	1,417	1,731*	10.4	13.1
497 BLACK BAPT EST[2]	NA	489	597*	3.6	4.5
FULTON	**409**	**298,493**	**422,840***	**65.2**	**100.0**
005 AME ZION	1	810	910	.1	.2
019 AMER BAPT USA	6	3,905	4,836*	.7	1.1
053 ASSEMB OF GOD	6	599	893	.1	.2
081 CATHOLIC	14	NA	29,062	4.5	6.9
081d *LATIN*	*13*	*NA*	*28,786*	*4.4*	*6.8*
081e *MARONITE*	*1*	*NA*	*276*	*-*	*.1*
089 CHR & MISS AL	2	104	181	-	-
093 CHR CH (DISC)	3	1,706	2,556	.4	.6
097 CHR CHS&CHS CR	19	7,017	8,690*	1.3	2.1
105 CHRISTIAN REF	1	0	0	-	-
111 CH CR,SCIENTST	5	NR	NR	-	-
123 CH GOD (ANDER)	2	314	393	.1	.1
127 CH GOD (CLEVE)	13	12,373	15,323*	2.4	3.6
133 CH GOD(7TH)DEN	1	0	0	-	-
145 CH GOD PROPHCY	3	110	136*	-	-
151 L-D SAINTS	3	NA	1,103	.2	.3
157 CH OF BRETHREN	1	32	40*	-	-
165 CH OF NAZARENE	2	130	202	-	-
167 CHS OF CHRIST	22	3,170	4,702	.7	1.1
193 EPISCOPAL	15	13,233	17,860	2.8	4.2
207 E.L.C.A.	11	3,016	3,839	.6	.9
246 GREEK ORTHODOX	1	NR	NR	-	-
265 INT PENT C CHR	2	59	60	-	-
269 JASPER&PVB ASC	1	166	206*	-	-
283 LUTH—MO SYNOD	5	1,012	1,280	.2	.3
287 MENN GEN CONF	1	0	0	-	-
339 PENT CH OF GOD	1	34	77	-	-
355 PRESB CH (USA)	30	22,848	28,296*	4.4	6.7
356 PRESB CH AMER	6	1,190	1,343	.2	.3
361 PRIM BAPT ASCS	7	344	426*	.1	.1
371 REF CH IN AM	1	167	249	-	.1
403 SALVATION ARMY	6	801	871	.1	.2
413 S.D.A.	12	8,182	10,133*	1.6	2.4
419 SO BAPT CONV	97	72,940	90,331*	13.9	21.4
423 SYRIAN ANTIOCH	1	NA	500	.1	.1
435 UNITARIAN-UNIV	2	190	293	-	.1
443 UN C OF CHRIST	4	592	733*	.1	.2
449 UN METHODIST	83	50,649	62,725*	9.7	14.8
496 JEWISH EST[1]	9	NA	14,915	2.3	3.5
497 BLACK BAPT EST[2]	NA	92,800	114,926*	17.7	27.2
498 INDEP.CHARIS.[3]	6	NA	2,700	.4	.6
499 INDEP.NON-CHAR[3]	4	NA	2,050	.3	.5
GILMER	**29**	**5,180**	**6,533***	**48.9**	**100.0**
081 CATHOLIC	1	NA	63	.5	1.0
081d *LATIN*	*1*	*NA*	*63*	*.5*	*1.0*
127 CH GOD (CLEVE)	1	217	269*	2.0	4.1
145 CH GOD PROPHCY	1	37	46*	.3	.7
167 CHS OF CHRIST	3	243	354	2.6	5.4
269 JASPER&PVB ASC	1	216	268*	2.0	4.1
361 PRIM BAPT ASCS	1	77	95*	.7	1.5
413 S.D.A.	1	162	201*	1.5	3.1
419 SO BAPT CONV	14	3,556	4,405*	33.0	67.4
449 UN METHODIST	6	672	832*	6.2	12.7
GLASCOCK	**16**	**1,558**	**1,903***	**80.7**	**100.0**
123 CH GOD (ANDER)	1	10	10	.4	.5
127 CH GOD (CLEVE)	2	89	109*	4.6	5.7
361 PRIM BAPT ASCS	2	64	78*	3.3	4.1
419 SO BAPT CONV	7	1,090	1,333*	56.6	70.0
449 UN METHODIST	4	305	373*	15.8	19.6

NA–Not applicable   NR–Not reported   *Total adherents estimated from known number of communicant, confirmed, full members.   - Represents a percent less than 0.1.   Percentages may not total due to rounding.

[1]See Appendix E   [2]See Appendix F   [3]See Appendix G   Lines in *italic* represent a breakdown of Catholic rites or Friends affiliations. They are included in their respective denominational total.

Table 4. Churches and Church Membership by County and Denomination: 1990

County and Denomination	Number of churches	Communicant, confirmed, full members	Total adherents Number	Percent of total population	Percent of total adherents
GLYNN	86	23,687	33,842*	54.2	100.0
001 ADVENT CHR CH	1	66	83*	.1	.2
053 ASSEMB OF GOD	2	74	118	.2	.3
081 CATHOLIC	2	NA	3,159	5.1	9.3
081d *LATIN*	2	NA	3,159	5.1	9.3
097 CHR CHS&CHS CR	1	40	50*	.1	.1
111 CH CR,SCIENTST	1	NR	NR	-	-
123 CH GOD (ANDER)	1	16	30	-	.1
127 CH GOD (CLEVE)	6	928	1,167*	1.9	3.4
145 CH GOD PROPHCY	2	74	93*	.1	.3
151 L-D SAINTS	1	NA	413	.7	1.2
165 CH OF NAZARENE	3	244	353	.6	1.0
167 CHS OF CHRIST	4	110	135	.2	.4
193 EPISCOPAL	7	1,322	1,558	2.5	4.6
207 E.L.C.A.	2	554	745	1.2	2.2
223 FREE WILL BAPT	1	68	85*	.1	.3
226 FRIENDS-USA	1	0	6*	-	-
226d *FGC & FUM*	1	0	6*	-	-
246 GREEK ORTHODOX	1	NR	NR	-	-
263 INT FOURSQ GOS	1	22	28*	-	.1
349 PENT HOLINESS	1	46	58*	.1	.2
355 PRESB CH (USA)	5	1,546	1,944*	3.1	5.7
356 PRESB CH AMER	1	24	24	-	.1
361 PRIM BAPT ASCS	1	77	97*	.2	.3
403 SALVATION ARMY	1	75	77	.1	.2
413 S.D.A.	2	154	194*	.3	.6
419 SO BAPT CONV	19	9,589	12,056*	19.3	35.6
449 UN METHODIST	15	4,533	5,699*	9.1	16.8
467 WESLEYAN	2	65	165	.3	.5
496 JEWISH EST[1]	1	NA	100	.2	.3
497 BLACK BAPT EST[2]	NA	4,060	5,105*	8.2	15.1
499 INDEP.NON-CHAR[3]	1	NA	300	.5	.9
GORDON	77	15,712	20,223*	57.7	100.0
053 ASSEMB OF GOD	2	73	120	.3	.6
081 CATHOLIC	1	NA	399	1.1	2.0
081d *LATIN*	1	NA	399	1.1	2.0
127 CH GOD (CLEVE)	10	1,332	1,676*	4.8	8.3
145 CH GOD PROPHCY	2	74	93*	.3	.5
165 CH OF NAZARENE	1	31	92	.3	.5
167 CHS OF CHRIST	3	328	388	1.1	1.9
185 CUMBER PRESB	1	25	25	.1	.1
193 EPISCOPAL	1	50	63	.2	.3
269 JASPER&PVB ASC	1	363	457*	1.3	2.3
331 ORTH CH IN AM	1	NR	NR	-	-
355 PRESB CH (USA)	1	172	216*	.6	1.1
361 PRIM BAPT ASCS	1	14	18*	.1	.1
413 S.D.A.	2	489	615*	1.8	3.0
419 SO BAPT CONV	36	10,729	13,503*	38.5	66.8
449 UN METHODIST	14	1,612	2,029*	5.8	10.0
497 BLACK BAPT EST[2]	NA	420	529*	1.5	2.6
GRADY	56	12,020	15,543*	76.6	100.0
053 ASSEMB OF GOD	3	111	176	.9	1.1
081 CATHOLIC	1	NA	25	.1	.2
081d *LATIN*	1	NA	25	.1	.2
127 CH GOD (CLEVE)	1	142	181*	.9	1.2
145 CH GOD PROPHCY	1	37	47*	.2	.3
151 L-D SAINTS	1	NA	131	.6	.8
165 CH OF NAZARENE	1	65	105	.5	.7
167 CHS OF CHRIST	3	87	104	.5	.7
223 FREE WILL BAPT	1	70	89*	.4	.6
349 PENT HOLINESS	1	110	140*	.7	.9
355 PRESB CH (USA)	1	111	142*	.7	.9
361 PRIM BAPT ASCS	5	195	249*	1.2	1.6
419 SO BAPT CONV	24	6,731	8,589*	42.4	55.3
443 UN C OF CHRIST	1	68	87*	.4	.6
449 UN METHODIST	12	1,321	1,686*	8.3	10.8
497 BLACK BAPT EST[2]	NA	2,972	3,792*	18.7	24.4
GREENE	30	6,670	8,768*	74.3	100.0
081 CATHOLIC	0	NA	5	-	.1
081d *LATIN*	0	NA	5	-	.1
127 CH GOD (CLEVE)	1	125	165*	1.4	1.9
167 CHS OF CHRIST	1	7	8	.1	.1
193 EPISCOPAL	1	40	60	.5	.7
355 PRESB CH (USA)	3	153	201*	1.7	2.3
356 PRESB CH AMER	2	34	34	.3	.4
413 S.D.A.	1	14	18*	.2	.2
419 SO BAPT CONV	12	2,493	3,281*	27.8	37.4
449 UN METHODIST	7	1,020	1,343*	11.4	15.3
467 WESLEYAN	2	48	52	.4	.6
497 BLACK BAPT EST[2]	NA	2,736	3,601*	30.5	41.1

County and Denomination	Number of churches	Communicant, confirmed, full members	Total adherents Number	Percent of total population	Percent of total adherents
GWINNETT	197	88,597	154,860*	43.9	100.0
005 AME ZION	2	248	283	.1	.2
053 ASSEMB OF GOD	7	849	1,076	.3	.7
055 AS REF PRES CH	1	75	105	-	.1
075 BRETHREN IN CR	1	26	52	-	-
081 CATHOLIC	6	NA	22,028	6.2	14.2
081d *LATIN*	6	NA	22,028	6.2	14.2
089 CHR & MISS AL	4	608	1,332	.4	.9
093 CHR CH (DISC)	3	740	843	.2	.5
097 CHR CHS&CHS CR	6	1,880	2,428*	.7	1.6
111 CH CR,SCIENTST	1	NR	NR	-	-
127 CH GOD (CLEVE)	8	1,896	2,449*	.7	1.6
145 CH GOD PROPHCY	2	74	96*	-	.1
151 L-D SAINTS	6	NA	2,597	.7	1.7
165 CH OF NAZARENE	2	177	268	.1	.2
167 CHS OF CHRIST	8	1,650	2,352	.7	1.5
176 CCC, NOT NAT'L	1	100	129*	-	.1
185 CUMBER PRESB	1	59	77	-	-
193 EPISCOPAL	3	1,153	2,001	.6	1.3
203 EVAN FREE CH	1	70	70	-	-
207 E.L.C.A.	7	2,946	4,292	1.2	2.8
226 FRIENDS-USA	1	0	11	-	-
226c *FGC*	1	0	11	-	-
283 LUTH—MO SYNOD	1	209	307	.1	.2
295 MORAV CH-SOUTH	1	136	192	.1	.1
329 OPEN BIBLE STD	1	NR	NR	-	-
331 ORTH CH IN AM	1	NR	NR	-	-
355 PRESB CH (USA)	9	3,783	4,886*	1.4	3.2
356 PRESB CH AMER	3	1,125	1,400	.4	.9
361 PRIM BAPT ASCS	4	59	76*	-	-
403 SALVATION ARMY	1	45	46	-	-
413 S.D.A.	4	434	560*	.2	.4
419 SO BAPT CONV	53	42,820	55,300*	15.7	35.7
435 UNITARIAN-UNIV	1	100	210	.1	.1
443 UN C OF CHRIST	1	78	101*	-	.1
449 UN METHODIST	33	21,146	27,309*	7.7	17.6
469 WELS	1	213	321	.1	.2
496 JEWISH EST[1]	1	NA	8,096	2.3	5.2
497 BLACK BAPT EST[2]	NA	5,898	7,617*	2.2	4.9
498 INDEP.CHARIS.[3]	4	NA	2,000	.6	1.3
499 INDEP.NON-CHAR[3]	7	NA	3,950	1.1	2.6
HABERSHAM	55	12,954	16,416*	59.4	100.0
053 ASSEMB OF GOD	2	52	67	.2	.4
081 CATHOLIC	1	NA	495	1.8	3.0
081d *LATIN*	1	NA	495	1.8	3.0
089 CHR & MISS AL	1	17	37	.1	.2
097 CHR CHS&CHS CR	2	344	421*	1.5	2.6
127 CH GOD (CLEVE)	3	240	294*	1.1	1.8
145 CH GOD PROPHCY	1	37	45*	.2	.3
167 CHS OF CHRIST	1	35	45	.2	.3
193 EPISCOPAL	1	217	298	1.1	1.8
329 OPEN BIBLE STD	1	NR	NR	-	-
355 PRESB CH (USA)	2	478	585*	2.1	3.6
419 SO BAPT CONV	30	9,741	11,932*	43.2	72.7
443 UN C OF CHRIST	1	17	21*	.1	.1
449 UN METHODIST	9	1,377	1,687*	6.1	10.3
497 BLACK BAPT EST[2]	NA	399	489*	1.8	3.0
HALL	115	40,638	54,887*	57.5	100.0
053 ASSEMB OF GOD	4	648	855	.9	1.6
081 CATHOLIC	1	NA	2,835	3.0	5.2
081d *LATIN*	1	NA	2,835	3.0	5.2
089 CHR & MISS AL	1	37	72	.1	.1
093 CHR CH (DISC)	1	70	90	.1	.2
097 CHR CHS&CHS CR	1	85	106*	.1	.2
111 CH CR,SCIENTST	1	NR	NR	-	-
127 CH GOD (CLEVE)	7	1,537	1,925*	2.0	3.5
145 CH GOD PROPHCY	1	37	46*	-	.1
151 L-D SAINTS	1	NA	402	.4	.7
165 CH OF NAZARENE	2	219	395	.4	.7
167 CHS OF CHRIST	3	159	212	.2	.4
179 CONSRV BAPT	1	NR	NR	-	-
193 EPISCOPAL	1	581	689	.7	1.3
207 E.L.C.A.	1	175	241	.3	.4
221 FREE METHODIST	1	52	52	.1	.1
223 FREE WILL BAPT	1	65	81*	.1	.1
283 LUTH—MO SYNOD	1	172	224	.2	.4
329 OPEN BIBLE STD	1	NR	NR	-	-
355 PRESB CH (USA)	2	1,029	1,289*	1.4	2.3
356 PRESB CH AMER	2	374	552	.6	1.0
403 SALVATION ARMY	1	104	107	.1	.2
413 S.D.A.	2	275	344*	.4	.6
419 SO BAPT CONV	53	27,057	33,888*	35.5	61.7
449 UN METHODIST	24	5,858	7,337*	7.7	13.4
497 BLACK BAPT EST[2]	NA	2,104	2,635*	2.8	4.8

NA–Not applicable   NR–Not reported   *Total adherents estimated from known number of communicant, confirmed, full members.   - Represents a percent less than 0.1.   Percentages may not total due to rounding.
[1]See Appendix E   [2]See Appendix F   [3]See Appendix G   Lines in *italic* represent a breakdown of Catholic rites or Friends affiliations. They are included in their respective denominational total.

Table 4. Churches and Church Membership by County and Denomination: 1990

County and Denomination	Number of churches	Communicant, confirmed, full members	Total adherents — Number	Percent of total population	Percent of total adherents
499 INDEP.NON-CHAR[3]	1	NA	510	.5	.9
HANCOCK	**30**	**4,860**	**6,409***	**71.9**	**100.0**
093 CHR CH (DISC)	1	41	58	.7	.9
127 CH GOD (CLEVE)	1	26	34*	.4	.5
167 CHS OF CHRIST	2	71	89	1.0	1.4
356 PRESB CH AMER	1	19	29	.3	.5
419 SO BAPT CONV	13	1,000	1,318*	14.8	20.6
449 UN METHODIST	12	414	546*	6.1	8.5
497 BLACK BAPT EST[2]	NA	3,289	4,335*	48.7	67.6
HARALSON	**52**	**10,514**	**13,687***	**62.3**	**100.0**
053 ASSEM OF GOD	1	47	90	.4	.7
081 CATHOLIC	0	NA	110	.5	.8
081d *LATIN*	*0*	*NA*	*110*	*.5*	*.8*
097 CHR CHS&CHS CR	2	245	309*	1.4	2.3
127 CH GOD (CLEVE)	3	456	576*	2.6	4.2
151 L-D SAINTS	1	NA	173	.8	1.3
167 CHS OF CHRIST	3	454	673	3.1	4.9
289 NEW HOPE B ASC	5	506	639*	2.9	4.7
349 PENT HOLINESS	1	31	39*	.2	.3
355 PRESB CH (USA)	2	42	53*	.2	.4
361 PRIM BAPT ASCS	2	15	19*	.1	.1
419 SO BAPT CONV	23	7,007	8,846*	40.3	64.6
449 UN METHODIST	9	1,296	1,636*	7.4	12.0
497 BLACK BAPT EST[2]	NA	415	524*	2.4	3.8
HARRIS	**38**	**5,767**	**7,326***	**41.2**	**100.0**
053 ASSEM OF GOD	1	12	24	.1	.3
081 CATHOLIC	1	NA	100	.6	1.4
081d *LATIN*	*1*	*NA*	*100*	*.6*	*1.4*
127 CH GOD (CLEVE)	1	102	127*	.7	1.7
167 CHS OF CHRIST	2	57	74	.4	1.0
339 PENT CH OF GOD	1	18	75	.4	1.0
361 PRIM BAPT ASCS	1	5	6*	-	.1
413 S.D.A.	1	86	107*	.6	1.5
419 SO BAPT CONV	20	3,475	4,315*	24.3	58.9
449 UN METHODIST	10	1,072	1,331*	7.5	18.2
497 BLACK BAPT EST[2]	NA	940	1,167*	6.6	15.9
HART	**40**	**10,232**	**13,045***	**66.2**	**100.0**
081 CATHOLIC	1	NA	382	1.9	2.9
081d *LATIN*	*1*	*NA*	*382*	*1.9*	*2.9*
089 CHR & MISS AL	1	0	49	.2	.4
097 CHR CHS&CHS CR	1	30	37*	.2	.3
127 CH GOD (CLEVE)	2	130	160*	.8	1.2
145 CH GOD PROPHCY	1	37	46*	.2	.4
167 CHS OF CHRIST	1	30	41	.2	.3
193 EPISCOPAL	1	105	121	.6	.9
349 PENT HOLINESS	1	84	104*	.5	.8
355 PRESB CH (USA)	2	146	180*	.9	1.4
419 SO BAPT CONV	18	6,901	8,512*	43.2	65.3
435 UNITARIAN-UNIV	1	10	10	.1	.1
449 UN METHODIST	10	1,595	1,967*	10.0	15.1
497 BLACK BAPT EST[2]	NA	1,164	1,436*	7.3	11.0
HEARD	**31**	**3,136**	**4,001***	**46.4**	**100.0**
081 CATHOLIC	0	NA	7	.1	.2
081d *LATIN*	*0*	*NA*	*7*	*.1*	*.2*
097 CHR CHS&CHS CR	1	50	64*	.7	1.6
127 CH GOD (CLEVE)	2	191	243*	2.8	6.1
167 CHS OF CHRIST	2	30	36	.4	.9
361 PRIM BAPT ASCS	1	4	5*	.1	.1
419 SO BAPT CONV	12	1,754	2,235*	25.9	55.9
449 UN METHODIST	13	769	980*	11.4	24.5
497 BLACK BAPT EST[2]	NA	338	431*	5.0	10.8
HENRY	**61**	**19,801**	**27,382***	**46.6**	**100.0**
053 ASSEM OF GOD	4	469	654	1.1	2.4
081 CATHOLIC	1	NA	576	1.0	2.1
081d *LATIN*	*1*	*NA*	*576*	*1.0*	*2.1*
097 CHR CHS&CHS CR	3	640	820*	1.4	3.0
123 CH GOD (ANDER)	1	0	21	-	.1
127 CH GOD (CLEVE)	3	337	432*	.7	1.6
145 CH GOD PROPHCY	1	37	47*	.1	.2
167 CHS OF CHRIST	2	212	272	.5	1.0
175 CONGR CHR CHS	1	93	119*	.2	.4
193 EPISCOPAL	1	139	203	.3	.7
355 PRESB CH (USA)	5	884	1,132*	1.9	4.1
356 PRESB CH AMER	1	40	47	.1	.2
361 PRIM BAPT ASCS	2	12	15*	-	.1
413 S.D.A.	1	102	131*	.2	.5
419 SO BAPT CONV	17	10,445	13,379*	22.8	48.9
449 UN METHODIST	18	4,422	5,664*	9.6	20.7
496 JEWISH EST[1]	0	NA	1,348	2.3	4.9
497 BLACK BAPT EST[2]	NA	1,969	2,522*	4.3	9.2
HOUSTON	**81**	**39,037**	**54,757***	**61.4**	**100.0**
053 ASSEM OF GOD	4	499	760	.9	1.4
059 BAPT MISS ASSN	1	153	197*	.2	.4
081 CATHOLIC	2	NA	2,715	3.0	5.0
081d *LATIN*	*2*	*NA*	*2,715*	*3.0*	*5.0*
089 CHR & MISS AL	1	45	76	.1	.1
093 CHR CH (DISC)	1	136	212	.2	.4
111 CH CR,SCIENTST	1	NR	NR	-	-
127 CH GOD (CLEVE)	6	1,158	1,490*	1.7	2.7
145 CH GOD PROPHCY	1	37	48*	.1	.1
151 L-D SAINTS	2	NA	706	.8	1.3
165 CH OF NAZARENE	1	188	226	.3	.4
167 CHS OF CHRIST	5	453	596	.7	1.1
193 EPISCOPAL	2	433	683	.8	1.2
207 E.L.C.A.	1	213	289	.3	.5
223 FREE WILL BAPT	2	61	78*	.1	.1
263 INT FOURSQ GOS	1	20	26*	-	-
283 LUTH—MO SYNOD	1	351	479	.5	.9
349 PENT HOLINESS	1	19	24*	-	-
355 PRESB CH (USA)	3	369	475*	.5	.9
356 PRESB CH AMER	2	356	447	.5	.8
361 PRIM BAPT ASCS	2	73	94*	.1	.2
403 SALVATION ARMY	1	105	121	.1	.2
413 S.D.A.	2	160	206*	.2	.4
419 SO BAPT CONV	25	21,446	27,598*	30.9	50.4
449 UN METHODIST	12	6,474	8,331*	9.3	15.2
496 JEWISH EST[1]	0	NA	288	.3	.5
497 BLACK BAPT EST[2]	NA	6,288	8,092*	9.1	14.8
499 INDEP.NON-CHAR[3]	1	NA	500	.6	.9
IRWIN	**19**	**4,295**	**5,565***	**64.3**	**100.0**
127 CH GOD (CLEVE)	1	202	262*	3.0	4.7
361 PRIM BAPT ASCS	6	529	685*	7.9	12.3
419 SO BAPT CONV	10	2,015	2,611*	30.2	46.9
449 UN METHODIST	2	327	424*	4.9	7.6
497 BLACK BAPT EST[2]	NA	1,222	1,583*	18.3	28.4
JACKSON	**61**	**11,142**	**14,420***	**48.1**	**100.0**
053 ASSEM OF GOD	1	39	63	.2	.4
081 CATHOLIC	1	NA	50	.2	.3
081d *LATIN*	*1*	*NA*	*50*	*.2*	*.3*
093 CHR CH (DISC)	1	130	224	.7	1.6
097 CHR CHS&CHS CR	3	555	700*	2.3	4.9
127 CH GOD (CLEVE)	2	151	191*	.6	1.3
145 CH GOD PROPHCY	3	110	139*	.5	1.0
151 L-D SAINTS	1	NA	238	.8	1.7
167 CHS OF CHRIST	1	50	62	.2	.4
355 PRESB CH (USA)	5	284	358*	1.2	2.5
361 PRIM BAPT ASCS	1	7	9*	-	.1
419 SO BAPT CONV	25	6,888	8,691*	29.0	60.3
443 UN C OF CHRIST	1	41	52*	.2	.4
449 UN METHODIST	16	1,945	2,454*	8.2	17.0
497 BLACK BAPT EST[2]	NA	942	1,189*	4.0	8.2
JASPER	**19**	**3,800**	**4,868***	**57.6**	**100.0**
167 CHS OF CHRIST	1	15	19	.2	.4
355 PRESB CH (USA)	1	163	209*	2.5	4.3
361 PRIM BAPT ASCS	1	7	9*	.1	.2
419 SO BAPT CONV	10	1,772	2,270*	26.9	46.6
449 UN METHODIST	6	477	611*	7.2	12.6
497 BLACK BAPT EST[2]	NA	1,366	1,750*	20.7	35.9
JEFF DAVIS	**34**	**7,473**	**9,836***	**81.7**	**100.0**
081 CATHOLIC	1	NA	85	.7	.9
081d *LATIN*	*1*	*NA*	*85*	*.7*	*.9*
089 CHR & MISS AL	1	74	78	.6	.8
127 CH GOD (CLEVE)	4	721	918*	7.6	9.3
145 CH GOD PROPHCY	1	37	47*	.4	.5
151 L-D SAINTS	1	NA	236	2.0	2.4
167 CHS OF CHRIST	2	49	77	.6	.8
223 FREE WILL BAPT	2	199	253*	2.1	2.6
361 PRIM BAPT ASCS	2	42	53*	.4	.5
413 S.D.A.	1	8	10*	.1	.1
419 SO BAPT CONV	16	5,189	6,609*	54.9	67.2
449 UN METHODIST	3	621	791*	6.6	8.0
497 BLACK BAPT EST[2]	NA	533	679*	5.6	6.9
JEFFERSON	**44**	**10,270**	**13,519***	**77.7**	**100.0**
053 ASSEM OF GOD	1	5	11	.1	.1
055 AS REF PRES CH	3	266	285	1.6	2.1
081 CATHOLIC	1	NA	100	.6	.7

NA–Not applicable   NR–Not reported   *Total adherents estimated from known number of communicant, confirmed, full members.   - Represents a percent less than 0.1.   Percentages may not total due to rounding.

[1]See Appendix E   [2]See Appendix F   [3]See Appendix G   Lines in *italic* represent a breakdown of Catholic rites or Friends affiliations. They are included in their respective denominational total.

Table 4. Churches and Church Membership by County and Denomination: 1990

County and Denomination	Number of churches	Communicant, confirmed, full members	Total adherents		
			Number	Percent of total population	Percent of total adherents
081d *LATIN*	*1*	*NA*	*100*	*.6*	*.7*
123 CH GOD (ANDER)	1	42	50	.3	.4
127 CH GOD (CLEVE)	2	146	190*	1.1	1.4
143 CG IN CR(MENN)	1	244	318*	1.8	2.4
151 L-D SAINTS	1	NA	71	.4	.5
165 CH OF NAZARENE	2	111	123	.7	.9
167 CHS OF CHRIST	1	15	18	.1	.1
193 EPISCOPAL	1	55	98	.6	.7
353 CHR BRETHREN	1	25	60	.3	.4
361 PRIM BAPT ASCS	1	47	61*	.4	.5
413 S.D.A.	0	76	99*	.6	.7
419 SO BAPT CONV	16	3,202	4,171*	24.0	30.9
449 UN METHODIST	12	1,528	1,991*	11.4	14.7
497 BLACK BAPT EST[2]	NA	4,508	5,873*	33.7	43.4
JENKINS	**20**	**5,071**	**6,647***	**80.6**	**100.0**
081 CATHOLIC	1	NA	40	.5	.6
081d *LATIN*	*1*	*NA*	*40*	*.5*	*.6*
123 CH GOD (ANDER)	1	14	17	.2	.3
167 CHS OF CHRIST	1	6	8	.1	.1
223 FREE WILL BAPT	1	110	143*	1.7	2.2
361 PRIM BAPT ASCS	1	15	20*	.2	.3
419 SO BAPT CONV	10	3,038	3,959*	48.0	59.6
449 UN METHODIST	5	608	792*	9.6	11.9
497 BLACK BAPT EST[2]	NA	1,280	1,668*	20.2	25.1
JOHNSON	**38**	**4,755**	**6,424***	**77.1**	**100.0**
001 ADVENT CHR CH	1	55	71*	.9	1.1
053 ASSEMB OF GOD	2	82	118	1.4	1.8
127 CH GOD (CLEVE)	2	239	309*	3.7	4.8
165 CH OF NAZARENE	2	263	598	7.2	9.3
349 PENT HOLINESS	1	7	9*	.1	.1
361 PRIM BAPT ASCS	4	135	175*	2.1	2.7
419 SO BAPT CONV	14	1,794	2,322*	27.9	36.1
449 UN METHODIST	12	860	1,113*	13.4	17.3
497 BLACK BAPT EST[2]	NA	1,320	1,709*	20.5	26.6
JONES	**23**	**5,097**	**6,593***	**31.8**	**100.0**
127 CH GOD (CLEVE)	1	121	155*	.7	2.4
167 CHS OF CHRIST	1	25	32	.2	.5
355 PRESB CH (USA)	1	47	60*	.3	.9
361 PRIM BAPT ASCS	4	60	77*	.4	1.2
419 SO BAPT CONV	11	2,707	3,468*	16.7	52.6
449 UN METHODIST	5	895	1,147*	5.5	17.4
496 JEWISH EST[1]	0	NA	63	.3	1.0
497 BLACK BAPT EST[2]	NA	1,242	1,591*	7.7	24.1
LAMAR	**35**	**6,498**	**8,369***	**64.2**	**100.0**
053 ASSEMB OF GOD	1	63	114	.9	1.4
081 CATHOLIC	1	NA	110	.8	1.3
081d *LATIN*	*1*	*NA*	*110*	*.8*	*1.3*
127 CH GOD (CLEVE)	1	40	50*	.4	.6
145 CH GOD PROPHCY	1	37	46*	.4	.5
165 CH OF NAZARENE	1	132	252	1.9	3.0
167 CHS OF CHRIST	1	65	72	.6	.9
349 PENT HOLINESS	3	66	83*	.6	1.0
355 PRESB CH (USA)	1	75	94*	.7	1.1
361 PRIM BAPT ASCS	3	109	137*	1.1	1.6
419 SO BAPT CONV	9	2,727	3,419*	26.2	40.9
443 UN C OF CHRIST	1	32	40*	.3	.5
449 UN METHODIST	12	1,087	1,363*	10.5	16.3
497 BLACK BAPT EST[2]	NA	2,065	2,589*	19.9	30.9
LANIER	**14**	**2,860**	**3,758***	**67.9**	**100.0**
081 CATHOLIC	1	NA	47	.8	1.3
081d *LATIN*	*1*	*NA*	*47*	*.8*	*1.3*
127 CH GOD (CLEVE)	2	110	143*	2.6	3.8
145 CH GOD PROPHCY	1	37	48*	.9	1.3
167 CHS OF CHRIST	2	71	94	1.7	2.5
413 S.D.A.	2	183	237*	4.3	6.3
419 SO BAPT CONV	3	1,118	1,450*	26.2	38.6
449 UN METHODIST	3	658	853*	15.4	22.7
497 BLACK BAPT EST[2]	NA	683	886*	16.0	23.6
LAURENS	**96**	**22,403**	**29,465***	**73.7**	**100.0**
053 ASSEMB OF GOD	5	239	334	.8	1.1
081 CATHOLIC	1	NA	320	.8	1.1
081d *LATIN*	*1*	*NA*	*320*	*.8*	*1.1*
093 CHR CH (DISC)	3	154	185	.5	.6
123 CH GOD (ANDER)	2	81	115	.3	.4
127 CH GOD (CLEVE)	3	315	404*	1.0	1.4
145 CH GOD PROPHCY	2	74	95*	.2	.3
151 L-D SAINTS	1	NA	239	.6	.8
165 CH OF NAZARENE	3	430	673	1.7	2.3
167 CHS OF CHRIST	4	232	307	.8	1.0

County and Denomination	Number of churches	Communicant, confirmed, full members	Total adherents		
			Number	Percent of total population	Percent of total adherents
193 EPISCOPAL	1	139	188	.5	.6
223 FREE WILL BAPT	1	46	59*	.1	.2
286 E.PA MENNONITE	1	68	87*	.2	.3
355 PRESB CH (USA)	2	230	295*	.7	1.0
361 PRIM BAPT ASCS	2	59	76*	.2	.3
413 S.D.A.	2	180	231*	.6	.8
419 SO BAPT CONV	43	11,651	14,946*	37.4	50.7
449 UN METHODIST	20	3,475	4,458*	11.1	15.1
497 BLACK BAPT EST[2]	NA	5,030	6,453*	16.1	21.9
LEE	**13**	**3,468**	**5,172***	**31.8**	**100.0**
127 CH GOD (CLEVE)	1	91	121*	.7	2.3
151 L-D SAINTS	1	NA	545	3.4	10.5
167 CHS OF CHRIST	1	31	56	.3	1.1
355 PRESB CH (USA)	1	20	27*	.2	.5
413 S.D.A.	1	39	52*	.3	1.0
419 SO BAPT CONV	5	1,779	2,365*	14.6	45.7
449 UN METHODIST	2	481	640*	3.9	12.4
467 WESLEYAN	1	10	14	.1	.3
497 BLACK BAPT EST[2]	NA	1,017	1,352*	8.3	26.1
LIBERTY	**31**	**12,916**	**18,159***	**34.4**	**100.0**
053 ASSEMB OF GOD	2	125	254	.5	1.4
081 CATHOLIC	1	NA	50	.1	.3
081d *LATIN*	*1*	*NA*	*50*	*.1*	*.3*
123 CH GOD (ANDER)	1	27	81	.2	.4
127 CH GOD (CLEVE)	2	441	595*	1.1	3.3
151 L-D SAINTS	1	NA	425	.8	2.3
165 CH OF NAZARENE	1	3	30	.1	.2
167 CHS OF CHRIST	2	150	185	.4	1.0
193 EPISCOPAL	1	46	81	.2	.4
355 PRESB CH (USA)	6	458	618*	1.2	3.4
419 SO BAPT CONV	8	3,925	5,296*	10.0	29.2
443 UN C OF CHRIST	1	105	142*	.3	.8
449 UN METHODIST	4	1,357	1,831*	3.5	10.1
467 WESLEYAN	1	20	125	.2	.7
497 BLACK BAPT EST[2]	NA	6,259	8,446*	16.0	46.5
LINCOLN	**20**	**4,002**	**5,058***	**68.0**	**100.0**
053 ASSEMB OF GOD	1	87	150	2.0	3.0
081 CATHOLIC	0	NA	6	.1	.1
081d *LATIN*	*0*	*NA*	*6*	*.1*	*.1*
127 CH GOD (CLEVE)	1	33	41*	.6	.8
355 PRESB CH (USA)	1	10	13*	.2	.3
419 SO BAPT CONV	10	1,874	2,346*	31.5	46.4
449 UN METHODIST	7	685	858*	11.5	17.0
497 BLACK BAPT EST[2]	NA	1,313	1,644*	22.1	32.5
LONG	**8**	**2,049**	**2,695***	**43.5**	**100.0**
127 CH GOD (CLEVE)	1	70	92*	1.5	3.4
419 SO BAPT CONV	5	1,404	1,847*	29.8	68.5
449 UN METHODIST	2	185	243*	3.9	9.0
497 BLACK BAPT EST[2]	NA	390	513*	8.3	19.0
LOWNDES	**109**	**31,995**	**45,596***	**60.0**	**100.0**
005 AME ZION	1	150	167	.2	.4
053 ASSEMB OF GOD	3	272	425	.6	.9
081 CATHOLIC	2	NA	3,539	4.7	7.8
081d *LATIN*	*2*	*NA*	*3,539*	*4.7*	*7.8*
093 CHR CH (DISC)	3	294	423	.6	.9
111 CH CR,SCIENTST	1	NR	NR	-	-
123 CH GOD (ANDER)	1	12	14	-	-
127 CH GOD (CLEVE)	11	1,276	1,638*	2.2	3.6
145 CH GOD PROPHCY	3	110	141*	.2	.3
151 L-D SAINTS	1	NA	553	.7	1.2
165 CH OF NAZARENE	2	218	386	.5	.8
167 CHS OF CHRIST	17	2,410	3,217	4.2	7.1
193 EPISCOPAL	3	620	844	1.1	1.9
207 E.L.C.A.	1	74	105	.1	.2
223 FREE WILL BAPT	2	131	168*	.2	.4
283 LUTH—MO SYNOD	1	158	225	.3	.5
349 PENT HOLINESS	1	26	33*	-	.1
353 CHR BRETHREN	1	45	60	.1	.1
355 PRESB CH (USA)	4	700	898*	1.2	2.0
356 PRESB CH AMER	1	192	192	.3	.4
361 PRIM BAPT ASCS	3	84	108*	.1	.2
403 SALVATION ARMY	1	78	81	.1	.2
413 S.D.A.	2	241	309*	.4	.7
419 SO BAPT CONV	27	12,309	15,798*	20.8	34.6
435 UNITARIAN-UNIV	1	18	20	-	-
449 UN METHODIST	14	5,232	6,715*	8.8	14.7
496 JEWISH EST[1]	2	NA	110	.1	.2
497 BLACK BAPT EST[2]	NA	7,345	9,427*	12.4	20.7

NA–Not applicable   NR–Not reported   *Total adherents estimated from known number of communicant, confirmed, full members.   - Represents a percent less than 0.1.   Percentages may not total due to rounding.
[1]See Appendix E   [2]See Appendix F   [3]See Appendix G   Lines in *italic* represent a breakdown of Catholic rites or Friends affiliations. They are included in their respective denominational total.

Table 4. Churches and Church Membership by County and Denomination: 1990

County and Denomination	Number of churches	Communicant, confirmed, full members	Total adherents Number	Percent of total population	Percent of total adherents
LUMPKIN	**16**	**2,019**	**2,947***	**20.2**	**100.0**
053 ASSEMB OF GOD	1	45	60	.4	2.0
081 CATHOLIC	1	NA	206	1.4	7.0
081d *LATIN*	*1*	*NA*	*206*	*1.4*	*7.0*
127 CH GOD (CLEVE)	1	199	247*	1.7	8.4
145 CH GOD PROPHCY	1	37	46*	.3	1.6
151 L-D SAINTS	1	NA	226	1.6	7.7
167 CHS OF CHRIST	2	30	46	.3	1.6
193 EPISCOPAL	1	40	49	.3	1.7
355 PRESB CH (USA)	1	72	89*	.6	3.0
419 SO BAPT CONV	3	992	1,229*	8.4	41.7
449 UN METHODIST	4	604	749*	5.1	25.4
MC DUFFIE	**30**	**8,685**	**11,972***	**59.5**	**100.0**
001 ADVENT CHR CH	1	25	33*	.2	.3
053 ASSEMB OF GOD	1	38	42	.2	.4
081 CATHOLIC	1	NA	350	1.7	2.9
081d *LATIN*	*1*	*NA*	*350*	*1.7*	*2.9*
127 CH GOD (CLEVE)	2	140	182*	.9	1.5
151 L-D SAINTS	1	NA	321	1.6	2.7
167 CHS OF CHRIST	2	130	168	.8	1.4
193 EPISCOPAL	1	54	60	.3	.5
223 FREE WILL BAPT	1	90	117*	.6	1.0
356 PRESB CH AMER	1	247	280	1.4	2.3
419 SO BAPT CONV	13	4,664	6,064*	30.1	50.7
449 UN METHODIST	6	1,587	2,064*	10.3	17.2
496 JEWISH EST[1]	0	NA	68	.3	.6
497 BLACK BAPT EST[2]	NA	1,710	2,223*	11.0	18.6
MC INTOSH	**20**	**3,934**	**5,253***	**60.8**	**100.0**
053 ASSEMB OF GOD	1	49	75	.9	1.4
081 CATHOLIC	1	NA	50	.6	1.0
081d *LATIN*	*1*	*NA*	*50*	*.6*	*1.0*
127 CH GOD (CLEVE)	2	165	210*	2.4	4.0
145 CH GOD PROPHCY	2	74	94*	1.1	1.8
151 L-D SAINTS	1	NA	179	2.1	3.4
167 CHS OF CHRIST	1	25	33	.4	.6
193 EPISCOPAL	2	131	175	2.0	3.3
355 PRESB CH (USA)	2	136	173*	2.0	3.3
419 SO BAPT CONV	6	1,150	1,462*	16.9	27.8
449 UN METHODIST	2	248	315*	3.6	6.0
497 BLACK BAPT EST[2]	NA	1,956	2,487*	28.8	47.3
MACON	**28**	**7,587**	**10,048***	**76.6**	**100.0**
061 BEACHY AMISH	1	217	287*	2.2	2.9
081 CATHOLIC	1	NA	30	.2	.3
081d *LATIN*	*1*	*NA*	*30*	*.2*	*.3*
145 CH GOD PROPHCY	1	37	49*	.4	.5
167 CHS OF CHRIST	2	53	58	.4	.6
193 EPISCOPAL	1	20	34	.3	.3
207 E.L.C.A.	1	156	203	1.5	2.0
223 FREE WILL BAPT	3	203	268*	2.0	2.7
361 PRIM BAPT ASCS	1	30	40*	.3	.4
419 SO BAPT CONV	11	2,507	3,313*	25.3	33.0
449 UN METHODIST	6	788	1,041*	7.9	10.4
497 BLACK BAPT EST[2]	NA	3,576	4,725*	36.0	47.0
MADISON	**38**	**8,554**	**10,843***	**51.5**	**100.0**
081 CATHOLIC	0	NA	34	.2	.3
081d *LATIN*	*0*	*NA*	*34*	*.2*	*.3*
097 CHR CHS&CHS CR	1	30	38*	.2	.4
127 CH GOD (CLEVE)	1	3	4*	-	-
167 CHS OF CHRIST	1	15	24	.1	.2
215 EVAN METH CH	1	175	221*	1.0	2.0
349 PENT HOLINESS	1	13	16*	.1	.1
355 PRESB CH (USA)	2	91	115*	.5	1.1
361 PRIM BAPT ASCS	1	32	40*	.2	.4
419 SO BAPT CONV	23	6,375	8,052*	38.3	74.3
449 UN METHODIST	7	1,220	1,541*	7.3	14.2
497 BLACK BAPT EST[2]	NA	600	758*	3.6	7.0
MARION	**20**	**2,669**	**3,436***	**61.5**	**100.0**
053 ASSEMB OF GOD	1	12	20	.4	.6
167 CHS OF CHRIST	1	35	38	.7	1.1
361 PRIM BAPT ASCS	3	41	53*	.9	1.5
413 S.D.A.	1	18	23*	.4	.7
419 SO BAPT CONV	9	1,001	1,290*	23.1	37.5
449 UN METHODIST	5	490	631*	11.3	18.4
497 BLACK BAPT EST[2]	NA	1,072	1,381*	24.7	40.2
MERIWETHER	**53**	**12,529**	**16,305***	**72.8**	**100.0**
053 ASSEMB OF GOD	1	48	58	.3	.4
081 CATHOLIC	1	NA	60	.3	.4
081d *LATIN*	*1*	*NA*	*60*	*.3*	*.4*

County and Denomination	Number of churches	Communicant, confirmed, full members	Total adherents Number	Percent of total population	Percent of total adherents
127 CH GOD (CLEVE)	1	37	48*	.2	.3
145 CH GOD PROPHCY	1	37	48*	.2	.3
165 CH OF NAZARENE	2	147	287	1.3	1.8
167 CHS OF CHRIST	2	135	180	.8	1.1
355 PRESB CH (USA)	2	88	113*	.5	.7
361 PRIM BAPT ASCS	2	40	52*	.2	.3
419 SO BAPT CONV	21	5,168	6,659*	29.7	40.8
443 UN C OF CHRIST	1	138	178*	.8	1.1
449 UN METHODIST	19	2,048	2,639*	11.8	16.2
497 BLACK BAPT EST[2]	NA	4,643	5,983*	26.7	36.7
MILLER	**23**	**3,514**	**4,467***	**71.1**	**100.0**
053 ASSEMB OF GOD	2	51	82	1.3	1.8
127 CH GOD (CLEVE)	4	156	197*	3.1	4.4
167 CHS OF CHRIST	2	66	84	1.3	1.9
223 FREE WILL BAPT	8	578	732*	11.7	16.4
285 MENNONITE CH	1	11	16	.3	.4
419 SO BAPT CONV	4	1,291	1,634*	26.0	36.6
449 UN METHODIST	2	559	707*	11.3	15.8
497 BLACK BAPT EST[2]	NA	802	1,015*	16.2	22.7
MITCHELL	**43**	**12,656**	**16,804***	**82.9**	**100.0**
053 ASSEMB OF GOD	2	89	140	.7	.8
081 CATHOLIC	1	NA	50	.2	.3
081d *LATIN*	*1*	*NA*	*50*	*.2*	*.3*
097 CHR CHS&CHS CR	1	78	103*	.5	.6
127 CH GOD (CLEVE)	2	49	65*	.3	.4
167 CHS OF CHRIST	2	70	98	.5	.6
193 EPISCOPAL	1	34	46	.2	.3
223 FREE WILL BAPT	3	191	252*	1.2	1.5
285 MENNONITE CH	1	38	75	.4	.4
355 PRESB CH (USA)	2	58	77*	.4	.5
361 PRIM BAPT ASCS	1	58	77*	.4	.5
419 SO BAPT CONV	20	6,262	8,262*	40.7	49.2
449 UN METHODIST	7	1,245	1,643*	8.1	9.8
497 BLACK BAPT EST[2]	NA	4,484	5,916*	29.2	35.2
MONROE	**37**	**7,729**	**9,845***	**57.5**	**100.0**
005 AME ZION	1	185	260	1.5	2.6
053 ASSEMB OF GOD	1	22	31	.2	.3
081 CATHOLIC	1	NA	18	.1	.2
081d *LATIN*	*1*	*NA*	*18*	*.1*	*.2*
127 CH GOD (CLEVE)	1	94	119*	.7	1.2
145 CH GOD PROPHCY	1	37	47*	.3	.5
167 CHS OF CHRIST	1	75	90	.5	.9
355 PRESB CH (USA)	1	87	110*	.6	1.1
356 PRESB CH AMER	1	82	124	.7	1.3
361 PRIM BAPT ASCS	3	136	172*	1.0	1.7
419 SO BAPT CONV	16	3,308	4,187*	24.5	42.5
449 UN METHODIST	10	1,190	1,506*	8.8	15.3
497 BLACK BAPT EST[2]	NA	2,513	3,181*	18.6	32.3
MONTGOMERY	**25**	**3,672**	**4,592***	**64.1**	**100.0**
001 ADVENT CHR CH	1	70	88*	1.2	1.9
127 CH GOD (CLEVE)	3	243	304*	4.2	6.6
355 PRESB CH (USA)	2	37	46*	.6	1.0
419 SO BAPT CONV	11	1,753	2,192*	30.6	47.7
449 UN METHODIST	8	627	784*	10.9	17.1
497 BLACK BAPT EST[2]	NA	942	1,178*	16.4	25.7
MORGAN	**30**	**6,341**	**9,286***	**72.1**	**100.0**
081 CATHOLIC	1	NA	95	.7	1.0
081d *LATIN*	*1*	*NA*	*95*	*.7*	*1.0*
127 CH GOD (CLEVE)	1	123	157*	1.2	1.7
151 L-D SAINTS	1	NA	399	3.1	4.3
167 CHS OF CHRIST	1	100	168	1.3	1.8
193 EPISCOPAL	1	101	107	.8	1.2
283 LUTH—MO SYNOD	1	13	19	.1	.2
355 PRESB CH (USA)	1	181	230*	1.8	2.5
361 PRIM BAPT ASCS	1	31	39*	.3	.4
413 S.D.A.	1	31	39*	.3	.4
419 SO BAPT CONV	10	2,715	3,456*	26.8	37.2
449 UN METHODIST	10	974	1,240*	9.6	13.4
497 BLACK BAPT EST[2]	NA	2,072	2,637*	20.5	28.4
499 INDEP.NON-CHAR[3]	1	NA	700	5.4	7.5
MURRAY	**31**	**6,803**	**8,812***	**33.7**	**100.0**
081 CATHOLIC	0	NA	114	.4	1.3
081d *LATIN*	*0*	*NA*	*114*	*.4*	*1.3*
127 CH GOD (CLEVE)	5	380	489*	1.9	5.5
145 CH GOD PROPHCY	1	37	48*	.2	.5
167 CHS OF CHRIST	1	100	110	.4	1.2
185 CUMBER PRESB	1	183	203	.8	2.3
361 PRIM BAPT ASCS	1	66	85*	.3	1.0
419 SO BAPT CONV	15	5,362	6,895*	26.4	78.2

NA–Not applicable NR–Not reported *Total adherents estimated from known number of communicant, confirmed, full members. - Represents a percent less than 0.1. Percentages may not total due to rounding.
[1]See Appendix E [2]See Appendix F [3]See Appendix G Lines in *italic* represent a breakdown of Catholic rites or Friends affiliations. They are included in their respective denominational total.

Table 4. Churches and Church Membership by County and Denomination: 1990

County and Denomination		Number of churches	Communicant, confirmed, full members	Total adherents		
				Number	Percent of total population	Percent of total adherents
449	UN METHODIST	7	675	868*	3.3	9.9
MUSCOGEE		**160**	**77,390**	**108,841***	**60.7**	**100.0**
005	AME ZION	1	492	542	.3	.5
019	AMER BAPT USA	2	685	872*	.5	.8
053	ASSEMB OF GOD	14	2,742	5,801	3.2	5.3
055	AS REF PRES CH	1	81	81	-	.1
081	CATHOLIC	4	NA	4,942	2.8	4.5
081d	*LATIN*	*4*	*NA*	*4,942*	*2.8*	*4.5*
093	CHR CH (DISC)	1	211	273	.2	.3
111	CH CR,SCIENTST	1	NR	NR	-	-
123	CH GOD (ANDER)	2	68	68	-	.1
127	CH GOD (CLEVE)	5	964	1,227*	.7	1.1
145	CH GOD PROPHCY	4	147	187*	.1	.2
151	L-D SAINTS	4	NA	1,321	.7	1.2
165	CH OF NAZARENE	3	391	508	.3	.5
167	CHS OF CHRIST	9	814	1,351	.8	1.2
193	EPISCOPAL	3	1,105	1,282	.7	1.2
207	E.L.C.A.	1	458	599	.3	.6
223	FREE WILL BAPT	3	291	370*	.2	.3
263	INT FOURSQ GOS	1	180	229*	.1	.2
283	LUTH—MO SYNOD	2	574	668	.4	.6
339	PENT CH OF GOD	4	79	176	.1	.2
355	PRESB CH (USA)	9	2,018	2,569*	1.4	2.4
356	PRESB CH AMER	3	115	182	.1	.2
361	PRIM BAPT ASCS	3	115	146*	.1	.1
403	SALVATION ARMY	1	213	234	.1	.2
413	S.D.A.	3	800	1,018*	.6	.9
419	SO BAPT CONV	44	36,132	45,990*	25.7	42.3
435	UNITARIAN-UNIV	1	44	48	-	-
443	UN C OF CHRIST	1	13	17*	-	-
449	UN METHODIST	27	12,733	16,207*	9.0	14.9
496	JEWISH EST[1]	2	NA	913	.5	.8
497	BLACK BAPT EST[2]	NA	15,925	20,270*	11.3	18.6
499	INDEP.NON-CHAR[3]	1	NA	750	.4	.7
NEWTON		**63**	**20,122**	**28,658***	**68.5**	**100.0**
053	ASSEMB OF GOD	1	17	24	.1	.1
055	AS REF PRES CH	1	73	73	.2	.3
081	CATHOLIC	1	NA	244	.6	.9
081d	*LATIN*	*1*	*NA*	*244*	*.6*	*.9*
097	CHR CHS&CHS CR	1	415	532*	1.3	1.9
127	CH GOD (CLEVE)	1	34	44*	.1	.2
151	L-D SAINTS	1	NA	701	1.7	2.4
165	CH OF NAZARENE	1	82	91	.2	.3
167	CHS OF CHRIST	2	96	125	.3	.4
193	EPISCOPAL	1	118	138	.3	.5
355	PRESB CH (USA)	6	629	806*	1.9	2.8
356	PRESB CH AMER	1	68	70	.2	.2
361	PRIM BAPT ASCS	1	24	31*	.1	.1
413	S.D.A.	1	129	165*	.4	.6
419	SO BAPT CONV	17	7,977	10,218*	24.4	35.7
449	UN METHODIST	25	5,884	7,537*	18.0	26.3
467	WESLEYAN	1	51	104	.2	.4
496	JEWISH EST[1]	0	NA	959	2.3	3.3
497	BLACK BAPT EST[2]	NA	4,525	5,796*	13.9	20.2
499	INDEP.NON-CHAR[3]	1	NA	1,000	2.4	3.5
OCONEE		**28**	**6,036**	**9,960***	**56.5**	**100.0**
093	CHR CH (DISC)	5	589	899	5.1	9.0
167	CHS OF CHRIST	1	64	83	.5	.8
349	PENT HOLINESS	1	29	38*	.2	.4
355	PRESB CH (USA)	1	199	258*	1.5	2.6
356	PRESB CH AMER	1	170	211	1.2	2.1
419	SO BAPT CONV	10	3,609	4,685*	26.6	47.0
449	UN METHODIST	8	949	1,232*	7.0	12.4
497	BLACK BAPT EST[2]	NA	427	554*	3.1	5.6
498	INDEP.CHARIS.[3]	1	NA	2,000	11.4	20.1
OGLETHORPE		**31**	**3,595**	**4,516***	**46.3**	**100.0**
005	AME ZION	1	125	150	1.5	3.3
081	CATHOLIC	0	NA	3	-	.1
081d	*LATIN*	*0*	*NA*	*3*	*-*	*.1*
093	CHR CH (DISC)	1	50	73	.7	1.6
127	CH GOD (CLEVE)	1	17	21*	.2	.5
167	CHS OF CHRIST	1	0	0	-	-
215	EVAN METH CH	1	42	53*	.5	1.2
355	PRESB CH (USA)	1	14	18*	.2	.4
413	S.D.A.	1	51	64*	.7	1.4
419	SO BAPT CONV	15	2,059	2,582*	26.4	57.2
449	UN METHODIST	9	534	670*	6.9	14.8
497	BLACK BAPT EST[2]	NA	703	882*	9.0	19.5
PAULDING		**53**	**11,626**	**16,240***	**39.0**	**100.0**
053	ASSEMB OF GOD	1	64	81	.2	.5

County and Denomination		Number of churches	Communicant, confirmed, full members	Total adherents		
				Number	Percent of total population	Percent of total adherents
081	CATHOLIC	1	NA	115	.3	.7
081d	*LATIN*	*1*	*NA*	*115*	*.3*	*.7*
097	CHR CHS&CHS CR	1	250	326*	.8	2.0
127	CH GOD (CLEVE)	2	269	351*	.8	2.2
167	CHS OF CHRIST	3	106	157	.4	1.0
289	NEW HOPE B ASC	9	1,377	1,795*	4.3	11.1
361	PRIM BAPT ASCS	2	9	12*	-	.1
415	S-D BAPTIST GC	1	35	46*	.1	.3
419	SO BAPT CONV	22	7,557	9,849*	23.7	60.6
449	UN METHODIST	11	1,424	1,856*	4.5	11.4
496	JEWISH EST[1]	0	NA	955	2.3	5.9
497	BLACK BAPT EST[2]	NA	535	697*	1.7	4.3
PEACH		**21**	**6,417**	**8,486***	**40.0**	**100.0**
053	ASSEMB OF GOD	1	42	90	.4	1.1
081	CATHOLIC	1	NA	183	.9	2.2
081d	*LATIN*	*1*	*NA*	*183*	*.9*	*2.2*
127	CH GOD (CLEVE)	1	19	24*	.1	.3
151	L-D SAINTS	1	NA	94	.4	1.1
165	CH OF NAZARENE	1	57	73	.3	.9
167	CHS OF CHRIST	3	143	177	.8	2.1
193	EPISCOPAL	2	171	181	.9	2.1
355	PRESB CH (USA)	1	90	114*	.5	1.3
361	PRIM BAPT ASCS	1	12	15*	.1	.2
413	S.D.A.	1	10	13*	.1	.2
419	SO BAPT CONV	4	2,164	2,745*	13.0	32.3
449	UN METHODIST	4	1,355	1,719*	8.1	20.3
496	JEWISH EST[1]	0	NA	72	.3	.8
497	BLACK BAPT EST[2]	NA	2,354	2,986*	14.1	35.2
PICKENS		**39**	**7,264**	**9,478***	**65.7**	**100.0**
053	ASSEMB OF GOD	1	58	110	.8	1.2
081	CATHOLIC	2	NA	430	3.0	4.5
081d	*LATIN*	*2*	*NA*	*430*	*3.0*	*4.5*
097	CHR CHS&CHS CR	1	115	143*	1.0	1.5
127	CH GOD (CLEVE)	2	181	224*	1.6	2.4
145	CH GOD PROPHCY	1	37	46*	.3	.5
167	CHS OF CHRIST	4	174	225	1.6	2.4
193	EPISCOPAL	1	38	40	.3	.4
269	JASPER&PVB ASC	17	3,636	4,509*	31.2	47.6
355	PRESB CH (USA)	1	77	95*	.7	1.0
419	SO BAPT CONV	6	2,327	2,886*	20.0	30.4
449	UN METHODIST	3	621	770*	5.3	8.1
PIERCE		**36**	**6,437**	**8,513***	**63.9**	**100.0**
053	ASSEMB OF GOD	1	43	63	.5	.7
127	CH GOD (CLEVE)	2	276	348*	2.6	4.1
145	CH GOD PROPHCY	1	37	47*	.4	.6
151	L-D SAINTS	1	NA	373	2.8	4.4
167	CHS OF CHRIST	1	14	21	.2	.2
223	FREE WILL BAPT	1	50	63*	.5	.7
355	PRESB CH (USA)	1	159	201*	1.5	2.4
361	PRIM BAPT ASCS	5	44	56*	.4	.7
419	SO BAPT CONV	16	4,628	5,843*	43.8	68.6
449	UN METHODIST	7	730	922*	6.9	10.8
497	BLACK BAPT EST[2]	NA	456	576*	4.3	6.8
PIKE		**31**	**5,419**	**6,962***	**68.1**	**100.0**
053	ASSEMB OF GOD	1	28	63	.6	.9
081	CATHOLIC	0	NA	24	.2	.3
081d	*LATIN*	*0*	*NA*	*24*	*.2*	*.3*
093	CHR CH (DISC)	1	15	20	.2	.3
165	CH OF NAZARENE	2	139	203	2.0	2.9
349	PENT HOLINESS	1	17	22*	.2	.3
355	PRESB CH (USA)	1	60	76*	.7	1.1
361	PRIM BAPT ASCS	1	9	11*	.1	.2
419	SO BAPT CONV	15	3,902	4,957*	48.5	71.2
449	UN METHODIST	9	652	828*	8.1	11.9
497	BLACK BAPT EST[2]	NA	597	758*	7.4	10.9
POLK		**63**	**16,986**	**21,844***	**64.6**	**100.0**
053	ASSEMB OF GOD	1	0	0	-	-
081	CATHOLIC	1	NA	373	1.1	1.7
081d	*LATIN*	*1*	*NA*	*373*	*1.1*	*1.7*
127	CH GOD (CLEVE)	3	347	435*	1.3	2.0
145	CH GOD PROPHCY	1	37	46*	.1	.2
151	L-D SAINTS	1	NA	149	.4	.7
167	CHS OF CHRIST	3	282	377	1.1	1.7
193	EPISCOPAL	1	65	74	.2	.3
289	NEW HOPE B ASC	3	230	288*	.9	1.3
355	PRESB CH (USA)	2	244	306*	.9	1.4
356	PRESB CH AMER	1	64	83	.2	.4
361	PRIM BAPT ASCS	2	8	10*	-	-
413	S.D.A.	1	26	33*	.1	.2
419	SO BAPT CONV	34	13,315	16,700*	49.4	76.5

NA–Not applicable   NR–Not reported   *Total adherents estimated from known number of communicant, confirmed, full members.   - Represents a percent less than 0.1.   Percentages may not total due to rounding.
[1] See Appendix E   [2] See Appendix F   [3] See Appendix G   Lines in *italic* represent a breakdown of Catholic rites or Friends affiliations. They are included in their respective denominational total.

Table 4. Churches and Church Membership by County and Denomination: 1990

County and Denomination	Number of churches	Communicant, confirmed, full members	Total adherents — Number	Total adherents — Percent of total population	Total adherents — Percent of total adherents
449 UN METHODIST	9	1,703	2,136*	6.3	9.8
497 BLACK BAPT EST[2]	NA	665	834*	2.5	3.8
PULASKI	**17**	**5,532**	**6,997***	**86.3**	**100.0**
127 CH GOD (CLEVE)	1	27	34*	.4	.5
167 CHS OF CHRIST	1	15	18	.2	.3
193 EPISCOPAL	1	44	65	.8	.9
349 PENT HOLINESS	1	63	80*	1.0	1.1
419 SO BAPT CONV	12	3,616	4,568*	56.3	65.3
449 UN METHODIST	1	544	687*	8.5	9.8
497 BLACK BAPT EST[2]	NA	1,223	1,545*	19.1	22.1
PUTNAM	**22**	**4,913**	**6,245***	**44.2**	**100.0**
081 CATHOLIC	1	NA	100	.7	1.6
081d *LATIN*	*1*	*NA*	*100*	*.7*	*1.6*
123 CH GOD (ANDER)	1	21	21	.1	.3
127 CH GOD (CLEVE)	1	68	85*	.6	1.4
145 CH GOD PROPHCY	1	37	46*	.3	.7
167 CHS OF CHRIST	1	20	27	.2	.4
349 PENT HOLINESS	1	144	180*	1.3	2.9
355 PRESB CH (USA)	1	71	89*	.6	1.4
361 PRIM BAPT ASCS	1	8	10*	.1	.2
419 SO BAPT CONV	5	1,460	1,827*	12.9	29.3
449 UN METHODIST	9	877	1,098*	7.8	17.6
497 BLACK BAPT EST[2]	NA	2,207	2,762*	19.5	44.2
QUITMAN	**5**	**1,142**	**1,432***	**64.8**	**100.0**
167 CHS OF CHRIST	1	83	106	4.8	7.4
419 SO BAPT CONV	2	422	528*	23.9	36.9
449 UN METHODIST	2	122	153*	6.9	10.7
497 BLACK BAPT EST[2]	NA	515	645*	29.2	45.0
RABUN	**41**	**5,183**	**6,339***	**54.4**	**100.0**
053 ASSEMB OF GOD	1	12	18	.2	.3
081 CATHOLIC	1	NA	145	1.2	2.3
081d *LATIN*	*1*	*NA*	*145*	*1.2*	*2.3*
097 CHR CHS&CHS CR	1	31	37*	.3	.6
127 CH GOD (CLEVE)	4	275	329*	2.8	5.2
193 EPISCOPAL	1	95	110	.9	1.7
355 PRESB CH (USA)	6	302	361*	3.1	5.7
419 SO BAPT CONV	20	3,690	4,409*	37.9	69.6
449 UN METHODIST	7	778	930*	8.0	14.7
RANDOLPH	**26**	**5,138**	**6,697***	**83.5**	**100.0**
053 ASSEMB OF GOD	1	24	32	.4	.5
081 CATHOLIC	1	NA	20	.2	.3
081d *LATIN*	*1*	*NA*	*20*	*.2*	*.3*
127 CH GOD (CLEVE)	1	27	35*	.4	.5
285 MENNONITE CH	1	27	42	.5	.6
355 PRESB CH (USA)	1	59	77*	1.0	1.1
419 SO BAPT CONV	14	2,326	3,019*	37.6	45.1
449 UN METHODIST	7	516	670*	8.4	10.0
497 BLACK BAPT EST[2]	NA	2,159	2,802*	34.9	41.8
RICHMOND	**166**	**81,082**	**121,548***	**64.1**	**100.0**
001 ADVENT CHR CH	2	194	247*	.1	.2
005 AME ZION	2	1,144	1,294	.7	1.1
019 AMER BAPT USA	3	665	847*	.4	.7
053 ASSEMB OF GOD	8	1,423	1,421	.7	1.2
055 AS REF PRES CH	1	37	37	-	-
081 CATHOLIC	5	NA	10,167	5.4	8.4
081d *LATIN*	*4*	*NA*	*9,644*	*5.1*	*7.9*
081f *MELKITE-GK*	*1*	*NA*	*523*	*.3*	*.4*
089 CHR & MISS AL	1	46	106	.1	.1
093 CHR CH (DISC)	2	649	927	.5	.8
097 CHR CHS&CHS CR	2	247	315*	.2	.3
111 CH CR,SCIENTST	1	NR	NR	-	-
123 CH GOD (ANDER)	1	65	65	-	.1
127 CH GOD (CLEVE)	6	1,738	2,214*	1.2	1.8
145 CH GOD PROPHCY	1	37	47*	-	-
151 L-D SAINTS	3	NA	1,085	.6	.9
165 CH OF NAZARENE	2	207	118	.1	.1
167 CHS OF CHRIST	4	814	1,148	.6	.9
193 EPISCOPAL	7	2,658	3,255	1.7	2.7
207 E.L.C.A.	4	1,577	2,123	1.1	1.7
223 FREE WILL BAPT	1	31	39*	-	-
226 FRIENDS-USA	1	18	23*	-	-
226d *FGC & FUM*	*1*	*18*	*23**	-	-
246 GREEK ORTHODOX	1	NR	NR	-	-
259 IFCA	1	NR	NR	-	-
263 INT FOURSQ GOS	1	35	45*	-	-
283 LUTH—MO SYNOD	1	482	688	.4	.6
285 MENNONITE CH	1	36	66	-	.1
349 PENT HOLINESS	5	384	489*	.3	.4
353 CHR BRETHREN	4	295	565	.3	.5
355 PRESB CH (USA)	7	2,281	2,905*	1.5	2.4
356 PRESB CH AMER	4	1,815	2,416	1.3	2.0
361 PRIM BAPT ASCS	2	271	345*	.2	.3
403 SALVATION ARMY	1	219	233	.1	.2
413 S.D.A.	2	737	939*	.5	.8
419 SO BAPT CONV	45	34,215	43,578*	23.0	35.9
435 UNITARIAN-UNIV	1	133	183	.1	.2
449 UN METHODIST	22	9,981	12,712*	6.7	10.5
467 WESLEYAN	1	41	61	-	.1
496 JEWISH EST[1]	1	NA	996	.5	.8
497 BLACK BAPT EST[2]	NA	18,607	23,699*	12.5	19.5
498 INDEP.CHARIS.[3]	4	NA	2,100	1.1	1.7
499 INDEP.NON-CHAR[3]	5	NA	4,050	2.1	3.3
ROCKDALE	**38**	**17,431**	**26,423***	**48.8**	**100.0**
053 ASSEMB OF GOD	2	87	116	.2	.4
081 CATHOLIC	1	NA	2,260	4.2	8.6
081d *LATIN*	*1*	*NA*	*2,260*	*4.2*	*8.6*
089 CHR & MISS AL	1	96	130	.2	.5
097 CHR CHS&CHS CR	3	952	1,221*	2.3	4.6
111 CH CR,SCIENTST	1	NR	NR	-	-
127 CH GOD (CLEVE)	2	632	811*	1.5	3.1
167 CHS OF CHRIST	2	143	233	.4	.9
193 EPISCOPAL	1	216	294	.5	1.1
207 E.L.C.A.	1	378	527	1.0	2.0
215 EVAN METH CH	1	13	17*	-	.1
355 PRESB CH (USA)	3	1,215	1,558*	2.9	5.9
356 PRESB CH AMER	1	60	72	.1	.3
413 S.D.A.	1	145	186*	.3	.7
419 SO BAPT CONV	11	7,889	10,118*	18.7	38.3
449 UN METHODIST	6	3,386	4,343*	8.0	16.4
496 JEWISH EST[1]	0	NA	1,241	2.3	4.7
497 BLACK BAPT EST[2]	NA	2,219	2,846*	5.3	10.8
498 INDEP.CHARIS.[3]	1	NA	450	.8	1.7
SCHLEY	**8**	**1,738**	**2,230***	**62.2**	**100.0**
223 FREE WILL BAPT	1	25	32*	.9	1.4
419 SO BAPT CONV	2	526	675*	18.8	30.3
449 UN METHODIST	5	619	794*	22.1	35.6
497 BLACK BAPT EST[2]	NA	568	729*	20.3	32.7
SCREVEN	**56**	**8,758**	**11,564***	**83.5**	**100.0**
053 ASSEMB OF GOD	2	27	38	.3	.3
055 AS REF PRES CH	1	14	14	.1	.1
081 CATHOLIC	1	NA	120	.9	1.0
081d *LATIN*	*1*	*NA*	*120*	*.9*	*1.0*
093 CHR CH (DISC)	2	45	70	.5	.6
097 CHR CHS&CHS CR	1	13	17*	.1	.1
123 CH GOD (ANDER)	2	49	95	.7	.8
127 CH GOD (CLEVE)	1	27	35*	.3	.3
167 CHS OF CHRIST	1	25	32	.2	.3
263 INT FOURSQ GOS	1	111	145*	1.0	1.3
349 PENT HOLINESS	1	120	156*	1.1	1.3
356 PRESB CH AMER	1	43	56	.4	.5
419 SO BAPT CONV	20	3,706	4,825*	34.9	41.7
449 UN METHODIST	22	2,518	3,279*	23.7	28.4
497 BLACK BAPT EST[2]	NA	2,060	2,682*	19.4	23.2
SEMINOLE	**24**	**4,252**	**5,593***	**62.1**	**100.0**
053 ASSEMB OF GOD	2	48	83	.9	1.5
081 CATHOLIC	1	NA	31	.3	.6
081d *LATIN*	*1*	*NA*	*31*	*.3*	*.6*
127 CH GOD (CLEVE)	4	281	351*	3.9	6.3
151 L-D SAINTS	1	NA	203	2.3	3.6
165 CH OF NAZARENE	1	47	83	.9	1.5
167 CHS OF CHRIST	1	64	81	.9	1.4
223 FREE WILL BAPT	5	180	225*	2.5	4.0
355 PRESB CH (USA)	1	188	235*	2.6	4.2
419 SO BAPT CONV	4	1,434	1,791*	19.9	32.0
449 UN METHODIST	4	642	802*	8.9	14.3
497 BLACK BAPT EST[2]	NA	1,368	1,708*	19.0	30.5
SPALDING	**79**	**25,026**	**33,994***	**62.4**	**100.0**
019 AMER BAPT USA	2	1,125	1,438*	2.6	4.2
053 ASSEMB OF GOD	7	763	1,348	2.5	4.0
081 CATHOLIC	1	NA	350	.6	1.0
081d *LATIN*	*1*	*NA*	*350*	*.6*	*1.0*
089 CHR & MISS AL	1	40	70	.1	.2
093 CHR CH (DISC)	2	258	420	.8	1.2
127 CH GOD (CLEVE)	3	1,025	1,310*	2.4	3.9
145 CH GOD PROPHCY	1	37	47*	.1	.1
165 CH OF NAZARENE	1	117	119	.2	.4
167 CHS OF CHRIST	3	216	267	.5	.8
193 EPISCOPAL	2	485	596	1.1	1.8
207 E.L.C.A.	1	136	189	.3	.6

NA–Not applicable   NR–Not reported   *Total adherents estimated from known number of communicant, confirmed, full members.   - Represents a percent less than 0.1.   Percentages may not total due to rounding.

[1] See Appendix E   [2] See Appendix F   [3] See Appendix G   Lines in *italic* represent a breakdown of Catholic rites or Friends affiliations. They are included in their respective denominational total.

Table 4. Churches and Church Membership by County and Denomination: 1990

County and Denomination		Number of churches	Communicant, confirmed, full members	Total adherents		
				Number	Percent of total population	Percent of total adherents
349	PENT HOLINESS	1	11	14*	-	-
355	PRESB CH (USA)	1	590	754*	1.4	2.2
356	PRESB CH AMER	1	0	0	-	-
361	PRIM BAPT ASCS	1	30	38*	.1	.1
403	SALVATION ARMY	1	83	83	.2	.2
413	S.D.A.	2	128	164*	.3	.5
419	SO BAPT CONV	28	12,554	16,049*	29.5	47.2
449	UN METHODIST	19	3,691	4,718*	8.7	13.9
467	WESLEYAN	1	49	56	.1	.2
496	JEWISH EST[1]	0	NA	1,249	2.3	3.7
497	BLACK BAPT EST[2]	NA	3,688	4,715*	8.7	13.9
STEPHENS		**47**	**12,651**	**16,844***	**72.4**	**100.0**
053	ASSEMB OF GOD	2	292	662	2.8	3.9
081	CATHOLIC	1	NA	300	1.3	1.8
081d	*LATIN*	*1*	*NA*	*300*	*1.3*	*1.8*
089	CHR & MISS AL	2	233	833	3.6	4.9
123	CH GOD (ANDER)	1	40	40	.2	.2
127	CH GOD (CLEVE)	4	493	606*	2.6	3.6
145	CH GOD PROPHCY	1	37	45*	.2	.3
151	L-D SAINTS	1	NA	188	.8	1.1
165	CH OF NAZARENE	1	38	43	.2	.3
167	CHS OF CHRIST	1	50	65	.3	.4
193	EPISCOPAL	1	126	156	.7	.9
283	LUTH—MO SYNOD	1	80	87	.4	.5
355	PRESB CH (USA)	1	209	257*	1.1	1.5
403	SALVATION ARMY	1	70	71	.3	.4
413	S.D.A.	1	34	42*	.2	.2
419	SO BAPT CONV	21	8,877	10,904*	46.9	64.7
449	UN METHODIST	7	1,262	1,550*	6.7	9.2
497	BLACK BAPT EST[2]	NA	810	995*	4.3	5.9
STEWART		**17**	**3,088**	**3,932***	**69.5**	**100.0**
053	ASSEMB OF GOD	1	23	43	.8	1.1
361	PRIM BAPT ASCS	2	11	14*	.2	.4
419	SO BAPT CONV	8	911	1,156*	20.4	29.4
449	UN METHODIST	6	480	609*	10.8	15.5
497	BLACK BAPT EST[2]	NA	1,663	2,110*	37.3	53.7
SUMTER		**49**	**14,858**	**19,639***	**65.0**	**100.0**
053	ASSEMB OF GOD	1	81	109	.4	.6
081	CATHOLIC	1	NA	400	1.3	2.0
081d	*LATIN*	*1*	*NA*	*400*	*1.3*	*2.0*
093	CHR CH (DISC)	1	28	39	.1	.2
127	CH GOD (CLEVE)	2	74	96*	.3	.5
145	CH GOD PROPHCY	2	74	96*	.3	.5
167	CHS OF CHRIST	3	194	265	.9	1.3
193	EPISCOPAL	1	126	188	.6	1.0
207	E.L.C.A.	1	72	77	.3	.4
226	FRIENDS-USA	1	2	5	-	-
226c	*FGC*	*1*	*2*	*5*	*-*	*-*
285	MENNONITE CH	1	32	32	.1	.2
355	PRESB CH (USA)	1	316	409*	1.4	2.1
356	PRESB CH AMER	1	63	72	.2	.4
361	PRIM BAPT ASCS	1	38	49*	.2	.2
413	S.D.A.	2	257	333*	1.1	1.7
419	SO BAPT CONV	19	6,391	8,275*	27.4	42.1
449	UN METHODIST	10	2,794	3,618*	12.0	18.4
467	WESLEYAN	1	60	65	.2	.3
497	BLACK BAPT EST[2]	NA	4,256	5,511*	18.2	28.1
TALBOT		**23**	**3,349**	**4,235***	**64.9**	**100.0**
127	CH GOD (CLEVE)	1	80	100*	1.5	2.4
167	CHS OF CHRIST	1	40	52	.8	1.2
339	PENT CH OF GOD	1	34	77	1.2	1.8
355	PRESB CH (USA)	1	11	14*	.2	.3
361	PRIM BAPT ASCS	3	32	40*	.6	.9
419	SO BAPT CONV	6	808	1,013*	15.5	23.9
449	UN METHODIST	10	454	569*	8.7	13.4
497	BLACK BAPT EST[2]	NA	1,890	2,370*	36.3	56.0
TALIAFERRO		**14**	**1,245**	**1,589***	**83.0**	**100.0**
081	CATHOLIC	1	NA	6	.3	.4
081d	*LATIN*	*1*	*NA*	*6*	*.3*	*.4*
355	PRESB CH (USA)	2	29	37*	1.9	2.3
419	SO BAPT CONV	7	568	722*	37.7	45.4
449	UN METHODIST	4	106	135*	7.0	8.5
497	BLACK BAPT EST[2]	NA	542	689*	36.0	43.4
TATTNALL		**54**	**9,719**	**12,133***	**68.5**	**100.0**
053	ASSEMB OF GOD	1	65	98	.6	.8
081	CATHOLIC	2	NA	50	.3	.4
081d	*LATIN*	*2*	*NA*	*50*	*.3*	*.4*
093	CHR CH (DISC)	1	141	196	1.1	1.6
123	CH GOD (ANDER)	2	38	90	.5	.7

County and Denomination		Number of churches	Communicant, confirmed, full members	Total adherents		
				Number	Percent of total population	Percent of total adherents
127	CH GOD (CLEVE)	3	117	144*	.8	1.2
145	CH GOD PROPHCY	1	37	46*	.3	.4
167	CHS OF CHRIST	1	15	20	.1	.2
223	FREE WILL BAPT	7	879	1,085*	6.1	8.9
349	PENT HOLINESS	2	185	228*	1.3	1.9
361	PRIM BAPT ASCS	9	560	691*	3.9	5.7
419	SO BAPT CONV	16	3,871	4,779*	27.0	39.4
449	UN METHODIST	9	1,405	1,735*	9.8	14.3
497	BLACK BAPT EST[2]	NA	2,406	2,971*	16.8	24.5
TAYLOR		**27**	**3,976**	**5,049***	**66.1**	**100.0**
127	CH GOD (CLEVE)	2	194	246*	3.2	4.9
145	CH GOD PROPHCY	1	37	47*	.6	.9
361	PRIM BAPT ASCS	6	48	61*	.8	1.2
419	SO BAPT CONV	9	1,436	1,824*	23.9	36.1
449	UN METHODIST	9	727	923*	12.1	18.3
497	BLACK BAPT EST[2]	NA	1,534	1,948*	25.5	38.6
TELFAIR		**41**	**6,515**	**8,414***	**76.5**	**100.0**
081	CATHOLIC	1	NA	80	.7	1.0
081d	*LATIN*	*1*	*NA*	*80*	*.7*	*1.0*
123	CH GOD (ANDER)	1	17	17	.2	.2
127	CH GOD (CLEVE)	6	379	485*	4.4	5.8
167	CHS OF CHRIST	1	15	25	.2	.3
355	PRESB CH (USA)	1	71	91*	.8	1.1
419	SO BAPT CONV	17	2,974	3,804*	34.6	45.2
449	UN METHODIST	14	1,305	1,669*	15.2	19.8
497	BLACK BAPT EST[2]	NA	1,754	2,243*	20.4	26.7
TERRELL		**25**	**7,520**	**9,856***	**92.5**	**100.0**
053	ASSEMB OF GOD	1	98	130	1.2	1.3
127	CH GOD (CLEVE)	1	5	7*	.1	.1
167	CHS OF CHRIST	2	73	122	1.1	1.2
193	EPISCOPAL	1	50	81	.8	.8
355	PRESB CH (USA)	1	82	107*	1.0	1.1
361	PRIM BAPT ASCS	3	27	35*	.3	.4
419	SO BAPT CONV	8	1,723	2,248*	21.1	22.8
449	UN METHODIST	8	837	1,092*	10.3	11.1
497	BLACK BAPT EST[2]	NA	4,625	6,034*	56.6	61.2
THOMAS		**82**	**20,517**	**26,623***	**68.3**	**100.0**
053	ASSEMB OF GOD	4	546	551	1.4	2.1
081	CATHOLIC	1	NA	80	.2	.3
081d	*LATIN*	*1*	*NA*	*80*	*.2*	*.3*
093	CHR CH (DISC)	1	21	28	.1	.1
097	CHR CHS&CHS CR	1	200	257*	.7	1.0
111	CH CR,SCIENTST	1	NR	NR	-	-
127	CH GOD (CLEVE)	8	521	670*	1.7	2.5
145	CH GOD PROPHCY	1	37	48*	.1	.2
151	L-D SAINTS	1	NA	280	.7	1.1
165	CH OF NAZARENE	1	107	148	.4	.6
167	CHS OF CHRIST	5	311	483	1.2	1.8
193	EPISCOPAL	3	475	557	1.4	2.1
349	PENT HOLINESS	1	22	28*	.1	.1
355	PRESB CH (USA)	5	709	912*	2.3	3.4
356	PRESB CH AMER	1	0	0	-	-
361	PRIM BAPT ASCS	3	86	111*	.3	.4
403	SALVATION ARMY	1	61	62	.2	.2
413	S.D.A.	2	268	345*	.9	1.3
419	SO BAPT CONV	27	10,208	13,130*	33.7	49.3
443	UN C OF CHRIST	1	40	51*	.1	.2
449	UN METHODIST	14	2,433	3,130*	8.0	11.8
497	BLACK BAPT EST[2]	NA	4,472	5,752*	14.8	21.6
TIFT		**54**	**18,523**	**24,160***	**69.0**	**100.0**
053	ASSEMB OF GOD	1	332	308	.9	1.3
081	CATHOLIC	1	NA	450	1.3	1.9
081d	*LATIN*	*1*	*NA*	*450*	*1.3*	*1.9*
097	CHR CHS&CHS CR	1	375	483*	1.4	2.0
127	CH GOD (CLEVE)	6	930	1,198*	3.4	5.0
145	CH GOD PROPHCY	2	74	95*	.3	.4
165	CH OF NAZARENE	1	157	212	.6	.9
167	CHS OF CHRIST	2	134	179	.5	.7
193	EPISCOPAL	1	326	353	1.0	1.5
223	FREE WILL BAPT	2	113	146*	.4	.6
283	LUTH—MO SYNOD	1	107	151	.4	.6
355	PRESB CH (USA)	1	242	312*	.9	1.3
356	PRESB CH AMER	1	0	0	-	-
361	PRIM BAPT ASCS	4	207	267*	.8	1.1
413	S.D.A.	1	35	45*	.1	.2
419	SO BAPT CONV	20	10,172	13,107*	37.5	54.3
449	UN METHODIST	9	2,479	3,194*	9.1	13.2
497	BLACK BAPT EST[2]	NA	2,840	3,660*	10.5	15.1

NA–Not applicable   NR–Not reported   *Total adherents estimated from known number of communicant, confirmed, full members.   - Represents a percent less than 0.1.   Percentages may not total due to rounding.
[1]See Appendix E   [2]See Appendix F   [3]See Appendix G   Lines in *italic* represent a breakdown of Catholic rites or Friends affiliations. They are included in their respective denominational total.

Table 4. Churches and Church Membership by County and Denomination: 1990

County and Denomination	Number of churches	Communicant, confirmed, full members	Total adherents Number	Percent of total population	Percent of total adherents
TOOMBS	56	10,821	15,109*	62.8	100.0
001 ADVENT CHR CH	1	32	42*	.2	.3
053 ASSEMB OF GOD	2	190	240	1.0	1.6
081 CATHOLIC	1	NA	550	2.3	3.6
081d *LATIN*	*1*	*NA*	*550*	*2.3*	*3.6*
127 CH GOD (CLEVE)	6	496	645*	2.7	4.3
145 CH GOD PROPHCY	4	147	191*	.8	1.3
151 L-D SAINTS	1	NA	333	1.4	2.2
165 CH OF NAZARENE	1	41	95	.4	.6
167 CHS OF CHRIST	2	26	57	.2	.4
193 EPISCOPAL	1	76	152	.6	1.0
223 FREE WILL BAPT	2	219	285*	1.2	1.9
323 OLD ORD AMISH	1	NA	50	.2	.3
355 PRESB CH (USA)	2	342	444*	1.8	2.9
361 PRIM BAPT ASCS	3	49	64*	.3	.4
403 SALVATION ARMY	1	10	14	.1	.1
419 SO BAPT CONV	17	5,414	7,036*	29.2	46.6
449 UN METHODIST	11	2,140	2,781*	11.6	18.4
497 BLACK BAPT EST[2]	NA	1,639	2,130*	8.8	14.1
TOWNS	23	3,892	4,547*	67.3	100.0
081 CATHOLIC	0	NA	53	.8	1.2
081d *LATIN*	*0*	*NA*	*53*	*.8*	*1.2*
127 CH GOD (CLEVE)	3	195	225*	3.3	4.9
167 CHS OF CHRIST	2	17	21	.3	.5
355 PRESB CH (USA)	1	61	70*	1.0	1.5
419 SO BAPT CONV	14	3,148	3,634*	53.8	79.9
449 UN METHODIST	3	471	544*	8.1	12.0
TREUTLEN	18	2,919	3,752*	62.6	100.0
001 ADVENT CHR CH	1	55	70*	1.2	1.9
127 CH GOD (CLEVE)	1	32	41*	.7	1.1
165 CH OF NAZARENE	1	9	36	.6	1.0
167 CHS OF CHRIST	1	10	13	.2	.3
349 PENT HOLINESS	1	15	19*	.3	.5
361 PRIM BAPT ASCS	2	28	36*	.6	1.0
419 SO BAPT CONV	8	1,480	1,890*	31.5	50.4
449 UN METHODIST	3	368	470*	7.8	12.5
497 BLACK BAPT EST[2]	NA	922	1,177*	19.6	31.4
TROUP	111	28,680	38,276*	68.9	100.0
053 ASSEMB OF GOD	3	302	406	.7	1.1
081 CATHOLIC	1	NA	861	1.6	2.2
081d *LATIN*	*1*	*NA*	*861*	*1.6*	*2.2*
097 CHR CHS&CHS CR	1	110	141*	.3	.4
123 CH GOD (ANDER)	1	45	67	.1	.2
127 CH GOD (CLEVE)	6	664	849*	1.5	2.2
151 L-D SAINTS	1	NA	222	.4	.6
165 CH OF NAZARENE	1	34	31	.1	.1
167 CHS OF CHRIST	8	545	736	1.3	1.9
193 EPISCOPAL	2	382	628	1.1	1.6
207 E.L.C.A.	1	174	267	.5	.7
349 PENT HOLINESS	1	46	59*	.1	.2
355 PRESB CH (USA)	6	1,020	1,303*	2.3	3.4
361 PRIM BAPT ASCS	2	28	36*	.1	.1
413 S.D.A.	3	134	171*	.3	.4
419 SO BAPT CONV	33	14,164	18,101*	32.6	47.3
443 UN C OF CHRIST	3	465	594*	1.1	1.6
449 UN METHODIST	36	5,357	6,846*	12.3	17.9
496 JEWISH EST[1]	1	NA	0	-	-
497 BLACK BAPT EST[2]	NA	5,210	6,658*	12.0	17.4
498 INDEP.CHARIS.[3]	1	NA	300	.5	.8
TURNER	26	6,492	8,597*	98.8	100.0
053 ASSEMB OF GOD	1	30	40	.5	.5
127 CH GOD (CLEVE)	1	20	27*	.3	.3
145 CH GOD PROPHCY	1	37	49*	.6	.6
167 CHS OF CHRIST	1	54	61	.7	.7
223 FREE WILL BAPT	1	106	141*	1.6	1.6
361 PRIM BAPT ASCS	1	5	7*	.1	.1
419 SO BAPT CONV	15	3,923	5,204*	59.8	60.5
449 UN METHODIST	4	669	887*	10.2	10.3
467 WESLEYAN	1	5	2	-	-
497 BLACK BAPT EST[2]	NA	1,643	2,179*	25.0	25.3
TWIGGS	16	4,778	6,361*	64.9	100.0
053 ASSEMB OF GOD	1	49	86	.9	1.4
127 CH GOD (CLEVE)	1	86	114*	1.2	1.8
361 PRIM BAPT ASCS	1	120	159*	1.6	2.5
419 SO BAPT CONV	8	2,073	2,751*	28.1	43.2
449 UN METHODIST	5	358	475*	4.8	7.5
497 BLACK BAPT EST[2]	NA	2,092	2,776*	28.3	43.6
UNION	34	5,445	6,756*	56.3	100.0
081 CATHOLIC	1	NA	210	1.8	3.1
081d *LATIN*	*1*	*NA*	*210*	*1.8*	*3.1*
127 CH GOD (CLEVE)	3	183	221*	1.8	3.3
165 CH OF NAZARENE	1	73	43	.4	.6
167 CHS OF CHRIST	1	75	97	.8	1.4
193 EPISCOPAL	1	42	64	.5	.9
419 SO BAPT CONV	21	4,349	5,248*	43.8	77.7
449 UN METHODIST	6	723	873*	7.3	12.9
UPSON	48	14,597	18,537*	70.5	100.0
053 ASSEMB OF GOD	1	176	164	.6	.9
081 CATHOLIC	1	NA	456	1.7	2.5
081d *LATIN*	*1*	*NA*	*456*	*1.7*	*2.5*
127 CH GOD (CLEVE)	1	422	525*	2.0	2.8
165 CH OF NAZARENE	1	30	22	.1	.1
167 CHS OF CHRIST	2	159	207	.8	1.1
223 FREE WILL BAPT	2	247	307*	1.2	1.7
349 PENT HOLINESS	1	55	68*	.3	.4
355 PRESB CH (USA)	1	360	447*	1.7	2.4
361 PRIM BAPT ASCS	5	206	256*	1.0	1.4
413 S.D.A.	2	132	164*	.6	.9
419 SO BAPT CONV	24	8,872	11,027*	41.9	59.5
449 UN METHODIST	7	1,734	2,155*	8.2	11.6
497 BLACK BAPT EST[2]	NA	2,204	2,739*	10.4	14.8
WALKER	118	23,593	31,193*	53.5	100.0
005 AME ZION	4	284	374	.6	1.2
053 ASSEMB OF GOD	2	125	220	.4	.7
081 CATHOLIC	1	NA	723	1.2	2.3
081d *LATIN*	*1*	*NA*	*723*	*1.2*	*2.3*
123 CH GOD (ANDER)	3	142	182	.3	.6
127 CH GOD (CLEVE)	10	1,432	1,786*	3.1	5.7
145 CH GOD PROPHCY	6	221	276*	.5	.9
146 CH GOD MTN ASM	1	48	60*	.1	.2
151 L-D SAINTS	1	NA	264	.5	.8
165 CH OF NAZARENE	6	475	772	1.3	2.5
167 CHS OF CHRIST	11	1,235	1,471	2.5	4.7
207 E.L.C.A.	1	76	103	.2	.3
355 PRESB CH (USA)	2	152	190*	.3	.6
356 PRESB CH AMER	3	186	233	.4	.7
413 S.D.A.	2	101	126*	.2	.4
419 SO BAPT CONV	48	15,708	19,586*	33.6	62.8
449 UN METHODIST	16	2,679	3,340*	5.7	10.7
496 JEWISH EST[1]	0	NA	228	.4	.7
497 BLACK BAPT EST[2]	NA	729	909*	1.6	2.9
499 INDEP.NON-CHAR[3]	1	NA	350	.6	1.1
WALTON	55	13,589	18,678*	48.4	100.0
005 AME ZION	6	778	1,028	2.7	5.5
053 ASSEMB OF GOD	2	124	253	.7	1.4
081 CATHOLIC	1	NA	272	.7	1.5
081d *LATIN*	*1*	*NA*	*272*	*.7*	*1.5*
093 CHR CH (DISC)	3	295	421	1.1	2.3
097 CHR CHS&CHS CR	1	183	234*	.6	1.3
127 CH GOD (CLEVE)	3	701	897*	2.3	4.8
167 CHS OF CHRIST	2	45	72	.2	.4
193 EPISCOPAL	1	126	137	.4	.7
349 PENT HOLINESS	1	57	73*	.2	.4
355 PRESB CH (USA)	1	227	291*	.8	1.6
361 PRIM BAPT ASCS	3	51	65*	.2	.3
419 SO BAPT CONV	20	6,580	8,421*	21.8	45.1
449 UN METHODIST	11	2,116	2,708*	7.0	14.5
496 JEWISH EST[1]	0	NA	855	2.2	4.6
497 BLACK BAPT EST[2]	NA	2,306	2,951*	7.6	15.8
WARE	77	17,561	23,432*	66.1	100.0
001 ADVENT CHR CH	2	150	188*	.5	.8
053 ASSEMB OF GOD	2	207	260	.7	1.1
081 CATHOLIC	1	NA	570	1.6	2.4
081d *LATIN*	*1*	*NA*	*570*	*1.6*	*2.4*
093 CHR CH (DISC)	1	170	272	.8	1.2
111 CH CR,SCIENTST	1	NR	NR	-	-
127 CH GOD (CLEVE)	6	760	954*	2.7	4.1
145 CH GOD PROPHCY	6	221	277*	.8	1.2
151 L-D SAINTS	1	NA	444	1.3	1.9
165 CH OF NAZARENE	1	82	96	.3	.4
167 CHS OF CHRIST	3	134	173	.5	.7
193 EPISCOPAL	1	232	280	.8	1.2
215 EVAN METH CH	1	37	46*	.1	.2
223 FREE WILL BAPT	4	200	251*	.7	1.1
349 PENT HOLINESS	3	232	291*	.8	1.2
355 PRESB CH (USA)	1	305	383*	1.1	1.6
361 PRIM BAPT ASCS	5	95	119*	.3	.5
403 SALVATION ARMY	1	115	116	.3	.5

NA–Not applicable   NR–Not reported   *Total adherents estimated from known number of communicant, confirmed, full members.   - Represents a percent less than 0.1.   Percentages may not total due to rounding.
[1]See Appendix E   [2]See Appendix F   [3]See Appendix G   Lines in *italic* represent a breakdown of Catholic rites or Friends affiliations. They are included in their respective denominational total.

Table 4. Churches and Church Membership by County and Denomination: 1990

County and Denomination		Number of churches	Communicant, confirmed, full members	Total adherents		
				Number	Percent of total population	Percent of total adherents
413	S.D.A.	2	161	202*	.6	.9
419	SO BAPT CONV	22	8,344	10,471*	29.5	44.7
449	UN METHODIST	12	3,317	4,162*	11.7	17.8
497	BLACK BAPT EST[2]	NA	2,799	3,512*	9.9	15.0
499	INDEP.NON-CHAR[3]	1	NA	365	1.0	1.6
WARREN		**15**	**3,521**	**4,546***	**74.8**	**100.0**
081	CATHOLIC	0	NA	3	-	.1
081d	LATIN	0	NA	3	-	.1
419	SO BAPT CONV	8	1,108	1,430*	23.5	31.5
449	UN METHODIST	7	714	921*	15.2	20.3
497	BLACK BAPT EST[2]	NA	1,699	2,192*	36.1	48.2
WASHINGTON		**53**	**11,265**	**14,924***	**78.1**	**100.0**
081	CATHOLIC	1	NA	55	.3	.4
081d	LATIN	1	NA	55	.3	.4
093	CHR CH (DISC)	3	166	213	1.1	1.4
097	CHR CHS&CHS CR	1	190	247*	1.3	1.7
123	CH GOD (ANDER)	1	15	25	.1	.2
127	CH GOD (CLEVE)	4	229	298*	1.6	2.0
165	CH OF NAZARENE	1	341	648	3.4	4.3
167	CHS OF CHRIST	3	60	79	.4	.5
193	EPISCOPAL	1	29	35	.2	.2
356	PRESB CH AMER	1	16	16	.1	.1
361	PRIM BAPT ASCS	1	74	96*	.5	.6
413	S.D.A.	1	31	40*	.2	.3
419	SO BAPT CONV	23	3,997	5,206*	27.2	34.9
449	UN METHODIST	11	1,523	1,984*	10.4	13.3
467	WESLEYAN	1	5	5	-	-
497	BLACK BAPT EST[2]	NA	4,589	5,977*	31.3	40.0
WAYNE		**56**	**12,145**	**16,724***	**74.8**	**100.0**
053	ASSEMB OF GOD	1	138	195	.9	1.2
061	BEACHY AMISH	1	46	59*	.3	.4
081	CATHOLIC	1	NA	750	3.4	4.5
081d	LATIN	1	NA	750	3.4	4.5
097	CHR CHS&CHS CR	1	50	65*	.3	.4
123	CH GOD (ANDER)	1	25	36	.2	.2
127	CH GOD (CLEVE)	10	1,697	2,191*	9.8	13.1
145	CH GOD PROPHCY	1	37	48*	.2	.3
151	L-D SAINTS	1	NA	270	1.2	1.6
167	CHS OF CHRIST	2	15	21	.1	.1
193	EPISCOPAL	1	130	169	.8	1.0
223	FREE WILL BAPT	3	561	724*	3.2	4.3
355	PRESB CH (USA)	2	101	130*	.6	.8
361	PRIM BAPT ASCS	4	255	329*	1.5	2.0
419	SO BAPT CONV	20	6,502	8,395*	37.6	50.2
449	UN METHODIST	7	1,321	1,706*	7.6	10.2
497	BLACK BAPT EST[2]	NA	1,267	1,636*	7.3	9.8
WEBSTER		**12**	**1,702**	**2,184***	**96.5**	**100.0**
123	CH GOD (ANDER)	1	16	30	1.3	1.4
167	CHS OF CHRIST	1	32	54	2.4	2.5
355	PRESB CH (USA)	1	5	6*	.3	.3
361	PRIM BAPT ASCS	2	36	46*	2.0	2.1
419	SO BAPT CONV	5	901	1,144*	50.6	52.4
449	UN METHODIST	2	186	236*	10.4	10.8
497	BLACK BAPT EST[2]	NA	526	668*	29.5	30.6
WHEELER		**21**	**2,922**	**3,711***	**75.7**	**100.0**
123	CH GOD (ANDER)	1	22	22	.4	.6
127	CH GOD (CLEVE)	3	164	209*	4.3	5.6
361	PRIM BAPT ASCS	1	60	76*	1.6	2.0
419	SO BAPT CONV	10	1,377	1,752*	35.7	47.2
449	UN METHODIST	6	614	781*	15.9	21.0
497	BLACK BAPT EST[2]	NA	685	871*	17.8	23.5
WHITE		**30**	**3,902**	**4,937***	**38.0**	**100.0**
053	ASSEMB OF GOD	1	45	60	.5	1.2
081	CATHOLIC	1	NA	191	1.5	3.9
081d	LATIN	1	NA	191	1.5	3.9
127	CH GOD (CLEVE)	1	39	47*	.4	1.0
167	CHS OF CHRIST	1	7	7	.1	.1
355	PRESB CH (USA)	2	195	237*	1.8	4.8
413	S.D.A.	1	96	116*	.9	2.3
419	SO BAPT CONV	13	2,482	3,011*	23.2	61.0
449	UN METHODIST	9	1,024	1,242*	9.5	25.2
467	WESLEYAN	1	14	26	.2	.5
WHITFIELD		**99**	**27,651**	**35,886***	**49.5**	**100.0**
053	ASSEMB OF GOD	4	209	279	.4	.8
081	CATHOLIC	1	NA	896	1.2	2.5
081d	LATIN	1	NA	896	1.2	2.5
097	CHR CHS&CHS CR	1	115	144*	.2	.4

County and Denomination		Number of churches	Communicant, confirmed, full members	Total adherents		
				Number	Percent of total population	Percent of total adherents
127	CH GOD (CLEVE)	8	2,120	2,651*	3.7	7.4
145	CH GOD PROPHCY	6	221	276*	.4	.8
146	CH GOD MTN ASM	1	72	90*	.1	.3
151	L-D SAINTS	2	NA	292	.4	.8
165	CH OF NAZARENE	2	175	247	.3	.7
167	CHS OF CHRIST	7	804	973	1.3	2.7
193	EPISCOPAL	1	513	568	.8	1.6
207	E.L.C.A.	1	105	146	.2	.4
215	EVAN METH CH	1	262	328*	.5	.9
355	PRESB CH (USA)	2	963	1,204*	1.7	3.4
356	PRESB CH AMER	1	206	206	.3	.6
403	SALVATION ARMY	1	77	88	.1	.2
413	S.D.A.	2	500	625*	.9	1.7
419	SO BAPT CONV	40	15,950	19,946*	27.5	55.6
449	UN METHODIST	17	4,614	5,770*	8.0	16.1
496	JEWISH EST[1]	1	NA	225	.3	.6
497	BLACK BAPT EST[2]	NA	745	932*	1.3	2.6
WILCOX		**35**	**4,994**	**6,380***	**91.0**	**100.0**
127	CH GOD (CLEVE)	2	221	282*	4.0	4.4
223	FREE WILL BAPT	1	85	109*	1.6	1.7
361	PRIM BAPT ASCS	4	39	50*	.7	.8
419	SO BAPT CONV	22	3,159	4,035*	57.6	63.2
449	UN METHODIST	6	456	583*	8.3	9.1
497	BLACK BAPT EST[2]	NA	1,034	1,321*	18.8	20.7
WILKES		**31**	**6,292**	**8,082***	**76.3**	**100.0**
005	AME ZION	1	75	80	.8	1.0
081	CATHOLIC	1	NA	73	.7	.9
081d	LATIN	1	NA	73	.7	.9
127	CH GOD (CLEVE)	1	37	47*	.4	.6
167	CHS OF CHRIST	2	64	114	1.1	1.4
193	EPISCOPAL	1	79	95	.9	1.2
353	CHR BRETHREN	1	80	150	1.4	1.9
355	PRESB CH (USA)	2	126	159*	1.5	2.0
419	SO BAPT CONV	15	2,758	3,483*	32.9	43.1
449	UN METHODIST	7	791	999*	9.4	12.4
497	BLACK BAPT EST[2]	NA	2,282	2,882*	27.2	35.7
WILKINSON		**32**	**5,314**	**6,987***	**68.3**	**100.0**
081	CATHOLIC	1	NA	15	.1	.2
081d	LATIN	1	NA	15	.1	.2
145	CH GOD PROPHCY	1	37	48*	.5	.7
167	CHS OF CHRIST	2	48	75	.7	1.1
361	PRIM BAPT ASCS	4	52	68*	.7	1.0
419	SO BAPT CONV	14	2,465	3,211*	31.4	46.0
449	UN METHODIST	9	690	899*	8.8	12.9
467	WESLEYAN	1	22	65	.6	.9
497	BLACK BAPT EST[2]	NA	2,000	2,606*	25.5	37.3
WORTH		**48**	**10,225**	**13,395***	**67.8**	**100.0**
053	ASSEMB OF GOD	1	35	43	.2	.3
127	CH GOD (CLEVE)	1	93	122*	.6	.9
145	CH GOD PROPHCY	1	37	48*	.2	.4
167	CHS OF CHRIST	2	46	60	.3	.4
223	FREE WILL BAPT	4	309	404*	2.0	3.0
339	PENT CH OF GOD	1	35	77	.4	.6
355	PRESB CH (USA)	1	89	116*	.6	.9
361	PRIM BAPT ASCS	3	69	90*	.5	.7
419	SO BAPT CONV	26	5,588	7,305*	37.0	54.5
449	UN METHODIST	8	1,112	1,454*	7.4	10.9
497	BLACK BAPT EST[2]	NA	2,812	3,676*	18.6	27.4

HAWAII

County and Denomination		Number of churches	Communicant, confirmed, full members	Total adherents		
				Number	Percent of total population	Percent of total adherents
THE STATE.....		758	87,579	390,827*	35.3	100.0
HAWAII		**156**	**10,760**	**48,900***	**40.6**	**100.0**
053	ASSEMB OF GOD	15	1,188	1,742	1.4	3.6
057	BAPT GEN CONF	1	20	26*	-	.1
081	CATHOLIC	29	NA	28,556	23.7	58.4
081d	LATIN	29	NA	28,556	23.7	58.4
089	CHR & MISS AL	1	0	76	.1	.2
111	CH CR,SCIENTST	1	NR	NR	-	-
127	CH GOD (CLEVE)	3	230	299*	.2	.6
145	CH GOD PROPHCY	1	24	31*	-	.1
151	L-D SAINTS	17	NA	5,721	4.8	11.7
165	CH OF NAZARENE	3	175	475	.4	1.0
167	CHS OF CHRIST	4	73	121	.1	.2
176	CCC, NOT NAT'L	10	429	558*	.5	1.1

NA–Not applicable   NR–Not reported   *Total adherents estimated from known number of communicant, confirmed, full members.   - Represents a percent less than 0.1.   Percentages may not total due to rounding.
[1]See Appendix E   [2]See Appendix F   [3]See Appendix G   Lines in *italic* represent a breakdown of Catholic rites or Friends affiliations. They are included in their respective denominational total.

Table 4. Churches and Church Membership by County and Denomination: 1990

County and Denomination	Number of churches	Communicant, confirmed, full members	Total adherents		
			Number	Percent of total population	Percent of total adherents
193 EPISCOPAL	7	513	651	.5	1.3
207 E.L.C.A.	1	74	121	.1	.2
226 FRIENDS-USA	2	9	22	-	-
226f INDEPENDNT	*2*	*9*	*22*	-	-
263 INT FOURSQ GOS	6	1,471	1,912*	1.6	3.9
283 LUTH—MO SYNOD	2	86	115	.1	.2
291 MISSIONARY CH	1	69	168	.1	.3
339 PENT CH OF GOD	1	32	46	-	.1
349 PENT HOLINESS	3	92	120*	.1	.2
355 PRESB CH (USA)	4	1,181	1,535*	1.3	3.1
403 SALVATION ARMY	3	213	261	.2	.5
413 S.D.A.	4	647	841*	.7	1.7
419 SO BAPT CONV	11	1,552	2,017*	1.7	4.1
443 UN C OF CHRIST	19	2,115	2,749*	2.3	5.6
449 UN METHODIST	5	461	599*	.5	1.2
496 JEWISH EST[1]	2	NA	0	-	-
497 BLACK BAPT EST[2]	NA	106	138*	.1	.3
HONOLULU	**434**	**65,839**	**288,507***	**34.5**	**100.0**
019 AMER BAPT USA	4	697	866*	.1	.3
053 ASSEMB OF GOD	46	5,870	8,648	1.0	3.0
057 BAPT GEN CONF	2	132	164*	-	.1
081 CATHOLIC	41	NA	172,563	20.6	59.8
081d LATIN	*41*	*NA*	*172,563*	*20.6*	*59.8*
089 CHR & MISS AL	8	848	1,409	.2	.5
093 CHR CH (DISC)	3	230	305	-	.1
097 CHR CHS&CHS CR	10	1,110	1,380*	.2	.5
105 CHRISTIAN REF	1	53	72	-	-
111 CH CR,SCIENTST	3	NR	NR	-	-
123 CH GOD (ANDER)	1	31	34	-	-
127 CH GOD (CLEVE)	6	862	1,072*	.1	.4
145 CH GOD PROPHCY	3	73	91*	-	-
151 L-D SAINTS	74	NA	26,754	3.2	9.3
165 CH OF NAZARENE	13	1,487	1,746	.2	.6
167 CHS OF CHRIST	7	680	847	.1	.3
175 CONGR CHR CHS	1	19	24*	-	-
176 CCC, NOT NAT'L	1	36	45*	-	-
179 CONSRV BAPT	2	NR	NR	-	-
193 EPISCOPAL	23	5,216	7,527	.9	2.6
203 EVAN FREE CH	2	35	40	-	-
207 E.L.C.A.	9	2,531	3,419	.4	1.2
223 FREE WILL BAPT	1	50	62*	-	-
226 FRIENDS-USA	2	74	92	-	-
226f INDEPENDNT	*2*	*74*	*92*	-	-
246 GREEK ORTHODOX	1	NR	NR	-	-
249 AP CATH ASSYR	0	3	11	-	-
263 INT FOURSQ GOS	12	2,034	2,529*	.3	.9
283 LUTH—MO SYNOD	7	1,094	1,507	.2	.5
291 MISSIONARY CH	5	294	563	.1	.2
349 PENT HOLINESS	3	642	798*	.1	.3
353 CHR BRETHREN	3	125	200	-	.1
355 PRESB CH (USA)	2	184	229*	-	.1
356 PRESB CH AMER	1	71	97	-	-
403 SALVATION ARMY	3	563	600	.1	.2
413 S.D.A.	13	3,386	4,209*	.5	1.5
419 SO BAPT CONV	35	13,230	16,447*	2.0	5.7
435 UNITARIAN-UNIV	1	176	204	-	.1
443 UN C OF CHRIST	54	12,839	15,961*	1.9	5.5
449 UN METHODIST	20	5,578	6,934*	.8	2.4
469 WELS	1	66	96	-	-
496 JEWISH EST[1]	4	NA	0	-	-
497 BLACK BAPT EST[2]	NA	5,520	6,862*	.8	2.4
498 INDEP.CHARIS.[3]	5	NA	3,600	.4	1.2
499 INDEP.NON-CHAR[3]	1	NA	500	.1	.2
KALAWAO	**2**	**25**	**90***	**69.2**	**100.0**
081 CATHOLIC	1	NA	65	50.0	72.2
081d LATIN	*1*	*NA*	*65*	*50.0*	*72.2*
443 UN C OF CHRIST	1	25	25*	19.2	27.8
KAUAI	**59**	**4,278**	**17,051***	**33.3**	**100.0**
053 ASSEMB OF GOD	4	297	453	.9	2.7
081 CATHOLIC	8	NA	8,729	17.1	51.2
081d LATIN	*8*	*NA*	*8,729*	*17.1*	*51.2*
097 CHR CHS&CHS CR	1	26	33*	.1	.2
111 CH CR,SCIENTST	1	NR	NR	-	-
151 L-D SAINTS	5	NA	2,132	4.2	12.5
165 CH OF NAZARENE	1	65	158	.3	.9
167 CHS OF CHRIST	1	39	71	.1	.4
175 CONGR CHR CHS	1	24	31*	.1	.2
176 CCC, NOT NAT'L	1	41	53*	.1	.3
181 CONSRV CONGR	1	20	26*	.1	.2
193 EPISCOPAL	5	509	920	1.8	5.4
207 E.L.C.A.	1	177	265	.5	1.6
226 FRIENDS-USA	1	2	5	-	-
226f INDEPENDNT	*1*	*2*	*5*	-	-

County and Denomination	Number of churches	Communicant, confirmed, full members	Total adherents		
			Number	Percent of total population	Percent of total adherents
263 INT FOURSQ GOS	3	222	285*	.6	1.7
291 MISSIONARY CH	3	235	593	1.2	3.5
403 SALVATION ARMY	3	267	274	.5	1.6
413 S.D.A.	2	369	474*	.9	2.8
419 SO BAPT CONV	2	421	541*	1.1	3.2
443 UN C OF CHRIST	12	1,299	1,668*	3.3	9.8
449 UN METHODIST	3	265	340*	.7	2.0
MAUI	**107**	**6,677**	**36,279***	**36.1**	**100.0**
053 ASSEMB OF GOD	4	1,120	2,162	2.2	6.0
081 CATHOLIC	23	NA	22,867	22.8	63.0
081d LATIN	*23*	*NA*	*22,867*	*22.8*	*63.0*
111 CH CR,SCIENTST	1	NR	NR	-	-
127 CH GOD (CLEVE)	3	163	207*	.2	.6
145 CH GOD PROPHCY	1	24	31*	-	.1
151 L-D SAINTS	13	NA	3,696	3.7	10.2
165 CH OF NAZARENE	3	115	177	.2	.5
167 CHS OF CHRIST	1	19	37	-	.1
176 CCC, NOT NAT'L	5	437	556*	.6	1.5
179 CONSRV BAPT	1	NR	NR	-	-
193 EPISCOPAL	5	752	1,298	1.3	3.6
207 E.L.C.A.	1	97	139	.1	.4
221 FREE METHODIST	1	0	15	-	-
226 FRIENDS-USA	2	6	18	-	-
226f INDEPENDNT	*2*	*6*	*18*	-	-
283 LUTH—MO SYNOD	2	143	230	.2	.6
291 MISSIONARY CH	1	20	44	-	.1
349 PENT HOLINESS	1	10	13*	-	-
403 SALVATION ARMY	2	112	132	.1	.4
413 S.D.A.	2	320	407*	.4	1.1
419 SO BAPT CONV	8	1,042	1,326*	1.3	3.7
443 UN C OF CHRIST	24	1,924	2,449*	2.4	6.8
449 UN METHODIST	3	373	475*	.5	1.3

IDAHO

County and Denomination	Number of churches	Communicant, confirmed, full members	Total adherents		
			Number	Percent of total population	Percent of total adherents
THE STATE.....	1,600	114,833	507,426*	50.4	100.0
ADA	**191**	**26,759**	**88,076***	**42.8**	**100.0**
019 AMER BAPT USA	6	1,902	2,456*	1.2	2.8
053 ASSEMB OF GOD	6	1,060	3,154	1.5	3.6
081 CATHOLIC	8	NA	15,583	7.6	17.7
081d LATIN	*8*	*NA*	*15,583*	*7.6*	*17.7*
089 CHR & MISS AL	1	0	504	.2	.6
093 CHR CH (DISC)	3	1,043	1,654	.8	1.9
097 CHR CHS&CHS CR	16	4,412	5,696*	2.8	6.5
105 CHRISTIAN REF	1	102	195	.1	.2
111 CH CR,SCIENTST	2	NR	NR	-	-
123 CH GOD (ANDER)	1	145	145	.1	.2
127 CH GOD (CLEVE)	1	251	324*	.2	.4
145 CH GOD PROPHCY	1	25	32*	-	-
151 L-D SAINTS	69	NA	32,517	15.8	36.9
157 CH OF BRETHREN	2	180	232*	.1	.3
165 CH OF NAZARENE	8	1,720	2,314	1.1	2.6
167 CHS OF CHRIST	4	437	630	.3	.7
179 CONSRV BAPT	2	NR	NR	-	-
193 EPISCOPAL	4	1,409	2,122	1.0	2.4
203 EVAN FREE CH	1	60	125	.1	.1
207 E.L.C.A.	5	1,546	2,324	1.1	2.6
221 FREE METHODIST	1	0	54	-	.1
226 FRIENDS-USA	5	474	679*	.3	.8
226b EFI	*4*	*462*	*664*	*.3*	*.8*
226f INDEPENDNT	*1*	*12*	*15*	* -	-
246 GREEK ORTHODOX	1	NR	NR	-	-
263 INT FOURSQ GOS	4	165	213*	.1	.2
283 LUTH—MO SYNOD	4	1,204	1,643	.8	1.9
285 MENNONITE CH	1	43	73	-	.1
339 PENT CH OF GOD	1	4	20	-	-
353 CHR BRETHREN	1	90	95	-	.1
355 PRESB CH (USA)	4	1,803	2,328*	1.1	2.6
403 SALVATION ARMY	1	139	165	.1	.2
413 S.D.A.	5	1,238	1,598*	.8	1.8
419 SO BAPT CONV	4	1,838	2,373*	1.2	2.7
435 UNITARIAN-UNIV	1	168	275	.1	.3
438 UN BRETH IN CR	1	26	37	-	-
443 UN C OF CHRIST	2	592	764*	.4	.9
449 UN METHODIST	8	4,479	5,783*	2.8	6.6
496 JEWISH EST[1]	2	NA	220	.1	.2
497 BLACK BAPT EST[2]	NA	204	263*	.1	.3
498 INDEP.CHARIS.[3]	1	NA	700	.3	.8
499 INDEP.NON-CHAR[3]	2	NA	786	.4	.9

Table 4. Churches and Church Membership by County and Denomination: 1990

County and Denomination	Number of churches	Communicant, confirmed, full members	Total adherents Number	Percent of total population	Percent of total adherents
ADAMS	**7**	**258**	**605***	**18.6**	**100.0**
053 ASSEMB OF GOD	2	90	140	4.3	23.1
081 CATHOLIC	1	NA	100	3.1	16.5
081d *LATIN*	*1*	*NA*	*100*	*3.1*	*16.5*
151 L-D SAINTS	1	NA	157	4.8	26.0
165 CH OF NAZARENE	1	48	53	1.6	8.8
175 CONGR CHR CHS	1	80	103*	3.2	17.0
449 UN METHODIST	1	40	52*	1.6	8.6
BANNOCK	**102**	**4,436**	**41,946***	**63.5**	**100.0**
019 AMER BAPT USA	1	215	290*	.4	.7
053 ASSEMB OF GOD	2	168	210	.3	.5
081 CATHOLIC	5	NA	3,734	5.7	8.9
081d *LATIN*	*5*	*NA*	*3,734*	*5.7*	*8.9*
089 CHR & MISS AL	1	78	128	.2	.3
093 CHR CH (DISC)	1	200	298	.5	.7
111 CH CR,SCIENTST	1	NR	NR	-	-
127 CH GOD (CLEVE)	1	30	40*	.1	.1
145 CH GOD PROPHCY	1	25	34*	.1	.1
151 L-D SAINTS	70	NA	31,830	48.2	75.9
165 CH OF NAZARENE	1	138	226	.3	.5
167 CHS OF CHRIST	1	75	123	.2	.3
193 EPISCOPAL	1	157	325	.5	.8
207 E.L.C.A.	1	283	385	.6	.9
246 GREEK ORTHODOX	1	NR	NR	-	-
259 IFCA	2	NR	NR	-	-
263 INT FOURSQ GOS	1	57	77*	.1	.2
283 LUTH—MO SYNOD	2	776	1,218	1.8	2.9
355 PRESB CH (USA)	1	363	490*	.7	1.2
403 SALVATION ARMY	1	38	50	.1	.1
413 S.D.A.	1	132	178*	.3	.4
419 SO BAPT CONV	2	758	1,022*	1.5	2.4
435 UNITARIAN-UNIV	1	70	110	.2	.3
443 UN C OF CHRIST	1	189	255*	.4	.6
449 UN METHODIST	2	684	923*	1.4	2.2
BEAR LAKE	**20**	**47**	**5,450***	**89.6**	**100.0**
081 CATHOLIC	1	NA	135	2.2	2.5
081d *LATIN*	*1*	*NA*	*135*	*2.2*	*2.5*
151 L-D SAINTS	17	NA	5,248	86.3	96.3
263 INT FOURSQ GOS	1	28	40*	.7	.7
355 PRESB CH (USA)	1	19	27*	.4	.5
BENEWAH	**17**	**1,012**	**3,806***	**48.0**	**100.0**
053 ASSEMB OF GOD	2	116	246	3.1	6.5
081 CATHOLIC	5	NA	2,100	26.5	55.2
081d *LATIN*	*5*	*NA*	*2,100*	*26.5*	*55.2*
151 L-D SAINTS	1	NA	217	2.7	5.7
165 CH OF NAZARENE	1	145	259	3.3	6.8
167 CHS OF CHRIST	1	12	16	.2	.4
179 CONSRV BAPT	1	NR	NR	-	-
207 E.L.C.A.	1	161	228	2.9	6.0
221 FREE METHODIST	1	24	24	.3	.6
263 INT FOURSQ GOS	1	89	115*	1.4	3.0
355 PRESB CH (USA)	1	194	251*	3.2	6.6
413 S.D.A.	1	75	97*	1.2	2.5
419 SO BAPT CONV	1	196	253*	3.2	6.6
BINGHAM	**78**	**1,800**	**27,598***	**73.4**	**100.0**
019 AMER BAPT USA	1	181	260*	.7	.9
053 ASSEMB OF GOD	3	132	226	.6	.8
081 CATHOLIC	5	NA	1,824	4.9	6.6
081d *LATIN*	*5*	*NA*	*1,824*	*4.9*	*6.6*
151 L-D SAINTS	57	NA	23,082	61.4	83.6
167 CHS OF CHRIST	1	30	39	.1	.1
193 EPISCOPAL	2	148	370	1.0	1.3
207 E.L.C.A.	2	296	416	1.1	1.5
283 LUTH—MO SYNOD	1	91	124	.3	.4
287 MENN GEN CONF	1	281	335	.9	1.2
419 SO BAPT CONV	2	282	406*	1.1	1.5
449 UN METHODIST	3	359	516*	1.4	1.9
BLAINE	**17**	**682**	**3,842***	**28.4**	**100.0**
019 AMER BAPT USA	1	41	52*	.4	1.4
053 ASSEMB OF GOD	1	62	195	1.4	5.1
081 CATHOLIC	2	NA	875	6.5	22.8
081d *LATIN*	*2*	*NA*	*875*	*6.5*	*22.8*
111 CH CR,SCIENTST	1	NR	NR	-	-
151 L-D SAINTS	5	NA	1,869	13.8	48.6
193 EPISCOPAL	2	186	330	2.4	8.6
263 INT FOURSQ GOS	1	49	63*	.5	1.6
283 LUTH—MO SYNOD	1	104	152	1.1	4.0
355 PRESB CH (USA)	1	156	199*	1.5	5.2
413 S.D.A.	1	52	66*	.5	1.7

County and Denomination	Number of churches	Communicant, confirmed, full members	Total adherents Number	Percent of total population	Percent of total adherents
419 SO BAPT CONV	1	32	41*	.3	1.1
BOISE	**13**	**747**	**1,520***	**43.3**	**100.0**
053 ASSEMB OF GOD	2	45	97	2.8	6.4
081 CATHOLIC	3	NA	263	7.5	17.3
081d *LATIN*	*3*	*NA*	*263*	*7.5*	*17.3*
097 CHR CHS&CHS CR	4	639	822*	23.4	54.1
151 L-D SAINTS	2	NA	246	7.0	16.2
207 E.L.C.A.	1	26	44	1.3	2.9
419 SO BAPT CONV	1	37	48*	1.4	3.2
BONNER	**35**	**2,258**	**5,399***	**20.3**	**100.0**
053 ASSEMB OF GOD	2	149	272	1.0	5.0
081 CATHOLIC	4	NA	1,260	4.7	23.3
081d *LATIN*	*4*	*NA*	*1,260*	*4.7*	*23.3*
111 CH CR,SCIENTST	1	NR	NR	-	-
123 CH GOD (ANDER)	1	30	30	.1	.6
127 CH GOD (CLEVE)	1	28	36*	.1	.7
151 L-D SAINTS	2	NA	602	2.3	11.2
165 CH OF NAZARENE	1	75	135	.5	2.5
167 CHS OF CHRIST	1	3	10	-	.2
179 CONSRV BAPT	2	NR	NR	-	-
181 CONSRV CONGR	1	126	163*	.6	3.0
193 EPISCOPAL	1	75	83	.3	1.5
203 EVAN FREE CH	1	30	30	.1	.6
207 E.L.C.A.	2	429	642	2.4	11.9
221 FREE METHODIST	1	28	39	.1	.7
226 FRIENDS-USA	1	6	24	.1	.4
226f *INDEPENDNT*	*1*	*6*	*24*	*.1*	*.4*
263 INT FOURSQ GOS	1	46	59*	.2	1.1
283 LUTH—MO SYNOD	1	65	92	.3	1.7
355 PRESB CH (USA)	1	199	257*	1.0	4.8
413 S.D.A.	3	487	628*	2.4	11.6
419 SO BAPT CONV	3	151	195*	.7	3.6
449 UN METHODIST	3	331	427*	1.6	7.9
498 INDEP.CHARIS.[3]	1	NA	415	1.6	7.7
BONNEVILLE	**114**	**6,598**	**56,156***	**77.8**	**100.0**
019 AMER BAPT USA	1	441	613*	.8	1.1
053 ASSEMB OF GOD	2	267	394	.5	.7
081 CATHOLIC	2	NA	5,522	7.6	9.8
081d *LATIN*	*2*	*NA*	*5,522*	*7.6*	*9.8*
089 CHR & MISS AL	1	139	293	.4	.5
093 CHR CH (DISC)	1	124	154	.2	.3
111 CH CR,SCIENTST	1	NR	NR	-	-
127 CH GOD (CLEVE)	1	2	3*	-	-
151 L-D SAINTS	87	NA	41,108	56.9	73.2
165 CH OF NAZARENE	1	146	292	.4	.5
167 CHS OF CHRIST	1	132	202	.3	.4
193 EPISCOPAL	2	195	369	.5	.7
207 E.L.C.A.	1	719	1,060	1.5	1.9
263 INT FOURSQ GOS	1	130	181*	.3	.3
283 LUTH—MO SYNOD	2	648	914	1.3	1.6
313 N AM BAPT CONF	1	50	69*	.1	.1
355 PRESB CH (USA)	2	910	1,264*	1.8	2.3
403 SALVATION ARMY	1	87	93	.1	.2
413 S.D.A.	1	104	144*	.2	.3
419 SO BAPT CONV	1	1,251	1,738*	2.4	3.1
435 UNITARIAN-UNIV	1	39	56	.1	.1
443 UN C OF CHRIST	1	107	149*	.2	.3
449 UN METHODIST	2	1,107	1,538*	2.1	2.7
BOUNDARY	**14**	**1,340**	**2,889***	**34.7**	**100.0**
053 ASSEMB OF GOD	1	45	80	1.0	2.8
081 CATHOLIC	3	NA	495	5.9	17.1
081d *LATIN*	*3*	*NA*	*495*	*5.9*	*17.1*
143 CG IN CR(MENN)	1	270	358*	4.3	12.4
151 L-D SAINTS	1	NA	528	6.3	18.3
167 CHS OF CHRIST	1	40	60	.7	2.1
193 EPISCOPAL	1	12	14	.2	.5
207 E.L.C.A.	1	264	397	4.8	13.7
221 FREE METHODIST	1	39	73	.9	2.5
285 MENNONITE CH	1	15	15	.2	.5
413 S.D.A.	1	111	147*	1.8	5.1
419 SO BAPT CONV	1	291	386*	4.6	13.4
449 UN METHODIST	1	253	336*	4.0	11.6
BUTTE	**6**	**313**	**1,479***	**50.7**	**100.0**
019 AMER BAPT USA	1	298	407*	13.9	27.5
081 CATHOLIC	1	NA	76	2.6	5.1
081d *LATIN*	*1*	*NA*	*76*	*2.6*	*5.1*
151 L-D SAINTS	3	NA	980	33.6	66.3
193 EPISCOPAL	1	15	16	.5	1.1

NA–Not applicable   NR–Not reported   *Total adherents estimated from known number of communicant, confirmed, full members.   - Represents a percent less than 0.1.   Percentages may not total due to rounding.
[1]See Appendix E   [2]See Appendix F   [3]See Appendix G   Lines in *italic* represent a breakdown of Catholic rites or Friends affiliations. They are included in their respective denominational total.

Table 4. Churches and Church Membership by County and Denomination: 1990

County and Denomination	Number of churches	Communicant, confirmed, full members	Total adherents Number	Percent of total population	Percent of total adherents
CAMAS	**2**	**0**	**123***	**16.9**	**100.0**
081 CATHOLIC	1	NA	25	3.4	20.3
081d *LATIN*	*1*	*NA*	*25*	*3.4*	*20.3*
151 L-D SAINTS	1	NA	98	13.5	79.7
CANYON	**120**	**14,569**	**39,398***	**43.7**	**100.0**
019 AMER BAPT USA	4	529	698*	.8	1.8
053 ASSEMB OF GOD	7	785	1,310	1.5	3.3
081 CATHOLIC	5	NA	8,851	9.8	22.5
081d *LATIN*	*5*	*NA*	*8,851*	*9.8*	*22.5*
089 CHR & MISS AL	1	27	57	.1	.1
093 CHR CH (DISC)	2	513	804	.9	2.0
111 CH CR,SCIENTST	1	NR	NR	-	-
123 CH GOD (ANDER)	2	179	179	.2	.5
127 CH GOD (CLEVE)	3	101	133*	.1	.3
133 CH GOD(7TH)DEN	1	46	58	.1	.1
145 CH GOD PROPHCY	4	100	132*	.1	.3
151 L-D SAINTS	26	NA	11,421	12.7	29.0
157 CH OF BRETHREN	2	286	377*	.4	1.0
163 CH OF LUTH BR	1	65	157	.2	.4
165 CH OF NAZARENE	12	4,361	4,832	5.4	12.3
167 CHS OF CHRIST	5	328	422	.5	1.1
179 CONSRV BAPT	3	NR	NR	-	-
193 EPISCOPAL	2	268	285	.3	.7
207 E.L.C.A.	2	366	533	.6	1.4
221 FREE METHODIST	2	362	490	.5	1.2
226 FRIENDS-USA	3	454	554	.6	1.4
226b *EFI*	*3*	*454*	*554*	*.6*	*1.4*
263 INT FOURSQ GOS	2	115	152*	.2	.4
283 LUTH—MO SYNOD	3	740	1,098	1.2	2.8
285 MENNONITE CH	2	96	153	.2	.4
339 PENT CH OF GOD	1	66	71	.1	.2
355 PRESB CH (USA)	4	945	1,247*	1.4	3.2
403 SALVATION ARMY	2	150	169	.2	.4
413 S.D.A.	6	1,167	1,540*	1.7	3.9
419 SO BAPT CONV	3	859	1,133*	1.3	2.9
443 UN C OF CHRIST	1	173	228*	.3	.6
449 UN METHODIST	6	1,360	1,794*	2.0	4.6
469 WELS	1	128	170	.2	.4
498 INDEP.CHARIS.*3*	1	NA	350	.4	.9
CARIBOU	**18**	**219**	**5,908***	**84.8**	**100.0**
081 CATHOLIC	1	NA	460	6.6	7.8
081d *LATIN*	*1*	*NA*	*460*	*6.6*	*7.8*
151 L-D SAINTS	13	NA	5,129	73.7	86.8
263 INT FOURSQ GOS	1	40	57*	.8	1.0
283 LUTH—MO SYNOD	1	26	44	.6	.7
355 PRESB CH (USA)	1	110	157*	2.3	2.7
419 SO BAPT CONV	1	43	61*	.9	1.0
CASSIA	**46**	**1,757**	**14,872***	**76.1**	**100.0**
053 ASSEMB OF GOD	3	243	414	2.1	2.8
081 CATHOLIC	1	NA	1,350	6.9	9.1
081d *LATIN*	*1*	*NA*	*1,350*	*6.9*	*9.1*
089 CHR & MISS AL	1	14	34	.2	.2
093 CHR CH (DISC)	1	163	236	1.2	1.6
151 L-D SAINTS	31	NA	10,970	56.2	73.8
165 CH OF NAZARENE	1	5	0	-	-
167 CHS OF CHRIST	1	18	23	.1	.2
179 CONSRV BAPT	1	NR	NR	-	-
193 EPISCOPAL	1	77	107	.5	.7
283 LUTH—MO SYNOD	1	267	373	1.9	2.5
355 PRESB CH (USA)	1	238	335*	1.7	2.3
413 S.D.A.	1	89	125*	.6	.8
419 SO BAPT CONV	1	285	401*	2.1	2.7
449 UN METHODIST	1	358	504*	2.6	3.4
CLARK	**3**	**23**	**543***	**71.3**	**100.0**
019 AMER BAPT USA	1	23	31*	4.1	5.7
151 L-D SAINTS	2	NA	512	67.2	94.3
CLEARWATER	**24**	**1,413**	**2,909***	**34.2**	**100.0**
053 ASSEMB OF GOD	2	54	76	.9	2.6
081 CATHOLIC	2	NA	320	3.8	11.0
081d *LATIN*	*2*	*NA*	*320*	*3.8*	*11.0*
089 CHR & MISS AL	1	33	93	1.1	3.2
093 CHR CH (DISC)	1	39	57	.7	2.0
123 CH GOD (ANDER)	1	75	75	.9	2.6
151 L-D SAINTS	1	NA	370	4.4	12.7
164 CH LUTH CONF	1	26	31	.4	1.1
165 CH OF NAZARENE	2	55	123	1.4	4.2
207 E.L.C.A.	2	109	194	2.3	6.7
339 PENT CH OF GOD	2	69	153	1.8	5.3
355 PRESB CH (USA)	1	7	9*	.1	.3

County and Denomination	Number of churches	Communicant, confirmed, full members	Total adherents Number	Percent of total population	Percent of total adherents
413 S.D.A.	2	152	188*	2.2	6.5
419 SO BAPT CONV	2	452	558*	6.6	19.2
438 UN BRETH IN CR	1	29	29	.3	1.0
449 UN METHODIST	2	274	338*	4.0	11.6
467 WESLEYAN	1	39	295	3.5	10.1
CUSTER	**9**	**144**	**1,761***	**42.6**	**100.0**
053 ASSEMB OF GOD	1	83	111	2.7	6.3
081 CATHOLIC	2	NA	20	.5	1.1
081d *LATIN*	*2*	*NA*	*20*	*.5*	*1.1*
151 L-D SAINTS	4	NA	1,550	37.5	88.0
167 CHS OF CHRIST	1	2	3	.1	.2
443 UN C OF CHRIST	1	59	77*	1.9	4.4
ELMORE	**29**	**3,224**	**8,275***	**39.0**	**100.0**
019 AMER BAPT USA	1	132	179*	.8	2.2
053 ASSEMB OF GOD	2	65	156	.7	1.9
081 CATHOLIC	2	NA	1,728	8.1	20.9
081d *LATIN*	*2*	*NA*	*1,728*	*8.1*	*20.9*
089 CHR & MISS AL	1	12	35	.2	.4
093 CHR CH (DISC)	1	96	132	.6	1.6
127 CH GOD (CLEVE)	1	36	49*	.2	.6
145 CH GOD PROPHCY	1	25	34*	.2	.4
151 L-D SAINTS	5	NA	1,945	9.2	23.5
165 CH OF NAZARENE	1	56	93	.4	1.1
167 CHS OF CHRIST	1	50	80	.4	1.0
193 EPISCOPAL	2	83	134	.6	1.6
203 EVAN FREE CH	1	50	100	.5	1.2
207 E.L.C.A.	1	84	128	.6	1.5
283 LUTH—MO SYNOD	1	210	293	1.4	3.5
339 PENT CH OF GOD	1	0	40	.2	.5
355 PRESB CH (USA)	1	21	28*	.1	.3
413 S.D.A.	1	68	92*	.4	1.1
419 SO BAPT CONV	3	1,695	2,296*	10.8	27.7
443 UN C OF CHRIST	1	317	429*	2.0	5.2
449 UN METHODIST	1	92	125*	.6	1.5
497 BLACK BAPT EST*2*	NA	132	179*	.8	2.2
FRANKLIN	**26**	**25**	**8,367***	**90.6**	**100.0**
081 CATHOLIC	1	NA	50	.5	.6
081d *LATIN*	*1*	*NA*	*50*	*.5*	*.6*
151 L-D SAINTS	24	NA	8,281	89.7	99.0
355 PRESB CH (USA)	1	25	36*	.4	.4
FREMONT	**24**	**627**	**7,740***	**70.8**	**100.0**
081 CATHOLIC	1	NA	205	1.9	2.6
081d *LATIN*	*1*	*NA*	*205*	*1.9*	*2.6*
151 L-D SAINTS	17	NA	6,711	61.4	86.7
167 CHS OF CHRIST	1	30	39	.4	.5
193 EPISCOPAL	1	24	14	.1	.2
263 INT FOURSQ GOS	1	44	62*	.6	.8
283 LUTH—MO SYNOD	1	308	397	3.6	5.1
355 PRESB CH (USA)	1	82	116*	1.1	1.5
449 UN METHODIST	1	139	196*	1.8	2.5
GEM	**19**	**1,352**	**4,273***	**36.1**	**100.0**
019 AMER BAPT USA	1	176	225*	1.9	5.3
081 CATHOLIC	1	NA	550	4.6	12.9
081d *LATIN*	*1*	*NA*	*550*	*4.6*	*12.9*
145 CH GOD PROPHCY	1	25	32*	.3	.7
151 L-D SAINTS	5	NA	1,861	15.7	43.6
165 CH OF NAZARENE	2	211	381	3.2	8.9
167 CHS OF CHRIST	1	40	52	.4	1.2
179 CONSRV BAPT	1	NR	NR	-	-
193 EPISCOPAL	1	80	91	.8	2.1
263 INT FOURSQ GOS	1	118	151*	1.3	3.5
283 LUTH—MO SYNOD	1	211	301	2.5	7.0
355 PRESB CH (USA)	1	118	151*	1.3	3.5
413 S.D.A.	1	68	87*	.7	2.0
419 SO BAPT CONV	1	117	150*	1.3	3.5
449 UN METHODIST	2	188	241*	2.0	5.6
GOODING	**25**	**1,461**	**5,609***	**48.2**	**100.0**
019 AMER BAPT USA	1	75	98*	.8	1.7
053 ASSEMB OF GOD	1	39	103	.9	1.8
081 CATHOLIC	2	NA	911	7.8	16.2
081d *LATIN*	*2*	*NA*	*911*	*7.8*	*16.2*
097 CHR CHS&CHS CR	1	165	216*	1.9	3.9
151 L-D SAINTS	7	NA	2,580	22.2	46.0
165 CH OF NAZARENE	1	82	125	1.1	2.2
167 CHS OF CHRIST	2	68	100	.9	1.8
193 EPISCOPAL	1	34	64	.6	1.1
221 FREE METHODIST	1	9	35	.3	.6
283 LUTH—MO SYNOD	2	172	235	2.0	4.2
355 PRESB CH (USA)	1	114	149*	1.3	2.7

NA–Not applicable NR–Not reported *Total adherents estimated from known number of communicant, confirmed, full members. - Represents a percent less than 0.1. Percentages may not total due to rounding.
[1]See Appendix E [2]See Appendix F [3]See Appendix G Lines in *italic* represent a breakdown of Catholic rites or Friends affiliations. They are included in their respective denominational total.

Table 4. Churches and Church Membership by County and Denomination: 1990

County and Denomination	Number of churches	Communicant, confirmed, full members	Total adherents		
			Number	Percent of total population	Percent of total adherents
371 REF CH IN AM	1	56	147	1.3	2.6
419 SO BAPT CONV	1	149	195*	1.7	3.5
449 UN METHODIST	3	498	651*	5.6	11.6
IDAHO	**40**	**1,359**	**4,658***	**33.8**	**100.0**
019 AMER BAPT USA	1	95	121*	.9	2.6
053 ASSEMB OF GOD	3	149	263	1.9	5.6
081 CATHOLIC	8	NA	2,101	15.2	45.1
081d LATIN	8	NA	2,101	15.2	45.1
089 CHR & MISS AL	1	0	18	.1	.4
105 CHRISTIAN REF	1	76	107	.8	2.3
127 CH GOD (CLEVE)	2	25	32*	.2	.7
151 L-D SAINTS	3	NA	646	4.7	13.9
165 CH OF NAZARENE	2	164	220	1.6	4.7
167 CHS OF CHRIST	1	10	13	.1	.3
193 EPISCOPAL	1	21	21	.2	.5
226 FRIENDS-USA	1	32	59	.4	1.3
226b EFI	1	32	59	.4	1.3
259 IFCA	2	NR	NR	-	-
283 LUTH—MO SYNOD	1	107	124	.9	2.7
339 PENT CH OF GOD	2	70	154	1.1	3.3
355 PRESB CH (USA)	2	74	94*	.7	2.0
413 S.D.A.	1	20	26*	.2	.6
419 SO BAPT CONV	6	365	466*	3.4	10.0
449 UN METHODIST	2	151	193*	1.4	4.1
JEFFERSON	**35**	**284**	**12,162***	**73.5**	**100.0**
019 AMER BAPT USA	1	58	85*	.5	.7
081 CATHOLIC	3	NA	160	1.0	1.3
081d LATIN	3	NA	160	1.0	1.3
151 L-D SAINTS	28	NA	11,583	70.0	95.2
223 FREE WILL BAPT	1	120	176*	1.1	1.4
283 LUTH—MO SYNOD	1	46	70	.4	.6
355 PRESB CH (USA)	1	60	88*	.5	.7
JEROME	**25**	**1,858**	**8,286***	**54.7**	**100.0**
019 AMER BAPT USA	1	230	309*	2.0	3.7
053 ASSEMB OF GOD	2	154	256	1.7	3.1
081 CATHOLIC	1	NA	2,114	14.0	25.5
081d LATIN	1	NA	2,114	14.0	25.5
093 CHR CH (DISC)	1	79	145	1.0	1.7
123 CH GOD (ANDER)	1	65	130	.9	1.6
151 L-D SAINTS	7	NA	3,378	22.3	40.8
165 CH OF NAZARENE	1	119	263	1.7	3.2
167 CHS OF CHRIST	2	80	103	.7	1.2
193 EPISCOPAL	1	36	47	.3	.6
203 EVAN FREE CH	1	50	140	.9	1.7
223 FREE WILL BAPT	1	49	66*	.4	.8
283 LUTH—MO SYNOD	2	465	622	4.1	7.5
355 PRESB CH (USA)	2	295	396*	2.6	4.8
413 S.D.A.	1	9	12*	.1	.1
449 UN METHODIST	1	227	305*	2.0	3.7
KOOTENAI	**66**	**9,516**	**22,346***	**32.0**	**100.0**
019 AMER BAPT USA	2	324	412*	.6	1.8
053 ASSEMB OF GOD	4	639	1,171	1.7	5.2
057 BAPT GEN CONF	1	691	879*	1.3	3.9
081 CATHOLIC	5	NA	4,644	6.7	20.8
081d LATIN	5	NA	4,644	6.7	20.8
093 CHR CH (DISC)	1	67	130	.2	.6
111 CH CR,SCIENTST	1	NR	NR	-	-
123 CH GOD (ANDER)	2	40	55	.1	.2
127 CH GOD (CLEVE)	1	27	34*	-	.2
151 L-D SAINTS	8	NA	3,552	5.1	15.9
165 CH OF NAZARENE	2	257	384	.6	1.7
167 CHS OF CHRIST	2	332	499	.7	2.2
193 EPISCOPAL	1	306	418	.6	1.9
207 E.L.C.A.	4	1,348	1,901	2.7	8.5
221 FREE METHODIST	1	32	80	.1	.4
226 FRIENDS-USA	3	283	669	1.0	3.0
226b EFI	3	283	669	1.0	3.0
263 INT FOURSQ GOS	2	72	92*	.1	.4
283 LUTH—MO SYNOD	3	1,476	1,961	2.8	8.8
285 MENNONITE CH	1	12	33	-	.1
339 PENT CH OF GOD	3	92	194	.3	.9
353 CHR BRETHREN	1	50	93	.1	.4
355 PRESB CH (USA)	4	848	1,079*	1.5	4.8
413 S.D.A.	3	691	879*	1.3	3.9
419 SO BAPT CONV	5	1,151	1,464*	2.1	6.6
449 UN METHODIST	3	718	913*	1.3	4.1
467 WESLEYAN	2	60	160	.2	.7
499 INDEP.NON-CHAR[3]	1	NA	650	.9	2.9
LATAH	**44**	**4,256**	**9,930***	**32.4**	**100.0**
019 AMER BAPT USA	1	202	248*	.8	2.5

County and Denomination	Number of churches	Communicant, confirmed, full members	Total adherents		
			Number	Percent of total population	Percent of total adherents
053 ASSEMB OF GOD	2	73	175	.6	1.8
081 CATHOLIC	5	NA	2,225	7.3	22.4
081d LATIN	5	NA	2,225	7.3	22.4
093 CHR CH (DISC)	2	240	338	1.1	3.4
111 CH CR,SCIENTST	1	NR	NR	-	-
123 CH GOD (ANDER)	1	31	31	.1	.3
151 L-D SAINTS	6	NA	1,768	5.8	17.8
165 CH OF NAZARENE	4	590	1,168	3.8	11.8
167 CHS OF CHRIST	1	15	25	.1	.3
193 EPISCOPAL	1	152	203	.7	2.0
207 E.L.C.A.	7	1,193	1,564	5.1	15.8
226 FRIENDS-USA	1	8	20	.1	.2
226f INDEPENDNT	1	8	20	.1	.2
263 INT FOURSQ GOS	1	0	0*	-	-
355 PRESB CH (USA)	3	433	531*	1.7	5.3
413 S.D.A.	4	365	448*	1.5	4.5
419 SO BAPT CONV	1	353	433*	1.4	4.4
435 UNITARIAN-UNIV	1	85	120	.4	1.2
449 UN METHODIST	2	516	633*	2.1	6.4
LEMHI	**15**	**746**	**2,782***	**40.3**	**100.0**
053 ASSEMB OF GOD	1	26	35	.5	1.3
081 CATHOLIC	2	NA	352	5.1	12.7
081d LATIN	2	NA	352	5.1	12.7
151 L-D SAINTS	4	NA	1,444	20.9	51.9
167 CHS OF CHRIST	1	11	15	.2	.5
193 EPISCOPAL	1	74	119	1.7	4.3
263 INT FOURSQ GOS	1	156	199*	2.9	7.2
283 LUTH—MO SYNOD	1	121	160	2.3	5.8
355 PRESB CH (USA)	1	38	49*	.7	1.8
419 SO BAPT CONV	1	140	179*	2.6	6.4
449 UN METHODIST	2	180	230*	3.3	8.3
LEWIS	**19**	**738**	**1,725***	**49.1**	**100.0**
053 ASSEMB OF GOD	1	26	35	1.0	2.0
081 CATHOLIC	3	NA	649	18.5	37.6
081d LATIN	3	NA	649	18.5	37.6
093 CHR CH (DISC)	2	138	203	5.8	11.8
157 CH OF BRETHREN	1	8	10*	.3	.6
167 CHS OF CHRIST	1	20	25	.7	1.4
179 CONSRV BAPT	1	NR	NR	-	-
207 E.L.C.A.	2	133	172	4.9	10.0
355 PRESB CH (USA)	5	217	279*	7.9	16.2
413 S.D.A.	1	62	80*	2.3	4.6
419 SO BAPT CONV	1	87	112*	3.2	6.5
449 UN METHODIST	1	47	60*	1.7	3.5
496 JEWISH EST[1]	0	NA	100	2.8	5.8
LINCOLN	**12**	**432**	**1,815***	**54.9**	**100.0**
019 AMER BAPT USA	1	53	70*	2.1	3.9
053 ASSEMB OF GOD	2	105	155	4.7	8.5
081 CATHOLIC	1	NA	285	8.6	15.7
081d LATIN	1	NA	285	8.6	15.7
151 L-D SAINTS	4	NA	956	28.9	52.7
193 EPISCOPAL	1	49	50	1.5	2.8
413 S.D.A.	1	112	149*	4.5	8.2
449 UN METHODIST	2	113	150*	4.5	8.3
MADISON	**71**	**84**	**21,720***	**91.7**	**100.0**
081 CATHOLIC	1	NA	40	.2	.2
081d LATIN	1	NA	40	.2	.2
151 L-D SAINTS	68	NA	21,567	91.1	99.3
263 INT FOURSQ GOS	1	32	43*	.2	.2
355 PRESB CH (USA)	1	52	70*	.3	.3
MINIDOKA	**36**	**2,068**	**12,441***	**64.3**	**100.0**
019 AMER BAPT USA	1	56	77*	.4	.6
053 ASSEMB OF GOD	2	89	191	1.0	1.5
081 CATHOLIC	1	NA	2,050	10.6	16.5
081d LATIN	1	NA	2,050	10.6	16.5
127 CH GOD (CLEVE)	1	26	36*	.2	.3
151 L-D SAINTS	18	NA	7,380	38.1	59.3
165 CH OF NAZARENE	1	61	62	.3	.5
167 CHS OF CHRIST	1	75	97	.5	.8
181 CONSRV CONGR	1	280	386*	2.0	3.1
193 EPISCOPAL	1	70	123	.6	1.0
223 FREE WILL BAPT	1	81	112*	.6	.9
263 INT FOURSQ GOS	1	49	68*	.4	.5
283 LUTH—MO SYNOD	1	338	559	2.9	4.5
313 N AM BAPT CONF	1	266	367*	1.9	2.9
329 OPEN BIBLE STD	2	NR	NR	-	-
419 SO BAPT CONV	1	111	153*	.8	1.2
449 UN METHODIST	2	566	780*	4.0	6.3

NA–Not applicable   NR–Not reported   *Total adherents estimated from known number of communicant, confirmed, full members.   - Represents a percent less than 0.1.   Percentages may not total due to rounding.
[1]See Appendix E   [2]See Appendix F   [3]See Appendix G   Lines in *italic* represent a breakdown of Catholic rites or Friends affiliations. They are included in their respective denominational total.

Table 4. Churches and Church Membership by County and Denomination: 1990

County and Denomination		Number of churches	Communicant, confirmed, full members	Total adherents		
				Number	Percent of total population	Percent of total adherents
NEZ PERCE		**40**	**4,815**	**12,184***	**36.1**	**100.0**
001	ADVENT CHR CH	1	33	41*	.1	.3
019	AMER BAPT USA	1	91	113*	.3	.9
053	ASSEMB OF GOD	3	596	1,490	4.4	12.2
081	CATHOLIC	4	NA	2,947	8.7	24.2
081d	LATIN	4	NA	2,947	8.7	24.2
089	CHR & MISS AL	1	76	155	.5	1.3
097	CHR CHS&CHS CR	1	118	147*	.4	1.2
111	CH CR,SCIENTST	1	NR	NR	-	-
123	CH GOD (ANDER)	1	20	40	.1	.3
145	CH GOD PROPHCY	1	25	31*	.1	.3
151	L-D SAINTS	3	NA	1,602	4.7	13.1
165	CH OF NAZARENE	2	463	853	2.5	7.0
167	CHS OF CHRIST	1	95	145	.4	1.2
193	EPISCOPAL	1	259	314	.9	2.6
207	E.L.C.A.	4	997	1,230	3.6	10.1
283	LUTH—MO SYNOD	1	109	144	.4	1.2
329	OPEN BIBLE STD	1	NR	NR	-	-
339	PENT CH OF GOD	1	34	77	.2	.6
355	PRESB CH (USA)	3	334	415*	1.2	3.4
403	SALVATION ARMY	1	68	78	.2	.6
413	S.D.A.	1	241	300*	.9	2.5
419	SO BAPT CONV	1	427	531*	1.6	4.4
435	UNITARIAN-UNIV	1	2	2	-	-
443	UN C OF CHRIST	1	73	91*	.3	.7
449	UN METHODIST	3	754	938*	2.8	7.7
498	INDEP.CHARIS.[3]	1	NA	500	1.5	4.1
ONEIDA		**9**	**45**	**2,952***	**84.5**	**100.0**
081	CATHOLIC	1	NA	20	.6	.7
081d	LATIN	1	NA	20	.6	.7
151	L-D SAINTS	7	NA	2,868	82.1	97.2
355	PRESB CH (USA)	1	45	64*	1.8	2.2
OWYHEE		**20**	**545**	**3,319***	**39.5**	**100.0**
053	ASSEMB OF GOD	2	103	235	2.8	7.1
081	CATHOLIC	6	NA	1,180	14.1	35.6
081d	LATIN	6	NA	1,180	14.1	35.6
093	CHR CH (DISC)	1	32	52	.6	1.6
151	L-D SAINTS	3	NA	1,140	13.6	34.3
165	CH OF NAZARENE	2	118	277	3.3	8.3
167	CHS OF CHRIST	1	20	30	.4	.9
226	FRIENDS-USA	2	116	193	2.3	5.8
226b	EFI	2	116	193	2.3	5.8
283	LUTH—MO SYNOD	1	62	81	1.0	2.4
285	MENNONITE CH	1	33	50	.6	1.5
355	PRESB CH (USA)	1	61	81*	1.0	2.4
PAYETTE		**33**	**2,688**	**7,087***	**43.1**	**100.0**
019	AMER BAPT USA	2	709	932*	5.7	13.2
053	ASSEMB OF GOD	3	276	498	3.0	7.0
081	CATHOLIC	2	NA	1,211	7.4	17.1
081d	LATIN	2	NA	1,211	7.4	17.1
111	CH CR,SCIENTST	1	NR	NR	-	-
143	CG IN CR(MENN)	1	18	24*	.1	.3
151	L-D SAINTS	6	NA	2,099	12.8	29.6
157	CH OF BRETHREN	1	145	191*	1.2	2.7
165	CH OF NAZARENE	2	174	271	1.6	3.8
167	CHS OF CHRIST	2	95	121	.7	1.7
179	CONSRV BAPT	1	NR	NR	-	-
193	EPISCOPAL	1	20	54	.3	.8
221	FREE METHODIST	1	82	118	.7	1.7
283	LUTH—MO SYNOD	1	93	123	.7	1.7
339	PENT CH OF GOD	1	35	77	.5	1.1
413	S.D.A.	3	369	485*	3.0	6.8
419	SO BAPT CONV	1	127	167*	1.0	2.4
443	UN C OF CHRIST	2	143	188*	1.1	2.7
449	UN METHODIST	2	402	528*	3.2	7.5
POWER		**14**	**708**	**4,215***	**59.5**	**100.0**
053	ASSEMB OF GOD	1	134	300	4.2	7.1
081	CATHOLIC	1	NA	750	10.6	17.8
081d	LATIN	1	NA	750	10.6	17.8
151	L-D SAINTS	6	NA	2,384	33.6	56.6
193	EPISCOPAL	1	5	7	.1	.2
207	E.L.C.A.	1	368	499	7.0	11.8
419	SO BAPT CONV	1	39	53*	.7	1.3
443	UN C OF CHRIST	2	97	133*	1.9	3.2
449	UN METHODIST	1	65	89*	1.3	2.1
SHOSHONE		**26**	**2,104**	**5,375***	**38.6**	**100.0**
019	AMER BAPT USA	1	55	68*	.5	1.3
053	ASSEMB OF GOD	3	178	323	2.3	6.0
081	CATHOLIC	3	NA	1,877	13.5	34.9
081d	LATIN	3	NA	1,877	13.5	34.9
127	CH GOD (CLEVE)	1	25	31*	.2	.6
151	L-D SAINTS	2	NA	565	4.1	10.5
165	CH OF NAZARENE	1	59	115	.8	2.1
167	CHS OF CHRIST	1	80	120	.9	2.2
193	EPISCOPAL	2	76	107	.8	2.0
203	EVAN FREE CH	1	25	35	.3	.7
207	E.L.C.A.	2	458	690	5.0	12.8
283	LUTH—MO SYNOD	2	180	244	1.8	4.5
413	S.D.A.	1	87	108*	.8	2.0
419	SO BAPT CONV	2	448	555*	4.0	10.3
443	UN C OF CHRIST	2	267	331*	2.4	6.2
449	UN METHODIST	2	166	206*	1.5	3.8
TETON		**8**	**0**	**2,492***	**72.5**	**100.0**
081	CATHOLIC	1	NA	30	.9	1.2
081d	LATIN	1	NA	30	.9	1.2
151	L-D SAINTS	7	NA	2,462	71.6	98.8
TWIN FALLS		**83**	**9,163**	**26,979***	**50.4**	**100.0**
019	AMER BAPT USA	5	1,463	1,914*	3.6	7.1
053	ASSEMB OF GOD	6	524	985	1.8	3.7
081	CATHOLIC	3	NA	3,625	6.8	13.4
081d	LATIN	3	NA	3,625	6.8	13.4
089	CHR & MISS AL	1	20	110	.2	.4
093	CHR CH (DISC)	1	107	125	.2	.5
097	CHR CHS&CHS CR	2	524	685*	1.3	2.5
111	CH CR,SCIENTST	1	NR	NR	-	-
143	CG IN CR(MENN)	1	156	204*	.4	.8
145	CH GOD PROPHCY	1	25	33*	.1	.1
151	L-D SAINTS	25	NA	10,918	20.4	40.5
157	CH OF BRETHREN	1	42	55*	.1	.2
165	CH OF NAZARENE	4	653	803	1.5	3.0
167	CHS OF CHRIST	2	158	206	.4	.8
179	CONSRV BAPT	1	NR	NR	-	-
193	EPISCOPAL	2	347	409	.8	1.5
207	E.L.C.A.	1	237	304	.6	1.1
223	FREE WILL BAPT	1	85	111*	.2	.4
263	INT FOURSQ GOS	1	25	33*	.1	.1
283	LUTH—MO SYNOD	5	1,516	1,990	3.7	7.4
285	MENNONITE CH	1	64	90	.2	.3
291	MISSIONARY CH	1	56	62	.1	.2
355	PRESB CH (USA)	3	578	756*	1.4	2.8
371	REF CH IN AM	1	393	730	1.4	2.7
403	SALVATION ARMY	1	64	67	.1	.2
413	S.D.A.	2	274	358*	.7	1.3
419	SO BAPT CONV	3	238	311*	.6	1.2
438	UN BRETH IN CR	1	51	51	.1	.2
449	UN METHODIST	6	1,563	2,044*	3.8	7.6
VALLEY		**18**	**706**	**1,792***	**29.3**	**100.0**
053	ASSEMB OF GOD	2	125	158	2.6	8.8
081	CATHOLIC	3	NA	200	3.3	11.2
081d	LATIN	3	NA	200	3.3	11.2
151	L-D SAINTS	2	NA	584	9.6	32.6
165	CH OF NAZARENE	1	99	151	2.5	8.4
167	CHS OF CHRIST	1	15	20	.3	1.1
179	CONSRV BAPT	1	NR	NR	-	-
193	EPISCOPAL	1	50	69	1.1	3.9
226	FRIENDS-USA	1	15	35	.6	2.0
226b	EFI	1	15	35	.6	2.0
263	INT FOURSQ GOS	1	12	15*	.2	.8
283	LUTH—MO SYNOD	2	188	301	4.9	16.8
413	S.D.A.	1	87	111*	1.8	6.2
419	SO BAPT CONV	1	52	67*	1.1	3.7
443	UN C OF CHRIST	1	63	81*	1.3	4.5
WASHINGTON		**27**	**1,654**	**4,622***	**54.1**	**100.0**
001	ADVENT CHR CH	1	11	14*	.2	.3
019	AMER BAPT USA	3	380	488*	5.7	10.6
053	ASSEMB OF GOD	2	214	327	3.8	7.1
081	CATHOLIC	2	NA	1,000	11.7	21.6
081d	LATIN	2	NA	1,000	11.7	21.6
151	L-D SAINTS	4	NA	1,352	15.8	29.3
165	CH OF NAZARENE	1	79	160	1.9	3.5
167	CHS OF CHRIST	2	66	91	1.1	2.0
179	CONSRV BAPT	1	NR	NR	-	-
193	EPISCOPAL	1	40	73	.9	1.6
263	INT FOURSQ GOS	1	18	23*	.3	.5
283	LUTH—MO SYNOD	1	30	40	.5	.9
339	PENT CH OF GOD	1	0	6	.1	.1
355	PRESB CH (USA)	1	136	175*	2.0	3.8
413	S.D.A.	3	254	326*	3.8	7.1
419	SO BAPT CONV	1	43	55*	.6	1.2
436	UNITED BAPT	1	5	6*	.1	.1
449	UN METHODIST	1	378	486*	5.7	10.5

NA–Not applicable   NR–Not reported   *Total adherents estimated from known number of communicant, confirmed, full members.   - Represents a percent less than 0.1.   Percentages may not total due to rounding.

[1]See Appendix E   [2]See Appendix F   [3]See Appendix G   Lines in italic represent a breakdown of Catholic rites or Friends affiliations. They are included in their respective denominational total.

Table 4. Churches and Church Membership by County and Denomination: 1990

County and Denomination	Number of churches	Communicant, confirmed, full members	Total adherents Number	Percent of total population	Percent of total adherents
ILLINOIS					
THE STATE.....	9,799	2,175,908	6,848,422*	59.9	100.0
ADAMS	**96**	**18,967**	**43,111***	**65.2**	**100.0**
019 AMER BAPT USA	4	1,069	1,343*	2.0	3.1
053 ASSEMB OF GOD	3	667	921	1.4	2.1
057 BAPT GEN CONF	1	53	67*	.1	.2
081 CATHOLIC	12	NA	17,492	26.5	40.6
081d LATIN	12	NA	17,492	26.5	40.6
093 CHR CH (DISC)	6	728	1,411	2.1	3.3
097 CHR CHS&CHS CR	10	2,857	3,589*	5.4	8.3
111 CH CR,SCIENTST	1	NR	NR	-	-
151 L-D SAINTS	1	NA	422	.6	1.0
157 CH OF BRETHREN	1	61	77*	.1	.2
165 CH OF NAZARENE	1	79	177	.3	.4
167 CHS OF CHRIST	2	96	133	.2	.3
175 CONGR CHR CHS	1	325	408*	.6	.9
207 E.L.C.A.	8	2,125	2,677	4.1	6.2
221 FREE METHODIST	1	18	36	.1	.1
226 FRIENDS-USA	1	14	18*	-	-
226c FGC	1	14	18*	-	-
283 LUTH—MO SYNOD	5	2,011	2,701	4.1	6.3
339 PENT CH OF GOD	1	34	76	.1	.2
355 PRESB CH (USA)	4	882	1,108*	1.7	2.6
403 SALVATION ARMY	1	367	425	.6	1.0
413 S.D.A.	1	84	106*	.2	.2
419 SO BAPT CONV	3	512	643*	1.0	1.5
435 UNITARIAN-UNIV	1	62	80	.1	.2
443 UN C OF CHRIST	7	2,922	3,670*	5.6	8.5
449 UN METHODIST	18	3,663	4,601*	7.0	10.7
496 JEWISH EST[1]	1	NA	125	.2	.3
497 BLACK BAPT EST[2]	NA	338	425*	.6	1.0
499 INDEP.NON-CHAR[3]	1	NA	380	.6	.9
ALEXANDER	**33**	**4,218**	**6,141***	**57.8**	**100.0**
019 AMER BAPT USA	1	325	420*	4.0	6.8
053 ASSEMB OF GOD	3	100	154	1.4	2.5
081 CATHOLIC	1	NA	581	5.5	9.5
081d LATIN	1	NA	581	5.5	9.5
093 CHR CH (DISC)	1	38	41	.4	.7
097 CHR CHS&CHS CR	1	87	112*	1.1	1.8
167 CHS OF CHRIST	1	23	30	.3	.5
193 EPISCOPAL	1	106	227	2.1	3.7
207 E.L.C.A.	1	59	80	.8	1.3
223 FREE WILL BAPT	2	345	446*	4.2	7.3
259 IFCA	1	NR	NR	-	-
355 PRESB CH (USA)	1	41	53*	.5	.9
413 S.D.A.	1	22	28*	.3	.5
419 SO BAPT CONV	9	1,795	2,320*	21.8	37.8
443 UN C OF CHRIST	1	15	19*	.2	.3
449 UN METHODIST	7	292	377*	3.5	6.1
496 JEWISH EST[1]	1	NA	0	-	-
497 BLACK BAPT EST[2]	NA	970	1,253*	11.8	20.4
BOND	**43**	**5,239**	**7,476***	**49.9**	**100.0**
019 AMER BAPT USA	1	359	443*	3.0	5.9
053 ASSEMB OF GOD	3	170	322	2.1	4.3
081 CATHOLIC	3	NA	766	5.1	10.2
081d LATIN	3	NA	766	5.1	10.2
097 CHR CHS&CHS CR	5	1,157	1,427*	9.5	19.1
123 CH GOD (ANDER)	1	18	32	.2	.4
151 L-D SAINTS	1	NA	79	.5	1.1
157 CH OF BRETHREN	1	15	19*	.1	.3
167 CHS OF CHRIST	1	88	95	.6	1.3
185 CUMBER PRESB	2	65	65	.4	.9
221 FREE METHODIST	2	423	563	3.8	7.5
283 LUTH—MO SYNOD	1	119	145	1.0	1.9
339 PENT CH OF GOD	1	34	77	.5	1.0
355 PRESB CH (USA)	3	414	511*	3.4	6.8
419 SO BAPT CONV	11	1,556	1,919*	12.8	25.7
443 UN C OF CHRIST	1	68	84*	.6	1.1
449 UN METHODIST	6	753	929*	6.2	12.4
BOONE	**25**	**6,283**	**11,628***	**37.7**	**100.0**
019 AMER BAPT USA	1	316	404*	1.3	3.5
053 ASSEMB OF GOD	1	30	50	.2	.4
081 CATHOLIC	1	NA	3,311	10.7	28.5
081d LATIN	1	NA	3,311	10.7	28.5
111 CH CR,SCIENTST	1	NR	NR	-	-
165 CH OF NAZARENE	1	0	0	-	-
167 CHS OF CHRIST	1	50	80	.3	.7
175 CONGR CHR CHS	1	50	64*	.2	.6
193 EPISCOPAL	1	124	200	.6	1.7
207 E.L.C.A.	2	1,031	1,349	4.4	11.6

County and Denomination	Number of churches	Communicant, confirmed, full members	Total adherents Number	Percent of total population	Percent of total adherents
283 LUTH—MO SYNOD	1	1,355	1,816	5.9	15.6
329 OPEN BIBLE STD	1	NR	NR	-	-
355 PRESB CH (USA)	2	851	1,088*	3.5	9.4
375 REF EPISCOPAL	1	5	5	-	-
403 SALVATION ARMY	1	54	58	.2	.5
419 SO BAPT CONV	1	151	193*	.6	1.7
443 UN C OF CHRIST	2	483	618*	2.0	5.3
449 UN METHODIST	5	1,672	2,138*	6.9	18.4
469 WELS	1	111	145	.5	1.2
496 JEWISH EST[1]	0	NA	109	.4	.9
BROWN	**13**	**1,694**	**3,151***	**54.0**	**100.0**
019 AMER BAPT USA	3	531	643*	11.0	20.4
081 CATHOLIC	1	NA	900	15.4	28.6
081d LATIN	1	NA	900	15.4	28.6
093 CHR CH (DISC)	2	174	393	6.7	12.5
097 CHR CHS&CHS CR	2	325	393*	6.7	12.5
121 CH GOD (ABR)	1	77	93*	1.6	3.0
165 CH OF NAZARENE	1	69	97	1.7	3.1
283 LUTH—MO SYNOD	1	62	81	1.4	2.6
355 PRESB CH (USA)	1	83	100*	1.7	3.2
449 UN METHODIST	1	267	323*	5.5	10.3
497 BLACK BAPT EST[2]	NA	106	128*	2.2	4.1
BUREAU	**78**	**9,220**	**23,000***	**64.4**	**100.0**
019 AMER BAPT USA	5	663	833*	2.3	3.6
053 ASSEMB OF GOD	2	14	24	.1	.1
081 CATHOLIC	17	NA	10,832	30.4	47.1
081d LATIN	17	NA	10,832	30.4	47.1
093 CHR CH (DISC)	3	421	622	1.7	2.7
111 CH CR,SCIENTST	1	NR	NR	-	-
145 CH GOD PROPHCY	1	38	48*	.1	.2
151 L-D SAINTS	1	NA	159	.4	.7
165 CH OF NAZARENE	1	54	90	.3	.4
167 CHS OF CHRIST	1	18	24	.1	.1
171 CH GOD-GEN CON	1	204	256*	.7	1.1
175 CONGR CHR CHS	3	161	202*	.6	.9
207 E.L.C.A.	6	2,346	3,062	8.6	13.3
259 IFCA	1	NR	NR	-	-
283 LUTH—MO SYNOD	1	110	138	.4	.6
285 MENNONITE CH	2	125	255	.7	1.1
287 MENN GEN CONF	1	17	32	.1	.1
291 MISSIONARY CH	1	66	70	.2	.3
353 CHR BRETHREN	2	220	320	.9	1.4
355 PRESB CH (USA)	2	259	325*	.9	1.4
413 S.D.A.	1	12	15*	-	.1
419 SO BAPT CONV	1	157	197*	.6	.9
438 UN BRETH IN CR	1	20	20	.1	.1
443 UN C OF CHRIST	8	1,443	1,813*	5.1	7.9
449 UN METHODIST	13	2,788	3,503*	9.8	15.2
467 WESLEYAN	2	84	160	.4	.7
CALHOUN	**23**	**1,003**	**3,862***	**72.6**	**100.0**
081 CATHOLIC	7	NA	2,617	49.2	67.8
081d LATIN	7	NA	2,617	49.2	67.8
165 CH OF NAZARENE	2	34	38	.7	1.0
167 CHS OF CHRIST	5	259	330	6.2	8.5
207 E.L.C.A.	1	86	111	2.1	2.9
283 LUTH—MO SYNOD	3	384	471	8.9	12.2
355 PRESB CH (USA)	2	188	231*	4.3	6.0
449 UN METHODIST	3	52	64*	1.2	1.7
CARROLL	**44**	**6,608**	**10,183***	**60.6**	**100.0**
019 AMER BAPT USA	2	239	296*	1.8	2.9
053 ASSEMB OF GOD	2	81	220	1.3	2.2
071 BRETHREN (ASH)	2	469	581*	3.5	5.7
081 CATHOLIC	3	NA	1,877	11.2	18.4
081d LATIN	3	NA	1,877	11.2	18.4
097 CHR CHS&CHS CR	1	40	50*	.3	.5
111 CH CR,SCIENTST	1	NR	NR	-	-
157 CH OF BRETHREN	3	414	513*	3.1	5.0
171 CH GOD-GEN CON	3	418	518*	3.1	5.1
175 CONGR CHR CHS	1	33	41*	.2	.4
193 EPISCOPAL	1	12	15	.1	.1
203 EVAN FREE CH	1	44	45	.3	.4
207 E.L.C.A.	4	1,184	1,481	8.8	14.5
355 PRESB CH (USA)	2	263	326*	1.9	3.2
371 REF CH IN AM	1	49	97	.6	1.0
413 S.D.A.	1	26	32*	.2	.3
419 SO BAPT CONV	1	112	139*	.8	1.4
438 UN BRETH IN CR	2	50	50	.3	.5
443 UN C OF CHRIST	1	254	315*	1.9	3.1
449 UN METHODIST	10	2,555	3,167*	18.8	31.1
469 WELS	2	365	420	2.5	4.1

NA–Not applicable   NR–Not reported   *Total adherents estimated from known number of communicant, confirmed, full members.   - Represents a percent less than 0.1.   Percentages may not total due to rounding.
[1]See Appendix E   [2]See Appendix F   [3]See Appendix G   Lines in *italic* represent a breakdown of Catholic rites or Friends affiliations. They are included in their respective denominational total.

115

Table 4. Churches and Church Membership by County and Denomination: 1990

County and Denomination	Number of churches	Communicant, confirmed, full members	Total adherents Number	Percent of total population	Percent of total adherents
CASS	36	5,758	8,784*	65.4	100.0
019 AMER BAPT USA	1	214	268*	2.0	3.1
053 ASSEMB OF GOD	2	96	196	1.5	2.2
081 CATHOLIC	5	NA	1,252	9.3	14.3
081d *LATIN*	5	*NA*	*1,252*	*9.3*	*14.3*
093 CHR CH (DISC)	2	170	288	2.1	3.3
097 CHR CHS&CHS CR	2	500	626*	4.7	7.1
123 CH GOD (ANDER)	1	30	55	.4	.6
165 CH OF NAZARENE	2	222	326	2.4	3.7
167 CHS OF CHRIST	1	16	25	.2	.3
185 CUMBER PRESB	1	104	118	.9	1.3
207 E.L.C.A.	4	1,215	1,579	11.8	18.0
283 LUTH—MO SYNOD	4	1,021	1,336	9.9	15.2
355 PRESB CH (USA)	2	248	310*	2.3	3.5
419 SO BAPT CONV	4	590	738*	5.5	8.4
443 UN C OF CHRIST	1	110	138*	1.0	1.6
449 UN METHODIST	4	1,222	1,529*	11.4	17.4
CHAMPAIGN	161	37,391	70,527*	40.8	100.0
019 AMER BAPT USA	5	1,229	1,494*	.9	2.1
040 AP CHR CH-AMER	1	46	81	-	.1
053 ASSEMB OF GOD	3	808	1,123	.6	1.6
081 CATHOLIC	17	NA	18,371	10.6	26.0
081d *LATIN*	17	*NA*	*18,371*	*10.6*	*26.0*
089 CHR & MISS AL	1	41	71	-	.1
093 CHR CH (DISC)	4	826	1,369	.8	1.9
097 CHR CHS&CHS CR	13	2,758	3,352*	1.9	4.8
105 CHRISTIAN REF	1	76	117	.1	.2
111 CH CR,SCIENTST	2	NR	NR	-	-
123 CH GOD (ANDER)	1	31	31	-	-
127 CH GOD (CLEVE)	2	330	401*	.2	.6
151 L-D SAINTS	3	NA	1,037	.6	1.5
157 CH OF BRETHREN	1	65	79*	-	.1
165 CH OF NAZARENE	8	613	933	.5	1.3
167 CHS OF CHRIST	6	615	835	.5	1.2
179 CONSRV BAPT	1	NR	NR	-	-
193 EPISCOPAL	3	707	1,074	.6	1.5
203 EVAN FREE CH	1	38	95	.1	.1
207 E.L.C.A.	11	5,330	7,166	4.1	10.2
221 FREE METHODIST	2	174	177	.1	.3
226 FRIENDS-USA	1	73	89*	.1	.1
226c *FGC*	1	*73*	*89**	*.1*	*.1*
246 GREEK ORTHODOX	1	NR	NR	-	-
263 INT FOURSQ GOS	3	585	711*	.4	1.0
283 LUTH—MO SYNOD	6	2,673	3,605	2.1	5.1
285 MENNONITE CH	3	496	596	.3	.8
287 MENN GEN CONF	1	48	77	-	.1
353 CHR BRETHREN	1	150	200	.1	.3
355 PRESB CH (USA)	9	2,772	3,369*	1.9	4.8
361 PRIM BAPT ASCS	1	34	41*	-	.1
403 SALVATION ARMY	1	178	205	.1	.3
413 S.D.A.	2	147	179*	.1	.3
419 SO BAPT CONV	8	1,911	2,323*	1.3	3.3
435 UNITARIAN-UNIV	1	231	333	.2	.5
443 UN C OF CHRIST	3	1,139	1,384*	.8	2.0
449 UN METHODIST	29	9,066	11,019*	6.4	15.6
467 WESLEYAN	1	56	170	.1	.2
469 WELS	1	84	109	.1	.2
496 JEWISH EST[1]	1	NA	1,700	1.0	2.4
497 BLACK BAPT EST[2]	NA	4,061	4,936*	2.9	7.0
498 INDEP.CHARIS.[3]	1	NA	1,200	.7	1.7
499 INDEP.NON-CHAR[3]	1	NA	475	.3	.7
CHRISTIAN	64	10,069	20,146*	58.5	100.0
001 ADVENT CHR CH	1	31	39*	.1	.2
019 AMER BAPT USA	4	1,157	1,441*	4.2	7.2
053 ASSEMB OF GOD	4	241	315	.9	1.6
081 CATHOLIC	6	NA	6,604	19.2	32.8
081d *LATIN*	6	*NA*	*6,604*	*19.2*	*32.8*
093 CHR CH (DISC)	2	488	903	2.6	4.5
097 CHR CHS&CHS CR	7	1,270	1,582*	4.6	7.9
127 CH GOD (CLEVE)	1	194	242*	.7	1.2
165 CH OF NAZARENE	5	366	561	1.6	2.8
167 CHS OF CHRIST	2	68	87	.3	.4
171 CH GOD-GEN CON	1	130	162*	.5	.8
203 EVAN FREE CH	1	136	150	.4	.7
221 FREE METHODIST	2	74	75	.2	.4
283 LUTH—MO SYNOD	4	1,026	1,395	4.1	6.9
355 PRESB CH (USA)	5	917	1,142*	3.3	5.7
419 SO BAPT CONV	3	507	632*	1.8	3.1
443 UN C OF CHRIST	1	353	440*	1.3	2.2
449 UN METHODIST	14	3,111	3,876*	11.3	19.2
499 INDEP.NON-CHAR[3]	1	NA	500	1.5	2.5
CLARK	63	7,354	9,917*	62.3	100.0
081 CATHOLIC	2	NA	668	4.2	6.7
081d *LATIN*	2	*NA*	*668*	*4.2*	*6.7*
093 CHR CH (DISC)	1	225	294	1.8	3.0
097 CHR CHS&CHS CR	7	1,047	1,297*	8.1	13.1
111 CH CR,SCIENTST	1	NR	NR	-	-
121 CH GOD (ABR)	1	8	10*	.1	.1
165 CH OF NAZARENE	3	216	380	2.4	3.8
167 CHS OF CHRIST	4	236	306	1.9	3.1
171 CH GOD-GEN CON	5	438	543*	3.4	5.5
185 CUMBER PRESB	4	220	235	1.5	2.4
259 IFCA	1	NR	NR	-	-
283 LUTH—MO SYNOD	2	163	229	1.4	2.3
419 SO BAPT CONV	12	2,636	3,266*	20.5	32.9
443 UN C OF CHRIST	1	130	161*	1.0	1.6
449 UN METHODIST	16	1,994	2,470*	15.5	24.9
467 WESLEYAN	3	41	58	.4	.6
CLAY	47	6,454	9,487*	65.6	100.0
019 AMER BAPT USA	1	316	394*	2.7	4.2
053 ASSEMB OF GOD	1	60	141	1.0	1.5
081 CATHOLIC	2	NA	1,317	9.1	13.9
081d *LATIN*	2	*NA*	*1,317*	*9.1*	*13.9*
097 CHR CHS&CHS CR	14	2,386	2,978*	20.6	31.4
123 CH GOD (ANDER)	1	127	127	.9	1.3
127 CH GOD (CLEVE)	1	57	71*	.5	.7
145 CH GOD PROPHCY	1	38	47*	.3	.5
165 CH OF NAZARENE	1	134	277	1.9	2.9
167 CHS OF CHRIST	1	33	42	.3	.4
215 EVAN METH CH	1	15	19*	.1	.2
283 LUTH—MO SYNOD	1	177	191	1.3	2.0
355 PRESB CH (USA)	1	79	99*	.7	1.0
361 PRIM BAPT ASCS	1	22	27*	.2	.3
419 SO BAPT CONV	10	1,833	2,288*	15.8	24.1
443 UN C OF CHRIST	1	50	62*	.4	.7
449 UN METHODIST	9	1,127	1,407*	9.7	14.8
CLINTON	45	5,030	24,742*	72.9	100.0
053 ASSEMB OF GOD	1	12	31	.1	.1
081 CATHOLIC	14	NA	17,150	50.5	69.3
081d *LATIN*	14	*NA*	*17,150*	*50.5*	*69.3*
097 CHR CHS&CHS CR	1	70	89*	.3	.4
127 CH GOD (CLEVE)	1	29	37*	.1	.1
151 L-D SAINTS	1	NA	245	.7	1.0
165 CH OF NAZARENE	1	69	195	.6	.8
283 LUTH—MO SYNOD	4	1,117	1,522	4.5	6.2
313 N AM BAPT CONF	1	67	85*	.3	.3
413 S.D.A.	1	26	33*	.1	.1
419 SO BAPT CONV	4	1,152	1,462*	4.3	5.9
443 UN C OF CHRIST	5	1,036	1,315*	3.9	5.3
449 UN METHODIST	10	1,202	1,525*	4.5	6.2
496 JEWISH EST[1]	1	NA	736	2.2	3.0
497 BLACK BAPT EST[2]	NA	250	317*	.9	1.3
COLES	70	13,149	20,549*	39.8	100.0
019 AMER BAPT USA	4	1,526	1,826*	3.5	8.9
053 ASSEMB OF GOD	3	120	273	.5	1.3
081 CATHOLIC	2	NA	3,406	6.6	16.6
081d *LATIN*	2	*NA*	*3,406*	*6.6*	*16.6*
089 CHR & MISS AL	2	103	163	.3	.8
093 CHR CH (DISC)	3	1,278	1,822	3.5	8.9
097 CHR CHS&CHS CR	8	1,510	1,807*	3.5	8.8
111 CH CR,SCIENTST	1	NR	NR	-	-
123 CH GOD (ANDER)	1	98	209	.4	1.0
151 L-D SAINTS	1	NA	305	.6	1.5
165 CH OF NAZARENE	3	386	648	1.3	3.2
167 CHS OF CHRIST	4	163	215	.4	1.0
171 CH GOD-GEN CON	2	527	631*	1.2	3.1
185 CUMBER PRESB	1	142	142	.3	.7
193 EPISCOPAL	1	135	155	.3	.8
207 E.L.C.A.	1	95	128	.2	.6
221 FREE METHODIST	1	31	58	.1	.3
259 IFCA	1	NR	NR	-	-
283 LUTH—MO SYNOD	3	1,432	2,002	3.9	9.7
285 MENNONITE CH	1	63	65	.1	.3
355 PRESB CH (USA)	4	1,144	1,369*	2.7	6.7
403 SALVATION ARMY	1	100	107	.2	.5
413 S.D.A.	1	26	31*	.1	.2
419 SO BAPT CONV	6	1,433	1,715*	3.3	8.3
435 UNITARIAN-UNIV	1	8	8	-	-
449 UN METHODIST	11	2,618	3,133*	6.1	15.2
467 WESLEYAN	2	27	111	.2	.5
496 JEWISH EST[1]	1	NA	0	-	-
497 BLACK BAPT EST[2]	NA	184	220*	.4	1.1
COOK	2,181	647,322	3,229,739*	63.3	100.0
001 ADVENT CHR CH	2	242	302*	-	-
005 AME ZION	8	12,785	16,090	.3	.5

NA–Not applicable   NR–Not reported   *Total adherents estimated from known number of communicant, confirmed, full members.   - Represents a percent less than 0.1.   Percentages may not total due to rounding.

[1] See Appendix E   [2] See Appendix F   [3] See Appendix G   Lines in *italic* represent a breakdown of Catholic rites or Friends affiliations. They are included in their respective denominational total.

Table 4. Churches and Church Membership by County and Denomination: 1990

County and Denomination	Number of churches	Communicant, confirmed, full members	Total adherents		
			Number	Percent of total population	Percent of total adherents
009 ALBAN ORTH DIO	1	NR	NR	-	-
019 AMER BAPT USA	56	17,004	21,210*	.4	.7
022 EASTERN ORTH	1	242	242	-	-
040 AP CHR CH-AMER	1	122	217	-	-
049 ARMEN AP CH AM	1	400	3,000	.1	.1
053 ASSEMB OF GOD	71	9,673	15,886	.3	.5
057 BAPT GEN CONF	41	7,164	8,936*	.2	.3
059 BAPT MISS ASSN	1	37	46*	-	-
075 BRETHREN IN CR	1	0	0	-	-
080 BYELORSSN ORTH	1	NR	NR	-	-
081 CATHOLIC	308	NA	2,121,152	41.5	65.7
081b BYZAN RUTH	*1*	*NA*	*720*		
081c CHALDEAN	*2*	*NA*	*4,000*	*.1*	*.1*
081d LATIN	*298*	*NA*	*2,106,650*	*41.3*	*65.2*
081f MELKITE-GK	*1*	*NA*	*351*	-	-
081h UKRAINIAN	*6*	*NA*	*9,431*	*.2*	*.3*
089 CHR & MISS AL	23	2,053	2,734	.1	.1
093 CHR CH (DISC)	20	3,065	4,954	.1	.2
097 CHR CHS&CHS CR	24	3,356	4,186*	.1	.1
105 CHRISTIAN REF	35	7,991	12,298	.2	.4
111 CH CR,SCIENTST	38	NR	NR	-	-
123 CH GOD (ANDER)	17	2,512	2,616	.1	.1
127 CH GOD (CLEVE)	32	3,010	3,755*	.1	.1
133 CH GOD(7TH)DEN	3	167	245	-	-
145 CH GOD PROPHCY	6	233	291*	-	-
151 L-D SAINTS	17	NA	6,988	.1	.2
157 CH OF BRETHREN	5	437	545*	-	-
165 CH OF NAZARENE	39	2,992	3,881	.1	.1
167 CHS OF CHRIST	51	8,238	11,189	.2	.3
175 CONGR CHR CHS	7	1,469	1,832*	-	.1
176 CCC, NOT NAT'L	1	897	1,119*	-	-
179 CONSRV BAPT	18	NR	NR	-	-
185 CUMBER PRESB	2	74	82	-	-
193 EPISCOPAL	79	16,381	23,311	.5	.7
195 ESTONIAN ELC	1	140	175*	-	-
199 EVAN CONGR CH	1	54	94	-	-
203 EVAN FREE CH	28	3,082	5,039	.1	.2
207 E.L.C.A.	181	61,376	80,710	1.6	2.5
209 EVAN LUTH SYN	2	103	144	-	-
213 EVAN MENN INC	1	74	92*	-	-
221 FREE METHODIST	7	307	358	-	-
223 FREE WILL BAPT	2	81	101*	-	-
226 FRIENDS-USA	7	486	574*	-	-
226c FGC	*3*	*80*	*100**		
226d FGC & FUM	*2*	*268*	*302*		
226e FUM	*2*	*138*	*172**		
237 GC MENN BR CHS	1	20	25*	-	-
246 GREEK ORTHODOX	18	NR	NR	-	-
249 AP CATH ASSYR	2	5,380	25,937	.5	.8
259 IFCA	24	NR	NR	-	-
263 INT FOURSQ GOS	3	673	839*	-	-
274 LAT EVAN LUTH	2	666	764	-	-
283 LUTH—MO SYNOD	144	63,821	83,205	1.6	2.6
284 LUTH CH-AM ASC	1	126	163	-	-
285 MENNONITE CH	13	741	1,249	-	-
287 MENN GEN CONF	9	292	379	-	-
291 MISSIONARY CH	3	142	327	-	-
307 NETH REF CONGR	1	10	16	-	-
313 N AM BAPT CONF	7	885	1,104*	-	-
325 OLD REG BAPT	1	6	7*	-	-
329 OPEN BIBLE STD	1	NR	NR	-	-
331 ORTH CH IN AM	7	NR	NR	-	-
349 PENT HOLINESS	2	45	56*	-	-
353 CHR BRETHREN	22	1,437	2,225	-	.1
355 PRESB CH (USA)	103	32,797	40,909*	.8	1.3
356 PRESB CH AMER	2	52	80	-	-
371 REF CH IN AM	24	6,768	10,692	.2	.3
375 REF EPISCOPAL	1	240	276	-	-
397 ROMANIAN ORTH	2	NR	NR	-	-
403 SALVATION ARMY	18	1,863	2,071	-	.1
413 S.D.A.	56	12,031	15,007*	.3	.5
419 SO BAPT CONV	101	25,808	32,192*	.6	1.0
423 SYRIAN ANTIOCH	3	NA	1,900	-	.1
435 UNITARIAN-UNIV	14	2,338	3,090	.1	.1
443 UN C OF CHRIST	116	44,094	55,001*	1.1	1.7
449 UN METHODIST	159	46,146	57,560*	1.1	1.8
467 WESLEYAN	7	381	1,165	-	-
469 WELS	7	1,745	2,335	-	.1
496 JEWISH EST[1]	140	NA	208,577	4.1	6.5
497 BLACK BAPT EST[2]	NA	232,568	290,094*	5.7	9.0
498 INDEP.CHARIS.[3]	9	NA	9,450	.2	.3
499 INDEP.NON-CHAR[3]	18	NA	28,650	.6	.9
CRAWFORD	**64**	**7,856**	**11,720***	**60.2**	**100.0**
011 A.W.M.C.	1	15	19*	.1	.2
019 AMER BAPT USA	2	636	788*	4.0	6.7
053 ASSEMB OF GOD	2	183	268	1.4	2.3

County and Denomination	Number of churches	Communicant, confirmed, full members	Total adherents		
			Number	Percent of total population	Percent of total adherents
081 CATHOLIC	2	NA	1,150	5.9	9.8
081d LATIN	*2*	*NA*	*1,150*	*5.9*	*9.8*
093 CHR CH (DISC)	2	579	1,198	6.2	10.2
097 CHR CHS&CHS CR	8	1,617	2,002*	10.3	17.1
111 CH CR,SCIENTST	1	NR	NR	-	-
165 CH OF NAZARENE	1	44	112	.6	1.0
167 CHS OF CHRIST	3	142	185	1.0	1.6
185 CUMBER PRESB	1	46	49	.3	.4
193 EPISCOPAL	1	26	35	.2	.3
221 FREE METHODIST	2	47	73	.4	.6
226 FRIENDS-USA	1	62	77*	.4	.7
226e FUM	*1*	*62*	*77**	*.4*	*.7*
259 IFCA	1	NR	NR	-	-
283 LUTH—MO SYNOD	1	41	66	.3	.6
355 PRESB CH (USA)	2	236	292*	1.5	2.5
419 SO BAPT CONV	8	1,412	1,748*	9.0	14.9
443 UN C OF CHRIST	1	83	103*	.5	.9
449 UN METHODIST	21	2,597	3,216*	16.5	27.4
467 WESLEYAN	3	90	339	1.7	2.9
CUMBERLAND	**31**	**2,197**	**3,814***	**35.7**	**100.0**
081 CATHOLIC	3	NA	975	9.1	25.6
081d LATIN	*3*	*NA*	*975*	*9.1*	*25.6*
097 CHR CHS&CHS CR	3	558	717*	6.7	18.8
167 CHS OF CHRIST	2	66	85	.8	2.2
171 CH GOD-GEN CON	2	171	220*	2.1	5.8
221 FREE METHODIST	2	91	133	1.2	3.5
226 FRIENDS-USA	1	25	32*	.3	.8
226e FUM	*1*	*25*	*32**	*.3*	*.8*
355 PRESB CH (USA)	2	161	207*	1.9	5.4
419 SO BAPT CONV	6	381	489*	4.6	12.8
449 UN METHODIST	9	744	956*	9.0	25.1
467 WESLEYAN	1	0	0	-	-
DE KALB	**87**	**20,258**	**41,133***	**52.8**	**100.0**
001 ADVENT CHR CH	1	37	45*	.1	.1
019 AMER BAPT USA	3	909	1,098*	1.4	2.7
053 ASSEMB OF GOD	3	316	525	.7	1.3
057 BAPT GEN CONF	1	210	254*	.3	.6
059 BAPT MISS ASSN	1	40	48*	.1	.1
081 CATHOLIC	6	NA	14,038	18.0	34.1
081d LATIN	*6*	*NA*	*14,038*	*18.0*	*34.1*
097 CHR CHS&CHS CR	1	219	265*	.3	.6
111 CH CR,SCIENTST	2	NR	NR	-	-
127 CH GOD (CLEVE)	1	134	162*	.2	.4
151 L-D SAINTS	1	NA	358	.5	.9
165 CH OF NAZARENE	2	163	388	.5	.9
167 CHS OF CHRIST	3	216	276	.4	.7
179 CONSRV BAPT	1	NR	NR	-	-
193 EPISCOPAL	2	408	565	.7	1.4
203 EVAN FREE CH	1	95	170	.2	.4
207 E.L.C.A.	9	4,678	6,241	8.0	15.2
220 FREE LUTHERAN	1	98	124	.2	.3
226 FRIENDS-USA	1	10	12*	-	-
226c FGC	*1*	*10*	*12**	-	-
246 GREEK ORTHODOX	1	NR	NR	-	-
249 AP CATH ASSYR	1	153	379	.5	.9
259 IFCA	1	NR	NR	-	-
263 INT FOURSQ GOS	2	334	404*	.5	1.0
283 LUTH—MO SYNOD	4	1,989	2,589	3.3	6.3
355 PRESB CH (USA)	4	705	852*	1.1	2.1
403 SALVATION ARMY	1	90	113	.1	.3
413 S.D.A.	1	80	97*	.1	.2
419 SO BAPT CONV	3	626	756*	1.0	1.8
435 UNITARIAN-UNIV	2	593	758	1.0	1.8
443 UN C OF CHRIST	9	2,552	3,083*	4.0	7.5
449 UN METHODIST	16	5,145	6,216*	8.0	15.1
467 WESLEYAN	1	47	240	.3	.6
496 JEWISH EST[1]	0	NA	200	.3	.5
497 BLACK BAPT EST[2]	NA	411	497*	.6	1.2
499 INDEP.NON-CHAR[3]	1	NA	380	.5	.9
DE WITT	**32**	**5,228**	**8,488***	**51.4**	**100.0**
053 ASSEMB OF GOD	1	189	350	2.1	4.1
081 CATHOLIC	3	NA	1,627	9.9	19.2
081d LATIN	*3*	*NA*	*1,627*	*9.9*	*19.2*
097 CHR CHS&CHS CR	8	2,153	2,703*	16.4	31.8
123 CH GOD (ANDER)	1	27	52	.3	.6
127 CH GOD (CLEVE)	2	111	139*	.8	1.6
165 CH OF NAZARENE	2	287	508	3.1	6.0
167 CHS OF CHRIST	1	35	52	.3	.6
185 CUMBER PRESB	1	64	68	.4	.8
221 FREE METHODIST	1	34	34	.2	.4
283 LUTH—MO SYNOD	1	169	245	1.5	2.9
355 PRESB CH (USA)	1	207	260*	1.6	3.1
419 SO BAPT CONV	3	215	270*	1.6	3.2

NA–Not applicable NR–Not reported *Total adherents estimated from known number of communicant, confirmed, full members. - Represents a percent less than 0.1. Percentages may not total due to rounding.
[1]See Appendix E [2]See Appendix F [3]See Appendix G Lines in *italic* represent a breakdown of Catholic rites or Friends affiliations. They are included in their respective denominational total.

Table 4. Churches and Church Membership by County and Denomination: 1990

County and Denomination	Number of churches	Communicant, confirmed, full members	Total adherents — Number	Percent of total population	Percent of total adherents
449 UN METHODIST	7	1,737	2,180*	13.2	25.7
DOUGLAS	**60**	**6,351**	**12,716***	**65.3**	**100.0**
019 AMER BAPT USA	5	567	727*	3.7	5.7
053 ASSEMB OF GOD	1	111	258	1.3	2.0
061 BEACHY AMISH	1	129	165*	.8	1.3
081 CATHOLIC	3	NA	2,118	10.9	16.7
081d LATIN	*3*	*NA*	*2,118*	*10.9*	*16.7*
093 CHR CH (DISC)	2	362	544	2.8	4.3
097 CHR CHS&CHS CR	4	1,157	1,484*	7.6	11.7
123 CH GOD (ANDER)	2	45	76	.4	.6
165 CH OF NAZARENE	4	180	311	1.6	2.4
167 CHS OF CHRIST	1	98	127	.7	1.0
221 FREE METHODIST	1	31	39	.2	.3
259 IFCA	1	NR	NR	-	-
283 LUTH—MO SYNOD	1	309	412	2.1	3.2
285 MENNONITE CH	2	279	401	2.1	3.2
323 OLD ORD AMISH	14	NA	2,100	10.8	16.5
355 PRESB CH (USA)	3	137	176*	.9	1.4
361 PRIM BAPT ASCS	1	10	13*	.1	.1
419 SO BAPT CONV	2	79	101*	.5	.8
443 UN C OF CHRIST	3	525	673*	3.5	5.3
449 UN METHODIST	9	2,332	2,991*	15.4	23.5
DU PAGE	**349**	**108,325**	**483,537***	**61.9**	**100.0**
001 ADVENT CHR CH	1	343	436*	.1	.1
019 AMER BAPT USA	3	517	657*	.1	.1
053 ASSEMB OF GOD	10	3,275	7,991	1.0	1.7
057 BAPT GEN CONF	6	712	904*	.1	.2
081 CATHOLIC	49	NA	292,175	37.4	60.4
081d LATIN	*46*	*NA*	*290,574*	*37.2*	*60.1*
081e MARONITE	*1*	*NA*	*957*	*.1*	*.2*
081g ROMANIAN	*2*	*NA*	*644*	*.1*	*.1*
089 CHR & MISS AL	13	921	1,607	.2	.3
093 CHR CH (DISC)	2	325	456	.1	.1
097 CHR CHS&CHS CR	8	1,457	1,851*	.2	.4
105 CHRISTIAN REF	7	2,012	3,199	.4	.7
111 CH CR,SCIENTST	8	NR	NR	-	-
121 CH GOD (ABR)	1	20	25*	-	-
123 CH GOD (ANDER)	2	145	191	-	-
127 CH GOD (CLEVE)	2	80	102*	-	-
145 CH GOD PROPHCY	1	38	48*	-	-
151 L-D SAINTS	7	NA	2,777	.4	.6
157 CH OF BRETHREN	3	450	572*	.1	.1
164 CH LUTH CONF	1	46	65	-	-
165 CH OF NAZARENE	2	303	396	.1	.1
167 CHS OF CHRIST	6	593	850	.1	.2
175 CONGR CHR CHS	3	426	541*	.1	.1
179 CONSRV BAPT	3	NR	NR	-	-
193 EPISCOPAL	13	5,226	6,899	.9	1.4
203 EVAN FREE CH	7	1,477	2,141	.3	.4
207 E.L.C.A.	29	17,681	24,576	3.1	5.1
209 EVAN LUTH SYN	1	181	258	-	.1
216 EVAN PRESBY CH	1	197	198	-	-
221 FREE METHODIST	1	75	75	-	-
226 FRIENDS-USA	1	114	126	-	-
226d FGC & FUM	*1*	*114*	*126*	*-*	*-*
246 GREEK ORTHODOX	1	NR	NR	-	-
249 AP CATH ASSYR	0	27	297	-	.1
259 IFCA	4	NR	NR	-	-
274 LAT EVAN LUTH	2	501	556	.1	.1
283 LUTH—MO SYNOD	28	19,123	26,762	3.4	5.5
284 LUTH CH-AM ASC	1	214	246	-	.1
285 MENNONITE CH	1	155	234	-	-
313 N AM BAPT CONF	2	391	497*	.1	.1
353 CHR BRETHREN	5	540	1,192	.2	.2
355 PRESB CH (USA)	16	9,105	11,564*	1.5	2.4
356 PRESB CH AMER	6	816	887	.1	.2
371 REF CH IN AM	4	459	891	.1	.2
403 SALVATION ARMY	1	271	280	-	.1
413 S.D.A.	9	2,572	3,267*	.4	.7
419 SO BAPT CONV	10	1,770	2,248*	.3	.5
431 UKRANIAN AMER	1	NR	NR	-	-
435 UNITARIAN-UNIV	3	712	1,002	.1	.2
443 UN C OF CHRIST	23	12,991	16,500*	2.1	3.4
449 UN METHODIST	30	17,648	22,414*	2.9	4.6
467 WESLEYAN	1	212	396	.1	.1
469 WELS	2	412	586	.1	.1
496 JEWISH EST[1]	4	NA	31,936	4.1	6.6
497 BLACK BAPT EST[2]	NA	3,792	4,816*	.6	1.0
499 INDEP.NON-CHAR[3]	4	NA	7,850	1.0	1.6
EDGAR	**53**	**6,886**	**10,842***	**55.3**	**100.0**
019 AMER BAPT USA	2	612	760*	3.9	7.0
053 ASSEMB OF GOD	1	67	154	.8	1.4
081 CATHOLIC	4	NA	1,611	8.2	14.9
081d LATIN	*4*	*NA*	*1,611*	*8.2*	*14.9*
093 CHR CH (DISC)	2	364	675	3.4	6.2
097 CHR CHS&CHS CR	9	2,119	2,631*	13.4	24.3
111 CH CR,SCIENTST	1	NR	NR	-	-
127 CH GOD (CLEVE)	1	83	103*	.5	1.0
151 L-D SAINTS	1	NA	86	.4	.8
165 CH OF NAZARENE	3	262	553	2.8	5.1
167 CHS OF CHRIST	3	126	164	.8	1.5
193 EPISCOPAL	1	19	26	.1	.2
259 IFCA	1	NR	NR	-	-
283 LUTH—MO SYNOD	1	377	498	2.5	4.6
339 PENT CH OF GOD	1	35	77	.4	.7
355 PRESB CH (USA)	4	430	534*	2.7	4.9
413 S.D.A.	1	44	55*	.3	.5
449 UN METHODIST	17	2,348	2,915*	14.9	26.9
EDWARDS	**32**	**4,462**	**5,682***	**76.4**	**100.0**
093 CHR CH (DISC)	1	162	282	3.8	5.0
097 CHR CHS&CHS CR	8	1,508	1,874*	25.2	33.0
127 CH GOD (CLEVE)	1	55	68*	.9	1.2
157 CH OF BRETHREN	1	150	186*	2.5	3.3
175 CONGR CHR CHS	2	92	114*	1.5	2.0
193 EPISCOPAL	1	26	31	.4	.5
221 FREE METHODIST	2	78	108	1.5	1.9
293 MORAV CH-NORTH	1	321	447	6.0	7.9
355 PRESB CH (USA)	1	35	43*	.6	.8
419 SO BAPT CONV	3	917	1,140*	15.3	20.1
443 UN C OF CHRIST	1	50	62*	.8	1.1
449 UN METHODIST	10	1,068	1,327*	17.8	23.4
EFFINGHAM	**67**	**9,484**	**24,869***	**78.4**	**100.0**
053 ASSEMB OF GOD	1	79	110	.3	.4
081 CATHOLIC	10	NA	11,979	37.8	48.2
081d LATIN	*10*	*NA*	*11,979*	*37.8*	*48.2*
093 CHR CH (DISC)	2	264	458	1.4	1.8
097 CHR CHS&CHS CR	10	865	1,145*	3.6	4.6
123 CH GOD (ANDER)	1	0	183	.6	.7
151 L-D SAINTS	1	NA	66	.2	.3
165 CH OF NAZARENE	2	124	143	.5	.6
167 CHS OF CHRIST	1	68	88	.3	.4
193 EPISCOPAL	1	23	30	.1	.1
207 E.L.C.A.	2	343	447	1.4	1.8
223 FREE WILL BAPT	1	38	50*	.2	.2
283 LUTH—MO SYNOD	10	2,831	3,754	11.8	15.1
355 PRESB CH (USA)	2	320	423*	1.3	1.7
419 SO BAPT CONV	7	2,534	3,353*	10.6	13.5
449 UN METHODIST	16	1,995	2,640*	8.3	10.6
FAYETTE	**73**	**9,596**	**13,234***	**63.3**	**100.0**
053 ASSEMB OF GOD	2	100	186	.9	1.4
081 CATHOLIC	4	NA	1,132	5.4	8.6
081d LATIN	*4*	*NA*	*1,132*	*5.4*	*8.6*
093 CHR CH (DISC)	1	97	182	.9	1.4
097 CHR CHS&CHS CR	10	895	1,112*	5.3	8.4
123 CH GOD (ANDER)	3	102	102	.5	.8
157 CH OF BRETHREN	1	85	106*	.5	.8
167 CHS OF CHRIST	3	112	145	.7	1.1
185 CUMBER PRESB	1	14	16	.1	.1
207 E.L.C.A.	2	357	454	2.2	3.4
221 FREE METHODIST	3	115	123	.6	.9
283 LUTH—MO SYNOD	4	1,582	2,051	9.8	15.5
355 PRESB CH (USA)	1	130	162*	.8	1.2
413 S.D.A.	1	46	57*	.3	.4
419 SO BAPT CONV	20	4,048	5,029*	24.1	38.0
443 UN C OF CHRIST	1	163	203*	1.0	1.5
449 UN METHODIST	16	1,633	2,029*	9.7	15.3
497 BLACK BAPT EST[2]	NA	117	145*	.7	1.1
FORD	**39**	**5,664**	**9,540***	**66.8**	**100.0**
053 ASSEMB OF GOD	1	31	60	.4	.6
081 CATHOLIC	6	NA	2,179	15.3	22.8
081d LATIN	*6*	*NA*	*2,179*	*15.3*	*22.8*
093 CHR CH (DISC)	2	247	341	2.4	3.6
097 CHR CHS&CHS CR	2	270	339*	2.4	3.6
165 CH OF NAZARENE	3	80	228	1.6	2.4
167 CHS OF CHRIST	1	57	65	.5	.7
175 CONGR CHR CHS	1	51	64*	.4	.7
207 E.L.C.A.	6	1,430	1,883	13.2	19.7
355 PRESB CH (USA)	3	410	514*	3.6	5.4
356 PRESB CH AMER	1	74	85	.6	.9
419 SO BAPT CONV	2	537	674*	4.7	7.1
443 UN C OF CHRIST	1	54	68*	.5	.7
449 UN METHODIST	10	2,423	3,040*	21.3	31.9

NA–Not applicable NR–Not reported *Total adherents estimated from known number of communicant, confirmed, full members. - Represents a percent less than 0.1. Percentages may not total due to rounding.
[1]See Appendix E [2]See Appendix F [3]See Appendix G Lines in *italic* represent a breakdown of Catholic rites or Friends affiliations. They are included in their respective denominational total.

Table 4. Churches and Church Membership by County and Denomination: 1990

County and Denomination	Number of churches	Communicant, confirmed, full members	Total adherents Number	Percent of total population	Percent of total adherents
FRANKLIN	**122**	**19,420**	**27,044***	**67.1**	**100.0**
019 AMER BAPT USA	6	1,213	1,482*	3.7	5.5
053 ASSEMB OF GOD	2	56	159	.4	.6
081 CATHOLIC	6	NA	2,414	6.0	8.9
081d *LATIN*	*6*	*NA*	*2,414*	*6.0*	*8.9*
093 CHR CH (DISC)	1	280	480	1.2	1.8
097 CHR CHS&CHS CR	11	1,851	2,262*	5.6	8.4
111 CH CR,SCIENTST	1	NR	NR	-	-
123 CH GOD (ANDER)	3	141	233	.6	.9
127 CH GOD (CLEVE)	8	1,031	1,260*	3.1	4.7
151 L-D SAINTS	1	NA	391	1.0	1.4
165 CH OF NAZARENE	3	210	420	1.0	1.6
167 CHS OF CHRIST	7	322	419	1.0	1.5
193 EPISCOPAL	1	62	95	.2	.4
223 FREE WILL BAPT	6	748	914*	2.3	3.4
283 LUTH—MO SYNOD	1	135	181	.4	.7
286 E.PA MENNONITE	1	34	42*	.1	.2
331 ORTH CH IN AM	2	NR	NR	-	-
355 PRESB CH (USA)	1	75	92*	.2	.3
356 PRESB CH AMER	1	13	13	-	-
403 SALVATION ARMY	1	47	59	.1	.2
413 S.D.A.	1	79	97*	.2	.4
419 SO BAPT CONV	42	11,660	14,247*	35.3	52.7
449 UN METHODIST	14	1,444	1,764*	4.4	6.5
467 WESLEYAN	1	19	20	-	.1
496 JEWISH EST[1]	1	NA	0	-	-
FULTON	**83**	**10,516**	**17,826***	**46.8**	**100.0**
019 AMER BAPT USA	2	1,146	1,410*	3.7	7.9
053 ASSEMB OF GOD	4	231	396	1.0	2.2
081 CATHOLIC	4	NA	2,980	7.8	16.7
081d *LATIN*	*4*	*NA*	*2,980*	*7.8*	*16.7*
093 CHR CH (DISC)	5	742	1,675	4.4	9.4
097 CHR CHS&CHS CR	5	837	1,030*	2.7	5.8
111 CH CR,SCIENTST	1	NR	NR	-	-
145 CH GOD PROPHCY	1	38	47*	.1	.3
151 L-D SAINTS	1	NA	164	.4	.9
157 CH OF BRETHREN	3	346	426*	1.1	2.4
165 CH OF NAZARENE	10	511	1,330	3.5	7.5
167 CHS OF CHRIST	3	70	120	.3	.7
203 EVAN FREE CH	1	123	204	.5	1.1
207 E.L.C.A.	2	391	500	1.3	2.8
221 FREE METHODIST	2	90	93	.2	.5
339 PENT CH OF GOD	1	34	77	.2	.4
355 PRESB CH (USA)	4	858	1,056*	2.8	5.9
361 PRIM BAPT ASCS	1	20	25*	.1	.1
371 REF CH IN AM	1	141	242	.6	1.4
403 SALVATION ARMY	1	117	117	.3	.7
413 S.D.A.	1	87	107*	.3	.6
419 SO BAPT CONV	1	120	148*	.4	.8
443 UN C OF CHRIST	3	649	799*	2.1	4.5
449 UN METHODIST	26	3,832	4,716*	12.4	26.5
497 BLACK BAPT EST[2]	NA	133	164*	.4	.9
GALLATIN	**23**	**1,390**	**2,814***	**40.7**	**100.0**
081 CATHOLIC	4	NA	1,112	16.1	39.5
081d *LATIN*	*4*	*NA*	*1,112*	*16.1*	*39.5*
097 CHR CHS&CHS CR	1	50	61*	.9	2.2
123 CH GOD (ANDER)	1	26	26	.4	.9
127 CH GOD (CLEVE)	3	62	75*	1.1	2.7
165 CH OF NAZARENE	1	35	69	1.0	2.5
185 CUMBER PRESB	2	40	40	.6	1.4
355 PRESB CH (USA)	5	189	230*	3.3	8.2
419 SO BAPT CONV	3	733	891*	12.9	31.7
449 UN METHODIST	3	255	310*	4.5	11.0
GREENE	**45**	**7,074**	**11,104***	**72.5**	**100.0**
019 AMER BAPT USA	11	2,600	3,278*	21.4	29.5
053 ASSEMB OF GOD	2	72	144	.9	1.3
081 CATHOLIC	3	NA	1,992	13.0	17.9
081d *LATIN*	*3*	*NA*	*1,992*	*13.0*	*17.9*
093 CHR CH (DISC)	2	245	432	2.8	3.9
167 CHS OF CHRIST	2	24	32	.2	.3
283 LUTH—MO SYNOD	1	215	286	1.9	2.6
355 PRESB CH (USA)	2	167	211*	1.4	1.9
419 SO BAPT CONV	16	2,807	3,539*	23.1	31.9
449 UN METHODIST	6	944	1,190*	7.8	10.7
GRUNDY	**33**	**6,361**	**17,013***	**52.6**	**100.0**
019 AMER BAPT USA	1	359	457*	1.4	2.7
053 ASSEMB OF GOD	2	190	361	1.1	2.1
081 CATHOLIC	6	NA	8,093	25.0	47.6
081d *LATIN*	*6*	*NA*	*8,093*	*25.0*	*47.6*
097 CHR CHS&CHS CR	1	574	731*	2.3	4.3
151 L-D SAINTS	1	NA	599	1.9	3.5
165 CH OF NAZARENE	1	94	123	.4	.7
167 CHS OF CHRIST	1	40	45	.1	.3
193 EPISCOPAL	1	87	124	.4	.7
207 E.L.C.A.	3	893	1,184	3.7	7.0
220 FREE LUTHERAN	1	375	450	1.4	2.6
221 FREE METHODIST	1	23	27	.1	.2
283 LUTH—MO SYNOD	1	73	93	.3	.5
355 PRESB CH (USA)	3	909	1,158*	3.6	6.8
419 SO BAPT CONV	2	279	356*	1.1	2.1
443 UN C OF CHRIST	1	259	330*	1.0	1.9
449 UN METHODIST	7	2,206	2,811*	8.7	16.5
496 JEWISH EST[1]	0	NA	71	.2	.4
HAMILTON	**40**	**3,243**	**5,069***	**59.6**	**100.0**
053 ASSEMB OF GOD	1	41	59	.7	1.2
081 CATHOLIC	3	NA	1,089	12.8	21.5
081d *LATIN*	*3*	*NA*	*1,089*	*12.8*	*21.5*
097 CHR CHS&CHS CR	2	160	196*	2.3	3.9
127 CH GOD (CLEVE)	1	85	104*	1.2	2.1
167 CHS OF CHRIST	2	87	113	1.3	2.2
185 CUMBER PRESB	2	87	87	1.0	1.7
193 EPISCOPAL	1	18	29	.3	.6
283 LUTH—MO SYNOD	1	48	56	.7	1.1
355 PRESB CH (USA)	1	71	87*	1.0	1.7
419 SO BAPT CONV	18	2,320	2,849*	33.5	56.2
449 UN METHODIST	8	326	400*	4.7	7.9
HANCOCK	**65**	**7,179**	**12,094***	**56.6**	**100.0**
019 AMER BAPT USA	2	289	361*	1.7	3.0
053 ASSEMB OF GOD	5	247	415	1.9	3.4
081 CATHOLIC	6	NA	2,218	10.4	18.3
081d *LATIN*	*6*	*NA*	*2,218*	*10.4*	*18.3*
093 CHR CH (DISC)	4	653	1,109	5.2	9.2
097 CHR CHS&CHS CR	6	970	1,213*	5.7	10.0
151 L-D SAINTS	1	NA	434	2.0	3.6
165 CH OF NAZARENE	1	17	21	.1	.2
175 CONGR CHR CHS	1	170	213*	1.0	1.8
207 E.L.C.A.	4	924	1,181	5.5	9.8
221 FREE METHODIST	1	17	30	.1	.2
259 IFCA	3	NR	NR	-	-
283 LUTH—MO SYNOD	2	277	346	1.6	2.9
339 PENT CH OF GOD	1	35	77	.4	.6
355 PRESB CH (USA)	7	793	991*	4.6	8.2
361 PRIM BAPT ASCS	2	77	96*	.4	.8
413 S.D.A.	1	12	15*	.1	.1
419 SO BAPT CONV	1	126	158*	.7	1.3
443 UN C OF CHRIST	2	426	533*	2.5	4.4
449 UN METHODIST	15	2,146	2,683*	12.6	22.2
HARDIN	**14**	**1,033**	**1,459***	**28.1**	**100.0**
081 CATHOLIC	1	NA	180	3.5	12.3
081d *LATIN*	*1*	*NA*	*180*	*3.5*	*12.3*
097 CHR CHS&CHS CR	2	220	269*	5.2	18.4
123 CH GOD (ANDER)	1	22	22	.4	1.5
167 CHS OF CHRIST	3	118	164	3.2	11.2
419 SO BAPT CONV	4	532	651*	12.5	44.6
449 UN METHODIST	3	141	173*	3.3	11.9
HENDERSON	**20**	**2,305**	**3,487***	**43.1**	**100.0**
019 AMER BAPT USA	1	194	242*	3.0	6.9
053 ASSEMB OF GOD	1	30	83	1.0	2.4
081 CATHOLIC	2	NA	515	6.4	14.8
081d *LATIN*	*2*	*NA*	*515*	*6.4*	*14.8*
093 CHR CH (DISC)	1	120	189	2.3	5.4
097 CHR CHS&CHS CR	1	210	261*	3.2	7.5
165 CH OF NAZARENE	1	38	52	.6	1.5
207 E.L.C.A.	1	176	200	2.5	5.7
355 PRESB CH (USA)	3	382	476*	5.9	13.7
371 REF CH IN AM	1	60	106	1.3	3.0
449 UN METHODIST	8	1,095	1,363*	16.8	39.1
HENRY	**85**	**17,848**	**35,685***	**69.8**	**100.0**
019 AMER BAPT USA	5	1,570	1,985*	3.9	5.6
053 ASSEMB OF GOD	5	205	352	.7	1.0
057 BAPT GEN CONF	1	99	125*	.2	.4
081 CATHOLIC	11	NA	12,576	24.6	35.2
081d *LATIN*	*11*	*NA*	*12,576*	*24.6*	*35.2*
097 CHR CHS&CHS CR	3	750	948*	1.9	2.7
111 CH CR,SCIENTST	1	NR	NR	-	-
127 CH GOD (CLEVE)	2	112	142*	.3	.4
165 CH OF NAZARENE	2	140	299	.6	.8
167 CHS OF CHRIST	3	112	125	.2	.4
199 EVAN CONGR CH	1	99	139	.3	.4
203 EVAN FREE CH	2	216	385	.8	1.1
207 E.L.C.A.	10	4,224	5,315	10.4	14.9

NA–Not applicable NR–Not reported *Total adherents estimated from known number of communicant, confirmed, full members. - Represents a percent less than 0.1. Percentages may not total due to rounding.
[1]See Appendix E [2]See Appendix F [3]See Appendix G Lines in *italic* represent a breakdown of Catholic rites or Friends affiliations. They are included in their respective denominational total.

Table 4. Churches and Church Membership by County and Denomination: 1990

County and Denomination	Number of churches	Communicant, confirmed, full members	Total adherents		
			Number	Percent of total population	Percent of total adherents
221 FREE METHODIST	1	28	40	.1	.1
263 INT FOURSQ GOS	1	14	18*	-	.1
283 LUTH—MO SYNOD	4	1,574	2,060	4.0	5.8
329 OPEN BIBLE STD	1	NR	NR	-	-
355 PRESB CH (USA)	4	1,114	1,408*	2.8	3.9
403 SALVATION ARMY	1	73	81	.2	.2
413 S.D.A.	2	24	30*	.1	.1
419 SO BAPT CONV	2	436	551*	1.1	1.5
443 UN C OF CHRIST	6	1,536	1,942*	3.8	5.4
449 UN METHODIST	17	5,361	6,778*	13.2	19.0
496 JEWISH EST[1]	0	NA	182	.4	.5
497 BLACK BAPT EST[2]	NA	161	204*	.4	.6
IROQUOIS	**74**	**11,085**	**19,115***	**62.1**	**100.0**
040 AP CHR CH-AMER	1	253	448	1.5	2.3
053 ASSEMB OF GOD	1	60	107	.3	.6
081 CATHOLIC	11	NA	4,741	15.4	24.8
081d LATIN	11	NA	4,741	15.4	24.8
093 CHR CH (DISC)	2	319	474	1.5	2.5
097 CHR CHS&CHS CR	7	790	988*	3.2	5.2
123 CH GOD (ANDER)	1	29	29	.1	.2
165 CH OF NAZARENE	4	126	294	1.0	1.5
175 CONGR CHR CHS	1	75	94*	.3	.5
193 EPISCOPAL	1	26	31	.1	.2
203 EVAN FREE CH	1	62	133	.4	.7
207 E.L.C.A.	5	1,689	2,128	6.9	11.1
220 FREE LUTHERAN	1	235	278	.9	1.5
283 LUTH—MO SYNOD	10	2,866	3,634	11.8	19.0
284 LUTH CH-AM ASC	1	295	388	1.3	2.0
349 PENT HOLINESS	1	135	169*	.5	.9
355 PRESB CH (USA)	2	155	194*	.6	1.0
371 REF CH IN AM	1	107	170	.6	.9
419 SO BAPT CONV	2	43	54*	.2	.3
438 UN BRETH IN CR	1	29	29	.1	.2
443 UN C OF CHRIST	3	562	703*	2.3	3.7
449 UN METHODIST	16	3,184	3,980*	12.9	20.8
467 WESLEYAN	1	45	49	.2	.3
JACKSON	**95**	**18,457**	**26,694***	**43.7**	**100.0**
019 AMER BAPT USA	9	2,150	2,537*	4.2	9.5
053 ASSEMB OF GOD	4	309	514	.8	1.9
059 BAPT MISS ASSN	1	77	91*	.1	.3
081 CATHOLIC	6	NA	3,365	5.5	12.6
081d LATIN	6	NA	3,365	5.5	12.6
089 CHR & MISS AL	1	0	17	-	.1
093 CHR CH (DISC)	1	336	740	1.2	2.8
097 CHR CHS&CHS CR	5	1,370	1,616*	2.6	6.1
111 CH CR,SCIENTST	2	NR	NR	-	-
123 CH GOD (ANDER)	4	81	100	.2	.4
127 CH GOD (CLEVE)	1	110	130*	.2	.5
151 L-D SAINTS	1	NA	371	.6	1.4
165 CH OF NAZARENE	3	198	360	.6	1.3
167 CHS OF CHRIST	3	273	359	.6	1.3
193 EPISCOPAL	1	122	143	.2	.5
207 E.L.C.A.	5	1,238	1,618	2.6	6.1
226 FRIENDS-USA	1	9	11*	-	-
226c FGC	1	9	11*	-	-
283 LUTH—MO SYNOD	5	1,660	2,112	3.5	7.9
353 CHR BRETHREN	2	107	175	.3	.7
355 PRESB CH (USA)	4	496	585*	1.0	2.2
356 PRESB CH AMER	1	89	116	.2	.4
419 SO BAPT CONV	17	5,846	6,897*	11.3	25.8
435 UNITARIAN-UNIV	1	94	144	.2	.5
443 UN C OF CHRIST	2	232	274*	.4	1.0
449 UN METHODIST	14	2,400	2,832*	4.6	10.6
496 JEWISH EST[1]	1	NA	100	.2	.4
497 BLACK BAPT EST[2]	NA	1,260	1,487*	2.4	5.6
JASPER	**35**	**2,777**	**6,054***	**57.1**	**100.0**
019 AMER BAPT USA	1	314	405*	3.8	6.7
053 ASSEMB OF GOD	1	41	39	.4	.6
081 CATHOLIC	3	NA	2,464	23.2	40.7
081d LATIN	3	NA	2,464	23.2	40.7
097 CHR CHS&CHS CR	6	726	936*	8.8	15.5
151 L-D SAINTS	1	NA	48	.5	.8
167 CHS OF CHRIST	4	113	147	1.4	2.4
185 CUMBER PRESB	1	76	76	.7	1.3
207 E.L.C.A.	1	43	51	.5	.8
221 FREE METHODIST	1	51	51	.5	.8
283 LUTH—MO SYNOD	1	72	109	1.0	1.8
355 PRESB CH (USA)	1	113	146*	1.4	2.4
419 SO BAPT CONV	4	403	519*	4.9	8.6
449 UN METHODIST	10	825	1,063*	10.0	17.6
JEFFERSON	**87**	**15,776**	**22,461***	**60.7**	**100.0**
005 AME ZION	1	340	515	1.4	2.3

County and Denomination	Number of churches	Communicant, confirmed, full members	Total adherents		
			Number	Percent of total population	Percent of total adherents
019 AMER BAPT USA	2	289	367*	1.0	1.6
053 ASSEMB OF GOD	1	49	111	.3	.5
081 CATHOLIC	2	NA	2,000	5.4	8.9
081d LATIN	2	NA	2,000	5.4	8.9
097 CHR CHS&CHS CR	10	1,748	2,220*	6.0	9.9
123 CH GOD (ANDER)	3	85	212	.6	.9
127 CH GOD (CLEVE)	2	243	309*	.8	1.4
165 CH OF NAZARENE	2	109	127	.3	.6
167 CHS OF CHRIST	2	205	265	.7	1.2
193 EPISCOPAL	1	150	239	.6	1.1
207 E.L.C.A.	1	228	304	.8	1.4
223 FREE WILL BAPT	6	792	1,006*	2.7	4.5
283 LUTH—MO SYNOD	1	277	386	1.0	1.7
323 OLD ORD AMISH	1	NA	100	.3	.4
355 PRESB CH (USA)	1	367	466*	1.3	2.1
413 S.D.A.	1	23	29*	.1	.1
419 SO BAPT CONV	32	8,348	10,604*	28.6	47.2
435 UNITARIAN-UNIV	1	36	42	.1	.2
443 UN C OF CHRIST	1	107	136*	.4	.6
449 UN METHODIST	16	1,998	2,538*	6.9	11.3
497 BLACK BAPT EST[2]	NA	382	485*	1.3	2.2
JERSEY	**31**	**4,593**	**13,710***	**66.8**	**100.0**
019 AMER BAPT USA	3	1,189	1,506*	7.3	11.0
053 ASSEMB OF GOD	4	394	839	4.1	6.1
081 CATHOLIC	5	NA	7,067	34.4	51.5
081d LATIN	5	NA	7,067	34.4	51.5
097 CHR CHS&CHS CR	1	35	44*	.2	.3
111 CH CR,SCIENTST	2	NR	NR	-	-
165 CH OF NAZARENE	1	68	95	.5	.7
167 CHS OF CHRIST	1	101	131	.6	1.0
283 LUTH—MO SYNOD	1	284	389	1.9	2.8
355 PRESB CH (USA)	1	258	327*	1.6	2.4
419 SO BAPT CONV	5	1,055	1,336*	6.5	9.7
443 UN C OF CHRIST	2	544	689*	3.4	5.0
449 UN METHODIST	5	665	842*	4.1	6.1
496 JEWISH EST[1]	0	NA	445	2.2	3.2
JO DAVIESS	**44**	**5,289**	**16,788***	**76.9**	**100.0**
053 ASSEMB OF GOD	2	85	119	.5	.7
081 CATHOLIC	10	NA	9,889	45.3	58.9
081d LATIN	10	NA	9,889	45.3	58.9
165 CH OF NAZARENE	1	51	128	.6	.8
193 EPISCOPAL	1	65	103	.5	.6
203 EVAN FREE CH	1	0	0	-	-
207 E.L.C.A.	8	1,816	2,459	11.3	14.6
259 IFCA	1	NR	NR	-	-
283 LUTH—MO SYNOD	1	238	304	1.4	1.8
355 PRESB CH (USA)	6	729	911*	4.2	5.4
419 SO BAPT CONV	1	45	56*	.3	.3
435 UNITARIAN-UNIV	1	94	113	.5	.7
449 UN METHODIST	10	2,071	2,589*	11.9	15.4
469 WELS	1	95	117	.5	.7
JOHNSON	**34**	**3,725**	**4,682***	**41.3**	**100.0**
019 AMER BAPT USA	1	94	111*	1.0	2.4
053 ASSEMB OF GOD	2	52	76	.7	1.6
081 CATHOLIC	1	NA	295	2.6	6.3
081d LATIN	1	NA	295	2.6	6.3
097 CHR CHS&CHS CR	1	150	177*	1.6	3.8
123 CH GOD (ANDER)	1	8	8	.1	.2
167 CHS OF CHRIST	3	118	144	1.3	3.1
185 CUMBER PRESB	1	95	95	.8	2.0
419 SO BAPT CONV	15	2,305	2,713*	23.9	57.9
449 UN METHODIST	9	699	823*	7.3	17.6
497 BLACK BAPT EST[2]	NA	204	240*	2.1	5.1
KANE	**211**	**62,054**	**172,618***	**54.4**	**100.0**
019 AMER BAPT USA	7	2,629	3,453*	1.1	2.0
039 AP CHR CH(NAZ)	1	26	34*	-	-
040 AP CHR CH-AMER	1	230	405	.1	.2
053 ASSEMB OF GOD	6	901	1,725	.5	1.0
057 BAPT GEN CONF	3	142	186*	.1	.1
081 CATHOLIC	26	NA	87,399	27.5	50.6
081d LATIN	26	NA	87,399	27.5	50.6
097 CHR CHS&CHS CR	4	875	1,149*	.4	.7
111 CH CR,SCIENTST	3	NR	NR	-	-
123 CH GOD (ANDER)	2	112	114	-	.1
127 CH GOD (CLEVE)	6	736	967*	.3	.6
145 CH GOD PROPHCY	2	77	101*	-	.1
151 L-D SAINTS	4	NA	1,690	.5	1.0
157 CH OF BRETHREN	3	689	905*	.3	.5
165 CH OF NAZARENE	2	158	164	.1	.1
167 CHS OF CHRIST	4	249	329	.1	.2
179 CONSRV BAPT	1	NR	NR	-	-
181 CONSRV CONGR	1	417	548*	.2	.3

NA–Not applicable   NR–Not reported   *Total adherents estimated from known number of communicant, confirmed, full members.   - Represents a percent less than 0.1.   Percentages may not total due to rounding.
[1]See Appendix E   [2]See Appendix F   [3]See Appendix G   Lines in *italic* represent a breakdown of Catholic rites or Friends affiliations. They are included in their respective denominational total.

Table 4. Churches and Church Membership by County and Denomination: 1990

County and Denomination	Number of churches	Communicant, confirmed, full members	Total adherents Number	Total adherents Percent of total population	Total adherents Percent of total adherents
193 EPISCOPAL	8	2,188	2,903	.9	1.7
203 EVAN FREE CH	2	101	190	.1	.1
207 E.L.C.A.	18	10,660	14,496	4.6	8.4
221 FREE METHODIST	2	103	103	-	.1
223 FREE WILL BAPT	2	251	330*	.1	.2
249 AP CATH ASSYR	0	32	157	-	.1
259 IFCA	1	NR	NR	-	-
263 INT FOURSQ GOS	4	733	963*	.3	.6
283 LUTH—MO SYNOD	19	10,380	13,774	4.3	8.0
313 N AM BAPT CONF	1	35	46*	-	-
329 OPEN BIBLE STD	1	NR	NR	-	-
331 ORTH CH IN AM	1	NR	NR	-	-
339 PENT CH OF GOD	1	34	77	-	-
353 CHR BRETHREN	2	79	145	-	.1
355 PRESB CH (USA)	6	2,781	3,652*	1.2	2.1
356 PRESB CH AMER	1	264	314	.1	.2
403 SALVATION ARMY	3	303	327	.1	.2
413 S.D.A.	4	793	1,041*	.3	.6
419 SO BAPT CONV	14	2,970	3,901*	1.2	2.3
435 UNITARIAN-UNIV	2	289	438	.1	.3
443 UN C OF CHRIST	15	6,464	8,490*	2.7	4.9
449 UN METHODIST	24	11,455	15,045*	4.7	8.7
469 WELS	2	237	401	.1	.2
496 JEWISH EST[1]	2	NA	534	.2	.3
497 BLACK BAPT EST[2]	NA	4,661	6,122*	1.9	3.5
KANKAKEE	**106**	**22,342**	**52,692***	**54.7**	**100.0**
005 AME ZION	1	363	488	.5	.9
019 AMER BAPT USA	2	747	959*	1.0	1.8
053 ASSEMB OF GOD	1	42	60	.1	.1
081 CATHOLIC	17	NA	21,404	22.2	40.6
081d LATIN	*17*	*NA*	*21,404*	*22.2*	*40.6*
093 CHR CH (DISC)	2	342	445	.5	.8
097 CHR CHS&CHS CR	2	180	231*	.2	.4
105 CHRISTIAN REF	1	146	245	.3	.5
111 CH CR,SCIENTST	1	NR	NR	-	-
123 CH GOD (ANDER)	2	40	65	.1	.1
127 CH GOD (CLEVE)	1	247	317*	.3	.6
151 L-D SAINTS	1	NA	378	.4	.7
165 CH OF NAZARENE	10	2,121	3,622	3.8	6.9
167 CHS OF CHRIST	4	226	296	.3	.6
179 CONSRV BAPT	1	NR	NR	-	-
193 EPISCOPAL	2	375	450	.5	.9
203 EVAN FREE CH	1	101	158	.2	.3
207 E.L.C.A.	3	910	1,140	1.2	2.2
223 FREE WILL BAPT	1	20	26*	-	-
246 GREEK ORTHODOX	1	NR	NR	-	-
263 INT FOURSQ GOS	1	69	89*	.1	.2
283 LUTH—MO SYNOD	8	3,438	4,460	4.6	8.5
285 MENNONITE CH	1	45	65	.1	.1
313 N AM BAPT CONF	1	377	484*	.5	.9
329 OPEN BIBLE STD	1	NR	NR	-	-
355 PRESB CH (USA)	3	694	891*	.9	1.7
371 REF CH IN AM	3	517	834	.9	1.6
403 SALVATION ARMY	1	120	126	.1	.2
413 S.D.A.	2	236	303*	.3	.6
419 SO BAPT CONV	3	985	1,265*	1.3	2.4
443 UN C OF CHRIST	3	962	1,235*	1.3	2.3
449 UN METHODIST	20	5,258	6,750*	7.0	12.8
469 WELS	2	250	313	.3	.6
496 JEWISH EST[1]	1	NA	200	.2	.4
497 BLACK BAPT EST[2]	NA	3,531	4,533*	4.7	8.6
499 INDEP.NON-CHAR[3]	2	NA	860	.9	1.6
KENDALL	**37**	**7,979**	**18,874***	**47.9**	**100.0**
019 AMER BAPT USA	1	319	416*	1.1	2.2
053 ASSEMB OF GOD	1	256	500	1.3	2.6
057 BAPT GEN CONF	1	159	207*	.5	1.1
059 BAPT MISS ASSN	1	157	205*	.5	1.1
081 CATHOLIC	3	NA	7,691	19.5	40.7
081d LATIN	*3*	*NA*	*7,691*	*19.5*	*40.7*
097 CHR CHS&CHS CR	2	300	391*	1.0	2.1
127 CH GOD (CLEVE)	1	35	46*	.1	.2
167 CHS OF CHRIST	1	75	97	.2	.5
207 E.L.C.A.	3	788	999	2.5	5.3
220 FREE LUTHERAN	2	727	1,044	2.6	5.5
246 GREEK ORTHODOX	1	NR	NR	-	-
259 IFCA	1	NR	NR	-	-
283 LUTH—MO SYNOD	2	1,248	1,771	4.5	9.4
284 LUTH CH-AM ASC	2	461	636	1.6	3.4
349 PENT HOLINESS	1	12	16*	-	.1
355 PRESB CH (USA)	2	727	948*	2.4	5.0
419 SO BAPT CONV	2	222	290*	.7	1.5
443 UN C OF CHRIST	1	514	670*	1.7	3.5
449 UN METHODIST	8	1,979	2,581*	6.5	13.7
496 JEWISH EST[1]	0	NA	66	.2	.3
499 INDEP.NON-CHAR[3]	1	NA	300	.8	1.6

County and Denomination	Number of churches	Communicant, confirmed, full members	Total adherents Number	Total adherents Percent of total population	Total adherents Percent of total adherents
KNOX	**64**	**13,683**	**23,864***	**42.3**	**100.0**
001 ADVENT CHR CH	1	35	43*	.1	.2
019 AMER BAPT USA	1	474	581*	1.0	2.4
053 ASSEMB OF GOD	2	202	285	.5	1.2
057 BAPT GEN CONF	2	890	1,090*	1.9	4.6
081 CATHOLIC	7	NA	5,821	10.3	24.4
081d LATIN	*7*	*NA*	*5,821*	*10.3*	*24.4*
093 CHR CH (DISC)	3	972	1,433	2.5	6.0
111 CH CR,SCIENTST	1	NR	NR	-	-
123 CH GOD (ANDER)	1	250	250	.4	1.0
127 CH GOD (CLEVE)	1	98	120*	.2	.5
145 CH GOD PROPHCY	1	38	47*	.1	.2
151 L-D SAINTS	1	NA	351	.6	1.5
165 CH OF NAZARENE	2	283	680	1.2	2.8
167 CHS OF CHRIST	2	80	101	.2	.4
175 CONGR CHR CHS	2	455	557*	1.0	2.3
207 E.L.C.A.	6	2,804	3,571	6.3	15.0
226 FRIENDS-USA	1	18	22*	-	.1
226c FGC	*1*	*18*	*22**	*-*	*.1*
263 INT FOURSQ GOS	1	110	135*	.2	.6
283 LUTH—MO SYNOD	1	326	435	.8	1.8
329 OPEN BIBLE STD	1	NR	NR	-	-
355 PRESB CH (USA)	5	1,519	1,861*	3.3	7.8
403 SALVATION ARMY	1	73	75	.1	.3
413 S.D.A.	1	63	77*	.1	.3
419 SO BAPT CONV	1	211	259*	.5	1.1
443 UN C OF CHRIST	2	287	352*	.6	1.5
449 UN METHODIST	15	3,895	4,772*	8.5	20.0
467 WESLEYAN	1	32	150	.3	.6
496 JEWISH EST[1]	1	NA	100	.2	.4
497 BLACK BAPT EST[2]	NA	568	696*	1.2	2.9
LAKE	**253**	**64,900**	**335,886***	**65.0**	**100.0**
019 AMER BAPT USA	3	857	1,103*	.2	.3
049 ARMEN AP CH AM	1	100	450	.1	.1
053 ASSEMB OF GOD	12	1,625	3,202	.6	1.0
057 BAPT GEN CONF	9	1,572	2,023*	.4	.6
059 BAPT MISS ASSN	1	41	53*	-	-
081 CATHOLIC	29	NA	243,350	47.1	72.5
081d LATIN	*29*	*NA*	*243,350*	*47.1*	*72.5*
089 CHR & MISS AL	3	111	209	-	.1
093 CHR CH (DISC)	3	644	1,015	.2	.3
097 CHR CHS&CHS CR	3	330	425*	.1	.1
111 CH CR,SCIENTST	7	NR	NR	-	-
127 CH GOD (CLEVE)	5	508	654*	.1	.2
145 CH GOD PROPHCY	2	77	99*	-	-
151 L-D SAINTS	6	NA	2,428	.5	.7
165 CH OF NAZARENE	4	283	513	.1	.2
167 CHS OF CHRIST	7	344	467	.1	.1
193 EPISCOPAL	11	5,163	7,164	1.4	2.1
199 EVAN CONGR CH	1	69	99	-	-
203 EVAN FREE CH	11	1,716	3,117	.6	.9
207 E.L.C.A.	21	10,071	14,631	2.8	4.4
221 FREE METHODIST	1	166	323	.1	.1
223 FREE WILL BAPT	1	22	28*	-	-
226 FRIENDS-USA	1	123	158*	-	-
226c FGC	*1*	*123*	*158**	*-*	*-*
246 GREEK ORTHODOX	1	NR	NR	-	-
249 AP CATH ASSYR	0	53	333	.1	.1
259 IFCA	5	NR	NR	-	-
263 INT FOURSQ GOS	3	27	35*	-	-
283 LUTH—MO SYNOD	8	4,008	5,339	1.0	1.6
285 MENNONITE CH	1	18	30	-	-
291 MISSIONARY CH	3	495	763	.1	.2
313 N AM BAPT CONF	1	61	79*	-	-
339 PENT CH OF GOD	1	34	77	-	-
353 CHR BRETHREN	3	158	255	-	.1
355 PRESB CH (USA)	9	8,071	10,388*	2.0	3.1
356 PRESB CH AMER	1	59	84	-	-
371 REF CH IN AM	1	60	147	-	-
403 SALVATION ARMY	1	78	88	-	-
413 S.D.A.	3	384	494*	.1	.1
419 SO BAPT CONV	16	4,825	6,210*	1.2	1.8
435 UNITARIAN-UNIV	2	356	516	.1	.2
443 UN C OF CHRIST	13	4,607	5,930*	1.1	1.8
449 UN METHODIST	19	6,954	8,951*	1.7	2.7
467 WESLEYAN	1	0	10	-	-
469 WELS	7	2,303	3,171	.6	.9
496 JEWISH EST[1]	12	NA	500	.1	.1
497 BLACK BAPT EST[2]	NA	8,527	10,975*	2.1	3.3
LA SALLE	**140**	**20,918**	**76,023***	**71.1**	**100.0**
001 ADVENT CHR CH	1	32	40*	-	.1
019 AMER BAPT USA	3	595	744*	.7	1.0
053 ASSEMB OF GOD	6	318	650	.6	.9
081 CATHOLIC	31	NA	47,777	44.7	62.8

NA–Not applicable NR–Not reported *Total adherents estimated from known number of communicant, confirmed, full members. - Represents a percent less than 0.1. Percentages may not total due to rounding.
[1]See Appendix E [2]See Appendix F [3]See Appendix G Lines in *italic* represent a breakdown of Catholic rites or Friends affiliations. They are included in their respective denominational total.

Table 4. Churches and Church Membership by County and Denomination: 1990

County and Denomination	Number of churches	Communicant, confirmed, full members	Total adherents Number	Percent of total population	Percent of total adherents
081d *LATIN*	31	NA	47,777	44.7	62.8
089 CHR & MISS AL	1	0	14	-	-
097 CHR CHS&CHS CR	4	874	1,092*	1.0	1.4
111 CH CR,SCIENTST	1	NR	NR	-	-
123 CH GOD (ANDER)	2	82	132	.1	.2
151 L-D SAINTS	1	NA	290	.3	.4
163 CH OF LUTH BR	1	72	97	.1	.1
165 CH OF NAZARENE	7	632	1,223	1.1	1.6
167 CHS OF CHRIST	2	96	133	.1	.2
179 CONSRV BAPT	1	NR	NR	-	-
193 EPISCOPAL	3	209	320	.3	.4
203 EVAN FREE CH	1	32	65	.1	.1
207 E.L.C.A.	12	5,024	6,739	6.3	8.9
220 FREE LUTHERAN	4	444	620	.6	.8
259 IFCA	1	NR	NR	-	-
263 INT FOURSQ GOS	1	55	69*	.1	.1
283 LUTH—MO SYNOD	3	1,208	1,569	1.5	2.1
329 OPEN BIBLE STD	1	NR	NR	-	-
339 PENT CH OF GOD	1	34	77	.1	.1
355 PRESB CH (USA)	7	1,734	2,167*	2.0	2.9
363 PRIMITIVE METH	1	90	142	.1	.2
403 SALVATION ARMY	2	157	167	.2	.2
413 S.D.A.	3	184	230*	.2	.3
419 SO BAPT CONV	7	844	1,055*	1.0	1.4
443 UN C OF CHRIST	6	1,512	1,890	1.8	2.5
449 UN METHODIST	25	6,461	8,075*	7.6	10.6
497 BLACK BAPT EST[2]	NA	229	286*	.3	.4
498 INDEP.CHARIS.[3]	1	NA	360	.3	.5
LAWRENCE	**55**	**5,845**	**9,557***	**59.8**	**100.0**
053 ASSEMB OF GOD	1	60	81	.5	.8
081 CATHOLIC	3	NA	807	5.1	8.4
081d *LATIN*	3	NA	807	5.1	8.4
093 CHR CH (DISC)	1	390	547	3.4	5.7
097 CHR CHS&CHS CR	5	1,190	1,465*	9.2	15.3
123 CH GOD (ANDER)	1	40	43	.3	.4
127 CH GOD (CLEVE)	3	256	315*	2.0	3.3
145 CH GOD PROPHCY	1	38	47*	.3	.5
151 L-D SAINTS	1	NA	358	2.2	3.7
157 CH OF BRETHREN	1	66	81*	.5	.8
165 CH OF NAZARENE	1	33	120	.8	1.3
167 CHS OF CHRIST	2	29	39	.2	.4
175 CONGR CHR CHS	2	81	100*	.6	1.0
221 FREE METHODIST	6	308	334	2.1	3.5
283 LUTH—MO SYNOD	1	53	72	.5	.8
355 PRESB CH (USA)	4	277	341*	2.1	3.6
419 SO BAPT CONV	2	705	868*	5.4	9.1
449 UN METHODIST	18	2,233	2,749*	17.2	28.8
467 WESLEYAN	1	86	190	1.2	2.0
499 INDEP.NON-CHAR[3]	1	NA	1,000	6.3	10.5
LEE	**65**	**9,394**	**21,983***	**63.9**	**100.0**
019 AMER BAPT USA	3	416	523*	1.5	2.4
053 ASSEMB OF GOD	1	68	145	.4	.7
081 CATHOLIC	9	NA	9,618	28.0	43.8
081d *LATIN*	9	NA	9,618	28.0	43.8
089 CHR & MISS AL	3	119	268	.8	1.2
093 CHR CH (DISC)	1	133	140	.4	.6
097 CHR CHS&CHS CR	3	259	326*	.9	1.5
111 CH CR,SCIENTST	1	NR	NR	-	-
121 CH GOD (ABR)	1	22	28*	.1	.1
123 CH GOD (ANDER)	1	30	86	.3	.4
151 L-D SAINTS	1	NA	242	.7	1.1
157 CH OF BRETHREN	2	422	530*	1.5	2.4
165 CH OF NAZARENE	1	41	77	.2	.4
167 CHS OF CHRIST	1	26	34	.1	.2
193 EPISCOPAL	1	101	122	.4	.6
199 EVAN CONGR CH	3	321	321	.9	1.5
203 EVAN FREE CH	1	42	95	.3	.4
207 E.L.C.A.	8	2,888	3,747	10.9	17.0
259 IFCA	1	NR	NR	-	-
263 INT FOURSQ GOS	1	83	104*	.3	.5
283 LUTH—MO SYNOD	1	110	157	.5	.7
329 OPEN BIBLE STD	1	NR	NR	-	-
355 PRESB CH (USA)	3	562	706*	2.1	3.2
419 SO BAPT CONV	3	426	535*	1.6	2.4
443 UN C OF CHRIST	2	192	241*	.7	1.1
449 UN METHODIST	12	2,890	3,633*	10.6	16.5
497 BLACK BAPT EST[2]	NA	243	305*	.9	1.4
LIVINGSTON	**80**	**13,005**	**24,457***	**62.2**	**100.0**
019 AMER BAPT USA	6	1,082	1,346*	3.4	5.5
040 AP CHR CH-AMER	2	527	932	2.4	3.8
053 ASSEMB OF GOD	3	207	414	1.1	1.7
081 CATHOLIC	13	NA	7,273	18.5	29.7
081d *LATIN*	13	NA	7,273	18.5	29.7

County and Denomination	Number of churches	Communicant, confirmed, full members	Total adherents Number	Percent of total population	Percent of total adherents
093 CHR CH (DISC)	4	214	374	1.0	1.5
097 CHR CHS&CHS CR	2	168	209*	.5	.9
111 CH CR,SCIENTST	1	NR	NR	-	-
123 CH GOD (ANDER)	1	21	21	.1	.1
127 CH GOD (CLEVE)	2	69	86*	.2	.4
151 L-D SAINTS	1	NA	72	.2	.3
165 CH OF NAZARENE	3	116	190	.5	.8
167 CHS OF CHRIST	3	122	157	.4	.6
193 EPISCOPAL	1	112	167	.4	.7
207 E.L.C.A.	10	3,231	4,255	10.8	17.4
213 EVAN MENN INC	1	171	213*	.5	.9
221 FREE METHODIST	1	11	17	.1	.1
283 LUTH—MO SYNOD	2	702	941	2.4	3.8
285 MENNONITE CH	1	88	126	.3	.5
287 MENN GEN CONF	1	79	99	.3	.4
355 PRESB CH (USA)	2	775	964*	2.5	3.9
403 SALVATION ARMY	1	36	39	.1	.2
443 UN C OF CHRIST	3	480	597*	1.5	2.4
449 UN METHODIST	16	4,374	5,442*	13.8	22.3
497 BLACK BAPT EST[2]	NA	420	523*	1.3	2.1
LOGAN	**55**	**9,122**	**18,028***	**58.5**	**100.0**
019 AMER BAPT USA	1	282	347*	1.1	1.9
053 ASSEMB OF GOD	1	41	73	.2	.4
081 CATHOLIC	5	NA	6,128	19.9	34.0
081d *LATIN*	5	NA	6,128	19.9	34.0
093 CHR CH (DISC)	1	90	156	.5	.9
097 CHR CHS&CHS CR	12	849	1,046*	3.4	5.8
127 CH GOD (CLEVE)	1	43	53*	.2	.3
165 CH OF NAZARENE	1	71	498	1.6	2.8
167 CHS OF CHRIST	1	42	53	.2	.3
185 CUMBER PRESB	2	202	215	.7	1.2
193 EPISCOPAL	1	104	135	.4	.7
207 E.L.C.A.	4	1,782	2,291	7.4	12.7
221 FREE METHODIST	1	45	49	.2	.3
259 IFCA	1	NR	NR	-	-
283 LUTH—MO SYNOD	5	1,807	2,340	7.6	13.0
355 PRESB CH (USA)	2	329	405*	1.3	2.2
403 SALVATION ARMY	1	65	88	.3	.5
413 S.D.A.	1	19	23*	.1	.1
419 SO BAPT CONV	1	103	127*	.4	.7
443 UN C OF CHRIST	1	480	591*	1.9	3.3
449 UN METHODIST	12	2,511	3,093*	10.0	17.2
497 BLACK BAPT EST[2]	NA	257	317*	1.0	1.8
MC DONOUGH	**63**	**8,758**	**14,609***	**41.5**	**100.0**
019 AMER BAPT USA	4	913	1,067*	3.0	7.3
053 ASSEMB OF GOD	3	399	1,454	4.1	10.0
081 CATHOLIC	3	NA	2,310	6.6	15.8
081d *LATIN*	3	NA	2,310	6.6	15.8
093 CHR CH (DISC)	5	660	1,352	3.8	9.3
097 CHR CHS&CHS CR	6	1,018	1,189*	3.4	8.1
111 CH CR,SCIENTST	1	NR	NR	-	-
121 CH GOD (ABR)	1	115	134*	.4	.9
123 CH GOD (ANDER)	1	20	24	.1	.2
133 CH GOD(7TH)DEN	1	55	80	.2	.5
151 L-D SAINTS	1	NA	274	.8	1.9
165 CH OF NAZARENE	2	113	179	.5	1.2
167 CHS OF CHRIST	1	93	121	.3	.8
207 E.L.C.A.	1	279	360	1.0	2.5
221 FREE METHODIST	1	23	35	.1	.2
259 IFCA	1	NR	NR	-	-
283 LUTH—MO SYNOD	1	230	326	.9	2.2
329 OPEN BIBLE STD	1	NR	NR	-	-
339 PENT CH OF GOD	1	34	77	.2	.5
355 PRESB CH (USA)	7	1,366	1,596*	4.5	10.9
356 PRESB CH AMER	1	34	43	.1	.3
403 SALVATION ARMY	1	67	71	.2	.5
419 SO BAPT CONV	1	164	192*	.5	1.3
435 UNITARIAN-UNIV	1	43	66	.2	.5
449 UN METHODIST	17	2,883	3,368*	9.6	23.1
497 BLACK BAPT EST[2]	NA	249	291*	.8	2.0
MC HENRY	**107**	**32,929**	**107,228***	**58.5**	**100.0**
019 AMER BAPT USA	2	205	268*	.1	.2
053 ASSEMB OF GOD	4	553	920	.5	.9
057 BAPT GEN CONF	1	102	133*	.1	.1
081 CATHOLIC	17	NA	53,288	29.1	49.7
081d *LATIN*	17	NA	53,288	29.1	49.7
089 CHR & MISS AL	1	123	269	.1	.3
097 CHR CHS&CHS CR	2	190	248*	.1	.2
105 CHRISTIAN REF	1	60	102	.1	.1
111 CH CR,SCIENTST	3	NR	NR	-	-
127 CH GOD (CLEVE)	1	14	18*	-	-
151 L-D SAINTS	2	NA	923	.5	.9
165 CH OF NAZARENE	1	47	123	.1	.1

NA–Not applicable   NR–Not reported   *Total adherents estimated from known number of communicant, confirmed, full members.   - Represents a percent less than 0.1.   Percentages may not total due to rounding.

[1]See Appendix E   [2]See Appendix F   [3]See Appendix G   Lines in *italic* represent a breakdown of Catholic rites or Friends affiliations. They are included in their respective denominational total.

122

Table 4. Churches and Church Membership by County and Denomination: 1990

County and Denomination	Number of churches	Communicant, confirmed, full members	Total adherents Number	Total adherents Percent of total population	Total adherents Percent of total adherents
167 CHS OF CHRIST	1	70	110	.1	.1
193 EPISCOPAL	5	973	1,699	.9	1.6
195 ESTONIAN ELC	1	170	222*	.1	.2
203 EVAN FREE CH	4	553	1,092	.6	1.0
207 E.L.C.A.	10	7,911	11,338	6.2	10.6
221 FREE METHODIST	1	115	115	.1	.1
226 FRIENDS-USA	1	34	44*	-	-
226c FGC	*1*	*34*	*44**	*-*	*-*
249 AP CATH ASSYR	0	13	79	-	.1
259 IFCA	1	NR	NR	-	-
263 INT FOURSQ GOS	1	202	264*	.1	.2
283 LUTH—MO SYNOD	11	8,010	10,684	5.8	10.0
339 PENT CH OF GOD	1	34	77	-	.1
355 PRESB CH (USA)	5	1,677	2,191*	1.2	2.0
419 SO BAPT CONV	5	1,459	1,906*	1.0	1.8
435 UNITARIAN-UNIV	1	117	158	.1	.1
443 UN C OF CHRIST	9	5,205	6,801*	3.7	6.3
449 UN METHODIST	14	4,867	6,359*	3.5	5.9
469 WELS	1	225	310	.2	.3
496 JEWISH EST[1]	0	NA	7,487	4.1	7.0
MC LEAN	**139**	**33,825**	**63,601***	**49.2**	**100.0**
001 ADVENT CHR CH	1	0	30*	-	-
019 AMER BAPT USA	7	1,027	1,261*	1.0	2.0
040 AP CHR CH-AMER	2	440	780	.6	1.2
053 ASSEMB OF GOD	2	372	749	.6	1.2
057 BAPT GEN CONF	1	53	65*	.1	.1
081 CATHOLIC	10	NA	16,893	13.1	26.6
081d LATIN	*10*	*NA*	*16,893*	*13.1*	*26.6*
083 CHRIST CATH CH	1	5	5	-	-
089 CHR & MISS AL	1	54	104	.1	.2
093 CHR CH (DISC)	14	2,317	3,619	2.8	5.7
097 CHR CHS&CHS CR	7	3,231	3,966*	3.1	6.2
111 CH CR,SCIENTST	1	NR	NR	-	-
123 CH GOD (ANDER)	3	176	222	.2	.3
127 CH GOD (CLEVE)	2	485	595*	.5	.9
151 L-D SAINTS	1	NA	643	.5	1.0
165 CH OF NAZARENE	2	295	466	.4	.7
167 CHS OF CHRIST	5	431	561	.4	.9
193 EPISCOPAL	2	454	562	.4	.9
203 EVAN FREE CH	1	147	272	.2	.4
207 E.L.C.A.	6	2,909	3,937	3.0	6.2
213 EVAN MENN INC	1	36	44*	-	.1
221 FREE METHODIST	1	53	56	-	.1
223 FREE WILL BAPT	1	10	12*	-	-
226 FRIENDS-USA	1	20	25*	-	-
226c FGC	*1*	*20*	*25**	*-*	*-*
259 IFCA	2	NR	NR	-	-
263 INT FOURSQ GOS	1	177	217*	.2	.3
283 LUTH—MO SYNOD	7	4,036	5,405	4.2	8.5
285 MENNONITE CH	1	279	408	.3	.6
287 MENN GEN CONF	4	548	671	.5	1.1
339 PENT CH OF GOD	1	35	76	.1	.1
355 PRESB CH (USA)	9	3,956	4,856*	3.8	7.6
356 PRESB CH AMER	1	58	88	.1	.1
403 SALVATION ARMY	1	186	201	.2	.3
413 S.D.A.	1	88	108*	.1	.2
419 SO BAPT CONV	4	1,098	1,348*	1.0	2.1
443 UN C OF CHRIST	2	374	459*	.4	.7
449 UN METHODIST	26	9,033	11,088*	8.6	17.4
467 WESLEYAN	3	21	77	.1	.1
469 WELS	1	57	88	.1	.1
496 JEWISH EST[1]	1	NA	170	.1	.3
497 BLACK BAPT EST[2]	NA	1,364	1,674*	1.3	2.6
499 INDEP.NON-CHAR[3]	1	NA	1,800	1.4	2.8
MACON	**134**	**37,938**	**64,342***	**54.9**	**100.0**
019 AMER BAPT USA	1	570	714*	.6	1.1
053 ASSEMB OF GOD	4	887	1,520	1.3	2.4
081 CATHOLIC	8	NA	13,618	11.6	21.2
081d LATIN	*8*	*NA*	*13,618*	*11.6*	*21.2*
083 CHRIST CATH CH	1	12	12	-	-
089 CHR & MISS AL	1	26	49	-	.1
093 CHR CH (DISC)	9	2,967	5,250	4.5	8.2
097 CHR CHS&CHS CR	5	1,307	1,637*	1.4	2.5
111 CH CR,SCIENTST	1	NR	NR	-	-
123 CH GOD (ANDER)	6	523	587	.5	.9
127 CH GOD (CLEVE)	1	148	185*	.2	.3
151 L-D SAINTS	2	NA	581	.5	.9
157 CH OF BRETHREN	1	116	145*	.1	.2
165 CH OF NAZARENE	5	1,322	1,965	1.7	3.1
167 CHS OF CHRIST	4	660	789	.7	1.2
171 CH GOD-GEN CON	11	1,308	1,638*	1.4	2.5
193 EPISCOPAL	1	446	607	.5	.9
207 E.L.C.A.	3	1,197	1,620	1.4	2.5
221 FREE METHODIST	1	296	328	.3	.5
223 FREE WILL BAPT	1	256	321*	.3	.5

County and Denomination	Number of churches	Communicant, confirmed, full members	Total adherents Number	Total adherents Percent of total population	Total adherents Percent of total adherents
226 FRIENDS-USA	1	12	15*	-	-
226c FGC	*1*	*12*	*15**	*-*	*-*
246 GREEK ORTHODOX	1	NR	NR	-	-
259 IFCA	2	NR	NR	-	-
263 INT FOURSQ GOS	3	1,709	2,141*	1.8	3.3
283 LUTH—MO SYNOD	8	5,151	6,566	5.6	10.2
355 PRESB CH (USA)	7	2,629	3,293*	2.8	5.1
403 SALVATION ARMY	1	199	203	.2	.3
413 S.D.A.	3	128	160*	.1	.2
419 SO BAPT CONV	12	3,610	4,522*	3.9	7.0
435 UNITARIAN-UNIV	1	87	109	.1	.2
443 UN C OF CHRIST	2	553	693*	.6	1.1
449 UN METHODIST	25	8,344	10,452*	8.9	16.2
467 WESLEYAN	1	9	70	.1	.1
496 JEWISH EST[1]	1	NA	210	.2	.3
497 BLACK BAPT EST[2]	NA	3,466	4,342*	3.7	6.7
MACOUPIN	**103**	**14,661**	**26,597***	**55.8**	**100.0**
019 AMER BAPT USA	4	693	867*	1.8	3.3
053 ASSEMB OF GOD	5	461	1,123	2.4	4.2
081 CATHOLIC	16	NA	7,023	14.7	26.4
081d LATIN	*16*	*NA*	*7,023*	*14.7*	*26.4*
093 CHR CH (DISC)	4	542	1,095	2.3	4.1
097 CHR CHS&CHS CR	6	458	573*	1.2	2.2
157 CH OF BRETHREN	2	339	424*	.9	1.6
165 CH OF NAZARENE	2	158	254	.5	1.0
167 CHS OF CHRIST	4	124	159	.3	.6
193 EPISCOPAL	2	127	177	.4	.7
207 E.L.C.A.	4	773	983	2.1	3.7
283 LUTH—MO SYNOD	6	2,490	3,251	6.8	12.2
339 PENT CH OF GOD	1	34	76	.2	.3
355 PRESB CH (USA)	4	391	489*	1.0	1.8
361 PRIM BAPT ASCS	1	46	58*	.1	.2
419 SO BAPT CONV	19	3,802	4,759*	10.0	17.9
443 UN C OF CHRIST	4	1,262	1,580*	3.3	5.9
449 UN METHODIST	19	2,961	3,706*	7.8	13.9
MADISON	**276**	**71,117**	**146,360***	**58.7**	**100.0**
019 AMER BAPT USA	15	3,728	4,671*	1.9	3.2
039 AP CHR CH(NAZ)	1	3	4*	-	-
049 ARMEN AP CH AM	1	200	600	.2	.4
053 ASSEMB OF GOD	26	3,079	5,885	2.4	4.0
081 CATHOLIC	27	NA	46,451	18.6	31.7
081d LATIN	*26*	*NA*	*46,429*	*18.6*	*31.7*
081h UKRAINIAN	*1*	*NA*	*22*		
093 CHR CH (DISC)	3	497	637	.3	.4
097 CHR CHS&CHS CR	10	1,889	2,367*	.9	1.6
111 CH CR,SCIENTST	3	NR	NR	-	-
123 CH GOD (ANDER)	6	206	550	.2	.4
127 CH GOD (CLEVE)	4	896	1,123*	.5	.8
145 CH GOD PROPHCY	2	77	96*	-	.1
151 L-D SAINTS	2	NA	840	.3	.6
165 CH OF NAZARENE	7	936	1,402	.6	1.0
167 CHS OF CHRIST	15	1,330	1,720	.7	1.2
175 CONGR CHR CHS	2	130	163*	.1	.1
179 CONSRV BAPT	1	NR	NR	-	-
181 CONSRV CONGR	1	277	347*	.1	.2
193 EPISCOPAL	5	755	937	.4	.6
203 EVAN FREE CH	1	63	95	-	.1
207 E.L.C.A.	4	852	1,097	.4	.7
221 FREE METHODIST	2	123	137	.1	.1
223 FREE WILL BAPT	2	306	383*	.2	.3
263 INT FOURSQ GOS	2	115	144*	.1	.1
283 LUTH—MO SYNOD	22	10,475	13,591	5.5	9.3
331 ORTH CH IN AM	2	NR	NR	-	-
339 PENT CH OF GOD	3	121	242	.1	.2
353 CHR BRETHREN	1	150	225	.1	.2
355 PRESB CH (USA)	17	4,648	5,824*	2.3	4.0
356 PRESB CH AMER	3	146	197	.1	.1
403 SALVATION ARMY	2	242	246	.1	.2
413 S.D.A.	1	89	112*	-	.1
419 SO BAPT CONV	34	18,012	22,569*	9.1	15.4
435 UNITARIAN-UNIV	1	93	118	-	.1
443 UN C OF CHRIST	17	9,674	12,121*	4.9	8.3
449 UN METHODIST	26	8,048	10,084*	4.0	6.9
496 JEWISH EST[1]	2	NA	5,404	2.2	3.7
497 BLACK BAPT EST[2]	NA	3,957	4,958*	2.0	3.4
498 INDEP.CHARIS.[3]	3	NA	1,020	.4	.7
MARION	**103**	**18,785**	**28,585***	**68.8**	**100.0**
005 AME ZION	1	375	540	1.3	1.9
019 AMER BAPT USA	1	1,458	1,842*	4.4	6.4
053 ASSEMB OF GOD	3	319	641	1.5	2.2
059 BAPT MISS ASSN	1	11	14*	-	-
081 CATHOLIC	4	NA	3,510	8.4	12.3
081d LATIN	*4*	*NA*	*3,510*	*8.4*	*12.3*

NA–Not applicable   NR–Not reported   *Total adherents estimated from known number of communicant, confirmed, full members.   - Represents a percent less than 0.1.   Percentages may not total due to rounding.
[1]See Appendix E   [2]See Appendix F   [3]See Appendix G   Lines in *italic* represent a breakdown of Catholic rites or Friends affiliations. They are included in their respective denominational total.

ILLINOIS

Table 4. Churches and Church Membership by County and Denomination: 1990

County and Denomination	Number of churches	Communicant, confirmed, full members	Total adherents Number	Percent of total population	Percent of total adherents
093 CHR CH (DISC)	3	431	756	1.8	2.6
097 CHR CHS&CHS CR	14	3,360	4,245*	10.2	14.9
111 CH CR,SCIENTST	1	NR	NR	-	-
123 CH GOD (ANDER)	2	64	83	.2	.3
127 CH GOD (CLEVE)	3	255	322*	.8	1.1
151 L-D SAINTS	1	NA	296	.7	1.0
157 CH OF BRETHREN	1	27	34*	.1	.1
165 CH OF NAZARENE	1	116	325	.8	1.1
167 CHS OF CHRIST	5	378	490	1.2	1.7
193 EPISCOPAL	2	101	111	.3	.4
207 E.L.C.A.	1	120	148	.4	.5
221 FREE METHODIST	2	159	188	.5	.7
223 FREE WILL BAPT	2	141	178*	.4	.6
283 LUTH—MO SYNOD	3	1,652	2,149	5.2	7.5
355 PRESB CH (USA)	5	524	662*	1.6	2.3
361 PRIM BAPT ASCS	1	9	11*	-	-
403 SALVATION ARMY	1	97	100	.2	.3
419 SO BAPT CONV	22	5,696	7,197*	17.3	25.2
443 UN C OF CHRIST	2	488	617*	1.5	2.2
449 UN METHODIST	20	2,702	3,414*	8.2	11.9
497 BLACK BAPT EST[2]	NA	302	382*	.9	1.3
499 INDEP.NON-CHAR[3]	1	NA	330	.8	1.2
MARSHALL	**32**	**3,933**	**8,355***	**65.0**	**100.0**
019 AMER BAPT USA	1	128	158*	1.2	1.9
053 ASSEMB OF GOD	1	32	43	.3	.5
081 CATHOLIC	6	NA	3,396	26.4	40.6
081d LATIN	6	NA	3,396	26.4	40.6
093 CHR CH (DISC)	1	125	230	1.8	2.8
097 CHR CHS&CHS CR	2	363	449*	3.5	5.4
165 CH OF NAZARENE	1	30	49	.4	.6
207 E.L.C.A.	4	789	963	7.5	11.5
283 LUTH—MO SYNOD	3	534	654	5.1	7.8
285 MENNONITE CH	1	29	59	.5	.7
329 OPEN BIBLE STD	1	NR	NR	-	-
355 PRESB CH (USA)	4	397	491*	3.8	5.9
443 UN C OF CHRIST	1	292	361*	2.8	4.3
449 UN METHODIST	6	1,214	1,502*	11.7	18.0
MASON	**35**	**6,601**	**9,718***	**59.7**	**100.0**
019 AMER BAPT USA	2	599	749*	4.6	7.7
053 ASSEMB OF GOD	2	194	426	2.6	4.4
081 CATHOLIC	3	NA	980	6.0	10.1
081d LATIN	3	NA	980	6.0	10.1
093 CHR CH (DISC)	2	647	1,031	6.3	10.6
097 CHR CHS&CHS CR	2	552	690*	4.2	7.1
165 CH OF NAZARENE	2	125	212	1.3	2.2
193 EPISCOPAL	1	64	86	.5	.9
283 LUTH—MO SYNOD	7	1,791	2,298	14.1	23.6
291 MISSIONARY CH	2	165	166	1.0	1.7
355 PRESB CH (USA)	1	232	290*	1.8	3.0
419 SO BAPT CONV	4	543	679*	4.2	7.0
449 UN METHODIST	7	1,689	2,111*	13.0	21.7
MASSAC	**42**	**8,736**	**11,428***	**77.5**	**100.0**
053 ASSEMB OF GOD	2	175	272	1.8	2.4
081 CATHOLIC	1	NA	500	3.4	4.4
081d LATIN	1	NA	500	3.4	4.4
093 CHR CH (DISC)	1	154	257	1.7	2.2
097 CHR CHS&CHS CR	3	777	949*	6.4	8.3
123 CH GOD (ANDER)	1	40	95	.6	.8
127 CH GOD (CLEVE)	1	165	202*	1.4	1.8
165 CH OF NAZARENE	1	56	137	.9	1.2
167 CHS OF CHRIST	6	413	545	3.7	4.8
185 CUMBER PRESB	1	88	89	.6	.8
207 E.L.C.A.	4	759	922	6.2	8.1
355 PRESB CH (USA)	1	83	101*	.7	.9
413 S.D.A.	1	39	48*	.3	.4
419 SO BAPT CONV	12	4,652	5,681*	38.5	49.7
443 UN C OF CHRIST	2	368	449*	3.0	3.9
449 UN METHODIST	5	798	975*	6.6	8.5
497 BLACK BAPT EST[2]	NA	169	206*	1.4	1.8
MENARD	**25**	**4,687**	**7,113***	**63.7**	**100.0**
081 CATHOLIC	2	NA	1,082	9.7	15.2
081d LATIN	2	NA	1,082	9.7	15.2
093 CHR CH (DISC)	2	155	263	2.4	3.7
097 CHR CHS&CHS CR	3	977	1,242*	11.1	17.5
185 CUMBER PRESB	1	15	18	.2	.3
263 INT FOURSQ GOS	1	85	108*	1.0	1.5
283 LUTH—MO SYNOD	2	594	763	6.8	10.7
355 PRESB CH (USA)	4	864	1,098*	9.8	15.4
413 S.D.A.	1	11	14*	.1	.2
419 SO BAPT CONV	5	995	1,265*	11.3	17.8
443 UN C OF CHRIST	1	368	468*	4.2	6.6
449 UN METHODIST	3	623	792*	7.1	11.1
MERCER	**34**	**5,076**	**8,225***	**47.6**	**100.0**
019 AMER BAPT USA	2	671	844*	4.9	10.3
053 ASSEMB OF GOD	2	103	192	1.1	2.3
081 CATHOLIC	5	NA	1,587	9.2	19.3
081d LATIN	5	NA	1,587	9.2	19.3
093 CHR CH (DISC)	1	222	386	2.2	4.7
165 CH OF NAZARENE	1	52	94	.5	1.1
203 EVAN FREE CH	1	61	92	.5	1.1
207 E.L.C.A.	4	1,057	1,371	7.9	16.7
329 OPEN BIBLE STD	1	NR	NR	-	-
355 PRESB CH (USA)	8	1,172	1,473*	8.5	17.9
413 S.D.A.	1	26	33*	.2	.4
419 SO BAPT CONV	1	76	96*	.6	1.2
449 UN METHODIST	7	1,636	2,057*	11.9	25.0
MONROE	**31**	**6,875**	**20,205***	**90.1**	**100.0**
053 ASSEMB OF GOD	2	51	91	.4	.5
081 CATHOLIC	7	NA	9,010	40.2	44.6
081d LATIN	7	NA	9,010	40.2	44.6
127 CH GOD (CLEVE)	1	55	70*	.3	.3
165 CH OF NAZARENE	1	14	0	-	-
167 CHS OF CHRIST	1	33	35	.2	.2
283 LUTH—MO SYNOD	4	1,586	2,079	9.3	10.3
356 PRESB CH AMER	1	68	98	.4	.5
419 SO BAPT CONV	3	1,060	1,350*	6.0	6.7
443 UN C OF CHRIST	8	3,917	4,990*	22.3	24.7
449 UN METHODIST	1	91	116*	.5	.6
496 JEWISH EST[1]	0	NA	486	2.2	2.4
499 INDEP.NON-CHAR[3]	2	NA	1,880	8.4	9.3
MONTGOMERY	**80**	**10,995**	**19,106***	**62.2**	**100.0**
019 AMER BAPT USA	3	613	767*	2.5	4.0
053 ASSEMB OF GOD	4	272	503	1.6	2.6
081 CATHOLIC	7	NA	4,692	15.3	24.6
081d LATIN	7	NA	4,692	15.3	24.6
093 CHR CH (DISC)	5	563	750	2.4	3.9
097 CHR CHS&CHS CR	5	507	634*	2.1	3.3
151 L-D SAINTS	1	NA	230	.7	1.2
207 E.L.C.A.	9	1,182	1,578	5.1	8.3
221 FREE METHODIST	3	43	98	.3	.5
283 LUTH—MO SYNOD	5	1,800	2,334	7.6	12.2
355 PRESB CH (USA)	7	689	862*	2.8	4.5
413 S.D.A.	1	14	18*	.1	.1
419 SO BAPT CONV	18	3,294	4,119*	13.4	21.6
435 UNITARIAN-UNIV	1	14	14	-	.1
443 UN C OF CHRIST	1	62	78*	.3	.4
449 UN METHODIST	10	1,831	2,290*	7.5	12.0
497 BLACK BAPT EST[2]	NA	111	139*	.5	.7
MORGAN	**69**	**11,727**	**22,441***	**61.7**	**100.0**
019 AMER BAPT USA	3	1,159	1,432*	3.9	6.4
053 ASSEMB OF GOD	1	160	213	.6	.9
081 CATHOLIC	5	NA	4,880	13.4	21.7
081d LATIN	5	NA	4,880	13.4	21.7
093 CHR CH (DISC)	6	978	2,382	6.5	10.6
097 CHR CHS&CHS CR	4	866	1,070*	2.9	4.8
123 CH GOD (ANDER)	1	9	10	-	-
151 L-D SAINTS	1	NA	269	.7	1.2
165 CH OF NAZARENE	1	16	55	.2	.2
167 CHS OF CHRIST	2	213	271	.7	1.2
193 EPISCOPAL	1	203	279	.8	1.2
207 E.L.C.A.	3	428	558	1.5	2.5
263 INT FOURSQ GOS	1	50	62*	.2	.3
283 LUTH—MO SYNOD	5	1,761	2,351	6.5	10.5
355 PRESB CH (USA)	3	705	871*	2.4	3.9
403 SALVATION ARMY	1	86	94	.3	.4
413 S.D.A.	1	16	20*	.1	.1
419 SO BAPT CONV	9	1,621	2,003*	5.5	8.9
443 UN C OF CHRIST	2	239	295*	.8	1.3
449 UN METHODIST	16	2,888	3,568*	9.8	15.9
469 WELS	1	29	37	.1	.2
497 BLACK BAPT EST[2]	NA	300	371*	1.0	1.7
499 INDEP.NON-CHAR[3]	2	NA	1,350	3.7	6.0
MOULTRIE	**41**	**4,804**	**7,845***	**56.3**	**100.0**
019 AMER BAPT USA	1	232	291*	2.1	3.7
053 ASSEMB OF GOD	1	8	15	.1	.2
061 BEACHY AMISH	1	40	50*	.4	.6
081 CATHOLIC	3	NA	568	4.1	7.2
081d LATIN	3	NA	568	4.1	7.2
093 CHR CH (DISC)	6	1,299	2,273	16.3	29.0
097 CHR CHS&CHS CR	3	367	461*	3.3	5.9
123 CH GOD (ANDER)	3	162	255	1.8	3.3
167 CHS OF CHRIST	3	87	113	.8	1.4
171 CH GOD-GEN CON	1	15	19*	.1	.2

NA–Not applicable   NR–Not reported   *Total adherents estimated from known number of communicant, confirmed, full members.   - Represents a percent less than 0.1.   Percentages may not total due to rounding.
[1]See Appendix E   [2]See Appendix F   [3]See Appendix G   Lines in *italic* represent a breakdown of Catholic rites or Friends affiliations. They are included in their respective denominational total.

Table 4. Churches and Church Membership by County and Denomination: 1990

County and Denomination	Number of churches	Communicant, confirmed, full members	Total adherents Number	Percent of total population	Percent of total adherents
185 CUMBER PRESB	1	326	333	2.4	4.2
221 FREE METHODIST	1	27	32	.2	.4
283 LUTH—MO SYNOD	2	294	391	2.8	5.0
323 OLD ORD AMISH	4	NA	600	4.3	7.6
355 PRESB CH (USA)	1	57	72*	.5	.9
419 SO BAPT CONV	4	724	909*	6.5	11.6
449 UN METHODIST	6	1,166	1,463*	10.5	18.6
OGLE	**76**	**12,391**	**22,308***	**48.5**	**100.0**
053 ASSEMB OF GOD	4	142	217	.5	1.0
057 BAPT GEN CONF	2	194	248*	.5	1.1
081 CATHOLIC	4	NA	5,826	12.7	26.1
081d LATIN	*4*	*NA*	*5,826*	*12.7*	*26.1*
089 CHR & MISS AL	1	0	0	-	-
093 CHR CH (DISC)	1	65	89	.2	.4
097 CHR CHS&CHS CR	4	294	375*	.8	1.7
111 CH CR,SCIENTST	1	NR	NR	-	-
121 CH GOD (ABR)	3	302	385*	.8	1.7
123 CH GOD (ANDER)	1	20	50	.1	.2
127 CH GOD (CLEVE)	1	175	223*	.5	1.0
151 L-D SAINTS	1	NA	177	.4	.8
157 CH OF BRETHREN	3	736	939*	2.0	4.2
165 CH OF NAZARENE	2	88	150	.3	.7
167 CHS OF CHRIST	1	75	97	.2	.4
179 CONSRV BAPT	1	NR	NR	-	-
181 CONSRV CONGR	1	59	75*	.2	.3
193 EPISCOPAL	2	143	158	.3	.7
203 EVAN FREE CH	1	125	145	.3	.6
207 E.L.C.A.	9	2,733	3,643	7.9	16.3
263 INT FOURSQ GOS	1	126	161*	.4	.7
283 LUTH—MO SYNOD	2	916	1,286	2.8	5.8
329 OPEN BIBLE STD	2	NR	NR	-	-
355 PRESB CH (USA)	7	1,334	1,703*	3.7	7.6
371 REF CH IN AM	4	653	997	2.2	4.5
419 SO BAPT CONV	2	322	411*	.9	1.8
438 UN BRETH IN CR	2	37	37	.1	.2
443 UN C OF CHRIST	1	620	791*	1.7	3.5
449 UN METHODIST	12	3,232	4,125*	9.0	18.5
PEORIA	**170**	**45,887**	**96,007***	**52.5**	**100.0**
019 AMER BAPT USA	3	1,183	1,484*	.8	1.5
039 AP CHR CH(NAZ)	1	37	46*	-	-
040 AP CHR CH-AMER	2	866	1,531	.8	1.6
053 ASSEMB OF GOD	7	745	1,203	.7	1.3
059 BAPT MISS ASSN	1	16	20*	-	-
081 CATHOLIC	21	NA	34,713	19.0	36.2
081d LATIN	*20*	*NA*	*33,997*	*18.6*	*35.4*
081e MARONITE	*1*	*NA*	*716*	*.4*	*.7*
093 CHR CH (DISC)	5	1,325	2,540	1.4	2.6
097 CHR CHS&CHS CR	4	560	702*	.4	.7
111 CH CR,SCIENTST	2	NR	NR	-	-
123 CH GOD (ANDER)	2	234	238	.1	.2
127 CH GOD (CLEVE)	1	100	125*	.1	.1
151 L-D SAINTS	1	NA	678	.4	.7
157 CH OF BRETHREN	1	186	233*	.1	.2
165 CH OF NAZARENE	6	292	591	.3	.6
167 CHS OF CHRIST	5	468	611	.3	.6
179 CONSRV BAPT	1	NR	NR	-	-
203 EVAN FREE CH	4	215	346	.2	.4
207 E.L.C.A.	11	5,250	6,740	3.7	7.0
213 EVAN MENN INC	1	0	0*	-	-
220 FREE LUTHERAN	1	36	63	-	.1
221 FREE METHODIST	2	186	186	.1	.2
223 FREE WILL BAPT	1	17	21*	-	-
246 GREEK ORTHODOX	1	NR	NR	-	-
259 IFCA	2	NR	NR	-	-
283 LUTH—MO SYNOD	9	4,326	5,835	3.2	6.1
285 MENNONITE CH	4	216	286	.2	.3
287 MENN GEN CONF	4	496	593	.3	.6
291 MISSIONARY CH	3	582	687	.4	.7
313 N AM BAPT CONF	1	60	75*	-	.1
355 PRESB CH (USA)	10	3,777	4,738*	2.6	4.9
356 PRESB CH AMER	3	2,648	2,691	1.5	2.8
371 REF CH IN AM	1	51	83	-	.1
403 SALVATION ARMY	1	200	208	.1	.2
413 S.D.A.	2	376	472*	.3	.5
419 SO BAPT CONV	8	3,148	3,949*	2.2	4.1
435 UNITARIAN-UNIV	1	179	237	.1	.2
438 UN BRETH IN CR	1	52	60	-	.1
443 UN C OF CHRIST	6	1,793	2,249*	1.2	2.3
449 UN METHODIST	26	10,163	12,749*	7.0	13.3
496 JEWISH EST[1]	2	NA	567	.3	.6
497 BLACK BAPT EST[2]	NA	6,104	7,657*	4.2	8.0
498 INDEP.CHARIS.[3]	1	NA	500	.3	.5
499 INDEP.NON-CHAR[3]	1	NA	300	.2	.3

County and Denomination	Number of churches	Communicant, confirmed, full members	Total adherents Number	Percent of total population	Percent of total adherents
PERRY	**47**	**9,085**	**14,908***	**69.6**	**100.0**
005 AME ZION	1	150	235	1.1	1.6
019 AMER BAPT USA	3	291	366*	1.7	2.5
053 ASSEMB OF GOD	2	152	270	1.3	1.8
081 CATHOLIC	4	NA	3,177	14.8	21.3
081d LATIN	*4*	*NA*	*3,177*	*14.8*	*21.3*
093 CHR CH (DISC)	1	240	530	2.5	3.6
097 CHR CHS&CHS CR	3	360	452*	2.1	3.0
127 CH GOD (CLEVE)	1	7	9*	-	.1
165 CH OF NAZARENE	1	61	47	.2	.3
167 CHS OF CHRIST	1	35	46	.2	.3
283 LUTH—MO SYNOD	3	267	307	1.4	2.1
355 PRESB CH (USA)	3	351	441*	2.1	3.0
356 PRESB CH AMER	1	45	72	.3	.5
413 S.D.A.	1	15	19*	.1	.1
419 SO BAPT CONV	17	5,550	6,975*	32.6	46.8
443 UN C OF CHRIST	2	663	833*	3.9	5.6
449 UN METHODIST	3	898	1,129*	5.3	7.6
PIATT	**38**	**5,448**	**8,100***	**52.1**	**100.0**
019 AMER BAPT USA	1	206	257*	1.7	3.2
053 ASSEMB OF GOD	2	54	53	.3	.7
071 BRETHREN (ASH)	2	72	90*	.6	1.1
081 CATHOLIC	2	NA	1,066	6.9	13.2
081d LATIN	*2*	*NA*	*1,066*	*6.9*	*13.2*
089 CHR & MISS AL	1	0	70	.5	.9
093 CHR CH (DISC)	1	68	118	.8	1.5
097 CHR CHS&CHS CR	3	433	540*	3.5	6.7
157 CH OF BRETHREN	2	219	273*	1.8	3.4
165 CH OF NAZARENE	2	163	328	2.1	4.0
167 CHS OF CHRIST	2	100	123	.8	1.5
171 CH GOD-GEN CON	1	175	218*	1.4	2.7
207 E.L.C.A.	1	259	352	2.3	4.3
355 PRESB CH (USA)	2	322	401*	2.6	5.0
419 SO BAPT CONV	5	404	504*	3.2	6.2
443 UN C OF CHRIST	2	282	352*	2.3	4.3
449 UN METHODIST	9	2,691	3,355*	21.6	41.4
PIKE	**56**	**6,373**	**9,057***	**51.5**	**100.0**
019 AMER BAPT USA	3	470	583*	3.3	6.4
053 ASSEMB OF GOD	2	185	320	1.8	3.5
081 CATHOLIC	3	NA	529	3.0	5.8
081d LATIN	*3*	*NA*	*529*	*3.0*	*5.8*
093 CHR CH (DISC)	2	430	844	4.8	9.3
097 CHR CHS&CHS CR	13	1,546	1,919*	10.9	21.2
165 CH OF NAZARENE	5	332	594	3.4	6.6
167 CHS OF CHRIST	6	286	380	2.2	4.2
283 LUTH—MO SYNOD	1	140	184	1.0	2.0
355 PRESB CH (USA)	2	29	36*	.2	.4
419 SO BAPT CONV	4	826	1,025*	5.8	11.3
449 UN METHODIST	15	2,129	2,643*	15.0	29.2
POPE	**20**	**1,686**	**2,030***	**46.4**	**100.0**
127 CH GOD (CLEVE)	1	71	85*	1.9	4.2
167 CHS OF CHRIST	1	19	24	.5	1.2
283 LUTH—MO SYNOD	1	77	101	2.3	5.0
355 PRESB CH (USA)	1	38	46*	1.1	2.3
419 SO BAPT CONV	12	1,243	1,489*	34.0	73.3
449 UN METHODIST	4	238	285*	6.5	14.0
PULASKI	**32**	**3,652**	**5,240***	**69.7**	**100.0**
053 ASSEMB OF GOD	1	74	132	1.8	2.5
081 CATHOLIC	3	NA	446	5.9	8.5
081d LATIN	*3*	*NA*	*446*	*5.9*	*8.5*
093 CHR CH (DISC)	1	55	95	1.3	1.8
097 CHR CHS&CHS CR	2	225	292*	3.9	5.6
167 CHS OF CHRIST	3	111	143	1.9	2.7
181 CONSRV CONGR	2	190	246*	3.3	4.7
283 LUTH—MO SYNOD	1	70	89	1.2	1.7
419 SO BAPT CONV	8	1,727	2,240*	29.8	42.7
443 UN C OF CHRIST	2	107	139*	1.8	2.7
449 UN METHODIST	9	409	531*	7.1	10.1
497 BLACK BAPT EST[2]	NA	684	887*	11.8	16.9
PUTNAM	**11**	**983**	**2,721***	**47.5**	**100.0**
081 CATHOLIC	3	NA	1,485	25.9	54.6
081d LATIN	*3*	*NA*	*1,485*	*25.9*	*54.6*
207 E.L.C.A.	2	259	335	5.8	12.3
226 FRIENDS-USA	1	70	88*	1.5	3.2
226c FGC	*1*	*70*	*88***	*1.5*	*3.2*
435 UNITARIAN-UNIV	1	25	25	.4	.9
443 UN C OF CHRIST	1	325	407*	7.1	15.0
449 UN METHODIST	3	304	381*	6.6	14.0

NA–Not applicable   NR–Not reported   *Total adherents estimated from known number of communicant, confirmed, full members.   - Represents a percent less than 0.1.   Percentages may not total due to rounding.
[1]See Appendix E   [2]See Appendix F   [3]See Appendix G   Lines in *italic* represent a breakdown of Catholic rites or Friends affiliations. They are included in their respective denominational total.

Table 4. Churches and Church Membership by County and Denomination: 1990

County and Denomination	Number of churches	Communicant, confirmed, full members	Total adherents Number	Percent of total population	Percent of total adherents
RANDOLPH	**69**	**14,008**	**25,607***	**74.0**	**100.0**
019 AMER BAPT USA	1	103	127*	.4	.5
053 ASSEMB OF GOD	3	127	316	.9	1.2
059 BAPT MISS ASSN	1	75	93*	.3	.4
081 CATHOLIC	11	NA	7,799	22.6	30.5
081d LATIN	11	NA	7,799	22.6	30.5
097 CHR CHS&CHS CR	2	110	136*	.4	.5
151 L-D SAINTS	1	NA	88	.3	.3
165 CH OF NAZARENE	3	93	223	.6	.9
167 CHS OF CHRIST	2	30	37	.1	.1
207 E.L.C.A.	5	1,642	2,022	5.8	7.9
216 EVAN PRESBY CH	1	43	45	.1	.2
283 LUTH—MO SYNOD	9	5,026	6,380	18.4	24.9
353 CHR BRETHREN	1	20	25	.1	.1
355 PRESB CH (USA)	7	1,316	1,624*	4.7	6.3
356 PRESB CH AMER	2	343	424	1.2	1.7
419 SO BAPT CONV	9	2,497	3,081*	8.9	12.0
443 UN C OF CHRIST	2	667	823*	2.4	3.2
449 UN METHODIST	9	1,349	1,664*	4.8	6.5
497 BLACK BAPT EST2	NA	567	700*	2.0	2.7
RICHLAND	**43**	**5,248**	**9,344***	**56.5**	**100.0**
019 AMER BAPT USA	1	244	308*	1.9	3.3
053 ASSEMB OF GOD	1	68	135	.8	1.4
081 CATHOLIC	2	NA	2,356	14.2	25.2
081d LATIN	2	NA	2,356	14.2	25.2
089 CHR & MISS AL	1	0	15	.1	.2
093 CHR CH (DISC)	1	44	76	.5	.8
097 CHR CHS&CHS CR	7	996	1,256*	7.6	13.4
127 CH GOD (CLEVE)	1	30	38*	.2	.4
151 L-D SAINTS	1	NA	110	.7	1.2
157 CH OF BRETHREN	1	33	42*	.3	.4
165 CH OF NAZARENE	1	130	310	1.9	3.3
167 CHS OF CHRIST	5	245	318	1.9	3.4
193 EPISCOPAL	1	44	67	.4	.7
207 E.L.C.A.	1	484	644	3.9	6.9
221 FREE METHODIST	1	165	183	1.1	2.0
355 PRESB CH (USA)	1	248	313*	1.9	3.3
413 S.D.A.	1	47	59*	.4	.6
419 SO BAPT CONV	3	506	638*	3.9	6.8
443 UN C OF CHRIST	2	139	175*	1.1	1.9
449 UN METHODIST	11	1,825	2,301*	13.9	24.6
ROCK ISLAND	**132**	**36,271**	**84,407***	**56.8**	**100.0**
019 AMER BAPT USA	4	1,142	1,428*	1.0	1.7
053 ASSEMB OF GOD	6	773	1,034	.7	1.2
057 BAPT GEN CONF	1	334	418*	.3	.5
081 CATHOLIC	15	NA	33,944	22.8	40.2
081d LATIN	15	NA	33,944	22.8	40.2
089 CHR & MISS AL	1	18	19	-	-
093 CHR CH (DISC)	4	1,448	3,445	2.3	4.1
097 CHR CHS&CHS CR	2	192	240*	.2	.3
111 CH CR,SCIENTST	2	NR	NR	-	-
123 CH GOD (ANDER)	1	18	18	-	-
127 CH GOD (CLEVE)	1	57	71*	-	.1
145 CH GOD PROPHCY	1	38	48*	-	.1
151 L-D SAINTS	1	NA	565	.4	.7
165 CH OF NAZARENE	6	411	1,008	.7	1.2
167 CHS OF CHRIST	2	240	305	.2	.4
175 CONGR CHR CHS	1	67	84*	.1	.1
179 CONSRV BAPT	1	NR	NR	-	-
203 EVAN FREE CH	3	872	1,031	.7	1.2
207 E.L.C.A.	11	5,848	7,551	5.1	8.9
223 FREE WILL BAPT	3	299	374*	.3	.4
246 GREEK ORTHODOX	3	NR	NR	-	-
263 INT FOURSQ GOS	3	3,407	4,261*	2.9	5.0
283 LUTH—MO SYNOD	7	4,127	5,767	3.9	6.8
285 MENNONITE CH	2	161	219	.1	.3
329 OPEN BIBLE STD	1	NR	NR	-	-
353 CHR BRETHREN	2	177	445	.3	.5
355 PRESB CH (USA)	12	3,646	4,560*	3.1	5.4
403 SALVATION ARMY	2	244	278	.2	.3
413 S.D.A.	1	134	168*	.1	.2
419 SO BAPT CONV	4	772	965*	.6	1.1
431 UKRANIAN AMER	1	NR	NR	-	-
443 UN C OF CHRIST	4	2,478	3,099*	2.1	3.7
449 UN METHODIST	20	6,518	8,151*	5.5	9.7
467 WESLEYAN	1	81	477	.3	.6
469 WELS	1	197	288	.2	.3
496 JEWISH EST1	1	NA	530	.4	.6
497 BLACK BAPT EST2	NA	2,572	3,216*	2.2	3.8
499 INDEP.NON-CHAR3	1	NA	400	.3	.5
SAINT CLAIR	**209**	**60,830**	**137,229***	**52.2**	**100.0**
005 AME ZION	2	410	558	.2	.4
019 AMER BAPT USA	5	1,224	1,576*	.6	1.1
053 ASSEMB OF GOD	10	1,159	1,741	.7	1.3
059 BAPT MISS ASSN	2	1,122	1,445*	.5	1.1
081 CATHOLIC	34	NA	50,809	19.3	37.0
081d LATIN	34	NA	50,809	19.3	37.0
089 CHR & MISS AL	1	56	122	-	.1
093 CHR CH (DISC)	2	253	326	.1	.2
097 CHR CHS&CHS CR	5	1,230	1,584*	.6	1.2
111 CH CR,SCIENTST	2	NR	NR	-	-
123 CH GOD (ANDER)	5	363	405	.2	.3
127 CH GOD (CLEVE)	2	134	173*	.1	.1
145 CH GOD PROPHCY	1	38	49*	-	-
151 L-D SAINTS	3	NA	945	.4	.7
165 CH OF NAZARENE	7	499	803	.3	.6
167 CHS OF CHRIST	7	1,199	1,826	.7	1.3
193 EPISCOPAL	2	298	564	.2	.4
203 EVAN FREE CH	1	24	40	-	-
207 E.L.C.A.	7	1,729	2,289	.9	1.7
223 FREE WILL BAPT	1	48	62*	-	-
246 GREEK ORTHODOX	1	NR	NR	-	-
259 IFCA	4	NR	NR	-	-
263 INT FOURSQ GOS	1	47	61*	-	-
283 LUTH—MO SYNOD	11	3,841	5,046	1.9	3.7
325 OLD REG BAPT	1	48	62*	-	-
353 CHR BRETHREN	1	50	70	-	.1
355 PRESB CH (USA)	2	1,193	1,536*	.6	1.1
356 PRESB CH AMER	2	294	301	.1	.2
403 SALVATION ARMY	2	227	234	.1	.2
413 S.D.A.	2	331	426*	.2	.3
419 SO BAPT CONV	37	16,051	20,669*	7.9	15.1
436 UNITED BAPT	1	29	37*	-	-
443 UN C OF CHRIST	24	10,098	13,003*	4.9	9.5
449 UN METHODIST	17	6,212	7,999*	3.0	5.8
469 WELS	1	38	62	-	-
496 JEWISH EST1	2	NA	5,700	2.2	4.2
497 BLACK BAPT EST2	NA	12,585	16,206*	6.2	11.8
499 INDEP.NON-CHAR3	1	NA	500	.2	.4
SALINE	**77**	**13,045**	**17,531***	**66.0**	**100.0**
019 AMER BAPT USA	1	94	115*	.4	.7
053 ASSEMB OF GOD	1	51	68	.3	.4
081 CATHOLIC	2	NA	1,230	4.6	7.0
081d LATIN	2	NA	1,230	4.6	7.0
097 CHR CHS&CHS CR	2	490	599*	2.3	3.4
121 CH GOD (ABR)	1	40	49*	.2	.3
123 CH GOD (ANDER)	3	180	260	1.0	1.5
127 CH GOD (CLEVE)	4	340	416*	1.6	2.4
145 CH GOD PROPHCY	1	38	46*	.2	.3
151 L-D SAINTS	1	NA	207	.8	1.2
165 CH OF NAZARENE	2	89	258	1.0	1.5
167 CHS OF CHRIST	2	54	73	.3	.4
185 CUMBER PRESB	5	322	330	1.2	1.9
193 EPISCOPAL	1	32	34	.1	.2
207 E.L.C.A.	1	115	152	.6	.9
221 FREE METHODIST	1	9	15	.1	.1
355 PRESB CH (USA)	2	293	358*	1.3	2.0
413 S.D.A.	2	50	61*	.2	.3
415 S-D BAPTIST GC	1	55	67*	.3	.4
419 SO BAPT CONV	33	9,379	11,465*	43.2	65.4
449 UN METHODIST	11	1,229	1,502*	5.7	8.6
497 BLACK BAPT EST2	NA	185	226*	.9	1.3
SANGAMON	**177**	**48,974**	**103,981***	**58.3**	**100.0**
019 AMER BAPT USA	10	3,523	4,424*	2.5	4.3
053 ASSEMB OF GOD	6	4,393	7,967	4.5	7.7
057 BAPT GEN CONF	1	30	38*	-	-
081 CATHOLIC	21	NA	35,589	20.0	34.2
081d LATIN	21	NA	35,589	20.0	34.2
089 CHR & MISS AL	1	0	17	-	-
093 CHR CH (DISC)	4	821	1,346	.8	1.3
097 CHR CHS&CHS CR	18	6,974	8,757*	4.9	8.4
105 CHRISTIAN REF	1	40	61	-	.1
111 CH CR,SCIENTST	1	NR	NR	-	-
123 CH GOD (ANDER)	4	160	450	.3	.4
127 CH GOD (CLEVE)	2	181	227*	.1	.2
151 L-D SAINTS	1	NA	610	.3	.6
157 CH OF BRETHREN	1	84	105*	.1	.1
165 CH OF NAZARENE	6	708	1,165	.7	1.1
167 CHS OF CHRIST	4	356	455	.3	.4
193 EPISCOPAL	3	776	1,046	.6	1.0
203 EVAN FREE CH	1	180	352	.2	.3
207 E.L.C.A.	5	2,750	3,811	2.1	3.7
221 FREE METHODIST	1	72	81	-	.1
223 FREE WILL BAPT	1	26	33*	-	-
226 FRIENDS-USA	1	7	9*	-	-
226c FGC	1	7	9*	-	-
246 GREEK ORTHODOX	1	NR	NR	-	-
259 IFCA	2	NR	NR	-	-

NA–Not applicable   NR–Not reported   *Total adherents estimated from known number of communicant, confirmed, full members.   - Represents a percent less than 0.1.   Percentages may not total due to rounding.
1See Appendix E   2See Appendix F   3See Appendix G   Lines in italic represent a breakdown of Catholic rites or Friends affiliations. They are included in their respective denominational total.

Table 4. Churches and Church Membership by County and Denomination: 1990

County and Denomination	Number of churches	Communicant, confirmed, full members	Total adherents		
			Number	Percent of total population	Percent of total adherents
263 INT FOURSQ GOS	2	146	183*	.1	.2
283 LUTH—MO SYNOD	12	5,614	7,759	4.3	7.5
353 CHR BRETHREN	1	80	120	.1	.1
355 PRESB CH (USA)	13	4,130	5,186*	2.9	5.0
403 SALVATION ARMY	1	165	177	.1	.2
413 S.D.A.	2	126	158*	.1	.2
419 SO BAPT CONV	11	3,367	4,228*	2.4	4.1
435 UNITARIAN-UNIV	1	118	163	.1	.2
443 UN C OF CHRIST	2	718	902*	.5	.9
449 UN METHODIST	32	9,906	12,438*	7.0	12.0
496 JEWISH EST[1]	2	NA	1,000	.6	1.0
497 BLACK BAPT EST[2]	NA	3,523	4,424*	2.5	4.3
498 INDEP.CHARIS.[3]	2	NA	700	.4	.7
SCHUYLER	**26**	**2,305**	**3,196***	**42.6**	**100.0**
053 ASSEMB OF GOD	2	68	85	1.1	2.7
081 CATHOLIC	1	NA	211	2.8	6.6
081d LATIN	1	NA	211	2.8	6.6
093 CHR CH (DISC)	2	228	396	5.3	12.4
097 CHR CHS&CHS CR	2	245	303*	4.0	9.5
165 CH OF NAZARENE	1	32	43	.6	1.3
167 CHS OF CHRIST	1	15	19	.3	.6
221 FREE METHODIST	1	130	152	2.0	4.8
283 LUTH—MO SYNOD	1	90	127	1.7	4.0
353 CHR BRETHREN	1	8	20	.3	.6
355 PRESB CH (USA)	1	139	172*	2.3	5.4
419 SO BAPT CONV	1	221	273*	3.6	8.5
449 UN METHODIST	12	1,129	1,395*	18.6	43.6
SCOTT	**24**	**2,943**	**4,226***	**74.9**	**100.0**
019 AMER BAPT USA	3	898	1,129*	20.0	26.7
053 ASSEMB OF GOD	1	35	57	1.0	1.3
081 CATHOLIC	2	NA	380	6.7	9.0
081d LATIN	2	NA	380	6.7	9.0
093 CHR CH (DISC)	2	162	313	5.5	7.4
207 E.L.C.A.	1	140	175	3.1	4.1
283 LUTH—MO SYNOD	2	406	535	9.5	12.7
419 SO BAPT CONV	8	799	1,005*	17.8	23.8
449 UN METHODIST	5	503	632*	11.2	15.0
SHELBY	**71**	**9,199**	**12,898***	**57.9**	**100.0**
019 AMER BAPT USA	1	360	450*	2.0	3.5
053 ASSEMB OF GOD	1	41	81	.4	.6
081 CATHOLIC	4	NA	1,076	4.8	8.3
081d LATIN	4	NA	1,076	4.8	8.3
093 CHR CH (DISC)	2	519	825	3.7	6.4
097 CHR CHS&CHS CR	10	2,395	2,993*	13.4	23.2
127 CH GOD (CLEVE)	1	36	45*	.2	.3
165 CH OF NAZARENE	1	234	388	1.7	3.0
167 CHS OF CHRIST	10	316	404	1.8	3.1
171 CH GOD-GEN CON	1	44	55*	.2	.4
207 E.L.C.A.	2	244	309	1.4	2.4
221 FREE METHODIST	3	171	184	.8	1.4
283 LUTH—MO SYNOD	5	1,360	1,752	7.9	13.6
285 MENNONITE CH	1	41	41	.2	.3
355 PRESB CH (USA)	1	100	125*	.6	1.0
413 S.D.A.	1	46	57*	.3	.4
419 SO BAPT CONV	7	662	827*	3.7	6.4
443 UN C OF CHRIST	1	90	112*	.5	.9
449 UN METHODIST	19	2,540	3,174*	14.3	24.6
STARK	**18**	**1,995**	**3,773***	**57.7**	**100.0**
019 AMER BAPT USA	1	222	277*	4.2	7.3
040 AP CHR CH-AMER	1	104	184	2.8	4.9
081 CATHOLIC	3	NA	1,132	17.3	30.0
081d LATIN	3	NA	1,132	17.3	30.0
165 CH OF NAZARENE	1	69	170	2.6	4.5
175 CONGR CHR CHS	1	150	187*	2.9	5.0
176 CCC, NOT NAT'L	1	50	62*	.9	1.6
179 CONSRV BAPT	1	NR	NR	-	-
207 E.L.C.A.	1	100	139	2.1	3.7
355 PRESB CH (USA)	1	87	109*	1.7	2.9
443 UN C OF CHRIST	2	255	318*	4.9	8.4
449 UN METHODIST	5	958	1,195*	18.3	31.7
STEPHENSON	**80**	**16,045**	**28,700***	**59.7**	**100.0**
053 ASSEMB OF GOD	1	336	1,000	2.1	3.5
081 CATHOLIC	6	NA	6,923	14.4	24.1
081d LATIN	6	NA	6,923	14.4	24.1
105 CHRISTIAN REF	1	104	139	.3	.5
111 CH CR,SCIENTST	1	NR	NR	-	-
123 CH GOD (ANDER)	1	35	60	.1	.2
151 L-D SAINTS	1	NA	290	.6	1.0
157 CH OF BRETHREN	3	197	247*	.5	.9
165 CH OF NAZARENE	1	171	385	.8	1.3

County and Denomination	Number of churches	Communicant, confirmed, full members	Total adherents		
			Number	Percent of total population	Percent of total adherents
167 CHS OF CHRIST	1	105	137	.3	.5
171 CH GOD-GEN CON	1	96	120*	.2	.4
181 CONSRV CONGR	1	384	481*	1.0	1.7
193 EPISCOPAL	1	278	404	.8	1.4
199 EVAN CONGR CH	2	292	292	.6	1.0
203 EVAN FREE CH	5	808	1,056	2.2	3.7
207 E.L.C.A.	8	2,396	3,174	6.6	11.1
221 FREE METHODIST	3	103	183	.4	.6
226 FRIENDS-USA	1	3	6	-	-
226c FGC	1	3	6	-	-
283 LUTH—MO SYNOD	3	1,347	1,822	3.8	6.3
285 MENNONITE CH	1	143	221	.5	.8
329 OPEN BIBLE STD	1	NR	NR	-	-
355 PRESB CH (USA)	3	746	935*	1.9	3.3
371 REF CH IN AM	2	362	628	1.3	2.2
403 SALVATION ARMY	1	87	95	.2	.3
413 S.D.A.	1	49	61*	.1	.2
419 SO BAPT CONV	1	88	110*	.2	.4
443 UN C OF CHRIST	6	1,935	2,426*	5.0	8.5
449 UN METHODIST	22	5,275	6,614*	13.8	23.0
469 WELS	1	93	124	.3	.4
497 BLACK BAPT EST[2]	NA	612	767*	1.6	2.7
TAZEWELL	**135**	**32,622**	**60,817***	**49.2**	**100.0**
019 AMER BAPT USA	4	1,245	1,565*	1.3	2.6
039 AP CHR CH(NAZ)	1	166	209*	.2	.3
040 AP CHR CH-AMER	3	955	1,690	1.4	2.8
053 ASSEMB OF GOD	5	1,234	2,262	1.8	3.7
059 BAPT MISS ASSN	1	80	101*	.1	.2
081 CATHOLIC	7	NA	14,461	11.7	23.8
081d LATIN	7	NA	14,461	11.7	23.8
093 CHR CH (DISC)	4	1,461	2,282	1.8	3.8
097 CHR CHS&CHS CR	7	1,975	2,482*	2.0	4.1
121 CH GOD (ABR)	1	36	45*	-	.1
123 CH GOD (ANDER)	3	199	363	.3	.6
127 CH GOD (CLEVE)	1	38	48*	-	.1
145 CH GOD PROPHCY	2	77	97*	.1	.2
151 L-D SAINTS	1	NA	616	.5	1.0
165 CH OF NAZARENE	6	805	1,904	1.5	3.1
167 CHS OF CHRIST	4	530	681	.6	1.1
176 CCC, NOT NAT'L	1	170	214*	.2	.4
179 CONSRV BAPT	2	NR	NR	-	-
193 EPISCOPAL	2	268	372	.3	.6
207 E.L.C.A.	4	1,784	2,467	2.0	4.1
213 EVAN MENN INC	3	689	866*	.7	1.4
217 FIRE BAPTIZED	1	17	21*	-	-
221 FREE METHODIST	2	143	184	.1	.3
259 IFCA	2	NR	NR	-	-
283 LUTH—MO SYNOD	9	4,546	6,566	5.3	10.8
285 MENNONITE CH	6	895	1,331	1.1	2.2
287 MENN GEN CONF	2	129	161	.1	.3
291 MISSIONARY CH	5	408	477	.4	.8
329 OPEN BIBLE STD	1	NR	NR	-	-
339 PENT CH OF GOD	2	68	154	.1	.3
355 PRESB CH (USA)	6	964	1,212*	1.0	2.0
371 REF CH IN AM	2	306	543	.4	.9
403 SALVATION ARMY	1	93	101	.1	.2
419 SO BAPT CONV	12	3,101	3,897*	3.2	6.4
443 UN C OF CHRIST	6	2,368	2,976*	2.4	4.9
449 UN METHODIST	14	7,716	9,697*	7.8	15.9
467 WESLEYAN	1	61	250	.2	.4
469 WELS	1	95	139	.1	.2
496 JEWISH EST[1]	0	NA	383	.3	.6
UNION	**53**	**9,535**	**12,836***	**72.9**	**100.0**
019 AMER BAPT USA	2	147	179*	1.0	1.4
053 ASSEMB OF GOD	1	40	33	.2	.3
081 CATHOLIC	2	NA	1,150	6.5	9.0
081d LATIN	2	NA	1,150	6.5	9.0
097 CHR CHS&CHS CR	1	300	365*	2.1	2.8
123 CH GOD (ANDER)	1	50	76	.4	.6
127 CH GOD (CLEVE)	1	62	75*	.4	.6
165 CH OF NAZARENE	1	198	385	2.2	3.0
167 CHS OF CHRIST	2	135	175	1.0	1.4
185 CUMBER PRESB	4	117	121	.7	.9
207 E.L.C.A.	4	675	801	4.5	6.2
216 EVAN PRESBY CH	1	133	134	.8	1.0
259 IFCA	1	NR	NR	-	-
283 LUTH—MO SYNOD	1	134	168	1.0	1.3
286 E.PA MENNONITE	1	33	40*	.2	.3
355 PRESB CH (USA)	1	124	151*	.9	1.2
419 SO BAPT CONV	22	6,808	8,279*	47.0	64.5
449 UN METHODIST	7	579	704*	4.0	5.5
VERMILION	**137**	**23,943**	**41,969***	**47.6**	**100.0**
019 AMER BAPT USA	4	1,170	1,465*	1.7	3.5

NA–Not applicable   NR–Not reported   *Total adherents estimated from known number of communicant, confirmed, full members.   - Represents a percent less than 0.1.   Percentages may not total due to rounding.
[1]See Appendix E   [2]See Appendix F   [3]See Appendix G   Lines in *italic* represent a breakdown of Catholic rites or Friends affiliations. They are included in their respective denominational total.

127

Table 4. Churches and Church Membership by County and Denomination: 1990

County and Denomination	Number of churches	Communicant, confirmed, full members	Total adherents Number	Percent of total population	Percent of total adherents
053 ASSEM OF GOD	3	379	712	.8	1.7
081 CATHOLIC	7	NA	8,560	9.7	20.4
081d *LATIN*	7	NA	8,560	9.7	20.4
089 CHR & MISS AL	1	76	141	.2	.3
093 CHR CH (DISC)	5	1,315	2,707	3.1	6.4
097 CHR CHS&CHS CR	27	5,420	6,786*	7.7	16.2
111 CH CR,SCIENTST	1	NR	NR	-	-
123 CH GOD (ANDER)	3	141	201	.2	.5
127 CH GOD (CLEVE)	2	194	243*	.3	.6
151 L-D SAINTS	1	NA	284	.3	.7
165 CH OF NAZARENE	16	1,849	3,220	3.6	7.7
167 CHS OF CHRIST	3	306	385	.4	.9
175 CONGR CHR CHS	2	168	210*	.2	.5
185 CUMBER PRESB	1	86	86	.1	.2
193 EPISCOPAL	1	131	177	.2	.4
207 E.L.C.A.	2	443	563	.6	1.3
215 EVAN METH CH	1	44	55*	.1	.1
221 FREE METHODIST	1	106	106	.1	.3
226 FRIENDS-USA	4	551	690*	.8	1.6
226e *FUM*	4	551	690*	.8	1.6
263 INT FOURSQ GOS	2	44	55*	.1	.1
283 LUTH—MO SYNOD	3	2,163	2,789	3.2	6.6
339 PENT CH OF GOD	1	53	90	.1	.2
355 PRESB CH (USA)	4	933	1,168*	1.3	2.8
403 SALVATION ARMY	1	95	101	.1	.2
413 S.D.A.	2	96	120*	.1	.3
419 SO BAPT CONV	1	289	362*	.4	.9
443 UN C OF CHRIST	4	791	990*	1.1	2.4
449 UN METHODIST	30	5,519	6,909*	7.8	16.5
467 WESLEYAN	1	23	43	-	.1
496 JEWISH EST[1]	1	NA	0	-	-
497 BLACK BAPT EST[2]	NA	1,558	1,951*	2.2	4.6
498 INDEP.CHARIS.[3]	2	NA	800	.9	1.9
WABASH	**31**	**3,777**	**7,217***	**55.0**	**100.0**
081 CATHOLIC	2	NA	2,073	15.8	28.7
081d *LATIN*	2	NA	2,073	15.8	28.7
093 CHR CH (DISC)	3	522	825	6.3	11.4
097 CHR CHS&CHS CR	4	640	805*	6.1	11.2
123 CH GOD (ANDER)	1	191	248	1.9	3.4
151 L-D SAINTS	1	NA	131	1.0	1.8
165 CH OF NAZARENE	1	94	132	1.0	1.8
167 CHS OF CHRIST	1	350	500	3.8	6.9
193 EPISCOPAL	1	66	91	.7	1.3
207 E.L.C.A.	1	209	268	2.0	3.7
221 FREE METHODIST	2	110	132	1.0	1.8
283 LUTH—MO SYNOD	1	40	56	.4	.8
355 PRESB CH (USA)	2	124	156*	1.2	2.2
419 SO BAPT CONV	1	325	409*	3.1	5.7
449 UN METHODIST	10	1,106	1,391*	10.6	19.3
WARREN	**36**	**6,593**	**10,188***	**53.1**	**100.0**
019 AMER BAPT USA	3	352	442*	2.3	4.3
053 ASSEM OF GOD	2	31	50	.3	.5
057 BAPT GEN CONF	2	321	403*	2.1	4.0
081 CATHOLIC	2	NA	1,614	8.4	15.8
081d *LATIN*	2	NA	1,614	8.4	15.8
093 CHR CH (DISC)	3	425	698	3.6	6.9
097 CHR CHS&CHS CR	3	1,104	1,385*	7.2	13.6
165 CH OF NAZARENE	2	102	240	1.3	2.4
207 E.L.C.A.	1	596	761	4.0	7.5
263 INT FOURSQ GOS	1	112	141*	.7	1.4
355 PRESB CH (USA)	7	1,351	1,695*	8.8	16.6
413 S.D.A.	1	59	74*	.4	.7
419 SO BAPT CONV	1	114	143*	.7	1.4
449 UN METHODIST	8	2,026	2,542*	13.3	25.0
WASHINGTON	**41**	**6,167**	**12,417***	**83.0**	**100.0**
053 ASSEM OF GOD	1	31	51	.3	.4
081 CATHOLIC	6	NA	4,588	30.7	36.9
081d *LATIN*	6	NA	4,588	30.7	36.9
097 CHR CHS&CHS CR	1	40	50*	.3	.4
165 CH OF NAZARENE	1	28	42	.3	.3
283 LUTH—MO SYNOD	7	2,259	2,888	19.3	23.3
355 PRESB CH (USA)	2	267	336*	2.2	2.7
419 SO BAPT CONV	6	970	1,222*	8.2	9.8
443 UN C OF CHRIST	11	1,882	2,371*	15.8	19.1
449 UN METHODIST	6	690	869*	5.8	7.0
WAYNE	**64**	**7,957**	**10,123***	**58.7**	**100.0**
053 ASSEM OF GOD	1	81	200	1.2	2.0
081 CATHOLIC	1	NA	246	1.4	2.4
081d *LATIN*	1	NA	246	1.4	2.4
097 CHR CHS&CHS CR	7	1,460	1,803*	10.5	17.8
123 CH GOD (ANDER)	1	12	12	.1	.1
127 CH GOD (CLEVE)	2	129	159*	.9	1.6

County and Denomination	Number of churches	Communicant, confirmed, full members	Total adherents Number	Percent of total population	Percent of total adherents
157 CH OF BRETHREN	1	22	27*	.2	.3
165 CH OF NAZARENE	2	120	223	1.3	2.2
167 CHS OF CHRIST	1	75	97	.6	1.0
175 CONGR CHR CHS	1	92	114*	.7	1.1
185 CUMBER PRESB	5	624	637	3.7	6.3
223 FREE WILL BAPT	3	294	363*	2.1	3.6
283 LUTH—MO SYNOD	1	25	36	.2	.4
285 MENNONITE CH	1	26	33	.2	.3
286 E.PA MENNONITE	1	43	53*	.3	.5
419 SO BAPT CONV	20	3,489	4,310*	25.0	42.6
449 UN METHODIST	16	1,465	1,810*	10.5	17.9
WHITE	**58**	**7,728**	**10,515***	**63.6**	**100.0**
053 ASSEM OF GOD	1	36	40	.2	.4
081 CATHOLIC	2	NA	987	6.0	9.4
081d *LATIN*	2	NA	987	6.0	9.4
097 CHR CHS&CHS CR	4	1,221	1,499*	9.1	14.3
123 CH GOD (ANDER)	1	25	35	.2	.3
127 CH GOD (CLEVE)	2	226	277*	1.7	2.6
165 CH OF NAZARENE	1	57	148	.9	1.4
167 CHS OF CHRIST	4	356	455	2.8	4.3
185 CUMBER PRESB	4	280	293	1.8	2.8
283 LUTH—MO SYNOD	1	43	47	.3	.4
355 PRESB CH (USA)	3	265	325*	2.0	3.1
361 PRIM BAPT ASCS	1	42	52*	.3	.5
419 SO BAPT CONV	13	3,296	4,047*	24.5	38.5
449 UN METHODIST	18	1,881	2,310*	14.0	22.0
WHITESIDE	**93**	**20,668**	**40,078***	**66.6**	**100.0**
001 ADVENT CHR CH	1	67	84*	.1	.2
019 AMER BAPT USA	4	591	745*	1.2	1.9
053 ASSEM OF GOD	3	397	797	1.3	2.0
075 BRETHREN IN CR	1	41	71	.1	.2
081 CATHOLIC	9	NA	12,173	20.2	30.4
081d *LATIN*	9	NA	12,173	20.2	30.4
093 CHR CH (DISC)	2	428	835	1.4	2.1
097 CHR CHS&CHS CR	6	816	1,028*	1.7	2.6
105 CHRISTIAN REF	3	650	963	1.6	2.4
123 CH GOD (ANDER)	1	60	75	.1	.2
165 CH OF NAZARENE	3	588	898	1.5	2.2
179 CONSRV BAPT	1	NR	NR	-	-
193 EPISCOPAL	2	259	372	.6	.9
199 EVAN CONGR CH	1	64	64	.1	.2
203 EVAN FREE CH	1	44	107	.2	.3
207 E.L.C.A.	7	3,810	4,795	8.0	12.0
221 FREE METHODIST	1	28	32	.1	.1
263 INT FOURSQ GOS	1	88	111*	.2	.3
283 LUTH—MO SYNOD	4	1,431	1,831	3.0	4.6
285 MENNONITE CH	3	380	678	1.1	1.7
329 OPEN BIBLE STD	1	NR	NR	-	-
355 PRESB CH (USA)	4	1,198	1,510*	2.5	3.8
371 REF CH IN AM	8	2,406	3,709	6.2	9.3
403 SALVATION ARMY	1	123	126	.2	.3
413 S.D.A.	1	49	62*	.1	.2
419 SO BAPT CONV	5	1,396	1,759*	2.9	4.4
438 UN BRETH IN CR	1	48	62	.1	.2
443 UN C OF CHRIST	3	845	1,065*	1.8	2.7
449 UN METHODIST	14	4,861	6,126*	10.2	15.3
496 JEWISH EST[1]	1	NA	0	-	-
WILL	**206**	**51,415**	**182,363***	**51.0**	**100.0**
019 AMER BAPT USA	6	1,524	1,993*	.6	1.1
053 ASSEM OF GOD	5	883	2,541	.7	1.4
057 BAPT GEN CONF	3	367	480*	.1	.3
081 CATHOLIC	39	NA	110,614	31.0	60.7
081b *BYZAN RUTH*	1	NA	296	-	.2
081d *LATIN*	38	NA	110,318	30.9	60.5
089 CHR & MISS AL	2	96	229	.1	.1
097 CHR CHS&CHS CR	10	2,308	3,019*	.8	1.7
105 CHRISTIAN REF	1	129	266	.1	.1
111 CH CR,SCIENTST	2	NR	NR	-	-
123 CH GOD (ANDER)	3	93	166	-	.1
127 CH GOD (CLEVE)	2	196	256*	.1	.1
145 CH GOD PROPHCY	2	77	101*	-	.1
151 L-D SAINTS	1	NA	374	.1	.2
165 CH OF NAZARENE	6	557	1,043	.3	.6
167 CHS OF CHRIST	7	539	695	.2	.4
175 CONGR CHR CHS	1	143	187*	.1	.1
181 CONSRV CONGR	1	245	320*	.1	.2
193 EPISCOPAL	5	702	913	.3	.5
207 E.L.C.A.	12	5,230	7,540	2.1	4.1
215 EVAN METH CH	1	74	97*	-	.1
221 FREE METHODIST	1	78	78	-	-
223 FREE WILL BAPT	1	45	59*	-	-
246 GREEK ORTHODOX	1	NR	NR	-	-
283 LUTH—MO SYNOD	14	6,333	8,759	2.5	4.8

NA–Not applicable   NR–Not reported   *Total adherents estimated from known number of communicant, confirmed, full members.   - Represents a percent less than 0.1.   Percentages may not total due to rounding.
[1]See Appendix E   [2]See Appendix F   [3]See Appendix G   Lines in *italic* represent a breakdown of Catholic rites or Friends affiliations. They are included in their respective denominational total.

Table 4. Churches and Church Membership by County and Denomination: 1990

County and Denomination	Number of churches	Communicant, confirmed, full members	Total adherents Number	Total adherents Percent of total population	Total adherents Percent of total adherents
331 ORTH CH IN AM	1	NR	NR	-	-
339 PENT CH OF GOD	1	34	77	-	-
349 PENT HOLINESS	1	32	42*	-	-
353 CHR BRETHREN	1	25	35	-	-
355 PRESB CH (USA)	11	2,602	3,403*	1.0	1.9
371 REF CH IN AM	2	418	780	.2	.4
403 SALVATION ARMY	1	100	103	-	.1
413 S.D.A.	2	187	245*	.1	.1
419 SO BAPT CONV	19	4,877	6,379*	1.8	3.5
435 UNITARIAN-UNIV	1	87	100	-	.1
443 UN C OF CHRIST	12	4,770	6,239*	1.7	3.4
449 UN METHODIST	24	7,922	10,361*	2.9	5.7
467 WESLEYAN	1	18	48	-	-
469 WELS	2	1,316	1,737	.5	1.0
496 JEWISH EST[1]	1	NA	779	.2	.4
497 BLACK BAPT EST[2]	NA	9,408	12,305*	3.4	6.7
WILLIAMSON	**107**	**21,554**	**32,264***	**55.9**	**100.0**
019 AMER BAPT USA	10	1,741	2,137*	3.7	6.6
053 ASSEMB OF GOD	3	132	360	.6	1.1
059 BAPT MISS ASSN	1	90	110*	.2	.3
081 CATHOLIC	5	NA	5,495	9.5	17.0
081d LATIN	5	NA	5,495	9.5	17.0
093 CHR CH (DISC)	1	217	293	.5	.9
097 CHR CHS&CHS CR	8	1,435	1,761*	3.1	5.5
111 CH CR,SCIENTST	1	NR	NR	-	-
123 CH GOD (ANDER)	3	329	341	.6	1.1
127 CH GOD (CLEVE)	3	365	448*	.8	1.4
145 CH GOD PROPHCY	2	77	95*	.2	.3
165 CH OF NAZARENE	2	136	205	.4	.6
193 EPISCOPAL	1	67	85	.1	.3
207 E.L.C.A.	1	200	262	.5	.8
221 FREE METHODIST	2	56	88	.2	.3
223 FREE WILL BAPT	3	473	581*	1.0	1.8
283 LUTH—MO SYNOD	2	192	276	.5	.9
339 PENT CH OF GOD	1	35	77	.1	.2
355 PRESB CH (USA)	4	444	545*	.9	1.7
413 S.D.A.	2	146	179*	.3	.6
419 SO BAPT CONV	32	11,827	14,517*	25.1	45.0
443 UN C OF CHRIST	2	564	692*	1.2	2.1
449 UN METHODIST	17	2,800	3,437*	6.0	10.7
496 JEWISH EST[1]	1	NA	0	-	-
497 BLACK BAPT EST[2]	NA	228	280*	.5	.9
WINNEBAGO	**182**	**57,118**	**127,070***	**50.2**	**100.0**
019 AMER BAPT USA	3	909	1,146*	.5	.9
022 EASTERN ORTH	1	113	113	-	.1
053 ASSEMB OF GOD	9	2,199	4,371	1.7	3.4
057 BAPT GEN CONF	3	850	1,072*	.4	.8
081 CATHOLIC	16	NA	47,689	18.9	37.5
081d LATIN	16	NA	47,689	18.9	37.5
089 CHR & MISS AL	1	0	0	-	-
093 CHR CH (DISC)	3	226	439	.2	.3
097 CHR CHS&CHS CR	4	992	1,251*	.5	1.0
111 CH CR,SCIENTST	1	NR	NR	-	-
121 CH GOD (ABR)	2	54	68*	-	.1
123 CH GOD (ANDER)	3	33	93	-	.1
127 CH GOD (CLEVE)	2	62	78*	-	.1
145 CH GOD PROPHCY	1	38	48*	-	-
151 L-D SAINTS	2	NA	883	.3	.7
157 CH OF BRETHREN	1	99	125*	-	.1
165 CH OF NAZARENE	5	480	853	.3	.7
167 CHS OF CHRIST	9	798	1,109	.4	.9
179 CONSRV BAPT	1	NR	NR	-	-
193 EPISCOPAL	3	821	1,359	.5	1.1
199 EVAN CONGR CH	1	36	76	-	.1
203 EVAN FREE CH	6	2,728	2,986	1.2	2.3
207 E.L.C.A.	23	17,721	23,436	9.3	18.4
221 FREE METHODIST	1	45	64	-	.1
223 FREE WILL BAPT	1	17	21*	-	-
226 FRIENDS-USA	1	13	16*	-	-
226c FGC	1	13	16*	-	-
246 GREEK ORTHODOX	1	NR	NR	-	-
263 INT FOURSQ GOS	1	31	39*	-	-
283 LUTH—MO SYNOD	9	3,715	4,984	2.0	3.9
329 OPEN BIBLE STD	1	NR	NR	-	-
349 PENT HOLINESS	1	67	84*	-	.1
355 PRESB CH (USA)	8	3,481	4,388*	1.7	3.5
371 REF CH IN AM	1	163	277	.1	.2
403 SALVATION ARMY	2	408	445	.2	.4
413 S.D.A.	2	329	415*	.2	.3
419 SO BAPT CONV	9	2,207	2,782*	1.1	2.2
435 UNITARIAN-UNIV	2	544	680	.3	.5
438 UN BRETH IN CR	1	35	35	-	-
443 UN C OF CHRIST	8	2,982	3,759*	1.5	3.0
449 UN METHODIST	24	8,955	11,289*	4.5	8.9
467 WESLEYAN	1	52	181	.1	.1
469 WELS	2	212	307	.1	.2
496 JEWISH EST[1]	2	NA	891	.4	.7
497 BLACK BAPT EST[2]	NA	5,703	7,189*	2.8	5.7
498 INDEP.CHARIS.[3]	3	NA	900	.4	.7
499 INDEP.NON-CHAR[3]	1	NA	1,100	.4	.9
WOODFORD	**61**	**9,637**	**18,445***	**56.5**	**100.0**
019 AMER BAPT USA	3	508	655*	2.0	3.6
040 AP CHR CH-AMER	4	1,220	2,160	6.6	11.7
053 ASSEMB OF GOD	1	35	46	.1	.2
081 CATHOLIC	8	NA	5,366	16.4	29.1
081d LATIN	8	NA	5,366	16.4	29.1
093 CHR CH (DISC)	2	657	801	2.5	4.3
097 CHR CHS&CHS CR	2	126	162*	.5	.9
157 CH OF BRETHREN	2	67	86*	.3	.5
165 CH OF NAZARENE	2	222	392	1.2	2.1
167 CHS OF CHRIST	2	100	127	.4	.7
193 EPISCOPAL	1	34	58	.2	.3
207 E.L.C.A.	3	918	1,111	3.4	6.0
213 EVAN MENN INC	1	99	128*	.4	.7
259 IFCA	1	NR	NR	-	-
283 LUTH—MO SYNOD	5	1,202	1,560	4.8	8.5
285 MENNONITE CH	7	811	1,127	3.5	6.1
287 MENN GEN CONF	1	167	192	.6	1.0
355 PRESB CH (USA)	3	272	351*	1.1	1.9
419 SO BAPT CONV	1	136	175*	.5	.9
443 UN C OF CHRIST	4	1,405	1,811*	5.5	9.8
449 UN METHODIST	8	1,658	2,137*	6.5	11.6

INDIANA

County and Denomination	Number of churches	Communicant, confirmed, full members	Total adherents Number	Total adherents Percent of total population	Total adherents Percent of total adherents
THE STATE.....	7,134	1,306,718	2,634,841*	47.5	100.0
ADAMS	**76**	**11,068**	**22,283***	**71.7**	**100.0**
019 AMER BAPT USA	2	218	291*	.9	1.3
053 ASSEMB OF GOD	1	28	46	.1	.2
061 BEACHY AMISH	1	13	17*	.1	.1
081 CATHOLIC	2	NA	4,394	14.1	19.7
081d LATIN	2	NA	4,394	14.1	19.7
097 CHR CHS&CHS CR	2	250	334*	1.1	1.5
123 CH GOD (ANDER)	1	410	466	1.5	2.1
151 L-D SAINTS	1	NA	85	.3	.4
157 CH OF BRETHREN	1	287	383*	1.2	1.7
165 CH OF NAZARENE	4	390	681	2.2	3.1
193 EPISCOPAL	1	27	27	.1	.1
213 EVAN MENN INC	1	175	234*	.8	1.1
259 IFCA	2	NR	NR	-	-
283 LUTH—MO SYNOD	7	2,852	3,800	12.2	17.1
287 MENN GEN CONF	1	1,117	1,417	4.6	6.4
291 MISSIONARY CH	4	827	920	3.0	4.1
323 OLD ORD AMISH	22	NA	3,300	10.6	14.8
349 PENT HOLINESS	1	22	29*	.1	.1
355 PRESB CH (USA)	1	187	250*	.8	1.1
438 UN BRETH IN CR	4	363	363	1.2	1.6
443 UN C OF CHRIST	4	1,396	1,864*	6.0	8.4
449 UN METHODIST	12	2,447	3,267*	10.5	14.7
467 WESLEYAN	1	59	115	.4	.5
ALLEN	**268**	**79,056**	**165,657***	**55.1**	**100.0**
019 AMER BAPT USA	8	2,105	2,698*	.9	1.6
040 AP CHR CH-AMER	1	109	194	.1	.1
053 ASSEMB OF GOD	4	733	1,158	.4	.7
061 BEACHY AMISH	1	51	65*	-	-
071 BRETHREN (ASH)	1	37	47*	-	-
081 CATHOLIC	24	NA	51,000	17.0	30.8
081d LATIN	24	NA	51,000	17.0	30.8
089 CHR & MISS AL	2	198	336	.1	.2
093 CHR CH (DISC)	3	1,042	1,485	.5	.9
097 CHR CHS&CHS CR	9	3,254	4,171*	1.4	2.5
105 CHRISTIAN REF	2	433	656	.2	.4
111 CH CR,SCIENTST	1	NR	NR	-	-
123 CH GOD (ANDER)	7	527	727	.2	.4
127 CH GOD (CLEVE)	2	247	317*	.1	.2
145 CH GOD PROPHCY	1	33	42*	-	-
151 L-D SAINTS	2	NA	976	.3	.6
157 CH OF BRETHREN	3	752	964*	.3	.6
165 CH OF NAZARENE	10	1,158	1,667	.6	1.0
167 CHS OF CHRIST	6	720	990	.3	.6
171 CH GOD-GEN CON	4	751	963*	.3	.6
193 EPISCOPAL	3	1,166	1,657	.6	1.0
207 E.L.C.A.	21	10,274	13,653	4.5	8.2
213 EVAN MENN INC	5	655	840*	.3	.5

NA–Not applicable NR–Not reported *Total adherents estimated from known number of communicant, confirmed, full members. - Represents a percent less than 0.1. Percentages may not total due to rounding.
[1]See Appendix E [2]See Appendix F [3]See Appendix G Lines in *italic* represent a breakdown of Catholic rites or Friends affiliations. They are included in their respective denominational total.

Table 4. Churches and Church Membership by County and Denomination: 1990

County and Denomination	Number of churches	Communicant, confirmed, full members	Total adherents		
			Number	Percent of total population	Percent of total adherents
221 FREE METHODIST	1	113	149	-	.1
223 FREE WILL BAPT	1	52	67*	-	-
226 FRIENDS-USA	2	44	57*	-	-
226c FGC	1	17	22*	-	-
226e FUM	1	27	35*	-	-
246 GREEK ORTHODOX	1	NR	NR	-	-
263 INT FOURSQ GOS	1	0	0*	-	-
283 LUTH—MO SYNOD	29	18,865	25,455	8.5	15.4
285 MENNONITE CH	9	995	1,482	.5	.9
287 MENN GEN CONF	1	175	220	.1	.1
291 MISSIONARY CH	14	3,005	4,225	1.4	2.6
323 OLD ORD AMISH	11	NA	1,650	.5	1.0
331 ORTH CH IN AM	1	NR	NR	-	-
353 CHR BRETHREN	1	15	30	-	-
355 PRESB CH (USA)	8	3,639	4,664*	1.6	2.8
361 PRIM BAPT ASCS	1	9	12*	-	-
397 ROMANIAN ORTH	1	NR	NR	-	-
403 SALVATION ARMY	2	221	252	.1	.2
413 S.D.A.	2	370	474*	.2	.3
419 SO BAPT CONV	5	1,638	2,099*	.7	1.3
435 UNITARIAN-UNIV	1	205	271	.1	.2
436 UNITED BAPT	1	25	32*	-	-
438 UN BRETH IN CR	4	343	478	.2	.3
443 UN C OF CHRIST	5	2,818	3,612*	1.2	2.2
449 UN METHODIST	37	13,602	17,434*	5.8	10.5
467 WESLEYAN	3	383	715	.2	.4
469 WELS	2	279	390	.1	.2
496 JEWISH EST[1]	2	NA	910	.3	.5
497 BLACK BAPT EST[2]	NA	8,015	10,273*	3.4	6.2
498 INDEP.CHARIS.[3]	2	NA	6,100	2.0	3.7
BARTHOLOMEW	**86**	**22,282**	**34,440***	**54.1**	**100.0**
019 AMER BAPT USA	5	3,292	4,109*	6.5	11.9
053 ASSEMB OF GOD	2	249	544	.9	1.6
081 CATHOLIC	2	NA	3,562	5.6	10.3
081d LATIN	2	NA	3,562	5.6	10.3
089 CHR & MISS AL	1	34	95	.1	.3
093 CHR CH (DISC)	1	384	721	1.1	2.1
097 CHR CHS&CHS CR	9	4,832	6,031*	9.5	17.5
111 CH CR,SCIENTST	1	NR	NR	-	-
123 CH GOD (ANDER)	1	91	91	.1	.3
127 CH GOD (CLEVE)	1	191	238*	.4	.7
146 CH GOD MTN ASM	1	84	105*	.2	.3
151 L-D SAINTS	2	NA	579	.9	1.7
165 CH OF NAZARENE	4	378	633	1.0	1.8
167 CHS OF CHRIST	4	282	362	.6	1.1
193 EPISCOPAL	1	168	249	.4	.7
207 E.L.C.A.	1	320	368	.6	1.1
215 EVAN METH CH	1	28	35*	.1	.1
221 FREE METHODIST	1	130	163	.3	.5
226 FRIENDS-USA	1	167	208*	.3	.6
226e FUM	1	167	208*	.3	.6
263 INT FOURSQ GOS	1	0	0*	-	-
283 LUTH—MO SYNOD	7	4,081	5,204	8.2	15.1
293 MORAV CH-NORTH	1	346	422	.7	1.2
355 PRESB CH (USA)	3	851	1,062*	1.7	3.1
403 SALVATION ARMY	1	15	18	-	.1
413 S.D.A.	1	96	120*	.2	.3
419 SO BAPT CONV	4	866	1,081*	1.7	3.1
435 UNITARIAN-UNIV	1	44	63	.1	.2
436 UNITED BAPT	1	75	94*	.1	.3
438 UN BRETH IN CR	1	41	41	.1	.1
443 UN C OF CHRIST	1	63	79*	.1	.2
449 UN METHODIST	17	4,592	5,732*	9.0	16.6
467 WESLEYAN	7	367	1,163	1.8	3.4
497 BLACK BAPT EST[2]	NA	215	268*	.4	.8
499 INDEP.NON-CHAR[3]	1	NA	1,000	1.6	2.9
BENTON	**32**	**3,115**	**7,249***	**76.8**	**100.0**
081 CATHOLIC	6	NA	3,124	33.1	43.1
081d LATIN	6	NA	3,124	33.1	43.1
093 CHR CH (DISC)	1	45	57	.6	.8
097 CHR CHS&CHS CR	6	897	1,150*	12.2	15.9
151 L-D SAINTS	1	NA	69	.7	1.0
165 CH OF NAZARENE	1	20	30	.3	.4
207 E.L.C.A.	1	246	313	3.3	4.3
221 FREE METHODIST	1	7	52	.6	.7
283 LUTH—MO SYNOD	1	28	43	.5	.6
355 PRESB CH (USA)	3	329	422*	4.5	5.8
419 SO BAPT CONV	3	264	338*	3.6	4.7
449 UN METHODIST	7	1,261	1,617*	17.1	22.3
467 WESLEYAN	1	18	34	.4	.5
BLACKFORD	**28**	**2,955**	**5,224***	**37.1**	**100.0**
019 AMER BAPT USA	1	203	252*	1.8	4.8
053 ASSEMB OF GOD	2	64	123	.9	2.4

County and Denomination	Number of churches	Communicant, confirmed, full members	Total adherents		
			Number	Percent of total population	Percent of total adherents
081 CATHOLIC	2	NA	713	5.1	13.6
081d LATIN	2	NA	713	5.1	13.6
093 CHR CH (DISC)	1	145	382	2.7	7.3
097 CHR CHS&CHS CR	2	175	217*	1.5	4.2
123 CH GOD (ANDER)	1	9	22	.2	.4
157 CH OF BRETHREN	1	48	59*	.4	1.1
165 CH OF NAZARENE	3	330	787	5.6	15.1
207 E.L.C.A.	1	338	419	3.0	8.0
355 PRESB CH (USA)	1	136	169*	1.2	3.2
413 S.D.A.	1	9	11*	.1	.2
438 UN BRETH IN CR	1	45	45	.3	.9
449 UN METHODIST	10	1,352	1,675*	11.9	32.1
467 WESLEYAN	1	101	350	2.5	6.7
BOONE	**56**	**9,153**	**16,596***	**43.5**	**100.0**
019 AMER BAPT USA	2	574	730*	1.9	4.4
053 ASSEMB OF GOD	2	100	151	.4	.9
057 BAPT GEN CONF	1	28	36*	.1	.2
081 CATHOLIC	2	NA	3,206	8.4	19.3
081d LATIN	2	NA	3,206	8.4	19.3
093 CHR CH (DISC)	2	859	1,501	3.9	9.0
097 CHR CHS&CHS CR	6	1,828	2,326*	6.1	14.0
111 CH CR,SCIENTST	1	NR	NR	-	-
123 CH GOD (ANDER)	1	15	15	-	.1
145 CH GOD PROPHCY	2	67	85*	.2	.5
151 L-D SAINTS	1	NA	373	1.0	2.2
165 CH OF NAZARENE	1	90	250	.7	1.5
167 CHS OF CHRIST	3	195	271	.7	1.6
176 CCC, NOT NAT'L	1	89	113*	.3	.7
193 EPISCOPAL	2	237	385	1.0	2.3
207 E.L.C.A.	3	470	629	1.6	3.8
226 FRIENDS-USA	1	57	73*	.2	.4
226e FUM	1	57	73*	.2	.4
339 PENT CH OF GOD	2	86	180	.5	1.1
355 PRESB CH (USA)	3	1,308	1,664*	4.4	10.0
419 SO BAPT CONV	2	205	261*	.7	1.6
443 UN C OF CHRIST	4	431	548*	1.4	3.3
449 UN METHODIST	11	2,412	3,069*	8.0	18.5
467 WESLEYAN	2	102	425	1.1	2.6
496 JEWISH EST[1]	0	NA	305	.8	1.8
BROWN	**20**	**1,586**	**2,757***	**19.6**	**100.0**
019 AMER BAPT USA	1	223	275*	2.0	10.0
053 ASSEMB OF GOD	1	17	23	.2	.8
081 CATHOLIC	1	NA	709	5.0	25.7
081d LATIN	1	NA	709	5.0	25.7
097 CHR CHS&CHS CR	1	250	308*	2.2	11.2
111 CH CR,SCIENTST	1	NR	NR	-	-
165 CH OF NAZARENE	1	149	216	1.5	7.8
167 CHS OF CHRIST	2	75	100	.7	3.6
193 EPISCOPAL	1	57	69	.5	2.5
283 LUTH—MO SYNOD	1	174	237	1.7	8.6
285 MENNONITE CH	1	35	60	.4	2.2
419 SO BAPT CONV	1	15	18*	.1	.7
449 UN METHODIST	6	566	697*	5.0	25.3
467 WESLEYAN	2	25	45	.3	1.6
CARROLL	**40**	**5,464**	**7,785***	**41.4**	**100.0**
019 AMER BAPT USA	3	424	532*	2.8	6.8
053 ASSEMB OF GOD	1	41	90	.5	1.2
071 BRETHREN (ASH)	2	271	340*	1.8	4.4
081 CATHOLIC	1	NA	570	3.0	7.3
081d LATIN	1	NA	570	3.0	7.3
093 CHR CH (DISC)	2	297	546	2.9	7.0
097 CHR CHS&CHS CR	4	887	1,113*	5.9	14.3
127 CH GOD (CLEVE)	1	35	44*	.2	.6
157 CH OF BRETHREN	5	631	792*	4.2	10.2
167 CHS OF CHRIST	1	15	30	.2	.4
207 E.L.C.A.	3	382	570	3.0	7.3
355 PRESB CH (USA)	6	883	1,108*	5.9	14.2
443 UN C OF CHRIST	1	251	315*	1.7	4.0
449 UN METHODIST	11	1,308	1,641*	8.7	21.1
467 WESLEYAN	2	39	94	.5	1.2
CASS	**71**	**11,695**	**19,224***	**50.0**	**100.0**
019 AMER BAPT USA	5	1,587	1,987*	5.2	10.3
053 ASSEMB OF GOD	1	294	435	1.1	2.3
071 BRETHREN (ASH)	1	115	144*	.4	.7
081 CATHOLIC	2	NA	3,324	8.7	17.3
081d LATIN	2	NA	3,324	8.7	17.3
089 CHR & MISS AL	1	81	170	.4	.9
093 CHR CH (DISC)	2	567	744	1.9	3.9
097 CHR CHS&CHS CR	10	2,461	3,082*	8.0	16.0
111 CH CR,SCIENTST	1	NR	NR	-	-
123 CH GOD (ANDER)	2	141	141	.4	.7
127 CH GOD (CLEVE)	1	198	248*	.6	1.3

NA–Not applicable   NR–Not reported   *Total adherents estimated from known number of communicant, confirmed, full members.   - Represents a percent less than 0.1.   Percentages may not total due to rounding.
[1]See Appendix E   [2]See Appendix F   [3]See Appendix G   Lines in *italic* represent a breakdown of Catholic rites or Friends affiliations. They are included in their respective denominational total.

Table 4. Churches and Church Membership by County and Denomination: 1990

County and Denomination	Number of churches	Communicant, confirmed, full members	Total adherents Number	Percent of total population	Percent of total adherents
151 L-D SAINTS	2	NA	787	2.0	4.1
157 CH OF BRETHREN	1	103	129*	.3	.7
165 CH OF NAZARENE	1	181	318	.8	1.7
167 CHS OF CHRIST	3	130	190	.5	1.0
176 CCC, NOT NAT'L	2	179	224*	.6	1.2
193 EPISCOPAL	1	142	220	.6	1.1
207 E.L.C.A.	2	518	715	1.9	3.7
263 INT FOURSQ GOS	1	60	75*	.2	.4
283 LUTH—MO SYNOD	1	338	436	1.1	2.3
353 CHR BRETHREN	1	10	14	-	.1
355 PRESB CH (USA)	5	943	1,181*	3.1	6.1
403 SALVATION ARMY	1	136	175	.5	.9
413 S.D.A.	1	55	69*	.2	.4
443 UN C OF CHRIST	2	321	402*	1.0	2.1
449 UN METHODIST	20	3,074	3,849*	10.0	20.0
467 WESLEYAN	1	61	165	.4	.9
CLARK	**113**	**19,984**	**37,749***	**43.0**	**100.0**
001 ADVENT CHR CH	1	67	83*	.1	.2
019 AMER BAPT USA	5	1,176	1,464*	1.7	3.9
053 ASSEMB OF GOD	2	245	330	.4	.9
081 CATHOLIC	8	NA	10,633	12.1	28.2
081d LATIN	*8*	*NA*	*10,633*	*12.1*	*28.2*
093 CHR CH (DISC)	5	892	1,815	2.1	4.8
097 CHR CHS&CHS CR	10	1,201	1,495*	1.7	4.0
123 CH GOD (ANDER)	4	710	710	.8	1.9
127 CH GOD (CLEVE)	1	28	35*	-	.1
145 CH GOD PROPHECY	1	33	41*	-	.1
151 L-D SAINTS	1	NA	417	.5	1.1
165 CH OF NAZARENE	5	251	502	.6	1.3
167 CHS OF CHRIST	12	1,471	1,890	2.2	5.0
193 EPISCOPAL	1	121	171	.2	.5
203 EVAN FREE CH	1	29	71	.1	.2
207 E.L.C.A.	1	264	366	.4	1.0
283 LUTH—MO SYNOD	1	98	123	.1	.3
325 OLD REG BAPT	5	98	122*	.1	.3
355 PRESB CH (USA)	7	855	1,064*	1.2	2.8
413 S.D.A.	2	96	120*	.1	.3
419 SO BAPT CONV	14	6,887	8,574*	9.8	22.7
436 UNITED BAPT	1	92	115*	.1	.3
443 UN C OF CHRIST	2	457	569*	.6	1.5
449 UN METHODIST	23	3,670	4,569*	5.2	12.1
496 JEWISH EST[1]	0	NA	922	1.1	2.4
497 BLACK BAPT EST[2]	NA	1,243	1,548*	1.8	4.1
CLAY	**63**	**8,505**	**12,025***	**48.7**	**100.0**
019 AMER BAPT USA	5	1,223	1,536*	6.2	12.8
053 ASSEMB OF GOD	2	122	318	1.3	2.6
081 CATHOLIC	2	NA	745	3.0	6.2
081d LATIN	*2*	*NA*	*745*	*3.0*	*6.2*
093 CHR CH (DISC)	1	66	106	.4	.9
097 CHR CHS&CHS CR	4	2,210	2,776*	11.2	23.1
111 CH CR,SCIENTST	1	NR	NR	-	-
127 CH GOD (CLEVE)	1	23	29*	.1	.2
145 CH GOD PROPHECY	1	33	41*	.2	.3
165 CH OF NAZARENE	4	445	898	3.6	7.5
167 CHS OF CHRIST	6	281	382	1.5	3.2
175 CONGR CHR CHS	1	132	166*	.7	1.4
221 FREE METHODIST	1	31	57	.2	.5
259 IFCA	1	NR	NR	-	-
283 LUTH—MO SYNOD	1	141	162	.7	1.3
355 PRESB CH (USA)	2	352	442*	1.8	3.7
419 SO BAPT CONV	2	199	250*	1.0	2.1
443 UN C OF CHRIST	4	764	960*	3.9	8.0
449 UN METHODIST	23	2,465	3,097*	12.5	25.8
467 WESLEYAN	1	18	60	.2	.5
CLINTON	**61**	**9,038**	**13,384***	**43.2**	**100.0**
019 AMER BAPT USA	5	1,037	1,322*	4.3	9.9
053 ASSEMB OF GOD	2	164	280	.9	2.1
081 CATHOLIC	1	NA	1,052	3.4	7.9
081d LATIN	*1*	*NA*	*1,052*	*3.4*	*7.9*
093 CHR CH (DISC)	1	611	776	2.5	5.8
097 CHR CHS&CHS CR	6	1,249	1,592*	5.1	11.9
121 CH GOD (ABR)	1	32	41*	.1	.3
123 CH GOD (ANDER)	2	44	60	.2	.4
151 L-D SAINTS	1	NA	187	.6	1.4
157 CH OF BRETHREN	1	177	226*	.7	1.7
165 CH OF NAZARENE	2	344	538	1.7	4.0
167 CHS OF CHRIST	1	50	100	.3	.7
176 CCC, NOT NAT'L	1	69	88*	.3	.7
181 CONSRV CONGR	1	352	449*	1.4	3.4
207 E.L.C.A.	2	363	445	1.4	3.3
339 PENT CH OF GOD	1	35	77	.2	.6
355 PRESB CH (USA)	5	990	1,262*	4.1	9.4
413 S.D.A.	1	57	73*	.2	.5
419 SO BAPT CONV	4	545	695*	2.2	5.2
443 UN C OF CHRIST	2	248	316*	1.0	2.4
449 UN METHODIST	14	2,369	3,021*	9.8	22.6
467 WESLEYAN	7	302	784	2.5	5.9
CRAWFORD	**28**	**2,718**	**4,215***	**42.5**	**100.0**
019 AMER BAPT USA	3	186	234*	2.4	5.6
075 BRETHREN IN CR	1	12	35	.4	.8
081 CATHOLIC	1	NA	204	2.1	4.8
081d LATIN	*1*	*NA*	*204*	*2.1*	*4.8*
093 CHR CH (DISC)	1	77	124	1.3	2.9
097 CHR CHS&CHS CR	5	1,345	1,693*	17.1	40.2
151 L-D SAINTS	1	NA	213	2.1	5.1
165 CH OF NAZARENE	2	25	61	.6	1.4
221 FREE METHODIST	1	53	53	.5	1.3
355 PRESB CH (USA)	1	133	167*	1.7	4.0
436 UNITED BAPT	1	28	35*	.4	.8
449 UN METHODIST	8	649	817*	8.2	19.4
467 WESLEYAN	3	210	579	5.8	13.7
DAVIESS	**79**	**8,793**	**17,506***	**63.6**	**100.0**
019 AMER BAPT USA	4	1,162	1,504*	5.5	8.6
053 ASSEMB OF GOD	2	140	195	.7	1.1
061 BEACHY AMISH	1	50	65*	.2	.4
081 CATHOLIC	7	NA	3,703	13.4	21.2
081d LATIN	*7*	*NA*	*3,703*	*13.4*	*21.2*
093 CHR CH (DISC)	1	204	498	1.8	2.8
097 CHR CHS&CHS CR	8	2,510	3,249*	11.8	18.6
123 CH GOD (ANDER)	1	49	67	.2	.4
127 CH GOD (CLEVE)	1	46	60*	.2	.3
165 CH OF NAZARENE	2	131	298	1.1	1.7
167 CHS OF CHRIST	4	213	311	1.1	1.8
171 CH GOD-GEN CON	1	59	76*	.3	.4
185 CUMBER PRESB	1	40	50	.2	.3
193 EPISCOPAL	1	34	35	.1	.2
207 E.L.C.A.	1	126	184	.7	1.1
221 FREE METHODIST	1	121	124	.5	.7
285 MENNONITE CH	7	891	1,219	4.4	7.0
323 OLD ORD AMISH	11	NA	1,650	6.0	9.4
355 PRESB CH (USA)	1	169	219*	.8	1.3
413 S.D.A.	2	24	31*	.1	.2
419 SO BAPT CONV	3	420	544*	2.0	3.1
449 UN METHODIST	16	2,303	2,981*	10.8	17.0
467 WESLEYAN	3	101	443	1.6	2.5
DEARBORN	**57**	**9,098**	**18,352***	**47.3**	**100.0**
019 AMER BAPT USA	8	2,338	3,014*	7.8	16.4
081 CATHOLIC	6	NA	5,727	14.7	31.2
081d LATIN	*6*	*NA*	*5,727*	*14.7*	*31.2*
089 CHR & MISS AL	1	91	218	.6	1.2
097 CHR CHS&CHS CR	7	1,704	2,197*	5.7	12.0
111 CH CR,SCIENTST	1	NR	NR	-	-
123 CH GOD (ANDER)	1	40	45	.1	.2
165 CH OF NAZARENE	1	37	80	.2	.4
167 CHS OF CHRIST	1	17	30	.1	.2
193 EPISCOPAL	1	45	92	.2	.5
207 E.L.C.A.	4	859	1,079	2.8	5.9
223 FREE WILL BAPT	2	83	107*	.3	.6
283 LUTH—MO SYNOD	4	1,085	1,506	3.9	8.2
355 PRESB CH (USA)	4	377	486*	1.3	2.6
419 SO BAPT CONV	1	42	54*	.1	.3
443 UN C OF CHRIST	3	267	344*	.9	1.9
449 UN METHODIST	10	2,012	2,594*	6.7	14.1
467 WESLEYAN	2	101	151	.4	.8
496 JEWISH EST[1]	0	NA	628	1.6	3.4
DECATUR	**60**	**7,566**	**14,872***	**62.9**	**100.0**
019 AMER BAPT USA	11	3,058	3,931*	16.6	26.4
053 ASSEMB OF GOD	3	124	171	.7	1.1
081 CATHOLIC	5	NA	4,718	20.0	31.7
081d LATIN	*5*	*NA*	*4,718*	*20.0*	*31.7*
093 CHR CH (DISC)	2	425	540	2.3	3.6
097 CHR CHS&CHS CR	6	884	1,136*	4.8	7.6
123 CH GOD (ANDER)	1	206	206	.9	1.4
127 CH GOD (CLEVE)	1	45	58*	.2	.4
165 CH OF NAZARENE	1	30	161	.7	1.1
167 CHS OF CHRIST	1	20	20	.1	.1
207 E.L.C.A.	2	173	231	1.0	1.6
221 FREE METHODIST	1	58	71	.3	.5
283 LUTH—MO SYNOD	1	131	194	.8	1.3
355 PRESB CH (USA)	4	475	611*	2.6	4.1
419 SO BAPT CONV	5	417	536*	2.3	3.6
449 UN METHODIST	11	1,420	1,825*	7.7	12.3
467 WESLEYAN	4	100	163	.7	1.1
499 INDEP.NON-CHAR[3]	1	NA	300	1.3	2.0

NA–Not applicable   NR–Not reported   *Total adherents estimated from known number of communicant, confirmed, full members.   - Represents a percent less than 0.1.   Percentages may not total due to rounding.
[1]See Appendix E   [2]See Appendix F   [3]See Appendix G   Lines in *italic* represent a breakdown of Catholic rites or Friends affiliations. They are included in their respective denominational total.

INDIANA

Table 4. Churches and Church Membership by County and Denomination: 1990

County and Denomination	Number of churches	Communicant, confirmed, full members	Total adherents Number	Percent of total population	Percent of total adherents
DE KALB	**61**	**8,644**	**15,603***	**44.2**	**100.0**
019 AMER BAPT USA	1	391	506*	1.4	3.2
053 ASSEMB OF GOD	3	178	235	.7	1.5
075 BRETHREN IN CR	1	52	52	.1	.3
081 CATHOLIC	3	NA	3,647	10.3	23.4
081d *LATIN*	*3*	*NA*	*3,647*	*10.3*	*23.4*
089 CHR & MISS AL	1	44	96	.3	.6
093 CHR CH (DISC)	1	285	450	1.3	2.9
097 CHR CHS&CHS CR	6	1,091	1,412*	4.0	9.0
123 CH GOD (ANDER)	3	465	530	1.5	3.4
133 CH GOD(7TH)DEN	1	15	20	.1	.1
157 CH OF BRETHREN	3	318	412*	1.2	2.6
165 CH OF NAZARENE	5	432	827	2.3	5.3
167 CHS OF CHRIST	1	45	62	.2	.4
171 CH GOD-GEN CON	1	169	219*	.6	1.4
207 E.L.C.A.	5	760	1,198	3.4	7.7
265 INT PENT C CHR	1	59	59	.2	.4
283 LUTH—MO SYNOD	3	766	1,068	3.0	6.8
291 MISSIONARY CH	1	163	326	.9	2.1
355 PRESB CH (USA)	2	715	926*	2.6	5.9
419 SO BAPT CONV	1	74	96*	.3	.6
438 UN BRETH IN CR	2	152	152	.4	1.0
449 UN METHODIST	15	2,458	3,182*	9.0	20.4
467 WESLEYAN	1	12	21	.1	.1
496 JEWISH EST[1]	0	NA	107	.3	.7
DELAWARE	**140**	**25,291**	**44,922***	**37.5**	**100.0**
019 AMER BAPT USA	3	1,610	1,940*	1.6	4.3
053 ASSEMB OF GOD	3	435	795	.7	1.8
071 BRETHREN (ASH)	2	236	284*	.2	.6
081 CATHOLIC	2	NA	5,621	4.7	12.5
081d *LATIN*	*2*	*NA*	*5,621*	*4.7*	*12.5*
089 CHR & MISS AL	1	37	109	.1	.2
093 CHR CH (DISC)	5	991	1,766	1.5	3.9
097 CHR CHS&CHS CR	2	636	766*	.6	1.7
111 CH CR,SCIENTST	1	NR	NR	-	-
123 CH GOD (ANDER)	9	731	985	.8	2.2
127 CH GOD (CLEVE)	1	114	137*	.1	.3
145 CH GOD PROPHCY	1	33	40*	-	.1
146 CH GOD MTN ASM	1	64	77*	.1	.2
151 L-D SAINTS	2	NA	672	.6	1.5
157 CH OF BRETHREN	3	156	188*	.2	.4
165 CH OF NAZARENE	16	2,032	3,462	2.9	7.7
167 CHS OF CHRIST	9	1,130	1,472	1.2	3.3
193 EPISCOPAL	1	133	156	.1	.3
207 E.L.C.A.	3	788	1,086	.9	2.4
226 FRIENDS-USA	2	433	522*	.4	1.2
226e *FUM*	*2*	*433*	*522**	*.4*	*1.2*
263 INT FOURSQ GOS	2	383	462*	.4	1.0
283 LUTH—MO SYNOD	1	373	472	.4	1.1
285 MENNONITE CH	1	3	14	-	-
287 MENN GEN CONF	1	7	12	-	-
296 MIDW CONGR FEL	3	149	180*	.2	.4
353 CHR BRETHREN	1	15	20	-	-
355 PRESB CH (USA)	2	1,097	1,322*	1.1	2.9
356 PRESB CH AMER	1	345	418	.3	.9
403 SALVATION ARMY	1	56	63	.1	.1
413 S.D.A.	2	99	119*	.1	.3
419 SO BAPT CONV	9	1,948	2,348*	2.0	5.2
435 UNITARIAN-UNIV	1	212	304	.3	.7
436 UNITED BAPT	3	930	1,121*	.9	2.5
438 UN BRETH IN CR	2	96	117	.1	.3
443 UN C OF CHRIST	4	910	1,097*	.9	2.4
449 UN METHODIST	32	7,075	8,526*	7.1	19.0
467 WESLEYAN	3	139	355	.3	.8
496 JEWISH EST[1]	1	NA	160	.1	.4
497 BLACK BAPT EST[2]	NA	1,895	2,284*	1.9	5.1
498 INDEP.CHARIS.[3]	1	NA	4,000	3.3	8.9
499 INDEP.NON-CHAR[3]	2	NA	1,450	1.2	3.2
DUBOIS	**45**	**6,321**	**27,710***	**75.7**	**100.0**
053 ASSEMB OF GOD	1	84	240	.7	.9
081 CATHOLIC	11	NA	19,110	52.2	69.0
081d *LATIN*	*11*	*NA*	*19,110*	*52.2*	*69.0*
093 CHR CH (DISC)	1	40	64	.2	.2
097 CHR CHS&CHS CR	4	646	833*	2.3	3.0
151 L-D SAINTS	1	NA	100	.3	.4
165 CH OF NAZARENE	2	130	315	.9	1.1
167 CHS OF CHRIST	2	82	126	.3	.5
207 E.L.C.A.	7	2,196	2,850	7.8	10.3
355 PRESB CH (USA)	1	96	124*	.3	.4
413 S.D.A.	1	21	27*	.1	.1
419 SO BAPT CONV	2	357	460*	1.3	1.7
443 UN C OF CHRIST	6	1,731	2,231*	6.1	8.1
449 UN METHODIST	5	931	1,200*	3.3	4.3
467 WESLEYAN	1	7	30	.1	.1

County and Denomination	Number of churches	Communicant, confirmed, full members	Total adherents Number	Percent of total population	Percent of total adherents
ELKHART	**227**	**39,868**	**70,640***	**45.2**	**100.0**
005 AME ZION	1	60	72	-	.1
053 ASSEMB OF GOD	6	1,605	2,535	1.6	3.6
061 BEACHY AMISH	4	462	598*	.4	.8
071 BRETHREN (ASH)	6	1,491	1,929*	1.2	2.7
075 BRETHREN IN CR	2	169	180	.1	.3
081 CATHOLIC	5	NA	11,461	7.3	16.2
081d *LATIN*	*5*	*NA*	*11,461*	*7.3*	*16.2*
089 CHR & MISS AL	2	0	52	-	.1
093 CHR CH (DISC)	2	458	568	.4	.8
097 CHR CHS&CHS CR	1	250	323*	.2	.5
105 CHRISTIAN REF	1	168	248	.2	.4
111 CH CR,SCIENTST	2	NR	NR	-	-
123 CH GOD (ANDER)	4	1,126	1,147	.7	1.6
127 CH GOD (CLEVE)	4	312	404*	.3	.6
145 CH GOD PROPHCY	1	33	43*	-	.1
151 L-D SAINTS	2	NA	536	.3	.8
157 CH OF BRETHREN	19	3,310	4,283*	2.7	6.1
165 CH OF NAZARENE	7	949	1,611	1.0	2.3
167 CHS OF CHRIST	3	355	380	.2	.5
171 CH GOD-GEN CON	1	184	238*	.2	.3
193 EPISCOPAL	4	900	1,322	.8	1.9
203 EVAN FREE CH	1	38	130	.1	.2
207 E.L.C.A.	10	2,941	3,811	2.4	5.4
221 FREE METHODIST	2	134	195	.1	.3
223 FREE WILL BAPT	1	60	78*	-	.1
259 IFCA	2	NR	NR	-	-
283 LUTH—MO SYNOD	3	842	1,179	.8	1.7
285 MENNONITE CH	40	6,978	10,157	6.5	14.4
287 MENN GEN CONF	8	959	1,123	.7	1.6
291 MISSIONARY CH	15	2,419	3,584	2.3	5.1
323 OLD ORD AMISH	18	NA	2,700	1.7	3.8
339 PENT CH OF GOD	4	73	227	.1	.3
355 PRESB CH (USA)	3	1,511	1,955*	1.3	2.8
361 PRIM BAPT ASCS	2	18	23*	-	-
403 SALVATION ARMY	2	198	211	.1	.3
413 S.D.A.	2	192	248*	.2	.4
419 SO BAPT CONV	2	202	261*	.2	.4
435 UNITARIAN-UNIV	1	123	178	.1	.3
438 UN BRETH IN CR	1	66	66	-	.1
443 UN C OF CHRIST	6	1,362	1,762*	1.1	2.5
449 UN METHODIST	22	8,019	10,376*	6.6	14.7
467 WESLEYAN	1	22	105	.1	.1
497 BLACK BAPT EST[2]	NA	1,879	2,431*	1.6	3.4
499 INDEP.NON-CHAR[3]	4	NA	1,910	1.2	2.7
FAYETTE	**39**	**5,149**	**10,446***	**40.2**	**100.0**
019 AMER BAPT USA	1	755	938*	3.6	9.0
053 ASSEMB OF GOD	1	90	109	.4	1.0
081 CATHOLIC	1	NA	2,196	8.4	21.0
081d *LATIN*	*1*	*NA*	*2,196*	*8.4*	*21.0*
093 CHR CH (DISC)	3	548	713	2.7	6.8
097 CHR CHS&CHS CR	1	218	271*	1.0	2.6
111 CH CR,SCIENTST	1	NR	NR	-	-
123 CH GOD (ANDER)	1	185	185	.7	1.8
127 CH GOD (CLEVE)	1	101	126*	.5	1.2
145 CH GOD PROPHCY	1	33	41*	.2	.4
151 L-D SAINTS	1	NA	213	.8	2.0
165 CH OF NAZARENE	2	174	348	1.3	3.3
167 CHS OF CHRIST	3	100	127	.5	1.2
193 EPISCOPAL	1	34	57	.2	.5
207 E.L.C.A.	1	228	296	1.1	2.8
283 LUTH—MO SYNOD	1	62	90	.3	.9
355 PRESB CH (USA)	1	291	362*	1.4	3.5
361 PRIM BAPT ASCS	1	48	60*	.2	.6
403 SALVATION ARMY	1	86	86	.3	.8
413 S.D.A.	1	21	26*	.1	.2
419 SO BAPT CONV	1	588	731*	2.8	7.0
449 UN METHODIST	9	1,573	1,955*	7.5	18.7
467 WESLEYAN	1	14	16	.1	.2
499 INDEP.NON-CHAR[3]	2	NA	1,500	5.8	14.4
FLOYD	**67**	**22,186**	**39,998***	**62.1**	**100.0**
001 ADVENT CHR CH	1	109	137*	.2	.3
019 AMER BAPT USA	4	1,407	1,772*	2.8	4.4
053 ASSEMB OF GOD	1	77	101	.2	.3
081 CATHOLIC	5	NA	10,627	16.5	26.6
081d *LATIN*	*5*	*NA*	*10,627*	*16.5*	*26.6*
093 CHR CH (DISC)	5	1,122	1,650	2.6	4.1
097 CHR CHS&CHS CR	4	1,635	2,059*	3.2	5.1
111 CH CR,SCIENTST	1	NR	NR	-	-
123 CH GOD (ANDER)	2	357	357	.6	.9
145 CH GOD PROPHCY	1	33	42*	.1	.1
165 CH OF NAZARENE	3	528	1,020	1.6	2.6
167 CHS OF CHRIST	3	373	465	.7	1.2
193 EPISCOPAL	1	268	389	.6	1.0

NA–Not applicable   NR–Not reported   *Total adherents estimated from known number of communicant, confirmed, full members.   - Represents a percent less than 0.1.   Percentages may not total due to rounding.

[1]See Appendix E   [2]See Appendix F   [3]See Appendix G   Lines in *italic* represent a breakdown of Catholic rites or Friends affiliations. They are included in their respective denominational total.

Table 4. Churches and Church Membership by County and Denomination: 1990

County and Denomination	Number of churches	Communicant, confirmed, full members	Total adherents Number	Percent of total population	Percent of total adherents
207 E.L.C.A.	1	192	285	.4	.7
283 LUTH—MO SYNOD	2	842	1,164	1.8	2.9
355 PRESB CH (USA)	2	567	714*	1.1	1.8
403 SALVATION ARMY	1	74	83	.1	.2
413 S.D.A.	1	108	136*	.2	.3
419 SO BAPT CONV	9	7,948	10,009*	15.5	25.0
436 UNITED BAPT	1	66	83*	.1	.2
443 UN C OF CHRIST	1	1,085	1,366*	2.1	3.4
449 UN METHODIST	15	4,665	5,875*	9.1	14.7
467 WESLEYAN	3	31	105	.2	.3
496 JEWISH EST[1]	0	NA	679	1.1	1.7
497 BLACK BAPT EST[2]	NA	699	880*	1.4	2.2
FOUNTAIN	**43**	**4,402**	**6,578***	**36.9**	**100.0**
053 ASSEMB OF GOD	2	176	377	2.1	5.7
081 CATHOLIC	2	NA	753	4.2	11.4
081d LATIN	2	NA	753	4.2	11.4
093 CHR CH (DISC)	3	256	357	2.0	5.4
097 CHR CHS&CHS CR	8	1,267	1,582*	8.9	24.0
123 CH GOD (ANDER)	1	60	125	.7	1.9
127 CH GOD (CLEVE)	1	21	26*	.1	.4
165 CH OF NAZARENE	4	290	460	2.6	7.0
167 CHS OF CHRIST	1	48	69	.4	1.0
176 CCC, NOT NAT'L	3	313	391*	2.2	5.9
207 E.L.C.A.	2	212	269	1.5	4.1
221 FREE METHODIST	1	107	107	.6	1.6
355 PRESB CH (USA)	2	193	241*	1.4	3.7
419 SO BAPT CONV	1	62	77*	.4	1.2
443 UN C OF CHRIST	2	104	130*	.7	2.0
449 UN METHODIST	10	1,293	1,614*	9.1	24.5
FRANKLIN	**39**	**3,120**	**10,515***	**53.7**	**100.0**
081 CATHOLIC	7	NA	5,261	26.9	50.0
081d LATIN	7	NA	5,261	26.9	50.0
097 CHR CHS&CHS CR	5	480	620*	3.2	5.9
146 CH GOD MTN ASM	1	49	63*	.3	.6
151 L-D SAINTS	1	NA	259	1.3	2.5
165 CH OF NAZARENE	2	30	122	.6	1.2
207 E.L.C.A.	2	415	519	2.7	4.9
325 OLD REG BAPT	1	14	18*	.1	.2
355 PRESB CH (USA)	1	26	34*	.2	.3
419 SO BAPT CONV	5	759	980*	5.0	9.3
443 UN C OF CHRIST	2	513	662*	3.4	6.3
449 UN METHODIST	10	834	1,077*	5.5	10.2
499 INDEP.NON-CHAR[3]	2	NA	900	4.6	8.6
FULTON	**35**	**3,936**	**5,885***	**31.2**	**100.0**
019 AMER BAPT USA	2	501	632*	3.4	10.7
053 ASSEMB OF GOD	1	47	69	.4	1.2
071 BRETHREN (ASH)	1	67	85*	.5	1.4
081 CATHOLIC	2	NA	746	4.0	12.7
081d LATIN	2	NA	746	4.0	12.7
093 CHR CH (DISC)	1	342	581	3.1	9.9
097 CHR CHS&CHS CR	1	85	107*	.6	1.8
123 CH GOD (ANDER)	3	431	503	2.7	8.5
127 CH GOD (CLEVE)	1	48	61*	.3	1.0
157 CH OF BRETHREN	1	71	90*	.5	1.5
165 CH OF NAZARENE	1	77	144	.8	2.4
167 CHS OF CHRIST	1	80	85	.5	1.4
259 IFCA	2	NR	NR	-	-
283 LUTH—MO SYNOD	1	261	341	1.8	5.8
355 PRESB CH (USA)	1	162	205*	1.1	3.5
413 S.D.A.	1	9	11*	.1	.2
449 UN METHODIST	14	1,721	2,173*	11.5	36.9
467 WESLEYAN	1	34	52	.3	.9
GIBSON	**67**	**6,634**	**15,186***	**47.6**	**100.0**
053 ASSEMB OF GOD	2	216	319	1.0	2.1
081 CATHOLIC	7	NA	6,367	20.0	41.9
081d LATIN	7	NA	6,367	20.0	41.9
093 CHR CH (DISC)	2	223	350	1.1	2.3
097 CHR CHS&CHS CR	3	486	608*	1.9	4.0
111 CH CR,SCIENTST	1	NR	NR	-	-
123 CH GOD (ANDER)	2	200	205	.6	1.3
157 CH OF BRETHREN	1	132	165*	.5	1.1
165 CH OF NAZARENE	6	604	1,160	3.6	7.6
167 CHS OF CHRIST	2	48	62	.2	.4
185 CUMBER PRESB	1	26	28	.1	.2
207 E.L.C.A.	1	206	267	.8	1.8
259 IFCA	1	NR	NR	-	-
355 PRESB CH (USA)	7	588	736*	2.3	4.8
403 SALVATION ARMY	1	54	59	.2	.4
419 SO BAPT CONV	5	677	847*	2.7	5.6
443 UN C OF CHRIST	5	529	662*	2.1	4.4
449 UN METHODIST	17	2,433	3,044*	9.5	20.0
467 WESLEYAN	3	84	147	.5	1.0

County and Denomination	Number of churches	Communicant, confirmed, full members	Total adherents Number	Percent of total population	Percent of total adherents
497 BLACK BAPT EST[2]	NA	128	160*	.5	1.1
GRANT	**127**	**19,112**	**31,504***	**42.5**	**100.0**
019 AMER BAPT USA	3	827	1,019*	1.4	3.2
053 ASSEMB OF GOD	5	680	1,256	1.7	4.0
071 BRETHREN (ASH)	1	16	20*	-	.1
081 CATHOLIC	3	NA	3,225	4.3	10.2
081d LATIN	3	NA	3,225	4.3	10.2
089 CHR & MISS AL	1	92	100	.1	.3
093 CHR CH (DISC)	6	984	2,296	3.1	7.3
097 CHR CHS&CHS CR	4	895	1,103*	1.5	3.5
111 CH CR,SCIENTST	1	NR	NR	-	-
123 CH GOD (ANDER)	4	268	285	.4	.9
127 CH GOD (CLEVE)	1	45	55*	.1	.2
145 CH GOD PROPHCY	1	33	41*	.1	.1
151 L-D SAINTS	1	NA	353	.5	1.1
157 CH OF BRETHREN	1	145	179*	.2	.6
165 CH OF NAZARENE	7	462	836	1.1	2.7
167 CHS OF CHRIST	4	273	331	.4	1.1
176 CCC, NOT NAT'L	1	104	128*	.2	.4
193 EPISCOPAL	2	290	385	.5	1.2
207 E.L.C.A.	2	349	491	.7	1.6
213 EVAN MENN INC	1	228	281*	.4	.9
223 FREE WILL BAPT	2	82	101*	.1	.3
226 FRIENDS-USA	10	1,313	1,618*	2.2	5.1
226e FUM	10	1,313	1,618*	2.2	5.1
283 LUTH—MO SYNOD	1	326	466	.6	1.5
339 PENT CH OF GOD	1	12	38	.1	.1
355 PRESB CH (USA)	3	624	769*	1.0	2.4
361 PRIM BAPT ASCS	2	62	76*	.1	.2
403 SALVATION ARMY	1	102	115	.2	.4
413 S.D.A.	2	217	267*	.4	.8
419 SO BAPT CONV	4	2,344	2,889*	3.9	9.2
438 UN BRETH IN CR	1	33	35	-	.1
443 UN C OF CHRIST	1	152	187*	.3	.6
449 UN METHODIST	29	4,262	5,254*	7.1	16.7
467 WESLEYAN	20	2,811	5,872	7.9	18.6
496 JEWISH EST[1]	1	NA	100	.1	.3
497 BLACK BAPT EST[2]	NA	1,081	1,333*	1.8	4.2
GREENE	**82**	**9,115**	**13,256***	**43.6**	**100.0**
019 AMER BAPT USA	9	2,843	3,532*	11.6	26.6
053 ASSEMB OF GOD	5	468	846	2.8	6.4
081 CATHOLIC	3	NA	720	2.4	5.4
081d LATIN	3	NA	720	2.4	5.4
093 CHR CH (DISC)	6	615	1,218	4.0	9.2
097 CHR CHS&CHS CR	6	1,005	1,249*	4.1	9.4
123 CH GOD (ANDER)	1	60	68	.2	.5
127 CH GOD (CLEVE)	4	361	449*	1.5	3.4
151 L-D SAINTS	1	NA	225	.7	1.7
165 CH OF NAZARENE	4	151	324	1.1	2.4
167 CHS OF CHRIST	9	483	624	2.1	4.7
171 CH GOD-GEN CON	3	102	127*	.4	1.0
207 E.L.C.A.	1	148	191	.6	1.4
221 FREE METHODIST	1	19	28	.1	.2
339 PENT CH OF GOD	2	19	54	.2	.4
355 PRESB CH (USA)	2	152	189*	.6	1.4
403 SALVATION ARMY	1	47	56	.2	.4
413 S.D.A.	1	59	73*	.2	.6
443 UN C OF CHRIST	1	299	372*	1.2	2.8
449 UN METHODIST	18	2,242	2,786*	9.2	21.0
467 WESLEYAN	4	42	125	.4	.9
HAMILTON	**98**	**22,606**	**50,239***	**46.1**	**100.0**
019 AMER BAPT USA	2	146	190*	.2	.4
053 ASSEMB OF GOD	3	958	2,788	2.6	5.5
057 BAPT GEN CONF	1	103	134*	.1	.3
071 BRETHREN (ASH)	1	51	66*	.1	.1
081 CATHOLIC	5	NA	16,156	14.8	32.2
081d LATIN	5	NA	16,156	14.8	32.2
082 CENTRAL BAPT	2	155	201*	.2	.4
093 CHR CH (DISC)	5	1,674	2,910	2.7	5.8
097 CHR CHS&CHS CR	13	3,904	5,073*	4.7	10.1
111 CH CR,SCIENTST	1	NR	NR	-	-
123 CH GOD (ANDER)	3	259	317	.3	.6
127 CH GOD (CLEVE)	1	142	185*	.2	.4
145 CH GOD PROPHCY	1	33	43*	-	.1
151 L-D SAINTS	1	NA	335	.3	.7
157 CH OF BRETHREN	1	94	122*	.1	.2
165 CH OF NAZARENE	2	198	329	.3	.7
167 CHS OF CHRIST	3	262	296	.3	.6
193 EPISCOPAL	2	682	1,082	1.0	2.2
207 E.L.C.A.	3	1,665	2,308	2.1	4.6
221 FREE METHODIST	1	0	54	-	.1
226 FRIENDS-USA	8	1,157	1,503*	1.4	3.0
226e FUM	7	1,104	1,434*	1.3	2.9

NA–Not applicable NR–Not reported *Total adherents estimated from known number of communicant, confirmed, full members. - Represents a percent less than 0.1. Percentages may not total due to rounding.
[1]See Appendix E [2]See Appendix F [3]See Appendix G Lines in *italic* represent a breakdown of Catholic rites or Friends affiliations. They are included in their respective denominational total.

Table 4. Churches and Church Membership by County and Denomination: 1990

County and Denomination	Number of churches	Communicant, confirmed, full members	Total adherents Number	Percent of total population	Percent of total adherents
226g INDEP EVAN	1	53	69*	.1	.1
283 LUTH—MO SYNOD	3	1,400	1,922	1.8	3.8
355 PRESB CH (USA)	1	332	431*	.4	.9
356 PRESB CH AMER	1	0	0	-	-
371 REF CH IN AM	1	75	232	.2	.5
413 S.D.A.	3	491	638*	.6	1.3
419 SO BAPT CONV	6	1,011	1,314*	1.2	2.6
443 UN C OF CHRIST	1	353	459*	.4	.9
449 UN METHODIST	16	6,988	9,080*	8.3	18.1
467 WESLEYAN	6	294	641	.6	1.3
496 JEWISH EST[1]	0	NA	872	.8	1.7
497 BLACK BAPT EST[2]	NA	179	233*	.2	.5
499 INDEP.NON-CHAR[3]	1	NA	325	.3	.6
HANCOCK	**61**	**10,019**	**17,794***	**39.1**	**100.0**
053 ASSEMB OF GOD	1	70	94	.2	.5
081 CATHOLIC	2	NA	3,001	6.6	16.9
081d LATIN	2	NA	3,001	6.6	16.9
093 CHR CH (DISC)	3	587	1,073	2.4	6.0
097 CHR CHS&CHS CR	8	1,918	2,424*	5.3	13.6
123 CH GOD (ANDER)	1	85	157	.3	.9
145 CH GOD PROPHCY	1	33	42*	.1	.2
151 L-D SAINTS	1	NA	353	.8	2.0
165 CH OF NAZARENE	6	581	1,287	2.8	7.2
167 CHS OF CHRIST	2	135	176	.4	1.0
207 E.L.C.A.	1	254	332	.7	1.9
223 FREE WILL BAPT	1	12	15*		.1
226 FRIENDS-USA	2	142	179*	.4	1.0
226e FUM	2	142	179*	.4	1.0
283 LUTH—MO SYNOD	2	738	1,026	2.3	5.8
325 OLD REG BAPT	1	20	25*	.1	.1
355 PRESB CH (USA)	1	135	171*	.4	1.0
361 PRIM BAPT ASCS	1	19	24*	.1	.1
413 S.D.A.	1	43	54*	.1	.3
419 SO BAPT CONV	2	489	618*	1.4	3.5
443 UN C OF CHRIST	1	147	186*	.4	1.0
449 UN METHODIST	21	4,541	5,740*	12.6	32.3
467 WESLEYAN	2	70	453	1.0	2.5
496 JEWISH EST[1]	0	NA	364	.8	2.0
HARRISON	**78**	**7,965**	**15,816***	**52.9**	**100.0**
019 AMER BAPT USA	1	128	164*	.5	1.0
053 ASSEMB OF GOD	4	456	646	2.2	4.1
081 CATHOLIC	6	NA	4,685	15.7	29.6
081d LATIN	6	NA	4,685	15.7	29.6
093 CHR CH (DISC)	1	212	554	1.9	3.5
097 CHR CHS&CHS CR	5	480	615*	2.1	3.9
145 CH GOD PROPHCY	2	67	86*	.3	.5
151 L-D SAINTS	1	NA	368	1.2	2.3
165 CH OF NAZARENE	2	185	345	1.2	2.2
167 CHS OF CHRIST	4	330	454	1.5	2.9
207 E.L.C.A.	2	263	368	1.2	2.3
283 LUTH—MO SYNOD	2	684	944	3.2	6.0
355 PRESB CH (USA)	5	406	520*	1.7	3.3
419 SO BAPT CONV	8	1,199	1,536*	5.1	9.7
443 UN C OF CHRIST	1	49	63*	.2	.4
449 UN METHODIST	33	3,488	4,468*	14.9	28.2
467 WESLEYAN	1	18	0	-	-
HENDRICKS	**78**	**13,894**	**27,243***	**36.0**	**100.0**
019 AMER BAPT USA	5	1,234	1,565*	2.1	5.7
053 ASSEMB OF GOD	3	241	490	.6	1.8
081 CATHOLIC	3	NA	6,908	9.1	25.4
081d LATIN	3	NA	6,908	9.1	25.4
089 CHR & MISS AL	1	29	73	.1	.3
093 CHR CH (DISC)	8	1,134	2,135	2.8	7.8
097 CHR CHS&CHS CR	8	3,135	3,975*	5.2	14.6
123 CH GOD (ANDER)	2	52	55	.1	.2
127 CH GOD (CLEVE)	1	16	20*	-	.1
145 CH GOD PROPHCY	1	33	42*	.1	.2
151 L-D SAINTS	2	NA	755	1.0	2.8
165 CH OF NAZARENE	4	214	494	.7	1.8
167 CHS OF CHRIST	7	610	831	1.1	3.1
193 EPISCOPAL	2	296	463	.6	1.7
207 E.L.C.A.	1	260	376	.5	1.4
209 EVAN LUTH SYN	1	46	69	.1	.3
221 FREE METHODIST	1	104	121	.2	.4
226 FRIENDS-USA	4	750	951*	1.3	3.5
226e FUM	4	750	951*	1.3	3.5
283 LUTH—MO SYNOD	2	241	340	.4	1.2
355 PRESB CH (USA)	4	404	512*	.7	1.9
361 PRIM BAPT ASCS	1	11	14*	-	.1
413 S.D.A.	1	32	41*	.1	.2
419 SO BAPT CONV	4	1,357	1,721*	2.3	6.3
449 UN METHODIST	12	3,514	4,456*	5.9	16.4
496 JEWISH EST[1]	0	NA	606	.8	2.2

County and Denomination	Number of churches	Communicant, confirmed, full members	Total adherents Number	Percent of total population	Percent of total adherents
497 BLACK BAPT EST[2]	NA	181	230*	.3	.8
HENRY	**96**	**12,482**	**20,129***	**41.8**	**100.0**
019 AMER BAPT USA	1	705	863*	1.8	4.3
053 ASSEMB OF GOD	1	191	231	.5	1.1
081 CATHOLIC	2	NA	1,105	2.3	5.5
081d LATIN	2	NA	1,105	2.3	5.5
089 CHR & MISS AL	1	40	72	.1	.4
093 CHR CH (DISC)	4	905	1,835	3.8	9.1
097 CHR CHS&CHS CR	7	645	790*	1.6	3.9
123 CH GOD (ANDER)	2	384	519	1.1	2.6
127 CH GOD (CLEVE)	1	100	122*	.3	.6
146 CH GOD MTN ASM	1	30	37*	.1	.2
151 L-D SAINTS	1	NA	145	.3	.7
157 CH OF BRETHREN	2	90	110*	.2	.5
165 CH OF NAZARENE	9	1,163	2,672	5.6	13.3
167 CHS OF CHRIST	7	337	459	1.0	2.3
193 EPISCOPAL	1	75	131	.3	.7
207 E.L.C.A.	1	291	382	.8	1.9
221 FREE METHODIST	1	98	104	.2	.5
223 FREE WILL BAPT	1	130	159*	.3	.8
226 FRIENDS-USA	10	1,029	1,260*	2.6	6.3
226e FUM	10	1,029	1,260*	2.6	6.3
263 INT FOURSQ GOS	1	841	1,029*	2.1	5.1
296 MIDW CONGR FEL	1	50	61*	.1	.3
355 PRESB CH (USA)	4	756	925*	1.9	4.6
403 SALVATION ARMY	1	60	69	.1	.3
413 S.D.A.	1	24	29*	.1	.1
419 SO BAPT CONV	9	1,492	1,826*	3.8	9.1
436 UNITED BAPT	2	312	382*	.8	1.9
438 UN BRETH IN CR	1	52	52	.1	.3
443 UN C OF CHRIST	1	221	271*	.6	1.3
449 UN METHODIST	15	2,215	2,711*	5.6	13.5
467 WESLEYAN	5	246	903	1.9	4.5
499 INDEP.NON-CHAR[3]	2	NA	875	1.8	4.3
HOWARD	**109**	**20,819**	**35,924***	**44.4**	**100.0**
005 AME ZION	1	200	275	.3	.8
019 AMER BAPT USA	4	989	1,245*	1.5	3.5
053 ASSEMB OF GOD	4	748	1,461	1.8	4.1
061 BEACHY AMISH	1	68	86*	.1	.2
071 BRETHREN (ASH)	1	24	30*	-	.1
081 CATHOLIC	2	NA	7,320	9.1	20.4
081d LATIN	2	NA	7,320	9.1	20.4
083 CHRIST CATH CH	1	7	7	-	-
089 CHR & MISS AL	1	42	104	.1	.3
093 CHR CH (DISC)	3	1,046	1,567	1.9	4.4
097 CHR CHS&CHS CR	7	1,851	2,329*	2.9	6.5
111 CH CR,SCIENTST	1	NR	NR	-	-
121 CH GOD (ABR)	1	42	53*	.1	.1
123 CH GOD (ANDER)	1	0	163	.2	.5
127 CH GOD (CLEVE)	3	383	482*	.6	1.3
145 CH GOD PROPHCY	1	33	42*	.1	.1
146 CH GOD MTN ASM	1	87	109*	.1	.3
151 L-D SAINTS	1	NA	426	.5	1.2
157 CH OF BRETHREN	2	264	332*	.4	.9
165 CH OF NAZARENE	4	824	893	1.1	2.5
167 CHS OF CHRIST	2	354	460	.6	1.3
193 EPISCOPAL	1	295	376	.5	1.0
207 E.L.C.A.	2	484	630	.8	1.8
221 FREE METHODIST	1	136	178	.2	.5
226 FRIENDS-USA	13	1,550	1,951*	2.4	5.4
226e FUM	12	1,531	1,927*	2.4	5.4
226g INDEP EVAN	1	19	24*	-	.1
259 IFCA	1	NR	NR	-	-
263 INT FOURSQ GOS	2	644	810*	1.0	2.3
283 LUTH—MO SYNOD	3	1,141	1,477	1.8	4.1
285 MENNONITE CH	2	114	164	.2	.5
323 OLD ORD AMISH	2	NA	300	.4	.8
339 PENT CH OF GOD	1	34	76	.1	.2
355 PRESB CH (USA)	2	1,298	1,634*	2.0	4.5
403 SALVATION ARMY	1	223	251	.3	.7
413 S.D.A.	2	140	176*	.2	.5
419 SO BAPT CONV	4	1,290	1,623*	2.0	4.5
435 UNITARIAN-UNIV	1	29	33	-	.1
438 UN BRETH IN CR	1	372	372	.5	1.0
443 UN C OF CHRIST	1	392	493*	.6	1.4
449 UN METHODIST	17	4,094	5,152*	6.4	14.3
467 WESLEYAN	7	389	877	1.1	2.4
469 WELS	1	69	103	.1	.3
496 JEWISH EST[1]	1	NA	0	-	-
497 BLACK BAPT EST[2]	NA	1,163	1,464*	1.8	4.1
499 INDEP.NON-CHAR[3]	1	NA	400	.5	1.1
HUNTINGTON	**74**	**9,962**	**19,621***	**55.4**	**100.0**
019 AMER BAPT USA	3	333	427*	1.2	2.2

NA–Not applicable NR–Not reported *Total adherents estimated from known number of communicant, confirmed, full members. - Represents a percent less than 0.1. Percentages may not total due to rounding.
[1]See Appendix E [2]See Appendix F [3]See Appendix G Lines in *italic* represent a breakdown of Catholic rites or Friends affiliations. They are included in their respective denominational total.

Table 4. Churches and Church Membership by County and Denomination: 1990

County and Denomination	Number of churches	Communicant, confirmed, full members	Total adherents Number	Percent of total population	Percent of total adherents
053 ASSEMB OF GOD	1	123	320	.9	1.6
071 BRETHREN (ASH)	2	149	191*	.5	1.0
081 CATHOLIC	3	NA	5,104	14.4	26.0
081d LATIN	*3*	*NA*	*5,104*	*14.4*	*26.0*
089 CHR & MISS AL	2	51	94	.3	.5
093 CHR CH (DISC)	4	759	1,120	3.2	5.7
097 CHR CHS&CHS CR	2	0	0*	-	-
111 CH CR,SCIENTST	1	NR	NR	-	-
123 CH GOD (ANDER)	1	0	303	.9	1.5
127 CH GOD (CLEVE)	1	17	22*	.1	.1
145 CH GOD PROPHCY	1	33	42*	.1	.2
151 L-D SAINTS	1	NA	400	1.1	2.0
157 CH OF BRETHREN	6	579	742*	2.1	3.8
165 CH OF NAZARENE	4	672	1,438	4.1	7.3
167 CHS OF CHRIST	3	132	210	.6	1.1
193 EPISCOPAL	1	83	114	.3	.6
223 FREE WILL BAPT	3	127	163*	.5	.8
283 LUTH—MO SYNOD	1	772	1,152	3.3	5.9
355 PRESB CH (USA)	1	274	351*	1.0	1.8
403 SALVATION ARMY	1	133	141	.4	.7
419 SO BAPT CONV	1	125	160*	.5	.8
438 UN BRETH IN CR	4	927	927	2.6	4.7
443 UN C OF CHRIST	5	1,298	1,663*	4.7	8.5
449 UN METHODIST	17	3,140	4,022*	11.4	20.5
467 WESLEYAN	5	235	515	1.5	2.6
JACKSON	**78**	**15,972**	**22,081***	**58.5**	**100.0**
019 AMER BAPT USA	7	2,054	2,591*	6.9	11.7
053 ASSEMB OF GOD	1	129	163	.4	.7
081 CATHOLIC	2	NA	1,044	2.8	4.7
081d LATIN	*2*	*NA*	*1,044*	*2.8*	*4.7*
089 CHR & MISS AL	1	26	46	.1	.2
093 CHR CH (DISC)	1	685	798	2.1	3.6
097 CHR CHS&CHS CR	15	2,451	3,091*	8.2	14.0
123 CH GOD (ANDER)	1	62	70	.2	.3
127 CH GOD (CLEVE)	2	190	240*	.6	1.1
157 CH OF BRETHREN	1	25	32*	.1	.1
165 CH OF NAZARENE	6	1,390	2,565	6.8	11.6
167 CHS OF CHRIST	2	119	143	.4	.6
193 EPISCOPAL	1	32	41	.1	.2
207 E.L.C.A.	1	355	468	1.2	2.1
221 FREE METHODIST	1	33	46	.1	.2
263 INT FOURSQ GOS	1	17	21*	.1	.1
283 LUTH—MO SYNOD	9	5,165	6,586	17.5	29.8
325 OLD REG BAPT	1	31	39*	.1	.2
355 PRESB CH (USA)	3	447	564*	1.5	2.6
413 S.D.A.	1	39	49*	.1	.2
419 SO BAPT CONV	2	605	763*	2.0	3.5
443 UN C OF CHRIST	2	156	197*	.5	.9
449 UN METHODIST	15	1,936	2,442*	6.5	11.1
467 WESLEYAN	2	25	82	.2	.4
JASPER	**43**	**6,317**	**12,472***	**50.0**	**100.0**
019 AMER BAPT USA	2	338	434*	1.7	3.5
040 AP CHR CH-AMER	1	92	162	.6	1.3
053 ASSEMB OF GOD	2	204	319	1.3	2.6
081 CATHOLIC	4	NA	3,286	13.2	26.3
081d LATIN	*4*	*NA*	*3,286*	*13.2*	*26.3*
093 CHR CH (DISC)	2	539	797	3.2	6.4
097 CHR CHS&CHS CR	3	440	566*	2.3	4.5
105 CHRISTIAN REF	2	722	1,160	4.6	9.3
123 CH GOD (ANDER)	1	12	17	.1	.1
165 CH OF NAZARENE	2	139	281	1.1	2.3
167 CHS OF CHRIST	2	75	105	.4	.8
193 EPISCOPAL	1	18	30	.1	.2
203 EVAN FREE CH	2	89	128	.5	1.0
283 LUTH—MO SYNOD	4	637	850	3.4	6.8
285 MENNONITE CH	1	70	114	.5	.9
339 PENT CH OF GOD	2	54	239	1.0	1.9
355 PRESB CH (USA)	2	270	347*	1.4	2.8
361 PRIM BAPT ASCS	1	26	33*	.1	.3
371 REF CH IN AM	2	1,018	1,581	6.3	12.7
419 SO BAPT CONV	1	111	143*	.6	1.1
449 UN METHODIST	6	1,463	1,880*	7.5	15.1
JAY	**56**	**4,970**	**8,857***	**41.2**	**100.0**
019 AMER BAPT USA	1	65	82*	.4	.9
053 ASSEMB OF GOD	1	28	82	.4	.9
081 CATHOLIC	3	NA	1,667	7.7	18.8
081d LATIN	*3*	*NA*	*1,667*	*7.7*	*18.8*
089 CHR & MISS AL	1	0	0	-	-
097 CHR CHS&CHS CR	6	824	1,034*	4.8	11.7
123 CH GOD (ANDER)	1	7	7	-	.1
145 CH GOD PROPHCY	1	33	41*	.2	.5
157 CH OF BRETHREN	2	57	72*	.3	.8
165 CH OF NAZARENE	6	552	1,242	5.8	14.0

County and Denomination	Number of churches	Communicant, confirmed, full members	Total adherents Number	Percent of total population	Percent of total adherents
167 CHS OF CHRIST	1	58	61	.3	.7
207 E.L.C.A.	3	504	743	3.5	8.4
215 EVAN METH CH	1	47	59*	.3	.7
226 FRIENDS-USA	3	* 116	146*	.7	1.6
226e FUM	*3*	*116*	*146*￼*	*.7*	*1.6*
296 MIDW CONGR FEL	3	91	114*	.5	1.3
355 PRESB CH (USA)	1	285	358*	1.7	4.0
413 S.D.A.	1	13	16*	.1	.2
419 SO BAPT CONV	1	445	559*	2.6	6.3
443 UN C OF CHRIST	2	146	183*	.9	2.1
449 UN METHODIST	17	1,638	2,056*	9.6	23.2
467 WESLEYAN	1	61	335	1.6	3.8
JEFFERSON	**68**	**9,424**	**14,838***	**49.8**	**100.0**
019 AMER BAPT USA	17	4,141	5,132*	17.2	34.6
053 ASSEMB OF GOD	1	349	700	2.3	4.7
081 CATHOLIC	4	NA	2,414	8.1	16.3
081d LATIN	*4*	*NA*	*2,414*	*8.1*	*16.3*
089 CHR & MISS AL	1	58	108	.4	.7
093 CHR CH (DISC)	1	150	204	.7	1.4
097 CHR CHS&CHS CR	7	1,065	1,320*	4.4	8.9
111 CH CR,SCIENTST	1	NR	NR	-	-
123 CH GOD (ANDER)	1	29	31	.1	.2
145 CH GOD PROPHCY	1	33	41*	.1	.3
146 CH GOD MTN ASM	1	20	25*	.1	.2
151 L-D SAINTS	1	NA	233	.8	1.6
165 CH OF NAZARENE	1	58	140	.5	.9
167 CHS OF CHRIST	1	82	107	.4	.7
193 EPISCOPAL	1	127	208	.7	1.4
207 E.L.C.A.	1	136	175	.6	1.2
283 LUTH—MO SYNOD	1	105	156	.5	1.1
285 MENNONITE CH	1	15	21	.1	.1
325 OLD REG BAPT	2	63	78*	.3	.5
355 PRESB CH (USA)	4	514	637*	2.1	4.3
403 SALVATION ARMY	1	81	85	.3	.6
413 S.D.A.	1	44	55*	.2	.4
419 SO BAPT CONV	1	501	621*	2.1	4.2
443 UN C OF CHRIST	1	105	130*	.4	.9
449 UN METHODIST	14	1,648	2,042*	6.9	13.8
467 WESLEYAN	2	100	175	.6	1.2
JENNINGS	**54**	**6,184**	**10,517***	**44.4**	**100.0**
019 AMER BAPT USA	15	3,289	4,137*	17.5	39.3
053 ASSEMB OF GOD	1	34	73	.3	.7
081 CATHOLIC	4	NA	1,844	7.8	17.5
081d LATIN	*4*	*NA*	*1,844*	*7.8*	*17.5*
097 CHR CHS&CHS CR	3	625	786*	3.3	7.5
123 CH GOD (ANDER)	4	124	360	1.5	3.4
127 CH GOD (CLEVE)	1	83	104*	.4	1.0
151 L-D SAINTS	1	NA	180	.8	1.7
165 CH OF NAZARENE	1	210	643	2.7	6.1
167 CHS OF CHRIST	2	80	104	.4	1.0
283 LUTH—MO SYNOD	1	92	134	.6	1.3
285 MENNONITE CH	1	48	74	.3	.7
325 OLD REG BAPT	1	11	14*	.1	.1
355 PRESB CH (USA)	4	205	258*	1.1	2.5
413 S.D.A.	1	46	58*	.2	.6
419 SO BAPT CONV	2	326	410*	1.7	3.9
449 UN METHODIST	11	979	1,231*	5.2	11.7
467 WESLEYAN	1	32	107	.5	1.0
JOHNSON	**83**	**18,693**	**35,622***	**40.4**	**100.0**
019 AMER BAPT USA	5	1,758	2,220*	2.5	6.2
053 ASSEMB OF GOD	5	210	402	.5	1.1
057 BAPT GEN CONF	1	39	49*	.1	.1
081 CATHOLIC	3	NA	6,295	7.1	17.7
081d LATIN	*3*	*NA*	*6,295*	*7.1*	*17.7*
093 CHR CH (DISC)	9	1,544	2,674	3.0	7.5
097 CHR CHS&CHS CR	9	5,234	6,609*	7.5	18.6
123 CH GOD (ANDER)	1	45	80	.1	.2
127 CH GOD (CLEVE)	2	304	384*	.4	1.1
145 CH GOD PROPHCY	1	33	42*	-	.1
151 L-D SAINTS	1	NA	527	.6	1.5
157 CH OF BRETHREN	1	81	102*	.1	.3
165 CH OF NAZARENE	3	292	504	.6	1.4
167 CHS OF CHRIST	3	467	599	.7	1.7
175 CONGR CHR CHS	1	402	508*	.6	1.4
193 EPISCOPAL	1	157	209	.2	.6
207 E.L.C.A.	1	138	170	.2	.5
215 EVAN METH CH	1	67	85*	.1	.2
221 FREE METHODIST	1	13	42	-	.1
283 LUTH—MO SYNOD	2	685	979	1.1	2.7
339 PENT CH OF GOD	1	34	77	.1	.2
355 PRESB CH (USA)	6	1,431	1,807*	2.1	5.1
361 PRIM BAPT ASCS	1	23	29*	-	.1
413 S.D.A.	1	62	78*	.1	.2

NA–Not applicable   NR–Not reported   *Total adherents estimated from known number of communicant, confirmed, full members.   - Represents a percent less than 0.1.   Percentages may not total due to rounding.
[1]See Appendix E   [2]See Appendix F   [3]See Appendix G   Lines in *italic* represent a breakdown of Catholic rites or Friends affiliations. They are included in their respective denominational total.

INDIANA

Table 4. Churches and Church Membership by County and Denomination: 1990

County and Denomination	Number of churches	Communicant, confirmed, full members	Total adherents Number	Percent of total population	Percent of total adherents
419 SO BAPT CONV	5	1,766	2,230*	2.5	6.3
443 UN C OF CHRIST	1	95	120*	.1	.3
449 UN METHODIST	10	3,499	4,418*	5.0	12.4
467 WESLEYAN	4	91	296	.3	.8
496 JEWISH EST[1]	0	NA	705	.8	2.0
497 BLACK BAPT EST[2]	NA	223	282*	.3	.8
499 INDEP.NON-CHAR[3]	3	NA	3,100	3.5	8.7
KNOX	**81**	**11,140**	**20,072***	**50.3**	**100.0**
019 AMER BAPT USA	5	1,722	2,105*	5.3	10.5
053 ASSEMB OF GOD	2	72	133	.3	.7
081 CATHOLIC	6	NA	5,380	13.5	26.8
081d LATIN	6	NA	5,380	13.5	26.8
093 CHR CH (DISC)	4	739	1,199	3.0	6.0
097 CHR CHS&CHS CR	4	734	897*	2.2	4.5
111 CH CR,SCIENTST	1	NR	NR	-	-
123 CH GOD (ANDER)	2	372	499	1.3	2.5
127 CH GOD (CLEVE)	1	15	18*	-	.1
145 CH GOD PROPHCY	1	33	40*	.1	.2
165 CH OF NAZARENE	3	347	868	2.2	4.3
167 CHS OF CHRIST	4	212	308	.8	1.5
179 CONSRV BAPT	1	NR	NR	-	-
185 CUMBER PRESB	1	91	95	.2	.5
193 EPISCOPAL	1	98	127	.3	.6
207 E.L.C.A.	1	146	235	.6	1.2
221 FREE METHODIST	1	177	212	.5	1.1
263 INT FOURSQ GOS	1	256	313*	.8	1.6
283 LUTH—MO SYNOD	2	669	919	2.3	4.6
355 PRESB CH (USA)	8	542	663*	1.7	3.3
356 PRESB CH AMER	1	34	45	.1	.2
403 SALVATION ARMY	1	59	88	.2	.4
413 S.D.A.	1	45	55*	.1	.3
419 SO BAPT CONV	1	703	859*	2.2	4.3
443 UN C OF CHRIST	3	1,271	1,554*	3.9	7.7
449 UN METHODIST	21	2,736	3,345*	8.4	16.7
467 WESLEYAN	4	67	115	.3	.6
KOSCIUSKO	**88**	**11,161**	**19,901***	**30.5**	**100.0**
019 AMER BAPT USA	1	133	173*	.3	.9
040 AP CHR CH-AMER	1	109	194	.3	1.0
053 ASSEMB OF GOD	1	78	200	.3	1.0
061 BEACHY AMISH	1	33	43*	.1	.2
071 BRETHREN (ASH)	3	436	567*	.9	2.8
081 CATHOLIC	4	NA	3,010	4.6	15.1
081d LATIN	4	NA	3,010	4.6	15.1
097 CHR CHS&CHS CR	1	500	650*	1.0	3.3
111 CH CR,SCIENTST	1	NR	NR	-	-
123 CH GOD (ANDER)	2	606	665	1.0	3.3
127 CH GOD (CLEVE)	1	12	16*	-	.1
151 L-D SAINTS	1	NA	268	.4	1.3
157 CH OF BRETHREN	8	846	1,099*	1.7	5.5
165 CH OF NAZARENE	2	234	414	.6	2.1
167 CHS OF CHRIST	2	75	112	.2	.6
171 CH GOD-GEN CON	3	270	351*	.5	1.8
193 EPISCOPAL	2	310	464	.7	2.3
207 E.L.C.A.	2	131	182	.3	.9
221 FREE METHODIST	2	367	367	.6	1.8
226 FRIENDS-USA	1	48	62*	.1	.3
226e FUM	1	48	62*	.1	.3
259 IFCA	1	NR	NR	-	-
263 INT FOURSQ GOS	1	0	0*	-	-
283 LUTH—MO SYNOD	1	295	371	.6	1.9
285 MENNONITE CH	5	375	550	.8	2.8
291 MISSIONARY CH	1	21	54	.1	.3
323 OLD ORD AMISH	4	NA	600	.9	3.0
325 OLD REG BAPT	1	37	48*	.1	.2
339 PENT CH OF GOD	2	48	180	.3	.9
353 CHR BRETHREN	1	77	100	.2	.5
355 PRESB CH (USA)	3	891	1,158*	1.8	5.8
356 PRESB CH AMER	1	40	41	.1	.2
361 PRIM BAPT ASCS	1	11	14*	-	.1
403 SALVATION ARMY	1	137	142	.2	.7
413 S.D.A.	1	32	42*	.1	.2
449 UN METHODIST	23	4,752	6,176*	9.5	31.0
467 WESLEYAN	2	257	1,588	2.4	8.0
LAGRANGE	**101**	**4,869**	**15,605***	**52.9**	**100.0**
019 AMER BAPT USA	1	106	146*	.5	.9
053 ASSEMB OF GOD	1	26	35	.1	.2
061 BEACHY AMISH	1	52	72*	.2	.5
081 CATHOLIC	2	NA	566	1.9	3.6
081d LATIN	2	NA	566	1.9	3.6
123 CH GOD (ANDER)	2	250	315	1.1	2.0
146 CH GOD MTN ASM	1	4	6*	-	-
157 CH OF BRETHREN	1	52	72*	.2	.5
165 CH OF NAZARENE	2	152	441	1.5	2.8
167 CHS OF CHRIST	1	74	100	.3	.6
193 EPISCOPAL	1	57	64	.2	.4
207 E.L.C.A.	1	449	583	2.0	3.7
283 LUTH—MO SYNOD	2	267	329	1.1	2.1
285 MENNONITE CH	9	1,426	1,767	6.0	11.3
287 MENN GEN CONF	1	124	156	.5	1.0
291 MISSIONARY CH	2	102	175	.6	1.1
323 OLD ORD AMISH	56	NA	8,400	28.5	53.8
355 PRESB CH (USA)	2	197	271*	.9	1.7
419 SO BAPT CONV	1	45	62*	.2	.4
436 UNITED BAPT	1	13	18*	.1	.1
449 UN METHODIST	13	1,473	2,027*	6.9	13.0
LAKE	**349**	**94,785**	**346,097***	**72.8**	**100.0**
005 AME ZION	5	8,150	10,187	2.1	2.9
019 AMER BAPT USA	8	1,996	2,548*	.5	.7
022 EASTERN ORTH	2	286	286	.1	.1
053 ASSEMB OF GOD	20	2,311	3,712	.8	1.1
057 BAPT GEN CONF	1	187	239*	.1	.1
059 BAPT MISS ASSN	1	41	52*	-	-
081 CATHOLIC	64	NA	138,830	29.2	40.1
081b BYZAN RUTH	4	NA	1,686	.4	.5
081d LATIN	57	NA	136,236	28.6	39.4
081f MELKITE-GK	1	NA	522	.1	.2
081g ROMANIAN	1	NA	322	.1	.1
081h UKRAINIAN	1	NA	64	-	-
089 CHR & MISS AL	1	20	35	-	-
093 CHR CH (DISC)	6	530	799	.2	.2
097 CHR CHS&CHS CR	13	3,066	3,914*	.8	1.1
105 CHRISTIAN REF	6	1,370	2,636	.6	.8
111 CH CR,SCIENTST	4	NR	NR	-	-
123 CH GOD (ANDER)	8	956	1,046	.2	.3
127 CH GOD (CLEVE)	6	824	1,052*	.2	.3
145 CH GOD PROPHCY	3	111	142*	-	-
151 L-D SAINTS	1	NA	595	.1	.2
165 CH OF NAZARENE	16	1,977	2,609	.5	.8
167 CHS OF CHRIST	11	948	1,221	.3	.4
175 CONGR CHR CHS	2	125	160*	-	-
179 CONSRV BAPT	1	NR	NR	-	-
191 ENTRPR BPT ASC	1	56	71*	-	-
193 EPISCOPAL	6	833	1,144	.2	.3
203 EVAN FREE CH	2	37	110	-	-
207 E.L.C.A.	15	4,017	5,462	1.1	1.6
221 FREE METHODIST	2	161	161	-	-
246 GREEK ORTHODOX	3	NR	NR	-	-
249 AP CATH ASSYR	1	53	329	.1	.1
259 IFCA	5	NR	NR	-	-
283 LUTH—MO SYNOD	23	8,146	10,674	2.2	3.1
331 ORTH CH IN AM	2	NR	NR	-	-
339 PENT CH OF GOD	3	86	189	-	.1
349 PENT HOLINESS	1	25	32*	-	-
355 PRESB CH (USA)	13	3,814	4,869*	1.0	1.4
356 PRESB CH AMER	2	788	1,019	.2	.3
371 REF CH IN AM	3	571	953	.2	.3
397 ROMANIAN ORTH	1	NR	NR	-	-
403 SALVATION ARMY	3	307	355	.1	.1
413 S.D.A.	6	1,361	1,737*	.4	.5
419 SO BAPT CONV	31	9,950	12,702*	2.7	3.7
435 UNITARIAN-UNIV	2	148	170	-	-
443 UN C OF CHRIST	8	2,142	2,735*	.6	.8
449 UN METHODIST	24	8,376	10,693*	2.2	3.1
467 WESLEYAN	2	54	92	-	-
469 WELS	1	111	168	-	-
496 JEWISH EST[1]	6	NA	1,809	.4	.5
497 BLACK BAPT EST[2]	NA	30,851	39,385*	8.3	11.4
498 INDEP.CHARIS.[3]	2	NA	3,800	.8	1.1
499 INDEP.NON-CHAR[3]	2	NA	77,375	16.3	22.4
LA PORTE	**105**	**20,988**	**47,187***	**44.1**	**100.0**
019 AMER BAPT USA	2	720	896*	.8	1.9
040 AP CHR CH-AMER	1	115	205	.2	.4
053 ASSEMB OF GOD	4	411	727	.7	1.5
057 BAPT GEN CONF	1	155	193*	.2	.4
059 BAPT MISS ASSN	1	123	153*	.1	.3
081 CATHOLIC	13	NA	18,958	17.7	40.2
081d LATIN	13	NA	18,958	17.7	40.2
093 CHR CH (DISC)	2	310	815	.8	1.7
097 CHR CHS&CHS CR	6	1,335	1,662*	1.6	3.5
111 CH CR,SCIENTST	2	NR	NR	-	-
123 CH GOD (ANDER)	1	110	133	.1	.3
127 CH GOD (CLEVE)	2	144	179*	.2	.4
145 CH GOD PROPHCY	1	33	41*	-	.1
151 L-D SAINTS	2	NA	361	.3	.8
157 CH OF BRETHREN	2	121	151*	.1	.3
165 CH OF NAZARENE	2	127	277	.3	.6
167 CHS OF CHRIST	3	165	216	.2	.5
175 CONGR CHR CHS	1	53	66*	.1	.1

NA–Not applicable   NR–Not reported   *Total adherents estimated from known number of communicant, confirmed, full members.   - Represents a percent less than 0.1.   Percentages may not total due to rounding.

[1]See Appendix E   [2]See Appendix F   [3]See Appendix G   Lines in *italic* represent a breakdown of Catholic rites or Friends affiliations. They are included in their respective denominational total.

Table 4. Churches and Church Membership by County and Denomination: 1990

County and Denomination	Number of churches	Communicant, confirmed, full members	Total adherents Number	Total adherents Percent of total population	Total adherents Percent of total adherents
193 EPISCOPAL	3	650	731	.7	1.5
207 E.L.C.A.	5	2,513	3,401	3.2	7.2
221 FREE METHODIST	2	204	204	.2	.4
223 FREE WILL BAPT	2	102	127*	.1	.3
259 IFCA	2	NR	NR	-	-
283 LUTH—MO SYNOD	9	3,060	4,138	3.9	8.8
285 MENNONITE CH	2	133	221	.2	.5
291 MISSIONARY CH	1	72	133	.1	.3
339 PENT CH OF GOD	2	68	154	.1	.3
355 PRESB CH (USA)	3	1,512	1,882*	1.8	4.0
403 SALVATION ARMY	2	243	259	.2	.5
413 S.D.A.	2	183	228*	.2	.5
419 SO BAPT CONV	3	467	581*	.5	1.2
431 UKRANIAN AMER	1	NR	NR	-	-
436 UNITED BAPT	1	61	76*	.1	.2
443 UN C OF CHRIST	3	2,117	2,635*	2.5	5.6
449 UN METHODIST	13	3,511	4,370*	4.1	9.3
467 WESLEYAN	2	118	180	.2	.4
496 JEWISH EST[1]	1	NA	280	.3	.6
497 BLACK BAPT EST[2]	NA	2,052	2,554*	2.4	5.4
LAWRENCE	**86**	**13,445**	**19,881***	**46.4**	**100.0**
019 AMER BAPT USA	16	4,459	5,526*	12.9	27.8
053 ASSEMB OF GOD	1	154	187	.4	.9
081 CATHOLIC	2	NA	1,907	4.5	9.6
081d LATIN	*2*	*NA*	*1,907*	*4.5*	*9.6*
093 CHR CH (DISC)	3	607	1,480	3.5	7.4
097 CHR CHS&CHS CR	10	2,687	3,330*	7.8	16.7
123 CH GOD (ANDER)	4	504	593	1.4	3.0
127 CH GOD (CLEVE)	2	246	305*	.7	1.5
145 CH GOD PROPHCY	1	33	41*	.1	.2
151 L-D SAINTS	1	NA	280	.7	1.4
165 CH OF NAZARENE	4	606	1,060	2.5	5.3
167 CHS OF CHRIST	16	1,140	1,453	3.4	7.3
193 EPISCOPAL	1	143	171	.4	.9
221 FREE METHODIST	1	444	444	1.0	2.2
283 LUTH—MO SYNOD	2	299	427	1.0	2.1
339 PENT CH OF GOD	1	57	121	.3	.6
355 PRESB CH (USA)	2	303	375*	.9	1.9
403 SALVATION ARMY	2	144	165	.4	.8
413 S.D.A.	1	111	138*	.3	.7
419 SO BAPT CONV	1	23	29*	.1	.1
449 UN METHODIST	13	1,370	1,698*	4.0	8.5
467 WESLEYAN	2	115	151	.4	.8
MADISON	**150**	**32,192**	**50,726***	**38.8**	**100.0**
005 AME ZION	1	292	438	.3	.9
019 AMER BAPT USA	9	3,440	4,243*	3.2	8.4
053 ASSEMB OF GOD	3	601	1,017	.8	2.0
081 CATHOLIC	4	NA	7,153	5.5	14.1
081d LATIN	*4*	*NA*	*7,153*	*5.5*	*14.1*
089 CHR & MISS AL	1	76	185	.1	.4
093 CHR CH (DISC)	10	3,241	4,757	3.6	9.4
097 CHR CHS&CHS CR	7	3,245	4,003*	3.1	7.9
111 CH CR,SCIENTST	1	NR	NR	-	-
123 CH GOD (ANDER)	17	4,160	4,967	3.8	9.8
127 CH GOD (CLEVE)	3	349	430*	.3	.8
145 CH GOD PROPHCY	1	33	41*	-	.1
151 L-D SAINTS	2	NA	562	.4	1.1
157 CH OF BRETHREN	2	320	395*	.3	.8
165 CH OF NAZARENE	10	1,803	2,733	2.1	5.4
167 CHS OF CHRIST	7	983	1,280	1.0	2.5
193 EPISCOPAL	2	362	661	.5	1.3
207 E.L.C.A.	4	792	1,067	.8	2.1
221 FREE METHODIST	2	187	281	.2	.6
223 FREE WILL BAPT	2	137	169*	.1	.3
226 FRIENDS-USA	5	279	344*	.3	.7
226c FGC	*1*	*19*	*23**	*-*	*-*
226e FUM	*3*	*225*	*278**	*.2*	*.5*
226g INDEP EVAN	*1*	*35*	*43**	*-*	*.1*
263 INT FOURSQ GOS	2	68	84*	.1	.2
283 LUTH—MO SYNOD	2	519	629	.5	1.2
296 MIDW CONGR FEL	1	48	59*	-	.1
355 PRESB CH (USA)	2	939	1,158*	.9	2.3
356 PRESB CH AMER	1	0	0	-	-
403 SALVATION ARMY	1	114	118	.1	.2
413 S.D.A.	2	253	312*	.2	.6
419 SO BAPT CONV	3	415	512*	.4	1.0
438 UN BRETH IN CR	1	35	38	-	.1
443 UN C OF CHRIST	1	376	464*	.4	.9
449 UN METHODIST	27	5,756	7,100*	5.4	14.0
467 WESLEYAN	14	759	2,307	1.8	4.5
497 BLACK BAPT EST[2]	NA	2,610	3,219*	2.5	6.3
MARION	**523**	**193,869**	**361,192***	**45.3**	**100.0**
005 AME ZION	6	7,945	10,328	1.3	2.9

County and Denomination	Number of churches	Communicant, confirmed, full members	Total adherents Number	Total adherents Percent of total population	Total adherents Percent of total adherents
019 AMER BAPT USA	29	9,132	11,483*	1.4	3.2
040 AP CHR CH-AMER	1	42	72	-	-
053 ASSEMB OF GOD	13	4,384	10,229	1.3	2.8
081 CATHOLIC	43	NA	84,033	10.5	23.3
081b BYZAN RUTH	*1*	*NA*	*40*		
081d LATIN	*42*	*NA*	*83,993*	*10.5*	*23.3*
089 CHR & MISS AL	3	294	472	.1	.1
093 CHR CH (DISC)	30	14,071	20,596	2.6	5.7
097 CHR CHS&CHS CR	35	18,160	22,836*	2.9	6.3
105 CHRISTIAN REF	1	67	124	-	-
111 CH CR,SCIENTST	6	NR	NR	-	-
123 CH GOD (ANDER)	14	1,700	2,158	.3	.6
127 CH GOD (CLEVE)	5	1,004	1,263*	.2	.3
145 CH GOD PROPHCY	2	67	84*	-	-
151 L-D SAINTS	6	NA	2,116	.3	.6
157 CH OF BRETHREN	1	150	189*	-	.1
165 CH OF NAZARENE	24	3,687	8,570	1.1	2.4
167 CHS OF CHRIST	36	6,449	8,687	1.1	2.4
179 CONSRV BAPT	2	NR	NR	-	-
185 CUMBER PRESB	1	138	138	-	-
193 EPISCOPAL	10	3,211	4,630	.6	1.3
195 ESTONIAN ELC	1	26	33*	-	-
203 EVAN FREE CH	1	673	1,000	.1	.3
207 E.L.C.A.	19	5,825	7,553	.9	2.1
220 FREE LUTHERAN	1	158	206	-	.1
221 FREE METHODIST	6	1,002	1,230	.2	.3
223 FREE WILL BAPT	1	225	283*	-	.1
226 FRIENDS-USA	8	1,257	1,581*	.2	.4
226c FGC	*1*	*46*	*58**	*-*	*-*
226e FUM	*7*	*1,211*	*1,523**	*.2*	*.4*
246 GREEK ORTHODOX	1	NR	NR	-	-
263 INT FOURSQ GOS	3	297	373*	-	.1
274 LAT EVAN LUTH	1	373	409	.1	.1
283 LUTH—MO SYNOD	15	5,474	7,474	.9	2.1
284 LUTH CH-AM ASC	1	263	351	-	.1
285 MENNONITE CH	1	149	317	-	.1
291 MISSIONARY CH	1	72	32	-	-
293 MORAV CH-NORTH	3	207	271	-	.1
313 N AM BAPT CONF	1	66	83*	-	-
329 OPEN BIBLE STD	1	NR	NR	-	-
339 PENT CH OF GOD	3	103	192	-	.1
353 CHR BRETHREN	1	45	70	-	-
355 PRESB CH (USA)	23	14,306	17,990*	2.3	5.0
356 PRESB CH AMER	2	122	172	-	-
371 REF CH IN AM	1	154	220	-	.1
397 ROMANIAN ORTH	1	NR	NR	-	-
403 SALVATION ARMY	3	305	315	-	.1
413 S.D.A.	9	2,360	2,968*	.4	.8
419 SO BAPT CONV	25	7,438	9,353*	1.2	2.6
435 UNITARIAN-UNIV	4	919	1,151	.1	.3
443 UN C OF CHRIST	15	5,946	7,477*	.9	2.1
449 UN METHODIST	64	29,445	37,027*	4.6	10.3
467 WESLEYAN	14	848	1,951	.2	.5
469 WELS	2	456	638	.1	.2
496 JEWISH EST[1]	5	NA	6,379	.8	1.8
497 BLACK BAPT EST[2]	NA	44,854	56,403*	7.1	15.6
498 INDEP.CHARIS.[3]	6	NA	2,535	.3	.7
499 INDEP.NON-CHAR[3]	12	NA	7,147	.9	2.0
MARSHALL	**71**	**7,618**	**15,642***	**37.1**	**100.0**
053 ASSEMB OF GOD	3	106	160	.4	1.0
081 CATHOLIC	3	NA	2,970	7.0	19.0
081d LATIN	*3*	*NA*	*2,970*	*7.0*	*19.0*
097 CHR CHS&CHS CR	1	75	97*	.2	.6
111 CH CR,SCIENTST	1	NR	NR	-	-
121 CH GOD (ABR)	1	29	37*	.1	.2
123 CH GOD (ANDER)	2	118	168	.4	1.1
151 L-D SAINTS	1	NA	161	.4	1.0
157 CH OF BRETHREN	6	835	1,078*	2.6	6.9
165 CH OF NAZARENE	1	82	181	.4	1.2
167 CHS OF CHRIST	2	70	95	.2	.6
193 EPISCOPAL	1	197	265	.6	1.7
207 E.L.C.A.	1	255	328	.8	2.1
283 LUTH—MO SYNOD	3	763	1,062	2.5	6.8
285 MENNONITE CH	2	170	259	.6	1.7
291 MISSIONARY CH	2	132	229	.5	1.5
323 OLD ORD AMISH	16	NA	2,400	5.7	15.3
329 OPEN BIBLE STD	1	NR	NR	-	-
355 PRESB CH (USA)	1	200	258*	.6	1.6
361 PRIM BAPT ASCS	1	47	61*	.1	.4
413 S.D.A.	1	25	32*	.1	.2
419 SO BAPT CONV	1	57	74*	.2	.5
443 UN C OF CHRIST	4	1,210	1,562*	3.7	10.0
449 UN METHODIST	14	2,980	3,846*	9.1	24.6
467 WESLEYAN	2	267	319	.8	2.0

NA–Not applicable NR–Not reported *Total adherents estimated from known number of communicant, confirmed, full members. - Represents a percent less than 0.1. Percentages may not total due to rounding.
[1]See Appendix E [2]See Appendix F [3]See Appendix G Lines in *italic* represent a breakdown of Catholic rites or Friends affiliations. They are included in their respective denominational total.

Table 4. Churches and Church Membership by County and Denomination: 1990

County and Denomination	Number of churches	Communicant, confirmed, full members	Total adherents Number	Percent of total population	Percent of total adherents
MARTIN	**33**	**2,631**	**6,176***	**59.6**	**100.0**
053 ASSEMB OF GOD	1	53	101	1.0	1.6
081 CATHOLIC	5	NA	2,782	26.8	45.0
081d LATIN	*5*	*NA*	*2,782*	*26.8*	*45.0*
097 CHR CHS&CHS CR	3	803	1,017*	9.8	16.5
165 CH OF NAZARENE	2	54	109	1.1	1.8
167 CHS OF CHRIST	5	191	255	2.5	4.1
207 E.L.C.A.	1	302	382	3.7	6.2
285 MENNONITE CH	2	61	61	.6	1.0
419 SO BAPT CONV	2	145	184*	1.8	3.0
449 UN METHODIST	10	1,004	1,271*	12.3	20.6
467 WESLEYAN	2	18	14	.1	.2
MIAMI	**60**	**9,850**	**14,819***	**40.2**	**100.0**
019 AMER BAPT USA	7	2,277	2,930*	7.9	19.8
053 ASSEMB OF GOD	1	233	275	.7	1.9
071 BRETHREN (ASH)	5	319	410*	1.1	2.8
081 CATHOLIC	1	NA	1,879	5.1	12.7
081d LATIN	*1*	*NA*	*1,879*	*5.1*	*12.7*
089 CHR & MISS AL	1	49	184	.5	1.2
093 CHR CH (DISC)	1	769	1,032	2.8	7.0
097 CHR CHS&CHS CR	2	297	382*	1.0	2.6
111 CH CR,SCIENTST	1	NR	NR	-	-
123 CH GOD (ANDER)	1	61	81	.2	.5
127 CH GOD (CLEVE)	1	46	59*	.2	.4
146 CH GOD MTN ASM	1	10	13*	-	.1
157 CH OF BRETHREN	3	658	847*	2.3	5.7
165 CH OF NAZARENE	1	202	242	.7	1.6
167 CHS OF CHRIST	1	47	61	.2	.4
221 FREE METHODIST	1	47	94	.3	.6
223 FREE WILL BAPT	1	16	21*	.1	.1
226 FRIENDS-USA	1	286	368*	1.0	2.5
226e FUM	*1*	*286*	*368*￼*	*1.0*	*2.5*
263 INT FOURSQ GOS	1	179	230*	.6	1.6
283 LUTH—MO SYNOD	1	840	1,164	3.2	7.9
285 MENNONITE CH	2	266	408	1.1	2.8
291 MISSIONARY CH	1	55	39	.1	.3
355 PRESB CH (USA)	1	385	495*	1.3	3.3
403 SALVATION ARMY	1	112	112	.3	.8
419 SO BAPT CONV	1	137	176*	.5	1.2
449 UN METHODIST	21	2,288	2,944*	8.0	19.9
467 WESLEYAN	1	32	65	.2	.4
497 BLACK BAPT EST[2]	NA	239	308*	.8	2.1
MONROE	**103**	**19,338**	**37,345***	**34.3**	**100.0**
019 AMER BAPT USA	8	2,771	3,249*	3.0	8.7
053 ASSEMB OF GOD	7	756	1,237	1.1	3.3
059 BAPT MISS ASSN	1	100	117*	.1	.3
081 CATHOLIC	3	NA	9,294	8.5	24.9
081d LATIN	*3*	*NA*	*9,294*	*8.5*	*24.9*
093 CHR CH (DISC)	3	869	1,507	1.4	4.0
097 CHR CHS&CHS CR	11	2,970	3,482*	3.2	9.3
111 CH CR,SCIENTST	1	NR	NR	-	-
121 CH GOD (ABR)	1	9	11*	-	-
123 CH GOD (ANDER)	2	165	172	.2	.5
145 CH GOD PROPHCY	1	33	39*	-	.1
151 L-D SAINTS	3	NA	963	.9	2.6
165 CH OF NAZARENE	5	798	1,387	1.3	3.7
167 CHS OF CHRIST	21	1,658	2,024	1.9	5.4
193 EPISCOPAL	1	358	616	.6	1.6
203 EVAN FREE CH	1	14	35	-	.1
207 E.L.C.A.	1	347	460	.4	1.2
221 FREE METHODIST	1	337	337	.3	.9
223 FREE WILL BAPT	1	17	20*	-	.1
226 FRIENDS-USA	1	94	110*	.1	.3
226e FUM	*1*	*94*	*110*￼*	*.1*	*.3*
283 LUTH—MO SYNOD	2	379	488	.4	1.3
355 PRESB CH (USA)	2	590	692*	.6	1.9
356 PRESB CH AMER	1	45	60	.1	.2
361 PRIM BAPT ASCS	1	12	14*	-	-
403 SALVATION ARMY	1	119	132	.1	.4
413 S.D.A.	1	150	176*	.2	.5
419 SO BAPT CONV	3	557	653*	.6	1.7
435 UNITARIAN-UNIV	1	322	402	.4	1.1
443 UN C OF CHRIST	1	817	958*	.9	2.6
449 UN METHODIST	13	4,259	4,993*	4.6	13.4
467 WESLEYAN	2	42	138	.1	.4
496 JEWISH EST[1]	0	NA	1,000	.9	2.7
497 BLACK BAPT EST[2]	NA	750	879*	.8	2.4
499 INDEP.NON-CHAR[3]	2	NA	1,700	1.6	4.6
MONTGOMERY	**62**	**10,668**	**16,059***	**46.6**	**100.0**
019 AMER BAPT USA	5	1,930	2,403*	7.0	15.0
053 ASSEMB OF GOD	1	105	190	.6	1.2
081 CATHOLIC	1	NA	1,836	5.3	11.4
081d LATIN	*1*	*NA*	*1,836*	*5.3*	*11.4*
093 CHR CH (DISC)	4	800	1,462	4.2	9.1
097 CHR CHS&CHS CR	12	2,891	3,599*	10.5	22.4
123 CH GOD (ANDER)	1	38	51	.1	.3
127 CH GOD (CLEVE)	1	49	61*	.2	.4
151 L-D SAINTS	1	NA	228	.7	1.4
165 CH OF NAZARENE	2	269	356	1.0	2.2
167 CHS OF CHRIST	4	219	270*	.8	1.7
176 CCC, NOT NAT'L	1	73	91*	.3	.6
181 CONSRV CONGR	1	157	195*	.6	1.2
193 EPISCOPAL	1	102	166	.5	1.0
207 E.L.C.A.	1	289	404	1.2	2.5
226 FRIENDS-USA	1	22	27*	.1	.2
226e FUM	*1*	*22*	*27*￼*	*.1*	*.2*
283 LUTH—MO SYNOD	1	166	224	.7	1.4
355 PRESB CH (USA)	4	516	642*	1.9	4.0
413 S.D.A.	1	16	20*	.1	.1
419 SO BAPT CONV	3	338	421*	1.2	2.6
443 UN C OF CHRIST	1	35	44*	.1	.3
449 UN METHODIST	14	2,622	3,264*	9.5	20.3
467 WESLEYAN	1	31	105	.3	.7
MORGAN	**82**	**12,845**	**21,806***	**39.0**	**100.0**
019 AMER BAPT USA	10	1,999	2,543*	4.5	11.7
053 ASSEMB OF GOD	3	237	419	.7	1.9
081 CATHOLIC	2	NA	2,151	3.8	9.9
081d LATIN	*2*	*NA*	*2,151*	*3.8*	*9.9*
093 CHR CH (DISC)	4	1,120	1,943	3.5	8.9
097 CHR CHS&CHS CR	13	2,842	3,616*	6.5	16.6
123 CH GOD (ANDER)	3	299	465	.8	2.1
127 CH GOD (CLEVE)	1	48	61*	.1	.3
151 L-D SAINTS	1	NA	335	.6	1.5
165 CH OF NAZARENE	6	477	1,217	2.2	5.6
167 CHS OF CHRIST	6	469	605	1.1	2.8
193 EPISCOPAL	1	62	75	.1	.3
215 EVAN METH CH	1	21	27*	-	.1
221 FREE METHODIST	1	76	108	.2	.5
226 FRIENDS-USA	3	464	590*	1.1	2.7
226e FUM	*3*	*464*	*590*￼*	*1.1*	*2.7*
283 LUTH—MO SYNOD	1	118	154	.3	.7
291 MISSIONARY CH	2	219	377	.7	1.7
355 PRESB CH (USA)	1	337	429*	.8	2.0
413 S.D.A.	1	19	24*	-	.1
419 SO BAPT CONV	7	2,219	2,823*	5.0	12.9
449 UN METHODIST	9	1,749	2,225*	4.0	10.2
467 WESLEYAN	4	70	322	.6	1.5
496 JEWISH EST[1]	0	NA	447	.8	2.0
499 INDEP.NON-CHAR[3]	2	NA	850	1.5	3.9
NEWTON	**26**	**3,268**	**6,179***	**45.6**	**100.0**
019 AMER BAPT USA	2	429	553*	4.1	8.9
053 ASSEMB OF GOD	1	33	50	.4	.8
057 BAPT GEN CONF	1	0	0*	-	-
081 CATHOLIC	3	NA	1,762	13.0	28.5
081d LATIN	*3*	*NA*	*1,762*	*13.0*	*28.5*
093 CHR CH (DISC)	2	246	441	3.3	7.1
097 CHR CHS&CHS CR	1	310	400*	3.0	6.5
105 CHRISTIAN REF	1	131	247	1.8	4.0
283 LUTH—MO SYNOD	1	84	111	.8	1.8
287 MENN GEN CONF	1	43	46	.3	.7
355 PRESB CH (USA)	3	363	468*	3.5	7.6
419 SO BAPT CONV	2	387	499*	3.7	8.1
449 UN METHODIST	8	1,242	1,602*	11.8	25.9
NOBLE	**65**	**7,677**	**14,441***	**38.1**	**100.0**
019 AMER BAPT USA	2	132	171*	.5	1.2
053 ASSEMB OF GOD	4	250	412	1.1	2.9
081 CATHOLIC	6	NA	3,092	8.2	21.4
081d LATIN	*6*	*NA*	*3,092*	*8.2*	*21.4*
093 CHR CH (DISC)	1	250	405	1.1	2.8
097 CHR CHS&CHS CR	2	160	208*	.5	1.4
111 CH CR,SCIENTST	1	NR	NR	-	-
121 CH GOD (ABR)	1	52	68*	.2	.5
123 CH GOD (ANDER)	1	90	140	.4	1.0
151 L-D SAINTS	1	NA	199	.5	1.4
157 CH OF BRETHREN	1	86	112*	.3	.8
165 CH OF NAZARENE	3	169	466	1.2	3.2
167 CHS OF CHRIST	2	45	51	.1	.4
207 E.L.C.A.	4	536	669	1.8	4.6
283 LUTH—MO SYNOD	3	1,554	2,174	5.7	15.1
291 MISSIONARY CH	2	42	71	.2	.5
325 OLD REG BAPT	1	40	52*	.1	.4
355 PRESB CH (USA)	4	505	656*	1.7	4.5
413 S.D.A.	1	31	40*	.1	.3
436 UNITED BAPT	1	42	55*	.1	.4
443 UN C OF CHRIST	1	90	117*	.3	.8
449 UN METHODIST	20	3,407	4,423*	11.7	30.6

NA–Not applicable   NR–Not reported   *Total adherents estimated from known number of communicant, confirmed, full members.   - Represents a percent less than 0.1.   Percentages may not total due to rounding.
[1]See Appendix E   [2]See Appendix F   [3]See Appendix G   Lines in *italic* represent a breakdown of Catholic rites or Friends affiliations. They are included in their respective denominational total.

Table 4. Churches and Church Membership by County and Denomination: 1990

County and Denomination	Number of churches	Communicant, confirmed, full members	Total adherents		
			Number	Percent of total population	Percent of total adherents
467 WESLEYAN	3	196	860	2.3	6.0
OHIO	**13**	**1,811**	**2,288***	**43.0**	**100.0**
019 AMER BAPT USA	3	467	590*	11.1	25.8
097 CHR CHS&CHS CR	1	500	632*	11.9	27.6
165 CH OF NAZARENE	1	74	97	1.8	4.2
207 E.L.C.A.	2	174	217	4.1	9.5
419 SO BAPT CONV	1	112	142*	2.7	6.2
443 UN C OF CHRIST	1	170	215*	4.0	9.4
449 UN METHODIST	3	299	378*	7.1	16.5
467 WESLEYAN	1	15	17	.3	.7
ORANGE	**58**	**6,448**	**9,105***	**49.5**	**100.0**
019 AMER BAPT USA	5	1,369	1,719*	9.3	18.9
053 ASSEMB OF GOD	1	29	25	.1	.3
081 CATHOLIC	2	NA	550	3.0	6.0
081d *LATIN*	*2*	*NA*	*550*	*3.0*	*6.0*
093 CHR CH (DISC)	2	160	225	1.2	2.5
097 CHR CHS&CHS CR	9	1,895	2,380*	12.9	26.1
127 CH GOD (CLEVE)	1	87	109*	.6	1.2
165 CH OF NAZARENE	3	211	413	2.2	4.5
167 CHS OF CHRIST	8	330	439	2.4	4.8
226 FRIENDS-USA	4	279	350*	1.9	3.8
226e *FUM*	*4*	*279*	*350**	*1.9*	*3.8*
285 MENNONITE CH	1	75	146	.8	1.6
287 MENN GEN CONF	1	80	80	.4	.9
323 OLD ORD AMISH	1	NA	150	.8	1.6
355 PRESB CH (USA)	1	89	112*	.6	1.2
413 S.D.A.	1	51	64*	.3	.7
419 SO BAPT CONV	1	374	470*	2.6	5.2
449 UN METHODIST	13	1,259	1,581*	8.6	17.4
467 WESLEYAN	4	160	292	1.6	3.2
OWEN	**47**	**4,758**	**6,947***	**40.2**	**100.0**
019 AMER BAPT USA	9	1,699	2,142*	12.4	30.8
053 ASSEMB OF GOD	2	65	106	.6	1.5
081 CATHOLIC	1	NA	210	1.2	3.0
081d *LATIN*	*1*	*NA*	*210*	*1.2*	*3.0*
093 CHR CH (DISC)	1	55	89	.5	1.3
097 CHR CHS&CHS CR	4	825	1,040*	6.0	15.0
127 CH GOD (CLEVE)	1	15	19*	.1	.3
145 CH GOD PROPHCY	1	33	42*	.2	.6
165 CH OF NAZARENE	5	337	491	2.8	7.1
167 CHS OF CHRIST	5	459	593	3.4	8.5
207 E.L.C.A.	1	29	31	.2	.4
355 PRESB CH (USA)	2	162	204*	1.2	2.9
361 PRIM BAPT ASCS	1	24	30*	.2	.4
413 S.D.A.	1	66	83*	.5	1.2
443 UN C OF CHRIST	1	48	61*	.4	.9
449 UN METHODIST	10	931	1,174*	6.8	16.9
467 WESLEYAN	1	10	32	.2	.5
499 INDEP.NON-CHAR[3]	1	NA	600	3.5	8.6
PARKE	**44**	**3,979**	**5,443***	**35.3**	**100.0**
019 AMER BAPT USA	5	525	647*	4.2	11.9
053 ASSEMB OF GOD	1	75	100	.6	1.8
081 CATHOLIC	2	NA	476	3.1	8.7
081d *LATIN*	*2*	*NA*	*476*	*3.1*	*8.7*
093 CHR CH (DISC)	1	155	197	1.3	3.6
097 CHR CHS&CHS CR	7	966	1,191*	7.7	21.9
111 CH CR,SCIENTST	1	NR	NR	-	-
165 CH OF NAZARENE	3	98	178	1.2	3.3
167 CHS OF CHRIST	3	188	237	1.5	4.4
226 FRIENDS-USA	4	489	603*	3.9	11.1
226e *FUM*	*4*	*489*	*603**	*3.9*	*11.1*
259 IFCA	2	NR	NR	-	-
325 OLD REG BAPT	1	23	28*	.2	.5
339 PENT CH OF GOD	1	12	25	.2	.5
355 PRESB CH (USA)	2	228	281*	1.8	5.2
419 SO BAPT CONV	1	180	222*	1.4	4.1
449 UN METHODIST	8	967	1,193*	7.7	21.9
467 WESLEYAN	2	73	65	.4	1.2
PERRY	**35**	**3,355**	**9,566***	**50.1**	**100.0**
019 AMER BAPT USA	4	751	940*	4.9	9.8
053 ASSEMB OF GOD	1	53	70	.4	.7
081 CATHOLIC	8	NA	5,320	27.8	55.6
081d *LATIN*	*8*	*NA*	*5,320*	*27.8*	*55.6*
093 CHR CH (DISC)	1	35	56	.3	.6
097 CHR CHS&CHS CR	1	150	188*	1.0	2.0
127 CH GOD (CLEVE)	1	18	23*	.1	.2
145 CH GOD PROPHCY	1	33	41*	.2	.4
151 L-D SAINTS	1	NA	117	.6	1.2
165 CH OF NAZARENE	1	106	120	.6	1.3
167 CHS OF CHRIST	2	460	495	2.6	5.2

County and Denomination	Number of churches	Communicant, confirmed, full members	Total adherents		
			Number	Percent of total population	Percent of total adherents
193 EPISCOPAL	1	24	29	.2	.3
283 LUTH—MO SYNOD	1	289	363	1.9	3.8
361 PRIM BAPT ASCS	1	9	11*	.1	.1
413 S.D.A.	1	56	70*	.4	.7
443 UN C OF CHRIST	2	756	946*	5.0	9.9
449 UN METHODIST	7	606	758*	4.0	7.9
467 WESLEYAN	1	9	19	.1	.2
PIKE	**36**	**2,612**	**3,848***	**30.8**	**100.0**
019 AMER BAPT USA	1	310	382*	3.1	9.9
053 ASSEMB OF GOD	2	42	109	.9	2.8
081 CATHOLIC	1	NA	400	3.2	10.4
081d *LATIN*	*1*	*NA*	*400*	*3.2*	*10.4*
093 CHR CH (DISC)	1	35	56	.4	1.5
097 CHR CHS&CHS CR	3	310	382*	3.1	9.9
123 CH GOD (ANDER)	3	191	246	2.0	6.4
165 CH OF NAZARENE	2	108	251	2.0	6.5
167 CHS OF CHRIST	5	159	206	1.6	5.4
185 CUMBER PRESB	1	102	102	.8	2.7
207 E.L.C.A.	1	175	223	1.8	5.8
221 FREE METHODIST	2	95	114	.9	3.0
355 PRESB CH (USA)	1	146	180*	1.4	4.7
361 PRIM BAPT ASCS	1	10	12*	.1	.3
419 SO BAPT CONV	1	50	62*	.5	1.6
449 UN METHODIST	9	861	1,060*	8.5	27.5
467 WESLEYAN	2	18	63	.5	1.6
PORTER	**95**	**19,747**	**48,205***	**37.4**	**100.0**
040 AP CHR CH-AMER	1	70	125	.1	.3
053 ASSEMB OF GOD	6	474	951	.7	2.0
081 CATHOLIC	8	NA	19,866	15.4	41.2
081d *LATIN*	*8*	*NA*	*19,866*	*15.4*	*41.2*
093 CHR CH (DISC)	2	397	908	.7	1.9
097 CHR CHS&CHS CR	3	600	762*	.6	1.6
111 CH CR,SCIENTST	2	NR	NR	-	-
123 CH GOD (ANDER)	1	100	100	.1	.2
127 CH GOD (CLEVE)	2	440	559*	.4	1.2
145 CH GOD PROPHCY	2	67	85*	.1	.2
151 L-D SAINTS	2	NA	740	.6	1.5
165 CH OF NAZARENE	6	1,349	2,093	1.6	4.3
167 CHS OF CHRIST	4	466	604	.5	1.3
193 EPISCOPAL	2	276	406	.3	.8
203 EVAN FREE CH	2	600	1,218	.9	2.5
207 E.L.C.A.	7	2,907	3,903	3.0	8.1
226 FRIENDS-USA	1	9	11*	-	-
226c *FGC*	*1*	*9*	*11**	-	-
246 GREEK ORTHODOX	1	NR	NR	-	-
259 IFCA	1	NR	NR	-	-
283 LUTH—MO SYNOD	9	4,315	5,410	4.2	11.2
285 MENNONITE CH	3	282	307	.2	.6
325 OLD REG BAPT	1	4	5*	-	-
339 PENT CH OF GOD	1	8	30	-	.1
355 PRESB CH (USA)	6	1,874	2,382*	1.8	4.9
356 PRESB CH AMER	1	61	95	.1	.2
363 PRIMITIVE METH	1	39	69	.1	.1
403 SALVATION ARMY	1	43	44	-	.1
413 S.D.A.	2	63	80*	.1	.2
419 SO BAPT CONV	6	1,850	2,351*	1.8	4.9
443 UN C OF CHRIST	2	201	255*	.2	.5
449 UN METHODIST	7	3,193	4,058*	3.1	8.4
467 WESLEYAN	1	59	297	.2	.6
496 JEWISH EST[1]	1	NA	491	.4	1.0
POSEY	**45**	**6,246**	**13,444***	**51.8**	**100.0**
053 ASSEMB OF GOD	2	273	540	2.1	4.0
081 CATHOLIC	4	NA	4,798	18.5	35.7
081d *LATIN*	*4*	*NA*	*4,798*	*18.5*	*35.7*
093 CHR CH (DISC)	2	224	402	1.5	3.0
097 CHR CHS&CHS CR	4	615	790*	3.0	5.9
127 CH GOD (CLEVE)	1	56	72*	.3	.5
151 L-D SAINTS	1	NA	57	.2	.4
165 CH OF NAZARENE	4	270	599	2.3	4.5
167 CHS OF CHRIST	1	28	35	.1	.3
193 EPISCOPAL	2	120	166	.6	1.2
355 PRESB CH (USA)	2	122	157*	.6	1.2
413 S.D.A.	1	5	6*	-	-
419 SO BAPT CONV	2	1,044	1,341*	5.2	10.0
443 UN C OF CHRIST	6	1,601	2,056*	7.9	15.3
449 UN METHODIST	13	1,888	2,425*	9.3	18.0
PULASKI	**31**	**3,128**	**6,681***	**52.8**	**100.0**
019 AMER BAPT USA	1	49	63*	.5	.9
040 AP CHR CH-AMER	1	262	462	3.7	6.9
053 ASSEMB OF GOD	2	29	79	.6	1.2
081 CATHOLIC	5	NA	2,105	16.6	31.5
081d *LATIN*	*5*	*NA*	*2,105*	*16.6*	*31.5*

NA–Not applicable   NR–Not reported   *Total adherents estimated from known number of communicant, confirmed, full members.   - Represents a percent less than 0.1.   Percentages may not total due to rounding.
[1]See Appendix E   [2]See Appendix F   [3]See Appendix G   Lines in *italic* represent a breakdown of Catholic rites or Friends affiliations. They are included in their respective denominational total.

Table 4. Churches and Church Membership by County and Denomination: 1990

County and Denomination		Number of churches	Communicant, confirmed, full members	Total adherents		
				Number	Percent of total population	Percent of total adherents
093	CHR CH (DISC)	2	180	466	3.7	7.0
097	CHR CHS&CHS CR	2	525	675*	5.3	10.1
145	CH GOD PROPHCY	1	33	42*	.3	.6
165	CH OF NAZARENE	1	265	441	3.5	6.6
167	CHS OF CHRIST	1	15	25	.2	.4
176	CCC, NOT NAT'L	1	46	59*	.5	.9
223	FREE WILL BAPT	1	33	42*	.3	.6
283	LUTH—MO SYNOD	3	418	568	4.5	8.5
353	CHR BRETHREN	1	25	50	.4	.7
355	PRESB CH (USA)	2	185	238*	1.9	3.6
443	UN C OF CHRIST	2	194	249*	2.0	3.7
449	UN METHODIST	5	869	1,117*	8.8	16.7
PUTNAM		**49**	**8,303**	**11,359***	**37.5**	**100.0**
019	AMER BAPT USA	7	1,737	2,116*	7.0	18.6
053	ASSEMB OF GOD	1	184	300	1.0	2.6
081	CATHOLIC	1	NA	626	2.1	5.5
081d	LATIN	1	NA	626	2.1	5.5
093	CHR CH (DISC)	4	1,201	1,626	5.4	14.3
097	CHR CHS&CHS CR	6	1,440	1,754*	5.8	15.4
123	CH GOD (ANDER)	1	15	18	.1	.2
127	CH GOD (CLEVE)	1	114	139*	.5	1.2
151	L-D SAINTS	1	NA	97	.3	.9
165	CH OF NAZARENE	3	218	426	1.4	3.8
167	CHS OF CHRIST	4	313	412	1.4	3.6
175	CONGR CHR CHS	1	40	49*	.2	.4
193	EPISCOPAL	1	111	175	.6	1.5
226	FRIENDS-USA	1	44	54*	.2	.5
226e	FUM	1	44	54*	.2	.5
283	LUTH—MO SYNOD	1	141	224	.7	2.0
355	PRESB CH (USA)	3	299	364*	1.2	3.2
413	S.D.A.	0	19	23*	.1	.2
419	SO BAPT CONV	2	448	546*	1.8	4.8
426	2SEED-SPRT BPT	1	20	24*	.1	.2
443	UN C OF CHRIST	1	275	335*	1.1	2.9
449	UN METHODIST	9	1,507	1,835*	6.1	16.2
497	BLACK BAPT EST[2]	NA	177	216*	.7	1.9
RANDOLPH		**74**	**6,666**	**10,311***	**38.0**	**100.0**
053	ASSEMB OF GOD	2	195	518	1.9	5.0
081	CATHOLIC	2	NA	641	2.4	6.2
081d	LATIN	2	NA	641	2.4	6.2
093	CHR CH (DISC)	3	721	1,462	5.4	14.2
097	CHR CHS&CHS CR	3	530	658*	2.4	6.4
123	CH GOD (ANDER)	2	100	104	.4	1.0
165	CH OF NAZARENE	7	798	1,436	5.3	13.9
167	CHS OF CHRIST	2	84	109	.4	1.1
176	CCC, NOT NAT'L	1	11	14*	.1	.1
207	E.L.C.A.	2	340	456	1.7	4.4
226	FRIENDS-USA	13	892	1,107*	4.1	10.7
226e	FUM	11	820	1,018*	3.7	9.9
226g	INDEP EVAN	2	72	89*	.3	.9
296	MIDW CONGR FEL	12	638	792*	2.9	7.7
355	PRESB CH (USA)	2	175	217*	.8	2.1
419	SO BAPT CONV	2	213	264*	1.0	2.6
449	UN METHODIST	19	1,921	2,385*	8.8	23.1
467	WESLEYAN	2	48	148	.5	1.4
RIPLEY		**55**	**7,367**	**15,870***	**64.5**	**100.0**
019	AMER BAPT USA	12	2,635	3,369*	13.7	21.2
053	ASSEMB OF GOD	2	78	128	.5	.8
081	CATHOLIC	8	NA	6,375	25.9	40.2
081d	LATIN	8	NA	6,375	25.9	40.2
097	CHR CHS&CHS CR	3	430	550*	2.2	3.5
165	CH OF NAZARENE	1	17	50	.2	.3
167	CHS OF CHRIST	1	48	63	.3	.4
207	E.L.C.A.	6	1,734	2,157*	8.8	13.6
283	LUTH—MO SYNOD	1	181	245	1.0	1.5
325	OLD REG BAPT	2	43	55*	.2	.3
419	SO BAPT CONV	3	319	408*	1.7	2.6
443	UN C OF CHRIST	2	280	358*	1.5	2.3
449	UN METHODIST	11	1,539	1,967*	8.0	12.4
467	WESLEYAN	3	63	145	.6	.9
RUSH		**46**	**5,709**	**9,609***	**53.0**	**100.0**
019	AMER BAPT USA	1	500	632*	3.5	6.6
053	ASSEMB OF GOD	1	20	45	.2	.5
081	CATHOLIC	1	NA	1,344	7.4	14.0
081d	LATIN	1	NA	1,344	7.4	14.0
093	CHR CH (DISC)	7	825	1,424	7.9	14.8
097	CHR CHS&CHS CR	9	1,706	2,158*	11.9	22.5
123	CH GOD (ANDER)	1	104	150	.8	1.6
165	CH OF NAZARENE	2	121	235	1.3	2.4
167	CHS OF CHRIST	2	85	105	.6	1.1
193	EPISCOPAL	1	19	26	.1	.3
226	FRIENDS-USA	3	149	188*	1.0	2.0

County and Denomination		Number of churches	Communicant, confirmed, full members	Total adherents		
				Number	Percent of total population	Percent of total adherents
226e	FUM	3	149	188*	1.0	2.0
283	LUTH—MO SYNOD	1	27	31	.2	.3
323	OLD ORD AMISH	2	NA	300	1.7	3.1
355	PRESB CH (USA)	2	317	401*	2.2	4.2
403	SALVATION ARMY	1	59	69	.4	.7
419	SO BAPT CONV	2	556	703*	3.9	7.3
449	UN METHODIST	7	1,145	1,448*	8.0	15.1
467	WESLEYAN	3	76	350	1.9	3.6
SAINT JOSEPH		**198**	**37,494**	**119,120***	**48.2**	**100.0**
005	AME ZION	2	810	972	.4	.8
019	AMER BAPT USA	3	481	602*	.2	.5
040	AP CHR CH-AMER	1	27	47	-	-
053	ASSEMB OF GOD	6	905	1,666	.7	1.4
071	BRETHREN (ASH)	5	415	519*	.2	.4
081	CATHOLIC	30	NA	62,723	25.4	52.7
081d	LATIN	28	NA	62,418	25.3	52.4
081f	MELKITE-GK	1	NA	252	.1	.2
081h	UKRAINIAN	1	NA	53	-	-
093	CHR CH (DISC)	4	1,031	1,386	.6	1.2
097	CHR CHS&CHS CR	5	1,465	1,833*	.7	1.5
105	CHRISTIAN REF	1	179	272	.1	.2
111	CH CR,SCIENTST	2	NR	NR	-	-
121	CH GOD (ABR)	1	108	135*	.1	.1
123	CH GOD (ANDER)	3	311	359	.1	.3
127	CH GOD (CLEVE)	2	218	273*	.1	.2
145	CH GOD PROPHCY	1	33	41*	-	-
151	L-D SAINTS	1	NA	631	.3	.5
157	CH OF BRETHREN	6	691	864*	.3	.7
165	CH OF NAZARENE	3	462	758	.3	.6
167	CHS OF CHRIST	4	340	442	.2	.4
175	CONGR CHR CHS	1	131	164*	.1	.1
193	EPISCOPAL	4	796	1,097	.4	.9
203	EVAN FREE CH	1	298	612	.2	.5
207	E.L.C.A.	9	2,728	3,909	1.6	3.3
226	FRIENDS-USA	1	4	17	-	-
226f	INDEPENDNT	1	4	17	-	-
246	GREEK ORTHODOX	1	NR	NR	-	-
259	IFCA	2	NR	NR	-	-
283	LUTH—MO SYNOD	6	1,922	2,523	1.0	2.1
285	MENNONITE CH	3	190	249	.1	.2
287	MENN GEN CONF	1	8	14	-	-
291	MISSIONARY CH	17	1,485	2,493	1.0	2.1
339	PENT CH OF GOD	1	15	40	-	-
353	CHR BRETHREN	1	15	25	-	-
355	PRESB CH (USA)	8	3,003	3,757*	1.5	3.2
403	SALVATION ARMY	2	203	227	.1	.2
413	S.D.A.	2	722	903*	.4	.8
419	SO BAPT CONV	2	602	753*	.3	.6
435	UNITARIAN-UNIV	1	81	117	-	.1
438	UN BRETH IN CR	1	69	84	-	.1
443	UN C OF CHRIST	7	1,558	1,949*	.8	1.6
449	UN METHODIST	31	9,378	11,731*	4.7	9.8
467	WESLEYAN	6	171	569	.2	.5
469	WELS	1	243	313	.1	.3
496	JEWISH EST[1]	5	NA	1,800	.7	1.5
497	BLACK BAPT EST[2]	NA	6,396	8,001*	3.2	6.7
498	INDEP.CHARIS.[3]	1	NA	2,000	.8	1.7
499	INDEP.NON-CHAR[3]	3	NA	2,250	.9	1.9
SCOTT		**45**	**7,521**	**10,163***	**48.4**	**100.0**
019	AMER BAPT USA	9	2,623	3,323*	15.8	32.7
053	ASSEMB OF GOD	1	25	50	.2	.5
081	CATHOLIC	1	NA	503	2.4	4.9
081d	LATIN	1	NA	503	2.4	4.9
082	CENTRAL BAPT	1	71	90*	.4	.9
097	CHR CHS&CHS CR	7	2,670	3,383*	16.1	33.3
123	CH GOD (ANDER)	1	103	103	.5	1.0
127	CH GOD (CLEVE)	3	369	468*	2.2	4.6
145	CH GOD PROPHCY	1	33	42*	.2	.4
165	CH OF NAZARENE	1	56	154	.7	1.5
167	CHS OF CHRIST	2	134	160	.8	1.6
283	LUTH—MO SYNOD	1	40	49	.2	.5
285	MENNONITE CH	1	15	15	.1	.1
355	PRESB CH (USA)	2	162	205*	1.0	2.0
413	S.D.A.	1	64	81*	.4	.8
419	SO BAPT CONV	2	275	348*	1.7	3.4
436	UNITED BAPT	1	85	108*	.5	1.1
449	UN METHODIST	8	755	957*	4.6	9.4
467	WESLEYAN	2	41	124	.6	1.2
SHELBY		**63**	**10,435**	**18,268***	**45.3**	**100.0**
019	AMER BAPT USA	10	2,952	3,742*	9.3	20.5
053	ASSEMB OF GOD	1	89	170	.4	.9
081	CATHOLIC	2	NA	3,056	7.6	16.7
081d	LATIN	2	NA	3,056	7.6	16.7

NA–Not applicable   NR–Not reported   *Total adherents estimated from known number of communicant, confirmed, full members.   - Represents a percent less than 0.1.   Percentages may not total due to rounding.

[1]See Appendix E   [2]See Appendix F   [3]See Appendix G   Lines in italic represent a breakdown of Catholic rites or Friends affiliations. They are included in their respective denominational total.

Table 4. Churches and Church Membership by County and Denomination: 1990

County and Denomination	Number of churches	Communicant, confirmed, full members	Total adherents Number	Percent of total population	Percent of total adherents
093 CHR CH (DISC)	1	527	841	2.1	4.6
097 CHR CHS&CHS CR	6	1,275	1,616*	4.0	8.8
111 CH CR,SCIENTST	1	NR	NR	-	-
123 CH GOD (ANDER)	1	40	40	.1	.2
151 L-D SAINTS	1	NA	245	.6	1.3
165 CH OF NAZARENE	3	397	875	2.2	4.8
167 CHS OF CHRIST	1	17	22	.1	.1
193 EPISCOPAL	1	51	71	.2	.4
207 E.L.C.A.	2	233	306	.8	1.7
215 EVAN METH CH	1	133	169*	.4	.9
283 LUTH—MO SYNOD	1	95	135	.3	.7
355 PRESB CH (USA)	2	472	598*	1.5	3.3
403 SALVATION ARMY	1	68	70	.2	.4
413 S.D.A.	2	97	123*	.3	.7
419 SO BAPT CONV	3	594	753*	1.9	4.1
443 UN C OF CHRIST	2	466	591*	1.5	3.2
449 UN METHODIST	18	2,818	3,573*	8.9	19.6
467 WESLEYAN	2	111	350	.9	1.9
496 JEWISH EST[1]	0	NA	322	.8	1.8
499 INDEP.NON-CHAR[3]	1	NA	600	1.5	3.3
SPENCER	**48**	**6,702**	**12,255***	**62.9**	**100.0**
019 AMER BAPT USA	5	722	916*	4.7	7.5
081 CATHOLIC	6	NA	3,512	18.0	28.7
081d LATIN	6	NA	3,512	18.0	28.7
097 CHR CHS&CHS CR	4	2,430	3,084*	15.8	25.2
165 CH OF NAZARENE	3	183	377	1.9	3.1
167 CHS OF CHRIST	1	40	75	.4	.6
207 E.L.C.A.	1	101	138	.7	1.1
283 LUTH—MO SYNOD	1	293	375	1.9	3.1
355 PRESB CH (USA)	1	64	81*	.4	.7
361 PRIM BAPT ASCS	1	8	10*	.1	.1
419 SO BAPT CONV	4	598	759*	3.9	6.2
443 UN C OF CHRIST	4	375	476*	2.4	3.9
449 UN METHODIST	16	1,881	2,387*	12.2	19.5
467 WESLEYAN	1	7	65	.3	.5
STARKE	**31**	**3,258**	**6,848***	**30.1**	**100.0**
053 ASSEMB OF GOD	2	99	218	1.0	3.2
081 CATHOLIC	5	NA	2,050	9.0	29.9
081d LATIN	5	NA	2,050	9.0	29.9
097 CHR CHS&CHS CR	1	160	204*	.9	3.0
127 CH GOD (CLEVE)	1	17	22*	.1	.3
165 CH OF NAZARENE	1	54	123	.5	1.8
223 FREE WILL BAPT	2	188	240*	1.1	3.5
259 IFCA	1	NR	NR	-	-
283 LUTH—MO SYNOD	3	1,123	1,485	6.5	21.7
285 MENNONITE CH	2	163	338	1.5	4.9
339 PENT CH OF GOD	1	9	20	.1	.3
353 CHR BRETHREN	1	50	70	.3	1.0
413 S.D.A.	1	41	52*	.2	.8
436 UNITED BAPT	4	549	700*	3.1	10.2
443 UN C OF CHRIST	1	148	189*	.8	2.8
449 UN METHODIST	4	657	837*	3.7	12.2
499 INDEP.NON-CHAR[3]	1	NA	300	1.3	4.4
STEUBEN	**48**	**5,553**	**9,905***	**36.1**	**100.0**
019 AMER BAPT USA	2	163	205*	.7	2.1
053 ASSEMB OF GOD	2	201	434	1.6	4.4
081 CATHOLIC	2	NA	1,773	6.5	17.9
081d LATIN	2	NA	1,773	6.5	17.9
097 CHR CHS&CHS CR	4	777	976*	3.6	9.9
123 CH GOD (ANDER)	1	22	52	.2	.5
151 L-D SAINTS	1	NA	120	.4	1.2
165 CH OF NAZARENE	2	112	246	.9	2.5
167 CHS OF CHRIST	1	45	48	.2	.5
176 CCC, NOT NAT'L	1	78	98*	.4	1.0
193 EPISCOPAL	1	57	88	.3	.9
207 E.L.C.A.	1	512	635	2.3	6.4
283 LUTH—MO SYNOD	3	512	596	2.2	6.0
291 MISSIONARY CH	3	321	716	2.6	7.2
323 OLD ORD AMISH	2	NA	300	1.1	3.0
339 PENT CH OF GOD	1	39	150	.5	1.5
355 PRESB CH (USA)	2	209	263*	1.0	2.7
413 S.D.A.	1	31	39*	.1	.4
419 SO BAPT CONV	1	360	452*	1.6	4.6
438 UN BRETH IN CR	2	90	90	.3	.9
443 UN C OF CHRIST	2	330	415*	1.5	4.2
449 UN METHODIST	12	1,655	2,079*	7.6	21.0
467 WESLEYAN	1	39	130	.5	1.3
SULLIVAN	**65**	**6,520**	**8,829***	**46.5**	**100.0**
019 AMER BAPT USA	6	1,658	2,057*	10.8	23.3
053 ASSEMB OF GOD	4	214	347	1.8	3.9
081 CATHOLIC	1	NA	459	2.4	5.2
081d LATIN	1	NA	459	2.4	5.2

County and Denomination	Number of churches	Communicant, confirmed, full members	Total adherents Number	Percent of total population	Percent of total adherents
093 CHR CH (DISC)	1	94	116	.6	1.3
097 CHR CHS&CHS CR	4	1,338	1,660*	8.7	18.8
127 CH GOD (CLEVE)	3	170	211*	1.1	2.4
145 CH GOD PROPHCY	1	33	41*	.2	.5
165 CH OF NAZARENE	1	91	189	1.0	2.1
167 CHS OF CHRIST	11	642	894	4.7	10.1
215 EVAN METH CH	1	106	131*	.7	1.5
226 FRIENDS-USA	1	8	10*	.1	.1
226g INDEP EVAN	1	8	10*	.1	.1
355 PRESB CH (USA)	2	224	278*	1.5	3.1
413 S.D.A.	1	6	7*	-	.1
419 SO BAPT CONV	3	252	313*	1.6	3.5
443 UN C OF CHRIST	1	30	37*	.2	.4
449 UN METHODIST	21	1,612	2,000*	10.5	22.7
467 WESLEYAN	3	42	79	.4	.9
SWITZERLAND	**28**	**2,341**	**3,270***	**42.3**	**100.0**
019 AMER BAPT USA	12	1,765	2,232*	28.8	68.3
081 CATHOLIC	1	NA	229	3.0	7.0
081d LATIN	1	NA	229	3.0	7.0
123 CH GOD (ANDER)	1	31	31	.4	.9
165 CH OF NAZARENE	2	26	45	.6	1.4
323 OLD ORD AMISH	1	NA	100	1.3	3.1
355 PRESB CH (USA)	1	57	72*	.9	2.2
419 SO BAPT CONV	2	127	161*	2.1	4.9
449 UN METHODIST	7	316	400*	5.2	12.2
467 WESLEYAN	1	19	0	-	-
TIPPECANOE	**102**	**22,665**	**44,629***	**34.2**	**100.0**
019 AMER BAPT USA	3	1,513	1,818*	1.4	4.1
053 ASSEMB OF GOD	3	1,190	3,209	2.5	7.2
081 CATHOLIC	5	NA	11,094	8.5	24.9
081d LATIN	5	NA	11,094	8.5	24.9
089 CHR & MISS AL	1	32	100	.1	.2
093 CHR CH (DISC)	2	1,128	2,295	1.8	5.1
097 CHR CHS&CHS CR	1	240	288*	.2	.6
111 CH CR,SCIENTST	1	NR	NR	-	-
123 CH GOD (ANDER)	2	125	125	.1	.3
127 CH GOD (CLEVE)	1	9	11*	-	-
151 L-D SAINTS	3	NA	922	.7	2.1
157 CH OF BRETHREN	1	78	94*	.1	.2
165 CH OF NAZARENE	1	228	406	.3	.9
167 CHS OF CHRIST	3	430	720	.6	1.6
193 EPISCOPAL	2	386	737	.6	1.7
199 EVAN CONGR CH	1	31	113	.1	.3
207 E.L.C.A.	3	1,024	1,375	1.1	3.1
213 EVAN MENN INC	1	26	31*	-	.1
221 FREE METHODIST	1	34	51	-	.1
226 FRIENDS-USA	2	39	47*	-	.1
226c FGC	1	25	30*	-	.1
226e FUM	1	14	17*	-	-
259 IFCA	2	NR	NR	-	-
263 INT FOURSQ GOS	1	87	105*	.1	.2
283 LUTH—MO SYNOD	4	1,850	2,450	1.9	5.5
285 MENNONITE CH	1	24	33	-	.1
287 MENN GEN CONF	1	13	16	-	-
339 PENT CH OF GOD	2	71	205	.2	.5
353 CHR BRETHREN	1	30	50	-	.1
355 PRESB CH (USA)	9	3,971	4,772*	3.7	10.7
371 REF CH IN AM	2	276	432	.3	1.0
403 SALVATION ARMY	1	100	112	.1	.3
413 S.D.A.	1	221	266*	.2	.6
419 SO BAPT CONV	8	1,400	1,682*	1.3	3.8
435 UNITARIAN-UNIV	1	102	164	.1	.4
438 UN BRETH IN CR	1	157	157	.1	.4
443 UN C OF CHRIST	2	747	898*	.7	2.0
449 UN METHODIST	21	6,221	7,476*	5.7	16.8
467 WESLEYAN	2	147	657	.5	1.5
469 WELS	1	32	48	-	.1
496 JEWISH EST[1]	3	NA	500	.4	1.1
497 BLACK BAPT EST[2]	NA	703	845*	.6	1.9
499 INDEP.NON-CHAR[3]	1	NA	325	.2	.7
TIPTON	**25**	**3,774**	**6,826***	**42.3**	**100.0**
019 AMER BAPT USA	1	204	255*	1.6	3.7
053 ASSEMB OF GOD	1	16	26	.2	.4
081 CATHOLIC	1	NA	1,243	7.7	18.2
081d LATIN	1	NA	1,243	7.7	18.2
093 CHR CH (DISC)	2	706	1,429	8.9	20.9
097 CHR CHS&CHS CR	4	865	1,079*	6.7	15.8
127 CH GOD (CLEVE)	1	58	72*	.4	1.1
146 CH GOD MTN ASM	1	68	85*	.5	1.2
165 CH OF NAZARENE	1	85	144	.9	2.1
167 CHS OF CHRIST	1	117	152	.9	2.2
226 FRIENDS-USA	1	10	12*	.1	.2
226e FUM	1	10	12*	.1	.2

NA–Not applicable   NR–Not reported   *Total adherents estimated from known number of communicant, confirmed, full members.   - Represents a percent less than 0.1.   Percentages may not total due to rounding.
[1]See Appendix E   [2]See Appendix F   [3]See Appendix G   Lines in *italic* represent a breakdown of Catholic rites or Friends affiliations. They are included in their respective denominational total.

Table 4. Churches and Church Membership by County and Denomination: 1990

County and Denomination	Number of churches	Communicant, confirmed, full members	Total adherents Number	Percent of total population	Percent of total adherents
283 LUTH—MO SYNOD	1	422	506	3.1	7.4
355 PRESB CH (USA)	1	162	202*	1.3	3.0
419 SO BAPT CONV	1	46	57*	.4	.8
449 UN METHODIST	5	843	1,052*	6.5	15.4
467 WESLEYAN	3	172	512	3.2	7.5
UNION	**11**	**1,167**	**1,823***	**26.1**	**100.0**
081 CATHOLIC	1	NA	360	5.2	19.7
081d LATIN	*1*	*NA*	*360*	*5.2*	*19.7*
165 CH OF NAZARENE	2	137	159	2.3	8.7
226 FRIENDS-USA	1	31	39*	.6	2.1
226e FUM	*1*	*31*	*39*	*.6*	*2.1*
355 PRESB CH (USA)	1	121	153*	2.2	8.4
361 PRIM BAPT ASCS	1	12	15*	.2	.8
419 SO BAPT CONV	1	113	143*	2.0	7.8
449 UN METHODIST	4	753	954*	13.7	52.3
VANDERBURGH	**158**	**49,766**	**95,612***	**57.9**	**100.0**
005 AME ZION	1	300	389	.2	.4
019 AMER BAPT USA	5	1,616	1,997*	1.2	2.1
053 ASSEMB OF GOD	7	1,022	1,474	.9	1.5
071 BRETHREN (ASH)	1	128	158*	.1	.2
081 CATHOLIC	20	NA	29,867	18.1	31.2
081d LATIN	*20*	*NA*	*29,867*	*18.1*	*31.2*
093 CHR CH (DISC)	3	727	1,019	.6	1.1
097 CHR CHS&CHS CR	2	1,545	1,910*	1.2	2.0
111 CH CR,SCIENTST	1	NR	NR	-	-
123 CH GOD (ANDER)	2	118	149	.1	.2
127 CH GOD (CLEVE)	2	108	133*	.1	.1
145 CH GOD PROPHCY	1	33	41*	-	-
151 L-D SAINTS	1	NA	500	.3	.5
165 CH OF NAZARENE	6	517	739	.4	.8
167 CHS OF CHRIST	6	1,090	1,354	.8	1.4
179 CONSRV BAPT	1	NR	NR	-	-
185 CUMBER PRESB	2	698	738	.4	.8
193 EPISCOPAL	1	246	402	.2	.4
203 EVAN FREE CH	1	206	206	.1	.2
207 E.L.C.A.	6	1,422	1,842	1.1	1.9
221 FREE METHODIST	1	90	98	.1	.1
226 FRIENDS-USA	1	10	12*	-	-
226e FUM	*1*	*10*	*12*	-	-
283 LUTH—MO SYNOD	8	2,733	3,543	2.1	3.7
355 PRESB CH (USA)	9	2,005	2,478*	1.5	2.6
403 SALVATION ARMY	2	257	298	.2	.3
413 S.D.A.	2	235	290*	.2	.3
419 SO BAPT CONV	24	16,692	20,630*	12.5	21.6
435 UNITARIAN-UNIV	1	88	103	.1	.1
443 UN C OF CHRIST	14	7,048	8,711*	5.3	9.1
449 UN METHODIST	18	6,955	8,596*	5.2	9.0
467 WESLEYAN	3	596	1,940	1.2	2.0
496 JEWISH EST[1]	3	NA	520	.3	.5
497 BLACK BAPT EST[2]	NA	3,281	4,055*	2.5	4.2
498 INDEP.CHARIS.[3]	2	NA	1,120	.7	1.2
499 INDEP.NON-CHAR[3]	1	NA	300	.2	.3
VERMILLION	**31**	**3,411**	**6,093***	**36.3**	**100.0**
019 AMER BAPT USA	3	733	905*	5.4	14.9
053 ASSEMB OF GOD	3	143	320	1.9	5.3
081 CATHOLIC	2	NA	1,321	7.9	21.7
081d LATIN	*2*	*NA*	*1,321*	*7.9*	*21.7*
093 CHR CH (DISC)	1	218	350	2.1	5.7
097 CHR CHS&CHS CR	2	501	618*	3.7	10.1
127 CH GOD (CLEVE)	1	49	60*	.4	1.0
165 CH OF NAZARENE	4	233	623	3.7	10.2
167 CHS OF CHRIST	1	40	52	.3	.9
226 FRIENDS-USA	2	146	180*	1.1	3.0
226e FUM	*2*	*146*	*180*	*1.1*	*3.0*
355 PRESB CH (USA)	2	237	293*	1.7	4.8
449 UN METHODIST	10	1,111	1,371*	8.2	22.5
VIGO	**119**	**20,267**	**34,817***	**32.8**	**100.0**
019 AMER BAPT USA	7	2,263	2,760*	2.6	7.9
053 ASSEMB OF GOD	5	1,333	2,110	2.0	6.1
081 CATHOLIC	9	NA	6,764	6.4	19.4
081d LATIN	*9*	*NA*	*6,764*	*6.4*	*19.4*
089 CHR & MISS AL	1	29	74	.1	.2
093 CHR CH (DISC)	1	232	412	.4	1.2
097 CHR CHS&CHS CR	9	2,892	3,528*	3.3	10.1
111 CH CR,SCIENTST	1	NR	NR	-	-
123 CH GOD (ANDER)	2	13	68	.1	.2
127 CH GOD (CLEVE)	1	62	76*	.1	.2
145 CH GOD PROPHCY	2	67	82*	.1	.2
151 L-D SAINTS	3	NA	723	.7	2.1
165 CH OF NAZARENE	5	483	725	.7	2.1
167 CHS OF CHRIST	8	901	1,183	1.1	3.4
175 CONGR CHR CHS	2	167	204*	.2	.6
176 CCC, NOT NAT'L	1	100	122*	.1	.4
193 EPISCOPAL	2	473	733	.7	2.1
207 E.L.C.A.	3	600	852	.8	2.4
221 FREE METHODIST	1	44	101	.1	.3
226 FRIENDS-USA	2	33	43*	-	.1
226f INDEPENDNT	*1*	*6*	*10*	-	-
226g INDEP EVAN	*1*	*27*	*33*	-	*.1*
259 IFCA	1	NR	NR	-	-
263 INT FOURSQ GOS	2	318	388*	.4	1.1
283 LUTH—MO SYNOD	1	379	527	.5	1.5
353 CHR BRETHREN	1	25	50	-	.1
355 PRESB CH (USA)	3	808	986*	.9	2.8
403 SALVATION ARMY	1	130	172	.2	.5
413 S.D.A.	3	201	245*	.2	.7
419 SO BAPT CONV	3	904	1,103*	1.0	3.2
435 UNITARIAN-UNIV	1	43	58	.1	.2
443 UN C OF CHRIST	2	639	779*	.7	2.2
449 UN METHODIST	24	5,228	6,377*	6.0	18.3
467 WESLEYAN	10	336	939	.9	2.7
496 JEWISH EST[1]	1	NA	325	.3	.9
497 BLACK BAPT EST[2]	NA	1,564	1,908*	1.8	5.5
499 INDEP.NON-CHAR[3]	1	NA	400	.4	1.1
WABASH	**71**	**9,720**	**14,476***	**41.3**	**100.0**
053 ASSEMB OF GOD	2	145	350	1.0	2.4
071 BRETHREN (ASH)	4	413	517*	1.5	3.6
081 CATHOLIC	3	NA	1,305	3.7	9.0
081d LATIN	*3*	*NA*	*1,305*	*3.7*	*9.0*
089 CHR & MISS AL	1	108	208	.6	1.4
093 CHR CH (DISC)	2	461	716	2.0	4.9
097 CHR CHS&CHS CR	3	455	570*	1.6	3.9
123 CH GOD (ANDER)	1	59	93	.3	.6
127 CH GOD (CLEVE)	1	66	83*	.2	.6
146 CH GOD MTN ASM	1	32	40*	.1	.3
157 CH OF BRETHREN	5	1,338	1,676*	4.8	11.6
165 CH OF NAZARENE	2	152	346	1.0	2.4
167 CHS OF CHRIST	2	130	167	.5	1.2
171 CH GOD-GEN CON	1	214	268*	.8	1.9
175 CONGR CHR CHS	1	165	207*	.6	1.4
207 E.L.C.A.	2	693	871	2.5	6.0
213 EVAN MENN INC	1	25	31*	.1	.2
223 FREE WILL BAPT	4	528	661*	1.9	4.6
226 FRIENDS-USA	1	408	511*	1.5	3.5
226e FUM	*1*	*408*	*511*	*1.5*	*3.5*
259 IFCA	1	NR	NR	-	-
283 LUTH—MO SYNOD	1	92	129	.4	.9
291 MISSIONARY CH	1	103	205	.6	1.4
355 PRESB CH (USA)	2	400	501*	1.4	3.5
413 S.D.A.	1	18	23*	.1	.2
436 UNITED BAPT	1	37	46*	.1	.3
443 UN C OF CHRIST	3	547	685*	2.0	4.7
449 UN METHODIST	20	2,966	3,716*	10.6	25.7
467 WESLEYAN	4	165	551	1.6	3.8
WARREN	**19**	**1,840**	**2,351***	**28.8**	**100.0**
053 ASSEMB OF GOD	1	23	32	.4	1.4
097 CHR CHS&CHS CR	3	685	857*	10.5	36.5
121 CH GOD (ABR)	1	36	45*	.6	1.9
165 CH OF NAZARENE	2	110	181	2.2	7.7
221 FREE METHODIST	1	8	12	.1	.5
355 PRESB CH (USA)	2	174	218*	2.7	9.3
449 UN METHODIST	9	804	1,006*	12.3	42.8
WARRICK	**53**	**7,960**	**19,420***	**43.2**	**100.0**
019 AMER BAPT USA	1	355	453*	1.0	2.3
053 ASSEMB OF GOD	2	97	160	.4	.8
081 CATHOLIC	5	NA	7,269	16.2	37.4
081d LATIN	*5*	*NA*	*7,269*	*16.2*	*37.4*
093 CHR CH (DISC)	1	112	181	.4	.9
097 CHR CHS&CHS CR	1	109	139*	.3	.7
111 CH CR,SCIENTST	1	NR	NR	-	-
151 L-D SAINTS	1	NA	158	.4	.8
165 CH OF NAZARENE	3	209	379	.8	2.0
167 CHS OF CHRIST	1	50	85	.2	.4
185 CUMBER PRESB	1	296	343	.8	1.8
207 E.L.C.A.	2	162	212	.5	1.1
221 FREE METHODIST	1	35	35	.1	.2
223 FREE WILL BAPT	1	36	46*	.1	.2
259 IFCA	1	NR	NR	-	-
283 LUTH—MO SYNOD	1	208	249	.6	1.3
355 PRESB CH (USA)	2	598	764*	1.7	3.9
413 S.D.A.	1	39	50*	.1	.3
419 SO BAPT CONV	4	1,918	2,449*	5.5	12.6
443 UN C OF CHRIST	5	1,313	1,677*	3.7	8.6
449 UN METHODIST	15	2,370	3,026*	6.7	15.6
467 WESLEYAN	1	53	245	.5	1.3

NA–Not applicable   NR–Not reported   *Total adherents estimated from known number of communicant, confirmed, full members.   - Represents a percent less than 0.1.   Percentages may not total due to rounding.
[1]See Appendix E   [2]See Appendix F   [3]See Appendix G   Lines in italic represent a breakdown of Catholic rites or Friends affiliations. They are included in their respective denominational total.

Table 4. Churches and Church Membership by County and Denomination: 1990

County and Denomination	Number of churches	Communicant, confirmed, full members	Total adherents Number	Percent of total population	Percent of total adherents
498 INDEP.CHARIS.[3]	1	NA	300	.7	1.5
499 INDEP.NON-CHAR[3]	1	NA	1,200	2.7	6.2
WASHINGTON	**68**	**6,733**	**10,442***	**44.0**	**100.0**
019 AMER BAPT USA	9	1,618	2,050*	8.6	19.6
053 ASSEMB OF GOD	1	44	125	.5	1.2
081 CATHOLIC	1	NA	421	1.8	4.0
081d LATIN	*1*	*NA*	*421*	*1.8*	*4.0*
093 CHR CH (DISC)	1	454	969	4.1	9.3
097 CHR CHS&CHS CR	7	875	1,109*	4.7	10.6
123 CH GOD (ANDER)	1	60	80	.3	.8
127 CH GOD (CLEVE)	2	54	68*	.3	.7
145 CH GOD PROPHCY	1	33	42*	.2	.4
146 CH GOD MTN ASM	1	2	3*	-	-
151 L-D SAINTS	1	NA	239	1.0	2.3
165 CH OF NAZARENE	3	175	508	2.1	4.9
167 CHS OF CHRIST	14	1,093	1,438	6.1	13.8
226 FRIENDS-USA	1	85	108*	.5	1.0
226e FUM	*1*	*85*	*108***	*.5*	*1.0*
283 LUTH—MO SYNOD	1	37	67	.3	.6
323 OLD ORD AMISH	2	NA	300	1.3	2.9
355 PRESB CH (USA)	2	213	270*	1.1	2.6
413 S.D.A.	1	13	16*	.1	.2
419 SO BAPT CONV	4	628	796*	3.4	7.6
436 UNITED BAPT	1	120	152*	.6	1.5
449 UN METHODIST	12	1,208	1,530*	6.5	14.7
467 WESLEYAN	2	21	151	.6	1.4
WAYNE	**109**	**17,295**	**27,706***	**38.5**	**100.0**
011 A.W.M.C.	1	15	19*	-	.1
019 AMER BAPT USA	3	1,663	2,060*	2.9	7.4
053 ASSEMB OF GOD	3	249	373	.5	1.3
081 CATHOLIC	4	NA	4,652	6.5	16.8
081d LATIN	*4*	*NA*	*4,652*	*6.5*	*16.8*
089 CHR & MISS AL	2	76	154	.2	.6
093 CHR CH (DISC)	2	599	935	1.3	3.4
097 CHR CHS&CHS CR	7	875	1,084*	1.5	3.9
111 CH CR,SCIENTST	1	NR	NR	-	-
123 CH GOD (ANDER)	2	84	87	.1	.3
127 CH GOD (CLEVE)	1	337	417*	.6	1.5
146 CH GOD MTN ASM	1	67	83*	.1	.3
151 L-D SAINTS	1	NA	518	.7	1.9
157 CH OF BRETHREN	5	339	420*	.6	1.5
165 CH OF NAZARENE	8	852	1,533	2.1	5.5
167 CHS OF CHRIST	5	223	336	.5	1.2
193 EPISCOPAL	1	102	190	.3	.7
207 E.L.C.A.	6	2,027	2,529	3.5	9.1
226 FRIENDS-USA	12	1,065	1,317*	1.8	4.8
226d FGC & FUM	*1*	*166*	*203*	*.3*	*.7*
226e FUM	*10*	*870*	*1,078***	*1.5*	*3.9*
226g INDEP EVAN	*1*	*29*	*36***	*.1*	*.1*
283 LUTH—MO SYNOD	1	40	44	.1	.2
355 PRESB CH (USA)	5	930	1,152*	1.6	4.2
356 PRESB CH AMER	1	129	151	.2	.5
361 PRIM BAPT ASCS	1	32	40*	.1	.1
403 SALVATION ARMY	1	157	158	.2	.6
413 S.D.A.	1	149	185*	.3	.7
419 SO BAPT CONV	10	2,464	3,052*	4.2	11.0
435 UNITARIAN-UNIV	1	24	24	-	.1
443 UN C OF CHRIST	2	167	207*	.3	.7
449 UN METHODIST	18	3,705	4,589*	6.4	16.6
467 WESLEYAN	2	112	390	.5	1.4
496 JEWISH EST[1]	1	NA	0	-	-
497 BLACK BAPT EST[2]	NA	813	1,007*	1.4	3.6
WELLS	**51**	**8,019**	**12,624***	**48.7**	**100.0**
019 AMER BAPT USA	3	559	722*	2.8	5.7
040 AP CHR CH-AMER	2	1,205	2,135	8.2	16.9
081 CATHOLIC	1	NA	750	2.9	5.9
081d LATIN	*1*	*NA*	*750*	*2.9*	*5.9*
123 CH GOD (ANDER)	1	47	58	.2	.5
127 CH GOD (CLEVE)	1	63	81*	.3	.6
157 CH OF BRETHREN	1	54	70*	.3	.6
165 CH OF NAZARENE	2	293	463	1.8	3.7
167 CHS OF CHRIST	1	30	65	.3	.5
171 CH GOD-GEN CON	1	110	142*	.5	1.1
207 E.L.C.A.	3	735	1,032	4.0	8.2
226 FRIENDS-USA	1	6	8*	-	.1
226e FUM	*1*	*6*	*8***	*-*	*.1*
283 LUTH—MO SYNOD	2	565	783	3.0	6.2
291 MISSIONARY CH	2	185	430	1.7	3.4
355 PRESB CH (USA)	2	572	739*	2.8	5.9
413 S.D.A.	1	24	31*	.1	.2
438 UN BRETH IN CR	3	416	416	1.6	3.3
443 UN C OF CHRIST	2	693	895*	3.4	7.1
449 UN METHODIST	19	2,217	2,864*	11.0	22.7

County and Denomination	Number of churches	Communicant, confirmed, full members	Total adherents Number	Percent of total population	Percent of total adherents
467 WESLEYAN	3	245	940	3.6	7.4
WHITE	**40**	**6,152**	**9,441***	**40.6**	**100.0**
019 AMER BAPT USA	7	1,582	2,000*	8.6	21.2
040 AP CHR CH-AMER	1	101	181	.8	1.9
053 ASSEMB OF GOD	1	156	250	1.1	2.6
081 CATHOLIC	2	NA	1,394	6.0	14.8
081d LATIN	*2*	*NA*	*1,394*	*6.0*	*14.8*
093 CHR CH (DISC)	2	542	694	3.0	7.4
097 CHR CHS&CHS CR	3	390	493*	2.1	5.2
157 CH OF BRETHREN	4	289	365*	1.6	3.9
165 CH OF NAZARENE	1	44	64	.3	.7
167 CHS OF CHRIST	2	98	153	.7	1.6
171 CH GOD-GEN CON	1	155	196*	.8	2.1
207 E.L.C.A.	1	133	178	.8	1.9
283 LUTH—MO SYNOD	2	502	665	2.9	7.0
355 PRESB CH (USA)	3	547	691*	3.0	7.3
413 S.D.A.	1	40	51*	.2	.5
449 UN METHODIST	8	1,559	1,971*	8.5	20.9
467 WESLEYAN	1	14	95	.4	1.0
WHITLEY	**52**	**6,491**	**11,405***	**41.2**	**100.0**
019 AMER BAPT USA	1	28	36*	.1	.3
053 ASSEMB OF GOD	1	23	23	.1	.2
057 BAPT GEN CONF	1	135	173*	.6	1.5
081 CATHOLIC	3	NA	2,182	7.9	19.1
081d LATIN	*3*	*NA*	*2,182*	*7.9*	*19.1*
093 CHR CH (DISC)	2	160	267	1.0	2.3
123 CH GOD (ANDER)	2	195	234	.8	2.1
127 CH GOD (CLEVE)	1	20	26*	.1	.2
157 CH OF BRETHREN	4	448	574*	2.1	5.0
165 CH OF NAZARENE	2	411	752	2.7	6.6
167 CHS OF CHRIST	1	39	62	.2	.5
171 CH GOD-GEN CON	6	949	1,216*	4.4	10.7
207 E.L.C.A.	3	773	948	3.4	8.3
216 EVAN PRESBY CH	1	200	207	.7	1.8
221 FREE METHODIST	1	31	57	.2	.5
223 FREE WILL BAPT	1	41	53*	.2	.5
283 LUTH—MO SYNOD	3	835	1,084	3.9	9.5
323 OLD ORD AMISH	1	NA	150	.5	1.3
339 PENT CH OF GOD	1	32	47	.2	.4
355 PRESB CH (USA)	2	247	316*	1.1	2.8
449 UN METHODIST	12	1,881	2,410*	8.7	21.1
467 WESLEYAN	2	43	155	.6	1.4
496 JEWISH EST[1]	0	NA	83	.3	.7
499 INDEP.NON-CHAR[3]	1	NA	350	1.3	3.1

IOWA

County and Denomination	Number of churches	Communicant, confirmed, full members	Total adherents Number	Percent of total population	Percent of total adherents
THE STATE.....	4,560	845,107	1,681,062*	60.5	100.0
ADAIR	**23**	**3,629**	**5,912***	**70.3**	**100.0**
081 CATHOLIC	3	NA	1,327	15.8	22.4
081d LATIN	*3*	*NA*	*1,327*	*15.8*	*22.4*
093 CHR CH (DISC)	1	50	65	.8	1.1
207 E.L.C.A.	2	708	923	11.0	15.6
226 FRIENDS-USA	1	66	83*	1.0	1.4
226e FUM	*1*	*66*	*83***	*1.0*	*1.4*
283 LUTH—MO SYNOD	2	599	741	8.8	12.5
353 CHR BRETHREN	1	76	110	1.3	1.9
355 PRESB CH (USA)	2	257	321*	3.8	5.4
443 UN C OF CHRIST	2	94	118*	1.4	2.0
449 UN METHODIST	9	1,779	2,224*	26.4	37.6
ADAMS	**15**	**1,486**	**2,463***	**50.6**	**100.0**
081 CATHOLIC	1	NA	500	10.3	20.3
081d LATIN	*1*	*NA*	*500*	*10.3*	*20.3*
093 CHR CH (DISC)	2	257	380	7.8	15.4
097 CHR CHS&CHS CR	1	0	0*	-	-
157 CH OF BRETHREN	2	62	77*	1.6	3.1
207 E.L.C.A.	1	110	157	3.2	6.4
283 LUTH—MO SYNOD	1	179	262	5.4	10.6
355 PRESB CH (USA)	1	207	256*	5.3	10.4
449 UN METHODIST	6	671	831*	17.1	33.7
ALLAMAKEE	**39**	**5,592**	**12,256***	**88.5**	**100.0**
057 BAPT GEN CONF	1	75	96*	.7	.8
081 CATHOLIC	11	NA	5,236	37.8	42.7
081d LATIN	*11*	*NA*	*5,236*	*37.8*	*42.7*
179 CONSRV BAPT	1	NR	NR	-	-

NA–Not applicable NR–Not reported *Total adherents estimated from known number of communicant, confirmed, full members. - Represents a percent less than 0.1. Percentages may not total due to rounding.
[1]See Appendix E [2]See Appendix F [3]See Appendix G Lines in *italic* represent a breakdown of Catholic rites or Friends affiliations. They are included in their respective denominational total.

143

Table 4. Churches and Church Membership by County and Denomination: 1990

County and Denomination	Number of churches	Communicant, confirmed, full members	Total adherents Number	Percent of total population	Percent of total adherents
207 E.L.C.A.	7	2,785	3,458	25.0	28.2
209 EVAN LUTH SYN	2	79	87	.6	.7
355 PRESB CH (USA)	7	1,165	1,484*	10.7	12.1
413 S.D.A.	1	58	74*	.5	.6
443 UN C OF CHRIST	4	884	1,126*	8.1	9.2
449 UN METHODIST	5	546	695*	5.0	5.7
APPANOOSE	**36**	**3,115**	**6,508***	**47.4**	**100.0**
019 AMER BAPT USA	1	487	605*	4.4	9.3
053 ASSEMB OF GOD	1	53	70	.5	1.1
081 CATHOLIC	3	NA	1,634	11.9	25.1
081d LATIN	3	NA	1,634	11.9	25.1
093 CHR CH (DISC)	5	542	1,025	7.5	15.7
097 CHR CHS&CHS CR	6	373	463*	3.4	7.1
127 CH GOD (CLEVE)	1	101	125*	.9	1.9
157 CH OF BRETHREN	1	94	117*	.9	1.8
165 CH OF NAZARENE	2	103	226	1.6	3.5
193 EPISCOPAL	1	10	10	.1	.2
207 E.L.C.A.	1	110	275	2.0	4.2
329 OPEN BIBLE STD	1	NR	NR	-	-
353 CHR BRETHREN	1	20	40	.3	.6
355 PRESB CH (USA)	1	106	132*	1.0	2.0
413 S.D.A.	1	40	50*	.4	.8
449 UN METHODIST	9	1,076	1,336*	9.7	20.5
499 INDEP.NON-CHAR3	1	NA	400	2.9	6.1
AUDUBON	**19**	**3,907**	**5,789***	**78.9**	**100.0**
081 CATHOLIC	2	NA	848	11.6	14.6
081d LATIN	2	NA	848	11.6	14.6
093 CHR CH (DISC)	1	217	285	3.9	4.9
207 E.L.C.A.	7	2,135	2,709	36.9	46.8
283 LUTH—MO SYNOD	2	339	423	5.8	7.3
355 PRESB CH (USA)	1	341	427*	5.8	7.4
413 S.D.A.	2	50	63*	.9	1.1
443 UN C OF CHRIST	1	78	98*	1.3	1.7
449 UN METHODIST	3	747	936*	12.8	16.2
BENTON	**48**	**7,781**	**14,180***	**63.2**	**100.0**
019 AMER BAPT USA	2	174	223*	1.0	1.6
053 ASSEMB OF GOD	2	102	251	1.1	1.8
081 CATHOLIC	8	NA	3,951	17.6	27.9
081d LATIN	8	NA	3,951	17.6	27.9
093 CHR CH (DISC)	4	594	785	3.5	5.5
121 CH GOD (ABR)	2	46	59*	.3	.4
157 CH OF BRETHREN	1	33	42*	.2	.3
207 E.L.C.A.	2	386	539	2.4	3.8
283 LUTH—MO SYNOD	10	3,545	4,607	20.5	32.5
355 PRESB CH (USA)	5	963	1,236*	5.5	8.7
443 UN C OF CHRIST	1	219	281*	1.3	2.0
449 UN METHODIST	11	1,719	2,206*	9.8	15.6
BLACK HAWK	**138**	**36,746**	**76,224***	**61.6**	**100.0**
019 AMER BAPT USA	4	1,234	1,544*	1.2	2.0
053 ASSEMB OF GOD	4	352	644	.5	.8
057 BAPT GEN CONF	1	246	308*	.2	.4
071 BRETHREN (ASH)	1	178	223*	.2	.3
081 CATHOLIC	15	NA	25,633	20.7	33.6
081d LATIN	15	NA	25,633	20.7	33.6
089 CHR & MISS AL	1	29	71	.1	.1
093 CHR CH (DISC)	2	498	782	.6	1.0
097 CHR CHS&CHS CR	3	330	413*	.3	.5
105 CHRISTIAN REF	1	92	119	.1	.2
111 CH CR,SCIENTST	1	NR	NR	-	-
121 CH GOD (ABR)	1	14	18*	-	-
151 L-D SAINTS	2	NA	692	.6	.9
157 CH OF BRETHREN	2	492	615*	.5	.8
165 CH OF NAZARENE	2	257	610	.5	.8
167 CHS OF CHRIST	2	187	243	.2	.3
193 EPISCOPAL	2	515	700	.6	.9
203 EVAN FREE CH	1	57	60	-	.1
207 E.L.C.A.	18	10,074	13,432	10.8	17.6
209 EVAN LUTH SYN	1	89	106	.1	.1
221 FREE METHODIST	1	75	75	.1	.1
226 FRIENDS-USA	1	3	5	-	-
226f INDEPENDNT	1	3	5	-	-
246 GREEK ORTHODOX	1	NR	NR	-	-
259 IFCA	2	NR	NR	-	-
263 INT FOURSQ GOS	1	105	131*	.1	.2
283 LUTH—MO SYNOD	8	3,528	5,155	4.2	6.8
284 LUTH CH-AM ASC	1	333	424	.3	.6
285 MENNONITE CH	1	17	32	-	-
287 MENN GEN CONF	1	9	19	-	-
313 N AM BAPT CONF	1	34	43*	-	.1
329 OPEN BIBLE STD	1	NR	NR	-	-
353 CHR BRETHREN	5	377	450	.4	.6
355 PRESB CH (USA)	10	3,520	4,403*	3.6	5.8

County and Denomination	Number of churches	Communicant, confirmed, full members	Total adherents Number	Percent of total population	Percent of total adherents
371 REF CH IN AM	3	568	868	.7	1.1
403 SALVATION ARMY	3	299	383	.3	.5
413 S.D.A.	1	159	199*	.2	.3
419 SO BAPT CONV	4	847	1,059*	.9	1.4
435 UNITARIAN-UNIV	1	155	210	.2	.3
443 UN C OF CHRIST	3	1,242	1,554*	1.3	2.0
449 UN METHODIST	18	6,820	8,531*	6.9	11.2
467 WESLEYAN	6	1,760	3,454	2.8	4.5
496 JEWISH EST1	1	NA	200	.2	.3
497 BLACK BAPT EST2	NA	2,251	2,816*	2.3	3.7
BOONE	**49**	**8,656**	**14,584***	**57.9**	**100.0**
019 AMER BAPT USA	2	776	967*	3.8	6.6
053 ASSEMB OF GOD	1	44	70	.3	.5
081 CATHOLIC	3	NA	2,752	10.9	18.9
081d LATIN	3	NA	2,752	10.9	18.9
089 CHR & MISS AL	2	183	370	1.5	2.5
093 CHR CH (DISC)	2	402	923	3.7	6.3
111 CH CR,SCIENTST	1	NR	NR	-	-
123 CH GOD (ANDER)	1	0	94	.4	.6
145 CH GOD PROPHCY	1	22	27*	.1	.2
151 L-D SAINTS	1	NA	224	.9	1.5
157 CH OF BRETHREN	1	42	52*	.2	.4
165 CH OF NAZARENE	1	34	112	.4	.8
167 CHS OF CHRIST	2	80	103	.4	.7
193 EPISCOPAL	1	79	89	.4	.6
203 EVAN FREE CH	2	389	504	2.0	3.5
207 E.L.C.A.	5	1,880	2,401	9.5	16.5
221 FREE METHODIST	1	16	26	.1	.2
283 LUTH—MO SYNOD	3	1,451	1,818	7.2	12.5
329 OPEN BIBLE STD	2	NR	NR	-	-
355 PRESB CH (USA)	1	348	434*	1.7	3.0
363 PRIMITIVE METH	2	16	24	.1	.2
403 SALVATION ARMY	1	83	92	.4	.6
413 S.D.A.	1	28	35*	.1	.2
443 UN C OF CHRIST	2	339	422*	1.7	2.9
449 UN METHODIST	10	2,444	3,045*	12.1	20.9
BREMER	**41**	**12,257**	**18,423***	**80.8**	**100.0**
019 AMER BAPT USA	1	161	200*	.9	1.1
053 ASSEMB OF GOD	1	14	18	.1	.1
057 BAPT GEN CONF	2	269	334*	1.5	1.8
081 CATHOLIC	3	NA	2,725	11.9	14.8
081d LATIN	3	NA	2,725	11.9	14.8
193 EPISCOPAL	1	32	45	.2	.2
207 E.L.C.A.	12	6,056	7,918	34.7	43.0
283 LUTH—MO SYNOD	7	2,043	2,577	11.3	14.0
313 N AM BAPT CONF	1	81	101*	.4	.5
329 OPEN BIBLE STD	1	NR	NR	-	-
443 UN C OF CHRIST	5	1,562	1,939*	8.5	10.5
449 UN METHODIST	7	2,039	2,531*	11.1	13.7
496 JEWISH EST1	0	NA	35	.2	.2
BUCHANAN	**44**	**5,396**	**15,335***	**73.6**	**100.0**
019 AMER BAPT USA	4	360	475*	2.3	3.1
053 ASSEMB OF GOD	1	39	52	.2	.3
081 CATHOLIC	8	NA	7,257	34.8	47.3
081d LATIN	8	NA	7,257	34.8	47.3
097 CHR CHS&CHS CR	1	50	66*	.3	.4
193 EPISCOPAL	1	40	43	.2	.3
207 E.L.C.A.	3	1,422	1,950	9.4	12.7
263 INT FOURSQ GOS	1	142	187*	.9	1.2
283 LUTH—MO SYNOD	3	386	492	2.4	3.2
284 LUTH CH-AM ASC	1	88	127	.6	.8
323 OLD ORD AMISH	6	NA	900	4.3	5.9
355 PRESB CH (USA)	5	768	1,013*	4.9	6.6
443 UN C OF CHRIST	1	159	210*	1.0	1.4
449 UN METHODIST	9	1,942	2,563*	12.3	16.7
BUENA VISTA	**41**	**9,843**	**15,490***	**77.6**	**100.0**
019 AMER BAPT USA	1	277	349*	1.7	2.3
053 ASSEMB OF GOD	1	107	190	1.0	1.2
081 CATHOLIC	2	NA	2,781	13.9	18.0
081d LATIN	2	NA	2,781	13.9	18.0
097 CHR CHS&CHS CR	2	267	336*	1.7	2.2
193 EPISCOPAL	1	39	58	.3	.4
203 EVAN FREE CH	3	179	341	1.7	2.2
207 E.L.C.A.	10	2,845	3,728	18.7	24.1
283 LUTH—MO SYNOD	7	2,326	2,917	14.6	18.8
355 PRESB CH (USA)	3	999	1,258*	6.3	8.1
419 SO BAPT CONV	1	26	33*	.2	.2
443 UN C OF CHRIST	4	384	484*	2.4	3.1
449 UN METHODIST	6	2,394	3,015*	15.1	19.5

NA–Not applicable   NR–Not reported   *Total adherents estimated from known number of communicant, confirmed, full members.   - Represents a percent less than 0.1.   Percentages may not total due to rounding.
1See Appendix E   2See Appendix F   3See Appendix G   Lines in *italic* represent a breakdown of Catholic rites or Friends affiliations. They are included in their respective denominational total.

Table 4. Churches and Church Membership by County and Denomination: 1990

County and Denomination	Number of churches	Communicant, confirmed, full members	Total adherents Number	Total adherents Percent of total population	Total adherents Percent of total adherents
BUTLER	**49**	**8,404**	**12,154***	**77.3**	**100.0**
081 CATHOLIC	5	NA	942	6.0	7.8
081d *LATIN*	*5*	*NA*	*942*	*6.0*	*7.8*
097 CHR CHS&CHS CR	2	125	157*	1.0	1.3
105 CHRISTIAN REF	2	293	407	2.6	3.3
157 CH OF BRETHREN	1	50	63*	.4	.5
181 CONSRV CONGR	1	281	353*	2.2	2.9
207 E.L.C.A.	7	2,651	3,477	22.1	28.6
209 EVAN LUTH SYN	1	97	117	.7	1.0
259 IFCA	1	NR	NR	-	-
283 LUTH—MO SYNOD	1	128	173	1.1	1.4
313 N AM BAPT CONF	2	394	495*	3.1	4.1
353 CHR BRETHREN	2	66	140	.9	1.2
355 PRESB CH (USA)	5	649	816*	5.2	6.7
371 REF CH IN AM	6	1,113	1,776	11.3	14.6
443 UN C OF CHRIST	4	1,040	1,307*	8.3	10.8
449 UN METHODIST	8	1,465	1,841*	11.7	15.1
467 WESLEYAN	1	52	90	.6	.7
CALHOUN	**37**	**6,214**	**9,792***	**85.1**	**100.0**
019 AMER BAPT USA	1	168	209*	1.8	2.1
057 BAPT GEN CONF	1	17	21*	.2	.2
081 CATHOLIC	6	NA	1,793	15.6	18.3
081d *LATIN*	*6*	*NA*	*1,793*	*15.6*	*18.3*
093 CHR CH (DISC)	2	238	476	4.1	4.9
097 CHR CHS&CHS CR	1	133	166*	1.4	1.7
207 E.L.C.A.	4	1,764	2,303	20.0	23.5
283 LUTH—MO SYNOD	5	1,190	1,504	13.1	15.4
285 MENNONITE CH	1	188	208	1.8	2.1
355 PRESB CH (USA)	2	430	535*	4.6	5.5
413 S.D.A.	1	32	40*	.3	.4
443 UN C OF CHRIST	3	307	382*	3.3	3.9
449 UN METHODIST	9	1,731	2,155*	18.7	22.0
467 WESLEYAN	1	16	0	-	-
CARROLL	**38**	**4,928**	**19,958***	**93.2**	**100.0**
053 ASSEMB OF GOD	1	54	92	.4	.5
081 CATHOLIC	15	NA	13,363	62.4	67.0
081d *LATIN*	*15*	*NA*	*13,363*	*62.4*	*67.0*
093 CHR CH (DISC)	1	128	247	1.2	1.2
097 CHR CHS&CHS CR	1	63	83*	.4	.4
151 L-D SAINTS	1	NA	57	.3	.3
167 CHS OF CHRIST	1	7	8	-	-
193 EPISCOPAL	1	23	36	.2	.2
207 E.L.C.A.	2	368	529	2.5	2.7
283 LUTH—MO SYNOD	5	2,074	2,643	12.3	13.2
355 PRESB CH (USA)	5	646	847*	4.0	4.2
449 UN METHODIST	5	1,565	2,053*	9.6	10.3
CASS	**45**	**7,628**	**12,044***	**79.6**	**100.0**
019 AMER BAPT USA	1	160	201*	1.3	1.7
053 ASSEMB OF GOD	1	101	181	1.2	1.5
081 CATHOLIC	5	NA	2,029	13.4	16.8
081d *LATIN*	*5*	*NA*	*2,029*	*13.4*	*16.8*
093 CHR CH (DISC)	3	568	753	5.0	6.3
097 CHR CHS&CHS CR	4	695	871*	5.8	7.2
145 CH GOD PROPHCY	1	22	28*	.2	.2
151 L-D SAINTS	1	NA	77	.5	.6
165 CH OF NAZARENE	1	44	111	.7	.9
167 CHS OF CHRIST	1	37	44	.3	.4
203 EVAN FREE CH	1	85	85	.6	.7
207 E.L.C.A.	2	896	1,181	7.8	9.8
283 LUTH—MO SYNOD	3	1,240	1,600	10.6	13.3
353 CHR BRETHREN	3	190	383	2.5	3.2
355 PRESB CH (USA)	1	407	510*	3.4	4.2
413 S.D.A.	1	43	54*	.4	.4
443 UN C OF CHRIST	5	885	1,109*	7.3	9.2
449 UN METHODIST	11	2,255	2,827*	18.7	23.5
CEDAR	**31**	**6,149**	**9,813***	**56.5**	**100.0**
019 AMER BAPT USA	1	69	87*	.5	.9
081 CATHOLIC	3	NA	1,765	10.2	18.0
081d *LATIN*	*3*	*NA*	*1,765*	*10.2*	*18.0*
151 L-D SAINTS	1	NA	144	.8	1.5
157 CH OF BRETHREN	1	11	14*	.1	.1
193 EPISCOPAL	1	151	225	1.3	2.3
207 E.L.C.A.	3	892	1,268	7.3	12.9
226 FRIENDS-USA	2	219	278*	1.6	2.8
226a *CONSERV*	*1*	*100*	*127*	*.7*	*1.3*
226e *FUM*	*1*	*119*	*151*	*.9*	*1.5*
263 INT FOURSQ GOS	1	24	30*	.2	.3
283 LUTH—MO SYNOD	3	827	988	5.7	10.1
355 PRESB CH (USA)	3	220	279*	1.6	2.8
443 UN C OF CHRIST	4	2,035	2,579*	14.8	26.3
449 UN METHODIST	8	1,701	2,156*	12.4	22.0

County and Denomination	Number of churches	Communicant, confirmed, full members	Total adherents Number	Total adherents Percent of total population	Total adherents Percent of total adherents
CERRO GORDO	**61**	**16,457**	**29,696***	**63.5**	**100.0**
019 AMER BAPT USA	2	424	528*	1.1	1.8
053 ASSEMB OF GOD	1	68	163	.3	.5
081 CATHOLIC	5	NA	7,617	16.3	25.6
081d *LATIN*	*5*	*NA*	*7,617*	*16.3*	*25.6*
089 CHR & MISS AL	1	25	80	.2	.3
093 CHR CH (DISC)	2	272	442	.9	1.5
097 CHR CHS&CHS CR	2	163	203*	.4	.7
105 CHRISTIAN REF	1	81	142	.3	.5
111 CH CR,SCIENTST	2	NR	NR	-	-
151 L-D SAINTS	1	NA	199	.4	.7
165 CH OF NAZARENE	1	59	138	.3	.5
167 CHS OF CHRIST	1	33	42	.1	.1
175 CONGR CHR CHS	2	262	326*	.7	1.1
193 EPISCOPAL	1	227	313	.7	1.1
203 EVAN FREE CH	2	314	568	1.2	1.9
207 E.L.C.A.	8	6,920	9,321	19.9	31.4
209 EVAN LUTH SYN	1	120	163	.3	.5
221 FREE METHODIST	1	33	59	.1	.2
226 FRIENDS-USA	1	38	47*	.1	.2
226e *FUM*	*1*	*38*	*47*	*.1*	*.2*
246 GREEK ORTHODOX	1	NR	NR	-	-
283 LUTH—MO SYNOD	2	977	1,258	2.7	4.2
329 OPEN BIBLE STD	3	NR	NR	-	-
355 PRESB CH (USA)	1	511	637*	1.4	2.1
371 REF CH IN AM	1	228	357	.8	1.2
403 SALVATION ARMY	1	169	176	.4	.6
413 S.D.A.	1	107	133*	.3	.4
419 SO BAPT CONV	1	149	186*	.4	.6
435 UNITARIAN-UNIV	1	14	14	-	-
443 UN C OF CHRIST	1	487	607*	1.3	2.0
449 UN METHODIST	11	4,663	5,809*	12.4	19.6
469 WELS	1	113	168	.4	.6
496 JEWISH EST[1]	1	NA	0	-	-
CHEROKEE	**32**	**6,264**	**11,725***	**83.2**	**100.0**
019 AMER BAPT USA	2	152	193*	1.4	1.6
081 CATHOLIC	4	NA	3,371	23.9	28.8
081d *LATIN*	*4*	*NA*	*3,371*	*23.9*	*28.8*
093 CHR CH (DISC)	1	13	21	.1	.2
097 CHR CHS&CHS CR	1	400	507*	3.6	4.3
151 L-D SAINTS	1	NA	213	1.5	1.8
203 EVAN FREE CH	2	234	298	2.1	2.5
207 E.L.C.A.	2	888	1,149	8.2	9.8
283 LUTH—MO SYNOD	5	1,547	2,131	15.1	18.2
329 OPEN BIBLE STD	1	NR	NR	-	-
355 PRESB CH (USA)	3	619	785*	5.6	6.7
413 S.D.A.	1	3	4*	-	-
419 SO BAPT CONV	1	63	80*	.6	.7
443 UN C OF CHRIST	1	144	183*	1.3	1.6
449 UN METHODIST	7	2,201	2,790*	19.8	23.8
CHICKASAW	**32**	**4,670**	**10,461***	**78.7**	**100.0**
019 AMER BAPT USA	2	304	389*	2.9	3.7
057 BAPT GEN CONF	1	32	41*	.3	.4
081 CATHOLIC	8	NA	4,494	33.8	43.0
081d *LATIN*	*8*	*NA*	*4,494*	*33.8*	*43.0*
157 CH OF BRETHREN	1	215	275*	2.1	2.6
176 CCC, NOT NAT'L	1	105	134*	1.0	1.3
207 E.L.C.A.	6	1,914	2,489	18.7	23.8
209 EVAN LUTH SYN	3	382	448	3.4	4.3
283 LUTH—MO SYNOD	1	220	272	2.0	2.6
443 UN C OF CHRIST	4	575	737*	5.5	7.0
449 UN METHODIST	5	923	1,182*	8.9	11.3
CLARKE	**18**	**2,225**	**3,634***	**43.9**	**100.0**
053 ASSEMB OF GOD	1	74	226	2.7	6.2
081 CATHOLIC	1	NA	350	4.2	9.6
081d *LATIN*	*1*	*NA*	*350*	*4.2*	*9.6*
093 CHR CH (DISC)	2	464	687	8.3	18.9
097 CHR CHS&CHS CR	1	350	439*	5.3	12.1
151 L-D SAINTS	1	NA	202	2.4	5.6
167 CHS OF CHRIST	1	56	84	1.0	2.3
259 IFCA	1	NR	NR	-	-
263 INT FOURSQ GOS	1	5	6*	.1	.2
283 LUTH—MO SYNOD	1	241	341	4.1	9.4
355 PRESB CH (USA)	1	33	41*	.5	1.1
413 S.D.A.	1	28	35*	.4	1.0
419 SO BAPT CONV	1	61	77*	.9	2.1
449 UN METHODIST	5	913	1,146*	13.8	31.5
CLAY	**34**	**7,178**	**11,997***	**68.2**	**100.0**
019 AMER BAPT USA	1	80	102*	.6	.9
053 ASSEMB OF GOD	1	59	100	.6	.8
081 CATHOLIC	3	NA	2,373	13.5	19.8

NA–Not applicable   NR–Not reported   *Total adherents estimated from known number of communicant, confirmed, full members.   - Represents a percent less than 0.1.   Percentages may not total due to rounding.
[1]See Appendix E   [2]See Appendix F   [3]See Appendix G   Lines in *italic* represent a breakdown of Catholic rites or Friends affiliations. They are included in their respective denominational total.

Table 4. Churches and Church Membership by County and Denomination: 1990

County and Denomination	Number of churches	Communicant, confirmed, full members	Total adherents Number	Percent of total population	Percent of total adherents
081d LATIN	3	NA	2,373	13.5	19.8
093 CHR CH (DISC)	1	339	378	2.1	3.2
165 CH OF NAZARENE	1	17	58	.3	.5
167 CHS OF CHRIST	1	28	36	.2	.3
175 CONGR CHR CHS	2	610	782*	4.4	6.5
193 EPISCOPAL	1	34	42	.2	.4
207 E.L.C.A.	4	1,878	2,592	14.7	21.6
283 LUTH—MO SYNOD	3	1,065	1,482	8.4	12.4
371 REF CH IN AM	2	435	678	3.9	5.7
413 S.D.A.	1	72	92*	.5	.8
419 SO BAPT CONV	1	41	53*	.3	.4
443 UN C OF CHRIST	2	141	181*	1.0	1.5
449 UN METHODIST	10	2,379	3,048*	17.3	25.4
CLAYTON	**43**	**7,582**	**15,057***	**79.0**	**100.0**
081 CATHOLIC	9	NA	5,439	28.5	36.1
081d LATIN	9	NA	5,439	28.5	36.1
175 CONGR CHR CHS	2	117	149*	.8	1.0
203 EVAN FREE CH	1	46	80	.4	.5
207 E.L.C.A.	20	4,979	6,260	32.9	41.6
283 LUTH—MO SYNOD	2	269	346	1.8	2.3
353 CHR BRETHREN	1	70	100	.5	.7
443 UN C OF CHRIST	2	763	974*	5.1	6.5
449 UN METHODIST	6	1,338	1,709*	9.0	11.4
CLINTON	**75**	**13,841**	**29,733***	**58.3**	**100.0**
019 AMER BAPT USA	2	561	709*	1.4	2.4
053 ASSEMB OF GOD	2	40	55	.1	.2
081 CATHOLIC	13	NA	11,069	21.7	37.2
081d LATIN	13	NA	11,069	21.7	37.2
097 CHR CHS&CHS CR	1	300	379*	.7	1.3
111 CH CR,SCIENTST	1	NR	NR	-	-
123 CH GOD (ANDER)	2	84	89	.2	.3
151 L-D SAINTS	1	NA	309	.6	1.0
163 CH OF LUTH BR	1	76	122	.2	.4
165 CH OF NAZARENE	1	29	94	.2	.3
167 CHS OF CHRIST	1	55	62	.1	.2
193 EPISCOPAL	2	279	560	1.1	1.9
203 EVAN FREE CH	2	188	508	1.0	1.7
207 E.L.C.A.	11	3,402	4,387	8.6	14.8
220 FREE LUTHERAN	1	84	116	.2	.4
263 INT FOURSQ GOS	2	404	511*	1.0	1.7
283 LUTH—MO SYNOD	5	2,558	3,380	6.6	11.4
329 OPEN BIBLE STD	1	NR	NR	-	-
355 PRESB CH (USA)	4	752	951*	1.9	3.2
371 REF CH IN AM	1	128	249	.5	.8
403 SALVATION ARMY	1	84	97	.2	.3
413 S.D.A.	1	53	67*	.1	.2
419 SO BAPT CONV	3	577	730*	1.4	2.5
435 UNITARIAN-UNIV	1	22	22	-	.1
443 UN C OF CHRIST	5	1,597	2,019*	4.0	6.8
449 UN METHODIST	10	2,411	3,049*	6.0	10.3
497 BLACK BAPT EST[2]	NA	157	199*	.4	.7
CRAWFORD	**39**	**8,051**	**13,971***	**83.3**	**100.0**
019 AMER BAPT USA	1	83	105*	.6	.8
053 ASSEMB OF GOD	1	30	40	.2	.3
057 BAPT GEN CONF	2	269	340*	2.0	2.4
081 CATHOLIC	6	NA	3,752	22.4	26.9
081d LATIN	6	NA	3,752	22.4	26.9
167 CHS OF CHRIST	1	2	2	-	-
193 EPISCOPAL	1	21	23	.1	.2
207 E.L.C.A.	1	149	187	1.1	1.3
283 LUTH—MO SYNOD	12	4,933	6,149	36.7	44.0
355 PRESB CH (USA)	4	837	1,058*	6.3	7.6
419 SO BAPT CONV	1	90	114*	.7	.8
443 UN C OF CHRIST	3	621	785*	4.7	5.6
449 UN METHODIST	5	988	1,249*	7.4	8.9
467 WESLEYAN	1	28	167	1.0	1.2
DALLAS	**61**	**8,223**	**16,085***	**54.1**	**100.0**
053 ASSEMB OF GOD	3	86	128	.4	.8
075 BRETHREN IN CR	1	32	39	.1	.2
081 CATHOLIC	5	NA	4,161	14.0	25.9
081d LATIN	5	NA	4,161	14.0	25.9
093 CHR CH (DISC)	6	940	1,694	5.7	10.5
097 CHR CHS&CHS CR	2	91	117*	.4	.7
111 CH CR,SCIENTST	1	NR	NR	-	-
151 L-D SAINTS	1	NA	420	1.4	2.6
157 CH OF BRETHREN	2	335	431*	1.4	2.7
167 CHS OF CHRIST	1	33	75	.3	.5
193 EPISCOPAL	1	91	132	.4	.8
207 E.L.C.A.	5	953	1,282	4.3	8.0
226 FRIENDS-USA	3	220	283*	1.0	1.8
226a CONSERV	1	95	122*	.4	.8
226e FUM	2	125	161*	.5	1.0
283 LUTH—MO SYNOD	4	960	1,338	4.5	8.3
324 OLD ORD RVR BR	1	38	64	.2	.4
329 OPEN BIBLE STD	1	NR	NR	-	-
353 CHR BRETHREN	1	45	68	.2	.4
355 PRESB CH (USA)	4	445	572*	1.9	3.6
419 SO BAPT CONV	3	202	260*	.9	1.6
449 UN METHODIST	16	3,752	4,823*	16.2	30.0
496 JEWISH EST[1]	0	NA	198	.7	1.2
DAVIS	**21**	**1,954**	**3,426***	**41.2**	**100.0**
040 AP CHR CH-AMER	1	43	78	.9	2.3
081 CATHOLIC	1	NA	90	1.1	2.6
081d LATIN	1	NA	90	1.1	2.6
093 CHR CH (DISC)	5	691	1,210	14.6	35.3
097 CHR CHS&CHS CR	1	140	178*	2.1	5.2
165 CH OF NAZARENE	1	51	111	1.3	3.2
167 CHS OF CHRIST	1	5	5	.1	.1
207 E.L.C.A.	1	93	126	1.5	3.7
287 MENN GEN CONF	1	68	83	1.0	2.4
323 OLD ORD AMISH	3	NA	450	5.4	13.1
329 OPEN BIBLE STD	1	NR	NR	-	-
449 UN METHODIST	5	863	1,095*	13.2	32.0
DECATUR	**30**	**1,554**	**2,243***	**26.9**	**100.0**
019 AMER BAPT USA	1	38	46*	.6	2.1
040 AP CHR CH-AMER	1	12	22	.3	1.0
053 ASSEMB OF GOD	5	141	215	2.6	9.6
061 BEACHY AMISH	1	75	91*	1.1	4.1
081 CATHOLIC	2	NA	250	3.0	11.1
081d LATIN	2	NA	250	3.0	11.1
093 CHR CH (DISC)	1	35	60	.7	2.7
097 CHR CHS&CHS CR	1	104	127*	1.5	5.7
167 CHS OF CHRIST	4	70	91	1.1	4.1
259 IFCA	1	NR	NR	-	-
283 LUTH—MO SYNOD	1	80	122	1.5	5.4
285 MENNONITE CH	1	17	21	.3	.9
355 PRESB CH (USA)	2	100	122*	1.5	5.4
419 SO BAPT CONV	2	347	423*	5.1	18.9
449 UN METHODIST	7	535	653*	7.8	29.1
DELAWARE	**37**	**4,038**	**13,271***	**73.6**	**100.0**
053 ASSEMB OF GOD	1	47	98	.5	.7
081 CATHOLIC	11	NA	7,678	42.6	57.9
081d LATIN	11	NA	7,678	42.6	57.9
179 CONSRV BAPT	1	NR	NR	-	-
207 E.L.C.A.	7	1,151	1,527	8.5	11.5
283 LUTH—MO SYNOD	2	414	591	3.3	4.5
323 OLD ORD AMISH	1	NA	150	.8	1.1
353 CHR BRETHREN	1	52	80	.4	.6
355 PRESB CH (USA)	2	304	403*	2.2	3.0
443 UN C OF CHRIST	3	288	382*	2.1	2.9
449 UN METHODIST	8	1,782	2,362*	13.1	17.8
DES MOINES	**68**	**12,475**	**23,886***	**56.1**	**100.0**
019 AMER BAPT USA	3	483	606*	1.4	2.5
040 AP CHR CH-AMER	1	60	105	.2	.4
053 ASSEMB OF GOD	1	291	565	1.3	2.4
057 BAPT GEN CONF	1	334	419*	1.0	1.8
081 CATHOLIC	6	NA	7,042	16.5	29.5
081d LATIN	6	NA	7,042	16.5	29.5
093 CHR CH (DISC)	1	592	911	2.1	3.8
097 CHR CHS&CHS CR	1	185	232*	.5	1.0
111 CH CR,SCIENTST	1	NR	NR	-	-
165 CH OF NAZARENE	2	232	556	1.3	2.3
167 CHS OF CHRIST	1	73	82	.2	.3
175 CONGR CHR CHS	1	247	310*	.7	1.3
185 CUMBER PRESB	1	111	124	.3	.5
193 EPISCOPAL	1	269	275	.6	1.2
203 EVAN FREE CH	5	585	782	1.8	3.3
207 E.L.C.A.	6	2,342	3,113	7.3	13.0
221 FREE METHODIST	1	20	28	.1	.1
263 INT FOURSQ GOS	1	32	40*	.1	.2
283 LUTH—MO SYNOD	1	103	155	.4	.6
285 MENNONITE CH	1	0	6	-	-
313 N AM BAPT CONF	1	671	842*	2.0	3.5
329 OPEN BIBLE STD	1	NR	NR	-	-
355 PRESB CH (USA)	4	804	1,009*	2.4	4.2
403 SALVATION ARMY	1	91	100	.2	.4
413 S.D.A.	1	111	139*	.3	.6
419 SO BAPT CONV	1	202	253*	.6	1.1
435 UNITARIAN-UNIV	1	36	45	.1	.2
443 UN C OF CHRIST	8	1,400	1,757*	4.1	7.4
449 UN METHODIST	11	2,841	3,564*	8.4	14.9
469 WELS	1	76	120	.3	.5
496 JEWISH EST[1]	1	NA	0	-	-
497 BLACK BAPT EST[2]	NA	284	356*	.8	1.5

NA–Not applicable   NR–Not reported   *Total adherents estimated from known number of communicant, confirmed, full members.   - Represents a percent less than 0.1.   Percentages may not total due to rounding.
[1]See Appendix E   [2]See Appendix F   [3]See Appendix G   Lines in *italic* represent a breakdown of Catholic rites or Friends affiliations. They are included in their respective denominational total.

Table 4. Churches and Church Membership by County and Denomination: 1990

County and Denomination	Number of churches	Communicant, confirmed, full members	Total adherents		
			Number	Percent of total population	Percent of total adherents
498 INDEP.CHARIS.[3]	1	NA	350	.8	1.5
DICKINSON	**26**	**5,791**	**9,683***	**64.9**	**100.0**
019 AMER BAPT USA	1	35	43*	.3	.4
057 BAPT GEN CONF	1	98	120*	.8	1.2
081 CATHOLIC	2	NA	2,522	16.9	26.0
081d *LATIN*	*2*	*NA*	*2,522*	*16.9*	*26.0*
111 CH CR,SCIENTST	1	NR	NR	-	-
193 EPISCOPAL	1	103	127	.9	1.3
203 EVAN FREE CH	1	87	155	1.0	1.6
207 E.L.C.A.	3	1,240	1,621	10.9	16.7
226 FRIENDS-USA	1	47	57*	.4	.6
226e *FUM*	*1*	*47*	*57**	*.4*	*.6*
263 INT FOURSQ GOS	1	11	13*	.1	.1
283 LUTH—MO SYNOD	3	958	1,098	7.4	11.3
355 PRESB CH (USA)	2	804	983*	6.6	10.2
413 S.D.A.	1	33	40*	.3	.4
443 UN C OF CHRIST	1	235	287*	1.9	3.0
449 UN METHODIST	7	2,140	2,617*	17.6	27.0
DUBUQUE	**77**	**8,519**	**61,248***	**70.9**	**100.0**
019 AMER BAPT USA	1	70	89*	.1	.1
053 ASSEMB OF GOD	1	30	50	.1	.1
081 CATHOLIC	31	NA	49,669	57.5	81.1
081d *LATIN*	*31*	*NA*	*49,669*	*57.5*	*81.1*
151 L-D SAINTS	1	NA	248	.3	.4
165 CH OF NAZARENE	1	35	98	.1	.2
167 CHS OF CHRIST	1	19	24	-	-
193 EPISCOPAL	1	351	370	.4	.6
203 EVAN FREE CH	1	80	225	.3	.4
207 E.L.C.A.	8	2,418	3,115	3.6	5.1
226 FRIENDS-USA	1	2	15	-	-
226c *FGC*	*1*	*2*	*15*	*-*	*-*
246 GREEK ORTHODOX	1	NR	NR	-	-
259 IFCA	1	NR	NR	-	-
283 LUTH—MO SYNOD	3	959	1,398	1.6	2.3
329 OPEN BIBLE STD	1	NR	NR	-	-
353 CHR BRETHREN	2	115	305	.4	.5
355 PRESB CH (USA)	5	1,326	1,681*	1.9	2.7
403 SALVATION ARMY	1	82	113	.1	.2
413 S.D.A.	1	40	51*	.1	.1
419 SO BAPT CONV	2	81	103*	.1	.2
435 UNITARIAN-UNIV	1	25	35	-	.1
443 UN C OF CHRIST	4	1,225	1,553*	1.8	2.5
449 UN METHODIST	7	1,661	2,106*	2.4	3.4
496 JEWISH EST[1]	1	NA	0	-	-
EMMET	**26**	**5,991**	**9,489***	**82.0**	**100.0**
057 BAPT GEN CONF	1	203	254*	2.2	2.7
081 CATHOLIC	2	NA	1,738	15.0	18.3
081d *LATIN*	*2*	*NA*	*1,738*	*15.0*	*18.3*
093 CHR CH (DISC)	1	257	377	3.3	4.0
165 CH OF NAZARENE	1	22	93	.8	1.0
167 CHS OF CHRIST	1	28	50	.4	.5
207 E.L.C.A.	9	2,777	3,569	30.8	37.6
221 FREE METHODIST	1	31	46	.4	.5
283 LUTH—MO SYNOD	2	711	903	7.8	9.5
355 PRESB CH (USA)	4	877	1,099*	9.5	11.6
449 UN METHODIST	4	1,085	1,360*	11.8	14.3
FAYETTE	**58**	**9,399**	**17,850***	**81.7**	**100.0**
019 AMER BAPT USA	2	423	534*	2.4	3.0
040 AP CHR CH-AMER	1	41	71	.3	.4
053 ASSEMB OF GOD	1	61	147	.7	.8
081 CATHOLIC	7	NA	5,391	24.7	30.2
081d *LATIN*	*7*	*NA*	*5,391*	*24.7*	*30.2*
097 CHR CHS&CHS CR	2	180	227*	1.0	1.3
151 L-D SAINTS	1	NA	127	.6	.7
163 CH OF LUTH BR	1	105	195	.9	1.1
167 CHS OF CHRIST	1	19	34	.2	.2
193 EPISCOPAL	2	14	15	.1	.1
207 E.L.C.A.	12	4,187	5,441	24.9	30.5
263 INT FOURSQ GOS	1	26	33*	.2	.2
283 LUTH—MO SYNOD	3	726	940	4.3	5.3
284 LUTH CH-AM ASC	1	53	62	.3	.3
313 N AM BAPT CONF	1	147	185*	.8	1.0
353 CHR BRETHREN	1	35	50	.2	.3
355 PRESB CH (USA)	4	957	1,207*	5.5	6.8
413 S.D.A.	1	45	57*	.3	.3
449 UN METHODIST	14	2,268	2,861*	13.1	16.0
467 WESLEYAN	2	112	273	1.2	1.5
FLOYD	**29**	**5,723**	**10,306***	**60.4**	**100.0**
019 AMER BAPT USA	1	257	322*	1.9	3.1
053 ASSEMB OF GOD	1	26	32	.2	.3

County and Denomination	Number of churches	Communicant, confirmed, full members	Total adherents		
			Number	Percent of total population	Percent of total adherents
081 CATHOLIC	3	NA	2,793	16.4	27.1
081d *LATIN*	*3*	*NA*	*2,793*	*16.4*	*27.1*
089 CHR & MISS AL	1	94	198	1.2	1.9
093 CHR CH (DISC)	2	147	263	1.5	2.6
193 EPISCOPAL	1	34	45	.3	.4
207 E.L.C.A.	5	2,080	2,652	15.5	25.7
355 PRESB CH (USA)	1	170	213*	1.2	2.1
413 S.D.A.	1	12	15*	.1	.1
443 UN C OF CHRIST	2	521	652*	3.8	6.3
449 UN METHODIST	7	2,172	2,718*	15.9	26.4
467 WESLEYAN	3	141	317	1.9	3.1
469 WELS	1	69	86	.5	.8
FRANKLIN	**35**	**5,871**	**8,596***	**75.6**	**100.0**
019 AMER BAPT USA	1	91	114*	1.0	1.3
053 ASSEMB OF GOD	1	108	113	1.0	1.3
057 BAPT GEN CONF	1	91	114*	1.0	1.3
081 CATHOLIC	4	NA	1,004	8.8	11.7
081d *LATIN*	*4*	*NA*	*1,004*	*8.8*	*11.7*
093 CHR CH (DISC)	1	131	222	2.0	2.6
097 CHR CHS&CHS CR	1	167	210*	1.8	2.4
111 CH CR,SCIENTST	1	NR	NR	-	-
207 E.L.C.A.	4	1,155	1,466	12.9	17.1
283 LUTH—MO SYNOD	2	884	1,087	9.6	12.6
313 N AM BAPT CONF	1	61	77*	.7	.9
371 REF CH IN AM	2	392	681	6.0	7.9
413 S.D.A.	1	25	31*	.3	.4
443 UN C OF CHRIST	3	863	1,085*	9.5	12.6
449 UN METHODIST	12	1,903	2,392*	21.0	27.8
FREMONT	**28**	**2,720**	**4,402***	**53.5**	**100.0**
019 AMER BAPT USA	1	224	281*	3.4	6.4
053 ASSEMB OF GOD	1	32	90	1.1	2.0
081 CATHOLIC	2	NA	866	10.5	19.7
081d *LATIN*	*2*	*NA*	*866*	*10.5*	*19.7*
097 CHR CHS&CHS CR	4	292	366*	4.4	8.3
165 CH OF NAZARENE	1	84	156	1.9	3.5
176 CCC, NOT NAT'L	1	75	94*	1.1	2.1
221 FREE METHODIST	1	28	34	.4	.8
283 LUTH—MO SYNOD	1	69	112	1.4	2.5
355 PRESB CH (USA)	3	323	405*	4.9	9.2
443 UN C OF CHRIST	4	287	360*	4.4	8.2
449 UN METHODIST	9	1,306	1,638*	19.9	37.2
GREENE	**31**	**4,532**	**7,717***	**76.8**	**100.0**
019 AMER BAPT USA	2	322	400*	4.0	5.2
053 ASSEMB OF GOD	1	72	160	1.6	2.1
081 CATHOLIC	6	NA	1,674	16.7	21.7
081d *LATIN*	*6*	*NA*	*1,674*	*16.7*	*21.7*
093 CHR CH (DISC)	1	350	700	7.0	9.1
097 CHR CHS&CHS CR	1	125	155*	1.5	2.0
167 CHS OF CHRIST	1	70	91	.9	1.2
207 E.L.C.A.	1	46	82	.8	1.1
226 FRIENDS-USA	2	259	322*	3.2	4.2
226e *FUM*	*2*	*259*	*322**	*3.2*	*4.2*
283 LUTH—MO SYNOD	2	512	684	6.8	8.9
329 OPEN BIBLE STD	1	NR	NR	-	-
355 PRESB CH (USA)	3	350	435*	4.3	5.6
449 UN METHODIST	10	2,426	3,014*	30.0	39.1
GRUNDY	**36**	**6,819**	**9,220***	**76.6**	**100.0**
053 ASSEMB OF GOD	2	77	120	1.0	1.3
081 CATHOLIC	4	NA	256	2.1	2.8
081d *LATIN*	*4*	*NA*	*256*	*2.1*	*2.8*
105 CHRISTIAN REF	4	571	849	7.1	9.2
157 CH OF BRETHREN	1	210	262*	2.2	2.8
171 CH GOD-GEN CON	1	85	106*	.9	1.1
207 E.L.C.A.	3	1,032	1,367	11.4	14.8
283 LUTH—MO SYNOD	2	343	424	3.5	4.6
353 CHR BRETHREN	1	25	50	.4	.5
355 PRESB CH (USA)	5	1,190	1,487*	12.4	16.1
356 PRESB CH AMER	1	269	357	3.0	3.9
371 REF CH IN AM	3	639	963	8.0	10.4
438 UN BRETH IN CR	1	2	10	.1	.1
443 UN C OF CHRIST	2	660	825*	6.9	8.9
449 UN METHODIST	6	1,716	2,144*	17.8	23.3
GUTHRIE	**36**	**3,614**	**5,773***	**52.8**	**100.0**
053 ASSEMB OF GOD	1	34	45	.4	.8
081 CATHOLIC	6	NA	1,107	10.1	19.2
081d *LATIN*	*6*	*NA*	*1,107*	*10.1*	*19.2*
093 CHR CH (DISC)	3	350	516	4.7	8.9
097 CHR CHS&CHS CR	4	237	294*	2.7	5.1
157 CH OF BRETHREN	1	215	267*	2.4	4.6
167 CHS OF CHRIST	1	14	18	.2	.3

NA–Not applicable   NR–Not reported   *Total adherents estimated from known number of communicant, confirmed, full members.   - Represents a percent less than 0.1.   Percentages may not total due to rounding.
[1]See Appendix E   [2]See Appendix F   [3]See Appendix G   Lines in *italic* represent a breakdown of Catholic rites or Friends affiliations. They are included in their respective denominational total.

147

Table 4. Churches and Church Membership by County and Denomination: 1990

County and Denomination	Number of churches	Communicant, confirmed, full members	Total adherents Number	Total adherents Percent of total population	Total adherents Percent of total adherents
176 CCC, NOT NAT'L	1	44	55*	.5	1.0
283 LUTH—MO SYNOD	4	705	926	8.5	16.0
329 OPEN BIBLE STD	1	NR	NR		
355 PRESB CH (USA)	1	93	116*	1.1	2.0
413 S.D.A.	1	37	46*	.4	.8
449 UN METHODIST	11	1,862	2,313*	21.2	40.1
467 WESLEYAN	1	23	70	.6	1.2
HAMILTON	**36**	**7,793**	**12,346***	**76.8**	**100.0**
019 AMER BAPT USA	1	331	413*	2.6	3.3
053 ASSEMB OF GOD	1	50	75	.5	.6
057 BAPT GEN CONF	1	82	102*	.6	.8
081 CATHOLIC	3	NA	2,214	13.8	17.9
081d LATIN	3	NA	2,214	13.8	17.9
089 CHR & MISS AL	1	102	304	1.9	2.5
093 CHR CH (DISC)	1	73	125	.8	1.0
097 CHR CHS&CHS CR	2	440	549*	3.4	4.4
193 EPISCOPAL	1	48	62	.4	.5
207 E.L.C.A.	7	2,922	3,756	23.4	30.4
220 FREE LUTHERAN	1	133	137	.9	1.1
283 LUTH—MO SYNOD	1	508	687	4.3	5.6
353 CHR BRETHREN	2	100	175	1.1	1.4
355 PRESB CH (USA)	1	113	141*	.9	1.1
443 UN C OF CHRIST	3	773	964*	6.0	7.8
449 UN METHODIST	10	2,118	2,642*	16.4	21.4
HANCOCK	**36**	**6,023**	**10,128***	**80.1**	**100.0**
019 AMER BAPT USA	1	40	51*	.4	.5
081 CATHOLIC	5	NA	2,232	17.7	22.0
081d LATIN	5	NA	2,232	17.7	22.0
105 CHRISTIAN REF	4	514	709	5.6	7.0
165 CH OF NAZARENE	1	130	130	1.0	1.3
203 EVAN FREE CH	2	195	272	2.2	2.7
207 E.L.C.A.	7	1,277	1,647	13.0	16.3
283 LUTH—MO SYNOD	2	733	1,044	8.3	10.3
284 LUTH CH-AM ASC	1	36	64	.5	.6
355 PRESB CH (USA)	2	251	322*	2.5	3.2
373 REF CH IN U.S.	1	151	196	1.6	1.9
443 UN C OF CHRIST	3	716	919*	7.3	9.1
449 UN METHODIST	7	1,980	2,542*	20.1	25.1
HARDIN	**50**	**10,277**	**14,398***	**75.4**	**100.0**
019 AMER BAPT USA	1	83	102*	.5	.7
053 ASSEMB OF GOD	1	43	65	.3	.5
081 CATHOLIC	3	NA	1,234	6.5	8.6
081d LATIN	3	NA	1,234	6.5	8.6
093 CHR CH (DISC)	3	381	675	3.5	4.7
097 CHR CHS&CHS CR	1	60	74*	.4	.5
105 CHRISTIAN REF	2	119	179	.9	1.2
123 CH GOD (ANDER)	1	16	20	.1	.1
165 CH OF NAZARENE	1	35	70	.4	.5
193 EPISCOPAL	1	36	37	.2	.3
203 EVAN FREE CH	1	88	140	.7	1.0
207 E.L.C.A.	4	1,052	1,330	7.0	9.2
220 FREE LUTHERAN	2	234	306	1.6	2.1
226 FRIENDS-USA	2	437	538*	2.8	3.7
226e FUM	2	437	538*	2.8	3.7
283 LUTH—MO SYNOD	5	1,956	2,455	12.9	17.1
313 N AM BAPT CONF	1	255	314*	1.6	2.2
329 OPEN BIBLE STD	1	NR	NR	-	-
355 PRESB CH (USA)	3	407	501*	2.6	3.5
356 PRESB CH AMER	2	240	294	1.5	2.0
371 REF CH IN AM	1	161	309	1.6	2.1
443 UN C OF CHRIST	6	1,945	2,395*	12.5	16.6
449 UN METHODIST	8	2,729	3,360*	17.6	23.3
HARRISON	**37**	**4,350**	**8,476***	**57.5**	**100.0**
019 AMER BAPT USA	1	50	63*	.4	.7
053 ASSEMB OF GOD	2	83	240	1.6	2.8
081 CATHOLIC	5	NA	2,443	16.6	28.8
081d LATIN	5	NA	2,443	16.6	28.8
093 CHR CH (DISC)	1	185	298	2.0	3.5
097 CHR CHS&CHS CR	6	1,091	1,381*	9.4	16.3
151 L-D SAINTS	1	NA	137	.9	1.6
165 CH OF NAZARENE	1	57	115	.8	1.4
179 CONSRV BAPT	1	NR	NR	-	-
207 E.L.C.A.	3	580	813	5.5	9.6
283 LUTH—MO SYNOD	4	703	960	6.5	11.3
355 PRESB CH (USA)	2	188	238*	1.6	2.8
449 UN METHODIST	10	1,413	1,788*	12.1	21.1
HENRY	**41**	**6,090**	**9,316***	**48.5**	**100.0**
019 AMER BAPT USA	3	521	649*	3.4	7.0
053 ASSEMB OF GOD	1	23	34	.2	.4
081 CATHOLIC	1	NA	1,265	6.6	13.6
081d LATIN	1	NA	1,265	6.6	13.6
097 CHR CHS&CHS CR	2	238	296*	1.5	3.2
111 CH CR,SCIENTST	1	NR	NR	-	-
151 L-D SAINTS	1	NA	314	1.6	3.4
165 CH OF NAZARENE	1	28	43	.2	.5
171 CH GOD-GEN CON	1	39	49*	.3	.5
175 CONGR CHR CHS	1	79	98*	.5	1.1
193 EPISCOPAL	1	146	197	1.0	2.1
203 EVAN FREE CH	1	49	61	.3	.7
207 E.L.C.A.	1	416	569	3.0	6.1
226 FRIENDS-USA	2	159	198*	1.0	2.1
226e FUM	2	159	198*	1.0	2.1
283 LUTH—MO SYNOD	1	272	401	2.1	4.3
285 MENNONITE CH	3	456	604	3.1	6.5
287 MENN GEN CONF	2	277	320	1.7	3.4
291 MISSIONARY CH	2	41	52	.3	.6
329 OPEN BIBLE STD	2	NR	NR	-	-
355 PRESB CH (USA)	3	720	896*	4.7	9.6
419 SO BAPT CONV	1	69	86*	.4	.9
443 UN C OF CHRIST	1	203	253*	1.3	2.7
449 UN METHODIST	9	2,354	2,931*	15.2	31.5
HOWARD	**25**	**2,962**	**8,865***	**90.4**	**100.0**
019 AMER BAPT USA	1	39	50*	.5	.6
053 ASSEMB OF GOD	1	33	31	.3	.3
081 CATHOLIC	8	NA	5,087	51.9	57.4
081d LATIN	8	NA	5,087	51.9	57.4
207 E.L.C.A.	6	1,712	2,195	22.4	24.8
283 LUTH—MO SYNOD	1	142	187	1.9	2.1
355 PRESB CH (USA)	1	41	52*	.5	.6
443 UN C OF CHRIST	1	70	89*	.9	1.0
449 UN METHODIST	6	925	1,174*	12.0	13.2
HUMBOLDT	**22**	**5,818**	**8,804***	**81.9**	**100.0**
019 AMER BAPT USA	1	74	93*	.9	1.1
057 BAPT GEN CONF	1	244	306*	2.8	3.5
081 CATHOLIC	2	NA	1,381	12.8	15.7
081d LATIN	2	NA	1,381	12.8	15.7
207 E.L.C.A.	8	2,473	3,117	29.0	35.4
283 LUTH—MO SYNOD	2	740	999	9.3	11.3
413 S.D.A.	1	25	31*	.3	.4
443 UN C OF CHRIST	1	402	503*	4.7	5.7
449 UN METHODIST	5	1,774	2,221*	20.6	25.2
467 WESLEYAN	1	86	153	1.4	1.7
IDA	**15**	**4,447**	**6,926***	**82.8**	**100.0**
081 CATHOLIC	2	NA	1,184	14.2	17.1
081d LATIN	2	NA	1,184	14.2	17.1
171 CH GOD-GEN CON	1	139	178*	2.1	2.6
203 EVAN FREE CH	1	117	176	2.1	2.5
207 E.L.C.A.	1	696	903	10.8	13.0
283 LUTH—MO SYNOD	3	1,641	2,106	25.2	30.4
355 PRESB CH (USA)	2	590	757*	9.0	10.9
449 UN METHODIST	5	1,264	1,622*	19.4	23.4
IOWA	**34**	**5,787**	**9,846***	**67.3**	**100.0**
081 CATHOLIC	6	NA	2,300	15.7	23.4
081d LATIN	6	NA	2,300	15.7	23.4
093 CHR CH (DISC)	1	111	268	1.8	2.7
165 CH OF NAZARENE	1	35	76	.5	.8
203 EVAN FREE CH	1	9	27	.2	.3
207 E.L.C.A.	1	150	219	1.5	2.2
283 LUTH—MO SYNOD	8	2,903	3,748	25.6	38.1
285 MENNONITE CH	2	340	387	2.6	3.9
313 N AM BAPT CONF	1	88	111*	.8	1.1
355 PRESB CH (USA)	2	616	776*	5.3	7.9
443 UN C OF CHRIST	1	183	231*	1.6	2.3
449 UN METHODIST	10	1,352	1,703*	11.6	17.3
JACKSON	**36**	**4,724**	**10,867***	**54.5**	**100.0**
019 AMER BAPT USA	1	144	184*	.9	1.7
053 ASSEMB OF GOD	1	17	23	.1	.2
081 CATHOLIC	13	NA	4,494	22.5	41.4
081d LATIN	13	NA	4,494	22.5	41.4
193 EPISCOPAL	1	46	151	.8	1.4
207 E.L.C.A.	8	2,844	3,842	19.3	35.4
283 LUTH—MO SYNOD	1	83	143	.7	1.3
355 PRESB CH (USA)	3	412	526*	2.6	4.8
443 UN C OF CHRIST	3	376	480*	2.4	4.4
449 UN METHODIST	5	802	1,024*	5.1	9.4
JASPER	**62**	**11,586**	**18,621***	**53.5**	**100.0**
019 AMER BAPT USA	1	492	613*	1.8	3.3
053 ASSEMB OF GOD	2	300	606	1.7	3.3
081 CATHOLIC	3	NA	2,770	8.0	14.9

NA–Not applicable NR–Not reported *Total adherents estimated from known number of communicant, confirmed, full members. - Represents a percent less than 0.1. Percentages may not total due to rounding.
[1]See Appendix E [2]See Appendix F [3]See Appendix G Lines in *italic* represent a breakdown of Catholic rites or Friends affiliations. They are included in their respective denominational total.

Table 4. Churches and Church Membership by County and Denomination: 1990

County and Denomination	Number of churches	Communicant, confirmed, full members	Total adherents Number	Total adherents Percent of total population	Total adherents Percent of total adherents
081d *LATIN*	3	*NA*	*2,770*	*8.0*	*14.9*
089 CHR & MISS AL	1	216	700	2.0	3.8
093 CHR CH (DISC)	5	980	1,376	4.0	7.4
105 CHRISTIAN REF	3	878	1,386	4.0	7.4
127 CH GOD (CLEVE)	2	87	108*	.3	.6
157 CH OF BRETHREN	1	165	206*	.6	1.1
165 CH OF NAZARENE	1	136	213	.6	1.1
167 CHS OF CHRIST	3	49	59	.2	.3
179 CONSRV BAPT	1	NR	NR	-	-
193 EPISCOPAL	1	104	139	.4	.7
203 EVAN FREE CH	1	55	68	.2	.4
207 E.L.C.A.	4	1,048	1,255	3.6	6.7
226 FRIENDS-USA	2	196	244*	.7	1.3
226e *FUM*	2	*196*	*244**	*.7*	*1.3*
259 IFCA	1	NR	NR	-	-
263 INT FOURSQ GOS	1	260	324*	.9	1.7
283 LUTH—MO SYNOD	1	316	404	1.2	2.2
355 PRESB CH (USA)	4	912	1,137*	3.3	6.1
371 REF CH IN AM	3	840	1,359	3.9	7.3
403 SALVATION ARMY	1	131	137	.4	.7
413 S.D.A.	1	43	54*	.2	.3
419 SO BAPT CONV	2	65	81*	.2	.4
443 UN C OF CHRIST	4	1,113	1,388*	4.0	7.5
449 UN METHODIST	12	3,155	3,934*	11.3	21.1
469 WELS	1	45	60	.2	.3
JEFFERSON	**29**	**4,251**	**7,120***	**43.7**	**100.0**
019 AMER BAPT USA	3	540	671*	4.1	9.4
053 ASSEMB OF GOD	1	31	75	.5	1.1
081 CATHOLIC	2	NA	1,364	8.4	19.2
081d *LATIN*	2	*NA*	*1,364*	*8.4*	*19.2*
093 CHR CH (DISC)	2	420	759	4.7	10.7
097 CHR CHS&CHS CR	1	0	0*	-	-
151 L-D SAINTS	1	NA	121	.7	1.7
157 CH OF BRETHREN	1	60	75*	.5	1.1
165 CH OF NAZARENE	1	92	126	.8	1.8
193 EPISCOPAL	1	12	12	.1	.2
207 E.L.C.A.	2	711	941	5.8	13.2
221 FREE METHODIST	1	107	107	.7	1.5
226 FRIENDS-USA	2	183	227*	1.4	3.2
226e *FUM*	2	*183*	*227**	*1.4*	*3.2*
263 INT FOURSQ GOS	1	175	217*	1.3	3.0
283 LUTH—MO SYNOD	1	124	193	1.2	2.7
355 PRESB CH (USA)	1	372	462*	2.8	6.5
413 S.D.A.	1	30	37*	.2	.5
443 UN C OF CHRIST	1	53	66*	.4	.9
449 UN METHODIST	6	1,341	1,667*	10.2	23.4
JOHNSON	**81**	**14,901**	**35,552***	**37.0**	**100.0**
019 AMER BAPT USA	1	208	249*	.3	.7
040 AP CHR CH-AMER	1	18	33	-	.1
053 ASSEMB OF GOD	2	148	264	.3	.7
057 BAPT GEN CONF	1	157	188*	.2	.5
061 BEACHY AMISH	1	127	152*	.2	.4
081 CATHOLIC	12	NA	13,559	14.1	38.1
081d *LATIN*	12	*NA*	*13,559*	*14.1*	*38.1*
089 CHR & MISS AL	1	0	14	-	-
093 CHR CH (DISC)	1	219	233	.2	.7
097 CHR CHS&CHS CR	2	110	132*	.1	.4
105 CHRISTIAN REF	2	133	191	.2	.5
111 CH CR,SCIENTST	1	NR	NR	-	-
151 L-D SAINTS	1	NA	596	.6	1.7
165 CH OF NAZARENE	1	151	147	.2	.4
167 CHS OF CHRIST	1	82	104	.1	.3
171 CH GOD-GEN CON	1	32	38*	-	.1
193 EPISCOPAL	2	526	634	.7	1.8
203 EVAN FREE CH	1	200	580	.6	1.6
207 E.L.C.A.	3	2,783	3,805	4.0	10.7
221 FREE METHODIST	1	23	40	-	.1
226 FRIENDS-USA	1	28	34*	-	.1
226a *CONSERV*	1	*28*	*34**	-	*.1*
263 INT FOURSQ GOS	1	27	32*	-	.1
283 LUTH—MO SYNOD	4	1,002	1,358	1.4	3.8
285 MENNONITE CH	6	1,134	1,483	1.5	4.2
291 MISSIONARY CH	1	22	15	-	-
323 OLD ORD AMISH	7	NA	1,050	1.1	3.0
355 PRESB CH (USA)	4	1,924	2,306*	2.4	6.5
356 PRESB CH AMER	1	24	46	-	.1
403 SALVATION ARMY	1	13	22	-	.1
413 S.D.A.	1	59	71*	.1	.2
419 SO BAPT CONV	2	413	495*	.5	1.4
435 UNITARIAN-UNIV	1	248	380	.4	1.1
443 UN C OF CHRIST	3	473	567*	.6	1.6
449 UN METHODIST	10	4,094	4,907*	5.1	13.8
496 JEWISH EST[1]	2	NA	1,200	1.2	3.4
497 BLACK BAPT EST[2]	NA	523	627*	.7	1.8

County and Denomination	Number of churches	Communicant, confirmed, full members	Total adherents Number	Total adherents Percent of total population	Total adherents Percent of total adherents
JONES	**39**	**6,245**	**12,331***	**63.4**	**100.0**
019 AMER BAPT USA	1	135	169*	.9	1.4
053 ASSEMB OF GOD	1	19	34	.2	.3
081 CATHOLIC	6	NA	4,278	22.0	34.7
081d *LATIN*	6	*NA*	*4,278*	*22.0*	*34.7*
097 CHR CHS&CHS CR	1	0	0*	-	-
157 CH OF BRETHREN	1	115	144*	.7	1.2
165 CH OF NAZARENE	1	51	52	.3	.4
193 EPISCOPAL	1	18	22	.1	.2
207 E.L.C.A.	7	2,559	3,423	17.6	27.8
259 IFCA	1	NR	NR	-	-
263 INT FOURSQ GOS	1	9	11*	.1	.1
283 LUTH—MO SYNOD	1	353	468	2.4	3.8
355 PRESB CH (USA)	4	545	681*	3.5	5.5
419 SO BAPT CONV	1	59	74*	.4	.6
443 UN C OF CHRIST	3	832	1,039*	5.3	8.4
449 UN METHODIST	9	1,550	1,936*	10.0	15.7
KEOKUK	**42**	**3,237**	**6,805***	**58.5**	**100.0**
019 AMER BAPT USA	3	150	189*	1.6	2.8
053 ASSEMB OF GOD	1	8	16	.1	.2
081 CATHOLIC	8	NA	2,573	22.1	37.8
081d *LATIN*	8	*NA*	*2,573*	*22.1*	*37.8*
093 CHR CH (DISC)	6	380	572	4.9	8.4
157 CH OF BRETHREN	1	20	25*	.2	.4
207 E.L.C.A.	1	66	83	.7	1.2
215 EVAN METH CH	1	8	10*	.1	.1
226 FRIENDS-USA	2	233	294*	2.5	4.3
226e *FUM*	2	*233*	*294**	*2.5*	*4.3*
283 LUTH—MO SYNOD	1	104	161	1.4	2.4
285 MENNONITE CH	1	69	106	.9	1.6
355 PRESB CH (USA)	4	506	639*	5.5	9.4
449 UN METHODIST	13	1,693	2,137*	18.4	31.4
KOSSUTH	**43**	**7,367**	**16,804***	**90.4**	**100.0**
019 AMER BAPT USA	1	58	74*	.4	.4
053 ASSEMB OF GOD	1	60	108	.6	.6
057 BAPT GEN CONF	1	128	164*	.9	1.0
081 CATHOLIC	7	NA	7,245	39.0	43.1
081d *LATIN*	7	*NA*	*7,245*	*39.0*	*43.1*
179 CONSRV BAPT	1	NR	NR	-	-
193 EPISCOPAL	1	94	135	.7	.8
203 EVAN FREE CH	2	75	116	.6	.7
207 E.L.C.A.	4	1,469	1,927	10.4	11.5
283 LUTH—MO SYNOD	7	2,101	2,684	14.4	16.0
329 OPEN BIBLE STD	1	NR	NR	-	-
355 PRESB CH (USA)	5	637	816*	4.4	4.9
371 REF CH IN AM	1	236	319	1.7	1.9
443 UN C OF CHRIST	2	565	724*	3.9	4.3
449 UN METHODIST	9	1,944	2,492*	13.4	14.8
LEE	**64**	**10,557**	**24,185***	**62.5**	**100.0**
019 AMER BAPT USA	2	1,235	1,550*	4.0	6.4
053 ASSEMB OF GOD	3	347	709	1.8	2.9
081 CATHOLIC	9	NA	9,637	24.9	39.8
081d *LATIN*	9	*NA*	*9,637*	*24.9*	*39.8*
093 CHR CH (DISC)	2	706	1,355	3.5	5.6
097 CHR CHS&CHS CR	2	720	904*	2.3	3.7
111 CH CR,SCIENTST	1	NR	NR	-	-
165 CH OF NAZARENE	3	250	447	1.2	1.8
167 CHS OF CHRIST	3	46	87	.2	.4
193 EPISCOPAL	2	250	340	.9	1.4
203 EVAN FREE CH	1	110	180	.5	.7
207 E.L.C.A.	2	621	803	2.1	3.3
263 INT FOURSQ GOS	2	68	85*	.2	.4
283 LUTH—MO SYNOD	2	158	199	.5	.8
285 MENNONITE CH	1	13	40	.1	.2
287 MENN GEN CONF	1	144	181	.5	.7
355 PRESB CH (USA)	6	691	867*	2.2	3.6
403 SALVATION ARMY	1	88	88	.2	.4
413 S.D.A.	2	91	114*	.3	.5
419 SO BAPT CONV	3	943	1,183*	3.1	4.9
443 UN C OF CHRIST	6	1,563	1,962*	5.1	8.1
449 UN METHODIST	9	2,275	2,855*	7.4	11.8
497 BLACK BAPT EST[2]	NA	238	299*	.8	1.2
499 INDEP.NON-CHAR[3]	1	NA	300	.8	1.2
LINN	**160**	**39,476**	**95,066***	**56.3**	**100.0**
019 AMER BAPT USA	4	908	1,133*	.7	1.2
053 ASSEMB OF GOD	2	608	1,480	.9	1.6
057 BAPT GEN CONF	2	270	337*	.2	.4
081 CATHOLIC	19	NA	38,980	23.1	41.0
081d *LATIN*	19	*NA*	*38,980*	*23.1*	*41.0*
089 CHR & MISS AL	1	38	91	.1	.1
093 CHR CH (DISC)	7	1,665	3,010	1.8	3.2

NA–Not applicable   NR–Not reported   *Total adherents estimated from known number of communicant, confirmed, full members.   - Represents a percent less than 0.1.   Percentages may not total due to rounding.

[1]See Appendix E   [2]See Appendix F   [3]See Appendix G   Lines in *italic* represent a breakdown of Catholic rites or Friends affiliations. They are included in their respective denominational total.

149

Table 4. Churches and Church Membership by County and Denomination: 1990

County and Denomination	Number of churches	Communicant, confirmed, full members	Total adherents Number	Percent of total population	Percent of total adherents
097 CHR CHS&CHS CR	3	380	474*	.3	.5
105 CHRISTIAN REF	1	99	171	.1	.2
111 CH CR,SCIENTST	1	NR	NR	-	-
123 CH GOD (ANDER)	1	100	110	.1	.1
127 CH GOD (CLEVE)	1	50	62*	-	.1
133 CH GOD(7TH)DEN	1	59	73	-	.1
145 CH GOD PROPHCY	1	22	27*	-	-
151 L-D SAINTS	3	NA	930	.6	1.0
157 CH OF BRETHREN	2	90	112*	.1	.1
165 CH OF NAZARENE	3	735	1,226	.7	1.3
167 CHS OF CHRIST	3	222	279	.2	.3
175 CONGR CHR CHS	1	77	96*	.1	.1
179 CONSRV BAPT	3	NR	NR	-	-
193 EPISCOPAL	3	579	942	.6	1.0
203 EVAN FREE CH	1	97	190	.1	.2
207 E.L.C.A.	13	7,456	10,051	6.0	10.6
221 FREE METHODIST	3	153	179	.1	.2
226 FRIENDS-USA	2	101	126*	.1	.1
226a CONSERV	1	65	81*	-	.1
226e FUM	1	36	45*	-	-
246 GREEK ORTHODOX	1	NR	NR	-	-
259 IFCA	1	NR	NR	-	-
263 INT FOURSQ GOS	2	355	443*	.3	.5
283 LUTH—MO SYNOD	9	4,886	6,335	3.8	6.7
313 N AM BAPT CONF	1	52	65*	-	.1
329 OPEN BIBLE STD	1	NR	NR	-	-
353 CHR BRETHREN	2	52	95	.1	.1
355 PRESB CH (USA)	15	5,161	6,440*	3.8	6.8
356 PRESB CH AMER	1	54	54	-	.1
371 REF CH IN AM	1	170	325	.2	.3
403 SALVATION ARMY	1	138	155	.1	.2
413 S.D.A.	2	406	507*	.3	.5
419 SO BAPT CONV	1	798	996*	.6	1.0
435 UNITARIAN-UNIV	1	271	361	.2	.4
443 UN C OF CHRIST	4	1,471	1,835*	1.1	1.9
449 UN METHODIST	27	10,555	13,170*	7.8	13.9
467 WESLEYAN	2	296	611	.4	.6
469 WELS	1	221	316	.2	.3
496 JEWISH EST[1]	2	NA	430	.3	.5
497 BLACK BAPT EST[2]	NA	881	1,099*	.7	1.2
499 INDEP.NON-CHAR[3]	4	NA	1,750	1.0	1.8
LOUISA	**21**	**2,948**	**4,467***	**38.5**	**100.0**
040 AP CHR CH-AMER	1	226	401	3.5	9.0
081 CATHOLIC	2	NA	590	5.1	13.2
081d LATIN	2	NA	590	5.1	13.2
165 CH OF NAZARENE	1	38	52	.4	1.2
171 CH GOD-GEN CON	2	87	110*	.9	2.5
221 FREE METHODIST	1	34	50	.4	1.1
259 IFCA	1	NR	NR	-	-
283 LUTH—MO SYNOD	1	93	135	1.2	3.0
355 PRESB CH (USA)	5	728	922*	8.0	20.6
449 UN METHODIST	7	1,742	2,207*	19.0	49.4
LUCAS	**23**	**2,667**	**4,569***	**50.4**	**100.0**
019 AMER BAPT USA	1	596	738*	8.1	16.2
053 ASSEMB OF GOD	3	73	212	2.3	4.6
081 CATHOLIC	1	NA	787	8.7	17.2
081d LATIN	1	NA	787	8.7	17.2
093 CHR CH (DISC)	2	244	404	4.5	8.8
127 CH GOD (CLEVE)	1	21	26*	.3	.6
165 CH OF NAZARENE	1	224	481	5.3	10.5
167 CHS OF CHRIST	1	20	25	.3	.5
193 EPISCOPAL	1	22	32	.4	.7
207 E.L.C.A.	1	285	401	4.4	8.8
226 FRIENDS-USA	1	51	63*	.7	1.4
226e FUM	1	51	63*	.7	1.4
259 IFCA	1	NR	NR	-	-
283 LUTH—MO SYNOD	1	0	0	-	-
355 PRESB CH (USA)	2	133	165*	1.8	3.6
449 UN METHODIST	6	998	1,235*	13.6	27.0
LYON	**36**	**5,770**	**9,558***	**80.0**	**100.0**
040 AP CHR CH-AMER	1	250	445	3.7	4.7
053 ASSEMB OF GOD	1	41	78	.7	.8
081 CATHOLIC	3	NA	1,100	9.2	11.5
081d LATIN	3	NA	1,100	9.2	11.5
093 CHR CH (DISC)	1	76	92	.8	1.0
105 CHRISTIAN REF	3	552	938	7.8	9.8
176 CCC, NOT NAT'L	1	60	79*	.7	.8
207 E.L.C.A.	5	1,275	1,649	13.8	17.3
283 LUTH—MO SYNOD	2	531	671	5.6	7.0
313 N AM BAPT CONF	3	326	429*	3.6	4.5
355 PRESB CH (USA)	4	728	958*	8.0	10.0
371 REF CH IN AM	6	1,192	2,146	18.0	22.5
443 UN C OF CHRIST	2	241	317*	2.7	3.3

County and Denomination	Number of churches	Communicant, confirmed, full members	Total adherents Number	Percent of total population	Percent of total adherents
449 UN METHODIST	4	498	656*	5.5	6.9
MADISON	**30**	**3,931**	**6,119***	**49.0**	**100.0**
081 CATHOLIC	2	NA	806	6.5	13.2
081d LATIN	2	NA	806	6.5	13.2
089 CHR & MISS AL	1	17	21	.2	.3
093 CHR CH (DISC)	3	467	842	6.7	13.8
097 CHR CHS&CHS CR	1	338	430*	3.4	7.0
145 CH GOD PROPHCY	1	22	28*	.2	.5
165 CH OF NAZARENE	1	49	116	.9	1.9
176 CCC, NOT NAT'L	1	36	46*	.4	.8
193 EPISCOPAL	1	12	12	.1	.2
207 E.L.C.A.	1	258	347	2.8	5.7
226 FRIENDS-USA	1	170	216*	1.7	3.5
226e FUM	1	170	216*	1.7	3.5
263 INT FOURSQ GOS	1	73	93*	.7	1.5
283 LUTH—MO SYNOD	1	277	350	2.8	5.7
355 PRESB CH (USA)	2	324	412*	3.3	6.7
413 S.D.A.	1	31	39*	.3	.6
419 SO BAPT CONV	1	295	375*	3.0	6.1
443 UN C OF CHRIST	1	68	86*	.7	1.4
449 UN METHODIST	10	1,494	1,900*	15.2	31.1
MAHASKA	**43**	**7,008**	**11,755***	**54.6**	**100.0**
019 AMER BAPT USA	2	128	161*	.7	1.4
053 ASSEMB OF GOD	2	379	672	3.1	5.7
081 CATHOLIC	1	NA	1,150	5.3	9.8
081d LATIN	1	NA	1,150	5.3	9.8
089 CHR & MISS AL	1	26	74	.3	.6
093 CHR CH (DISC)	3	550	1,187	5.5	10.1
097 CHR CHS&CHS CR	1	151	190*	.9	1.6
105 CHRISTIAN REF	6	1,218	1,906	8.9	16.2
165 CH OF NAZARENE	2	581	1,201	5.6	10.2
167 CHS OF CHRIST	1	38	45	.2	.4
193 EPISCOPAL	1	52	85	.4	.7
221 FREE METHODIST	1	37	39	.2	.3
226 FRIENDS-USA	2	370	466*	2.2	4.0
226e FUM	2	370	466*	2.2	4.0
259 IFCA	1	NR	NR	-	-
283 LUTH—MO SYNOD	1	254	322	1.5	2.7
329 OPEN BIBLE STD	1	NR	NR	-	-
353 CHR BRETHREN	1	60	80	.4	.7
355 PRESB CH (USA)	2	292	368*	1.7	3.1
371 REF CH IN AM	2	693	989	4.6	8.4
443 UN C OF CHRIST	1	235	296*	1.4	2.5
449 UN METHODIST	9	1,800	2,269*	10.5	19.3
467 WESLEYAN	1	11	60	.3	.5
469 WELS	1	133	195	.9	1.7
MARION	**58**	**10,692**	**17,719***	**59.1**	**100.0**
019 AMER BAPT USA	2	856	1,071*	3.6	6.0
053 ASSEMB OF GOD	3	134	258	.9	1.5
057 BAPT GEN CONF	1	31	39*	.1	.2
081 CATHOLIC	4	NA	2,558	8.5	14.4
081d LATIN	4	NA	2,558	8.5	14.4
089 CHR & MISS AL	1	35	35	.1	.2
093 CHR CH (DISC)	3	322	634	2.1	3.6
097 CHR CHS&CHS CR	3	661	827*	2.8	4.7
105 CHRISTIAN REF	5	2,007	2,991	10.0	16.9
127 CH GOD (CLEVE)	1	64	80*	.3	.5
151 L-D SAINTS	1	NA	108	.4	.6
165 CH OF NAZARENE	2	184	456	1.5	2.6
167 CHS OF CHRIST	1	40	58	.2	.3
207 E.L.C.A.	2	376	547	1.8	3.1
221 FREE METHODIST	1	28	28	.1	.2
259 IFCA	1	NR	NR	-	-
263 INT FOURSQ GOS	1	38	48*	.2	.3
283 LUTH—MO SYNOD	3	482	665	2.2	3.8
329 OPEN BIBLE STD	2	NR	NR	-	-
353 CHR BRETHREN	1	45	65	.2	.4
355 PRESB CH (USA)	1	210	263*	.9	1.5
371 REF CH IN AM	6	2,855	4,080	13.6	23.0
413 S.D.A.	1	95	119*	.4	.7
449 UN METHODIST	12	2,229	2,789*	9.3	15.7
MARSHALL	**63**	**12,823**	**22,062***	**57.6**	**100.0**
019 AMER BAPT USA	1	942	1,170*	3.1	5.3
053 ASSEMB OF GOD	1	117	156	.4	.7
081 CATHOLIC	5	NA	5,398	14.1	24.5
081d LATIN	5	NA	5,398	14.1	24.5
089 CHR & MISS AL	1	0	35	.1	.2
093 CHR CH (DISC)	3	757	1,102	2.9	5.0
097 CHR CHS&CHS CR	2	500	621*	1.6	2.8
123 CH GOD (ANDER)	1	35	35	.1	.2
151 L-D SAINTS	1	NA	201	.5	.9
157 CH OF BRETHREN	1	108	134*	.4	.6

NA–Not applicable   NR–Not reported   *Total adherents estimated from known number of communicant, confirmed, full members.   - Represents a percent less than 0.1.   Percentages may not total due to rounding.
[1] See Appendix E   [2] See Appendix F   [3] See Appendix G   Lines in *italic* represent a breakdown of Catholic rites or Friends affiliations. They are included in their respective denominational total.

Table 4. Churches and Church Membership by County and Denomination: 1990

County and Denomination	Number of churches	Communicant, confirmed, full members	Total adherents Number	Percent of total population	Percent of total adherents
165 CH OF NAZARENE	1	160	278	.7	1.3
167 CHS OF CHRIST	1	84	120	.3	.5
175 CONGR CHR CHS	2	502	624*	1.6	2.8
193 EPISCOPAL	1	156	209	.5	.9
207 E.L.C.A.	4	1,647	2,180	5.7	9.9
226 FRIENDS-USA	4	840	1,044*	2.7	4.7
226e FUM	*4*	*840*	*1,044**	*2.7*	*4.7*
283 LUTH—MO SYNOD	4	1,305	1,658	4.3	7.5
329 OPEN BIBLE STD	1	NR	NR	-	-
339 PENT CH OF GOD	2	69	153	.4	.7
355 PRESB CH (USA)	3	832	1,034*	2.7	4.7
403 SALVATION ARMY	1	150	185	.5	.8
413 S.D.A.	1	73	91*	.2	.4
419 SO BAPT CONV	1	44	55*	.1	.2
443 UN C OF CHRIST	7	890	1,106*	2.9	5.0
449 UN METHODIST	13	3,585	4,454*	11.6	20.2
467 WESLEYAN	1	27	19	-	.1
MILLS	**28**	**4,012**	**6,120***	**46.4**	**100.0**
019 AMER BAPT USA	3	628	793*	6.0	13.0
081 CATHOLIC	1	NA	927	7.0	15.1
081d LATIN	*1*	*NA*	*927*	*7.0*	*15.1*
093 CHR CH (DISC)	1	315	420	3.2	6.9
097 CHR CHS&CHS CR	1	150	189*	1.4	3.1
165 CH OF NAZARENE	1	47	86	.7	1.4
179 CONSRV BAPT	1	NR	NR	-	-
193 EPISCOPAL	1	10	17	.1	.3
203 EVAN FREE CH	1	45	115	.9	1.9
207 E.L.C.A.	1	366	465	3.5	7.6
263 INT FOURSQ GOS	1	12	15*	.1	.2
283 LUTH—MO SYNOD	2	465	602	4.6	9.8
355 PRESB CH (USA)	1	73	92*	.7	1.5
413 S.D.A.	1	15	19*	.1	.3
419 SO BAPT CONV	1	142	179*	1.4	2.9
443 UN C OF CHRIST	1	172	217*	1.6	3.5
449 UN METHODIST	10	1,572	1,984*	15.0	32.4
MITCHELL	**32**	**5,080**	**11,105***	**101.6**	**100.0**
019 AMER BAPT USA	3	208	261*	2.4	2.4
081 CATHOLIC	6	NA	4,131	37.8	37.2
081d LATIN	*6*	*NA*	*4,131*	*37.8*	*37.2*
089 CHR & MISS AL	1	80	230	2.1	2.1
207 E.L.C.A.	7	2,374	3,128	28.6	28.2
209 EVAN LUTH SYN	1	27	37	.3	.3
221 FREE METHODIST	1	12	26	.2	.2
283 LUTH—MO SYNOD	4	1,168	1,475	13.5	13.3
323 OLD ORD AMISH	2	NA	300	2.7	2.7
443 UN C OF CHRIST	3	396	496*	4.5	4.5
449 UN METHODIST	4	815	1,021*	9.3	9.2
MONONA	**28**	**4,229**	**6,752***	**67.3**	**100.0**
081 CATHOLIC	4	NA	1,362	13.6	20.2
081d LATIN	*4*	*NA*	*1,362*	*13.6*	*20.2*
093 CHR CH (DISC)	1	143	232	2.3	3.4
097 CHR CHS&CHS CR	3	640	790*	7.9	11.7
203 EVAN FREE CH	1	31	33	.3	.5
207 E.L.C.A.	3	936	1,281	12.8	19.0
283 LUTH—MO SYNOD	2	946	1,161	11.6	17.2
413 S.D.A.	2	47	58*	.6	.9
419 SO BAPT CONV	1	35	43*	.4	.6
443 UN C OF CHRIST	6	643	794*	7.9	11.8
449 UN METHODIST	5	808	998*	9.9	14.8
MONROE	**19**	**1,817**	**5,302***	**65.3**	**100.0**
019 AMER BAPT USA	1	28	35*	.4	.7
081 CATHOLIC	5	NA	2,902	35.8	54.7
081d LATIN	*5*	*NA*	*2,902*	*35.8*	*54.7*
093 CHR CH (DISC)	1	425	650	8.0	12.3
157 CH OF BRETHREN	1	20	25*	.3	.5
165 CH OF NAZARENE	1	28	35	.4	.7
193 EPISCOPAL	1	15	18	.2	.3
207 E.L.C.A.	1	164	204	2.5	3.8
329 OPEN BIBLE STD	1	NR	NR	-	-
353 CHR BRETHREN	1	6	20	.2	.4
413 S.D.A.	1	51	64*	.8	1.2
419 SO BAPT CONV	1	103	129*	1.6	2.4
449 UN METHODIST	3	970	1,210*	14.9	22.8
467 WESLEYAN	1	7	10	.1	.2
MONTGOMERY	**30**	**4,541**	**6,915***	**57.3**	**100.0**
001 ADVENT CHR CH	1	71	88*	.7	1.3
019 AMER BAPT USA	1	296	366*	3.0	5.3
053 ASSEMB OF GOD	1	49	89	.7	1.3
081 CATHOLIC	2	NA	799	6.6	11.6
081d LATIN	*2*	*NA*	*799*	*6.6*	*11.6*

County and Denomination	Number of churches	Communicant, confirmed, full members	Total adherents Number	Percent of total population	Percent of total adherents
089 CHR & MISS AL	1	28	78	.6	1.1
093 CHR CH (DISC)	1	212	434	3.6	6.3
097 CHR CHS&CHS CR	2	175	217*	1.8	3.1
145 CH GOD PROPHCY	1	22	27*	.2	.4
151 L-D SAINTS	1	NA	121	1.0	1.7
165 CH OF NAZARENE	1	70	223	1.8	3.2
193 EPISCOPAL	1	21	25	.2	.4
207 E.L.C.A.	3	1,300	1,574	13.0	22.8
283 LUTH—MO SYNOD	2	223	307	2.5	4.4
355 PRESB CH (USA)	3	473	585*	4.8	8.5
443 UN C OF CHRIST	1	97	120*	1.0	1.7
449 UN METHODIST	8	1,504	1,862*	15.4	26.9
MUSCATINE	**61**	**10,452**	**19,036***	**47.7**	**100.0**
019 AMER BAPT USA	1	678	870*	2.2	4.6
053 ASSEMB OF GOD	3	132	284	.7	1.5
057 BAPT GEN CONF	2	99	127*	.3	.7
081 CATHOLIC	7	NA	4,953	12.4	26.0
081d LATIN	*7*	*NA*	*4,953*	*12.4*	*26.0*
093 CHR CH (DISC)	3	609	748	1.9	3.9
097 CHR CHS&CHS CR	1	30	38*	.1	.2
127 CH GOD (CLEVE)	1	47	60*	.2	.3
151 L-D SAINTS	1	NA	258	.6	1.4
165 CH OF NAZARENE	1	58	125	.3	.7
167 CHS OF CHRIST	1	100	130	.3	.7
179 CONSRV BAPT	2	NR	NR	-	-
193 EPISCOPAL	1	134	198	.5	1.0
203 EVAN FREE CH	1	231	234	.6	1.2
207 E.L.C.A.	6	2,006	2,643	6.6	13.9
226 FRIENDS-USA	2	267	342*	.9	1.8
226e FUM	*2*	*267*	*342**	*.9*	*1.8*
263 INT FOURSQ GOS	1	109	140*	.4	.7
283 LUTH—MO SYNOD	2	765	1,240	3.1	6.5
285 MENNONITE CH	1	35	50	.1	.3
355 PRESB CH (USA)	4	1,006	1,290*	3.2	6.8
403 SALVATION ARMY	1	65	72	.2	.4
413 S.D.A.	1	201	258*	.6	1.4
443 UN C OF CHRIST	4	610	782*	2.0	4.1
449 UN METHODIST	14	3,270	4,194*	10.5	22.0
O'BRIEN	**39**	**9,167**	**14,381***	**93.1**	**100.0**
053 ASSEMB OF GOD	1	125	166	1.1	1.2
081 CATHOLIC	5	NA	1,903	12.3	13.2
081d LATIN	*5*	*NA*	*1,903*	*12.3*	*13.2*
097 CHR CHS&CHS CR	3	262	332*	2.1	2.3
105 CHRISTIAN REF	4	921	1,511	9.8	10.5
171 CH GOD-GEN CON	1	38	48*	.3	.3
207 E.L.C.A.	3	923	1,209	7.8	8.4
226 FRIENDS-USA	1	97	123*	.8	.9
226a CONSERV	*1*	*97*	*123**	*.8*	*.9*
283 LUTH—MO SYNOD	5	1,955	2,460	15.9	17.1
355 PRESB CH (USA)	2	447	567*	3.7	3.9
371 REF CH IN AM	5	1,691	2,628	17.0	18.3
443 UN C OF CHRIST	3	877	1,112*	7.2	7.7
449 UN METHODIST	6	1,831	2,322*	15.0	16.1
OSCEOLA	**23**	**3,587**	**5,975***	**82.2**	**100.0**
081 CATHOLIC	2	NA	1,100	15.1	18.4
081d LATIN	*2*	*NA*	*1,100*	*15.1*	*18.4*
089 CHR & MISS AL	1	28	70	1.0	1.2
105 CHRISTIAN REF	2	394	637	8.8	10.7
179 CONSRV BAPT	1	NR	NR	-	-
207 E.L.C.A.	2	789	1,028	14.1	17.2
259 IFCA	1	NR	NR	-	-
283 LUTH—MO SYNOD	4	615	756	10.4	12.7
355 PRESB CH (USA)	2	452	576*	7.9	9.6
371 REF CH IN AM	3	498	775	10.7	13.0
443 UN C OF CHRIST	1	96	122*	1.7	2.0
449 UN METHODIST	4	715	911*	12.5	15.2
PAGE	**45**	**7,215**	**11,031***	**65.4**	**100.0**
019 AMER BAPT USA	2	330	408*	2.4	3.7
053 ASSEMB OF GOD	2	84	444	2.6	4.0
081 CATHOLIC	2	NA	1,193	7.1	10.8
081d LATIN	*2*	*NA*	*1,193*	*7.1*	*10.8*
093 CHR CH (DISC)	3	474	845	5.0	7.7
111 CH CR,SCIENTST	1	NR	NR	-	-
127 CH GOD (CLEVE)	1	74	92*	.5	.8
145 CH GOD PROPHCY	1	22	27*	.2	.2
165 CH OF NAZARENE	2	88	125	.7	1.1
171 CH GOD-GEN CON	1	62	77*	.5	.7
193 EPISCOPAL	1	102	122	.7	1.1
207 E.L.C.A.	5	938	1,172	6.9	10.6
221 FREE METHODIST	1	22	54	.3	.5
283 LUTH—MO SYNOD	4	1,405	1,889	11.2	17.1
291 MISSIONARY CH	2	80	211	1.3	1.9

NA–Not applicable NR–Not reported *Total adherents estimated from known number of communicant, confirmed, full members. - Represents a percent less than 0.1. Percentages may not total due to rounding.
[1] See Appendix E [2] See Appendix F [3] See Appendix G Lines in *italic* represent a breakdown of Catholic rites or Friends affiliations. They are included in their respective denominational total.

Table 4. Churches and Church Membership by County and Denomination: 1990

County and Denomination	Number of churches	Communicant, confirmed, full members	Total adherents Number	Percent of total population	Percent of total adherents
355 PRESB CH (USA)	5	984	1,218*	7.2	11.0
419 SO BAPT CONV	2	323	400*	2.4	3.6
443 UN C OF CHRIST	1	262	324*	1.9	2.9
449 UN METHODIST	8	1,944	2,406*	14.3	21.8
469 WELS	1	21	24	.1	.2
PALO ALTO	**29**	**4,642**	**9,970***	**93.4**	**100.0**
040 AP CHR CH–AMER	1	163	288	2.7	2.9
053 ASSEMB OF GOD	1	39	75	.7	.8
081 CATHOLIC	6	NA	3,981	37.3	39.9
081d LATIN	6	NA	3,981	37.3	39.9
193 EPISCOPAL	1	37	60	.6	.6
207 E.L.C.A.	5	1,417	1,772	16.6	17.8
283 LUTH—MO SYNOD	5	1,012	1,282	12.0	12.9
353 CHR BRETHREN	1	25	50	.5	.5
413 S.D.A.	1	10	13*	.1	.1
443 UN C OF CHRIST	1	88	111*	1.0	1.1
449 UN METHODIST	7	1,851	2,338*	21.9	23.5
PLYMOUTH	**49**	**7,797**	**18,307***	**78.3**	**100.0**
019 AMER BAPT USA	2	268	348*	1.5	1.9
053 ASSEMB OF GOD	1	42	95	.4	.5
081 CATHOLIC	11	NA	8,086	34.6	44.2
081d LATIN	11	NA	8,086	34.6	44.2
097 CHR CHS&CHS CR	2	204	265*	1.1	1.4
105 CHRISTIAN REF	1	181	270	1.2	1.5
157 CH OF BRETHREN	1	28	36*	.2	.2
165 CH OF NAZARENE	1	26	63	.3	.3
167 CHS OF CHRIST	1	33	41	.2	.2
193 EPISCOPAL	1	18	25	.1	.1
207 E.L.C.A.	9	3,040	3,959	16.9	21.6
283 LUTH—MO SYNOD	4	1,453	1,872	8.0	10.2
355 PRESB CH (USA)	3	368	477*	2.0	2.6
443 UN C OF CHRIST	3	244	316*	1.4	1.7
449 UN METHODIST	9	1,892	2,454*	10.5	13.4
POCAHONTAS	**28**	**4,316**	**8,685***	**91.2**	**100.0**
081 CATHOLIC	6	NA	3,193	33.5	36.8
081d LATIN	6	NA	3,193	33.5	36.8
093 CHR CH (DISC)	1	185	282	3.0	3.2
097 CHR CHS&CHS CR	1	20	25*	.3	.3
207 E.L.C.A.	7	1,911	2,410	25.3	27.7
283 LUTH—MO SYNOD	1	44	50	.5	.6
284 LUTH CH–AM ASC	1	153	197	2.1	2.3
355 PRESB CH (USA)	3	270	341*	3.6	3.9
443 UN C OF CHRIST	1	97	122*	1.3	1.4
449 UN METHODIST	7	1,636	2,065*	21.7	23.8
POLK	**268**	**72,879**	**164,819***	**50.4**	**100.0**
005 AME ZION	1	254	269	.1	.2
019 AMER BAPT USA	7	1,284	1,609*	.5	1.0
053 ASSEMB OF GOD	13	2,685	6,060	1.9	3.7
057 BAPT GEN CONF	4	612	767*	.2	.5
075 BRETHREN IN CR	1	25	29	-	-
081 CATHOLIC	21	NA	55,214	16.9	33.5
081d LATIN	21	NA	55,214	16.9	33.5
089 CHR & MISS AL	3	159	169	.1	.1
093 CHR CH (DISC)	18	6,362	9,764	3.0	5.9
097 CHR CHS&CHS CR	8	1,830	2,293*	.7	1.4
105 CHRISTIAN REF	1	209	332	.1	.2
111 CH CR,SCIENTST	2	NR	NR	-	-
123 CH GOD (ANDER)	1	59	75	-	-
127 CH GOD (CLEVE)	3	174	218*	.1	.1
145 CH GOD PROPHCY	1	22	28*	-	-
151 L-D SAINTS	3	NA	1,074	.3	.7
157 CH OF BRETHREN	2	190	238*	.1	.1
165 CH OF NAZARENE	6	677	1,249	.4	.8
167 CHS OF CHRIST	9	549	704	.2	.4
179 CONSRV BAPT	1	NR	NR	-	-
193 EPISCOPAL	6	1,968	2,550	.8	1.5
203 EVAN FREE CH	4	302	498	.2	.3
207 E.L.C.A.	26	15,805	21,683	6.6	13.2
216 EVAN PRESBY CH	1	209	209	.1	.1
221 FREE METHODIST	1	81	114	-	.1
226 FRIENDS-USA	2	231	290*	.1	.2
226a CONSERV	1	70	88*	-	.1
226e FUM	1	161	202*	.1	.1
246 GREEK ORTHODOX	1	NR	NR	-	-
259 IFCA	2	NR	NR	-	-
263 INT FOURSQ GOS	1	218	273*	.1	.2
274 LAT EVAN LUTH	1	74	75	-	-
283 LUTH—MO SYNOD	10	4,226	5,717	1.7	3.5
285 MENNONITE CH	1	86	266	.1	.2
329 OPEN BIBLE STD	13	NR	NR	-	-
339 PENT CH OF GOD	1	34	77	-	-
353 CHR BRETHREN	2	107	214	.1	.1

County and Denomination	Number of churches	Communicant, confirmed, full members	Total adherents Number	Percent of total population	Percent of total adherents
355 PRESB CH (USA)	16	6,732	8,436*	2.6	5.1
356 PRESB CH AMER	1	17	17	-	-
371 REF CH IN AM	4	1,371	2,298	.7	1.4
403 SALVATION ARMY	2	390	431	.1	.3
413 S.D.A.	4	1,069	1,340*	.4	.8
419 SO BAPT CONV	6	1,172	1,469*	.4	.9
435 UNITARIAN-UNIV	1	260	360	.1	.2
438 UN BRETH IN CR	1	26	26	-	-
443 UN C OF CHRIST	6	4,094	5,130*	1.6	3.1
449 UN METHODIST	38	15,152	18,988*	5.8	11.5
467 WESLEYAN	2	97	210	.1	.1
469 WELS	1	154	188	.1	.1
496 JEWISH EST[1]	6	NA	2,164	.7	1.3
497 BLACK BAPT EST[2]	NA	3,913	4,904*	1.5	3.0
498 INDEP.CHARIS.[3]	1	NA	4,200	1.3	2.5
499 INDEP.NON-CHAR[3]	2	NA	2,600	.8	1.6
POTTAWATTAMIE	**95**	**20,415**	**39,185***	**47.4**	**100.0**
019 AMER BAPT USA	2	705	898*	1.1	2.3
053 ASSEMB OF GOD	4	302	573	.7	1.5
081 CATHOLIC	9	NA	9,531	11.5	24.3
081d LATIN	9	NA	9,531	11.5	24.3
089 CHR & MISS AL	1	114	350	.4	.9
093 CHR CH (DISC)	2	401	998	1.2	2.5
097 CHR CHS&CHS CR	4	2,329	2,968*	3.6	7.6
111 CH CR,SCIENTST	1	NR	NR	-	-
127 CH GOD (CLEVE)	2	268	342*	.4	.9
145 CH GOD PROPHCY	1	22	28*	-	.1
151 L-D SAINTS	2	NA	736	.9	1.9
157 CH OF BRETHREN	1	52	66*	.1	.2
165 CH OF NAZARENE	3	392	746	.9	1.9
167 CHS OF CHRIST	1	130	165	.2	.4
179 CONSRV BAPT	2	NR	NR	-	-
193 EPISCOPAL	1	141	165	.2	.4
203 EVAN FREE CH	1	19	75	.1	.2
207 E.L.C.A.	8	4,305	5,707	6.9	14.6
283 LUTH—MO SYNOD	6	2,011	2,842	3.4	7.3
291 MISSIONARY CH	1	23	34	-	.1
329 OPEN BIBLE STD	1	NR	NR	-	-
339 PENT CH OF GOD	1	35	76	.1	.2
353 CHR BRETHREN	1	18	30	-	.1
355 PRESB CH (USA)	11	2,197	2,800*	3.4	7.1
403 SALVATION ARMY	1	150	157	.2	.4
413 S.D.A.	1	95	121*	.1	.3
419 SO BAPT CONV	2	364	464*	.6	1.2
443 UN C OF CHRIST	9	2,419	3,082*	3.7	7.9
449 UN METHODIST	13	3,838	4,891*	5.9	12.5
469 WELS	1	85	122	.1	.3
496 JEWISH EST[1]	1	NA	868	1.1	2.2
499 INDEP.NON-CHAR[3]	1	NA	350	.4	.9
POWESHIEK	**42**	**5,529**	**9,821***	**51.6**	**100.0**
019 AMER BAPT USA	1	214	264*	1.4	2.7
053 ASSEMB OF GOD	1	48	65	.3	.7
081 CATHOLIC	2	NA	2,581	13.6	26.3
081d LATIN	2	NA	2,581	13.6	26.3
089 CHR & MISS AL	1	0	61	.3	.6
093 CHR CH (DISC)	1	23	25	.1	.3
097 CHR CHS&CHS CR	2	814	1,005*	5.3	10.2
111 CH CR,SCIENTST	1	NR	NR	-	-
151 L-D SAINTS	1	NA	95	.5	1.0
157 CH OF BRETHREN	1	44	54*	.3	.5
165 CH OF NAZARENE	2	36	198	1.0	2.0
167 CHS OF CHRIST	4	83	102	.5	1.0
193 EPISCOPAL	1	64	118	.6	1.2
207 E.L.C.A.	2	539	662	3.5	6.7
226 FRIENDS-USA	3	122	164*	.9	1.7
226e FUM	2	117	144*	.8	1.5
226f INDEPENDNT	1	5	20	.1	.2
259 IFCA	1	NR	NR	-	-
283 LUTH—MO SYNOD	2	315	443	2.3	4.5
355 PRESB CH (USA)	6	893	1,102*	5.8	11.2
413 S.D.A.	1	12	15*	.1	.2
443 UN C OF CHRIST	2	386	477*	2.5	4.9
449 UN METHODIST	7	1,936	2,390*	12.6	24.3
RINGGOLD	**25**	**1,967**	**2,687***	**49.6**	**100.0**
001 ADVENT CHR CH	1	20	25*	.5	.9
019 AMER BAPT USA	1	228	280*	5.2	10.4
053 ASSEMB OF GOD	2	71	107	2.0	4.0
081 CATHOLIC	2	NA	219	4.0	8.2
081d LATIN	2	NA	219	4.0	8.2
093 CHR CH (DISC)	4	426	559	10.3	20.8
221 FREE METHODIST	1	26	26	.5	1.0
283 LUTH—MO SYNOD	1	71	89	1.6	3.3
355 PRESB CH (USA)	3	140	172*	3.2	6.4

NA–Not applicable   NR–Not reported   *Total adherents estimated from known number of communicant, confirmed, full members.   - Represents a percent less than 0.1.   Percentages may not total due to rounding.
[1]See Appendix E   [2]See Appendix F   [3]See Appendix G   Lines in *italic* represent a breakdown of Catholic rites or Friends affiliations. They are included in their respective denominational total.

Table 4. Churches and Church Membership by County and Denomination: 1990

County and Denomination	Number of churches	Communicant, confirmed, full members	Total adherents Number	Percent of total population	Percent of total adherents
449 UN METHODIST	10	985	1,210*	22.3	45.0
SAC	**36**	**6,231**	**10,952***	**88.9**	**100.0**
019 AMER BAPT USA	1	142	180*	1.5	1.6
081 CATHOLIC	6	NA	2,897	23.5	26.5
081d *LATIN*	*6*	*NA*	*2,897*	*23.5*	*26.5*
093 CHR CH (DISC)	1	264	471	3.8	4.3
167 CHS OF CHRIST	1	9	12	.1	.1
207 E.L.C.A.	2	642	823	6.7	7.5
283 LUTH—MO SYNOD	8	2,161	2,745	22.3	25.1
355 PRESB CH (USA)	8	1,089	1,382*	11.2	12.6
443 UN C OF CHRIST	2	259	329*	2.7	3.0
449 UN METHODIST	7	1,665	2,113*	17.1	19.3
SCOTT	**113**	**32,298**	**77,514***	**51.3**	**100.0**
019 AMER BAPT USA	2	428	550*	.4	.7
053 ASSEMB OF GOD	5	791	1,046	.7	1.3
057 BAPT GEN CONF	4	845	1,086*	.7	1.4
081 CATHOLIC	14	NA	30,718	20.3	39.6
081d *LATIN*	*14*	*NA*	*30,718*	*20.3*	*39.6*
089 CHR & MISS AL	2	25	85	.1	.1
093 CHR CH (DISC)	3	1,038	1,445	1.0	1.9
097 CHR CHS&CHS CR	3	508	653*	.4	.8
105 CHRISTIAN REF	1	60	112	.1	.1
111 CH CR,SCIENTST	1	NR	NR	-	-
123 CH GOD (ANDER)	1	18	27	-	-
127 CH GOD (CLEVE)	2	148	190*	.1	.2
145 CH GOD PROPHCY	1	22	28*	-	-
151 L-D SAINTS	2	NA	928	.6	1.2
165 CH OF NAZARENE	2	218	427	.3	.6
167 CHS OF CHRIST	2	244	310	.2	.4
193 EPISCOPAL	3	964	1,624	1.1	2.1
203 EVAN FREE CH	1	94	175	.1	.2
207 E.L.C.A.	13	9,588	13,690	9.1	17.7
223 FREE WILL BAPT	1	79	102*	.1	.1
226 FRIENDS-USA	1	114	147*	.1	.2
226e *FUM*	*1*	*114*	*147**	*.1*	*.2*
263 INT FOURSQ GOS	1	131	168*	.1	.2
283 LUTH—MO SYNOD	6	3,264	4,552	3.0	5.9
284 LUTH CH-AM ASC	2	248	427	.3	.6
329 OPEN BIBLE STD	2	NR	NR	-	-
353 CHR BRETHREN	1	100	150	.1	.2
355 PRESB CH (USA)	10	3,595	4,620*	3.1	6.0
371 REF CH IN AM	1	194	294	.2	.4
403 SALVATION ARMY	1	114	114	.1	.1
413 S.D.A.	2	352	452*	.3	.6
419 SO BAPT CONV	5	1,522	1,956*	1.3	2.5
435 UNITARIAN-UNIV	1	199	274	.2	.4
443 UN C OF CHRIST	2	548	704*	.5	.9
449 UN METHODIST	11	4,669	6,001*	4.0	7.7
469 WELS	1	71	113	.1	.1
496 JEWISH EST[1]	1	NA	538	.4	.7
497 BLACK BAPT EST[2]	NA	2,107	2,708*	1.8	3.5
499 INDEP.NON-CHAR[3]	2	NA	1,100	.7	1.4
SHELBY	**32**	**4,613**	**10,876***	**82.2**	**100.0**
019 AMER BAPT USA	2	442	559*	4.2	5.1
053 ASSEMB OF GOD	1	36	70	.5	.6
081 CATHOLIC	6	NA	5,002	37.8	46.0
081d *LATIN*	*6*	*NA*	*5,002*	*37.8*	*46.0*
097 CHR CHS&CHS CR	3	277	350*	2.6	3.2
167 CHS OF CHRIST	2	92	122	.9	1.1
179 CONSRV BAPT	1	NR	NR	-	-
193 EPISCOPAL	1	28	35	.3	.3
207 E.L.C.A.	5	1,938	2,448	18.5	22.5
283 LUTH—MO SYNOD	1	58	87	.7	.8
355 PRESB CH (USA)	1	102	129*	1.0	1.2
413 S.D.A.	1	14	18*	.1	.2
443 UN C OF CHRIST	1	260	329*	2.5	3.0
449 UN METHODIST	7	1,366	1,727*	13.1	15.9
SIOUX	**67**	**16,765**	**28,137***	**94.1**	**100.0**
019 AMER BAPT USA	1	256	337*	1.1	1.2
053 ASSEMB OF GOD	1	8	18	.1	.1
081 CATHOLIC	6	NA	2,479	8.3	8.8
081d *LATIN*	*6*	*NA*	*2,479*	*8.3*	*8.8*
089 CHR & MISS AL	1	148	412	1.4	1.5
105 CHRISTIAN REF	16	4,982	7,897	26.4	28.1
157 CH OF BRETHREN	1	59	78*	.3	.3
167 CHS OF CHRIST	1	14	18	.1	.1
203 EVAN FREE CH	1	0	91	.3	.3
207 E.L.C.A.	6	1,133	1,494	5.0	5.3
283 LUTH—MO SYNOD	4	1,072	1,415	4.7	5.0
307 NETH REF CONGR	2	787	1,525	5.1	5.4
355 PRESB CH (USA)	4	494	650*	2.2	2.3
371 REF CH IN AM	18	7,076	10,755	36.0	38.2

County and Denomination	Number of churches	Communicant, confirmed, full members	Total adherents Number	Percent of total population	Percent of total adherents
413 S.D.A.	1	7	9*	-	-
443 UN C OF CHRIST	1	130	171*	.6	.6
449 UN METHODIST	3	599	788*	2.6	2.8
STORY	**79**	**21,445**	**35,002***	**47.1**	**100.0**
019 AMER BAPT USA	1	224	267*	.4	.8
053 ASSEMB OF GOD	4	266	517	.7	1.5
081 CATHOLIC	6	NA	5,594	7.5	16.0
081d *LATIN*	*6*	*NA*	*5,594*	*7.5*	*16.0*
093 CHR CH (DISC)	5	928	1,447	1.9	4.1
097 CHR CHS&CHS CR	1	210	250*	.3	.7
105 CHRISTIAN REF	2	116	180	.2	.5
111 CH CR,SCIENTST	1	NR	NR	-	-
145 CH GOD PROPHCY	1	22	26*	-	.1
151 L-D SAINTS	1	NA	437	.6	1.2
157 CH OF BRETHREN	1	14	17*	-	-
165 CH OF NAZARENE	1	79	168	.2	.5
167 CHS OF CHRIST	1	57	79	.1	.2
193 EPISCOPAL	1	748	1,510	2.0	4.3
203 EVAN FREE CH	1	291	700	.9	2.0
207 E.L.C.A.	16	7,976	10,776	14.5	30.8
209 EVAN LUTH SYN	1	53	70	.1	.2
226 FRIENDS-USA	1	39	46*	.1	.1
226a *CONSERV*	*1*	*39*	*46**	*.1*	*.1*
283 LUTH—MO SYNOD	3	1,215	1,677	2.3	4.8
284 LUTH CH-AM ASC	1	332	402	.5	1.1
287 MENN GEN CONF	1	7	10	-	-
329 OPEN BIBLE STD	1	NR	NR	-	-
353 CHR BRETHREN	1	10	18	-	.1
355 PRESB CH (USA)	5	1,491	1,774*	2.4	5.1
413 S.D.A.	2	222	264*	.4	.8
419 SO BAPT CONV	2	867	1,032*	1.4	2.9
435 UNITARIAN-UNIV	1	230	345	.5	1.0
443 UN C OF CHRIST	1	359	427*	.6	1.2
449 UN METHODIST	15	5,434	6,466*	8.7	18.5
496 JEWISH EST[1]	1	NA	200	.3	.6
497 BLACK BAPT EST[2]	NA	255	303*	.4	.9
TAMA	**38**	**5,775**	**11,380***	**65.3**	**100.0**
053 ASSEMB OF GOD	2	59	138	.8	1.2
081 CATHOLIC	7	NA	3,978	22.8	35.0
081d *LATIN*	*7*	*NA*	*3,978*	*22.8*	*35.0*
089 CHR & MISS AL	2	89	149	.9	1.3
093 CHR CH (DISC)	1	54	88	.5	.8
121 CH GOD (ABR)	1	20	25*	.1	.2
207 E.L.C.A.	4	1,149	1,460	8.4	12.8
283 LUTH—MO SYNOD	1	86	124	.7	1.1
355 PRESB CH (USA)	3	514	645*	3.7	5.7
443 UN C OF CHRIST	4	1,076	1,350*	7.8	11.9
449 UN METHODIST	13	2,728	3,423*	19.7	30.1
TAYLOR	**29**	**3,077**	**4,267***	**60.0**	**100.0**
019 AMER BAPT USA	1	629	786*	11.0	18.4
081 CATHOLIC	2	NA	280	3.9	6.6
081d *LATIN*	*2*	*NA*	*280*	*3.9*	*6.6*
093 CHR CH (DISC)	3	188	355	5.0	8.3
097 CHR CHS&CHS CR	4	450	562*	7.9	13.2
165 CH OF NAZARENE	1	19	34	.5	.8
167 CHS OF CHRIST	2	33	42	.6	1.0
283 LUTH—MO SYNOD	1	28	30	.4	.7
291 MISSIONARY CH	1	36	64	.9	1.5
355 PRESB CH (USA)	3	237	296*	4.2	6.9
413 S.D.A.	1	54	67*	.9	1.6
419 SO BAPT CONV	1	70	87*	1.2	2.0
443 UN C OF CHRIST	1	38	47*	.7	1.1
449 UN METHODIST	8	1,295	1,617*	22.7	37.9
UNION	**28**	**3,515**	**6,450***	**50.6**	**100.0**
019 AMER BAPT USA	1	53	66*	.5	1.0
053 ASSEMB OF GOD	2	88	180	1.4	2.8
081 CATHOLIC	2	NA	1,401	11.0	21.7
081d *LATIN*	*2*	*NA*	*1,401*	*11.0*	*21.7*
093 CHR CH (DISC)	2	419	1,022	8.0	15.8
111 CH CR,SCIENTST	1	NR	NR	-	-
123 CH GOD (ANDER)	1	20	20	.2	.3
165 CH OF NAZARENE	1	21	64	.5	1.0
176 CCC, NOT NAT'L	1	29	36*	.3	.6
193 EPISCOPAL	1	24	27	.2	.4
207 E.L.C.A.	1	387	514	4.0	8.0
283 LUTH—MO SYNOD	1	268	371	2.9	5.8
355 PRESB CH (USA)	2	376	469*	3.7	7.3
413 S.D.A.	1	10	12*	.1	.2
419 SO BAPT CONV	1	51	64*	.5	1.0
443 UN C OF CHRIST	3	467	582*	4.6	9.0
449 UN METHODIST	7	1,302	1,622*	12.7	25.1

NA–Not applicable   NR–Not reported   *Total adherents estimated from known number of communicant, confirmed, full members.   - Represents a percent less than 0.1.   Percentages may not total due to rounding.
[1]See Appendix E   [2]See Appendix F   [3]See Appendix G   Lines in *italic* represent a breakdown of Catholic rites or Friends affiliations. They are included in their respective denominational total.

Table 4. Churches and Church Membership by County and Denomination: 1990

County and Denomination	Number of churches	Communicant, confirmed, full members	Total adherents Number	Percent of total population	Percent of total adherents
VAN BUREN	**29**	**2,143**	**3,518***	**45.8**	**100.0**
019 AMER BAPT USA	1	29	37*	.5	1.1
053 ASSEMB OF GOD	1	49	65	.8	1.8
081 CATHOLIC	1	NA	330	4.3	9.4
081d LATIN	1	NA	330	4.3	9.4
097 CHR CHS&CHS CR	3	345	436*	5.7	12.4
165 CH OF NAZARENE	1	33	60	.8	1.7
221 FREE METHODIST	1	22	28	.4	.8
283 LUTH—MO SYNOD	1	36	54	.7	1.5
323 OLD ORD AMISH	3	NA	450	5.9	12.8
355 PRESB CH (USA)	4	235	297*	3.9	8.4
443 UN C OF CHRIST	1	50	63*	.8	1.8
449 UN METHODIST	12	1,344	1,698*	22.1	48.3
WAPELLO	**70**	**8,451**	**16,563***	**46.4**	**100.0**
019 AMER BAPT USA	2	474	583*	1.6	3.5
053 ASSEMB OF GOD	4	322	641	1.8	3.9
081 CATHOLIC	5	NA	3,237	9.1	19.5
081d LATIN	5	NA	3,237	9.1	19.5
089 CHR & MISS AL	1	74	179	.5	1.1
093 CHR CH (DISC)	6	993	2,249	6.3	13.6
097 CHR CHS&CHS CR	2	365	449*	1.3	2.7
111 CH CR,SCIENTST	1	NR	NR	-	-
123 CH GOD (ANDER)	2	65	200	.6	1.2
145 CH GOD PROPHCY	1	22	27*	.1	.2
151 L-D SAINTS	1	NA	259	.7	1.6
157 CH OF BRETHREN	1	118	145*	.4	.9
165 CH OF NAZARENE	2	267	468	1.3	2.8
167 CHS OF CHRIST	2	85	116	.3	.7
193 EPISCOPAL	1	92	152	.4	.9
203 EVAN FREE CH	1	22	60	.2	.4
207 E.L.C.A.	3	1,091	1,549	4.3	9.4
221 FREE METHODIST	1	54	56	.2	.3
263 INT FOURSQ GOS	3	292	359*	1.0	2.2
283 LUTH—MO SYNOD	1	230	302	.8	1.8
329 OPEN BIBLE STD	3	NR	NR	-	-
339 PENT CH OF GOD	2	109	172	.5	1.0
353 CHR BRETHREN	2	70	125	.4	.8
355 PRESB CH (USA)	3	727	894*	2.5	5.4
371 REF CH IN AM	1	35	62	.2	.4
403 SALVATION ARMY	1	113	121	.3	.7
413 S.D.A.	1	90	111*	.3	.7
419 SO BAPT CONV	1	323	397*	1.1	2.4
443 UN C OF CHRIST	3	156	192*	.5	1.2
449 UN METHODIST	11	2,262	2,783*	7.8	16.8
499 INDEP.NON-CHAR[3]	2	NA	675	1.9	4.1
WARREN	**47**	**7,758**	**14,444***	**40.1**	**100.0**
019 AMER BAPT USA	1	800	1,025*	2.8	7.1
053 ASSEMB OF GOD	1	159	300	.8	2.1
057 BAPT GEN CONF	1	64	82*	.2	.6
081 CATHOLIC	6	NA	3,389	9.4	23.5
081d LATIN	6	NA	3,389	9.4	23.5
093 CHR CH (DISC)	4	468	743	2.1	5.1
097 CHR CHS&CHS CR	1	95	122*	.3	.8
165 CH OF NAZARENE	2	108	298	.8	2.1
167 CHS OF CHRIST	2	58	76	.2	.5
203 EVAN FREE CH	1	0	40	.1	.3
207 E.L.C.A.	3	862	1,193	3.3	8.3
226 FRIENDS-USA	5	346	444*	1.2	3.1
226e FUM	5	346	444*	1.2	3.1
283 LUTH—MO SYNOD	2	536	681	1.9	4.7
355 PRESB CH (USA)	3	865	1,109*	3.1	7.7
413 S.D.A.	1	28	36*	.1	.2
419 SO BAPT CONV	1	122	156*	.4	1.1
449 UN METHODIST	12	3,247	4,162*	11.6	28.8
496 JEWISH EST[1]	0	NA	238	.7	1.6
499 INDEP.NON-CHAR[3]	1	NA	350	1.0	2.4
WASHINGTON	**44**	**6,875**	**11,655***	**59.4**	**100.0**
019 AMER BAPT USA	3	739	939*	4.8	8.1
053 ASSEMB OF GOD	1	56	112	.6	1.0
057 BAPT GEN CONF	1	161	204*	1.0	1.8
081 CATHOLIC	4	NA	2,465	12.6	21.1
081d LATIN	4	NA	2,465	12.6	21.1
093 CHR CH (DISC)	3	439	645	3.3	5.5
097 CHR CHS&CHS CR	1	42	53*	.3	.5
127 CH GOD (CLEVE)	1	25	32*	.2	.3
165 CH OF NAZARENE	1	54	156	.8	1.3
167 CHS OF CHRIST	1	12	18	.1	.2
171 CH GOD-GEN CON	2	41	52*	.3	.4
176 CCC, NOT NAT'L	1	14	18*	.1	.2
207 E.L.C.A.	2	517	726	3.7	6.2
226 FRIENDS-USA	1	27	34*	.2	.3
226e FUM	1	27	34*	.2	.3
283 LUTH—MO SYNOD	1	48	61	.3	.5

County and Denomination	Number of churches	Communicant, confirmed, full members	Total adherents Number	Percent of total population	Percent of total adherents
285 MENNONITE CH	7	1,102	1,420	7.2	12.2
323 OLD ORD AMISH	1	NA	150	.8	1.3
355 PRESB CH (USA)	5	1,244	1,580*	8.1	13.6
449 UN METHODIST	8	2,354	2,990*	15.2	25.7
WAYNE	**28**	**2,607**	**3,457***	**48.9**	**100.0**
019 AMER BAPT USA	4	515	631*	8.9	18.3
053 ASSEMB OF GOD	3	132	243	3.4	7.0
081 CATHOLIC	1	NA	60	.8	1.7
081d LATIN	1	NA	60	.8	1.7
093 CHR CH (DISC)	4	203	376	5.3	10.9
097 CHR CHS&CHS CR	1	100	122*	1.7	3.5
145 CH GOD PROPHCY	1	22	27*	.4	.8
167 CHS OF CHRIST	2	56	65	.9	1.9
355 PRESB CH (USA)	1	91	111*	1.6	3.2
419 SO BAPT CONV	1	289	354*	5.0	10.2
449 UN METHODIST	10	1,199	1,468*	20.8	42.5
WEBSTER	**69**	**14,255**	**29,108***	**72.2**	**100.0**
019 AMER BAPT USA	3	554	700*	1.7	2.4
053 ASSEMB OF GOD	1	160	195	.5	.7
057 BAPT GEN CONF	1	144	182*	.5	.6
081 CATHOLIC	10	NA	9,937	24.6	34.1
081d LATIN	10	NA	9,937	24.6	34.1
093 CHR CH (DISC)	2	146	352	.9	1.2
097 CHR CHS&CHS CR	1	65	82*	.2	.3
111 CH CR,SCIENTST	1	NR	NR	-	-
151 L-D SAINTS	1	NA	220	.5	.8
157 CH OF BRETHREN	1	23	29*	.1	.1
165 CH OF NAZARENE	1	69	114	.3	.4
167 CHS OF CHRIST	1	59	76	.2	.3
176 CCC, NOT NAT'L	1	54	68*	.2	.2
193 EPISCOPAL	1	109	121	.3	.4
203 EVAN FREE CH	1	162	242	.6	.8
207 E.L.C.A.	12	4,321	5,608	13.9	19.3
283 LUTH—MO SYNOD	6	3,080	4,172	10.3	14.3
285 MENNONITE CH	1	58	68	.2	.2
353 CHR BRETHREN	1	10	20	-	.1
355 PRESB CH (USA)	3	744	940*	2.3	3.2
403 SALVATION ARMY	1	95	105	.3	.4
413 S.D.A.	0	18	23*	.1	.1
419 SO BAPT CONV	1	180	227*	.6	.8
438 UN BRETH IN CR	2	38	46	.1	.2
443 UN C OF CHRIST	2	340	429*	1.1	1.5
449 UN METHODIST	12	3,637	4,593*	11.4	15.8
496 JEWISH EST[1]	1	NA	0	-	-
497 BLACK BAPT EST[2]	NA	189	239*	.6	.8
498 INDEP.CHARIS.[3]	1	NA	320	.8	1.1
WINNEBAGO	**38**	**7,539**	**10,896***	**89.9**	**100.0**
053 ASSEMB OF GOD	1	17	22	.2	.2
057 BAPT GEN CONF	1	231	289*	2.4	2.7
081 CATHOLIC	3	NA	1,225	10.1	11.2
081d LATIN	3	NA	1,225	10.1	11.2
163 CH OF LUTH BR	3	82	120	1.0	1.1
175 CONGR CHR CHS	1	70	88*	.7	.8
181 CONSRV CONGR	1	155	194*	1.6	1.8
203 EVAN FREE CH	1	64	150	1.2	1.4
207 E.L.C.A.	11	4,840	6,076	50.1	55.8
209 EVAN LUTH SYN	6	421	543	4.5	5.0
263 INT FOURSQ GOS	1	36	45*	.4	.4
284 LUTH CH-AM ASC	1	100	107	.9	1.0
313 N AM BAPT CONF	1	96	120*	1.0	1.1
371 REF CH IN AM	1	225	412	3.4	3.8
413 S.D.A.	1	17	21*	.2	.2
449 UN METHODIST	5	1,185	1,484*	12.2	13.6
WINNESHIEK	**41**	**8,058**	**17,926***	**86.0**	**100.0**
053 ASSEMB OF GOD	1	35	47	.2	.3
081 CATHOLIC	8	NA	7,543	36.2	42.1
081d LATIN	8	NA	7,543	36.2	42.1
167 CHS OF CHRIST	1	11	17	.1	.1
193 EPISCOPAL	1	35	37	.2	.2
207 E.L.C.A.	21	6,767	8,767	42.1	48.9
209 EVAN LUTH SYN	1	69	75	.4	.4
226 FRIENDS-USA	2	68	105*	.5	.6
226e FUM	1	60	75*	.4	.4
226f INDEPENDNT	1	8	30	.1	.2
355 PRESB CH (USA)	1	80	100*	.5	.6
443 UN C OF CHRIST	1	157	195*	.9	1.1
449 UN METHODIST	4	836	1,040*	5.0	5.8
WOODBURY	**118**	**27,031**	**58,263***	**59.3**	**100.0**
019 AMER BAPT USA	3	422	543*	.6	.9
053 ASSEMB OF GOD	4	533	943	1.0	1.6

NA–Not applicable   NR–Not reported   *Total adherents estimated from known number of communicant, confirmed, full members.   - Represents a percent less than 0.1.   Percentages may not total due to rounding.
[1]See Appendix E   [2]See Appendix F   [3]See Appendix G   Lines in *italic* represent a breakdown of Catholic rites or Friends affiliations. They are included in their respective denominational total.

Table 4. Churches and Church Membership by County and Denomination: 1990

County and Denomination	Number of churches	Communicant, confirmed, full members	Total adherents Number	Percent of total population	Percent of total adherents
057 BAPT GEN CONF	1	66	85*	.1	.1
081 CATHOLIC	16	NA	19,803	20.2	34.0
081d *LATIN*	*16*	*NA*	*19,803*	*20.2*	*34.0*
089 CHR & MISS AL	1	55	95	.1	.2
093 CHR CH (DISC)	3	331	487	.5	.8
097 CHR CHS&CHS CR	3	335	431*	.4	.7
105 CHRISTIAN REF	1	123	202	.2	.3
111 CH CR,SCIENTST	1	NR	NR	-	-
151 L-D SAINTS	2	NA	936	1.0	1.6
165 CH OF NAZARENE	3	257	439	.4	.8
167 CHS OF CHRIST	2	33	42	-	.1
179 CONSRV BAPT	1	NR	NR	-	-
193 EPISCOPAL	3	967	1,277	1.3	2.2
203 EVAN FREE CH	1	101	101	.1	.2
207 E.L.C.A.	14	7,188	9,522	9.7	16.3
221 FREE METHODIST	1	25	58	.1	.1
246 GREEK ORTHODOX	1	NR	NR	-	-
263 INT FOURSQ GOS	1	45	58*	.1	.1
283 LUTH—MO SYNOD	12	4,367	5,951	6.1	10.2
329 OPEN BIBLE STD	1	NR	NR	-	-
353 CHR BRETHREN	2	85	150	.2	.3
355 PRESB CH (USA)	7	2,439	3,139*	3.2	5.4
371 REF CH IN AM	1	362	696	.7	1.2
403 SALVATION ARMY	1	231	246	.3	.4
413 S.D.A.	1	184	237*	.2	.4
419 SO BAPT CONV	1	223	287*	.3	.5
435 UNITARIAN-UNIV	1	86	111	.1	.2
443 UN C OF CHRIST	4	922	1,187*	1.2	2.0
449 UN METHODIST	20	6,958	8,955*	9.1	15.4
467 WESLEYAN	1	34	160	.2	.3
469 WELS	1	163	204	.2	.4
496 JEWISH EST[1]	2	NA	630	.6	1.1
497 BLACK BAPT EST[2]	NA	496	638*	.6	1.1
498 INDEP.CHARIS.[3]	1	NA	650	.7	1.1
WORTH	**21**	**4,952**	**6,469***	**81.0**	**100.0**
081 CATHOLIC	1	NA	300	3.8	4.6
081d *LATIN*	*1*	*NA*	*300*	*3.8*	*4.6*
097 CHR CHS&CHS CR	1	200	248*	3.1	3.8
163 CH OF LUTH BR	1	37	46	.6	.7
207 E.L.C.A.	11	3,733	4,665	58.4	72.1
209 EVAN LUTH SYN	2	122	149	1.9	2.3
449 UN METHODIST	4	838	1,040*	13.0	16.1
467 WESLEYAN	1	22	21	.3	.3
WRIGHT	**40**	**7,122**	**10,995***	**77.1**	**100.0**
019 AMER BAPT USA	1	102	126*	.9	1.1
053 ASSEMB OF GOD	2	57	104	.7	.9
081 CATHOLIC	3	NA	1,738	12.2	15.8
081d *LATIN*	*3*	*NA*	*1,738*	*12.2*	*15.8*
097 CHR CHS&CHS CR	2	315	390*	2.7	3.5
165 CH OF NAZARENE	1	37	264	1.9	2.4
203 EVAN FREE CH	2	77	126	.9	1.1
207 E.L.C.A.	10	2,703	3,418	24.0	31.1
283 LUTH—MO SYNOD	3	190	244	1.7	2.2
355 PRESB CH (USA)	3	453	561*	3.9	5.1
371 REF CH IN AM	2	195	318	2.2	2.9
443 UN C OF CHRIST	4	827	1,024*	7.2	9.3
449 UN METHODIST	7	2,166	2,682*	18.8	24.4

KANSAS

County and Denomination	Number of churches	Communicant, confirmed, full members	Total adherents Number	Percent of total population	Percent of total adherents
THE STATE.....	3,958	704,542	1,354,657*	54.7	100.0
ALLEN	**37**	**5,582**	**8,786***	**60.0**	**100.0**
019 AMER BAPT USA	2	991	1,266*	8.6	14.4
053 ASSEMB OF GOD	2	129	270	1.8	3.1
081 CATHOLIC	2	NA	1,300	8.9	14.8
081d *LATIN*	*2*	*NA*	*1,300*	*8.9*	*14.8*
093 CHR CH (DISC)	1	190	341	2.3	3.9
097 CHR CHS&CHS CR	3	460	588*	4.0	6.7
133 CH GOD(7TH)DEN	1	16	20	.1	.2
151 L-D SAINTS	1	NA	292	2.0	3.3
165 CH OF NAZARENE	2	195	167	1.1	1.9
167 CHS OF CHRIST	1	33	42	.3	.5
193 EPISCOPAL	1	40	40	.3	.5
207 E.L.C.A.	1	121	156	1.1	1.8
259 IFCA	1	NR	NR	-	-
283 LUTH—MO SYNOD	2	419	498	3.4	5.7
355 PRESB CH (USA)	3	306	391*	2.7	4.5
413 S.D.A.	1	91	116*	.8	1.3
419 SO BAPT CONV	2	847	1,082*	7.4	12.3
449 UN METHODIST	10	1,700	2,172*	14.8	24.7
467 WESLEYAN	1	44	45	.3	.5
ANDERSON	**30**	**2,409**	**6,198***	**79.4**	**100.0**
019 AMER BAPT USA	2	515	648*	8.3	10.5
053 ASSEMB OF GOD	1	38	50	.6	.8
081 CATHOLIC	5	NA	2,808	36.0	45.3
081d *LATIN*	*5*	*NA*	*2,808*	*36.0*	*45.3*
097 CHR CHS&CHS CR	3	706	889*	11.4	14.3
157 CH OF BRETHREN	2	52	65*	.8	1.0
165 CH OF NAZARENE	1	40	105	1.3	1.7
167 CHS OF CHRIST	2	20	27	.3	.4
283 LUTH—MO SYNOD	1	55	72	.9	1.2
285 MENNONITE CH	1	6	10	.1	.2
323 OLD ORD AMISH	2	NA	300	3.8	4.8
355 PRESB CH (USA)	1	66	83*	1.1	1.3
438 UN BRETH IN CR	1	23	23	.3	.4
449 UN METHODIST	8	888	1,118*	14.3	18.0
ATCHISON	**33**	**4,653**	**10,676***	**63.1**	**100.0**
019 AMER BAPT USA	1	258	326*	1.9	3.1
053 ASSEMB OF GOD	1	31	50	.3	.5
081 CATHOLIC	7	NA	4,623	27.3	43.3
081d *LATIN*	*6*	*NA*	*4,563*	*26.9*	*42.7*
081h *UKRAINIAN*	*1*	*NA*	*60*	*.4*	*.6*
093 CHR CH (DISC)	3	947	1,251	7.4	11.7
097 CHR CHS&CHS CR	5	310	392*	2.3	3.7
165 CH OF NAZARENE	1	36	62	.4	.6
193 EPISCOPAL	1	142	190	1.1	1.8
207 E.L.C.A.	2	426	532	3.1	5.0
259 IFCA	1	NR	NR	-	-
283 LUTH—MO SYNOD	1	855	1,152	6.8	10.8
339 PENT CH OF GOD	1	26	71	.4	.7
355 PRESB CH (USA)	2	458	578*	3.4	5.4
403 SALVATION ARMY	1	101	106	.6	1.0
413 S.D.A.	1	80	101*	.6	.9
449 UN METHODIST	5	782	988*	5.8	9.3
497 BLACK BAPT EST[2]	NA	201	254*	1.5	2.4
BARBER	**24**	**2,246**	**3,880***	**66.1**	**100.0**
019 AMER BAPT USA	1	56	71*	1.2	1.8
040 AP CHR CH-AMER	1	54	94	1.6	2.4
053 ASSEMB OF GOD	2	68	182	3.1	4.7
081 CATHOLIC	3	NA	856	14.6	22.1
081d *LATIN*	*3*	*NA*	*856*	*14.6*	*22.1*
093 CHR CH (DISC)	1	30	48	.8	1.2
097 CHR CHS&CHS CR	2	536	684*	11.6	17.6
167 CHS OF CHRIST	2	55	65	1.1	1.7
193 EPISCOPAL	1	17	16	.3	.4
283 LUTH—MO SYNOD	1	112	183	3.1	4.7
355 PRESB CH (USA)	2	62	79*	1.3	2.0
443 UN C OF CHRIST	2	132	168*	2.9	4.3
449 UN METHODIST	6	1,124	1,434*	24.4	37.0
BARTON	**58**	**9,553**	**20,873***	**71.0**	**100.0**
019 AMER BAPT USA	1	460	590*	2.0	2.8
053 ASSEMB OF GOD	2	349	759	2.6	3.6
081 CATHOLIC	9	NA	7,546	25.7	36.2
081d *LATIN*	*9*	*NA*	*7,546*	*25.7*	*36.2*
093 CHR CH (DISC)	2	446	755	2.6	3.6
097 CHR CHS&CHS CR	2	190	244*	.8	1.2
123 CH GOD (ANDER)	1	85	100	.3	.5
165 CH OF NAZARENE	2	295	490	1.7	2.3
167 CHS OF CHRIST	4	192	262	.9	1.3
193 EPISCOPAL	1	83	118	.4	.6
207 E.L.C.A.	4	1,503	2,080	7.1	10.0
226 FRIENDS-USA	1	38	49*	.2	.2
226b *EFI*	*1*	*38*	*49*	*.2*	*.2*
259 IFCA	2	NR	NR	-	-
263 INT FOURSQ GOS	2	56	72*	.2	.3
283 LUTH—MO SYNOD	4	796	1,023	3.5	4.9
313 N AM BAPT CONF	1	263	337*	1.1	1.6
355 PRESB CH (USA)	1	399	511*	1.7	2.4
413 S.D.A.	1	73	94*	.3	.5
419 SO BAPT CONV	6	1,065	1,365*	4.6	6.5
443 UN C OF CHRIST	2	551	706*	2.4	3.4
449 UN METHODIST	9	2,709	3,472*	11.8	16.6
499 INDEP.NON-CHAR[3]	1	NA	300	1.0	1.4
BOURBON	**38**	**4,652**	**7,640***	**51.0**	**100.0**
019 AMER BAPT USA	4	986	1,241*	8.3	16.2
040 AP CHR CH-AMER	1	37	67	.4	.9
053 ASSEMB OF GOD	2	158	351	2.3	4.6
059 BAPT MISS ASSN	1	121	152*	1.0	2.0
071 BRETHREN (ASH)	1	26	33*	.2	.4

NA–Not applicable   NR–Not reported   *Total adherents estimated from known number of communicant, confirmed, full members.   - Represents a percent less than 0.1.   Percentages may not total due to rounding.
[1]See Appendix E   [2]See Appendix F   [3]See Appendix G   Lines in *italic* represent a breakdown of Catholic rites or Friends affiliations. They are included in their respective denominational total.

KANSAS

Table 4. Churches and Church Membership by County and Denomination: 1990

County and Denomination	Number of churches	Communicant, confirmed, full members	Total adherents Number	Percent of total population	Percent of total adherents
081 CATHOLIC	2	NA	870	5.8	11.4
081d *LATIN*	2	*NA*	*870*	*5.8*	*11.4*
093 CHR CH (DISC)	2	268	351	2.3	4.6
097 CHR CHS&CHS CR	1	478	602*	4.0	7.9
127 CH GOD (CLEVE)	1	13	16*	.1	.2
157 CH OF BRETHREN	1	23	29*	.2	.4
165 CH OF NAZARENE	2	310	594	4.0	7.8
167 CHS OF CHRIST	2	67	83	.6	1.1
193 EPISCOPAL	1	47	56	.4	.7
259 IFCA	1	NR	NR	-	-
283 LUTH—MO SYNOD	1	109	168	1.1	2.2
355 PRESB CH (USA)	1	354	445*	3.0	5.8
413 S.D.A.	1	51	64*	.4	.8
419 SO BAPT CONV	1	141	177*	1.2	2.3
449 UN METHODIST	11	1,463	1,841*	12.3	24.1
499 INDEP.NON-CHAR[3]	1	NA	500	3.3	6.5
BROWN	**32**	**4,066**	**7,277***	**65.4**	**100.0**
019 AMER BAPT USA	5	715	917*	8.2	12.6
053 ASSEMB OF GOD	1	52	75	.7	1.0
081 CATHOLIC	3	NA	1,755	15.8	24.1
081d *LATIN*	3	*NA*	*1,755*	*15.8*	*24.1*
093 CHR CH (DISC)	3	338	679	6.1	9.3
097 CHR CHS&CHS CR	1	68	87*	.8	1.2
167 CHS OF CHRIST	1	15	19	.2	.3
207 E.L.C.A.	2	301	418	3.8	5.7
283 LUTH—MO SYNOD	4	467	588	5.3	8.1
339 PENT CH OF GOD	1	34	76	.7	1.0
355 PRESB CH (USA)	1	128	164*	1.5	2.3
443 UN C OF CHRIST	2	259	332*	3.0	4.6
449 UN METHODIST	8	1,689	2,167*	19.5	29.8
BUTLER	**79**	**13,970**	**23,688***	**46.8**	**100.0**
019 AMER BAPT USA	8	3,419	4,436*	8.8	18.7
053 ASSEMB OF GOD	4	229	479	.9	2.0
059 BAPT MISS ASSN	1	26	34*	.1	.1
081 CATHOLIC	3	NA	4,288	8.5	18.1
081d *LATIN*	3	*NA*	*4,288*	*8.5*	*18.1*
093 CHR CH (DISC)	6	1,245	1,731	3.4	7.3
097 CHR CHS&CHS CR	5	485	629*	1.2	2.7
123 CH GOD (ANDER)	2	255	284	.6	1.2
127 CH GOD (CLEVE)	1	7	9*	-	-
145 CH GOD PROPHCY	1	33	43*	.1	.2
151 L-D SAINTS	1	NA	369	.7	1.6
165 CH OF NAZARENE	3	253	435	.9	1.8
167 CHS OF CHRIST	5	405	483	1.0	2.0
193 EPISCOPAL	1	126	211	.4	.9
226 FRIENDS-USA	1	140	182*	.4	.8
226b *EFI*	1	*140*	*182*	*.4*	*.8*
259 IFCA	1	NR	NR	-	-
283 LUTH—MO SYNOD	3	594	812	1.6	3.4
287 MENN GEN CONF	1	159	201	.4	.8
355 PRESB CH (USA)	3	398	516*	1.0	2.2
403 SALVATION ARMY	1	45	48	.1	.2
413 S.D.A.	1	35	45*	.1	.2
419 SO BAPT CONV	8	1,993	2,586*	5.1	10.9
438 UN BRETH IN CR	1	39	66	.1	.3
443 UN C OF CHRIST	2	179	232*	.5	1.0
449 UN METHODIST	14	3,889	5,045*	10.0	21.3
467 WESLEYAN	1	16	40	.1	.2
496 JEWISH EST[1]	0	NA	104	.2	.4
499 INDEP.NON-CHAR[3]	1	NA	380	.8	1.6
CHASE	**17**	**1,338**	**1,944***	**64.3**	**100.0**
081 CATHOLIC	1	NA	250	8.3	12.9
081d *LATIN*	1	*NA*	*250*	*8.3*	*12.9*
093 CHR CH (DISC)	1	55	88	2.9	4.5
097 CHR CHS&CHS CR	2	55	69*	2.3	3.5
167 CHS OF CHRIST	1	7	7	.2	.4
226 FRIENDS-USA	1	53	66*	2.2	3.4
226b *EFI*	1	*53*	*66*	*2.2*	*3.4*
283 LUTH—MO SYNOD	1	60	79	2.6	4.1
355 PRESB CH (USA)	1	172	215*	7.1	11.1
419 SO BAPT CONV	1	175	219*	7.2	11.3
443 UN C OF CHRIST	1	22	27*	.9	1.4
449 UN METHODIST	7	739	924*	30.6	47.5
CHAUTAUQUA	**23**	**1,952**	**2,544***	**57.7**	**100.0**
019 AMER BAPT USA	2	642	785*	17.8	30.9
053 ASSEMB OF GOD	2	77	130	2.9	5.1
081 CATHOLIC	2	NA	57	1.3	2.2
081d *LATIN*	2	*NA*	*57*	*1.3*	*2.2*
093 CHR CH (DISC)	1	105	144	3.3	5.7
097 CHR CHS&CHS CR	2	205	251*	5.7	9.9
151 L-D SAINTS	1	NA	37	.8	1.5
167 CHS OF CHRIST	3	88	117	2.7	4.6
193 EPISCOPAL	2	76	95	2.2	3.7
413 S.D.A.	1	41	50*	1.1	2.0
419 SO BAPT CONV	1	246	301*	6.8	11.8
449 UN METHODIST	6	472	577*	13.1	22.7
CHEROKEE	**58**	**7,765**	**11,261***	**52.7**	**100.0**
019 AMER BAPT USA	1	200	252*	1.2	2.2
053 ASSEMB OF GOD	5	383	718	3.4	6.4
059 BAPT MISS ASSN	1	421	530*	2.5	4.7
081 CATHOLIC	6	NA	939	4.4	8.3
081d *LATIN*	6	*NA*	*939*	*4.4*	*8.3*
093 CHR CH (DISC)	3	580	992	4.6	8.8
097 CHR CHS&CHS CR	6	710	893*	4.2	7.9
145 CH GOD PROPHCY	1	33	42*	.2	.4
165 CH OF NAZARENE	3	148	233	1.1	2.1
167 CHS OF CHRIST	2	65	83	.4	.7
193 EPISCOPAL	2	47	64	.3	.6
217 FIRE BAPTIZED	1	10	13*	.1	.1
226 FRIENDS-USA	4	447	562*	2.6	5.0
226b *EFI*	4	*447*	*562*	*2.6*	*5.0*
355 PRESB CH (USA)	4	263	331*	1.5	2.9
413 S.D.A.	1	63	79*	.4	.7
419 SO BAPT CONV	11	3,307	4,161*	19.5	37.0
449 UN METHODIST	7	1,088	1,369*	6.4	12.2
CHEYENNE	**14**	**1,972**	**2,728***	**84.1**	**100.0**
053 ASSEMB OF GOD	1	29	40	1.2	1.5
081 CATHOLIC	2	NA	252	7.8	9.2
081d *LATIN*	2	*NA*	*252*	*7.8*	*9.2*
093 CHR CH (DISC)	1	274	280	8.6	10.3
167 CHS OF CHRIST	1	42	55	1.7	2.0
207 E.L.C.A.	3	691	909	28.0	33.3
413 S.D.A.	1	33	41*	1.3	1.5
419 SO BAPT CONV	1	94	116*	3.6	4.3
449 UN METHODIST	2	774	951*	29.3	34.9
467 WESLEYAN	2	35	84	2.6	3.1
CLARK	**11**	**1,411**	**2,155***	**89.1**	**100.0**
019 AMER BAPT USA	1	51	64*	2.6	3.0
053 ASSEMB OF GOD	1	11	33	1.4	1.5
081 CATHOLIC	1	NA	400	16.5	18.6
081d *LATIN*	1	*NA*	*400*	*16.5*	*18.6*
097 CHR CHS&CHS CR	3	486	605*	25.0	28.1
123 CH GOD (ANDER)	1	101	101	4.2	4.7
167 CHS OF CHRIST	1	19	26	1.1	1.2
355 PRESB CH (USA)	1	141	176*	7.3	8.2
449 UN METHODIST	2	602	750*	31.0	34.8
CLAY	**29**	**4,337**	**6,215***	**67.9**	**100.0**
005 AME ZION	2	165	189	2.1	3.0
019 AMER BAPT USA	1	336	421*	4.6	6.8
053 ASSEMB OF GOD	1	37	50	.5	.8
081 CATHOLIC	1	NA	674	7.4	10.8
081d *LATIN*	1	*NA*	*674*	*7.4*	*10.8*
097 CHR CHS&CHS CR	2	275	345*	3.8	5.6
167 CHS OF CHRIST	1	20	25	.3	.4
193 EPISCOPAL	2	137	204	2.2	3.3
207 E.L.C.A.	1	103	126	1.4	2.0
259 IFCA	1	NR	NR	-	-
283 LUTH—MO SYNOD	1	584	764	8.3	12.3
355 PRESB CH (USA)	3	720	902*	9.8	14.5
443 UN C OF CHRIST	1	48	60*	.7	1.0
449 UN METHODIST	10	1,795	2,249*	24.6	36.2
467 WESLEYAN	2	117	206	2.2	3.3
CLOUD	**30**	**3,653**	**8,111***	**73.6**	**100.0**
019 AMER BAPT USA	2	739	905*	8.2	11.2
053 ASSEMB OF GOD	1	49	66	.6	.8
081 CATHOLIC	7	NA	3,387	30.7	41.8
081d *LATIN*	7	*NA*	*3,387*	*30.7*	*41.8*
097 CHR CHS&CHS CR	4	434	531*	4.8	6.5
167 CHS OF CHRIST	1	11	20	.2	.2
193 EPISCOPAL	1	103	110	1.0	1.4
207 E.L.C.A.	2	277	363	3.3	4.5
355 PRESB CH (USA)	2	199	244*	2.2	3.0
449 UN METHODIST	7	1,489	1,822*	16.5	22.5
467 WESLEYAN	3	352	663	6.0	8.2
COFFEY	**30**	**3,958**	**6,172***	**73.4**	**100.0**
019 AMER BAPT USA	3	587	744*	8.9	12.1
040 AP CHR CH-AMER	1	49	89	1.1	1.4
053 ASSEMB OF GOD	2	159	390	4.6	6.3
081 CATHOLIC	2	NA	526	6.3	8.5
081d *LATIN*	2	*NA*	*526*	*6.3*	*8.5*
097 CHR CHS&CHS CR	4	682	865*	10.3	14.0

NA–Not applicable   NR–Not reported   *Total adherents estimated from known number of communicant, confirmed, full members.   - Represents a percent less than 0.1.   Percentages may not total due to rounding.
[1]See Appendix E   [2]See Appendix F   [3]See Appendix G   Lines in *italic* represent a breakdown of Catholic rites or Friends affiliations. They are included in their respective denominational total.

Table 4. Churches and Church Membership by County and Denomination: 1990

County and Denomination	Number of churches	Communicant, confirmed, full members	Total adherents Number	Percent of total population	Percent of total adherents
151 L-D SAINTS	1	NA	392	4.7	6.4
165 CH OF NAZARENE	1	20	20	.2	.3
167 CHS OF CHRIST	3	69	85	1.0	1.4
283 LUTH—MO SYNOD	2	274	375	4.5	6.1
419 SO BAPT CONV	1	297	377*	4.5	6.1
449 UN METHODIST	10	1,821	2,309*	27.5	37.4
COMANCHE	**12**	**1,747**	**2,386***	**103.2**	**100.0**
019 AMER BAPT USA	1	300	373*	16.1	15.6
053 ASSEMB OF GOD	1	40	90	3.9	3.8
081 CATHOLIC	1	NA	60	2.6	2.5
081d LATIN	1	NA	60	2.6	2.5
093 CHR CH (DISC)	2	312	501	21.7	21.0
097 CHR CHS&CHS CR	2	384	478*	20.7	20.0
285 MENNONITE CH	1	118	146	6.3	6.1
355 PRESB CH (USA)	1	90	112*	4.8	4.7
449 UN METHODIST	3	503	626*	27.1	26.2
COWLEY	**72**	**13,048**	**21,200***	**57.4**	**100.0**
019 AMER BAPT USA	4	1,743	2,206*	6.0	10.4
053 ASSEMB OF GOD	2	279	741	2.0	3.5
081 CATHOLIC	2	NA	2,165	5.9	10.2
081d LATIN	2	NA	2,165	5.9	10.2
089 CHR & MISS AL	1	0	32	.1	.2
093 CHR CH (DISC)	4	1,154	1,525	4.1	7.2
097 CHR CHS&CHS CR	4	340	430*	1.2	2.0
111 CH CR,SCIENTST	1	NR	NR	-	-
121 CH GOD (ABR)	1	11	14*	-	.1
123 CH GOD (ANDER)	1	0	0	-	-
127 CH GOD (CLEVE)	2	148	187*	.5	.9
151 L-D SAINTS	1	NA	288	.8	1.4
165 CH OF NAZARENE	3	324	704	1.9	3.3
167 CHS OF CHRIST	5	244	379	1.0	1.8
193 EPISCOPAL	2	216	352	1.0	1.7
203 EVAN FREE CH	1	85	160	.4	.8
221 FREE METHODIST	1	31	49	.1	.2
226 FRIENDS-USA	2	60	76*	.2	.4
226b EFI	2	60	76*	.2	.4
263 INT FOURSQ GOS	2	399	505*	1.4	2.4
283 LUTH—MO SYNOD	2	837	1,222	3.3	5.8
355 PRESB CH (USA)	4	906	1,147*	3.1	5.4
403 SALVATION ARMY	1	95	102	.3	.5
419 SO BAPT CONV	8	2,379	3,011*	8.2	14.2
443 UN C OF CHRIST	1	61	77*	.2	.4
449 UN METHODIST	14	3,509	4,441*	12.0	20.9
497 BLACK BAPT EST[2]	NA	227	287*	.8	1.4
498 INDEP.CHARIS.[3]	1	NA	400	1.1	1.9
499 INDEP.NON-CHAR[3]	2	NA	700	1.9	3.3
CRAWFORD	**65**	**8,333**	**16,544***	**46.5**	**100.0**
019 AMER BAPT USA	3	554	679*	1.9	4.1
053 ASSEMB OF GOD	1	98	300	.8	1.8
059 BAPT MISS ASSN	2	231	283*	.8	1.7
081 CATHOLIC	10	NA	4,994	14.0	30.2
081d LATIN	10	NA	4,994	14.0	30.2
093 CHR CH (DISC)	4	838	1,807	5.1	10.9
097 CHR CHS&CHS CR	3	471	578*	1.6	3.5
111 CH CR,SCIENTST	1	NR	NR	-	-
127 CH GOD (CLEVE)	2	99	121*	.3	.7
145 CH GOD PROPHCY	1	33	40*	.1	.2
151 L-D SAINTS	1	NA	198	.6	1.2
165 CH OF NAZARENE	3	281	436	1.2	2.6
167 CHS OF CHRIST	2	158	207	.6	1.3
193 EPISCOPAL	1	106	138	.4	.8
207 E.L.C.A.	1	213	251	.7	1.5
283 LUTH—MO SYNOD	5	525	714	2.0	4.3
355 PRESB CH (USA)	4	628	770*	2.2	4.7
403 SALVATION ARMY	1	100	120	.3	.7
413 S.D.A.	2	130	159*	.4	1.0
419 SO BAPT CONV	4	1,101	1,350*	3.8	8.2
449 UN METHODIST	13	2,687	3,295*	9.3	19.9
469 WELS	1	80	104	.3	.6
DECATUR	**18**	**1,512**	**2,669***	**66.4**	**100.0**
019 AMER BAPT USA	1	88	111*	2.8	4.2
053 ASSEMB OF GOD	1	38	71	1.8	2.7
081 CATHOLIC	2	NA	633	15.7	23.7
081d LATIN	2	NA	633	15.7	23.7
093 CHR CH (DISC)	1	57	88	2.2	3.3
167 CHS OF CHRIST	1	42	55	1.4	2.1
207 E.L.C.A.	2	127	201	5.0	7.5
283 LUTH—MO SYNOD	1	215	314	7.8	11.8
355 PRESB CH (USA)	1	41	52*	1.3	1.9
413 S.D.A.	1	16	20*	.5	.7
419 SO BAPT CONV	1	31	39*	1.0	1.5
449 UN METHODIST	6	857	1,085*	27.0	40.7

County and Denomination	Number of churches	Communicant, confirmed, full members	Total adherents Number	Percent of total population	Percent of total adherents
DICKINSON	**64**	**8,139**	**12,643***	**66.7**	**100.0**
019 AMER BAPT USA	4	516	648*	3.4	5.1
053 ASSEMB OF GOD	1	31	35	.2	.3
075 BRETHREN IN CR	3	284	284	1.5	2.2
081 CATHOLIC	6	NA	2,105	11.1	16.6
081d LATIN	6	NA	2,105	11.1	16.6
093 CHR CH (DISC)	1	137	199	1.0	1.6
097 CHR CHS&CHS CR	3	670	842*	4.4	6.7
123 CH GOD (ANDER)	1	14	23	.1	.2
151 L-D SAINTS	1	NA	389	2.1	3.1
157 CH OF BRETHREN	2	87	109*	.6	.9
165 CH OF NAZARENE	1	24	32	.2	.3
167 CHS OF CHRIST	2	25	28	.1	.2
193 EPISCOPAL	1	51	51	.3	.4
207 E.L.C.A.	4	1,025	1,297	6.8	10.3
263 INT FOURSQ GOS	1	49	62*	.3	.5
283 LUTH—MO SYNOD	4	794	985	5.2	7.8
313 N AM BAPT CONF	2	148	186*	1.0	1.5
353 CHR BRETHREN	1	30	50	.3	.4
355 PRESB CH (USA)	5	524	658*	3.5	5.2
413 S.D.A.	1	197	248*	1.3	2.0
419 SO BAPT CONV	1	125	157*	.8	1.2
438 UN BRETH IN CR	1	70	70	.4	.6
443 UN C OF CHRIST	2	253	318*	1.7	2.5
449 UN METHODIST	15	3,040	3,820*	20.1	30.2
467 WESLEYAN	1	45	47	.2	.4
DONIPHAN	**25**	**2,729**	**4,823***	**59.3**	**100.0**
019 AMER BAPT USA	3	883	1,107*	13.6	23.0
053 ASSEMB OF GOD	2	82	119	1.5	2.5
081 CATHOLIC	5	NA	1,228	15.1	25.5
081d LATIN	5	NA	1,228	15.1	25.5
093 CHR CH (DISC)	2	223	363	4.5	7.5
097 CHR CHS&CHS CR	1	200	251*	3.1	5.2
207 E.L.C.A.	1	215	300	3.7	6.2
283 LUTH—MO SYNOD	1	194	287	3.5	6.0
355 PRESB CH (USA)	1	56	70*	.9	1.5
413 S.D.A.	1	26	33*	.4	.7
419 SO BAPT CONV	1	38	48*	.6	1.0
443 UN C OF CHRIST	1	112	140*	1.7	2.9
449 UN METHODIST	6	700	877*	10.8	18.2
DOUGLAS	**75**	**14,768**	**26,582***	**32.5**	**100.0**
019 AMER BAPT USA	1	430	516*	.6	1.9
053 ASSEMB OF GOD	4	299	643	.8	2.4
081 CATHOLIC	5	NA	5,616	6.9	21.1
081d LATIN	5	NA	5,616	6.9	21.1
093 CHR CH (DISC)	2	503	828	1.0	3.1
097 CHR CHS&CHS CR	2	330	396*	.5	1.5
111 CH CR,SCIENTST	1	NR	NR	-	-
123 CH GOD (ANDER)	1	112	112	.1	.4
151 L-D SAINTS	2	NA	756	.9	2.8
157 CH OF BRETHREN	2	135	162*	.2	.6
165 CH OF NAZARENE	2	261	336	.4	1.3
167 CHS OF CHRIST	7	400	565	.7	2.1
193 EPISCOPAL	2	623	952	1.2	3.6
207 E.L.C.A.	2	1,411	1,900	2.3	7.1
216 EVAN PRESBY CH	1	83	91	.1	.3
221 FREE METHODIST	1	188	424	.5	1.6
226 FRIENDS-USA	3	184	222*	.3	.8
226b EFI	2	175	210*	.3	.8
226c FGC	1	9	12	-	-
283 LUTH—MO SYNOD	2	672	888	1.1	3.3
285 MENNONITE CH	1	38	78	.1	.3
287 MENN GEN CONF	1	20	30	-	.1
329 OPEN BIBLE STD	1	NR	NR	-	-
331 ORTH CH IN AM	1	NR	NR	-	-
353 CHR BRETHREN	2	168	280	.3	1.1
355 PRESB CH (USA)	3	823	987*	1.2	3.7
403 SALVATION ARMY	1	103	106	.1	.4
413 S.D.A.	1	40	48*	.1	.2
419 SO BAPT CONV	5	1,925	2,308*	2.8	8.7
435 UNITARIAN-UNIV	1	100	150	.2	.6
443 UN C OF CHRIST	3	1,322	1,585*	1.9	6.0
449 UN METHODIST	13	3,698	4,434*	5.4	16.7
467 WESLEYAN	1	21	190	.2	.7
496 JEWISH EST[1]	0	NA	175	.2	.7
497 BLACK BAPT EST[2]	NA	879	1,054*	1.3	4.0
498 INDEP.CHARIS.[3]	1	NA	750	.9	2.8
EDWARDS	**18**	**1,197**	**2,659***	**70.2**	**100.0**
019 AMER BAPT USA	2	60	75*	2.0	2.8
053 ASSEMB OF GOD	1	32	100	2.6	3.8
081 CATHOLIC	4	NA	961	25.4	36.1
081d LATIN	4	NA	961	25.4	36.1
093 CHR CH (DISC)	2	98	242	6.4	9.1

NA–Not applicable   NR–Not reported   *Total adherents estimated from known number of communicant, confirmed, full members.   - Represents a percent less than 0.1.   Percentages may not total due to rounding.
[1]See Appendix E   [2]See Appendix F   [3]See Appendix G   Lines in *italic* represent a breakdown of Catholic rites or Friends affiliations. They are included in their respective denominational total.

Table 4. Churches and Church Membership by County and Denomination: 1990

County and Denomination	Number of churches	Communicant, confirmed, full members	Total adherents Number	Percent of total population	Percent of total adherents
165 CH OF NAZARENE	1	27	66	1.7	2.5
193 EPISCOPAL	1	21	25	.7	.9
283 LUTH—MO SYNOD	1	130	158	4.2	5.9
443 UN C OF CHRIST	1	120	149*	3.9	5.6
449 UN METHODIST	5	709	883*	23.3	33.2
ELK	**16**	**1,270**	**1,693***	**50.9**	**100.0**
019 AMER BAPT USA	3	375	450*	13.5	26.6
053 ASSEMB OF GOD	1	38	58	1.7	3.4
081 CATHOLIC	1	NA	132	4.0	7.8
081d *LATIN*	*1*	*NA*	*132*	*4.0*	*7.8*
093 CHR CH (DISC)	1	30	61	1.8	3.6
097 CHR CHS&CHS CR	2	180	216*	6.5	12.8
167 CHS OF CHRIST	1	28	36	1.1	2.1
217 FIRE BAPTIZED	1	4	5*	.2	.3
449 UN METHODIST	5	598	718*	21.6	42.4
467 WESLEYAN	1	17	17	.5	1.0
ELLIS	**31**	**3,660**	**19,275***	**74.1**	**100.0**
019 AMER BAPT USA	2	125	158*	.6	.8
053 ASSEMB OF GOD	1	125	250	1.0	1.3
081 CATHOLIC	13	NA	14,253	54.8	73.9
081d *LATIN*	*13*	*NA*	*14,253*	*54.8*	*73.9*
097 CHR CHS&CHS CR	1	60	76*	.3	.4
165 CH OF NAZARENE	1	129	349	1.3	1.8
167 CHS OF CHRIST	1	50	64	.2	.3
193 EPISCOPAL	2	144	208	.8	1.1
207 E.L.C.A.	3	788	1,063	4.1	5.5
237 GC MENN BR CHS	1	54	68*	.3	.4
283 LUTH—MO SYNOD	1	314	426	1.6	2.2
355 PRESB CH (USA)	1	505	637*	2.4	3.3
419 SO BAPT CONV	2	50	63*	.2	.3
449 UN METHODIST	2	1,316	1,660*	6.4	8.6
ELLSWORTH	**20**	**2,543**	**4,437***	**67.4**	**100.0**
053 ASSEMB OF GOD	1	22	73	1.1	1.6
081 CATHOLIC	4	NA	1,196	18.2	27.0
081d *LATIN*	*4*	*NA*	*1,196*	*18.2*	*27.0*
193 EPISCOPAL	1	29	22	.3	.5
203 EVAN FREE CH	1	0	60	.9	1.4
207 E.L.C.A.	2	228	298	4.5	6.7
283 LUTH—MO SYNOD	3	920	1,146	17.4	25.8
313 N AM BAPT CONF	1	159	194*	2.9	4.4
355 PRESB CH (USA)	2	514	628*	9.5	14.2
443 UN C OF CHRIST	1	175	214*	3.2	4.8
449 UN METHODIST	4	496	606*	9.2	13.7
FINNEY	**30**	**6,837**	**16,800***	**50.8**	**100.0**
019 AMER BAPT USA	1	186	258*	.8	1.5
053 ASSEMB OF GOD	2	256	465	1.4	2.8
081 CATHOLIC	2	NA	6,546	19.8	39.0
081d *LATIN*	*2*	*NA*	*6,546*	*19.8*	*39.0*
093 CHR CH (DISC)	1	499	718	2.2	4.3
097 CHR CHS&CHS CR	1	350	486*	1.5	2.9
151 L-D SAINTS	1	NA	255	.8	1.5
157 CH OF BRETHREN	2	400	556*	1.7	3.3
165 CH OF NAZARENE	1	301	341	1.0	2.0
167 CHS OF CHRIST	1	117	152	.5	.9
193 EPISCOPAL	1	131	219	.7	1.3
207 E.L.C.A.	1	232	309	.9	1.8
237 GC MENN BR CHS	1	298	414*	1.3	2.5
283 LUTH—MO SYNOD	1	664	948	2.9	5.6
355 PRESB CH (USA)	2	361	501*	1.5	3.0
403 SALVATION ARMY	1	32	36	.1	.2
413 S.D.A.	1	113	157*	.5	.9
419 SO BAPT CONV	3	703	976*	3.0	5.8
443 UN C OF CHRIST	1	356	494*	1.5	2.9
449 UN METHODIST	4	1,817	2,524*	7.6	15.0
467 WESLEYAN	1	21	45	.1	.3
499 INDEP.NON-CHAR[3]	1	NA	400	1.2	2.4
FORD	**34**	**7,286**	**14,398***	**52.4**	**100.0**
019 AMER BAPT USA	1	453	593*	2.2	4.1
053 ASSEMB OF GOD	2	116	200	.7	1.4
081 CATHOLIC	6	NA	4,514	16.4	31.4
081d *LATIN*	*6*	*NA*	*4,514*	*16.4*	*31.4*
097 CHR CHS&CHS CR	4	1,769	2,314*	8.4	16.1
123 CH GOD (ANDER)	1	55	68	.2	.5
151 L-D SAINTS	1	NA	200	.7	1.4
165 CH OF NAZARENE	2	266	490	1.8	3.4
167 CHS OF CHRIST	1	217	296	1.1	2.1
193 EPISCOPAL	1	166	257	.9	1.8
207 E.L.C.A.	1	368	534	1.9	3.7
221 FREE METHODIST	1	12	28	.1	.2
283 LUTH—MO SYNOD	3	760	917	3.3	6.4
291 MISSIONARY CH	1	177	178	.6	1.2
355 PRESB CH (USA)	3	524	685*	2.5	4.8
403 SALVATION ARMY	1	61	61	.2	.4
419 SO BAPT CONV	1	449	587*	2.1	4.1
443 UN C OF CHRIST	1	62	81*	.3	.6
449 UN METHODIST	3	1,831	2,395*	8.7	16.6
FRANKLIN	**45**	**5,890**	**10,150***	**46.1**	**100.0**
019 AMER BAPT USA	8	1,669	2,153*	9.8	21.2
053 ASSEMB OF GOD	3	260	370	1.7	3.6
059 BAPT MISS ASSN	1	33	43*	.2	.4
081 CATHOLIC	2	NA	2,106	9.6	20.7
081d *LATIN*	*2*	*NA*	*2,106*	*9.6*	*20.7*
093 CHR CH (DISC)	3	329	427	1.9	4.2
097 CHR CHS&CHS CR	1	20	26*	.1	.3
111 CH CR,SCIENTST	1	NR	NR	-	-
151 L-D SAINTS	1	NA	149	.7	1.5
157 CH OF BRETHREN	2	260	335*	1.5	3.3
165 CH OF NAZARENE	1	87	185	.8	1.8
167 CHS OF CHRIST	2	81	120	.5	1.2
193 EPISCOPAL	1	89	105	.5	1.0
221 FREE METHODIST	1	11	30	.1	.3
263 INT FOURSQ GOS	1	119	154*	.7	1.5
283 LUTH—MO SYNOD	1	267	406	1.8	4.0
353 CHR BRETHREN	1	25	50	.2	.5
355 PRESB CH (USA)	2	406	524*	2.4	5.2
413 S.D.A.	1	78	101*	.5	1.0
419 SO BAPT CONV	2	148	191*	.9	1.9
449 UN METHODIST	9	1,919	2,475*	11.3	24.4
467 WESLEYAN	1	89	200	.9	2.0
GEARY	**33**	**7,672**	**14,106***	**46.3**	**100.0**
019 AMER BAPT USA	2	1,284	1,710*	5.6	12.1
053 ASSEMB OF GOD	1	143	179	.6	1.3
081 CATHOLIC	2	NA	2,998	9.8	21.3
081d *LATIN*	*2*	*NA*	*2,998*	*9.8*	*21.3*
097 CHR CHS&CHS CR	1	400	533*	1.8	3.8
123 CH GOD (ANDER)	1	65	100	.3	.7
127 CH GOD (CLEVE)	1	45	60*	.2	.4
145 CH GOD PROPHCY	1	33	44*	.1	.3
151 L-D SAINTS	1	NA	601	2.0	4.3
165 CH OF NAZARENE	2	185	362	1.2	2.6
167 CHS OF CHRIST	2	72	125	.4	.9
181 CONSRV CONGR	1	51	68*	.2	.5
193 EPISCOPAL	1	188	352	1.2	2.5
207 E.L.C.A.	1	152	228	.7	1.6
221 FREE METHODIST	1	2	8	-	.1
283 LUTH—MO SYNOD	2	490	589	1.9	4.2
313 N AM BAPT CONF	1	124	165*	.5	1.2
355 PRESB CH (USA)	1	641	854*	2.8	6.1
403 SALVATION ARMY	1	50	52	.2	.4
413 S.D.A.	1	33	44*	.1	.3
415 S-D BAPTIST GC	1	30	40*	.1	.3
419 SO BAPT CONV	2	899	1,198*	3.9	8.5
443 UN C OF CHRIST	2	300	400*	1.3	2.8
449 UN METHODIST	3	900	1,199*	3.9	8.5
467 WESLEYAN	1	43	143	.5	1.0
497 BLACK BAPT EST[2]	NA	1,542	2,054*	6.7	14.6
GOVE	**8**	**944**	**2,715***	**84.0**	**100.0**
081 CATHOLIC	3	NA	1,522	47.1	56.1
081d *LATIN*	*3*	*NA*	*1,522*	*47.1*	*56.1*
157 CH OF BRETHREN	1	388	490*	15.2	18.0
449 UN METHODIST	4	556	703*	21.8	25.9
GRAHAM	**15**	**1,309**	**2,459***	**69.4**	**100.0**
019 AMER BAPT USA	1	233	293*	8.3	11.9
053 ASSEMB OF GOD	2	108	158	4.5	6.4
081 CATHOLIC	2	NA	816	23.0	33.2
081d *LATIN*	*2*	*NA*	*816*	*23.0*	*33.2*
097 CHR CHS&CHS CR	1	200	252*	7.1	10.2
123 CH GOD (ANDER)	1	60	60	1.7	2.4
127 CH GOD (CLEVE)	1	3	4*	.1	.2
283 LUTH—MO SYNOD	1	69	75	2.1	3.1
355 PRESB CH (USA)	1	88	111*	3.1	4.5
419 SO BAPT CONV	1	35	44*	1.2	1.8
449 UN METHODIST	4	513	646*	18.2	26.3
GRANT	**16**	**2,566**	**4,199***	**58.7**	**100.0**
019 AMER BAPT USA	1	190	263*	3.7	6.3
053 ASSEMB OF GOD	1	57	100	1.4	2.4
081 CATHOLIC	1	NA	600	8.4	14.3
081d *LATIN*	*1*	*NA*	*600*	*8.4*	*14.3*
093 CHR CH (DISC)	1	214	308	4.3	7.3
123 CH GOD (ANDER)	1	159	167	2.3	4.0

NA–Not applicable   NR–Not reported   *Total adherents estimated from known number of communicant, confirmed, full members.   - Represents a percent less than 0.1.   Percentages may not total due to rounding.

[1]See Appendix E   [2]See Appendix F   [3]See Appendix G   Lines in *italic* represent a breakdown of Catholic rites or Friends affiliations. They are included in their respective denominational total.

Table 4. Churches and Church Membership by County and Denomination: 1990

County and Denomination	Number of churches	Communicant, confirmed, full members	Total adherents		
			Number	Percent of total population	Percent of total adherents
127 CH GOD (CLEVE)	1	67	93*	1.3	2.2
143 CG IN CR(MENN)	1	181	250*	3.5	6.0
165 CH OF NAZARENE	1	23	90	1.3	2.1
167 CHS OF CHRIST	1	107	146	2.0	3.5
193 EPISCOPAL	1	73	105	1.5	2.5
223 FREE WILL BAPT	1	34	47*	.7	1.1
237 GC MENN BR CHS	1	159	220*	3.1	5.2
283 LUTH—MO SYNOD	1	135	196	2.7	4.7
349 PENT HOLINESS	1	14	19*	.3	.5
419 SO BAPT CONV	1	461	638*	8.9	15.2
449 UN METHODIST	1	692	957*	13.4	22.8
GRAY	**18**	**2,356**	**3,787***	**70.2**	**100.0**
081 CATHOLIC	1	NA	520	9.6	13.7
081d LATIN	*1*	*NA*	*520*	*9.6*	*13.7*
093 CHR CH (DISC)	1	154	265	4.9	7.0
097 CHR CHS&CHS CR	1	60	81*	1.5	2.1
143 CG IN CR(MENN)	4	867	1,165*	21.6	30.8
165 CH OF NAZARENE	1	167	271	5.0	7.2
237 GC MENN BR CHS	1	115	155*	2.9	4.1
285 MENNONITE CH	1	35	47	.9	1.2
287 MENN GEN CONF	1	18	21	.4	.6
349 PENT HOLINESS	2	71	95*	1.8	2.5
419 SO BAPT CONV	1	126	169*	3.1	4.5
449 UN METHODIST	4	743	998*	18.5	26.4
GREELEY	**6**	**639**	**1,054***	**59.4**	**100.0**
019 AMER BAPT USA	1	243	328*	18.5	31.1
053 ASSEMB OF GOD	1	43	75	4.2	7.1
081 CATHOLIC	1	NA	170	9.6	16.1
081d LATIN	*1*	*NA*	*170*	*9.6*	*16.1*
207 E.L.C.A.	1	42	61	3.4	5.8
355 PRESB CH (USA)	1	103	139*	7.8	13.2
449 UN METHODIST	1	208	281*	15.8	26.7
GREENWOOD	**32**	**3,292**	**5,061***	**64.5**	**100.0**
040 AP CHR CH-AMER	1	26	46	.6	.9
053 ASSEMB OF GOD	1	20	30	.4	.6
081 CATHOLIC	3	NA	548	7.0	10.8
081d LATIN	*3*	*NA*	*548*	*7.0*	*10.8*
093 CHR CH (DISC)	3	395	728	9.3	14.4
097 CHR CHS&CHS CR	1	56	69*	.9	1.4
123 CH GOD (ANDER)	1	8	9	.1	.2
157 CH OF BRETHREN	1	18	22*	.3	.4
165 CH OF NAZARENE	2	89	137	1.7	2.7
167 CHS OF CHRIST	1	25	35	.4	.7
203 EVAN FREE CH	1	42	61	.8	1.2
207 E.L.C.A.	1	280	351	4.5	6.9
355 PRESB CH (USA)	1	54	66*	.8	1.3
413 S.D.A.	1	72	88*	1.1	1.7
419 SO BAPT CONV	3	721	883*	11.3	17.4
443 UN C OF CHRIST	1	286	350*	4.5	6.9
449 UN METHODIST	9	1,174	1,438*	18.3	28.4
467 WESLEYAN	1	26	200	2.5	4.0
HAMILTON	**8**	**978**	**1,629***	**68.2**	**100.0**
081 CATHOLIC	1	NA	230	9.6	14.1
081d LATIN	*1*	*NA*	*230*	*9.6*	*14.1*
097 CHR CHS&CHS CR	2	237	297*	12.4	18.2
165 CH OF NAZARENE	1	16	57	2.4	3.5
355 PRESB CH (USA)	1	175	219*	9.2	13.4
419 SO BAPT CONV	1	42	53*	2.2	3.3
449 UN METHODIST	1	432	541*	22.7	33.2
467 WESLEYAN	1	76	232	9.7	14.2
HARPER	**33**	**3,373**	**5,286***	**74.2**	**100.0**
019 AMER BAPT USA	2	297	372*	5.2	7.0
053 ASSEMB OF GOD	3	123	285	4.0	5.4
081 CATHOLIC	3	NA	720	10.1	13.6
081d LATIN	*3*	*NA*	*720*	*10.1*	*13.6*
093 CHR CH (DISC)	2	504	810	11.4	15.3
097 CHR CHS&CHS CR	3	670	840*	11.8	15.9
123 CH GOD (ANDER)	1	20	20	.3	.4
165 CH OF NAZARENE	1	46	122	1.7	2.3
167 CHS OF CHRIST	4	152	217	3.0	4.1
193 EPISCOPAL	1	18	18	.3	.3
285 MENNONITE CH	2	205	205	2.9	3.9
355 PRESB CH (USA)	3	155	194*	2.7	3.7
413 S.D.A.	1	28	35*	.5	.7
443 UN C OF CHRIST	2	220	276*	3.9	5.2
449 UN METHODIST	5	935	1,172*	16.5	22.2
HARVEY	**68**	**12,954**	**19,675***	**63.4**	**100.0**
019 AMER BAPT USA	1	725	914*	2.9	4.6
053 ASSEMB OF GOD	1	63	90	.3	.5
081 CATHOLIC	3	NA	2,923	9.4	14.9
081d LATIN	*3*	*NA*	*2,923*	*9.4*	*14.9*
093 CHR CH (DISC)	2	433	724	2.3	3.7
097 CHR CHS&CHS CR	1	65	82*	.3	.4
111 CH CR,SCIENTST	1	NR	NR	-	-
123 CH GOD (ANDER)	1	70	89	.3	.5
127 CH GOD (CLEVE)	1	5	6*	-	-
143 CG IN CR(MENN)	3	514	648*	2.1	3.3
151 L-D SAINTS	1	NA	219	.7	1.1
157 CH OF BRETHREN	1	88	111*	.4	.6
165 CH OF NAZARENE	2	406	482	1.6	2.4
167 CHS OF CHRIST	3	175	218	.7	1.1
193 EPISCOPAL	1	268	378	1.2	1.9
207 E.L.C.A.	1	198	293	.9	1.5
213 EVAN MENN INC	1	90	114*	.4	.6
221 FREE METHODIST	1	35	37	.1	.2
237 GC MENN BR CHS	3	388	489*	1.6	2.5
263 INT FOURSQ GOS	1	155	195*	.6	1.0
283 LUTH—MO SYNOD	1	420	516	1.7	2.6
285 MENNONITE CH	6	960	1,138	3.7	5.8
287 MENN GEN CONF	13	3,206	4,029	13.0	20.5
291 MISSIONARY CH	1	29	36	.1	.2
355 PRESB CH (USA)	3	539	680*	2.2	3.5
413 S.D.A.	1	27	34*	.1	.2
419 SO BAPT CONV	2	390	492*	1.6	2.5
443 UN C OF CHRIST	3	311	392*	1.3	2.0
449 UN METHODIST	9	3,248	4,097*	13.2	20.8
496 JEWISH EST[1]	0	NA	65	.2	.3
497 BLACK BAPT EST[2]	NA	146	184*	.6	.9
HASKELL	**10**	**1,726**	**2,870***	**73.9**	**100.0**
081 CATHOLIC	1	NA	550	14.2	19.2
081d LATIN	*1*	*NA*	*550*	*14.2*	*19.2*
097 CHR CHS&CHS CR	1	350	473*	12.2	16.5
123 CH GOD (ANDER)	1	66	126	3.2	4.4
165 CH OF NAZARENE	1	131	130	3.3	4.5
167 CHS OF CHRIST	2	44	57	1.5	2.0
419 SO BAPT CONV	2	504	681*	17.5	23.7
449 UN METHODIST	2	631	853*	22.0	29.7
HODGEMAN	**14**	**779**	**1,388***	**63.8**	**100.0**
019 AMER BAPT USA	2	111	144*	6.6	10.4
081 CATHOLIC	4	NA	390	17.9	28.1
081d LATIN	*4*	*NA*	*390*	*17.9*	*28.1*
167 CHS OF CHRIST	1	5	6	.3	.4
263 INT FOURSQ GOS	1	18	23*	1.1	1.7
283 LUTH—MO SYNOD	1	30	34	1.6	2.4
287 MENN GEN CONF	1	29	33	1.5	2.4
355 PRESB CH (USA)	1	146	189*	8.7	13.6
413 S.D.A.	1	42	54*	2.5	3.9
449 UN METHODIST	2	398	515*	23.7	37.1
JACKSON	**28**	**3,887**	**6,023***	**52.3**	**100.0**
019 AMER BAPT USA	3	514	667*	5.8	11.1
081 CATHOLIC	3	NA	877	7.6	14.6
081d LATIN	*3*	*NA*	*877*	*7.6*	*14.6*
093 CHR CH (DISC)	2	183	296	2.6	4.9
097 CHR CHS&CHS CR	3	581	754*	6.5	12.5
165 CH OF NAZARENE	1	13	59	.5	1.0
283 LUTH—MO SYNOD	2	331	399	3.5	6.6
313 N AM BAPT CONF	1	54	70*	.6	1.2
339 PENT CH OF GOD	1	35	77	.7	1.3
355 PRESB CH (USA)	2	228	296*	2.6	4.9
449 UN METHODIST	10	1,948	2,528*	21.9	42.0
JEFFERSON	**29**	**3,684**	**7,721***	**48.5**	**100.0**
019 AMER BAPT USA	1	224	287*	1.8	3.7
053 ASSEMB OF GOD	2	148	253	1.6	3.3
081 CATHOLIC	5	NA	2,808	17.7	36.4
081d LATIN	*5*	*NA*	*2,808*	*17.7*	*36.4*
097 CHR CHS&CHS CR	4	410	525*	3.3	6.8
165 CH OF NAZARENE	1	43	149	.9	1.9
167 CHS OF CHRIST	1	16	24	.2	.3
207 E.L.C.A.	1	69	94	.6	1.2
283 LUTH—MO SYNOD	1	200	286	1.8	3.7
355 PRESB CH (USA)	1	146	187*	1.2	2.4
415 S-D BAPTIST GC	1	103	132*	.8	1.7
419 SO BAPT CONV	1	149	191*	1.2	2.5
449 UN METHODIST	10	2,176	2,785*	17.5	36.1
JEWELL	**23**	**1,910**	**2,950***	**69.4**	**100.0**
019 AMER BAPT USA	1	149	184*	4.3	6.2
053 ASSEMB OF GOD	1	15	20	.5	.7
081 CATHOLIC	2	NA	421	9.9	14.3
081d LATIN	*2*	*NA*	*421*	*9.9*	*14.3*

NA–Not applicable   NR–Not reported   *Total adherents estimated from known number of communicant, confirmed, full members.   - Represents a percent less than 0.1.   Percentages may not total due to rounding.
[1]See Appendix E   [2]See Appendix F   [3]See Appendix G   Lines in *italic* represent a breakdown of Catholic rites or Friends affiliations. They are included in their respective denominational total.

KANSAS

Table 4. Churches and Church Membership by County and Denomination: 1990

County and Denomination	Number of churches	Communicant, confirmed, full members	Total adherents Number	Percent of total population	Percent of total adherents
093 CHR CH (DISC)	1	120	259	6.1	8.8
097 CHR CHS&CHS CR	2	110	136*	3.2	4.6
165 CH OF NAZARENE	1	49	53	1.2	1.8
167 CHS OF CHRIST	1	14	18	.4	.6
207 E.L.C.A.	1	127	220	5.2	7.5
226 FRIENDS-USA	1	133	164*	3.9	5.6
226b *EFI*	*1*	*133*	*164**	*3.9*	*5.6*
419 SO BAPT CONV	1	50	62*	1.5	2.1
449 UN METHODIST	11	1,143	1,413*	33.2	47.9
JOHNSON	**203**	**74,369**	**174,875***	**49.3**	**100.0**
019 AMER BAPT USA	14	5,125	6,533*	1.8	3.7
053 ASSEMB OF GOD	7	1,021	2,113	.6	1.2
063 BEREAN FUND CH	1	66	176	-	.1
081 CATHOLIC	15	NA	61,260	17.3	35.0
081d *LATIN*	*15*	*NA*	*61,260*	*17.3*	*35.0*
093 CHR CH (DISC)	10	4,607	6,104	1.7	3.5
097 CHR CHS&CHS CR	4	1,825	2,326*	.7	1.3
111 CH CR,SCIENTST	4	NR	NR	-	-
123 CH GOD (ANDER)	2	330	330	.1	.2
145 CH GOD PROPHCY	4	131	167*	-	.1
151 L-D SAINTS	8	NA	3,370	.9	1.9
157 CH OF BRETHREN	2	59	75*	-	-
165 CH OF NAZARENE	10	4,711	6,866	1.9	3.9
167 CHS OF CHRIST	8	1,714	2,329	.7	1.3
193 EPISCOPAL	6	3,396	4,420	1.2	2.5
203 EVAN FREE CH	2	151	362	.1	.2
207 E.L.C.A.	13	5,749	7,513	2.1	4.3
216 EVAN PRESBY CH	3	428	482	.1	.3
226 FRIENDS-USA	1	74	94*	-	.1
226b *EFI*	*1*	*74*	*94**	-	*.1*
237 GC MENN BR CHS	1	108	138*	-	.1
246 GREEK ORTHODOX	1	NR	NR	-	-
259 IFCA	1	NR	NR	-	-
283 LUTH—MO SYNOD	7	5,493	7,262	2.0	4.2
284 LUTH CH-AM ASC	1	19	28	-	-
313 N AM BAPT CONF	1	0	0*	-	-
349 PENT HOLINESS	1	18	23*	-	-
353 CHR BRETHREN	1	90	135	-	.1
355 PRESB CH (USA)	14	14,027	17,881*	5.0	10.2
356 PRESB CH AMER	2	328	425	.1	.2
371 REF CH IN AM	1	160	384	.1	.2
403 SALVATION ARMY	1	22	24	-	-
413 S.D.A.	2	290	370*	.1	.2
419 SO BAPT CONV	16	7,503	9,564*	2.7	5.5
435 UNITARIAN-UNIV	2	209	299	.1	.2
443 UN C OF CHRIST	3	953	1,215*	.3	.7
449 UN METHODIST	20	13,503	17,213*	4.8	9.8
467 WESLEYAN	2	150	942	.3	.5
469 WELS	2	280	366	.1	.2
496 JEWISH EST[1]	3	NA	4,330	1.2	2.5
497 BLACK BAPT EST[2]	NA	1,829	2,331*	.7	1.3
498 INDEP.CHARIS.[3]	3	NA	4,550	1.3	2.6
499 INDEP.NON-CHAR[3]	4	NA	2,875	.8	1.6
KEARNY	**15**	**1,370**	**2,692***	**66.8**	**100.0**
019 AMER BAPT USA	1	90	123*	3.1	4.6
053 ASSEMB OF GOD	1	14	33	.8	1.2
081 CATHOLIC	2	NA	715	17.8	26.6
081d *LATIN*	*2*	*NA*	*715*	*17.8*	*26.6*
093 CHR CH (DISC)	1	35	56	1.4	2.1
097 CHR CHS&CHS CR	1	120	164*	4.1	6.1
143 CG IN CR(MENN)	1	24	33*	.8	1.2
167 CHS OF CHRIST	1	42	55	1.4	2.0
283 LUTH—MO SYNOD	1	154	202	5.0	7.5
355 PRESB CH (USA)	1	128	175*	4.3	6.5
419 SO BAPT CONV	1	120	164*	4.1	6.1
449 UN METHODIST	3	620	847*	21.0	31.5
467 WESLEYAN	1	23	125	3.1	4.6
KINGMAN	**30**	**2,882**	**6,007***	**72.4**	**100.0**
019 AMER BAPT USA	2	438	559*	6.7	9.3
053 ASSEMB OF GOD	1	45	75	.9	1.2
081 CATHOLIC	7	NA	2,295	27.7	38.2
081d *LATIN*	*7*	*NA*	*2,295*	*27.7*	*38.2*
093 CHR CH (DISC)	2	446	577	7.0	9.6
097 CHR CHS&CHS CR	2	160	204*	2.5	3.4
165 CH OF NAZARENE	1	60	83	1.0	1.4
167 CHS OF CHRIST	3	121	183	2.2	3.0
193 EPISCOPAL	1	13	15	.2	.2
283 LUTH—MO SYNOD	1	127	162	2.0	2.7
287 MENN GEN CONF	1	157	174	2.1	2.9
355 PRESB CH (USA)	2	179	229*	2.8	3.8
449 UN METHODIST	7	1,136	1,451*	17.5	24.2

County and Denomination	Number of churches	Communicant, confirmed, full members	Total adherents Number	Percent of total population	Percent of total adherents
KIOWA	**13**	**2,242**	**3,239***	**88.5**	**100.0**
019 AMER BAPT USA	1	190	237*	6.5	7.3
053 ASSEMB OF GOD	1	49	85	2.3	2.6
081 CATHOLIC	1	NA	75	2.0	2.3
081d *LATIN*	*1*	*NA*	*75*	*2.0*	*2.3*
093 CHR CH (DISC)	1	145	463	12.7	14.3
143 CG IN CR(MENN)	1	81	101*	2.8	3.1
167 CHS OF CHRIST	1	45	60	1.6	1.9
226 FRIENDS-USA	1	500	623*	17.0	19.2
226b *EFI*	*1*	*500*	*623**	*17.0*	*19.2*
283 LUTH—MO SYNOD	1	44	55	1.5	1.7
285 MENNONITE CH	1	113	200	5.5	6.2
449 UN METHODIST	4	1,075	1,340*	36.6	41.4
LABETTE	**62**	**8,661**	**14,882***	**62.8**	**100.0**
019 AMER BAPT USA	4	1,322	1,670*	7.0	11.2
053 ASSEMB OF GOD	4	283	581	2.5	3.9
081 CATHOLIC	4	NA	3,610	15.2	24.3
081d *LATIN*	*4*	*NA*	*3,610*	*15.2*	*24.3*
093 CHR CH (DISC)	1	576	644	2.7	4.3
097 CHR CHS&CHS CR	7	890	1,124*	4.7	7.6
123 CH GOD (ANDER)	1	5	5	-	-
127 CH GOD (CLEVE)	3	157	198*	.8	1.3
151 L-D SAINTS	1	NA	113	.5	.8
157 CH OF BRETHREN	1	65	82*	.3	.6
165 CH OF NAZARENE	2	248	429	1.8	2.9
167 CHS OF CHRIST	1	93	121	.5	.8
193 EPISCOPAL	1	242	268	1.1	1.8
217 FIRE BAPTIZED	3	77	97*	.4	.7
223 FREE WILL BAPT	1	60	76*	.3	.5
263 INT FOURSQ GOS	1	292	369*	1.6	2.5
283 LUTH—MO SYNOD	2	286	361	1.5	2.4
329 OPEN BIBLE STD	1	NR	NR	-	-
355 PRESB CH (USA)	2	264	333*	1.4	2.2
413 S.D.A.	2	48	61*	.3	.4
419 SO BAPT CONV	5	1,152	1,455*	6.1	9.8
449 UN METHODIST	15	2,385	3,012*	12.7	20.2
497 BLACK BAPT EST[2]	NA	216	273*	1.2	1.8
LANE	**7**	**1,015**	**1,732***	**72.9**	**100.0**
081 CATHOLIC	1	NA	106	4.5	6.1
081d *LATIN*	*1*	*NA*	*106*	*4.5*	*6.1*
093 CHR CH (DISC)	1	250	545	22.9	31.5
151 L-D SAINTS	1	NA	100	4.2	5.8
283 LUTH—MO SYNOD	1	35	43	1.8	2.5
419 SO BAPT CONV	1	189	243*	10.2	14.0
449 UN METHODIST	2	541	695*	29.3	40.1
LEAVENWORTH	**65**	**11,451**	**26,840***	**41.7**	**100.0**
019 AMER BAPT USA	6	1,394	1,772*	2.8	6.6
053 ASSEMB OF GOD	3	208	360	.6	1.3
059 BAPT MISS ASSN	1	44	56*	.1	.2
081 CATHOLIC	10	NA	9,653	15.0	36.0
081d *LATIN*	*10*	*NA*	*9,653*	*15.0*	*36.0*
093 CHR CH (DISC)	2	554	983	1.5	3.7
097 CHR CHS&CHS CR	2	575	731*	1.1	2.7
111 CH CR,SCIENTST	1	NR	NR	-	-
123 CH GOD (ANDER)	1	10	10	-	-
145 CH GOD PROPHCY	1	33	42*	.1	.2
151 L-D SAINTS	2	NA	741	1.2	2.8
165 CH OF NAZARENE	1	107	288	.4	1.1
167 CHS OF CHRIST	2	160	221	.3	.8
193 EPISCOPAL	1	474	667	1.0	2.5
226 FRIENDS-USA	3	182	231*	.4	.9
226b *EFI*	*3*	*182*	*231**	*.4*	*.9*
283 LUTH—MO SYNOD	4	1,221	1,678	2.6	6.3
287 MENN GEN CONF	1	0	0	-	-
355 PRESB CH (USA)	1	289	367*	.6	1.4
403 SALVATION ARMY	1	140	163	.3	.6
413 S.D.A.	2	182	231*	.4	.9
419 SO BAPT CONV	4	1,685	2,142*	3.3	8.0
438 UN BRETH IN CR	1	31	41	.1	.2
443 UN C OF CHRIST	2	206	262*	.4	1.0
449 UN METHODIST	11	2,051	2,608*	4.1	9.7
467 WESLEYAN	1	19	35	.1	.1
496 JEWISH EST[1]	0	NA	785	1.2	2.9
497 BLACK BAPT EST[2]	NA	1,886	2,398*	3.7	8.9
499 INDEP.NON-CHAR[3]	1	NA	375	.6	1.4
LINCOLN	**18**	**1,804**	**2,538***	**69.5**	**100.0**
019 AMER BAPT USA	1	110	135*	3.7	5.3
081 CATHOLIC	1	NA	246	6.7	9.7
081d *LATIN*	*1*	*NA*	*246*	*6.7*	*9.7*
093 CHR CH (DISC)	1	40	64	1.8	2.5
167 CHS OF CHRIST	1	18	23	.6	.9

NA–Not applicable   NR–Not reported   *Total adherents estimated from known number of communicant, confirmed, full members.   - Represents a percent less than 0.1.   Percentages may not total due to rounding.
[1]See Appendix E   [2]See Appendix F   [3]See Appendix G   Lines in *italic* represent a breakdown of Catholic rites or Friends affiliations. They are included in their respective denominational total.

Table 4. Churches and Church Membership by County and Denomination: 1990

County and Denomination	Number of churches	Communicant, confirmed, full members	Total adherents Number	Percent of total population	Percent of total adherents
181 CONSRV CONGR	1	35	43*	1.2	1.7
207 E.L.C.A.	1	40	49	1.3	1.9
283 LUTH—MO SYNOD	3	835	1,079	29.5	42.5
355 PRESB CH (USA)	3	268	329*	9.0	13.0
443 UN C OF CHRIST	1	25	31*	.8	1.2
449 UN METHODIST	4	419	514*	14.1	20.3
467 WESLEYAN	1	14	25	.7	1.0
LINN	**25**	**2,336**	**3,404***	**41.2**	**100.0**
019 AMER BAPT USA	3	246	307*	3.7	9.0
053 ASSEMB OF GOD	1	26	55	.7	1.6
059 BAPT MISS ASSN	1	90	112*	1.4	3.3
081 CATHOLIC	2	NA	351	4.3	10.3
081d LATIN	2	NA	351	4.3	10.3
093 CHR CH (DISC)	2	275	434	5.3	12.7
097 CHR CHS&CHS CR	3	500	624*	7.6	18.3
145 CH GOD PROPHCY	1	33	41*	.5	1.2
165 CH OF NAZARENE	1	64	106	1.3	3.1
263 INT FOURSQ GOS	1	32	40*	.5	1.2
355 PRESB CH (USA)	1	59	74*	.9	2.2
413 S.D.A.	1	20	25*	.3	.7
419 SO BAPT CONV	1	81	101*	1.2	3.0
443 UN C OF CHRIST	1	107	133*	1.6	3.9
449 UN METHODIST	6	803	1,001*	12.1	29.4
LOGAN	**8**	**810**	**2,230***	**72.4**	**100.0**
081 CATHOLIC	1	NA	1,171	38.0	52.5
081d LATIN	1	NA	1,171	38.0	52.5
167 CHS OF CHRIST	1	35	46	1.5	2.1
193 EPISCOPAL	1	10	24	.8	1.1
207 E.L.C.A.	1	20	27	.9	1.2
283 LUTH—MO SYNOD	1	123	161	5.2	7.2
449 UN METHODIST	2	571	721*	23.4	32.3
467 WESLEYAN	1	51	80	2.6	3.6
LYON	**54**	**8,808**	**17,109***	**49.3**	**100.0**
019 AMER BAPT USA	2	232	297*	.9	1.7
053 ASSEMB OF GOD	3	196	409	1.2	2.4
081 CATHOLIC	5	NA	5,090	14.7	29.8
081d LATIN	5	NA	5,090	14.7	29.8
093 CHR CH (DISC)	1	411	530	1.5	3.1
097 CHR CHS&CHS CR	2	620	793*	2.3	4.6
111 CH CR,SCIENTST	1	NR	NR	-	-
123 CH GOD (ANDER)	1	18	18	.1	.1
145 CH GOD PROPHCY	1	33	42*	.1	.2
165 CH OF NAZARENE	1	226	237	.7	1.4
167 CHS OF CHRIST	1	128	153	.4	.9
175 CONGR CHR CHS	1	275	352*	1.0	2.1
176 CCC, NOT NAT'L	2	99	127*	.4	.7
193 EPISCOPAL	1	214	270	.8	1.6
207 E.L.C.A.	1	379	472	1.4	2.8
221 FREE METHODIST	1	31	56	.2	.3
223 FREE WILL BAPT	1	38	49*	.1	.3
226 FRIENDS-USA	3	254	325*	.9	1.9
226b EFI	3	254	325*	.9	1.9
283 LUTH—MO SYNOD	2	721	1,074	3.1	6.3
355 PRESB CH (USA)	4	575	735*	2.1	4.3
403 SALVATION ARMY	1	84	115	.3	.7
413 S.D.A.	1	17	22*	.1	.1
419 SO BAPT CONV	5	586	749*	2.2	4.4
449 UN METHODIST	12	3,514	4,493*	12.9	26.3
497 BLACK BAPT EST[2]	NA	157	201*	.6	1.2
498 INDEP.CHARIS.[3]	1	NA	500	1.4	2.9
MC PHERSON	**59**	**13,766**	**18,981***	**69.6**	**100.0**
019 AMER BAPT USA	3	949	1,203*	4.4	6.3
053 ASSEMB OF GOD	1	39	68	.2	.4
081 CATHOLIC	2	NA	1,194	4.4	6.3
081d LATIN	2	NA	1,194	4.4	6.3
093 CHR CH (DISC)	3	598	957	3.5	5.0
097 CHR CHS&CHS CR	1	75	95*	.3	.5
111 CH CR,SCIENTST	1	NR	NR	-	-
127 CH GOD (CLEVE)	1	11	14*	.1	.1
143 CG IN CR(MENN)	4	988	1,253*	4.6	6.6
157 CH OF BRETHREN	2	486	616*	2.3	3.2
165 CH OF NAZARENE	1	76	169	.6	.9
167 CHS OF CHRIST	3	163	186	.7	1.0
193 EPISCOPAL	1	83	114	.4	.6
207 E.L.C.A.	7	2,744	3,483	12.8	18.3
221 FREE METHODIST	1	574	653	2.4	3.4
237 GC MENN BR CHS	1	288	365*	1.3	1.9
263 INT FOURSQ GOS	1	90	114*	.4	.6
283 LUTH—MO SYNOD	3	586	782	2.9	4.1
285 MENNONITE CH	1	59	69	.3	.4
287 MENN GEN CONF	8	2,555	3,333	12.2	17.6
355 PRESB CH (USA)	2	379	480*	1.8	2.5

County and Denomination	Number of churches	Communicant, confirmed, full members	Total adherents Number	Percent of total population	Percent of total adherents
413 S.D.A.	1	35	44*	.2	.2
419 SO BAPT CONV	1	171	217*	.8	1.1
443 UN C OF CHRIST	2	339	430*	1.6	2.3
449 UN METHODIST	8	2,478	3,142*	11.5	16.6
MARION	**48**	**6,993**	**9,880***	**76.7**	**100.0**
019 AMER BAPT USA	1	97	119*	.9	1.2
081 CATHOLIC	5	NA	1,226	9.5	12.4
081d LATIN	5	NA	1,226	9.5	12.4
093 CHR CH (DISC)	1	211	233	1.8	2.4
097 CHR CHS&CHS CR	2	261	320*	2.5	3.2
123 CH GOD (ANDER)	1	16	16	.1	.2
143 CG IN CR(MENN)	3	330	405*	3.1	4.1
167 CHS OF CHRIST	1	25	38	.3	.4
207 E.L.C.A.	1	74	119	.9	1.2
237 GC MENN BR CHS	4	1,170	1,436*	11.1	14.5
283 LUTH—MO SYNOD	6	729	859	6.7	8.7
287 MENN GEN CONF	8	2,086	2,661	20.6	26.9
313 N AM BAPT CONF	3	315	387*	3.0	3.9
355 PRESB CH (USA)	1	116	142*	1.1	1.4
419 SO BAPT CONV	2	39	48*	.4	.5
449 UN METHODIST	9	1,524	1,871*	14.5	18.9
MARSHALL	**39**	**4,304**	**9,754***	**83.3**	**100.0**
019 AMER BAPT USA	1	53	68*	.6	.7
063 BEREAN FUND CH	1	17	52	.4	.5
081 CATHOLIC	8	NA	4,212	36.0	43.2
081d LATIN	8	NA	4,212	36.0	43.2
093 CHR CH (DISC)	1	210	285	2.4	2.9
097 CHR CHS&CHS CR	1	80	102*	.9	1.0
167 CHS OF CHRIST	1	45	60	.5	.6
193 EPISCOPAL	2	39	63	.5	.6
207 E.L.C.A.	3	535	639	5.5	6.6
221 FREE METHODIST	1	7	14	.1	.1
283 LUTH—MO SYNOD	6	985	1,280	10.9	13.1
355 PRESB CH (USA)	4	466	595*	5.1	6.1
413 S.D.A.	1	3	4*	-	-
443 UN C OF CHRIST	1	289	369*	3.2	3.8
449 UN METHODIST	8	1,575	2,011*	17.2	20.6
MEADE	**19**	**2,207**	**3,397***	**80.0**	**100.0**
019 AMER BAPT USA	2	451	573*	13.5	16.9
081 CATHOLIC	3	NA	563	13.3	16.6
081d LATIN	3	NA	563	13.3	16.6
097 CHR CHS&CHS CR	2	180	229*	5.4	6.7
165 CH OF NAZARENE	1	135	184	4.3	5.4
167 CHS OF CHRIST	1	40	56	1.3	1.6
211 FEL EVG BIB CH	1	86	86	2.0	2.5
226 FRIENDS-USA	2	243	309*	7.3	9.1
226b EFI	2	243	309*	7.3	9.1
283 LUTH—MO SYNOD	1	253	357	8.4	10.5
349 PENT HOLINESS	2	74	94*	2.2	2.8
355 PRESB CH (USA)	1	17	22*	.5	.6
449 UN METHODIST	3	728	924*	21.8	27.2
MIAMI	**40**	**5,528**	**11,513***	**49.1**	**100.0**
019 AMER BAPT USA	5	1,038	1,325*	5.6	11.5
053 ASSEMB OF GOD	3	277	629	2.7	5.5
081 CATHOLIC	4	NA	2,808	12.0	24.4
081d LATIN	4	NA	2,808	12.0	24.4
093 CHR CH (DISC)	2	236	384	1.6	3.3
097 CHR CHS&CHS CR	2	230	294*	1.3	2.6
151 L-D SAINTS	1	NA	481	2.0	4.2
165 CH OF NAZARENE	1	89	155	.7	1.3
167 CHS OF CHRIST	3	58	85	.4	.7
226 FRIENDS-USA	1	20	26*	.1	.2
226b EFI	1	20	26*	.1	.2
283 LUTH—MO SYNOD	2	973	1,368	5.8	11.9
355 PRESB CH (USA)	5	533	680*	2.9	5.9
419 SO BAPT CONV	2	408	521*	2.2	4.5
449 UN METHODIST	7	1,493	1,906*	8.1	16.6
467 WESLEYAN	1	24	75	.3	.7
496 JEWISH EST[1]	0	NA	286	1.2	2.5
497 BLACK BAPT EST[2]	NA	149	190*	.8	1.7
499 INDEP.NON-CHAR[3]	1	NA	300	1.3	2.6
MITCHELL	**23**	**2,851**	**6,607***	**91.7**	**100.0**
019 AMER BAPT USA	3	297	371*	5.2	5.6
053 ASSEMB OF GOD	1	74	159	2.2	2.4
081 CATHOLIC	3	NA	2,835	39.4	42.9
081d LATIN	3	NA	2,835	39.4	42.9
093 CHR CH (DISC)	1	293	436	6.1	6.6
097 CHR CHS&CHS CR	1	148	185*	2.6	2.8
167 CHS OF CHRIST	2	88	114	1.6	1.7
193 EPISCOPAL	1	7	7	.1	.1

NA–Not applicable   NR–Not reported   *Total adherents estimated from known number of communicant, confirmed, full members.   - Represents a percent less than 0.1.   Percentages may not total due to rounding.
[1]See Appendix E   [2]See Appendix F   [3]See Appendix G   Lines in *italic* represent a breakdown of Catholic rites or Friends affiliations. They are included in their respective denominational total.

Table 4. Churches and Church Membership by County and Denomination: 1990

County and Denomination	Number of churches	Communicant, confirmed, full members	Total adherents — Number	Total adherents — Percent of total population	Total adherents — Percent of total adherents
207 E.L.C.A.	1	332	477	6.6	7.2
226 FRIENDS-USA	1	87	109*	1.5	1.6
226b *EFI*	*1*	*87*	*109**	*1.5*	*1.6*
283 LUTH—MO SYNOD	1	106	143	2.0	2.2
313 N AM BAPT CONF	1	73	91*	1.3	1.4
355 PRESB CH (USA)	1	164	205*	2.8	3.1
449 UN METHODIST	6	1,182	1,475*	20.5	22.3
MONTGOMERY	**97**	**16,032**	**24,463***	**63.0**	**100.0**
019 AMER BAPT USA	4	1,932	2,430*	6.3	9.9
053 ASSEMB OF GOD	5	423	742	1.9	3.0
059 BAPT MISS ASSN	1	200	252*	.6	1.0
081 CATHOLIC	5	NA	2,888	7.4	11.8
081d *LATIN*	*5*	*NA*	*2,888*	*7.4*	*11.8*
093 CHR CH (DISC)	5	1,158	1,824	4.7	7.5
097 CHR CHS&CHS CR	7	1,490	1,874*	4.8	7.7
123 CH GOD (ANDER)	1	58	94	.2	.4
127 CH GOD (CLEVE)	3	273	343*	.9	1.4
145 CH GOD PROPHCY	1	33	42*	.1	.2
151 L-D SAINTS	2	NA	288	.7	1.2
157 CH OF BRETHREN	1	69	87*	.2	.4
165 CH OF NAZARENE	6	738	1,303	3.4	5.3
167 CHS OF CHRIST	5	436	566	1.5	2.3
193 EPISCOPAL	2	294	384	1.0	1.6
217 FIRE BAPTIZED	5	152	191*	.5	.8
226 FRIENDS-USA	3	99	125*	.3	.5
226b *EFI*	*3*	*99*	*125**	*.3*	*.5*
283 LUTH—MO SYNOD	3	1,031	1,406	3.6	5.7
349 PENT HOLINESS	3	337	424*	1.1	1.7
355 PRESB CH (USA)	3	847	1,066*	2.7	4.4
403 SALVATION ARMY	1	125	133	.3	.5
413 S.D.A.	4	181	228*	.6	.9
419 SO BAPT CONV	10	2,501	3,146*	8.1	12.9
443 UN C OF CHRIST	1	30	38*	.1	.2
449 UN METHODIST	15	3,090	3,887*	10.0	15.9
467 WESLEYAN	1	13	45	.1	.2
497 BLACK BAPT EST[2]	NA	522	657*	1.7	2.7
MORRIS	**19**	**2,534**	**3,584***	**57.8**	**100.0**
019 AMER BAPT USA	1	78	97*	1.6	2.7
081 CATHOLIC	1	NA	350	5.6	9.8
081d *LATIN*	*1*	*NA*	*350*	*5.6*	*9.8*
093 CHR CH (DISC)	1	255	410	6.6	11.4
097 CHR CHS&CHS CR	3	589	732*	11.8	20.4
207 E.L.C.A.	2	157	184	3.0	5.1
283 LUTH—MO SYNOD	2	230	288	4.6	8.0
355 PRESB CH (USA)	1	68	85*	1.4	2.4
443 UN C OF CHRIST	1	160	199*	3.2	5.6
449 UN METHODIST	7	997	1,239*	20.0	34.6
MORTON	**14**	**1,256**	**2,540***	**73.0**	**100.0**
019 AMER BAPT USA	1	56	73*	2.1	2.9
053 ASSEMB OF GOD	2	22	52	1.5	2.0
081 CATHOLIC	1	NA	560	16.1	22.0
081d *LATIN*	*1*	*NA*	*560*	*16.1*	*22.0*
097 CHR CHS&CHS CR	1	100	131*	3.8	5.2
123 CH GOD (ANDER)	1	94	254	7.3	10.0
151 L-D SAINTS	1	NA	118	3.4	4.6
165 CH OF NAZARENE	1	120	211	6.1	8.3
167 CHS OF CHRIST	1	19	24	.7	.9
283 LUTH—MO SYNOD	1	64	94	2.7	3.7
419 SO BAPT CONV	1	233	305*	8.8	12.0
449 UN METHODIST	3	548	718*	20.6	28.3
NEMAHA	**30**	**3,015**	**9,666***	**92.5**	**100.0**
019 AMER BAPT USA	2	200	260*	2.5	2.7
040 AP CHR CH-AMER	2	281	496	4.7	5.1
081 CATHOLIC	7	NA	5,616	53.8	58.1
081d *LATIN*	*7*	*NA*	*5,616*	*53.8*	*58.1*
111 CH CR,SCIENTST	1	NR	NR	-	-
157 CH OF BRETHREN	1	69	90*	.9	.9
167 CHS OF CHRIST	1	50	65	.6	.7
175 CONGR CHR CHS	1	343	446*	4.3	4.6
283 LUTH—MO SYNOD	1	194	276	2.6	2.9
419 SO BAPT CONV	1	44	57*	.5	.6
438 UN BRETH IN CR	1	55	55	.5	.6
443 UN C OF CHRIST	3	502	653*	6.3	6.8
449 UN METHODIST	8	1,239	1,612*	15.4	16.7
467 WESLEYAN	1	38	40	.4	.4
NEOSHO	**40**	**5,297**	**8,828***	**51.8**	**100.0**
019 AMER BAPT USA	4	800	1,008*	5.9	11.4
053 ASSEMB OF GOD	1	208	480	2.8	5.4
081 CATHOLIC	3	NA	1,537	9.0	17.4
081d *LATIN*	*3*	*NA*	*1,537*	*9.0*	*17.4*

County and Denomination	Number of churches	Communicant, confirmed, full members	Total adherents — Number	Total adherents — Percent of total population	Total adherents — Percent of total adherents
093 CHR CH (DISC)	3	479	915	5.4	10.4
097 CHR CHS&CHS CR	2	419	528*	3.1	6.0
123 CH GOD (ANDER)	1	18	29	.2	.3
127 CH GOD (CLEVE)	1	111	140*	.8	1.6
165 CH OF NAZARENE	2	188	243	1.4	2.8
167 CHS OF CHRIST	2	57	74	.4	.8
193 EPISCOPAL	1	77	154	.9	1.7
217 FIRE BAPTIZED	1	22	28*	.2	.3
226 FRIENDS-USA	1	41	52*	.3	.6
226b *EFI*	*1*	*41*	*52**	*.3*	*.6*
283 LUTH—MO SYNOD	2	448	593	3.5	6.7
355 PRESB CH (USA)	2	241	304*	1.8	3.4
413 S.D.A.	2	61	77*	.5	.9
419 SO BAPT CONV	1	227	286*	1.7	3.2
438 UN BRETH IN CR	2	96	96	.6	1.1
449 UN METHODIST	8	1,782	2,246*	13.2	25.4
467 WESLEYAN	1	22	38	.2	.4
NESS	**20**	**1,896**	**3,596***	**89.2**	**100.0**
019 AMER BAPT USA	2	334	422*	10.5	11.7
053 ASSEMB OF GOD	1	16	21	.5	.6
063 BEREAN FUND CH	1	9	25	.6	.7
081 CATHOLIC	2	NA	1,200	29.8	33.4
081d *LATIN*	*2*	*NA*	*1,200*	*29.8*	*33.4*
111 CH CR,SCIENTST	1	NR	NR	-	-
167 CHS OF CHRIST	2	63	82	2.0	2.3
207 E.L.C.A.	1	71	94	2.3	2.6
283 LUTH—MO SYNOD	1	105	131	3.2	3.6
287 MENN GEN CONF	1	104	111	2.8	3.1
413 S.D.A.	1	40	51*	1.3	1.4
449 UN METHODIST	7	1,154	1,459*	36.2	40.6
NORTON	**21**	**2,519**	**4,028***	**67.7**	**100.0**
019 AMER BAPT USA	1	46	55*	.9	1.4
057 BAPT GEN CONF	1	24	29*	.5	.7
081 CATHOLIC	3	NA	1,007	16.9	25.0
081d *LATIN*	*3*	*NA*	*1,007*	*16.9*	*25.0*
097 CHR CHS&CHS CR	2	968	1,167*	19.6	29.0
123 CH GOD (ANDER)	2	145	150	2.5	3.7
157 CH OF BRETHREN	1	54	65*	1.1	1.6
167 CHS OF CHRIST	1	28	36	.6	.9
193 EPISCOPAL	1	55	71	1.2	1.8
283 LUTH—MO SYNOD	1	108	134	2.3	3.3
413 S.D.A.	1	16	19*	.3	.5
443 UN C OF CHRIST	1	114	137*	2.3	3.4
449 UN METHODIST	5	907	1,093*	18.4	27.1
469 WELS	1	54	65	1.1	1.6
OSAGE	**27**	**2,950**	**4,650***	**30.5**	**100.0**
053 ASSEMB OF GOD	2	60	87	.6	1.9
081 CATHOLIC	2	NA	877	5.8	18.9
081d *LATIN*	*2*	*NA*	*877*	*5.8*	*18.9*
093 CHR CH (DISC)	1	315	365	2.4	7.8
097 CHR CHS&CHS CR	1	15	19*	.1	.4
123 CH GOD (ANDER)	1	53	54	.4	1.2
167 CHS OF CHRIST	3	93	126	.8	2.7
207 E.L.C.A.	1	149	199	1.3	4.3
221 FREE METHODIST	1	13	20	.1	.4
259 IFCA	1	NR	NR	-	-
263 INT FOURSQ GOS	1	22	28*	.2	.6
283 LUTH—MO SYNOD	1	201	305	2.0	6.6
355 PRESB CH (USA)	2	190	241*	1.6	5.2
419 SO BAPT CONV	2	207	263*	1.7	5.7
443 UN C OF CHRIST	1	87	110*	.7	2.4
449 UN METHODIST	6	1,530	1,941*	12.7	41.7
467 WESLEYAN	1	15	15	.1	.3
OSBORNE	**26**	**2,383**	**3,584***	**73.6**	**100.0**
019 AMER BAPT USA	1	123	152*	3.1	4.2
053 ASSEMB OF GOD	1	67	120	2.5	3.3
081 CATHOLIC	3	NA	577	11.9	16.1
081d *LATIN*	*3*	*NA*	*577*	*11.9*	*16.1*
093 CHR CH (DISC)	1	185	230	4.7	6.4
097 CHR CHS&CHS CR	2	260	321*	6.6	9.0
165 CH OF NAZARENE	1	30	47	1.0	1.3
207 E.L.C.A.	1	79	99	2.0	2.8
221 FREE METHODIST	1	33	50	1.0	1.4
226 FRIENDS-USA	1	60	74*	1.5	2.1
226b *EFI*	*1*	*60*	*74**	*1.5*	*2.1*
283 LUTH—MO SYNOD	2	397	497	10.2	13.9
355 PRESB CH (USA)	1	30	37*	.8	1.0
413 S.D.A.	1	41	51*	1.0	1.4
443 UN C OF CHRIST	2	142	175*	3.6	4.9
449 UN METHODIST	8	936	1,154*	23.7	32.2

NA–Not applicable NR–Not reported *Total adherents estimated from known number of communicant, confirmed, full members. - Represents a percent less than 0.1. Percentages may not total due to rounding.
[1]See Appendix E [2]See Appendix F [3]See Appendix G Lines in *italic* represent a breakdown of Catholic rites or Friends affiliations. They are included in their respective denominational total.

Table 4. Churches and Church Membership by County and Denomination: 1990

County and Denomination	Number of churches	Communicant, confirmed, full members	Total adherents Number	Percent of total population	Percent of total adherents
OTTAWA	**22**	**1,550**	**2,456***	**43.6**	**100.0**
019 AMER BAPT USA	2	158	199*	3.5	8.1
081 CATHOLIC	3	NA	385	6.8	15.7
081d *LATIN*	*3*	*NA*	*385*	*6.8*	*15.7*
165 CH OF NAZARENE	1	37	144	2.6	5.9
193 EPISCOPAL	1	22	38	.7	1.5
207 E.L.C.A.	1	120	146	2.6	5.9
221 FREE METHODIST	2	46	76	1.3	3.1
355 PRESB CH (USA)	4	376	473*	8.4	19.3
449 UN METHODIST	8	791	995*	17.7	40.5
PAWNEE	**19**	**2,853**	**5,092***	**67.4**	**100.0**
019 AMER BAPT USA	2	238	295*	3.9	5.8
053 ASSEMB OF GOD	1	46	70	.9	1.4
081 CATHOLIC	1	NA	1,200	15.9	23.6
081d *LATIN*	*1*	*NA*	*1,200*	*15.9*	*23.6*
093 CHR CH (DISC)	1	263	545	7.2	10.7
165 CH OF NAZARENE	1	87	212	2.8	4.2
167 CHS OF CHRIST	1	54	76	1.0	1.5
193 EPISCOPAL	1	40	51	.7	1.0
207 E.L.C.A.	1	58	71	.9	1.4
283 LUTH—MO SYNOD	1	252	349	4.6	6.9
287 MENN GEN CONF	1	131	138	1.8	2.7
355 PRESB CH (USA)	1	253	313*	4.1	6.1
413 S.D.A.	1	49	61*	.8	1.2
419 SO BAPT CONV	1	162	201*	2.7	3.9
449 UN METHODIST	5	1,220	1,510*	20.0	29.7
PHILLIPS	**29**	**2,830**	**4,439***	**67.4**	**100.0**
019 AMER BAPT USA	1	120	150*	2.3	3.4
053 ASSEMB OF GOD	2	73	143	2.2	3.2
081 CATHOLIC	2	NA	468	7.1	10.5
081d *LATIN*	*2*	*NA*	*468*	*7.1*	*10.5*
093 CHR CH (DISC)	1	186	294	4.5	6.6
097 CHR CHS&CHS CR	1	130	162*	2.5	3.6
105 CHRISTIAN REF	1	178	230	3.5	5.2
123 CH GOD (ANDER)	1	47	60	.9	1.4
151 L-D SAINTS	1	NA	132	2.0	3.0
165 CH OF NAZARENE	2	49	121	1.8	2.7
167 CHS OF CHRIST	2	45	58	.9	1.3
193 EPISCOPAL	1	29	30	.5	.7
207 E.L.C.A.	2	477	604	9.2	13.6
283 LUTH—MO SYNOD	1	167	222	3.4	5.0
353 CHR BRETHREN	1	8	16	.2	.4
355 PRESB CH (USA)	1	133	166*	2.5	3.7
371 REF CH IN AM	1	154	228	3.5	5.1
413 S.D.A.	1	11	14*	.2	.3
449 UN METHODIST	6	976	1,216*	18.5	27.4
467 WESLEYAN	1	47	125	1.9	2.8
POTTAWATOMIE	**33**	**3,789**	**9,133***	**56.6**	**100.0**
019 AMER BAPT USA	3	260	340*	2.1	3.7
053 ASSEMB OF GOD	1	81	158	1.0	1.7
081 CATHOLIC	7	NA	4,036	25.0	44.2
081d *LATIN*	*7*	*NA*	*4,036*	*25.0*	*44.2*
097 CHR CHS&CHS CR	2	230	301*	1.9	3.3
193 EPISCOPAL	1	76	107	.7	1.2
207 E.L.C.A.	2	169	227	1.4	2.5
283 LUTH—MO SYNOD	3	699	987	6.1	10.8
355 PRESB CH (USA)	1	134	175*	1.1	1.9
419 SO BAPT CONV	1	176	230*	1.4	2.5
443 UN C OF CHRIST	3	538	705*	4.4	7.7
449 UN METHODIST	9	1,426	1,867*	11.6	20.4
PRATT	**28**	**3,708**	**6,379***	**65.7**	**100.0**
019 AMER BAPT USA	2	264	331*	3.4	5.2
053 ASSEMB OF GOD	1	210	325	3.3	5.1
081 CATHOLIC	1	NA	1,133	11.7	17.8
081d *LATIN*	*1*	*NA*	*1,133*	*11.7*	*17.8*
093 CHR CH (DISC)	2	254	604	6.2	9.5
123 CH GOD (ANDER)	1	56	65	.7	1.0
151 L-D SAINTS	1	NA	110	1.1	1.7
165 CH OF NAZARENE	1	118	207	2.1	3.2
167 CHS OF CHRIST	2	135	176	1.8	2.8
193 EPISCOPAL	1	34	44	.5	.7
221 FREE METHODIST	1	53	80	.8	1.3
226 FRIENDS-USA	2	88	110*	1.1	1.7
226b *EFI*	*2*	*88*	*110**	*1.1*	*1.7*
283 LUTH—MO SYNOD	2	454	633	6.5	9.9
349 PENT HOLINESS	1	52	65*	.7	1.0
355 PRESB CH (USA)	1	199	250*	2.6	3.9
419 SO BAPT CONV	1	345	433*	4.5	6.8
449 UN METHODIST	8	1,446	1,813*	18.7	28.4

County and Denomination	Number of churches	Communicant, confirmed, full members	Total adherents Number	Percent of total population	Percent of total adherents
RAWLINS	**9**	**985**	**2,761***	**81.1**	**100.0**
081 CATHOLIC	3	NA	1,339	39.3	48.5
081d *LATIN*	*3*	*NA*	*1,339*	*39.3*	*48.5*
093 CHR CH (DISC)	1	174	374	11.0	13.5
165 CH OF NAZARENE	1	37	43	1.3	1.6
283 LUTH—MO SYNOD	2	322	429	12.6	15.5
443 UN C OF CHRIST	1	50	64*	1.9	2.3
449 UN METHODIST	1	402	512*	15.0	18.5
RENO	**98**	**20,187**	**34,388***	**55.1**	**100.0**
019 AMER BAPT USA	4	1,279	1,603*	2.6	4.7
053 ASSEMB OF GOD	3	327	405	.6	1.2
061 BEACHY AMISH	2	283	355*	.6	1.0
081 CATHOLIC	5	NA	6,339	10.2	18.4
081d *LATIN*	*5*	*NA*	*6,339*	*10.2*	*18.4*
093 CHR CH (DISC)	5	893	2,301	3.7	6.7
097 CHR CHS&CHS CR	2	591	741*	1.2	2.2
111 CH CR,SCIENTST	1	NR	NR	-	-
123 CH GOD (ANDER)	2	345	345	.6	1.0
127 CH GOD (CLEVE)	1	32	40*	.1	.1
151 L-D SAINTS	1	NA	325	.5	.9
157 CH OF BRETHREN	2	279	350*	.6	1.0
165 CH OF NAZARENE	5	1,075	1,487	2.4	4.3
167 CHS OF CHRIST	5	686	863	1.4	2.5
175 CONGR CHR CHS	1	231	290*	.5	.8
193 EPISCOPAL	1	423	533	.9	1.5
203 EVAN FREE CH	1	33	140	.2	.4
207 E.L.C.A.	3	727	991	1.6	2.9
221 FREE METHODIST	1	20	20	-	.1
223 FREE WILL BAPT	1	27	34*	.1	.1
226 FRIENDS-USA	1	164	206*	.3	.6
226b *EFI*	*1*	*164*	*206**	*.3*	*.6*
237 GC MENN BR CHS	1	391	490*	.8	1.4
259 IFCA	1	NR	NR	-	-
263 INT FOURSQ GOS	1	12	15*	-	-
283 LUTH—MO SYNOD	3	1,076	1,411	2.3	4.1
285 MENNONITE CH	5	737	861	1.4	2.5
287 MENN GEN CONF	4	1,191	1,455	2.3	4.2
291 MISSIONARY CH	1	24	29	-	.1
323 OLD ORD AMISH	3	NA	450	.7	1.3
339 PENT CH OF GOD	1	34	77	.1	.2
349 PENT HOLINESS	1	390	489*	.8	1.4
353 CHR BRETHREN	1	25	50	.1	.1
355 PRESB CH (USA)	4	1,350	1,692*	2.7	4.9
403 SALVATION ARMY	1	97	98	.2	.3
413 S.D.A.	1	166	208*	.3	.6
419 SO BAPT CONV	3	1,105	1,385*	2.2	4.0
443 UN C OF CHRIST	2	230	288*	.5	.8
449 UN METHODIST	15	5,493	6,887*	11.0	20.0
467 WESLEYAN	2	84	175	.3	.5
497 BLACK BAPT EST[2]	NA	367	460*	.7	1.3
499 INDEP.NON-CHAR[3]	1	NA	500	.8	1.5
REPUBLIC	**23**	**2,808**	**4,298***	**66.3**	**100.0**
019 AMER BAPT USA	1	116	141*	2.2	3.3
053 ASSEMB OF GOD	1	27	52	.8	1.2
081 CATHOLIC	3	NA	657	10.1	15.3
081d *LATIN*	*3*	*NA*	*657*	*10.1*	*15.3*
097 CHR CHS&CHS CR	1	223	272*	4.2	6.3
207 E.L.C.A.	4	602	864	13.3	20.1
355 PRESB CH (USA)	3	430	524*	8.1	12.2
413 S.D.A.	1	22	27*	.4	.6
449 UN METHODIST	8	1,273	1,551*	23.9	36.1
467 WESLEYAN	1	115	210	3.2	4.9
RICE	**33**	**4,828**	**7,489***	**70.6**	**100.0**
019 AMER BAPT USA	4	620	785*	7.4	10.5
053 ASSEMB OF GOD	2	126	176	1.7	2.4
081 CATHOLIC	4	NA	1,173	11.1	15.7
081d *LATIN*	*4*	*NA*	*1,173*	*11.1*	*15.7*
093 CHR CH (DISC)	1	239	434	4.1	5.8
097 CHR CHS&CHS CR	1	50	63*	.6	.8
111 CH CR,SCIENTST	1	NR	NR	-	-
165 CH OF NAZARENE	1	68	150	1.4	2.0
167 CHS OF CHRIST	1	51	58	.5	.8
193 EPISCOPAL	1	15	15	.1	.2
213 EVAN MENN INC	1	219	277*	2.6	3.7
283 LUTH—MO SYNOD	1	179	229	2.2	3.1
355 PRESB CH (USA)	4	463	586*	5.5	7.8
419 SO BAPT CONV	1	222	281*	2.6	3.8
443 UN C OF CHRIST	2	297	376*	3.5	5.0
449 UN METHODIST	8	2,279	2,886*	27.2	38.5
RILEY	**51**	**12,014**	**21,270***	**31.7**	**100.0**
019 AMER BAPT USA	2	615	751*	1.1	3.5

NA–Not applicable   NR–Not reported   *Total adherents estimated from known number of communicant, confirmed, full members.   - Represents a percent less than 0.1.   Percentages may not total due to rounding.
[1]See Appendix E   [2]See Appendix F   [3]See Appendix G   Lines in *italic* represent a breakdown of Catholic rites or Friends affiliations. They are included in their respective denominational total.

Table 4. Churches and Church Membership by County and Denomination: 1990

County and Denomination		Number of churches	Communicant, confirmed, full members	Total adherents		
				Number	Percent of total population	Percent of total adherents
053	ASSEM OF GOD	1	69	96	.1	.5
081	CATHOLIC	4	NA	4,846	7.2	22.8
081d	*LATIN*	*4*	*NA*	*4,846*	*7.2*	*22.8*
089	CHR & MISS AL	1	0	25	-	.1
093	CHR CH (DISC)	1	689	743	1.1	3.5
097	CHR CHS&CHS CR	1	100	122*	.2	.6
111	CH CR,SCIENTST	1	NR	NR	-	-
123	CH GOD (ANDER)	1	25	25	-	.1
127	CH GOD (CLEVE)	1	45	55*	.1	.3
151	L-D SAINTS	2	NA	721	1.1	3.4
165	CH OF NAZARENE	1	90	221	.3	1.0
167	CHS OF CHRIST	2	199	245	.4	1.2
193	EPISCOPAL	1	159	280	.4	1.3
203	EVAN FREE CH	1	30	118	.2	.6
207	E.L.C.A.	3	1,338	1,779	2.6	8.4
221	FREE METHODIST	1	27	53	.1	.2
226	FRIENDS-USA	1	7	15	-	.1
226c	*FGC*	*1*	*7*	*15*	*-*	*.1*
237	GC MENN BR CHS	1	63	77*	.1	.4
283	LUTH—MO SYNOD	1	695	1,009	1.5	4.7
285	MENNONITE CH	1	61	135	.2	.6
287	MENN GEN CONF	1	35	48	.1	.2
355	PRESB CH (USA)	5	1,370	1,673*	2.5	7.9
413	S.D.A.	1	71	87*	.1	.4
419	SO BAPT CONV	1	882	1,077*	1.6	5.1
435	UNITARIAN-UNIV	1	35	57	.1	.3
443	UN C OF CHRIST	1	253	309*	.5	1.5
449	UN METHODIST	10	3,494	4,268*	6.4	20.1
467	WESLEYAN	1	204	204	.3	1.0
496	JEWISH EST[1]	1	NA	100	.1	.5
497	BLACK BAPT EST[2]	NA	1,458	1,781*	2.7	8.4
498	INDEP.CHARIS.[3]	1	NA	350	.5	1.6
ROOKS		**19**	**2,500**	**4,997***	**82.7**	**100.0**
019	AMER BAPT USA	1	61	77*	1.3	1.5
053	ASSEMB OF GOD	2	125	151	2.5	3.0
081	CATHOLIC	4	NA	1,734	28.7	34.7
081d	*LATIN*	*4*	*NA*	*1,734*	*28.7*	*34.7*
097	CHR CHS&CHS CR	2	555	704*	11.7	14.1
123	CH GOD (ANDER)	1	67	123	2.0	2.5
165	CH OF NAZARENE	2	100	181	3.0	3.6
283	LUTH—MO SYNOD	1	95	128	2.1	2.6
419	SO BAPT CONV	1	288	365*	6.0	7.3
443	UN C OF CHRIST	1	123	156*	2.6	3.1
449	UN METHODIST	4	1,086	1,378*	22.8	27.6
RUSH		**17**	**1,560**	**3,086***	**80.3**	**100.0**
081	CATHOLIC	4	NA	1,206	31.4	39.1
081d	*LATIN*	*4*	*NA*	*1,206*	*31.4*	*39.1*
097	CHR CHS&CHS CR	1	110	134*	3.5	4.3
207	E.L.C.A.	4	529	627	16.3	20.3
313	N AM BAPT CONF	1	39	47*	1.2	1.5
413	S.D.A.	2	82	100*	2.6	3.2
449	UN METHODIST	5	800	972*	25.3	31.5
RUSSELL		**31**	**3,739**	**6,385***	**81.5**	**100.0**
019	AMER BAPT USA	2	120	147*	1.9	2.3
053	ASSEMB OF GOD	1	47	108	1.4	1.7
081	CATHOLIC	4	NA	1,575	20.1	24.7
081d	*LATIN*	*4*	*NA*	*1,575*	*20.1*	*24.7*
097	CHR CHS&CHS CR	1	70	86*	1.1	1.3
151	L-D SAINTS	1	NA	141	1.8	2.2
165	CH OF NAZARENE	1	20	46	.6	.7
167	CHS OF CHRIST	1	51	67	.9	1.0
193	EPISCOPAL	1	14	15	.2	.2
207	E.L.C.A.	5	1,326	1,628	20.8	25.5
259	IFCA	1	NR	NR	-	-
419	SO BAPT CONV	1	355	435*	5.6	6.8
443	UN C OF CHRIST	2	236	289*	3.7	4.5
449	UN METHODIST	9	1,442	1,766*	22.5	27.7
469	WELS	1	58	82	1.0	1.3
SALINE		**59**	**14,535**	**27,285***	**55.3**	**100.0**
019	AMER BAPT USA	2	507	642*	1.3	2.4
053	ASSEMB OF GOD	2	193	424	.9	1.6
081	CATHOLIC	5	NA	7,661	15.5	28.1
081d	*LATIN*	*5*	*NA*	*7,661*	*15.5*	*28.1*
093	CHR CH (DISC)	2	507	702	1.4	2.6
097	CHR CHS&CHS CR	1	120	152*	.3	.6
111	CH CR,SCIENTST	1	NR	NR	-	-
123	CH GOD (ANDER)	1	23	25	.1	.1
127	CH GOD (CLEVE)	1	3	4*	-	-
133	CH GOD(7TH)DEN	1	16	20	-	.1
165	CH OF NAZARENE	2	550	976	2.0	3.6
167	CHS OF CHRIST	1	150	191	.4	.7
193	EPISCOPAL	2	535	725	1.5	2.7

County and Denomination		Number of churches	Communicant, confirmed, full members	Total adherents		
				Number	Percent of total population	Percent of total adherents
207	E.L.C.A.	7	2,429	3,112	6.3	11.4
221	FREE METHODIST	1	48	60	.1	.2
223	FREE WILL BAPT	1	63	80*	.2	.3
259	IFCA	2	NR	NR	-	-
263	INT FOURSQ GOS	2	658	833*	1.7	3.1
283	LUTH—MO SYNOD	2	1,203	1,600	3.2	5.9
287	MENN GEN CONF	1	33	61	.1	.2
353	CHR BRETHREN	1	32	46	.1	.2
355	PRESB CH (USA)	3	1,493	1,891*	3.8	6.9
403	SALVATION ARMY	1	108	119	.2	.4
413	S.D.A.	1	129	163*	.3	.6
419	SO BAPT CONV	2	1,146	1,451*	2.9	5.3
443	UN C OF CHRIST	1	67	85*	.2	.3
449	UN METHODIST	9	4,065	5,148*	10.4	18.9
467	WESLEYAN	2	74	297	.6	1.1
469	WELS	1	58	80	.2	.3
497	BLACK BAPT EST[2]	NA	325	412*	.8	1.5
499	INDEP.NON-CHAR[3]	1	NA	325	.7	1.2
SCOTT		**12**	**2,516**	**4,145***	**78.4**	**100.0**
019	AMER BAPT USA	1	544	702*	13.3	16.9
053	ASSEMB OF GOD	1	28	70	1.3	1.7
081	CATHOLIC	1	NA	350	6.6	8.4
081d	*LATIN*	*1*	*NA*	*350*	*6.6*	*8.4*
093	CHR CH (DISC)	1	241	775	14.7	18.7
097	CHR CHS&CHS CR	1	120	155*	2.9	3.7
143	CG IN CR(MENN)	1	167	216*	4.1	5.2
165	CH OF NAZARENE	1	73	152	2.9	3.7
167	CHS OF CHRIST	1	93	121	2.3	2.9
193	EPISCOPAL	1	62	84	1.6	2.0
283	LUTH—MO SYNOD	1	304	379	7.2	9.1
419	SO BAPT CONV	1	135	174*	3.3	4.2
449	UN METHODIST	1	749	967*	18.3	23.3
SEDGWICK		**367**	**113,223**	**218,938***	**54.2**	**100.0**
011	A.W.M.C.	1	0	0*	-	-
019	AMER BAPT USA	20	4,318	5,572*	1.4	2.5
040	AP CHR CH-AMER	1	32	57	-	-
053	ASSEMB OF GOD	14	2,464	4,584	1.1	2.1
059	BAPT MISS ASSN	1	28	36*	-	-
071	BRETHREN (ASH)	1	95	123*	-	.1
081	CATHOLIC	28	NA	56,513	14.0	25.8
081d	*LATIN*	*28*	*NA*	*56,513*	*14.0*	*25.8*
089	CHR & MISS AL	1	0	0	-	-
093	CHR CH (DISC)	20	4,499	6,759	1.7	3.1
097	CHR CHS&CHS CR	15	7,906	10,202*	2.5	4.7
111	CH CR,SCIENTST	2	NR	NR	-	-
123	CH GOD (ANDER)	6	4,308	4,413	1.1	2.0
127	CH GOD (CLEVE)	5	653	843*	.2	.4
133	CH GOD(7TH)DEN	1	16	20	-	-
145	CH GOD PROPHCY	1	33	43*	-	-
151	L-D SAINTS	7	NA	2,737	.7	1.3
157	CH OF BRETHREN	1	529	683*	.2	.3
165	CH OF NAZARENE	16	2,902	3,880	1.0	1.8
167	CHS OF CHRIST	21	3,414	4,240	1.1	1.9
175	CONGR CHR CHS	3	1,269	1,638*	.4	.7
193	EPISCOPAL	8	2,445	3,334	.8	1.5
203	EVAN FREE CH	5	890	1,714	.4	.8
207	E.L.C.A.	7	2,351	3,208	.8	1.5
215	EVAN METH CH	3	120	155*	-	.1
217	FIRE BAPTIZED	1	11	14*	-	-
221	FREE METHODIST	3	150	220	.1	.1
223	FREE WILL BAPT	1	76	98*	-	-
226	FRIENDS-USA	6	1,233	1,591*	.4	.7
226b	*EFI*	*4*	*551*	*711**	*.2*	*.3*
226d	*FGC & FUM*	*1*	*18*	*23**	*-*	*-*
226e	*FUM*	*1*	*664*	*857**	*.2*	*.4*
237	GC MENN BR CHS	2	457	590*	.1	.3
246	GREEK ORTHODOX	1	NR	NR	-	-
259	IFCA	1	NR	NR	-	-
263	INT FOURSQ GOS	2	255	329*	.1	.2
283	LUTH—MO SYNOD	11	5,462	7,303	1.8	3.3
285	MENNONITE CH	1	27	48	-	-
287	MENN GEN CONF	3	575	726	.2	.3
291	MISSIONARY CH	3	74	157	-	.1
313	N AM BAPT CONF	1	76	98*	-	-
339	PENT CH OF GOD	1	34	77	-	-
349	PENT HOLINESS	4	404	521*	.1	.2
353	CHR BRETHREN	3	250	510	.1	.2
355	PRESB CH (USA)	20	7,125	9,194*	2.3	4.2
356	PRESB CH AMER	1	58	84	-	-
403	SALVATION ARMY	4	537	591*	.1	.3
413	S.D.A.	4	1,308	1,688*	.4	.8
419	SO BAPT CONV	29	23,874	30,807*	7.6	14.1
435	UNITARIAN-UNIV	1	176	211	.1	.1
438	UN BRETH IN CR	1	58	58	-	-
443	UN C OF CHRIST	6	1,002	1,293*	.3	.6

NA–Not applicable   NR–Not reported   *Total adherents estimated from known number of communicant, confirmed, full members.   - Represents a percent less than 0.1.   Percentages may not total due to rounding.

[1]See Appendix E   [2]See Appendix F   [3]See Appendix G   Lines in *italic* represent a breakdown of Catholic rites or Friends affiliations. They are included in their respective denominational total.

164

Table 4. Churches and Church Membership by County and Denomination: 1990

County and Denomination	Number of churches	Communicant, confirmed, full members	Total adherents Number	Percent of total population	Percent of total adherents
449 UN METHODIST	48	21,914	28,278*	7.0	12.9
467 WESLEYAN	4	169	423	.1	.2
469 WELS	1	112	156	-	.1
496 JEWISH EST[1]	2	NA	831	.2	.4
497 BLACK BAPT EST[2]	NA	9,534	12,303*	3.0	5.6
498 INDEP.CHARIS.[3]	4	NA	1,835	.5	.8
499 INDEP.NON-CHAR[3]	10	NA	8,150	2.0	3.7
SEWARD	**24**	**5,617**	**9,043***	**48.2**	**100.0**
019 AMER BAPT USA	1	1,140	1,535*	8.2	17.0
053 ASSEMB OF GOD	1	61	135	.7	1.5
081 CATHOLIC	1	NA	1,000	5.3	11.1
081d LATIN	*1*	*NA*	*1,000*	*5.3*	*11.1*
093 CHR CH (DISC)	1	225	265	1.4	2.9
097 CHR CHS&CHS CR	1	380	512*	2.7	5.7
111 CH CR,SCIENTST	1	NR	NR	-	-
123 CH GOD (ANDER)	2	157	213	1.1	2.4
151 L-D SAINTS	1	NA	181	1.0	2.0
165 CH OF NAZARENE	1	119	171	.9	1.9
167 CHS OF CHRIST	1	252	300	1.6	3.3
193 EPISCOPAL	1	101	147	.8	1.6
207 E.L.C.A.	1	70	94	.5	1.0
226 FRIENDS-USA	1	80	108*	.6	1.2
226b EFI	*1*	*80*	*108*/*	*.6*	*1.2*
283 LUTH—MO SYNOD	1	269	361	1.9	4.0
287 MENN GEN CONF	1	58	78	.4	.9
355 PRESB CH (USA)	1	198	267*	1.4	3.0
413 S.D.A.	1	34	46*	.2	.5
419 SO BAPT CONV	2	1,019	1,372*	7.3	15.2
449 UN METHODIST	3	1,222	1,646*	8.8	18.2
497 BLACK BAPT EST[2]	NA	232	312*	1.7	3.5
499 INDEP.NON-CHAR[3]	1	NA	300	1.6	3.3
SHAWNEE	**151**	**43,646**	**93,224***	**57.9**	**100.0**
011 A.W.M.C.	1	17	21*	-	-
019 AMER BAPT USA	12	4,451	5,605*	3.5	6.0
053 ASSEMB OF GOD	5	859	1,340	.8	1.4
081 CATHOLIC	9	NA	30,716	19.1	32.9
081d LATIN	*9*	*NA*	*30,716*	*19.1*	*32.9*
093 CHR CH (DISC)	6	1,608	2,981	1.9	3.2
097 CHR CHS&CHS CR	4	501	631*	.4	.7
111 CH CR,SCIENTST	1	NR	NR	-	-
123 CH GOD (ANDER)	2	44	46	-	-
145 CH GOD PROPHCY	1	33	42*	-	-
151 L-D SAINTS	4	NA	1,465	.9	1.6
157 CH OF BRETHREN	1	147	185*	.1	.2
165 CH OF NAZARENE	5	1,104	1,920	1.2	2.1
167 CHS OF CHRIST	7	1,082	1,393	.9	1.5
193 EPISCOPAL	3	1,672	2,332	1.4	2.5
203 EVAN FREE CH	1	35	60	-	.1
207 E.L.C.A.	4	1,552	2,075	1.3	2.2
221 FREE METHODIST	1	79	97	.1	.1
223 FREE WILL BAPT	1	47	59*	-	.1
226 FRIENDS-USA	2	131	178*	.1	.2
226b EFI	*1*	*114*	*144*/*	*.1*	*.2*
226c FGC	*1*	*17*	*34*	-	-
237 GC MENN BR CHS	1	73	92*	.1	.1
263 INT FOURSQ GOS	1	135	170*	.1	.2
283 LUTH—MO SYNOD	7	3,478	4,716	2.9	5.1
287 MENN GEN CONF	1	101	126	.1	.1
329 OPEN BIBLE STD	1	NR	NR	-	-
339 PENT CH OF GOD	1	34	77	-	.1
353 CHR BRETHREN	1	30	40	-	-
355 PRESB CH (USA)	12	3,695	4,653*	2.9	5.0
403 SALVATION ARMY	1	124	142	.1	.2
413 S.D.A.	3	728	917*	.6	1.0
419 SO BAPT CONV	13	5,460	6,875*	4.3	7.4
435 UNITARIAN-UNIV	1	108	143	.1	.2
443 UN C OF CHRIST	5	1,928	2,428*	1.5	2.6
449 UN METHODIST	23	10,477	13,192*	8.2	14.2
467 WESLEYAN	4	282	1,032	.6	1.1
469 WELS	1	97	125	.1	.1
496 JEWISH EST[1]	1	NA	500	.3	.5
497 BLACK BAPT EST[2]	NA	3,534	4,450*	2.8	4.8
498 INDEP.CHARIS.[3]	1	NA	350	.2	.4
499 INDEP.NON-CHAR[3]	3	NA	2,050	1.3	2.2
SHERIDAN	**12**	**725**	**2,417***	**79.4**	**100.0**
081 CATHOLIC	4	NA	1,394	45.8	57.7
081d LATIN	*4*	*NA*	*1,394*	*45.8*	*57.7*
093 CHR CH (DISC)	1	111	231	7.6	9.6
167 CHS OF CHRIST	1	23	30	1.0	1.2
283 LUTH—MO SYNOD	1	111	143	4.7	5.9
355 PRESB CH (USA)	1	180	232*	7.6	9.6
449 UN METHODIST	4	300	387*	12.7	16.0

County and Denomination	Number of churches	Communicant, confirmed, full members	Total adherents Number	Percent of total population	Percent of total adherents
SHERMAN	**14**	**1,718**	**3,109***	**44.9**	**100.0**
019 AMER BAPT USA	1	85	108*	1.6	3.5
081 CATHOLIC	1	NA	1,020	14.7	32.8
081d LATIN	*1*	*NA*	*1,020*	*14.7*	*32.8*
093 CHR CH (DISC)	1	251	275	4.0	8.8
097 CHR CHS&CHS CR	1	30	38*	.5	1.2
111 CH CR,SCIENTST	1	NR	NR	-	-
165 CH OF NAZARENE	1	35	32	.5	1.0
167 CHS OF CHRIST	1	25	35	.5	1.1
193 EPISCOPAL	1	78	97	1.4	3.1
207 E.L.C.A.	1	347	402	5.8	12.9
259 IFCA	1	NR	NR	-	-
413 S.D.A.	1	38	48*	.7	1.5
419 SO BAPT CONV	1	63	80*	1.2	2.6
449 UN METHODIST	2	766	974*	14.1	31.3
SMITH	**25**	**2,719**	**3,865***	**76.1**	**100.0**
053 ASSEMB OF GOD	1	27	35	.7	.9
081 CATHOLIC	2	NA	194	3.8	5.0
081d LATIN	*2*	*NA*	*194*	*3.8*	*5.0*
093 CHR CH (DISC)	3	351	576	11.3	14.9
097 CHR CHS&CHS CR	1	75	91*	1.8	2.4
105 CHRISTIAN REF	1	134	201	4.0	5.2
165 CH OF NAZARENE	2	103	196	3.9	5.1
203 EVAN FREE CH	1	45	83	1.6	2.1
207 E.L.C.A.	3	827	1,065	21.0	27.6
283 LUTH—MO SYNOD	1	145	199	3.9	5.1
355 PRESB CH (USA)	1	101	122*	2.4	3.2
443 UN C OF CHRIST	2	127	154*	3.0	4.0
449 UN METHODIST	7	784	949*	18.7	24.6
STAFFORD	**26**	**2,505**	**3,683***	**68.6**	**100.0**
019 AMER BAPT USA	2	254	320*	6.0	8.7
081 CATHOLIC	2	NA	150	2.8	4.1
081d LATIN	*2*	*NA*	*150*	*2.8*	*4.1*
093 CHR CH (DISC)	2	367	597	11.1	16.2
151 L-D SAINTS	1	NA	201	3.7	5.5
157 CH OF BRETHREN	1	63	79*	1.5	2.1
165 CH OF NAZARENE	1	75	124	2.3	3.4
167 CHS OF CHRIST	2	170	218	4.1	5.9
217 FIRE BAPTIZED	1	2	3*	.1	.1
221 FREE METHODIST	1	19	31	.6	.8
226 FRIENDS-USA	1	38	48*	.9	1.3
226b EFI	*1*	*38*	*48*/*	*.9*	*1.3*
313 N AM BAPT CONF	1	185	233*	4.3	6.3
355 PRESB CH (USA)	2	85	107*	2.0	2.9
419 SO BAPT CONV	1	51	64*	1.2	1.7
443 UN C OF CHRIST	2	298	376*	7.0	10.2
449 UN METHODIST	6	898	1,132*	21.1	30.7
STANTON	**8**	**626**	**1,211***	**51.9**	**100.0**
081 CATHOLIC	1	NA	100	4.3	8.3
081d LATIN	*1*	*NA*	*100*	*4.3*	*8.3*
151 L-D SAINTS	1	NA	141	6.0	11.6
165 CH OF NAZARENE	1	54	71	3.0	5.9
167 CHS OF CHRIST	1	10	13	.6	1.1
449 UN METHODIST	2	485	654*	28.0	54.0
467 WESLEYAN	2	77	232	9.9	19.2
STEVENS	**15**	**2,245**	**3,473***	**68.8**	**100.0**
019 AMER BAPT USA	1	148	195*	3.9	5.6
053 ASSEMB OF GOD	1	89	210	4.2	6.0
081 CATHOLIC	1	NA	312	6.2	9.0
081d LATIN	*1*	*NA*	*312*	*6.2*	*9.0*
097 CHR CHS&CHS CR	1	525	692*	13.7	19.9
123 CH GOD (ANDER)	1	69	114	2.3	3.3
165 CH OF NAZARENE	1	36	80	1.6	2.3
167 CHS OF CHRIST	1	54	78	1.5	2.2
193 EPISCOPAL	1	27	56	1.1	1.6
226 FRIENDS-USA	2	229	302*	6.0	8.7
226b EFI	*2*	*229*	*302*/*	*6.0*	*8.7*
283 LUTH—MO SYNOD	1	92	147	2.9	4.2
349 PENT HOLINESS	1	34	45*	.9	1.3
419 SO BAPT CONV	1	220	290*	5.7	8.4
449 UN METHODIST	2	722	952*	18.9	27.4
SUMNER	**67**	**10,190**	**17,112***	**66.2**	**100.0**
019 AMER BAPT USA	6	978	1,266*	4.9	7.4
053 ASSEMB OF GOD	3	213	450	1.7	2.6
071 BRETHREN (ASH)	1	54	70*	.3	.4
081 CATHOLIC	6	NA	3,533	13.7	20.6
081d LATIN	*6*	*NA*	*3,533*	*13.7*	*20.6*
093 CHR CH (DISC)	6	1,093	1,597	6.2	9.3
097 CHR CHS&CHS CR	1	1,000	1,294*	5.0	7.6

NA–Not applicable NR–Not reported *Total adherents estimated from known number of communicant, confirmed, full members. - Represents a percent less than 0.1. Percentages may not total due to rounding.
[1]See Appendix E [2]See Appendix F [3]See Appendix G Lines in *italic* represent a breakdown of Catholic rites or Friends affiliations. They are included in their respective denominational total.

165

KANSAS

Table 4. Churches and Church Membership by County and Denomination: 1990

County and Denomination	Number of churches	Communicant, confirmed, full members	Total adherents		
			Number	Percent of total population	Percent of total adherents
123 CH GOD (ANDER)	1	59	59	.2	.3
151 L-D SAINTS	1	NA	257	1.0	1.5
165 CH OF NAZARENE	1	136	114	.4	.7
167 CHS OF CHRIST	9	718	795	3.1	4.6
193 EPISCOPAL	1	22	22	.1	.1
207 E.L.C.A.	1	158	197	.8	1.2
223 FREE WILL BAPT	1	111	144*	.6	.8
226 FRIENDS-USA	1	170	220*	.9	1.3
226b *EFI*	1	*170*	*220**	*.9*	*1.3*
283 LUTH—MO SYNOD	2	208	269	1.0	1.6
355 PRESB CH (USA)	5	566	732*	2.8	4.3
413 S.D.A.	2	67	87*	.3	.5
419 SO BAPT CONV	6	1,187	1,536*	5.9	9.0
449 UN METHODIST	12	3,427	4,435*	17.2	25.9
467 WESLEYAN	1	23	35	.1	.2
THOMAS	**17**	**2,215**	**4,624***	**56.0**	**100.0**
019 AMER BAPT USA	2	217	280*	3.4	6.1
053 ASSEMB OF GOD	1	118	300	3.6	6.5
063 BEREAN FUND CH	1	48	97	1.2	2.1
081 CATHOLIC	1	NA	1,381	16.7	29.9
081d *LATIN*	1	*NA*	*1,381*	*16.7*	*29.9*
093 CHR CH (DISC)	1	157	216	2.6	4.7
151 L-D SAINTS	1	NA	91	1.1	2.0
167 CHS OF CHRIST	1	28	36	.4	.8
193 EPISCOPAL	1	18	28	.3	.6
207 E.L.C.A.	1	75	95	1.2	2.1
283 LUTH—MO SYNOD	1	307	402	4.9	8.7
355 PRESB CH (USA)	1	221	285*	3.5	6.2
419 SO BAPT CONV	1	93	120*	1.5	2.6
449 UN METHODIST	3	898	1,159*	14.0	25.1
467 WESLEYAN	1	35	134	1.6	2.9
TREGO	**12**	**1,230**	**2,718***	**73.6**	**100.0**
053 ASSEMB OF GOD	1	27	44	1.2	1.6
081 CATHOLIC	2	NA	1,074	29.1	39.5
081d *LATIN*	2	*NA*	*1,074*	*29.1*	*39.5*
097 CHR CHS&CHS CR	1	119	150*	4.1	5.5
123 CH GOD (ANDER)	1	0	83	2.2	3.1
207 E.L.C.A.	4	607	766	20.7	28.2
355 PRESB CH (USA)	1	134	169*	4.6	6.2
419 SO BAPT CONV	1	16	20*	.5	.7
449 UN METHODIST	1	327	412*	11.2	15.2
WABAUNSEE	**24**	**2,246**	**3,624***	**54.9**	**100.0**
019 AMER BAPT USA	1	48	61*	.9	1.7
053 ASSEMB OF GOD	1	38	50	.8	1.4
081 CATHOLIC	3	NA	702	10.6	19.4
081d *LATIN*	3	*NA*	*702*	*10.6*	*19.4*
097 CHR CHS&CHS CR	1	80	102*	1.5	2.8
167 CHS OF CHRIST	3	67	87	1.3	2.4
175 CONGR CHR CHS	1	90	115*	1.7	3.2
283 LUTH—MO SYNOD	3	780	1,048	15.9	28.9
355 PRESB CH (USA)	1	76	97*	1.5	2.7
419 SO BAPT CONV	2	65	83*	1.3	2.3
443 UN C OF CHRIST	2	207	264*	4.0	7.3
449 UN METHODIST	6	795	1,015*	15.4	28.0
WALLACE	**11**	**649**	**1,254***	**68.9**	**100.0**
019 AMER BAPT USA	2	156	203*	11.1	16.2
053 ASSEMB OF GOD	1	23	23	1.3	1.8
081 CATHOLIC	2	NA	344	18.9	27.4
081d *LATIN*	2	*NA*	*344*	*18.9*	*27.4*
143 CG IN CR(MENN)	1	42	55*	3.0	4.4
207 E.L.C.A.	2	95	129	7.1	10.3
449 UN METHODIST	2	285	370*	20.3	29.5
467 WESLEYAN	1	48	130	7.1	10.4
WASHINGTON	**37**	**3,859**	**6,821***	**96.4**	**100.0**
019 AMER BAPT USA	1	102	125*	1.8	1.8
081 CATHOLIC	6	NA	1,990	28.1	29.2
081d *LATIN*	6	*NA*	*1,990*	*28.1*	*29.2*
097 CHR CHS&CHS CR	3	413	508*	7.2	7.4
145 CH GOD PROPHCY	1	33	41*	.6	.6
157 CH OF BRETHREN	1	25	31*	.4	.5
207 E.L.C.A.	8	847	1,057	14.9	15.5
283 LUTH—MO SYNOD	6	1,356	1,740	24.6	25.5
355 PRESB CH (USA)	3	342	420*	5.9	6.2
419 SO BAPT CONV	1	105	129*	1.8	1.9
449 UN METHODIST	6	627	771*	10.9	11.3
469 WELS	1	9	9	.1	.1
WICHITA	**10**	**850**	**1,827***	**66.2**	**100.0**
019 AMER BAPT USA	1	240	324*	11.7	17.7
053 ASSEMB OF GOD	1	61	139	5.0	7.6
081 CATHOLIC	2	NA	618	22.4	33.8
081d *LATIN*	2	*NA*	*618*	*22.4*	*33.8*
221 FREE METHODIST	1	51	73	2.6	4.0
355 PRESB CH (USA)	2	150	203*	7.4	11.1
449 UN METHODIST	3	348	470*	17.0	25.7
WILSON	**36**	**3,176**	**4,977***	**48.4**	**100.0**
019 AMER BAPT USA	2	202	252*	2.4	5.1
053 ASSEMB OF GOD	1	126	228	2.2	4.6
081 CATHOLIC	2	NA	581	5.6	11.7
081d *LATIN*	2	*NA*	*581*	*5.6*	*11.7*
093 CHR CH (DISC)	2	392	697	6.8	14.0
097 CHR CHS&CHS CR	5	281	351*	3.4	7.1
123 CH GOD (ANDER)	1	42	50	.5	1.0
127 CH GOD (CLEVE)	1	6	7*	.1	.1
143 CG IN CR(MENN)	1	115	143*	1.4	2.9
157 CH OF BRETHREN	1	48	60*	.6	1.2
165 CH OF NAZARENE	3	246	431	4.2	8.7
167 CHS OF CHRIST	1	28	36	.3	.7
171 CH GOD-GEN CON	1	62	77*	.7	1.5
193 EPISCOPAL	1	51	55	.5	1.1
207 E.L.C.A.	1	16	27	.3	.5
217 FIRE BAPTIZED	1	13	16*	.2	.3
355 PRESB CH (USA)	2	107	134*	1.3	2.7
413 S.D.A.	1	31	39*	.4	.8
419 SO BAPT CONV	1	74	92*	.9	1.8
449 UN METHODIST	7	1,263	1,576*	15.3	31.7
467 WESLEYAN	1	73	125	1.2	2.5
WOODSON	**20**	**1,693**	**2,639***	**64.1**	**100.0**
053 ASSEMB OF GOD	1	30	36	.9	1.4
081 CATHOLIC	2	NA	450	10.9	17.1
081d *LATIN*	2	*NA*	*450*	*10.9*	*17.1*
093 CHR CH (DISC)	2	342	507	12.3	19.2
097 CHR CHS&CHS CR	1	40	49*	1.2	1.9
165 CH OF NAZARENE	1	41	61	1.5	2.3
167 CHS OF CHRIST	1	20	25	.6	.9
171 CH GOD-GEN CON	1	85	105*	2.6	4.0
193 EPISCOPAL	1	54	76	1.8	2.9
283 LUTH—MO SYNOD	1	34	41	1.0	1.6
355 PRESB CH (USA)	2	128	158*	3.8	6.0
419 SO BAPT CONV	2	322	397*	9.6	15.0
449 UN METHODIST	4	588	725*	17.6	27.5
467 WESLEYAN	1	9	9	.2	.3
WYANDOTTE	**168**	**35,184**	**78,546***	**48.5**	**100.0**
005 AME ZION	2	116	178	.1	.2
019 AMER BAPT USA	22	4,236	5,487*	3.4	7.0
053 ASSEMB OF GOD	7	1,096	1,753	1.1	2.2
059 BAPT MISS ASSN	1	145	188*	.1	.2
081 CATHOLIC	16	NA	27,912	17.2	35.5
081d *LATIN*	16	*NA*	*27,912*	*17.2*	*35.5*
089 CHR & MISS AL	1	498	508	.3	.6
093 CHR CH (DISC)	12	2,114	3,593	2.2	4.6
097 CHR CHS&CHS CR	1	20	26*	-	-
111 CH CR,SCIENTST	1	NR	NR	-	-
123 CH GOD (ANDER)	4	640	678	.4	.9
127 CH GOD (CLEVE)	1	94	122*	.1	.2
145 CH GOD PROPHCY	1	33	43*	-	.1
151 L-D SAINTS	2	NA	1,083	.7	1.4
157 CH OF BRETHREN	1	67	87*	.1	.1
165 CH OF NAZARENE	9	1,065	1,443	.9	1.8
167 CHS OF CHRIST	8	1,017	1,314	.8	1.7
193 EPISCOPAL	3	433	554	.3	.7
207 E.L.C.A.	3	501	635	.4	.8
217 FIRE BAPTIZED	1	5	6*	-	-
221 FREE METHODIST	1	63	106	.1	.1
223 FREE WILL BAPT	1	45	58*	-	.1
226 FRIENDS-USA	1	34	44*	-	.1
226b *EFI*	1	*34*	*44**	*-*	*.1*
259 IFCA	2	NR	NR	-	-
283 LUTH—MO SYNOD	7	2,097	2,590	1.6	3.3
285 MENNONITE CH	2	184	236	.1	.3
287 MENN GEN CONF	2	101	101	.1	.1
331 ORTH CH IN AM	1	NR	NR	-	-
353 CHR BRETHREN	2	36	72	-	.1
355 PRESB CH (USA)	6	634	821*	.5	1.0
403 SALVATION ARMY	1	112	112	.1	.1
413 S.D.A.	4	1,704	2,207*	1.4	2.8
419 SO BAPT CONV	16	4,509	5,841*	3.6	7.4
443 UN C OF CHRIST	5	835	1,082*	.7	1.4
449 UN METHODIST	16	4,223	5,470*	3.4	7.0
467 WESLEYAN	2	62	143	.1	.2
496 JEWISH EST[1]	0	NA	1,975	1.4	2.5
497 BLACK BAPT EST[2]	NA	8,465	10,965*	6.8	14.0
499 INDEP.NON-CHAR[3]	3	NA	1,113	.7	1.4

NA–Not applicable   NR–Not reported   *Total adherents estimated from known number of communicant, confirmed, full members.   - Represents a percent less than 0.1.   Percentages may not total due to rounding.
[1]See Appendix E   [2]See Appendix F   [3]See Appendix G   Lines in *italic* represent a breakdown of Catholic rites or Friends affiliations. They are included in their respective denominational total.

Table 4. Churches and Church Membership by County and Denomination: 1990

County and Denomination	Number of churches	Communicant, confirmed, full members	Total adherents Number	Total adherents Percent of total population	Total adherents Percent of total adherents
KENTUCKY					
THE STATE.....	7,255	1,439,334	2,227,747*	60.4	100.0
ADAIR	**69**	**6,514**	**8,463***	**55.1**	**100.0**
005 AME ZION	1	75	82	.5	1.0
053 ASSEMB OF GOD	1	45	62	.4	.7
075 BRETHREN IN CR	4	166	225	1.5	2.7
081 CATHOLIC	1	NA	59	.4	.7
081d LATIN	1	NA	59	.4	.7
097 CHR CHS&CHS CR	8	1,190	1,463*	9.5	17.3
123 CH GOD (ANDER)	1	52	52	.3	.6
127 CH GOD (CLEVE)	1	82	101*	.7	1.2
145 CH GOD PROPHCY	2	86	106*	.7	1.3
165 CH OF NAZARENE	3	321	656	4.3	7.8
167 CHS OF CHRIST	1	210	231	1.5	2.7
185 CUMBER PRESB	1	18	18	.1	.2
193 EPISCOPAL	1	19	32	.2	.4
323 OLD ORD AMISH	1	NA	150	1.0	1.8
355 PRESB CH (USA)	1	73	90*	.6	1.1
413 S.D.A.	1	72	89*	.6	1.1
419 SO BAPT CONV	18	1,817	2,234*	14.5	26.4
449 UN METHODIST	23	2,288	2,813*	18.3	33.2
ALLEN	**43**	**5,450**	**6,953***	**47.5**	**100.0**
060 BRN RVR MB ASC	1	57	72*	.5	1.0
081 CATHOLIC	1	NA	88	.6	1.3
081d LATIN	1	NA	88	.6	1.3
145 CH GOD PROPHCY	2	86	108*	.7	1.6
165 CH OF NAZARENE	1	57	95	.6	1.4
167 CHS OF CHRIST	2	203	253	1.7	3.6
185 CUMBER PRESB	1	0	0	-	-
221 FREE METHODIST	1	82	102	.7	1.5
320 "OLD" MB ASCS	4	762	957*	6.5	13.8
419 SO BAPT CONV	15	2,528	3,175*	21.7	45.7
436 UNITED BAPT	2	189	237*	1.6	3.4
449 UN METHODIST	13	1,486	1,866*	12.8	26.8
ANDERSON	**37**	**6,893**	**9,494***	**65.2**	**100.0**
053 ASSEMB OF GOD	1	92	90	.6	.9
081 CATHOLIC	1	NA	401	2.8	4.2
081d LATIN	1	NA	401	2.8	4.2
093 CHR CH (DISC)	4	659	1,232	8.5	13.0
097 CHR CHS&CHS CR	8	1,144	1,437*	9.9	15.1
127 CH GOD (CLEVE)	1	87	109*	.7	1.1
167 CHS OF CHRIST	3	145	185	1.3	1.9
329 OPEN BIBLE STD	1	NR	NR	-	-
339 PENT CH OF GOD	1	68	138	.9	1.5
355 PRESB CH (USA)	1	76	95*	.7	1.0
419 SO BAPT CONV	13	4,118	5,174*	35.5	54.5
449 UN METHODIST	3	504	633*	4.3	6.7
BALLARD	**31**	**5,081**	**6,348***	**80.3**	**100.0**
081 CATHOLIC	1	NA	201	2.5	3.2
081d LATIN	1	NA	201	2.5	3.2
093 CHR CH (DISC)	2	88	122	1.5	1.9
167 CHS OF CHRIST	1	19	24	.3	.4
185 CUMBER PRESB	2	250	261	3.3	4.1
419 SO BAPT CONV	17	3,910	4,751*	60.1	74.8
449 UN METHODIST	8	814	989*	12.5	15.6
BARREN	**85**	**16,343**	**20,699***	**60.9**	**100.0**
053 ASSEMB OF GOD	1	97	150	.4	.7
060 BRN RVR MB ASC	3	385	477*	1.4	2.3
081 CATHOLIC	1	NA	138	.4	.7
081d LATIN	1	NA	138	.4	.7
093 CHR CH (DISC)	2	594	711	2.1	3.4
097 CHR CHS&CHS CR	2	395	489*	1.4	2.4
123 CH GOD (ANDER)	1	48	48	.1	.2
127 CH GOD (CLEVE)	2	122	151*	.4	.7
151 L-D SAINTS	1	NA	148	.4	.7
165 CH OF NAZARENE	2	241	262	.8	1.3
167 CHS OF CHRIST	12	1,415	1,802	5.3	8.7
185 CUMBER PRESB	3	478	486	1.4	2.3
193 EPISCOPAL	1	50	75	.2	.4
223 FREE WILL BAPT	1	207	256*	.8	1.2
320 "OLD" MB ASCS	1	163	202*	.6	1.0
323 OLD ORD AMISH	2	NA	300	.9	1.4
355 PRESB CH (USA)	1	140	173*	.5	.8
413 S.D.A.	1	65	80*	.2	.4
419 SO BAPT CONV	25	8,592	10,634*	31.3	51.4
436 UNITED BAPT	4	684	847*	2.5	4.1
449 UN METHODIST	17	2,195	2,717*	8.0	13.1
467 WESLEYAN	2	60	43	.1	.2
497 BLACK BAPT EST[2]	NA	412	510*	1.5	2.5

County and Denomination	Number of churches	Communicant, confirmed, full members	Total adherents Number	Total adherents Percent of total population	Total adherents Percent of total adherents
BATH	**40**	**2,928**	**3,921***	**40.5**	**100.0**
081 CATHOLIC	1	NA	40	.4	1.0
081d LATIN	1	NA	40	.4	1.0
093 CHR CH (DISC)	5	360	707	7.3	18.0
097 CHR CHS&CHS CR	6	586	726*	7.5	18.5
123 CH GOD (ANDER)	7	345	493	5.1	12.6
127 CH GOD (CLEVE)	1	98	121*	1.2	3.1
167 CHS OF CHRIST	3	171	211	2.2	5.4
171 CH GOD-GEN CON	1	223	276*	2.8	7.0
185 CUMBER PRESB	6	429	459	4.7	11.7
223 FREE WILL BAPT	1	100	124*	1.3	3.2
259 IFCA	1	NR	NR	-	-
355 PRESB CH (USA)	3	141	175*	1.8	4.5
419 SO BAPT CONV	2	179	222*	2.3	5.7
449 UN METHODIST	3	296	367*	3.8	9.4
BELL	**91**	**15,843**	**20,758***	**65.9**	**100.0**
005 AME ZION	1	240	265	.8	1.3
019 AMER BAPT USA	1	0	0*	-	-
053 ASSEMB OF GOD	1	84	80	.3	.4
081 CATHOLIC	2	NA	382	1.2	1.8
081d LATIN	2	NA	382	1.2	1.8
093 CHR CH (DISC)	2	242	326	1.0	1.6
127 CH GOD (CLEVE)	3	272	341*	1.1	1.6
145 CH GOD PROPHCY	4	172	216*	.7	1.0
146 CH GOD MTN ASM	2	110	138*	.4	.7
165 CH OF NAZARENE	2	55	111	.4	.5
167 CHS OF CHRIST	1	74	105	.3	.5
193 EPISCOPAL	1	85	105	.3	.5
355 PRESB CH (USA)	2	206	258*	.8	1.2
361 PRIM BAPT ASCS	4	240	301*	1.0	1.5
403 SALVATION ARMY	1	59	61	.2	.3
413 S.D.A.	0	11	14*	-	.1
419 SO BAPT CONV	58	13,100	16,435*	52.2	79.2
449 UN METHODIST	5	696	873*	2.8	4.2
497 BLACK BAPT EST[2]	NA	197	247*	.8	1.2
498 INDEP.CHARIS.[3]	1	NA	500	1.6	2.4
BOONE	**59**	**16,395**	**34,212***	**59.4**	**100.0**
053 ASSEMB OF GOD	2	935	1,460	2.5	4.3
081 CATHOLIC	4	NA	9,395	16.3	27.5
081d LATIN	4	NA	9,395	16.3	27.5
089 CHR & MISS AL	1	0	46	.1	.1
093 CHR CH (DISC)	6	1,114	2,015	3.5	5.9
097 CHR CHS&CHS CR	5	1,126	1,473*	2.6	4.3
123 CH GOD (ANDER)	1	0	97	.2	.3
127 CH GOD (CLEVE)	1	164	215*	.4	.6
145 CH GOD PROPHCY	1	43	56*	.1	.2
151 L-D SAINTS	1	NA	354	.6	1.0
157 CH OF BRETHREN	1	82	107*	.2	.3
165 CH OF NAZARENE	2	100	132	.2	.4
167 CHS OF CHRIST	4	263	373	.6	1.1
193 EPISCOPAL	1	196	262	.5	.8
207 E.L.C.A.	2	893	1,178	2.0	3.4
223 FREE WILL BAPT	1	30	39*	.1	.1
355 PRESB CH (USA)	2	248	324*	.6	.9
356 PRESB CH AMER	1	0	0	-	-
419 SO BAPT CONV	16	9,664	12,640*	21.9	36.9
449 UN METHODIST	5	1,521	1,989*	3.5	5.8
467 WESLEYAN	1	16	96	.2	.3
496 JEWISH EST[1]	0	NA	911	1.6	2.7
499 INDEP.NON-CHAR[3]	1	NA	1,050	1.8	3.1
BOURBON	**42**	**7,656**	**11,708***	**60.9**	**100.0**
053 ASSEMB OF GOD	1	145	225	1.2	1.9
081 CATHOLIC	1	NA	800	4.2	6.8
081d LATIN	1	NA	800	4.2	6.8
093 CHR CH (DISC)	8	1,186	2,032	10.6	17.4
097 CHR CHS&CHS CR	4	785	984*	5.1	8.4
123 CH GOD (ANDER)	2	293	335	1.7	2.9
127 CH GOD (CLEVE)	1	40	50*	.3	.4
151 L-D SAINTS	1	NA	342	1.8	2.9
165 CH OF NAZARENE	3	140	236	1.2	2.0
167 CHS OF CHRIST	2	103	133	.7	1.1
193 EPISCOPAL	1	270	373	1.9	3.2
339 PENT CH OF GOD	1	34	77	.4	.7
355 PRESB CH (USA)	3	291	365*	1.9	3.1
419 SO BAPT CONV	5	2,628	3,295*	17.1	28.1
449 UN METHODIST	8	1,212	1,520*	7.9	13.0
467 WESLEYAN	1	26	200	1.0	1.7
496 JEWISH EST[1]	0	NA	110	.6	.9
497 BLACK BAPT EST[2]	NA	503	631*	3.3	5.4
BOYD	**95**	**24,285**	**32,879***	**64.3**	**100.0**
053 ASSEMB OF GOD	1	94	177	.3	.5

NA–Not applicable   NR–Not reported   *Total adherents estimated from known number of communicant, confirmed, full members.   - Represents a percent less than 0.1.   Percentages may not total due to rounding.
[1] See Appendix E   [2] See Appendix F   [3] See Appendix G   Lines in *italic* represent a breakdown of Catholic rites or Friends affiliations. They are included in their respective denominational total.

Table 4. Churches and Church Membership by County and Denomination: 1990

County and Denomination	Number of churches	Communicant, confirmed, full members	Total adherents Number	Percent of total population	Percent of total adherents
081 CATHOLIC	1	NA	2,397	4.7	7.3
081d *LATIN*	*1*	*NA*	*2,397*	*4.7*	*7.3*
093 CHR CH (DISC)	1	516	784	1.5	2.4
097 CHR CHS&CHS CR	4	600	731*	1.4	2.2
123 CH GOD (ANDER)	4	382	632	1.2	1.9
127 CH GOD (CLEVE)	4	606	738*	1.4	2.2
165 CH OF NAZARENE	10	1,441	2,037	4.0	6.2
167 CHS OF CHRIST	5	184	236	.5	.7
191 ENTRPR BPT ASC	1	58	71*	.1	.2
193 EPISCOPAL	1	358	484	.9	1.5
223 FREE WILL BAPT	12	1,238	1,507*	2.9	4.6
265 INT PENT C CHR	2	94	159	.3	.5
283 LUTH—MO SYNOD	1	207	264	.5	.8
325 OLD REG BAPT	2	96	117*	.2	.4
355 PRESB CH (USA)	4	715	871*	1.7	2.6
403 SALVATION ARMY	1	87	90	.2	.3
419 SO BAPT CONV	22	11,757	14,315*	28.0	43.5
436 UNITED BAPT	3	536	653*	1.3	2.0
449 UN METHODIST	14	4,916	5,986*	11.7	18.2
467 WESLEYAN	2	85	246	.5	.7
497 BLACK BAPT EST[2]	NA	315	384*	.8	1.2
BOYLE	**48**	**15,004**	**19,926***	**77.7**	**100.0**
053 ASSEMB OF GOD	1	59	79	.3	.4
081 CATHOLIC	3	NA	1,375	5.4	6.9
081d *LATIN*	*3*	*NA*	*1,375*	*5.4*	*6.9*
093 CHR CH (DISC)	3	770	898	3.5	4.5
097 CHR CHS&CHS CR	1	350	429*	1.7	2.2
123 CH GOD (ANDER)	3	190	351	1.4	1.8
127 CH GOD (CLEVE)	3	284	348*	1.4	1.7
165 CH OF NAZARENE	1	83	141	.5	.7
167 CHS OF CHRIST	5	447	567	2.2	2.8
193 EPISCOPAL	1	207	267	1.0	1.3
283 LUTH—MO SYNOD	1	115	155	.6	.8
339 PENT CH OF GOD	1	34	76	.3	.4
355 PRESB CH (USA)	2	842	1,031*	4.0	5.2
403 SALVATION ARMY	1	90	96	.4	.5
419 SO BAPT CONV	17	9,866	12,084*	47.1	60.6
449 UN METHODIST	4	1,057	1,295*	5.1	6.5
467 WESLEYAN	1	11	0	-	-
497 BLACK BAPT EST[2]	NA	599	734*	2.9	3.7
BRACKEN	**33**	**3,575**	**5,342***	**68.8**	**100.0**
053 ASSEMB OF GOD	1	22	40	.5	.7
081 CATHOLIC	2	NA	768	9.9	14.4
081d *LATIN*	*2*	*NA*	*768*	*9.9*	*14.4*
093 CHR CH (DISC)	1	62	100	1.3	1.9
097 CHR CHS&CHS CR	8	1,088	1,362*	17.5	25.5
165 CH OF NAZARENE	1	84	170	2.2	3.2
207 E.L.C.A.	1	74	101	1.3	1.9
355 PRESB CH (USA)	2	124	155*	2.0	2.9
419 SO BAPT CONV	7	1,312	1,642*	21.1	30.7
449 UN METHODIST	9	802	1,004*	12.9	18.8
467 WESLEYAN	1	7	0	-	-
BREATHITT	**41**	**3,144**	**4,423***	**28.2**	**100.0**
053 ASSEMB OF GOD	2	60	126	.8	2.8
071 BRETHREN (ASH)	3	29	37*	.2	.8
081 CATHOLIC	1	NA	52	.3	1.2
081d *LATIN*	*1*	*NA*	*52*	*.3*	*1.2*
097 CHR CHS&CHS CR	1	220	281*	1.8	6.4
123 CH GOD (ANDER)	1	0	80	.5	1.8
127 CH GOD (CLEVE)	1	85	108*	.7	2.4
151 L-D SAINTS	1	NA	117	.7	2.6
167 CHS OF CHRIST	1	20	26	.2	.6
203 EVAN FREE CH	1	0	0	-	-
221 FREE METHODIST	2	51	106	.7	2.4
285 MENNONITE CH	4	78	173	1.1	3.9
325 OLD REG BAPT	9	688	877*	5.6	19.8
329 OPEN BIBLE STD	1	NR	NR	-	-
355 PRESB CH (USA)	1	56	71*	.5	1.6
413 S.D.A.	0	11	14*	.1	.3
419 SO BAPT CONV	2	768	980*	6.2	22.2
436 UNITED BAPT	7	751	958*	6.1	21.7
449 UN METHODIST	3	327	417*	2.7	9.4
BRECKINRIDGE	**59**	**7,177**	**11,272***	**69.1**	**100.0**
053 ASSEMB OF GOD	1	20	54	.3	.5
081 CATHOLIC	5	NA	2,067	12.7	18.3
081d *LATIN*	*5*	*NA*	*2,067*	*12.7*	*18.3*
097 CHR CHS&CHS CR	1	110	138*	.8	1.2
123 CH GOD (ANDER)	1	0	39	.2	.3
145 CH GOD PROPHCY	1	43	54*	.3	.5
167 CHS OF CHRIST	2	66	84	.5	.7
291 MISSIONARY CH	1	40	31	.2	.3
419 SO BAPT CONV	21	4,425	5,567*	34.1	49.4

County and Denomination	Number of churches	Communicant, confirmed, full members	Total adherents Number	Percent of total population	Percent of total adherents
449 UN METHODIST	24	2,270	2,856*	17.5	25.3
467 WESLEYAN	2	63	206	1.3	1.8
497 BLACK BAPT EST[2]	NA	140	176*	1.1	1.6
BULLITT	**64**	**15,087**	**23,748***	**49.9**	**100.0**
053 ASSEMB OF GOD	4	365	451	.9	1.9
081 CATHOLIC	3	NA	3,985	8.4	16.8
081d *LATIN*	*3*	*NA*	*3,985*	*8.4*	*16.8*
082 CENTRAL BAPT	1	148	190*	.4	.8
093 CHR CH (DISC)	1	98	160	.3	.7
097 CHR CHS&CHS CR	3	607	779*	1.6	3.3
127 CH GOD (CLEVE)	2	156	200*	.4	.8
145 CH GOD PROPHCY	3	129	166*	.3	.7
151 L-D SAINTS	1	NA	438	.9	1.8
165 CH OF NAZARENE	2	98	85	.2	.4
167 CHS OF CHRIST	5	306	387	.8	1.6
283 LUTH—MO SYNOD	1	0	0	-	-
355 PRESB CH (USA)	1	93	119*	.3	.5
419 SO BAPT CONV	27	11,213	14,395*	30.3	60.6
436 UNITED BAPT	2	483	620*	1.3	2.6
449 UN METHODIST	7	1,381	1,773*	3.7	7.5
467 WESLEYAN	1	10	0	-	-
BUTLER	**50**	**6,364**	**8,273***	**73.6**	**100.0**
081 CATHOLIC	1	NA	50	.4	.6
081d *LATIN*	*1*	*NA*	*50*	*.4*	*.6*
097 CHR CHS&CHS CR	1	200	251*	2.2	3.0
151 L-D SAINTS	1	NA	205	1.8	2.5
165 CH OF NAZARENE	1	37	61	.5	.7
167 CHS OF CHRIST	11	448	582	5.2	7.0
185 CUMBER PRESB	3	86	87	.8	1.1
285 MENNONITE CH	1	6	15	.1	.2
419 SO BAPT CONV	25	5,205	6,542*	58.2	79.1
449 UN METHODIST	6	382	480*	4.3	5.8
CALDWELL	**48**	**10,887**	**13,504***	**102.1**	**100.0**
053 ASSEMB OF GOD	1	84	121	.9	.9
081 CATHOLIC	1	NA	76	.6	.6
081d *LATIN*	*1*	*NA*	*76*	*.6*	*.6*
093 CHR CH (DISC)	2	176	310	2.3	2.3
097 CHR CHS&CHS CR	2	225	276*	2.1	2.0
167 CHS OF CHRIST	1	75	150	1.1	1.1
185 CUMBER PRESB	6	359	361	2.7	2.7
355 PRESB CH (USA)	1	112	137*	1.0	1.0
419 SO BAPT CONV	27	8,667	10,616*	80.2	78.6
449 UN METHODIST	7	1,004	1,230*	9.3	9.1
497 BLACK BAPT EST[2]	NA	185	227*	1.7	1.7
CALLOWAY	**81**	**15,406**	**19,450***	**63.3**	**100.0**
053 ASSEMB OF GOD	1	106	150	.5	.8
081 CATHOLIC	1	NA	630	2.0	3.2
081d *LATIN*	*1*	*NA*	*630*	*2.0*	*3.2*
093 CHR CH (DISC)	1	300	408	1.3	2.1
111 CH CR,SCIENTST	1	NR	NR	-	-
127 CH GOD (CLEVE)	1	10	12*	-	.1
151 L-D SAINTS	1	NA	119	.4	.6
165 CH OF NAZARENE	2	65	54	.2	.3
167 CHS OF CHRIST	17	2,492	3,327	10.8	17.1
185 CUMBER PRESB	3	244	261	.8	1.3
193 EPISCOPAL	1	101	141	.5	.7
283 LUTH—MO SYNOD	1	190	249	.8	1.3
339 PENT CH OF GOD	2	69	154	.5	.8
355 PRESB CH (USA)	1	161	190*	.6	1.0
413 S.D.A.	1	49	58*	.2	.3
419 SO BAPT CONV	27	8,404	9,907*	32.2	50.9
449 UN METHODIST	20	2,979	3,512*	11.4	18.1
497 BLACK BAPT EST[2]	NA	236	278*	.9	1.4
CAMPBELL	**84**	**18,361**	**50,882***	**60.7**	**100.0**
053 ASSEMB OF GOD	3	411	412	.5	.8
081 CATHOLIC	16	NA	26,288	31.3	51.7
081d *LATIN*	*16*	*NA*	*26,288*	*31.3*	*51.7*
093 CHR CH (DISC)	2	232	300	.4	.6
097 CHR CHS&CHS CR	3	375	477*	.6	.9
111 CH CR,SCIENTST	1	NR	NR	-	-
123 CH GOD (ANDER)	2	17	96	.1	.2
127 CH GOD (CLEVE)	4	449	572*	.7	1.1
146 CH GOD MTN ASM	1	24	31*	-	.1
165 CH OF NAZARENE	4	555	709	.8	1.4
167 CHS OF CHRIST	1	120	159	.2	.3
193 EPISCOPAL	2	590	704	.8	1.4
207 E.L.C.A.	4	508	618	.7	1.2
325 OLD REG BAPT	1	213	271*	.3	.5
355 PRESB CH (USA)	2	497	633*	.8	1.2
403 SALVATION ARMY	1	51	56	.1	.1

NA–Not applicable   NR–Not reported   *Total adherents estimated from known number of communicant, confirmed, full members.   - Represents a percent less than 0.1.   Percentages may not total due to rounding.

[1] See Appendix E   [2] See Appendix F   [3] See Appendix G   Lines in *italic* represent a breakdown of Catholic rites or Friends affiliations. They are included in their respective denominational total.

Table 4. Churches and Church Membership by County and Denomination: 1990

County and Denomination	Number of churches	Communicant, confirmed, full members	Total adherents Number	Percent of total population	Percent of total adherents
419 SO BAPT CONV	19	8,968	11,417*	13.6	22.4
443 UN C OF CHRIST	7	2,555	3,253*	3.9	6.4
449 UN METHODIST	11	2,538	3,231*	3.9	6.3
496 JEWISH EST[1]	0	NA	1,327	1.6	2.6
497 BLACK BAPT EST[2]	NA	258	328*	.4	.6
CARLISLE	**25**	**3,305**	**4,677***	**89.3**	**100.0**
053 ASSEMB OF GOD	1	85	80	1.5	1.7
081 CATHOLIC	1	NA	310	5.9	6.6
081d LATIN	*1*	*NA*	*310*	*5.9*	*6.6*
093 CHR CH (DISC)	2	128	176	3.4	3.8
151 L-D SAINTS	1	NA	318	6.1	6.8
167 CHS OF CHRIST	4	190	247	4.7	5.3
419 SO BAPT CONV	11	2,486	3,038*	58.0	65.0
449 UN METHODIST	5	416	508*	9.7	10.9
CARROLL	**21**	**3,941**	**5,336***	**57.4**	**100.0**
053 ASSEMB OF GOD	1	64	49	.5	.9
081 CATHOLIC	1	NA	350	3.8	6.6
081d LATIN	*1*	*NA*	*350*	*3.8*	*6.6*
093 CHR CH (DISC)	2	223	318	3.4	6.0
097 CHR CHS&CHS CR	2	136	172*	1.9	3.2
167 CHS OF CHRIST	1	23	30	.3	.6
207 E.L.C.A.	1	64	80	.9	1.5
419 SO BAPT CONV	9	2,840	3,595*	38.7	67.4
449 UN METHODIST	3	464	587*	6.3	11.0
467 WESLEYAN	1	127	155	1.7	2.9
CARTER	**50**	**3,889**	**5,311***	**21.8**	**100.0**
053 ASSEMB OF GOD	1	22	47	.2	.9
081 CATHOLIC	1	NA	104	.4	2.0
081d LATIN	*1*	*NA*	*104*	*.4*	*2.0*
097 CHR CHS&CHS CR	4	200	250*	1.0	4.7
123 CH GOD (ANDER)	1	0	63	.3	1.2
127 CH GOD (CLEVE)	1	64	80*	.3	1.5
145 CH GOD PROPHCY	1	43	54*	.2	1.0
151 L-D SAINTS	1	NA	46	.2	.9
165 CH OF NAZARENE	3	125	365	1.5	6.9
167 CHS OF CHRIST	1	32	44	.2	.8
223 FREE WILL BAPT	8	455	568*	2.3	10.7
325 OLD REG BAPT	2	68	85*	.3	1.6
355 PRESB CH (USA)	1	71	89*	.4	1.7
361 PRIM BAPT ASCS	1	20	25*	.1	.5
419 SO BAPT CONV	10	1,917	2,395*	9.8	45.1
436 UNITED BAPT	3	119	149*	.6	2.8
449 UN METHODIST	6	560	700*	2.9	13.2
467 WESLEYAN	5	193	247	1.0	4.7
CASEY	**49**	**5,159**	**7,253***	**51.0**	**100.0**
061 BEACHY AMISH	1	40	50*	.4	.7
081 CATHOLIC	2	NA	413	2.9	5.7
081d LATIN	*2*	*NA*	*413*	*2.9*	*5.7*
093 CHR CH (DISC)	2	220	449	3.2	6.2
097 CHR CHS&CHS CR	3	320	400*	2.8	5.5
123 CH GOD (ANDER)	3	70	150	1.1	2.1
127 CH GOD (CLEVE)	1	52	65*	.5	.9
165 CH OF NAZARENE	1	30	42	.3	.6
167 CHS OF CHRIST	8	266	339	2.4	4.7
323 OLD ORD AMISH	1	NA	150	1.1	2.1
419 SO BAPT CONV	13	2,524	3,151*	22.2	43.4
436 UNITED BAPT	1	168	210*	1.5	2.9
449 UN METHODIST	13	1,469	1,834*	12.9	25.3
CHRISTIAN	**100**	**26,962**	**36,458***	**52.9**	**100.0**
005 AME ZION	1	75	90	.1	.2
053 ASSEMB OF GOD	3	377	417	.6	1.1
081 CATHOLIC	1	NA	1,136	1.6	3.1
081d LATIN	*1*	*NA*	*1,136*	*1.6*	*3.1*
093 CHR CH (DISC)	8	1,013	1,539	2.2	4.2
111 CH CR,SCIENTST	1	NR	NR	-	-
127 CH GOD (CLEVE)	1	87	111*	.2	.3
145 CH GOD PROPHCY	1	43	55*	.1	.2
151 L-D SAINTS	2	NA	789	1.1	2.2
165 CH OF NAZARENE	1	64	123	.2	.3
167 CHS OF CHRIST	9	891	1,167	1.7	3.2
185 CUMBER PRESB	4	503	505	.7	1.4
193 EPISCOPAL	1	254	301	.4	.8
223 FREE WILL BAPT	1	71	90*	.1	.2
263 INT FOURSQ GOS	1	20	25*	-	.1
283 LUTH—MO SYNOD	1	94	134	.2	.4
323 OLD ORD AMISH	2	NA	200	.3	.5
355 PRESB CH (USA)	4	507	644*	.9	1.8
403 SALVATION ARMY	1	147	149	.2	.4
413 S.D.A.	2	97	123*	.2	.3
419 SO BAPT CONV	38	14,713	18,687*	27.1	51.3

County and Denomination	Number of churches	Communicant, confirmed, full members	Total adherents Number	Percent of total population	Percent of total adherents
435 UNITARIAN-UNIV	1	7	13	-	-
449 UN METHODIST	16	2,875	3,652*	5.3	10.0
497 BLACK BAPT EST[2]	NA	5,124	6,508*	9.4	17.9
CLARK	**57**	**13,394**	**18,155***	**61.6**	**100.0**
053 ASSEMB OF GOD	1	98	155	.5	.9
081 CATHOLIC	1	NA	640	2.2	3.5
081d LATIN	*1*	*NA*	*640*	*2.2*	*3.5*
093 CHR CH (DISC)	5	892	1,085	3.7	6.0
097 CHR CHS&CHS CR	12	1,702	2,128*	7.2	11.7
123 CH GOD (ANDER)	2	340	524	1.8	2.9
127 CH GOD (CLEVE)	2	791	989*	3.4	5.4
145 CH GOD PROPHCY	1	43	54*	.2	.3
151 L-D SAINTS	1	NA	318	1.1	1.8
165 CH OF NAZARENE	1	89	182	.6	1.0
167 CHS OF CHRIST	5	307	391	1.3	2.2
193 EPISCOPAL	2	159	257	.9	1.4
216 EVAN PRESBY CH	1	46	46	.2	.3
263 INT FOURSQ GOS	1	31	39*	.1	.2
283 LUTH—MO SYNOD	1	105	141	.5	.8
355 PRESB CH (USA)	2	380	475*	1.6	2.6
413 S.D.A.	1	56	70*	.2	.4
419 SO BAPT CONV	11	5,638	7,050*	23.9	38.8
449 UN METHODIST	6	2,171	2,715*	9.2	15.0
467 WESLEYAN	1	57	115	.4	.6
496 JEWISH EST[1]	0	NA	169	.6	.9
497 BLACK BAPT EST[2]	NA	489	612*	2.1	3.4
CLAY	**47**	**9,586**	**12,605***	**58.0**	**100.0**
081 CATHOLIC	1	NA	100	.5	.8
081d LATIN	*1*	*NA*	*100*	*.5*	*.8*
089 CHR & MISS AL	1	27	58	.3	.5
097 CHR CHS&CHS CR	2	240	312*	1.4	2.5
127 CH GOD (CLEVE)	3	347	452*	2.1	3.6
157 CH OF BRETHREN	3	233	303*	1.4	2.4
167 CHS OF CHRIST	1	28	36	.2	.3
263 INT FOURSQ GOS	1	26	34*	.2	.3
285 MENNONITE CH	2	46	66	.3	.5
355 PRESB CH (USA)	3	84	109*	.5	.9
413 S.D.A.	1	141	184*	.8	1.5
419 SO BAPT CONV	20	7,303	9,505*	43.7	75.4
436 UNITED BAPT	5	858	1,117*	5.1	8.9
449 UN METHODIST	4	253	329*	1.5	2.6
CLINTON	**37**	**4,368**	**5,584***	**61.1**	**100.0**
081 CATHOLIC	1	NA	59	.6	1.1
081d LATIN	*1*	*NA*	*59*	*.6*	*1.1*
093 CHR CH (DISC)	1	53	71	.8	1.3
097 CHR CHS&CHS CR	1	81	100*	1.1	1.8
127 CH GOD (CLEVE)	1	8	10*	.1	.2
165 CH OF NAZARENE	3	231	409	4.5	7.3
167 CHS OF CHRIST	2	124	178	1.9	3.2
223 FREE WILL BAPT	2	132	162*	1.8	2.9
419 SO BAPT CONV	7	1,756	2,158*	23.6	38.6
436 UNITED BAPT	4	411	505*	5.5	9.0
449 UN METHODIST	15	1,572	1,932*	21.1	34.6
CRITTENDEN	**34**	**3,904**	**5,162***	**56.1**	**100.0**
053 ASSEMB OF GOD	1	13	16	.2	.3
081 CATHOLIC	1	NA	142	1.5	2.8
081d LATIN	*1*	*NA*	*142*	*1.5*	*2.8*
093 CHR CH (DISC)	1	30	40	.4	.8
123 CH GOD (ANDER)	1	0	0	-	-
145 CH GOD PROPHCY	1	43	53*	.6	1.0
167 CHS OF CHRIST	1	21	24	.3	.5
185 CUMBER PRESB	4	485	492	5.4	9.5
323 OLD ORD AMISH	2	NA	300	3.3	5.8
355 PRESB CH (USA)	3	106	131*	1.4	2.5
419 SO BAPT CONV	16	2,758	3,410*	37.1	66.1
449 UN METHODIST	3	448	554*	6.0	10.7
CUMBERLAND	**46**	**3,130**	**3,949***	**58.2**	**100.0**
053 ASSEMB OF GOD	1	36	63	.9	1.6
060 BRN RVR MB ASC	1	74	91*	1.3	2.3
081 CATHOLIC	1	NA	59	.9	1.5
081d LATIN	*1*	*NA*	*59*	*.9*	*1.5*
093 CHR CH (DISC)	1	120	144	2.1	3.6
097 CHR CHS&CHS CR	1	45	55*	.8	1.4
165 CH OF NAZARENE	1	62	94	1.4	2.4
167 CHS OF CHRIST	13	577	728	10.7	18.4
185 CUMBER PRESB	1	25	25	.4	.6
353 CHR BRETHREN	1	20	20	.3	.5
355 PRESB CH (USA)	1	36	44*	.6	1.1
419 SO BAPT CONV	4	561	690*	10.2	17.5
436 UNITED BAPT	1	112	138*	2.0	3.5

NA–Not applicable   NR–Not reported   *Total adherents estimated from known number of communicant, confirmed, full members.   - Represents a percent less than 0.1.   Percentages may not total due to rounding.
[1]See Appendix E   [2]See Appendix F   [3]See Appendix G   Lines in *italic* represent a breakdown of Catholic rites or Friends affiliations. They are included in their respective denominational total.

Table 4. Churches and Church Membership by County and Denomination: 1990

County and Denomination	Number of churches	Communicant, confirmed, full members	Total adherents Number	Percent of total population	Percent of total adherents
449 UN METHODIST	19	1,462	1,798*	26.5	45.5
DAVIESS	**128**	**38,288**	**68,637***	**78.7**	**100.0**
005 AME ZION	1	67	82	.1	.1
053 ASSEMB OF GOD	3	1,451	1,801	2.1	2.6
081 CATHOLIC	17	NA	18,728	21.5	27.3
081d *LATIN*	*17*	*NA*	*18,728*	*21.5*	*27.3*
089 CHR & MISS AL	1	0	7	-	-
093 CHR CH (DISC)	3	933	1,337	1.5	1.9
097 CHR CHS&CHS CR	2	1,040	1,322*	1.5	1.9
123 CH GOD (ANDER)	2	103	153	.2	.2
127 CH GOD (CLEVE)	2	167	212*	.2	.3
145 CH GOD PROPHCY	3	129	164*	.2	.2
151 L-D SAINTS	1	NA	183	.2	.3
165 CH OF NAZARENE	2	213	337	.4	.5
167 CHS OF CHRIST	6	511	666	.8	1.0
185 CUMBER PRESB	4	610	677	.8	1.0
193 EPISCOPAL	1	295	455	.5	.7
207 E.L.C.A.	1	178	251	.3	.4
223 FREE WILL BAPT	1	136	173*	.2	.3
283 LUTH—MO SYNOD	1	82	112	.1	.2
353 CHR BRETHREN	1	30	40	-	.1
355 PRESB CH (USA)	3	676	859*	1.0	1.3
356 PRESB CH AMER	1	38	49	.1	.1
403 SALVATION ARMY	1	230	255	.3	.4
413 S.D.A.	2	257	327*	.4	.5
419 SO BAPT CONV	47	24,969	31,729*	36.4	46.2
435 UNITARIAN-UNIV	1	29	33	-	-
436 UNITED BAPT	1	96	122*	.1	.2
443 UN C OF CHRIST	1	334	424*	.5	.6
449 UN METHODIST	17	4,582	5,823*	6.7	8.5
467 WESLEYAN	1	37	175	.2	.3
497 BLACK BAPT EST[2]	NA	1,095	1,391*	1.6	2.0
499 INDEP.NON-CHAR[3]	1	NA	750	.9	1.1
EDMONSON	**40**	**6,824**	**8,564***	**82.7**	**100.0**
081 CATHOLIC	1	NA	150	1.4	1.8
081d *LATIN*	*1*	*NA*	*150*	*1.4*	*1.8*
167 CHS OF CHRIST	3	250	303	2.9	3.5
185 CUMBER PRESB	1	83	89	.9	1.0
419 SO BAPT CONV	15	1,182	1,461*	14.1	17.1
436 UNITED BAPT	19	5,258	6,498*	62.7	75.9
449 UN METHODIST	1	51	63*	.6	.7
ELLIOTT	**13**	**1,046**	**1,350***	**20.9**	**100.0**
191 ENTRPR BPT ASC	6	575	742*	11.5	55.0
361 PRIM BAPT ASCS	1	9	12*	.2	.9
419 SO BAPT CONV	1	161	208*	3.2	15.4
436 UNITED BAPT	3	100	129*	2.0	9.6
449 UN METHODIST	2	201	259*	4.0	19.2
ESTILL	**41**	**4,808**	**6,434***	**44.0**	**100.0**
053 ASSEMB OF GOD	1	67	65	.4	1.0
081 CATHOLIC	1	NA	55	.4	.9
081d *LATIN*	*1*	*NA*	*55*	*.4*	*.9*
093 CHR CH (DISC)	2	205	335	2.3	5.2
097 CHR CHS&CHS CR	3	660	825*	5.6	12.8
123 CH GOD (ANDER)	3	15	213	1.5	3.3
127 CH GOD (CLEVE)	1	282	353*	2.4	5.5
145 CH GOD PROPHCY	1	43	54*	.4	.8
151 L-D SAINTS	1	NA	107	.7	1.7
165 CH OF NAZARENE	3	232	295	2.0	4.6
167 CHS OF CHRIST	5	120	155	1.1	2.4
193 EPISCOPAL	1	6	7	-	.1
221 FREE METHODIST	1	36	42	.3	.7
419 SO BAPT CONV	14	2,676	3,345*	22.9	52.0
449 UN METHODIST	4	466	583*	4.0	9.1
FAYETTE	**159**	**80,582**	**126,012***	**55.9**	**100.0**
040 AP CHR CH-AMER	1	7	12	-	-
053 ASSEMB OF GOD	6	1,185	2,315	1.0	1.8
081 CATHOLIC	7	NA	22,299	9.9	17.7
081d *LATIN*	*7*	*NA*	*22,299*	*9.9*	*17.7*
089 CHR & MISS AL	1	221	412	.2	.3
093 CHR CH (DISC)	12	5,283	7,275	3.2	5.8
097 CHR CHS&CHS CR	14	11,641	14,178*	6.3	11.3
111 CH CR,SCIENTST	1	NR	NR	-	-
123 CH GOD (ANDER)	2	421	477	.2	.4
127 CH GOD (CLEVE)	5	852	1,038*	.5	.8
145 CH GOD PROPHCY	1	43	52*	-	-
151 L-D SAINTS	2	NA	1,345	.6	1.1
165 CH OF NAZARENE	6	1,043	1,677	.7	1.3
167 CHS OF CHRIST	8	1,081	1,510	.7	1.2
185 CUMBER PRESB	1	80	89	-	.1
193 EPISCOPAL	7	2,567	3,500	1.6	2.8
207 E.L.C.A.	3	1,121	1,469	.7	1.2
215 EVAN METH CH	2	129	157*	.1	.1
221 FREE METHODIST	1	16	41	-	-
223 FREE WILL BAPT	1	150	183*	.1	.1
226 FRIENDS-USA	1	32	39*	-	-
226c *FGC*	*1*	*32*	*39*￪	-	-
246 GREEK ORTHODOX	1	NR	NR	-	-
283 LUTH—MO SYNOD	3	580	790	.4	.6
285 MENNONITE CH	1	28	74	-	.1
355 PRESB CH (USA)	12	3,962	4,825*	2.1	3.8
356 PRESB CH AMER	2	226	285	.1	.2
403 SALVATION ARMY	1	145	152	.1	.1
413 S.D.A.	2	502	611*	.3	.5
419 SO BAPT CONV	32	27,124	33,035*	14.7	26.2
435 UNITARIAN-UNIV	1	187	264	.1	.2
436 UNITED BAPT	1	87	106*	-	.1
443 UN C OF CHRIST	1	41	50*	-	-
449 UN METHODIST	14	12,495	15,218*	6.8	12.1
467 WESLEYAN	2	183	97	-	.1
469 WELS	1	26	31	-	-
496 JEWISH EST[1]	3	NA	1,294	.6	1.0
497 BLACK BAPT EST[2]	NA	9,124	11,112*	4.9	8.8
FLEMING	**44**	**3,876**	**5,221***	**42.5**	**100.0**
053 ASSEMB OF GOD	3	150	249	2.0	4.8
081 CATHOLIC	1	NA	140	1.1	2.7
081d *LATIN*	*1*	*NA*	*140*	*1.1*	*2.7*
093 CHR CH (DISC)	3	400	684	5.6	13.1
097 CHR CHS&CHS CR	7	630	781*	6.4	15.0
123 CH GOD (ANDER)	3	180	190	1.5	3.6
165 CH OF NAZARENE	1	70	149	1.2	2.9
191 ENTRPR BPT ASC	1	31	38*	.3	.7
193 EPISCOPAL	1	20	22	.2	.4
325 OLD REG BAPT	1	37	46*	.4	.9
355 PRESB CH (USA)	2	25	31*	.3	.6
419 SO BAPT CONV	4	601	745*	6.1	14.3
436 UNITED BAPT	1	22	27*	.2	.5
449 UN METHODIST	16	1,710	2,119*	17.2	40.6
FLOYD	**115**	**10,581**	**14,034***	**32.2**	**100.0**
053 ASSEMB OF GOD	3	186	348	.8	2.5
081 CATHOLIC	1	NA	250	.6	1.8
081d *LATIN*	*1*	*NA*	*250*	*.6*	*1.8*
097 CHR CHS&CHS CR	3	345	440*	1.0	3.1
123 CH GOD (ANDER)	1	70	85	.2	.6
127 CH GOD (CLEVE)	5	155	198*	.5	1.4
145 CH GOD PROPHCY	5	215	274*	.6	2.0
151 L-D SAINTS	1	NA	75	.2	.5
167 CHS OF CHRIST	10	787	1,072	2.5	7.6
193 EPISCOPAL	1	25	44	.1	.3
221 FREE METHODIST	1	0	23	.1	.2
223 FREE WILL BAPT	18	2,023	2,581*	5.9	18.4
325 OLD REG BAPT	24	1,530	1,952*	4.5	13.9
355 PRESB CH (USA)	2	191	244*	.6	1.7
413 S.D.A.	1	33	42*	.1	.3
419 SO BAPT CONV	13	2,367	3,020*	6.9	21.5
436 UNITED BAPT	13	743	948*	2.2	6.8
449 UN METHODIST	13	1,911	2,438*	5.6	17.4
FRANKLIN	**67**	**21,411**	**30,146***	**68.9**	**100.0**
053 ASSEMB OF GOD	1	253	465	1.1	1.5
081 CATHOLIC	1	NA	2,334	5.3	7.7
081d *LATIN*	*1*	*NA*	*2,334*	*5.3*	*7.7*
089 CHR & MISS AL	1	32	80	.2	.3
093 CHR CH (DISC)	4	1,815	2,871	6.6	9.5
097 CHR CHS&CHS CR	4	1,202	1,475*	3.4	4.9
111 CH CR,SCIENTST	1	NR	NR	-	-
123 CH GOD (ANDER)	1	0	70	.2	.2
127 CH GOD (CLEVE)	2	236	290*	.7	1.0
165 CH OF NAZARENE	2	351	556	1.3	1.8
167 CHS OF CHRIST	5	365	468	1.1	1.6
193 EPISCOPAL	1	421	584	1.3	1.9
207 E.L.C.A.	1	197	264	.6	.9
339 PENT CH OF GOD	3	356	502	1.1	1.7
355 PRESB CH (USA)	2	835	1,024*	2.3	3.4
403 SALVATION ARMY	1	46	50	.1	.2
413 S.D.A.	2	98	120*	.3	.4
419 SO BAPT CONV	28	12,387	15,196*	34.7	50.4
449 UN METHODIST	5	1,980	2,429*	5.5	8.1
467 WESLEYAN	1	27	44	.1	.1
497 BLACK BAPT EST[2]	NA	810	994*	2.3	3.3
499 INDEP.NON-CHAR[3]	1	NA	330	.8	1.1
FULTON	**37**	**6,603**	**8,402***	**101.6**	**100.0**
053 ASSEMB OF GOD	2	67	86	1.0	1.0
081 CATHOLIC	2	NA	288	3.5	3.4

NA–Not applicable   NR–Not reported   *Total adherents estimated from known number of communicant, confirmed, full members.   - Represents a percent less than 0.1.   Percentages may not total due to rounding.

[1]See Appendix E   [2]See Appendix F   [3]See Appendix G   Lines in *italic* represent a breakdown of Catholic rites or Friends affiliations. They are included in their respective denominational total.

Table 4. Churches and Church Membership by County and Denomination: 1990

County and Denomination	Number of churches	Communicant, confirmed, full members	Total adherents Number	Percent of total population	Percent of total adherents
081d LATIN	*2*	*NA*	*288*	*3.5*	*3.4*
093 CHR CH (DISC)	1	63	75	.9	.9
097 CHR CHS&CHS CR	1	100	124*	1.5	1.5
111 CH CR,SCIENTST	1	NR	NR	-	-
123 CH GOD (ANDER)	1	60	60	.7	.7
165 CH OF NAZARENE	1	78	80	1.0	1.0
167 CHS OF CHRIST	2	187	243	2.9	2.9
185 CUMBER PRESB	1	217	227	2.7	2.7
193 EPISCOPAL	2	75	86	1.0	1.0
413 S.D.A.	1	41	51*	.6	.6
419 SO BAPT CONV	13	3,825	4,740*	57.3	56.4
449 UN METHODIST	9	1,521	1,885*	22.8	22.4
497 BLACK BAPT EST[2]	NA	369	457*	5.5	5.4
GALLATIN	**16**	**2,652**	**3,647***	**67.6**	**100.0**
081 CATHOLIC	1	NA	120	2.2	3.3
081d LATIN	*1*	*NA*	*120*	*2.2*	*3.3*
093 CHR CH (DISC)	2	121	296	5.5	8.1
097 CHR CHS&CHS CR	1	100	128*	2.4	3.5
127 CH GOD (CLEVE)	1	26	33*	.6	.9
167 CHS OF CHRIST	1	17	21	.4	.6
419 SO BAPT CONV	8	2,174	2,776*	51.5	76.1
449 UN METHODIST	2	214	273*	5.1	7.5
GARRARD	**29**	**4,701**	**6,173***	**53.3**	**100.0**
081 CATHOLIC	1	NA	138	1.2	2.2
081d LATIN	*1*	*NA*	*138*	*1.2*	*2.2*
093 CHR CH (DISC)	4	320	581	5.0	9.4
127 CH GOD (CLEVE)	2	220	269*	2.3	4.4
165 CH OF NAZARENE	1	183	332	2.9	5.4
167 CHS OF CHRIST	2	119	134	1.2	2.2
355 PRESB CH (USA)	2	154	188*	1.6	3.0
419 SO BAPT CONV	11	3,060	3,742*	32.3	60.6
449 UN METHODIST	6	645	789*	6.8	12.8
GRANT	**34**	**6,933**	**9,593***	**61.0**	**100.0**
053 ASSEMB OF GOD	1	62	88	.6	.9
081 CATHOLIC	1	NA	512	3.3	5.3
081d LATIN	*1*	*NA*	*512*	*3.3*	*5.3*
093 CHR CH (DISC)	2	195	365	2.3	3.8
097 CHR CHS&CHS CR	7	1,016	1,308*	8.3	13.6
127 CH GOD (CLEVE)	1	63	81*	.5	.8
339 PENT CH OF GOD	1	34	77	.5	.8
355 PRESB CH (USA)	1	30	39*	.2	.4
419 SO BAPT CONV	17	5,291	6,811*	43.3	71.0
449 UN METHODIST	3	242	312*	2.0	3.3
GRAVES	**107**	**20,973**	**28,295***	**84.3**	**100.0**
053 ASSEMB OF GOD	1	648	600	1.8	2.1
061 BEACHY AMISH	1	68	84*	.3	.3
081 CATHOLIC	2	NA	2,620	7.8	9.3
081d LATIN	*2*	*NA*	*2,620*	*7.8*	*9.3*
093 CHR CH (DISC)	2	570	748	2.2	2.6
097 CHR CHS&CHS CR	1	60	74*	.2	.3
127 CH GOD (CLEVE)	2	108	133*	.4	.5
143 CG IN CR(MENN)	1	46	57*	.2	.2
145 CH GOD PROPHCY	1	43	53*	.2	.2
165 CH OF NAZARENE	1	93	89	.3	.3
167 CHS OF CHRIST	22	2,646	3,355	10.0	11.9
185 CUMBER PRESB	5	287	299	.9	1.1
193 EPISCOPAL	1	27	35	.1	.1
349 PENT HOLINESS	1	87	107*	.3	.4
355 PRESB CH (USA)	1	142	175*	.5	.6
413 S.D.A.	1	27	33*	.1	.1
419 SO BAPT CONV	44	13,553	16,660*	49.7	58.9
449 UN METHODIST	19	2,179	2,679*	8.0	9.5
467 WESLEYAN	1	16	35	.1	.1
497 BLACK BAPT EST[2]	NA	373	459*	1.4	1.6
GRAYSON	**74**	**7,896**	**11,709***	**55.6**	**100.0**
053 ASSEMB OF GOD	1	26	35	.2	.3
081 CATHOLIC	6	NA	1,881	8.9	16.1
081d LATIN	*6*	*NA*	*1,881*	*8.9*	*16.1*
093 CHR CH (DISC)	1	100	150	.7	1.3
097 CHR CHS&CHS CR	5	674	842*	4.0	7.2
127 CH GOD (CLEVE)	1	76	95*	.5	.8
145 CH GOD PROPHCY	4	172	215*	1.0	1.8
165 CH OF NAZARENE	1	33	0	-	-
167 CHS OF CHRIST	11	548	710	3.4	6.1
185 CUMBER PRESB	5	267	285	1.4	2.4
283 LUTH—MO SYNOD	1	17	20	.1	.2
320 "OLD" MB ASCS	2	107	134*	.6	1.1
413 S.D.A.	1	36	45*	.2	.4
419 SO BAPT CONV	17	3,662	4,576*	21.7	39.1
436 UNITED BAPT	8	1,319	1,648*	7.8	14.1
449 UN METHODIST	10	859	1,073*	5.1	9.2
GREEN	**47**	**7,677**	**9,365***	**90.3**	**100.0**
081 CATHOLIC	1	NA	79	.8	.8
081d LATIN	*1*	*NA*	*79*	*.8*	*.8*
097 CHR CHS&CHS CR	1	50	61*	.6	.7
165 CH OF NAZARENE	2	126	193	1.9	2.1
167 CHS OF CHRIST	6	266	327	3.2	3.5
185 CUMBER PRESB	3	459	467	4.5	5.0
355 PRESB CH (USA)	2	195	237*	2.3	2.5
419 SO BAPT CONV	22	5,575	6,778*	65.4	72.4
449 UN METHODIST	10	1,006	1,223*	11.8	13.1
GREENUP	**76**	**10,980**	**14,907***	**40.6**	**100.0**
053 ASSEMB OF GOD	1	129	170	.5	1.1
081 CATHOLIC	1	NA	40	.1	.3
081d LATIN	*1*	*NA*	*40*	*.1*	*.3*
097 CHR CHS&CHS CR	7	2,321	2,869*	7.8	19.2
123 CH GOD (ANDER)	2	240	291	.8	2.0
127 CH GOD (CLEVE)	4	249	308*	.8	2.1
145 CH GOD PROPHCY	1	43	53*	.1	.4
146 CH GOD MTN ASM	1	17	21*	.1	.1
151 L-D SAINTS	1	NA	527	1.4	3.5
165 CH OF NAZARENE	7	819	1,391	3.8	9.3
191 ENTRPR BPT ASC	5	239	295*	.8	2.0
207 E.L.C.A.	1	98	121	.3	.8
223 FREE WILL BAPT	5	442	546*	1.5	3.7
265 INT PENT C CHR	2	97	107	.3	.7
325 OLD REG BAPT	5	199	246*	.7	1.7
355 PRESB CH (USA)	1	20	25*	.1	.2
413 S.D.A.	1	99	122*	.3	.8
419 SO BAPT CONV	10	3,462	4,280*	11.6	28.7
436 UNITED BAPT	3	87	108*	.3	.7
449 UN METHODIST	16	2,407	2,976*	8.1	20.0
467 WESLEYAN	1	12	0	-	-
499 INDEP.NON-CHAR[3]	1	NA	411	1.1	2.8
HANCOCK	**26**	**4,451**	**6,633***	**84.3**	**100.0**
081 CATHOLIC	2	NA	928	11.8	14.0
081d LATIN	*2*	*NA*	*928*	*11.8*	*14.0*
097 CHR CHS&CHS CR	1	35	45*	.6	.7
165 CH OF NAZARENE	1	29	62	.8	.9
185 CUMBER PRESB	1	33	33	.4	.5
419 SO BAPT CONV	13	3,339	4,284*	54.5	64.6
449 UN METHODIST	7	998	1,281*	16.3	19.3
467 WESLEYAN	1	17	0	-	-
HARDIN	**112**	**31,325**	**47,720***	**53.5**	**100.0**
053 ASSEMB OF GOD	6	776	1,035	1.2	2.2
081 CATHOLIC	7	NA	5,785	6.5	12.1
081d LATIN	*7*	*NA*	*5,785*	*6.5*	*12.1*
089 CHR & MISS AL	1	73	100	.1	.2
093 CHR CH (DISC)	1	69	79	.1	.2
097 CHR CHS&CHS CR	8	1,762	2,268*	2.5	4.8
123 CH GOD (ANDER)	1	79	100	.1	.2
127 CH GOD (CLEVE)	4	285	367*	.4	.8
145 CH GOD PROPHCY	3	129	166*	.2	.3
151 L-D SAINTS	2	NA	752	.8	1.6
165 CH OF NAZARENE	2	123	163	.2	.3
167 CHS OF CHRIST	6	645	829	.9	1.7
185 CUMBER PRESB	3	116	119	.1	.2
193 EPISCOPAL	1	173	257	.3	.5
207 E.L.C.A.	1	196	259	.3	.5
223 FREE WILL BAPT	1	54	70*	.1	.1
283 LUTH—MO SYNOD	1	119	147	.2	.3
323 OLD ORD AMISH	1	NA	150	.2	.3
355 PRESB CH (USA)	1	322	415*	.5	.9
413 S.D.A.	1	82	106*	.1	.2
419 SO BAPT CONV	37	19,236	24,764*	27.7	51.9
436 UNITED BAPT	1	153	197*	.2	.4
449 UN METHODIST	19	4,428	5,701*	6.4	11.9
467 WESLEYAN	3	74	191	.2	.4
497 BLACK BAPT EST[2]	NA	2,431	3,130*	3.5	6.6
499 INDEP.NON-CHAR[3]	1	NA	570	.6	1.2
HARLAN	**113**	**15,313**	**20,089***	**54.9**	**100.0**
005 AME ZION	2	216	281	.8	1.4
053 ASSEMB OF GOD	2	38	141	.4	.7
081 CATHOLIC	3	NA	386	1.1	1.9
081d LATIN	*3*	*NA*	*386*	*1.1*	*1.9*
082 CENTRAL BAPT	1	174	222*	.6	1.1
093 CHR CH (DISC)	1	175	211	.6	1.1
097 CHR CHS&CHS CR	6	445	568*	1.6	2.8
123 CH GOD (ANDER)	1	60	67	.2	.3
127 CH GOD (CLEVE)	14	1,410	1,799*	4.9	9.0

NA–Not applicable   NR–Not reported   *Total adherents estimated from known number of communicant, confirmed, full members.   - Represents a percent less than 0.1.   Percentages may not total due to rounding.
[1]See Appendix E   [2]See Appendix F   [3]See Appendix G   Lines in *italic* represent a breakdown of Catholic rites or Friends affiliations. They are included in their respective denominational total.

Table 4. Churches and Church Membership by County and Denomination: 1990

County and Denomination	Number of churches	Communicant, confirmed, full members	Total adherents Number	Percent of total population	Percent of total adherents
145 CH GOD PROPHCY	3	129	165*	.5	.8
146 CH GOD MTN ASM	4	114	145*	.4	.7
151 L-D SAINTS	1	NA	90	.2	.4
165 CH OF NAZARENE	2	85	102	.3	.5
167 CHS OF CHRIST	7	292	361	1.0	1.8
193 EPISCOPAL	1	42	66	.2	.3
285 MENNONITE CH	2	14	24	.1	.1
325 OLD REG BAPT	1	33	42*	.1	.2
355 PRESB CH (USA)	3	191	244*	.7	1.2
361 PRIM BAPT ASCS	2	264	337*	.9	1.7
413 S.D.A.	1	37	47*	.1	.2
419 SO BAPT CONV	43	9,955	12,704*	34.7	63.2
436 UNITED BAPT	1	74	94*	.3	.5
438 UN BRETH IN CR	2	51	61	.2	.3
449 UN METHODIST	10	1,217	1,553*	4.2	7.7
497 BLACK BAPT EST[2]	NA	297	379*	1.0	1.9
HARRISON	**51**	**7,921**	**10,844***	**66.7**	**100.0**
053 ASSEMB OF GOD	1	18	46	.3	.4
081 CATHOLIC	1	NA	562	3.5	5.2
081d LATIN	*1*	*NA*	*562*	*3.5*	*5.2*
093 CHR CH (DISC)	5	720	1,058	6.5	9.8
097 CHR CHS&CHS CR	9	2,015	2,530*	15.6	23.3
123 CH GOD (ANDER)	1	0	155	1.0	1.4
127 CH GOD (CLEVE)	1	20	25*	.2	.2
165 CH OF NAZARENE	1	20	0	-	-
167 CHS OF CHRIST	1	93	113	.7	1.0
193 EPISCOPAL	1	46	72	.4	.7
339 PENT CH OF GOD	1	34	77	.5	.7
355 PRESB CH (USA)	2	182	229*	1.4	2.1
356 PRESB CH AMER	1	144	164	1.0	1.5
413 S.D.A.	1	34	43*	.3	.4
419 SO BAPT CONV	9	2,314	2,906*	17.9	26.8
449 UN METHODIST	16	2,281	2,864*	17.6	26.4
HART	**60**	**8,705**	**10,947***	**73.5**	**100.0**
081 CATHOLIC	1	NA	99	.7	.9
081d LATIN	*1*	*NA*	*99*	*.7*	*.9*
097 CHR CHS&CHS CR	1	75	93*	.6	.8
127 CH GOD (CLEVE)	1	20	25*	.2	.2
145 CH GOD PROPHCY	1	43	54*	.4	.5
167 CHS OF CHRIST	7	309	387	2.6	3.5
185 CUMBER PRESB	4	219	219	1.5	2.0
323 OLD ORD AMISH	1	NA	50	.3	.5
355 PRESB CH (USA)	1	16	20*	.1	.2
419 SO BAPT CONV	26	5,819	7,253*	48.7	66.3
436 UNITED BAPT	4	676	843*	5.7	7.7
449 UN METHODIST	13	1,272	1,585*	10.6	14.5
497 BLACK BAPT EST[2]	NA	256	319*	2.1	2.9
HENDERSON	**64**	**19,846**	**29,343***	**68.2**	**100.0**
005 AME ZION	1	255	270	.6	.9
053 ASSEMB OF GOD	2	337	880	2.0	3.0
081 CATHOLIC	2	NA	3,461	8.0	11.8
081d LATIN	*2*	*NA*	*3,461*	*8.0*	*11.8*
093 CHR CH (DISC)	2	408	551	1.3	1.9
097 CHR CHS&CHS CR	3	330	418*	1.0	1.4
127 CH GOD (CLEVE)	1	25	32*	.1	.1
145 CH GOD PROPHCY	2	86	109*	.3	.4
151 L-D SAINTS	1	NA	149	.3	.5
165 CH OF NAZARENE	3	217	359	.8	1.2
167 CHS OF CHRIST	2	291	378	.9	1.3
193 EPISCOPAL	1	192	316	.7	1.1
283 LUTH—MO SYNOD	1	101	153	.4	.5
355 PRESB CH (USA)	1	364	461*	1.1	1.6
403 SALVATION ARMY	1	78	80	.2	.3
413 S.D.A.	1	116	147*	.3	.5
419 SO BAPT CONV	28	12,210	15,457*	35.9	52.7
443 UN C OF CHRIST	1	69	87*	.2	.3
449 UN METHODIST	11	3,843	4,865*	11.3	16.6
497 BLACK BAPT EST[2]	NA	924	1,170*	2.7	4.0
HENRY	**42**	**6,710**	**9,035***	**70.5**	**100.0**
081 CATHOLIC	1	NA	158	1.2	1.7
081d LATIN	*1*	*NA*	*158*	*1.2*	*1.7*
093 CHR CH (DISC)	11	885	1,486	11.6	16.4
097 CHR CHS&CHS CR	1	110	137*	1.1	1.5
127 CH GOD (CLEVE)	1	81	101*	.8	1.1
151 L-D SAINTS	1	NA	103	.8	1.1
167 CHS OF CHRIST	1	28	36	.3	.4
355 PRESB CH (USA)	1	88	109*	.9	1.2
419 SO BAPT CONV	15	4,284	5,329*	41.6	59.0
449 UN METHODIST	9	1,086	1,351*	10.5	15.0
467 WESLEYAN	1	19	65	.5	.7
497 BLACK BAPT EST[2]	NA	129	160*	1.2	1.8

County and Denomination	Number of churches	Communicant, confirmed, full members	Total adherents Number	Percent of total population	Percent of total adherents
HICKMAN	**29**	**3,717**	**4,927***	**88.5**	**100.0**
053 ASSEMB OF GOD	1	98	180	3.2	3.7
081 CATHOLIC	2	NA	334	6.0	6.8
081d LATIN	*2*	*NA*	*334*	*6.0*	*6.8*
093 CHR CH (DISC)	1	23	36	.6	.7
167 CHS OF CHRIST	1	56	73	1.3	1.5
419 SO BAPT CONV	13	2,394	2,911*	52.3	59.1
449 UN METHODIST	11	1,025	1,246*	22.4	25.3
497 BLACK BAPT EST[2]	NA	121	147*	2.6	3.0
HOPKINS	**95**	**20,728**	**27,867***	**60.4**	**100.0**
005 AME ZION	5	390	428	.9	1.5
053 ASSEMB OF GOD	3	465	724	1.6	2.6
081 CATHOLIC	3	NA	1,269	2.8	4.6
081d LATIN	*3*	*NA*	*1,269*	*2.8*	*4.6*
093 CHR CH (DISC)	5	848	1,428	3.1	5.1
097 CHR CHS&CHS CR	4	775	968*	2.1	3.5
111 CH CR,SCIENTST	1	NR	NR	-	-
123 CH GOD (ANDER)	1	175	175	.4	.6
127 CH GOD (CLEVE)	1	78	97*	.2	.3
145 CH GOD PROPHCY	1	43	54*	.1	.2
151 L-D SAINTS	1	NA	311	.7	1.1
165 CH OF NAZARENE	1	31	69	.1	.2
167 CHS OF CHRIST	4	421	528	1.1	1.9
185 CUMBER PRESB	4	378	391	.8	1.4
193 EPISCOPAL	1	149	199	.4	.7
203 EVAN FREE CH	1	82	120	.3	.4
207 E.L.C.A.	1	87	121	.3	.4
355 PRESB CH (USA)	1	368	460*	1.0	1.7
361 PRIM BAPT ASCS	4	208	260*	.6	.9
403 SALVATION ARMY	1	59	66	.1	.2
413 S.D.A.	1	44	55*	.1	.2
419 SO BAPT CONV	34	12,550	15,676*	34.0	56.3
449 UN METHODIST	17	2,827	3,531*	7.7	12.7
497 BLACK BAPT EST[2]	NA	750	937*	2.0	3.4
JACKSON	**27**	**3,189**	**4,255***	**35.6**	**100.0**
081 CATHOLIC	1	NA	39	.3	.9
081d LATIN	*1*	*NA*	*39*	*.3*	*.9*
127 CH GOD (CLEVE)	1	68	87*	.7	2.0
167 CHS OF CHRIST	3	103	131	1.1	3.1
371 REF CH IN AM	3	173	367	3.1	8.6
419 SO BAPT CONV	19	2,845	3,631*	30.4	85.3
JEFFERSON	**571**	**230,412**	**451,514***	**67.9**	**100.0**
005 AME ZION	8	12,380	13,180	2.0	2.9
011 A.W.M.C.	1	25	31*	-	-
019 AMER BAPT USA	3	742	918*	.1	.2
053 ASSEMB OF GOD	14	8,249	7,596	1.1	1.7
055 AS REF PRES CH	1	128	133	-	-
081 CATHOLIC	83	NA	156,307	23.5	34.6
081d LATIN	*83*	*NA*	*156,307*	*23.5*	*34.6*
082 CENTRAL BAPT	1	20	25*	-	-
089 CHR & MISS AL	4	395	592	.1	.1
093 CHR CH (DISC)	17	5,369	9,013	1.4	2.0
097 CHR CHS&CHS CR	22	10,894	13,477*	2.0	3.0
111 CH CR,SCIENTST	2	NR	NR	-	-
123 CH GOD (ANDER)	5	570	630	.1	.1
127 CH GOD (CLEVE)	18	2,142	2,650*	.4	.6
145 CH GOD PROPHCY	6	255	315*	-	.1
146 CH GOD MTN ASM	1	25	31*	-	-
151 L-D SAINTS	3	NA	1,174	.2	.3
165 CH OF NAZARENE	13	1,393	2,363	.4	.5
167 CHS OF CHRIST	50	5,195	6,656	1.0	1.5
185 CUMBER PRESB	2	593	625	.1	.1
193 EPISCOPAL	18	5,171	6,715	1.0	1.5
203 EVAN FREE CH	1	64	105	-	-
207 E.L.C.A.	16	3,365	4,317	.6	1.0
216 EVAN PRESBY CH	1	27	27	-	-
221 FREE METHODIST	1	11	20	-	-
223 FREE WILL BAPT	1	128	158*	-	-
226 FRIENDS-USA	1	58	72*	-	-
226c FGC	*1*	*58*	*72**	*-*	*-*
246 GREEK ORTHODOX	1	NR	NR	-	-
283 LUTH—MO SYNOD	6	1,608	1,985	.3	.4
285 MENNONITE CH	1	43	88	-	-
291 MISSIONARY CH	1	0	14	-	-
320 "OLD" MB ASCS	1	363	449*	.1	.1
325 OLD REG BAPT	1	42	52*	-	-
329 OPEN BIBLE STD	1	NR	NR	-	-
353 CHR BRETHREN	1	25	50	-	-
355 PRESB CH (USA)	31	11,710	14,486*	2.2	3.2
356 PRESB CH AMER	1	31	56	-	-
403 SALVATION ARMY	4	416	480	.1	.1
413 S.D.A.	4	1,571	1,943*	.3	.4
419 SO BAPT CONV	126	91,766	113,523*	17.1	25.1

NA–Not applicable NR–Not reported *Total adherents estimated from known number of communicant, confirmed, full members. - Represents a percent less than 0.1. Percentages may not total due to rounding.

[1]See Appendix E [2]See Appendix F [3]See Appendix G

Lines in *italic* represent a breakdown of Catholic rites or Friends affiliations. They are included in their respective denominational total.

Table 4. Churches and Church Membership by County and Denomination: 1990

County and Denomination		Number of churches	Communicant, confirmed, full members	Total adherents		
				Number	Percent of total population	Percent of total adherents
435	UNITARIAN-UNIV	3	469	624	.1	.1
436	UNITED BAPT	7	2,374	2,937*	.4	.7
443	UN C OF CHRIST	20	5,662	7,004*	1.1	1.6
449	UN METHODIST	52	22,620	27,983*	4.2	6.2
467	WESLEYAN	3	103	0	-	-
469	WELS	1	74	93	-	-
496	JEWISH EST[1]	7	NA	6,990	1.1	1.5
497	BLACK BAPT EST[2]	NA	34,336	42,477*	6.4	9.4
498	INDEP.CHARIS.[3]	1	NA	400	.1	.1
499	INDEP.NON-CHAR[3]	5	NA	2,750	.4	.6
JESSAMINE		**41**	**7,036**	**10,361***	**34.0**	**100.0**
053	ASSEMB OF GOD	2	106	239	.8	2.3
075	BRETHREN IN CR	1	0	12	-	.1
081	CATHOLIC	1	NA	675	2.2	6.5
081d	LATIN	1	NA	675	2.2	6.5
089	CHR & MISS AL	1	29	97	.3	.9
093	CHR CH (DISC)	4	728	1,081	3.5	10.4
097	CHR CHS&CHS CR	2	147	187*	.6	1.8
127	CH GOD (CLEVE)	1	141	180*	.6	1.7
146	CH GOD MTN ASM	1	17	22*	.1	.2
165	CH OF NAZARENE	2	82	148	.5	1.4
167	CHS OF CHRIST	3	157	280	.9	2.7
193	EPISCOPAL	1	93	132	.4	1.3
207	E.L.C.A.	1	66	81	.3	.8
221	FREE METHODIST	2	177	316	1.0	3.0
291	MISSIONARY CH	1	62	77	.3	.7
355	PRESB CH (USA)	4	216	275*	.9	2.7
419	SO BAPT CONV	8	3,184	4,053*	13.3	39.1
449	UN METHODIST	6	1,532	1,950*	6.4	18.8
496	JEWISH EST[1]	0	NA	175	.6	1.7
497	BLACK BAPT EST[2]	NA	299	381*	1.2	3.7
JOHNSON		**86**	**9,021**	**11,912***	**51.2**	**100.0**
053	ASSEMB OF GOD	1	17	44	.2	.4
081	CATHOLIC	1	NA	125	.5	1.0
081d	LATIN	1	NA	125	.5	1.0
097	CHR CHS&CHS CR	2	255	320*	1.4	2.7
123	CH GOD (ANDER)	4	215	355	1.5	3.0
127	CH GOD (CLEVE)	1	28	35*	.2	.3
151	L-D SAINTS	1	NA	165	.7	1.4
165	CH OF NAZARENE	1	22	182	.8	1.5
167	CHS OF CHRIST	8	466	588	2.5	4.9
191	ENTRPR BPT ASC	9	891	1,119*	4.8	9.4
223	FREE WILL BAPT	26	3,529	4,431*	19.1	37.2
265	INT PENT C CHR	3	145	215	.9	1.8
283	LUTH—MO SYNOD	1	16	18	.1	.2
325	OLD REG BAPT	1	16	20*	.1	.2
361	PRIM BAPT ASCS	1	27	34*	.1	.3
419	SO BAPT CONV	3	983	1,234*	5.3	10.4
436	UNITED BAPT	19	1,644	2,064*	8.9	17.3
449	UN METHODIST	4	767	963*	4.1	8.1
KENTON		**122**	**29,261**	**79,684***	**56.1**	**100.0**
005	AME ZION	1	336	400	.3	.5
057	BAPT GEN CONF	1	46	59*	-	.1
081	CATHOLIC	20	NA	38,341	27.0	48.1
081d	LATIN	20	NA	38,341	27.0	48.1
093	CHR CH (DISC)	8	1,591	3,064	2.2	3.8
097	CHR CHS&CHS CR	11	2,998	3,849*	2.7	4.8
111	CH CR,SCIENTST	1	NR	NR	-	-
123	CH GOD (ANDER)	2	55	200	.1	.3
127	CH GOD (CLEVE)	5	434	557*	.4	.7
146	CH GOD MTN ASM	1	38	49*	-	.1
151	L-D SAINTS	1	NA	547	.4	.7
165	CH OF NAZARENE	4	971	934	.7	1.2
167	CHS OF CHRIST	2	175	228	.2	.3
193	EPISCOPAL	2	552	801	.6	1.0
207	E.L.C.A.	1	457	637	.4	.8
215	EVAN METH CH	1	78	100*	.1	.1
223	FREE WILL BAPT	1	27	35*	-	-
283	LUTH—MO SYNOD	1	126	174	.1	.2
355	PRESB CH (USA)	5	1,261	1,619*	1.1	2.0
403	SALVATION ARMY	1	105	127	.1	.2
413	S.D.A.	2	284	365*	.3	.5
419	SO BAPT CONV	29	13,534	17,377*	12.2	21.8
443	UN C OF CHRIST	4	756	971*	.7	1.2
449	UN METHODIST	15	4,054	5,205*	3.7	6.5
467	WESLEYAN	2	124	181	.1	.2
496	JEWISH EST[1]	0	NA	2,248	1.6	2.8
497	BLACK BAPT EST[2]	NA	1,259	1,616*	1.1	2.0
KNOTT		**41**	**3,645**	**5,344***	**29.8**	**100.0**
151	L-D SAINTS	1	NA	340	1.9	6.4
167	CHS OF CHRIST	2	50	60	.3	1.1
203	EVAN FREE CH	1	13	35	.2	.7

County and Denomination		Number of churches	Communicant, confirmed, full members	Total adherents		
				Number	Percent of total population	Percent of total adherents
285	MENNONITE CH	2	60	93	.5	1.7
325	OLD REG BAPT	23	944	1,210*	6.8	22.6
419	SO BAPT CONV	6	2,011	2,579*	14.4	48.3
436	UNITED BAPT	4	385	494*	2.8	9.2
449	UN METHODIST	1	182	233*	1.3	4.4
499	INDEP.NON-CHAR[3]	1	NA	300	1.7	5.6
KNOX		**73**	**14,931**	**19,541***	**65.8**	**100.0**
001	ADVENT CHR CH	1	23	29*	.1	.1
053	ASSEMB OF GOD	1	46	60	.2	.3
081	CATHOLIC	2	NA	475	1.6	2.4
081d	LATIN	2	NA	475	1.6	2.4
093	CHR CH (DISC)	1	94	146	.5	.7
097	CHR CHS&CHS CR	2	293	374*	1.3	1.9
127	CH GOD (CLEVE)	2	142	181*	.6	.9
146	CH GOD MTN ASM	1	35	45*	.2	.2
165	CH OF NAZARENE	1	128	164	.6	.8
193	EPISCOPAL	1	35	43	.1	.2
419	SO BAPT CONV	56	13,442	17,140*	57.8	87.7
436	UNITED BAPT	2	148	189*	.6	1.0
449	UN METHODIST	3	545	695*	2.3	3.6
LARUE		**33**	**6,488**	**8,347***	**71.5**	**100.0**
053	ASSEMB OF GOD	2	63	131	1.1	1.6
081	CATHOLIC	1	NA	217	1.9	2.6
081d	LATIN	1	NA	217	1.9	2.6
093	CHR CH (DISC)	1	66	99	.8	1.2
097	CHR CHS&CHS CR	2	354	438*	3.8	5.2
127	CH GOD (CLEVE)	1	81	100*	.9	1.2
145	CH GOD PROPHCY	1	43	53*	.5	.6
165	CH OF NAZARENE	1	53	132	1.1	1.6
167	CHS OF CHRIST	2	72	93	.8	1.1
185	CUMBER PRESB	1	219	226	1.9	2.7
419	SO BAPT CONV	17	5,050	6,255*	53.6	74.9
449	UN METHODIST	4	487	603*	5.2	7.2
LAUREL		**93**	**16,358**	**21,214***	**48.8**	**100.0**
053	ASSEMB OF GOD	2	151	215	.5	1.0
081	CATHOLIC	3	NA	370	.9	1.7
081d	LATIN	3	NA	370	.9	1.7
093	CHR CH (DISC)	2	338	397	.9	1.9
097	CHR CHS&CHS CR	5	550	697*	1.6	3.3
123	CH GOD (ANDER)	1	26	54	.1	.3
127	CH GOD (CLEVE)	2	204	258*	.6	1.2
145	CH GOD PROPHCY	1	43	54*	.1	.3
165	CH OF NAZARENE	1	66	160	.4	.8
167	CHS OF CHRIST	6	488	648	1.5	3.1
325	OLD REG BAPT	1	22	28*	.1	.1
355	PRESB CH (USA)	1	193	245*	.6	1.2
413	S.D.A.	1	90	114*	.3	.5
419	SO BAPT CONV	41	10,587	13,413*	30.9	63.2
436	UNITED BAPT	18	2,798	3,545*	8.2	16.7
449	UN METHODIST	8	802	1,016*	2.3	4.8
LAWRENCE		**61**	**6,084**	**7,869***	**56.2**	**100.0**
081	CATHOLIC	1	NA	65	.5	.8
081d	LATIN	1	NA	65	.5	.8
093	CHR CH (DISC)	1	250	334	2.4	4.2
097	CHR CHS&CHS CR	1	80	102*	.7	1.3
123	CH GOD (ANDER)	1	60	95	.7	1.2
127	CH GOD (CLEVE)	1	142	180*	1.3	2.3
165	CH OF NAZARENE	1	18	62	.4	.8
167	CHS OF CHRIST	1	35	45	.3	.6
191	ENTRPR BPT ASC	4	279	354*	2.5	4.5
223	FREE WILL BAPT	19	1,733	2,202*	15.7	28.0
325	OLD REG BAPT	1	29	37*	.3	.5
361	PRIM BAPT ASCS	2	281	357*	2.6	4.5
419	SO BAPT CONV	6	986	1,253*	9.0	15.9
436	UNITED BAPT	11	1,218	1,547*	11.1	19.7
449	UN METHODIST	11	973	1,236*	8.8	15.7
LEE		**30**	**2,153**	**2,895***	**39.0**	**100.0**
053	ASSEMB OF GOD	1	39	62	.8	2.1
081	CATHOLIC	2	NA	118	1.6	4.1
081d	LATIN	2	NA	118	1.6	4.1
093	CHR CH (DISC)	1	30	40	.5	1.4
097	CHR CHS&CHS CR	2	197	252*	3.4	8.7
123	CH GOD (ANDER)	4	304	379	5.1	13.1
127	CH GOD (CLEVE)	1	71	91*	1.2	3.1
145	CH GOD PROPHCY	1	43	55*	.7	1.9
165	CH OF NAZARENE	1	64	95	1.3	3.3
167	CHS OF CHRIST	7	272	322	4.3	11.1
193	EPISCOPAL	1	44	59	.8	2.0
199	EVAN CONGR CH	1	33	73	1.0	2.5
355	PRESB CH (USA)	2	77	98*	1.3	3.4

NA–Not applicable NR–Not reported *Total adherents estimated from known number of communicant, confirmed, full members. - Represents a percent less than 0.1. Percentages may not total due to rounding.
[1]See Appendix E [2]See Appendix F [3]See Appendix G Lines in *italic* represent a breakdown of Catholic rites or Friends affiliations. They are included in their respective denominational total.

Table 4. Churches and Church Membership by County and Denomination: 1990

Left Column

County and Denomination	Number of churches	Communicant, confirmed, full members	Total adherents — Number	Total adherents — Percent of total population	Total adherents — Percent of total adherents
419 SO BAPT CONV	5	933	1,192*	16.1	41.2
449 UN METHODIST	1	46	59*	.8	2.0
LESLIE	**31**	**2,377**	**3,618***	**26.5**	**100.0**
081 CATHOLIC	1	NA	20	.1	.6
081d LATIN	*1*	*NA*	*20*	*.1*	*.6*
089 CHR & MISS AL	1	7	13	.1	.4
127 CH GOD (CLEVE)	6	423	551*	4.0	15.2
167 CHS OF CHRIST	7	353	459	3.4	12.7
355 PRESB CH (USA)	3	196	255*	1.9	7.0
419 SO BAPT CONV	6	1,041	1,355*	9.9	37.5
449 UN METHODIST	6	357	465*	3.4	12.9
498 INDEP.CHARIS.[3]	1	NA	500	3.7	13.8
LETCHER	**79**	**6,594**	**8,470***	**31.4**	**100.0**
005 AME ZION	1	85	98	.4	1.2
081 CATHOLIC	2	NA	95	.4	1.1
081d LATIN	*2*	*NA*	*95*	*.4*	*1.1*
089 CHR & MISS AL	1	46	47	.2	.6
097 CHR CHS&CHS CR	1	30	38*	.1	.4
123 CH GOD (ANDER)	1	110	110	.4	1.3
127 CH GOD (CLEVE)	3	219	279*	1.0	3.3
145 CH GOD PROPHCY	2	86	110*	.4	1.3
146 CH GOD MTN ASM	1	60	76*	.3	.9
165 CH OF NAZARENE	1	31	61	.2	.7
167 CHS OF CHRIST	9	249	319	1.2	3.8
263 INT FOURSQ GOS	1	54	69*	.3	.8
287 MENN GEN CONF	1	6	12	-	.1
325 OLD REG BAPT	30	1,744	2,221*	8.2	26.2
355 PRESB CH (USA)	4	251	320*	1.2	3.8
361 PRIM BAPT ASCS	4	236	301*	1.1	3.6
413 S.D.A.	1	18	23*	.1	.3
419 SO BAPT CONV	10	2,858	3,640*	13.5	43.0
449 UN METHODIST	6	511	651*	2.4	7.7
LEWIS	**34**	**3,231**	**4,155***	**31.9**	**100.0**
081 CATHOLIC	1	NA	76	.6	1.8
081d LATIN	*1*	*NA*	*76*	*.6*	*1.8*
097 CHR CHS&CHS CR	12	1,238	1,560*	12.0	37.5
123 CH GOD (ANDER)	1	25	25	.2	.6
127 CH GOD (CLEVE)	2	203	256*	2.0	6.2
145 CH GOD PROPHCY	1	43	54*	.4	1.3
165 CH OF NAZARENE	1	34	57	.4	1.4
355 PRESB CH (USA)	1	6	8*	.1	.2
419 SO BAPT CONV	5	894	1,126*	8.6	27.1
449 UN METHODIST	10	788	993*	7.6	23.9
LINCOLN	**72**	**10,469**	**13,371***	**66.7**	**100.0**
081 CATHOLIC	1	NA	93	.5	.7
081d LATIN	*1*	*NA*	*93*	*.5*	*.7*
093 CHR CH (DISC)	2	235	399	2.0	3.0
097 CHR CHS&CHS CR	4	400	502*	2.5	3.8
123 CH GOD (ANDER)	6	228	309	1.5	2.3
127 CH GOD (CLEVE)	3	252	317*	1.6	2.4
145 CH GOD PROPHCY	1	43	54*	.3	.4
165 CH OF NAZARENE	2	96	123	.6	.9
167 CHS OF CHRIST	11	350	440	2.2	3.3
283 LUTH—MO SYNOD	1	22	26	.1	.2
325 OLD REG BAPT	4	73	92*	.5	.7
355 PRESB CH (USA)	1	115	144*	.7	1.1
413 S.D.A.	1	46	58*	.3	.4
419 SO BAPT CONV	26	7,687	9,656*	48.2	72.2
449 UN METHODIST	9	773	971*	4.8	7.3
497 BLACK BAPT EST[2]	NA	149	187*	.9	1.4
LIVINGSTON	**47**	**5,563**	**6,765***	**74.7**	**100.0**
081 CATHOLIC	1	NA	34	.4	.5
081d LATIN	*1*	*NA*	*34*	*.4*	*.5*
093 CHR CH (DISC)	1	18	28	.3	.4
167 CHS OF CHRIST	3	151	196	2.2	2.9
185 CUMBER PRESB	2	74	74	.8	1.1
419 SO BAPT CONV	26	4,230	5,115*	56.4	75.6
449 UN METHODIST	14	1,090	1,318*	14.5	19.5
LOGAN	**80**	**15,265**	**19,834***	**81.2**	**100.0**
005 AME ZION	4	432	560	2.3	2.8
061 BEACHY AMISH	1	61	77*	.3	.4
081 CATHOLIC	1	NA	420	1.7	2.1
081d LATIN	*1*	*NA*	*420*	*1.7*	*2.1*
093 CHR CH (DISC)	3	221	308	1.3	1.6
097 CHR CHS&CHS CR	2	350	440*	1.8	2.2
145 CH GOD PROPHCY	1	43	54*	.2	.3
151 L-D SAINTS	1	NA	105	.4	.5
165 CH OF NAZARENE	0	0	87	.4	.4
167 CHS OF CHRIST	12	737	1,005	4.1	5.1

Right Column

County and Denomination	Number of churches	Communicant, confirmed, full members	Total adherents — Number	Total adherents — Percent of total population	Total adherents — Percent of total adherents
185 CUMBER PRESB	5	376	387	1.6	2.0
193 EPISCOPAL	1	88	112	.5	.6
283 LUTH—MO SYNOD	1	14	15	.1	.1
355 PRESB CH (USA)	2	215	270*	1.1	1.4
419 SO BAPT CONV	31	10,426	13,101*	53.7	66.1
449 UN METHODIST	15	1,801	2,263*	9.3	11.4
497 BLACK BAPT EST[2]	NA	501	630*	2.6	3.2
LYON	**22**	**3,754**	**4,453***	**67.2**	**100.0**
053 ASSEMB OF GOD	1	64	130	2.0	2.9
081 CATHOLIC	1	NA	102	1.5	2.3
081d LATIN	*1*	*NA*	*102*	*1.5*	*2.3*
167 CHS OF CHRIST	2	117	151	2.3	3.4
419 SO BAPT CONV	12	2,874	3,274*	49.4	73.5
449 UN METHODIST	6	699	796*	12.0	17.9
MC CRACKEN	**94**	**31,299**	**46,418***	**73.8**	**100.0**
053 ASSEMB OF GOD	1	69	80	.1	.2
081 CATHOLIC	4	NA	4,759	7.6	10.3
081d LATIN	*4*	*NA*	*4,759*	*7.6*	*10.3*
093 CHR CH (DISC)	4	643	991	1.6	2.1
097 CHR CHS&CHS CR	1	120	148*	.2	.3
111 CH CR,SCIENTST	1	NR	NR	-	-
123 CH GOD (ANDER)	4	36	103	.2	.2
127 CH GOD (CLEVE)	1	54	67*	.1	.1
145 CH GOD PROPHCY	1	43	53*	.1	.1
151 L-D SAINTS	1	NA	335	.5	.7
165 CH OF NAZARENE	1	95	238	.4	.5
167 CHS OF CHRIST	11	1,968	2,524	4.0	5.4
185 CUMBER PRESB	5	1,817	1,928	3.1	4.2
193 EPISCOPAL	1	351	582	.9	1.3
207 E.L.C.A.	1	184	241	.4	.5
223 FREE WILL BAPT	1	21	26*	-	.1
283 LUTH—MO SYNOD	1	430	567	.9	1.2
355 PRESB CH (USA)	3	653	806*	1.3	1.7
403 SALVATION ARMY	1	111	112	.2	.2
413 S.D.A.	2	215	265*	.4	.6
419 SO BAPT CONV	30	18,037	22,256*	35.4	47.9
443 UN C OF CHRIST	1	158	195*	.3	.4
449 UN METHODIST	15	4,744	5,854*	9.3	12.6
496 JEWISH EST[1]	0	NA	725	1.2	1.6
497 BLACK BAPT EST[2]	NA	1,550	1,913*	3.0	4.1
499 INDEP.NON-CHAR[3]	3	NA	1,650	2.6	3.6
MC CREARY	**30**	**5,251**	**6,846***	**43.9**	**100.0**
081 CATHOLIC	1	NA	64	.4	.9
081d LATIN	*1*	*NA*	*64*	*.4*	*.9*
093 CHR CH (DISC)	1	30	32	.2	.5
127 CH GOD (CLEVE)	1	48	62*	.4	.9
145 CH GOD PROPHCY	1	43	56*	.4	.8
146 CH GOD MTN ASM	2	563	728*	4.7	10.6
167 CHS OF CHRIST	2	45	57	.4	.8
413 S.D.A.	1	85	110*	.7	1.6
419 SO BAPT CONV	9	2,434	3,147*	20.2	46.0
436 UNITED BAPT	9	1,792	2,317*	14.8	33.8
449 UN METHODIST	3	211	273*	1.7	4.0
MC LEAN	**35**	**5,155**	**6,601***	**68.6**	**100.0**
081 CATHOLIC	2	NA	345	3.6	5.2
081d LATIN	*2*	*NA*	*345*	*3.6*	*5.2*
093 CHR CH (DISC)	1	79	82	.9	1.2
097 CHR CHS&CHS CR	1	227	281*	2.9	4.3
145 CH GOD PROPHCY	2	86	106*	1.1	1.6
167 CHS OF CHRIST	1	51	67	.7	1.0
185 CUMBER PRESB	3	432	432	4.5	6.5
221 FREE METHODIST	1	7	16	.2	.2
355 PRESB CH (USA)	1	12	15*	.2	.2
419 SO BAPT CONV	12	2,832	3,503*	36.4	53.1
449 UN METHODIST	10	1,418	1,754*	18.2	26.6
467 WESLEYAN	1	11	0	-	-
MADISON	**99**	**19,998**	**26,979***	**46.9**	**100.0**
053 ASSEMB OF GOD	3	244	322	.6	1.2
081 CATHOLIC	3	NA	1,889	3.3	7.0
081d LATIN	*3*	*NA*	*1,889*	*3.3*	*7.0*
089 CHR & MISS AL	2	57	147	.3	.5
093 CHR CH (DISC)	7	1,391	2,158	3.8	8.0
097 CHR CHS&CHS CR	11	1,968	2,379*	4.1	8.8
123 CH GOD (ANDER)	1	72	72	.1	.3
127 CH GOD (CLEVE)	4	566	684*	1.2	2.5
151 L-D SAINTS	1	NA	197	.3	.7
165 CH OF NAZARENE	4	447	640	1.1	2.4
167 CHS OF CHRIST	6	371	475	.8	1.8
193 EPISCOPAL	1	80	103	.2	.4
207 E.L.C.A.	1	115	167	.3	.6

NA–Not applicable   NR–Not reported   *Total adherents estimated from known number of communicant, confirmed, full members.   - Represents a percent less than 0.1.   Percentages may not total due to rounding.

[1]See Appendix E   [2]See Appendix F   [3]See Appendix G   Lines in *italic* represent a breakdown of Catholic rites or Friends affiliations. They are included in their respective denominational total.

174

Table 4. Churches and Church Membership by County and Denomination: 1990

County and Denomination	Number of churches	Communicant, confirmed, full members	Total adherents Number	Percent of total population	Percent of total adherents
226 FRIENDS-USA	1	47	57	.1	.2
226c FGC	1	47	57	.1	.2
355 PRESB CH (USA)	3	492	595*	1.0	2.2
403 SALVATION ARMY	1	30	32	.1	.1
413 S.D.A.	3	63	76*	.1	.3
419 SO BAPT CONV	37	11,682	14,122*	24.6	52.3
435 UNITARIAN-UNIV	1	26	26	-	.1
449 UN METHODIST	9	1,631	1,972*	3.4	7.3
497 BLACK BAPT EST[2]	NA	716	866*	1.5	3.2
MAGOFFIN	**42**	**3,320**	**4,487***	**34.3**	**100.0**
053 ASSEMB OF GOD	2	42	48	.4	1.1
081 CATHOLIC	1	NA	30	.2	.7
081d LATIN	1	NA	30	.2	.7
097 CHR CHS&CHS CR	1	83	109*	.8	2.4
123 CH GOD (ANDER)	1	0	26	.2	.6
146 CH GOD MTN ASM	1	11	14*	.1	.3
151 L-D SAINTS	1	NA	29	.2	.6
167 CHS OF CHRIST	2	90	123	.9	2.7
223 FREE WILL BAPT	3	228	298*	2.3	6.6
265 INT PENT C CHR	3	100	160	1.2	3.6
325 OLD REG BAPT	1	18	24*	.2	.5
339 PENT CH OF GOD	1	34	77	.6	1.7
361 PRIM BAPT ASCS	3	79	103*	.8	2.3
419 SO BAPT CONV	4	597	781*	6.0	17.4
436 UNITED BAPT	17	1,789	2,339*	17.9	52.1
449 UN METHODIST	1	249	326*	2.5	7.3
MARION	**38**	**5,841**	**16,284***	**98.7**	**100.0**
005 AME ZION	3	287	310	1.9	1.9
053 ASSEMB OF GOD	1	29	59	.4	.4
081 CATHOLIC	7	NA	8,736	52.9	53.6
081d LATIN	7	NA	8,736	52.9	53.6
093 CHR CH (DISC)	1	80	85	.5	.5
097 CHR CHS&CHS CR	2	190	242*	1.5	1.5
127 CH GOD (CLEVE)	1	98	125*	.8	.8
167 CHS OF CHRIST	2	100	127	.8	.8
355 PRESB CH (USA)	2	147	187*	1.1	1.1
419 SO BAPT CONV	11	3,662	4,667*	28.3	28.7
449 UN METHODIST	7	860	1,096*	6.6	6.7
467 WESLEYAN	1	35	200	1.2	1.2
497 BLACK BAPT EST[2]	NA	353	450*	2.7	2.8
MARSHALL	**70**	**12,971**	**17,385***	**63.9**	**100.0**
053 ASSEMB OF GOD	1	15	21	.1	.1
081 CATHOLIC	2	NA	586	2.2	3.4
081d LATIN	2	NA	586	2.2	3.4
093 CHR CH (DISC)	1	105	135	.5	.8
097 CHR CHS&CHS CR	1	35	43*	.2	.2
151 L-D SAINTS	1	NA	186	.7	1.1
165 CH OF NAZARENE	1	59	55	.2	.3
167 CHS OF CHRIST	12	1,836	2,501	9.2	14.4
185 CUMBER PRESB	5	434	453	1.7	2.6
193 EPISCOPAL	1	20	71	.3	.4
207 E.L.C.A.	1	119	196	.7	1.1
223 FREE WILL BAPT	2	101	123*	.5	.7
339 PENT CH OF GOD	1	35	77	.3	.4
355 PRESB CH (USA)	1	64	78*	.3	.4
419 SO BAPT CONV	25	7,968	9,705*	35.7	55.8
449 UN METHODIST	14	2,180	2,655*	9.8	15.3
498 INDEP.CHARIS.[3]	1	NA	500	1.8	2.9
MARTIN	**42**	**3,556**	**4,878***	**38.9**	**100.0**
081 CATHOLIC	1	NA	22	.2	.5
081d LATIN	1	NA	22	.2	.5
127 CH GOD (CLEVE)	4	170	225*	1.8	4.6
157 CH OF BRETHREN	1	13	17*	.1	.3
165 CH OF NAZARENE	3	243	469	3.7	9.6
167 CHS OF CHRIST	4	158	216	1.7	4.4
223 FREE WILL BAPT	6	584	772*	6.2	15.8
325 OLD REG BAPT	3	110	145*	1.2	3.0
419 SO BAPT CONV	2	645	853*	6.8	17.5
436 UNITED BAPT	16	1,451	1,918*	15.3	39.3
449 UN METHODIST	2	182	241*	1.9	4.9
MASON	**54**	**7,925**	**13,035***	**78.2**	**100.0**
053 ASSEMB OF GOD	2	147	274	1.6	2.1
081 CATHOLIC	3	NA	2,617	15.7	20.1
081d LATIN	3	NA	2,617	15.7	20.1
093 CHR CH (DISC)	6	681	1,053	6.3	8.1
097 CHR CHS&CHS CR	5	620	773*	4.6	5.9
127 CH GOD (CLEVE)	1	43	54*	.3	.4
151 L-D SAINTS	1	NA	234	1.4	1.8
165 CH OF NAZARENE	1	250	296	1.8	2.3
167 CHS OF CHRIST	1	20	26	.2	.2

County and Denomination	Number of churches	Communicant, confirmed, full members	Total adherents Number	Percent of total population	Percent of total adherents
193 EPISCOPAL	1	91	122	.7	.9
283 LUTH—MO SYNOD	1	63	76	.5	.6
355 PRESB CH (USA)	3	174	217*	1.3	1.7
419 SO BAPT CONV	10	2,068	2,577*	15.5	19.8
449 UN METHODIST	18	3,400	4,237*	25.4	32.5
467 WESLEYAN	1	64	100	.6	.8
497 BLACK BAPT EST[2]	NA	304	379*	2.3	2.9
MEADE	**36**	**6,958**	**13,219***	**54.7**	**100.0**
053 ASSEMB OF GOD	2	192	284	1.2	2.1
081 CATHOLIC	4	NA	3,591	14.9	27.2
081d LATIN	4	NA	3,591	14.9	27.2
097 CHR CHS&CHS CR	2	120	165*	.7	1.2
127 CH GOD (CLEVE)	1	29	40*	.2	.3
145 CH GOD PROPHCY	1	43	59*	.2	.4
146 CH GOD MTN ASM	1	5	7*	-	.1
165 CH OF NAZARENE	1	37	60	.2	.5
167 CHS OF CHRIST	2	63	92	.4	.7
193 EPISCOPAL	1	25	33	.1	.2
339 PENT CH OF GOD	1	35	77	.3	.6
355 PRESB CH (USA)	1	95	131*	.5	1.0
419 SO BAPT CONV	14	4,903	6,741*	27.9	51.0
449 UN METHODIST	5	839	1,153*	4.8	8.7
497 BLACK BAPT EST[2]	NA	572	786*	3.3	5.9
MENIFEE	**10**	**496**	**641***	**12.6**	**100.0**
081 CATHOLIC	1	NA	41	.8	6.4
081d LATIN	1	NA	41	.8	6.4
097 CHR CHS&CHS CR	1	25	31*	.6	4.8
123 CH GOD (ANDER)	2	88	90	1.8	14.0
127 CH GOD (CLEVE)	1	17	21*	.4	3.3
167 CHS OF CHRIST	1	5	6	.1	.9
179 CONSRV BAPT	1	NR	NR	-	-
216 EVAN PRESBY CH	1	0	0	-	-
355 PRESB CH (USA)	1	25	31*	.6	4.8
419 SO BAPT CONV	1	336	421*	8.3	65.7
MERCER	**54**	**12,514**	**16,659***	**87.0**	**100.0**
053 ASSEMB OF GOD	1	20	40	.2	.2
081 CATHOLIC	1	NA	410	2.1	2.5
081d LATIN	1	NA	410	2.1	2.5
093 CHR CH (DISC)	5	710	1,163	6.1	7.0
097 CHR CHS&CHS CR	5	1,080	1,331*	7.0	8.0
127 CH GOD (CLEVE)	2	177	218*	1.1	1.3
151 L-D SAINTS	1	NA	256	1.3	1.5
165 CH OF NAZARENE	1	124	122	.6	.7
167 CHS OF CHRIST	4	276	346	1.8	2.1
185 CUMBER PRESB	2	248	256	1.3	1.5
193 EPISCOPAL	1	37	68	.4	.4
339 PENT CH OF GOD	1	50	55	.3	.3
355 PRESB CH (USA)	3	296	365*	1.9	2.2
419 SO BAPT CONV	18	8,537	10,518*	54.9	63.1
449 UN METHODIST	8	763	940*	4.9	5.6
497 BLACK BAPT EST[2]	NA	196	241*	1.3	1.4
499 INDEP.NON-CHAR[3]	1	NA	330	1.7	2.0
METCALFE	**42**	**3,754**	**4,877***	**54.4**	**100.0**
060 BRN RVR MB ASC	3	340	419*	4.7	8.6
081 CATHOLIC	1	NA	40	.4	.8
081d LATIN	1	NA	40	.4	.8
097 CHR CHS&CHS CR	1	107	132*	1.5	2.7
127 CH GOD (CLEVE)	1	29	36*	.4	.7
151 L-D SAINTS	1	NA	214	2.4	4.4
167 CHS OF CHRIST	8	509	666	7.4	13.7
185 CUMBER PRESB	8	176	176	2.0	3.6
419 SO BAPT CONV	9	1,668	2,055*	22.9	42.1
436 UNITED BAPT	2	152	187*	2.1	3.8
449 UN METHODIST	8	773	952*	10.6	19.5
MONROE	**47**	**4,542**	**6,172***	**54.1**	**100.0**
060 BRN RVR MB ASC	3	283	349*	3.1	5.7
081 CATHOLIC	1	NA	39	.3	.6
081d LATIN	1	NA	39	.3	.6
145 CH GOD PROPHCY	1	43	53*	.5	.9
151 L-D SAINTS	1	NA	280	2.5	4.5
167 CHS OF CHRIST	27	1,300	1,858	16.3	30.1
419 SO BAPT CONV	9	2,484	3,061*	26.8	49.6
449 UN METHODIST	5	432	532*	4.7	8.6
MONTGOMERY	**41**	**6,693**	**8,869***	**45.3**	**100.0**
005 AME ZION	1	120	150	.8	1.7
053 ASSEMB OF GOD	2	155	237	1.2	2.7
081 CATHOLIC	1	NA	350	1.8	3.9
081d LATIN	1	NA	350	1.8	3.9
093 CHR CH (DISC)	3	844	1,170	6.0	13.2

NA–Not applicable   NR–Not reported   *Total adherents estimated from known number of communicant, confirmed, full members.   - Represents a percent less than 0.1.   Percentages may not total due to rounding.
[1]See Appendix E   [2]See Appendix F   [3]See Appendix G   Lines in *italic* represent a breakdown of Catholic rites or Friends affiliations. They are included in their respective denominational total.

Table 4. Churches and Church Membership by County and Denomination: 1990

County and Denomination	Number of churches	Communicant, confirmed, full members	Total adherents Number	Percent of total population	Percent of total adherents
097 CHR CHS&CHS CR	2	300	373*	1.9	4.2
123 CH GOD (ANDER)	5	846	1,098	5.6	12.4
127 CH GOD (CLEVE)	1	167	208*	1.1	2.3
145 CH GOD PROPHCY	1	43	54*	.3	.6
165 CH OF NAZARENE	1	170	159	.8	1.8
167 CHS OF CHRIST	8	482	633	3.2	7.1
193 EPISCOPAL	1	103	125	.6	1.4
325 OLD REG BAPT	2	65	81*	.4	.9
355 PRESB CH (USA)	1	166	207*	1.1	2.3
419 SO BAPT CONV	6	2,339	2,912*	14.9	32.8
436 UNITED BAPT	3	96	120*	.6	1.4
449 UN METHODIST	3	601	748*	3.8	8.4
497 BLACK BAPT EST2	NA	196	244*	1.2	2.8
MORGAN	**37**	**2,848**	**3,845***	**33.0**	**100.0**
081 CATHOLIC	1	NA	68	.6	1.8
081d LATIN	*1*	*NA*	*68*	*.6*	*1.8*
093 CHR CH (DISC)	3	296	414	3.6	10.8
097 CHR CHS&CHS CR	1	230	290*	2.5	7.5
123 CH GOD (ANDER)	4	196	275	2.4	7.2
127 CH GOD (CLEVE)	1	113	142*	1.2	3.7
167 CHS OF CHRIST	4	100	173	1.5	4.5
191 ENTRPR BPT ASC	8	730	920*	7.9	23.9
285 MENNONITE CH	2	80	172	1.5	4.5
325 OLD REG BAPT	1	52	66*	.6	1.7
355 PRESB CH (USA)	1	78	98*	.8	2.5
361 PRIM BAPT ASCS	5	253	319*	2.7	8.3
419 SO BAPT CONV	2	430	542*	4.7	14.1
436 UNITED BAPT	3	121	153*	1.3	4.0
449 UN METHODIST	1	169	213*	1.8	5.5
MUHLENBERG	**94**	**18,892**	**23,977***	**76.6**	**100.0**
005 AME ZION	3	463	613	2.0	2.6
053 ASSEMB OF GOD	2	63	106	.3	.4
081 CATHOLIC	1	NA	237	.8	1.0
081d LATIN	*1*	*NA*	*237*	*.8*	*1.0*
093 CHR CH (DISC)	2	157	252	.8	1.1
097 CHR CHS&CHS CR	2	210	260*	.8	1.1
127 CH GOD (CLEVE)	1	106	131*	.4	.5
145 CH GOD PROPHCY	1	43	53*	.2	.2
151 L-D SAINTS	1	NA	181	.6	.8
165 CH OF NAZARENE	1	50	87	.3	.4
167 CHS OF CHRIST	11	672	880	2.8	3.7
185 CUMBER PRESB	3	241	261	.8	1.1
355 PRESB CH (USA)	6	245	303*	1.0	1.3
413 S.D.A.	1	46	57*	.2	.2
419 SO BAPT CONV	45	14,657	18,155*	58.0	75.7
449 UN METHODIST	14	1,623	2,010*	6.4	8.4
497 BLACK BAPT EST2	NA	316	391*	1.2	1.6
NELSON	**56**	**9,135**	**20,872***	**70.3**	**100.0**
005 AME ZION	3	538	623	2.1	3.0
053 ASSEMB OF GOD	2	58	80	.3	.4
081 CATHOLIC	10	NA	8,983	30.2	43.0
081d LATIN	*10*	*NA*	*8,983*	*30.2*	*43.0*
093 CHR CH (DISC)	5	536	799	2.7	3.8
097 CHR CHS&CHS CR	3	327	424*	1.4	2.0
127 CH GOD (CLEVE)	2	267	346*	1.2	1.7
145 CH GOD PROPHCY	1	43	56*	.2	.3
167 CHS OF CHRIST	4	239	311	1.0	1.5
193 EPISCOPAL	1	41	56	.2	.3
355 PRESB CH (USA)	3	129	167*	.6	.8
419 SO BAPT CONV	15	5,586	7,248*	24.4	34.7
449 UN METHODIST	7	927	1,203*	4.0	5.8
497 BLACK BAPT EST2	NA	444	576*	1.9	2.8
NICHOLAS	**20**	**1,997**	**2,763***	**41.1**	**100.0**
053 ASSEMB OF GOD	1	109	190	2.8	6.9
081 CATHOLIC	1	NA	130	1.9	4.7
081d LATIN	*1*	*NA*	*130*	*1.9*	*4.7*
093 CHR CH (DISC)	3	141	241	3.6	8.7
097 CHR CHS&CHS CR	1	80	99*	1.5	3.6
165 CH OF NAZARENE	1	13	57	.8	2.1
167 CHS OF CHRIST	1	28	36	.5	1.3
355 PRESB CH (USA)	1	63	78*	1.2	2.8
419 SO BAPT CONV	3	686	848*	12.6	30.7
449 UN METHODIST	8	877	1,084*	16.1	39.2
OHIO	**91**	**12,494**	**16,150***	**76.5**	**100.0**
053 ASSEMB OF GOD	3	113	205	1.0	1.3
081 CATHOLIC	2	NA	334	1.6	2.1
081d LATIN	*2*	*NA*	*334*	*1.6*	*2.1*
097 CHR CHS&CHS CR	3	469	592*	2.8	3.7
127 CH GOD (CLEVE)	3	329	415*	2.0	2.6
145 CH GOD PROPHCY	4	172	217*	1.0	1.3
167 CHS OF CHRIST	7	505	643	3.0	4.0
185 CUMBER PRESB	2	98	106	.5	.7
355 PRESB CH (USA)	1	9	11*	.1	.1
413 S.D.A.	1	60	76*	.4	.5
419 SO BAPT CONV	43	9,253	11,676*	55.3	72.3
449 UN METHODIST	21	1,486	1,875*	8.9	11.6
OLDHAM	**38**	**10,261**	**16,795***	**50.5**	**100.0**
053 ASSEMB OF GOD	3	270	332	1.0	2.0
081 CATHOLIC	3	NA	2,637	7.9	15.7
081d LATIN	*3*	*NA*	*2,637*	*7.9*	*15.7*
093 CHR CH (DISC)	2	329	703	2.1	4.2
097 CHR CHS&CHS CR	2	164	211*	.6	1.3
127 CH GOD (CLEVE)	1	115	148*	.4	.9
151 L-D SAINTS	1	NA	363	1.1	2.2
165 CH OF NAZARENE	1	17	66	.2	.4
167 CHS OF CHRIST	2	77	99	.3	.6
193 EPISCOPAL	1	228	222	.7	1.3
283 LUTH—MO SYNOD	1	87	117	.4	.7
355 PRESB CH (USA)	2	523	673*	2.0	4.0
413 S.D.A.	1	216	278*	.8	1.7
419 SO BAPT CONV	11	5,329	6,857*	20.6	40.8
449 UN METHODIST	7	2,544	3,274*	9.8	19.5
496 JEWISH EST1	0	NA	349	1.0	2.1
497 BLACK BAPT EST2	NA	362	466*	1.4	2.8
OWEN	**39**	**6,197**	**8,394***	**92.9**	**100.0**
053 ASSEMB OF GOD	3	181	308	3.4	3.7
081 CATHOLIC	2	NA	75	.8	.9
081d LATIN	*2*	*NA*	*75*	*.8*	*.9*
093 CHR CH (DISC)	3	183	288	3.2	3.4
097 CHR CHS&CHS CR	1	160	201*	2.2	2.4
413 S.D.A.	1	84	105*	1.2	1.3
419 SO BAPT CONV	25	5,343	6,708*	74.2	79.9
449 UN METHODIST	3	246	309*	3.4	3.7
498 INDEP.CHARIS.3	1	NA	400	4.4	4.8
OWSLEY	**15**	**1,088**	**1,381***	**27.4**	**100.0**
081 CATHOLIC	1	NA	36	.7	2.6
081d LATIN	*1*	*NA*	*36*	*.7*	*2.6*
127 CH GOD (CLEVE)	1	38	48*	1.0	3.5
167 CHS OF CHRIST	1	100	105	2.1	7.6
325 OLD REG BAPT	2	117	147*	2.9	10.6
355 PRESB CH (USA)	3	208	261*	5.2	18.9
419 SO BAPT CONV	4	429	538*	10.7	39.0
449 UN METHODIST	3	196	246*	4.9	17.8
PENDLETON	**45**	**6,918**	**9,978***	**82.9**	**100.0**
053 ASSEMB OF GOD	1	100	155	1.3	1.6
081 CATHOLIC	2	NA	614	5.1	6.2
081d LATIN	*2*	*NA*	*614*	*5.1*	*6.2*
093 CHR CH (DISC)	5	502	872	7.2	8.7
097 CHR CHS&CHS CR	8	1,345	1,742*	14.5	17.5
127 CH GOD (CLEVE)	1	49	63*	.5	.6
165 CH OF NAZARENE	1	14	35	.3	.4
355 PRESB CH (USA)	1	50	65*	.5	.7
419 SO BAPT CONV	19	4,122	5,340*	44.4	53.5
449 UN METHODIST	6	702	909*	7.6	9.1
467 WESLEYAN	1	34	183	1.5	1.8
PERRY	**77**	**9,072**	**11,895***	**39.3**	**100.0**
053 ASSEMB OF GOD	1	41	40	.1	.3
081 CATHOLIC	1	NA	207	.7	1.7
081d LATIN	*1*	*NA*	*207*	*.7*	*1.7*
082 CENTRAL BAPT	1	30	38*	.1	.3
093 CHR CH (DISC)	1	15	45	.1	.4
123 CH GOD (ANDER)	1	0	105	.3	.9
127 CH GOD (CLEVE)	12	981	1,247*	4.1	10.5
145 CH GOD PROPHCY	2	86	109*	.4	.9
167 CHS OF CHRIST	12	459	606	2.0	5.1
193 EPISCOPAL	1	29	36	.1	.3
203 EVAN FREE CH	3	64	100	.3	.8
325 OLD REG BAPT	9	737	937*	3.1	7.9
355 PRESB CH (USA)	5	470	597*	2.0	5.0
361 PRIM BAPT ASCS	1	41	52*	.2	.4
419 SO BAPT CONV	23	5,617	7,138*	23.6	60.0
436 UNITED BAPT	1	66	84*	.3	.7
449 UN METHODIST	3	308	391*	1.3	3.3
497 BLACK BAPT EST2	NA	128	163*	.5	1.4
PIKE	**182**	**17,311**	**22,525***	**31.0**	**100.0**
053 ASSEMB OF GOD	2	90	150	.2	.7
081 CATHOLIC	3	NA	335	.5	1.5
081d LATIN	*3*	*NA*	*335*	*.5*	*1.5*
089 CHR & MISS AL	4	88	205	.3	.9

NA–Not applicable   NR–Not reported   *Total adherents estimated from known number of communicant, confirmed, full members.   - Represents a percent less than 0.1.   Percentages may not total due to rounding.

1See Appendix E   2See Appendix F   3See Appendix G   Lines in *italic* represent a breakdown of Catholic rites or Friends affiliations. They are included in their respective denominational total.

Table 4. Churches and Church Membership by County and Denomination: 1990

County and Denomination	Number of churches	Communicant, confirmed, full members	Total adherents — Number	Percent of total population	Percent of total adherents
093 CHR CH (DISC)	1	184	257	.4	1.1
097 CHR CHS&CHS CR	10	1,192	1,503*	2.1	6.7
123 CH GOD (ANDER)	4	187	256	.4	1.1
127 CH GOD (CLEVE)	9	606	764*	1.1	3.4
145 CH GOD PROPHCY	1	43	54*	.1	.2
151 L-D SAINTS	1	NA	64	.1	.3
167 CHS OF CHRIST	23	958	1,236	1.7	5.5
193 EPISCOPAL	1	27	27	-	.1
223 FREE WILL BAPT	14	1,422	1,793*	2.5	8.0
325 OLD REG BAPT	56	2,724	3,434*	4.7	15.2
355 PRESB CH (USA)	6	547	690*	1.0	3.1
361 PRIM BAPT ASCS	12	835	1,053*	1.5	4.7
413 S.D.A.	1	24	30*	-	.1
419 SO BAPT CONV	20	6,787	8,557*	11.8	38.0
436 UNITED BAPT	1	59	74*	.1	.3
449 UN METHODIST	11	1,496	1,886*	2.6	8.4
467 WESLEYAN	2	42	157	.2	.7
POWELL	**28**	**2,991**	**3,784***	**32.4**	**100.0**
053 ASSEMB OF GOD	1	29	43	.4	1.1
081 CATHOLIC	1	NA	38	.3	1.0
081d LATIN	*1*	*NA*	*38*	*.3*	*1.0*
097 CHR CHS&CHS CR	3	593	769*	6.6	20.3
123 CH GOD (ANDER)	7	553	594	5.1	15.7
127 CH GOD (CLEVE)	1	134	174*	1.5	4.6
145 CH GOD PROPHCY	1	43	56*	.5	1.5
167 CHS OF CHRIST	6	261	322	2.8	8.5
355 PRESB CH (USA)	1	163	212*	1.8	5.6
419 SO BAPT CONV	3	949	1,231*	10.5	32.5
449 UN METHODIST	4	266	345*	3.0	9.1
PULASKI	**155**	**28,648**	**37,345***	**75.5**	**100.0**
053 ASSEMB OF GOD	2	101	139	.3	.4
081 CATHOLIC	1	NA	558	1.1	1.5
081d LATIN	*1*	*NA*	*558*	*1.1*	*1.5*
093 CHR CH (DISC)	2	468	693	1.4	1.9
097 CHR CHS&CHS CR	4	320	394*	.8	1.1
123 CH GOD (ANDER)	3	40	194	.4	.5
127 CH GOD (CLEVE)	7	484	595*	1.2	1.6
145 CH GOD PROPHCY	5	215	265*	.5	.7
151 L-D SAINTS	1	NA	122	.2	.3
165 CH OF NAZARENE	7	798	1,104	2.2	3.0
167 CHS OF CHRIST	14	681	944	1.9	2.5
193 EPISCOPAL	1	189	217	.4	.6
207 E.L.C.A.	1	121	159	.3	.4
339 PENT CH OF GOD	1	34	76	.2	.2
355 PRESB CH (USA)	2	340	418*	.8	1.1
419 SO BAPT CONV	62	17,293	21,277*	43.0	57.0
436 UNITED BAPT	25	5,319	6,544*	13.2	17.5
449 UN METHODIST	15	2,093	2,575*	5.2	6.9
467 WESLEYAN	1	5	40	.1	.1
497 BLACK BAPT EST[2]	NA	147	181*	.4	.5
499 INDEP.NON-CHAR[3]	1	NA	850	1.7	2.3
ROBERTSON	**7**	**823**	**1,024***	**48.2**	**100.0**
053 ASSEMB OF GOD	1	49	70	3.3	6.8
097 CHR CHS&CHS CR	2	345	425*	20.0	41.5
419 SO BAPT CONV	1	198	244*	11.5	23.8
449 UN METHODIST	3	231	285*	13.4	27.8
ROCKCASTLE	**44**	**6,764**	**8,512***	**57.5**	**100.0**
053 ASSEMB OF GOD	1	45	59	.4	.7
081 CATHOLIC	1	NA	31	.2	.4
081d LATIN	*1*	*NA*	*31*	*.2*	*.4*
097 CHR CHS&CHS CR	3	531	665*	4.5	7.8
127 CH GOD (CLEVE)	3	173	217*	1.5	2.5
165 CH OF NAZARENE	1	24	44	.3	.5
167 CHS OF CHRIST	7	328	401	2.7	4.7
419 SO BAPT CONV	25	5,531	6,930*	46.8	81.4
436 UNITED BAPT	2	87	109*	.7	1.3
449 UN METHODIST	1	45	56*	.4	.7
ROWAN	**26**	**2,824**	**4,435***	**21.8**	**100.0**
081 CATHOLIC	1	NA	250	1.2	5.6
081d LATIN	*1*	*NA*	*250*	*1.2*	*5.6*
093 CHR CH (DISC)	1	222	327	1.6	7.4
097 CHR CHS&CHS CR	3	269	319*	1.6	7.2
123 CH GOD (ANDER)	5	412	826	4.1	18.6
127 CH GOD (CLEVE)	1	63	75*	.4	1.7
151 L-D SAINTS	1	NA	436	2.1	9.8
165 CH OF NAZARENE	1	70	75	.4	1.7
167 CHS OF CHRIST	1	70	80	.4	1.8
191 ENTRPR BPT ASC	1	43	51*	.3	1.1
193 EPISCOPAL	1	34	49	.2	1.1
223 FREE WILL BAPT	1	200	237*	1.2	5.3
355 PRESB CH (USA)	1	61	72*	.4	1.6
361 PRIM BAPT ASCS	2	82	97*	.5	2.2
413 S.D.A.	1	45	53*	.3	1.2
419 SO BAPT CONV	2	640	760*	3.7	17.1
436 UNITED BAPT	2	85	101*	.5	2.3
449 UN METHODIST	1	528	627*	3.1	14.1
RUSSELL	**56**	**6,492**	**8,091***	**55.0**	**100.0**
081 CATHOLIC	1	NA	98	.7	1.2
081d LATIN	*1*	*NA*	*98*	*.7*	*1.2*
097 CHR CHS&CHS CR	4	700	852*	5.8	10.5
127 CH GOD (CLEVE)	6	392	477*	3.2	5.9
145 CH GOD PROPHCY	2	86	105*	.7	1.3
165 CH OF NAZARENE	2	81	177	1.2	2.2
167 CHS OF CHRIST	6	202	266	1.8	3.3
413 S.D.A.	1	63	77*	.5	1.0
419 SO BAPT CONV	16	2,729	3,323*	22.6	41.1
436 UNITED BAPT	6	890	1,084*	7.4	13.4
449 UN METHODIST	10	1,340	1,632*	11.1	20.2
467 WESLEYAN	2	9	0	-	-
SCOTT	**48**	**9,312**	**13,375***	**56.0**	**100.0**
053 ASSEMB OF GOD	1	169	325	1.4	2.4
081 CATHOLIC	2	NA	650	2.7	4.9
081d LATIN	*2*	*NA*	*650*	*2.7*	*4.9*
093 CHR CH (DISC)	5	697	1,337	5.6	10.0
097 CHR CHS&CHS CR	6	803	1,019*	4.3	7.6
123 CH GOD (ANDER)	3	60	339	1.4	2.5
127 CH GOD (CLEVE)	2	168	213*	.9	1.6
165 CH OF NAZARENE	1	483	506	2.1	3.8
167 CHS OF CHRIST	4	114	148	.6	1.1
193 EPISCOPAL	1	136	190	.8	1.4
339 PENT CH OF GOD	1	34	77	.3	.6
355 PRESB CH (USA)	4	232	294*	1.2	2.2
419 SO BAPT CONV	13	5,020	6,369*	26.7	47.6
449 UN METHODIST	5	939	1,191*	5.0	8.9
496 JEWISH EST[1]	0	NA	137	.6	1.0
497 BLACK BAPT EST[2]	NA	457	580*	2.4	4.3
SHELBY	**47**	**14,001**	**18,697***	**75.3**	**100.0**
053 ASSEMB OF GOD	1	146	350	1.4	1.9
081 CATHOLIC	2	NA	444	1.8	2.4
081d LATIN	*2*	*NA*	*444*	*1.8*	*2.4*
093 CHR CH (DISC)	4	639	1,175	4.7	6.3
097 CHR CHS&CHS CR	2	1,010	1,251*	5.0	6.7
127 CH GOD (CLEVE)	1	58	72*	.3	.4
165 CH OF NAZARENE	1	47	38	.2	.2
167 CHS OF CHRIST	2	98	138	.6	.7
193 EPISCOPAL	1	61	94	.4	.5
283 LUTH—MO SYNOD	1	19	25	.1	.1
355 PRESB CH (USA)	1	355	440*	1.8	2.4
419 SO BAPT CONV	24	9,686	11,997*	48.3	64.2
449 UN METHODIST	6	1,068	1,323*	5.3	7.1
467 WESLEYAN	1	71	170	.7	.9
496 JEWISH EST[1]	0	NA	260	1.0	1.4
497 BLACK BAPT EST[2]	NA	743	920*	3.7	4.9
SIMPSON	**41**	**8,063**	**10,405***	**68.7**	**100.0**
053 ASSEMB OF GOD	1	79	95	.6	.9
061 BEACHY AMISH	2	104	131*	.9	1.3
081 CATHOLIC	1	NA	250	1.7	2.4
081d LATIN	*1*	*NA*	*250*	*1.7*	*2.4*
145 CH GOD PROPHCY	1	43	54*	.4	.5
165 CH OF NAZARENE	1	83	80	.5	.8
167 CHS OF CHRIST	9	882	1,130	7.5	10.9
193 EPISCOPAL	1	31	37	.2	.4
207 E.L.C.A.	1	96	123	.8	1.2
320 "OLD" MB ASCS	3	403	508*	3.4	4.9
355 PRESB CH (USA)	2	209	264*	1.7	2.5
413 S.D.A.	1	31	39*	.3	.4
419 SO BAPT CONV	11	4,598	5,798*	38.3	55.7
449 UN METHODIST	7	1,104	1,392*	9.2	13.4
497 BLACK BAPT EST[2]	NA	400	504*	3.3	4.8
SPENCER	**18**	**3,363**	**4,583***	**67.4**	**100.0**
053 ASSEMB OF GOD	1	95	275	4.0	6.0
081 CATHOLIC	1	NA	138	2.0	3.0
081d LATIN	*1*	*NA*	*138*	*2.0*	*3.0*
093 CHR CH (DISC)	1	75	140	2.1	3.1
097 CHR CHS&CHS CR	4	575	726*	10.7	15.8
145 CH GOD PROPHCY	1	43	54*	.8	1.2
167 CHS OF CHRIST	1	51	62	.9	1.4
325 OLD REG BAPT	1	5	6*	.1	.1
419 SO BAPT CONV	7	2,432	3,072*	45.2	67.0
449 UN METHODIST	1	87	110*	1.6	2.4

NA–Not applicable   NR–Not reported   *Total adherents estimated from known number of communicant, confirmed, full members.   - Represents a percent less than 0.1.   Percentages may not total due to rounding.

[1]See Appendix E   [2]See Appendix F   [3]See Appendix G   Lines in *italic* represent a breakdown of Catholic rites or Friends affiliations. They are included in their respective denominational total.

Table 4. Churches and Church Membership by County and Denomination: 1990

County and Denomination	Number of churches	Communicant, confirmed, full members	Total adherents Number	Percent of total population	Percent of total adherents
TAYLOR	**61**	**12,624**	**16,542***	**78.2**	**100.0**
005 AME ZION	1	100	125	.6	.8
053 ASSEMB OF GOD	1	17	21	.1	.1
075 BRETHREN IN CR	1	34	34	.2	.2
081 CATHOLIC	4	NA	836	4.0	5.1
081d LATIN	*4*	*NA*	*836*	*4.0*	*5.1*
097 CHR CHS&CHS CR	3	711	883*	4.2	5.3
123 CH GOD (ANDER)	2	150	185	.9	1.1
127 CH GOD (CLEVE)	1	40	50*	.2	.3
165 CH OF NAZARENE	1	90	214	1.0	1.3
167 CHS OF CHRIST	3	195	263	1.2	1.6
185 CUMBER PRESB	4	437	455	2.2	2.8
355 PRESB CH (USA)	1	216	268*	1.3	1.6
413 S.D.A.	1	12	15*	.1	.1
419 SO BAPT CONV	23	7,960	9,887*	46.8	59.8
449 UN METHODIST	15	2,402	2,983*	14.1	18.0
497 BLACK BAPT EST[2]	NA	260	323*	1.5	2.0
TODD	**45**	**5,974**	**8,337***	**76.2**	**100.0**
053 ASSEMB OF GOD	1	37	80	.7	1.0
081 CATHOLIC	2	NA	127	1.2	1.5
081d LATIN	*2*	*NA*	*127*	*1.2*	*1.5*
093 CHR CH (DISC)	2	124	202	1.8	2.4
151 L-D SAINTS	1	NA	155	1.4	1.9
165 CH OF NAZARENE	1	78	296	2.7	3.6
167 CHS OF CHRIST	7	358	468	4.3	5.6
185 CUMBER PRESB	2	53	58	.5	.7
323 OLD ORD AMISH	2	NA	300	2.7	3.6
355 PRESB CH (USA)	1	34	43*	.4	.5
419 SO BAPT CONV	14	3,621	4,549*	41.6	54.6
449 UN METHODIST	11	1,351	1,697*	15.5	20.4
467 WESLEYAN	1	30	0	-	-
497 BLACK BAPT EST[2]	NA	288	362*	3.3	4.3
TRIGG	**35**	**6,746**	**8,338***	**80.5**	**100.0**
081 CATHOLIC	1	NA	220	2.1	2.6
081d LATIN	*1*	*NA*	*220*	*2.1*	*2.6*
093 CHR CH (DISC)	2	250	284	2.7	3.4
167 CHS OF CHRIST	2	144	187	1.8	2.2
223 FREE WILL BAPT	1	20	24*	.2	.3
419 SO BAPT CONV	19	5,092	6,130*	59.2	73.5
449 UN METHODIST	10	945	1,138*	11.0	13.6
497 BLACK BAPT EST[2]	NA	295	355*	3.4	4.3
TRIMBLE	**19**	**2,624**	**3,344***	**54.9**	**100.0**
081 CATHOLIC	1	NA	17	.3	.5
081d LATIN	*1*	*NA*	*17*	*.3*	*.5*
093 CHR CH (DISC)	1	91	212	3.5	6.3
097 CHR CHS&CHS CR	2	383	479*	7.9	14.3
419 SO BAPT CONV	8	1,473	1,841*	30.2	55.1
449 UN METHODIST	6	636	795*	13.1	23.8
467 WESLEYAN	1	41	0	-	-
UNION	**46**	**7,216**	**12,552***	**75.8**	**100.0**
053 ASSEMB OF GOD	1	52	61	.4	.5
081 CATHOLIC	6	NA	3,606	21.8	28.7
081d LATIN	*6*	*NA*	*3,606*	*21.8*	*28.7*
093 CHR CH (DISC)	2	344	418	2.5	3.3
097 CHR CHS&CHS CR	3	440	548*	3.3	4.4
145 CH GOD PROPHCY	2	86	107*	.6	.9
167 CHS OF CHRIST	5	200	257	1.6	2.0
185 CUMBER PRESB	2	264	295	1.8	2.4
193 EPISCOPAL	1	16	25	.2	.2
355 PRESB CH (USA)	2	99	123*	.7	1.0
419 SO BAPT CONV	16	4,209	5,238*	31.6	41.7
449 UN METHODIST	6	895	1,114*	6.7	8.9
497 BLACK BAPT EST[2]	NA	611	760*	4.6	6.1
WARREN	**132**	**31,616**	**43,015***	**56.1**	**100.0**
005 AME ZION	1	83	98	.1	.2
053 ASSEMB OF GOD	2	301	407	.5	.9
059 BAPT MISS ASSN	1	33	41*	.1	.1
081 CATHOLIC	2	NA	2,700	3.5	6.3
081d LATIN	*2*	*NA*	*2,700*	*3.5*	*6.3*
089 CHR & MISS AL	1	0	0	-	-
093 CHR CH (DISC)	4	607	875	1.1	2.0
097 CHR CHS&CHS CR	3	241	297*	.4	.7
111 CH CR,SCIENTST	1	NR	NR	-	-
123 CH GOD (ANDER)	1	25	48	.1	.1
127 CH GOD (CLEVE)	2	106	131*	.2	.3
145 CH GOD PROPHCY	1	43	53*	.1	.1
151 L-D SAINTS	1	NA	568	.7	1.3
165 CH OF NAZARENE	3	320	419	.5	1.0
167 CHS OF CHRIST	22	2,883	3,629	4.7	8.4
185 CUMBER PRESB	2	445	504	.7	1.2
193 EPISCOPAL	1	490	654	.9	1.5
221 FREE METHODIST	2	97	180	.2	.4
223 FREE WILL BAPT	1	58	72*	.1	.2
283 LUTH—MO SYNOD	1	351	469	.6	1.1
320 "OLD" MB ASCS	5	1,232	1,520*	2.0	3.5
355 PRESB CH (USA)	6	1,211	1,494*	1.9	3.5
403 SALVATION ARMY	1	105	109	.1	.3
413 S.D.A.	3	242	298*	.4	.7
419 SO BAPT CONV	41	16,393	20,219*	26.4	47.0
435 UNITARIAN-UNIV	1	11	11	-	-
436 UNITED BAPT	1	108	133*	.2	.3
449 UN METHODIST	21	4,698	5,795*	7.6	13.5
497 BLACK BAPT EST[2]	NA	1,533	1,891*	2.5	4.4
499 INDEP.NON-CHAR[3]	1	NA	400	.5	.9
WASHINGTON	**36**	**5,668**	**11,300***	**108.2**	**100.0**
005 AME ZION	3	393	478	4.6	4.2
081 CATHOLIC	5	NA	3,817	36.6	33.8
081d LATIN	*5*	*NA*	*3,817*	*36.6*	*33.8*
097 CHR CHS&CHS CR	4	710	898*	8.6	7.9
127 CH GOD (CLEVE)	1	81	102*	1.0	.9
145 CH GOD PROPHCY	1	43	54*	.5	.5
151 L-D SAINTS	1	NA	286	2.7	2.5
167 CHS OF CHRIST	3	131	163	1.6	1.4
323 OLD ORD AMISH	1	NA	50	.5	.4
355 PRESB CH (USA)	2	139	176*	1.7	1.6
419 SO BAPT CONV	12	3,687	4,664*	44.7	41.3
449 UN METHODIST	3	265	335*	3.2	3.0
497 BLACK BAPT EST[2]	NA	219	277*	2.7	2.5
WAYNE	**58**	**10,687**	**13,672***	**78.3**	**100.0**
053 ASSEMB OF GOD	1	43	36	.2	.3
081 CATHOLIC	1	NA	70	.4	.5
081d LATIN	*1*	*NA*	*70*	*.4*	*.5*
097 CHR CHS&CHS CR	2	355	447*	2.6	3.3
123 CH GOD (ANDER)	1	68	128	.7	.9
127 CH GOD (CLEVE)	1	66	83*	.5	.6
165 CH OF NAZARENE	1	151	299	1.7	2.2
167 CHS OF CHRIST	5	232	298	1.7	2.2
419 SO BAPT CONV	24	6,732	8,481*	48.6	62.0
436 UNITED BAPT	13	2,157	2,718*	15.6	19.9
449 UN METHODIST	9	883	1,112*	6.4	8.1
WEBSTER	**53**	**7,744**	**9,877***	**70.8**	**100.0**
005 AME ZION	3	375	418	3.0	4.2
053 ASSEMB OF GOD	1	201	370	2.7	3.7
081 CATHOLIC	2	NA	143	1.0	1.4
081d LATIN	*2*	*NA*	*143*	*1.0*	*1.4*
093 CHR CH (DISC)	3	198	247	1.8	2.5
097 CHR CHS&CHS CR	3	225	282*	2.0	2.9
145 CH GOD PROPHCY	3	129	162*	1.2	1.6
167 CHS OF CHRIST	4	247	322	2.3	3.3
185 CUMBER PRESB	5	278	292	2.1	3.0
361 PRIM BAPT ASCS	2	61	77*	.6	.8
419 SO BAPT CONV	18	4,456	5,590*	40.1	56.6
449 UN METHODIST	9	1,385	1,737*	12.4	17.6
497 BLACK BAPT EST[2]	NA	189	237*	1.7	2.4
WHITLEY	**95**	**18,419**	**23,764***	**71.3**	**100.0**
001 ADVENT CHR CH	1	20	25*	.1	.1
053 ASSEMB OF GOD	1	53	112	.3	.5
081 CATHOLIC	3	NA	246	.7	1.0
081d LATIN	*3*	*NA*	*246*	*.7*	*1.0*
093 CHR CH (DISC)	2	479	599	1.8	2.5
127 CH GOD (CLEVE)	6	668	842*	2.5	3.5
145 CH GOD PROPHCY	1	43	54*	.2	.2
146 CH GOD MTN ASM	6	237	299*	.9	1.3
151 L-D SAINTS	1	NA	242	.7	1.0
167 CHS OF CHRIST	4	286	388	1.2	1.6
355 PRESB CH (USA)	1	139	175*	.5	.7
413 S.D.A.	1	26	33*	.1	.1
419 SO BAPT CONV	60	15,190	19,139*	57.4	80.5
436 UNITED BAPT	1	280	353*	1.1	1.5
449 UN METHODIST	7	998	1,257*	3.8	5.3
WOLFE	**10**	**789**	**1,166***	**17.9**	**100.0**
081 CATHOLIC	1	NA	15	.2	1.3
081d LATIN	*1*	*NA*	*15*	*.2*	*1.3*
093 CHR CH (DISC)	1	69	96	1.5	8.2
123 CH GOD (ANDER)	2	93	255	3.9	21.9
127 CH GOD (CLEVE)	1	35	45*	.7	3.9
145 CH GOD PROPHCY	1	43	55*	.8	4.7
167 CHS OF CHRIST	1	45	58	.9	5.0
419 SO BAPT CONV	1	303	386*	5.9	33.1

NA–Not applicable   NR–Not reported   *Total adherents estimated from known number of communicant, confirmed, full members.   - Represents a percent less than 0.1.   Percentages may not total due to rounding.

[1]See Appendix E   [2]See Appendix F   [3]See Appendix G   Lines in *italic* represent a breakdown of Catholic rites or Friends affiliations. They are included in their respective denominational total.

Table 4. Churches and Church Membership by County and Denomination: 1990

County and Denomination	Number of churches	Communicant, confirmed, full members	Total adherents Number	Percent of total population	Percent of total adherents
449 UN METHODIST	2	201	256*	3.9	22.0
WOODFORD	**39**	**9,051**	**13,423***	**67.3**	**100.0**
053 ASSEMB OF GOD	3	286	406	2.0	3.0
081 CATHOLIC	1	NA	1,148	5.8	8.6
081d LATIN	1	NA	1,148	5.8	8.6
093 CHR CH (DISC)	5	561	1,051	5.3	7.8
097 CHR CHS&CHS CR	1	425	534*	2.7	4.0
127 CH GOD (CLEVE)	1	50	63*	.3	.5
145 CH GOD PROPHCY	1	43	54*	.3	.4
151 L-D SAINTS	1	NA	271	1.4	2.0
165 CH OF NAZARENE	2	96	196	1.0	1.5
167 CHS OF CHRIST	2	97	136	.7	1.0
193 EPISCOPAL	1	350	438	2.2	3.3
339 PENT CH OF GOD	1	35	77	.4	.6
355 PRESB CH (USA)	4	778	978*	4.9	7.3
419 SO BAPT CONV	11	4,684	5,887*	29.5	43.9
449 UN METHODIST	5	1,254	1,576*	7.9	11.7
496 JEWISH EST[1]	0	NA	115	.6	.9
497 BLACK BAPT EST[2]	NA	392	493*	2.5	3.7

LOUISIANA

County and Denomination	Number of churches	Communicant, confirmed, full members	Total adherents Number	Percent of total population	Percent of total adherents
THE STATE.....	4,025	1,193,779	2,975,409*	70.5	100.0
ACADIA	**58**	**7,947**	**48,917***	**87.5**	**100.0**
053 ASSEMB OF GOD	4	854	1,465	2.6	3.0
081 CATHOLIC	22	NA	37,806	67.7	77.3
081d LATIN	22	NA	37,806	67.7	77.3
093 CHR CH (DISC)	1	45	60	.1	.1
097 CHR CHS&CHS CR	2	220	295*	.5	.6
151 L-D SAINTS	1	NA	105	.2	.2
165 CH OF NAZARENE	3	258	369	.7	.8
167 CHS OF CHRIST	2	138	179	.3	.4
193 EPISCOPAL	1	108	143	.3	.3
283 LUTH—MO SYNOD	2	154	218	.4	.4
355 PRESB CH (USA)	1	98	131*	.2	.3
419 SO BAPT CONV	9	2,782	3,732*	6.7	7.6
449 UN METHODIST	10	1,018	1,366*	2.4	2.8
497 BLACK BAPT EST[2]	NA	2,272	3,048*	5.5	6.2
ALLEN	**46**	**7,020**	**13,745***	**64.8**	**100.0**
053 ASSEMB OF GOD	5	155	224	1.1	1.6
081 CATHOLIC	7	NA	4,636	21.8	33.7
081d LATIN	7	NA	4,636	21.8	33.7
127 CH GOD (CLEVE)	1	58	75*	.4	.5
151 L-D SAINTS	1	NA	35	.2	.3
165 CH OF NAZARENE	1	0	0	-	-
167 CHS OF CHRIST	3	145	203	1.0	1.5
193 EPISCOPAL	1	14	17	.1	.1
259 IFCA	1	NR	NR	-	-
356 PRESB CH AMER	1	25	25	.1	.2
419 SO BAPT CONV	17	5,097	6,565*	30.9	47.8
449 UN METHODIST	8	543	699*	3.3	5.1
497 BLACK BAPT EST[2]	NA	983	1,266*	6.0	9.2
ASCENSION	**40**	**9,478**	**43,684***	**75.0**	**100.0**
053 ASSEMB OF GOD	2	230	338	.6	.8
081 CATHOLIC	10	NA	30,321	52.1	69.4
081d LATIN	10	NA	30,321	52.1	69.4
127 CH GOD (CLEVE)	3	183	246*	.4	.6
151 L-D SAINTS	1	NA	504	.9	1.2
167 CHS OF CHRIST	2	120	147	.3	.3
193 EPISCOPAL	1	48	58	.1	.1
283 LUTH—MO SYNOD	1	57	86	.1	.2
355 PRESB CH (USA)	1	95	127*	.2	.3
413 S.D.A.	1	81	109*	.2	.2
419 SO BAPT CONV	10	4,048	5,433*	9.3	12.4
449 UN METHODIST	8	960	1,288*	2.2	2.9
496 JEWISH EST[1]	0	NA	120	.2	.3
497 BLACK BAPT EST[2]	NA	3,656	4,907*	8.4	11.2
ASSUMPTION	**17**	**3,565**	**18,868***	**82.9**	**100.0**
053 ASSEMB OF GOD	1	24	33	.1	.2
081 CATHOLIC	9	NA	14,115	62.0	74.8
081d LATIN	9	NA	14,115	62.0	74.8
145 CH GOD PROPHCY	1	25	33*	.1	.2
419 SO BAPT CONV	3	949	1,265*	5.6	6.7
449 UN METHODIST	3	276	368*	1.6	2.0
497 BLACK BAPT EST[2]	NA	2,291	3,054*	13.4	16.2

County and Denomination	Number of churches	Communicant, confirmed, full members	Total adherents Number	Percent of total population	Percent of total adherents
AVOYELLES	**57**	**6,600**	**27,868***	**71.2**	**100.0**
053 ASSEMB OF GOD	1	26	48	.1	.2
081 CATHOLIC	22	NA	19,141	48.9	68.7
081d LATIN	22	NA	19,141	48.9	68.7
097 CHR CHS&CHS CR	1	20	26*	.1	.1
151 L-D SAINTS	1	NA	100	.3	.4
165 CH OF NAZARENE	1	100	150	.4	.5
167 CHS OF CHRIST	2	72	95	.2	.3
193 EPISCOPAL	1	68	85	.2	.3
215 EVAN METH CH	2	59	77*	.2	.3
283 LUTH—MO SYNOD	1	57	74	.2	.3
419 SO BAPT CONV	15	3,143	4,093*	10.5	14.7
449 UN METHODIST	10	691	900*	2.3	3.2
497 BLACK BAPT EST[2]	NA	2,364	3,079*	7.9	11.0
BEAUREGARD	**58**	**13,080**	**19,213***	**63.9**	**100.0**
053 ASSEMB OF GOD	1	56	90	.3	.5
081 CATHOLIC	4	NA	2,025	6.7	10.5
081d LATIN	4	NA	2,025	6.7	10.5
123 CH GOD (ANDER)	1	12	12	-	.1
143 CG IN CR(MENN)	1	230	298*	1.0	1.6
145 CH GOD PROPHCY	1	25	32*	.1	.2
151 L-D SAINTS	1	NA	215	.7	1.1
165 CH OF NAZARENE	1	121	152	.5	.8
167 CHS OF CHRIST	9	499	680	2.3	3.5
176 CCC, NOT NAT'L	1	40	52*	.2	.3
193 EPISCOPAL	1	101	120	.4	.6
283 LUTH—MO SYNOD	1	128	170	.6	.9
355 PRESB CH (USA)	1	105	136*	.5	.7
356 PRESB CH AMER	1	12	12	-	.1
413 S.D.A.	1	65	84*	.3	.4
419 SO BAPT CONV	29	9,767	12,649*	42.0	65.8
449 UN METHODIST	4	917	1,188*	3.9	6.2
497 BLACK BAPT EST[2]	NA	1,002	1,298*	4.3	6.8
BIENVILLE	**42**	**9,165**	**11,868***	**74.3**	**100.0**
053 ASSEMB OF GOD	5	236	250	1.6	2.1
059 BAPT MISS ASSN	3	537	691*	4.3	5.8
081 CATHOLIC	1	NA	126	.8	1.1
081d LATIN	1	NA	126	.8	1.1
167 CHS OF CHRIST	2	73	95	.6	.8
361 PRIM BAPT ASCS	2	116	149*	.9	1.3
419 SO BAPT CONV	22	5,274	6,787*	42.5	57.2
449 UN METHODIST	7	763	982*	6.1	8.3
497 BLACK BAPT EST[2]	NA	2,166	2,788*	17.4	23.5
BOSSIER	**82**	**33,600**	**51,685***	**60.0**	**100.0**
053 ASSEMB OF GOD	12	1,133	1,684	2.0	3.3
059 BAPT MISS ASSN	2	205	267*	.3	.5
081 CATHOLIC	4	NA	6,272	7.3	12.1
081d LATIN	4	NA	6,272	7.3	12.1
093 CHR CH (DISC)	1	38	60	.1	.1
097 CHR CHS&CHS CR	5	478	623*	.7	1.2
123 CH GOD (ANDER)	1	50	65	.1	.1
127 CH GOD (CLEVE)	1	43	56*	.1	.1
151 L-D SAINTS	2	NA	789	.9	1.5
165 CH OF NAZARENE	2	80	158	.2	.3
167 CHS OF CHRIST	6	1,059	1,340	1.6	2.6
193 EPISCOPAL	1	224	269	.3	.5
216 EVAN PRESBY CH	1	51	51	.1	.1
263 INT FOURSQ GOS	1	53	69*	.1	.1
283 LUTH—MO SYNOD	1	254	335	.4	.6
355 PRESB CH (USA)	6	550	717*	.8	1.4
413 S.D.A.	1	30	39*	-	.1
419 SO BAPT CONV	23	21,375	27,867*	32.4	53.9
449 UN METHODIST	10	3,095	4,035*	4.7	7.8
467 WESLEYAN	1	93	189	.2	.4
496 JEWISH EST[1]	0	NA	257	.3	.5
497 BLACK BAPT EST[2]	NA	4,789	6,243*	7.3	12.1
499 INDEP.NON-CHAR[3]	1	NA	300	.3	.6
CADDO	**212**	**112,985**	**167,071***	**67.3**	**100.0**
005 AME ZION	1	50	75	-	-
053 ASSEMB OF GOD	11	3,210	4,332	1.7	2.6
059 BAPT MISS ASSN	2	425	549*	.2	.3
081 CATHOLIC	12	NA	15,836	6.4	9.5
081d LATIN	12	NA	15,836	6.4	9.5
093 CHR CH (DISC)	4	1,284	1,800	.7	1.1
097 CHR CHS&CHS CR	5	458	591*	.2	.4
111 CH CR,SCIENTST	1	NR	NR	-	-
123 CH GOD (ANDER)	3	385	515	.2	.3
127 CH GOD (CLEVE)	2	188	243*	.1	.1
145 CH GOD PROPHCY	2	51	66*	-	-
151 L-D SAINTS	2	NA	827	.3	.5
165 CH OF NAZARENE	8	860	1,083	.4	.6

NA–Not applicable   NR–Not reported   *Total adherents estimated from known number of communicant, confirmed, full members.   - Represents a percent less than 0.1.   Percentages may not total due to rounding.
[1]See Appendix E   [2]See Appendix F   [3]See Appendix G   Lines in *italic* represent a breakdown of Catholic rites or Friends affiliations. They are included in their respective denominational total.

LOUISIANA

Table 4. Churches and Church Membership by County and Denomination: 1990

County and Denomination	Number of churches	Communicant, confirmed, full members	Total adherents Number	Percent of total population	Percent of total adherents
167 CHS OF CHRIST	18	2,358	3,050	1.2	1.8
193 EPISCOPAL	5	4,037	4,731	1.9	2.8
207 E.L.C.A.	3	612	820	.3	.5
221 FREE METHODIST	2	112	112	-	.1
223 FREE WILL BAPT	1	38	49*	-	-
226 FRIENDS-USA	1	6	24	-	-
226c *FGC*	*1*	*6*	*24*	-	-
246 GREEK ORTHODOX	1	NR	NR	-	-
263 INT FOURSQ GOS	1	66	85*	-	.1
283 LUTH—MO SYNOD	4	658	861	.3	.5
355 PRESB CH (USA)	10	2,467	3,186*	1.3	1.9
356 PRESB CH AMER	1	0	0	-	-
361 PRIM BAPT ASCS	2	91	118*	-	.1
403 SALVATION ARMY	1	242	246	.1	.1
413 S.D.A.	6	1,165	1,505*	.6	.9
419 SO BAPT CONV	59	57,068	73,700*	29.7	44.1
435 UNITARIAN-UNIV	1	201	251	.1	.2
449 UN METHODIST	35	17,210	22,226*	9.0	13.3
496 JEWISH EST[1]	2	NA	743	.3	.4
497 BLACK BAPT EST[2]	NA	19,743	25,497*	10.3	15.3
498 INDEP.CHARIS.[3]	2	NA	2,000	.8	1.2
499 INDEP.NON-CHAR[3]	4	NA	1,950	.8	1.2
CALCASIEU	**150**	**52,611**	**127,739***	**76.0**	**100.0**
053 ASSEMB OF GOD	13	1,572	2,859	1.7	2.2
081 CATHOLIC	28	NA	57,496	34.2	45.0
081d *LATIN*	*28*	*NA*	*57,496*	*34.2*	*45.0*
093 CHR CH (DISC)	2	467	706	.4	.6
097 CHR CHS&CHS CR	3	335	436*	.3	.3
111 CH CR,SCIENTST	1	NR	NR	-	-
123 CH GOD (ANDER)	4	409	478	.3	.4
151 L-D SAINTS	1	NA	495	.3	.4
165 CH OF NAZARENE	6	326	517	.3	.4
167 CHS OF CHRIST	8	1,165	1,507	.9	1.2
193 EPISCOPAL	6	1,183	1,491	.9	1.2
207 E.L.C.A.	1	85	123	.1	.1
259 IFCA	3	NR	NR	-	-
283 LUTH—MO SYNOD	4	577	809	.5	.6
355 PRESB CH (USA)	3	835	1,088*	.6	.9
356 PRESB CH AMER	1	100	118	.1	.1
403 SALVATION ARMY	1	123	127	.1	.1
413 S.D.A.	2	270	352*	.2	.3
419 SO BAPT CONV	44	27,826	36,250*	21.6	28.4
443 UN C OF CHRIST	1	58	76*	-	.1
449 UN METHODIST	17	6,686	8,710*	5.2	6.8
496 JEWISH EST[1]	1	NA	300	.2	.2
497 BLACK BAPT EST[2]	NA	10,594	13,801*	8.2	10.8
CALDWELL	**27**	**4,719**	**6,162***	**62.8**	**100.0**
053 ASSEMB OF GOD	2	71	95	1.0	1.5
081 CATHOLIC	1	NA	61	.6	1.0
081d *LATIN*	*1*	*NA*	*61*	*.6*	*1.0*
123 CH GOD (ANDER)	2	27	87	.9	1.4
127 CH GOD (CLEVE)	2	122	156*	1.6	2.5
167 CHS OF CHRIST	1	42	55	.6	.9
419 SO BAPT CONV	15	3,629	4,648*	47.4	75.4
449 UN METHODIST	4	443	567*	5.8	9.2
497 BLACK BAPT EST[2]	NA	385	493*	5.0	8.0
CAMERON	**17**	**1,454**	**6,882***	**74.3**	**100.0**
081 CATHOLIC	10	NA	4,957	53.5	72.0
081d *LATIN*	*10*	*NA*	*4,957*	*53.5*	*72.0*
419 SO BAPT CONV	5	1,183	1,566*	16.9	22.8
449 UN METHODIST	2	161	213*	2.3	3.1
497 BLACK BAPT EST[2]	NA	110	146*	1.6	2.1
CATAHOULA	**35**	**5,309**	**7,047***	**63.7**	**100.0**
053 ASSEMB OF GOD	3	90	103	.9	1.5
081 CATHOLIC	1	NA	75	.7	1.1
081d *LATIN*	*1*	*NA*	*75*	*.7*	*1.1*
123 CH GOD (ANDER)	1	60	75	.7	1.1
167 CHS OF CHRIST	2	31	45	.4	.6
221 FREE METHODIST	1	42	42	.4	.6
355 PRESB CH (USA)	1	101	133*	1.2	1.9
356 PRESB CH AMER	1	39	50	.5	.7
419 SO BAPT CONV	22	3,700	4,880*	44.1	69.2
449 UN METHODIST	3	350	462*	4.2	6.6
497 BLACK BAPT EST[2]	NA	896	1,182*	10.7	16.8
CLAIBORNE	**42**	**8,632**	**11,160***	**64.1**	**100.0**
053 ASSEMB OF GOD	3	153	230	1.3	2.1
081 CATHOLIC	2	NA	258	1.5	2.3
081d *LATIN*	*2*	*NA*	*258*	*1.5*	*2.3*
167 CHS OF CHRIST	7	305	408	2.3	3.7
355 PRESB CH (USA)	3	261	328*	1.9	2.9

County and Denomination	Number of churches	Communicant, confirmed, full members	Total adherents Number	Percent of total population	Percent of total adherents
361 PRIM BAPT ASCS	1	15	19*	.1	.2
419 SO BAPT CONV	15	4,123	5,177*	29.7	46.4
449 UN METHODIST	11	1,268	1,592*	9.1	14.3
497 BLACK BAPT EST[2]	NA	2,507	3,148*	18.1	28.2
CONCORDIA	**40**	**9,353**	**13,229***	**63.5**	**100.0**
053 ASSEMB OF GOD	3	161	196	.9	1.5
059 BAPT MISS ASSN	1	436	574*	2.8	4.3
081 CATHOLIC	3	NA	818	3.9	6.2
081d *LATIN*	*3*	*NA*	*818*	*3.9*	*6.2*
093 CHR CH (DISC)	2	30	80	.4	.6
123 CH GOD (ANDER)	5	105	205	1.0	1.5
127 CH GOD (CLEVE)	1	75	99*	.5	.7
145 CH GOD PROPHCY	1	25	33*	.2	.2
167 CHS OF CHRIST	2	125	170	.8	1.3
221 FREE METHODIST	1	20	20	.1	.2
355 PRESB CH (USA)	2	213	281*	1.3	2.1
419 SO BAPT CONV	16	5,237	6,899*	33.1	52.2
449 UN METHODIST	3	558	735*	3.5	5.6
497 BLACK BAPT EST[2]	NA	2,368	3,119*	15.0	23.6
DE SOTO	**64**	**11,762**	**16,217***	**64.0**	**100.0**
053 ASSEMB OF GOD	3	120	128	.5	.8
081 CATHOLIC	4	NA	871	3.4	5.4
081d *LATIN*	*4*	*NA*	*871*	*3.4*	*5.4*
093 CHR CH (DISC)	1	6	10	-	.1
167 CHS OF CHRIST	5	211	283	1.1	1.7
193 EPISCOPAL	1	92	106	.4	.7
355 PRESB CH (USA)	5	183	239*	.9	1.5
361 PRIM BAPT ASCS	1	32	42*	.2	.3
413 S.D.A.	1	44	58*	.2	.4
419 SO BAPT CONV	27	7,191	9,403*	37.1	58.0
449 UN METHODIST	16	1,395	1,824*	7.2	11.2
497 BLACK BAPT EST[2]	NA	2,488	3,253*	12.8	20.1
EAST BATON ROUGE	**214**	**115,402**	**257,613***	**67.8**	**100.0**
005 AME ZION	1	150	165	-	.1
019 AMER BAPT USA	4	1,934	2,475*	.7	1.0
053 ASSEMB OF GOD	9	1,232	2,008	.5	.8
059 BAPT MISS ASSN	3	1,242	1,589*	.4	.6
081 CATHOLIC	25	NA	97,051	25.5	37.7
081d *LATIN*	*25*	*NA*	*97,051*	*25.5*	*37.7*
093 CHR CH (DISC)	1	438	811	.2	.3
097 CHR CHS&CHS CR	4	240	307*	.1	.1
111 CH CR,SCIENTST	1	NR	NR	-	-
121 CH GOD (ABR)	1	23	29*	-	-
123 CH GOD (ANDER)	3	140	177	-	.1
127 CH GOD (CLEVE)	3	416	532*	.1	.2
145 CH GOD PROPHCY	3	78	100*	-	-
151 L-D SAINTS	6	NA	2,387	.6	.9
165 CH OF NAZARENE	3	284	338	.1	.1
167 CHS OF CHRIST	11	1,523	1,968	.5	.8
193 EPISCOPAL	9	3,452	4,675	1.2	1.8
207 E.L.C.A.	2	588	753	.2	.3
216 EVAN PRESBY CH	1	66	68	-	-
223 FREE WILL BAPT	1	45	58*	-	-
226 FRIENDS-USA	1	17	26	-	-
226c *FGC*	*1*	*17*	*26*	-	-
246 GREEK ORTHODOX	1	NR	NR	-	-
249 AP CATH ASSYR	0	10	52	-	-
266 INTRSTAT & ASC	1	38	49*	-	-
283 LUTH—MO SYNOD	6	1,298	1,663	.4	.6
331 ORTH CH IN AM	1	NR	NR	-	-
355 PRESB CH (USA)	10	3,744	4,791*	1.3	1.9
356 PRESB CH AMER	3	890	1,068*	.3	.4
361 PRIM BAPT ASCS	2	60	77*	-	-
403 SALVATION ARMY	1	165	167	-	.1
413 S.D.A.	4	872	1,116*	.3	.4
419 SO BAPT CONV	50	51,599	66,033*	17.4	25.6
435 UNITARIAN-UNIV	1	243	347	.1	.1
443 UN C OF CHRIST	1	190	243*	.1	.1
449 UN METHODIST	30	18,083	23,141*	6.1	9.0
467 WESLEYAN	1	46	60	-	-
469 WELS	1	42	68	-	-
496 JEWISH EST[1]	2	NA	873	.2	.3
497 BLACK BAPT EST[2]	NA	26,254	33,598*	8.8	13.0
498 INDEP.CHARIS.[3]	4	NA	6,600	1.7	2.6
499 INDEP.NON-CHAR[3]	3	NA	2,150	.6	.8
EAST CARROLL	**21**	**5,227**	**7,632***	**78.6**	**100.0**
053 ASSEMB OF GOD	1	35	61	.6	.8
081 CATHOLIC	1	NA	355	3.7	4.7
081d *LATIN*	*1*	*NA*	*355*	*3.7*	*4.7*
097 CHR CHS&CHS CR	1	30	42*	.4	.6
143 CG IN CR(MENN)	1	62	86*	.9	1.1
167 CHS OF CHRIST	2	103	140	1.4	1.8

NA–Not applicable   NR–Not reported   *Total adherents estimated from known number of communicant, confirmed, full members.   - Represents a percent less than 0.1.   Percentages may not total due to rounding.
[1]See Appendix E   [2]See Appendix F   [3]See Appendix G   Lines in *italic* represent a breakdown of Catholic rites or Friends affiliations. They are included in their respective denominational total.

Table 4. Churches and Church Membership by County and Denomination: 1990

County and Denomination	Number of churches	Communicant, confirmed, full members	Total adherents Number	Percent of total population	Percent of total adherents
193 EPISCOPAL	1	72	80	.8	1.0
223 FREE WILL BAPT	1	115	160*	1.6	2.1
355 PRESB CH (USA)	1	53	74*	.8	1.0
419 SO BAPT CONV	10	2,520	3,514*	36.2	46.0
449 UN METHODIST	2	276	385*	4.0	5.0
497 BLACK BAPT EST[2]	NA	1,961	2,735*	28.2	35.8
EAST FELICIANA	**29**	**8,219**	**11,139***	**58.0**	**100.0**
081 CATHOLIC	1	NA	400	2.1	3.6
081d LATIN	1	NA	400	2.1	3.6
167 CHS OF CHRIST	1	45	60	.3	.5
193 EPISCOPAL	1	73	86	.4	.8
283 LUTH—MO SYNOD	1	112	162	.8	1.5
355 PRESB CH (USA)	3	82	107*	.6	1.0
419 SO BAPT CONV	10	3,704	4,836*	25.2	43.4
449 UN METHODIST	12	1,371	1,790*	9.3	16.1
497 BLACK BAPT EST[2]	NA	2,832	3,698*	19.2	33.2
EVANGELINE	**34**	**5,625**	**27,405***	**82.4**	**100.0**
053 ASSEMB OF GOD	2	145	221	.7	.8
081 CATHOLIC	12	NA	19,811	59.5	72.3
081d LATIN	12	NA	19,811	59.5	72.3
097 CHR CHS&CHS CR	1	40	53*	.2	.2
151 L-D SAINTS	1	NA	91	.3	.3
167 CHS OF CHRIST	3	266	343	1.0	1.3
419 SO BAPT CONV	13	3,191	4,247*	12.8	15.5
449 UN METHODIST	2	40	53*	.2	.2
497 BLACK BAPT EST[2]	NA	1,943	2,586*	7.8	9.4
FRANKLIN	**54**	**13,031**	**17,354***	**77.5**	**100.0**
053 ASSEMB OF GOD	3	113	146	.7	.8
081 CATHOLIC	2	NA	281	1.3	1.6
081d LATIN	2	NA	281	1.3	1.6
097 CHR CHS&CHS CR	1	0	0*	-	-
151 L-D SAINTS	1	NA	56	.3	.3
165 CH OF NAZARENE	1	37	53	.2	.3
167 CHS OF CHRIST	2	103	133	.6	.8
193 EPISCOPAL	1	20	21	.1	.1
221 FREE METHODIST	1	23	23	.1	.1
353 CHR BRETHREN	1	10	20	.1	.1
355 PRESB CH (USA)	3	68	89*	.4	.5
419 SO BAPT CONV	32	9,747	12,731*	56.9	73.4
449 UN METHODIST	6	715	934*	4.2	5.4
497 BLACK BAPT EST[2]	NA	2,195	2,867*	12.8	16.5
GRANT	**48**	**8,327**	**11,359***	**64.8**	**100.0**
053 ASSEMB OF GOD	2	85	137	.8	1.2
081 CATHOLIC	3	NA	395	2.3	3.5
081d LATIN	3	NA	395	2.3	3.5
127 CH GOD (CLEVE)	1	30	39*	.2	.3
165 CH OF NAZARENE	1	12	0	-	-
167 CHS OF CHRIST	4	192	252	1.4	2.2
361 PRIM BAPT ASCS	1	14	18*	.1	.2
419 SO BAPT CONV	26	6,912	9,039*	51.6	79.6
449 UN METHODIST	9	499	653*	3.7	5.7
467 WESLEYAN	1	28	100	.6	.9
497 BLACK BAPT EST[2]	NA	555	726*	4.1	6.4
IBERIA	**39**	**10,447**	**59,611***	**87.3**	**100.0**
053 ASSEMB OF GOD	1	349	500	.7	.8
081 CATHOLIC	13	NA	45,592	66.8	76.5
081d LATIN	13	NA	45,592	66.8	76.5
089 CHR & MISS AL	1	0	34	-	.1
097 CHR CHS&CHS CR	1	200	269*	.4	.5
145 CH GOD PROPHCY	1	25	34*	-	.1
165 CH OF NAZARENE	1	46	13	-	-
167 CHS OF CHRIST	2	201	251	.4	.4
193 EPISCOPAL	1	319	385	.6	.6
355 PRESB CH (USA)	2	72	97*	.1	.2
413 S.D.A.	1	34	46*	.1	.1
419 SO BAPT CONV	4	2,929	3,944*	5.8	6.6
443 UN C OF CHRIST	3	167	225*	.3	.4
449 UN METHODIST	7	1,604	2,160*	3.2	3.6
496 JEWISH EST[1]	1	NA	0	-	-
497 BLACK BAPT EST[2]	NA	4,501	6,061*	8.9	10.2
IBERVILLE	**35**	**5,758**	**20,473***	**65.9**	**100.0**
019 AMER BAPT USA	1	75	98*	.3	.5
053 ASSEMB OF GOD	3	122	150	.5	.7
081 CATHOLIC	9	NA	12,784	41.2	62.4
081d LATIN	9	NA	12,784	41.2	62.4
123 CH GOD (ANDER)	1	25	42	.1	.2
145 CH GOD PROPHCY	1	25	33*	.1	.2
151 L-D SAINTS	1	NA	123	.4	.6
167 CHS OF CHRIST	1	17	25	.1	.1
193 EPISCOPAL	2	143	194*	.6	.9
419 SO BAPT CONV	7	1,288	1,691*	5.4	8.3
449 UN METHODIST	9	850	1,116*	3.6	5.5
497 BLACK BAPT EST[2]	NA	3,213	4,217*	13.6	20.6
JACKSON	**47**	**8,561**	**11,271***	**71.8**	**100.0**
053 ASSEMB OF GOD	2	340	399	2.5	3.5
081 CATHOLIC	1	NA	240	1.5	2.1
081d LATIN	1	NA	240	1.5	2.1
123 CH GOD (ANDER)	3	212	242	1.5	2.1
151 L-D SAINTS	1	NA	82	.5	.7
165 CH OF NAZARENE	1	12	38	.2	.3
167 CHS OF CHRIST	1	65	85	.5	.8
185 CUMBER PRESB	1	63	69	.4	.6
361 PRIM BAPT ASCS	1	29	37*	.2	.3
413 S.D.A.	1	17	22*	.1	.2
419 SO BAPT CONV	26	5,470	7,032*	44.8	62.4
449 UN METHODIST	9	922	1,185*	7.5	10.5
497 BLACK BAPT EST[2]	NA	1,431	1,840*	11.7	16.3
JEFFERSON	**145**	**61,423**	**305,156***	**68.1**	**100.0**
005 AME ZION	1	225	320	.1	.1
053 ASSEMB OF GOD	11	5,220	8,620	1.9	2.8
059 BAPT MISS ASSN	1	311	394*	.1	.1
081 CATHOLIC	41	NA	218,962	48.8	71.8
081d LATIN	41	NA	218,962	48.8	71.8
093 CHR CH (DISC)	1	150	191	-	.1
111 CH CR,SCIENTST	1	NR	NR	-	-
121 CH GOD (ABR)	1	7	9*	-	-
123 CH GOD (ANDER)	1	81	81	-	-
127 CH GOD (CLEVE)	3	364	461*	.1	.2
145 CH GOD PROPHCY	2	51	65*	-	-
151 L-D SAINTS	3	NA	1,092	.2	.4
165 CH OF NAZARENE	1	103	125	-	-
167 CHS OF CHRIST	6	720	947	.2	.3
185 CUMBER PRESB	1	422	457	.1	.1
193 EPISCOPAL	6	1,953	2,673	.6	.9
207 E.L.C.A.	4	812	1,090	.2	.4
259 IFCA	1	NR	NR	-	-
283 LUTH—MO SYNOD	6	2,720	3,486	.8	1.1
353 CHR BRETHREN	1	42	80	-	-
355 PRESB CH (USA)	6	1,762	2,232*	.5	.7
356 PRESB CH AMER	1	129	193	-	.1
361 PRIM BAPT ASCS	1	44	56*	-	-
413 S.D.A.	3	536	679*	.2	.2
419 SO BAPT CONV	23	18,071	22,896*	5.1	7.5
443 UN C OF CHRIST	3	524	664*	.1	.2
449 UN METHODIST	12	5,395	6,835*	1.5	2.2
496 JEWISH EST[1]	3	NA	4,352	1.0	1.4
497 BLACK BAPT EST[2]	NA	21,781	27,596*	6.2	9.0
498 INDEP.CHARIS.[3]	1	NA	600	.1	.2
JEFFERSON DAVIS	**40**	**6,395**	**23,651***	**77.0**	**100.0**
053 ASSEMB OF GOD	3	361	456	1.5	1.9
081 CATHOLIC	12	NA	14,595	47.5	61.7
081d LATIN	12	NA	14,595	47.5	61.7
097 CHR CHS&CHS CR	1	212	281*	.9	1.2
151 L-D SAINTS	1	NA	97	.3	.4
157 CH OF BRETHREN	1	74	98*	.3	.4
176 CCC, NOT NAT'L	1	99	131*	.4	.6
193 EPISCOPAL	1	47	47	.2	.2
283 LUTH—MO SYNOD	1	74	98	.3	.4
349 PENT HOLINESS	1	71	94*	.3	.4
355 PRESB CH (USA)	2	155	205*	.7	.9
419 SO BAPT CONV	7	2,717	3,600*	11.7	15.2
449 UN METHODIST	8	1,282	1,698*	5.5	7.2
497 BLACK BAPT EST[2]	NA	1,303	1,726*	5.6	7.3
499 INDEP.NON-CHAR[3]	1	NA	525	1.7	2.2
LAFAYETTE	**73**	**29,923**	**130,510***	**79.2**	**100.0**
053 ASSEMB OF GOD	3	1,007	1,630	1.0	1.2
081 CATHOLIC	29	NA	90,100	54.7	69.0
081d LATIN	29	NA	90,100	54.7	69.0
093 CHR CH (DISC)	1	115	131	.1	.1
097 CHR CHS&CHS CR	1	90	118*	.1	.1
111 CH CR,SCIENTST	1	NR	NR	-	-
123 CH GOD (ANDER)	1	23	25	-	-
127 CH GOD (CLEVE)	1	104	136*	.1	.1
151 L-D SAINTS	1	NA	515	.3	.4
165 CH OF NAZARENE	1	31	18	-	-
167 CHS OF CHRIST	3	400	508	.3	.4
193 EPISCOPAL	3	1,185	1,690	1.0	1.3
207 E.L.C.A.	1	316	540	.3	.4
283 LUTH—MO SYNOD	2	238	353	.2	.3
349 PENT HOLINESS	1	1,100	1,437*	.9	1.1
353 CHR BRETHREN	1	55	120	.1	.1

NA–Not applicable   NR–Not reported   *Total adherents estimated from known number of communicant, confirmed, full members.   - Represents a percent less than 0.1.   Percentages may not total due to rounding.
[1]See Appendix E   [2]See Appendix F   [3]See Appendix G   Lines in *italic* represent a breakdown of Catholic rites or Friends affiliations. They are included in their respective denominational total.

181

Table 4. Churches and Church Membership by County and Denomination: 1990

County and Denomination	Number of churches	Communicant, confirmed, full members	Total adherents Number	Percent of total population	Percent of total adherents
355 PRESB CH (USA)	3	827	1,080*	.7	.8
356 PRESB CH AMER	1	40	62	-	-
403 SALVATION ARMY	1	50	58	-	-
413 S.D.A.	1	80	105*	.1	.1
419 SO BAPT CONV	9	10,416	13,607*	8.3	10.4
435 UNITARIAN-UNIV	1	25	25	-	-
449 UN METHODIST	5	3,668	4,792*	2.9	3.7
496 JEWISH EST[1]	2	NA	197	.1	.2
497 BLACK BAPT EST[2]	NA	10,153	13,263*	8.0	10.2
LAFOURCHE	**48**	**8,454**	**58,739***	**68.4**	**100.0**
053 ASSEMB OF GOD	5	556	837	1.0	1.4
081 CATHOLIC	14	NA	47,447	55.3	80.8
081d LATIN	*14*	*NA*	*47,447*	*55.3*	*80.8*
145 CH GOD PROPHCY	1	25	33*	-	.1
167 CHS OF CHRIST	3	100	114	.1	.2
176 CCC, NOT NAT'L	1	61	80*	.1	.1
193 EPISCOPAL	1	145	278	.3	.5
355 PRESB CH (USA)	4	341	448*	.5	.8
413 S.D.A.	1	25	33*	-	.1
419 SO BAPT CONV	9	2,999	3,943*	4.6	6.7
449 UN METHODIST	9	1,253	1,648*	1.9	2.8
497 BLACK BAPT EST[2]	NA	2,949	3,878*	4.5	6.6
LA SALLE	**51**	**9,978**	**12,737***	**93.2**	**100.0**
053 ASSEMB OF GOD	3	265	268	2.0	2.1
081 CATHOLIC	1	NA	149	1.1	1.2
081d LATIN	*1*	*NA*	*149*	*1.1*	*1.2*
127 CH GOD (CLEVE)	2	103	131*	1.0	1.0
165 CH OF NAZARENE	2	54	71	.5	.6
167 CHS OF CHRIST	2	101	131	1.0	1.0
221 FREE METHODIST	3	56	67	.5	.5
419 SO BAPT CONV	32	8,424	10,683*	78.2	83.9
449 UN METHODIST	6	700	888*	6.5	7.0
497 BLACK BAPT EST[2]	NA	275	349*	2.6	2.7
LINCOLN	**54**	**18,931**	**25,871***	**62.0**	**100.0**
053 ASSEMB OF GOD	1	74	105	.3	.4
081 CATHOLIC	2	NA	2,370	5.7	9.2
081d LATIN	*2*	*NA*	*2,370*	*5.7*	*9.2*
111 CH CR,SCIENTST	1	NR	NR	-	-
123 CH GOD (ANDER)	1	69	75	.2	.3
145 CH GOD PROPHCY	1	25	31*	.1	.1
151 L-D SAINTS	1	NA	227	.5	.9
165 CH OF NAZARENE	1	39	140	.3	.5
167 CHS OF CHRIST	4	294	388	.9	1.5
193 EPISCOPAL	1	173	233	.6	.9
226 FRIENDS-USA	1	1	2	-	-
226c FGC	*1*	*1*	*2*	*-*	*-*
283 LUTH—MO SYNOD	1	45	50	.1	.2
355 PRESB CH (USA)	2	489	598*	1.4	2.3
356 PRESB CH AMER	1	89	98	.2	.4
361 PRIM BAPT ASCS	1	4	5*	-	-
419 SO BAPT CONV	24	10,503	12,841*	30.8	49.6
435 UNITARIAN-UNIV	1	19	19	-	.1
449 UN METHODIST	10	3,402	4,159*	10.0	16.1
497 BLACK BAPT EST[2]	NA	3,705	4,530*	10.9	17.5
LIVINGSTON	**92**	**27,126**	**54,039***	**76.6**	**100.0**
053 ASSEMB OF GOD	3	247	282	.4	.5
059 BAPT MISS ASSN	3	587	781*	1.1	1.4
081 CATHOLIC	8	NA	17,445	24.7	32.3
081d LATIN	*8*	*NA*	*17,445*	*24.7*	*32.3*
121 CH GOD (ABR)	1	106	141*	.2	.3
127 CH GOD (CLEVE)	1	33	44*	.1	.1
145 CH GOD PROPHCY	2	51	68*	.1	.1
151 L-D SAINTS	1	NA	291	.4	.5
165 CH OF NAZARENE	1	14	26	-	-
167 CHS OF CHRIST	4	181	245	.3	.5
193 EPISCOPAL	1	307	391	.6	.7
266 INTRSTAT & ASC	1	89	118*	.2	.2
339 PENT CH OF GOD	3	103	231	.3	.4
355 PRESB CH (USA)	3	137	182*	.3	.3
413 S.D.A.	1	125	166*	.2	.3
419 SO BAPT CONV	46	21,563	28,698*	40.7	53.1
449 UN METHODIST	13	2,503	3,331*	4.7	6.2
496 JEWISH EST[1]	0	NA	162	.2	.3
497 BLACK BAPT EST[2]	NA	1,080	1,437*	2.0	2.7
MADISON	**16**	**6,382**	**8,944***	**71.8**	**100.0**
005 AME ZION	2	351	546	4.4	6.1
081 CATHOLIC	1	NA	210	1.7	2.3
081d LATIN	*1*	*NA*	*210*	*1.7*	*2.3*
167 CHS OF CHRIST	1	32	42	.3	.5
193 EPISCOPAL	1	91	125	1.0	1.4
355 PRESB CH (USA)	1	56	76*	.6	.8
413 S.D.A.	1	20	27*	.2	.3
419 SO BAPT CONV	8	3,134	4,255*	34.1	47.6
449 UN METHODIST	1	386	524*	4.2	5.9
497 BLACK BAPT EST[2]	NA	2,312	3,139*	25.2	35.1
MOREHOUSE	**67**	**15,206**	**20,786***	**65.1**	**100.0**
005 AME ZION	2	162	347	1.1	1.7
053 ASSEMB OF GOD	6	644	719	2.3	3.5
059 BAPT MISS ASSN	1	186	244*	.8	1.2
081 CATHOLIC	3	NA	698	2.2	3.4
081d LATIN	*3*	*NA*	*698*	*2.2*	*3.4*
123 CH GOD (ANDER)	4	250	309	1.0	1.5
127 CH GOD (CLEVE)	2	216	284*	.9	1.4
145 CH GOD PROPHCY	1	25	33*	.1	.2
151 L-D SAINTS	2	NA	188	.6	.9
167 CHS OF CHRIST	3	463	600	1.9	2.9
193 EPISCOPAL	3	306	351	1.1	1.7
223 FREE WILL BAPT	1	78	102*	.3	.5
355 PRESB CH (USA)	2	172	226*	.7	1.1
361 PRIM BAPT ASCS	1	8	11*	-	.1
413 S.D.A.	0	8	11*	-	.1
419 SO BAPT CONV	25	8,408	11,042*	34.6	53.1
449 UN METHODIST	11	1,318	1,731*	5.4	8.3
497 BLACK BAPT EST[2]	NA	2,962	3,890*	12.2	18.7
NATCHITOCHES	**80**	**14,692**	**24,417***	**66.6**	**100.0**
001 ADVENT CHR CH	1	12	16*	-	.1
053 ASSEMB OF GOD	4	504	593	1.6	2.4
059 BAPT MISS ASSN	1	118	153*	.4	.6
081 CATHOLIC	10	NA	4,740	12.9	19.4
081d LATIN	*10*	*NA*	*4,740*	*12.9*	*19.4*
123 CH GOD (ANDER)	1	10	20	.1	.1
151 L-D SAINTS	3	NA	647	1.8	2.6
165 CH OF NAZARENE	1	39	67	.2	.3
167 CHS OF CHRIST	2	205	274	.7	1.1
185 CUMBER PRESB	1	105	113	.3	.5
193 EPISCOPAL	1	86	119	.3	.5
221 FREE METHODIST	1	20	20	.1	.1
283 LUTH—MO SYNOD	1	69	87	.2	.4
355 PRESB CH (USA)	1	87	113*	.3	.5
413 S.D.A.	2	98	127*	.3	.5
419 SO BAPT CONV	34	8,556	11,115*	30.3	45.5
449 UN METHODIST	16	1,706	2,216*	6.0	9.1
497 BLACK BAPT EST[2]	NA	3,077	3,997*	10.9	16.4
ORLEANS	**262**	**117,123**	**329,770***	**66.4**	**100.0**
005 AME ZION	3	1,985	2,280	.5	.7
019 AMER BAPT USA	1	350	446*	.1	.1
053 ASSEMB OF GOD	8	1,572	2,051	.4	.6
081 CATHOLIC	74	NA	171,328	34.5	52.0
081d LATIN	*74*	*NA*	*171,328*	*34.5*	*52.0*
093 CHR CH (DISC)	2	184	287	.1	.1
111 CH CR,SCIENTST	4	NR	NR	-	-
123 CH GOD (ANDER)	1	58	85	-	-
127 CH GOD (CLEVE)	1	194	247*	-	.1
145 CH GOD PROPHCY	1	25	32*	-	-
151 L-D SAINTS	3	NA	1,130	.2	.3
165 CH OF NAZARENE	3	125	91	-	-
167 CHS OF CHRIST	6	1,113	1,514	.3	.5
193 EPISCOPAL	12	5,357	6,672	1.3	2.0
207 E.L.C.A.	4	791	1,012	.2	.3
226 FRIENDS-USA	1	26	39	-	-
226c FGC	*1*	*26*	*39*	*-*	*-*
246 GREEK ORTHODOX	1	NR	NR	-	-
259 IFCA	1	NR	NR	-	-
283 LUTH—MO SYNOD	18	5,132	6,653	1.3	2.0
285 MENNONITE CH	1	100	115	-	-
331 ORTH CH IN AM	1	NR	NR	-	-
353 CHR BRETHREN	3	140	275	.1	.1
355 PRESB CH (USA)	15	3,648	4,650*	.9	1.4
356 PRESB CH AMER	1	0	0	-	-
403 SALVATION ARMY	1	136	138	-	-
413 S.D.A.	7	2,730	3,480*	.7	1.1
419 SO BAPT CONV	29	19,061	24,295*	4.9	7.4
435 UNITARIAN-UNIV	2	302	373	.1	.1
443 UN C OF CHRIST	8	2,032	2,590*	.5	.8
449 UN METHODIST	38	10,904	13,898*	2.8	4.2
467 WESLEYAN	1	38	63	-	-
469 WELS	1	66	92	-	-
496 JEWISH EST[1]	8	NA	4,814	1.0	1.5
497 BLACK BAPT EST[2]	NA	61,054	77,820*	15.7	23.6
498 INDEP.CHARIS.[3]	1	NA	2,800	.6	.8
499 INDEP.NON-CHAR[3]	1	NA	500	.1	.2

NA–Not applicable   NR–Not reported   *Total adherents estimated from known number of communicant, confirmed, full members.   - Represents a percent less than 0.1.   Percentages may not total due to rounding.

[1] See Appendix E   [2] See Appendix F   [3] See Appendix G   Lines in *italic* represent a breakdown of Catholic rites or Friends affiliations. They are included in their respective denominational total.

Table 4. Churches and Church Membership by County and Denomination: 1990

County and Denomination	Number of churches	Communicant, confirmed, full members	Total adherents		
			Number	Percent of total population	Percent of total adherents
OUACHITA	**157**	**65,910**	**94,870***	**66.7**	**100.0**
053 ASSEMB OF GOD	20	2,635	3,522	2.5	3.7
059 BAPT MISS ASSN	3	245	318*	.2	.3
081 CATHOLIC	8	NA	7,404	5.2	7.8
081d LATIN	8	NA	7,404	5.2	7.8
093 CHR CH (DISC)	1	467	691	.5	.7
111 CH CR,SCIENTST	1	NR	NR	-	-
123 CH GOD (ANDER)	6	250	414	.3	.4
127 CH GOD (CLEVE)	4	1,063	1,380*	1.0	1.5
151 L-D SAINTS	2	NA	684	.5	.7
165 CH OF NAZARENE	2	258	256	.2	.3
167 CHS OF CHRIST	16	2,150	3,098	2.2	3.3
185 CUMBER PRESB	1	19	19	-	-
193 EPISCOPAL	4	1,397	1,907	1.3	2.0
207 E.L.C.A.	1	90	127	.1	.1
217 FIRE BAPTIZED	1	2	3*	-	-
246 GREEK ORTHODOX	1	NR	NR	-	-
263 INT FOURSQ GOS	1	4	5*	-	-
283 LUTH—MO SYNOD	2	332	464	.3	.5
355 PRESB CH (USA)	6	1,146	1,488*	1.0	1.6
356 PRESB CH AMER	1	102	122	.1	.1
361 PRIM BAPT ASCS	1	12	16*	-	-
403 SALVATION ARMY	1	92	96	.1	.1
413 S.D.A.	2	261	339*	.2	.4
419 SO BAPT CONV	49	37,594	48,810*	34.3	51.4
443 UN C OF CHRIST	1	88	114*	.1	.1
449 UN METHODIST	20	8,903	11,559*	8.1	12.2
467 WESLEYAN	1	51	150	.1	.2
496 JEWISH EST[1]	1	NA	525	.4	.6
497 BLACK BAPT EST[2]	NA	8,749	11,359*	8.0	12.0
PLAQUEMINES	**25**	**4,664**	**16,432***	**64.3**	**100.0**
053 ASSEMB OF GOD	3	179	239	.9	1.5
081 CATHOLIC	6	NA	10,040	39.3	61.1
081d LATIN	6	NA	10,040	39.3	61.1
151 L-D SAINTS	1	NA	60	.2	.4
165 CH OF NAZARENE	1	58	151	.6	.9
167 CHS OF CHRIST	2	42	60	.2	.4
285 MENNONITE CH	1	27	79	.3	.5
355 PRESB CH (USA)	1	7	9*	-	.1
419 SO BAPT CONV	7	2,752	3,665*	14.3	22.3
449 UN METHODIST	3	272	362*	1.4	2.2
497 BLACK BAPT EST[2]	NA	1,327	1,767*	6.9	10.8
POINTE COUPEE	**24**	**4,551**	**22,098***	**98.0**	**100.0**
053 ASSEMB OF GOD	2	110	132	.6	.6
081 CATHOLIC	8	NA	16,113	71.5	72.9
081d LATIN	8	NA	16,113	71.5	72.9
193 EPISCOPAL	3	191	253	1.1	1.1
419 SO BAPT CONV	6	1,200	1,581*	7.0	7.2
449 UN METHODIST	5	159	210*	.9	1.0
497 BLACK BAPT EST[2]	NA	2,891	3,809*	16.9	17.2
RAPIDES	**194**	**51,997**	**89,479***	**68.0**	**100.0**
053 ASSEMB OF GOD	8	1,066	1,575	1.2	1.8
081 CATHOLIC	25	NA	20,376	15.5	22.8
081d LATIN	25	NA	20,376	15.5	22.8
093 CHR CH (DISC)	1	70	103	.1	.1
097 CHR CHS&CHS CR	2	200	260*	.2	.3
111 CH CR,SCIENTST	1	NR	NR	-	-
123 CH GOD (ANDER)	5	151	184	.1	.2
127 CH GOD (CLEVE)	1	106	138*	.1	.2
145 CH GOD PROPHCY	1	25	32*	-	-
151 L-D SAINTS	2	NA	589	.4	.7
165 CH OF NAZARENE	3	194	187	.1	.2
167 CHS OF CHRIST	6	514	824	.6	.9
193 EPISCOPAL	6	1,215	1,453	1.1	1.6
221 FREE METHODIST	3	163	178	.1	.2
223 FREE WILL BAPT	1	69	90*	.1	.1
283 LUTH—MO SYNOD	3	382	516	.4	.6
355 PRESB CH (USA)	2	147	191*	.1	.2
356 PRESB CH AMER	1	267	267	.2	.3
361 PRIM BAPT ASCS	1	39	51*	-	.1
403 SALVATION ARMY	1	80	83	.1	.1
413 S.D.A.	2	585	760*	.6	.8
419 SO BAPT CONV	87	34,035	44,229*	33.6	49.4
435 UNITARIAN-UNIV	1	11	11	-	-
449 UN METHODIST	25	5,253	6,826*	5.2	7.6
467 WESLEYAN	2	66	323	.2	.4
469 WELS	1	57	94	.1	.1
496 JEWISH EST[1]	2	NA	350	.3	.4
497 BLACK BAPT EST[2]	NA	7,302	9,489*	7.2	10.6
499 INDEP.NON-CHAR[3]	1	NA	300	.2	.3

County and Denomination	Number of churches	Communicant, confirmed, full members	Total adherents		
			Number	Percent of total population	Percent of total adherents
RED RIVER	**23**	**4,797**	**6,650***	**70.8**	**100.0**
053 ASSEMB OF GOD	2	152	123	1.3	1.8
059 BAPT MISS ASSN	1	171	228*	2.4	3.4
081 CATHOLIC	1	NA	170	1.8	2.6
081d LATIN	1	NA	170	1.8	2.6
123 CH GOD (ANDER)	1	15	15	.2	.2
151 L-D SAINTS	1	NA	177	1.9	2.7
167 CHS OF CHRIST	1	12	16	.2	.2
413 S.D.A.	1	74	99*	1.1	1.5
419 SO BAPT CONV	11	2,891	3,849*	41.0	57.9
449 UN METHODIST	4	363	483*	5.1	7.3
497 BLACK BAPT EST[2]	NA	1,119	1,490*	15.9	22.4
RICHLAND	**58**	**12,966**	**17,403***	**84.4**	**100.0**
053 ASSEMB OF GOD	6	188	254	1.2	1.5
081 CATHOLIC	2	NA	325	1.6	1.9
081d LATIN	2	NA	325	1.6	1.9
127 CH GOD (CLEVE)	4	226	298*	1.4	1.7
167 CHS OF CHRIST	5	361	492	2.4	2.8
193 EPISCOPAL	1	87	110	.5	.6
349 PENT HOLINESS	1	50	66*	.3	.4
355 PRESB CH (USA)	2	41	54*	.3	.3
356 PRESB CH AMER	1	195	234	1.1	1.3
419 SO BAPT CONV	29	8,421	11,095*	53.8	63.8
449 UN METHODIST	7	1,047	1,379*	6.7	7.9
497 BLACK BAPT EST[2]	NA	2,350	3,096*	15.0	17.8
SABINE	**78**	**11,043**	**18,768***	**82.9**	**100.0**
053 ASSEMB OF GOD	2	191	201	.9	1.1
081 CATHOLIC	5	NA	4,533	20.0	24.2
081d LATIN	5	NA	4,533	20.0	24.2
123 CH GOD (ANDER)	1	31	65	.3	.3
145 CH GOD PROPHCY	1	25	32*	.1	.2
165 CH OF NAZARENE	5	231	295	1.3	1.6
167 CHS OF CHRIST	3	122	153	.7	.8
185 CUMBER PRESB	1	49	49	.2	.3
419 SO BAPT CONV	51	8,883	11,486*	50.7	61.2
449 UN METHODIST	9	640	828*	3.7	4.4
497 BLACK BAPT EST[2]	NA	871	1,126*	5.0	6.0
SAINT BERNARD	**31**	**4,638**	**48,835***	**73.3**	**100.0**
053 ASSEMB OF GOD	4	523	1,260	1.9	2.6
059 BAPT MISS ASSN	1	39	50*	.1	.1
081 CATHOLIC	8	NA	41,350	62.1	84.7
081d LATIN	8	NA	41,350	62.1	84.7
127 CH GOD (CLEVE)	1	373	475*	.7	1.0
151 L-D SAINTS	1	NA	349	.5	.7
167 CHS OF CHRIST	2	77	101	.2	.2
193 EPISCOPAL	1	115	143	.2	.3
207 E.L.C.A.	1	373	505	.8	1.0
283 LUTH—MO SYNOD	1	339	394	.6	.8
355 PRESB CH (USA)	2	196	249*	.4	.5
413 S.D.A.	1	51	65*	.1	.1
419 SO BAPT CONV	6	1,363	1,735*	2.6	3.6
449 UN METHODIST	2	332	423*	.6	.9
496 JEWISH EST[1]	0	NA	645	1.0	1.3
497 BLACK BAPT EST[2]	NA	857	1,091*	1.6	2.2
SAINT CHARLES	**25**	**7,643**	**34,689***	**81.7**	**100.0**
053 ASSEMB OF GOD	3	296	655	1.5	1.9
081 CATHOLIC	8	NA	23,716	55.9	68.4
081d LATIN	8	NA	23,716	55.9	68.4
167 CHS OF CHRIST	1	93	121	.3	.3
193 EPISCOPAL	1	45	51	.1	.1
285 MENNONITE CH	1	125	200	.5	.6
355 PRESB CH (USA)	2	210	283*	.7	.8
419 SO BAPT CONV	6	3,626	4,881*	11.5	14.1
449 UN METHODIST	3	423	569*	1.3	1.6
496 JEWISH EST[1]	0	NA	411	1.0	1.2
497 BLACK BAPT EST[2]	NA	2,825	3,802*	9.0	11.0
SAINT HELENA	**24**	**6,070**	**8,353***	**84.6**	**100.0**
005 AME ZION	1	75	110	1.1	1.3
081 CATHOLIC	1	NA	250	2.5	3.0
081d LATIN	1	NA	250	2.5	3.0
419 SO BAPT CONV	13	3,700	4,933*	50.0	59.1
449 UN METHODIST	9	697	929*	9.4	11.1
497 BLACK BAPT EST[2]	NA	1,598	2,131*	21.6	25.5
SAINT JAMES	**15**	**3,831**	**22,725***	**108.8**	**100.0**
053 ASSEMB OF GOD	2	75	96	.5	.4
081 CATHOLIC	7	NA	17,575	84.2	77.3
081d LATIN	7	NA	17,575	84.2	77.3
419 SO BAPT CONV	2	147	198*	.9	.9

NA–Not applicable   NR–Not reported   *Total adherents estimated from known number of communicant, confirmed, full members.   - Represents a percent less than 0.1.   Percentages may not total due to rounding.
[1]See Appendix E   [2]See Appendix F   [3]See Appendix G   Lines in *italic* represent a breakdown of Catholic rites or Friends affiliations. They are included in their respective denominational total.

LOUISIANA

Table 4. Churches and Church Membership by County and Denomination: 1990

County and Denomination	Number of churches	Communicant, confirmed, full members	Total adherents Number	Percent of total population	Percent of total adherents
449 UN METHODIST	4	380	511*	2.4	2.2
497 BLACK BAPT EST2	NA	3,229	4,345*	20.8	19.1
SAINT JOHN THE BAPTIST	**16**	**4,829**	**30,590***	**76.5**	**100.0**
053 ASSEMB OF GOD	1	86	166	.4	.5
081 CATHOLIC	6	NA	23,278	58.2	76.1
081d LATIN	6	NA	23,278	58.2	76.1
151 L-D SAINTS	1	NA	148	.4	.5
165 CH OF NAZARENE	1	0	0	-	-
167 CHS OF CHRIST	1	50	65	.2	.2
193 EPISCOPAL	1	63	92	.2	.3
207 E.L.C.A.	1	103	161	.4	.5
266 INTRSTAT & ASC	1	11	15*	-	-
355 PRESB CH (USA)	1	67	93*	.2	.3
419 SO BAPT CONV	1	1,209	1,681*	4.2	5.5
449 UN METHODIST	1	379	527*	1.3	1.7
496 JEWISH EST1	0	NA	387	1.0	1.3
497 BLACK BAPT EST2	NA	2,861	3,977*	9.9	13.0
SAINT LANDRY	**69**	**14,051**	**78,578***	**97.8**	**100.0**
053 ASSEMB OF GOD	1	189	200	.2	.3
081 CATHOLIC	35	NA	59,904	74.6	76.2
081d LATIN	35	NA	59,904	74.6	76.2
123 CH GOD (ANDER)	1	56	64	.1	.1
167 CHS OF CHRIST	3	118	156	.2	.2
193 EPISCOPAL	2	138	185	.2	.2
313 N AM BAPT CONF	1	67	90*	.1	.1
356 PRESB CH AMER	2	201	220	.3	.3
419 SO BAPT CONV	15	4,692	6,274*	7.8	8.0
449 UN METHODIST	9	1,356	1,813*	2.3	2.3
497 BLACK BAPT EST2	NA	7,234	9,672*	12.0	12.3
SAINT MARTIN	**18**	**3,541**	**36,728***	**83.5**	**100.0**
053 ASSEMB OF GOD	1	50	60	.1	.2
081 CATHOLIC	13	NA	31,903	72.5	86.9
081d LATIN	13	NA	31,903	72.5	86.9
167 CHS OF CHRIST	1	25	34	.1	.1
419 SO BAPT CONV	2	487	657*	1.5	1.8
449 UN METHODIST	1	96	130*	.3	.4
496 JEWISH EST1	0	NA	53	.1	.1
497 BLACK BAPT EST2	NA	2,883	3,891*	8.8	10.6
SAINT MARY	**59**	**12,445**	**45,587***	**78.5**	**100.0**
053 ASSEMB OF GOD	3	463	706	1.2	1.5
081 CATHOLIC	18	NA	28,460	49.0	62.4
081d LATIN	18	NA	28,460	49.0	62.4
089 CHR & MISS AL	1	39	69	.1	.2
111 CH CR,SCIENTST	1	NR	NR	-	-
123 CH GOD (ANDER)	1	10	30	.1	.1
145 CH GOD PROPHCY	2	51	69*	.1	.2
151 L-D SAINTS	2	NA	212	.4	.5
167 CHS OF CHRIST	3	128	194	.3	.4
193 EPISCOPAL	2	187	267	.5	.6
283 LUTH—MO SYNOD	1	63	92	.2	.2
355 PRESB CH (USA)	3	129	174*	.3	.4
419 SO BAPT CONV	10	5,308	7,146*	12.3	15.7
449 UN METHODIST	11	1,972	2,655*	4.6	5.8
496 JEWISH EST1	1	NA	0	-	-
497 BLACK BAPT EST2	NA	4,095	5,513*	9.5	12.1
SAINT TAMMANY	**118**	**31,847**	**85,939***	**59.5**	**100.0**
005 AME ZION	1	145	216	.1	.3
053 ASSEMB OF GOD	6	775	1,106	.8	1.3
059 BAPT MISS ASSN	2	685	903*	.6	1.1
081 CATHOLIC	14	NA	40,557	28.1	47.2
081d LATIN	14	NA	40,557	28.1	47.2
093 CHR CH (DISC)	2	541	661	.5	.8
097 CHR CHS&CHS CR	1	41	54*	-	.1
111 CH CR,SCIENTST	2	NR	NR	-	-
123 CH GOD (ANDER)	2	75	76	.1	.1
127 CH GOD (CLEVE)	6	845	1,114*	.8	1.3
145 CH GOD PROPHCY	3	78	103*	.1	.1
151 L-D SAINTS	4	NA	1,069	.7	1.2
165 CH OF NAZARENE	3	138	320	.2	.4
167 CHS OF CHRIST	3	401	605	.4	.7
193 EPISCOPAL	3	896	1,570	1.1	1.8
203 EVAN FREE CH	1	0	170	.1	.2
207 E.L.C.A.	2	336	516	.4	.6
266 INTRSTAT & ASC	6	536	706*	.5	.8
283 LUTH—MO SYNOD	3	1,238	1,649	1.1	1.9
353 CHR BRETHREN	3	139	199	.1	.2
355 PRESB CH (USA)	5	1,306	1,721*	1.2	2.0
356 PRESB CH AMER	1	72	98	.1	.1
413 S.D.A.	3	303	399*	.3	.5
419 SO BAPT CONV	27	13,033	17,177*	11.9	20.0

County and Denomination	Number of churches	Communicant, confirmed, full members	Total adherents Number	Percent of total population	Percent of total adherents
435 UNITARIAN-UNIV	1	110	175	.1	.2
449 UN METHODIST	13	5,666	7,467*	5.2	8.7
469 WELS	1	102	137	.1	.2
496 JEWISH EST1	0	NA	1,391	1.0	1.6
497 BLACK BAPT EST2	NA	4,386	5,780*	4.0	6.7
TANGIPAHOA	**121**	**32,990**	**49,335***	**57.6**	**100.0**
005 AME ZION	11	5,595	6,660	7.8	13.5
053 ASSEMB OF GOD	4	728	996	1.2	2.0
059 BAPT MISS ASSN	4	299	393*	.5	.8
081 CATHOLIC	8	NA	5,874	6.9	11.9
081d LATIN	8	NA	5,874	6.9	11.9
093 CHR CH (DISC)	1	109	165	.2	.3
111 CH CR,SCIENTST	1	NR	NR	-	-
121 CH GOD (ABR)	1	52	68*	.1	.1
123 CH GOD (ANDER)	2	136	146	.2	.3
127 CH GOD (CLEVE)	3	192	252*	.3	.5
145 CH GOD PROPHCY	2	51	67*	.1	.1
151 L-D SAINTS	2	NA	719	.8	1.5
165 CH OF NAZARENE	1	2	0	-	-
167 CHS OF CHRIST	10	466	592	.7	1.2
171 CH GOD-GEN CON	1	62	81*	.1	.2
193 EPISCOPAL	3	380	546	.6	1.1
266 INTRSTAT & ASC	4	341	448*	.5	.9
283 LUTH—MO SYNOD	1	195	262	.3	.5
339 PENT CH OF GOD	1	35	76	.1	.2
355 PRESB CH (USA)	3	423	556*	.6	1.1
413 S.D.A.	2	463	608*	.7	1.2
419 SO BAPT CONV	45	15,965	20,977*	24.5	42.5
449 UN METHODIST	11	2,018	2,651*	3.1	5.4
497 BLACK BAPT EST2	NA	5,478	7,198*	8.4	14.6
TENSAS	**21**	**3,649**	**4,935***	**69.5**	**100.0**
081 CATHOLIC	1	NA	79	1.1	1.6
081d LATIN	1	NA	79	1.1	1.6
123 CH GOD (ANDER)	1	0	0	-	-
145 CH GOD PROPHCY	1	25	33*	.5	.7
167 CHS OF CHRIST	2	55	80	1.1	1.6
193 EPISCOPAL	2	90	113	1.6	2.3
355 PRESB CH (USA)	2	84	112*	1.6	2.3
419 SO BAPT CONV	8	1,935	2,575*	36.3	52.2
449 UN METHODIST	4	280	373*	5.3	7.6
497 BLACK BAPT EST2	NA	1,180	1,570*	22.1	31.8
TERREBONNE	**51**	**14,945**	**66,031***	**68.1**	**100.0**
053 ASSEMB OF GOD	4	363	532	.5	.8
081 CATHOLIC	21	NA	45,243	46.7	68.5
081d LATIN	21	NA	45,243	46.7	68.5
127 CH GOD (CLEVE)	3	220	297*	.3	.4
145 CH GOD PROPHCY	1	25	34*		.1
151 L-D SAINTS	1	NA	296	.3	.4
165 CH OF NAZARENE	1	10	0	-	-
167 CHS OF CHRIST	2	263	305	.3	.5
176 CCC, NOT NAT'L	2	95	128*	.1	.2
193 EPISCOPAL	2	272	718	.7	1.1
216 EVAN PRESBY CH	1	124	129	.1	.2
283 LUTH—MO SYNOD	1	235	360	.4	.5
403 SALVATION ARMY	1	33	37	-	.1
413 S.D.A.	1	72	97*	.1	.1
419 SO BAPT CONV	7	7,451	10,054*	10.4	15.2
449 UN METHODIST	3	1,364	1,840*	1.9	2.8
497 BLACK BAPT EST2	NA	4,418	5,961*	6.1	9.0
UNION	**77**	**13,535**	**17,656***	**85.3**	**100.0**
053 ASSEMB OF GOD	5	478	635	3.1	3.6
059 BAPT MISS ASSN	5	890	1,140*	5.5	6.5
081 CATHOLIC	1	NA	150	.7	.8
081d LATIN	1	NA	150	.7	.8
151 L-D SAINTS	1	NA	143	.7	.8
167 CHS OF CHRIST	15	980	1,265	6.1	7.2
259 IFCA	1	NR	NR	-	-
361 PRIM BAPT ASCS	2	48	61*	.3	.3
419 SO BAPT CONV	38	8,548	10,945*	52.9	62.0
449 UN METHODIST	9	793	1,015*	4.9	5.7
497 BLACK BAPT EST2	NA	1,798	2,302*	11.1	13.0
VERMILION	**39**	**4,694**	**42,974***	**85.9**	**100.0**
053 ASSEMB OF GOD	2	252	439	.9	1.0
081 CATHOLIC	17	NA	36,648	73.2	85.3
081d LATIN	17	NA	36,648	73.2	85.3
097 CHR CHS&CHS CR	1	30	40*	.1	.1
127 CH GOD (CLEVE)	1	10	13*	-	-
167 CHS OF CHRIST	2	71	110	.2	.3
193 EPISCOPAL	1	94	110	.2	.3
355 PRESB CH (USA)	1	37	49*	.1	.1

NA–Not applicable   NR–Not reported   *Total adherents estimated from known number of communicant, confirmed, full members.   - Represents a percent less than 0.1.   Percentages may not total due to rounding.
[1]See Appendix E   [2]See Appendix F   [3]See Appendix G   Lines in *italic* represent a breakdown of Catholic rites or Friends affiliations. They are included in their respective denominational total.

Table 4. Churches and Church Membership by County and Denomination: 1990

County and Denomination	Number of churches	Communicant, confirmed, full members	Total adherents: Number	Percent of total population	Percent of total adherents
419 SO BAPT CONV	5	1,541	2,042*	4.1	4.8
443 UN C OF CHRIST	3	112	148*	.3	.3
449 UN METHODIST	6	994	1,317*	2.6	3.1
497 BLACK BAPT EST[2]	NA	1,553	2,058*	4.1	4.8
VERNON	**79**	**19,683**	**27,981***	**45.2**	**100.0**
053 ASSEMB OF GOD	6	695	834	1.3	3.0
081 CATHOLIC	1	NA	1,500	2.4	5.4
081d LATIN	*1*	*NA*	*1,500*	*2.4*	*5.4*
093 CHR CH (DISC)	1	128	288	.5	1.0
123 CH GOD (ANDER)	2	92	105	.2	.4
151 L-D SAINTS	1	NA	458	.7	1.6
165 CH OF NAZARENE	1	24	53	.1	.2
167 CHS OF CHRIST	4	247	321	.5	1.1
193 EPISCOPAL	1	109	125	.2	.4
283 LUTH—MO SYNOD	1	89	131	.2	.5
361 PRIM BAPT ASCS	2	3	4*	-	-
419 SO BAPT CONV	53	14,779	19,518*	31.5	69.8
449 UN METHODIST	6	644	850*	1.4	3.0
497 BLACK BAPT EST[2]	NA	2,873	3,794*	6.1	13.6
WASHINGTON	**78**	**20,470**	**28,942***	**67.0**	**100.0**
053 ASSEMB OF GOD	2	57	81	.2	.3
059 BAPT MISS ASSN	2	301	387*	.9	1.3
081 CATHOLIC	2	NA	2,600	6.0	9.0
081d LATIN	*2*	*NA*	*2,600*	*6.0*	*9.0*
127 CH GOD (CLEVE)	2	43	55*	.1	.2
145 CH GOD PROPHCY	1	25	32*	.1	.1
167 CHS OF CHRIST	2	56	72	.2	.2
193 EPISCOPAL	1	74	80	.2	.3
266 INTRSTAT & ASC	17	2,168	2,789*	6.5	9.6
283 LUTH—MO SYNOD	1	89	129	.3	.4
355 PRESB CH (USA)	1	201	259*	.6	.9
413 S.D.A.	1	37	48*	.1	.2
419 SO BAPT CONV	33	12,712	16,354*	37.9	56.5
449 UN METHODIST	12	1,720	2,213*	5.1	7.6
496 JEWISH EST[1]	1	NA	0	-	-
497 BLACK BAPT EST[2]	NA	2,987	3,843*	8.9	13.3
WEBSTER	**78**	**21,451**	**28,339***	**67.5**	**100.0**
053 ASSEMB OF GOD	9	715	1,033	2.5	3.6
059 BAPT MISS ASSN	6	1,632	2,074*	4.9	7.3
081 CATHOLIC	3	NA	772	1.8	2.7
081d LATIN	*3*	*NA*	*772*	*1.8*	*2.7*
093 CHR CH (DISC)	1	20	29	.1	.1
097 CHR CHS&CHS CR	1	93	118*	.3	.4
127 CH GOD (CLEVE)	1	23	29*	.1	.1
151 L-D SAINTS	1	NA	103	.2	.4
165 CH OF NAZARENE	2	12	0	-	-
167 CHS OF CHRIST	9	535	742	1.8	2.6
193 EPISCOPAL	1	177	249	.6	.9
355 PRESB CH (USA)	2	258	328*	.8	1.2
413 S.D.A.	2	112	142*	.3	.5
419 SO BAPT CONV	24	12,238	15,556*	37.0	54.9
449 UN METHODIST	16	2,671	3,395*	8.1	12.0
497 BLACK BAPT EST[2]	NA	2,965	3,769*	9.0	13.3
WEST BATON ROUGE	**9**	**3,287**	**10,720***	**55.2**	**100.0**
081 CATHOLIC	2	NA	6,346	32.7	59.2
081d LATIN	*2*	*NA*	*6,346*	*32.7*	*59.2*
167 CHS OF CHRIST	1	84	114	.6	1.1
355 PRESB CH (USA)	1	87	115*	.6	1.1
419 SO BAPT CONV	4	1,541	2,028*	10.4	18.9
449 UN METHODIST	1	188	247*	1.3	2.3
496 JEWISH EST[1]	0	NA	45	.2	.4
497 BLACK BAPT EST[2]	NA	1,387	1,825*	9.4	17.0
WEST CARROLL	**37**	**7,355**	**9,938***	**82.2**	**100.0**
053 ASSEMB OF GOD	3	156	275	2.3	2.8
081 CATHOLIC	1	NA	270	2.2	2.7
081d LATIN	*1*	*NA*	*270*	*2.2*	*2.7*
123 CH GOD (ANDER)	5	349	531	4.4	5.3
167 CHS OF CHRIST	3	152	198	1.6	2.0
361 PRIM BAPT ASCS	1	38	49*	.4	.5
419 SO BAPT CONV	17	5,680	7,347*	60.8	73.9
449 UN METHODIST	7	538	696*	5.8	7.0
497 BLACK BAPT EST[2]	NA	442	572*	4.7	5.8
WEST FELICIANA	**9**	**3,776**	**8,250***	**63.9**	**100.0**
081 CATHOLIC	1	NA	3,726	28.9	45.2
081d LATIN	*1*	*NA*	*3,726*	*28.9*	*45.2*
193 EPISCOPAL	1	248	347	2.7	4.2
419 SO BAPT CONV	3	957	1,133*	8.8	13.7
449 UN METHODIST	4	342	405*	3.1	4.9
497 BLACK BAPT EST[2]	NA	2,229	2,639*	20.4	32.0
WINN	**56**	**9,611**	**12,752***	**78.4**	**100.0**
053 ASSEMB OF GOD	5	271	387	2.4	3.0
081 CATHOLIC	2	NA	225	1.4	1.8
081d LATIN	*2*	*NA*	*225*	*1.4*	*1.8*
127 CH GOD (CLEVE)	1	93	119*	.7	.9
151 L-D SAINTS	1	NA	179	1.1	1.4
165 CH OF NAZARENE	1	46	45	.3	.4
167 CHS OF CHRIST	4	196	257	1.6	2.0
193 EPISCOPAL	1	52	64	.4	.5
355 PRESB CH (USA)	1	70	90*	.6	.7
419 SO BAPT CONV	35	6,832	8,757*	53.8	68.7
449 UN METHODIST	5	555	711*	4.4	5.6
497 BLACK BAPT EST[2]	NA	1,496	1,918*	11.8	15.0

MAINE

County and Denomination	Number of churches	Communicant, confirmed, full members	Total adherents: Number	Percent of total population	Percent of total adherents
THE STATE.....	1,336	123,672	447,053*	36.4	100.0
ANDROSCOGGIN	**71**	**6,912**	**46,620***	**44.3**	**100.0**
001 ADVENT CHR CH	2	115	144*	.1	.3
019 AMER BAPT USA	7	1,741	2,187*	2.1	4.7
053 ASSEMB OF GOD	2	295	445	.4	1.0
081 CATHOLIC	14	NA	35,130	33.4	75.4
081d LATIN	*14*	*NA*	*35,130*	*33.4*	*75.4*
111 CH CR,SCIENTST	1	NR	NR	-	-
127 CH GOD (CLEVE)	1	34	43*	-	.1
151 L-D SAINTS	2	NA	631	.6	1.4
157 CH OF BRETHREN	1	51	64*	.1	.1
165 CH OF NAZARENE	5	288	779	.7	1.7
176 CCC, NOT NAT'L	3	151	190*	.2	.4
179 CONSRV BAPT	2	NR	NR	-	-
193 EPISCOPAL	3	387	872	.8	1.9
207 E.L.C.A.	1	152	263	.2	.6
226 FRIENDS-USA	2	178	200	.2	.4
226d FGC & FUM	*2*	*178*	*200*	*.2*	*.4*
246 GREEK ORTHODOX	1	NR	NR	-	-
355 PRESB CH (USA)	3	341	428*	.4	.9
403 SALVATION ARMY	1	101	122	.1	.3
413 S.D.A.	1	102	128*	.1	.3
419 SO BAPT CONV	1	326	410*	.4	.9
435 UNITARIAN-UNIV	1	138	218	.2	.5
443 UN C OF CHRIST	5	787	989*	.9	2.1
449 UN METHODIST	8	1,725	2,167*	2.1	4.6
496 JEWISH EST[1]	2	NA	500	.5	1.1
499 INDEP.NON-CHAR[3]	2	NA	710	.7	1.5
AROOSTOOK	**121**	**10,462**	**47,424***	**54.6**	**100.0**
001 ADVENT CHR CH	6	411	513*	.6	1.1
019 AMER BAPT USA	16	3,612	4,506*	5.2	9.5
053 ASSEMB OF GOD	7	561	791	.9	1.7
057 BAPT GEN CONF	2	163	203*	.2	.4
081 CATHOLIC	33	NA	32,706	37.6	69.0
081d LATIN	*33*	*NA*	*32,706*	*37.6*	*69.0*
089 CHR & MISS AL	1	25	50	.1	.1
111 CH CR,SCIENTST	1	NR	NR	-	-
151 L-D SAINTS	2	NA	441	.5	.9
165 CH OF NAZARENE	2	28	104	.1	.2
167 CHS OF CHRIST	2	57	90	.1	.2
179 CONSRV BAPT	1	NR	NR	-	-
193 EPISCOPAL	6	600	999	1.1	2.1
207 E.L.C.A.	3	495	655	.8	1.4
223 FREE WILL BAPT	1	87	109*	.1	.2
349 PENT HOLINESS	1	10	12*	-	-
403 SALVATION ARMY	1	53	55	.1	.1
413 S.D.A.	2	116	145*	.2	.3
419 SO BAPT CONV	1	282	352*	.4	.7
435 UNITARIAN-UNIV	3	143	163	.2	.3
443 UN C OF CHRIST	10	701	875*	1.0	1.8
449 UN METHODIST	14	2,579	3,218*	3.7	6.8
467 WESLEYAN	6	393	1,255	1.4	2.6
497 BLACK BAPT EST[2]	NA	146	182*	.2	.4
CUMBERLAND	**200**	**27,604**	**85,743***	**35.3**	**100.0**
001 ADVENT CHR CH	3	187	230*	.1	.3
005 AME ZION	1	209	254	.1	.3
019 AMER BAPT USA	15	2,466	3,029*	1.2	3.5
053 ASSEMB OF GOD	8	683	1,303	.5	1.5
081 CATHOLIC	30	NA	43,197	17.8	50.4
081d LATIN	*30*	*NA*	*43,197*	*17.8*	*50.4*
089 CHR & MISS AL	4	164	348	.1	.4
097 CHR CHS&CHS CR	3	96	118*	-	.1

NA–Not applicable NR–Not reported *Total adherents estimated from known number of communicant, confirmed, full members. - Represents a percent less than 0.1. Percentages may not total due to rounding.
[1]See Appendix E [2]See Appendix F [3]See Appendix G Lines in *italic* represent a breakdown of Catholic rites or Friends affiliations. They are included in their respective denominational total.

Table 4. Churches and Church Membership by County and Denomination: 1990

County and Denomination	Number of churches	Communicant, confirmed, full members	Total adherents Number	Total adherents Percent of total population	Total adherents Percent of total adherents
111 CH CR,SCIENTST	2	NR	NR	-	-
127 CH GOD (CLEVE)	1	237	291*	.1	.3
145 CH GOD PROPHCY	1	28	34*	-	-
151 L-D SAINTS	3	NA	1,299	.5	1.5
157 CH OF BRETHREN	1	17	21*	-	-
165 CH OF NAZARENE	9	1,030	1,546	.6	1.8
167 CHS OF CHRIST	4	109	167	.1	.2
175 CONGR CHR CHS	2	330	405*	.2	.5
176 CCC, NOT NAT'L	1	544	668*	.3	.8
179 CONSRV BAPT	7	NR	NR	-	-
193 EPISCOPAL	11	2,652	4,388	1.8	5.1
203 EVAN FREE CH	2	142	250	.1	.3
207 E.L.C.A.	6	1,124	1,578	.6	1.8
221 FREE METHODIST	1	23	30	-	-
226 FRIENDS-USA	3	150	150	.1	.2
226d FGC & FUM	3	150	150	.1	.2
246 GREEK ORTHODOX	1	NR	NR	-	-
283 LUTH—MO SYNOD	1	213	386	.2	.5
285 MENNONITE CH	1	40	82	-	.1
353 CHR BRETHREN	1	45	75	-	.1
403 SALVATION ARMY	1	170	183	.1	.2
413 S.D.A.	6	805	989*	.4	1.2
419 SO BAPT CONV	2	648	796*	.3	.9
435 UNITARIAN-UNIV	5	996	1,413	.6	1.6
443 UN C OF CHRIST	33	9,245	11,354*	4.7	13.2
449 UN METHODIST	26	4,888	6,003*	2.5	7.0
469 WELS	1	60	84	-	.1
496 JEWISH EST[1]	3	NA	3,900	1.6	4.5
497 BLACK BAPT EST[2]	NA	303	372*	.2	.4
499 INDEP.NON-CHAR[3]	1	NA	800	.3	.9
FRANKLIN	**47**	**3,025**	**10,467***	**36.1**	**100.0**
019 AMER BAPT USA	3	397	499*	1.7	4.8
053 ASSEMB OF GOD	2	80	153	.5	1.5
081 CATHOLIC	8	NA	5,886	20.3	56.2
081d LATIN	8	NA	5,886	20.3	56.2
097 CHR CHS&CHS CR	1	0	0*	-	-
111 CH CR,SCIENTST	1	NR	NR	-	-
151 L-D SAINTS	1	NA	296	1.0	2.8
165 CH OF NAZARENE	2	133	252	.9	2.4
167 CHS OF CHRIST	2	34	57	.2	.5
176 CCC, NOT NAT'L	1	33	41*	.1	.4
179 CONSRV BAPT	1	NR	NR	-	-
181 CONSRV CONGR	1	13	16*	.1	.2
193 EPISCOPAL	2	344	742	2.6	7.1
226 FRIENDS-USA	1	3	26	.1	.2
226d FGC & FUM	1	3	26	.1	.2
355 PRESB CH (USA)	2	91	114*	.4	1.1
413 S.D.A.	3	93	117*	.4	1.1
443 UN C OF CHRIST	8	906	1,139*	3.9	10.9
449 UN METHODIST	8	898	1,129*	3.9	10.8
HANCOCK	**97**	**5,965**	**11,422***	**24.3**	**100.0**
001 ADVENT CHR CH	2	110	136*	.3	1.2
019 AMER BAPT USA	16	1,506	1,864*	4.0	16.3
053 ASSEMB OF GOD	2	93	188	.4	1.6
081 CATHOLIC	8	NA	3,446	7.3	30.2
081d LATIN	8	NA	3,446	7.3	30.2
111 CH CR,SCIENTST	3	NR	NR	-	-
127 CH GOD (CLEVE)	4	113	140*	.3	1.2
151 L-D SAINTS	1	NA	129	.3	1.1
165 CH OF NAZARENE	2	89	183	.4	1.6
167 CHS OF CHRIST	1	14	21	-	.2
176 CCC, NOT NAT'L	3	280	347*	.7	3.0
179 CONSRV BAPT	1	NR	NR	-	-
193 EPISCOPAL	8	719	1,210	2.6	10.6
207 E.L.C.A.	1	121	153	.3	1.3
226 FRIENDS-USA	3	77	95*	.2	.8
226d FGC & FUM	3	77	95*	.2	.8
259 IFCA	1	NR	NR	-	-
413 S.D.A.	1	30	37*	.1	.3
435 UNITARIAN-UNIV	2	156	184	.4	1.6
443 UN C OF CHRIST	21	1,707	2,113*	4.5	18.5
449 UN METHODIST	17	950	1,176*	2.5	10.3
KENNEBEC	**116**	**11,957**	**49,846***	**43.0**	**100.0**
001 ADVENT CHR CH	2	235	293*	.3	.6
019 AMER BAPT USA	22	3,239	4,035*	3.5	8.1
053 ASSEMB OF GOD	2	263	290	.3	.6
081 CATHOLIC	19	NA	32,570	28.1	65.3
081d LATIN	18	NA	31,454	27.1	63.1
081e MARONITE	1	NA	1,116	1.0	2.2
089 CHR & MISS AL	1	28	67	.1	.1
111 CH CR,SCIENTST	2	NR	NR	-	-
127 CH GOD (CLEVE)	3	207	258*	.2	.5
151 L-D SAINTS	2	NA	549	.5	1.1

County and Denomination	Number of churches	Communicant, confirmed, full members	Total adherents Number	Total adherents Percent of total population	Total adherents Percent of total adherents
165 CH OF NAZARENE	4	398	591	.5	1.2
167 CHS OF CHRIST	2	69	88	.1	.2
176 CCC, NOT NAT'L	1	18	22*	-	-
179 CONSRV BAPT	3	NR	NR	-	-
181 CONSRV CONGR	1	39	49*	-	.1
193 EPISCOPAL	6	926	1,447	1.2	2.9
203 EVAN FREE CH	1	37	80	.1	.2
207 E.L.C.A.	1	345	555	.5	1.1
221 FREE METHODIST	1	50	62	.1	.1
226 FRIENDS-USA	4	180	219	.2	.4
226d FGC & FUM	4	180	219	.2	.4
263 INT FOURSQ GOS	1	155	193*	.2	.4
283 LUTH—MO SYNOD	1	85	104	.1	.2
285 MENNONITE CH	1	28	44	-	.1
353 CHR BRETHREN	1	13	60	.1	.1
403 SALVATION ARMY	2	87	100	.1	.2
413 S.D.A.	1	79	98*	.1	.2
419 SO BAPT CONV	1	34	42*	-	.1
435 UNITARIAN-UNIV	4	327	497	.4	1.0
443 UN C OF CHRIST	9	1,572	1,959*	1.7	3.9
449 UN METHODIST	16	3,543	4,414*	3.8	8.9
496 JEWISH EST[1]	1	NA	800	.7	1.6
499 INDEP.NON-CHAR[3]	1	NA	360	.3	.7
KNOX	**53**	**5,308**	**10,943***	**30.1**	**100.0**
001 ADVENT CHR CH	2	126	156*	-	1.4
019 AMER BAPT USA	11	1,710	2,117*	5.8	19.3
053 ASSEMB OF GOD	1	116	250	.7	2.3
059 BAPT MISS ASSN	1	24	30*	.1	.3
081 CATHOLIC	5	NA	3,710	10.2	33.9
081d LATIN	5	NA	3,710	10.2	33.9
111 CH CR,SCIENTST	3	NR	NR	-	-
127 CH GOD (CLEVE)	1	7	9*	-	.1
151 L-D SAINTS	1	NA	200	.6	1.8
165 CH OF NAZARENE	2	148	190	.5	1.7
175 CONGR CHR CHS	2	474	587*	1.6	5.4
176 CCC, NOT NAT'L	2	35	43*	.1	.4
179 CONSRV BAPT	1	NR	NR	-	-
193 EPISCOPAL	3	685	1,050	2.9	9.6
207 E.L.C.A.	1	135	163	.4	1.5
226 FRIENDS-USA	1	2	12	-	.1
226d FGC & FUM	1	2	12	-	.1
353 CHR BRETHREN	1	22	33	.1	.3
403 SALVATION ARMY	1	51	56	.2	.5
413 S.D.A.	1	82	102*	.3	.9
419 SO BAPT CONV	2	38	47*	.1	.4
435 UNITARIAN-UNIV	1	137	202	.6	1.8
443 UN C OF CHRIST	3	556	688*	1.9	6.3
449 UN METHODIST	7	960	1,188*	3.3	10.9
496 JEWISH EST[1]	0	NA	110	.3	1.0
LINCOLN	**46**	**3,557**	**16,654***	**54.9**	**100.0**
019 AMER BAPT USA	8	617	767*	2.5	4.6
053 ASSEMB OF GOD	1	63	89	.3	.5
081 CATHOLIC	7	NA	11,803	38.9	70.9
081d LATIN	7	NA	11,803	38.9	70.9
111 CH CR,SCIENTST	2	NR	NR	-	-
165 CH OF NAZARENE	2	110	157	.5	.9
179 CONSRV BAPT	2	NR	NR	-	-
193 EPISCOPAL	4	658	875	2.9	5.3
226 FRIENDS-USA	1	48	60*	.2	.4
226d FGC & FUM	1	48	60*	.2	.4
435 UNITARIAN-UNIV	1	51	63	.2	.4
443 UN C OF CHRIST	9	968	1,204*	4.0	7.2
449 UN METHODIST	8	1,042	1,296*	4.3	7.8
499 INDEP.NON-CHAR[3]	1	NA	340	1.1	2.0
OXFORD	**76**	**5,143**	**15,760***	**30.0**	**100.0**
001 ADVENT CHR CH	1	86	108*	.2	.7
019 AMER BAPT USA	8	572	721*	1.4	4.6
053 ASSEMB OF GOD	3	239	362	.7	2.3
081 CATHOLIC	5	NA	8,527	16.2	54.1
081d LATIN	5	NA	8,527	16.2	54.1
089 CHR & MISS AL	2	46	96	.2	.6
097 CHR CHS&CHS CR	1	35	44*	.1	.3
111 CH CR,SCIENTST	1	NR	NR	-	-
127 CH GOD (CLEVE)	1	31	39*	.1	.2
151 L-D SAINTS	3	NA	476	.9	3.0
165 CH OF NAZARENE	3	156	216	.4	1.4
167 CHS OF CHRIST	1	79	110	.2	.7
175 CONGR CHR CHS	3	406	512*	1.0	3.2
176 CCC, NOT NAT'L	2	67	84*	.2	.5
181 CONSRV CONGR	2	78	98*	.2	.6
193 EPISCOPAL	2	230	387	.7	2.5
207 E.L.C.A.	1	128	160	.3	1.0
226 FRIENDS-USA	1	3	17	-	.1

NA–Not applicable NR–Not reported *Total adherents estimated from known number of communicant, confirmed, full members. - Represents a percent less than 0.1. Percentages may not total due to rounding.
[1]See Appendix E [2]See Appendix F [3]See Appendix G Lines in *italic* represent a breakdown of Catholic rites or Friends affiliations. They are included in their respective denominational total.

Table 4. Churches and Church Membership by County and Denomination: 1990

County and Denomination	Number of churches	Communicant, confirmed, full members	Total adherents		
			Number	Percent of total population	Percent of total adherents
226d *FGC & FUM*	*1*	*3*	*17*	-	*.1*
355 PRESB CH (USA)	1	61	77*	.1	.5
413 S.D.A.	3	376	474*	.9	3.0
435 UNITARIAN-UNIV	6	156	234	.4	1.5
443 UN C OF CHRIST	19	1,579	1,991*	3.8	12.6
449 UN METHODIST	7	815	1,027*	2.0	6.5
PENOBSCOT	**131**	**13,705**	**45,421***	**31.0**	**100.0**
001 ADVENT CHR CH	1	40	49*	-	.1
019 AMER BAPT USA	16	3,070	3,785*	2.6	8.3
053 ASSEMB OF GOD	5	371	724	.5	1.6
081 CATHOLIC	21	NA	24,062	16.4	53.0
081d *LATIN*	*21*	*NA*	*24,062*	*16.4*	*53.0*
089 CHR & MISS AL	2	53	91	.1	.2
111 CH CR,SCIENTST	2	NR	NR	-	-
127 CH GOD (CLEVE)	6	396	488*	.3	1.1
151 L-D SAINTS	2	NA	725	.5	1.6
165 CH OF NAZARENE	4	458	803	.5	1.8
167 CHS OF CHRIST	3	85	120	.1	.3
175 CONGR CHR CHS	3	510	629*	.4	1.4
176 CCC, NOT NAT'L	1	97	120*	.1	.3
179 CONSRV BAPT	5	NR	NR	-	-
193 EPISCOPAL	6	953	1,265	.9	2.8
207 E.L.C.A.	1	256	398	.3	.9
226 FRIENDS-USA	1	30	34	-	.1
226d *FGC & FUM*	*1*	*30*	*34*	-	*.1*
246 GREEK ORTHODOX	1	NR	NR	-	-
263 INT FOURSQ GOS	1	42	52*	-	.1
403 SALVATION ARMY	1	107	140	.1	.3
413 S.D.A.	3	182	224*	.2	.5
435 UNITARIAN-UNIV	3	350	463	.3	1.0
443 UN C OF CHRIST	15	2,424	2,988*	2.0	6.6
449 UN METHODIST	20	4,163	5,132*	3.5	11.3
467 WESLEYAN	2	14	101	.1	.2
496 JEWISH EST[1]	3	NA	1,250	.9	2.8
497 BLACK BAPT EST[2]	NA	104	128*	.1	.3
498 INDEP.CHARIS.[3]	2	NA	1,250	.9	2.8
499 INDEP.NON-CHAR[3]	1	NA	400	.3	.9
PISCATAQUIS	**34**	**2,886**	**6,223***	**33.4**	**100.0**
001 ADVENT CHR CH	1	25	31*	.2	.5
019 AMER BAPT USA	3	665	831*	4.5	13.4
053 ASSEMB OF GOD	3	104	150	.8	2.4
081 CATHOLIC	7	NA	2,255	12.1	36.2
081d *LATIN*	*7*	*NA*	*2,255*	*12.1*	*36.2*
151 L-D SAINTS	1	NA	212	1.1	3.4
165 CH OF NAZARENE	2	70	175	.9	2.8
176 CCC, NOT NAT'L	1	1	1*	-	-
193 EPISCOPAL	2	124	158	.8	2.5
203 EVAN FREE CH	1	40	80	.4	1.3
435 UNITARIAN-UNIV	2	69	95	.5	1.5
443 UN C OF CHRIST	4	556	695*	3.7	11.2
449 UN METHODIST	7	1,232	1,540*	8.3	24.7
SAGADAHOC	**38**	**3,005**	**8,640***	**25.8**	**100.0**
019 AMER BAPT USA	8	1,002	1,275*	3.8	14.8
053 ASSEMB OF GOD	1	53	100	.3	1.2
081 CATHOLIC	3	NA	3,315	9.9	38.4
081d *LATIN*	*3*	*NA*	*3,315*	*9.9*	*38.4*
089 CHR & MISS AL	1	20	39	.1	.5
111 CH CR,SCIENTST	1	NR	NR	-	-
165 CH OF NAZARENE	5	175	648	1.9	7.5
176 CCC, NOT NAT'L	1	7	9*	-	.1
179 CONSRV BAPT	1	NR	NR	-	-
193 EPISCOPAL	1	224	530	1.6	6.1
226 FRIENDS-USA	1	20	25*	.1	.3
226d *FGC & FUM*	*1*	*20*	*25**	*.1*	*.3*
263 INT FOURSQ GOS	1	74	94*	.3	1.1
331 ORTH CH IN AM	1	NR	NR	-	-
355 PRESB CH (USA)	1	106	135*	.4	1.6
403 SALVATION ARMY	1	58	60	.2	.7
413 S.D.A.	2	145	184*	.5	2.1
443 UN C OF CHRIST	3	713	907*	2.7	10.5
449 UN METHODIST	5	408	519*	1.5	6.0
496 JEWISH EST[1]	1	NA	800	2.4	9.3
SOMERSET	**60**	**4,060**	**11,398***	**22.9**	**100.0**
019 AMER BAPT USA	6	978	1,237*	2.5	10.9
053 ASSEMB OF GOD	3	240	314	.6	2.8
081 CATHOLIC	5	NA	5,417	10.9	47.5
081d *LATIN*	*5*	*NA*	*5,417*	*10.9*	*47.5*
097 CHR CHS&CHS CR	1	0	0*	-	-
127 CH GOD (CLEVE)	1	31	39*	.1	.3
151 L-D SAINTS	1	NA	236	.5	2.1
165 CH OF NAZARENE	6	440	1,046	2.1	9.2
167 CHS OF CHRIST	1	40	62	.1	.5

County and Denomination	Number of churches	Communicant, confirmed, full members	Total adherents		
			Number	Percent of total population	Percent of total adherents
175 CONGR CHR CHS	4	279	353*	.7	3.1
179 CONSRV BAPT	3	NR	NR	-	-
193 EPISCOPAL	4	166	228	.5	2.0
203 EVAN FREE CH	1	50	125	.3	1.1
226 FRIENDS-USA	1	20	20	-	.2
226d *FGC & FUM*	*1*	*20*	*20*	-	*.2*
263 INT FOURSQ GOS	1	69	87*	.2	.8
355 PRESB CH (USA)	3	51	65*	.1	.6
413 S.D.A.	2	323	409*	.8	3.6
435 UNITARIAN-UNIV	1	50	86	.2	.8
443 UN C OF CHRIST	7	416	526*	1.1	4.6
449 UN METHODIST	9	907	1,148*	2.3	10.1
WALDO	**39**	**2,394**	**5,534***	**16.8**	**100.0**
019 AMER BAPT USA	5	526	667*	2.0	12.1
053 ASSEMB OF GOD	1	6	13	-	.2
081 CATHOLIC	3	NA	2,160	6.5	39.0
081d *LATIN*	*3*	*NA*	*2,160*	*6.5*	*39.0*
111 CH CR,SCIENTST	1	NR	NR	-	-
127 CH GOD (CLEVE)	1	207	262*	.8	4.7
145 CH GOD PROPHCY	1	28	35*	.1	.6
151 L-D SAINTS	1	NA	168	.5	3.0
165 CH OF NAZARENE	1	92	215	.7	3.9
167 CHS OF CHRIST	1	35	45	.1	.8
175 CONGR CHR CHS	2	96	122*	.4	2.2
176 CCC, NOT NAT'L	1	63	80*	.2	1.4
179 CONSRV BAPT	1	NR	NR	-	-
193 EPISCOPAL	1	83	152	.5	2.7
203 EVAN FREE CH	1	20	40	.1	.7
226 FRIENDS-USA	1	14	24	.1	.4
226d *FGC & FUM*	*1*	*14*	*24*	*.1*	*.4*
413 S.D.A.	1	26	33*	.1	.6
419 SO BAPT CONV	1	27	34*	.1	.6
443 UN C OF CHRIST	8	478	606*	1.8	11.0
449 UN METHODIST	7	693	878*	2.7	15.9
WASHINGTON	**79**	**3,813**	**8,733***	**24.7**	**100.0**
001 ADVENT CHR CH	3	115	144*	.4	1.6
011 A.W.M.C.	1	0	0*	-	-
019 AMER BAPT USA	2	399	499*	1.4	5.7
053 ASSEMB OF GOD	4	74	112	.3	1.3
081 CATHOLIC	11	NA	3,550	10.1	40.7
081d *LATIN*	*11*	*NA*	*3,550*	*10.1*	*40.7*
093 CHR CH (DISC)	1	94	115	.3	1.3
111 CH CR,SCIENTST	1	NR	NR	-	-
127 CH GOD (CLEVE)	2	119	149*	.4	1.7
151 L-D SAINTS	2	NA	153	.4	1.8
165 CH OF NAZARENE	1	19	53	.2	.6
167 CHS OF CHRIST	2	85	114	.3	1.3
175 CONGR CHR CHS	5	204	255*	.7	2.9
176 CCC, NOT NAT'L	4	177	221*	.6	2.5
179 CONSRV BAPT	1	NR	NR	-	-
193 EPISCOPAL	3	193	391	1.1	4.5
226 FRIENDS-USA	2	18	46	.1	.5
226d *FGC & FUM*	*2*	*18*	*46*	*.1*	*.5*
413 S.D.A.	2	61	76*	.2	.9
419 SO BAPT CONV	1	24	30*	.1	.3
435 UNITARIAN-UNIV	1	21	25	.1	.3
443 UN C OF CHRIST	10	684	855*	2.4	9.8
449 UN METHODIST	17	1,392	1,739*	4.9	19.9
467 WESLEYAN	3	134	206	.6	2.4
YORK	**128**	**13,876**	**66,225***	**40.2**	**100.0**
001 ADVENT CHR CH	5	353	445*	.3	.7
019 AMER BAPT USA	19	3,594	4,530*	2.8	6.8
053 ASSEMB OF GOD	7	650	1,169	.7	1.8
081 CATHOLIC	21	NA	46,709	28.4	70.5
081d *LATIN*	*21*	*NA*	*46,709*	*28.4*	*70.5*
083 CHRIST CATH CH	1	29	35	-	.1
111 CH CR,SCIENTST	3	NR	NR	-	-
151 L-D SAINTS	1	NA	441	.3	.7
165 CH OF NAZARENE	4	157	249	.2	.4
167 CHS OF CHRIST	2	75	135	.1	.2
175 CONGR CHR CHS	1	130	164*	.1	.2
176 CCC, NOT NAT'L	3	325	410*	.2	.6
179 CONSRV BAPT	3	NR	NR	-	-
181 CONSRV CONGR	1	53	67*	-	.1
193 EPISCOPAL	6	1,125	1,681	1.0	2.5
203 EVAN FREE CH	1	25	70	-	.1
207 E.L.C.A.	1	144	224	.1	.3
226 FRIENDS-USA	1	14	16	-	-
226d *FGC & FUM*	*1*	*14*	*16*	-	-
246 GREEK ORTHODOX	1	NR	NR	-	-
263 INT FOURSQ GOS	1	0	0*	-	-
403 SALVATION ARMY	2	297	321	.2	.5
413 S.D.A.	2	104	131*	.1	.2

NA–Not applicable   NR–Not reported   *Total adherents estimated from known number of communicant, confirmed, full members.   - Represents a percent less than 0.1.   Percentages may not total due to rounding.

[1] See Appendix E   [2] See Appendix F   [3] See Appendix G   Lines in *italic* represent a breakdown of Catholic rites or Friends affiliations. They are included in their respective denominational total.

Table 4. Churches and Church Membership by County and Denomination: 1990

County and Denomination	Number of churches	Communicant, confirmed, full members	Total adherents Number	Percent of total population	Percent of total adherents
419 SO BAPT CONV	1	34	43*	-	.1
435 UNITARIAN-UNIV	3	360	509	.3	.8
443 UN C OF CHRIST	19	3,472	4,376*	2.7	6.6
449 UN METHODIST	17	2,848	3,590*	2.2	5.4
496 JEWISH EST[1]	2	NA	800	.5	1.2
497 BLACK BAPT EST[2]	NA	87	110*	.1	.2
MARYLAND					
THE STATE.....	3,519	938,574	2,311,614*	48.3	100.0
ALLEGANY	143	24,027	45,483*	60.7	100.0
053 ASSEMB OF GOD	12	1,274	3,306	4.4	7.3
061 BEACHY AMISH	1	32	38*	.1	.1
071 BRETHREN (ASH)	1	15	18*	-	-
081 CATHOLIC	8	NA	11,867	15.8	26.1
081d LATIN	8	NA	11,867	15.8	26.1
093 CHR CH (DISC)	1	75	148	.2	.3
097 CHR CHS&CHS CR	1	135	162*	.2	.4
111 CH CR,SCIENTST	1	NR	NR	-	-
123 CH GOD (ANDER)	1	46	88	.1	.2
127 CH GOD (CLEVE)	1	401	482*	.6	1.1
151 L-D SAINTS	1	NA	678	.9	1.5
157 CH OF BRETHREN	5	747	898*	1.2	2.0
165 CH OF NAZARENE	4	509	806	1.1	1.8
167 CHS OF CHRIST	1	93	121	.2	.3
175 CONGR CHR CHS	1	90	108*	.1	.2
193 EPISCOPAL	6	1,037	1,574	2.1	3.5
207 E.L.C.A.	6	2,472	3,355	4.5	7.4
226 FRIENDS-USA	1	0	8	-	-
226c FGC	1	0	8	-	-
259 IFCA	1	NR	NR	-	-
283 LUTH—MO SYNOD	1	181	212	.3	.5
285 MENNONITE CH	2	153	196	.3	.4
349 PENT HOLINESS	2	113	136*	.2	.3
353 CHR BRETHREN	2	55	80	.1	.2
355 PRESB CH (USA)	7	1,107	1,331*	1.8	2.9
356 PRESB CH AMER	1	47	81	.1	.2
403 SALVATION ARMY	1	108	112	.1	.2
413 S.D.A.	1	166	200*	.3	.4
419 SO BAPT CONV	11	3,008	3,617*	4.8	8.0
435 UNITARIAN-UNIV	1	30	34	-	.1
443 UN C OF CHRIST	7	674	810*	1.1	1.8
449 UN METHODIST	49	10,912	13,121*	17.5	28.8
467 WESLEYAN	2	210	826	1.1	1.8
496 JEWISH EST[1]	2	NA	265	.4	.6
497 BLACK BAPT EST[2]	NA	337	405*	.5	.9
499 INDEP.NON-CHAR[3]	1	NA	400	.5	.9
ANNE ARUNDEL	228	72,415	173,623*	40.6	100.0
005 AME ZION	1	124	189	-	.1
019 AMER BAPT USA	1	0	0*	-	-
053 ASSEMB OF GOD	5	662	1,168	.3	.7
057 BAPT GEN CONF	1	27	34*	-	-
081 CATHOLIC	19	NA	72,508	17.0	41.8
081d LATIN	19	NA	72,508	17.0	41.8
089 CHR & MISS AL	2	61	93	-	.1
097 CHR CHS&CHS CR	2	390	485*	.1	.3
111 CH CR,SCIENTST	2	NR	NR	-	-
123 CH GOD (ANDER)	2	161	195	-	.1
127 CH GOD (CLEVE)	8	1,284	1,596*	.4	.9
145 CH GOD PROPHCY	1	30	37*	-	-
151 L-D SAINTS	6	NA	2,604	.6	1.5
157 CH OF BRETHREN	2	265	329*	.1	.2
165 CH OF NAZARENE	4	513	774	.2	.4
167 CHS OF CHRIST	3	363	412	.1	.2
193 EPISCOPAL	15	5,496	8,596	2.0	5.0
207 E.L.C.A.	12	6,502	10,121	2.4	5.8
221 FREE METHODIST	1	65	65	-	-
226 FRIENDS-USA	1	38	47*	-	-
226c FGC	1	38	47*	-	-
246 GREEK ORTHODOX	1	NR	NR	-	-
259 IFCA	1	NR	NR	-	-
265 INT PENT C CHR	1	42	42	-	-
283 LUTH—MO SYNOD	6	2,926	4,238	1.0	2.4
339 PENT CH OF GOD	1	170	300	.1	.2
355 PRESB CH (USA)	5	3,654	4,541*	1.1	2.6
356 PRESB CH AMER	7	1,494	1,787	.4	1.0
403 SALVATION ARMY	1	64	68	-	-
413 S.D.A.	6	626	778*	.2	.4
419 SO BAPT CONV	26	9,882	12,280*	2.9	7.1
435 UNITARIAN-UNIV	1	278	430	.1	.2

County and Denomination	Number of churches	Communicant, confirmed, full members	Total adherents Number	Percent of total population	Percent of total adherents
438 UN BRETH IN CR	1	119	119	-	.1
443 UN C OF CHRIST	1	114	142*	-	.1
449 UN METHODIST	72	25,840	32,111*	7.5	18.5
467 WESLEYAN	3	125	270	.1	.2
496 JEWISH EST[1]	3	NA	2,000	.5	1.2
497 BLACK BAPT EST[2]	NA	11,100	13,794*	3.2	7.9
498 INDEP.CHARIS.[3]	2	NA	600	.1	.3
499 INDEP.NON-CHAR[3]	2	NA	870	.2	.5
BALTIMORE	374	109,627	364,351*	52.6	100.0
005 AME ZION	1	57	100	-	-
019 AMER BAPT USA	1	512	621*	.1	.2
053 ASSEMB OF GOD	16	3,001	5,586	.8	1.5
055 AS REF PRES CH	1	150	172	-	-
075 BRETHREN IN CR	1	19	25	-	-
081 CATHOLIC	37	NA	164,219	23.7	45.1
081b BYZAN RUTH	1	NA	130	-	-
081d LATIN	34	NA	163,134	23.6	44.8
081h UKRAINIAN	2	NA	955	.1	.3
089 CHR & MISS AL	1	24	47	-	-
093 CHR CH (DISC)	1	80	105	-	-
097 CHR CHS&CHS CR	6	464	562*	.1	.2
111 CH CR,SCIENTST	3	NR	NR	-	-
123 CH GOD (ANDER)	3	220	250	-	.1
127 CH GOD (CLEVE)	7	1,101	1,335*	.2	.4
145 CH GOD PROPHCY	1	30	36*	-	-
151 L-D SAINTS	4	NA	2,155	.3	.6
157 CH OF BRETHREN	3	215	261*	-	.1
165 CH OF NAZARENE	2	169	306	-	.1
167 CHS OF CHRIST	7	2,273	2,607	.4	.7
193 EPISCOPAL	24	7,532	11,056	1.6	3.0
199 EVAN CONGR CH	2	123	278	-	.1
203 EVAN FREE CH	1	40	50	-	-
207 E.L.C.A.	28	12,717	18,868	2.7	5.2
216 EVAN PRESBY CH	1	274	281	-	.1
223 FREE WILL BAPT	1	183	222*	-	.1
226 FRIENDS-USA	2	54	65*	-	-
226d FGC & FUM	2	54	65*	-	-
265 INT PENT C CHR	1	31	31	-	-
283 LUTH—MO SYNOD	14	4,718	6,792	1.0	1.9
285 MENNONITE CH	2	60	137	-	-
329 OPEN BIBLE STD	1	NR	NR	-	-
349 PENT HOLINESS	1	388	470*	.1	.1
353 CHR BRETHREN	5	516	780	.1	.2
355 PRESB CH (USA)	8	1,446	1,753*	.3	.5
356 PRESB CH AMER	8	2,205	2,570	.4	.7
375 REF EPISCOPAL	3	694	794	.1	.2
403 SALVATION ARMY	4	399	422	.1	.1
413 S.D.A.	4	495	600*	.1	.2
419 SO BAPT CONV	37	13,461	16,316*	2.4	4.5
435 UNITARIAN-UNIV	3	692	865	.1	.2
443 UN C OF CHRIST	6	2,245	2,721*	.4	.7
449 UN METHODIST	101	34,109	41,345*	6.0	11.3
469 WELS	1	156	210	-	-
496 JEWISH EST[1]	9	NA	48,701	7.0	13.4
497 BLACK BAPT EST[2]	NA	18,774	22,757*	3.3	6.2
498 INDEP.CHARIS.[3]	6	NA	3,375	.5	.9
499 INDEP.NON-CHAR[3]	6	NA	4,505	.7	1.2
BALTIMORE CITY	423	157,037	340,680*	46.3	100.0
005 AME ZION	4	5,175	5,817	.8	1.7
019 AMER BAPT USA	17	10,980	13,704*	1.9	4.0
053 ASSEMB OF GOD	4	310	674	.1	.2
081 CATHOLIC	57	NA	93,032	12.6	27.3
081d LATIN	57	NA	93,032	12.6	27.3
089 CHR & MISS AL	3	338	585	.1	.2
093 CHR CH (DISC)	9	902	1,322	.2	.4
097 CHR CHS&CHS CR	1	300	374*	.1	.1
111 CH CR,SCIENTST	4	NR	NR	-	-
123 CH GOD (ANDER)	3	357	357	-	.1
127 CH GOD (CLEVE)	14	2,570	3,208*	.4	.9
145 CH GOD PROPHCY	3	91	114*	-	-
157 CH OF BRETHREN	2	284	354*	-	.1
165 CH OF NAZARENE	2	101	69	-	-
181 CONSRV CONGR	1	43	54*	-	-
193 EPISCOPAL	32	9,167	14,028	1.9	4.1
195 ESTONIAN ELC	1	224	280*	-	.1
207 E.L.C.A.	36	10,853	16,019	2.2	4.7
221 FREE METHODIST	3	190	218	-	.1
223 FREE WILL BAPT	1	22	27*	-	-
226 FRIENDS-USA	2	613	765*	.1	.2
226c FGC	1	484	604*	.1	.2
226d FGC & FUM	1	129	161*	-	-
246 GREEK ORTHODOX	3	NR	NR	-	-
259 IFCA	1	NR	NR	-	-
283 LUTH—MO SYNOD	11	3,308	4,675	.6	1.4
331 ORTH CH IN AM	1	NR	NR	-	-

NA–Not applicable   NR–Not reported   *Total adherents estimated from known number of communicant, confirmed, full members.   - Represents a percent less than 0.1.   Percentages may not total due to rounding.
[1]See Appendix E   [2]See Appendix F   [3]See Appendix G   Lines in italic represent a breakdown of Catholic rites or Friends affiliations. They are included in their respective denominational total.

188

Table 4. Churches and Church Membership by County and Denomination: 1990

County and Denomination	Number of churches	Communicant, confirmed, full members	Total adherents		
			Number	Percent of total population	Percent of total adherents
353 CHR BRETHREN	4	259	405	.1	.1
355 PRESB CH (USA)	29	9,707	12,115*	1.6	3.6
356 PRESB CH AMER	12	1,751	2,054	.3	.6
413 S.D.A.	8	2,032	2,536*	.3	.7
419 SO BAPT CONV	24	4,589	5,727*	.8	1.7
423 SYRIAN ANTIOCH	1	NA	500	.1	.1
435 UNITARIAN-UNIV	1	10	10	-	-
443 UN C OF CHRIST	14	2,906	3,627*	.5	1.1
449 UN METHODIST	72	20,944	26,139*	3.6	7.7
467 WESLEYAN	2	79	61	-	-
496 JEWISH EST[1]	41	NA	45,799	6.2	13.4
497 BLACK BAPT EST[2]	NA	68,932	86,031*	11.7	25.3
CALVERT	**43**	**8,872**	**17,957***	**35.0**	**100.0**
053 ASSEMB OF GOD	2	138	251	.5	1.4
081 CATHOLIC	5	NA	6,000	11.7	33.4
081d LATIN	5	NA	6,000	11.7	33.4
151 L-D SAINTS	1	NA	323	.6	1.8
167 CHS OF CHRIST	1	64	83	.2	.5
193 EPISCOPAL	4	859	1,257	2.4	7.0
259 IFCA	1	NR	NR	-	-
283 LUTH—MO SYNOD	1	187	233	.5	1.3
356 PRESB CH AMER	1	216	236	.5	1.3
413 S.D.A.	2	154	199*	.4	1.1
419 SO BAPT CONV	3	415	536*	1.0	3.0
449 UN METHODIST	21	5,048	6,523*	12.7	36.3
467 WESLEYAN	1	23	31	.1	.2
497 BLACK BAPT EST[2]	NA	1,768	2,285*	4.4	12.7
CAROLINE	**52**	**6,976**	**11,470***	**42.4**	**100.0**
081 CATHOLIC	3	NA	1,962	7.3	17.1
081d LATIN	3	NA	1,962	7.3	17.1
123 CH GOD (ANDER)	1	58	82	.3	.7
127 CH GOD (CLEVE)	3	422	534*	2.0	4.7
145 CH GOD PROPHCY	1	30	38*	.1	.3
157 CH OF BRETHREN	2	171	216*	.8	1.9
165 CH OF NAZARENE	1	124	268	1.0	2.3
167 CHS OF CHRIST	1	19	24	.1	.2
193 EPISCOPAL	2	97	190	.7	1.7
283 LUTH—MO SYNOD	1	354	492	1.8	4.3
339 PENT CH OF GOD	1	60	150	.6	1.3
413 S.D.A.	1	58	73*	.3	.6
419 SO BAPT CONV	3	413	522*	1.9	4.6
449 UN METHODIST	27	4,194	5,306*	19.6	46.3
467 WESLEYAN	5	182	609	2.3	5.3
497 BLACK BAPT EST[2]	NA	794	1,004*	3.7	8.8
CARROLL	**131**	**28,109**	**56,126***	**45.5**	**100.0**
053 ASSEMB OF GOD	2	274	685	.6	1.2
055 AS REF PRES CH	1	35	54	-	.1
071 BRETHREN (ASH)	1	103	131*	.1	.2
081 CATHOLIC	4	NA	18,258	14.8	32.5
081d LATIN	4	NA	18,258	14.8	32.5
097 CHR CHS&CHS CR	1	132	167*	.1	.3
111 CH CR,SCIENTST	1	NR	NR	-	-
127 CH GOD (CLEVE)	2	212	269*	.2	.5
151 L-D SAINTS	1	NA	277	.2	.5
157 CH OF BRETHREN	8	1,543	1,958*	1.6	3.5
165 CH OF NAZARENE	2	105	246	.2	.4
167 CHS OF CHRIST	1	73	120	.1	.2
171 CH GOD-GEN CON	3	158	200*	.2	.4
193 EPISCOPAL	3	725	1,308	1.1	2.3
207 E.L.C.A.	23	6,707	9,475*	7.7	16.9
221 FREE METHODIST	1	18	31	-	.1
226 FRIENDS-USA	1	19	24*	-	-
226d FGC & FUM	1	19	24*	-	-
263 INT FOURSQ GOS	1	57	72*	.1	.1
283 LUTH—MO SYNOD	1	185	266	.2	.5
284 LUTH CH-AM ASC	1	47	65	.1	.1
285 MENNONITE CH	2	22	34	-	.1
286 E.PA MENNONITE	1	42	53*	-	.1
355 PRESB CH (USA)	3	479	608*	.5	1.1
356 PRESB CH AMER	1	51	68	.1	.1
375 REF EPISCOPAL	1	91	146	.1	.3
413 S.D.A.	1	181	230*	.2	.4
419 SO BAPT CONV	9	2,849	3,615*	2.9	6.4
443 UN C OF CHRIST	10	2,532	3,213*	2.6	5.7
449 UN METHODIST	44	10,825	13,736*	11.1	24.5
496 JEWISH EST[1]	1	NA	0	-	-
497 BLACK BAPT EST[2]	NA	644	817*	.7	1.5
CECIL	**81**	**13,794**	**23,628***	**33.1**	**100.0**
001 ADVENT CHR CH	1	26	33*	-	.1
053 ASSEMB OF GOD	1	335	250	.4	1.1
081 CATHOLIC	7	NA	5,378	7.5	22.8
081d LATIN	6	NA	5,228	7.3	22.1

County and Denomination	Number of churches	Communicant, confirmed, full members	Total adherents		
			Number	Percent of total population	Percent of total adherents
081h UKRAINIAN	1	NA	150	.2	.6
127 CH GOD (CLEVE)	3	208	264*	.4	1.1
145 CH GOD PROPHCY	1	30	38*	.1	.2
157 CH OF BRETHREN	1	14	18*	-	.1
165 CH OF NAZARENE	3	294	397	.6	1.7
167 CHS OF CHRIST	4	116	157	.2	.7
193 EPISCOPAL	5	1,008	1,324	1.9	5.6
203 EVAN FREE CH	1	34	75	.1	.3
207 E.L.C.A.	1	122	157	.2	.7
285 MENNONITE CH	1	17	23	-	.1
325 OLD REG BAPT	1	48	61*	.1	.3
355 PRESB CH (USA)	6	811	1,031*	1.4	4.4
356 PRESB CH AMER	1	76	150	.2	.6
386 REGULAR BAPT	1	104	132*	.2	.6
413 S.D.A.	3	339	431*	.6	1.8
419 SO BAPT CONV	8	3,983	5,064*	7.1	21.4
449 UN METHODIST	30	5,517	7,015d	9.8	29.7
497 BLACK BAPT EST[2]	NA	712	905*	1.3	3.8
499 INDEP.NON-CHAR[3]	2	NA	725	1.0	3.1
CHARLES	**65**	**15,250**	**46,666***	**46.1**	**100.0**
053 ASSEMB OF GOD	3	172	238	.2	.5
081 CATHOLIC	11	NA	25,500	25.2	54.6
081d LATIN	11	NA	25,500	25.2	54.6
089 CHR & MISS AL	1	31	91	.1	.2
123 CH GOD (ANDER)	2	98	111	.1	.2
127 CH GOD (CLEVE)	1	341	445*	.4	1.0
151 L-D SAINTS	1	NA	575	.6	1.2
165 CH OF NAZARENE	2	179	223	.2	.5
167 CHS OF CHRIST	1	170	221	.2	.5
193 EPISCOPAL	6	819	1,250	1.2	2.7
207 E.L.C.A.	1	217	338	.3	.7
283 LUTH—MO SYNOD	3	640	893	.9	1.9
355 PRESB CH (USA)	1	233	304*	.3	.7
356 PRESB CH AMER	1	54	84	.1	.2
413 S.D.A.	2	246	321*	.3	.7
419 SO BAPT CONV	13	4,617	6,027*	6.0	12.9
449 UN METHODIST	14	3,361	4,387*	4.3	9.4
467 WESLEYAN	1	25	75	.1	.2
497 BLACK BAPT EST[2]	NA	4,047	5,283*	5.2	11.3
498 INDEP.CHARIS.[3]	1	NA	300	.3	.6
DORCHESTER	**84**	**10,415**	**14,514***	**48.0**	**100.0**
005 AME ZION	1	17	28	.1	.2
081 CATHOLIC	4	NA	1,281	4.2	8.8
081d LATIN	4	NA	1,281	4.2	8.8
089 CHR & MISS AL	2	75	204	.7	1.4
097 CHR CHS&CHS CR	1	90	110*	.4	.8
127 CH GOD (CLEVE)	3	354	434*	1.4	3.0
145 CH GOD PROPHCY	2	61	75*	.2	.5
165 CH OF NAZARENE	1	66	104	.3	.7
167 CHS OF CHRIST	1	50	67	.2	.5
193 EPISCOPAL	6	527	632	2.1	4.4
259 IFCA	1	NR	NR	-	-
283 LUTH—MO SYNOD	1	78	101	.3	.7
403 SALVATION ARMY	1	107	116	.4	.8
413 S.D.A.	2	96	118*	.4	.8
419 SO BAPT CONV	3	888	1,088*	3.6	7.5
443 UN C OF CHRIST	1	178	218*	.7	1.5
449 UN METHODIST	50	6,140	7,521*	24.9	51.8
467 WESLEYAN	4	188	580	1.9	4.0
497 BLACK BAPT EST[2]	NA	1,500	1,837*	6.1	12.7
FREDERICK	**183**	**37,852**	**70,496***	**46.9**	**100.0**
019 AMER BAPT USA	1	63	80*	.1	.1
053 ASSEMB OF GOD	4	341	655	.4	.9
055 AS REF PRES CH	1	81	95	.1	.1
075 BRETHREN IN CR	2	37	91	.1	.1
081 CATHOLIC	11	NA	18,018	12.0	25.6
081d LATIN	11	NA	18,018	12.0	25.6
089 CHR & MISS AL	3	166	343	.2	.5
097 CHR CHS&CHS CR	1	150	191*	.1	.3
111 CH CR,SCIENTST	1	NR	NR	-	-
127 CH GOD (CLEVE)	3	780	991*	.7	1.4
145 CH GOD PROPHCY	3	91	116*	.1	.2
151 L-D SAINTS	4	NA	1,378	.9	2.0
157 CH OF BRETHREN	11	2,612	3,318*	2.2	4.7
165 CH OF NAZARENE	2	245	319	.2	.5
167 CHS OF CHRIST	1	141	183	.1	.3
171 CH GOD-GEN CON	7	464	589*	.4	.8
193 EPISCOPAL	8	1,127	2,094	1.4	3.0
207 E.L.C.A.	30	9,917	13,863	9.2	19.7
226 FRIENDS-USA	1	18	23*	-	-
226d FGC & FUM	1	18	23*	-	-
263 INT FOURSQ GOS	1	92	117*	.1	.2
283 LUTH—MO SYNOD	1	123	176	.1	.2

NA–Not applicable   NR–Not reported   *Total adherents estimated from known number of communicant, confirmed, full members.   - Represents a percent less than 0.1.   Percentages may not total due to rounding.
[1]See Appendix E   [2]See Appendix F   [3]See Appendix G   Lines in *italic* represent a breakdown of Catholic rites or Friends affiliations. They are included in their respective denominational total.

Table 4. Churches and Church Membership by County and Denomination: 1990

County and Denomination	Number of churches	Communicant, confirmed, full members	Total adherents Number	Percent of total population	Percent of total adherents
285 MENNONITE CH	1	25	25	-	-
293 MORAV CH-NORTH	1	289	387	.3	.5
339 PENT CH OF GOD	1	29	75	-	.1
355 PRESB CH (USA)	3	531	674*	.4	1.0
356 PRESB CH AMER	1	71	103	.1	.1
403 SALVATION ARMY	1	126	126	.1	.2
413 S.D.A.	3	620	788*	.5	1.1
419 SO BAPT CONV	7	3,159	4,012*	2.7	5.7
435 UNITARIAN-UNIV	1	78	138	.1	.2
443 UN C OF CHRIST	15	3,517	4,467*	3.0	6.3
449 UN METHODIST	52	11,199	14,225*	9.5	20.2
496 JEWISH EST[1]	1	NA	600	.4	.9
497 BLACK BAPT EST[2]	NA	1,760	2,236*	1.5	3.2
GARRETT	**97**	**8,318**	**13,519***	**48.0**	**100.0**
053 ASSEMB OF GOD	10	568	1,165	4.1	8.6
061 BEACHY AMISH	1	0	0*	-	-
081 CATHOLIC	5	NA	1,920	6.8	14.2
081d *LATIN*	*5*	*NA*	*1,920*	*6.8*	*14.2*
093 CHR CH (DISC)	1	220	367	1.3	2.7
097 CHR CHS&CHS CR	1	30	38*	.1	.3
123 CH GOD (ANDER)	1	0	53	.2	.4
127 CH GOD (CLEVE)	3	236	298*	1.1	2.2
145 CH GOD PROPHCY	1	30	38*	.1	.3
151 L-D SAINTS	1	NA	104	.4	.8
157 CH OF BRETHREN	10	871	1,102*	3.9	8.2
165 CH OF NAZARENE	1	73	125	.4	.9
167 CHS OF CHRIST	1	40	52	.2	.4
171 CH GOD-GEN CON	2	201	254*	.9	1.9
175 CONGR CHR CHS	1	64	81*	.3	.6
193 EPISCOPAL	2	169	248	.9	1.8
203 EVAN FREE CH	1	109	150	.5	1.1
207 E.L.C.A.	9	1,319	1,785	6.3	13.2
283 LUTH—MO SYNOD	2	408	515	1.8	3.8
285 MENNONITE CH	8	689	847	3.0	6.3
323 OLD ORD AMISH	1	NA	150	.5	1.1
413 S.D.A.	2	177	224*	.8	1.7
419 SO BAPT CONV	4	376	476*	1.7	3.5
438 UN BRETH IN CR	2	171	171	.6	1.3
443 UN C OF CHRIST	2	263	333*	1.2	2.5
449 UN METHODIST	24	2,286	2,891*	10.3	21.4
467 WESLEYAN	1	18	132	.5	1.0
HARFORD	**122**	**31,271**	**73,599***	**40.4**	**100.0**
053 ASSEMB OF GOD	4	343	524	.3	.7
081 CATHOLIC	9	NA	29,132	16.0	39.6
081d *LATIN*	*9*	*NA*	*29,132*	*16.0*	*39.6*
089 CHR & MISS AL	1	48	91	-	.1
097 CHR CHS&CHS CR	4	1,634	2,082*	1.1	2.8
111 CH CR,SCIENTST	1	NR	NR	-	-
127 CH GOD (CLEVE)	4	314	400*	.2	.5
145 CH GOD PROPHCY	1	30	38*	-	.1
151 L-D SAINTS	2	NA	800	.4	1.1
165 CH OF NAZARENE	2	465	744	.4	1.0
167 CHS OF CHRIST	2	130	205	.1	.3
193 EPISCOPAL	10	1,662	2,612	1.4	3.5
207 E.L.C.A.	7	2,966	4,660	2.6	6.3
226 FRIENDS-USA	2	105	134*	.1	.2
226c *FGC*	*1*	*55*	*70**	*-*	*.1*
226d *FGC & FUM*	*1*	*50*	*64**	*-*	*.1*
283 LUTH—MO SYNOD	1	1,037	1,474	.8	2.0
355 PRESB CH (USA)	11	3,267	4,162*	2.3	5.7
356 PRESB CH AMER	1	149	224	.1	.3
375 REF EPISCOPAL	1	62	68	-	.1
386 REGULAR BAPT	1	147	187*	.1	.3
403 SALVATION ARMY	1	69	69	-	.1
413 S.D.A.	2	252	321*	.2	.4
419 SO BAPT CONV	11	5,656	7,206*	4.0	9.8
435 UNITARIAN-UNIV	1	104	163	.1	.2
443 UN C OF CHRIST	1	108	138*	.1	.2
449 UN METHODIST	37	9,311	11,863*	6.5	16.1
496 JEWISH EST[1]	3	NA	1,000	.5	1.4
497 BLACK BAPT EST[2]	NA	3,412	4,347*	2.4	5.9
499 INDEP.NON-CHAR[3]	2	NA	955	.5	1.3
HOWARD	**114**	**29,634**	**77,322***	**41.3**	**100.0**
019 AMER BAPT USA	1	360	455*	.2	.6
053 ASSEMB OF GOD	5	457	1,035	.6	1.3
081 CATHOLIC	8	NA	29,184	15.6	37.7
081d *LATIN*	*8*	*NA*	*29,184*	*15.6*	*37.7*
089 CHR & MISS AL	1	4	37	-	-
093 CHR CH (DISC)	1	48	70	-	.1
111 CH CR,SCIENTST	1	NR	NR	-	-
123 CH GOD (ANDER)	3	588	598	.3	.8
145 CH GOD PROPHCY	1	30	38*	-	-
151 L-D SAINTS	3	NA	1,274	.7	1.6
157 CH OF BRETHREN	2	115	145*	.1	.2
165 CH OF NAZARENE	2	409	459	.2	.6
167 CHS OF CHRIST	1	75	100	.1	.1
193 EPISCOPAL	8	1,993	3,555	1.9	4.6
203 EVAN FREE CH	1	30	60	-	.1
207 E.L.C.A.	9	3,380	4,633	2.5	6.0
259 IFCA	1	NR	NR	-	-
263 INT FOURSQ GOS	1	71	90*	-	.1
283 LUTH—MO SYNOD	2	387	495	.3	.6
285 MENNONITE CH	2	57	103	.1	.1
331 ORTH CH IN AM	1	NR	NR	-	-
355 PRESB CH (USA)	4	1,971	2,491*	1.3	3.2
356 PRESB CH AMER	2	1,088	1,288	.7	1.7
413 S.D.A.	5	901	1,139*	.6	1.5
419 SO BAPT CONV	12	3,972	5,020*	2.7	6.5
435 UNITARIAN-UNIV	1	383	626	.3	.8
443 UN C OF CHRIST	1	92	116*	.1	.2
449 UN METHODIST	30	8,385	10,597*	5.7	13.7
496 JEWISH EST[1]	4	NA	7,200	3.8	9.3
497 BLACK BAPT EST[2]	NA	4,838	6,114*	3.3	7.9
499 INDEP.NON-CHAR[3]	1	NA	400	.2	.5
KENT	**46**	**6,049**	**10,946***	**61.3**	**100.0**
053 ASSEMB OF GOD	1	37	50	.3	.5
061 BEACHY AMISH	1	55	66*	.4	.6
081 CATHOLIC	3	NA	2,097	11.8	19.2
081d *LATIN*	*3*	*NA*	*2,097*	*11.8*	*19.2*
193 EPISCOPAL	5	741	1,121	6.3	10.2
215 EVAN METH CH	1	23	28*	.2	.3
226 FRIENDS-USA	1	35	42*	.2	.4
226c *FGC*	*1*	*35*	*42**	*.2*	*.4*
283 LUTH—MO SYNOD	1	241	306	1.7	2.8
285 MENNONITE CH	1	14	49	.3	.4
355 PRESB CH (USA)	1	109	131*	.7	1.2
413 S.D.A.	2	195	234*	1.3	2.1
419 SO BAPT CONV	1	144	173*	1.0	1.6
449 UN METHODIST	27	3,839	4,609*	25.8	42.1
497 BLACK BAPT EST[2]	NA	616	740*	4.1	6.8
499 INDEP.NON-CHAR[3]	1	NA	1,300	7.3	11.9
MONTGOMERY	**390**	**126,586**	**399,477***	**52.8**	**100.0**
005 AME ZION	5	1,195	1,985	.3	.5
019 AMER BAPT USA	15	6,437	7,939*	1.0	2.0
022 EASTERN ORTH	1	135	135	-	-
049 ARMEN AP CH AM	1	1,000	4,000	.5	1.0
053 ASSEMB OF GOD	10	1,165	1,659	.2	.4
055 AS REF PRES CH	2	640	842	.1	.2
081 CATHOLIC	34	NA	170,000	22.5	42.6
081d *LATIN*	*34*	*NA*	*170,000*	*22.5*	*42.6*
089 CHR & MISS AL	6	502	1,351	.2	.3
093 CHR CH (DISC)	5	1,077	1,440	.2	.4
097 CHR CHS&CHS CR	1	275	339*	-	.1
105 CHRISTIAN REF	1	128	178	-	-
111 CH CR,SCIENTST	4	NR	NR	-	-
123 CH GOD (ANDER)	2	475	475	.1	.1
127 CH GOD (CLEVE)	5	433	534*	.1	.1
133 CH GOD(7TH)DEN	1	52	68	-	-
145 CH GOD PROPHCY	1	30	37*	-	-
151 L-D SAINTS	14	NA	6,287	.8	1.6
157 CH OF BRETHREN	2	178	220*	-	.1
165 CH OF NAZARENE	2	232	577	.1	.1
167 CHS OF CHRIST	5	483	627	.1	.2
179 CONSRV BAPT	1	NR	NR	-	-
193 EPISCOPAL	24	8,458	14,413	1.9	3.6
207 E.L.C.A.	15	6,894	8,803	1.2	2.2
216 EVAN PRESBY CH	1	2,174	2,211	.3	.6
221 FREE METHODIST	5	256	279	-	.1
226 FRIENDS-USA	4	863	1,064*	.1	.3
226d *FGC & FUM*	*4*	*863*	*1,064**	*.1*	*.3*
246 GREEK ORTHODOX	1	NR	NR	-	-
263 INT FOURSQ GOS	4	384	474*	.1	.1
274 LAT EVAN LUTH	1	442	517	.1	.1
283 LUTH—MO SYNOD	7	2,920	3,839	.5	1.0
285 MENNONITE CH	3	91	138	-	-
313 N AM BAPT CONF	1	44	54*	-	-
331 ORTH CH IN AM	1	NR	NR	-	-
349 PENT HOLINESS	1	54	67*	-	-
353 CHR BRETHREN	3	230	315	-	.1
355 PRESB CH (USA)	27	7,190	8,867*	1.2	2.2
356 PRESB CH AMER	2	134	210	-	.1
413 S.D.A.	17	9,054	11,166*	1.5	2.8
419 SO BAPT CONV	46	18,832	23,225*	3.1	5.8
435 UNITARIAN-UNIV	5	2,264	3,112	.4	.8
443 UN C OF CHRIST	7	2,496	3,078*	.4	.8
449 UN METHODIST	63	28,969	35,727*	4.7	8.9
467 WESLEYAN	3	129	350	-	.1
496 JEWISH EST[1]	25	NA	53,225	7.0	13.3

NA–Not applicable   NR–Not reported   *Total adherents estimated from known number of communicant, confirmed, full members.   - Represents a percent less than 0.1.   Percentages may not total due to rounding.
[1]See Appendix E   [2]See Appendix F   [3]See Appendix G   Lines in *italic* represent a breakdown of Catholic rites or Friends affiliations. They are included in their respective denominational total.

Table 4. Churches and Church Membership by County and Denomination: 1990

County and Denomination	Number of churches	Communicant, confirmed, full members	Total adherents		
			Number	Percent of total population	Percent of total adherents
497 BLACK BAPT EST[2]	NA	20,271	25,000*	3.3	6.3
498 INDEP.CHARIS.[3]	4	NA	3,400	.4	.9
499 INDEP.NON-CHAR[3]	2	NA	1,250	.2	.3
PRINCE GEORGES	**365**	**148,790**	**394,515***	**54.1**	**100.0**
001 ADVENT CHR CH	1	31	39*	-	-
005 AME ZION	4	7,631	7,906	1.1	2.0
019 AMER BAPT USA	30	11,552	14,353*	2.0	3.6
039 AP CHR CH(NAZ)	1	36	45*	-	-
053 ASSEMB OF GOD	12	1,747	2,777	.4	.7
081 CATHOLIC	35	NA	142,876	19.6	36.2
081b BYZAN RUTH	*1*	*NA*	*376*	*.1*	*.1*
081d LATIN	*34*	*NA*	*142,500*	*19.5*	*36.1*
089 CHR & MISS AL	1	53	144	-	-
093 CHR CH (DISC)	8	1,029	1,683	.2	.4
097 CHR CHS&CHS CR	2	254	316*	-	.1
111 CH CR,SCIENTST	3	NR	NR	-	-
123 CH GOD (ANDER)	3	118	123	-	-
127 CH GOD (CLEVE)	8	5,097	6,333*	.9	1.6
133 CH GOD(7TH)DEN	1	51	67	-	-
145 CH GOD PROPHCY	4	128	159*	-	-
151 L-D SAINTS	9	NA	3,339	.5	.8
157 CH OF BRETHREN	1	119	148*	-	-
165 CH OF NAZARENE	5	565	637	.1	.2
167 CHS OF CHRIST	7	1,312	1,762	.2	.4
179 CONSRV BAPT	2	NR	NR	-	-
193 EPISCOPAL	24	4,629	7,642	1.0	1.9
207 E.L.C.A.	13	3,279	4,330	.6	1.1
220 FREE LUTHERAN	1	15	29	-	-
221 FREE METHODIST	2	95	102	-	-
223 FREE WILL BAPT	1	197	245*	-	.1
226 FRIENDS-USA	3	271	337*	-	.1
226d FGC & FUM	*3*	*271*	*337**	*-*	*.1*
246 GREEK ORTHODOX	1	NR	NR	-	-
259 IFCA	5	NR	NR	-	-
263 INT FOURSQ GOS	2	316	393*	.1	.1
283 LUTH—MO SYNOD	9	2,974	3,932	.5	1.0
285 MENNONITE CH	2	175	315	-	.1
287 MENN GEN CONF	1	58	75	-	-
293 MORAV CH-NORTH	2	365	502	.1	.1
329 OPEN BIBLE STD	1	NR	NR	-	-
349 PENT HOLINESS	2	101	125*	-	-
353 CHR BRETHREN	5	425	631	.1	.2
355 PRESB CH (USA)	21	4,069	5,056*	.7	1.3
356 PRESB CH AMER	2	842	1,086	.1	.3
413 S.D.A.	6	2,526	3,138*	.4	.8
415 S-D BAPTIST GC	1	31	39*	-	-
419 SO BAPT CONV	55	20,563	25,548*	3.5	6.5
435 UNITARIAN-UNIV	3	491	696	.1	.2
443 UN C OF CHRIST	4	668	830*	.1	.2
449 UN METHODIST	44	18,267	22,696*	3.1	5.8
467 WESLEYAN	1	51	170	-	-
469 WELS	1	164	258	-	.1
496 JEWISH EST[1]	5	NA	51,275	7.0	13.0
497 BLACK BAPT EST[2]	NA	58,495	72,677*	10.0	18.4
498 INDEP.CHARIS.[3]	4	NA	4,050	.6	1.0
499 INDEP.NON-CHAR[3]	7	NA	5,631	.8	1.4
QUEEN ANNES	**44**	**6,558**	**10,517***	**31.0**	**100.0**
053 ASSEMB OF GOD	1	31	77	.2	.7
081 CATHOLIC	3	NA	1,961	5.8	18.6
081d LATIN	*3*	*NA*	*1,961*	*5.8*	*18.6*
089 CHR & MISS AL	1	31	101	.3	1.0
127 CH GOD (CLEVE)	3	287	358*	1.1	3.4
151 L-D SAINTS	1	NA	120	.4	1.1
165 CH OF NAZARENE	1	81	129	.4	1.2
167 CHS OF CHRIST	1	30	56	.2	.5
193 EPISCOPAL	3	594	834	2.5	7.9
283 LUTH—MO SYNOD	1	145	213	.6	2.0
413 S.D.A.	1	147	184*	.5	1.7
419 SO BAPT CONV	1	123	154*	.5	1.5
449 UN METHODIST	25	4,207	5,254*	15.5	50.0
467 WESLEYAN	2	39	23	.1	.2
497 BLACK BAPT EST[2]	NA	843	1,053*	3.1	10.0
SAINT MARYS	**60**	**9,166**	**34,642***	**45.6**	**100.0**
053 ASSEMB OF GOD	3	567	558	.7	1.6
081 CATHOLIC	15	NA	21,000	27.6	60.6
081d LATIN	*15*	*NA*	*21,000*	*27.6*	*60.6*
111 CH CR,SCIENTST	1	NR	NR	-	-
127 CH GOD (CLEVE)	2	263	341*	.4	1.0
151 L-D SAINTS	1	NA	436	.6	1.3
165 CH OF NAZARENE	1	225	175	.2	.5
167 CHS OF CHRIST	1	125	163	.2	.5
193 EPISCOPAL	7	1,205	2,087	2.7	6.0
226 FRIENDS-USA	1	3	23	-	.1

County and Denomination	Number of churches	Communicant, confirmed, full members	Total adherents		
			Number	Percent of total population	Percent of total adherents
226c FGC	*1*	*3*	*23*	*-*	*.1*
263 INT FOURSQ GOS	1	0	0*	-	-
283 LUTH—MO SYNOD	2	668	1,010	1.3	2.9
285 MENNONITE CH	1	78	78	.1	.2
286 E.PA MENNONITE	1	31	40*	.1	.1
323 OLD ORD AMISH	5	NA	750	1.0	2.2
353 CHR BRETHREN	1	200	450	.6	1.3
355 PRESB CH (USA)	1	199	258*	.3	.7
413 S.D.A.	1	45	58*	.1	.2
419 SO BAPT CONV	3	1,686	2,189*	2.9	6.3
449 UN METHODIST	11	2,042	2,651*	3.5	7.7
496 JEWISH EST[1]	1	NA	0	-	-
497 BLACK BAPT EST[2]	NA	1,829	2,375*	3.1	6.9
SOMERSET	**62**	**8,992**	**10,913***	**46.6**	**100.0**
005 AME ZION	1	225	373	1.6	3.4
053 ASSEMB OF GOD	1	74	85	.4	.8
081 CATHOLIC	1	NA	56	.2	.5
081d LATIN	*1*	*NA*	*56*	*.2*	*.5*
093 CHR CH (DISC)	1	29	70	.3	.6
127 CH GOD (CLEVE)	2	592	702*	3.0	6.4
145 CH GOD PROPHCY	1	30	36*	.2	.3
157 CH OF BRETHREN	1	128	152*	.6	1.4
193 EPISCOPAL	3	136	189	.8	1.7
285 MENNONITE CH	1	106	122	.5	1.1
355 PRESB CH (USA)	2	221	262*	1.1	2.4
419 SO BAPT CONV	4	994	1,179*	5.0	10.8
449 UN METHODIST	43	4,204	4,984*	21.3	45.7
467 WESLEYAN	1	30	67	.3	.6
497 BLACK BAPT EST[2]	NA	2,223	2,636*	11.2	24.2
TALBOT	**56**	**9,405**	**14,837***	**48.6**	**100.0**
053 ASSEMB OF GOD	1	17	15	-	.1
081 CATHOLIC	3	NA	2,506	8.2	16.9
081d LATIN	*3*	*NA*	*2,506*	*8.2*	*16.9*
097 CHR CHS&CHS CR	1	70	84*	.3	.6
111 CH CR,SCIENTST	1	NR	NR	-	-
127 CH GOD (CLEVE)	1	419	506*	1.7	3.4
151 L-D SAINTS	1	NA	174	.6	1.2
157 CH OF BRETHREN	2	332	401*	1.3	2.7
165 CH OF NAZARENE	1	139	203	.7	1.4
193 EPISCOPAL	7	1,952	2,883	9.4	19.4
207 E.L.C.A.	2	297	399	1.3	2.7
226 FRIENDS-USA	1	131	158*	.5	1.1
226c FGC	*1*	*131*	*158**	*.5*	*1.1*
283 LUTH—MO SYNOD	1	354	495	1.6	3.3
355 PRESB CH (USA)	1	310	374*	1.2	2.5
419 SO BAPT CONV	3	636	768*	2.5	5.2
435 UNITARIAN-UNIV	1	58	68	.2	.5
449 UN METHODIST	25	3,582	4,323*	14.2	29.1
467 WESLEYAN	3	129	198	.6	1.3
496 JEWISH EST[1]	1	NA	100	.3	.7
497 BLACK BAPT EST[2]	NA	979	1,182*	3.9	8.0
WASHINGTON	**177**	**35,906**	**55,742***	**45.9**	**100.0**
011 A.W.M.C.	1	0	0*	-	-
019 AMER BAPT USA	1	135	165*	.1	.3
053 ASSEMB OF GOD	7	1,062	1,884	1.6	3.4
071 BRETHREN (ASH)	2	554	675*	.6	1.2
075 BRETHREN IN CR	2	159	159	.1	.3
081 CATHOLIC	8	NA	8,723	7.2	15.6
081d LATIN	*8*	*NA*	*8,723*	*7.2*	*15.6*
093 CHR CH (DISC)	6	1,441	1,873	1.5	3.4
097 CHR CHS&CHS CR	3	480	585*	.5	1.0
111 CH CR,SCIENTST	1	NR	NR	-	-
127 CH GOD (CLEVE)	7	1,104	1,346*	1.1	2.4
145 CH GOD PROPHCY	1	30	37*	-	.1
151 L-D SAINTS	1	NA	556	.5	1.0
157 CH OF BRETHREN	11	1,855	2,261*	1.9	4.1
165 CH OF NAZARENE	2	130	287	.2	.5
167 CHS OF CHRIST	1	117	152	.1	.3
171 CH GOD-GEN CON	7	587	716*	.6	1.3
193 EPISCOPAL	7	1,076	1,443	1.2	2.6
203 EVAN FREE CH	1	100	160	.1	.3
207 E.L.C.A.	20	6,996	8,752	7.2	15.7
283 LUTH—MO SYNOD	2	361	485	.4	.9
285 MENNONITE CH	16	1,341	1,477	1.2	2.6
291 MISSIONARY CH	1	15	25	-	-
331 ORTH CH IN AM	1	NR	NR	-	-
339 PENT CH OF GOD	1	44	75	.1	.1
353 CHR BRETHREN	1	25	50	-	.1
355 PRESB CH (USA)	5	896	1,092*	.9	2.0
356 PRESB CH AMER	2	65	98	.1	.2
403 SALVATION ARMY	1	132	132	.1	.2
413 S.D.A.	5	1,219	1,486*	1.2	2.7
419 SO BAPT CONV	7	1,538	1,875*	1.5	3.4

NA–Not applicable   NR–Not reported   *Total adherents estimated from known number of communicant, confirmed, full members.   - Represents a percent less than 0.1.   Percentages may not total due to rounding.
[1]See Appendix E   [2]See Appendix F   [3]See Appendix G   Lines in *italic* represent a breakdown of Catholic rites or Friends affiliations. They are included in their respective denominational total.

Table 4. Churches and Church Membership by County and Denomination: 1990

County and Denomination	Number of churches	Communicant, confirmed, full members	Total adherents		
			Number	Percent of total population	Percent of total adherents
435 UNITARIAN-UNIV	1	64	69	.1	.1
438 UN BRETH IN CR	3	170	170	.1	.3
443 UN C OF CHRIST	11	3,055	3,724*	3.1	6.7
449 UN METHODIST	28	9,531	11,619*	9.6	20.8
467 WESLEYAN	1	32	50	-	.1
496 JEWISH EST[1]	1	NA	300	.2	.5
497 BLACK BAPT EST[2]	NA	1,592	1,941*	1.6	3.5
499 INDEP.NON-CHAR[3]	1	NA	1,300	1.1	2.3
WICOMICO	**99**	**21,479**	**34,122***	**45.9**	**100.0**
005 AME ZION	2	907	1,203	1.6	3.5
053 ASSEMB OF GOD	1	63	74	.1	.2
081 CATHOLIC	2	NA	3,731	5.0	10.9
081d *LATIN*	2	*NA*	*3,731*	*5.0*	*10.9*
089 CHR & MISS AL	1	0	47	.1	.1
097 CHR CHS&CHS CR	4	260	323*	.4	.9
111 CH CR,SCIENTST	1	NR	NR	-	-
123 CH GOD (ANDER)	1	4	4	-	-
127 CH GOD (CLEVE)	2	624	775*	1.0	2.3
145 CH GOD PROPHCY	3	91	113*	.2	.3
151 L-D SAINTS	1	NA	425	.6	1.2
165 CH OF NAZARENE	1	385	633	.9	1.9
167 CHS OF CHRIST	2	57	95	.1	.3
193 EPISCOPAL	5	1,144	1,397	1.9	4.1
207 E.L.C.A.	1	160	198	.3	.6
226 FRIENDS-USA	1	16	20*	-	.1
226c *FGC*	1	*16*	*20*	-	*.1*
263 INT FOURSQ GOS	1	0	0*	-	-
283 LUTH—MO SYNOD	1	400	551	.7	1.6
285 MENNONITE CH	1	28	43	.1	.1
355 PRESB CH (USA)	1	401	498*	.7	1.5
356 PRESB CH AMER	1	62	97	.1	.3
403 SALVATION ARMY	1	92	105	.1	.3
413 S.D.A.	2	274	340*	.5	1.0
419 SO BAPT CONV	6	1,874	2,326*	3.1	6.8
435 UNITARIAN-UNIV	1	30	44	.1	.1
449 UN METHODIST	50	11,342	14,078*	18.9	41.3
467 WESLEYAN	4	315	2,240	3.0	6.6
496 JEWISH EST[1]	1	NA	400	.5	1.2
497 BLACK BAPT EST[2]	NA	2,950	3,662*	4.9	10.7
499 INDEP.NON-CHAR[3]	1	NA	700	.9	2.1
WORCESTER	**80**	**12,046**	**16,469***	**47.0**	**100.0**
053 ASSEMB OF GOD	2	125	216	.6	1.3
081 CATHOLIC	4	NA	1,554	4.4	9.4
081d *LATIN*	4	*NA*	*1,554*	*4.4*	*9.4*
093 CHR CH (DISC)	1	61	98	.3	.6
097 CHR CHS&CHS CR	2	70	85*	.2	.5
127 CH GOD (CLEVE)	2	171	208*	.6	1.3
145 CH GOD PROPHCY	3	91	110*	.3	.7
165 CH OF NAZARENE	1	32	98	.3	.6
193 EPISCOPAL	5	796	981	2.8	6.0
207 E.L.C.A.	1	368	432	1.2	2.6
246 GREEK ORTHODOX	1	NR	NR	-	-
285 MENNONITE CH	2	76	135	.4	.8
355 PRESB CH (USA)	6	669	812*	2.3	4.9
413 S.D.A.	1	45	55*	.2	.3
419 SO BAPT CONV	8	2,211	2,684*	7.7	16.3
449 UN METHODIST	40	6,002	7,287*	20.8	44.2
496 JEWISH EST[1]	1	NA	100	.3	.6
497 BLACK BAPT EST[2]	NA	1,329	1,614*	4.6	9.8

MASSACHUSETTS

County and Denomination	Number of churches	Communicant, confirmed, full members	Total adherents		
			Number	Percent of total population	Percent of total adherents
THE STATE.....	3,382	500,580	3,942,101*	65.5	100.0
BARNSTABLE	**129**	**19,520**	**119,830***	**64.2**	**100.0**
019 AMER BAPT USA	7	1,152	1,387*	.7	1.2
053 ASSEMB OF GOD	4	339	686	.4	.6
057 BAPT GEN CONF	1	116	140*	.1	.1
081 CATHOLIC	29	NA	89,000	47.7	74.3
081d *LATIN*	29	*NA*	*89,000*	*47.7*	*74.3*
089 CHR & MISS AL	3	84	204	.1	.2
111 CH CR,SCIENTST	6	NR	NR	-	-
151 L-D SAINTS	2	NA	505	.3	.4
165 CH OF NAZARENE	2	162	207	.1	.2
167 CHS OF CHRIST	1	53	83	-	.1
175 CONGR CHR CHS	1	624	752*	.4	.6
179 CONSRV BAPT	5	NR	NR	-	-
193 EPISCOPAL	11	4,159	8,028	4.3	6.7
207 E.L.C.A.	3	1,083	1,358	.7	1.1
209 EVAN LUTH SYN	1	86	104	.1	.1

County and Denomination	Number of churches	Communicant, confirmed, full members	Total adherents		
			Number	Percent of total population	Percent of total adherents
226 FRIENDS-USA	4	161	194*	.1	.2
226d *FGC & FUM*	4	*161*	*194*	*.1*	*.2*
246 GREEK ORTHODOX	1	NR	NR	-	-
283 LUTH—MO SYNOD	1	42	48	-	-
331 ORTH CH IN AM	1	NR	NR	-	-
403 SALVATION ARMY	1	61	68	-	.1
413 S.D.A.	1	111	134*	.1	.1
419 SO BAPT CONV	1	177	213*	.1	.2
435 UNITARIAN-UNIV	8	1,676	2,157	1.2	1.8
443 UN C OF CHRIST	17	5,609	6,755*	3.6	5.6
449 UN METHODIST	15	3,382	4,073*	2.2	3.4
496 JEWISH EST[1]	2	NA	2,900	1.6	2.4
497 BLACK BAPT EST[2]	NA	443	534*	.3	.4
499 INDEP.NON-CHAR[3]	1	NA	300	.2	.3
BERKSHIRE	**146**	**14,887**	**109,176***	**78.3**	**100.0**
001 ADVENT CHR CH	1	115	140*	.1	.1
005 AME ZION	4	415	859	.6	.8
019 AMER BAPT USA	12	2,408	2,923*	2.1	2.7
053 ASSEMB OF GOD	3	369	561	.4	.5
081 CATHOLIC	41	NA	85,097	61.1	77.9
081d *LATIN*	40	*NA*	*85,000*	*61.0*	*77.9*
081h *UKRAINIAN*	1	*NA*	*97*	*.1*	*.1*
083 CHRIST CATH CH	1	6	6	-	-
111 CH CR,SCIENTST	2	NR	NR	-	-
151 L-D SAINTS	1	NA	282	.2	.3
165 CH OF NAZARENE	1	83	160	.1	.1
167 CHS OF CHRIST	2	105	166	.1	.2
175 CONGR CHR CHS	7	394	478*	.3	.4
176 CCC, NOT NAT'L	2	159	193*	.1	.2
179 CONSRV BAPT	1	NR	NR	-	-
181 CONSRV CONGR	1	66	80*	.1	.1
193 EPISCOPAL	15	2,477	4,271	3.1	3.9
203 EVAN FREE CH	1	70	106	.1	.1
207 E.L.C.A.	1	797	957	.7	.9
226 FRIENDS-USA	2	27	33	-	-
226d *FGC & FUM*	2	*27*	*33*	-	-
246 GREEK ORTHODOX	1	NR	NR	-	-
331 ORTH CH IN AM	1	NR	NR	-	-
403 SALVATION ARMY	2	125	141	.1	.1
413 S.D.A.	1	132	160*	.1	.1
419 SO BAPT CONV	1	34	41*	-	-
435 UNITARIAN-UNIV	2	141	203	.1	.2
443 UN C OF CHRIST	24	3,900	4,735*	3.4	4.3
449 UN METHODIST	10	2,479	3,010*	2.2	2.8
469 WELS	1	94	128	.1	.1
496 JEWISH EST[1]	5	NA	3,850	2.8	3.5
497 BLACK BAPT EST[2]	NA	491	596*	.4	.5
BRISTOL	**274**	**28,491**	**293,200***	**57.9**	**100.0**
001 ADVENT CHR CH	3	125	155*	-	.1
005 AME ZION	2	210	348	.1	.1
019 AMER BAPT USA	21	3,910	4,834*	1.0	1.6
053 ASSEMB OF GOD	9	1,368	2,070	.4	.7
057 BAPT GEN CONF	2	199	246*	-	.1
081 CATHOLIC	87	NA	245,216	48.4	83.6
081d *LATIN*	85	*NA*	*243,000*	*48.0*	*82.9*
081e *MARONITE*	2	*NA*	*2,216*	*.4*	*.8*
089 CHR & MISS AL	4	144	287	.1	.1
111 CH CR,SCIENTST	3	NR	NR	-	-
127 CH GOD (CLEVE)	4	186	230*	-	.1
145 CH GOD PROPHCY	1	28	35*	-	-
151 L-D SAINTS	2	NA	591	.1	.2
165 CH OF NAZARENE	3	879	1,238	.2	.4
167 CHS OF CHRIST	4	234	358	.1	.1
175 CONGR CHR CHS	6	674	833*	.2	.3
176 CCC, NOT NAT'L	1	144	178*	-	.1
179 CONSRV BAPT	5	NR	NR	-	-
181 CONSRV CONGR	3	482	596*	.1	.2
193 EPISCOPAL	19	5,342	9,889	2.0	3.4
207 E.L.C.A.	3	937	1,330	.3	.5
220 FREE LUTHERAN	1	17	24	-	-
221 FREE METHODIST	1	14	39	-	-
226 FRIENDS-USA	7	411	508*	.1	.2
226d *FGC & FUM*	7	*411*	*508*	*.1*	*.2*
246 GREEK ORTHODOX	2	NR	NR	-	-
263 INT FOURSQ GOS	3	290	359*	.1	.1
283 LUTH—MO SYNOD	1	82	123	-	-
353 CHR BRETHREN	3	250	315	.1	.1
355 PRESB CH (USA)	2	141	174*	-	.1
363 PRIMITIVE METH	2	79	111	-	-
403 SALVATION ARMY	2	160	212	-	.1
413 S.D.A.	8	874	1,081*	.2	.4
419 SO BAPT CONV	2	132	163*	-	.1
435 UNITARIAN-UNIV	7	1,164	1,474	.3	.5
443 UN C OF CHRIST	20	4,974	6,150*	1.2	2.1
449 UN METHODIST	18	3,481	4,304*	.9	1.5

NA–Not applicable   NR–Not reported   *Total adherents estimated from known number of communicant, confirmed, full members.   - Represents a percent less than 0.1.   Percentages may not total due to rounding.
[1]See Appendix E   [2]See Appendix F   [3]See Appendix G   Lines in *italic* represent a breakdown of Catholic rites or Friends affiliations. They are included in their respective denominational total.

Table 4. Churches and Church Membership by County and Denomination: 1990

County and Denomination	Number of churches	Communicant, confirmed, full members	Total adherents		
			Number	Percent of total population	Percent of total adherents
496 JEWISH EST[1]	9	NA	6,180	1.2	2.1
497 BLACK BAPT EST[2]	NA	1,560	1,929*	.4	.7
499 INDEP.NON-CHAR[3]	4	NA	1,620	.3	.6
DUKES	**24**	**1,715**	**7,541***	**64.8**	**100.0**
019 AMER BAPT USA	3	327	403*	3.5	5.3
053 ASSEMB OF GOD	1	41	69	.6	.9
057 BAPT GEN CONF	1	50	62*	.5	.8
081 CATHOLIC	3	NA	5,000	43.0	66.3
081d LATIN	3	NA	5,000	43.0	66.3
111 CH CR,SCIENTST	1	NR	NR	-	-
151 L-D SAINTS	1	NA	27	.2	.4
176 CCC, NOT NAT'L	1	244	300*	2.6	4.0
193 EPISCOPAL	3	340	562	4.8	7.5
226 FRIENDS-USA	1	18	22*	.2	.3
226d FGC & FUM	1	18	22*	.2	.3
435 UNITARIAN-UNIV	1	83	83	.7	1.1
443 UN C OF CHRIST	1	135	166*	1.4	2.2
449 UN METHODIST	6	477	587*	5.0	7.8
496 JEWISH EST[1]	1	NA	260	2.2	3.4
ESSEX	**375**	**50,941**	**446,947***	**66.7**	**100.0**
001 ADVENT CHR CH	2	60	74*	-	-
019 AMER BAPT USA	27	4,786	5,898*	.9	1.3
049 ARMEN AP CH AM	1	250	800	.1	.2
053 ASSEMB OF GOD	14	1,126	1,989	.3	.4
057 BAPT GEN CONF	1	275	339*	.1	.1
081 CATHOLIC	89	NA	329,929	49.2	73.8
081d LATIN	86	NA	327,640	48.9	73.3
081e MARONITE	1	NA	1,216	.2	.3
081f MELKITE-GK	1	NA	1,000	.1	.2
081h UKRAINIAN	1	NA	73	-	-
089 CHR & MISS AL	3	241	709	.1	.2
093 CHR CH (DISC)	2	98	124	-	-
111 CH CR,SCIENTST	9	NR	NR	-	-
127 CH GOD (CLEVE)	3	297	366*	.1	.1
145 CH GOD PROPHCY	1	28	35*	-	-
151 L-D SAINTS	2	NA	477	.1	.1
165 CH OF NAZARENE	5	515	672	.1	.2
167 CHS OF CHRIST	2	90	145	-	-
175 CONGR CHR CHS	1	260	320*	-	.1
176 CCC, NOT NAT'L	1	405	499*	.1	.1
179 CONSRV BAPT	3	NR	NR	-	-
181 CONSRV CONGR	5	753	928*	.1	.2
193 EPISCOPAL	28	10,456	18,456	2.8	4.1
207 E.L.C.A.	6	1,498	2,052	.3	.5
221 FREE METHODIST	5	210	437	.1	.1
226 FRIENDS-USA	4	112	142	-	-
226d FGC & FUM	4	112	142	-	-
246 GREEK ORTHODOX	7	NR	NR	-	-
283 LUTH—MO SYNOD	2	452	619	.1	.1
331 ORTH CH IN AM	1	NR	NR	-	-
353 CHR BRETHREN	4	197	313	-	.1
355 PRESB CH (USA)	4	591	728*	.1	.2
363 PRIMITIVE METH	4	196	295	-	.1
403 SALVATION ARMY	5	384	408	.1	.1
413 S.D.A.	7	380	468*	.1	.1
419 SO BAPT CONV	2	323	398*	.1	.1
435 UNITARIAN-UNIV	15	2,280	3,160	.5	.7
443 UN C OF CHRIST	52	13,114	16,160*	2.4	3.6
449 UN METHODIST	34	8,503	10,478*	1.6	2.3
496 JEWISH EST[1]	22	NA	45,007	6.7	10.1
497 BLACK BAPT EST[2]	NA	3,061	3,772*	.6	.8
499 INDEP.NON-CHAR[3]	2	NA	750	.1	.2
FRANKLIN	**89**	**6,743**	**60,205***	**85.9**	**100.0**
019 AMER BAPT USA	6	433	539*	.8	.9
053 ASSEMB OF GOD	4	162	280	.4	.5
057 BAPT GEN CONF	1	98	122*	.2	.2
081 CATHOLIC	19	NA	50,098	71.5	83.2
081d LATIN	18	NA	50,000	71.3	83.0
081h UKRAINIAN	1	NA	98	.1	.2
089 CHR & MISS AL	1	257	547	.8	.9
111 CH CR,SCIENTST	1	NR	NR	-	-
165 CH OF NAZARENE	1	40	36	.1	.1
167 CHS OF CHRIST	1	11	15	-	-
176 CCC, NOT NAT'L	2	130	162*	.2	.3
181 CONSRV CONGR	1	106	132*	.2	.2
193 EPISCOPAL	4	507	1,109	1.6	1.8
207 E.L.C.A.	2	374	496	.7	.8
226 FRIENDS-USA	2	8	10*	-	-
226d FGC & FUM	2	8	10*	-	-
403 SALVATION ARMY	1	83	96	.1	.2
413 S.D.A.	2	108	134*	.2	.2
419 SO BAPT CONV	1	21	26*	-	-
435 UNITARIAN-UNIV	6	464	601	.9	1.0

County and Denomination	Number of churches	Communicant, confirmed, full members	Total adherents		
			Number	Percent of total population	Percent of total adherents
443 UN C OF CHRIST	26	3,206	3,988*	5.7	6.6
449 UN METHODIST	6	735	914*	1.3	1.5
496 JEWISH EST[1]	2	NA	900	1.3	1.5
HAMPDEN	**241**	**40,534**	**216,569***	**47.5**	**100.0**
001 ADVENT CHR CH	2	87	109*	-	.1
005 AME ZION	2	235	298	.1	.1
019 AMER BAPT USA	18	4,837	6,037*	1.3	2.8
049 ARMEN AP CH AM	1	300	1,400	.3	.6
053 ASSEMB OF GOD	8	1,919	3,187	.7	1.5
081 CATHOLIC	72	NA	152,254	33.4	70.3
081d LATIN	70	NA	150,000	32.9	69.3
081e MARONITE	1	NA	2,166	.5	1.0
081h UKRAINIAN	1	NA	88	-	-
089 CHR & MISS AL	1	48	145	-	.1
111 CH CR,SCIENTST	3	NR	NR	-	-
127 CH GOD (CLEVE)	5	465	580*	.1	.3
145 CH GOD PROPHCY	1	28	35*	-	-
151 L-D SAINTS	2	NA	855	.2	.4
165 CH OF NAZARENE	2	182	164	-	.1
167 CHS OF CHRIST	3	287	404	.1	.2
175 CONGR CHR CHS	2	419	523*	.1	.2
179 CONSRV BAPT	2	NR	NR	-	-
181 CONSRV CONGR	1	91	114*	-	.1
193 EPISCOPAL	15	3,368	5,657	1.2	2.6
203 EVAN FREE CH	1	60	150	-	.1
207 E.L.C.A.	5	1,499	2,032	.4	.9
221 FREE METHODIST	1	7	15	-	-
246 GREEK ORTHODOX	4	NR	NR	-	-
263 INT FOURSQ GOS	1	7	9*	-	-
283 LUTH—MO SYNOD	4	1,486	2,024	.4	.9
331 ORTH CH IN AM	1	NR	NR	-	-
339 PENT CH OF GOD	1	19	50	-	-
353 CHR BRETHREN	1	18	25	-	-
355 PRESB CH (USA)	4	534	667*	.1	.3
356 PRESB CH AMER	1	77	119	-	.1
403 SALVATION ARMY	2	249	283	.1	.1
413 S.D.A.	3	613	765*	.2	.4
419 SO BAPT CONV	4	393	491*	.1	.2
435 UNITARIAN-UNIV	3	334	502	.1	.2
443 UN C OF CHRIST	34	11,879	14,827*	3.2	6.8
449 UN METHODIST	18	4,389	5,478*	1.2	2.5
467 WESLEYAN	1	64	207	-	.1
496 JEWISH EST[1]	12	NA	8,875	1.9	4.1
497 BLACK BAPT EST[2]	NA	6,640	8,288*	1.8	3.8
HAMPSHIRE	**90**	**10,633**	**84,817***	**57.9**	**100.0**
005 AME ZION	1	201	289	.2	.3
019 AMER BAPT USA	2	267	315*	.2	.4
053 ASSEMB OF GOD	2	220	325	.2	.4
081 CATHOLIC	27	NA	66,150	45.1	78.0
081b BYZAN RUTH	1	NA	150	.1	.2
081d LATIN	26	NA	66,000	45.0	77.8
089 CHR & MISS AL	1	0	18	-	-
111 CH CR,SCIENTST	1	NR	NR	-	-
151 L-D SAINTS	1	NA	471	.3	.6
175 CONGR CHR CHS	2	263	310*	.2	.4
176 CCC, NOT NAT'L	1	26	31*	-	-
193 EPISCOPAL	6	1,346	2,310	1.6	2.7
207 E.L.C.A.	3	671	882	.6	1.0
226 FRIENDS-USA	2	188	222*	.2	.3
226d FGC & FUM	2	188	222*	.2	.3
283 LUTH—MO SYNOD	1	213	222	.2	.3
331 ORTH CH IN AM	1	NR	NR	-	-
435 UNITARIAN-UNIV	3	350	521	.4	.6
443 UN C OF CHRIST	27	5,327	6,284*	4.3	7.4
449 UN METHODIST	5	1,067	1,259*	.9	1.5
496 JEWISH EST[1]	3	NA	4,125	2.8	4.9
497 BLACK BAPT EST[2]	NA	494	583*	.4	.7
499 INDEP.NON-CHAR[3]	1	NA	500	.3	.6
MIDDLESEX	**656**	**102,496**	**993,075***	**71.0**	**100.0**
001 ADVENT CHR CH	1	57	68*	-	-
005 AME ZION	2	201	335	-	-
007 ALBAN ORTH ARC	1	NR	NR	-	-
019 AMER BAPT USA	63	13,537	16,200*	1.2	1.6
049 ARMEN AP CH AM	1	2,000	12,000	.9	1.2
053 ASSEMB OF GOD	13	1,481	2,280	.2	.2
057 BAPT GEN CONF	1	54	65*	-	-
081 CATHOLIC	143	NA	754,988	54.0	76.0
081d LATIN	143	NA	754,988	54.0	76.0
089 CHR & MISS AL	4	105	190	-	-
097 CHR CHS&CHS CR	2	170	203*	-	-
105 CHRISTIAN REF	1	91	143	-	-
111 CH CR,SCIENTST	18	NR	NR	-	-
123 CH GOD (ANDER)	1	12	12	-	-

NA–Not applicable NR–Not reported *Total adherents estimated from known number of communicant, confirmed, full members. - Represents a percent less than 0.1. Percentages may not total due to rounding.
[1] See Appendix E [2] See Appendix F [3] See Appendix G Lines in italic represent a breakdown of Catholic rites or Friends affiliations. They are included in their respective denominational total.

Table 4. Churches and Church Membership by County and Denomination: 1990

County and Denomination	Number of churches	Communicant, confirmed, full members	Total adherents Number	Percent of total population	Percent of total adherents
127 CH GOD (CLEVE)	5	235	281*	-	-
145 CH GOD PROPHCY	1	28	34*	-	-
151 L-D SAINTS	13	NA	4,678	.3	.5
165 CH OF NAZARENE	12	1,288	1,825	.1	.2
167 CHS OF CHRIST	6	386	576	-	.1
175 CONGR CHR CHS	1	85	102*	-	-
176 CCC, NOT NAT'L	3	501	600*	-	.1
179 CONSRV BAPT	8	NR	NR	-	-
181 CONSRV CONGR	4	419	501*	-	.1
193 EPISCOPAL	55	15,554	25,282	1.8	2.5
203 EVAN FREE CH	3	197	309	-	-
207 E.L.C.A.	14	4,501	5,860	.4	.6
209 EVAN LUTH SYN	1	90	111	-	-
226 FRIENDS-USA	5	733	877*	.1	.1
226d *FGC & FUM*	*5*	*733*	*877**	*.1*	*.1*
246 GREEK ORTHODOX	11	NR	NR	-	-
263 INT FOURSQ GOS	3	30	36*	-	-
283 LUTH—MO SYNOD	2	690	1,013	.1	.1
285 MENNONITE CH	1	33	65	-	-
331 ORTH CH IN AM	1	NR	NR	-	-
353 CHR BRETHREN	4	221	355	-	-
355 PRESB CH (USA)	8	1,426	1,707*	.1	.2
363 PRIMITIVE METH	2	189	244	-	-
371 REF CH IN AM	1	79	166	-	-
403 SALVATION ARMY	5	367	434	-	-
413 S.D.A.	12	1,483	1,775*	.1	.2
419 SO BAPT CONV	9	1,990	2,381*	.2	.2
435 UNITARIAN-UNIV	38	7,789	10,916	.8	1.1
443 UN C OF CHRIST	77	22,442	26,857*	1.9	2.7
449 UN METHODIST	50	16,241	19,436*	1.4	2.0
496 JEWISH EST[1]	48	NA	86,267	6.2	8.7
497 BLACK BAPT EST[2]	NA	7,791	9,324*	.7	.9
499 INDEP.NON-CHAR[3]	2	NA	4,579	.3	.5
NANTUCKET	**8**	**1,246**	**4,438***	**73.8**	**100.0**
019 AMER BAPT USA	1	55	66*	1.1	1.5
081 CATHOLIC	1	NA	3,000	49.9	67.6
081d *LATIN*	*1*	*NA*	*3,000*	*49.9*	*67.6*
111 CH CR,SCIENTST	1	NR	NR	-	-
175 CONGR CHR CHS	1	302	364*	6.1	8.2
193 EPISCOPAL	1	651	719	12.0	16.2
226 FRIENDS-USA	1	1	4	.1	.1
226f *INDEPENDNT*	*1*	*1*	*4*	*.1*	*.1*
435 UNITARIAN-UNIV	1	210	252	4.2	5.7
449 UN METHODIST	1	27	33*	.5	.7
NORFOLK	**289**	**46,324**	**435,707***	**70.7**	**100.0**
019 AMER BAPT USA	18	3,339	4,000*	.6	.9
053 ASSEMB OF GOD	3	571	1,353	.2	.3
057 BAPT GEN CONF	5	845	1,012*	.2	.2
081 CATHOLIC	63	NA	336,797	54.7	77.3
081d *LATIN*	*63*	*NA*	*336,797*	*54.7*	*77.3*
089 CHR & MISS AL	1	116	307	-	.1
097 CHR CHS&CHS CR	1	50	60*	-	-
111 CH CR,SCIENTST	7	NR	NR	-	-
151 L-D SAINTS	2	NA	648	.1	.1
165 CH OF NAZARENE	4	787	911	.1	.2
167 CHS OF CHRIST	1	50	60	-	-
175 CONGR CHR CHS	5	2,303	2,759*	.4	.6
176 CCC, NOT NAT'L	1	223	267*	-	.1
179 CONSRV BAPT	4	NR	NR	-	-
181 CONSRV CONGR	1	153	183*	-	-
193 EPISCOPAL	30	8,195	12,905	2.1	3.0
203 EVAN FREE CH	1	75	116	-	-
207 E.L.C.A.	7	1,633	2,083	.3	.5
226 FRIENDS-USA	1	159	190*	-	-
226d *FGC & FUM*	*1*	*159*	*190**	-	-
246 GREEK ORTHODOX	3	NR	NR	-	-
263 INT FOURSQ GOS	2	24	29*	-	-
283 LUTH—MO SYNOD	3	613	760	.1	.2
285 MENNONITE CH	1	40	88	-	-
353 CHR BRETHREN	1	25	50	-	-
355 PRESB CH (USA)	6	1,130	1,354*	.2	.3
356 PRESB CH AMER	1	58	70	-	-
403 SALVATION ARMY	1	68	81	-	-
413 S.D.A.	7	2,421	2,900*	.5	.7
435 UNITARIAN-UNIV	17	3,235	4,591	.7	1.1
443 UN C OF CHRIST	36	13,196	15,807*	2.6	3.6
449 UN METHODIST	14	4,674	5,599*	.9	1.3
496 JEWISH EST[1]	41	NA	37,123	6.0	8.5
497 BLACK BAPT EST[2]	NA	2,341	2,804*	.5	.6
499 INDEP.NON-CHAR[3]	1	NA	800	.1	.2
PLYMOUTH	**230**	**33,537**	**427,177***	**98.1**	**100.0**
001 ADVENT CHR CH	1	89	112*	-	-
005 AME ZION	1	150	208	-	-

County and Denomination	Number of churches	Communicant, confirmed, full members	Total adherents Number	Percent of total population	Percent of total adherents
019 AMER BAPT USA	18	3,106	3,912*	.9	.9
053 ASSEMB OF GOD	10	875	1,781	.4	.4
057 BAPT GEN CONF	3	584	736*	.2	.2
081 CATHOLIC	45	NA	344,319	79.1	80.6
081d *LATIN*	*44*	*NA*	*344,018*	*79.0*	*80.5*
081e *MARONITE*	*1*	*NA*	*301*	*.1*	*.1*
089 CHR & MISS AL	4	218	485	.1	.1
111 CH CR,SCIENTST	7	NR	NR	-	-
123 CH GOD (ANDER)	1	41	60	-	-
127 CH GOD (CLEVE)	2	86	108*	-	-
145 CH GOD PROPHCY	1	28	35*	-	-
151 L-D SAINTS	2	NA	798	.2	.2
165 CH OF NAZARENE	5	647	1,007	.2	.2
167 CHS OF CHRIST	1	48	68	-	-
175 CONGR CHR CHS	5	1,048	1,320*	.3	.3
176 CCC, NOT NAT'L	2	513	646*	.1	.2
179 CONSRV BAPT	3	NR	NR	-	-
181 CONSRV CONGR	2	181	228*	.1	.1
193 EPISCOPAL	15	5,476	9,180	2.1	2.1
207 E.L.C.A.	5	1,324	1,895	.4	.4
226 FRIENDS-USA	4	27	47	-	-
226d *FGC & FUM*	*4*	*27*	*47*	-	-
246 GREEK ORTHODOX	1	NR	NR	-	-
263 INT FOURSQ GOS	4	476	599*	.1	.1
283 LUTH—MO SYNOD	2	340	483	.1	.1
331 ORTH CH IN AM	1	NR	NR	-	-
403 SALVATION ARMY	2	119	143	-	-
413 S.D.A.	4	306	385*	.1	.1
419 SO BAPT CONV	4	286	360*	.1	.1
435 UNITARIAN-UNIV	14	1,974	2,853	.7	.7
443 UN C OF CHRIST	27	8,348	10,514*	2.4	2.5
449 UN METHODIST	23	4,048	5,098*	1.2	1.2
496 JEWISH EST[1]	9	NA	34,728	8.0	8.1
497 BLACK BAPT EST[2]	NA	3,199	4,029*	.9	.9
499 INDEP.NON-CHAR[3]	2	NA	1,040	.2	.2
SUFFOLK	**325**	**78,918**	**311,840***	**47.0**	**100.0**
005 AME ZION	7	6,159	6,955	1.0	2.2
007 ALBAN ORTH ARC	2	NR	NR	-	-
009 ALBAN ORTH DIO	1	NR	NR	-	-
019 AMER BAPT USA	35	9,428	11,158*	1.7	3.6
053 ASSEMB OF GOD	9	1,971	1,940	.3	.6
057 BAPT GEN CONF	2	259	307*	-	.1
081 CATHOLIC	80	NA	173,825	26.2	55.7
081a *ARMENIAN*	*1*	*NA*	*3,100*	*.5*	*1.0*
081d *LATIN*	*76*	*NA*	*167,248*	*25.2*	*53.6*
081e *MARONITE*	*1*	*NA*	*1,866*	*.3*	*.6*
081f *MELKITE-GK*	*1*	*NA*	*1,298*	*.2*	*.4*
081h *UKRAINIAN*	*1*	*NA*	*313*	-	*.1*
089 CHR & MISS AL	5	382	490	.1	.2
105 CHRISTIAN REF	1	0	0	-	-
111 CH CR,SCIENTST	4	NR	NR	-	-
123 CH GOD (ANDER)	2	925	975	.1	.3
127 CH GOD (CLEVE)	6	781	924*	.1	.3
145 CH GOD PROPHCY	5	140	166*	-	.1
151 L-D SAINTS	1	NA	129	-	-
165 CH OF NAZARENE	3	141	199	-	.1
167 CHS OF CHRIST	4	3,417	4,443	.7	1.4
175 CONGR CHR CHS	3	1,834	2,170*	.3	.7
176 CCC, NOT NAT'L	1	345	408*	.1	.1
179 CONSRV BAPT	6	NR	NR	-	-
181 CONSRV CONGR	4	1,876	2,220*	.3	.7
193 EPISCOPAL	25	7,345	12,183	1.8	3.9
207 E.L.C.A.	6	691	1,037	.2	.3
221 FREE METHODIST	1	6	13	-	-
226 FRIENDS-USA	2	52	70	-	-
226d *FGC & FUM*	*2*	*52*	*70*	-	-
246 GREEK ORTHODOX	3	NR	NR	-	-
263 INT FOURSQ GOS	1	3	4*	-	-
274 LAT EVAN LUTH	2	820	883	.1	.3
283 LUTH—MO SYNOD	2	521	685	.1	.2
285 MENNONITE CH	2	89	99	-	-
287 MENN GEN CONF	1	20	25	-	-
331 ORTH CH IN AM	2	NR	NR	-	-
353 CHR BRETHREN	3	124	217	-	.1
355 PRESB CH (USA)	6	298	353*	.1	.1
356 PRESB CH AMER	1	0	0	-	-
403 SALVATION ARMY	3	342	362	.1	.1
413 S.D.A.	4	454	537*	.1	.2
419 SO BAPT CONV	12	3,198	3,785*	.6	1.2
423 SYRIAN ANTIOCH	1	NA	600	.1	.2
435 UNITARIAN-UNIV	10	3,882	4,517	.7	1.4
443 UN C OF CHRIST	19	2,524	2,987*	.4	1.0
449 UN METHODIST	10	1,995	2,361*	.4	.8
467 WESLEYAN	1	12	25	-	-
496 JEWISH EST[1]	27	NA	40,005	6.0	12.8
497 BLACK BAPT EST[2]	NA	28,884	34,183*	5.1	11.0

NA–Not applicable   NR–Not reported   *Total adherents estimated from known number of communicant, confirmed, full members.   - Represents a percent less than 0.1.   Percentages may not total due to rounding.
[1]See Appendix E   [2]See Appendix F   [3]See Appendix G   Lines in *italic* represent a breakdown of Catholic rites or Friends affiliations. They are included in their respective denominational total.

Table 4. Churches and Church Membership by County and Denomination: 1990

Left column table:

County and Denomination	Number of churches	Communicant, confirmed, full members	Total adherents Number	Percent of total population	Percent of total adherents
499 INDEP.NON-CHAR[3]	1	NA	600	.1	.2
WORCESTER	**506**	**64,595**	**431,579***	**60.8**	**100.0**
001 ADVENT CHR CH	2	176	219*	-	.1
005 AME ZION	2	1,110	1,418	.2	.3
007 ALBAN ORTH ARC	2	NR	NR	-	-
019 AMER BAPT USA	30	6,832	8,484*	1.2	2.0
045 APOSTOLIC LUTH	1	80	400	.1	.1
049 ARMEN AP CH AM	2	525	2,450	.3	.6
053 ASSEMB OF GOD	20	1,722	3,639	.5	.8
057 BAPT GEN CONF	9	1,117	1,387*	.2	.3
081 CATHOLIC	133	NA	325,686	45.9	75.5
081d LATIN	131	NA	324,446	45.7	75.2
081e MARONITE	1	NA	710	.1	.2
081f MELKITE-GK	1	NA	530	.1	.1
089 CHR & MISS AL	4	166	267	-	.1
093 CHR CH (DISC)	1	30	30	-	-
097 CHR CHS&CHS CR	1	58	72*	-	-
105 CHRISTIAN REF	2	855	1,229	.2	.3
111 CH CR,SCIENTST	6	NR	NR	-	-
127 CH GOD (CLEVE)	5	177	220*	-	.1
145 CH GOD PROPHCY	3	84	104*	-	-
151 L-D SAINTS	4	NA	1,632	.2	.4
165 CH OF NAZARENE	3	312	629	.1	.1
167 CHS OF CHRIST	4	182	303	-	.1
176 CCC, NOT NAT'L	2	573	712*	.1	.2
179 CONSRV BAPT	8	NR	NR	-	-
181 CONSRV CONGR	4	282	350*	-	.1
193 EPISCOPAL	30	6,989	11,639	1.6	2.7
207 E.L.C.A.	16	6,300	8,287	1.2	1.9
226 FRIENDS-USA	1	64	79*	-	-
226d FGC & FUM	1	64	79*	-	-
246 GREEK ORTHODOX	5	NR	NR	-	-
263 INT FOURSQ GOS	1	0	0*	-	-
283 LUTH—MO SYNOD	3	736	1,076	.2	.2
355 PRESB CH (USA)	3	503	625*	.1	.1
403 SALVATION ARMY	5	364	381	.1	.1
413 S.D.A.	16	3,642	4,523*	.6	1.0
419 SO BAPT CONV	10	1,707	2,120*	.3	.5
423 SYRIAN ANTIOCH	1	NA	800	.1	.2
435 UNITARIAN-UNIV	28	2,943	3,957	.6	.9
443 UN C OF CHRIST	77	16,712	20,753*	2.9	4.8
449 UN METHODIST	36	7,431	9,228*	1.3	2.1
496 JEWISH EST[1]	23	NA	13,700	1.9	3.2
497 BLACK BAPT EST[2]	NA	2,923	3,630*	.5	.8
499 INDEP.NON-CHAR[3]	3	NA	1,550	.2	.4

MICHIGAN

County and Denomination	Number of churches	Communicant, confirmed, full members	Total adherents Number	Percent of total population	Percent of total adherents
THE STATE.....	7,229	1,583,261	4,686,550*	50.4	100.0
ALCONA	**19**	**1,040**	**2,410***	**23.8**	**100.0**
019 AMER BAPT USA	1	100	119*	1.2	4.9
081 CATHOLIC	4	NA	1,175	11.6	48.8
081d LATIN	4	NA	1,175	11.6	48.8
127 CH GOD (CLEVE)	1	42	50*	.5	2.1
181 CONSRV CONGR	1	25	30*	.3	1.2
193 EPISCOPAL	1	35	35	.3	1.5
207 E.L.C.A.	2	185	225	2.2	9.3
283 LUTH—MO SYNOD	1	30	36	.4	1.5
355 PRESB CH (USA)	2	168	200*	2.0	8.3
413 S.D.A.	1	12	14*	.1	.6
449 UN METHODIST	4	330	392*	3.9	16.3
469 WELS	1	113	134	1.3	5.6
ALGER	**18**	**1,410**	**3,993***	**44.5**	**100.0**
081 CATHOLIC	4	NA	2,032	22.6	50.9
081d LATIN	4	NA	2,032	22.6	50.9
193 EPISCOPAL	1	49	110	1.2	2.8
207 E.L.C.A.	3	498	686	7.6	17.2
220 FREE LUTHERAN	1	120	170	1.9	4.3
283 LUTH—MO SYNOD	2	322	424	4.7	10.6
285 MENNONITE CH	1	22	54	.6	1.4
355 PRESB CH (USA)	1	105	130*	1.4	3.3
413 S.D.A.	1	67	83*	.9	2.1
449 UN METHODIST	3	173	214*	2.4	5.4
467 WESLEYAN	1	54	90	1.0	2.3
ALLEGAN	**140**	**25,568**	**47,504***	**52.5**	**100.0**
019 AMER BAPT USA	1	130	170*	.2	.4
053 ASSEMB OF GOD	4	162	303	.3	.6

Right column table:

County and Denomination	Number of churches	Communicant, confirmed, full members	Total adherents Number	Percent of total population	Percent of total adherents
081 CATHOLIC	8	NA	8,983	9.9	18.9
081d LATIN	8	NA	8,983	9.9	18.9
093 CHR CH (DISC)	1	220	410	.5	.9
105 CHRISTIAN REF	31	7,695	11,540	12.8	24.3
111 CH CR,SCIENTST	1	NR	NR	-	-
123 CH GOD (ANDER)	2	332	445	.5	.9
151 L-D SAINTS	2	NA	443	.5	.9
165 CH OF NAZARENE	1	21	71	.1	.1
167 CHS OF CHRIST	3	91	145	.2	.3
175 CONGR CHR CHS	4	812	1,063*	1.2	2.2
179 CONSRV BAPT	3	NR	NR	-	-
193 EPISCOPAL	3	311	421	.5	.9
207 E.L.C.A.	2	482	714	.8	1.5
221 FREE METHODIST	1	13	29	-	.1
259 IFCA	6	NR	NR	-	-
339 PENT CH OF GOD	1	14	25	-	.1
355 PRESB CH (USA)	2	259	339*	.4	.7
371 REF CH IN AM	25	9,914	15,192	16.8	32.0
403 SALVATION ARMY	1	99	102	.1	.2
413 S.D.A.	3	191	250*	.3	.5
419 SO BAPT CONV	1	39	51*	.1	.1
438 UN BRETH IN CR	2	69	93	.1	.2
443 UN C OF CHRIST	2	251	329*	.4	.7
449 UN METHODIST	20	2,650	3,471*	3.8	7.3
467 WESLEYAN	5	529	1,181	1.3	2.5
469 WELS	5	952	1,299	1.4	2.7
497 BLACK BAPT EST[2]	NA	332	435*	.5	.9
ALPENA	**42**	**7,421**	**20,104***	**65.7**	**100.0**
019 AMER BAPT USA	2	225	283*	.9	1.4
053 ASSEMB OF GOD	1	126	150	.5	.7
081 CATHOLIC	6	NA	10,233	33.4	50.9
081d LATIN	6	NA	10,233	33.4	50.9
097 CHR CHS&CHS CR	1	0	0*	-	-
123 CH GOD (ANDER)	1	67	68	.2	.3
145 CH GOD PROPHCY	1	35	44*	.1	.2
165 CH OF NAZARENE	1	40	71	.2	.4
167 CHS OF CHRIST	1	19	24	.1	.1
175 CONGR CHR CHS	1	131	164*	.5	.8
193 EPISCOPAL	2	781	1,000	3.3	5.0
207 E.L.C.A.	5	2,507	3,468	11.3	17.3
209 EVAN LUTH SYN	1	25	35	.1	.2
221 FREE METHODIST	1	87	131	.4	.7
259 IFCA	1	NR	NR	-	-
283 LUTH—MO SYNOD	3	1,606	2,216	7.2	11.0
284 LUTH CH-AM ASC	1	29	34	.1	.2
313 N AM BAPT CONF	1	280	352*	1.2	1.8
355 PRESB CH (USA)	1	174	218*	.7	1.1
403 SALVATION ARMY	1	122	129	.4	.6
413 S.D.A.	1	84	105*	.3	.5
419 SO BAPT CONV	1	43	54*	.2	.3
438 UN BRETH IN CR	1	35	63	.2	.3
443 UN C OF CHRIST	1	336	422*	1.4	2.1
449 UN METHODIST	5	669	840*	2.7	4.2
496 JEWISH EST[1]	1	NA	0	-	-
ANTRIM	**36**	**2,702**	**5,640***	**31.0**	**100.0**
081 CATHOLIC	4	NA	1,537	8.5	27.3
081d LATIN	4	NA	1,537	8.5	27.3
097 CHR CHS&CHS CR	1	140	175*	1.0	3.1
105 CHRISTIAN REF	2	206	318	1.7	5.6
165 CH OF NAZARENE	1	12	35	.2	.6
175 CONGR CHR CHS	1	196	245*	1.3	4.3
193 EPISCOPAL	1	117	184	1.0	3.3
207 E.L.C.A.	1	87	113	.6	2.0
221 FREE METHODIST	2	38	109	.6	1.9
283 LUTH—MO SYNOD	3	309	412	2.3	7.3
285 MENNONITE CH	1	35	60	.3	1.1
291 MISSIONARY CH	1	104	169	.9	3.0
339 PENT CH OF GOD	2	68	153	.8	2.7
349 PENT HOLINESS	1	34	42*	.2	.7
355 PRESB CH (USA)	2	303	378*	2.1	6.7
371 REF CH IN AM	1	173	296	1.6	5.2
413 S.D.A.	2	54	67*	.4	1.2
449 UN METHODIST	8	706	881*	4.8	15.6
467 WESLEYAN	2	120	466	2.6	8.3
ARENAC	**27**	**2,110**	**7,751***	**51.9**	**100.0**
053 ASSEMB OF GOD	1	74	166	1.1	2.1
081 CATHOLIC	3	NA	4,700	31.5	60.6
081b BYZAN RUTH	1	NA	30	.2	.4
081d LATIN	2	NA	4,670	31.3	60.3
193 EPISCOPAL	1	58	81	.5	1.0
207 E.L.C.A.	1	156	195	1.3	2.5
221 FREE METHODIST	3	65	126	.8	1.6
283 LUTH—MO SYNOD	2	446	609	4.1	7.9

NA–Not applicable   NR–Not reported   *Total adherents estimated from known number of communicant, confirmed, full members.   - Represents a percent less than 0.1.   Percentages may not total due to rounding.
[1]See Appendix E   [2]See Appendix F   [3]See Appendix G   Lines in *italic* represent a breakdown of Catholic rites or Friends affiliations. They are included in their respective denominational total.

MICHIGAN

Table 4. Churches and Church Membership by County and Denomination: 1990

County and Denomination	Number of churches	Communicant, confirmed, full members	Total adherents Number	Percent of total population	Percent of total adherents
285 MENNONITE CH	1	137	262	1.8	3.4
339 PENT CH OF GOD	1	34	76	.5	1.0
353 CHR BRETHREN	1	190	300	2.0	3.9
355 PRESB CH (USA)	1	51	64*	.4	.8
419 SO BAPT CONV	1	38	48*	.3	.6
443 UN C OF CHRIST	1	49	62*	.4	.8
449 UN METHODIST	6	652	823*	5.5	10.6
467 WESLEYAN	2	43	89	.6	1.1
469 WELS	2	117	150	1.0	1.9
BARAGA	**13**	**2,141**	**4,613***	**58.0**	**100.0**
045 APOSTOLIC LUTH	1	27	42	.5	.9
081 CATHOLIC	3	NA	1,892	23.8	41.0
081d LATIN	3	NA	1,892	23.8	41.0
207 E.L.C.A.	5	1,607	2,043	25.7	44.3
220 FREE LUTHERAN	1	66	72	.9	1.6
283 LUTH—MO SYNOD	1	250	324	4.1	7.0
413 S.D.A.	0	24	30*	.4	.7
449 UN METHODIST	2	167	210*	2.6	4.6
BARRY	**55**	**5,867**	**12,077***	**24.1**	**100.0**
053 ASSEMB OF GOD	3	170	423	.8	3.5
081 CATHOLIC	4	NA	2,410	4.8	20.0
081d LATIN	4	NA	2,410	4.8	20.0
093 CHR CH (DISC)	1	95	95	.2	.8
105 CHRISTIAN REF	1	93	158	.3	1.3
123 CH GOD (ANDER)	1	52	79	.2	.7
127 CH GOD (CLEVE)	1	27	35*	.1	.3
133 CH GOD(7TH)DEN	1	31	39	.1	.3
151 L-D SAINTS	3	NA	986	2.0	8.2
157 CH OF BRETHREN	2	176	225*	.4	1.9
165 CH OF NAZARENE	2	186	291	.6	2.4
167 CHS OF CHRIST	1	27	37	.1	.3
193 EPISCOPAL	1	158	243	.5	2.0
207 E.L.C.A.	2	457	605	1.2	5.0
221 FREE METHODIST	1	68	83	.2	.7
259 IFCA	2	NR	NR	-	-
283 LUTH—MO SYNOD	1	71	105	.2	.9
339 PENT CH OF GOD	1	34	76	.2	.6
355 PRESB CH (USA)	1	605	775*	1.5	6.4
371 REF CH IN AM	1	604	1,172	2.3	9.7
413 S.D.A.	2	173	221*	.4	1.8
419 SO BAPT CONV	2	87	111*	.2	.9
438 UN BRETH IN CR	3	185	220	.4	1.8
449 UN METHODIST	15	2,291	2,933*	5.9	24.3
467 WESLEYAN	3	277	755	1.5	6.3
BAY	**93**	**21,254**	**74,064***	**66.3**	**100.0**
019 AMER BAPT USA	3	863	1,085*	1.0	1.5
040 AP CHR CH-AMER	1	160	285	.3	.4
053 ASSEMB OF GOD	3	233	605	.5	.8
081 CATHOLIC	23	NA	44,406	39.7	60.0
081b BYZAN RUTH	1	NA	80	.1	.1
081d LATIN	22	NA	44,326	39.7	59.8
111 CH CR,SCIENTST	1	NR	NR	-	-
123 CH GOD (ANDER)	2	185	266	.2	.4
127 CH GOD (CLEVE)	1	62	78*	.1	.1
151 L-D SAINTS	1	NA	213	.2	.3
165 CH OF NAZARENE	2	164	429	.4	.6
167 CHS OF CHRIST	2	106	137	.1	.2
193 EPISCOPAL	2	1,146	1,326	1.2	1.8
203 EVAN FREE CH	1	140	210	.2	.3
207 E.L.C.A.	1	577	745	.7	1.0
221 FREE METHODIST	1	89	89	.1	.1
263 INT FOURSQ GOS	1	0	0*	-	-
283 LUTH—MO SYNOD	11	9,112	11,961	10.7	16.1
291 MISSIONARY CH	1	101	137	.1	.2
313 N AM BAPT CONF	1	138	173*	.2	.2
339 PENT CH OF GOD	1	60	110	.1	.1
353 CHR BRETHREN	3	65	120	.1	.2
355 PRESB CH (USA)	5	1,875	2,357*	2.1	3.2
403 SALVATION ARMY	1	103	127	.1	.2
413 S.D.A.	1	67	84*	.1	.1
419 SO BAPT CONV	2	215	270*	.2	.4
443 UN C OF CHRIST	2	194	244*	.2	.3
449 UN METHODIST	10	2,288	2,877*	2.6	3.9
467 WESLEYAN	3	309	1,256	1.1	1.7
469 WELS	5	2,651	3,403	3.0	4.6
496 JEWISH EST[1]	1	NA	280	.3	.4
497 BLACK BAPT EST[2]	NA	351	441*	.4	.6
499 INDEP.NON-CHAR[3]	1	NA	350	.3	.5
BENZIE	**28**	**2,528**	**3,977***	**32.6**	**100.0**
053 ASSEMB OF GOD	1	88	90	.7	2.3
081 CATHOLIC	1	NA	588	4.8	14.8
081d LATIN	1	NA	588	4.8	14.8

County and Denomination	Number of churches	Communicant, confirmed, full members	Total adherents Number	Percent of total population	Percent of total adherents
093 CHR CH (DISC)	2	178	242	2.0	6.1
097 CHR CHS&CHS CR	1	90	111*	.9	2.8
111 CH CR,SCIENTST	1	NR	NR	-	-
127 CH GOD (CLEVE)	1	5	6*	-	.2
165 CH OF NAZARENE	1	20	80	.7	2.0
167 CHS OF CHRIST	1	33	42	.3	1.1
175 CONGR CHR CHS	1	148	183*	1.5	4.6
181 CONSRV CONGR	2	204	252*	2.1	6.3
193 EPISCOPAL	1	111	150	1.2	3.8
207 E.L.C.A.	1	311	409	3.4	10.3
226 FRIENDS-USA	1	5	35	.3	.9
226e FUM	1	5	35	.3	.9
259 IFCA	2	NR	NR	-	-
283 LUTH—MO SYNOD	1	184	264	2.2	6.6
413 S.D.A.	1	23	28*	.2	.7
443 UN C OF CHRIST	1	369	457*	3.7	11.5
449 UN METHODIST	5	675	835*	6.8	21.0
467 WESLEYAN	3	84	205	1.7	5.2
BERRIEN	**179**	**46,456**	**83,979***	**52.0**	**100.0**
019 AMER BAPT USA	3	1,091	1,382*	.9	1.6
053 ASSEMB OF GOD	5	1,068	1,985	1.2	2.4
057 BAPT GEN CONF	2	314	398*	.2	.5
059 BAPT MISS ASSN	1	25	32*	-	-
081 CATHOLIC	12	NA	22,424	13.9	26.7
081d LATIN	12	NA	22,424	13.9	26.7
093 CHR CH (DISC)	1	134	218	.1	.3
097 CHR CHS&CHS CR	5	1,145	1,450*	.9	1.7
105 CHRISTIAN REF	1	192	332	.2	.4
111 CH CR,SCIENTST	2	NR	NR	-	-
123 CH GOD (ANDER)	9	878	969	.6	1.2
127 CH GOD (CLEVE)	5	515	652*	.4	.8
145 CH GOD PROPHCY	3	107	135*	.1	.2
151 L-D SAINTS	2	NA	382	.2	.5
164 CH LUTH CONF	1	175	230	.1	.3
165 CH OF NAZARENE	4	232	426	.3	.5
167 CHS OF CHRIST	5	495	642	.4	.8
175 CONGR CHR CHS	2	277	351*	.2	.4
181 CONSRV CONGR	1	165	209*	.1	.2
193 EPISCOPAL	4	489	654	.4	.8
203 EVAN FREE CH	1	96	275	.2	.3
207 E.L.C.A.	4	1,085	1,397	.9	1.7
221 FREE METHODIST	3	112	210	.1	.3
223 FREE WILL BAPT	1	35	44*	-	.1
246 GREEK ORTHODOX	1	NR	NR	-	-
259 IFCA	4	NR	NR	-	-
283 LUTH—MO SYNOD	10	7,434	9,768	6.1	11.6
291 MISSIONARY CH	1	9	27	-	-
313 N AM BAPT CONF	5	1,250	1,583*	1.0	1.9
339 PENT CH OF GOD	2	69	154	.1	.2
355 PRESB CH (USA)	5	1,576	1,996*	1.2	2.4
371 REF CH IN AM	2	160	293	.2	.3
403 SALVATION ARMY	1	124	134	.1	.2
413 S.D.A.	14	6,482	8,208*	5.1	9.8
419 SO BAPT CONV	7	730	924*	.6	1.1
435 UNITARIAN-UNIV	1	46	48	-	.1
443 UN C OF CHRIST	15	3,515	4,451*	2.8	5.3
449 UN METHODIST	26	5,506	6,972*	4.3	8.3
469 WELS	6	3,886	4,910	3.0	5.8
496 JEWISH EST[1]	1	NA	500	.3	.6
497 BLACK BAPT EST[2]	NA	7,039	8,914*	5.5	10.6
499 INDEP.NON-CHAR[3]	1	NA	300	.2	.4
BRANCH	**45**	**4,786**	**11,997***	**28.9**	**100.0**
019 AMER BAPT USA	2	644	827*	2.0	6.9
053 ASSEMB OF GOD	2	176	396	1.0	3.3
071 BRETHREN (ASH)	1	10	13*	-	.1
081 CATHOLIC	3	NA	4,372	10.5	36.4
081d LATIN	3	NA	4,372	10.5	36.4
097 CHR CHS&CHS CR	2	195	251*	.6	2.1
123 CH GOD (ANDER)	1	37	37	.1	.3
151 L-D SAINTS	1	NA	265	.6	2.2
165 CH OF NAZARENE	1	130	177	.4	1.5
167 CHS OF CHRIST	1	33	42	.1	.4
193 EPISCOPAL	1	139	166	.4	1.4
207 E.L.C.A.	1	182	243	.6	2.0
221 FREE METHODIST	2	148	258	.6	2.2
283 LUTH—MO SYNOD	3	392	520	1.3	4.3
291 MISSIONARY CH	2	143	203	.5	1.7
323 OLD ORD AMISH	5	NA	750	1.8	6.3
339 PENT CH OF GOD	1	34	77	.2	.6
353 CHR BRETHREN	1	50	100	.2	.8
355 PRESB CH (USA)	2	481	618*	1.5	5.2
413 S.D.A.	1	148	190*	.5	1.6
438 UN BRETH IN CR	1	44	66	.2	.6
443 UN C OF CHRIST	3	440	565*	1.4	4.7
449 UN METHODIST	6	1,069	1,373*	3.3	11.4

NA–Not applicable   NR–Not reported   *Total adherents estimated from known number of communicant, confirmed, full members.   - Represents a percent less than 0.1.   Percentages may not total due to rounding.
[1]See Appendix E   [2]See Appendix F   [3]See Appendix G   Lines in *italic* represent a breakdown of Catholic rites or Friends affiliations. They are included in their respective denominational total.

Table 4. Churches and Church Membership by County and Denomination: 1990

County and Denomination	Number of churches	Communicant, confirmed, full members	Total adherents		
			Number	Percent of total population	Percent of total adherents
467　WESLEYAN	2	129	280	.7	2.3
497　BLACK BAPT EST[2]	NA	162	208*	.5	1.7
CALHOUN	**137**	**25,883**	**52,105***	**38.3**	**100.0**
005　AME ZION	1	435	492	.4	.9
019　AMER BAPT USA	6	901	1,138*	.8	2.2
053　ASSEMB OF GOD	6	803	1,537	1.1	2.9
059　BAPT MISS ASSN	2	39	49*	-	.1
081　CATHOLIC	5	NA	15,654	11.5	30.0
081d　*LATIN*	*5*	*NA*	*15,654*	*11.5*	*30.0*
093　CHR CH (DISC)	1	26	55	-	.1
097　CHR CHS&CHS CR	3	410	518*	.4	1.0
105　CHRISTIAN REF	1	208	344	.3	.7
111　CH CR,SCIENTST	3	NR	NR	-	-
123　CH GOD (ANDER)	6	366	419	.3	.8
127　CH GOD (CLEVE)	3	295	373*	.3	.7
145　CH GOD PROPHCY	2	71	90*	.1	.2
157　CH OF BRETHREN	1	57	72*	.1	.1
165　CH OF NAZARENE	4	446	767	.6	1.5
167　CHS OF CHRIST	5	442	590	.4	1.1
171　CH GOD-GEN CON	1	31	39*	-	.1
176　CCC, NOT NAT'L	1	47	59*	-	.1
179　CONSRV BAPT	1	NR	NR	-	-
193　EPISCOPAL	4	934	1,408	1.0	2.7
207　E.L.C.A.	2	478	661	.5	1.3
221　FREE METHODIST	2	87	126	.1	.2
226　FRIENDS-USA	1	172	252	.2	.5
226b　*EFI*	*1*	*172*	*252*	*.2*	*.5*
246　GREEK ORTHODOX	1	NR	NR	-	-
259　IFCA	5	NR	NR	-	-
263　INT FOURSQ GOS	1	46	58*	-	.1
283　LUTH—MO SYNOD	6	2,766	3,908	2.9	7.5
285　MENNONITE CH	1	45	80	.1	.2
291　MISSIONARY CH	2	142	243	.2	.5
323　OLD ORD AMISH	1	NA	50	-	.1
325　OLD REG BAPT	2	35	44*	-	.1
331　ORTH CH IN AM	1	NR	NR	-	-
339　PENT CH OF GOD	2	134	377	.3	.7
353　CHR BRETHREN	1	22	30	-	.1
355　PRESB CH (USA)	6	2,402	3,034*	2.2	5.8
371　REF CH IN AM	1	118	186	.1	.4
403　SALVATION ARMY	1	199	243	.2	.5
413　S.D.A.	5	1,400	1,768*	1.3	3.4
415　S-D BAPTIST GC	1	163	206*	.2	.4
419　SO BAPT CONV	8	1,543	1,949*	1.4	3.7
438　UN BRETH IN CR	1	39	73	.1	.1
443　UN C OF CHRIST	4	1,628	2,056*	1.5	3.9
449　UN METHODIST	18	4,175	5,273*	3.9	10.1
467　WESLEYAN	5	600	2,118	1.6	4.1
469　WELS	1	108	146	.1	.3
496　JEWISH EST[1]	1	NA	180	.1	.3
497　BLACK BAPT EST[2]	NA	4,070	5,140*	3.8	9.9
499　INDEP.NON-CHAR[3]	1	NA	300	.2	.6
CASS	**50**	**5,028**	**11,219***	**22.7**	**100.0**
019　AMER BAPT USA	2	335	424*	.9	3.8
059　BAPT MISS ASSN	1	69	87*	.2	.8
081　CATHOLIC	5	NA	4,077	8.2	36.3
081d　*LATIN*	*5*	*NA*	*4,077*	*8.2*	*36.3*
093　CHR CH (DISC)	1	80	430	.9	3.8
097　CHR CHS&CHS CR	2	0	0*	-	-
111　CH CR,SCIENTST	1	NR	NR	-	-
123　CH GOD (ANDER)	3	120	190	.4	1.7
165　CH OF NAZARENE	1	117	239	.5	2.1
167　CHS OF CHRIST	1	47	61	.1	.5
193　EPISCOPAL	1	101	177	.4	1.6
203　EVAN FREE CH	1	96	185	.4	1.6
226　FRIENDS-USA	1	38	48*	.1	.4
226e　*FUM*	*1*	*38*	*48*￼*	*.1*	*.4*
259　IFCA	1	NR	NR	-	-
283　LUTH—MO SYNOD	1	167	239	.5	2.1
285　MENNONITE CH	1	51	88	.2	.8
291　MISSIONARY CH	4	211	348	.7	3.1
339　PENT CH OF GOD	1	35	77	.2	.7
353　CHR BRETHREN	1	15	15	-	.1
355　PRESB CH (USA)	2	321	407*	.8	3.6
403　SALVATION ARMY	1	80	86	.2	.8
413　S.D.A.	5	499	632*	1.3	5.6
419　SO BAPT CONV	1	110	139*	.3	1.2
443　UN C OF CHRIST	2	255	323*	.7	2.9
449　UN METHODIST	9	1,080	1,368*	2.8	12.2
469　WELS	1	347	497	1.0	4.4
497　BLACK BAPT EST[2]	NA	854	1,082*	2.2	9.6
CHARLEVOIX	**44**	**3,428**	**8,697***	**40.5**	**100.0**
019　AMER BAPT USA	1	77	98*	.5	1.1
053　ASSEMB OF GOD	3	179	327	1.5	3.8
081　CATHOLIC	6	NA	3,835	17.9	44.1
081d　*LATIN*	*6*	*NA*	*3,835*	*17.9*	*44.1*
111　CH CR,SCIENTST	1	NR	NR	-	-
123　CH GOD (ANDER)	1	130	130	.6	1.5
127　CH GOD (CLEVE)	1	20	25*	.1	.3
151　L-D SAINTS	1	NA	166	.8	1.9
165　CH OF NAZARENE	2	40	85	.4	1.0
167　CHS OF CHRIST	1	28	36	.2	.4
193　EPISCOPAL	2	106	134	.6	1.5
207　E.L.C.A.	1	150	211	1.0	2.4
209　EVAN LUTH SYN	1	45	54	.3	.6
221　FREE METHODIST	1	76	94	.4	1.1
259　IFCA	1	NR	NR	-	-
283　LUTH—MO SYNOD	2	416	516	2.4	5.9
285　MENNONITE CH	1	12	14	.1	.2
291　MISSIONARY CH	1	68	149	.7	1.7
339　PENT CH OF GOD	1	34	77	.4	.9
355　PRESB CH (USA)	3	500	636*	3.0	7.3
371　REF CH IN AM	1	334	567	2.6	6.5
413　S.D.A.	1	85	108*	.5	1.2
419　SO BAPT CONV	1	5	6*	-	.1
443　UN C OF CHRIST	2	429	546*	2.5	6.3
449　UN METHODIST	8	694	883*	4.1	10.2
CHEBOYGAN	**32**	**2,616**	**9,291***	**43.4**	**100.0**
053　ASSEMB OF GOD	2	160	361	1.7	3.9
081　CATHOLIC	6	NA	5,425	25.4	58.4
081d　*LATIN*	*6*	*NA*	*5,425*	*25.4*	*58.4*
093　CHR CH (DISC)	1	118	169	.8	1.8
111　CH CR,SCIENTST	1	NR	NR	-	-
151　L-D SAINTS	1	NA	73	.3	.8
167　CHS OF CHRIST	1	28	36	.2	.4
193　EPISCOPAL	2	248	332	1.6	3.6
207　E.L.C.A.	1	544	782	3.7	8.4
221　FREE METHODIST	2	37	84	.4	.9
259　IFCA	2	NR	NR	-	-
283　LUTH—MO SYNOD	1	267	371	1.7	4.0
339　PENT CH OF GOD	1	34	77	.4	.8
355　PRESB CH (USA)	1	105	132*	.6	1.4
403　SALVATION ARMY	1	68	70	.3	.8
413　S.D.A.	1	29	36*	.2	.4
419　SO BAPT CONV	1	22	28*	.1	.3
443　UN C OF CHRIST	2	152	191*	.9	2.1
449　UN METHODIST	3	672	843*	3.9	9.1
467　WESLEYAN	1	77	208	1.0	2.2
469　WELS	1	55	73	.3	.8
CHIPPEWA	**58**	**5,386**	**12,196***	**35.2**	**100.0**
019　AMER BAPT USA	1	110	135*	.4	1.1
045　APOSTOLIC LUTH	1	10	15	-	.1
053　ASSEMB OF GOD	3	90	203	.6	1.7
081　CATHOLIC	14	NA	5,079	14.7	41.6
081d　*LATIN*	*14*	*NA*	*5,079*	*14.7*	*41.6*
097　CHR CHS&CHS CR	2	400	491*	1.4	4.0
105　CHRISTIAN REF	2	220	370	1.1	3.0
165　CH OF NAZARENE	2	120	227	.7	1.9
167　CHS OF CHRIST	1	23	32	.1	.3
193　EPISCOPAL	4	252	307	.9	2.5
207　E.L.C.A.	2	660	862	2.5	7.1
221　FREE METHODIST	1	34	72	.2	.6
246　GREEK ORTHODOX	1	NR	NR	-	-
283　LUTH—MO SYNOD	1	40	49	.1	.4
285　MENNONITE CH	1	24	36	.1	.3
339　PENT CH OF GOD	1	34	77	.2	.6
353　CHR BRETHREN	1	18	34	.1	.3
355　PRESB CH (USA)	8	955	1,171*	3.4	9.6
403　SALVATION ARMY	1	74	95	.3	.8
413　S.D.A.	1	49	60*	.2	.5
419　SO BAPT CONV	2	617	757*	2.2	6.2
443　UN C OF CHRIST	1	37	45*	.1	.4
449　UN METHODIST	5	867	1,064*	3.1	8.7
467　WESLEYAN	1	75	160	.5	1.3
469　WELS	1	176	240	.7	2.0
497　BLACK BAPT EST[2]	NA	501	615*	1.8	5.0
CLARE	**33**	**3,172**	**6,992***	**28.0**	**100.0**
053　ASSEMB OF GOD	2	226	490	2.0	7.0
081　CATHOLIC	2	NA	1,982	7.9	28.3
081d　*LATIN*	*2*	*NA*	*1,982*	*7.9*	*28.3*
097　CHR CHS&CHS CR	2	200	252*	1.0	3.6
111　CH CR,SCIENTST	1	NR	NR	-	-
123　CH GOD (ANDER)	1	40	40	.2	.6
151　L-D SAINTS	1	NA	178	.7	2.5
165　CH OF NAZARENE	2	113	223	.9	3.2
167　CHS OF CHRIST	2	56	71	.3	1.0

NA–Not applicable　　NR–Not reported　　*Total adherents estimated from known number of communicant, confirmed, full members.　　- Represents a percent less than 0.1.　　Percentages may not total due to rounding.
[1]See Appendix E　　[2]See Appendix F　　[3]See Appendix G　　Lines in *italic* represent a breakdown of Catholic rites or Friends affiliations. They are included in their respective denominational total.

Table 4. Churches and Church Membership by County and Denomination: 1990

County and Denomination	Number of churches	Communicant, confirmed, full members	Total adherents Number	Percent of total population	Percent of total adherents
171 CH GOD-GEN CON	4	110	139*	.6	2.0
203 EVAN FREE CH	1	25	35	.1	.5
283 LUTH—MO SYNOD	2	370	480	1.9	6.9
323 OLD ORD AMISH	2	NA	300	1.2	4.3
419 SO BAPT CONV	1	80	101*	.4	1.4
438 UN BRETH IN CR	2	201	325	1.3	4.6
443 UN C OF CHRIST	2	531	669*	2.7	9.6
449 UN METHODIST	2	736	928*	3.7	13.3
467 WESLEYAN	1	187	415	1.7	5.9
469 WELS	3	297	364	1.5	5.2
CLINTON	**49**	**6,397**	**21,076***	**36.4**	**100.0**
019 AMER BAPT USA	2	178	230*	.4	1.1
053 ASSEMB OF GOD	1	73	138	.2	.7
081 CATHOLIC	4	NA	11,964	20.7	56.8
081d LATIN	*4*	*NA*	*11,964*	*20.7*	*56.8*
097 CHR CHS&CHS CR	3	690	890*	1.5	4.2
105 CHRISTIAN REF	1	145	286	.5	1.4
123 CH GOD (ANDER)	1	0	127	.2	.6
165 CH OF NAZARENE	2	201	362	.6	1.7
167 CHS OF CHRIST	2	59	77	.1	.4
175 CONGR CHR CHS	1	406	524*	.9	2.5
181 CONSRV CONGR	2	229	295*	.5	1.4
193 EPISCOPAL	2	118	219	.4	1.0
221 FREE METHODIST	1	18	32	.1	.2
263 INT FOURSQ GOS	2	65	84*	.1	.4
283 LUTH—MO SYNOD	4	1,291	1,681	2.9	8.0
323 OLD ORD AMISH	1	NA	100	.2	.5
371 REF CH IN AM	1	186	255	.4	1.2
413 S.D.A.	1	100	129*	.2	.6
419 SO BAPT CONV	1	150	193*	.3	.9
443 UN C OF CHRIST	1	256	330*	.6	1.6
449 UN METHODIST	16	2,232	2,879*	5.0	13.7
496 JEWISH EST[1]	0	NA	281	.5	1.3
CRAWFORD	**12**	**1,406**	**3,309***	**27.0**	**100.0**
053 ASSEMB OF GOD	1	63	200	1.6	6.0
081 CATHOLIC	1	NA	1,150	9.4	34.8
081d LATIN	*1*	*NA*	*1,150*	*9.4*	*34.8*
123 CH GOD (ANDER)	1	12	15	.1	.5
151 L-D SAINTS	1	NA	135	1.1	4.1
167 CHS OF CHRIST	1	30	35	.3	1.1
193 EPISCOPAL	1	171	310	2.5	9.4
207 E.L.C.A.	1	129	173	1.4	5.2
221 FREE METHODIST	1	65	93	.8	2.8
283 LUTH—MO SYNOD	1	356	465	3.8	14.1
413 S.D.A.	1	45	57*	.5	1.7
419 SO BAPT CONV	1	82	104*	.8	3.1
449 UN METHODIST	1	453	572*	4.7	17.3
DELTA	**58**	**7,283**	**24,054***	**63.7**	**100.0**
053 ASSEMB OF GOD	1	160	265	.7	1.1
057 BAPT GEN CONF	3	369	466*	1.2	1.9
081 CATHOLIC	13	NA	14,545	38.5	60.5
081d LATIN	*13*	*NA*	*14,545*	*38.5*	*60.5*
097 CHR CHS&CHS CR	1	30	38*	.1	.2
111 CH CR,SCIENTST	1	NR	NR	-	-
127 CH GOD (CLEVE)	1	58	73*	.2	.3
151 L-D SAINTS	1	NA	82	.2	.3
165 CH OF NAZARENE	0	6	25	.1	.1
167 CHS OF CHRIST	1	35	48	.1	.2
175 CONGR CHR CHS	1	110	139*	.4	.6
193 EPISCOPAL	3	292	499	1.3	2.1
203 EVAN FREE CH	1	45	65	.2	.3
207 E.L.C.A.	10	3,542	4,362	11.5	18.1
220 FREE LUTHERAN	1	31	38	.1	.2
221 FREE METHODIST	1	9	22	.1	.1
259 IFCA	1	NR	NR	-	-
283 LUTH—MO SYNOD	1	122	181	.5	.8
285 MENNONITE CH	1	28	95	.3	.4
353 CHR BRETHREN	1	25	80	.2	.3
355 PRESB CH (USA)	1	337	425*	1.1	1.8
403 SALVATION ARMY	1	144	162	.4	.7
413 S.D.A.	2	128	162*	.4	.7
419 SO BAPT CONV	1	12	15*	-	.1
443 UN C OF CHRIST	2	57	72*	.2	.3
449 UN METHODIST	4	1,197	1,510*	4.0	6.3
469 WELS	4	546	685	1.8	2.8
DICKINSON	**35**	**5,217**	**16,084***	**59.9**	**100.0**
053 ASSEMB OF GOD	1	117	187	.7	1.2
057 BAPT GEN CONF	3	466	587*	2.2	3.6
081 CATHOLIC	9	NA	8,955	33.4	55.7
081d LATIN	*9*	*NA*	*8,955*	*33.4*	*55.7*
097 CHR CHS&CHS CR	1	120	151*	.6	.9
111 CH CR,SCIENTST	1	NR	NR		

County and Denomination	Number of churches	Communicant, confirmed, full members	Total adherents Number	Percent of total population	Percent of total adherents
151 L-D SAINTS	1	NA	148	.6	.9
167 CHS OF CHRIST	1	11	14	.1	.1
193 EPISCOPAL	1	157	397	1.5	2.5
207 E.L.C.A.	5	2,209	2,922	10.9	18.2
211 FEL EVG BIB CH	1	12	20	.1	.1
283 LUTH—MO SYNOD	1	269	350	1.3	2.2
355 PRESB CH (USA)	2	594	748*	2.8	4.7
413 S.D.A.	1	52	65*	.2	.4
419 SO BAPT CONV	1	131	165*	.6	1.0
449 UN METHODIST	4	972	1,224*	4.6	7.6
469 WELS	1	107	151	.6	.9
496 JEWISH EST[1]	1	NA	0	-	-
EATON	**81**	**13,685**	**25,248***	**27.2**	**100.0**
019 AMER BAPT USA	1	581	739*	.8	2.9
053 ASSEMB OF GOD	7	2,411	5,842	6.3	23.1
081 CATHOLIC	1	NA	2,990	3.2	11.8
081d LATIN	*1*	*NA*	*2,990*	*3.2*	*11.8*
097 CHR CHS&CHS CR	1	105	134*	.1	.5
105 CHRISTIAN REF	1	34	53	.1	.2
111 CH CR,SCIENTST	1	NR	NR	-	-
123 CH GOD (ANDER)	1	79	79	.1	.3
127 CH GOD (CLEVE)	2	222	283*	.3	1.1
151 L-D SAINTS	1	NA	374	.4	1.5
157 CH OF BRETHREN	1	34	43*	-	.2
165 CH OF NAZARENE	5	611	1,125	1.2	4.5
167 CHS OF CHRIST	2	46	61	.1	.2
175 CONGR CHR CHS	2	254	323*	.3	1.3
193 EPISCOPAL	3	401	561	.6	2.2
207 E.L.C.A.	2	410	560	.6	2.2
221 FREE METHODIST	2	109	154	.2	.6
259 IFCA	4	NR	NR	-	-
283 LUTH—MO SYNOD	2	683	935	1.0	3.7
323 OLD ORD AMISH	2	NA	300	.3	1.2
325 OLD REG BAPT	1	20	25*	-	.1
339 PENT CH OF GOD	1	34	77	.1	.3
355 PRESB CH (USA)	1	240	305*	.3	1.2
413 S.D.A.	6	962	1,224*	1.3	4.8
419 SO BAPT CONV	2	384	489*	.5	1.9
438 UN BRETH IN CR	4	296	361	.4	1.4
443 UN C OF CHRIST	4	958	1,219*	1.3	4.8
449 UN METHODIST	17	3,522	4,483*	4.8	17.8
467 WESLEYAN	1	70	220	.2	.9
469 WELS	2	282	365	.4	1.4
496 JEWISH EST[1]	0	NA	451	.5	1.8
497 BLACK BAPT EST[2]	NA	937	1,193*	1.3	4.7
498 INDEP.CHARIS.[3]	1	NA	280	.3	1.1
EMMET	**43**	**4,480**	**12,493***	**49.9**	**100.0**
053 ASSEMB OF GOD	1	121	240	1.0	1.9
081 CATHOLIC	6	NA	5,917	23.6	47.4
081d LATIN	*6*	*NA*	*5,917*	*23.6*	*47.4*
093 CHR CH (DISC)	1	135	405	1.6	3.2
097 CHR CHS&CHS CR	1	0	0*	-	-
111 CH CR,SCIENTST	1	NR	NR	-	-
123 CH GOD (ANDER)	1	33	40	.2	.3
165 CH OF NAZARENE	2	199	450	1.8	3.6
167 CHS OF CHRIST	1	32	43	.2	.3
193 EPISCOPAL	1	264	300	1.2	2.4
207 E.L.C.A.	1	141	205	.8	1.6
259 IFCA	1	NR	NR	-	-
283 LUTH—MO SYNOD	1	537	686	2.7	5.5
285 MENNONITE CH	3	181	330	1.3	2.6
291 MISSIONARY CH	2	99	185	.7	1.5
339 PENT CH OF GOD	2	61	104	.4	.8
355 PRESB CH (USA)	2	738	937*	3.7	7.5
403 SALVATION ARMY	1	72	78	.3	.6
413 S.D.A.	2	147	187*	.7	1.5
419 SO BAPT CONV	2	193	245*	1.0	2.0
443 UN C OF CHRIST	1	42	53*	.2	.4
449 UN METHODIST	6	1,071	1,360*	5.4	10.9
467 WESLEYAN	2	383	686	2.7	5.5
469 WELS	1	31	42	.2	.3
496 JEWISH EST[1]	1	NA	0	-	-
GENESEE	**316**	**81,940**	**182,431***	**42.4**	**100.0**
005 AME ZION	1	539	646	.2	.4
019 AMER BAPT USA	11	2,902	3,715*	.9	2.0
053 ASSEMB OF GOD	16	1,680	3,114	.7	1.7
059 BAPT MISS ASSN	4	839	1,074*	.2	.6
075 BRETHREN IN CR	1	62	81	-	-
081 CATHOLIC	29	NA	67,251	15.6	36.9
081b BYZAN RUTH	*1*	*NA*	*627*	*.1*	*.3*
081d LATIN	*26*	*NA*	*65,148*	*15.1*	*35.7*
081e MARONITE	*1*	*NA*	*1,416*	*.3*	*.8*
081h UKRAINIAN	*1*	*NA*	*60*		-

Table 4. Churches and Church Membership by County and Denomination: 1990

County and Denomination	Number of churches	Communicant, confirmed, full members	Total adherents		
			Number	Percent of total population	Percent of total adherents
089 CHR & MISS AL	1	50	137	-	.1
093 CHR CH (DISC)	3	434	565	.1	.3
097 CHR CHS&CHS CR	4	480	614*	.1	.3
105 CHRISTIAN REF	1	84	152	-	.1
111 CH CR,SCIENTST	2	NR	NR	-	-
123 CH GOD (ANDER)	9	1,130	1,374	.3	.8
127 CH GOD (CLEVE)	4	744	952*	.2	.5
145 CH GOD PROPHCY	1	35	45*	-	-
151 L-D SAINTS	2	NA	926	.2	.5
157 CH OF BRETHREN	1	45	58*	-	-
165 CH OF NAZARENE	17	2,509	4,098	1.0	2.2
167 CHS OF CHRIST	13	2,615	3,237	.8	1.8
179 CONSRV BAPT	1	NR	NR	-	-
181 CONSRV CONGR	3	472	604*	.1	.3
193 EPISCOPAL	7	1,708	2,405	.6	1.3
207 E.L.C.A.	6	1,276	1,713	.4	.9
216 EVAN PRESBY CH	1	541	578	.1	.3
221 FREE METHODIST	11	887	1,241	.3	.7
223 FREE WILL BAPT	2	259	332*	.1	.2
246 GREEK ORTHODOX	1	NR	NR	-	-
249 AP CATH ASSYR	1	79	316	.1	.2
259 IFCA	5	NR	NR	-	-
265 INT PENT C CHR	1	33	45	-	-
283 LUTH—MO SYNOD	17	7,968	10,423	2.4	5.7
285 MENNONITE CH	2	52	90	-	-
291 MISSIONARY CH	4	322	439	.1	.2
331 ORTH CH IN AM	1	NR	NR	-	-
339 PENT CH OF GOD	9	357	806	.2	.4
349 PENT HOLINESS	1	35	45*	-	-
353 CHR BRETHREN	1	59	89	-	-
355 PRESB CH (USA)	16	5,964	7,634*	1.8	4.2
356 PRESB CH AMER	1	366	424	.1	.2
371 REF CH IN AM	1	219	368	.1	.2
403 SALVATION ARMY	3	448	495	.1	.3
413 S.D.A.	5	1,071	1,371*	.3	.8
419 SO BAPT CONV	27	7,610	9,741*	2.3	5.3
435 UNITARIAN-UNIV	1	129	181	-	.1
438 UN BRETH IN CR	2	153	294	.1	.2
443 UN C OF CHRIST	3	1,327	1,699*	.4	.9
449 UN METHODIST	41	10,728	13,733*	3.2	7.5
467 WESLEYAN	8	633	1,026	.2	.6
469 WELS	6	1,251	1,702	.4	.9
496 JEWISH EST[1]	2	NA	1,825	.4	1.0
497 BLACK BAPT EST[2]	NA	23,845	30,523*	7.1	16.7
499 INDEP.NON-CHAR[3]	6	NA	4,250	1.0	2.3
GLADWIN	**31**	**2,885**	**6,451***	**29.5**	**100.0**
053 ASSEMB OF GOD	2	110	240	1.1	3.7
057 BAPT GEN CONF	1	49	62*	.3	1.0
081 CATHOLIC	2	NA	1,824	8.3	28.3
081d LATIN	*2*	*NA*	*1,824*	*8.3*	*28.3*
123 CH GOD (ANDER)	1	0	62	.3	1.0
157 CH OF BRETHREN	1	98	123*	.6	1.9
165 CH OF NAZARENE	2	221	432	2.0	6.7
167 CHS OF CHRIST	1	89	124	.6	1.9
193 EPISCOPAL	1	127	165	.8	2.6
207 E.L.C.A.	2	338	478	2.2	7.4
221 FREE METHODIST	2	137	170	.8	2.6
283 LUTH—MO SYNOD	1	527	653	3.0	10.1
291 MISSIONARY CH	1	18	42	.2	.7
313 N AM BAPT CONF	1	247	311*	1.4	4.8
323 OLD ORD AMISH	4	NA	600	2.7	9.3
355 PRESB CH (USA)	1	85	107*	.5	1.7
413 S.D.A.	2	87	109*	.5	1.7
449 UN METHODIST	5	632	795*	3.6	12.3
469 WELS	1	120	154	.7	2.4
GOGEBIC	**29**	**4,675**	**10,788***	**59.8**	**100.0**
045 APOSTOLIC LUTH	1	50	125	.7	1.2
053 ASSEMB OF GOD	1	53	122	.7	1.1
057 BAPT GEN CONF	1	122	147*	.8	1.4
081 CATHOLIC	6	NA	4,687	26.0	43.4
081d LATIN	*6*	*NA*	*4,687*	*26.0*	*43.4*
089 CHR & MISS AL	1	8	9	-	.1
151 L-D SAINTS	1	NA	138	.8	1.3
193 EPISCOPAL	1	61	83	.5	.8
207 E.L.C.A.	6	2,849	3,555	19.7	33.0
220 FREE LUTHERAN	1	44	55	.3	.5
283 LUTH—MO SYNOD	4	889	1,144	6.3	10.6
355 PRESB CH (USA)	3	155	187*	1.0	1.7
413 S.D.A.	1	36	43*	.2	.4
449 UN METHODIST	2	408	493*	2.7	4.6
GRAND TRAVERSE	**60**	**9,615**	**27,413***	**42.7**	**100.0**
019 AMER BAPT USA	2	107	137*	.2	.5
053 ASSEMB OF GOD	1	60	80	.1	.3

County and Denomination	Number of churches	Communicant, confirmed, full members	Total adherents		
			Number	Percent of total population	Percent of total adherents
081 CATHOLIC	7	NA	13,747	21.4	50.1
081d LATIN	*7*	*NA*	*13,747*	*21.4*	*50.1*
093 CHR CH (DISC)	1	203	302	.5	1.1
097 CHR CHS&CHS CR	2	130	166*	.3	.6
105 CHRISTIAN REF	1	63	113	.2	.4
111 CH CR,SCIENTST	1	NR	NR	-	-
123 CH GOD (ANDER)	1	50	62	.1	.2
127 CH GOD (CLEVE)	1	76	97*	.2	.4
151 L-D SAINTS	1	NA	390	.6	1.4
165 CH OF NAZARENE	1	118	286	.4	1.0
167 CHS OF CHRIST	1	75	97	.2	.4
179 CONSRV BAPT	1	NR	NR	-	-
193 EPISCOPAL	1	280	460	.7	1.7
203 EVAN FREE CH	1	36	72	.1	.3
207 E.L.C.A.	3	1,328	1,744	2.7	6.4
221 FREE METHODIST	1	13	26	-	.1
259 IFCA	2	NR	NR	-	-
283 LUTH—MO SYNOD	4	1,423	2,062	3.2	7.5
285 MENNONITE CH	1	29	54	.1	.2
291 MISSIONARY CH	2	31	66	.1	.2
339 PENT CH OF GOD	1	34	77	.1	.3
355 PRESB CH (USA)	1	812	1,037*	1.6	3.8
371 REF CH IN AM	1	587	943	1.5	3.4
403 SALVATION ARMY	1	127	141	.2	.5
413 S.D.A.	1	123	157*	.2	.6
419 SO BAPT CONV	3	253	323*	.5	1.2
435 UNITARIAN-UNIV	1	126	156	.2	.6
443 UN C OF CHRIST	2	1,139	1,454*	2.3	5.3
449 UN METHODIST	9	2,229	2,846*	4.4	10.4
467 WESLEYAN	1	92	224	.3	.8
469 WELS	1	71	94	.1	.3
496 JEWISH EST[1]	2	NA	0	-	-
GRATIOT	**71**	**7,964**	**15,117***	**38.8**	**100.0**
019 AMER BAPT USA	1	111	141*	.4	.9
053 ASSEMB OF GOD	2	79	150	.4	1.0
081 CATHOLIC	5	NA	4,036	10.4	26.7
081d LATIN	*5*	*NA*	*4,036*	*10.4*	*26.7*
097 CHR CHS&CHS CR	4	1,155	1,464*	3.8	9.7
111 CH CR,SCIENTST	1	NR	NR	-	-
123 CH GOD (ANDER)	3	375	606	1.6	4.0
127 CH GOD (CLEVE)	1	74	94*	.2	.6
143 CG IN CR(MENN)	1	216	274*	.7	1.8
157 CH OF BRETHREN	1	102	129*	.3	.9
165 CH OF NAZARENE	4	352	834	2.1	5.5
171 CH GOD-GEN CON	2	30	38*	.1	.3
193 EPISCOPAL	1	237	283	.7	1.9
221 FREE METHODIST	2	90	106	.3	.7
263 INT FOURSQ GOS	1	18	23*	.1	.2
265 INT PENT C CHR	3	67	83	.2	.5
283 LUTH—MO SYNOD	2	636	835	2.1	5.5
285 MENNONITE CH	1	142	172	.4	1.1
339 PENT CH OF GOD	2	42	88	.2	.6
355 PRESB CH (USA)	5	858	1,088*	2.8	7.2
403 SALVATION ARMY	1	77	79	.2	.5
413 S.D.A.	3	228	289*	.7	1.9
419 SO BAPT CONV	1	123	156*	.4	1.0
438 UN BRETH IN CR	3	175	184	.5	1.2
443 UN C OF CHRIST	1	130	165*	.4	1.1
449 UN METHODIST	13	2,107	2,671*	6.9	17.7
467 WESLEYAN	5	189	675	1.7	4.5
469 WELS	2	351	454	1.2	3.0
HILLSDALE	**63**	**5,830**	**10,163***	**23.4**	**100.0**
019 AMER BAPT USA	4	469	602*	1.4	5.9
053 ASSEMB OF GOD	1	314	418	1.0	4.1
081 CATHOLIC	1	NA	1,666	3.8	16.4
081d LATIN	*1*	*NA*	*1,666*	*3.8*	*16.4*
097 CHR CHS&CHS CR	2	170	218*	.5	2.1
111 CH CR,SCIENTST	1	NR	NR	-	-
145 CH GOD PROPHCY	1	35	45*	.1	.4
165 CH OF NAZARENE	2	116	286	.7	2.8
167 CHS OF CHRIST	1	50	75	.2	.7
175 CONGR CHR CHS	3	232	298*	.7	2.9
193 EPISCOPAL	2	169	197	.5	1.9
207 E.L.C.A.	1	127	172	.4	1.7
221 FREE METHODIST	1	173	223	.5	2.2
259 IFCA	4	NR	NR	-	-
283 LUTH—MO SYNOD	1	233	329	.8	3.2
285 MENNONITE CH	2	111	175	.4	1.7
291 MISSIONARY CH	1	40	60	.1	.6
323 OLD ORD AMISH	3	NA	450	1.0	4.4
325 OLD REG BAPT	1	11	14*	-	.1
339 PENT CH OF GOD	2	60	165	.4	1.6
355 PRESB CH (USA)	3	774	994*	2.3	9.8
403 SALVATION ARMY	1	91	142	.3	1.4
413 S.D.A.	2	124	159*	.4	1.6

MICHIGAN

Table 4. Churches and Church Membership by County and Denomination: 1990

County and Denomination	Number of churches	Communicant, confirmed, full members	Total adherents		
			Number	Percent of total population	Percent of total adherents
419 SO BAPT CONV	1	212	272*	.6	2.7
438 UN BRETH IN CR	5	454	520	1.2	5.1
443 UN C OF CHRIST	2	270	347*	.8	3.4
449 UN METHODIST	13	1,367	1,756*	4.0	17.3
467 WESLEYAN	2	228	580	1.3	5.7
HOUGHTON	**59**	**6,076**	**15,018***	**42.4**	**100.0**
045 APOSTOLIC LUTH	8	612	1,181	3.3	7.9
053 ASSEMB OF GOD	1	116	246	.7	1.6
081 CATHOLIC	12	NA	6,594	18.6	43.9
081d LATIN	*12*	*NA*	*6,594*	*18.6*	*43.9*
097 CHR CHS&CHS CR	1	44	53*	.1	.4
111 CH CR,SCIENTST	1	NR	NR	-	-
151 L-D SAINTS	1	NA	124	.3	.8
167 CHS OF CHRIST	1	25	33	.1	.2
193 EPISCOPAL	2	193	265	.7	1.8
207 E.L.C.A.	8	2,503	3,311	9.3	22.0
220 FREE LUTHERAN	1	62	68	.2	.5
226 FRIENDS-USA	1	10	27	.1	.2
226c FGC	*1*	*10*	*27*	*.1*	*.2*
283 LUTH—MO SYNOD	3	696	871	2.5	5.8
353 CHR BRETHREN	1	9	18	.1	.1
355 PRESB CH (USA)	2	104	126*	.4	.8
403 SALVATION ARMY	1	51	67	.2	.4
413 S.D.A.	1	54	65*	.2	.4
419 SO BAPT CONV	1	32	39*	.1	.3
435 UNITARIAN-UNIV	1	33	42	.1	.3
443 UN C OF CHRIST	2	208	252*	.7	1.7
449 UN METHODIST	7	1,045	1,266*	3.6	8.4
469 WELS	2	279	370	1.0	2.5
496 JEWISH EST[1]	1	NA	0	-	-
HURON	**71**	**9,427**	**25,756***	**73.7**	**100.0**
019 AMER BAPT USA	2	215	272*	.8	1.1
053 ASSEMB OF GOD	3	82	189	.5	.7
081 CATHOLIC	15	NA	13,358	38.2	51.9
081d LATIN	*15*	*NA*	*13,358*	*38.2*	*51.9*
165 CH OF NAZARENE	2	104	200	.6	.8
167 CHS OF CHRIST	1	10	19	.1	.1
193 EPISCOPAL	2	94	133	.4	.5
207 E.L.C.A.	1	446	591	1.7	2.3
221 FREE METHODIST	2	77	166	.5	.6
249 AP CATH ASSYR	0	1	4	-	-
283 LUTH—MO SYNOD	9	4,089	5,325	15.2	20.7
285 MENNONITE CH	3	348	428	1.2	1.7
291 MISSIONARY CH	2	114	166	.5	.6
355 PRESB CH (USA)	5	331	419*	1.2	1.6
356 PRESB CH AMER	1	290	333	1.0	1.3
413 S.D.A.	1	25	32*	.1	.1
449 UN METHODIST	18	2,389	3,027*	8.7	11.8
467 WESLEYAN	1	44	135	.4	.5
469 WELS	3	768	959	2.7	3.7
INGHAM	**199**	**47,311**	**113,481***	**40.3**	**100.0**
019 AMER BAPT USA	12	3,783	4,703*	1.7	4.1
053 ASSEMB OF GOD	7	629	1,152	.4	1.0
057 BAPT GEN CONF	2	384	477*	.2	.4
059 BAPT MISS ASSN	1	223	277*	.1	.2
081 CATHOLIC	17	NA	43,976	15.6	38.8
081d LATIN	*16*	*NA*	*43,724*	*15.5*	*38.5*
081f MELKITE-GK	*1*	*NA*	*252*	*.1*	*.2*
089 CHR & MISS AL	2	95	174	.1	.2
093 CHR CH (DISC)	1	367	447	.2	.4
097 CHR CHS&CHS CR	5	1,166	1,450*	.5	1.3
105 CHRISTIAN REF	2	628	948	.3	.8
111 CH CR,SCIENTST	4	NR	NR	-	-
123 CH GOD (ANDER)	2	640	650	.2	.6
127 CH GOD (CLEVE)	4	213	265*	.1	.2
145 CH GOD PROPHCY	1	35	44*	-	-
151 L-D SAINTS	3	NA	948	.3	.8
157 CH OF BRETHREN	1	45	56*	-	-
165 CH OF NAZARENE	10	1,110	1,605	.6	1.4
167 CHS OF CHRIST	4	345	463	.2	.4
175 CONGR CHR CHS	1	1,341	1,667*	.6	1.5
193 EPISCOPAL	5	1,322	1,808	.6	1.6
203 EVAN FREE CH	1	55	110	-	.1
207 E.L.C.A.	9	3,372	4,591	1.6	4.0
215 EVAN METH CH	1	4	5*	-	-
221 FREE METHODIST	5	559	833	.3	.7
226 FRIENDS-USA	1	47	58*	-	.1
226c FGC	*1*	*47*	*58**	*-*	*.1*
246 GREEK ORTHODOX	1	NR	NR	-	-
259 IFCA	2	NR	NR	-	-
274 LAT EVAN LUTH	1	67	76	-	.1
283 LUTH—MO SYNOD	8	2,463	3,393	1.2	3.0
285 MENNONITE CH	1	39	61	-	.1

County and Denomination	Number of churches	Communicant, confirmed, full members	Total adherents		
			Number	Percent of total population	Percent of total adherents
287 MENN GEN CONF	1	15	25	-	-
291 MISSIONARY CH	1	30	60	-	.1
313 N AM BAPT CONF	1	261	324*	.1	.3
325 OLD REG BAPT	1	19	24*	-	-
339 PENT CH OF GOD	1	35	77	-	.1
353 CHR BRETHREN	1	25	50	-	-
355 PRESB CH (USA)	10	3,674	4,567*	1.6	4.0
371 REF CH IN AM	1	206	416	.1	.4
403 SALVATION ARMY	2	224	246	.1	.2
413 S.D.A.	5	491	610*	.2	.5
419 SO BAPT CONV	4	1,552	1,929*	.7	1.7
435 UNITARIAN-UNIV	1	339	479	.2	.4
438 UN BRETH IN CR	2	206	260	.1	.2
443 UN C OF CHRIST	9	3,527	4,385*	1.6	3.9
449 UN METHODIST	28	7,695	9,566*	3.4	8.4
467 WESLEYAN	5	420	1,153	.4	1.0
469 WELS	3	1,782	2,311	.8	2.0
496 JEWISH EST[1]	2	NA	1,368	.5	1.2
497 BLACK BAPT EST[2]	NA	7,878	9,794*	3.5	8.6
498 INDEP.CHARIS.[3]	2	NA	800	.3	.7
499 INDEP.NON-CHAR[3]	5	NA	4,800	1.7	4.2
IONIA	**61**	**6,022**	**19,951***	**35.0**	**100.0**
019 AMER BAPT USA	3	330	424*	.7	2.1
053 ASSEMB OF GOD	2	66	187	.3	.9
081 CATHOLIC	6	NA	11,461	20.1	57.4
081d LATIN	*6*	*NA*	*11,461*	*20.1*	*57.4*
093 CHR CH (DISC)	2	155	232	.4	1.2
097 CHR CHS&CHS CR	2	45	58*	.1	.3
105 CHRISTIAN REF	3	257	438	.8	2.2
123 CH GOD (ANDER)	1	61	105	.2	.5
127 CH GOD (CLEVE)	2	138	177*	.3	.9
165 CH OF NAZARENE	4	167	395	.7	2.0
175 CONGR CHR CHS	1	40	51*	.1	.3
179 CONSRV BAPT	1	NR	NR	-	-
193 EPISCOPAL	1	121	179	.3	.9
221 FREE METHODIST	3	81	108	.2	.5
259 IFCA	1	NR	NR	-	-
283 LUTH—MO SYNOD	3	689	940	1.6	4.7
285 MENNONITE CH	1	33	74	.1	.4
329 OPEN BIBLE STD	1	NR	NR	-	-
355 PRESB CH (USA)	2	279	358*	.6	1.8
413 S.D.A.	2	201	258*	.5	1.3
438 UN BRETH IN CR	2	139	139	.2	.7
443 UN C OF CHRIST	3	507	651*	1.1	3.3
449 UN METHODIST	12	1,883	2,417*	4.2	12.1
467 WESLEYAN	2	83	335	.6	1.7
469 WELS	1	58	80	.1	.4
497 BLACK BAPT EST[2]	NA	689	884*	1.6	4.4
IOSCO	**39**	**5,056**	**12,302***	**40.7**	**100.0**
019 AMER BAPT USA	2	148	189*	.6	1.5
053 ASSEMB OF GOD	3	234	410	1.4	3.3
057 BAPT GEN CONF	1	152	194*	.6	1.6
081 CATHOLIC	5	NA	5,200	17.2	42.3
081d LATIN	*5*	*NA*	*5,200*	*17.2*	*42.3*
111 CH CR,SCIENTST	1	NR	NR	-	-
151 L-D SAINTS	1	NA	226	.7	1.8
165 CH OF NAZARENE	2	78	224	.7	1.8
167 CHS OF CHRIST	1	90	100	.3	.8
193 EPISCOPAL	2	282	364	1.2	3.0
207 E.L.C.A.	2	373	464	1.5	3.8
221 FREE METHODIST	1	16	37	.1	.3
283 LUTH—MO SYNOD	4	1,097	1,437	4.8	11.7
285 MENNONITE CH	1	15	35	.1	.3
323 OLD ORD AMISH	1	NA	150	.5	1.2
413 S.D.A.	2	55	70*	.2	.6
419 SO BAPT CONV	2	511	651*	2.2	5.3
449 UN METHODIST	7	1,404	1,790*	5.9	14.6
469 WELS	1	456	576	1.9	4.7
497 BLACK BAPT EST[2]	NA	145	185*	.6	1.5
IRON	**25**	**2,434**	**5,913***	**44.9**	**100.0**
053 ASSEMB OF GOD	1	41	75	.6	1.3
057 BAPT GEN CONF	2	144	174*	1.3	2.9
081 CATHOLIC	5	NA	2,762	21.0	46.7
081d LATIN	*5*	*NA*	*2,762*	*21.0*	*46.7*
164 CH LUTH CONF	1	54	63	.5	1.1
165 CH OF NAZARENE	1	5	26	.2	.4
193 EPISCOPAL	2	86	104	.8	1.8
207 E.L.C.A.	4	1,251	1,662	12.6	28.1
259 IFCA	1	NR	NR	-	-
283 LUTH—MO SYNOD	2	179	236	1.8	4.0
355 PRESB CH (USA)	1	342	413*	3.1	7.0
413 S.D.A.	1	26	31*	.2	.5
449 UN METHODIST	3	257	310*	2.4	5.2

Table 4. Churches and Church Membership by County and Denomination: 1990

County and Denomination	Number of churches	Communicant, confirmed, full members	Total adherents Number	Percent of total population	Percent of total adherents
469 WELS	1	49	57	.4	1.0
ISABELLA	**53**	**5,618**	**19,099***	**35.0**	**100.0**
019 AMER BAPT USA	1	45	55*	.1	.3
053 ASSEMB OF GOD	1	24	50	.1	.3
081 CATHOLIC	6	NA	10,988	20.1	57.5
081d LATIN	6	NA	10,988	20.1	57.5
089 CHR & MISS AL	1	38	57	.1	.3
097 CHR CHS&CHS CR	3	525	642*	1.2	3.4
105 CHRISTIAN REF	1	66	103	.2	.5
121 CH GOD (ABR)	1	155	190*	.3	1.0
123 CH GOD (ANDER)	1	69	69	.1	.4
127 CH GOD (CLEVE)	1	13	16*	-	.1
151 L-D SAINTS	1	NA	370	.7	1.9
157 CH OF BRETHREN	1	60	73*	.1	.4
165 CH OF NAZARENE	3	173	290	.5	1.5
167 CHS OF CHRIST	2	145	187	.3	1.0
179 CONSRV BAPT	1	NR	NR	-	-
193 EPISCOPAL	1	209	257	.5	1.3
207 E.L.C.A.	1	499	707	1.3	3.7
216 EVAN PRESBY CH	1	247	262	.5	1.4
221 FREE METHODIST	1	51	159	.3	.8
226 FRIENDS-USA	1	15	18*	-	.1
226c FGC	1	15	18*	-	.1
283 LUTH—MO SYNOD	2	375	519	1.0	2.7
291 MISSIONARY CH	1	18	46	.1	.2
323 OLD ORD AMISH	2	NA	300	.5	1.6
355 PRESB CH (USA)	2	506	619*	1.1	3.2
403 SALVATION ARMY	1	3	3	-	-
413 S.D.A.	1	111	136*	.2	.7
419 SO BAPT CONV	1	31	38*	.1	.2
449 UN METHODIST	11	1,862	2,278*	4.2	11.9
467 WESLEYAN	1	43	105	.2	.5
469 WELS	2	189	263	.5	1.4
496 JEWISH EST[1]	0	NA	120	.2	.6
497 BLACK BAPT EST[2]	NA	146	179*	.3	.9
JACKSON	**114**	**21,023**	**59,486***	**39.7**	**100.0**
019 AMER BAPT USA	4	768	963*	.6	1.6
053 ASSEMB OF GOD	5	258	387	.3	.7
057 BAPT GEN CONF	1	25	31*	-	.1
081 CATHOLIC	10	NA	29,459	19.7	49.5
081d LATIN	10	NA	29,459	19.7	49.5
097 CHR CHS&CHS CR	1	388	487*	.3	.8
105 CHRISTIAN REF	1	75	123	.1	.2
111 CH CR,SCIENTST	1	NR	NR	-	-
123 CH GOD (ANDER)	3	336	343	.2	.6
127 CH GOD (CLEVE)	1	101	127*	.1	.2
145 CH GOD PROPHCY	1	35	44*	-	.1
151 L-D SAINTS	2	NA	576	.4	1.0
165 CH OF NAZARENE	4	337	668	.4	1.1
167 CHS OF CHRIST	3	387	534	.4	.9
175 CONGR CHR CHS	1	321	403*	.3	.7
179 CONSRV BAPT	3	NR	NR	-	-
193 EPISCOPAL	5	1,275	2,144	1.4	3.6
207 E.L.C.A.	3	981	1,324	.9	2.2
221 FREE METHODIST	3	848	1,257	.8	2.1
259 IFCA	1	NR	NR	-	-
283 LUTH—MO SYNOD	2	1,618	2,282	1.5	3.8
285 MENNONITE CH	1	46	74	-	.1
291 MISSIONARY CH	4	172	287	.2	.5
331 ORTH CH IN AM	1	NR	NR	-	-
339 PENT CH OF GOD	1	0	400	.3	.7
353 CHR BRETHREN	1	85	100	.1	.2
355 PRESB CH (USA)	4	1,767	2,216*	1.5	3.7
361 PRIM BAPT ASCS	1	0	0*	-	-
397 ROMANIAN ORTH	2	NR	NR	-	-
403 SALVATION ARMY	1	107	122	.1	.2
413 S.D.A.	2	384	482*	.3	.8
419 SO BAPT CONV	5	1,535	1,925*	1.3	3.2
435 UNITARIAN-UNIV	3	79	109	.1	.2
438 UN BRETH IN CR	2	327	339	.2	.6
443 UN C OF CHRIST	5	802	1,006*	.7	1.7
449 UN METHODIST	18	3,979	4,991*	3.3	8.4
467 WESLEYAN	5	391	1,418	.9	2.4
469 WELS	2	205	287	.2	.5
496 JEWISH EST[1]	1	NA	325	.2	.5
497 BLACK BAPT EST[2]	NA	3,391	4,253*	2.8	7.1
KALAMAZOO	**163**	**39,611**	**85,521***	**38.3**	**100.0**
019 AMER BAPT USA	5	2,030	2,521*	1.1	2.9
053 ASSEMB OF GOD	6	987	2,217	1.0	2.6
057 BAPT GEN CONF	2	212	263*	.1	.3
059 BAPT MISS ASSN	1	105	130*	.1	.2
075 BRETHREN IN CR	1	31	40	-	-
081 CATHOLIC	9	NA	26,642	11.9	31.2
081d LATIN	9	NA	26,642	11.9	31.2
093 CHR CH (DISC)	1	172	223	.1	.3
097 CHR CHS&CHS CR	3	474	589*	.3	.7
105 CHRISTIAN REF	17	4,022	6,163	2.8	7.2
111 CH CR,SCIENTST	1	NR	NR	-	-
123 CH GOD (ANDER)	4	484	524	.2	.6
127 CH GOD (CLEVE)	1	151	188*	.1	.2
145 CH GOD PROPHCY	1	35	43*	-	.1
151 L-D SAINTS	1	NA	410	.2	.5
157 CH OF BRETHREN	1	62	77*	-	.1
165 CH OF NAZARENE	4	726	950	.4	1.1
167 CHS OF CHRIST	4	390	544	.2	.6
175 CONGR CHR CHS	1	75	93*	-	.1
193 EPISCOPAL	5	1,722	2,517	1.1	2.9
203 EVAN FREE CH	2	0	50	-	.1
207 E.L.C.A.	6	1,876	2,577	1.2	3.0
221 FREE METHODIST	2	302	511	.2	.6
223 FREE WILL BAPT	1	60	75*	-	.1
226 FRIENDS-USA	1	36	45*	-	.1
226c FGC	1	36	45*	-	.1
246 GREEK ORTHODOX	1	NR	NR	-	-
249 AP CATH ASSYR	0	3	16	-	-
259 IFCA	5	NR	NR	-	-
263 INT FOURSQ GOS	1	73	91*	-	.1
274 LAT EVAN LUTH	2	522	588	.3	.7
283 LUTH—MO SYNOD	5	1,711	2,231	1.0	2.6
291 MISSIONARY CH	2	67	141	.1	.2
307 NETH REF CONGR	1	207	360	.2	.4
349 PENT HOLINESS	1	20	25*	-	-
355 PRESB CH (USA)	5	2,347	2,914*	1.3	3.4
371 REF CH IN AM	16	5,417	8,977	4.0	10.5
403 SALVATION ARMY	1	131	159	.1	.2
413 S.D.A.	2	504	626*	.3	.7
419 SO BAPT CONV	4	544	676*	.3	.8
435 UNITARIAN-UNIV	1	283	442	.2	.5
443 UN C OF CHRIST	6	1,399	1,737*	.8	2.0
449 UN METHODIST	21	6,329	7,859*	3.5	9.2
467 WESLEYAN	2	304	630	.3	.7
469 WELS	1	172	246	.1	.3
496 JEWISH EST[1]	2	NA	1,000	.4	1.2
497 BLACK BAPT EST[2]	NA	5,626	6,986*	3.1	8.2
498 INDEP.CHARIS.[3]	1	NA	600	.3	.7
499 INDEP.NON-CHAR[3]	3	NA	1,825	.8	2.1
KALKASKA	**17**	**1,440**	**2,669***	**19.8**	**100.0**
019 AMER BAPT USA	1	160	208*	1.5	7.8
053 ASSEMB OF GOD	2	91	123	.9	4.6
081 CATHOLIC	1	NA	750	5.6	28.1
081d LATIN	1	NA	750	5.6	28.1
097 CHR CHS&CHS CR	4	639	832*	6.2	31.2
127 CH GOD (CLEVE)	1	39	51*	.4	1.9
165 CH OF NAZARENE	1	25	44	.3	1.6
167 CHS OF CHRIST	1	16	24	.2	.9
283 LUTH—MO SYNOD	1	250	351	2.6	13.2
413 S.D.A.	1	54	70*	.5	2.6
419 SO BAPT CONV	1	9	12*	.1	.4
449 UN METHODIST	3	157	204*	1.5	7.6
KENT	**381**	**105,814**	**258,043***	**51.5**	**100.0**
005 AME ZION	2	1,670	1,912	.4	.7
019 AMER BAPT USA	2	162	210*	-	.1
040 AP CHR CH-AMER	1	78	138	-	.1
053 ASSEMB OF GOD	9	3,882	9,021	1.8	3.5
057 BAPT GEN CONF	3	440	572*	.1	.2
081 CATHOLIC	38	NA	86,135	17.2	33.4
081d LATIN	37	NA	86,103	17.2	33.4
081h UKRAINIAN	1	NA	32	-	-
089 CHR & MISS AL	1	49	148	-	.1
093 CHR CH (DISC)	2	1,269	1,539	.3	.6
097 CHR CHS&CHS CR	4	235	305*	.1	.1
105 CHRISTIAN REF	78	28,511	43,473	8.7	16.8
111 CH CR,SCIENTST	2	NR	NR	-	-
121 CH GOD (ABR)	4	250	325*	.1	.1
123 CH GOD (ANDER)	6	504	618	.1	.2
127 CH GOD (CLEVE)	3	299	388*	.1	.2
133 CH GOD(7TH)DEN	1	31	39	-	-
151 L-D SAINTS	4	NA	1,322	.3	.5
165 CH OF NAZARENE	6	927	1,421	.3	.6
167 CHS OF CHRIST	8	672	944	.2	.4
175 CONGR CHR CHS	1	923	1,199*	.2	.5
179 CONSRV BAPT	2	NR	NR	-	-
193 EPISCOPAL	9	2,270	3,218	.6	1.2
203 EVAN FREE CH	3	176	344	.1	.1
207 E.L.C.A.	12	5,906	8,246	1.6	3.2
221 FREE METHODIST	4	297	404	.1	.2
226 FRIENDS-USA	1	19	25*	-	-
226c FGC	1	19	25*	-	-

NA–Not applicable   NR–Not reported   *Total adherents estimated from known number of communicant, confirmed, full members.   - Represents a percent less than 0.1.   Percentages may not total due to rounding.
[1]See Appendix E   [2]See Appendix F   [3]See Appendix G   Lines in italic represent a breakdown of Catholic rites or Friends affiliations. They are included in their respective denominational total.

Table 4. Churches and Church Membership by County and Denomination: 1990

County and Denomination	Number of churches	Communicant, confirmed, full members	Total adherents Number	Percent of total population	Percent of total adherents
246 GREEK ORTHODOX	1	NR	NR	-	-
259 IFCA	14	NR	NR	-	-
274 LAT EVAN LUTH	1	397	408	.1	.2
283 LUTH—MO SYNOD	16	5,325	7,351	1.5	2.8
285 MENNONITE CH	1	39	89	-	-
291 MISSIONARY CH	1	19	33	-	-
307 NETH REF CONGR	2	818	1,457	.3	.6
349 PENT HOLINESS	1	12	16*	-	-
353 CHR BRETHREN	4	290	530	.1	.2
355 PRESB CH (USA)	7	4,243	5,512*	1.1	2.1
356 PRESB CH AMER	2	252	359	.1	.1
371 REF CH IN AM	38	13,138	20,738	4.1	8.0
403 SALVATION ARMY	2	310	320	.1	.1
413 S.D.A.	7	1,679	2,181*	.4	.8
419 SO BAPT CONV	4	1,540	2,001*	.4	.8
438 UN BRETH IN CR	3	362	415	.1	.2
443 UN C OF CHRIST	16	7,731	10,043*	2.0	3.9
449 UN METHODIST	32	8,578	11,143*	2.2	4.3
467 WESLEYAN	5	625	3,038	.6	1.2
469 WELS	2	477	702	.1	.3
496 JEWISH EST[1]	3	NA	1,090	.2	.4
497 BLACK BAPT EST[2]	NA	11,409	14,821*	3.0	5.7
498 INDEP.CHARIS.[3]	3	NA	2,700	.5	1.0
499 INDEP.NON-CHAR[3]	10	NA	11,150	2.2	4.3
KEWEENAW	**4**	**320**	**720***	**42.3**	**100.0**
081 CATHOLIC	2	NA	284	16.7	39.4
081d LATIN	*2*	*NA*	*284*	*16.7*	*39.4*
207 E.L.C.A.	1	257	361	21.2	50.1
449 UN METHODIST	1	63	75*	4.4	10.4
LAKE	**15**	**1,046**	**2,290***	**26.7**	**100.0**
081 CATHOLIC	3	NA	735	8.6	32.1
081d LATIN	*3*	*NA*	*735*	*8.6*	*32.1*
093 CHR CH (DISC)	1	45	70	.8	3.1
097 CHR CHS&CHS CR	1	150	187*	2.2	8.2
167 CHS OF CHRIST	1	36	47	.5	2.1
259 IFCA	1	NR	NR	-	-
283 LUTH—MO SYNOD	1	87	128	1.5	5.6
413 S.D.A.	2	74	92*	1.1	4.0
443 UN C OF CHRIST	1	167	208*	2.4	9.1
449 UN METHODIST	3	187	233*	2.7	10.2
467 WESLEYAN	1	43	270	3.1	11.8
497 BLACK BAPT EST[2]	NA	257	320*	3.7	14.0
LAPEER	**60**	**8,040**	**28,646***	**38.3**	**100.0**
019 AMER BAPT USA	2	219	284*	.4	1.0
053 ASSEMB OF GOD	3	302	469	.6	1.6
081 CATHOLIC	6	NA	14,932	20.0	52.1
081d LATIN	*6*	*NA*	*14,932*	*20.0*	*52.1*
097 CHR CHS&CHS CR	2	290	376*	.5	1.3
105 CHRISTIAN REF	1	293	513	.7	1.8
123 CH GOD (ANDER)	1	25	25	-	.1
127 CH GOD (CLEVE)	1	195	253*	.3	.9
151 L-D SAINTS	1	NA	257	.3	.9
165 CH OF NAZARENE	3	150	244	.3	.9
167 CHS OF CHRIST	2	110	167	.2	.6
176 CCC, NOT NAT'L	1	441	572*	.8	2.0
193 EPISCOPAL	3	494	683	.9	2.4
207 E.L.C.A.	1	328	442	.6	1.5
221 FREE METHODIST	2	104	163	.2	.6
249 AP CATH ASSYR	0	1	7	-	-
259 IFCA	1	NR	NR	-	-
283 LUTH—MO SYNOD	4	1,807	2,515	3.4	8.8
285 MENNONITE CH	1	23	25	-	.1
355 PRESB CH (USA)	1	540	700*	.9	2.4
413 S.D.A.	2	121	157*	.2	.5
419 SO BAPT CONV	1	26	34*	-	.1
443 UN C OF CHRIST	1	140	182*	.2	.6
449 UN METHODIST	14	1,908	2,474*	3.3	8.6
467 WESLEYAN	3	265	802	1.1	2.8
469 WELS	2	258	366	.5	1.3
496 JEWISH EST[1]	0	NA	1,604	2.1	5.6
499 INDEP.NON-CHAR[3]	1	NA	400	.5	1.4
LEELANAU	**27**	**1,952**	**6,053***	**36.6**	**100.0**
081 CATHOLIC	8	NA	3,329	20.1	55.0
081d LATIN	*8*	*NA*	*3,329*	*20.1*	*55.0*
111 CH CR,SCIENTST	1	NR	NR	-	-
175 CONGR CHR CHS	1	211	267*	1.6	4.4
207 E.L.C.A.	2	246	333	2.0	5.5
209 EVAN LUTH SYN	1	85	119	.7	2.0
226 FRIENDS-USA	2	103	123	.7	2.0
226e FUM	*2*	*103*	*123*	*.7*	*2.0*
283 LUTH—MO SYNOD	3	405	523	3.2	8.6
355 PRESB CH (USA)	1	17	21*	.1	.3

County and Denomination	Number of churches	Communicant, confirmed, full members	Total adherents Number	Percent of total population	Percent of total adherents
371 REF CH IN AM	1	218	334	2.0	5.5
419 SO BAPT CONV	1	18	23*	.1	.4
438 UN BRETH IN CR	1	13	22	.1	.4
443 UN C OF CHRIST	1	195	246*	1.5	4.1
449 UN METHODIST	3	386	488*	3.0	8.1
467 WESLEYAN	1	55	225	1.4	3.7
LENAWEE	**112**	**17,008**	**35,789***	**39.1**	**100.0**
019 AMER BAPT USA	6	1,031	1,315*	1.4	3.7
053 ASSEMB OF GOD	3	800	1,485	1.6	4.1
081 CATHOLIC	8	NA	11,058	12.1	30.9
081d LATIN	*8*	*NA*	*11,058*	*12.1*	*30.9*
093 CHR CH (DISC)	1	80	110	.1	.3
111 CH CR,SCIENTST	1	NR	NR	-	-
123 CH GOD (ANDER)	2	88	91	.1	.3
127 CH GOD (CLEVE)	4	349	445*	.5	1.2
145 CH GOD PROPHCY	1	35	45*	-	.1
151 L-D SAINTS	2	NA	498	.5	1.4
157 CH OF BRETHREN	2	45	57*	.1	.2
165 CH OF NAZARENE	5	681	1,114	1.2	3.1
167 CHS OF CHRIST	2	231	318	.3	.9
175 CONGR CHR CHS	3	486	620*	.7	1.7
193 EPISCOPAL	4	571	1,208	1.3	3.4
203 EVAN FREE CH	1	90	180	.2	.5
207 E.L.C.A.	5	1,446	1,990	2.2	5.6
213 EVAN MENN INC	1	55	70*	.1	.2
221 FREE METHODIST	2	66	110	.1	.3
223 FREE WILL BAPT	1	65	83*	.1	.2
226 FRIENDS-USA	4	338	368	.4	1.0
226b EFI	*4*	*338*	*368*	*.4*	*1.0*
259 IFCA	2	NR	NR	-	-
283 LUTH—MO SYNOD	6	1,762	2,503	2.7	7.0
355 PRESB CH (USA)	6	1,158	1,477*	1.6	4.1
403 SALVATION ARMY	1	88	99	.1	.3
413 S.D.A.	2	164	209*	.2	.6
419 SO BAPT CONV	6	910	1,161*	1.3	3.2
438 UN BRETH IN CR	4	514	514	.6	1.4
443 UN C OF CHRIST	4	810	1,033*	1.1	2.9
449 UN METHODIST	17	3,413	4,354*	4.8	12.2
467 WESLEYAN	1	44	137	.1	.4
469 WELS	4	1,360	1,719	1.9	4.8
497 BLACK BAPT EST[2]	NA	328	418*	.5	1.2
499 INDEP.NON-CHAR[3]	1	NA	1,000	1.1	2.8
LIVINGSTON	**68**	**12,059**	**38,616***	**33.4**	**100.0**
019 AMER BAPT USA	3	638	819*	.7	2.1
045 APOSTOLIC LUTH	1	30	52	-	.1
053 ASSEMB OF GOD	2	106	225	.2	.6
081 CATHOLIC	7	NA	18,498	16.0	47.9
081d LATIN	*7*	*NA*	*18,498*	*16.0*	*47.9*
097 CHR CHS&CHS CR	2	272	349*	.3	.9
111 CH CR,SCIENTST	1	NR	NR	-	-
123 CH GOD (ANDER)	1	120	120	.1	.3
127 CH GOD (CLEVE)	1	73	94*	.1	.2
145 CH GOD PROPHCY	1	35	45*	-	.1
151 L-D SAINTS	1	NA	375	.3	1.0
165 CH OF NAZARENE	3	688	1,250	1.1	3.2
167 CHS OF CHRIST	2	198	327	.3	.8
193 EPISCOPAL	3	443	644	.6	1.7
203 EVAN FREE CH	1	96	175	.2	.5
207 E.L.C.A.	5	1,924	2,797	2.4	7.2
216 EVAN PRESBY CH	1	288	300	.3	.8
221 FREE METHODIST	3	141	260	.2	.7
283 LUTH—MO SYNOD	6	2,232	3,183	2.8	8.2
285 MENNONITE CH	1	13	23	-	.1
313 N AM BAPT CONF	1	0	0*	-	-
355 PRESB CH (USA)	3	1,186	1,523*	1.3	3.9
361 PRIM BAPT ASCS	1	42	54*	-	.1
403 SALVATION ARMY	1	79	89	.1	.2
413 S.D.A.	1	25	32*	-	.1
419 SO BAPT CONV	2	202	259*	.2	.7
438 UN BRETH IN CR	1	72	242	.2	.6
443 UN C OF CHRIST	1	245	315*	.3	.8
449 UN METHODIST	8	2,335	2,998*	2.6	7.8
467 WESLEYAN	1	243	329	.3	.9
469 WELS	1	143	214	.2	.6
496 JEWISH EST[1]	1	NA	2,481	2.1	6.4
497 BLACK BAPT EST[2]	NA	190	244*	.2	.6
499 INDEP.NON-CHAR[3]	1	NA	300	.3	.8
LUCE	**11**	**879**	**1,978***	**34.3**	**100.0**
053 ASSEMB OF GOD	1	50	85	1.5	4.3
081 CATHOLIC	1	NA	848	14.7	42.9
081d LATIN	*1*	*NA*	*848*	*14.7*	*42.9*
167 CHS OF CHRIST	1	25	33	.6	1.7
193 EPISCOPAL	1	52	55	1.0	2.8

NA–Not applicable   NR–Not reported   *Total adherents estimated from known number of communicant, confirmed, full members.   - Represents a percent less than 0.1.   Percentages may not total due to rounding.
[1]See Appendix E   [2]See Appendix F   [3]See Appendix G   Lines in *italic* represent a breakdown of Catholic rites or Friends affiliations. They are included in their respective denominational total.

Table 4. Churches and Church Membership by County and Denomination: 1990

County and Denomination		Number of churches	Communicant, confirmed, full members	Total adherents		
				Number	Percent of total population	Percent of total adherents
207	E.L.C.A.	1	283	378	6.6	19.1
283	LUTH—MO SYNOD	1	182	228	4.0	11.5
355	PRESB CH (USA)	1	107	134*	2.3	6.8
413	S.D.A.	1	20	25*	.4	1.3
449	UN METHODIST	2	153	192*	3.3	9.7
467	WESLEYAN	1	7	0	-	-
MACKINAC		**28**	**1,208**	**3,446***	**32.3**	**100.0**
053	ASSEMB OF GOD	1	24	40	.4	1.2
081	CATHOLIC	7	NA	1,849	17.3	53.7
081d	LATIN	7	NA	1,849	17.3	53.7
165	CH OF NAZARENE	1	22	38	.4	1.1
175	CONGR CHR CHS	1	35	44*	.4	1.3
193	EPISCOPAL	4	79	123	1.2	3.6
203	EVAN FREE CH	1	25	55	.5	1.6
207	E.L.C.A.	4	296	380	3.6	11.0
283	LUTH—MO SYNOD	1	207	235	2.2	6.8
285	MENNONITE CH	3	82	138	1.3	4.0
355	PRESB CH (USA)	2	55	69*	.6	2.0
449	UN METHODIST	2	369	461*	4.3	13.4
469	WELS	1	14	14	.1	.4
MACOMB		**271**	**66,047**	**484,786***	**67.6**	**100.0**
001	ADVENT CHR CH	1	43	53*	-	-
005	AME ZION	1	400	448	.1	.1
019	AMER BAPT USA	3	607	747*	.1	.2
053	ASSEMB OF GOD	14	2,292	4,136	.6	.9
057	BAPT GEN CONF	2	118	145*	-	-
081	CATHOLIC	59	NA	373,485	52.1	77.0
081b	BYZAN RUTH	1	NA	555	.1	.1
081d	LATIN	56	NA	371,797	51.8	76.7
081f	MELKITE-GK	1	NA	522	.1	.1
081h	UKRAINIAN	1	NA	611	.1	.1
089	CHR & MISS AL	2	73	232	-	-
097	CHR CHS&CHS CR	1	500	615*	.1	.1
105	CHRISTIAN REF	1	55	85	-	-
111	CH CR,SCIENTST	2	NR	NR	-	-
123	CH GOD (ANDER)	4	278	304	-	.1
127	CH GOD (CLEVE)	6	1,820	2,239*	.3	.5
145	CH GOD PROPHCY	1	35	43*	-	-
151	L-D SAINTS	2	NA	613	.1	.1
165	CH OF NAZARENE	7	1,024	1,798	.3	.4
167	CHS OF CHRIST	12	2,096	2,787	.4	.6
179	CONSRV BAPT	1	NR	NR	-	-
181	CONSRV CONGR	1	94	116*	-	-
185	CUMBER PRESB	2	197	205	-	-
193	EPISCOPAL	7	1,202	1,908	.3	.4
195	ESTONIAN ELC	1	90	111*	-	-
207	E.L.C.A.	23	8,795	12,896	1.8	2.7
209	EVAN LUTH SYN	1	220	296	-	.1
216	EVAN PRESBY CH	1	461	477	.1	.1
223	FREE WILL BAPT	3	289	356*	-	.1
246	GREEK ORTHODOX	2	NR	NR	-	-
265	INT PENT C CHR	1	6	15	-	-
283	LUTH—MO SYNOD	25	21,884	30,290	4.2	6.2
291	MISSIONARY CH	3	179	222	-	-
313	N AM BAPT CONF	8	1,883	2,317*	.3	.5
320	"OLD" MB ASCS	1	121	149*	-	-
325	OLD REG BAPT	1	43	53*	-	-
355	PRESB CH (USA)	10	4,039	4,970*	.7	1.0
371	REF CH IN AM	1	120	210	-	-
397	ROMANIAN ORTH	1	NR	NR	-	-
403	SALVATION ARMY	3	257	321	-	.1
413	S.D.A.	1	324	399*	.1	.1
419	SO BAPT CONV	12	4,138	5,091*	.7	1.1
443	UN C OF CHRIST	9	2,878	3,541*	.5	.7
449	UN METHODIST	22	5,692	7,003*	1.0	1.4
467	WESLEYAN	3	260	902	.1	.2
469	WELS	5	591	799	.1	.2
496	JEWISH EST[1]	2	NA	15,388	2.1	3.2
497	BLACK BAPT EST[2]	NA	2,943	3,621*	.5	.7
498	INDEP.CHARIS.[3]	1	NA	3,500	.5	.7
499	INDEP.NON-CHAR[3]	2	NA	1,900	.3	.4
MANISTEE		**32**	**4,837**	**12,037***	**56.6**	**100.0**
053	ASSEMB OF GOD	1	61	120	.6	1.0
057	BAPT GEN CONF	1	179	220*	1.0	1.8
081	CATHOLIC	5	NA	5,512	25.9	45.8
081d	LATIN	5	NA	5,512	25.9	45.8
097	CHR CHS&CHS CR	1	24	29*	.1	.2
151	L-D SAINTS	1	NA	184	.9	1.5
157	CH OF BRETHREN	3	233	286*	1.3	2.4
165	CH OF NAZARENE	1	41	89	.4	.7
193	EPISCOPAL	1	159	165	.8	1.4
207	E.L.C.A.	2	1,347	1,838	8.6	15.3
283	LUTH—MO SYNOD	4	1,587	2,132	10.0	17.7

County and Denomination		Number of churches	Communicant, confirmed, full members	Total adherents		
				Number	Percent of total population	Percent of total adherents
285	MENNONITE CH	1	18	34	.2	.3
403	SALVATION ARMY	1	51	55	.3	.5
413	S.D.A.	1	39	48*	.2	.4
419	SO BAPT CONV	1	46	57*	.3	.5
443	UN C OF CHRIST	2	325	399*	1.9	3.3
449	UN METHODIST	4	599	736*	3.5	6.1
467	WESLEYAN	1	13	0	-	-
469	WELS	1	115	133	.6	1.1
MARQUETTE		**83**	**13,539**	**32,745***	**46.2**	**100.0**
019	AMER BAPT USA	1	100	126*	.2	.4
045	APOSTOLIC LUTH	3	160	182	.3	.6
053	ASSEMB OF GOD	1	191	350	.5	1.1
057	BAPT GEN CONF	3	333	419*	.6	1.3
081	CATHOLIC	15	NA	13,961	19.7	42.6
081d	LATIN	15	NA	13,961	19.7	42.6
097	CHR CHS&CHS CR	1	120	151*	.2	.5
111	CH CR,SCIENTST	1	NR	NR	-	-
121	CH GOD (ABR)	2	23	29*	-	.1
127	CH GOD (CLEVE)	1	16	20*	-	.1
151	L-D SAINTS	1	NA	325	.5	1.0
164	CH LUTH CONF	1	201	249	.4	.8
165	CH OF NAZARENE	1	48	115	.2	.4
167	CHS OF CHRIST	2	78	135	.2	.4
193	EPISCOPAL	5	486	837	1.2	2.6
207	E.L.C.A.	15	6,670	8,988	12.7	27.4
220	FREE LUTHERAN	1	142	228	.3	.7
226	FRIENDS-USA	1	4	14	-	-
226c	FGC	1	4	14	-	-
246	GREEK ORTHODOX	1	NR	NR	-	-
259	IFCA	1	NR	NR	-	-
283	LUTH—MO SYNOD	2	747	1,119	1.6	3.4
291	MISSIONARY CH	1	62	107	.2	.3
353	CHR BRETHREN	1	16	32	-	.1
355	PRESB CH (USA)	3	582	733*	1.0	2.2
403	SALVATION ARMY	2	134	152	.2	.5
413	S.D.A.	1	48	60*	.1	.2
419	SO BAPT CONV	3	525	661*	.9	2.0
449	UN METHODIST	10	2,444	3,078*	4.3	9.4
469	WELS	2	141	186	.3	.6
496	JEWISH EST[1]	1	NA	150	.2	.5
497	BLACK BAPT EST[2]	NA	268	338*	.5	1.0
MASON		**38**	**4,762**	**11,290***	**44.2**	**100.0**
053	ASSEMB OF GOD	1	112	150	.6	1.3
057	BAPT GEN CONF	2	332	418*	1.6	3.7
081	CATHOLIC	7	NA	4,799	18.8	42.5
081d	LATIN	7	NA	4,799	18.8	42.5
097	CHR CHS&CHS CR	1	60	76*	.3	.7
111	CH CR,SCIENTST	1	NR	NR	-	-
123	CH GOD (ANDER)	1	96	114	.4	1.0
151	L-D SAINTS	2	NA	202	.8	1.8
157	CH OF BRETHREN	1	50	63*	.2	.6
165	CH OF NAZARENE	1	71	141	.6	1.2
167	CHS OF CHRIST	1	70	80	.3	.7
176	CCC, NOT NAT'L	1	680	856*	3.4	7.6
193	EPISCOPAL	1	117	125	.5	1.1
203	EVAN FREE CH	1	145	246	1.0	2.2
207	E.L.C.A.	3	972	1,218	4.8	10.8
221	FREE METHODIST	1	34	50	.2	.4
283	LUTH—MO SYNOD	2	513	661	2.6	5.9
323	OLD ORD AMISH	1	NA	150	.6	1.3
371	REF CH IN AM	1	186	285	1.1	2.5
403	SALVATION ARMY	1	84	87	.3	.8
413	S.D.A.	1	71	89*	.3	.8
449	UN METHODIST	5	1,017	1,280*	5.0	11.3
467	WESLEYAN	1	23	44	.2	.4
469	WELS	1	129	156	.6	1.4
MECOSTA		**51**	**5,249**	**12,140***	**32.5**	**100.0**
001	ADVENT CHR CH	1	50	60*	.2	.5
053	ASSEMB OF GOD	1	91	195	.5	1.6
081	CATHOLIC	4	NA	4,700	12.6	38.7
081d	LATIN	4	NA	4,700	12.6	38.7
097	CHR CHS&CHS CR	3	280	338*	.9	2.8
105	CHRISTIAN REF	1	116	164	.4	1.4
111	CH CR,SCIENTST	1	NR	NR	-	-
123	CH GOD (ANDER)	3	165	210	.6	1.7
127	CH GOD (CLEVE)	1	106	128*	.3	1.1
151	L-D SAINTS	1	NA	181	.5	1.5
157	CH OF BRETHREN	1	10	12*	-	.1
165	CH OF NAZARENE	1	34	77	.2	.6
167	CHS OF CHRIST	1	28	43	.1	.4
179	CONSRV BAPT	1	NR	NR	-	-
193	EPISCOPAL	1	201	227	.6	1.9
203	EVAN FREE CH	1	103	200	.5	1.6

NA–Not applicable NR–Not reported *Total adherents estimated from known number of communicant, confirmed, full members. - Represents a percent less than 0.1. Percentages may not total due to rounding.
[1]See Appendix E [2]See Appendix F [3]See Appendix G Lines in *italic* represent a breakdown of Catholic rites or Friends affiliations. They are included in their respective denominational total.

Table 4. Churches and Church Membership by County and Denomination: 1990

County and Denomination	Number of churches	Communicant, confirmed, full members	Total adherents		
			Number	Percent of total population	Percent of total adherents
207 E.L.C.A.	1	318	407	1.1	3.4
221 FREE METHODIST	4	199	387	1.0	3.2
283 LUTH—MO SYNOD	3	1,037	1,394	3.7	11.5
284 LUTH CH-AM ASC	1	32	52	.1	.4
323 OLD ORD AMISH	2	NA	300	.8	2.5
355 PRESB CH (USA)	1	251	303*	.8	2.5
413 S.D.A.	1	33	40*	.1	.3
419 SO BAPT CONV	1	186	225*	.6	1.9
435 UNITARIAN-UNIV	1	29	44	.1	.4
438 UN BRETH IN CR	1	49	49	.1	.4
443 UN C OF CHRIST	1	225	272*	.7	2.2
449 UN METHODIST	9	1,231	1,487*	4.0	12.2
467 WESLEYAN	1	20	75	.2	.6
469 WELS	2	231	299	.8	2.5
497 BLACK BAPT EST[2]	NA	224	271*	.7	2.2
MENOMINEE	**39**	**4,817**	**15,192***	**61.0**	**100.0**
053 ASSEMB OF GOD	2	65	142	.6	.9
057 BAPT GEN CONF	1	131	165*	.7	1.1
081 CATHOLIC	11	NA	8,686	34.9	57.2
081d LATIN	11	NA	8,686	34.9	57.2
127 CH GOD (CLEVE)	1	34	43*	.2	.3
151 L-D SAINTS	1	NA	102	.4	.7
165 CH OF NAZARENE	1	9	53	.2	.3
167 CHS OF CHRIST	1	14	24	.1	.2
193 EPISCOPAL	2	121	192	.8	1.3
203 EVAN FREE CH	1	100	146	.6	1.0
207 E.L.C.A.	5	2,207	2,937	11.8	19.3
293 MORAV CH-NORTH	1	118	141	.6	.9
355 PRESB CH (USA)	1	396	499*	2.0	3.3
413 S.D.A.	2	279	352*	1.4	2.3
419 SO BAPT CONV	1	28	35*	.1	.2
449 UN METHODIST	4	552	696*	2.8	4.6
469 WELS	4	763	979	3.9	6.4
MIDLAND	**81**	**17,036**	**38,239***	**50.5**	**100.0**
019 AMER BAPT USA	1	385	490*	.6	1.3
053 ASSEMB OF GOD	3	553	932	1.2	2.4
081 CATHOLIC	7	NA	12,568	16.6	32.9
081d LATIN	7	NA	12,568	16.6	32.9
097 CHR CHS&CHS CR	1	115	146*	.2	.4
111 CH CR,SCIENTST	1	NR	NR	-	-
123 CH GOD (ANDER)	6	769	853	1.1	2.2
127 CH GOD (CLEVE)	1	334	425*	.6	1.1
151 L-D SAINTS	2	NA	601	.8	1.6
157 CH OF BRETHREN	1	37	47*	.1	.1
165 CH OF NAZARENE	3	370	477	.6	1.2
167 CHS OF CHRIST	1	165	165	.2	.4
193 EPISCOPAL	2	725	984	1.3	2.6
203 EVAN FREE CH	1	40	85	.1	.2
207 E.L.C.A.	2	1,399	1,858	2.5	4.9
209 EVAN LUTH SYN	1	214	300	.4	.8
213 EVAN MENN INC	1	62	79*	.1	.2
221 FREE METHODIST	3	164	363	.5	.9
283 LUTH—MO SYNOD	4	2,616	3,409	4.5	8.9
285 MENNONITE CH	1	69	289	.4	.8
291 MISSIONARY CH	1	42	107	.1	.3
339 PENT CH OF GOD	3	50	345	.5	.9
355 PRESB CH (USA)	2	2,060	2,623*	3.5	6.9
371 REF CH IN AM	1	193	338	.4	.9
403 SALVATION ARMY	1	121	245	.3	.6
413 S.D.A.	2	271	345*	.5	.9
419 SO BAPT CONV	5	613	781*	1.0	2.0
435 UNITARIAN-UNIV	1	108	160	.2	.4
438 UN BRETH IN CR	1	92	92	.1	.2
443 UN C OF CHRIST	1	422	537*	.7	1.4
449 UN METHODIST	13	4,323	5,505*	7.3	14.4
467 WESLEYAN	5	330	1,727	2.3	4.5
469 WELS	1	191	305	.4	.8
496 JEWISH EST[1]	1	NA	200	.3	.5
497 BLACK BAPT EST[2]	NA	203	258*	.3	.7
498 INDEP.CHARIS.[3]	1	NA	600	.8	1.6
MISSAUKEE	**25**	**2,433**	**4,397***	**36.2**	**100.0**
053 ASSEMB OF GOD	1	19	28	.2	.6
081 CATHOLIC	1	NA	700	5.8	15.9
081d LATIN	1	NA	700	5.8	15.9
097 CHR CHS&CHS CR	1	40	53*	.4	1.2
105 CHRISTIAN REF	6	1,088	1,758	14.5	40.0
207 E.L.C.A.	1	204	266	2.2	6.0
216 EVAN PRESBY CH	1	71	71	.6	1.6
221 FREE METHODIST	2	30	55	.5	1.3
355 PRESB CH (USA)	2	192	252*	2.1	5.7
371 REF CH IN AM	3	404	708	5.8	16.1
413 S.D.A.	1	51	67*	.6	1.5
419 SO BAPT CONV	1	37	49*	.4	1.1

County and Denomination	Number of churches	Communicant, confirmed, full members	Total adherents		
			Number	Percent of total population	Percent of total adherents
449 UN METHODIST	5	297	390*	3.2	8.9
MONROE	**117**	**22,725**	**82,215***	**61.5**	**100.0**
019 AMER BAPT USA	4	674	866*	.6	1.1
053 ASSEMB OF GOD	3	147	271	.2	.3
057 BAPT GEN CONF	2	596	766*	.6	.9
081 CATHOLIC	13	NA	47,781	35.8	58.1
081d LATIN	13	NA	47,781	35.8	58.1
089 CHR & MISS AL	4	245	504	.4	.6
097 CHR CHS&CHS CR	1	65	84*	.1	.1
111 CH CR,SCIENTST	1	NR	NR	-	-
123 CH GOD (ANDER)	1	36	45	-	.1
127 CH GOD (CLEVE)	4	1,340	1,722*	1.3	2.1
133 CH GOD(7TH)DEN	1	31	40	-	-
145 CH GOD PROPHCY	1	35	45*	-	.1
146 CH GOD MTN ASM	2	232	298*	.2	.4
151 L-D SAINTS	1	NA	259	.2	.3
165 CH OF NAZARENE	2	388	662	.5	.8
167 CHS OF CHRIST	2	142	186	.1	.2
181 CONSRV CONGR	1	158	203*	.2	.2
193 EPISCOPAL	2	346	426	.3	.5
207 E.L.C.A.	11	4,231	5,951	4.5	7.2
221 FREE METHODIST	3	243	598	.4	.7
263 INT FOURSQ GOS	1	35	45*	-	.1
283 LUTH—MO SYNOD	6	4,043	5,695	4.3	6.9
291 MISSIONARY CH	1	0	0	-	-
325 OLD REG BAPT	1	56	72*	.1	.1
355 PRESB CH (USA)	5	804	1,033*	.8	1.3
403 SALVATION ARMY	1	50	61	-	.1
413 S.D.A.	2	143	184*	.1	.2
419 SO BAPT CONV	16	3,682	4,733*	3.5	5.8
438 UN BRETH IN CR	2	57	57	-	.1
449 UN METHODIST	17	3,166	4,070*	3.0	5.0
467 WESLEYAN	3	193	545	.4	.7
469 WELS	3	925	1,296	1.0	1.6
496 JEWISH EST[1]	0	NA	2,866	2.1	3.5
497 BLACK BAPT EST[2]	NA	662	851*	.6	1.0
MONTCALM	**80**	**7,857**	**13,543***	**25.5**	**100.0**
019 AMER BAPT USA	2	186	240*	.5	1.8
053 ASSEMB OF GOD	3	193	352	.7	2.6
081 CATHOLIC	5	NA	2,782	5.2	20.5
081d LATIN	5	NA	2,782	5.2	20.5
093 CHR CH (DISC)	1	70	108	.2	.8
097 CHR CHS&CHS CR	4	220	283*	.5	2.1
105 CHRISTIAN REF	1	93	156	.3	1.2
123 CH GOD (ANDER)	4	262	287	.5	2.1
127 CH GOD (CLEVE)	1	55	71*	.1	.5
143 CG IN CR(MENN)	1	139	179*	.3	1.3
157 CH OF BRETHREN	1	17	22*	-	.2
165 CH OF NAZARENE	1	50	84	.2	.6
167 CHS OF CHRIST	1	16	23	-	.2
171 CH GOD-GEN CON	1	29	37*	.1	.3
175 CONGR CHR CHS	2	475	612*	1.2	4.5
193 EPISCOPAL	1	89	107	.2	.8
203 EVAN FREE CH	1	56	82	.2	.6
207 E.L.C.A.	6	1,246	1,698	3.2	12.5
221 FREE METHODIST	3	124	282	.5	2.1
259 IFCA	5	NR	NR	-	-
265 INT PENT C CHR	1	19	37	.1	.3
283 LUTH—MO SYNOD	5	1,058	1,400	2.6	10.3
323 OLD ORD AMISH	1	NA	150	.3	1.1
339 PENT CH OF GOD	1	35	77	.1	.6
413 S.D.A.	7	689	888*	1.7	6.6
438 UN BRETH IN CR	1	102	102	.2	.8
443 UN C OF CHRIST	6	760	979*	1.8	7.2
449 UN METHODIST	13	1,612	2,077*	3.9	15.3
467 WESLEYAN	1	42	145	.3	1.1
497 BLACK BAPT EST[2]	NA	220	283*	.5	2.1
MONTMORENCY	**20**	**1,732**	**3,709***	**41.5**	**100.0**
053 ASSEMB OF GOD	2	60	105	1.2	2.8
075 BRETHREN IN CR	1	20	34	.4	.9
081 CATHOLIC	3	NA	1,517	17.0	40.9
081d LATIN	3	NA	1,517	17.0	40.9
167 CHS OF CHRIST	1	18	23	.3	.6
181 CONSRV CONGR	1	111	136*	1.5	3.7
193 EPISCOPAL	2	133	161	1.8	4.3
209 EVAN LUTH SYN	1	60	70	.8	1.9
221 FREE METHODIST	2	66	102	1.1	2.8
283 LUTH—MO SYNOD	2	714	887	9.9	23.9
419 SO BAPT CONV	2	56	69*	.8	1.9
443 UN C OF CHRIST	2	374	458*	5.1	12.3
449 UN METHODIST	1	120	147*	1.6	4.0

NA–Not applicable   NR–Not reported   *Total adherents estimated from known number of communicant, confirmed, full members.   - Represents a percent less than 0.1.   Percentages may not total due to rounding.
[1]See Appendix E   [2]See Appendix F   [3]See Appendix G   Lines in *italic* represent a breakdown of Catholic rites or Friends affiliations. They are included in their respective denominational total.

Table 4. Churches and Church Membership by County and Denomination: 1990

County and Denomination	Number of churches	Communicant, confirmed, full members	Total adherents Number	Percent of total population	Percent of total adherents
MUSKEGON	**133**	**32,565**	**62,706***	**39.4**	**100.0**
005 AME ZION	1	1,510	1,812	1.1	2.9
019 AMER BAPT USA	2	683	880*	.6	1.4
053 ASSEMB OF GOD	6	962	1,926	1.2	3.1
057 BAPT GEN CONF	8	1,772	2,283*	1.4	3.6
081 CATHOLIC	12	NA	16,181	10.2	25.8
081d *LATIN*	*12*	*NA*	*16,181*	*10.2*	*25.8*
089 CHR & MISS AL	1	50	154	.1	.2
093 CHR CH (DISC)	1	88	126	.1	.2
097 CHR CHS&CHS CR	2	474	611*	.4	1.0
105 CHRISTIAN REF	7	1,909	2,781	1.7	4.4
111 CH CR,SCIENTST	1	NR	NR	-	-
123 CH GOD (ANDER)	4	387	416	.3	.7
127 CH GOD (CLEVE)	2	236	304*	.2	.5
133 CH GOD(7TH)DEN	1	31	39	-	.1
151 L-D SAINTS	1	NA	547	.3	.9
157 CH OF BRETHREN	1	24	31*	-	-
165 CH OF NAZARENE	2	334	503	.3	.8
167 CHS OF CHRIST	2	223	285	.2	.5
175 CONGR CHR CHS	1	83	107*	.1	.2
176 CCC, NOT NAT'L	1	404	520*	.3	.8
181 CONSRV CONGR	1	121	156*	.1	.2
193 EPISCOPAL	4	900	1,609	1.0	2.6
203 EVAN FREE CH	1	161	287	.2	.5
207 E.L.C.A.	10	3,317	4,425	2.8	7.1
209 EVAN LUTH SYN	1	266	405	.3	.6
221 FREE METHODIST	4	159	271	.2	.4
246 GREEK ORTHODOX	1	NR	NR	-	-
259 IFCA	3	NR	NR	-	-
283 LUTH—MO SYNOD	5	2,434	3,226	2.0	5.1
291 MISSIONARY CH	1	113	165	.1	.3
353 CHR BRETHREN	3	124	175	.1	.3
355 PRESB CH (USA)	1	457	589*	.4	.9
371 REF CH IN AM	15	3,196	5,715	3.6	9.1
403 SALVATION ARMY	1	129	153	.1	.2
413 S.D.A.	2	334	430*	.3	.7
419 SO BAPT CONV	1	10	13*	-	-
435 UNITARIAN-UNIV	1	46	54	-	.1
443 UN C OF CHRIST	3	1,496	1,927*	1.2	3.1
449 UN METHODIST	13	3,506	4,517*	2.8	7.2
467 WESLEYAN	4	261	631	.4	1.0
469 WELS	1	247	335	.2	.5
496 JEWISH EST[1]	1	NA	235	.1	.4
497 BLACK BAPT EST[2]	NA	6,118	7,882*	5.0	12.6
NEWAYGO	**47**	**5,822**	**13,490***	**35.3**	**100.0**
053 ASSEMB OF GOD	3	186	410	1.1	3.0
081 CATHOLIC	6	NA	4,206	11.0	31.2
081d *LATIN*	*6*	*NA*	*4,206*	*11.0*	*31.2*
093 CHR CH (DISC)	1	135	194	.5	1.4
097 CHR CHS&CHS CR	1	95	124*	.3	.9
105 CHRISTIAN REF	7	1,545	2,243	5.9	16.6
111 CH CR,SCIENTST	1	NR	NR	-	-
127 CH GOD (CLEVE)	1	157	205*	.5	1.5
165 CH OF NAZARENE	0	0	287	.8	2.1
193 EPISCOPAL	2	139	185	.5	1.4
221 FREE METHODIST	1	7	21	.1	.2
259 IFCA	3	NR	NR	-	-
283 LUTH—MO SYNOD	2	507	693	1.8	5.1
285 MENNONITE CH	1	43	43	.1	.3
323 OLD ORD AMISH	1	NA	50	.1	.4
371 REF CH IN AM	3	897	1,488	3.9	11.0
413 S.D.A.	1	69	90*	.2	.7
415 S-D BAPTIST GC	1	54	71*	.2	.5
443 UN C OF CHRIST	3	587	767*	2.0	5.7
449 UN METHODIST	6	1,166	1,523*	4.0	11.3
467 WESLEYAN	3	235	890	2.3	6.6
OAKLAND	**522**	**139,125**	**481,835***	**44.5**	**100.0**
007 ALBAN ORTH ARC	1	NR	NR	-	-
019 AMER BAPT USA	13	4,111	5,105*	.5	1.1
039 AP CHR CH(NAZ)	1	69	86*	-	-
045 APOSTOLIC LUTH	1	175	450	-	.1
053 ASSEMB OF GOD	18	3,379	6,028	.6	1.3
057 BAPT GEN CONF	2	152	189*	-	-
075 BRETHREN IN CR	1	26	44	-	-
081 CATHOLIC	63	NA	269,878	24.9	56.0
081c *CHALDEAN*	*4*	*NA*	*25,000*	*2.3*	*5.2*
081d *LATIN*	*59*	*NA*	*244,878*	*22.6*	*50.8*
089 CHR & MISS AL	6	1,075	1,424	.1	.3
093 CHR CH (DISC)	3	340	410	-	.1
097 CHR CHS&CHS CR	6	589	731*	.1	.2
105 CHRISTIAN REF	2	269	474	-	.1
111 CH CR,SCIENTST	9	NR	NR	-	-
123 CH GOD (ANDER)	9	1,455	1,524	.1	.3
127 CH GOD (CLEVE)	12	2,703	3,356*	.3	.7

County and Denomination	Number of churches	Communicant, confirmed, full members	Total adherents Number	Percent of total population	Percent of total adherents
145 CH GOD PROPHCY	1	35	43*	-	-
151 L-D SAINTS	7	NA	3,214	.3	.7
157 CH OF BRETHREN	1	30	37*	-	-
165 CH OF NAZARENE	15	2,065	2,968	.3	.6
167 CHS OF CHRIST	22	3,801	4,798	.4	1.0
175 CONGR CHR CHS	7	2,509	3,115*	.3	.6
179 CONSRV BAPT	7	NR	NR	-	-
181 CONSRV CONGR	1	179	222*	-	-
193 EPISCOPAL	23	7,974	12,714	1.2	2.6
203 EVAN FREE CH	1	64	130	-	-
207 E.L.C.A.	30	11,444	15,575	1.4	3.2
216 EVAN PRESBY CH	6	1,098	1,189	.1	.2
221 FREE METHODIST	6	862	968	.1	.2
223 FREE WILL BAPT	4	543	674*	.1	.1
226 FRIENDS-USA	1	25	31*	-	-
226c *FGC*	*1*	*25*	*31**	-	-
246 GREEK ORTHODOX	2	NR	NR	-	-
249 AP CATH ASSYR	0	3	26	-	-
259 IFCA	2	NR	NR	-	-
263 INT FOURSQ GOS	2	364	452*	-	.1
283 LUTH—MO SYNOD	33	18,661	25,211	2.3	5.2
291 MISSIONARY CH	7	535	879	.1	.2
313 N AM BAPT CONF	2	368	457*	-	.1
329 OPEN BIBLE STD	1	NR	NR	-	-
331 ORTH CH IN AM	1	NR	NR	-	-
339 PENT CH OF GOD	2	69	153	-	-
353 CHR BRETHREN	3	290	650	.1	.1
355 PRESB CH (USA)	30	17,240	21,406*	2.0	4.4
371 REF CH IN AM	2	92	244	-	.1
397 ROMANIAN ORTH	1	NR	NR	-	-
403 SALVATION ARMY	3	676	779	.1	.2
413 S.D.A.	8	1,572	1,952*	.2	.4
419 SO BAPT CONV	26	4,995	6,202*	.6	1.3
423 SYRIAN ANTIOCH	1	NA	1,100	.1	.2
435 UNITARIAN-UNIV	4	912	1,234	.1	.3
443 UN C OF CHRIST	8	3,097	3,845*	.4	.8
449 UN METHODIST	59	22,564	28,017*	2.6	5.8
467 WESLEYAN	3	314	996	.1	.2
469 WELS	3	471	632	.1	.1
496 JEWISH EST[1]	36	NA	23,243	2.1	4.8
497 BLACK BAPT EST[2]	NA	21,930	27,230*	2.5	5.7
498 INDEP.CHARIS.[3]	1	NA	500	-	.1
499 INDEP.NON-CHAR[3]	3	NA	1,250	.1	.3
OCEANA	**38**	**3,200**	**7,370***	**32.8**	**100.0**
053 ASSEMB OF GOD	1	28	67	.3	.9
057 BAPT GEN CONF	1	71	93*	.4	1.3
081 CATHOLIC	8	NA	2,753	12.3	37.4
081d *LATIN*	*8*	*NA*	*2,753*	*12.3*	*37.4*
105 CHRISTIAN REF	2	247	371	1.7	5.0
165 CH OF NAZARENE	1	18	52	.2	.7
167 CHS OF CHRIST	1	23	30	.1	.4
193 EPISCOPAL	1	78	85	.4	1.2
207 E.L.C.A.	1	244	332	1.5	4.5
209 EVAN LUTH SYN	1	29	46	.2	.6
283 LUTH—MO SYNOD	1	237	284	1.3	3.9
355 PRESB CH (USA)	1	153	200*	.9	2.7
371 REF CH IN AM	1	205	334	1.5	4.5
413 S.D.A.	1	59	77*	.3	1.0
443 UN C OF CHRIST	2	429	560*	2.5	7.6
449 UN METHODIST	9	1,061	1,384*	6.2	18.8
467 WESLEYAN	5	206	544	2.4	7.4
469 WELS	1	112	158	.7	2.1
OGEMAW	**24**	**2,465**	**6,329***	**33.9**	**100.0**
011 A.W.M.C.	1	0	0*	-	-
053 ASSEMB OF GOD	1	30	57	.3	.9
081 CATHOLIC	3	NA	2,897	15.5	45.8
081d *LATIN*	*3*	*NA*	*2,897*	*15.5*	*45.8*
127 CH GOD (CLEVE)	1	39	49*	.3	.8
157 CH OF BRETHREN	1	72	91*	.5	1.4
165 CH OF NAZARENE	2	63	225	1.2	3.6
167 CHS OF CHRIST	1	64	90	.5	1.4
193 EPISCOPAL	2	137	218	1.2	3.4
207 E.L.C.A.	1	166	223	1.2	3.5
221 FREE METHODIST	1	72	132	.7	2.1
226 FRIENDS-USA	1	71	79	.4	1.2
226b *EFI*	*1*	*71*	*79*	*.4*	*1.2*
283 LUTH—MO SYNOD	2	791	1,039	5.6	16.4
413 S.D.A.	1	24	30*	.2	.5
419 SO BAPT CONV	2	272	343*	1.8	5.4
449 UN METHODIST	3	656	826*	4.4	13.1
467 WESLEYAN	1	8	30	.2	.5
ONTONAGON	**31**	**2,163**	**4,433***	**50.1**	**100.0**
045 APOSTOLIC LUTH	3	69	107	1.2	2.4

NA–Not applicable   NR–Not reported   *Total adherents estimated from known number of communicant, confirmed, full members.   - Represents a percent less than 0.1.   Percentages may not total due to rounding.
[1]See Appendix E   [2]See Appendix F   [3]See Appendix G   Lines in *italic* represent a breakdown of Catholic rites or Friends affiliations. They are included in their respective denominational total.

Table 4. Churches and Church Membership by County and Denomination: 1990

County and Denomination	Number of churches	Communicant, confirmed, full members	Total adherents		
			Number	Percent of total population	Percent of total adherents
053 ASSEMB OF GOD	2	71	108	1.2	2.4
081 CATHOLIC	6	NA	1,663	18.8	37.5
081d LATIN	*6*	*NA*	*1,663*	*18.8*	*37.5*
193 EPISCOPAL	2	57	126	1.4	2.8
207 E.L.C.A.	7	906	1,156	13.1	26.1
220 FREE LUTHERAN	1	69	81	.9	1.8
283 LUTH—MO SYNOD	2	411	484	5.5	10.9
355 PRESB CH (USA)	1	37	45*	.5	1.0
413 S.D.A.	0	35	43*	.5	1.0
449 UN METHODIST	6	374	455*	5.1	10.3
469 WELS	1	134	165	1.9	3.7
OSCEOLA	**48**	**3,500**	**6,707***	**33.3**	**100.0**
053 ASSEMB OF GOD	2	113	234	1.2	3.5
057 BAPT GEN CONF	2	86	112*	.6	1.7
081 CATHOLIC	5	NA	1,548	7.7	23.1
081d LATIN	*5*	*NA*	*1,548*	*7.7*	*23.1*
105 CHRISTIAN REF	1	257	446	2.2	6.6
123 CH GOD (ANDER)	1	85	89	.4	1.3
127 CH GOD (CLEVE)	1	25	32*	.2	.5
165 CH OF NAZARENE	2	145	173	.9	2.6
181 CONSRV CONGR	1	25	32*	.2	.5
207 E.L.C.A.	4	665	893	4.4	13.3
221 FREE METHODIST	4	123	208	1.0	3.1
259 IFCA	1	NR	NR	-	-
283 LUTH—MO SYNOD	1	412	547	2.7	8.2
323 OLD ORD AMISH	2	NA	200	1.0	3.0
355 PRESB CH (USA)	1	14	18*	.1	.3
413 S.D.A.	3	109	141*	.7	2.1
443 UN C OF CHRIST	2	113	147*	.7	2.2
449 UN METHODIST	12	1,239	1,607*	8.0	24.0
467 WESLEYAN	3	89	280	1.4	4.2
OSCODA	**17**	**1,291**	**2,586***	**33.0**	**100.0**
053 ASSEMB OF GOD	1	39	60	.8	2.3
081 CATHOLIC	1	NA	637	8.1	24.6
081d LATIN	*1*	*NA*	*637*	*8.1*	*24.6*
123 CH GOD (ANDER)	1	138	149	1.9	5.8
167 CHS OF CHRIST	2	60	79	1.0	3.1
193 EPISCOPAL	1	29	31	.4	1.2
285 MENNONITE CH	3	445	595	7.6	23.0
287 MENN GEN CONF	1	106	144	1.8	5.6
323 OLD ORD AMISH	2	NA	300	3.8	11.6
413 S.D.A.	1	115	143*	1.8	5.5
443 UN C OF CHRIST	1	39	48*	.6	1.9
449 UN METHODIST	1	182	226*	2.9	8.7
467 WESLEYAN	1	27	45	.6	1.7
469 WELS	1	111	129	1.6	5.0
OTSEGO	**19**	**2,071**	**10,141***	**56.5**	**100.0**
053 ASSEMB OF GOD	1	85	200	1.1	2.0
081 CATHOLIC	3	NA	7,025	39.1	69.3
081d LATIN	*3*	*NA*	*7,025*	*39.1*	*69.3*
105 CHRISTIAN REF	1	52	91	.5	.9
111 CH CR,SCIENTST	1	NR	NR	-	-
123 CH GOD (ANDER)	1	25	47	.3	.5
165 CH OF NAZARENE	1	31	66	.4	.7
167 CHS OF CHRIST	1	35	45	.3	.4
193 EPISCOPAL	1	115	127	.7	1.3
203 EVAN FREE CH	1	170	450	2.5	4.4
207 E.L.C.A.	1	240	351	2.0	3.5
283 LUTH—MO SYNOD	1	323	447	2.5	4.4
355 PRESB CH (USA)	1	70	91*	.5	.9
413 S.D.A.	1	59	76*	.4	.7
419 SO BAPT CONV	1	80	104*	.6	1.0
443 UN C OF CHRIST	1	226	293*	1.6	2.9
449 UN METHODIST	1	540	699*	3.9	6.9
469 WELS	1	20	29	.2	.3
OTTAWA	**162**	**47,114**	**100,790***	**53.7**	**100.0**
053 ASSEMB OF GOD	6	547	792	.4	.8
057 BAPT GEN CONF	1	43	56*	-	.1
081 CATHOLIC	10	NA	22,146	11.8	22.0
081d LATIN	*10*	*NA*	*22,146*	*11.8*	*22.0*
089 CHR & MISS AL	1	50	100	.1	.1
097 CHR CHS&CHS CR	2	240	314*	.2	.3
105 CHRISTIAN REF	50	15,959	24,506	13.1	24.3
111 CH CR,SCIENTST	1	NR	NR	-	-
123 CH GOD (ANDER)	1	71	78	-	.1
127 CH GOD (CLEVE)	2	256	335*	.2	.3
133 CH GOD(7TH)DEN	1	31	39	-	-
145 CH GOD PROPHCY	1	35	46*	-	-
151 L-D SAINTS	1	NA	219	.1	.2
165 CH OF NAZARENE	2	206	322	.2	.3
167 CHS OF CHRIST	3	246	321	.2	.3
179 CONSRV BAPT	1	NR	NR	-	-
193 EPISCOPAL	2	689	901	.5	.9
207 E.L.C.A.	1	567	727	.4	.7
221 FREE METHODIST	1	77	114	.1	.1
259 IFCA	4	NR	NR	-	-
283 LUTH—MO SYNOD	10	4,481	6,178	3.3	6.1
353 CHR BRETHREN	2	149	207	.1	.2
355 PRESB CH (USA)	4	2,406	3,150*	1.7	3.1
356 PRESB CH AMER	1	0	0	-	-
371 REF CH IN AM	33	15,038	26,514	14.1	26.3
403 SALVATION ARMY	1	112	140	.1	.1
413 S.D.A.	5	582	762*	.4	.8
419 SO BAPT CONV	1	130	170*	.1	.2
443 UN C OF CHRIST	2	792	1,037*	.6	1.0
449 UN METHODIST	5	2,834	3,711*	2.0	3.7
467 WESLEYAN	6	1,291	6,801	3.6	6.7
496 JEWISH EST [1]	0	NA	410	.2	.4
497 BLACK BAPT EST [2]	NA	282	369*	.2	.4
499 INDEP.NON-CHAR [3]	1	NA	325	.2	.3
PRESQUE ISLE	**23**	**3,229**	**8,701***	**63.3**	**100.0**
053 ASSEMB OF GOD	2	53	117	.9	1.3
081 CATHOLIC	4	NA	4,593	33.4	52.8
081d LATIN	*4*	*NA*	*4,593*	*33.4*	*52.8*
193 EPISCOPAL	1	55	62	.5	.7
207 E.L.C.A.	4	338	436	3.2	5.0
283 LUTH—MO SYNOD	6	1,883	2,369	17.2	27.2
355 PRESB CH (USA)	1	282	352*	2.6	4.0
413 S.D.A.	1	76	95*	.7	1.1
419 SO BAPT CONV	2	188	235*	1.7	2.7
449 UN METHODIST	2	354	442*	3.2	5.1
ROSCOMMON	**30**	**2,586**	**6,828***	**34.5**	**100.0**
019 AMER BAPT USA	2	254	304*	1.5	4.5
053 ASSEMB OF GOD	3	131	320	1.6	4.7
081 CATHOLIC	5	NA	3,179	16.1	46.6
081d LATIN	*5*	*NA*	*3,179*	*16.1*	*46.6*
111 CH CR,SCIENTST	1	NR	NR	-	-
151 L-D SAINTS	1	NA	110	.6	1.6
165 CH OF NAZARENE	1	24	45	.2	.7
167 CHS OF CHRIST	1	35	46	.2	.7
175 CONGR CHR CHS	1	250	300*	1.5	4.4
193 EPISCOPAL	2	168	325	1.6	4.8
207 E.L.C.A.	1	167	194	1.0	2.8
221 FREE METHODIST	1	24	63	.3	.9
259 IFCA	1	NR	NR	-	-
283 LUTH—MO SYNOD	2	577	686	3.5	10.0
355 PRESB CH (USA)	1	85	102*	.5	1.5
413 S.D.A.	1	36	43*	.2	.6
419 SO BAPT CONV	3	275	330*	1.7	4.8
449 UN METHODIST	2	503	603*	3.0	8.8
467 WESLEYAN	1	57	178	.9	2.6
SAGINAW	**181**	**51,771**	**121,646***	**57.4**	**100.0**
019 AMER BAPT USA	6	1,682	2,150*	1.0	1.8
053 ASSEMB OF GOD	12	1,293	2,984	1.4	2.5
059 BAPT MISS ASSN	1	76	97*	-	.1
075 BRETHREN IN CR	1	19	31	-	-
081 CATHOLIC	36	NA	52,068	24.6	42.8
081d LATIN	*36*	*NA*	*52,068*	*24.6*	*42.8*
089 CHR & MISS AL	2	66	181	.1	.1
093 CHR CH (DISC)	2	196	275	.1	.2
097 CHR CHS&CHS CR	1	100	128*	.1	.1
105 CHRISTIAN REF	1	84	140	.1	.1
111 CH CR,SCIENTST	1	NR	NR	-	-
123 CH GOD (ANDER)	1	104	104	-	.1
127 CH GOD (CLEVE)	1	57	73*	-	.1
133 CH GOD(7TH)DEN	2	62	78	-	.1
151 L-D SAINTS	1	NA	402	.2	.3
164 CH LUTH CONF	1	198	268	.1	.2
165 CH OF NAZARENE	6	671	844	.4	.7
167 CHS OF CHRIST	3	267	345	.2	.3
175 CONGR CHR CHS	1	100	128*	.1	.1
179 CONSRV BAPT	1	NR	NR	-	-
193 EPISCOPAL	6	952	1,620	.8	1.3
207 E.L.C.A.	12	5,620	7,292	3.4	6.0
209 EVAN LUTH SYN	1	165	224	.1	.2
221 FREE METHODIST	3	131	177	.1	.1
246 GREEK ORTHODOX	1	NR	NR	-	-
249 AP CATH ASSYR	0	7	39	-	-
259 IFCA	1	NR	NR	-	-
274 LAT EVAN LUTH	1	161	166	.1	.1
283 LUTH—MO SYNOD	15	13,789	17,898	8.4	14.7
285 MENNONITE CH	2	128	206	.1	.2
339 PENT CH OF GOD	1	34	77	-	.1
353 CHR BRETHREN	1	23	90	-	.1
355 PRESB CH (USA)	8	2,657	3,396*	1.6	2.8

NA–Not applicable NR–Not reported *Total adherents estimated from known number of communicant, confirmed, full members. - Represents a percent less than 0.1. Percentages may not total due to rounding.

[1]See Appendix E [2]See Appendix F [3]See Appendix G Lines in *italic* represent a breakdown of Catholic rites or Friends affiliations. They are included in their respective denominational total.

Table 4. Churches and Church Membership by County and Denomination: 1990

County and Denomination	Number of churches	Communicant, confirmed, full members	Total adherents		
			Number	Percent of total population	Percent of total adherents
367 PROT CONF (LU)	1	50	65	-	.1
403 SALVATION ARMY	1	140	181	.1	.1
413 S.D.A.	4	573	732*	.3	.6
419 SO BAPT CONV	1	215	275*	.1	.2
431 UKRANIAN AMER	1	NR	NR	-	-
435 UNITARIAN-UNIV	1	10	15	-	-
438 UN BRETH IN CR	1	94	94	-	.1
443 UN C OF CHRIST	4	1,302	1,664*	.8	1.4
449 UN METHODIST	18	4,897	6,258*	3.0	5.1
467 WESLEYAN	3	213	686	.3	.6
469 WELS	12	5,206	6,667	3.1	5.5
496 JEWISH EST[1]	2	NA	200	.1	.2
497 BLACK BAPT EST[2]	NA	10,429	13,328*	6.3	11.0
SAINT CLAIR	**109**	**18,042**	**81,566***	**56.0**	**100.0**
011 A.W.M.C.	1	0	0*	-	-
019 AMER BAPT USA	3	369	471*	.3	.6
053 ASSEMB OF GOD	3	314	436	.3	.5
081 CATHOLIC	17	NA	52,261	35.9	64.1
081d LATIN	17	NA	52,261	35.9	64.1
089 CHR & MISS AL	1	14	22	-	-
097 CHR CHS&CHS CR	2	375	479*	.3	.6
111 CH CR,SCIENTST	1	NR	NR	-	-
127 CH GOD (CLEVE)	1	272	347*	.2	.4
151 L-D SAINTS	1	NA	375	.3	.5
165 CH OF NAZARENE	4	272	404	.3	.5
167 CHS OF CHRIST	3	98	129	.1	.2
175 CONGR CHR CHS	2	113	144*	.1	.2
176 CCC, NOT NAT'L	1	680	869*	.6	1.1
181 CONSRV CONGR	1	38	49*	-	.1
193 EPISCOPAL	8	1,187	1,972	1.4	2.4
207 E.L.C.A.	8	2,539	3,797	2.6	4.7
221 FREE METHODIST	3	190	276	.2	.3
283 LUTH—MO SYNOD	6	3,084	4,351	3.0	5.3
291 MISSIONARY CH	2	440	1,118	.8	1.4
353 CHR BRETHREN	1	40	65	-	.1
355 PRESB CH (USA)	4	924	1,180*	.8	1.4
403 SALVATION ARMY	1	351	370	.3	.5
413 S.D.A.	1	114	146*	.1	.2
419 SO BAPT CONV	2	143	183*	.1	.2
443 UN C OF CHRIST	5	1,430	1,826*	1.3	2.2
449 UN METHODIST	20	3,380	4,317*	3.0	5.3
467 WESLEYAN	4	474	1,316	.9	1.6
469 WELS	2	356	461	.3	.6
496 JEWISH EST[1]	1	NA	3,123	2.1	3.8
497 BLACK BAPT EST[2]	NA	845	1,079*	.7	1.3
SAINT JOSEPH	**91**	**10,120**	**22,236***	**37.7**	**100.0**
019 AMER BAPT USA	2	237	307*	.5	1.4
053 ASSEMB OF GOD	3	239	430	.7	1.9
057 BAPT GEN CONF	1	48	62*	.1	.3
059 BAPT MISS ASSN	2	172	223*	.4	1.0
061 BEACHY AMISH	1	44	57*	.1	.3
081 CATHOLIC	6	NA	6,138	10.4	27.6
081d LATIN	6	NA	6,138	10.4	27.6
097 CHR CHS&CHS CR	3	275	356*	.6	1.6
105 CHRISTIAN REF	1	45	80	.1	.4
111 CH CR,SCIENTST	2	NR	NR	-	-
123 CH GOD (ANDER)	3	206	231	.4	1.0
146 CH GOD MTN ASM	1	12	16*	-	.1
151 L-D SAINTS	1	NA	216	.4	1.0
157 CH OF BRETHREN	1	52	67*	.1	.3
165 CH OF NAZARENE	2	387	878	1.5	3.9
167 CHS OF CHRIST	1	51	67	.1	.3
179 CONSRV BAPT	1	NR	NR	-	-
193 EPISCOPAL	2	376	540	.9	2.4
207 E.L.C.A.	3	829	1,187	2.0	5.3
259 IFCA	4	NR	NR	-	-
283 LUTH—MO SYNOD	6	1,427	1,952	3.3	8.8
285 MENNONITE CH	8	829	1,256	2.1	5.6
291 MISSIONARY CH	5	274	663	1.1	3.0
323 OLD ORD AMISH	6	NA	900	1.5	4.0
339 PENT CH OF GOD	2	79	197	.3	.9
353 CHR BRETHREN	1	25	50	.1	.2
355 PRESB CH (USA)	3	1,173	1,519*	2.6	6.8
403 SALVATION ARMY	1	68	76	.1	.3
413 S.D.A.	3	222	287*	.5	1.3
443 UN C OF CHRIST	1	74	96*	.2	.4
449 UN METHODIST	13	2,205	2,855*	4.8	12.8
467 WESLEYAN	1	202	800	1.4	3.6
469 WELS	1	202	255	.4	1.1
497 BLACK BAPT EST[2]	NA	367	475*	.8	2.1
SANILAC	**81**	**6,578**	**15,219***	**38.1**	**100.0**
019 AMER BAPT USA	2	252	323*	.8	2.1
053 ASSEMB OF GOD	3	119	278	.7	1.8

County and Denomination	Number of churches	Communicant, confirmed, full members	Total adherents		
			Number	Percent of total population	Percent of total adherents
075 BRETHREN IN CR	1	43	80	.2	.5
081 CATHOLIC	9	NA	5,616	14.1	36.9
081d LATIN	9	NA	5,616	14.1	36.9
089 CHR & MISS AL	1	73	151	.4	1.0
127 CH GOD (CLEVE)	1	74	95*	.2	.6
165 CH OF NAZARENE	2	66	137	.3	.9
167 CHS OF CHRIST	1	28	36	.1	.2
193 EPISCOPAL	3	242	312	.8	2.1
207 E.L.C.A.	2	410	605	1.5	4.0
221 FREE METHODIST	2	191	241	.6	1.6
246 GREEK ORTHODOX	1	NR	NR	-	-
259 IFCA	1	NR	NR	-	-
283 LUTH—MO SYNOD	7	1,527	1,975	4.9	13.0
291 MISSIONARY CH	7	326	657	1.6	4.3
323 OLD ORD AMISH	2	NA	200	.5	1.3
353 CHR BRETHREN	1	12	25	.1	.2
355 PRESB CH (USA)	6	778	998*	2.5	6.6
413 S.D.A.	1	22	28*	.1	.2
443 UN C OF CHRIST	1	31	40*	.1	.3
449 UN METHODIST	25	2,137	2,741*	6.9	18.0
467 WESLEYAN	2	247	681	1.7	4.5
SCHOOLCRAFT	**19**	**874**	**2,715***	**32.7**	**100.0**
019 AMER BAPT USA	1	247	307*	3.7	11.3
081 CATHOLIC	4	NA	1,509	18.2	55.6
081d LATIN	4	NA	1,509	18.2	55.6
123 CH GOD (ANDER)	1	22	25	.3	.9
151 L-D SAINTS	1	NA	36	.4	1.3
193 EPISCOPAL	1	35	43	.5	1.6
263 INT FOURSQ GOS	1	58	72*	.9	2.7
283 LUTH—MO SYNOD	1	67	89	1.1	3.3
285 MENNONITE CH	4	80	180	2.2	6.6
355 PRESB CH (USA)	1	126	157*	1.9	5.8
413 S.D.A.	1	21	26*	.3	1.0
443 UN C OF CHRIST	1	40	50*	.6	1.8
449 UN METHODIST	2	178	221*	2.7	8.1
SHIAWASSEE	**86**	**10,452**	**26,550***	**38.1**	**100.0**
019 AMER BAPT USA	2	281	360*	.5	1.4
053 ASSEMB OF GOD	3	144	246	.4	.9
075 BRETHREN IN CR	1	15	30	-	.1
081 CATHOLIC	6	NA	10,333	14.8	38.9
081d LATIN	6	NA	10,333	14.8	38.9
097 CHR CHS&CHS CR	4	1,265	1,622*	2.3	6.1
111 CH CR,SCIENTST	1	NR	NR	-	-
123 CH GOD (ANDER)	1	135	135	.2	.5
127 CH GOD (CLEVE)	2	157	201*	.3	.8
133 CH GOD(7TH)DEN	1	31	40	.1	.2
151 L-D SAINTS	2	NA	822	1.2	3.1
165 CH OF NAZARENE	6	701	1,377	2.0	5.2
167 CHS OF CHRIST	1	65	85	.1	.3
175 CONGR CHR CHS	2	468	600*	.9	2.3
181 CONSRV CONGR	2	206	264*	.4	1.0
193 EPISCOPAL	2	219	314	.5	1.2
203 EVAN FREE CH	1	84	104	.1	.4
207 E.L.C.A.	1	193	298	.4	1.1
216 EVAN PRESBY CH	1	70	70	.1	.3
221 FREE METHODIST	4	269	282	.4	1.1
259 IFCA	2	NR	NR	-	-
283 LUTH—MO SYNOD	1	24	43	.1	.2
339 PENT CH OF GOD	1	35	77	.1	.3
353 CHR BRETHREN	1	50	130	.2	.5
403 SALVATION ARMY	1	91	95	.1	.4
413 S.D.A.	2	237	304*	.4	1.1
419 SO BAPT CONV	3	356	456*	.7	1.7
443 UN C OF CHRIST	3	897	1,150*	1.6	4.3
449 UN METHODIST	23	2,567	3,291*	4.7	12.4
467 WESLEYAN	3	336	1,676	2.4	6.3
469 WELS	3	1,556	2,145	3.1	8.1
TUSCOLA	**84**	**12,831**	**24,145***	**43.5**	**100.0**
019 AMER BAPT USA	1	21	27*	-	.1
053 ASSEMB OF GOD	4	220	498	.9	2.1
081 CATHOLIC	8	NA	6,564	11.8	27.2
081d LATIN	8	NA	6,564	11.8	27.2
089 CHR & MISS AL	1	24	60	.1	.2
097 CHR CHS&CHS CR	2	267	342*	.6	1.4
111 CH CR,SCIENTST	1	NR	NR	-	-
123 CH GOD (ANDER)	1	210	210	.4	.9
127 CH GOD (CLEVE)	1	68	87*	.2	.4
151 L-D SAINTS	1	NA	148	.3	.6
165 CH OF NAZARENE	8	478	801	1.4	3.3
167 CHS OF CHRIST	3	149	206	.4	.9
203 EVAN FREE CH	1	138	225	.4	.9
207 E.L.C.A.	2	312	414	.7	1.7
221 FREE METHODIST	1	19	37	.1	.2

NA–Not applicable   NR–Not reported   *Total adherents estimated from known number of communicant, confirmed, full members.   - Represents a percent less than 0.1.   Percentages may not total due to rounding.
[1]See Appendix E   [2]See Appendix F   [3]See Appendix G   Lines in *italic* represent a breakdown of Catholic rites or Friends affiliations. They are included in their respective denominational total.

MICHIGAN

Table 4. Churches and Church Membership by County and Denomination: 1990

County and Denomination	Number of churches	Communicant, confirmed, full members	Total adherents		
			Number	Percent of total population	Percent of total adherents
259 IFCA	4	NR	NR	-	-
283 LUTH—MO SYNOD	8	5,353	7,103	12.8	29.4
285 MENNONITE CH	1	44	44	.1	.2
291 MISSIONARY CH	3	105	151	.3	.6
293 MORAV CH-NORTH	1	332	421	.8	1.7
353 CHR BRETHREN	2	28	50	.1	.2
355 PRESB CH (USA)	4	829	1,061*	1.9	4.4
413 S.D.A.	2	127	163*	.3	.7
419 SO BAPT CONV	1	35	45*	.1	.2
438 UN BRETH IN CR	1	156	178	.3	.7
449 UN METHODIST	19	2,965	3,795*	6.8	15.7
467 WESLEYAN	1	142	428	.8	1.8
469 WELS	2	809	1,087	2.0	4.5
VAN BUREN	**86**	**9,349**	**20,387***	**29.1**	**100.0**
019 AMER BAPT USA	1	160	207*	.3	1.0
053 ASSEMB OF GOD	2	56	99	.1	.5
059 BAPT MISS ASSN	2	115	149*	.2	.7
081 CATHOLIC	7	NA	7,412	10.6	36.4
081d LATIN	7	NA	7,412	10.6	36.4
093 CHR CH (DISC)	1	40	53	.1	.3
097 CHR CHS&CHS CR	1	300	389*	.6	1.9
105 CHRISTIAN REF	3	151	245	.3	1.2
111 CH CR,SCIENTST	1	NR	NR	-	-
123 CH GOD (ANDER)	2	70	70	.1	.3
127 CH GOD (CLEVE)	1	31	40*	.1	.2
133 CH GOD(7TH)DEN	2	62	78	.1	.4
151 L-D SAINTS	2	NA	268	.4	1.3
164 CH LUTH CONF	1	76	121	.2	.6
165 CH OF NAZARENE	0	7	32	-	.2
167 CHS OF CHRIST	2	109	144	.2	.7
175 CONGR CHR CHS	1	24	31*	-	.2
176 CCC, NOT NAT'L	1	70	91*	.1	.4
179 CONSRV BAPT	1	NR	NR	-	-
181 CONSRV CONGR	2	148	192*	.3	.9
193 EPISCOPAL	2	192	298	.4	1.5
207 E.L.C.A.	1	469	570	.8	2.8
213 EVAN MENN INC	1	140	182*	.3	.9
221 FREE METHODIST	2	62	95	.1	.5
223 FREE WILL BAPT	1	40	52*	.1	.3
259 IFCA	2	NR	NR	-	-
265 INT PENT C CHR	2	90	128	.2	.6
283 LUTH—MO SYNOD	1	633	849	1.2	4.2
339 PENT CH OF GOD	3	129	240	.3	1.2
349 PENT HOLINESS	1	9	12*	-	.1
353 CHR BRETHREN	1	20	55	.1	.3
355 PRESB CH (USA)	3	728	944*	1.3	4.6
371 REF CH IN AM	3	620	1,090	1.6	5.3
413 S.D.A.	7	626	812*	1.2	4.0
419 SO BAPT CONV	3	189	245*	.3	1.2
443 UN C OF CHRIST	2	513	665*	.9	3.3
449 UN METHODIST	14	1,888	2,448*	3.5	12.0
469 WELS	3	507	687	1.0	3.4
496 JEWISH EST[1]	1	NA	0	-	-
497 BLACK BAPT EST[2]	NA	1,075	1,394*	2.0	6.8
WASHTENAW	**187**	**48,432**	**104,216***	**36.8**	**100.0**
001 ADVENT CHR CH	1	18	22*	-	-
019 AMER BAPT USA	9	3,411	4,128*	1.5	4.0
053 ASSEMB OF GOD	8	938	1,897	.7	1.8
057 BAPT GEN CONF	2	319	386*	.1	.4
081 CATHOLIC	14	NA	34,376	12.1	33.0
081d LATIN	14	NA	34,376	12.1	33.0
089 CHR & MISS AL	1	16	167	.1	.2
093 CHR CH (DISC)	1	151	188	.1	.2
097 CHR CHS&CHS CR	2	80	97*	-	.1
105 CHRISTIAN REF	3	448	645	.2	.6
111 CH CR,SCIENTST	2	NR	NR	-	-
123 CH GOD (ANDER)	3	328	341	.1	.3
127 CH GOD (CLEVE)	3	328	397*	.1	.4
145 CH GOD PROPHCY	1	35	42*	-	-
146 CH GOD MTN ASM	1	50	61*	-	.1
151 L-D SAINTS	3	NA	1,019	.4	1.0
157 CH OF BRETHREN	1	26	31*	-	-
165 CH OF NAZARENE	3	196	283	.1	.3
167 CHS OF CHRIST	6	670	884	.3	.8
175 CONGR CHR CHS	1	913	1,105*	.4	1.1
181 CONSRV CONGR	1	7	8*	-	-
193 EPISCOPAL	8	1,743	3,386	1.2	3.2
203 EVAN FREE CH	1	35	80	-	.1
207 E.L.C.A.	10	4,796	6,112	2.2	5.9
216 EVAN PRESBY CH	1	134	144	.1	.1
221 FREE METHODIST	4	531	987	.3	.9
223 FREE WILL BAPT	5	720	871*	.3	.8
226 FRIENDS-USA	3	231	338*	.1	.3
226b EFI	2	72	146	.1	.1
226c FGC	1	159	192*	.1	.2

County and Denomination	Number of churches	Communicant, confirmed, full members	Total adherents		
			Number	Percent of total population	Percent of total adherents
246 GREEK ORTHODOX	1	NR	NR	-	-
259 IFCA	2	NR	NR	-	-
283 LUTH—MO SYNOD	11	3,024	4,132	1.5	4.0
285 MENNONITE CH	2	34	64	-	.1
287 MENN GEN CONF	2	15	32	-	-
291 MISSIONARY CH	1	8	13	-	-
325 OLD REG BAPT	1	67	81*	-	.1
329 OPEN BIBLE STD	1	NR	NR	-	-
339 PENT CH OF GOD	3	103	230	.1	.2
353 CHR BRETHREN	1	15	15	-	-
355 PRESB CH (USA)	7	3,695	4,471*	1.6	4.3
371 REF CH IN AM	1	45	105	-	.1
403 SALVATION ARMY	2	167	237	.1	.2
413 S.D.A.	2	404	489*	.2	.5
419 SO BAPT CONV	6	2,851	3,450*	1.2	3.3
435 UNITARIAN-UNIV	2	456	715	.3	.7
436 UNITED BAPT	1	26	31*	-	-
443 UN C OF CHRIST	12	4,650	5,627*	2.0	5.4
449 UN METHODIST	19	6,200	7,503*	2.7	7.2
467 WESLEYAN	1	28	68	-	.1
469 WELS	6	1,543	1,995	.7	1.9
496 JEWISH EST[1]	3	NA	4,500	1.6	4.3
497 BLACK BAPT EST[2]	NA	8,977	10,863*	3.8	10.4
498 INDEP.CHARIS.[3]	2	NA	850	.3	.8
499 INDEP.NON-CHAR[3]	2	NA	750	.3	.7
WAYNE	**923**	**401,097**	**1,367,836***	**64.8**	**100.0**
005 AME ZION	12	35,220	41,873	2.0	3.1
019 AMER BAPT USA	33	21,018	26,658*	1.3	1.9
039 AP CHR CH(NAZ)	1	15	19*	-	-
040 AP CHR CH-AMER	1	90	160	-	-
049 ARMEN AP CH AM	1	1,000	5,000	.2	.4
053 ASSEMB OF GOD	30	4,968	8,783	.4	.6
057 BAPT GEN CONF	3	362	459*	-	-
081 CATHOLIC	186	NA	778,340	36.9	56.9
081a ARMENIAN	1	NA	600	-	-
081b BYZAN RUTH	3	NA	1,155	.1	.1
081c CHALDEAN	1	NA	6,000	.3	.4
081d LATIN	173	NA	761,510	36.1	55.7
081e MARONITE	1	NA	2,041	.1	.1
081f MELKITE-GK	1	NA	1,500	.1	.1
081g ROMANIAN	2	NA	644	-	-
081h UKRAINIAN	4	NA	4,890	.2	.4
089 CHR & MISS AL	6	386	793	-	.1
093 CHR CH (DISC)	5	1,437	2,069	.1	.2
097 CHR CHS&CHS CR	8	1,349	1,711*	.1	.1
105 CHRISTIAN REF	2	494	769	-	.1
111 CH CR,SCIENTST	14	NR	NR	-	-
123 CH GOD (ANDER)	15	1,417	2,035	.1	.1
127 CH GOD (CLEVE)	26	4,017	5,095*	.2	.4
133 CH GOD(7TH)DEN	1	31	39	-	-
145 CH GOD PROPHCY	10	357	453*	-	-
146 CH GOD MTN ASM	4	116	147*	-	-
151 L-D SAINTS	7	NA	3,627	.2	.3
157 CH OF BRETHREN	2	153	194*	-	-
164 CH LUTH CONF	1	7	12	-	-
165 CH OF NAZARENE	12	1,185	1,224	.1	.1
167 CHS OF CHRIST	40	7,339	10,034	.5	.7
175 CONGR CHR CHS	7	2,946	3,737*	.2	.3
179 CONSRV BAPT	2	NR	NR	-	-
185 CUMBER PRESB	1	35	40	-	-
193 EPISCOPAL	44	10,759	15,284	.7	1.1
207 E.L.C.A.	56	18,303	24,474	1.2	1.8
216 EVAN PRESBY CH	4	6,450	6,620	.3	.5
221 FREE METHODIST	8	816	1,083	.1	.1
223 FREE WILL BAPT	15	1,987	2,520*	.1	.2
226 FRIENDS-USA	1	28	36*	-	-
226c FGC	1	28	36*	-	-
246 GREEK ORTHODOX	6	NR	NR	-	-
249 AP CATH ASSYR	1	37	272	-	-
259 IFCA	1	NR	NR	-	-
274 LAT EVAN LUTH	1	345	402	-	-
283 LUTH—MO SYNOD	61	26,752	36,873	1.7	2.7
285 MENNONITE CH	3	49	62	-	-
287 MENN GEN CONF	1	6	6	-	-
291 MISSIONARY CH	4	223	309	-	-
293 MORAV CH-NORTH	2	183	236	-	-
313 N AM BAPT CONF	2	926	1,175*	.1	.1
325 OLD REG BAPT	3	161	204*	-	-
331 ORTH CH IN AM	5	NR	NR	-	-
339 PENT CH OF GOD	2	37	106	-	-
349 PENT HOLINESS	1	26	33*	-	-
353 CHR BRETHREN	14	1,665	2,374	.1	.2
355 PRESB CH (USA)	44	22,668	28,751*	1.4	2.1
361 PRIM BAPT ASCS	2	96	122*	-	-
371 REF CH IN AM	8	759	1,631	.1	.1
397 ROMANIAN ORTH	2	NR	NR	-	-

NA–Not applicable   NR–Not reported   *Total adherents estimated from known number of communicant, confirmed, full members.   - Represents a percent less than 0.1.   Percentages may not total due to rounding.
[1]See Appendix E   [2]See Appendix F   [3]See Appendix G   Lines in *italic* represent a breakdown of Catholic rites or Friends affiliations. They are included in their respective denominational total.

Table 4. Churches and Church Membership by County and Denomination: 1990

County and Denomination	Number of churches	Communicant, confirmed, full members	Total adherents Number	Percent of total population	Percent of total adherents
403 SALVATION ARMY	9	1,512	1,639	.1	.1
413 S.D.A.	15	5,821	7,383*	.3	.5
419 SO BAPT CONV	41	10,416	13,211*	.6	1.0
423 SYRIAN ANTIOCH	1	NA	600	-	-
431 UKRANIAN AMER	1	NR	NR	-	-
435 UNITARIAN-UNIV	2	479	587	-	-
438 UN BRETH IN CR	2	101	101	-	-
443 UN C OF CHRIST	24	9,796	12,425*	.6	.9
449 UN METHODIST	62	19,396	24,601*	1.2	1.8
467 WESLEYAN	7	321	644	-	-
469 WELS	12	4,020	5,432	.3	.4
496 JEWISH EST[1]	5	NA	45,296	2.1	3.3
497 BLACK BAPT EST[2]	NA	173,017	219,448*	10.4	16.0
498 INDEP.CHARIS.[3]	9	NA	11,000	.5	.8
499 INDEP.NON-CHAR[3]	12	NA	9,625	.5	.7
WEXFORD	**47**	**5,033**	**9,812***	**37.2**	**100.0**
019 AMER BAPT USA	2	781	1,011*	3.8	10.3
053 ASSEMB OF GOD	1	120	260	1.0	2.6
057 BAPT GEN CONF	1	309	400*	1.5	4.1
081 CATHOLIC	3	NA	2,400	9.1	24.5
081d LATIN	*3*	*NA*	*2,400*	*9.1*	*24.5*
093 CHR CH (DISC)	3	158	235	.9	2.4
105 CHRISTIAN REF	1	188	299	1.1	3.0
111 CH CR,SCIENTST	1	NR	NR	-	-
123 CH GOD (ANDER)	2	81	81	.3	.8
127 CH GOD (CLEVE)	1	29	38*	.1	.4
145 CH GOD PROPHCY	1	35	45*	.2	.5
165 CH OF NAZARENE	2	191	609	2.3	6.2
167 CHS OF CHRIST	1	35	55	.2	.6
175 CONGR CHR CHS	1	45	58*	.2	.6
193 EPISCOPAL	1	71	134	.5	1.4
207 E.L.C.A.	2	736	1,083	4.1	11.0
221 FREE METHODIST	4	79	187	.7	1.9
259 IFCA	3	NR	NR	-	-
283 LUTH—MO SYNOD	2	354	528	2.0	5.4
339 PENT CH OF GOD	1	35	77	.3	.8
353 CHR BRETHREN	1	12	40	.2	.4
355 PRESB CH (USA)	1	383	496*	1.9	5.1
403 SALVATION ARMY	1	109	117	.4	1.2
413 S.D.A.	3	242	313*	1.2	3.2
419 SO BAPT CONV	1	78	101*	.4	1.0
443 UN C OF CHRIST	1	148	192*	.7	2.0
449 UN METHODIST	5	766	992*	3.8	10.1
467 WESLEYAN	1	48	61	.2	.6

MINNESOTA

County and Denomination	Number of churches	Communicant, confirmed, full members	Total adherents Number	Percent of total population	Percent of total adherents
THE STATE.....	4,981	1,222,359	2,837,418*	64.9	100.0
AITKIN	**49**	**5,970**	**9,577***	**77.1**	**100.0**
053 ASSEMB OF GOD	3	128	256	2.1	2.7
057 BAPT GEN CONF	1	63	77*	.6	.8
081 CATHOLIC	5	NA	1,655	13.3	17.3
081d LATIN	*5*	*NA*	*1,655*	*13.3*	*17.3*
089 CHR & MISS AL	1	12	52	.4	.5
097 CHR CHS&CHS CR	1	45	55*	.4	.6
111 CH CR,SCIENTST	1	NR	NR	-	-
163 CH OF LUTH BR	1	60	70	.6	.7
179 CONSRV BAPT	1	NR	NR	-	-
193 EPISCOPAL	1	22	23	.2	.2
207 E.L.C.A.	15	3,587	4,825	38.8	50.4
220 FREE LUTHERAN	1	25	25	.2	.3
283 LUTH—MO SYNOD	4	883	1,135	9.1	11.9
355 PRESB CH (USA)	3	145	178*	1.4	1.9
413 S.D.A.	1	29	36*	.3	.4
419 SO BAPT CONV	1	59	72*	.6	.8
443 UN C OF CHRIST	1	90	110*	.9	1.1
449 UN METHODIST	7	813	998*	8.0	10.4
469 WELS	1	9	10	.1	.1
ANOKA	**95**	**42,945**	**129,831***	**53.3**	**100.0**
053 ASSEMB OF GOD	7	1,837	2,925	1.2	2.3
057 BAPT GEN CONF	4	1,030	1,364*	.6	1.1
081 CATHOLIC	9	NA	60,488	24.8	46.6
081d LATIN	*9*	*NA*	*60,488*	*24.8*	*46.6*
089 CHR & MISS AL	3	242	669	.3	.5
093 CHR CH (DISC)	1	167	205	.1	.2
097 CHR CHS&CHS CR	2	120	159*	.1	.1
127 CH GOD (CLEVE)	1	187	248*	.1	.2
145 CH GOD PROPHCY	1	24	32*	-	-
151 L-D SAINTS	3	NA	868	.4	.7

County and Denomination	Number of churches	Communicant, confirmed, full members	Total adherents Number	Percent of total population	Percent of total adherents
164 CH LUTH CONF	1	240	323	.1	.2
167 CHS OF CHRIST	1	18	40	-	-
179 CONSRV BAPT	2	NR	NR	-	-
193 EPISCOPAL	2	365	653	.3	.5
203 EVAN FREE CH	3	615	1,158	.5	.9
207 E.L.C.A.	19	24,831	36,723	15.1	28.3
220 FREE LUTHERAN	1	38	51	-	-
263 INT FOURSQ GOS	1	0	0*	-	-
283 LUTH—MO SYNOD	10	6,648	9,328	3.8	7.2
331 ORTH CH IN AM	1	NR	NR	-	-
355 PRESB CH (USA)	2	410	543*	.2	.4
413 S.D.A.	1	190	252*	.1	.2
419 SO BAPT CONV	2	211	279*	.1	.2
435 UNITARIAN-UNIV	1	65	83	-	.1
443 UN C OF CHRIST	1	411	544*	.2	.4
449 UN METHODIST	10	4,384	5,805*	2.4	4.5
467 WESLEYAN	2	124	353	.1	.3
469 WELS	1	447	624	.3	.5
496 JEWISH EST[1]	0	NA	3,312	1.4	2.6
497 BLACK BAPT EST[2]	NA	341	452*	.2	.3
498 INDEP.CHARIS.[3]	1	NA	1,300	.5	1.0
499 INDEP.NON-CHAR[3]	2	NA	1,050	.4	.8
BECKER	**58**	**10,607**	**19,405***	**69.6**	**100.0**
053 ASSEMB OF GOD	2	181	385	1.4	2.0
081 CATHOLIC	10	NA	5,096	18.3	26.3
081d LATIN	*10*	*NA*	*5,096*	*18.3*	*26.3*
089 CHR & MISS AL	1	115	265	1.0	1.4
164 CH LUTH CONF	2	86	115	.4	.6
165 CH OF NAZARENE	1	22	78	.3	.4
176 CCC, NOT NAT'L	1	245	318*	1.1	1.6
179 CONSRV BAPT	2	NR	NR	-	-
193 EPISCOPAL	3	299	534	1.9	2.8
203 EVAN FREE CH	1	40	70	.3	.4
207 E.L.C.A.	17	5,562	7,282	26.1	37.5
209 EVAN LUTH SYN	1	166	205	.7	1.1
220 FREE LUTHERAN	1	30	43	.2	.2
283 LUTH—MO SYNOD	10	3,021	3,907	14.0	20.1
285 MENNONITE CH	2	67	105	.4	.5
413 S.D.A.	1	186	241*	.9	1.2
443 UN C OF CHRIST	1	61	79*	.3	.4
449 UN METHODIST	2	526	682*	2.4	3.5
BELTRAMI	**58**	**7,621**	**16,531***	**48.1**	**100.0**
053 ASSEMB OF GOD	2	122	328	1.0	2.0
057 BAPT GEN CONF	1	26	34*	.1	.2
081 CATHOLIC	7	NA	4,929	14.3	29.8
081d LATIN	*7*	*NA*	*4,929*	*14.3*	*29.8*
097 CHR CHS&CHS CR	1	30	39*	.1	.2
111 CH CR,SCIENTST	1	NR	NR	-	-
145 CH GOD PROPHCY	1	24	32*	.1	.2
151 L-D SAINTS	2	NA	421	1.2	2.5
165 CH OF NAZARENE	2	79	135	.4	.8
179 CONSRV BAPT	1	NR	NR	-	-
193 EPISCOPAL	3	190	511	1.5	3.1
203 EVAN FREE CH	3	283	490	1.4	3.0
207 E.L.C.A.	15	4,233	6,002	17.5	36.3
220 FREE LUTHERAN	1	42	67	.2	.4
221 FREE METHODIST	1	28	60	.2	.4
226 FRIENDS-USA	1	2	28	.1	.2
226c FGC	*1*	*2*	*28*	*.1*	*.2*
283 LUTH—MO SYNOD	2	752	979	2.8	5.9
284 LUTH CH-AM ASC	2	76	88	.3	.5
285 MENNONITE CH	1	30	61	.2	.4
339 PENT CH OF GOD	2	68	152	.4	.9
355 PRESB CH (USA)	3	574	753*	2.2	4.6
413 S.D.A.	2	216	284*	.8	1.7
419 SO BAPT CONV	1	143	188*	.5	1.1
435 UNITARIAN-UNIV	1	0	0	-	-
449 UN METHODIST	1	590	774*	2.3	4.7
469 WELS	1	113	176	.5	1.1
BENTON	**27**	**3,218**	**19,054***	**63.1**	**100.0**
057 BAPT GEN CONF	1	79	105*	.3	.6
081 CATHOLIC	9	NA	14,398	47.7	75.6
081d LATIN	*9*	*NA*	*14,398*	*47.7*	*75.6*
089 CHR & MISS AL	1	105	275	.9	1.4
097 CHR CHS&CHS CR	1	15	20*	.1	.1
203 EVAN FREE CH	1	84	175	.6	.9
207 E.L.C.A.	3	556	683	2.3	3.6
283 LUTH—MO SYNOD	4	1,488	2,171	7.2	11.4
355 PRESB CH (USA)	3	423	561*	1.9	2.9
403 SALVATION ARMY	1	81	85	.3	.4
443 UN C OF CHRIST	1	8	11*	-	.1
449 UN METHODIST	1	193	256*	.8	1.3
469 WELS	1	186	314	1.0	1.6

NA–Not applicable   NR–Not reported   *Total adherents estimated from known number of communicant, confirmed, full members.   - Represents a percent less than 0.1.   Percentages may not total due to rounding.
[1]See Appendix E   [2]See Appendix F   [3]See Appendix G   Lines in *italic* represent a breakdown of Catholic rites or Friends affiliations. They are included in their respective denominational total.

Table 4. Churches and Church Membership by County and Denomination: 1990

County and Denomination	Number of churches	Communicant, confirmed, full members	Total adherents Number	Percent of total population	Percent of total adherents
BIG STONE	**28**	**4,269**	**7,293***	**116.0**	**100.0**
053 ASSEMB OF GOD	1	32	43	.7	.6
057 BAPT GEN CONF	1	90	113*	1.8	1.5
081 CATHOLIC	3	NA	1,698	27.0	23.3
081d LATIN	3	NA	1,698	27.0	23.3
179 CONSRV BAPT	1	NR	NR	-	-
207 E.L.C.A.	7	2,162	2,849	45.3	39.1
220 FREE LUTHERAN	1	63	90	1.4	1.2
257 HUTTERIAN BR	1	NA	100	1.6	1.4
283 LUTH—MO SYNOD	4	1,026	1,256	20.0	17.2
413 S.D.A.	1	30	38*	.6	.5
443 UN C OF CHRIST	2	246	310*	4.9	4.3
449 UN METHODIST	4	443	559*	8.9	7.7
469 WELS	2	177	237	3.8	3.2
BLUE EARTH	**73**	**18,653**	**37,184***	**68.8**	**100.0**
019 AMER BAPT USA	2	600	736*	1.4	2.0
053 ASSEMB OF GOD	1	68	90	.2	.2
057 BAPT GEN CONF	1	176	216*	.4	.6
081 CATHOLIC	9	NA	12,350	22.9	33.2
081d LATIN	9	NA	12,350	22.9	33.2
093 CHR CH (DISC)	2	234	337	.6	.9
097 CHR CHS&CHS CR	2	98	120*	.2	.3
111 CH CR,SCIENTST	1	NR	NR	-	-
145 CH GOD PROPHCY	1	24	29*	.1	.1
151 L-D SAINTS	1	NA	295	.5	.8
164 CH LUTH CONF	2	785	1,048	1.9	2.8
165 CH OF NAZARENE	1	37	65	.1	.2
167 CHS OF CHRIST	1	51	86	.2	.2
179 CONSRV BAPT	1	NR	NR	-	-
193 EPISCOPAL	1	251	316	.6	.8
207 E.L.C.A.	12	6,957	9,404	17.4	25.3
209 EVAN LUTH SYN	1	425	646	1.2	1.7
220 FREE LUTHERAN	1	50	80	.1	.2
226 FRIENDS-USA	1	3	10	-	-
226f INDEPENDNT	1	3	10	-	-
283 LUTH—MO SYNOD	12	3,827	5,069	9.4	13.6
355 PRESB CH (USA)	4	1,555	1,909*	3.5	5.1
403 SALVATION ARMY	1	71	77	.1	.2
413 S.D.A.	1	108	133*	.2	.4
419 SO BAPT CONV	1	91	112*	.2	.3
435 UNITARIAN-UNIV	1	48	70	.1	.2
443 UN C OF CHRIST	2	672	825*	1.5	2.2
449 UN METHODIST	7	1,786	2,192*	4.1	5.9
469 WELS	3	736	969	1.8	2.6
BROWN	**35**	**9,487**	**23,919***	**88.6**	**100.0**
053 ASSEMB OF GOD	2	85	134	.5	.6
081 CATHOLIC	7	NA	11,542	42.8	48.3
081d LATIN	7	NA	11,542	42.8	48.3
097 CHR CHS&CHS CR	1	0	0*	-	-
193 EPISCOPAL	1	48	48	.2	.2
207 E.L.C.A.	10	3,821	5,114	19.0	21.4
283 LUTH—MO SYNOD	2	850	1,143	4.2	4.8
435 UNITARIAN-UNIV	1	135	148	.5	.6
443 UN C OF CHRIST	3	675	866*	3.2	3.6
449 UN METHODIST	4	1,108	1,421*	5.3	5.9
469 WELS	4	2,765	3,503	13.0	14.6
CARLTON	**50**	**7,473**	**16,141***	**55.2**	**100.0**
045 APOSTOLIC LUTH	3	255	479	1.6	3.0
053 ASSEMB OF GOD	1	46	99	.3	.6
057 BAPT GEN CONF	2	199	255*	.9	1.6
081 CATHOLIC	9	NA	5,705	19.5	35.3
081d LATIN	9	NA	5,705	19.5	35.3
089 CHR & MISS AL	1	21	91	.3	.6
193 EPISCOPAL	2	77	121	.4	.7
203 EVAN FREE CH	1	22	30	.1	.2
207 E.L.C.A.	14	4,060	5,618	19.2	34.8
220 FREE LUTHERAN	1	700	1,000	3.4	6.2
283 LUTH—MO SYNOD	7	1,112	1,487	5.1	9.2
287 MENN GEN CONF	1	18	24	.1	.1
355 PRESB CH (USA)	3	529	677*	2.3	4.2
413 S.D.A.	1	23	29*	.1	.2
449 UN METHODIST	4	411	526*	1.8	3.3
CARVER	**47**	**13,902**	**31,331***	**65.4**	**100.0**
053 ASSEMB OF GOD	1	20	36	.1	.1
057 BAPT GEN CONF	1	30	40*	.1	.1
081 CATHOLIC	9	NA	11,349	23.7	36.2
081d LATIN	9	NA	11,349	23.7	36.2
089 CHR & MISS AL	1	160	308	.6	1.0
203 EVAN FREE CH	2	247	540	1.1	1.7
207 E.L.C.A.	8	3,700	5,577	11.6	17.8
283 LUTH—MO SYNOD	12	7,653	10,060	21.0	32.1

County and Denomination	Number of churches	Communicant, confirmed, full members	Total adherents Number	Percent of total population	Percent of total adherents
293 MORAV CH-NORTH	3	620	789	1.6	2.5
355 PRESB CH (USA)	1	149	198*	.4	.6
443 UN C OF CHRIST	5	991	1,318*	2.8	4.2
449 UN METHODIST	3	212	282*	.6	.9
469 WELS	1	120	183	.4	.6
496 JEWISH EST[1]	0	NA	651	1.4	2.1
CASS	**49**	**4,655**	**9,310***	**42.7**	**100.0**
045 APOSTOLIC LUTH	1	25	50	.2	.5
053 ASSEMB OF GOD	4	146	262	1.2	2.8
057 BAPT GEN CONF	2	143	182*	.8	2.0
081 CATHOLIC	8	NA	2,484	11.4	26.7
081d LATIN	8	NA	2,484	11.4	26.7
089 CHR & MISS AL	4	132	289	1.3	3.1
165 CH OF NAZARENE	1	131	304	1.4	3.3
193 EPISCOPAL	2	188	373	1.7	4.0
203 EVAN FREE CH	1	55	120	.6	1.3
207 E.L.C.A.	14	2,474	3,413	15.7	36.7
283 LUTH—MO SYNOD	3	469	620	2.8	6.7
285 MENNONITE CH	1	8	19	.1	.2
339 PENT CH OF GOD	2	68	154	.7	1.7
413 S.D.A.	1	22	28*	.1	.3
443 UN C OF CHRIST	3	612	780*	3.6	8.4
449 UN METHODIST	2	182	232*	1.1	2.5
CHIPPEWA	**27**	**7,866**	**11,824***	**89.4**	**100.0**
057 BAPT GEN CONF	2	135	172*	1.3	1.5
081 CATHOLIC	1	NA	1,473	11.1	12.5
081d LATIN	1	NA	1,473	11.1	12.5
105 CHRISTIAN REF	1	277	394	3.0	3.3
207 E.L.C.A.	14	5,267	6,847	51.8	57.9
283 LUTH—MO SYNOD	3	738	933	7.1	7.9
355 PRESB CH (USA)	1	41	52*	.4	.4
371 REF CH IN AM	2	802	1,180	8.9	10.0
443 UN C OF CHRIST	1	168	214*	1.6	1.8
449 UN METHODIST	2	438	559*	4.2	4.7
CHISAGO	**31**	**8,002**	**16,162***	**53.0**	**100.0**
053 ASSEMB OF GOD	2	185	243	.8	1.5
057 BAPT GEN CONF	2	246	326*	1.1	2.0
081 CATHOLIC	5	NA	4,719	15.5	29.2
081d LATIN	5	NA	4,719	15.5	29.2
179 CONSRV BAPT	2	NR	NR	-	-
203 EVAN FREE CH	3	245	438	1.4	2.7
207 E.L.C.A.	10	6,220	8,502	27.9	52.6
220 FREE LUTHERAN	1	47	93	.3	.6
283 LUTH—MO SYNOD	2	298	417	1.4	2.6
449 UN METHODIST	4	761	1,010*	3.3	6.2
496 JEWISH EST[1]	0	NA	414	1.4	2.6
CLAY	**62**	**18,940**	**33,582***	**66.6**	**100.0**
053 ASSEMB OF GOD	2	185	479	.9	1.4
081 CATHOLIC	8	NA	7,059	14.0	21.0
081d LATIN	8	NA	7,059	14.0	21.0
089 CHR & MISS AL	1	38	93	.2	.3
097 CHR CHS&CHS CR	1	95	119*	.2	.4
151 L-D SAINTS	2	NA	506	1.0	1.5
163 CH OF LUTH BR	2	249	731	1.4	2.2
165 CH OF NAZARENE	1	45	236	.5	.7
193 EPISCOPAL	1	43	45	.1	.1
203 EVAN FREE CH	1	67	99	.2	.3
207 E.L.C.A.	25	14,135	18,803	37.3	56.0
209 EVAN LUTH SYN	2	230	306	.6	.9
220 FREE LUTHERAN	1	80	132	.3	.4
226 FRIENDS-USA	0	2	3	-	-
226c FGC	0	2	3	-	-
257 HUTTERIAN BR	1	NA	100	.2	.3
283 LUTH—MO SYNOD	4	1,519	1,854	3.7	5.5
355 PRESB CH (USA)	3	510	638*	1.3	1.9
443 UN C OF CHRIST	4	1,021	1,278*	2.5	3.8
449 UN METHODIST	2	577	722*	1.4	2.1
469 WELS	1	144	212	.4	.6
496 JEWISH EST[1]	0	NA	167	.3	.5
CLEARWATER	**25**	**2,715**	**4,599***	**55.3**	**100.0**
053 ASSEMB OF GOD	1	12	40	.5	.9
057 BAPT GEN CONF	1	88	114*	1.4	2.5
081 CATHOLIC	3	NA	543	6.5	11.8
081d LATIN	3	NA	543	6.5	11.8
151 L-D SAINTS	1	NA	59	.7	1.3
163 CH OF LUTH BR	1	85	147	1.8	3.2
193 EPISCOPAL	1	83	260	3.1	5.7
203 EVAN FREE CH	1	54	70	.8	1.5
207 E.L.C.A.	9	1,724	2,426	29.2	52.8
209 EVAN LUTH SYN	1	107	162	1.9	3.5

NA–Not applicable   NR–Not reported   *Total adherents estimated from known number of communicant, confirmed, full members.   - Represents a percent less than 0.1.   Percentages may not total due to rounding.

[1]See Appendix E   [2]See Appendix F   [3]See Appendix G   Lines in *italic* represent a breakdown of Catholic rites or Friends affiliations. They are included in their respective denominational total.

Table 4. Churches and Church Membership by County and Denomination: 1990

County and Denomination	Number of churches	Communicant, confirmed, full members	Total adherents Number	Percent of total population	Percent of total adherents
220 FREE LUTHERAN	5	358	502	6.0	10.9
283 LUTH—MO SYNOD	1	204	276	3.3	6.0
COOK	**11**	**1,205**	**1,857***	**48.0**	**100.0**
053 ASSEMB OF GOD	1	64	58	1.5	3.1
057 BAPT GEN CONF	2	78	97*	2.5	5.2
081 CATHOLIC	2	NA	345	8.9	18.6
081d LATIN	*2*	*NA*	*345*	*8.9*	*18.6*
203 EVAN FREE CH	1	105	130	3.4	7.0
207 E.L.C.A.	4	690	894	23.1	48.1
413 S.D.A.	0	11	14*	.4	.8
443 UN C OF CHRIST	1	257	319*	8.2	17.2
COTTONWOOD	**40**	**7,844**	**11,367***	**89.5**	**100.0**
053 ASSEMB OF GOD	2	92	200	1.6	1.8
081 CATHOLIC	4	NA	1,540	12.1	13.5
081d LATIN	*4*	*NA*	*1,540*	*12.1*	*13.5*
089 CHR & MISS AL	2	154	304	2.4	2.7
105 CHRISTIAN REF	1	28	46	.4	.4
179 CONSRV BAPT	2	NR	NR	-	-
193 EPISCOPAL	1	61	105	.8	.9
203 EVAN FREE CH	1	55	80	.6	.7
207 E.L.C.A.	8	3,169	3,921	30.9	34.5
211 FEL EVG BIB CH	1	192	192	1.5	1.7
237 GC MENN BR CHS	2	205	256*	2.0	2.3
283 LUTH—MO SYNOD	2	1,380	1,729	13.6	15.2
284 LUTH CH-AM ASC	1	57	70	.6	.6
287 MENN GEN CONF	4	1,099	1,235	9.7	10.9
355 PRESB CH (USA)	3	408	510*	4.0	4.5
413 S.D.A.	1	17	21*	.2	.2
449 UN METHODIST	5	927	1,158*	9.1	10.2
CROW WING	**64**	**12,441**	**27,091***	**61.2**	**100.0**
053 ASSEMB OF GOD	3	390	740	1.7	2.7
057 BAPT GEN CONF	1	90	115*	.3	.4
081 CATHOLIC	12	NA	9,818	22.2	36.2
081d LATIN	*12*	*NA*	*9,818*	*22.2*	*36.2*
089 CHR & MISS AL	3	85	209	.5	.8
097 CHR CHS&CHS CR	2	90	115*	.3	.4
111 CH CR,SCIENTST	1	NR	NR	-	-
127 CH GOD (CLEVE)	1	15	19*	-	.1
151 L-D SAINTS	1	NA	428	1.0	1.6
165 CH OF NAZARENE	2	162	337	.8	1.2
167 CHS OF CHRIST	1	40	60	.1	.2
179 CONSRV BAPT	1	NR	NR	-	-
193 EPISCOPAL	1	260	390	.9	1.4
203 EVAN FREE CH	2	261	405	.9	1.5
207 E.L.C.A.	12	6,396	8,328	18.8	30.7
226 FRIENDS-USA	1	0	12	-	-
226c FGC	*1*	*0*	*12*	*-*	*-*
283 LUTH—MO SYNOD	7	2,025	2,669	6.0	9.9
355 PRESB CH (USA)	3	725	923*	2.1	3.4
403 SALVATION ARMY	1	117	137	.3	.5
413 S.D.A.	1	168	214*	.5	.8
443 UN C OF CHRIST	1	362	461*	1.0	1.7
449 UN METHODIST	5	1,063	1,354*	3.1	5.0
467 WESLEYAN	1	75	209	.5	.8
469 WELS	1	117	148	.3	.5
DAKOTA	**144**	**49,016**	**151,416***	**55.0**	**100.0**
019 AMER BAPT USA	2	167	221*	.1	.1
039 AP CHR CH(NAZ)	1	7	9*	-	-
040 AP CHR CH-AMER	1	39	69	-	-
053 ASSEMB OF GOD	6	762	1,910	.7	1.3
057 BAPT GEN CONF	6	1,347	1,781*	.6	1.2
081 CATHOLIC	20	NA	75,188	27.3	49.7
081d LATIN	*20*	*NA*	*75,188*	*27.3*	*49.7*
089 CHR & MISS AL	4	190	435	.2	.3
097 CHR CHS&CHS CR	1	200	265*	.1	.2
105 CHRISTIAN REF	1	90	133	-	.1
111 CH CR,SCIENTST	1	NR	NR	-	-
127 CH GOD (CLEVE)	1	166	220*	.1	.1
151 L-D SAINTS	3	NA	1,207	.4	.8
163 CH OF LUTH BR	1	99	229	.1	.2
164 CH LUTH CONF	1	140	206	.1	.1
165 CH OF NAZARENE	2	103	222	.1	.1
167 CHS OF CHRIST	2	121	185	.1	.1
179 CONSRV BAPT	1	NR	NR	-	-
193 EPISCOPAL	5	780	1,302	.5	.9
203 EVAN FREE CH	5	434	1,070	.4	.7
207 E.L.C.A.	25	25,646	36,814	13.4	24.3
263 INT FOURSQ GOS	1	0	0*	-	-
283 LUTH—MO SYNOD	12	5,992	8,041	2.9	5.3
313 N AM BAPT CONF	3	533	705*	.3	.5
339 PENT CH OF GOD	1	35	77	-	.1
355 PRESB CH (USA)	3	612	809*	.3	.5

County and Denomination	Number of churches	Communicant, confirmed, full members	Total adherents Number	Percent of total population	Percent of total adherents
356 PRESB CH AMER	1	56	104	-	.1
371 REF CH IN AM	3	668	1,331	.5	.9
413 S.D.A.	1	18	24*	-	-
419 SO BAPT CONV	3	379	501*	.2	.3
435 UNITARIAN-UNIV	1	26	26	-	-
443 UN C OF CHRIST	3	732	968*	.4	.6
449 UN METHODIST	13	5,026	6,647*	2.4	4.4
467 WESLEYAN	1	34	50	-	-
469 WELS	7	3,712	4,983	1.8	3.3
496 JEWISH EST[1]	0	NA	3,741	1.4	2.5
497 BLACK BAPT EST[2]	NA	902	1,193*	.4	.8
498 INDEP.CHARIS.[3]	2	NA	750	.3	.5
DODGE	**33**	**7,034**	**11,595***	**73.7**	**100.0**
053 ASSEMB OF GOD	1	38	68	.4	.6
081 CATHOLIC	5	NA	2,185	13.9	18.8
081d LATIN	*5*	*NA*	*2,185*	*13.9*	*18.8*
097 CHR CHS&CHS CR	1	175	235*	1.5	2.0
179 CONSRV BAPT	1	NR	NR	-	-
181 CONSRV CONGR	1	165	221*	1.4	1.9
193 EPISCOPAL	1	102	120	.8	1.0
207 E.L.C.A.	6	4,012	5,373	34.2	46.3
220 FREE LUTHERAN	1	34	45	.3	.4
283 LUTH—MO SYNOD	3	456	582	3.7	5.0
284 LUTH CH-AM ASC	1	78	122	.8	1.1
285 MENNONITE CH	1	18	20	.1	.2
355 PRESB CH (USA)	3	558	748*	4.8	6.5
413 S.D.A.	1	102	137*	.9	1.2
415 S-D BAPTIST GC	1	97	130*	.8	1.1
443 UN C OF CHRIST	2	371	498*	3.2	4.3
449 UN METHODIST	4	828	1,111*	7.1	9.6
DOUGLAS	**51**	**11,698**	**22,249***	**77.6**	**100.0**
053 ASSEMB OF GOD	1	120	217	.8	1.0
057 BAPT GEN CONF	1	287	367*	1.3	1.6
081 CATHOLIC	6	NA	6,631	23.1	29.8
081d LATIN	*6*	*NA*	*6,631*	*23.1*	*29.8*
097 CHR CHS&CHS CR	1	68	87*	.3	.4
111 CH CR,SCIENTST	1	NR	NR	-	-
143 CG IN CR(MENN)	1	15	19*	.1	.1
151 L-D SAINTS	1	NA	153	.5	.7
163 CH OF LUTH BR	1	53	139	.5	.6
193 EPISCOPAL	1	126	161	.6	.7
203 EVAN FREE CH	1	30	60	.2	.3
207 E.L.C.A.	19	7,246	9,577	33.4	43.0
220 FREE LUTHERAN	1	152	200	.7	.9
221 FREE METHODIST	1	36	55	.2	.2
283 LUTH—MO SYNOD	9	2,264	2,877	10.0	12.9
355 PRESB CH (USA)	1	140	179*	.6	.8
371 REF CH IN AM	1	65	129	.4	.6
443 UN C OF CHRIST	1	396	506*	1.8	2.3
449 UN METHODIST	2	572	731*	2.5	3.3
469 WELS	1	128	161	.6	.7
FARIBAULT	**48**	**9,407**	**17,443***	**103.0**	**100.0**
019 AMER BAPT USA	1	252	318*	1.9	1.8
053 ASSEMB OF GOD	2	99	180	1.1	1.0
081 CATHOLIC	7	NA	5,129	30.3	29.4
081d LATIN	*7*	*NA*	*5,129*	*30.3*	*29.4*
145 CH GOD PROPHCY	1	24	30*	.2	.2
163 CH OF LUTH BR	1	57	164	1.0	.9
179 CONSRV BAPT	1	NR	NR	-	-
207 E.L.C.A.	13	4,273	5,673	33.5	32.5
283 LUTH—MO SYNOD	7	1,720	2,171	12.8	12.4
284 LUTH CH-AM ASC	1	112	154	.9	.9
355 PRESB CH (USA)	2	376	475*	2.8	2.7
443 UN C OF CHRIST	2	435	549*	3.2	3.1
449 UN METHODIST	10	2,059	2,600*	15.4	14.9
FILLMORE	**64**	**12,735**	**19,741***	**95.0**	**100.0**
053 ASSEMB OF GOD	1	86	140	.7	.7
081 CATHOLIC	9	NA	2,642	12.7	13.4
081d LATIN	*9*	*NA*	*2,642*	*12.7*	*13.4*
143 CG IN CR(MENN)	1	12	15*	.1	.1
157 CH OF BRETHREN	1	132	169*	.8	.9
193 EPISCOPAL	2	84	120	.6	.6
207 E.L.C.A.	27	8,574	11,232	54.1	56.9
221 FREE METHODIST	1	37	69	.3	.3
283 LUTH—MO SYNOD	4	1,307	1,677	8.1	8.5
323 OLD ORD AMISH	3	NA	450	2.2	2.3
355 PRESB CH (USA)	3	366	468*	2.3	2.4
371 REF CH IN AM	1	272	374	1.8	1.9
449 UN METHODIST	11	1,865	2,385*	11.5	12.1

NA–Not applicable   NR–Not reported   *Total adherents estimated from known number of communicant, confirmed, full members.   - Represents a percent less than 0.1.   Percentages may not total due to rounding.
[1]See Appendix E   [2]See Appendix F   [3]See Appendix G   Lines in *italic* represent a breakdown of Catholic rites or Friends affiliations. They are included in their respective denominational total.

Table 4. Churches and Church Membership by County and Denomination: 1990

County and Denomination	Number of churches	Communicant, confirmed, full members	Total adherents Number	Percent of total population	Percent of total adherents
FREEBORN	**55**	**17,107**	**27,834***	**84.2**	**100.0**
019 AMER BAPT USA	3	1,144	1,435*	4.3	5.2
053 ASSEMB OF GOD	1	71	168	.5	.6
081 CATHOLIC	3	NA	4,899	14.8	17.6
081d LATIN	3	NA	4,899	14.8	17.6
097 CHR CHS&CHS CR	1	140	176*	.5	.6
105 CHRISTIAN REF	1	146	250	.8	.9
111 CH CR,SCIENTST	1	NR	NR	-	-
145 CH GOD PROPHCY	1	24	30*	.1	.1
167 CHS OF CHRIST	1	30	39	.1	.1
181 CONSRV CONGR	1	53	66*	.2	.2
193 EPISCOPAL	1	128	247	.7	.9
207 E.L.C.A.	24	11,686	15,755	47.7	56.6
209 EVAN LUTH SYN	3	509	694	2.1	2.5
283 LUTH—MO SYNOD	2	650	843	2.5	3.0
284 LUTH CH-AM ASC	1	22	33	.1	.1
355 PRESB CH (USA)	1	612	768*	2.3	2.8
371 REF CH IN AM	1	214	331	1.0	1.2
403 SALVATION ARMY	1	88	93	.3	.3
413 S.D.A.	1	56	70*	.2	.3
443 UN C OF CHRIST	1	167	209*	.6	.8
449 UN METHODIST	5	1,339	1,680*	5.1	6.0
467 WESLEYAN	1	28	48	.1	.2
GOODHUE	**72**	**20,734**	**34,479***	**84.7**	**100.0**
053 ASSEMB OF GOD	3	154	236	.6	.7
057 BAPT GEN CONF	1	194	250*	.6	.7
081 CATHOLIC	6	NA	6,737	16.6	19.5
081d LATIN	6	NA	6,737	16.6	19.5
089 CHR & MISS AL	1	26	51	.1	.1
097 CHR CHS&CHS CR	1	40	52*	.1	.2
151 L-D SAINTS	1	NA	197	.5	.6
164 CH LUTH CONF	1	97	151	.4	.4
165 CH OF NAZARENE	1	0	0	-	-
167 CHS OF CHRIST	1	15	20	-	.1
193 EPISCOPAL	5	493	701	1.7	2.0
207 E.L.C.A.	26	13,555	17,981	44.2	52.2
220 FREE LUTHERAN	3	421	547	1.3	1.6
283 LUTH—MO SYNOD	3	782	1,047	2.6	3.0
284 LUTH CH-AM ASC	1	17	31	.1	.1
355 PRESB CH (USA)	1	260	335*	.8	1.0
413 S.D.A.	1	50	64*	.2	.2
443 UN C OF CHRIST	2	314	404*	1.0	1.2
449 UN METHODIST	4	1,449	1,866*	4.6	5.4
467 WESLEYAN	1	15	60	.1	.2
469 WELS	9	2,852	3,749	9.2	10.9
GRANT	**27**	**4,264**	**6,040***	**96.7**	**100.0**
053 ASSEMB OF GOD	1	16	28	.4	.5
081 CATHOLIC	2	NA	587	9.4	9.7
081d LATIN	2	NA	587	9.4	9.7
203 EVAN FREE CH	1	55	81	1.3	1.3
207 E.L.C.A.	14	3,026	3,867	61.9	64.0
283 LUTH—MO SYNOD	3	494	616	9.9	10.2
355 PRESB CH (USA)	3	310	390*	6.2	6.5
371 REF CH IN AM	1	34	57	.9	.9
449 UN METHODIST	2	329	414*	6.6	6.9
HENNEPIN	**616**	**257,537**	**591,225***	**57.3**	**100.0**
001 ADVENT CHR CH	1	49	60*	-	-
019 AMER BAPT USA	11	3,597	4,435*	.4	.8
045 APOSTOLIC LUTH	2	230	595	.1	.1
053 ASSEMB OF GOD	32	4,658	8,825	.9	1.5
057 BAPT GEN CONF	19	6,149	7,582*	.7	1.3
081 CATHOLIC	78	NA	215,426	20.9	36.4
081b BYZAN RUTH	1	NA	250	-	-
081d LATIN	75	NA	214,435	20.8	36.3
081e MARONITE	1	NA	341	-	.1
081h UKRAINIAN	1	NA	400	-	.1
089 CHR & MISS AL	11	1,370	5,935	.6	1.0
093 CHR CH (DISC)	3	747	1,095	.1	.2
097 CHR CHS&CHS CR	4	555	684*	.1	.1
105 CHRISTIAN REF	3	454	666	.1	.1
111 CH CR,SCIENTST	7	NR	NR	-	-
121 CH GOD (ABR)	1	49	60*	-	-
123 CH GOD (ANDER)	1	63	75	-	-
127 CH GOD (CLEVE)	2	232	286*	-	-
145 CH GOD PROPHCY	2	49	60*	-	-
151 L-D SAINTS	9	NA	4,458	.4	.8
163 CH OF LUTH BR	2	314	485	-	.1
165 CH OF NAZARENE	7	675	1,210	.1	.2
167 CHS OF CHRIST	7	873	1,283	.1	.2
175 CONGR CHR CHS	2	5,843	7,204*	.7	1.2
179 CONSRV BAPT	7	NR	NR	-	-
193 EPISCOPAL	23	7,445	11,031	1.1	1.9
195 ESTONIAN ELC	1	100	123*	-	-
203 EVAN FREE CH	22	4,530	6,727	.7	1.1
207 E.L.C.A.	126	118,705	160,979	15.6	27.2
209 EVAN LUTH SYN	2	672	897	.1	.2
220 FREE LUTHERAN	10	1,958	2,651	.3	.4
221 FREE METHODIST	3	73	115	-	-
226 FRIENDS-USA	2	98	235	-	-
226c FGC	2	98	235	-	-
237 GC MENN BR CHS	1	102	126*	-	-
246 GREEK ORTHODOX	1	NR	NR	-	-
263 INT FOURSQ GOS	2	123	152*	-	-
274 LAT EVAN LUTH	2	862	949	.1	.2
283 LUTH—MO SYNOD	35	18,825	24,735	2.4	4.2
284 LUTH CH-AM ASC	2	405	548	.1	.1
285 MENNONITE CH	1	149	204	-	-
287 MENN GEN CONF	1	67	92	-	-
293 MORAV CH-NORTH	1	171	270	-	-
313 N AM BAPT CONF	3	520	641*	.1	.1
331 ORTH CH IN AM	1	NR	NR	-	-
339 PENT CH OF GOD	1	34	77	-	-
353 CHR BRETHREN	4	254	425	-	.1
355 PRESB CH (USA)	26	14,520	17,903*	1.7	3.0
356 PRESB CH AMER	1	58	101	-	-
371 REF CH IN AM	2	246	435	-	.1
403 SALVATION ARMY	5	753	834	.1	.1
413 S.D.A.	9	1,609	1,984*	.2	.3
419 SO BAPT CONV	7	1,369	1,688*	.2	.3
435 UNITARIAN-UNIV	6	1,924	2,694	.3	.5
443 UN C OF CHRIST	22	12,747	15,717*	1.5	2.7
449 UN METHODIST	43	23,641	29,149*	2.8	4.9
467 WESLEYAN	2	174	356	-	.1
469 WELS	10	3,603	4,613	.4	.8
496 JEWISH EST[1]	14	NA	14,034	1.4	2.4
497 BLACK BAPT EST[2]	NA	15,893	19,596*	1.9	3.3
498 INDEP.CHARIS.[3]	8	NA	5,250	.5	.9
499 INDEP.NON-CHAR[3]	6	NA	5,470	.5	.9
HOUSTON	**29**	**6,846**	**15,818***	**85.5**	**100.0**
081 CATHOLIC	5	NA	6,870	37.1	43.4
081d LATIN	5	NA	6,870	37.1	43.4
203 EVAN FREE CH	2	97	139	.8	.9
207 E.L.C.A.	8	4,143	5,388	29.1	34.1
355 PRESB CH (USA)	2	86	112*	.6	.7
443 UN C OF CHRIST	2	465	604*	3.3	3.8
449 UN METHODIST	5	814	1,057*	5.7	6.7
469 WELS	5	1,241	1,648	8.9	10.4
HUBBARD	**32**	**3,987**	**7,130***	**47.7**	**100.0**
053 ASSEMB OF GOD	1	67	110	.7	1.5
081 CATHOLIC	4	NA	1,755	11.7	24.6
081d LATIN	4	NA	1,755	11.7	24.6
089 CHR & MISS AL	2	35	83	.6	1.2
097 CHR CHS&CHS CR	1	85	108*	.7	1.5
111 CH CR,SCIENTST	1	NR	NR	-	-
163 CH OF LUTH BR	1	24	59	.4	.8
165 CH OF NAZARENE	1	25	32	.2	.4
167 CHS OF CHRIST	2	77	92	.6	1.3
179 CONSRV BAPT	2	NR	NR	-	-
193 EPISCOPAL	1	35	44	.3	.6
203 EVAN FREE CH	1	12	22	.1	.3
207 E.L.C.A.	4	1,433	1,928	12.9	27.0
221 FREE METHODIST	2	39	50	.3	.7
283 LUTH—MO SYNOD	4	1,303	1,759	11.8	24.7
413 S.D.A.	1	59	75*	.5	1.1
435 UNITARIAN-UNIV	1	12	20	.1	.3
449 UN METHODIST	3	781	993*	6.6	13.9
ISANTI	**30**	**8,560**	**14,453***	**55.8**	**100.0**
053 ASSEMB OF GOD	1	39	71	.3	.5
057 BAPT GEN CONF	7	1,595	2,116*	8.2	14.6
081 CATHOLIC	3	NA	2,458	9.5	17.0
081d LATIN	3	NA	2,458	9.5	17.0
127 CH GOD (CLEVE)	1	33	44*	.2	.3
203 EVAN FREE CH	2	175	249	1.0	1.7
207 E.L.C.A.	8	4,861	6,686	25.8	46.3
283 LUTH—MO SYNOD	4	1,290	1,702	6.6	11.8
413 S.D.A.	1	24	32*	.1	.2
449 UN METHODIST	2	495	657*	2.5	4.5
469 WELS	1	48	86	.3	.6
496 JEWISH EST[1]	0	NA	352	1.4	2.4
ITASCA	**79**	**8,486**	**17,372***	**42.5**	**100.0**
045 APOSTOLIC LUTH	1	31	70	.2	.4
053 ASSEMB OF GOD	2	162	406	1.0	2.3
057 BAPT GEN CONF	2	87	111*	.3	.6
081 CATHOLIC	14	NA	5,681	13.9	32.7
081d LATIN	14	NA	5,681	13.9	32.7

NA–Not applicable NR–Not reported *Total adherents estimated from known number of communicant, confirmed, full members. - Represents a percent less than 0.1. Percentages may not total due to rounding.
[1]See Appendix E [2]See Appendix F [3]See Appendix G Lines in *italic* represent a breakdown of Catholic rites or Friends affiliations. They are included in their respective denominational total.

Table 4. Churches and Church Membership by County and Denomination: 1990

County and Denomination	Number of churches	Communicant, confirmed, full members	Total adherents Number	Percent of total population	Percent of total adherents
089 CHR & MISS AL	3	109	304	.7	1.7
111 CH CR,SCIENTST	1	NR	NR	-	-
123 CH GOD (ANDER)	1	94	100	.2	.6
127 CH GOD (CLEVE)	2	111	142*	.3	.8
151 L-D SAINTS	1	NA	171	.4	1.0
163 CH OF LUTH BR	2	71	167	.4	1.0
165 CH OF NAZARENE	1	130	220	.5	1.3
193 EPISCOPAL	2	275	343	.8	2.0
203 EVAN FREE CH	2	31	89	.2	.5
207 E.L.C.A.	13	2,869	3,777	9.2	21.7
226 FRIENDS-USA	1	0	21	.1	.1
226c *FGC*	*1*	*0*	*21*	*.1*	*.1*
259 IFCA	1	NR	NR	-	-
283 LUTH—MO SYNOD	6	1,746	2,230	5.5	12.8
285 MENNONITE CH	1	25	30	.1	.2
355 PRESB CH (USA)	10	1,468	1,873*	4.6	10.8
413 S.D.A.	2	94	120*	.3	.7
419 SO BAPT CONV	3	176	225*	.6	1.3
435 UNITARIAN-UNIV	1	16	22	.1	.1
449 UN METHODIST	5	926	1,182*	2.9	6.8
469 WELS	1	65	88	.2	.5
JACKSON	**31**	**6,138**	**10,001***	**85.6**	**100.0**
053 ASSEMB OF GOD	1	18	51	.4	.5
081 CATHOLIC	3	NA	2,134	18.3	21.3
081d *LATIN*	*3*	*NA*	*2,134*	*18.3*	*21.3*
164 CH LUTH CONF	1	147	184	1.6	1.8
179 CONSRV BAPT	1	NR	NR	-	-
207 E.L.C.A.	9	2,342	3,002	25.7	30.0
283 LUTH—MO SYNOD	9	2,380	3,028	25.9	30.3
285 MENNONITE CH	1	67	97	.8	1.0
355 PRESB CH (USA)	1	427	543*	4.7	5.4
413 S.D.A.	1	2	3*	-	-
449 UN METHODIST	4	755	959*	8.2	9.6
KANABEC	**17**	**4,299**	**7,213***	**56.3**	**100.0**
053 ASSEMB OF GOD	1	104	199	1.6	2.8
057 BAPT GEN CONF	3	395	519*	4.1	7.2
081 CATHOLIC	2	NA	1,403	11.0	19.5
081d *LATIN*	*2*	*NA*	*1,403*	*11.0*	*19.5*
165 CH OF NAZARENE	1	43	23	.2	.3
207 E.L.C.A.	4	1,905	2,641	20.6	36.6
283 LUTH—MO SYNOD	3	1,314	1,721	13.4	23.9
355 PRESB CH (USA)	1	172	226*	1.8	3.1
449 UN METHODIST	2	366	481*	3.8	6.7
KANDIYOHI	**65**	**18,414**	**30,139***	**77.8**	**100.0**
053 ASSEMB OF GOD	2	618	1,034	2.7	3.4
057 BAPT GEN CONF	3	535	693*	1.8	2.3
081 CATHOLIC	5	NA	5,262	13.6	17.5
081d *LATIN*	*5*	*NA*	*5,262*	*13.6*	*17.5*
105 CHRISTIAN REF	4	1,014	1,532	4.0	5.1
111 CH CR,SCIENTST	1	NR	NR	-	-
123 CH GOD (ANDER)	1	65	65	.2	.2
165 CH OF NAZARENE	1	71	150	.4	.5
167 CHS OF CHRIST	1	35	51	.1	.2
193 EPISCOPAL	1	64	97	.3	.3
203 EVAN FREE CH	1	220	479	1.2	1.6
207 E.L.C.A.	23	11,251	14,795	38.2	49.1
220 FREE LUTHERAN	4	404	472	1.2	1.6
283 LUTH—MO SYNOD	3	1,103	1,461	3.8	4.8
353 CHR BRETHREN	1	25	50	.1	.2
355 PRESB CH (USA)	3	1,138	1,473*	3.8	4.9
371 REF CH IN AM	2	476	712	1.8	2.4
403 SALVATION ARMY	1	51	54	.1	.2
413 S.D.A.	1	54	70*	.2	.2
435 UNITARIAN-UNIV	1	30	35	.1	.1
449 UN METHODIST	5	1,107	1,433*	3.7	4.8
469 WELS	1	153	221	.6	.7
KITTSON	**20**	**3,071**	**4,402***	**76.3**	**100.0**
053 ASSEMB OF GOD	2	58	96	1.7	2.2
057 BAPT GEN CONF	1	121	152*	2.6	3.5
081 CATHOLIC	2	NA	344	6.0	7.8
081d *LATIN*	*2*	*NA*	*344*	*6.0*	*7.8*
193 EPISCOPAL	1	20	20	.3	.5
207 E.L.C.A.	9	2,432	3,231	56.0	73.4
284 LUTH CH-AM ASC	1	38	52	.9	1.2
355 PRESB CH (USA)	1	233	294*	5.1	6.7
413 S.D.A.	1	66	83*	1.4	1.9
419 SO BAPT CONV	1	29	37*	.6	.8
449 UN METHODIST	1	74	93*	1.6	2.1
KOOCHICHING	**31**	**3,574**	**8,163***	**50.1**	**100.0**
053 ASSEMB OF GOD	2	75	150	.9	1.8
057 BAPT GEN CONF	2	97	120*	.7	1.5
081 CATHOLIC	3	NA	3,063	18.8	37.5
081d *LATIN*	*3*	*NA*	*3,063*	*18.8*	*37.5*
089 CHR & MISS AL	1	27	61	.4	.7
165 CH OF NAZARENE	1	40	40	.2	.5
193 EPISCOPAL	1	90	166	1.0	2.0
203 EVAN FREE CH	1	22	28	.2	.3
207 E.L.C.A.	7	2,055	3,000	18.4	36.8
220 FREE LUTHERAN	2	210	269	1.7	3.3
283 LUTH—MO SYNOD	1	303	424	2.6	5.2
285 MENNONITE CH	3	64	119	.7	1.5
403 SALVATION ARMY	1	60	66	.4	.8
413 S.D.A.	1	27	33*	.2	.4
419 SO BAPT CONV	1	55	68*	.4	.8
443 UN C OF CHRIST	2	391	484*	3.0	5.9
449 UN METHODIST	2	58	72*	.4	.9
LAC QUI PARLE	**31**	**6,457**	**9,770***	**109.5**	**100.0**
057 BAPT GEN CONF	1	27	34*	.4	.3
081 CATHOLIC	4	NA	1,442	16.2	14.8
081d *LATIN*	*4*	*NA*	*1,442*	*16.2*	*14.8*
163 CH OF LUTH BR	1	0	85	1.0	.9
165 CH OF NAZARENE	1	18	34	.4	.3
207 E.L.C.A.	12	5,137	6,568	73.6	67.2
283 LUTH—MO SYNOD	4	713	885	9.9	9.1
284 LUTH CH-AM ASC	1	14	22	.2	.2
355 PRESB CH (USA)	1	172	217*	2.4	2.2
371 REF CH IN AM	1	34	49	.5	.5
443 UN C OF CHRIST	2	195	246*	2.8	2.5
449 UN METHODIST	2	130	164*	1.8	1.7
469 WELS	1	17	24	.3	.2
LAKE	**23**	**3,127**	**6,161***	**59.2**	**100.0**
019 AMER BAPT USA	1	200	247*	2.4	4.0
053 ASSEMB OF GOD	2	125	229	2.2	3.7
057 BAPT GEN CONF	1	62	76*	.7	1.2
081 CATHOLIC	2	NA	1,575	15.1	25.6
081d *LATIN*	*2*	*NA*	*1,575*	*15.1*	*25.6*
179 CONSRV BAPT	2	NR	NR	-	-
203 EVAN FREE CH	1	52	60	.6	1.0
207 E.L.C.A.	6	1,873	2,553	24.5	41.4
283 LUTH—MO SYNOD	2	173	185	1.8	3.0
355 PRESB CH (USA)	2	168	207*	2.0	3.4
371 REF CH IN AM	1	89	160	1.5	2.6
403 SALVATION ARMY	1	20	20	.2	.3
443 UN C OF CHRIST	1	204	251*	2.4	4.1
449 UN METHODIST	1	161	198*	1.9	3.2
496 JEWISH EST[1]	0	NA	400	3.8	6.5
LAKE OF THE WOODS	**14**	**1,154**	**2,402***	**58.9**	**100.0**
053 ASSEMB OF GOD	1	42	112	2.7	4.7
081 CATHOLIC	2	NA	501	12.3	20.9
081d *LATIN*	*2*	*NA*	*501*	*12.3*	*20.9*
203 EVAN FREE CH	1	9	30	.7	1.2
207 E.L.C.A.	4	790	1,277	31.3	53.2
283 LUTH—MO SYNOD	1	92	116	2.8	4.8
353 CHR BRETHREN	1	22	110	2.7	4.6
413 S.D.A.	1	27	35*	.9	1.5
419 SO BAPT CONV	1	27	35*	.9	1.5
443 UN C OF CHRIST	2	145	186*	4.6	7.7
LE SUEUR	**43**	**6,895**	**19,294***	**83.0**	**100.0**
053 ASSEMB OF GOD	1	25	60	.3	.3
081 CATHOLIC	13	NA	9,890	42.6	51.3
081d *LATIN*	*13*	*NA*	*9,890*	*42.6*	*51.3*
089 CHR & MISS AL	1	32	72	.3	.4
097 CHR CHS&CHS CR	1	135	176*	.8	.9
163 CH OF LUTH BR	1	54	151	.6	.8
193 EPISCOPAL	2	48	64	.3	.3
207 E.L.C.A.	6	2,830	3,878	16.7	20.1
283 LUTH—MO SYNOD	4	922	1,261	5.4	6.5
355 PRESB CH (USA)	2	360	470*	2.0	2.4
413 S.D.A.	1	21	27*	.1	.1
419 SO BAPT CONV	1	146	191*	.8	1.0
443 UN C OF CHRIST	1	825	1,078*	4.6	5.6
449 UN METHODIST	7	1,014	1,324*	5.7	6.9
469 WELS	2	483	652	2.8	3.4
LINCOLN	**23**	**3,456**	**6,614***	**96.0**	**100.0**
081 CATHOLIC	5	NA	2,255	32.7	34.1
081d *LATIN*	*5*	*NA*	*2,255*	*32.7*	*34.1*
089 CHR & MISS AL	1	33	83	1.2	1.3
163 CH OF LUTH BR	1	36	72	1.0	1.1
207 E.L.C.A.	9	2,591	3,221	46.7	48.7
449 UN METHODIST	4	385	480*	7.0	7.3

NA–Not applicable NR–Not reported *Total adherents estimated from known number of communicant, confirmed, full members. - Represents a percent less than 0.1. Percentages may not total due to rounding.
[1]See Appendix E [2]See Appendix F [3]See Appendix G Lines in *italic* represent a breakdown of Catholic rites or Friends affiliations. They are included in their respective denominational total.

Table 4. Churches and Church Membership by County and Denomination: 1990

County and Denomination	Number of churches	Communicant, confirmed, full members	Total adherents Number	Percent of total population	Percent of total adherents
469 WELS	3	411	503	7.3	7.6
LYON	**46**	**7,478**	**18,731***	**75.6**	**100.0**
053 ASSEMB OF GOD	1	87	150	.6	.8
057 BAPT GEN CONF	1	23	29*	.1	.2
081 CATHOLIC	7	NA	8,662	34.9	46.2
081d *LATIN*	7	NA	8,662	34.9	46.2
089 CHR & MISS AL	1	20	40	.2	.2
097 CHR CHS&CHS CR	1	0	0*	-	-
151 L-D SAINTS	1	NA	116	.5	.6
167 CHS OF CHRIST	1	14	26	.1	.1
193 EPISCOPAL	1	92	122	.5	.7
203 EVAN FREE CH	3	275	475	1.9	2.5
207 E.L.C.A.	11	3,259	4,258	17.2	22.7
209 EVAN LUTH SYN	2	322	432	1.7	2.3
283 LUTH—MO SYNOD	2	339	479	1.9	2.6
355 PRESB CH (USA)	4	658	840*	3.4	4.5
413 S.D.A.	0	10	13*	.1	.1
419 SO BAPT CONV	1	87	111*	.4	.6
443 UN C OF CHRIST	1	84	107*	.4	.6
449 UN METHODIST	5	1,371	1,751*	7.1	9.3
469 WELS	3	837	1,120	4.5	6.0
MC LEOD	**46**	**15,656**	**28,923***	**90.3**	**100.0**
053 ASSEMB OF GOD	1	177	500	1.6	1.7
057 BAPT GEN CONF	2	260	338*	1.1	1.2
081 CATHOLIC	6	NA	8,198	25.6	28.3
081d *LATIN*	6	NA	8,198	25.6	28.3
193 EPISCOPAL	1	19	19	.1	.1
207 E.L.C.A.	8	4,168	5,795	18.1	20.0
283 LUTH—MO SYNOD	9	6,909	8,735	27.3	30.2
313 N AM BAPT CONF	1	94	122*	.4	.4
355 PRESB CH (USA)	2	299	389*	1.2	1.3
413 S.D.A.	1	315	410*	1.3	1.4
443 UN C OF CHRIST	7	1,548	2,013*	6.3	7.0
449 UN METHODIST	3	949	1,234*	3.9	4.3
467 WESLEYAN	1	22	40	.1	.1
469 WELS	4	896	1,130	3.5	3.9
MAHNOMEN	**17**	**1,344**	**4,308***	**85.4**	**100.0**
053 ASSEMB OF GOD	1	21	26	.5	.6
081 CATHOLIC	5	NA	2,494	49.4	57.9
081d *LATIN*	5	NA	2,494	49.4	57.9
105 CHRISTIAN REF	1	15	15	.3	.3
193 EPISCOPAL	1	102	192	3.8	4.5
207 E.L.C.A.	5	903	1,184	23.5	27.5
283 LUTH—MO SYNOD	1	110	143	2.8	3.3
443 UN C OF CHRIST	2	136	179*	3.5	4.2
449 UN METHODIST	1	57	75*	1.5	1.7
MARSHALL	**44**	**5,023**	**10,281***	**93.5**	**100.0**
053 ASSEMB OF GOD	1	20	30	.3	.3
057 BAPT GEN CONF	2	50	64*	.6	.6
081 CATHOLIC	9	NA	3,759	34.2	36.6
081d *LATIN*	9	NA	3,759	34.2	36.6
203 EVAN FREE CH	1	49	93	.8	.9
207 E.L.C.A.	17	3,569	4,604	41.9	44.8
209 EVAN LUTH SYN	1	34	63	.6	.6
220 FREE LUTHERAN	6	444	586	5.3	5.7
283 LUTH—MO SYNOD	2	359	460	4.2	4.5
284 LUTH CH-AM ASC	1	120	139	1.3	1.4
355 PRESB CH (USA)	2	159	203*	1.8	2.0
413 S.D.A.	1	57	73*	.7	.7
449 UN METHODIST	1	162	207*	1.9	2.0
MARTIN	**54**	**12,760**	**20,119***	**87.8**	**100.0**
019 AMER BAPT USA	1	191	243*	1.1	1.2
053 ASSEMB OF GOD	3	151	232	1.0	1.2
081 CATHOLIC	5	NA	3,623	15.8	18.0
081d *LATIN*	5	NA	3,623	15.8	18.0
097 CHR CHS&CHS CR	3	242	308*	1.3	1.5
151 L-D SAINTS	1	NA	100	.4	.5
193 EPISCOPAL	1	112	136	.6	.7
203 EVAN FREE CH	2	348	570	2.5	2.8
207 E.L.C.A.	9	3,481	4,515	19.7	22.4
259 IFCA	1	NR	NR	-	-
283 LUTH—MO SYNOD	12	4,922	6,175	26.9	30.7
403 SALVATION ARMY	1	46	50	.2	.2
413 S.D.A.	1	10	13*	.1	.1
443 UN C OF CHRIST	7	1,701	2,161*	9.4	10.7
449 UN METHODIST	6	1,499	1,905*	8.3	9.5
469 WELS	1	57	88	.4	.4
MEEKER	**41**	**8,250**	**15,236***	**73.1**	**100.0**
045 APOSTOLIC LUTH	1	34	67	.3	.4

County and Denomination	Number of churches	Communicant, confirmed, full members	Total adherents Number	Percent of total population	Percent of total adherents
053 ASSEMB OF GOD	1	68	83	.4	.5
057 BAPT GEN CONF	2	276	359*	1.7	2.4
061 BEACHY AMISH	1	46	60*	.3	.4
081 CATHOLIC	6	NA	4,446	21.3	29.2
081d *LATIN*	6	NA	4,446	21.3	29.2
097 CHR CHS&CHS CR	2	205	267*	1.3	1.8
121 CH GOD (ABR)	2	137	178*	.9	1.2
151 L-D SAINTS	1	NA	123	.6	.8
165 CH OF NAZARENE	1	139	234	1.1	1.5
193 EPISCOPAL	1	126	126	.6	.8
203 EVAN FREE CH	1	39	70	.3	.5
207 E.L.C.A.	12	5,116	6,574	31.5	43.1
283 LUTH—MO SYNOD	2	543	704	3.4	4.6
355 PRESB CH (USA)	1	123	160*	.8	1.1
413 S.D.A.	1	30	39*	.2	.3
443 UN C OF CHRIST	2	154	201*	1.0	1.3
449 UN METHODIST	2	467	608*	2.9	4.0
469 WELS	2	747	937	4.5	6.1
MILLE LACS	**42**	**7,140**	**14,427***	**77.3**	**100.0**
053 ASSEMB OF GOD	3	165	345	1.8	2.4
057 BAPT GEN CONF	3	379	494*	2.6	3.4
081 CATHOLIC	6	NA	4,072	21.8	28.2
081d *LATIN*	6	NA	4,072	21.8	28.2
089 CHR & MISS AL	4	149	437	2.3	3.0
105 CHRISTIAN REF	2	544	808	4.3	5.6
203 EVAN FREE CH	6	336	573	3.1	4.0
207 E.L.C.A.	8	3,687	5,138	27.5	35.6
209 EVAN LUTH SYN	1	371	531	2.8	3.7
283 LUTH—MO SYNOD	3	635	857	4.6	5.9
339 PENT CH OF GOD	1	34	77	.4	.5
355 PRESB CH (USA)	1	55	72*	.4	.5
443 UN C OF CHRIST	1	135	176*	.9	1.2
449 UN METHODIST	3	650	847*	4.5	5.9
MORRISON	**51**	**4,756**	**24,191***	**81.7**	**100.0**
053 ASSEMB OF GOD	1	124	300	1.0	1.2
057 BAPT GEN CONF	1	43	57*	.2	.2
081 CATHOLIC	19	NA	17,316	58.5	71.6
081d *LATIN*	19	NA	17,316	58.5	71.6
089 CHR & MISS AL	3	105	242	.8	1.0
097 CHR CHS&CHS CR	1	15	20*	.1	.1
127 CH GOD (CLEVE)	1	5	7*	-	-
165 CH OF NAZARENE	1	21	56	.2	.2
181 CONSRV CONGR	1	71	95*	.3	.4
193 EPISCOPAL	2	94	123	.4	.5
203 EVAN FREE CH	1	57	125	.4	.5
207 E.L.C.A.	5	1,531	2,134	7.2	8.8
220 FREE LUTHERAN	1	35	47	.2	.2
221 FREE METHODIST	1	14	19	.1	.1
283 LUTH—MO SYNOD	8	1,812	2,514	8.5	10.4
339 PENT CH OF GOD	1	35	77	.3	.3
355 PRESB CH (USA)	1	119	159*	.5	.7
443 UN C OF CHRIST	1	234	312*	1.1	1.3
449 UN METHODIST	2	441	588*	2.0	2.4
MOWER	**60**	**14,671**	**28,532***	**76.3**	**100.0**
081 CATHOLIC	10	NA	9,254	24.8	32.4
081d *LATIN*	10	NA	9,254	24.8	32.4
089 CHR & MISS AL	1	11	28	.1	.1
093 CHR CH (DISC)	1	32	53	.1	.2
097 CHR CHS&CHS CR	2	391	490*	1.3	1.7
151 L-D SAINTS	1	NA	263	.7	.9
164 CH LUTH CONF	1	134	185	.5	.6
167 CHS OF CHRIST	1	20	30	.1	.1
193 EPISCOPAL	1	168	235	.6	.8
203 EVAN FREE CH	1	33	68	.2	.2
207 E.L.C.A.	14	8,509	11,124	29.8	39.0
220 FREE LUTHERAN	1	45	56	.1	.2
221 FREE METHODIST	1	81	119	.3	.4
257 HUTTERIAN BR	1	NA	100	.3	.4
283 LUTH—MO SYNOD	6	1,564	1,964	5.3	6.9
329 OPEN BIBLE STD	1	NR	NR	-	-
355 PRESB CH (USA)	2	838	1,050*	2.8	3.7
403 SALVATION ARMY	1	235	240	.6	.8
413 S.D.A.	1	28	35*	.1	.1
443 UN C OF CHRIST	3	421	527*	1.4	1.8
449 UN METHODIST	8	1,917	2,402*	6.4	8.4
469 WELS	2	244	309	.8	1.1
MURRAY	**26**	**4,275**	**8,568***	**88.7**	**100.0**
053 ASSEMB OF GOD	1	25	45	.5	.5
057 BAPT GEN CONF	1	151	192*	2.0	2.2
081 CATHOLIC	5	NA	2,896	30.0	33.8
081d *LATIN*	5	NA	2,896	30.0	33.8
105 CHRISTIAN REF	1	204	315	3.3	3.7

NA–Not applicable NR–Not reported *Total adherents estimated from known number of communicant, confirmed, full members. - Represents a percent less than 0.1. Percentages may not total due to rounding.

[1]See Appendix E [2]See Appendix F [3]See Appendix G Lines in *italic* represent a breakdown of Catholic rites or Friends affiliations. They are included in their respective denominational total.

Table 4. Churches and Church Membership by County and Denomination: 1990

County and Denomination	Number of churches	Communicant, confirmed, full members	Total adherents Number	Percent of total population	Percent of total adherents
207 E.L.C.A.	8	1,792	2,373	24.6	27.7
283 LUTH—MO SYNOD	2	882	1,104	11.4	12.9
355 PRESB CH (USA)	4	543	689*	7.1	8.0
371 REF CH IN AM	2	299	473	4.9	5.5
449 UN METHODIST	2	379	481*	5.0	5.6
NICOLLET	**27**	**8,243**	**17,066***	**60.8**	**100.0**
053 ASSEMB OF GOD	1	147	380	1.4	2.2
081 CATHOLIC	6	NA	5,961	21.2	34.9
081d *LATIN*	*6*	*NA*	*5,961*	*21.2*	*34.9*
089 CHR & MISS AL	1	58	171	.6	1.0
164 CH LUTH CONF	1	40	48	.2	.3
193 EPISCOPAL	1	53	116	.4	.7
207 E.L.C.A.	7	3,993	5,365	19.1	31.4
209 EVAN LUTH SYN	1	201	254	.9	1.5
263 INT FOURSQ GOS	1	30	38*	.1	.2
283 LUTH—MO SYNOD	1	371	485	1.7	2.8
355 PRESB CH (USA)	1	287	364*	1.3	2.1
449 UN METHODIST	2	607	769*	2.7	4.5
469 WELS	4	2,456	3,115	11.1	18.3
NOBLES	**42**	**8,953**	**17,698***	**88.1**	**100.0**
053 ASSEMB OF GOD	1	140	276	1.4	1.6
057 BAPT GEN CONF	1	154	195*	1.0	1.1
081 CATHOLIC	7	NA	5,675	28.2	32.1
081d *LATIN*	*7*	*NA*	*5,675*	*28.2*	*32.1*
097 CHR CHS&CHS CR	1	400	506*	2.5	2.9
105 CHRISTIAN REF	3	571	842	4.2	4.8
157 CH OF BRETHREN	1	74	94*	.5	.5
179 CONSRV BAPT	1	NR	NR	-	-
193 EPISCOPAL	1	13	18	.1	.1
207 E.L.C.A.	5	2,234	2,988	14.9	16.9
283 LUTH—MO SYNOD	4	1,710	2,253	11.2	12.7
355 PRESB CH (USA)	11	2,124	2,685*	13.4	15.2
371 REF CH IN AM	3	670	1,075	5.3	6.1
449 UN METHODIST	3	863	1,091*	5.4	6.2
NORMAN	**33**	**5,629**	**7,850***	**98.4**	**100.0**
081 CATHOLIC	3	NA	752	9.4	9.6
081d *LATIN*	*3*	*NA*	*752*	*9.4*	*9.6*
163 CH OF LUTH BR	2	161	226	2.8	2.9
207 E.L.C.A.	23	4,518	5,678	71.2	72.3
283 LUTH—MO SYNOD	3	709	890	11.2	11.3
443 UN C OF CHRIST	1	55	69*	.9	.9
449 UN METHODIST	1	186	235*	2.9	3.0
OLMSTED	**88**	**32,416**	**70,674***	**66.4**	**100.0**
053 ASSEMB OF GOD	3	495	968	.9	1.4
057 BAPT GEN CONF	1	141	182*	.2	.3
063 BEREAN FUND CH	1	59	151	.1	.2
081 CATHOLIC	10	NA	24,494	23.0	34.7
081d *LATIN*	*10*	*NA*	*24,494*	*23.0*	*34.7*
089 CHR & MISS AL	1	66	126	.1	.2
093 CHR CH (DISC)	1	105	117	.1	.2
097 CHR CHS&CHS CR	4	605	782*	.7	1.1
111 CH CR,SCIENTST	1	NR	NR	-	-
151 L-D SAINTS	2	NA	910	.9	1.3
163 CH OF LUTH BR	1	73	204	.2	.3
164 CH LUTH CONF	1	9	13	-	-
165 CH OF NAZARENE	1	133	294	.3	.4
167 CHS OF CHRIST	4	74	101	.1	.1
193 EPISCOPAL	2	1,030	1,546	1.5	2.2
203 EVAN FREE CH	2	249	522	.5	.7
207 E.L.C.A.	10	11,930	16,468	15.5	23.3
226 FRIENDS-USA	1	3	17	-	-
226c *FGC*	*1*	*3*	*17*	-	-
246 GREEK ORTHODOX	1	NR	NR	-	-
259 IFCA	1	NR	NR	-	-
263 INT FOURSQ GOS	1	8	10*	-	-
283 LUTH—MO SYNOD	9	5,546	7,295	6.9	10.3
287 MENN GEN CONF	1	30	40	-	.1
355 PRESB CH (USA)	2	1,412	1,826*	1.7	2.6
356 PRESB CH AMER	1	48	80	.1	.1
371 REF CH IN AM	1	189	271	.3	.4
403 SALVATION ARMY	1	168	171	.2	.2
413 S.D.A.	1	221	286*	.3	.4
419 SO BAPT CONV	2	459	593*	.6	.8
435 UNITARIAN-UNIV	1	175	311	.3	.4
443 UN C OF CHRIST	3	1,801	2,329*	2.2	3.3
449 UN METHODIST	10	6,048	7,820*	7.3	11.1
467 WESLEYAN	1	81	100	.1	.1
469 WELS	4	1,050	1,478	1.4	2.1
496 JEWISH EST[1]	1	NA	400	.4	.6
497 BLACK BAPT EST[2]	NA	208	269*	.3	.4
499 INDEP.NON-CHAR[3]	1	NA	500	.5	.7

County and Denomination	Number of churches	Communicant, confirmed, full members	Total adherents Number	Percent of total population	Percent of total adherents
OTTER TAIL	**126**	**24,346**	**40,452***	**79.8**	**100.0**
019 AMER BAPT USA	1	19	24*	-	.1
045 APOSTOLIC LUTH	1	219	1,000	2.0	2.5
053 ASSEMB OF GOD	3	102	178	.4	.4
057 BAPT GEN CONF	4	493	624*	1.2	1.5
081 CATHOLIC	14	NA	7,552	14.9	18.7
081d *LATIN*	*14*	*NA*	*7,552*	*14.9*	*18.7*
089 CHR & MISS AL	2	72	179	.4	.4
111 CH CR,SCIENTST	1	NR	NR	-	-
151 L-D SAINTS	1	NA	112	.2	.3
163 CH OF LUTH BR	3	526	1,181	2.3	2.9
165 CH OF NAZARENE	1	161	256	.5	.6
167 CHS OF CHRIST	1	20	35	.1	.1
179 CONSRV BAPT	1	NR	NR	-	-
193 EPISCOPAL	1	118	138	.3	.3
203 EVAN FREE CH	1	80	150	.3	.4
207 E.L.C.A.	41	12,949	16,745	33.0	41.4
220 FREE LUTHERAN	4	647	835	1.6	2.1
283 LUTH—MO SYNOD	21	5,771	7,432	14.7	18.4
284 LUTH CH-AM ASC	1	70	81	.2	.2
355 PRESB CH (USA)	3	538	681*	1.3	1.7
403 SALVATION ARMY	1	54	61	.1	.2
413 S.D.A.	3	103	130*	.3	.3
435 UNITARIAN-UNIV	1	41	67	.1	.2
443 UN C OF CHRIST	6	737	933*	1.8	2.3
449 UN METHODIST	10	1,626	2,058*	4.1	5.1
PENNINGTON	**23**	**5,934**	**10,170***	**76.4**	**100.0**
053 ASSEMB OF GOD	1	100	140	1.1	1.4
057 BAPT GEN CONF	1	106	134*	1.0	1.3
081 CATHOLIC	2	NA	2,088	15.7	20.5
081d *LATIN*	*2*	*NA*	*2,088*	*15.7*	*20.5*
163 CH OF LUTH BR	2	48	154	1.2	1.5
203 EVAN FREE CH	1	149	260	2.0	2.6
207 E.L.C.A.	11	4,348	5,846	43.9	57.5
220 FREE LUTHERAN	2	346	488	3.7	4.8
283 LUTH—MO SYNOD	1	327	417	3.1	4.1
413 S.D.A.	1	118	149*	1.1	1.5
449 UN METHODIST	1	392	494*	3.7	4.9
PINE	**50**	**5,426**	**10,569***	**49.7**	**100.0**
045 APOSTOLIC LUTH	1	32	57	.3	.5
053 ASSEMB OF GOD	3	137	238	1.1	2.3
057 BAPT GEN CONF	2	194	249*	1.2	2.4
081 CATHOLIC	8	NA	2,999	14.1	28.4
081d *LATIN*	*8*	*NA*	*2,999*	*14.1*	*28.4*
165 CH OF NAZARENE	1	18	62	.3	.6
167 CHS OF CHRIST	1	14	28	.1	.3
193 EPISCOPAL	1	62	63	.3	.6
203 EVAN FREE CH	3	234	433	2.0	4.1
207 E.L.C.A.	10	2,285	3,094	14.6	29.3
220 FREE LUTHERAN	2	129	147	.7	1.4
221 FREE METHODIST	1	29	63	.3	.6
283 LUTH—MO SYNOD	5	1,431	1,919	9.0	18.2
323 OLD ORD AMISH	1	NA	150	.7	1.4
355 PRESB CH (USA)	4	238	305*	1.4	2.9
356 PRESB CH AMER	1	132	132	.6	1.2
413 S.D.A.	2	67	86*	.4	.8
443 UN C OF CHRIST	1	127	163*	.8	1.5
449 UN METHODIST	3	297	381*	1.8	3.6
PIPESTONE	**31**	**6,301**	**10,056***	**95.9**	**100.0**
053 ASSEMB OF GOD	1	50	80	.8	.8
057 BAPT GEN CONF	1	132	170*	1.6	1.7
081 CATHOLIC	3	NA	1,578	15.0	15.7
081d *LATIN*	*3*	*NA*	*1,578*	*15.0*	*15.7*
105 CHRISTIAN REF	4	1,074	1,676	16.0	16.7
207 E.L.C.A.	3	1,286	1,725	16.4	17.2
209 EVAN LUTH SYN	1	58	74	.7	.7
220 FREE LUTHERAN	1	246	288	2.7	2.9
283 LUTH—MO SYNOD	6	1,522	1,846	17.6	18.4
355 PRESB CH (USA)	3	631	813*	7.7	8.1
371 REF CH IN AM	2	576	871	8.3	8.7
413 S.D.A.	1	54	70*	.7	.7
449 UN METHODIST	5	672	865*	8.2	8.6
POLK	**85**	**13,081**	**25,222***	**77.6**	**100.0**
053 ASSEMB OF GOD	3	170	265	.8	1.1
057 BAPT GEN CONF	2	207	267*	.8	1.1
081 CATHOLIC	9	NA	7,685	23.6	30.5
081d *LATIN*	*9*	*NA*	*7,685*	*23.6*	*30.5*
097 CHR CHS&CHS CR	1	80	103*	.3	.4
105 CHRISTIAN REF	2	37	55	.2	.2
151 L-D SAINTS	1	NA	318	1.0	1.3
163 CH OF LUTH BR	1	18	18	.1	.1

NA–Not applicable   NR–Not reported   *Total adherents estimated from known number of communicant, confirmed, full members.   - Represents a percent less than 0.1.   Percentages may not total due to rounding.
[1]See Appendix E   [2]See Appendix F   [3]See Appendix G   Lines in *italic* represent a breakdown of Catholic rites or Friends affiliations. They are included in their respective denominational total.

Table 4. Churches and Church Membership by County and Denomination: 1990

County and Denomination	Number of churches	Communicant, confirmed, full members	Total adherents Number	Percent of total population	Percent of total adherents
167 CHS OF CHRIST	1	32	44	.1	.2
179 CONSRV BAPT	1	NR	NR	-	-
207 E.L.C.A.	33	8,187	10,869	33.4	43.1
209 EVAN LUTH SYN	5	419	462	1.4	1.8
220 FREE LUTHERAN	9	762	1,038	3.2	4.1
283 LUTH—MO SYNOD	7	1,771	2,292	7.1	9.1
284 LUTH CH-AM ASC	1	36	47	.1	.2
355 PRESB CH (USA)	4	843	1,089*	3.4	4.3
413 S.D.A.	1	41	53*	.2	.2
449 UN METHODIST	4	478	617*	1.9	2.4
POPE	**31**	**5,419**	**8,879***	**82.6**	**100.0**
057 BAPT GEN CONF	1	100	129*	1.2	1.5
081 CATHOLIC	4	NA	1,785	16.6	20.1
081d *LATIN*	*4*	*NA*	*1,785*	*16.6*	*20.1*
207 E.L.C.A.	17	4,398	5,729	53.3	64.5
220 FREE LUTHERAN	1	58	98	.9	1.1
283 LUTH—MO SYNOD	2	348	478	4.4	5.4
413 S.D.A.	2	44	57*	.5	.6
443 UN C OF CHRIST	1	132	170*	1.6	1.9
449 UN METHODIST	2	274	352*	3.3	4.0
469 WELS	1	65	81	.8	.9
RAMSEY	**295**	**104,539**	**312,318***	**64.3**	**100.0**
019 AMER BAPT USA	10	3,253	4,078*	.8	1.3
053 ASSEMB OF GOD	14	1,865	5,050	1.0	1.6
057 BAPT GEN CONF	11	4,604	5,772*	1.2	1.8
081 CATHOLIC	49	NA	157,945	32.5	50.6
081d *LATIN*	*47*	*NA*	*157,523*	*32.4*	*50.4*
081e *MARONITE*	*1*	*NA*	*366*	*.1*	*.1*
081h *UKRAINIAN*	*1*	*NA*	*56*	-	-
089 CHR & MISS AL	9	2,752	3,425	.7	1.1
093 CHR CH (DISC)	2	239	353	.1	.1
097 CHR CHS&CHS CR	2	260	326*	.1	.1
105 CHRISTIAN REF	1	318	499	.1	.2
111 CH CR,SCIENTST	4	NR	NR	-	-
133 CH GOD(7TH)DEN	1	67	96	-	-
151 L-D SAINTS	5	NA	1,243	.3	.4
165 CH OF NAZARENE	3	240	314	.1	.1
167 CHS OF CHRIST	3	221	358	.1	.1
179 CONSRV BAPT	3	NR	NR	-	-
181 CONSRV CONGR	1	77	97*	-	-
193 EPISCOPAL	13	4,283	6,031	1.2	1.9
203 EVAN FREE CH	4	601	1,005	.2	.3
207 E.L.C.A.	54	47,478	66,037	13.6	21.1
226 FRIENDS-USA	1	64	189	-	.1
226c *FGC*	*1*	*64*	*189*	-	*.1*
246 GREEK ORTHODOX	1	NR	NR	-	-
259 IFCA	1	NR	NR	-	-
263 INT FOURSQ GOS	1	11	14*	-	-
283 LUTH—MO SYNOD	15	8,166	10,749	2.2	3.4
284 LUTH CH-AM ASC	1	250	300	.1	.1
285 MENNONITE CH	1	26	48	-	-
287 MENN GEN CONF	1	0	0	-	-
313 N AM BAPT CONF	1	184	231*	-	.1
331 ORTH CH IN AM	1	NR	NR	-	-
353 CHR BRETHREN	2	147	170	-	.1
355 PRESB CH (USA)	16	5,877	7,367*	1.5	2.4
397 ROMANIAN ORTH	1	NR	NR	-	-
403 SALVATION ARMY	2	426	468	.1	.1
413 S.D.A.	4	371	465*	.1	.1
419 SO BAPT CONV	2	448	562*	.1	.2
435 UNITARIAN-UNIV	3	1,194	1,821	.4	.6
443 UN C OF CHRIST	10	4,337	5,437*	1.1	1.7
449 UN METHODIST	21	7,599	9,526*	2.0	3.1
467 WESLEYAN	1	70	171	-	.1
469 WELS	7	3,116	4,227	.9	1.4
496 JEWISH EST[1]	7	NA	6,604	1.4	2.1
497 BLACK BAPT EST[2]	NA	5,995	7,515*	1.5	2.4
498 INDEP.CHARIS.[3]	4	NA	2,025	.4	.6
499 INDEP.NON-CHAR[3]	2	NA	1,800	.4	.6
RED LAKE	**17**	**1,321**	**4,253***	**94.0**	**100.0**
081 CATHOLIC	6	NA	2,422	53.5	56.9
081d *LATIN*	*6*	*NA*	*2,422*	*53.5*	*56.9*
207 E.L.C.A.	4	749	1,070	23.6	25.2
209 EVAN LUTH SYN	2	164	246	5.4	5.8
283 LUTH—MO SYNOD	3	315	394	8.7	9.3
355 PRESB CH (USA)	2	93	121*	2.7	2.8
REDWOOD	**56**	**8,274**	**16,371***	**94.9**	**100.0**
053 ASSEMB OF GOD	1	59	80	.5	.5
081 CATHOLIC	12	NA	5,963	34.6	36.4
081d *LATIN*	*12*	*NA*	*5,963*	*34.6*	*36.4*
097 CHR CHS&CHS CR	2	165	212*	1.2	1.3
165 CH OF NAZARENE	1	19	17	.1	.1
207 E.L.C.A.	14	3,971	4,975	28.8	30.4
209 EVAN LUTH SYN	2	359	425	2.5	2.6
283 LUTH—MO SYNOD	4	312	388	2.2	2.4
355 PRESB CH (USA)	4	444	570*	3.3	3.5
413 S.D.A.	1	29	37*	.2	.2
449 UN METHODIST	9	1,219	1,564*	9.1	9.6
469 WELS	6	1,697	2,140	12.4	13.1
RENVILLE	**50**	**8,666**	**16,575***	**93.8**	**100.0**
081 CATHOLIC	8	NA	5,264	29.8	31.8
081d *LATIN*	*8*	*NA*	*5,264*	*29.8*	*31.8*
089 CHR & MISS AL	1	16	32	.2	.2
105 CHRISTIAN REF	1	157	233	1.3	1.4
121 CH GOD (ABR)	1	27	35*	.2	.2
165 CH OF NAZARENE	2	21	42	.2	.3
193 EPISCOPAL	1	88	236	1.3	1.4
203 EVAN FREE CH	1	26	50	.3	.3
207 E.L.C.A.	16	4,767	6,167	34.9	37.2
355 PRESB CH (USA)	1	185	238*	1.3	1.4
449 UN METHODIST	10	1,645	2,115*	12.0	12.8
469 WELS	8	1,734	2,163	12.2	13.0
RICE	**53**	**13,762**	**32,425***	**65.9**	**100.0**
053 ASSEMB OF GOD	2	188	391	.8	1.2
057 BAPT GEN CONF	1	144	182*	.4	.6
081 CATHOLIC	8	NA	13,887	28.2	42.8
081d *LATIN*	*8*	*NA*	*13,887*	*28.2*	*42.8*
089 CHR & MISS AL	1	60	115	.2	.4
097 CHR CHS&CHS CR	1	60	76*	.2	.2
163 CH OF LUTH BR	1	48	98	.2	.3
165 CH OF NAZARENE	1	12	27	.1	.1
167 CHS OF CHRIST	1	21	38	.1	.1
193 EPISCOPAL	3	404	623	1.3	1.9
203 EVAN FREE CH	2	52	120	.2	.4
207 E.L.C.A.	11	6,082	8,223	16.7	25.4
226 FRIENDS-USA	1	20	50	.1	.2
226c *FGC*	*1*	*20*	*50*	*.1*	*.2*
283 LUTH—MO SYNOD	6	3,337	4,391	8.9	13.5
293 MORAV CH-NORTH	1	68	77	.2	.2
413 S.D.A.	1	64	81*	.2	.2
435 UNITARIAN-UNIV	1	17	20	-	.1
443 UN C OF CHRIST	4	1,280	1,618*	3.3	5.0
449 UN METHODIST	7	1,905	2,408*	4.9	7.4
ROCK	**18**	**5,180**	**7,932***	**80.9**	**100.0**
053 ASSEMB OF GOD	1	36	48	.5	.6
081 CATHOLIC	1	NA	988	10.1	12.5
081d *LATIN*	*1*	*NA*	*988*	*10.1*	*12.5*
105 CHRISTIAN REF	2	333	543	5.5	6.8
179 CONSRV BAPT	1	NR	NR	-	-
193 EPISCOPAL	1	7	7	.1	.1
207 E.L.C.A.	3	1,625	2,034	20.7	25.6
209 EVAN LUTH SYN	1	280	352	3.6	4.4
283 LUTH—MO SYNOD	2	963	1,205	12.3	15.2
355 PRESB CH (USA)	2	653	840*	8.6	10.6
371 REF CH IN AM	2	701	1,166	11.9	14.7
449 UN METHODIST	2	582	749*	7.6	9.4
ROSEAU	**43**	**5,275**	**9,779***	**65.1**	**100.0**
053 ASSEMB OF GOD	2	128	291	1.9	3.0
057 BAPT GEN CONF	2	173	232*	1.5	2.4
081 CATHOLIC	7	NA	2,339	15.6	23.9
081d *LATIN*	*7*	*NA*	*2,339*	*15.6*	*23.9*
151 L-D SAINTS	1	NA	107	.7	1.1
175 CONGR CHR CHS	1	138	185*	1.2	1.9
193 EPISCOPAL	1	56	67	.4	.7
207 E.L.C.A.	17	3,650	5,111	34.0	52.3
209 EVAN LUTH SYN	1	22	50	.3	.5
220 FREE LUTHERAN	10	1,002	1,255	8.4	12.8
413 S.D.A.	0	1	1*	-	-
449 UN METHODIST	1	105	141*	.9	1.4
SAINT LOUIS	**231**	**42,552**	**106,729***	**53.8**	**100.0**
019 AMER BAPT USA	3	147	181*	.1	.2
045 APOSTOLIC LUTH	3	89	123	.1	.1
053 ASSEMB OF GOD	11	996	2,562	1.3	2.4
057 BAPT GEN CONF	15	2,259	2,788*	1.4	2.6
081 CATHOLIC	41	NA	48,383	24.4	45.3
081d *LATIN*	*41*	*NA*	*48,383*	*24.4*	*45.3*
089 CHR & MISS AL	2	264	464	.2	.4
093 CHR CH (DISC)	1	70	122	.1	.1
111 CH CR,SCIENTST	2	NR	NR	-	-
123 CH GOD (ANDER)	1	50	60	-	.1
151 L-D SAINTS	3	NA	759	.4	.7
165 CH OF NAZARENE	2	0	0	-	-

NA–Not applicable   NR–Not reported   *Total adherents estimated from known number of communicant, confirmed, full members.   - Represents a percent less than 0.1.   Percentages may not total due to rounding.
[1]See Appendix E   [2]See Appendix F   [3]See Appendix G   Lines in *italic* represent a breakdown of Catholic rites or Friends affiliations. They are included in their respective denominational total.

Table 4. Churches and Church Membership by County and Denomination: 1990

County and Denomination	Number of churches	Communicant, confirmed, full members	Total adherents Number	Percent of total population	Percent of total adherents
167 CHS OF CHRIST	5	170	245	.1	.2
175 CONGR CHR CHS	1	149	184*	.1	.2
181 CONSRV CONGR	3	579	715*	.4	.7
193 EPISCOPAL	10	1,318	2,105	1.1	2.0
203 EVAN FREE CH	3	109	202	.1	.2
207 E.L.C.A.	47	20,453	27,750	14.0	26.0
211 FEL EVG BIB CH	1	17	17	-	-
220 FREE LUTHERAN	3	135	193	.1	.2
226 FRIENDS-USA	1	13	56	-	.1
226c FGC	*1*	*13*	*56*	*-*	*.1*
246 GREEK ORTHODOX	1	NR	NR	-	-
263 INT FOURSQ GOS	3	31	38*	-	-
283 LUTH—MO SYNOD	12	3,230	4,327	2.2	4.1
284 LUTH CH-AM ASC	1	512	687	.3	.6
331 ORTH CH IN AM	1	NR	NR	-	-
353 CHR BRETHREN	2	75	90	-	.1
355 PRESB CH (USA)	10	3,222	3,977*	2.0	3.7
403 SALVATION ARMY	3	500	567	.3	.5
413 S.D.A.	2	256	316*	.2	.3
419 SO BAPT CONV	3	344	425*	.2	.4
435 UNITARIAN-UNIV	3	146	222	.1	.2
443 UN C OF CHRIST	4	1,447	1,786*	.9	1.7
449 UN METHODIST	23	5,570	6,875*	3.5	6.4
469 WELS	1	109	150	.1	.1
496 JEWISH EST[1]	4	NA	0	-	-
497 BLACK BAPT EST[2]	NA	292	360*	.2	.3
SCOTT	**45**	**10,123**	**48,906***	**84.5**	**100.0**
053 ASSEMB OF GOD	4	275	585	1.0	1.2
057 BAPT GEN CONF	2	229	307*	.5	.6
081 CATHOLIC	12	NA	33,795	58.4	69.1
081d LATIN	*12*	*NA*	*33,795*	*58.4*	*69.1*
089 CHR & MISS AL	1	59	160	.3	.3
207 E.L.C.A.	8	4,456	6,363	11.0	13.0
220 FREE LUTHERAN	1	247	332	.6	.7
283 LUTH—MO SYNOD	4	1,557	2,072	3.6	4.2
313 N AM BAPT CONF	1	68	91*	.2	.2
355 PRESB CH (USA)	2	424	568*	1.0	1.2
371 REF CH IN AM	1	139	296	.5	.6
449 UN METHODIST	5	987	1,321*	2.3	2.7
469 WELS	4	1,682	2,230	3.9	4.6
496 JEWISH EST[1]	0	NA	786	1.4	1.6
SHERBURNE	**30**	**7,089**	**21,076***	**50.2**	**100.0**
053 ASSEMB OF GOD	1	557	1,300	3.1	6.2
057 BAPT GEN CONF	1	64	86*	.2	.4
081 CATHOLIC	5	NA	9,608	22.9	45.6
081d LATIN	*5*	*NA*	*9,608*	*22.9*	*45.6*
089 CHR & MISS AL	2	300	653	1.6	3.1
145 CH GOD PROPHCY	1	24	32*	.1	.2
193 EPISCOPAL	1	71	141	.3	.7
203 EVAN FREE CH	3	254	534	1.3	2.5
207 E.L.C.A.	6	3,671	5,792	13.8	27.5
209 EVAN LUTH SYN	1	189	229	.5	1.1
283 LUTH—MO SYNOD	4	990	1,369	3.3	6.5
443 UN C OF CHRIST	1	334	448*	1.1	2.1
449 UN METHODIST	3	545	732*	1.7	3.5
469 WELS	1	90	152	.4	.7
SIBLEY	**40**	**7,645**	**12,376***	**86.1**	**100.0**
040 AP CHR CH-AMER	1	58	103	.7	.8
053 ASSEMB OF GOD	1	53	70	.5	.6
057 BAPT GEN CONF	2	62	80*	.6	.6
081 CATHOLIC	8	NA	2,662	18.5	21.5
081d LATIN	*8*	*NA*	*2,662*	*18.5*	*21.5*
179 CONSRV BAPT	1	NR	NR	-	-
207 E.L.C.A.	9	2,696	3,436	23.9	27.8
209 EVAN LUTH SYN	1	99	130	.9	1.1
257 HUTTERIAN BR	1	NA	100	.7	.8
283 LUTH—MO SYNOD	8	2,271	2,827	19.7	22.8
413 S.D.A.	1	24	31*	.2	.3
443 UN C OF CHRIST	3	656	846*	5.9	6.8
449 UN METHODIST	1	229	295*	2.1	2.4
469 WELS	3	1,497	1,796	12.5	14.5
STEARNS	**115**	**17,159**	**93,204***	**78.5**	**100.0**
053 ASSEMB OF GOD	4	672	1,433	1.2	1.5
057 BAPT GEN CONF	2	379	487*	.4	.5
081 CATHOLIC	51	NA	69,481	58.5	74.5
081d LATIN	*51*	*NA*	*69,481*	*58.5*	*74.5*
097 CHR CHS&CHS CR	2	211	271*	.2	.3
105 CHRISTIAN REF	1	112	164	.1	.2
111 CH CR,SCIENTST	1	NR	NR	-	-
121 CH GOD (ABR)	1	14	18*	-	-
151 L-D SAINTS	1	NA	288	.2	.3
167 CHS OF CHRIST	1	78	122	.1	.1
179 CONSRV BAPT	1	NR	NR	-	-
181 CONSRV CONGR	1	25	32*	-	-
193 EPISCOPAL	3	308	377	.3	.4
203 EVAN FREE CH	2	118	240	.2	.3
207 E.L.C.A.	12	7,438	10,402	8.8	11.2
220 FREE LUTHERAN	3	219	229	.2	.2
226 FRIENDS-USA	1	7	21	-	-
226c FGC	*1*	*7*	*21*	*-*	*-*
283 LUTH—MO SYNOD	11	3,698	4,620	3.9	5.0
331 ORTH CH IN AM	2	NR	NR	-	-
355 PRESB CH (USA)	3	1,137	1,462*	1.2	1.6
413 S.D.A.	1	109	140*	.1	.2
419 SO BAPT CONV	1	86	111*	.1	.1
435 UNITARIAN-UNIV	1	78	130	.1	.1
443 UN C OF CHRIST	2	380	489*	.4	.5
449 UN METHODIST	7	2,090	2,687*	2.3	2.9
STEELE	**39**	**12,801**	**25,055***	**81.5**	**100.0**
019 AMER BAPT USA	1	244	316*	1.0	1.3
053 ASSEMB OF GOD	2	157	239	.8	1.0
057 BAPT GEN CONF	1	328	425*	1.4	1.7
081 CATHOLIC	7	NA	8,243	26.8	32.9
081d LATIN	*7*	*NA*	*8,243*	*26.8*	*32.9*
097 CHR CHS&CHS CR	1	60	78*	.3	.3
123 CH GOD (ANDER)	1	33	34	.1	.1
167 CHS OF CHRIST	1	13	18	.1	.1
193 EPISCOPAL	1	141	210	.7	.8
207 E.L.C.A.	12	7,446	9,811	31.9	39.2
283 LUTH—MO SYNOD	4	1,649	2,117	6.9	8.4
355 PRESB CH (USA)	1	647	839*	2.7	3.3
413 S.D.A.	1	32	41*	.1	.2
443 UN C OF CHRIST	2	887	1,150*	3.7	4.6
449 UN METHODIST	3	1,026	1,330*	4.3	5.3
469 WELS	1	138	204	.7	.8
STEVENS	**26**	**4,395**	**8,127***	**76.4**	**100.0**
040 AP CHR CH-AMER	1	245	435	4.1	5.4
053 ASSEMB OF GOD	1	33	45	.4	.6
081 CATHOLIC	3	NA	2,220	20.9	27.3
081d LATIN	*3*	*NA*	*2,220*	*20.9*	*27.3*
105 CHRISTIAN REF	1	78	142	1.3	1.7
164 CH LUTH CONF	1	34	40	.4	.5
165 CH OF NAZARENE	1	50	83	.8	1.0
203 EVAN FREE CH	2	80	246	2.3	3.0
207 E.L.C.A.	7	2,664	3,396	31.9	41.8
283 LUTH—MO SYNOD	1	280	344	3.2	4.2
284 LUTH CH-AM ASC	1	35	77	.7	.9
443 UN C OF CHRIST	2	249	306*	2.9	3.8
449 UN METHODIST	3	311	383*	3.6	4.7
469 WELS	2	336	410	3.9	5.0
SWIFT	**39**	**6,387**	**10,741***	**100.2**	**100.0**
053 ASSEMB OF GOD	1	52	86	.8	.8
057 BAPT GEN CONF	2	179	227*	2.1	2.1
081 CATHOLIC	7	NA	2,608	24.3	24.3
081d LATIN	*7*	*NA*	*2,608*	*24.3*	*24.3*
164 CH LUTH CONF	2	225	290	2.7	2.7
193 EPISCOPAL	1	16	16	.1	.1
203 EVAN FREE CH	3	175	258	2.4	2.4
207 E.L.C.A.	12	3,859	4,867	45.4	45.3
283 LUTH—MO SYNOD	5	1,161	1,477	13.8	13.8
313 N AM BAPT CONF	1	57	72*	.7	.7
355 PRESB CH (USA)	1	116	147*	1.4	1.4
413 S.D.A.	1	49	62*	.6	.6
443 UN C OF CHRIST	2	351	445*	4.1	4.1
449 UN METHODIST	1	147	186*	1.7	1.7
TODD	**54**	**6,840**	**16,699***	**71.5**	**100.0**
053 ASSEMB OF GOD	3	221	447	1.9	2.7
057 BAPT GEN CONF	1	40	52*	.2	.3
061 BEACHY AMISH	1	20	26*	.1	.2
081 CATHOLIC	8	NA	7,093	30.4	42.5
081d LATIN	*8*	*NA*	*7,093*	*30.4*	*42.5*
089 CHR & MISS AL	2	90	223	1.0	1.3
123 CH GOD (ANDER)	1	80	111	.5	.7
165 CH OF NAZARENE	2	64	215	.9	1.3
179 CONSRV BAPT	1	NR	NR	-	-
181 CONSRV CONGR	1	20	26*	.1	.2
203 EVAN FREE CH	1	48	65	.3	.4
207 E.L.C.A.	11	2,411	3,181	13.6	19.0
221 FREE METHODIST	2	29	43	.2	.3
283 LUTH—MO SYNOD	8	2,612	3,487	14.9	20.9
323 OLD ORD AMISH	1	NA	150	.6	.9
443 UN C OF CHRIST	3	360	472*	2.0	2.8
449 UN METHODIST	8	845	1,108*	4.7	6.6

NA–Not applicable   NR–Not reported   *Total adherents estimated from known number of communicant, confirmed, full members.   - Represents a percent less than 0.1.   Percentages may not total due to rounding.
[1]See Appendix E   [2]See Appendix F   [3]See Appendix G   Lines in *italic* represent a breakdown of Catholic rites or Friends affiliations. They are included in their respective denominational total.

MINNESOTA

Table 4. Churches and Church Membership by County and Denomination: 1990

| County and Denomination | Number of churches | Communicant, confirmed, full members | Total adherents | | |
			Number	Percent of total population	Percent of total adherents
TRAVERSE	**18**	**2,365**	**4,802***	**107.6**	**100.0**
081 CATHOLIC	5	NA	1,903	42.6	39.6
081d LATIN	5	NA	1,903	42.6	39.6
127 CH GOD (CLEVE)	1	3	4*	.1	.1
207 E.L.C.A.	2	592	706	15.8	14.7
283 LUTH—MO SYNOD	4	1,161	1,420	31.8	29.6
355 PRESB CH (USA)	3	272	344*	7.7	7.2
443 UN C OF CHRIST	1	63	80*	1.8	1.7
449 UN METHODIST	1	103	130*	2.9	2.7
469 WELS	1	171	215	4.8	4.5
WABASHA	**45**	**7,541**	**17,290***	**87.6**	**100.0**
053 ASSEM OF GOD	1	49	68	.3	.4
057 BAPT GEN CONF	1	51	66*	.3	.4
081 CATHOLIC	10	NA	7,149	36.2	41.3
081d LATIN	10	NA	7,149	36.2	41.3
097 CHR CHS&CHS CR	1	115	150*	.8	.9
151 L-D SAINTS	1	NA	201	1.0	1.2
193 EPISCOPAL	2	144	262	1.3	1.5
203 EVAN FREE CH	1	27	55	.3	.3
207 E.L.C.A.	3	1,210	1,651	8.4	9.5
283 LUTH—MO SYNOD	4	1,839	2,420	12.3	14.0
353 CHR BRETHREN	1	60	90	.5	.5
355 PRESB CH (USA)	1	127	166*	.8	1.0
443 UN C OF CHRIST	4	613	799*	4.0	4.6
449 UN METHODIST	8	852	1,111*	5.6	6.4
467 WESLEYAN	1	5	18	.1	.1
469 WELS	6	2,449	3,084	15.6	17.8
WADENA	**36**	**5,003**	**9,946***	**75.6**	**100.0**
045 APOSTOLIC LUTH	2	200	314	2.4	3.2
053 ASSEM OF GOD	3	158	299	2.3	3.0
081 CATHOLIC	4	NA	2,764	21.0	27.8
081d LATIN	4	NA	2,764	21.0	27.8
089 CHR & MISS AL	4	170	603	4.6	6.1
167 CHS OF CHRIST	1	45	55	.4	.6
193 EPISCOPAL	1	30	53	.4	.5
207 E.L.C.A.	4	1,614	2,176	16.5	21.9
220 FREE LUTHERAN	2	233	267	2.0	2.7
283 LUTH—MO SYNOD	6	1,579	2,010	15.3	20.2
323 OLD ORD AMISH	1	NA	150	1.1	1.5
413 S.D.A.	1	86	111*	.8	1.1
443 UN C OF CHRIST	2	233	300*	2.3	3.0
449 UN METHODIST	5	655	844*	6.4	8.5
WASECA	**32**	**8,041**	**15,999***	**88.5**	**100.0**
053 ASSEM OF GOD	1	41	75	.4	.5
081 CATHOLIC	4	NA	5,321	29.4	33.3
081d LATIN	4	NA	5,321	29.4	33.3
175 CONGR CHR CHS	1	200	259*	1.4	1.6
193 EPISCOPAL	2	30	42	.2	.3
203 EVAN FREE CH	1	97	216	1.2	1.4
207 E.L.C.A.	9	3,547	4,809	26.6	30.1
220 FREE LUTHERAN	1	60	65	.4	.4
283 LUTH—MO SYNOD	5	2,567	3,272	18.1	20.5
443 UN C OF CHRIST	2	290	376*	2.1	2.4
449 UN METHODIST	4	982	1,272*	7.0	8.0
467 WESLEYAN	1	23	21	.1	.1
469 WELS	1	204	271	1.5	1.7
WASHINGTON	**94**	**32,351**	**86,891***	**59.6**	**100.0**
019 AMER BAPT USA	1	147	194*	.1	.2
053 ASSEM OF GOD	4	434	742	.5	.9
057 BAPT GEN CONF	3	213	281*	.2	.3
081 CATHOLIC	11	NA	36,789	25.2	42.3
081d LATIN	11	NA	36,789	25.2	42.3
089 CHR & MISS AL	3	274	822	.6	.9
097 CHR CHS&CHS CR	2	233	308*	.2	.4
111 CH CR,SCIENTST	1	NR	NR	-	-
123 CH GOD (ANDER)	2	65	80	.1	.1
151 L-D SAINTS	1	NA	496	.3	.6
167 CHS OF CHRIST	2	83	152	.1	.2
175 CONGR CHR CHS	1	324	428*	.3	.5
179 CONSRV BAPT	3	NR	NR	-	-
181 CONSRV CONGR	1	46	61*	-	.1
193 EPISCOPAL	4	619	815	.6	.9
203 EVAN FREE CH	3	181	405	.3	.5
207 E.L.C.A.	21	19,860	29,916	20.5	34.4
226 FRIENDS-USA	1	10	30	-	-
226c FGC	1	10	30	-	-
283 LUTH—MO SYNOD	7	2,765	3,962	2.7	4.6
339 PENT CH OF GOD	1	34	77	.1	.1
355 PRESB CH (USA)	3	1,515	2,000*	1.4	2.3
413 S.D.A.	1	44	58*	-	.1
443 UN C OF CHRIST	4	933	1,231*	.8	1.4

| County and Denomination | Number of churches | Communicant, confirmed, full members | Total adherents | | |
			Number	Percent of total population	Percent of total adherents
449 UN METHODIST	6	2,555	3,372*	2.3	3.9
467 WESLEYAN	1	49	116	.1	.1
469 WELS	7	1,544	2,014	1.4	2.3
496 JEWISH EST [1]	0	NA	1,984	1.4	2.3
497 BLACK BAPT EST [2]	NA	423	558*	.4	.6
WATONWAN	**31**	**6,301**	**10,156***	**86.9**	**100.0**
053 ASSEM OF GOD	1	61	95	.8	.9
081 CATHOLIC	2	NA	2,053	17.6	20.2
081d LATIN	2	NA	2,053	17.6	20.2
097 CHR CHS&CHS CR	1	125	162*	1.4	1.6
203 EVAN FREE CH	1	9	9	.1	.1
207 E.L.C.A.	12	3,484	4,531	38.8	44.6
220 FREE LUTHERAN	1	31	38	.3	.4
283 LUTH—MO SYNOD	4	840	1,034	8.9	10.2
287 MENN GEN CONF	2	116	156	1.3	1.5
355 PRESB CH (USA)	2	500	647*	5.5	6.4
449 UN METHODIST	2	364	471*	4.0	4.6
469 WELS	3	771	960	8.2	9.5
WILKIN	**22**	**2,780**	**5,736***	**76.3**	**100.0**
019 AMER BAPT USA	1	57	74*	1.0	1.3
057 BAPT GEN CONF	1	62	80*	1.1	1.4
081 CATHOLIC	3	NA	1,845	24.5	32.2
081d LATIN	3	NA	1,845	24.5	32.2
179 CONSRV BAPT	1	NR	NR	-	-
203 EVAN FREE CH	1	49	89	1.2	1.6
207 E.L.C.A.	5	1,462	2,200	29.3	38.4
220 FREE LUTHERAN	1	28	34	.5	.6
283 LUTH—MO SYNOD	4	600	741	9.9	12.9
355 PRESB CH (USA)	1	66	85*	1.1	1.5
443 UN C OF CHRIST	1	28	36*	.5	.6
449 UN METHODIST	3	428	552*	7.3	9.6
WINONA	**71**	**13,435**	**31,815***	**66.5**	**100.0**
019 AMER BAPT USA	1	118	147*	.3	.5
053 ASSEM OF GOD	1	124	300	.6	.9
057 BAPT GEN CONF	1	40	50*	.1	.2
081 CATHOLIC	15	NA	13,503	28.2	42.4
081d LATIN	15	NA	13,503	28.2	42.4
097 CHR CHS&CHS CR	1	40	50*	.1	.2
151 L-D SAINTS	1	NA	154	.3	.5
157 CH OF BRETHREN	1	132	164*	.3	.5
165 CH OF NAZARENE	1	99	95	.2	.3
167 CHS OF CHRIST	2	96	128	.3	.4
193 EPISCOPAL	2	195	329	.7	1.0
203 EVAN FREE CH	1	160	260	.5	.8
207 E.L.C.A.	5	2,958	3,940	8.2	12.4
226 FRIENDS-USA	1	2	8	-	-
226c FGC	1	2	8	-	-
259 IFCA	2	NR	NR	-	-
283 LUTH—MO SYNOD	6	3,409	4,533	9.5	14.2
293 MORAV CH-NORTH	2	259	329	.7	1.0
323 OLD ORD AMISH	2	NA	300	.6	.9
355 PRESB CH (USA)	3	320	398*	.8	1.3
413 S.D.A.	1	56	70*	.1	.2
419 SO BAPT CONV	1	16	20*	-	.1
443 UN C OF CHRIST	3	712	885*	1.9	2.8
449 UN METHODIST	8	1,438	1,788*	3.7	5.6
469 WELS	10	3,261	4,364	9.1	13.7
WRIGHT	**76**	**16,713**	**42,615***	**62.0**	**100.0**
053 ASSEM OF GOD	5	447	698	1.0	1.6
057 BAPT GEN CONF	2	248	337*	.5	.8
081 CATHOLIC	11	NA	17,583	25.6	41.3
081d LATIN	11	NA	17,583	25.6	41.3
089 CHR & MISS AL	3	60	173	.3	.4
097 CHR CHS&CHS CR	1	130	177*	.3	.4
151 L-D SAINTS	2	NA	623	.9	1.5
167 CHS OF CHRIST	1	13	19	-	-
193 EPISCOPAL	1	29	37	.1	.1
203 EVAN FREE CH	5	349	645	.9	1.5
207 E.L.C.A.	16	7,579	10,762	15.7	25.3
220 FREE LUTHERAN	1	107	157	.2	.4
283 LUTH—MO SYNOD	7	3,227	4,412	6.4	10.4
355 PRESB CH (USA)	4	603	819*	1.2	1.9
443 UN C OF CHRIST	2	251	341*	.5	.8
449 UN METHODIST	9	1,863	2,530*	3.7	5.9
469 WELS	6	1,807	2,368	3.4	5.6
496 JEWISH EST [1]	0	NA	934	1.4	2.2
YELLOW MEDICINE	**35**	**6,911**	**10,638***	**91.0**	**100.0**
053 ASSEM OF GOD	2	67	129	1.1	1.2
081 CATHOLIC	3	NA	1,723	14.7	16.2
081d LATIN	3	NA	1,723	14.7	16.2

NA–Not applicable NR–Not reported *Total adherents estimated from known number of communicant, confirmed, full members. - Represents a percent less than 0.1. Percentages may not total due to rounding.
[1] See Appendix E [2] See Appendix F [3] See Appendix G Lines in *italic* represent a breakdown of Catholic rites or Friends affiliations. They are included in their respective denominational total.

Table 4. Churches and Church Membership by County and Denomination: 1990

County and Denomination	Number of churches	Communicant, confirmed, full members	Total adherents Number	Percent of total population	Percent of total adherents
089 CHR & MISS AL	2	63	172	1.5	1.6
097 CHR CHS&CHS CR	1	152	194*	1.7	1.8
179 CONSRV BAPT	1	NR	NR	-	-
203 EVAN FREE CH	1	23	50	.4	.5
207 E.L.C.A.	12	4,258	5,453	46.7	51.3
283 LUTH—MO SYNOD	4	914	1,157	9.9	10.9
355 PRESB CH (USA)	2	291	370*	3.2	3.5
443 UN C OF CHRIST	1	233	297*	2.5	2.8
449 UN METHODIST	2	232	295*	2.5	2.8
469 WELS	4	678	798	6.8	7.5

MISSISSIPPI

County and Denomination	Number of churches	Communicant, confirmed, full members	Total adherents Number	Percent of total population	Percent of total adherents
THE STATE.....	5,433	1,307,928	1,806,049*	70.2	100.0
ADAMS	**50**	**16,557**	**24,095***	**68.1**	**100.0**
053 ASSEMB OF GOD	1	165	195	.6	.8
059 BAPT MISS ASSN	1	144	186*	.5	.8
081 CATHOLIC	4	NA	2,746	7.8	11.4
081d LATIN	4	NA	2,746	7.8	11.4
111 CH CR,SCIENTST	1	NR	NR	-	-
123 CH GOD (ANDER)	1	154	154	.4	.6
127 CH GOD (CLEVE)	2	582	752*	2.1	3.1
145 CH GOD PROPHCY	1	33	43*	.1	.2
151 L-D SAINTS	1	NA	132	.4	.5
165 CH OF NAZARENE	1	55	0	-	-
167 CHS OF CHRIST	3	479	670	1.9	2.8
193 EPISCOPAL	1	443	535	1.5	2.2
215 EVAN METH CH	1	70	90*	.3	.4
283 LUTH—MO SYNOD	1	58	73	.2	.3
355 PRESB CH (USA)	3	472	610*	1.7	2.5
356 PRESB CH AMER	1	97	97	.3	.4
361 PRIM BAPT ASCS	1	53	68*	.2	.3
403 SALVATION ARMY	1	75	81	.2	.3
413 S.D.A.	2	161	208*	.6	.9
419 SO BAPT CONV	15	7,470	9,647*	27.3	40.0
449 UN METHODIST	7	1,824	2,356*	6.7	9.8
496 JEWISH EST[1]	1	NA	0	-	-
497 BLACK BAPT EST[2]	NA	4,222	5,452*	15.4	22.6
ALCORN	**88**	**18,094**	**22,881***	**72.1**	**100.0**
053 ASSEMB OF GOD	2	239	215	.7	.9
059 BAPT MISS ASSN	2	829	1,029*	3.2	4.5
081 CATHOLIC	1	NA	400	1.3	1.7
081d LATIN	1	NA	400	1.3	1.7
097 CHR CHS&CHS CR	4	485	602*	1.9	2.6
127 CH GOD (CLEVE)	1	64	79*	.2	.3
145 CH GOD PROPHCY	1	33	41*	.1	.2
167 CHS OF CHRIST	20	1,726	2,254*	7.1	9.9
185 CUMBER PRESB	1	45	54	.2	.2
193 EPISCOPAL	1	74	80	.3	.3
223 FREE WILL BAPT	2	106	132*	.4	.6
283 LUTH—MO SYNOD	1	106	141	.4	.6
355 PRESB CH (USA)	3	514	638*	2.0	2.8
361 PRIM BAPT ASCS	2	79	98*	.3	.4
413 S.D.A.	1	79	98*	.3	.4
419 SO BAPT CONV	31	10,302	12,785*	40.3	55.9
449 UN METHODIST	15	2,545	3,158*	10.0	13.8
497 BLACK BAPT EST[2]	NA	868	1,077*	3.4	4.7
AMITE	**45**	**7,598**	**10,293***	**77.2**	**100.0**
053 ASSEMB OF GOD	1	14	18	.1	.2
081 CATHOLIC	1	NA	49	.4	.5
081d LATIN	1	NA	49	.4	.5
127 CH GOD (CLEVE)	1	28	36*	.3	.3
145 CH GOD PROPHCY	2	68	88*	.7	.9
151 L-D SAINTS	2	NA	408	3.1	4.0
165 CH OF NAZARENE	1	50	48	.4	.5
339 PENT CH OF GOD	1	34	77	.6	.7
355 PRESB CH (USA)	1	9	12*	.1	.1
356 PRESB CH AMER	2	38	43	.3	.4
361 PRIM BAPT ASCS	1	21	27*	.2	.3
419 SO BAPT CONV	25	4,734	6,122*	45.9	59.5
449 UN METHODIST	7	534	691*	5.2	6.7
497 BLACK BAPT EST[2]	NA	2,068	2,674*	20.1	26.0
ATTALA	**78**	**11,650**	**14,752***	**79.8**	**100.0**
005 AME ZION	1	126	173	.9	1.2
053 ASSEMB OF GOD	1	41	49	.3	.3
059 BAPT MISS ASSN	1	48	61*	.3	.4
081 CATHOLIC	1	NA	85	.5	.6

County and Denomination	Number of churches	Communicant, confirmed, full members	Total adherents Number	Percent of total population	Percent of total adherents
081d LATIN	1	NA	85	.5	.6
123 CH GOD (ANDER)	2	38	48	.3	.3
127 CH GOD (CLEVE)	2	125	158*	.9	1.1
145 CH GOD PROPHCY	1	33	42*	.2	.3
165 CH OF NAZARENE	1	56	38	.2	.3
167 CHS OF CHRIST	6	211	292	1.6	2.0
193 EPISCOPAL	1	20	22	.1	.1
207 E.L.C.A.	1	68	91	.5	.6
355 PRESB CH (USA)	2	74	94*	.5	.6
356 PRESB CH AMER	2	317	317	1.7	2.1
361 PRIM BAPT ASCS	1	12	15*	.1	.1
419 SO BAPT CONV	30	6,036	7,641*	41.3	51.8
449 UN METHODIST	25	1,946	2,463*	13.3	16.7
497 BLACK BAPT EST[2]	NA	2,499	3,163*	17.1	21.4
BENTON	**28**	**3,970**	**5,331***	**66.3**	**100.0**
097 CHR CHS&CHS CR	1	35	46*	.6	.9
167 CHS OF CHRIST	5	353	625	7.8	11.7
185 CUMBER PRESB	1	61	64	.8	1.2
193 EPISCOPAL	1	19	26	.3	.5
355 PRESB CH (USA)	1	33	43*	.5	.8
419 SO BAPT CONV	11	2,080	2,714*	33.7	50.9
449 UN METHODIST	8	304	397*	4.9	7.4
497 BLACK BAPT EST[2]	NA	1,085	1,416*	17.6	26.6
BOLIVAR	**77**	**17,579**	**25,285***	**60.4**	**100.0**
019 AMER BAPT USA	1	200	271*	.6	1.1
053 ASSEMB OF GOD	3	142	201	.5	.8
059 BAPT MISS ASSN	1	40	54*	.1	.2
081 CATHOLIC	5	NA	1,212	2.9	4.8
081d LATIN	5	NA	1,212	2.9	4.8
093 CHR CH (DISC)	3	113	243	.6	1.0
127 CH GOD (CLEVE)	1	151	205*	.5	.8
145 CH GOD PROPHCY	1	33	45*	.1	.2
151 L-D SAINTS	1	NA	177	.4	.7
165 CH OF NAZARENE	2	138	192	.5	.8
167 CHS OF CHRIST	5	864	1,074	2.6	4.2
193 EPISCOPAL	2	183	241	.6	1.0
263 INT FOURSQ GOS	1	60	81*	.2	.3
283 LUTH—MO SYNOD	1	57	66	.2	.3
355 PRESB CH (USA)	4	243	330*	.8	1.3
356 PRESB CH AMER	1	269	317	.8	1.3
361 PRIM BAPT ASCS	1	25	34*	.1	.1
413 S.D.A.	2	80	108*	.3	.4
419 SO BAPT CONV	24	6,832	9,264*	22.1	36.6
449 UN METHODIST	17	1,691	2,293*	5.5	9.1
496 JEWISH EST[1]	1	NA	120	.3	.5
497 BLACK BAPT EST[2]	NA	6,458	8,757*	20.9	34.6
CALHOUN	**70**	**11,415**	**14,301***	**95.9**	**100.0**
127 CH GOD (CLEVE)	1	73	91*	.6	.6
145 CH GOD PROPHCY	3	101	126*	.8	.9
165 CH OF NAZARENE	1	29	72	.5	.5
167 CHS OF CHRIST	2	64	75	.5	.5
223 FREE WILL BAPT	1	123	154*	1.0	1.1
361 PRIM BAPT ASCS	1	13	16*	.1	.1
419 SO BAPT CONV	50	8,814	11,019*	73.9	77.1
449 UN METHODIST	11	819	1,024*	6.9	7.2
497 BLACK BAPT EST[2]	NA	1,379	1,724*	11.6	12.1
CARROLL	**48**	**6,320**	**8,081***	**87.5**	**100.0**
001 ADVENT CHR CH	1	22	28*	.3	.3
093 CHR CH (DISC)	2	110	153	1.7	1.9
097 CHR CHS&CHS CR	1	100	128*	1.4	1.6
167 CHS OF CHRIST	1	45	55	.6	.7
193 EPISCOPAL	1	16	20	.2	.2
356 PRESB CH AMER	3	159	187	2.0	2.3
419 SO BAPT CONV	19	3,470	4,441*	48.1	55.0
449 UN METHODIST	20	1,147	1,468*	15.9	18.2
497 BLACK BAPT EST[2]	NA	1,251	1,601*	17.3	19.8
CHICKASAW	**67**	**10,169**	**13,379***	**74.0**	**100.0**
053 ASSEMB OF GOD	1	23	50	.3	.4
081 CATHOLIC	2	NA	96	.5	.7
081d LATIN	2	NA	96	.5	.7
127 CH GOD (CLEVE)	3	207	271*	1.5	2.0
143 CG IN CR(MENN)	1	124	162*	.9	1.2
145 CH GOD PROPHCY	4	135	177*	1.0	1.3
165 CH OF NAZARENE	3	226	270	1.5	2.0
167 CHS OF CHRIST	5	298	378	2.1	2.8
193 EPISCOPAL	1	11	11	.1	.1
355 PRESB CH (USA)	4	134	175*	1.0	1.3
356 PRESB CH AMER	1	31	31	.2	.2
419 SO BAPT CONV	19	4,752	6,222*	34.4	46.5
449 UN METHODIST	22	1,837	2,405*	13.3	18.0

NA–Not applicable   NR–Not reported   *Total adherents estimated from known number of communicant, confirmed, full members.   - Represents a percent less than 0.1.   Percentages may not total due to rounding.
[1]See Appendix E   [2]See Appendix F   [3]See Appendix G   Lines in *italic* represent a breakdown of Catholic rites or Friends affiliations. They are included in their respective denominational total.

Table 4. Churches and Church Membership by County and Denomination: 1990

County and Denomination	Number of churches	Communicant, confirmed, full members	Total adherents — Number	Percent of total population	Percent of total adherents
497 BLACK BAPT EST²	NA	2,391	3,131*	17.3	23.4
CHOCTAW	**49**	**6,124**	**7,980***	**88.0**	**100.0**
005 AME ZION	1	160	207	2.3	2.6
151 L-D SAINTS	1	NA	103	1.1	1.3
167 CHS OF CHRIST	1	88	112	1.2	1.4
185 CUMBER PRESB	1	212	221	2.4	2.8
349 PENT HOLINESS	1	19	25*	.3	.3
355 PRESB CH (USA)	8	271	352*	3.9	4.4
356 PRESB CH AMER	1	38	38	.4	.5
419 SO BAPT CONV	23	3,687	4,783*	52.7	59.9
449 UN METHODIST	12	714	926*	10.2	11.6
497 BLACK BAPT EST²	NA	935	1,213*	13.4	15.2
CLAIBORNE	**34**	**5,813**	**7,584***	**66.7**	**100.0**
005 AME ZION	1	240	293	2.6	3.9
081 CATHOLIC	1	NA	110	1.0	1.5
081d *LATIN*	*1*	*NA*	*110*	*1.0*	*1.5*
093 CHR CH (DISC)	14	577	810	7.1	10.7
167 CHS OF CHRIST	2	25	45	.4	.6
185 CUMBER PRESB	1	42	45	.4	.6
193 EPISCOPAL	1	72	84	.7	1.1
355 PRESB CH (USA)	1	166	212*	1.9	2.8
413 S.D.A.	1	69	88*	.8	1.2
419 SO BAPT CONV	5	997	1,272*	11.2	16.8
449 UN METHODIST	6	427	545*	4.8	7.2
496 JEWISH EST¹	1	NA	0	-	-
497 BLACK BAPT EST²	NA	3,198	4,080*	35.9	53.8
CLARKE	**81**	**11,770**	**15,255***	**88.1**	**100.0**
053 ASSEMB OF GOD	4	248	312	1.8	2.0
081 CATHOLIC	1	NA	40	.2	.3
081d *LATIN*	*1*	*NA*	*40*	*.2*	*.3*
123 CH GOD (ANDER)	6	97	217	1.3	1.4
165 CH OF NAZARENE	1	208	241	1.4	1.6
167 CHS OF CHRIST	2	64	93	.5	.6
193 EPISCOPAL	1	24	25	.1	.2
266 INTRSTAT & ASC	1	75	97*	.6	.6
349 PENT HOLINESS	5	355	457*	2.6	3.0
413 S.D.A.	1	21	27*	.2	.2
419 SO BAPT CONV	28	5,850	7,531*	43.5	49.4
449 UN METHODIST	31	2,781	3,580*	20.7	23.5
497 BLACK BAPT EST²	NA	2,047	2,635*	15.2	17.3
CLAY	**42**	**11,498**	**15,639***	**74.0**	**100.0**
053 ASSEMB OF GOD	1	20	25	.1	.2
059 BAPT MISS ASSN	1	184	242*	1.1	1.5
081 CATHOLIC	1	NA	209	1.0	1.3
081d *LATIN*	*1*	*NA*	*209*	*1.0*	*1.3*
093 CHR CH (DISC)	3	301	370	1.8	2.4
127 CH GOD (CLEVE)	2	229	301*	1.4	1.9
143 CG IN CR(MENN)	1	81	107*	.5	.7
145 CH GOD PROPHCY	1	33	43*	.2	.3
151 L-D SAINTS	1	NA	340	1.6	2.2
167 CHS OF CHRIST	4	244	329	1.6	2.1
193 EPISCOPAL	1	75	96	.5	.6
216 EVAN PRESBY CH	1	164	167	.8	1.1
339 PENT CH OF GOD	1	34	77	.4	.5
355 PRESB CH (USA)	2	25	33*	.2	.2
413 S.D.A.	1	41	54*	.3	.3
419 SO BAPT CONV	11	4,573	6,017*	28.5	38.5
449 UN METHODIST	10	1,636	2,153*	10.2	13.8
497 BLACK BAPT EST²	NA	3,858	5,076*	24.0	32.5
COAHOMA	**37**	**13,097**	**18,980***	**59.9**	**100.0**
005 AME ZION	1	43	68	.2	.4
053 ASSEMB OF GOD	1	35	89	.3	.5
081 CATHOLIC	2	NA	1,271	4.0	6.7
081d *LATIN*	*2*	*NA*	*1,271*	*4.0*	*6.7*
093 CHR CH (DISC)	1	85	90	.3	.5
097 CHR CHS&CHS CR	1	75	102*	.3	.5
111 CH CR,SCIENTST	1	NR	NR	-	-
127 CH GOD (CLEVE)	1	81	110*	.3	.6
143 CG IN CR(MENN)	1	149	203*	.6	1.1
165 CH OF NAZARENE	1	76	70	.2	.4
167 CHS OF CHRIST	2	160	195	.6	1.0
193 EPISCOPAL	1	526	600	1.9	3.2
356 PRESB CH AMER	1	408	475	1.5	2.5
413 S.D.A.	1	68	93*	.3	.5
419 SO BAPT CONV	10	4,675	6,367*	20.1	33.5
449 UN METHODIST	11	1,698	2,313*	7.3	12.2
496 JEWISH EST¹	1	NA	100	.3	.5
497 BLACK BAPT EST²	NA	5,018	6,834*	21.6	36.0
COPIAH	**73**	**16,089**	**21,338***	**77.3**	**100.0**
005 AME ZION	1	240	270	1.0	1.3
053 ASSEMB OF GOD	1	33	50	.2	.2
081 CATHOLIC	2	NA	164	.6	.8
081d *LATIN*	*2*	*NA*	*164*	*.6*	*.8*
093 CHR CH (DISC)	1	10	13	-	.1
151 L-D SAINTS	2	NA	345	1.3	1.6
165 CH OF NAZARENE	1	42	65	.2	.3
167 CHS OF CHRIST	3	54	94	.3	.4
193 EPISCOPAL	2	30	33	.1	.2
349 PENT HOLINESS	1	218	283*	1.0	1.3
356 PRESB CH AMER	3	327	360	1.3	1.7
413 S.D.A.	1	121	157*	.6	.7
419 SO BAPT CONV	31	9,241	12,005*	43.5	56.3
449 UN METHODIST	24	2,358	3,063*	11.1	14.4
497 BLACK BAPT EST²	NA	3,415	4,436*	16.1	20.8
COVINGTON	**50**	**9,506**	**12,681***	**76.7**	**100.0**
053 ASSEMB OF GOD	1	24	41	.2	.3
059 BAPT MISS ASSN	2	410	538*	3.3	4.2
081 CATHOLIC	0	NA	98	.6	.8
081d *LATIN*	*0*	*NA*	*98*	*.6*	*.8*
151 L-D SAINTS	1	NA	149	.9	1.2
167 CHS OF CHRIST	3	72	106	.6	.8
193 EPISCOPAL	1	38	38	.2	.3
266 INTRSTAT & ASC	10	1,023	1,343*	8.1	10.6
356 PRESB CH AMER	5	275	307	1.9	2.4
419 SO BAPT CONV	18	4,905	6,439*	39.0	50.8
449 UN METHODIST	9	775	1,017*	6.2	8.0
497 BLACK BAPT EST²	NA	1,984	2,605*	15.8	20.5
DE SOTO	**95**	**29,390**	**40,359***	**59.4**	**100.0**
053 ASSEMB OF GOD	4	527	715	1.1	1.8
055 AS REF PRES CH	1	103	121	.2	.3
059 BAPT MISS ASSN	2	635	819*	1.2	2.0
081 CATHOLIC	4	NA	1,363	2.0	3.4
081d *LATIN*	*4*	*NA*	*1,363*	*2.0*	*3.4*
097 CHR CHS&CHS CR	2	140	181*	.3	.4
127 CH GOD (CLEVE)	4	481	621*	.9	1.5
151 L-D SAINTS	1	NA	247	.4	.6
165 CH OF NAZARENE	1	72	120	.2	.3
167 CHS OF CHRIST	12	1,599	2,144	3.2	5.3
193 EPISCOPAL	2	208	246	.4	.6
223 FREE WILL BAPT	1	15	19*	-	-
283 LUTH—MO SYNOD	1	123	179	.3	.4
349 PENT HOLINESS	1	29	37*	.1	.1
355 PRESB CH (USA)	6	561	724*	1.1	1.8
413 S.D.A.	2	88	114*	.2	.3
419 SO BAPT CONV	34	18,585	23,985*	35.3	59.4
449 UN METHODIST	17	3,598	4,643*	6.8	11.5
496 JEWISH EST¹	0	NA	692	1.0	1.7
497 BLACK BAPT EST²	NA	2,626	3,389*	5.0	8.4
FORREST	**106**	**38,456**	**53,307***	**78.0**	**100.0**
053 ASSEMB OF GOD	5	277	380	.6	.7
059 BAPT MISS ASSN	6	859	1,080*	1.6	2.0
081 CATHOLIC	3	NA	3,328	4.9	6.2
081d *LATIN*	*3*	*NA*	*3,328*	*4.9*	*6.2*
093 CHR CH (DISC)	1	130	233	.3	.4
111 CH CR,SCIENTST	1	NR	NR	-	-
123 CH GOD (ANDER)	2	122	140	.2	.3
127 CH GOD (CLEVE)	4	518	651*	1.0	1.2
145 CH GOD PROPHCY	1	33	41*	.1	.1
151 L-D SAINTS	2	NA	770	1.1	1.4
165 CH OF NAZARENE	1	97	102	.1	.2
167 CHS OF CHRIST	5	438	577	.8	1.1
193 EPISCOPAL	2	841	1,006	1.5	1.9
223 FREE WILL BAPT	1	44	55*	.1	.1
263 INT FOURSQ GOS	1	34	43*	.1	.1
266 INTRSTAT & ASC	6	624	785*	1.1	1.5
283 LUTH—MO SYNOD	1	210	256	.4	.5
355 PRESB CH (USA)	2	353	444*	.6	.8
356 PRESB CH AMER	4	1,095	1,339	2.0	2.5
403 SALVATION ARMY	1	84	91	.1	.2
413 S.D.A.	2	250	314*	.5	.6
419 SO BAPT CONV	36	21,866	27,496*	40.2	51.6
449 UN METHODIST	17	5,429	6,827*	10.0	12.8
496 JEWISH EST¹	1	NA	120	.2	.2
497 BLACK BAPT EST²	NA	5,152	6,479*	9.5	12.2
499 INDEP.NON-CHAR³	1	NA	750	1.1	1.4
FRANKLIN	**46**	**6,122**	**7,993***	**95.4**	**100.0**
053 ASSEMB OF GOD	1	19	21	.3	.3
081 CATHOLIC	1	NA	16	.2	.2
081d *LATIN*	*1*	*NA*	*16*	*.2*	*.2*

NA–Not applicable   NR–Not reported   *Total adherents estimated from known number of communicant, confirmed, full members.   - Represents a percent less than 0.1.   Percentages may not total due to rounding.
¹See Appendix E   ²See Appendix F   ³See Appendix G   Lines in *italic* represent a breakdown of Catholic rites or Friends affiliations. They are included in their respective denominational total.

Table 4. Churches and Church Membership by County and Denomination: 1990

County and Denomination	Number of churches	Communicant, confirmed, full members	Total adherents		
			Number	Percent of total population	Percent of total adherents
127 CH GOD (CLEVE)	3	226	294*	3.5	3.7
167 CHS OF CHRIST	2	58	103	1.2	1.3
356 PRESB CH AMER	2	48	58	.7	.7
361 PRIM BAPT ASCS	3	359	467*	5.6	5.8
419 SO BAPT CONV	22	3,487	4,532*	54.1	56.7
449 UN METHODIST	12	871	1,132*	13.5	14.2
497 BLACK BAPT EST[2]	NA	1,054	1,370*	16.4	17.1
GEORGE	**57**	**10,152**	**13,471***	**80.8**	**100.0**
053 ASSEMB OF GOD	4	218	304	1.8	2.3
059 BAPT MISS ASSN	13	1,572	2,040*	12.2	15.1
081 CATHOLIC	1	NA	165	1.0	1.2
081d LATIN	1	NA	165	1.0	1.2
127 CH GOD (CLEVE)	2	228	296*	1.8	2.2
151 L-D SAINTS	1	NA	90	.5	.7
165 CH OF NAZARENE	1	20	47	.3	.3
167 CHS OF CHRIST	3	172	224	1.3	1.7
266 INTRSTAT & ASC	9	1,179	1,530*	9.2	11.4
355 PRESB CH (USA)	1	47	61*	.4	.5
419 SO BAPT CONV	11	4,944	6,415*	38.5	47.6
449 UN METHODIST	11	1,391	1,805*	10.8	13.4
497 BLACK BAPT EST[2]	NA	381	494*	3.0	3.7
GREENE	**50**	**5,367**	**6,960***	**68.1**	**100.0**
053 ASSEMB OF GOD	2	129	160	1.6	2.3
059 BAPT MISS ASSN	4	423	548*	5.4	7.9
081 CATHOLIC	1	NA	31	.3	.4
081d LATIN	1	NA	31	.3	.4
123 CH GOD (ANDER)	1	5	20	.2	.3
127 CH GOD (CLEVE)	5	271	351*	3.4	5.0
167 CHS OF CHRIST	2	57	74	.7	1.1
223 FREE WILL BAPT	2	140	181*	1.8	2.6
266 INTRSTAT & ASC	2	247	320*	3.1	4.6
355 PRESB CH (USA)	1	73	95*	.9	1.4
356 PRESB CH AMER	1	117	119	1.2	1.7
419 SO BAPT CONV	19	2,585	3,350*	32.8	48.1
449 UN METHODIST	10	793	1,028*	10.1	14.8
497 BLACK BAPT EST[2]	NA	527	683*	6.7	9.8
GRENADA	**34**	**10,915**	**14,675***	**68.1**	**100.0**
053 ASSEMB OF GOD	1	29	50	.2	.3
081 CATHOLIC	1	NA	473	2.2	3.2
081d LATIN	1	NA	473	2.2	3.2
127 CH GOD (CLEVE)	1	189	245*	1.1	1.7
145 CH GOD PROPHCY	2	67	87*	.4	.6
165 CH OF NAZARENE	1	136	271	1.3	1.8
167 CHS OF CHRIST	4	457	603	2.8	4.1
193 EPISCOPAL	1	174	223	1.0	1.5
355 PRESB CH (USA)	2	117	151*	.7	1.0
356 PRESB CH AMER	1	151	155	.7	1.1
413 S.D.A.	1	20	26*	.1	.2
419 SO BAPT CONV	12	5,212	6,745*	31.3	46.0
449 UN METHODIST	7	1,310	1,695*	7.9	11.6
497 BLACK BAPT EST[2]	NA	3,053	3,951*	18.3	26.9
HANCOCK	**38**	**5,410**	**15,515***	**48.9**	**100.0**
053 ASSEMB OF GOD	2	241	315	1.0	2.0
059 BAPT MISS ASSN	5	882	1,117*	3.5	7.2
081 CATHOLIC	8	NA	8,133	25.6	52.4
081d LATIN	8	NA	8,133	25.6	52.4
127 CH GOD (CLEVE)	1	36	46*	.1	.3
151 L-D SAINTS	1	NA	387	1.2	2.5
167 CHS OF CHRIST	1	56	73	.2	.5
193 EPISCOPAL	2	339	553	1.7	3.6
283 LUTH—MO SYNOD	1	99	136	.4	.9
355 PRESB CH (USA)	2	246	311*	1.0	2.0
419 SO BAPT CONV	9	1,994	2,524*	7.9	16.3
449 UN METHODIST	6	677	857*	2.7	5.5
497 BLACK BAPT EST[2]	NA	840	1,063*	3.3	6.9
HARRISON	**169**	**56,464**	**102,508***	**62.0**	**100.0**
053 ASSEMB OF GOD	6	1,225	2,248	1.4	2.2
059 BAPT MISS ASSN	8	1,931	2,472*	1.5	2.4
081 CATHOLIC	22	NA	27,390	16.6	26.7
081d LATIN	22	NA	27,390	16.6	26.7
093 CHR CH (DISC)	1	103	141	.1	.1
097 CHR CHS&CHS CR	1	63	81*	-	.1
111 CH CR,SCIENTST	1	NR	NR	-	-
123 CH GOD (ANDER)	1	50	65	-	.1
127 CH GOD (CLEVE)	4	308	394*	.2	.4
145 CH GOD PROPHCY	1	33	42*	-	-
151 L-D SAINTS	3	NA	1,414	.9	1.4
165 CH OF NAZARENE	3	215	395	.2	.4
167 CHS OF CHRIST	7	550	738	.4	.7
193 EPISCOPAL	5	1,744	2,024	1.2	2.0

County and Denomination	Number of churches	Communicant, confirmed, full members	Total adherents		
			Number	Percent of total population	Percent of total adherents
207 E.L.C.A.	4	503	693	.4	.7
223 FREE WILL BAPT	1	40	51*	-	-
246 GREEK ORTHODOX	1	NR	NR	-	-
266 INTRSTAT & ASC	4	520	666*	.4	.6
283 LUTH—MO SYNOD	3	610	746	.5	.7
285 MENNONITE CH	1	81	86	.1	.1
355 PRESB CH (USA)	5	719	921*	.6	.9
356 PRESB CH AMER	3	972	1,118	.7	1.1
403 SALVATION ARMY	2	146	151	.1	.1
413 S.D.A.	2	221	283*	.2	.3
419 SO BAPT CONV	43	26,622	34,084*	20.6	33.3
435 UNITARIAN-UNIV	1	20	20	-	-
449 UN METHODIST	33	10,017	12,825*	7.8	12.5
496 JEWISH EST[1]	1	NA	150	.1	.1
497 BLACK BAPT EST[2]	NA	9,771	12,510*	7.6	12.2
499 INDEP.NON-CHAR[3]	2	NA	800	.5	.8
HINDS	**215**	**129,028**	**177,907***	**69.9**	**100.0**
005 AME ZION	1	500	565	.2	.3
053 ASSEMB OF GOD	7	1,823	1,808	.7	1.0
059 BAPT MISS ASSN	4	915	1,173*	.5	.7
081 CATHOLIC	8	NA	7,739	3.0	4.4
081d LATIN	8	NA	7,739	3.0	4.4
093 CHR CH (DISC)	5	847	1,053	.4	.6
097 CHR CHS&CHS CR	1	226	290*	.1	.2
111 CH CR,SCIENTST	1	NR	NR	-	-
123 CH GOD (ANDER)	3	215	275	.1	.2
127 CH GOD (CLEVE)	1	130	167*	.1	.1
145 CH GOD PROPHCY	2	67	86*	-	-
151 L-D SAINTS	2	NA	882	.3	.5
165 CH OF NAZARENE	4	463	837	.3	.5
167 CHS OF CHRIST	15	1,833	2,633	1.0	1.5
185 CUMBER PRESB	1	83	83	-	-
193 EPISCOPAL	11	4,787	5,778	2.3	3.2
207 E.L.C.A.	2	280	354	.1	.2
246 GREEK ORTHODOX	1	NR	NR	-	-
263 INT FOURSQ GOS	1	97	124*	-	.1
283 LUTH—MO SYNOD	5	645	831	.3	.5
285 MENNONITE CH	1	27	53	-	-
331 ORTH CH IN AM	1	NR	NR	-	-
339 PENT CH OF GOD	1	34	77	-	-
349 PENT HOLINESS	2	111	142*	.1	.1
355 PRESB CH (USA)	7	1,795	2,301*	.9	1.3
356 PRESB CH AMER	15	4,619	5,577	2.2	3.1
361 PRIM BAPT ASCS	1	163	209*	.1	.1
403 SALVATION ARMY	1	155	160	.1	.1
413 S.D.A.	3	1,362	1,746*	.7	1.0
419 SO BAPT CONV	60	61,647	79,029*	31.1	44.4
435 UNITARIAN-UNIV	1	42	53	-	-
449 UN METHODIST	40	17,872	22,911*	9.0	12.9
467 WESLEYAN	1	55	125	-	.1
496 JEWISH EST[1]	0	NA	450	.2	.3
497 BLACK BAPT EST[2]	NA	28,235	36,196*	14.2	20.3
498 INDEP.CHARIS.[3]	1	NA	700	.3	.4
499 INDEP.NON-CHAR[3]	5	NA	3,500	1.4	2.0
HOLMES	**61**	**11,182**	**15,361***	**71.1**	**100.0**
001 ADVENT CHR CH	1	26	36*	.2	.2
005 AME ZION	2	130	195	.9	1.3
081 CATHOLIC	1	NA	50	.2	.3
081d LATIN	1	NA	50	.2	.3
145 CH GOD PROPHCY	1	33	45*	.2	.3
165 CH OF NAZARENE	1	56	69	.3	.4
167 CHS OF CHRIST	4	106	131	.6	.9
193 EPISCOPAL	1	31	38	.2	.2
355 PRESB CH (USA)	1	11	15*	.1	.1
356 PRESB CH AMER	7	245	290	1.3	1.9
419 SO BAPT CONV	19	3,234	4,445*	20.6	28.9
449 UN METHODIST	22	1,703	2,341*	10.8	15.2
496 JEWISH EST[1]	1	NA	0	-	-
497 BLACK BAPT EST[2]	NA	5,607	7,706*	35.7	50.2
HUMPHREYS	**25**	**6,519**	**9,152***	**75.4**	**100.0**
059 BAPT MISS ASSN	2	141	196*	1.6	2.1
081 CATHOLIC	1	NA	125	1.0	1.4
081d LATIN	1	NA	125	1.0	1.4
123 CH GOD (ANDER)	1	18	20	.2	.2
127 CH GOD (CLEVE)	2	103	143*	1.2	1.6
167 CHS OF CHRIST	2	80	102	.8	1.1
193 EPISCOPAL	1	18	27	.2	.3
356 PRESB CH AMER	1	172	205	1.7	2.2
413 S.D.A.	1	34	47*	.4	.5
419 SO BAPT CONV	8	2,528	3,519*	29.0	38.5
449 UN METHODIST	6	609	848*	7.0	9.3
497 BLACK BAPT EST[2]	NA	2,816	3,920*	32.3	42.8

NA–Not applicable   NR–Not reported   *Total adherents estimated from known number of communicant, confirmed, full members.   - Represents a percent less than 0.1.   Percentages may not total due to rounding.
[1]See Appendix E   [2]See Appendix F   [3]See Appendix G   Lines in *italic* represent a breakdown of Catholic rites or Friends affiliations. They are included in their respective denominational total.

Table 4. Churches and Church Membership by County and Denomination: 1990

County and Denomination	Number of churches	Communicant, confirmed, full members	Total adherents		
			Number	Percent of total population	Percent of total adherents
ISSAQUENA	**3**	**570**	**755***	**39.5**	**100.0**
145 CH GOD PROPHCY	1	33	44*	2.3	5.8
419 SO BAPT CONV	1	139	184*	9.6	24.4
449 UN METHODIST	1	31	41*	2.1	5.4
497 BLACK BAPT EST[2]	NA	367	486*	25.5	64.4
ITAWAMBA	**70**	**9,601**	**11,883***	**59.4**	**100.0**
059 BAPT MISS ASSN	12	2,618	3,196*	16.0	26.9
081 CATHOLIC	1	NA	68	.3	.6
081d LATIN	1	NA	68	.3	.6
097 CHR CHS&CHS CR	1	59	72*	.4	.6
145 CH GOD PROPHCY	3	101	123*	.6	1.0
167 CHS OF CHRIST	12	763	1,030	5.1	8.7
223 FREE WILL BAPT	2	333	406*	2.0	3.4
356 PRESB CH AMER	1	134	161	.8	1.4
361 PRIM BAPT ASCS	1	39	48*	.2	.4
419 SO BAPT CONV	16	2,997	3,658*	18.3	30.8
449 UN METHODIST	21	2,231	2,723*	13.6	22.9
497 BLACK BAPT EST[2]	NA	326	398*	2.0	3.3
JACKSON	**149**	**47,543**	**73,578***	**63.8**	**100.0**
005 AME ZION	3	1,230	1,265	1.1	1.7
053 ASSEMB OF GOD	18	1,939	3,108	2.7	4.2
059 BAPT MISS ASSN	8	1,049	1,358*	1.2	1.8
081 CATHOLIC	10	NA	11,244	9.8	15.3
081d LATIN	10	NA	11,244	9.8	15.3
093 CHR CH (DISC)	1	80	126	.1	.2
123 CH GOD (ANDER)	2	65	83	.1	.1
127 CH GOD (CLEVE)	1	50	65*	.1	.1
145 CH GOD PROPHCY	1	33	43*	-	.1
151 L-D SAINTS	1	NA	326	.3	.4
165 CH OF NAZARENE	2	202	169	.1	.2
167 CHS OF CHRIST	10	695	1,068	.9	1.5
193 EPISCOPAL	3	784	1,064	.9	1.4
207 E.L.C.A.	2	412	547	.5	.7
249 AP CATH ASSYR	0	17	72	.1	.1
266 INTRSTAT & ASC	2	128	166*	.1	.2
283 LUTH—MO SYNOD	2	217	289	.3	.4
349 PENT HOLINESS	2	127	164*	.1	.2
355 PRESB CH (USA)	3	836	1,082*	.9	1.5
356 PRESB CH AMER	2	215	266	.2	.4
403 SALVATION ARMY	1	79	97	.1	.1
413 S.D.A.	1	43	56*	-	.1
419 SO BAPT CONV	43	24,554	31,780*	27.6	43.2
449 UN METHODIST	31	7,650	9,901*	8.6	13.5
497 BLACK BAPT EST[2]	NA	7,138	9,239*	8.0	12.6
JASPER	**73**	**11,429**	**14,914***	**87.1**	**100.0**
053 ASSEMB OF GOD	3	83	119	.7	.8
059 BAPT MISS ASSN	6	1,031	1,343*	7.8	9.0
081 CATHOLIC	1	NA	60	.4	.4
081d LATIN	1	NA	60	.4	.4
123 CH GOD (ANDER)	2	94	130	.8	.9
167 CHS OF CHRIST	1	50	60	.4	.4
355 PRESB CH (USA)	4	117	152*	.9	1.0
356 PRESB CH AMER	2	163	163	1.0	1.1
361 PRIM BAPT ASCS	3	90	117*	.7	.8
419 SO BAPT CONV	22	3,892	5,071*	29.6	34.0
449 UN METHODIST	29	2,934	3,823*	22.3	25.6
497 BLACK BAPT EST[2]	NA	2,975	3,876*	22.6	26.0
JEFFERSON	**28**	**4,255**	**6,123***	**70.8**	**100.0**
081 CATHOLIC	2	NA	270	3.1	4.4
081d LATIN	2	NA	270	3.1	4.4
093 CHR CH (DISC)	1	20	27	.3	.4
167 CHS OF CHRIST	1	8	11	.1	.2
193 EPISCOPAL	1	6	6	.1	.1
355 PRESB CH (USA)	1	14	19*	.2	.3
356 PRESB CH AMER	1	30	30	.3	.5
361 PRIM BAPT ASCS	1	17	23*	.3	.4
413 S.D.A.	1	64	88*	1.0	1.4
419 SO BAPT CONV	7	530	731*	8.4	11.9
449 UN METHODIST	12	1,011	1,394*	16.1	22.8
497 BLACK BAPT EST[2]	NA	2,555	3,524*	40.7	57.6
JEFFERSON DAVIS	**28**	**7,135**	**9,796***	**69.7**	**100.0**
081 CATHOLIC	3	NA	500	3.6	5.1
081d LATIN	3	NA	500	3.6	5.1
165 CH OF NAZARENE	1	57	47	.3	.5
171 CH GOD-GEN CON	1	16	21*	.1	.2
266 INTRSTAT & ASC	2	219	287*	2.0	2.9
356 PRESB CH AMER	1	155	181	1.3	1.8
419 SO BAPT CONV	14	3,502	4,587*	32.6	46.8
449 UN METHODIST	6	558	731*	5.2	7.5

County and Denomination	Number of churches	Communicant, confirmed, full members	Total adherents		
			Number	Percent of total population	Percent of total adherents
497 BLACK BAPT EST[2]	NA	2,628	3,442*	24.5	35.1
JONES	**141**	**37,834**	**49,113***	**79.2**	**100.0**
005 AME ZION	2	315	410	.7	.8
053 ASSEMB OF GOD	9	488	772	1.2	1.6
059 BAPT MISS ASSN	21	4,317	5,477*	8.8	11.2
081 CATHOLIC	1	NA	775	1.2	1.6
081d LATIN	1	NA	775	1.2	1.6
123 CH GOD (ANDER)	4	195	238	.4	.5
127 CH GOD (CLEVE)	3	292	370*	.6	.8
151 L-D SAINTS	1	NA	155	.2	.3
165 CH OF NAZARENE	2	104	247	.4	.5
167 CHS OF CHRIST	3	279	377	.6	.8
193 EPISCOPAL	1	271	309	.5	.6
207 E.L.C.A.	1	62	74	.1	.2
216 EVAN PRESBY CH	1	285	286	.5	.6
223 FREE WILL BAPT	2	64	81*	.1	.2
266 INTRSTAT & ASC	3	289	367*	.6	.7
355 PRESB CH (USA)	3	411	521*	.8	1.1
356 PRESB CH AMER	2	106	110	.2	.2
361 PRIM BAPT ASCS	1	51	65*	.1	.1
403 SALVATION ARMY	1	88	92	.1	.2
413 S.D.A.	3	174	221*	.4	.4
419 SO BAPT CONV	50	22,214	28,184*	45.4	57.4
435 UNITARIAN-UNIV	2	40	55	.1	.1
449 UN METHODIST	24	3,959	5,023*	8.1	10.2
467 WESLEYAN	1	32	85	.1	.2
497 BLACK BAPT EST[2]	NA	3,798	4,819*	7.8	9.8
KEMPER	**50**	**5,993**	**7,803***	**75.3**	**100.0**
053 ASSEMB OF GOD	2	115	134	1.3	1.7
123 CH GOD (ANDER)	1	7	23	.2	.3
151 L-D SAINTS	1	NA	136	1.3	1.7
167 CHS OF CHRIST	1	25	34	.3	.4
223 FREE WILL BAPT	1	53	68*	.7	.9
356 PRESB CH AMER	5	190	197	1.9	2.5
419 SO BAPT CONV	15	1,762	2,268*	21.9	29.1
449 UN METHODIST	24	1,876	2,414*	23.3	30.9
497 BLACK BAPT EST[2]	NA	1,965	2,529*	24.4	32.4
LAFAYETTE	**65**	**13,775**	**18,316***	**57.6**	**100.0**
053 ASSEMB OF GOD	1	36	73	.2	.4
059 BAPT MISS ASSN	1	44	52*	.2	.3
081 CATHOLIC	2	NA	1,476	4.6	8.1
081d LATIN	2	NA	1,476	4.6	8.1
151 L-D SAINTS	1	NA	184	.6	1.0
165 CH OF NAZARENE	1	30	40	.1	.2
167 CHS OF CHRIST	7	485	677	2.1	3.7
193 EPISCOPAL	1	298	463	1.5	2.5
223 FREE WILL BAPT	2	414	493*	1.5	2.7
283 LUTH—MO SYNOD	1	57	71	.2	.4
355 PRESB CH (USA)	2	570	679*	2.1	3.7
356 PRESB CH AMER	1	0	0	-	-
361 PRIM BAPT ASCS	2	63	75*	.2	.4
419 SO BAPT CONV	23	7,465	8,894*	27.9	48.6
449 UN METHODIST	20	2,355	2,806*	8.8	15.3
497 BLACK BAPT EST[2]	NA	1,958	2,333*	7.3	12.7
LAMAR	**52**	**12,205**	**16,752***	**55.1**	**100.0**
059 BAPT MISS ASSN	6	1,152	1,503*	4.9	9.0
081 CATHOLIC	1	NA	821	2.7	4.9
081d LATIN	1	NA	821	2.7	4.9
123 CH GOD (ANDER)	1	7	12	-	.1
127 CH GOD (CLEVE)	2	103	134*	.4	.8
167 CHS OF CHRIST	1	51	67	.2	.4
266 INTRSTAT & ASC	9	885	1,155*	3.8	6.9
361 PRIM BAPT ASCS	2	91	119*	.4	.7
413 S.D.A.	1	255	333*	1.1	2.0
419 SO BAPT CONV	18	7,252	9,464*	31.1	56.5
449 UN METHODIST	11	1,517	1,980*	6.5	11.8
497 BLACK BAPT EST[2]	NA	892	1,164*	3.8	6.9
LAUDERDALE	**152**	**43,937**	**58,957***	**78.0**	**100.0**
005 AME ZION	3	540	681	.9	1.2
053 ASSEMB OF GOD	8	864	1,134	1.5	1.9
059 BAPT MISS ASSN	2	204	261*	.3	.4
081 CATHOLIC	2	NA	2,050	2.7	3.5
081d LATIN	2	NA	2,050	2.7	3.5
093 CHR CH (DISC)	1	374	555	.7	.9
097 CHR CHS&CHS CR	1	40	51*	.1	.1
111 CH CR,SCIENTST	1	NR	NR	-	-
123 CH GOD (ANDER)	10	534	743	1.0	1.3
145 CH GOD PROPHCY	2	67	86*	.1	.1
151 L-D SAINTS	1	NA	357	.5	.6
165 CH OF NAZARENE	2	509	762	1.0	1.3

Table 4. Churches and Church Membership by County and Denomination: 1990

County and Denomination		Number of churches	Communicant, confirmed, full members	Total adherents		
				Number	Percent of total population	Percent of total adherents
167	CHS OF CHRIST	6	327	440	.6	.7
171	CH GOD–GEN CON	1	54	69*	.1	.1
193	EPISCOPAL	2	827	1,133	1.5	1.9
263	INT FOURSQ GOS	1	126	161*	.2	.3
283	LUTH—MO SYNOD	2	112	159	.2	.3
285	MENNONITE CH	1	31	44	.1	.1
349	PENT HOLINESS	4	236	302*	.4	.5
355	PRESB CH (USA)	6	1,072	1,373*	1.8	2.3
356	PRESB CH AMER	4	232	235	.3	.4
361	PRIM BAPT ASCS	1	15	19*	-	-
403	SALVATION ARMY	1	158	172	.2	.3
413	S.D.A.	3	484	620*	.8	1.1
419	SO BAPT CONV	48	23,156	29,654*	39.2	50.3
449	UN METHODIST	37	7,528	9,640*	12.8	16.4
496	JEWISH EST[1]	2	NA	0	-	-
497	BLACK BAPT EST[2]	NA	6,447	8,256*	10.9	14.0
LAWRENCE		**35**	**7,665**	**9,976***	**80.1**	**100.0**
053	ASSEMB OF GOD	1	8	26	.2	.3
081	CATHOLIC	0	NA	30	.2	.3
081d	*LATIN*	*0*	*NA*	*30*	*.2*	*.3*
123	CH GOD (ANDER)	1	30	60	.5	.6
145	CH GOD PROPHCY	1	33	43*	.3	.4
165	CH OF NAZARENE	1	30	0	-	-
167	CHS OF CHRIST	2	52	63	.5	.6
356	PRESB CH AMER	1	12	26	.2	.3
419	SO BAPT CONV	23	5,590	7,251*	58.2	72.7
449	UN METHODIST	5	495	642*	5.2	6.4
497	BLACK BAPT EST[2]	NA	1,415	1,835*	14.7	18.4
LEAKE		**74**	**10,742**	**13,950***	**75.7**	**100.0**
005	AME ZION	2	140	195	1.1	1.4
053	ASSEMB OF GOD	2	55	52	.3	.4
081	CATHOLIC	1	NA	214	1.2	1.5
081d	*LATIN*	*1*	*NA*	*214*	*1.2*	*1.5*
093	CHR CH (DISC)	1	45	48	.3	.3
097	CHR CHS&CHS CR	1	40	51*	.3	.4
123	CH GOD (ANDER)	2	106	121	.7	.9
127	CH GOD (CLEVE)	1	87	111*	.6	.8
151	L-D SAINTS	1	NA	91	.5	.7
167	CHS OF CHRIST	1	30	65	.4	.5
171	CH GOD-GEN CON	1	0	0*	-	-
185	CUMBER PRESB	2	238	242	1.3	1.7
356	PRESB CH AMER	3	254	271	1.5	1.9
361	PRIM BAPT ASCS	3	109	140*	.8	1.0
419	SO BAPT CONV	37	6,195	7,937*	43.1	56.9
449	UN METHODIST	16	1,197	1,534*	8.3	11.0
497	BLACK BAPT EST[2]	NA	2,246	2,878*	15.6	20.6
LEE		**133**	**35,109**	**46,802***	**71.4**	**100.0**
053	ASSEMB OF GOD	4	286	353	.5	.8
055	AS REF PRES CH	1	22	22	-	-
059	BAPT MISS ASSN	8	1,213	1,560*	2.4	3.3
081	CATHOLIC	2	NA	993	1.5	2.1
081d	*LATIN*	*2*	*NA*	*993*	*1.5*	*2.1*
093	CHR CH (DISC)	2	291	354	.5	.8
097	CHR CHS&CHS CR	5	526	676*	1.0	1.4
127	CH GOD (CLEVE)	1	233	300*	.5	.6
145	CH GOD PROPHCY	5	168	216*	.3	.5
151	L-D SAINTS	1	NA	204	.3	.4
165	CH OF NAZARENE	1	68	110	.2	.2
167	CHS OF CHRIST	11	1,483	2,065	3.1	4.4
193	EPISCOPAL	1	217	305	.5	.7
223	FREE WILL BAPT	3	533	685*	1.0	1.5
283	LUTH—MO SYNOD	1	138	184	.3	.4
355	PRESB CH (USA)	8	784	1,008*	1.5	2.2
356	PRESB CH AMER	2	235	281	.4	.6
403	SALVATION ARMY	1	124	124	.2	.3
413	S.D.A.	2	96	123*	.2	.3
419	SO BAPT CONV	45	19,609	25,211*	38.4	53.9
449	UN METHODIST	27	5,638	7,249*	11.1	15.5
496	JEWISH EST[1]	1	NA	0	-	-
497	BLACK BAPT EST[2]	NA	3,445	4,429*	6.8	9.5
498	INDEP.CHARIS.[3]	1	NA	350	.5	.7
LEFLORE		**49**	**17,223**	**24,076***	**64.5**	**100.0**
053	ASSEMB OF GOD	1	33	75	.2	.3
081	CATHOLIC	2	NA	840	2.2	3.5
081d	*LATIN*	*2*	*NA*	*840*	*2.2*	*3.5*
093	CHR CH (DISC)	3	358	521	1.4	2.2
127	CH GOD (CLEVE)	2	248	331*	.9	1.4
145	CH GOD PROPHCY	2	67	89*	.2	.4
151	L-D SAINTS	1	NA	169	.5	.7
167	CHS OF CHRIST	3	318	413	1.1	1.7
193	EPISCOPAL	1	367	509	1.4	2.1
223	FREE WILL BAPT	1	30	40*	.1	.2

County and Denomination		Number of churches	Communicant, confirmed, full members	Total adherents		
				Number	Percent of total population	Percent of total adherents
283	LUTH—MO SYNOD	1	43	46	.1	.2
339	PENT CH OF GOD	1	35	77	.2	.3
355	PRESB CH (USA)	1	375	501*	1.3	2.1
356	PRESB CH AMER	2	247	331	.9	1.4
403	SALVATION ARMY	1	98	103	.3	.4
413	S.D.A.	1	264	352*	.9	1.5
419	SO BAPT CONV	13	6,942	9,268*	24.8	38.5
449	UN METHODIST	11	2,243	2,995*	8.0	12.4
496	JEWISH EST[1]	2	NA	0	-	-
497	BLACK BAPT EST[2]	NA	5,555	7,416*	19.9	30.8
LINCOLN		**86**	**21,188**	**28,383***	**93.7**	**100.0**
053	ASSEMB OF GOD	3	199	315	1.0	1.1
081	CATHOLIC	1	NA	495	1.6	1.7
081d	*LATIN*	*1*	*NA*	*495*	*1.6*	*1.7*
123	CH GOD (ANDER)	1	75	100	.3	.4
127	CH GOD (CLEVE)	1	31	39*	.1	.1
151	L-D SAINTS	1	NA	190	.6	.7
165	CH OF NAZARENE	1	74	179	.6	.6
167	CHS OF CHRIST	14	1,210	1,720	5.7	6.1
193	EPISCOPAL	1	71	86	.3	.3
355	PRESB CH (USA)	1	31	39*	.1	.1
356	PRESB CH AMER	1	386	465	1.5	1.6
361	PRIM BAPT ASCS	2	237	301*	1.0	1.1
413	S.D.A.	2	100	127*	.4	.4
419	SO BAPT CONV	39	14,198	18,019*	59.5	63.5
449	UN METHODIST	16	2,359	2,994*	9.9	10.5
496	JEWISH EST[1]	1	NA	0	-	-
497	BLACK BAPT EST[2]	NA	2,217	2,814*	9.3	9.9
499	INDEP.NON-CHAR[3]	1	NA	500	1.7	1.8
LOWNDES		**88**	**27,707**	**37,952***	**64.0**	**100.0**
053	ASSEMB OF GOD	4	666	1,159	2.0	3.1
059	BAPT MISS ASSN	2	363	473*	.8	1.2
081	CATHOLIC	1	NA	730	1.2	1.9
081d	*LATIN*	*1*	*NA*	*730*	*1.2*	*1.9*
097	CHR CHS&CHS CR	1	220	287*	.5	.8
111	CH CR,SCIENTST	1	NR	NR	-	-
145	CH GOD PROPHCY	1	33	43*	.1	.1
151	L-D SAINTS	1	NA	295	.5	.8
165	CH OF NAZARENE	1	137	161	.3	.4
167	CHS OF CHRIST	9	1,156	1,547	2.6	4.1
185	CUMBER PRESB	4	410	449	.8	1.2
193	EPISCOPAL	2	463	616	1.0	1.6
207	E.L.C.A.	1	111	159	.3	.4
216	EVAN PRESBY CH	1	83	89	.2	.2
223	FREE WILL BAPT	3	330	430*	.7	1.1
266	INTRSTAT & ASC	1	7	9*	-	-
283	LUTH—MO SYNOD	1	76	100	.2	.3
285	MENNONITE CH	1	25	40	.1	.1
339	PENT CH OF GOD	1	78	150	.3	.4
355	PRESB CH (USA)	3	224	292*	.5	.8
356	PRESB CH AMER	1	278	340	.6	.9
403	SALVATION ARMY	1	85	96	.2	.3
413	S.D.A.	2	213	278*	.5	.7
419	SO BAPT CONV	23	13,456	17,541*	29.6	46.2
449	UN METHODIST	19	3,852	5,022*	8.5	13.2
469	WELS	1	34	47	.1	.1
496	JEWISH EST[1]	1	NA	0	-	-
497	BLACK BAPT EST[2]	NA	5,407	7,049*	11.9	18.6
498	INDEP.CHARIS.[3]	1	NA	550	.9	1.4
MADISON		**69**	**21,039**	**29,272***	**54.4**	**100.0**
005	AME ZION	10	3,225	3,706	6.9	12.7
053	ASSEMB OF GOD	2	64	90	.2	.3
081	CATHOLIC	5	NA	2,153	4.0	7.4
081d	*LATIN*	*5*	*NA*	*2,153*	*4.0*	*7.4*
093	CHR CH (DISC)	1	50	68	.1	.2
123	CH GOD (ANDER)	1	46	46	.1	.2
145	CH GOD PROPHCY	1	33	43*	.1	.1
165	CH OF NAZARENE	1	33	49	.1	.2
167	CHS OF CHRIST	5	360	473	.9	1.6
193	EPISCOPAL	2	333	458	.9	1.6
355	PRESB CH (USA)	1	321	420*	.8	1.4
356	PRESB CH AMER	4	661	850	1.6	2.9
413	S.D.A.	1	188	246*	.5	.8
419	SO BAPT CONV	16	7,635	9,995*	18.6	34.1
443	UN C OF CHRIST	1	36	47*	.1	.2
449	UN METHODIST	16	2,809	3,677*	6.8	12.6
467	WESLEYAN	1	73	85	.2	.3
496	JEWISH EST[1]	1	NA	95	.2	.3
497	BLACK BAPT EST[2]	NA	5,172	6,771*	12.6	23.1
MARION		**69**	**16,130**	**21,522***	**84.3**	**100.0**
053	ASSEMB OF GOD	2	138	150	.6	.7
059	BAPT MISS ASSN	4	865	1,125*	4.4	5.2

NA–Not applicable   NR–Not reported   *Total adherents estimated from known number of communicant, confirmed, full members.   - Represents a percent less than 0.1.   Percentages may not total due to rounding.
[1]See Appendix E   [2]See Appendix F   [3]See Appendix G   Lines in *italic* represent a breakdown of Catholic rites or Friends affiliations. They are included in their respective denominational total.

MISSISSIPPI

Table 4. Churches and Church Membership by County and Denomination: 1990

County and Denomination	Number of churches	Communicant, confirmed, full members	Total adherents Number	Percent of total population	Percent of total adherents
081 CATHOLIC	1	NA	217	.8	1.0
081d *LATIN*	*1*	*NA*	*217*	*.8*	*1.0*
127 CH GOD (CLEVE)	9	716	931*	3.6	4.3
145 CH GOD PROPHCY	1	33	43*	.2	.2
151 L-D SAINTS	1	NA	361	1.4	1.7
165 CH OF NAZARENE	1	42	70	.3	.3
167 CHS OF CHRIST	2	47	61	.2	.3
193 EPISCOPAL	1	45	55	.2	.3
266 INTRSTAT & ASC	8	983	1,278*	5.0	5.9
356 PRESB CH AMER	1	114	136	.5	.6
413 S.D.A.	2	59	77*	.3	.4
419 SO BAPT CONV	22	9,281	12,068*	47.2	56.1
449 UN METHODIST	14	1,913	2,487*	9.7	11.6
497 BLACK BAPT EST[2]	NA	1,894	2,463*	9.6	11.4
MARSHALL	**56**	**11,345**	**15,136***	**49.9**	**100.0**
053 ASSEMB OF GOD	2	83	116	.4	.8
081 CATHOLIC	1	NA	220	.7	1.5
081d *LATIN*	*1*	*NA*	*220*	*.7*	*1.5*
151 L-D SAINTS	1	NA	155	.5	1.0
167 CHS OF CHRIST	8	511	638	2.1	4.2
193 EPISCOPAL	1	64	77	.3	.5
283 LUTH—MO SYNOD	1	29	29	.1	.2
355 PRESB CH (USA)	4	181	236*	.8	1.6
361 PRIM BAPT ASCS	1	39	51*	.2	.3
419 SO BAPT CONV	19	5,131	6,692*	22.0	44.2
449 UN METHODIST	18	1,534	2,001*	6.6	13.2
497 BLACK BAPT EST[2]	NA	3,773	4,921*	16.2	32.5
MONROE	**104**	**19,068**	**24,732***	**67.6**	**100.0**
053 ASSEMB OF GOD	3	180	301	.8	1.2
059 BAPT MISS ASSN	1	348	446*	1.2	1.8
081 CATHOLIC	2	NA	201	.5	.8
081d *LATIN*	*2*	*NA*	*201*	*.5*	*.8*
089 CHR & MISS AL	1	33	58	.2	.2
097 CHR CHS&CHS CR	2	451	578*	1.6	2.3
127 CH GOD (CLEVE)	3	183	235*	.6	1.0
145 CH GOD PROPHCY	4	135	173*	.5	.7
167 CHS OF CHRIST	14	1,114	1,446	4.0	5.8
193 EPISCOPAL	1	74	88	.2	.4
223 FREE WILL BAPT	6	614	787*	2.2	3.2
285 MENNONITE CH	1	26	35	.1	.1
355 PRESB CH (USA)	3	199	255*	.7	1.0
356 PRESB CH AMER	1	57	57	.2	.2
361 PRIM BAPT ASCS	2	184	236*	.6	1.0
413 S.D.A.	1	60	77*	.2	.3
419 SO BAPT CONV	32	9,002	11,543*	31.6	46.7
449 UN METHODIST	27	3,686	4,726*	12.9	19.1
497 BLACK BAPT EST[2]	NA	2,722	3,490*	9.5	14.1
MONTGOMERY	**42**	**8,335**	**10,759***	**86.9**	**100.0**
001 ADVENT CHR CH	1	25	32*	.3	.3
081 CATHOLIC	1	NA	70	.6	.7
081d *LATIN*	*1*	*NA*	*70*	*.6*	*.7*
127 CH GOD (CLEVE)	3	174	223*	1.8	2.1
167 CHS OF CHRIST	4	230	305	2.5	2.8
193 EPISCOPAL	1	7	12	.1	.1
339 PENT CH OF GOD	1	34	77	.6	.7
356 PRESB CH AMER	1	121	132	1.1	1.2
419 SO BAPT CONV	18	4,484	5,737*	46.3	53.3
449 UN METHODIST	12	1,397	1,787*	14.4	16.6
497 BLACK BAPT EST[2]	NA	1,863	2,384*	19.2	22.2
NESHOBA	**94**	**13,405**	**18,140***	**73.1**	**100.0**
053 ASSEMB OF GOD	3	134	257	1.0	1.4
059 BAPT MISS ASSN	1	89	115*	.5	.6
081 CATHOLIC	2	NA	650	2.6	3.6
081d *LATIN*	*2*	*NA*	*650*	*2.6*	*3.6*
123 CH GOD (ANDER)	3	71	111	.4	.6
127 CH GOD (CLEVE)	1	55	71*	.3	.4
145 CH GOD PROPHCY	1	33	43*	.2	.2
165 CH OF NAZARENE	2	58	126	.5	.7
167 CHS OF CHRIST	2	167	225	.9	1.2
185 CUMBER PRESB	2	89	99	.4	.5
193 EPISCOPAL	1	27	24	.1	.1
223 FREE WILL BAPT	1	6	8*	-	-
285 MENNONITE CH	2	103	126	.5	.7
339 PENT CH OF GOD	1	34	77	.3	.4
355 PRESB CH (USA)	1	27	35*	.1	.2
356 PRESB CH AMER	1	130	134	.5	.7
419 SO BAPT CONV	43	8,536	11,057*	44.6	61.0
449 UN METHODIST	27	2,738	3,547*	14.3	19.6
497 BLACK BAPT EST[2]	NA	1,108	1,435*	5.8	7.9

County and Denomination	Number of churches	Communicant, confirmed, full members	Total adherents Number	Percent of total population	Percent of total adherents
NEWTON	**66**	**11,560**	**14,761***	**72.7**	**100.0**
053 ASSEMB OF GOD	1	26	30	.1	.2
081 CATHOLIC	2	NA	154	.8	1.0
081d *LATIN*	*2*	*NA*	*154*	*.8*	*1.0*
097 CHR CHS&CHS CR	2	160	202*	1.0	1.4
123 CH GOD (ANDER)	3	155	177	.9	1.2
127 CH GOD (CLEVE)	6	402	507*	2.5	3.4
167 CHS OF CHRIST	3	100	206	1.0	1.4
185 CUMBER PRESB	1	122	131	.6	.9
193 EPISCOPAL	1	11	11	.1	.1
339 PENT CH OF GOD	1	35	77	.4	.5
355 PRESB CH (USA)	1	25	32*	.2	.2
356 PRESB CH AMER	3	137	137	.7	.9
361 PRIM BAPT ASCS	1	8	10*	-	.1
419 SO BAPT CONV	29	6,742	8,501*	41.9	57.6
449 UN METHODIST	12	1,640	2,068*	10.2	14.0
497 BLACK BAPT EST[2]	NA	1,997	2,518*	12.4	17.1
NOXUBEE	**48**	**6,753**	**9,254***	**73.4**	**100.0**
005 AME ZION	1	83	148	1.2	1.6
081 CATHOLIC	1	NA	34	.3	.4
081d *LATIN*	*1*	*NA*	*34*	*.3*	*.4*
123 CH GOD (ANDER)	1	12	22	.2	.2
143 CG IN CR(MENN)	2	319	437*	3.5	4.7
167 CHS OF CHRIST	2	44	51	.4	.6
185 CUMBER PRESB	2	69	70	.6	.8
193 EPISCOPAL	2	27	29	.2	.3
285 MENNONITE CH	4	193	261	2.1	2.8
356 PRESB CH AMER	3	115	138	1.1	1.5
419 SO BAPT CONV	11	1,511	2,068*	16.4	22.3
449 UN METHODIST	19	1,439	1,970*	15.6	21.3
497 BLACK BAPT EST[2]	NA	2,941	4,026*	31.9	43.5
OKTIBBEHA	**59**	**17,868**	**23,648***	**61.6**	**100.0**
053 ASSEMB OF GOD	1	30	35	.1	.1
059 BAPT MISS ASSN	1	39	47*	.1	.2
081 CATHOLIC	2	NA	1,800	4.7	7.6
081d *LATIN*	*2*	*NA*	*1,800*	*4.7*	*7.6*
093 CHR CH (DISC)	1	12	16	-	.1
123 CH GOD (ANDER)	1	8	16	-	.1
127 CH GOD (CLEVE)	2	183	223*	.6	.9
145 CH GOD PROPHCY	1	33	40*	.1	.2
165 CH OF NAZARENE	0	0	28	.1	.1
167 CHS OF CHRIST	5	457	605	1.6	2.6
193 EPISCOPAL	1	251	314	.8	1.3
283 LUTH—MO SYNOD	1	95	129	.3	.5
355 PRESB CH (USA)	4	892	1,085*	2.8	4.6
356 PRESB CH AMER	1	88	110	.3	.5
419 SO BAPT CONV	19	8,586	10,447*	27.2	44.2
449 UN METHODIST	19	3,963	4,822*	12.6	20.4
497 BLACK BAPT EST[2]	NA	3,231	3,931*	10.2	16.6
PANOLA	**85**	**16,608**	**22,182***	**73.9**	**100.0**
005 AME ZION	12	1,902	2,478	8.3	11.2
053 ASSEMB OF GOD	2	97	207	.7	.9
081 CATHOLIC	2	NA	140	.5	.6
081d *LATIN*	*2*	*NA*	*140*	*.5*	*.6*
123 CH GOD (ANDER)	1	50	93	.3	.4
127 CH GOD (CLEVE)	2	78	104*	.3	.5
165 CH OF NAZARENE	1	27	54	.2	.2
167 CHS OF CHRIST	7	625	772	2.6	3.5
193 EPISCOPAL	2	84	102	.3	.5
355 PRESB CH (USA)	4	410	544*	1.8	2.5
356 PRESB CH AMER	1	62	69	.2	.3
413 S.D.A.	1	31	41*	.1	.2
419 SO BAPT CONV	26	7,088	9,409*	31.4	42.4
449 UN METHODIST	24	2,589	3,437*	11.5	15.5
497 BLACK BAPT EST[2]	NA	3,565	4,732*	15.8	21.3
PEARL RIVER	**81**	**21,871**	**29,793***	**77.0**	**100.0**
053 ASSEMB OF GOD	2	126	220	.6	.7
059 BAPT MISS ASSN	18	3,123	4,021*	10.4	13.5
081 CATHOLIC	1	NA	1,209	3.1	4.1
081d *LATIN*	*1*	*NA*	*1,209*	*3.1*	*4.1*
127 CH GOD (CLEVE)	2	278	358*	.9	1.2
145 CH GOD PROPHCY	1	33	42*	.1	.1
151 L-D SAINTS	1	NA	322	.8	1.1
167 CHS OF CHRIST	2	72	91	.2	.3
193 EPISCOPAL	1	65	112	.3	.4
266 INTRSTAT & ASC	10	1,202	1,548*	4.0	5.2
283 LUTH—MO SYNOD	1	174	269	.7	.9
355 PRESB CH (USA)	1	18	23*	.1	.1
356 PRESB CH AMER	1	93	93	.2	.3
413 S.D.A.	1	12	15*	-	.1
419 SO BAPT CONV	32	13,697	17,636*	45.6	59.2

NA–Not applicable   NR–Not reported   *Total adherents estimated from known number of communicant, confirmed, full members.   - Represents a percent less than 0.1.   Percentages may not total due to rounding.
[1]See Appendix E   [2]See Appendix F   [3]See Appendix G   Lines in *italic* represent a breakdown of Catholic rites or Friends affiliations. They are included in their respective denominational total.

Table 4. Churches and Church Membership by County and Denomination: 1990

County and Denomination	Number of churches	Communicant, confirmed, full members	Total adherents Number	Percent of total population	Percent of total adherents
449 UN METHODIST	7	1,618	2,083*	5.4	7.0
497 BLACK BAPT EST2	NA	1,360	1,751*	4.5	5.9
PERRY	**46**	**6,113**	**8,231***	**75.8**	**100.0**
059 BAPT MISS ASSN	5	541	712*	6.6	8.7
081 CATHOLIC	0	NA	55	.5	.7
081d LATIN	0	NA	55	.5	.7
123 CH GOD (ANDER)	1	30	40	.4	.5
127 CH GOD (CLEVE)	4	200	263*	2.4	3.2
145 CH GOD PROPHCY	1	33	43*	.4	.5
151 L-D SAINTS	1	NA	130	1.2	1.6
167 CHS OF CHRIST	1	15	23	.2	.3
223 FREE WILL BAPT	3	113	149*	1.4	1.8
266 INTRSTAT & ASC	3	358	471*	4.3	5.7
356 PRESB CH AMER	1	18	20	.2	.2
419 SO BAPT CONV	18	3,552	4,676*	43.0	56.8
449 UN METHODIST	8	665	875*	8.1	10.6
497 BLACK BAPT EST2	NA	588	774*	7.1	9.4
PIKE	**68**	**19,872**	**26,948***	**73.1**	**100.0**
005 AME ZION	1	75	113	.3	.4
053 ASSEMB OF GOD	2	190	200	.5	.7
059 BAPT MISS ASSN	1	0	0*	-	-
081 CATHOLIC	3	NA	1,031	2.8	3.8
081d LATIN	3	NA	1,031	2.8	3.8
093 CHR CH (DISC)	1	85	112	.3	.4
111 CH CR,SCIENTST	1	NR	NR	-	-
127 CH GOD (CLEVE)	1	48	62*	.2	.2
145 CH GOD PROPHCY	1	33	43*	.1	.2
165 CH OF NAZARENE	2	365	490	1.3	1.8
167 CHS OF CHRIST	4	236	428	1.2	1.6
193 EPISCOPAL	1	204	237	.6	.9
216 EVAN PRESBY CH	1	17	19	.1	.1
283 LUTH—MO SYNOD	1	31	50	.1	.2
353 CHR BRETHREN	1	35	75	.2	.3
355 PRESB CH (USA)	3	448	582*	1.6	2.2
403 SALVATION ARMY	1	14	14	-	.1
413 S.D.A.	2	83	108*	.3	.4
415 S-D BAPTIST GC	1	31	40*	.1	.1
419 SO BAPT CONV	28	11,578	15,034*	40.8	55.8
449 UN METHODIST	12	2,267	2,944*	8.0	10.9
497 BLACK BAPT EST2	NA	4,132	5,366*	14.5	19.9
PONTOTOC	**82**	**14,299**	**18,121***	**81.5**	**100.0**
053 ASSEMB OF GOD	1	0	0	-	-
081 CATHOLIC	1	NA	54	.2	.3
081d LATIN	1	NA	54	.2	.3
145 CH GOD PROPHCY	1	33	42*	.2	.2
165 CH OF NAZARENE	1	59	69	.3	.4
167 CHS OF CHRIST	4	188	243	1.1	1.3
223 FREE WILL BAPT	5	373	472*	2.1	2.6
355 PRESB CH (USA)	3	90	114*	.5	.6
356 PRESB CH AMER	1	48	48	.2	.3
419 SO BAPT CONV	48	11,212	14,176*	63.7	78.2
449 UN METHODIST	17	1,516	1,917*	8.6	10.6
497 BLACK BAPT EST2	NA	780	986*	4.4	5.4
PRENTISS	**80**	**11,853**	**15,324***	**65.8**	**100.0**
053 ASSEMB OF GOD	1	51	73	.3	.5
059 BAPT MISS ASSN	4	503	627*	2.7	4.1
081 CATHOLIC	1	NA	57	.2	.4
081d LATIN	1	NA	57	.2	.4
097 CHR CHS&CHS CR	2	260	324*	1.4	2.1
127 CH GOD (CLEVE)	2	96	120*	.5	.8
145 CH GOD PROPHCY	1	33	41*	.2	.3
151 L-D SAINTS	1	NA	446	1.9	2.9
167 CHS OF CHRIST	16	1,244	1,586	6.8	10.3
223 FREE WILL BAPT	9	638	795*	3.4	5.2
355 PRESB CH (USA)	1	31	39*	.2	.3
361 PRIM BAPT ASCS	1	15	19*	.1	.1
419 SO BAPT CONV	24	5,817	7,252*	31.2	47.3
449 UN METHODIST	17	2,507	3,125*	13.4	20.4
497 BLACK BAPT EST2	NA	658	820*	3.5	5.4
QUITMAN	**30**	**7,196**	**9,569***	**91.2**	**100.0**
005 AME ZION	4	561	749	7.1	7.8
019 AMER BAPT USA	1	150	200*	1.9	2.1
053 ASSEMB OF GOD	1	32	39	.4	.4
093 CHR CH (DISC)	1	5	12	.1	.1
127 CH GOD (CLEVE)	1	108	144*	1.4	1.5
167 CHS OF CHRIST	2	65	90	.9	.9
356 PRESB CH AMER	1	97	117	1.1	1.2
419 SO BAPT CONV	11	3,392	4,512*	43.0	47.2
449 UN METHODIST	8	665	885*	8.4	9.2
497 BLACK BAPT EST2	NA	2,121	2,821*	26.9	29.5

County and Denomination	Number of churches	Communicant, confirmed, full members	Total adherents Number	Percent of total population	Percent of total adherents
RANKIN	**122**	**41,062**	**55,246***	**63.4**	**100.0**
053 ASSEMB OF GOD	5	388	541	.6	1.0
059 BAPT MISS ASSN	4	738	938*	1.1	1.7
081 CATHOLIC	2	NA	1,980	2.3	3.6
081d LATIN	2	NA	1,980	2.3	3.6
127 CH GOD (CLEVE)	4	947	1,204*	1.4	2.2
145 CH GOD PROPHCY	1	33	42*	-	.1
151 L-D SAINTS	1	NA	407	.5	.7
167 CHS OF CHRIST	5	240	332	.4	.6
193 EPISCOPAL	2	275	378	.4	.7
207 E.L.C.A.	1	147	188	.2	.3
216 EVAN PRESBY CH	1	462	478	.5	.9
223 FREE WILL BAPT	1	229	291*	.3	.5
266 INTRSTAT & ASC	1	48	61*	.1	.1
283 LUTH—MO SYNOD	1	64	89	.1	.2
339 PENT CH OF GOD	1	34	76	.1	.1
349 PENT HOLINESS	1	70	89*	.1	.2
356 PRESB CH AMER	2	421	465	.5	.8
413 S.D.A.	1	127	161*	.2	.3
419 SO BAPT CONV	57	26,126	33,206*	38.1	60.1
449 UN METHODIST	29	6,291	7,996*	9.2	14.5
496 JEWISH EST1	1	NA	154	.2	.3
497 BLACK BAPT EST2	NA	4,422	5,620*	6.4	10.2
498 INDEP.CHARIS.3	1	NA	550	.6	1.0
SCOTT	**78**	**14,553**	**19,140***	**79.3**	**100.0**
053 ASSEMB OF GOD	4	128	210	.9	1.1
059 BAPT MISS ASSN	1	137	178*	.7	.9
081 CATHOLIC	1	NA	100	.4	.5
081d LATIN	1	NA	100	.4	.5
097 CHR CHS&CHS CR	2	75	98*	.4	.5
127 CH GOD (CLEVE)	1	117	152*	.6	.8
151 L-D SAINTS	1	NA	96	.4	.5
167 CHS OF CHRIST	3	107	127	.5	.7
185 CUMBER PRESB	2	58	58	.2	.3
207 E.L.C.A.	1	23	24	.1	.1
356 PRESB CH AMER	2	93	112	.5	.6
361 PRIM BAPT ASCS	1	38	49*	.2	.3
419 SO BAPT CONV	38	7,925	10,317*	42.7	53.9
449 UN METHODIST	21	2,712	3,531*	14.6	18.4
497 BLACK BAPT EST2	NA	3,140	4,088*	16.9	21.4
SHARKEY	**18**	**4,009**	**5,653***	**80.0**	**100.0**
059 BAPT MISS ASSN	1	66	92*	1.3	1.6
081 CATHOLIC	1	NA	105	1.5	1.9
081d LATIN	1	NA	105	1.5	1.9
145 CH GOD PROPHCY	2	67	93*	1.3	1.6
167 CHS OF CHRIST	1	115	146	2.1	2.6
193 EPISCOPAL	1	73	82	1.2	1.5
356 PRESB CH AMER	1	14	14	.2	.2
413 S.D.A.	1	43	60*	.8	1.1
419 SO BAPT CONV	6	1,485	2,070*	29.3	36.6
449 UN METHODIST	4	541	754*	10.7	13.3
497 BLACK BAPT EST2	NA	1,605	2,237*	31.7	39.6
SIMPSON	**72**	**16,561**	**21,596***	**90.2**	**100.0**
053 ASSEMB OF GOD	3	129	123	.5	.6
059 BAPT MISS ASSN	1	54	70*	.3	.3
081 CATHOLIC	1	NA	123	.5	.6
081d LATIN	1	NA	123	.5	.6
127 CH GOD (CLEVE)	3	410	531*	2.2	2.5
145 CH GOD PROPHCY	2	67	87*	.4	.4
151 L-D SAINTS	1	NA	103	.4	.5
167 CHS OF CHRIST	3	80	129	.5	.6
353 CHR BRETHREN	1	132	133	.6	.6
356 PRESB CH AMER	2	182	211	.9	1.0
361 PRIM BAPT ASCS	2	173	224*	.9	1.0
419 SO BAPT CONV	45	11,578	14,997*	62.6	69.4
449 UN METHODIST	8	1,107	1,434*	6.0	6.6
497 BLACK BAPT EST2	NA	2,649	3,431*	14.3	15.9
SMITH	**69**	**9,906**	**12,734***	**86.1**	**100.0**
053 ASSEMB OF GOD	1	30	40	.3	.3
059 BAPT MISS ASSN	4	377	482*	3.3	3.8
081 CATHOLIC	1	NA	100	.7	.8
081d LATIN	1	NA	100	.7	.8
127 CH GOD (CLEVE)	1	23	29*	.2	.2
167 CHS OF CHRIST	1	11	20	.1	.2
207 E.L.C.A.	1	25	27	.2	.2
266 INTRSTAT & ASC	1	116	148*	1.0	1.2
356 PRESB CH AMER	2	120	133	.9	1.0
361 PRIM BAPT ASCS	1	45	57*	.4	.4
413 S.D.A.	1	29	37*	.3	.3
419 SO BAPT CONV	43	7,125	9,100*	61.5	71.5
449 UN METHODIST	12	1,226	1,566*	10.6	12.3

NA–Not applicable   NR–Not reported   *Total adherents estimated from known number of communicant, confirmed, full members.   - Represents a percent less than 0.1.   Percentages may not total due to rounding.
[1]See Appendix E   [2]See Appendix F   [3]See Appendix G   Lines in *italic* represent a breakdown of Catholic rites or Friends affiliations. They are included in their respective denominational total.

MISSISSIPPI

Table 4. Churches and Church Membership by County and Denomination: 1990

County and Denomination	Number of churches	Communicant, confirmed, full members	Total adherents Number	Percent of total population	Percent of total adherents
497 BLACK BAPT EST²	NA	779	995*	6.7	7.8
STONE	**29**	**5,703**	**7,550***	**70.2**	**100.0**
053 ASSEMB OF GOD	1	22	29	.3	.4
059 BAPT MISS ASSN	6	1,468	1,881*	17.5	24.9
081 CATHOLIC	1	NA	145	1.3	1.9
081d LATIN	1	NA	145	1.3	1.9
127 CH GOD (CLEVE)	1	61	78*	.7	1.0
151 L-D SAINTS	1	NA	92	.9	1.2
167 CHS OF CHRIST	1	42	57	.5	.8
266 INTRSTAT & ASC	6	665	852*	7.9	11.3
355 PRESB CH (USA)	1	60	77*	.7	1.0
419 SO BAPT CONV	5	1,953	2,503*	23.3	33.2
449 UN METHODIST	6	869	1,114*	10.4	14.8
497 BLACK BAPT EST²	NA	563	722*	6.7	9.6
SUNFLOWER	**56**	**14,826**	**20,096***	**61.1**	**100.0**
053 ASSEMB OF GOD	1	72	90	.3	.4
059 BAPT MISS ASSN	1	73	97*	.3	.5
081 CATHOLIC	2	NA	417	1.3	2.1
081d LATIN	2	NA	417	1.3	2.1
093 CHR CH (DISC)	4	86	116	.4	.6
123 CH GOD (ANDER)	2	44	52	.2	.3
127 CH GOD (CLEVE)	6	312	415*	1.3	2.1
165 CH OF NAZARENE	1	79	84	.3	.4
167 CHS OF CHRIST	5	424	579	1.8	2.9
193 EPISCOPAL	2	173	242	.7	1.2
356 PRESB CH AMER	1	193	221	.7	1.1
413 S.D.A.	1	147	196*	.6	1.0
419 SO BAPT CONV	17	6,044	8,039*	24.5	40.0
449 UN METHODIST	13	2,005	2,667*	8.1	13.3
497 BLACK BAPT EST²	NA	5,174	6,881*	20.9	34.2
TALLAHATCHIE	**51**	**8,316**	**11,176***	**73.5**	**100.0**
005 AME ZION	1	200	243	1.6	2.2
081 CATHOLIC	1	NA	62	.4	.6
081d LATIN	1	NA	62	.4	.6
097 CHR CHS&CHS CR	1	20	27*	.2	.2
127 CH GOD (CLEVE)	5	486	650*	4.3	5.8
145 CH GOD PROPHCY	5	168	225*	1.5	2.0
165 CH OF NAZARENE	1	60	116	.8	1.0
167 CHS OF CHRIST	6	212	281	1.8	2.5
193 EPISCOPAL	1	95	103	.7	.9
355 PRESB CH (USA)	6	276	369*	2.4	3.3
419 SO BAPT CONV	16	3,082	4,125*	27.1	36.9
449 UN METHODIST	8	676	905*	6.0	8.1
497 BLACK BAPT EST²	NA	3,041	4,070*	26.8	36.4
TATE	**54**	**12,592**	**16,722***	**78.0**	**100.0**
053 ASSEMB OF GOD	1	47	65	.3	.4
081 CATHOLIC	1	NA	116	.5	.7
081d LATIN	1	NA	116	.5	.7
123 CH GOD (ANDER)	1	100	100	.5	.6
127 CH GOD (CLEVE)	1	62	80*	.4	.5
151 L-D SAINTS	1	NA	336	1.6	2.0
165 CH OF NAZARENE	1	19	24	.1	.1
167 CHS OF CHRIST	15	2,062	2,704	12.6	16.2
207 E.L.C.A.	1	20	23	.1	.1
355 PRESB CH (USA)	1	126	163*	.8	1.0
419 SO BAPT CONV	21	6,447	8,323*	38.8	49.8
449 UN METHODIST	10	1,169	1,509*	7.0	9.0
497 BLACK BAPT EST²	NA	2,540	3,279*	15.3	19.6
TIPPAH	**73**	**11,439**	**14,724***	**75.4**	**100.0**
053 ASSEMB OF GOD	2	148	216	1.1	1.5
055 AS REF PRES CH	1	84	89	.5	.6
127 CH GOD (CLEVE)	1	35	44*	.2	.3
151 L-D SAINTS	1	NA	92	.5	.6
167 CHS OF CHRIST	8	597	1,003	5.1	6.8
185 CUMBER PRESB	1	144	144	.7	1.0
355 PRESB CH (USA)	5	415	523*	2.7	3.6
356 PRESB CH AMER	1	41	41	.2	.3
419 SO BAPT CONV	32	7,629	9,615*	49.2	65.3
449 UN METHODIST	21	1,569	1,978*	10.1	13.4
497 BLACK BAPT EST²	NA	777	979*	5.0	6.6
TISHOMINGO	**75**	**8,556**	**10,879***	**61.5**	**100.0**
053 ASSEMB OF GOD	1	9	14	.1	.1
059 BAPT MISS ASSN	6	374	458*	2.6	4.2
081 CATHOLIC	1	NA	26	.1	.2
081d LATIN	1	NA	26	.1	.2
127 CH GOD (CLEVE)	2	113	138*	.8	1.3
145 CH GOD PROPHCY	3	101	124*	.7	1.1
167 CHS OF CHRIST	10	781	1,035	5.9	9.5

County and Denomination	Number of churches	Communicant, confirmed, full members	Total adherents Number	Percent of total population	Percent of total adherents
223 FREE WILL BAPT	4	349	427*	2.4	3.9
361 PRIM BAPT ASCS	2	44	54*	.3	.5
419 SO BAPT CONV	26	5,127	6,274*	35.5	57.7
449 UN METHODIST	19	1,506	1,843*	10.4	16.9
497 BLACK BAPT EST²	NA	152	186*	1.1	1.7
499 INDEP.NON-CHAR³	1	NA	300	1.7	2.8
TUNICA	**11**	**3,573**	**5,082***	**62.2**	**100.0**
081 CATHOLIC	1	NA	24	.3	.5
081d LATIN	1	NA	24	.3	.5
145 CH GOD PROPHCY	1	33	47*	.6	.9
167 CHS OF CHRIST	2	129	162	2.0	3.2
193 EPISCOPAL	1	57	89	1.1	1.8
355 PRESB CH (USA)	1	140	199*	2.4	3.9
413 S.D.A.	1	36	51*	.6	1.0
419 SO BAPT CONV	2	698	991*	12.1	19.5
449 UN METHODIST	2	375	532*	6.5	10.5
497 BLACK BAPT EST²	NA	2,105	2,987*	36.6	58.8
UNION	**70**	**16,426**	**20,609***	**93.3**	**100.0**
053 ASSEMB OF GOD	2	163	180	.8	.9
055 AS REF PRES CH	3	391	434	2.0	2.1
081 CATHOLIC	1	NA	101	.5	.5
081d LATIN	1	NA	101	.5	.5
127 CH GOD (CLEVE)	2	160	200*	.9	1.0
165 CH OF NAZARENE	1	33	81	.4	.4
167 CHS OF CHRIST	5	368	455	2.1	2.2
355 PRESB CH (USA)	1	90	113*	.5	.5
419 SO BAPT CONV	39	12,324	15,420*	69.8	74.8
449 UN METHODIST	16	2,125	2,659*	12.0	12.9
497 BLACK BAPT EST²	NA	772	966*	4.4	4.7
WALTHALL	**30**	**8,123**	**10,940***	**76.2**	**100.0**
081 CATHOLIC	1	NA	167	1.2	1.5
081d LATIN	1	NA	167	1.2	1.5
167 CHS OF CHRIST	1	11	15	.1	.1
266 INTRSTAT & ASC	4	597	792*	5.5	7.2
285 MENNONITE CH	1	35	42	.3	.4
353 CHR BRETHREN	1	8	16	.1	.1
361 PRIM BAPT ASCS	2	84	111*	.8	1.0
419 SO BAPT CONV	13	4,394	5,827*	40.6	53.3
449 UN METHODIST	7	921	1,221*	8.5	11.2
497 BLACK BAPT EST²	NA	2,073	2,749*	19.2	25.1
WARREN	**62**	**23,509**	**33,690***	**70.4**	**100.0**
053 ASSEMB OF GOD	2	113	157	.3	.5
059 BAPT MISS ASSN	3	383	497*	1.0	1.5
081 CATHOLIC	3	NA	2,952	6.2	8.8
081d LATIN	3	NA	2,952	6.2	8.8
093 CHR CH (DISC)	2	188	200	.4	.6
111 CH CR,SCIENTST	1	NR	NR	-	-
123 CH GOD (ANDER)	1	8	19	-	.1
127 CH GOD (CLEVE)	1	57	74*	.2	.2
145 CH GOD PROPHCY	2	67	87*	.2	.3
151 L-D SAINTS	1	NA	260	.5	.8
165 CH OF NAZARENE	1	113	87	.2	.3
167 CHS OF CHRIST	7	658	864	1.8	2.6
193 EPISCOPAL	4	699	872	1.8	2.6
283 LUTH—MO SYNOD	1	143	221	.5	.7
339 PENT CH OF GOD	1	35	77	.2	.2
355 PRESB CH (USA)	2	550	714*	1.5	2.1
356 PRESB CH AMER	1	250	250	.5	.7
403 SALVATION ARMY	1	106	107	.2	.3
413 S.D.A.	2	226	293*	.6	.9
419 SO BAPT CONV	14	11,583	15,039*	31.4	44.6
449 UN METHODIST	11	3,751	4,870*	10.2	14.5
496 JEWISH EST¹	1	NA	105	.2	.3
497 BLACK BAPT EST²	NA	4,579	5,945*	12.4	17.6
WASHINGTON	**76**	**29,084**	**43,996***	**64.8**	**100.0**
053 ASSEMB OF GOD	6	818	793	1.2	1.8
059 BAPT MISS ASSN	2	219	298*	.4	.7
081 CATHOLIC	4	NA	3,605	5.3	8.2
081d LATIN	4	NA	3,605	5.3	8.2
093 CHR CH (DISC)	1	100	129	.2	.3
111 CH CR,SCIENTST	1	NR	NR	-	-
127 CH GOD (CLEVE)	3	567	772*	1.1	1.8
143 CG IN CR(MENN)	1	142	193*	.3	.4
145 CH GOD PROPHCY	1	33	45*	.1	.1
165 CH OF NAZARENE	1	40	49	.1	.1
167 CHS OF CHRIST	5	496	656	1.0	1.5
193 EPISCOPAL	4	597	784	1.2	1.8
223 FREE WILL BAPT	1	40	54*	.1	.1
266 INTRSTAT & ASC	1	80	109*	.2	.2
283 LUTH—MO SYNOD	1	82	119	.2	.3

NA–Not applicable   NR–Not reported   *Total adherents estimated from known number of communicant, confirmed, full members.   - Represents a percent less than 0.1.   Percentages may not total due to rounding.
[1]See Appendix E   [2]See Appendix F   [3]See Appendix G   Lines in *italic* represent a breakdown of Catholic rites or Friends affiliations. They are included in their respective denominational total.

Table 4. Churches and Church Membership by County and Denomination: 1990

County and Denomination	Number of churches	Communicant, confirmed, full members	Total adherents Number	Percent of total population	Percent of total adherents
339 PENT CH OF GOD	1	34	77	.1	.2
355 PRESB CH (USA)	4	787	1,071*	1.6	2.4
356 PRESB CH AMER	1	50	68	.1	.2
403 SALVATION ARMY	1	86	90	.1	.2
413 S.D.A.	4	471	641*	.9	1.5
419 SO BAPT CONV	20	12,123	16,498*	24.3	37.5
449 UN METHODIST	10	2,703	3,679*	5.4	8.4
496 JEWISH EST[1]	1	NA	480	.7	1.1
497 BLACK BAPT EST[2]	NA	9,616	13,086*	19.3	29.7
499 INDEP.NON-CHAR[3]	2	NA	700	1.0	1.6
WAYNE	**67**	**9,978**	**13,480***	**69.1**	**100.0**
053 ASSEMB OF GOD	11	557	1,022	5.2	7.6
059 BAPT MISS ASSN	1	114	150*	.8	1.1
081 CATHOLIC	1	NA	82	.4	.6
081d LATIN	*1*	*NA*	*82*	*.4*	*.6*
127 CH GOD (CLEVE)	1	163	215*	1.1	1.6
165 CH OF NAZARENE	1	34	27	.1	.2
167 CHS OF CHRIST	2	135	175	.9	1.3
223 FREE WILL BAPT	5	288	380*	1.9	2.8
266 INTRSTAT & ASC	1	15	20*	.1	.1
356 PRESB CH AMER	3	119	127	.7	.9
361 PRIM BAPT ASCS	1	7	9*	-	.1
419 SO BAPT CONV	23	4,767	6,288*	32.2	46.6
449 UN METHODIST	17	1,397	1,843*	9.4	13.7
497 BLACK BAPT EST[2]	NA	2,382	3,142*	16.1	23.3
WEBSTER	**49**	**6,708**	**8,488***	**83.0**	**100.0**
081 CATHOLIC	1	NA	18	.2	.2
081d LATIN	*1*	*NA*	*18*	*.2*	*.2*
127 CH GOD (CLEVE)	4	141	178*	1.7	2.1
145 CH GOD PROPHCY	1	33	42*	.4	.5
167 CHS OF CHRIST	1	19	24	.2	.3
223 FREE WILL BAPT	2	44	56*	.5	.7
419 SO BAPT CONV	28	5,035	6,357*	62.2	74.9
449 UN METHODIST	12	895	1,130*	11.1	13.3
497 BLACK BAPT EST[2]	NA	541	683*	6.7	8.0
WILKINSON	**24**	**5,237**	**7,163***	**74.0**	**100.0**
081 CATHOLIC	2	NA	210	2.2	2.9
081d LATIN	*2*	*NA*	*210*	*2.2*	*2.9*
093 CHR CH (DISC)	2	108	144	1.5	2.0
167 CHS OF CHRIST	3	253	391	4.0	5.5
193 EPISCOPAL	1	77	77	.8	1.1
356 PRESB CH AMER	1	29	29	.3	.4
413 S.D.A.	1	4	5*	.1	.1
419 SO BAPT CONV	5	1,401	1,854*	19.2	25.9
449 UN METHODIST	9	1,128	1,493*	15.4	20.8
497 BLACK BAPT EST[2]	NA	2,237	2,960*	30.6	41.3
WINSTON	**62**	**12,419**	**16,074***	**82.7**	**100.0**
053 ASSEMB OF GOD	4	163	265	1.4	1.6
081 CATHOLIC	1	NA	96	.5	.6
081d LATIN	*1*	*NA*	*96*	*.5*	*.6*
167 CHS OF CHRIST	1	28	36	.2	.2
207 E.L.C.A.	2	62	84	.4	.5
216 EVAN PRESBY CH	1	65	67	.3	.4
285 MENNONITE CH	1	37	42	.2	.3
356 PRESB CH AMER	2	242	301	1.5	1.9
419 SO BAPT CONV	27	6,571	8,439*	43.4	52.5
449 UN METHODIST	23	2,479	3,184*	16.4	19.8
497 BLACK BAPT EST[2]	NA	2,772	3,560*	18.3	22.1
YALOBUSHA	**53**	**8,630**	**11,013***	**91.5**	**100.0**
005 AME ZION	3	543	772	6.4	7.0
053 ASSEMB OF GOD	1	40	50	.4	.5
097 CHR CHS&CHS CR	1	365	463*	3.8	4.2
127 CH GOD (CLEVE)	2	86	109*	.9	1.0
145 CH GOD PROPHCY	2	67	85*	.7	.8
167 CHS OF CHRIST	6	383	493	4.1	4.5
193 EPISCOPAL	1	17	17	.1	.2
355 PRESB CH (USA)	3	66	84*	.7	.8
356 PRESB CH AMER	2	94	102	.8	.9
361 PRIM BAPT ASCS	2	20	25*	.2	.2
413 S.D.A.	1	23	29*	.2	.3
419 SO BAPT CONV	20	4,564	5,788*	48.1	52.6
449 UN METHODIST	9	812	1,030*	8.6	9.4
497 BLACK BAPT EST[2]	NA	1,550	1,966*	16.3	17.9
YAZOO	**64**	**13,238**	**18,414***	**72.2**	**100.0**
053 ASSEMB OF GOD	1	69	110	.4	.6
059 BAPT MISS ASSN	2	211	283*	1.1	1.5
081 CATHOLIC	2	NA	615	2.4	3.3
081d LATIN	*2*	*NA*	*615*	*2.4*	*3.3*
123 CH GOD (ANDER)	1	175	175	.7	1.0

County and Denomination	Number of churches	Communicant, confirmed, full members	Total adherents Number	Percent of total population	Percent of total adherents
127 CH GOD (CLEVE)	1	65	87*	.3	.5
145 CH GOD PROPHCY	2	67	90*	.4	.5
151 L-D SAINTS	1	NA	66	.3	.4
167 CHS OF CHRIST	3	129	170	.7	.9
193 EPISCOPAL	1	150	194	.8	1.1
266 INTRSTAT & ASC	1	38	51*	.2	.3
339 PENT CH OF GOD	2	68	153	.6	.8
356 PRESB CH AMER	2	377	454	1.8	2.5
413 S.D.A.	1	151	203*	.8	1.1
419 SO BAPT CONV	24	5,938	7,974*	31.3	43.3
449 UN METHODIST	20	2,502	3,360*	13.2	18.2
497 BLACK BAPT EST[2]	NA	3,298	4,429*	17.4	24.1

MISSOURI

County and Denomination	Number of churches	Communicant, confirmed, full members	Total adherents Number	Percent of total population	Percent of total adherents
THE STATE.....	7,666	1,542,347	2,944,890*	57.6	100.0
ADAIR	**38**	**6,547**	**10,272***	**41.8**	**100.0**
053 ASSEMB OF GOD	2	138	267	1.1	2.6
081 CATHOLIC	2	NA	1,713	7.0	16.7
081d LATIN	*2*	*NA*	*1,713*	*7.0*	*16.7*
093 CHR CH (DISC)	2	623	837	3.4	8.1
097 CHR CHS&CHS CR	2	125	149*	.6	1.5
123 CH GOD (ANDER)	1	0	105	.4	1.0
145 CH GOD PROPHCY	1	25	30*	.1	.3
151 L-D SAINTS	1	NA	409	1.7	4.0
165 CH OF NAZARENE	1	304	250	1.0	2.4
167 CHS OF CHRIST	2	109	139	.6	1.4
193 EPISCOPAL	1	67	103	.4	1.0
203 EVAN FREE CH	1	60	190	.8	1.8
223 FREE WILL BAPT	2	193	230*	.9	2.2
283 LUTH—MO SYNOD	1	237	311	1.3	3.0
355 PRESB CH (USA)	1	351	417*	1.7	4.1
361 PRIM BAPT ASCS	1	12	14*	.1	.1
403 SALVATION ARMY	1	62	65	.3	.6
413 S.D.A.	1	55	65*	.3	.6
419 SO BAPT CONV	7	2,848	3,387*	13.8	33.0
449 UN METHODIST	8	1,338	1,591*	6.5	15.5
ANDREW	**28**	**3,802**	**5,990***	**40.9**	**100.0**
081 CATHOLIC	1	NA	544	3.7	9.1
081d LATIN	*1*	*NA*	*544*	*3.7*	*9.1*
093 CHR CH (DISC)	4	669	1,134	7.8	18.9
097 CHR CHS&CHS CR	2	100	127*	.9	2.1
123 CH GOD (ANDER)	1	30	30	.2	.5
127 CH GOD (CLEVE)	1	91	116*	.8	1.9
167 CHS OF CHRIST	1	56	73	.5	1.2
185 CUMBER PRESB	1	5	5	-	.1
193 EPISCOPAL	1	17	37	.3	.6
355 PRESB CH (USA)	1	74	94*	.6	1.6
419 SO BAPT CONV	6	1,441	1,830*	12.5	30.6
443 UN C OF CHRIST	2	392	498*	3.4	8.3
449 UN METHODIST	6	927	1,177*	8.0	19.6
498 INDEP.CHARIS.[3]	1	NA	325	2.2	5.4
ATCHISON	**24**	**4,184**	**5,453***	**73.1**	**100.0**
053 ASSEMB OF GOD	2	85	150	2.0	2.8
081 CATHOLIC	1	NA	172	2.3	3.2
081d LATIN	*1*	*NA*	*172*	*2.3*	*3.2*
093 CHR CH (DISC)	3	222	394	5.3	7.2
097 CHR CHS&CHS CR	1	98	119*	1.6	2.2
127 CH GOD (CLEVE)	1	16	19*	.3	.3
185 CUMBER PRESB	1	5	5	.1	.1
193 EPISCOPAL	1	18	23	.3	.4
207 E.L.C.A.	2	728	918	12.3	16.8
283 LUTH—MO SYNOD	1	21	32	.4	.6
355 PRESB CH (USA)	2	359	435*	5.8	8.0
419 SO BAPT CONV	4	1,311	1,587*	21.3	29.1
449 UN METHODIST	5	1,321	1,599*	21.4	29.3
AUDRAIN	**60**	**11,265**	**17,018***	**72.1**	**100.0**
053 ASSEMB OF GOD	2	102	206	.9	1.2
081 CATHOLIC	4	NA	2,250	9.5	13.2
081d LATIN	*4*	*NA*	*2,250*	*9.5*	*13.2*
093 CHR CH (DISC)	7	1,040	1,702	7.2	10.0
097 CHR CHS&CHS CR	9	1,500	1,886*	8.0	11.1
165 CH OF NAZARENE	2	141	318	1.3	1.9
167 CHS OF CHRIST	1	68	70	.3	.4
193 EPISCOPAL	1	70	81	.3	.5
217 FIRE BAPTIZED	1	11	14*	.1	.1
283 LUTH—MO SYNOD	2	363	471	2.0	2.8

NA–Not applicable   NR–Not reported   *Total adherents estimated from known number of communicant, confirmed, full members.   - Represents a percent less than 0.1.   Percentages may not total due to rounding.

[1]See Appendix E   [2]See Appendix F   [3]See Appendix G   Lines in *italic* represent a breakdown of Catholic rites or Friends affiliations. They are included in their respective denominational total.

Table 4. Churches and Church Membership by County and Denomination: 1990

County and Denomination	Number of churches	Communicant, confirmed, full members	Total adherents Number	Percent of total population	Percent of total adherents
355 PRESB CH (USA)	7	1,337	1,681*	7.1	9.9
413 S.D.A.	1	48	60*	.3	.4
419 SO BAPT CONV	16	5,156	6,482*	27.5	38.1
443 UN C OF CHRIST	1	55	69*	.3	.4
449 UN METHODIST	6	1,076	1,353*	5.7	8.0
497 BLACK BAPT EST²	NA	298	375*	1.6	2.2
BARRY	**92**	**13,426**	**18,887***	**68.6**	**100.0**
053 ASSEMB OF GOD	8	313	665	2.4	3.5
059 BAPT MISS ASSN	3	130	162*	.6	.9
081 CATHOLIC	4	NA	1,460	5.3	7.7
081d LATIN	4	NA	1,460	5.3	7.7
093 CHR CH (DISC)	1	163	196	.7	1.0
097 CHR CHS&CHS CR	5	726	904*	3.3	4.8
133 CH GOD(7TH)DEN	1	42	55	.2	.3
151 L-D SAINTS	1	NA	120	.4	.6
165 CH OF NAZARENE	2	144	310	1.1	1.6
167 CHS OF CHRIST	13	745	1,006	3.7	5.3
193 EPISCOPAL	1	92	114	.4	.6
223 FREE WILL BAPT	2	242	301*	1.1	1.6
230 FUND METHODIST	2	112	174	.6	.9
283 LUTH—MO SYNOD	3	293	380	1.4	2.0
339 PENT CH OF GOD	2	31	95	.3	.5
355 PRESB CH (USA)	2	290	361*	1.3	1.9
413 S.D.A.	1	98	122*	.4	.6
419 SO BAPT CONV	31	8,433	10,504*	38.1	55.6
449 UN METHODIST	10	1,572	1,958*	7.1	10.4
BARTON	**37**	**4,801**	**6,476***	**57.2**	**100.0**
040 AP CHR CH-AMER	1	71	126	1.1	1.9
053 ASSEMB OF GOD	2	112	190	1.7	2.9
061 BEACHY AMISH	1	35	44*	.4	.7
081 CATHOLIC	2	NA	226	2.0	3.5
081d LATIN	2	NA	226	2.0	3.5
093 CHR CH (DISC)	1	139	218	1.9	3.4
097 CHR CHS&CHS CR	1	856	1,086*	9.6	16.8
127 CH GOD (CLEVE)	1	55	70*	.6	1.1
145 CH GOD PROPHCY	2	50	63*	.6	1.0
165 CH OF NAZARENE	1	81	160	1.4	2.5
167 CHS OF CHRIST	1	85	108	1.0	1.7
185 CUMBER PRESB	1	113	118	1.0	1.8
223 FREE WILL BAPT	3	187	237*	2.1	3.7
283 LUTH—MO SYNOD	1	142	181	1.6	2.8
355 PRESB CH (USA)	1	36	46*	.4	.7
413 S.D.A.	1	31	39*	.3	.6
419 SO BAPT CONV	10	1,689	2,144*	19.0	33.1
449 UN METHODIST	7	1,119	1,420*	12.6	21.9
BATES	**59**	**6,990**	**9,557***	**63.6**	**100.0**
053 ASSEMB OF GOD	4	195	348	2.3	3.6
081 CATHOLIC	2	NA	336	2.2	3.5
081d LATIN	2	NA	336	2.2	3.5
093 CHR CH (DISC)	3	779	1,121	7.5	11.7
097 CHR CHS&CHS CR	9	1,130	1,426*	9.5	14.9
143 CG IN CR(MENN)	1	146	184*	1.2	1.9
165 CH OF NAZARENE	1	59	199	1.3	2.1
167 CHS OF CHRIST	5	193	239	1.6	2.5
207 E.L.C.A.	1	33	38	.3	.4
283 LUTH—MO SYNOD	1	271	357	2.4	3.7
339 PENT CH OF GOD	1	0	30	.2	.3
355 PRESB CH (USA)	3	221	279*	1.9	2.9
419 SO BAPT CONV	14	2,637	3,327*	22.1	34.8
443 UN C OF CHRIST	1	42	53*	.4	.6
449 UN METHODIST	13	1,284	1,620*	10.8	17.0
BENTON	**42**	**6,038**	**7,905***	**57.0**	**100.0**
053 ASSEMB OF GOD	3	108	259	1.9	3.3
081 CATHOLIC	2	NA	500	3.6	6.3
081d LATIN	2	NA	500	3.6	6.3
093 CHR CH (DISC)	1	98	106	.8	1.3
157 CH OF BRETHREN	1	16	19*	.1	.2
165 CH OF NAZARENE	1	50	48	.3	.6
167 CHS OF CHRIST	3	70	88	.6	1.1
207 E.L.C.A.	3	488	597	4.3	7.6
283 LUTH—MO SYNOD	7	1,452	1,803	13.0	22.8
285 MENNONITE CH	1	24	49	.4	.6
419 SO BAPT CONV	12	2,491	2,961*	21.4	37.5
449 UN METHODIST	8	1,241	1,475*	10.6	18.7
BOLLINGER	**39**	**3,134**	**4,884***	**46.0**	**100.0**
053 ASSEMB OF GOD	2	51	96	.9	2.0
059 BAPT MISS ASSN	1	13	16*	.2	.3
081 CATHOLIC	2	NA	886	8.3	18.1
081d LATIN	2	NA	886	8.3	18.1
123 CH GOD (ANDER)	1	25	25	.2	.5
127 CH GOD (CLEVE)	1	18	23*	.2	.5
167 CHS OF CHRIST	2	60	77	.7	1.6
207 E.L.C.A.	2	184	229	2.2	4.7
353 CHR BRETHREN	1	30	60	.6	1.2
355 PRESB CH (USA)	3	147	185*	1.7	3.8
419 SO BAPT CONV	13	1,955	2,466*	23.2	50.5
449 UN METHODIST	11	651	821*	7.7	16.8
BOONE	**107**	**29,167**	**52,957***	**47.1**	**100.0**
019 AMER BAPT USA	2	1,164	1,428*	1.3	2.7
053 ASSEMB OF GOD	5	590	1,241	1.1	2.3
059 BAPT MISS ASSN	1	14	17*	-	-
081 CATHOLIC	4	NA	11,720	10.4	22.1
081d LATIN	4	NA	11,720	10.4	22.1
093 CHR CH (DISC)	12	2,647	4,829	4.3	9.1
097 CHR CHS&CHS CR	4	668	820*	.7	1.5
105 CHRISTIAN REF	1	32	60	.1	.1
111 CH CR,SCIENTST	1	NR	NR	-	-
123 CH GOD (ANDER)	1	55	98	.1	.2
151 L-D SAINTS	4	NA	943	.8	1.8
157 CH OF BRETHREN	1	11	13*	-	-
165 CH OF NAZARENE	2	179	227	.2	.4
167 CHS OF CHRIST	6	527	662	.6	1.3
193 EPISCOPAL	2	653	855	.8	1.6
203 EVAN FREE CH	1	300	450	.4	.8
207 E.L.C.A.	1	574	830	.7	1.6
223 FREE WILL BAPT	1	41	50*	-	.1
226 FRIENDS-USA	1	42	52*	-	.1
226c FGC	1	42	52*	-	.1
263 INT FOURSQ GOS	1	42	52*	-	.1
283 LUTH—MO SYNOD	3	1,022	1,360	1.2	2.6
355 PRESB CH (USA)	2	1,086	1,333*	1.2	2.5
356 PRESB CH AMER	1	11	15	-	-
361 PRIM BAPT ASCS	1	75	92*	.1	.2
403 SALVATION ARMY	1	83	85	.1	.2
413 S.D.A.	3	749	919*	.8	1.7
419 SO BAPT CONV	26	10,676	13,102*	11.7	24.7
435 UNITARIAN-UNIV	1	174	244	.2	.5
443 UN C OF CHRIST	2	759	931*	.8	1.8
449 UN METHODIST	13	4,730	5,805*	5.2	11.0
469 WELS	1	48	56	-	.1
496 JEWISH EST¹	0	NA	350	.3	.7
497 BLACK BAPT EST²	NA	2,215	2,718*	2.4	5.1
498 INDEP.CHARIS.³	2	NA	1,600	1.4	3.0
BUCHANAN	**105**	**27,013**	**46,505***	**56.0**	**100.0**
053 ASSEMB OF GOD	3	572	824	1.0	1.8
081 CATHOLIC	10	NA	9,782	11.8	21.0
081d LATIN	9	NA	9,746	11.7	21.0
081h UKRAINIAN	1	NA	36	-	.1
093 CHR CH (DISC)	5	1,744	2,396	2.9	5.2
097 CHR CHS&CHS CR	8	1,868	2,348*	2.8	5.0
111 CH CR,SCIENTST	1	NR	NR	-	-
127 CH GOD (CLEVE)	3	260	327*	.4	.7
133 CH GOD(7TH)DEN	1	42	55	.1	.1
151 L-D SAINTS	1	NA	687	.8	1.5
157 CH OF BRETHREN	1	36	45*	.1	.1
165 CH OF NAZARENE	2	245	513	.6	1.1
167 CHS OF CHRIST	1	130	165	.2	.4
185 CUMBER PRESB	1	68	76	.1	.2
193 EPISCOPAL	1	275	309	.4	.7
207 E.L.C.A.	1	569	711	.9	1.5
223 FREE WILL BAPT	1	52	65*	.1	.1
263 INT FOURSQ GOS	2	293	368*	.4	.8
283 LUTH—MO SYNOD	2	841	1,087	1.3	2.3
329 OPEN BIBLE STD	1	NR	NR	-	-
339 PENT CH OF GOD	4	137	306	.4	.7
355 PRESB CH (USA)	8	1,654	2,079*	2.5	4.5
403 SALVATION ARMY	1	164	183	.2	.4
413 S.D.A.	2	319	401*	.5	.9
419 SO BAPT CONV	19	11,108	13,962*	16.8	30.0
438 UN BRETH IN CR	1	56	56	.1	.1
443 UN C OF CHRIST	2	596	749*	.9	1.6
449 UN METHODIST	18	5,287	6,645*	8.0	14.3
496 JEWISH EST¹	2	NA	265	.3	.6
497 BLACK BAPT EST²	NA	697	876*	1.1	1.9
498 INDEP.CHARIS.³	1	NA	400	.5	.9
499 INDEP.NON-CHAR³	2	NA	825	1.0	1.8
BUTLER	**88**	**11,937**	**17,095***	**44.1**	**100.0**
053 ASSEMB OF GOD	5	336	580	1.5	3.4
059 BAPT MISS ASSN	10	499	621*	1.6	3.6
081 CATHOLIC	1	NA	1,383	3.6	8.1
081d LATIN	1	NA	1,383	3.6	8.1
093 CHR CH (DISC)	2	460	637	1.6	3.7
097 CHR CHS&CHS CR	1	0	0*	-	-

NA–Not applicable NR–Not reported *Total adherents estimated from known number of communicant, confirmed, full members. - Represents a percent less than 0.1. Percentages may not total due to rounding.
¹See Appendix E ²See Appendix F ³See Appendix G Lines in *italic* represent a breakdown of Catholic rites or Friends affiliations. They are included in their respective denominational total.

Table 4. Churches and Church Membership by County and Denomination: 1990

County and Denomination	Number of churches	Communicant, confirmed, full members	Total adherents Number	Percent of total population	Percent of total adherents
111 CH CR,SCIENTST	1	NR	NR	-	-
123 CH GOD (ANDER)	4	450	461	1.2	2.7
127 CH GOD (CLEVE)	1	80	100*	.3	.6
145 CH GOD PROPHCY	1	25	31*	.1	.2
151 L-D SAINTS	1	NA	254	.7	1.5
165 CH OF NAZARENE	3	93	174	.4	1.0
167 CHS OF CHRIST	14	792	1,011	2.6	5.9
193 EPISCOPAL	1	100	135	.3	.8
223 FREE WILL BAPT	2	68	85*	.2	.5
283 LUTH—MO SYNOD	1	349	443	1.1	2.6
339 PENT CH OF GOD	1	7	25	.1	.1
349 PENT HOLINESS	1	32	40*	.1	.2
355 PRESB CH (USA)	2	332	413*	1.1	2.4
413 S.D.A.	1	97	121*	.3	.7
419 SO BAPT CONV	23	6,143	7,648*	19.7	44.7
443 UN C OF CHRIST	1	76	95*	.2	.6
449 UN METHODIST	9	1,548	1,927*	5.0	11.3
467 WESLEYAN	1	25	82	.2	.5
497 BLACK BAPT EST2	NA	425	529*	1.4	3.1
499 INDEP.NON-CHAR3	1	NA	300	.8	1.8
CALDWELL	**31**	**3,788**	**5,320***	**63.5**	**100.0**
053 ASSEMB OF GOD	3	55	117	1.4	2.2
081 CATHOLIC	1	NA	192	2.3	3.6
081d LATIN	1	NA	192	2.3	3.6
093 CHR CH (DISC)	2	175	281	3.4	5.3
097 CHR CHS&CHS CR	2	182	229*	2.7	4.3
151 L-D SAINTS	1	NA	273	3.3	5.1
165 CH OF NAZARENE	1	95	109	1.3	2.0
167 CHS OF CHRIST	4	153	187	2.2	3.5
419 SO BAPT CONV	8	1,813	2,279*	27.2	42.8
443 UN C OF CHRIST	1	121	152*	1.8	2.9
449 UN METHODIST	8	1,194	1,501*	17.9	28.2
CALLAWAY	**69**	**9,868**	**16,047***	**48.9**	**100.0**
053 ASSEMB OF GOD	3	100	266	.8	1.7
081 CATHOLIC	3	NA	2,579	7.9	16.1
081d LATIN	3	NA	2,579	7.9	16.1
093 CHR CH (DISC)	11	1,098	1,946	5.9	12.1
097 CHR CHS&CHS CR	1	10	13*	-	.1
151 L-D SAINTS	1	NA	202	.6	1.3
165 CH OF NAZARENE	1	85	173	.5	1.1
167 CHS OF CHRIST	1	130	165	.5	1.0
193 EPISCOPAL	2	69	81	.2	.5
221 FREE METHODIST	1	7	14	-	.1
283 LUTH—MO SYNOD	2	230	284	.9	1.8
339 PENT CH OF GOD	1	15	75	.2	.5
355 PRESB CH (USA)	5	841	1,061*	3.2	6.6
419 SO BAPT CONV	19	5,308	6,697*	20.4	41.7
443 UN C OF CHRIST	1	66	83*	.3	.5
449 UN METHODIST	17	1,571	1,982*	6.0	12.4
497 BLACK BAPT EST2	NA	338	426*	1.3	2.7
CAMDEN	**46**	**7,027**	**10,073***	**36.6**	**100.0**
053 ASSEMB OF GOD	4	228	392	1.4	3.9
081 CATHOLIC	1	NA	872	3.2	8.7
081d LATIN	1	NA	872	3.2	8.7
093 CHR CH (DISC)	3	692	1,068	3.9	10.6
097 CHR CHS&CHS CR	2	48	58*	.2	.6
151 L-D SAINTS	1	NA	299	1.1	3.0
165 CH OF NAZARENE	1	30	47	.2	.5
167 CHS OF CHRIST	4	175	221	.8	2.2
193 EPISCOPAL	1	69	82	.3	.8
207 E.L.C.A.	2	470	568	2.1	5.6
283 LUTH—MO SYNOD	2	253	293	1.1	2.9
339 PENT CH OF GOD	1	23	108	.4	1.1
355 PRESB CH (USA)	2	115	138*	.5	1.4
413 S.D.A.	1	68	82*	.3	.8
419 SO BAPT CONV	17	3,741	4,503*	16.4	44.7
449 UN METHODIST	4	1,115	1,342*	4.9	13.3
CAPE GIRARDEAU	**95**	**26,758**	**42,501***	**69.0**	**100.0**
053 ASSEMB OF GOD	4	625	1,521	2.5	3.6
059 BAPT MISS ASSN	1	21	26*	-	.1
081 CATHOLIC	4	NA	7,247	11.8	17.1
081d LATIN	4	NA	7,247	11.8	17.1
093 CHR CH (DISC)	2	793	994	1.6	2.3
097 CHR CHS&CHS CR	1	195	240*	.4	.6
111 CH CR,SCIENTST	1	NR	NR	-	-
123 CH GOD (ANDER)	2	140	151	.2	.4
127 CH GOD (CLEVE)	1	96	118*	.2	.3
145 CH GOD PROPHCY	2	50	62*	.1	.1
151 L-D SAINTS	1	NA	338	.5	.8
165 CH OF NAZARENE	1	305	334	.5	.8
167 CHS OF CHRIST	4	340	371	.6	.9
193 EPISCOPAL	1	97	144	.2	.3

County and Denomination	Number of churches	Communicant, confirmed, full members	Total adherents Number	Percent of total population	Percent of total adherents
203 EVAN FREE CH	1	46	65	.1	.2
207 E.L.C.A.	2	382	513	.8	1.2
209 EVAN LUTH SYN	1	145	180	.3	.4
216 EVAN PRESBY CH	1	46	48	.1	.1
223 FREE WILL BAPT	1	130	160*	.3	.4
263 INT FOURSQ GOS	1	97	119*	.2	.3
283 LUTH—MO SYNOD	14	6,479	8,318	13.5	19.6
353 CHR BRETHREN	2	235	420	.7	1.0
355 PRESB CH (USA)	3	878	1,080*	1.8	2.5
403 SALVATION ARMY	1	87	94	.2	.2
413 S.D.A.	1	35	43*	.1	.1
419 SO BAPT CONV	19	8,878	10,923*	17.7	25.7
443 UN C OF CHRIST	4	963	1,185*	1.9	2.8
449 UN METHODIST	18	5,056	6,221*	10.1	14.6
497 BLACK BAPT EST2	NA	639	786*	1.3	1.8
499 INDEP.NON-CHAR3	1	NA	800	1.3	1.9
CARROLL	**46**	**5,856**	**8,224***	**76.5**	**100.0**
053 ASSEMB OF GOD	1	44	92	.9	1.1
081 CATHOLIC	2	NA	616	5.7	7.5
081d LATIN	2	NA	616	5.7	7.5
093 CHR CH (DISC)	7	202	440	4.1	5.4
097 CHR CHS&CHS CR	1	75	94*	.9	1.1
157 CH OF BRETHREN	1	54	68*	.6	.8
165 CH OF NAZARENE	1	40	42	.4	.5
167 CHS OF CHRIST	5	150	192	1.8	2.3
283 LUTH—MO SYNOD	2	579	710	6.6	8.6
323 OLD ORD AMISH	1	NA	50	.5	.6
355 PRESB CH (USA)	1	37	46*	.4	.6
419 SO BAPT CONV	14	3,328	4,174*	38.8	50.8
449 UN METHODIST	9	1,328	1,666*	15.5	20.3
469 WELS	1	19	34	.3	.4
CARTER	**21**	**1,478**	**2,052***	**37.2**	**100.0**
053 ASSEMB OF GOD	2	176	260	4.7	12.7
059 BAPT MISS ASSN	2	69	88*	1.6	4.3
081 CATHOLIC	2	NA	148	2.7	7.2
081d LATIN	2	NA	148	2.7	7.2
123 CH GOD (ANDER)	1	30	40	.7	1.9
145 CH GOD PROPHCY	3	75	95*	1.7	4.6
167 CHS OF CHRIST	2	55	69	1.3	3.4
283 LUTH—MO SYNOD	1	19	25	.5	1.2
285 MENNONITE CH	1	43	43	.8	2.1
419 SO BAPT CONV	4	918	1,166*	21.1	56.8
443 UN C OF CHRIST	1	10	13*	.2	.6
449 UN METHODIST	2	83	105*	1.9	5.1
CASS	**83**	**19,372**	**29,885***	**46.8**	**100.0**
053 ASSEMB OF GOD	7	484	1,139	1.8	3.8
081 CATHOLIC	3	NA	2,187	3.4	7.3
081d LATIN	3	NA	2,187	3.4	7.3
093 CHR CH (DISC)	10	1,662	2,474	3.9	8.3
097 CHR CHS&CHS CR	1	35	45*	.1	.2
121 CH GOD (ABR)	1	60	78*	.1	.3
127 CH GOD (CLEVE)	1	20	26*	-	.1
151 L-D SAINTS	1	NA	283	.4	.9
165 CH OF NAZARENE	3	167	257	.4	.9
167 CHS OF CHRIST	5	254	341	.5	1.1
193 EPISCOPAL	1	127	177	.3	.6
203 EVAN FREE CH	1	24	65	.1	.2
207 E.L.C.A.	2	307	402	.6	1.3
223 FREE WILL BAPT	2	186	242*	.4	.8
283 LUTH—MO SYNOD	3	301	450	.7	1.5
285 MENNONITE CH	2	306	379	.6	1.3
355 PRESB CH (USA)	4	298	387*	.6	1.3
419 SO BAPT CONV	24	11,537	14,981*	23.5	50.1
449 UN METHODIST	10	3,272	4,249*	6.7	14.2
469 WELS	1	151	210	.3	.7
496 JEWISH EST1	0	NA	778	1.2	2.6
497 BLACK BAPT EST2	NA	181	235*	.4	.8
498 INDEP.CHARIS.3	1	NA	500	.8	1.7
CEDAR	**28**	**3,888**	**5,469***	**45.2**	**100.0**
053 ASSEMB OF GOD	2	181	429	3.5	7.8
081 CATHOLIC	2	NA	321	2.7	5.9
081d LATIN	2	NA	321	2.7	5.9
093 CHR CH (DISC)	1	140	356	2.9	6.5
097 CHR CHS&CHS CR	5	780	949*	7.8	17.4
165 CH OF NAZARENE	1	43	68	.6	1.2
167 CHS OF CHRIST	3	123	161	1.3	2.9
223 FREE WILL BAPT	2	52	63*	.5	1.2
283 LUTH—MO SYNOD	1	96	114	.9	2.1
285 MENNONITE CH	1	30	35	.3	.6
355 PRESB CH (USA)	2	132	161*	1.3	2.9
419 SO BAPT CONV	4	1,683	2,048*	16.9	37.4
449 UN METHODIST	3	628	764*	6.3	14.0

NA–Not applicable   NR–Not reported   *Total adherents estimated from known number of communicant, confirmed, full members.   - Represents a percent less than 0.1.   Percentages may not total due to rounding.
[1]See Appendix E   [2]See Appendix F   [3]See Appendix G   Lines in *italic* represent a breakdown of Catholic rites or Friends affiliations. They are included in their respective denominational total.

Table 4. Churches and Church Membership by County and Denomination: 1990

County and Denomination	Number of churches	Communicant, confirmed, full members	Total adherents Number	Percent of total population	Percent of total adherents
CHARITON	**34**	**3,704**	**5,088***	**55.3**	**100.0**
053 ASSEMB OF GOD	1	14	14	.2	.3
081 CATHOLIC	6	NA	351	3.8	6.9
081d LATIN	6	NA	351	3.8	6.9
093 CHR CH (DISC)	5	285	433	4.7	8.5
097 CHR CHS&CHS CR	1	70	88*	1.0	1.7
283 LUTH—MO SYNOD	3	828	1,055	11.5	20.7
419 SO BAPT CONV	6	1,336	1,677*	18.2	33.0
449 UN METHODIST	12	1,171	1,470*	16.0	28.9
CHRISTIAN	**63**	**8,775**	**13,948***	**42.7**	**100.0**
053 ASSEMB OF GOD	4	688	1,205	3.7	8.6
081 CATHOLIC	2	NA	1,117	3.4	8.0
081d LATIN	2	NA	1,117	3.4	8.0
083 CHRIST CATH CH	1	23	62	.2	.4
093 CHR CH (DISC)	5	522	788	2.4	5.6
097 CHR CHS&CHS CR	1	0	0*	-	-
151 L-D SAINTS	1	NA	612	1.9	4.4
165 CH OF NAZARENE	2	177	201	.6	1.4
167 CHS OF CHRIST	7	382	483	1.5	3.5
221 FREE METHODIST	1	38	85	.3	.6
283 LUTH—MO SYNOD	1	85	117	.4	.8
355 PRESB CH (USA)	1	107	138*	.4	1.0
419 SO BAPT CONV	30	6,059	7,808*	23.9	56.0
443 UN C OF CHRIST	1	125	161*	.5	1.2
449 UN METHODIST	5	569	733*	2.2	5.3
496 JEWISH EST[1]	0	NA	38	.1	.3
498 INDEP.CHARIS.[3]	1	NA	400	1.2	2.9
CLARK	**33**	**2,903**	**4,879***	**64.6**	**100.0**
081 CATHOLIC	3	NA	528	7.0	10.8
081d LATIN	3	NA	528	7.0	10.8
093 CHR CH (DISC)	3	334	467	6.2	9.6
151 L-D SAINTS	2	NA	471	6.2	9.7
167 CHS OF CHRIST	1	35	40	.5	.8
323 OLD ORD AMISH	1	NA	150	2.0	3.1
355 PRESB CH (USA)	2	115	146*	1.9	3.0
413 S.D.A.	1	61	78*	1.0	1.6
419 SO BAPT CONV	12	1,273	1,619*	21.5	33.2
443 UN C OF CHRIST	1	360	458*	6.1	9.4
449 UN METHODIST	7	725	922*	12.2	18.9
CLAY	**131**	**39,069**	**72,400***	**47.2**	**100.0**
019 AMER BAPT USA	1	239	301*	.2	.4
053 ASSEMB OF GOD	12	1,100	2,901	1.9	4.0
057 BAPT GEN CONF	1	24	30*	-	-
081 CATHOLIC	7	NA	14,029	9.1	19.4
081d LATIN	7	NA	14,029	9.1	19.4
089 CHR & MISS AL	2	161	221	.1	.3
093 CHR CH (DISC)	10	3,356	5,478	3.6	7.6
097 CHR CHS&CHS CR	2	115	145*	.1	.2
111 CH CR,SCIENTST	2	NR	NR	-	-
123 CH GOD (ANDER)	1	71	71	-	.1
127 CH GOD (CLEVE)	1	54	68*	-	.1
145 CH GOD PROPHCY	1	25	31*	-	-
151 L-D SAINTS	5	NA	1,767	1.2	2.4
165 CH OF NAZARENE	4	543	860	.6	1.2
167 CHS OF CHRIST	9	1,030	1,382	.9	1.9
193 EPISCOPAL	3	535	686	.4	.9
207 E.L.C.A.	3	908	1,259	.8	1.7
259 IFCA	1	NR	NR	-	-
283 LUTH—MO SYNOD	5	2,214	2,942	1.9	4.1
339 PENT CH OF GOD	1	34	77	.1	.1
355 PRESB CH (USA)	3	931	1,171*	.8	1.6
361 PRIM BAPT ASCS	1	62	78*	.1	.1
373 REF CH IN U.S.	1	41	47	-	.1
413 S.D.A.	1	108	136*	.1	.2
419 SO BAPT CONV	33	18,925	23,806*	15.5	32.9
443 UN C OF CHRIST	1	247	311*	.2	.4
449 UN METHODIST	14	7,538	9,482*	6.2	13.1
467 WESLEYAN	1	96	144	.1	.2
496 JEWISH EST[1]	0	NA	1,871	1.2	2.6
497 BLACK BAPT EST[2]	NA	712	896*	.6	1.2
499 INDEP.NON-CHAR[3]	5	NA	2,210	1.4	3.1
CLINTON	**33**	**5,681**	**8,704***	**52.4**	**100.0**
053 ASSEMB OF GOD	4	152	207	1.2	2.4
081 CATHOLIC	2	NA	1,020	6.1	11.7
081d LATIN	2	NA	1,020	6.1	11.7
093 CHR CH (DISC)	4	874	1,499	9.0	17.2
097 CHR CHS&CHS CR	1	100	128*	.8	1.5
127 CH GOD (CLEVE)	1	16	20*	.1	.2
157 CH OF BRETHREN	1	23	29*	.2	.3
167 CHS OF CHRIST	2	131	170	1.0	2.0
223 FREE WILL BAPT	1	25	32*	.2	.4

County and Denomination	Number of churches	Communicant, confirmed, full members	Total adherents Number	Percent of total population	Percent of total adherents
339 PENT CH OF GOD	1	34	77	.5	.9
355 PRESB CH (USA)	2	56	71*	.4	.8
361 PRIM BAPT ASCS	1	9	11*	.1	.1
419 SO BAPT CONV	7	2,909	3,714*	22.4	42.7
449 UN METHODIST	6	1,352	1,726*	10.4	19.8
COLE	**71**	**20,435**	**46,985***	**73.9**	**100.0**
005 AME ZION	1	150	183	.3	.4
053 ASSEMB OF GOD	3	517	922	1.5	2.0
059 BAPT MISS ASSN	1	57	71*	.1	.2
081 CATHOLIC	9	NA	19,965	31.4	42.5
081d LATIN	9	NA	19,965	31.4	42.5
093 CHR CH (DISC)	3	889	1,354	2.1	2.9
097 CHR CHS&CHS CR	3	1,028	1,281*	2.0	2.7
111 CH CR,SCIENTST	1	NR	NR	-	-
123 CH GOD (ANDER)	2	150	159	.3	.3
151 L-D SAINTS	1	NA	364	.6	.8
165 CH OF NAZARENE	1	82	159	.3	.3
167 CHS OF CHRIST	3	190	252	.4	.5
193 EPISCOPAL	1	345	506	.8	1.1
203 EVAN FREE CH	1	16	20	-	-
207 E.L.C.A.	3	718	909	1.4	1.9
209 EVAN LUTH SYN	1	36	54	.1	.1
221 FREE METHODIST	1	32	32	.1	.1
283 LUTH—MO SYNOD	5	3,064	3,906	6.1	8.3
339 PENT CH OF GOD	2	64	245	.4	.5
353 CHR BRETHREN	1	40	50	.1	.1
355 PRESB CH (USA)	1	1,034	1,289*	2.0	2.7
403 SALVATION ARMY	1	115	122	.2	.3
413 S.D.A.	1	102	127*	.2	.3
415 S-D BAPTIST GC	1	30	37*	.1	.1
419 SO BAPT CONV	17	7,557	9,419*	14.8	20.0
443 UN C OF CHRIST	2	1,062	1,324*	2.1	2.8
449 UN METHODIST	3	2,123	2,646*	4.2	5.6
496 JEWISH EST[1]	1	NA	0	-	-
497 BLACK BAPT EST[2]	NA	1,034	1,289*	2.0	2.7
499 INDEP.NON-CHAR[3]	1	NA	300	.5	.6
COOPER	**49**	**5,792**	**10,611***	**71.5**	**100.0**
053 ASSEMB OF GOD	1	36	65	.4	.6
081 CATHOLIC	4	NA	3,010	20.3	28.4
081d LATIN	4	NA	3,010	20.3	28.4
093 CHR CH (DISC)	2	216	370	2.5	3.5
151 L-D SAINTS	1	NA	48	.3	.5
167 CHS OF CHRIST	3	125	181	1.2	1.7
193 EPISCOPAL	1	35	47	.3	.4
263 INT FOURSQ GOS	1	93	115*	.8	1.1
283 LUTH—MO SYNOD	4	783	1,038	7.0	9.8
323 OLD ORD AMISH	1	NA	150	1.0	1.4
339 PENT CH OF GOD	1	20	35	.2	.3
355 PRESB CH (USA)	5	230	285*	1.9	2.7
356 PRESB CH AMER	1	69	82	.6	.8
419 SO BAPT CONV	14	2,583	3,200*	21.6	30.2
443 UN C OF CHRIST	4	548	679*	4.6	6.4
449 UN METHODIST	6	813	1,007*	6.8	9.5
497 BLACK BAPT EST[2]	NA	241	299*	2.0	2.8
CRAWFORD	**46**	**6,439**	**9,524***	**49.7**	**100.0**
053 ASSEMB OF GOD	8	503	967	5.0	10.2
059 BAPT MISS ASSN	3	684	868*	4.5	9.1
081 CATHOLIC	3	NA	1,015	5.3	10.7
081d LATIN	3	NA	1,015	5.3	10.7
097 CHR CHS&CHS CR	2	50	63*	.3	.7
127 CH GOD (CLEVE)	2	244	310*	1.6	3.3
167 CHS OF CHRIST	1	59	76	.4	.8
223 FREE WILL BAPT	2	118	150*	.8	1.6
283 LUTH—MO SYNOD	2	301	389	2.0	4.1
339 PENT CH OF GOD	1	18	25	.1	.3
355 PRESB CH (USA)	3	356	452*	2.4	4.7
413 S.D.A.	1	86	109*	.6	1.1
419 SO BAPT CONV	14	3,534	4,483*	23.4	47.1
436 UNITED BAPT	2	36	46*	.2	.5
449 UN METHODIST	2	450	571*	3.0	6.0
DADE	**44**	**4,181**	**5,619***	**75.4**	**100.0**
053 ASSEMB OF GOD	2	78	145	1.9	2.6
081 CATHOLIC	1	NA	109	1.5	1.9
081d LATIN	1	NA	109	1.5	1.9
093 CHR CH (DISC)	7	462	714	9.6	12.7
097 CHR CHS&CHS CR	3	280	349*	4.7	6.2
121 CH GOD (ABR)	2	25	31*	.4	.6
151 L-D SAINTS	1	NA	74	1.0	1.3
167 CHS OF CHRIST	4	300	387	5.2	6.9
185 CUMBER PRESB	1	28	28	.4	.5
223 FREE WILL BAPT	1	21	26*	.3	.5
283 LUTH—MO SYNOD	1	468	616	8.3	11.0

NA–Not applicable NR–Not reported *Total adherents estimated from known number of communicant, confirmed, full members. - Represents a percent less than 0.1. Percentages may not total due to rounding.
[1]See Appendix E [2]See Appendix F [3]See Appendix G Lines in italic represent a breakdown of Catholic rites or Friends affiliations. They are included in their respective denominational total.

Table 4. Churches and Church Membership by County and Denomination: 1990

County and Denomination	Number of churches	Communicant, confirmed, full members	Total adherents Number	Percent of total population	Percent of total adherents
355 PRESB CH (USA)	4	148	185*	2.5	3.3
419 SO BAPT CONV	14	2,138	2,665*	35.8	47.4
449 UN METHODIST	3	233	290*	3.9	5.2
DALLAS	**41**	**4,277**	**5,997***	**47.4**	**100.0**
053 ASSEMB OF GOD	2	175	321	2.5	5.4
081 CATHOLIC	1	NA	175	1.4	2.9
081d LATIN	1	NA	175	1.4	2.9
093 CHR CH (DISC)	4	303	569	4.5	9.5
097 CHR CHS&CHS CR	2	145	183*	1.4	3.1
133 CH GOD(7TH)DEN	1	42	55	.4	.9
167 CHS OF CHRIST	3	112	145	1.1	2.4
207 E.L.C.A.	1	64	79	.6	1.3
223 FREE WILL BAPT	7	746	941*	7.4	15.7
285 MENNONITE CH	2	268	475	3.8	7.9
419 SO BAPT CONV	15	2,004	2,527*	20.0	42.1
449 UN METHODIST	3	418	527*	4.2	8.8
DAVIESS	**37**	**3,325**	**5,534***	**70.4**	**100.0**
053 ASSEMB OF GOD	1	37	110	1.4	2.0
081 CATHOLIC	1	NA	104	1.3	1.9
081d LATIN	1	NA	104	1.3	1.9
093 CHR CH (DISC)	3	311	631	8.0	11.4
097 CHR CHS&CHS CR	1	20	25*	.3	.5
167 CHS OF CHRIST	3	89	113	1.4	2.0
323 OLD ORD AMISH	6	NA	900	11.4	16.3
339 PENT CH OF GOD	1	35	77	1.0	1.4
355 PRESB CH (USA)	2	45	57*	.7	1.0
413 S.D.A.	1	32	40*	.5	.7
419 SO BAPT CONV	9	2,031	2,562*	32.6	46.3
449 UN METHODIST	9	725	915*	11.6	16.5
DE KALB	**31**	**3,536**	**4,399***	**44.1**	**100.0**
081 CATHOLIC	1	NA	79	.8	1.8
081d LATIN	1	NA	79	.8	1.8
093 CHR CH (DISC)	2	131	264	2.6	6.0
097 CHR CHS&CHS CR	3	245	295*	3.0	6.7
165 CH OF NAZARENE	1	87	68	.7	1.5
185 CUMBER PRESB	1	67	67	.7	1.5
283 LUTH—MO SYNOD	1	95	122	1.2	2.8
355 PRESB CH (USA)	2	70	84*	.8	1.9
419 SO BAPT CONV	10	1,728	2,080*	20.9	47.3
449 UN METHODIST	10	958	1,153*	11.6	26.2
497 BLACK BAPT EST[2]	NA	155	187*	1.9	4.3
DENT	**43**	**7,698**	**10,479***	**76.5**	**100.0**
053 ASSEMB OF GOD	3	328	603	4.4	5.8
059 BAPT MISS ASSN	1	21	26*	.2	.2
081 CATHOLIC	2	NA	485	3.5	4.6
081d LATIN	2	NA	485	3.5	4.6
097 CHR CHS&CHS CR	2	426	532*	3.9	5.1
123 CH GOD (ANDER)	1	40	40	.3	.4
151 L-D SAINTS	1	NA	118	.9	1.1
167 CHS OF CHRIST	3	259	330	2.4	3.1
185 CUMBER PRESB	1	40	40	.3	.4
207 E.L.C.A.	1	64	81	.6	.8
223 FREE WILL BAPT	1	32	40*	.3	.4
283 LUTH—MO SYNOD	1	137	207	1.5	2.0
339 PENT CH OF GOD	1	8	50	.4	.5
413 S.D.A.	1	47	59*	.4	.6
419 SO BAPT CONV	16	5,592	6,988*	51.0	66.7
436 UNITED BAPT	4	212	265*	1.9	2.5
449 UN METHODIST	4	492	615*	4.5	5.9
DOUGLAS	**22**	**2,155**	**3,000***	**25.3**	**100.0**
053 ASSEMB OF GOD	1	40	65	.5	2.2
081 CATHOLIC	2	NA	160	1.3	5.3
081d LATIN	2	NA	160	1.3	5.3
089 CHR & MISS AL	1	0	7	.1	.2
123 CH GOD (ANDER)	1	22	28	.2	.9
165 CH OF NAZARENE	3	385	506	4.3	16.9
167 CHS OF CHRIST	4	200	264	2.2	8.8
207 E.L.C.A.	1	56	72	.6	2.4
223 FREE WILL BAPT	1	55	69*	.6	2.3
339 PENT CH OF GOD	2	69	154	1.3	5.1
413 S.D.A.	1	56	71*	.6	2.4
419 SO BAPT CONV	4	918	1,158*	9.8	38.6
449 UN METHODIST	1	354	446*	3.8	14.9
DUNKLIN	**88**	**15,485**	**20,386***	**61.6**	**100.0**
053 ASSEMB OF GOD	10	588	1,111	3.4	5.4
059 BAPT MISS ASSN	2	70	87*	.3	.4
081 CATHOLIC	3	NA	655	2.0	3.2
081d LATIN	3	NA	655	2.0	3.2
093 CHR CH (DISC)	1	110	136	.4	.7

County and Denomination	Number of churches	Communicant, confirmed, full members	Total adherents Number	Percent of total population	Percent of total adherents
097 CHR CHS&CHS CR	2	190	237*	.7	1.2
123 CH GOD (ANDER)	1	119	127	.4	.6
127 CH GOD (CLEVE)	2	101	126*	.4	.6
145 CH GOD PROPHCY	2	50	62*	.2	.3
165 CH OF NAZARENE	2	210	265	.8	1.3
167 CHS OF CHRIST	12	1,090	1,366	4.1	6.7
193 EPISCOPAL	1	7	7	-	-
283 LUTH—MO SYNOD	2	65	104	.3	.5
349 PENT HOLINESS	3	138	172*	.5	.8
355 PRESB CH (USA)	3	224	280*	.8	1.4
413 S.D.A.	1	19	24*	.1	.1
419 SO BAPT CONV	29	10,236	12,792*	38.6	62.7
449 UN METHODIST	12	1,705	2,131*	6.4	10.5
497 BLACK BAPT EST[2]	NA	563	704*	2.1	3.5
FRANKLIN	**139**	**23,042**	**52,902***	**65.6**	**100.0**
053 ASSEMB OF GOD	10	691	1,162	1.4	2.2
059 BAPT MISS ASSN	7	1,558	2,013*	2.5	3.8
081 CATHOLIC	19	NA	20,359	25.3	38.5
081d LATIN	19	NA	20,359	25.3	38.5
093 CHR CH (DISC)	1	40	62	.1	.1
097 CHR CHS&CHS CR	5	1,107	1,430*	1.8	2.7
111 CH CR,SCIENTST	2	NR	NR	-	-
151 L-D SAINTS	1	NA	403	.5	.8
165 CH OF NAZARENE	3	257	367	.5	.7
167 CHS OF CHRIST	4	244	318	.4	.6
193 EPISCOPAL	2	91	118	.1	.2
203 EVAN FREE CH	1	29	45	.1	.1
207 E.L.C.A.	2	280	399	.5	.8
223 FREE WILL BAPT	1	90	116*	.1	.2
283 LUTH—MO SYNOD	9	2,454	3,287	4.1	6.2
339 PENT CH OF GOD	1	15	40	-	.1
353 CHR BRETHREN	1	63	93	.1	.2
355 PRESB CH (USA)	6	830	1,072*	1.3	2.0
356 PRESB CH AMER	2	133	220	.3	.4
413 S.D.A.	1	92	119*	.1	.2
419 SO BAPT CONV	32	9,074	11,723*	14.5	22.2
443 UN C OF CHRIST	13	3,383	4,371*	5.4	8.3
449 UN METHODIST	15	2,385	3,081*	3.8	5.8
467 WESLEYAN	1	28	100	.1	.2
496 JEWISH EST[1]	0	NA	1,748	2.2	3.3
497 BLACK BAPT EST[2]	NA	198	256*	.3	.5
GASCONADE	**47**	**6,216**	**9,923***	**70.8**	**100.0**
053 ASSEMB OF GOD	1	40	55	.4	.6
081 CATHOLIC	3	NA	2,109	15.1	21.3
081d LATIN	3	NA	2,109	15.1	21.3
097 CHR CHS&CHS CR	2	225	280*	2.0	2.8
127 CH GOD (CLEVE)	1	16	20*	.1	.2
167 CHS OF CHRIST	1	70	91	.6	.9
259 IFCA	1	NR	NR	-	-
283 LUTH—MO SYNOD	4	587	797	5.7	8.0
313 N AM BAPT CONF	1	51	63*	.4	.6
355 PRESB CH (USA)	3	114	142*	1.0	1.4
413 S.D.A.	1	20	25*	.2	.3
419 SO BAPT CONV	8	1,935	2,405*	17.2	24.2
443 UN C OF CHRIST	11	2,420	3,008*	21.5	30.3
449 UN METHODIST	9	690	858*	6.1	8.6
469 WELS	1	48	70	.5	.7
GENTRY	**34**	**4,111**	**5,773***	**84.3**	**100.0**
053 ASSEMB OF GOD	2	50	77	1.1	1.3
081 CATHOLIC	2	NA	359	5.2	6.2
081d LATIN	2	NA	359	5.2	6.2
093 CHR CH (DISC)	4	461	798	11.7	13.8
133 CH GOD(7TH)DEN	1	42	55	.8	1.0
151 L-D SAINTS	1	NA	62	.9	1.1
167 CHS OF CHRIST	3	100	127	1.9	2.2
185 CUMBER PRESB	1	8	8	.1	.1
355 PRESB CH (USA)	2	185	230*	3.4	4.0
413 S.D.A.	1	11	14*	.2	.2
419 SO BAPT CONV	11	2,388	2,967*	43.3	51.4
449 UN METHODIST	6	866	1,076*	15.7	18.6
GREENE	**257**	**76,983**	**120,652***	**58.0**	**100.0**
019 AMER BAPT USA	1	806	983*	.5	.8
053 ASSEMB OF GOD	38	5,958	12,068	5.8	10.0
059 BAPT MISS ASSN	2	142	173*	.1	.1
081 CATHOLIC	6	NA	10,920	5.3	9.1
081d LATIN	6	NA	10,920	5.3	9.1
089 CHR & MISS AL	1	25	65	-	.1
093 CHR CH (DISC)	9	3,045	3,989	1.9	3.3
097 CHR CHS&CHS CR	7	1,495	1,824*	.9	1.5
111 CH CR,SCIENTST	1	NR	NR	-	-
121 CH GOD (ABR)	1	13	16*	-	-
123 CH GOD (ANDER)	3	306	326	.2	.3

NA–Not applicable   NR–Not reported   *Total adherents estimated from known number of communicant, confirmed, full members.   - Represents a percent less than 0.1.   Percentages may not total due to rounding.
[1]See Appendix E   [2]See Appendix F   [3]See Appendix G   Lines in *italic* represent a breakdown of Catholic rites or Friends affiliations. They are included in their respective denominational total.

231

MISSOURI

Table 4. Churches and Church Membership by County and Denomination: 1990

County and Denomination	Number of churches	Communicant, confirmed, full members	Total adherents — Number	Percent of total population	Percent of total adherents
127 CH GOD (CLEVE)	1	226	276*	.1	.2
145 CH GOD PROPHCY	1	25	31*	-	-
151 L-D SAINTS	2	NA	1,030	.5	.9
157 CH OF BRETHREN	2	30	37*	-	-
165 CH OF NAZARENE	6	934	1,250	.6	1.0
167 CHS OF CHRIST	18	3,320	4,102	2.0	3.4
185 CUMBER PRESB	1	190	195	.1	.2
193 EPISCOPAL	4	1,440	1,774	.9	1.5
207 E.L.C.A.	2	715	1,030	.5	.9
215 EVAN METH CH	1	29	35*	-	-
220 FREE LUTHERAN	1	54	69	-	.1
221 FREE METHODIST	1	3	3	-	-
223 FREE WILL BAPT	6	837	1,021*	.5	.8
226 FRIENDS-USA	1	6	24	-	-
226c FGC	*1*	*6*	*24*	*-*	*-*
230 FUND METHODIST	4	175	235	.1	.2
259 IFCA	2	NR	NR	-	-
263 INT FOURSQ GOS	3	120	146*	.1	.1
283 LUTH—MO SYNOD	4	1,842	2,458	1.2	2.0
339 PENT CH OF GOD	2	95	195	.1	.2
349 PENT HOLINESS	1	25	31*	-	-
353 CHR BRETHREN	1	50	75	-	.1
355 PRESB CH (USA)	12	3,791	4,625*	2.2	3.8
356 PRESB CH AMER	2	164	187	.1	.2
403 SALVATION ARMY	1	118	118	.1	.1
413 S.D.A.	2	414	505*	.2	.4
419 SO BAPT CONV	64	38,221	46,633*	22.4	38.7
435 UNITARIAN-UNIV	1	176	237	.1	.2
443 UN C OF CHRIST	2	405	494*	.2	.4
449 UN METHODIST	28	10,735	13,098*	6.3	10.9
467 WESLEYAN	1	31	71	-	.1
469 WELS	1	31	40	-	-
496 JEWISH EST[1]	1	NA	246	.1	.2
497 BLACK BAPT EST[2]	NA	991	1,209*	.6	1.0
498 INDEP.CHARIS.[3]	1	NA	825	.4	.7
499 INDEP.NON-CHAR[3]	8	NA	7,983	3.8	6.6
GRUNDY	**41**	**6,556**	**8,813***	**83.6**	**100.0**
053 ASSEMB OF GOD	3	223	586	5.6	6.6
081 CATHOLIC	1	NA	185	1.8	2.1
081d LATIN	*1*	*NA*	*185*	*1.8*	*2.1*
093 CHR CH (DISC)	3	537	782	7.4	8.9
097 CHR CHS&CHS CR	4	547	667*	6.3	7.6
151 L-D SAINTS	1	NA	199	1.9	2.3
165 CH OF NAZARENE	1	117	203	1.9	2.3
167 CHS OF CHRIST	2	340	345	3.3	3.9
193 EPISCOPAL	1	24	32	.3	.4
263 INT FOURSQ GOS	1	48	59*	.6	.7
283 LUTH—MO SYNOD	1	114	135	1.3	1.5
355 PRESB CH (USA)	1	123	150*	1.4	1.7
419 SO BAPT CONV	13	3,532	4,310*	40.9	48.9
449 UN METHODIST	9	951	1,160*	11.0	13.2
HARRISON	**51**	**4,667**	**6,497***	**76.7**	**100.0**
053 ASSEMB OF GOD	5	181	347	4.1	5.3
081 CATHOLIC	2	NA	219	2.6	3.4
081d LATIN	*2*	*NA*	*219*	*2.6*	*3.4*
093 CHR CH (DISC)	7	624	1,197	14.1	18.4
097 CHR CHS&CHS CR	2	90	110*	1.3	1.7
167 CHS OF CHRIST	4	98	145	1.7	2.2
283 LUTH—MO SYNOD	1	56	72	.9	1.1
419 SO BAPT CONV	13	2,036	2,480*	29.3	38.2
449 UN METHODIST	17	1,582	1,927*	22.8	29.7
HENRY	**65**	**9,032**	**13,611***	**67.9**	**100.0**
053 ASSEMB OF GOD	2	221	340	1.7	2.5
081 CATHOLIC	5	NA	1,451	7.2	10.7
081d LATIN	*5*	*NA*	*1,451*	*7.2*	*10.7*
093 CHR CH (DISC)	4	657	1,190	5.9	8.7
097 CHR CHS&CHS CR	2	95	117*	.6	.9
123 CH GOD (ANDER)	1	18	25	.1	.2
151 L-D SAINTS	1	NA	185	.9	1.4
157 CH OF BRETHREN	1	44	54*	.3	.4
165 CH OF NAZARENE	2	105	338	1.7	2.5
167 CHS OF CHRIST	2	146	185	.9	1.4
185 CUMBER PRESB	3	167	168	.8	1.2
193 EPISCOPAL	1	24	37	.2	.3
283 LUTH—MO SYNOD	1	186	252	1.3	1.9
323 OLD ORD AMISH	1	NA	150	.7	1.1
339 PENT CH OF GOD	1	16	55	.3	.4
355 PRESB CH (USA)	4	356	439*	2.2	3.2
413 S.D.A.	1	88	108*	.5	.8
419 SO BAPT CONV	20	5,133	6,328*	31.6	46.5
449 UN METHODIST	13	1,776	2,189*	10.9	16.1

County and Denomination	Number of churches	Communicant, confirmed, full members	Total adherents — Number	Percent of total population	Percent of total adherents
HICKORY	**28**	**2,138**	**2,820***	**38.4**	**100.0**
053 ASSEMB OF GOD	2	73	95	1.3	3.4
081 CATHOLIC	1	NA	228	3.1	8.1
081d LATIN	*1*	*NA*	*228*	*3.1*	*8.1*
093 CHR CH (DISC)	5	266	395	5.4	14.0
097 CHR CHS&CHS CR	1	150	176*	2.4	6.2
121 CH GOD (ABR)	2	13	15*	.2	.5
157 CH OF BRETHREN	1	63	74*	1.0	2.6
165 CH OF NAZARENE	1	36	36	.5	1.3
223 FREE WILL BAPT	1	93	109*	1.5	3.9
263 INT FOURSQ GOS	1	25	29*	.4	1.0
283 LUTH—MO SYNOD	1	0	0	-	-
419 SO BAPT CONV	6	1,161	1,361*	18.6	48.3
443 UN C OF CHRIST	1	18	21*	.3	.7
449 UN METHODIST	5	240	281*	3.8	10.0
HOLT	**33**	**3,097**	**4,349***	**72.1**	**100.0**
081 CATHOLIC	1	NA	179	3.0	4.1
081d LATIN	*1*	*NA*	*179*	*3.0*	*4.1*
093 CHR CH (DISC)	3	414	672	11.1	15.5
097 CHR CHS&CHS CR	4	523	652*	10.8	15.0
123 CH GOD (ANDER)	1	40	51	.8	1.2
165 CH OF NAZARENE	3	153	306	5.1	7.0
283 LUTH—MO SYNOD	3	336	456	7.6	10.5
355 PRESB CH (USA)	6	258	322*	5.3	7.4
419 SO BAPT CONV	5	383	477*	7.9	11.0
449 UN METHODIST	7	990	1,234*	20.5	28.4
HOWARD	**34**	**4,348**	**7,219***	**75.0**	**100.0**
053 ASSEMB OF GOD	1	43	80	.8	1.1
081 CATHOLIC	2	NA	1,450	15.1	20.1
081d LATIN	*2*	*NA*	*1,450*	*15.1*	*20.1*
093 CHR CH (DISC)	7	466	894	9.3	12.4
167 CHS OF CHRIST	1	28	48	.5	.7
193 EPISCOPAL	1	17	19	.2	.3
263 INT FOURSQ GOS	1	49	61*	.6	.8
283 LUTH—MO SYNOD	1	63	86	.9	1.2
355 PRESB CH (USA)	1	28	35*	.4	.5
419 SO BAPT CONV	10	2,166	2,695*	28.0	37.3
443 UN C OF CHRIST	1	288	358*	3.7	5.0
449 UN METHODIST	8	1,046	1,301*	13.5	18.0
497 BLACK BAPT EST[2]	NA	154	192*	2.0	2.7
HOWELL	**91**	**11,325**	**15,891***	**50.5**	**100.0**
053 ASSEMB OF GOD	7	489	678	2.2	4.3
059 BAPT MISS ASSN	1	131	165*	.5	1.0
081 CATHOLIC	4	NA	1,176	3.7	7.4
081d LATIN	*4*	*NA*	*1,176*	*3.7*	*7.4*
093 CHR CH (DISC)	1	287	411	1.3	2.6
097 CHR CHS&CHS CR	5	476	598*	1.9	3.8
123 CH GOD (ANDER)	6	303	447	1.4	2.8
145 CH GOD PROPHCY	2	50	63*	.2	.4
157 CH OF BRETHREN	1	103	129*	.4	.8
165 CH OF NAZARENE	3	128	240	.8	1.5
167 CHS OF CHRIST	15	1,235	1,611	5.1	10.1
185 CUMBER PRESB	1	94	94	.3	.6
193 EPISCOPAL	1	77	104	.3	.7
207 E.L.C.A.	2	145	197	.6	1.2
217 FIRE BAPTIZED	1	2	3*	-	-
223 FREE WILL BAPT	5	513	645*	2.1	4.1
283 LUTH—MO SYNOD	1	137	185	.6	1.2
339 PENT CH OF GOD	2	102	283	.9	1.8
355 PRESB CH (USA)	3	247	310*	1.0	2.0
361 PRIM BAPT ASCS	2	22	28*	.1	.2
413 S.D.A.	2	103	129*	.4	.8
419 SO BAPT CONV	20	5,964	7,494*	23.8	47.2
449 UN METHODIST	4	717	901*	2.9	5.7
IRON	**35**	**3,936**	**5,572***	**51.9**	**100.0**
053 ASSEMB OF GOD	6	293	468	4.4	8.4
059 BAPT MISS ASSN	1	20	25*	.2	.4
081 CATHOLIC	2	NA	475	4.4	8.5
081d LATIN	*2*	*NA*	*475*	*4.4*	*8.5*
165 CH OF NAZARENE	2	120	193	1.8	3.5
167 CHS OF CHRIST	1	54	60	.6	1.1
193 EPISCOPAL	1	29	34	.3	.6
223 FREE WILL BAPT	1	40	50*	.5	.9
283 LUTH—MO SYNOD	2	119	152	1.4	2.7
339 PENT CH OF GOD	1	12	25	.2	.4
353 CHR BRETHREN	1	25	50	.5	.9
355 PRESB CH (USA)	1	82	103*	1.0	1.8
419 SO BAPT CONV	10	2,415	3,026*	28.2	54.3
436 UNITED BAPT	3	197	247*	2.3	4.4
449 UN METHODIST	3	530	664*	6.2	11.9

NA–Not applicable NR–Not reported *Total adherents estimated from known number of communicant, confirmed, full members. - Represents a percent less than 0.1. Percentages may not total due to rounding.

[1]See Appendix E [2]See Appendix F [3]See Appendix G Lines in italic represent a breakdown of Catholic rites or Friends affiliations. They are included in their respective denominational total.

Table 4. Churches and Church Membership by County and Denomination: 1990

County and Denomination	Number of churches	Communicant, confirmed, full members	Total adherents Number	Percent of total population	Percent of total adherents
JACKSON	**512**	**187,046**	**340,773***	**53.8**	**100.0**
005 AME ZION	4	1,720	2,150	.3	.6
019 AMER BAPT USA	6	2,066	2,592*	.4	.8
040 AP CHR CH-AMER	1	23	43	-	-
053 ASSEMB OF GOD	33	5,891	10,812	1.7	3.2
057 BAPT GEN CONF	1	128	161*	-	-
059 BAPT MISS ASSN	3	392	492*	.1	.1
081 CATHOLIC	53	NA	73,120	11.5	21.5
081b *BYZAN RUTH*	1	NA	60	-	-
081d *LATIN*	52	NA	73,060	11.5	21.4
093 CHR CH (DISC)	30	11,449	18,777	3.0	5.5
097 CHR CHS&CHS CR	12	1,885	2,365*	.4	.7
105 CHRISTIAN REF	1	67	114	-	-
111 CH CR,SCIENTST	5	NR	NR	-	-
123 CH GOD (ANDER)	8	550	631	.1	.2
127 CH GOD (CLEVE)	5	343	430*	.1	.1
133 CH GOD(7TH)DEN	1	42	56	-	-
145 CH GOD PROPHCY	2	50	63*	-	-
151 L-D SAINTS	10	NA	4,467	.7	1.3
157 CH OF BRETHREN	1	184	231*	-	.1
165 CH OF NAZARENE	14	3,135	3,961	.6	1.2
167 CHS OF CHRIST	24	3,549	4,603	.7	1.4
175 CONGR CHR CHS	1	94	118*	-	-
185 CUMBER PRESB	2	147	166	-	-
193 EPISCOPAL	13	5,357	6,150	1.0	1.8
203 EVAN FREE CH	1	22	60	-	-
207 E.L.C.A.	12	2,184	2,739	.4	.8
221 FREE METHODIST	1	33	58	-	-
223 FREE WILL BAPT	6	648	813*	.1	.2
226 FRIENDS-USA	2	96	120*	-	-
226a *CONSERV*	1	53	66*	-	-
226b *EFI*	1	43	54*	-	-
246 GREEK ORTHODOX	1	NR	NR	-	-
259 IFCA	1	NR	NR	-	-
263 INT FOURSQ GOS	1	169	212*	-	.1
283 LUTH—MO SYNOD	18	6,499	8,785	1.4	2.6
339 PENT CH OF GOD	3	103	231	-	.1
353 CHR BRETHREN	1	30	60	-	-
355 PRESB CH (USA)	33	10,832	13,590*	2.1	4.0
356 PRESB CH AMER	1	23	25	-	-
361 PRIM BAPT ASCS	2	79	99*	-	-
371 REF CH IN AM	1	85	150	-	-
403 SALVATION ARMY	5	700	758	.1	.2
413 S.D.A.	9	2,495	3,130*	.5	.9
419 SO BAPT CONV	92	62,964	78,997*	12.5	23.2
435 UNITARIAN-UNIV	1	435	525	.1	.2
443 UN C OF CHRIST	9	2,183	2,739*	.4	.8
449 UN METHODIST	59	24,363	30,567*	4.8	9.0
467 WESLEYAN	3	117	455	.1	.1
469 WELS	1	50	80	-	-
496 JEWISH EST[1]	6	NA	7,722	1.2	2.3
497 BLACK BAPT EST[2]	NA	35,864	44,996*	7.1	13.2
498 INDEP.CHARIS.[3]	8	NA	6,500	1.0	1.9
499 INDEP.NON-CHAR[3]	5	NA	5,860	.9	1.7
JASPER	**171**	**38,969**	**57,930***	**64.0**	**100.0**
053 ASSEMB OF GOD	15	2,914	6,199	6.9	10.7
059 BAPT MISS ASSN	2	134	168*	.2	.3
081 CATHOLIC	4	NA	4,256	4.7	7.3
081d *LATIN*	4	NA	4,256	4.7	7.3
093 CHR CH (DISC)	3	587	809	.9	1.4
097 CHR CHS&CHS CR	26	6,412	8,018*	8.9	13.8
111 CH CR,SCIENTST	1	NR	NR	-	-
123 CH GOD (ANDER)	2	33	190	.2	.3
127 CH GOD (CLEVE)	2	276	345*	.4	.6
133 CH GOD(7TH)DEN	1	42	55	.1	.1
145 CH GOD PROPHCY	1	25	31*	-	.1
151 L-D SAINTS	3	NA	961	1.1	1.7
157 CH OF BRETHREN	1	21	26*	-	-
165 CH OF NAZARENE	6	1,154	1,489	1.6	2.6
167 CHS OF CHRIST	6	651	877	1.0	1.5
175 CONGR CHR CHS	1	250	313*	.3	.5
193 EPISCOPAL	2	853	1,129	1.2	1.9
207 E.L.C.A.	1	155	178	.2	.3
217 FIRE BAPTIZED	1	16	20*	-	-
221 FREE METHODIST	1	25	30	-	.1
223 FREE WILL BAPT	2	249	311*	.3	.5
226 FRIENDS-USA	2	96	120*	.1	.2
226b *EFI*	2	96	120*	.1	.2
259 IFCA	1	NR	NR	-	-
263 INT FOURSQ GOS	1	33	41*	-	.1
283 LUTH—MO SYNOD	4	1,096	1,505	1.7	2.6
339 PENT CH OF GOD	5	132	358	.4	.6
355 PRESB CH (USA)	9	1,668	2,086*	2.3	3.6
375 REF EPISCOPAL	1	34	35	-	.1
403 SALVATION ARMY	2	182	189	.2	.3
413 S.D.A.	2	162	203*	.2	.4

County and Denomination	Number of churches	Communicant, confirmed, full members	Total adherents Number	Percent of total population	Percent of total adherents
419 SO BAPT CONV	37	16,159	20,206*	22.3	34.9
443 UN C OF CHRIST	1	14	18*	-	-
449 UN METHODIST	23	5,291	6,616*	7.3	11.4
496 JEWISH EST[1]	1	NA	67	.1	.1
497 BLACK BAPT EST[2]	NA	305	381*	.4	.7
498 INDEP.CHARIS.[3]	1	NA	700	.8	1.2
JEFFERSON	**133**	**33,793**	**78,389***	**45.7**	**100.0**
053 ASSEMB OF GOD	9	1,400	2,051	1.2	2.6
059 BAPT MISS ASSN	6	516	677*	.4	.9
081 CATHOLIC	11	NA	27,851	16.3	35.5
081d *LATIN*	11	NA	27,851	16.3	35.5
093 CHR CH (DISC)	2	267	432	.3	.6
097 CHR CHS&CHS CR	3	380	499*	.3	.6
111 CH CR,SCIENTST	1	NR	NR	-	-
121 CH GOD (ABR)	1	26	34*	-	-
123 CH GOD (ANDER)	1	185	214	.1	.3
127 CH GOD (CLEVE)	3	268	352*	.2	.4
151 L-D SAINTS	1	NA	415	.2	.5
165 CH OF NAZARENE	5	404	1,019	.6	1.3
167 CHS OF CHRIST	6	753	942	.5	1.2
171 CH GOD-GEN CON	1	21	28*	-	-
193 EPISCOPAL	1	75	76	-	.1
207 E.L.C.A.	1	336	419	.2	.5
223 FREE WILL BAPT	4	567	744*	.4	.9
259 IFCA	1	NR	NR	-	-
283 LUTH—MO SYNOD	10	4,162	5,845	3.4	7.5
339 PENT CH OF GOD	2	39	284	.2	.4
353 CHR BRETHREN	1	25	50	-	.1
355 PRESB CH (USA)	6	744	977*	.6	1.2
361 PRIM BAPT ASCS	1	21	28*	-	-
419 SO BAPT CONV	33	18,438	24,205*	14.1	30.9
436 UNITED BAPT	1	94	123*	.1	.2
443 UN C OF CHRIST	5	1,642	2,156*	1.3	2.8
449 UN METHODIST	15	3,112	4,085*	2.4	5.2
496 JEWISH EST[1]	0	NA	3,716	2.2	4.7
497 BLACK BAPT EST[2]	NA	318	417*	.2	.5
498 INDEP.CHARIS.[3]	2	NA	750	.4	1.0
JOHNSON	**74**	**13,069**	**20,314***	**47.8**	**100.0**
053 ASSEMB OF GOD	3	257	608	1.4	3.0
081 CATHOLIC	2	NA	1,415	3.3	7.0
081d *LATIN*	2	NA	1,415	3.3	7.0
093 CHR CH (DISC)	6	933	1,214	2.9	6.0
097 CHR CHS&CHS CR	3	575	719*	1.7	3.5
151 L-D SAINTS	1	NA	352	.8	1.7
157 CH OF BRETHREN	2	96	120*	.3	.6
165 CH OF NAZARENE	2	84	197	.5	1.0
167 CHS OF CHRIST	3	171	251	.6	1.2
185 CUMBER PRESB	3	221	229	.5	1.1
193 EPISCOPAL	1	109	175	.4	.9
203 EVAN FREE CH	1	16	36	.1	.2
221 FREE METHODIST	1	17	17	-	.1
283 LUTH—MO SYNOD	3	379	496	1.2	2.4
339 PENT CH OF GOD	1	41	125	.3	.6
355 PRESB CH (USA)	5	522	652*	1.5	3.2
413 S.D.A.	1	55	69*	.2	.3
419 SO BAPT CONV	22	6,982	8,726*	20.5	43.0
449 UN METHODIST	12	2,086	2,607*	6.1	12.8
497 BLACK BAPT EST[2]	NA	525	656*	1.5	3.2
499 INDEP.NON-CHAR[3]	2	NA	1,650	3.9	8.1
KNOX	**24**	**1,614**	**2,690***	**60.0**	**100.0**
053 ASSEMB OF GOD	3	166	332	7.4	12.3
081 CATHOLIC	2	NA	513	11.4	19.1
081d *LATIN*	2	NA	513	11.4	19.1
093 CHR CH (DISC)	2	92	188	4.2	7.0
097 CHR CHS&CHS CR	2	210	256*	5.7	9.5
165 CH OF NAZARENE	1	29	39	.9	1.4
167 CHS OF CHRIST	1	25	32	.7	1.2
419 SO BAPT CONV	8	561	683*	15.2	25.4
449 UN METHODIST	5	531	647*	14.4	24.1
LACLEDE	**66**	**10,026**	**14,084***	**51.9**	**100.0**
053 ASSEMB OF GOD	4	342	627	2.3	4.5
081 CATHOLIC	2	NA	953	3.5	6.8
081d *LATIN*	2	NA	953	3.5	6.8
093 CHR CH (DISC)	1	219	313	1.2	2.2
097 CHR CHS&CHS CR	5	1,003	1,274*	4.7	9.0
123 CH GOD (ANDER)	2	131	182	.7	1.3
151 L-D SAINTS	1	NA	157	.6	1.1
165 CH OF NAZARENE	1	200	303	1.1	2.2
167 CHS OF CHRIST	3	377	491	1.8	3.5
185 CUMBER PRESB	2	277	298	1.1	2.1
193 EPISCOPAL	1	112	125	.5	.9
223 FREE WILL BAPT	6	465	591*	2.2	4.2

NA–Not applicable   NR–Not reported   *Total adherents estimated from known number of communicant, confirmed, full members.   - Represents a percent less than 0.1.   Percentages may not total due to rounding.
[1]See Appendix E   [2]See Appendix F   [3]See Appendix G   Lines in *italic* represent a breakdown of Catholic rites or Friends affiliations. They are included in their respective denominational total.

Table 4. Churches and Church Membership by County and Denomination: 1990

County and Denomination	Number of churches	Communicant, confirmed, full members	Total adherents Number	Percent of total population	Percent of total adherents
259 IFCA	2	NR	NR	-	-
283 LUTH—MO SYNOD	1	251	325	1.2	2.3
339 PENT CH OF GOD	1	27	34	.1	.2
413 S.D.A.	1	61	77*	.3	.5
419 SO BAPT CONV	22	5,215	6,624*	24.4	47.0
443 UN C OF CHRIST	1	163	207*	.8	1.5
449 UN METHODIST	10	1,183	1,503*	5.5	10.7
LAFAYETTE	**67**	**14,809**	**21,562***	**69.3**	**100.0**
053 ASSEMB OF GOD	5	220	375	1.2	1.7
081 CATHOLIC	5	NA	1,839	5.9	8.5
081d *LATIN*	*5*	*NA*	*1,839*	*5.9*	*8.5*
093 CHR CH (DISC)	6	909	1,460	4.7	6.8
097 CHR CHS&CHS CR	1	140	177*	.6	.8
151 L-D SAINTS	1	NA	228	.7	1.1
167 CHS OF CHRIST	2	164	227	.7	1.1
193 EPISCOPAL	1	67	79	.3	.4
283 LUTH—MO SYNOD	8	3,517	4,411	14.2	20.5
355 PRESB CH (USA)	4	390	493*	1.6	2.3
419 SO BAPT CONV	16	5,057	6,397*	20.6	29.7
443 UN C OF CHRIST	7	2,031	2,569*	8.3	11.9
449 UN METHODIST	11	2,081	2,633*	8.5	12.2
496 JEWISH EST[1]	0	NA	379	1.2	1.8
497 BLACK BAPT EST[2]	NA	233	295*	.9	1.4
LAWRENCE	**85**	**12,359**	**18,321***	**60.6**	**100.0**
053 ASSEMB OF GOD	5	436	730	2.4	4.0
081 CATHOLIC	4	NA	1,799	5.9	9.8
081d *LATIN*	*4*	*NA*	*1,799*	*5.9*	*9.8*
093 CHR CH (DISC)	4	386	735	2.4	4.0
097 CHR CHS&CHS CR	5	556	703*	2.3	3.8
151 L-D SAINTS	1	NA	308	1.0	1.7
165 CH OF NAZARENE	5	223	314	1.0	1.7
167 CHS OF CHRIST	3	313	428	1.4	2.3
171 CH GOD-GEN CON	1	79	100*	.3	.5
185 CUMBER PRESB	3	73	73	.2	.4
203 EVAN FREE CH	1	20	25	.1	.1
221 FREE METHODIST	2	44	65	.2	.4
223 FREE WILL BAPT	2	194	245*	.8	1.3
230 FUND METHODIST	2	256	370	1.2	2.0
283 LUTH—MO SYNOD	3	1,006	1,340	4.4	7.3
355 PRESB CH (USA)	4	486	614*	2.0	3.4
419 SO BAPT CONV	25	6,658	8,413*	27.8	45.9
443 UN C OF CHRIST	3	112	142*	.5	.8
449 UN METHODIST	12	1,517	1,917*	6.3	10.5
LEWIS	**38**	**4,647**	**6,940***	**67.8**	**100.0**
053 ASSEMB OF GOD	2	58	120	1.2	1.7
081 CATHOLIC	3	NA	719	7.0	10.4
081d *LATIN*	*3*	*NA*	*719*	*7.0*	*10.4*
093 CHR CH (DISC)	5	533	950	9.3	13.7
097 CHR CHS&CHS CR	2	160	196*	1.9	2.8
167 CHS OF CHRIST	1	8	10	.1	.1
283 LUTH—MO SYNOD	1	262	345	3.4	5.0
323 OLD ORD AMISH	1	NA	150	1.5	2.2
355 PRESB CH (USA)	1	7	9*	.1	.1
419 SO BAPT CONV	13	2,909	3,570*	34.9	51.4
449 UN METHODIST	9	710	871*	8.5	12.6
LINCOLN	**60**	**8,339**	**16,152***	**55.9**	**100.0**
053 ASSEMB OF GOD	4	246	590	2.0	3.7
055 AS REF PRES CH	2	137	157	.5	1.0
081 CATHOLIC	5	NA	4,289	14.8	26.6
081d *LATIN*	*5*	*NA*	*4,289*	*14.8*	*26.6*
093 CHR CH (DISC)	4	610	788	2.7	4.9
097 CHR CHS&CHS CR	2	294	388*	1.3	2.4
151 L-D SAINTS	1	NA	240	.8	1.5
167 CHS OF CHRIST	1	110	120	.4	.7
217 FIRE BAPTIZED	4	123	162*	.6	1.0
283 LUTH—MO SYNOD	1	395	586	2.0	3.6
355 PRESB CH (USA)	4	326	430*	1.5	2.7
413 S.D.A.	1	25	33*	.1	.2
419 SO BAPT CONV	14	3,707	4,889*	16.9	30.3
443 UN C OF CHRIST	3	524	691*	2.4	4.3
449 UN METHODIST	13	1,716	2,263*	7.8	14.0
497 BLACK BAPT EST[2]	NA	126	166*	.6	1.0
499 INDEP.NON-CHAR[3]	1	NA	360	1.2	2.2
LINN	**48**	**6,967**	**10,350***	**74.5**	**100.0**
053 ASSEMB OF GOD	3	187	321	2.3	3.1
061 BEACHY AMISH	1	52	65*	.5	.6
081 CATHOLIC	2	NA	1,377	9.9	13.3
081d *LATIN*	*2*	*NA*	*1,377*	*9.9*	*13.3*
093 CHR CH (DISC)	4	671	978	7.0	9.4
097 CHR CHS&CHS CR	1	124	154*	1.1	1.5

County and Denomination	Number of churches	Communicant, confirmed, full members	Total adherents Number	Percent of total population	Percent of total adherents
165 CH OF NAZARENE	1	83	155	1.1	1.5
167 CHS OF CHRIST	4	160	203	1.5	2.0
283 LUTH—MO SYNOD	1	28	36	.3	.3
353 CHR BRETHREN	1	25	50	.4	.5
355 PRESB CH (USA)	1	112	139*	1.0	1.3
413 S.D.A.	1	22	27*	.2	.3
419 SO BAPT CONV	14	3,390	4,217*	30.4	40.7
449 UN METHODIST	14	2,113	2,628*	18.9	25.4
LIVINGSTON	**46**	**7,947**	**11,672***	**80.0**	**100.0**
019 AMER BAPT USA	1	104	130*	.9	1.1
053 ASSEMB OF GOD	2	112	189	1.3	1.6
081 CATHOLIC	4	NA	1,543	10.6	13.2
081d *LATIN*	*4*	*NA*	*1,543*	*10.6*	*13.2*
093 CHR CH (DISC)	4	388	641	4.4	5.5
127 CH GOD (CLEVE)	1	37	46*	.3	.4
165 CH OF NAZARENE	1	15	12	.1	.1
167 CHS OF CHRIST	1	250	325	2.2	2.8
193 EPISCOPAL	1	57	69	.5	.6
221 FREE METHODIST	1	120	120	.8	1.0
283 LUTH—MO SYNOD	1	122	158	1.1	1.4
339 PENT CH OF GOD	1	34	77	.5	.7
355 PRESB CH (USA)	3	432	539*	3.7	4.6
403 SALVATION ARMY	1	57	59	.4	.5
413 S.D.A.	1	22	27*	.2	.2
419 SO BAPT CONV	14	4,486	5,601*	38.4	48.0
443 UN C OF CHRIST	1	129	161*	1.1	1.4
449 UN METHODIST	8	1,582	1,975*	13.5	16.9
MC DONALD	**52**	**5,099**	**7,092***	**41.9**	**100.0**
053 ASSEMB OF GOD	3	65	107	.6	1.5
081 CATHOLIC	1	NA	130	.8	1.8
081d *LATIN*	*1*	*NA*	*130*	*.8*	*1.8*
093 CHR CH (DISC)	1	89	139	.8	2.0
097 CHR CHS&CHS CR	2	230	295*	1.7	4.2
151 L-D SAINTS	1	NA	201	1.2	2.8
165 CH OF NAZARENE	2	111	313	1.8	4.4
167 CHS OF CHRIST	11	312	386	2.3	5.4
193 EPISCOPAL	1	66	78	.5	1.1
223 FREE WILL BAPT	2	147	188*	1.1	2.7
230 FUND METHODIST	1	39	75	.4	1.1
339 PENT CH OF GOD	1	25	35	.2	.5
349 PENT HOLINESS	1	20	26*	.2	.4
355 PRESB CH (USA)	1	12	15*	.1	.2
361 PRIM BAPT ASCS	1	13	17*	.1	.2
413 S.D.A.	1	30	38*	.2	.5
419 SO BAPT CONV	15	3,333	4,271*	25.2	60.2
449 UN METHODIST	7	607	778*	4.6	11.0
MACON	**60**	**7,576**	**11,393***	**74.2**	**100.0**
053 ASSEMB OF GOD	3	109	190	1.2	1.7
081 CATHOLIC	2	NA	1,292	8.4	11.3
081d *LATIN*	*2*	*NA*	*1,292*	*8.4*	*11.3*
093 CHR CH (DISC)	3	630	1,007	6.6	8.8
097 CHR CHS&CHS CR	9	865	1,065*	6.9	9.3
151 L-D SAINTS	1	NA	168	1.1	1.5
165 CH OF NAZARENE	1	75	92	.6	.8
167 CHS OF CHRIST	3	82	105	.7	.9
283 LUTH—MO SYNOD	1	269	348	2.3	3.1
323 OLD ORD AMISH	2	NA	300	2.0	2.6
355 PRESB CH (USA)	5	562	692*	4.5	6.1
361 PRIM BAPT ASCS	2	40	49*	.3	.4
413 S.D.A.	2	83	102*	.7	.9
419 SO BAPT CONV	16	3,775	4,647*	30.3	40.8
443 UN C OF CHRIST	2	162	199*	1.3	1.7
449 UN METHODIST	8	924	1,137*	7.4	10.0
MADISON	**48**	**4,536**	**6,442***	**57.9**	**100.0**
053 ASSEMB OF GOD	2	99	135	1.2	2.1
059 BAPT MISS ASSN	1	53	66*	.6	1.0
081 CATHOLIC	1	NA	571	5.1	8.9
081d *LATIN*	*1*	*NA*	*571*	*5.1*	*8.9*
093 CHR CH (DISC)	1	137	305	2.7	4.7
097 CHR CHS&CHS CR	1	0	0*	-	-
121 CH GOD (ABR)	1	38	47*	.4	.7
123 CH GOD (ANDER)	1	9	14	.1	.2
145 CH GOD PROPHCY	1	25	31*	.3	.5
165 CH OF NAZARENE	1	113	146	1.3	2.3
167 CHS OF CHRIST	2	74	96	.9	1.5
223 FREE WILL BAPT	10	598	747*	6.7	11.6
283 LUTH—MO SYNOD	1	143	181	1.6	2.8
339 PENT CH OF GOD	2	61	122	1.1	1.9
355 PRESB CH (USA)	1	0	0*	-	-
361 PRIM BAPT ASCS	1	17	21*	.2	.3
413 S.D.A.	1	29	36*	.3	.6
419 SO BAPT CONV	12	2,199	2,748*	24.7	42.7

NA–Not applicable   NR–Not reported   *Total adherents estimated from known number of communicant, confirmed, full members.   - Represents a percent less than 0.1.   Percentages may not total due to rounding.
[1]See Appendix E   [2]See Appendix F   [3]See Appendix G   Lines in *italic* represent a breakdown of Catholic rites or Friends affiliations. They are included in their respective denominational total.

Table 4. Churches and Church Membership by County and Denomination: 1990

County and Denomination	Number of churches	Communicant, confirmed, full members	Total adherents Number	Total adherents Percent of total population	Total adherents Percent of total adherents
436 UNITED BAPT	5	340	425*	3.8	6.6
449 UN METHODIST	3	601	751*	6.7	11.7
MARIES	**32**	**3,194**	**4,801***	**60.2**	**100.0**
053 ASSEMB OF GOD	3	56	87	1.1	1.8
081 CATHOLIC	3	NA	802	10.1	16.7
081d *LATIN*	*3*	*NA*	*802*	*10.1*	*16.7*
097 CHR CHS&CHS CR	1	375	467*	5.9	9.7
165 CH OF NAZARENE	1	18	21	.3	.4
167 CHS OF CHRIST	7	305	400	5.0	8.3
283 LUTH—MO SYNOD	1	84	104	1.3	2.2
353 CHR BRETHREN	1	54	54	.7	1.1
419 SO BAPT CONV	10	1,911	2,379*	29.8	49.6
449 UN METHODIST	5	391	487*	6.1	10.1
MARION	**65**	**12,885**	**21,274***	**76.9**	**100.0**
040 AP CHR CH-AMER	1	86	151	.5	.7
053 ASSEMB OF GOD	4	628	867	3.1	4.1
059 BAPT MISS ASSN	1	42	54*	.2	.3
081 CATHOLIC	2	NA	4,338	15.7	20.4
081d *LATIN*	*2*	*NA*	*4,338*	*15.7*	*20.4*
093 CHR CH (DISC)	7	817	1,166	4.2	5.5
097 CHR CHS&CHS CR	3	690	879*	3.2	4.1
111 CH CR,SCIENTST	1	NR	NR	-	-
151 L-D SAINTS	1	NA	215	.8	1.0
165 CH OF NAZARENE	2	318	368	1.3	1.7
167 CHS OF CHRIST	2	87	120	.4	.6
193 EPISCOPAL	2	183	273	1.0	1.3
221 FREE METHODIST	1	24	32	.1	.2
223 FREE WILL BAPT	1	30	38*	.1	.2
283 LUTH—MO SYNOD	3	1,375	1,795	6.5	8.4
285 MENNONITE CH	2	108	174	.6	.8
355 PRESB CH (USA)	3	627	799*	2.9	3.8
403 SALVATION ARMY	1	95	100	.4	.5
413 S.D.A.	1	66	84*	.3	.4
419 SO BAPT CONV	17	5,805	7,396*	26.7	34.8
449 UN METHODIST	10	1,636	2,084*	7.5	9.8
497 BLACK BAPT EST[2]	NA	268	341*	1.2	1.6
MERCER	**21**	**2,389**	**3,119***	**83.8**	**100.0**
053 ASSEMB OF GOD	2	90	163	4.4	5.2
081 CATHOLIC	1	NA	66	1.8	2.1
081d *LATIN*	*1*	*NA*	*66*	*1.8*	*2.1*
093 CHR CH (DISC)	2	129	254	6.8	8.1
097 CHR CHS&CHS CR	1	0	0*	-	-
167 CHS OF CHRIST	1	25	30	.8	1.0
283 LUTH—MO SYNOD	1	25	40	1.1	1.3
349 PENT HOLINESS	1	39	47*	1.3	1.5
419 SO BAPT CONV	8	1,605	1,943*	52.2	62.3
449 UN METHODIST	4	476	576*	15.5	18.5
MILLER	**54**	**7,151**	**13,068***	**63.1**	**100.0**
001 ADVENT CHR CH	1	65	83*	.4	.6
053 ASSEMB OF GOD	4	265	409	2.0	3.1
081 CATHOLIC	5	NA	3,420	16.5	26.2
081d *LATIN*	*5*	*NA*	*3,420*	*16.5*	*26.2*
093 CHR CH (DISC)	1	319	349	1.7	2.7
097 CHR CHS&CHS CR	3	541	694*	3.4	5.3
111 CH CR,SCIENTST	1	NR	NR	-	-
165 CH OF NAZARENE	2	264	496	2.4	3.8
167 CHS OF CHRIST	12	474	598	2.9	4.6
283 LUTH—MO SYNOD	1	223	294	1.4	2.2
339 PENT CH OF GOD	1	12	30	.1	.2
413 S.D.A.	1	24	31*	.1	.2
419 SO BAPT CONV	18	4,533	5,812*	28.1	44.5
443 UN C OF CHRIST	1	43	55*	.3	.4
449 UN METHODIST	2	388	497*	2.4	3.8
499 INDEP.NON-CHAR[3]	1	NA	300	1.4	2.3
MISSISSIPPI	**35**	**6,079**	**8,522***	**59.0**	**100.0**
053 ASSEMB OF GOD	2	168	364	2.5	4.3
081 CATHOLIC	1	NA	530	3.7	6.2
081d *LATIN*	*1*	*NA*	*530*	*3.7*	*6.2*
093 CHR CH (DISC)	1	45	70	.5	.8
097 CHR CHS&CHS CR	2	382	491*	3.4	5.8
123 CH GOD (ANDER)	2	163	214	1.5	2.5
145 CH GOD PROPHCY	2	50	64*	.4	.8
165 CH OF NAZARENE	1	29	59	.4	.7
167 CHS OF CHRIST	2	90	104	.7	1.2
223 FREE WILL BAPT	1	42	54*	.4	.6
349 PENT HOLINESS	2	105	135*	.9	1.6
413 S.D.A.	1	82	105*	.7	1.2
419 SO BAPT CONV	12	3,513	4,519*	31.3	53.0
449 UN METHODIST	6	822	1,057*	7.3	12.4
497 BLACK BAPT EST[2]	NA	588	756*	5.2	8.9
MONITEAU	**44**	**6,435**	**10,527***	**85.6**	**100.0**
053 ASSEMB OF GOD	3	138	320	2.6	3.0
081 CATHOLIC	3	NA	1,828	14.9	17.4
081d *LATIN*	*3*	*NA*	*1,828*	*14.9*	*17.4*
093 CHR CH (DISC)	3	218	500	4.1	4.7
145 CH GOD PROPHCY	1	25	32*	.3	.3
151 L-D SAINTS	1	NA	83	.7	.8
167 CHS OF CHRIST	1	37	48	.4	.5
283 LUTH—MO SYNOD	1	365	484	3.9	4.6
287 MENN GEN CONF	1	207	285	2.3	2.7
339 PENT CH OF GOD	1	10	30	.2	.3
355 PRESB CH (USA)	1	4	5*	-	-
419 SO BAPT CONV	17	3,921	4,990*	40.6	47.4
443 UN C OF CHRIST	4	785	999*	8.1	9.5
449 UN METHODIST	7	725	923*	7.5	8.8
MONROE	**36**	**3,228**	**5,883***	**64.6**	**100.0**
053 ASSEMB OF GOD	1	25	71	.8	1.2
061 BEACHY AMISH	1	42	54*	.6	.9
081 CATHOLIC	3	NA	1,392	15.3	23.7
081d *LATIN*	*3*	*NA*	*1,392*	*15.3*	*23.7*
093 CHR CH (DISC)	9	753	1,272	14.0	21.6
123 CH GOD (ANDER)	1	13	22	.2	.4
193 EPISCOPAL	1	16	16	.2	.3
283 LUTH—MO SYNOD	1	94	126	1.4	2.1
355 PRESB CH (USA)	2	124	159*	1.7	2.7
419 SO BAPT CONV	11	1,537	1,971*	21.6	33.5
449 UN METHODIST	6	624	800*	8.8	13.6
MONTGOMERY	**48**	**4,645**	**7,363***	**64.8**	**100.0**
053 ASSEMB OF GOD	1	26	49	.4	.7
081 CATHOLIC	5	NA	1,264	11.1	17.2
081d *LATIN*	*5*	*NA*	*1,264*	*11.1*	*17.2*
093 CHR CH (DISC)	3	204	480	4.2	6.5
097 CHR CHS&CHS CR	3	220	277*	2.4	3.8
165 CH OF NAZARENE	1	29	67	.6	.9
167 CHS OF CHRIST	1	50	64	.6	.9
217 FIRE BAPTIZED	2	34	43*	.4	.6
259 IFCA	1	NR	NR	-	-
283 LUTH—MO SYNOD	3	534	658	5.8	8.9
355 PRESB CH (USA)	3	407	512*	4.5	7.0
419 SO BAPT CONV	11	1,574	1,979*	17.4	26.9
443 UN C OF CHRIST	2	254	319*	2.8	4.3
449 UN METHODIST	12	1,313	1,651*	14.5	22.4
MORGAN	**45**	**6,467**	**8,773***	**56.3**	**100.0**
019 AMER BAPT USA	1	45	55*	.4	.6
053 ASSEMB OF GOD	3	380	570	3.7	6.5
081 CATHOLIC	2	NA	733	4.7	8.4
081d *LATIN*	*2*	*NA*	*733*	*4.7*	*8.4*
093 CHR CH (DISC)	3	101	120	.8	1.4
097 CHR CHS&CHS CR	2	250	305*	2.0	3.5
123 CH GOD (ANDER)	1	60	60	.4	.7
143 CG IN CR(MENN)	1	101	123*	.8	1.4
167 CHS OF CHRIST	1	28	36	.2	.4
207 E.L.C.A.	2	329	394	2.5	4.5
283 LUTH—MO SYNOD	2	433	551	3.5	6.3
285 MENNONITE CH	1	52	57	.4	.6
286 E.PA MENNONITE	1	33	40*	.3	.5
339 PENT CH OF GOD	2	20	64	.4	.7
355 PRESB CH (USA)	3	187	229*	1.5	2.6
419 SO BAPT CONV	13	3,048	3,725*	23.9	42.5
443 UN C OF CHRIST	1	95	116*	.7	1.3
449 UN METHODIST	6	1,305	1,595*	10.2	18.2
NEW MADRID	**53**	**8,012**	**11,889***	**56.8**	**100.0**
053 ASSEMB OF GOD	7	261	455	2.2	3.8
059 BAPT MISS ASSN	2	375	485*	2.3	4.1
081 CATHOLIC	2	NA	1,018	4.9	8.6
081d *LATIN*	*2*	*NA*	*1,018*	*4.9*	*8.6*
093 CHR CH (DISC)	1	50	90	.4	.8
123 CH GOD (ANDER)	3	102	286	1.4	2.4
127 CH GOD (CLEVE)	1	45	58*	.3	.5
145 CH GOD PROPHCY	1	25	32*	.2	.3
151 L-D SAINTS	1	NA	231	1.1	1.9
157 CH OF BRETHREN	2	54	70*	.3	.6
165 CH OF NAZARENE	1	24	18	.1	.2
167 CHS OF CHRIST	7	341	437	2.1	3.7
355 PRESB CH (USA)	1	33	43*	.2	.4
361 PRIM BAPT ASCS	1	20	26*	.1	.2
413 S.D.A.	1	13	17*	.1	.1
419 SO BAPT CONV	14	5,210	6,736*	32.2	56.7
449 UN METHODIST	8	771	997*	4.8	8.4
497 BLACK BAPT EST[2]	NA	688	890*	4.3	7.5

NA–Not applicable   NR–Not reported   *Total adherents estimated from known number of communicant, confirmed, full members.   - Represents a percent less than 0.1.   Percentages may not total due to rounding.
[1]See Appendix E   [2]See Appendix F   [3]See Appendix G   Lines in *italic* represent a breakdown of Catholic rites or Friends affiliations. They are included in their respective denominational total.

Table 4. Churches and Church Membership by County and Denomination: 1990

County and Denomination		Number of churches	Communicant, confirmed, full members	Total adherents		
				Number	Percent of total population	Percent of total adherents
NEWTON		**102**	**17,360**	**24,128***	**54.3**	**100.0**
053	ASSEMB OF GOD	5	661	1,267	2.9	5.3
061	BEACHY AMISH	1	73	92*	.2	.4
081	CATHOLIC	3	NA	1,072	2.4	4.4
081d	LATIN	3	NA	1,072	2.4	4.4
093	CHR CH (DISC)	1	442	516	1.2	2.1
097	CHR CHS&CHS CR	5	1,183	1,492*	3.4	6.2
123	CH GOD (ANDER)	2	133	201	.5	.8
151	L-D SAINTS	2	NA	351	.8	1.5
157	CH OF BRETHREN	1	0	0*	-	-
165	CH OF NAZARENE	3	207	291	.7	1.2
167	CHS OF CHRIST	18	1,237	1,800	4.0	7.5
175	CONGR CHR CHS	1	111	140*	.3	.6
193	EPISCOPAL	1	112	112	.3	.5
203	EVAN FREE CH	1	32	70	.2	.3
217	FIRE BAPTIZED	2	20	25*	.1	.1
223	FREE WILL BAPT	4	321	405*	.9	1.7
230	FUND METHODIST	1	4	8	-	-
283	LUTH—MO SYNOD	1	251	329	.7	1.4
329	OPEN BIBLE STD	1	NR	NR	-	-
339	PENT CH OF GOD	1	15	35	.1	.1
355	PRESB CH (USA)	2	204	257*	.6	1.1
361	PRIM BAPT ASCS	1	24	30*	.1	.1
413	S.D.A.	1	28	35*	.1	.1
419	SO BAPT CONV	34	10,923	13,779*	31.0	57.1
449	UN METHODIST	9	1,362	1,718*	3.9	7.1
467	WESLEYAN	1	17	70	.2	.3
496	JEWISH EST[1]	0	NA	33	.1	.1
NODAWAY		**44**	**6,943**	**12,328***	**56.8**	**100.0**
053	ASSEMB OF GOD	1	140	260	1.2	2.1
081	CATHOLIC	4	NA	3,221	14.8	26.1
081d	LATIN	4	NA	3,221	14.8	26.1
093	CHR CH (DISC)	6	1,134	1,700	7.8	13.8
097	CHR CHS&CHS CR	6	620	756*	3.5	6.1
151	L-D SAINTS	1	NA	176	.8	1.4
165	CH OF NAZARENE	1	34	63	.3	.5
167	CHS OF CHRIST	3	120	149	.7	1.2
193	EPISCOPAL	1	57	81	.4	.7
283	LUTH—MO SYNOD	1	190	256	1.2	2.1
355	PRESB CH (USA)	1	222	271*	1.2	2.2
419	SO BAPT CONV	3	1,776	2,165*	10.0	17.6
449	UN METHODIST	16	2,650	3,230*	14.9	26.2
OREGON		**59**	**4,574**	**5,838***	**61.6**	**100.0**
053	ASSEMB OF GOD	6	235	385	4.1	6.6
059	BAPT MISS ASSN	1	36	44*	.5	.8
081	CATHOLIC	1	NA	144	1.5	2.5
081d	LATIN	1	NA	144	1.5	2.5
093	CHR CH (DISC)	1	25	27	.3	.5
123	CH GOD (ANDER)	1	62	83	.9	1.4
145	CH GOD PROPHCY	1	25	30*	.3	.5
167	CHS OF CHRIST	7	460	593	6.3	10.2
185	CUMBER PRESB	1	14	14	.1	.2
207	E.L.C.A.	1	31	38	.4	.7
223	FREE WILL BAPT	23	1,517	1,844*	19.5	31.6
419	SO BAPT CONV	12	1,825	2,218*	23.4	38.0
449	UN METHODIST	4	344	418*	4.4	7.2
OSAGE		**34**	**2,084**	**10,569***	**87.9**	**100.0**
053	ASSEMB OF GOD	1	93	76	.6	.7
061	BEACHY AMISH	1	35	45*	.4	.4
081	CATHOLIC	12	NA	7,947	66.1	75.2
081d	LATIN	12	NA	7,947	66.1	75.2
097	CHR CHS&CHS CR	5	351	448*	3.7	4.2
283	LUTH—MO SYNOD	2	126	166	1.4	1.6
419	SO BAPT CONV	7	958	1,222*	10.2	11.6
443	UN C OF CHRIST	3	136	174*	1.4	1.6
449	UN METHODIST	3	385	491*	4.1	4.6
OZARK		**29**	**1,647**	**2,753***	**32.0**	**100.0**
053	ASSEMB OF GOD	3	168	305	3.5	11.1
081	CATHOLIC	1	NA	203	2.4	7.4
081d	LATIN	1	NA	203	2.4	7.4
093	CHR CH (DISC)	1	134	241	2.8	8.8
123	CH GOD (ANDER)	1	35	55	.6	2.0
151	L-D SAINTS	1	NA	335	3.9	12.2
165	CH OF NAZARENE	1	22	17	.2	.6
167	CHS OF CHRIST	15	592	763	8.9	27.7
283	LUTH—MO SYNOD	1	52	55	.6	2.0
413	S.D.A.	1	23	28*	.3	1.0
419	SO BAPT CONV	3	458	554*	6.4	20.1
449	UN METHODIST	1	163	197*	2.3	7.2*

County and Denomination		Number of churches	Communicant, confirmed, full members	Total adherents		
				Number	Percent of total population	Percent of total adherents
PEMISCOT		**63**	**11,262**	**15,683***	**71.5**	**100.0**
053	ASSEMB OF GOD	4	235	414	1.9	2.6
059	BAPT MISS ASSN	1	123	162*	.7	1.0
081	CATHOLIC	1	NA	295	1.3	1.9
081d	LATIN	1	NA	295	1.3	1.9
097	CHR CHS&CHS CR	1	125	164*	.7	1.0
127	CH GOD (CLEVE)	3	227	298*	1.4	1.9
145	CH GOD PROPHCY	1	25	33*	.2	.2
151	L-D SAINTS	1	NA	299	1.4	1.9
165	CH OF NAZARENE	2	97	193	.9	1.2
167	CHS OF CHRIST	10	544	651	3.0	4.2
193	EPISCOPAL	1	11	14	.1	.1
339	PENT CH OF GOD	2	82	90	.4	.6
349	PENT HOLINESS	3	149	196*	.9	1.2
355	PRESB CH (USA)	1	327	430*	2.0	2.7
413	S.D.A.	1	94	124*	.6	.8
419	SO BAPT CONV	19	6,625	8,705*	39.7	55.5
449	UN METHODIST	10	864	1,135*	5.2	7.2
467	WESLEYAN	2	60	280	1.3	1.8
497	BLACK BAPT EST[2]	NA	1,674	2,200*	10.0	14.0
PERRY		**30**	**4,622**	**13,398***	**80.5**	**100.0**
053	ASSEMB OF GOD	1	43	83	.5	.6
081	CATHOLIC	10	NA	7,557	45.4	56.4
081d	LATIN	10	NA	7,557	45.4	56.4
165	CH OF NAZARENE	1	24	0	-	-
167	CHS OF CHRIST	1	10	15	.1	.1
283	LUTH—MO SYNOD	8	3,267	4,107	24.7	30.7
355	PRESB CH (USA)	2	155	198*	1.2	1.5
419	SO BAPT CONV	4	752	963*	5.8	7.2
449	UN METHODIST	3	371	475*	2.9	3.5
PETTIS		**77**	**17,168**	**26,132***	**73.7**	**100.0**
053	ASSEMB OF GOD	4	169	338	1.0	1.3
081	CATHOLIC	4	NA	3,380	9.5	12.9
081d	LATIN	4	NA	3,380	9.5	12.9
093	CHR CH (DISC)	1	722	1,243	3.5	4.8
097	CHR CHS&CHS CR	3	886	1,116*	3.1	4.3
111	CH CR,SCIENTST	1	NR	NR	-	-
127	CH GOD (CLEVE)	1	80	101*	.3	.4
151	L-D SAINTS	1	NA	434	1.2	1.7
165	CH OF NAZARENE	1	62	99	.3	.4
167	CHS OF CHRIST	1	60	84	.2	.3
193	EPISCOPAL	1	270	309	.9	1.2
207	E.L.C.A.	2	329	404	1.1	1.5
223	FREE WILL BAPT	1	82	103*	.3	.4
283	LUTH—MO SYNOD	2	1,298	1,780	5.0	6.8
329	OPEN BIBLE STD	1	NR	NR	-	-
339	PENT CH OF GOD	2	50	175	.5	.7
355	PRESB CH (USA)	3	721	908*	2.6	3.5
403	SALVATION ARMY	1	72	76	.2	.3
413	S.D.A.	2	157	198*	.6	.8
419	SO BAPT CONV	27	8,858	11,161*	31.5	42.7
443	UN C OF CHRIST	1	305	384*	1.1	1.5
449	UN METHODIST	16	2,797	3,524*	9.9	13.5
496	JEWISH EST[1]	1	NA	0	-	-
497	BLACK BAPT EST[2]	NA	250	315*	.9	1.2
PHELPS		**64**	**11,663**	**18,186***	**51.6**	**100.0**
053	ASSEMB OF GOD	5	494	1,153	3.3	6.3
059	BAPT MISS ASSN	1	32	39*	.1	.2
081	CATHOLIC	3	NA	2,460	7.0	13.5
081d	LATIN	3	NA	2,460	7.0	13.5
089	CHR & MISS AL	1	10	40	.1	.2
093	CHR CH (DISC)	1	27	42	.1	.2
097	CHR CHS&CHS CR	4	1,633	2,007*	5.7	11.0
111	CH CR,SCIENTST	1	NR	NR	-	-
123	CH GOD (ANDER)	3	376	498	1.4	2.7
151	L-D SAINTS	1	NA	295	.8	1.6
165	CH OF NAZARENE	1	101	118	.3	.6
167	CHS OF CHRIST	8	479	620	1.8	3.4
193	EPISCOPAL	2	335	433	1.2	2.4
223	FREE WILL BAPT	1	35	43*	.1	.2
226	FRIENDS-USA	1	4	10	-	.1
226c	FGC	1	4	10	-	.1
259	IFCA	1	NR	NR	-	-
283	LUTH—MO SYNOD	4	990	1,209	3.4	6.6
339	PENT CH OF GOD	1	35	77	.2	.4
355	PRESB CH (USA)	1	571	702*	2.0	3.9
361	PRIM BAPT ASCS	1	26	32*	.1	.2
413	S.D.A.	1	118	145*	.4	.8
419	SO BAPT CONV	17	5,437	6,683*	19.0	36.7
435	UNITARIAN-UNIV	1	17	21	.1	.1
449	UN METHODIST	3	943	1,159*	3.3	6.4
498	INDEP.CHARIS.[3]	1	NA	400	1.1	2.2

NA–Not applicable   NR–Not reported   *Total adherents estimated from known number of communicant, confirmed, full members.   - Represents a percent less than 0.1.   Percentages may not total due to rounding.
[1]See Appendix E   [2]See Appendix F   [3]See Appendix G   Lines in *italic* represent a breakdown of Catholic rites or Friends affiliations. They are included in their respective denominational total.

Table 4. Churches and Church Membership by County and Denomination: 1990

County and Denomination	Number of churches	Communicant, confirmed, full members	Total adherents Number	Percent of total population	Percent of total adherents
PIKE	**66**	**6,210**	**11,358***	**71.1**	**100.0**
053 ASSEMB OF GOD	2	32	88	.6	.8
081 CATHOLIC	3	NA	2,745	17.2	24.2
081d LATIN	*3*	*NA*	*2,745*	*17.2*	*24.2*
093 CHR CH (DISC)	10	497	860	5.4	7.6
165 CH OF NAZARENE	1	59	80	.5	.7
167 CHS OF CHRIST	4	98	123	.8	1.1
193 EPISCOPAL	3	123	144	.9	1.3
217 FIRE BAPTIZED	1	14	18*	.1	.2
221 FREE METHODIST	1	4	4	-	-
283 LUTH—MO SYNOD	2	159	206	1.3	1.8
323 OLD ORD AMISH	3	NA	450	2.8	4.0
355 PRESB CH (USA)	10	733	932*	5.8	8.2
419 SO BAPT CONV	20	3,781	4,806*	30.1	42.3
449 UN METHODIST	6	533	677*	4.2	6.0
497 BLACK BAPT EST[2]	NA	177	225*	1.4	2.0
PLATTE	**61**	**12,588**	**23,746***	**41.0**	**100.0**
019 AMER BAPT USA	1	35	44*	.1	.2
053 ASSEMB OF GOD	3	585	593	1.0	2.5
081 CATHOLIC	2	NA	5,476	9.5	23.1
081d LATIN	*2*	*NA*	*5,476*	*9.5*	*23.1*
093 CHR CH (DISC)	13	1,824	2,805	4.8	11.8
097 CHR CHS&CHS CR	3	387	488*	.8	2.1
151 L-D SAINTS	1	NA	397	.7	1.7
165 CH OF NAZARENE	1	49	50	.1	.2
167 CHS OF CHRIST	4	153	196	.3	.8
193 EPISCOPAL	1	207	346	.6	1.5
203 EVAN FREE CH	1	40	100	.2	.4
207 E.L.C.A.	1	330	465	.8	2.0
223 FREE WILL BAPT	1	104	131*	.2	.6
283 LUTH—MO SYNOD	3	843	1,097	1.9	4.6
331 ORTH CH IN AM	1	NR	NR	-	-
355 PRESB CH (USA)	1	366	461*	.8	1.9
419 SO BAPT CONV	14	4,784	6,030*	10.4	25.4
443 UN C OF CHRIST	1	44	55*	.1	.2
449 UN METHODIST	6	2,434	3,068*	5.3	12.9
469 WELS	1	81	132	.2	.6
496 JEWISH EST[1]	0	NA	706	1.2	3.0
497 BLACK BAPT EST[2]	NA	322	406*	.7	1.7
498 INDEP.CHARIS.[3]	1	NA	300	.5	1.3
499 INDEP.NON-CHAR[3]	1	NA	400	.7	1.7
POLK	**49**	**6,454**	**9,034***	**41.4**	**100.0**
053 ASSEMB OF GOD	9	595	926	4.2	10.3
081 CATHOLIC	2	NA	532	2.4	5.9
081d LATIN	*2*	*NA*	*532*	*2.4*	*5.9*
093 CHR CH (DISC)	3	347	548	2.5	6.1
097 CHR CHS&CHS CR	1	150	185*	.8	2.0
123 CH GOD (ANDER)	1	25	46	.2	.5
165 CH OF NAZARENE	1	62	44	.2	.5
167 CHS OF CHRIST	2	148	181	.8	2.0
185 CUMBER PRESB	2	66	70	.3	.8
283 LUTH—MO SYNOD	1	139	208	1.0	2.3
323 OLD ORD AMISH	1	NA	100	.5	1.1
339 PENT CH OF GOD	1	33	150	.7	1.7
413 S.D.A.	1	47	58*	.3	.6
419 SO BAPT CONV	13	3,801	4,699*	21.5	52.0
449 UN METHODIST	11	1,041	1,287*	5.9	14.2
PULASKI	**69**	**13,922**	**19,676***	**47.6**	**100.0**
053 ASSEMB OF GOD	5	326	605	1.5	3.1
081 CATHOLIC	4	NA	648	1.6	3.3
081d LATIN	*4*	*NA*	*648*	*1.6*	*3.3*
093 CHR CH (DISC)	1	100	157	.4	.8
097 CHR CHS&CHS CR	9	1,311	1,713*	4.1	8.7
123 CH GOD (ANDER)	3	131	248	.6	1.3
127 CH GOD (CLEVE)	1	71	93*	.2	.5
145 CH GOD PROPHCY	1	25	33*	.1	.2
151 L-D SAINTS	1	NA	392	.9	2.0
165 CH OF NAZARENE	1	89	128	.3	.7
167 CHS OF CHRIST	8	371	481	1.2	2.4
217 FIRE BAPTIZED	1	9	12*	-	.1
223 FREE WILL BAPT	1	43	56*	.1	.3
283 LUTH—MO SYNOD	1	163	217	.5	1.1
323 OLD ORD AMISH	1	NA	150	.4	.8
355 PRESB CH (USA)	1	100	131*	.3	.7
413 S.D.A.	1	21	27*	.1	.1
419 SO BAPT CONV	26	9,395	12,276*	29.7	62.4
449 UN METHODIST	3	566	740*	1.8	3.8
497 BLACK BAPT EST[2]	NA	1,201	1,569*	3.8	8.0
PUTNAM	**18**	**2,146**	**2,730***	**53.8**	**100.0**
053 ASSEMB OF GOD	1	28	63	1.2	2.3
081 CATHOLIC	1	NA	99	1.9	3.6
081d LATIN	*1*	*NA*	*99*	*1.9*	*3.6*
097 CHR CHS&CHS CR	4	585	707*	13.9	25.9
167 CHS OF CHRIST	4	81	107	2.1	3.9
419 SO BAPT CONV	5	1,191	1,439*	28.3	52.7
449 UN METHODIST	3	261	315*	6.2	11.5
RALLS	**24**	**2,490**	**3,939***	**46.5**	**100.0**
081 CATHOLIC	2	NA	333	3.9	8.5
081d LATIN	*2*	*NA*	*333*	*3.9*	*8.5*
093 CHR CH (DISC)	7	387	962	11.3	24.4
097 CHR CHS&CHS CR	1	125	157*	1.9	4.0
283 LUTH—MO SYNOD	1	35	47	.6	1.2
355 PRESB CH (USA)	2	69	87*	1.0	2.2
419 SO BAPT CONV	8	1,643	2,063*	24.3	52.4
449 UN METHODIST	3	231	290*	3.4	7.4
RANDOLPH	**56**	**9,867**	**15,861***	**65.1**	**100.0**
053 ASSEMB OF GOD	3	172	258	1.1	1.6
081 CATHOLIC	1	NA	2,136	8.8	13.5
081d LATIN	*1*	*NA*	*2,136*	*8.8*	*13.5*
093 CHR CH (DISC)	7	1,173	1,628	6.7	10.3
097 CHR CHS&CHS CR	3	673	838*	3.4	5.3
123 CH GOD (ANDER)	1	41	41	.2	.3
145 CH GOD PROPHCY	1	25	31*	.1	.2
151 L-D SAINTS	1	NA	266	1.1	1.7
165 CH OF NAZARENE	1	82	197	.8	1.2
167 CHS OF CHRIST	3	125	151	.6	1.0
185 CUMBER PRESB	1	59	59	.2	.4
193 EPISCOPAL	1	107	110	.5	.7
223 FREE WILL BAPT	1	40	50*	.2	.3
283 LUTH—MO SYNOD	1	291	379	1.6	2.4
323 OLD ORD AMISH	6	NA	900	3.7	5.7
355 PRESB CH (USA)	1	173	215*	.9	1.4
361 PRIM BAPT ASCS	1	42	52*	.2	.3
413 S.D.A.	1	153	191*	.8	1.2
419 SO BAPT CONV	14	4,777	5,950*	24.4	37.5
449 UN METHODIST	8	1,549	1,929*	7.9	12.2
497 BLACK BAPT EST[2]	NA	385	480*	2.0	3.0
RAY	**50**	**9,318**	**14,122***	**64.3**	**100.0**
053 ASSEMB OF GOD	4	406	732	3.3	5.2
081 CATHOLIC	1	NA	500	2.3	3.5
081d LATIN	*1*	*NA*	*500*	*2.3*	*3.5*
093 CHR CH (DISC)	5	603	1,036	4.7	7.3
097 CHR CHS&CHS CR	1	100	129*	.6	.9
157 CH OF BRETHREN	1	56	72*	.3	.5
165 CH OF NAZARENE	2	141	309	1.4	2.2
167 CHS OF CHRIST	3	86	110	.5	.8
171 CH GOD-GEN CON	1	145	186*	.8	1.3
283 LUTH—MO SYNOD	1	156	242	1.1	1.7
339 PENT CH OF GOD	1	34	77	.4	.5
355 PRESB CH (USA)	2	216	278*	1.3	2.0
419 SO BAPT CONV	16	5,873	7,552*	34.4	53.5
449 UN METHODIST	11	1,502	1,931*	8.8	13.7
496 JEWISH EST[1]	0	NA	268	1.2	1.9
498 INDEP.CHARIS.[3]	1	NA	700	3.2	5.0
REYNOLDS	**29**	**3,109**	**3,963***	**59.5**	**100.0**
053 ASSEMB OF GOD	4	106	141	2.1	3.6
059 BAPT MISS ASSN	4	232	290*	4.4	7.3
081 CATHOLIC	2	NA	45	.7	1.1
081d LATIN	*2*	*NA*	*45*	*.7*	*1.1*
165 CH OF NAZARENE	1	36	64	1.0	1.6
167 CHS OF CHRIST	1	13	17	.3	.4
419 SO BAPT CONV	10	1,762	2,205*	33.1	55.6
436 UNITED BAPT	6	872	1,091*	16.4	27.5
449 UN METHODIST	1	88	110*	1.7	2.8
RIPLEY	**42**	**2,794**	**3,721***	**30.2**	**100.0**
053 ASSEMB OF GOD	1	73	130	1.1	3.5
059 BAPT MISS ASSN	7	312	392*	3.2	10.5
081 CATHOLIC	1	NA	141	1.1	3.8
081d LATIN	*1*	*NA*	*141*	*1.1*	*3.8*
093 CHR CH (DISC)	2	195	260	2.1	7.0
097 CHR CHS&CHS CR	1	0	0*	-	-
121 CH GOD (ABR)	1	16	20*	.2	.5
123 CH GOD (ANDER)	4	274	318	2.6	8.5
127 CH GOD (CLEVE)	1	36	45*	.4	1.2
167 CHS OF CHRIST	8	349	471	3.8	12.7
283 LUTH—MO SYNOD	1	75	104	.8	2.8
355 PRESB CH (USA)	1	63	79*	.6	2.1
413 S.D.A.	1	40	50*	.4	1.3
415 S-D BAPTIST GC	1	35	44*	.4	1.2
419 SO BAPT CONV	7	1,090	1,370*	11.1	36.8
449 UN METHODIST	5	236	297*	2.4	8.0

NA–Not applicable   NR–Not reported   *Total adherents estimated from known number of communicant, confirmed, full members.   - Represents a percent less than 0.1.   Percentages may not total due to rounding.
[1]See Appendix E   [2]See Appendix F   [3]See Appendix G   Lines in *italic* represent a breakdown of Catholic rites or Friends affiliations. They are included in their respective denominational total.

Table 4. Churches and Church Membership by County and Denomination: 1990

County and Denomination	Number of churches	Communicant, confirmed, full members	Total adherents Number	Percent of total population	Percent of total adherents
ST CHARLES	**135**	**38,502**	**118,020***	**55.4**	**100.0**
019 AMER BAPT USA	1	0	0*	-	-
053 ASSEMB OF GOD	6	776	1,528	.7	1.3
059 BAPT MISS ASSN	3	253	335*	.2	.3
081 CATHOLIC	19	NA	55,495	26.1	47.0
081d LATIN	19	NA	55,495	26.1	47.0
089 CHR & MISS AL	1	0	19	-	-
093 CHR CH (DISC)	1	367	490	.2	.4
097 CHR CHS&CHS CR	6	1,485	1,966*	.9	1.7
111 CH CR,SCIENTST	1	NR	NR	-	-
121 CH GOD (ABR)	1	12	16*	-	-
123 CH GOD (ANDER)	3	85	135	.1	.1
127 CH GOD (CLEVE)	2	219	290*	.1	.2
145 CH GOD PROPHCY	1	25	33*	-	-
151 L-D SAINTS	3	NA	1,383	.6	1.2
165 CH OF NAZARENE	3	447	838	.4	.7
167 CHS OF CHRIST	6	558	834	.4	.7
193 EPISCOPAL	2	406	605	.3	.5
203 EVAN FREE CH	1	318	446	.2	.4
207 E.L.C.A.	3	960	1,388	.7	1.2
216 EVAN PRESBY CH	1	51	58	-	-
223 FREE WILL BAPT	2	200	265*	.1	.2
259 IFCA	1	NR	NR	-	-
263 INT FOURSQ GOS	1	219	290*	.1	.2
283 LUTH—MO SYNOD	12	8,104	11,242	5.3	9.5
339 PENT CH OF GOD	1	34	77	-	.1
353 CHR BRETHREN	4	91	150	.1	.1
355 PRESB CH (USA)	2	1,994	2,640*	1.2	2.2
356 PRESB CH AMER	1	50	74	-	.1
403 SALVATION ARMY	1	96	102	-	.1
413 S.D.A.	3	136	180*	.1	.2
419 SO BAPT CONV	18	11,970	15,847*	7.4	13.4
443 UN C OF CHRIST	13	4,001	5,297*	2.5	4.5
449 UN METHODIST	7	4,209	5,572*	2.6	4.7
467 WESLEYAN	1	49	210	.1	.2
469 WELS	1	75	111	.1	.1
496 JEWISH EST[1]	1	NA	4,617	2.2	3.9
497 BLACK BAPT EST[2]	NA	1,312	1,737*	.8	1.5
498 INDEP.CHARIS.[3]	1	NA	1,800	.8	1.5
499 INDEP.NON-CHAR[3]	3	NA	1,950	.9	1.7
ST CLAIR	**29**	**3,471**	**4,912***	**58.1**	**100.0**
053 ASSEMB OF GOD	2	90	250	3.0	5.1
081 CATHOLIC	1	NA	55	.7	1.1
081d LATIN	1	NA	55	.7	1.1
093 CHR CH (DISC)	2	182	394	4.7	8.0
097 CHR CHS&CHS CR	3	125	152*	1.8	3.1
151 L-D SAINTS	1	NA	283	3.3	5.8
157 CH OF BRETHREN	1	34	41*	.5	.8
283 LUTH—MO SYNOD	1	147	187	2.2	3.8
339 PENT CH OF GOD	1	35	77	.9	1.6
355 PRESB CH (USA)	1	32	39*	.5	.8
419 SO BAPT CONV	9	2,147	2,609*	30.9	53.1
443 UN C OF CHRIST	1	66	80*	.9	1.6
449 UN METHODIST	6	613	745*	8.8	15.2
STE GENEVIEVE	**25**	**2,590**	**11,597***	**72.3**	**100.0**
053 ASSEMB OF GOD	1	49	150	.9	1.3
081 CATHOLIC	9	NA	8,176	51.0	70.5
081d LATIN	9	NA	8,176	51.0	70.5
283 LUTH—MO SYNOD	1	177	242	1.5	2.1
355 PRESB CH (USA)	1	185	237*	1.5	2.0
419 SO BAPT CONV	13	2,179	2,792*	17.4	24.1
ST FRANCOIS	**109**	**20,297**	**31,249***	**63.9**	**100.0**
053 ASSEMB OF GOD	14	882	1,663	3.4	5.3
059 BAPT MISS ASSN	2	54	67*	.1	.2
081 CATHOLIC	5	NA	4,764	9.7	15.2
081d LATIN	5	NA	4,764	9.7	15.2
093 CHR CH (DISC)	3	408	583	1.2	1.9
097 CHR CHS&CHS CR	2	160	199*	.4	.6
111 CH CR,SCIENTST	1	NR	NR	-	-
123 CH GOD (ANDER)	3	148	148	.3	.5
127 CH GOD (CLEVE)	7	716	892*	1.8	2.9
145 CH GOD PROPHCY	1	25	31*	.1	.1
165 CH OF NAZARENE	3	422	710	1.5	2.3
167 CHS OF CHRIST	5	241	308	.6	1.0
171 CH GOD-GEN CON	5	673	839*	1.7	2.7
193 EPISCOPAL	2	38	58	.1	.2
223 FREE WILL BAPT	8	2,138	2,665*	5.4	8.5
283 LUTH—MO SYNOD	4	1,028	1,341	2.7	4.3
331 ORTH CH IN AM	1	NR	NR	-	-
355 PRESB CH (USA)	2	244	304*	.6	1.0
413 S.D.A.	1	105	131*	.3	.4
419 SO BAPT CONV	21	9,699	12,088*	24.7	38.7
436 UNITED BAPT	5	491	612*	1.3	2.0

County and Denomination	Number of churches	Communicant, confirmed, full members	Total adherents Number	Percent of total population	Percent of total adherents
443 UN C OF CHRIST	1	222	277*	.6	.9
449 UN METHODIST	12	2,397	2,987*	6.1	9.6
497 BLACK BAPT EST[2]	NA	206	257*	.5	.8
499 INDEP.NON-CHAR[3]	1	NA	325	.7	1.0
ST LOUIS	**559**	**209,023**	**623,220***	**62.7**	**100.0**
001 ADVENT CHR CH	1	35	43*	-	-
005 AME ZION	3	2,334	2,801	.3	.4
039 AP CHR CH(NAZ)	1	26	32*	-	-
053 ASSEMB OF GOD	21	2,309	3,122	.3	.5
057 BAPT GEN CONF	2	212	263*	-	-
059 BAPT MISS ASSN	8	755	938*	.1	.2
081 CATHOLIC	104	NA	317,562	32.0	51.0
081b BYZAN RUTH	1	NA	45	-	-
081d LATIN	102	NA	316,051	31.8	50.7
081e MARONITE	1	NA	1,466	.1	.2
093 CHR CH (DISC)	3	724	995	.1	.2
097 CHR CHS&CHS CR	10	2,721	3,380*	.3	.5
111 CH CR,SCIENTST	11	NR	NR	-	-
123 CH GOD (ANDER)	7	479	588	.1	.1
127 CH GOD (CLEVE)	2	566	703*	.1	.1
145 CH GOD PROPHCY	2	50	62*	-	-
151 L-D SAINTS	12	NA	4,564	.5	.7
164 CH LUTH CONF	1	46	70	-	-
165 CH OF NAZARENE	11	1,846	2,297	.2	.4
167 CHS OF CHRIST	22	3,846	5,338	.5	.9
193 EPISCOPAL	17	7,008	9,906	1.0	1.6
203 EVAN FREE CH	1	365	616	.1	.1
207 E.L.C.A.	14	5,856	7,485	.8	1.2
216 EVAN PRESBY CH	2	233	237	-	-
223 FREE WILL BAPT	7	1,038	1,289*	.1	.2
226 FRIENDS-USA	1	154	191*	-	-
226c FGC	1	154	191*	-	-
246 GREEK ORTHODOX	1	NR	NR	-	-
259 IFCA	5	NR	NR	-	-
263 INT FOURSQ GOS	3	616	765*	.1	.1
283 LUTH—MO SYNOD	47	31,362	41,026	4.1	6.6
285 MENNONITE CH	2	104	152	-	-
287 MENN GEN CONF	1	27	50	-	-
339 PENT CH OF GOD	2	100	290	-	-
349 PENT HOLINESS	1	24	30*	-	-
353 CHR BRETHREN	10	844	1,360	.1	.2
355 PRESB CH (USA)	34	16,630	20,656*	2.1	3.3
356 PRESB CH AMER	8	1,148	1,445	.1	.2
403 SALVATION ARMY	1	214	232	-	-
413 S.D.A.	5	462	574*	.1	.1
415 S-D BAPTIST GC	1	18	22*	-	-
419 SO BAPT CONV	66	46,624	57,911*	5.8	9.3
435 UNITARIAN-UNIV	3	506	842	.1	.1
436 UNITED BAPT	2	117	145*	-	-
443 UN C OF CHRIST	35	19,972	24,807*	2.5	4.0
449 UN METHODIST	41	22,539	27,995*	2.8	4.5
469 WELS	2	279	366	-	.1
496 JEWISH EST[1]	6	NA	21,689	2.2	3.5
497 BLACK BAPT EST[2]	NA	36,834	45,751*	4.6	7.3
498 INDEP.CHARIS.[3]	11	NA	10,740	1.1	1.7
499 INDEP.NON-CHAR[3]	9	NA	3,890	.4	.6
ST LOUIS CITY	**310**	**102,964**	**230,869***	**58.2**	**100.0**
005 AME ZION	3	1,672	1,807	.5	.8
019 AMER BAPT USA	7	4,910	6,160*	1.6	2.7
053 ASSEMB OF GOD	9	1,112	2,128	.5	.9
057 BAPT GEN CONF	1	32	40*	-	-
081 CATHOLIC	64	NA	90,846	22.9	39.3
081d LATIN	63	NA	90,715	22.9	39.3
081h UKRAINIAN	1	NA	131	-	.1
089 CHR & MISS AL	1	61	110	-	-
093 CHR CH (DISC)	13	2,970	5,276	1.3	2.3
097 CHR CHS&CHS CR	6	1,070	1,342*	.3	.6
105 CHRISTIAN REF	1	132	213	.1	.1
111 CH CR,SCIENTST	4	NR	NR	-	-
123 CH GOD (ANDER)	5	406	465	.1	.2
127 CH GOD (CLEVE)	3	427	536*	.1	.2
145 CH GOD PROPHCY	2	50	63*	-	-
165 CH OF NAZARENE	6	857	1,064	.3	.5
167 CHS OF CHRIST	6	679	810	.2	.4
171 CH GOD-GEN CON	1	0	0*	-	-
181 CONSRV CONGR	1	73	92*	-	-
193 EPISCOPAL	11	1,997	2,582	.7	1.1
203 EVAN FREE CH	1	110	200	.1	.1
207 E.L.C.A.	11	4,818	6,243	1.6	2.7
216 EVAN PRESBY CH	2	2,673	2,720	.7	1.2
221 FREE METHODIST	4	101	175	-	.1
246 GREEK ORTHODOX	1	NR	NR	-	-
259 IFCA	1	NR	NR	-	-
274 LAT EVAN LUTH	1	21	21	-	-
283 LUTH—MO SYNOD	27	9,704	13,027	3.3	5.6

Table 4. Churches and Church Membership by County and Denomination: 1990

County and Denomination	Number of churches	Communicant, confirmed, full members	Total adherents Number	Percent of total population	Percent of total adherents
331 ORTH CH IN AM	1	NR	NR	-	-
339 PENT CH OF GOD	1	34	77	-	-
353 CHR BRETHREN	2	101	135	-	.1
355 PRESB CH (USA)	18	3,181	3,991*	1.0	1.7
356 PRESB CH AMER	7	1,615	1,694	.4	.7
397 ROMANIAN ORTH	1	NR	NR	-	-
403 SALVATION ARMY	6	847	964	.2	.4
413 S.D.A.	4	2,283	2,864*	.7	1.2
419 SO BAPT CONV	19	14,053	17,631*	4.4	7.6
435 UNITARIAN-UNIV	1	445	558	.1	.2
436 UNITED BAPT	1	61	77*	-	-
443 UN C OF CHRIST	23	5,826	7,309*	1.8	3.2
449 UN METHODIST	15	4,687	5,880*	1.5	2.5
467 WESLEYAN	3	91	175	-	.1
496 JEWISH EST[1]	16	NA	8,599	2.2	3.7
497 BLACK BAPT EST[2]	NA	35,865	44,995*	11.3	19.5
SALINE	**72**	**10,695**	**16,258***	**69.1**	**100.0**
053 ASSEMB OF GOD	5	277	497	2.1	3.1
081 CATHOLIC	3	NA	2,427	10.3	14.9
081d LATIN	3	NA	2,427	10.3	14.9
093 CHR CH (DISC)	5	921	1,265	5.4	7.8
123 CH GOD (ANDER)	1	35	36	.2	.2
151 L-D SAINTS	1	NA	100	.4	.6
165 CH OF NAZARENE	1	115	231	1.0	1.4
167 CHS OF CHRIST	2	55	68	.3	.4
185 CUMBER PRESB	1	217	236	1.0	1.5
193 EPISCOPAL	1	50	66	.3	.4
223 FREE WILL BAPT	1	198	246*	1.0	1.5
259 IFCA	1	NR	NR	-	-
283 LUTH—MO SYNOD	7	1,313	1,748	7.4	10.8
355 PRESB CH (USA)	7	664	825*	3.5	5.1
413 S.D.A.	1	26	32*	.1	.2
419 SO BAPT CONV	18	4,273	5,311*	22.6	32.7
443 UN C OF CHRIST	4	438	544*	2.3	3.3
449 UN METHODIST	13	1,829	2,273*	9.7	14.0
497 BLACK BAPT EST[2]	NA	284	353*	1.5	2.2
SCHUYLER	**20**	**1,989**	**2,529***	**59.7**	**100.0**
053 ASSEMB OF GOD	1	62	96	2.3	3.8
081 CATHOLIC	1	NA	40	.9	1.6
081d LATIN	1	NA	40	.9	1.6
093 CHR CH (DISC)	1	30	47	1.1	1.9
097 CHR CHS&CHS CR	4	760	944*	22.3	37.3
167 CHS OF CHRIST	1	10	13	.3	.5
207 E.L.C.A.	1	110	126	3.0	5.0
223 FREE WILL BAPT	1	35	43*	1.0	1.7
419 SO BAPT CONV	5	760	944*	22.3	37.3
449 UN METHODIST	5	222	276*	6.5	10.9
SCOTLAND	**20**	**2,054**	**2,906***	**60.3**	**100.0**
053 ASSEMB OF GOD	1	12	50	1.0	1.7
081 CATHOLIC	1	NA	260	5.4	8.9
081d LATIN	1	NA	260	5.4	8.9
093 CHR CH (DISC)	1	12	20	.4	.7
097 CHR CHS&CHS CR	1	415	519*	10.8	17.9
151 L-D SAINTS	1	NA	28	.6	1.0
283 LUTH—MO SYNOD	1	37	54	1.1	1.9
355 PRESB CH (USA)	1	92	115*	2.4	4.0
419 SO BAPT CONV	6	810	1,014*	21.0	34.9
449 UN METHODIST	7	676	846*	17.5	29.1
SCOTT	**72**	**14,171**	**25,250***	**64.1**	**100.0**
053 ASSEMB OF GOD	4	680	1,274	3.2	5.0
059 BAPT MISS ASSN	2	233	300*	.8	1.2
081 CATHOLIC	7	NA	6,024	15.3	23.9
081d LATIN	7	NA	6,024	15.3	23.9
093 CHR CH (DISC)	2	418	642	1.6	2.5
123 CH GOD (ANDER)	3	370	698	1.8	2.8
127 CH GOD (CLEVE)	1	179	230*	.6	.9
145 CH GOD PROPHCY	2	50	64*	.2	.3
151 L-D SAINTS	1	NA	63	.2	.2
165 CH OF NAZARENE	2	188	289	.7	1.1
167 CHS OF CHRIST	6	715	933	2.4	3.7
193 EPISCOPAL	1	107	144	.4	.6
223 FREE WILL BAPT	2	86	111*	.3	.4
283 LUTH—MO SYNOD	3	626	813	2.1	3.2
355 PRESB CH (USA)	1	228	293*	.7	1.2
413 S.D.A.	2	102	131*	.3	.5
419 SO BAPT CONV	22	7,345	9,443*	24.0	37.4
449 UN METHODIST	10	2,038	2,620*	6.7	10.4
467 WESLEYAN	1	57	215	.5	.9
497 BLACK BAPT EST[2]	NA	749	963*	2.4	3.8

County and Denomination	Number of churches	Communicant, confirmed, full members	Total adherents Number	Percent of total population	Percent of total adherents
SHANNON	**27**	**2,254**	**3,367***	**44.2**	**100.0**
053 ASSEMB OF GOD	3	127	263	3.5	7.8
081 CATHOLIC	1	NA	33	.4	1.0
081d LATIN	1	NA	33	.4	1.0
097 CHR CHS&CHS CR	2	230	290*	3.8	8.6
145 CH GOD PROPHCY	5	119	150*	2.0	4.5
151 L-D SAINTS	1	NA	371	4.9	11.0
167 CHS OF CHRIST	2	43	55	.7	1.6
285 MENNONITE CH	1	9	25	.3	.7
419 SO BAPT CONV	6	1,405	1,774*	23.3	52.7
443 UN C OF CHRIST	1	21	27*	.4	.8
449 UN METHODIST	5	300	379*	5.0	11.3
SHELBY	**40**	**3,996**	**5,627***	**81.1**	**100.0**
053 ASSEMB OF GOD	2	28	25	.4	.4
081 CATHOLIC	5	NA	610	8.8	10.8
081d LATIN	5	NA	610	8.8	10.8
093 CHR CH (DISC)	3	47	84	1.2	1.5
097 CHR CHS&CHS CR	6	1,501	1,880*	27.1	33.4
157 CH OF BRETHREN	1	33	41*	.6	.7
165 CH OF NAZARENE	1	44	47	.7	.8
167 CHS OF CHRIST	1	20	20	.3	.4
221 FREE METHODIST	1	5	7	.1	.1
283 LUTH—MO SYNOD	1	101	121	1.7	2.2
285 MENNONITE CH	1	47	74	1.1	1.3
419 SO BAPT CONV	9	1,320	1,653*	23.8	29.4
449 UN METHODIST	9	850	1,065*	15.3	18.9
STODDARD	**61**	**8,372**	**11,528***	**39.9**	**100.0**
053 ASSEMB OF GOD	8	617	1,086	3.8	9.4
059 BAPT MISS ASSN	1	98	121*	.4	1.0
081 CATHOLIC	2	NA	659	2.3	5.7
081d LATIN	2	NA	659	2.3	5.7
089 CHR & MISS AL	1	20	61	.2	.5
093 CHR CH (DISC)	1	223	288	1.0	2.5
097 CHR CHS&CHS CR	3	180	222*	.8	1.9
123 CH GOD (ANDER)	1	63	90	.3	.8
127 CH GOD (CLEVE)	1	96	118*	.4	1.0
145 CH GOD PROPHCY	1	25	31*	.1	.3
165 CH OF NAZARENE	3	295	377	1.3	3.3
167 CHS OF CHRIST	10	824	1,076	3.7	9.3
283 LUTH—MO SYNOD	1	123	158	.5	1.4
323 OLD ORD AMISH	1	NA	50	.2	.4
339 PENT CH OF GOD	1	24	56	.2	.5
355 PRESB CH (USA)	1	59	73*	.3	.6
419 SO BAPT CONV	15	4,473	5,518*	19.1	47.9
449 UN METHODIST	10	1,252	1,544*	5.3	13.4
STONE	**52**	**5,507**	**7,556***	**39.6**	**100.0**
053 ASSEMB OF GOD	5	230	393	2.1	5.2
081 CATHOLIC	1	NA	742	3.9	9.8
081d LATIN	1	NA	742	3.9	9.8
093 CHR CH (DISC)	2	125	188	1.0	2.5
097 CHR CHS&CHS CR	3	255	305*	1.6	4.0
127 CH GOD (CLEVE)	2	96	115*	.6	1.5
165 CH OF NAZARENE	1	12	24	.1	.3
167 CHS OF CHRIST	5	207	278	1.5	3.7
171 CH GOD-GEN CON	1	78	93*	.5	1.2
185 CUMBER PRESB	1	26	26	.1	.3
193 EPISCOPAL	1	31	50	.3	.7
223 FREE WILL BAPT	2	141	169*	.9	2.2
230 FUND METHODIST	3	121	175	.9	2.3
283 LUTH—MO SYNOD	1	294	340	1.8	4.5
355 PRESB CH (USA)	2	323	387*	2.0	5.1
361 PRIM BAPT ASCS	1	22	26*	.1	.3
413 S.D.A.	1	21	25*	.1	.3
419 SO BAPT CONV	17	2,667	3,193*	16.7	42.3
449 UN METHODIST	3	858	1,027*	5.4	13.6
SULLIVAN	**36**	**2,995**	**3,956***	**62.5**	**100.0**
053 ASSEMB OF GOD	2	64	92	1.5	2.3
081 CATHOLIC	1	NA	200	3.2	5.1
081d LATIN	1	NA	200	3.2	5.1
093 CHR CH (DISC)	3	48	110	1.7	2.8
097 CHR CHS&CHS CR	4	555	666*	10.5	16.8
123 CH GOD (ANDER)	1	25	33	.5	.8
167 CHS OF CHRIST	2	45	58	.9	1.5
283 LUTH—MO SYNOD	1	29	37	.6	.9
323 OLD ORD AMISH	1	NA	50	.8	1.3
339 PENT CH OF GOD	1	34	77	1.2	1.9
355 PRESB CH (USA)	2	74	89*	1.4	2.2
361 PRIM BAPT ASCS	1	40	48*	.8	1.2
419 SO BAPT CONV	10	1,457	1,748*	27.6	44.2
449 UN METHODIST	7	624	748*	11.8	18.9

NA–Not applicable   NR–Not reported   *Total adherents estimated from known number of communicant, confirmed, full members.   - Represents a percent less than 0.1.   Percentages may not total due to rounding.

[1]See Appendix E   [2]See Appendix F   [3]See Appendix G   Lines in *italic* represent a breakdown of Catholic rites or Friends affiliations. They are included in their respective denominational total.

Table 4. Churches and Church Membership by County and Denomination: 1990

County and Denomination	Number of churches	Communicant, confirmed, full members	Total adherents Number	Percent of total population	Percent of total adherents
TANEY	**41**	**5,973**	**9,264***	**36.2**	**100.0**
053 ASSEMB OF GOD	3	214	676	2.6	7.3
081 CATHOLIC	2	NA	1,210	4.7	13.1
081d *LATIN*	2	*NA*	*1,210*	*4.7*	*13.1*
093 CHR CH (DISC)	2	379	525	2.1	5.7
097 CHR CHS&CHS CR	3	500	596*	2.3	6.4
111 CH CR,SCIENTST	1	NR	NR	-	-
127 CH GOD (CLEVE)	1	24	29*	.1	.3
151 L-D SAINTS	1	NA	251	1.0	2.7
165 CH OF NAZARENE	3	157	280	1.1	3.0
167 CHS OF CHRIST	4	204	260	1.0	2.8
193 EPISCOPAL	1	175	205	.8	2.2
203 EVAN FREE CH	1	16	110	.4	1.2
207 E.L.C.A.	1	89	107	.4	1.2
223 FREE WILL BAPT	1	65	77*	.3	.8
259 IFCA	2	NR	NR	-	-
283 LUTH—MO SYNOD	1	99	111	.4	1.2
355 PRESB CH (USA)	4	733	873*	3.4	9.4
413 S.D.A.	1	20	24*	.1	.3
419 SO BAPT CONV	7	2,494	2,972*	11.6	32.1
449 UN METHODIST	2	804	958*	3.7	10.3
TEXAS	**77**	**10,567**	**14,092***	**65.6**	**100.0**
053 ASSEMB OF GOD	6	234	399	1.9	2.8
081 CATHOLIC	4	NA	414	1.9	2.9
081d *LATIN*	4	*NA*	*414*	*1.9*	*2.9*
093 CHR CH (DISC)	1	25	39	.2	.3
097 CHR CHS&CHS CR	8	1,022	1,293*	6.0	9.2
123 CH GOD (ANDER)	2	82	132	.6	.9
145 CH GOD PROPHCY	2	50	63*	.3	.4
151 L-D SAINTS	1	NA	197	.9	1.4
157 CH OF BRETHREN	2	83	105*	.5	.7
167 CHS OF CHRIST	7	471	569	2.6	4.0
223 FREE WILL BAPT	9	835	1,056*	4.9	7.5
283 LUTH—MO SYNOD	1	97	129	.6	.9
285 MENNONITE CH	1	21	23	.1	.2
349 PENT HOLINESS	6	423	535*	2.5	3.8
419 SO BAPT CONV	23	6,362	8,048*	37.5	57.1
449 UN METHODIST	4	862	1,090*	5.1	7.7
VERNON	**48**	**7,059**	**10,349***	**54.4**	**100.0**
053 ASSEMB OF GOD	2	136	213	1.1	2.1
059 BAPT MISS ASSN	1	156	196*	1.0	1.9
081 CATHOLIC	1	NA	870	4.6	8.4
081d *LATIN*	1	*NA*	*870*	*4.6*	*8.4*
093 CHR CH (DISC)	1	388	529	2.8	5.1
097 CHR CHS&CHS CR	7	1,045	1,314*	6.9	12.7
111 CH CR,SCIENTST	1	NR	NR	-	-
143 CG IN CR(MENN)	1	80	101*	.5	1.0
151 L-D SAINTS	1	NA	262	1.4	2.5
165 CH OF NAZARENE	1	135	303	1.6	2.9
167 CHS OF CHRIST	2	112	145	.8	1.4
193 EPISCOPAL	1	114	178	.9	1.7
207 E.L.C.A.	1	95	140	.7	1.4
283 LUTH—MO SYNOD	1	39	113	.6	1.1
355 PRESB CH (USA)	1	133	167*	.9	1.6
413 S.D.A.	1	148	186*	1.0	1.8
419 SO BAPT CONV	17	3,450	4,339*	22.8	41.9
449 UN METHODIST	8	1,028	1,293*	6.8	12.5
WARREN	**27**	**4,760**	**10,082***	**51.6**	**100.0**
053 ASSEMB OF GOD	2	45	72	.4	.7
081 CATHOLIC	4	NA	3,553	18.2	35.2
081d *LATIN*	4	*NA*	*3,553*	*18.2*	*35.2*
097 CHR CHS&CHS CR	1	33	43*	.2	.4
127 CH GOD (CLEVE)	1	37	48*	.2	.5
165 CH OF NAZARENE	1	63	127	.7	1.3
167 CHS OF CHRIST	1	50	53	.3	.5
259 IFCA	1	NR	NR	-	-
283 LUTH—MO SYNOD	1	415	550	2.8	5.5
419 SO BAPT CONV	4	1,020	1,322*	6.8	13.1
443 UN C OF CHRIST	5	1,881	2,438*	12.5	24.2
449 UN METHODIST	5	877	1,136*	5.8	11.3
467 WESLEYAN	1	231	600	3.1	6.0
497 BLACK BAPT EST[2]	NA	108	140*	.7	1.4
WASHINGTON	**54**	**4,652**	**10,316***	**50.6**	**100.0**
053 ASSEMB OF GOD	6	231	537	2.6	5.2
059 BAPT MISS ASSN	11	1,337	1,735*	8.5	16.8
081 CATHOLIC	4	NA	3,923	19.2	38.0
081d *LATIN*	4	*NA*	*3,923*	*19.2*	*38.0*
097 CHR CHS&CHS CR	1	137	178*	.9	1.7
127 CH GOD (CLEVE)	3	222	288*	1.4	2.8
165 CH OF NAZARENE	2	57	87	.4	.8
167 CHS OF CHRIST	1	100	127	.6	1.2

County and Denomination	Number of churches	Communicant, confirmed, full members	Total adherents Number	Percent of total population	Percent of total adherents
171 CH GOD-GEN CON	5	196	254*	1.2	2.5
223 FREE WILL BAPT	2	74	96*	.5	.9
283 LUTH—MO SYNOD	1	31	40	.2	.4
339 PENT CH OF GOD	3	50	175	.9	1.7
355 PRESB CH (USA)	2	128	166*	.8	1.6
419 SO BAPT CONV	7	1,471	1,908*	9.4	18.5
449 UN METHODIST	6	618	802*	3.9	7.8
WAYNE	**42**	**3,250**	**4,546***	**39.4**	**100.0**
053 ASSEMB OF GOD	5	184	359	3.1	7.9
081 CATHOLIC	2	NA	365	3.2	8.0
081d *LATIN*	2	*NA*	*365*	*3.2*	*8.0*
097 CHR CHS&CHS CR	1	42	51*	.4	1.1
165 CH OF NAZARENE	2	190	282	2.4	6.2
167 CHS OF CHRIST	2	77	98	.8	2.2
209 EVAN LUTH SYN	1	52	64	.6	1.4
283 LUTH—MO SYNOD	2	40	51	.4	1.1
339 PENT CH OF GOD	1	25	45	.4	1.0
413 S.D.A.	1	39	48*	.4	1.1
419 SO BAPT CONV	17	2,066	2,528*	21.9	55.6
436 UNITED BAPT	1	94	115*	1.0	2.5
449 UN METHODIST	7	441	540*	4.7	11.9
WEBSTER	**89**	**9,285**	**14,253***	**60.0**	**100.0**
053 ASSEMB OF GOD	6	214	436	1.8	3.1
081 CATHOLIC	1	NA	444	1.9	3.1
081d *LATIN*	1	*NA*	*444*	*1.9*	*3.1*
093 CHR CH (DISC)	3	319	584	2.5	4.1
097 CHR CHS&CHS CR	1	112	144*	.6	1.0
127 CH GOD (CLEVE)	1	8	10*	-	.1
151 L-D SAINTS	1	NA	263	1.1	1.8
165 CH OF NAZARENE	3	117	148	.6	1.0
167 CHS OF CHRIST	9	336	450	1.9	3.2
185 CUMBER PRESB	2	128	128	.5	.9
215 EVAN METH CH	1	119	153*	.6	1.1
223 FREE WILL BAPT	14	771	994*	4.2	7.0
283 LUTH—MO SYNOD	3	438	601	2.5	4.2
285 MENNONITE CH	1	99	109	.5	.8
323 OLD ORD AMISH	4	NA	600	2.5	4.2
361 PRIM BAPT ASCS	1	9	12*	.1	.1
413 S.D.A.	2	161	208*	.9	1.5
419 SO BAPT CONV	23	5,008	6,455*	27.2	45.3
449 UN METHODIST	12	1,446	1,864*	7.8	13.1
499 INDEP.NON-CHAR[3]	1	NA	650	2.7	4.6
WORTH	**16**	**1,762**	**2,316***	**94.9**	**100.0**
053 ASSEMB OF GOD	1	53	100	4.1	4.3
093 CHR CH (DISC)	2	233	379	15.5	16.4
097 CHR CHS&CHS CR	3	330	411*	16.8	17.7
167 CHS OF CHRIST	1	25	32	1.3	1.4
355 PRESB CH (USA)	1	25	31*	1.3	1.3
419 SO BAPT CONV	5	747	929*	38.1	40.1
449 UN METHODIST	3	349	434*	17.8	18.7
WRIGHT	**63**	**7,412**	**10,195***	**60.8**	**100.0**
053 ASSEMB OF GOD	5	353	592	3.5	5.8
081 CATHOLIC	2	NA	373	2.2	3.7
081d *LATIN*	2	*NA*	*373*	*2.2*	*3.7*
093 CHR CH (DISC)	1	22	34	.2	.3
097 CHR CHS&CHS CR	2	35	45*	.3	.4
123 CH GOD (ANDER)	2	30	75	.4	.7
145 CH GOD PROPHCY	1	25	32*	.2	.3
157 CH OF BRETHREN	1	25	32*	.2	.3
165 CH OF NAZARENE	3	231	460	2.7	4.5
167 CHS OF CHRIST	6	311	400	2.4	3.9
185 CUMBER PRESB	1	99	99	.6	1.0
193 EPISCOPAL	1	42	48	.3	.5
223 FREE WILL BAPT	16	1,302	1,670*	10.0	16.4
349 PENT HOLINESS	1	260	334*	2.0	3.3
413 S.D.A.	1	55	71*	.4	.7
419 SO BAPT CONV	16	4,017	5,154*	30.8	50.6
449 UN METHODIST	4	605	776*	4.6	7.6

NA–Not applicable   NR–Not reported   *Total adherents estimated from known number of communicant, confirmed, full members.   - Represents a percent less than 0.1.   Percentages may not total due to rounding.
[1]See Appendix E   [2]See Appendix F   [3]See Appendix G   Lines in *italic* represent a breakdown of Catholic rites or Friends affiliations. They are included in their respective denominational total.

Table 4. Churches and Church Membership by County and Denomination: 1990

County and Denomination	Number of churches	Communicant, confirmed, full members	Total adherents		
			Number	Percent of total population	Percent of total adherents
MONTANA					
THE STATE.....	1,415	125,160	341,247*	42.7	100.0
BEAVERHEAD	16	768	3,314*	39.3	100.0
053 ASSEMB OF GOD	1	27	79	.9	2.4
081 CATHOLIC	2	NA	1,100	13.1	33.2
081d *LATIN*	*2*	*NA*	*1,100*	*13.1*	*33.2*
151 L-D SAINTS	3	NA	963	11.4	29.1
167 CHS OF CHRIST	1	26	48	.6	1.4
193 EPISCOPAL	1	77	295	3.5	8.9
207 E.L.C.A.	1	154	200	2.4	6.0
226 FRIENDS-USA	1	4	10	.1	.3
226f *INDEPENDNT*	*1*	*4*	*10*	*.1*	*.3*
263 INT FOURSQ GOS	1	28	36*	.4	1.1
355 PRESB CH (USA)	2	288	372*	4.4	11.2
413 S.D.A.	1	22	28*	.3	.8
419 SO BAPT CONV	1	24	31*	.4	.9
449 UN METHODIST	1	118	152*	1.8	4.6
BIG HORN	33	1,379	4,095*	36.1	100.0
019 AMER BAPT USA	5	410	583*	5.1	14.2
053 ASSEMB OF GOD	1	11	120	1.1	2.9
081 CATHOLIC	7	NA	1,725	15.2	42.1
081d *LATIN*	*7*	*NA*	*1,725*	*15.2*	*42.1*
089 CHR & MISS AL	1	16	43	.4	1.1
123 CH GOD (ANDER)	1	0	35	.3	.9
151 L-D SAINTS	1	NA	139	1.2	3.4
179 CONSRV BAPT	1	NR	NR	-	-
193 EPISCOPAL	1	15	36	.3	.9
207 E.L.C.A.	1	122	169	1.5	4.1
257 HUTTERIAN BR	1	NA	70	.6	1.7
263 INT FOURSQ GOS	1	54	77*	.7	1.9
283 LUTH—MO SYNOD	2	146	207	1.8	5.1
287 MENN GEN CONF	1	58	58	.5	1.4
329 OPEN BIBLE STD	1	NR	NR	-	-
339 PENT CH OF GOD	2	69	154	1.4	3.8
413 S.D.A.	1	39	55*	.5	1.3
419 SO BAPT CONV	2	85	121*	1.1	3.0
443 UN C OF CHRIST	2	289	411*	3.6	10.0
449 UN METHODIST	1	65	92*	.8	2.2
BLAINE	27	1,127	3,061*	45.5	100.0
053 ASSEMB OF GOD	4	158	301	4.5	9.8
081 CATHOLIC	7	NA	1,100	16.3	35.9
081d *LATIN*	*7*	*NA*	*1,100*	*16.3*	*35.9*
089 CHR & MISS AL	2	20	56	.8	1.8
097 CHR CHS&CHS CR	1	86	117*	1.7	3.8
151 L-D SAINTS	1	NA	202	3.0	6.6
167 CHS OF CHRIST	1	10	13	.2	.4
207 E.L.C.A.	4	512	677	10.1	22.1
257 HUTTERIAN BR	2	NA	140	2.1	4.6
283 LUTH—MO SYNOD	1	79	99	1.5	3.2
355 PRESB CH (USA)	2	110	149*	2.2	4.9
449 UN METHODIST	2	152	207*	3.1	6.8
BROADWATER	10	580	1,873*	56.4	100.0
081 CATHOLIC	2	NA	345	10.4	18.4
081d *LATIN*	*2*	*NA*	*345*	*10.4*	*18.4*
089 CHR & MISS AL	1	26	70	2.1	3.7
151 L-D SAINTS	2	NA	722	21.8	38.5
193 EPISCOPAL	1	38	49	1.5	2.6
207 E.L.C.A.	1	148	211	6.4	11.3
419 SO BAPT CONV	2	174	225*	6.8	12.0
449 UN METHODIST	1	194	251*	7.6	13.4
CARBON	27	1,221	2,905*	36.0	100.0
053 ASSEMB OF GOD	1	20	26	.3	.9
081 CATHOLIC	5	NA	960	11.9	33.0
081d *LATIN*	*5*	*NA*	*960*	*11.9*	*33.0*
089 CHR & MISS AL	1	22	52	.6	1.8
093 CHR CH (DISC)	1	82	115	1.4	4.0
151 L-D SAINTS	2	NA	226	2.8	7.8
167 CHS OF CHRIST	1	22	24	.3	.8
193 EPISCOPAL	3	79	94	1.2	3.2
207 E.L.C.A.	2	225	356	4.4	12.3
283 LUTH—MO SYNOD	2	180	223	2.8	7.7
413 S.D.A.	1	79	100*	1.2	3.4
419 SO BAPT CONV	2	51	64*	.8	2.2
443 UN C OF CHRIST	1	157	198*	2.5	6.8
449 UN METHODIST	4	274	345*	4.3	11.9
467 WESLEYAN	1	30	122	1.5	4.2
CARTER	7	64	235*	15.6	100.0
081 CATHOLIC	2	NA	135	9.0	57.4
081d *LATIN*	*2*	*NA*	*135*	*9.0*	*57.4*
151 L-D SAINTS	1	NA	20	1.3	8.5
207 E.L.C.A.	1	20	25	1.7	10.6
329 OPEN BIBLE STD	1	NR	NR	-	-
413 S.D.A.	1	19	24*	1.6	10.2
443 UN C OF CHRIST	1	25	31*	2.1	13.2
CASCADE	81	10,620	30,856*	39.7	100.0
019 AMER BAPT USA	1	369	476*	.6	1.5
053 ASSEMB OF GOD	2	349	670	.9	2.2
081 CATHOLIC	15	NA	12,192	15.7	39.5
081d *LATIN*	*15*	*NA*	*12,192*	*15.7*	*39.5*
089 CHR & MISS AL	1	59	209	.3	.7
093 CHR CH (DISC)	1	219	388	.5	1.3
097 CHR CHS&CHS CR	2	45	58*	.1	.2
111 CH CR,SCIENTST	1	NR	NR	-	-
123 CH GOD (ANDER)	1	0	25	-	.1
127 CH GOD (CLEVE)	1	39	50*	.1	.2
151 L-D SAINTS	11	NA	2,987	3.8	9.7
163 CH OF LUTH BR	1	26	61	.1	.2
165 CH OF NAZARENE	1	204	236	.3	.8
167 CHS OF CHRIST	3	263	338	.4	1.1
193 EPISCOPAL	2	471	566	.7	1.8
203 EVAN FREE CH	1	62	62	.1	.2
207 E.L.C.A.	6	2,927	4,167	5.4	13.5
226 FRIENDS-USA	1	1	7	-	-
226f *INDEPENDNT*	*1*	*1*	*7*	*-*	*-*
246 GREEK ORTHODOX	1	NR	NR	-	-
257 HUTTERIAN BR	4	NA	355	.5	1.2
263 INT FOURSQ GOS	1	350	451*	.6	1.5
283 LUTH—MO SYNOD	3	818	1,053	1.4	3.4
355 PRESB CH (USA)	2	1,058	1,364*	1.8	4.4
371 REF CH IN AM	1	58	120	.2	.4
403 SALVATION ARMY	1	106	106	.1	.3
413 S.D.A.	1	222	286*	.4	.9
419 SO BAPT CONV	4	926	1,194*	1.5	3.9
435 UNITARIAN-UNIV	1	15	15	-	-
443 UN C OF CHRIST	1	454	585*	.8	1.9
449 UN METHODIST	7	1,282	1,653*	2.1	5.4
469 WELS	1	71	91	.1	.3
497 BLACK BAPT EST[2]	NA	226	291*	.4	.9
498 INDEP.CHARIS.[3]	1	NA	400	.5	1.3
499 INDEP.NON-CHAR[3]	1	NA	400	.5	1.3
CHOUTEAU	17	1,080	4,332*	79.5	100.0
053 ASSEMB OF GOD	1	12	23	.4	.5
081 CATHOLIC	7	NA	2,933	53.8	67.7
081d *LATIN*	*7*	*NA*	*2,933*	*53.8*	*67.7*
097 CHR CHS&CHS CR	1	200	256*	4.7	5.9
123 CH GOD (ANDER)	1	81	81	1.5	1.9
193 EPISCOPAL	1	40	60	1.1	1.4
207 E.L.C.A.	1	162	227	4.2	5.2
283 LUTH—MO SYNOD	1	58	78	1.4	1.8
449 UN METHODIST	4	527	674*	12.4	15.6
CUSTER	20	2,383	5,606*	47.9	100.0
019 AMER BAPT USA	1	184	232*	2.0	4.1
053 ASSEMB OF GOD	1	115	220	1.9	3.9
081 CATHOLIC	3	NA	2,050	17.5	36.6
081d *LATIN*	*3*	*NA*	*2,050*	*17.5*	*36.6*
089 CHR & MISS AL	1	6	16	.1	.3
093 CHR CH (DISC)	1	74	104	.9	1.9
151 L-D SAINTS	1	NA	160	1.4	2.9
167 CHS OF CHRIST	2	27	41	.4	.7
193 EPISCOPAL	1	79	98	.8	1.7
207 E.L.C.A.	1	414	610	5.2	10.9
263 INT FOURSQ GOS	1	52	66*	.6	1.2
283 LUTH—MO SYNOD	1	421	651	5.6	11.6
355 PRESB CH (USA)	1	324	408*	3.5	7.3
413 S.D.A.	1	69	87*	.7	1.6
419 SO BAPT CONV	1	100	126*	1.1	2.2
443 UN C OF CHRIST	1	61	77*	.7	1.4
449 UN METHODIST	1	440	555*	4.7	9.9
467 WESLEYAN	1	17	105	.9	1.9
DANIELS	13	891	2,072*	91.4	100.0
053 ASSEMB OF GOD	1	34	52	2.3	2.5
081 CATHOLIC	4	NA	800	35.3	38.6
081d *LATIN*	*4*	*NA*	*800*	*35.3*	*38.6*
089 CHR & MISS AL	2	8	63	2.8	3.0
207 E.L.C.A.	5	739	1,022	45.1	49.3
449 UN METHODIST	1	110	135*	6.0	6.5

NA–Not applicable   NR–Not reported   *Total adherents estimated from known number of communicant, confirmed, full members.   - Represents a percent less than 0.1.   Percentages may not total due to rounding.
[1]See Appendix E   [2]See Appendix F   [3]See Appendix G   Lines in *italic* represent a breakdown of Catholic rites or Friends affiliations. They are included in their respective denominational total.

Table 4. Churches and Church Membership by County and Denomination: 1990

County and Denomination		Number of churches	Communicant, confirmed, full members	Total adherents		
				Number	Percent of total population	Percent of total adherents
DAWSON		**23**	**2,540**	**4,613***	**48.5**	**100.0**
053	ASSEMB OF GOD	1	46	90	.9	2.0
081	CATHOLIC	4	NA	1,108	11.7	24.0
081d	*LATIN*	*4*	*NA*	*1,108*	*11.7*	*24.0*
089	CHR & MISS AL	2	97	192	2.0	4.2
167	CHS OF CHRIST	1	39	62	.7	1.3
193	EPISCOPAL	1	11	11	.1	.2
207	E.L.C.A.	3	661	1,008	10.6	21.9
283	LUTH—MO SYNOD	1	822	1,049	11.0	22.7
285	MENNONITE CH	2	92	108	1.1	2.3
287	MENN GEN CONF	2	101	131	1.4	2.8
413	S.D.A.	1	45	57*	.6	1.2
419	SO BAPT CONV	1	158	201*	2.1	4.4
443	UN C OF CHRIST	2	183	233*	2.5	5.1
449	UN METHODIST	2	285	363*	3.8	7.9
DEER LODGE		**12**	**960**	**6,403***	**62.3**	**100.0**
053	ASSEMB OF GOD	1	77	151	1.5	2.4
057	BAPT GEN CONF	1	150	180*	1.8	2.8
081	CATHOLIC	1	NA	4,600	44.8	71.8
081d	*LATIN*	*1*	*NA*	*4,600*	*44.8*	*71.8*
093	CHR CH (DISC)	1	19	21	.2	.3
151	L-D SAINTS	1	NA	521	5.1	8.1
167	CHS OF CHRIST	1	33	48	.5	.7
193	EPISCOPAL	1	77	137	1.3	2.1
207	E.L.C.A.	1	353	444	4.3	6.9
263	INT FOURSQ GOS	1	7	8*	.1	.1
283	LUTH—MO SYNOD	1	34	41	.4	.6
355	PRESB CH (USA)	1	151	181*	1.8	2.8
419	SO BAPT CONV	1	59	71*	.7	1.1
FALLON		**12**	**1,040**	**2,115***	**68.2**	**100.0**
053	ASSEMB OF GOD	1	101	182	5.9	8.6
081	CATHOLIC	2	NA	600	19.3	28.4
081d	*LATIN*	*2*	*NA*	*600*	*19.3*	*28.4*
151	L-D SAINTS	1	NA	33	1.1	1.6
203	EVAN FREE CH	1	115	115	3.7	5.4
207	E.L.C.A.	2	472	687	22.1	32.5
313	N AM BAPT CONF	1	80	105*	3.4	5.0
419	SO BAPT CONV	1	137	180*	5.8	8.5
443	UN C OF CHRIST	1	113	148*	4.8	7.0
467	WESLEYAN	2	22	65	2.1	3.1
FERGUS		**34**	**2,120**	**5,739***	**47.5**	**100.0**
053	ASSEMB OF GOD	1	73	120	1.0	2.1
081	CATHOLIC	8	NA	2,154	17.8	37.5
081d	*LATIN*	*8*	*NA*	*2,154*	*17.8*	*37.5*
089	CHR & MISS AL	1	41	125	1.0	2.2
097	CHR CHS&CHS CR	1	225	285*	2.4	5.0
111	CH CR,SCIENTST	1	NR	NR	-	-
127	CH GOD (CLEVE)	1	37	47*	.4	.8
151	L-D SAINTS	1	NA	334	2.8	5.8
165	CH OF NAZARENE	1	37	92	.8	1.6
167	CHS OF CHRIST	1	31	40	.3	.7
179	CONSRV BAPT	1	NR	NR	-	-
193	EPISCOPAL	1	83	101	.8	1.8
207	E.L.C.A.	2	510	712	5.9	12.4
257	HUTTERIAN BR	5	NA	350	2.9	6.1
283	LUTH—MO SYNOD	2	197	256	2.1	4.5
355	PRESB CH (USA)	2	303	384*	3.2	6.7
413	S.D.A.	1	65	82*	.7	1.4
419	SO BAPT CONV	1	52	66*	.5	1.2
449	UN METHODIST	3	466	591*	4.9	10.3
FLATHEAD		**79**	**9,234**	**22,171***	**37.4**	**100.0**
019	AMER BAPT USA	1	97	125*	.2	.6
053	ASSEMB OF GOD	6	1,191	2,911	4.9	13.1
057	BAPT GEN CONF	1	53	68*	.1	.3
081	CATHOLIC	8	NA	6,047	10.2	27.3
081d	*LATIN*	*8*	*NA*	*6,047*	*10.2*	*27.3*
089	CHR & MISS AL	7	286	720	1.2	3.2
093	CHR CH (DISC)	3	236	294	.5	1.3
097	CHR CHS&CHS CR	3	178	229*	.4	1.0
111	CH CR,SCIENTST	1	NR	NR	-	-
123	CH GOD (ANDER)	2	144	168	.3	.8
145	CH GOD PROPHCY	1	18	23*	-	.1
151	L-D SAINTS	6	NA	2,050	3.5	9.2
165	CH OF NAZARENE	2	348	712	1.2	3.2
167	CHS OF CHRIST	4	126	192	.3	.9
193	EPISCOPAL	3	294	344	.6	1.6
207	E.L.C.A.	7	2,641	3,520	5.9	15.9
226	FRIENDS-USA	1	3	8	-	-
226f	*INDEPENDNT*	*1*	*3*	*8*	*-*	*-*
263	INT FOURSQ GOS	3	180	232*	.4	1.0
283	LUTH—MO SYNOD	3	955	1,314	2.2	5.9

County and Denomination		Number of churches	Communicant, confirmed, full members	Total adherents		
				Number	Percent of total population	Percent of total adherents
285	MENNONITE CH	1	72	76	.1	.3
339	PENT CH OF GOD	2	34	100	.2	.5
353	CHR BRETHREN	1	10	20	-	.1
355	PRESB CH (USA)	2	677	872*	1.5	3.9
403	SALVATION ARMY	1	104	111	.2	.5
413	S.D.A.	2	257	331*	.6	1.5
419	SO BAPT CONV	2	217	279*	.5	1.3
435	UNITARIAN-UNIV	1	28	28	-	.1
449	UN METHODIST	5	1,085	1,397*	2.4	6.3
GALLATIN		**64**	**8,067**	**19,153***	**38.0**	**100.0**
019	AMER BAPT USA	2	318	396*	.8	2.1
053	ASSEMB OF GOD	3	212	329	.7	1.7
081	CATHOLIC	7	NA	4,393	8.7	22.9
081d	*LATIN*	*7*	*NA*	*4,393*	*8.7*	*22.9*
089	CHR & MISS AL	1	82	182	.4	1.0
093	CHR CH (DISC)	1	321	518	1.0	2.7
097	CHR CHS&CHS CR	1	150	187*	.4	1.0
105	CHRISTIAN REF	4	997	1,679	3.3	8.8
111	CH CR,SCIENTST	1	NR	NR	-	-
127	CH GOD (CLEVE)	2	67	84*	.2	.4
151	L-D SAINTS	6	NA	1,749	3.5	9.1
165	CH OF NAZARENE	1	150	251	.5	1.3
167	CHS OF CHRIST	5	437	629	1.2	3.3
193	EPISCOPAL	2	253	360	.7	1.9
203	EVAN FREE CH	1	190	465	.9	2.4
207	E.L.C.A.	3	1,102	1,817	3.6	9.5
226	FRIENDS-USA	1	3	12	-	.1
226f	*INDEPENDNT*	*1*	*3*	*12*	*-*	*.1*
263	INT FOURSQ GOS	1	177	221*	.4	1.2
283	LUTH—MO SYNOD	2	560	846	1.7	4.4
355	PRESB CH (USA)	5	823	1,026*	2.0	5.4
403	SALVATION ARMY	1	16	19	-	.1
413	S.D.A.	3	463	577*	1.1	3.0
419	SO BAPT CONV	4	754	940*	1.9	4.9
435	UNITARIAN-UNIV	1	26	32	.1	.2
443	UN C OF CHRIST	1	209	261*	.5	1.4
449	UN METHODIST	2	703	876*	1.7	4.6
469	WELS	1	54	74	.1	.4
498	INDEP.CHARIS.[3]	1	NA	580	1.1	3.0
499	INDEP.NON-CHAR[3]	1	NA	650	1.3	3.4
GARFIELD		**8**	**313**	**748***	**47.1**	**100.0**
053	ASSEMB OF GOD	1	40	71	4.5	9.5
081	CATHOLIC	1	NA	225	14.2	30.1
081d	*LATIN*	*1*	*NA*	*225*	*14.2*	*30.1*
151	L-D SAINTS	1	NA	64	4.0	8.6
167	CHS OF CHRIST	1	22	39	2.5	5.2
207	E.L.C.A.	1	117	155	9.8	20.7
353	CHR BRETHREN	1	25	50	3.1	6.7
355	PRESB CH (USA)	1	72	95*	6.0	12.7
413	S.D.A.	1	37	49*	3.1	6.6
GLACIER		**22**	**986**	**8,998***	**74.2**	**100.0**
053	ASSEMB OF GOD	1	73	206	1.7	2.3
081	CATHOLIC	7	NA	6,784	56.0	75.4
081d	*LATIN*	*7*	*NA*	*6,784*	*56.0*	*75.4*
151	L-D SAINTS	2	NA	293	2.4	3.3
203	EVAN FREE CH	1	29	65	.5	.7
207	E.L.C.A.	1	454	675	5.6	7.5
257	HUTTERIAN BR	4	NA	356	2.9	4.0
263	INT FOURSQ GOS	1	13	19*	.2	.2
285	MENNONITE CH	1	2	6	-	.1
355	PRESB CH (USA)	1	232	332*	2.7	3.7
419	SO BAPT CONV	1	102	146*	1.2	1.6
449	UN METHODIST	2	81	116*	1.0	1.3
GOLDEN VALLEY		**11**	**131**	**544***	**59.6**	**100.0**
053	ASSEMB OF GOD	1	20	26	2.9	4.8
081	CATHOLIC	3	NA	154	16.9	28.3
081d	*LATIN*	*3*	*NA*	*154*	*16.9*	*28.3*
151	L-D SAINTS	1	NA	111	12.2	20.4
207	E.L.C.A.	2	39	70	7.7	12.9
257	HUTTERIAN BR	1	NA	89	9.8	16.4
419	SO BAPT CONV	1	16	20*	2.2	3.7
449	UN METHODIST	1	25	32*	3.5	5.9
469	WELS	1	31	42	4.6	7.7
GRANITE		**6**	**62**	**645***	**25.3**	**100.0**
081	CATHOLIC	2	NA	313	12.3	48.5
081d	*LATIN*	*2*	*NA*	*313*	*12.3*	*48.5*
151	L-D SAINTS	2	NA	236	9.3	36.6
193	EPISCOPAL	1	29	55	2.2	8.5
355	PRESB CH (USA)	1	33	41*	1.6	6.4

NA–Not applicable   NR–Not reported   *Total adherents estimated from known number of communicant, confirmed, full members.   - Represents a percent less than 0.1.   Percentages may not total due to rounding.
[1]See Appendix E   [2]See Appendix F   [3]See Appendix G   Lines in *italic* represent a breakdown of Catholic rites or Friends affiliations. They are included in their respective denominational total.

Table 4. Churches and Church Membership by County and Denomination: 1990

County and Denomination	Number of churches	Communicant, confirmed, full members	Total adherents		
			Number	Percent of total population	Percent of total adherents
HILL	**33**	**3,424**	**8,562***	**48.5**	**100.0**
019 AMER BAPT USA	2	117	155*	.9	1.8
053 ASSEMB OF GOD	2	126	321	1.8	3.7
081 CATHOLIC	2	NA	3,000	17.0	35.0
081d LATIN	2	NA	3,000	17.0	35.0
089 CHR & MISS AL	1	38	103	.6	1.2
097 CHR CHS&CHS CR	1	400	530*	3.0	6.2
111 CH CR,SCIENTST	1	NR	NR	-	-
151 L-D SAINTS	1	NA	344	1.9	4.0
165 CH OF NAZARENE	1	31	63	.4	.7
167 CHS OF CHRIST	1	12	16	.1	.2
193 EPISCOPAL	1	47	187	1.1	2.2
207 E.L.C.A.	8	1,527	2,084	11.8	24.3
257 HUTTERIAN BR	3	NA	248	1.4	2.9
263 INT FOURSQ GOS	2	94	125*	.7	1.5
283 LUTH—MO SYNOD	1	252	366	2.1	4.3
355 PRESB CH (USA)	1	128	170*	1.0	2.0
403 SALVATION ARMY	1	43	43	.2	.5
413 S.D.A.	1	80	106*	.6	1.2
419 SO BAPT CONV	1	127	168*	1.0	2.0
449 UN METHODIST	2	402	533*	3.0	6.2
JEFFERSON	**17**	**700**	**1,802***	**22.7**	**100.0**
053 ASSEMB OF GOD	2	63	120	1.5	6.7
081 CATHOLIC	3	NA	553	7.0	30.7
081d LATIN	3	NA	553	7.0	30.7
093 CHR CH (DISC)	1	130	133	1.7	7.4
151 L-D SAINTS	2	NA	313	3.9	17.4
165 CH OF NAZARENE	1	19	45	.6	2.5
283 LUTH—MO SYNOD	2	89	120	1.5	6.7
413 S.D.A.	1	24	31*	.4	1.7
419 SO BAPT CONV	2	167	217*	2.7	12.0
449 UN METHODIST	3	208	270*	3.4	15.0
JUDITH BASIN	**5**	**194**	**574***	**25.2**	**100.0**
081 CATHOLIC	1	NA	250	11.0	43.6
081d LATIN	1	NA	250	11.0	43.6
257 HUTTERIAN BR	1	NA	70	3.1	12.2
283 LUTH—MO SYNOD	1	55	81	3.5	14.1
355 PRESB CH (USA)	2	139	173*	7.6	30.1
LAKE	**40**	**2,661**	**7,275***	**34.6**	**100.0**
053 ASSEMB OF GOD	2	74	98	.5	1.3
081 CATHOLIC	6	NA	2,145	10.2	29.5
081d LATIN	6	NA	2,145	10.2	29.5
089 CHR & MISS AL	4	150	405	1.9	5.6
093 CHR CH (DISC)	1	62	105	.5	1.4
097 CHR CHS&CHS CR	4	249	326*	1.5	4.5
151 L-D SAINTS	4	NA	1,163	5.5	16.0
165 CH OF NAZARENE	1	50	145	.7	2.0
167 CHS OF CHRIST	2	36	55	.3	.8
193 EPISCOPAL	2	248	397	1.9	5.5
207 E.L.C.A.	2	685	919	4.4	12.6
283 LUTH—MO SYNOD	3	362	508	2.4	7.0
285 MENNONITE CH	1	13	28	.1	.4
355 PRESB CH (USA)	2	237	310*	1.5	4.3
413 S.D.A.	1	122	160*	.8	2.2
419 SO BAPT CONV	1	94	123*	.6	1.7
449 UN METHODIST	3	277	363*	1.7	5.0
467 WESLEYAN	1	2	25	.1	.3
LEWIS AND CLARK	**53**	**6,487**	**19,954***	**42.0**	**100.0**
019 AMER BAPT USA	1	119	153*	.3	.8
053 ASSEMB OF GOD	1	536	1,434	3.0	7.2
057 BAPT GEN CONF	1	31	40*	.1	.2
081 CATHOLIC	10	NA	8,960	18.9	44.9
081d LATIN	10	NA	8,960	18.9	44.9
089 CHR & MISS AL	1	23	73	.2	.4
093 CHR CH (DISC)	1	174	296	.6	1.5
097 CHR CHS&CHS CR	1	16	21*	-	.1
105 CHRISTIAN REF	1	53	110	.2	.6
111 CH CR,SCIENTST	1	NR	NR	-	-
127 CH GOD (CLEVE)	1	101	130*	.3	.7
145 CH GOD PROPHCY	1	18	23*	-	.1
151 L-D SAINTS	3	NA	1,237	2.6	6.2
165 CH OF NAZARENE	1	62	152	.3	.8
167 CHS OF CHRIST	2	99	128	.3	.6
179 CONSRV BAPT	1	NR	NR	-	-
193 EPISCOPAL	2	454	640	1.3	3.2
207 E.L.C.A.	3	1,186	1,703	3.6	8.5
226 FRIENDS-USA	1	5	8	-	-
226f INDEPENDNT	1	5	8	-	-
257 HUTTERIAN BR	1	NA	89	.2	.4
263 INT FOURSQ GOS	1	70	90*	.2	.5
283 LUTH—MO SYNOD	1	408	636	1.3	3.2

County and Denomination	Number of churches	Communicant, confirmed, full members	Total adherents		
			Number	Percent of total population	Percent of total adherents
349 PENT HOLINESS	1	22	28*	.1	.1
353 CHR BRETHREN	1	10	20	-	.1
355 PRESB CH (USA)	1	501	643*	1.4	3.2
403 SALVATION ARMY	1	102	106	.2	.5
413 S.D.A.	1	127	163*	.3	.8
419 SO BAPT CONV	4	463	594*	1.3	3.0
435 UNITARIAN-UNIV	1	15	19	-	.1
443 UN C OF CHRIST	1	459	589*	1.2	3.0
449 UN METHODIST	4	1,368	1,756*	3.7	8.8
467 WESLEYAN	1	0	15	-	.1
469 WELS	1	65	98	.2	.5
LIBERTY	**14**	**693**	**2,059***	**89.7**	**100.0**
053 ASSEMB OF GOD	1	45	60	2.6	2.9
081 CATHOLIC	4	NA	825	35.9	40.1
081d LATIN	4	NA	825	35.9	40.1
089 CHR & MISS AL	1	49	139	6.1	6.8
151 L-D SAINTS	1	NA	58	2.5	2.8
207 E.L.C.A.	3	430	570	24.8	27.7
257 HUTTERIAN BR	2	NA	178	7.8	8.6
355 PRESB CH (USA)	1	22	30*	1.3	1.5
449 UN METHODIST	1	147	199*	8.7	9.7
LINCOLN	**36**	**2,818**	**6,199***	**35.5**	**100.0**
019 AMER BAPT USA	1	220	287*	1.6	4.6
053 ASSEMB OF GOD	3	236	415	2.4	6.7
081 CATHOLIC	3	NA	1,200	6.9	19.4
081d LATIN	3	NA	1,200	6.9	19.4
089 CHR & MISS AL	2	59	194	1.1	3.1
097 CHR CHS&CHS CR	2	273	356*	2.0	5.7
123 CH GOD (ANDER)	3	75	147	.8	2.4
127 CH GOD (CLEVE)	1	12	16*	.1	.3
151 L-D SAINTS	3	NA	650	3.7	10.5
165 CH OF NAZARENE	1	75	135	.8	2.2
167 CHS OF CHRIST	1	65	100	.6	1.6
193 EPISCOPAL	3	82	136	.8	2.2
203 EVAN FREE CH	1	60	121	.7	2.0
207 E.L.C.A.	1	477	643	3.7	10.4
283 LUTH—MO SYNOD	3	511	772	4.4	12.5
323 OLD ORD AMISH	1	NA	150	.9	2.4
355 PRESB CH (USA)	1	62	81*	.5	1.3
413 S.D.A.	3	113	147*	.8	2.4
419 SO BAPT CONV	1	230	300*	1.7	4.8
449 UN METHODIST	2	268	349*	2.0	5.6
MC CONE	**11**	**590**	**1,281***	**56.3**	**100.0**
019 AMER BAPT USA	1	19	24*	1.1	1.9
053 ASSEMB OF GOD	1	43	75	3.3	5.9
081 CATHOLIC	4	NA	480	21.1	37.5
081d LATIN	4	NA	480	21.1	37.5
207 E.L.C.A.	1	366	491	21.6	38.3
419 SO BAPT CONV	1	74	95*	4.2	7.4
443 UN C OF CHRIST	2	46	59*	2.6	4.6
469 WELS	1	42	57	2.5	4.4
MADISON	**16**	**527**	**1,398***	**23.3**	**100.0**
053 ASSEMB OF GOD	2	86	211	3.5	15.1
081 CATHOLIC	1	NA	321	5.4	23.0
081d LATIN	1	NA	321	5.4	23.0
111 CH CR,SCIENTST	1	NR	NR	-	-
151 L-D SAINTS	2	NA	306	5.1	21.9
167 CHS OF CHRIST	1	9	14	.2	1.0
193 EPISCOPAL	3	145	173	2.9	12.4
203 EVAN FREE CH	1	24	50	.8	3.6
283 LUTH—MO SYNOD	2	40	48	.8	3.4
355 PRESB CH (USA)	1	78	96*	1.6	6.9
449 UN METHODIST	2	145	179*	3.0	12.8
MEAGHER	**9**	**241**	**1,102***	**60.6**	**100.0**
053 ASSEMB OF GOD	1	6	16	.9	1.5
081 CATHOLIC	1	NA	586	32.2	53.2
081d LATIN	1	NA	586	32.2	53.2
089 CHR & MISS AL	1	32	36	2.0	3.3
207 E.L.C.A.	2	140	207	11.4	18.8
257 HUTTERIAN BR	2	NA	178	9.8	16.2
355 PRESB CH (USA)	1	52	65*	3.6	5.9
413 S.D.A.	1	11	14*	.8	1.3
MINERAL	**6**	**187**	**511***	**15.4**	**100.0**
053 ASSEMB OF GOD	1	47	72	2.2	14.1
081 CATHOLIC	1	NA	125	3.8	24.5
081d LATIN	1	NA	125	3.8	24.5
151 L-D SAINTS	1	NA	122	3.7	23.9
167 CHS OF CHRIST	1	10	13	.4	2.5
283 LUTH—MO SYNOD	1	94	132	4.0	25.8

NA–Not applicable   NR–Not reported   *Total adherents estimated from known number of communicant, confirmed, full members.   - Represents a percent less than 0.1.   Percentages may not total due to rounding.

[1]See Appendix E   [2]See Appendix F   [3]See Appendix G   Lines in *italic* represent a breakdown of Catholic rites or Friends affiliations. They are included in their respective denominational total.

Table 4. Churches and Church Membership by County and Denomination: 1990

County and Denomination	Number of churches	Communicant, confirmed, full members	Total adherents Number	Percent of total population	Percent of total adherents
413 S.D.A.	1	36	47*	1.4	9.2
MISSOULA	**70**	**8,908**	**23,994***	**30.5**	**100.0**
011 A.W.M.C.	2	46	58*	.1	.2
019 AMER BAPT USA	1	204	257*	.3	1.1
053 ASSEMB OF GOD	2	768	1,431	1.8	6.0
081 CATHOLIC	10	NA	8,057	10.2	33.6
081d *LATIN*	*10*	*NA*	*8,057*	*10.2*	*33.6*
089 CHR & MISS AL	1	185	521	.7	2.2
093 CHR CH (DISC)	1	176	282	.4	1.2
097 CHR CHS&CHS CR	1	75	94*	.1	.4
111 CH CR,SCIENTST	1	NR	NR	-	-
123 CH GOD (ANDER)	1	36	45	.1	.2
127 CH GOD (CLEVE)	1	15	19*	-	.1
145 CH GOD PROPHCY	1	18	23*	-	.1
151 L-D SAINTS	9	NA	2,963	3.8	12.3
165 CH OF NAZARENE	2	114	152	.2	.6
167 CHS OF CHRIST	4	164	212	.3	.9
193 EPISCOPAL	1	523	740	.9	3.1
203 EVAN FREE CH	1	19	35	-	.1
207 E.L.C.A.	6	2,140	3,324	4.2	13.9
221 FREE METHODIST	1	11	33	-	.1
226 FRIENDS-USA	1	18	23*	-	.1
226f *INDEPENDNT*	*1*	*18*	*23**	*-*	*.1*
246 GREEK ORTHODOX	1	NR	NR	-	-
263 INT FOURSQ GOS	1	268	338*	.4	1.4
283 LUTH—MO SYNOD	5	838	1,175	1.5	4.9
313 N AM BAPT CONF	1	263	331*	.4	1.4
339 PENT CH OF GOD	2	110	180	.2	.8
353 CHR BRETHREN	1	25	50	.1	.2
355 PRESB CH (USA)	2	663	835*	1.1	3.5
403 SALVATION ARMY	1	79	89	.1	.4
413 S.D.A.	1	269	339*	.4	1.4
419 SO BAPT CONV	3	588	741*	.9	3.1
435 UNITARIAN-UNIV	1	28	39	-	.2
443 UN C OF CHRIST	1	316	398*	.5	1.7
449 UN METHODIST	2	863	1,087*	1.4	4.5
469 WELS	1	86	123	.2	.5
MUSSELSHELL	**18**	**684**	**1,528***	**37.2**	**100.0**
019 AMER BAPT USA	1	100	123*	3.0	8.0
053 ASSEMB OF GOD	1	24	68	1.7	4.5
081 CATHOLIC	5	NA	520	12.7	34.0
081d *LATIN*	*5*	*NA*	*520*	*12.7*	*34.0*
167 CHS OF CHRIST	2	39	57	1.4	3.7
193 EPISCOPAL	1	23	31	.8	2.0
203 EVAN FREE CH	1	10	16	.4	1.0
207 E.L.C.A.	1	163	246	6.0	16.1
257 HUTTERIAN BR	1	NA	70	1.7	4.6
283 LUTH—MO SYNOD	1	41	47	1.1	3.1
413 S.D.A.	1	18	22*	.5	1.4
419 SO BAPT CONV	1	36	44*	1.1	2.9
449 UN METHODIST	1	181	223*	5.4	14.6
469 WELS	1	49	61	1.5	4.0
PARK	**22**	**1,468**	**3,866***	**26.5**	**100.0**
019 AMER BAPT USA	1	110	138*	.9	3.6
053 ASSEMB OF GOD	1	87	225	1.5	5.8
081 CATHOLIC	4	NA	1,388	9.5	35.9
081d *LATIN*	*4*	*NA*	*1,388*	*9.5*	*35.9*
127 CH GOD (CLEVE)	1	9	11*	.1	.3
151 L-D SAINTS	2	NA	359	2.5	9.3
165 CH OF NAZARENE	1	27	80	.5	2.1
167 CHS OF CHRIST	1	36	46	.3	1.2
175 CONGR CHR CHS	1	43	54*	.4	1.4
193 EPISCOPAL	2	100	191	1.3	4.9
207 E.L.C.A.	3	475	639	4.4	16.5
413 S.D.A.	1	93	117*	.8	3.0
419 SO BAPT CONV	1	58	73*	.5	1.9
449 UN METHODIST	2	349	439*	3.0	11.4
469 WELS	1	81	106	.7	2.7
PETROLEUM	**3**	**74**	**157***	**30.3**	**100.0**
081 CATHOLIC	1	NA	50	9.6	31.8
081d *LATIN*	*1*	*NA*	*50*	*9.6*	*31.8*
449 UN METHODIST	1	32	40*	7.7	25.5
469 WELS	1	42	67	12.9	42.7
PHILLIPS	**22**	**917**	**2,785***	**53.9**	**100.0**
053 ASSEMB OF GOD	2	90	187	3.6	6.7
081 CATHOLIC	4	NA	1,200	23.2	43.1
081d *LATIN*	*4*	*NA*	*1,200*	*23.2*	*43.1*
097 CHR CHS&CHS CR	1	35	46*	.9	1.7
151 L-D SAINTS	1	NA	110	2.1	3.9
163 CH OF LUTH BR	1	28	84	1.6	3.0
167 CHS OF CHRIST	1	9	10	.2	.4
193 EPISCOPAL	1	14	22	.4	.8
207 E.L.C.A.	5	622	831	16.1	29.8
257 HUTTERIAN BR	2	NA	140	2.7	5.0
259 IFCA	1	NR	NR	-	-
263 INT FOURSQ GOS	1	17	22*	.4	.8
419 SO BAPT CONV	1	9	12*	.2	.4
443 UN C OF CHRIST	1	93	121*	2.3	4.3
PONDERA	**19**	**1,603**	**4,269***	**66.4**	**100.0**
053 ASSEMB OF GOD	1	57	145	2.3	3.4
081 CATHOLIC	3	NA	1,562	24.3	36.6
081d *LATIN*	*3*	*NA*	*1,562*	*24.3*	*36.6*
093 CHR CH (DISC)	1	64	79	1.2	1.9
105 CHRISTIAN REF	1	61	104	1.6	2.4
151 L-D SAINTS	1	NA	200	3.1	4.7
207 E.L.C.A.	3	775	1,057	16.4	24.8
257 HUTTERIAN BR	3	NA	266	4.1	6.2
355 PRESB CH (USA)	1	235	311*	4.8	7.3
419 SO BAPT CONV	3	224	297*	4.6	7.0
449 UN METHODIST	2	187	248*	3.9	5.8
POWDER RIVER	**10**	**238**	**691***	**33.1**	**100.0**
053 ASSEMB OF GOD	1	16	28	1.3	4.1
081 CATHOLIC	4	NA	350	16.7	50.7
081d *LATIN*	*4*	*NA*	*350*	*16.7*	*50.7*
089 CHR & MISS AL	1	12	24	1.1	3.5
179 CONSRV BAPT	1	NR	NR	-	-
207 E.L.C.A.	1	113	166	7.9	24.0
443 UN C OF CHRIST	2	97	123*	5.9	17.8
POWELL	**13**	**588**	**1,477***	**22.3**	**100.0**
053 ASSEMB OF GOD	1	81	158	2.4	10.7
081 CATHOLIC	4	NA	312	4.7	21.1
081d *LATIN*	*4*	*NA*	*312*	*4.7*	*21.1*
093 CHR CH (DISC)	1	41	74	1.1	5.0
151 L-D SAINTS	1	NA	279	4.2	18.9
167 CHS OF CHRIST	1	8	8	.1	.5
193 EPISCOPAL	1	51	99	1.5	6.7
203 EVAN FREE CH	1	25	55	.8	3.7
283 LUTH—MO SYNOD	1	148	208	3.1	14.1
355 PRESB CH (USA)	1	144	175*	2.6	11.8
419 SO BAPT CONV	1	90	109*	1.6	7.4
PRAIRIE	**8**	**422**	**860***	**62.2**	**100.0**
081 CATHOLIC	1	NA	225	16.3	26.2
081d *LATIN*	*1*	*NA*	*225*	*16.3*	*26.2*
207 E.L.C.A.	1	63	79	5.7	9.2
283 LUTH—MO SYNOD	1	115	176	12.7	20.5
355 PRESB CH (USA)	1	125	150*	10.8	17.4
413 S.D.A.	1	4	5*	.4	.6
467 WESLEYAN	2	67	167	12.1	19.4
469 WELS	1	48	58	4.2	6.7
RAVALLI	**47**	**3,426**	**7,670***	**30.7**	**100.0**
019 AMER BAPT USA	4	385	489*	2.0	6.4
053 ASSEMB OF GOD	2	289	486	1.9	6.3
081 CATHOLIC	4	NA	1,484	5.9	19.3
081d *LATIN*	*4*	*NA*	*1,484*	*5.9*	*19.3*
093 CHR CH (DISC)	1	93	133	.5	1.7
097 CHR CHS&CHS CR	1	30	38*	.2	.5
111 CH CR,SCIENTST	1	NR	NR	-	-
151 L-D SAINTS	5	NA	1,449	5.8	18.9
165 CH OF NAZARENE	1	54	80	.3	1.0
167 CHS OF CHRIST	3	109	161	.6	2.1
193 EPISCOPAL	2	91	147	.6	1.9
207 E.L.C.A.	1	421	541	2.2	7.1
259 IFCA	3	NR	NR	-	-
263 INT FOURSQ GOS	3	113	143*	.6	1.9
283 LUTH—MO SYNOD	2	432	573	2.3	7.5
285 MENNONITE CH	1	32	33	.1	.4
353 CHR BRETHREN	1	25	50	.2	.7
355 PRESB CH (USA)	2	283	359*	1.4	4.7
413 S.D.A.	3	269	341*	1.4	4.4
419 SO BAPT CONV	2	345	438*	1.8	5.7
449 UN METHODIST	3	378	480*	1.9	6.3
467 WESLEYAN	2	77	245	1.0	3.2
RICHLAND	**27**	**3,547**	**7,943***	**74.1**	**100.0**
053 ASSEMB OF GOD	1	191	438	4.1	5.5
081 CATHOLIC	3	NA	2,132	19.9	26.8
081d *LATIN*	*3*	*NA*	*2,132*	*19.9*	*26.8*
089 CHR & MISS AL	4	122	368	3.4	4.6
151 L-D SAINTS	2	NA	440	4.1	5.5
163 CH OF LUTH BR	1	61	167	1.6	2.1

NA–Not applicable   NR–Not reported   *Total adherents estimated from known number of communicant, confirmed, full members.   - Represents a percent less than 0.1.   Percentages may not total due to rounding.

[1]See Appendix E   [2]See Appendix F   [3]See Appendix G   Lines in *italic* represent a breakdown of Catholic rites or Friends affiliations. They are included in their respective denominational total.

Table 4. Churches and Church Membership by County and Denomination: 1990

County and Denomination	Number of churches	Communicant, confirmed, full members	Total adherents Number	Percent of total population	Percent of total adherents
165 CH OF NAZARENE	1	80	198	1.8	2.5
167 CHS OF CHRIST	1	60	95	.9	1.2
181 CONSRV CONGR	1	135	179*	1.7	2.3
207 E.L.C.A.	4	1,548	2,185	20.4	27.5
283 LUTH—MO SYNOD	2	388	442	4.1	5.6
284 LUTH CH-AM ASC	1	162	237	2.2	3.0
355 PRESB CH (USA)	1	123	163*	1.5	2.1
413 S.D.A.	1	23	31*	.3	.4
419 SO BAPT CONV	1	31	41*	.4	.5
443 UN C OF CHRIST	2	263	349*	3.3	4.4
449 UN METHODIST	1	360	478*	4.5	6.0
ROOSEVELT	**47**	**2,782**	**7,337***	**66.7**	**100.0**
019 AMER BAPT USA	1	47	66*	.6	.9
053 ASSEMB OF GOD	2	116	210	1.9	2.9
081 CATHOLIC	11	NA	2,753	25.0	37.5
081d *LATIN*	*11*	*NA*	*2,753*	*25.0*	*37.5*
151 L-D SAINTS	2	NA	727	6.6	9.9
157 CH OF BRETHREN	1	47	66*	.6	.9
165 CH OF NAZARENE	1	13	66	.6	.9
167 CHS OF CHRIST	1	21	28	.3	.4
207 E.L.C.A.	8	1,171	1,533	13.9	20.9
220 FREE LUTHERAN	2	67	75	.7	1.0
237 GC MENN BR CHS	1	30	42*	.4	.6
283 LUTH—MO SYNOD	1	139	190	1.7	2.6
287 MENN GEN CONF	1	59	59	.5	.8
339 PENT CH OF GOD	1	34	77	.7	1.0
355 PRESB CH (USA)	7	543	758*	6.9	10.3
419 SO BAPT CONV	3	317	443*	4.0	6.0
443 UN C OF CHRIST	1	80	112*	1.0	1.5
449 UN METHODIST	2	77	108*	1.0	1.5
469 WELS	1	21	24	.2	.3
ROSEBUD	**31**	**1,532**	**6,064***	**57.7**	**100.0**
053 ASSEMB OF GOD	1	38	54	.5	.9
081 CATHOLIC	8	NA	2,735	26.0	45.1
081d *LATIN*	*8*	*NA*	*2,735*	*26.0*	*45.1*
089 CHR & MISS AL	1	38	50	.5	.8
151 L-D SAINTS	2	NA	760	7.2	12.5
167 CHS OF CHRIST	2	32	48	.5	.8
193 EPISCOPAL	1	17	26	.2	.4
263 INT FOURSQ GOS	1	38	53*	.5	.9
283 LUTH—MO SYNOD	3	437	723	6.9	11.9
287 MENN GEN CONF	2	60	65	.6	1.1
339 PENT CH OF GOD	1	35	77	.7	1.3
355 PRESB CH (USA)	2	290	405*	3.9	6.7
419 SO BAPT CONV	4	442	617*	5.9	10.2
443 UN C OF CHRIST	1	45	63*	.6	1.0
449 UN METHODIST	1	24	33*	.3	.5
467 WESLEYAN	1	36	355	3.4	5.9
SANDERS	**25**	**1,145**	**2,381***	**27.5**	**100.0**
053 ASSEMB OF GOD	2	126	172	2.0	7.2
081 CATHOLIC	4	NA	519	6.0	21.8
081d *LATIN*	*4*	*NA*	*519*	*6.0*	*21.8*
089 CHR & MISS AL	1	36	65	.7	2.7
097 CHR CHS&CHS CR	1	90	116*	1.3	4.9
123 CH GOD (ANDER)	1	60	60	.7	2.5
151 L-D SAINTS	2	NA	266	3.1	11.2
175 CONGR CHR CHS	1	118	151*	1.7	6.3
207 E.L.C.A.	3	309	419	4.8	17.6
339 PENT CH OF GOD	1	0	70	.8	2.9
353 CHR BRETHREN	1	60	100	1.2	4.2
355 PRESB CH (USA)	1	53	68*	.8	2.9
413 S.D.A.	2	79	101*	1.2	4.2
419 SO BAPT CONV	1	47	60*	.7	2.5
449 UN METHODIST	4	167	214*	2.5	9.0
SHERIDAN	**25**	**1,977**	**3,441***	**72.7**	**100.0**
053 ASSEMB OF GOD	2	84	165	3.5	4.8
081 CATHOLIC	3	NA	824	17.4	23.9
081d *LATIN*	*3*	*NA*	*824*	*17.4*	*23.9*
167 CHS OF CHRIST	1	17	23	.5	.7
207 E.L.C.A.	11	1,427	1,857	39.2	54.0
283 LUTH—MO SYNOD	1	82	100	2.1	2.9
285 MENNONITE CH	1	20	35	.7	1.0
413 S.D.A.	1	13	16*	.3	.5
419 SO BAPT CONV	1	41	52*	1.1	1.5
443 UN C OF CHRIST	2	198	249*	5.3	7.2
449 UN METHODIST	2	95	120*	2.5	3.5
SILVER BOW	**34**	**2,901**	**16,404***	**48.3**	**100.0**
019 AMER BAPT USA	2	110	137*	.4	.8
045 APOSTOLIC LUTH	1	6	10	-	.1
053 ASSEMB OF GOD	1	100	300	.9	1.8

County and Denomination	Number of churches	Communicant, confirmed, full members	Total adherents Number	Percent of total population	Percent of total adherents
081 CATHOLIC	5	NA	11,133	32.8	67.9
081d *LATIN*	*5*	*NA*	*11,133*	*32.8*	*67.9*
093 CHR CH (DISC)	1	42	67	.2	.4
111 CH CR,SCIENTST	1	NR	NR	-	-
127 CH GOD (CLEVE)	1	25	31*	.1	.2
145 CH GOD PROPHCY	1	18	22*	.1	.1
151 L-D SAINTS	2	NA	1,084	3.2	6.6
165 CH OF NAZARENE	1	28	68	.2	.4
167 CHS OF CHRIST	2	77	93	.3	.6
179 CONSRV BAPT	1	NR	NR	-	-
193 EPISCOPAL	1	226	324	1.0	2.0
207 E.L.C.A.	2	567	893	2.6	5.4
263 INT FOURSQ GOS	1	119	148*	.4	.9
283 LUTH—MO SYNOD	1	130	182	.5	1.1
349 PENT HOLINESS	1	21	26*	.1	.2
355 PRESB CH (USA)	1	245	304*	.9	1.9
403 SALVATION ARMY	1	21	25	.1	.2
413 S.D.A.	1	96	119*	.4	.7
419 SO BAPT CONV	2	369	458*	1.3	2.8
443 UN C OF CHRIST	1	125	155*	.5	.9
449 UN METHODIST	2	576	715*	2.1	4.4
496 JEWISH EST[1]	1	NA	110	.3	.7
STILLWATER	**14**	**1,074**	**1,999***	**30.6**	**100.0**
053 ASSEMB OF GOD	1	45	184	2.8	9.2
081 CATHOLIC	1	NA	335	5.1	16.8
081d *LATIN*	*1*	*NA*	*335*	*5.1*	*16.8*
111 CH CR,SCIENTST	1	NR	NR	-	-
151 L-D SAINTS	1	NA	178	2.7	8.9
193 EPISCOPAL	1	21	31	.5	1.6
207 E.L.C.A.	2	364	467	7.1	23.4
283 LUTH—MO SYNOD	2	232	277	4.2	13.9
419 SO BAPT CONV	1	35	45*	.7	2.3
443 UN C OF CHRIST	3	338	432*	6.6	21.6
449 UN METHODIST	1	39	50*	.8	2.5
SWEET GRASS	**10**	**744**	**1,116***	**35.4**	**100.0**
081 CATHOLIC	1	NA	125	4.0	11.2
081d *LATIN*	*1*	*NA*	*125*	*4.0*	*11.2*
127 CH GOD (CLEVE)	1	70	87*	2.8	7.8
167 CHS OF CHRIST	1	5	6	.2	.5
193 EPISCOPAL	1	57	84	2.7	7.5
203 EVAN FREE CH	1	24	39	1.2	3.5
207 E.L.C.A.	2	424	570	18.1	51.1
413 S.D.A.	1	32	40*	1.3	3.6
419 SO BAPT CONV	1	12	15*	.5	1.3
443 UN C OF CHRIST	1	120	150*	4.8	13.4
TETON	**23**	**1,742**	**4,048***	**64.6**	**100.0**
053 ASSEMB OF GOD	2	79	130	2.1	3.2
081 CATHOLIC	4	NA	952	15.2	23.5
081d *LATIN*	*4*	*NA*	*952*	*15.2*	*23.5*
151 L-D SAINTS	2	NA	504	8.0	12.5
207 E.L.C.A.	4	781	1,040	16.6	25.7
257 HUTTERIAN BR	3	NA	267	4.3	6.6
283 LUTH—MO SYNOD	2	202	276	4.4	6.8
413 S.D.A.	1	63	81*	1.3	2.0
443 UN C OF CHRIST	2	221	286*	4.6	7.1
449 UN METHODIST	3	396	512*	8.2	12.6
TOOLE	**18**	**1,370**	**3,278***	**65.0**	**100.0**
053 ASSEMB OF GOD	1	68	120	2.4	3.7
081 CATHOLIC	2	NA	900	17.8	27.5
081d *LATIN*	*2*	*NA*	*900*	*17.8*	*27.5*
151 L-D SAINTS	1	NA	126	2.5	3.8
207 E.L.C.A.	5	720	1,111	22.0	33.9
257 HUTTERIAN BR	3	NA	265	5.3	8.1
413 S.D.A.	1	74	96*	1.9	2.9
419 SO BAPT CONV	1	194	252*	5.0	7.7
449 UN METHODIST	4	314	408*	8.1	12.4
TREASURE	**5**	**189**	**481***	**55.0**	**100.0**
081 CATHOLIC	1	NA	150	17.2	31.2
081d *LATIN*	*1*	*NA*	*150*	*17.2*	*31.2*
151 L-D SAINTS	1	NA	68	7.8	14.1
283 LUTH—MO SYNOD	1	49	86	9.8	17.9
355 PRESB CH (USA)	1	98	124*	14.2	25.8
419 SO BAPT CONV	1	42	53*	6.1	11.0
VALLEY	**27**	**2,065**	**3,893***	**47.3**	**100.0**
053 ASSEMB OF GOD	1	64	136	1.7	3.5
081 CATHOLIC	4	NA	1,000	12.1	25.7
081d *LATIN*	*4*	*NA*	*1,000*	*12.1*	*25.7*
151 L-D SAINTS	1	NA	103	1.3	2.6
165 CH OF NAZARENE	1	15	17	.2	.4

NA–Not applicable   NR–Not reported   *Total adherents estimated from known number of communicant, confirmed, full members.   - Represents a percent less than 0.1.   Percentages may not total due to rounding.
[1]See Appendix E   [2]See Appendix F   [3]See Appendix G   Lines in *italic* represent a breakdown of Catholic rites or Friends affiliations. They are included in their respective denominational total.

Table 4. Churches and Church Membership by County and Denomination: 1990

County and Denomination	Number of churches	Communicant, confirmed, full members	Total adherents Number	Percent of total population	Percent of total adherents
167 CHS OF CHRIST	1	11	15	.2	.4
179 CONSRV BAPT	1	NR	NR	-	-
193 EPISCOPAL	1	27	27	.3	.7
207 E.L.C.A.	6	1,157	1,528	18.5	39.2
211 FEL EVG BIB CH	1	85	115	1.4	3.0
237 GC MENN BR CHS	1	123	156*	1.9	4.0
283 LUTH—MO SYNOD	1	60	100	1.2	2.6
339 PENT CH OF GOD	1	34	77	.9	2.0
355 PRESB CH (USA)	1	0	0*	-	-
413 S.D.A.	1	37	47*	.6	1.2
419 SO BAPT CONV	2	122	154*	1.9	4.0
443 UN C OF CHRIST	1	85	108*	1.3	2.8
449 UN METHODIST	2	245	310*	3.8	8.0
WHEATLAND	**13**	**429**	**1,044***	**46.5**	**100.0**
053 ASSEMB OF GOD	1	44	76	3.4	7.3
081 CATHOLIC	2	NA	253	11.3	24.2
081d LATIN	*2*	*NA*	*253*	*11.3*	*24.2*
151 L-D SAINTS	1	NA	49	2.2	4.7
207 E.L.C.A.	1	90	138	6.1	13.2
257 HUTTERIAN BR	2	NA	176	7.8	16.9
283 LUTH—MO SYNOD	1	45	51	2.3	4.9
355 PRESB CH (USA)	1	76	96*	4.3	9.2
419 SO BAPT CONV	1	56	71*	3.2	6.8
449 UN METHODIST	2	106	134*	6.0	12.8
467 WESLEYAN	1	12	0	-	-
WIBAUX	**6**	**246**	**740***	**62.1**	**100.0**
053 ASSEMB OF GOD	1	36	70	5.9	9.5
081 CATHOLIC	2	NA	400	33.6	54.1
081d LATIN	*2*	*NA*	*400*	*33.6*	*54.1*
207 E.L.C.A.	2	153	198	16.6	26.8
449 UN METHODIST	1	57	72*	6.0	9.7
YELLOWSTONE	**115**	**20,996**	**53,580***	**47.2**	**100.0**
019 AMER BAPT USA	1	512	653*	.6	1.2
053 ASSEMB OF GOD	6	1,061	3,053	2.7	5.7
057 BAPT GEN CONF	2	132	168*	.1	.3
081 CATHOLIC	9	NA	18,277	16.1	34.1
081d LATIN	*9*	*NA*	*18,277*	*16.1*	*34.1*
089 CHR & MISS AL	3	232	652	.6	1.2
093 CHR CH (DISC)	2	392	613	.5	1.1
097 CHR CHS&CHS CR	2	120	153*	.1	.3
111 CH CR,SCIENTST	1	NR	NR	-	-
123 CH GOD (ANDER)	1	40	40	-	.1
127 CH GOD (CLEVE)	1	88	112*	.1	.2
145 CH GOD PROPHCY	2	35	45*	-	.1
151 L-D SAINTS	10	NA	3,952	3.5	7.4
163 CH OF LUTH BR	1	54	126	.1	.2
165 CH OF NAZARENE	4	311	450	.4	.8
167 CHS OF CHRIST	2	216	307	.3	.6
179 CONSRV BAPT	2	NR	NR	-	-
193 EPISCOPAL	4	871	1,183	1.0	2.2
203 EVAN FREE CH	1	55	104	.1	.2
207 E.L.C.A.	11	4,922	6,915	6.1	12.9
223 FREE WILL BAPT	2	43	55*	-	.1
226 FRIENDS-USA	1	7	9*	-	-
226f INDEPENDNT	*1*	*7*	*9**	-	-
246 GREEK ORTHODOX	1	NR	NR	-	-
263 INT FOURSQ GOS	1	1,740	2,219*	2.0	4.1
283 LUTH—MO SYNOD	6	2,193	3,086	2.7	5.8
284 LUTH CH-AM ASC	1	76	116	.1	.2
329 OPEN BIBLE STD	3	NR	NR	-	-
355 PRESB CH (USA)	2	717	915*	.8	1.7
403 SALVATION ARMY	1	34	52	-	.1
413 S.D.A.	2	346	441*	.4	.8
419 SO BAPT CONV	12	2,070	2,640*	2.3	4.9
435 UNITARIAN-UNIV	1	78	85	.1	.2
443 UN C OF CHRIST	7	2,177	2,777*	2.4	5.2
449 UN METHODIST	5	2,118	2,702*	2.4	5.0
467 WESLEYAN	1	62	0	-	-
469 WELS	1	185	266	.2	.5
496 JEWISH EST[1]	1	NA	200	.2	.4
497 BLACK BAPT EST[2]	NA	109	139*	.1	.3
499 INDEP.NON-CHAR[3]	2	NA	1,075	.9	2.0
YELLOWSTONE NAT'L PARK	**1**	**5**	**6***	**11.5**	**100.0**
263 INT FOURSQ GOS	1	5	6*	11.5	100.0

County and Denomination	Number of churches	Communicant, confirmed, full members	Total adherents Number	Percent of total population	Percent of total adherents
NEBRASKA					
THE STATE.....	2,629	477,349	1,006,572*	63.8	100.0
ADAMS	**44**	**11,868**	**21,258***	**71.8**	**100.0**
019 AMER BAPT USA	2	540	674*	2.3	3.2
053 ASSEMB OF GOD	1	195	453	1.5	2.1
063 BEREAN FUND CH	1	97	161	.5	.8
081 CATHOLIC	5	NA	5,461	18.4	25.7
081d LATIN	*5*	*NA*	*5,461*	*18.4*	*25.7*
093 CHR CH (DISC)	1	210	275	.9	1.3
097 CHR CHS&CHS CR	1	60	75*	.3	.4
123 CH GOD (ANDER)	1	24	51	.2	.2
151 L-D SAINTS	1	NA	233	.8	1.1
165 CH OF NAZARENE	1	204	385	1.3	1.8
167 CHS OF CHRIST	1	80	115	.4	.5
193 EPISCOPAL	1	340	424	1.4	2.0
203 EVAN FREE CH	1	104	190	.6	.9
207 E.L.C.A.	4	2,372	3,034	10.2	14.3
283 LUTH—MO SYNOD	7	2,647	3,507	11.8	16.5
355 PRESB CH (USA)	3	1,539	1,922*	6.5	9.0
373 REF CH IN U.S.	1	15	20	.1	.1
403 SALVATION ARMY	1	66	67	.2	.3
413 S.D.A.	1	56	70*	.2	.3
419 SO BAPT CONV	1	101	126*	.4	.6
443 UN C OF CHRIST	2	322	402*	1.4	1.9
449 UN METHODIST	6	2,774	3,465*	11.7	16.3
469 WELS	1	122	148	.5	.7
ANTELOPE	**29**	**3,410**	**6,862***	**86.2**	**100.0**
081 CATHOLIC	4	NA	2,204	27.7	32.1
081d LATIN	*4*	*NA*	*2,204*	*27.7*	*32.1*
089 CHR & MISS AL	1	48	110	1.4	1.6
097 CHR CHS&CHS CR	3	243	320*	4.0	4.7
193 EPISCOPAL	1	26	36	.5	.5
203 EVAN FREE CH	1	63	100	1.3	1.5
283 LUTH—MO SYNOD	6	1,412	1,940	24.4	28.3
413 S.D.A.	1	75	99*	1.2	1.4
443 UN C OF CHRIST	4	568	749*	9.4	10.9
449 UN METHODIST	7	946	1,248*	15.7	18.2
467 WESLEYAN	1	29	56	.7	.8
ARTHUR	**2**	**206**	**266***	**57.6**	**100.0**
019 AMER BAPT USA	1	199	248*	53.7	93.2
467 WESLEYAN	1	7	18	3.9	6.8
BANNER	**2**	**126**	**187***	**21.9**	**100.0**
193 EPISCOPAL	1	17	45	5.3	24.1
449 UN METHODIST	1	109	142*	16.7	75.9
BLAINE	**5**	**230**	**291***	**43.1**	**100.0**
329 OPEN BIBLE STD	1	NR	NR	-	-
443 UN C OF CHRIST	3	186	236*	35.0	81.1
469 WELS	1	44	55	8.1	18.9
BOONE	**25**	**2,354**	**6,111***	**91.7**	**100.0**
019 AMER BAPT USA	1	185	242*	3.6	4.0
053 ASSEMB OF GOD	1	44	97	1.5	1.6
081 CATHOLIC	6	NA	3,082	46.2	50.4
081d LATIN	*6*	*NA*	*3,082*	*46.2*	*50.4*
165 CH OF NAZARENE	1	9	16	.2	.3
167 CHS OF CHRIST	1	25	30	.4	.5
193 EPISCOPAL	1	20	20	.3	.3
207 E.L.C.A.	2	717	861	12.9	14.1
283 LUTH—MO SYNOD	3	249	320	4.8	5.2
355 PRESB CH (USA)	3	215	281*	4.2	4.6
413 S.D.A.	1	24	31*	.5	.5
443 UN C OF CHRIST	1	40	52*	.8	.9
449 UN METHODIST	4	826	1,079*	16.2	17.7
BOX BUTTE	**25**	**3,696**	**8,478***	**64.6**	**100.0**
019 AMER BAPT USA	1	120	162*	1.2	1.9
053 ASSEMB OF GOD	1	90	210	1.6	2.5
063 BEREAN FUND CH	1	58	146	1.1	1.7
081 CATHOLIC	2	NA	3,040	23.2	35.9
081d LATIN	*2*	*NA*	*3,040*	*23.2*	*35.9*
093 CHR CH (DISC)	1	95	128	1.0	1.5
097 CHR CHS&CHS CR	1	45	61*	.5	.7
111 CH CR,SCIENTST	1	NR	NR	-	-
123 CH GOD (ANDER)	1	16	35	.3	.4
151 L-D SAINTS	1	NA	126	1.0	1.5
165 CH OF NAZARENE	2	59	127	1.0	1.5
167 CHS OF CHRIST	2	42	54	.4	.6

NA–Not applicable   NR–Not reported   *Total adherents estimated from known number of communicant, confirmed, full members.   - Represents a percent less than 0.1.   Percentages may not total due to rounding.

[1]See Appendix E   [2]See Appendix F   [3]See Appendix G   Lines in *italic* represent a breakdown of Catholic rites or Friends affiliations. They are included in their respective denominational total.

Table 4. Churches and Church Membership by County and Denomination: 1990

County and Denomination	Number of churches	Communicant, confirmed, full members	Total adherents Number	Percent of total population	Percent of total adherents
193 EPISCOPAL	1	236	345	2.6	4.1
203 EVAN FREE CH	1	19	55	.4	.6
207 E.L.C.A.	1	496	719	5.5	8.5
283 LUTH—MO SYNOD	1	524	699	5.3	8.2
355 PRESB CH (USA)	1	492	663*	5.0	7.8
413 S.D.A.	2	172	232*	1.8	2.7
443 UN C OF CHRIST	1	92	124*	.9	1.5
449 UN METHODIST	2	1,118	1,507*	11.5	17.8
467 WESLEYAN	1	22	45	.3	.5
BOYD	**17**	**953**	**2,112***	**74.5**	**100.0**
053 ASSEMB OF GOD	1	43	40	1.4	1.9
081 CATHOLIC	4	NA	887	31.3	42.0
081d LATIN	4	NA	887	31.3	42.0
207 E.L.C.A.	2	210	271	9.6	12.8
283 LUTH—MO SYNOD	3	209	285	10.1	13.5
443 UN C OF CHRIST	1	127	161*	5.7	7.6
449 UN METHODIST	3	209	264*	9.3	12.5
467 WESLEYAN	2	47	75	2.6	3.6
469 WELS	1	108	129	4.6	6.1
BROWN	**11**	**1,221**	**2,458***	**67.2**	**100.0**
053 ASSEMB OF GOD	2	39	80	2.2	3.3
063 BEREAN FUND CH	1	43	43	1.2	1.7
081 CATHOLIC	1	NA	750	20.5	30.5
081d LATIN	1	NA	750	20.5	30.5
165 CH OF NAZARENE	1	96	153	4.2	6.2
203 EVAN FREE CH	1	28	90	2.5	3.7
283 LUTH—MO SYNOD	1	327	473	12.9	19.2
443 UN C OF CHRIST	1	185	234*	6.4	9.5
449 UN METHODIST	3	503	635*	17.4	25.8
BUFFALO	**66**	**11,849**	**22,757***	**60.8**	**100.0**
019 AMER BAPT USA	2	736	924*	2.5	4.1
053 ASSEMB OF GOD	3	308	722	1.9	3.2
063 BEREAN FUND CH	1	22	40	.1	.2
081 CATHOLIC	8	NA	6,327	16.9	27.8
081d LATIN	8	NA	6,327	16.9	27.8
093 CHR CH (DISC)	2	380	603	1.6	2.6
097 CHR CHS&CHS CR	3	188	236*	.6	1.0
111 CH CR,SCIENTST	1	NR	NR	-	-
123 CH GOD (ANDER)	1	52	66	.2	.3
145 CH GOD PROPHCY	2	53	67*	.2	.3
151 L-D SAINTS	1	NA	245	.7	1.1
165 CH OF NAZARENE	1	91	173	.5	.8
167 CHS OF CHRIST	2	89	114	.3	.5
193 EPISCOPAL	1	229	336	.9	1.5
203 EVAN FREE CH	2	300	770	2.1	3.4
207 E.L.C.A.	2	1,327	1,855	5.0	8.2
263 INT FOURSQ GOS	1	79	99*	.3	.4
283 LUTH—MO SYNOD	8	2,342	3,110	8.3	13.7
329 OPEN BIBLE STD	2	NR	NR	-	-
355 PRESB CH (USA)	1	574	720*	1.9	3.2
356 PRESB CH AMER	1	113	113	.3	.5
403 SALVATION ARMY	1	100	106	.3	.5
413 S.D.A.	2	97	122*	.3	.5
419 SO BAPT CONV	1	163	205*	.5	.9
435 UNITARIAN-UNIV	1	15	15	-	.1
443 UN C OF CHRIST	1	65	82*	.2	.4
449 UN METHODIST	13	4,470	5,610*	15.0	24.7
467 WESLEYAN	1	2	15	-	.1
469 WELS	1	54	82	.2	.4
BURT	**24**	**4,435**	**6,392***	**81.2**	**100.0**
019 AMER BAPT USA	2	439	555*	7.1	8.7
053 ASSEMB OF GOD	1	69	130	1.7	2.0
057 BAPT GEN CONF	1	38	48*	.6	.8
081 CATHOLIC	3	NA	744	9.5	11.6
081d LATIN	3	NA	744	9.5	11.6
203 EVAN FREE CH	1	50	90	1.1	1.4
207 E.L.C.A.	3	1,556	1,940	24.7	30.4
283 LUTH—MO SYNOD	2	306	385	4.9	6.0
355 PRESB CH (USA)	3	670	847*	10.8	13.3
413 S.D.A.	1	18	23*	.3	.4
449 UN METHODIST	7	1,289	1,630*	20.7	25.5
BUTLER	**26**	**1,451**	**7,299***	**84.9**	**100.0**
019 AMER BAPT USA	2	54	69*	.8	.9
081 CATHOLIC	11	NA	5,334	62.0	73.1
081d LATIN	11	NA	5,334	62.0	73.1
093 CHR CH (DISC)	1	5	9	.1	.1
151 L-D SAINTS	1	NA	107	1.2	1.5
207 E.L.C.A.	1	152	196	2.3	2.7
283 LUTH—MO SYNOD	2	310	418	4.9	5.7
443 UN C OF CHRIST	1	46	59*	.7	.8

County and Denomination	Number of churches	Communicant, confirmed, full members	Total adherents Number	Percent of total population	Percent of total adherents
449 UN METHODIST	5	717	919*	10.7	12.6
469 WELS	2	167	188	2.2	2.6
CASS	**42**	**5,460**	**11,075***	**52.0**	**100.0**
019 AMER BAPT USA	1	39	50*	.2	.5
063 BEREAN FUND CH	1	39	49	.2	.4
081 CATHOLIC	5	NA	3,269	15.3	29.5
081d LATIN	5	NA	3,269	15.3	29.5
093 CHR CH (DISC)	5	319	800	3.8	7.2
097 CHR CHS&CHS CR	1	50	65*	.3	.6
151 L-D SAINTS	1	NA	227	1.1	2.0
167 CHS OF CHRIST	1	31	40	.2	.4
193 EPISCOPAL	1	88	121	.6	1.1
207 E.L.C.A.	2	338	458	2.1	4.1
283 LUTH—MO SYNOD	5	1,177	1,524	7.1	13.8
291 MISSIONARY CH	1	89	173	.8	1.6
355 PRESB CH (USA)	2	525	679*	3.2	6.1
419 SO BAPT CONV	1	280	362*	1.7	3.3
443 UN C OF CHRIST	3	428	554*	2.6	5.0
449 UN METHODIST	11	2,043	2,643*	12.4	23.9
467 WESLEYAN	1	14	61	.3	.6
CEDAR	**27**	**2,799**	**9,541***	**94.2**	**100.0**
053 ASSEMB OF GOD	1	29	40	.4	.4
081 CATHOLIC	11	NA	5,866	57.9	61.5
081d LATIN	11	NA	5,866	57.9	61.5
097 CHR CHS&CHS CR	1	18	24*	.2	.3
207 E.L.C.A.	4	1,453	1,873	18.5	19.6
283 LUTH—MO SYNOD	1	179	253	2.5	2.7
329 OPEN BIBLE STD	1	NR	NR	-	-
355 PRESB CH (USA)	2	267	354*	3.5	3.7
443 UN C OF CHRIST	2	288	382*	3.8	4.0
449 UN METHODIST	4	565	749*	7.4	7.9
CHASE	**16**	**1,749**	**2,933***	**66.9**	**100.0**
053 ASSEMB OF GOD	1	52	105	2.4	3.6
063 BEREAN FUND CH	1	24	59	1.3	2.0
081 CATHOLIC	2	NA	502	11.5	17.1
081d LATIN	2	NA	502	11.5	17.1
157 CH OF BRETHREN	1	35	45*	1.0	1.5
165 CH OF NAZARENE	1	13	23	.5	.8
167 CHS OF CHRIST	3	65	100	2.3	3.4
283 LUTH—MO SYNOD	2	619	828	18.9	28.2
291 MISSIONARY CH	1	40	42	1.0	1.4
449 UN METHODIST	3	879	1,139*	26.0	38.8
467 WESLEYAN	1	22	90	2.1	3.1
CHERRY	**26**	**1,790**	**3,578***	**56.7**	**100.0**
019 AMER BAPT USA	1	7	9*	.1	.3
053 ASSEMB OF GOD	1	89	125	2.0	3.5
063 BEREAN FUND CH	1	30	60	1.0	1.7
081 CATHOLIC	4	NA	1,100	17.4	30.7
081d LATIN	4	NA	1,100	17.4	30.7
151 L-D SAINTS	1	NA	94	1.5	2.6
164 CH LUTH CONF	1	86	128	2.0	3.6
165 CH OF NAZARENE	1	23	0	-	-
193 EPISCOPAL	3	128	165	2.6	4.6
283 LUTH—MO SYNOD	4	244	371	5.9	10.4
355 PRESB CH (USA)	1	378	488*	7.7	13.6
413 S.D.A.	1	38	49*	.8	1.4
419 SO BAPT CONV	1	89	115*	1.8	3.2
449 UN METHODIST	4	473	610*	9.7	17.0
467 WESLEYAN	1	14	0	-	-
469 WELS	1	191	264	4.2	7.4
CHEYENNE	**31**	**4,125**	**7,135***	**75.2**	**100.0**
053 ASSEMB OF GOD	2	53	111	1.2	1.6
081 CATHOLIC	3	NA	1,500	15.8	21.0
081d LATIN	3	NA	1,500	15.8	21.0
093 CHR CH (DISC)	1	82	128	1.3	1.8
097 CHR CHS&CHS CR	1	11	14*	.1	.2
151 L-D SAINTS	1	NA	100	1.1	1.4
165 CH OF NAZARENE	1	24	61	.6	.9
167 CHS OF CHRIST	1	45	58	.6	.8
193 EPISCOPAL	1	85	132	1.4	1.9
203 EVAN FREE CH	1	65	165	1.7	2.3
207 E.L.C.A.	6	1,329	1,703	17.9	23.9
263 INT FOURSQ GOS	1	111	142*	1.5	2.0
283 LUTH—MO SYNOD	4	646	905	9.5	12.7
355 PRESB CH (USA)	2	333	426*	4.5	6.0
413 S.D.A.	1	62	79*	.8	1.1
419 SO BAPT CONV	1	104	133*	1.4	1.9
449 UN METHODIST	3	1,154	1,478*	15.6	20.7
467 WESLEYAN	1	21	0	-	-

NA–Not applicable   NR–Not reported   *Total adherents estimated from known number of communicant, confirmed, full members.   - Represents a percent less than 0.1.   Percentages may not total due to rounding.
[1]See Appendix E   [2]See Appendix F   [3]See Appendix G   Lines in *italic* represent a breakdown of Catholic rites or Friends affiliations. They are included in their respective denominational total.

NEBRASKA

Table 4. Churches and Church Membership by County and Denomination: 1990

County and Denomination	Number of churches	Communicant, confirmed, full members	Total adherents Number	Percent of total population	Percent of total adherents
CLAY	**32**	**3,579**	**5,596***	**78.6**	**100.0**
081 CATHOLIC	3	NA	1,025	14.4	18.3
081d *LATIN*	*3*	*NA*	*1,025*	*14.4*	*18.3*
093 CHR CH (DISC)	1	40	65	.9	1.2
097 CHR CHS&CHS CR	3	310	393*	5.5	7.0
123 CH GOD (ANDER)	1	14	14	.2	.3
193 EPISCOPAL	1	11	11	.2	.2
203 EVAN FREE CH	1	37	51	.7	.9
207 E.L.C.A.	4	673	850	11.9	15.2
355 PRESB CH (USA)	3	483	613*	8.6	11.0
373 REF CH IN U.S.	2	401	524	7.4	9.4
419 SO BAPT CONV	1	75	95*	1.3	1.7
443 UN C OF CHRIST	3	668	848*	11.9	15.2
449 UN METHODIST	8	817	1,037*	14.6	18.5
469 WELS	1	50	70	1.0	1.3
COLFAX	**20**	**2,352**	**7,782***	**85.2**	**100.0**
081 CATHOLIC	9	NA	4,690	51.3	60.3
081d *LATIN*	*9*	*NA*	*4,690*	*51.3*	*60.3*
193 EPISCOPAL	1	19	19	.2	.2
207 E.L.C.A.	2	604	793	8.7	10.2
283 LUTH—MO SYNOD	4	589	808	8.8	10.4
355 PRESB CH (USA)	2	811	1,047*	11.5	13.5
443 UN C OF CHRIST	1	68	88*	1.0	1.1
449 UN METHODIST	1	261	337*	3.7	4.3
CUMING	**28**	**4,784**	**10,133***	**100.2**	**100.0**
053 ASSEMB OF GOD	1	90	103	1.0	1.0
057 BAPT GEN CONF	1	24	31*	.3	.3
081 CATHOLIC	7	NA	4,178	41.3	41.2
081d *LATIN*	*7*	*NA*	*4,178*	*41.3*	*41.2*
167 CHS OF CHRIST	1	12	27	.3	.3
207 E.L.C.A.	2	888	1,082	10.7	10.7
283 LUTH—MO SYNOD	9	2,965	3,722	36.8	36.7
285 MENNONITE CH	1	163	168	1.7	1.7
355 PRESB CH (USA)	1	98	125*	1.2	1.2
443 UN C OF CHRIST	2	231	296*	2.9	2.9
449 UN METHODIST	3	313	401*	4.0	4.0
CUSTER	**51**	**4,603**	**8,195***	**66.8**	**100.0**
019 AMER BAPT USA	4	506	640*	5.2	7.8
053 ASSEMB OF GOD	1	46	98	.8	1.2
057 BAPT GEN CONF	1	61	77*	.6	.9
063 BEREAN FUND CH	1	69	162	1.3	2.0
081 CATHOLIC	9	NA	2,052	16.7	25.0
081d *LATIN*	*9*	*NA*	*2,052*	*16.7*	*25.0*
093 CHR CH (DISC)	1	80	108	.9	1.3
097 CHR CHS&CHS CR	4	332	420*	3.4	5.1
123 CH GOD (ANDER)	1	0	56	.5	.7
165 CH OF NAZARENE	2	48	45	.4	.5
167 CHS OF CHRIST	1	40	70	.6	.9
193 EPISCOPAL	2	75	81	.7	1.0
203 EVAN FREE CH	2	152	310	2.5	3.8
207 E.L.C.A.	2	252	321	2.6	3.9
283 LUTH—MO SYNOD	3	170	250	2.0	3.1
285 MENNONITE CH	1	23	28	.2	.3
329 OPEN BIBLE STD	1	NR	NR	-	-
355 PRESB CH (USA)	1	179	226*	1.8	2.8
413 S.D.A.	1	67	85*	.7	1.0
449 UN METHODIST	12	2,392	3,024*	24.6	36.9
469 WELS	1	111	142	1.2	1.7
DAKOTA	**21**	**3,937**	**8,910***	**53.2**	**100.0**
053 ASSEMB OF GOD	1	170	300	1.8	3.4
081 CATHOLIC	5	NA	3,452	20.6	38.7
081d *LATIN*	*5*	*NA*	*3,452*	*20.6*	*38.7*
089 CHR & MISS AL	1	0	30	.2	.3
097 CHR CHS&CHS CR	1	115	152*	.9	1.7
207 E.L.C.A.	4	1,866	2,581	15.4	29.0
283 LUTH—MO SYNOD	1	596	824	4.9	9.2
313 N AM BAPT CONF	1	22	29*	.2	.3
329 OPEN BIBLE STD	1	NR	NR	-	-
355 PRESB CH (USA)	2	350	462*	2.8	5.2
419 SO BAPT CONV	1	196	259*	1.5	2.9
449 UN METHODIST	3	622	821*	4.9	9.2
DAWES	**23**	**2,336**	**5,012***	**55.6**	**100.0**
019 AMER BAPT USA	1	317	396*	4.4	7.9
053 ASSEMB OF GOD	2	86	395	4.4	7.9
063 BEREAN FUND CH	1	38	70	.8	1.4
081 CATHOLIC	2	NA	1,505	16.7	30.0
081d *LATIN*	*2*	*NA*	*1,505*	*16.7*	*30.0*
097 CHR CHS&CHS CR	1	75	94*	1.0	1.9
151 L-D SAINTS	1	NA	103	1.1	2.1
165 CH OF NAZARENE	2	41	133	1.5	2.7
167 CHS OF CHRIST	1	15	19	.2	.4
193 EPISCOPAL	1	150	229	2.5	4.6
207 E.L.C.A.	1	201	264	2.9	5.3
283 LUTH—MO SYNOD	2	372	505	5.6	10.1
413 S.D.A.	2	108	135*	1.5	2.7
419 SO BAPT CONV	1	12	15*	.2	.3
443 UN C OF CHRIST	2	191	238*	2.6	4.7
449 UN METHODIST	3	730	911*	10.1	18.2
DAWSON	**51**	**8,882**	**14,531***	**72.9**	**100.0**
019 AMER BAPT USA	2	241	308*	1.5	2.1
053 ASSEMB OF GOD	2	128	185	.9	1.3
057 BAPT GEN CONF	1	159	203*	1.0	1.4
063 BEREAN FUND CH	2	109	178	.9	1.2
081 CATHOLIC	6	NA	2,623	13.2	18.1
081d *LATIN*	*6*	*NA*	*2,623*	*13.2*	*18.1*
093 CHR CH (DISC)	1	35	44	.2	.3
097 CHR CHS&CHS CR	3	641	818*	4.1	5.6
123 CH GOD (ANDER)	2	59	75	.4	.5
133 CH GOD(7TH)DEN	1	9	9	-	.1
151 L-D SAINTS	1	NA	101	.5	.7
165 CH OF NAZARENE	2	149	338	1.7	2.3
167 CHS OF CHRIST	2	44	57	.3	.4
193 EPISCOPAL	1	45	45	.2	.3
203 EVAN FREE CH	4	248	371	1.9	2.6
207 E.L.C.A.	5	1,863	2,484	12.5	17.1
283 LUTH—MO SYNOD	3	891	1,255	6.3	8.6
355 PRESB CH (USA)	4	1,057	1,349*	6.8	9.3
413 S.D.A.	1	80	102*	.5	.7
419 SO BAPT CONV	1	175	223*	1.1	1.5
449 UN METHODIST	7	2,949	3,763*	18.9	25.9
DEUEL	**10**	**1,356**	**1,980***	**88.5**	**100.0**
053 ASSEMB OF GOD	2	130	185	8.3	9.3
081 CATHOLIC	1	NA	262	11.7	13.2
081d *LATIN*	*1*	*NA*	*262*	*11.7*	*13.2*
207 E.L.C.A.	2	219	279	12.5	14.1
263 INT FOURSQ GOS	1	28	35*	1.6	1.8
283 LUTH—MO SYNOD	2	332	408	18.2	20.6
449 UN METHODIST	2	647	811*	36.3	41.0
DIXON	**26**	**3,790**	**5,841***	**95.1**	**100.0**
081 CATHOLIC	4	NA	984	16.0	16.8
081d *LATIN*	*4*	*NA*	*984*	*16.0*	*16.8*
097 CHR CHS&CHS CR	1	100	128*	2.1	2.2
203 EVAN FREE CH	2	124	201	3.3	3.4
207 E.L.C.A.	7	2,046	2,587	42.1	44.3
226 FRIENDS-USA	1	67	86*	1.4	1.5
226b *EFI*	*1*	*67*	*86**	*1.4*	*1.5*
283 LUTH—MO SYNOD	5	747	953	15.5	16.3
355 PRESB CH (USA)	2	137	175*	2.8	3.0
443 UN C OF CHRIST	1	62	79*	1.3	1.4
449 UN METHODIST	3	507	648*	10.5	11.1
DODGE	**53**	**13,557**	**26,228***	**76.0**	**100.0**
019 AMER BAPT USA	1	411	518*	1.5	2.0
053 ASSEMB OF GOD	1	78	142	.4	.5
063 BEREAN FUND CH	1	0	100	.3	.4
081 CATHOLIC	6	NA	8,305	24.1	31.7
081d *LATIN*	*6*	*NA*	*8,305*	*24.1*	*31.7*
089 CHR & MISS AL	1	300	507	1.5	1.9
093 CHR CH (DISC)	1	260	443	1.3	1.7
097 CHR CHS&CHS CR	1	41	52*	.2	.2
127 CH GOD (CLEVE)	1	19	24*	.1	.1
165 CH OF NAZARENE	1	78	155	.4	.6
167 CHS OF CHRIST	1	45	58	.2	.2
193 EPISCOPAL	1	225	384	1.1	1.5
203 EVAN FREE CH	1	81	140	.4	.5
207 E.L.C.A.	15	4,984	6,361	18.4	24.3
263 INT FOURSQ GOS	1	96	121*	.4	.5
283 LUTH—MO SYNOD	7	3,044	4,017	11.6	15.3
355 PRESB CH (USA)	2	1,179	1,486*	4.3	5.7
403 SALVATION ARMY	1	125	145	.4	.6
413 S.D.A.	1	49	62*	.2	.2
419 SO BAPT CONV	1	175	221*	.6	.8
443 UN C OF CHRIST	3	728	918*	2.7	3.5
449 UN METHODIST	4	1,625	2,048*	5.9	7.8
469 WELS	1	14	21	.1	.1
DOUGLAS	**285**	**86,739**	**254,393***	**61.1**	**100.0**
005 AME ZION	1	200	268	.1	.1
019 AMER BAPT USA	11	2,294	2,923*	.7	1.1
053 ASSEMB OF GOD	5	953	1,728	.4	.7
057 BAPT GEN CONF	7	1,068	1,361*	.3	.5

NA–Not applicable   NR–Not reported   *Total adherents estimated from known number of communicant, confirmed, full members.   - Represents a percent less than 0.1.   Percentages may not total due to rounding.

[1]See Appendix E   [2]See Appendix F   [3]See Appendix G   Lines in *italic* represent a breakdown of Catholic rites or Friends affiliations. They are included in their respective denominational total.

Table 4. Churches and Church Membership by County and Denomination: 1990

County and Denomination	Number of churches	Communicant, confirmed, full members	Total adherents Number	Total adherents Percent of total population	Total adherents Percent of total adherents
063 BEREAN FUND CH	1	12	51	-	-
081 CATHOLIC	53	NA	119,453	28.7	47.0
081d *LATIN*	*52*	*NA*	*119,381*	*28.7*	*46.9*
081h *UKRAINIAN*	*1*	*NA*	*72*	-	-
089 CHR & MISS AL	6	1,599	4,400	1.1	1.7
093 CHR CH (DISC)	4	1,120	1,902	.5	.7
097 CHR CHS&CHS CR	6	1,150	1,466*	.4	.6
105 CHRISTIAN REF	1	100	170	-	.1
111 CH CR,SCIENTST	4	NR	NR	-	-
121 CH GOD (ABR)	1	83	106*	-	-
123 CH GOD (ANDER)	2	64	129	-	.1
127 CH GOD (CLEVE)	4	420	535*	.1	.2
145 CH GOD PROPHCY	1	22	28*	-	-
151 L-D SAINTS	7	NA	3,905	.9	1.5
165 CH OF NAZARENE	2	257	373	.1	.1
167 CHS OF CHRIST	5	820	1,086	.3	.4
179 CONSRV BAPT	1	NR	NR	-	-
193 EPISCOPAL	8	2,838	3,744	.9	1.5
203 EVAN FREE CH	2	220	670	.2	.3
207 E.L.C.A.	29	17,820	24,797	6.0	9.7
211 FEL EVG BIB CH	2	331	693	.2	.3
221 FREE METHODIST	1	61	72	-	-
223 FREE WILL BAPT	1	28	36*	-	-
226 FRIENDS-USA	2	96	124*	-	-
226b *EFI*	*1*	*92*	*117*	-	-
226f *INDEPENDNT*	*1*	*4*	*7*	-	-
237 GC MENN BR CHS	3	72	92*	-	-
246 GREEK ORTHODOX	1	NR	NR	-	-
263 INT FOURSQ GOS	3	480	612*	.1	.2
274 LAT EVAN LUTH	1	58	61	-	-
283 LUTH—MO SYNOD	18	9,688	13,074	3.1	5.1
284 LUTH CH-AM ASC	1	442	572	.1	.2
285 MENNONITE CH	1	17	39	-	-
329 OPEN BIBLE STD	1	NR	NR	-	-
353 CHR BRETHREN	3	150	250	.1	.1
355 PRESB CH (USA)	27	9,762	12,440*	3.0	4.9
356 PRESB CH AMER	1	58	96	-	-
371 REF CH IN AM	1	293	574	.1	.2
403 SALVATION ARMY	4	563	617	.1	.2
413 S.D.A.	3	1,424	1,815*	.4	.7
419 SO BAPT CONV	4	3,426	4,366*	1.0	1.7
435 UNITARIAN-UNIV	2	318	429	.1	.2
443 UN C OF CHRIST	6	3,922	4,998*	1.2	2.0
449 UN METHODIST	21	11,750	14,974*	3.6	5.9
467 WESLEYAN	1	31	100	-	-
469 WELS	4	689	966	.2	.4
496 JEWISH EST[1]	5	NA	4,380	1.1	1.7
497 BLACK BAPT EST[2]	NA	12,040	15,343*	3.7	6.0
498 INDEP.CHARIS.[3]	5	NA	4,650	1.1	1.8
499 INDEP.NON-CHAR[3]	2	NA	3,925	.9	1.5
DUNDY	**11**	**1,102**	**1,576***	**61.0**	**100.0**
081 CATHOLIC	1	NA	189	7.3	12.0
081d *LATIN*	*1*	*NA*	*189*	*7.3*	*12.0*
207 E.L.C.A.	2	274	355	13.7	22.5
226 FRIENDS-USA	1	60	78	3.0	4.9
226b *EFI*	*1*	*60*	*78*	*3.0*	*4.9*
283 LUTH—MO SYNOD	1	127	163	6.3	10.3
355 PRESB CH (USA)	1	57	70*	2.7	4.4
413 S.D.A.	1	22	27*	1.0	1.7
419 SO BAPT CONV	1	73	90*	3.5	5.7
449 UN METHODIST	3	489	604*	23.4	38.3
FILLMORE	**24**	**2,965**	**5,272***	**74.2**	**100.0**
053 ASSEMB OF GOD	1	44	99	1.4	1.9
081 CATHOLIC	5	NA	1,391	19.6	26.4
081d *LATIN*	*5*	*NA*	*1,391*	*19.6*	*26.4*
203 EVAN FREE CH	1	61	127	1.8	2.4
207 E.L.C.A.	4	499	667	9.4	12.7
283 LUTH—MO SYNOD	1	129	163	2.3	3.1
285 MENNONITE CH	1	206	277	3.9	5.3
287 MENN GEN CONF	1	29	36	.5	.7
443 UN C OF CHRIST	2	430	539*	7.6	10.2
449 UN METHODIST	6	1,383	1,733*	24.4	32.9
469 WELS	2	184	240	3.4	4.6
FRANKLIN	**22**	**2,279**	**3,255***	**82.7**	**100.0**
053 ASSEMB OF GOD	1	19	40	1.0	1.2
081 CATHOLIC	4	NA	372	9.4	11.4
081d *LATIN*	*4*	*NA*	*372*	*9.4*	*11.4*
207 E.L.C.A.	4	751	939	23.8	28.8
283 LUTH—MO SYNOD	3	353	418	10.6	12.8
291 MISSIONARY CH	1	71	96	2.4	2.9
355 PRESB CH (USA)	1	164	200*	5.1	6.1
443 UN C OF CHRIST	2	309	378*	9.6	11.6
449 UN METHODIST	4	591	722*	18.3	22.2

County and Denomination	Number of churches	Communicant, confirmed, full members	Total adherents Number	Total adherents Percent of total population	Total adherents Percent of total adherents
467 WESLEYAN	2	21	90	2.3	2.8
FRONTIER	**13**	**1,577**	**2,177***	**70.2**	**100.0**
063 BEREAN FUND CH	1	36	66	2.1	3.0
081 CATHOLIC	1	NA	117	3.8	5.4
081d *LATIN*	*1*	*NA*	*117*	*3.8*	*5.4*
097 CHR CHS&CHS CR	1	80	103*	3.3	4.7
165 CH OF NAZARENE	1	20	45	1.5	2.1
207 E.L.C.A.	1	496	617	19.9	28.3
283 LUTH—MO SYNOD	1	234	316	10.2	14.5
413 S.D.A.	1	18	23*	.7	1.1
443 UN C OF CHRIST	2	62	80*	2.6	3.7
449 UN METHODIST	4	631	810*	26.1	37.2
FURNAS	**28**	**3,226**	**4,534***	**81.6**	**100.0**
019 AMER BAPT USA	3	296	362*	6.5	8.0
053 ASSEMB OF GOD	1	11	14	.3	.3
057 BAPT GEN CONF	1	57	70*	1.3	1.5
081 CATHOLIC	2	NA	510	9.2	11.2
081d *LATIN*	*2*	*NA*	*510*	*9.2*	*11.2*
093 CHR CH (DISC)	1	40	87	1.6	1.9
097 CHR CHS&CHS CR	3	315	385*	6.9	8.5
121 CH GOD (ABR)	1	29	35*	.6	.8
193 EPISCOPAL	1	47	51	.9	1.1
203 EVAN FREE CH	1	13	35	.6	.8
221 FREE METHODIST	1	18	26	.5	.6
283 LUTH—MO SYNOD	2	753	945	17.0	20.8
355 PRESB CH (USA)	1	109	133*	2.4	2.9
413 S.D.A.	1	28	34*	.6	.7
443 UN C OF CHRIST	1	213	261*	4.7	5.8
449 UN METHODIST	8	1,297	1,586*	28.6	35.0
GAGE	**61**	**11,908**	**17,991***	**78.9**	**100.0**
019 AMER BAPT USA	1	163	202*	.9	1.1
053 ASSEMB OF GOD	1	76	115	.5	.6
081 CATHOLIC	5	NA	2,092	9.2	11.6
081d *LATIN*	*5*	*NA*	*2,092*	*9.2*	*11.6*
093 CHR CH (DISC)	2	509	713	3.1	4.0
097 CHR CHS&CHS CR	2	500	619*	2.7	3.4
123 CH GOD (ANDER)	1	59	59	.3	.3
157 CH OF BRETHREN	1	94	116*	.5	.6
165 CH OF NAZARENE	1	75	115	.5	.6
167 CHS OF CHRIST	3	79	103	.5	.6
193 EPISCOPAL	2	123	146	.6	.8
207 E.L.C.A.	11	4,608	6,218	27.3	34.6
283 LUTH—MO SYNOD	4	1,530	2,026	8.9	11.3
287 MENN GEN CONF	2	405	535	2.3	3.0
313 N AM BAPT CONF	1	96	119*	.5	.7
329 OPEN BIBLE STD	1	NR	NR	-	-
355 PRESB CH (USA)	5	581	719*	3.2	4.0
371 REF CH IN AM	1	160	240	1.1	1.3
403 SALVATION ARMY	1	129	147	.6	.8
413 S.D.A.	1	30	37*	.2	.2
443 UN C OF CHRIST	1	122	151*	.7	.8
449 UN METHODIST	10	2,215	2,743*	12.0	15.2
469 WELS	3	354	459	2.0	2.6
499 INDEP.NON-CHAR[3]	1	NA	317	1.4	1.8
GARDEN	**13**	**1,028**	**1,725***	**70.1**	**100.0**
053 ASSEMB OF GOD	1	21	30	1.2	1.7
081 CATHOLIC	2	NA	400	16.3	23.2
081d *LATIN*	*2*	*NA*	*400*	*16.3*	*23.2*
167 CHS OF CHRIST	1	3	4	.2	.2
193 EPISCOPAL	1	20	20	.8	1.2
207 E.L.C.A.	2	414	512	20.8	29.7
355 PRESB CH (USA)	1	72	89*	3.6	5.2
413 S.D.A.	1	15	19*	.8	1.1
449 UN METHODIST	2	404	500*	20.3	29.0
467 WESLEYAN	2	79	151	6.1	8.8
GARFIELD	**9**	**880**	**1,468***	**68.6**	**100.0**
053 ASSEMB OF GOD	1	48	81	3.8	5.5
063 BEREAN FUND CH	1	24	38	1.8	2.6
081 CATHOLIC	1	NA	328	15.3	22.3
081d *LATIN*	*1*	*NA*	*328*	*15.3*	*22.3*
097 CHR CHS&CHS CR	2	190	236*	11.0	16.1
283 LUTH—MO SYNOD	1	151	206	9.6	14.0
419 SO BAPT CONV	1	65	81*	3.8	5.5
443 UN C OF CHRIST	1	167	207*	9.7	14.1
449 UN METHODIST	1	235	291*	13.6	19.8
GOSPER	**5**	**944**	**1,281***	**66.4**	**100.0**
081 CATHOLIC	1	NA	78	4.0	6.1
081d *LATIN*	*1*	*NA*	*78*	*4.0*	*6.1*
093 CHR CH (DISC)	1	99	122	6.3	9.5

NA–Not applicable   NR–Not reported   *Total adherents estimated from known number of communicant, confirmed, full members.   - Represents a percent less than 0.1.   Percentages may not total due to rounding.
[1]See Appendix E   [2]See Appendix F   [3]See Appendix G   Lines in *italic* represent a breakdown of Catholic rites or Friends affiliations. They are included in their respective denominational total.

Table 4. Churches and Church Membership by County and Denomination: 1990

County and Denomination	Number of churches	Communicant, confirmed, full members	Total adherents Number	Percent of total population	Percent of total adherents
207 E.L.C.A.	1	348	466	24.2	36.4
283 LUTH—MO SYNOD	1	282	350	18.2	27.3
449 UN METHODIST	1	215	265*	13.7	20.7
GRANT	**6**	**461**	**722***	**93.9**	**100.0**
081 CATHOLIC	1	NA	65	8.5	9.0
081d LATIN	*1*	*NA*	*65*	*8.5*	*9.0*
193 EPISCOPAL	1	82	130	16.9	18.0
283 LUTH—MO SYNOD	1	70	121	15.7	16.8
413 S.D.A.	1	28	37*	4.8	5.1
443 UN C OF CHRIST	2	281	369*	48.0	51.1
GREELEY	**13**	**847**	**3,236***	**107.7**	**100.0**
057 BAPT GEN CONF	1	46	60*	2.0	1.9
081 CATHOLIC	5	NA	2,142	71.3	66.2
081d LATIN	*5*	*NA*	*2,142*	*71.3*	*66.2*
207 E.L.C.A.	1	248	315	10.5	9.7
283 LUTH—MO SYNOD	1	162	207	6.9	6.4
355 PRESB CH (USA)	1	17	22*	.7	.7
449 UN METHODIST	4	374	490*	16.3	15.1
HALL	**54**	**16,185**	**34,189***	**69.9**	**100.0**
019 AMER BAPT USA	1	458	590*	1.2	1.7
053 ASSEMB OF GOD	3	498	1,611	3.3	4.7
057 BAPT GEN CONF	1	56	72*	.1	.2
081 CATHOLIC	6	NA	10,771	22.0	31.5
081d LATIN	*6*	*NA*	*10,771*	*22.0*	*31.5*
089 CHR & MISS AL	1	17	48	.1	.1
093 CHR CH (DISC)	1	271	382	.8	1.1
097 CHR CHS&CHS CR	1	115	148*	.3	.4
111 CH CR,SCIENTST	1	NR	NR	-	-
127 CH GOD (CLEVE)	1	120	154*	.3	.5
145 CH GOD PROPHCY	1	22	28*	.1	.1
151 L-D SAINTS	2	NA	625	1.3	1.8
165 CH OF NAZARENE	1	102	412	.8	1.2
167 CHS OF CHRIST	2	127	168	.3	.5
193 EPISCOPAL	1	318	378	.8	1.1
203 EVAN FREE CH	1	278	575	1.2	1.7
207 E.L.C.A.	3	3,092	3,919	8.0	11.5
246 GREEK ORTHODOX	1	NR	NR	-	-
263 INT FOURSQ GOS	1	30	39*	.1	.1
283 LUTH—MO SYNOD	6	3,447	4,649	9.5	13.6
285 MENNONITE CH	1	93	118	.2	.3
355 PRESB CH (USA)	2	1,218	1,568*	3.2	4.6
356 PRESB CH AMER	1	19	35	.1	.1
403 SALVATION ARMY	1	127	136	.3	.4
413 S.D.A.	2	270	348*	.7	1.0
419 SO BAPT CONV	1	90	116*	.2	.3
443 UN C OF CHRIST	1	273	351*	.7	1.0
449 UN METHODIST	8	4,945	6,366*	13.0	18.6
467 WESLEYAN	1	12	50	.1	.1
469 WELS	1	187	257	.5	.8
496 JEWISH EST[1]	0	NA	275	.6	.8
HAMILTON	**22**	**3,379**	**5,151***	**58.1**	**100.0**
053 ASSEMB OF GOD	1	40	49	.6	1.0
057 BAPT GEN CONF	1	62	81*	.9	1.6
081 CATHOLIC	2	NA	521	5.9	10.1
081d LATIN	*2*	*NA*	*521*	*5.9*	*10.1*
093 CHR CH (DISC)	1	190	325	3.7	6.3
203 EVAN FREE CH	3	180	324	3.7	6.3
207 E.L.C.A.	3	493	709	8.0	13.8
283 LUTH—MO SYNOD	3	668	859	9.7	16.7
355 PRESB CH (USA)	1	111	145*	1.6	2.8
413 S.D.A.	1	62	81*	.9	1.6
443 UN C OF CHRIST	1	72	94*	1.1	1.8
449 UN METHODIST	4	1,451	1,896*	21.4	36.8
469 WELS	1	50	67	.8	1.3
HARLAN	**20**	**1,700**	**2,660***	**69.8**	**100.0**
081 CATHOLIC	3	NA	393	10.3	14.8
081d LATIN	*3*	*NA*	*393*	*10.3*	*14.8*
093 CHR CH (DISC)	1	86	135	3.5	5.1
203 EVAN FREE CH	3	129	191	5.0	7.2
207 E.L.C.A.	3	436	573	15.0	21.5
221 FREE METHODIST	1	15	24	.6	.9
283 LUTH—MO SYNOD	1	220	308	8.1	11.6
355 PRESB CH (USA)	2	147	183*	4.8	6.9
449 UN METHODIST	5	634	788*	20.7	29.6
467 WESLEYAN	1	33	65	1.7	2.4
HAYES	**5**	**202**	**439***	**35.9**	**100.0**
057 BAPT GEN CONF	1	51	64*	5.2	14.6
081 CATHOLIC	1	NA	125	10.2	28.5
081d LATIN	*1*	*NA*	*125*	*10.2*	*28.5*
089 CHR & MISS AL	1	46	117	9.6	26.7
167 CHS OF CHRIST	1	13	17	1.4	3.9
443 UN C OF CHRIST	1	92	116*	9.5	26.4
HITCHCOCK	**15**	**1,396**	**2,305***	**61.5**	**100.0**
081 CATHOLIC	3	NA	372	9.9	16.1
081d LATIN	*3*	*NA*	*372*	*9.9*	*16.1*
089 CHR & MISS AL	1	44	116	3.1	5.0
123 CH GOD (ANDER)	1	0	31	.8	1.3
167 CHS OF CHRIST	1	28	36	1.0	1.6
283 LUTH—MO SYNOD	2	284	381	10.2	16.5
291 MISSIONARY CH	1	22	43	1.1	1.9
353 CHR BRETHREN	1	25	50	1.3	2.2
443 UN C OF CHRIST	1	47	60*	1.6	2.6
449 UN METHODIST	4	946	1,216*	32.4	52.8
HOLT	**36**	**3,014**	**9,071***	**72.0**	**100.0**
053 ASSEMB OF GOD	4	284	425	3.4	4.7
081 CATHOLIC	6	NA	4,744	37.7	52.3
081d LATIN	*6*	*NA*	*4,744*	*37.7*	*52.3*
097 CHR CHS&CHS CR	2	150	198*	1.6	2.2
151 L-D SAINTS	1	NA	45	.4	.5
207 E.L.C.A.	1	168	249	2.0	2.7
221 FREE METHODIST	1	19	25	.2	.3
283 LUTH—MO SYNOD	3	685	965	7.7	10.6
355 PRESB CH (USA)	6	525	694*	5.5	7.7
413 S.D.A.	1	10	13*	.1	.1
449 UN METHODIST	7	1,029	1,361*	10.8	15.0
467 WESLEYAN	3	116	311	2.5	3.4
469 WELS	1	28	41	.3	.5
HOOKER	**4**	**285**	**711***	**89.7**	**100.0**
053 ASSEMB OF GOD	1	38	77	9.7	10.8
081 CATHOLIC	1	NA	300	37.8	42.2
081d LATIN	*1*	*NA*	*300*	*37.8*	*42.2*
193 EPISCOPAL	1	39	76	9.6	10.7
449 UN METHODIST	1	208	258*	32.5	36.3
HOWARD	**16**	**1,491**	**3,800***	**62.8**	**100.0**
057 BAPT GEN CONF	2	107	137*	2.3	3.6
081 CATHOLIC	5	NA	1,884	31.1	49.6
081d LATIN	*5*	*NA*	*1,884*	*31.1*	*49.6*
207 E.L.C.A.	2	460	582	9.6	15.3
220 FREE LUTHERAN	1	31	38	.6	1.0
283 LUTH—MO SYNOD	1	255	344	5.7	9.1
355 PRESB CH (USA)	1	152	194*	3.2	5.1
449 UN METHODIST	4	486	621*	10.3	16.3
JEFFERSON	**31**	**4,577**	**6,671***	**76.2**	**100.0**
019 AMER BAPT USA	1	161	199*	2.3	3.0
053 ASSEMB OF GOD	1	27	100	1.1	1.5
081 CATHOLIC	1	NA	592	6.8	8.9
081d LATIN	*1*	*NA*	*592*	*6.8*	*8.9*
093 CHR CH (DISC)	1	135	295	3.4	4.4
111 CH CR,SCIENTST	1	NR	NR	-	-
123 CH GOD (ANDER)	1	43	73	.8	1.1
151 L-D SAINTS	1	NA	37	.4	.6
165 CH OF NAZARENE	1	44	43	.5	.6
167 CHS OF CHRIST	1	12	12	.1	.2
193 EPISCOPAL	1	50	69	.8	1.0
207 E.L.C.A.	4	721	985	11.2	14.8
211 FEL EVG BIB CH	1	76	100	1.1	1.5
220 FREE LUTHERAN	1	241	292	3.3	4.4
263 INT FOURSQ GOS	1	81	100*	1.1	1.5
283 LUTH—MO SYNOD	4	1,216	1,568	17.9	23.5
355 PRESB CH (USA)	2	385	476*	5.4	7.1
413 S.D.A.	1	47	58*	.7	.9
443 UN C OF CHRIST	3	268	331*	3.8	5.0
449 UN METHODIST	3	748	924*	10.5	13.9
469 WELS	1	322	417	4.8	6.3
JOHNSON	**16**	**2,183**	**3,420***	**73.2**	**100.0**
019 AMER BAPT USA	1	248	307*	6.6	9.0
081 CATHOLIC	2	NA	726	15.5	21.2
081d LATIN	*2*	*NA*	*726*	*15.5*	*21.2*
193 EPISCOPAL	1	6	6	.1	.2
207 E.L.C.A.	2	686	857	18.3	25.1
283 LUTH—MO SYNOD	2	483	583	12.5	17.0
355 PRESB CH (USA)	1	123	152*	3.3	4.4
443 UN C OF CHRIST	1	126	156*	3.3	4.6
449 UN METHODIST	6	511	633*	13.5	18.5
KEARNEY	**20**	**3,268**	**4,646***	**70.1**	**100.0**
081 CATHOLIC	2	NA	401	6.0	8.6

NA–Not applicable   NR–Not reported   *Total adherents estimated from known number of communicant, confirmed, full members.   - Represents a percent less than 0.1.   Percentages may not total due to rounding.
[1]See Appendix E   [2]See Appendix F   [3]See Appendix G   Lines in *italic* represent a breakdown of Catholic rites or Friends affiliations. They are included in their respective denominational total.

Table 4. Churches and Church Membership by County and Denomination: 1990

County and Denomination		Number of churches	Communicant, confirmed, full members	Total adherents		
				Number	Percent of total population	Percent of total adherents
081d	*LATIN*	2	NA	401	6.0	8.6
093	CHR CH (DISC)	1	132	214	3.2	4.6
203	EVAN FREE CH	3	188	235	3.5	5.1
207	E.L.C.A.	5	952	1,235	18.6	26.6
283	LUTH—MO SYNOD	3	632	827	12.5	17.8
329	OPEN BIBLE STD	1	NR	NR	-	-
355	PRESB CH (USA)	2	565	718*	10.8	15.5
413	S.D.A.	1	5	6*	.1	.1
449	UN METHODIST	2	794	1,010*	15.2	21.7
KEITH		**20**	**3,034**	**5,966***	**69.5**	**100.0**
053	ASSEMB OF GOD	1	36	75	.9	1.3
057	BAPT GEN CONF	1	80	103*	1.2	1.7
063	BEREAN FUND CH	1	50	88	1.0	1.5
081	CATHOLIC	2	NA	1,837	21.4	30.8
081d	*LATIN*	2	NA	1,837	21.4	30.8
123	CH GOD (ANDER)	1	0	30	.3	.5
167	CHS OF CHRIST	1	121	158	1.8	2.6
193	EPISCOPAL	1	84	97	1.1	1.6
203	EVAN FREE CH	1	50	80	.9	1.3
207	E.L.C.A.	1	194	241	2.8	4.0
283	LUTH—MO SYNOD	3	989	1,421	16.6	23.8
355	PRESB CH (USA)	2	39	50*	.6	.8
413	S.D.A.	1	14	18*	.2	.3
443	UN C OF CHRIST	2	367	471*	5.5	7.9
449	UN METHODIST	2	1,010	1,297*	15.1	21.7
KEYA PAHA		**6**	**509**	**640***	**62.2**	**100.0**
053	ASSEMB OF GOD	1	45	55	5.3	8.6
283	LUTH—MO SYNOD	2	205	264	25.7	41.2
413	S.D.A.	1	29	36*	3.5	5.6
449	UN METHODIST	2	230	285*	27.7	44.5
KIMBALL		**10**	**1,410**	**2,464***	**60.0**	**100.0**
053	ASSEMB OF GOD	1	29	84	2.0	3.4
081	CATHOLIC	1	NA	600	14.6	24.4
081d	*LATIN*	1	NA	600	14.6	24.4
165	CH OF NAZARENE	1	35	72	1.8	2.9
193	EPISCOPAL	1	31	31	.8	1.3
207	E.L.C.A.	1	342	442	10.8	17.9
283	LUTH—MO SYNOD	1	209	267	6.5	10.8
355	PRESB CH (USA)	2	209	265*	6.5	10.8
449	UN METHODIST	2	555	703*	17.1	28.5
KNOX		**30**	**4,110**	**8,251***	**86.5**	**100.0**
081	CATHOLIC	5	NA	2,939	30.8	35.6
081d	*LATIN*	5	NA	2,939	30.8	35.6
193	EPISCOPAL	3	107	167	1.8	2.0
207	E.L.C.A.	6	1,874	2,456	25.8	29.8
259	IFCA	1	NR	NR	-	-
283	LUTH—MO SYNOD	4	929	1,185	12.4	14.4
355	PRESB CH (USA)	2	116	145*	1.5	1.8
443	UN C OF CHRIST	4	277	347*	3.6	4.2
449	UN METHODIST	5	807	1,012*	10.6	12.3
LANCASTER		**174**	**57,223**	**110,985***	**51.9**	**100.0**
019	AMER BAPT USA	3	895	1,109*	.5	1.0
053	ASSEMB OF GOD	6	1,630	1,980	.9	1.8
057	BAPT GEN CONF	1	84	104*	-	.1
063	BEREAN FUND CH	2	361	1,060	.5	1.0
081	CATHOLIC	15	NA	29,297	13.7	26.4
081d	*LATIN*	14	NA	29,260	13.7	26.4
081h	*UKRAINIAN*	1	NA	37	-	-
093	CHR CH (DISC)	6	1,427	2,900	1.4	2.6
097	CHR CHS&CHS CR	4	1,030	1,276*	.6	1.1
111	CH CR,SCIENTST	2	NR	NR	-	-
123	CH GOD (ANDER)	2	140	143	.1	.1
127	CH GOD (CLEVE)	1	64	79*	-	.1
151	L-D SAINTS	4	NA	1,727	.8	1.6
157	CH OF BRETHREN	1	130	161*	.1	.1
165	CH OF NAZARENE	2	374	694	.3	.6
167	CHS OF CHRIST	2	408	566	.3	.5
193	EPISCOPAL	4	1,441	1,759	.8	1.6
203	EVAN FREE CH	1	204	680	.3	.6
207	E.L.C.A.	15	9,032	12,188	5.7	11.0
211	FEL EVG BIB CH	1	28	50	-	-
221	FREE METHODIST	1	25	41	-	-
223	FREE WILL BAPT	1	30	37*	-	-
226	FRIENDS-USA	1	34	42*	-	-
226a	*CONSERV*	1	34	42*	-	-
246	GREEK ORTHODOX	1	NR	NR	-	-
263	INT FOURSQ GOS	1	146	181*	.1	.2
274	LAT EVAN LUTH	2	274	288	.1	.3
283	LUTH—MO SYNOD	15	8,305	11,325	5.3	10.2
285	MENNONITE CH	1	44	83	-	.1

County and Denomination		Number of churches	Communicant, confirmed, full members	Total adherents		
				Number	Percent of total population	Percent of total adherents
287	MENN GEN CONF	1	24	29	-	-
291	MISSIONARY CH	1	77	99	-	.1
329	OPEN BIBLE STD	1	NR	NR	-	-
353	CHR BRETHREN	1	30	60	-	.1
355	PRESB CH (USA)	10	5,561	6,890*	3.2	6.2
356	PRESB CH AMER	1	128	183	.1	.2
371	REF CH IN AM	3	614	939	.4	.8
373	REF CH IN U.S.	1	82	107	.1	.1
403	SALVATION ARMY	1	216	236	.1	.2
413	S.D.A.	7	2,916	3,613*	1.7	3.3
419	SO BAPT CONV	4	937	1,161*	.5	1.0
431	UKRANIAN AMER	1	NR	NR	-	-
435	UNITARIAN-UNIV	1	460	575	.3	.5
443	UN C OF CHRIST	10	4,061	5,032*	2.4	4.5
449	UN METHODIST	27	14,366	17,799*	8.3	16.0
467	WESLEYAN	1	29	120	.1	.1
469	WELS	2	384	521	.2	.5
496	JEWISH EST[1]	2	NA	825	.4	.7
497	BLACK BAPT EST[2]	NA	1,232	1,526*	.7	1.4
499	INDEP.NON-CHAR[3]	4	NA	3,500	1.6	3.2
LINCOLN		**51**	**9,716**	**20,114***	**61.9**	**100.0**
019	AMER BAPT USA	1	768	993*	3.1	4.9
053	ASSEMB OF GOD	4	283	606	1.9	3.0
057	BAPT GEN CONF	1	119	154*	.5	.8
063	BEREAN FUND CH	2	289	292	.9	1.5
081	CATHOLIC	7	NA	6,100	18.8	30.3
081d	*LATIN*	7	NA	6,100	18.8	30.3
093	CHR CH (DISC)	1	248	761	2.3	3.8
097	CHR CHS&CHS CR	1	150	194*	.6	1.0
111	CH CR,SCIENTST	1	NR	NR	-	-
123	CH GOD (ANDER)	1	0	0	-	-
151	L-D SAINTS	2	NA	529	1.6	2.6
165	CH OF NAZARENE	1	195	272	.8	1.4
167	CHS OF CHRIST	1	84	109	.3	.5
193	EPISCOPAL	1	196	307	.9	1.5
203	EVAN FREE CH	1	185	345	1.1	1.7
207	E.L.C.A.	4	1,942	2,543	7.8	12.6
259	IFCA	1	NR	NR	-	-
263	INT FOURSQ GOS	1	167	216*	.7	1.1
283	LUTH—MO SYNOD	3	985	1,360	4.2	6.8
329	OPEN BIBLE STD	2	NR	NR	-	-
355	PRESB CH (USA)	2	849	1,097*	3.4	5.5
403	SALVATION ARMY	1	200	230	.7	1.1
413	S.D.A.	1	134	173*	.5	.9
419	SO BAPT CONV	1	173	224*	.7	1.1
449	UN METHODIST	8	2,589	3,346*	10.3	16.6
467	WESLEYAN	1	70	140	.4	.7
469	WELS	1	90	123	.4	.6
LOGAN		**5**	**205**	**664***	**75.6**	**100.0**
053	ASSEMB OF GOD	1	21	28	3.2	4.2
063	BEREAN FUND CH	2	80	215	24.5	32.4
081	CATHOLIC	1	NA	279	31.8	42.0
081d	*LATIN*	1	NA	279	31.8	42.0
355	PRESB CH (USA)	1	104	142*	16.2	21.4
LOUP		**3**	**117**	**172***	**25.2**	**100.0**
053	ASSEMB OF GOD	1	39	52	7.6	30.2
203	EVAN FREE CH	1	8	30	4.4	17.4
449	UN METHODIST	1	70	90*	13.2	52.3
MC PHERSON		**3**	**78**	**160***	**29.3**	**100.0**
221	FREE METHODIST	1	20	72	13.2	45.0
449	UN METHODIST	1	53	68*	12.5	42.5
467	WESLEYAN	1	5	20	3.7	12.5
MADISON		**56**	**14,479**	**28,224***	**86.4**	**100.0**
019	AMER BAPT USA	1	420	547*	1.7	1.9
053	ASSEMB OF GOD	1	66	117	.4	.4
081	CATHOLIC	5	NA	8,618	26.4	30.5
081d	*LATIN*	5	NA	8,618	26.4	30.5
089	CHR & MISS AL	2	27	107	.3	.4
097	CHR CHS&CHS CR	5	792	1,032*	3.2	3.7
111	CH CR,SCIENTST	1	NR	NR	-	-
127	CH GOD (CLEVE)	1	79	103*	.3	.4
145	CH GOD PROPHCY	1	22	29*	.1	.1
151	L-D SAINTS	1	NA	166	.5	.6
165	CH OF NAZARENE	2	50	101	.3	.4
167	CHS OF CHRIST	1	47	61	.2	.2
181	CONSRV CONGR	1	6	8*	-	-
193	EPISCOPAL	1	148	245	.8	.9
203	EVAN FREE CH	2	94	170	.5	.6
207	E.L.C.A.	5	1,845	2,511	7.7	8.9
283	LUTH—MO SYNOD	9	6,208	8,293	25.4	29.4

Table 4. Churches and Church Membership by County and Denomination: 1990

County and Denomination	Number of churches	Communicant, confirmed, full members	Total adherents Number	Percent of total population	Percent of total adherents
355 PRESB CH (USA)	2	488	636*	1.9	2.3
403 SALVATION ARMY	1	3	24	.1	.1
413 S.D.A.	1	33	43*	.1	.2
419 SO BAPT CONV	2	135	176*	.5	.6
443 UN C OF CHRIST	1	367	478*	1.5	1.7
449 UN METHODIST	8	2,924	3,809*	11.7	13.5
469 WELS	2	725	950	2.9	3.4
MERRICK	**27**	**3,251**	**5,738***	**71.4**	**100.0**
019 AMER BAPT USA	1	103	131*	1.6	2.3
063 BEREAN FUND CH	1	50	105	1.3	1.8
081 CATHOLIC	3	NA	1,448	18.0	25.2
081d LATIN	3	NA	1,448	18.0	25.2
097 CHR CHS&CHS CR	2	190	242*	3.0	4.2
133 CH GOD(7TH)DEN	1	9	9	.1	.2
165 CH OF NAZARENE	1	3	7	.1	.1
181 CONSRV CONGR	1	62	79*	1.0	1.4
193 EPISCOPAL	1	31	45	.6	.8
203 EVAN FREE CH	1	70	173	2.2	3.0
207 E.L.C.A.	1	108	132	1.6	2.3
226 FRIENDS-USA	1	109	139*	1.7	2.4
226e FUM	1	109	139*	1.7	2.4
283 LUTH—MO SYNOD	3	878	1,120	13.9	19.5
355 PRESB CH (USA)	1	129	164*	2.0	2.9
449 UN METHODIST	8	1,494	1,902*	23.7	33.1
467 WESLEYAN	1	15	42	.5	.7
MORRILL	**22**	**1,992**	**3,451***	**63.6**	**100.0**
019 AMER BAPT USA	1	132	169*	3.1	4.9
053 ASSEMB OF GOD	3	182	276	5.1	8.0
081 CATHOLIC	3	NA	847	15.6	24.5
081d LATIN	3	NA	847	15.6	24.5
097 CHR CHS&CHS CR	2	221	282*	5.2	8.2
181 CONSRV CONGR	1	134	171*	3.2	5.0
193 EPISCOPAL	2	24	28	.5	.8
207 E.L.C.A.	1	182	238	4.4	6.9
246 GREEK ORTHODOX	1	NR	NR	-	-
283 LUTH—MO SYNOD	2	321	424	7.8	12.3
355 PRESB CH (USA)	3	375	479*	8.8	13.9
413 S.D.A.	1	19	24*	.4	.7
443 UN C OF CHRIST	1	294	375*	6.9	10.9
449 UN METHODIST	1	108	138*	2.5	4.0
NANCE	**11**	**1,367**	**3,474***	**81.3**	**100.0**
081 CATHOLIC	3	NA	1,705	39.9	49.1
081d LATIN	3	NA	1,705	39.9	49.1
207 E.L.C.A.	1	319	384	9.0	11.1
283 LUTH—MO SYNOD	2	291	401	9.4	11.5
355 PRESB CH (USA)	1	157	204*	4.8	5.9
443 UN C OF CHRIST	1	43	56*	1.3	1.6
449 UN METHODIST	3	557	724*	16.9	20.8
NEMAHA	**27**	**3,545**	**5,218***	**65.4**	**100.0**
053 ASSEMB OF GOD	1	47	100	1.3	1.9
063 BEREAN FUND CH	1	44	78	1.0	1.5
081 CATHOLIC	1	NA	475	6.0	9.1
081d LATIN	1	NA	475	6.0	9.1
093 CHR CH (DISC)	4	237	499	6.3	9.6
097 CHR CHS&CHS CR	1	480	596*	7.5	11.4
145 CH GOD PROPHCY	1	22	27*	.3	.5
167 CHS OF CHRIST	1	28	36	.5	.7
207 E.L.C.A.	7	1,601	2,050	25.7	39.3
283 LUTH—MO SYNOD	1	207	266	3.3	5.1
355 PRESB CH (USA)	1	99	123*	1.5	2.4
419 SO BAPT CONV	1	37	46*	.6	.9
449 UN METHODIST	7	743	922*	11.6	17.7
NUCKOLLS	**24**	**2,508**	**4,781***	**82.6**	**100.0**
019 AMER BAPT USA	1	238	299*	5.2	6.3
081 CATHOLIC	5	NA	1,477	25.5	30.9
081d LATIN	5	NA	1,477	25.5	30.9
097 CHR CHS&CHS CR	4	138	173*	3.0	3.6
165 CH OF NAZARENE	1	46	106	1.8	2.2
167 CHS OF CHRIST	1	20	30	.5	.6
207 E.L.C.A.	4	636	822	14.2	17.2
283 LUTH—MO SYNOD	2	446	598	10.3	12.5
355 PRESB CH (USA)	1	179	225*	3.9	4.7
413 S.D.A.	1	38	48*	.8	1.0
443 UN C OF CHRIST	1	313	393*	6.8	8.2
449 UN METHODIST	2	449	563*	9.7	11.8
467 WESLEYAN	1	5	47	.8	1.0
OTOE	**41**	**6,013**	**10,898***	**76.5**	**100.0**
057 BAPT GEN CONF	1	15	19*	.1	.2
081 CATHOLIC	7	NA	2,883	20.2	26.5

County and Denomination	Number of churches	Communicant, confirmed, full members	Total adherents Number	Percent of total population	Percent of total adherents
081d LATIN	7	NA	2,883	20.2	26.5
093 CHR CH (DISC)	2	315	812	5.7	7.5
097 CHR CHS&CHS CR	1	75	94*	.7	.9
167 CHS OF CHRIST	1	33	42	.3	.4
193 EPISCOPAL	1	71	195	1.4	1.8
203 EVAN FREE CH	1	0	0	-	-
207 E.L.C.A.	8	2,371	2,914	20.4	26.7
263 INT FOURSQ GOS	1	9	11*	.1	.1
283 LUTH—MO SYNOD	1	91	110	.8	1.0
355 PRESB CH (USA)	4	588	740*	5.2	6.8
413 S.D.A.	1	18	23*	.2	.2
419 SO BAPT CONV	1	42	53*	.4	.5
443 UN C OF CHRIST	5	1,175	1,479*	10.4	13.6
449 UN METHODIST	6	1,210	1,523*	10.7	14.0
PAWNEE	**15**	**1,451**	**2,414***	**72.8**	**100.0**
019 AMER BAPT USA	1	38	46*	1.4	1.9
081 CATHOLIC	2	NA	597	18.0	24.7
081d LATIN	2	NA	597	18.0	24.7
093 CHR CH (DISC)	1	75	130	3.9	5.4
097 CHR CHS&CHS CR	1	132	161*	4.9	6.7
167 CHS OF CHRIST	1	4	5	.2	.2
207 E.L.C.A.	1	21	30	.9	1.2
283 LUTH—MO SYNOD	2	364	449	13.5	18.6
355 PRESB CH (USA)	1	106	129*	3.9	5.3
443 UN C OF CHRIST	1	242	295*	8.9	12.2
449 UN METHODIST	4	469	572*	17.2	23.7
PERKINS	**13**	**1,527**	**2,443***	**72.6**	**100.0**
081 CATHOLIC	2	NA	477	14.2	19.5
081d LATIN	2	NA	477	14.2	19.5
143 CG IN CR(MENN)	1	90	117*	3.5	4.8
203 EVAN FREE CH	1	31	62	1.8	2.5
237 GC MENN BR CHS	1	94	122*	3.6	5.0
263 INT FOURSQ GOS	1	40	52*	1.5	2.1
283 LUTH—MO SYNOD	3	368	438	13.0	17.9
443 UN C OF CHRIST	1	114	148*	4.4	6.1
449 UN METHODIST	3	790	1,027*	30.5	42.0
PHELPS	**25**	**5,160**	**7,783***	**80.1**	**100.0**
019 AMER BAPT USA	1	469	598*	6.2	7.7
053 ASSEMB OF GOD	1	130	375	3.9	4.8
081 CATHOLIC	1	NA	821	8.5	10.5
081d LATIN	1	NA	821	8.5	10.5
097 CHR CHS&CHS CR	1	13	17*	.2	.2
165 CH OF NAZARENE	0	17	108	1.1	1.4
167 CHS OF CHRIST	1	33	42	.4	.5
193 EPISCOPAL	1	103	115	1.2	1.5
203 EVAN FREE CH	5	622	837	8.6	10.8
207 E.L.C.A.	5	1,555	1,992	20.5	25.6
283 LUTH—MO SYNOD	2	605	821	8.5	10.5
355 PRESB CH (USA)	1	293	374*	3.8	4.8
413 S.D.A.	1	38	48*	.5	.6
449 UN METHODIST	5	1,282	1,635*	16.8	21.0
PIERCE	**19**	**3,942**	**6,560***	**83.8**	**100.0**
081 CATHOLIC	3	NA	1,412	18.0	21.5
081d LATIN	3	NA	1,412	18.0	21.5
207 E.L.C.A.	2	561	718	9.2	10.9
226 FRIENDS-USA	1	42	55*	.7	.8
226b EFI	1	42	55*	.7	.8
283 LUTH—MO SYNOD	5	2,064	2,721	34.8	41.5
443 UN C OF CHRIST	2	360	475*	6.1	7.2
449 UN METHODIST	5	721	951*	12.2	14.5
469 WELS	1	194	228	2.9	3.5
PLATTE	**42**	**9,054**	**25,527***	**85.6**	**100.0**
019 AMER BAPT USA	2	424	565*	1.9	2.2
053 ASSEMB OF GOD	1	142	285	1.0	1.1
081 CATHOLIC	8	NA	12,971	43.5	50.8
081d LATIN	8	NA	12,971	43.5	50.8
097 CHR CHS&CHS CR	1	40	53*	.2	.2
165 CH OF NAZARENE	1	53	64	.2	.3
167 CHS OF CHRIST	1	31	57	.2	.2
193 EPISCOPAL	1	139	180	.6	.7
203 EVAN FREE CH	1	177	376	1.3	1.5
207 E.L.C.A.	7	2,310	3,426	11.5	13.4
283 LUTH—MO SYNOD	6	2,864	3,708	12.4	14.5
313 N AM BAPT CONF	3	101	135*	.5	.5
355 PRESB CH (USA)	1	603	804*	2.7	3.1
413 S.D.A.	1	62	83*	.3	.3
419 SO BAPT CONV	1	64	85*	.3	.3
443 UN C OF CHRIST	2	658	877*	2.9	3.4
449 UN METHODIST	4	1,359	1,812*	6.1	7.1
469 WELS	1	27	46	.2	.2

NA–Not applicable   NR–Not reported   *Total adherents estimated from known number of communicant, confirmed, full members.   - Represents a percent less than 0.1.   Percentages may not total due to rounding.

[1]See Appendix E   [2]See Appendix F   [3]See Appendix G   Lines in *italic* represent a breakdown of Catholic rites or Friends affiliations. They are included in their respective denominational total.

Table 4. Churches and Church Membership by County and Denomination: 1990

| County and Denomination | Number of churches | Communicant, confirmed, full members | Total adherents | | |
			Number	Percent of total population	Percent of total adherents
POLK	**18**	**2,684**	**3,929***	**69.2**	**100.0**
019 AMER BAPT USA	1	170	214*	3.8	5.4
057 BAPT GEN CONF	2	296	373*	6.6	9.5
081 CATHOLIC	4	NA	511	9.0	13.0
081d LATIN	4	NA	511	9.0	13.0
203 EVAN FREE CH	2	143	195	3.4	5.0
207 E.L.C.A.	4	947	1,215	21.4	30.9
449 UN METHODIST	5	1,128	1,421*	25.0	36.2
RED WILLOW	**31**	**4,368**	**8,742***	**74.7**	**100.0**
019 AMER BAPT USA	1	150	192*	1.6	2.2
053 ASSEMB OF GOD	1	109	275	2.3	3.1
063 BEREAN FUND CH	1	18	53	.5	.6
081 CATHOLIC	4	NA	2,710	23.2	31.0
081d LATIN	4	NA	2,710	23.2	31.0
093 CHR CH (DISC)	1	88	144	1.2	1.6
097 CHR CHS&CHS CR	3	365	466*	4.0	5.3
111 CH CR,SCIENTST	1	NR	NR	-	-
123 CH GOD (ANDER)	1	60	60	.5	.7
151 L-D SAINTS	1	NA	145	1.2	1.7
165 CH OF NAZARENE	1	65	86	.7	1.0
167 CHS OF CHRIST	1	85	136	1.2	1.6
175 CONGR CHR CHS	1	402	514*	4.4	5.9
193 EPISCOPAL	1	196	259	2.2	3.0
203 EVAN FREE CH	1	105	235	2.0	2.7
207 E.L.C.A.	1	181	256	2.2	2.9
283 LUTH—MO SYNOD	2	848	1,047	8.9	12.0
355 PRESB CH (USA)	2	51	65*	.6	.7
413 S.D.A.	1	34	43*	.4	.5
419 SO BAPT CONV	1	68	87*	.7	1.0
449 UN METHODIST	3	1,521	1,943*	16.6	22.2
467 WESLEYAN	1	0	0	-	-
469 WELS	1	22	26	.2	.3
RICHARDSON	**36**	**3,668**	**6,932***	**69.8**	**100.0**
019 AMER BAPT USA	1	30	37*	.4	.5
053 ASSEMB OF GOD	1	86	127	1.3	1.8
063 BEREAN FUND CH	1	27	35	.4	.5
071 BRETHREN (ASH)	1	44	55*	.6	.8
081 CATHOLIC	5	NA	1,770	17.8	25.5
081d LATIN	5	NA	1,770	17.8	25.5
093 CHR CH (DISC)	4	395	885	8.9	12.8
165 CH OF NAZARENE	1	120	147	1.5	2.1
167 CHS OF CHRIST	1	37	48	.5	.7
175 CONGR CHR CHS	1	15	19*	.2	.3
193 EPISCOPAL	1	81	136	1.4	2.0
207 E.L.C.A.	3	814	1,131	11.4	16.3
283 LUTH—MO SYNOD	3	566	732	7.4	10.6
355 PRESB CH (USA)	2	169	211*	2.1	3.0
413 S.D.A.	1	23	29*	.3	.4
419 SO BAPT CONV	1	54	67*	.7	1.0
443 UN C OF CHRIST	2	192	239*	2.4	3.4
449 UN METHODIST	7	1,015	1,264*	12.7	18.2
ROCK	**7**	**529**	**881***	**43.6**	**100.0**
053 ASSEMB OF GOD	1	28	45	2.2	5.1
081 CATHOLIC	1	NA	150	7.4	17.0
081d LATIN	1	NA	150	7.4	17.0
193 EPISCOPAL	1	25	69	3.4	7.8
207 E.L.C.A.	1	147	197	9.8	22.4
449 UN METHODIST	3	329	420*	20.8	47.7
SALINE	**22**	**4,321**	**7,099***	**55.8**	**100.0**
063 BEREAN FUND CH	1	29	47	.4	.7
081 CATHOLIC	4	NA	1,672	13.1	23.6
081d LATIN	4	NA	1,672	13.1	23.6
193 EPISCOPAL	2	59	68	.5	1.0
207 E.L.C.A.	2	636	799	6.3	11.3
283 LUTH—MO SYNOD	2	1,057	1,353	10.6	19.1
443 UN C OF CHRIST	4	857	1,066*	8.4	15.0
449 UN METHODIST	7	1,683	2,094*	16.5	29.5
SARPY	**47**	**15,549**	**39,673***	**38.7**	**100.0**
019 AMER BAPT USA	1	247	333*	.3	.8
053 ASSEMB OF GOD	3	1,025	3,369	3.3	8.5
057 BAPT GEN CONF	1	53	71*	.1	.2
063 BEREAN FUND CH	1	99	146	.1	.4
081 CATHOLIC	4	NA	13,005	12.7	32.8
081d LATIN	4	NA	13,005	12.7	32.8
089 CHR & MISS AL	3	99	445	.4	1.1
093 CHR CH (DISC)	1	171	206	.2	.5
097 CHR CHS&CHS CR	2	985	1,327*	1.3	3.3
151 L-D SAINTS	4	NA	1,647	1.6	4.2
165 CH OF NAZARENE	1	82	155	.2	.4

| County and Denomination | Number of churches | Communicant, confirmed, full members | Total adherents | | |
			Number	Percent of total population	Percent of total adherents
167 CHS OF CHRIST	1	230	330	.3	.8
193 EPISCOPAL	1	255	512	.5	1.3
207 E.L.C.A.	5	2,705	3,694	3.6	9.3
221 FREE METHODIST	1	17	42	-	.1
263 INT FOURSQ GOS	1	14	19*	-	-
283 LUTH—MO SYNOD	4	1,632	2,300	2.2	5.8
355 PRESB CH (USA)	3	1,412	1,903*	1.9	4.8
413 S.D.A.	1	160	216*	.2	.5
419 SO BAPT CONV	4	2,732	3,682*	3.6	9.3
449 UN METHODIST	4	2,220	2,992*	2.9	7.5
496 JEWISH EST[1]	0	NA	1,078	1.1	2.7
497 BLACK BAPT EST[2]	NA	1,411	1,901*	1.9	4.8
499 INDEP.NON-CHAR[3]	1	NA	300	.3	.8
SAUNDERS	**45**	**4,817**	**14,056***	**76.9**	**100.0**
019 AMER BAPT USA	1	50	64*	.4	.5
053 ASSEMB OF GOD	1	21	79	.4	.6
057 BAPT GEN CONF	3	83	107*	.6	.8
081 CATHOLIC	12	NA	7,418	40.6	52.8
081d LATIN	12	NA	7,418	40.6	52.8
089 CHR & MISS AL	1	0	36	.2	.3
093 CHR CH (DISC)	1	254	649	3.5	4.6
097 CHR CHS&CHS CR	1	40	52*	.3	.4
175 CONGR CHR CHS	2	145	187*	1.0	1.3
207 E.L.C.A.	9	2,016	2,612	14.3	18.6
283 LUTH—MO SYNOD	2	405	526	2.9	3.7
355 PRESB CH (USA)	4	637	822*	4.5	5.8
443 UN C OF CHRIST	1	82	106*	.6	.8
449 UN METHODIST	7	1,084	1,398*	7.6	9.9
SCOTTS BLUFF	**70**	**11,220**	**20,032***	**55.6**	**100.0**
019 AMER BAPT USA	1	350	448*	1.2	2.2
053 ASSEMB OF GOD	6	525	845	2.3	4.2
057 BAPT GEN CONF	1	150	192*	.5	1.0
063 BEREAN FUND CH	2	193	225	.6	1.1
081 CATHOLIC	7	NA	4,663	12.9	23.3
081d LATIN	7	NA	4,663	12.9	23.3
093 CHR CH (DISC)	2	270	375	1.0	1.9
097 CHR CHS&CHS CR	9	1,181	1,510*	4.2	7.5
111 CH CR,SCIENTST	1	NR	NR	-	-
123 CH GOD (ANDER)	2	10	130	.4	.6
127 CH GOD (CLEVE)	1	13	17*	-	.1
151 L-D SAINTS	1	NA	313	.9	1.6
165 CH OF NAZARENE	2	78	258	.7	1.3
167 CHS OF CHRIST	1	42	55	.2	.3
179 CONSRV BAPT	1	NR	NR	-	-
181 CONSRV CONGR	2	909	1,162*	3.2	5.8
193 EPISCOPAL	3	561	692	1.9	3.5
203 EVAN FREE CH	2	214	300	.8	1.5
207 E.L.C.A.	2	755	1,003	2.8	5.0
263 INT FOURSQ GOS	1	30	38*	.1	.2
283 LUTH—MO SYNOD	4	1,235	1,633	4.5	8.2
355 PRESB CH (USA)	3	736	941*	2.6	4.7
413 S.D.A.	2	256	327*	.9	1.6
419 SO BAPT CONV	1	128	164*	.5	.8
443 UN C OF CHRIST	3	590	754*	2.1	3.8
449 UN METHODIST	8	2,919	3,732*	10.4	18.6
467 WESLEYAN	1	24	180	.5	.9
469 WELS	1	51	75	.2	.4
SEWARD	**40**	**7,744**	**12,098***	**78.3**	**100.0**
053 ASSEMB OF GOD	1	125	265	1.7	2.2
081 CATHOLIC	4	NA	1,727	11.2	14.3
081d LATIN	4	NA	1,727	11.2	14.3
093 CHR CH (DISC)	1	17	40	.3	.3
167 CHS OF CHRIST	1	28	36	.2	.3
193 EPISCOPAL	1	46	52	.3	.4
203 EVAN FREE CH	1	24	70	.5	.6
207 E.L.C.A.	2	536	689	4.5	5.7
283 LUTH—MO SYNOD	9	3,907	5,272	34.1	43.6
285 MENNONITE CH	6	786	1,050	6.8	8.7
291 MISSIONARY CH	1	38	61	.4	.5
355 PRESB CH (USA)	1	98	124*	.8	1.0
413 S.D.A.	1	3	4*	-	-
443 UN C OF CHRIST	3	288	366*	2.4	3.0
449 UN METHODIST	6	1,738	2,208*	14.3	18.3
469 WELS	2	110	134	.9	1.1
SHERIDAN	**26**	**2,183**	**4,137***	**61.3**	**100.0**
081 CATHOLIC	4	NA	999	14.8	24.1
081d LATIN	4	NA	999	14.8	24.1
123 CH GOD (ANDER)	2	108	135	2.0	3.3
151 L-D SAINTS	1	NA	81	1.2	2.0
193 EPISCOPAL	2	76	315	4.7	7.6
207 E.L.C.A.	2	157	206	3.1	5.0
226 FRIENDS-USA	1	39	50*	.7	1.2

NA–Not applicable   NR–Not reported   *Total adherents estimated from known number of communicant, confirmed, full members.   - Represents a percent less than 0.1.   Percentages may not total due to rounding.
[1]See Appendix E   [2]See Appendix F   [3]See Appendix G   Lines in *italic* represent a breakdown of Catholic rites or Friends affiliations. They are included in their respective denominational total.

Table 4. Churches and Church Membership by County and Denomination: 1990

County and Denomination	Number of churches	Communicant, confirmed, full members	Total adherents		
			Number	Percent of total population	Percent of total adherents
226b EFI	*1*	*39*	*50**	*.7*	*1.2*
283 LUTH—MO SYNOD	3	491	671	9.9	16.2
355 PRESB CH (USA)	1	303	386*	5.7	9.3
413 S.D.A.	2	39	50*	.7	1.2
443 UN C OF CHRIST	1	31	39*	.6	.9
449 UN METHODIST	5	892	1,136*	16.8	27.5
467 WESLEYAN	1	35	50	.7	1.2
469 WELS	1	12	19	.3	.5
SHERMAN	**11**	**685**	**1,961***	**52.7**	**100.0**
081 CATHOLIC	4	NA	1,059	28.5	54.0
081d LATIN	*4*	*NA*	*1,059*	*28.5*	*54.0*
097 CHR CHS&CHS CR	1	80	101*	2.7	5.2
207 E.L.C.A.	1	95	128	3.4	6.5
283 LUTH—MO SYNOD	1	216	300	8.1	15.3
355 PRESB CH (USA)	1	52	66*	1.8	3.4
443 UN C OF CHRIST	1	29	37*	1.0	1.9
449 UN METHODIST	2	213	270*	7.3	13.8
SIOUX	**3**	**214**	**448***	**28.9**	**100.0**
081 CATHOLIC	1	NA	180	11.6	40.2
081d LATIN	*1*	*NA*	*180*	*11.6*	*40.2*
283 LUTH—MO SYNOD	1	43	53	3.4	11.8
449 UN METHODIST	1	171	215*	13.9	48.0
STANTON	**11**	**1,730**	**2,745***	**44.0**	**100.0**
081 CATHOLIC	1	NA	454	7.3	16.5
081d LATIN	*1*	*NA*	*454*	*7.3*	*16.5*
203 EVAN FREE CH	1	19	56	.9	2.0
207 E.L.C.A.	2	279	320	5.1	11.7
283 LUTH—MO SYNOD	2	504	657	10.5	23.9
443 UN C OF CHRIST	2	408	553*	8.9	20.1
449 UN METHODIST	2	261	354*	5.7	12.9
469 WELS	1	259	351	5.6	12.8
THAYER	**31**	**4,816**	**6,721***	**101.3**	**100.0**
053 ASSEMB OF GOD	1	20	36	.5	.5
081 CATHOLIC	2	NA	712	10.7	10.6
081d LATIN	*2*	*NA*	*712*	*10.7*	*10.6*
093 CHR CH (DISC)	1	125	160	2.4	2.4
097 CHR CHS&CHS CR	2	205	253*	3.8	3.8
157 CH OF BRETHREN	1	113	139*	2.1	2.1
167 CHS OF CHRIST	1	37	48	.7	.7
207 E.L.C.A.	8	2,062	2,571	38.7	38.3
283 LUTH—MO SYNOD	6	1,148	1,439	21.7	21.4
355 PRESB CH (USA)	3	227	280*	4.2	4.2
443 UN C OF CHRIST	1	62	76*	1.1	1.1
449 UN METHODIST	5	817	1,007*	15.2	15.0
THOMAS	**6**	**357**	**524***	**61.6**	**100.0**
053 ASSEMB OF GOD	1	89	105	12.3	20.0
081 CATHOLIC	1	NA	55	6.5	10.5
081d LATIN	*1*	*NA*	*55*	*6.5*	*10.5*
283 LUTH—MO SYNOD	1	45	71	8.3	13.5
443 UN C OF CHRIST	3	223	293*	34.4	55.9
THURSTON	**20**	**1,940**	**3,428***	**49.4**	**100.0**
053 ASSEMB OF GOD	2	92	140	2.0	4.1
081 CATHOLIC	4	NA	564	8.1	16.5
081d LATIN	*4*	*NA*	*564*	*8.1*	*16.5*
123 CH GOD (ANDER)	1	0	30	.4	.9
193 EPISCOPAL	1	30	47	.7	1.4
207 E.L.C.A.	3	938	1,178	17.0	34.4
283 LUTH—MO SYNOD	1	223	305	4.4	8.9
355 PRESB CH (USA)	3	249	352*	5.1	10.3
371 REF CH IN AM	2	70	335	4.8	9.8
449 UN METHODIST	3	338	477*	6.9	13.9
VALLEY	**17**	**1,750**	**3,248***	**62.8**	**100.0**
053 ASSEMB OF GOD	1	75	110	2.1	3.4
057 BAPT GEN CONF	2	118	147*	2.8	4.5
081 CATHOLIC	3	NA	1,007	19.5	31.0
081d LATIN	*3*	*NA*	*1,007*	*19.5*	*31.0*
097 CHR CHS&CHS CR	1	150	187*	3.6	5.8
203 EVAN FREE CH	1	40	67	1.3	2.1
207 E.L.C.A.	1	160	206	4.0	6.3
283 LUTH—MO SYNOD	1	174	234	4.5	7.2
355 PRESB CH (USA)	1	96	120*	2.3	3.7
415 S-D BAPTIST GC	1	189	236*	4.6	7.3
443 UN C OF CHRIST	1	12	15*	.3	.5
449 UN METHODIST	4	736	919*	17.8	28.3
WASHINGTON	**22**	**5,451**	**8,975***	**54.0**	**100.0**
019 AMER BAPT USA	2	167	212*	1.3	2.4

County and Denomination	Number of churches	Communicant, confirmed, full members	Total adherents		
			Number	Percent of total population	Percent of total adherents
053 ASSEMB OF GOD	1	19	50	.3	.6
057 BAPT GEN CONF	1	84	106*	.6	1.2
081 CATHOLIC	2	NA	1,741	10.5	19.4
081d LATIN	*2*	*NA*	*1,741*	*10.5*	*19.4*
097 CHR CHS&CHS CR	1	250	317*	1.9	3.5
167 CHS OF CHRIST	1	24	32	.2	.4
193 EPISCOPAL	1	151	199	1.2	2.2
207 E.L.C.A.	4	1,769	2,302	13.9	25.6
283 LUTH—MO SYNOD	3	1,135	1,496	9.0	16.7
355 PRESB CH (USA)	1	144	182*	1.1	2.0
443 UN C OF CHRIST	2	379	480*	2.9	5.3
449 UN METHODIST	3	1,329	1,684*	10.1	18.8
496 JEWISH EST [1]	0	NA	174	1.0	1.9
WAYNE	**22**	**4,281**	**6,145***	**65.6**	**100.0**
019 AMER BAPT USA	1	62	77*	.8	1.3
053 ASSEMB OF GOD	1	27	54	.6	.9
081 CATHOLIC	1	NA	848	9.1	13.8
081d LATIN	*1*	*NA*	*848*	*9.1*	*13.8*
097 CHR CHS&CHS CR	1	50	62*	.7	1.0
193 EPISCOPAL	1	5	7	.1	.1
203 EVAN FREE CH	1	23	58	.6	.9
207 E.L.C.A.	3	1,208	1,451	15.5	23.6
283 LUTH—MO SYNOD	6	1,447	1,742	18.6	28.3
355 PRESB CH (USA)	2	299	369*	3.9	6.0
443 UN C OF CHRIST	1	22	27*	.3	.4
449 UN METHODIST	3	884	1,092*	11.7	17.8
469 WELS	1	254	358	3.8	5.8
WEBSTER	**18**	**2,069**	**2,932***	**68.5**	**100.0**
019 AMER BAPT USA	1	34	42*	1.0	1.4
053 ASSEMB OF GOD	1	38	71	1.7	2.4
081 CATHOLIC	2	NA	324	7.6	11.1
081d LATIN	*2*	*NA*	*324*	*7.6*	*11.1*
097 CHR CHS&CHS CR	1	70	86*	2.0	2.9
207 E.L.C.A.	1	259	334	7.8	11.4
283 LUTH—MO SYNOD	3	525	641	15.0	21.9
443 UN C OF CHRIST	1	113	139*	3.2	4.7
449 UN METHODIST	7	1,004	1,231*	28.8	42.0
467 WESLEYAN	1	26	64	1.5	2.2
WHEELER	**4**	**205**	**406***	**42.8**	**100.0**
081 CATHOLIC	1	NA	122	12.9	30.0
081d LATIN	*1*	*NA*	*122*	*12.9*	*30.0*
283 LUTH—MO SYNOD	1	41	63	6.6	15.5
449 UN METHODIST	2	164	221*	23.3	54.4
YORK	**36**	**7,543**	**11,899***	**82.5**	**100.0**
019 AMER BAPT USA	1	46	59*	.4	.5
053 ASSEMB OF GOD	1	49	85	.6	.7
057 BAPT GEN CONF	1	95	122*	.8	1.0
081 CATHOLIC	2	NA	1,790	12.4	15.0
081d LATIN	*2*	*NA*	*1,790*	*12.4*	*15.0*
093 CHR CH (DISC)	1	200	266	1.8	2.2
165 CH OF NAZARENE	2	106	148	1.0	1.2
167 CHS OF CHRIST	1	217	516	3.6	4.3
193 EPISCOPAL	1	31	37	.3	.3
207 E.L.C.A.	3	612	781	5.4	6.6
211 FEL EVG BIB CH	1	121	185	1.3	1.6
237 GC MENN BR CHS	1	210	269*	1.9	2.3
283 LUTH—MO SYNOD	6	2,288	3,005	20.8	25.3
287 MENN GEN CONF	1	1,095	1,463	10.1	12.3
355 PRESB CH (USA)	2	498	637*	4.4	5.4
413 S.D.A.	1	14	18*	.1	.2
419 SO BAPT CONV	1	18	23*	.2	.2
443 UN C OF CHRIST	2	104	133*	.9	1.1
449 UN METHODIST	7	1,783	2,282*	15.8	19.2
469 WELS	1	56	80	.6	.7

NEVADA

County and Denomination	Number of churches	Communicant, confirmed, full members	Total adherents		
			Number	Percent of total population	Percent of total adherents
THE STATE.....	664	86,694	386,312*	32.1	100.0
CHURCHILL	**17**	**1,240**	**5,040***	**28.1**	**100.0**
053 ASSEMB OF GOD	1	172	410	2.3	8.1
081 CATHOLIC	1	NA	1,127	6.3	22.4
081d LATIN	*1*	*NA*	*1,127*	*6.3*	*22.4*
151 L-D SAINTS	5	NA	1,918	10.7	38.1
165 CH OF NAZARENE	1	129	253	1.4	5.0
167 CHS OF CHRIST	1	48	62	.3	1.2

NA–Not applicable NR–Not reported *Total adherents estimated from known number of communicant, confirmed, full members. - Represents a percent less than 0.1. Percentages may not total due to rounding.
[1] See Appendix E [2] See Appendix F [3] See Appendix G Lines in *italic* represent a breakdown of Catholic rites or Friends affiliations. They are included in their respective denominational total.

Table 4. Churches and Church Membership by County and Denomination: 1990

County and Denomination	Number of churches	Communicant, confirmed, full members	Total adherents Number	Percent of total population	Percent of total adherents
193 EPISCOPAL	1	49	60	.3	1.2
259 IFCA	1	NR	NR	-	-
283 LUTH—MO SYNOD	1	135	263	1.5	5.2
339 PENT CH OF GOD	1	34	77	.4	1.5
413 S.D.A.	1	141	182*	1.0	3.6
419 SO BAPT CONV	2	276	357*	2.0	7.1
449 UN METHODIST	1	256	331*	1.8	6.6
CLARK	**303**	**57,403**	**265,293***	**35.8**	**100.0**
019 AMER BAPT USA	13	4,639	5,784*	.8	2.2
053 ASSEMB OF GOD	11	2,403	4,272	.6	1.6
059 BAPT MISS ASSN	1	81	101*	-	-
081 CATHOLIC	18	NA	109,057	14.7	41.1
081b *BYZAN RUTH*	1	*NA*	*256*	-	*.1*
081d *LATIN*	17	*NA*	*108,801*	*14.7*	*41.0*
089 CHR & MISS AL	1	25	35	-	-
093 CHR CH (DISC)	1	421	491	.1	.2
097 CHR CHS&CHS CR	5	1,565	1,951*	.3	.7
105 CHRISTIAN REF	1	40	55	-	-
111 CH CR,SCIENTST	2	NR	NR	-	-
123 CH GOD (ANDER)	2	38	71	-	-
127 CH GOD (CLEVE)	5	254	317*	-	.1
133 CH GOD(7TH)DEN	1	29	44	-	-
145 CH GOD PROPHCY	1	34	42*	-	-
151 L-D SAINTS	123	NA	59,081	8.0	22.3
165 CH OF NAZARENE	4	417	482	.1	.2
167 CHS OF CHRIST	9	1,125	1,485	.2	.6
179 CONSRV BAPT	2	NR	NR	-	-
193 EPISCOPAL	8	1,316	1,930	.3	.7
203 EVAN FREE CH	1	60	110	-	-
207 E.L.C.A.	8	4,398	6,138	.8	2.3
246 GREEK ORTHODOX	1	NR	NR	-	-
249 AP CATH ASSYR	0	12	72	-	-
259 IFCA	1	NR	NR	-	-
263 INT FOURSQ GOS	8	1,710	2,132*	.3	.8
283 LUTH—MO SYNOD	6	2,170	2,962	.4	1.1
331 ORTH CH IN AM	1	NR	NR	-	-
355 PRESB CH (USA)	5	1,885	2,350*	.3	.9
356 PRESB CH AMER	1	0	0	-	-
403 SALVATION ARMY	2	347	368	-	.1
413 S.D.A.	5	969	1,208*	.2	.5
419 SO BAPT CONV	30	14,169	17,667*	2.4	6.7
435 UNITARIAN-UNIV	1	66	76	-	-
443 UN C OF CHRIST	2	298	372*	.1	.1
449 UN METHODIST	10	3,493	4,355*	.6	1.6
469 WELS	2	349	470	.1	.2
496 JEWISH EST[1]	4	NA	19,000	2.6	7.2
497 BLACK BAPT EST[2]	NA	15,090	18,815*	2.5	7.1
498 INDEP.CHARIS.[3]	3	NA	2,300	.3	.9
499 INDEP.NON-CHAR[3]	4	NA	1,700	.2	.6
DOUGLAS	**18**	**1,354**	**5,599***	**20.3**	**100.0**
053 ASSEMB OF GOD	1	18	25	.1	.4
081 CATHOLIC	2	NA	2,265	8.2	40.5
081d *LATIN*	2	*NA*	*2,265*	*8.2*	*40.5*
097 CHR CHS&CHS CR	1	40	50*	.2	.9
151 L-D SAINTS	3	NA	1,436	5.2	25.6
165 CH OF NAZARENE	1	42	156	.6	2.8
193 EPISCOPAL	2	138	253	.9	4.5
263 INT FOURSQ GOS	1	18	23*	.1	.4
283 LUTH—MO SYNOD	1	395	481	1.7	8.6
339 PENT CH OF GOD	1	17	45	.2	.8
419 SO BAPT CONV	3	426	537*	1.9	9.6
449 UN METHODIST	2	260	328*	1.2	5.9
ELKO	**36**	**1,880**	**10,757***	**32.1**	**100.0**
019 AMER BAPT USA	1	68	92*	.3	.9
053 ASSEMB OF GOD	3	94	142	.4	1.3
081 CATHOLIC	3	NA	3,357	10.0	31.2
081d *LATIN*	3	*NA*	*3,357*	*10.0*	*31.2*
151 L-D SAINTS	11	NA	4,620	13.8	42.9
165 CH OF NAZARENE	1	30	96	.3	.9
167 CHS OF CHRIST	2	15	18	.1	.2
193 EPISCOPAL	2	268	489	1.5	4.5
263 INT FOURSQ GOS	1	0	0*	-	-
283 LUTH—MO SYNOD	2	206	291	.9	2.7
339 PENT CH OF GOD	1	35	77	.2	.7
355 PRESB CH (USA)	4	565	764*	2.3	7.1
413 S.D.A.	1	44	60*	.2	.6
419 SO BAPT CONV	3	499	675*	2.0	6.3
449 UN METHODIST	1	56	76*	.2	.7
ESMERALDA	**3**	**174**	**1,002***	**74.6**	**100.0**
081 CATHOLIC	1	NA	300	22.3	29.9
081d *LATIN*	1	*NA*	*300*	*22.3*	*29.9*
151 L-D SAINTS	1	NA	487	36.2	48.6
419 SO BAPT CONV	1	174	215*	16.0	21.5
EUREKA	**6**	**108**	**380***	**24.6**	**100.0**
081 CATHOLIC	1	NA	59	3.8	15.5
081d *LATIN*	1	*NA*	*59*	*3.8*	*15.5*
145 CH GOD PROPHCY	1	31	40*	2.6	10.5
151 L-D SAINTS	1	NA	185	12.0	48.7
193 EPISCOPAL	1	14	14	.9	3.7
419 SO BAPT CONV	2	63	82*	5.3	21.6
HUMBOLDT	**18**	**1,108**	**4,794***	**37.3**	**100.0**
053 ASSEMB OF GOD	2	86	168	1.3	3.5
081 CATHOLIC	2	NA	1,939	15.1	40.4
081d *LATIN*	2	*NA*	*1,939*	*15.1*	*40.4*
111 CH CR,SCIENTST	1	NR	NR	-	-
151 L-D SAINTS	3	NA	1,295	10.1	27.0
167 CHS OF CHRIST	1	11	14	.1	.3
193 EPISCOPAL	1	37	65	.5	1.4
259 IFCA	2	NR	NR	-	-
263 INT FOURSQ GOS	1	42	56*	.4	1.2
283 LUTH—MO SYNOD	1	108	165	1.3	3.4
413 S.D.A.	1	92	122*	.9	2.5
419 SO BAPT CONV	2	551	730*	5.7	15.2
449 UN METHODIST	1	181	240*	1.9	5.0
LANDER	**12**	**518**	**2,620***	**41.8**	**100.0**
053 ASSEMB OF GOD	1	94	125	2.0	4.8
081 CATHOLIC	1	NA	900	14.4	34.4
081d *LATIN*	1	*NA*	*900*	*14.4*	*34.4*
151 L-D SAINTS	3	NA	1,003	16.0	38.3
167 CHS OF CHRIST	1	19	26	.4	1.0
193 EPISCOPAL	1	6	12	.2	.5
283 LUTH—MO SYNOD	1	20	31	.5	1.2
419 SO BAPT CONV	3	356	491*	7.8	18.7
449 UN METHODIST	1	23	32*	.5	1.2
LINCOLN	**12**	**375**	**3,207***	**85.0**	**100.0**
053 ASSEMB OF GOD	1	11	20	.5	.6
081 CATHOLIC	1	NA	910	24.1	28.4
081d *LATIN*	1	*NA*	*910*	*24.1*	*28.4*
151 L-D SAINTS	5	NA	1,785	47.3	55.7
193 EPISCOPAL	1	24	44	1.2	1.4
263 INT FOURSQ GOS	1	100	132*	3.5	4.1
419 SO BAPT CONV	2	225	296*	7.8	9.2
449 UN METHODIST	1	15	20*	.5	.6
LYON	**19**	**878**	**3,879***	**19.4**	**100.0**
053 ASSEMB OF GOD	1	35	77	.4	2.0
081 CATHOLIC	3	NA	1,446	7.2	37.3
081d *LATIN*	3	*NA*	*1,446*	*7.2*	*37.3*
151 L-D SAINTS	4	NA	1,233	6.2	31.8
165 CH OF NAZARENE	1	9	12	.1	.3
167 CHS OF CHRIST	1	20	28	.1	.7
193 EPISCOPAL	1	8	16	.1	.4
203 EVAN FREE CH	1	25	45	.2	1.2
221 FREE METHODIST	1	23	49	.2	1.3
283 LUTH—MO SYNOD	1	27	35	.2	.9
413 S.D.A.	1	47	60*	.3	1.5
419 SO BAPT CONV	3	574	737*	3.7	19.0
449 UN METHODIST	1	110	141*	.7	3.6
MINERAL	**16**	**934**	**1,978***	**30.5**	**100.0**
053 ASSEMB OF GOD	1	42	107	1.7	5.4
081 CATHOLIC	2	NA	100	1.5	5.1
081d *LATIN*	2	*NA*	*100*	*1.5*	*5.1*
151 L-D SAINTS	2	NA	533	8.2	26.9
165 CH OF NAZARENE	1	48	116	1.8	5.9
167 CHS OF CHRIST	1	10	13	.2	.7
193 EPISCOPAL	1	14	14	.2	.7
283 LUTH—MO SYNOD	1	62	82	1.3	4.1
339 PENT CH OF GOD	1	34	77	1.2	3.9
355 PRESB CH (USA)	1	57	74*	1.1	3.7
413 S.D.A.	1	13	17*	.3	.9
419 SO BAPT CONV	3	619	800*	12.4	40.4
449 UN METHODIST	1	35	45*	.7	2.3
NYE	**25**	**1,265**	**3,603***	**20.3**	**100.0**
019 AMER BAPT USA	2	100	125*	.7	3.5
053 ASSEMB OF GOD	5	161	315	1.8	8.7
081 CATHOLIC	2	NA	886	5.0	24.6
081d *LATIN*	2	*NA*	*886*	*5.0*	*24.6*
151 L-D SAINTS	4	NA	1,034	5.8	28.7
167 CHS OF CHRIST	2	30	39	.2	1.1
193 EPISCOPAL	3	62	65	.4	1.8

NA–Not applicable NR–Not reported *Total adherents estimated from known number of communicant, confirmed, full members. - Represents a percent less than 0.1. Percentages may not total due to rounding.
[1]See Appendix E [2]See Appendix F [3]See Appendix G Lines in *italic* represent a breakdown of Catholic rites or Friends affiliations. They are included in their respective denominational total.

Table 4. Churches and Church Membership by County and Denomination: 1990

County and Denomination	Number of churches	Communicant, confirmed, full members	Total adherents		
			Number	Percent of total population	Percent of total adherents
283 LUTH—MO SYNOD	1	14	16	.1	.4
355 PRESB CH (USA)	1	43	54*	.3	1.5
419 SO BAPT CONV	4	746	933*	5.2	25.9
449 UN METHODIST	1	109	136*	.8	3.8
PERSHING	**10**	**426**	**1,368***	**31.5**	**100.0**
053 ASSEMB OF GOD	2	94	133	3.1	9.7
081 CATHOLIC	1	NA	400	9.2	29.2
081d LATIN	*1*	*NA*	*400*	*9.2*	*29.2*
151 L-D SAINTS	1	NA	369	8.5	27.0
167 CHS OF CHRIST	1	10	13	.3	1.0
193 EPISCOPAL	1	23	54	1.2	3.9
349 PENT HOLINESS	1	100	134*	3.1	9.8
419 SO BAPT CONV	1	132	177*	4.1	12.9
449 UN METHODIST	1	39	52*	1.2	3.8
469 WELS	1	28	36	.8	2.6
STOREY	**4**	**91**	**387***	**15.3**	**100.0**
081 CATHOLIC	1	NA	263	10.4	68.0
081d LATIN	*1*	*NA*	*263*	*10.4*	*68.0*
193 EPISCOPAL	1	11	25	1.0	6.5
355 PRESB CH (USA)	1	34	42*	1.7	10.9
413 S.D.A.	1	46	57*	2.3	14.7
WASHOE	**116**	**14,056**	**57,924***	**22.7**	**100.0**
019 AMER BAPT USA	4	507	624*	.2	1.1
053 ASSEMB OF GOD	5	486	956	.4	1.7
081 CATHOLIC	9	NA	26,128	10.3	45.1
081d LATIN	*9*	*NA*	*26,128*	*10.3*	*45.1*
089 CHR & MISS AL	1	0	32	-	.1
093 CHR CH (DISC)	2	157	160	.1	.3
097 CHR CHS&CHS CR	2	465	572*	.2	1.0
111 CH CR,SCIENTST	1	NR	NR	-	-
123 CH GOD (ANDER)	2	200	206	.1	.4
127 CH GOD (CLEVE)	2	64	79*	-	.1
145 CH GOD PROPHCY	1	31	38*	-	.1
151 L-D SAINTS	21	NA	9,808	3.9	16.9
165 CH OF NAZARENE	4	376	613	.2	1.1
167 CHS OF CHRIST	5	336	389	.2	.7
179 CONSRV BAPT	2	NR	NR	-	-
193 EPISCOPAL	7	1,301	2,028	.8	3.5
203 EVAN FREE CH	2	196	368	.1	.6
207 E.L.C.A.	4	1,210	1,692	.7	2.9
221 FREE METHODIST	1	0	31	-	.1
226 FRIENDS-USA	1	20	49	-	.1
226f INDEPENDNT	*1*	*20*	*49*	-	*.1*
246 GREEK ORTHODOX	1	NR	NR	-	-
259 IFCA	1	NR	NR	-	-
263 INT FOURSQ GOS	3	252	310*	.1	.5
283 LUTH—MO SYNOD	2	847	1,186	.5	2.0
339 PENT CH OF GOD	2	69	154	.1	.3
355 PRESB CH (USA)	5	1,332	1,639*	.6	2.8
403 SALVATION ARMY	1	121	135	.1	.2
413 S.D.A.	3	737	907*	.4	1.6
419 SO BAPT CONV	11	2,216	2,727*	1.1	4.7
435 UNITARIAN-UNIV	1	113	135	.1	.2
443 UN C OF CHRIST	2	269	331*	.1	.6
449 UN METHODIST	4	1,378	1,696*	.7	2.9
469 WELS	1	161	239	.1	.4
496 JEWISH EST[1]	2	NA	1,400	.5	2.4
497 BLACK BAPT EST[2]	NA	1,212	1,492*	.6	2.6
499 INDEP.NON-CHAR[3]	1	NA	1,800	.7	3.1
WHITE PINE	**18**	**529**	**4,679***	**50.5**	**100.0**
053 ASSEMB OF GOD	1	71	95	1.0	2.0
081 CATHOLIC	2	NA	1,449	15.6	31.0
081d LATIN	*2*	*NA*	*1,449*	*15.6*	*31.0*
151 L-D SAINTS	7	NA	2,539	27.4	54.3
165 CH OF NAZARENE	1	19	33	.4	.7
193 EPISCOPAL	1	57	73	.8	1.6
246 GREEK ORTHODOX	2	NR	NR	-	-
283 LUTH—MO SYNOD	1	41	52	.6	1.1
419 SO BAPT CONV	1	227	292*	3.2	6.2
449 UN METHODIST	2	114	146*	1.6	3.1
CARSON CITY	**31**	**4,355**	**13,802***	**34.1**	**100.0**
019 AMER BAPT USA	1	60	73*	.2	.5
053 ASSEMB OF GOD	1	153	240	.6	1.7
081 CATHOLIC	3	NA	6,370	15.8	46.2
081d LATIN	*3*	*NA*	*6,370*	*15.8*	*46.2*
097 CHR CHS&CHS CR	1	225	273*	.7	2.0
111 CH CR,SCIENTST	1	NR	NR	-	-
127 CH GOD (CLEVE)	1	17	21*	.1	.2
151 L-D SAINTS	4	NA	1,707	4.2	12.4
165 CH OF NAZARENE	1	44	82	.2	.6

County and Denomination	Number of churches	Communicant, confirmed, full members	Total adherents		
			Number	Percent of total population	Percent of total adherents
167 CHS OF CHRIST	2	83	99	.2	.7
193 EPISCOPAL	1	277	382	.9	2.8
207 E.L.C.A.	1	221	367	.9	2.7
259 IFCA	2	NR	NR	-	-
263 INT FOURSQ GOS	2	135	164*	.4	1.2
283 LUTH—MO SYNOD	1	461	655	1.6	4.7
355 PRESB CH (USA)	1	591	718*	1.8	5.2
403 SALVATION ARMY	1	2	2	-	-
413 S.D.A.	1	189	230*	.6	1.7
419 SO BAPT CONV	3	965	1,173*	2.9	8.5
449 UN METHODIST	2	766	931*	2.3	6.7
467 WESLEYAN	1	45	168	.4	1.2
497 BLACK BAPT EST[2]	NA	121	147*	.4	1.1
NEW HAMPSHIRE					
THE STATE.....	896	94,202	438,374*	39.5	100.0
BELKNAP	**61**	**5,499**	**21,676***	**44.0**	**100.0**
001 ADVENT CHR CH	4	189	237*	.5	1.1
019 AMER BAPT USA	11	1,786	2,239*	4.5	10.3
053 ASSEMB OF GOD	1	35	131	.3	.6
081 CATHOLIC	15	NA	13,790	28.0	63.6
081d LATIN	*15*	*NA*	*13,790*	*28.0*	*63.6*
089 CHR & MISS AL	1	50	104	.2	.5
111 CH CR,SCIENTST	1	NR	NR	-	-
151 L-D SAINTS	1	NA	384	.8	1.8
167 CHS OF CHRIST	1	26	42	.1	.2
175 CONGR CHR CHS	3	46	58*	.1	.3
176 CCC, NOT NAT'L	1	221	277*	.6	1.3
179 CONSRV BAPT	2	NR	NR	-	-
193 EPISCOPAL	3	472	765	1.6	3.5
207 E.L.C.A.	1	157	228	.5	1.1
246 GREEK ORTHODOX	1	NR	NR	-	-
356 PRESB CH AMER	1	72	90	.2	.4
403 SALVATION ARMY	1	47	47	.1	.2
413 S.D.A.	1	46	58*	.1	.3
435 UNITARIAN-UNIV	1	81	109	.2	.5
443 UN C OF CHRIST	7	1,537	1,927*	3.9	8.9
449 UN METHODIST	3	734	920*	1.9	4.2
496 JEWISH EST[1]	1	NA	270	.5	1.2
CARROLL	**53**	**4,041**	**9,728***	**27.5**	**100.0**
001 ADVENT CHR CH	2	120	149*	.4	1.5
019 AMER BAPT USA	6	687	852*	2.4	8.8
081 CATHOLIC	11	NA	4,132	11.7	42.5
081d LATIN	*11*	*NA*	*4,132*	*11.7*	*42.5*
089 CHR & MISS AL	1	62	132	.4	1.4
111 CH CR,SCIENTST	2	NR	NR	-	-
151 L-D SAINTS	1	NA	120	.3	1.2
165 CH OF NAZARENE	1	51	68	.2	.7
167 CHS OF CHRIST	1	70	90	.3	.9
175 CONGR CHR CHS	2	102	126*	.4	1.3
176 CCC, NOT NAT'L	1	15	19*	.1	.2
179 CONSRV BAPT	1	NR	NR	-	-
181 CONSRV CONGR	1	86	107*	.3	1.1
193 EPISCOPAL	4	702	1,272	3.6	13.1
226 FRIENDS-USA	1	32	40*	.1	.4
226d FGC & FUM	*1*	*32*	*40*	*.1*	*.4*
413 S.D.A.	1	35	43*	.1	.4
443 UN C OF CHRIST	9	1,521	1,886*	5.3	19.4
449 UN METHODIST	8	558	692*	2.0	7.1
CHESHIRE	**86**	**7,340**	**23,197***	**33.1**	**100.0**
019 AMER BAPT USA	4	311	386*	.6	1.7
053 ASSEMB OF GOD	3	170	282	.4	1.2
081 CATHOLIC	24	NA	13,025	18.6	56.1
081d LATIN	*24*	*NA*	*13,025*	*18.6*	*56.1*
089 CHR & MISS AL	1	33	79	.1	.3
105 CHRISTIAN REF	1	29	46	.1	.2
111 CH CR,SCIENTST	1	NR	NR	-	-
151 L-D SAINTS	1	NA	230	.3	1.0
165 CH OF NAZARENE	1	60	161	.2	.7
167 CHS OF CHRIST	1	74	90	.1	.4
175 CONGR CHR CHS	2	271	337*	.5	1.5
176 CCC, NOT NAT'L	1	11	14*	-	.1
193 EPISCOPAL	2	674	1,099	1.6	4.7
203 EVAN FREE CH	1	55	110	.2	.5
207 E.L.C.A.	1	74	107	.2	.5
226 FRIENDS-USA	1	14	24	-	.1
226d FGC & FUM	*1*	*14*	*24*	-	*.1*
246 GREEK ORTHODOX	1	NR	NR	-	-

NA–Not applicable   NR–Not reported   *Total adherents estimated from known number of communicant, confirmed, full members.   - Represents a percent less than 0.1.   Percentages may not total due to rounding.
[1]See Appendix E   [2]See Appendix F   [3]See Appendix G   Lines in *italic* represent a breakdown of Catholic rites or Friends affiliations. They are included in their respective denominational total.

Table 4. Churches and Church Membership by County and Denomination: 1990

County and Denomination	Number of churches	Communicant, confirmed, full members	Total adherents Number	Percent of total population	Percent of total adherents
283 LUTH—MO SYNOD	2	562	776	1.1	3.3
353 CHR BRETHREN	1	35	70	.1	.3
403 SALVATION ARMY	1	53	64	.1	.3
413 S.D.A.	2	176	219*	.3	.9
419 SO BAPT CONV	1	31	39*	.1	.2
435 UNITARIAN-UNIV	6	638	834	1.2	3.6
443 UN C OF CHRIST	17	3,474	4,316*	6.2	18.6
449 UN METHODIST	10	595	739*	1.1	3.2
496 JEWISH EST[1]	0	NA	150	.2	.6
COOS	**54**	**3,079**	**16,029***	**46.0**	**100.0**
001 ADVENT CHR CH	1	57	70*	.2	.4
019 AMER BAPT USA	3	292	360*	1.0	2.2
053 ASSEMB OF GOD	3	192	350	1.0	2.2
081 CATHOLIC	13	NA	11,901	34.2	74.2
081d LATIN	13	NA	11,901	34.2	74.2
111 CH CR,SCIENTST	2	NR	NR	-	-
167 CHS OF CHRIST	1	45	80	.2	.5
193 EPISCOPAL	4	346	616	1.8	3.8
207 E.L.C.A.	1	216	265	.8	1.7
226 FRIENDS-USA	1	4	12	-	.1
226d FGC & FUM	1	4	12	-	.1
331 ORTH CH IN AM	1	NR	NR	-	-
356 PRESB CH AMER	1	8	11	-	.1
403 SALVATION ARMY	1	43	50	.1	.3
413 S.D.A.	1	19	23*	.1	.1
443 UN C OF CHRIST	6	479	591*	1.7	3.7
449 UN METHODIST	13	1,378	1,700*	4.9	10.6
496 JEWISH EST[1]	2	NA	0	-	-
GRAFTON	**108**	**8,036**	**18,476***	**24.7**	**100.0**
001 ADVENT CHR CH	2	46	56*	.1	.3
019 AMER BAPT USA	9	1,317	1,613*	2.2	8.7
053 ASSEMB OF GOD	6	275	430	.6	2.3
057 BAPT GEN CONF	1	4	5*	-	-
081 CATHOLIC	23	NA	7,053	9.4	38.2
081d LATIN	23	NA	7,053	9.4	38.2
089 CHR & MISS AL	1	54	77	.1	.4
111 CH CR,SCIENTST	3	NR	NR	-	-
151 L-D SAINTS	2	NA	484	.6	2.6
165 CH OF NAZARENE	1	52	102	.1	.6
175 CONGR CHR CHS	1	19	23*	-	.1
176 CCC, NOT NAT'L	2	63	77*	.1	.4
179 CONSRV BAPT	2	NR	NR	-	-
193 EPISCOPAL	7	829	1,429	1.9	7.7
207 E.L.C.A.	2	218	304	.4	1.6
226 FRIENDS-USA	1	147	180*	.2	1.0
226d FGC & FUM	1	147	180*	.2	1.0
259 IFCA	1	NR	NR	-	-
413 S.D.A.	2	130	159*	.2	.9
419 SO BAPT CONV	1	46	56*	.1	.3
435 UNITARIAN-UNIV	2	143	220	.3	1.2
443 UN C OF CHRIST	19	2,755	3,374*	4.5	18.3
449 UN METHODIST	19	1,938	2,374*	3.2	12.8
496 JEWISH EST[1]	1	NA	460	.6	2.5
HILLSBOROUGH	**155**	**22,467**	**155,723***	**46.3**	**100.0**
001 ADVENT CHR CH	1	47	59*	-	-
019 AMER BAPT USA	13	1,951	2,457*	.7	1.6
045 APOSTOLIC LUTH	1	0	1,030	.3	.7
053 ASSEMB OF GOD	9	723	1,093	.3	.7
057 BAPT GEN CONF	1	22	28*	-	-
081 CATHOLIC	11	NA	117,237	34.9	75.3
081d LATIN	9	NA	116,939	34.8	75.1
081f MELKITE-GK	1	NA	207	.1	.1
081h UKRAINIAN	1	NA	91	-	.1
089 CHR & MISS AL	4	49	202	.1	.1
097 CHR CHS&CHS CR	1	119	150*	-	.1
111 CH CR,SCIENTST	4	NR	NR	-	-
127 CH GOD (CLEVE)	2	311	392*	.1	.3
145 CH GOD PROPHCY	1	28	35*	-	-
151 L-D SAINTS	4	NA	1,375	.4	.9
165 CH OF NAZARENE	1	372	324	.1	.2
167 CHS OF CHRIST	3	280	388	.1	.2
175 CONGR CHR CHS	2	233	293*	.1	.2
176 CCC, NOT NAT'L	4	386	486*	.1	.3
179 CONSRV BAPT	6	NR	NR	-	-
181 CONSRV CONGR	1	242	305*	.1	.2
193 EPISCOPAL	8	1,951	3,693	1.1	2.4
207 E.L.C.A.	3	527	805	.2	.5
226 FRIENDS-USA	1	65	82*	-	.1
226d FGC & FUM	1	65	82*	-	.1
246 GREEK ORTHODOX	4	NR	NR	-	-
263 INT FOURSQ GOS	1	9	11*	-	-
283 LUTH—MO SYNOD	4	602	900	.3	.6
349 PENT HOLINESS	1	40	50*	-	-

County and Denomination	Number of churches	Communicant, confirmed, full members	Total adherents Number	Percent of total population	Percent of total adherents
353 CHR BRETHREN	2	250	275	.1	.2
355 PRESB CH (USA)	6	1,056	1,330*	.4	.9
356 PRESB CH AMER	1	57	74	-	-
403 SALVATION ARMY	2	299	330	.1	.2
413 S.D.A.	3	248	312*	.1	.2
419 SO BAPT CONV	2	650	819*	.2	.5
435 UNITARIAN-UNIV	5	855	1,212	.4	.8
443 UN C OF CHRIST	24	7,342	9,247*	2.8	5.9
449 UN METHODIST	11	3,075	3,873*	1.2	2.5
467 WESLEYAN	1	3	30	-	-
469 WELS	1	94	144	-	.1
496 JEWISH EST[1]	3	NA	3,500	1.0	2.2
497 BLACK BAPT EST[2]	NA	581	732*	.2	.5
498 INDEP.CHARIS.[3]	1	NA	1,600	.5	1.0
499 INDEP.NON-CHAR[3]	2	NA	850	.3	.5
MERRIMACK	**101**	**12,713**	**38,709***	**32.3**	**100.0**
001 ADVENT CHR CH	3	117	147*	.1	.4
019 AMER BAPT USA	15	3,246	4,074*	3.4	10.5
053 ASSEMB OF GOD	2	116	228	.2	.6
081 CATHOLIC	15	NA	20,627	17.2	53.3
081d LATIN	15	NA	20,627	17.2	53.3
111 CH CR,SCIENTST	2	NR	NR	-	-
127 CH GOD (CLEVE)	1	38	48*	-	.1
151 L-D SAINTS	2	NA	564	.5	1.5
165 CH OF NAZARENE	2	126	159	.1	.4
167 CHS OF CHRIST	1	87	118	.1	.3
175 CONGR CHR CHS	1	155	195*	.2	.5
176 CCC, NOT NAT'L	3	339	426*	.4	1.1
179 CONSRV BAPT	5	NR	NR	-	-
181 CONSRV CONGR	1	93	117*	.1	.3
193 EPISCOPAL	7	1,458	2,426	2.0	6.3
207 E.L.C.A.	1	222	293	.2	.8
226 FRIENDS-USA	1	46	70	.1	.2
226d FGC & FUM	1	46	70	.1	.2
246 GREEK ORTHODOX	2	NR	NR	-	-
353 CHR BRETHREN	2	43	75	.1	.2
355 PRESB CH (USA)	1	131	164*	.1	.4
403 SALVATION ARMY	1	90	103	.1	.3
413 S.D.A.	1	70	88*	.1	.2
419 SO BAPT CONV	1	67	84*	.1	.2
435 UNITARIAN-UNIV	4	523	691	.6	1.8
443 UN C OF CHRIST	20	4,154	5,214*	4.3	13.5
449 UN METHODIST	6	1,592	1,998*	1.7	5.2
496 JEWISH EST[1]	1	NA	450	.4	1.2
499 INDEP.NON-CHAR[3]	1	NA	350	.3	.9
ROCKINGHAM	**141**	**20,261**	**87,761***	**35.7**	**100.0**
001 ADVENT CHR CH	3	136	172*	.1	.2
005 AME ZION	1	50	87	-	.1
019 AMER BAPT USA	21	3,853	4,876*	2.0	5.6
053 ASSEMB OF GOD	6	775	1,330	.5	1.5
081 CATHOLIC	19	NA	57,763	23.5	65.8
081d LATIN	19	NA	57,763	23.5	65.8
097 CHR CHS&CHS CR	2	194	246*	.1	.3
111 CH CR,SCIENTST	2	NR	NR	-	-
145 CH GOD PROPHCY	1	28	35*	-	-
151 L-D SAINTS	3	NA	867	.4	1.0
165 CH OF NAZARENE	2	54	109	-	.1
167 CHS OF CHRIST	3	119	167	.1	.2
175 CONGR CHR CHS	3	496	628*	.3	.7
176 CCC, NOT NAT'L	4	900	1,139*	.5	1.3
179 CONSRV BAPT	3	NR	NR	-	-
181 CONSRV CONGR	1	80	101*	-	.1
193 EPISCOPAL	8	1,755	3,359	1.4	3.8
203 EVAN FREE CH	1	60	80	-	.1
207 E.L.C.A.	2	565	898	.4	1.0
226 FRIENDS-USA	1	1	7	-	-
226d FGC & FUM	1	1	7	-	-
246 GREEK ORTHODOX	1	NR	NR	-	-
283 LUTH—MO SYNOD	2	164	232	.1	.3
355 PRESB CH (USA)	2	524	663*	.3	.8
403 SALVATION ARMY	1	69	83	-	.1
413 S.D.A.	1	74	94*	-	.1
419 SO BAPT CONV	3	1,305	1,652*	.7	1.9
435 UNITARIAN-UNIV	4	703	1,023	.4	1.2
443 UN C OF CHRIST	22	4,574	5,789*	2.4	6.6
449 UN METHODIST	17	3,332	4,217*	1.7	4.8
496 JEWISH EST[1]	1	NA	1,100	.4	1.3
497 BLACK BAPT EST[2]	NA	450	569*	.2	.6
499 INDEP.NON-CHAR[3]	1	NA	475	.2	.5
STRAFFORD	**77**	**6,846**	**48,086***	**46.1**	**100.0**
001 ADVENT CHR CH	3	259	320*	.3	.7
019 AMER BAPT USA	4	486	601*	.6	1.2
053 ASSEMB OF GOD	3	337	607	.6	1.3

NA–Not applicable   NR–Not reported   *Total adherents estimated from known number of communicant, confirmed, full members.   - Represents a percent less than 0.1.   Percentages may not total due to rounding.
[1]See Appendix E   [2]See Appendix F   [3]See Appendix G   Lines in *italic* represent a breakdown of Catholic rites or Friends affiliations. They are included in their respective denominational total.

Table 4. Churches and Church Membership by County and Denomination: 1990

County and Denomination	Number of churches	Communicant, confirmed, full members	Total adherents		
			Number	Percent of total population	Percent of total adherents
081 CATHOLIC	24	NA	37,795	36.3	78.6
081d LATIN	23	NA	37,544	36.0	78.1
081e MARONITE	1	NA	251	.2	.5
111 CH CR,SCIENTST	1	NR	NR	-	-
123 CH GOD (ANDER)	1	40	55	.1	.1
127 CH GOD (CLEVE)	1	11	14*	-	-
145 CH GOD PROPHCY	1	28	35*	-	.1
151 L-D SAINTS	2	NA	611	.6	1.3
167 CHS OF CHRIST	2	92	142	.1	.3
179 CONSRV BAPT	7	NR	NR	-	-
193 EPISCOPAL	3	665	1,119	1.1	2.3
203 EVAN FREE CH	1	85	150	.1	.3
207 E.L.C.A.	1	132	215	.2	.4
223 FREE WILL BAPT	1	98	121*	.1	.3
226 FRIENDS-USA	2	126	156*	.1	.3
226d FGC & FUM	2	126	156*	.1	.3
246 GREEK ORTHODOX	2	NR	NR	-	-
249 AP CATH ASSYR	0	9	27	-	.1
403 SALVATION ARMY	1	78	86	.1	.2
413 S.D.A.	1	136	168*	.2	.3
419 SO BAPT CONV	1	94	116*	.1	.2
435 UNITARIAN-UNIV	1	56	63	.1	.1
443 UN C OF CHRIST	8	2,562	3,167*	3.0	6.6
449 UN METHODIST	5	1,441	1,781*	1.7	3.7
496 JEWISH EST[1]	1	NA	600	.6	1.2
497 BLACK BAPT EST[2]	NA	111	137*	.1	.3
SULLIVAN	**60**	**3,920**	**18,989***	**49.2**	**100.0**
019 AMER BAPT USA	7	963	1,205*	3.1	6.3
053 ASSEMB OF GOD	2	161	247	.6	1.3
081 CATHOLIC	15	NA	13,739	35.6	72.4
081d LATIN	15	NA	13,739	35.6	72.4
165 CH OF NAZARENE	1	55	51	.1	.3
167 CHS OF CHRIST	1	3	3	-	-
175 CONGR CHR CHS	1	102	128*	.3	.7
176 CCC, NOT NAT'L	1	113	141*	.4	.7
179 CONSRV BAPT	2	NR	NR	-	-
193 EPISCOPAL	4	302	523	1.4	2.8
207 E.L.C.A.	1	69	96	.2	.5
226 FRIENDS-USA	1	2	15	-	.1
226d FGC & FUM	1	2	15	-	.1
246 GREEK ORTHODOX	1	NR	NR	-	-
263 INT FOURSQ GOS	1	32	40*	.1	.2
331 ORTH CH IN AM	1	NR	NR	-	-
413 S.D.A.	2	66	83*	.2	.4
419 SO BAPT CONV	1	15	19*	-	.1
435 UNITARIAN-UNIV	1	30	37	.1	.2
443 UN C OF CHRIST	7	1,181	1,478*	3.8	7.8
449 UN METHODIST	9	826	1,034*	2.7	5.4
496 JEWISH EST[1]	1	NA	150	.4	.8

NEW JERSEY

County and Denomination	Number of churches	Communicant, confirmed, full members	Total adherents		
			Number	Percent of total population	Percent of total adherents
THE STATE.....	4,183	813,759	4,734,822*	61.3	100.0
ATLANTIC	**146**	**21,574**	**113,736***	**50.7**	**100.0**
005 AME ZION	2	647	691	.3	.6
019 AMER BAPT USA	3	923	1,127*	.5	1.0
053 ASSEMB OF GOD	6	430	640	.3	.6
081 CATHOLIC	24	NA	66,328	29.6	58.3
081d LATIN	24	NA	66,328	29.6	58.3
089 CHR & MISS AL	4	212	533	.2	.5
111 CH CR,SCIENTST	1	NR	NR	-	-
123 CH GOD (ANDER)	3	92	107	-	.1
127 CH GOD (CLEVE)	2	81	99*	-	.1
145 CH GOD PROPHCY	1	27	33*	-	-
151 L-D SAINTS	1	NA	410	.2	.4
165 CH OF NAZARENE	1	75	104	-	.1
167 CHS OF CHRIST	2	90	113	.1	.1
193 EPISCOPAL	8	1,390	1,979	.9	1.7
203 EVAN FREE CH	1	108	197	.1	.2
207 E.L.C.A.	7	1,783	3,025	1.3	2.7
226 FRIENDS-USA	1	31	38*	-	-
226c FGC	1	31	38*	-	-
246 GREEK ORTHODOX	2	NR	NR	-	-
259 IFCA	1	NR	NR	-	-
285 MENNONITE CH	1	61	81	-	.1
293 MORAV CH-NORTH	1	343	443	.2	.4
331 ORTH CH IN AM	1	NR	NR	-	-
353 CHR BRETHREN	2	100	130	.1	.1
355 PRESB CH (USA)	8	1,311	1,601*	.7	1.4
356 PRESB CH AMER	1	22	25	-	-
375 REF EPISCOPAL	2	76	91	-	.1
403 SALVATION ARMY	1	65	81	-	.1
413 S.D.A.	5	345	421*	.2	.4
419 SO BAPT CONV	1	285	348*	.2	.3
443 UN C OF CHRIST	4	838	1,024*	.5	.9
449 UN METHODIST	28	4,496	5,492*	2.4	4.8
467 WESLEYAN	2	179	335	.1	.3
496 JEWISH EST[1]	13	NA	15,800	7.0	13.9
497 BLACK BAPT EST[2]	NA	7,564	9,240*	4.1	8.1
498 INDEP.CHARIS.[3]	1	NA	400	.2	.4
499 INDEP.NON-CHAR[3]	4	NA	2,800	1.2	2.5
BERGEN	**447**	**76,160**	**658,388***	**79.8**	**100.0**
005 AME ZION	9	6,985	8,270	1.0	1.3
019 AMER BAPT USA	16	2,692	3,198*	.4	.5
039 AP CHR CH(NAZ)	1	80	95*	-	-
049 ARMEN AP CH AM	1	1,500	9,000	1.1	1.4
053 ASSEMB OF GOD	18	1,446	2,265	.3	.3
081 CATHOLIC	77	NA	455,930	55.2	69.2
081b BYZAN RUTH	1	NA	182	-	-
081d LATIN	74	NA	455,390	55.2	69.2
081h UKRAINIAN	2	NA	358	-	.1
089 CHR & MISS AL	3	177	212	-	-
105 CHRISTIAN REF	6	2,179	3,037	.4	.5
111 CH CR,SCIENTST	6	NR	NR	-	-
123 CH GOD (ANDER)	1	0	61	-	-
127 CH GOD (CLEVE)	1	56	67*	-	-
145 CH GOD PROPHCY	1	27	32*	-	-
151 L-D SAINTS	4	NA	1,123	.1	.2
163 CH OF LUTH BR	2	193	398	-	.1
165 CH OF NAZARENE	5	684	479	.1	.1
167 CHS OF CHRIST	2	135	170	-	-
179 CONSRV BAPT	1	NR	NR	-	-
193 EPISCOPAL	39	8,847	13,420	1.6	2.0
195 ESTONIAN ELC	1	109	136*	-	-
203 EVAN FREE CH	4	659	842	.1	.1
207 E.L.C.A.	32	8,466	11,246	1.4	1.7
221 FREE METHODIST	1	21	47	-	-
226 FRIENDS-USA	1	71	84*	-	-
226d FGC & FUM	1	71	84*	-	-
246 GREEK ORTHODOX	4	NR	NR	-	-
259 IFCA	4	NR	NR	-	-
283 LUTH—MO SYNOD	12	4,519	5,857	.7	.9
307 NETH REF CONGR	1	416	753	.1	.1
331 ORTH CH IN AM	2	NR	NR	-	-
349 PENT HOLINESS	1	76	90*	-	-
353 CHR BRETHREN	5	480	676	.1	.1
355 PRESB CH (USA)	34	8,839	10,499*	1.3	1.6
356 PRESB CH AMER	1	97	97	-	-
371 REF CH IN AM	36	6,810	12,596	1.5	1.9
403 SALVATION ARMY	2	57	60	-	-
413 S.D.A.	7	814	967*	.1	.1
419 SO BAPT CONV	5	807	959*	.1	.1
423 SYRIAN ANTIOCH	2	NA	7,700	.9	1.2
435 UNITARIAN-UNIV	3	541	769	.1	.1
443 UN C OF CHRIST	12	2,227	2,645*	.3	.4
449 UN METHODIST	29	8,399	9,976*	1.2	1.5
496 JEWISH EST[1]	54	NA	85,000	10.3	12.9
497 BLACK BAPT EST[2]	NA	7,751	9,207*	1.1	1.4
499 INDEP.NON-CHAR[3]	1	NA	425	.1	.1
BURLINGTON	**201**	**46,194**	**178,478***	**45.2**	**100.0**
005 AME ZION	2	493	522	.1	.3
019 AMER BAPT USA	14	3,782	4,704*	1.2	2.6
053 ASSEMB OF GOD	11	2,461	5,119	1.3	2.9
081 CATHOLIC	26	NA	105,907	26.8	59.3
081b BYZAN RUTH	1	NA	285	.1	.2
081d LATIN	24	NA	105,300	26.7	59.0
081g ROMANIAN	1	NA	322	.1	.2
089 CHR & MISS AL	1	215	640	.2	.4
097 CHR CHS&CHS CR	1	60	75*	-	-
111 CH CR,SCIENTST	2	NR	NR	-	-
123 CH GOD (ANDER)	1	16	20	-	-
127 CH GOD (CLEVE)	2	135	168*	-	.1
145 CH GOD PROPHCY	1	27	34*	-	-
151 L-D SAINTS	2	NA	727	.2	.4
163 CH OF LUTH BR	1	123	212	.1	.1
165 CH OF NAZARENE	3	377	440	.1	.2
167 CHS OF CHRIST	2	280	322	.1	.2
193 EPISCOPAL	17	4,425	6,371	1.6	3.6
203 EVAN FREE CH	1	68	80	-	-
207 E.L.C.A.	10	4,833	7,032	1.8	3.9
226 FRIENDS-USA	11	1,139	1,417*	.4	.8
226c FGC	11	1,139	1,417*	.4	.8
259 IFCA	2	NR	NR	-	-
263 INT FOURSQ GOS	1	6	7*	-	-
283 LUTH—MO SYNOD	2	322	654	.2	.4

NA–Not applicable   NR–Not reported   *Total adherents estimated from known number of communicant, confirmed, full members.   - Represents a percent less than 0.1.   Percentages may not total due to rounding.
[1]See Appendix E   [2]See Appendix F   [3]See Appendix G   Lines in *italic* represent a breakdown of Catholic rites or Friends affiliations. They are included in their respective denominational total.

Table 4. Churches and Church Membership by County and Denomination: 1990

County and Denomination	Number of churches	Communicant, confirmed, full members	Total adherents Number	Percent of total population	Percent of total adherents
293 MORAV CH-NORTH	2	390	482	.1	.3
331 ORTH CH IN AM	1	NR	NR	-	-
353 CHR BRETHREN	1	31	50	-	-
355 PRESB CH (USA)	17	4,301	5,350*	1.4	3.0
356 PRESB CH AMER	2	113	164	-	.1
371 REF CH IN AM	1	70	152	-	.1
375 REF EPISCOPAL	1	36	43	-	-
413 S.D.A.	5	291	362*	.1	.2
419 SO BAPT CONV	5	1,444	1,796*	.5	1.0
435 UNITARIAN-UNIV	1	20	25	-	-
443 UN C OF CHRIST	2	322	400*	.1	.2
449 UN METHODIST	42	9,427	11,725*	3.0	6.6
467 WESLEYAN	1	38	53	-	-
496 JEWISH EST[1]	7	NA	9,807	2.5	5.5
497 BLACK BAPT EST[2]	NA	10,949	13,618*	3.4	7.6
CAMDEN	**250**	**56,563**	**277,512***	**55.2**	**100.0**
005 AME ZION	3	1,256	1,635	.3	.6
019 AMER BAPT USA	23	5,606	7,106*	1.4	2.6
053 ASSEMB OF GOD	10	1,342	2,469	.5	.9
081 CATHOLIC	52	NA	186,838	37.2	67.3
081d LATIN	51	NA	186,251	37.0	67.1
081h UKRAINIAN	1	NA	587	.1	.2
089 CHR & MISS AL	2	98	302	.1	.1
111 CH CR,SCIENTST	2	NR	NR	-	-
123 CH GOD (ANDER)	2	130	166	-	.1
127 CH GOD (CLEVE)	1	30	38*	-	-
145 CH GOD PROPHCY	2	55	70*	-	-
151 L-D SAINTS	2	NA	819	.2	.3
165 CH OF NAZARENE	1	49	125	-	-
167 CHS OF CHRIST	4	249	321	.1	.1
179 CONSRV BAPT	4	NR	NR	-	-
193 EPISCOPAL	21	5,241	7,324	1.5	2.6
207 E.L.C.A.	21	5,758	9,326	1.9	3.4
216 EVAN PRESBY CH	1	409	420	.1	.2
226 FRIENDS-USA	2	248	314*	.1	.1
226c FGC	2	248	314*	.1	.1
246 GREEK ORTHODOX	1	NR	NR	-	-
259 IFCA	4	NR	NR	-	-
283 LUTH—MO SYNOD	2	762	1,104	.2	.4
285 MENNONITE CH	2	128	216	-	.1
353 CHR BRETHREN	3	84	153	-	.1
355 PRESB CH (USA)	16	5,917	7,500*	1.5	2.7
356 PRESB CH AMER	1	273	414	.1	.1
403 SALVATION ARMY	1	86	88	-	-
413 S.D.A.	4	694	880*	.2	.3
435 UNITARIAN-UNIV	1	329	442	.1	.2
449 UN METHODIST	50	11,923	15,112*	3.0	5.4
467 WESLEYAN	2	83	230	-	.1
496 JEWISH EST[1]	6	NA	12,482	2.5	4.5
497 BLACK BAPT EST[2]	NA	15,813	20,043*	4.0	7.2
499 INDEP.NON-CHAR[3]	4	NA	1,575	.3	.6
CAPE MAY	**82**	**11,038**	**42,568***	**44.8**	**100.0**
019 AMER BAPT USA	6	1,043	1,269*	1.3	3.0
053 ASSEMB OF GOD	2	363	476	.5	1.1
081 CATHOLIC	15	NA	27,957	29.4	65.7
081d LATIN	14	NA	27,757	29.2	65.2
081h UKRAINIAN	1	NA	200	.2	.5
089 CHR & MISS AL	1	0	45	-	.1
111 CH CR,SCIENTST	1	NR	NR	-	-
151 L-D SAINTS	1	NA	128	.1	.3
165 CH OF NAZARENE	2	124	253	.3	.6
167 CHS OF CHRIST	1	35	45	-	.1
193 EPISCOPAL	7	1,093	1,498	1.6	3.5
207 E.L.C.A.	6	1,528	2,118	2.2	5.0
226 FRIENDS-USA	2	44	54*	.1	.1
226c FGC	2	44	54*	.1	.1
246 GREEK ORTHODOX	1	NR	NR	-	-
353 CHR BRETHREN	2	55	80	.1	.2
355 PRESB CH (USA)	4	843	1,025*	1.1	2.4
356 PRESB CH AMER	1	81	103	.1	.2
413 S.D.A.	3	215	262*	.3	.6
449 UN METHODIST	25	4,581	5,573*	5.9	13.1
496 JEWISH EST[1]	2	NA	425	.4	1.0
497 BLACK BAPT EST[2]	NA	1,033	1,257*	1.3	3.0
CUMBERLAND	**133**	**23,028**	**69,757***	**50.5**	**100.0**
005 AME ZION	2	418	507	.4	.7
019 AMER BAPT USA	8	2,381	2,988*	2.2	4.3
053 ASSEMB OF GOD	7	1,232	2,227	1.6	3.2
081 CATHOLIC	16	NA	34,944	25.3	50.1
081d LATIN	15	NA	34,394	24.9	49.3
081h UKRAINIAN	1	NA	550	.4	.8
089 CHR & MISS AL	1	143	332	.2	.5
097 CHR CHS&CHS CR	1	31	39*	-	.1
111 CH CR,SCIENTST	1	NR	NR	-	-
127 CH GOD (CLEVE)	7	839	1,053*	.8	1.5
145 CH GOD PROPHCY	2	55	69*	-	.1
151 L-D SAINTS	1	NA	469	.3	.7
165 CH OF NAZARENE	4	844	1,414	1.0	2.0
167 CHS OF CHRIST	2	55	71	.1	.1
193 EPISCOPAL	4	941	1,372	1.0	2.0
195 ESTONIAN ELC	1	150	188*	.1	.3
207 E.L.C.A.	3	1,179	1,705	1.2	2.4
223 FREE WILL BAPT	1	30	38*	-	.1
226 FRIENDS-USA	2	74	93*	.1	.1
226c FGC	2	74	93*	.1	.1
246 GREEK ORTHODOX	1	NR	NR	-	-
283 LUTH—MO SYNOD	1	301	416	.3	.6
285 MENNONITE CH	1	60	60	-	.1
286 E.PA MENNONITE	1	37	46*	-	.1
355 PRESB CH (USA)	9	1,644	2,063*	1.5	3.0
356 PRESB CH AMER	1	102	137	.1	.2
403 SALVATION ARMY	1	46	55	-	.1
413 S.D.A.	6	633	794*	.6	1.1
415 S-D BAPTIST GC	2	370	464*	.3	.7
419 SO BAPT CONV	1	185	232*	.2	.3
449 UN METHODIST	38	6,709	8,420*	6.1	12.1
467 WESLEYAN	2	54	245	.2	.4
496 JEWISH EST[1]	5	NA	2,960	2.1	4.2
497 BLACK BAPT EST[2]	NA	4,515	5,666*	4.1	8.1
499 INDEP.NON-CHAR[3]	1	NA	690	.5	1.0
ESSEX	**385**	**107,416**	**522,415***	**67.1**	**100.0**
005 AME ZION	4	8,265	10,575	1.4	2.0
019 AMER BAPT USA	45	13,486	16,622*	2.1	3.2
053 ASSEMB OF GOD	9	1,105	1,523	.2	.3
057 BAPT GEN CONF	1	159	196*	-	-
081 CATHOLIC	68	NA	308,459	39.6	59.0
081b BYZAN RUTH	1	NA	401	.1	.1
081d LATIN	67	NA	308,058	39.6	59.0
089 CHR & MISS AL	2	183	216	-	-
093 CHR CH (DISC)	5	538	698	.1	.1
097 CHR CHS&CHS CR	1	600	740*	.1	.1
111 CH CR,SCIENTST	2	NR	NR	-	-
123 CH GOD (ANDER)	1	85	85	-	-
127 CH GOD (CLEVE)	8	666	821*	.1	.2
145 CH GOD PROPHCY	2	55	68*	-	-
151 L-D SAINTS	3	NA	993	.1	.2
165 CH OF NAZARENE	3	279	261	-	-
167 CHS OF CHRIST	4	945	1,122	.1	.2
179 CONSRV BAPT	3	NR	NR	-	-
193 EPISCOPAL	30	6,842	10,995	1.4	2.1
203 EVAN FREE CH	2	610	725	.1	.1
207 E.L.C.A.	8	1,815	2,552	.3	.5
221 FREE METHODIST	2	6	6	-	-
226 FRIENDS-USA	1	114	141*	-	-
226d FGC & FUM	1	114	141*	-	-
246 GREEK ORTHODOX	2	NR	NR	-	-
283 LUTH—MO SYNOD	6	851	1,103	.1	.2
313 N AM BAPT CONF	1	98	121*	-	-
331 ORTH CH IN AM	1	NR	NR	-	-
353 CHR BRETHREN	6	364	468	.1	.1
355 PRESB CH (USA)	46	10,438	12,865*	1.7	2.5
356 PRESB CH AMER	4	109	142	-	-
371 REF CH IN AM	11	726	1,875	.2	.4
403 SALVATION ARMY	4	365	393	.1	.1
413 S.D.A.	11	2,832	3,491*	.4	.7
419 SO BAPT CONV	9	795	980*	.1	.2
435 UNITARIAN-UNIV	2	447	589	.1	.1
443 UN C OF CHRIST	13	5,205	6,415*	.8	1.2
449 UN METHODIST	22	5,302	6,535*	.8	1.3
467 WESLEYAN	1	39	94	-	-
496 JEWISH EST[1]	42	NA	76,200	9.8	14.6
497 BLACK BAPT EST[2]	NA	44,092	54,346*	7.0	10.4
GLOUCESTER	**155**	**24,758**	**110,666***	**48.1**	**100.0**
019 AMER BAPT USA	6	924	1,174*	.5	1.1
053 ASSEMB OF GOD	12	1,723	2,386	1.0	2.2
059 BAPT MISS ASSN	1	38	48*	-	-
081 CATHOLIC	23	NA	69,044	30.0	62.4
081d LATIN	22	NA	68,852	29.9	62.2
081h UKRAINIAN	1	NA	192	.1	.2
089 CHR & MISS AL	2	109	280	.1	.3
111 CH CR,SCIENTST	1	NR	NR	-	-
127 CH GOD (CLEVE)	3	92	117*	.1	.1
151 L-D SAINTS	2	NA	645	.3	.6
165 CH OF NAZARENE	2	129	208	.1	.2
167 CHS OF CHRIST	3	218	290	.1	.3
179 CONSRV BAPT	5	NR	NR	-	-
193 EPISCOPAL	10	2,184	3,486	1.5	3.2
207 E.L.C.A.	6	2,275	3,601	1.6	3.3

NA–Not applicable NR–Not reported *Total adherents estimated from known number of communicant, confirmed, full members. - Represents a percent less than 0.1. Percentages may not total due to rounding.
[1] See Appendix E [2] See Appendix F [3] See Appendix G Lines in *italic* represent a breakdown of Catholic rites or Friends affiliations. They are included in their respective denominational total.

Table 4. Churches and Church Membership by County and Denomination: 1990

County and Denomination	Number of churches	Communicant, confirmed, full members	Total adherents Number	Percent of total population	Percent of total adherents
223 FREE WILL BAPT	1	48	61*	-	.1
226 FRIENDS-USA	3	269	342*	.1	.3
226c *FGC*	*3*	*269*	*342**	*.1*	*.3*
259 IFCA	3	NR	NR	-	-
263 INT FOURSQ GOS	2	183	232*	.1	.2
355 PRESB CH (USA)	12	2,384	3,028*	1.3	2.7
356 PRESB CH AMER	1	38	77	-	.1
413 S.D.A.	4	358	455*	.2	.4
435 UNITARIAN-UNIV	1	32	55	-	-
443 UN C OF CHRIST	1	110	140*	.1	.1
449 UN METHODIST	45	9,713	12,338*	5.4	11.1
467 WESLEYAN	1	71	245	.1	.2
496 JEWISH EST[1]	2	NA	5,711	2.5	5.2
497 BLACK BAPT EST[2]	NA	3,860	4,903*	2.1	4.4
498 INDEP.CHARIS.[3]	1	NA	400	.2	.4
499 INDEP.NON-CHAR[3]	2	NA	1,400	.6	1.3
HUDSON	**254**	**34,581**	**384,725***	**69.6**	**100.0**
005 AME ZION	2	2,476	2,579	.5	.7
019 AMER BAPT USA	12	3,939	4,764*	.9	1.2
022 EASTERN ORTH	1	57	57	-	-
040 AP CHR CH-AMER	1	11	21	-	-
053 ASSEMB OF GOD	12	1,152	1,806	.3	.5
081 CATHOLIC	63	NA	324,245	58.6	84.3
081b *BYZAN RUTH*	*2*	*NA*	*1,019*	*.2*	*.3*
081d *LATIN*	*59*	*NA*	*321,451*	*58.1*	*83.6*
081h *UKRAINIAN*	*2*	*NA*	*1,775*	*.3*	*.5*
089 CHR & MISS AL	4	111	263	-	.1
111 CH CR,SCIENTST	2	NR	NR	-	-
123 CH GOD (ANDER)	2	130	130	-	-
127 CH GOD (CLEVE)	3	158	191*	-	-
145 CH GOD PROPHCY	1	27	33*	-	-
151 L-D SAINTS	1	NA	539	.1	.1
165 CH OF NAZARENE	2	114	164	-	-
179 CONSRV BAPT	3	NR	NR	-	-
193 EPISCOPAL	16	1,475	2,230	.4	.6
203 EVAN FREE CH	3	136	189	-	-
207 E.L.C.A.	21	3,516	4,780	.9	1.2
221 FREE METHODIST	2	87	183	-	-
246 GREEK ORTHODOX	2	NR	NR	-	-
283 LUTH—MO SYNOD	3	320	425	.1	.1
313 N AM BAPT CONF	2	36	44*	-	-
331 ORTH CH IN AM	2	NR	NR	-	-
353 CHR BRETHREN	5	250	340	.1	.1
355 PRESB CH (USA)	10	985	1,191*	.2	.3
371 REF CH IN AM	14	841	1,658	.3	.4
375 REF EPISCOPAL	1	70	90	-	-
403 SALVATION ARMY	3	309	351	.1	.1
413 S.D.A.	10	932	1,127*	.2	.3
419 SO BAPT CONV	4	245	296*	.1	.1
443 UN C OF CHRIST	1	31	37*	-	-
449 UN METHODIST	19	1,672	2,022*	.4	.5
467 WESLEYAN	1	55	340	.1	.1
496 JEWISH EST[1]	26	NA	15,950	2.9	4.1
497 BLACK BAPT EST[2]	NA	15,446	18,680*	3.4	4.9
HUNTERDON	**99**	**13,788**	**46,742***	**43.4**	**100.0**
019 AMER BAPT USA	7	1,328	1,639*	1.5	3.5
053 ASSEMB OF GOD	4	581	921	.9	2.0
071 BRETHREN (ASH)	2	40	49*	-	.1
081 CATHOLIC	11	NA	27,000	25.1	57.8
081d *LATIN*	*11*	*NA*	*27,000*	*25.1*	*57.8*
097 CHR CHS&CHS CR	1	75	93*	.1	.2
111 CH CR,SCIENTST	1	NR	NR	-	-
151 L-D SAINTS	1	NA	244	.2	.5
157 CH OF BRETHREN	1	126	156*	.1	.3
165 CH OF NAZARENE	1	34	62	.1	.1
179 CONSRV BAPT	3	NR	NR	-	-
193 EPISCOPAL	4	695	1,218	1.1	2.6
203 EVAN FREE CH	1	24	50	-	.1
207 E.L.C.A.	2	649	846	.8	1.8
226 FRIENDS-USA	1	40	49*	-	.1
226c *FGC*	*1*	*40*	*49**	*-*	*.1*
283 LUTH—MO SYNOD	2	768	1,074	1.0	2.3
331 ORTH CH IN AM	1	NR	NR	-	-
355 PRESB CH (USA)	17	4,251	5,247*	4.9	11.2
356 PRESB CH AMER	1	18	19	-	-
371 REF CH IN AM	8	1,184	2,168	2.0	4.6
435 UNITARIAN-UNIV	1	24	38	-	.1
443 UN C OF CHRIST	1	324	400*	.4	.9
449 UN METHODIST	26	3,139	3,875*	3.6	8.3
467 WESLEYAN	1	59	164	.2	.4
496 JEWISH EST[1]	1	NA	900	.8	1.9
497 BLACK BAPT EST[2]	NA	429	530*	.5	1.1

County and Denomination	Number of churches	Communicant, confirmed, full members	Total adherents Number	Percent of total population	Percent of total adherents
MERCER	**181**	**47,814**	**184,229***	**56.5**	**100.0**
005 AME ZION	1	2,340	2,495	.8	1.4
019 AMER BAPT USA	17	4,648	5,652*	1.7	3.1
053 ASSEMB OF GOD	9	1,319	2,957	.9	1.6
081 CATHOLIC	35	NA	112,756	34.6	61.2
081b *BYZAN RUTH*	*2*	*NA*	*3,966*	*1.2*	*2.2*
081d *LATIN*	*31*	*NA*	*107,000*	*32.8*	*58.1*
081g *ROMANIAN*	*1*	*NA*	*322*	*.1*	*.2*
081h *UKRAINIAN*	*1*	*NA*	*1,468*	*.5*	*.8*
089 CHR & MISS AL	1	102	202	.1	.1
111 CH CR,SCIENTST	2	NR	NR	-	-
123 CH GOD (ANDER)	1	130	140	-	.1
127 CH GOD (CLEVE)	3	393	478*	.1	.3
151 L-D SAINTS	1	NA	341	.1	.2
165 CH OF NAZARENE	1	169	255	.1	.1
167 CHS OF CHRIST	3	390	465	.1	.3
179 CONSRV BAPT	3	NR	NR	-	-
193 EPISCOPAL	11	5,070	7,647	2.3	4.2
203 EVAN FREE CH	1	49	120	-	.1
207 E.L.C.A.	11	3,233	4,612	1.4	2.5
226 FRIENDS-USA	2	255	310*	.1	.2
226c *FGC*	*2*	*255*	*310**	*.1*	*.2*
246 GREEK ORTHODOX	1	NR	NR	-	-
283 LUTH—MO SYNOD	4	661	858	.3	.5
285 MENNONITE CH	1	71	121	-	.1
331 ORTH CH IN AM	2	NR	NR	-	-
353 CHR BRETHREN	1	70	100	-	.1
355 PRESB CH (USA)	22	9,467	11,512*	3.5	6.2
356 PRESB CH AMER	3	182	182	.1	.1
371 REF CH IN AM	1	137	270	.1	.1
403 SALVATION ARMY	1	54	65	-	-
413 S.D.A.	8	1,079	1,312*	.4	.7
419 SO BAPT CONV	1	344	418*	.1	.2
435 UNITARIAN-UNIV	2	534	754	.2	.4
443 UN C OF CHRIST	1	78	95*	-	.1
449 UN METHODIST	17	5,094	6,195*	1.9	3.4
467 WESLEYAN	1	40	90	-	-
496 JEWISH EST[1]	12	NA	9,000	2.8	4.9
497 BLACK BAPT EST[2]	NA	11,905	14,477*	4.4	7.9
499 INDEP.NON-CHAR[3]	1	NA	350	.1	.2
MIDDLESEX	**270**	**47,353**	**460,006***	**68.5**	**100.0**
005 AME ZION	2	592	717	.1	.2
019 AMER BAPT USA	13	4,298	5,176*	.8	1.1
022 EASTERN ORTH	1	800	800	.1	.2
053 ASSEMB OF GOD	9	1,180	1,779	.3	.4
059 BAPT MISS ASSN	1	12	14*	-	-
080 BYELORSSN ORTH	1	NR	NR	-	-
081 CATHOLIC	72	NA	331,632	49.4	72.1
081b *BYZAN RUTH*	*7*	*NA*	*4,210*	*.6*	*.9*
081d *LATIN*	*62*	*NA*	*324,000*	*48.2*	*70.4*
081h *UKRAINIAN*	*3*	*NA*	*3,422*	*.5*	*.7*
089 CHR & MISS AL	4	280	670	.1	.1
093 CHR CH (DISC)	2	945	1,232	.2	.3
111 CH CR,SCIENTST	1	NR	NR	-	-
127 CH GOD (CLEVE)	1	175	211*	-	-
151 L-D SAINTS	1	NA	476	.1	.1
165 CH OF NAZARENE	1	74	74	-	-
167 CHS OF CHRIST	2	58	73	-	-
179 CONSRV BAPT	2	NR	NR	-	-
193 EPISCOPAL	19	3,377	4,979	.7	1.1
207 E.L.C.A.	14	3,891	5,253	.8	1.1
226 FRIENDS-USA	1	65	78*	-	-
226d *FGC & FUM*	*1*	*65*	*78**	*-*	*-*
246 GREEK ORTHODOX	2	NR	NR	-	-
259 IFCA	3	NR	NR	-	-
274 LAT EVAN LUTH	1	300	321	-	.1
283 LUTH—MO SYNOD	4	1,575	2,481	.4	.5
313 N AM BAPT CONF	1	118	142*	-	-
331 ORTH CH IN AM	1	NR	NR	-	-
353 CHR BRETHREN	2	141	289	-	.1
355 PRESB CH (USA)	22	7,978	9,608*	1.4	2.1
356 PRESB CH AMER	1	0	0	-	-
371 REF CH IN AM	11	1,685	3,573	.5	.8
403 SALVATION ARMY	2	150	178	-	-
413 S.D.A.	9	968	1,166*	.2	.3
419 SO BAPT CONV	3	558	672*	.1	.1
431 UKRANIAN AMER	1	NR	NR	-	-
435 UNITARIAN-UNIV	1	185	257	-	.1
443 UN C OF CHRIST	7	1,730	2,083*	.3	.5
449 UN METHODIST	20	5,713	6,880*	1.0	1.5
467 WESLEYAN	1	0	14	-	-
469 WELS	1	120	171	-	-
496 JEWISH EST[1]	29	NA	58,000	8.6	12.6
497 BLACK BAPT EST[2]	NA	10,385	12,507*	1.9	2.7
498 INDEP.CHARIS.[3]	1	NA	8,500	1.3	1.8

NA–Not applicable   NR–Not reported   *Total adherents estimated from known number of communicant, confirmed, full members.   - Represents a percent less than 0.1.   Percentages may not total due to rounding.
[1]See Appendix E   [2]See Appendix F   [3]See Appendix G   Lines in *italic* represent a breakdown of Catholic rites or Friends affiliations. They are included in their respective denominational total.

Table 4. Churches and Church Membership by County and Denomination: 1990

County and Denomination	Number of churches	Communicant, confirmed, full members	Total adherents		
			Number	Percent of total population	Percent of total adherents
MONMOUTH	**284**	**61,945**	**316,892***	**57.3**	**100.0**
005 AME ZION	8	5,935	7,716	1.4	2.4
019 AMER BAPT USA	23	6,382	7,889*	1.4	2.5
022 EASTERN ORTH	1	39	39	-	-
053 ASSEMB OF GOD	9	983	2,041	.4	.6
081 CATHOLIC	49	NA	198,687	35.9	62.7
081d *LATIN*	*47*	*NA*	*197,800*	*35.8*	*62.4*
081f *MELKITE-GK*	*1*	*NA*	*522*	*.1*	*.2*
081h *UKRAINIAN*	*1*	*NA*	*365*	*.1*	*.1*
111 CH CR,SCIENTST	4	NR	NR	-	-
123 CH GOD (ANDER)	2	137	137	-	-
127 CH GOD (CLEVE)	4	273	337*	.1	.1
145 CH GOD PROPHCY	2	55	68*	-	-
151 L-D SAINTS	3	NA	1,457	.3	.5
165 CH OF NAZARENE	1	27	102	-	-
167 CHS OF CHRIST	2	270	239	-	.1
179 CONSRV BAPT	4	NR	NR	-	-
193 EPISCOPAL	24	5,744	8,183	1.5	2.6
203 EVAN FREE CH	1	35	90	-	-
207 E.L.C.A.	11	4,558	6,821	1.2	2.2
226 FRIENDS-USA	2	121	150*	-	-
226d *FGC & FUM*	*2*	*121*	*150***	*-*	*-*
246 GREEK ORTHODOX	2	NR	NR	-	-
265 INT PENT C CHR	1	57	57	-	-
283 LUTH—MO SYNOD	3	1,035	1,473	.3	.5
353 CHR BRETHREN	3	199	315	.1	.1
355 PRESB CH (USA)	20	7,697	9,515*	1.7	3.0
356 PRESB CH AMER	1	49	61	-	-
371 REF CH IN AM	10	1,678	3,602	.7	1.1
403 SALVATION ARMY	2	391	426	.1	.1
413 S.D.A.	2	376	465*	.1	.1
419 SO BAPT CONV	5	1,227	1,517*	.3	.5
435 UNITARIAN-UNIV	1	252	394	.1	.1
443 UN C OF CHRIST	2	208	257*	-	.1
449 UN METHODIST	49	15,053	18,609*	3.4	5.9
467 WESLEYAN	1	19	40	-	-
496 JEWISH EST[1]	30	NA	33,600	6.1	10.6
497 BLACK BAPT EST[2]	NA	9,145	11,305*	2.0	3.6
498 INDEP.CHARIS.[3]	1	NA	800	.1	.3
499 INDEP.NON-CHAR[3]	1	NA	500	.1	.2
MORRIS	**237**	**41,384**	**261,512***	**62.1**	**100.0**
019 AMER BAPT USA	5	663	805*	.2	.3
022 EASTERN ORTH	1	119	119	-	-
053 ASSEMB OF GOD	8	552	794	.2	.3
081 CATHOLIC	50	NA	171,714	40.8	65.7
081b *BYZAN RUTH*	*1*	*NA*	*135*	*-*	*.1*
081d *LATIN*	*48*	*NA*	*171,000*	*40.6*	*65.4*
081h *UKRAINIAN*	*1*	*NA*	*579*	*.1*	*.2*
089 CHR & MISS AL	7	1,119	2,410	.6	.9
097 CHR CHS&CHS CR	1	100	121*	-	-
105 CHRISTIAN REF	2	290	451	.1	.2
111 CH CR,SCIENTST	3	NR	NR	-	-
123 CH GOD (ANDER)	1	20	20	-	-
151 L-D SAINTS	3	NA	1,109	.3	.4
163 CH OF LUTH BR	1	167	679	.2	.3
165 CH OF NAZARENE	2	276	247	.1	.1
167 CHS OF CHRIST	5	318	403	.1	.2
175 CONGR CHR CHS	2	193	234*	.1	.1
179 CONSRV BAPT	1	NR	NR	-	-
193 EPISCOPAL	19	5,514	8,308	2.0	3.2
203 EVAN FREE CH	3	153	300	.1	.1
207 E.L.C.A.	12	3,069	4,262	1.0	1.6
221 FREE METHODIST	1	32	32	-	-
226 FRIENDS-USA	3	211	256*	.1	.1
226d *FGC & FUM*	*3*	*211*	*256***	*.1*	*.1*
246 GREEK ORTHODOX	1	NR	NR	-	-
259 IFCA	1	NR	NR	-	-
283 LUTH—MO SYNOD	4	1,110	1,378	.3	.5
285 MENNONITE CH	1	24	53	-	-
331 ORTH CH IN AM	1	NR	NR	-	-
355 PRESB CH (USA)	34	11,356	13,795*	3.3	5.3
356 PRESB CH AMER	1	0	0	-	-
371 REF CH IN AM	5	1,014	2,113	.5	.8
403 SALVATION ARMY	2	92	110	-	-
413 S.D.A.	3	242	294*	.1	.1
419 SO BAPT CONV	3	1,253	1,522*	.4	.6
435 UNITARIAN-UNIV	2	316	469	.1	.2
443 UN C OF CHRIST	3	1,211	1,471*	.3	.6
449 UN METHODIST	31	9,476	11,511*	2.7	4.4
469 WELS	1	75	93	-	-
496 JEWISH EST[1]	14	NA	33,500	8.0	12.8
497 BLACK BAPT EST[2]	NA	2,419	2,939*	.7	1.1
OCEAN	**163**	**31,923**	**222,443***	**51.3**	**100.0**
005 AME ZION	2	269	319	.1	.1
019 AMER BAPT USA	5	674	821*	.2	.4
053 ASSEMB OF GOD	9	1,274	3,471	.8	1.6
081 CATHOLIC	34	NA	168,885	39.0	75.9
081b *BYZAN RUTH*	*1*	*NA*	*160*	*-*	*.1*
081d *LATIN*	*32*	*NA*	*168,300*	*38.9*	*75.7*
081h *UKRAINIAN*	*1*	*NA*	*425*	*.1*	*.2*
089 CHR & MISS AL	1	22	44	-	-
105 CHRISTIAN REF	1	0	0	-	-
111 CH CR,SCIENTST	2	NR	NR	-	-
127 CH GOD (CLEVE)	2	143	174*	-	.1
165 CH OF NAZARENE	1	86	229	.1	.1
167 CHS OF CHRIST	2	126	159	-	.1
179 CONSRV BAPT	7	NR	NR	-	-
193 EPISCOPAL	12	3,871	5,759	1.3	2.6
195 ESTONIAN ELC	1	383	467*	.1	.2
199 EVAN CONGR CH	1	266	266	.1	.1
203 EVAN FREE CH	1	279	279	.1	.1
207 E.L.C.A.	10	4,684	6,861	1.6	3.1
226 FRIENDS-USA	2	41	50*	-	-
226c *FGC*	*2*	*41*	*50***	*-*	*-*
246 GREEK ORTHODOX	1	NR	NR	-	-
283 LUTH—MO SYNOD	4	950	1,245	.3	.6
293 MORAV CH-NORTH	1	107	145	-	.1
331 ORTH CH IN AM	2	NR	NR	-	-
353 CHR BRETHREN	3	305	545	.1	.2
355 PRESB CH (USA)	10	5,885	7,170*	1.7	3.2
356 PRESB CH AMER	1	126	195	-	.1
371 REF CH IN AM	3	1,210	1,699	.4	.8
403 SALVATION ARMY	1	28	28	-	-
413 S.D.A.	2	222	270*	.1	.1
419 SO BAPT CONV	1	82	100*	-	-
435 UNITARIAN-UNIV	1	27	27	-	-
443 UN C OF CHRIST	1	112	136*	-	.1
449 UN METHODIST	28	8,421	10,260*	2.4	4.6
496 JEWISH EST[1]	10	NA	9,500	2.2	4.3
497 BLACK BAPT EST[2]	NA	2,330	2,839*	.7	1.3
499 INDEP.NON-CHAR[3]	1	NA	500	.1	.2
PASSAIC	**242**	**39,323**	**240,992***	**53.2**	**100.0**
005 AME ZION	2	2,775	2,870	.6	1.2
019 AMER BAPT USA	17	2,893	3,564*	.8	1.5
053 ASSEMB OF GOD	17	2,185	4,039	.9	1.7
081 CATHOLIC	51	NA	168,121	37.1	69.8
081a *ARMENIAN*	*1*	*NA*	*1,500*	*.3*	*.6*
081b *BYZAN RUTH*	*1*	*NA*	*3,021*	*.7*	*1.3*
081d *LATIN*	*47*	*NA*	*157,000*	*34.7*	*65.1*
081f *MELKITE-GK*	*1*	*NA*	*2,600*	*.6*	*1.1*
081h *UKRAINIAN*	*1*	*NA*	*4,000*	*.9*	*1.7*
089 CHR & MISS AL	1	0	186	-	.1
105 CHRISTIAN REF	10	1,717	2,424	.5	1.0
111 CH CR,SCIENTST	1	NR	NR	-	-
123 CH GOD (ANDER)	4	49	101	-	-
127 CH GOD (CLEVE)	6	519	639*	.1	.3
145 CH GOD PROPHCY	2	55	68*	-	-
151 L-D SAINTS	1	NA	248	.1	.1
165 CH OF NAZARENE	3	334	233	.1	.1
193 EPISCOPAL	13	2,384	3,648	.8	1.5
195 ESTONIAN ELC	1	30	37*	-	-
207 E.L.C.A.	3	653	876	.2	.4
221 FREE METHODIST	2	108	254	.1	.1
246 GREEK ORTHODOX	1	NR	NR	-	-
259 IFCA	2	NR	NR	-	-
283 LUTH—MO SYNOD	7	1,386	1,990	.4	.8
307 NETH REF CONGR	1	122	211	-	.1
331 ORTH CH IN AM	3	NR	NR	-	-
339 PENT CH OF GOD	1	35	55	-	-
355 PRESB CH (USA)	14	2,704	3,331*	.7	1.4
371 REF CH IN AM	18	2,510	4,475	1.0	1.9
403 SALVATION ARMY	2	129	143	-	.1
413 S.D.A.	5	944	1,163*	.3	.5
419 SO BAPT CONV	3	293	361*	.1	.1
435 UNITARIAN-UNIV	1	65	77	-	-
443 UN C OF CHRIST	3	683	841*	.2	.3
449 UN METHODIST	18	3,955	4,873*	1.1	2.0
496 JEWISH EST[1]	28	NA	18,700	4.1	7.8
497 BLACK BAPT EST[2]	NA	12,795	15,764*	3.5	6.5
499 INDEP.NON-CHAR[3]	1	NA	1,700	.4	.7
SALEM	**74**	**11,892**	**24,822***	**38.0**	**100.0**
019 AMER BAPT USA	5	1,488	1,858*	2.8	7.5
053 ASSEMB OF GOD	5	407	760	1.2	3.1
081 CATHOLIC	6	NA	9,014	13.8	36.3
081d *LATIN*	*6*	*NA*	*9,014*	*13.8*	*36.3*
111 CH CR,SCIENTST	1	NR	NR	-	-
127 CH GOD (CLEVE)	1	14	17*	-	.1
151 L-D SAINTS	1	NA	110	.2	.4
165 CH OF NAZARENE	3	266	396	.6	1.6

NA–Not applicable   NR–Not reported   *Total adherents estimated from known number of communicant, confirmed, full members.   - Represents a percent less than 0.1.   Percentages may not total due to rounding.

[1]See Appendix E   [2]See Appendix F   [3]See Appendix G   Lines in *italic* represent a breakdown of Catholic rites or Friends affiliations. They are included in their respective denominational total.

Table 4. Churches and Church Membership by County and Denomination: 1990

County and Denomination	Number of churches	Communicant, confirmed, full members	Total adherents Number	Percent of total population	Percent of total adherents
179 CONSRV BAPT	3	NR	NR	-	-
193 EPISCOPAL	4	592	997	1.5	4.0
207 E.L.C.A.	2	426	570	.9	2.3
226 FRIENDS-USA	2	378	472*	.7	1.9
226c FGC	*2*	*378*	*472**	*.7*	*1.9*
259 IFCA	1	NR	NR	-	-
283 LUTH—MO SYNOD	1	160	181	.3	.7
285 MENNONITE CH	2	56	118	.2	.5
355 PRESB CH (USA)	5	1,489	1,859*	2.8	7.5
413 S.D.A.	2	222	277*	.4	1.1
419 SO BAPT CONV	1	409	511*	.8	2.1
449 UN METHODIST	25	4,064	5,074*	7.8	20.4
467 WESLEYAN	1	68	195	.3	.8
496 JEWISH EST[1]	3	NA	100	.2	.4
497 BLACK BAPT EST[2]	NA	1,853	2,313*	3.5	9.3
SOMERSET	**140**	**25,032**	**135,760***	**56.5**	**100.0**
005 AME ZION	1	525	590	.2	.4
019 AMER BAPT USA	1	302	366*	.2	.3
022 EASTERN ORTH	1	172	172	.1	.1
053 ASSEMB OF GOD	3	506	756	.3	.6
081 CATHOLIC	29	NA	91,406	38.0	67.3
081b BYZAN RUTH	*2*	*NA*	*1,350*	*.6*	*1.0*
081d LATIN	*25*	*NA*	*89,000*	*37.0*	*65.6*
081e MARONITE	*1*	*NA*	*716*	*.3*	*.5*
081h UKRAINIAN	*1*	*NA*	*340*	*.1*	*.3*
089 CHR & MISS AL	2	102	282	.1	.2
093 CHR CH (DISC)	1	20	38	-	-
111 CH CR,SCIENTST	2	NR	NR	-	-
123 CH GOD (ANDER)	1	25	40	-	-
127 CH GOD (CLEVE)	1	17	21*	-	-
151 L-D SAINTS	4	NA	1,214	.5	.9
163 CH OF LUTH BR	1	74	281	.1	.2
167 CHS OF CHRIST	2	145	194	.1	.1
175 CONGR CHR CHS	1	222	269*	.1	.2
179 CONSRV BAPT	3	NR	NR	-	-
193 EPISCOPAL	9	3,198	5,481	2.3	4.0
203 EVAN FREE CH	3	249	408	.2	.3
207 E.L.C.A.	4	1,121	1,521	.6	1.1
259 IFCA	1	NR	NR	-	-
283 LUTH—MO SYNOD	4	1,155	1,471	.6	1.1
331 ORTH CH IN AM	1	NR	NR	-	-
355 PRESB CH (USA)	14	5,637	6,827*	2.8	5.0
356 PRESB CH AMER	3	174	217	.1	.2
371 REF CH IN AM	19	3,267	6,585	2.7	4.9
375 REF EPISCOPAL	2	161	231	.1	.2
415 S-D BAPTIST GC	1	26	31*	-	-
419 SO BAPT CONV	3	543	658*	.3	.5
443 UN C OF CHRIST	2	234	283*	.1	.2
449 UN METHODIST	16	4,287	5,192*	2.2	3.8
496 JEWISH EST[1]	5	NA	7,750	3.2	5.7
497 BLACK BAPT EST[2]	NA	2,870	3,476*	1.4	2.6
SUSSEX	**78**	**11,613**	**55,651***	**42.5**	**100.0**
019 AMER BAPT USA	4	557	716*	.5	1.3
053 ASSEMB OF GOD	3	349	545	.4	1.0
081 CATHOLIC	16	NA	35,000	26.7	62.9
081d LATIN	*16*	*NA*	*35,000*	*26.7*	*62.9*
089 CHR & MISS AL	1	0	61	-	.1
105 CHRISTIAN REF	2	379	631	.5	1.1
111 CH CR,SCIENTST	1	NR	NR	-	-
151 L-D SAINTS	2	NA	343	.3	.6
165 CH OF NAZARENE	1	83	63	-	.1
175 CONGR CHR CHS	1	250	322*	.2	.6
193 EPISCOPAL	4	960	1,526	1.2	2.7
203 EVAN FREE CH	1	61	155	.1	.3
207 E.L.C.A.	3	505	791	.6	1.4
249 AP CATH ASSYR	0	3	11	-	-
283 LUTH—MO SYNOD	3	926	1,560	1.2	2.8
331 ORTH CH IN AM	1	NR	NR	-	-
353 CHR BRETHREN	1	14	16	-	-
355 PRESB CH (USA)	12	3,406	4,380*	3.3	7.9
371 REF CH IN AM	1	55	156	.1	.3
413 S.D.A.	2	265	341*	.3	.6
435 UNITARIAN-UNIV	1	17	28	-	.1
449 UN METHODIST	13	3,495	4,495*	3.4	8.1
467 WESLEYAN	1	48	102	.1	.2
496 JEWISH EST[1]	4	NA	4,100	3.1	7.4
497 BLACK BAPT EST[2]	NA	240	309*	.2	.6
UNION	**269**	**66,500**	**372,963***	**75.5**	**100.0**
005 AME ZION	5	1,307	1,386	.3	.4
019 AMER BAPT USA	24	9,400	11,357*	2.3	3.0
022 EASTERN ORTH	2	450	450	.1	.1
053 ASSEMB OF GOD	14	1,432	2,010	.4	.5
081 CATHOLIC	47	NA	259,678	52.6	69.6

County and Denomination	Number of churches	Communicant, confirmed, full members	Total adherents Number	Percent of total population	Percent of total adherents
081b BYZAN RUTH	*3*	*NA*	*2,555*	*.5*	*.7*
081d LATIN	*42*	*NA*	*254,482*	*51.5*	*68.2*
081h UKRAINIAN	*2*	*NA*	*2,641*	*.5*	*.7*
089 CHR & MISS AL	5	295	638	.1	.2
097 CHR CHS&CHS CR	1	60	72*	-	-
111 CH CR,SCIENTST	3	NR	NR	-	-
123 CH GOD (ANDER)	2	235	265	.1	.1
127 CH GOD (CLEVE)	2	111	134*	-	-
145 CH GOD PROPHCY	2	55	66*	-	-
151 L-D SAINTS	1	NA	411	.1	.1
165 CH OF NAZARENE	2	71	107	-	-
167 CHS OF CHRIST	2	86	112	-	-
179 CONSRV BAPT	2	NR	NR	-	-
193 EPISCOPAL	16	5,596	7,391	1.5	2.0
207 E.L.C.A.	14	4,124	5,692	1.2	1.5
221 FREE METHODIST	1	0	21	-	-
226 FRIENDS-USA	1	174	210*	-	.1
226d FGC & FUM	*1*	*174*	*210**	*-*	*.1*
246 GREEK ORTHODOX	2	NR	NR	-	-
263 INT FOURSQ GOS	1	59	71*	-	-
274 LAT EVAN LUTH	1	110	120	-	-
283 LUTH—MO SYNOD	5	1,247	1,581	.3	.4
293 MORAV CH-NORTH	1	133	153	-	-
331 ORTH CH IN AM	1	NR	NR	-	-
349 PENT HOLINESS	1	80	97*	-	-
353 CHR BRETHREN	6	551	841	.2	.2
355 PRESB CH (USA)	30	13,108	15,836*	3.2	4.2
371 REF CH IN AM	2	249	470	.1	.1
375 REF EPISCOPAL	1	56	74	-	-
403 SALVATION ARMY	2	111	130	-	-
413 S.D.A.	6	689	832*	.2	.2
415 S-D BAPTIST GC	1	78	94*	-	-
419 SO BAPT CONV	3	423	511*	.1	.1
435 UNITARIAN-UNIV	2	813	970	.2	.3
443 UN C OF CHRIST	5	1,697	2,050*	.4	.5
449 UN METHODIST	19	5,729	6,921*	1.4	1.9
496 JEWISH EST[1]	33	NA	30,000	6.1	8.0
497 BLACK BAPT EST[2]	NA	17,971	21,712*	4.4	5.8
498 INDEP.CHARIS.[3]	1	NA	500	.1	.1
WARREN	**93**	**13,880**	**54,565***	**59.6**	**100.0**
039 AP CHR CH(NAZ)	1	8	10*	-	.7
053 ASSEMB OF GOD	3	264	390	.4	.7
081 CATHOLIC	12	NA	35,770	39.0	65.6
081b BYZAN RUTH	*1*	*NA*	*350*	*.4*	*.6*
081d LATIN	*10*	*NA*	*35,000*	*38.2*	*64.1*
081h UKRAINIAN	*1*	*NA*	*420*	*.5*	*.8*
089 CHR & MISS AL	4	145	373	.4	.7
097 CHR CHS&CHS CR	1	56	70*	.1	.1
165 CH OF NAZARENE	3	62	132	.1	.2
167 CHS OF CHRIST	1	40	50	.1	.1
179 CONSRV BAPT	2	NR	NR	-	-
193 EPISCOPAL	7	1,185	1,795	2.0	3.3
203 EVAN FREE CH	1	118	205	.2	.4
207 E.L.C.A.	5	2,463	3,335	3.6	6.1
259 IFCA	2	NR	NR	-	-
283 LUTH—MO SYNOD	2	398	536	.6	1.0
285 MENNONITE CH	2	131	210	.2	.4
331 ORTH CH IN AM	1	NR	NR	-	-
353 CHR BRETHREN	1	125	200	.2	.4
355 PRESB CH (USA)	17	3,656	4,561*	5.0	8.4
356 PRESB CH AMER	1	132	170	.2	.3
413 S.D.A.	3	394	492*	.5	.9
443 UN C OF CHRIST	1	103	128*	.1	.2
449 UN METHODIST	23	4,348	5,424*	5.9	9.9
496 JEWISH EST[1]	0	NA	400	.4	.7
497 BLACK BAPT EST[2]	NA	252	314*	.3	.6

NEW MEXICO

County and Denomination	Number of churches	Communicant, confirmed, full members	Total adherents Number	Percent of total population	Percent of total adherents
THE STATE.....	1,824	259,196	889,298*	58.7	100.0
BERNALILLO	**270**	**70,346**	**257,061***	**53.5**	**100.0**
019 AMER BAPT USA	3	664	840*	.2	.3
053 ASSEMB OF GOD	15	2,687	5,573	1.2	2.2
075 BRETHREN IN CR	1	55	55	-	-
081 CATHOLIC	44	NA	132,122	27.5	51.4
081b BYZAN RUTH	*1*	*NA*	*221*	*-*	*.1*
081d LATIN	*42*	*NA*	*131,379*	*27.3*	*51.1*
081f MELKITE-GK	*1*	*NA*	*522*	*.1*	*.2*
089 CHR & MISS AL	1	8	48	-	-
093 CHR CH (DISC)	3	1,041	1,545	.3	.6

NA–Not applicable   NR–Not reported   *Total adherents estimated from known number of communicant, confirmed, full members.   - Represents a percent less than 0.1.   Percentages may not total due to rounding.
[1]See Appendix E   [2]See Appendix F   [3]See Appendix G   Lines in *italic* represent a breakdown of Catholic rites or Friends affiliations. They are included in their respective denominational total.

Table 4. Churches and Church Membership by County and Denomination: 1990

County and Denomination	Number of churches	Communicant, confirmed, full members	Total adherents Number	Percent of total population	Percent of total adherents
097 CHR CHS&CHS CR	6	1,309	1,657*	.3	.6
105 CHRISTIAN REF	3	160	255	.1	.1
111 CH CR,SCIENTST	1	NR	NR	-	-
123 CH GOD (ANDER)	3	272	277	.1	.1
127 CH GOD (CLEVE)	2	46	58*	-	-
133 CH GOD(7TH)DEN	1	12	15	-	-
145 CH GOD PROPHCY	1	22	28*	-	-
151 L-D SAINTS	18	NA	7,897	1.6	3.1
164 CH LUTH CONF	1	8	15	-	-
165 CH OF NAZARENE	9	1,781	1,667	.3	.6
167 CHS OF CHRIST	14	2,097	3,047	.6	1.2
179 CONSRV BAPT	2	NR	NR	-	-
185 CUMBER PRESB	1	2,224	2,224	.5	.9
193 EPISCOPAL	7	2,888	4,013	.8	1.6
203 EVAN FREE CH	1	160	300	.1	.1
207 E.L.C.A.	9	5,502	7,983	1.7	3.1
221 FREE METHODIST	1	24	24	-	-
223 FREE WILL BAPT	1	23	29*	-	-
226 FRIENDS-USA	2	153	193*	-	.1
226b EFI	1	34	42	-	-
226f INDEPENDNT	1	119	151*	-	.1
246 GREEK ORTHODOX	1	NR	NR	-	-
259 IFCA	1	NR	NR	-	-
263 INT FOURSQ GOS	5	441	558*	.1	.2
265 INT PENT C CHR	1	25	25	-	-
283 LUTH—MO SYNOD	8	2,380	3,209	.7	1.2
285 MENNONITE CH	4	125	249	.1	.1
331 ORTH CH IN AM	1	NR	NR	-	-
339 PENT CH OF GOD	2	42	75	-	-
349 PENT HOLINESS	1	88	111*	-	-
353 CHR BRETHREN	2	65	100	-	-
355 PRESB CH (USA)	11	4,142	5,242*	1.1	2.0
356 PRESB CH AMER	1	65	93	-	-
403 SALVATION ARMY	2	196	255	.1	.1
413 S.D.A.	5	1,197	1,515*	.3	.6
419 SO BAPT CONV	35	24,039	30,425*	6.3	11.8
435 UNITARIAN-UNIV	1	549	679	.1	.3
443 UN C OF CHRIST	3	588	744*	.2	.3
449 UN METHODIST	18	12,273	15,534*	3.2	6.0
467 WESLEYAN	1	19	75	-	-
469 WELS	1	160	219	-	.1
496 JEWISH EST[1]	2	NA	4,400	.9	1.7
497 BLACK BAPT EST[2]	NA	2,816	3,564*	.7	1.4
498 INDEP.CHARIS.[3]	3	NA	2,000	.4	.8
499 INDEP.NON-CHAR[3]	11	NA	18,124	3.8	7.1
CATRON	**16**	**484**	**1,552***	**60.6**	**100.0**
081 CATHOLIC	3	NA	374	14.6	24.1
081d LATIN	3	NA	374	14.6	24.1
151 L-D SAINTS	3	NA	571	22.3	36.8
167 CHS OF CHRIST	1	14	18	.7	1.2
355 PRESB CH (USA)	4	72	90*	3.5	5.8
413 S.D.A.	1	8	10*	.4	.6
419 SO BAPT CONV	4	390	489*	19.1	31.5
CHAVES	**81**	**15,032**	**38,971***	**67.4**	**100.0**
053 ASSEMB OF GOD	10	650	1,283	2.2	3.3
081 CATHOLIC	4	NA	16,660	28.8	42.7
081d LATIN	4	NA	16,660	28.8	42.7
093 CHR CH (DISC)	1	369	395	.7	1.0
097 CHR CHS&CHS CR	1	50	66*	.1	.2
111 CH CR,SCIENTST	1	NR	NR	-	-
127 CH GOD (CLEVE)	3	95	125*	.2	.3
133 CH GOD(7TH)DEN	1	11	13	-	-
145 CH GOD PROPHCY	1	22	29*	.1	.1
151 L-D SAINTS	2	NA	801	1.4	2.1
165 CH OF NAZARENE	3	312	659	1.1	1.7
167 CHS OF CHRIST	11	1,228	1,624	2.8	4.2
193 EPISCOPAL	2	457	708	1.2	1.8
203 EVAN FREE CH	1	75	125	.2	.3
207 E.L.C.A.	1	177	230	.4	.6
223 FREE WILL BAPT	1	10	13*	-	-
263 INT FOURSQ GOS	1	80	105*	.2	.3
283 LUTH—MO SYNOD	1	206	266	.5	.7
339 PENT CH OF GOD	1	25	40	.1	.1
355 PRESB CH (USA)	4	775	1,022*	1.8	2.6
403 SALVATION ARMY	1	107	110	.2	.3
413 S.D.A.	3	163	215*	.4	.6
419 SO BAPT CONV	16	7,689	10,137*	17.5	26.0
449 UN METHODIST	7	2,295	3,026*	5.2	7.8
469 WELS	1	29	46	.1	.1
496 JEWISH EST[1]	1	NA	0	-	-
497 BLACK BAPT EST[2]	NA	207	273*	.5	.7
499 INDEP.NON-CHAR[3]	2	NA	1,000	1.7	2.6

County and Denomination	Number of churches	Communicant, confirmed, full members	Total adherents Number	Percent of total population	Percent of total adherents
CIBOLA	**38**	**830**	**12,467***	**52.4**	**100.0**
011 A.W.M.C.	1	9	12*	.1	.1
053 ASSEMB OF GOD	2	94	181	.8	1.5
081 CATHOLIC	15	NA	8,827	37.1	70.8
081d LATIN	15	NA	8,827	37.1	70.8
127 CH GOD (CLEVE)	2	194	265*	1.1	2.1
151 L-D SAINTS	6	NA	2,336	9.8	18.7
165 CH OF NAZARENE	4	141	233	1.0	1.9
167 CHS OF CHRIST	1	210	273	1.1	2.2
193 EPISCOPAL	1	24	64	.3	.5
221 FREE METHODIST	1	2	7	-	.1
283 LUTH—MO SYNOD	1	39	51	.2	.4
339 PENT CH OF GOD	2	70	154	.6	1.2
449 UN METHODIST	2	47	64*	.3	.5
COLFAX	**37**	**2,198**	**9,812***	**75.9**	**100.0**
053 ASSEMB OF GOD	2	83	191	1.5	1.9
081 CATHOLIC	10	NA	6,905	53.4	70.4
081d LATIN	10	NA	6,905	53.4	70.4
093 CHR CH (DISC)	1	35	75	.6	.8
145 CH GOD PROPHCY	1	22	28*	.2	.3
167 CHS OF CHRIST	4	90	124	1.0	1.3
193 EPISCOPAL	1	47	53	.4	.5
283 LUTH—MO SYNOD	2	20	26	.2	.3
355 PRESB CH (USA)	1	144	183*	1.4	1.9
413 S.D.A.	1	30	38*	.3	.4
419 SO BAPT CONV	10	1,124	1,425*	11.0	14.5
449 UN METHODIST	4	603	764*	5.9	7.8
CURRY	**59**	**17,459**	**31,606***	**74.9**	**100.0**
001 ADVENT CHR CH	1	179	238*	.6	.8
053 ASSEMB OF GOD	4	450	637	1.5	2.0
059 BAPT MISS ASSN	1	53	70*	.2	.2
081 CATHOLIC	4	NA	7,790	18.5	24.6
081d LATIN	4	NA	7,790	18.5	24.6
097 CHR CHS&CHS CR	2	600	797*	1.9	2.5
111 CH CR,SCIENTST	1	NR	NR	-	-
123 CH GOD (ANDER)	1	45	45	.1	.1
127 CH GOD (CLEVE)	1	33	44*	.1	.1
145 CH GOD PROPHCY	2	44	58*	.1	.2
151 L-D SAINTS	2	NA	617	1.5	2.0
157 CH OF BRETHREN	1	50	66*	.2	.2
165 CH OF NAZARENE	2	798	1,078	2.6	3.4
167 CHS OF CHRIST	8	1,254	1,599	3.8	5.1
193 EPISCOPAL	1	153	206	.5	.7
207 E.L.C.A.	1	95	126	.3	.4
283 LUTH—MO SYNOD	1	234	309	.7	1.0
353 CHR BRETHREN	2	74	150	.4	.5
355 PRESB CH (USA)	2	166	221*	.5	.7
403 SALVATION ARMY	1	97	102	.2	.3
413 S.D.A.	2	121	161*	.4	.5
419 SO BAPT CONV	14	10,239	13,606*	32.2	43.0
449 UN METHODIST	5	2,271	3,018*	7.2	9.5
497 BLACK BAPT EST[2]	NA	503	668*	1.6	2.1
DE BACA	**7**	**981**	**2,268***	**100.7**	**100.0**
053 ASSEMB OF GOD	1	19	25	1.1	1.1
081 CATHOLIC	1	NA	1,005	44.6	44.3
081d LATIN	1	NA	1,005	44.6	44.3
165 CH OF NAZARENE	1	18	40	1.8	1.8
167 CHS OF CHRIST	1	150	195	8.7	8.6
193 EPISCOPAL	1	16	27	1.2	1.2
419 SO BAPT CONV	1	553	694*	30.8	30.6
449 UN METHODIST	1	225	282*	12.5	12.4
DONA ANA	**120**	**16,706**	**79,464***	**58.6**	**100.0**
053 ASSEMB OF GOD	15	1,114	1,616	1.2	2.0
059 BAPT MISS ASSN	1	76	100*	.1	.1
081 CATHOLIC	17	NA	54,316	40.1	68.4
081b BYZAN RUTH	1	NA	35	-	-
081d LATIN	16	NA	54,281	40.1	68.3
083 CHRIST CATH CH	2	17	26	-	-
093 CHR CH (DISC)	1	178	195	.1	.2
097 CHR CHS&CHS CR	2	95	125*	.1	.2
111 CH CR,SCIENTST	1	NR	NR	-	-
123 CH GOD (ANDER)	2	112	126	.1	.2
127 CH GOD (CLEVE)	2	55	72*	.1	.1
145 CH GOD PROPHCY	3	68	89*	.1	.1
151 L-D SAINTS	8	NA	2,026	1.5	2.5
165 CH OF NAZARENE	2	158	221	.2	.3
167 CHS OF CHRIST	11	1,030	1,321	1.0	1.7
193 EPISCOPAL	4	738	975	.7	1.2
203 EVAN FREE CH	1	83	145	.1	.2
207 E.L.C.A.	2	587	743	.5	.9
226 FRIENDS-USA	1	27	36*	-	-

NA–Not applicable   NR–Not reported   *Total adherents estimated from known number of communicant, confirmed, full members.   - Represents a percent less than 0.1.   Percentages may not total due to rounding.
[1]See Appendix E   [2]See Appendix F   [3]See Appendix G   Lines in *italic* represent a breakdown of Catholic rites or Friends affiliations. They are included in their respective denominational total.

Table 4. Churches and Church Membership by County and Denomination: 1990

County and Denomination	Number of churches	Communicant, confirmed, full members	Total adherents Number	Percent of total population	Percent of total adherents
226f INDEPENDNT	1	27	36*	-	-
259 IFCA	1	NR	NR	-	-
283 LUTH—MO SYNOD	1	102	147	.1	.2
349 PENT HOLINESS	1	28	37*	-	-
353 CHR BRETHREN	1	125	300	.2	.4
355 PRESB CH (USA)	3	842	1,108*	.8	1.4
356 PRESB CH AMER	2	239	240	.2	.3
403 SALVATION ARMY	1	100	105	.1	.1
413 S.D.A.	3	141	186*	.1	.2
419 SO BAPT CONV	21	7,056	9,286*	6.9	11.7
435 UNITARIAN-UNIV	1	87	97	.1	.1
449 UN METHODIST	7	3,140	4,132*	3.0	5.2
469 WELS	1	45	60	-	.1
496 JEWISH EST[1]	1	NA	525	.4	.7
497 BLACK BAPT EST[2]	NA	463	609*	.4	.8
499 INDEP.NON-CHAR[3]	1	NA	500	.4	.6
EDDY	**83**	**16,380**	**46,540***	**95.8**	**100.0**
053 ASSEMB OF GOD	7	658	1,203	2.5	2.6
059 BAPT MISS ASSN	2	151	198*	.4	.4
081 CATHOLIC	5	NA	22,480	46.3	48.3
081d LATIN	5	NA	22,480	46.3	48.3
093 CHR CH (DISC)	2	275	571	1.2	1.2
097 CHR CHS&CHS CR	2	189	248*	.5	.5
111 CH CR,SCIENTST	1	NR	NR	-	-
127 CH GOD (CLEVE)	5	270	354*	.7	.8
145 CH GOD PROPHCY	1	22	29*	.1	.1
151 L-D SAINTS	2	NA	716	1.5	1.5
165 CH OF NAZARENE	3	230	370	.8	.8
167 CHS OF CHRIST	11	1,681	2,203	4.5	4.7
193 EPISCOPAL	2	248	340	.7	.7
207 E.L.C.A.	1	85	99	.2	.2
223 FREE WILL BAPT	2	77	101*	.2	.2
226 FRIENDS-USA	1	1	6	-	-
226f INDEPENDNT	1	1	6	-	-
259 IFCA	1	NR	NR	-	-
283 LUTH—MO SYNOD	2	156	195	.4	.4
285 MENNONITE CH	1	73	80	.2	.2
355 PRESB CH (USA)	2	470	617*	1.3	1.3
413 S.D.A.	1	29	38*	.1	.1
419 SO BAPT CONV	18	8,921	11,709*	24.1	25.2
449 UN METHODIST	9	2,701	3,545*	7.3	7.6
497 BLACK BAPT EST[2]	NA	143	188*	.4	.4
498 INDEP.CHARIS.[3]	1	NA	700	1.4	1.5
499 INDEP.NON-CHAR[3]	1	NA	550	1.1	1.2
GRANT	**41**	**3,793**	**18,628***	**67.3**	**100.0**
053 ASSEMB OF GOD	3	342	505	1.8	2.7
059 BAPT MISS ASSN	1	0	0*	-	-
081 CATHOLIC	5	NA	12,570	45.4	67.5
081d LATIN	5	NA	12,570	45.4	67.5
111 CH CR,SCIENTST	1	NR	NR	-	-
127 CH GOD (CLEVE)	1	68	89*	.3	.5
151 L-D SAINTS	4	NA	1,075	3.9	5.8
165 CH OF NAZARENE	1	29	27	.1	.1
167 CHS OF CHRIST	4	184	239	.9	1.3
179 CONSRV BAPT	1	NR	NR	-	-
193 EPISCOPAL	1	182	231	.8	1.2
226 FRIENDS-USA	1	22	29*	.1	.2
226f INDEPENDNT	1	22	29*	.1	.2
283 LUTH—MO SYNOD	1	125	144	.5	.8
355 PRESB CH (USA)	2	187	245*	.9	1.3
413 S.D.A.	1	52	68*	.2	.4
419 SO BAPT CONV	8	1,731	2,266*	8.2	12.2
443 UN C OF CHRIST	3	86	113*	.4	.6
449 UN METHODIST	3	785	1,027*	3.7	5.5
GUADALUPE	**25**	**251**	**4,149***	**99.8**	**100.0**
053 ASSEMB OF GOD	1	9	25	.6	.6
081 CATHOLIC	19	NA	3,800	91.4	91.6
081d LATIN	19	NA	3,800	91.4	91.6
167 CHS OF CHRIST	2	36	53	1.3	1.3
419 SO BAPT CONV	2	127	167*	4.0	4.0
449 UN METHODIST	1	79	104*	2.5	2.5
HARDING	**9**	**165**	**1,011***	**102.4**	**100.0**
081 CATHOLIC	6	NA	801	81.2	79.2
081d LATIN	6	NA	801	81.2	79.2
093 CHR CH (DISC)	1	12	16	1.6	1.6
419 SO BAPT CONV	1	122	155*	15.7	15.3
449 UN METHODIST	1	31	39*	4.0	3.9
HIDALGO	**11**	**841**	**2,213***	**37.1**	**100.0**
053 ASSEMB OF GOD	2	67	185	3.1	8.4
081 CATHOLIC	1	NA	653	11.0	29.5
081d LATIN	1	NA	653	11.0	29.5
097 CHR CHS&CHS CR	1	50	67*	1.1	3.0
151 L-D SAINTS	1	NA	338	5.7	15.3
167 CHS OF CHRIST	1	26	34	.6	1.5
419 SO BAPT CONV	4	563	755*	12.7	34.1
449 UN METHODIST	1	135	181*	3.0	8.2
LEA	**97**	**26,122**	**43,996***	**78.9**	**100.0**
053 ASSEMB OF GOD	11	611	1,029	1.8	2.3
059 BAPT MISS ASSN	2	75	102*	.2	.2
081 CATHOLIC	3	NA	6,700	12.0	15.2
081d LATIN	3	NA	6,700	12.0	15.2
093 CHR CH (DISC)	1	80	124	.2	.3
097 CHR CHS&CHS CR	3	672	912*	1.6	2.1
111 CH CR,SCIENTST	2	NR	NR	-	-
127 CH GOD (CLEVE)	4	113	153*	.3	.3
145 CH GOD PROPHCY	2	44	60*	.1	.1
151 L-D SAINTS	2	NA	507	.9	1.2
165 CH OF NAZARENE	3	259	378	.7	.9
167 CHS OF CHRIST	16	1,847	2,383	4.3	5.4
193 EPISCOPAL	2	254	301	.5	.7
207 E.L.C.A.	1	95	126	.2	.3
223 FREE WILL BAPT	1	36	49*	.1	.1
283 LUTH—MO SYNOD	2	185	233	.4	.5
349 PENT HOLINESS	2	52	71*	.1	.2
355 PRESB CH (USA)	3	285	387*	.7	.9
403 SALVATION ARMY	1	84	86	.2	.2
413 S.D.A.	3	79	107*	.2	.2
419 SO BAPT CONV	25	17,268	23,424*	42.0	53.2
449 UN METHODIST	6	3,632	4,927*	8.8	11.2
497 BLACK BAPT EST[2]	NA	451	612*	1.1	1.4
498 INDEP.CHARIS.[3]	1	NA	325	.6	.7
499 INDEP.NON-CHAR[3]	1	NA	1,000	1.8	2.3
LINCOLN	**27**	**2,813**	**5,415***	**44.3**	**100.0**
053 ASSEMB OF GOD	2	75	103	.8	1.9
081 CATHOLIC	1	NA	1,447	11.8	26.7
081d LATIN	1	NA	1,447	11.8	26.7
093 CHR CH (DISC)	1	188	502	4.1	9.3
151 L-D SAINTS	1	NA	148	1.2	2.7
165 CH OF NAZARENE	1	59	62	.5	1.1
167 CHS OF CHRIST	3	245	343	2.8	6.3
193 EPISCOPAL	1	182	222	1.8	4.1
263 INT FOURSQ GOS	1	30	37*	.3	.7
283 LUTH—MO SYNOD	1	117	157	1.3	2.9
355 PRESB CH (USA)	4	161	201*	1.6	3.7
413 S.D.A.	1	20	25*	.2	.5
419 SO BAPT CONV	7	1,291	1,612*	13.2	29.8
449 UN METHODIST	3	445	556*	4.6	10.3
LOS ALAMOS	**28**	**6,916**	**14,444***	**79.7**	**100.0**
019 AMER BAPT USA	1	838	1,045*	5.8	7.2
053 ASSEMB OF GOD	1	37	80	.4	.6
081 CATHOLIC	2	NA	4,250	23.5	29.4
081d LATIN	2	NA	4,250	23.5	29.4
089 CHR & MISS AL	1	51	117	.6	.8
093 CHR CH (DISC)	1	180	209	1.2	1.4
097 CHR CHS&CHS CR	1	400	499*	2.8	3.5
111 CH CR,SCIENTST	1	NR	NR	-	-
151 L-D SAINTS	2	NA	940	5.2	6.5
165 CH OF NAZARENE	1	54	134	.7	.9
167 CHS OF CHRIST	1	224	310	1.7	2.1
193 EPISCOPAL	1	431	520	2.9	3.6
203 EVAN FREE CH	1	21	50	.3	.3
207 E.L.C.A.	1	324	554	3.1	3.8
226 FRIENDS-USA	1	3	9	-	.1
226f INDEPENDNT	1	3	9	-	.1
353 CHR BRETHREN	1	30	60	.3	.4
355 PRESB CH (USA)	2	338	421*	2.3	2.9
356 PRESB CH AMER	1	69	84	.5	.6
419 SO BAPT CONV	2	1,814	2,262*	12.5	15.7
435 UNITARIAN-UNIV	1	153	206	1.1	1.4
443 UN C OF CHRIST	1	838	1,045*	5.8	7.2
449 UN METHODIST	2	1,034	1,289*	7.1	8.9
469 WELS	1	77	110	.6	.8
496 JEWISH EST[1]	1	NA	250	1.4	1.7
LUNA	**23**	**2,402**	**10,299***	**56.9**	**100.0**
053 ASSEMB OF GOD	2	69	85	.5	.8
081 CATHOLIC	2	NA	6,800	37.5	66.0
081d LATIN	2	NA	6,800	37.5	66.0
097 CHR CHS&CHS CR	1	135	174*	1.0	1.7
111 CH CR,SCIENTST	1	NR	NR	-	-
145 CH GOD PROPHCY	1	22	28*	.2	.3
151 L-D SAINTS	1	NA	443	2.4	4.3
165 CH OF NAZARENE	1	53	55	.3	.5

NA–Not applicable   NR–Not reported   *Total adherents estimated from known number of communicant, confirmed, full members.   - Represents a percent less than 0.1.   Percentages may not total due to rounding.
[1] See Appendix E   [2] See Appendix F   [3] See Appendix G   Lines in *italic* represent a breakdown of Catholic rites or Friends affiliations. They are included in their respective denominational total.

Table 4. Churches and Church Membership by County and Denomination: 1990

County and Denomination	Number of churches	Communicant, confirmed, full members	Total adherents Number	Percent of total population	Percent of total adherents
167 CHS OF CHRIST	3	100	131	.7	1.3
193 EPISCOPAL	1	47	58	.3	.6
263 INT FOURSQ GOS	1	28	36*	.2	.3
283 LUTH—MO SYNOD	1	121	134	.7	1.3
355 PRESB CH (USA)	1	120	155*	.9	1.5
413 S.D.A.	1	89	115*	.6	1.1
419 SO BAPT CONV	4	987	1,272*	7.0	12.4
449 UN METHODIST	2	631	813*	4.5	7.9
MC KINLEY	**84**	**4,668**	**19,023***	**31.3**	**100.0**
053 ASSEMB OF GOD	8	426	649	1.1	3.4
081 CATHOLIC	19	NA	7,593	12.5	39.9
081d LATIN	*19*	*NA*	*7,593*	*12.5*	*39.9*
097 CHR CHS&CHS CR	1	52	75*	.1	.4
105 CHRISTIAN REF	11	582	1,084	1.8	5.7
127 CH GOD (CLEVE)	6	411	596*	1.0	3.1
151 L-D SAINTS	8	NA	3,647	6.0	19.2
165 CH OF NAZARENE	3	176	399	.7	2.1
167 CHS OF CHRIST	3	198	240	.4	1.3
171 CH GOD-GEN CON	2	39	57*	.1	.3
179 CONSRV BAPT	1	NR	NR	-	-
193 EPISCOPAL	1	86	95	.2	.5
226 FRIENDS-USA	1	4	9	-	-
226f INDEPENDNT	*1*	*4*	*9*	*-*	*-*
263 INT FOURSQ GOS	1	24	35*	.1	.2
283 LUTH—MO SYNOD	2	103	161	.3	.8
339 PENT CH OF GOD	6	207	461	.8	2.4
349 PENT HOLINESS	1	12	17*	-	.1
355 PRESB CH (USA)	1	69	100*	.2	.5
413 S.D.A.	1	31	45*	.1	.2
419 SO BAPT CONV	6	1,848	2,680*	4.4	14.1
449 UN METHODIST	1	400	580*	1.0	3.0
499 INDEP.NON-CHAR3	1	NA	500	.8	2.6
MORA	**28**	**265**	**4,370***	**102.5**	**100.0**
053 ASSEMB OF GOD	1	51	49	1.1	1.1
081 CATHOLIC	20	NA	4,045	94.9	92.6
081d LATIN	*20*	*NA*	*4,045*	*94.9*	*92.6*
167 CHS OF CHRIST	4	104	134	3.1	3.1
355 PRESB CH (USA)	2	75	97*	2.3	2.2
419 SO BAPT CONV	1	35	45*	1.1	1.0
OTERO	**65**	**10,407**	**38,098***	**73.4**	**100.0**
053 ASSEMB OF GOD	5	667	1,125	2.2	3.0
081 CATHOLIC	6	NA	22,898	44.1	60.1
081d LATIN	*6*	*NA*	*22,898*	*44.1*	*60.1*
093 CHR CH (DISC)	1	60	66	.1	.2
097 CHR CHS&CHS CR	1	115	153*	.3	.4
111 CH CR,SCIENTST	1	NR	NR	-	-
127 CH GOD (CLEVE)	1	61	81*	.2	.2
145 CH GOD PROPHCY	1	22	29*	.1	.1
151 L-D SAINTS	3	NA	898	1.7	2.4
165 CH OF NAZARENE	2	123	206	.4	.5
167 CHS OF CHRIST	12	525	695	1.3	1.8
179 CONSRV BAPT	1	NR	NR	-	-
193 EPISCOPAL	2	156	261	.5	.7
207 E.L.C.A.	1	324	444	.9	1.2
263 INT FOURSQ GOS	1	0	0*	-	-
283 LUTH—MO SYNOD	1	261	348	.7	.9
355 PRESB CH (USA)	1	125	166*	.3	.4
356 PRESB CH AMER	1	92	110	.2	.3
371 REF CH IN AM	1	89	276	.5	.7
413 S.D.A.	1	91	121*	.2	.3
419 SO BAPT CONV	14	5,094	6,772*	13.0	17.8
435 UNITARIAN-UNIV	1	35	36	.1	.1
449 UN METHODIST	7	2,091	2,780*	5.4	7.3
497 BLACK BAPT EST2	NA	476	633*	1.2	1.7
QUAY	**35**	**4,824**	**9,640***	**89.1**	**100.0**
053 ASSEMB OF GOD	4	254	350	3.2	3.6
081 CATHOLIC	4	NA	3,365	31.1	34.9
081d LATIN	*4*	*NA*	*3,365*	*31.1*	*34.9*
097 CHR CHS&CHS CR	1	80	101*	.9	1.0
151 L-D SAINTS	1	NA	156	1.4	1.6
165 CH OF NAZARENE	1	28	12	.1	.1
167 CHS OF CHRIST	7	204	270	2.5	2.8
193 EPISCOPAL	1	17	28	.3	.3
355 PRESB CH (USA)	1	58	73*	.7	.8
413 S.D.A.	1	31	39*	.4	.4
419 SO BAPT CONV	9	3,479	4,396*	40.6	45.6
449 UN METHODIST	5	673	850*	7.9	8.8
RIO ARRIBA	**89**	**1,707**	**25,879***	**75.3**	**100.0**
053 ASSEMB OF GOD	12	537	935	2.7	3.6
081 CATHOLIC	53	NA	22,465	65.4	86.8
081d LATIN	*53*	*NA*	*22,465*	*65.4*	*86.8*
151 L-D SAINTS	2	NA	370	1.1	1.4
167 CHS OF CHRIST	3	111	143	.4	.6
193 EPISCOPAL	2	54	82	.2	.3
263 INT FOURSQ GOS	1	13	17*	-	.1
355 PRESB CH (USA)	4	267	359*	1.0	1.4
371 REF CH IN AM	1	86	299	.9	1.2
413 S.D.A.	3	103	138*	.4	.5
419 SO BAPT CONV	2	241	324*	.9	1.3
449 UN METHODIST	5	295	397*	1.2	1.5
498 INDEP.CHARIS.3	1	NA	350	1.0	1.4
ROOSEVELT	**40**	**7,303**	**13,250***	**79.3**	**100.0**
053 ASSEMB OF GOD	2	153	249	1.5	1.9
081 CATHOLIC	1	NA	3,070	18.4	23.2
081d LATIN	*1*	*NA*	*3,070*	*18.4*	*23.2*
097 CHR CHS&CHS CR	1	200	254*	1.5	1.9
127 CH GOD (CLEVE)	1	21	27*	.2	.2
145 CH GOD PROPHCY	1	22	28*	.2	.2
151 L-D SAINTS	1	NA	222	1.3	1.7
165 CH OF NAZARENE	1	67	98	.6	.7
167 CHS OF CHRIST	9	908	1,156	6.9	8.7
193 EPISCOPAL	1	36	57	.3	.4
355 PRESB CH (USA)	1	90	114*	.7	.9
413 S.D.A.	1	24	30*	.2	.2
419 SO BAPT CONV	15	4,956	6,296*	37.7	47.5
449 UN METHODIST	4	826	1,049*	6.3	7.9
498 INDEP.CHARIS.3	1	NA	600	3.6	4.5
SANDOVAL	**57**	**3,382**	**25,946***	**41.0**	**100.0**
053 ASSEMB OF GOD	4	251	406	.6	1.6
059 BAPT MISS ASSN	1	0	0*	-	-
081 CATHOLIC	22	NA	19,274	30.4	74.3
081d LATIN	*22*	*NA*	*19,274*	*30.4*	*74.3*
097 CHR CHS&CHS CR	2	227	308*	.5	1.2
111 CH CR,SCIENTST	1	NR	NR	-	-
127 CH GOD (CLEVE)	1	17	23*	-	.1
151 L-D SAINTS	6	NA	1,949	3.1	7.5
157 CH OF BRETHREN	1	33	45*	.1	.2
167 CHS OF CHRIST	3	97	159	.3	.6
193 EPISCOPAL	1	81	90	.1	.3
203 EVAN FREE CH	1	86	170	.3	.7
283 LUTH—MO SYNOD	1	193	269	.4	1.0
355 PRESB CH (USA)	4	546	741*	1.2	2.9
413 S.D.A.	1	177	240*	.4	.9
419 SO BAPT CONV	4	789	1,070*	1.7	4.1
443 UN C OF CHRIST	1	329	446*	.7	1.7
449 UN METHODIST	2	317	430*	.7	1.7
469 WELS	1	77	106	.2	.4
497 BLACK BAPT EST2	NA	162	220*	.3	.8
SAN JUAN	**128**	**17,350**	**44,590***	**48.7**	**100.0**
053 ASSEMB OF GOD	11	947	1,559	1.7	3.5
075 BRETHREN IN CR	1	43	43	-	.1
081 CATHOLIC	8	NA	7,181	7.8	16.1
081d LATIN	*8*	*NA*	*7,181*	*7.8*	*16.1*
093 CHR CH (DISC)	1	239	357	.4	.8
097 CHR CHS&CHS CR	3	205	289*	.3	.6
105 CHRISTIAN REF	5	198	351	.4	.8
111 CH CR,SCIENTST	1	NR	NR	-	-
123 CH GOD (ANDER)	2	65	88	.1	.2
127 CH GOD (CLEVE)	5	199	281*	.3	.6
151 L-D SAINTS	23	NA	10,863	11.9	24.4
165 CH OF NAZARENE	3	271	459	.5	1.0
167 CHS OF CHRIST	10	923	1,343	1.5	3.0
179 CONSRV BAPT	1	NR	NR	-	-
193 EPISCOPAL	6	289	678	.7	1.5
203 EVAN FREE CH	1	0	40	-	.1
207 E.L.C.A.	1	288	405	.4	.9
221 FREE METHODIST	8	324	324	.4	.7
263 INT FOURSQ GOS	1	55	78*	.1	.2
283 LUTH—MO SYNOD	1	205	292	.3	.7
285 MENNONITE CH	1	58	58	.1	.1
329 OPEN BIBLE STD	1	NR	NR	-	-
355 PRESB CH (USA)	3	602	850*	.9	1.9
403 SALVATION ARMY	1	47	50	.1	.1
413 S.D.A.	5	518	731*	.8	1.6
419 SO BAPT CONV	16	9,466	13,363*	14.6	30.0
435 UNITARIAN-UNIV	1	15	25	-	.1
449 UN METHODIST	6	2,393	3,378*	3.7	7.6
498 INDEP.CHARIS.3	1	NA	500	.5	1.1
499 INDEP.NON-CHAR3	1	NA	1,004	1.1	2.3
SAN MIGUEL	**48**	**1,347**	**15,639***	**60.8**	**100.0**
053 ASSEMB OF GOD	3	80	131	.5	.8
081 CATHOLIC	30	NA	13,690	53.2	87.5

NA–Not applicable   NR–Not reported   *Total adherents estimated from known number of communicant, confirmed, full members.   - Represents a percent less than 0.1.   Percentages may not total due to rounding.
[1]See Appendix E   [2]See Appendix F   [3]See Appendix G   Lines in *italic* represent a breakdown of Catholic rites or Friends affiliations. They are included in their respective denominational total.

Table 4. Churches and Church Membership by County and Denomination: 1990

County and Denomination		Number of churches	Communicant, confirmed, full members	Total adherents		
				Number	Percent of total population	Percent of total adherents
081d	LATIN	30	NA	13,690	53.2	87.5
093	CHR CH (DISC)	1	60	70	.3	.4
151	L-D SAINTS	1	NA	118	.5	.8
167	CHS OF CHRIST	5	177	268	1.0	1.7
193	EPISCOPAL	1	61	79	.3	.5
207	E.L.C.A.	1	31	35	.1	.2
226	FRIENDS-USA	1	4	10	-	.1
226f	INDEPENDNT	1	4	10	-	.1
283	LUTH—MO SYNOD	1	48	71	.3	.5
355	PRESB CH (USA)	1	129	170*	.7	1.1
419	SO BAPT CONV	2	559	736*	2.9	4.7
449	UN METHODIST	1	198	261*	1.0	1.7
SANTA FE		**74**	**8,672**	**47,849***	**48.4**	**100.0**
053	ASSEMB OF GOD	4	489	643	.6	1.3
081	CATHOLIC	26	NA	33,750	34.1	70.5
081d	LATIN	26	NA	33,750	34.1	70.5
093	CHR CH (DISC)	1	70	99	.1	.2
097	CHR CHS&CHS CR	2	90	113*	.1	.2
111	CH CR,SCIENTST	1	NR	NR	-	-
127	CH GOD (CLEVE)	1	24	30*	-	.1
133	CH GOD(7TH)DEN	1	11	13	-	-
151	L-D SAINTS	3	NA	1,240	1.3	2.6
165	CH OF NAZARENE	1	44	58	.1	.1
167	CHS OF CHRIST	3	180	244	.2	.5
193	EPISCOPAL	2	835	997	1.0	2.1
203	EVAN FREE CH	1	0	0	-	-
207	E.L.C.A.	2	231	320	.3	.7
226	FRIENDS-USA	2	65	77	.1	.2
226f	INDEPENDNT	2	65	77	.1	.2
246	GREEK ORTHODOX	1	NR	NR	-	-
283	LUTH—MO SYNOD	2	264	362	.4	.8
331	ORTH CH IN AM	1	NR	NR	-	-
355	PRESB CH (USA)	2	962	1,212*	1.2	2.5
403	SALVATION ARMY	1	80	88	.1	.2
413	S.D.A.	2	122	154*	.2	.3
419	SO BAPT CONV	7	2,855	3,598*	3.6	7.5
435	UNITARIAN-UNIV	1	213	258	.3	.5
443	UN C OF CHRIST	1	165	208*	.2	.4
449	UN METHODIST	3	1,841	2,320*	2.3	4.8
496	JEWISH EST[1]	1	NA	900	.9	1.9
497	BLACK BAPT EST[2]	NA	131	165*	.2	.3
498	INDEP.CHARIS.[3]	1	NA	600	.6	1.3
499	INDEP.NON-CHAR[3]	1	NA	400	.4	.8
SIERRA		**18**	**1,588**	**4,039***	**40.7**	**100.0**
053	ASSEMB OF GOD	2	95	240	2.4	5.9
081	CATHOLIC	1	NA	1,805	18.2	44.7
081d	LATIN	1	NA	1,805	18.2	44.7
089	CHR & MISS AL	1	0	50	.5	1.2
097	CHR CHS&CHS CR	1	125	148*	1.5	3.7
127	CH GOD (CLEVE)	1	4	5*	.1	.1
151	L-D SAINTS	1	NA	154	1.6	3.8
165	CH OF NAZARENE	1	34	52	.5	1.3
167	CHS OF CHRIST	3	128	160	1.6	4.0
193	EPISCOPAL	2	33	55	.6	1.4
283	LUTH—MO SYNOD	1	77	82	.8	2.0
284	LUTH CH-AM ASC	1	35	35	.4	.9
413	S.D.A.	1	59	70*	.7	1.7
419	SO BAPT CONV	1	633	750*	7.6	18.6
449	UN METHODIST	1	365	433*	4.4	10.7
SOCORRO		**36**	**1,266**	**9,415***	**63.8**	**100.0**
053	ASSEMB OF GOD	2	104	307	2.1	3.3
081	CATHOLIC	15	NA	7,200	48.8	76.5
081d	LATIN	15	NA	7,200	48.8	76.5
133	CH GOD(7TH)DEN	1	11	13	.1	.1
151	L-D SAINTS	1	NA	349	2.4	3.7
165	CH OF NAZARENE	1	20	30	.2	.3
167	CHS OF CHRIST	2	89	115	.8	1.2
193	EPISCOPAL	1	38	50	.3	.5
226	FRIENDS-USA	1	8	14	.1	.1
226f	INDEPENDNT	1	8	14	.1	.1
283	LUTH—MO SYNOD	1	17	22	.1	.2
339	PENT CH OF GOD	1	35	77	.5	.8
355	PRESB CH (USA)	2	130	170*	1.2	1.8
413	S.D.A.	1	42	55*	.4	.6
419	SO BAPT CONV	4	545	715*	4.8	7.6
449	UN METHODIST	3	227	298*	2.0	3.2
TAOS		**57**	**1,747**	**20,379***	**88.2**	**100.0**
053	ASSEMB OF GOD	5	232	324	1.4	1.6
081	CATHOLIC	29	NA	17,525	75.8	86.0
081d	LATIN	29	NA	17,525	75.8	86.0
111	CH CR,SCIENTST	1	NR	NR	-	-
151	L-D SAINTS	3	NA	442	1.9	2.2

County and Denomination		Number of churches	Communicant, confirmed, full members	Total adherents		
				Number	Percent of total population	Percent of total adherents
167	CHS OF CHRIST	4	152	196	.8	1.0
193	EPISCOPAL	1	285	423	1.8	2.1
226	FRIENDS-USA	2	5	13	.1	.1
226f	INDEPENDNT	2	5	13	.1	.1
263	INT FOURSQ GOS	1	191	248*	1.1	1.2
339	PENT CH OF GOD	2	68	153	.7	.8
355	PRESB CH (USA)	3	267	346*	1.5	1.7
413	S.D.A.	2	65	84*	.4	.4
419	SO BAPT CONV	3	391	507*	2.2	2.5
449	UN METHODIST	1	91	118*	.5	.6
TORRANCE		**30**	**2,302**	**5,031***	**48.9**	**100.0**
053	ASSEMB OF GOD	5	229	316	3.1	6.3
081	CATHOLIC	11	NA	1,890	18.4	37.6
081d	LATIN	11	NA	1,890	18.4	37.6
165	CH OF NAZARENE	2	123	195	1.9	3.9
167	CHS OF CHRIST	4	174	268	2.6	5.3
419	SO BAPT CONV	4	1,288	1,713*	16.7	34.0
449	UN METHODIST	4	488	649*	6.3	12.9
UNION		**14**	**1,417**	**3,130***	**75.9**	**100.0**
053	ASSEMB OF GOD	1	45	60	1.5	1.9
081	CATHOLIC	4	NA	1,300	31.5	41.5
081d	LATIN	4	NA	1,300	31.5	41.5
127	CH GOD (CLEVE)	1	29	37*	.9	1.2
167	CHS OF CHRIST	2	114	146	3.5	4.7
413	S.D.A.	1	16	21*	.5	.7
419	SO BAPT CONV	2	643	830*	20.1	26.5
449	UN METHODIST	3	570	736*	17.8	23.5
VALENCIA		**49**	**7,232**	**23,124***	**51.1**	**100.0**
053	ASSEMB OF GOD	5	394	777	1.7	3.4
081	CATHOLIC	12	NA	12,805	28.3	55.4
081d	LATIN	12	NA	12,805	28.3	55.4
097	CHR CHS&CHS CR	3	442	586*	1.3	2.5
111	CH CR,SCIENTST	1	NR	NR	-	-
151	L-D SAINTS	1	NA	606	1.3	2.6
165	CH OF NAZARENE	2	176	138	.3	.6
167	CHS OF CHRIST	3	245	346	.8	1.5
193	EPISCOPAL	1	126	78	.2	.3
207	E.L.C.A.	1	208	313	.7	1.4
283	LUTH—MO SYNOD	1	95	126	.3	.5
355	PRESB CH (USA)	3	332	440*	1.0	1.9
413	S.D.A.	4	239	317*	.7	1.4
419	SO BAPT CONV	9	4,071	5,394*	11.9	23.3
449	UN METHODIST	3	818	1,084*	2.4	4.7
497	BLACK BAPT EST[2]	NA	86	114*	.3	.5

NEW YORK

County and Denomination		Number of churches	Communicant, confirmed, full members	Total adherents		
				Number	Percent of total population	Percent of total adherents
THE STATE.....		10,878	1,974,175	11,813,403*	65.7	100.0
ALBANY		**184**	**32,398**	**217,774***	**74.4**	**100.0**
005	AME ZION	2	2,017	2,723	.9	1.3
019	AMER BAPT USA	8	909	1,094*	.4	.5
053	ASSEMB OF GOD	4	381	695	.2	.3
057	BAPT GEN CONF	1	0	0*	-	-
081	CATHOLIC	47	NA	168,414	57.6	77.3
081d	LATIN	45	NA	167,738	57.3	77.0
081h	UKRAINIAN	2	NA	676	.2	.3
089	CHR & MISS AL	4	319	699	.2	.3
111	CH CR,SCIENTST	2	NR	NR	-	-
127	CH GOD (CLEVE)	1	20	24*	-	-
145	CH GOD PROPHCY	1	54	65*	-	-
151	L-D SAINTS	2	NA	715	.2	.3
165	CH OF NAZARENE	1	41	50	-	-
167	CHS OF CHRIST	1	112	145	-	.1
176	CCC, NOT NAT'L	1	24	29*	-	-
181	CONSRV CONGR	1	99	119*	-	.1
193	EPISCOPAL	12	3,226	4,529	1.5	2.1
195	ESTONIAN ELC	1	47	57*	-	-
203	EVAN FREE CH	1	56	90	-	-
207	E.L.C.A.	8	2,589	3,916	1.3	1.8
226	FRIENDS-USA	1	82	99*	-	-
226d	FGC & FUM	1	82	99*	-	-
246	GREEK ORTHODOX	1	NR	NR	-	-
283	LUTH—MO SYNOD	6	1,806	2,356	.8	1.1
331	ORTH CH IN AM	2	NR	NR	-	-
355	PRESB CH (USA)	15	3,708	4,464*	1.5	2.0
371	REF CH IN AM	21	3,018	6,269	2.1	2.9
403	SALVATION ARMY	2	90	98	-	-

NA–Not applicable   NR–Not reported   *Total adherents estimated from known number of communicant, confirmed, full members.   - Represents a percent less than 0.1.   Percentages may not total due to rounding.
[1]See Appendix E   [2]See Appendix F   [3]See Appendix G   Lines in italic represent a breakdown of Catholic rites or Friends affiliations. They are included in their respective denominational total.

Table 4. Churches and Church Membership by County and Denomination: 1990

County and Denomination	Number of churches	Communicant, confirmed, full members	Total adherents Number	Percent of total population	Percent of total adherents
413 S.D.A.	2	386	465*	.2	.2
435 UNITARIAN-UNIV	1	400	544	.2	.2
443 UN C OF CHRIST	4	613	738*	.3	.3
449 UN METHODIST	20	8,225	9,903*	3.4	4.5
467 WESLEYAN	3	116	337	.1	.2
496 JEWISH EST[1]	7	NA	3,924	1.3	1.8
497 BLACK BAPT EST[2]	NA	4,060	4,888*	1.7	2.2
499 INDEP.NON-CHAR[3]	1	NA	325	.1	.1
ALLEGANY	**99**	**7,425**	**18,388***	**36.4**	**100.0**
019 AMER BAPT USA	6	724	904*	1.8	4.9
053 ASSEMB OF GOD	2	181	223	.4	1.2
081 CATHOLIC	14	NA	6,819	13.5	37.1
081d *LATIN*	*14*	*NA*	*6,819*	*13.5*	*37.1*
089 CHR & MISS AL	3	141	334	.7	1.8
093 CHR CH (DISC)	1	251	440	.9	2.4
097 CHR CHS&CHS CR	3	202	252*	.5	1.4
151 L-D SAINTS	1	NA	181	.4	1.0
167 CHS OF CHRIST	1	26	35	.1	.2
193 EPISCOPAL	7	354	494	1.0	2.7
215 EVAN METH CH	1	19	24*	-	.1
221 FREE METHODIST	1	29	74	.1	.4
226 FRIENDS-USA	1	39	49*	.1	.3
226d *FGC & FUM*	*1*	*39*	*49**	*.1*	*.3*
283 LUTH—MO SYNOD	2	562	675	1.3	3.7
285 MENNONITE CH	4	109	178	.4	1.0
323 OLD ORD AMISH	2	NA	250	.5	1.4
353 CHR BRETHREN	1	20	40	.1	.2
355 PRESB CH (USA)	5	268	335*	.7	1.8
356 PRESB CH AMER	1	29	49	.1	.3
403 SALVATION ARMY	1	73	84	.2	.5
413 S.D.A.	1	49	61*	.1	.3
415 S-D BAPTIST GC	4	360	449*	.9	2.4
419 SO BAPT CONV	1	38	47*	.1	.3
443 UN C OF CHRIST	1	105	131*	.3	.7
449 UN METHODIST	27	3,310	4,131*	8.2	22.5
467 WESLEYAN	6	536	1,409	2.8	7.7
499 INDEP.NON-CHAR[3]	2	NA	720	1.4	3.9
BRONX	**431**	**114,254**	**804,782***	**66.9**	**100.0**
005 AME ZION	11	12,869	15,623	1.3	1.9
019 AMER BAPT USA	28	11,429	14,645*	1.2	1.8
053 ASSEMB OF GOD	38	5,497	7,243	.6	.9
066 BIBLE CH OF CR	2	3,930	5,036*	.4	.6
075 BRETHREN IN CR	1	86	86	-	-
081 CATHOLIC	71	NA	568,814	47.3	70.7
081d *LATIN*	*70*	*NA*	*568,732*	*47.2*	*70.7*
081h *UKRAINIAN*	*1*	*NA*	*82*	*-*	*-*
089 CHR & MISS AL	7	496	582	-	.1
093 CHR CH (DISC)	4	644	835	.1	.1
097 CHR CHS&CHS CR	2	55	70*	-	-
111 CH CR,SCIENTST	1	NR	NR	-	-
123 CH GOD (ANDER)	2	126	129	-	-
127 CH GOD (CLEVE)	22	1,505	1,929*	.2	.2
133 CH GOD(7TH)DEN	1	39	52	-	-
145 CH GOD PROPHCY	3	165	211*	-	-
151 L-D SAINTS	3	NA	917	.1	.1
165 CH OF NAZARENE	3	343	288	-	-
167 CHS OF CHRIST	2	15	30	-	-
179 CONSRV BAPT	1	NR	NR	-	-
181 CONSRV CONGR	2	44	56*	-	-
193 EPISCOPAL	22	4,537	6,950	.6	.9
207 E.L.C.A.	17	2,201	3,538	.3	.4
246 GREEK ORTHODOX	2	NR	NR	-	-
283 LUTH—MO SYNOD	5	679	893	.1	.1
285 MENNONITE CH	5	154	253	-	-
293 MORAV CH-NORTH	1	133	183	-	-
329 OPEN BIBLE STD	2	NR	NR	-	-
331 ORTH CH IN AM	1	NR	NR	-	-
339 PENT CH OF GOD	2	93	175	-	-
353 CHR BRETHREN	3	190	283	-	-
355 PRESB CH (USA)	19	2,910	3,729*	.3	.5
371 REF CH IN AM	5	354	1,001	.1	.1
403 SALVATION ARMY	2	164	200	-	-
413 S.D.A.	18	5,370	6,881*	.6	.9
419 SO BAPT CONV	12	1,042	1,335*	.1	.2
438 UN BRETH IN CR	1	19	28	-	-
443 UN C OF CHRIST	10	1,204	1,543*	.1	.2
449 UN METHODIST	20	4,749	6,085*	.5	.8
467 WESLEYAN	2	25	184	-	-
496 JEWISH EST[1]	75	NA	85,000	7.1	10.6
497 BLACK BAPT EST[2]	NA	53,187	68,155*	5.7	8.5
498 INDEP.CHARIS.[3]	3	NA	1,820	.2	.2
BROOME	**173**	**35,258**	**113,467***	**53.5**	**100.0**
005 AME ZION	1	432	512	.2	.5

County and Denomination	Number of churches	Communicant, confirmed, full members	Total adherents Number	Percent of total population	Percent of total adherents
019 AMER BAPT USA	6	1,328	1,624*	.8	1.4
022 EASTERN ORTH	2	1,603	1,603	.8	1.4
053 ASSEMB OF GOD	3	1,445	2,723	1.3	2.4
081 CATHOLIC	32	NA	64,239	30.3	56.6
081b *BYZAN RUTH*	*1*	*NA*	*1,351*	*.6*	*1.2*
081d *LATIN*	*30*	*NA*	*62,520*	*29.5*	*55.1*
081h *UKRAINIAN*	*1*	*NA*	*368*	*.2*	*.3*
089 CHR & MISS AL	7	292	926	.4	.8
093 CHR CH (DISC)	1	130	160	.1	.1
097 CHR CHS&CHS CR	2	285	349*	.2	.3
105 CHRISTIAN REF	1	139	220	.1	.2
111 CH CR,SCIENTST	1	NR	NR	-	-
145 CH GOD PROPHCY	1	54	66*	-	.1
151 L-D SAINTS	3	NA	810	.4	.7
165 CH OF NAZARENE	2	263	359	.2	.3
167 CHS OF CHRIST	1	115	140	.1	.1
193 EPISCOPAL	9	2,390	3,713	1.8	3.3
203 EVAN FREE CH	1	65	110	.1	.1
207 E.L.C.A.	7	2,434	3,379	1.6	3.0
221 FREE METHODIST	3	116	176	.1	.2
226 FRIENDS-USA	1	11	13*	-	-
226d *FGC & FUM*	*1*	*11*	*13**	*-*	*-*
246 GREEK ORTHODOX	2	NR	NR	-	-
283 LUTH—MO SYNOD	2	533	670	.3	.6
331 ORTH CH IN AM	2	NR	NR	-	-
355 PRESB CH (USA)	17	4,206	5,145*	2.4	4.5
356 PRESB CH AMER	1	16	16	-	-
363 PRIMITIVE METH	1	283	457	.2	.4
403 SALVATION ARMY	1	100	115	.1	.1
413 S.D.A.	2	234	286*	.1	.3
419 SO BAPT CONV	1	281	344*	.2	.3
435 UNITARIAN-UNIV	1	225	280	.1	.2
443 UN C OF CHRIST	7	1,184	1,448*	.7	1.3
449 UN METHODIST	45	16,354	20,005*	9.4	17.6
467 WESLEYAN	2	28	302	.1	.3
496 JEWISH EST[1]	5	NA	2,406	1.1	2.1
497 BLACK BAPT EST[2]	NA	712	871*	.4	.8
CATTARAUGUS	**133**	**11,425**	**40,395***	**48.0**	**100.0**
019 AMER BAPT USA	4	1,236	1,578*	1.9	3.9
053 ASSEMB OF GOD	1	29	60	.1	.1
081 CATHOLIC	29	NA	22,556	26.8	55.8
081b *BYZAN RUTH*	*1*	*NA*	*50*	*.1*	*.1*
081d *LATIN*	*27*	*NA*	*21,354*	*25.4*	*52.9*
081e *MARONITE*	*1*	*NA*	*1,152*	*1.4*	*2.9*
089 CHR & MISS AL	3	134	397	.5	1.0
111 CH CR,SCIENTST	1	NR	NR	-	-
145 CH GOD PROPHCY	1	54	69*	.1	.2
151 L-D SAINTS	1	NA	306	.4	.8
165 CH OF NAZARENE	1	62	69	.1	.2
167 CHS OF CHRIST	1	16	33	-	.1
193 EPISCOPAL	6	643	1,080	1.3	2.7
207 E.L.C.A.	1	129	165	.2	.4
221 FREE METHODIST	9	560	882	1.0	2.2
263 INT FOURSQ GOS	1	45	57*	.1	.1
283 LUTH—MO SYNOD	7	1,666	2,583	3.1	6.4
323 OLD ORD AMISH	8	NA	1,200	1.4	3.0
329 OPEN BIBLE STD	1	NR	NR	-	-
353 CHR BRETHREN	1	35	50	.1	.1
355 PRESB CH (USA)	8	1,449	1,850*	2.2	4.6
403 SALVATION ARMY	2	78	92	.1	.2
413 S.D.A.	4	168	214*	.3	.5
419 SO BAPT CONV	1	46	59*	.1	.1
443 UN C OF CHRIST	4	475	606*	.7	1.5
449 UN METHODIST	31	4,288	5,473*	6.5	13.5
467 WESLEYAN	6	211	767	.9	1.9
496 JEWISH EST[1]	1	NA	120	.1	.3
497 BLACK BAPT EST[2]	NA	101	129*	.2	.3
CAYUGA	**100**	**9,723**	**35,491***	**43.1**	**100.0**
005 AME ZION	1	299	339	.4	1.0
019 AMER BAPT USA	10	1,296	1,640*	2.0	4.6
053 ASSEMB OF GOD	4	174	346	.4	1.0
081 CATHOLIC	24	NA	22,256	27.0	62.7
081d *LATIN*	*23*	*NA*	*21,006*	*25.5*	*59.2*
081h *UKRAINIAN*	*1*	*NA*	*1,250*	*1.5*	*3.5*
089 CHR & MISS AL	2	103	246	.3	.7
093 CHR CH (DISC)	1	160	208	.3	.6
111 CH CR,SCIENTST	1	NR	NR	-	-
127 CH GOD (CLEVE)	1	67	85*	.1	.2
151 L-D SAINTS	1	NA	234	.3	.7
165 CH OF NAZARENE	1	133	161	.2	.5
179 CONSRV BAPT	1	NR	NR	-	-
193 EPISCOPAL	4	428	727	.9	2.0
221 FREE METHODIST	1	21	46	.1	.1
226 FRIENDS-USA	1	72	91*	.1	.3
226d *FGC & FUM*	*1*	*72*	*91**	*.1*	*.3*

NA–Not applicable   NR–Not reported   *Total adherents estimated from known number of communicant, confirmed, full members.   - Represents a percent less than 0.1.   Percentages may not total due to rounding.
[1]See Appendix E   [2]See Appendix F   [3]See Appendix G   Lines in *italic* represent a breakdown of Catholic rites or Friends affiliations. They are included in their respective denominational total.

Table 4. Churches and Church Membership by County and Denomination: 1990

County and Denomination	Number of churches	Communicant, confirmed, full members	Total adherents Number	Percent of total population	Percent of total adherents
283 LUTH—MO SYNOD	1	173	235	.3	.7
331 ORTH CH IN AM	1	NR	NR	-	-
355 PRESB CH (USA)	13	1,579	1,998*	2.4	5.6
371 REF CH IN AM	2	145	298	.4	.8
403 SALVATION ARMY	1	91	106	.1	.3
413 S.D.A.	2	261	330*	.4	.9
419 SO BAPT CONV	1	35	44*	.1	.1
435 UNITARIAN-UNIV	1	30	35	-	.1
443 UN C OF CHRIST	2	109	138*	.2	.4
449 UN METHODIST	22	4,148	5,248*	6.4	14.8
496 JEWISH EST[1]	1	NA	175	.2	.5
497 BLACK BAPT EST[2]	NA	399	505*	.6	1.4
CHAUTAUQUA	**188**	**26,883**	**79,962***	**56.4**	**100.0**
005 AME ZION	1	524	630	.4	.8
007 ALBAN ORTH ARC	1	NR	NR	-	-
011 A.W.M.C.	2	32	40*	-	.1
019 AMER BAPT USA	9	1,182	1,475*	1.0	1.8
053 ASSEMB OF GOD	7	423	695	.5	.9
057 BAPT GEN CONF	3	679	847*	.6	1.1
081 CATHOLIC	26	NA	43,216	30.5	54.0
081d LATIN	26	NA	43,216	30.5	54.0
089 CHR & MISS AL	4	170	288	.2	.4
093 CHR CH (DISC)	1	22	26	-	-
111 CH CR,SCIENTST	3	NR	NR	-	-
123 CH GOD (ANDER)	4	368	430	.3	.5
151 L-D SAINTS	2	NA	560	.4	.7
165 CH OF NAZARENE	3	167	282	.2	.4
167 CHS OF CHRIST	1	42	65	-	.1
181 CONSRV CONGR	4	723	902*	.6	1.1
193 EPISCOPAL	7	1,687	2,204	1.6	2.8
207 E.L.C.A.	13	4,933	6,418	4.5	8.0
221 FREE METHODIST	4	315	485	.3	.6
226 FRIENDS-USA	2	39	49*	-	.1
226d FGC & FUM	2	39	49*	-	.1
246 GREEK ORTHODOX	1	NR	NR	-	-
263 INT FOURSQ GOS	2	75	94*	.1	.1
283 LUTH—MO SYNOD	3	455	587	.4	.7
323 OLD ORD AMISH	4	NA	600	.4	.8
329 OPEN BIBLE STD	1	NR	NR	-	-
353 CHR BRETHREN	1	17	40	-	.1
355 PRESB CH (USA)	8	2,133	2,662*	1.9	3.3
371 REF CH IN AM	2	350	624	.4	.8
403 SALVATION ARMY	2	288	295	.2	.4
413 S.D.A.	2	197	246*	.2	.3
419 SO BAPT CONV	2	251	313*	.2	.4
435 UNITARIAN-UNIV	2	81	135	.1	.2
443 UN C OF CHRIST	3	670	836*	.6	1.0
449 UN METHODIST	49	10,216	12,751*	9.0	15.9
467 WESLEYAN	6	449	1,454	1.0	1.8
496 JEWISH EST[1]	3	NA	220	.2	.3
497 BLACK BAPT EST[2]	NA	395	493*	.3	.6
CHEMUNG	**89**	**16,977**	**52,282***	**54.9**	**100.0**
005 AME ZION	2	683	827	.9	1.6
019 AMER BAPT USA	6	1,456	1,822*	1.9	3.5
053 ASSEMB OF GOD	4	896	1,204	1.3	2.3
081 CATHOLIC	12	NA	27,704	29.1	53.0
081d LATIN	11	NA	27,421	28.8	52.4
081h UKRAINIAN	1	NA	283	.3	.5
089 CHR & MISS AL	2	183	449	.5	.9
093 CHR CH (DISC)	1	115	122	.1	.2
111 CH CR,SCIENTST	1	NR	NR	-	-
151 L-D SAINTS	1	NA	526	.6	1.0
165 CH OF NAZARENE	3	250	533	.6	1.0
167 CHS OF CHRIST	1	62	95	.1	.2
193 EPISCOPAL	6	935	1,655	1.7	3.2
203 EVAN FREE CH	2	94	186	.2	.4
207 E.L.C.A.	3	1,130	1,474	1.5	2.8
221 FREE METHODIST	1	35	62	.1	.1
226 FRIENDS-USA	1	46	58*	.1	.1
226d FGC & FUM	1	46	58*	.1	.1
246 GREEK ORTHODOX	1	NR	NR	-	-
331 ORTH CH IN AM	1	NR	NR	-	-
355 PRESB CH (USA)	6	1,947	2,436*	2.6	4.7
403 SALVATION ARMY	1	96	130	.1	.2
413 S.D.A.	1	282	353*	.4	.7
419 SO BAPT CONV	1	382	478*	.5	.9
435 UNITARIAN-UNIV	1	35	59	.1	.1
443 UN C OF CHRIST	2	960	1,201*	1.3	2.3
449 UN METHODIST	22	6,179	7,732*	8.1	14.8
467 WESLEYAN	5	349	997	1.0	1.9
496 JEWISH EST[1]	2	NA	1,100	1.2	2.1
497 BLACK BAPT EST[2]	NA	862	1,079*	1.1	2.1
CHENANGO	**75**	**8,512**	**17,968***	**34.7**	**100.0**
005 AME ZION	1	179	220	.4	1.2
019 AMER BAPT USA	9	1,545	1,976*	3.8	11.0
053 ASSEMB OF GOD	3	151	328	.6	1.8
081 CATHOLIC	9	NA	6,299	12.2	35.1
081d LATIN	9	NA	6,299	12.2	35.1
089 CHR & MISS AL	2	58	178	.3	1.0
111 CH CR,SCIENTST	1	NR	NR	-	-
151 L-D SAINTS	1	NA	163	.3	.9
167 CHS OF CHRIST	1	10	13	-	.1
176 CCC, NOT NAT'L	2	21	27*	.1	.2
193 EPISCOPAL	9	864	1,387	2.7	7.7
207 E.L.C.A.	1	299	472	.9	2.6
221 FREE METHODIST	1	60	92	.2	.5
226 FRIENDS-USA	1	12	18	-	.1
226d FGC & FUM	1	12	18	-	.1
355 PRESB CH (USA)	3	257	329*	.6	1.8
413 S.D.A.	2	116	148*	.3	.8
419 SO BAPT CONV	2	155	198*	.4	1.1
443 UN C OF CHRIST	6	1,144	1,463*	2.8	8.1
449 UN METHODIST	20	3,641	4,657*	9.0	25.9
496 JEWISH EST[1]	1	NA	0	-	-
CLINTON	**77**	**5,069**	**50,818***	**59.1**	**100.0**
019 AMER BAPT USA	1	148	185*	.2	.4
053 ASSEMB OF GOD	2	218	426	.5	.8
081 CATHOLIC	32	NA	43,000	50.0	84.6
081d LATIN	32	NA	43,000	50.0	84.6
089 CHR & MISS AL	1	47	102	.1	.2
127 CH GOD (CLEVE)	1	30	37*	-	.1
165 CH OF NAZARENE	3	235	401	.5	.8
167 CHS OF CHRIST	1	23	30	-	.1
193 EPISCOPAL	2	516	759	.9	1.5
207 E.L.C.A.	1	81	106	.1	.2
263 INT FOURSQ GOS	1	12	15*	-	-
355 PRESB CH (USA)	6	689	861*	1.0	1.7
403 SALVATION ARMY	1	31	37	-	.1
413 S.D.A.	1	36	45*	.1	.1
419 SO BAPT CONV	1	121	151*	.2	.3
435 UNITARIAN-UNIV	1	46	61	.1	.1
449 UN METHODIST	14	2,092	2,613*	3.0	5.1
467 WESLEYAN	6	245	806	.9	1.6
496 JEWISH EST[1]	1	NA	260	.3	.5
497 BLACK BAPT EST[2]	NA	499	623*	.7	1.2
499 INDEP.NON-CHAR[3]	1	NA	300	.3	.6
COLUMBIA	**80**	**8,672**	**24,098***	**38.3**	**100.0**
005 AME ZION	1	275	323	.5	1.3
019 AMER BAPT USA	2	176	217*	.3	.9
053 ASSEMB OF GOD	2	139	233	.4	1.0
081 CATHOLIC	12	NA	10,287	16.3	42.7
081d LATIN	11	NA	10,219	16.2	42.4
081h UKRAINIAN	1	NA	68	.1	.3
111 CH CR,SCIENTST	1	NR	NR	-	-
151 L-D SAINTS	1	NA	108	.2	.4
167 CHS OF CHRIST	1	10	13	-	.1
181 CONSRV CONGR	1	245	303*	.5	1.3
193 EPISCOPAL	7	843	1,362	2.2	5.7
207 E.L.C.A.	12	1,782	2,441	3.9	10.1
226 FRIENDS-USA	2	38	47*	.1	.2
226d FGC & FUM	2	38	47*	.1	.2
283 LUTH—MO SYNOD	2	268	354	.6	1.5
355 PRESB CH (USA)	4	530	655*	1.0	2.7
371 REF CH IN AM	13	1,320	3,502	5.6	14.5
413 S.D.A.	1	211	261*	.4	1.1
443 UN C OF CHRIST	1	78	96*	.2	.4
449 UN METHODIST	16	2,410	2,978*	4.7	12.4
467 WESLEYAN	1	22	46	.1	.2
496 JEWISH EST[1]	0	NA	470	.7	2.0
497 BLACK BAPT EST[2]	NA	325	402*	.6	1.7
CORTLAND	**51**	**7,447**	**19,290***	**39.4**	**100.0**
019 AMER BAPT USA	4	1,410	1,754*	3.6	9.1
053 ASSEMB OF GOD	2	190	285	.6	1.5
081 CATHOLIC	7	NA	9,248	18.9	47.9
081d LATIN	7	NA	9,248	18.9	47.9
089 CHR & MISS AL	1	33	43	.1	.2
097 CHR CHS&CHS CR	1	27	34*	.1	.2
111 CH CR,SCIENTST	1	NR	NR	-	-
151 L-D SAINTS	1	NA	289	.6	1.5
165 CH OF NAZARENE	1	62	51	.1	.3
167 CHS OF CHRIST	1	6	8	-	-
193 EPISCOPAL	2	344	550	1.1	2.9
207 E.L.C.A.	1	81	109	.2	.6
221 FREE METHODIST	1	36	59	.1	.3
283 LUTH—MO SYNOD	1	178	262	.5	1.4

NA–Not applicable NR–Not reported *Total adherents estimated from known number of communicant, confirmed, full members. - Represents a percent less than 0.1. Percentages may not total due to rounding.

[1]See Appendix E [2]See Appendix F [3]See Appendix G Lines in italic represent a breakdown of Catholic rites or Friends affiliations. They are included in their respective denominational total.

Table 4. Churches and Church Membership by County and Denomination: 1990

County and Denomination	Number of churches	Communicant, confirmed, full members	Total adherents: Number	Total adherents: Percent of total population	Total adherents: Percent of total adherents
353 CHR BRETHREN	1	8	16	-	.1
355 PRESB CH (USA)	4	846	1,052*	2.1	5.5
403 SALVATION ARMY	1	58	61	.1	.3
413 S.D.A.	1	147	183*	.4	.9
419 SO BAPT CONV	1	78	97*	.2	.5
435 UNITARIAN-UNIV	1	17	22	-	.1
443 UN C OF CHRIST	3	998	1,241*	2.5	6.4
449 UN METHODIST	14	2,911	3,620*	7.4	18.8
467 WESLEYAN	1	17	106	.2	.5
496 JEWISH EST[1]	0	NA	200	.4	1.0
DELAWARE	**108**	**9,933**	**17,332***	**36.7**	**100.0**
001 ADVENT CHR CH	1	40	50*	.1	.3
019 AMER BAPT USA	8	813	1,011*	2.1	5.8
053 ASSEMB OF GOD	5	263	638	1.4	3.7
075 BRETHREN IN CR	2	92	95	.2	.5
081 CATHOLIC	15	NA	4,107	8.7	23.7
081b BYZAN RUTH	*1*	*NA*	*200*	*.4*	*1.2*
081d LATIN	*14*	*NA*	*3,907*	*8.3*	*22.5*
089 CHR & MISS AL	4	229	411	.9	2.4
167 CHS OF CHRIST	1	10	13	-	.1
179 CONSRV BAPT	2	NR	NR	-	-
193 EPISCOPAL	10	590	931	2.0	5.4
207 E.L.C.A.	2	343	541	1.1	3.1
221 FREE METHODIST	2	49	78	.2	.5
226 FRIENDS-USA	1	5	9	-	.1
226d FGC & FUM	*1*	*5*	*9*	*-*	*.1*
259 IFCA	1	NR	NR	-	-
283 LUTH—MO SYNOD	1	77	94	.2	.5
355 PRESB CH (USA)	22	2,239	2,785*	5.9	16.1
371 REF CH IN AM	1	129	282	.6	1.6
413 S.D.A.	1	126	157*	.3	.9
419 SO BAPT CONV	2	73	91*	.2	.5
443 UN C OF CHRIST	3	528	657*	1.4	3.8
449 UN METHODIST	23	4,327	5,382*	11.4	31.1
496 JEWISH EST[1]	1	NA	0	-	-
DUTCHESS	**165**	**29,254**	**153,674***	**59.2**	**100.0**
005 AME ZION	3	1,550	1,755	.7	1.1
019 AMER BAPT USA	11	1,925	2,373*	.9	1.5
053 ASSEMB OF GOD	4	660	2,059	.8	1.3
081 CATHOLIC	24	NA	105,628	40.7	68.7
081d LATIN	*23*	*NA*	*104,928*	*40.4*	*68.3*
081f MELKITE-GK	*1*	*NA*	*700*	*.3*	*.5*
089 CHR & MISS AL	4	222	637	.2	.4
097 CHR CHS&CHS CR	1	48	59*	-	-
105 CHRISTIAN REF	1	92	127	-	.1
111 CH CR,SCIENTST	2	NR	NR	-	-
127 CH GOD (CLEVE)	2	20	25*	-	-
151 L-D SAINTS	2	NA	557	.2	.4
165 CH OF NAZARENE	2	255	401	.2	.3
167 CHS OF CHRIST	2	80	104	-	.1
179 CONSRV BAPT	1	NR	NR	-	-
193 EPISCOPAL	24	3,460	4,887	1.9	3.2
203 EVAN FREE CH	1	130	225	.1	.1
207 E.L.C.A.	6	2,023	2,833	1.1	1.8
226 FRIENDS-USA	3	248	306*	.1	.2
226d FGC & FUM	*3*	*248*	*306**	*.1*	*.2*
246 GREEK ORTHODOX	1	NR	NR	-	-
259 IFCA	1	NR	NR	-	-
274 LAT EVAN LUTH	1	65	72	-	-
283 LUTH—MO SYNOD	4	907	1,237	.5	.8
331 ORTH CH IN AM	1	NR	NR	-	-
355 PRESB CH (USA)	14	3,118	3,844*	1.5	2.5
363 PRIMITIVE METH	1	11	17	-	-
371 REF CH IN AM	11	2,472	5,185	2.0	3.4
403 SALVATION ARMY	2	173	187	.1	.1
413 S.D.A.	2	319	393*	.2	.3
419 SO BAPT CONV	1	328	404*	.2	.3
435 UNITARIAN-UNIV	1	129	169	.1	.1
443 UN C OF CHRIST	2	389	480*	.2	.3
449 UN METHODIST	24	7,049	8,690*	3.3	5.7
496 JEWISH EST[1]	6	NA	6,605	2.5	4.3
497 BLACK BAPT EST[2]	NA	3,581	4,415*	1.7	2.9
ERIE	**599**	**133,786**	**768,735***	**79.4**	**100.0**
005 AME ZION	10	11,652	13,909	1.4	1.8
019 AMER BAPT USA	31	9,503	11,647*	1.2	1.5
022 EASTERN ORTH	1	138	138	-	-
053 ASSEMB OF GOD	24	8,699	11,210	1.2	1.5
075 BRETHREN IN CR	1	102	102	-	-
081 CATHOLIC	163	NA	572,878	59.1	74.5
081b BYZAN RUTH	*1*	*NA*	*220*	*-*	*-*
081d LATIN	*158*	*NA*	*570,249*	*58.9*	*74.2*
081e MARONITE	*1*	*NA*	*1,216*	*.1*	*.2*
081h UKRAINIAN	*3*	*NA*	*1,193*	*.1*	*.2*
089 CHR & MISS AL	5	318	658	.1	.1
093 CHR CH (DISC)	8	1,112	1,436	.1	.2
097 CHR CHS&CHS CR	3	420	515*	.1	.1
111 CH CR,SCIENTST	6	NR	NR	-	-
123 CH GOD (ANDER)	1	100	100	-	-
127 CH GOD (CLEVE)	3	291	357*	-	-
145 CH GOD PROPHCY	1	54	66*	-	-
151 L-D SAINTS	6	NA	1,592	.2	.2
165 CH OF NAZARENE	7	305	427	-	.1
167 CHS OF CHRIST	5	545	645	.1	.1
179 CONSRV BAPT	3	NR	NR	-	-
181 CONSRV CONGR	2	255	313*	-	-
193 EPISCOPAL	35	9,160	13,084	1.4	1.7
195 ESTONIAN ELC	1	102	125*	-	-
207 E.L.C.A.	43	15,545	22,459	2.3	2.9
221 FREE METHODIST	5	221	376	-	-
226 FRIENDS-USA	3	172	211*	-	-
226d FGC & FUM	*3*	*172*	*211**	*-*	*-*
246 GREEK ORTHODOX	1	NR	NR	-	-
283 LUTH—MO SYNOD	25	8,661	11,605	1.2	1.5
285 MENNONITE CH	3	318	443	-	.1
313 N AM BAPT CONF	4	700	858*	.1	.1
331 ORTH CH IN AM	2	NR	NR	-	-
353 CHR BRETHREN	7	345	540	.1	.1
355 PRESB CH (USA)	39	13,621	16,694*	1.7	2.2
356 PRESB CH AMER	1	85	88	-	-
403 SALVATION ARMY	4	337	410	-	.1
413 S.D.A.	2	273	335*	-	-
419 SO BAPT CONV	13	1,315	1,612*	.2	.2
431 UKRANIAN AMER	1	NR	NR	-	-
435 UNITARIAN-UNIV	4	871	1,059	.1	.1
443 UN C OF CHRIST	41	11,654	14,283*	1.5	1.9
449 UN METHODIST	53	18,204	22,311*	2.3	2.9
467 WESLEYAN	9	569	2,172	.2	.3
469 WELS	1	82	113	-	-
496 JEWISH EST[1]	19	NA	18,125	1.9	2.4
497 BLACK BAPT EST[2]	NA	18,057	22,131*	2.3	2.9
498 INDEP.CHARIS.[3]	2	NA	3,300	.3	.4
499 INDEP.NON-CHAR[3]	1	NA	408	-	.1
ESSEX	**68**	**5,632**	**24,640***	**66.3**	**100.0**
019 AMER BAPT USA	4	491	606*	1.6	2.5
053 ASSEMB OF GOD	3	133	142	.4	.6
081 CATHOLIC	13	NA	17,000	45.8	69.0
081d LATIN	*13*	*NA*	*17,000*	*45.8*	*69.0*
089 CHR & MISS AL	1	45	114	.3	.5
151 L-D SAINTS	2	NA	338	.9	1.4
165 CH OF NAZARENE	3	151	169	.5	.7
167 CHS OF CHRIST	1	17	22	.1	.1
175 CONGR CHR CHS	1	73	90*	.2	.4
193 EPISCOPAL	9	684	1,006	2.7	4.1
355 PRESB CH (USA)	2	98	121*	.3	.5
371 REF CH IN AM	1	85	271	.7	1.1
419 SO BAPT CONV	1	101	125*	.3	.5
443 UN C OF CHRIST	7	523	646*	1.7	2.6
449 UN METHODIST	20	3,091	3,817*	10.3	15.5
497 BLACK BAPT EST[2]	NA	140	173*	.5	.7
FRANKLIN	**66**	**4,559**	**32,200***	**69.2**	**100.0**
019 AMER BAPT USA	1	80	100*	.2	.3
053 ASSEMB OF GOD	2	71	131	.3	.4
081 CATHOLIC	20	NA	26,000	55.9	80.7
081d LATIN	*20*	*NA*	*26,000*	*55.9*	*80.7*
111 CH CR,SCIENTST	1	NR	NR	-	-
151 L-D SAINTS	1	NA	97	.2	.3
165 CH OF NAZARENE	1	38	83	.2	.3
176 CCC, NOT NAT'L	1	51	64*	.1	.2
193 EPISCOPAL	3	344	481	1.0	1.5
207 E.L.C.A.	1	51	76	.2	.2
221 FREE METHODIST	2	12	48	.1	.1
226 FRIENDS-USA	1	4	5*	-	-
226d FGC & FUM	*1*	*4*	*5**	*-*	*-*
355 PRESB CH (USA)	8	486	608*	1.3	1.9
371 REF CH IN AM	1	127	317	.7	1.0
413 S.D.A.	4	102	128*	.3	.4
419 SO BAPT CONV	4	513	642*	1.4	2.0
443 UN C OF CHRIST	1	392	491*	1.1	1.5
449 UN METHODIST	13	2,004	2,509*	5.4	7.8
467 WESLEYAN	1	52	130	.3	.4
497 BLACK BAPT EST[2]	NA	232	290*	.6	.9
FULTON	**55**	**8,152**	**22,538***	**41.6**	**100.0**
005 AME ZION	2	438	573	1.1	2.5
019 AMER BAPT USA	1	101	126*	.2	.6
053 ASSEMB OF GOD	1	66	110	.2	.5
055 AS REF PRES CH	1	35	50	.1	.2

NA–Not applicable NR–Not reported *Total adherents estimated from known number of communicant, confirmed, full members. - Represents a percent less than 0.1. Percentages may not total due to rounding.
[1]See Appendix E [2]See Appendix F [3]See Appendix G Lines in *italic* represent a breakdown of Catholic rites or Friends affiliations. They are included in their respective denominational total.

Table 4. Churches and Church Membership by County and Denomination: 1990

County and Denomination	Number of churches	Communicant, confirmed, full members	Total adherents Number	Percent of total population	Percent of total adherents
081 CATHOLIC	9	NA	9,468	17.5	42.0
081d LATIN	9	NA	9,468	17.5	42.0
089 CHR & MISS AL	1	0	0	-	-
093 CHR CH (DISC)	1	60	78	.1	.3
111 CH CR,SCIENTST	1	NR	NR	-	-
165 CH OF NAZARENE	1	13	64	.1	.3
167 CHS OF CHRIST	1	37	67	.1	.3
179 CONSRV BAPT	3	NR	NR	-	-
181 CONSRV CONGR	1	59	74*	.1	.3
193 EPISCOPAL	1	200	367	.7	1.6
207 E.L.C.A.	3	860	1,329	2.5	5.9
221 FREE METHODIST	2	89	89	.2	.4
246 GREEK ORTHODOX	1	NR	NR	-	-
355 PRESB CH (USA)	6	1,070	1,336*	2.5	5.9
371 REF CH IN AM	1	163	439	.8	1.9
403 SALVATION ARMY	1	30	30	.1	.1
413 S.D.A.	1	17	21*	-	.1
443 UN C OF CHRIST	1	143	178*	.3	.8
449 UN METHODIST	12	4,643	5,795*	10.7	25.7
467 WESLEYAN	1	42	67	.1	.3
496 JEWISH EST[1]	1	NA	870	1.6	3.9
497 BLACK BAPT EST[2]	NA	86	107*	.2	.5
499 INDEP.NON-CHAR[3]	1	NA	1,300	2.4	5.8
GENESEE	**73**	**10,908**	**39,260***	**65.4**	**100.0**
005 AME ZION	1	308	353	.6	.9
019 AMER BAPT USA	6	1,625	2,059*	3.4	5.2
053 ASSEMB OF GOD	1	194	400	.7	1.0
081 CATHOLIC	17	NA	24,240	40.4	61.7
081d LATIN	17	NA	24,240	40.4	61.7
089 CHR & MISS AL	1	18	70	.1	.2
093 CHR CH (DISC)	1	45	60	.1	.2
111 CH CR,SCIENTST	1	NR	NR	-	-
179 CONSRV BAPT	2	NR	NR	-	-
193 EPISCOPAL	4	749	1,537	2.6	3.9
221 FREE METHODIST	1	160	224	.4	.6
259 IFCA	1	NR	NR	-	-
283 LUTH—MO SYNOD	1	683	869	1.4	2.2
355 PRESB CH (USA)	13	2,753	3,489*	5.8	8.9
403 SALVATION ARMY	1	50	56	.1	.1
413 S.D.A.	4	1,074	1,361*	2.3	3.5
443 UN C OF CHRIST	2	117	148*	.2	.4
449 UN METHODIST	13	2,929	3,712*	6.2	9.5
467 WESLEYAN	1	61	202	.3	.5
496 JEWISH EST[1]	1	NA	0	-	-
497 BLACK BAPT EST[2]	NA	142	180*	.3	.5
499 INDEP.NON-CHAR[3]	1	NA	300	.5	.8
GREENE	**73**	**5,176**	**15,339***	**34.3**	**100.0**
019 AMER BAPT USA	2	87	106*	.2	.7
053 ASSEMB OF GOD	1	27	41	.1	.3
081 CATHOLIC	19	NA	6,568	14.7	42.8
081d LATIN	18	NA	6,478	14.5	42.2
081h UKRAINIAN	1	NA	90	.2	.6
151 L-D SAINTS	1	NA	74	.2	.5
193 EPISCOPAL	6	391	577	1.3	3.8
207 E.L.C.A.	2	387	495	1.1	3.2
221 FREE METHODIST	1	53	77	.2	.5
246 GREEK ORTHODOX	1	NR	NR	-	-
257 HUTTERIAN BR	1	NA	225	.5	1.5
283 LUTH—MO SYNOD	1	275	389	.9	2.5
355 PRESB CH (USA)	3	118	144*	.3	.9
371 REF CH IN AM	8	566	1,690	3.8	11.0
443 UN C OF CHRIST	2	155	189*	.4	1.2
449 UN METHODIST	22	2,711	3,310*	7.4	21.6
467 WESLEYAN	1	49	197	.4	1.3
496 JEWISH EST[1]	2	NA	821	1.8	5.4
497 BLACK BAPT EST[2]	NA	357	436*	1.0	2.8
HAMILTON	**20**	**830**	**3,309***	**62.7**	**100.0**
081 CATHOLIC	7	NA	2,200	41.7	66.5
081d LATIN	7	NA	2,200	41.7	66.5
179 CONSRV BAPT	1	NR	NR	-	-
193 EPISCOPAL	2	26	46	.9	1.4
355 PRESB CH (USA)	1	16	19*	.4	.6
419 SO BAPT CONV	1	50	60*	1.1	1.8
449 UN METHODIST	6	660	789*	14.9	23.8
467 WESLEYAN	2	78	195	3.7	5.9
HERKIMER	**86**	**9,312**	**29,959***	**45.5**	**100.0**
019 AMER BAPT USA	12	1,495	1,869*	2.8	6.2
053 ASSEMB OF GOD	3	226	392	.6	1.3
081 CATHOLIC	19	NA	16,630	25.3	55.5
081d LATIN	18	NA	16,566	25.2	55.3
081h UKRAINIAN	1	NA	64	.1	.2
089 CHR & MISS AL	2	61	100	.2	.3

County and Denomination	Number of churches	Communicant, confirmed, full members	Total adherents Number	Percent of total population	Percent of total adherents
151 L-D SAINTS	1	NA	126	.2	.4
179 CONSRV BAPT	1	NR	NR	-	-
193 EPISCOPAL	5	624	1,104	1.7	3.7
207 E.L.C.A.	5	1,211	1,599	2.4	5.3
221 FREE METHODIST	1	51	91	.1	.3
323 OLD ORD AMISH	1	NA	150	.2	.5
331 ORTH CH IN AM	1	NR	NR	-	-
355 PRESB CH (USA)	4	816	1,020*	1.6	3.4
371 REF CH IN AM	2	444	961	1.5	3.2
403 SALVATION ARMY	1	30	37	.1	.1
413 S.D.A.	1	41	51*	.1	.2
435 UNITARIAN-UNIV	2	145	184	.3	.6
443 UN C OF CHRIST	1	96	120*	.2	.4
449 UN METHODIST	23	4,072	5,090*	7.7	17.0
496 JEWISH EST[1]	1	NA	435	.7	1.5
JEFFERSON	**140**	**14,799**	**48,338***	**43.6**	**100.0**
005 AME ZION	1	37	54	-	.1
019 AMER BAPT USA	10	1,315	1,691*	1.5	3.5
053 ASSEMB OF GOD	5	330	605	.5	1.3
061 BEACHY AMISH	1	20	26*	-	.1
081 CATHOLIC	24	NA	27,000	24.3	55.9
081d LATIN	24	NA	27,000	24.3	55.9
089 CHR & MISS AL	3	113	285	.3	.6
093 CHR CH (DISC)	1	45	60	.1	.1
111 CH CR,SCIENTST	1	NR	NR	-	-
127 CH GOD (CLEVE)	1	29	37*	-	.1
151 L-D SAINTS	1	NA	591	.5	1.2
165 CH OF NAZARENE	3	328	605	.5	1.3
167 CHS OF CHRIST	1	45	65	.1	.1
176 CCC, NOT NAT'L	3	257	331*	.3	.7
179 CONSRV BAPT	1	NR	NR	-	-
193 EPISCOPAL	12	1,485	2,369	2.1	4.9
207 E.L.C.A.	3	584	862	.8	1.8
221 FREE METHODIST	1	67	106	.1	.2
246 GREEK ORTHODOX	1	NR	NR	-	-
285 MENNONITE CH	3	133	283	.3	.6
355 PRESB CH (USA)	10	1,604	2,063*	1.9	4.3
371 REF CH IN AM	1	77	375	.3	.8
403 SALVATION ARMY	1	52	69	.1	.1
413 S.D.A.	2	66	85*	.1	.2
415 S-D BAPTIST GC	1	24	31*	-	.1
419 SO BAPT CONV	4	413	531*	.5	1.1
435 UNITARIAN-UNIV	3	115	142	.1	.3
443 UN C OF CHRIST	5	821	1,056*	1.0	2.2
449 UN METHODIST	35	5,973	7,682*	6.9	15.9
467 WESLEYAN	1	0	50	-	.1
496 JEWISH EST[1]	1	NA	170	.2	.4
497 BLACK BAPT EST[2]	NA	866	1,114*	1.0	2.3
KINGS	**1,147**	**235,332**	**1,539,500***	**66.9**	**100.0**
019 AMER BAPT USA	54	48,917	61,722*	2.7	4.0
053 ASSEMB OF GOD	43	9,262	13,768	.6	.9
057 BAPT GEN CONF	2	95	120*	-	-
081 CATHOLIC	125	NA	807,100	35.1	52.4
081a ARMENIAN	1	NA	320	-	-
081b BYZAN RUTH	2	NA	804	-	.1
081d LATIN	118	NA	802,786	34.9	52.1
081e MARONITE	1	NA	1,116	-	.1
081f MELKITE-GK	1	NA	1,800	.1	.1
081h UKRAINIAN	2	NA	274	-	-
089 CHR & MISS AL	6	461	753	-	-
093 CHR CH (DISC)	23	4,977	6,434	.3	.4
097 CHR CHS&CHS CR	12	461	582*	-	-
105 CHRISTIAN REF	1	52	74	-	-
111 CH CR,SCIENTST	3	NR	NR	-	-
123 CH GOD (ANDER)	8	396	515	-	-
127 CH GOD (CLEVE)	23	2,989	3,771*	.2	.2
133 CH GOD(7TH)DEN	2	80	107	-	-
145 CH GOD PROPHCY	10	549	693*	-	-
151 L-D SAINTS	3	NA	1,941	.1	.1
157 CH OF BRETHREN	1	165	208*	-	-
163 CH OF LUTH BR	1	327	327	-	-
165 CH OF NAZARENE	12	1,553	2,307	.1	.1
167 CHS OF CHRIST	4	529	701	-	-
175 CONGR CHR CHS	4	910	1,148*	-	.1
176 CCC, NOT NAT'L	1	37	47*	-	-
179 CONSRV BAPT	7	NR	NR	-	-
193 EPISCOPAL	35	13,532	20,143	.9	1.3
203 EVAN FREE CH	3	340	425	-	-
207 E.L.C.A.	38	6,391	9,030	.4	.6
217 FIRE BAPTIZED	1	2	3*	-	-
221 FREE METHODIST	4	115	238	-	-
226 FRIENDS-USA	1	227	286*	-	-
226d FGC & FUM	1	227	286*	-	-
246 GREEK ORTHODOX	5	NR	NR	-	-
283 LUTH—MO SYNOD	8	1,371	1,965	.1	.1

NA–Not applicable NR–Not reported *Total adherents estimated from known number of communicant, confirmed, full members. - Represents a percent less than 0.1. Percentages may not total due to rounding.

[1]See Appendix E [2]See Appendix F [3]See Appendix G Lines in *italic* represent a breakdown of Catholic rites or Friends affiliations. They are included in their respective denominational total.

Table 4. Churches and Church Membership by County and Denomination: 1990

County and Denomination	Number of churches	Communicant, confirmed, full members	Total adherents Number	Percent of total population	Percent of total adherents
285 MENNONITE CH	7	228	374	-	-
291 MISSIONARY CH	2	114	121	-	-
293 MORAV CH-NORTH	2	487	945	-	.1
329 OPEN BIBLE STD	2	NR	NR	-	-
331 ORTH CH IN AM	2	NR	NR	-	-
353 CHR BRETHREN	10	1,446	2,115	.1	.1
355 PRESB CH (USA)	26	3,933	4,963*	.2	.3
371 REF CH IN AM	12	696	1,550	.1	.1
375 REF EPISCOPAL	1	6	6	-	-
397 ROMANIAN ORTH	1	NR	NR	-	-
403 SALVATION ARMY	6	687	770	-	.1
413 S.D.A.	36	15,490	19,545*	.8	1.3
415 S-D BAPTIST GC	1	38	48*	-	-
419 SO BAPT CONV	18	1,905	2,404*	.1	.2
435 UNITARIAN-UNIV	3	483	578	-	-
438 UN BRETH IN CR	1	41	43	-	-
443 UN C OF CHRIST	10	1,097	1,384*	.1	.1
449 UN METHODIST	31	11,502	14,513*	.6	.9
467 WESLEYAN	3	203	320	-	-
496 JEWISH EST[1]	526	NA	418,900	18.2	27.2
497 BLACK BAPT EST[2]	NA	103,238	130,263*	5.7	8.5
498 INDEP.CHARIS.[3]	6	NA	3,250	.1	.2
499 INDEP.NON-CHAR[3]	1	NA	3,000	.1	.2
LEWIS	**57**	**4,430**	**21,231***	**79.2**	**100.0**
019 AMER BAPT USA	2	246	324*	1.2	1.5
040 AP CHR CH-AMER	1	73	128	.5	.6
053 ASSEMB OF GOD	1	137	240	.9	1.1
081 CATHOLIC	18	NA	15,000	56.0	70.7
081d LATIN	18	NA	15,000	56.0	70.7
093 CHR CH (DISC)	1	50	65	.2	.3
151 L-D SAINTS	1	NA	157	.6	.7
165 CH OF NAZARENE	1	111	133	.5	.6
176 CCC, NOT NAT'L	1	9	12*	-	.1
193 EPISCOPAL	4	194	550	2.1	2.6
285 MENNONITE CH	7	1,294	1,523	5.7	7.2
286 E.PA MENNONITE	1	52	69*	.3	.3
355 PRESB CH (USA)	2	337	444*	1.7	2.1
371 REF CH IN AM	1	25	79	.3	.4
413 S.D.A.	2	61	80*	.3	.4
443 UN C OF CHRIST	3	129	170*	.6	.8
449 UN METHODIST	11	1,712	2,257*	8.4	10.6
LIVINGSTON	**67**	**7,225**	**25,759***	**41.3**	**100.0**
019 AMER BAPT USA	2	107	133*	.2	.5
053 ASSEMB OF GOD	3	187	341	.5	1.3
081 CATHOLIC	14	NA	14,359	23.0	55.7
081d LATIN	14	NA	14,359	23.0	55.7
093 CHR CH (DISC)	1	31	40	.1	.2
123 CH GOD (ANDER)	1	30	35	.1	.1
151 L-D SAINTS	1	NA	325	.5	1.3
165 CH OF NAZARENE	1	94	177	.3	.7
193 EPISCOPAL	5	549	895	1.4	3.5
207 E.L.C.A.	1	351	463	.7	1.8
221 FREE METHODIST	1	80	96	.2	.4
283 LUTH—MO SYNOD	1	116	134	.2	.5
355 PRESB CH (USA)	16	2,637	3,268*	5.2	12.7
419 SO BAPT CONV	1	88	109*	.2	.4
443 UN C OF CHRIST	2	264	327*	.5	1.3
449 UN METHODIST	15	2,344	2,905*	4.7	11.3
467 WESLEYAN	2	98	412	.7	1.6
496 JEWISH EST[1]	0	NA	1,431	2.3	5.6
497 BLACK BAPT EST[2]	NA	249	309*	.5	1.2
MADISON	**71**	**10,417**	**28,877***	**41.8**	**100.0**
019 AMER BAPT USA	11	1,896	2,369*	3.4	8.2
053 ASSEMB OF GOD	2	180	312	.5	1.1
081 CATHOLIC	8	NA	14,428	20.9	50.0
081d LATIN	8	NA	14,428	20.9	50.0
089 CHR & MISS AL	1	53	93	.1	.3
111 CH CR,SCIENTST	1	NR	NR	-	-
151 L-D SAINTS	1	NA	310	.4	1.1
165 CH OF NAZARENE	1	68	58	.1	.2
176 CCC, NOT NAT'L	1	106	132*	.2	.5
193 EPISCOPAL	5	706	925	1.3	3.2
221 FREE METHODIST	2	99	151	.2	.5
226 FRIENDS-USA	1	27	34*	-	.1
226d FGC & FUM	1	27	34*	-	.1
259 IFCA	1	NR	NR	-	-
283 LUTH—MO SYNOD	1	195	275	.4	1.0
355 PRESB CH (USA)	6	1,418	1,772*	2.6	6.1
403 SALVATION ARMY	1	50	56	.1	.2
415 S-D BAPTIST GC	1	31	39*	.1	.1
443 UN C OF CHRIST	3	385	481*	.7	1.7
449 UN METHODIST	24	5,079	6,346*	9.2	22.0
496 JEWISH EST[1]	0	NA	941	1.4	3.3

County and Denomination	Number of churches	Communicant, confirmed, full members	Total adherents Number	Percent of total population	Percent of total adherents
497 BLACK BAPT EST[2]	NA	124	155*	.2	.5
MONROE	**376**	**94,489**	**382,171***	**53.5**	**100.0**
005 AME ZION	2	1,205	1,338	.2	.4
007 ALBAN ORTH ARC	1	NR	NR	-	-
019 AMER BAPT USA	31	12,794	15,938*	2.2	4.2
039 AP CHR CH(NAZ)	1	41	51*	-	-
053 ASSEMB OF GOD	14	2,265	4,520	.6	1.2
081 CATHOLIC	78	NA	233,718	32.7	61.2
081d LATIN	75	NA	231,248	32.4	60.5
081f MELKITE-GK	1	NA	252	-	.1
081h UKRAINIAN	2	NA	2,218	.3	.6
089 CHR & MISS AL	2	184	322	-	.1
093 CHR CH (DISC)	2	184	188	-	-
097 CHR CHS&CHS CR	2	83	103*	-	-
105 CHRISTIAN REF	2	468	744	.1	.2
111 CH CR,SCIENTST	4	NR	NR	-	-
123 CH GOD (ANDER)	1	0	0	-	-
127 CH GOD (CLEVE)	6	330	411*	.1	.1
145 CH GOD PROPHCY	1	54	67*	-	-
151 L-D SAINTS	7	NA	2,641	.4	.7
164 CH LUTH CONF	1	49	60	-	-
165 CH OF NAZARENE	5	911	1,412	.2	.4
167 CHS OF CHRIST	7	1,045	1,518	.2	.4
193 EPISCOPAL	22	6,675	10,395	1.5	2.7
203 EVAN FREE CH	1	24	70	-	-
207 E.L.C.A.	19	9,121	12,210	1.7	3.2
221 FREE METHODIST	8	1,241	1,624	.2	.4
226 FRIENDS-USA	1	138	172*	-	-
226d FGC & FUM	1	138	172*	-	-
246 GREEK ORTHODOX	1	NR	NR	-	-
259 IFCA	2	NR	NR	-	-
263 INT FOURSQ GOS	2	155	193*	-	.1
274 LAT EVAN LUTH	1	144	161	-	-
283 LUTH—MO SYNOD	14	5,844	8,459	1.2	2.2
285 MENNONITE CH	1	24	25	-	-
313 N AM BAPT CONF	2	321	400*	.1	.1
331 ORTH CH IN AM	1	NR	NR	-	-
349 PENT HOLINESS	1	60	75*	-	-
353 CHR BRETHREN	2	194	338	-	.1
355 PRESB CH (USA)	34	14,461	18,015*	2.5	4.7
371 REF CH IN AM	4	747	1,259	.2	.3
403 SALVATION ARMY	2	214	276	-	.1
413 S.D.A.	6	1,420	1,769*	.2	.5
419 SO BAPT CONV	6	445	554*	.1	.1
435 UNITARIAN-UNIV	2	930	1,253	.2	.3
443 UN C OF CHRIST	17	5,884	7,330*	1.0	1.9
449 UN METHODIST	33	12,459	15,521*	2.2	4.1
467 WESLEYAN	5	357	992	.1	.3
469 WELS	1	39	58	-	-
496 JEWISH EST[1]	14	NA	16,382	2.3	4.3
497 BLACK BAPT EST[2]	NA	13,979	17,414*	2.4	4.6
498 INDEP.CHARIS.[3]	3	NA	1,425	.2	.4
499 INDEP.NON-CHAR[3]	4	NA	2,770	.4	.7
MONTGOMERY	**69**	**7,174**	**32,585***	**62.7**	**100.0**
005 AME ZION	1	27	34	.1	.1
019 AMER BAPT USA	1	280	348*	.7	1.1
053 ASSEMB OF GOD	3	210	360	.7	1.1
081 CATHOLIC	13	NA	20,618	39.7	63.3
081d LATIN	12	NA	20,489	39.4	62.9
081h UKRAINIAN	1	NA	129	.2	.4
089 CHR & MISS AL	2	68	159	.3	.5
145 CH GOD PROPHCY	1	54	67*	.1	.2
151 L-D SAINTS	1	NA	276	.5	.8
176 CCC, NOT NAT'L	1	12	15*	-	-
193 EPISCOPAL	2	318	458	.9	1.4
207 E.L.C.A.	7	2,037	3,136	6.0	9.6
259 IFCA	1	NR	NR	-	-
285 MENNONITE CH	1	18	29	.1	.1
323 OLD ORD AMISH	1	NA	150	.3	.5
355 PRESB CH (USA)	3	610	757*	1.5	2.3
371 REF CH IN AM	14	1,051	2,371	4.6	7.3
435 UNITARIAN-UNIV	1	25	25	-	.1
443 UN C OF CHRIST	1	99	123*	.2	.4
449 UN METHODIST	13	2,365	2,937*	5.7	9.0
496 JEWISH EST[1]	2	NA	722	1.4	2.2
NASSAU	**519**	**97,173**	**1,100,639***	**85.5**	**100.0**
005 AME ZION	10	7,373	8,216	.6	.7
019 AMER BAPT USA	8	1,973	2,372*	.2	.2
022 EASTERN ORTH	1	82	82	-	-
053 ASSEMB OF GOD	15	1,512	2,354	.2	.2
057 BAPT GEN CONF	2	176	212*	-	-
081 CATHOLIC	68	NA	662,155	51.4	60.2
081b BYZAN RUTH	1	NA	200	-	-

NA–Not applicable   NR–Not reported   *Total adherents estimated from known number of communicant, confirmed, full members.   - Represents a percent less than 0.1.   Percentages may not total due to rounding.
[1]See Appendix E   [2]See Appendix F   [3]See Appendix G   Lines in *italic* represent a breakdown of Catholic rites or Friends affiliations. They are included in their respective denominational total.

Table 4. Churches and Church Membership by County and Denomination: 1990

County and Denomination	Number of churches	Communicant, confirmed, full members	Total adherents Number	Percent of total population	Percent of total adherents
081d *LATIN*	66	NA	661,494	51.4	60.1
081h *UKRAINIAN*	1	NA	461	-	-
089 CHR & MISS AL	5	89	207	-	-
093 CHR CH (DISC)	1	80	104	-	-
097 CHR CHS&CHS CR	5	297	357*	-	-
111 CH CR,SCIENTST	13	NR	NR	-	-
123 CH GOD (ANDER)	2	107	182	-	-
127 CH GOD (CLEVE)	3	160	192*	-	-
133 CH GOD(7TH)DEN	1	39	52	-	-
145 CH GOD PROPHCY	4	220	265*	-	-
151 L-D SAINTS	3	NA	1,003	.1	.1
165 CH OF NAZARENE	8	616	1,257	.1	.1
167 CHS OF CHRIST	3	263	338	-	-
179 CONSRV BAPT	7	NR	NR	-	-
181 CONSRV CONGR	1	59	71*	-	-
193 EPISCOPAL	43	15,473	21,850	1.7	2.0
203 EVAN FREE CH	3	228	257	-	-
207 E.L.C.A.	37	14,581	19,942	1.5	1.8
220 FREE LUTHERAN	1	83	95	-	-
221 FREE METHODIST	1	0	23	-	-
226 FRIENDS-USA	5	416	500*	-	-
226d *FGC & FUM*	5	416	500*	-	-
246 GREEK ORTHODOX	7	NR	NR	-	-
263 INT FOURSQ GOS	1	0	0*	-	-
283 LUTH—MO SYNOD	10	4,183	5,535	.4	.5
284 LUTH CH-AM ASC	2	87	97	-	-
313 N AM BAPT CONF	1	65	78*	-	-
331 ORTH CH IN AM	3	NR	NR	-	-
353 CHR BRETHREN	3	175	255	-	-
355 PRESB CH (USA)	22	4,957	5,960*	.5	.5
371 REF CH IN AM	10	1,481	3,122	.2	.3
403 SALVATION ARMY	2	286	319	-	-
413 S.D.A.	12	2,083	2,504*	.2	.2
419 SO BAPT CONV	2	107	129*	-	-
431 UKRANIAN AMER	1	NR	NR	-	-
435 UNITARIAN-UNIV	4	1,008	1,317	.1	.1
443 UN C OF CHRIST	10	3,335	4,010*	.3	.4
449 UN METHODIST	40	17,324	20,829*	1.6	1.9
496 JEWISH EST[1]	137	NA	311,700	24.2	28.3
497 BLACK BAPT EST[2]	NA	18,255	21,948*	1.7	2.0
498 INDEP.CHARIS.[3]	1	NA	350	-	-
499 INDEP.NON-CHAR[3]	1	NA	400	-	-
NEW YORK	**669**	**217,124**	**1,137,816***	**76.5**	**100.0**
005 AME ZION	19	62,581	80,018	5.4	7.0
019 AMER BAPT USA	43	25,892	29,827*	2.0	2.6
022 EASTERN ORTH	2	389	389	-	-
049 ARMEN AP CH AM	1	800	10,000	.7	.9
053 ASSEMB OF GOD	39	4,230	16,288	1.1	1.4
057 BAPT GEN CONF	1	114	131*	-	-
081 CATHOLIC	101	NA	564,969	38.0	49.7
081a *ARMENIAN*	1	NA	6,050	.4	.5
081d *LATIN*	99	NA	556,719	37.4	48.9
081h *UKRAINIAN*	1	NA	2,200	.1	.2
089 CHR & MISS AL	8	903	1,050	.1	.1
093 CHR CH (DISC)	7	754	869	.1	.1
097 CHR CHS&CHS CR	7	145	167*	-	-
105 CHRISTIAN REF	1	56	80	-	-
111 CH CR,SCIENTST	10	NR	NR	-	-
123 CH GOD (ANDER)	4	478	478	-	-
127 CH GOD (CLEVE)	7	768	885*	.1	.1
145 CH GOD PROPHCY	2	110	127*	-	-
151 L-D SAINTS	4	NA	1,995	.1	.2
165 CH OF NAZARENE	4	318	194	-	-
167 CHS OF CHRIST	10	2,995	4,175	.3	.4
179 CONSRV BAPT	2	NR	NR	-	-
193 EPISCOPAL	45	16,123	23,627	1.6	2.1
195 ESTONIAN ELC	1	650	749*	.1	.1
207 E.L.C.A.	20	3,848	5,248	.4	.5
221 FREE METHODIST	1	74	100	-	-
226 FRIENDS-USA	2	337	388*	-	-
226d *FGC & FUM*	2	337	388*	-	-
246 GREEK ORTHODOX	11	NR	NR	-	-
283 LUTH—MO SYNOD	4	694	1,434	.1	.1
285 MENNONITE CH	3	61	144	-	-
287 MENN GEN CONF	1	0	0	-	-
293 MORAV CH-NORTH	2	720	1,309	.1	.1
331 ORTH CH IN AM	4	NR	NR	-	-
353 CHR BRETHREN	2	67	102	-	-
355 PRESB CH (USA)	28	9,585	11,042*	.7	1.0
356 PRESB CH AMER	1	160	162	-	-
371 REF CH IN AM	6	6,127	11,447	.8	1.0
375 REF EPISCOPAL	1	86	114	-	-
397 ROMANIAN ORTH	1	NR	NR	-	-
403 SALVATION ARMY	4	438	475	-	-
413 S.D.A.	18	5,540	6,382*	.4	.6
419 SO BAPT CONV	9	1,125	1,296*	.1	.1

County and Denomination	Number of churches	Communicant, confirmed, full members	Total adherents Number	Percent of total population	Percent of total adherents
423 SYRIAN ANTIOCH	1	NA	600	-	.1
431 UKRANIAN AMER	1	NR	NR	-	-
435 UNITARIAN-UNIV	3	1,761	2,014	.1	.2
443 UN C OF CHRIST	11	3,276	3,774*	.3	.3
449 UN METHODIST	24	12,137	13,982*	.9	1.2
469 WELS	1	36	46	-	-
496 JEWISH EST[1]	188	NA	274,300	18.4	24.1
497 BLACK BAPT EST[2]	NA	53,746	61,914*	4.2	5.4
498 INDEP.CHARIS.[3]	2	NA	4,200	.3	.4
499 INDEP.NON-CHAR[3]	2	NA	1,325	.1	.1
NIAGARA	**192**	**36,839**	**146,137***	**66.2**	**100.0**
005 AME ZION	1	620	667	.3	.5
019 AMER BAPT USA	11	1,805	2,249*	1.0	1.5
049 ARMEN AP CH AM	1	200	600	.3	.4
053 ASSEMB OF GOD	6	744	1,315	.6	.9
081 CATHOLIC	36	NA	93,869	42.5	64.2
081d *LATIN*	35	NA	93,818	42.5	64.2
081h *UKRAINIAN*	1	NA	51	-	-
089 CHR & MISS AL	3	288	693	.3	.5
093 CHR CH (DISC)	2	423	519	.2	.4
111 CH CR,SCIENTST	2	NR	NR	-	-
127 CH GOD (CLEVE)	2	227	283*	.1	.2
151 L-D SAINTS	3	NA	663	.3	.5
163 CH OF LUTH BR	1	10	149	.1	.1
165 CH OF NAZARENE	5	305	540	.2	.4
167 CHS OF CHRIST	3	163	234	.1	.2
193 EPISCOPAL	11	2,507	4,292	1.9	2.9
207 E.L.C.A.	13	3,963	5,424	2.5	3.7
221 FREE METHODIST	6	378	511	.2	.3
226 FRIENDS-USA	1	10	12*	-	-
226d *FGC & FUM*	1	10	12*	-	-
283 LUTH—MO SYNOD	20	8,641	12,044	5.5	8.2
331 ORTH CH IN AM	1	NR	NR	-	-
353 CHR BRETHREN	2	165	325	.1	.2
355 PRESB CH (USA)	14	4,355	5,426*	2.5	3.7
403 SALVATION ARMY	2	158	180	.1	.1
413 S.D.A.	3	157	196*	.1	.1
419 SO BAPT CONV	4	216	269*	.1	.2
435 UNITARIAN-UNIV	1	69	73	-	-
443 UN C OF CHRIST	9	2,054	2,559*	1.2	1.8
449 UN METHODIST	23	7,265	9,051*	4.1	6.2
467 WESLEYAN	2	126	515	.2	.4
496 JEWISH EST[1]	2	NA	400	.2	.3
497 BLACK BAPT EST[2]	NA	1,990	2,479*	1.1	1.7
498 INDEP.CHARIS.[3]	2	NA	600	.3	.4
ONEIDA	**232**	**30,393**	**143,147***	**57.1**	**100.0**
005 AME ZION	1	619	697	.3	.5
019 AMER BAPT USA	15	2,634	3,258*	1.3	2.3
053 ASSEMB OF GOD	5	594	1,093	.4	.8
081 CATHOLIC	59	NA	99,142	39.5	69.3
081d *LATIN*	55	NA	96,554	38.5	67.5
081e *MARONITE*	1	NA	2,103	.8	1.5
081f *MELKITE-GK*	1	NA	200	.1	.1
081h *UKRAINIAN*	2	NA	285	.1	.2
089 CHR & MISS AL	3	275	702	.3	.5
097 CHR CHS&CHS CR	1	0	0*	-	-
111 CH CR,SCIENTST	1	NR	NR	-	-
151 L-D SAINTS	2	NA	523	.2	.4
165 CH OF NAZARENE	2	83	100	-	.1
167 CHS OF CHRIST	2	143	193	.1	.1
179 CONSRV BAPT	3	NR	NR	-	-
193 EPISCOPAL	19	2,171	3,620	1.4	2.5
207 E.L.C.A.	4	1,661	2,300	.9	1.6
221 FREE METHODIST	1	17	18	-	-
226 FRIENDS-USA	1	20	25*	-	-
226d *FGC & FUM*	1	20	25*	-	-
263 INT FOURSQ GOS	1	90	111*	-	.1
283 LUTH—MO SYNOD	4	2,122	4,224	1.7	3.0
293 MORAV CH-NORTH	1	148	185	.1	.1
331 ORTH CH IN AM	1	NR	NR	-	-
355 PRESB CH (USA)	27	4,474	5,533*	2.2	3.9
371 REF CH IN AM	1	124	276	.1	.2
403 SALVATION ARMY	2	190	217	.1	.2
413 S.D.A.	5	321	397*	.2	.3
415 S-D BAPTIST GC	2	153	189*	.1	.1
419 SO BAPT CONV	6	803	993*	.4	.7
435 UNITARIAN-UNIV	2	171	229	.1	.2
443 UN C OF CHRIST	9	1,212	1,499*	.6	1.0
449 UN METHODIST	45	9,953	12,309*	4.9	8.6
467 WESLEYAN	3	169	676	.3	.5
496 JEWISH EST[1]	4	NA	1,860	.7	1.3
497 BLACK BAPT EST[2]	NA	2,246	2,778*	1.1	1.9

NA–Not applicable   NR–Not reported   *Total adherents estimated from known number of communicant, confirmed, full members.   - Represents a percent less than 0.1.   Percentages may not total due to rounding.
[1] See Appendix E   [2] See Appendix F   [3] See Appendix G   Lines in *italic* represent a breakdown of Catholic rites or Friends affiliations. They are included in their respective denominational total.

Table 4. Churches and Church Membership by County and Denomination: 1990

County and Denomination	Number of churches	Communicant, confirmed, full members	Total adherents		
			Number	Percent of total population	Percent of total adherents
ONONDAGA	**299**	**60,651**	**250,156***	**53.3**	**100.0**
005 AME ZION	3	859	1,036	.2	.4
019 AMER BAPT USA	22	6,019	7,491*	1.6	3.0
039 AP CHR CH(NAZ)	1	68	85*	-	-
049 ARMEN AP CH AM	1	150	450	.1	.2
053 ASSEMB OF GOD	11	1,440	2,414	.5	1.0
081 CATHOLIC	59	NA	159,183	33.9	63.6
081d *LATIN*	58	*NA*	*157,583*	*33.6*	*63.0*
081h *UKRAINIAN*	1	*NA*	*1,600*	*.3*	*.6*
089 CHR & MISS AL	4	622	1,305	.3	.5
093 CHR CH (DISC)	2	90	141	-	.1
097 CHR CHS&CHS CR	4	383	477*	.1	.2
105 CHRISTIAN REF	1	75	134	-	.1
111 CH CR,SCIENTST	2	NR	NR	-	-
127 CH GOD (CLEVE)	3	292	363*	.1	.1
145 CH GOD PROPHCY	1	54	67*	-	-
151 L-D SAINTS	3	NA	963	.2	.4
165 CH OF NAZARENE	3	352	611	.1	.2
167 CHS OF CHRIST	3	275	378	.1	.2
175 CONGR CHR CHS	1	128	159*	-	.1
179 CONSRV BAPT	3	NR	NR	-	-
193 EPISCOPAL	22	4,818	7,127	1.5	2.8
195 ESTONIAN ELC	1	32	40*	-	-
207 E.L.C.A.	13	5,591	7,642	1.6	3.1
221 FREE METHODIST	3	83	161	-	.1
226 FRIENDS-USA	1	140	174*	-	.1
226d *FGC & FUM*	1	*140*	*174*	-	*.1*
246 GREEK ORTHODOX	1	NR	NR	-	-
263 INT FOURSQ GOS	1	35	44*	-	-
274 LAT EVAN LUTH	2	263	282	.1	.1
283 LUTH—MO SYNOD	1	381	478	.1	.2
285 MENNONITE CH	1	11	24	-	-
329 OPEN BIBLE STD	1	NR	NR	-	-
331 ORTH CH IN AM	2	NR	NR	-	-
353 CHR BRETHREN	1	8	16	-	-
355 PRESB CH (USA)	25	5,806	7,226*	1.5	2.9
371 REF CH IN AM	2	389	646	.1	.3
403 SALVATION ARMY	1	176	193	-	.1
413 S.D.A.	4	731	910*	.2	.4
419 SO BAPT CONV	6	1,093	1,360*	.3	.5
435 UNITARIAN-UNIV	2	586	842	.2	.3
443 UN C OF CHRIST	7	1,461	1,818*	.4	.7
449 UN METHODIST	53	21,716	27,027*	5.8	10.8
467 WESLEYAN	5	281	1,619	.3	.6
469 WELS	1	42	57	-	-
496 JEWISH EST[1]	12	NA	6,396	1.4	2.6
497 BLACK BAPT EST[2]	NA	6,201	7,717*	1.6	3.1
498 INDEP.CHARIS.[3]	2	NA	1,550	.3	.6
499 INDEP.NON-CHAR[3]	2	NA	1,550	.3	.6
ONTARIO	**88**	**13,464**	**48,204***	**50.7**	**100.0**
019 AMER BAPT USA	9	1,191	1,488*	1.6	3.1
053 ASSEMB OF GOD	3	156	243	.3	.5
081 CATHOLIC	13	NA	25,161	26.5	52.2
081d *LATIN*	13	*NA*	*25,161*	*26.5*	*52.2*
089 CHR & MISS AL	2	32	92	.1	.2
097 CHR CHS&CHS CR	1	50	62*	.1	.1
111 CH CR,SCIENTST	1	NR	NR	-	-
127 CH GOD (CLEVE)	2	57	71*	.1	.1
151 L-D SAINTS	3	NA	828	.9	1.7
165 CH OF NAZARENE	1	61	81	.1	.2
179 CONSRV BAPT	2	NR	NR	-	-
193 EPISCOPAL	5	1,032	1,533	1.6	3.2
207 E.L.C.A.	2	511	736	.8	1.5
226 FRIENDS-USA	1	182	227*	.2	.5
226d *FGC & FUM*	1	*182*	*227*	*.2*	*.5*
259 IFCA	1	NR	NR	-	-
283 LUTH—MO SYNOD	2	591	939	1.0	1.9
355 PRESB CH (USA)	8	2,251	2,813*	3.0	5.8
403 SALVATION ARMY	2	166	189	.2	.4
413 S.D.A.	1	40	50*	.1	.1
419 SO BAPT CONV	2	118	147*	.2	.3
443 UN C OF CHRIST	7	1,341	1,676*	1.8	3.5
449 UN METHODIST	17	5,313	6,639*	7.0	13.8
467 WESLEYAN	1	90	195	.2	.4
496 JEWISH EST[1]	1	NA	2,482	2.6	5.1
497 BLACK BAPT EST[2]	NA	282	352*	.4	.7
498 INDEP.CHARIS.[3]	1	NA	2,200	2.3	4.6
ORANGE	**202**	**30,426**	**177,371***	**57.7**	**100.0**
005 AME ZION	4	2,038	2,713	.9	1.5
019 AMER BAPT USA	5	867	1,114*	.4	.6
053 ASSEMB OF GOD	9	958	1,638	.5	.9
081 CATHOLIC	29	NA	123,461	40.1	69.6
081d *LATIN*	28	*NA*	*123,366*	*40.1*	*69.6*
081h *UKRAINIAN*	1	*NA*	*95*	-	*.1*

County and Denomination	Number of churches	Communicant, confirmed, full members	Total adherents		
			Number	Percent of total population	Percent of total adherents
089 CHR & MISS AL	1	59	78	-	-
093 CHR CH (DISC)	1	160	208	.1	.1
105 CHRISTIAN REF	1	325	550	.2	.3
111 CH CR,SCIENTST	2	NR	NR	-	-
123 CH GOD (ANDER)	1	65	65	-	-
127 CH GOD (CLEVE)	3	363	466*	.2	.3
145 CH GOD PROPHCY	2	110	141*	-	.1
151 L-D SAINTS	3	NA	731	.2	.4
165 CH OF NAZARENE	3	148	361	.1	.2
167 CHS OF CHRIST	3	114	155	.1	.1
179 CONSRV BAPT	5	NR	NR	-	-
181 CONSRV CONGR	2	230	295*	.1	.2
193 EPISCOPAL	19	2,635	4,041	1.3	2.3
203 EVAN FREE CH	2	35	65	-	-
207 E.L.C.A.	5	1,452	2,303	.7	1.3
216 EVAN PRESBY CH	1	98	112	-	.1
226 FRIENDS-USA	1	39	50*	-	-
226d *FGC & FUM*	1	*39*	*50*	-	-
246 GREEK ORTHODOX	2	NR	NR	-	-
263 INT FOURSQ GOS	1	38	49*	-	-
283 LUTH—MO SYNOD	4	1,478	2,461	.8	1.4
331 ORTH CH IN AM	1	NR	NR	-	-
355 PRESB CH (USA)	26	5,052	6,490*	2.1	3.7
356 PRESB CH AMER	1	131	160	.1	.1
371 REF CH IN AM	8	1,198	2,795	.9	1.6
403 SALVATION ARMY	3	230	264	.1	.1
413 S.D.A.	3	322	414*	.1	.2
419 SO BAPT CONV	2	337	433*	.1	.2
423 SYRIAN ANTIOCH	1	NA	400	.1	.2
435 UNITARIAN-UNIV	2	68	101	-	.1
443 UN C OF CHRIST	4	678	871*	.3	.5
449 UN METHODIST	28	7,545	9,693*	3.2	5.5
496 JEWISH EST[1]	14	NA	10,000	3.3	5.6
497 BLACK BAPT EST[2]	NA	3,653	4,693*	1.5	2.6
ORLEANS	**49**	**6,747**	**23,235***	**55.5**	**100.0**
005 AME ZION	1	75	83	.2	.4
019 AMER BAPT USA	5	708	900*	2.2	3.9
053 ASSEMB OF GOD	3	358	663	1.6	2.9
081 CATHOLIC	8	NA	12,975	31.0	55.8
081d *LATIN*	8	*NA*	*12,975*	*31.0*	*55.8*
089 CHR & MISS AL	2	52	122	.3	.5
123 CH GOD (ANDER)	1	60	60	.1	.3
193 EPISCOPAL	3	367	622	1.5	2.7
207 E.L.C.A.	3	649	827	2.0	3.6
221 FREE METHODIST	1	74	141	.3	.6
283 LUTH—MO SYNOD	1	171	218	.5	.9
313 N AM BAPT CONF	1	60	76*	.2	.3
323 OLD ORD AMISH	1	NA	150	.4	.6
355 PRESB CH (USA)	5	1,146	1,456*	3.5	6.3
435 UNITARIAN-UNIV	1	37	58	.1	.2
443 UN C OF CHRIST	1	62	79*	.2	.3
449 UN METHODIST	11	2,419	3,074*	7.3	13.2
467 WESLEYAN	1	56	195	.5	.8
496 JEWISH EST[1]	0	NA	960	2.3	4.1
497 BLACK BAPT EST[2]	NA	453	576*	1.4	2.5
OSWEGO	**124**	**14,621**	**45,972***	**37.8**	**100.0**
019 AMER BAPT USA	8	1,266	1,625*	1.3	3.5
053 ASSEMB OF GOD	5	285	514	.4	1.1
081 CATHOLIC	23	NA	23,306	19.1	50.7
081d *LATIN*	23	*NA*	*23,306*	*19.1*	*50.7*
089 CHR & MISS AL	3	383	994	.8	2.2
097 CHR CHS&CHS CR	4	220	282*	.2	.6
111 CH CR,SCIENTST	1	NR	NR	-	-
151 L-D SAINTS	2	NA	507	.4	1.1
165 CH OF NAZARENE	2	152	313	.3	.7
167 CHS OF CHRIST	1	73	131	.1	.3
193 EPISCOPAL	5	699	948	.8	2.1
207 E.L.C.A.	2	800	1,166	1.0	2.5
221 FREE METHODIST	1	24	62	.1	.1
283 LUTH—MO SYNOD	1	71	91	.1	.2
355 PRESB CH (USA)	7	464	596*	.5	1.3
403 SALVATION ARMY	2	184	193	.2	.4
413 S.D.A.	3	231	297*	.2	.6
435 UNITARIAN-UNIV	1	60	65	.1	.1
443 UN C OF CHRIST	7	789	1,013*	.8	2.2
449 UN METHODIST	38	8,551	10,976*	9.0	23.9
467 WESLEYAN	7	267	1,099	.9	2.4
496 JEWISH EST[1]	1	NA	1,663	1.4	3.6
497 BLACK BAPT EST[2]	NA	102	131*	.1	.3
OTSEGO	**95**	**10,534**	**22,592***	**37.3**	**100.0**
019 AMER BAPT USA	7	1,035	1,266*	2.1	5.6
053 ASSEMB OF GOD	3	157	245	.4	1.1
081 CATHOLIC	11	NA	8,820	14.6	39.0

NA–Not applicable   NR–Not reported   *Total adherents estimated from known number of communicant, confirmed, full members.   - Represents a percent less than 0.1.   Percentages may not total due to rounding.
[1]See Appendix E   [2]See Appendix F   [3]See Appendix G   Lines in *italic* represent a breakdown of Catholic rites or Friends affiliations. They are included in their respective denominational total.

Table 4. Churches and Church Membership by County and Denomination: 1990

County and Denomination	Number of churches	Communicant, confirmed, full members	Total adherents Number	Percent of total population	Percent of total adherents
081d LATIN	11	NA	8,820	14.6	39.0
105 CHRISTIAN REF	1	75	136	.2	.6
111 CH CR,SCIENTST	1	NR	NR	-	-
151 L-D SAINTS	1	NA	218	.4	1.0
167 CHS OF CHRIST	1	33	42	.1	.2
179 CONSRV BAPT	4	NR	NR	-	-
193 EPISCOPAL	10	1,243	1,594	2.6	7.1
207 E.L.C.A.	4	703	1,052	1.7	4.7
226 FRIENDS-USA	2	12	17	-	.1
226d FGC & FUM	2	12	17	-	.1
353 CHR BRETHREN	1	22	40	.1	.2
355 PRESB CH (USA)	13	1,720	2,104*	3.5	9.3
403 SALVATION ARMY	1	55	69	.1	.3
413 S.D.A.	1	43	53*	.1	.2
435 UNITARIAN-UNIV	2	192	272	.4	1.2
449 UN METHODIST	31	5,136	6,282*	10.4	27.8
496 JEWISH EST[1]	1	NA	250	.4	1.1
497 BLACK BAPT EST[2]	NA	108	132*	.2	.6
PUTNAM	**45**	**5,783**	**51,480***	**61.3**	**100.0**
001 ADVENT CHR CH	1	10	13*	-	-
005 AME ZION	1	282	339	.4	.7
019 AMER BAPT USA	4	881	1,105*	1.3	2.1
053 ASSEMB OF GOD	2	122	207	.2	.4
081 CATHOLIC	5	NA	42,676	50.8	82.9
081d LATIN	5	NA	42,676	50.8	82.9
167 CHS OF CHRIST	1	28	36	-	.1
179 CONSRV BAPT	2	NR	NR	-	-
193 EPISCOPAL	5	661	1,040	1.2	2.0
207 E.L.C.A.	1	635	977	1.2	1.9
246 GREEK ORTHODOX	1	NR	NR	-	-
283 LUTH—MO SYNOD	1	367	578	.7	1.1
355 PRESB CH (USA)	5	632	793*	.9	1.5
413 S.D.A.	3	227	285*	.3	.6
449 UN METHODIST	8	1,798	2,255*	2.7	4.4
496 JEWISH EST[1]	5	NA	1,000	1.2	1.9
497 BLACK BAPT EST[2]	NA	140	176*	.2	.3
QUEENS	**703**	**147,994**	**1,242,861***	**63.7**	**100.0**
005 AME ZION	4	5,444	7,247	.4	.6
007 ALBAN ORTH ARC	1	NR	NR	-	-
019 AMER BAPT USA	33	11,970	14,311*	.7	1.2
039 AP CHR CH(NAZ)	1	57	68*	-	-
049 ARMEN AP CH AM	1	500	3,000	.2	.2
053 ASSEMB OF GOD	20	3,269	5,199	.3	.4
080 BYELORSSN ORTH	1	NR	NR	-	-
081 CATHOLIC	107	NA	731,454	37.5	58.9
081b BYZAN RUTH	2	NA	800	-	.1
081d LATIN	101	NA	729,072	37.4	58.7
081g ROMANIAN	1	NA	322	-	-
081h UKRAINIAN	3	NA	1,260	.1	.1
089 CHR & MISS AL	13	724	1,492	.1	.1
093 CHR CH (DISC)	2	170	220	-	-
097 CHR CHS&CHS CR	4	201	240*	-	-
105 CHRISTIAN REF	1	40	52	-	-
111 CH CR,SCIENTST	6	NR	NR	-	-
123 CH GOD (ANDER)	6	588	638	-	.1
127 CH GOD (CLEVE)	12	1,144	1,368*	.1	.1
145 CH GOD PROPHCY	2	110	132*	-	-
151 L-D SAINTS	5	NA	1,315	.1	.1
165 CH OF NAZARENE	13	794	1,069	.1	.1
167 CHS OF CHRIST	8	407	556	-	-
175 CONGR CHR CHS	1	241	288*	-	-
179 CONSRV BAPT	6	NR	NR	-	-
193 EPISCOPAL	33	10,585	13,741	.7	1.1
195 ESTONIAN ELC	1	297	355*	-	-
203 EVAN FREE CH	1	65	85	-	-
207 E.L.C.A.	38	7,023	9,666	.5	.8
221 FREE METHODIST	1	10	29	-	-
226 FRIENDS-USA	1	39	47*	-	-
226d FGC & FUM	1	39	47*	-	-
246 GREEK ORTHODOX	9	NR	NR	-	-
259 IFCA	1	NR	NR	-	-
263 INT FOURSQ GOS	1	0	0*	-	-
283 LUTH—MO SYNOD	23	4,254	6,256	.3	.5
285 MENNONITE CH	1	51	130	-	-
293 MORAV CH-NORTH	1	156	280	-	-
313 N AM BAPT CONF	2	233	279*	-	-
331 ORTH CH IN AM	2	NR	NR	-	-
353 CHR BRETHREN	4	375	495	-	-
355 PRESB CH (USA)	34	4,800	5,739*	.3	.5
356 PRESB CH AMER	3	530	637	-	.1
371 REF CH IN AM	25	2,531	4,989	.3	.4
397 ROMANIAN ORTH	2	NR	NR	-	-
403 SALVATION ARMY	5	258	299	-	-
413 S.D.A.	23	6,563	7,846*	.4	.6
419 SO BAPT CONV	19	3,820	4,567*	.2	.4

County and Denomination	Number of churches	Communicant, confirmed, full members	Total adherents Number	Percent of total population	Percent of total adherents
431 UKRANIAN AMER	1	NR	NR	-	-
435 UNITARIAN-UNIV	2	131	156	-	-
443 UN C OF CHRIST	15	2,380	2,845*	.1	.2
449 UN METHODIST	27	8,594	10,275*	.5	.8
467 WESLEYAN	1	73	125	-	-
496 JEWISH EST[1]	179	NA	321,200	16.5	25.8
497 BLACK BAPT EST[2]	NA	69,567	83,171*	4.3	6.7
498 INDEP.CHARIS.[3]	1	NA	1,000	.1	.1
RENSSELAER	**147**	**17,632**	**74,747***	**48.4**	**100.0**
005 AME ZION	1	656	741	.5	1.0
019 AMER BAPT USA	8	1,253	1,545*	1.0	2.1
049 ARMEN AP CH AM	1	200	600	.4	.8
053 ASSEMB OF GOD	4	232	350	.2	.5
057 BAPT GEN CONF	1	32	39*	-	.1
081 CATHOLIC	36	NA	46,819	30.3	62.6
081d LATIN	34	NA	46,325	30.0	62.0
081e MARONITE	1	NA	366	.2	.5
081h UKRAINIAN	1	NA	128	.1	.2
089 CHR & MISS AL	3	134	331	.2	.4
093 CHR CH (DISC)	2	82	124	.1	.2
097 CHR CHS&CHS CR	1	30	37*	-	-
111 CH CR,SCIENTST	1	NR	NR	-	-
123 CH GOD (ANDER)	1	24	47	-	.1
145 CH GOD PROPHCY	1	54	67*	-	.1
167 CHS OF CHRIST	1	10	13	-	-
179 CONSRV BAPT	3	NR	NR	-	-
193 EPISCOPAL	12	1,017	1,796	1.2	2.4
207 E.L.C.A.	11	2,500	3,689	2.4	4.9
246 GREEK ORTHODOX	1	NR	NR	-	-
283 LUTH—MO SYNOD	1	220	306	.2	.4
355 PRESB CH (USA)	10	1,764	2,175*	1.4	2.9
371 REF CH IN AM	8	1,325	2,833	1.8	3.8
403 SALVATION ARMY	1	85	105	.1	.1
415 S-D BAPTIST GC	1	71	88*	.1	.1
443 UN C OF CHRIST	4	441	544*	.4	.7
449 UN METHODIST	27	6,636	8,181*	5.3	10.9
467 WESLEYAN	1	16	25	-	-
496 JEWISH EST[1]	5	NA	2,944	1.9	3.9
497 BLACK BAPT EST[2]	NA	850	1,048*	.7	1.4
498 INDEP.CHARIS.[3]	1	NA	300	.2	.4
RICHMOND	**141**	**20,092**	**299,380***	**79.0**	**100.0**
005 AME ZION	2	637	819	.2	.3
019 AMER BAPT USA	2	558	692*	.2	.2
053 ASSEMB OF GOD	6	1,085	1,614	.4	.5
081 CATHOLIC	36	NA	240,619	63.5	80.4
081d LATIN	35	NA	240,449	63.4	80.3
081h UKRAINIAN	1	NA	170	-	.1
097 CHR CHS&CHS CR	1	43	53*	-	-
111 CH CR,SCIENTST	2	NR	NR	-	-
127 CH GOD (CLEVE)	1	41	51*	-	-
145 CH GOD PROPHCY	1	54	67*	-	-
151 L-D SAINTS	1	NA	243	.1	.1
163 CH OF LUTH BR	1	46	121	-	-
165 CH OF NAZARENE	1	11	33	-	-
167 CHS OF CHRIST	2	90	126	-	-
175 CONGR CHR CHS	1	114	141*	-	-
179 CONSRV BAPT	2	NR	NR	-	-
193 EPISCOPAL	10	2,208	3,123	.8	1.0
203 EVAN FREE CH	3	266	323	.1	.1
207 E.L.C.A.	9	2,887	4,082	1.1	1.4
226 FRIENDS-USA	1	7	9*	-	-
226d FGC & FUM	1	7	9*	-	-
246 GREEK ORTHODOX	1	NR	NR	-	-
283 LUTH—MO SYNOD	2	697	909	.2	.3
285 MENNONITE CH	1	0	30	-	-
293 MORAV CH-NORTH	4	984	1,363	.4	.5
331 ORTH CH IN AM	1	NR	NR	-	-
353 CHR BRETHREN	1	25	65	-	-
355 PRESB CH (USA)	4	767	952*	.3	.3
371 REF CH IN AM	5	509	1,091	.3	.4
403 SALVATION ARMY	2	57	66	-	-
413 S.D.A.	3	414	514*	.1	.2
419 SO BAPT CONV	3	516	640*	.2	.2
423 SYRIAN ANTIOCH	1	NA	600	.2	.2
435 UNITARIAN-UNIV	1	114	154	-	.1
443 UN C OF CHRIST	3	360	447*	.1	.1
449 UN METHODIST	9	2,567	3,185*	.8	1.1
496 JEWISH EST[1]	18	NA	31,000	8.2	10.4
497 BLACK BAPT EST[2]	NA	5,035	6,248*	1.6	2.1
ROCKLAND	**172**	**17,269**	**193,211***	**72.8**	**100.0**
005 AME ZION	8	1,640	2,221	.8	1.1
019 AMER BAPT USA	1	57	71*	-	-
053 ASSEMB OF GOD	5	280	500	.2	.3

NA–Not applicable   NR–Not reported   *Total adherents estimated from known number of communicant, confirmed, full members.   - Represents a percent less than 0.1.   Percentages may not total due to rounding.
[1]See Appendix E   [2]See Appendix F   [3]See Appendix G   Lines in *italic* represent a breakdown of Catholic rites or Friends affiliations. They are included in their respective denominational total.

Table 4. Churches and Church Membership by County and Denomination: 1990

County and Denomination	Number of churches	Communicant, confirmed, full members	Total adherents Number	Percent of total population	Percent of total adherents
081 CATHOLIC	19	NA	109,153	41.1	56.5
081d LATIN	18	NA	109,015	41.1	56.4
081h UKRAINIAN	1	NA	138	.1	.1
089 CHR & MISS AL	9	496	1,225	.5	.6
097 CHR CHS&CHS CR	1	20	25*	-	-
105 CHRISTIAN REF	1	49	70	-	-
111 CH CR,SCIENTST	2	NR	NR	-	-
127 CH GOD (CLEVE)	4	472	590*	.2	.3
145 CH GOD PROPHCY	1	54	67*	-	-
163 CH OF LUTH BR	1	42	112	-	.1
165 CH OF NAZARENE	1	24	56	-	-
179 CONSRV BAPT	2	NR	NR	-	-
181 CONSRV CONGR	1	46	57*	-	-
193 EPISCOPAL	10	1,494	2,122	.8	1.1
203 EVAN FREE CH	1	110	175	.1	.1
207 E.L.C.A.	4	1,973	2,633	1.0	1.4
226 FRIENDS-USA	1	51	64*	-	-
226d FGC & FUM	1	51	64*	-	-
246 GREEK ORTHODOX	1	NR	NR	-	-
283 LUTH—MO SYNOD	1	111	123	-	.1
331 ORTH CH IN AM	2	NR	NR	-	-
355 PRESB CH (USA)	12	1,812	2,264*	.9	1.2
371 REF CH IN AM	6	548	1,395	.5	.7
403 SALVATION ARMY	1	102	103	-	.1
413 S.D.A.	6	682	852*	.3	.4
419 SO BAPT CONV	1	116	145*	.1	.1
435 UNITARIAN-UNIV	1	80	115	-	.1
443 UN C OF CHRIST	1	186	232*	.1	.1
449 UN METHODIST	15	2,438	3,046*	1.1	1.6
467 WESLEYAN	1	35	33	-	-
496 JEWISH EST[1]	51	NA	60,000	22.6	31.1
497 BLACK BAPT EST[2]	NA	4,351	5,437*	2.0	2.8
498 INDEP.CHARIS.[3]	1	NA	325	.1	.2
ST LAWRENCE	**166**	**13,070**	**61,776***	**55.2**	**100.0**
001 ADVENT CHR CH	1	53	66*	.1	.1
019 AMER BAPT USA	4	433	539*	.5	.9
053 ASSEMB OF GOD	4	167	302	.3	.5
081 CATHOLIC	35	NA	43,000	38.4	69.6
081d LATIN	35	NA	43,000	38.4	69.6
111 CH CR,SCIENTST	1	NR	NR	-	-
133 CH GOD(7TH)DEN	1	40	53	-	.1
151 L-D SAINTS	1	NA	321	.3	.5
165 CH OF NAZARENE	3	194	219	.2	.4
167 CHS OF CHRIST	2	52	68	.1	.1
176 CCC, NOT NAT'L	2	88	109*	.1	.2
179 CONSRV BAPT	1	NR	NR	-	-
181 CONSRV CONGR	1	50	62*	.1	.1
193 EPISCOPAL	9	1,049	1,806	1.6	2.9
221 FREE METHODIST	1	25	39	-	.1
226 FRIENDS-USA	1	7	18	-	-
226d FGC & FUM	1	7	18	-	-
283 LUTH—MO SYNOD	1	100	121	.1	.2
323 OLD ORD AMISH	4	NA	600	.5	1.0
353 CHR BRETHREN	1	68	136	.1	.2
355 PRESB CH (USA)	19	2,597	3,231*	2.9	5.2
403 SALVATION ARMY	2	82	91	.1	.1
413 S.D.A.	2	99	123*	.1	.2
419 SO BAPT CONV	9	782	973*	.9	1.6
435 UNITARIAN-UNIV	1	278	363	.3	.6
443 UN C OF CHRIST	8	1,027	1,278*	1.1	2.1
449 UN METHODIST	38	5,356	6,663*	6.0	10.8
467 WESLEYAN	11	307	936	.8	1.5
496 JEWISH EST[1]	3	NA	390	.3	.6
497 BLACK BAPT EST[2]	NA	216	269*	.2	.4
SARATOGA	**112**	**18,956**	**68,099***	**37.6**	**100.0**
005 AME ZION	1	186	229	.1	.3
019 AMER BAPT USA	7	1,573	1,971*	1.1	2.9
053 ASSEMB OF GOD	4	163	258	.1	.4
055 AS REF PRES CH	1	149	205	.1	.3
057 BAPT GEN CONF	1	453	568*	.3	.8
059 BAPT MISS ASSN	2	93	117*	.1	.2
081 CATHOLIC	16	NA	37,133	20.5	54.5
081d LATIN	16	NA	37,133	20.5	54.5
089 CHR & MISS AL	2	236	565	.3	.8
111 CH CR,SCIENTST	1	NR	NR	-	-
151 L-D SAINTS	1	NA	409	.2	.6
165 CH OF NAZARENE	2	67	397	.2	.6
167 CHS OF CHRIST	2	116	172	.1	.3
193 EPISCOPAL	9	2,767	4,153	2.3	6.1
207 E.L.C.A.	3	518	810	.4	1.2
221 FREE METHODIST	2	52	67	-	.1
226 FRIENDS-USA	2	115	144*	.1	.2
226d FGC & FUM	2	115	144*	.1	.2
259 IFCA	1	NR	NR	-	-
283 LUTH—MO SYNOD	1	424	573	.3	.8

County and Denomination	Number of churches	Communicant, confirmed, full members	Total adherents Number	Percent of total population	Percent of total adherents
331 ORTH CH IN AM	1	NR	NR	-	-
355 PRESB CH (USA)	8	1,554	1,947*	1.1	2.9
356 PRESB CH AMER	1	122	195	.1	.3
371 REF CH IN AM	4	514	1,116	.6	1.6
403 SALVATION ARMY	1	54	62	-	.1
413 S.D.A.	3	146	183*	.1	.3
443 UN C OF CHRIST	1	88	110*	.1	.2
449 UN METHODIST	24	8,938	11,199*	6.2	16.4
467 WESLEYAN	3	142	495	.3	.7
469 WELS	1	112	156	.1	.2
496 JEWISH EST[1]	3	NA	3,016	1.7	4.4
497 BLACK BAPT EST[2]	NA	374	469*	.3	.7
498 INDEP.CHARIS.[3]	1	NA	300	.2	.4
499 INDEP.NON-CHAR[3]	3	NA	1,080	.6	1.6
SCHENECTADY	**111**	**20,393**	**86,017***	**57.6**	**100.0**
005 AME ZION	1	498	654	.4	.8
019 AMER BAPT USA	8	1,481	1,810*	1.2	2.1
053 ASSEMB OF GOD	2	147	304	.2	.4
059 BAPT MISS ASSN	2	68	83*	.1	.1
081 CATHOLIC	21	NA	49,219	33.0	57.2
081d LATIN	21	NA	49,219	33.0	57.2
111 CH CR,SCIENTST	1	NR	NR	-	-
127 CH GOD (CLEVE)	1	80	98*	.1	.1
151 L-D SAINTS	2	NA	652	.4	.8
165 CH OF NAZARENE	1	98	132	.1	.2
167 CHS OF CHRIST	1	100	123	.1	.1
181 CONSRV CONGR	2	482	589*	.4	.7
193 EPISCOPAL	6	1,341	2,180	1.5	2.5
207 E.L.C.A.	5	1,933	2,665	1.8	3.1
226 FRIENDS-USA	2	64	78*	.1	.1
226d FGC & FUM	2	64	78*	.1	.1
246 GREEK ORTHODOX	1	NR	NR	-	-
274 LAT EVAN LUTH	1	75	78	.1	.1
283 LUTH—MO SYNOD	3	1,396	1,811	1.2	2.1
353 CHR BRETHREN	1	73	90	.1	.1
355 PRESB CH (USA)	6	1,401	1,712*	1.1	2.0
356 PRESB CH AMER	2	557	626	.4	.7
371 REF CH IN AM	13	3,381	6,066	4.1	7.1
403 SALVATION ARMY	1	152	175	.1	.2
413 S.D.A.	2	110	134*	.1	.2
415 S-D BAPTIST GC	1	31	38*	-	-
419 SO BAPT CONV	1	318	389*	.3	.5
435 UNITARIAN-UNIV	1	489	639	.4	.7
443 UN C OF CHRIST	2	120	147*	.1	.2
449 UN METHODIST	15	4,955	6,057*	4.1	7.0
496 JEWISH EST[1]	4	NA	7,273	4.9	8.5
497 BLACK BAPT EST[2]	NA	1,043	1,275*	.9	1.5
498 INDEP.CHARIS.[3]	2	NA	920	.6	1.1
SCHOHARIE	**57**	**5,966**	**11,372***	**35.7**	**100.0**
019 AMER BAPT USA	2	156	192*	.6	1.7
053 ASSEMB OF GOD	1	41	91	.3	.8
081 CATHOLIC	5	NA	2,549	8.0	22.4
081d LATIN	5	NA	2,549	8.0	22.4
089 CHR & MISS AL	1	35	89	.3	.8
111 CH CR,SCIENTST	1	NR	NR	-	-
151 L-D SAINTS	1	NA	331	1.0	2.9
176 CCC, NOT NAT'L	1	16	20*	.1	.2
193 EPISCOPAL	2	91	126	.4	1.1
207 E.L.C.A.	7	1,640	2,465	7.7	21.7
221 FREE METHODIST	1	10	15	-	.1
355 PRESB CH (USA)	4	370	455*	1.4	4.0
371 REF CH IN AM	5	349	923	2.9	8.1
419 SO BAPT CONV	1	37	46*	.1	.4
443 UN C OF CHRIST	2	57	70*	.2	.6
449 UN METHODIST	22	3,128	3,850*	12.1	33.9
467 WESLEYAN	1	36	150	.5	1.3
SCHUYLER	**30**	**3,119**	**7,358***	**39.4**	**100.0**
019 AMER BAPT USA	6	718	912*	4.9	12.4
053 ASSEMB OF GOD	1	40	82	.4	1.1
081 CATHOLIC	2	NA	2,972	15.9	40.4
081d LATIN	2	NA	2,972	15.9	40.4
165 CH OF NAZARENE	1	37	135	.7	1.8
193 EPISCOPAL	3	323	419	2.2	5.7
226 FRIENDS-USA	1	19	24*	.1	.3
226d FGC & FUM	1	19	24*	.1	.3
355 PRESB CH (USA)	5	467	593*	3.2	8.1
449 UN METHODIST	10	1,469	1,866*	10.0	25.4
467 WESLEYAN	1	46	355	1.9	4.8
SENECA	**37**	**3,910**	**13,083***	**38.8**	**100.0**
019 AMER BAPT USA	1	145	182*	.5	1.4
053 ASSEMB OF GOD	3	122	199	.6	1.5
081 CATHOLIC	4	NA	7,539	22.4	57.6

NA–Not applicable NR–Not reported *Total adherents estimated from known number of communicant, confirmed, full members. - Represents a percent less than 0.1. Percentages may not total due to rounding.
[1]See Appendix E [2]See Appendix F [3]See Appendix G Lines in *italic* represent a breakdown of Catholic rites or Friends affiliations. They are included in their respective denominational total.

Table 4. Churches and Church Membership by County and Denomination: 1990

County and Denomination	Number of churches	Communicant, confirmed, full members	Total adherents Number	Percent of total population	Percent of total adherents
081d *LATIN*	4	NA	7,539	22.4	57.6
097 CHR CHS&CHS CR	1	64	80*	.2	.6
165 CH OF NAZARENE	1	45	58	.2	.4
179 CONSRV BAPT	2	NR	NR	-	-
193 EPISCOPAL	4	457	678	2.0	5.2
283 LUTH—MO SYNOD	2	364	520	1.5	4.0
286 E.PA MENNONITE	1	55	69*	.2	.5
323 OLD ORD AMISH	1	NA	150	.4	1.1
355 PRESB CH (USA)	8	912	1,144*	3.4	8.7
371 REF CH IN AM	2	248	541	1.6	4.1
443 UN C OF CHRIST	1	83	104*	.3	.8
449 UN METHODIST	5	1,305	1,637*	4.9	12.5
467 WESLEYAN	1	38	92	.3	.7
497 BLACK BAPT EST[2]	NA	72	90*	.3	.7
STEUBEN	**138**	**15,872**	**44,512***	**44.9**	**100.0**
019 AMER BAPT USA	13	1,943	2,472*	2.5	5.6
022 EASTERN ORTH	1	121	121	.1	.3
053 ASSEMB OF GOD	6	407	865	.9	1.9
081 CATHOLIC	18	NA	21,864	22.1	49.1
081d *LATIN*	17	NA	21,850	22.1	49.1
081h *UKRAINIAN*	1	NA	14	-	-
089 CHR & MISS AL	4	336	425	.4	1.0
097 CHR CHS&CHS CR	1	99	126*	.1	.3
111 CH CR,SCIENTST	1	NR	NR	-	-
127 CH GOD (CLEVE)	1	28	36*	-	.1
151 L-D SAINTS	2	NA	299	.3	.7
165 CH OF NAZARENE	2	145	298	.3	.7
179 CONSRV BAPT	1	NR	NR	-	-
193 EPISCOPAL	6	955	1,988	2.0	4.5
207 E.L.C.A.	2	290	432	.4	1.0
221 FREE METHODIST	1	42	80	.1	.2
283 LUTH—MO SYNOD	2	233	306	.3	.7
285 MENNONITE CH	3	164	301	.3	.7
323 OLD ORD AMISH	3	NA	450	.5	1.0
355 PRESB CH (USA)	16	2,374	3,020*	3.0	6.8
403 SALVATION ARMY	2	139	143	.1	.3
413 S.D.A.	2	165	210*	.2	.5
435 UNITARIAN-UNIV	1	26	35	-	.1
443 UN C OF CHRIST	5	625	795*	.8	1.8
449 UN METHODIST	37	6,980	8,881*	9.0	20.0
467 WESLEYAN	7	646	1,169	1.2	2.6
496 JEWISH EST[1]	1	NA	0	-	-
497 BLACK BAPT EST[2]	NA	154	196*	.2	.4
SUFFOLK	**447**	**106,479**	**941,127***	**71.2**	**100.0**
005 AME ZION	11	6,212	7,513	.6	.8
019 AMER BAPT USA	9	2,192	2,706*	.2	.3
053 ASSEMB OF GOD	23	2,082	3,195	.2	.3
081 CATHOLIC	70	NA	687,756	52.0	73.1
081b *BYZAN RUTH*	1	NA	725	.1	.1
081d *LATIN*	68	NA	686,808	52.0	73.0
081h *UKRAINIAN*	1	NA	223	-	-
089 CHR & MISS AL	1	105	305	-	-
097 CHR CHS&CHS CR	7	567	700*	.1	.1
105 CHRISTIAN REF	2	174	279	-	-
111 CH CR,SCIENTST	8	NR	NR	-	-
123 CH GOD (ANDER)	1	0	0	-	-
127 CH GOD (CLEVE)	14	1,968	2,430*	.2	.3
145 CH GOD PROPHCY	1	54	67*	-	-
151 L-D SAINTS	4	NA	1,234	.1	.1
163 CH OF LUTH BR	2	97	219	-	-
165 CH OF NAZARENE	5	445	599	-	.1
167 CHS OF CHRIST	8	728	989	.1	.1
176 CCC, NOT NAT'L	1	513	633*	-	.1
179 CONSRV BAPT	8	NR	NR	-	-
193 EPISCOPAL	41	13,960	19,519	1.5	2.1
203 EVAN FREE CH	3	212	335	-	-
207 E.L.C.A.	27	16,159	24,278	1.8	2.6
226 FRIENDS-USA	5	115	142*	-	-
226d *FGC & FUM*	5	115	142*	-	-
246 GREEK ORTHODOX	5	NR	NR	-	-
283 LUTH—MO SYNOD	15	9,481	13,547	1.0	1.4
313 N AM BAPT CONF	1	40	49*	-	-
331 ORTH CH IN AM	2	NR	NR	-	-
353 CHR BRETHREN	4	176	275	-	-
355 PRESB CH (USA)	36	10,283	12,695*	1.0	1.3
371 REF CH IN AM	3	837	1,752	.1	.2
403 SALVATION ARMY	1	48	49	-	-
413 S.D.A.	8	884	1,091*	.1	.1
419 SO BAPT CONV	9	936	1,156*	.1	.1
435 UNITARIAN-UNIV	7	757	1,073	.1	.1
443 UN C OF CHRIST	14	3,470	4,284*	.3	.5
449 UN METHODIST	49	20,263	25,016*	1.9	2.7
467 WESLEYAN	1	38	97	-	-
469 WELS	1	54	68	-	-
496 JEWISH EST[1]	36	NA	106,200	8.0	11.3

County and Denomination	Number of churches	Communicant, confirmed, full members	Total adherents Number	Percent of total population	Percent of total adherents
497 BLACK BAPT EST[2]	NA	13,629	16,826*	1.3	1.8
498 INDEP.CHARIS.[3]	4	NA	4,050	.3	.4
SULLIVAN	**99**	**7,068**	**35,296***	**50.9**	**100.0**
005 AME ZION	2	258	410	.6	1.2
019 AMER BAPT USA	1	20	25*	-	.1
053 ASSEMB OF GOD	4	213	355	.5	1.0
066 BIBLE CH OF CR	1	120	150*	.2	.4
080 BYELORSSN ORTH	1	NR	NR	-	-
081 CATHOLIC	12	NA	16,502	23.8	46.8
081d *LATIN*	11	NA	16,293	23.5	46.2
081h *UKRAINIAN*	1	NA	209	.3	.6
111 CH CR,SCIENTST	1	NR	NR	-	-
123 CH GOD (ANDER)	1	55	71	.1	.2
127 CH GOD (CLEVE)	1	33	41*	.1	.1
165 CH OF NAZARENE	1	61	80	.1	.2
176 CCC, NOT NAT'L	2	98	122*	.2	.3
193 EPISCOPAL	3	175	263	.4	.7
207 E.L.C.A.	4	747	1,001	1.4	2.8
221 FREE METHODIST	2	143	215	.3	.6
226 FRIENDS-USA	1	13	16*	-	-
226d *FGC & FUM*	1	13	16*	-	-
246 GREEK ORTHODOX	1	NR	NR	-	-
353 CHR BRETHREN	1	12	12	-	-
355 PRESB CH (USA)	8	919	1,145*	1.7	3.2
371 REF CH IN AM	6	356	955	1.4	2.7
413 S.D.A.	1	24	30*	-	.1
419 SO BAPT CONV	1	67	84*	.1	.2
443 UN C OF CHRIST	1	139	173*	.2	.5
449 UN METHODIST	28	2,831	3,529*	5.1	10.0
496 JEWISH EST[1]	15	NA	9,140	13.2	25.9
497 BLACK BAPT EST[2]	NA	784	977*	1.4	2.8
TIOGA	**58**	**8,893**	**20,724***	**39.6**	**100.0**
019 AMER BAPT USA	3	814	1,050*	2.0	5.1
053 ASSEMB OF GOD	1	33	38	.1	.2
081 CATHOLIC	5	NA	7,782	14.9	37.6
081d *LATIN*	5	NA	7,782	14.9	37.6
089 CHR & MISS AL	4	361	695	1.3	3.4
151 L-D SAINTS	1	NA	326	.6	1.6
165 CH OF NAZARENE	2	425	640	1.2	3.1
167 CHS OF CHRIST	1	30	35	.1	.2
179 CONSRV BAPT	1	NR	NR	-	-
181 CONSRV CONGR	1	149	192*	.4	.9
193 EPISCOPAL	3	270	548	1.0	2.6
207 E.L.C.A.	1	83	102	.2	.5
283 LUTH—MO SYNOD	1	152	243	.5	1.2
355 PRESB CH (USA)	4	992	1,280*	2.4	6.2
403 SALVATION ARMY	1	33	37	.1	.2
413 S.D.A.	1	19	25*	-	.1
419 SO BAPT CONV	2	196	253*	.5	1.2
443 UN C OF CHRIST	3	200	258*	.5	1.2
449 UN METHODIST	22	5,136	6,626*	12.7	32.0
496 JEWISH EST[1]	1	NA	594	1.1	2.9
TOMPKINS	**64**	**10,200**	**26,102***	**27.7**	**100.0**
005 AME ZION	1	556	701	.7	2.7
019 AMER BAPT USA	5	693	820*	.9	3.1
053 ASSEMB OF GOD	6	424	950	1.0	3.6
081 CATHOLIC	6	NA	11,119	11.8	42.6
081d *LATIN*	6	NA	11,119	11.8	42.6
089 CHR & MISS AL	2	86	171	.2	.7
111 CH CR,SCIENTST	1	NR	NR	-	-
151 L-D SAINTS	2	NA	697	.7	2.7
165 CH OF NAZARENE	1	60	100	.1	.4
167 CHS OF CHRIST	1	60	110	.1	.4
179 CONSRV BAPT	1	NR	NR	-	-
193 EPISCOPAL	4	452	670	.7	2.6
207 E.L.C.A.	1	461	621	.7	2.4
226 FRIENDS-USA	1	116	137*	.1	.5
226d *FGC & FUM*	1	116	137*	.1	.5
246 GREEK ORTHODOX	1	NR	NR	-	-
283 LUTH—MO SYNOD	1	263	340	.4	1.3
355 PRESB CH (USA)	3	1,426	1,687*	1.8	6.5
356 PRESB CH AMER	1	54	92	.1	.4
403 SALVATION ARMY	1	45	54	.1	.2
413 S.D.A.	1	68	80*	.1	.3
419 SO BAPT CONV	1	49	58*	.1	.2
435 UNITARIAN-UNIV	1	345	480	.5	1.8
443 UN C OF CHRIST	6	1,310	1,550*	1.6	5.9
449 UN METHODIST	15	3,315	3,922*	4.2	15.0
496 JEWISH EST[1]	1	NA	1,250	1.3	4.8
497 BLACK BAPT EST[2]	NA	417	493*	.5	1.9

NA–Not applicable   NR–Not reported   *Total adherents estimated from known number of communicant, confirmed, full members.   - Represents a percent less than 0.1.   Percentages may not total due to rounding.

[1]See Appendix E   [2]See Appendix F   [3]See Appendix G   Lines in *italic* represent a breakdown of Catholic rites or Friends affiliations. They are included in their respective denominational total.

Table 4. Churches and Church Membership by County and Denomination: 1990

County and Denomination	Number of churches	Communicant, confirmed, full members	Total adherents		
			Number	Percent of total population	Percent of total adherents
ULSTER	**159**	**16,806**	**86,111***	**52.1**	**100.0**
005 AME ZION	3	1,614	1,840	1.1	2.1
019 AMER BAPT USA	2	275	338*	.2	.4
053 ASSEMB OF GOD	6	223	411	.2	.5
081 CATHOLIC	22	NA	55,147	33.4	64.0
081d LATIN	*21*	*NA*	*54,864*	*33.2*	*63.7*
081h UKRAINIAN	*1*	*NA*	*283*	*.2*	*.3*
089 CHR & MISS AL	1	83	147	.1	.2
111 CH CR,SCIENTST	2	NR	NR	-	-
151 L-D SAINTS	1	NA	437	.3	.5
165 CH OF NAZARENE	3	170	163	.1	.2
167 CHS OF CHRIST	1	56	73	-	.1
175 CONGR CHR CHS	2	225	276*	.2	.3
193 EPISCOPAL	9	861	1,587	1.0	1.8
203 EVAN FREE CH	1	180	325	.2	.4
207 E.L.C.A.	10	2,384	3,420	2.1	4.0
226 FRIENDS-USA	3	138	169*	.1	.2
226d FGC & FUM	*3*	*138*	*169*	*.1*	*.2*
246 GREEK ORTHODOX	1	NR	NR	-	-
257 HUTTERIAN BR	2	NA	450	.3	.5
259 IFCA	1	NR	NR	-	-
283 LUTH—MO SYNOD	1	115	155	.1	.2
353 CHR BRETHREN	2	31	62	-	.1
355 PRESB CH (USA)	4	509	625*	.4	.7
371 REF CH IN AM	29	3,092	7,531	4.6	8.7
403 SALVATION ARMY	1	56	61	-	.1
413 S.D.A.	1	38	47*	-	.1
419 SO BAPT CONV	1	98	120*	.1	.1
431 UKRANIAN AMER	1	NR	NR	-	-
435 UNITARIAN-UNIV	1	64	76	-	.1
443 UN C OF CHRIST	1	94	115*	.1	.1
449 UN METHODIST	34	5,359	6,580*	4.0	7.6
467 WESLEYAN	3	68	138	.1	.2
496 JEWISH EST[1]	10	NA	4,500	2.7	5.2
497 BLACK BAPT EST[2]	NA	1,073	1,318*	.8	1.5
WARREN	**68**	**8,089**	**25,320***	**42.8**	**100.0**
019 AMER BAPT USA	5	812	1,005*	1.7	4.0
053 ASSEMB OF GOD	3	168	247	.4	1.0
081 CATHOLIC	13	NA	13,714	23.2	54.2
081d LATIN	*13*	*NA*	*13,714*	*23.2*	*54.2*
089 CHR & MISS AL	1	20	35	.1	.1
111 CH CR,SCIENTST	1	NR	NR	-	-
127 CH GOD (CLEVE)	1	95	118*	.2	.5
151 L-D SAINTS	1	NA	363	.6	1.4
167 CHS OF CHRIST	1	37	48	.1	.2
193 EPISCOPAL	9	1,034	1,870	3.2	7.4
221 FREE METHODIST	2	78	84	.1	.3
283 LUTH—MO SYNOD	1	437	567	1.0	2.2
355 PRESB CH (USA)	6	1,869	2,313*	3.9	9.1
403 SALVATION ARMY	1	83	105	.2	.4
413 S.D.A.	2	223	276*	.5	1.1
435 UNITARIAN-UNIV	1	70	125	.2	.5
449 UN METHODIST	14	2,970	3,676*	6.2	14.5
467 WESLEYAN	4	193	374	.6	1.5
496 JEWISH EST[1]	2	NA	400	.7	1.6
WASHINGTON	**82**	**8,843**	**20,866***	**35.2**	**100.0**
019 AMER BAPT USA	11	1,501	1,879*	3.2	9.0
053 ASSEMB OF GOD	4	396	743	1.3	3.6
081 CATHOLIC	13	NA	8,777	14.8	42.1
081b BYZAN RUTH	*1*	*NA*	*228*	*.4*	*1.1*
081d LATIN	*12*	*NA*	*8,549*	*14.4*	*41.0*
111 CH CR,SCIENTST	1	NR	NR	-	-
165 CH OF NAZARENE	1	49	73	.1	.3
167 CHS OF CHRIST	1	20	25	-	.1
176 CCC, NOT NAT'L	1	67	84*	.1	.4
179 CONSRV BAPT	1	NR	NR	-	-
181 CONSRV CONGR	1	88	110*	.2	.5
193 EPISCOPAL	7	540	745	1.3	3.6
226 FRIENDS-USA	1	46	58*	.1	.3
226d FGC & FUM	*1*	*46*	*58*	*.1*	*.3*
259 IFCA	1	NR	NR	-	-
285 MENNONITE CH	1	23	48	.1	.2
329 OPEN BIBLE STD	1	NR	NR	-	-
331 ORTH CH IN AM	1	NR	NR	-	-
355 PRESB CH (USA)	12	1,854	2,320*	3.9	11.1
371 REF CH IN AM	1	71	224	.4	1.1
419 SO BAPT CONV	1	26	33*	.1	.2
443 UN C OF CHRIST	1	46	58*	.1	.3
449 UN METHODIST	19	3,729	4,667*	7.9	22.4
467 WESLEYAN	2	50	200	.3	1.0
496 JEWISH EST[1]	0	NA	400	.7	1.9
497 BLACK BAPT EST[2]	NA	337	422*	.7	2.0

County and Denomination	Number of churches	Communicant, confirmed, full members	Total adherents		
			Number	Percent of total population	Percent of total adherents
WAYNE	**104**	**15,759**	**44,378***	**49.8**	**100.0**
019 AMER BAPT USA	13	2,661	3,428*	3.8	7.7
053 ASSEMB OF GOD	8	345	615	.7	1.4
081 CATHOLIC	13	NA	19,533	21.9	44.0
081d LATIN	*13*	*NA*	*19,533*	*21.9*	*44.0*
089 CHR & MISS AL	1	33	85	.1	.2
105 CHRISTIAN REF	1	203	313	.4	.7
111 CH CR,SCIENTST	1	NR	NR	-	-
123 CH GOD (ANDER)	2	95	95	.1	.2
151 L-D SAINTS	2	NA	793	.9	1.8
167 CHS OF CHRIST	1	25	35	-	.1
193 EPISCOPAL	5	724	1,246	1.4	2.8
207 E.L.C.A.	2	573	1,065	1.2	2.4
221 FREE METHODIST	5	170	367	.4	.8
226 FRIENDS-USA	1	1	4	-	-
226d FGC & FUM	*1*	*1*	*4*	*-*	*-*
283 LUTH—MO SYNOD	2	179	220	.2	.5
323 OLD ORD AMISH	1	NA	150	.2	.3
355 PRESB CH (USA)	12	2,552	3,288*	3.7	7.4
371 REF CH IN AM	8	1,155	2,023	2.3	4.6
413 S.D.A.	1	38	49*	.1	.1
419 SO BAPT CONV	1	54	70*	.1	.2
443 UN C OF CHRIST	2	164	211*	.2	.5
449 UN METHODIST	22	6,328	8,152*	9.1	18.4
496 JEWISH EST[1]	0	NA	2,045	2.3	4.6
497 BLACK BAPT EST[2]	NA	459	591*	.7	1.3
WESTCHESTER	**448**	**97,987**	**676,128***	**77.3**	**100.0**
005 AME ZION	9	15,401	18,654	2.1	2.8
019 AMER BAPT USA	20	6,725	8,109*	.9	1.2
022 EASTERN ORTH	1	278	278	-	-
053 ASSEMB OF GOD	18	1,754	2,817	.3	.4
066 BIBLE CH OF CR	1	1,980	2,387*	.3	.4
081 CATHOLIC	90	NA	427,885	48.9	63.3
081b BYZAN RUTH	*2*	*NA*	*500*	*.1*	*.1*
081d LATIN	*86*	*NA*	*426,150*	*48.7*	*63.0*
081f MELKITE-GK	*1*	*NA*	*252*	*-*	*-*
081h UKRAINIAN	*1*	*NA*	*983*	*.1*	*.1*
089 CHR & MISS AL	8	716	1,518	.2	.2
093 CHR CH (DISC)	1	40	52	-	-
097 CHR CHS&CHS CR	2	18	22*	-	-
111 CH CR,SCIENTST	10	NR	NR	-	-
123 CH GOD (ANDER)	1	8	10	-	-
127 CH GOD (CLEVE)	6	415	500*	.1	.1
145 CH GOD PROPHCY	3	165	199*	-	-
151 L-D SAINTS	3	NA	1,218	.1	.2
163 CH OF LUTH BR	1	133	395	-	.1
165 CH OF NAZARENE	2	83	181	-	-
167 CHS OF CHRIST	3	53	64	-	-
179 CONSRV BAPT	4	NR	NR	-	-
193 EPISCOPAL	49	10,572	16,946	1.9	2.5
207 E.L.C.A.	17	4,180	5,449	.6	.8
226 FRIENDS-USA	5	476	574*	.1	.1
226d FGC & FUM	*5*	*476*	*574*	*.1*	*.1*
246 GREEK ORTHODOX	4	NR	NR	-	-
249 AP CATH ASSYR	1	760	0	-	-
274 LAT EVAN LUTH	1	1,812	1,988	.2	.3
283 LUTH—MO SYNOD	10	2,374	2,896	.3	.4
331 ORTH CH IN AM	2	NR	NR	-	-
353 CHR BRETHREN	5	304	489	.1	.1
355 PRESB CH (USA)	29	10,855	13,089*	1.5	1.9
356 PRESB CH AMER	1	15	17	-	-
371 REF CH IN AM	11	2,403	3,667	.4	.5
403 SALVATION ARMY	5	124	153	-	-
413 S.D.A.	13	1,969	2,374*	.3	.4
419 SO BAPT CONV	2	131	158*	-	-
435 UNITARIAN-UNIV	5	636	915	.1	.1
443 UN C OF CHRIST	11	2,636	3,179*	.4	.5
449 UN METHODIST	34	11,214	13,522*	1.5	2.0
496 JEWISH EST[1]	60	NA	122,600	14.0	18.1
497 BLACK BAPT EST[2]	NA	19,757	23,823*	2.7	3.5
WYOMING	**62**	**5,818**	**19,237***	**45.3**	**100.0**
019 AMER BAPT USA	6	704	888*	2.1	4.6
081 CATHOLIC	16	NA	11,680	27.5	60.7
081d LATIN	*16*	*NA*	*11,680*	*27.5*	*60.7*
089 CHR & MISS AL	1	44	92	.2	.5
111 CH CR,SCIENTST	1	NR	NR	-	-
127 CH GOD (CLEVE)	2	81	102*	.2	.5
151 L-D SAINTS	1	NA	94	.2	.5
165 CH OF NAZARENE	1	75	101	.2	.5
167 CHS OF CHRIST	1	5	5	-	-
179 CONSRV BAPT	3	NR	NR	-	-
193 EPISCOPAL	3	361	457	1.1	2.4
221 FREE METHODIST	2	69	146	.3	.8
283 LUTH—MO SYNOD	1	218	300	.7	1.6

NA–Not applicable   NR–Not reported   *Total adherents estimated from known number of communicant, confirmed, full members.   - Represents a percent less than 0.1.   Percentages may not total due to rounding.

[1]See Appendix E   [2]See Appendix F   [3]See Appendix G   Lines in *italic* represent a breakdown of Catholic rites or Friends affiliations. They are included in their respective denominational total.

Table 4. Churches and Church Membership by County and Denomination: 1990

County and Denomination	Number of churches	Communicant, confirmed, full members	Total adherents Number	Percent of total population	Percent of total adherents
313 N AM BAPT CONF	1	111	140*	.3	.7
355 PRESB CH (USA)	5	688	867*	2.0	4.5
413 S.D.A.	0	16	20*	-	.1
443 UN C OF CHRIST	8	1,614	2,035*	4.8	10.6
449 UN METHODIST	10	1,557	1,963*	4.6	10.2
497 BLACK BAPT EST2	NA	275	347*	.8	1.8
YATES	**39**	**4,754**	**8,787***	**38.5**	**100.0**
019 AMER BAPT USA	7	838	1,061*	4.7	12.1
053 ASSEMB OF GOD	1	20	33	.1	.4
061 BEACHY AMISH	1	47	60*	.3	.7
081 CATHOLIC	2	NA	2,761	12.1	31.4
081d LATIN	*2*	*NA*	*2,761*	*12.1*	*31.4*
165 CH OF NAZARENE	1	36	16	.1	.2
179 CONSRV BAPT	1	NR	NR	-	-
193 EPISCOPAL	2	142	248	1.1	2.8
207 E.L.C.A.	2	418	505	2.2	5.7
226 FRIENDS-USA	1	17	22*	.1	.3
226d FGC & FUM	*1*	*17*	*22**	*.1*	*.3*
355 PRESB CH (USA)	5	538	681*	3.0	7.8
443 UN C OF CHRIST	2	91	115*	.5	1.3
449 UN METHODIST	13	2,538	3,214*	14.1	36.6
467 WESLEYAN	1	69	71	.3	.8

NORTH CAROLINA

County and Denomination	Number of churches	Communicant, confirmed, full members	Total adherents Number	Percent of total population	Percent of total adherents
THE STATE.....	11,331	3,004,855	3,977,923*	60.0	100.0
ALAMANCE	**160**	**47,523**	**61,017***	**56.4**	**100.0**
005 AME ZION	1	75	83	.1	.1
053 ASSEMB OF GOD	1	302	600	.6	1.0
055 AS REF PRES CH	1	322	361	.3	.6
081 CATHOLIC	1	NA	1,534	1.4	2.5
081d LATIN	*1*	*NA*	*1,534*	*1.4*	*2.5*
093 CHR CH (DISC)	1	58	110	.1	.2
097 CHR CHS&CHS CR	2	124	149*	.1	.2
127 CH GOD (CLEVE)	5	484	583*	.5	1.0
145 CH GOD PROPHCY	3	107	129*	.1	.2
151 L-D SAINTS	3	NA	761	.7	1.2
165 CH OF NAZARENE	3	536	571	.5	.9
167 CHS OF CHRIST	2	158	188	.2	.3
175 CONGR CHR CHS	1	25	30*	-	-
176 CCC, NOT NAT'L	3	137	165*	.2	.3
181 CONSRV CONGR	1	175	211*	.2	.3
193 EPISCOPAL	2	518	788	.7	1.3
207 E.L.C.A.	5	1,193	1,448	1.3	2.4
215 EVAN METH CH	2	126	152*	.1	.2
216 EVAN PRESBY CH	1	38	38	-	.1
226 FRIENDS-USA	6	461	590*	.5	1.0
226a CONSERV	*1*	*15*	*23*	*-*	*-*
226b EFI	*1*	*50*	*90*	*.1*	*.1*
226e FUM	*4*	*396*	*477**	*.4*	*.8*
246 GREEK ORTHODOX	1	NR	NR	-	-
283 LUTH—MO SYNOD	1	100	131	.1	.2
349 PENT HOLINESS	3	467	562*	.5	.9
353 CHR BRETHREN	2	240	412	.4	.7
355 PRESB CH (USA)	12	3,971	4,781*	4.4	7.8
356 PRESB CH AMER	1	382	481	.4	.8
361 PRIM BAPT ASCS	2	20	24*	-	-
403 SALVATION ARMY	1	105	108	.1	.2
413 S.D.A.	2	218	262*	.2	.4
419 SO BAPT CONV	30	13,113	15,788*	14.6	25.9
443 UN C OF CHRIST	27	5,536	6,665*	6.2	10.9
449 UN METHODIST	27	12,052	14,511*	13.4	23.8
467 WESLEYAN	5	277	383	.4	.6
497 BLACK BAPT EST2	NA	6,203	7,468*	6.9	12.2
499 INDEP.NON-CHAR3	1	NA	950	.9	1.6
ALEXANDER	**67**	**16,301**	**20,402***	**74.1**	**100.0**
001 ADVENT CHR CH	1	123	151*	.5	.7
005 AME ZION	1	103	148	.5	.7
053 ASSEMB OF GOD	1	10	15	.1	.1
055 AS REF PRES CH	2	91	106	.4	.5
081 CATHOLIC	1	NA	80	.3	.4
081d LATIN	*1*	*NA*	*80*	*.3*	*.4*
127 CH GOD (CLEVE)	2	86	106*	.4	.5
145 CH GOD PROPHCY	1	36	44*	.2	.2
167 CHS OF CHRIST	1	27	35	.1	.2
207 E.L.C.A.	6	1,882	2,501	9.1	12.3
283 LUTH—MO SYNOD	2	340	437	1.6	2.1
349 PENT HOLINESS	1	19	23*	.1	.1
355 PRESB CH (USA)	2	256	315*	1.1	1.5

County and Denomination	Number of churches	Communicant, confirmed, full members	Total adherents Number	Percent of total population	Percent of total adherents
419 SO BAPT CONV	34	11,243	13,844*	50.3	67.9
449 UN METHODIST	10	1,522	1,874*	6.8	9.2
467 WESLEYAN	2	65	110	.4	.5
497 BLACK BAPT EST2	NA	498	613*	2.2	3.0
ALLEGHANY	**31**	**2,489**	**3,310***	**34.5**	**100.0**
081 CATHOLIC	1	NA	90	.9	2.7
081d LATIN	*1*	*NA*	*90*	*.9*	*2.7*
151 L-D SAINTS	2	NA	260	2.7	7.9
157 CH OF BRETHREN	3	186	221*	2.3	6.7
349 PENT HOLINESS	1	37	44*	.5	1.3
355 PRESB CH (USA)	1	135	161*	1.7	4.9
361 PRIM BAPT ASCS	4	106	126*	1.3	3.8
386 REGULAR BAPT	3	111	132*	1.4	4.0
419 SO BAPT CONV	10	1,437	1,709*	17.8	51.6
449 UN METHODIST	6	477	567*	5.9	17.1
ANSON	**93**	**20,228**	**25,489***	**108.6**	**100.0**
005 AME ZION	16	6,420	8,168	34.8	32.0
081 CATHOLIC	1	NA	47	.2	.2
081d LATIN	*1*	*NA*	*47*	*.2*	*.2*
123 CH GOD (ANDER)	2	60	60	.3	.2
127 CH GOD (CLEVE)	2	136	170*	.7	.7
145 CH GOD PROPHCY	3	107	134*	.6	.5
167 CHS OF CHRIST	1	25	32	.1	.1
193 EPISCOPAL	2	129	164	.7	.6
223 FREE WILL BAPT	1	66	83*	.4	.3
349 PENT HOLINESS	1	34	43*	.2	.2
355 PRESB CH (USA)	5	365	457*	1.9	1.8
361 PRIM BAPT ASCS	4	74	93*	.4	.4
419 SO BAPT CONV	30	6,596	8,257*	35.2	32.4
449 UN METHODIST	25	2,473	3,096*	13.2	12.1
497 BLACK BAPT EST2	NA	3,743	4,685*	20.0	18.4
ASHE	**122**	**13,176**	**15,931***	**71.7**	**100.0**
053 ASSEMB OF GOD	1	30	45	.2	.3
081 CATHOLIC	1	NA	99	.4	.6
081d LATIN	*1*	*NA*	*99*	*.4*	*.6*
097 CHR CHS&CHS CR	2	130	155*	.7	1.0
145 CH GOD PROPHCY	1	36	43*	.2	.3
165 CH OF NAZARENE	1	35	76	.3	.5
167 CHS OF CHRIST	2	95	124	.6	.8
193 EPISCOPAL	1	79	100	.5	.6
265 INT PENT C CHR	1	14	29	.1	.2
285 MENNONITE CH	3	79	138	.6	.9
355 PRESB CH (USA)	6	342	408*	1.8	2.6
361 PRIM BAPT ASCS	7	179	214*	1.0	1.3
386 REGULAR BAPT	29	3,165	3,775*	17.0	23.7
413 S.D.A.	1	37	44*	.2	.3
419 SO BAPT CONV	46	7,301	8,708*	39.2	54.7
449 UN METHODIST	20	1,654	1,973*	8.9	12.4
AVERY	**62**	**5,528**	**6,719***	**45.2**	**100.0**
053 ASSEMB OF GOD	1	8	7	-	.1
081 CATHOLIC	1	NA	46	.3	.7
081d LATIN	*1*	*NA*	*46*	*.3*	*.7*
097 CHR CHS&CHS CR	3	135	163*	1.1	2.4
127 CH GOD (CLEVE)	1	51	61*	.4	.9
151 L-D SAINTS	1	NA	79	.5	1.2
167 CHS OF CHRIST	2	20	26	.2	.4
193 EPISCOPAL	1	18	17	.1	.3
207 E.L.C.A.	1	17	18	.1	.3
215 EVAN METH CH	1	23	28*	.2	.4
216 EVAN PRESBY CH	1	178	178	1.2	2.6
223 FREE WILL BAPT	1	54	65*	.4	1.0
237 GC MENN BR CHS	1	45	54*	.4	.8
355 PRESB CH (USA)	8	678	817*	5.5	12.2
356 PRESB CH AMER	2	109	109	.7	1.6
386 REGULAR BAPT	1	19	23*	.2	.3
413 S.D.A.	1	184	222*	1.5	3.3
419 SO BAPT CONV	25	3,527	4,249*	28.6	63.2
449 UN METHODIST	10	462	557*	3.7	8.3
BEAUFORT	**136**	**26,031**	**33,725***	**79.8**	**100.0**
005 AME ZION	21	7,640	9,168	21.7	27.2
053 ASSEMB OF GOD	2	110	170	.4	.5
081 CATHOLIC	1	NA	534	1.3	1.6
081d LATIN	*1*	*NA*	*534*	*1.3*	*1.6*
093 CHR CH (DISC)	22	1,819	3,141	7.4	9.3
097 CHR CHS&CHS CR	20	4,443	5,533*	13.1	16.4
105 CHRISTIAN REF	1	159	279	.7	.8
111 CH CR,SCIENTST	1	NR	NR	-	-
127 CH GOD (CLEVE)	9	695	865*	2.0	2.6
145 CH GOD PROPHCY	1	36	45*	.1	.1
151 L-D SAINTS	1	NA	142	.3	.4

NA–Not applicable NR–Not reported *Total adherents estimated from known number of communicant, confirmed, full members. - Represents a percent less than 0.1. Percentages may not total due to rounding.
[1]See Appendix E [2]See Appendix F [3]See Appendix G Lines in *italic* represent a breakdown of Catholic rites or Friends affiliations. They are included in their respective denominational total.

Table 4. Churches and Church Membership by County and Denomination: 1990

County and Denomination		Number of churches	Communicant, confirmed, full members	Total adherents		
				Number	Percent of total population	Percent of total adherents
167	CHS OF CHRIST	2	122	172	.4	.5
193	EPISCOPAL	9	717	881	2.1	2.6
223	FREE WILL BAPT	7	1,019	1,269*	3.0	3.8
349	PENT HOLINESS	8	299	372*	.9	1.1
355	PRESB CH (USA)	2	518	645*	1.5	1.9
356	PRESB CH AMER	1	75	75	.2	.2
361	PRIM BAPT ASCS	3	17	21*	-	.1
413	S.D.A.	1	37	46*	.1	.1
419	SO BAPT CONV	11	2,500	3,113*	7.4	9.2
449	UN METHODIST	13	2,639	3,286*	7.8	9.7
497	BLACK BAPT EST[2]	NA	3,186	3,968*	9.4	11.8
BERTIE		**45**	**11,768**	**15,540***	**76.2**	**100.0**
005	AME ZION	1	130	199	1.0	1.3
019	AMER BAPT USA	1	400	514*	2.5	3.3
053	ASSEMB OF GOD	5	407	580	2.8	3.7
093	CHR CH (DISC)	2	113	195	1.0	1.3
151	L-D SAINTS	1	NA	280	1.4	1.8
193	EPISCOPAL	3	178	238	1.2	1.5
349	PENT HOLINESS	2	33	42*	.2	.3
419	SO BAPT CONV	24	5,820	7,473*	36.7	48.1
449	UN METHODIST	6	464	596*	2.9	3.8
497	BLACK BAPT EST[2]	NA	4,223	5,423*	26.6	34.9
BLADEN		**92**	**20,913**	**26,422***	**92.2**	**100.0**
005	AME ZION	20	6,582	8,401	29.3	31.8
053	ASSEMB OF GOD	1	35	48	.2	.2
081	CATHOLIC	1	NA	62	.2	.2
081d	*LATIN*	*1*	*NA*	*62*	*.2*	*.2*
123	CH GOD (ANDER)	1	20	28	.1	.1
127	CH GOD (CLEVE)	2	124	155*	.5	.6
145	CH GOD PROPHCY	1	36	45*	.2	.2
167	CHS OF CHRIST	1	27	29	.1	.1
193	EPISCOPAL	1	43	63	.2	.2
349	PENT HOLINESS	2	91	114*	.4	.4
355	PRESB CH (USA)	8	624	779*	2.7	2.9
413	S.D.A.	2	113	141*	.5	.5
419	SO BAPT CONV	36	8,199	10,242*	35.7	38.8
449	UN METHODIST	15	2,105	2,629*	9.2	10.0
467	WESLEYAN	1	210	308	1.1	1.2
497	BLACK BAPT EST[2]	NA	2,704	3,378*	11.8	12.8
BRUNSWICK		**97**	**18,958**	**24,418***	**47.9**	**100.0**
005	AME ZION	9	2,430	2,916	5.7	11.9
053	ASSEMB OF GOD	1	45	64	.1	.3
081	CATHOLIC	2	NA	841	1.6	3.4
081d	*LATIN*	*2*	*NA*	*841*	*1.6*	*3.4*
089	CHR & MISS AL	1	41	120	.2	.5
127	CH GOD (CLEVE)	3	189	231*	.5	.9
145	CH GOD PROPHCY	1	36	44*	.1	.2
151	L-D SAINTS	2	NA	419	.8	1.7
167	CHS OF CHRIST	2	61	89	.2	.4
193	EPISCOPAL	3	315	426	.8	1.7
207	E.L.C.A.	2	260	276	.5	1.1
325	OLD REG BAPT	1	12	15*	-	.1
349	PENT HOLINESS	3	173	211*	.4	.9
355	PRESB CH (USA)	6	928	1,133*	2.2	4.6
361	PRIM BAPT ASCS	1	91	111*	.2	.5
403	SALVATION ARMY	1	193	204	.4	.8
413	S.D.A.	1	143	175*	.3	.7
419	SO BAPT CONV	47	9,443	11,529*	22.6	47.2
449	UN METHODIST	11	2,375	2,900*	5.7	11.9
497	BLACK BAPT EST[2]	NA	2,223	2,714*	5.3	11.1
BUNCOMBE		**301**	**80,994**	**117,631***	**67.3**	**100.0**
005	AME ZION	8	2,479	3,180	1.8	2.7
019	AMER BAPT USA	2	520	628*	.4	.5
053	ASSEMB OF GOD	3	454	881	.5	.7
081	CATHOLIC	5	NA	4,387	2.5	3.7
081d	*LATIN*	*5*	*NA*	*4,387*	*2.5*	*3.7*
089	CHR & MISS AL	3	267	342	.2	.3
093	CHR CH (DISC)	5	463	670	.4	.6
097	CHR CHS&CHS CR	6	298	360*	.2	.3
111	CH CR,SCIENTST	2	NR	NR	-	-
123	CH GOD (ANDER)	4	102	113	.1	.1
127	CH GOD (CLEVE)	9	1,057	1,277*	.7	1.1
145	CH GOD PROPHCY	1	36	43*	-	-
151	L-D SAINTS	2	NA	489	.3	.4
165	CH OF NAZARENE	4	321	488	.3	.4
167	CHS OF CHRIST	7	428	550	.3	.5
193	EPISCOPAL	10	1,907	2,823	1.6	2.4
207	E.L.C.A.	3	792	1,005	.6	.9
215	EVAN METH CH	1	22	27*	-	-
216	EVAN PRESBY CH	2	104	112	.1	.1
223	FREE WILL BAPT	12	1,221	1,475*	.8	1.3
226	FRIENDS-USA	1	83	140	.1	.1

County and Denomination		Number of churches	Communicant, confirmed, full members	Total adherents		
				Number	Percent of total population	Percent of total adherents
226c	FGC	1	83	140	.1	.1
246	GREEK ORTHODOX	1	NR	NR	-	-
263	INT FOURSQ GOS	1	25	30*	-	-
283	LUTH—MO SYNOD	1	395	486	.3	.4
285	MENNONITE CH	1	37	82	-	.1
349	PENT HOLINESS	2	94	114*	.1	.1
353	CHR BRETHREN	1	80	100	.1	.1
355	PRESB CH (USA)	16	3,989	4,820*	2.8	4.1
356	PRESB CH AMER	10	2,240	2,802	1.6	2.4
361	PRIM BAPT ASCS	1	17	21*	-	-
403	SALVATION ARMY	1	163	174	.1	.1
413	S.D.A.	6	1,596	1,928*	1.1	1.6
419	SO BAPT CONV	107	44,759	54,082*	30.9	46.0
435	UNITARIAN-UNIV	1	361	526	.3	.4
443	UN C OF CHRIST	1	137	166*	.1	.1
449	UN METHODIST	56	12,008	14,509*	8.3	12.3
467	WESLEYAN	2	268	290	.2	.2
496	JEWISH EST[1]	2	NA	13,050	7.5	11.1
497	BLACK BAPT EST[2]	NA	4,271	5,161*	3.0	4.4
499	INDEP.NON-CHAR[3]	1	NA	300	.2	.3
BURKE		**156**	**41,266**	**51,512***	**68.0**	**100.0**
001	ADVENT CHR CH	1	93	113*	.1	.2
005	AME ZION	1	234	349	.5	.7
053	ASSEMB OF GOD	4	455	600	.8	1.2
081	CATHOLIC	1	NA	369	.5	.7
081d	*LATIN*	*1*	*NA*	*369*	*.5*	*.7*
093	CHR CH (DISC)	1	32	32	-	.1
097	CHR CHS&CHS CR	1	30	36*	-	.1
123	CH GOD (ANDER)	3	540	643	.8	1.2
127	CH GOD (CLEVE)	3	599	727*	1.0	1.4
145	CH GOD PROPHCY	1	36	44*	.1	.1
151	L-D SAINTS	1	NA	331	.4	.6
167	CHS OF CHRIST	1	70	91	.1	.2
193	EPISCOPAL	4	444	564	.7	1.1
207	E.L.C.A.	3	777	984	1.3	1.9
215	EVAN METH CH	2	282	342*	.5	.7
223	FREE WILL BAPT	4	354	430*	.6	.8
283	LUTH—MO SYNOD	1	26	34	-	.1
349	PENT HOLINESS	2	96	117*	.2	.2
355	PRESB CH (USA)	7	1,466	1,780*	2.4	3.5
356	PRESB CH AMER	1	100	128	.2	.2
413	S.D.A.	2	223	271*	.4	.5
419	SO BAPT CONV	80	27,753	33,694*	44.5	65.4
449	UN METHODIST	29	5,842	7,093*	9.4	13.8
467	WESLEYAN	3	271	340	.4	.7
496	JEWISH EST[1]	0	NA	527	.7	1.0
497	BLACK BAPT EST[2]	NA	1,543	1,873*	2.5	3.6
CABARRUS		**228**	**59,967**	**78,157***	**79.0**	**100.0**
001	ADVENT CHR CH	1	56	69*	.1	.1
005	AME ZION	26	9,758	12,734	12.9	16.3
053	ASSEMB OF GOD	2	1,745	3,065	3.1	3.9
055	AS REF PRES CH	1	138	170	.2	.2
081	CATHOLIC	2	NA	1,617	1.6	2.1
081d	*LATIN*	*2*	*NA*	*1,617*	*1.6*	*2.1*
093	CHR CH (DISC)	3	286	420	.4	.5
097	CHR CHS&CHS CR	2	282	347*	.4	.4
123	CH GOD (ANDER)	2	185	200	.2	.3
127	CH GOD (CLEVE)	10	1,522	1,873*	1.9	2.4
145	CH GOD PROPHCY	6	214	263*	.3	.3
151	L-D SAINTS	1	NA	511	.5	.7
165	CH OF NAZARENE	3	251	353	.4	.5
167	CHS OF CHRIST	3	218	281	.3	.4
193	EPISCOPAL	1	419	538	.5	.7
207	E.L.C.A.	16	4,105	5,041	5.1	6.4
215	EVAN METH CH	2	124	153*	.2	.2
223	FREE WILL BAPT	15	1,266	1,558*	1.6	2.0
259	IFCA	1	NR	NR	-	-
263	INT FOURSQ GOS	4	893	1,099*	1.1	1.4
283	LUTH—MO SYNOD	3	553	737	.7	.9
349	PENT HOLINESS	4	456	561*	.6	.7
355	PRESB CH (USA)	19	3,962	4,876*	4.9	6.2
356	PRESB CH AMER	4	275	282	.3	.4
361	PRIM BAPT ASCS	2	58	71*	.1	.1
403	SALVATION ARMY	1	102	113	.1	.1
413	S.D.A.	2	175	215*	.2	.3
419	SO BAPT CONV	52	18,447	22,702*	22.9	29.0
435	UNITARIAN-UNIV	1	85	131	.1	.2
443	UN C OF CHRIST	8	1,265	1,557*	1.6	2.0
449	UN METHODIST	29	9,149	11,259*	11.4	14.4
467	WESLEYAN	2	149	182	.2	.2
496	JEWISH EST[1]	0	NA	467	.5	.6
497	BLACK BAPT EST[2]	NA	3,829	4,712*	4.8	6.0

NA–Not applicable   NR–Not reported   *Total adherents estimated from known number of communicant, confirmed, full members.   - Represents a percent less than 0.1.   Percentages may not total due to rounding.
[1]See Appendix E   [2]See Appendix F   [3]See Appendix G   Lines in *italic* represent a breakdown of Catholic rites or Friends affiliations. They are included in their respective denominational total.

Table 4. Churches and Church Membership by County and Denomination: 1990

County and Denomination	Number of churches	Communicant, confirmed, full members	Total adherents		
			Number	Percent of total population	Percent of total adherents
CALDWELL	**143**	**36,658**	**45,279***	**64.0**	**100.0**
001 ADVENT CHR CH	9	958	1,167*	1.7	2.6
053 ASSEMB OF GOD	1	16	24	-	.1
081 CATHOLIC	1	NA	464	.7	1.0
081d *LATIN*	*1*	*NA*	*464*	*.7*	*1.0*
097 CHR CHS&CHS CR	2	50	61*	.1	.1
121 CH GOD (ABR)	1	88	107*	.2	.2
123 CH GOD (ANDER)	1	155	155	.2	.3
127 CH GOD (CLEVE)	7	504	614*	.9	1.4
145 CH GOD PROPHCY	2	71	87*	.1	.2
151 L-D SAINTS	1	NA	122	.2	.3
167 CHS OF CHRIST	1	96	125	.2	.3
193 EPISCOPAL	1	152	176	.2	.4
207 E.L.C.A.	6	1,104	1,362	1.9	3.0
237 GC MENN BR CHS	3	80	97*	.1	.2
349 PENT HOLINESS	3	373	455*	.6	1.0
355 PRESB CH (USA)	5	1,046	1,275*	1.8	2.8
361 PRIM BAPT ASCS	2	45	55*	.1	.1
413 S.D.A.	2	127	155*	.2	.3
419 SO BAPT CONV	70	26,276	32,022*	45.3	70.7
443 UN C OF CHRIST	1	148	180*	.3	.4
449 UN METHODIST	23	4,373	5,329*	7.5	11.8
467 WESLEYAN	1	59	105	.1	.2
497 BLACK BAPT EST[2]	NA	937	1,142*	1.6	2.5
CAMDEN	**18**	**3,052**	**4,285***	**72.6**	**100.0**
005 AME ZION	1	50	68	1.2	1.6
097 CHR CHS&CHS CR	2	196	241*	4.1	5.6
151 L-D SAINTS	1	NA	514	8.7	12.0
349 PENT HOLINESS	2	167	205*	3.5	4.8
413 S.D.A.	1	106	130*	2.2	3.0
419 SO BAPT CONV	5	1,340	1,646*	27.9	38.4
449 UN METHODIST	5	678	833*	14.1	19.4
467 WESLEYAN	1	16	35	.6	.8
497 BLACK BAPT EST[2]	NA	499	613*	10.4	14.3
CARTERET	**90**	**17,954**	**24,590***	**46.8**	**100.0**
005 AME ZION	7	1,786	2,256	4.3	9.2
053 ASSEMB OF GOD	4	110	154	.3	.6
081 CATHOLIC	1	NA	1,270	2.4	5.2
081d *LATIN*	*1*	*NA*	*1,270*	*2.4*	*5.2*
093 CHR CH (DISC)	2	164	435	.8	1.8
127 CH GOD (CLEVE)	3	283	344*	.7	1.4
145 CH GOD PROPHCY	2	71	86*	.2	.3
151 L-D SAINTS	2	NA	625	1.2	2.5
165 CH OF NAZARENE	1	62	134	.3	.5
167 CHS OF CHRIST	2	100	160	.3	.7
193 EPISCOPAL	2	866	1,102	2.1	4.5
207 E.L.C.A.	1	200	284	.5	1.2
223 FREE WILL BAPT	4	540	655*	1.2	2.7
263 INT FOURSQ GOS	1	0	0*	-	-
349 PENT HOLINESS	5	757	919*	1.7	3.7
355 PRESB CH (USA)	3	818	993*	1.9	4.0
361 PRIM BAPT ASCS	4	20	24*	-	.1
419 SO BAPT CONV	19	5,315	6,451*	12.3	26.2
435 UNITARIAN-UNIV	1	59	70	.1	.3
443 UN C OF CHRIST	2	74	90*	.2	.4
449 UN METHODIST	22	5,626	6,829*	13.0	27.8
467 WESLEYAN	1	45	125	.2	.5
497 BLACK BAPT EST[2]	NA	1,058	1,284*	2.4	5.2
499 INDEP.NON-CHAR[3]	1	NA	300	.6	1.2
CASWELL	**43**	**7,621**	**9,251***	**44.7**	**100.0**
053 ASSEMB OF GOD	1	114	115	.6	1.2
157 CH OF BRETHREN	1	160	195*	.9	2.1
193 EPISCOPAL	1	13	12	.1	.1
349 PENT HOLINESS	2	67	82*	.4	.9
355 PRESB CH (USA)	7	326	397*	1.9	4.3
419 SO BAPT CONV	12	1,997	2,431*	11.7	26.3
443 UN C OF CHRIST	2	251	306*	1.5	3.3
449 UN METHODIST	17	1,850	2,252*	10.9	24.3
497 BLACK BAPT EST[2]	NA	2,843	3,461*	16.7	37.4
CATAWBA	**203**	**65,981**	**86,839***	**73.3**	**100.0**
001 ADVENT CHR CH	2	131	160*	.1	.2
005 AME ZION	11	2,140	3,022	2.6	3.5
019 AMER BAPT USA	2	1,034	1,266*	1.1	1.5
053 ASSEMB OF GOD	3	328	439	.4	.5
081 CATHOLIC	2	NA	2,610	2.2	3.0
081d *LATIN*	*2*	*NA*	*2,610*	*2.2*	*3.0*
089 CHR & MISS AL	1	0	135	.1	.2
111 CH CR,SCIENTST	1	NR	NR	-	-
123 CH GOD (ANDER)	3	362	515	.4	.6
127 CH GOD (CLEVE)	5	798	977*	.8	1.1
133 CH GOD(7TH)DEN	1	23	29		

County and Denomination	Number of churches	Communicant, confirmed, full members	Total adherents		
			Number	Percent of total population	Percent of total adherents
145 CH GOD PROPHCY	2	71	87*	.1	.1
151 L-D SAINTS	3	NA	984	.8	1.1
165 CH OF NAZARENE	1	57	73	.1	.1
167 CHS OF CHRIST	4	285	454	.4	.5
193 EPISCOPAL	3	1,058	1,283	1.1	1.5
207 E.L.C.A.	26	10,589	13,198	11.1	15.2
215 EVAN METH CH	1	37	45*	-	.1
223 FREE WILL BAPT	2	78	95*	.1	.1
226 FRIENDS-USA	1	4	10	-	-
226c *FGC*	*1*	*4*	*10*	*-*	*-*
283 LUTH—MO SYNOD	12	6,343	7,873	6.6	9.1
285 MENNONITE CH	2	123	171	.1	.2
295 MORAV CH-SOUTH	1	92	140	.1	.2
349 PENT HOLINESS	3	731	895*	.8	1.0
353 CHR BRETHREN	1	80	350	.3	.4
355 PRESB CH (USA)	6	1,811	2,217*	1.9	2.6
356 PRESB CH AMER	1	22	40	-	-
403 SALVATION ARMY	1	151	158	.1	.2
413 S.D.A.	1	376	460*	.4	.5
419 SO BAPT CONV	49	22,261	27,247*	23.0	31.4
435 UNITARIAN-UNIV	1	31	32	-	-
443 UN C OF CHRIST	11	3,049	3,732*	3.2	4.3
449 UN METHODIST	34	10,491	12,841*	10.8	14.8
467 WESLEYAN	4	241	281	.2	.3
496 JEWISH EST[1]	1	NA	823	.7	.9
497 BLACK BAPT EST[2]	NA	3,184	3,897*	3.3	4.5
499 INDEP.NON-CHAR[3]	1	NA	300	.3	.3
CHATHAM	**109**	**21,234**	**26,608***	**68.6**	**100.0**
005 AME ZION	16	4,708	6,152	15.9	23.1
053 ASSEMB OF GOD	1	35	55	.1	.2
081 CATHOLIC	1	NA	145	.4	.5
081d *LATIN*	*1*	*NA*	*145*	*.4*	*.5*
123 CH GOD (ANDER)	1	45	45	.1	.2
127 CH GOD (CLEVE)	1	67	82*	.2	.3
145 CH GOD PROPHCY	4	143	174*	.4	.7
165 CH OF NAZARENE	1	0	17	-	.1
167 CHS OF CHRIST	1	33	42	.1	.2
175 CONGR CHR CHS	1	50	61*	.2	.2
176 CCC, NOT NAT'L	3	263	320*	.8	1.2
193 EPISCOPAL	1	118	203	.5	.8
226 FRIENDS-USA	3	496	604*	1.6	2.3
226e *FUM*	*3*	*496*	*604**	*1.6*	*2.3*
349 PENT HOLINESS	1	149	182*	.5	.7
353 CHR BRETHREN	1	90	150	.4	.6
355 PRESB CH (USA)	4	266	324*	.8	1.2
361 PRIM BAPT ASCS	1	9	11*	-	-
413 S.D.A.	1	47	57*	.1	.2
419 SO BAPT CONV	33	7,910	9,636*	24.9	36.2
443 UN C OF CHRIST	6	782	953*	2.5	3.6
449 UN METHODIST	27	3,771	4,594*	11.9	17.3
467 WESLEYAN	1	117	200	.5	.8
497 BLACK BAPT EST[2]	NA	2,135	2,601*	6.7	9.8
CHEROKEE	**82**	**12,249**	**15,192***	**75.3**	**100.0**
053 ASSEMB OF GOD	1	50	83	.4	.5
081 CATHOLIC	2	NA	263	1.3	1.7
081d *LATIN*	*2*	*NA*	*263*	*1.3*	*1.7*
123 CH GOD (ANDER)	1	50	50	.2	.3
127 CH GOD (CLEVE)	4	156	188*	.9	1.2
145 CH GOD PROPHCY	2	71	85*	.4	.6
151 L-D SAINTS	1	NA	127	.6	.8
167 CHS OF CHRIST	2	56	74	.4	.5
193 EPISCOPAL	1	77	108	.5	.7
207 E.L.C.A.	1	101	136	.7	.9
221 FREE METHODIST	1	20	23	.1	.2
349 PENT HOLINESS	2	67	81*	.4	.5
355 PRESB CH (USA)	1	95	114*	.6	.8
356 PRESB CH AMER	2	142	163	.8	1.1
413 S.D.A.	2	213	256*	1.3	1.7
419 SO BAPT CONV	48	10,082	12,124*	60.1	79.8
449 UN METHODIST	10	1,053	1,266*	6.3	8.3
467 WESLEYAN	1	16	51	.3	.3
CHOWAN	**37**	**9,233**	**11,901***	**88.1**	**100.0**
005 AME ZION	14	2,650	3,408	25.2	28.6
053 ASSEMB OF GOD	1	98	120	.9	1.0
081 CATHOLIC	1	NA	234	1.7	2.0
081d *LATIN*	*1*	*NA*	*234*	*1.7*	*2.0*
093 CHR CH (DISC)	1	80	114	.8	1.0
097 CHR CHS&CHS CR	2	0	0*	-	-
167 CHS OF CHRIST	1	25	34	.3	.3
193 EPISCOPAL	2	304	341	2.5	2.9
349 PENT HOLINESS	3	237	298*	2.2	2.5
355 PRESB CH (USA)	1	86	108*	.8	.9
419 SO BAPT CONV	8	3,650	4,596*	34.0	38.6

NA–Not applicable   NR–Not reported   *Total adherents estimated from known number of communicant, confirmed, full members.   - Represents a percent less than 0.1.   Percentages may not total due to rounding.
[1] See Appendix E   [2] See Appendix F   [3] See Appendix G   Lines in *italic* represent a breakdown of Catholic rites or Friends affiliations. They are included in their respective denominational total.

Table 4. Churches and Church Membership by County and Denomination: 1990

County and Denomination	Number of churches	Communicant, confirmed, full members	Total adherents Number	Percent of total population	Percent of total adherents
449 UN METHODIST	3	389	490*	3.6	4.1
497 BLACK BAPT EST[2]	NA	1,714	2,158*	16.0	18.1
CLAY	**35**	**3,641**	**4,695***	**65.6**	**100.0**
053 ASSEMB OF GOD	2	114	270	3.8	5.8
081 CATHOLIC	1	NA	133	1.9	2.8
081d LATIN	*1*	*NA*	*133*	*1.9*	*2.8*
127 CH GOD (CLEVE)	5	271	325*	4.5	6.9
165 CH OF NAZARENE	1	38	81	1.1	1.7
167 CHS OF CHRIST	1	32	40	.6	.9
193 EPISCOPAL	1	114	161	2.3	3.4
355 PRESB CH (USA)	1	29	35*	.5	.7
419 SO BAPT CONV	16	2,452	2,941*	41.1	62.6
449 UN METHODIST	7	591	709*	9.9	15.1
CLEVELAND	**176**	**51,385**	**64,010***	**75.6**	**100.0**
005 AME ZION	7	2,187	2,236	2.6	3.5
053 ASSEMB OF GOD	2	65	82	.1	.1
055 AS REF PRES CH	1	369	423	.5	.7
081 CATHOLIC	2	NA	802	.9	1.3
081d LATIN	*2*	*NA*	*802*	*.9*	*1.3*
127 CH GOD (CLEVE)	5	662	815*	1.0	1.3
151 L-D SAINTS	1	NA	303	.4	.5
165 CH OF NAZARENE	2	131	214	.3	.3
167 CHS OF CHRIST	1	98	127	.1	.2
193 EPISCOPAL	2	226	352	.4	.5
207 E.L.C.A.	3	837	1,005	1.2	1.6
215 EVAN METH CH	1	49	60*	.1	.1
216 EVAN PRESBY CH	1	38	39	-	.1
223 FREE WILL BAPT	3	270	332*	.4	.5
263 INT FOURSQ GOS	1	117	144*	.2	.2
349 PENT HOLINESS	2	208	256*	.3	.4
355 PRESB CH (USA)	7	1,443	1,776*	2.1	2.8
361 PRIM BAPT ASCS	1	22	27*	-	-
403 SALVATION ARMY	1	50	50	.1	.1
413 S.D.A.	2	147	181*	.2	.3
419 SO BAPT CONV	90	32,703	40,251*	47.5	62.9
449 UN METHODIST	39	7,163	8,816*	10.4	13.8
467 WESLEYAN	2	318	449	.5	.7
497 BLACK BAPT EST[2]	NA	4,282	5,270*	6.2	8.2
COLUMBUS	**134**	**29,769**	**37,559***	**75.7**	**100.0**
001 ADVENT CHR CH	1	38	48*	.1	.1
005 AME ZION	11	4,967	5,710	11.5	15.2
053 ASSEMB OF GOD	1	92	83	.2	.2
081 CATHOLIC	2	NA	302	.6	.8
081d LATIN	*2*	*NA*	*302*	*.6*	*.8*
089 CHR & MISS AL	1	39	84	.2	.2
127 CH GOD (CLEVE)	6	496	626*	1.3	1.7
145 CH GOD PROPHCY	1	36	45*	.1	.1
151 L-D SAINTS	2	NA	190	.4	.5
167 CHS OF CHRIST	2	53	74	.1	.2
193 EPISCOPAL	1	75	84	.2	.2
207 E.L.C.A.	1	8	8	-	-
223 FREE WILL BAPT	1	56	71*	.1	.2
349 PENT HOLINESS	4	463	584*	1.2	1.6
355 PRESB CH (USA)	8	769	971*	2.0	2.6
371 REF CH IN AM	2	239	421	.8	1.1
413 S.D.A.	2	86	109*	.2	.3
419 SO BAPT CONV	66	15,692	19,808*	39.9	52.7
449 UN METHODIST	20	2,880	3,635*	7.3	9.7
467 WESLEYAN	1	115	80	.2	.2
496 JEWISH EST[1]	1	NA	0	-	-
497 BLACK BAPT EST[2]	NA	3,665	4,626*	9.3	12.3
CRAVEN	**117**	**36,582**	**51,747***	**63.4**	**100.0**
005 AME ZION	15	11,495	13,794	16.9	26.7
053 ASSEMB OF GOD	2	213	325	.4	.6
081 CATHOLIC	2	NA	4,552	5.6	8.8
081d LATIN	*2*	*NA*	*4,552*	*5.6*	*8.8*
093 CHR CH (DISC)	16	1,394	2,088	2.6	4.0
097 CHR CHS&CHS CR	2	208	266*	.3	.5
111 CH CR,SCIENTST	1	NR	NR	-	-
127 CH GOD (CLEVE)	4	384	491*	.6	.9
145 CH GOD PROPHCY	2	71	91*	.1	.2
151 L-D SAINTS	2	NA	768	.9	1.5
165 CH OF NAZARENE	2	83	208	.3	.4
167 CHS OF CHRIST	2	130	155	.2	.3
193 EPISCOPAL	4	1,278	1,696	2.1	3.3
207 E.L.C.A.	2	333	461	.6	.9
223 FREE WILL BAPT	6	588	752*	.9	1.5
283 LUTH—MO SYNOD	1	169	246	.3	.5
349 PENT HOLINESS	6	375	480*	.6	.9
355 PRESB CH (USA)	6	1,684	2,154*	2.6	4.2
356 PRESB CH AMER	1	108	120	.1	.2
403 SALVATION ARMY	1	103	106	.1	.2

County and Denomination	Number of churches	Communicant, confirmed, full members	Total adherents Number	Percent of total population	Percent of total adherents
413 S.D.A.	1	71	91*	.1	.2
419 SO BAPT CONV	14	5,873	7,514*	9.2	14.5
443 UN C OF CHRIST	3	371	475*	.6	.9
449 UN METHODIST	20	6,403	8,192*	10.0	15.8
467 WESLEYAN	1	150	200	.2	.4
496 JEWISH EST[1]	1	NA	0	-	-
497 BLACK BAPT EST[2]	NA	5,098	6,522*	8.0	12.6
CUMBERLAND	**249**	**88,060**	**122,964***	**44.8**	**100.0**
001 ADVENT CHR CH	3	194	251*	.1	.2
005 AME ZION	25	12,679	13,872	5.1	11.3
019 AMER BAPT USA	1	1,600	2,069*	.8	1.7
053 ASSEMB OF GOD	7	1,058	1,308	.5	1.1
081 CATHOLIC	5	NA	6,266	2.3	5.1
081d LATIN	*4*	*NA*	*5,900*	*2.1*	*4.8*
081e MARONITE	*1*	*NA*	*366*	*.1*	*.3*
089 CHR & MISS AL	1	88	128	-	.1
093 CHR CH (DISC)	8	597	869	.3	.7
097 CHR CHS&CHS CR	1	100	129*	-	.1
111 CH CR,SCIENTST	1	NR	NR	-	-
127 CH GOD (CLEVE)	20	2,919	3,774*	1.4	3.1
145 CH GOD PROPHCY	6	214	277*	.1	.2
151 L-D SAINTS	4	NA	1,940	.7	1.6
165 CH OF NAZARENE	1	190	268	.1	.2
167 CHS OF CHRIST	4	403	600	.2	.5
193 EPISCOPAL	6	1,439	1,993	.7	1.6
207 E.L.C.A.	2	544	690	.3	.6
223 FREE WILL BAPT	1	28	36*	-	-
226 FRIENDS-USA	1	12	18	-	-
226c FGC	*1*	*12*	*18*	*-*	*-*
246 GREEK ORTHODOX	1	NR	NR	-	-
283 LUTH—MO SYNOD	1	377	438	.2	.4
349 PENT HOLINESS	11	4,130	5,340*	1.9	4.3
353 CHR BRETHREN	2	70	145	.1	.1
355 PRESB CH (USA)	27	5,291	6,841*	2.5	5.6
356 PRESB CH AMER	1	76	95	-	.1
403 SALVATION ARMY	1	84	91	-	.1
413 S.D.A.	2	576	745*	.3	.6
419 SO BAPT CONV	66	25,839	33,407*	12.2	27.2
435 UNITARIAN-UNIV	1	22	27	-	-
443 UN C OF CHRIST	3	195	252*	.1	.2
449 UN METHODIST	28	10,459	13,522*	4.9	11.0
467 WESLEYAN	1	59	150	.1	.1
469 WELS	1	50	85	-	.1
496 JEWISH EST[1]	1	NA	0	-	-
497 BLACK BAPT EST[2]	NA	18,767	24,263*	8.8	19.7
498 INDEP.CHARIS.[3]	2	NA	1,125	.4	.9
499 INDEP.NON-CHAR[3]	3	NA	1,950	.7	1.6
CURRITUCK	**26**	**5,201**	**6,830***	**49.7**	**100.0**
005 AME ZION	4	765	1,020	7.4	14.9
053 ASSEMB OF GOD	2	201	325	2.4	4.8
093 CHR CH (DISC)	3	69	264	1.9	3.9
097 CHR CHS&CHS CR	2	250	313*	2.3	4.5
419 SO BAPT CONV	8	2,352	2,948*	21.5	43.2
449 UN METHODIST	7	1,199	1,503*	10.9	22.0
497 BLACK BAPT EST[2]	NA	365	457*	3.3	6.7
DARE	**43**	**5,944**	**8,789***	**38.6**	**100.0**
053 ASSEMB OF GOD	9	627	1,056	4.6	12.0
081 CATHOLIC	3	NA	978	4.3	11.1
081d LATIN	*3*	*NA*	*978*	*4.3*	*11.1*
093 CHR CH (DISC)	1	38	57	.3	.6
097 CHR CHS&CHS CR	1	51	62*	.3	.7
111 CH CR,SCIENTST	1	NR	NR	-	-
127 CH GOD (CLEVE)	1	26	32*	.1	.4
145 CH GOD PROPHCY	1	36	44*	.2	.5
151 L-D SAINTS	1	NA	185	.8	2.1
167 CHS OF CHRIST	1	15	20	.1	.2
193 EPISCOPAL	1	313	441	1.9	5.0
265 INT PENT C CHR	2	40	53	.2	.6
283 LUTH—MO SYNOD	1	83	109	.5	1.2
355 PRESB CH (USA)	1	266	324*	1.4	3.7
361 PRIM BAPT ASCS	1	2	2*	-	-
419 SO BAPT CONV	3	830	1,012*	4.4	11.5
435 UNITARIAN-UNIV	1	46	60	.3	.7
449 UN METHODIST	14	3,379	4,120*	18.1	46.9
497 BLACK BAPT EST[2]	NA	192	234*	1.0	2.7
DAVIDSON	**210**	**54,539**	**69,344***	**54.7**	**100.0**
005 AME ZION	5	1,248	1,667	1.3	2.4
019 AMER BAPT USA	1	275	337*	.3	.5
053 ASSEMB OF GOD	3	283	439	.3	.6
081 CATHOLIC	2	NA	764	.6	1.1
081d LATIN	*2*	*NA*	*764*	*.6*	*1.1*
089 CHR & MISS AL	3	742	1,032	.8	1.5

NA–Not applicable   NR–Not reported   *Total adherents estimated from known number of communicant, confirmed, full members.   - Represents a percent less than 0.1.   Percentages may not total due to rounding.
[1]See Appendix E   [2]See Appendix F   [3]See Appendix G   Lines in *italic* represent a breakdown of Catholic rites or Friends affiliations. They are included in their respective denominational total.

Table 4. Churches and Church Membership by County and Denomination: 1990

County and Denomination	Number of churches	Communicant, confirmed, full members	Total adherents Number	Percent of total population	Percent of total adherents
127 CH GOD (CLEVE)	5	656	804*	.6	1.2
145 CH GOD PROPHCY	4	143	175*	.1	.3
151 L-D SAINTS	1	NA	134	.1	.2
157 CH OF BRETHREN	1	64	78*	.1	.1
165 CH OF NAZARENE	1	58	75	.1	.1
167 CHS OF CHRIST	5	199	254	.2	.4
193 EPISCOPAL	2	312	425	.3	.6
207 E.L.C.A.	9	2,003	2,531	2.0	3.6
215 EVAN METH CH	2	94	115*	.1	.2
223 FREE WILL BAPT	11	867	1,062*	.8	1.5
226 FRIENDS-USA	1	107	131*	.1	.2
226e FUM	*1*	*107*	*131**	*.1*	*.2*
263 INT FOURSQ GOS	1	75	92*	.1	.1
295 MORAV CH-SOUTH	2	167	207	.2	.3
349 PENT HOLINESS	3	506	620*	.5	.9
355 PRESB CH (USA)	5	1,404	1,720*	1.4	2.5
356 PRESB CH AMER	1	116	116	.1	.2
361 PRIM BAPT ASCS	2	17	21*	-	-
403 SALVATION ARMY	3	255	275	.2	.4
413 S.D.A.	2	386	473*	.4	.7
419 SO BAPT CONV	43	16,650	20,400*	16.1	29.4
443 UN C OF CHRIST	20	6,413	7,857*	6.2	11.3
449 UN METHODIST	62	16,792	20,574*	16.2	29.7
467 WESLEYAN	9	1,039	1,674	1.3	2.4
496 JEWISH EST[1]	0	NA	408	.3	.6
497 BLACK BAPT EST[2]	NA	3,668	4,494*	3.5	6.5
499 INDEP.NON-CHAR[3]	1	NA	390	.3	.6
DAVIE	**65**	**12,030**	**14,912***	**53.5**	**100.0**
005 AME ZION	5	850	992	3.6	6.7
053 ASSEMB OF GOD	1	42	65	.2	.4
081 CATHOLIC	1	NA	170	.6	1.1
081d LATIN	*1*	*NA*	*170*	*.6*	*1.1*
127 CH GOD (CLEVE)	2	105	127*	.5	.9
145 CH GOD PROPHCY	1	36	44*	.2	.3
151 L-D SAINTS	1	NA	84	.3	.6
167 CHS OF CHRIST	3	458	563	2.0	3.8
193 EPISCOPAL	2	62	68	.2	.5
207 E.L.C.A.	1	61	73	.3	.5
295 MORAV CH-SOUTH	1	344	414	1.5	2.8
325 OLD REG BAPT	1	8	10*	-	.1
349 PENT HOLINESS	3	191	232*	.8	1.6
355 PRESB CH (USA)	5	952	1,156*	4.1	7.8
413 S.D.A.	1	41	50*	.2	.3
419 SO BAPT CONV	16	4,594	5,576*	20.0	37.4
449 UN METHODIST	20	3,506	4,256*	15.3	28.5
467 WESLEYAN	1	41	41	.1	.3
496 JEWISH EST[1]	0	NA	94	.3	.6
497 BLACK BAPT EST[2]	NA	739	897*	3.2	6.0
DUPLIN	**89**	**16,332**	**20,865***	**52.2**	**100.0**
005 AME ZION	5	655	786	2.0	3.8
053 ASSEMB OF GOD	1	199	240	.6	1.2
081 CATHOLIC	1	NA	68	.2	.3
081d LATIN	*1*	*NA*	*68*	*.2*	*.3*
093 CHR CH (DISC)	7	503	735	1.8	3.5
127 CH GOD (CLEVE)	1	117	146*	.4	.7
145 CH GOD PROPHCY	2	71	89*	.2	.4
151 L-D SAINTS	2	NA	311	.8	1.5
167 CHS OF CHRIST	2	35	46	.1	.2
223 FREE WILL BAPT	2	132	165*	.4	.8
263 INT FOURSQ GOS	1	19	24*	.1	.1
349 PENT HOLINESS	3	298	373*	.9	1.8
355 PRESB CH (USA)	17	1,781	2,227*	5.6	10.7
419 SO BAPT CONV	28	6,957	8,701*	21.8	41.7
435 UNITARIAN-UNIV	1	56	65	.2	.3
449 UN METHODIST	16	2,308	2,886*	7.2	13.8
497 BLACK BAPT EST[2]	NA	3,201	4,003*	10.0	19.2
DURHAM	**164**	**72,437**	**97,743***	**53.8**	**100.0**
001 ADVENT CHR CH	1	52	64*	-	.1
005 AME ZION	5	5,228	6,535	3.6	6.7
019 AMER BAPT USA	5	3,236	3,953*	2.2	4.0
053 ASSEMB OF GOD	3	275	407	.2	.4
081 CATHOLIC	3	NA	5,313	2.9	5.4
081d LATIN	*3*	*NA*	*5,313*	*2.9*	*5.4*
089 CHR & MISS AL	2	211	349	.2	.4
093 CHR CH (DISC)	2	60	125	.1	.1
097 CHR CHS&CHS CR	1	56	68*	-	.1
111 CH CR,SCIENTST	1	NR	NR	-	-
123 CH GOD (ANDER)	1	12	26	-	-
127 CH GOD (CLEVE)	2	277	338*	.2	.3
145 CH GOD PROPHCY	5	178	217*	.1	.2
151 L-D SAINTS	2	NA	740	.4	.8
165 CH OF NAZARENE	1	60	61	-	.1
167 CHS OF CHRIST	4	766	1,121	.6	1.1

County and Denomination	Number of churches	Communicant, confirmed, full members	Total adherents Number	Percent of total population	Percent of total adherents
193 EPISCOPAL	6	1,967	2,650	1.5	2.7
207 E.L.C.A.	4	954	1,239	.7	1.3
223 FREE WILL BAPT	6	830	1,014*	.6	1.0
226 FRIENDS-USA	1	59	140	.1	.1
226c FGC	*1*	*59*	*140*	*.1*	*.1*
246 GREEK ORTHODOX	1	NR	NR	-	-
263 INT FOURSQ GOS	1	3	4*	-	-
283 LUTH—MO SYNOD	1	315	436	.2	.4
285 MENNONITE CH	1	46	96	.1	.1
287 MENN GEN CONF	1	14	24	-	-
295 MORAV CH-SOUTH	1	51	58	-	.1
349 PENT HOLINESS	2	573	700*	.4	.7
353 CHR BRETHREN	2	263	526	.3	.5
355 PRESB CH (USA)	9	3,372	4,119*	2.3	4.2
356 PRESB CH AMER	1	15	21	-	-
361 PRIM BAPT ASCS	4	30	37*	-	-
403 SALVATION ARMY	1	128	130	.1	.1
413 S.D.A.	2	544	664*	.4	.7
419 SO BAPT CONV	42	25,618	31,291*	17.2	32.0
435 UNITARIAN-UNIV	1	475	691	.4	.7
443 UN C OF CHRIST	5	1,174	1,434*	.8	1.5
449 UN METHODIST	28	11,025	13,466*	7.4	13.8
467 WESLEYAN	1	59	59	-	.1
496 JEWISH EST[1]	4	NA	1,403	.8	1.4
497 BLACK BAPT EST[2]	NA	14,511	17,724*	9.7	18.1
499 INDEP.NON-CHAR[3]	1	NA	500	.3	.5
EDGECOMBE	**82**	**23,419**	**31,352***	**55.4**	**100.0**
001 ADVENT CHR CH	1	20	26*	-	.1
005 AME ZION	4	2,425	3,108	5.5	9.9
053 ASSEMB OF GOD	3	169	319	.6	1.0
081 CATHOLIC	2	NA	768	1.4	2.4
081d LATIN	*2*	*NA*	*768*	*1.4*	*2.4*
093 CHR CH (DISC)	4	739	1,097	1.9	3.5
097 CHR CHS&CHS CR	2	145	186*	.3	.6
127 CH GOD (CLEVE)	4	574	735*	1.3	2.3
145 CH GOD PROPHCY	1	36	46*	.1	.1
151 L-D SAINTS	2	NA	417	.7	1.3
167 CHS OF CHRIST	1	35	46	.1	.1
193 EPISCOPAL	7	754	931	1.6	3.0
207 E.L.C.A.	1	210	247	.4	.8
223 FREE WILL BAPT	2	220	282*	.5	.9
285 MENNONITE CH	1	27	43	.1	.1
349 PENT HOLINESS	3	697	892*	1.6	2.8
355 PRESB CH (USA)	10	1,011	1,294*	2.3	4.1
361 PRIM BAPT ASCS	1	18	23*	-	.1
403 SALVATION ARMY	1	95	96	.2	.3
413 S.D.A.	2	124	159*	.3	.5
419 SO BAPT CONV	21	6,682	8,554*	15.1	27.3
449 UN METHODIST	9	1,794	2,297*	4.1	7.3
497 BLACK BAPT EST[2]	NA	7,644	9,786*	17.3	31.2
FORSYTH	**301**	**121,034**	**165,697***	**62.3**	**100.0**
005 AME ZION	11	8,140	9,768	3.7	5.9
019 AMER BAPT USA	5	3,433	4,177*	1.6	2.5
053 ASSEMB OF GOD	4	1,909	3,008	1.1	1.8
081 CATHOLIC	6	NA	9,341	3.5	5.6
081d LATIN	*6*	*NA*	*9,341*	*3.5*	*5.6*
089 CHR & MISS AL	3	108	156	.1	.1
093 CHR CH (DISC)	8	1,441	1,947	.7	1.2
097 CHR CHS&CHS CR	12	2,139	2,603*	1.0	1.6
111 CH CR,SCIENTST	1	NR	NR	-	-
123 CH GOD (ANDER)	1	40	55	-	-
127 CH GOD (CLEVE)	5	389	473*	.2	.3
145 CH GOD PROPHCY	2	71	86*	-	.1
151 L-D SAINTS	3	NA	1,496	.6	.9
157 CH OF BRETHREN	1	279	339*	.1	.2
165 CH OF NAZARENE	2	92	134	.1	.1
167 CHS OF CHRIST	15	1,790	2,346	.9	1.4
193 EPISCOPAL	6	2,437	3,480	1.3	2.1
207 E.L.C.A.	7	1,895	2,370	.9	1.4
215 EVAN METH CH	1	52	63*	-	-
216 EVAN PRESBY CH	1	768	775	.3	.5
226 FRIENDS-USA	5	583	709*	.3	.4
226e FUM	*5*	*583*	*709**	*.3*	*.4*
246 GREEK ORTHODOX	1	NR	NR	-	-
263 INT FOURSQ GOS	2	0	0*	-	-
283 LUTH—MO SYNOD	4	708	886	.3	.5
285 MENNONITE CH	1	47	56	-	-
295 MORAV CH-SOUTH	32	12,552	15,410	5.8	9.3
349 PENT HOLINESS	7	514	625*	.2	.4
353 CHR BRETHREN	3	180	375	.1	.2
355 PRESB CH (USA)	14	5,280	6,424*	2.4	3.9
356 PRESB CH AMER	1	235	310	.1	.2
361 PRIM BAPT ASCS	2	75	91*	-	.1
403 SALVATION ARMY	1	85	90	-	.1
413 S.D.A.	2	1,183	1,439*	.5	.9

NA–Not applicable   NR–Not reported   *Total adherents estimated from known number of communicant, confirmed, full members.   - Represents a percent less than 0.1.   Percentages may not total due to rounding.

[1]See Appendix E   [2]See Appendix F   [3]See Appendix G   Lines in *italic* represent a breakdown of Catholic rites or Friends affiliations. They are included in their respective denominational total.

Table 4. Churches and Church Membership by County and Denomination: 1990

| County and Denomination | Number of churches | Communicant, confirmed, full members | Total adherents | | |
			Number	Percent of total population	Percent of total adherents
419 SO BAPT CONV	56	31,013	37,735*	14.2	22.8
435 UNITARIAN-UNIV	1	180	227	.1	.1
443 UN C OF CHRIST	6	690	840*	.3	.5
449 UN METHODIST	58	22,517	27,398*	10.3	16.5
467 WESLEYAN	6	517	694	.3	.4
496 JEWISH EST[1]	2	NA	911	.3	.5
497 BLACK BAPT EST[2]	NA	19,692	23,960*	9.0	14.5
498 INDEP.CHARIS.[3]	2	NA	1,900	.7	1.1
499 INDEP.NON-CHAR[3]	1	NA	3,000	1.1	1.8
FRANKLIN	**69**	**16,050**	**20,679***	**56.8**	**100.0**
005 AME ZION	3	298	451	1.2	2.2
093 CHR CH (DISC)	1	175	262	.7	1.3
127 CH GOD (CLEVE)	5	220	271*	.7	1.3
145 CH GOD PROPHCY	3	107	132*	.4	.6
151 L-D SAINTS	1	NA	472	1.3	2.3
176 CCC, NOT NAT'L	1	123	151*	.4	.7
193 EPISCOPAL	2	112	174	.5	.8
349 PENT HOLINESS	2	66	81*	.2	.4
355 PRESB CH (USA)	2	121	149*	.4	.7
419 SO BAPT CONV	32	9,774	12,033*	33.0	58.2
443 UN C OF CHRIST	7	763	939*	2.6	4.5
449 UN METHODIST	10	1,536	1,891*	5.2	9.1
496 JEWISH EST[1]	0	NA	281	.8	1.4
497 BLACK BAPT EST[2]	NA	2,755	3,392*	9.3	16.4
GASTON	**326**	**94,551**	**122,576***	**70.0**	**100.0**
001 ADVENT CHR CH	1	32	40*	-	-
005 AME ZION	26	7,676	9,714	5.5	7.9
053 ASSEMB OF GOD	7	1,218	1,855	1.1	1.5
055 AS REF PRES CH	6	1,546	1,797	1.0	1.5
081 CATHOLIC	3	NA	3,388	1.9	2.8
081d LATIN	3	NA	3,388	1.9	2.8
097 CHR CHS&CHS CR	1	0	0*	-	-
111 CH CR,SCIENTST	1	NR	NR	-	-
127 CH GOD (CLEVE)	27	4,054	5,021*	2.9	4.1
145 CH GOD PROPHCY	3	107	133*	.1	.1
151 L-D SAINTS	2	NA	682	.4	.6
165 CH OF NAZARENE	3	169	309	.2	.3
167 CHS OF CHRIST	2	150	218	.1	.2
193 EPISCOPAL	4	699	821	.5	.7
207 E.L.C.A.	15	4,731	5,883	3.4	4.8
216 EVAN PRESBY CH	2	135	138	.1	.1
223 FREE WILL BAPT	31	3,825	4,737*	2.7	3.9
263 INT FOURSQ GOS	4	1,087	1,346*	.8	1.1
283 LUTH—MO SYNOD	1	26	29	-	-
349 PENT HOLINESS	5	555	687*	.4	.6
353 CHR BRETHREN	1	25	50	-	-
355 PRESB CH (USA)	16	4,626	5,729*	3.3	4.7
356 PRESB CH AMER	8	899	1,052	.6	.9
403 SALVATION ARMY	1	205	207	.1	.2
413 S.D.A.	2	175	217*	.1	.2
419 SO BAPT CONV	107	43,118	53,399*	30.5	43.6
443 UN C OF CHRIST	1	93	115*	.1	.1
449 UN METHODIST	38	11,266	13,952*	8.0	11.4
467 WESLEYAN	7	1,379	1,671	1.0	1.4
496 JEWISH EST[1]	1	NA	1,020	.6	.8
497 BLACK BAPT EST[2]	NA	6,755	8,366*	4.8	6.8
GATES	**25**	**5,465**	**6,828***	**73.4**	**100.0**
005 AME ZION	4	500	591	6.4	8.7
053 ASSEMB OF GOD	1	17	26	.3	.4
176 CCC, NOT NAT'L	1	180	225*	2.4	3.3
193 EPISCOPAL	2	42	70	.8	1.0
419 SO BAPT CONV	9	2,341	2,930*	31.5	42.9
443 UN C OF CHRIST	2	429	537*	5.8	7.9
449 UN METHODIST	6	547	685*	7.4	10.0
497 BLACK BAPT EST[2]	NA	1,409	1,764*	19.0	25.8
GRAHAM	**20**	**3,615**	**4,421***	**61.4**	**100.0**
081 CATHOLIC	1	NA	24	.3	.5
081d LATIN	1	NA	24	.3	.5
127 CH GOD (CLEVE)	1	16	19*	.3	.4
167 CHS OF CHRIST	1	10	13	.2	.3
193 EPISCOPAL	1	24	26	.4	.6
207 E.L.C.A.	1	8	8	.1	.2
419 SO BAPT CONV	14	3,403	4,143*	57.6	93.7
449 UN METHODIST	1	154	188*	2.6	4.3
GRANVILLE	**68**	**19,179**	**23,786***	**62.0**	**100.0**
005 AME ZION	5	1,140	1,520	4.0	6.4
019 AMER BAPT USA	1	225	275*	.7	1.2
081 CATHOLIC	2	NA	152	.4	.6
081d LATIN	2	NA	152	.4	.6
127 CH GOD (CLEVE)	3	99	121*	.3	.5

| County and Denomination | Number of churches | Communicant, confirmed, full members | Total adherents | | |
			Number	Percent of total population	Percent of total adherents
145 CH GOD PROPHCY	1	36	44*	.1	.2
193 EPISCOPAL	2	299	413	1.1	1.7
355 PRESB CH (USA)	7	409	500*	1.3	2.1
419 SO BAPT CONV	30	10,951	13,396*	34.9	56.3
443 UN C OF CHRIST	3	169	207*	.5	.9
449 UN METHODIST	14	2,251	2,754*	7.2	11.6
497 BLACK BAPT EST[2]	NA	3,600	4,404*	11.5	18.5
GREENE	**24**	**6,600**	**7,991***	**51.9**	**100.0**
005 AME ZION	5	1,658	1,708	11.1	21.4
093 CHR CH (DISC)	4	221	395	2.6	4.9
223 FREE WILL BAPT	1	500	624*	4.1	7.8
349 PENT HOLINESS	1	47	59*	.4	.7
355 PRESB CH (USA)	2	90	112*	.7	1.4
419 SO BAPT CONV	2	470	586*	3.8	7.3
449 UN METHODIST	9	1,416	1,766*	11.5	22.1
497 BLACK BAPT EST[2]	NA	2,198	2,741*	17.8	34.3
GUILFORD	**384**	**155,069**	**205,490***	**59.1**	**100.0**
005 AME ZION	8	13,345	16,014	4.6	7.8
019 AMER BAPT USA	1	15	18*	-	-
053 ASSEMB OF GOD	8	546	929	.3	.5
055 AS REF PRES CH	2	583	829	.2	.4
081 CATHOLIC	7	NA	10,339	3.0	5.0
081d LATIN	7	NA	10,339	3.0	5.0
089 CHR & MISS AL	4	414	675	.2	.3
093 CHR CH (DISC)	3	521	935	.3	.5
097 CHR CHS&CHS CR	5	914	1,108*	.3	.5
111 CH CR,SCIENTST	2	NR	NR	-	-
123 CH GOD (ANDER)	5	235	274	.1	.1
127 CH GOD (CLEVE)	9	859	1,041*	.3	.5
145 CH GOD PROPHCY	9	321	389*	.1	.2
151 L-D SAINTS	6	NA	2,249	.6	1.1
165 CH OF NAZARENE	8	652	893	.3	.4
167 CHS OF CHRIST	6	1,290	1,868	.5	.9
176 CCC, NOT NAT'L	1	98	119*	-	.1
193 EPISCOPAL	9	3,904	4,874	1.4	2.4
207 E.L.C.A.	10	3,326	4,417	1.3	2.1
215 EVAN METH CH	3	271	329*	.1	.2
216 EVAN PRESBY CH	1	156	159	-	.1
223 FREE WILL BAPT	3	236	286*	.1	.1
226 FRIENDS-USA	17	3,646	4,445*	1.3	2.2
226b EFI	2	184	226	.1	.1
226c FGC	1	103	147	-	.1
226d FGC & FUM	1	424	514*	.1	.3
226e FUM	13	2,935	3,558*	1.0	1.7
246 GREEK ORTHODOX	1	NR	NR	-	-
263 INT FOURSQ GOS	3	518	628*	.2	.3
283 LUTH—MO SYNOD	6	936	1,089	.3	.5
295 MORAV CH-SOUTH	2	535	654	.2	.3
349 PENT HOLINESS	9	1,116	1,353*	.4	.7
353 CHR BRETHREN	1	475	660	.2	.3
355 PRESB CH (USA)	29	13,900	16,851*	4.9	8.2
356 PRESB CH AMER	1	64	64	-	-
361 PRIM BAPT ASCS	3	142	172*	-	.1
403 SALVATION ARMY	1	174	178	.1	.1
413 S.D.A.	3	1,342	1,627*	.5	.8
419 SO BAPT CONV	76	43,579	52,832*	15.2	25.7
435 UNITARIAN-UNIV	1	186	247	.1	.1
443 UN C OF CHRIST	14	3,148	3,816*	1.1	1.9
449 UN METHODIST	80	34,713	42,083*	12.1	20.5
467 WESLEYAN	18	3,250	4,451	1.3	2.2
496 JEWISH EST[1]	6	NA	1,162	.3	.6
497 BLACK BAPT EST[2]	NA	19,659	23,833*	6.9	11.6
498 INDEP.CHARIS.[3]	1	NA	800	.2	.4
499 INDEP.NON-CHAR[3]	2	NA	800	.2	.4
HALIFAX	**88**	**21,823**	**28,495***	**51.3**	**100.0**
053 ASSEMB OF GOD	1	10	24	-	.1
081 CATHOLIC	2	NA	390	.7	1.4
081d LATIN	2	NA	390	.7	1.4
097 CHR CHS&CHS CR	6	1,275	1,620*	2.9	5.7
123 CH GOD (ANDER)	1	5	20	-	.1
127 CH GOD (CLEVE)	4	232	295*	.5	1.0
151 L-D SAINTS	1	NA	238	.4	.8
165 CH OF NAZARENE	1	0	0	-	-
167 CHS OF CHRIST	2	36	45	.1	.2
193 EPISCOPAL	7	454	651	1.2	2.3
223 FREE WILL BAPT	1	80	102*	.2	.4
265 INT PENT C CHR	1	6	6	-	-
339 PENT CH OF GOD	1	36	85	.2	.3
349 PENT HOLINESS	5	307	390*	.7	1.4
355 PRESB CH (USA)	3	499	634*	1.1	2.2
361 PRIM BAPT ASCS	2	8	10*	-	-
413 S.D.A.	1	61	78*	.1	.3
419 SO BAPT CONV	26	7,323	9,305*	16.8	32.7

Table 4. Churches and Church Membership by County and Denomination: 1990

County and Denomination	Number of churches	Communicant, confirmed, full members	Total adherents Number	Percent of total population	Percent of total adherents
449 UN METHODIST	22	4,831	6,139*	11.1	21.5
496 JEWISH EST[1]	1	NA	0	-	-
497 BLACK BAPT EST[2]	NA	6,660	8,463*	15.2	29.7
HARNETT	**124**	**30,180**	**38,913***	**57.4**	**100.0**
001 ADVENT CHR CH	2	145	181*	.3	.5
005 AME ZION	17	4,415	5,876	8.7	15.1
053 ASSEMB OF GOD	2	228	294	.4	.8
081 CATHOLIC	1	NA	548	.8	1.4
081d LATIN	1	NA	548	.8	1.4
093 CHR CH (DISC)	3	474	734	1.1	1.9
127 CH GOD (CLEVE)	6	774	967*	1.4	2.5
145 CH GOD PROPHCY	7	250	312*	.5	.8
151 L-D SAINTS	1	NA	162	.2	.4
193 EPISCOPAL	1	123	151	.2	.4
223 FREE WILL BAPT	3	388	485*	.7	1.2
349 PENT HOLINESS	5	1,242	1,551*	2.3	4.0
355 PRESB CH (USA)	19	2,704	3,377*	5.0	8.7
361 PRIM BAPT ASCS	5	102	127*	.2	.3
413 S.D.A.	1	99	124*	.2	.3
419 SO BAPT CONV	34	11,928	14,897*	22.0	38.3
443 UN C OF CHRIST	1	139	174*	.3	.4
449 UN METHODIST	16	3,473	4,337*	6.4	11.1
497 BLACK BAPT EST[2]	NA	3,696	4,616*	6.8	11.9
HAYWOOD	**123**	**29,180**	**35,397***	**75.4**	**100.0**
005 AME ZION	2	105	155	.3	.4
053 ASSEMB OF GOD	1	32	68	.1	.2
081 CATHOLIC	3	NA	518	1.1	1.5
081d LATIN	3	NA	518	1.1	1.5
111 CH CR,SCIENTST	1	NR	NR	-	-
127 CH GOD (CLEVE)	4	338	401*	.9	1.1
145 CH GOD PROPHCY	3	107	127*	.3	.4
151 L-D SAINTS	1	NA	190	.4	.5
165 CH OF NAZARENE	1	42	94	.2	.3
167 CHS OF CHRIST	1	80	104	.2	.3
193 EPISCOPAL	2	302	424	.9	1.2
221 FREE METHODIST	1	22	22	-	.1
223 FREE WILL BAPT	5	452	536*	1.1	1.5
283 LUTH—MO SYNOD	1	130	152	.3	.4
353 CHR BRETHREN	1	80	90	.2	.3
355 PRESB CH (USA)	3	352	417*	.9	1.2
356 PRESB CH AMER	2	281	284	.6	.8
403 SALVATION ARMY	1	120	142	.3	.4
413 S.D.A.	1	104	123*	.3	.3
419 SO BAPT CONV	58	20,511	24,311*	51.8	68.7
449 UN METHODIST	28	5,725	6,786*	14.5	19.2
467 WESLEYAN	3	241	268	.6	.8
497 BLACK BAPT EST[2]	NA	156	185*	.4	.5
HENDERSON	**107**	**32,722**	**42,045***	**60.7**	**100.0**
005 AME ZION	1	21	32	-	.1
053 ASSEMB OF GOD	1	45	55	.1	.1
055 AS REF PRES CH	1	397	405	.6	1.0
081 CATHOLIC	1	NA	2,115	3.1	5.0
081d LATIN	1	NA	2,115	3.1	5.0
089 CHR & MISS AL	1	126	216	.3	.5
111 CH CR,SCIENTST	1	NR	NR	-	-
121 CH GOD (ABR)	1	18	21*	-	-
123 CH GOD (ANDER)	1	25	25	-	.1
127 CH GOD (CLEVE)	4	294	350*	.5	.8
151 L-D SAINTS	1	NA	365	.5	.9
164 CH LUTH CONF	1	29	35	.1	.1
165 CH OF NAZARENE	1	439	490	.7	1.2
167 CHS OF CHRIST	1	177	230	.3	.5
193 EPISCOPAL	6	1,797	2,574	3.7	6.1
207 E.L.C.A.	1	829	981	1.4	2.3
263 INT FOURSQ GOS	1	0	0*	-	-
283 LUTH—MO SYNOD	1	197	218	.3	.5
339 PENT CH OF GOD	1	35	77	.1	.2
349 PENT HOLINESS	1	201	240*	.3	.6
355 PRESB CH (USA)	5	2,000	2,384*	3.4	5.7
356 PRESB CH AMER	1	486	486	.7	1.2
403 SALVATION ARMY	1	54	56	.1	.1
413 S.D.A.	3	1,465	1,746*	2.5	4.2
419 SO BAPT CONV	51	18,513	22,068*	31.9	52.5
435 UNITARIAN-UNIV	1	95	107	.2	.3
443 UN C OF CHRIST	1	415	495*	.7	1.2
449 UN METHODIST	13	4,273	5,094*	7.4	12.1
467 WESLEYAN	2	152	282	.4	.7
469 WELS	1	69	84	.1	.2
496 JEWISH EST[1]	1	NA	135	.2	.3
497 BLACK BAPT EST[2]	NA	570	679*	1.0	1.6
HERTFORD	**40**	**11,783**	**15,050***	**66.8**	**100.0**
005 AME ZION	3	158	174	.8	1.2

County and Denomination	Number of churches	Communicant, confirmed, full members	Total adherents Number	Percent of total population	Percent of total adherents
053 ASSEMB OF GOD	2	108	164	.7	1.1
081 CATHOLIC	1	NA	153	.7	1.0
081d LATIN	1	NA	153	.7	1.0
097 CHR CHS&CHS CR	1	72	91*	.4	.6
123 CH GOD (ANDER)	1	24	24	.1	.2
127 CH GOD (CLEVE)	1	23	29*	.1	.2
193 EPISCOPAL	1	149	166	.7	1.1
223 FREE WILL BAPT	2	265	336*	1.5	2.2
349 PENT HOLINESS	2	348	441*	2.0	2.9
355 PRESB CH (USA)	1	85	108*	.5	.7
413 S.D.A.	1	67	85*	.4	.6
419 SO BAPT CONV	19	5,217	6,608*	29.3	43.9
449 UN METHODIST	5	896	1,135*	5.0	7.5
497 BLACK BAPT EST[2]	NA	4,371	5,536*	24.6	36.8
HOKE	**34**	**10,116**	**13,720***	**60.0**	**100.0**
005 AME ZION	5	1,646	2,469	10.8	18.0
053 ASSEMB OF GOD	1	21	51	.2	.4
081 CATHOLIC	1	NA	130	.6	.9
081d LATIN	1	NA	130	.6	.9
127 CH GOD (CLEVE)	1	73	96*	.4	.7
145 CH GOD PROPHCY	1	36	47*	.2	.3
215 EVAN METH CH	1	75	98*	.4	.7
353 CHR BRETHREN	1	50	75	.3	.5
355 PRESB CH (USA)	6	921	1,206*	5.3	8.8
419 SO BAPT CONV	12	2,902	3,799*	16.6	27.7
449 UN METHODIST	5	1,063	1,391*	6.1	10.1
497 BLACK BAPT EST[2]	NA	3,329	4,358*	19.1	31.8
HYDE	**36**	**2,205**	**2,933***	**54.2**	**100.0**
053 ASSEMB OF GOD	2	36	81	1.5	2.8
093 CHR CH (DISC)	9	225	436	8.1	14.9
097 CHR CHS&CHS CR	5	236	292*	5.4	10.0
167 CHS OF CHRIST	1	10	20	.4	.7
193 EPISCOPAL	4	49	79	1.5	2.7
285 MENNONITE CH	1	51	51	.9	1.7
349 PENT HOLINESS	1	18	22*	.4	.8
355 PRESB CH (USA)	1	54	67*	1.2	2.3
419 SO BAPT CONV	3	220	272*	5.0	9.3
449 UN METHODIST	9	706	872*	16.1	29.7
497 BLACK BAPT EST[2]	NA	600	741*	13.7	25.3
IREDELL	**209**	**50,718**	**64,530***	**69.4**	**100.0**
005 AME ZION	15	4,147	5,404	5.8	8.4
019 AMER BAPT USA	1	142	174*	.2	.3
053 ASSEMB OF GOD	4	387	433	.5	.7
055 AS REF PRES CH	9	2,353	2,674	2.9	4.1
081 CATHOLIC	2	NA	1,675	1.8	2.6
081d LATIN	2	NA	1,675	1.8	2.6
089 CHR & MISS AL	1	30	66	.1	.1
097 CHR CHS&CHS CR	1	29	36*	-	.1
127 CH GOD (CLEVE)	9	956	1,174*	1.3	1.8
145 CH GOD PROPHCY	1	36	44*	-	.1
151 L-D SAINTS	1	NA	369	.4	.6
165 CH OF NAZARENE	2	188	237	.3	.4
167 CHS OF CHRIST	5	800	1,064	1.1	1.6
193 EPISCOPAL	2	400	544	.6	.8
203 EVAN FREE CH	1	0	0	-	-
207 E.L.C.A.	7	2,111	2,597	2.8	4.0
215 EVAN METH CH	1	101	124*	.1	.2
223 FREE WILL BAPT	2	287	353*	.4	.5
226 FRIENDS-USA	2	129	158*	.2	.2
226e FUM	2	129	158*	.2	.2
263 INT FOURSQ GOS	3	167	205*	.2	.3
283 LUTH—MO SYNOD	1	174	215	.2	.3
349 PENT HOLINESS	1	35	43*	-	.1
355 PRESB CH (USA)	22	3,693	4,536*	4.9	7.0
356 PRESB CH AMER	2	288	361	.4	.6
403 SALVATION ARMY	1	38	38	-	.1
413 S.D.A.	1	85	104*	.1	.2
419 SO BAPT CONV	55	19,661	24,150*	26.0	37.4
443 UN C OF CHRIST	5	251	308*	.3	.5
449 UN METHODIST	46	10,196	12,524*	13.5	19.4
467 WESLEYAN	5	445	512	.6	.8
496 JEWISH EST[1]	1	NA	0	-	-
497 BLACK BAPT EST[2]	NA	3,589	4,408*	4.7	6.8
JACKSON	**88**	**13,292**	**16,395***	**61.1**	**100.0**
005 AME ZION	2	168	182	.7	1.1
053 ASSEMB OF GOD	1	26	35	.1	.2
081 CATHOLIC	3	NA	260	1.0	1.6
081d LATIN	3	NA	260	1.0	1.6
127 CH GOD (CLEVE)	5	238	280*	1.0	1.7
151 L-D SAINTS	1	NA	310	1.2	1.9
157 CH OF BRETHREN	1	92	108*	.4	.7
167 CHS OF CHRIST	2	151	196	.7	1.2

NA–Not applicable   NR–Not reported   *Total adherents estimated from known number of communicant, confirmed, full members.   - Represents a percent less than 0.1.   Percentages may not total due to rounding.
[1]See Appendix E   [2]See Appendix F   [3]See Appendix G   Lines in *italic* represent a breakdown of Catholic rites or Friends affiliations. They are included in their respective denominational total.

Table 4. Churches and Church Membership by County and Denomination: 1990

County and Denomination		Number of churches	Communicant, confirmed, full members	Total adherents		
				Number	Percent of total population	Percent of total adherents
193	EPISCOPAL	3	250	385	1.4	2.3
207	E.L.C.A.	1	110	117	.4	.7
355	PRESB CH (USA)	2	226	266*	1.0	1.6
356	PRESB CH AMER	1	0	0	-	-
413	S.D.A.	1	37	44*	.2	.3
419	SO BAPT CONV	50	10,294	12,127*	45.2	74.0
449	UN METHODIST	12	1,670	1,967*	7.3	12.0
467	WESLEYAN	3	30	118	.4	.7
JOHNSTON		**185**	**29,584**	**37,639***	**46.3**	**100.0**
001	ADVENT CHR CH	13	1,250	1,542*	1.9	4.1
005	AME ZION	4	196	263	.3	.7
053	ASSEMB OF GOD	2	306	515	.6	1.4
081	CATHOLIC	2	NA	419	.5	1.1
081d	*LATIN*	*2*	*NA*	*419*	*.5*	*1.1*
089	CHR & MISS AL	1	0	47	.1	.1
093	CHR CH (DISC)	19	1,905	2,789	3.4	7.4
123	CH GOD (ANDER)	1	50	56	.1	.1
127	CH GOD (CLEVE)	13	988	1,219*	1.5	3.2
145	CH GOD PROPHCY	11	392	484*	.6	1.3
151	L-D SAINTS	1	NA	116	.1	.3
167	CHS OF CHRIST	1	46	59	.1	.2
193	EPISCOPAL	1	136	159	.2	.4
223	FREE WILL BAPT	4	682	842*	1.0	2.2
226	FRIENDS-USA	1	89	110*	.1	.3
226e	*FUM*	*1*	*89*	*110***	*.1*	*.3*
349	PENT HOLINESS	10	779	961*	1.2	2.6
355	PRESB CH (USA)	15	1,131	1,396*	1.7	3.7
356	PRESB CH AMER	1	84	86	.1	.2
361	PRIM BAPT ASCS	13	146	180*	.2	.5
403	SALVATION ARMY	1	68	69	.1	.2
419	SO BAPT CONV	47	13,112	16,180*	19.9	43.0
443	UN C OF CHRIST	4	677	835*	1.0	2.2
449	UN METHODIST	20	4,074	5,027*	6.2	13.4
497	BLACK BAPT EST[2]	NA	3,473	4,285*	5.3	11.4
JONES		**28**	**4,330**	**5,452***	**57.9**	**100.0**
005	AME ZION	4	200	229	2.4	4.2
093	CHR CH (DISC)	5	378	511	5.4	9.4
097	CHR CHS&CHS CR	1	0	0*	-	-
193	EPISCOPAL	1	26	27	.3	.5
349	PENT HOLINESS	1	73	92*	1.0	1.7
355	PRESB CH (USA)	1	104	131*	1.4	2.4
419	SO BAPT CONV	5	1,303	1,638*	17.4	30.0
443	UN C OF CHRIST	3	171	215*	2.3	3.9
449	UN METHODIST	7	836	1,051*	11.2	19.3
497	BLACK BAPT EST[2]	NA	1,239	1,558*	16.5	28.6
LEE		**91**	**22,348**	**30,301***	**73.2**	**100.0**
005	AME ZION	17	4,651	6,076	14.7	20.1
053	ASSEMB OF GOD	1	133	200	.5	.7
081	CATHOLIC	1	NA	1,186	2.9	3.9
081d	*LATIN*	*1*	*NA*	*1,186*	*2.9*	*3.9*
093	CHR CH (DISC)	1	134	185	.4	.6
097	CHR CHS&CHS CR	1	17	21*	.1	.1
111	CH CR,SCIENTST	1	NR	NR	-	-
127	CH GOD (CLEVE)	1	362	455*	1.1	1.5
145	CH GOD PROPHCY	3	107	134*	.3	.4
151	L-D SAINTS	1	NA	177	.4	.6
165	CH OF NAZARENE	1	23	53	.1	.2
167	CHS OF CHRIST	2	61	78	.2	.3
176	CCC, NOT NAT'L	3	290	364*	.9	1.2
193	EPISCOPAL	1	359	491	1.2	1.6
207	E.L.C.A.	1	256	310	.7	1.0
223	FREE WILL BAPT	2	90	113*	.3	.4
263	INT FOURSQ GOS	1	32	40*	.1	.1
349	PENT HOLINESS	2	190	239*	.6	.8
353	CHR BRETHREN	1	150	200	.5	.7
355	PRESB CH (USA)	14	2,758	3,464*	8.4	11.4
419	SO BAPT CONV	15	5,585	7,015*	17.0	23.2
443	UN C OF CHRIST	7	1,175	1,476*	3.6	4.9
449	UN METHODIST	12	3,653	4,589*	11.1	15.1
467	WESLEYAN	1	53	85	.2	.3
497	BLACK BAPT EST[2]	NA	2,269	2,850*	6.9	9.4
499	INDEP.NON-CHAR[3]	1	NA	500	1.2	1.7
LENOIR		**105**	**25,894**	**34,755***	**60.7**	**100.0**
001	ADVENT CHR CH	1	87	108*	.2	.3
005	AME ZION	10	3,863	5,150	9.0	14.8
053	ASSEMB OF GOD	1	45	60	.1	.2
081	CATHOLIC	2	NA	559	1.0	1.6
081d	*LATIN*	*2*	*NA*	*559*	*1.0*	*1.6*
093	CHR CH (DISC)	22	3,325	4,509	7.9	13.0
111	CH CR,SCIENTST	1	NR	NR	-	-
127	CH GOD (CLEVE)	3	429	532*	.9	1.5
145	CH GOD PROPHCY	2	71	88*	.2	.3

County and Denomination		Number of churches	Communicant, confirmed, full members	Total adherents		
				Number	Percent of total population	Percent of total adherents
151	L-D SAINTS	4	NA	1,458	2.5	4.2
165	CH OF NAZARENE	1	34	0	-	-
167	CHS OF CHRIST	1	57	79	.1	.2
193	EPISCOPAL	3	660	779	1.4	2.2
207	E.L.C.A.	1	40	54	.1	.2
223	FREE WILL BAPT	4	1,360	1,686*	2.9	4.9
263	INT FOURSQ GOS	1	56	69*	.1	.2
283	LUTH—MO SYNOD	1	133	160	.3	.5
349	PENT HOLINESS	3	685	849*	1.5	2.4
355	PRESB CH (USA)	7	963	1,194*	2.1	3.4
403	SALVATION ARMY	1	156	157	.3	.5
413	S.D.A.	3	274	340*	.6	1.0
419	SO BAPT CONV	16	4,369	5,416*	9.5	15.6
435	UNITARIAN-UNIV	1	18	18	-	.1
443	UN C OF CHRIST	2	124	154*	.3	.4
449	UN METHODIST	13	3,703	4,590*	8.0	13.2
496	JEWISH EST[1]	NA	NA	0	-	-
497	BLACK BAPT EST[2]	NA	5,442	6,746*	11.8	19.4
LINCOLN		**119**	**25,975**	**33,448***	**66.5**	**100.0**
005	AME ZION	4	977	1,178	2.3	3.5
053	ASSEMB OF GOD	2	41	66	.1	.2
081	CATHOLIC	2	NA	476	.9	1.4
081d	*LATIN*	*2*	*NA*	*476*	*.9*	*1.4*
093	CHR CH (DISC)	1	53	78	.2	.2
097	CHR CHS&CHS CR	1	18	22*	-	.1
127	CH GOD (CLEVE)	6	419	519*	1.0	1.6
145	CH GOD PROPHCY	2	71	88*	.2	.3
167	CHS OF CHRIST	2	60	76	.2	.2
193	EPISCOPAL	3	301	446	.9	1.3
207	E.L.C.A.	9	2,280	2,809	5.6	8.4
215	EVAN METH CH	1	39	48*	.1	.1
223	FREE WILL BAPT	1	163	202*	.4	.6
263	INT FOURSQ GOS	1	37	46*	.1	.1
283	LUTH—MO SYNOD	1	79	128	.3	.4
349	PENT HOLINESS	1	79	98*	.2	.3
355	PRESB CH (USA)	3	738	914*	1.8	2.7
356	PRESB CH AMER	1	142	155	.3	.5
413	S.D.A.	1	59	73*	.1	.2
419	SO BAPT CONV	35	11,341	14,049*	27.9	42.0
443	UN C OF CHRIST	2	227	281*	.6	.8
449	UN METHODIST	35	7,221	8,945*	17.8	26.7
467	WESLEYAN	4	406	518	1.0	1.5
496	JEWISH EST[1]	0	NA	207	.4	.6
497	BLACK BAPT EST[2]	NA	1,224	1,516*	3.0	4.5
499	INDEP.NON-CHAR[3]	1	NA	510	1.0	1.5
MC DOWELL		**104**	**17,131**	**21,250***	**59.6**	**100.0**
005	AME ZION	2	328	369	1.0	1.7
053	ASSEMB OF GOD	1	42	72	.2	.3
081	CATHOLIC	1	NA	145	.4	.7
081d	*LATIN*	*1*	*NA*	*145*	*.4*	*.7*
089	CHR & MISS AL	1	39	57	.2	.3
097	CHR CHS&CHS CR	1	25	30*	.1	.1
127	CH GOD (CLEVE)	5	350	426*	1.2	2.0
145	CH GOD PROPHCY	1	36	44*	.1	.2
146	CH GOD MTN ASM	1	109	133*	.4	.6
151	L-D SAINTS	1	NA	241	.7	1.1
167	CHS OF CHRIST	2	84	109	.3	.5
193	EPISCOPAL	1	92	119	.3	.6
223	FREE WILL BAPT	9	1,442	1,755*	4.9	8.3
283	LUTH—MO SYNOD	1	47	55	.2	.3
349	PENT HOLINESS	6	341	415*	1.2	2.0
355	PRESB CH (USA)	5	573	697*	2.0	3.3
356	PRESB CH AMER	2	242	242	.7	1.1
413	S.D.A.	1	73	89*	.2	.4
419	SO BAPT CONV	42	10,550	12,837*	36.0	60.4
449	UN METHODIST	19	2,263	2,754*	7.7	13.0
467	WESLEYAN	2	138	227	.6	1.1
497	BLACK BAPT EST[2]	NA	357	434*	1.2	2.0
MACON		**95**	**13,748**	**17,222***	**73.3**	**100.0**
005	AME ZION	1	13	29	.1	.2
053	ASSEMB OF GOD	6	673	972	4.1	5.6
081	CATHOLIC	2	NA	554	2.4	3.2
081d	*LATIN*	*2*	*NA*	*554*	*2.4*	*3.2*
089	CHR & MISS AL	1	19	54	.2	.3
111	CH CR,SCIENTST	1	NR	NR	-	-
127	CH GOD (CLEVE)	6	393	464*	2.0	2.7
151	L-D SAINTS	1	NA	210	.9	1.2
165	CH OF NAZARENE	1	20	37	.2	.2
167	CHS OF CHRIST	2	50	65	.3	.4
193	EPISCOPAL	4	421	511	2.2	3.0
216	EVAN PRESBY CH	3	187	189	.8	1.1
226	FRIENDS-USA	1	3	4*	-	-
226c	*FGC*	*1*	*3*	*4***	*-*	*-*

NA–Not applicable   NR–Not reported   *Total adherents estimated from known number of communicant, confirmed, full members.   - Represents a percent less than 0.1.   Percentages may not total due to rounding.
[1]See Appendix E   [2]See Appendix F   [3]See Appendix G   Lines in *italic* represent a breakdown of Catholic rites or Friends affiliations. They are included in their respective denominational total.

Table 4. Churches and Church Membership by County and Denomination: 1990

County and Denomination	Number of churches	Communicant, confirmed, full members	Total adherents Number	Percent of total population	Percent of total adherents
283 LUTH—MO SYNOD	1	131	164	.7	1.0
355 PRESB CH (USA)	3	423	499*	2.1	2.9
356 PRESB CH AMER	1	31	37	.2	.2
413 S.D.A.	1	105	124*	.5	.7
419 SO BAPT CONV	44	9,124	10,768*	45.8	62.5
435 UNITARIAN-UNIV	1	36	40	.2	.2
449 UN METHODIST	15	2,119	2,501*	10.6	14.5
MADISON	**83**	**9,875**	**11,963***	**70.6**	**100.0**
081 CATHOLIC	2	NA	132	.8	1.1
081d LATIN	*2*	*NA*	*132*	*.8*	*1.1*
097 CHR CHS&CHS CR	2	53	63*	.4	.5
123 CH GOD (ANDER)	7	244	269	1.6	2.2
127 CH GOD (CLEVE)	2	45	54*	.3	.5
193 EPISCOPAL	1	62	148	.9	1.2
223 FREE WILL BAPT	3	252	301*	1.8	2.5
355 PRESB CH (USA)	4	164	196*	1.2	1.6
403 SALVATION ARMY	1	82	84	.5	.7
419 SO BAPT CONV	50	8,456	10,098*	59.6	84.4
449 UN METHODIST	10	489	584*	3.4	4.9
467 WESLEYAN	1	28	34	.2	.3
MARTIN	**78**	**13,292**	**17,168***	**68.5**	**100.0**
005 AME ZION	5	1,095	1,460	5.8	8.5
053 ASSEMB OF GOD	2	55	92	.4	.5
081 CATHOLIC	1	NA	68	.3	.4
081d LATIN	*1*	*NA*	*68*	*.3*	*.4*
093 CHR CH (DISC)	17	1,482	2,199	8.8	12.8
097 CHR CHS&CHS CR	13	2,379	2,982*	11.9	17.4
127 CH GOD (CLEVE)	2	107	134*	.5	.8
167 CHS OF CHRIST	1	14	14	.1	.1
193 EPISCOPAL	1	129	152	.6	.9
223 FREE WILL BAPT	1	65	81*	.3	.5
226 FRIENDS-USA	1	21	26*	.1	.2
226g INDEP EVAN	*1*	*21*	*26**	*.1*	*.2*
259 IFCA	1	NR	NR	-	-
349 PENT HOLINESS	5	477	598*	2.4	3.5
355 PRESB CH (USA)	3	256	321*	1.3	1.9
361 PRIM BAPT ASCS	5	23	29*	.1	.2
419 SO BAPT CONV	11	3,373	4,228*	16.9	24.6
449 UN METHODIST	9	1,115	1,398*	5.6	8.1
497 BLACK BAPT EST[2]	NA	2,701	3,386*	13.5	19.7
MECKLENBURG	**454**	**227,126**	**328,378***	**64.2**	**100.0**
001 ADVENT CHR CH	1	330	409*	.1	.1
005 AME ZION	37	32,680	39,794	7.8	12.1
019 AMER BAPT USA	8	6,548	8,117*	1.6	2.5
053 ASSEMB OF GOD	10	1,669	2,205	.4	.7
055 AS REF PRES CH	12	2,548	2,896	.6	.9
081 CATHOLIC	11	NA	27,017	5.3	8.2
081d LATIN	*11*	*NA*	*27,017*	*5.3*	*8.2*
089 CHR & MISS AL	4	210	310	.1	.1
093 CHR CH (DISC)	3	589	900	.2	.3
097 CHR CHS&CHS CR	3	414	513*	.1	.2
111 CH CR,SCIENTST	2	NR	NR	-	-
123 CH GOD (ANDER)	4	300	305	.1	.1
127 CH GOD (CLEVE)	17	4,996	6,193*	1.2	1.9
145 CH GOD PROPHCY	4	143	177*	-	.1
151 L-D SAINTS	7	NA	3,319	.6	1.0
165 CH OF NAZARENE	6	1,070	1,273	.2	.4
167 CHS OF CHRIST	10	1,633	2,318	.5	.7
179 CONSRV BAPT	1	NR	NR	-	-
193 EPISCOPAL	14	6,586	9,071	1.8	2.8
203 EVAN FREE CH	1	326	350	.1	.1
207 E.L.C.A.	14	6,138	7,896	1.5	2.4
215 EVAN METH CH	1	15	19*	-	-
216 EVAN PRESBY CH	2	450	454	.1	.1
223 FREE WILL BAPT	4	212	263*	.1	.1
226 FRIENDS-USA	3	110	147*	-	-
226d FGC & FUM	*2*	*58*	*83*	*-*	*-*
226e FUM	*1*	*52*	*64**	*-*	*-*
246 GREEK ORTHODOX	1	NR	NR	-	-
263 INT FOURSQ GOS	4	932	1,155*	.2	.4
283 LUTH—MO SYNOD	7	2,061	2,744	.5	.8
295 MORAV CH-SOUTH	2	628	772	.2	.2
331 ORTH CH IN AM	1	NR	NR	-	-
339 PENT CH OF GOD	1	34	76	-	-
349 PENT HOLINESS	4	354	439*	.1	.1
353 CHR BRETHREN	1	125	185	-	.1
355 PRESB CH (USA)	72	32,017	39,689*	7.8	12.1
356 PRESB CH AMER	7	1,244	1,823	.4	.6
403 SALVATION ARMY	1	167	189	-	.1
413 S.D.A.	5	1,995	2,473*	.5	.8
419 SO BAPT CONV	94	57,484	71,259*	13.9	21.7
435 UNITARIAN-UNIV	1	555	730	.1	.2
443 UN C OF CHRIST	3	395	490*	.1	.1

County and Denomination	Number of churches	Communicant, confirmed, full members	Total adherents Number	Percent of total population	Percent of total adherents
449 UN METHODIST	53	32,974	40,876*	8.0	12.4
467 WESLEYAN	3	286	455	.1	.1
469 WELS	1	66	93	-	-
496 JEWISH EST[1]	4	NA	2,105	.4	.6
497 BLACK BAPT EST[2]	NA	28,842	35,754*	7.0	10.9
498 INDEP.CHARIS.[3]	4	NA	2,175	.4	.7
499 INDEP.NON-CHAR[3]	6	NA	10,950	2.1	3.3
MITCHELL	**54**	**9,074**	**11,100***	**76.9**	**100.0**
053 ASSEMB OF GOD	1	39	60	.4	.5
081 CATHOLIC	1	NA	173	1.2	1.6
081d LATIN	*1*	*NA*	*173*	*1.2*	*1.6*
097 CHR CHS&CHS CR	2	0	0*	-	-
127 CH GOD (CLEVE)	2	94	113*	.8	1.0
157 CH OF BRETHREN	1	38	46*	.3	.4
167 CHS OF CHRIST	1	60	76	.5	.7
193 EPISCOPAL	1	107	144	1.0	1.3
223 FREE WILL BAPT	1	150	180*	1.2	1.6
355 PRESB CH (USA)	5	396	475*	3.3	4.3
419 SO BAPT CONV	35	7,765	9,323*	64.6	84.0
449 UN METHODIST	4	425	510*	3.5	4.6
MONTGOMERY	**88**	**14,611**	**18,134***	**77.7**	**100.0**
005 AME ZION	14	3,642	3,906	16.7	21.5
053 ASSEMB OF GOD	1	45	60	.3	.3
081 CATHOLIC	1	NA	240	1.0	1.3
081d LATIN	*1*	*NA*	*240*	*1.0*	*1.3*
127 CH GOD (CLEVE)	3	123	153*	.7	.8
145 CH GOD PROPHCY	2	71	88*	.4	.5
167 CHS OF CHRIST	1	19	24	.1	.1
193 EPISCOPAL	1	20	23	.1	.1
349 PENT HOLINESS	5	270	336*	1.4	1.9
355 PRESB CH (USA)	6	639	795*	3.4	4.4
419 SO BAPT CONV	28	4,619	5,746*	24.6	31.7
443 UN C OF CHRIST	3	127	158*	.7	.9
449 UN METHODIST	20	2,704	3,364*	14.4	18.6
467 WESLEYAN	3	310	726	3.1	4.0
497 BLACK BAPT EST[2]	NA	2,022	2,515*	10.8	13.9
MOORE	**123**	**26,207**	**33,632***	**57.0**	**100.0**
005 AME ZION	16	4,689	5,071	8.6	15.1
053 ASSEMB OF GOD	2	172	257	.4	.8
081 CATHOLIC	2	NA	1,959	3.3	5.8
081d LATIN	*2*	*NA*	*1,959*	*3.3*	*5.8*
089 CHR & MISS AL	1	38	82	.1	.2
111 CH CR,SCIENTST	1	NR	NR	-	-
127 CH GOD (CLEVE)	3	123	149*	.3	.4
145 CH GOD PROPHCY	5	178	216*	.4	.6
151 L-D SAINTS	1	NA	236	.4	.7
167 CHS OF CHRIST	1	35	46	.1	.1
175 CONGR CHR CHS	1	50	61*	.1	.2
176 CCC, NOT NAT'L	3	302	366*	.6	1.1
193 EPISCOPAL	1	872	1,072	1.8	3.2
203 EVAN FREE CH	1	20	45	.1	.1
207 E.L.C.A.	1	404	476	.8	1.4
226 FRIENDS-USA	6	248	330*	.6	1.0
226b EFI	*4*	*154*	*216*	*.4*	*.6*
226e FUM	*2*	*94*	*114**	*.2*	*.3*
283 LUTH—MO SYNOD	1	90	125	.2	.4
355 PRESB CH (USA)	22	3,682	4,462*	7.6	13.3
356 PRESB CH AMER	2	81	92	.2	.3
361 PRIM BAPT ASCS	1	27	33*	.1	.1
413 S.D.A.	1	54	65*	.1	.2
419 SO BAPT CONV	24	7,033	8,523*	14.4	25.3
443 UN C OF CHRIST	5	793	961*	1.6	2.9
449 UN METHODIST	20	4,603	5,578*	9.5	16.6
467 WESLEYAN	2	87	245	.4	.7
497 BLACK BAPT EST[2]	NA	2,626	3,182*	5.4	9.5
NASH	**114**	**32,018**	**40,472***	**52.8**	**100.0**
005 AME ZION	2	382	571	.7	1.4
053 ASSEMB OF GOD	2	176	180	.2	.4
081 CATHOLIC	1	NA	456	.6	1.1
081d LATIN	*1*	*NA*	*456*	*.6*	*1.1*
089 CHR & MISS AL	1	22	43	.1	.1
093 CHR CH (DISC)	3	317	455	.6	1.1
097 CHR CHS&CHS CR	1	275	342*	.4	.8
111 CH CR,SCIENTST	1	NR	NR	-	-
127 CH GOD (CLEVE)	10	1,481	1,842*	2.4	4.6
145 CH GOD PROPHCY	6	214	266*	.3	.7
165 CH OF NAZARENE	1	84	91	.1	.2
167 CHS OF CHRIST	1	45	68	.1	.2
193 EPISCOPAL	2	946	1,222	1.6	3.0
207 E.L.C.A.	1	107	142	.2	.4
223 FREE WILL BAPT	2	303	377*	.5	.9
263 INT FOURSQ GOS	1	70	87*	.1	.2

NA—Not applicable   NR—Not reported   *Total adherents estimated from known number of communicant, confirmed, full members.   - Represents a percent less than 0.1.   Percentages may not total due to rounding.
[1]See Appendix E   [2]See Appendix F   [3]See Appendix G   Lines in *italic* represent a breakdown of Catholic rites or Friends affiliations. They are included in their respective denominational total.

Table 4. Churches and Church Membership by County and Denomination: 1990

County and Denomination	Number of churches	Communicant, confirmed, full members	Total adherents Number	Percent of total population	Percent of total adherents
339　PENT CH OF GOD	2	75	89	.1	.2
349　PENT HOLINESS	9	712	885*	1.2	2.2
355　PRESB CH (USA)	5	1,243	1,546*	2.0	3.8
361　PRIM BAPT ASCS	2	9	11*	-	-
419　SO BAPT CONV	40	14,287	17,766*	23.2	43.9
449　UN METHODIST	19	5,395	6,709*	8.7	16.6
467　WESLEYAN	1	46	75	.1	.2
496　JEWISH EST¹	1	NA	0	-	-
497　BLACK BAPT EST²	NA	5,829	7,249*	9.5	17.9
NEW HANOVER	**133**	**58,034**	**76,924***	**64.0**	**100.0**
001　ADVENT CHR CH	6	484	587*	.5	.8
005　AME ZION	11	8,390	10,068	8.4	13.1
053　ASSEMB OF GOD	3	276	372	.3	.5
081　CATHOLIC	6	NA	4,901	4.1	6.4
081d　*LATIN*	*6*	*NA*	*4,901*	*4.1*	*6.4*
089　CHR & MISS AL	3	42	134	.1	.2
093　CHR CH (DISC)	1	392	623	.5	.8
097　CHR CHS&CHS CR	1	100	121*	.1	.2
111　CH CR,SCIENTST	1	NR	NR	-	-
127　CH GOD (CLEVE)	5	868	1,053*	.9	1.4
145　CH GOD PROPHCY	2	71	86*	.1	.1
151　L-D SAINTS	2	NA	873	.7	1.1
165　CH OF NAZARENE	1	168	324	.3	.4
167　CHS OF CHRIST	3	234	349	.3	.5
193　EPISCOPAL	7	2,901	3,495	2.9	4.5
207　E.L.C.A.	4	1,635	2,140	1.8	2.8
216　EVAN PRESBY CH	1	1,538	1,555	1.3	2.0
223　FREE WILL BAPT	1	21	25*	-	-
226　FRIENDS-USA	1	14	34	-	-
226a　*CONSERV*	*1*	*14*	*34*	*-*	*-*
246　GREEK ORTHODOX	1	NR	NR	-	-
283　LUTH—MO SYNOD	1	121	151	.1	.2
295　MORAV CH-SOUTH	1	140	175	.1	.2
349　PENT HOLINESS	2	275	334*	.3	.4
353　CHR BRETHREN	1	130	200	.2	.3
355　PRESB CH (USA)	14	4,880	5,919*	4.9	7.7
356　PRESB CH AMER	1	63	82	.1	.1
361　PRIM BAPT ASCS	1	3	4*	-	-
413　S.D.A.	2	484	587*	.5	.8
419　SO BAPT CONV	31	20,721	25,133*	20.9	32.7
435　UNITARIAN-UNIV	1	101	114	.1	.1
443　UN C OF CHRIST	2	119	144*	.1	.2
449　UN METHODIST	13	6,634	8,046*	6.7	10.5
467　WESLEYAN	1	50	88	.1	.1
496　JEWISH EST¹	2	NA	500	.4	.6
497　BLACK BAPT EST²	NA	7,179	8,707*	7.2	11.3
NORTHAMPTON	**44**	**10,593**	**13,128***	**63.1**	**100.0**
053　ASSEMB OF GOD	1	16	13	.1	.1
097　CHR CHS&CHS CR	1	70	87*	.4	.7
127　CH GOD (CLEVE)	1	16	20*	.1	.2
145　CH GOD PROPHCY	1	36	45*	.2	.3
193　EPISCOPAL	2	37	55	.3	.4
226　FRIENDS-USA	1	71	91	.4	.7
226a　*CONSERV*	*1*	*71*	*91*	*.4*	*.7*
419　SO BAPT CONV	18	3,866	4,789*	23.0	36.5
443　UN C OF CHRIST	1	75	93*	.4	.7
449　UN METHODIST	18	2,251	2,788*	13.4	21.2
497　BLACK BAPT EST²	NA	4,155	5,147*	24.7	39.2
ONSLOW	**102**	**34,125**	**50,298***	**33.6**	**100.0**
005　AME ZION	6	2,652	3,536	2.4	7.0
053　ASSEMB OF GOD	4	349	670	.4	1.3
081　CATHOLIC	2	NA	4,556	3.0	9.1
081d　*LATIN*	*2*	*NA*	*4,556*	*3.0*	*9.1*
093　CHR CH (DISC)	3	458	1,344	.9	2.7
097　CHR CHS&CHS CR	2	170	214*	.1	.4
123　CH GOD (ANDER)	4	160	168	.1	.3
127　CH GOD (CLEVE)	3	149	187*	.1	.4
151　L-D SAINTS	3	NA	1,075	.7	2.1
165　CH OF NAZARENE	1	43	112	.1	.2
167　CHS OF CHRIST	3	477	585	.4	1.2
193　EPISCOPAL	3	527	1,141	.8	2.3
207　E.L.C.A.	1	264	366	.2	.7
223　FREE WILL BAPT	8	1,103	1,386*	.9	2.8
263　INT FOURSQ GOS	1	144	181*	.1	.4
283　LUTH—MO SYNOD	1	210	296	.2	.6
349　PENT HOLINESS	5	353	444*	.3	.9
355　PRESB CH (USA)	2	483	607*	.4	1.2
356　PRESB CH AMER	1	0	0	-	-
361　PRIM BAPT ASCS	5	60	75*	.1	.1
403　SALVATION ARMY	1	10	11	-	-
413　S.D.A.	2	105	132*	.1	.3
419　SO BAPT CONV	24	12,324	15,490*	10.3	30.8
443　UN C OF CHRIST	1	26	33*	-	.1

County and Denomination	Number of churches	Communicant, confirmed, full members	Total adherents Number	Percent of total population	Percent of total adherents
449　UN METHODIST	14	5,146	6,468*	4.3	12.9
467　WESLEYAN	1	32	60	-	.1
496　JEWISH EST¹	1	NA	0	-	-
497　BLACK BAPT EST²	NA	8,880	11,161*	7.4	22.2
ORANGE	**93**	**24,723**	**35,185***	**37.5**	**100.0**
005　AME ZION	3	136	158	.2	.4
019　AMER BAPT USA	2	990	1,167*	1.2	3.3
053　ASSEMB OF GOD	1	36	55	.1	.2
059　BAPT MISS ASSN	1	0	0*	-	-
081　CATHOLIC	3	NA	4,087	4.4	11.6
081d　*LATIN*	*3*	*NA*	*4,087*	*4.4*	*11.6*
111　CH CR,SCIENTST	1	NR	NR	-	-
123　CH GOD (ANDER)	2	35	40	-	.1
127　CH GOD (CLEVE)	2	289	341*	.4	1.0
145　CH GOD PROPHCY	3	107	126*	.1	.4
151　L-D SAINTS	2	NA	540	.6	1.5
165　CH OF NAZARENE	1	19	41	-	.1
167　CHS OF CHRIST	2	55	80	.1	.2
176　CCC, NOT NAT'L	1	22	26*	-	.1
193　EPISCOPAL	3	1,436	2,166	2.3	6.2
207　E.L.C.A.	1	561	715	.8	2.0
216　EVAN PRESBY CH	1	0	0	-	-
226　FRIENDS-USA	1	100	118*	.1	.3
226c　*FGC*	*1*	*100*	*118*￼*	*.1*	*.3*
283　LUTH—MO SYNOD	1	45	52	.1	.1
349　PENT HOLINESS	1	68	80*	.1	.2
355　PRESB CH (USA)	9	1,911	2,252*	2.4	6.4
356　PRESB CH AMER	1	211	266	.3	.8
413　S.D.A.	1	19	22*	-	.1
419　SO BAPT CONV	22	7,392	8,712*	9.3	24.8
443　UN C OF CHRIST	5	789	930*	1.0	2.6
449　UN METHODIST	21	5,997	7,068*	7.5	20.1
467　WESLEYAN	2	68	190	.2	.5
496　JEWISH EST¹	0	NA	724	.8	2.1
497　BLACK BAPT EST²	NA	4,437	5,229*	5.6	14.9
PAMLICO	**40**	**4,353**	**5,535***	**48.7**	**100.0**
005　AME ZION	3	594	820	7.2	14.8
053　ASSEMB OF GOD	1	12	16	.1	.3
093　CHR CH (DISC)	7	453	687	6.0	12.4
097　CHR CHS&CHS CR	1	56	69*	.6	1.2
127　CH GOD (CLEVE)	1	63	77*	.7	1.4
145　CH GOD PROPHCY	1	36	44*	.4	.8
176　CCC, NOT NAT'L	1	49	60*	.5	1.1
193　EPISCOPAL	1	114	115	1.0	2.1
349　PENT HOLINESS	7	202	248*	2.2	4.5
356　PRESB CH AMER	1	22	24	.2	.4
361　PRIM BAPT ASCS	2	12	15*	.1	.3
419　SO BAPT CONV	2	313	384*	3.4	6.9
443　UN C OF CHRIST	4	318	390*	3.4	7.0
449　UN METHODIST	8	1,114	1,366*	12.0	24.7
497　BLACK BAPT EST²	NA	995	1,220*	10.7	22.0
PASQUOTANK	**48**	**17,122**	**22,637***	**72.3**	**100.0**
005　AME ZION	11	5,500	6,781	21.7	30.0
053　ASSEMB OF GOD	1	177	280	.9	1.2
081　CATHOLIC	1	NA	755	2.4	3.3
081d　*LATIN*	*1*	*NA*	*755*	*2.4*	*3.3*
093　CHR CH (DISC)	3	382	615	2.0	2.7
097　CHR CHS&CHS CR	2	280	358*	1.1	1.6
127　CH GOD (CLEVE)	1	44	56*	.2	.2
145　CH GOD PROPHCY	1	36	46*	.1	.2
165　CH OF NAZARENE	1	37	80	.3	.4
167　CHS OF CHRIST	1	28	36	.1	.2
193　EPISCOPAL	1	271	359	1.1	1.6
215　EVAN METH CH	2	241	308*	1.0	1.4
265　INT PENT C CHR	1	77	133	.4	.6
349　PENT HOLINESS	1	270	345*	1.1	1.5
355　PRESB CH (USA)	1	225	288*	.9	1.3
403　SALVATION ARMY	1	107	123	.4	.5
413　S.D.A.	1	43	55*	.2	.2
419　SO BAPT CONV	9	4,165	5,323*	17.0	23.5
449　UN METHODIST	9	2,442	3,121*	10.0	13.8
497　BLACK BAPT EST²	NA	2,797	3,575*	11.4	15.8
PENDER	**52**	**10,860**	**13,801***	**47.8**	**100.0**
001　ADVENT CHR CH	2	130	160*	.6	1.2
005　AME ZION	2	21	33	.1	.2
053　ASSEMB OF GOD	2	90	164	.6	1.2
081　CATHOLIC	2	NA	173	.6	1.3
081d　*LATIN*	*2*	*NA*	*173*	*.6*	*1.3*
093　CHR CH (DISC)	1	36	54	.2	.4
151　L-D SAINTS	1	NA	200	.7	1.4
193　EPISCOPAL	2	140	136	.5	1.0
349　PENT HOLINESS	1	72	89*	.3	.6

NA–Not applicable　　NR–Not reported　　*Total adherents estimated from known number of communicant, confirmed, full members.　　- Represents a percent less than 0.1.　　Percentages may not total due to rounding.
¹See Appendix E　　²See Appendix F　　³See Appendix G　　Lines in *italic* represent a breakdown of Catholic rites or Friends affiliations. They are included in their respective denominational total.

Table 4. Churches and Church Membership by County and Denomination: 1990

County and Denomination	Number of churches	Communicant, confirmed, full members	Total adherents Number	Percent of total population	Percent of total adherents
355 PRESB CH (USA)	8	1,135	1,400*	4.9	10.1
361 PRIM BAPT ASCS	1	3	4*	-	-
413 S.D.A.	1	42	52*	.2	.4
419 SO BAPT CONV	21	5,587	6,891*	23.9	49.9
449 UN METHODIST	8	1,487	1,834*	6.4	13.3
497 BLACK BAPT EST²	NA	2,117	2,611*	9.0	18.9
PERQUIMANS	**35**	**6,442**	**7,800***	**74.7**	**100.0**
005 AME ZION	5	1,531	1,607	15.4	20.6
053 ASSEMB OF GOD	2	64	120	1.1	1.5
081 CATHOLIC	1	NA	23	.2	.3
081d LATIN	1	NA	23	.2	.3
093 CHR CH (DISC)	1	13	33	.3	.4
097 CHR CHS&CHS CR	2	265	329*	3.1	4.2
193 EPISCOPAL	1	78	85	.8	1.1
226 FRIENDS-USA	2	309	384*	3.7	4.9
226e FUM	2	309	384*	3.7	4.9
265 INT PENT C CHR	1	27	30	.3	.4
349 PENT HOLINESS	3	166	206*	2.0	2.6
419 SO BAPT CONV	8	1,433	1,780*	17.0	22.8
449 UN METHODIST	8	1,330	1,652*	15.8	21.2
467 WESLEYAN	1	71	116	1.1	1.5
497 BLACK BAPT EST²	NA	1,155	1,435*	13.7	18.4
PERSON	**51**	**13,801**	**17,448***	**57.8**	**100.0**
081 CATHOLIC	1	NA	180	.6	1.0
081d LATIN	1	NA	180	.6	1.0
127 CH GOD (CLEVE)	1	163	201*	.7	1.2
151 L-D SAINTS	1	NA	196	.6	1.1
167 CHS OF CHRIST	1	40	49	.2	.3
193 EPISCOPAL	1	99	137	.5	.8
355 PRESB CH (USA)	1	153	189*	.6	1.1
361 PRIM BAPT ASCS	6	98	121*	.4	.7
419 SO BAPT CONV	23	7,548	9,304*	30.8	53.3
449 UN METHODIST	15	3,476	4,285*	14.2	24.6
467 WESLEYAN	1	25	75	.2	.4
497 BLACK BAPT EST²	NA	2,199	2,711*	9.0	15.5
PITT	**128**	**32,927**	**44,461***	**41.2**	**100.0**
001 ADVENT CHR CH	1	12	15*	-	-
005 AME ZION	5	775	843	.8	1.9
019 AMER BAPT USA	1	400	494*	.5	1.1
053 ASSEMB OF GOD	1	134	275	.3	.6
081 CATHOLIC	3	NA	1,756	1.6	3.9
081d LATIN	3	NA	1,756	1.6	3.9
093 CHR CH (DISC)	21	3,324	4,654*	4.3	10.5
097 CHR CHS&CHS CR	3	371	459*	.4	1.0
111 CH CR,SCIENTST	1	NR	NR	-	-
127 CH GOD (CLEVE)	6	576	712*	.7	1.6
133 CH GOD(7TH)DEN	1	24	30	-	.1
143 CG IN CR(MENN)	1	25	31*	-	.1
145 CH GOD PROPHCY	2	71	88*	.1	.2
151 L-D SAINTS	1	NA	480	.4	1.1
167 CHS OF CHRIST	2	75	113	.1	.3
193 EPISCOPAL	4	932	1,264	1.2	2.8
207 E.L.C.A.	1	240	303	.3	.7
223 FREE WILL BAPT	12	2,424	2,997*	2.8	6.7
226 FRIENDS-USA	1	8	20	-	-
226a CONSERV	1	8	20	-	-
263 INT FOURSQ GOS	1	91	112*	.1	.3
283 LUTH—MO SYNOD	1	43	62	.1	.1
349 PENT HOLINESS	13	1,175	1,453*	1.3	3.3
355 PRESB CH (USA)	9	1,672	2,067*	1.9	4.6
356 PRESB CH AMER	1	94	137	.1	.3
361 PRIM BAPT ASCS	5	43	53*	-	.1
403 SALVATION ARMY	1	33	42	-	.1
413 S.D.A.	2	141	174*	.2	.4
419 SO BAPT CONV	13	4,719	5,834*	5.4	13.1
435 UNITARIAN-UNIV	1	28	35	-	.1
449 UN METHODIST	13	6,824	8,436*	7.8	19.0
496 JEWISH EST¹	0	NA	300	.3	.7
497 BLACK BAPT EST²	NA	8,673	10,722*	9.9	24.1
499 INDEP.NON-CHAR³	1	NA	500	.5	1.1
POLK	**52**	**8,663**	**10,709***	**74.3**	**100.0**
005 AME ZION	1	89	105	.7	1.0
053 ASSEMB OF GOD	1	24	22	.2	.2
055 AS REF PRES CH	1	121	141	1.0	1.3
081 CATHOLIC	1	NA	324	2.2	3.0
081d LATIN	1	NA	324	2.2	3.0
111 CH CR,SCIENTST	1	NR	NR	-	-
127 CH GOD (CLEVE)	1	30	35*	.2	.3
151 L-D SAINTS	1	NA	213	1.5	2.0
157 CH OF BRETHREN	1	121	142*	1.0	1.3
167 CHS OF CHRIST	1	20	28	.2	.3
193 EPISCOPAL	3	794	914	6.3	8.5
226 FRIENDS-USA	1	0	11	.1	.1
226c FGC	1	0	11	.1	.1
283 LUTH—MO SYNOD	1	60	72	.5	.7
355 PRESB CH (USA)	3	495	582*	4.0	5.4
413 S.D.A.	2	302	355*	2.5	3.3
419 SO BAPT CONV	25	5,164	6,069*	42.1	56.7
443 UN C OF CHRIST	1	521	612*	4.2	5.7
449 UN METHODIST	7	673	791*	5.5	7.4
497 BLACK BAPT EST²	NA	249	293*	2.0	2.7
RANDOLPH	**226**	**38,120**	**49,831***	**46.8**	**100.0**
005 AME ZION	2	654	1,031	1.0	2.1
053 ASSEMB OF GOD	3	678	1,109	1.0	2.2
081 CATHOLIC	1	NA	384	.4	.8
081d LATIN	1	NA	384	.4	.8
123 CH GOD (ANDER)	1	92	95	.1	.2
127 CH GOD (CLEVE)	8	903	1,112*	1.0	2.2
145 CH GOD PROPHCY	6	214	264*	.2	.5
151 L-D SAINTS	1	NA	239	.2	.5
165 CH OF NAZARENE	2	102	168	.2	.3
167 CHS OF CHRIST	1	55	100	.1	.2
176 CCC, NOT NAT'L	2	444	547*	.5	1.1
193 EPISCOPAL	1	221	248	.2	.5
207 E.L.C.A.	3	503	632	.6	1.3
215 EVAN METH CH	1	35	43*	-	.1
226 FRIENDS-USA	15	2,436	3,000*	2.8	6.0
226e FUM	15	2,436	3,000*	2.8	6.0
246 GREEK ORTHODOX	1	NR	NR	-	-
349 PENT HOLINESS	6	294	362*	.3	.7
353 CHR BRETHREN	1	25	50	-	.1
355 PRESB CH (USA)	4	836	1,030*	1.0	2.1
361 PRIM BAPT ASCS	3	64	79*	.1	.2
403 SALVATION ARMY	1	6	6	-	-
413 S.D.A.	1	73	90*	.1	.2
419 SO BAPT CONV	51	14,181	17,464*	16.4	35.0
443 UN C OF CHRIST	16	1,543	1,900*	1.8	3.8
449 UN METHODIST	73	11,341	13,966*	13.1	28.0
467 WESLEYAN	21	1,523	2,781	2.6	5.6
496 JEWISH EST¹	0	NA	345	.3	.7
497 BLACK BAPT EST²	NA	1,897	2,336*	2.2	4.7
499 INDEP.NON-CHAR³	1	NA	450	.4	.9
RICHMOND	**135**	**28,251**	**35,246***	**79.2**	**100.0**
005 AME ZION	18	7,570	9,084	20.4	25.8
053 ASSEMB OF GOD	1	87	122	.3	.3
081 CATHOLIC	1	NA	272	.6	.8
081d LATIN	1	NA	272	.6	.8
097 CHR CHS&CHS CR	1	30	37*	.1	.1
127 CH GOD (CLEVE)	3	173	216*	.5	.6
145 CH GOD PROPHCY	7	250	312*	.7	.9
151 L-D SAINTS	1	NA	104	.2	.3
167 CHS OF CHRIST	1	93	121	.3	.3
193 EPISCOPAL	2	81	109	.2	.3
207 E.L.C.A.	1	119	142	.3	.4
223 FREE WILL BAPT	22	1,623	2,025*	4.5	5.7
349 PENT HOLINESS	8	371	463*	1.0	1.3
355 PRESB CH (USA)	12	1,360	1,697*	3.8	4.8
356 PRESB CH AMER	1	165	176	.4	.5
419 SO BAPT CONV	28	7,754	9,674*	21.7	27.4
443 UN C OF CHRIST	1	106	132*	.3	.4
449 UN METHODIST	24	5,116	6,383*	14.3	18.1
467 WESLEYAN	3	246	301	.7	.9
497 BLACK BAPT EST²	NA	3,107	3,876*	8.7	11.0
ROBESON	**219**	**44,772**	**59,858***	**56.9**	**100.0**
005 AME ZION	15	1,195	1,434	1.4	2.4
053 ASSEMB OF GOD	7	587	990	.9	1.7
081 CATHOLIC	2	NA	693	.7	1.2
081d LATIN	2	NA	693	.7	1.2
089 CHR & MISS AL	2	199	266	.3	.4
093 CHR CH (DISC)	1	34	50	-	.1
127 CH GOD (CLEVE)	17	1,588	2,073*	2.0	3.5
145 CH GOD PROPHCY	2	71	93*	.1	.2
151 L-D SAINTS	3	NA	605	.6	1.0
167 CHS OF CHRIST	2	116	168	.2	.3
193 EPISCOPAL	1	184	242	.2	.4
207 E.L.C.A.	1	112	130	.1	.2
349 PENT HOLINESS	7	882	1,151*	1.1	1.9
353 CHR BRETHREN	2	220	295	.3	.5
355 PRESB CH (USA)	22	2,574	3,360*	3.2	5.6
413 S.D.A.	1	54	70*	.1	.1
419 SO BAPT CONV	99	23,947	31,258*	29.7	52.2
449 UN METHODIST	34	6,689	8,731*	8.3	14.6
496 JEWISH EST¹	1	NA	0	-	-
497 BLACK BAPT EST²	NA	6,320	8,249*	7.8	13.8

NA–Not applicable   NR–Not reported   *Total adherents estimated from known number of communicant, confirmed, full members.   - Represents a percent less than 0.1.   Percentages may not total due to rounding.
¹See Appendix E   ²See Appendix F   ³See Appendix G   Lines in *italic* represent a breakdown of Catholic rites or Friends affiliations. They are included in their respective denominational total.

Table 4. Churches and Church Membership by County and Denomination: 1990

County and Denomination	Number of churches	Communicant, confirmed, full members	Total adherents Number	Percent of total population	Percent of total adherents
ROCKINGHAM	**162**	**31,808**	**40,222***	**46.7**	**100.0**
019 AMER BAPT USA	1	200	244*	.3	.6
053 ASSEMB OF GOD	4	218	360	.4	.9
081 CATHOLIC	2	NA	545	.6	1.4
081d LATIN	2	NA	545	.6	1.4
089 CHR & MISS AL	1	102	260	.3	.6
093 CHR CH (DISC)	7	903	1,337	1.6	3.3
097 CHR CHS&CHS CR	8	1,559	1,904*	2.2	4.7
127 CH GOD (CLEVE)	6	286	349*	.4	.9
145 CH GOD PROPHCY	5	178	217*	.3	.5
151 L-D SAINTS	1	NA	135	.2	.3
157 CH OF BRETHREN	1	222	271*	.3	.7
167 CHS OF CHRIST	2	48	70	.1	.2
176 CCC, NOT NAT'L	1	94	115*	.1	.3
193 EPISCOPAL	5	656	825	1.0	2.1
207 E.L.C.A.	1	62	72	.1	.2
215 EVAN METH CH	1	114	139*	.2	.3
226 FRIENDS-USA	2	97	137*	.2	.3
226b EFI	1	57	88	.1	.2
226e FGC & FUM	1	40	49*	.1	.1
263 INT FOURSQ GOS	1	0	0*	-	-
295 MORAV CH-SOUTH	2	441	543	.6	1.4
349 PENT HOLINESS	8	809	988*	1.1	2.5
355 PRESB CH (USA)	11	1,362	1,663*	1.9	4.1
361 PRIM BAPT ASCS	6	71	87*	.1	.2
403 SALVATION ARMY	2	126	144	.2	.4
413 S.D.A.	0	22	27*	-	.1
419 SO BAPT CONV	36	11,720	14,314*	16.6	35.6
443 UN C OF CHRIST	3	713	871*	1.0	2.2
449 UN METHODIST	39	6,910	8,439*	9.8	21.0
467 WESLEYAN	6	660	994	1.2	2.5
497 BLACK BAPT EST[2]	NA	4,235	5,172*	6.0	12.9
ROWAN	**211**	**64,603**	**79,579***	**71.9**	**100.0**
005 AME ZION	14	11,578	12,323	11.1	15.5
053 ASSEMB OF GOD	2	483	538	.5	.7
055 AS REF PRES CH	1	112	132	.1	.2
081 CATHOLIC	1	NA	1,072	1.0	1.3
081d LATIN	1	NA	1,072	1.0	1.3
089 CHR & MISS AL	2	216	294	.3	.4
097 CHR CHS&CHS CR	2	145	178*	.2	.2
111 CHR CR,SCIENTST	1	NR	NR	-	-
123 CH GOD (ANDER)	1	25	25	-	-
127 CH GOD (CLEVE)	8	681	838*	.8	1.1
145 CH GOD PROPHCY	2	71	87*	.1	.1
151 L-D SAINTS	1	NA	202	.2	.3
165 CH OF NAZARENE	1	78	101	.1	.1
167 CHS OF CHRIST	6	306	445	.4	.6
193 EPISCOPAL	5	897	1,033	.9	1.3
207 E.L.C.A.	33	11,183	14,080	12.7	17.7
223 FREE WILL BAPT	2	58	71*	.1	.1
263 INT FOURSQ GOS	2	303	373*	.3	.5
283 LUTH—MO SYNOD	1	97	135	.1	.2
349 PENT HOLINESS	2	72	89*	.1	.1
353 CHR BRETHREN	1	22	32	-	-
355 PRESB CH (USA)	16	3,243	3,990*	3.6	5.0
356 PRESB CH AMER	1	126	138	.1	.2
403 SALVATION ARMY	1	113	122	.1	.2
413 S.D.A.	2	252	310*	.3	.4
419 SO BAPT CONV	51	16,591	20,411*	18.5	25.6
443 UN C OF CHRIST	11	2,792	3,435*	3.1	4.3
449 UN METHODIST	33	8,884	10,929*	9.9	13.7
467 WESLEYAN	6	920	1,149	1.0	1.4
469 WELS	1	60	78	.1	.1
496 JEWISH EST[1]	1	NA	455	.4	.6
497 BLACK BAPT EST[2]	NA	5,295	6,514*	5.9	8.2
RUTHERFORD	**149**	**36,815**	**45,625***	**80.2**	**100.0**
005 AME ZION	7	785	906	1.6	2.0
019 AMER BAPT USA	1	210	258*	.5	.6
053 ASSEMB OF GOD	1	50	50	.1	.1
081 CATHOLIC	1	NA	335	.6	.7
081d LATIN	1	NA	335	.6	.7
089 CHR & MISS AL	1	0	0	-	-
127 CH GOD (CLEVE)	4	191	235*	.4	.5
145 CH GOD PROPHCY	1	36	44*	.1	.1
157 CH OF BRETHREN	1	124	152*	.3	.3
165 CH OF NAZARENE	1	34	66	.1	.1
167 CHS OF CHRIST	1	33	42	.1	.1
193 EPISCOPAL	2	238	357	.6	.8
207 E.L.C.A.	1	89	119	.2	.3
223 FREE WILL BAPT	2	214	263*	.5	.6
263 INT FOURSQ GOS	1	136	167*	.3	.4
355 PRESB CH (USA)	8	847	1,041*	1.8	2.3
413 S.D.A.	1	89	109*	.2	.2
419 SO BAPT CONV	87	27,706	34,048*	59.8	74.6

County and Denomination	Number of churches	Communicant, confirmed, full members	Total adherents Number	Percent of total population	Percent of total adherents
449 UN METHODIST	26	4,285	5,266*	9.3	11.5
467 WESLEYAN	2	176	235	.4	.5
497 BLACK BAPT EST[2]	NA	1,572	1,932*	3.4	4.2
SAMPSON	**139**	**28,420**	**36,262***	**76.7**	**100.0**
005 AME ZION	11	4,060	4,872	10.3	13.4
019 AMER BAPT USA	1	499	623*	1.3	1.7
053 ASSEMB OF GOD	1	33	44	.1	.1
066 BIBLE CH OF CR	1	180	225*	.5	.6
081 CATHOLIC	2	NA	575	1.2	1.6
081d LATIN	2	NA	575	1.2	1.6
093 CHR CH (DISC)	16	2,417	3,265	6.9	9.0
127 CH GOD (CLEVE)	6	350	437*	.9	1.2
145 CH GOD PROPHCY	7	250	312*	.7	.9
151 L-D SAINTS	1	NA	133	.3	.4
167 CHS OF CHRIST	1	22	35	.1	.1
193 EPISCOPAL	1	90	120	.3	.3
223 FREE WILL BAPT	2	352	440*	.9	1.2
226 FRIENDS-USA	1	110	137*	.3	.4
226e FUM	1	110	137*	.3	.4
349 PENT HOLINESS	9	913	1,140*	2.4	3.1
355 PRESB CH (USA)	5	666	832*	1.8	2.3
361 PRIM BAPT ASCS	5	45	56*	.1	.2
413 S.D.A.	2	86	107*	.2	.3
419 SO BAPT CONV	44	11,090	13,847*	29.3	38.2
449 UN METHODIST	23	3,470	4,333*	9.2	11.9
497 BLACK BAPT EST[2]	NA	3,787	4,729*	10.0	13.0
SCOTLAND	**70**	**16,018**	**21,616***	**64.0**	**100.0**
005 AME ZION	9	3,589	4,660	13.8	21.6
053 ASSEMB OF GOD	1	21	30	.1	.1
081 CATHOLIC	1	NA	350	1.0	1.6
081d LATIN	1	NA	350	1.0	1.6
097 CHR CHS&CHS CR	1	70	90*	.3	.4
127 CH GOD (CLEVE)	4	759	975*	2.9	4.5
145 CH GOD PROPHCY	2	71	91*	.3	.4
165 CH OF NAZARENE	1	46	91	.3	.4
193 EPISCOPAL	1	80	129	.4	.6
207 E.L.C.A.	1	104	147	.4	.7
223 FREE WILL BAPT	2	74	95*	.3	.4
349 PENT HOLINESS	8	492	632*	1.9	2.9
353 CHR BRETHREN	1	85	125	.4	.6
355 PRESB CH (USA)	8	1,572	2,020*	6.0	9.3
413 S.D.A.	1	106	136*	.4	.6
419 SO BAPT CONV	12	2,529	3,249*	9.6	15.0
449 UN METHODIST	14	3,437	4,415*	13.1	20.4
467 WESLEYAN	2	43	204	.6	.9
497 BLACK BAPT EST[2]	NA	2,940	3,777*	11.2	17.5
499 INDEP.NON-CHAR[3]	1	NA	400	1.2	1.9
STANLY	**134**	**30,526**	**39,195***	**75.7**	**100.0**
005 AME ZION	7	1,842	2,456	4.7	6.3
053 ASSEMB OF GOD	1	251	204	.4	.5
081 CATHOLIC	1	NA	426	.8	1.1
081d LATIN	1	NA	426	.8	1.1
127 CH GOD (CLEVE)	6	424	524*	1.0	1.3
145 CH GOD PROPHCY	3	107	132*	.3	.3
151 L-D SAINTS	1	NA	184	.4	.5
165 CH OF NAZARENE	2	145	218	.4	.6
167 CHS OF CHRIST	1	40	68	.1	.2
193 EPISCOPAL	1	334	496	1.0	1.3
207 E.L.C.A.	4	931	1,132	2.2	2.9
263 INT FOURSQ GOS	1	11	14*	-	-
349 PENT HOLINESS	1	47	58*	.1	.1
355 PRESB CH (USA)	7	1,152	1,424*	2.8	3.6
356 PRESB CH AMER	2	442	493	1.0	1.3
361 PRIM BAPT ASCS	3	201	248*	.5	.6
413 S.D.A.	1	130	161*	.3	.4
419 SO BAPT CONV	58	16,932	20,929*	40.4	53.4
443 UN C OF CHRIST	2	376	465*	.9	1.2
449 UN METHODIST	30	5,616	6,942*	13.4	17.7
467 WESLEYAN	1	104	140	.3	.4
497 BLACK BAPT EST[2]	NA	1,441	1,781*	3.4	4.5
499 INDEP.NON-CHAR[3]	1	NA	700	1.4	1.8
STOKES	**73**	**12,052**	**15,361***	**41.3**	**100.0**
081 CATHOLIC	1	NA	264	.7	1.7
081d LATIN	1	NA	264	.7	1.7
093 CHR CH (DISC)	2	237	338	.9	2.2
097 CHR CHS&CHS CR	7	1,740	2,130*	5.7	13.9
127 CH GOD (CLEVE)	3	153	187*	.5	1.2
151 L-D SAINTS	1	NA	174	.5	1.1
167 CHS OF CHRIST	1	46	64	.2	.4
193 EPISCOPAL	2	81	107	.3	.7
226 FRIENDS-USA	1	12	15*	-	.1
226e FUM	1	12	15*	-	.1

NA–Not applicable   NR–Not reported   *Total adherents estimated from known number of communicant, confirmed, full members.   - Represents a percent less than 0.1.   Percentages may not total due to rounding.
[1]See Appendix E   [2]See Appendix F   [3]See Appendix G   Lines in *italic* represent a breakdown of Catholic rites or Friends affiliations. They are included in their respective denominational total.

Table 4. Churches and Church Membership by County and Denomination: 1990

County and Denomination		Number of churches	Communicant, confirmed, full members	Total adherents		
				Number	Percent of total population	Percent of total adherents
295	MORAV CH-SOUTH	2	458	542	1.5	3.5
349	PENT HOLINESS	2	183	224*	.6	1.5
355	PRESB CH (USA)	6	377	461*	1.2	3.0
361	PRIM BAPT ASCS	8	283	346*	.9	2.3
419	SO BAPT CONV	19	5,689	6,964*	18.7	45.3
443	UN C OF CHRIST	1	72	88*	.2	.6
449	UN METHODIST	17	2,105	2,577*	6.9	16.8
496	JEWISH EST[1]	0	NA	126	.3	.8
497	BLACK BAPT EST[2]	NA	616	754*	2.0	4.9
SURRY		**163**	**27,075**	**33,597***	**54.4**	**100.0**
005	AME ZION	1	17	29	-	.1
053	ASSEMB OF GOD	3	119	118	.2	.4
081	CATHOLIC	2	NA	362	.6	1.1
081d	*LATIN*	*2*	*NA*	*362*	*.6*	*1.1*
093	CHR CH (DISC)	1	140	188	.3	.6
097	CHR CHS&CHS CR	4	455	550*	.9	1.6
127	CH GOD (CLEVE)	3	290	351*	.6	1.0
145	CH GOD PROPHCY	2	71	86*	.1	.3
151	L-D SAINTS	1	NA	275	.4	.8
157	CH OF BRETHREN	1	52	63*	.1	.2
167	CHS OF CHRIST	3	126	163	.3	.5
193	EPISCOPAL	2	161	212	.3	.6
207	E.L.C.A.	1	83	117	.2	.3
226	FRIENDS-USA	8	1,007	1,218*	2.0	3.6
226e	*FUM*	*8*	*1,007*	*1,218***	*2.0*	*3.6*
265	INT PENT C CHR	1	29	44	.1	.1
295	MORAV CH-SOUTH	1	430	540	.9	1.6
349	PENT HOLINESS	6	412	498*	.8	1.5
355	PRESB CH (USA)	7	954	1,154*	1.9	3.4
361	PRIM BAPT ASCS	14	204	247*	.4	.7
403	SALVATION ARMY	1	84	94	.2	.3
419	SO BAPT CONV	69	17,805	21,535*	34.9	64.1
449	UN METHODIST	29	3,701	4,476*	7.3	13.3
467	WESLEYAN	3	264	465	.8	1.4
497	BLACK BAPT EST[2]	NA	671	812*	1.3	2.4
SWAIN		**36**	**3,904**	**5,039***	**44.7**	**100.0**
053	ASSEMB OF GOD	1	50	55	.5	1.1
081	CATHOLIC	2	NA	168	1.5	3.3
081d	*LATIN*	*2*	*NA*	*168*	*1.5*	*3.3*
127	CH GOD (CLEVE)	4	158	196*	1.7	3.9
167	CHS OF CHRIST	1	20	26	.2	.5
193	EPISCOPAL	1	10	13	.1	.3
355	PRESB CH (USA)	1	98	121*	1.1	2.4
413	S.D.A.	1	40	49*	.4	1.0
419	SO BAPT CONV	21	3,144	3,890*	34.5	77.2
449	UN METHODIST	2	361	447*	4.0	8.9
467	WESLEYAN	2	23	74	.7	1.5
TRANSYLVANIA		**55**	**12,135**	**15,335***	**60.1**	**100.0**
053	ASSEMB OF GOD	1	38	50	.2	.3
081	CATHOLIC	1	NA	594	2.3	3.9
081d	*LATIN*	*1*	*NA*	*594*	*2.3*	*3.9*
089	CHR & MISS AL	1	27	44	.2	.3
123	CH GOD (ANDER)	1	30	30	.1	.2
127	CH GOD (CLEVE)	4	223	266*	1.0	1.7
145	CH GOD PROPHCY	1	36	43*	.2	.3
151	L-D SAINTS	1	NA	169	.7	1.1
165	CH OF NAZARENE	1	29	54	.2	.4
167	CHS OF CHRIST	1	38	50	.2	.3
193	EPISCOPAL	1	350	430	1.7	2.8
207	E.L.C.A.	1	199	237	.9	1.5
226	FRIENDS-USA	1	12	17	.1	.1
226c	*FGC*	*1*	*12*	*17*	*.1*	*.1*
356	PRESB CH AMER	1	120	164	.6	1.1
413	S.D.A.	1	49	59*	.2	.4
419	SO BAPT CONV	31	9,130	10,904*	42.7	71.1
449	UN METHODIST	6	1,366	1,631*	6.4	10.6
467	WESLEYAN	1	201	250	1.0	1.6
497	BLACK BAPT EST[2]	NA	287	343*	1.3	2.2
TYRRELL		**22**	**2,093**	**3,042***	**78.9**	**100.0**
053	ASSEMB OF GOD	1	60	75	1.9	2.5
081	CATHOLIC	1	NA	12	.3	.4
081d	*LATIN*	*1*	*NA*	*12*	*.3*	*.4*
093	CHR CH (DISC)	8	472	966	25.1	31.8
097	CHR CHS&CHS CR	2	150	191*	5.0	6.3
193	EPISCOPAL	2	31	41	1.1	1.3
223	FREE WILL BAPT	1	150	191*	5.0	6.3
361	PRIM BAPT ASCS	1	1	1*	-	-
419	SO BAPT CONV	2	350	446*	11.6	14.7
449	UN METHODIST	4	359	457*	11.9	15.0
497	BLACK BAPT EST[2]	NA	520	662*	17.2	21.8

County and Denomination		Number of churches	Communicant, confirmed, full members	Total adherents		
				Number	Percent of total population	Percent of total adherents
UNION		**168**	**40,131**	**52,855***	**62.8**	**100.0**
001	ADVENT CHR CH	2	188	239*	.3	.5
005	AME ZION	17	3,388	4,367	5.2	8.3
053	ASSEMB OF GOD	1	64	90	.1	.2
081	CATHOLIC	1	NA	986	1.2	1.9
081d	*LATIN*	*1*	*NA*	*986*	*1.2*	*1.9*
089	CHR & MISS AL	1	0	30	-	.1
123	CH GOD (ANDER)	3	93	100	.1	.2
127	CH GOD (CLEVE)	3	135	172*	.2	.3
145	CH GOD PROPHCY	3	107	136*	.2	.3
165	CH OF NAZARENE	1	222	333	.4	.6
167	CHS OF CHRIST	2	68	87	.1	.2
193	EPISCOPAL	1	343	413	.5	.8
203	EVAN FREE CH	1	65	125	.1	.2
207	E.L.C.A.	1	222	282	.3	.5
216	EVAN PRESBY CH	1	97	97	.1	.2
223	FREE WILL BAPT	1	70	89*	.1	.2
263	INT FOURSQ GOS	2	291	370*	.4	.7
349	PENT HOLINESS	2	72	91*	.1	.2
355	PRESB CH (USA)	19	2,714	3,449*	4.1	6.5
361	PRIM BAPT ASCS	4	331	421*	.5	.8
419	SO BAPT CONV	65	20,572	26,141*	31.0	49.5
443	UN C OF CHRIST	1	75	95*	.1	.2
449	UN METHODIST	35	7,014	8,913*	10.6	16.9
496	JEWISH EST[1]	0	NA	346	.4	.7
497	BLACK BAPT EST[2]	NA	4,000	5,083*	6.0	9.6
499	INDEP.NON-CHAR[3]	1	NA	400	.5	.8
VANCE		**77**	**20,291**	**25,929***	**66.7**	**100.0**
005	AME ZION	6	1,665	2,048	5.3	7.9
053	ASSEMB OF GOD	1	31	43	.1	.2
081	CATHOLIC	1	NA	315	.8	1.2
081d	*LATIN*	*1*	*NA*	*315*	*.8*	*1.2*
127	CH GOD (CLEVE)	4	532	669*	1.7	2.6
145	CH GOD PROPHCY	1	36	45*	.1	.2
151	L-D SAINTS	1	NA	199	.5	.8
165	CH OF NAZARENE	1	73	36	.1	.1
167	CHS OF CHRIST	2	83	114	.3	.4
193	EPISCOPAL	3	306	385	1.0	1.5
223	FREE WILL BAPT	1	75	94*	.2	.4
349	PENT HOLINESS	3	412	518*	1.3	2.0
355	PRESB CH (USA)	6	601	756*	1.9	2.9
403	SALVATION ARMY	1	79	82	.2	.3
419	SO BAPT CONV	20	6,126	7,705*	19.8	29.7
443	UN C OF CHRIST	8	1,893	2,381*	6.1	9.2
449	UN METHODIST	18	4,151	5,221*	13.4	20.1
497	BLACK BAPT EST[2]	NA	4,228	5,318*	13.7	20.5
WAKE		**350**	**163,743**	**239,501***	**56.6**	**100.0**
001	ADVENT CHR CH	1	194	238*	.1	.1
005	AME ZION	7	7,306	9,270	2.2	3.9
019	AMER BAPT USA	3	2,485	3,047*	.7	1.3
053	ASSEMB OF GOD	7	1,241	2,276	.5	1.0
055	AS REF PRES CH	1	0	0	-	-
081	CATHOLIC	13	NA	24,218	5.7	10.1
081d	*LATIN*	*13*	*NA*	*24,218*	*5.7*	*10.1*
089	CHR & MISS AL	5	623	1,148	.3	.5
093	CHR CH (DISC)	9	1,477	1,944	.5	.8
097	CHR CHS&CHS CR	6	348	427*	.1	.2
111	CH CR,SCIENTST	2	NR	NR	-	-
123	CH GOD (ANDER)	3	173	205	-	.1
127	CH GOD (CLEVE)	13	1,337	1,639*	.4	.7
133	CH GOD(7TH)DEN	1	23	29	-	-
145	CH GOD PROPHCY	7	250	307*	.1	.1
151	L-D SAINTS	6	NA	2,029	.5	.8
165	CH OF NAZARENE	3	459	853	.2	.4
167	CHS OF CHRIST	8	1,281	1,816	.4	.8
176	CCC, NOT NAT'L	6	958	1,175*	.3	.5
193	EPISCOPAL	11	6,710	8,246	1.9	3.4
207	E.L.C.A.	6	3,493	4,767	1.1	2.0
223	FREE WILL BAPT	7	1,385	1,698*	.4	.7
226	FRIENDS-USA	1	20	50	-	-
226c	*FGC*	*1*	*20*	*50*	*-*	*-*
246	GREEK ORTHODOX	1	NR	NR	-	-
263	INT FOURSQ GOS	2	82	101*	-	-
283	LUTH—MO SYNOD	2	777	1,079	.3	.5
285	MENNONITE CH	1	28	60	-	-
287	MENN GEN CONF	1	17	30	-	-
295	MORAV CH-SOUTH	1	302	409	.1	.2
331	ORTH CH IN AM	1	NR	NR	-	-
349	PENT HOLINESS	8	962	1,180*	.3	.5
353	CHR BRETHREN	6	449	789	.2	.3
355	PRESB CH (USA)	23	13,196	16,182*	3.8	6.8
356	PRESB CH AMER	3	496	688	.2	.3
361	PRIM BAPT ASCS	4	53	65*	-	-
371	REF CH IN AM	1	122	205	-	.1

NA–Not applicable   NR–Not reported   *Total adherents estimated from known number of communicant, confirmed, full members.   - Represents a percent less than 0.1.   Percentages may not total due to rounding.

[1]See Appendix E   [2]See Appendix F   [3]See Appendix G   Lines in *italic* represent a breakdown of Catholic rites or Friends affiliations. They are included in their respective denominational total.

Table 4. Churches and Church Membership by County and Denomination: 1990

County and Denomination	Number of churches	Communicant, confirmed, full members	Total adherents Number	Percent of total population	Percent of total adherents
403 SALVATION ARMY	1	205	217	.1	.1
413 S.D.A.	2	653	801*	.2	.3
419 SO BAPT CONV	93	56,500	69,283*	16.4	28.9
435 UNITARIAN-UNIV	1	290	434	.1	.2
443 UN C OF CHRIST	22	3,930	4,819*	1.1	2.0
449 UN METHODIST	36	29,593	36,288*	8.6	15.2
469 WELS	1	93	140	-	.1
496 JEWISH EST[1]	3	NA	3,267	.8	1.4
497 BLACK BAPT EST[2]	NA	26,232	32,167*	7.6	13.4
498 INDEP.CHARIS.[3]	3	NA	1,225	.3	.5
499 INDEP.NON-CHAR[3]	8	NA	4,690	1.1	2.0
WARREN	**45**	**10,319**	**12,869***	**74.5**	**100.0**
081 CATHOLIC	1	NA	38	.2	.3
081d LATIN	*1*	*NA*	*38*	*.2*	*.3*
127 CH GOD (CLEVE)	1	44	55*	.3	.4
145 CH GOD PROPHCY	1	36	45*	.3	.3
176 CCC, NOT NAT'L	3	335	415*	2.4	3.2
193 EPISCOPAL	3	100	118	.7	.9
283 LUTH—MO SYNOD	1	245	311	1.8	2.4
349 PENT HOLINESS	1	34	42*	.2	.3
355 PRESB CH (USA)	2	65	81*	.5	.6
419 SO BAPT CONV	16	3,610	4,476*	25.9	34.8
443 UN C OF CHRIST	4	844	1,047*	6.1	8.1
449 UN METHODIST	11	1,626	2,016*	11.7	15.7
467 WESLEYAN	1	61	110	.6	.9
497 BLACK BAPT EST[2]	NA	3,319	4,115*	23.8	32.0
WASHINGTON	**43**	**7,169**	**9,352***	**66.8**	**100.0**
005 AME ZION	2	162	188	1.3	2.0
053 ASSEMB OF GOD	1	25	46	.3	.5
081 CATHOLIC	1	NA	83	.6	.9
081d LATIN	*1*	*NA*	*83*	*.6*	*.9*
093 CHR CH (DISC)	4	442	688	4.9	7.4
097 CHR CHS&CHS CR	8	1,435	1,823*	13.0	19.5
127 CH GOD (CLEVE)	2	154	196*	1.4	2.1
151 L-D SAINTS	1	NA	149	1.1	1.6
165 CH OF NAZARENE	1	171	144	1.0	1.5
167 CHS OF CHRIST	1	45	57	.4	.6
193 EPISCOPAL	3	162	169	1.2	1.8
223 FREE WILL BAPT	2	255	324*	2.3	3.5
349 PENT HOLINESS	2	164	208*	1.5	2.2
355 PRESB CH (USA)	1	60	76*	.5	.8
361 PRIM BAPT ASCS	1	1	1*	-	-
413 S.D.A.	1	25	32*	.2	.3
419 SO BAPT CONV	6	1,160	1,474*	10.5	15.8
449 UN METHODIST	6	763	969*	6.9	10.4
497 BLACK BAPT EST[2]	NA	2,145	2,725*	19.5	29.1
WATAUGA	**86**	**15,064**	**18,785***	**50.8**	**100.0**
001 ADVENT CHR CH	2	145	168*	.5	.9
053 ASSEMB OF GOD	3	114	146	.4	.8
055 AS REF PRES CH	1	0	0	-	-
081 CATHOLIC	1	NA	783	2.1	4.2
081d LATIN	*1*	*NA*	*783*	*2.1*	*4.2*
089 CHR & MISS AL	1	87	226	.6	1.2
097 CHR CHS&CHS CR	2	284	328*	.9	1.7
127 CH GOD (CLEVE)	2	44	51*	.1	.3
151 L-D SAINTS	1	NA	140	.4	.7
167 CHS OF CHRIST	1	61	79	.2	.4
193 EPISCOPAL	3	430	688	1.9	3.7
207 E.L.C.A.	3	775	976	2.6	5.2
226 FRIENDS-USA	1	0	12	-	.1
226c FGC	*1*	*0*	*12*	*-*	*.1*
237 GC MENN BR CHS	1	58	67*	.2	.4
263 INT FOURSQ GOS	1	93	108*	.3	.6
355 PRESB CH (USA)	3	528	610*	1.7	3.2
356 PRESB CH AMER	1	66	78	.2	.4
413 S.D.A.	1	29	34*	.1	.2
419 SO BAPT CONV	46	10,247	11,846*	32.1	63.1
435 UNITARIAN-UNIV	1	91	119	.3	.6
449 UN METHODIST	11	1,827	2,112*	5.7	11.2
497 BLACK BAPT EST[2]	NA	185	214*	.6	1.1
WAYNE	**146**	**38,347**	**51,439***	**49.1**	**100.0**
001 ADVENT CHR CH	1	97	122*	.1	.2
005 AME ZION	13	3,655	3,780	3.6	7.3
053 ASSEMB OF GOD	2	468	740	.7	1.4
081 CATHOLIC	2	NA	1,818	1.7	3.5
081d LATIN	*2*	*NA*	*1,818*	*1.7*	*3.5*
089 CHR & MISS AL	1	22	49	-	.1
093 CHR CH (DISC)	21	3,315	4,526	4.3	8.8
127 CH GOD (CLEVE)	7	924	1,162*	1.1	2.3
145 CH GOD PROPHCY	5	177	223*	.2	.4
151 L-D SAINTS	3	NA	1,134	1.1	2.2
165 CH OF NAZARENE	1	30	51	-	.1

County and Denomination	Number of churches	Communicant, confirmed, full members	Total adherents Number	Percent of total population	Percent of total adherents
167 CHS OF CHRIST	1	149	194	.2	.4
193 EPISCOPAL	3	551	757	.7	1.5
207 E.L.C.A.	1	270	364	.3	.7
223 FREE WILL BAPT	4	1,352	1,701*	1.6	3.3
226 FRIENDS-USA	7	898	1,130*	1.1	2.2
226e FUM	*7*	*898*	*1,130**	*1.1*	*2.2*
283 LUTH—MO SYNOD	1	43	60	.1	.1
349 PENT HOLINESS	10	1,128	1,419*	1.4	2.8
353 CHR BRETHREN	1	34	68	.1	.1
355 PRESB CH (USA)	5	1,448	1,822*	1.7	3.5
356 PRESB CH AMER	2	222	252	.2	.5
361 PRIM BAPT ASCS	2	21	26*	-	.1
403 SALVATION ARMY	1	163	170	.2	.3
413 S.D.A.	2	206	259*	.2	.5
419 SO BAPT CONV	18	7,387	9,293*	8.9	18.1
435 UNITARIAN-UNIV	1	32	44	-	.1
443 UN C OF CHRIST	1	110	138*	.1	.3
449 UN METHODIST	27	7,474	9,403*	9.0	18.3
467 WESLEYAN	1	12	50	-	.1
496 JEWISH EST[1]	1	NA	120	.1	.2
497 BLACK BAPT EST[2]	NA	8,159	10,264*	9.8	20.0
499 INDEP.NON-CHAR[3]	1	NA	300	.3	.6
WILKES	**136**	**31,193**	**38,630***	**65.0**	**100.0**
001 ADVENT CHR CH	2	55	67*	.1	.2
005 AME ZION	3	426	487	.8	1.3
053 ASSEMB OF GOD	1	64	80	.1	.2
081 CATHOLIC	1	NA	288	.5	.7
081d LATIN	*1*	*NA*	*288*	*.5*	*.7*
127 CH GOD (CLEVE)	3	123	150*	.3	.4
145 CH GOD PROPHCY	1	36	44*	.1	.1
151 L-D SAINTS	1	NA	293	.5	.8
157 CH OF BRETHREN	2	94	114*	.2	.3
167 CHS OF CHRIST	3	164	237	.4	.6
193 EPISCOPAL	1	166	251	.4	.6
207 E.L.C.A.	1	160	223	.4	.6
226 FRIENDS-USA	1	3	7	-	-
226c FGC	*1*	*3*	*7*	*-*	*-*
237 GC MENN BR CHS	1	15	18*	-	-
265 INT PENT C CHR	1	54	106	.2	.3
349 PENT HOLINESS	2	138	168*	.3	.4
355 PRESB CH (USA)	2	560	681*	1.1	1.8
361 PRIM BAPT ASCS	5	87	106*	.2	.3
413 S.D.A.	1	49	60*	.1	.2
419 SO BAPT CONV	88	25,748	31,298*	52.7	81.0
449 UN METHODIST	16	2,569	3,123*	5.3	8.1
497 BLACK BAPT EST[2]	NA	682	829*	1.4	2.1
WILSON	**84**	**26,314**	**34,292***	**51.9**	**100.0**
001 ADVENT CHR CH	2	111	139*	.2	.4
005 AME ZION	5	2,182	2,784	4.2	8.1
053 ASSEMB OF GOD	1	42	60	.1	.2
081 CATHOLIC	1	NA	842	1.3	2.5
081d LATIN	*1*	*NA*	*842*	*1.3*	*2.5*
093 CHR CH (DISC)	10	1,799	2,461	3.7	7.2
097 CHR CHS&CHS CR	1	57	71*	.1	.2
123 CH GOD (ANDER)	1	30	30	-	.1
127 CH GOD (CLEVE)	4	590	737*	1.1	2.1
145 CH GOD PROPHCY	3	107	134*	.2	.4
151 L-D SAINTS	1	NA	214	.3	.6
167 CHS OF CHRIST	1	30	44	.1	.1
193 EPISCOPAL	2	427	584	.9	1.7
207 E.L.C.A.	1	128	144	.2	.4
216 EVAN PRESBY CH	1	88	90	.1	.3
223 FREE WILL BAPT	6	1,876	2,344*	3.5	6.8
263 INT FOURSQ GOS	1	23	29*	-	.1
283 LUTH—MO SYNOD	1	127	165	.2	.5
349 PENT HOLINESS	8	734	917*	1.4	2.7
355 PRESB CH (USA)	7	1,359	1,698*	2.6	5.0
403 SALVATION ARMY	1	181	198	.3	.6
413 S.D.A.	2	165	206*	.3	.6
419 SO BAPT CONV	12	5,773	7,212*	10.9	21.0
449 UN METHODIST	11	4,419	5,520*	8.4	16.1
467 WESLEYAN	1	55	160	.2	.5
497 BLACK BAPT EST[2]	NA	6,011	7,509*	11.4	21.9
YADKIN	**84**	**14,876**	**18,404***	**60.4**	**100.0**
005 AME ZION	4	552	690	2.3	3.7
053 ASSEMB OF GOD	2	74	142	.5	.8
081 CATHOLIC	1	NA	0	-	-
081d LATIN	*1*	*NA*	*0*	*-*	*-*
127 CH GOD (CLEVE)	2	154	186*	.6	1.0
151 L-D SAINTS	1	NA	118	.4	.6
167 CHS OF CHRIST	3	184	255	.8	1.4
207 E.L.C.A.	1	59	74	.2	.4
215 EVAN METH CH	1	21	25*	.1	.1

NA–Not applicable NR–Not reported *Total adherents estimated from known number of communicant, confirmed, full members. - Represents a percent less than 0.1. Percentages may not total due to rounding.
[1]See Appendix E [2]See Appendix F [3]See Appendix G Lines in *italic* represent a breakdown of Catholic rites or Friends affiliations. They are included in their respective denominational total.

Table 4. Churches and Church Membership by County and Denomination: 1990

County and Denomination	Number of churches	Communicant, confirmed, full members	Total adherents Number	Percent of total population	Percent of total adherents
226 FRIENDS-USA	10	1,396	1,683*	5.5	9.1
226e FUM	*10*	*1,396*	*1,683**	*5.5*	*9.1*
323 OLD ORD AMISH	1	NA	150	.5	.8
349 PENT HOLINESS	5	479	577*	1.9	3.1
355 PRESB CH (USA)	2	104	125*	.4	.7
361 PRIM BAPT ASCS	2	16	19*	.1	.1
386 REGULAR BAPT	1	26	31*	.1	.2
419 SO BAPT CONV	27	8,633	10,405*	34.1	56.5
443 UN C OF CHRIST	1	67	81*	.3	.4
449 UN METHODIST	20	2,725	3,284*	10.8	17.8
496 JEWISH EST[1]	0	NA	94	.3	.5
497 BLACK BAPT EST[2]	NA	386	465*	1.5	2.5
YANCEY	**48**	**5,915**	**7,245***	**47.0**	**100.0**
005 AME ZION	1	136	207	1.3	2.9
081 CATHOLIC	1	NA	80	.5	1.1
081d LATIN	*1*	*NA*	*80*	*.5*	*1.1*
127 CH GOD (CLEVE)	1	94	113*	.7	1.6
145 CH GOD PROPHCY	1	36	43*	.3	.6
157 CH OF BRETHREN	2	84	101*	.7	1.4
167 CHS OF CHRIST	1	11	15	.1	.2
207 E.L.C.A.	1	66	86	.6	1.2
226 FRIENDS-USA	1	61	97	.6	1.3
226c FGC	*1*	*61*	*97*	*.6*	*1.3*
355 PRESB CH (USA)	7	346	415*	2.7	5.7
413 S.D.A.	1	42	50*	.3	.7
419 SO BAPT CONV	23	4,231	5,070*	32.9	70.0
449 UN METHODIST	8	808	968*	6.3	13.4

NORTH DAKOTA

County and Denomination	Number of churches	Communicant, confirmed, full members	Total adherents Number	Percent of total population	Percent of total adherents
THE STATE.....	1,622	228,131	484,628*	75.9	100.0
ADAMS	**11**	**1,217**	**2,140***	**67.4**	**100.0**
053 ASSEMB OF GOD	1	42	91	2.9	4.3
081 CATHOLIC	2	NA	486	15.3	22.7
081d LATIN	*2*	*NA*	*486*	*15.3*	*22.7*
203 EVAN FREE CH	1	22	35	1.1	1.6
207 E.L.C.A.	3	909	1,229	38.7	57.4
443 UN C OF CHRIST	2	129	161*	5.1	7.5
449 UN METHODIST	1	90	112*	3.5	5.2
469 WELS	1	25	26	.8	1.2
BARNES	**41**	**5,528**	**9,812***	**78.2**	**100.0**
053 ASSEMB OF GOD	2	123	233	1.9	2.4
081 CATHOLIC	6	NA	2,624	20.9	26.7
081d LATIN	*6*	*NA*	*2,624*	*20.9*	*26.7*
165 CH OF NAZARENE	1	137	200	1.6	2.0
193 EPISCOPAL	1	25	35	.3	.4
203 EVAN FREE CH	2	59	100	.8	1.0
207 E.L.C.A.	14	3,284	4,247	33.9	43.3
220 FREE LUTHERAN	2	282	345	2.8	3.5
263 INT FOURSQ GOS	1	0	0*	-	-
283 LUTH—MO SYNOD	1	190	234	1.9	2.4
313 N AM BAPT CONF	1	86	107*	.9	1.1
353 CHR BRETHREN	1	33	50	.4	.5
371 REF CH IN AM	1	38	56	.4	.6
413 S.D.A.	1	14	17*	.1	.2
443 UN C OF CHRIST	1	369	457*	3.6	4.7
449 UN METHODIST	5	810	1,004*	8.0	10.2
469 WELS	1	78	103	.8	1.0
BENSON	**34**	**2,279**	**7,814***	**108.6**	**100.0**
053 ASSEMB OF GOD	1	56	74	1.0	.9
081 CATHOLIC	8	NA	4,785	66.5	61.2
081d LATIN	*8*	*NA*	*4,785*	*66.5*	*61.2*
157 CH OF BRETHREN	1	47	65*	.9	.8
163 CH OF LUTH BR	1	21	150	2.1	1.9
193 EPISCOPAL	1	50	87	1.2	1.1
203 EVAN FREE CH	1	51	54	.8	.7
207 E.L.C.A.	15	1,720	2,174	30.2	27.8
220 FREE LUTHERAN	3	240	294	4.1	3.8
355 PRESB CH (USA)	2	69	96*	1.3	1.2
419 SO BAPT CONV	1	25	35*	.5	.4
BILLINGS	**4**	**43**	**144***	**13.0**	**100.0**
081 CATHOLIC	2	NA	85	7.7	59.0
081d LATIN	*1*	*NA*	*20*	*1.8*	*13.9*
081h UKRAINIAN	*1*	*NA*	*65*	*5.9*	*45.1*
207 E.L.C.A.	1	34	47	4.2	32.6

County and Denomination	Number of churches	Communicant, confirmed, full members	Total adherents Number	Percent of total population	Percent of total adherents
443 UN C OF CHRIST	1	9	12*	1.1	8.3
BOTTINEAU	**30**	**4,362**	**6,823***	**85.2**	**100.0**
019 AMER BAPT USA	1	82	102*	1.3	1.5
053 ASSEMB OF GOD	1	19	18	.2	.3
081 CATHOLIC	3	NA	912	11.4	13.4
081d LATIN	*3*	*NA*	*912*	*11.4*	*13.4*
163 CH OF LUTH BR	2	183	513	6.4	7.5
167 CHS OF CHRIST	1	2	2	-	-
207 E.L.C.A.	10	2,790	3,673	45.8	53.8
283 LUTH—MO SYNOD	5	678	848	10.6	12.4
355 PRESB CH (USA)	3	336	417*	5.2	6.1
413 S.D.A.	1	46	57*	.7	.8
449 UN METHODIST	3	226	281*	3.5	4.1
BOWMAN	**16**	**1,645**	**3,317***	**92.2**	**100.0**
053 ASSEMB OF GOD	2	121	214	6.0	6.5
081 CATHOLIC	4	NA	1,104	30.7	33.3
081d LATIN	*4*	*NA*	*1,104*	*30.7*	*33.3*
167 CHS OF CHRIST	1	2	7	.2	.2
207 E.L.C.A.	6	1,296	1,706	47.4	51.4
355 PRESB CH (USA)	1	10	13*	.4	.4
413 S.D.A.	1	49	62*	1.7	1.9
449 UN METHODIST	1	167	211*	5.9	6.4
BURKE	**20**	**2,013**	**3,179***	**105.9**	**100.0**
019 AMER BAPT USA	1	200	244*	8.1	7.7
053 ASSEMB OF GOD	1	29	45	1.5	1.4
081 CATHOLIC	5	NA	586	19.5	18.4
081d LATIN	*5*	*NA*	*586*	*19.5*	*18.4*
127 CH GOD (CLEVE)	1	22	27*	.9	.8
207 E.L.C.A.	7	1,372	1,779	59.3	56.0
283 LUTH—MO SYNOD	2	79	94	3.1	3.0
284 LUTH CH-AM ASC	1	116	166	5.5	5.2
355 PRESB CH (USA)	1	59	72*	2.4	2.3
449 UN METHODIST	1	136	166*	5.5	5.2
BURLEIGH	**63**	**19,015**	**43,846***	**72.9**	**100.0**
019 AMER BAPT USA	1	357	459*	.8	1.0
053 ASSEMB OF GOD	2	535	1,004	1.7	2.3
081 CATHOLIC	8	NA	17,179	28.6	39.2
081d LATIN	*8*	*NA*	*17,179*	*28.6*	*39.2*
089 CHR & MISS AL	1	37	68	.1	.2
111 CH CR,SCIENTST	1	NR	NR	-	-
127 CH GOD (CLEVE)	1	83	107*	.2	.2
145 CH GOD PROPHCY	1	20	26*	-	.1
151 L-D SAINTS	1	NA	461	.8	1.1
163 CH OF LUTH BR	1	62	200	.3	.5
164 CH LUTH CONF	1	19	26	-	.1
165 CH OF NAZARENE	1	72	96	.2	.2
167 CHS OF CHRIST	1	58	88	.1	.2
181 CONSRV CONGR	1	33	42*	.1	.1
193 EPISCOPAL	1	302	461	.8	1.1
203 EVAN FREE CH	1	130	310	.5	.7
207 E.L.C.A.	12	10,352	14,000	23.3	31.9
220 FREE LUTHERAN	1	32	51	.1	.1
226 FRIENDS-USA	1	5	14	-	-
226c FGC	*1*	*5*	*14*	*-*	*-*
237 GC MENN BR CHS	1	44	57*	.1	.1
263 INT FOURSQ GOS	1	222	285*	.5	.7
283 LUTH—MO SYNOD	3	1,173	1,526	2.5	3.5
313 N AM BAPT CONF	2	823	1,057*	1.8	2.4
355 PRESB CH (USA)	2	991	1,273*	2.1	2.9
371 REF CH IN AM	1	259	607	1.0	1.4
403 SALVATION ARMY	1	90	91	.2	.2
413 S.D.A.	2	365	469*	.8	1.1
419 SO BAPT CONV	1	118	152*	.3	.3
435 UNITARIAN-UNIV	1	44	59	.1	.1
443 UN C OF CHRIST	2	390	501*	.8	1.1
449 UN METHODIST	6	2,171	2,788*	4.6	6.4
467 WESLEYAN	1	23	110	.2	.3
469 WELS	1	205	279	.5	.6
496 JEWISH EST[1]	1	NA	0	-	-
CASS	**119**	**33,845**	**67,952***	**66.1**	**100.0**
019 AMER BAPT USA	1	163	204*	.2	.3
053 ASSEMB OF GOD	2	1,038	1,888	1.8	2.8
081 CATHOLIC	15	NA	21,488	20.9	31.6
081d LATIN	*15*	*NA*	*21,488*	*20.9*	*31.6*
089 CHR & MISS AL	1	0	40	-	.1
111 CH CR,SCIENTST	1	NR	NR	-	-
133 CH GOD(7TH)DEN	1	18	23	-	-
145 CH GOD PROPHCY	1	20	25*	-	-
163 CH OF LUTH BR	1	102	191	.2	.3
165 CH OF NAZARENE	1	28	72	.1	.1

NA–Not applicable   NR–Not reported   *Total adherents estimated from known number of communicant, confirmed, full members.   - Represents a percent less than 0.1.   Percentages may not total due to rounding.
[1]See Appendix E   [2]See Appendix F   [3]See Appendix G   Lines in *italic* represent a breakdown of Catholic rites or Friends affiliations. They are included in their respective denominational total.

Table 4. Churches and Church Membership by County and Denomination: 1990

County and Denomination	Number of churches	Communicant, confirmed, full members	Total adherents Number	Percent of total population	Percent of total adherents
167 CHS OF CHRIST	1	50	75	.1	.1
179 CONSRV BAPT	2	NR	NR	-	-
193 EPISCOPAL	2	590	848	.8	1.2
203 EVAN FREE CH	2	401	833	.8	1.2
207 E.L.C.A.	36	22,300	30,188	29.3	44.4
220 FREE LUTHERAN	1	198	237	.2	.3
221 FREE METHODIST	1	16	30	-	-
226 FRIENDS-USA	1	3	12	-	-
226c FGC	*1*	*3*	*12*	-	-
283 LUTH—MO SYNOD	5	2,115	2,921	2.8	4.3
285 MENNONITE CH	2	67	76	.1	.1
287 MENN GEN CONF	3	39	39	-	.1
293 MORAV CH-NORTH	4	464	563	.5	.8
313 N AM BAPT CONF	2	219	274*	.3	.4
353 CHR BRETHREN	1	25	50	-	.1
355 PRESB CH (USA)	10	2,174	2,723*	2.6	4.0
371 REF CH IN AM	1	45	104	.1	.2
403 SALVATION ARMY	1	62	62	.1	.1
413 S.D.A.	1	130	163*	.2	.2
419 SO BAPT CONV	1	148	185*	.2	.3
435 UNITARIAN-UNIV	1	54	76	.1	.1
443 UN C OF CHRIST	4	874	1,095*	1.1	1.6
449 UN METHODIST	12	2,502	3,134*	3.0	4.6
496 JEWISH EST[1]	1	NA	333	.3	.5
CAVALIER	**31**	**2,287**	**5,317***	**87.7**	**100.0**
053 ASSEMB OF GOD	1	22	41	.7	.8
081 CATHOLIC	8	NA	2,389	39.4	44.9
081d LATIN	*8*	*NA*	*2,389*	*39.4*	*44.9*
193 EPISCOPAL	1	28	34	.6	.6
207 E.L.C.A.	7	1,073	1,407	23.2	26.5
237 GC MENN BR CHS	1	56	71*	1.2	1.3
283 LUTH—MO SYNOD	2	223	277	4.6	5.2
287 MENN GEN CONF	2	231	272	4.5	5.1
355 PRESB CH (USA)	6	331	418*	6.9	7.9
419 SO BAPT CONV	1	66	83*	1.4	1.6
449 UN METHODIST	2	257	325*	5.4	6.1
DICKEY	**25**	**2,951**	**4,864***	**79.6**	**100.0**
019 AMER BAPT USA	1	71	88*	1.4	1.8
053 ASSEMB OF GOD	1	71	130	2.1	2.7
081 CATHOLIC	3	NA	930	15.2	19.1
081d LATIN	*3*	*NA*	*930*	*15.2*	*19.1*
165 CH OF NAZARENE	2	153	277	4.5	5.7
193 EPISCOPAL	1	31	32	.5	.7
207 E.L.C.A.	4	819	1,065	17.4	21.9
257 HUTTERIAN BR	1	NA	100	1.6	2.1
283 LUTH—MO SYNOD	4	1,074	1,337	21.9	27.5
355 PRESB CH (USA)	2	170	210*	3.4	4.3
413 S.D.A.	1	68	84*	1.4	1.7
443 UN C OF CHRIST	1	17	21*	.3	.4
449 UN METHODIST	4	477	590*	9.7	12.1
DIVIDE	**19**	**1,370**	**2,081***	**71.8**	**100.0**
053 ASSEMB OF GOD	2	54	119	4.1	5.7
081 CATHOLIC	2	NA	258	8.9	12.4
081d LATIN	*2*	*NA*	*258*	*8.9*	*12.4*
163 CH OF LUTH BR	1	18	50	1.7	2.4
207 E.L.C.A.	12	1,203	1,538	53.1	73.9
284 LUTH CH-AM ASC	1	37	45	1.6	2.2
355 PRESB CH (USA)	1	58	71*	2.4	3.4
DUNN	**14**	**1,239**	**2,321***	**58.0**	**100.0**
019 AMER BAPT USA	1	19	25*	.6	1.1
057 BAPT GEN CONF	1	24	32*	.8	1.4
081 CATHOLIC	2	NA	751	18.8	32.4
081d LATIN	*2*	*NA*	*751*	*18.8*	*32.4*
207 E.L.C.A.	6	1,029	1,303	32.5	56.1
283 LUTH—MO SYNOD	1	70	79	2.0	3.4
356 PRESB CH AMER	1	17	25	.6	1.1
443 UN C OF CHRIST	2	80	106*	2.6	4.6
EDDY	**11**	**1,339**	**2,318***	**78.5**	**100.0**
081 CATHOLIC	1	NA	570	19.3	24.6
081d LATIN	*1*	*NA*	*570*	*19.3*	*24.6*
165 CH OF NAZARENE	1	19	49	1.7	2.1
181 CONSRV CONGR	1	86	106*	3.6	4.6
203 EVAN FREE CH	1	35	48	1.6	2.1
207 E.L.C.A.	4	966	1,254	42.5	54.1
283 LUTH—MO SYNOD	1	84	106	3.6	4.6
449 UN METHODIST	2	149	185*	6.3	8.0
EMMONS	**20**	**1,274**	**4,380***	**90.7**	**100.0**
053 ASSEMB OF GOD	1	22	40	.8	.9
081 CATHOLIC	8	NA	2,716	56.2	62.0

County and Denomination	Number of churches	Communicant, confirmed, full members	Total adherents Number	Percent of total population	Percent of total adherents
081d LATIN	*8*	*NA*	*2,716*	*56.2*	*62.0*
105 CHRISTIAN REF	1	86	126	2.6	2.9
207 E.L.C.A.	2	495	637	13.2	14.5
313 N AM BAPT CONF	1	97	120*	2.5	2.7
355 PRESB CH (USA)	1	36	45*	.9	1.0
371 REF CH IN AM	2	167	236	4.9	5.4
413 S.D.A.	1	8	10*	.2	.2
449 UN METHODIST	2	204	253*	5.2	5.8
469 WELS	1	159	197	4.1	4.5
FOSTER	**14**	**2,026**	**3,625***	**91.0**	**100.0**
081 CATHOLIC	2	NA	959	24.1	26.5
081d LATIN	*2*	*NA*	*959*	*24.1*	*26.5*
165 CH OF NAZARENE	1	26	54	1.4	1.5
207 E.L.C.A.	5	1,147	1,509	37.9	41.6
283 LUTH—MO SYNOD	1	295	392	9.8	10.8
313 N AM BAPT CONF	1	138	176*	4.4	4.9
413 S.D.A.	1	61	78*	2.0	2.2
443 UN C OF CHRIST	1	135	172*	4.3	4.7
449 UN METHODIST	2	224	285*	7.2	7.9
GOLDEN VALLEY	**10**	**576**	**1,641***	**77.8**	**100.0**
081 CATHOLIC	3	NA	866	41.1	52.8
081d LATIN	*3*	*NA*	*866*	*41.1*	*52.8*
207 E.L.C.A.	2	283	388	18.4	23.6
283 LUTH—MO SYNOD	1	175	234	11.1	14.3
413 S.D.A.	1	20	26*	1.2	1.6
443 UN C OF CHRIST	2	82	106*	5.0	6.5
449 UN METHODIST	1	16	21*	1.0	1.3
GRAND FORKS	**75**	**18,617**	**40,941***	**57.9**	**100.0**
019 AMER BAPT USA	1	200	254*	.4	.6
053 ASSEMB OF GOD	2	136	395	.6	1.0
081 CATHOLIC	8	NA	14,650	20.7	35.8
081d LATIN	*8*	*NA*	*14,650*	*20.7*	*35.8*
097 CHR CHS&CHS CR	1	60	76*	.1	.2
111 CH CR,SCIENTST	1	NR	NR	-	-
123 CH GOD (ANDER)	1	50	50	.1	.1
127 CH GOD (CLEVE)	1	41	52*	.1	.1
145 CH GOD PROPHCY	1	20	25*	-	.1
163 CH OF LUTH BR	1	118	419	.6	1.0
165 CH OF NAZARENE	2	122	344	.5	.8
167 CHS OF CHRIST	2	64	110	.2	.3
193 EPISCOPAL	1	281	377	.5	.9
203 EVAN FREE CH	1	213	470	.7	1.1
207 E.L.C.A.	24	11,222	15,646	22.1	38.2
220 FREE LUTHERAN	3	336	472	.7	1.2
226 FRIENDS-USA	1	0	7	-	-
226c FGC	*1*	*0*	*7*	-	-
263 INT FOURSQ GOS	1	58	74*	.1	.2
283 LUTH—MO SYNOD	4	934	1,298	1.8	3.2
284 LUTH CH-AM ASC	1	138	204	.3	.5
313 N AM BAPT CONF	1	325	413*	.6	1.0
355 PRESB CH (USA)	5	948	1,206*	1.7	2.9
403 SALVATION ARMY	1	71	77	.1	.2
413 S.D.A.	1	187	238*	.3	.6
419 SO BAPT CONV	2	1,284	1,633*	2.3	4.0
443 UN C OF CHRIST	2	199	253*	.4	.6
449 UN METHODIST	5	1,228	1,562*	2.2	3.8
496 JEWISH EST[1]	1	NA	150	.2	.4
497 BLACK BAPT EST[2]	NA	382	486*	.7	1.2
GRANT	**21**	**1,706**	**2,960***	**83.4**	**100.0**
053 ASSEMB OF GOD	1	56	111	3.1	3.8
081 CATHOLIC	4	NA	817	23.0	27.6
081d LATIN	*4*	*NA*	*817*	*23.0*	*27.6*
181 CONSRV CONGR	1	100	125*	3.5	4.2
207 E.L.C.A.	3	852	1,057	29.8	35.7
313 N AM BAPT CONF	1	113	141*	4.0	4.8
355 PRESB CH (USA)	1	41	51*	1.4	1.7
413 S.D.A.	1	10	13*	.4	.4
443 UN C OF CHRIST	4	152	190*	5.4	6.4
449 UN METHODIST	2	147	184*	5.2	6.2
469 WELS	3	235	271	7.6	9.2
GRIGGS	**20**	**1,587**	**2,496***	**75.6**	**100.0**
053 ASSEMB OF GOD	1	32	45	1.4	1.8
081 CATHOLIC	2	NA	415	12.6	16.6
081d LATIN	*2*	*NA*	*415*	*12.6*	*16.6*
163 CH OF LUTH BR	1	64	135	4.1	5.4
203 EVAN FREE CH	3	91	104	3.1	4.2
207 E.L.C.A.	8	1,058	1,349	40.8	54.0
220 FREE LUTHERAN	1	95	121	3.7	4.8
283 LUTH—MO SYNOD	2	180	243	7.4	9.7
355 PRESB CH (USA)	1	47	59*	1.8	2.4

NA–Not applicable   NR–Not reported   *Total adherents estimated from known number of communicant, confirmed, full members.   - Represents a percent less than 0.1.   Percentages may not total due to rounding.
[1]See Appendix E   [2]See Appendix F   [3]See Appendix G   Lines in *italic* represent a breakdown of Catholic rites or Friends affiliations. They are included in their respective denominational total.

Table 4. Churches and Church Membership by County and Denomination: 1990

County and Denomination	Number of churches	Communicant, confirmed, full members	Total adherents Number	Percent of total population	Percent of total adherents
449 UN METHODIST	1	20	25*	.8	1.0
HETTINGER	**17**	**1,395**	**3,806***	**110.5**	**100.0**
053 ASSEMB OF GOD	2	58	107	3.1	2.8
081 CATHOLIC	3	NA	2,058	59.7	54.1
081d LATIN	3	NA	2,058	59.7	54.1
165 CH OF NAZARENE	1	13	38	1.1	1.0
181 CONSRV CONGR	1	132	166*	4.8	4.4
203 EVAN FREE CH	1	73	73	2.1	1.9
207 E.L.C.A.	6	970	1,176	34.1	30.9
443 UN C OF CHRIST	3	149	188*	5.5	4.9
KIDDER	**21**	**1,596**	**2,952***	**88.6**	**100.0**
081 CATHOLIC	3	NA	460	13.8	15.6
081d LATIN	3	NA	460	13.8	15.6
151 L-D SAINTS	1	NA	370	11.1	12.5
165 CH OF NAZARENE	1	27	69	2.1	2.3
207 E.L.C.A.	5	795	996	29.9	33.7
283 LUTH—MO SYNOD	1	171	255*	7.7	8.6
355 PRESB CH (USA)	1	32	40*	1.2	1.4
443 UN C OF CHRIST	4	87	110*	3.3	3.7
449 UN METHODIST	4	264	333*	10.0	11.3
469 WELS	1	220	319	9.6	10.8
LA MOURE	**38**	**2,964**	**5,532***	**102.8**	**100.0**
053 ASSEMB OF GOD	1	75	123	2.3	2.2
057 BAPT GEN CONF	1	114	144*	2.7	2.6
081 CATHOLIC	6	NA	1,387	25.8	25.1
081d LATIN	6	NA	1,387	25.8	25.1
133 CH GOD(7TH)DEN	1	18	24	.4	.4
165 CH OF NAZARENE	1	45	170	3.2	3.1
207 E.L.C.A.	10	1,185	1,502	27.9	27.2
257 HUTTERIAN BR	2	NA	200	3.7	3.6
283 LUTH—MO SYNOD	4	609	801	14.9	14.5
355 PRESB CH (USA)	2	158	199*	3.7	3.6
371 REF CH IN AM	1	71	113	2.1	2.0
413 S.D.A.	2	80	101*	1.9	1.8
443 UN C OF CHRIST	1	39	49*	.9	.9
449 UN METHODIST	6	570	719*	13.4	13.0
LOGAN	**17**	**1,334**	**2,759***	**96.9**	**100.0**
053 ASSEMB OF GOD	2	56	76	2.7	2.8
081 CATHOLIC	4	NA	1,125	39.5	40.8
081d LATIN	4	NA	1,125	39.5	40.8
207 E.L.C.A.	3	678	823	28.9	29.8
283 LUTH—MO SYNOD	1	76	93	3.3	3.4
313 N AM BAPT CONF	3	196	240*	8.4	8.7
413 S.D.A.	1	17	21*	.7	.8
443 UN C OF CHRIST	2	191	234*	8.2	8.5
449 UN METHODIST	1	120	147*	5.2	5.3
MC HENRY	**37**	**3,289**	**6,276***	**96.1**	**100.0**
019 AMER BAPT USA	2	42	53*	.8	.8
081 CATHOLIC	8	NA	2,034	31.2	32.4
081d LATIN	8	NA	2,034	31.2	32.4
165 CH OF NAZARENE	1	31	19	.3	.3
207 E.L.C.A.	12	2,230	2,908	44.5	46.3
283 LUTH—MO SYNOD	5	527	690	10.6	11.0
313 N AM BAPT CONF	2	94	119*	1.8	1.9
355 PRESB CH (USA)	1	91	115*	1.8	1.8
373 REF CH IN U.S.	1	36	38	.6	.6
443 UN C OF CHRIST	2	100	126*	1.9	2.0
449 UN METHODIST	3	138	174*	2.7	2.8
MC INTOSH	**20**	**3,173**	**4,286***	**106.6**	**100.0**
053 ASSEMB OF GOD	1	25	40	1.0	.9
057 BAPT GEN CONF	1	14	17*	.4	.4
081 CATHOLIC	3	NA	528	13.1	12.3
081d LATIN	3	NA	528	13.1	12.3
207 E.L.C.A.	3	1,641	1,914	47.6	44.7
283 LUTH—MO SYNOD	1	85	101	2.5	2.4
313 N AM BAPT CONF	4	531	642*	16.0	15.0
373 REF CH IN U.S.	1	70	77	1.9	1.8
413 S.D.A.	1	43	52*	1.3	1.2
443 UN C OF CHRIST	1	235	284*	7.1	6.6
449 UN METHODIST	3	399	482*	12.0	11.2
469 WELS	1	130	149	3.7	3.5
MC KENZIE	**33**	**2,399**	**4,538***	**71.1**	**100.0**
053 ASSEMB OF GOD	1	52	120	1.9	2.6
081 CATHOLIC	6	NA	1,274	20.0	28.1
081d LATIN	6	NA	1,274	20.0	28.1
165 CH OF NAZARENE	1	10	15	.2	.3
193 EPISCOPAL	1	37	39	.6	.9
207 E.L.C.A.	13	1,760	2,395	37.5	52.8
283 LUTH—MO SYNOD	2	163	223	3.5	4.9
355 PRESB CH (USA)	1	58	79*	1.2	1.7
413 S.D.A.	2	89	121*	1.9	2.7
419 SO BAPT CONV	1	54	73*	1.1	1.6
443 UN C OF CHRIST	2	63	85*	1.3	1.9
449 UN METHODIST	1	14	19*	.3	.4
467 WESLEYAN	2	99	95	1.5	2.1
MC LEAN	**52**	**4,818**	**8,201***	**78.4**	**100.0**
053 ASSEMB OF GOD	3	92	147	1.4	1.8
081 CATHOLIC	8	NA	1,771	16.9	21.6
081d LATIN	7	NA	1,690	16.2	20.6
081h UKRAINIAN	1	NA	81	.8	1.0
127 CH GOD (CLEVE)	2	28	36*	.3	.4
151 L-D SAINTS	1	NA	32	.3	.4
181 CONSRV CONGR	1	28	36*	.3	.4
193 EPISCOPAL	1	27	154	1.5	1.9
203 EVAN FREE CH	1	70	95	.9	1.2
207 E.L.C.A.	15	2,793	3,643	34.8	44.4
283 LUTH—MO SYNOD	3	493	628	6.0	7.7
313 N AM BAPT CONF	2	383	493*	4.7	6.0
353 CHR BRETHREN	1	12	25	.2	.3
355 PRESB CH (USA)	1	108	139*	1.3	1.7
356 PRESB CH AMER	1	67	79	.8	1.0
413 S.D.A.	3	103	133*	1.3	1.6
443 UN C OF CHRIST	3	325	418*	4.0	5.1
449 UN METHODIST	4	289	372*	3.6	4.5
MERCER	**27**	**4,871**	**8,225***	**83.9**	**100.0**
053 ASSEMB OF GOD	3	114	203	2.1	2.5
081 CATHOLIC	2	NA	1,678	17.1	20.4
081d LATIN	2	NA	1,678	17.1	20.4
127 CH GOD (CLEVE)	1	81	110*	1.1	1.3
145 CH GOD PROPHCY	2	42	57*	.6	.7
165 CH OF NAZARENE	1	24	51	.5	.6
167 CHS OF CHRIST	1	2	6	.1	.1
207 E.L.C.A.	7	3,005	4,070	41.5	49.5
283 LUTH—MO SYNOD	5	1,085	1,346	13.7	16.4
313 N AM BAPT CONF	1	173	235*	2.4	2.9
413 S.D.A.	1	48	65*	.7	.8
419 SO BAPT CONV	1	69	94*	1.0	1.1
449 UN METHODIST	2	228	310*	3.2	3.8
MORTON	**45**	**6,315**	**20,195***	**85.2**	**100.0**
053 ASSEMB OF GOD	2	132	288	1.2	1.4
081 CATHOLIC	12	NA	11,339	47.8	56.1
081d LATIN	12	NA	11,339	47.8	56.1
165 CH OF NAZARENE	1	124	319	1.3	1.6
181 CONSRV CONGR	1	35	46*	.2	.2
193 EPISCOPAL	1	24	26	.1	.1
207 E.L.C.A.	5	2,197	3,279	13.8	16.2
283 LUTH—MO SYNOD	3	576	731	3.1	3.6
313 N AM BAPT CONF	1	183	239*	1.0	1.2
355 PRESB CH (USA)	2	393	512*	2.2	2.5
413 S.D.A.	2	75	98*	.4	.5
419 SO BAPT CONV	2	332	433*	1.8	2.1
443 UN C OF CHRIST	6	1,330	1,734*	7.3	8.6
449 UN METHODIST	4	604	787*	3.3	3.9
467 WESLEYAN	1	8	0	-	-
469 WELS	2	302	364	1.5	1.8
MOUNTRAIL	**32**	**2,941**	**5,140***	**73.2**	**100.0**
019 AMER BAPT USA	1	109	142*	2.0	2.8
045 APOSTOLIC LUTH	1	0	30	.4	.6
053 ASSEMB OF GOD	2	88	163	2.3	3.2
081 CATHOLIC	5	NA	1,107	15.8	21.5
081d LATIN	5	NA	1,107	15.8	21.5
151 L-D SAINTS	1	NA	221	3.1	4.3
193 EPISCOPAL	1	5	10	.1	.2
207 E.L.C.A.	12	1,733	2,214	31.5	43.1
220 FREE LUTHERAN	2	263	330	4.7	6.4
284 LUTH CH-AM ASC	2	485	587	8.4	11.4
355 PRESB CH (USA)	1	39	51*	.7	1.0
413 S.D.A.	1	29	38*	.5	.7
443 UN C OF CHRIST	3	190	247*	3.5	4.8
NELSON	**24**	**2,620**	**4,033***	**91.5**	**100.0**
081 CATHOLIC	4	NA	836	19.0	20.7
081d LATIN	4	NA	836	19.0	20.7
193 EPISCOPAL	1	16	20	.5	.5
207 E.L.C.A.	14	2,265	2,776	62.9	68.8
220 FREE LUTHERAN	1	147	163	3.7	4.0
283 LUTH—MO SYNOD	2	86	108	2.4	2.7
443 UN C OF CHRIST	2	106	130*	2.9	3.2

NA–Not applicable   NR–Not reported   *Total adherents estimated from known number of communicant, confirmed, full members.   - Represents a percent less than 0.1.   Percentages may not total due to rounding.

[1] See Appendix E   [2] See Appendix F   [3] See Appendix G   Lines in *italic* represent a breakdown of Catholic rites or Friends affiliations. They are included in their respective denominational total.

Table 4. Churches and Church Membership by County and Denomination: 1990

County and Denomination		Number of churches	Communicant, confirmed, full members	Total adherents		
				Number	Percent of total population	Percent of total adherents
OLIVER		**5**	**646**	**1,506***	**63.3**	**100.0**
081	CATHOLIC	1	NA	574	24.1	38.1
081d	*LATIN*	*1*	*NA*	*574*	*24.1*	*38.1*
165	CH OF NAZARENE	1	5	18	.8	1.2
207	E.L.C.A.	1	310	453	19.0	30.1
283	LUTH—MO SYNOD	1	252	353	14.8	23.4
449	UN METHODIST	1	79	108*	4.5	7.2
PEMBINA		**44**	**4,279**	**7,859***	**85.1**	**100.0**
053	ASSEMB OF GOD	3	121	222	2.4	2.8
081	CATHOLIC	9	NA	2,124	23.0	27.0
081d	*LATIN*	*9*	*NA*	*2,124*	*23.0*	*27.0*
193	EPISCOPAL	1	37	46	.5	.6
203	EVAN FREE CH	2	88	163	1.8	2.1
207	E.L.C.A.	8	1,905	2,605	28.2	33.1
220	FREE LUTHERAN	1	26	38	.4	.5
283	LUTH—MO SYNOD	4	540	662	7.2	8.4
355	PRESB CH (USA)	4	586	750*	8.1	9.5
419	SO BAPT CONV	1	19	24*	.3	.3
449	UN METHODIST	11	957	1,225*	13.3	15.6
PIERCE		**17**	**1,584**	**4,101***	**81.2**	**100.0**
053	ASSEMB OF GOD	1	64	131	2.6	3.2
081	CATHOLIC	4	NA	2,017	39.9	49.2
081d	*LATIN*	*4*	*NA*	*2,017*	*39.9*	*49.2*
203	EVAN FREE CH	1	15	58	1.1	1.4
207	E.L.C.A.	6	1,213	1,497	29.6	36.5
220	FREE LUTHERAN	1	44	55	1.1	1.3
283	LUTH—MO SYNOD	1	159	232	4.6	5.7
355	PRESB CH (USA)	2	40	50*	1.0	1.2
449	UN METHODIST	1	49	61*	1.2	1.5
RAMSEY		**35**	**4,778**	**11,015***	**86.9**	**100.0**
053	ASSEMB OF GOD	1	38	73	.6	.7
081	CATHOLIC	5	NA	4,675	36.9	42.4
081d	*LATIN*	*5*	*NA*	*4,675*	*36.9*	*42.4*
127	CH GOD (CLEVE)	1	13	16*	.1	.1
133	CH GOD(7TH)DEN	1	18	23	.2	.2
151	L-D SAINTS	1	NA	45	.4	.4
167	CHS OF CHRIST	1	3	7	.1	.1
193	EPISCOPAL	1	23	24	.2	.2
203	EVAN FREE CH	1	53	75	.6	.7
207	E.L.C.A.	11	3,386	4,513	35.6	41.0
220	FREE LUTHERAN	4	249	294	2.3	2.7
283	LUTH—MO SYNOD	1	236	309	2.4	2.8
355	PRESB CH (USA)	2	166	210*	1.7	1.9
413	S.D.A.	1	19	24*	.2	.2
419	SO BAPT CONV	1	146	185*	1.5	1.7
449	UN METHODIST	3	428	542*	4.3	4.9
RANSOM		**22**	**3,333**	**5,612***	**94.8**	**100.0**
019	AMER BAPT USA	1	78	98*	1.7	1.7
053	ASSEMB OF GOD	1	67	130	2.2	2.3
081	CATHOLIC	3	NA	1,181	19.9	21.0
081d	*LATIN*	*3*	*NA*	*1,181*	*19.9*	*21.0*
207	E.L.C.A.	10	2,466	3,291	55.6	58.6
220	FREE LUTHERAN	1	28	40	.7	.7
283	LUTH—MO SYNOD	1	261	330	5.6	5.9
355	PRESB CH (USA)	1	52	65*	1.1	1.2
413	S.D.A.	1	31	39*	.7	.7
449	UN METHODIST	3	350	438*	7.4	7.8
RENVILLE		**17**	**1,593**	**2,986***	**94.5**	**100.0**
019	AMER BAPT USA	1	116	147*	4.7	4.9
081	CATHOLIC	5	NA	900	28.5	30.1
081d	*LATIN*	*5*	*NA*	*900*	*28.5*	*30.1*
165	CH OF NAZARENE	1	32	122	3.9	4.1
207	E.L.C.A.	7	1,152	1,460	46.2	48.9
283	LUTH—MO SYNOD	1	101	114	3.6	3.8
449	UN METHODIST	2	192	243*	7.7	8.1
RICHLAND		**54**	**7,349**	**16,283***	**89.7**	**100.0**
053	ASSEMB OF GOD	1	126	260	1.4	1.6
081	CATHOLIC	8	NA	6,451	35.5	39.6
081d	*LATIN*	*8*	*NA*	*6,451*	*35.5*	*39.6*
127	CH GOD (CLEVE)	1	49	63*	.3	.4
151	L-D SAINTS	1	NA	88	.5	.5
163	CH OF LUTH BR	1	43	142	.8	.9
176	CCC, NOT NAT'L	1	28	36*	.2	.2
193	EPISCOPAL	1	72	72	.4	.4
203	EVAN FREE CH	1	37	104	.6	.6
207	E.L.C.A.	18	3,408	4,445	24.5	27.3
220	FREE LUTHERAN	1	74	110	.6	.7
283	LUTH—MO SYNOD	8	2,136	2,754	15.2	16.9
413	S.D.A.	1	107	137*	.8	.8
443	UN C OF CHRIST	3	473	604*	3.3	3.7
449	UN METHODIST	8	796	1,017*	5.6	6.2
ROLETTE		**30**	**1,752**	**17,349***	**135.8**	**100.0**
053	ASSEMB OF GOD	3	92	161	1.3	.9
081	CATHOLIC	8	NA	14,850	116.3	85.6
081d	*LATIN*	*8*	*NA*	*14,850*	*116.3*	*85.6*
089	CHR & MISS AL	1	23	42	.3	.2
127	CH GOD (CLEVE)	1	9	13*	.1	.1
151	L-D SAINTS	1	NA	55	.4	.3
163	CH OF LUTH BR	1	46	130	1.0	.7
193	EPISCOPAL	1	49	72	.6	.4
207	E.L.C.A.	7	885	1,185	9.3	6.8
283	LUTH—MO SYNOD	1	161	204	1.6	1.2
285	MENNONITE CH	2	152	152	1.2	.9
355	PRESB CH (USA)	2	226	327*	2.6	1.9
449	UN METHODIST	2	109	158*	1.2	.9
SARGENT		**23**	**2,499**	**4,280***	**94.1**	**100.0**
019	AMER BAPT USA	1	19	24*	.5	.6
081	CATHOLIC	6	NA	972	21.4	22.7
081d	*LATIN*	*6*	*NA*	*972*	*21.4*	*22.7*
097	CHR CHS&CHS CR	1	10	13*	.3	.3
207	E.L.C.A.	9	2,008	2,608	57.3	60.9
257	HUTTERIAN BR	1	NA	100	2.2	2.3
283	LUTH—MO SYNOD	2	308	370	8.1	8.6
443	UN C OF CHRIST	1	17	21*	.5	.5
449	UN METHODIST	2	137	172*	3.8	4.0
SHERIDAN		**16**	**1,167**	**1,605***	**74.7**	**100.0**
053	ASSEMB OF GOD	1	32	40	1.9	2.5
081	CATHOLIC	1	NA	96	4.5	6.0
081d	*LATIN*	*1*	*NA*	*96*	*4.5*	*6.0*
165	CH OF NAZARENE	1	7	14	.7	.9
207	E.L.C.A.	2	361	517	24.1	32.2
237	GC MENN BR CHS	1	8	10*	.5	.6
283	LUTH—MO SYNOD	1	181	218	10.1	13.6
313	N AM BAPT CONF	3	288	356*	16.6	22.2
373	REF CH IN U.S.	1	36	41	1.9	2.6
413	S.D.A.	2	100	123*	5.7	7.7
449	UN METHODIST	3	154	190*	8.8	11.8
SIOUX		**12**	**298**	**1,513***	**40.2**	**100.0**
053	ASSEMB OF GOD	2	43	86	2.3	5.7
081	CATHOLIC	5	NA	793	21.1	52.4
081d	*LATIN*	*5*	*NA*	*793*	*21.1*	*52.4*
193	EPISCOPAL	2	88	378	10.1	25.0
419	SO BAPT CONV	1	124	190*	5.1	12.6
443	UN C OF CHRIST	2	43	66*	1.8	4.4
SLOPE		**3**	**146**	**280***	**30.9**	**100.0**
081	CATHOLIC	1	NA	50	5.5	17.9
081d	*LATIN*	*1*	*NA*	*50*	*5.5*	*17.9*
207	E.L.C.A.	1	69	129	14.2	46.1
443	UN C OF CHRIST	1	77	101*	11.1	36.1
STARK		**39**	**3,871**	**18,215***	**79.8**	**100.0**
019	AMER BAPT USA	1	38	50*	.2	.3
053	ASSEMB OF GOD	1	135	280	1.2	1.5
081	CATHOLIC	14	NA	12,522	54.8	68.7
081d	*LATIN*	*13*	*NA*	*12,387*	*54.3*	*68.0*
081h	*UKRAINIAN*	*1*	*NA*	*135*	*.6*	*.7*
111	CH CR,SCIENTST	1	NR	NR	-	-
127	CH GOD (CLEVE)	1	11	14*	.1	.1
151	L-D SAINTS	1	NA	128	.6	.7
165	CH OF NAZARENE	1	37	122	.5	.7
167	CHS OF CHRIST	1	13	33	.1	.2
181	CONSRV CONGR	1	65	85*	.4	.5
193	EPISCOPAL	1	67	96	.4	.5
207	E.L.C.A.	6	1,806	2,600	11.4	14.3
220	FREE LUTHERAN	1	304	396	1.7	2.2
283	LUTH—MO SYNOD	2	323	483	2.1	2.7
313	N AM BAPT CONF	1	136	178*	.8	1.0
355	PRESB CH (USA)	1	41	54*	.2	.3
413	S.D.A.	1	28	37*	.2	.2
419	SO BAPT CONV	1	167	219*	1.0	1.2
443	UN C OF CHRIST	2	382	501*	2.2	2.8
449	UN METHODIST	1	318	417*	1.8	2.3
STEELE		**22**	**1,824**	**2,558***	**105.7**	**100.0**
053	ASSEMB OF GOD	1	20	26	1.1	1.0
081	CATHOLIC	2	NA	286	11.8	11.2
081d	*LATIN*	*2*	*NA*	*286*	*11.8*	*11.2*

NA–Not applicable   NR–Not reported   *Total adherents estimated from known number of communicant, confirmed, full members.   - Represents a percent less than 0.1.   Percentages may not total due to rounding.
[1]See Appendix E   [2]See Appendix F   [3]See Appendix G   Lines in *italic* represent a breakdown of Catholic rites or Friends affiliations. They are included in their respective denominational total.

Table 4. Churches and Church Membership by County and Denomination: 1990

County and Denomination	Number of churches	Communicant, confirmed, full members	Total adherents — Number	Percent of total population	Percent of total adherents
207 E.L.C.A.	13	1,502	1,872	77.4	73.2
283 LUTH—MO SYNOD	1	74	85	3.5	3.3
355 PRESB CH (USA)	1	49	62*	2.6	2.4
443 UN C OF CHRIST	1	41	52*	2.1	2.0
449 UN METHODIST	2	86	108*	4.5	4.2
469 WELS	1	52	67	2.8	2.6
STUTSMAN	**49**	**8,947**	**16,401***	**73.7**	**100.0**
053 ASSEM OF GOD	2	146	311	1.4	1.9
057 BAPT GEN CONF	1	156	196*	.9	1.2
081 CATHOLIC	8	NA	4,311	19.4	26.3
081d LATIN	*8*	*NA*	*4,311*	*19.4*	*26.3*
151 L-D SAINTS	1	NA	76	.3	.5
163 CH OF LUTH BR	1	30	124	.6	.8
164 CH LUTH CONF	1	129	171	.8	1.0
165 CH OF NAZARENE	1	168	266	1.2	1.6
176 CCC, NOT NAT'L	1	22	28*	.1	.2
193 EPISCOPAL	1	113	175	.8	1.1
207 E.L.C.A.	11	4,599	6,171	27.7	37.6
221 FREE METHODIST	1	26	34	.2	.2
263 INT FOURSQ GOS	1	9	11*	-	.1
283 LUTH—MO SYNOD	3	807	1,087	4.9	6.6
313 N AM BAPT CONF	2	142	179*	.8	1.1
355 PRESB CH (USA)	1	342	431*	1.9	2.6
403 SALVATION ARMY	1	59	60	.3	.4
413 S.D.A.	3	339	427*	1.9	2.6
443 UN C OF CHRIST	3	501	631*	2.8	3.8
449 UN METHODIST	6	1,359	1,712*	7.7	10.4
TOWNER	**15**	**1,688**	**3,177***	**87.6**	**100.0**
053 ASSEM OF GOD	1	71	120	3.3	3.8
081 CATHOLIC	4	NA	861	23.7	27.1
081d LATIN	*4*	*NA*	*861*	*23.7*	*27.1*
157 CH OF BRETHREN	1	97	124*	3.4	3.9
207 E.L.C.A.	4	931	1,275	35.2	40.1
283 LUTH—MO SYNOD	1	275	396	10.9	12.5
355 PRESB CH (USA)	2	57	73*	2.0	2.3
449 UN METHODIST	2	257	328*	9.0	10.3
TRAILL	**32**	**5,367**	**7,748***	**88.5**	**100.0**
081 CATHOLIC	2	NA	748	8.5	9.7
081d LATIN	*2*	*NA*	*748*	*8.5*	*9.7*
151 L-D SAINTS	1	NA	199	2.3	2.6
163 CH OF LUTH BR	1	58	124	1.4	1.6
203 EVAN FREE CH	1	56	100	1.1	1.3
207 E.L.C.A.	19	4,462	5,573	63.7	71.9
209 EVAN LUTH SYN	1	110	136	1.6	1.8
220 FREE LUTHERAN	3	162	201	2.3	2.6
283 LUTH—MO SYNOD	1	208	278	3.2	3.6
443 UN C OF CHRIST	2	221	276*	3.2	3.6
449 UN METHODIST	1	90	113*	1.3	1.5
WALSH	**50**	**4,972**	**12,042***	**87.0**	**100.0**
053 ASSEM OF GOD	1	62	110	.8	.9
057 BAPT GEN CONF	1	40	51*	.4	.4
081 CATHOLIC	12	NA	5,503	39.8	45.7
081d LATIN	*12*	*NA*	*5,503*	*39.8*	*45.7*
143 CG IN CR(MENN)	1	78	100*	.7	.8
165 CH OF NAZARENE	1	8	39	.3	.3
193 EPISCOPAL	1	17	17	.1	.1
203 EVAN FREE CH	1	24	24	.2	.2
207 E.L.C.A.	18	3,721	4,752	34.3	39.5
220 FREE LUTHERAN	4	229	317	2.3	2.6
257 HUTTERIAN BR	1	NA	100	.7	.8
283 LUTH—MO SYNOD	1	166	226	1.6	1.9
355 PRESB CH (USA)	5	428	548*	4.0	4.6
449 UN METHODIST	3	199	255*	1.8	2.1
WARD	**92**	**17,022**	**33,596***	**58.0**	**100.0**
019 AMER BAPT USA	5	362	469*	.8	1.4
053 ASSEM OF GOD	3	464	1,174	2.0	3.5
057 BAPT GEN CONF	1	9	12*	-	-
081 CATHOLIC	13	NA	9,244	16.0	27.5
081d LATIN	*13*	*NA*	*9,244*	*16.0*	*27.5*
089 CHR & MISS AL	1	44	125	.2	.4
097 CHR CHS&CHS CR	1	100	129*	.2	.4
111 CH CR,SCIENTST	1	NR	NR	-	-
127 CH GOD (CLEVE)	1	302	391*	.7	1.2
145 CH GOD PROPHCY	1	20	26*	-	.1
151 L-D SAINTS	1	NA	488	.8	1.5
157 CH OF BRETHREN	1	42	54*	.1	.2
163 CH OF LUTH BR	1	294	890	1.5	2.6
165 CH OF NAZARENE	4	234	541	.9	1.6
167 CHS OF CHRIST	2	69	103	.2	.3
193 EPISCOPAL	1	129	211	.4	.6
203 EVAN FREE CH	1	63	135	.2	.4
207 E.L.C.A.	23	8,616	11,342	19.6	33.8
220 FREE LUTHERAN	1	169	203	.4	.6
237 GC MENN BR CHS	2	85	110*	.2	.3
246 GREEK ORTHODOX	1	NR	NR	-	-
283 LUTH—MO SYNOD	5	1,975	2,617	4.5	7.8
284 LUTH CH-AM ASC	1	43	77	.1	.2
285 MENNONITE CH	1	35	48	.1	.1
313 N AM BAPT CONF	1	434	562*	1.0	1.7
331 ORTH CH IN AM	1	NR	NR	-	-
355 PRESB CH (USA)	2	1,019	1,319*	2.3	3.9
373 REF CH IN U.S.	1	30	46	.1	.1
403 SALVATION ARMY	1	106	109	.2	.3
413 S.D.A.	2	238	308*	.5	.9
419 SO BAPT CONV	3	506	655*	1.1	1.9
443 UN C OF CHRIST	1	274	355*	.6	1.1
449 UN METHODIST	5	1,033	1,337*	2.3	4.0
467 WESLEYAN	1	25	125	.2	.4
496 JEWISH EST[1]	2	NA	0	-	-
497 BLACK BAPT EST[2]	NA	302	391*	.7	1.2
WELLS	**38**	**2,793**	**5,425***	**92.5**	**100.0**
053 ASSEM OF GOD	1	40	75	1.3	1.4
081 CATHOLIC	5	NA	1,656	28.2	30.5
081d LATIN	*5*	*NA*	*1,656*	*28.2*	*30.5*
123 CH GOD (ANDER)	1	35	56	1.0	1.0
163 CH OF LUTH BR	1	0	11	.2	.2
165 CH OF NAZARENE	2	62	141	2.4	2.6
207 E.L.C.A.	10	1,463	1,905	32.5	35.1
237 GC MENN BR CHS	1	156	192*	3.3	3.5
283 LUTH—MO SYNOD	1	102	126	2.1	2.3
313 N AM BAPT CONF	3	302	372*	6.3	6.9
353 CHR BRETHREN	2	24	35	.6	.6
413 S.D.A.	5	303	374*	6.4	6.9
443 UN C OF CHRIST	2	41	51*	.9	.9
449 UN METHODIST	3	187	231*	3.9	4.3
467 WESLEYAN	1	78	200	3.4	3.7
WILLIAMS	**46**	**9,589**	**17,163***	**81.2**	**100.0**
053 ASSEM OF GOD	2	254	530	2.5	3.1
081 CATHOLIC	5	NA	3,451	16.3	20.1
081d LATIN	*5*	*NA*	*3,451*	*16.3*	*20.1*
089 CHR & MISS AL	1	12	26	.1	.2
151 L-D SAINTS	1	NA	195	.9	1.1
163 CH OF LUTH BR	1	76	310	1.5	1.8
165 CH OF NAZARENE	1	55	102	.5	.6
167 CHS OF CHRIST	1	36	69	.3	.4
193 EPISCOPAL	1	133	158	.7	.9
203 EVAN FREE CH	1	55	135	.6	.8
207 E.L.C.A.	18	5,591	7,626	36.1	44.4
220 FREE LUTHERAN	4	675	863	4.1	5.0
283 LUTH—MO SYNOD	1	202	282	1.3	1.6
284 LUTH CH-AM ASC	1	1,013	1,461	6.9	8.5
355 PRESB CH (USA)	1	214	282*	1.3	1.6
403 SALVATION ARMY	1	37	44	.2	.3
413 S.D.A.	2	85	112*	.5	.7
419 SO BAPT CONV	1	386	509*	2.4	3.0
443 UN C OF CHRIST	1	214	282*	1.3	1.6
449 UN METHODIST	2	551	726*	3.4	4.2

OHIO

County and Denomination	Number of churches	Communicant, confirmed, full members	Total adherents — Number	Percent of total population	Percent of total adherents
THE STATE.....	11,086	2,278,892	5,437,630*	50.1	100.0
ADAMS	**59**	**3,768**	**5,968***	**23.5**	**100.0**
019 AMER BAPT USA	2	164	210*	.8	3.5
061 BEACHY AMISH	1	13	17*	.1	.3
081 CATHOLIC	4	NA	580	2.3	9.7
081d LATIN	*4*	*NA*	*580*	*2.3*	*9.7*
097 CHR CHS&CHS CR	10	1,025	1,313*	5.2	22.0
123 CH GOD (ANDER)	1	50	56	.2	.9
127 CH GOD (CLEVE)	2	80	102*	.4	1.7
151 L-D SAINTS	1	NA	200	.8	3.4
157 CH OF BRETHREN	3	40	51*	.2	.9
165 CH OF NAZARENE	2	163	280	1.1	4.7
167 CHS OF CHRIST	1	10	15	.1	.3
323 OLD ORD AMISH	2	NA	300	1.2	5.0
355 PRESB CH (USA)	7	547	701*	2.8	11.7
413 S.D.A.	1	36	46*	.2	.8
419 SO BAPT CONV	3	286	366*	1.4	6.1
438 UN BRETH IN CR	1	13	13	.1	.2
449 UN METHODIST	18	1,341	1,718*	6.8	28.8

NA–Not applicable   NR–Not reported   *Total adherents estimated from known number of communicant, confirmed, full members.   - Represents a percent less than 0.1.   Percentages may not total due to rounding.
[1]See Appendix E   [2]See Appendix F   [3]See Appendix G   Lines in *italic* represent a breakdown of Catholic rites or Friends affiliations. They are included in their respective denominational total.

Table 4. Churches and Church Membership by County and Denomination: 1990

County and Denomination	Number of churches	Communicant, confirmed, full members	Total adherents Number	Percent of total population	Percent of total adherents
ALLEN	**135**	**27,952**	**54,193***	**49.4**	**100.0**
019 AMER BAPT USA	3	993	1,264*	1.2	2.3
053 ASSEMB OF GOD	2	338	568	.5	1.0
081 CATHOLIC	9	NA	14,076	12.8	26.0
081d LATIN	*9*	*NA*	*14,076*	*12.8*	*26.0*
089 CHR & MISS AL	3	453	1,011	.9	1.9
093 CHR CH (DISC)	2	847	1,232	1.1	2.3
097 CHR CHS&CHS CR	5	530	675*	.6	1.2
111 CH CR,SCIENTST	1	NR	NR	-	-
123 CH GOD (ANDER)	4	201	640	.6	1.2
145 CH GOD PROPHCY	1	36	46*	-	.1
151 L-D SAINTS	1	NA	538	.5	1.0
157 CH OF BRETHREN	4	871	1,109*	1.0	2.0
165 CH OF NAZARENE	5	868	1,641	1.5	3.0
167 CHS OF CHRIST	2	244	297	.3	.5
171 CH GOD-GEN CON	1	54	69*	.1	.1
175 CONGR CHR CHS	1	100	127*	.1	.2
193 EPISCOPAL	1	193	325	.3	.6
207 E.L.C.A.	9	2,890	3,868	3.5	7.1
221 FREE METHODIST	1	20	21	-	-
226 FRIENDS-USA	2	45	65*	.1	.1
226c FGC	*1*	*8*	*18*	*-*	*-*
226e FUM	*1*	*37*	*47***	*-*	*.1*
283 LUTH—MO SYNOD	1	353	457	.4	.8
285 MENNONITE CH	4	386	477	.4	.9
287 MENN GEN CONF	2	616	813	.7	1.5
291 MISSIONARY CH	4	265	312	.3	.6
329 OPEN BIBLE STD	1	NR	NR	-	-
339 PENT CH OF GOD	1	34	76	.1	.1
355 PRESB CH (USA)	5	1,125	1,432*	1.3	2.6
403 SALVATION ARMY	1	119	128	.1	.2
413 S.D.A.	2	183	233*	.2	.4
419 SO BAPT CONV	4	647	824*	.8	1.5
435 UNITARIAN-UNIV	1	25	30	-	.1
436 UNITED BAPT	2	22	28*	-	.1
443 UN C OF CHRIST	10	2,536	3,228*	2.9	6.0
449 UN METHODIST	33	8,642	11,001*	10.0	20.3
466 WAYN TR MB ASC	2	884	1,125*	1.0	2.1
467 WESLEYAN	3	91	144	.1	.3
496 JEWISH EST[1]	1	NA	260	.2	.5
497 BLACK BAPT EST[2]	NA	3,341	4,253*	3.9	7.8
499 INDEP.NON-CHAR[3]	1	NA	1,800	1.6	3.3
ASHLAND	**86**	**13,083**	**21,780***	**45.8**	**100.0**
019 AMER BAPT USA	2	600	760*	1.6	3.5
053 ASSEMB OF GOD	1	215	516	1.1	2.4
071 BRETHREN (ASH)	2	495	627*	1.3	2.9
075 BRETHREN IN CR	1	79	107	.2	.5
081 CATHOLIC	2	NA	2,519	5.3	11.6
081d LATIN	*2*	*NA*	*2,519*	*5.3*	*11.6*
089 CHR & MISS AL	2	112	237	.5	1.1
093 CHR CH (DISC)	1	320	1,015	2.1	4.7
097 CHR CHS&CHS CR	5	663	840*	1.8	3.9
111 CH CR,SCIENTST	1	NR	NR	-	-
123 CH GOD (ANDER)	2	48	54	.1	.2
127 CH GOD (CLEVE)	2	140	177*	.4	.8
151 L-D SAINTS	1	NA	227	.5	1.0
157 CH OF BRETHREN	3	520	659*	1.4	3.0
165 CH OF NAZARENE	3	308	436	.9	2.0
167 CHS OF CHRIST	3	290	422	.9	1.9
171 CH GOD-GEN CON	1	43	54*	.1	.2
175 CONGR CHR CHS	1	90	114*	.2	.5
193 EPISCOPAL	1	102	164	.3	.8
203 EVAN FREE CH	1	55	116	.2	.5
207 E.L.C.A.	10	3,421	4,310	9.1	19.8
246 GREEK ORTHODOX	1	NR	NR	-	-
263 INT FOURSQ GOS	1	0	0*	-	-
323 OLD ORD AMISH	6	NA	850	1.8	3.9
325 OLD REG BAPT	1	22	28*	.1	.1
329 OPEN BIBLE STD	1	NR	NR	-	-
355 PRESB CH (USA)	5	853	1,081*	2.3	5.0
403 SALVATION ARMY	1	53	55	.1	.3
419 SO BAPT CONV	1	80	101*	.2	.5
438 UN BRETH IN CR	1	7	12	-	.1
443 UN C OF CHRIST	3	395	500*	1.1	2.3
449 UN METHODIST	17	4,120	5,220*	11.0	24.0
467 WESLEYAN	1	20	35	.1	.2
469 WELS	1	32	44	.1	.2
499 INDEP.NON-CHAR[3]	1	NA	500	1.1	2.3
ASHTABULA	**128**	**18,410**	**45,620***	**45.7**	**100.0**
011 A.W.M.C.	2	43	55*	.1	.1
019 AMER BAPT USA	6	1,588	2,017*	2.0	4.4
053 ASSEMB OF GOD	5	760	1,486	1.5	3.3
081 CATHOLIC	12	NA	19,541	19.6	42.8
081b BYZAN RUTH	*1*	*NA*	*405*	*.4*	*.9*
081d LATIN	*11*	*NA*	*19,136*	*19.2*	*41.9*
089 CHR & MISS AL	1	98	233	.2	.5
093 CHR CH (DISC)	3	313	506	.5	1.1
097 CHR CHS&CHS CR	5	571	725*	.7	1.6
111 CH CR,SCIENTST	1	NR	NR	-	-
123 CH GOD (ANDER)	2	68	89	.1	.2
127 CH GOD (CLEVE)	4	295	375*	.4	.8
145 CH GOD PROPHCY	1	36	46*	-	.1
151 L-D SAINTS	1	NA	303	.3	.7
165 CH OF NAZARENE	7	1,091	1,601	1.6	3.5
167 CHS OF CHRIST	2	210	245	.2	.5
181 CONSRV CONGR	2	197	250*	.3	.5
193 EPISCOPAL	4	412	864	.9	1.9
207 E.L.C.A.	5	2,249	3,040	3.0	6.7
221 FREE METHODIST	2	23	65	.1	.1
263 INT FOURSQ GOS	2	88	112*	.1	.2
283 LUTH—MO SYNOD	2	553	739	.7	1.6
325 OLD REG BAPT	1	24	30*	-	.1
349 PENT HOLINESS	1	49	62*	.1	.1
355 PRESB CH (USA)	10	1,881	2,389*	2.4	5.2
403 SALVATION ARMY	1	54	58	.1	.1
413 S.D.A.	2	112	142*	.1	.3
419 SO BAPT CONV	4	474	602*	.6	1.3
443 UN C OF CHRIST	10	1,908	2,423*	2.4	5.3
449 UN METHODIST	27	4,623	5,871*	5.9	12.9
496 JEWISH EST[1]	1	NA	0	-	-
497 BLACK BAPT EST[2]	NA	690	876*	.9	1.9
498 INDEP.CHARIS.[3]	1	NA	400	.4	.9
499 INDEP.NON-CHAR[3]	1	NA	475	.5	1.0
ATHENS	**94**	**8,706**	**13,417***	**22.5**	**100.0**
011 A.W.M.C.	1	0	0*	-	-
019 AMER BAPT USA	2	256	305*	.5	2.3
053 ASSEMB OF GOD	1	133	247	.4	1.8
081 CATHOLIC	7	NA	2,103	3.5	15.7
081d LATIN	*7*	*NA*	*2,103*	*3.5*	*15.7*
093 CHR CH (DISC)	7	647	897	1.5	6.7
097 CHR CHS&CHS CR	11	1,341	1,600*	2.7	11.9
111 CH CR,SCIENTST	1	NR	NR	-	-
123 CH GOD (ANDER)	2	69	136	.2	1.0
127 CH GOD (CLEVE)	2	85	101*	.2	.8
145 CH GOD PROPHCY	1	36	43*	.1	.3
151 L-D SAINTS	1	NA	206	.3	1.5
165 CH OF NAZARENE	3	277	330	.6	2.5
167 CHS OF CHRIST	2	151	178	.3	1.3
193 EPISCOPAL	2	274	309	.5	2.3
207 E.L.C.A.	1	310	399	.7	3.0
221 FREE METHODIST	1	26	28	-	.2
226 FRIENDS-USA	1	38	45*	.1	.3
226c FGC	*1*	*38*	*45***	*.1*	*.3*
355 PRESB CH (USA)	5	941	1,123*	1.9	8.4
403 SALVATION ARMY	1	34	39	.1	.3
413 S.D.A.	1	73	87*	.1	.6
419 SO BAPT CONV	3	457	545*	.9	4.1
435 UNITARIAN-UNIV	1	57	87	.1	.6
449 UN METHODIST	31	2,742	3,272*	5.5	24.4
467 WESLEYAN	6	390	797	1.3	5.9
496 JEWISH EST[1]	0	NA	100	.2	.7
497 BLACK BAPT EST[2]	NA	369	440*	.7	3.3
AUGLAIZE	**64**	**11,912**	**29,971***	**67.2**	**100.0**
019 AMER BAPT USA	2	265	345*	.8	1.2
053 ASSEMB OF GOD	2	120	229	.5	.8
081 CATHOLIC	7	NA	13,500	30.3	45.0
081d LATIN	*7*	*NA*	*13,500*	*30.3*	*45.0*
089 CHR & MISS AL	1	82	209	.5	.7
097 CHR CHS&CHS CR	4	330	430*	1.0	1.4
123 CH GOD (ANDER)	1	23	45	.1	.2
146 CH GOD MTN ASM	1	13	17*	-	.1
165 CH OF NAZARENE	5	477	1,173	2.6	3.9
167 CHS OF CHRIST	3	80	124	.3	.4
207 E.L.C.A.	5	1,983	2,632	5.9	8.8
226 FRIENDS-USA	1	20	26*	.1	.1
226e FUM	*1*	*20*	*26***	*.1*	*.1*
283 LUTH—MO SYNOD	1	138	176	.4	.6
329 OPEN BIBLE STD	1	NR	NR	-	-
355 PRESB CH (USA)	1	71	92*	.2	.3
419 SO BAPT CONV	2	301	392*	.9	1.3
438 UN BRETH IN CR	2	52	56	.1	.2
443 UN C OF CHRIST	7	3,941	5,131*	11.5	17.1
449 UN METHODIST	15	3,766	4,903*	11.0	16.4
466 WAYN TR MB ASC	2	216	281*	.6	.9
467 WESLEYAN	1	34	105	.2	.4
496 JEWISH EST[1]	0	NA	105	.2	.4

NA–Not applicable   NR–Not reported   *Total adherents estimated from known number of communicant, confirmed, full members.   - Represents a percent less than 0.1.   Percentages may not total due to rounding.

[1]See Appendix E   [2]See Appendix F   [3]See Appendix G   Lines in *italic* represent a breakdown of Catholic rites or Friends affiliations. They are included in their respective denominational total.

Table 4. Churches and Church Membership by County and Denomination: 1990

County and Denomination	Number of churches	Communicant, confirmed, full members	Total adherents Number	Percent of total population	Percent of total adherents
BELMONT	**152**	**18,151**	**36,117***	**50.8**	**100.0**
019 AMER BAPT USA	1	350	427*	.6	1.2
022 EASTERN ORTH	1	106	106	.1	.3
053 ASSEMB OF GOD	3	308	431	.6	1.2
081 CATHOLIC	20	NA	12,384	17.4	34.3
081d LATIN	20	NA	12,384	17.4	34.3
089 CHR & MISS AL	1	73	140	.2	.4
093 CHR CH (DISC)	4	399	1,012	1.4	2.8
097 CHR CHS&CHS CR	11	1,890	2,308*	3.2	6.4
123 CH GOD (ANDER)	1	109	122	.2	.3
151 L-D SAINTS	1	NA	297	.4	.8
165 CH OF NAZARENE	7	372	484	.7	1.3
167 CHS OF CHRIST	18	1,129	1,508	2.1	4.2
193 EPISCOPAL	2	166	234	.3	.6
207 E.L.C.A.	4	1,095	1,635	2.3	4.5
226 FRIENDS-USA	3	622	757*	1.1	2.1
226a CONSERV	2	209	255*	.4	.7
226b EFI	1	413	502	.7	1.4
246 GREEK ORTHODOX	1	NR	NR	-	-
285 MENNONITE CH	1	50	76	.1	.2
331 ORTH CH IN AM	1	NR	NR	-	-
355 PRESB CH (USA)	23	3,600	4,396*	6.2	12.2
403 SALVATION ARMY	1	44	62	.1	.2
419 SO BAPT CONV	2	369	451*	.6	1.2
435 UNITARIAN-UNIV	1	11	13	-	-
443 UN C OF CHRIST	1	149	182*	.3	.5
449 UN METHODIST	42	6,924	8,455*	11.9	23.4
467 WESLEYAN	1	30	70	.1	.2
496 JEWISH EST[1]	1	NA	134	.2	.4
497 BLACK BAPT EST[2]	NA	355	433*	.6	1.2
BROWN	**70**	**7,323**	**16,636***	**47.6**	**100.0**
053 ASSEMB OF GOD	2	70	94	.3	.6
081 CATHOLIC	7	NA	5,620	16.1	33.8
081d LATIN	7	NA	5,620	16.1	33.8
093 CHR CH (DISC)	1	20	80	.2	.5
097 CHR CHS&CHS CR	13	2,487	3,200*	9.2	19.2
.127 CH GOD (CLEVE)	1	58	75*	.2	.5
151 L-D SAINTS	1	NA	259	.7	1.6
165 CH OF NAZARENE	4	328	738	2.1	4.4
167 CHS OF CHRIST	3	97	130	.4	.8
207 E.L.C.A.	1	394	480	1.4	2.9
355 PRESB CH (USA)	5	484	623*	1.8	3.7
419 SO BAPT CONV	8	1,521	1,957*	5.6	11.8
443 UN C OF CHRIST	4	349	449*	1.3	2.7
449 UN METHODIST	16	1,470	1,891*	5.4	11.4
467 WESLEYAN	2	45	140	.4	.8
499 INDEP.NON-CHAR[3]	2	NA	900	2.6	5.4
BUTLER	**231**	**56,489**	**118,749***	**40.7**	**100.0**
019 AMER BAPT USA	4	2,646	3,340*	1.1	2.8
053 ASSEMB OF GOD	5	1,732	3,571	1.2	3.0
081 CATHOLIC	14	NA	39,110	13.4	32.9
081d LATIN	14	NA	39,110	13.4	32.9
089 CHR & MISS AL	2	139	232	.1	.2
093 CHR CH (DISC)	4	912	1,333	.5	1.1
097 CHR CHS&CHS CR	7	841	1,061*	.4	.9
111 CH CR,SCIENTST	3	NR	NR	-	-
123 CH GOD (ANDER)	19	2,451	4,665	1.6	3.9
127 CH GOD (CLEVE)	13	4,275	5,395*	1.9	4.5
145 CH GOD PROPHCY	2	72	91*	-	.1
151 L-D SAINTS	3	NA	1,059	.4	.9
157 CH OF BRETHREN	1	37	47*	-	-
165 CH OF NAZARENE	11	2,557	4,275	1.5	3.6
167 CHS OF CHRIST	9	751	923	.3	.8
191 ENTRPR BPT ASC	1	120	151*	.1	.1
193 EPISCOPAL	4	1,078	1,635	.6	1.4
207 E.L.C.A.	9	2,698	3,697	1.3	3.1
223 FREE WILL BAPT	1	60	76*	-	.1
226 FRIENDS-USA	1	15	34	-	-
226d FGC & FUM	1	15	34	-	-
246 GREEK ORTHODOX	1	NR	NR	-	-
263 INT FOURSQ GOS	1	74	93*	-	.1
283 LUTH—MO SYNOD	3	1,006	1,418	.5	1.2
287 MENN GEN CONF	1	140	170	.1	.1
291 MISSIONARY CH	3	138	121	-	.1
325 OLD REG BAPT	2	108	136*	-	.1
339 PENT CH OF GOD	1	34	77	-	.1
353 CHR BRETHREN	1	52	80	-	.1
355 PRESB CH (USA)	15	4,711	5,946*	2.0	5.0
403 SALVATION ARMY	3	290	307	.1	.3
413 S.D.A.	2	270	341*	.1	.3
419 SO BAPT CONV	42	13,594	17,157*	5.9	14.4
435 UNITARIAN-UNIV	1	65	100	-	.1
436 UNITED BAPT	6	809	1,021*	.4	.9
443 UN C OF CHRIST	5	2,148	2,711*	.9	2.3
449 UN METHODIST	24	8,753	11,047*	3.8	9.3
467 WESLEYAN	3	350	882	.3	.7
496 JEWISH EST[1]	1	NA	900	.3	.8
497 BLACK BAPT EST[2]	NA	3,563	4,497*	1.5	3.8
499 INDEP.NON-CHAR[3]	3	NA	1,050	.4	.9
CARROLL	**47**	**5,052**	**9,727***	**36.7**	**100.0**
053 ASSEMB OF GOD	2	107	185	.7	1.9
061 BEACHY AMISH	1	31	39*	.1	.4
081 CATHOLIC	4	NA	2,290	8.6	23.5
081d LATIN	4	NA	2,290	8.6	23.5
093 CHR CH (DISC)	1	175	281	1.1	2.9
097 CHR CHS&CHS CR	2	390	494*	1.9	5.1
151 L-D SAINTS	1	NA	216	.8	2.2
165 CH OF NAZARENE	2	79	156	.6	1.6
167 CHS OF CHRIST	1	40	60	.2	.6
207 E.L.C.A.	5	1,079	1,452	5.5	14.9
263 INT FOURSQ GOS	1	70	89*	.3	.9
285 MENNONITE CH	1	36	36	.1	.4
355 PRESB CH (USA)	7	663	840*	3.2	8.6
413 S.D.A.	1	34	43*	.2	.4
449 UN METHODIST	16	2,312	2,930*	11.0	30.1
467 WESLEYAN	1	36	98	.4	1.0
496 JEWISH EST[1]	0	NA	168	.6	1.7
499 INDEP.NON-CHAR[3]	1	NA	350	1.3	3.6
CHAMPAIGN	**55**	**7,735**	**13,168***	**36.6**	**100.0**
019 AMER BAPT USA	5	1,271	1,598*	4.4	12.1
081 CATHOLIC	4	NA	2,230	6.2	16.9
081d LATIN	4	NA	2,230	6.2	16.9
097 CHR CHS&CHS CR	1	124	156*	.4	1.2
121 CH GOD (ABR)	1	10	13*	-	.1
123 CH GOD (ANDER)	3	193	293	.8	2.2
145 CH GOD PROPHCY	2	72	91*	.3	.7
151 L-D SAINTS	1	NA	611	1.7	4.6
165 CH OF NAZARENE	3	250	497	1.4	3.8
167 CHS OF CHRIST	3	150	192	.5	1.5
193 EPISCOPAL	2	209	290	.8	2.2
207 E.L.C.A.	2	598	808	2.2	6.1
221 FREE METHODIST	1	42	52	.1	.4
223 FREE WILL BAPT	3	250	314*	.9	2.4
226 FRIENDS-USA	3	123	220	.6	1.7
226b EFI	3	123	220	.6	1.7
257 HUTTERIAN BR	1	NA	100	.3	.8
285 MENNONITE CH	2	224	334	.9	2.5
291 MISSIONARY CH	1	55	132	.4	1.0
355 PRESB CH (USA)	2	655	824*	2.3	6.3
361 PRIM BAPT ASCS	1	32	40*	.1	.3
419 SO BAPT CONV	1	18	23*	.1	.2
436 UNITED BAPT	2	156	196*	.5	1.5
449 UN METHODIST	11	3,085	3,880*	10.8	29.5
497 BLACK BAPT EST[2]	NA	218	274*	.8	2.1
CLARK	**168**	**33,640**	**58,447***	**39.6**	**100.0**
019 AMER BAPT USA	6	1,224	1,530*	1.0	2.6
053 ASSEMB OF GOD	2	197	295	.2	.5
075 BRETHREN IN CR	1	59	60	-	.1
081 CATHOLIC	7	NA	13,350	9.0	22.8
081d LATIN	7	NA	13,350	9.0	22.8
093 CHR CH (DISC)	3	453	565	.4	1.0
097 CHR CHS&CHS CR	6	2,345	2,932*	2.0	5.0
111 CH CR,SCIENTST	1	NR	NR	-	-
121 CH GOD (ABR)	2	163	204*	.1	.3
123 CH GOD (ANDER)	9	1,626	2,021	1.4	3.5
127 CH GOD (CLEVE)	4	391	489*	.3	.8
157 CH OF BRETHREN	3	814	1,018*	.7	1.7
165 CH OF NAZARENE	7	1,241	2,342	1.6	4.0
167 CHS OF CHRIST	6	409	493	.3	.8
191 ENTRPR BPT ASC	1	47	59*	-	.1
193 EPISCOPAL	1	286	359	.2	.6
207 E.L.C.A.	15	5,544	7,066	4.8	12.1
223 FREE WILL BAPT	7	700	875*	.6	1.5
226 FRIENDS-USA	1	22	36	-	.1
226b EFI	1	22	36	-	.1
246 GREEK ORTHODOX	1	NR	NR	-	-
263 INT FOURSQ GOS	1	61	76*	.1	.1
265 INT PENT C CHR	2	161	228	.2	.4
283 LUTH—MO SYNOD	1	121	161	.1	.3
285 MENNONITE CH	3	281	487	.3	.8
291 MISSIONARY CH	3	203	201	.1	.3
329 OPEN BIBLE STD	1	NR	NR	-	-
339 PENT CH OF GOD	3	97	204	.1	.3
355 PRESB CH (USA)	6	1,772	2,215*	1.5	3.8
403 SALVATION ARMY	1	92	103	.1	.2
413 S.D.A.	3	430	538*	.4	.9
419 SO BAPT CONV	8	2,170	2,713*	1.8	4.6

NA–Not applicable   NR–Not reported   *Total adherents estimated from known number of communicant, confirmed, full members.   - Represents a percent less than 0.1.   Percentages may not total due to rounding.
[1]See Appendix E   [2]See Appendix F   [3]See Appendix G   Lines in *italic* represent a breakdown of Catholic rites or Friends affiliations. They are included in their respective denominational total.

298

Table 4. Churches and Church Membership by County and Denomination: 1990

County and Denomination	Number of churches	Communicant, confirmed, full members	Total adherents		
			Number	Percent of total population	Percent of total adherents
436 UNITED BAPT	1	24	30*	-	.1
438 UN BRETH IN CR	2	91	100	.1	.2
443 UN C OF CHRIST	10	1,407	1,759*	1.2	3.0
449 UN METHODIST	34	7,493	9,368*	6.3	16.0
467 WESLEYAN	2	96	315	.2	.5
469 WELS	1	85	125	.1	.2
496 JEWISH EST[1]	2	NA	1,210	.8	2.1
497 BLACK BAPT EST[2]	NA	3,535	4,420*	3.0	7.6
499 INDEP.NON-CHAR[3]	1	NA	500	.3	.9
CLERMONT	**132**	**22,278**	**59,152***	**39.4**	**100.0**
019 AMER BAPT USA	1	481	627*	.4	1.1
053 ASSEMB OF GOD	6	597	830	.6	1.4
081 CATHOLIC	13	NA	23,370	15.6	39.5
081d *LATIN*	*13*	*NA*	*23,370*	*15.6*	*39.5*
097 CHR CHS&CHS CR	12	3,998	5,211*	3.5	8.8
123 CH GOD (ANDER)	2	175	175	.1	.3
127 CH GOD (CLEVE)	5	577	752*	.5	1.3
145 CH GOD PROPHCY	1	36	47*	-	.1
146 CH GOD MTN ASM	3	322	420*	.3	.7
151 L-D SAINTS	2	NA	766	.5	1.3
165 CH OF NAZARENE	10	1,082	1,482	1.0	2.5
167 CHS OF CHRIST	5	445	705	.5	1.2
171 CH GOD-GEN CON	1	61	80*	.1	.1
193 EPISCOPAL	1	28	46	-	.1
203 EVAN FREE CH	1	320	818	.5	1.4
207 E.L.C.A.	1	276	444	.3	.8
283 LUTH—MO SYNOD	1	428	676	.5	1.1
325 OLD REG BAPT	1	96	125*	.1	.2
353 CHR BRETHREN	2	137	200	.1	.3
355 PRESB CH (USA)	7	772	1,006*	.7	1.7
403 SALVATION ARMY	1	37	41	-	.1
413 S.D.A.	1	175	228*	.2	.4
419 SO BAPT CONV	19	5,484	7,148*	4.8	12.1
443 UN C OF CHRIST	1	37	48*	-	.1
449 UN METHODIST	30	6,183	8,060*	5.4	13.6
467 WESLEYAN	3	181	315	.2	.5
496 JEWISH EST[1]	0	NA	2,376	1.6	4.0
497 BLACK BAPT EST[2]	NA	350	456*	.3	.8
499 INDEP.NON-CHAR[3]	2	NA	2,700	1.8	4.6
CLINTON	**63**	**9,172**	**14,513***	**41.0**	**100.0**
019 AMER BAPT USA	2	372	473*	1.3	3.3
053 ASSEMB OF GOD	1	128	233	.7	1.6
081 CATHOLIC	3	NA	2,250	6.4	15.5
081d *LATIN*	*3*	*NA*	*2,250*	*6.4*	*15.5*
093 CHR CH (DISC)	1	303	506	1.4	3.5
097 CHR CHS&CHS CR	7	1,865	2,373*	6.7	16.4
123 CH GOD (ANDER)	3	175	261	.7	1.8
127 CH GOD (CLEVE)	2	194	247*	.7	1.7
151 L-D SAINTS	1	NA	167	.5	1.2
165 CH OF NAZARENE	3	298	560	1.6	3.9
167 CHS OF CHRIST	2	51	66	.2	.5
193 EPISCOPAL	1	30	37	.1	.3
207 E.L.C.A.	1	250	338	1.0	2.3
226 FRIENDS-USA	10	1,139	1,445*	4.1	10.0
226d *FGC & FUM*	*1*	*54*	*64*	*.2*	*.4*
226e *FUM*	*9*	*1,085*	*1,381**	*3.9*	*9.5*
325 OLD REG BAPT	1	17	22*	.1	.2
329 OPEN BIBLE STD	1	NR	NR	-	-
355 PRESB CH (USA)	1	382	486*	1.4	3.3
361 PRIM BAPT ASCS	1	34	43*	.1	.3
413 S.D.A.	1	59	75*	.2	.5
419 SO BAPT CONV	6	748	952*	2.7	6.6
443 UN C OF CHRIST	1	155	197*	.6	1.4
449 UN METHODIST	14	2,815	3,582*	10.1	24.7
497 BLACK BAPT EST[2]	NA	157	200*	.6	1.4
COLUMBIANA	**163**	**28,543**	**49,582***	**45.8**	**100.0**
005 AME ZION	2	120	144	.1	.3
011 A.W.M.C.	1	63	79*	.1	.2
019 AMER BAPT USA	2	608	764*	.7	1.5
053 ASSEMB OF GOD	5	568	943	.9	1.9
071 BRETHREN (ASH)	1	80	101*	.1	.2
081 CATHOLIC	11	NA	12,277	11.3	24.8
081d *LATIN*	*11*	*NA*	*12,277*	*11.3*	*24.8*
093 CHR CH (DISC)	3	1,058	1,690	1.6	3.4
097 CHR CHS&CHS CR	15	3,766	4,735*	4.4	9.5
111 CH CR,SCIENTST	1	NR	NR	-	-
123 CH GOD (ANDER)	1	25	72	.1	.1
127 CH GOD (CLEVE)	2	112	141*	.1	.3
143 CG IN CR(MENN)	1	86	108*	.1	.2
145 CH GOD PROPHCY	1	36	45*	-	.1
151 L-D SAINTS	2	NA	551	.5	1.1
157 CH OF BRETHREN	2	185	233*	.2	.5
165 CH OF NAZARENE	9	1,952	2,358	2.2	4.8

County and Denomination	Number of churches	Communicant, confirmed, full members	Total adherents		
			Number	Percent of total population	Percent of total adherents
167 CHS OF CHRIST	8	563	732	.7	1.5
193 EPISCOPAL	3	394	453	.4	.9
207 E.L.C.A.	8	3,314	4,228	3.9	8.5
221 FREE METHODIST	4	243	296	.3	.6
226 FRIENDS-USA	8	1,345	1,500*	1.4	3.0
226a *CONSERV*	*3*	*258*	*324**	*.3*	*.7*
226b *EFI*	*5*	*1,087*	*1,176*	*1.1*	*2.4*
263 INT FOURSQ GOS	1	38	48*	-	.1
285 MENNONITE CH	1	93	131	.1	.3
329 OPEN BIBLE STD	1	NR	NR	-	-
355 PRESB CH (USA)	27	5,317	6,685*	6.2	13.5
356 PRESB CH AMER	1	270	310	.3	.6
397 ROMANIAN ORTH	1	NR	NR	-	-
403 SALVATION ARMY	2	97	115	.1	.2
413 S.D.A.	1	63	79*	.1	.2
419 SO BAPT CONV	3	204	256*	.2	.5
438 UN BRETH IN CR	1	72	112	.1	.2
443 UN C OF CHRIST	2	618	777*	.7	1.6
449 UN METHODIST	29	6,943	8,729*	8.1	17.6
496 JEWISH EST[1]	2	NA	200	.2	.4
497 BLACK BAPT EST[2]	NA	310	390*	.4	.8
499 INDEP.NON-CHAR[3]	1	NA	300	.3	.6
COSHOCTON	**69**	**9,884**	**14,931***	**42.1**	**100.0**
019 AMER BAPT USA	5	739	943*	2.7	6.3
053 ASSEMB OF GOD	1	79	135	.4	.9
061 BEACHY AMISH	1	25	32*	.1	.2
081 CATHOLIC	2	NA	2,008	5.7	13.4
081d *LATIN*	*2*	*NA*	*2,008*	*5.7*	*13.4*
089 CHR & MISS AL	1	18	20	.1	.1
093 CHR CH (DISC)	2	365	467	1.3	3.1
097 CHR CHS&CHS CR	1	30	38*	.1	.3
123 CH GOD (ANDER)	2	22	116	.3	.8
165 CH OF NAZARENE	4	490	684	1.9	4.6
167 CHS OF CHRIST	6	349	452	1.3	3.0
193 EPISCOPAL	1	127	128	.4	.9
207 E.L.C.A.	2	588	727	2.1	4.9
263 INT FOURSQ GOS	1	4	5*	-	-
285 MENNONITE CH	1	17	40	.1	.3
339 PENT CH OF GOD	2	40	170	.5	1.1
355 PRESB CH (USA)	5	1,044	1,332*	3.8	8.9
403 SALVATION ARMY	1	233	279	.8	1.9
413 S.D.A.	1	51	65*	.2	.4
419 SO BAPT CONV	2	300	383*	1.1	2.6
443 UN C OF CHRIST	3	474	605*	1.7	4.1
449 UN METHODIST	23	4,766	6,080*	17.2	40.7
467 WESLEYAN	2	123	222	.6	1.5
CRAWFORD	**91**	**14,790**	**24,816***	**51.8**	**100.0**
019 AMER BAPT USA	2	157	198*	.4	.8
053 ASSEMB OF GOD	2	104	178	.4	.7
081 CATHOLIC	5	NA	4,806	10.0	19.4
081d *LATIN*	*5*	*NA*	*4,806*	*10.0*	*19.4*
089 CHR & MISS AL	2	282	572	1.2	2.3
093 CHR CH (DISC)	1	137	177	.4	.7
097 CHR CHS&CHS CR	4	540	680*	1.4	2.7
111 CH CR,SCIENTST	2	NR	NR	-	-
127 CH GOD (CLEVE)	2	128	161*	.3	.6
145 CH GOD PROPHCY	2	72	91*	.2	.4
165 CH OF NAZARENE	3	707	1,146	2.4	4.6
167 CHS OF CHRIST	2	154	200	.4	.8
179 CONSRV BAPT	1	NR	NR	-	-
193 EPISCOPAL	2	55	70	.1	.3
207 E.L.C.A.	16	4,980	6,697	14.0	27.0
221 FREE METHODIST	1	79	105	.2	.4
263 INT FOURSQ GOS	1	40	50*	.1	.2
265 INT PENT C CHR	1	26	40	.1	.2
329 OPEN BIBLE STD	2	NR	NR	-	-
339 PENT CH OF GOD	1	34	76	.2	.3
355 PRESB CH (USA)	3	549	692*	1.4	2.8
403 SALVATION ARMY	1	74	82	.2	.3
413 S.D.A.	2	186	234*	.5	.9
419 SO BAPT CONV	2	564	710*	1.5	2.9
443 UN C OF CHRIST	6	1,864	2,348*	4.9	9.5
449 UN METHODIST	22	4,043	5,093*	10.6	20.5
467 WESLEYAN	2	15	85	.2	.3
499 INDEP.NON-CHAR[3]	1	NA	325	.7	1.3
CUYAHOGA	**757**	**265,618**	**942,069***	**66.7**	**100.0**
005 AME ZION	7	13,730	16,476	1.2	1.7
007 ALBAN ORTH ARC	1	NR	NR	-	-
019 AMER BAPT USA	41	22,824	28,176*	2.0	3.0
022 EASTERN ORTH	1	104	104	-	-
039 AP CHR CH(NAZ)	3	115	142*	-	-
049 ARMEN AP CH AM	1	150	350	-	-
053 ASSEMB OF GOD	17	2,402	10,850	.8	1.2

NA–Not applicable   NR–Not reported   *Total adherents estimated from known number of communicant, confirmed, full members.   - Represents a percent less than 0.1.   Percentages may not total due to rounding.
[1]See Appendix E   [2]See Appendix F   [3]See Appendix G   Lines in *italic* represent a breakdown of Catholic rites or Friends affiliations. They are included in their respective denominational total.

299

Table 4. Churches and Church Membership by County and Denomination: 1990

County and Denomination	Number of churches	Communicant, confirmed, full members	Total adherents Number	Percent of total population	Percent of total adherents
057 BAPT GEN CONF	3	183	226*	-	-
071 BRETHREN (ASH)	1	1,105	1,364*	.1	.1
081 CATHOLIC	158	NA	534,785	37.9	56.8
081b *BYZAN RUTH*	11	NA	7,876	.6	.8
081d *LATIN*	139	NA	521,313	36.9	55.3
081e *MARONITE*	1	NA	1,266	.1	.1
081f *MELKITE-GK*	1	NA	950	.1	.1
081g *ROMANIAN*	1	NA	322	-	-
081h *UKRAINIAN*	5	NA	3,058	.2	.3
089 CHR & MISS AL	5	431	1,280	.1	.1
093 CHR CH (DISC)	22	4,268	7,438	.5	.8
097 CHR CHS&CHS CR	5	830	1,025*	.1	.1
105 CHRISTIAN REF	3	394	597	-	.1
111 CH CR,SCIENTST	12	NR	NR	-	-
121 CH GOD (ABR)	2	50	62*	-	-
123 CH GOD (ANDER)	8	771	1,033	.1	.1
127 CH GOD (CLEVE)	7	1,924	2,375*	.2	.3
145 CH GOD PROPHCY	6	209	258*	-	-
146 CH GOD MTN ASM	1	97	120*	-	-
151 L-D SAINTS	6	NA	1,947	.1	.2
157 CH OF BRETHREN	1	220	272*	-	-
163 CH OF LUTH BR	1	22	54	-	-
165 CH OF NAZARENE	14	1,272	3,525	.2	.4
167 CHS OF CHRIST	12	1,152	1,907	.1	.2
175 CONGR CHR CHS	2	291	359*	-	-
191 ENTRPR BPT ASC	1	53	65*	-	-
193 EPISCOPAL	26	8,668	11,993	.8	1.3
195 ESTONIAN ELC	1	102	126*	-	-
207 E.L.C.A.	43	16,829	22,432	1.6	2.4
221 FREE METHODIST	2	92	129	-	-
223 FREE WILL BAPT	9	450	556*	-	.1
226 FRIENDS-USA	5	335	575*	-	.1
226b *EFI*	4	246	465	-	-
226c *FGC*	1	89	110*	-	-
246 GREEK ORTHODOX	4	NR	NR	-	-
259 IFCA	1	NR	NR	-	-
263 INT FOURSQ GOS	7	757	934*	.1	.1
274 LAT EVAN LUTH	1	672	735	.1	.1
283 LUTH—MO SYNOD	43	18,334	24,098	1.7	2.6
285 MENNONITE CH	4	469	617	-	.1
291 MISSIONARY CH	3	97	108	-	-
313 N AM BAPT CONF	3	1,188	1,467*	.1	.2
331 ORTH CH IN AM	6	NR	NR	-	-
353 CHR BRETHREN	5	240	420	-	-
355 PRESB CH (USA)	35	14,670	18,110*	1.3	1.9
356 PRESB CH AMER	1	37	57	-	-
363 PRIMITIVE METH	1	21	25	-	-
371 REF CH IN AM	5	534	932	.1	.1
375 REF EPISCOPAL	1	33	33	-	-
397 ROMANIAN ORTH	1	NR	NR	-	-
403 SALVATION ARMY	6	628	735	.1	.1
413 S.D.A.	12	3,590	4,432*	.3	.5
419 SO BAPT CONV	24	4,403	5,435*	.4	.6
431 UKRANIAN AMER	2	NR	NR	-	-
435 UNITARIAN-UNIV	5	1,338	1,853	.1	.2
443 UN C OF CHRIST	43	17,130	21,146*	1.5	2.2
449 UN METHODIST	59	27,224	33,607*	2.4	3.6
467 WESLEYAN	3	112	246	-	-
469 WELS	1	62	86	-	-
496 JEWISH EST[1]	50	NA	50,050	3.5	5.3
497 BLACK BAPT EST[2]	NA	95,006	117,282*	8.3	12.4
498 INDEP.CHARIS.[3]	2	NA	6,660	.5	.7
499 INDEP.NON-CHAR[3]	2	NA	2,400	.2	.3
DARKE	**91**	**13,221**	**25,095***	**46.8**	**100.0**
053 ASSEMB OF GOD	1	144	228	.4	.9
081 CATHOLIC	5	NA	7,540	14.1	30.0
081d *LATIN*	5	NA	7,540	14.1	30.0
089 CHR & MISS AL	1	98	148	.3	.6
097 CHR CHS&CHS CR	3	540	688*	1.3	2.7
123 CH GOD (ANDER)	2	650	650	1.2	2.6
127 CH GOD (CLEVE)	1	89	113*	.2	.5
146 CH GOD MTN ASM	1	41	52*	.1	.2
151 L-D SAINTS	1	NA	181	.3	.7
157 CH OF BRETHREN	9	1,556	1,983*	3.7	7.9
165 CH OF NAZARENE	2	184	408	.8	1.6
167 CHS OF CHRIST	1	23	30	.1	.1
193 EPISCOPAL	1	172	231	.4	.9
207 E.L.C.A.	8	2,096	2,809	5.2	11.2
291 MISSIONARY CH	2	206	262	.5	1.0
296 MIDW CONGR FEL	6	342	436*	.8	1.7
324 OLD ORD RVR BR	1	5	8	-	-
329 OPEN BIBLE STD	1	NR	NR	-	-
355 PRESB CH (USA)	3	560	714*	1.3	2.8
419 SO BAPT CONV	6	799	1,018*	1.9	4.1
436 UNITED BAPT	1	62	79*	.1	.3
443 UN C OF CHRIST	7	1,434	1,827*	3.4	7.3
449 UN METHODIST	23	4,020	5,122*	9.6	20.4
467 WESLEYAN	5	200	568	1.1	2.3
DEFIANCE	**67**	**13,341**	**23,937***	**60.8**	**100.0**
019 AMER BAPT USA	1	415	533*	1.4	2.2
040 AP CHR CH-AMER	1	62	112	.3	.5
053 ASSEMB OF GOD	3	181	341	.9	1.4
081 CATHOLIC	8	NA	6,000	15.2	25.1
081d *LATIN*	8	NA	6,000	15.2	25.1
097 CHR CHS&CHS CR	4	1,024	1,316*	3.3	5.5
123 CH GOD (ANDER)	2	500	500	1.3	2.1
127 CH GOD (CLEVE)	2	73	94*	.2	.4
157 CH OF BRETHREN	2	175	225*	.6	.9
165 CH OF NAZARENE	2	202	450	1.1	1.9
167 CHS OF CHRIST	1	80	104	.3	.4
171 CH GOD-GEN CON	2	150	193*	.5	.8
193 EPISCOPAL	1	90	136	.3	.6
207 E.L.C.A.	6	2,360	3,086	7.8	12.9
226 FRIENDS-USA	0	6	8*	-	-
226c *FGC*	0	6	8*	-	-
283 LUTH—MO SYNOD	4	2,545	3,642	9.3	15.2
285 MENNONITE CH	2	161	161	.4	.7
323 OLD ORD AMISH	1	NA	150	.4	.6
329 OPEN BIBLE STD	1	NR	NR	-	-
339 PENT CH OF GOD	2	54	130	.3	.5
355 PRESB CH (USA)	2	535	688*	1.7	2.9
361 PRIM BAPT ASCS	1	8	10*	-	-
413 S.D.A.	3	122	157*	.4	.7
419 SO BAPT CONV	2	484	622*	1.6	2.6
438 UN BRETH IN CR	1	31	31	.1	.1
443 UN C OF CHRIST	1	384	494*	1.3	2.1
449 UN METHODIST	12	3,699	4,754*	12.1	19.9
DELAWARE	**70**	**10,742**	**18,129***	**27.1**	**100.0**
019 AMER BAPT USA	4	705	897*	1.3	4.9
053 ASSEMB OF GOD	1	40	33	-	.2
081 CATHOLIC	1	NA	2,775	4.1	15.3
081d *LATIN*	1	NA	2,775	4.1	15.3
093 CHR CH (DISC)	1	219	240	.4	1.3
097 CHR CHS&CHS CR	5	616	784*	1.2	4.3
111 CH CR,SCIENTST	1	NR	NR	-	-
123 CH GOD (ANDER)	1	45	49	.1	.3
127 CH GOD (CLEVE)	1	65	83*	.1	.5
151 L-D SAINTS	1	NA	366	.5	2.0
157 CH OF BRETHREN	1	52	66*	.1	.4
165 CH OF NAZARENE	2	281	237	.4	1.3
167 CHS OF CHRIST	1	68	87	.1	.5
193 EPISCOPAL	1	203	364	.5	2.0
207 E.L.C.A.	2	719	977	1.5	5.4
223 FREE WILL BAPT	4	350	445*	.7	2.5
226 FRIENDS-USA	3	86	158*	.2	.9
226b *EFI*	2	78	148	.2	.8
226c *FGC*	1	8	10*	-	.1
283 LUTH—MO SYNOD	2	194	264	.4	1.5
285 MENNONITE CH	1	13	26	-	.1
355 PRESB CH (USA)	7	1,777	2,261*	3.4	12.5
361 PRIM BAPT ASCS	1	10	13*	-	.1
403 SALVATION ARMY	1	25	27	-	.1
413 S.D.A.	2	115	146*	.2	.8
419 SO BAPT CONV	1	150	191*	.3	1.1
435 UNITARIAN-UNIV	1	15	17	-	.1
443 UN C OF CHRIST	2	487	620*	.9	3.4
449 UN METHODIST	17	4,027	5,125*	7.7	28.3
467 WESLEYAN	4	94	227	.3	1.3
496 JEWISH EST[1]	0	NA	760	1.1	4.2
497 BLACK BAPT EST[2]	NA	386	491*	.7	2.7
498 INDEP.CHARIS.[3]	1	NA	400	.6	2.2
ERIE	**76**	**17,138**	**40,841***	**53.2**	**100.0**
005 AME ZION	1	85	102	.1	.2
019 AMER BAPT USA	1	247	310*	.4	.8
053 ASSEMB OF GOD	3	692	1,012	1.3	2.5
081 CATHOLIC	8	NA	17,481	22.8	42.8
081d *LATIN*	8	NA	17,481	22.8	42.8
089 CHR & MISS AL	2	48	116	.2	.3
097 CHR CHS&CHS CR	1	280	352*	.5	.9
127 CH GOD (CLEVE)	3	223	280*	.4	.7
145 CH GOD PROPHCY	2	72	90*	.1	.2
146 CH GOD MTN ASM	1	34	43*	.1	.1
165 CH OF NAZARENE	2	262	513	.7	1.3
167 CHS OF CHRIST	3	255	320	.4	.8
193 EPISCOPAL	3	717	1,223	1.6	3.0
207 E.L.C.A.	8	4,272	5,927	7.7	14.5
223 FREE WILL BAPT	1	50	63*	.1	.2
226 FRIENDS-USA	1	38	75	.1	.2
226b *EFI*	1	38	75	.1	.2

NA–Not applicable   NR–Not reported   *Total adherents estimated from known number of communicant, confirmed, full members.   - Represents a percent less than 0.1.   Percentages may not total due to rounding.
[1]See Appendix E   [2]See Appendix F   [3]See Appendix G   Lines in *italic* represent a breakdown of Catholic rites or Friends affiliations. They are included in their respective denominational total.

Table 4. Churches and Church Membership by County and Denomination: 1990

County and Denomination	Number of churches	Communicant, confirmed, full members	Total adherents		
			Number	Percent of total population	Percent of total adherents
263 INT FOURSQ GOS	1	184	231*	.3	.6
283 LUTH—MO SYNOD	1	114	167	.2	.4
355 PRESB CH (USA)	3	775	974*	1.3	2.4
403 SALVATION ARMY	1	20	20	-	-
413 S.D.A.	1	40	50*	.1	.1
419 SO BAPT CONV	4	984	1,237*	1.6	3.0
435 UNITARIAN-UNIV	1	35	45	.1	.1
436 UNITED BAPT	1	9	11*	-	-
443 UN C OF CHRIST	10	3,899	4,900*	6.4	12.0
449 UN METHODIST	10	2,351	2,954*	3.8	7.2
466 WAYN TR MB ASC	1	65	82*	.1	.2
496 JEWISH EST[1]	1	NA	130	.2	.3
497 BLACK BAPT EST[2]	NA	1,387	1,743*	2.3	4.3
499 INDEP.NON-CHAR[3]	1	NA	390	.5	1.0
FAIRFIELD	**121**	**22,154**	**36,667***	**35.4**	**100.0**
019 AMER BAPT USA	1	37	47*	-	.1
053 ASSEMB OF GOD	2	87	150	.1	.4
081 CATHOLIC	5	NA	6,822	6.6	18.6
081d LATIN	5	NA	6,822	6.6	18.6
097 CHR CHS&CHS CR	5	1,392	1,761*	1.7	4.8
111 CH CR,SCIENTST	1	NR	NR	-	-
123 CH GOD (ANDER)	1	0	150	.1	.4
127 CH GOD (CLEVE)	3	312	395*	.4	1.1
145 CH GOD PROPHCY	1	36	46*	-	.1
151 L-D SAINTS	1	NA	389	.4	1.1
165 CH OF NAZARENE	6	690	735	.7	2.0
167 CHS OF CHRIST	4	285	410	.4	1.1
179 CONSRV BAPT	1	NR	NR	-	-
193 EPISCOPAL	2	264	364	.4	1.0
207 E.L.C.A.	17	3,578	4,750	4.6	13.0
221 FREE METHODIST	1	25	50	-	.1
223 FREE WILL BAPT	2	175	221*	.2	.6
283 LUTH—MO SYNOD	3	888	1,206*	1.2	3.3
323 OLD ORD AMISH	1	NA	50	-	.1
355 PRESB CH (USA)	6	1,277	1,615*	1.6	4.4
361 PRIM BAPT ASCS	1	9	11*	-	-
403 SALVATION ARMY	1	100	108	.1	.3
413 S.D.A.	1	75	95*	.1	.3
419 SO BAPT CONV	4	1,160	1,467*	1.4	4.0
435 UNITARIAN-UNIV	1	23	23	-	.1
438 UN BRETH IN CR	3	908	908	.9	2.5
443 UN C OF CHRIST	7	1,128	1,427*	1.4	3.9
449 UN METHODIST	39	9,328	11,798*	11.4	32.2
467 WESLEYAN	1	64	57	.1	.2
496 JEWISH EST[1]	0	NA	1,216	1.2	3.3
497 BLACK BAPT EST[2]	NA	313	396*	.4	1.1
FAYETTE	**35**	**4,769**	**7,021***	**25.6**	**100.0**
019 AMER BAPT USA	2	484	609*	2.2	8.7
053 ASSEMB OF GOD	1	159	180	.7	2.6
081 CATHOLIC	1	NA	725	2.6	10.3
081d LATIN	1	NA	725	2.6	10.3
097 CHR CHS&CHS CR	2	350	440*	1.6	6.3
111 CH CR,SCIENTST	1	NR	NR	-	-
123 CH GOD (ANDER)	1	40	60	.2	.9
127 CH GOD (CLEVE)	1	37	47*	.2	.7
165 CH OF NAZARENE	1	160	356	1.3	5.1
167 CHS OF CHRIST	1	75	95	.3	1.4
193 EPISCOPAL	1	63	120	.4	1.7
207 E.L.C.A.	1	221	279	1.0	4.0
265 INT PENT C CHR	1	6	20	.1	.3
355 PRESB CH (USA)	3	715	900*	3.3	12.8
361 PRIM BAPT ASCS	2	27	34*	.1	.5
413 S.D.A.	1	19	24*	.1	.3
419 SO BAPT CONV	1	53	67*	.2	1.0
449 UN METHODIST	12	2,178	2,741*	10.0	39.0
467 WESLEYAN	2	36	140	.5	2.0
497 BLACK BAPT EST[2]	NA	146	184*	.7	2.6
FRANKLIN	**598**	**202,783**	**402,447***	**41.9**	**100.0**
001 ADVENT CHR CH	1	22	27*	-	-
005 AME ZION	3	2,076	2,638	.3	.7
011 A.W.M.C.	1	0	0*	-	-
019 AMER BAPT USA	25	10,312	12,851*	1.3	3.2
039 AP CHR CH(NAZ)	1	33	41*	-	-
053 ASSEMB OF GOD	12	1,688	3,452	.4	.9
057 BAPT GEN CONF	2	169	211*	-	.1
071 BRETHREN (ASH)	2	99	123*	-	-
081 CATHOLIC	54	NA	114,514	11.9	28.5
081b BYZAN RUTH	1	NA	249	-	.1
081d LATIN	52	NA	114,013	11.9	28.3
081f MELKITE-GK	1	NA	252	-	.1
089 CHR & MISS AL	6	636	1,240	.1	.3
093 CHR CH (DISC)	10	1,890	3,068	.3	.8
097 CHR CHS&CHS CR	30	9,977	12,434*	1.3	3.1

County and Denomination	Number of churches	Communicant, confirmed, full members	Total adherents		
			Number	Percent of total population	Percent of total adherents
105 CHRISTIAN REF	1	100	158	-	-
111 CH CR,SCIENTST	4	NR	NR	-	-
121 CH GOD (ABR)	1	16	20*	-	-
123 CH GOD (ANDER)	9	1,693	1,875	.2	.5
127 CH GOD (CLEVE)	10	2,432	3,031*	.3	.8
145 CH GOD PROPHCY	4	143	178*	-	-
146 CH GOD MTN ASM	2	71	88*	-	-
151 L-D SAINTS	10	NA	3,721	.4	.9
165 CH OF NAZARENE	25	4,154	6,131	.6	1.5
167 CHS OF CHRIST	23	2,775	3,645	.4	.9
171 CH GOD-GEN CON	2	54	67*	-	-
175 CONGR CHR CHS	2	310	386*	-	.1
181 CONSRV CONGR	1	35	44*	-	-
191 ENTRPR BPT ASC	5	360	449*	-	.1
193 EPISCOPAL	12	3,989	6,783	.7	1.7
199 EVAN CONGR CH	1	43	158	-	-
203 EVAN FREE CH	1	51	120	-	-
207 E.L.C.A.	46	20,490	27,887	2.9	6.9
221 FREE METHODIST	2	143	178	-	-
223 FREE WILL BAPT	20	2,500	3,116*	.3	.8
226 FRIENDS-USA	5	472	523*	.1	.1
226b EFI	4	362	386	-	.1
226c FGC	1	110	137*	-	-
246 GREEK ORTHODOX	1	NR	NR	-	-
259 IFCA	1	NR	NR	-	-
263 INT FOURSQ GOS	1	50	62*	-	-
265 INT PENT C CHR	2	97	163	-	-
274 LAT EVAN LUTH	1	95	98	-	-
283 LUTH—MO SYNOD	8	2,028	2,674*	.3	.7
285 MENNONITE CH	2	135	192	-	-
287 MENN GEN CONF	1	52	70	-	-
293 MORAV CH-NORTH	1	125	176	-	-
325 OLD REG BAPT	2	60	75*	-	-
331 ORTH CH IN AM	1	NR	NR	-	-
355 PRESB CH (USA)	34	16,341	20,365*	2.1	5.1
356 PRESB CH AMER	1	18	25	-	-
361 PRIM BAPT ASCS	1	84	105*	-	-
371 REF CH IN AM	2	377	781	.1	.2
403 SALVATION ARMY	4	370	404	-	.1
413 S.D.A.	10	2,891	3,603*	.4	.9
415 S-D BAPTIST GC	1	26	32*	-	-
419 SO BAPT CONV	42	18,783	23,408*	2.4	5.8
435 UNITARIAN-UNIV	2	612	832	.1	.2
436 UNITED BAPT	3	197	246*	-	.1
438 UN BRETH IN CR	5	1,277	1,277	.1	.3
443 UN C OF CHRIST	12	8,369	10,430*	1.1	2.6
449 UN METHODIST	91	41,031	51,135*	5.3	12.7
467 WESLEYAN	5	514	998	.1	.2
469 WELS	5	1,052	1,474	.2	.4
496 JEWISH EST[1]	11	NA	10,488	1.1	2.6
497 BLACK BAPT EST[2]	NA	41,466	51,677*	5.4	12.8
498 INDEP.CHARIS.[3]	6	NA	7,675	.8	1.9
499 INDEP.NON-CHAR[3]	9	NA	4,825	.5	1.2
FULTON	**65**	**13,261**	**23,949***	**62.2**	**100.0**
053 ASSEMB OF GOD	2	152	267	.7	1.1
081 CATHOLIC	7	NA	5,487	14.3	22.9
081d LATIN	6	NA	5,165	13.4	21.6
081g ROMANIAN	1	NA	322	.8	1.3
089 CHR & MISS AL	1	94	114	.3	.5
093 CHR CH (DISC)	5	994	1,669	4.3	7.0
097 CHR CHS&CHS CR	4	523	677*	1.8	2.8
123 CH GOD (ANDER)	1	175	209	.5	.9
157 CH OF BRETHREN	1	53	69*	.2	.3
165 CH OF NAZARENE	6	433	896	2.3	3.7
207 E.L.C.A.	5	1,810	2,379	6.2	9.9
213 EVAN MENN INC	2	1,112	1,439*	3.7	6.0
283 LUTH—MO SYNOD	3	1,067	1,443	3.7	6.0
285 MENNONITE CH	7	1,903	2,470	6.4	10.3
291 MISSIONARY CH	2	236	289	.8	1.2
419 SO BAPT CONV	2	255	330*	.9	1.4
435 UNITARIAN-UNIV	1	17	37	.1	.2
443 UN C OF CHRIST	3	739	956*	2.5	4.0
449 UN METHODIST	12	3,660	4,736*	12.3	19.8
466 WAYN TR MB ASC	1	38	49*	.1	.2
496 JEWISH EST[1]	0	NA	433	1.1	1.8
GALLIA	**53**	**5,452**	**8,276***	**26.7**	**100.0**
019 AMER BAPT USA	5	1,006	1,271*	4.1	15.4
053 ASSEMB OF GOD	1	27	47	.2	.6
081 CATHOLIC	1	NA	589	1.9	7.1
081d LATIN	1	NA	589	1.9	7.1
097 CHR CHS&CHS CR	2	400	505*	1.6	6.1
123 CH GOD (ANDER)	2	15	156	.5	1.9
127 CH GOD (CLEVE)	2	107	135*	.4	1.6
145 CH GOD PROPHCY	1	36	45*	.1	.5
151 L-D SAINTS	1	NA	227	.7	2.7

NA–Not applicable   NR–Not reported   *Total adherents estimated from known number of communicant, confirmed, full members.   - Represents a percent less than 0.1.   Percentages may not total due to rounding.
[1]See Appendix E   [2]See Appendix F   [3]See Appendix G   Lines in *italic* represent a breakdown of Catholic rites or Friends affiliations. They are included in their respective denominational total.

OHIO

Table 4. Churches and Church Membership by County and Denomination: 1990

County and Denomination	Number of churches	Communicant, confirmed, full members	Total adherents Number	Percent of total population	Percent of total adherents
165 CH OF NAZARENE	1	317	633	2.0	7.6
167 CHS OF CHRIST	1	150	160	.5	1.9
175 CONGR CHR CHS	1	28	35*	.1	.4
191 ENTRPR BPT ASC	2	83	105*	.3	1.3
193 EPISCOPAL	1	206	285	.9	3.4
207 E.L.C.A.	1	83	116	.4	1.4
223 FREE WILL BAPT	3	175	221*	.7	2.7
265 INT PENT C CHR	1	10	15	-	.2
285 MENNONITE CH	2	92	134	.4	1.6
325 OLD REG BAPT	1	20	25*	.1	.3
355 PRESB CH (USA)	1	268	339*	1.1	4.1
419 SO BAPT CONV	2	393	496*	1.6	6.0
436 UNITED BAPT	1	26	33*	.1	.4
449 UN METHODIST	18	1,768	2,233*	7.2	27.0
467 WESLEYAN	2	51	230	.7	2.8
497 BLACK BAPT EST[2]	NA	191	241*	.8	2.9
GEAUGA	**106**	**8,916**	**40,705***	**50.2**	**100.0**
011 A.W.M.C.	1	13	17*	-	-
019 AMER BAPT USA	1	370	477*	.6	1.2
053 ASSEMB OF GOD	3	383	585	.7	1.4
061 BEACHY AMISH	1	34	44*	.1	.1
081 CATHOLIC	8	NA	17,477	21.5	42.9
081b BYZAN RUTH	*1*	*NA*	*50*	*.1*	*.1*
081d LATIN	*7*	*NA*	*17,427*	*21.5*	*42.8*
089 CHR & MISS AL	1	23	63	.1	.2
093 CHR CH (DISC)	2	356	573	.7	1.4
097 CHR CHS&CHS CR	2	340	438*	.5	1.1
111 CH CR,SCIENTST	1	NR	NR	-	-
127 CH GOD (CLEVE)	1	21	27*		.1
151 L-D SAINTS	4	NA	1,194	1.5	2.9
167 CHS OF CHRIST	1	16	20	-	-
181 CONSRV CONGR	1	76	98*	.1	.2
193 EPISCOPAL	1	138	224	.3	.6
207 E.L.C.A.	2	464	655	.8	1.6
283 LUTH—MO SYNOD	3	604	739	.9	1.8
285 MENNONITE CH	3	249	459	.6	1.1
323 OLD ORD AMISH	50	NA	7,500	9.2	18.4
355 PRESB CH (USA)	2	791	1,020*	1.3	2.5
413 S.D.A.	1	199	257*	.3	.6
419 SO BAPT CONV	2	391	504*	.6	1.2
443 UN C OF CHRIST	9	2,543	3,278*	4.0	8.1
449 UN METHODIST	6	1,619	2,087*	2.6	5.1
496 JEWISH EST[1]	0	NA	2,600	3.2	6.4
497 BLACK BAPT EST[2]	NA	286	369*	.5	.9
GREENE	**126**	**28,476**	**53,840***	**39.4**	**100.0**
019 AMER BAPT USA	2	146	182*	.1	.3
053 ASSEMB OF GOD	2	192	265	.2	.5
081 CATHOLIC	5	NA	13,360	9.8	24.8
081d LATIN	*5*	*NA*	*13,360*	*9.8*	*24.8*
089 CHR & MISS AL	1	374	996	.7	1.8
093 CHR CH (DISC)	1	90	189	.1	.4
097 CHR CHS&CHS CR	8	2,560	3,195*	2.3	5.9
111 CH CR,SCIENTST	1	NR	NR	-	-
123 CH GOD (ANDER)	5	513	598	.4	1.1
127 CH GOD (CLEVE)	3	518	646*	.5	1.2
151 L-D SAINTS	3	NA	897	.7	1.7
157 CH OF BRETHREN	1	153	191*	.1	.4
165 CH OF NAZARENE	7	1,511	3,001	2.2	5.6
167 CHS OF CHRIST	6	635	811	.6	1.5
179 CONSRV BAPT	1	NR	NR	-	-
191 ENTRPR BPT ASC	2	138	172*	.1	.3
193 EPISCOPAL	2	282	407	.3	.8
207 E.L.C.A.	5	1,993	2,654	1.9	4.9
221 FREE METHODIST	1	19	38	-	.1
223 FREE WILL BAPT	3	250	312*	.2	.6
226 FRIENDS-USA	5	439	548*	.4	1.0
226c FGC	*1*	*93*	*116*de*	*.1*	*.2*
226e FUM	*4*	*346*	*432*de*	*.3*	*.8*
265 INT PENT C CHR	1	53	109	.1	.2
283 LUTH—MO SYNOD	1	313	404	.3	.8
291 MISSIONARY CH	4	318	412	.3	.8
313 N AM BAPT CONF	1	84	105*	.1	.2
325 OLD REG BAPT	1	63	79*	.1	.1
329 OPEN BIBLE STD	2	NR	NR	-	-
355 PRESB CH (USA)	10	3,499	4,366*	3.2	8.1
361 PRIM BAPT ASCS	2	302	377*	.3	.7
403 SALVATION ARMY	1	59	67	-	.1
413 S.D.A.	2	196	245*	.2	.5
419 SO BAPT CONV	11	5,410	6,751*	4.9	12.5
435 UNITARIAN-UNIV	1	105	120	.1	.2
436 UNITED BAPT	1	72	90*	.1	.2
443 UN C OF CHRIST	5	2,143	2,674*	2.0	5.0
449 UN METHODIST	17	3,430	4,280*	3.1	7.9
467 WESLEYAN	1	9	56	-	.1
496 JEWISH EST[1]	0	NA	840	.6	1.6
497 BLACK BAPT EST[2]	NA	2,607	3,253*	2.4	6.0
499 INDEP.NON-CHAR[3]	1	NA	1,150	.8	2.1
GUERNSEY	**89**	**8,953**	**15,723***	**40.3**	**100.0**
019 AMER BAPT USA	6	679	858*	2.2	5.5
053 ASSEMB OF GOD	1	231	600	1.5	3.8
061 BEACHY AMISH	1	34	43*	.1	.3
081 CATHOLIC	4	NA	3,056	7.8	19.4
081b BYZAN RUTH	*1*	*NA*	*644*	*1.7*	*4.1*
081d LATIN	*3*	*NA*	*2,412*	*6.2*	*15.3*
089 CHR & MISS AL	1	23	48	.1	.3
093 CHR CH (DISC)	2	207	315	.8	2.0
097 CHR CHS&CHS CR	1	60	76*	.2	.5
123 CH GOD (ANDER)	2	44	57	.1	.4
127 CH GOD (CLEVE)	1	35	44*	.1	.3
145 CH GOD PROPHCY	1	36	46*	.1	.3
151 L-D SAINTS	1	NA	239	.6	1.5
165 CH OF NAZARENE	2	199	246	.6	1.6
167 CHS OF CHRIST	7	597	938	2.4	6.0
193 EPISCOPAL	1	71	93	.2	.6
207 E.L.C.A.	3	528	648	1.7	4.1
221 FREE METHODIST	1	36	39	.1	.2
263 INT FOURSQ GOS	1	117	148*	.4	.9
283 LUTH—MO SYNOD	1	102	134	.3	.9
285 MENNONITE CH	1	25	28	.1	.2
323 OLD ORD AMISH	1	NA	150	.4	1.0
331 ORTH CH IN AM	1	NR	NR	-	-
339 PENT CH OF GOD	1	37	300	.8	1.9
355 PRESB CH (USA)	10	1,231	1,556*	4.0	9.9
403 SALVATION ARMY	3	292	308	.8	2.0
419 SO BAPT CONV	1	452	571*	1.5	3.6
449 UN METHODIST	32	3,722	4,705*	12.1	29.9
467 WESLEYAN	2	60	306	.8	1.9
497 BLACK BAPT EST[2]	NA	135	171*	.4	1.1
HAMILTON	**599**	**176,585**	**521,382***	**60.2**	**100.0**
005 AME ZION	11	5,570	6,684	.8	1.3
019 AMER BAPT USA	22	8,334	10,529*	1.2	2.0
053 ASSEMB OF GOD	6	1,312	2,312	.3	.4
057 BAPT GEN CONF	2	637	805*	.1	.2
075 BRETHREN IN CR	1	40	45	-	-
081 CATHOLIC	96	NA	267,806	30.9	51.4
081d LATIN	*95*	*NA*	*266,510*	*30.8*	*51.1*
081e MARONITE	*1*	*NA*	*1,296*	*.2*	*.2*
089 CHR & MISS AL	4	249	448	.1	.1
093 CHR CH (DISC)	14	1,881	3,028	.3	.6
097 CHR CHS&CHS CR	33	12,271	15,503*	1.8	3.0
105 CHRISTIAN REF	1	78	125	-	-
111 CH CR,SCIENTST	6	NR	NR	-	-
123 CH GOD (ANDER)	13	1,128	1,370	.2	.3
127 CH GOD (CLEVE)	16	2,154	2,721*	.3	.5
145 CH GOD PROPHCY	1	36	45*	-	-
146 CH GOD MTN ASM	8	409	517*	.1	.1
151 L-D SAINTS	4	NA	1,851	.2	.4
165 CH OF NAZARENE	20	2,514	6,018	.7	1.2
167 CHS OF CHRIST	21	2,431	3,327	.4	.6
176 CCC, NOT NAT'L	1	58	73*	-	-
179 CONSRV BAPT	2	NR	NR	-	-
193 EPISCOPAL	23	6,288	8,854	1.0	1.7
203 EVAN FREE CH	3	132	255	-	-
207 E.L.C.A.	15	3,966	5,570	.6	1.1
221 FREE METHODIST	1	9	25	-	-
226 FRIENDS-USA	3	273	341*	-	.1
226d FGC & FUM	*2*	*124*	*153*	*-*	*-*
226e FUM	*1*	*149*	*188*de*	*-*	*-*
246 GREEK ORTHODOX	1	NR	NR	-	-
263 INT FOURSQ GOS	1	60	76*	-	-
274 LAT EVAN LUTH	1	43	51	-	-
283 LUTH—MO SYNOD	12	3,797	5,176	.6	1.0
285 MENNONITE CH	3	115	175	-	-
287 MENN GEN CONF	1	30	39	-	-
329 OPEN BIBLE STD	2	NR	NR	-	-
331 ORTH CH IN AM	1	NR	NR	-	-
353 CHR BRETHREN	2	115	210	-	-
355 PRESB CH (USA)	50	20,181	25,496*	2.9	4.9
356 PRESB CH AMER	2	220	360	-	.1
375 REF EPISCOPAL	1	30	30	-	-
413 S.D.A.	6	1,377	1,740*	.2	.3
419 SO BAPT CONV	40	13,610	17,195*	2.0	3.3
435 UNITARIAN-UNIV	4	739	995	.1	.2
436 UNITED BAPT	1	203	256*	-	-
443 UN C OF CHRIST	28	7,951	10,045*	1.2	1.9
449 UN METHODIST	72	28,778	36,358*	4.2	7.0
467 WESLEYAN	7	254	547	.1	.1
469 WELS	1	167	217	-	-
496 JEWISH EST[1]	24	NA	13,709	1.6	2.6
497 BLACK BAPT EST[2]	NA	49,145	62,089*	7.2	11.9

NA–Not applicable   NR–Not reported   *Total adherents estimated from known number of communicant, confirmed, full members.   - Represents a percent less than 0.1.   Percentages may not total due to rounding.
[1]See Appendix E   [2]See Appendix F   [3]See Appendix G   Lines in *italic* represent a breakdown of Catholic rites or Friends affiliations. They are included in their respective denominational total.

Table 4. Churches and Church Membership by County and Denomination: 1990

County and Denomination	Number of churches	Communicant, confirmed, full members	Total adherents		
			Number	Percent of total population	Percent of total adherents
498 INDEP.CHARIS.[3]	5	NA	2,105	.2	.4
499 INDEP.NON-CHAR[3]	7	NA	6,261	.7	1.2
HANCOCK	**83**	**19,547**	**33,607***	**51.3**	**100.0**
053 ASSEMB OF GOD	2	224	600	.9	1.8
071 BRETHREN (ASH)	1	35	44*	.1	.1
081 CATHOLIC	1	NA	6,401	9.8	19.0
081d LATIN	1	NA	6,401	9.8	19.0
089 CHR & MISS AL	1	27	33	.1	.1
093 CHR CH (DISC)	1	230	280	.4	.8
097 CHR CHS&CHS CR	5	1,170	1,483*	2.3	4.4
111 CH CR,SCIENTST	1	NR	NR	-	-
123 CH GOD (ANDER)	1	320	320	.5	1.0
127 CH GOD (CLEVE)	1	262	332*	.5	1.0
151 L-D SAINTS	1	NA	351	.5	1.0
165 CH OF NAZARENE	3	251	574	.9	1.7
167 CHS OF CHRIST	1	79	103	.2	.3
171 CH GOD-GEN CON	2	681	863*	1.3	2.6
193 EPISCOPAL	1	201	282	.4	.8
199 EVAN CONGR CH	1	106	106	.2	.3
203 EVAN FREE CH	1	30	95	.1	.3
207 E.L.C.A.	7	3,194	4,579	7.0	13.6
226 FRIENDS-USA	1	7	14	-	-
226c FGC	1	7	14	-	-
263 INT FOURSQ GOS	1	0	0*	-	-
283 LUTH—MO SYNOD	1	151	218	.3	.6
339 PENT CH OF GOD	1	35	130	.2	.4
355 PRESB CH (USA)	5	2,109	2,674*	4.1	8.0
361 PRIM BAPT ASCS	2	31	39*	.1	.1
403 SALVATION ARMY	1	127	149	.2	.4
413 S.D.A.	1	112	142*	.2	.4
419 SO BAPT CONV	1	133	169*	.3	.5
436 UNITED BAPT	1	48	61*	.1	.2
438 UN BRETH IN CR	1	162	231	.4	.7
443 UN C OF CHRIST	1	149	189*	.3	.6
449 UN METHODIST	32	8,716	11,051*	16.9	32.9
469 WELS	2	827	1,129	1.7	3.4
497 BLACK BAPT EST[2]	NA	130	165*	.3	.5
499 INDEP.NON-CHAR[3]	1	NA	800	1.2	2.4
HARDIN	**74**	**8,784**	**13,345***	**42.9**	**100.0**
019 AMER BAPT USA	2	555	691*	2.2	5.2
053 ASSEMB OF GOD	3	193	314	1.0	2.4
081 CATHOLIC	2	NA	1,182	3.8	8.9
081d LATIN	2	NA	1,182	3.8	8.9
089 CHR & MISS AL	1	77	188	.6	1.4
093 CHR CH (DISC)	2	167	615	2.0	4.6
097 CHR CHS&CHS CR	6	852	1,061*	3.4	8.0
123 CH GOD (ANDER)	1	47	68	.2	.5
157 CH OF BRETHREN	1	62	77*	.2	.6
165 CH OF NAZARENE	1	115	85	.3	.6
167 CHS OF CHRIST	2	128	163	.5	1.2
171 CH GOD-GEN CON	2	46	57*	.2	.4
207 E.L.C.A.	3	577	751	2.4	5.6
223 FREE WILL BAPT	1	50	62*	.2	.5
263 INT FOURSQ GOS	1	121	151*	.5	1.1
323 OLD ORD AMISH	4	NA	600	1.9	4.5
325 OLD REG BAPT	1	11	14*	-	.1
339 PENT CH OF GOD	3	120	213	.7	1.6
355 PRESB CH (USA)	4	352	438*	1.4	3.3
419 SO BAPT CONV	1	123	153*	.5	1.1
436 UNITED BAPT	2	87	108*	.3	.8
443 UN C OF CHRIST	5	979	1,219*	3.9	9.1
449 UN METHODIST	24	4,026	5,014*	16.1	37.6
467 WESLEYAN	1	20	25	.1	.2
469 WELS	1	76	96	.3	.7
HARRISON	**58**	**4,797**	**6,518***	**40.5**	**100.0**
053 ASSEMB OF GOD	3	141	171	1.1	2.6
081 CATHOLIC	5	NA	527	3.3	8.1
081d LATIN	5	NA	527	3.3	8.1
097 CHR CHS&CHS CR	3	475	585*	3.6	9.0
123 CH GOD (ANDER)	1	0	40	.2	.6
151 L-D SAINTS	1	NA	110	.7	1.7
165 CH OF NAZARENE	4	187	109	.7	1.7
167 CHS OF CHRIST	3	196	249	1.5	3.8
207 E.L.C.A.	1	66	131	.8	2.0
226 FRIENDS-USA	1	88	108*	.7	1.7
226a CONSERV	1	88	108*	.7	1.7
355 PRESB CH (USA)	11	1,130	1,392*	8.7	21.4
419 SO BAPT CONV	1	15	18*	.1	.3
449 UN METHODIST	24	2,499	3,078*	19.1	47.2
HENRY	**61**	**13,405**	**20,746***	**71.3**	**100.0**
053 ASSEMB OF GOD	2	72	121	.4	.6

County and Denomination	Number of churches	Communicant, confirmed, full members	Total adherents		
			Number	Percent of total population	Percent of total adherents
081 CATHOLIC	6	NA	2,817	9.7	13.6
081d LATIN	6	NA	2,817	9.7	13.6
097 CHR CHS&CHS CR	1	130	168*	.6	.8
151 L-D SAINTS	1	NA	133	.5	.6
157 CH OF BRETHREN	1	21	27*	.1	.1
165 CH OF NAZARENE	1	86	260	.9	1.3
171 CH GOD-GEN CON	1	53	68*	.2	.3
193 EPISCOPAL	1	114	151	.5	.7
207 E.L.C.A.	11	3,852	4,993	17.2	24.1
209 EVAN LUTH SYN	1	365	511	1.8	2.5
283 LUTH—MO SYNOD	9	4,165	5,554	19.1	26.8
355 PRESB CH (USA)	2	356	460*	1.6	2.2
373 REF CH IN U.S.	1	110	141	.5	.7
413 S.D.A.	2	65	84*	.3	.4
419 SO BAPT CONV	3	330	426*	1.5	2.1
438 UN BRETH IN CR	1	46	63	.2	.3
443 UN C OF CHRIST	2	651	841*	2.9	4.1
449 UN METHODIST	13	2,943	3,800*	13.1	18.3
467 WESLEYAN	2	46	128	.4	.6
HIGHLAND	**84**	**10,264**	**15,550***	**43.5**	**100.0**
019 AMER BAPT USA	3	804	1,019*	2.9	6.6
053 ASSEMB OF GOD	1	57	75	.2	.5
081 CATHOLIC	2	NA	1,690	4.7	10.9
081d LATIN	2	NA	1,690	4.7	10.9
097 CHR CHS&CHS CR	12	3,018	3,827*	10.7	24.6
111 CH CR,SCIENTST	1	NR	NR	-	-
123 CH GOD (ANDER)	1	19	30	.1	.2
127 CH GOD (CLEVE)	2	260	330*	.9	2.1
145 CH GOD PROPHCY	1	36	46*	.1	.3
146 CH GOD MTN ASM	1	43	55*	.2	.4
151 L-D SAINTS	1	NA	88	.2	.6
165 CH OF NAZARENE	2	327	599	1.7	3.9
167 CHS OF CHRIST	3	278	376	1.1	2.4
193 EPISCOPAL	1	69	107	.3	.7
203 EVAN FREE CH	1	27	65	.2	.4
207 E.L.C.A.	2	143	161	.5	1.0
223 FREE WILL BAPT	2	300	380*	1.1	2.4
226 FRIENDS-USA	6	547	694*	1.9	4.5
226e FUM	6	547	694*	1.9	4.5
265 INT PENT C CHR	2	64	64	.2	.4
291 MISSIONARY CH	1	23	29	.1	.2
339 PENT CH OF GOD	1	34	77	.2	.5
355 PRESB CH (USA)	4	591	749*	2.1	4.8
413 S.D.A.	1	59	75*	.2	.5
419 SO BAPT CONV	3	309	392*	1.1	2.5
438 UN BRETH IN CR	1	129	129	.4	.8
449 UN METHODIST	26	2,925	3,709*	10.4	23.9
467 WESLEYAN	2	50	115	.3	.7
497 BLACK BAPT EST[2]	NA	152	193*	.5	1.2
499 INDEP.NON-CHAR[3]	1	NA	476	1.3	3.1
HOCKING	**62**	**4,747**	**7,556***	**29.6**	**100.0**
001 ADVENT CHR CH	1	28	35*	.1	.5
053 ASSEMB OF GOD	1	15	20	.1	.3
081 CATHOLIC	2	NA	1,074	4.2	14.2
081d LATIN	2	NA	1,074	4.2	14.2
089 CHR & MISS AL	1	38	108	.4	1.4
093 CHR CH (DISC)	1	38	82	.3	1.1
097 CHR CHS&CHS CR	1	250	315*	1.2	4.2
123 CH GOD (ANDER)	1	0	171	.7	2.3
127 CH GOD (CLEVE)	1	85	107*	.4	1.4
165 CH OF NAZARENE	2	163	341	1.3	4.5
167 CHS OF CHRIST	2	70	104	.4	1.4
193 EPISCOPAL	1	21	21	.1	.3
207 E.L.C.A.	3	469	629	2.5	8.3
223 FREE WILL BAPT	1	100	126*	.5	1.7
283 LUTH—MO SYNOD	1	122	168	.7	2.2
285 MENNONITE CH	2	64	97	.4	1.3
355 PRESB CH (USA)	1	281	354*	1.4	4.7
361 PRIM BAPT ASCS	1	10	13*	.1	.2
419 SO BAPT CONV	1	480	605*	2.4	8.0
438 UN BRETH IN CR	2	99	99	.4	1.3
449 UN METHODIST	33	2,384	3,007*	11.8	39.8
467 WESLEYAN	3	30	80	.3	1.1
HOLMES	**130**	**7,202**	**21,271***	**64.8**	**100.0**
061 BEACHY AMISH	5	322	451*	1.4	2.1
081 CATHOLIC	2	NA	477	1.5	2.2
081d LATIN	2	NA	477	1.5	2.2
097 CHR CHS&CHS CR	7	1,926	2,700*	8.2	12.7
127 CH GOD (CLEVE)	1	51	71*	.2	.3
165 CH OF NAZARENE	1	56	70	.2	.3
167 CHS OF CHRIST	3	135	173	.5	.8
207 E.L.C.A.	1	216	274	.8	1.3
259 IFCA	1	NR	NR	-	-

NA–Not applicable   NR–Not reported   *Total adherents estimated from known number of communicant, confirmed, full members.   - Represents a percent less than 0.1.   Percentages may not total due to rounding.
[1]See Appendix E   [2]See Appendix F   [3]See Appendix G   Lines in *italic* represent a breakdown of Catholic rites or Friends affiliations. They are included in their respective denominational total.

Table 4. Churches and Church Membership by County and Denomination: 1990

County and Denomination	Number of churches	Communicant, confirmed, full members	Total adherents Number	Percent of total population	Percent of total adherents
283 LUTH—MO SYNOD	1	57	70	.2	.3
285 MENNONITE CH	18	2,472	2,978	9.1	14.0
323 OLD ORD AMISH	75	NA	11,250	34.2	52.9
355 PRESB CH (USA)	2	225	315*	1.0	1.5
413 S.D.A.	1	47	66*	.2	.3
443 UN C OF CHRIST	5	727	1,019*	3.1	4.8
449 UN METHODIST	7	968	1,357*	4.1	6.4
HURON	**77**	**10,668**	**25,616***	**45.5**	**100.0**
019 AMER BAPT USA	2	529	685*	1.2	2.7
053 ASSEMB OF GOD	2	210	337	.6	1.3
081 CATHOLIC	10	NA	10,193	18.1	39.8
081d LATIN	10	NA	10,193	18.1	39.8
089 CHR & MISS AL	4	468	1,489	2.6	5.8
093 CHR CH (DISC)	1	58	90	.2	.4
097 CHR CHS&CHS CR	3	175	227*	.4	.9
105 CHRISTIAN REF	1	193	296	.5	1.2
127 CH GOD (CLEVE)	4	430	557*	1.0	2.2
145 CH GOD PROPHCY	3	108	140*	.2	.5
151 L-D SAINTS	1	NA	330	.6	1.3
165 CH OF NAZARENE	3	209	431	.8	1.7
167 CHS OF CHRIST	4	215	280	.5	1.1
176 CCC, NOT NAT'L	1	24	31*	.1	.1
193 EPISCOPAL	2	95	131	.2	.5
207 E.L.C.A.	6	2,361	3,168	5.6	12.4
223 FREE WILL BAPT	1	25	32*	.1	.1
263 INT FOURSQ GOS	1	0	0*	-	-
355 PRESB CH (USA)	3	681	882*	1.6	3.4
403 SALVATION ARMY	1	39	41	.1	.2
413 S.D.A.	2	150	194*	.3	.8
419 SO BAPT CONV	3	370	479*	.9	1.9
435 UNITARIAN-UNIV	1	14	14	-	.1
436 UNITED BAPT	1	32	41*	.1	.2
443 UN C OF CHRIST	4	799	1,035*	1.8	4.0
449 UN METHODIST	13	3,352	4,343*	7.7	17.0
497 BLACK BAPT EST[2]	NA	131	170*	.3	.7
JACKSON	**68**	**6,731**	**9,605***	**31.8**	**100.0**
019 AMER BAPT USA	4	997	1,264*	4.2	13.2
053 ASSEMB OF GOD	1	26	42	.1	.4
081 CATHOLIC	2	NA	763	2.5	7.9
081d LATIN	2	NA	763	2.5	7.9
093 CHR CH (DISC)	2	133	270	.9	2.8
097 CHR CHS&CHS CR	4	144	182*	.6	1.9
127 CH GOD (CLEVE)	2	177	224*	.7	2.3
145 CH GOD PROPHCY	2	72	91*	.3	.9
151 L-D SAINTS	1	NA	96	.3	1.0
165 CH OF NAZARENE	3	331	694	2.3	7.2
167 CHS OF CHRIST	4	123	173	.6	1.8
191 ENTRPR BPT ASC	1	22	28*	.1	.3
207 E.L.C.A.	1	108	142	.5	1.5
223 FREE WILL BAPT	8	350	444*	1.5	4.6
285 MENNONITE CH	1	23	43	.1	.4
325 OLD REG BAPT	1	36	46*	.2	.5
355 PRESB CH (USA)	7	716	907*	3.0	9.4
413 S.D.A.	1	56	71*	.2	.7
419 SO BAPT CONV	4	531	673*	2.2	7.0
449 UN METHODIST	17	2,554	3,237*	10.7	33.7
467 WESLEYAN	2	332	215	.7	2.2
JEFFERSON	**146**	**16,841**	**39,825***	**49.6**	**100.0**
019 AMER BAPT USA	2	212	258*	.3	.6
053 ASSEMB OF GOD	5	453	940	1.2	2.4
081 CATHOLIC	27	NA	18,337	22.8	46.0
081b BYZAN RUTH	2	NA	1,434	1.8	3.6
081d LATIN	25	NA	16,903	21.1	42.4
093 CHR CH (DISC)	3	255	294	.4	.7
097 CHR CHS&CHS CR	8	2,458	2,988*	3.7	7.5
111 CH CR,SCIENTST	1	NR	NR	-	-
123 CH GOD (ANDER)	2	270	276	.3	.7
151 L-D SAINTS	1	NA	166	.2	.4
165 CH OF NAZARENE	8	604	888	1.1	2.2
167 CHS OF CHRIST	3	260	338	.4	.8
193 EPISCOPAL	2	278	402	.5	1.0
207 E.L.C.A.	2	320	440	.5	1.1
216 EVAN PRESBY CH	2	165	172	.2	.4
226 FRIENDS-USA	3	143	166	.2	.4
226b EFI	3	143	166	.2	.4
246 GREEK ORTHODOX	1	NR	NR	-	-
283 LUTH—MO SYNOD	1	159	181	.2	.5
331 ORTH CH IN AM	3	NR	NR	-	-
353 CHR BRETHREN	1	40	50	.1	.1
355 PRESB CH (USA)	19	2,841	3,454*	4.3	8.7
356 PRESB CH AMER	1	316	316	.4	.8
403 SALVATION ARMY	1	76	89	.1	.2
413 S.D.A.	1	41	50*	.1	.1

County and Denomination	Number of churches	Communicant, confirmed, full members	Total adherents Number	Percent of total population	Percent of total adherents
419 SO BAPT CONV	1	243	295*	.4	.7
438 UN BRETH IN CR	1	69	69	.1	.2
443 UN C OF CHRIST	1	189	230*	.3	.6
449 UN METHODIST	42	6,187	7,522*	9.4	18.9
467 WESLEYAN	2	44	248	.3	.6
496 JEWISH EST[1]	2	NA	175	.2	.4
497 BLACK BAPT EST[2]	NA	1,218	1,481*	1.8	3.7
KNOX	**91**	**12,235**	**19,729***	**41.6**	**100.0**
001 ADVENT CHR CH	1	35	43*	.1	.2
019 AMER BAPT USA	5	1,176	1,459*	3.1	7.4
053 ASSEMB OF GOD	1	153	238	.5	1.2
081 CATHOLIC	2	NA	2,232	4.7	11.3
081d LATIN	2	NA	2,232	4.7	11.3
089 CHR & MISS AL	1	59	108	.2	.5
093 CHR CH (DISC)	1	421	654	1.4	3.3
097 CHR CHS&CHS CR	12	1,395	1,730*	3.6	8.8
123 CH GOD (ANDER)	2	130	215	.5	1.1
127 CH GOD (CLEVE)	1	155	192*	.4	1.0
151 L-D SAINTS	1	NA	173	.4	.9
157 CH OF BRETHREN	1	116	144*	.3	.7
165 CH OF NAZARENE	4	1,136	1,803	3.8	9.1
167 CHS OF CHRIST	3	266	345	.7	1.7
191 ENTRPR BPT ASC	1	34	42*	.1	.2
193 EPISCOPAL	2	411	701	1.5	3.6
207 E.L.C.A.	2	463	674	1.4	3.4
223 FREE WILL BAPT	1	35	43*	.1	.2
263 INT FOURSQ GOS	3	163	202*	.4	1.0
323 OLD ORD AMISH	9	NA	1,200	2.5	6.1
355 PRESB CH (USA)	3	478	593*	1.2	3.0
403 SALVATION ARMY	1	120	142	.3	.7
413 S.D.A.	4	1,003	1,244*	2.6	6.3
419 SO BAPT CONV	1	274	340*	.7	1.7
443 UN C OF CHRIST	1	298	370*	.8	1.9
449 UN METHODIST	26	3,797	4,710*	9.9	23.9
467 WESLEYAN	2	117	132	.3	.7
LAKE	**117**	**25,885**	**127,279***	**59.1**	**100.0**
005 AME ZION	1	225	300	.1	.2
019 AMER BAPT USA	5	961	1,194*	.6	.9
053 ASSEMB OF GOD	5	951	2,617	1.2	2.1
057 BAPT GEN CONF	1	141	175*	.1	.1
081 CATHOLIC	16	NA	83,582	38.8	65.7
081b BYZAN RUTH	2	NA	207	.1	.2
081d LATIN	14	NA	83,375	38.7	65.5
089 CHR & MISS AL	2	176	301	.1	.2
093 CHR CH (DISC)	4	449	841	.4	.7
097 CHR CHS&CHS CR	3	1,110	1,379*	.6	1.1
111 CH CR,SCIENTST	2	NR	NR	-	-
123 CH GOD (ANDER)	1	28	28	-	-
127 CH GOD (CLEVE)	5	410	509*	.2	.4
145 CH GOD PROPHCY	1	36	45*	-	-
146 CH GOD MTN ASM	1	38	47*	-	-
151 L-D SAINTS	1	NA	348	.2	.3
157 CH OF BRETHREN	1	165	205*	.1	.2
163 CH OF LUTH BR	1	50	135	.1	.1
165 CH OF NAZARENE	3	382	530	.2	.4
167 CHS OF CHRIST	4	281	403	.2	.3
193 EPISCOPAL	5	1,147	1,619	.8	1.3
207 E.L.C.A.	5	1,488	2,008	.9	1.6
216 EVAN PRESBY CH	1	157	157	.1	.1
226 FRIENDS-USA	1	316	933	.4	.7
226b EFI	1	316	933	.4	.7
283 LUTH—MO SYNOD	8	2,848	3,724	1.7	2.9
285 MENNONITE CH	1	24	64	-	.1
331 ORTH CH IN AM	1	NR	NR	-	-
353 CHR BRETHREN	1	51	85	-	.1
355 PRESB CH (USA)	3	853	1,060*	.5	.8
403 SALVATION ARMY	1	85	89	-	.1
413 S.D.A.	2	220	273*	.1	.2
419 SO BAPT CONV	5	2,136	2,654*	1.2	2.1
435 UNITARIAN-UNIV	2	180	216	.1	.2
443 UN C OF CHRIST	9	2,906	3,610*	1.7	2.8
449 UN METHODIST	11	7,043	8,750*	4.1	6.9
469 WELS	1	71	109	.1	.1
496 JEWISH EST[1]	2	NA	7,800	3.6	6.1
497 BLACK BAPT EST[2]	NA	957	1,189*	.6	.9
499 INDEP.NON-CHAR[3]	1	NA	300	.1	.2
LAWRENCE	**91**	**9,407**	**14,437***	**23.3**	**100.0**
019 AMER BAPT USA	3	1,196	1,505*	2.4	10.4
053 ASSEMB OF GOD	1	26	34	.1	.2
081 CATHOLIC	4	NA	1,980	3.2	13.7
081d LATIN	4	NA	1,980	3.2	13.7
097 CHR CHS&CHS CR	3	465	585*	.9	4.1
123 CH GOD (ANDER)	1	20	28	-	.2

NA–Not applicable   NR–Not reported   *Total adherents estimated from known number of communicant, confirmed, full members.   - Represents a percent less than 0.1.   Percentages may not total due to rounding.
[1]See Appendix E   [2]See Appendix F   [3]See Appendix G   Lines in *italic* represent a breakdown of Catholic rites or Friends affiliations. They are included in their respective denominational total.

Table 4. Churches and Church Membership by County and Denomination: 1990

County and Denomination	Number of churches	Communicant, confirmed, full members	Total adherents Number	Percent of total population	Percent of total adherents
145 CH GOD PROPHCY	1	36	45*	.1	.3
165 CH OF NAZARENE	10	959	1,480	2.4	10.3
167 CHS OF CHRIST	9	613	770	1.2	5.3
191 ENTRPR BPT ASC	2	120	151*	.2	1.0
193 EPISCOPAL	1	71	123	.2	.9
207 E.L.C.A.	1	144	168	.3	1.2
223 FREE WILL BAPT	10	500	629*	1.0	4.4
265 INT PENT C CHR	1	12	41	.1	.3
285 MENNONITE CH	1	45	55	.1	.4
349 PENT HOLINESS	2	34	43*	.1	.3
355 PRESB CH (USA)	2	147	185*	.3	1.3
419 SO BAPT CONV	3	828	1,042*	1.7	7.2
436 UNITED BAPT	6	808	1,017*	1.6	7.0
449 UN METHODIST	29	2,960	3,724*	6.0	25.8
497 BLACK BAPT EST[2]	NA	423	532*	.9	3.7
499 INDEP.NON-CHAR[3]	1	NA	300	.5	2.1
LICKING	**157**	**28,789**	**49,965***	**38.9**	**100.0**
019 AMER BAPT USA	11	2,353	2,964*	2.3	5.9
053 ASSEMB OF GOD	2	171	242	.2	.5
061 BEACHY AMISH	1	80	101*	.1	.2
071 BRETHREN (ASH)	1	43	54*	-	.1
081 CATHOLIC	7	NA	8,981	7.0	18.0
081d LATIN	*7*	*NA*	*8,981*	*7.0*	*18.0*
093 CHR CH (DISC)	1	649	940	.7	1.9
097 CHR CHS&CHS CR	14	2,865	3,609*	2.8	7.2
111 CH CR,SCIENTST	1	NR	NR	-	-
123 CH GOD (ANDER)	2	15	21	-	-
127 CH GOD (CLEVE)	3	272	343*	.3	.7
145 CH GOD PROPHCY	1	36	45*	-	.1
151 L-D SAINTS	2	NA	962	.7	1.9
165 CH OF NAZARENE	8	982	2,062	1.6	4.1
167 CHS OF CHRIST	7	390	498	.4	1.0
175 CONGR CHR CHS	1	326	411*	.3	.8
193 EPISCOPAL	2	405	498	.4	1.0
207 E.L.C.A.	7	2,161	2,969	2.3	5.9
221 FREE METHODIST	1	24	35	-	.1
223 FREE WILL BAPT	2	200	252*	.2	.5
226 FRIENDS-USA	1	3	9	-	-
226c FGC	*1*	*3*	*9*	*-*	*-*
263 INT FOURSQ GOS	1	80	101*	.1	.2
283 LUTH—MO SYNOD	2	340	448	.3	.9
323 OLD ORD AMISH	1	NA	150	.1	.3
329 OPEN BIBLE STD	1	NR	NR	-	-
339 PENT CH OF GOD	1	50	176	.1	.4
355 PRESB CH (USA)	12	3,008	3,789*	3.0	7.6
361 PRIM BAPT ASCS	3	31	39*	-	.1
403 SALVATION ARMY	1	87	92	.1	.2
413 S.D.A.	2	301	379*	.3	.8
419 SO BAPT CONV	10	3,085	3,886*	3.0	7.8
435 UNITARIAN-UNIV	1	10	20	-	-
438 UN BRETH IN CR	1	119	123	.1	.2
443 UN C OF CHRIST	4	1,076	1,356*	1.1	2.7
449 UN METHODIST	37	8,937	11,259*	8.8	22.5
467 WESLEYAN	1	89	171	.1	.3
496 JEWISH EST[1]	1	NA	1,473	1.1	2.9
497 BLACK BAPT EST[2]	NA	601	757*	.6	1.5
499 INDEP.NON-CHAR[3]	1	NA	750	.6	1.5
LOGAN	**70**	**11,245**	**18,423***	**43.5**	**100.0**
019 AMER BAPT USA	1	100	127*	.3	.7
053 ASSEMB OF GOD	1	125	255	.6	1.4
071 BRETHREN (ASH)	1	153	195*	.5	1.1
081 CATHOLIC	2	NA	2,500	5.9	13.6
081d LATIN	*2*	*NA*	*2,500*	*5.9*	*13.6*
093 CHR CH (DISC)	2	720	1,143	2.7	6.2
097 CHR CHS&CHS CR	5	491	625*	1.5	3.4
123 CH GOD (ANDER)	3	368	619	1.5	3.4
127 CH GOD (CLEVE)	2	1,258	1,602*	3.8	8.7
151 L-D SAINTS	1	NA	262	.6	1.4
157 CH OF BRETHREN	2	153	195*	.5	1.1
165 CH OF NAZARENE	3	246	712	1.7	3.9
167 CHS OF CHRIST	2	197	236	.6	1.3
193 EPISCOPAL	1	172	241	.6	1.3
207 E.L.C.A.	4	836	1,130	2.7	6.1
226 FRIENDS-USA	4	164	300	.7	1.6
226b EFI	*4*	*164*	*300*	*.7*	*1.6*
285 MENNONITE CH	3	494	643	1.5	3.5
291 MISSIONARY CH	1	13	12	-	.1
323 OLD ORD AMISH	2	NA	300	.7	1.6
329 OPEN BIBLE STD	1	NR	NR	-	-
355 PRESB CH (USA)	5	882	1,123*	2.7	6.1
413 S.D.A.	1	50	64*	.1	.3
419 SO BAPT CONV	1	527	671*	1.6	3.6
443 UN C OF CHRIST	1	269	342*	.8	1.9
449 UN METHODIST	21	3,850	4,901*	11.6	26.6
497 BLACK BAPT EST[2]	NA	177	225*	.5	1.2

County and Denomination	Number of churches	Communicant, confirmed, full members	Total adherents Number	Percent of total population	Percent of total adherents
LORAIN	**228**	**46,000**	**130,769***	**48.2**	**100.0**
005 AME ZION	1	350	445	.2	.3
019 AMER BAPT USA	7	956	1,214*	.4	.9
053 ASSEMB OF GOD	10	1,790	2,995	1.1	2.3
057 BAPT GEN CONF	2	164	208*	.1	.2
081 CATHOLIC	39	NA	68,070	25.1	52.1
081b BYZAN RUTH	*2*	*NA*	*840*	*.3*	*.6*
081d LATIN	*35*	*NA*	*66,801*	*24.6*	*51.1*
081g ROMANIAN	*1*	*NA*	*322*	*.1*	*.2*
081h UKRAINIAN	*1*	*NA*	*107*	*-*	*.1*
089 CHR & MISS AL	4	33	114	-	.1
093 CHR CH (DISC)	4	987	1,867	.7	1.4
097 CHR CHS&CHS CR	1	80	102*	-	.1
111 CH CR,SCIENTST	3	NR	NR	-	-
121 CH GOD (ABR)	1	44	56*	-	-
123 CH GOD (ANDER)	2	120	120	-	.1
127 CH GOD (CLEVE)	6	986	1,252*	.5	1.0
133 CH GOD(7TH)DEN	1	25	30	-	-
145 CH GOD PROPHCY	2	72	91*	-	.1
146 CH GOD MTN ASM	1	36	46*	-	-
151 L-D SAINTS	2	NA	738	.3	.6
157 CH OF BRETHREN	1	42	53*	-	-
165 CH OF NAZARENE	5	519	993	.4	.8
167 CHS OF CHRIST	7	549	683	.3	.5
181 CONSRV CONGR	1	63	80*	-	.1
191 ENTRPR BPT ASC	1	81	103*	-	.1
193 EPISCOPAL	3	751	1,125	.4	.9
207 E.L.C.A.	8	2,379	3,143	1.2	2.4
223 FREE WILL BAPT	5	250	317*	.1	.2
226 FRIENDS-USA	1	11	14	-	-
226c FGC	*1*	*11*	*14*	*-*	*-*
246 GREEK ORTHODOX	1	NR	NR	-	-
263 INT FOURSQ GOS	2	455	578*	.2	.4
283 LUTH—MO SYNOD	13	3,684	4,838	1.8	3.7
285 MENNONITE CH	1	50	104	-	.1
325 OLD REG BAPT	1	21	27*	-	-
331 ORTH CH IN AM	2	NR	NR	-	-
339 PENT CH OF GOD	2	55	109	-	.1
349 PENT HOLINESS	1	53	67*	-	.1
353 CHR BRETHREN	2	37	74	-	.1
355 PRESB CH (USA)	5	1,043	1,324*	.5	1.0
403 SALVATION ARMY	2	219	234	.1	.2
413 S.D.A.	4	432	548*	.2	.4
419 SO BAPT CONV	16	5,892	7,479*	2.8	5.7
435 UNITARIAN-UNIV	1	19	27	-	-
443 UN C OF CHRIST	25	9,451	11,997*	4.4	9.2
449 UN METHODIST	28	8,444	10,718*	4.0	8.2
467 WESLEYAN	1	97	275	.1	.2
496 JEWISH EST[1]	2	NA	850	.3	.7
497 BLACK BAPT EST[2]	NA	5,760	7,311*	2.7	5.6
499 INDEP.NON-CHAR[3]	1	NA	350	.1	.3
LUCAS	**305**	**94,403**	**225,551***	**48.8**	**100.0**
005 AME ZION	3	2,861	3,125	.7	1.4
019 AMER BAPT USA	15	3,402	4,299*	.9	1.9
040 AP CHR CH-AMER	1	47	82	-	-
053 ASSEMB OF GOD	5	923	1,775	.4	.8
057 BAPT GEN CONF	1	35	44*	-	-
059 BAPT MISS ASSN	1	150	190*	-	.1
081 CATHOLIC	49	NA	88,991	19.2	39.5
081b BYZAN RUTH	*1*	*NA*	*150*	*-*	*.1*
081d LATIN	*48*	*NA*	*88,841*	*19.2*	*39.4*
089 CHR & MISS AL	6	1,296	2,515	.5	1.1
093 CHR CH (DISC)	5	1,113	1,372	.3	.6
097 CHR CHS&CHS CR	6	1,757	2,220*	.5	1.0
105 CHRISTIAN REF	1	81	143	-	.1
111 CH CR,SCIENTST	4	NR	NR	-	-
123 CH GOD (ANDER)	6	1,220	1,325	.3	.6
127 CH GOD (CLEVE)	4	295	373*	.1	.2
133 CH GOD(7TH)DEN	1	25	31	-	-
145 CH GOD PROPHCY	1	36	45*	-	-
151 L-D SAINTS	2	NA	795	.2	.4
157 CH OF BRETHREN	1	89	112*	-	-
165 CH OF NAZARENE	5	737	1,100	.2	.5
167 CHS OF CHRIST	5	1,408	1,876	.4	.8
171 CH GOD-GEN CON	1	58	73*	-	-
175 CONGR CHR CHS	3	1,334	1,686*	.4	.7
193 EPISCOPAL	8	3,090	5,810	1.3	2.6
207 E.L.C.A.	39	23,779	35,165	7.6	15.6
221 FREE METHODIST	2	203	273	.1	.1
223 FREE WILL BAPT	2	150	190*	-	.1
226 FRIENDS-USA	1	3	12	-	-
226c FGC	*1*	*3*	*12*	*-*	*-*
246 GREEK ORTHODOX	1	NR	NR	-	-
283 LUTH—MO SYNOD	10	2,785	3,535	.8	1.6
285 MENNONITE CH	2	116	210	-	.1
291 MISSIONARY CH	1	27	42	-	-

NA–Not applicable   NR–Not reported   *Total adherents estimated from known number of communicant, confirmed, full members.   - Represents a percent less than 0.1.   Percentages may not total due to rounding.
[1]See Appendix E   [2]See Appendix F   [3]See Appendix G   Lines in *italic* represent a breakdown of Catholic rites or Friends affiliations. They are included in their respective denominational total.

Table 4. Churches and Church Membership by County and Denomination: 1990

County and Denomination	Number of churches	Communicant, confirmed, full members	Total adherents Number	Percent of total population	Percent of total adherents
313 N AM BAPT CONF	1	202	255*	.1	.1
329 OPEN BIBLE STD	2	NR	NR	-	-
331 ORTH CH IN AM	1	NR	NR	-	-
349 PENT HOLINESS	4	325	411*	.1	.2
353 CHR BRETHREN	2	191	361	.1	.2
355 PRESB CH (USA)	10	4,000	5,054*	1.1	2.2
403 SALVATION ARMY	1	133	137	-	.1
413 S.D.A.	2	429	542*	.1	.2
419 SO BAPT CONV	12	3,412	4,311*	.9	1.9
435 UNITARIAN-UNIV	1	375	475	.1	.2
438 UN BRETH IN CR	3	322	322	.1	.1
443 UN C OF CHRIST	13	4,390	5,547*	1.2	2.5
449 UN METHODIST	40	14,014	17,707*	3.8	7.9
466 WAYN TR MB ASC	1	156	197*	-	.1
467 WESLEYAN	3	126	264	.1	.1
469 WELS	6	736	957	.2	.4
496 JEWISH EST[1]	4	NA	4,635	1.0	2.1
497 BLACK BAPT EST[2]	NA	18,572	23,467*	5.1	10.4
498 INDEP.CHARIS.[3]	1	NA	400	.1	.2
499 INDEP.NON-CHAR[3]	6	NA	3,100	.7	1.4
MADISON	**58**	**9,828**	**15,520***	**41.9**	**100.0**
019 AMER BAPT USA	1	194	240*	.6	1.5
053 ASSEMB OF GOD	1	150	200	.5	1.3
061 BEACHY AMISH	3	286	354*	1.0	2.3
081 CATHOLIC	3	NA	2,158	5.8	13.9
081d *LATIN*	3	*NA*	*2,158*	*5.8*	*13.9*
097 CHR CHS&CHS CR	2	166	206*	.6	1.3
123 CH GOD (ANDER)	1	58	59	.2	.4
127 CH GOD (CLEVE)	1	144	178*	.5	1.1
145 CH GOD PROPHCY	1	36	45*	.1	.3
165 CH OF NAZARENE	3	424	873	2.4	5.6
167 CHS OF CHRIST	1	25	40	.1	.3
191 ENTRPR BPT ASC	3	88	109*	.3	.7
193 EPISCOPAL	1	106	199	.5	1.3
207 E.L.C.A.	2	857	1,059	2.9	6.8
223 FREE WILL BAPT	4	200	248*	.7	1.6
265 INT PENT C CHR	1	30	58	.2	.4
285 MENNONITE CH	6	793	1,120	3.0	7.2
323 OLD ORD AMISH	1	NA	150	.4	1.0
355 PRESB CH (USA)	3	908	1,125*	3.0	7.2
419 SO BAPT CONV	3	681	844*	2.3	5.4
436 UNITED BAPT	1	118	146*	.4	.9
443 UN C OF CHRIST	2	298	369*	1.0	2.4
449 UN METHODIST	14	3,516	4,355*	11.7	28.1
496 JEWISH EST[1]	0	NA	456	1.2	2.9
497 BLACK BAPT EST[2]	NA	750	929*	2.5	6.0
MAHONING	**251**	**57,062**	**187,851***	**70.9**	**100.0**
005 AME ZION	2	1,097	1,524	.6	.8
011 A.W.M.C.	1	17	21*	-	-
019 AMER BAPT USA	9	2,754	3,398*	1.3	1.8
022 EASTERN ORTH	1	136	136	.1	.1
053 ASSEMB OF GOD	15	3,546	4,795	1.8	2.6
057 BAPT GEN CONF	4	1,103	1,361*	.5	.7
081 CATHOLIC	44	NA	109,985	41.5	58.5
081b *BYZAN RUTH*	6	*NA*	*16,776*	*6.3*	*8.9*
081d *LATIN*	35	*NA*	*90,724*	*34.3*	*48.3*
081e *MARONITE*	2	*NA*	*1,675*	*.6*	*.9*
081h *UKRAINIAN*	1	*NA*	*810*	*.3*	*.4*
089 CHR & MISS AL	1	38	58	-	-
093 CHR CH (DISC)	7	1,544	2,535	1.0	1.3
097 CHR CHS&CHS CR	10	2,682	3,309*	1.2	1.8
111 CH CR,SCIENTST	1	NR	NR	-	-
123 CH GOD (ANDER)	3	267	323	.1	.2
127 CH GOD (CLEVE)	3	191	236*	.1	.1
151 L-D SAINTS	1	NA	242	.1	.1
157 CH OF BRETHREN	2	143	176*	.1	.1
165 CH OF NAZARENE	6	761	1,159	.4	.6
167 CHS OF CHRIST	7	530	703	.3	.4
181 CONSRV CONGR	1	206	254*	.1	.1
193 EPISCOPAL	5	1,185	1,617	.6	.9
199 EVAN CONGR CH	1	102	252	.1	.1
207 E.L.C.A.	19	6,465	8,290	3.1	4.4
216 EVAN PRESBY CH	1	428	435	.2	.2
221 FREE METHODIST	3	189	244	.1	.1
226 FRIENDS-USA	4	625	696	.3	.4
226b *EFI*	4	*625*	*696*	*.3*	*.4*
246 GREEK ORTHODOX	3	NR	NR	-	-
263 INT FOURSQ GOS	1	7	9*	-	-
283 LUTH—MO SYNOD	6	1,151	1,636	.6	.9
285 MENNONITE CH	5	342	456	.2	.2
329 OPEN BIBLE STD	1	NR	NR	-	-
331 ORTH CH IN AM	2	NR	NR	-	-
353 CHR BRETHREN	1	7	7	-	-
355 PRESB CH (USA)	23	7,246	8,941*	3.4	4.8
356 PRESB CH AMER	1	123	123	-	.1
363 PRIMITIVE METH	1	129	149	.1	.1
397 ROMANIAN ORTH	1	NR	NR	-	-
403 SALVATION ARMY	1	148	195	.1	.1
413 S.D.A.	5	641	791*	.3	.4
419 SO BAPT CONV	8	1,426	1,759*	.7	.9
435 UNITARIAN-UNIV	1	140	200	.1	.1
443 UN C OF CHRIST	9	3,519	4,342*	1.6	2.3
449 UN METHODIST	21	7,408	9,140*	3.5	4.9
496 JEWISH EST[1]	5	NA	2,020	.8	1.1
497 BLACK BAPT EST[2]	NA	10,766	13,284*	5.0	7.1
498 INDEP.CHARIS.[3]	1	NA	300	.1	.2
499 INDEP.NON-CHAR[3]	4	NA	2,750	1.0	1.5
MARION	**80**	**16,766**	**28,065***	**43.7**	**100.0**
011 A.W.M.C.	1	0	0*	-	-
019 AMER BAPT USA	7	1,813	2,289*	3.6	8.2
053 ASSEMB OF GOD	1	182	213	.3	.8
081 CATHOLIC	2	NA	4,118	6.4	14.7
081d *LATIN*	2	*NA*	*4,118*	*6.4*	*14.7*
089 CHR & MISS AL	1	210	533	.8	1.9
093 CHR CH (DISC)	1	297	557	.9	2.0
097 CHR CHS&CHS CR	3	620	783*	1.2	2.8
111 CH CR,SCIENTST	1	NR	NR	-	-
123 CH GOD (ANDER)	1	50	85	.1	.3
127 CH GOD (CLEVE)	1	74	93*	.1	.3
145 CH GOD PROPHCY	1	36	45*	.1	.2
151 L-D SAINTS	1	NA	207	.3	.7
157 CH OF BRETHREN	1	105	133*	.2	.5
165 CH OF NAZARENE	3	924	1,166	1.8	4.2
167 CHS OF CHRIST	1	210	265	.4	.9
191 ENTRPR BPT ASC	3	233	294*	.5	1.0
193 EPISCOPAL	1	101	149	.2	.5
203 EVAN FREE CH	1	60	70	.1	.2
207 E.L.C.A.	7	3,106	4,875	7.6	17.4
226 FRIENDS-USA	1	22	42	.1	.1
226b *EFI*	1	*22*	*42*	*.1*	*.1*
263 INT FOURSQ GOS	1	13	16*	-	.1
265 INT PENT C CHR	1	53	53	.1	.2
339 PENT CH OF GOD	2	26	110	.2	.4
355 PRESB CH (USA)	3	1,016	1,283*	2.0	4.6
361 PRIM BAPT ASCS	1	19	24*	-	.1
403 SALVATION ARMY	1	118	125	.2	.4
413 S.D.A.	1	130	164*	.3	.6
443 UN C OF CHRIST	5	1,039	1,312*	2.0	4.7
449 UN METHODIST	20	5,607	7,080*	11.0	25.2
467 WESLEYAN	3	107	370	.6	1.3
496 JEWISH EST[1]	1	NA	110	.2	.4
497 BLACK BAPT EST[2]	NA	595	751*	1.2	2.7
499 INDEP.NON-CHAR[3]	2	NA	750	1.2	2.7
MEDINA	**112**	**20,385**	**66,207***	**54.1**	**100.0**
019 AMER BAPT USA	2	179	230*	.2	.3
039 AP CHR CH(NAZ)	1	26	33*	-	-
053 ASSEMB OF GOD	4	507	880	.7	1.3
081 CATHOLIC	10	NA	31,323	25.6	47.3
081b *BYZAN RUTH*	1	*NA*	*200*	*.2*	*.3*
081d *LATIN*	9	*NA*	*31,123*	*25.4*	*47.0*
089 CHR & MISS AL	2	235	570	.5	.9
093 CHR CH (DISC)	4	1,148	1,754	1.4	2.6
097 CHR CHS&CHS CR	1	275	353*	.3	.5
111 CH CR,SCIENTST	1	NR	NR	-	-
123 CH GOD (ANDER)	1	0	0	-	-
127 CH GOD (CLEVE)	1	58	74*	.1	.1
145 CH GOD PROPHCY	1	36	46*	-	.1
146 CH GOD MTN ASM	1	50	64*	.1	.1
151 L-D SAINTS	1	NA	375	.3	.6
157 CH OF BRETHREN	2	51	65*	.1	.1
165 CH OF NAZARENE	3	409	551	.5	.8
167 CHS OF CHRIST	3	232	285	.2	.4
193 EPISCOPAL	3	353	749	.6	1.1
207 E.L.C.A.	10	4,249	5,711	4.7	8.6
226 FRIENDS-USA	1	51	80	.1	.1
226b *EFI*	1	*51*	*80*	*.1*	*.1*
263 INT FOURSQ GOS	1	66	85*	.1	.1
283 LUTH—MO SYNOD	4	1,556	2,176	1.8	3.3
285 MENNONITE CH	1	83	116	.1	.2
287 MENN GEN CONF	1	113	132	.1	.2
323 OLD ORD AMISH	6	NA	900	.7	1.4
325 OLD REG BAPT	1	83	107*	.1	.2
355 PRESB CH (USA)	3	343	440*	.4	.7
356 PRESB CH AMER	1	69	86	.1	.1
371 REF CH IN AM	1	214	397	.3	.6
403 SALVATION ARMY	1	44	47	-	.1
413 S.D.A.	1	82	105*	.1	.2
419 SO BAPT CONV	5	794	1,019*	.8	1.5
431 UKRANIAN AMER	1	NR	NR	-	-

NA–Not applicable   NR–Not reported   *Total adherents estimated from known number of communicant, confirmed, full members.   - Represents a percent less than 0.1.   Percentages may not total due to rounding.

[1]See Appendix E   [2]See Appendix F   [3]See Appendix G   Lines in *italic* represent a breakdown of Catholic rites or Friends affiliations. They are included in their respective denominational total.

Table 4. Churches and Church Membership by County and Denomination: 1990

County and Denomination	Number of churches	Communicant, confirmed, full members	Total adherents		
			Number	Percent of total population	Percent of total adherents
435 UNITARIAN-UNIV	1	35	47	-	.1
443 UN C OF CHRIST	9	2,920	3,748*	3.1	5.7
449 UN METHODIST	18	5,769	7,405*	6.1	11.2
467 WESLEYAN	2	113	193	.2	.3
496 JEWISH EST[1]	0	NA	4,550	3.7	6.9
497 BLACK BAPT EST[2]	NA	231	297*	.2	.4
499 INDEP.NON-CHAR[3]	2	NA	1,200	1.0	1.8
MEIGS	**76**	**5,005**	**7,073***	**30.8**	**100.0**
019 AMER BAPT USA	4	860	1,084*	4.7	15.3
081 CATHOLIC	2	NA	384	1.7	5.4
081d LATIN	*2*	*NA*	*384*	*1.7*	*5.4*
093 CHR CH (DISC)	1	70	109	.5	1.5
097 CHR CHS&CHS CR	10	907	1,143*	5.0	16.2
123 CH GOD (ANDER)	1	15	22	.1	.3
127 CH GOD (CLEVE)	3	151	190*	.8	2.7
165 CH OF NAZARENE	9	399	836	3.6	11.8
167 CHS OF CHRIST	7	267	338	1.5	4.8
175 CONGR CHR CHS	1	228	287*	1.2	4.1
193 EPISCOPAL	1	63	82	.4	1.2
207 E.L.C.A.	2	112	183	.8	2.6
221 FREE METHODIST	1	46	71	.3	1.0
223 FREE WILL BAPT	1	35	44*	.2	.6
329 OPEN BIBLE STD	1	NR	NR	-	-
355 PRESB CH (USA)	3	111	140*	.6	2.0
403 SALVATION ARMY	1	11	15	.1	.2
413 S.D.A.	1	26	33*	.1	.5
419 SO BAPT CONV	2	190	239*	1.0	3.4
438 UN BRETH IN CR	2	133	133	.6	1.9
449 UN METHODIST	23	1,381	1,740*	7.6	24.6
MERCER	**70**	**6,981**	**31,633***	**80.2**	**100.0**
053 ASSEMB OF GOD	1	53	65	.2	.2
081 CATHOLIC	20	NA	22,140	56.1	70.0
081d LATIN	*20*	*NA*	*22,140*	*56.1*	*70.0*
097 CHR CHS&CHS CR	1	150	199*	.5	.6
111 CH CR,SCIENTST	1	NR	NR	-	-
127 CH GOD (CLEVE)	1	51	68*	.2	.2
146 CH GOD MTN ASM	1	35	46*	.1	.1
157 CH OF BRETHREN	1	34	45*	.1	.1
165 CH OF NAZARENE	2	322	603	1.5	1.9
167 CHS OF CHRIST	1	17	22	.1	.1
171 CH GOD-GEN CON	5	425	564*	1.4	1.8
207 E.L.C.A.	6	1,574	2,036	5.2	6.4
215 EVAN METH CH	1	6	8*	-	-
226 FRIENDS-USA	2	21	28*	.1	.1
226e FUM	*1*	*6*	*8***	*-*	*-*
226g INDEP EVAN	*1*	*15*	*20***	*.1*	*.1*
291 MISSIONARY CH	1	227	482	1.2	1.5
296 MIDW CONGR FEL	2	68	90*	.2	.3
355 PRESB CH (USA)	2	288	382*	1.0	1.2
419 SO BAPT CONV	1	50	66*	.2	.2
438 UN BRETH IN CR	4	259	259	.7	.8
443 UN C OF CHRIST	2	441	585*	1.5	1.8
449 UN METHODIST	14	2,960	3,925*	10.0	12.4
467 WESLEYAN	1	0	20	.1	.1
MIAMI	**112**	**22,765**	**43,645***	**46.8**	**100.0**
019 AMER BAPT USA	5	1,819	2,299*	2.5	5.3
053 ASSEMB OF GOD	2	108	225	.2	.5
071 BRETHREN (ASH)	1	169	214*	.2	.5
075 BRETHREN IN CR	4	315	343	.4	.8
081 CATHOLIC	7	NA	12,530	13.4	28.7
081d LATIN	*7*	*NA*	*12,530*	*13.4*	*28.7*
097 CHR CHS&CHS CR	2	370	468*	.5	1.1
111 CH CR,SCIENTST	1	NR	NR	-	-
121 CH GOD (ABR)	3	221	279*	.3	.6
123 CH GOD (ANDER)	3	250	250	.3	.6
127 CH GOD (CLEVE)	1	81	102*	.1	.2
146 CH GOD MTN ASM	2	78	99*	.1	.2
151 L-D SAINTS	1	NA	529	.6	1.2
157 CH OF BRETHREN	9	2,047	2,587*	2.8	5.9
165 CH OF NAZARENE	5	709	1,350	1.4	3.1
167 CHS OF CHRIST	3	286	368	.4	.8
171 CH GOD-GEN CON	1	328	415*	.4	1.0
193 EPISCOPAL	2	258	480	.5	1.1
207 E.L.C.A.	8	2,384	3,071	3.3	7.0
223 FREE WILL BAPT	2	125	158*	.2	.4
226 FRIENDS-USA	2	147	186*	.2	.4
226e FUM	*2*	*147*	*186***	*.2*	*.4*
259 IFCA	2	NR	NR	-	-
291 MISSIONARY CH	2	126	125	.1	.3
296 MIDW CONGR FEL	1	24	30*	-	.1
323 OLD ORD AMISH	1	NA	150	.2	.3
329 OPEN BIBLE STD	1	NR	NR	-	-
339 PENT CH OF GOD	1	30	65	.1	.1

County and Denomination	Number of churches	Communicant, confirmed, full members	Total adherents		
			Number	Percent of total population	Percent of total adherents
355 PRESB CH (USA)	4	1,192	1,506*	1.6	3.5
403 SALVATION ARMY	1	78	82	.1	.2
413 S.D.A.	1	102	129*	.1	.3
419 SO BAPT CONV	4	1,246	1,575*	1.7	3.6
443 UN C OF CHRIST	13	4,360	5,510*	5.9	12.6
449 UN METHODIST	13	5,424	6,855*	7.4	15.7
467 WESLEYAN	2	5	5	-	-
496 JEWISH EST[1]	1	NA	600	.6	1.4
497 BLACK BAPT EST[2]	NA	483	610*	.7	1.4
499 INDEP.NON-CHAR[3]	1	NA	450	.5	1.0
MONROE	**78**	**6,333**	**9,385***	**60.6**	**100.0**
019 AMER BAPT USA	3	166	206*	1.3	2.2
040 AP CHR CH-AMER	1	29	49	.3	.5
081 CATHOLIC	4	NA	1,044	6.7	11.1
081d LATIN	*4*	*NA*	*1,044*	*6.7*	*11.1*
097 CHR CHS&CHS CR	4	415	516*	3.3	5.5
123 CH GOD (ANDER)	1	13	21	.1	.2
127 CH GOD (CLEVE)	1	48	60*	.4	.6
165 CH OF NAZARENE	1	50	104	.7	1.1
167 CHS OF CHRIST	30	1,695	2,333	15.1	24.9
221 FREE METHODIST	1	439	628	4.1	6.7
323 OLD ORD AMISH	1	NA	100	.6	1.1
355 PRESB CH (USA)	3	145	180*	1.2	1.9
419 SO BAPT CONV	1	522	649*	4.2	6.9
443 UN C OF CHRIST	6	1,162	1,445*	9.3	15.4
449 UN METHODIST	21	1,649	2,050*	13.2	21.8
MONTGOMERY	**445**	**133,331**	**277,086***	**48.3**	**100.0**
005 AME ZION	2	662	950	.2	.3
019 AMER BAPT USA	19	5,193	6,477*	1.1	2.3
053 ASSEMB OF GOD	12	2,982	7,306	1.3	2.6
071 BRETHREN (ASH)	2	403	503*	.1	.2
075 BRETHREN IN CR	2	168	168	-	.1
081 CATHOLIC	36	NA	92,390	16.1	33.3
081b BYZAN RUTH	*1*	*NA*	*100*	*-*	*-*
081d LATIN	*35*	*NA*	*92,290*	*16.1*	*33.3*
089 CHR & MISS AL	6	773	2,285	.4	.8
093 CHR CH (DISC)	4	1,278	1,653	.3	.6
097 CHR CHS&CHS CR	7	900	1,123*	.2	.4
111 CH CR,SCIENTST	3	NR	NR	-	-
121 CH GOD (ABR)	1	22	27*	-	-
123 CH GOD (ANDER)	15	2,695	2,950	.5	1.1
127 CH GOD (CLEVE)	14	2,307	2,877*	.5	1.0
145 CH GOD PROPHCY	3	108	135*	-	-
146 CH GOD MTN ASM	2	73	91*	-	-
151 L-D SAINTS	7	NA	2,774	.5	1.0
157 CH OF BRETHREN	11	2,514	3,136*	.5	1.1
165 CH OF NAZARENE	20	2,511	4,100	.7	1.5
167 CHS OF CHRIST	26	2,795	3,616	.6	1.3
191 ENTRPR BPT ASC	1	21	26*	-	-
193 EPISCOPAL	7	2,995	3,913	.7	1.4
207 E.L.C.A.	32	11,288	14,706	2.6	5.3
221 FREE METHODIST	1	35	46	-	-
223 FREE WILL BAPT	5	500	624*	.1	.2
226 FRIENDS-USA	2	77	96*	-	-
226c FGC	*1*	*39*	*49***	*-*	*-*
226e FUM	*1*	*38*	*47***	*-*	*-*
246 GREEK ORTHODOX	1	NR	NR	-	-
263 INT FOURSQ GOS	1	0	0*	-	-
274 LAT EVAN LUTH	1	89	106	-	-
283 LUTH—MO SYNOD	4	1,160	1,566	.3	.6
291 MISSIONARY CH	2	106	129	-	-
313 N AM BAPT CONF	1	196	244*	-	.1
325 OLD REG BAPT	1	15	19*	-	-
329 OPEN BIBLE STD	8	NR	NR	-	-
331 ORTH CH IN AM	1	NR	NR	-	-
339 PENT CH OF GOD	1	27	125	-	-
349 PENT HOLINESS	1	25	31*	-	-
353 CHR BRETHREN	1	25	50	-	-
355 PRESB CH (USA)	13	4,651	5,801*	1.0	2.1
356 PRESB CH AMER	1	45	85	-	-
361 PRIM BAPT ASCS	1	41	51*	-	-
403 SALVATION ARMY	2	227	255	-	.1
413 S.D.A.	4	1,773	2,211*	.4	.8
419 SO BAPT CONV	50	23,935	29,853*	5.2	10.8
435 UNITARIAN-UNIV	4	342	467	.1	.2
436 UNITED BAPT	1	20	25*	-	-
438 UN BRETH IN CR	3	312	312	.1	.1
443 UN C OF CHRIST	22	6,917	8,627*	1.5	3.1
449 UN METHODIST	57	25,093	31,297*	5.5	11.3
467 WESLEYAN	7	350	759	.1	.3
469 WELS	1	59	73	-	-
496 JEWISH EST[1]	6	NA	2,000	.3	.7
497 BLACK BAPT EST[2]	NA	27,623	34,453*	6.0	12.4
498 INDEP.CHARIS.[3]	2	NA	1,350	.2	.5
499 INDEP.NON-CHAR[3]	8	NA	5,225	.9	1.9

NA–Not applicable   NR–Not reported   *Total adherents estimated from known number of communicant, confirmed, full members.   - Represents a percent less than 0.1.   Percentages may not total due to rounding.
[1]See Appendix E   [2]See Appendix F   [3]See Appendix G   Lines in *italic* represent a breakdown of Catholic rites or Friends affiliations. They are included in their respective denominational total.

Table 4. Churches and Church Membership by County and Denomination: 1990

County and Denomination	Number of churches	Communicant, confirmed, full members	Total adherents Number	Percent of total population	Percent of total adherents
MORGAN	**42**	**4,617**	**6,439***	**45.4**	**100.0**
061 BEACHY AMISH	1	55	71*	.5	1.1
081 CATHOLIC	1	NA	359	2.5	5.6
081d LATIN	1	NA	359	2.5	5.6
093 CHR CH (DISC)	1	91	102	.7	1.6
097 CHR CHS&CHS CR	6	922	1,189*	8.4	18.5
165 CH OF NAZARENE	2	88	99	.7	1.5
167 CHS OF CHRIST	6	388	469	3.3	7.3
207 E.L.C.A.	2	90	140	1.0	2.2
221 FREE METHODIST	1	5	20	.1	.3
226 FRIENDS-USA	1	27	35*	.2	.5
226a CONSERV	1	27	35*	.2	.5
323 OLD ORD AMISH	1	NA	150	1.1	2.3
355 PRESB CH (USA)	2	173	223*	1.6	3.5
413 S.D.A.	2	750	967*	6.8	15.0
419 SO BAPT CONV	1	309	398*	2.8	6.2
449 UN METHODIST	15	1,596	2,058*	14.5	32.0
497 BLACK BAPT EST[2]	NA	123	159*	1.1	2.5
MORROW	**51**	**5,605**	**7,701***	**27.8**	**100.0**
001 ADVENT CHR CH	2	68	88*	.3	1.1
019 AMER BAPT USA	3	490	631*	2.3	8.2
081 CATHOLIC	1	NA	320	1.2	4.2
081d LATIN	1	NA	320	1.2	4.2
089 CHR & MISS AL	1	21	120	.4	1.6
097 CHR CHS&CHS CR	3	540	695*	2.5	9.0
165 CH OF NAZARENE	3	308	432	1.6	5.6
191 ENTRPR BPT ASC	2	122	157*	.6	2.0
207 E.L.C.A.	2	350	429	1.5	5.6
226 FRIENDS-USA	3	288	300	1.1	3.9
226b EFI	3	288	300	1.1	3.9
285 MENNONITE CH	2	89	129	.5	1.7
325 OLD REG BAPT	1	24	31*	.1	.4
355 PRESB CH (USA)	2	294	378*	1.4	4.9
361 PRIM BAPT ASCS	2	34	44*	.2	.6
413 S.D.A.	1	22	28*	.1	.4
419 SO BAPT CONV	1	145	187*	.7	2.4
443 UN C OF CHRIST	1	53	68*	.2	.9
449 UN METHODIST	20	2,691	3,464*	12.5	45.0
467 WESLEYAN	1	66	200	.7	2.6
MUSKINGUM	**133**	**21,441**	**37,828***	**46.1**	**100.0**
011 A.W.M.C.	1	21	27*	-	.1
019 AMER BAPT USA	7	1,458	1,844*	2.2	4.9
053 ASSEMB OF GOD	2	113	314	.4	.8
081 CATHOLIC	6	NA	8,691	10.6	23.0
081d LATIN	5	NA	8,439	10.3	22.3
081f MELKITE-GK	1	NA	252	.3	.7
089 CHR & MISS AL	2	120	325	.4	.9
093 CHR CH (DISC)	1	730	981	1.2	2.6
097 CHR CHS&CHS CR	3	500	632*	.8	1.7
111 CH CR,SCIENTST	1	NR	NR	-	-
123 CH GOD (ANDER)	2	141	166	.2	.4
151 L-D SAINTS	1	NA	379	.5	1.0
157 CH OF BRETHREN	1	98	124*	.2	.3
165 CH OF NAZARENE	5	509	762	.9	2.0
167 CHS OF CHRIST	9	628	833	1.0	2.2
179 CONSRV BAPT	1	NR	NR	-	-
193 EPISCOPAL	1	178	212	.3	.6
207 E.L.C.A.	7	1,297	1,663	2.0	4.4
221 FREE METHODIST	3	192	192	.2	.5
223 FREE WILL BAPT	1	40	51*	.1	.1
226 FRIENDS-USA	1	3	9	-	-
226c FGC	1	3	9	-	-
283 LUTH—MO SYNOD	1	982	1,251	1.5	3.3
285 MENNONITE CH	1	54	85	.1	.2
329 OPEN BIBLE STD	1	NR	NR	-	-
339 PENT CH OF GOD	2	76	214	.3	.6
355 PRESB CH (USA)	17	2,737	3,462*	4.2	9.2
356 PRESB CH AMER	1	3	3	-	-
361 PRIM BAPT ASCS	1	8	10*	-	-
403 SALVATION ARMY	1	63	69	.1	.2
413 S.D.A.	2	213	269*	.3	.7
419 SO BAPT CONV	4	492	622*	.8	1.6
443 UN C OF CHRIST	2	456	577*	.7	1.5
449 UN METHODIST	40	9,467	11,976*	14.6	31.7
467 WESLEYAN	3	100	301	.4	.8
496 JEWISH EST[1]	2	NA	120	.1	.3
497 BLACK BAPT EST[2]	NA	762	964*	1.2	2.5
499 INDEP.NON-CHAR[3]	1	NA	700	.9	1.9
NOBLE	**40**	**2,533**	**5,009***	**44.2**	**100.0**
053 ASSEMB OF GOD	1	30	45	.4	.9
081 CATHOLIC	5	NA	1,724	15.2	34.4
081d LATIN	5	NA	1,724	15.2	34.4
097 CHR CHS&CHS CR	1	400	520*	4.6	10.4

County and Denomination	Number of churches	Communicant, confirmed, full members	Total adherents Number	Percent of total population	Percent of total adherents
123 CH GOD (ANDER)	1	85	85	.7	1.7
165 CH OF NAZARENE	1	93	97	.9	1.9
167 CHS OF CHRIST	6	476	612	5.4	12.2
207 E.L.C.A.	1	104	146	1.3	2.9
221 FREE METHODIST	3	127	198	1.7	4.0
355 PRESB CH (USA)	1	147	191*	1.7	3.8
419 SO BAPT CONV	1	0	0*	-	-
443 UN C OF CHRIST	1	35	45*	.4	.9
449 UN METHODIST	18	1,036	1,346*	11.9	26.9
OTTAWA	**57**	**12,032**	**21,962***	**54.9**	**100.0**
053 ASSEMB OF GOD	1	108	213	.5	1.0
081 CATHOLIC	5	NA	5,748	14.4	26.2
081b BYZAN RUTH	1	NA	339	.8	1.5
081d LATIN	4	NA	5,409	13.5	24.6
089 CHR & MISS AL	2	125	413	1.0	1.9
093 CHR CH (DISC)	2	77	148	.4	.7
111 CH CR,SCIENTST	1	NR	NR	-	-
123 CH GOD (ANDER)	1	69	95	.2	.4
127 CH GOD (CLEVE)	1	35	43*	.1	.2
145 CH GOD PROPHCY	1	36	45*	.1	.2
165 CH OF NAZARENE	1	47	90	.2	.4
167 CHS OF CHRIST	2	45	57	.1	.3
193 EPISCOPAL	2	168	303	.8	1.4
207 E.L.C.A.	12	4,874	6,725	16.8	30.6
283 LUTH—MO SYNOD	1	315	399	1.0	1.8
331 ORTH CH IN AM	1	NR	NR	-	-
339 PENT CH OF GOD	1	35	77	.2	.4
355 PRESB CH (USA)	2	175	217*	.5	1.0
413 S.D.A.	1	263	326*	.8	1.5
419 SO BAPT CONV	3	601	744*	1.9	3.4
438 UN BRETH IN CR	2	161	168	.4	.8
443 UN C OF CHRIST	6	2,394	2,963*	7.4	13.5
449 UN METHODIST	8	2,487	3,078*	7.7	14.0
467 WESLEYAN	1	17	110	.3	.5
PAULDING	**42**	**4,937**	**9,338***	**45.6**	**100.0**
040 AP CHR CH-AMER	1	242	427	2.1	4.6
081 CATHOLIC	5	NA	2,458	12.0	26.3
081d LATIN	5	NA	2,458	12.0	26.3
093 CHR CH (DISC)	1	250	286	1.4	3.1
097 CHR CHS&CHS CR	3	225	293*	1.4	3.1
123 CH GOD (ANDER)	3	190	227	1.1	2.4
127 CH GOD (CLEVE)	1	50	65*	.3	.7
165 CH OF NAZARENE	3	348	795	3.9	8.5
167 CHS OF CHRIST	1	73	95	.5	1.0
207 E.L.C.A.	3	627	835	4.1	8.9
283 LUTH—MO SYNOD	1	194	288	1.4	3.1
355 PRESB CH (USA)	3	291	379*	1.8	4.1
419 SO BAPT CONV	1	102	133*	.6	1.4
443 UN C OF CHRIST	2	92	120*	.6	1.3
449 UN METHODIST	13	2,029	2,645*	12.9	28.3
466 WAYN TR MB ASC	1	224	292*	1.4	3.1
PERRY	**69**	**5,974**	**11,763***	**37.3**	**100.0**
019 AMER BAPT USA	3	288	372*	1.2	3.2
061 BEACHY AMISH	1	50	65*	.2	.6
081 CATHOLIC	9	NA	3,665	11.6	31.2
081d LATIN	9	NA	3,665	11.6	31.2
093 CHR CH (DISC)	2	166	414	1.3	3.5
097 CHR CHS&CHS CR	1	40	52*	.2	.4
123 CH GOD (ANDER)	1	40	40	.1	.3
157 CH OF BRETHREN	1	122	158*	.5	1.3
165 CH OF NAZARENE	1	186	255	.8	2.2
167 CHS OF CHRIST	6	290	398	1.3	3.4
207 E.L.C.A.	6	1,028	1,345	4.3	11.4
221 FREE METHODIST	1	69	74	.2	.6
285 MENNONITE CH	1	29	31	.1	.3
323 OLD ORD AMISH	1	NA	50	.2	.4
355 PRESB CH (USA)	2	128	165*	.5	1.4
419 SO BAPT CONV	1	38	49*	.2	.4
438 UN BRETH IN CR	2	160	160	.5	1.4
443 UN C OF CHRIST	3	270	349*	1.1	3.0
449 UN METHODIST	25	3,014	3,895*	12.3	33.1
467 WESLEYAN	2	56	226	.7	1.9
PICKAWAY	**55**	**10,384**	**15,784***	**32.7**	**100.0**
053 ASSEMB OF GOD	1	45	82	.2	.5
081 CATHOLIC	1	NA	1,301	2.7	8.2
081d LATIN	1	NA	1,301	2.7	8.2
097 CHR CHS&CHS CR	3	271	334*	.7	2.1
123 CH GOD (ANDER)	2	90	145	.3	.9
127 CH GOD (CLEVE)	1	115	142*	.3	.9
157 CH OF BRETHREN	1	65	80*	.2	.5
165 CH OF NAZARENE	3	524	1,228	2.5	7.8
167 CHS OF CHRIST	1	159	257	.5	1.6

NA–Not applicable   NR–Not reported   *Total adherents estimated from known number of communicant, confirmed, full members.   - Represents a percent less than 0.1.   Percentages may not total due to rounding.

[1]See Appendix E   [2]See Appendix F   [3]See Appendix G   Lines in *italic* represent a breakdown of Catholic rites or Friends affiliations. They are included in their respective denominational total.

Table 4. Churches and Church Membership by County and Denomination: 1990

County and Denomination	Number of churches	Communicant, confirmed, full members	Total adherents Number	Percent of total population	Percent of total adherents
193 EPISCOPAL	1	203	203	.4	1.3
207 E.L.C.A.	5	1,603	1,982	4.1	12.6
223 FREE WILL BAPT	1	50	62*	.1	.4
323 OLD ORD AMISH	1	NA	100	.2	.6
355 PRESB CH (USA)	2	463	570*	1.2	3.6
419 SO BAPT CONV	3	985	1,213*	2.5	7.7
449 UN METHODIST	27	4,844	5,966*	12.4	37.8
467 WESLEYAN	2	143	424	.9	2.7
496 JEWISH EST[1]	0	NA	680	1.4	4.3
497 BLACK BAPT EST[2]	NA	824	1,015*	2.1	6.4
PIKE	**38**	**3,988**	**5,603***	**23.1**	**100.0**
081 CATHOLIC	1	NA	348	1.4	6.2
081d LATIN	1	NA	348	1.4	6.2
097 CHR CHS&CHS CR	3	483	619*	2.6	11.0
127 CH GOD (CLEVE)	1	60	77*	.3	1.4
157 CH OF BRETHREN	1	33	42*	.2	.7
165 CH OF NAZARENE	1	72	225	.9	4.0
167 CHS OF CHRIST	3	191	257	1.1	4.6
191 ENTRPR BPT ASC	3	108	138*	.6	2.5
223 FREE WILL BAPT	3	350	449*	1.9	8.0
265 INT PENT C CHR	1	16	17	.1	.3
283 LUTH—MO SYNOD	1	48	58	.2	1.0
285 MENNONITE CH	1	21	33	.1	.6
355 PRESB CH (USA)	1	270	346*	1.4	6.2
361 PRIM BAPT ASCS	1	29	37*	.2	.7
419 SO BAPT CONV	2	925	1,186*	4.9	21.2
436 UNITED BAPT	5	269	345*	1.4	6.2
443 UN C OF CHRIST	1	19	24*	.1	.4
449 UN METHODIST	9	1,094	1,402*	5.8	25.0
PORTAGE	**95**	**15,751**	**45,162***	**31.7**	**100.0**
019 AMER BAPT USA	1	150	186*	.1	.4
053 ASSEMB OF GOD	4	584	1,373	1.0	3.0
075 BRETHREN IN CR	1	62	62	-	.1
081 CATHOLIC	11	NA	20,424	14.3	45.2
081d LATIN	11	NA	20,424	14.3	45.2
089 CHR & MISS AL	3	273	519	.4	1.1
093 CHR CH (DISC)	6	1,286	1,969	1.4	4.4
097 CHR CHS&CHS CR	1	60	74*	.1	.2
111 CH CR,SCIENTST	1	NR	NR	-	-
123 CH GOD (ANDER)	4	306	318	.2	.7
127 CH GOD (CLEVE)	2	220	272*	.2	.6
145 CH GOD PROPHCY	1	36	45*	-	.1
146 CH GOD MTN ASM	1	3	4*	-	-
151 L-D SAINTS	1	NA	403	.3	.9
157 CH OF BRETHREN	1	143	177*	.1	.4
165 CH OF NAZARENE	4	402	553	.4	1.2
167 CHS OF CHRIST	4	305	453	.3	1.0
193 EPISCOPAL	2	431	538	.4	1.2
203 EVAN FREE CH	1	135	190	.1	.4
207 E.L.C.A.	3	944	1,345	.9	3.0
221 FREE METHODIST	1	12	21	-	-
226 FRIENDS-USA	2	136	206*	.1	.5
226b EFI	1	96	156*	.1	.3
226c FGC	1	40	50*	-	.1
283 LUTH—MO SYNOD	3	877	1,245	.9	2.8
285 MENNONITE CH	1	109	135	.1	.3
331 ORTH CH IN AM	1	NR	NR	-	-
355 PRESB CH (USA)	1	347	430*	.3	1.0
363 PRIMITIVE METH	1	95	119	.1	.3
413 S.D.A.	1	31	38*	-	.1
419 SO BAPT CONV	5	537	665*	.5	1.5
435 UNITARIAN-UNIV	1	72	108	.1	.2
443 UN C OF CHRIST	7	2,403	2,975*	2.1	6.6
449 UN METHODIST	16	4,732	5,858*	4.1	13.0
496 JEWISH EST[1]	0	NA	1,320	.9	2.9
497 BLACK BAPT EST[2]	NA	1,060	1,312*	.9	2.9
498 INDEP.CHARIS.[3]	2	NA	1,025	.7	2.3
499 INDEP.NON-CHAR[3]	1	NA	800	.6	1.8
PREBLE	**68**	**10,525**	**15,921***	**39.7**	**100.0**
053 ASSEMB OF GOD	1	46	65	.2	.4
071 BRETHREN (ASH)	2	261	333*	.8	2.1
081 CATHOLIC	3	NA	1,970	4.9	12.4
081d LATIN	3	NA	1,970	4.9	12.4
097 CHR CHS&CHS CR	3	385	491*	1.2	3.1
123 CH GOD (ANDER)	3	302	366	.9	2.3
127 CH GOD (CLEVE)	3	256	326*	.8	2.0
157 CH OF BRETHREN	6	1,407	1,794*	4.5	11.3
165 CH OF NAZARENE	1	91	223	.6	1.4
167 CHS OF CHRIST	2	90	114	.3	.7
176 CCC, NOT NAT'L	1	35	45*	.1	.3
207 E.L.C.A.	6	1,550	2,063	5.1	13.0
226 FRIENDS-USA	1	90	115*	.3	.7
226e FUM	1	90	115*	.3	.7

County and Denomination	Number of churches	Communicant, confirmed, full members	Total adherents Number	Percent of total population	Percent of total adherents
355 PRESB CH (USA)	4	450	574*	1.4	3.6
413 S.D.A.	1	80	102*	.3	.6
419 SO BAPT CONV	9	2,252	2,871*	7.2	18.0
443 UN C OF CHRIST	7	1,086	1,385*	3.5	8.7
449 UN METHODIST	14	2,144	2,734*	6.8	17.2
499 INDEP.NON-CHAR[3]	1	NA	350	.9	2.2
PUTNAM	**55**	**4,703**	**23,457***	**69.4**	**100.0**
053 ASSEMB OF GOD	1	30	40	.1	.2
081 CATHOLIC	15	NA	16,696	49.4	71.2
081d LATIN	15	NA	16,696	49.4	71.2
093 CHR CH (DISC)	1	115	153	.5	.7
097 CHR CHS&CHS CR	1	50	67*	.2	.3
123 CH GOD (ANDER)	1	0	27	.1	.1
127 CH GOD (CLEVE)	1	5	7*	-	-
157 CH OF BRETHREN	1	273	366*	1.1	1.6
165 CH OF NAZARENE	1	52	87	.3	.4
207 E.L.C.A.	3	295	387	1.1	1.6
221 FREE METHODIST	1	25	27	.1	.1
285 MENNONITE CH	1	64	149	.4	.6
287 MENN GEN CONF	2	644	1,159	3.4	4.9
291 MISSIONARY CH	2	111	158	.5	.7
339 PENT CH OF GOD	2	48	127	.4	.5
355 PRESB CH (USA)	2	224	300*	.9	1.3
361 PRIM BAPT ASCS	1	16	21*	.1	.1
413 S.D.A.	1	43	58*	.2	.2
443 UN C OF CHRIST	1	235	315*	.9	1.3
449 UN METHODIST	16	2,403	3,219*	9.5	13.7
466 WAYN TR MB ASC	1	70	94*	.3	.4
RICHLAND	**147**	**28,832**	**50,985***	**40.4**	**100.0**
005 AME ZION	1	155	186	.1	.4
019 AMER BAPT USA	4	745	933*	.7	1.8
039 AP CHR CH(NAZ)	2	503	630*	.5	1.2
040 AP CHR CH-AMER	1	124	219	.2	.4
053 ASSEMB OF GOD	2	238	430	.3	.8
057 BAPT GEN CONF	1	297	372*	.3	.7
071 BRETHREN (ASH)	1	23	29*	-	.1
081 CATHOLIC	5	NA	10,372	8.2	20.3
081d LATIN	5	NA	10,372	8.2	20.3
089 CHR & MISS AL	4	936	1,389	1.1	2.7
093 CHR CH (DISC)	4	939	1,742	1.4	3.4
097 CHR CHS&CHS CR	4	641	803*	.6	1.6
111 CH CR,SCIENTST	1	NR	NR	-	-
123 CH GOD (ANDER)	3	367	480	.4	.9
127 CH GOD (CLEVE)	4	779	976*	.8	1.9
145 CH GOD PROPHCY	1	36	45*	-	.1
151 L-D SAINTS	2	NA	551	.4	1.1
157 CH OF BRETHREN	3	303	380*	.3	.7
165 CH OF NAZARENE	4	363	649	.5	1.3
167 CHS OF CHRIST	6	397	515	.4	1.0
171 CH GOD-GEN CON	1	97	122*	.1	.2
175 CONGR CHR CHS	2	980	1,228*	1.0	2.4
179 CONSRV BAPT	1	NR	NR	-	-
193 EPISCOPAL	2	611	1,007	.8	2.0
199 EVAN CONGR CH	1	61	61	-	.1
203 EVAN FREE CH	1	20	60	-	.1
207 E.L.C.A.	18	6,477	8,255	6.5	16.2
221 FREE METHODIST	1	170	170	.1	.3
223 FREE WILL BAPT	3	350	439*	.3	.9
226 FRIENDS-USA	2	34	66	.1	.1
226b EFI	1	31	52	-	.1
226c FGC	1	3	14	-	-
246 GREEK ORTHODOX	1	NR	NR	-	-
259 IFCA	2	NR	NR	-	-
263 INT FOURSQ GOS	2	177	222*	.2	.4
283 LUTH—MO SYNOD	1	57	78	.1	.2
323 OLD ORD AMISH	1	NA	150	.1	.3
325 OLD REG BAPT	1	59	74*	.1	.1
329 OPEN BIBLE STD	4	NR	NR	-	-
353 CHR BRETHREN	1	20	20	-	-
355 PRESB CH (USA)	7	1,981	2,482*	2.0	4.9
403 SALVATION ARMY	1	85	92	.1	.2
413 S.D.A.	2	189	237*	.2	.5
419 SO BAPT CONV	6	1,065	1,334*	1.1	2.6
435 UNITARIAN-UNIV	1	20	26	-	.1
436 UNITED BAPT	2	63	79*	.1	.2
443 UN C OF CHRIST	4	1,215	1,522*	1.2	3.0
449 UN METHODIST	20	5,485	6,872*	5.4	13.5
467 WESLEYAN	1	62	145	.1	.3
496 JEWISH EST[1]	2	NA	250	.2	.5
497 BLACK BAPT EST[2]	NA	2,708	3,393*	2.7	6.7
498 INDEP.CHARIS.[3]	1	NA	350	.3	.7
499 INDEP.NON-CHAR[3]	2	NA	1,550	1.2	3.0

Table 4. Churches and Church Membership by County and Denomination: 1990

County and Denomination		Number of churches	Communicant, confirmed, full members	Total adherents		
				Number	Percent of total population	Percent of total adherents
ROSS		**84**	**13,543**	**20,121***	**29.0**	**100.0**
019	AMER BAPT USA	1	1,164	1,443*	2.1	7.2
053	ASSEMB OF GOD	1	60	159	.2	.8
081	CATHOLIC	2	NA	2,347	3.4	11.7
081d	*LATIN*	*2*	*NA*	*2,347*	*3.4*	*11.7*
093	CHR CH (DISC)	1	78	184	.3	.9
097	CHR CHS&CHS CR	3	461	572*	.8	2.8
111	CH CR,SCIENTST	1	NR	NR	-	-
123	CH GOD (ANDER)	2	175	271	.4	1.3
127	CH GOD (CLEVE)	3	260	322*	.5	1.6
145	CH GOD PROPHCY	1	36	45*	.1	.2
151	L-D SAINTS	1	NA	184	.3	.9
157	CH OF BRETHREN	1	25	31*	-	.2
165	CH OF NAZARENE	4	405	643	.9	3.2
167	CHS OF CHRIST	2	164	234	.3	1.2
175	CONGR CHR CHS	1	276	342*	.5	1.7
191	ENTRPR BPT ASC	2	177	219*	.3	1.1
193	EPISCOPAL	1	190	355	.5	1.8
207	E.L.C.A.	1	421	526	.8	2.6
223	FREE WILL BAPT	2	175	217*	.3	1.1
226	FRIENDS-USA	1	15	19*	-	.1
226e	*FUM*	*1*	*15*	*19**	*-*	*.1*
265	INT PENT C CHR	2	33	51	.1	.3
283	LUTH—MO SYNOD	1	115	153	.2	.8
329	OPEN BIBLE STD	1	NR	NR	-	-
355	PRESB CH (USA)	7	1,090	1,351*	1.9	6.7
403	SALVATION ARMY	1	105	110	.2	.5
413	S.D.A.	1	161	200*	.3	1.0
419	SO BAPT CONV	2	1,125	1,395*	2.0	6.9
436	UNITED BAPT	1	66	82*	.1	.4
438	UN BRETH IN CR	1	25	25	-	.1
443	UN C OF CHRIST	2	400	496*	.7	2.5
449	UN METHODIST	32	5,059	6,273*	9.0	31.2
467	WESLEYAN	2	300	654	.9	3.3
497	BLACK BAPT EST[2]	NA	982	1,218*	1.8	6.1
SANDUSKY		**75**	**14,595**	**31,446***	**50.7**	**100.0**
053	ASSEMB OF GOD	4	222	514	.8	1.6
071	BRETHREN (ASH)	1	38	49*	.1	.2
081	CATHOLIC	8	NA	11,693	18.9	37.2
081d	*LATIN*	*8*	*NA*	*11,693*	*18.9*	*37.2*
089	CHR & MISS AL	1	66	169	.3	.5
093	CHR CH (DISC)	2	203	298	.5	.9
097	CHR CHS&CHS CR	1	100	128*	.2	.4
111	CH CR,SCIENTST	1	NR	NR	-	-
123	CH GOD (ANDER)	1	25	55	.1	.2
127	CH GOD (CLEVE)	2	142	182*	.3	.6
145	CH GOD PROPHCY	1	36	46*	.1	.1
151	L-D SAINTS	1	NA	165	.3	.5
165	CH OF NAZARENE	3	189	290	.5	.9
167	CHS OF CHRIST	3	118	152	.2	.5
193	EPISCOPAL	2	339	489	.8	1.6
207	E.L.C.A.	11	5,511	7,376	11.9	23.5
223	FREE WILL BAPT	1	60	77*	.1	.2
285	MENNONITE CH	1	19	49	.1	.2
291	MISSIONARY CH	1	67	128	.2	.4
313	N AM BAPT CONF	1	85	109*	.2	.3
329	OPEN BIBLE STD	1	NR	NR	-	-
353	CHR BRETHREN	1	23	50	.1	.2
355	PRESB CH (USA)	3	791	1,014*	1.6	3.2
413	S.D.A.	1	28	36*	.1	.1
419	SO BAPT CONV	4	826	1,058*	1.7	3.4
443	UN C OF CHRIST	2	819	1,050*	1.7	3.3
449	UN METHODIST	15	4,516	5,787*	9.3	18.4
467	WESLEYAN	1	31	45	.1	.1
496	JEWISH EST[1]	1	NA	0	-	-
497	BLACK BAPT EST[2]	NA	341	437*	.7	1.4
SCIOTO		**135**	**14,254**	**22,086***	**27.5**	**100.0**
019	AMER BAPT USA	1	402	505*	.6	2.3
053	ASSEMB OF GOD	1	36	115	.1	.5
081	CATHOLIC	7	NA	3,281	4.1	14.9
081d	*LATIN*	*7*	*NA*	*3,281*	*4.1*	*14.9*
093	CHR CH (DISC)	1	251	318	.4	1.4
097	CHR CHS&CHS CR	8	1,795	2,256*	2.8	10.2
123	CH GOD (ANDER)	2	55	179	.2	.8
127	CH GOD (CLEVE)	5	664	834*	1.0	3.8
145	CH GOD PROPHCY	2	72	90*	.1	.4
151	L-D SAINTS	1	NA	269	.3	1.2
165	CH OF NAZARENE	10	1,334	1,987	2.5	9.0
167	CHS OF CHRIST	7	363	485	.6	2.2
191	ENTRPR BPT ASC	2	46	58*	.1	.3
193	EPISCOPAL	1	184	227	.3	1.0
207	E.L.C.A.	2	341	446	.6	2.0
223	FREE WILL BAPT	28	1,500	1,885*	2.3	8.5
265	INT PENT C CHR	4	65	163	.2	.7

County and Denomination		Number of churches	Communicant, confirmed, full members	Total adherents		
				Number	Percent of total population	Percent of total adherents
355	PRESB CH (USA)	3	821	1,032*	1.3	4.7
403	SALVATION ARMY	1	85	99	.1	.4
413	S.D.A.	1	124	156*	.2	.7
419	SO BAPT CONV	2	163	205*	.3	.9
436	UNITED BAPT	5	353	444*	.6	2.0
443	UN C OF CHRIST	1	430	540*	.7	2.4
449	UN METHODIST	37	4,546	5,713*	7.1	25.9
467	WESLEYAN	2	84	120	.1	.5
496	JEWISH EST[1]	1	NA	0	-	-
497	BLACK BAPT EST[2]	NA	540	679*	.8	3.1
SENECA		**93**	**14,297**	**35,371***	**59.2**	**100.0**
019	AMER BAPT USA	2	237	305*	.5	.9
053	ASSEMB OF GOD	2	141	339	.6	1.0
081	CATHOLIC	15	NA	16,375	27.4	46.3
081d	*LATIN*	*15*	*NA*	*16,375*	*27.4*	*46.3*
089	CHR & MISS AL	1	62	107	.2	.3
093	CHR CH (DISC)	2	272	382	.6	1.1
097	CHR CHS&CHS CR	2	275	354*	.6	1.0
111	CH CR,SCIENTST	1	NR	NR	-	-
127	CH GOD (CLEVE)	1	34	44*	.1	.1
145	CH GOD PROPHCY	2	72	93*	.2	.3
151	L-D SAINTS	1	NA	168	.3	.5
157	CH OF BRETHREN	2	68	87*	.1	.2
165	CH OF NAZARENE	2	514	580	1.0	1.6
167	CHS OF CHRIST	2	76	98	.2	.3
171	CH GOD-GEN CON	1	60	77*	.1	.2
193	EPISCOPAL	2	286	337	.6	1.0
207	E.L.C.A.	4	2,055	2,915	4.9	8.2
263	INT FOURSQ GOS	2	237	305*	.5	.9
283	LUTH—MO SYNOD	1	108	167	.3	.5
325	OLD REG BAPT	1	21	27*	-	.1
339	PENT CH OF GOD	2	69	154	.3	.4
355	PRESB CH (USA)	2	632	813*	1.4	2.3
361	PRIM BAPT ASCS	1	9	12*	-	-
403	SALVATION ARMY	1	69	70	.1	.2
419	SO BAPT CONV	1	56	72*	.1	.2
436	UNITED BAPT	1	28	36*	.1	.1
438	UN BRETH IN CR	1	35	35	.1	.1
443	UN C OF CHRIST	14	3,517	4,522*	7.6	12.8
449	UN METHODIST	23	5,106	6,565*	11.0	18.6
466	WAYN TR MB ASC	1	0	0*	-	-
497	BLACK BAPT EST[2]	NA	258	332*	.6	.9
SHELBY		**57**	**10,018**	**27,089***	**60.3**	**100.0**
019	AMER BAPT USA	3	538	703*	1.6	2.6
053	ASSEMB OF GOD	1	69	74	.2	.3
081	CATHOLIC	8	NA	13,330	29.7	49.2
081d	*LATIN*	*8*	*NA*	*13,330*	*29.7*	*49.2*
093	CHR CH (DISC)	1	200	367	.8	1.4
097	CHR CHS&CHS CR	1	80	105*	.2	.4
111	CH CR,SCIENTST	1	NR	NR	-	-
123	CH GOD (ANDER)	1	181	333	.7	1.2
127	CH GOD (CLEVE)	1	203	265*	.6	1.0
146	CH GOD MTN ASM	1	89	116*	.3	.4
157	CH OF BRETHREN	1	99	129*	.3	.5
165	CH OF NAZARENE	2	132	375	.8	1.4
193	EPISCOPAL	1	66	119	.3	.4
207	E.L.C.A.	6	2,673	3,519	7.8	13.0
283	LUTH—MO SYNOD	1	46	55	.1	.2
291	MISSIONARY CH	1	41	106	.2	.4
296	MIDW CONGR FEL	1	90	118*	.3	.4
329	OPEN BIBLE STD	1	NR	NR	-	-
355	PRESB CH (USA)	1	364	476*	1.1	1.8
403	SALVATION ARMY	1	79	91	.2	.3
419	SO BAPT CONV	4	832	1,088*	2.4	4.0
436	UNITED BAPT	2	237	310*	.7	1.1
443	UN C OF CHRIST	4	1,037	1,356*	3.0	5.0
449	UN METHODIST	12	2,814	3,680*	8.2	13.6
467	WESLEYAN	1	13	197	.4	.7
497	BLACK BAPT EST[2]	NA	135	177*	.4	.7
STARK		**339**	**84,569**	**181,494***	**49.4**	**100.0**
005	AME ZION	1	394	488	.1	.3
011	A.W.M.C.	8	171	213*	.1	.1
019	AMER BAPT USA	8	2,338	2,909*	.8	1.6
053	ASSEMB OF GOD	10	1,162	1,846	.5	1.0
061	BEACHY AMISH	1	110	137*	-	.1
071	BRETHREN (ASH)	3	293	365*	.1	.2
075	BRETHREN IN CR	3	177	188	.1	.1
081	CATHOLIC	31	NA	59,350	16.1	32.7
081d	*LATIN*	*28*	*NA*	*58,608*	*15.9*	*32.3*
081g	*ROMANIAN*	*2*	*NA*	*644*	*.2*	*.4*
081h	*UKRAINIAN*	*1*	*NA*	*98*	*-*	*.1*
089	CHR & MISS AL	3	258	443	.1	.2
093	CHR CH (DISC)	4	2,073	2,783	.8	1.5

NA–Not applicable NR–Not reported *Total adherents estimated from known number of communicant, confirmed, full members. - Represents a percent less than 0.1. Percentages may not total due to rounding.
[1]See Appendix E [2]See Appendix F [3]See Appendix G Lines in *italic* represent a breakdown of Catholic rites or Friends affiliations. They are included in their respective denominational total.

Table 4. Churches and Church Membership by County and Denomination: 1990

County and Denomination	Number of churches	Communicant, confirmed, full members	Total adherents		
			Number	Percent of total population	Percent of total adherents
097 CHR CHS&CHS CR	16	7,310	9,096*	2.5	5.0
111 CH CR,SCIENTST	3	NR	NR	-	-
123 CH GOD (ANDER)	9	863	1,073	.3	.6
127 CH GOD (CLEVE)	6	931	1,158*	.3	.6
145 CH GOD PROPHCY	1	36	45*	-	-
151 L-D SAINTS	2	NA	721	.2	.4
157 CH OF BRETHREN	9	1,421	1,768*	.5	1.0
165 CH OF NAZARENE	12	1,866	2,540	.7	1.4
167 CHS OF CHRIST	17	2,153	2,815	.8	1.6
171 CH GOD-GEN CON	1	17	21*	-	-
179 CONSRV BAPT	1	NR	NR	-	-
181 CONSRV CONGR	2	331	412*	.1	.2
193 EPISCOPAL	5	1,916	2,518	.7	1.4
199 EVAN CONGR CH	1	56	74	-	-
207 E.L.C.A.	26	9,757	13,196	3.6	7.3
221 FREE METHODIST	2	126	146	-	.1
226 FRIENDS-USA	4	1,315	1,572	.4	.9
226b EFI	*4*	*1,315*	*1,572*	*.4*	*.9*
246 GREEK ORTHODOX	3	NR	NR	-	-
263 INT FOURSQ GOS	2	184	229*	.1	.1
265 INT PENT C CHR	1	66	166	-	.1
274 LAT EVAN LUTH	1	20	21	-	-
283 LUTH—MO SYNOD	3	1,125	1,492	.4	.8
285 MENNONITE CH	14	1,743	2,289	.6	1.3
323 OLD ORD AMISH	2	NA	300	.1	.2
329 OPEN BIBLE STD	1	NR	NR	-	-
331 ORTH CH IN AM	2	NR	NR	-	-
339 PENT CH OF GOD	1	34	77	-	-
355 PRESB CH (USA)	14	6,510	8,100*	2.2	4.5
397 ROMANIAN ORTH	1	NR	NR	-	-
403 SALVATION ARMY	3	443	500	.1	.3
413 S.D.A.	2	285	355*	.1	.2
419 SO BAPT CONV	3	600	747*	.2	.4
443 UN C OF CHRIST	25	10,565	13,146*	3.6	7.2
449 UN METHODIST	58	21,085	26,235*	7.1	14.5
467 WESLEYAN	1	38	71	-	-
496 JEWISH EST[1]	4	NA	2,232	.6	1.2
497 BLACK BAPT EST[2]	NA	6,797	8,457*	2.3	4.7
498 INDEP.CHARIS.[3]	.2	NA	1,120	.3	.6
499 INDEP.NON-CHAR[3]	7	NA	10,080	2.7	5.6
SUMMIT	**388**	**98,477**	**268,050***	**52.0**	**100.0**
005 AME ZION	1	1,522	2,244	.4	.8
011 A.W.M.C.	4	53	66*	-	-
019 AMER BAPT USA	13	4,462	5,528*	1.1	2.1
022 EASTERN ORTH	1	52	52	-	-
039 AP CHR CH(NAZ)	5	491	608*	.1	.2
040 AP CHR CH-AMER	1	86	151	-	.1
053 ASSEMB OF GOD	14	1,833	3,536	.7	1.3
057 BAPT GEN CONF	1	82	102*	-	-
081 CATHOLIC	43	NA	98,600	19.1	36.8
081b BYZAN RUTH	*2*	*NA*	*662*	*.1*	*.2*
081d LATIN	*38*	*NA*	*95,510*	*18.5*	*35.6*
081e MARONITE	*1*	*NA*	*1,216*	*.2*	*.5*
081f MELKITE-GK	*1*	*NA*	*800*	*.2*	*.3*
081h UKRAINIAN	*1*	*NA*	*412*	*.1*	*.2*
089 CHR & MISS AL	12	1,399	3,169	.6	1.2
093 CHR CH (DISC)	15	3,898	5,279	1.0	2.0
097 CHR CHS&CHS CR	15	3,957	4,903*	1.0	1.8
105 CHRISTIAN REF	1	93	99	-	-
111 CH CR,SCIENTST	3	NR	NR	-	-
123 CH GOD (ANDER)	9	874	999	.2	.4
127 CH GOD (CLEVE)	6	682	845*	.2	.3
145 CH GOD PROPHCY	1	36	45*	-	-
146 CH GOD MTN ASM	1	51	63*	-	-
151 L-D SAINTS	2	NA	1,107	.2	.4
157 CH OF BRETHREN	3	507	628*	.1	.2
165 CH OF NAZARENE	15	2,248	2,850	.6	1.1
167 CHS OF CHRIST	15	1,747	2,208	.4	.8
175 CONGR CHR CHS	1	963	1,193*	.2	.4
179 CONSRV BAPT	2	NR	NR	-	-
181 CONSRV CONGR	1	67	83*	-	-
193 EPISCOPAL	11	4,313	5,852	1.1	2.2
199 EVAN CONGR CH	4	484	624	.1	.2
203 EVAN FREE CH	1	0	0	-	-
207 E.L.C.A.	17	6,190	8,154	1.6	3.0
221 FREE METHODIST	1	131	252	-	.1
223 FREE WILL BAPT	2	250	310*	.1	.1
226 FRIENDS-USA	4	234	286*	.1	.1
226b EFI	*3*	*199*	*243*	*-*	*.1*
226c FGC	*1*	*35*	*43*$	*-*	*-*
246 GREEK ORTHODOX	1	NR	NR	-	-
259 IFCA	1	NR	NR	-	-
263 INT FOURSQ GOS	3	545	675*	.1	.3
265 INT PENT C CHR	1	113	178	-	.1
283 LUTH—MO SYNOD	12	4,925	6,443	1.3	2.4
285 MENNONITE CH	1	33	33	-	-

County and Denomination	Number of churches	Communicant, confirmed, full members	Total adherents		
			Number	Percent of total population	Percent of total adherents
320 "OLD" MB ASCS	1	69	85*	-	-
325 OLD REG BAPT	1	18	22*	-	-
329 OPEN BIBLE STD	1	NR	NR	-	-
331 ORTH CH IN AM	2	NR	NR	-	-
353 CHR BRETHREN	2	125	175	-	.1
355 PRESB CH (USA)	16	6,506	8,061*	1.6	3.0
356 PRESB CH AMER	2	145	215	-	.1
361 PRIM BAPT ASCS	1	5	6*	-	-
397 ROMANIAN ORTH	1	NR	NR	-	-
403 SALVATION ARMY	3	234	341	.1	.1
413 S.D.A.	4	877	1,087*	.2	.4
419 SO BAPT CONV	12	1,657	2,053*	.4	.8
435 UNITARIAN-UNIV	1	380	520	.1	.2
436 UNITED BAPT	1	27	33*	-	-
443 UN C OF CHRIST	23	11,126	13,785*	2.7	5.1
449 UN METHODIST	47	18,136	22,470*	4.4	8.4
467 WESLEYAN	3	191	422	.1	.2
469 WELS	1	60	93	-	-
496 JEWISH EST[1]	7	NA	4,680	.9	1.7
497 BLACK BAPT EST[2]	NA	16,600	20,567*	4.0	7.7
498 INDEP.CHARIS.[3]	3	NA	970	.2	.4
499 INDEP.NON-CHAR[3]	12	NA	35,300	6.9	13.2
TRUMBULL	**200**	**40,938**	**112,109***	**49.2**	**100.0**
011 A.W.M.C.	2	36	45*	-	-
019 AMER BAPT USA	5	876	1,086*	.5	1.0
022 EASTERN ORTH	1	148	148	.1	.1
039 AP CHR CH(NAZ)	1	29	36*	-	-
053 ASSEMB OF GOD	8	1,070	1,724	.8	1.5
081 CATHOLIC	24	NA	55,021	24.2	49.1
081b BYZAN RUTH	*2*	*NA*	*6,843*	*3.0*	*6.1*
081d LATIN	*20*	*NA*	*47,016*	*20.6*	*41.9*
081g ROMANIAN	*1*	*NA*	*322*	*.1*	*.3*
081h UKRAINIAN	*1*	*NA*	*840*	*.4*	*.7*
089 CHR & MISS AL	3	442	898	.4	.8
093 CHR CH (DISC)	16	4,614	6,868	3.0	6.1
097 CHR CHS&CHS CR	7	1,872	2,322*	1.0	2.1
111 CH CR,SCIENTST	1	NR	NR	-	-
123 CH GOD (ANDER)	7	945	1,213	.5	1.1
127 CH GOD (CLEVE)	4	490	608*	.3	.5
145 CH GOD PROPHCY	1	36	45*	-	-
151 L-D SAINTS	1	NA	347	.2	.3
157 CH OF BRETHREN	1	102	127*	.1	.1
165 CH OF NAZARENE	10	1,431	2,307	1.0	2.1
167 CHS OF CHRIST	2	476	564	.2	.5
175 CONGR CHR CHS	2	321	398*	.2	.4
179 CONSRV BAPT	1	NR	NR	-	-
193 EPISCOPAL	2	759	926	.4	.8
199 EVAN CONGR CH	2	198	407	.2	.4
207 E.L.C.A.	13	3,853	4,997	2.2	4.5
221 FREE METHODIST	1	83	102	-	.1
223 FREE WILL BAPT	2	200	248*	.1	.2
246 GREEK ORTHODOX	1	NR	NR	-	-
263 INT FOURSQ GOS	2	120	149*	.1	.1
283 LUTH—MO SYNOD	1	136	168	.1	.1
323 OLD ORD AMISH	5	NA	750	.3	.7
331 ORTH CH IN AM	1	NR	NR	-	-
355 PRESB CH (USA)	11	3,148	3,904*	1.7	3.5
397 ROMANIAN ORTH	2	NR	NR	-	-
403 SALVATION ARMY	1	153	200	.1	.2
413 S.D.A.	1	116	144*	.1	.1
419 SO BAPT CONV	15	2,398	2,974*	1.3	2.7
443 UN C OF CHRIST	4	1,718	2,131*	.9	1.9
449 UN METHODIST	36	10,986	13,625*	6.0	12.2
469 WELS	1	52	65	-	.1
496 JEWISH EST[1]	1	NA	1,740	.8	1.6
497 BLACK BAPT EST[2]	NA	4,130	5,122*	2.2	4.6
499 INDEP.NON-CHAR[3]	1	NA	700	.3	.6
TUSCARAWAS	**164**	**27,498**	**48,079***	**57.2**	**100.0**
005 AME ZION	1	100	121	.1	.3
019 AMER BAPT USA	1	217	273*	.3	.6
053 ASSEMB OF GOD	3	258	491	.6	1.0
061 BEACHY AMISH	1	115	145*	.2	.3
081 CATHOLIC	10	NA	8,257	9.8	17.2
081d LATIN	*10*	*NA*	*8,257*	*9.8*	*17.2*
089 CHR & MISS AL	2	150	382	.5	.8
093 CHR CH (DISC)	1	199	257	.3	.5
097 CHR CHS&CHS CR	4	1,431	1,803*	2.1	3.8
123 CH GOD (ANDER)	4	257	311	.4	.6
127 CH GOD (CLEVE)	6	395	498*	.6	1.0
157 CH OF BRETHREN	3	307	387*	.5	.8
165 CH OF NAZARENE	6	1,018	1,548	1.8	3.2
167 CHS OF CHRIST	6	416	550	.7	1.1
179 CONSRV BAPT	1	NR	NR	-	-
193 EPISCOPAL	1	92	146	.2	.3
207 E.L.C.A.	15	5,169	6,794	8.1	14.1

NA–Not applicable   NR–Not reported   *Total adherents estimated from known number of communicant, confirmed, full members.   - Represents a percent less than 0.1.   Percentages may not total due to rounding.
[1]See Appendix E   [2]See Appendix F   [3]See Appendix G   Lines in *italic* represent a breakdown of Catholic rites or Friends affiliations. They are included in their respective denominational total.

Table 4. Churches and Church Membership by County and Denomination: 1990

County and Denomination		Number of churches	Communicant, confirmed, full members	Total adherents		
				Number	Percent of total population	Percent of total adherents
221	FREE METHODIST	1	107	259	.3	.5
223	FREE WILL BAPT	1	30	38*	-	.1
263	INT FOURSQ GOS	4	631	795*	.9	1.7
265	INT PENT C CHR	2	46	85	.1	.2
287	MENN GEN CONF	1	247	287	.3	.6
293	MORAV CH-NORTH	6	1,759	2,233	2.7	4.6
323	OLD ORD AMISH	19	NA	2,850	3.4	5.9
355	PRESB CH (USA)	5	773	974*	1.2	2.0
403	SALVATION ARMY	1	108	138	.2	.3
413	S.D.A.	1	57	72*	.1	.1
419	SO BAPT CONV	3	336	423*	.5	.9
443	UN C OF CHRIST	15	5,665	7,138*	8.5	14.8
449	UN METHODIST	38	7,394	9,316*	11.1	19.4
467	WESLEYAN	1	84	335	.4	.7
497	BLACK BAPT EST[2]	NA	137	173*	.2	.4
499	INDEP.NON-CHAR[3]	1	NA	1,000	1.2	2.1
UNION		**42**	**8,377**	**12,663***	**39.6**	**100.0**
001	ADVENT CHR CH	1	13	16*	.1	.1
019	AMER BAPT USA	3	500	630*	2.0	5.0
053	ASSEMB OF GOD	1	22	27	.1	.2
081	CATHOLIC	2	NA	930	2.9	7.3
081d	*LATIN*	*2*	*NA*	*930*	*2.9*	*7.3*
097	CHR CHS&CHS CR	2	240	303*	.9	2.4
123	CH GOD (ANDER)	1	20	35	.1	.3
145	CH GOD PROPHCY	1	36	45*	.1	.4
165	CH OF NAZARENE	1	179	332	1.0	2.6
167	CHS OF CHRIST	2	190	242	.8	1.9
191	ENTRPR BPT ASC	1	11	14*	-	.1
207	E.L.C.A.	2	992	1,422	4.4	11.2
226	FRIENDS-USA	2	138	197	.6	1.6
226b	*EFI*	*2*	*138*	*197*	*.6*	*1.6*
263	INT FOURSQ GOS	1	49	62*	.2	.5
283	LUTH—MO SYNOD	2	1,403	1,923	6.0	15.2
355	PRESB CH (USA)	2	846	1,067*	3.3	8.4
419	SO BAPT CONV	1	167	211*	.7	1.7
443	UN C OF CHRIST	1	233	294*	.9	2.3
449	UN METHODIST	15	3,021	3,809*	11.9	30.1
496	JEWISH EST[1]	0	NA	304	1.0	2.4
497	BLACK BAPT EST[2]	NA	317	400*	1.3	3.2
499	INDEP.NON-CHAR[3]	1	NA	400	1.3	3.2
VAN WERT		**53**	**8,701**	**23,380***	**76.7**	**100.0**
053	ASSEMB OF GOD	2	214	520	1.7	2.2
081	CATHOLIC	1	NA	11,634	38.2	49.8
081d	*LATIN*	*1*	*NA*	*11,634*	*38.2*	*49.8*
097	CHR CHS&CHS CR	1	150	192*	.6	.8
123	CH GOD (ANDER)	2	120	128	.4	.5
165	CH OF NAZARENE	2	87	193	.6	.8
171	CH GOD-GEN CON	2	169	216*	.7	.9
193	EPISCOPAL	1	16	18	.1	.1
207	E.L.C.A.	4	974	1,332	4.4	5.7
226	FRIENDS-USA	3	315	701*	2.3	3.0
226b	*EFI*	*1*	*224*	*585*	*1.9*	*2.5*
226e	*FUM*	*2*	*91*	*116*	*.4*	*.5*
283	LUTH—MO SYNOD	4	1,107	1,414	4.6	6.0
285	MENNONITE CH	1	19	41	.1	.2
339	PENT CH OF GOD	1	34	76	.2	.3
355	PRESB CH (USA)	3	850	1,085*	3.6	4.6
413	S.D.A.	1	16	20*	.1	.1
419	SO BAPT CONV	1	52	66*	.2	.3
438	UN BRETH IN CR	7	368	368	1.2	1.6
443	UN C OF CHRIST	1	427	545*	1.8	2.3
449	UN METHODIST	16	3,783	4,831*	15.9	20.7
VINTON		**32**	**1,581**	**2,501***	**22.5**	**100.0**
053	ASSEMB OF GOD	1	60	85	.8	3.4
081	CATHOLIC	1	NA	171	1.5	6.8
081d	*LATIN*	*1*	*NA*	*171*	*1.5*	*6.8*
093	CHR CH (DISC)	3	119	362	3.3	14.5
165	CH OF NAZARENE	3	145	283	2.6	11.3
167	CHS OF CHRIST	2	46	59	.5	2.4
193	EPISCOPAL	1	10	24	.2	1.0
223	FREE WILL BAPT	4	300	379*	3.4	15.2
226	FRIENDS-USA	1	6	8*	.1	.3
226e	*FUM*	*1*	*6*	*8*	*.1*	*.3*
325	OLD REG BAPT	1	41	52*	.5	2.1
355	PRESB CH (USA)	2	86	109*	1.0	4.4
419	SO BAPT CONV	2	203	256*	2.3	10.2
449	UN METHODIST	11	565	713*	6.4	28.5
WARREN		**115**	**22,622**	**40,558***	**35.6**	**100.0**
011	A.W.M.C.	1	15	19*	-	-
019	AMER BAPT USA	3	915	1,163*	1.0	2.9
053	ASSEMB OF GOD	5	369	480	.4	1.2
071	BRETHREN (ASH)	1	0	0*	-	-

County and Denomination		Number of churches	Communicant, confirmed, full members	Total adherents		
				Number	Percent of total population	Percent of total adherents
081	CATHOLIC	6	NA	8,770	7.7	21.6
081d	*LATIN*	*6*	*NA*	*8,770*	*7.7*	*21.6*
097	CHR CHS&CHS CR	8	1,807	2,296*	2.0	5.7
111	CH CR,SCIENTST	1	NR	NR	-	-
123	CH GOD (ANDER)	7	327	500	.4	1.2
127	CH GOD (CLEVE)	6	1,150	1,461*	1.3	3.6
145	CH GOD PROPHCY	2	72	91*	.1	.2
151	L-D SAINTS	1	NA	439	.4	1.1
157	CH OF BRETHREN	1	63	80*	.1	.2
165	CH OF NAZARENE	5	642	1,208	1.1	3.0
167	CHS OF CHRIST	4	179	223	.2	.5
193	EPISCOPAL	3	342	505	.4	1.2
203	EVAN FREE CH	1	45	170	.1	.4
207	E.L.C.A.	3	542	786	.7	1.9
223	FREE WILL BAPT	1	50	64*	.1	.2
226	FRIENDS-USA	1	101	128*	.1	.3
226c	*FGC*	*1*	*101*	*128*	*.1*	*.3*
283	LUTH—MO SYNOD	1	139	212	.2	.5
325	OLD REG BAPT	1	17	22*	-	.1
329	OPEN BIBLE STD	1	NR	NR	-	-
355	PRESB CH (USA)	7	1,674	2,127*	1.9	5.2
413	S.D.A.	1	109	138*	.1	.3
419	SO BAPT CONV	18	8,175	10,387*	9.1	25.6
436	UNITED BAPT	1	36	46*	-	.1
443	UN C OF CHRIST	6	1,079	1,371*	1.2	3.4
449	UN METHODIST	18	4,063	5,162*	4.5	12.7
469	WELS	1	56	77	.1	.2
496	JEWISH EST[1]	0	NA	1,801	1.6	4.4
497	BLACK BAPT EST[2]	NA	655	832*	.7	2.1
WASHINGTON		**129**	**16,821**	**27,111***	**43.5**	**100.0**
019	AMER BAPT USA	10	3,127	3,903*	6.3	14.4
053	ASSEMB OF GOD	1	43	80	.1	.3
075	BRETHREN IN CR	1	5	5	-	-
081	CATHOLIC	6	NA	5,367	8.6	19.8
081d	*LATIN*	*6*	*NA*	*5,367*	*8.6*	*19.8*
093	CHR CH (DISC)	1	100	138	.2	.5
097	CHR CHS&CHS CR	6	965	1,204*	1.9	4.4
111	CH CR,SCIENTST	1	NR	NR	-	-
127	CH GOD (CLEVE)	2	196	245*	.4	.9
145	CH GOD PROPHCY	1	36	45*	.1	.2
151	L-D SAINTS	1	NA	168	.3	.6
165	CH OF NAZARENE	5	607	831	1.3	3.1
167	CHS OF CHRIST	14	1,631	2,200	3.5	8.1
181	CONSRV CONGR	1	275	343*	.6	1.3
193	EPISCOPAL	1	104	169	.3	.6
207	E.L.C.A.	1	467	615	1.0	2.3
215	EVAN METH CH	1	35	44*	.1	.2
226	FRIENDS-USA	1	4	6	-	-
226f	*INDEPENDNT*	*1*	*4*	*6*	-	-
259	IFCA	1	NR	NR	-	-
323	OLD ORD AMISH	1	NA	150	.2	.6
349	PENT HOLINESS	2	613	765*	1.2	2.8
355	PRESB CH (USA)	8	1,087	1,357*	2.2	5.0
403	SALVATION ARMY	1	67	91	.1	.3
413	S.D.A.	1	64	80*	.1	.3
419	SO BAPT CONV	3	561	700*	1.1	2.6
435	UNITARIAN-UNIV	1	50	65	.1	.2
438	UN BRETH IN CR	1	16	17	-	.1
443	UN C OF CHRIST	9	1,188	1,483*	2.4	5.5
449	UN METHODIST	41	5,188	6,475*	10.4	23.9
467	WESLEYAN	4	120	198	.3	.7
469	WELS	1	62	105	.2	.4
496	JEWISH EST[1]	NA	NA	0	-	-
497	BLACK BAPT EST[2]	NA	210	262*	.4	1.0
WAYNE		**194**	**31,121**	**58,041***	**57.2**	**100.0**
001	ADVENT CHR CH	1	20	26*	-	-
019	AMER BAPT USA	1	65	84*	.1	.1
040	AP CHR CH-AMER	2	568	1,003	1.0	1.7
053	ASSEMB OF GOD	2	338	495	.5	.9
071	BRETHREN (ASH)	1	208	268*	.3	.5
081	CATHOLIC	5	NA	7,586	7.5	13.1
081d	*LATIN*	*5*	*NA*	*7,586*	*7.5*	*13.1*
089	CHR & MISS AL	2	382	766	.8	1.3
093	CHR CH (DISC)	2	791	1,304	1.3	2.2
097	CHR CHS&CHS CR	5	1,123	1,446*	1.4	2.5
111	CH CR,SCIENTST	1	NR	NR	-	-
123	CH GOD (ANDER)	2	160	210	.2	.4
127	CH GOD (CLEVE)	3	305	393*	.4	.7
143	CG IN CR(MENN)	1	136	175*	.2	.3
145	CH GOD PROPHCY	1	36	46*	-	.1
146	CH GOD MTN ASM	1	89	115*	.1	.2
151	L-D SAINTS	1	NA	250	.2	.4
157	CH OF BRETHREN	5	831	1,070*	1.1	1.8
165	CH OF NAZARENE	4	563	779	.8	1.3
167	CHS OF CHRIST	5	256	317	.3	.5

NA–Not applicable NR–Not reported *Total adherents estimated from known number of communicant, confirmed, full members. - Represents a percent less than 0.1. Percentages may not total due to rounding.
[1]See Appendix E [2]See Appendix F [3]See Appendix G Lines in *italic* represent a breakdown of Catholic rites or Friends affiliations. They are included in their respective denominational total.

Table 4. Churches and Church Membership by County and Denomination: 1990

County and Denomination	Number of churches	Communicant, confirmed, full members	Total adherents Number	Percent of total population	Percent of total adherents
171 CH GOD-GEN CON	5	767	988*	1.0	1.7
193 EPISCOPAL	1	171	197	.2	.3
207 E.L.C.A.	11	3,488	4,694	4.6	8.1
221 FREE METHODIST	1	27	82	.1	.1
223 FREE WILL BAPT	2	125	161*	.2	.3
226 FRIENDS-USA	1	39	50*	-	.1
226c FGC	1	39	50*	-	.1
263 INT FOURSQ GOS	2	336	433*	.4	.7
283 LUTH—MO SYNOD	1	74	90	.1	.2
285 MENNONITE CH	17	3,264	4,053	4.0	7.0
287 MENN GEN CONF	2	422	558	.5	1.0
323 OLD ORD AMISH	46	NA	6,900	6.8	11.9
355 PRESB CH (USA)	12	4,903	6,314*	6.2	10.9
403 SALVATION ARMY	1	20	24	-	-
413 S.D.A.	1	132	170*	.2	.3
419 SO BAPT CONV	7	1,817	2,340*	2.3	4.0
435 UNITARIAN-UNIV	1	48	58	.1	.1
438 UN BRETH IN CR	1	35	35	-	.1
443 UN C OF CHRIST	8	2,953	3,803*	3.7	6.6
449 UN METHODIST	25	6,236	8,030*	7.9	13.8
467 WESLEYAN	1	51	88	.1	.2
496 JEWISH EST[1]	1	NA	125	.1	.2
497 BLACK BAPT EST[2]	NA	342	440*	.4	.8
499 INDEP.NON-CHAR[3]	2	NA	2,075	2.0	3.6
WILLIAMS	**65**	**11,056**	**17,958***	**48.6**	**100.0**
053 ASSEMB OF GOD	1	83	104	.3	.6
071 BRETHREN (ASH)	1	255	328*	.9	1.8
081 CATHOLIC	5	NA	3,254	8.8	18.1
081d LATIN	5	NA	3,254	8.8	18.1
089 CHR & MISS AL	2	198	415	1.1	2.3
097 CHR CHS&CHS CR	6	1,715	2,205*	6.0	12.3
151 L-D SAINTS	1	NA	160	.4	.9
157 CH OF BRETHREN	2	215	276*	.7	1.5
165 CH OF NAZARENE	3	308	506	1.4	2.8
167 CHS OF CHRIST	1	10	13	-	.1
171 CH GOD-GEN CON	2	23	30*	.1	.2
193 EPISCOPAL	1	43	88	.2	.5
207 E.L.C.A.	6	1,888	2,481	6.7	13.8
213 EVAN MENN INC	1	104	134*	.4	.7
221 FREE METHODIST	1	25	55	.1	.3
285 MENNONITE CH	2	520	571	1.5	3.2
339 PENT CH OF GOD	2	70	154	.4	.9
355 PRESB CH (USA)	6	992	1,275*	3.5	7.1
419 SO BAPT CONV	1	273	351*	.9	2.0
438 UN BRETH IN CR	6	326	405	1.1	2.3
449 UN METHODIST	15	4,008	5,153*	13.9	28.7
WOOD	**138**	**24,345**	**45,778***	**40.4**	**100.0**
019 AMER BAPT USA	1	203	251*	.2	.5
053 ASSEMB OF GOD	3	704	1,475	1.3	3.2
081 CATHOLIC	11	NA	11,077	9.8	24.2
081d LATIN	10	NA	10,977	9.7	24.0
081h UKRAINIAN	1	NA	100	.1	.2
089 CHR & MISS AL	3	344	810	.7	1.8
093 CHR CH (DISC)	4	626	993	.9	2.2
097 CHR CHS&CHS CR	5	829	1,025*	.9	2.2
123 CH GOD (ANDER)	2	145	232	.2	.5
127 CH GOD (CLEVE)	1	39	48*	-	.1
151 L-D SAINTS	2	NA	577	.5	1.3
157 CH OF BRETHREN	1	148	183*	.2	.4
165 CH OF NAZARENE	4	291	538	.5	1.2
167 CHS OF CHRIST	4	311	366	.3	.8
171 CH GOD-GEN CON	2	101	125*	.1	.3
175 CONGR CHR CHS	2	236	292*	.3	.6
193 EPISCOPAL	2	328	678	.6	1.5
207 E.L.C.A.	18	7,674	10,155	9.0	22.2
209 EVAN LUTH SYN	1	253	421	.4	.9
213 EVAN MENN INC	1	54	67*	.1	.1
223 FREE WILL BAPT	1	76	94*	.1	.2
226 FRIENDS-USA	1	3	4*	-	-
226c FGC	1	3	4*	-	-
263 INT FOURSQ GOS	4	217	268*	.2	.6
283 LUTH—MO SYNOD	1	157	212	.2	.5
285 MENNONITE CH	1	25	25	-	.1
287 MENN GEN CONF	1	0	0	-	-
291 MISSIONARY CH	1	0	32	-	.1
320 "OLD" MB ASCS	1	67	83*	.1	.2
339 PENT CH OF GOD	3	80	179	.2	.4
355 PRESB CH (USA)	10	1,440	1,780*	1.6	3.9
419 SO BAPT CONV	2	620	766*	.7	1.7
435 UNITARIAN-UNIV	1	96	136	.1	.3
438 UN BRETH IN CR	4	541	541	.5	1.2
443 UN C OF CHRIST	2	444	549*	.5	1.2
449 UN METHODIST	36	7,642	9,445*	8.3	20.6
466 WAYN TR MB ASC	1	281	347*	.3	.8
467 WESLEYAN	1	53	380	.3	.8

County and Denomination	Number of churches	Communicant, confirmed, full members	Total adherents Number	Percent of total population	Percent of total adherents
496 JEWISH EST[1]	0	NA	1,232	1.1	2.7
497 BLACK BAPT EST[2]	NA	317	392*	.3	.9
WYANDOT	**47**	**7,054**	**13,718***	**61.6**	**100.0**
019 AMER BAPT USA	1	21	27*	.1	.2
081 CATHOLIC	6	NA	4,358	19.6	31.8
081d LATIN	6	NA	4,358	19.6	31.8
123 CH GOD (ANDER)	1	19	20	.1	.1
145 CH GOD PROPHCY	1	36	46*	.2	.3
165 CH OF NAZARENE	2	233	569	2.6	4.1
167 CHS OF CHRIST	1	21	27	.1	.2
171 CH GOD-GEN CON	2	209	267*	1.2	1.9
207 E.L.C.A.	5	2,205	2,852	12.8	20.8
325 OLD REG BAPT	1	29	37*	.2	.3
339 PENT CH OF GOD	1	34	70	.3	.5
355 PRESB CH (USA)	2	272	347*	1.6	2.5
419 SO BAPT CONV	1	201	256*	1.2	1.9
443 UN C OF CHRIST	3	744	949*	4.3	6.9
449 UN METHODIST	19	3,013	3,843*	17.3	28.0
467 WESLEYAN	1	17	50	.2	.4

OKLAHOMA

County and Denomination	Number of churches	Communicant, confirmed, full members	Total adherents Number	Percent of total population	Percent of total adherents
THE STATE.....	5,707	1,473,855	2,102,290*	66.8	100.0
ADAIR	**53**	**7,022**	**9,360***	**50.8**	**100.0**
053 ASSEMB OF GOD	3	153	234	1.3	2.5
059 BAPT MISS ASSN	2	78	102*	.6	1.1
081 CATHOLIC	1	NA	75	.4	.8
081d LATIN	1	NA	75	.4	.8
097 CHR CHS&CHS CR	1	315	412*	2.2	4.4
123 CH GOD (ANDER)	1	5	5	-	.1
167 CHS OF CHRIST	6	345	436	2.4	4.7
339 PENT CH OF GOD	3	74	184	1.0	2.0
349 PENT HOLINESS	3	256	335*	1.8	3.6
355 PRESB CH (USA)	1	7	9*	-	.1
413 S.D.A.	1	23	30*	.2	.3
419 SO BAPT CONV	26	5,153	6,737*	36.6	72.0
449 UN METHODIST	5	613	801*	4.3	8.6
ALFALFA	**35**	**3,783**	**5,071***	**79.0**	**100.0**
053 ASSEMB OF GOD	2	50	64	1.0	1.3
081 CATHOLIC	2	NA	403	6.3	7.9
081d LATIN	2	NA	403	6.3	7.9
093 CHR CH (DISC)	5	491	675	10.5	13.3
097 CHR CHS&CHS CR	3	290	346*	5.4	6.8
143 CG IN CR(MENN)	1	47	56*	.9	1.1
157 CH OF BRETHREN	1	49	59*	.9	1.2
165 CH OF NAZARENE	3	77	122	1.9	2.4
167 CHS OF CHRIST	5	181	243	3.8	4.8
226 FRIENDS-USA	1	123	147*	2.3	2.9
226b EFI	1	123	147*	2.3	2.9
313 N AM BAPT CONF	1	58	69*	1.1	1.4
419 SO BAPT CONV	3	942	1,125*	17.5	22.2
443 UN C OF CHRIST	1	61	73*	1.1	1.4
449 UN METHODIST	7	1,414	1,689*	26.3	33.3
ATOKA	**54**	**8,119**	**10,340***	**80.9**	**100.0**
053 ASSEMB OF GOD	3	102	194	1.5	1.9
059 BAPT MISS ASSN	2	251	311*	2.4	3.0
081 CATHOLIC	1	NA	94	.7	.9
081d LATIN	1	NA	94	.7	.9
093 CHR CH (DISC)	1	44	62	.5	.6
133 CH GOD(7TH)DEN	1	37	50	.4	.5
165 CH OF NAZARENE	1	39	84	.7	.8
167 CHS OF CHRIST	7	463	584	4.6	5.6
185 CUMBER PRESB	3	83	83	.6	.8
223 FREE WILL BAPT	4	245	304*	2.4	2.9
339 PENT CH OF GOD	2	69	154	1.2	1.5
349 PENT HOLINESS	3	127	158*	1.2	1.5
355 PRESB CH (USA)	1	9	11*	.1	.1
419 SO BAPT CONV	20	6,166	7,651*	59.9	74.0
449 UN METHODIST	5	301	373*	2.9	3.6
497 BLACK BAPT EST[2]	NA	183	227*	1.8	2.2
BEAVER	**29**	**3,413**	**4,490***	**74.5**	**100.0**
053 ASSEMB OF GOD	1	6	10	.2	.2
081 CATHOLIC	1	NA	75	1.2	1.7
081d LATIN	1	NA	75	1.2	1.7
097 CHR CHS&CHS CR	2	340	431*	7.2	9.6

NA–Not applicable   NR–Not reported   *Total adherents estimated from known number of communicant, confirmed, full members.   - Represents a percent less than 0.1.   Percentages may not total due to rounding.
[1]See Appendix E   [2]See Appendix F   [3]See Appendix G   Lines in *italic* represent a breakdown of Catholic rites or Friends affiliations. They are included in their respective denominational total.

Table 4. Churches and Church Membership by County and Denomination: 1990

County and Denomination	Number of churches	Communicant, confirmed, full members	Total adherents Number	Percent of total population	Percent of total adherents
123 CH GOD (ANDER)	2	25	64	1.1	1.4
165 CH OF NAZARENE	2	34	88	1.5	2.0
167 CHS OF CHRIST	3	121	158	2.6	3.5
226 FRIENDS-USA	1	109	138*	2.3	3.1
226b *EFI*	*1*	*109*	*138**	*2.3*	*3.1*
237 GC MENN BR CHS	1	103	131*	2.2	2.9
283 LUTH—MO SYNOD	1	25	32	.5	.7
287 MENN GEN CONF	1	93	117	1.9	2.6
355 PRESB CH (USA)	1	28	36*	.6	.8
413 S.D.A.	1	8	10*	.2	.2
419 SO BAPT CONV	7	1,351	1,715*	28.5	38.2
449 UN METHODIST	5	1,170	1,485*	24.7	33.1
BECKHAM	**46**	**11,878**	**16,933***	**90.0**	**100.0**
053 ASSEM OF GOD	5	603	861	4.6	5.1
081 CATHOLIC	2	NA	1,476	7.8	8.7
081d *LATIN*	*2*	*NA*	*1,476*	*7.8*	*8.7*
093 CHR CH (DISC)	2	370	500	2.7	3.0
097 CHR CHS&CHS CR	1	75	97*	.5	.6
123 CH GOD (ANDER)	1	75	75	.4	.4
145 CH GOD PROPHCY	1	32	41*	.2	.2
165 CH OF NAZARENE	3	227	323	1.7	1.9
167 CHS OF CHRIST	6	966	1,176	6.3	6.9
223 FREE WILL BAPT	1	90	116*	.6	.7
257 HUTTERIAN BR	1	NA	100	.5	.6
283 LUTH—MO SYNOD	1	39	66	.4	.4
349 PENT HOLINESS	1	17	22*	.1	.1
355 PRESB CH (USA)	1	109	140*	.7	.8
413 S.D.A.	1	44	57*	.3	.3
419 SO BAPT CONV	16	7,463	9,607*	51.1	56.7
449 UN METHODIST	3	1,768	2,276*	12.1	13.4
BLAINE	**50**	**6,145**	**8,673***	**75.6**	**100.0**
019 AMER BAPT USA	2	187	240*	2.1	2.8
053 ASSEM OF GOD	6	153	214	1.9	2.5
081 CATHOLIC	3	NA	560	4.9	6.5
081d *LATIN*	*3*	*NA*	*560*	*4.9*	*6.5*
093 CHR CH (DISC)	2	166	284	2.5	3.3
097 CHR CHS&CHS CR	3	634	814*	7.1	9.4
123 CH GOD (ANDER)	2	45	49	.4	.6
165 CH OF NAZARENE	2	144	287	2.5	3.3
167 CHS OF CHRIST	4	234	280	2.4	3.2
221 FREE METHODIST	1	23	33	.3	.4
237 GC MENN BR CHS	1	47	60*	.5	.7
283 LUTH—MO SYNOD	1	142	188	1.6	2.2
285 MENNONITE CH	1	168	249	2.2	2.9
287 MENN GEN CONF	2	54	59	.5	.7
313 N AM BAPT CONF	1	93	119*	1.0	1.4
339 PENT CH OF GOD	1	34	77	.7	.9
349 PENT HOLINESS	1	11	14*	.1	.2
413 S.D.A.	2	185	237*	2.1	2.7
419 SO BAPT CONV	8	2,204	2,829*	24.7	32.6
443 UN C OF CHRIST	1	43	55*	.5	.6
449 UN METHODIST	6	1,578	2,025*	17.7	23.3
BRYAN	**86**	**16,560**	**21,451***	**66.8**	**100.0**
053 ASSEM OF GOD	5	215	469	1.5	2.2
081 CATHOLIC	1	NA	200	.6	.9
081d *LATIN*	*1*	*NA*	*200*	*.6*	*.9*
093 CHR CH (DISC)	1	276	290	.9	1.4
123 CH GOD (ANDER)	1	20	20	.1	.1
151 L-D SAINTS	1	NA	207	.6	1.0
165 CH OF NAZARENE	3	401	632	2.0	2.9
167 CHS OF CHRIST	13	1,135	1,522	4.7	7.1
193 EPISCOPAL	1	108	138	.4	.6
207 E.L.C.A.	1	170	213	.7	1.0
223 FREE WILL BAPT	3	65	81*	.3	.4
339 PENT CH OF GOD	3	88	209	.7	1.0
349 PENT HOLINESS	2	675	837*	2.6	3.9
355 PRESB CH (USA)	6	329	408*	1.3	1.9
413 S.D.A.	1	66	82*	.3	.4
419 SO BAPT CONV	36	11,333	14,060*	43.8	65.5
449 UN METHODIST	8	1,679	2,083*	6.5	9.7
CADDO	**116**	**20,034**	**27,213***	**92.1**	**100.0**
019 AMER BAPT USA	3	385	496*	1.7	1.8
053 ASSEM OF GOD	9	510	766	2.6	2.8
081 CATHOLIC	5	NA	686	2.3	2.5
081d *LATIN*	*5*	*NA*	*686*	*2.3*	*2.5*
093 CHR CH (DISC)	5	648	834	2.8	3.1
097 CHR CHS&CHS CR	8	655	844*	2.9	3.1
127 CH GOD (CLEVE)	2	259	334*	1.1	1.2
151 L-D SAINTS	1	NA	256	.9	.9
165 CH OF NAZARENE	3	213	375	1.3	1.4
167 CHS OF CHRIST	11	806	1,048	3.5	3.9
207 E.L.C.A.	2	97	150	.5	.6

County and Denomination	Number of churches	Communicant, confirmed, full members	Total adherents Number	Percent of total population	Percent of total adherents
283 LUTH—MO SYNOD	2	151	192	.6	.7
287 MENN GEN CONF	2	104	138	.5	.5
339 PENT CH OF GOD	3	81	194	.7	.7
349 PENT HOLINESS	8	720	927*	3.1	3.4
355 PRESB CH (USA)	1	71	91*	.3	.3
371 REF CH IN AM	1	64	213	.7	.8
419 SO BAPT CONV	25	11,181	14,402*	48.7	52.9
443 UN C OF CHRIST	1	76	98*	.3	.4
449 UN METHODIST	24	3,829	4,932*	16.7	18.1
497 BLACK BAPT EST[2]	NA	184	237*	.8	.9
CANADIAN	**80**	**23,116**	**36,819***	**49.5**	**100.0**
053 ASSEM OF GOD	5	696	1,531	2.1	4.2
081 CATHOLIC	5	NA	4,246	5.7	11.5
081d *LATIN*	*5*	*NA*	*4,246*	*5.7*	*11.5*
093 CHR CH (DISC)	5	654	1,287	1.7	3.5
097 CHR CHS&CHS CR	2	510	668*	.9	1.8
123 CH GOD (ANDER)	1	0	44	.1	.1
127 CH GOD (CLEVE)	1	87	114*	.2	.3
145 CH GOD PROPHCY	1	33	43*	.1	.1
151 L-D SAINTS	1	NA	259	.3	.7
165 CH OF NAZARENE	8	794	1,311	1.8	3.6
167 CHS OF CHRIST	11	1,198	1,944	2.6	5.3
193 EPISCOPAL	2	92	129	.2	.4
207 E.L.C.A.	1	245	374	.5	1.0
221 FREE METHODIST	1	12	12	-	-
223 FREE WILL BAPT	1	168	220*	.3	.6
283 LUTH—MO SYNOD	3	914	1,265	1.7	3.4
339 PENT CH OF GOD	2	70	154	.2	.4
349 PENT HOLINESS	3	338	443*	.6	1.2
355 PRESB CH (USA)	2	202	265*	.4	.7
413 S.D.A.	2	66	86*	.1	.2
419 SO BAPT CONV	14	11,479	15,038*	20.2	40.8
449 UN METHODIST	9	5,008	6,561*	8.8	17.8
496 JEWISH EST[1]	0	NA	104	.1	.3
497 BLACK BAPT EST[2]	NA	550	721*	1.0	2.0
CARTER	**92**	**26,649**	**37,046***	**86.3**	**100.0**
053 ASSEM OF GOD	8	1,187	2,555	6.0	6.9
059 BAPT MISS ASSN	1	364	461*	1.1	1.2
081 CATHOLIC	2	NA	1,900	4.4	5.1
081d *LATIN*	*2*	*NA*	*1,900*	*4.4*	*5.1*
089 CHR & MISS AL	1	7	17	-	-
093 CHR CH (DISC)	2	384	523	1.2	1.4
097 CHR CHS&CHS CR	1	100	127*	.3	.3
111 CH CR,SCIENTST	1	NR	NR	-	-
165 CH OF NAZARENE	1	142	194	.5	.5
167 CHS OF CHRIST	12	1,280	1,650	3.8	4.5
193 EPISCOPAL	1	291	355	.8	1.0
223 FREE WILL BAPT	8	1,052	1,333*	3.1	3.6
283 LUTH—MO SYNOD	1	116	151	.4	.4
339 PENT CH OF GOD	7	227	536	1.2	1.4
349 PENT HOLINESS	5	189	240*	.6	.6
355 PRESB CH (USA)	1	304	385*	.9	1.0
403 SALVATION ARMY	1	78	92	.2	.2
413 S.D.A.	1	299	379*	.9	1.0
419 SO BAPT CONV	29	14,794	18,752*	43.7	50.6
449 UN METHODIST	8	4,957	6,283*	14.6	17.0
496 JEWISH EST[1]	1	NA	0	-	-
497 BLACK BAPT EST[2]	NA	878	1,113*	2.6	3.0
CHEROKEE	**61**	**8,919**	**12,273***	**36.0**	**100.0**
053 ASSEM OF GOD	3	331	660	1.9	5.4
081 CATHOLIC	2	NA	344	1.0	2.8
081d *LATIN*	*2*	*NA*	*344*	*1.0*	*2.8*
093 CHR CH (DISC)	2	232	272	.8	2.2
097 CHR CHS&CHS CR	1	120	152*	.4	1.2
123 CH GOD (ANDER)	1	60	60	.2	.5
127 CH GOD (CLEVE)	1	54	69*	.2	.6
133 CH GOD(7TH)DEN	1	38	50	.1	.4
151 L-D SAINTS	1	NA	259	.8	2.1
165 CH OF NAZARENE	1	89	121	.4	1.0
167 CHS OF CHRIST	7	593	725	2.1	5.9
193 EPISCOPAL	1	79	102	.3	.8
203 EVAN FREE CH	1	41	107	.3	.9
223 FREE WILL BAPT	2	89	113*	.3	.9
283 LUTH—MO SYNOD	1	134	185	.5	1.5
339 PENT CH OF GOD	2	32	139	.4	1.1
349 PENT HOLINESS	2	115	146*	.4	1.2
355 PRESB CH (USA)	2	219	278*	.8	2.3
413 S.D.A.	1	37	47*	.1	.4
419 SO BAPT CONV	23	5,179	6,570*	19.3	53.5
449 UN METHODIST	6	1,477	1,874*	5.5	15.3
CHOCTAW	**62**	**10,693**	**14,215***	**92.9**	**100.0**
053 ASSEM OF GOD	4	215	573	3.7	4.0

NA–Not applicable   NR–Not reported   *Total adherents estimated from known number of communicant, confirmed, full members.   - Represents a percent less than 0.1.   Percentages may not total due to rounding.
[1]See Appendix E   [2]See Appendix F   [3]See Appendix G   Lines in *italic* represent a breakdown of Catholic rites or Friends affiliations. They are included in their respective denominational total.

Table 4. Churches and Church Membership by County and Denomination: 1990

County and Denomination	Number of churches	Communicant, confirmed, full members	Total adherents		
			Number	Percent of total population	Percent of total adherents
081 CATHOLIC	3	NA	168	1.1	1.2
081d LATIN	3	NA	168	1.1	1.2
093 CHR CH (DISC)	1	127	160	1.0	1.1
127 CH GOD (CLEVE)	1	108	138*	.9	1.0
165 CH OF NAZARENE	2	46	119	.8	.8
167 CHS OF CHRIST	8	375	489	3.2	3.4
185 CUMBER PRESB	1	25	29	.2	.2
193 EPISCOPAL	1	32	58	.4	.4
339 PENT CH OF GOD	1	34	77	.5	.5
355 PRESB CH (USA)	3	98	125*	.8	.9
413 S.D.A.	1	35	45*	.3	.3
419 SO BAPT CONV	28	8,264	10,534*	68.8	74.1
449 UN METHODIST	8	864	1,101*	7.2	7.7
497 BLACK BAPT EST[2]	NA	470	599*	3.9	4.2
CIMARRON	**18**	**2,400**	**3,190***	**96.6**	**100.0**
081 CATHOLIC	1	NA	150	4.5	4.7
081d LATIN	1	NA	150	4.5	4.7
097 CHR CHS&CHS CR	1	114	144*	4.4	4.5
123 CH GOD (ANDER)	1	22	26	.8	.8
165 CH OF NAZARENE	1	22	19	.6	.6
167 CHS OF CHRIST	2	87	107	3.2	3.4
283 LUTH—MO SYNOD	1	56	86	2.6	2.7
349 PENT HOLINESS	1	24	30*	.9	.9
419 SO BAPT CONV	5	1,261	1,597*	48.4	50.1
449 UN METHODIST	5	814	1,031*	31.2	32.3
CLEVELAND	**115**	**47,764**	**69,666***	**40.0**	**100.0**
053 ASSEMB OF GOD	5	457	655	.4	.9
059 BAPT MISS ASSN	1	883	1,115*	.6	1.6
081 CATHOLIC	4	NA	6,519	3.7	9.4
081d LATIN	4	NA	6,519	3.7	9.4
093 CHR CH (DISC)	3	1,125	1,278	.7	1.8
097 CHR CHS&CHS CR	3	818	1,033*	.6	1.5
111 CH CR,SCIENTST	1	NR	NR	-	-
123 CH GOD (ANDER)	3	492	631	.4	.9
127 CH GOD (CLEVE)	3	360	455*	.3	.7
151 L-D SAINTS	4	NA	1,172	.7	1.7
165 CH OF NAZARENE	5	529	614	.4	.9
167 CHS OF CHRIST	11	2,000	2,650	1.5	3.8
171 CH GOD-GEN CON	1	181	229*	.1	.3
193 EPISCOPAL	3	768	1,294	.7	1.9
207 E.L.C.A.	1	333	449	.3	.6
223 FREE WILL BAPT	4	574	725*	.4	1.0
226 FRIENDS-USA	1	8	18	-	-
226c FGC	1	8	18	-	-
283 LUTH—MO SYNOD	2	891	1,224	.7	1.8
339 PENT CH OF GOD	4	136	277	.2	.4
349 PENT HOLINESS	5	398	503*	.3	.7
355 PRESB CH (USA)	3	1,372	1,733*	1.0	2.5
403 SALVATION ARMY	1	44	45	-	.1
413 S.D.A.	2	174	220*	.1	.3
419 SO BAPT CONV	33	26,228	33,125*	19.0	47.5
435 UNITARIAN-UNIV	1	45	60	-	.1
449 UN METHODIST	8	8,210	10,369*	6.0	14.9
469 WELS	1	143	195	.1	.3
496 JEWISH EST[1]	0	NA	414	.2	.6
497 BLACK BAPT EST[2]	NA	1,595	2,014*	1.2	2.9
498 INDEP.CHARIS.[3]	1	NA	350	.2	.5
499 INDEP.NON-CHAR[3]	1	NA	300	.2	.4
COAL	**25**	**2,550**	**3,654***	**63.2**	**100.0**
059 BAPT MISS ASSN	1	63	79*	1.4	2.2
081 CATHOLIC	2	NA	230	4.0	6.3
081d LATIN	2	NA	230	4.0	6.3
165 CH OF NAZARENE	1	47	134	2.3	3.7
167 CHS OF CHRIST	3	180	229	4.0	6.3
171 CH GOD-GEN CON	1	32	40*	.7	1.1
185 CUMBER PRESB	1	32	35	.6	1.0
193 EPISCOPAL	1	56	58	1.0	1.6
323 OLD ORD AMISH	1	NA	150	2.6	4.1
339 PENT CH OF GOD	1	8	35	.6	1.0
349 PENT HOLINESS	1	19	24*	.4	.7
355 PRESB CH (USA)	1	21	26*	.4	.7
413 S.D.A.	1	28	35*	.6	1.0
419 SO BAPT CONV	6	1,470	1,837*	31.8	50.3
449 UN METHODIST	4	594	742*	12.8	20.3
COMANCHE	**144**	**53,964**	**76,570***	**68.7**	**100.0**
019 AMER BAPT USA	2	130	168*	.2	.2
053 ASSEMB OF GOD	15	1,653	2,162	1.9	2.8
081 CATHOLIC	4	NA	4,783	4.3	6.2
081d LATIN	4	NA	4,783	4.3	6.2
093 CHR CH (DISC)	4	670	983	.9	1.3
097 CHR CHS&CHS CR	4	1,100	1,424*	1.3	1.9
111 CH CR,SCIENTST	1	NR	NR	-	-
123 CH GOD (ANDER)	1	159	159	.1	.2
127 CH GOD (CLEVE)	5	210	272*	.2	.4
145 CH GOD PROPHCY	1	33	43*	-	.1
151 L-D SAINTS	2	NA	966	.9	1.3
165 CH OF NAZARENE	5	422	562	.5	.7
167 CHS OF CHRIST	17	1,791	2,218	2.0	2.9
193 EPISCOPAL	2	452	579	.5	.8
207 E.L.C.A.	1	89	103	.1	.1
223 FREE WILL BAPT	4	388	502*	.5	.7
237 GC MENN BR CHS	2	127	164*	.1	.2
283 LUTH—MO SYNOD	2	503	706	.6	.9
339 PENT CH OF GOD	2	68	152	.1	.2
349 PENT HOLINESS	2	253	328*	.3	.4
355 PRESB CH (USA)	4	659	853*	.8	1.1
356 PRESB CH AMER	1	81	108	.1	.1
371 REF CH IN AM	1	62	118	.1	.2
403 SALVATION ARMY	1	186	188	.2	.2
413 S.D.A.	2	331	429*	.4	.6
419 SO BAPT CONV	34	31,768	41,138*	36.9	53.7
443 UN C OF CHRIST	1	126	163*	.1	.2
449 UN METHODIST	22	6,677	8,646*	7.8	11.3
497 BLACK BAPT EST[2]	NA	6,026	7,803*	7.0	10.2
498 INDEP.CHARIS.[3]	1	NA	400	.4	.5
499 INDEP.NON-CHAR[3]	1	NA	450	.4	.6
COTTON	**27**	**4,967**	**6,370***	**95.8**	**100.0**
053 ASSEMB OF GOD	2	64	96	1.4	1.5
081 CATHOLIC	1	NA	108	1.6	1.7
081d LATIN	1	NA	108	1.6	1.7
093 CHR CH (DISC)	1	87	114	1.7	1.8
127 CH GOD (CLEVE)	1	67	83*	1.2	1.3
165 CH OF NAZARENE	2	103	155	2.3	2.4
167 CHS OF CHRIST	3	160	230	3.5	3.6
355 PRESB CH (USA)	2	62	77*	1.2	1.2
419 SO BAPT CONV	10	3,527	4,390*	66.0	68.9
449 UN METHODIST	5	897	1,117*	16.8	17.5
CRAIG	**39**	**7,567**	**9,959***	**70.6**	**100.0**
053 ASSEMB OF GOD	3	180	289	2.0	2.9
081 CATHOLIC	2	NA	430	3.0	4.3
081d LATIN	2	NA	430	3.0	4.3
093 CHR CH (DISC)	1	233	281	2.0	2.8
097 CHR CHS&CHS CR	2	255	310*	2.2	3.1
111 CH CR,SCIENTST	1	NR	NR	-	-
123 CH GOD (ANDER)	1	0	152	1.1	1.5
165 CH OF NAZARENE	1	44	164	1.2	1.6
167 CHS OF CHRIST	2	169	219	1.6	2.2
193 EPISCOPAL	1	65	78	.6	.8
223 FREE WILL BAPT	1	20	24*	.2	.2
263 INT FOURSQ GOS	3	193	234*	1.7	2.3
355 PRESB CH (USA)	1	175	212*	1.5	2.1
413 S.D.A.	1	14	17*	.1	.2
419 SO BAPT CONV	15	4,676	5,676*	40.2	57.0
449 UN METHODIST	4	1,543	1,873*	13.3	18.8
CREEK	**115**	**27,898**	**37,763***	**62.0**	**100.0**
001 ADVENT CHR CH	1	56	71*	.1	.2
053 ASSEMB OF GOD	9	1,165	1,999	3.3	5.3
059 BAPT MISS ASSN	2	170	217*	.4	.6
081 CATHOLIC	4	NA	1,000	1.6	2.6
081d LATIN	4	NA	1,000	1.6	2.6
093 CHR CH (DISC)	4	219	303	.5	.8
097 CHR CHS&CHS CR	6	1,393	1,777*	2.9	4.7
123 CH GOD (ANDER)	4	370	519	.9	1.4
145 CH GOD PROPHCY	2	65	83*	.1	.2
151 L-D SAINTS	2	NA	260	.4	.7
165 CH OF NAZARENE	4	690	887	1.5	2.3
167 CHS OF CHRIST	8	731	960	1.6	2.5
193 EPISCOPAL	1	151	177	.3	.5
223 FREE WILL BAPT	16	0	0*	-	-
339 PENT CH OF GOD	2	69	154	.3	.4
349 PENT HOLINESS	4	275	351*	.6	.9
355 PRESB CH (USA)	2	710	906*	1.5	2.4
403 SALVATION ARMY	1	55	65	.1	.2
413 S.D.A.	3	283	361*	.6	1.0
419 SO BAPT CONV	28	17,098	21,814*	35.8	57.8
449 UN METHODIST	12	3,817	4,870*	8.0	12.9
496 JEWISH EST[1]	0	NA	248	.4	.7
497 BLACK BAPT EST[2]	NA	581	741*	1.2	2.0
CUSTER	**71**	**16,816**	**23,426***	**87.1**	**100.0**
053 ASSEMB OF GOD	5	362	732	2.7	3.1
059 BAPT MISS ASSN	1	117	149*	.6	.6
061 BEACHY AMISH	1	45	57*	.2	.2
075 BRETHREN IN CR	1	148	148	.6	.6
081 CATHOLIC	3	NA	1,564	5.8	6.7

NA–Not applicable   NR–Not reported   *Total adherents estimated from known number of communicant, confirmed, full members.   - Represents a percent less than 0.1.   Percentages may not total due to rounding.
[1]See Appendix E   [2]See Appendix F   [3]See Appendix G   Lines in italic represent a breakdown of Catholic rites or Friends affiliations. They are included in their respective denominational total.

Table 4. Churches and Church Membership by County and Denomination: 1990

County and Denomination	Number of churches	Communicant, confirmed, full members	Total adherents Number	Percent of total population	Percent of total adherents
081d *LATIN*	3	NA	1,564	5.8	6.7
089 CHR & MISS AL	1	0	0	-	-
093 CHR CH (DISC)	2	361	501	1.9	2.1
097 CHR CHS&CHS CR	5	881	1,122*	4.2	4.8
123 CH GOD (ANDER)	1	229	229	.9	1.0
143 CG IN CR(MENN)	1	15	19*	.1	.1
157 CH OF BRETHREN	1	40	51*	.2	.2
165 CH OF NAZARENE	3	93	280	1.0	1.2
167 CHS OF CHRIST	6	782	1,090	4.1	4.7
185 CUMBER PRESB	1	197	218	.8	.9
193 EPISCOPAL	2	68	123	.5	.5
203 EVAN FREE CH	1	123	123	.5	.5
207 E.L.C.A.	2	348	437	1.6	1.9
223 FREE WILL BAPT	4	313	399*	1.5	1.7
237 GC MENN BR CHS	1	141	180*	.7	.8
287 MENN GEN CONF	2	171	199	.7	.8
339 PENT CH OF GOD	2	49	102	.4	.4
349 PENT HOLINESS	2	76	97*	.4	.4
355 PRESB CH (USA)	2	87	111*	.4	.5
413 S.D.A.	1	18	23*	.1	.1
419 SO BAPT CONV	11	8,391	10,684*	39.7	45.6
443 UN C OF CHRIST	1	191	243*	.9	1.0
449 UN METHODIST	8	3,342	4,255*	15.8	18.2
497 BLACK BAPT EST[2]	NA	228	290*	1.1	1.2
DELAWARE	**67**	**9,239**	**11,922***	**42.5**	**100.0**
053 ASSEM OF GOD	6	437	530	1.9	4.4
059 BAPT MISS ASSN	2	185	228*	.8	1.9
081 CATHOLIC	1	NA	214	.8	1.8
081d *LATIN*	1	NA	214	.8	1.8
097 CHR CHS&CHS CR	3	750	922*	3.3	7.7
127 CH GOD (CLEVE)	1	34	42*	.1	.4
145 CH GOD PROPHCY	1	32	39*	.1	.3
165 CH OF NAZARENE	1	14	22	.1	.2
167 CHS OF CHRIST	6	376	476	1.7	4.0
193 EPISCOPAL	1	74	101	.4	.8
207 E.L.C.A.	2	93	138	.5	1.2
223 FREE WILL BAPT	1	92	113*	.4	.9
226 FRIENDS-USA	1	61	75*	.3	.6
226e *FUM*	1	61	75*	.3	.6
259 IFCA	1	NR	NR	-	-
349 PENT HOLINESS	1	16	20*	.1	.2
355 PRESB CH (USA)	1	73	90*	.3	.8
413 S.D.A.	1	70	86*	.3	.7
419 SO BAPT CONV	31	5,511	6,778*	24.1	56.9
449 UN METHODIST	5	1,421	1,748*	6.2	14.7
499 INDEP.NON-CHAR[3]	1	NA	300	1.1	2.5
DEWEY	**43**	**3,935**	**5,352***	**96.4**	**100.0**
053 ASSEM OF GOD	5	176	286	5.2	5.3
075 BRETHREN IN CR	1	30	32	.6	.6
081 CATHOLIC	1	NA	60	1.1	1.1
081d *LATIN*	1	NA	60	1.1	1.1
093 CHR CH (DISC)	5	448	789	14.2	14.7
097 CHR CHS&CHS CR	6	672	846*	15.2	15.8
165 CH OF NAZARENE	3	108	190	3.4	3.6
167 CHS OF CHRIST	3	144	188	3.4	3.5
223 FREE WILL BAPT	2	71	89*	1.6	1.7
226 FRIENDS-USA	1	67	84*	1.5	1.6
226b *EFI*	1	67	84*	1.5	1.6
287 MENN GEN CONF	1	45	47	.8	.9
339 PENT CH OF GOD	1	3	9	.2	.2
419 SO BAPT CONV	6	1,249	1,572*	28.3	29.4
449 UN METHODIST	8	922	1,160*	20.9	21.7
ELLIS	**26**	**2,708**	**3,546***	**78.9**	**100.0**
053 ASSEM OF GOD	3	121	158	3.5	4.5
081 CATHOLIC	1	NA	75	1.7	2.1
081d *LATIN*	1	NA	75	1.7	2.1
093 CHR CH (DISC)	2	89	149	3.3	4.2
097 CHR CHS&CHS CR	1	160	198*	4.4	5.6
123 CH GOD (ANDER)	1	16	16	.4	.5
165 CH OF NAZARENE	3	125	233	5.2	6.6
167 CHS OF CHRIST	3	92	103	2.3	2.9
283 LUTH—MO SYNOD	1	64	89	2.0	2.5
313 N AM BAPT CONF	1	53	66*	1.5	1.9
413 S.D.A.	1	96	119*	2.6	3.4
419 SO BAPT CONV	4	1,165	1,441*	32.0	40.6
449 UN METHODIST	5	727	899*	20.0	25.4
GARFIELD	**90**	**26,826**	**39,280***	**69.2**	**100.0**
053 ASSEM OF GOD	5	1,074	1,628	2.9	4.1
059 BAPT MISS ASSN	1	58	73*	.1	.2
081 CATHOLIC	3	NA	4,075	7.2	10.4
081d *LATIN*	3	NA	4,075	7.2	10.4
093 CHR CH (DISC)	8	2,258	3,445	6.1	8.8

County and Denomination	Number of churches	Communicant, confirmed, full members	Total adherents Number	Percent of total population	Percent of total adherents
097 CHR CHS&CHS CR	3	1,376	1,739*	3.1	4.4
111 CH CR,SCIENTST	1	NR	NR	-	-
123 CH GOD (ANDER)	1	0	24	-	.1
127 CH GOD (CLEVE)	1	33	42*	.1	.1
145 CH GOD PROPHCY	1	33	42*	.1	.1
151 L-D SAINTS	1	NA	302	.5	.8
157 CH OF BRETHREN	1	72	91*	.2	.2
165 CH OF NAZARENE	4	601	625	1.1	1.6
167 CHS OF CHRIST	4	594	693	1.2	1.8
193 EPISCOPAL	1	259	301	.5	.8
207 E.L.C.A.	1	111	138	.2	.4
221 FREE METHODIST	1	29	29	.1	.1
223 FREE WILL BAPT	1	86	109*	.2	.3
226 FRIENDS-USA	1	15	19*	-	-
226b *EFI*	1	15	19*	-	-
237 GC MENN BR CHS	1	397	502*	.9	1.3
259 IFCA	1	NR	NR	-	-
283 LUTH—MO SYNOD	8	2,291	3,022	5.3	7.7
287 MENN GEN CONF	1	139	188	.3	.5
339 PENT CH OF GOD	1	34	76	.1	.2
349 PENT HOLINESS	2	214	270*	.5	.7
355 PRESB CH (USA)	1	760	960*	1.7	2.4
403 SALVATION ARMY	1	145	151	.3	.4
413 S.D.A.	2	200	253*	.4	.6
419 SO BAPT CONV	15	8,051	10,173*	17.9	25.9
443 UN C OF CHRIST	2	210	265*	.5	.7
449 UN METHODIST	13	7,002	8,848*	15.6	22.5
467 WESLEYAN	3	173	425	.7	1.1
497 BLACK BAPT EST[2]	NA	611	772*	1.4	2.0
GARVIN	**75**	**16,870**	**22,107***	**83.1**	**100.0**
053 ASSEM OF GOD	6	379	727	2.7	3.3
059 BAPT MISS ASSN	6	791	982*	3.7	4.4
081 CATHOLIC	2	NA	330	1.2	1.5
081d *LATIN*	2	NA	330	1.2	1.5
093 CHR CH (DISC)	2	239	340	1.3	1.5
097 CHR CHS&CHS CR	1	110	137*	.5	.6
123 CH GOD (ANDER)	1	0	136	.5	.6
127 CH GOD (CLEVE)	1	72	89*	.3	.4
145 CH GOD PROPHCY	1	33	41*	.2	.2
165 CH OF NAZARENE	2	83	153	.6	.7
167 CHS OF CHRIST	15	1,262	1,867	7.0	8.4
193 EPISCOPAL	2	53	74	.3	.3
223 FREE WILL BAPT	2	40	50*	.2	.2
339 PENT CH OF GOD	1	35	77	.3	.3
349 PENT HOLINESS	2	140	174*	.7	.8
355 PRESB CH (USA)	1	192	238*	.9	1.1
413 S.D.A.	1	35	43*	.2	.2
419 SO BAPT CONV	21	10,587	13,148*	49.4	59.5
449 UN METHODIST	8	2,641	3,280*	12.3	14.8
497 BLACK BAPT EST[2]	NA	178	221*	.8	1.0
GRADY	**83**	**21,728**	**29,700***	**71.1**	**100.0**
053 ASSEM OF GOD	6	791	1,236	3.0	4.2
059 BAPT MISS ASSN	4	432	555*	1.3	1.9
081 CATHOLIC	2	NA	651	1.6	2.2
081d *LATIN*	2	NA	651	1.6	2.2
093 CHR CH (DISC)	3	496	694	1.7	2.3
097 CHR CHS&CHS CR	3	620	796*	1.9	2.7
111 CH CR,SCIENTST	1	NR	NR	-	-
127 CH GOD (CLEVE)	1	98	126*	.3	.4
143 CG IN CR(MENN)	1	214	275*	.7	.9
151 L-D SAINTS	1	NA	129	.3	.4
165 CH OF NAZARENE	2	145	204	.5	.7
167 CHS OF CHRIST	10	1,400	1,600	3.8	5.4
193 EPISCOPAL	1	105	169	.4	.6
207 E.L.C.A.	1	53	70	.2	.2
223 FREE WILL BAPT	2	65	83*	.2	.3
283 LUTH—MO SYNOD	2	156	198	.5	.7
339 PENT CH OF GOD	3	90	229	.5	.8
349 PENT HOLINESS	2	79	101*	.2	.3
355 PRESB CH (USA)	1	158	203*	.5	.7
356 PRESB CH AMER	1	34	43	.1	.1
403 SALVATION ARMY	1	80	81	.2	.3
413 S.D.A.	1	34	44*	.1	.1
419 SO BAPT CONV	22	13,338	17,125*	41.0	57.7
449 UN METHODIST	10	2,963	3,804*	9.1	12.8
497 BLACK BAPT EST[2]	NA	377	484*	1.2	1.6
499 INDEP.NON-CHAR[3]	2	NA	800	1.9	2.7
GRANT	**38**	**4,303**	**6,032***	**106.0**	**100.0**
053 ASSEM OF GOD	4	66	105	1.8	1.7
081 CATHOLIC	3	NA	526	9.2	8.7
081d *LATIN*	3	NA	526	9.2	8.7
093 CHR CH (DISC)	5	735	998	17.5	16.5
097 CHR CHS&CHS CR	4	395	493*	8.7	8.2

NA–Not applicable   NR–Not reported   *Total adherents estimated from known number of communicant, confirmed, full members.   - Represents a percent less than 0.1.   Percentages may not total due to rounding.

[1]See Appendix E   [2]See Appendix F   [3]See Appendix G   Lines in *italic* represent a breakdown of Catholic rites or Friends affiliations. They are included in their respective denominational total.

316

Table 4. Churches and Church Membership by County and Denomination: 1990

County and Denomination	Number of churches	Communicant, confirmed, full members	Total adherents: Number	Total adherents: Percent of total population	Total adherents: Percent of total adherents
165 CH OF NAZARENE	2	68	112	2.0	1.9
167 CHS OF CHRIST	2	70	100	1.8	1.7
283 LUTH—MO SYNOD	1	41	56	1.0	.9
287 MENN GEN CONF	2	103	116	2.0	1.9
419 SO BAPT CONV	6	1,240	1,548*	27.2	25.7
443 UN C OF CHRIST	1	37	46*	.8	.8
449 UN METHODIST	8	1,548	1,932*	34.0	32.0
GREER	**25**	**4,685**	**5,897***	**89.9**	**100.0**
053 ASSEMB OF GOD	2	132	177	2.7	3.0
081 CATHOLIC	1	NA	300	4.6	5.1
081d LATIN	*1*	*NA*	*300*	*4.6*	*5.1*
093 CHR CH (DISC)	1	83	142	2.2	2.4
165 CH OF NAZARENE	1	31	65	1.0	1.1
167 CHS OF CHRIST	5	493	550	8.4	9.3
185 CUMBER PRESB	1	69	83	1.3	1.4
283 LUTH—MO SYNOD	1	112	130	2.0	2.2
419 SO BAPT CONV	7	2,975	3,516*	53.6	59.6
449 UN METHODIST	6	790	934*	14.2	15.8
HARMON	**18**	**3,187**	**4,405***	**116.1**	**100.0**
053 ASSEMB OF GOD	1	14	26	.7	.6
081 CATHOLIC	1	NA	326	8.6	7.4
081d LATIN	*1*	*NA*	*326*	*8.6*	*7.4*
165 CH OF NAZARENE	3	47	69	1.8	1.6
167 CHS OF CHRIST	4	492	639	16.8	14.5
419 SO BAPT CONV	7	2,201	2,795*	73.7	63.5
449 UN METHODIST	2	433	550*	14.5	12.5
HARPER	**17**	**2,864**	**3,803***	**93.6**	**100.0**
053 ASSEMB OF GOD	2	100	207	5.1	5.4
081 CATHOLIC	1	NA	75	1.8	2.0
081d LATIN	*1*	*NA*	*75*	*1.8*	*2.0*
093 CHR CH (DISC)	2	190	309	7.6	8.1
097 CHR CHS&CHS CR	1	200	247*	6.1	6.5
165 CH OF NAZARENE	2	25	36	.9	.9
167 CHS OF CHRIST	2	73	90	2.2	2.4
283 LUTH—MO SYNOD	1	111	161	4.0	4.2
419 SO BAPT CONV	3	1,229	1,520*	37.4	40.0
449 UN METHODIST	3	936	1,158*	28.5	30.4
HASKELL	**48**	**5,322**	**6,847***	**62.6**	**100.0**
053 ASSEMB OF GOD	5	352	632	5.8	9.2
081 CATHOLIC	1	NA	60	.5	.9
081d LATIN	*1*	*NA*	*60*	*.5*	*.9*
097 CHR CHS&CHS CR	1	50	62*	.6	.9
167 CHS OF CHRIST	4	244	275	2.5	4.0
223 FREE WILL BAPT	13	495	616*	5.6	9.0
259 IFCA	1	NR	NR	-	-
349 PENT HOLINESS	1	42	52*	.5	.8
419 SO BAPT CONV	18	3,519	4,379*	40.0	64.0
449 UN METHODIST	4	620	771*	7.0	11.3
HUGHES	**65**	**7,864**	**9,753***	**74.9**	**100.0**
001 ADVENT CHR CH	1	35	43*	.3	.4
053 ASSEMB OF GOD	3	166	244	1.9	2.5
059 BAPT MISS ASSN	2	57	70*	.5	.7
081 CATHOLIC	1	NA	125	1.0	1.3
081d LATIN	*1*	*NA*	*125*	*1.0*	*1.3*
093 CHR CH (DISC)	2	120	156	1.2	1.6
123 CH GOD (ANDER)	2	113	118	.9	1.2
145 CH GOD PROPHCY	1	32	39*	.3	.4
165 CH OF NAZARENE	2	153	158	1.2	1.6
167 CHS OF CHRIST	8	450	548	4.2	5.6
193 EPISCOPAL	1	37	49	.4	.5
223 FREE WILL BAPT	4	495	606*	4.7	6.2
263 INT FOURSQ GOS	1	6	7*	.1	.1
349 PENT HOLINESS	4	168	206*	1.6	2.1
355 PRESB CH (USA)	1	12	15*	.1	.2
419 SO BAPT CONV	21	4,799	5,874*	45.1	60.2
449 UN METHODIST	11	1,221	1,495*	11.5	15.3
JACKSON	**51**	**16,929**	**24,287***	**84.4**	**100.0**
053 ASSEMB OF GOD	5	550	681	2.4	2.8
059 BAPT MISS ASSN	1	46	60*	.2	.2
081 CATHOLIC	1	NA	1,000	3.5	4.1
081d LATIN	*1*	*NA*	*1,000*	*3.5*	*4.1*
093 CHR CH (DISC)	1	94	191	.7	.8
127 CH GOD (CLEVE)	1	76	100*	.3	.4
145 CH GOD PROPHCY	1	33	43*	.1	.2
151 L-D SAINTS	1	NA	349	1.2	1.4
165 CH OF NAZARENE	2	98	126	.4	.5
167 CHS OF CHRIST	8	955	1,242	4.3	5.1
193 EPISCOPAL	1	133	231	.8	1.0
207 E.L.C.A.	1	102	151	.5	.6
283 LUTH—MO SYNOD	1	105	154	.5	.6
349 PENT HOLINESS	1	5	7*	-	-
355 PRESB CH (USA)	1	168	221*	.8	.9
403 SALVATION ARMY	1	125	136	.5	.6
413 S.D.A.	1	63	83*	.3	.3
419 SO BAPT CONV	13	10,642	13,970*	48.6	57.5
449 UN METHODIST	8	3,073	4,034*	14.0	16.6
497 BLACK BAPT EST[2]	NA	661	868*	3.0	3.6
499 INDEP.NON-CHAR[3]	2	NA	640	2.2	2.6
JEFFERSON	**27**	**4,100**	**5,421***	**77.3**	**100.0**
053 ASSEMB OF GOD	5	309	586	8.4	10.8
081 CATHOLIC	2	NA	150	2.1	2.8
081d LATIN	*2*	*NA*	*150*	*2.1*	*2.8*
093 CHR CH (DISC)	1	42	60	.9	1.1
145 CH GOD PROPHCY	1	33	41*	.6	.8
165 CH OF NAZARENE	2	62	74	1.1	1.4
167 CHS OF CHRIST	5	444	568	8.1	10.5
413 S.D.A.	1	49	60*	.9	1.1
419 SO BAPT CONV	7	2,530	3,107*	44.3	57.3
449 UN METHODIST	3	631	775*	11.1	14.3
JOHNSTON	**45**	**5,727**	**7,319***	**73.0**	**100.0**
053 ASSEMB OF GOD	3	193	274	2.7	3.7
059 BAPT MISS ASSN	1	47	59*	.6	.8
081 CATHOLIC	1	NA	60	.6	.8
081d LATIN	*1*	*NA*	*60*	*.6*	*.8*
093 CHR CH (DISC)	1	73	104	1.0	1.4
127 CH GOD (CLEVE)	3	183	229*	2.3	3.1
145 CH GOD PROPHCY	1	32	40*	.4	.5
165 CH OF NAZARENE	2	253	341	3.4	4.7
167 CHS OF CHRIST	7	306	397	4.0	5.4
193 EPISCOPAL	1	16	16	.2	.2
223 FREE WILL BAPT	1	140	176*	1.8	2.4
349 PENT HOLINESS	1	79	99*	1.0	1.4
355 PRESB CH (USA)	2	46	58*	.6	.8
419 SO BAPT CONV	14	3,765	4,721*	47.1	64.5
449 UN METHODIST	7	594	745*	7.4	10.2
KAY	**90**	**25,775**	**37,861***	**78.8**	**100.0**
019 AMER BAPT USA	1	50	63*	.1	.2
053 ASSEMB OF GOD	4	416	719	1.5	1.9
081 CATHOLIC	4	NA	3,335	6.9	8.8
081d LATIN	*4*	*NA*	*3,335*	*6.9*	*8.8*
093 CHR CH (DISC)	9	2,921	4,606	9.6	12.2
097 CHR CHS&CHS CR	3	557	705*	1.5	1.9
123 CH GOD (ANDER)	2	132	174	.4	.5
151 L-D SAINTS	2	NA	626	1.3	1.7
165 CH OF NAZARENE	7	575	837	1.7	2.2
167 CHS OF CHRIST	6	973	1,290	2.7	3.4
193 EPISCOPAL	2	306	337	.7	.9
207 E.L.C.A.	1	177	271	.6	.7
223 FREE WILL BAPT	1	127	161*	.3	.4
259 IFCA	1	NR	NR	-	-
263 INT FOURSQ GOS	1	65	82*	.2	.2
283 LUTH—MO SYNOD	4	1,113	1,371	2.9	3.6
339 PENT CH OF GOD	2	32	74	.2	.2
349 PENT HOLINESS	3	73	92*	.2	.2
355 PRESB CH (USA)	4	1,105	1,399*	2.9	3.7
403 SALVATION ARMY	1	121	136	.3	.4
413 S.D.A.	1	43	54*	.1	.1
419 SO BAPT CONV	15	10,132	12,830*	26.7	33.9
449 UN METHODIST	13	6,598	8,355*	17.4	22.1
467 WESLEYAN	2	49	78	.2	.2
496 JEWISH EST[1]	1	NA	0	-	-
497 BLACK BAPT EST[2]	NA	210	266*	.6	.7
KINGFISHER	**43**	**6,677**	**10,968***	**83.0**	**100.0**
053 ASSEMB OF GOD	2	114	113	.9	1.0
081 CATHOLIC	4	NA	2,298	17.4	21.0
081d LATIN	*4*	*NA*	*2,298*	*17.4*	*21.0*
093 CHR CH (DISC)	5	825	1,113	8.4	10.1
097 CHR CHS&CHS CR	3	190	246*	1.9	2.2
157 CH OF BRETHREN	1	45	58*	.4	.5
165 CH OF NAZARENE	3	406	448	3.4	4.1
167 CHS OF CHRIST	2	151	255	1.9	2.3
283 LUTH—MO SYNOD	1	219	286	2.2	2.6
313 N AM BAPT CONF	1	35	45*	.3	.4
339 PENT CH OF GOD	1	34	77	.6	.7
349 PENT HOLINESS	1	145	188*	1.4	1.7
355 PRESB CH (USA)	1	96	124*	.9	1.1
419 SO BAPT CONV	10	2,406	3,114*	23.6	28.4
443 UN C OF CHRIST	3	315	408*	3.1	3.7
449 UN METHODIST	5	1,696	2,195*	16.6	20.0

NA–Not applicable NR–Not reported *Total adherents estimated from known number of communicant, confirmed, full members. - Represents a percent less than 0.1. Percentages may not total due to rounding.
[1]See Appendix E [2]See Appendix F [3]See Appendix G Lines in *italic* represent a breakdown of Catholic rites or Friends affiliations. They are included in their respective denominational total.

OKLAHOMA

Table 4. Churches and Church Membership by County and Denomination: 1990

County and Denomination	Number of churches	Communicant, confirmed, full members	Total adherents Number	Total adherents Percent of total population	Total adherents Percent of total adherents
KIOWA	**46**	**8,303**	**11,042***	**97.3**	**100.0**
019 AMER BAPT USA	2	325	411*	3.6	3.7
053 ASSEMB OF GOD	6	153	285	2.5	2.6
081 CATHOLIC	1	NA	360	3.2	3.3
081d *LATIN*	*1*	*NA*	*360*	*3.2*	*3.3*
093 CHR CH (DISC)	3	154	220	1.9	2.0
097 CHR CHS&CHS CR	2	115	145*	1.3	1.3
111 CH CR,SCIENTST	1	NR	NR	-	-
165 CH OF NAZARENE	2	28	29	.3	.3
167 CHS OF CHRIST	8	489	640	5.6	5.8
207 E.L.C.A.	1	85	109	1.0	1.0
283 LUTH—MO SYNOD	1	155	189	1.7	1.7
339 PENT CH OF GOD	2	70	154	1.4	1.4
349 PENT HOLINESS	1	102	129*	1.1	1.2
355 PRESB CH (USA)	1	68	86*	.8	.8
419 SO BAPT CONV	9	5,247	6,628*	58.4	60.0
449 UN METHODIST	6	1,164	1,470*	13.0	13.3
497 BLACK BAPT EST[2]	NA	148	187*	1.6	1.7
LATIMER	**44**	**5,093**	**6,879***	**66.6**	**100.0**
053 ASSEMB OF GOD	4	185	360	3.5	5.2
081 CATHOLIC	2	NA	163	1.6	2.4
081d *LATIN*	*2*	*NA*	*163*	*1.6*	*2.4*
097 CHR CHS&CHS CR	1	50	64*	.6	.9
145 CH GOD PROPHCY	1	33	42*	.4	.6
151 L-D SAINTS	1	NA	94	.9	1.4
165 CH OF NAZARENE	1	18	45	.4	.7
167 CHS OF CHRIST	4	147	180	1.7	2.6
185 CUMBER PRESB	1	2	2	-	-
223 FREE WILL BAPT	4	227	289*	2.8	4.2
355 PRESB CH (USA)	1	20	25*	.2	.4
419 SO BAPT CONV	19	3,949	5,027*	48.6	73.1
449 UN METHODIST	5	462	588*	5.7	8.5
LE FLORE	**148**	**20,386**	**28,496***	**65.9**	**100.0**
053 ASSEMB OF GOD	23	1,614	3,815	8.8	13.4
081 CATHOLIC	3	NA	325	.8	1.1
081d *LATIN*	*3*	*NA*	*325*	*.8*	*1.1*
093 CHR CH (DISC)	2	175	392	.9	1.4
097 CHR CHS&CHS CR	5	310	393*	.9	1.4
133 CH GOD(7TH)DEN	1	38	50	.1	.2
145 CH GOD PROPHCY	1	33	42*	.1	.1
165 CH OF NAZARENE	5	378	577	1.3	2.0
167 CHS OF CHRIST	10	541	745	1.7	2.6
171 CH GOD-GEN CON	2	40	51*	.1	.2
185 CUMBER PRESB	1	40	44	.1	.2
193 EPISCOPAL	1	20	28	.1	.1
223 FREE WILL BAPT	14	714	905*	2.1	3.2
339 PENT CH OF GOD	6	204	483	1.1	1.7
349 PENT HOLINESS	1	227	288*	.7	1.0
355 PRESB CH (USA)	5	92	117*	.3	.4
361 PRIM BAPT ASCS	1	19	24*	.1	.1
413 S.D.A.	1	10	13*	-	-
419 SO BAPT CONV	53	13,587	17,231*	39.8	60.5
449 UN METHODIST	13	2,091	2,652*	6.1	9.3
497 BLACK BAPT EST[2]	NA	253	321*	.7	1.1
LINCOLN	**76**	**11,867**	**16,616***	**56.9**	**100.0**
053 ASSEMB OF GOD	11	791	1,511	5.2	9.1
081 CATHOLIC	4	NA	867	3.0	5.2
081d *LATIN*	*4*	*NA*	*867*	*3.0*	*5.2*
093 CHR CH (DISC)	5	605	789	2.7	4.7
097 CHR CHS&CHS CR	6	494	631*	2.2	3.8
111 CH CR,SCIENTST	1	NR	NR	-	-
165 CH OF NAZARENE	5	300	386	1.3	2.3
167 CHS OF CHRIST	7	550	746	2.6	4.5
171 CH GOD-GEN CON	1	11	14*	-	.1
207 E.L.C.A.	1	76	97	.3	.6
221 FREE METHODIST	1	31	35	.1	.2
223 FREE WILL BAPT	2	129	165*	.6	1.0
226 FRIENDS-USA	1	89	114*	.4	.7
226b *EFI*	*1*	*89*	*114* *	*.4*	*.7*
283 LUTH—MO SYNOD	1	137	170	.6	1.0
339 PENT CH OF GOD	1	35	77	.3	.5
355 PRESB CH (USA)	3	82	105*	.4	.6
413 S.D.A.	1	20	26*	.1	.2
419 SO BAPT CONV	18	6,608	8,443*	28.9	50.8
449 UN METHODIST	7	1,716	2,193*	7.5	13.2
497 BLACK BAPT EST[2]	NA	193	247*	.8	1.5
LOGAN	**50**	**8,274**	**12,395***	**42.7**	**100.0**
053 ASSEMB OF GOD	3	281	568	2.0	4.6
081 CATHOLIC	3	NA	1,015	3.5	8.2
081d *LATIN*	*3*	*NA*	*1,015*	*3.5*	*8.2*
093 CHR CH (DISC)	4	1,160	1,496	5.2	12.1
097 CHR CHS&CHS CR	2	250	316*	1.1	2.5
111 CH CR,SCIENTST	1	NR	NR	-	-
127 CH GOD (CLEVE)	1	38	48*	.2	.4
145 CH GOD PROPHCY	1	32	40*	.1	.3
165 CH OF NAZARENE	5	277	603	2.1	4.9
167 CHS OF CHRIST	7	402	513	1.8	4.1
193 EPISCOPAL	2	106	113	.4	.9
221 FREE METHODIST	1	11	21	.1	.2
283 LUTH—MO SYNOD	1	141	223	.8	1.8
353 CHR BRETHREN	1	40	75	.3	.6
355 PRESB CH (USA)	1	263	332*	1.1	2.7
361 PRIM BAPT ASCS	1	21	27*	.1	.2
413 S.D.A.	2	42	53*	.2	.4
419 SO BAPT CONV	4	2,308	2,916*	10.1	23.5
443 UN C OF CHRIST	1	54	68*	.2	.5
449 UN METHODIST	8	1,628	2,057*	7.1	16.6
496 JEWISH EST[1]	0	NA	70	.2	.6
497 BLACK BAPT EST[2]	NA	1,220	1,541*	5.3	12.4
499 INDEP.NON-CHAR[3]	1	NA	300	1.0	2.4
LOVE	**28**	**5,030**	**6,481***	**79.5**	**100.0**
053 ASSEMB OF GOD	2	54	53	.6	.8
093 CHR CH (DISC)	1	79	138	1.7	2.1
151 L-D SAINTS	1	NA	247	3.0	3.8
167 CHS OF CHRIST	4	567	710	8.7	11.0
349 PENT HOLINESS	5	295	363*	4.5	5.6
355 PRESB CH (USA)	1	15	18*	.2	.3
419 SO BAPT CONV	11	3,553	4,377*	53.7	67.5
449 UN METHODIST	3	467	575*	7.0	8.9
MC CLAIN	**65**	**11,494**	**15,500***	**68.0**	**100.0**
053 ASSEMB OF GOD	3	188	327	1.4	2.1
059 BAPT MISS ASSN	5	1,216	1,539*	6.8	9.9
081 CATHOLIC	1	NA	280	1.2	1.8
081d *LATIN*	*1*	*NA*	*280*	*1.2*	*1.8*
093 CHR CH (DISC)	2	123	232	1.0	1.5
151 L-D SAINTS	3	NA	466	2.0	3.0
165 CH OF NAZARENE	2	79	62	.3	.4
167 CHS OF CHRIST	11	815	1,032	4.5	6.7
223 FREE WILL BAPT	5	383	485*	2.1	3.1
339 PENT CH OF GOD	1	34	76	.3	.5
349 PENT HOLINESS	4	178	225*	1.0	1.5
355 PRESB CH (USA)	3	66	84*	.4	.5
361 PRIM BAPT ASCS	2	115	146*	.6	.9
419 SO BAPT CONV	17	7,103	8,988*	39.4	58.0
449 UN METHODIST	6	1,194	1,511*	6.6	9.7
496 JEWISH EST[1]	0	NA	47	.2	.3
MC CURTAIN	**119**	**12,395**	**16,727***	**50.0**	**100.0**
053 ASSEMB OF GOD	13	971	1,504	4.5	9.0
059 BAPT MISS ASSN	1	301	390*	1.2	2.3
081 CATHOLIC	1	NA	216	.6	1.3
081d *LATIN*	*1*	*NA*	*216*	*.6*	*1.3*
093 CHR CH (DISC)	2	50	58	.2	.3
097 CHR CHS&CHS CR	4	123	159*	.5	1.0
127 CH GOD (CLEVE)	5	294	381*	1.1	2.3
145 CH GOD PROPHCY	1	33	43*	.1	.3
151 L-D SAINTS	1	NA	160	.5	1.0
165 CH OF NAZARENE	2	72	141	.4	.8
167 CHS OF CHRIST	22	1,003	1,243	3.7	7.4
185 CUMBER PRESB	4	97	130	.4	.8
193 EPISCOPAL	1	40	83	.2	.5
223 FREE WILL BAPT	4	381	493*	1.5	2.9
339 PENT CH OF GOD	1	34	77	.2	.5
355 PRESB CH (USA)	17	457	592*	1.8	3.5
413 S.D.A.	1	14	18*	.1	.1
419 SO BAPT CONV	21	5,384	6,972*	20.9	41.7
449 UN METHODIST	18	2,294	2,970*	8.9	17.8
497 BLACK BAPT EST[2]	NA	847	1,097*	3.3	6.6
MC INTOSH	**52**	**7,471**	**9,462***	**56.4**	**100.0**
053 ASSEMB OF GOD	3	268	360	2.1	3.8
081 CATHOLIC	1	NA	240	1.4	2.5
081d *LATIN*	*1*	*NA*	*240*	*1.4*	*2.5*
093 CHR CH (DISC)	1	38	43	.3	.5
097 CHR CHS&CHS CR	3	224	272*	1.6	2.9
165 CH OF NAZARENE	1	21	41	.2	.4
167 CHS OF CHRIST	6	483	616	3.7	6.5
171 CH GOD-GEN CON	2	51	62*	.4	.7
193 EPISCOPAL	1	39	43	.3	.5
223 FREE WILL BAPT	3	270	328*	2.0	3.5
283 LUTH—MO SYNOD	1	51	65	.4	.7
339 PENT CH OF GOD	2	68	154	.9	1.6
349 PENT HOLINESS	1	44	53*	.3	.6
355 PRESB CH (USA)	1	34	41*	.2	.4
419 SO BAPT CONV	24	4,937	5,998*	35.7	63.4

NA–Not applicable   NR–Not reported   *Total adherents estimated from known number of communicant, confirmed, full members.   - Represents a percent less than 0.1.   Percentages may not total due to rounding.

[1]See Appendix E   [2]See Appendix F   [3]See Appendix G   Lines in *italic* represent a breakdown of Catholic rites or Friends affiliations. They are included in their respective denominational total.

Table 4. Churches and Church Membership by County and Denomination: 1990

County and Denomination	Number of churches	Communicant, confirmed, full members	Total adherents		
			Number	Percent of total population	Percent of total adherents
449 UN METHODIST	2	730	887*	5.3	9.4
497 BLACK BAPT EST²	NA	213	259*	1.5	2.7
MAJOR	**33**	**4,041**	**5,684***	**70.6**	**100.0**
053 ASSEMB OF GOD	3	97	192	2.4	3.4
081 CATHOLIC	1	NA	140	1.7	2.5
081d LATIN	*1*	*NA*	*140*	*1.7*	*2.5*
093 CHR CH (DISC)	4	374	459	5.7	8.1
097 CHR CHS&CHS CR	1	75	95*	1.2	1.7
133 CH GOD(7TH)DEN	1	37	50	.6	.9
143 CG IN CR(MENN)	1	229	290*	3.6	5.1
151 L-D SAINTS	1	NA	77	1.0	1.4
165 CH OF NAZARENE	4	251	560	7.0	9.9
167 CHS OF CHRIST	2	93	121	1.5	2.1
211 FEL EVG BIB CH	1	69	69	.9	1.2
237 GC MENN BR CHS	1	516	654*	8.1	11.5
287 MENN GEN CONF	2	188	213	2.6	3.7
355 PRESB CH (USA)	1	47	60*	.7	1.1
419 SO BAPT CONV	5	1,358	1,722*	21.4	30.3
449 UN METHODIST	4	644	817*	10.1	14.4
467 WESLEYAN	1	63	165	2.0	2.9
MARSHALL	**38**	**5,998**	**7,593***	**70.1**	**100.0**
053 ASSEMB OF GOD	2	93	127	1.2	1.7
081 CATHOLIC	2	NA	60	.6	.8
081d LATIN	*2*	*NA*	*60*	*.6*	*.8*
151 L-D SAINTS	1	NA	200	1.8	2.6
165 CH OF NAZARENE	2	87	185	1.7	2.4
167 CHS OF CHRIST	7	526	646	6.0	8.5
349 PENT HOLINESS	1	37	45*	.4	.6
355 PRESB CH (USA)	1	8	10*	.1	.1
413 S.D.A.	1	23	28*	.3	.4
419 SO BAPT CONV	17	4,044	4,871*	45.0	64.2
449 UN METHODIST	4	1,180	1,421*	13.1	18.7
MAYES	**96**	**14,847**	**20,075***	**60.2**	**100.0**
053 ASSEMB OF GOD	8	490	929	2.8	4.6
059 BAPT MISS ASSN	1	56	71*	.2	.4
081 CATHOLIC	2	NA	325	1.0	1.6
081d LATIN	*2*	*NA*	*325*	*1.0*	*1.6*
093 CHR CH (DISC)	2	327	478	1.4	2.4
097 CHR CHS&CHS CR	4	404	513*	1.5	2.6
123 CH GOD (ANDER)	2	246	347	1.0	1.7
127 CH GOD (CLEVE)	3	290	368*	1.1	1.8
145 CH GOD PROPHCY	1	33	42*	.1	.2
151 L-D SAINTS	1	NA	197	.6	1.0
165 CH OF NAZARENE	2	124	207	.6	1.0
167 CHS OF CHRIST	7	492	635	1.9	3.2
185 CUMBER PRESB	1	33	33	.1	.2
193 EPISCOPAL	1	95	107	.3	.5
223 FREE WILL BAPT	10	1,150	1,461*	4.4	7.3
283 LUTH—MO SYNOD	2	216	263	.8	1.3
285 MENNONITE CH	2	196	215	.6	1.1
323 OLD ORD AMISH	2	NA	300	.9	1.5
355 PRESB CH (USA)	2	172	218*	.7	1.1
413 S.D.A.	2	192	244*	.7	1.2
419 SO BAPT CONV	30	8,037	10,208*	30.6	50.8
449 UN METHODIST	11	2,294	2,914*	8.7	14.5
MURRAY	**37**	**6,137**	**7,984***	**66.3**	**100.0**
053 ASSEMB OF GOD	3	192	277	2.3	3.5
081 CATHOLIC	1	NA	200	1.7	2.5
081d LATIN	*1*	*NA*	*200*	*1.7*	*2.5*
093 CHR CH (DISC)	1	138	168	1.4	2.1
097 CHR CHS&CHS CR	1	125	156*	1.3	2.0
145 CH GOD PROPHCY	1	33	41*	.3	.5
151 L-D SAINTS	1	NA	113	.9	1.4
165 CH OF NAZARENE	1	20	48	.4	.6
167 CHS OF CHRIST	6	408	467	3.9	5.8
193 EPISCOPAL	1	9	11	.1	.1
223 FREE WILL BAPT	2	268	334*	2.8	4.2
283 LUTH—MO SYNOD	1	17	28	.2	.4
349 PENT HOLINESS	2	171	213*	1.8	2.7
355 PRESB CH (USA)	2	79	98*	.8	1.2
413 S.D.A.	1	32	40*	.3	.5
419 SO BAPT CONV	10	3,980	4,961*	41.2	62.1
449 UN METHODIST	3	665	829*	6.9	10.4
MUSKOGEE	**137**	**35,554**	**47,547***	**69.8**	**100.0**
019 AMER BAPT USA	1	40	51*	.1	.1
053 ASSEMB OF GOD	15	1,980	2,652	3.9	5.6
059 BAPT MISS ASSN	1	320	407*	.6	.9
081 CATHOLIC	3	NA	1,500	2.2	3.2
081d LATIN	*3*	*NA*	*1,500*	*2.2*	*3.2*
093 CHR CH (DISC)	2	95	112	.2	.2
097 CHR CHS&CHS CR	7	1,595	2,030*	3.0	4.3
111 CH CR,SCIENTST	1	NR	NR	-	-
123 CH GOD (ANDER)	2	206	281	.4	.6
127 CH GOD (CLEVE)	2	88	112*	.2	.2
145 CH GOD PROPHCY	2	65	83*	.1	.2
151 L-D SAINTS	1	NA	390	.6	.8
165 CH OF NAZARENE	2	312	423	.6	.9
167 CHS OF CHRIST	16	1,666	2,202	3.2	4.6
171 CH GOD-GEN CON	1	17	22*	-	-
185 CUMBER PRESB	1	28	32	-	.1
193 EPISCOPAL	2	280	427	.6	.9
223 FREE WILL BAPT	8	707	900*	1.3	1.9
283 LUTH—MO SYNOD	2	465	602	.9	1.3
339 PENT CH OF GOD	3	90	213	.3	.4
349 PENT HOLINESS	4	487	620*	.9	1.3
355 PRESB CH (USA)	4	752	957*	1.4	2.0
403 SALVATION ARMY	1	109	120	.2	.3
413 S.D.A.	2	320	407*	.6	.9
419 SO BAPT CONV	37	17,267	21,976*	32.3	46.2
449 UN METHODIST	16	6,329	8,055*	11.8	16.9
496 JEWISH EST¹	1	NA	0	-	-
497 BLACK BAPT EST²	NA	2,336	2,973*	4.4	6.3
NOBLE	**31**	**5,346**	**7,532***	**68.2**	**100.0**
053 ASSEMB OF GOD	2	107	181	1.6	2.4
081 CATHOLIC	2	NA	523	4.7	6.9
081d LATIN	*2*	*NA*	*523*	*4.7*	*6.9*
093 CHR CH (DISC)	5	714	1,045	9.5	13.9
097 CHR CHS&CHS CR	1	50	64*	.6	.8
157 CH OF BRETHREN	1	65	83*	.8	1.1
165 CH OF NAZARENE	1	100	131	1.2	1.7
167 CHS OF CHRIST	1	127	193	1.7	2.6
193 EPISCOPAL	1	22	26	.2	.3
207 E.L.C.A.	1	222	256	2.3	3.4
283 LUTH—MO SYNOD	1	525	684	6.2	9.1
355 PRESB CH (USA)	1	236	300*	2.7	4.0
413 S.D.A.	1	28	36*	.3	.5
419 SO BAPT CONV	8	2,033	2,588*	23.4	34.4
449 UN METHODIST	5	1,117	1,422*	12.9	18.9
NOWATA	**30**	**4,871**	**6,329***	**63.3**	**100.0**
053 ASSEMB OF GOD	2	129	249	2.5	3.9
081 CATHOLIC	1	NA	125	1.3	2.0
081d LATIN	*1*	*NA*	*125*	*1.3*	*2.0*
093 CHR CH (DISC)	1	151	205	2.1	3.2
097 CHR CHS&CHS CR	2	541	671*	6.7	10.6
123 CH GOD (ANDER)	3	193	245	2.5	3.9
127 CH GOD (CLEVE)	1	49	61*	.6	1.0
165 CH OF NAZARENE	1	44	108	1.1	1.7
167 CHS OF CHRIST	2	50	61	.6	1.0
193 EPISCOPAL	1	26	29	.3	.5
223 FREE WILL BAPT	1	41	51*	.5	.8
349 PENT HOLINESS	1	140	174*	1.7	2.7
355 PRESB CH (USA)	1	51	63*	.6	1.0
413 S.D.A.	1	46	57*	.6	.9
419 SO BAPT CONV	6	2,411	2,991*	29.9	47.3
449 UN METHODIST	6	999	1,239*	12.4	19.6
OKFUSKEE	**33**	**5,123**	**6,445***	**55.8**	**100.0**
053 ASSEMB OF GOD	3	154	210	1.8	3.3
059 BAPT MISS ASSN	1	52	65*	.6	1.0
081 CATHOLIC	1	NA	35	.3	.5
081d LATIN	*1*	*NA*	*35*	*.3*	*.5*
093 CHR CH (DISC)	2	105	123	1.1	1.9
097 CHR CHS&CHS CR	1	118	147*	1.3	2.3
123 CH GOD (ANDER)	2	44	78	.7	1.2
167 CHS OF CHRIST	5	323	386	3.3	6.0
349 PENT HOLINESS	1	32	40*	.3	.6
355 PRESB CH (USA)	1	8	10*	.1	.2
419 SO BAPT CONV	10	3,331	4,158*	36.0	64.5
449 UN METHODIST	6	636	794*	6.9	12.3
497 BLACK BAPT EST²	NA	320	399*	3.5	6.2
OKLAHOMA	**567**	**299,834**	**436,615***	**72.8**	**100.0**
005 AME ZION	2	542	733	.1	.2
053 ASSEMB OF GOD	45	20,027	23,275	3.9	5.3
059 BAPT MISS ASSN	5	1,147	1,449*	.2	.3
075 BRETHREN IN CR	1	60	60	-	-
081 CATHOLIC	22	NA	40,378	6.7	9.2
081d LATIN	*22*	*NA*	*40,378*	*6.7*	*9.2*
089 CHR & MISS AL	2	68	181	-	-
093 CHR CH (DISC)	26	9,660	14,963	2.5	3.4
097 CHR CHS&CHS CR	14	3,041	3,843*	.6	.9
105 CHRISTIAN REF	1	12	22	-	-
111 CH CR,SCIENTST	7	NR	NR	-	-
123 CH GOD (ANDER)	9	687	842	.1	.2

NA–Not applicable   NR–Not reported   *Total adherents estimated from known number of communicant, confirmed, full members.   - Represents a percent less than 0.1.   Percentages may not total due to rounding.
¹See Appendix E   ²See Appendix F   ³See Appendix G   Lines in *italic* represent a breakdown of Catholic rites or Friends affiliations. They are included in their respective denominational total.

Table 4. Churches and Church Membership by County and Denomination: 1990

County and Denomination	Number of churches	Communicant, confirmed, full members	Total adherents Number	Total adherents Percent of total population	Total adherents Percent of total adherents
127 CH GOD (CLEVE)	6	526	665*	.1	.2
133 CH GOD(7TH)DEN	2	76	100	-	-
145 CH GOD PROPHCY	4	131	166*	-	-
151 L-D SAINTS	11	NA	4,250	.7	1.0
165 CH OF NAZARENE	38	9,798	12,177	2.0	2.8
167 CHS OF CHRIST	58	13,774	17,316	2.9	4.0
171 CH GOD-GEN CON	1	37	47*	-	-
175 CONGR GHR CHS	2	360	455*	.1	.1
185 CUMBER PRESB	1	110	116	-	-
193 EPISCOPAL	12	4,379	5,505	.9	1.3
203 EVAN FREE CH	2	57	71	-	-
207 E.L.C.A.	12	2,769	3,817	.6	.9
220 FREE LUTHERAN	1	149	180	-	-
221 FREE METHODIST	4	336	336	.1	.1
223 FREE WILL BAPT	10	1,448	1,830*	.3	.4
226 FRIENDS-USA	2	89	116*	-	-
226b EFI	1	40	51*	-	-
226c FGC	1	49	65	-	-
237 GC MENN BR CHS	2	155	196*	-	-
246 GREEK ORTHODOX	1	NR	NR	-	-
263 INT FOURSQ GOS	3	167	211*	-	-
283 LUTH—MO SYNOD	9	2,864	3,756	.6	.9
339 PENT CH OF GOD	4	181	441	.1	.1
349 PENT HOLINESS	23	2,475	3,127*	.5	.7
353 CHR BRETHREN	2	85	150	-	-
355 PRESB CH (USA)	17	7,780	9,831*	1.6	2.3
356 PRESB CH AMER	1	193	270	-	.1
361 PRIM BAPT ASCS	2	188	238*	-	.1
371 REF CH IN AM	1	641	1,114	.2	.3
403 SALVATION ARMY	1	208	244	-	.1
413 S.D.A.	9	1,821	2,301*	.4	.5
415 S-D BAPTIST GC	1	30	38*	-	-
419 SO BAPT CONV	117	137,623	173,898*	29.0	39.8
423 SYRIAN ANTIOCH	1	NA	400	.1	.1
431 UKRANIAN AMER	1	NR	NR	-	-
435 UNITARIAN-UNIV	2	364	478	.1	.1
443 UN C OF CHRIST	2	596	753*	.1	.2
449 UN METHODIST	53	48,182	60,882*	10.2	13.9
467 WESLEYAN	1	51	145	-	-
469 WELS	2	187	287	-	.1
496 JEWISH EST[1]	2	NA	1,449	.2	.3
497 BLACK BAPT EST[2]	NA	26,760	33,813*	5.6	7.7
498 INDEP.CHARIS.[3]	5	NA	5,100	.9	1.2
499 INDEP.NON-CHAR[3]	5	NA	4,600	.8	1.1
OKMULGEE	**77**	**18,048**	**24,504***	**67.2**	**100.0**
005 AME ZION	1	649	723	2.0	3.0
053 ASSEMB OF GOD	7	515	876	2.4	3.6
081 CATHOLIC	3	NA	1,095	3.0	4.5
081d LATIN	3	NA	1,095	3.0	4.5
093 CHR CH (DISC)	4	417	595	1.6	2.4
097 CHR CHS&CHS CR	1	200	253*	.7	1.0
123 CH GOD (ANDER)	1	10	15	-	.1
145 CH GOD PROPHCY	2	65	82*	.2	.3
151 L-D SAINTS	1	NA	286	.8	1.2
165 CH OF NAZARENE	2	422	605	1.7	2.5
167 CHS OF CHRIST	7	537	700	1.9	2.9
193 EPISCOPAL	2	121	160	.4	.7
223 FREE WILL BAPT	5	386	488*	1.3	2.0
263 INT FOURSQ GOS	2	84	106*	.3	.4
283 LUTH—MO SYNOD	1	141	178	.5	.7
349 PENT HOLINESS	2	280	354*	1.0	1.4
355 PRESB CH (USA)	2	200	253*	.7	1.0
403 SALVATION ARMY	1	65	81	.2	.3
413 S.D.A.	3	84	106*	.3	.4
419 SO BAPT CONV	18	10,067	12,735*	34.9	52.0
449 UN METHODIST	12	2,721	3,442*	9.4	14.0
497 BLACK BAPT EST[2]	NA	1,084	1,371*	3.8	5.6
OSAGE	**76**	**13,015**	**18,357***	**44.1**	**100.0**
053 ASSEMB OF GOD	8	590	872	2.1	4.8
059 BAPT MISS ASSN	1	76	97*	.2	.5
081 CATHOLIC	6	NA	1,317	3.2	7.2
081d LATIN	6	NA	1,317	3.2	7.2
093 CHR CH (DISC)	2	260	354	.9	1.9
097 CHR CHS&CHS CR	3	140	178*	.4	1.0
111 CH CR,SCIENTST	1	NR	NR	-	-
127 CH GOD (CLEVE)	2	114	145*	.3	.8
145 CH GOD PROPHCY	1	32	41*	.1	.2
151 L-D SAINTS	1	NA	83	.2	.5
165 CH OF NAZARENE	4	207	310	.7	1.7
167 CHS OF CHRIST	7	361	467	1.1	2.5
193 EPISCOPAL	1	85	92	.2	.5
217 FIRE BAPTIZED	1	9	11*	-	.1
223 FREE WILL BAPT	2	199	254*	.6	1.4
226 FRIENDS-USA	1	46	59*	.1	.3
226e FUM	1	46	59*	.1	.3
339 PENT CH OF GOD	1	35	77	.2	.4
349 PENT HOLINESS	3	226	288*	.7	1.6
355 PRESB CH (USA)	3	253	322*	.8	1.8
413 S.D.A.	1	9	11*	-	.1
419 SO BAPT CONV	19	7,774	9,903*	23.8	53.9
449 UN METHODIST	8	1,325	1,688*	4.1	9.2
496 JEWISH EST[1]	0	NA	165	.4	.9
497 BLACK BAPT EST[2]	NA	1,274	1,623*	3.9	8.8
OTTAWA	**85**	**19,259**	**25,303***	**82.8**	**100.0**
053 ASSEMB OF GOD	14	987	1,707	5.6	6.7
081 CATHOLIC	1	NA	610	2.0	2.4
081d LATIN	1	NA	610	2.0	2.4
093 CHR CH (DISC)	1	143	259	.8	1.0
097 CHR CHS&CHS CR	10	1,860	2,282*	7.5	9.0
111 CH CR,SCIENTST	1	NR	NR	-	-
123 CH GOD (ANDER)	1	38	64	.2	.3
151 L-D SAINTS	2	NA	390	1.3	1.5
165 CH OF NAZARENE	2	230	268	.9	1.1
167 CHS OF CHRIST	4	295	355	1.2	1.4
193 EPISCOPAL	1	152	181	.6	.7
217 FIRE BAPTIZED	1	13	16*	.1	.1
223 FREE WILL BAPT	3	180	221*	.7	.9
226 FRIENDS-USA	2	153	188*	.6	.7
226b EFI	2	153	188*	.6	.7
283 LUTH—MO SYNOD	2	324	491	1.6	1.9
339 PENT CH OF GOD	1	13	30	.1	.1
355 PRESB CH (USA)	1	240	294*	1.0	1.2
413 S.D.A.	1	21	26*	.1	.1
419 SO BAPT CONV	29	11,970	14,683*	48.0	58.0
449 UN METHODIST	8	2,640	3,238*	10.6	12.8
PAWNEE	**43**	**7,801**	**9,963***	**64.0**	**100.0**
053 ASSEMB OF GOD	4	308	355	2.3	3.6
081 CATHOLIC	2	NA	80	.5	.8
081d LATIN	2	NA	80	.5	.8
093 CHR CH (DISC)	1	182	250	1.6	2.5
097 CHR CHS&CHS CR	2	410	518*	3.3	5.2
145 CH GOD PROPHCY	1	33	42*	.3	.4
165 CH OF NAZARENE	2	75	121	.8	1.2
167 CHS OF CHRIST	4	258	332	2.1	3.3
193 EPISCOPAL	2	47	69	.4	.7
223 FREE WILL BAPT	2	59	75*	.5	.8
259 IFCA	1	NR	NR	-	-
349 PENT HOLINESS	2	78	99*	.6	1.0
355 PRESB CH (USA)	1	141	178*	1.1	1.8
413 S.D.A.	1	27	34*	.2	.3
419 SO BAPT CONV	12	5,367	6,779*	43.5	68.0
449 UN METHODIST	6	816	1,031*	6.6	10.3
PAYNE	**97**	**22,260**	**32,856***	**53.4**	**100.0**
001 ADVENT CHR CH	1	30	36*	.1	.1
053 ASSEMB OF GOD	8	641	1,059	1.7	3.2
081 CATHOLIC	2	NA	3,462	5.6	10.5
081d LATIN	2	NA	3,462	5.6	10.5
089 CHR & MISS AL	1	30	67	.1	.2
093 CHR CH (DISC)	3	880	1,154	1.9	3.5
097 CHR CHS&CHS CR	7	922	1,110*	1.8	3.4
111 CH CR,SCIENTST	2	NR	NR	-	-
123 CH GOD (ANDER)	5	202	316	.5	1.0
127 CH GOD (CLEVE)	1	47	57*	.1	.2
151 L-D SAINTS	2	NA	790	1.3	2.4
157 CH OF BRETHREN	1	162	195*	.3	.6
165 CH OF NAZARENE	3	314	304	.5	.9
167 CHS OF CHRIST	7	990	1,526	2.5	4.6
193 EPISCOPAL	2	369	430	.7	1.3
207 E.L.C.A.	1	315	416	.7	1.3
221 FREE METHODIST	1	14	14	-	-
223 FREE WILL BAPT	4	316	380*	.6	1.2
226 FRIENDS-USA	2	61	95*	.2	.3
226b EFI	1	45	54*	.1	.2
226c FGC	1	16	41	.1	.1
283 LUTH—MO SYNOD	2	400	590	1.0	1.8
287 MENN GEN CONF	1	6	6	-	-
339 PENT CH OF GOD	4	90	208	.3	.6
349 PENT HOLINESS	2	30	36*	.1	.1
355 PRESB CH (USA)	2	896	1,079*	1.8	3.3
403 SALVATION ARMY	2	97	100	.2	.3
413 S.D.A.	3	104	125*	.2	.4
419 SO BAPT CONV	15	9,252	11,140*	18.1	33.9
435 UNITARIAN-UNIV	1	100	141	.2	.4
449 UN METHODIST	10	5,542	6,673*	10.8	20.3
469 WELS	1	13	21	-	.1
497 BLACK BAPT EST[2]	NA	437	526*	.9	1.6
499 INDEP.NON-CHAR[3]	1	NA	800	1.3	2.4

NA–Not applicable   NR–Not reported   *Total adherents estimated from known number of communicant, confirmed, full members.   - Represents a percent less than 0.1.   Percentages may not total due to rounding.
[1]See Appendix E   [2]See Appendix F   [3]See Appendix G   Lines in *italic* represent a breakdown of Catholic rites or Friends affiliations. They are included in their respective denominational total.

Table 4. Churches and Church Membership by County and Denomination: 1990

County and Denomination	Number of churches	Communicant, confirmed, full members	Total adherents		
			Number	Percent of total population	Percent of total adherents
PITTSBURG	**124**	**21,967**	**30,355***	**74.8**	**100.0**
053 ASSEMB OF GOD	10	439	1,042	2.6	3.4
059 BAPT MISS ASSN	1	147	181*	.4	.6
081 CATHOLIC	4	NA	2,187	5.4	7.2
081d LATIN	4	NA	2,187	5.4	7.2
093 CHR CH (DISC)	2	216	392	1.0	1.3
097 CHR CHS&CHS CR	5	791	974*	2.4	3.2
111 CH CR,SCIENTST	1	NR	NR	-	-
123 CH GOD (ANDER)	1	40	40	.1	.1
127 CH GOD (CLEVE)	1	75	92*	.2	.3
133 CH GOD(7TH)DEN	1	38	50	.1	.2
145 CH GOD PROPHCY	1	33	41*	.1	.1
151 L-D SAINTS	1	NA	276	.7	.9
165 CH OF NAZARENE	3	249	405	1.0	1.3
167 CHS OF CHRIST	15	1,086	1,391	3.4	4.6
171 CH GOD-GEN CON	1	62	76*	.2	.3
193 EPISCOPAL	1	69	66	.2	.2
223 FREE WILL BAPT	7	763	939*	2.3	3.1
283 LUTH—MO SYNOD	1	125	202	.5	.7
331 ORTH CH IN AM	1	NR	NR	-	-
339 PENT CH OF GOD	2	68	154	.4	.5
349 PENT HOLINESS	3	138	170*	.4	.6
355 PRESB CH (USA)	2	607	747*	1.8	2.5
361 PRIM BAPT ASCS	1	65	80*	.2	.3
403 SALVATION ARMY	1	96	97	.2	.3
413 S.D.A.	2	84	103*	.3	.3
419 SO BAPT CONV	42	13,827	17,020*	41.9	56.1
449 UN METHODIST	14	2,580	3,176*	7.8	10.5
497 BLACK BAPT EST[2]	NA	369	454*	1.1	1.5
PONTOTOC	**92**	**18,352**	**25,172***	**73.8**	**100.0**
053 ASSEMB OF GOD	6	318	640	1.9	2.5
059 BAPT MISS ASSN	5	476	591*	1.7	2.3
081 CATHOLIC	1	NA	690	2.0	2.7
081d LATIN	1	NA	690	2.0	2.7
093 CHR CH (DISC)	1	403	659	1.9	2.6
111 CH CR,SCIENTST	1	NR	NR	-	-
127 CH GOD (CLEVE)	1	194	241*	.7	1.0
145 CH GOD PROPHCY	3	98	122*	.4	.5
151 L-D SAINTS	1	NA	163	.5	.6
165 CH OF NAZARENE	1	263	270	.8	1.1
167 CHS OF CHRIST	11	1,389	1,746	5.1	6.9
185 CUMBER PRESB	1	133	163	.5	.6
193 EPISCOPAL	1	273	357	1.0	1.4
223 FREE WILL BAPT	13	1,746	2,167*	6.4	8.6
263 INT FOURSQ GOS	1	17	21*	.1	.1
283 LUTH—MO SYNOD	1	129	181	.5	.7
349 PENT HOLINESS	5	448	556*	1.6	2.2
355 PRESB CH (USA)	1	337	418*	1.2	1.7
361 PRIM BAPT ASCS	1	48	60*	.2	.2
403 SALVATION ARMY	1	106	117	.3	.5
413 S.D.A.	1	32	40*	.1	.2
419 SO BAPT CONV	23	9,203	11,421*	33.5	45.4
449 UN METHODIST	10	2,528	3,137*	9.2	12.5
497 BLACK BAPT EST[2]	NA	211	262*	.8	1.0
498 INDEP.CHARIS.[3]	1	NA	800	2.3	3.2
499 INDEP.NON-CHAR[3]	1	NA	350	1.0	1.4
POTTAWATOMIE	**127**	**31,170**	**42,708***	**72.7**	**100.0**
053 ASSEMB OF GOD	10	522	935	1.6	2.2
081 CATHOLIC	4	NA	2,126	3.6	5.0
081d LATIN	4	NA	2,126	3.6	5.0
093 CHR CH (DISC)	2	442	592	1.0	1.4
097 CHR CHS&CHS CR	2	108	136*	.2	.3
111 CH CR,SCIENTST	1	NR	NR	-	-
123 CH GOD (ANDER)	2	156	214	.4	.5
127 CH GOD (CLEVE)	3	275	347*	.6	.8
133 CH GOD(7TH)DEN	1	38	50	.1	.1
145 CH GOD PROPHCY	1	33	42*	.1	.1
151 L-D SAINTS	2	NA	512	.9	1.2
165 CH OF NAZARENE	3	282	504	.9	1.2
167 CHS OF CHRIST	18	1,551	1,973	3.4	4.6
171 CH GOD-GEN CON	3	82	104*	.2	.2
193 EPISCOPAL	1	193	273	.5	.6
203 EVAN FREE CH	1	30	50	.1	.1
207 E.L.C.A.	1	138	178	.3	.4
223 FREE WILL BAPT	5	358	452*	.8	1.1
283 LUTH—MO SYNOD	1	96	126	.2	.3
339 PENT CH OF GOD	2	54	127	.2	.3
349 PENT HOLINESS	5	317	400*	.7	.9
355 PRESB CH (USA)	3	336	424*	.7	1.0
361 PRIM BAPT ASCS	1	35	44*	.1	.1
403 SALVATION ARMY	1	86	95	.2	.2
413 S.D.A.	1	74	93*	.2	.2
419 SO BAPT CONV	42	21,521	27,165*	46.2	63.6
449 UN METHODIST	11	4,042	5,102*	8.7	11.9

County and Denomination	Number of churches	Communicant, confirmed, full members	Total adherents		
			Number	Percent of total population	Percent of total adherents
496 JEWISH EST[1]	0	NA	138	.2	.3
497 BLACK BAPT EST[2]	NA	401	506*	.9	1.2
PUSHMATAHA	**55**	**5,182**	**6,983***	**63.5**	**100.0**
053 ASSEMB OF GOD	6	393	910	8.3	13.0
081 CATHOLIC	2	NA	83	.8	1.2
081d LATIN	2	NA	83	.8	1.2
093 CHR CH (DISC)	1	35	51	.5	.7
097 CHR CHS&CHS CR	4	155	193*	1.8	2.8
165 CH OF NAZARENE	1	33	56	.5	.8
167 CHS OF CHRIST	5	333	415	3.8	5.9
193 EPISCOPAL	1	13	29	.3	.4
223 FREE WILL BAPT	5	112	139*	1.3	2.0
355 PRESB CH (USA)	1	40	50*	.5	.7
413 S.D.A.	1	25	31*	.3	.4
419 SO BAPT CONV	18	3,381	4,203*	38.2	60.2
449 UN METHODIST	10	662	823*	7.5	11.8
ROGER MILLS	**26**	**2,588**	**3,340***	**80.5**	**100.0**
053 ASSEMB OF GOD	4	107	160	3.9	4.8
165 CH OF NAZARENE	2	0	0	-	-
167 CHS OF CHRIST	6	234	299	7.2	9.0
287 MENN GEN CONF	1	25	47	1.1	1.4
349 PENT HOLINESS	2	51	65*	1.6	1.9
419 SO BAPT CONV	7	1,590	2,028*	48.9	60.7
449 UN METHODIST	4	581	741*	17.9	22.2
ROGERS	**84**	**20,562**	**29,717***	**53.9**	**100.0**
053 ASSEMB OF GOD	9	923	1,820	3.3	6.1
059 BAPT MISS ASSN	1	31	40*	.1	.1
081 CATHOLIC	1	NA	1,500	2.7	5.0
081d LATIN	1	NA	1,500	2.7	5.0
093 CHR CH (DISC)	2	469	662	1.2	2.2
097 CHR CHS&CHS CR	3	962	1,235*	2.2	4.2
123 CH GOD (ANDER)	1	65	80	.1	.3
127 CH GOD (CLEVE)	1	51	65*	.1	.2
133 CH GOD(7TH)DEN	1	37	50	.1	.2
145 CH GOD PROPHCY	2	65	83*	.2	.3
151 L-D SAINTS	1	NA	312	.6	1.0
165 CH OF NAZARENE	2	195	205	.4	.7
167 CHS OF CHRIST	8	613	805	1.5	2.7
193 EPISCOPAL	1	150	242	.4	.8
221 FREE METHODIST	1	29	51	.1	.2
223 FREE WILL BAPT	4	164	210*	.4	.7
263 INT FOURSQ GOS	1	17	22*	-	.1
283 LUTH—MO SYNOD	2	346	479	.9	1.6
287 MENN GEN CONF	1	184	237	.4	.8
339 PENT CH OF GOD	1	34	76	.1	.3
349 PENT HOLINESS	1	44	56*	.1	.2
355 PRESB CH (USA)	2	277	355*	.6	1.2
356 PRESB CH AMER	1	0	0	-	-
413 S.D.A.	1	117	150*	.3	.5
419 SO BAPT CONV	25	12,872	16,519*	29.9	55.6
449 UN METHODIST	10	2,917	3,743*	6.8	12.6
496 JEWISH EST[1]	0	NA	220	.4	.7
498 INDEP.CHARIS.[3]	1	NA	500	.9	1.7
SEMINOLE	**80**	**16,066**	**21,007***	**82.7**	**100.0**
005 AME ZION	1	100	116	.5	.6
053 ASSEMB OF GOD	10	548	958	3.8	4.6
081 CATHOLIC	2	NA	200	.8	1.0
081d LATIN	2	NA	200	.8	1.0
093 CHR CH (DISC)	2	183	300	1.2	1.4
123 CH GOD (ANDER)	3	95	162	.6	.8
127 CH GOD (CLEVE)	1	33	42*	.2	.2
165 CH OF NAZARENE	3	81	230	.9	1.1
167 CHS OF CHRIST	9	906	1,115	4.4	5.3
193 EPISCOPAL	1	56	68	.3	.3
223 FREE WILL BAPT	4	352	443*	1.7	2.1
339 PENT CH OF GOD	3	103	231	.9	1.1
349 PENT HOLINESS	4	251	316*	1.2	1.5
355 PRESB CH (USA)	6	205	258*	1.0	1.2
413 S.D.A.	1	27	34*	.1	.2
419 SO BAPT CONV	20	10,301	12,976*	51.1	61.8
449 UN METHODIST	10	2,350	2,960*	11.6	14.1
497 BLACK BAPT EST[2]	NA	475	598*	2.4	2.8
SEQUOYAH	**71**	**11,145**	**15,390***	**45.5**	**100.0**
053 ASSEMB OF GOD	12	749	1,254	3.7	8.1
059 BAPT MISS ASSN	1	256	327*	1.0	2.1
081 CATHOLIC	2	NA	360	1.1	2.3
081d LATIN	2	NA	360	1.1	2.3
097 CHR CHS&CHS CR	1	189	242*	.7	1.6
127 CH GOD (CLEVE)	1	24	31*	.1	.2
151 L-D SAINTS	1	NA	269	.8	1.7

NA–Not applicable NR–Not reported *Total adherents estimated from known number of communicant, confirmed, full members. - Represents a percent less than 0.1. Percentages may not total due to rounding.
[1]See Appendix E [2]See Appendix F [3]See Appendix G Lines in *italic* represent a breakdown of Catholic rites or Friends affiliations. They are included in their respective denominational total.

Table 4. Churches and Church Membership by County and Denomination: 1990

County and Denomination	Number of churches	Communicant, confirmed, full members	Total adherents Number	Percent of total population	Percent of total adherents
165 CH OF NAZARENE	3	262	475	1.4	3.1
167 CHS OF CHRIST	8	457	570	1.7	3.7
221 FREE METHODIST	1	15	15	-	.1
223 FREE WILL BAPT	5	563	720*	2.1	4.7
259 IFCA	1	NR	NR	-	-
283 LUTH—MO SYNOD	1	65	95	.3	.6
339 PENT CH OF GOD	3	103	214	.6	1.4
349 PENT HOLINESS	1	55	70*	.2	.5
355 PRESB CH (USA)	1	63	81*	.2	.5
413 S.D.A.	1	83	106*	.3	.7
419 SO BAPT CONV	22	6,694	8,557*	25.3	55.6
449 UN METHODIST	6	1,328	1,698*	5.0	11.0
497 BLACK BAPT EST[2]	NA	239	306*	.9	2.0
STEPHENS	**82**	**25,305**	**34,053***	**80.5**	**100.0**
053 ASSEMB OF GOD	9	781	1,790	4.2	5.3
081 CATHOLIC	3	NA	1,249	3.0	3.7
081d *LATIN*	*3*	*NA*	*1,249*	*3.0*	*3.7*
093 CHR CH (DISC)	2	704	945	2.2	2.8
097 CHR CHS&CHS CR	2	114	143*	.3	.4
111 CH CR,SCIENTST	1	NR	NR	-	-
123 CH GOD (ANDER)	1	53	53	.1	.2
127 CH GOD (CLEVE)	2	74	93*	.2	.3
145 CH GOD PROPHCY	1	33	41*	.1	.1
151 L-D SAINTS	1	NA	291	.7	.9
165 CH OF NAZARENE	4	375	477	1.1	1.4
167 CHS OF CHRIST	12	1,641	2,003	4.7	5.9
185 CUMBER PRESB	2	290	320	.8	.9
193 EPISCOPAL	1	61	70	.2	.2
223 FREE WILL BAPT	4	178	223*	.5	.7
283 LUTH—MO SYNOD	1	83	113	.3	.3
339 PENT CH OF GOD	2	68	154	.4	.5
355 PRESB CH (USA)	1	420	526*	1.2	1.5
413 S.D.A.	1	67	84*	.2	.2
419 SO BAPT CONV	24	16,276	20,365*	48.1	59.8
449 UN METHODIST	8	3,855	4,823*	11.4	14.2
497 BLACK BAPT EST[2]	NA	232	290*	.7	.9
TEXAS	**51**	**9,529**	**14,107***	**85.9**	**100.0**
053 ASSEMB OF GOD	1	60	80	.5	.6
081 CATHOLIC	2	NA	1,536	9.4	10.9
081d *LATIN*	*2*	*NA*	*1,536*	*9.4*	*10.9*
093 CHR CH (DISC)	3	296	597	3.6	4.2
097 CHR CHS&CHS CR	1	225	288*	1.8	2.0
123 CH GOD (ANDER)	3	106	124	.8	.9
165 CH OF NAZARENE	3	263	373	2.3	2.6
167 CHS OF CHRIST	6	398	585	3.6	4.1
193 EPISCOPAL	1	43	73	.4	.5
211 FEL EVG BIB CH	1	46	80	.5	.6
223 FREE WILL BAPT	1	77	98*	.6	.7
237 GC MENN BR CHS	1	74	95*	.6	.7
263 INT FOURSQ GOS	1	93	119*	.7	.8
283 LUTH—MO SYNOD	3	492	656	4.0	4.7
349 PENT HOLINESS	1	80	102*	.6	.7
355 PRESB CH (USA)	1	275	352*	2.1	2.5
413 S.D.A.	2	73	93*	.6	.7
419 SO BAPT CONV	11	3,891	4,974*	30.3	35.3
449 UN METHODIST	9	3,037	3,882*	23.6	27.5
TILLMAN	**33**	**7,647**	**10,561***	**101.7**	**100.0**
053 ASSEMB OF GOD	3	83	138	1.3	1.3
081 CATHOLIC	3	NA	800	7.7	7.6
081d *LATIN*	*3*	*NA*	*800*	*7.7*	*7.6*
093 CHR CH (DISC)	1	154	199	1.9	1.9
165 CH OF NAZARENE	1	47	47	.5	.4
167 CHS OF CHRIST	5	659	831	8.0	7.9
349 PENT HOLINESS	1	44	56*	.5	.5
355 PRESB CH (USA)	2	116	148*	1.4	1.4
361 PRIM BAPT ASCS	1	47	60*	.6	.6
419 SO BAPT CONV	11	5,152	6,567*	63.2	62.2
449 UN METHODIST	5	1,094	1,395*	13.4	13.2
497 BLACK BAPT EST[2]	NA	251	320*	3.1	3.0
TULSA	**465**	**212,368**	**332,630***	**66.1**	**100.0**
005 AME ZION	1	214	249	-	.1
019 AMER BAPT USA	2	780	987*	.2	.3
053 ASSEMB OF GOD	41	7,278	12,112	2.4	3.6
059 BAPT MISS ASSN	2	183	232*	-	.1
081 CATHOLIC	23	NA	35,032	7.0	10.5
081d *LATIN*	*23*	*NA*	*35,032*	*7.0*	*10.5*
089 CHR & MISS AL	2	95	136	-	-
093 CHR CH (DISC)	21	5,322	7,010	1.4	2.1
097 CHR CHS&CHS CR	23	6,268	7,929*	1.6	2.4
111 CH CR,SCIENTST	5	NR	NR	-	-
123 CH GOD (ANDER)	7	764	872	.2	.3
127 CH GOD (CLEVE)	5	394	498*	.1	.1

County and Denomination	Number of churches	Communicant, confirmed, full members	Total adherents Number	Percent of total population	Percent of total adherents
133 CH GOD(7TH)DEN	1	38	50	-	-
145 CH GOD PROPHCY	13	424	536*	.1	.2
151 L-D SAINTS	8	NA	3,423	.7	1.0
165 CH OF NAZARENE	14	2,257	3,145	.6	.9
167 CHS OF CHRIST	34	7,117	9,179	1.8	2.8
171 CH GOD-GEN CON	3	139	176*	-	.1
181 CONSRV CONGR	1	108	137*	-	-
185 CUMBER PRESB	2	367	425	.1	.1
193 EPISCOPAL	10	4,069	5,156	1.0	1.6
203 EVAN FREE CH	2	235	275	.1	.1
207 E.L.C.A.	8	2,473	3,395	.7	1.0
216 EVAN PRESBY CH	1	29	29	-	-
217 FIRE BAPTIZED	1	6	8*	-	-
221 FREE METHODIST	1	38	38	-	-
223 FREE WILL BAPT	30	3,654	4,622*	.9	1.4
226 FRIENDS-USA	1	22	30	-	-
226c *FGC*	*1*	*22*	*30*	-	-
237 GC MENN BR CHS	2	611	773*	.2	.2
246 GREEK ORTHODOX	1	NR	NR	-	-
259 IFCA	4	NR	NR	-	-
263 INT FOURSQ GOS	3	173	219*	-	.1
283 LUTH—MO SYNOD	7	3,044	4,258	.8	1.3
329 OPEN BIBLE STD	1	NR	NR	-	-
331 ORTH CH IN AM	1	NR	NR	-	-
339 PENT CH OF GOD	4	97	259	.1	.1
349 PENT HOLINESS	3	2,475	3,131*	.6	.9
353 CHR BRETHREN	1	50	110	-	-
355 PRESB CH (USA)	19	9,012	11,401*	2.3	3.4
356 PRESB CH AMER	1	492	623	.1	.2
403 SALVATION ARMY	1	299	339	.1	.1
413 S.D.A.	7	1,095	1,385*	.3	.4
419 SO BAPT CONV	87	88,378	111,802*	22.2	33.6
435 UNITARIAN-UNIV	3	1,401	2,095	.4	.6
443 UN C OF CHRIST	1	218	276*	.1	.1
449 UN METHODIST	47	47,565	60,172*	12.0	18.1
467 WESLEYAN	1	70	202	-	.1
469 WELS	1	95	127	-	-
496 JEWISH EST[1]	2	NA	1,925	.4	.6
497 BLACK BAPT EST[2]	NA	15,019	19,000*	3.8	5.7
498 INDEP.CHARIS.[3]	4	NA	15,262	3.0	4.6
499 INDEP.NON-CHAR[3]	5	NA	3,590	.7	1.1
WAGONER	**56**	**11,361**	**15,809***	**33.0**	**100.0**
053 ASSEMB OF GOD	4	307	506	1.1	3.2
081 CATHOLIC	2	NA	325	.7	2.1
081d *LATIN*	*2*	*NA*	*325*	*.7*	*2.1*
093 CHR CH (DISC)	1	161	235	.5	1.5
097 CHR CHS&CHS CR	2	434	561*	1.2	3.5
127 CH GOD (CLEVE)	1	103	133*	.3	.8
145 CH GOD PROPHCY	3	98	127*	.3	.8
151 L-D SAINTS	1	NA	351	.7	2.2
165 CH OF NAZARENE	3	124	287	.6	1.8
167 CHS OF CHRIST	6	498	600	1.3	3.8
193 EPISCOPAL	1	23	28	.1	.2
223 FREE WILL BAPT	6	448	579*	1.2	3.7
283 LUTH—MO SYNOD	1	34	40	.1	.3
339 PENT CH OF GOD	1	35	77	.2	.5
349 PENT HOLINESS	1	65	84*	.2	.5
355 PRESB CH (USA)	1	140	181*	.4	1.1
413 S.D.A.	1	20	26*	.1	.2
419 SO BAPT CONV	14	7,032	9,091*	19.0	57.5
449 UN METHODIST	7	1,238	1,601*	3.3	10.1
496 JEWISH EST[1]	0	NA	200	.4	1.3
497 BLACK BAPT EST[2]	NA	601	777*	1.6	4.9
WASHINGTON	**70**	**27,119**	**40,017***	**83.3**	**100.0**
053 ASSEMB OF GOD	5	587	1,107	2.3	2.8
081 CATHOLIC	3	NA	3,375	7.0	8.4
081d *LATIN*	*3*	*NA*	*3,375*	*7.0*	*8.4*
093 CHR CH (DISC)	2	657	932	1.9	2.3
097 CHR CHS&CHS CR	4	1,289	1,619*	3.4	4.0
111 CH CR,SCIENTST	1	NR	NR	-	-
123 CH GOD (ANDER)	1	105	186	.4	.5
127 CH GOD (CLEVE)	1	48	60*	.1	.1
145 CH GOD PROPHCY	1	33	41*	.1	.1
151 L-D SAINTS	2	NA	711	1.5	1.8
165 CH OF NAZARENE	2	536	556	1.2	1.4
167 CHS OF CHRIST	3	972	1,308	2.7	3.3
193 EPISCOPAL	1	656	679	1.4	1.7
207 E.L.C.A.	1	112	160	.3	.4
215 EVAN METH CH	1	35	44*	.1	.1
217 FIRE BAPTIZED	2	36	45*	.1	.1
223 FREE WILL BAPT	2	164	206*	.4	.5
226 FRIENDS-USA	2	110	138*	.3	.3
226b *EFI*	*2*	*110*	*138*	*.3*	*.3*
283 LUTH—MO SYNOD	1	568	703	1.5	1.8
353 CHR BRETHREN	1	23	60	.1	.1

NA–Not applicable   NR–Not reported   *Total adherents estimated from known number of communicant, confirmed, full members.   - Represents a percent less than 0.1.   Percentages may not total due to rounding.
[1]See Appendix E   [2]See Appendix F   [3]See Appendix G   Lines in *italic* represent a breakdown of Catholic rites or Friends affiliations. They are included in their respective denominational total.

Table 4. Churches and Church Membership by County and Denomination: 1990

County and Denomination	Number of churches	Communicant, confirmed, full members	Total adherents Number	Percent of total population	Percent of total adherents
355 PRESB CH (USA)	2	1,656	2,080*	4.3	5.2
403 SALVATION ARMY	1	171	176	.4	.4
413 S.D.A.	1	89	112*	.2	.3
419 SO BAPT CONV	19	11,338	14,243*	29.6	35.6
435 UNITARIAN-UNIV	1	21	21	-	.1
449 UN METHODIST	8	7,039	8,842*	18.4	22.1
467 WESLEYAN	2	561	2,220	4.6	5.5
497 BLACK BAPT EST[2]	NA	313	393*	.8	1.0
WASHITA	**39**	**7,328**	**9,584***	**83.8**	**100.0**
053 ASSEMB OF GOD	3	110	154	1.3	1.6
081 CATHOLIC	1	NA	125	1.1	1.3
081d LATIN	*1*	*NA*	*125*	*1.1*	*1.3*
151 L-D SAINTS	1	NA	208	1.8	2.2
165 CH OF NAZARENE	1	0	0	-	-
167 CHS OF CHRIST	9	803	941	8.2	9.8
185 CUMBER PRESB	1	47	63	.6	.7
207 E.L.C.A.	1	221	264	2.3	2.8
237 GC MENN BR CHS	2	668	848*	7.4	8.8
287 MENN GEN CONF	1	126	139	1.2	1.5
313 N AM BAPT CONF	1	108	137*	1.2	1.4
349 PENT HOLINESS	1	24	30*	.3	.3
355 PRESB CH (USA)	2	139	176*	1.5	1.8
419 SO BAPT CONV	7	3,429	4,351*	38.0	45.4
449 UN METHODIST	7	1,614	2,048*	17.9	21.4
467 WESLEYAN	1	39	100	.9	1.0
WOODS	**39**	**4,987**	**6,903***	**75.8**	**100.0**
053 ASSEMB OF GOD	2	107	195	2.1	2.8
081 CATHOLIC	2	NA	400	4.4	5.8
081d LATIN	*2*	*NA*	*400*	*4.4*	*5.8*
093 CHR CH (DISC)	4	380	546	6.0	7.9
097 CHR CHS&CHS CR	1	65	78*	.9	1.1
123 CH GOD (ANDER)	3	175	251	2.8	3.6
151 L-D SAINTS	1	NA	63	.7	.9
165 CH OF NAZARENE	3	114	208	2.3	3.0
167 CHS OF CHRIST	3	284	397	4.4	5.8
193 EPISCOPAL	1	29	53	.6	.8
221 FREE METHODIST	1	33	33	.4	.5
226 FRIENDS-USA	1	143	172*	1.9	2.5
226b EFI	*1*	*143*	*172**	*1.9*	*2.5*
259 IFCA	1	NR	NR	-	-
283 LUTH—MO SYNOD	1	324	409	4.5	5.9
355 PRESB CH (USA)	1	128	154*	1.7	2.2
413 S.D.A.	1	21	25*	.3	.4
419 SO BAPT CONV	4	1,242	1,497*	16.4	21.7
449 UN METHODIST	6	1,762	2,123*	23.3	30.8
467 WESLEYAN	3	180	299	3.3	4.3
WOODWARD	**36**	**9,736**	**14,587***	**76.9**	**100.0**
053 ASSEMB OF GOD	3	454	842	4.4	5.8
081 CATHOLIC	2	NA	1,665	8.8	11.4
081d LATIN	*2*	*NA*	*1,665*	*8.8*	*11.4*
093 CHR CH (DISC)	3	688	805	4.2	5.5
097 CHR CHS&CHS CR	3	149	191*	1.0	1.3
127 CH GOD (CLEVE)	1	51	65*	.3	.4
165 CH OF NAZARENE	1	238	492	2.6	3.4
167 CHS OF CHRIST	1	280	364	1.9	2.5
193 EPISCOPAL	1	85	141	.7	1.0
221 FREE METHODIST	1	6	13	.1	.1
223 FREE WILL BAPT	1	77	99*	.5	.7
283 LUTH—MO SYNOD	1	175	240	1.3	1.6
355 PRESB CH (USA)	1	169	217*	1.1	1.5
413 S.D.A.	1	71	91*	.5	.6
419 SO BAPT CONV	8	4,480	5,751*	30.3	39.4
449 UN METHODIST	8	2,813	3,611*	19.0	24.8

OREGON

County and Denomination	Number of churches	Communicant, confirmed, full members	Total adherents Number	Percent of total population	Percent of total adherents
THE STATE.....	2,908	365,034	915,285*	32.2	100.0
BAKER	**35**	**1,831**	**5,037***	**32.9**	**100.0**
053 ASSEMB OF GOD	3	134	439	2.9	8.7
081 CATHOLIC	5	NA	1,270	8.3	25.2
081d LATIN	*5*	*NA*	*1,270*	*8.3*	*25.2*
097 CHR CHS&CHS CR	2	239	301*	2.0	6.0
111 CH CR,SCIENTST	1	NR	NR	-	-
151 L-D SAINTS	3	NA	1,015	6.6	20.2
165 CH OF NAZARENE	2	231	428	2.8	8.5
167 CHS OF CHRIST	2	22	34	.2	.7
179 CONSRV BAPT	4	NR	NR	-	-

County and Denomination	Number of churches	Communicant, confirmed, full members	Total adherents Number	Percent of total population	Percent of total adherents
193 EPISCOPAL	1	56	115	.8	2.3
207 E.L.C.A.	1	202	245	1.6	4.9
263 INT FOURSQ GOS	1	43	54*	.4	1.1
339 PENT CH OF GOD	1	29	41	.3	.8
355 PRESB CH (USA)	2	217	273*	1.8	5.4
403 SALVATION ARMY	1	67	78	.5	1.5
413 S.D.A.	2	224	282*	1.8	5.6
449 UN METHODIST	4	367	462*	3.0	9.2
BENTON	**57**	**9,177**	**19,407***	**27.4**	**100.0**
019 AMER BAPT USA	1	31	38*	.1	.2
053 ASSEMB OF GOD	3	352	817	1.2	4.2
057 BAPT GEN CONF	1	25	30*	-	.2
081 CATHOLIC	2	NA	4,634	6.5	23.9
081d LATIN	*2*	*NA*	*4,634*	*6.5*	*23.9*
089 CHR & MISS AL	1	27	62	.1	.3
093 CHR CH (DISC)	1	335	505	.7	2.6
097 CHR CHS&CHS CR	2	295	358*	.5	1.8
105 CHRISTIAN REF	1	78	127	.2	.7
111 CH CR,SCIENTST	1	NR	NR	-	-
151 L-D SAINTS	5	NA	2,090	3.0	10.8
165 CH OF NAZARENE	2	463	548	.8	2.8
167 CHS OF CHRIST	3	154	232	.3	1.2
179 CONSRV BAPT	4	NR	NR	-	-
193 EPISCOPAL	1	896	1,033	1.5	5.3
207 E.L.C.A.	1	918	1,267	1.8	6.5
221 FREE METHODIST	1	24	30	-	.2
226 FRIENDS-USA	1	38	46*	.1	.2
226f INDEPENDNT	*1*	*38*	*46**	*.1*	*.2*
263 INT FOURSQ GOS	3	289	351*	.5	1.8
283 LUTH—MO SYNOD	3	774	1,012	1.4	5.2
284 LUTH CH-AM ASC	1	60	60	.1	.3
285 MENNONITE CH	1	88	206	.3	1.1
339 PENT CH OF GOD	2	33	110	.2	.6
355 PRESB CH (USA)	2	967	1,175*	1.7	6.1
413 S.D.A.	2	303	368*	.5	1.9
419 SO BAPT CONV	3	869	1,055*	1.5	5.4
435 UNITARIAN-UNIV	1	325	589	.8	3.0
438 UN BRETH IN CR	1	106	106	.1	.5
443 UN C OF CHRIST	1	346	420*	.6	2.2
449 UN METHODIST	4	1,214	1,475*	2.1	7.6
469 WELS	1	62	85	.1	.4
496 JEWISH EST[1]	0	NA	150	.2	.8
497 BLACK BAPT EST[2]	NA	105	128*	.2	.7
498 INDEP.CHARIS.[3]	1	NA	300	.4	1.5
CLACKAMAS	**202**	**31,644**	**78,178***	**28.0**	**100.0**
001 ADVENT CHR CH	2	68	86*	-	.1
019 AMER BAPT USA	6	1,230	1,554*	.6	2.0
053 ASSEMB OF GOD	15	1,828	3,017	1.1	3.9
081 CATHOLIC	9	NA	16,192	5.8	20.7
081d LATIN	*9*	*NA*	*16,192*	*5.8*	*20.7*
089 CHR & MISS AL	4	179	520	.2	.7
093 CHR CH (DISC)	1	421	593	.2	.8
097 CHR CHS&CHS CR	13	2,899	3,663*	1.3	4.7
111 CH CR,SCIENTST	2	NR	NR	-	-
123 CH GOD (ANDER)	1	0	46	-	.1
127 CH GOD (CLEVE)	1	170	215*	.1	.3
151 L-D SAINTS	20	NA	8,877	3.2	11.4
165 CH OF NAZARENE	8	1,033	1,312	.5	1.7
167 CHS OF CHRIST	7	495	662	.2	.8
175 CONGR CHR CHS	1	66	83*	-	.1
176 CCC, NOT NAT'L	1	20	25*	-	-
179 CONSRV BAPT	14	NR	NR	-	-
181 CONSRV CONGR	1	7	9*	-	-
193 EPISCOPAL	7	1,957	2,574	.9	3.3
203 EVAN FREE CH	2	215	420	.2	.5
207 E.L.C.A.	13	5,045	6,844	2.5	8.8
215 EVAN METH CH	1	42	53*	-	.1
221 FREE METHODIST	1	24	35	-	-
226 FRIENDS-USA	1	151	204	.1	.3
226b EFI	*1*	*151*	*204*	*.1*	*.3*
263 INT FOURSQ GOS	6	1,909	2,412*	.9	3.1
283 LUTH—MO SYNOD	8	2,055	2,757	1.0	3.5
285 MENNONITE CH	2	312	462	.2	.6
287 MENN GEN CONF	1	308	408	.1	.5
313 N AM BAPT CONF	2	178	225*	.1	.3
353 CHR BRETHREN	1	75	100	-	.1
355 PRESB CH (USA)	8	2,395	3,026*	1.1	3.9
361 PRIM BAPT ASCS	1	17	21*	-	-
413 S.D.A.	9	3,268	4,130*	1.5	5.3
419 SO BAPT CONV	8	1,166	1,473*	.5	1.9
435 UNITARIAN-UNIV	2	92	128	-	.2
443 UN C OF CHRIST	6	771	974*	.3	1.2
449 UN METHODIST	13	2,941	3,716*	1.3	4.8
467 WESLEYAN	1	65	160	.1	.2
496 JEWISH EST[1]	0	NA	1,396	.5	1.8

NA–Not applicable   NR–Not reported   *Total adherents estimated from known number of communicant, confirmed, full members.   - Represents a percent less than 0.1.   Percentages may not total due to rounding.
[1]See Appendix E   [2]See Appendix F   [3]See Appendix G   Lines in *italic* represent a breakdown of Catholic rites or Friends affiliations. They are included in their respective denominational total.

Table 4. Churches and Church Membership by County and Denomination: 1990

County and Denomination		Number of churches	Communicant, confirmed, full members	Total adherents		
				Number	Percent of total population	Percent of total adherents
497	BLACK BAPT EST[2]	NA	242	306*	.1	.4
498	INDEP.CHARIS.[3]	1	NA	5,100	1.8	6.5
499	INDEP.NON-CHAR[3]	2	NA	4,400	1.6	5.6
CLATSOP		**48**	**3,836**	**8,063***	**24.2**	**100.0**
019	AMER BAPT USA	1	135	169*	.5	2.1
045	APOSTOLIC LUTH	1	24	44	.1	.5
053	ASSEMB OF GOD	5	248	411	1.2	5.1
081	CATHOLIC	4	NA	1,619	4.9	20.1
081d	*LATIN*	4	*NA*	*1,619*	*4.9*	*20.1*
097	CHR CHS&CHS CR	3	294	369*	1.1	4.6
111	CH CR,SCIENTST	2	NR	NR	-	-
151	L-D SAINTS	3	NA	886	2.7	11.0
165	CH OF NAZARENE	3	125	357	1.1	4.4
167	CHS OF CHRIST	1	28	36	.1	.4
179	CONSRV BAPT	4	NR	NR	-	-
193	EPISCOPAL	3	300	519	1.6	6.4
207	E.L.C.A.	4	1,438	2,085	6.3	25.9
220	FREE LUTHERAN	1	136	161	.5	2.0
226	FRIENDS-USA	1	37	67	.2	.8
226b	*EFI*	1	*37*	*67*	*.2*	*.8*
263	INT FOURSQ GOS	2	119	149*	.4	1.8
283	LUTH—MO SYNOD	1	44	53	.2	.7
355	PRESB CH (USA)	3	340	426*	1.3	5.3
413	S.D.A.	2	129	162*	.5	2.0
443	UN C OF CHRIST	1	16	20*	.1	.2
449	UN METHODIST	3	423	530*	1.6	6.6
COLUMBIA		**55**	**4,185**	**9,668***	**25.7**	**100.0**
045	APOSTOLIC LUTH	1	41	55	.1	.6
053	ASSEMB OF GOD	6	416	881	2.3	9.1
057	BAPT GEN CONF	2	253	326*	.9	3.4
081	CATHOLIC	5	NA	2,121	5.6	21.9
081d	*LATIN*	5	*NA*	*2,121*	*5.6*	*21.9*
093	CHR CH (DISC)	1	138	253	.7	2.6
097	CHR CHS&CHS CR	2	150	193*	.5	2.0
123	CH GOD (ANDER)	3	428	646	1.7	6.7
151	L-D SAINTS	4	NA	1,466	3.9	15.2
165	CH OF NAZARENE	2	55	154	.4	1.6
167	CHS OF CHRIST	2	140	182	.5	1.9
176	CCC, NOT NAT'L	1	234	301*	.8	3.1
179	CONSRV BAPT	4	NR	NR	-	-
193	EPISCOPAL	2	96	153	.4	1.6
207	E.L.C.A.	3	562	737	2.0	7.6
221	FREE METHODIST	1	28	38	.1	.4
259	IFCA	1	NR	NR	-	-
263	INT FOURSQ GOS	3	211	272*	.7	2.8
283	LUTH—MO SYNOD	2	441	613	1.6	6.3
355	PRESB CH (USA)	2	239	308*	.8	3.2
413	S.D.A.	3	226	291*	.8	3.0
419	SO BAPT CONV	2	175	225*	.6	2.3
449	UN METHODIST	3	352	453*	1.2	4.7
COOS		**81**	**7,261**	**13,955***	**23.2**	**100.0**
019	AMER BAPT USA	2	283	352*	.6	2.5
053	ASSEMB OF GOD	7	559	1,021	1.7	7.3
081	CATHOLIC	3	NA	2,875	4.8	20.6
081d	*LATIN*	3	*NA*	*2,875*	*4.8*	*20.6*
089	CHR & MISS AL	1	41	80	.1	.6
093	CHR CH (DISC)	2	367	503	.8	3.6
097	CHR CHS&CHS CR	5	570	709*	1.2	5.1
105	CHRISTIAN REF	1	36	61	.1	.4
111	CH CR,SCIENTST	2	NR	NR	-	-
123	CH GOD (ANDER)	4	372	417	.7	3.0
127	CH GOD (CLEVE)	3	121	150*	.2	1.1
151	L-D SAINTS	4	NA	1,582	2.6	11.3
157	CH OF BRETHREN	1	25	31*	.1	.2
165	CH OF NAZARENE	4	457	479	.8	3.4
167	CHS OF CHRIST	2	191	229	.4	1.6
179	CONSRV BAPT	6	NR	NR	-	-
193	EPISCOPAL	5	422	583	1.0	4.2
207	E.L.C.A.	3	662	850	1.4	6.1
263	INT FOURSQ GOS	4	554	689*	1.1	4.9
283	LUTH—MO SYNOD	2	316	448	.7	3.2
329	OPEN BIBLE STD	1	NR	NR	-	-
339	PENT CH OF GOD	2	48	116	.2	.8
355	PRESB CH (USA)	5	561	698*	1.2	5.0
403	SALVATION ARMY	1	44	53	.1	.4
413	S.D.A.	4	651	810*	1.3	5.8
419	SO BAPT CONV	2	372	463*	.8	3.3
449	UN METHODIST	4	601	747*	1.2	5.4
469	WELS	1	8	9	-	.1
CROOK		**18**	**1,941**	**3,724***	**26.4**	**100.0**
053	ASSEMB OF GOD	1	114	200	1.4	5.4

County and Denomination		Number of churches	Communicant, confirmed, full members	Total adherents		
				Number	Percent of total population	Percent of total adherents
081	CATHOLIC	1	NA	573	4.1	15.4
081d	*LATIN*	1	*NA*	*573*	*4.1*	*15.4*
097	CHR CHS&CHS CR	2	381	484*	3.4	13.0
123	CH GOD (ANDER)	1	24	26	.2	.7
145	CH GOD PROPHCY	1	27	34*	.2	.9
151	L-D SAINTS	1	NA	552	3.9	14.8
165	CH OF NAZARENE	1	213	254	1.8	6.8
167	CHS OF CHRIST	1	55	125	.9	3.4
179	CONSRV BAPT	1	NR	NR	-	-
193	EPISCOPAL	1	90	146	1.0	3.9
207	E.L.C.A.	2	493	656	4.6	17.6
263	INT FOURSQ GOS	1	88	112*	.8	3.0
339	PENT CH OF GOD	1	65	65	.5	1.7
355	PRESB CH (USA)	1	54	69*	.5	1.9
413	S.D.A.	1	59	75*	.5	2.0
419	SO BAPT CONV	1	278	353*	2.5	9.5
CURRY		**30**	**2,023**	**4,528***	**23.4**	**100.0**
019	AMER BAPT USA	1	124	148*	.8	3.3
053	ASSEMB OF GOD	4	305	401	2.1	8.9
081	CATHOLIC	1	NA	1,367	7.1	30.2
081d	*LATIN*	1	*NA*	*1,367*	*7.1*	*30.2*
097	CHR CHS&CHS CR	1	150	179*	.9	4.0
111	CH CR,SCIENTST	2	NR	NR	-	-
151	L-D SAINTS	2	NA	575	3.0	12.7
165	CH OF NAZARENE	1	152	203	1.1	4.5
167	CHS OF CHRIST	2	92	126	.7	2.8
179	CONSRV BAPT	2	NR	NR	-	-
193	EPISCOPAL	3	124	134	.7	3.0
207	E.L.C.A.	3	342	481	2.5	10.6
263	INT FOURSQ GOS	2	136	163*	.8	3.6
339	PENT CH OF GOD	1	34	77	.4	1.7
355	PRESB CH (USA)	2	280	335*	1.7	7.4
413	S.D.A.	2	166	198*	1.0	4.4
419	SO BAPT CONV	1	118	141*	.7	3.1
DESCHUTES		**77**	**8,625**	**18,161***	**24.2**	**100.0**
053	ASSEMB OF GOD	4	599	1,095	1.5	6.0
081	CATHOLIC	4	NA	4,477	6.0	24.7
081d	*LATIN*	4	*NA*	*4,477*	*6.0*	*24.7*
089	CHR & MISS AL	2	7	30	-	.2
097	CHR CHS&CHS CR	5	555	697*	.9	3.8
111	CH CR,SCIENTST	1	NR	NR	-	-
123	CH GOD (ANDER)	1	34	34	-	.2
127	CH GOD (CLEVE)	1	45	57*	.1	.3
133	CH GOD(7TH)DEN	1	74	94	.1	.5
151	L-D SAINTS	7	NA	2,306	3.1	12.7
165	CH OF NAZARENE	4	420	510	.7	2.8
167	CHS OF CHRIST	4	242	476	.6	2.6
179	CONSRV BAPT	5	NR	NR	-	-
193	EPISCOPAL	3	693	789	1.1	4.3
203	EVAN FREE CH	1	250	250	.3	1.4
207	E.L.C.A.	4	628	808	1.1	4.4
221	FREE METHODIST	2	126	180	.2	1.0
226	FRIENDS-USA	2	11	59	.1	.3
226b	*EFI*	1	*7*	*43*	*.1*	*.2*
226f	*INDEPENDNT*	1	*4*	*16*	*-*	*.1*
259	IFCA	1	NR	NR	-	-
263	INT FOURSQ GOS	4	1,400	1,758*	2.3	9.7
283	LUTH—MO SYNOD	3	674	901	1.2	5.0
329	OPEN BIBLE STD	1	NR	NR	-	-
339	PENT CH OF GOD	2	70	120	.2	.7
355	PRESB CH (USA)	2	792	995*	1.3	5.5
403	SALVATION ARMY	1	22	25	-	.1
413	S.D.A.	2	355	446*	.6	2.5
419	SO BAPT CONV	7	1,094	1,374*	1.8	7.6
435	UNITARIAN-UNIV	1	30	35	-	.2
449	UN METHODIST	1	439	551*	.7	3.0
469	WELS	1	65	94	.1	.5
DOUGLAS		**142**	**13,932**	**25,296***	**26.7**	**100.0**
019	AMER BAPT USA	3	339	429*	.5	1.7
053	ASSEMB OF GOD	13	992	1,935	2.0	7.6
057	BAPT GEN CONF	1	40	51*	.1	.2
081	CATHOLIC	5	NA	3,880	4.1	15.3
081d	*LATIN*	5	*NA*	*3,880*	*4.1*	*15.3*
089	CHR & MISS AL	1	29	54	.1	.2
093	CHR CH (DISC)	2	105	141	.1	.6
097	CHR CHS&CHS CR	15	1,730	2,188*	2.3	8.6
111	CH CR,SCIENTST	1	NR	NR	-	-
123	CH GOD (ANDER)	3	287	319	.3	1.3
127	CH GOD (CLEVE)	3	204	258*	.3	1.0
145	CH GOD PROPHCY	3	81	102*	.1	.4
151	L-D SAINTS	8	NA	2,805	3.0	11.1
165	CH OF NAZARENE	5	562	513	.5	2.0
167	CHS OF CHRIST	8	641	824	.9	3.3

NA—Not applicable NR—Not reported *Total adherents estimated from known number of communicant, confirmed, full members. - Represents a percent less than 0.1. Percentages may not total due to rounding.
[1]See Appendix E [2]See Appendix F [3]See Appendix G Lines in *italic* represent a breakdown of Catholic rites or Friends affiliations. They are included in their respective denominational total.

Table 4. Churches and Church Membership by County and Denomination: 1990

County and Denomination	Number of churches	Communicant, confirmed, full members	Total adherents Number	Percent of total population	Percent of total adherents
179 CONSRV BAPT	4	NR	NR	-	-
193 EPISCOPAL	5	372	586	.6	2.3
203 EVAN FREE CH	2	125	273	.3	1.1
207 E.L.C.A.	1	507	622	.7	2.5
209 EVAN LUTH SYN	2	138	183	.2	.7
217 FIRE BAPTIZED	1	3	4*	-	-
221 FREE METHODIST	2	87	124	.1	.5
226 FRIENDS-USA	2	17	35	-	.1
226b EFI	*1*	*12*	*27*	*-*	*.1*
226f INDEPENDNT	*1*	*5*	*8*	*-*	*-*
259 IFCA	1	NR	NR	-	-
263 INT FOURSQ GOS	5	683	864*	.9	3.4
283 LUTH—MO SYNOD	3	801	1,085	1.1	4.3
285 MENNONITE CH	1	21	39	-	.2
291 MISSIONARY CH	3	157	272	.3	1.1
329 OPEN BIBLE STD	2	NR	NR	-	-
339 PENT CH OF GOD	1	12	70	.1	.3
355 PRESB CH (USA)	5	627	793*	.8	3.1
403 SALVATION ARMY	1	51	51	.1	.2
413 S.D.A.	9	1,776	2,246*	2.4	8.9
419 SO BAPT CONV	7	2,227	2,817*	3.0	11.1
435 UNITARIAN-UNIV	1	73	95	.1	.4
449 UN METHODIST	12	1,232	1,558*	1.6	6.2
467 WESLEYAN	1	13	80	.1	.3
GILLIAM	**8**	**255**	**572***	**33.3**	**100.0**
081 CATHOLIC	3	NA	238	13.9	41.6
081d LATIN	*3*	*NA*	*238*	*13.9*	*41.6*
165 CH OF NAZARENE	1	39	57	3.3	10.0
179 CONSRV BAPT	1	NR	NR	-	-
413 S.D.A.	1	19	24*	1.4	4.2
443 UN C OF CHRIST	1	137	176*	10.3	30.8
449 UN METHODIST	1	60	77*	4.5	13.5
GRANT	**25**	**761**	**1,885***	**24.0**	**100.0**
053 ASSEMB OF GOD	2	67	101	1.3	5.4
081 CATHOLIC	4	NA	350	4.5	18.6
081d LATIN	*4*	*NA*	*350*	*4.5*	*18.6*
093 CHR CH (DISC)	1	93	131	1.7	6.9
151 L-D SAINTS	2	NA	431	5.5	22.9
165 CH OF NAZARENE	1	66	176	2.2	9.3
167 CHS OF CHRIST	1	7	8	.1	.4
179 CONSRV BAPT	2	NR	NR	-	-
193 EPISCOPAL	1	29	40	.5	2.1
215 EVAN METH CH	1	23	29*	.4	1.5
263 INT FOURSQ GOS	1	56	71*	.9	3.8
283 LUTH—MO SYNOD	1	33	55	.7	2.9
355 PRESB CH (USA)	3	61	78*	1.0	4.1
413 S.D.A.	2	151	192*	2.4	10.2
419 SO BAPT CONV	1	33	42*	.5	2.2
449 UN METHODIST	2	142	181*	2.3	9.6
HARNEY	**17**	**740**	**2,488***	**35.2**	**100.0**
053 ASSEMB OF GOD	1	143	192	2.7	7.7
081 CATHOLIC	2	NA	1,103	15.6	44.3
081d LATIN	*2*	*NA*	*1,103*	*15.6*	*44.3*
093 CHR CH (DISC)	1	96	135	1.9	5.4
097 CHR CHS&CHS CR	1	53	68*	1.0	2.7
111 CH CR,SCIENTST	1	NR	NR	-	-
151 L-D SAINTS	2	NA	379	5.4	15.2
165 CH OF NAZARENE	1	81	89	1.3	3.6
167 CHS OF CHRIST	1	16	20	.3	.8
179 CONSRV BAPT	1	NR	NR	-	-
193 EPISCOPAL	1	48	69	1.0	2.8
207 E.L.C.A.	1	57	90	1.3	3.6
263 INT FOURSQ GOS	1	26	33*	.5	1.3
283 LUTH—MO SYNOD	1	57	101	1.4	4.1
355 PRESB CH (USA)	1	117	150*	2.1	6.0
413 S.D.A.	1	46	59*	.8	2.4
HOOD RIVER	**32**	**3,117**	**5,617***	**33.2**	**100.0**
053 ASSEMB OF GOD	3	290	489	2.9	8.7
081 CATHOLIC	1	NA	712	4.2	12.7
081d LATIN	*1*	*NA*	*712*	*4.2*	*12.7*
089 CHR & MISS AL	1	104	200	1.2	3.6
093 CHR CH (DISC)	1	231	347	2.1	6.2
111 CH CR,SCIENTST	1	NR	NR	-	-
151 L-D SAINTS	1	NA	563	3.3	10.0
165 CH OF NAZARENE	2	202	240	1.4	4.3
167 CHS OF CHRIST	3	129	187	1.1	3.3
179 CONSRV BAPT	2	NR	NR	-	-
193 EPISCOPAL	1	163	300	1.8	5.3
207 E.L.C.A.	1	83	133	.8	2.4
209 EVAN LUTH SYN	1	43	56	.3	1.0
226 FRIENDS-USA	1	3	13	.1	.2
226f INDEPENDNT	*1*	*3*	*13*	*.1*	*.2*

County and Denomination	Number of churches	Communicant, confirmed, full members	Total adherents Number	Percent of total population	Percent of total adherents
263 INT FOURSQ GOS	1	118	150*	.9	2.7
283 LUTH—MO SYNOD	1	148	185	1.1	3.3
355 PRESB CH (USA)	1	90	115*	.7	2.0
413 S.D.A.	1	190	242*	1.4	4.3
419 SO BAPT CONV	4	762	971*	5.7	17.3
443 UN C OF CHRIST	2	235	299*	1.8	5.3
449 UN METHODIST	3	326	415*	2.5	7.4
JACKSON	**139**	**15,898**	**48,636***	**33.2**	**100.0**
001 ADVENT CHR CH	1	17	21*	-	-
019 AMER BAPT USA	2	593	738*	.5	1.5
053 ASSEMB OF GOD	15	1,898	3,039	2.1	6.2
081 CATHOLIC	5	NA	13,931	9.5	28.6
081d LATIN	*5*	*NA*	*13,931*	*9.5*	*28.6*
089 CHR & MISS AL	2	70	131	.1	.3
093 CHR CH (DISC)	1	286	387	.3	.8
097 CHR CHS&CHS CR	9	1,187	1,478*	1.0	3.0
111 CH CR,SCIENTST	2	NR	NR	-	-
123 CH GOD (ANDER)	2	90	105	.1	.2
127 CH GOD (CLEVE)	1	19	24*	-	-
151 L-D SAINTS	11	NA	4,699	3.2	9.7
165 CH OF NAZARENE	8	995	2,237	1.5	4.6
167 CHS OF CHRIST	8	614	767	.5	1.6
179 CONSRV BAPT	6	NR	NR	-	-
193 EPISCOPAL	3	788	1,163	.8	2.4
203 EVAN FREE CH	1	0	45	-	.1
207 E.L.C.A.	2	1,005	1,180	.8	2.4
217 FIRE BAPTIZED	1	1	1*	-	-
221 FREE METHODIST	1	51	51	-	.1
226 FRIENDS-USA	3	286	369*	.3	.8
226b EFI	*2*	*259*	*335*	*.2*	*.7*
226f INDEPENDNT	*1*	*27*	*34**	*-*	*.1*
259 IFCA	1	NR	NR	-	-
263 INT FOURSQ GOS	3	333	415*	.3	.9
283 LUTH—MO SYNOD	5	843	1,045	.7	2.1
339 PENT CH OF GOD	5	156	440	.3	.9
353 CHR BRETHREN	1	12	18	-	-
355 PRESB CH (USA)	7	1,826	2,273*	1.6	4.7
403 SALVATION ARMY	1	144	161	.1	.3
413 S.D.A.	6	1,488	1,852*	1.3	3.8
419 SO BAPT CONV	8	1,423	1,771*	1.2	3.6
435 UNITARIAN-UNIV	1	185	291	.2	.6
443 UN C OF CHRIST	2	249	310*	.2	.6
449 UN METHODIST	5	1,243	1,547*	1.1	3.2
467 WESLEYAN	1	34	60	-	.1
469 WELS	1	62	87	.1	.2
496 JEWISH EST[1]	1	NA	500	.3	1.0
498 INDEP.CHARIS.[3]	1	NA	350	.2	.7
499 INDEP.NON-CHAR[3]	6	NA	7,150	4.9	14.7
JEFFERSON	**24**	**2,439**	**3,965***	**29.0**	**100.0**
053 ASSEMB OF GOD	1	50	70	.5	1.8
081 CATHOLIC	2	NA	629	4.6	15.9
081d LATIN	*2*	*NA*	*629*	*4.6*	*15.9*
093 CHR CH (DISC)	1	78	109	.8	2.7
097 CHR CHS&CHS CR	1	75	101*	.7	2.5
111 CH CR,SCIENTST	1	NR	NR	-	-
165 CH OF NAZARENE	2	43	98	.7	2.5
167 CHS OF CHRIST	1	23	30	.2	.8
179 CONSRV BAPT	2	NR	NR	-	-
193 EPISCOPAL	1	57	59	.4	1.5
207 E.L.C.A.	1	134	187	1.4	4.7
221 FREE METHODIST	1	99	144	1.1	3.6
226 FRIENDS-USA	1	85	131	1.0	3.3
226b EFI	*1*	*85*	*131*	*1.0*	*3.3*
263 INT FOURSQ GOS	1	34	46*	.3	1.2
285 MENNONITE CH	1	115	151	1.1	3.8
339 PENT CH OF GOD	1	2	5	-	.1
355 PRESB CH (USA)	1	43	58*	.4	1.5
413 S.D.A.	1	118	158*	1.2	4.0
419 SO BAPT CONV	3	1,193	1,600*	11.7	40.4
449 UN METHODIST	1	290	389*	2.8	9.8
JOSEPHINE	**58**	**7,537**	**18,432***	**29.4**	**100.0**
019 AMER BAPT USA	4	1,642	2,024*	3.2	11.0
053 ASSEMB OF GOD	3	527	3,538	5.6	19.2
075 BRETHREN IN CR	1	164	164	.3	.9
081 CATHOLIC	2	NA	3,378	5.4	18.3
081d LATIN	*2*	*NA*	*3,378*	*5.4*	*18.3*
089 CHR & MISS AL	2	79	188	.3	1.0
093 CHR CH (DISC)	1	195	209	.3	1.1
097 CHR CHS&CHS CR	2	362	446*	.7	2.4
111 CH CR,SCIENTST	2	NR	NR	-	-
123 CH GOD (ANDER)	1	40	40	.1	.2
127 CH GOD (CLEVE)	1	46	57*	.1	.3
151 L-D SAINTS	5	NA	2,208	3.5	12.0

NA–Not applicable   NR–Not reported   *Total adherents estimated from known number of communicant, confirmed, full members.   - Represents a percent less than 0.1.   Percentages may not total due to rounding.
[1]See Appendix E   [2]See Appendix F   [3]See Appendix G   Lines in *italic* represent a breakdown of Catholic rites or Friends affiliations. They are included in their respective denominational total.

OREGON

Table 4. Churches and Church Membership by County and Denomination: 1990

County and Denomination	Number of churches	Communicant, confirmed, full members	Total adherents		
			Number	Percent of total population	Percent of total adherents
157 CH OF BRETHREN	1	68	84*	.1	.5
165 CH OF NAZARENE	2	84	175	.3	.9
167 CHS OF CHRIST	4	271	332	.5	1.8
179 CONSRV BAPT	2	NR	NR	-	-
193 EPISCOPAL	2	268	426	.7	2.3
207 E.L.C.A.	2	466	524	.8	2.8
209 EVAN LUTH SYN	1	43	57	.1	.3
221 FREE METHODIST	1	31	110	.2	.6
259 IFCA	1	NR	NR	-	-
263 INT FOURSQ GOS	1	222	274*	.4	1.5
283 LUTH—MO SYNOD	1	307	380	.6	2.1
285 MENNONITE CH	1	64	104	.2	.6
339 PENT CH OF GOD	1	17	45	.1	.2
353 CHR BRETHREN	1	25	50	.1	.3
355 PRESB CH (USA)	1	348	429*	.7	2.3
413 S.D.A.	4	1,127	1,389*	2.2	7.5
419 SO BAPT CONV	3	586	722*	1.2	3.9
435 UNITARIAN-UNIV	1	22	22	-	.1
449 UN METHODIST	3	533	657*	1.0	3.6
498 INDEP.CHARIS.3	1	NA	400	.6	2.2
KLAMATH	**71**	**7,071**	**18,723***	**32.4**	**100.0**
053 ASSEMB OF GOD	8	610	1,373	2.4	7.3
081 CATHOLIC	6	NA	6,596	11.4	35.2
081d LATIN	6	NA	6,596	11.4	35.2
089 CHR & MISS AL	2	23	129	.2	.7
097 CHR CHS&CHS CR	4	1,363	1,720*	3.0	9.2
111 CH CR,SCIENTST	1	NR	NR	-	-
123 CH GOD (ANDER)	1	150	158	.3	.8
145 CH GOD PROPHCY	1	27	34*	.1	.2
151 L-D SAINTS	7	NA	2,146	3.7	11.5
157 CH OF BRETHREN	1	26	33*	.1	.2
165 CH OF NAZARENE	1	91	216	.4	1.2
167 CHS OF CHRIST	2	120	290	.5	1.5
179 CONSRV BAPT	2	NR	NR	-	-
193 EPISCOPAL	2	464	541	.9	2.9
203 EVAN FREE CH	1	143	300	.5	1.6
207 E.L.C.A.	2	634	866	1.5	4.6
209 EVAN LUTH SYN	1	71	90	.2	.5
226 FRIENDS-USA	2	74	157	.3	.8
226b EFI	2	74	157	.3	.8
263 INT FOURSQ GOS	2	238	300*	.5	1.6
283 LUTH—MO SYNOD	2	199	204	.4	1.1
329 OPEN BIBLE STD	3	NR	NR	-	-
355 PRESB CH (USA)	5	763	963*	1.7	5.1
403 SALVATION ARMY	1	29	29	.1	.2
413 S.D.A.	2	389	491*	.9	2.6
419 SO BAPT CONV	4	1,191	1,503*	2.6	8.0
435 UNITARIAN-UNIV	1	15	15	-	.1
443 UN C OF CHRIST	1	47	59*	.1	.3
449 UN METHODIST	6	404	510*	.9	2.7
LAKE	**20**	**797**	**2,445***	**34.0**	**100.0**
053 ASSEMB OF GOD	3	107	300	4.2	12.3
081 CATHOLIC	3	NA	935	13.0	38.2
081d LATIN	3	NA	935	13.0	38.2
127 CH GOD (CLEVE)	1	66	85*	1.2	3.5
151 L-D SAINTS	1	NA	303	4.2	12.4
165 CH OF NAZARENE	1	40	81	1.1	3.3
167 CHS OF CHRIST	1	42	50	.7	2.0
179 CONSRV BAPT	1	NR	NR	-	-
193 EPISCOPAL	2	44	45	.6	1.8
263 INT FOURSQ GOS	1	62	80*	1.1	3.3
283 LUTH—MO SYNOD	1	52	73	1.0	3.0
329 OPEN BIBLE STD	1	NR	NR	-	-
355 PRESB CH (USA)	1	153	197*	2.7	8.1
413 S.D.A.	0	40	51*	.7	2.1
419 SO BAPT CONV	1	117	150*	2.1	6.1
449 UN METHODIST	2	74	95*	1.3	3.9
LANE	**270**	**35,385**	**69,530***	**24.6**	**100.0**
019 AMER BAPT USA	4	813	1,009*	.4	1.5
053 ASSEMB OF GOD	21	2,374	4,842	1.7	7.0
059 BAPT MISS ASSN	1	33	41*	-	.1
081 CATHOLIC	15	NA	12,439	4.4	17.9
081d LATIN	14	NA	12,423	4.4	17.9
081h UKRAINIAN	1	NA	16	-	-
089 CHR & MISS AL	2	124	235	.1	.3
093 CHR CH (DISC)	8	1,244	1,600	.6	2.3
097 CHR CHS&CHS CR	28	4,047	5,024*	1.8	7.2
111 CH CR,SCIENTST	3	NR	NR	-	-
123 CH GOD (ANDER)	4	231	445	.2	.6
127 CH GOD (CLEVE)	2	103	128*	-	.2
133 CH GOD(7TH)DEN	1	73	94	-	.1
145 CH GOD PROPHCY	1	27	34*	-	-
151 L-D SAINTS	19	NA	7,537	2.7	10.8
157 CH OF BRETHREN	1	41	51*	-	.1
163 CH OF LUTH BR	1	48	128	-	.2
165 CH OF NAZARENE	13	1,602	1,771	.6	2.5
167 CHS OF CHRIST	15	1,009	1,280	.5	1.8
179 CONSRV BAPT	15	NR	NR	-	-
193 EPISCOPAL	7	1,276	1,832	.6	2.6
207 E.L.C.A.	11	3,168	4,356	1.5	6.3
215 EVAN METH CH	1	55	68*	-	.1
217 FIRE BAPTIZED	1	5	6*	-	-
220 FREE LUTHERAN	1	75	82	-	.1
221 FREE METHODIST	3	296	341	.1	.5
223 FREE WILL BAPT	1	122	151*	.1	.2
226 FRIENDS-USA	4	256	414*	.1	.6
226b EFI	2	170	307	.1	.4
226f INDEPENDNT	2	86	107*	-	.2
237 GC MENN BR CHS	1	90	112*	-	.2
246 GREEK ORTHODOX	1	NR	NR	-	-
263 INT FOURSQ GOS	10	3,984	4,946*	1.7	7.1
283 LUTH—MO SYNOD	9	1,974	2,643	.9	3.8
285 MENNONITE CH	1	41	66	-	.1
287 MENN GEN CONF	1	27	27	-	-
329 OPEN BIBLE STD	10	NR	NR	-	-
339 PENT CH OF GOD	5	149	456	.2	.7
349 PENT HOLINESS	1	72	89*	-	.1
353 CHR BRETHREN	1	70	120	-	.2
355 PRESB CH (USA)	8	1,654	2,053*	.7	3.0
356 PRESB CH AMER	1	42	42	-	.1
403 SALVATION ARMY	2	136	178	.1	.3
413 S.D.A.	9	1,920	2,384*	.8	3.4
419 SO BAPT CONV	10	3,490	4,333*	1.5	6.2
435 UNITARIAN-UNIV	1	237	279	.1	.4
443 UN C OF CHRIST	1	657	816*	.3	1.2
449 UN METHODIST	12	3,276	4,067*	1.4	5.8
467 WESLEYAN	1	17	48	-	.1
469 WELS	1	78	106	-	.2
496 JEWISH EST1	1	NA	2,300	.8	3.3
497 BLACK BAPT EST2	NA	449	557*	.2	.8
LINCOLN	**62**	**4,669**	**8,932***	**23.0**	**100.0**
019 AMER BAPT USA	1	30	37*	.1	.4
053 ASSEMB OF GOD	7	491	1,027	2.6	11.5
081 CATHOLIC	4	NA	1,630	4.2	18.2
081d LATIN	4	NA	1,630	4.2	18.2
097 CHR CHS&CHS CR	7	318	391*	1.0	4.4
111 CH CR,SCIENTST	2	NR	NR	-	-
151 L-D SAINTS	3	NA	925	2.4	10.4
165 CH OF NAZARENE	3	297	309	.8	3.5
167 CHS OF CHRIST	3	80	123	.3	1.4
179 CONSRV BAPT	2	NR	NR	-	-
193 EPISCOPAL	4	414	633	1.6	7.1
207 E.L.C.A.	1	244	330	.8	3.7
221 FREE METHODIST	1	43	51	.1	.6
263 INT FOURSQ GOS	3	447	550*	1.4	6.2
283 LUTH—MO SYNOD	3	448	578	1.5	6.5
285 MENNONITE CH	2	59	115	.3	1.3
339 PENT CH OF GOD	1	35	65	.2	.7
355 PRESB CH (USA)	4	530	652*	1.7	7.3
413 S.D.A.	3	319	392*	1.0	4.4
419 SO BAPT CONV	5	522	642*	1.7	7.2
435 UNITARIAN-UNIV	1	26	32	.1	.4
443 UN C OF CHRIST	1	231	284*	.7	3.2
449 UN METHODIST	1	135	166*	.4	1.9
LINN	**121**	**13,370**	**25,666***	**28.1**	**100.0**
053 ASSEMB OF GOD	8	1,979	4,879	5.3	19.0
059 BAPT MISS ASSN	2	109	138*	.2	.5
063 BEREAN FUND CH	1	30	30	-	.1
081 CATHOLIC	8	NA	3,378	3.7	13.2
081d LATIN	8	NA	3,378	3.7	13.2
089 CHR & MISS AL	1	29	54	.1	.2
093 CHR CH (DISC)	3	598	785	.9	3.1
097 CHR CHS&CHS CR	9	1,575	1,995*	2.2	7.8
111 CH CR,SCIENTST	2	NR	NR	-	-
123 CH GOD (ANDER)	3	274	282	.3	1.1
133 CH GOD(7TH)DEN	1	74	94	.1	.4
143 CG IN CR(MENN)	1	99	125*	.1	.5
145 CH GOD PROPHCY	1	27	34*	-	.1
151 L-D SAINTS	6	NA	2,433	2.7	9.5
165 CH OF NAZARENE	4	486	517	.6	2.0
167 CHS OF CHRIST	6	248	391	.4	1.5
179 CONSRV BAPT	10	NR	NR	-	-
193 EPISCOPAL	3	195	299	.3	1.2
207 E.L.C.A.	4	1,217	1,587	1.7	6.2
221 FREE METHODIST	3	220	293	.3	1.1
263 INT FOURSQ GOS	6	485	614*	.7	2.4
283 LUTH—MO SYNOD	4	662	861	.9	3.4
285 MENNONITE CH	11	1,126	1,692	1.9	6.6

NA–Not applicable   NR–Not reported   *Total adherents estimated from known number of communicant, confirmed, full members.   - Represents a percent less than 0.1.   Percentages may not total due to rounding.
[1]See Appendix E   [2]See Appendix F   [3]See Appendix G   Lines in italic represent a breakdown of Catholic rites or Friends affiliations. They are included in their respective denominational total.

Table 4. Churches and Church Membership by County and Denomination: 1990

County and Denomination	Number of churches	Communicant, confirmed, full members	Total adherents Number	Percent of total population	Percent of total adherents
329 OPEN BIBLE STD	1	NR	NR	-	-
339 PENT CH OF GOD	3	92	294	.3	1.1
355 PRESB CH (USA)	4	792	1,003*	1.1	3.9
403 SALVATION ARMY	1	56	93	.1	.4
413 S.D.A.	4	549	695*	.8	2.7
419 SO BAPT CONV	4	1,100	1,393*	1.5	5.4
449 UN METHODIST	7	1,348	1,707*	1.9	6.7
MALHEUR	**53**	**3,328**	**10,326***	**39.7**	**100.0**
019 AMER BAPT USA	1	160	210*	.8	2.0
053 ASSEMB OF GOD	4	171	286	1.1	2.8
081 CATHOLIC	6	NA	2,581	9.9	25.0
081d LATIN	6	NA	2,581	9.9	25.0
093 CHR CH (DISC)	1	300	355	1.4	3.4
097 CHR CHS&CHS CR	3	385	505*	1.9	4.9
111 CH CR,SCIENTST	1	NR	NR	-	-
145 CH GOD PROPHCY	1	27	35*	.1	.3
151 L-D SAINTS	10	NA	3,159	12.1	30.6
165 CH OF NAZARENE	4	598	990	3.8	9.6
167 CHS OF CHRIST	1	65	100	.4	1.0
179 CONSRV BAPT	4	NR	NR	-	-
193 EPISCOPAL	3	204	253	1.0	2.5
207 E.L.C.A.	2	150	200	.8	1.9
283 LUTH—MO SYNOD	1	261	331	1.3	3.2
355 PRESB CH (USA)	2	167	219*	.8	2.1
413 S.D.A.	2	106	139*	.5	1.3
419 SO BAPT CONV	3	173	227*	.9	2.2
449 UN METHODIST	4	561	736*	2.8	7.1
MARION	**217**	**34,877**	**109,456***	**47.9**	**100.0**
005 AME ZION	1	102	119	.1	.1
019 AMER BAPT USA	2	828	1,048*	.5	1.0
040 AP CHR CH-AMER	1	36	66	-	.1
053 ASSEMB OF GOD	15	3,224	5,543	2.4	5.1
059 BAPT MISS ASSN	1	17	22*	-	-
075 BRETHREN IN CR	1	48	48	-	-
081 CATHOLIC	17	NA	50,616	22.2	46.2
081d LATIN	17	NA	50,616	22.2	46.2
089 CHR & MISS AL	7	908	4,246	1.9	3.9
093 CHR CH (DISC)	5	1,859	2,277	1.0	2.1
097 CHR CHS&CHS CR	9	2,191	2,772*	1.2	2.5
105 CHRISTIAN REF	1	240	375	.2	.3
111 CH CR,SCIENTST	3	NR	NR	-	-
123 CH GOD (ANDER)	3	338	347	.2	.3
127 CH GOD (CLEVE)	5	138	175*	.1	.2
133 CH GOD(7TH)DEN	1	74	94	-	.1
145 CH GOD PROPHCY	3	81	102*	-	.1
151 L-D SAINTS	18	NA	6,579	2.9	6.0
163 CH OF LUTH BR	1	39	83	-	.1
165 CH OF NAZARENE	7	2,860	4,275	1.9	3.9
167 CHS OF CHRIST	7	517	684	.3	.6
179 CONSRV BAPT	12	NR	NR	-	-
193 EPISCOPAL	5	1,937	2,815	1.2	2.6
207 E.L.C.A.	10	4,321	6,025	2.6	5.5
221 FREE METHODIST	3	402	587	.3	.5
223 FREE WILL BAPT	1	91	115*	.1	.1
226 FRIENDS-USA	6	339	522*	.2	.5
226b EFI	5	308	483	.2	.4
226f INDEPENDNT	1	31	39*	-	-
237 GC MENN BR CHS	1	210	266*	.1	.2
259 IFCA	2	NR	NR	-	-
263 INT FOURSQ GOS	6	1,070	1,354*	.6	1.2
283 LUTH—MO SYNOD	7	1,523	1,921	.8	1.8
284 LUTH CH-AM ASC	1	111	142	.1	.1
285 MENNONITE CH	4	317	475	.2	.4
313 N AM BAPT CONF	1	243	307*	.1	.3
329 OPEN BIBLE STD	1	NR	NR	-	-
339 PENT CH OF GOD	5	148	372	.2	.3
349 PENT HOLINESS	2	76	96*	-	.1
353 CHR BRETHREN	2	58	121	.1	.1
355 PRESB CH (USA)	6	2,436	3,082*	1.3	2.8
403 SALVATION ARMY	1	178	189	.1	.2
413 S.D.A.	8	2,182	2,761*	1.2	2.5
419 SO BAPT CONV	3	553	700*	.3	.6
435 UNITARIAN-UNIV	1	168	253	.1	.2
443 UN C OF CHRIST	4	724	916*	.4	.8
449 UN METHODIST	10	3,617	4,577*	2.0	4.2
467 WESLEYAN	3	173	305	.1	.3
469 WELS	1	45	53	-	-
496 JEWISH EST[1]	1	NA	205	.1	.2
497 BLACK BAPT EST[2]	NA	455	576*	.3	.5
498 INDEP.CHARIS.[3]	1	NA	950	.4	.9
499 INDEP.NON-CHAR[3]	1	NA	300	.1	.3
MORROW	**19**	**840**	**2,062***	**27.0**	**100.0**
019 AMER BAPT USA	1	10	13*	.2	.6

County and Denomination	Number of churches	Communicant, confirmed, full members	Total adherents Number	Percent of total population	Percent of total adherents
053 ASSEMB OF GOD	3	82	158	2.1	7.7
081 CATHOLIC	2	NA	434	5.7	21.0
081d LATIN	2	NA	434	5.7	21.0
097 CHR CHS&CHS CR	1	75	98*	1.3	4.8
151 L-D SAINTS	2	NA	420	5.5	20.4
165 CH OF NAZARENE	1	26	26	.3	1.3
179 CONSRV BAPT	1	NR	NR	-	-
193 EPISCOPAL	1	64	155	2.0	7.5
207 E.L.C.A.	3	249	321	4.2	15.6
413 S.D.A.	2	130	170*	2.2	8.2
443 UN C OF CHRIST	1	109	143*	1.9	6.9
449 UN METHODIST	1	95	124*	1.6	6.0
MULTNOMAH	**442**	**78,677**	**209,096***	**35.8**	**100.0**
005 AME ZION	2	368	399	.1	.2
019 AMER BAPT USA	18	4,393	5,403*	.9	2.6
039 AP CHR CH(NAZ)	1	120	148*	-	.1
040 AP CHR CH-AMER	1	20	35	-	-
045 APOSTOLIC LUTH	1	56	98	-	-
053 ASSEMB OF GOD	15	2,393	3,956	.7	1.9
057 BAPT GEN CONF	5	1,013	1,246*	.2	.6
081 CATHOLIC	42	NA	77,732	13.3	37.2
081b BYZAN RUTH	1	NA	40	-	-
081d LATIN	40	NA	77,251	13.2	36.9
081e MARONITE	1	NA	441	.1	.2
089 CHR & MISS AL	4	424	626	.1	.3
093 CHR CH (DISC)	4	796	1,046	.2	.5
097 CHR CHS&CHS CR	14	4,265	5,245*	.9	2.5
105 CHRISTIAN REF	2	250	399	.1	.2
111 CH CR,SCIENTST	7	NR	NR	-	-
123 CH GOD (ANDER)	10	1,469	1,542	.3	.7
127 CH GOD (CLEVE)	2	495	609*	.1	.3
133 CH GOD(7TH)DEN	1	74	94	-	-
145 CH GOD PROPHCY	1	27	33*	-	-
151 L-D SAINTS	24	NA	11,657	2.0	5.6
157 CH OF BRETHREN	1	62	76*	-	-
163 CH OF LUTH BR	1	39	59	-	-
165 CH OF NAZARENE	9	2,315	2,657	.5	1.3
167 CHS OF CHRIST	10	1,477	1,903	.3	.9
179 CONSRV BAPT	27	NR	NR	-	-
181 CONSRV CONGR	1	50	61*	-	-
193 EPISCOPAL	16	4,687	6,930	1.2	3.3
195 ESTONIAN ELC	1	106	130*	-	.1
203 EVAN FREE CH	2	103	165	-	.1
207 E.L.C.A.	23	7,029	9,590	1.6	4.6
209 EVAN LUTH SYN	1	30	47	-	-
215 EVAN METH CH	2	88	108*	-	.1
221 FREE METHODIST	8	381	457	.1	.2
226 FRIENDS-USA	6	408	635*	.1	.3
226b EFI	4	327	535	.1	.3
226f INDEPENDNT	2	81	100*	-	-
237 GC MENN BR CHS	1	10	12*	-	-
246 GREEK ORTHODOX	1	NR	NR	-	-
263 INT FOURSQ GOS	8	4,528	5,569*	1.0	2.7
274 LAT EVAN LUTH	1	149	166	-	.1
283 LUTH—MO SYNOD	12	3,311	4,147	.7	2.0
284 LUTH CH-AM ASC	2	448	631	.1	.3
285 MENNONITE CH	2	215	372	.1	.2
291 MISSIONARY CH	1	64	70	-	-
313 N AM BAPT CONF	5	1,113	1,369*	.2	.7
329 OPEN BIBLE STD	4	NR	NR	-	-
331 ORTH CH IN AM	1	NR	NR	-	-
339 PENT CH OF GOD	2	44	92	-	-
349 PENT HOLINESS	1	44	54*	-	-
353 CHR BRETHREN	5	630	815	.1	.4
355 PRESB CH (USA)	31	10,807	13,291*	2.3	6.4
371 REF CH IN AM	1	16	29	-	-
375 REF EPISCOPAL	1	14	15	-	-
397 ROMANIAN ORTH	1	NR	NR	-	-
403 SALVATION ARMY	4	435	570	.1	.3
413 S.D.A.	12	4,922	6,053*	1.0	2.9
415 S-D BAPTIST GC	1	25	31*	-	-
419 SO BAPT CONV	20	4,146	5,099*	.9	2.4
423 SYRIAN ANTIOCH	1	NA	400	.1	.2
435 UNITARIAN-UNIV	3	870	1,305	.2	.6
443 UN C OF CHRIST	8	1,622	1,995*	.3	1.0
449 UN METHODIST	28	6,274	7,716*	1.3	3.7
467 WESLEYAN	3	103	323	.1	.2
469 WELS	2	447	665	.1	.3
496 JEWISH EST[1]	7	NA	3,704	.6	1.8
497 BLACK BAPT EST[2]	NA	5,502	6,767*	1.2	3.2
498 INDEP.CHARIS.[3]	4	NA	12,200	2.1	5.8
499 INDEP.NON-CHAR[3]	7	NA	2,550	.4	1.2
POLK	**57**	**4,948**	**20,120***	**40.6**	**100.0**
053 ASSEMB OF GOD	4	571	1,208	2.4	6.0
081 CATHOLIC	2	NA	10,916	22.0	54.3

NA–Not applicable   NR–Not reported   *Total adherents estimated from known number of communicant, confirmed, full members.   - Represents a percent less than 0.1.   Percentages may not total due to rounding.
[1]See Appendix E   [2]See Appendix F   [3]See Appendix G   Lines in *italic* represent a breakdown of Catholic rites or Friends affiliations. They are included in their respective denominational total.

Table 4. Churches and Church Membership by County and Denomination: 1990

County and Denomination		Number of churches	Communicant, confirmed, full members	Total adherents		
				Number	Percent of total population	Percent of total adherents
081d	LATIN	2	NA	10,916	22.0	54.3
089	CHR & MISS AL	1	124	174	.4	.9
093	CHR CH (DISC)	2	257	440	.9	2.2
097	CHR CHS&CHS CR	3	310	392*	.8	1.9
127	CH GOD (CLEVE)	1	45	57*	.1	.3
145	CH GOD PROPHCY	2	54	68*	.1	.3
151	L-D SAINTS	4	NA	1,433	2.9	7.1
165	CH OF NAZARENE	3	137	316	.6	1.6
167	CHS OF CHRIST	2	99	130	.3	.6
179	CONSRV BAPT	4	NR	NR	-	-
193	EPISCOPAL	2	178	290	.6	1.4
203	EVAN FREE CH	1	184	342	.7	1.7
207	E.L.C.A.	1	356	503	1.0	2.5
211	FEL EVG BIB CH	2	359	382	.8	1.9
221	FREE METHODIST	1	12	37	.1	.2
237	GC MENN BR CHS	1	104	132*	.3	.7
263	INT FOURSQ GOS	2	209	265*	.5	1.3
283	LUTH—MO SYNOD	2	354	498	1.0	2.5
285	MENNONITE CH	2	69	118	.2	.6
287	MENN GEN CONF	1	199	251	.5	1.2
339	PENT CH OF GOD	1	21	70	.1	.3
355	PRESB CH (USA)	2	301	381*	.8	1.9
413	S.D.A.	3	224	284*	.6	1.4
419	SO BAPT CONV	2	343	434*	.9	2.2
449	UN METHODIST	5	438	554*	1.1	2.8
496	JEWISH EST[1]	0	NA	45	.1	.2
498	INDEP.CHARIS.[3]	1	NA	400	.8	2.0
SHERMAN		**9**	**266**	**469***	**24.5**	**100.0**
081	CATHOLIC	3	NA	128	6.7	27.3
081d	LATIN	3	NA	128	6.7	27.3
097	CHR CHS&CHS CR	1	32	41*	2.1	8.7
179	CONSRV BAPT	2	NR	NR	-	-
355	PRESB CH (USA)	1	88	113*	5.9	24.1
419	SO BAPT CONV	1	44	56*	2.9	11.9
449	UN METHODIST	1	102	131*	6.8	27.9
TILLAMOOK		**31**	**2,792**	**5,301***	**24.6**	**100.0**
053	ASSEMB OF GOD	3	171	260	1.2	4.9
081	CATHOLIC	4	NA	1,116	5.2	21.1
081d	LATIN	4	NA	1,116	5.2	21.1
097	CHR CHS&CHS CR	2	495	609*	2.8	11.5
145	CH GOD PROPHCY	1	27	33*	.2	.6
151	L-D SAINTS	1	NA	475	2.2	9.0
165	CH OF NAZARENE	2	316	461	2.1	8.7
167	CHS OF CHRIST	1	27	37	.2	.7
179	CONSRV BAPT	1	NR	NR	-	-
193	EPISCOPAL	1	157	288	1.3	5.4
207	E.L.C.A.	1	56	100	.5	1.9
226	FRIENDS-USA	1	43	78	.4	1.5
226b	EFI	1	43	78	.4	1.5
259	IFCA	2	NR	NR	-	-
263	INT FOURSQ GOS	1	47	58*	.3	1.1
283	LUTH—MO SYNOD	1	210	257	1.2	4.8
355	PRESB CH (USA)	2	103	127*	.6	2.4
413	S.D.A.	2	278	342*	1.6	6.5
419	SO BAPT CONV	1	132	162*	.8	3.1
443	UN C OF CHRIST	1	114	140*	.6	2.6
449	UN METHODIST	3	616	758*	3.5	14.3
UMATILLA		**99**	**10,819**	**22,323***	**37.7**	**100.0**
019	AMER BAPT USA	5	1,155	1,480*	2.5	6.6
053	ASSEMB OF GOD	10	672	1,407	2.4	6.3
081	CATHOLIC	8	NA	3,975	6.7	17.8
081d	LATIN	8	NA	3,975	6.7	17.8
093	CHR CH (DISC)	3	725	1,321	2.2	5.9
097	CHR CHS&CHS CR	2	525	673*	1.1	3.0
111	CH CR,SCIENTST	2	NR	NR	-	-
123	CH GOD (ANDER)	2	120	120	.2	.5
127	CH GOD (CLEVE)	2	86	110*	.2	.5
145	CH GOD PROPHCY	1	27	35*	.1	.2
151	L-D SAINTS	8	NA	3,107	5.2	13.9
157	CH OF BRETHREN	1	116	149*	.3	.7
165	CH OF NAZARENE	4	256	522	.9	2.3
167	CHS OF CHRIST	4	126	206	.3	.9
179	CONSRV BAPT	6	NR	NR	-	-
193	EPISCOPAL	3	753	980	1.7	4.4
207	E.L.C.A.	3	755	942	1.6	4.2
221	FREE METHODIST	1	163	372	.6	1.7
263	INT FOURSQ GOS	2	179	229*	.4	1.0
283	LUTH—MO SYNOD	1	148	199	.3	.9
339	PENT CH OF GOD	2	69	153	.3	.7
355	PRESB CH (USA)	9	791	1,013*	1.7	4.5
403	SALVATION ARMY	1	64	73	.1	.3
413	S.D.A.	8	2,859	3,662*	6.2	16.4
419	SO BAPT CONV	4	339	434*	.7	1.9

County and Denomination		Number of churches	Communicant, confirmed, full members	Total adherents		
				Number	Percent of total population	Percent of total adherents
443	UN C OF CHRIST	1	119	152*	.3	.7
449	UN METHODIST	5	764	979*	1.7	4.4
467	WESLEYAN	1	8	30	.1	.1
UNION		**44**	**3,239**	**7,956***	**33.7**	**100.0**
053	ASSEMB OF GOD	2	152	200	.8	2.5
081	CATHOLIC	1	NA	1,382	5.9	17.4
081d	LATIN	1	NA	1,382	5.9	17.4
093	CHR CH (DISC)	1	376	476	2.0	6.0
097	CHR CHS&CHS CR	2	210	267*	1.1	3.4
111	CH CR,SCIENTST	1	NR	NR	-	-
123	CH GOD (ANDER)	1	40	46	.2	.6
151	L-D SAINTS	7	NA	2,075	8.8	26.1
165	CH OF NAZARENE	3	339	703	3.0	8.8
167	CHS OF CHRIST	2	64	94	.4	1.2
179	CONSRV BAPT	4	NR	NR	-	-
193	EPISCOPAL	1	127	211	.9	2.7
207	E.L.C.A.	1	217	279	1.2	3.5
215	EVAN METH CH	1	66	84*	.4	1.1
263	INT FOURSQ GOS	1	171	217*	.9	2.7
283	LUTH—MO SYNOD	1	139	196	.8	2.5
329	OPEN BIBLE STD	1	NR	NR	-	-
339	PENT CH OF GOD	1	19	50	.2	.6
355	PRESB CH (USA)	1	311	396*	1.7	5.0
403	SALVATION ARMY	1	51	53	.2	.7
413	S.D.A.	3	333	424*	1.8	5.3
419	SO BAPT CONV	2	156	198*	.8	2.5
435	UNITARIAN-UNIV	1	9	21	.1	.3
449	UN METHODIST	5	459	584*	2.5	7.3
WALLOWA		**20**	**1,039**	**2,260***	**32.7**	**100.0**
053	ASSEMB OF GOD	3	149	248	3.6	11.0
081	CATHOLIC	2	NA	489	7.1	21.6
081d	LATIN	2	NA	489	7.1	21.6
097	CHR CHS&CHS CR	3	348	441*	6.4	19.5
151	L-D SAINTS	1	NA	304	4.4	13.5
165	CH OF NAZARENE	1	37	94	1.4	4.2
167	CHS OF CHRIST	1	40	55	.8	2.4
179	CONSRV BAPT	2	NR	NR	-	-
193	EPISCOPAL	1	18	58	.8	2.6
207	E.L.C.A.	1	41	57	.8	2.5
355	PRESB CH (USA)	1	46	58*	.8	2.6
413	S.D.A.	1	80	101*	1.5	4.5
443	UN C OF CHRIST	1	113	143*	2.1	6.3
449	UN METHODIST	2	167	212*	3.1	9.4
WASCO		**33**	**3,103**	**7,442***	**34.3**	**100.0**
053	ASSEMB OF GOD	3	175	326	1.5	4.4
081	CATHOLIC	2	NA	1,967	9.1	26.4
081d	LATIN	2	NA	1,967	9.1	26.4
089	CHR & MISS AL	1	20	52	.2	.7
093	CHR CH (DISC)	2	185	262	1.2	3.5
097	CHR CHS&CHS CR	2	375	475*	2.2	6.4
111	CH CR,SCIENTST	1	NR	NR	-	-
151	L-D SAINTS	3	NA	1,179	5.4	15.8
165	CH OF NAZARENE	1	67	135	.6	1.8
167	CHS OF CHRIST	1	69	78	.4	1.0
179	CONSRV BAPT	3	NR	NR	-	-
193	EPISCOPAL	1	257	360	1.7	4.8
207	E.L.C.A.	1	539	794	3.7	10.7
209	EVAN LUTH SYN	1	57	81	.4	1.1
263	INT FOURSQ GOS	1	131	166*	.8	2.2
283	LUTH—MO SYNOD	1	110	142	.7	1.9
339	PENT CH OF GOD	1	0	15	.1	.2
355	PRESB CH (USA)	1	248	314*	1.4	4.2
403	SALVATION ARMY	1	42	47	.2	.6
413	S.D.A.	1	176	223*	1.0	3.0
419	SO BAPT CONV	1	218	276*	1.3	3.7
443	UN C OF CHRIST	1	179	227*	1.0	3.1
449	UN METHODIST	3	255	323*	1.5	4.3
WASHINGTON		**202**	**35,124**	**105,093***	**33.7**	**100.0**
019	AMER BAPT USA	7	1,066	1,359*	.4	1.3
053	ASSEMB OF GOD	10	1,224	1,875	.6	1.8
057	BAPT GEN CONF	1	132	168*	.1	.2
081	CATHOLIC	10	NA	39,560	12.7	37.6
081d	LATIN	10	NA	39,560	12.7	37.6
089	CHR & MISS AL	2	132	491	.2	.5
093	CHR CH (DISC)	4	878	1,408	.5	1.3
097	CHR CHS&CHS CR	7	2,536	3,233*	1.0	3.1
105	CHRISTIAN REF	1	13	20	-	-
111	CH CR,SCIENTST	4	NR	NR	-	-
123	CH GOD (ANDER)	5	493	575	.2	.5
151	L-D SAINTS	30	NA	13,312	4.3	12.7
165	CH OF NAZARENE	6	1,171	1,101	.4	1.0
167	CHS OF CHRIST	8	1,016	1,308	.4	1.2

NA—Not applicable   NR—Not reported   *Total adherents estimated from known number of communicant, confirmed, full members.   - Represents a percent less than 0.1.   Percentages may not total due to rounding.
[1]See Appendix E   [2]See Appendix F   [3]See Appendix G   Lines in *italic* represent a breakdown of Catholic rites or Friends affiliations. They are included in their respective denominational total.

Table 4. Churches and Church Membership by County and Denomination: 1990

County and Denomination	Number of churches	Communicant, confirmed, full members	Total adherents		
			Number	Percent of total population	Percent of total adherents
179 CONSRV BAPT	13	NR	NR	-	-
193 EPISCOPAL	5	1,172	2,004	.6	1.9
207 E.L.C.A.	8	3,912	5,368	1.7	5.1
221 FREE METHODIST	1	80	166	.1	.2
226 FRIENDS-USA	4	255	456	.1	.4
226b EFI	*3*	*246*	*438*	*.1*	*.4*
226f INDEPENDNT	*1*	*9*	*18*	-	-
259 IFCA	2	NR	NR	-	-
263 INT FOURSQ GOS	6	5,740	7,317*	2.3	7.0
283 LUTH—MO SYNOD	10	3,651	5,016	1.6	4.8
287 MENN GEN CONF	2	44	53	-	.1
313 N AM BAPT CONF	2	92	117*	-	.1
329 OPEN BIBLE STD	1	NR	NR	-	-
349 PENT HOLINESS	1	48	61*	-	.1
353 CHR BRETHREN	2	145	250	.1	.2
355 PRESB CH (USA)	9	1,850	2,358*	.8	2.2
403 SALVATION ARMY	1	10	12	-	-
413 S.D.A.	7	1,974	2,516*	.8	2.4
419 SO BAPT CONV	7	1,669	2,127*	.7	2.0
435 UNITARIAN-UNIV	1	109	187	.1	.2
443 UN C OF CHRIST	5	1,431	1,824*	.6	1.7
449 UN METHODIST	14	3,721	4,743*	1.5	4.5
467 WESLEYAN	1	7	24	-	-
469 WELS	1	114	148	-	.1
496 JEWISH EST[1]	0	NA	1,976	.6	1.9
497 BLACK BAPT EST[2]	NA	439	560*	.2	.5
498 INDEP.CHARIS.[3]	1	NA	1,200	.4	1.1
499 INDEP.NON-CHAR[3]	3	NA	2,200	.7	2.1
WHEELER	**4**	**108**	**274***	**19.6**	**100.0**
053 ASSEMB OF GOD	2	70	184	13.2	67.2
081 CATHOLIC	1	NA	44	3.2	16.1
081d LATIN	*1*	*NA*	*44*	*3.2*	*16.1*
449 UN METHODIST	1	38	46*	3.3	16.8
YAMHILL	**86**	**9,380**	**20,199***	**30.8**	**100.0**
019 AMER BAPT USA	2	697	901*	1.4	4.5
053 ASSEMB OF GOD	9	651	1,317	2.0	6.5
057 BAPT GEN CONF	1	30	39*	.1	.2
081 CATHOLIC	5	NA	4,383	6.7	21.7
081d LATIN	*5*	*NA*	*4,383*	*6.7*	*21.7*
093 CHR CH (DISC)	1	162	374	.6	1.9
097 CHR CHS&CHS CR	7	1,187	1,535*	2.3	7.6
105 CHRISTIAN REF	1	44	74	.1	.4
111 CH CR,SCIENTST	1	NR	NR	-	-
123 CH GOD (ANDER)	1	0	0	-	-
151 L-D SAINTS	6	NA	2,123	3.2	10.5
165 CH OF NAZARENE	3	590	873	1.3	4.3
167 CHS OF CHRIST	3	376	550	.8	2.7
179 CONSRV BAPT	5	NR	NR	-	-
193 EPISCOPAL	2	278	433	.7	2.1
207 E.L.C.A.	4	686	931	1.4	4.6
221 FREE METHODIST	3	368	478	.7	2.4
226 FRIENDS-USA	6	883	1,210	1.8	6.0
226b EFI	*6*	*883*	*1,210*	*1.8*	*6.0*
259 IFCA	1	NR	NR	-	-
263 INT FOURSQ GOS	2	220	285*	.4	1.4
283 LUTH—MO SYNOD	2	302	458	.7	2.3
285 MENNONITE CH	2	206	319	.5	1.6
291 MISSIONARY CH	1	19	31	-	.2
329 OPEN BIBLE STD	1	NR	NR	-	-
355 PRESB CH (USA)	2	514	665*	1.0	3.3
403 SALVATION ARMY	1	4	7	-	-
413 S.D.A.	4	662	856*	1.3	4.2
419 SO BAPT CONV	2	401	519*	.8	2.6
449 UN METHODIST	8	1,100	1,423*	2.2	7.0
496 JEWISH EST[1]	0	NA	415	.6	2.1

PENNSYLVANIA

County and Denomination	Number of churches	Communicant, confirmed, full members	Total adherents		
			Number	Percent of total population	Percent of total adherents
THE STATE.....	13,284	2,471,624	7,290,699*	61.4	100.0
ADAMS	**110**	**20,736**	**41,480***	**53.0**	**100.0**
005 AME ZION	1	113	209	.3	.5
019 AMER BAPT USA	2	462	576*	.7	1.4
053 ASSEMB OF GOD	3	560	1,221	1.6	2.9
075 BRETHREN IN CR	2	131	140	.2	.3
081 CATHOLIC	10	NA	13,727	17.5	33.1
081d LATIN	*10*	*NA*	*13,727*	*17.5*	*33.1*
123 CH GOD (ANDER)	1	150	170	.2	.4
127 CH GOD (CLEVE)	2	113	141*	.2	.3
145 CH GOD PROPHCY	2	71	88*	.1	.2

County and Denomination	Number of churches	Communicant, confirmed, full members	Total adherents		
			Number	Percent of total population	Percent of total adherents
151 L-D SAINTS	1	NA	478	.6	1.2
157 CH OF BRETHREN	4	577	719*	.9	1.7
165 CH OF NAZARENE	1	59	80	.1	.2
167 CHS OF CHRIST	1	60	70	.1	.2
179 CONSRV BAPT	1	NR	NR	-	-
193 EPISCOPAL	1	289	375	.5	.9
207 E.L.C.A.	26	8,408	10,974	14.0	26.5
223 FREE WILL BAPT	1	113	141*	.2	.3
226 FRIENDS-USA	2	72	90*	.1	.2
226c FGC	*1*	*52*	*65***	*.1*	*.2*
226d FGC & FUM	*1*	*20*	*25***	-	*.1*
263 INT FOURSQ GOS	1	475	592*	.8	1.4
285 MENNONITE CH	3	244	303	.4	.7
287 MENN GEN CONF	1	43	63	.1	.2
313 N AM BAPT CONF	1	48	60*	.1	.1
323 OLD ORD AMISH	1	NA	150	.2	.4
355 PRESB CH (USA)	3	848	1,056*	1.3	2.5
413 S.D.A.	2	141	176*	.2	.4
419 SO BAPT CONV	2	912	1,136*	1.5	2.7
438 UN BRETH IN CR	3	269	269	.3	.6
443 UN C OF CHRIST	15	3,888	4,844*	6.2	11.7
449 UN METHODIST	17	2,511	3,128*	4.0	7.5
496 JEWISH EST[1]	0	NA	281	.4	.7
497 BLACK BAPT EST[2]	NA	179	223*	.3	.5
ALLEGHENY	**1,088**	**225,136**	**1,013,336***	**75.8**	**100.0**
005 AME ZION	12	7,980	8,722	.7	.9
011 A.W.M.C.	1	30	36*	-	-
019 AMER BAPT USA	41	10,938	13,140*	1.0	1.3
022 EASTERN ORTH	5	1,392	1,392	.1	.1
053 ASSEMB OF GOD	24	3,603	6,337	.5	.6
055 AS REF PRES CH	1	208	265	-	-
057 BAPT GEN CONF	3	201	241*	-	-
071 BRETHREN (ASH)	1	87	105*	-	-
081 CATHOLIC	254	NA	695,911	52.1	68.7
081b BYZAN RUTH	*23*	*NA*	*48,727*	*3.6*	*4.8*
081d LATIN	*223*	*NA*	*643,359*	*48.1*	*63.5*
081e MARONITE	*1*	*NA*	*1,216*	*.1*	*.1*
081g ROMANIAN	*1*	*NA*	*322*	-	-
081h UKRAINIAN	*6*	*NA*	*2,287*	*.2*	*.2*
089 CHR & MISS AL	18	1,515	2,922	.2	.3
093 CHR CH (DISC)	7	676	959	.1	.1
097 CHR CHS&CHS CR	25	3,920	4,709*	.4	.5
111 CH CR,SCIENTST	9	NR	NR	-	-
123 CH GOD (ANDER)	5	455	464	-	-
127 CH GOD (CLEVE)	7	422	507*	-	.1
145 CH GOD PROPHCY	1	35	42*	-	-
151 L-D SAINTS	6	NA	2,049	.2	.2
157 CH OF BRETHREN	5	363	436*	-	-
165 CH OF NAZARENE	11	949	1,584	.1	.2
167 CHS OF CHRIST	10	578	858	.1	.1
171 CH GOD-GEN CON	2	50	60*	-	-
175 CONGR CHR CHS	6	512	615*	-	.1
179 CONSRV BAPT	5	NR	NR	-	-
181 CONSRV CONGR	1	35	42*	-	-
193 EPISCOPAL	38	10,285	15,167	1.1	1.5
203 EVAN FREE CH	5	459	927	.1	.1
207 E.L.C.A.	103	27,744	37,002	2.8	3.7
216 EVAN PRESBY CH	1	486	496	-	-
221 FREE METHODIST	6	240	317	-	-
226 FRIENDS-USA	1	255	306*	-	-
226c FGC	*1*	*255*	*306***	-	-
246 GREEK ORTHODOX	7	NR	NR	-	-
259 IFCA	1	NR	NR	-	-
263 INT FOURSQ GOS	1	67	80*	-	-
274 LAT EVAN LUTH	1	40	42	-	-
283 LUTH—MO SYNOD	29	5,472	6,985	.5	.7
285 MENNONITE CH	1	53	96	-	-
313 N AM BAPT CONF	2	304	365*	-	-
329 OPEN BIBLE STD	2	NR	NR	-	-
331 ORTH CH IN AM	10	NR	NR	-	-
353 CHR BRETHREN	8	527	979	.1	.1
355 PRESB CH (USA)	171	62,635	75,242*	5.6	7.4
356 PRESB CH AMER	8	1,378	1,899	.1	.2
363 PRIMITIVE METH	8	370	473	-	-
403 SALVATION ARMY	10	747	811	.1	.1
413 S.D.A.	3	331	398*	-	-
419 SO BAPT CONV	5	1,418	1,703*	.1	.2
435 UNITARIAN-UNIV	5	902	1,208	.1	.1
443 UN C OF CHRIST	23	2,856	3,431*	.3	.3
449 UN METHODIST	124	45,391	54,527*	4.1	5.4
467 WESLEYAN	3	185	366	-	-
469 WELS	1	84	117	-	-
496 JEWISH EST[1]	43	NA	26,816	2.0	2.6
497 BLACK BAPT EST[2]	NA	28,958	34,787*	2.6	3.4
498 INDEP.CHARIS.[3]	4	NA	4,800	.4	.5
499 INDEP.NON-CHAR[3]	4	NA	2,600	.2	.3

NA–Not applicable   NR–Not reported   *Total adherents estimated from known number of communicant, confirmed, full members.   - Represents a percent less than 0.1.   Percentages may not total due to rounding.
[1]See Appendix E   [2]See Appendix F   [3]See Appendix G   Lines in *italic* represent a breakdown of Catholic rites or Friends affiliations. They are included in their respective denominational total.

Table 4. Churches and Church Membership by County and Denomination: 1990

County and Denomination	Number of churches	Communicant, confirmed, full members	Total adherents Number	Percent of total population	Percent of total adherents
ARMSTRONG	**162**	**23,898**	**47,244***	**64.3**	**100.0**
011 A.W.M.C.	2	61	75*	.1	.2
019 AMER BAPT USA	6	1,482	1,819*	2.5	3.9
053 ASSEMB OF GOD	4	252	499	.7	1.1
071 BRETHREN (ASH)	1	191	234*	.3	.5
075 BRETHREN IN CR	1	0	0	-	-
081 CATHOLIC	17	NA	16,459	22.4	34.8
081b *BYZAN RUTH*	*1*	*NA*	*381*	*.5*	*.8*
081d *LATIN*	*15*	*NA*	*15,873*	*21.6*	*33.6*
081h *UKRAINIAN*	*1*	*NA*	*205*	*.3*	*.4*
089 CHR & MISS AL	1	50	135	.2	.3
123 CH GOD (ANDER)	6	860	1,184	1.6	2.5
127 CH GOD (CLEVE)	2	113	139*	.2	.3
145 CH GOD PROPHCY	2	71	87*	.1	.2
151 L-D SAINTS	1	NA	327	.4	.7
157 CH OF BRETHREN	2	386	474*	.6	1.0
165 CH OF NAZARENE	1	120	207	.3	.4
167 CHS OF CHRIST	2	122	184	.3	.4
171 CH GOD-GEN CON	4	292	358*	.5	.8
193 EPISCOPAL	5	399	489	.7	1.0
207 E.L.C.A.	24	6,381	8,514	11.6	18.0
221 FREE METHODIST	3	247	266	.4	.6
259 IFCA	2	NR	NR	-	-
355 PRESB CH (USA)	32	6,888	8,454*	11.5	17.9
356 PRESB CH AMER	2	90	121	.2	.3
403 SALVATION ARMY	1	111	123	.2	.3
413 S.D.A.	2	95	117*	.2	.2
419 SO BAPT CONV	2	111	136*	.2	.3
443 UN C OF CHRIST	9	1,325	1,626*	2.2	3.4
449 UN METHODIST	27	4,162	5,108*	7.0	10.8
496 JEWISH EST[1]	1	NA	0	-	-
497 BLACK BAPT EST[2]	NA	89	109*	.1	.2
BEAVER	**207**	**36,149**	**118,024***	**63.4**	**100.0**
005 AME ZION	1	438	544	.3	.5
011 A.W.M.C.	3	42	51*	-	-
019 AMER BAPT USA	7	1,244	1,522*	.8	1.3
022 EASTERN ORTH	1	263	263	.1	.2
053 ASSEMB OF GOD	4	303	688	.4	.6
081 CATHOLIC	29	NA	66,810	35.9	56.6
081b *BYZAN RUTH*	*2*	*NA*	*4,785*	*2.6*	*4.1*
081d *LATIN*	*25*	*NA*	*61,371*	*33.0*	*52.0*
081h *UKRAINIAN*	*2*	*NA*	*654*	*.4*	*.6*
089 CHR & MISS AL	10	722	1,418	.8	1.2
093 CHR CH (DISC)	1	95	243	.1	.2
097 CHR CHS&CHS CR	1	325	398*	.2	.3
123 CH GOD (ANDER)	1	85	87	-	.1
127 CH GOD (CLEVE)	1	68	83*	-	.1
151 L-D SAINTS	1	NA	445	.2	.4
165 CH OF NAZARENE	7	441	833	.4	.7
167 CHS OF CHRIST	3	279	340	.2	.3
171 CH GOD-GEN CON	2	203	248*	.1	.2
175 CONGR CHR CHS	1	40	49*	-	-
193 EPISCOPAL	6	737	953	.5	.8
203 EVAN FREE CH	1	170	475	.3	.4
207 E.L.C.A.	23	6,698	8,646	4.6	7.3
221 FREE METHODIST	7	484	660	.4	.6
246 GREEK ORTHODOX	2	NR	NR	-	-
283 LUTH—MO SYNOD	2	428	559	.3	.5
331 ORTH CH IN AM	2	NR	NR	-	-
355 PRESB CH (USA)	41	9,945	12,168*	6.5	10.3
356 PRESB CH AMER	5	589	753	.4	.6
363 PRIMITIVE METH	1	38	74	-	.1
403 SALVATION ARMY	3	277	334	.2	.3
413 S.D.A.	1	77	94*	.1	.1
419 SO BAPT CONV	2	181	221*	.1	.2
449 UN METHODIST	32	9,858	12,061*	6.5	10.2
467 WESLEYAN	2	91	265	.1	.2
496 JEWISH EST[1]	3	NA	3,933	2.1	3.3
497 BLACK BAPT EST[2]	NA	2,028	2,481*	1.3	2.1
499 INDEP.NON-CHAR[3]	1	NA	325	.2	.3
BEDFORD	**142**	**16,026**	**22,506***	**47.0**	**100.0**
005 AME ZION	1	137	153	.3	.7
022 EASTERN ORTH	1	92	92	.2	.4
053 ASSEMB OF GOD	10	527	1,185	2.5	5.3
057 BAPT GEN CONF	1	207	256*	.5	1.1
071 BRETHREN (ASH)	1	22	27*	.1	.1
075 BRETHREN IN CR	7	211	309	.6	1.4
081 CATHOLIC	3	NA	1,674	3.5	7.4
081d *LATIN*	*3*	*NA*	*1,674*	*3.5*	*7.4*
097 CHR CHS&CHS CR	2	40	50*	.1	.2
127 CH GOD (CLEVE)	4	709	878*	1.8	3.9
151 L-D SAINTS	1	NA	143	.3	.6
157 CH OF BRETHREN	17	2,798	3,464*	7.2	15.4
165 CH OF NAZARENE	2	196	343	.7	1.5

County and Denomination	Number of churches	Communicant, confirmed, full members	Total adherents Number	Percent of total population	Percent of total adherents
171 CH GOD-GEN CON	4	321	397*	.8	1.8
179 CONSRV BAPT	1	NR	NR	-	-
193 EPISCOPAL	1	88	99	.2	.4
207 E.L.C.A.	16	2,781	3,583	7.5	15.9
226 FRIENDS-USA	2	69	86*	.2	.4
226c *FGC*	*1*	*36*	*45**	*.1*	*.2*
226e *FUM*	*1*	*33*	*41**	*.1*	*.2*
285 MENNONITE CH	3	69	125	.3	.6
286 E.PA MENNONITE	1	42	52*	.1	.2
353 CHR BRETHREN	1	49	98	.2	.4
355 PRESB CH (USA)	2	438	542*	1.1	2.4
413 S.D.A.	2	111	137*	.3	.6
415 S-D BAPTIST GC	1	31	38*	.1	.2
443 UN C OF CHRIST	21	2,627	3,252*	6.8	14.4
449 UN METHODIST	37	4,461	5,523*	11.5	24.5
BERKS	**339**	**100,683**	**187,867***	**55.8**	**100.0**
019 AMER BAPT USA	2	424	520*	.2	.3
053 ASSEMB OF GOD	12	1,011	1,954	.6	1.0
075 BRETHREN IN CR	1	68	80	-	-
081 CATHOLIC	24	NA	54,882	16.3	29.2
081d *LATIN*	*23*	*NA*	*54,554*	*16.2*	*29.0*
081h *UKRAINIAN*	*1*	*NA*	*328*	*.1*	*.2*
089 CHR & MISS AL	2	40	91	-	-
097 CHR CHS&CHS CR	1	46	56*	-	-
111 CH CR,SCIENTST	1	NR	NR	-	-
123 CH GOD (ANDER)	6	335	442	.1	.2
127 CH GOD (CLEVE)	4	569	697*	.2	.4
143 CG IN CR(MENN)	1	86	105*	-	.1
151 L-D SAINTS	1	NA	675	.2	.4
157 CH OF BRETHREN	4	874	1,071*	.3	.6
165 CH OF NAZARENE	3	478	704	.2	.4
167 CHS OF CHRIST	5	201	278	.1	.1
179 CONSRV BAPT	1	NR	NR	-	-
193 EPISCOPAL	7	1,751	2,401	.7	1.3
199 EVAN CONGR CH	16	2,735	3,597	1.1	1.9
203 EVAN FREE CH	2	112	230	.1	.1
207 E.L.C.A.	83	42,294	54,953	16.3	29.3
226 FRIENDS-USA	3	115	141*	-	.1
226c *FGC*	*3*	*115*	*141**	*-*	*.1*
246 GREEK ORTHODOX	2	NR	NR	-	-
259 IFCA	4	NR	NR	-	-
285 MENNONITE CH	23	1,867	3,149	.9	1.7
286 E.PA MENNONITE	3	210	257*	.1	.1
287 MENN GEN CONF	1	164	238	.1	.1
291 MISSIONARY CH	1	54	53	-	-
293 MORAV CH-NORTH	1	146	266	.1	.1
331 ORTH CH IN AM	1	NR	NR	-	-
353 CHR BRETHREN	2	100	135	-	.1
355 PRESB CH (USA)	5	1,354	1,659*	.5	.9
403 SALVATION ARMY	1	128	144	-	.1
413 S.D.A.	8	1,883	2,308*	.7	1.2
419 SO BAPT CONV	1	157	192*	.1	.1
435 UNITARIAN-UNIV	1	145	230	.1	.1
443 UN C OF CHRIST	77	34,164	41,868*	12.4	22.3
449 UN METHODIST	22	7,213	8,840*	2.6	4.7
467 WESLEYAN	1	22	52	-	-
496 JEWISH EST[1]	5	NA	2,800	.8	1.5
497 BLACK BAPT EST[2]	NA	1,937	2,374*	.7	1.3
499 INDEP.NON-CHAR[3]	1	NA	425	.1	.2
BLAIR	**200**	**31,971**	**69,190***	**53.0**	**100.0**
005 AME ZION	1	165	266	.2	.4
019 AMER BAPT USA	2	338	417*	.3	.6
053 ASSEMB OF GOD	6	709	1,078	.8	1.6
075 BRETHREN IN CR	3	139	183	.1	.3
081 CATHOLIC	23	NA	26,028	19.9	37.6
081d *LATIN*	*22*	*NA*	*25,952*	*19.9*	*37.5*
081h *UKRAINIAN*	*1*	*NA*	*76*	*.1*	*.1*
089 CHR & MISS AL	7	397	755	.6	1.1
097 CHR CHS&CHS CR	1	550	678*	.5	1.0
111 CH CR,SCIENTST	1	NR	NR	-	-
127 CH GOD (CLEVE)	3	539	665*	.5	1.0
145 CH GOD PROPHCY	1	35	43*	-	.1
151 L-D SAINTS	1	NA	396	.3	.6
157 CH OF BRETHREN	20	4,107	5,064*	3.9	7.3
167 CHS OF CHRIST	1	70	91	.1	.1
171 CH GOD-GEN CON	7	738	910*	.7	1.3
179 CONSRV BAPT	1	NR	NR	-	-
193 EPISCOPAL	3	399	567	.4	.8
207 E.L.C.A.	24	8,104	10,946	8.4	15.8
221 FREE METHODIST	1	37	50	-	.1
246 GREEK ORTHODOX	1	NR	NR	-	-
259 IFCA	2	NR	NR	-	-
285 MENNONITE CH	4	246	371	.3	.5
287 MENN GEN CONF	2	40	53	-	.1
291 MISSIONARY CH	2	177	232	.2	.3

NA–Not applicable   NR–Not reported   *Total adherents estimated from known number of communicant, confirmed, full members.   - Represents a percent less than 0.1.   Percentages may not total due to rounding.
[1]See Appendix E   [2]See Appendix F   [3]See Appendix G   Lines in *italic* represent a breakdown of Catholic rites or Friends affiliations. They are included in their respective denominational total.

Table 4. Churches and Church Membership by County and Denomination: 1990

County and Denomination	Number of churches	Communicant, confirmed, full members	Total adherents — Number	Percent of total population	Percent of total adherents
323 OLD ORD AMISH	1	NA	100	.1	.1
331 ORTH CH IN AM	2	NR	NR	-	-
355 PRESB CH (USA)	10	2,096	2,584*	2.0	3.7
403 SALVATION ARMY	2	123	133	.1	.2
413 S.D.A.	1	42	52*	-	.1
419 SO BAPT CONV	2	64	79*	.1	.1
443 UN C OF CHRIST	13	1,470	1,813*	1.4	2.6
449 UN METHODIST	46	11,138	13,733*	10.5	19.8
469 WELS	1	40	67	.1	.1
496 JEWISH EST[1]	2	NA	480	.4	.7
497 BLACK BAPT EST[2]	NA	208	256*	.2	.4
499 INDEP.NON-CHAR[3]	2	NA	1,100	.8	1.6
BRADFORD	**127**	**13,974**	**27,628***	**45.3**	**100.0**
019 AMER BAPT USA	12	1,799	2,279*	3.7	8.2
053 ASSEMB OF GOD	1	61	125	.2	.5
081 CATHOLIC	14	NA	7,580	12.4	27.4
081d LATIN	*13*	*NA*	*7,160*	*11.7*	*25.9*
081h UKRAINIAN	*1*	*NA*	*420*	*.7*	*1.5*
089 CHR & MISS AL	2	34	108	.2	.4
093 CHR CH (DISC)	5	905	1,361	2.2	4.9
097 CHR CHS&CHS CR	5	587	744*	1.2	2.7
111 CH CR,SCIENTST	1	NR	NR	-	-
123 CH GOD (ANDER)	1	93	93	.2	.3
151 L-D SAINTS	1	NA	264	.4	1.0
175 CONGR CHR CHS	1	235	298*	.5	1.1
176 CCC, NOT NAT'L	1	100	127*	.2	.5
179 CONSRV BAPT	1	NR	NR	-	-
193 EPISCOPAL	4	605	876	1.4	3.2
207 E.L.C.A.	3	639	1,022	1.7	3.7
285 MENNONITE CH	3	97	203	.3	.7
323 OLD ORD AMISH	1	NA	150	.2	.5
355 PRESB CH (USA)	12	1,867	2,365*	3.9	8.6
413 S.D.A.	2	118	150*	.2	.5
419 SO BAPT CONV	1	85	108*	.2	.4
435 UNITARIAN-UNIV	3	101	122	.2	.4
443 UN C OF CHRIST	3	204	258*	.4	.9
449 UN METHODIST	43	5,931	7,515*	12.3	27.2
467 WESLEYAN	6	513	1,880	3.1	6.8
496 JEWISH EST[1]	1	NA	0	-	-
BUCKS	**305**	**69,955**	**328,874***	**60.8**	**100.0**
005 AME ZION	1	170	179	-	.1
019 AMER BAPT USA	7	1,021	1,280*	.2	.4
022 EASTERN ORTH	1	120	120	-	-
053 ASSEMB OF GOD	8	386	540	.1	.2
071 BRETHREN (ASH)	1	53	66*	-	-
075 BRETHREN IN CR	2	101	153	-	-
081 CATHOLIC	40	NA	195,996	36.2	59.6
081b BYZAN RUTH	*1*	*NA*	*763*	*.1*	*.2*
081d LATIN	*36*	*NA*	*190,236*	*35.2*	*57.8*
081h UKRAINIAN	*3*	*NA*	*4,997*	*.9*	*1.5*
089 CHR & MISS AL	4	81	167	-	.1
093 CHR CH (DISC)	1	40	45	-	-
097 CHR CHS&CHS CR	2	222	278*	.1	.1
111 CH CR,SCIENTST	2	NR	NR	-	-
127 CH GOD (CLEVE)	2	232	291*	.1	.1
145 CH GOD PROPHCY	1	35	44*	-	-
151 L-D SAINTS	3	NA	1,192	.2	.4
157 CH OF BRETHREN	1	115	144*	-	-
165 CH OF NAZARENE	3	190	273	.1	.1
167 CHS OF CHRIST	2	223	273	.1	.1
179 CONSRV BAPT	5	NR	NR	-	-
193 EPISCOPAL	18	4,081	6,313	1.2	1.9
203 EVAN FREE CH	2	107	205	-	.1
207 E.L.C.A.	40	19,164	25,856	4.8	7.9
226 FRIENDS-USA	12	1,510	1,893*	.3	.6
226c FGC	*12*	*1,510*	*1,893***	*.3*	*.6*
259 IFCA	2	NR	NR	-	-
263 INT FOURSQ GOS	1	0	0*	-	-
274 LAT EVAN LUTH	1	201	209	-	.1
283 LUTH—MO SYNOD	3	951	1,463	.3	.4
285 MENNONITE CH	15	2,326	3,298	.6	1.0
287 MENN GEN CONF	6	1,254	1,623	.3	.5
313 N AM BAPT CONF	1	134	168*	-	.1
331 ORTH CH IN AM	1	NR	NR	-	-
353 CHR BRETHREN	3	242	380	.1	.1
355 PRESB CH (USA)	18	10,184	12,770*	2.4	3.9
356 PRESB CH AMER	6	404	521	.1	.2
363 PRIMITIVE METH	6	483	612	.1	.2
371 REF CH IN AM	7	1,694	3,297	.6	1.0
375 REF EPISCOPAL	2	103	136	-	-
403 SALVATION ARMY	1	66	78	-	-
419 SO BAPT CONV	2	333	418*	.1	.1
435 UNITARIAN-UNIV	3	161	235	-	-
443 UN C OF CHRIST	23	7,455	9,348*	1.7	2.8
449 UN METHODIST	31	13,048	16,362*	3.0	5.0
467 WESLEYAN	1	61	95	-	-
469 WELS	1	39	52	-	-
496 JEWISH EST[1]	10	NA	36,283	6.7	11.0
497 BLACK BAPT EST[2]	NA	2,965	3,718*	.7	1.1
498 INDEP.CHARIS.[3]	2	NA	1,900	.4	.6
499 INDEP.NON-CHAR[3]	1	NA	600	.1	.2
BUTLER	**195**	**36,222**	**90,064***	**59.2**	**100.0**
011 A.W.M.C.	3	57	71*	-	.1
019 AMER BAPT USA	2	345	428*	.3	.5
053 ASSEMB OF GOD	5	639	2,276	1.5	2.5
071 BRETHREN (ASH)	1	33	41*	-	-
081 CATHOLIC	26	NA	40,538	26.7	45.0
081b BYZAN RUTH	*1*	*NA*	*2,391*	*1.6*	*2.7*
081d LATIN	*24*	*NA*	*37,992*	*25.0*	*42.2*
081h UKRAINIAN	*1*	*NA*	*155*	*.1*	*.2*
089 CHR & MISS AL	10	861	2,625	1.7	2.9
093 CHR CH (DISC)	1	113	121	.1	.1
097 CHR CHS&CHS CR	3	507	629*	.4	.7
111 CH CR,SCIENTST	1	NR	NR	-	-
123 CH GOD (ANDER)	1	1,092	1,092	.7	1.2
145 CH GOD PROPHCY	4	142	176*	.1	.2
151 L-D SAINTS	1	NA	370	.2	.4
157 CH OF BRETHREN	1	0	0*	-	-
165 CH OF NAZARENE	4	204	333	.2	.4
167 CHS OF CHRIST	2	68	120	.1	.1
193 EPISCOPAL	2	350	558	.4	.6
207 E.L.C.A.	22	8,209	11,066	7.3	12.3
216 EVAN PRESBY CH	1	295	295	.2	.3
221 FREE METHODIST	4	89	177	.1	.2
283 LUTH—MO SYNOD	3	842	1,263	.8	1.4
331 ORTH CH IN AM	2	NR	NR	-	-
353 CHR BRETHREN	1	10	10	-	-
355 PRESB CH (USA)	44	9,551	11,855*	7.8	13.2
356 PRESB CH AMER	4	1,182	1,316	.9	1.5
403 SALVATION ARMY	1	129	140	.1	.2
413 S.D.A.	4	1,026	1,273*	.8	1.4
419 SO BAPT CONV	5	643	798*	.5	.9
443 UN C OF CHRIST	5	1,707	2,119*	1.4	2.4
449 UN METHODIST	31	8,001	9,931*	6.5	11.0
496 JEWISH EST[1]	1	NA	285	.2	.3
497 BLACK BAPT EST[2]	NA	127	158*	.1	.2
CAMBRIA	**278**	**34,533**	**128,785***	**79.0**	**100.0**
011 A.W.M.C.	1	17	21*	-	-
019 AMER BAPT USA	5	1,556	1,889*	1.2	1.5
022 EASTERN ORTH	1	740	740	.5	.6
053 ASSEMB OF GOD	6	468	746	.5	.6
071 BRETHREN (ASH)	3	435	528*	.3	.4
075 BRETHREN IN CR	1	5	17	-	-
081 CATHOLIC	101	NA	83,942	51.5	65.2
081b BYZAN RUTH	*9*	*NA*	*14,846*	*9.1*	*11.5*
081d LATIN	*89*	*NA*	*68,128*	*41.8*	*52.9*
081h UKRAINIAN	*3*	*NA*	*968*	*.6*	*.8*
089 CHR & MISS AL	12	364	1,231	.8	1.0
093 CHR CH (DISC)	3	255	402	.2	.3
111 CH CR,SCIENTST	1	NR	NR	-	-
123 CH GOD (ANDER)	3	120	143	.1	.1
127 CH GOD (CLEVE)	1	119	144*	.1	.1
151 L-D SAINTS	2	NA	574	.4	.4
157 CH OF BRETHREN	11	2,492	3,025*	1.9	2.3
165 CH OF NAZARENE	4	204	282	.2	.2
167 CHS OF CHRIST	1	60	78	-	.1
171 CH GOD-GEN CON	2	39	47*	-	-
193 EPISCOPAL	3	397	512	.3	.4
199 EVAN CONGR CH	1	121	121	.1	.1
207 E.L.C.A.	18	6,662	9,170	5.6	7.1
246 GREEK ORTHODOX	1	NR	NR	-	-
259 IFCA	1	NR	NR	-	-
283 LUTH—MO SYNOD	1	90	96	.1	.1
285 MENNONITE CH	2	128	192	.1	.1
329 OPEN BIBLE STD	1	NR	NR	-	-
331 ORTH CH IN AM	5	NR	NR	-	-
355 PRESB CH (USA)	12	2,413	2,929*	1.8	2.3
356 PRESB CH AMER	1	72	111	.1	.1
403 SALVATION ARMY	1	109	110	.1	.1
413 S.D.A.	1	73	89*	.1	.1
419 SO BAPT CONV	2	264	320*	.2	.2
443 UN C OF CHRIST	6	848	1,029*	.6	.8
449 UN METHODIST	61	15,759	19,128*	11.7	14.9
496 JEWISH EST[1]	3	NA	291	.2	.2
497 BLACK BAPT EST[2]	NA	723	878*	.5	.7
CAMERON	**15**	**1,371**	**3,358***	**56.8**	**100.0**
019 AMER BAPT USA	1	123	154*	2.6	4.6
053 ASSEMB OF GOD	1	11	15	.3	.4

NA–Not applicable   NR–Not reported   *Total adherents estimated from known number of communicant, confirmed, full members.   - Represents a percent less than 0.1.   Percentages may not total due to rounding.
[1]See Appendix E   [2]See Appendix F   [3]See Appendix G   Lines in *italic* represent a breakdown of Catholic rites or Friends affiliations. They are included in their respective denominational total.

Table 4. Churches and Church Membership by County and Denomination: 1990

County and Denomination	Number of churches	Communicant, confirmed, full members	Total adherents Number	Percent of total population	Percent of total adherents
081 CATHOLIC	2	NA	1,500	25.4	44.7
081d LATIN	2	NA	1,500	25.4	44.7
089 CHR & MISS AL	1	42	133	2.2	4.0
193 EPISCOPAL	1	86	113	1.9	3.4
207 E.L.C.A.	1	85	110	1.9	3.3
221 FREE METHODIST	1	21	45	.8	1.3
355 PRESB CH (USA)	1	182	227*	3.8	6.8
419 SO BAPT CONV	1	100	125*	2.1	3.7
449 UN METHODIST	4	702	876*	14.8	26.1
467 WESLEYAN	1	19	60	1.0	1.8
CARBON	**101**	**16,496**	**38,361***	**67.5**	**100.0**
019 AMER BAPT USA	2	94	114*	.2	.3
022 EASTERN ORTH	2	495	495	.9	1.3
081 CATHOLIC	23	NA	16,382	28.8	42.7
081b BYZAN RUTH	4	NA	2,331	4.1	6.1
081d LATIN	18	NA	13,587	23.9	35.4
081h UKRAINIAN	1	NA	464	.8	1.2
123 CH GOD (ANDER)	1	12	12	-	-
157 CH OF BRETHREN	2	85	103*	.2	.3
167 CHS OF CHRIST	1	21	27	-	.1
193 EPISCOPAL	3	546	762	1.3	2.0
199 EVAN CONGR CH	5	814	1,029	1.8	2.7
203 EVAN FREE CH	1	258	345	.6	.9
207 E.L.C.A.	23	7,381	9,969	17.5	26.0
355 PRESB CH (USA)	3	595	722*	1.3	1.9
443 UN C OF CHRIST	18	4,677	5,678*	10.0	14.8
449 UN METHODIST	14	1,427	1,733*	3.0	4.5
467 WESLEYAN	2	91	185	.3	.5
496 JEWISH EST[1]	1	NA	805	1.4	2.1
CENTRE	**165**	**27,848**	**49,110***	**39.7**	**100.0**
019 AMER BAPT USA	3	1,065	1,245*	1.0	2.5
053 ASSEMB OF GOD	2	472	965	.8	2.0
057 BAPT GEN CONF	1	113	132*	.1	.3
075 BRETHREN IN CR	3	104	168	.1	.3
081 CATHOLIC	7	NA	12,216	9.9	24.9
081b BYZAN RUTH	1	NA	405	.3	.8
081d LATIN	6	NA	11,811	9.5	24.1
089 CHR & MISS AL	7	351	899	.7	1.8
097 CHR CHS&CHS CR	3	848	992*	.8	2.0
111 CH CR,SCIENTST	1	NR	NR	-	-
127 CH GOD (CLEVE)	2	195	228*	.2	.5
151 L-D SAINTS	1	NA	453	.4	.9
157 CH OF BRETHREN	1	429	502*	.4	1.0
165 CH OF NAZARENE	1	141	261	.2	.5
167 CHS OF CHRIST	5	138	195	.2	.4
179 CONSRV BAPT	2	NR	NR	-	-
193 EPISCOPAL	3	1,051	1,208	1.0	2.5
203 EVAN FREE CH	1	78	185	.1	.4
207 E.L.C.A.	19	5,244	6,783	5.5	13.8
221 FREE METHODIST	3	112	142	.1	.3
226 FRIENDS-USA	1	282	330*	.3	.7
226c FGC	1	282	330*	.3	.7
246 GREEK ORTHODOX	1	NR	NR	-	-
283 LUTH—MO SYNOD	1	42	53	-	.1
285 MENNONITE CH	2	92	102	.1	.2
323 OLD ORD AMISH	7	NA	1,050	.8	2.1
331 ORTH CH IN AM	2	NR	NR	-	-
355 PRESB CH (USA)	9	2,573	3,009*	2.4	6.1
356 PRESB CH AMER	1	0	0	-	-
413 S.D.A.	1	61	71*	.1	.1
419 SO BAPT CONV	1	60	70*	.1	.1
435 UNITARIAN-UNIV	1	183	244	.2	.5
443 UN C OF CHRIST	17	2,798	3,272*	2.6	6.7
449 UN METHODIST	54	10,828	12,661*	10.2	25.8
467 WESLEYAN	1	46	140	.1	.3
496 JEWISH EST[1]	0	NA	550	.4	1.1
497 BLACK BAPT EST[2]	NA	542	634*	.5	1.3
499 INDEP.NON-CHAR[3]	1	NA	350	.3	.7
CHESTER	**286**	**61,837**	**204,403***	**54.3**	**100.0**
005 AME ZION	2	372	609	.2	.3
019 AMER BAPT USA	18	4,486	5,594*	1.5	2.7
022 EASTERN ORTH	1	321	321	.1	.2
053 ASSEMB OF GOD	12	932	1,353	.4	.7
081 CATHOLIC	31	NA	94,255	25.0	46.1
081b BYZAN RUTH	1	NA	57	-	-
081d LATIN	29	NA	93,348	24.8	45.7
081h UKRAINIAN	1	NA	850	.2	.4
089 CHR & MISS AL	2	40	59	-	-
111 CH CR,SCIENTST	3	NR	NR	-	-
127 CH GOD (CLEVE)	3	138	172*	-	.1
151 L-D SAINTS	5	NA	1,628	.4	.8
157 CH OF BRETHREN	2	168	209*	.1	.1
165 CH OF NAZARENE	4	692	906	.2	.4
167 CHS OF CHRIST	7	410	511	.1	.2
179 CONSRV BAPT	1	NR	NR	-	-
193 EPISCOPAL	16	4,837	7,696	2.0	3.8
203 EVAN FREE CH	2	105	205	.1	.1
207 E.L.C.A.	14	7,296	10,263	2.7	5.0
223 FREE WILL BAPT	2	147	183*	-	.1
226 FRIENDS-USA	13	1,403	1,750*	.5	.9
226c FGC	13	1,403	1,750*	.5	.9
259 IFCA	5	NR	NR	-	-
263 INT FOURSQ GOS	1	117	146*	-	.1
283 LUTH—MO SYNOD	1	328	417	.1	.2
285 MENNONITE CH	18	1,523	2,347	.6	1.1
286 E.PA MENNONITE	1	92	115*	-	.1
323 OLD ORD AMISH	5	NA	750	.2	.4
331 ORTH CH IN AM	1	NR	NR	-	-
353 CHR BRETHREN	2	162	300	.1	.1
355 PRESB CH (USA)	31	12,766	15,919*	4.2	7.8
356 PRESB CH AMER	4	509	637	.2	.3
363 PRIMITIVE METH	1	121	206	.1	.1
386 REGULAR BAPT	1	29	36*	-	-
403 SALVATION ARMY	1	44	52	-	-
413 S.D.A.	3	272	339*	.1	.2
419 SO BAPT CONV	6	753	939*	.2	.5
435 UNITARIAN-UNIV	2	671	966	.3	.5
443 UN C OF CHRIST	14	3,493	4,356*	1.2	2.1
449 UN METHODIST	45	14,964	18,660*	5.0	9.1
496 JEWISH EST[1]	3	NA	25,235	6.7	12.3
497 BLACK BAPT EST[2]	NA	4,646	5,794*	1.5	2.8
499 INDEP.NON-CHAR[3]	3	NA	1,475	.4	.7
CLARION	**109**	**10,754**	**23,305***	**55.9**	**100.0**
011 A.W.M.C.	3	55	67*	.2	.3
019 AMER BAPT USA	3	535	652*	1.6	2.8
053 ASSEMB OF GOD	1	144	280	.7	1.2
081 CATHOLIC	9	NA	8,871	21.3	38.1
081d LATIN	9	NA	8,871	21.3	38.1
089 CHR & MISS AL	2	68	144	.3	.6
123 CH GOD (ANDER)	5	397	644	1.5	2.8
127 CH GOD (CLEVE)	1	18	22*	.1	.1
145 CH GOD PROPHCY	3	106	129*	.3	.6
151 L-D SAINTS	1	NA	80	.2	.3
165 CH OF NAZARENE	5	340	471	1.1	2.0
167 CHS OF CHRIST	1	45	75	.2	.3
179 CONSRV BAPT	2	NR	NR	-	-
193 EPISCOPAL	1	47	40	.1	.2
199 EVAN CONGR CH	4	456	1,023	2.5	4.4
207 E.L.C.A.	8	1,400	1,966	4.7	8.4
221 FREE METHODIST	3	45	78	.2	.3
355 PRESB CH (USA)	14	1,928	2,349*	5.6	10.1
443 UN C OF CHRIST	7	655	798*	1.9	3.4
449 UN METHODIST	34	4,461	5,434*	13.0	23.3
467 WESLEYAN	2	54	182	.4	.8
CLEARFIELD	**194**	**19,438**	**44,441***	**56.9**	**100.0**
019 AMER BAPT USA	1	195	242*	.3	.5
022 EASTERN ORTH	1	178	178	.2	.4
053 ASSEMB OF GOD	5	401	723	.9	1.6
057 BAPT GEN CONF	1	173	214*	.3	.5
081 CATHOLIC	20	NA	18,155	23.2	40.9
081b BYZAN RUTH	1	NA	644	.8	1.4
081d LATIN	18	NA	17,321	22.2	39.0
081h UKRAINIAN	1	NA	190	.2	.4
089 CHR & MISS AL	12	908	2,328	3.0	5.2
123 CH GOD (ANDER)	1	97	106	.1	.2
127 CH GOD (CLEVE)	1	14	17*	-	-
157 CH OF BRETHREN	3	148	183*	.2	.4
165 CH OF NAZARENE	3	207	307	.4	.7
167 CHS OF CHRIST	8	239	300	.4	.7
171 CH GOD-GEN CON	3	192	238*	.3	.5
179 CONSRV BAPT	1	NR	NR	-	-
193 EPISCOPAL	5	381	579	.7	1.3
203 EVAN FREE CH	2	138	218	.3	.5
207 E.L.C.A.	12	2,586	3,313	4.2	7.5
221 FREE METHODIST	5	111	159	.2	.4
226 FRIENDS-USA	1	107	133*	.2	.3
226c FGC & FUM	1	107	133*	.2	.3
283 LUTH—MO SYNOD	2	246	306	.4	.7
313 N AM BAPT CONF	2	478	592*	.8	1.3
323 OLD ORD AMISH	2	NA	300	.4	.7
331 ORTH CH IN AM	4	NR	NR	-	-
355 PRESB CH (USA)	16	2,288	2,835*	3.6	6.4
363 PRIMITIVE METH	2	65	100	.1	.2
403 SALVATION ARMY	2	118	126	.2	.3
413 S.D.A.	1	19	24*	-	.1
419 SO BAPT CONV	2	90	111*	.1	.2
443 UN C OF CHRIST	4	331	410*	.5	.9
449 UN METHODIST	70	9,651	11,957*	15.3	26.9

NA–Not applicable NR–Not reported *Total adherents estimated from known number of communicant, confirmed, full members. - Represents a percent less than 0.1. Percentages may not total due to rounding.
[1]See Appendix E [2]See Appendix F [3]See Appendix G Lines in *italic* represent a breakdown of Catholic rites or Friends affiliations. They are included in their respective denominational total.

Table 4. Churches and Church Membership by County and Denomination: 1990

County and Denomination	Number of churches	Communicant, confirmed, full members	Total adherents Number	Percent of total population	Percent of total adherents
467 WESLEYAN	3	77	287	.4	.6
CLINTON	**78**	**9,395**	**15,877***	**42.7**	**100.0**
053 ASSEMB OF GOD	2	95	164	.4	1.0
075 BRETHREN IN CR	1	106	106	.3	.7
081 CATHOLIC	2	NA	3,802	10.2	23.9
081d LATIN	2	NA	3,802	10.2	23.9
089 CHR & MISS AL	2	40	49	.1	.3
097 CHR CHS&CHS CR	5	1,052	1,280*	3.4	8.1
111 CH CR,SCIENTST	1	NR	NR	-	-
151 L-D SAINTS	1	NA	129	.3	.8
157 CH OF BRETHREN	1	80	97*	.3	.6
165 CH OF NAZARENE	1	45	32	.1	.2
167 CHS OF CHRIST	4	80	110	.3	.7
193 EPISCOPAL	2	185	206	.6	1.3
207 E.L.C.A.	8	1,169	1,515	4.1	9.5
221 FREE METHODIST	2	58	67	.2	.4
259 IFCA	1	NR	NR	-	-
285 MENNONITE CH	1	45	104	.3	.7
323 OLD ORD AMISH	2	NA	300	.8	1.9
353 CHR BRETHREN	1	22	33	.1	.2
355 PRESB CH (USA)	3	488	594*	1.6	3.7
403 SALVATION ARMY	1	101	124	.3	.8
413 S.D.A.	1	45	55*	.1	.3
419 SO BAPT CONV	1	50	61*	.2	.4
443 UN C OF CHRIST	4	809	985*	2.6	6.2
449 UN METHODIST	28	4,851	5,904*	15.9	37.2
467 WESLEYAN	2	74	160	.4	1.0
496 JEWISH EST[1]	1	NA	0	-	-
COLUMBIA	**114**	**19,258**	**33,146***	**52.4**	**100.0**
019 AMER BAPT USA	2	511	615*	1.0	1.9
053 ASSEMB OF GOD	4	569	939	1.5	2.8
081 CATHOLIC	8	NA	8,112	12.8	24.5
081d LATIN	7	NA	7,937	12.6	23.9
081h UKRAINIAN	1	NA	175	.3	.5
089 CHR & MISS AL	2	74	134	.2	.4
093 CHR CH (DISC)	3	417	667	1.1	2.0
097 CHR CHS&CHS CR	6	1,070	1,288*	2.0	3.9
111 CH CR,SCIENTST	1	NR	NR	-	-
151 L-D SAINTS	1	NA	257	.4	.8
165 CH OF NAZARENE	1	145	210	.3	.6
179 CONSRV BAPT	1	NR	NR	-	-
193 EPISCOPAL	3	380	553	.9	1.7
207 E.L.C.A.	14	4,603	5,968	9.4	18.0
226 FRIENDS-USA	1	82	99*	.2	.3
226c FGC	1	82	99*	.2	.3
259 IFCA	1	NR	NR	-	-
331 ORTH CH IN AM	1	NR	NR	-	-
355 PRESB CH (USA)	5	868	1,045*	1.7	3.2
403 SALVATION ARMY	1	74	88	.1	.3
413 S.D.A.	1	62	75*	.1	.2
419 SO BAPT CONV	1	215	259*	.4	.8
443 UN C OF CHRIST	11	1,797	2,163*	3.4	6.5
449 UN METHODIST	44	8,391	10,102*	16.0	30.5
496 JEWISH EST[1]	2	NA	572	.9	1.7
CRAWFORD	**168**	**17,818**	**38,848***	**45.1**	**100.0**
011 A.W.M.C.	5	166	208*	.2	.5
019 AMER BAPT USA	9	1,699	2,126*	2.5	5.5
053 ASSEMB OF GOD	2	213	415	.5	1.1
057 BAPT GEN CONF	1	76	95*	.1	.2
061 BEACHY AMISH	1	48	60*	.1	.2
081 CATHOLIC	15	NA	12,871	14.9	33.1
081d LATIN	15	NA	12,871	14.9	33.1
089 CHR & MISS AL	6	361	718	.8	1.8
097 CHR CHS&CHS CR	3	689	862*	1.0	2.2
111 CH CR,SCIENTST	1	NR	NR	-	-
123 CH GOD (ANDER)	3	137	159	.2	.4
151 L-D SAINTS	2	NA	294	.3	.8
165 CH OF NAZARENE	4	211	266	.3	.7
167 CHS OF CHRIST	2	35	46	.1	.1
175 CONGR CHR CHS	1	37	46*	.1	.1
193 EPISCOPAL	2	485	595	.7	1.5
203 EVAN FREE CH	2	347	467	.5	1.2
207 E.L.C.A.	6	1,232	1,693	2.0	4.4
221 FREE METHODIST	4	156	227	.3	.6
285 MENNONITE CH	5	220	390	.5	1.0
286 E.PA MENNONITE	1	29	36*	-	.1
323 OLD ORD AMISH	18	NA	2,650	3.1	6.8
331 ORTH CH IN AM	1	NR	NR	-	-
355 PRESB CH (USA)	13	3,020	3,778*	4.4	9.7
403 SALVATION ARMY	1	109	123	.1	.3
413 S.D.A.	1	5	6*	-	-
435 UNITARIAN-UNIV	1	106	131	.2	.3
438 UN BRETH IN CR	3	315	425	.5	1.1
443 UN C OF CHRIST	7	1,405	1,758*	2.0	4.5
449 UN METHODIST	48	6,549	8,193*	9.5	21.1
497 BLACK BAPT EST[2]	NA	168	210*	.2	.5
CUMBERLAND	**227**	**65,095**	**115,404***	**59.1**	**100.0**
005 AME ZION	3	447	765	.4	.7
019 AMER BAPT USA	1	591	712*	.4	.6
053 ASSEMB OF GOD	8	1,901	3,982	2.0	3.5
075 BRETHREN IN CR	10	2,265	2,545	1.3	2.2
081 CATHOLIC	9	NA	26,841	13.7	23.3
081d LATIN	9	NA	26,841	13.7	23.3
089 CHR & MISS AL	7	623	1,374	.7	1.2
093 CHR CH (DISC)	1	226	425	.2	.4
097 CHR CHS&CHS CR	1	90	108*	.1	.1
111 CH CR,SCIENTST	1	NR	NR	-	-
123 CH GOD (ANDER)	1	68	72	-	.1
127 CH GOD (CLEVE)	5	555	669*	.3	.6
143 CG IN CR(MENN)	1	34	41*	-	-
145 CH GOD PROPHCY	1	35	42*	-	-
151 L-D SAINTS	2	NA	671	.3	.6
157 CH OF BRETHREN	7	883	1,064*	.5	.9
165 CH OF NAZARENE	3	306	385	.2	.3
167 CHS OF CHRIST	4	380	445	.2	.4
171 CH GOD-GEN CON	22	3,888	4,686*	2.4	4.1
179 CONSRV BAPT	2	NR	NR	-	-
193 EPISCOPAL	4	1,719	2,198	1.1	1.9
203 EVAN FREE CH	3	403	795	.4	.7
207 E.L.C.A.	30	17,004	22,398	11.5	19.4
226 FRIENDS-USA	1	18	22*	-	-
226c FGC	1	18	22*	-	-
246 GREEK ORTHODOX	1	NR	NR	-	-
283 LUTH—MO SYNOD	1	231	305	.2	.3
285 MENNONITE CH	4	330	477	.2	.4
286 E.PA MENNONITE	2	99	119*	.1	.1
339 PENT CH OF GOD	1	31	43	-	-
355 PRESB CH (USA)	14	7,506	9,046*	4.6	7.8
356 PRESB CH AMER	3	379	497	.3	.4
403 SALVATION ARMY	1	108	116	.1	.1
413 S.D.A.	1	98	118*	.1	.1
419 SO BAPT CONV	4	1,381	1,664*	.9	1.4
438 UN BRETH IN CR	1	45	64	-	.1
443 UN C OF CHRIST	8	2,619	3,156*	1.6	2.7
449 UN METHODIST	52	19,948	24,041*	12.3	20.8
467 WESLEYAN	2	291	258	.1	.2
496 JEWISH EST[1]	1	NA	2,145	1.1	1.9
497 BLACK BAPT EST[2]	NA	593	715*	.4	.6
498 INDEP.CHARIS.[3]	1	NA	1,200	.6	1.0
499 INDEP.NON-CHAR[3]	3	NA	1,200	.6	1.0
DAUPHIN	**296**	**67,924**	**131,891***	**55.5**	**100.0**
005 AME ZION	2	531	733	.3	.6
019 AMER BAPT USA	6	484	594*	.2	.5
053 ASSEMB OF GOD	9	1,058	2,095	.9	1.6
075 BRETHREN IN CR	6	549	587	.2	.4
081 CATHOLIC	21	NA	37,317	15.7	28.3
081d LATIN	21	NA	37,317	15.7	28.3
089 CHR & MISS AL	4	302	519	.2	.4
111 CH CR,SCIENTST	3	NR	NR	-	-
123 CH GOD (ANDER)	3	133	158	.1	.1
127 CH GOD (CLEVE)	1	98	120*	.1	.1
133 CH GOD(7TH)DEN	1	13	23	-	-
145 CH GOD PROPHCY	1	35	43*	-	-
151 L-D SAINTS	3	NA	873	.4	.7
157 CH OF BRETHREN	8	1,706	2,095*	.9	1.6
165 CH OF NAZARENE	3	254	430	.2	.3
167 CHS OF CHRIST	2	146	241	.1	.2
171 CH GOD-GEN CON	15	2,401	2,949*	1.2	2.2
193 EPISCOPAL	6	1,766	2,090	.9	1.6
199 EVAN CONGR CH	11	1,260	2,135	.9	1.6
203 EVAN FREE CH	3	1,191	2,517	1.1	1.9
207 E.L.C.A.	42	15,190	20,055	8.4	15.2
226 FRIENDS-USA	1	93	114*	-	.1
226c FGC	1	93	114*	-	.1
259 IFCA	3	NR	NR	-	-
263 INT FOURSQ GOS	2	81	99*	-	.1
285 MENNONITE CH	10	432	610	.3	.5
323 OLD ORD AMISH	2	NA	300	.1	.2
331 ORTH CH IN AM	2	NR	NR	-	-
353 CHR BRETHREN	2	103	164	.1	.1
355 PRESB CH (USA)	11	5,305	6,516*	2.7	4.9
356 PRESB CH AMER	2	129	179	.1	.1
403 SALVATION ARMY	1	182	219	.1	.2
413 S.D.A.	5	619	760*	.3	.6
419 SO BAPT CONV	3	950	1,167*	.5	.9
435 UNITARIAN-UNIV	1	255	365	.2	.3
438 UN BRETH IN CR	1	189	191	.1	.1
441 UN CHRISTIAN	2	59	107	-	.1

NA–Not applicable NR–Not reported *Total adherents estimated from known number of communicant, confirmed, full members. - Represents a percent less than 0.1. Percentages may not total due to rounding.
[1] See Appendix E [2] See Appendix F [3] See Appendix G Lines in *italic* represent a breakdown of Catholic rites or Friends affiliations. They are included in their respective denominational total.

Table 4. Churches and Church Membership by County and Denomination: 1990

County and Denomination	Number of churches	Communicant, confirmed, full members	Total adherents Number	Percent of total population	Percent of total adherents
443 UN C OF CHRIST	17	5,052	6,205*	2.6	4.7
449 UN METHODIST	67	20,243	24,864*	10.5	18.9
467 WESLEYAN	2	92	415	.2	.3
469 WELS	1	128	197	.1	.1
496 JEWISH EST[1]	5	NA	2,626	1.1	2.0
497 BLACK BAPT EST[2]	NA	6,895	8,469*	3.6	6.4
498 INDEP.CHARIS.[3]	2	NA	1,300	.5	1.0
499 INDEP.NON-CHAR[3]	4	NA	1,450	.6	1.1
DELAWARE	**319**	**73,721**	**374,013***	**68.3**	**100.0**
005 AME ZION	2	462	684	.1	.2
019 AMER BAPT USA	21	4,099	5,025*	.9	1.3
053 ASSEM OF GOD	6	576	671	.1	.2
081 CATHOLIC	54	NA	240,787	44.0	64.4
081d *LATIN*	51	NA	237,946	43.4	63.6
081e *MARONITE*	1	NA	416	.1	.1
081h *UKRAINIAN*	2	NA	2,425	.4	.6
089 CHR & MISS AL	2	81	138	-	-
093 CHR CH (DISC)	1	105	151	-	-
097 CHR CHS&CHS CR	1	150	184*	-	-
111 CH CR,SCIENTST	3	NR	NR	-	-
123 CH GOD (ANDER)	1	45	45	-	-
127 CH GOD (CLEVE)	2	147	180*	-	-
145 CH GOD PROPHCY	1	35	43*	-	-
151 L-D SAINTS	3	NA	1,018	.2	.3
157 CH OF BRETHREN	1	112	137*	-	-
165 CH OF NAZARENE	3	357	567	.1	.2
167 CHS OF CHRIST	5	257	328	.1	.1
175 CONGR CHR CHS	1	168	206*	-	.1
179 CONSRV BAPT	1	NR	NR	-	-
193 EPISCOPAL	33	10,632	15,836	2.9	4.2
195 ESTONIAN ELC	1	76	94*	-	-
207 E.L.C.A.	22	6,932	9,637	1.8	2.6
226 FRIENDS-USA	14	1,900	2,329*	.4	.6
226c *FGC*	14	1,900	2,329*	.4	.6
246 GREEK ORTHODOX	3	NR	NR	-	-
259 IFCA	5	NR	NR	-	-
283 LUTH—MO SYNOD	3	580	794	.1	.2
285 MENNONITE CH	4	192	422	.1	.1
331 ORTH CH IN AM	1	NR	NR	-	-
353 CHR BRETHREN	3	130	213	-	.1
355 PRESB CH (USA)	35	15,060	18,463*	3.4	4.9
356 PRESB CH AMER	7	714	798	.1	.2
375 REF EPISCOPAL	2	163	217	-	.1
403 SALVATION ARMY	2	148	164	-	-
413 S.D.A.	2	289	354*	.1	.1
419 SO BAPT CONV	3	192	235*	-	.1
435 UNITARIAN-UNIV	1	257	362	.1	.1
443 UN C OF CHRIST	3	519	636*	.1	.2
449 UN METHODIST	54	17,330	21,247*	3.9	5.7
467 WESLEYAN	2	125	207	-	.1
496 JEWISH EST[1]	10	NA	36,716	6.7	9.8
497 BLACK BAPT EST[2]	NA	11,888	14,575*	2.7	3.9
499 INDEP.NON-CHAR[3]	1	NA	550	.1	.1
ELK	**46**	**5,261**	**26,110***	**74.9**	**100.0**
019 AMER BAPT USA	1	101	126*	.4	.5
053 ASSEM OF GOD	1	61	110	.3	.4
081 CATHOLIC	11	NA	18,979	54.4	72.7
081d *LATIN*	11	NA	18,979	54.4	72.7
089 CHR & MISS AL	2	44	99	.3	.4
097 CHR CHS&CHS CR	2	353	441*	1.3	1.7
151 L-D SAINTS	1	NA	88	.3	.3
165 CH OF NAZARENE	1	58	83	.2	.3
193 EPISCOPAL	2	93	122	.3	.5
207 E.L.C.A.	5	1,538	2,097	6.0	8.0
355 PRESB CH (USA)	4	548	685*	2.0	2.6
419 SO BAPT CONV	2	118	147*	.4	.6
443 UN C OF CHRIST	1	518	647*	1.9	2.5
449 UN METHODIST	12	1,709	2,136*	6.1	8.2
467 WESLEYAN	1	120	350	1.0	1.3
ERIE	**246**	**47,071**	**159,848***	**58.0**	**100.0**
005 AME ZION	1	450	523	.2	.3
011 A.W.M.C.	4	59	74*	-	-
019 AMER BAPT USA	11	2,845	3,572*	1.3	2.2
022 EASTERN ORTH	1	247	247	.1	.2
039 AP CHR CH(NAZ)	1	32	40*	-	-
053 ASSEM OF GOD	9	2,445	3,254	1.2	2.0
057 BAPT GEN CONF	3	552	693*	.3	.4
081 CATHOLIC	44	NA	95,190	34.5	59.6
081b *BYZAN RUTH*	2	NA	3,325	1.2	2.1
081d *LATIN*	42	NA	91,865	33.3	57.5
089 CHR & MISS AL	10	1,126	2,556	.9	1.6
093 CHR CH (DISC)	1	91	160	.1	.1
111 CH CR,SCIENTST	2	NR	NR	-	-

County and Denomination	Number of churches	Communicant, confirmed, full members	Total adherents Number	Percent of total population	Percent of total adherents
123 CH GOD (ANDER)	4	205	290	.1	.2
127 CH GOD (CLEVE)	2	574	721*	.3	.5
145 CH GOD PROPHCY	2	71	89*	-	.1
151 L-D SAINTS	2	NA	740	.3	.5
157 CH OF BRETHREN	1	132	166*	.1	.1
165 CH OF NAZARENE	7	675	1,078	.4	.7
167 CHS OF CHRIST	1	100	113	-	.1
193 EPISCOPAL	10	1,275	2,015	.7	1.3
203 EVAN FREE CH	2	129	200	.1	.1
207 E.L.C.A.	25	9,733	13,701	5.0	8.6
221 FREE METHODIST	5	122	180	.1	.1
226 FRIENDS-USA	1	5	18	-	-
226f *INDEPENDNT*	1	5	18	-	-
246 GREEK ORTHODOX	1	NR	NR	-	-
263 INT FOURSQ GOS	1	30	38*	-	-
283 LUTH—MO SYNOD	4	815	1,100	.4	.7
285 MENNONITE CH	2	148	217	.1	.1
313 N AM BAPT CONF	1	61	77*	-	-
323 OLD ORD AMISH	1	NA	150	.1	.1
331 ORTH CH IN AM	1	NR	NR	-	-
353 CHR BRETHREN	1	60	110	-	.1
355 PRESB CH (USA)	22	7,323	9,194*	3.3	5.8
356 PRESB CH AMER	1	39	53	-	-
403 SALVATION ARMY	2	287	305	.1	.2
413 S.D.A.	4	268	336*	.1	.2
419 SO BAPT CONV	3	341	428*	.2	.3
435 UNITARIAN-UNIV	2	116	144	.1	.1
443 UN C OF CHRIST	2	345	433*	.2	.3
449 UN METHODIST	45	13,562	17,026*	6.2	10.7
467 WESLEYAN	1	38	39	-	-
496 JEWISH EST[1]	2	NA	800	.3	.5
497 BLACK BAPT EST[2]	NA	2,770	3,478*	1.3	2.2
499 INDEP.NON-CHAR[3]	1	NA	300	.1	.2
FAYETTE	**253**	**28,641**	**94,452***	**65.0**	**100.0**
005 AME ZION	1	258	503	.3	.5
011 A.W.M.C.	2	39	48*	-	.1
019 AMER BAPT USA	14	2,644	3,240*	2.2	3.4
053 ASSEM OF GOD	4	444	905	.6	1.0
071 BRETHREN (ASH)	1	102	125*	.1	.1
075 BRETHREN IN CR	1	41	81	.1	.1
081 CATHOLIC	44	NA	52,483	36.1	55.6
081b *BYZAN RUTH*	6	NA	8,112	5.6	8.6
081d *LATIN*	37	NA	43,055	29.6	45.6
081e *MARONITE*	1	NA	1,316	.9	1.4
089 CHR & MISS AL	6	292	673	.5	.7
093 CHR CH (DISC)	7	1,921	3,262	2.2	3.5
097 CHR CHS&CHS CR	7	925	1,133*	.8	1.2
123 CH GOD (ANDER)	3	136	186	.1	.2
127 CH GOD (CLEVE)	5	387	474*	.3	.5
145 CH GOD PROPHCY	3	106	130*	.1	.1
151 L-D SAINTS	1	NA	160	.1	.2
157 CH OF BRETHREN	14	1,379	1,690*	1.2	1.8
165 CH OF NAZARENE	4	198	350	.2	.4
167 CHS OF CHRIST	3	169	247	.2	.3
171 CH GOD-GEN CON	6	721	883*	.6	.9
193 EPISCOPAL	3	177	315	.2	.3
203 EVAN FREE CH	1	75	90	.1	.1
207 E.L.C.A.	6	2,321	3,025	2.1	3.2
221 FREE METHODIST	12	530	827	.6	.9
226 FRIENDS-USA	1	10	12*	-	-
226a *CONSERV*	1	10	12*	-	-
257 HUTTERIAN BR	2	NA	450	.3	.5
263 INT FOURSQ GOS	1	84	103*	.1	.1
285 MENNONITE CH	3	241	294	.2	.3
329 OPEN BIBLE STD	1	NR	NR	-	-
331 ORTH CH IN AM	3	NR	NR	-	-
355 PRESB CH (USA)	30	4,744	5,813*	4.0	6.2
403 SALVATION ARMY	1	124	129	.1	.1
413 S.D.A.	2	125	153*	.1	.2
419 SO BAPT CONV	2	153	187*	.1	.2
449 UN METHODIST	55	9,304	11,401*	7.8	12.1
496 JEWISH EST[1]	2	NA	2,916	2.0	3.1
497 BLACK BAPT EST[2]	NA	991	1,214*	.8	1.3
499 INDEP.NON-CHAR[3]	2	NA	950	.7	1.0
FOREST	**18**	**983**	**1,583***	**33.0**	**100.0**
081 CATHOLIC	1	NA	150	3.1	9.5
081d *LATIN*	1	NA	150	3.1	9.5
089 CHR & MISS AL	1	32	59	1.2	3.7
123 CH GOD (ANDER)	3	82	175	3.6	11.1
207 E.L.C.A.	1	81	100	2.1	6.3
221 FREE METHODIST	2	10	23	.5	1.5
323 OLD ORD AMISH	1	NA	150	3.1	9.5
355 PRESB CH (USA)	3	214	255*	5.3	16.1
449 UN METHODIST	6	564	671*	14.0	42.4

NA–Not applicable   NR–Not reported   *Total adherents estimated from known number of communicant, confirmed, full members.   - Represents a percent less than 0.1.   Percentages may not total due to rounding.

[1]See Appendix E   [2]See Appendix F   [3]See Appendix G   Lines in *italic* represent a breakdown of Catholic rites or Friends affiliations. They are included in their respective denominational total.

Table 4. Churches and Church Membership by County and Denomination: 1990

County and Denomination	Number of churches	Communicant, confirmed, full members	Total adherents Number	Percent of total population	Percent of total adherents
FRANKLIN	**211**	**38,730**	**60,881***	**50.3**	**100.0**
005 AME ZION	1	175	311	.3	.5
019 AMER BAPT USA	1	121	149*	.1	.2
053 ASSEMB OF GOD	11	1,273	2,169	1.8	3.6
061 BEACHY AMISH	1	60	74*	.1	.1
071 BRETHREN (ASH)	1	54	66*	.1	.1
075 BRETHREN IN CR	12	2,200	2,391	2.0	3.9
081 CATHOLIC	7	NA	7,163	5.9	11.8
081d LATIN	7	NA	7,163	5.9	11.8
089 CHR & MISS AL	2	131	220	.2	.4
111 CH CR,SCIENTST	1	NR	NR	-	-
127 CH GOD (CLEVE)	5	711	875*	.7	1.4
151 L-D SAINTS	2	NA	1,043	.9	1.7
157 CH OF BRETHREN	11	2,214	2,725*	2.3	4.5
167 CHS OF CHRIST	1	34	44	-	.1
171 CH GOD-GEN CON	6	703	865*	.7	1.4
193 EPISCOPAL	4	467	568	.5	.9
203 EVAN FREE CH	2	65	86	.1	.1
207 E.L.C.A.	21	6,117	7,738	6.4	12.7
226 FRIENDS-USA	1	27	33*	-	.1
226c FGC	1	27	33*	-	.1
259 IFCA	1	NR	NR	-	-
263 INT FOURSQ GOS	1	73	90*	.1	.1
285 MENNONITE CH	16	1,737	2,216	1.8	3.6
286 E.PA MENNONITE	2	155	191*	.2	.3
323 OLD ORD AMISH	5	NA	750	.6	1.2
324 OLD ORD RVR BR	3	177	266	.2	.4
349 PENT HOLINESS	1	20	25*	-	-
353 CHR BRETHREN	3	266	412	.3	.7
355 PRESB CH (USA)	8	2,538	3,124*	2.6	5.1
403 SALVATION ARMY	1	49	55	-	.1
413 S.D.A.	2	269	331*	.3	.5
419 SO BAPT CONV	4	665	818*	.7	1.3
438 UN BRETH IN CR	19	5,767	5,767	4.8	9.5
443 UN C OF CHRIST	14	3,581	4,407*	3.6	7.2
449 UN METHODIST	37	8,604	10,589*	8.7	17.4
467 WESLEYAN	1	42	240	.2	.4
496 JEWISH EST[1]	1	NA	470	.4	.8
497 BLACK BAPT EST[2]	NA	435	535*	.4	.9
499 INDEP.NON-CHAR[3]	2	NA	4,075	3.4	6.7
FULTON	**44**	**3,443**	**4,580***	**33.1**	**100.0**
053 ASSEMB OF GOD	1	43	125	.9	2.7
081 CATHOLIC	1	NA	173	1.3	3.8
081d LATIN	1	NA	173	1.3	3.8
127 CH GOD (CLEVE)	1	29	36*	.3	.8
157 CH OF BRETHREN	4	267	336*	2.4	7.3
165 CH OF NAZARENE	2	124	124	.9	2.7
171 CH GOD-GEN CON	1	36	45*	.3	1.0
176 CCC, NOT NAT'L	3	229	288*	2.1	6.3
207 E.L.C.A.	3	575	717	5.2	15.7
285 MENNONITE CH	4	124	198	1.4	4.3
355 PRESB CH (USA)	4	447	563*	4.1	12.3
443 UN C OF CHRIST	3	209	263*	1.9	5.7
449 UN METHODIST	17	1,360	1,712*	12.4	37.4
GREENE	**107**	**10,497**	**18,547***	**46.9**	**100.0**
011 A.W.M.C.	1	13	16*	-	.1
019 AMER BAPT USA	13	1,895	2,352*	5.9	12.7
053 ASSEMB OF GOD	3	412	887	2.2	4.8
071 BRETHREN (ASH)	1	10	12*	-	.1
081 CATHOLIC	9	NA	4,595	11.6	24.8
081d LATIN	9	NA	4,595	11.6	24.8
093 CHR CH (DISC)	4	317	644	1.6	3.5
097 CHR CHS&CHS CR	5	643	798*	2.0	4.3
127 CH GOD (CLEVE)	3	330	410*	1.0	2.2
145 CH GOD PROPHCY	1	35	43*	.1	.2
165 CH OF NAZARENE	3	499	834	2.1	4.5
167 CHS OF CHRIST	4	109	139	.4	.7
171 CH GOD-GEN CON	6	187	232*	.6	1.3
193 EPISCOPAL	1	42	57	.1	.3
207 E.L.C.A.	1	170	222	.6	1.2
221 FREE METHODIST	1	32	37	.1	.2
291 MISSIONARY CH	2	49	63	.2	.3
353 CHR BRETHREN	1	50	100	.3	.5
355 PRESB CH (USA)	8	1,018	1,264*	3.2	6.8
356 PRESB CH AMER	1	388	506	1.3	2.7
413 S.D.A.	1	23	29*	.1	.2
419 SO BAPT CONV	1	193	240*	.6	1.3
449 UN METHODIST	37	4,082	5,067*	12.8	27.3
HUNTINGDON	**128**	**12,881**	**19,573***	**44.3**	**100.0**
019 AMER BAPT USA	5	457	556*	1.3	2.8
022 EASTERN ORTH	2	50	50	.1	.3
053 ASSEMB OF GOD	5	411	919	2.1	4.7
075 BRETHREN IN CR	2	40	58	.1	.3

County and Denomination	Number of churches	Communicant, confirmed, full members	Total adherents Number	Percent of total population	Percent of total adherents
081 CATHOLIC	4	NA	2,550	5.8	13.0
081d LATIN	4	NA	2,550	5.8	13.0
089 CHR & MISS AL	3	381	793	1.8	4.1
123 CH GOD (ANDER)	1	110	190	.4	1.0
127 CH GOD (CLEVE)	1	180	219*	.5	1.1
145 CH GOD PROPHCY	1	35	43*	.1	.2
151 L-D SAINTS	1	NA	186	.4	1.0
157 CH OF BRETHREN	9	1,441	1,754*	4.0	9.0
165 CH OF NAZARENE	4	301	569	1.3	2.9
167 CHS OF CHRIST	2	60	74	.2	.4
171 CH GOD-GEN CON	4	214	261*	.6	1.3
193 EPISCOPAL	1	90	144	.3	.7
207 E.L.C.A.	8	939	1,155	2.6	5.9
221 FREE METHODIST	1	28	59	.1	.3
226 FRIENDS-USA	1	3	15*	-	.1
226c FGC	1	3	15*	-	.1
285 MENNONITE CH	2	67	129	.3	.7
355 PRESB CH (USA)	13	1,449	1,764*	4.0	9.0
403 SALVATION ARMY	1	48	78	.2	.4
443 UN C OF CHRIST	8	872	1,062*	2.4	5.4
449 UN METHODIST	48	5,394	6,566*	14.9	33.5
496 JEWISH EST[1]	1	NA	0	-	-
497 BLACK BAPT EST[2]	NA	311	379*	.9	1.9
INDIANA	**182**	**20,454**	**44,806***	**49.8**	**100.0**
005 AME ZION	2	358	430	.5	1.0
011 A.W.M.C.	12	251	306*	.3	.7
019 AMER BAPT USA	7	648	791*	.9	1.8
022 EASTERN ORTH	2	382	382	.4	.9
053 ASSEMB OF GOD	5	352	632	.7	1.4
081 CATHOLIC	17	NA	16,139	17.9	36.0
081b BYZAN RUTH	2	NA	1,362	1.5	3.0
081d LATIN	15	NA	14,777	16.4	33.0
089 CHR & MISS AL	4	266	732	.8	1.6
093 CHR CH (DISC)	2	309	418	.5	.9
097 CHR CHS&CHS CR	3	170	207*	.2	.5
111 CH CR,SCIENTST	1	NR	NR	-	-
123 CH GOD (ANDER)	4	163	319	.4	.7
151 L-D SAINTS	1	NA	188	.2	.4
157 CH OF BRETHREN	6	704	859*	1.0	1.9
165 CH OF NAZARENE	4	306	620	.7	1.4
167 CHS OF CHRIST	5	395	612	.7	1.4
171 CH GOD-GEN CON	1	30	37*	-	.1
179 CONSRV BAPT	1	NR	NR	-	-
193 EPISCOPAL	2	239	380	.4	.8
203 EVAN FREE CH	1	81	140	.2	.3
207 E.L.C.A.	14	2,543	3,454	3.8	7.7
221 FREE METHODIST	2	71	123	.1	.3
226 FRIENDS-USA	1	4	14*	-	-
226c FGC	1	4	14*	-	-
259 IFCA	1	NR	NR	-	-
323 OLD ORD AMISH	9	NA	1,350	1.5	3.0
331 ORTH CH IN AM	2	NR	NR	-	-
353 CHR BRETHREN	1	35	60	.1	.1
355 PRESB CH (USA)	26	5,493	6,704*	7.4	15.0
403 SALVATION ARMY	1	70	75	.1	.2
413 S.D.A.	1	81	99*	.1	.2
419 SO BAPT CONV	2	181	221*	.2	.5
435 UNITARIAN-UNIV	1	41	59	.1	.1
449 UN METHODIST	38	7,059	8,616*	9.6	19.2
467 WESLEYAN	1	38	54	.1	.1
496 JEWISH EST[1]	1	NA	0	-	-
497 BLACK BAPT EST[2]	NA	184	225*	.3	.5
499 INDEP.NON-CHAR[3]	1	NA	560	.6	1.2
JEFFERSON	**133**	**11,714**	**29,691***	**64.4**	**100.0**
011 A.W.M.C.	1	19	24*	.1	.1
019 AMER BAPT USA	3	389	485*	1.1	1.6
053 ASSEMB OF GOD	3	396	650	1.4	2.2
081 CATHOLIC	15	NA	13,450	29.2	45.3
081b BYZAN RUTH	4	NA	5,527	12.0	18.6
081d LATIN	11	NA	7,923	17.2	26.7
089 CHR & MISS AL	6	376	1,116	2.4	3.8
097 CHR CHS&CHS CR	2	175	218*	.5	.7
123 CH GOD (ANDER)	3	172	455	1.0	1.5
151 L-D SAINTS	3	NA	293	.6	1.0
165 CH OF NAZARENE	2	102	217	.5	.7
167 CHS OF CHRIST	4	235	316	.7	1.1
171 CH GOD-GEN CON	2	88	110*	.2	.4
179 CONSRV BAPT	1	NR	NR	-	-
193 EPISCOPAL	2	85	103	.2	.3
207 E.L.C.A.	8	720	1,002	2.2	3.4
221 FREE METHODIST	3	28	46	.1	.2
283 LUTH—MO SYNOD	1	78	108	.2	.4
285 MENNONITE CH	1	6	6	-	-
353 CHR BRETHREN	1	15	100	.2	.3
355 PRESB CH (USA)	16	2,211	2,754*	6.0	9.3

NA–Not applicable NR–Not reported *Total adherents estimated from known number of communicant, confirmed, full members. - Represents a percent less than 0.1. Percentages may not total due to rounding.
[1]See Appendix E [2]See Appendix F [3]See Appendix G Lines in *italic* represent a breakdown of Catholic rites or Friends affiliations. They are included in their respective denominational total.

Table 4. Churches and Church Membership by County and Denomination: 1990

County and Denomination		Number of churches	Communicant, confirmed, full members	Total adherents		
				Number	Percent of total population	Percent of total adherents
403	SALVATION ARMY	1	96	112	.2	.4
413	S.D.A.	2	59	73*	.2	.2
443	UN C OF CHRIST	3	471	587*	1.3	2.0
449	UN METHODIST	49	5,993	7,466*	16.2	25.1
496	JEWISH EST[1]	1	NA	0	-	-
JUNIATA		**68**	**8,349**	**11,533***	**55.9**	**100.0**
053	ASSEMB OF GOD	2	108	214	1.0	1.9
075	BRETHREN IN CR	1	189	239	1.2	2.1
081	CATHOLIC	1	NA	292	1.4	2.5
081d	*LATIN*	*1*	*NA*	*292*	*1.4*	*2.5*
089	CHR & MISS AL	1	0	52	.3	.5
127	CH GOD (CLEVE)	1	70	88*	.4	.8
145	CH GOD PROPHCY	1	35	44*	.2	.4
157	CH OF BRETHREN	5	694	868*	4.2	7.5
179	CONSRV BAPT	2	NR	NR	-	-
207	E.L.C.A.	10	2,086	2,650	12.8	23.0
285	MENNONITE CH	3	297	392	1.9	3.4
286	E.PA MENNONITE	1	75	94*	.5	.8
323	OLD ORD AMISH	4	NA	600	2.9	5.2
355	PRESB CH (USA)	7	918	1,149*	5.6	10.0
413	S.D.A.	1	72	90*	.4	.8
419	SO BAPT CONV	1	73	91*	.4	.8
443	UN C OF CHRIST	2	136	170*	.8	1.5
449	UN METHODIST	25	3,596	4,500*	21.8	39.0
LACKAWANNA		**223**	**26,764**	**160,953***	**73.5**	**100.0**
019	AMER BAPT USA	11	2,219	2,672*	1.2	1.7
022	EASTERN ORTH	3	1,021	1,021	.5	.6
053	ASSEMB OF GOD	6	750	1,292	.6	.8
081	CATHOLIC	82	NA	125,510	57.3	78.0
081b	*BYZAN RUTH*	*7*	*NA*	*4,004*	*1.8*	*2.5*
081d	*LATIN*	*69*	*NA*	*115,511*	*52.7*	*71.8*
081e	*MARONITE*	*1*	*NA*	*866*	*.4*	*.5*
081f	*MELKITE-GK*	*1*	*NA*	*250*	*.1*	*.2*
081h	*UKRAINIAN*	*4*	*NA*	*4,879*	*2.2*	*3.0*
089	CHR & MISS AL	3	151	259	.1	.2
093	CHR CH (DISC)	2	126	215	.1	.1
111	CH CR,SCIENTST	1	NR	NR	-	-
123	CH GOD (ANDER)	1	40	110	.1	.1
151	L-D SAINTS	1	NA	460	.2	.3
167	CHS OF CHRIST	1	80	104	-	.1
193	EPISCOPAL	6	1,846	2,332	1.1	1.4
203	EVAN FREE CH	1	55	85	-	.1
207	E.L.C.A.	6	1,493	1,921	.9	1.2
221	FREE METHODIST	1	36	37	-	-
246	GREEK ORTHODOX	1	NR	NR	-	-
283	LUTH—MO SYNOD	3	839	993	.5	.6
285	MENNONITE CH	1	27	29	-	-
329	OPEN BIBLE STD	1	NR	NR	-	-
331	ORTH CH IN AM	6	NR	NR	-	-
355	PRESB CH (USA)	15	3,966	4,776*	2.2	3.0
363	PRIMITIVE METH	6	589	863	.4	.5
373	REF CH IN U.S.	1	15	21	-	-
375	REF EPISCOPAL	1	151	180	.1	.1
403	SALVATION ARMY	1	145	174	.1	.1
413	S.D.A.	1	81	98*	-	.1
419	SO BAPT CONV	1	92	111*	.1	.1
443	UN C OF CHRIST	9	1,686	2,030*	.9	1.3
449	UN METHODIST	40	11,052	13,310*	6.1	8.3
496	JEWISH EST[1]	11	NA	1,984	.9	1.2
497	BLACK BAPT EST[2]	NA	304	366*	.2	.2
LANCASTER		**589**	**120,692**	**213,327***	**50.5**	**100.0**
019	AMER BAPT USA	2	557	707*	.2	.3
053	ASSEMB OF GOD	10	1,729	2,971	.7	1.4
061	BEACHY AMISH	8	737	935*	.2	.4
075	BRETHREN IN CR	17	3,193	3,412	.8	1.6
081	CATHOLIC	20	NA	38,952	9.2	18.3
081b	*BYZAN RUTH*	*1*	*NA*	*150*	*-*	*.1*
081d	*LATIN*	*19*	*NA*	*38,802*	*9.2*	*18.2*
089	CHR & MISS AL	6	732	1,496	.4	.7
097	CHR CHS&CHS CR	2	332	421*	.1	.2
111	CH CR,SCIENTST	1	NR	NR	-	-
127	CH GOD (CLEVE)	3	434	551*	.1	.3
145	CH GOD PROPHCY	1	35	44*	-	-
151	L-D SAINTS	2	NA	871	.2	.4
157	CH OF BRETHREN	22	7,603	9,644*	2.3	4.5
165	CH OF NAZARENE	3	814	1,700	.4	.8
167	CHS OF CHRIST	2	95	107	-	.1
171	CH GOD-GEN CON	17	2,824	3,582*	.8	1.7
179	CONSRV BAPT	2	NR	NR	-	-
193	EPISCOPAL	10	3,192	4,725	1.1	2.2
199	EVAN CONGR CH	26	5,108	6,820	1.6	3.2
203	EVAN FREE CH	2	170	360	.1	.2
207	E.L.C.A.	44	21,207	27,686	6.5	13.0

County and Denomination		Number of churches	Communicant, confirmed, full members	Total adherents		
				Number	Percent of total population	Percent of total adherents
226	FRIENDS-USA	4	290	368*	.1	.2
226c	*FGC*	*4*	*290*	*368**	*.1*	*.2*
246	GREEK ORTHODOX	1	NR	NR	-	-
259	IFCA	11	NR	NR	-	-
263	INT FOURSQ GOS	1	45	57*	-	-
283	LUTH—MO SYNOD	2	486	639	.2	.3
284	LUTH CH-AM ASC	1	29	42	-	-
285	MENNONITE CH	108	14,964	20,225	4.8	9.5
286	E.PA MENNONITE	9	932	1,182*	.3	.6
287	MENN GEN CONF	5	688	874	.2	.4
293	MORAV CH-NORTH	2	1,453	1,781	.4	.8
323	OLD ORD AMISH	90	NA	13,500	3.2	6.3
324	OLD ORD RVR BR	2	99	176	-	.1
339	PENT CH OF GOD	1	17	21	-	-
353	CHR BRETHREN	1	50	75	-	-
355	PRESB CH (USA)	17	7,632	9,681*	2.3	4.5
356	PRESB CH AMER	4	1,157	1,536	.4	.7
403	SALVATION ARMY	1	114	120	-	.1
413	S.D.A.	3	309	392*	.1	.2
419	SO BAPT CONV	8	1,857	2,356*	.6	1.1
435	UNITARIAN-UNIV	1	464	674	.2	.3
438	UN BRETH IN CR	1	19	43	-	-
441	UN CHRISTIAN	2	70	169	-	.1
443	UN C OF CHRIST	35	13,490	17,112*	4.0	8.0
449	UN METHODIST	78	25,821	32,754*	7.7	15.4
496	JEWISH EST[1]	3	NA	2,100	.5	1.0
497	BLACK BAPT EST[2]	NA	1,944	2,466*	.6	1.2
LAWRENCE		**159**	**23,475**	**67,877***	**70.5**	**100.0**
005	AME ZION	2	535	474	.5	.7
011	A.W.M.C.	2	41	50*	.1	.1
019	AMER BAPT USA	3	416	509*	.5	.7
022	EASTERN ORTH	2	100	100	.1	.1
053	ASSEMB OF GOD	6	699	1,221	1.3	1.8
057	BAPT GEN CONF	1	858	1,050*	1.1	1.5
081	CATHOLIC	16	NA	35,518	36.9	52.3
081d	*LATIN*	*15*	*NA*	*34,652*	*36.0*	*51.1*
081e	*MARONITE*	*1*	*NA*	*866*	*.9*	*1.3*
089	CHR & MISS AL	9	485	1,098	1.1	1.6
093	CHR CH (DISC)	1	316	429	.4	.6
097	CHR CHS&CHS CR	6	845	1,034*	1.1	1.5
123	CH GOD (ANDER)	2	60	335	.3	.5
127	CH GOD (CLEVE)	1	150	183*	.2	.3
145	CH GOD PROPHCY	1	35	43*	-	.1
151	L-D SAINTS	1	NA	141	.1	.2
165	CH OF NAZARENE	2	161	233	.2	.3
167	CHS OF CHRIST	2	40	64	.1	.1
193	EPISCOPAL	1	551	701	.7	1.0
207	E.L.C.A.	4	1,325	1,679	1.7	2.5
215	EVAN METH CH	1	205	251*	.3	.4
221	FREE METHODIST	4	163	209	.2	.3
246	GREEK ORTHODOX	1	NR	NR	-	-
283	LUTH—MO SYNOD	1	165	195	.2	.3
285	MENNONITE CH	1	32	52	.1	.1
323	OLD ORD AMISH	13	NA	1,950	2.0	2.9
331	ORTH CH IN AM	2	NR	NR	-	-
349	PENT HOLINESS	2	38	46*	-	.1
355	PRESB CH (USA)	38	10,853	13,276*	13.8	19.6
356	PRESB CH AMER	2	192	270	.3	.4
363	PRIMITIVE METH	1	41	48	-	.1
397	ROMANIAN ORTH	2	NR	NR	-	-
403	SALVATION ARMY	1	80	80	.1	.1
413	S.D.A.	1	20	24*	-	-
438	UN BRETH IN CR	4	303	303	.3	.4
449	UN METHODIST	19	4,212	5,152*	5.4	7.6
467	WESLEYAN	1	97	400	.4	.6
496	JEWISH EST[1]	3	NA	200	.2	.3
497	BLACK BAPT EST[2]	NA	457	559*	.6	.8
LEBANON		**156**	**35,433**	**60,528***	**53.2**	**100.0**
053	ASSEMB OF GOD	4	437	649	.6	1.1
075	BRETHREN IN CR	2	542	542	.5	.9
081	CATHOLIC	10	NA	12,904	11.3	21.3
081d	*LATIN*	*10*	*NA*	*12,904*	*11.3*	*21.3*
089	CHR & MISS AL	1	44	82	.1	.1
127	CH GOD (CLEVE)	1	236	291*	.3	.5
151	L-D SAINTS	1	NA	287	.3	.5
157	CH OF BRETHREN	9	2,485	3,069*	2.7	5.1
165	CH OF NAZARENE	1	33	88	.1	.1
167	CHS OF CHRIST	1	55	60	.1	.1
193	EPISCOPAL	1	550	514	.5	.8
199	EVAN CONGR CH	9	1,639	2,330	2.0	3.8
203	EVAN FREE CH	1	29	75	.1	.1
207	E.L.C.A.	21	8,025	10,959	9.6	18.1
259	IFCA	5	NR	NR	-	-
263	INT FOURSQ GOS	1	55	68*	.1	.1
285	MENNONITE CH	10	810	975	.9	1.6

NA–Not applicable NR–Not reported *Total adherents estimated from known number of communicant, confirmed, full members. - Represents a percent less than 0.1. Percentages may not total due to rounding.
[1] See Appendix E [2] See Appendix F [3] See Appendix G Lines in *italic* represent a breakdown of Catholic rites or Friends affiliations. They are included in their respective denominational total.

Table 4. Churches and Church Membership by County and Denomination: 1990

County and Denomination	Number of churches	Communicant, confirmed, full members	Total adherents		
			Number	Percent of total population	Percent of total adherents
286 E.PA MENNONITE	5	451	557*	.5	.9
293 MORAV CH-NORTH	1	303	422	.4	.7
323 OLD ORD AMISH	3	NA	450	.4	.7
355 PRESB CH (USA)	2	807	997*	.9	1.6
403 SALVATION ARMY	1	56	60	.1	.1
413 S.D.A.	1	78	96*	.1	.2
419 SO BAPT CONV	1	104	128*	.1	.2
441 UN CHRISTIAN	7	251	494	.4	.8
443 UN C OF CHRIST	23	8,346	10,307*	9.1	17.0
449 UN METHODIST	33	9,960	12,300*	10.8	20.3
496 JEWISH EST[1]	1	NA	1,655	1.5	2.7
497 BLACK BAPT EST[2]	NA	137	169*	.1	.3
LEHIGH	**245**	**77,349**	**177,026***	**60.8**	**100.0**
005 AME ZION	1	272	290	.1	.2
019 AMER BAPT USA	2	488	595*	.2	.3
022 EASTERN ORTH	1	120	120	-	.1
053 ASSEMB OF GOD	9	1,182	1,964	.7	1.1
081 CATHOLIC	29	NA	71,428	24.5	40.3
081b *BYZAN RUTH*	2	NA	820	.3	.5
081d *LATIN*	26	NA	69,662	23.9	39.4
081h *UKRAINIAN*	1	NA	946	.3	.5
089 CHR & MISS AL	3	186	402	.1	.2
097 CHR CHS&CHS CR	1	121	147*	.1	.1
111 CH CR,SCIENTST	1	NR	NR	-	-
123 CH GOD (ANDER)	1	53	53	-	-
145 CH GOD PROPHCY	1	35	43*	-	-
151 L-D SAINTS	2	NA	817	.3	.5
157 CH OF BRETHREN	1	106	129*	-	.1
165 CH OF NAZARENE	2	424	662	.2	.4
167 CHS OF CHRIST	2	215	280	.1	.2
179 CONSRV BAPT	2	NR	NR	-	-
193 EPISCOPAL	7	1,901	2,992	1.0	1.7
199 EVAN CONGR CH	12	2,662	3,121	1.1	1.8
203 EVAN FREE CH	2	555	835	.3	.5
207 E.L.C.A.	55	30,388	41,145	14.1	23.2
221 FREE METHODIST	2	50	80	-	-
246 GREEK ORTHODOX	1	NR	NR	-	-
259 IFCA	2	NR	NR	-	-
283 LUTH—MO SYNOD	1	67	80	-	-
285 MENNONITE CH	5	59	114	-	.1
287 MENN GEN CONF	3	306	413	.1	.2
291 MISSIONARY CH	2	13	37	-	-
293 MORAV CH-NORTH	6	1,901	2,351	.8	1.3
331 ORTH CH IN AM	1	NR	NR	-	-
353 CHR BRETHREN	1	60	90	-	.1
355 PRESB CH (USA)	6	4,082	4,975*	1.7	2.8
356 PRESB CH AMER	1	59	68	-	-
363 PRIMITIVE METH	1	57	75	-	-
403 SALVATION ARMY	1	98	116	-	.1
413 S.D.A.	3	365	445*	.2	.3
419 SO BAPT CONV	1	198	241*	.1	.1
431 UKRANIAN AMER	1	NR	NR	-	-
443 UN C OF CHRIST	55	25,805	31,450*	10.8	17.8
449 UN METHODIST	9	3,713	4,525*	1.6	2.6
467 WESLEYAN	4	496	825	.3	.5
496 JEWISH EST[1]	4	NA	4,119	1.4	2.3
497 BLACK BAPT EST[2]	NA	1,312	1,599*	.5	.9
499 INDEP.NON-CHAR[3]	1	NA	400	.1	.2
LUZERNE	**406**	**47,704**	**241,660***	**73.6**	**100.0**
019 AMER BAPT USA	13	1,708	2,046*	.6	.8
022 EASTERN ORTH	1	187	187	.1	.1
053 ASSEMB OF GOD	11	883	1,494	.5	.6
075 BRETHREN IN CR	2	107	152	-	.1
081 CATHOLIC	139	NA	177,968	54.2	73.6
081b *BYZAN RUTH*	9	NA	8,371	2.6	3.5
081d *LATIN*	120	NA	162,951	49.7	67.4
081e *MARONITE*	2	NA	1,448	.4	.6
081h *UKRAINIAN*	8	NA	5,198	1.6	2.2
089 CHR & MISS AL	4	126	248	.1	.1
093 CHR CH (DISC)	2	305	536	.2	.2
097 CHR CHS&CHS CR	6	1,015	1,216*	.4	.5
111 CH CR,SCIENTST	1	NR	NR	-	-
151 L-D SAINTS	2	NA	451	.1	.2
167 CHS OF CHRIST	4	180	230	.1	.1
171 CH GOD-GEN CON	1	199	238*	.1	.1
175 CONGR CHR CHS	4	571	684*	.2	.3
176 CCC, NOT NAT'L	2	490	587*	.2	.2
181 CONSRV CONGR	1	146	175*	.1	.1
193 EPISCOPAL	10	1,991	2,714	.8	1.1
199 EVAN CONGR CH	1	81	310	.1	.1
203 EVAN FREE CH	1	100	210	.1	.1
207 E.L.C.A.	26	8,764	11,796	3.6	4.9
221 FREE METHODIST	5	137	247	.1	.1
226 FRIENDS-USA	1	34	41*	-	-
226c *FGC*	1	34	41*	-	-

County and Denomination	Number of churches	Communicant, confirmed, full members	Total adherents		
			Number	Percent of total population	Percent of total adherents
246 GREEK ORTHODOX	1	NR	NR	-	-
259 IFCA	1	NR	NR	-	-
263 INT FOURSQ GOS	1	107	128*	-	.1
283 LUTH—MO SYNOD	4	1,026	1,258	.4	.5
285 MENNONITE CH	2	65	95	-	-
331 ORTH CH IN AM	6	NR	NR	-	-
355 PRESB CH (USA)	27	4,812	5,764*	1.8	2.4
363 PRIMITIVE METH	11	1,225	1,802	.5	.7
375 REF EPISCOPAL	1	17	30	-	-
403 SALVATION ARMY	3	285	324	.1	.1
413 S.D.A.	4	227	272*	.1	.1
419 SO BAPT CONV	3	571	684*	.2	.3
431 UKRANIAN AMER	1	NR	NR	-	-
443 UN C OF CHRIST	23	3,937	4,716*	1.4	2.0
449 UN METHODIST	71	17,610	21,094*	6.4	8.7
467 WESLEYAN	1	32	73	-	-
496 JEWISH EST[1]	9	NA	2,972	.9	1.2
497 BLACK BAPT EST[2]	NA	766	918*	.3	.4
LYCOMING	**189**	**33,288**	**59,320***	**50.0**	**100.0**
005 AME ZION	1	387	416	.4	.7
019 AMER BAPT USA	12	2,172	2,700*	2.3	4.6
053 ASSEMB OF GOD	5	501	1,491	1.3	2.5
075 BRETHREN IN CR	1	27	58	-	.1
081 CATHOLIC	12	NA	14,639	12.3	24.7
081d *LATIN*	12	NA	14,639	12.3	24.7
089 CHR & MISS AL	5	301	531	.4	.9
093 CHR CH (DISC)	1	171	226	.2	.4
097 CHR CHS&CHS CR	5	865	1,075*	.9	1.8
111 CH CR,SCIENTST	1	NR	NR	-	-
123 CH GOD (ANDER)	1	85	85	.1	.1
151 L-D SAINTS	1	NA	342	.3	.6
165 CH OF NAZARENE	3	167	421	.4	.7
167 CHS OF CHRIST	1	85	135	.1	.2
179 CONSRV BAPT	1	NR	NR	-	-
193 EPISCOPAL	8	1,141	1,599	1.3	2.7
207 E.L.C.A.	23	8,264	10,742	9.0	18.1
221 FREE METHODIST	1	46	74	.1	.1
226 FRIENDS-USA	3	145	196*	.2	.3
226b *EFI*	2	130	177	.1	.3
226c *FGC*	1	15	19*	-	-
285 MENNONITE CH	2	94	201	.2	.3
323 OLD ORD AMISH	2	NA	300	.3	.5
331 ORTH CH IN AM	1	NR	NR	-	-
355 PRESB CH (USA)	11	2,191	2,723*	2.3	4.6
403 SALVATION ARMY	1	177	193	.2	.3
413 S.D.A.	2	180	224*	.2	.4
419 SO BAPT CONV	1	315	392*	.3	.7
443 UN C OF CHRIST	1	384	477*	.4	.8
449 UN METHODIST	78	14,838	18,443*	15.5	31.1
467 WESLEYAN	3	207	545	.5	.9
496 JEWISH EST[1]	2	NA	415	.3	.7
497 BLACK BAPT EST[2]	NA	545	677*	.6	1.1
MC KEAN	**86**	**10,644**	**22,156***	**47.0**	**100.0**
019 AMER BAPT USA	3	716	884*	1.9	4.0
053 ASSEMB OF GOD	2	111	156	.3	.7
081 CATHOLIC	11	NA	8,283	17.6	37.4
081d *LATIN*	11	NA	8,283	17.6	37.4
089 CHR & MISS AL	4	115	250	.5	1.1
111 CH CR,SCIENTST	1	NR	NR	-	-
123 CH GOD (ANDER)	2	113	142	.3	.6
151 L-D SAINTS	1	NA	46	.1	.2
165 CH OF NAZARENE	3	192	303	.6	1.4
167 CHS OF CHRIST	1	50	65	.1	.3
193 EPISCOPAL	6	447	618	1.3	2.8
207 E.L.C.A.	7	1,701	2,250	4.8	10.2
221 FREE METHODIST	7	272	312	.7	1.4
263 INT FOURSQ GOS	1	201	248*	.5	1.1
283 LUTH—MO SYNOD	1	314	469	1.0	2.1
285 MENNONITE CH	1	28	70	.1	.3
355 PRESB CH (USA)	4	1,131	1,397*	3.0	6.3
356 PRESB CH AMER	1	18	19	-	.1
403 SALVATION ARMY	1	92	98	.2	.4
413 S.D.A.	3	136	168*	.4	.8
419 SO BAPT CONV	1	497	614*	1.3	2.8
449 UN METHODIST	21	4,358	5,382*	11.4	24.3
467 WESLEYAN	2	70	171	.4	.8
496 JEWISH EST[1]	2	NA	110	.2	.5
497 BLACK BAPT EST[2]	NA	82	101*	.2	.5
MERCER	**181**	**32,486**	**74,474***	**61.5**	**100.0**
011 A.W.M.C.	7	124	151*	.1	.2
019 AMER BAPT USA	8	1,591	1,939*	1.6	2.6
022 EASTERN ORTH	1	484	484	.4	.6
039 AP CHR CH(NAZ)	1	25	30*	-	-

NA–Not applicable   NR–Not reported   *Total adherents estimated from known number of communicant, confirmed, full members.   - Represents a percent less than 0.1.   Percentages may not total due to rounding.
[1]See Appendix E   [2]See Appendix F   [3]See Appendix G   Lines in *italic* represent a breakdown of Catholic rites or Friends affiliations. They are included in their respective denominational total.

PENNSYLVANIA

Table 4. Churches and Church Membership by County and Denomination: 1990

County and Denomination	Number of churches	Communicant, confirmed, full members	Total adherents Number	Percent of total population	Percent of total adherents
053 ASSEMB OF GOD	3	91	125	.1	.2
057 BAPT GEN CONF	1	47	57*	-	.1
061 BEACHY AMISH	1	44	54*	-	.1
081 CATHOLIC	19	NA	32,288	26.7	43.4
081b BYZAN RUTH	1	NA	2,320	1.9	3.1
081d LATIN	17	NA	29,646	24.5	39.8
081g ROMANIAN	1	NA	322	.3	.4
089 CHR & MISS AL	6	339	763	.6	1.0
093 CHR CH (DISC)	2	336	702	.6	.9
097 CHR CHS&CHS CR	3	301	367*	.3	.5
111 CH CR,SCIENTST	2	NR	NR	-	-
123 CH GOD (ANDER)	6	379	493	.4	.7
145 CH GOD PROPHCY	3	106	129*	.1	.2
151 L-D SAINTS	2	NA	274	.2	.4
165 CH OF NAZARENE	6	455	922	.8	1.2
167 CHS OF CHRIST	2	160	217	.2	.3
171 CH GOD-GEN CON	1	45	55*	-	.1
193 EPISCOPAL	4	639	1,175	1.0	1.6
199 EVAN CONGR CH	2	252	328	.3	.4
207 E.L.C.A.	6	2,421	3,058	2.5	4.1
221 FREE METHODIST	4	92	159	.1	.2
246 GREEK ORTHODOX	1	NR	NR	-	-
283 LUTH—MO SYNOD	1	319	364	.3	.5
285 MENNONITE CH	1	84	129	.1	.2
323 OLD ORD AMISH	3	NA	350	.3	.5
349 PENT HOLINESS	5	425	518*	.4	.7
355 PRESB CH (USA)	32	9,882	12,046*	10.0	16.2
397 ROMANIAN ORTH	1	NR	NR	-	-
403 SALVATION ARMY	2	259	282	.2	.4
413 S.D.A.	1	43	52*	-	.1
419 SO BAPT CONV	2	213	260*	.2	.3
431 UKRANIAN AMER	1	NR	NR	-	-
438 UN BRETH IN CR	1	41	41	-	.1
443 UN C OF CHRIST	6	2,190	2,670*	2.2	3.6
449 UN METHODIST	31	9,846	12,003*	9.9	16.1
467 WESLEYAN	2	114	341	.3	.5
496 JEWISH EST[1]	1	NA	260	.2	.3
497 BLACK BAPT EST[2]	NA	1,139	1,388*	1.1	1.9
MIFFLIN	**113**	**16,631**	**25,887***	**56.0**	**100.0**
019 AMER BAPT USA	2	447	554*	1.2	2.1
053 ASSEMB OF GOD	1	141	200	.4	.8
061 BEACHY AMISH	3	306	379*	.8	1.5
075 BRETHREN IN CR	4	135	173	.4	.7
081 CATHOLIC	3	NA	2,107	4.6	8.1
081d LATIN	3	NA	2,107	4.6	8.1
089 CHR & MISS AL	6	516	1,052	2.3	4.1
127 CH GOD (CLEVE)	1	169	210*	.5	.8
143 CG IN CR(MENN)	1	121	150*	.3	.6
157 CH OF BRETHREN	6	1,066	1,322*	2.9	5.1
165 CH OF NAZARENE	1	38	87	.2	.3
167 CHS OF CHRIST	1	35	46	.1	.2
175 CONGR CHR CHS	1	60	74*	.2	.3
179 CONSRV BAPT	1	NR	NR	-	-
193 EPISCOPAL	1	259	330	.7	1.3
203 EVAN FREE CH	1	0	0	-	-
207 E.L.C.A.	10	3,116	4,055	8.8	15.7
285 MENNONITE CH	9	1,509	1,951	4.2	7.5
323 OLD ORD AMISH	16	NA	2,400	5.2	9.3
353 CHR BRETHREN	1	35	40	.1	.2
355 PRESB CH (USA)	9	1,520	1,885*	4.1	7.3
403 SALVATION ARMY	1	153	180	.4	.7
413 S.D.A.	1	36	45*	.1	.2
419 SO BAPT CONV	1	177	220*	.5	.8
443 UN C OF CHRIST	3	761	944*	2.0	3.6
449 UN METHODIST	28	6,015	7,459*	16.1	28.8
467 WESLEYAN	1	16	24	.1	.1
MONROE	**84**	**15,762**	**41,118***	**43.0**	**100.0**
053 ASSEMB OF GOD	4	564	855	.9	2.1
081 CATHOLIC	12	NA	18,917	19.8	46.0
081d LATIN	12	NA	18,917	19.8	46.0
089 CHR & MISS AL	1	13	13	-	-
111 CH CR,SCIENTST	1	NR	NR	-	-
151 L-D SAINTS	1	NA	371	.4	.9
167 CHS OF CHRIST	1	50	70	.1	.2
179 CONSRV BAPT	1	NR	NR	-	-
193 EPISCOPAL	2	408	631	.7	1.5
199 EVAN CONGR CH	1	194	194	.2	.5
207 E.L.C.A.	13	5,012	7,115	7.4	17.3
246 GREEK ORTHODOX	1	NR	NR	-	-
259 IFCA	1	NR	NR	-	-
283 LUTH—MO SYNOD	1	159	204	.2	.5
285 MENNONITE CH	2	75	126	.1	.3
293 MORAV CH-NORTH	1	60	75	.1	.2
331 ORTH CH IN AM	1	NR	NR	-	-
355 PRESB CH (USA)	5	1,349	1,685*	1.8	4.1

County and Denomination	Number of churches	Communicant, confirmed, full members	Total adherents Number	Percent of total population	Percent of total adherents
403 SALVATION ARMY	1	167	206	.2	.5
413 S.D.A.	1	145	181*	.2	.4
443 UN C OF CHRIST	6	1,454	1,816*	1.9	4.4
449 UN METHODIST	23	5,605	7,000*	7.3	17.0
467 WESLEYAN	2	173	375	.4	.9
496 JEWISH EST[1]	2	NA	867	.9	2.1
497 BLACK BAPT EST[2]	NA	334	417*	.4	1.0
MONTGOMERY	**462**	**130,701**	**450,999***	**66.5**	**100.0**
005 AME ZION	1	46	62	-	-
019 AMER BAPT USA	28	9,059	11,035*	1.6	2.4
053 ASSEMB OF GOD	15	1,128	2,133	.3	.5
057 BAPT GEN CONF	1	62	76*	-	-
075 BRETHREN IN CR	3	434	434	.1	.1
081 CATHOLIC	65	NA	235,352	34.7	52.2
081b BYZAN RUTH	2	NA	837	.1	.2
081d LATIN	59	NA	232,350	34.3	51.5
081h UKRAINIAN	4	NA	2,165	.3	.5
089 CHR & MISS AL	3	78	163	-	-
111 CH CR,SCIENTST	7	NR	NR	-	-
123 CH GOD (ANDER)	3	85	135	-	-
127 CH GOD (CLEVE)	1	128	156*	-	-
151 L-D SAINTS	1	NA	282	-	.1
157 CH OF BRETHREN	10	1,489	1,814*	.3	.4
165 CH OF NAZARENE	5	1,209	1,967	.3	.4
167 CHS OF CHRIST	3	309	427	.1	.1
179 CONSRV BAPT	2	NR	NR	-	-
193 EPISCOPAL	35	12,793	18,331	2.7	4.1
199 EVAN CONGR CH	8	852	943	.1	.2
207 E.L.C.A.	50	35,352	47,805	7.0	10.6
221 FREE METHODIST	1	30	30	-	-
226 FRIENDS-USA	10	1,766	2,150*	.3	.5
226a CONSERV	1	4	4	-	-
226c FGC	9	1,762	2,146*	.3	.5
246 GREEK ORTHODOX	2	NR	NR	-	-
259 IFCA	6	NR	NR	-	-
283 LUTH—MO SYNOD	3	221	301	-	.1
284 LUTH CH-AM ASC	1	25	37	-	-
285 MENNONITE CH	20	3,165	4,603	.7	1.0
286 E.PA MENNONITE	2	117	143*	-	-
287 MENN GEN CONF	6	1,491	1,826	.3	.4
291 MISSIONARY CH	1	10	11	-	-
331 ORTH CH IN AM	1	NR	NR	-	-
353 CHR BRETHREN	4	393	500	.1	.1
355 PRESB CH (USA)	30	17,088	20,815*	3.1	4.6
356 PRESB CH AMER	13	1,538	2,195	.3	.5
371 REF CH IN AM	1	330	562	.1	.1
375 REF EPISCOPAL	2	255	277	-	.1
403 SALVATION ARMY	2	136	147	-	-
405 SCHWENKFELDER	4	2,488	3,031*	.4	.7
413 S.D.A.	8	1,068	1,301*	.2	.3
419 SO BAPT CONV	3	573	698*	.1	.2
435 UNITARIAN-UNIV	2	73	93	-	-
443 UN C OF CHRIST	37	15,444	18,812*	2.8	4.2
449 UN METHODIST	35	13,706	16,695*	2.5	3.7
467 WESLEYAN	1	89	130	-	-
469 WELS	1	95	136	-	-
496 JEWISH EST[1]	25	NA	46,163	6.8	10.2
497 BLACK BAPT EST[2]	NA	7,576	9,228*	1.4	2.0
MONTOUR	**36**	**5,732**	**10,662***	**60.1**	**100.0**
019 AMER BAPT USA	1	101	125*	.7	1.2
081 CATHOLIC	1	NA	2,948	16.6	27.6
081d LATIN	1	NA	2,948	16.6	27.6
089 CHR & MISS AL	1	68	78	.4	.7
157 CH OF BRETHREN	2	369	456*	2.6	4.3
165 CH OF NAZARENE	1	62	133	.7	1.2
179 CONSRV BAPT	1	NR	NR	-	-
193 EPISCOPAL	2	209	271	1.5	2.5
207 E.L.C.A.	8	1,711	2,139	12.1	20.1
285 MENNONITE CH	3	207	351	2.0	3.3
286 E.PA MENNONITE	1	92	114*	.6	1.1
323 OLD ORD AMISH	3	NA	450	2.5	4.2
355 PRESB CH (USA)	3	580	716*	4.0	6.7
413 S.D.A.	1	76	94*	.5	.9
443 UN C OF CHRIST	4	1,310	1,618*	9.1	15.2
449 UN METHODIST	4	947	1,169*	6.6	11.0
NORTHAMPTON	**216**	**64,578**	**154,050***	**62.3**	**100.0**
005 AME ZION	1	250	266	.1	.2
019 AMER BAPT USA	3	891	1,092*	.4	.7
053 ASSEMB OF GOD	6	591	1,095	.4	.7
081 CATHOLIC	35	NA	66,445	26.9	43.1
081b BYZAN RUTH	1	NA	901	.4	.6
081d LATIN	31	NA	63,203	25.6	41.0
081e MARONITE	1	NA	226	.1	.1

NA–Not applicable   NR–Not reported   *Total adherents estimated from known number of communicant, confirmed, full members.   - Represents a percent less than 0.1.   Percentages may not total due to rounding.

[1]See Appendix E   [2]See Appendix F   [3]See Appendix G   Lines in *italic* represent a breakdown of Catholic rites or Friends affiliations. They are included in their respective denominational total.

Table 4. Churches and Church Membership by County and Denomination: 1990

County and Denomination	Number of churches	Communicant, confirmed, full members	Total adherents Number	Percent of total population	Percent of total adherents
081h *UKRAINIAN*	*2*	*NA*	*2,115*	*.9*	*1.4*
111 CH CR,SCIENTST	3	NR	NR	-	-
127 CH GOD (CLEVE)	1	36	44*	-	-
151 L-D SAINTS	2	NA	385	.2	.2
163 CH OF LUTH BR	1	78	255	.1	.2
165 CH OF NAZARENE	3	362	561	.2	.4
167 CHS OF CHRIST	2	71	92	-	.1
193 EPISCOPAL	5	2,161	2,805	1.1	1.8
199 EVAN CONGR CH	6	1,293	1,371	.6	.9
203 EVAN FREE CH	1	0	0	-	-
207 E.L.C.A.	47	24,311	32,575	13.2	21.1
226 FRIENDS-USA	1	116	142*	.1	.1
226c *FGC*	*1*	*116*	*142**	*.1*	*.1*
246 GREEK ORTHODOX	1	NR	NR	-	-
263 INT FOURSQ GOS	1	0	0*	-	-
283 LUTH—MO SYNOD	2	534	668	.3	.4
285 MENNONITE CH	6	466	753	.3	.5
293 MORAV CH-NORTH	10	4,630	5,893	2.4	3.8
331 ORTH CH IN AM	1	NR	NR	-	-
355 PRESB CH (USA)	8	4,921	6,029*	2.4	3.9
403 SALVATION ARMY	3	215	232	.1	.2
413 S.D.A.	3	215	263*	.1	.2
435 UNITARIAN-UNIV	1	272	378	.2	.2
443 UN C OF CHRIST	33	15,444	18,920*	7.7	12.3
449 UN METHODIST	23	6,106	7,480*	3.0	4.9
467 WESLEYAN	2	595	1,260	.5	.8
496 JEWISH EST[1]	4	NA	3,496	1.4	2.3
497 BLACK BAPT EST[2]	NA	1,020	1,250*	.5	.8
499 INDEP.NON-CHAR[3]	1	NA	300	.1	.2
NORTHUMBERLAND	**171**	**28,203**	**61,474***	**63.5**	**100.0**
019 AMER BAPT USA	3	624	759*	.8	1.2
053 ASSEMB OF GOD	4	209	539	.6	.9
081 CATHOLIC	26	NA	24,098	24.9	39.2
081d *LATIN*	*23*	*NA*	*22,021*	*22.8*	*35.8*
081h *UKRAINIAN*	*3*	*NA*	*2,077*	*2.1*	*3.4*
089 CHR & MISS AL	3	373	653	.7	1.1
165 CH OF NAZARENE	2	261	644	.7	1.0
171 CH GOD-GEN CON	1	70	85*	.1	.1
179 CONSRV BAPT	1	NR	NR	-	-
193 EPISCOPAL	5	455	716	.7	1.2
199 EVAN CONGR CH	5	746	948	1.0	1.5
203 EVAN FREE CH	2	115	198	.2	.3
207 E.L.C.A.	32	9,580	12,810	13.2	20.8
259 IFCA	1	NR	NR	-	-
283 LUTH—MO SYNOD	1	116	155	.2	.3
285 MENNONITE CH	1	101	186	.2	.3
323 OLD ORD AMISH	1	NA	150	.2	.2
331 ORTH CH IN AM	1	NR	NR	-	-
353 CHR BRETHREN	1	70	105	.1	.2
355 PRESB CH (USA)	9	1,589	1,934*	2.0	3.1
403 SALVATION ARMY	2	201	209	.2	.3
413 S.D.A.	1	37	45*	-	.1
443 UN C OF CHRIST	26	4,933	6,004*	6.2	9.8
449 UN METHODIST	35	8,266	10,060*	10.4	16.4
467 WESLEYAN	6	457	1,016	1.0	1.7
496 JEWISH EST[1]	2	NA	160	.2	.3
PERRY	**99**	**12,069**	**18,081***	**43.9**	**100.0**
005 AME ZION	3	629	789	1.9	4.4
053 ASSEMB OF GOD	4	562	1,059	2.6	5.9
075 BRETHREN IN CR	3	125	218	.5	1.2
081 CATHOLIC	3	NA	1,409	3.4	7.8
081d *LATIN*	*3*	*NA*	*1,409*	*3.4*	*7.8*
089 CHR & MISS AL	1	90	150	.4	.8
127 CH GOD (CLEVE)	1	37	47*	.1	.3
151 L-D SAINTS	1	NA	237	.6	1.3
157 CH OF BRETHREN	3	304	385*	.9	2.1
167 CHS OF CHRIST	1	8	14	-	.1
171 CH GOD-GEN CON	11	631	798*	1.9	4.4
179 CONSRV BAPT	1	NR	NR	-	-
193 EPISCOPAL	1	90	118	.3	.7
207 E.L.C.A.	15	3,120	4,018	9.8	22.2
259 IFCA	1	NR	NR	-	-
323 OLD ORD AMISH	1	NA	150	.4	.8
339 PENT CH OF GOD	1	34	78	.2	.4
355 PRESB CH (USA)	5	653	826*	2.0	4.6
413 S.D.A.	1	71	90*	.2	.5
443 UN C OF CHRIST	11	1,252	1,584*	3.8	8.8
449 UN METHODIST	30	4,425	5,600*	13.6	31.0
467 WESLEYAN	1	38	56	.1	.3
496 JEWISH EST[1]	0	NA	455	1.1	2.5
PHILADELPHIA	**812**	**209,065**	**932,721***	**58.8**	**100.0**
005 AME ZION	8	5,598	8,791	.6	.9
007 ALBAN ORTH ARC	2	NR	NR	-	-

County and Denomination	Number of churches	Communicant, confirmed, full members	Total adherents Number	Percent of total population	Percent of total adherents
019 AMER BAPT USA	72	18,199	22,471*	1.4	2.4
049 ARMEN AP CH AM	1	1,500	7,500	.5	.8
053 ASSEMB OF GOD	18	2,906	7,847	.5	.8
081 CATHOLIC	145	NA	537,699	33.9	57.6
081a *ARMENIAN*	*1*	*NA*	*250*	*-*	*-*
081b *BYZAN RUTH*	*2*	*NA*	*869*	*.1*	*.1*
081d *LATIN*	*133*	*NA*	*527,864*	*33.3*	*56.6*
081e *MARONITE*	*1*	*NA*	*816*	*.1*	*.1*
081h *UKRAINIAN*	*8*	*NA*	*7,900*	*.5*	*.8*
089 CHR & MISS AL	9	229	543	-	.1
093 CHR CH (DISC)	5	422	613	-	.1
097 CHR CHS&CHS CR	2	78	96*	-	-
105 CHRISTIAN REF	1	82	108	-	-
111 CH CR,SCIENTST	5	NR	NR	-	-
123 CH GOD (ANDER)	9	3,498	3,627	.2	.4
127 CH GOD (CLEVE)	10	839	1,036*	.1	.1
133 CH GOD(7TH)DEN	1	13	23	-	-
145 CH GOD PROPHCY	9	327	404*	-	-
151 L-D SAINTS	1	NA	674	-	.1
157 CH OF BRETHREN	5	289	357*	-	-
165 CH OF NAZARENE	2	110	112	-	-
167 CHS OF CHRIST	8	722	914	.1	.1
179 CONSRV BAPT	5	NR	NR	-	-
181 CONSRV CONGR	2	217	268*	-	-
193 EPISCOPAL	67	18,293	24,450	1.5	2.6
207 E.L.C.A.	58	15,904	22,564	1.4	2.4
223 FREE WILL BAPT	1	86	106*	-	-
226 FRIENDS-USA	9	1,354	1,672*	.1	.2
226c *FGC*	*9*	*1,354*	*1,672**	*.1*	*.2*
246 GREEK ORTHODOX	1	NR	NR	-	-
259 IFCA	3	NR	NR	-	-
274 LAT EVAN LUTH	1	318	337	-	-
283 LUTH—MO SYNOD	6	791	1,021	.1	.1
285 MENNONITE CH	10	516	840	.1	.1
287 MENN GEN CONF	4	90	90	-	-
293 MORAV CH-NORTH	2	249	359	-	-
313 N AM BAPT CONF	2	217	268*	-	-
331 ORTH CH IN AM	3	NR	NR	-	-
353 CHR BRETHREN	4	688	923	.1	.1
355 PRESB CH (USA)	70	13,087	16,159*	1.0	1.7
356 PRESB CH AMER	9	2,944	3,626	.2	.4
375 REF EPISCOPAL	8	382	450	-	-
397 ROMANIAN ORTH	1	NR	NR	-	-
403 SALVATION ARMY	8	709	840	.1	.1
405 SCHWENKFELDER	1	0	0*	-	-
413 S.D.A.	17	4,544	5,611*	.4	.6
415 S-D BAPTIST GC	1	34	42*	-	-
419 SO BAPT CONV	16	2,557	3,157*	.2	.3
423 SYRIAN ANTIOCH	1	NA	500	-	.1
435 UNITARIAN-UNIV	3	656	811	.1	.1
443 UN C OF CHRIST	23	3,542	4,373*	.3	.5
449 UN METHODIST	80	18,972	23,426*	1.5	2.5
496 JEWISH EST[1]	72	NA	106,303	6.7	11.4
497 BLACK BAPT EST[2]	NA	88,103	108,785*	6.9	11.7
498 INDEP.CHARIS.[3]	6	NA	10,900	.7	1.2
499 INDEP.NON-CHAR[3]	5	NA	2,025	.1	.2
PIKE	**28**	**2,437**	**7,479***	**26.7**	**100.0**
019 AMER BAPT USA	1	156	197*	.7	2.6
053 ASSEMB OF GOD	2	100	133	.5	1.8
081 CATHOLIC	9	NA	3,866	13.8	51.7
081d *LATIN*	*9*	*NA*	*3,866*	*13.8*	*51.7*
089 CHR & MISS AL	1	31	68	.2	.9
193 EPISCOPAL	1	124	209	.7	2.8
203 EVAN FREE CH	1	100	100	.4	1.3
207 E.L.C.A.	4	426	646	2.3	8.6
284 LUTH CH-AM ASC	1	65	72	.3	1.0
355 PRESB CH (USA)	1	116	146*	.5	2.0
371 REF CH IN AM	1	42	132	.5	1.8
449 UN METHODIST	6	1,277	1,610*	5.8	21.5
496 JEWISH EST[1]	0	NA	300	1.1	4.0
POTTER	**49**	**2,882**	**5,551***	**33.2**	**100.0**
019 AMER BAPT USA	4	320	407*	2.4	7.3
053 ASSEMB OF GOD	1	17	30	.2	.5
081 CATHOLIC	6	NA	1,648	9.9	29.7
081d *LATIN*	*6*	*NA*	*1,648*	*9.9*	*29.7*
089 CHR & MISS AL	4	224	426	2.5	7.7
097 CHR CHS&CHS CR	1	15	19*	.1	.3
167 CHS OF CHRIST	1	20	25	.1	.5
193 EPISCOPAL	2	228	282	1.7	5.1
207 E.L.C.A.	3	199	308	1.8	5.5
215 EVAN METH CH	1	8	10*	.1	.2
221 FREE METHODIST	4	76	141	.8	2.5
355 PRESB CH (USA)	2	248	315*	1.9	5.7
413 S.D.A.	1	97	123*	.7	2.2
415 S-D BAPTIST GC	1	64	81*	.5	1.5

NA–Not applicable   NR–Not reported   *Total adherents estimated from known number of communicant, confirmed, full members.   - Represents a percent less than 0.1.   Percentages may not total due to rounding.
[1]See Appendix E   [2]See Appendix F   [3]See Appendix G   Lines in *italic* represent a breakdown of Catholic rites or Friends affiliations. They are included in their respective denominational total.

PENNSYLVANIA

Table 4. Churches and Church Membership by County and Denomination: 1990

County and Denomination	Number of churches	Communicant, confirmed, full members	Total adherents Number	Percent of total population	Percent of total adherents
449　UN METHODIST	18	1,366	1,736*	10.4	31.3
SCHUYLKILL	**321**	**44,356**	**115,135***	**75.5**	**100.0**
019　AMER BAPT USA	6	401	483*	.3	.4
022　EASTERN ORTH	1	334	334	.2	.3
053　ASSEMB OF GOD	2	118	274	.2	.2
061　BEACHY AMISH	1	45	54*	-	-
075　BRETHREN IN CR	2	67	67	-	.1
081　CATHOLIC	85	NA	58,451	38.3	50.8
081b　　BYZAN RUTH	7	NA	2,966	1.9	2.6
081d　　LATIN	70	NA	51,872	34.0	45.1
081h　　UKRAINIAN	8	NA	3,613	2.4	3.1
097　CHR CHS&CHS CR	1	50	60*	-	.1
127　CH GOD (CLEVE)	1	70	84*	.1	.1
157　CH OF BRETHREN	1	272	327*	.2	.3
165　CH OF NAZARENE	3	293	365	.2	.3
167　CHS OF CHRIST	1	7	9	-	-
171　CH GOD-GEN CON	6	342	412*	.3	.4
175　CONGR CHR CHS	1	70	84*	.1	.1
193　EPISCOPAL	4	640	964	.6	.8
199　EVAN CONGR CH	17	2,621	3,461	2.3	3.0
203　EVAN FREE CH	2	92	176	.1	.2
207　E.L.C.A.	48	16,422	22,150	14.5	19.2
259　IFCA	2	NR	NR	-	-
263　INT FOURSQ GOS	4	537	646*	.4	.6
283　LUTH—MO SYNOD	1	86	108	.1	.1
285　MENNONITE CH	2	99	150	.1	.1
286　E.PA MENNONITE	2	74	89*	.1	.1
331　ORTH CH IN AM	5	NR	NR	-	-
355　PRESB CH (USA)	5	762	917*	.6	.8
363　PRIMITIVE METH	8	646	882	.6	.8
403　SALVATION ARMY	2	208	236	.2	.2
413　S.D.A.	2	48	58*	-	.1
419　SO BAPT CONV	2	58	70*	-	.1
443　UN C OF CHRIST	50	12,240	14,728*	9.7	12.8
449　UN METHODIST	50	7,452	8,967*	5.9	7.8
467　WESLEYAN	2	170	120	.1	.1
496　JEWISH EST[1]	2	NA	250	.2	.2
497　BLACK BAPT EST[2]	NA	132	159*	.1	.1
SNYDER	**78**	**13,005**	**17,942***	**48.9**	**100.0**
075　BRETHREN IN CR	1	12	31	.1	.2
081　CATHOLIC	1	NA	1,076	2.9	6.0
081d　　LATIN	1	NA	1,076	2.9	6.0
089　CHR & MISS AL	2	83	160	.4	.9
145　CH GOD PROPHCY	1	35	44*	.1	.2
157　CH OF BRETHREN	1	122	152*	.4	.8
165　CH OF NAZARENE	1	247	448	1.2	2.5
167　CHS OF CHRIST	1	170	220	.6	1.2
179　CONSRV BAPT	2	NR	NR	-	-
193　EPISCOPAL	1	132	110	.3	.6
207　E.L.C.A.	19	4,934	6,242	17.0	34.8
285　MENNONITE CH	5	259	384	1.0	2.1
287　MENN GEN CONF	1	407	407	1.1	2.3
323　OLD ORD AMISH	2	NA	300	.8	1.7
419　SO BAPT CONV	2	186	232*	.6	1.3
443　UN C OF CHRIST	10	2,496	3,115*	8.5	17.4
449　UN METHODIST	26	3,815	4,760*	13.0	26.5
467　WESLEYAN	2	107	261	.7	1.5
SOMERSET	**211**	**29,272**	**51,923***	**66.4**	**100.0**
019　AMER BAPT USA	2	70	87*	.1	.2
022　EASTERN ORTH	3	579	579	.7	1.1
053　ASSEMB OF GOD	6	234	467	.6	.9
061　BEACHY AMISH	1	184	228*	.3	.4
071　BRETHREN (ASH)	2	435	538*	.7	1.0
081　CATHOLIC	24	NA	12,997	16.6	25.0
081b　　BYZAN RUTH	2	NA	1,937	2.5	3.7
081d　　LATIN	22	NA	11,060	14.1	21.3
089　CHR & MISS AL	5	443	796	1.0	1.5
093　CHR CH (DISC)	1	20	30	-	.1
097　CHR CHS&CHS CR	5	1,124	1,391*	1.8	2.7
127　CH GOD (CLEVE)	7	659	816*	1.0	1.6
151　L-D SAINTS	1	NA	114	.1	.2
157　CH OF BRETHREN	23	4,265	5,279*	6.7	10.2
165　CH OF NAZARENE	5	514	864	1.1	1.7
167　CHS OF CHRIST	1	112	145	.2	.3
171　CH GOD-GEN CON	6	426	527*	.7	1.0
193　EPISCOPAL	1	99	193	.2	.4
207　E.L.C.A.	38	9,828	13,230	16.9	25.5
259　IFCA	1	NR	NR	-	-
265　INT PENT C CHR	1	10	24	-	-
283　LUTH—MO SYNOD	2	154	179	.2	.3
285　MENNONITE CH	9	984	1,247	1.6	2.4
323　OLD ORD AMISH	5	NA	750	1.0	1.4
331　ORTH CH IN AM	3	NR	NR	-	-

County and Denomination	Number of churches	Communicant, confirmed, full members	Total adherents Number	Percent of total population	Percent of total adherents
355　PRESB CH (USA)	3	441	546*	.7	1.1
403　SALVATION ARMY	1	2	2	-	-
413　S.D.A.	1	31	38*	-	.1
443　UN C OF CHRIST	18	3,153	3,903*	5.0	7.5
449　UN METHODIST	36	5,505	6,814*	8.7	13.1
496　JEWISH EST[1]	0	NA	139	.2	.3
SULLIVAN	**28**	**1,346**	**3,144***	**51.5**	**100.0**
019　AMER BAPT USA	1	10	12*	.2	.4
053　ASSEMB OF GOD	1	28	36	.6	1.1
081　CATHOLIC	7	NA	1,495	24.5	47.6
081b　　BYZAN RUTH	1	NA	200	3.3	6.4
081d　　LATIN	6	NA	1,295	21.2	41.2
207　E.L.C.A.	1	298	354	5.8	11.3
226　FRIENDS-USA	1	13	17	.3	.5
226c　　FGC	1	13	17	.3	.5
285　MENNONITE CH	2	79	170	2.8	5.4
331　ORTH CH IN AM	1	NR	NR	-	-
443　UN C OF CHRIST	2	118	142*	2.3	4.5
449　UN METHODIST	10	706	849*	13.9	27.0
467　WESLEYAN	2	94	69	1.1	2.2
SUSQUEHANNA	**81**	**6,625**	**16,392***	**40.6**	**100.0**
005　AME ZION	1	159	182	.5	1.1
019　AMER BAPT USA	4	405	514*	1.3	3.1
053　ASSEMB OF GOD	3	139	270	.7	1.6
081　CATHOLIC	18	NA	7,639	18.9	46.6
081d　　LATIN	18	NA	7,639	18.9	46.6
089　CHR & MISS AL	1	19	51	.1	.3
151　L-D SAINTS	1	NA	134	.3	.8
176　CCC, NOT NAT'L	1	58	74*	.2	.5
193　EPISCOPAL	3	345	544	1.3	3.3
221　FREE METHODIST	1	18	42	.1	.3
241　GEN SIX PR BPT	1	20	25*	.1	.2
283　LUTH—MO SYNOD	1	227	262	.6	1.6
285　MENNONITE CH	1	49	76	.2	.5
331　ORTH CH IN AM	2	NR	NR	-	-
355　PRESB CH (USA)	7	438	556*	1.4	3.4
413　S.D.A.	1	35	44*	.1	.3
435　UNITARIAN-UNIV	1	74	94	.2	.6
443　UN C OF CHRIST	1	273	346*	.9	2.1
449　UN METHODIST	33	4,366	5,539*	13.7	33.8
TIOGA	**99**	**8,426**	**14,367***	**34.9**	**100.0**
019　AMER BAPT USA	9	1,463	1,817*	4.4	12.6
053　ASSEMB OF GOD	4	263	399	1.0	2.8
075　BRETHREN IN CR	1	82	160	.4	1.1
081　CATHOLIC	11	NA	2,967	7.2	20.7
081d　　LATIN	11	NA	2,967	7.2	20.7
089　CHR & MISS AL	3	154	387	.9	2.7
093　CHR CH (DISC)	4	270	633	1.5	4.4
151　L-D SAINTS	1	NA	137	.3	1.0
167　CHS OF CHRIST	1	30	45	.1	.3
193　EPISCOPAL	5	390	531	1.3	3.7
207　E.L.C.A.	5	384	487	1.2	3.4
221　FREE METHODIST	2	67	88	.2	.6
283　LUTH—MO SYNOD	1	158	195	.5	1.4
285　MENNONITE CH	4	218	281	.7	2.0
353　CHR BRETHREN	1	30	60	.1	.4
355　PRESB CH (USA)	7	868	1,078*	2.6	7.5
413　S.D.A.	2	151	188*	.5	1.3
449　UN METHODIST	36	3,803	4,722*	11.5	32.9
467　WESLEYAN	2	95	192	.5	1.3
UNION	**64**	**10,430**	**15,449***	**42.7**	**100.0**
019　AMER BAPT USA	3	671	819*	2.3	5.3
053　ASSEMB OF GOD	3	250	465	1.3	3.0
061　BEACHY AMISH	1	107	131*	.4	.8
081　CATHOLIC	1	NA	1,160	3.2	7.5
081d　　LATIN	1	NA	1,160	3.2	7.5
089　CHR & MISS AL	1	105	198	.5	1.3
097　CHR CHS&CHS CR	2	212	259*	.7	1.7
143　CG IN CR(MENN)	1	64	78*	.2	.5
151　L-D SAINTS	1	NA	514	1.4	3.3
157　CH OF BRETHREN	1	175	214*	.6	1.4
165　CH OF NAZARENE	1	385	662	1.8	4.3
193　EPISCOPAL	1	115	207	.6	1.3
207　E.L.C.A.	10	3,079	3,922	10.8	25.4
226　FRIENDS-USA	1	28	34*	.1	.2
226c　　FGC	1	28	34*	.1	.2
263　INT FOURSQ GOS	1	129	157*	.4	1.0
285　MENNONITE CH	2	222	356	1.0	2.3
286　E.PA MENNONITE	1	115	140*	.4	.9
323　OLD ORD AMISH	2	NA	300	.8	1.9
355　PRESB CH (USA)	3	575	702*	1.9	4.5
403　SALVATION ARMY	1	76	91	.3	.6

NA–Not applicable　　NR–Not reported　　*Total adherents estimated from known number of communicant, confirmed, full members.　　- Represents a percent less than 0.1.　　Percentages may not total due to rounding.
[1]See Appendix E　　[2]See Appendix F　　[3]See Appendix G　　Lines in *italic* represent a breakdown of Catholic rites or Friends affiliations. They are included in their respective denominational total.

Table 4. Churches and Church Membership by County and Denomination: 1990

County and Denomination	Number of churches	Communicant, confirmed, full members	Total adherents Number	Percent of total population	Percent of total adherents
435 UNITARIAN-UNIV	1	31	46	.1	.3
443 UN C OF CHRIST	9	1,640	2,002*	5.5	13.0
449 UN METHODIST	17	2,299	2,806*	7.8	18.2
497 BLACK BAPT EST[2]	NA	152	186*	.5	1.2
VENANGO	**127**	**16,279**	**30,373***	**51.1**	**100.0**
011 A.W.M.C.	3	115	143*	.2	.5
019 AMER BAPT USA	4	524	654*	1.1	2.2
053 ASSEMB OF GOD	3	179	401	.7	1.3
081 CATHOLIC	7	NA	8,849	14.9	29.1
081d LATIN	7	NA	8,849	14.9	29.1
089 CHR & MISS AL	2	72	177	.3	.6
093 CHR CH (DISC)	1	60	66	.1	.2
123 CH GOD (ANDER)	6	641	679	1.1	2.2
145 CH GOD PROPHCY	2	71	89*	.1	.3
151 L-D SAINTS	1	NA	197	.3	.6
165 CH OF NAZARENE	2	375	760	1.3	2.5
167 CHS OF CHRIST	1	12	27	-	.1
171 CH GOD-GEN CON	5	427	533*	.9	1.8
193 EPISCOPAL	2	485	553	.9	1.8
199 EVAN CONGR CH	2	110	180	.3	.6
207 E.L.C.A.	5	1,038	1,411	2.4	4.6
221 FREE METHODIST	7	220	296	.5	1.0
263 INT FOURSQ GOS	1	34	42*	.1	.1
283 LUTH—MO SYNOD	1	286	386	.7	1.3
323 OLD ORD AMISH	2	NA	300	.5	1.0
355 PRESB CH (USA)	16	2,812	3,509*	5.9	11.6
403 SALVATION ARMY	2	176	189	.3	.6
413 S.D.A.	2	73	91*	.2	.3
435 UNITARIAN-UNIV	1	12	12	-	-
438 UN BRETH IN CR	2	244	311	.5	1.0
443 UN C OF CHRIST	1	36	45*	.1	.1
449 UN METHODIST	45	8,277	10,328*	17.4	34.0
496 JEWISH EST[1]	1	NA	145	.2	.5
WARREN	**80**	**11,320**	**22,557***	**50.1**	**100.0**
011 A.W.M.C.	2	52	65*	.1	.3
019 AMER BAPT USA	1	279	347*	.8	1.5
053 ASSEMB OF GOD	2	85	148	.3	.7
057 BAPT GEN CONF	2	206	257*	.6	1.1
081 CATHOLIC	8	NA	7,277	16.2	32.3
081b BYZAN RUTH	2	NA	1,434	3.2	6.4
081d LATIN	6	NA	5,843	13.0	25.9
089 CHR & MISS AL	2	77	156	.3	.7
111 CH CR,SCIENTST	1	NR	NR	-	-
123 CH GOD (ANDER)	1	0	90	.2	.4
127 CH GOD (CLEVE)	1	5	6*	-	-
151 L-D SAINTS	1	NA	189	.4	.8
165 CH OF NAZARENE	1	443	479	1.1	2.1
167 CHS OF CHRIST	1	58	73	.2	.3
175 CONGR CHR CHS	2	93	116*	.3	.5
181 CONSRV CONGR	2	86	107*	.2	.5
193 EPISCOPAL	2	364	450	1.0	2.0
207 E.L.C.A.	7	2,288	3,053	6.8	13.5
221 FREE METHODIST	5	207	362	.8	1.6
259 IFCA	1	NR	NR	-	-
323 OLD ORD AMISH	2	NA	300	.7	1.3
355 PRESB CH (USA)	6	1,489	1,854*	4.1	8.2
403 SALVATION ARMY	1	89	99	.2	.4
413 S.D.A.	1	32	40*	.1	.2
419 SO BAPT CONV	1	56	70*	.2	.3
443 UN C OF CHRIST	2	287	357*	.8	1.6
449 UN METHODIST	23	5,077	6,322*	14.0	28.0
467 WESLEYAN	1	47	340	.8	1.5
496 JEWISH EST[1]	1	NA	0	-	-
WASHINGTON	**275**	**41,685**	**119,473***	**58.4**	**100.0**
005 AME ZION	2	88	158	.1	.1
011 A.W.M.C.	1	0	0*	-	-
019 AMER BAPT USA	13	2,392	2,890*	1.4	2.4
022 EASTERN ORTH	1	132	132	.1	.1
053 ASSEMB OF GOD	3	797	1,305	.6	1.1
057 BAPT GEN CONF	1	97	117*	.1	.1
071 BRETHREN (ASH)	1	64	77*	-	.1
075 BRETHREN IN CR	1	30	38	-	-
081 CATHOLIC	41	NA	60,917	29.8	51.0
081b BYZAN RUTH	4	NA	7,896	3.9	6.6
081d LATIN	37	NA	53,021	25.9	44.4
089 CHR & MISS AL	4	275	649	.3	.5
093 CHR CH (DISC)	10	2,425	4,371	2.1	3.7
097 CHR CHS&CHS CR	10	1,735	2,096*	1.0	1.8
105 CHRISTIAN REF	1	45	63	-	.1
111 CH CR,SCIENTST	1	NR	NR	-	-
123 CH GOD (ANDER)	1	30	30	-	-
127 CH GOD (CLEVE)	1	245	296*	.1	.2
145 CH GOD PROPHCY	2	71	86*	-	.1

County and Denomination	Number of churches	Communicant, confirmed, full members	Total adherents Number	Percent of total population	Percent of total adherents
151 L-D SAINTS	3	NA	690	.3	.6
157 CH OF BRETHREN	1	30	36*	-	-
165 CH OF NAZARENE	9	722	944	.5	.8
167 CHS OF CHRIST	7	454	591	.3	.5
179 CONSRV BAPT	2	NR	NR	-	-
193 EPISCOPAL	6	1,123	1,883	.9	1.6
203 EVAN FREE CH	1	25	70	-	.1
207 E.L.C.A.	10	2,709	3,610	1.8	3.0
221 FREE METHODIST	2	153	281	.1	.2
246 GREEK ORTHODOX	1	NR	NR	-	-
283 LUTH—MO SYNOD	1	32	35	-	-
329 OPEN BIBLE STD	1	NR	NR	-	-
331 ORTH CH IN AM	5	NR	NR	-	-
353 CHR BRETHREN	1	15	25	-	-
355 PRESB CH (USA)	64	14,609	17,651*	8.6	14.8
356 PRESB CH AMER	1	73	91	-	.1
403 SALVATION ARMY	1	66	72	-	.1
413 S.D.A.	3	96	116*	.1	.1
419 SO BAPT CONV	3	739	893*	.4	.7
449 UN METHODIST	54	11,026	13,322*	6.5	11.2
467 WESLEYAN	2	73	245	.1	.2
496 JEWISH EST[1]	3	NA	4,105	2.0	3.4
497 BLACK BAPT EST[2]	NA	1,314	1,588*	.8	1.3
WAYNE	**80**	**7,406**	**20,818***	**52.1**	**100.0**
019 AMER BAPT USA	4	401	498*	1.2	2.4
053 ASSEMB OF GOD	2	253	585	1.5	2.8
081 CATHOLIC	17	NA	10,562	26.4	50.7
081d LATIN	17	NA	10,562	26.4	50.7
111 CH CR,SCIENTST	1	NR	NR	-	-
151 L-D SAINTS	1	NA	180	.5	.9
167 CHS OF CHRIST	1	15	20	.1	.1
193 EPISCOPAL	2	172	239	.6	1.1
207 E.L.C.A.	3	1,281	1,690	4.2	8.1
221 FREE METHODIST	2	173	197	.5	.9
226 FRIENDS-USA	1	16	30	.1	.1
226c FGC	1	16	30	.1	.1
259 IFCA	1	NR	NR	-	-
293 MORAV CH-NORTH	1	120	141	.4	.7
331 ORTH CH IN AM	2	NR	NR	-	-
355 PRESB CH (USA)	5	531	660*	1.7	3.2
413 S.D.A.	1	38	47*	.1	.2
419 SO BAPT CONV	1	14	17*	-	.1
435 UNITARIAN-UNIV	1	20	20	.1	.1
449 UN METHODIST	33	4,372	5,432*	13.6	26.1
496 JEWISH EST[1]	1	NA	500	1.3	2.4
WESTMORELAND	**435**	**82,904**	**264,548***	**71.4**	**100.0**
005 AME ZION	1	313	366	.1	.1
011 A.W.M.C.	3	44	53*	-	-
019 AMER BAPT USA	11	2,647	3,202*	.9	1.2
022 EASTERN ORTH	3	216	216	.1	.1
053 ASSEMB OF GOD	12	1,595	3,379	.9	1.3
071 BRETHREN (ASH)	3	223	270*	.1	.1
081 CATHOLIC	78	NA	150,593	40.7	56.9
081b BYZAN RUTH	9	NA	10,864	2.9	4.1
081d LATIN	64	NA	139,112	37.6	52.6
081h UKRAINIAN	5	NA	617	.2	.2
089 CHR & MISS AL	12	883	1,992	.5	.8
093 CHR CH (DISC)	3	665	940	.3	.4
097 CHR CHS&CHS CR	10	2,486	3,008*	.8	1.1
111 CH CR,SCIENTST	1	NR	NR	-	-
123 CH GOD (ANDER)	5	396	429	.1	.2
127 CH GOD (CLEVE)	1	62	75*	-	-
151 L-D SAINTS	1	NA	268	.1	.1
157 CH OF BRETHREN	5	1,122	1,357*	.4	.5
165 CH OF NAZARENE	5	480	572	.2	.2
167 CHS OF CHRIST	5	192	264	.1	.1
171 CH GOD-GEN CON	8	1,652	1,999*	.5	.8
179 CONSRV BAPT	1	NR	NR	-	-
193 EPISCOPAL	6	1,061	1,363	.4	.5
207 E.L.C.A.	52	18,867	25,326	6.8	9.6
221 FREE METHODIST	6	219	317	.1	.1
246 GREEK ORTHODOX	3	NR	NR	-	-
259 IFCA	4	NR	NR	-	-
283 LUTH—MO SYNOD	4	744	938	.3	.4
285 MENNONITE CH	1	182	232	.1	.1
291 MISSIONARY CH	1	27	27	-	-
313 N AM BAPT CONF	1	220	266*	.1	.1
329 OPEN BIBLE STD	3	NR	NR	-	-
331 ORTH CH IN AM	3	NR	NR	-	-
349 PENT HOLINESS	4	353	427*	.1	.2
353 CHR BRETHREN	1	90	135	-	-
355 PRESB CH (USA)	48	14,783	17,884*	4.8	6.8
356 PRESB CH AMER	3	311	373	.1	.1
363 PRIMITIVE METH	1	89	132	-	-
403 SALVATION ARMY	6	374	403	.1	.2

NA–Not applicable   NR–Not reported   *Total adherents estimated from known number of communicant, confirmed, full members.   - Represents a percent less than 0.1.   Percentages may not total due to rounding.
[1]See Appendix E   [2]See Appendix F   [3]See Appendix G   Lines in *italic* represent a breakdown of Catholic rites or Friends affiliations. They are included in their respective denominational total.

Table 4. Churches and Church Membership by County and Denomination: 1990

County and Denomination	Number of churches	Communicant, confirmed, full members	Total adherents Number	Percent of total population	Percent of total adherents
413 S.D.A.	1	60	73*	-	-
419 SO BAPT CONV	3	85	103*	-	-
435 UNITARIAN-UNIV	2	66	71	-	-
443 UN C OF CHRIST	26	5,679	6,870*	1.9	2.6
449 UN METHODIST	78	24,685	29,864*	8.1	11.3
467 WESLEYAN	3	539	818	.2	.3
469 WELS	1	152	189	.1	.1
496 JEWISH EST[1]	5	NA	7,430	2.0	2.8
497 BLACK BAPT EST[2]	NA	1,342	1,624*	.4	.6
499 INDEP.NON-CHAR[3]	1	NA	700	.2	.3
WYOMING	**38**	**4,706**	**11,757***	**41.9**	**100.0**
019 AMER BAPT USA	1	190	241*	.9	2.0
053 ASSEMB OF GOD	3	222	426	1.5	3.6
081 CATHOLIC	5	NA	4,989	17.8	42.4
081d LATIN	5	NA	4,989	17.8	42.4
151 L-D SAINTS	1	NA	151	.5	1.3
193 EPISCOPAL	1	153	322	1.1	2.7
207 E.L.C.A.	1	111	157	.6	1.3
221 FREE METHODIST	1	29	42	.1	.4
259 IFCA	1	NR	NR	-	-
283 LUTH—MO SYNOD	1	155	255	.9	2.2
355 PRESB CH (USA)	2	318	403*	1.4	3.4
413 S.D.A.	2	101	128*	.5	1.1
419 SO BAPT CONV	1	44	56*	.2	.5
449 UN METHODIST	18	3,383	4,287*	15.3	36.5
496 JEWISH EST[1]	0	NA	300	1.1	2.6
YORK	**402**	**109,707**	**182,719***	**53.8**	**100.0**
005 AME ZION	2	1,364	1,616	.5	.9
019 AMER BAPT USA	2	449	555*	.2	.3
053 ASSEMB OF GOD	18	1,818	3,091	.9	1.7
075 BRETHREN IN CR	4	481	640	.2	.4
081 CATHOLIC	12	NA	38,479	11.3	21.1
081d LATIN	12	NA	38,479	11.3	21.1
089 CHR & MISS AL	9	1,033	1,918	.6	1.0
097 CHR CHS&CHS CR	1	53	65*	-	-
111 CH CR,SCIENTST	2	NR	NR	-	-
127 CH GOD (CLEVE)	3	296	366*	.1	.2
145 CH GOD PROPHCY	1	35	43*	-	-
151 L-D SAINTS	3	NA	1,262	.4	.7
157 CH OF BRETHREN	18	4,566	5,642*	1.7	3.1
165 CH OF NAZARENE	4	780	1,350	.4	.7
167 CHS OF CHRIST	3	355	395	.1	.2
171 CH GOD-GEN CON	11	880	1,087*	.3	.6
179 CONSRV BAPT	1	NR	NR	-	-
193 EPISCOPAL	3	1,187	1,390	.4	.8
199 EVAN CONGR CH	6	1,180	1,670	.5	.9
203 EVAN FREE CH	4	212	372	.1	.2
207 E.L.C.A.	76	33,415	43,945	12.9	24.1
226 FRIENDS-USA	2	37	46*	-	-
226c FGC	2	37	46*	-	-
246 GREEK ORTHODOX	1	NR	NR	-	-
259 IFCA	4	NR	NR	-	-
263 INT FOURSQ GOS	11	638	788*	.2	.4
283 LUTH—MO SYNOD	3	1,332	1,696	.5	.9
285 MENNONITE CH	10	477	772	.2	.4
286 E.PA MENNONITE	1	26	32*	-	-
291 MISSIONARY CH	2	145	148	-	.1
293 MORAV CH-NORTH	2	339	436	.1	.2
323 OLD ORD AMISH	1	NA	150	-	.1
353 CHR BRETHREN	1	75	108	-	.1
355 PRESB CH (USA)	16	6,048	7,473*	2.2	4.1
356 PRESB CH AMER	3	212	273	.1	.1
361 PRIM BAPT ASCS	1	6	7*	-	-
386 REGULAR BAPT	1	66	82*	-	-
403 SALVATION ARMY	1	150	171	.1	.1
413 S.D.A.	3	425	525*	.2	.3
419 SO BAPT CONV	9	2,109	2,606*	.8	1.4
435 UNITARIAN-UNIV	1	120	190	.1	.1
438 UN BRETH IN CR	4	540	540	.2	.3
443 UN C OF CHRIST	44	18,905	23,360*	6.9	12.8
449 UN METHODIST	93	27,826	34,383*	10.1	18.8
496 JEWISH EST[1]	3	NA	1,219	.4	.7
497 BLACK BAPT EST[2]	NA	2,127	2,628*	.8	1.4
498 INDEP.CHARIS.[3]	1	NA	400	.1	.2
499 INDEP.NON-CHAR[3]	1	NA	800	.2	.4

County and Denomination	Number of churches	Communicant, confirmed, full members	Total adherents Number	Percent of total population	Percent of total adherents
RHODE ISLAND					
THE STATE.....	554	81,604	769,964*	76.7	100.0
BRISTOL	**28**	**3,902**	**40,209***	**82.3**	**100.0**
019 AMER BAPT USA	2	331	400*	.8	1.0
053 ASSEMB OF GOD	2	118	130	.3	.3
081 CATHOLIC	10	NA	33,834	69.2	84.1
081d LATIN	10	NA	33,834	69.2	84.1
179 CONSRV BAPT	1	NR	NR	-	-
193 EPISCOPAL	4	1,655	2,285	4.7	5.7
207 E.L.C.A.	1	278	366	.7	.9
355 PRESB CH (USA)	1	129	156*	.3	.4
443 UN C OF CHRIST	2	929	1,123*	2.3	2.8
449 UN METHODIST	2	462	559*	1.1	1.4
496 JEWISH EST[1]	2	NA	856	1.8	2.1
499 INDEP.NON-CHAR[3]	1	NA	500	1.0	1.2
KENT	**74**	**12,684**	**120,266***	**74.6**	**100.0**
001 ADVENT CHR CH	1	52	63*	-	.1
019 AMER BAPT USA	12	2,628	3,188*	2.0	2.7
053 ASSEMB OF GOD	2	442	739	.5	.6
057 BAPT GEN CONF	1	79	96*	.1	.1
081 CATHOLIC	24	NA	99,480	61.7	82.7
081d LATIN	24	NA	99,480	61.7	82.7
127 CH GOD (CLEVE)	1	106	129*	.1	.1
151 L-D SAINTS	1	NA	235	.1	.2
167 CHS OF CHRIST	1	43	80	-	.1
175 CONGR CHR CHS	1	106	129*	.1	.1
179 CONSRV BAPT	1	NR	NR	-	-
193 EPISCOPAL	9	3,991	6,171	3.8	5.1
207 E.L.C.A.	4	1,806	2,505	1.6	2.1
353 CHR BRETHREN	2	131	220	.1	.2
355 PRESB CH (USA)	2	963	1,168*	.7	1.0
435 UNITARIAN-UNIV	1	194	296	.2	.2
443 UN C OF CHRIST	3	172	209*	.1	.2
449 UN METHODIST	6	1,768	2,145*	1.3	1.8
496 JEWISH EST[1]	1	NA	2,567	1.6	2.1
497 BLACK BAPT EST[2]	NA	203	246*	.2	.2
499 INDEP.NON-CHAR[3]	1	NA	600	.4	.5
NEWPORT	**57**	**8,328**	**57,156***	**65.6**	**100.0**
019 AMER BAPT USA	7	1,453	1,769*	2.0	3.1
053 ASSEMB OF GOD	1	62	168	.2	.3
081 CATHOLIC	13	NA	44,564	51.1	78.0
081d LATIN	13	NA	44,564	51.1	78.0
111 CH CR,SCIENTST	1	NR	NR	-	-
151 L-D SAINTS	1	NA	332	.4	.6
167 CHS OF CHRIST	1	20	35	-	.1
176 CCC, NOT NAT'L	2	592	721*	.8	1.3
179 CONSRV BAPT	1	NR	NR	-	-
193 EPISCOPAL	11	2,726	4,397	5.0	7.7
207 E.L.C.A.	1	398	634	.7	1.1
226 FRIENDS-USA	4	138	238*	.3	.4
226b EFI	2	127	223	.3	.4
226d FGC & FUM	2	11	15	-	-
246 GREEK ORTHODOX	1	NR	NR	-	-
355 PRESB CH (USA)	1	427	520*	.6	.9
363 PRIMITIVE METH	1	50	90	.1	.2
403 SALVATION ARMY	1	74	77	.1	.1
419 SO BAPT CONV	1	434	528*	.6	.9
435 UNITARIAN-UNIV	1	117	147	.2	.3
443 UN C OF CHRIST	2	301	366*	.4	.6
449 UN METHODIST	3	1,003	1,221*	1.4	2.1
496 JEWISH EST[1]	3	NA	700	.8	1.2
497 BLACK BAPT EST[2]	NA	533	649*	.7	1.1
PROVIDENCE	**320**	**46,880**	**505,030***	**84.7**	**100.0**
001 ADVENT CHR CH	1	72	88*	-	-
005 AME ZION	2	330	495	.1	.1
019 AMER BAPT USA	41	10,760	13,095*	2.2	2.6
049 ARMEN AP CH AM	1	1,400	9,000	1.5	1.8
053 ASSEMB OF GOD	11	1,108	1,811	.3	.4
057 BAPT GEN CONF	1	15	18*	-	-
081 CATHOLIC	102	NA	423,608	71.0	83.9
081d LATIN	99	NA	421,404	70.7	83.4
081e MARONITE	1	NA	912	.2	.2
081f MELKITE-GK	1	NA	1,150	.2	.2
081h UKRAINIAN	1	NA	142	-	-
089 CHR & MISS AL	4	475	802	.1	.2
111 CH CR,SCIENTST	3	NR	NR	-	-
123 CH GOD (ANDER)	1	40	40	-	-
127 CH GOD (CLEVE)	6	451	549*	.1	.1
145 CH GOD PROPHCY	3	84	102*	-	-
151 L-D SAINTS	3	NA	871	.1	.2

NA–Not applicable   NR–Not reported   *Total adherents estimated from known number of communicant, confirmed, full members.   - Represents a percent less than 0.1.   Percentages may not total due to rounding.
[1] See Appendix E   [2] See Appendix F   [3] See Appendix G   Lines in italic represent a breakdown of Catholic rites or Friends affiliations. They are included in their respective denominational total.

Table 4. Churches and Church Membership by County and Denomination: 1990

County and Denomination	Number of churches	Communicant, confirmed, full members	Total adherents Number	Percent of total population	Percent of total adherents
163 CH OF LUTH BR	1	48	96	-	-
165 CH OF NAZARENE	3	207	358	.1	.1
167 CHS OF CHRIST	3	346	418	.1	.1
175 CONGR CHR CHS	1	35	43*	-	-
179 CONSRV BAPT	2	NR	NR	-	-
181 CONSRV CONGR	1	152	185*	-	-
193 EPISCOPAL	32	10,333	14,253	2.4	2.8
207 E.L.C.A.	4	1,187	1,557	.3	.3
221 FREE METHODIST	1	27	40	-	-
226 FRIENDS-USA	3	258	314*	.1	.1
226d *FGC & FUM*	*3*	*258*	*314**	*.1*	*.1*
246 GREEK ORTHODOX	2	NR	NR	-	-
263 INT FOURSQ GOS	3	48	58*	-	-
283 LUTH—MO SYNOD	3	815	988	.2	.2
331 ORTH CH IN AM	1	NR	NR	-	-
353 CHR BRETHREN	1	48	60	-	-
355 PRESB CH (USA)	3	466	567*	.1	.1
356 PRESB CH AMER	1	44	68	-	-
363 PRIMITIVE METH	3	199	293	-	.1
397 ROMANIAN ORTH	1	NR	NR	-	-
403 SALVATION ARMY	2	203	220	-	-
413 S.D.A.	5	529	644*	.1	.1
419 SO BAPT CONV	2	538	655*	.1	.1
423 SYRIAN ANTIOCH	1	NA	700	.1	.1
435 UNITARIAN-UNIV	6	915	1,218	.2	.2
443 UN C OF CHRIST	21	5,370	6,535*	1.1	1.3
449 UN METHODIST	12	3,869	4,708*	.8	.9
469 WELS	1	85	139	-	-
496 JEWISH EST[1]	17	NA	10,267	1.7	2.0
497 BLACK BAPT EST[2]	NA	6,423	7,817*	1.3	1.5
498 INDEP.CHARIS.[3]	1	NA	600	.1	.1
499 INDEP.NON-CHAR[3]	4	NA	1,750	.3	.3
WASHINGTON	**75**	**9,810**	**47,303***	**43.0**	**100.0**
001 ADVENT CHR CH	2	33	40*	-	.1
019 AMER BAPT USA	15	2,652	3,251*	3.0	6.9
053 ASSEMB OF GOD	2	192	355	.3	.8
081 CATHOLIC	16	NA	31,941	29.0	67.5
081d *LATIN*	*16*	*NA*	*31,941*	*29.0*	*67.5*
083 CHRIST CATH CH	1	43	47	-	.1
111 CH CR,SCIENTST	2	NR	NR	-	-
123 CH GOD (ANDER)	1	200	200	.2	.4
127 CH GOD (CLEVE)	1	37	45*	-	.1
165 CH OF NAZARENE	1	30	76	.1	.2
167 CHS OF CHRIST	1	40	72	.1	.2
179 CONSRV BAPT	1	NR	NR	-	-
181 CONSRV CONGR	1	21	26*	-	.1
193 EPISCOPAL	10	2,771	4,759	4.3	10.1
207 E.L.C.A.	2	329	438	.4	.9
223 FREE WILL BAPT	1	34	42*	-	.1
226 FRIENDS-USA	2	53	65*	.1	.1
226d *FGC & FUM*	*2*	*53*	*65**	*.1*	*.1*
241 GEN SIX PR BPT	1	120	147*	.1	.3
283 LUTH—MO SYNOD	1	267	427	.4	.9
355 PRESB CH (USA)	2	346	424*	.4	.9
413 S.D.A.	1	42	51*	-	.1
415 S-D BAPTIST GC	3	356	436*	.4	.9
419 SO BAPT CONV	2	374	458*	.4	1.0
443 UN C OF CHRIST	2	1,019	1,249*	1.1	2.6
449 UN METHODIST	3	646	792*	.7	1.7
496 JEWISH EST[1]	1	NA	1,711	1.6	3.6
497 BLACK BAPT EST[2]	NA	205	251*	.2	.5

SOUTH CAROLINA

County and Denomination	Number of churches	Communicant, confirmed, full members	Total adherents Number	Percent of total population	Percent of total adherents
THE STATE.....	5,509	1,612,322	2,157,828*	61.9	100.0
ABBEVILLE	**61**	**13,918**	**17,423***	**73.0**	**100.0**
055 AS REF PRES CH	4	481	552	2.3	3.2
061 BEACHY AMISH	1	118	147*	.6	.8
081 CATHOLIC	1	NA	119	.5	.7
081d *LATIN*	*1*	*NA*	*119*	*.5*	*.7*
127 CH GOD (CLEVE)	3	232	290*	1.2	1.7
145 CH GOD PROPHCY	1	33	41*	.2	.2
167 CHS OF CHRIST	1	349	475	2.0	2.7
193 EPISCOPAL	1	93	110	.5	.6
285 MENNONITE CH	1	124	126	.5	.7
349 PENT HOLINESS	2	353	441*	1.8	2.5
355 PRESB CH (USA)	10	881	1,100*	4.6	6.3
356 PRESB CH AMER	3	394	469	2.0	2.7
375 REF EPISCOPAL	1	25	25	.1	.1
419 SO BAPT CONV	20	6,510	8,128*	34.1	46.7

County and Denomination	Number of churches	Communicant, confirmed, full members	Total adherents Number	Percent of total population	Percent of total adherents
449 UN METHODIST	12	1,747	2,181*	9.1	12.5
497 BLACK BAPT EST[2]	NA	2,578	3,219*	13.5	18.5
AIKEN	**175**	**56,348**	**78,833***	**65.2**	**100.0**
053 ASSEMB OF GOD	2	51	135	.1	.2
081 CATHOLIC	4	NA	4,377	3.6	5.6
081d *LATIN*	*4*	*NA*	*4,377*	*3.6*	*5.6*
093 CHR CH (DISC)	5	268	401	.3	.5
111 CH CR,SCIENTST	1	NR	NR	-	-
123 CH GOD (ANDER)	4	117	160	.1	.2
127 CH GOD (CLEVE)	9	1,314	1,672*	1.4	2.1
145 CH GOD PROPHCY	1	33	42*	-	.1
151 L-D SAINTS	1	NA	519	.4	.7
165 CH OF NAZARENE	4	323	654	.5	.8
167 CHS OF CHRIST	9	559	779	.6	1.0
193 EPISCOPAL	5	1,238	1,676	1.4	2.1
207 E.L.C.A.	4	1,389	1,942	1.6	2.5
283 LUTH—MO SYNOD	1	148	194	.2	.2
349 PENT HOLINESS	9	1,066	1,356*	1.1	1.7
353 CHR BRETHREN	2	76	152	.1	.2
355 PRESB CH (USA)	3	1,791	2,279*	1.9	2.9
356 PRESB CH AMER	3	425	555	.5	.7
403 SALVATION ARMY	1	116	116	.1	.1
413 S.D.A.	3	178	226*	.2	.3
415 S-D BAPTIST GC	1	30	38*	-	-
419 SO BAPT CONV	81	31,434	39,993*	33.1	50.7
449 UN METHODIST	19	6,941	8,831*	7.3	11.2
496 JEWISH EST[1]	1	NA	0	-	-
497 BLACK BAPT EST[2]	NA	8,851	11,261*	9.3	14.3
499 INDEP.NON-CHAR[3]	2	NA	1,475	1.2	1.9
ALLENDALE	**24**	**6,208**	**8,125***	**69.3**	**100.0**
081 CATHOLIC	1	NA	40	.3	.5
081d *LATIN*	*1*	*NA*	*40*	*.3*	*.5*
093 CHR CH (DISC)	2	77	115	1.0	1.4
127 CH GOD (CLEVE)	1	34	44*	.4	.5
167 CHS OF CHRIST	1	7	12	.1	.1
193 EPISCOPAL	1	43	58	.5	.7
207 E.L.C.A.	2	110	148	1.3	1.8
355 PRESB CH (USA)	1	50	65*	.6	.8
419 SO BAPT CONV	9	2,092	2,716*	23.2	33.4
449 UN METHODIST	6	1,066	1,384*	11.8	17.0
497 BLACK BAPT EST[2]	NA	2,729	3,543*	30.2	43.6
ANDERSON	**243**	**76,518**	**97,525***	**67.2**	**100.0**
005 AME ZION	4	80	96	.1	.1
053 ASSEMB OF GOD	11	1,101	1,604	1.1	1.6
055 AS REF PRES CH	3	590	616	.4	.6
081 CATHOLIC	2	NA	1,226	.8	1.3
081d *LATIN*	*2*	*NA*	*1,226*	*.8*	*1.3*
097 CHR CHS&CHS CR	1	35	43*	-	-
121 CH GOD (ABR)	2	316	390*	.3	.4
127 CH GOD (CLEVE)	21	4,206	5,196*	3.6	5.3
145 CH GOD PROPHCY	14	458	566*	.4	.6
151 L-D SAINTS	1	NA	354	.2	.4
165 CH OF NAZARENE	1	41	60	-	.1
167 CHS OF CHRIST	2	93	121	.1	.1
193 EPISCOPAL	2	381	450	.3	.5
207 E.L.C.A.	1	251	325	.2	.3
216 EVAN PRESBY CH	1	55	65	-	.1
283 LUTH—MO SYNOD	1	194	253	.2	.3
285 MENNONITE CH	1	23	43	-	-
349 PENT HOLINESS	12	1,815	2,242*	1.5	2.3
353 CHR BRETHREN	1	70	100	.1	.1
355 PRESB CH (USA)	19	3,858	4,766*	3.3	4.9
356 PRESB CH AMER	2	180	228	.2	.2
403 SALVATION ARMY	1	88	90	.1	.1
413 S.D.A.	2	150	185*	.1	.2
419 SO BAPT CONV	95	47,604	58,808*	40.5	60.3
449 UN METHODIST	38	7,214	8,912*	6.1	9.1
467 WESLEYAN	6	405	755	.5	.8
496 JEWISH EST[1]	1	NA	0	-	-
497 BLACK BAPT EST[2]	NA	7,310	9,031*	6.2	9.3
499 INDEP.NON-CHAR[3]	1	NA	1,000	.7	1.0
BAMBERG	**55**	**10,522**	**13,537***	**80.1**	**100.0**
081 CATHOLIC	0	NA	14	.1	.1
081d *LATIN*	*0*	*NA*	*14*	*.1*	*.1*
093 CHR CH (DISC)	3	334	503	3.0	3.7
127 CH GOD (CLEVE)	3	53	68*	.4	.5
145 CH GOD PROPHCY	2	65	83*	.5	.6
165 CH OF NAZARENE	1	63	95	.6	.7
193 EPISCOPAL	2	88	128	.8	.9
207 E.L.C.A.	2	121	147	.9	1.1
349 PENT HOLINESS	2	132	168*	1.0	1.2
355 PRESB CH (USA)	2	64	82*	.5	.6

NA–Not applicable   NR–Not reported   *Total adherents estimated from known number of communicant, confirmed, full members.   - Represents a percent less than 0.1.   Percentages may not total due to rounding.
[1]See Appendix E   [2]See Appendix F   [3]See Appendix G   Lines in *italic* represent a breakdown of Catholic rites or Friends affiliations. They are included in their respective denominational total.

Table 4. Churches and Church Membership by County and Denomination: 1990

County and Denomination	Number of churches	Communicant, confirmed, full members	Total adherents Number	Percent of total population	Percent of total adherents
419 SO BAPT CONV	15	3,447	4,397*	26.0	32.5
449 UN METHODIST	23	2,604	3,322*	19.7	24.5
497 BLACK BAPT EST2	NA	3,551	4,530*	26.8	33.5
BARNWELL	**48**	**11,589**	**15,572***	**76.7**	**100.0**
053 ASSEMB OF GOD	1	18	47	.2	.3
061 BEACHY AMISH	1	45	59*	.3	.4
081 CATHOLIC	2	NA	191	.9	1.2
081d LATIN	2	NA	191	.9	1.2
089 CHR & MISS AL	1	24	39	.2	.3
097 CHR CHS&CHS CR	1	204	267*	1.3	1.7
123 CH GOD (ANDER)	1	9	16	.1	.1
127 CH GOD (CLEVE)	4	326	426*	2.1	2.7
151 L-D SAINTS	1	NA	169	.8	1.1
167 CHS OF CHRIST	3	161	241	1.2	1.5
193 EPISCOPAL	2	150	186	.9	1.2
285 MENNONITE CH	1	93	123	.6	.8
349 PENT HOLINESS	2	133	174*	.9	1.1
355 PRESB CH (USA)	3	329	430*	2.1	2.8
413 S.D.A.	0	19	25*	.1	.2
419 SO BAPT CONV	21	6,381	8,344*	41.1	53.6
449 UN METHODIST	4	720	942*	4.6	6.0
497 BLACK BAPT EST2	NA	2,977	3,893*	19.2	25.0
BEAUFORT	**68**	**22,338**	**33,680***	**39.0**	**100.0**
001 ADVENT CHR CH	1	36	45*	.1	.1
053 ASSEMB OF GOD	2	305	529	.6	1.6
081 CATHOLIC	5	NA	3,874	4.5	11.5
081d LATIN	5	NA	3,874	4.5	11.5
093 CHR CH (DISC)	4	247	362	.4	1.1
097 CHR CHS&CHS CR	1	60	76*	.1	.2
111 CH CR,SCIENTST	1	NR	NR	-	-
127 CH GOD (CLEVE)	2	197	249*	.3	.7
145 CH GOD PROPHCY	2	65	82*	.1	.2
151 L-D SAINTS	3	NA	949	1.1	2.8
165 CH OF NAZARENE	1	17	35	-	.1
167 CHS OF CHRIST	4	102	173	.2	.5
193 EPISCOPAL	5	2,047	2,955	3.4	8.8
207 E.L.C.A.	2	741	976	1.1	2.9
283 LUTH—MO SYNOD	1	71	100	.1	.3
349 PENT HOLINESS	1	23	29*	-	.1
353 CHR BRETHREN	2	53	79	.1	.2
355 PRESB CH (USA)	5	2,598	3,279*	3.8	9.7
356 PRESB CH AMER	1	51	79	.1	.2
403 SALVATION ARMY	2	176	187	.2	.6
413 S.D.A.	2	120	151*	.2	.4
419 SO BAPT CONV	11	6,813	8,600*	10.0	25.5
435 UNITARIAN-UNIV	1	51	59	.1	.2
449 UN METHODIST	8	2,535	3,200*	3.7	9.5
496 JEWISH EST1	1	NA	0		
497 BLACK BAPT EST2	NA	6,030	7,612*	8.8	22.6
BERKELEY	**148**	**34,279**	**52,281***	**40.6**	**100.0**
081 CATHOLIC	5	NA	3,036	2.4	5.8
081d LATIN	5	NA	3,036	2.4	5.8
093 CHR CH (DISC)	10	542	856	.7	1.6
097 CHR CHS&CHS CR	5	880	1,191*	.9	2.3
127 CH GOD (CLEVE)	2	246	333*	.3	.6
145 CH GOD PROPHCY	5	164	222*	.2	.4
151 L-D SAINTS	2	NA	1,177	.9	2.3
165 CH OF NAZARENE	2	224	449	.3	.9
167 CHS OF CHRIST	1	85	140	.1	.3
193 EPISCOPAL	6	498	669	.5	1.3
207 E.L.C.A.	4	786	1,128	.9	2.2
349 PENT HOLINESS	16	983	1,331*	1.0	2.5
355 PRESB CH (USA)	5	938	1,270*	1.0	2.4
375 REF EPISCOPAL	14	1,387	1,387	1.1	2.7
413 S.D.A.	1	37	50*	-	.1
419 SO BAPT CONV	33	12,881	17,435*	13.5	33.3
449 UN METHODIST	34	5,181	7,013*	5.4	13.4
467 WESLEYAN	1	30	21	-	-
496 JEWISH EST1	0	NA	1,152	.9	2.2
497 BLACK BAPT EST2	NA	9,417	12,746*	9.9	24.4
498 INDEP.CHARIS.3	1	NA	300	.2	.6
499 INDEP.NON-CHAR3	1	NA	375	.3	.7
CALHOUN	**26**	**5,509**	**7,254***	**56.9**	**100.0**
053 ASSEMB OF GOD	1	48	70	.5	1.0
081 CATHOLIC	0	NA	40	.3	.6
081d LATIN	0	NA	40	.3	.6
123 CH GOD (ANDER)	1	35	55	.4	.8
127 CH GOD (CLEVE)	1	26	33*	.3	.5
145 CH GOD PROPHCY	1	33	42*	.3	.6
151 L-D SAINTS	1	NA	238	1.9	3.3
193 EPISCOPAL	1	88	124	1.0	1.7
207 E.L.C.A.	5	427	540	4.2	7.4
356 PRESB CH AMER	1	121	121	.9	1.7
419 SO BAPT CONV	6	1,491	1,888*	14.8	26.0
449 UN METHODIST	8	988	1,251*	9.8	17.2
497 BLACK BAPT EST2	NA	2,252	2,852*	22.4	39.3
CHARLESTON	**257**	**106,365**	**160,857***	**54.5**	**100.0**
001 ADVENT CHR CH	1	32	40*	-	-
053 ASSEMB OF GOD	6	608	961	.3	.6
081 CATHOLIC	18	NA	17,271	5.9	10.7
081d LATIN	18	NA	17,271	5.9	10.7
089 CHR & MISS AL	1	45	113	-	.1
093 CHR CH (DISC)	2	291	513	.2	.3
097 CHR CHS&CHS CR	2	105	132*	-	.1
111 CH CR,SCIENTST	1	NR	NR	-	-
123 CH GOD (ANDER)	1	69	69	-	-
127 CH GOD (CLEVE)	6	1,203	1,511*	.5	.9
145 CH GOD PROPHCY	4	131	165*	.1	.1
151 L-D SAINTS	3	NA	1,077	.4	.7
165 CH OF NAZARENE	3	406	654	.2	.4
167 CHS OF CHRIST	8	1,653	1,971	.7	1.2
179 CONSRV BAPT	1	NR	NR		
193 EPISCOPAL	24	8,521	10,882	3.7	6.8
207 E.L.C.A.	14	5,516	7,187	2.4	4.5
215 EVAN METH CH	1	27	34*	-	-
223 FREE WILL BAPT	1	213	268*	.1	.2
226 FRIENDS-USA	1	37	50*	-	-
226d FGC & FUM	1	37	50*	-	-
246 GREEK ORTHODOX	1	NR	NR	-	-
259 IFCA	1	NR	NR	-	-
283 LUTH—MO SYNOD	1	331	457	.2	.3
285 MENNONITE CH	1	25	53	-	-
349 PENT HOLINESS	9	869	1,091*	.4	.7
353 CHR BRETHREN	3	57	120	-	.1
355 PRESB CH (USA)	25	8,512	10,690*	3.6	6.6
356 PRESB CH AMER	3	127	194	.1	.1
375 REF EPISCOPAL	15	1,408	1,408	.5	.9
403 SALVATION ARMY	1	165	172	.1	.1
413 S.D.A.	3	1,345	1,689*	.6	1.1
415 S-D BAPTIST GC	1	47	59*	-	-
419 SO BAPT CONV	50	36,575	45,934*	15.6	28.6
435 UNITARIAN-UNIV	1	192	226	.1	.1
443 UN C OF CHRIST	2	187	235*	.1	.1
449 UN METHODIST	35	15,183	19,068*	6.5	11.9
467 WESLEYAN	1	40	120	-	.1
496 JEWISH EST1	3	NA	2,655	.9	1.7
497 BLACK BAPT EST2	NA	22,445	28,188*	9.6	17.5
498 INDEP.CHARIS.3	2	NA	1,000	.3	.6
499 INDEP.NON-CHAR3	1	NA	4,600	1.6	2.9
CHEROKEE	**95**	**25,350**	**32,462***	**72.9**	**100.0**
005 AME ZION	2	493	606	1.4	1.9
053 ASSEMB OF GOD	2	61	109	.2	.3
055 AS REF PRES CH	1	71	79	.2	.2
081 CATHOLIC	1	NA	319	.7	1.0
081d LATIN	1	NA	319	.7	1.0
082 CENTRAL BAPT	1	0	0*	-	-
127 CH GOD (CLEVE)	4	460	574*	1.3	1.8
145 CH GOD PROPHCY	1	33	41*	.1	.1
151 L-D SAINTS	1	NA	528	1.2	1.6
167 CHS OF CHRIST	2	50	70	.2	.2
193 EPISCOPAL	1	114	145	.3	.4
207 E.L.C.A.	1	130	176	.4	.5
216 EVAN PRESBY CH	1	54	58	.1	.2
223 FREE WILL BAPT	3	173	216*	.5	.7
263 INT FOURSQ GOS	1	132	165*	.4	.5
355 PRESB CH (USA)	3	288	359*	.8	1.1
356 PRESB CH AMER	2	158	158	.4	.5
403 SALVATION ARMY	1	80	85	.2	.3
419 SO BAPT CONV	58	19,634	24,487*	55.0	75.4
449 UN METHODIST	8	1,136	1,417*	3.2	4.4
467 WESLEYAN	1	34	65	.1	.2
497 BLACK BAPT EST2	NA	2,249	2,805*	6.3	8.6
CHESTER	**105**	**24,286**	**29,364***	**91.3**	**100.0**
005 AME ZION	25	8,672	9,090	28.3	31.0
053 ASSEMB OF GOD	1	39	70	.2	.2
055 AS REF PRES CH	5	769	855	2.7	2.9
081 CATHOLIC	2	NA	174	.5	.6
081d LATIN	2	NA	174	.5	.6
127 CH GOD (CLEVE)	4	514	656*	2.0	2.2
145 CH GOD PROPHCY	3	98	125*	.4	.4
165 CH OF NAZARENE	2	386	806	2.5	2.7
167 CHS OF CHRIST	1	29	37	.1	.1
193 EPISCOPAL	2	69	91	.3	.3
207 E.L.C.A.	1	65	79	.2	.3
223 FREE WILL BAPT	3	303	387*	1.2	1.3

NA–Not applicable NR–Not reported *Total adherents estimated from known number of communicant, confirmed, full members. - Represents a percent less than 0.1. Percentages may not total due to rounding.

[1]See Appendix E [2]See Appendix F [3]See Appendix G Lines in *italic* represent a breakdown of Catholic rites or Friends affiliations. They are included in their respective denominational total.

Table 4. Churches and Church Membership by County and Denomination: 1990

County and Denomination	Number of churches	Communicant, confirmed, full members	Total adherents Number	Percent of total population	Percent of total adherents
263 INT FOURSQ GOS	1	101	129*	.4	.4
349 PENT HOLINESS	2	178	227*	.7	.8
355 PRESB CH (USA)	15	1,201	1,534*	4.8	5.2
356 PRESB CH AMER	2	282	314	1.0	1.1
419 SO BAPT CONV	19	6,325	8,078*	25.1	27.5
449 UN METHODIST	16	2,102	2,685*	8.3	9.1
497 BLACK BAPT EST[2]	NA	3,153	4,027*	12.5	13.7
CHESTERFIELD	**142**	**30,052**	**37,456***	**97.1**	**100.0**
005 AME ZION	17	8,086	9,036	23.4	24.1
081 CATHOLIC	2	NA	195	.5	.5
081d *LATIN*	*2*	*NA*	*195*	*.5*	*.5*
127 CH GOD (CLEVE)	6	578	733*	1.9	2.0
145 CH GOD PROPHCY	3	98	124*	.3	.3
151 L-D SAINTS	1	NA	329	.9	.9
165 CH OF NAZARENE	1	35	62	.2	.2
193 EPISCOPAL	1	176	259	.7	.7
223 FREE WILL BAPT	3	291	369*	1.0	1.0
349 PENT HOLINESS	1	76	96*	.2	.3
355 PRESB CH (USA)	13	1,031	1,308*	3.4	3.5
356 PRESB CH AMER	1	154	167	.4	.4
413 S.D.A.	1	33	42*	.1	.1
419 SO BAPT CONV	59	11,483	14,571*	37.8	38.9
449 UN METHODIST	33	4,846	6,149*	15.9	16.4
497 BLACK BAPT EST[2]	NA	3,165	4,016*	10.4	10.7
CLARENDON	**55**	**12,105**	**15,907***	**55.9**	**100.0**
053 ASSEMB OF GOD	1	18	30	.1	.2
081 CATHOLIC	1	NA	114	.4	.7
081d *LATIN*	*1*	*NA*	*114*	*.4*	*.7*
123 CH GOD (ANDER)	1	5	9	-	.1
127 CH GOD (CLEVE)	2	138	180*	.6	1.1
145 CH GOD PROPHCY	3	98	128*	.4	.8
167 CHS OF CHRIST	1	25	50	.2	.3
193 EPISCOPAL	1	62	122	.4	.8
223 FREE WILL BAPT	3	397	518*	1.8	3.3
349 PENT HOLINESS	11	1,069	1,394*	4.9	8.8
355 PRESB CH (USA)	7	1,168	1,523*	5.4	9.6
356 PRESB CH AMER	3	378	435	1.5	2.7
413 S.D.A.	1	63	82*	.3	.5
419 SO BAPT CONV	11	3,026	3,945*	13.9	24.8
449 UN METHODIST	9	1,714	2,235*	7.9	14.1
497 BLACK BAPT EST[2]	NA	3,944	5,142*	18.1	32.3
COLLETON	**92**	**16,731**	**22,301***	**64.9**	**100.0**
001 ADVENT CHR CH	4	481	622*	1.8	2.8
053 ASSEMB OF GOD	1	57	68	.2	.3
081 CATHOLIC	2	NA	433	1.3	1.9
081d *LATIN*	*2*	*NA*	*433*	*1.3*	*1.9*
093 CHR CH (DISC)	4	368	566	1.6	2.5
097 CHR CHS&CHS CR	2	125	162*	.5	.7
127 CH GOD (CLEVE)	1	120	155*	.5	.7
145 CH GOD PROPHCY	3	98	127*	.4	.6
151 L-D SAINTS	1	NA	196	.6	.9
167 CHS OF CHRIST	1	15	20	.1	.1
193 EPISCOPAL	2	210	256	.7	1.1
207 E.L.C.A.	1	120	127	.4	.6
263 INT FOURSQ GOS	1	84	109*	.3	.5
349 PENT HOLINESS	3	95	123*	.4	.6
355 PRESB CH (USA)	3	437	565*	1.6	2.5
419 SO BAPT CONV	27	6,576	8,501*	24.7	38.1
449 UN METHODIST	35	4,150	5,365*	15.6	24.1
496 JEWISH EST[1]	1	NA	0	-	-
497 BLACK BAPT EST[2]	NA	3,795	4,906*	14.3	22.0
DARLINGTON	**100**	**27,381**	**35,848***	**58.0**	**100.0**
001 ADVENT CHR CH	1	30	38*	.1	.1
053 ASSEMB OF GOD	2	258	315	.5	.9
081 CATHOLIC	3	NA	590	1.0	1.6
081d *LATIN*	*3*	*NA*	*590*	*1.0*	*1.6*
111 CH CR,SCIENTST	1	NR	NR	-	-
123 CH GOD (ANDER)	5	245	452	.7	1.3
127 CH GOD (CLEVE)	5	261	331*	.5	.9
145 CH GOD PROPHCY	4	131	166*	.3	.5
151 L-D SAINTS	1	NA	431	.7	1.2
165 CH OF NAZARENE	2	236	324	.5	.9
167 CHS OF CHRIST	1	21	27	-	.1
193 EPISCOPAL	2	412	523	.8	1.5
207 E.L.C.A.	1	95	110	.2	.3
223 FREE WILL BAPT	6	1,017	1,288*	2.1	3.6
349 PENT HOLINESS	6	443	561*	.9	1.6
355 PRESB CH (USA)	6	1,095	1,387*	2.2	3.9
413 S.D.A.	1	44	56*	.1	.2
419 SO BAPT CONV	30	11,553	14,633*	23.7	40.8
449 UN METHODIST	23	5,463	6,919*	11.2	19.3
497 BLACK BAPT EST[2]	NA	6,077	7,697*	12.4	21.5

County and Denomination	Number of churches	Communicant, confirmed, full members	Total adherents Number	Percent of total population	Percent of total adherents
DILLON	**59**	**14,148**	**18,695***	**64.2**	**100.0**
005 AME ZION	1	127	168	.6	.9
053 ASSEMB OF GOD	1	45	60	.2	.3
081 CATHOLIC	1	NA	193	.7	1.0
081d *LATIN*	*1*	*NA*	*193*	*.7*	*1.0*
127 CH GOD (CLEVE)	5	943	1,240*	4.3	6.6
145 CH GOD PROPHCY	1	33	43*	.1	.2
167 CHS OF CHRIST	1	21	28	.1	.1
193 EPISCOPAL	1	86	102	.4	.5
349 PENT HOLINESS	3	222	292*	1.0	1.6
355 PRESB CH (USA)	7	440	579*	2.0	3.1
356 PRESB CH AMER	2	330	336	1.2	1.8
419 SO BAPT CONV	23	7,111	9,354*	32.1	50.0
449 UN METHODIST	12	1,666	2,191*	7.5	11.7
496 JEWISH EST[1]	1	NA	0	-	-
497 BLACK BAPT EST[2]	NA	3,124	4,109*	14.1	22.0
DORCHESTER	**104**	**31,323**	**47,457***	**57.1**	**100.0**
005 AME ZION	1	183	233	.3	.5
053 ASSEMB OF GOD	1	359	600	.7	1.3
055 AS REF PRES CH	1	50	66	.1	.1
081 CATHOLIC	2	NA	3,772	4.5	7.9
081d *LATIN*	*2*	*NA*	*3,772*	*4.5*	*7.9*
093 CHR CH (DISC)	7	438	630	.8	1.3
097 CHR CHS&CHS CR	2	170	223*	.3	.5
123 CH GOD (ANDER)	2	265	299	.4	.6
127 CH GOD (CLEVE)	4	299	392*	.5	.8
145 CH GOD PROPHCY	3	98	129*	.2	.3
151 L-D SAINTS	2	NA	728	.9	1.5
165 CH OF NAZARENE	1	164	223	.3	.5
167 CHS OF CHRIST	3	359	524	.6	1.1
193 EPISCOPAL	2	861	1,247	1.5	2.6
207 E.L.C.A.	2	949	1,267	1.5	2.7
223 FREE WILL BAPT	1	43	56*	.1	.1
283 LUTH—MO SYNOD	1	248	352	.4	.7
349 PENT HOLINESS	4	180	236*	.3	.5
353 CHR BRETHREN	1	25	25	-	.1
355 PRESB CH (USA)	2	1,205	1,580*	1.9	3.3
356 PRESB CH AMER	1	53	102	.1	.2
375 REF EPISCOPAL	1	12	12	-	-
413 S.D.A.	2	240	315*	.4	.7
419 SO BAPT CONV	18	9,634	12,634*	15.2	26.6
449 UN METHODIST	37	9,634	12,634*	15.2	26.6
469 WELS	1	64	92	.1	.2
496 JEWISH EST[1]	0	NA	693	.8	1.5
497 BLACK BAPT EST[2]	NA	5,790	7,593*	9.1	16.0
498 INDEP.CHARIS.[3]	1	NA	300	.4	.6
499 INDEP.NON-CHAR[3]	1	NA	500	.6	1.1
EDGEFIELD	**35**	**8,773**	**12,503***	**68.0**	**100.0**
053 ASSEMB OF GOD	1	47	59	.3	.5
055 AS REF PRES CH	1	36	38	.2	.3
081 CATHOLIC	2	NA	1,253	6.8	10.0
081d *LATIN*	*2*	*NA*	*1,253*	*6.8*	*10.0*
127 CH GOD (CLEVE)	2	108	139*	.8	1.1
193 EPISCOPAL	1	179	208	1.1	1.7
207 E.L.C.A.	1	95	112	.6	.9
349 PENT HOLINESS	2	86	111*	.6	.9
355 PRESB CH (USA)	1	6	8*	-	.1
356 PRESB CH AMER	1	79	87	.5	.7
413 S.D.A.	1	35	45*	.2	.4
419 SO BAPT CONV	17	4,375	5,639*	30.7	45.1
449 UN METHODIST	5	811	1,045*	5.7	8.4
497 BLACK BAPT EST[2]	NA	2,916	3,759*	20.5	30.1
FAIRFIELD	**58**	**11,406**	**15,022***	**67.4**	**100.0**
005 AME ZION	7	733	999	4.5	6.7
053 ASSEMB OF GOD	1	42	50	.2	.3
055 AS REF PRES CH	3	295	338	1.5	2.3
081 CATHOLIC	1	NA	122	.5	.8
081d *LATIN*	*1*	*NA*	*122*	*.5*	*.8*
123 CH GOD (ANDER)	1	6	19	.1	.1
127 CH GOD (CLEVE)	1	138	176*	.8	1.2
145 CH GOD PROPHCY	2	65	83*	.4	.6
151 L-D SAINTS	1	NA	184	.8	1.2
165 CH OF NAZARENE	1	241	517	2.3	3.4
167 CHS OF CHRIST	1	60	100	.4	.7
193 EPISCOPAL	3	217	273	1.2	1.8
349 PENT HOLINESS	1	40	51*	.2	.3
355 PRESB CH (USA)	8	606	772*	3.5	5.1
356 PRESB CH AMER	4	545	599	2.7	4.0
419 SO BAPT CONV	15	3,106	3,955*	17.7	26.3
449 UN METHODIST	7	836	1,065*	4.8	7.1
467 WESLEYAN	1	26	53	.2	.4
497 BLACK BAPT EST[2]	NA	4,450	5,666*	25.4	37.7

NA–Not applicable NR–Not reported *Total adherents estimated from known number of communicant, confirmed, full members. - Represents a percent less than 0.1. Percentages may not total due to rounding.
[1]See Appendix E [2]See Appendix F [3]See Appendix G Lines in *italic* represent a breakdown of Catholic rites or Friends affiliations. They are included in their respective denominational total.

SOUTH CAROLINA

Table 4. Churches and Church Membership by County and Denomination: 1990

County and Denomination	Number of churches	Communicant, confirmed, full members	Total adherents Number	Percent of total population	Percent of total adherents
FLORENCE	**186**	**48,568**	**66,892***	**58.5**	**100.0**
053 ASSEMB OF GOD	3	265	444	.4	.7
055 AS REF PRES CH	1	162	189	.2	.3
081 CATHOLIC	4	NA	2,280	2.0	3.4
081d *LATIN*	*4*	*NA*	*2,280*	*2.0*	*3.4*
097 CHR CHS&CHS CR	1	20	26*	-	-
123 CH GOD (ANDER)	3	63	77	.1	.1
127 CH GOD (CLEVE)	13	997	1,276*	1.1	1.9
145 CH GOD PROPHCY	8	262	335*	.3	.5
151 L-D SAINTS	1	NA	515	.5	.8
165 CH OF NAZARENE	2	214	346	.3	.5
167 CHS OF CHRIST	5	223	284	.2	.4
193 EPISCOPAL	3	884	1,313	1.1	2.0
207 E.L.C.A.	2	517	640	.6	1.0
216 EVAN PRESBY CH	2	514	527	.5	.8
223 FREE WILL BAPT	29	3,057	3,913*	3.4	5.8
246 GREEK ORTHODOX	1	NR	NR	-	-
263 INT FOURSQ GOS	1	2	3*	-	-
283 LUTH—MO SYNOD	1	93	122	.1	.2
353 CHR BRETHREN	2	233	366	.3	.5
355 PRESB CH (USA)	9	2,005	2,566*	2.2	3.8
356 PRESB CH AMER	1	37	37	-	.1
403 SALVATION ARMY	1	111	119	.1	.2
413 S.D.A.	2	401	513*	.4	.8
419 SO BAPT CONV	43	18,016	23,061*	20.2	34.5
449 UN METHODIST	45	10,843	13,879*	12.1	20.7
467 WESLEYAN	1	0	0	-	-
496 JEWISH EST[1]	1	NA	210	.2	.3
497 BLACK BAPT EST[2]	NA	9,649	12,351*	10.8	18.5
499 INDEP.NON-CHAR[3]	1	NA	1,500	1.3	2.2
GEORGETOWN	**88**	**19,361**	**26,547***	**57.3**	**100.0**
053 ASSEMB OF GOD	3	240	505	1.1	1.9
081 CATHOLIC	4	NA	1,079	2.3	4.1
081d *LATIN*	*4*	*NA*	*1,079*	*2.3*	*4.1*
123 CH GOD (ANDER)	3	30	139	.3	.5
127 CH GOD (CLEVE)	5	592	770*	1.7	2.9
145 CH GOD PROPHCY	1	33	43*	.1	.2
165 CH OF NAZARENE	1	66	120	.3	.5
167 CHS OF CHRIST	3	307	400	.9	1.5
193 EPISCOPAL	4	772	1,013	2.2	3.8
207 E.L.C.A.	2	306	374	.8	1.4
223 FREE WILL BAPT	5	373	485*	1.0	1.8
349 PENT HOLINESS	14	1,185	1,542*	3.3	5.8
355 PRESB CH (USA)	4	888	1,155*	2.5	4.4
356 PRESB CH AMER	1	124	129	.3	.5
413 S.D.A.	1	22	29*	.1	.1
419 SO BAPT CONV	20	5,665	7,370*	15.9	27.8
449 UN METHODIST	16	3,857	5,018*	10.8	18.9
496 JEWISH EST[1]	1	NA	0	-	-
497 BLACK BAPT EST[2]	NA	4,901	6,376*	13.8	24.0
GREENVILLE	**398**	**157,247**	**207,720***	**64.9**	**100.0**
005 AME ZION	1	80	103	-	-
053 ASSEMB OF GOD	15	1,234	2,158	.7	1.0
055 AS REF PRES CH	3	950	1,095	.3	.5
081 CATHOLIC	7	NA	7,904	2.5	3.8
081d *LATIN*	*7*	*NA*	*7,904*	*2.5*	*3.8*
089 CHR & MISS AL	2	59	168	.1	.1
093 CHR CH (DISC)	1	98	160	-	.1
097 CHR CHS&CHS CR	1	180	223*	.1	.1
111 CH CR,SCIENTST	1	NR	NR	-	-
121 CH GOD (ABR)	1	24	30*	-	-
123 CH GOD (ANDER)	2	111	117	-	.1
127 CH GOD (CLEVE)	24	5,911	7,330*	2.3	3.5
145 CH GOD PROPHCY	17	556	690*	.2	.3
151 L-D SAINTS	4	NA	1,454	.5	.7
157 CH OF BRETHREN	1	48	60*	-	-
165 CH OF NAZARENE	2	288	425	.1	.2
167 CHS OF CHRIST	12	1,453	2,034	.6	1.0
193 EPISCOPAL	9	4,790	5,985	1.9	2.9
207 E.L.C.A.	6	2,654	3,583	1.1	1.7
223 FREE WILL BAPT	5	269	334*	.1	.2
246 GREEK ORTHODOX	1	NR	NR	-	-
283 LUTH—MO SYNOD	2	264	322	.1	.2
349 PENT HOLINESS	15	1,623	2,013*	.6	1.0
353 CHR BRETHREN	2	102	164	.1	.1
355 PRESB CH (USA)	17	8,662	10,742*	3.4	5.2
356 PRESB CH AMER	12	3,055	3,828	1.2	1.8
361 PRIM BAPT ASCS	1	30	37*	-	-
403 SALVATION ARMY	1	139	149	-	.1
413 S.D.A.	2	427	530*	.2	.3
419 SO BAPT CONV	155	87,627	108,668*	33.9	52.3
435 UNITARIAN-UNIV	1	162	217	.1	.1
449 UN METHODIST	63	18,590	23,054*	7.2	11.1
467 WESLEYAN	7	353	512	.2	.2
469 WELS	1	59	82	-	-
496 JEWISH EST[1]	2	NA	580	.2	.3
497 BLACK BAPT EST[2]	NA	17,449	21,639*	6.8	10.4
499 INDEP.NON-CHAR[3]	2	NA	1,330	.4	.6
GREENWOOD	**106**	**32,942**	**42,283***	**71.0**	**100.0**
053 ASSEMB OF GOD	2	178	247	.4	.6
055 AS REF PRES CH	2	367	406	.7	1.0
081 CATHOLIC	1	NA	959	1.6	2.3
081d *LATIN*	*1*	*NA*	*959*	*1.6*	*2.3*
127 CH GOD (CLEVE)	9	2,287	2,849*	4.8	6.7
145 CH GOD PROPHCY	6	196	244*	.4	.6
151 L-D SAINTS	1	NA	243	.4	.6
167 CHS OF CHRIST	2	88	111	.2	.3
193 EPISCOPAL	1	267	344	.6	.8
207 E.L.C.A.	1	314	402	.7	1.0
223 FREE WILL BAPT	1	117	146*	.2	.3
349 PENT HOLINESS	10	883	1,100*	1.8	2.6
355 PRESB CH (USA)	7	1,742	2,170*	3.6	5.1
356 PRESB CH AMER	1	111	142	.2	.3
403 SALVATION ARMY	1	72	79	.1	.2
413 S.D.A.	1	74	92*	.2	.2
419 SO BAPT CONV	33	15,413	19,203*	32.2	45.4
449 UN METHODIST	26	6,368	7,934*	13.3	18.8
467 WESLEYAN	1	57	120	.2	.3
497 BLACK BAPT EST[2]	NA	4,408	5,492*	9.2	13.0
HAMPTON	**56**	**9,852**	**13,284***	**73.0**	**100.0**
081 CATHOLIC	1	NA	91	.5	.7
081d *LATIN*	*1*	*NA*	*91*	*.5*	*.7*
093 CHR CH (DISC)	10	650	954	5.2	7.2
097 CHR CHS&CHS CR	1	110	146*	.8	1.1
123 CH GOD (ANDER)	1	68	85	.5	.6
127 CH GOD (CLEVE)	3	102	136*	.7	1.0
145 CH GOD PROPHCY	3	98	130*	.7	1.0
193 EPISCOPAL	2	63	78	.4	.6
355 PRESB CH (USA)	3	147	196*	1.1	1.5
361 PRIM BAPT ASCS	2	50	67*	.4	.5
419 SO BAPT CONV	19	4,327	5,761*	31.7	43.4
449 UN METHODIST	11	852	1,134*	6.2	8.5
497 BLACK BAPT EST[2]	NA	3,385	4,506*	24.8	33.9
HORRY	**239**	**53,720**	**73,017***	**50.7**	**100.0**
053 ASSEMB OF GOD	6	308	551	.4	.8
055 AS REF PRES CH	1	72	80	.1	.1
081 CATHOLIC	5	NA	5,369	3.7	7.4
081d *LATIN*	*5*	*NA*	*5,369*	*3.7*	*7.4*
089 CHR & MISS AL	1	87	145	.1	.2
097 CHR CHS&CHS CR	2	296	364*	.3	.5
111 CH CR,SCIENTST	1	NR	NR	-	-
123 CH GOD (ANDER)	1	52	55	-	.1
127 CH GOD (CLEVE)	7	619	760*	.5	1.0
145 CH GOD PROPHCY	1	33	41*	-	.1
151 L-D SAINTS	2	NA	537	.4	.7
165 CH OF NAZARENE	1	71	96	.1	.1
167 CHS OF CHRIST	2	172	244	.2	.3
193 EPISCOPAL	4	1,708	2,122	1.5	2.9
207 E.L.C.A.	4	1,299	1,586	1.1	2.2
223 FREE WILL BAPT	14	1,378	1,693*	1.2	2.3
226 FRIENDS-USA	1	0	9	-	-
226f *INDEPENDNT*	*1*	*0*	*9*	*-*	*-*
246 GREEK ORTHODOX	1	NR	NR	-	-
283 LUTH—MO SYNOD	2	234	277	.2	.4
349 PENT HOLINESS	39	2,834	3,482*	2.4	4.8
353 CHR BRETHREN	2	67	114	.1	.2
355 PRESB CH (USA)	5	2,493	3,063*	2.1	4.2
356 PRESB CH AMER	3	309	441	.3	.6
403 SALVATION ARMY	1	44	44	-	.1
413 S.D.A.	3	203	249*	.2	.3
419 SO BAPT CONV	98	26,466	32,515*	22.6	44.5
435 UNITARIAN-UNIV	1	15	15	-	-
449 UN METHODIST	28	8,778	10,784*	7.5	14.8
467 WESLEYAN	1	12	26	-	-
496 JEWISH EST[1]	1	NA	425	.3	.6
497 BLACK BAPT EST[2]	NA	6,170	7,580*	5.3	10.4
499 INDEP.NON-CHAR[3]	1	NA	350	.2	.5
JASPER	**29**	**7,095**	**9,703***	**62.7**	**100.0**
053 ASSEMB OF GOD	2	183	360	2.3	3.7
055 AS REF PRES CH	1	20	22	.1	.2
081 CATHOLIC	2	NA	119	.8	1.2
081d *LATIN*	*2*	*NA*	*119*	*.8*	*1.2*
127 CH GOD (CLEVE)	1	71	95*	.6	1.0
145 CH GOD PROPHCY	3	98	131*	.8	1.4
167 CHS OF CHRIST	1	24	27	.2	.3
193 EPISCOPAL	1	123	159	1.0	1.6

NA–Not applicable NR–Not reported *Total adherents estimated from known number of communicant, confirmed, full members. - Represents a percent less than 0.1. Percentages may not total due to rounding.
[1] See Appendix E [2] See Appendix F [3] See Appendix G Lines in *italic* represent a breakdown of Catholic rites or Friends affiliations. They are included in their respective denominational total.

Table 4. Churches and Church Membership by County and Denomination: 1990

County and Denomination	Number of churches	Communicant, confirmed, full members	Total adherents Number	Percent of total population	Percent of total adherents
413 S.D.A.	1	65	87*	.6	.9
419 SO BAPT CONV	12	2,909	3,888*	25.1	40.1
449 UN METHODIST	5	558	746*	4.8	7.7
497 BLACK BAPT EST[2]	NA	3,044	4,069*	26.3	41.9
KERSHAW	**106**	**25,460**	**33,473***	**76.8**	**100.0**
005 AME ZION	7	783	1,049	2.4	3.1
053 ASSEMB OF GOD	1	40	75	.2	.2
055 AS REF PRES CH	1	194	222	.5	.7
081 CATHOLIC	1	NA	550	1.3	1.6
081d LATIN	1	NA	550	1.3	1.6
123 CH GOD (ANDER)	2	124	208	.5	.6
127 CH GOD (CLEVE)	5	441	555*	1.3	1.7
145 CH GOD PROPHCY	4	131	165*	.4	.5
151 L-D SAINTS	2	NA	678	1.6	2.0
165 CH OF NAZARENE	1	148	242	.6	.7
167 CHS OF CHRIST	3	180	217	.5	.6
193 EPISCOPAL	1	290	419	1.0	1.3
207 E.L.C.A.	1	314	385	.9	1.2
223 FREE WILL BAPT	1	67	84*	.2	.3
349 PENT HOLINESS	2	215	271*	.6	.8
355 PRESB CH (USA)	6	952	1,198*	2.7	3.6
413 S.D.A.	1	106	133*	.3	.4
419 SO BAPT CONV	41	13,996	17,611*	40.4	52.6
449 UN METHODIST	25	4,452	5,602*	12.8	16.7
496 JEWISH EST[1]	1	NA	0	-	-
497 BLACK BAPT EST[2]	NA	3,027	3,809*	8.7	11.4
LANCASTER	**134**	**43,528**	**52,885***	**97.0**	**100.0**
005 AME ZION	25	13,413	14,687	26.9	27.8
053 ASSEMB OF GOD	2	90	103	.2	.2
055 AS REF PRES CH	5	1,102	1,197	2.2	2.3
081 CATHOLIC	1	NA	390	.7	.7
081d LATIN	1	NA	390	.7	.7
127 CH GOD (CLEVE)	4	373	470*	.9	.9
145 CH GOD PROPHCY	2	65	82*	.2	.2
165 CH OF NAZARENE	1	89	134	.2	.3
167 CHS OF CHRIST	1	30	35	.1	.1
193 EPISCOPAL	1	129	172	.3	.3
207 E.L.C.A.	1	183	242	.4	.5
223 FREE WILL BAPT	6	938	1,183*	2.2	2.2
349 PENT HOLINESS	4	492	621*	1.1	1.2
355 PRESB CH (USA)	10	1,139	1,437*	2.6	2.7
356 PRESB CH AMER	1	93	106	.2	.2
419 SO BAPT CONV	54	17,891	22,565*	41.4	42.7
449 UN METHODIST	16	4,111	5,185*	9.5	9.8
497 BLACK BAPT EST[2]	NA	3,390	4,276*	7.8	8.1
LAURENS	**134**	**28,960**	**36,496***	**62.8**	**100.0**
005 AME ZION	6	332	369	.6	1.0
053 ASSEMB OF GOD	3	233	295	.5	.8
055 AS REF PRES CH	2	214	255	.4	.7
081 CATHOLIC	2	NA	179	.3	.5
081d LATIN	2	NA	179	.3	.5
123 CH GOD (ANDER)	1	30	65	.1	.2
127 CH GOD (CLEVE)	6	570	706*	1.2	1.9
145 CH GOD PROPHCY	4	131	162*	.3	.4
165 CH OF NAZARENE	1	42	74	.1	.2
167 CHS OF CHRIST	2	61	78	.1	.2
193 EPISCOPAL	2	188	251	.4	.7
207 E.L.C.A.	2	222	267	.5	.7
223 FREE WILL BAPT	2	98	121*	.2	.3
349 PENT HOLINESS	7	565	700*	1.2	1.9
355 PRESB CH (USA)	16	1,998	2,475*	4.3	6.8
356 PRESB CH AMER	6	494	569	1.0	1.6
413 S.D.A.	1	47	58*	.1	.2
419 SO BAPT CONV	46	15,873	19,660*	33.8	53.9
449 UN METHODIST	22	3,734	4,625*	8.0	12.7
467 WESLEYAN	2	108	108	.2	.3
497 BLACK BAPT EST[2]	NA	4,020	4,979*	8.6	13.6
499 INDEP.NON-CHAR[3]	1	NA	500	.9	1.4
LEE	**43**	**8,765**	**11,547***	**62.6**	**100.0**
001 ADVENT CHR CH	1	89	117*	.6	1.0
081 CATHOLIC	0	NA	12	.1	.1
081d LATIN	0	NA	12	.1	.1
089 CHR & MISS AL	1	91	106	.6	.9
123 CH GOD (ANDER)	1	47	103	.6	.9
127 CH GOD (CLEVE)	1	60	79*	.4	.7
145 CH GOD PROPHCY	1	33	43*	.2	.4
165 CH OF NAZARENE	2	148	178	1.0	1.5
167 CHS OF CHRIST	1	50	90	.5	.8
259 IFCA	1	NR	NR	-	-
355 PRESB CH (USA)	6	388	509*	2.8	4.4
419 SO BAPT CONV	12	1,896	2,487*	13.5	21.5
449 UN METHODIST	16	2,020	2,650*	14.4	22.9

County and Denomination	Number of churches	Communicant, confirmed, full members	Total adherents Number	Percent of total population	Percent of total adherents
497 BLACK BAPT EST[2]	NA	3,943	5,173*	28.1	44.8
LEXINGTON	**200**	**70,083**	**97,203***	**58.0**	**100.0**
005 AME ZION	1	197	235	.1	.2
053 ASSEMB OF GOD	6	973	1,914	1.1	2.0
055 AS REF PRES CH	2	221	278	.2	.3
081 CATHOLIC	4	NA	4,012	2.4	4.1
081d LATIN	4	NA	4,012	2.4	4.1
089 CHR & MISS AL	2	113	231	.1	.2
097 CHR CHS&CHS CR	1	0	0*	-	-
123 CH GOD (ANDER)	1	86	104	.1	.1
127 CH GOD (CLEVE)	8	698	878*	.5	.9
145 CH GOD PROPHCY	2	65	82*	-	.1
151 L-D SAINTS	4	NA	1,475	.9	1.5
164 CH LUTH CONF	1	258	334	.2	.3
165 CH OF NAZARENE	6	751	1,223	.7	1.3
167 CHS OF CHRIST	4	572	745	.4	.8
193 EPISCOPAL	4	1,135	1,571	.9	1.6
207 E.L.C.A.	37	13,624	17,218	10.3	17.7
283 LUTH—MO SYNOD	1	270	362	.2	.4
285 MENNONITE CH	1	20	20	-	-
331 ORTH CH IN AM	1	NR	NR	-	-
349 PENT HOLINESS	7	390	491*	.3	.5
355 PRESB CH (USA)	5	1,565	1,968*	1.2	2.0
356 PRESB CH AMER	2	490	607	.4	.6
413 S.D.A.	1	42	53*	-	.1
419 SO BAPT CONV	67	30,552	38,429*	22.9	39.5
449 UN METHODIST	28	12,396	15,592*	9.3	16.0
467 WESLEYAN	1	21	35	-	-
469 WELS	1	41	59	-	.1
496 JEWISH EST[1]	0	NA	739	.4	.8
497 BLACK BAPT EST[2]	NA	5,603	7,048*	4.2	7.3
499 INDEP.NON-CHAR[3]	2	NA	1,500	.9	1.5
MC CORMICK	**18**	**3,916**	**4,767***	**53.8**	**100.0**
055 AS REF PRES CH	3	64	68	.8	1.4
081 CATHOLIC	2	NA	21	.2	.4
081d LATIN	2	NA	21	.2	.4
355 PRESB CH (USA)	1	13	16*	.2	.3
419 SO BAPT CONV	8	1,401	1,701*	19.2	35.7
449 UN METHODIST	4	661	803*	9.1	16.8
497 BLACK BAPT EST[2]	NA	1,777	2,158*	24.3	45.3
MARION	**50**	**14,936**	**19,871***	**58.6**	**100.0**
081 CATHOLIC	1	NA	163	.5	.8
081d LATIN	1	NA	163	.5	.8
127 CH GOD (CLEVE)	4	402	527*	1.6	2.7
151 L-D SAINTS	1	NA	120	.4	.6
167 CHS OF CHRIST	1	42	57	.2	.3
193 EPISCOPAL	1	86	107	.3	.5
223 FREE WILL BAPT	2	379	497*	1.5	2.5
349 PENT HOLINESS	4	133	174*	.5	.9
355 PRESB CH (USA)	1	263	345*	1.0	1.7
356 PRESB CH AMER	1	197	266	.8	1.3
413 S.D.A.	1	81	106*	.3	.5
419 SO BAPT CONV	17	5,993	7,858*	23.2	39.5
449 UN METHODIST	16	2,820	3,698*	10.9	18.6
497 BLACK BAPT EST[2]	NA	4,540	5,953*	17.6	30.0
MARLBORO	**78**	**16,343**	**20,906***	**71.2**	**100.0**
005 AME ZION	9	3,702	4,568	15.6	21.9
081 CATHOLIC	1	NA	117	.4	.6
081d LATIN	1	NA	117	.4	.6
123 CH GOD (ANDER)	1	38	38	.1	.2
127 CH GOD (CLEVE)	4	519	664*	2.3	3.2
165 CH OF NAZARENE	2	252	370	1.3	1.8
167 CHS OF CHRIST	1	31	40	.1	.2
193 EPISCOPAL	1	139	169	.6	.8
223 FREE WILL BAPT	1	30	38*	.1	.2
349 PENT HOLINESS	4	361	462*	1.6	2.2
355 PRESB CH (USA)	3	456	583*	2.0	2.8
413 S.D.A.	1	11	14*	-	.1
419 SO BAPT CONV	12	2,912	3,723*	12.7	17.8
449 UN METHODIST	37	4,367	5,583*	19.0	26.7
467 WESLEYAN	1	29	68	.2	.3
497 BLACK BAPT EST[2]	NA	3,496	4,469*	15.2	21.4
NEWBERRY	**88**	**18,822**	**23,814***	**71.8**	**100.0**
005 AME ZION	4	456	691	2.1	2.9
053 ASSEMB OF GOD	3	63	77	.2	.3
055 AS REF PRES CH	2	286	329	1.0	1.4
081 CATHOLIC	1	NA	157	.5	.7
081d LATIN	1	NA	157	.5	.7
082 CENTRAL BAPT	1	200	248*	.7	1.0
097 CHR CHS&CHS CR	1	60	74*	.2	.3

Table 4. Churches and Church Membership by County and Denomination: 1990

County and Denomination	Number of churches	Communicant, confirmed, full members	Total adherents		
			Number	Percent of total population	Percent of total adherents
123 CH GOD (ANDER)	1	40	40	.1	.2
127 CH GOD (CLEVE)	3	163	202*	.6	.8
145 CH GOD PROPHCY	1	33	41*	.1	.2
151 L-D SAINTS	1	NA	178	.5	.7
167 CHS OF CHRIST	1	28	36	.1	.2
193 EPISCOPAL	1	130	168	.5	.7
207 E.L.C.A.	25	6,130	7,579	22.8	31.8
349 PENT HOLINESS	3	185	230*	.7	1.0
355 PRESB CH (USA)	6	736	914*	2.8	3.8
356 PRESB CH AMER	1	180	214	.6	.9
419 SO BAPT CONV	14	3,493	4,336*	13.1	18.2
435 UNITARIAN-UNIV	1	25	25	.1	.1
449 UN METHODIST	16	3,696	4,588*	13.8	19.3
467 WESLEYAN	2	95	183	.6	.8
497 BLACK BAPT EST[2]	NA	2,823	3,504*	10.6	14.7
OCONEE	**135**	**27,692**	**35,124***	**61.1**	**100.0**
053 ASSEMB OF GOD	2	133	230	.4	.7
055 AS REF PRES CH	1	120	140	.2	.4
081 CATHOLIC	1	NA	348	.6	1.0
081d LATIN	1	NA	348	.6	1.0
089 CHR & MISS AL	1	0	0	-	-
111 CH CR,SCIENTST	1	NR	NR	-	-
127 CH GOD (CLEVE)	16	1,511	1,860*	3.2	5.3
145 CH GOD PROPHCY	9	295	363*	.6	1.0
151 L-D SAINTS	1	NA	317	.6	.9
165 CH OF NAZARENE	1	58	140	.2	.4
167 CHS OF CHRIST	2	165	197	.3	.6
193 EPISCOPAL	1	282	314	.5	.9
207 E.L.C.A.	1	345	473	.8	1.3
283 LUTH—MO SYNOD	1	85	112	.2	.3
285 MENNONITE CH	1	87	137	.2	.4
349 PENT HOLINESS	2	101	124*	.2	.4
355 PRESB CH (USA)	6	1,021	1,257*	2.2	3.6
413 S.D.A.	2	185	228*	.4	.6
419 SO BAPT CONV	65	19,860	24,446*	42.5	69.6
449 UN METHODIST	14	1,745	2,148*	3.7	6.1
467 WESLEYAN	7	458	762	1.3	2.2
497 BLACK BAPT EST[2]	NA	1,241	1,528*	2.7	4.4
ORANGEBURG	**150**	**41,514**	**54,535***	**64.3**	**100.0**
053 ASSEMB OF GOD	2	82	102	.1	.2
081 CATHOLIC	4	NA	691	.8	1.3
081d LATIN	4	NA	691	.8	1.3
093 CHR CH (DISC)	2	426	624	.7	1.1
097 CHR CHS&CHS CR	1	150	192*	.2	.4
123 CH GOD (ANDER)	2	19	26	-	-
127 CH GOD (CLEVE)	9	659	843*	1.0	1.5
145 CH GOD PROPHCY	3	98	125*	.1	.2
165 CH OF NAZARENE	3	365	696	.8	1.3
167 CHS OF CHRIST	2	131	210	.2	.4
193 EPISCOPAL	3	541	638	.8	1.2
207 E.L.C.A.	3	699	841	1.0	1.5
223 FREE WILL BAPT	1	47	60*	.1	.1
349 PENT HOLINESS	4	126	161*	.2	.3
355 PRESB CH (USA)	3	732	937*	1.1	1.7
356 PRESB CH AMER	1	311	390	.5	.7
403 SALVATION ARMY	1	86	86	.1	.2
413 S.D.A.	3	249	319*	.4	.6
419 SO BAPT CONV	41	12,688	16,239*	19.1	29.8
449 UN METHODIST	61	12,021	15,385*	18.1	28.2
496 JEWISH EST[1]	0	NA	105	.1	.2
497 BLACK BAPT EST[2]	NA	12,084	15,465*	18.2	28.4
499 INDEP.NON-CHAR[3]	1	NA	400	.5	.7
PICKENS	**152**	**42,274**	**53,729***	**57.2**	**100.0**
005 AME ZION	1	90	105	.1	.2
053 ASSEMB OF GOD	4	134	169	.2	.3
081 CATHOLIC	3	NA	1,582	1.7	2.9
081d LATIN	3	NA	1,582	1.7	2.9
127 CH GOD (CLEVE)	15	1,617	1,951*	2.1	3.6
145 CH GOD PROPHCY	8	262	316*	.3	.6
167 CHS OF CHRIST	3	97	151	.2	.3
193 EPISCOPAL	2	871	1,010	1.1	1.9
207 E.L.C.A.	2	587	829	.9	1.5
285 MENNONITE CH	1	21	40	-	.1
355 PRESB CH (USA)	6	1,866	2,252*	2.4	4.2
356 PRESB CH AMER	2	402	488	.5	.9
413 S.D.A.	1	60	72*	.1	.1
419 SO BAPT CONV	63	27,967	33,752*	35.9	62.8
435 UNITARIAN-UNIV	1	91	116	.1	.2
449 UN METHODIST	26	5,060	6,107*	6.5	11.4
467 WESLEYAN	14	1,086	2,119	2.3	3.9
496 JEWISH EST[1]	0	NA	180	.2	.3
497 BLACK BAPT EST[2]	NA	2,063	2,490*	2.7	4.6

County and Denomination	Number of churches	Communicant, confirmed, full members	Total adherents		
			Number	Percent of total population	Percent of total adherents
RICHLAND	**248**	**115,243**	**154,586***	**54.1**	**100.0**
001 ADVENT CHR CH	1	72	89*	-	.1
005 AME ZION	2	800	1,283	.4	.8
019 AMER BAPT USA	3	1,294	1,591*	.6	1.0
053 ASSEMB OF GOD	8	388	569	.2	.4
055 AS REF PRES CH	6	2,856	3,513	1.2	2.3
081 CATHOLIC	8	NA	7,530	2.6	4.9
081d LATIN	8	NA	7,530	2.6	4.9
093 CHR CH (DISC)	2	215	274	.1	.2
097 CHR CHS&CHS CR	2	297	365*	.1	.2
111 CH CR,SCIENTST	1	NR	NR	-	-
123 CH GOD (ANDER)	4	515	540	.2	.3
127 CH GOD (CLEVE)	6	787	968*	.3	.6
133 CH GOD(7TH)DEN	1	24	37	-	-
145 CH GOD PROPHCY	2	65	80*	-	.1
151 L-D SAINTS	4	NA	1,616	.6	1.0
165 CH OF NAZARENE	3	708	764	.3	.5
167 CHS OF CHRIST	9	929	1,271	.4	.8
179 CONSRV BAPT	1	NR	NR	-	-
193 EPISCOPAL	12	5,883	7,662	2.7	5.0
207 E.L.C.A.	22	6,918	8,406	2.9	5.4
223 FREE WILL BAPT	2	156	192*	.1	.1
226 FRIENDS-USA	1	15	30	-	-
226c FGC	1	15	30	-	-
246 GREEK ORTHODOX	1	NR	NR	-	-
263 INT FOURSQ GOS	1	31	38*	-	-
283 LUTH—MO SYNOD	2	206	365	.1	.2
349 PENT HOLINESS	10	1,030	1,267*	.4	.8
353 CHR BRETHREN	2	87	174	.1	.1
355 PRESB CH (USA)	13	7,284	8,956*	3.1	5.8
356 PRESB CH AMER	10	3,488	4,248	1.5	2.7
361 PRIM BAPT ASCS	1	16	20*	-	-
375 REF EPISCOPAL	1	16	16	-	-
403 SALVATION ARMY	1	101	111	-	.1
413 S.D.A.	4	975	1,199*	.4	.8
419 SO BAPT CONV	56	36,442	44,810*	15.7	29.0
435 UNITARIAN-UNIV	1	285	426	.1	.3
449 UN METHODIST	36	17,225	21,180*	7.4	13.7
467 WESLEYAN	2	115	317	.1	.2
496 JEWISH EST[1]	3	NA	1,264	.4	.8
497 BLACK BAPT EST[2]	NA	26,020	31,995*	11.2	20.7
499 INDEP.NON-CHAR[3]	4	NA	1,420	.5	.9
SALUDA	**43**	**8,681**	**10,977***	**67.1**	**100.0**
001 ADVENT CHR CH	1	60	75*	.5	.7
081 CATHOLIC	1	NA	106	.6	1.0
081d LATIN	1	NA	106	.6	1.0
111 CH CR,SCIENTST	1	NR	NR	-	-
127 CH GOD (CLEVE)	2	120	151*	.9	1.4
207 E.L.C.A.	6	765	932	5.7	8.5
349 PENT HOLINESS	5	354	444*	2.7	4.0
355 PRESB CH (USA)	1	64	80*	.5	.7
419 SO BAPT CONV	15	3,567	4,479*	27.4	40.8
449 UN METHODIST	11	1,896	2,381*	14.6	21.7
497 BLACK BAPT EST[2]	NA	1,855	2,329*	14.2	21.2
SPARTANBURG	**358**	**121,712**	**158,501***	**69.9**	**100.0**
005 AME ZION	8	1,493	1,607	.7	1.0
053 ASSEMB OF GOD	8	789	1,627	.7	1.0
055 AS REF PRES CH	2	196	207	.1	.1
081 CATHOLIC	3	NA	3,487	1.5	2.2
081d LATIN	3	NA	3,487	1.5	2.2
089 CHR & MISS AL	1	41	61	-	-
097 CHR CHS&CHS CR	1	74	91*	-	.1
111 CH CR,SCIENTST	1	NR	NR	-	-
123 CH GOD (ANDER)	1	90	92	-	.1
127 CH GOD (CLEVE)	16	2,379	2,937*	1.3	1.9
145 CH GOD PROPHCY	11	359	443*	.2	.3
151 L-D SAINTS	3	NA	772	.3	.5
165 CH OF NAZARENE	1	109	199	.1	.1
167 CHS OF CHRIST	6	714	929	.4	.6
193 EPISCOPAL	6	1,926	2,498	1.1	1.6
207 E.L.C.A.	3	1,320	1,662	.7	1.0
215 EVAN METH CH	1	115	142*	.1	.1
223 FREE WILL BAPT	13	3,551	4,384*	1.9	2.8
246 GREEK ORTHODOX	1	NR	NR	-	-
283 LUTH—MO SYNOD	1	88	110	-	.1
349 PENT HOLINESS	6	265	327*	.1	.2
353 CHR BRETHREN	1	25	50	-	-
355 PRESB CH (USA)	15	4,723	5,831*	2.6	3.7
356 PRESB CH AMER	9	994	1,127	.5	.7
403 SALVATION ARMY	1	113	118	.1	.1
413 S.D.A.	3	678	837*	.4	.5
419 SO BAPT CONV	148	71,101	87,775*	38.7	55.4
435 UNITARIAN-UNIV	1	100	145	.1	.1
449 UN METHODIST	70	15,223	18,793*	8.3	11.9

NA–Not applicable NR–Not reported *Total adherents estimated from known number of communicant, confirmed, full members. - Represents a percent less than 0.1. Percentages may not total due to rounding.
[1]See Appendix E [2]See Appendix F [3]See Appendix G Lines in *italic* represent a breakdown of Catholic rites or Friends affiliations. They are included in their respective denominational total.

Table 4. Churches and Church Membership by County and Denomination: 1990

County and Denomination	Number of churches	Communicant, confirmed, full members	Total adherents		
			Number	Percent of total population	Percent of total adherents
467 WESLEYAN	15	1,059	2,056	.9	1.3
496 JEWISH EST[1]	1	NA	380	.2	.2
497 BLACK BAPT EST[2]	NA	14,187	17,514*	7.7	11.0
498 INDEP.CHARIS.[3]	1	NA	2,300	1.0	1.5
SUMTER	**119**	**39,163**	**53,703***	**52.3**	**100.0**
001 ADVENT CHR CH	1	12	16*	-	-
005 AME ZION	1	150	225	.2	.4
053 ASSEMB OF GOD	2	252	476	.5	.9
055 AS REF PRES CH	3	275	321	.3	.6
081 CATHOLIC	2	NA	1,501	1.5	2.8
081d *LATIN*	*2*	*NA*	*1,501*	*1.5*	*2.8*
097 CHR CHS&CHS CR	1	75	97*	.1	.2
111 CH CR,SCIENTST	1	NR	NR	-	-
123 CH GOD (ANDER)	2	227	302	.3	.6
127 CH GOD (CLEVE)	2	266	345*	.3	.6
145 CH GOD PROPHCY	2	65	84*	.1	.2
151 L-D SAINTS	2	NA	784	.8	1.5
165 CH OF NAZARENE	3	681	1,142	1.1	2.1
167 CHS OF CHRIST	3	135	228	.2	.4
193 EPISCOPAL	6	776	970	.9	1.8
207 E.L.C.A.	1	517	712	.7	1.3
223 FREE WILL BAPT	2	261	339*	.3	.6
259 IFCA	1	NR	NR	-	-
349 PENT HOLINESS	4	175	227*	.2	.4
355 PRESB CH (USA)	16	2,836	3,679*	3.6	6.9
356 PRESB CH AMER	1	182	230	.2	.4
403 SALVATION ARMY	1	115	128	.1	.2
413 S.D.A.	2	307	398*	.4	.7
419 SO BAPT CONV	32	13,170	17,084*	16.6	31.8
449 UN METHODIST	27	7,809	10,130*	9.9	18.9
496 JEWISH EST[1]	1	NA	175	.2	.3
497 BLACK BAPT EST[2]	NA	10,877	14,110*	13.7	26.3
UNION	**75**	**19,727**	**24,573***	**81.0**	**100.0**
005 AME ZION	6	761	995	3.3	4.0
053 ASSEMB OF GOD	2	64	88	.3	.4
081 CATHOLIC	1	NA	81	.3	.3
081d *LATIN*	*1*	*NA*	*81*	*.3*	*.3*
127 CH GOD (CLEVE)	3	300	371*	1.2	1.5
145 CH GOD PROPHCY	2	65	80*	.3	.3
151 L-D SAINTS	1	NA	82	.3	.3
167 CHS OF CHRIST	2	178	228	.8	.9
193 EPISCOPAL	1	60	75	.2	.3
207 E.L.C.A.	1	63	79	.3	.3
223 FREE WILL BAPT	2	354	437*	1.4	1.8
355 PRESB CH (USA)	7	517	639*	2.1	2.6
356 PRESB CH AMER	1	104	104	.3	.4
403 SALVATION ARMY	1	62	65	.2	.3
413 S.D.A.	1	48	59*	.2	.2
419 SO BAPT CONV	27	11,558	14,280*	47.1	58.1
449 UN METHODIST	17	3,365	4,157*	13.7	16.9
497 BLACK BAPT EST[2]	NA	2,228	2,753*	9.1	11.2
WILLIAMSBURG	**87**	**17,120**	**22,820***	**62.0**	**100.0**
005 AME ZION	1	202	235	.6	1.0
053 ASSEMB OF GOD	2	76	111	.3	.5
081 CATHOLIC	1	NA	88	.2	.4
081d *LATIN*	*1*	*NA*	*88*	*.2*	*.4*
127 CH GOD (CLEVE)	5	434	576*	1.6	2.5
145 CH GOD PROPHCY	1	33	44*	.1	.2
165 CH OF NAZARENE	1	18	67	.2	.3
167 CHS OF CHRIST	2	40	50	.1	.2
193 EPISCOPAL	1	84	141	.4	.6
223 FREE WILL BAPT	3	216	287*	.8	1.3
349 PENT HOLINESS	12	657	871*	2.4	3.8
353 CHR BRETHREN	1	25	50	.1	.2
355 PRESB CH (USA)	5	692	918*	2.5	4.0
356 PRESB CH AMER	5	474	586	1.6	2.6
413 S.D.A.	2	161	214*	.6	.9
419 SO BAPT CONV	14	3,001	3,981*	10.8	17.4
449 UN METHODIST	30	5,207	6,907*	18.8	30.3
496 JEWISH EST[1]	1	NA	0	-	-
497 BLACK BAPT EST[2]	NA	5,800	7,694*	20.9	33.7
YORK	**239**	**74,449**	**96,770***	**73.6**	**100.0**
005 AME ZION	41	16,260	18,742	14.3	19.4
053 ASSEMB OF GOD	5	793	1,237	.9	1.3
055 AS REF PRES CH	11	3,206	3,758	2.9	3.9
081 CATHOLIC	4	NA	2,599	2.0	2.7
081d *LATIN*	*4*	*NA*	*2,599*	*2.0*	*2.7*
089 CHR & MISS AL	1	38	58	-	.1
097 CHR CHS&CHS CR	3	190	238*	.2	.2
127 CH GOD (CLEVE)	10	2,173	2,725*	2.1	2.8
145 CH GOD PROPHCY	6	196	246*	.2	.3
151 L-D SAINTS	3	NA	1,246	.9	1.3

County and Denomination	Number of churches	Communicant, confirmed, full members	Total adherents		
			Number	Percent of total population	Percent of total adherents
165 CH OF NAZARENE	7	1,225	2,108	1.6	2.2
167 CHS OF CHRIST	2	324	431	.3	.4
193 EPISCOPAL	3	856	1,012	.8	1.0
207 E.L.C.A.	3	758	1,015	.8	1.0
223 FREE WILL BAPT	8	394	494*	.4	.5
263 INT FOURSQ GOS	4	247	310*	.2	.3
349 PENT HOLINESS	4	544	682*	.5	.7
355 PRESB CH (USA)	21	4,985	6,252*	4.8	6.5
356 PRESB CH AMER	8	2,226	2,631	2.0	2.7
403 SALVATION ARMY	1	76	77	.1	.1
413 S.D.A.	1	111	139*	.1	.1
419 SO BAPT CONV	51	21,264	26,668*	20.3	27.6
449 UN METHODIST	36	10,400	13,043*	9.9	13.5
467 WESLEYAN	4	207	356	.3	.4
497 BLACK BAPT EST[2]	NA	7,976	10,003*	7.6	10.3
499 INDEP.NON-CHAR[3]	2	NA	700	.5	.7
SOUTH DAKOTA					
THE STATE.....	1,781	234,370	474,010*	68.1	100.0
AURORA	**14**	**1,244**	**3,243***	**103.4**	**100.0**
081 CATHOLIC	4	NA	1,617	51.6	49.9
081d *LATIN*	*4*	*NA*	*1,617*	*51.6*	*49.9*
207 E.L.C.A.	2	340	444	14.2	13.7
283 LUTH—MO SYNOD	2	319	379	12.1	11.7
355 PRESB CH (USA)	1	0	0*	-	-
371 REF CH IN AM	1	139	239	7.6	7.4
449 UN METHODIST	4	446	564*	18.0	17.4
BEADLE	**45**	**7,494**	**13,083***	**71.7**	**100.0**
019 AMER BAPT USA	1	267	339*	1.9	2.6
053 ASSEMB OF GOD	1	145	240	1.3	1.8
081 CATHOLIC	4	NA	2,537	13.9	19.4
081d *LATIN*	*4*	*NA*	*2,537*	*13.9*	*19.4*
089 CHR & MISS AL	1	87	212	1.2	1.6
097 CHR CHS&CHS CR	1	180	229*	1.3	1.8
151 L-D SAINTS	1	NA	123	.7	.9
165 CH OF NAZARENE	1	41	53	.3	.4
167 CHS OF CHRIST	1	27	35	.2	.3
193 EPISCOPAL	1	101	195	1.1	1.5
207 E.L.C.A.	3	1,504	2,156	11.8	16.5
237 GC MENN BR CHS	2	419	532*	2.9	4.1
257 HUTTERIAN BR	3	NA	300	1.6	2.3
283 LUTH—MO SYNOD	4	1,253	1,659	9.1	12.7
287 MENN GEN CONF	2	371	450	2.5	3.4
291 MISSIONARY CH	1	25	20	.1	.2
329 OPEN BIBLE STD	1	NR	NR	-	-
355 PRESB CH (USA)	5	889	1,129*	6.2	8.6
403 SALVATION ARMY	1	89	99	.5	.8
413 S.D.A.	1	55	70*	.4	.5
419 SO BAPT CONV	2	56	71*	.4	.5
443 UN C OF CHRIST	1	312	396*	2.2	3.0
449 UN METHODIST	5	1,523	1,934*	10.6	14.8
467 WESLEYAN	1	82	199	1.1	1.5
469 WELS	1	68	105	.6	.8
BENNETT	**13**	**458**	**1,738***	**54.2**	**100.0**
081 CATHOLIC	4	NA	668	20.8	38.4
081d *LATIN*	*4*	*NA*	*668*	*20.8*	*38.4*
123 CH GOD (ANDER)	1	0	35	1.1	2.0
151 L-D SAINTS	1	NA	27	.8	1.6
193 EPISCOPAL	3	188	615	19.2	35.4
355 PRESB CH (USA)	2	172	241*	7.5	13.9
413 S.D.A.	1	16	22*	.7	1.3
469 WELS	1	82	130	4.1	7.5
BON HOMME	**26**	**2,988**	**5,819***	**82.1**	**100.0**
057 BAPT GEN CONF	1	14	17*	.2	.3
081 CATHOLIC	5	NA	1,842	26.0	31.7
081d *LATIN*	*5*	*NA*	*1,842*	*26.0*	*31.7*
207 E.L.C.A.	1	279	362	5.1	6.2
257 HUTTERIAN BR	1	NA	100	1.4	1.7
283 LUTH—MO SYNOD	4	502	611	8.6	10.5
287 MENN GEN CONF	1	83	83	1.2	1.4
313 N AM BAPT CONF	3	401	497*	7.0	8.5
355 PRESB CH (USA)	4	514	638*	9.0	11.0
371 REF CH IN AM	1	314	574	8.1	9.9
443 UN C OF CHRIST	2	642	796*	11.2	13.7
449 UN METHODIST	2	225	279*	3.9	4.8
467 WESLEYAN	1	14	20	.3	.3

NA–Not applicable   NR–Not reported   *Total adherents estimated from known number of communicant, confirmed, full members.   - Represents a percent less than 0.1.   Percentages may not total due to rounding.
[1]See Appendix E   [2]See Appendix F   [3]See Appendix G   Lines in *italic* represent a breakdown of Catholic rites or Friends affiliations. They are included in their respective denominational total.

Table 4. Churches and Church Membership by County and Denomination: 1990

County and Denomination	Number of churches	Communicant, confirmed, full members	Total adherents		
			Number	Percent of total population	Percent of total adherents
BROOKINGS	**44**	**9,106**	**15,996***	**63.5**	**100.0**
019 AMER BAPT USA	1	145	178*	.7	1.1
053 ASSEMB OF GOD	1	146	291	1.2	1.8
057 BAPT GEN CONF	1	134	164*	.7	1.0
081 CATHOLIC	5	NA	3,980	15.8	24.9
081d LATIN	5	NA	3,980	15.8	24.9
097 CHR CHS&CHS CR	1	40	49*	.2	.3
105 CHRISTIAN REF	1	184	269	1.1	1.7
123 CH GOD (ANDER)	1	208	208	.8	1.3
151 L-D SAINTS	1	NA	128	.5	.8
167 CHS OF CHRIST	1	32	45	.2	.3
193 EPISCOPAL	1	153	209	.8	1.3
207 E.L.C.A.	6	3,956	5,288	21.0	33.1
220 FREE LUTHERAN	1	303	429	1.7	2.7
257 HUTTERIAN BR	2	NA	200	.8	1.3
283 LUTH—MO SYNOD	3	639	795	3.2	5.0
287 MENN GEN CONF	1	0	0	-	-
355 PRESB CH (USA)	2	527	646*	2.6	4.0
371 REF CH IN AM	2	215	362	1.4	2.3
419 SO BAPT CONV	1	74	91*	.4	.6
435 UNITARIAN-UNIV	1	5	5	-	-
443 UN C OF CHRIST	2	164	201*	.8	1.3
449 UN METHODIST	6	1,552	1,901*	7.5	11.9
467 WESLEYAN	1	225	0	-	-
469 WELS	2	404	557	2.2	3.5
BROWN	**67**	**14,375**	**29,288***	**82.3**	**100.0**
019 AMER BAPT USA	1	980	1,233*	3.5	4.2
053 ASSEMB OF GOD	1	264	480	1.3	1.6
081 CATHOLIC	6	NA	9,736	27.4	33.2
081d LATIN	6	NA	9,736	27.4	33.2
089 CHR & MISS AL	2	71	188	.5	.6
097 CHR CHS&CHS CR	1	35	44*	.1	.2
127 CH GOD (CLEVE)	1	56	70*	.2	.2
133 CH GOD(7TH)DEN	1	14	18	.1	.1
151 L-D SAINTS	1	NA	174	.5	.6
164 CH LUTH CONF	1	37	49	.1	.2
165 CH OF NAZARENE	1	53	170	.5	.6
167 CHS OF CHRIST	1	40	70	.2	.2
193 EPISCOPAL	1	232	292	.8	1.0
203 EVAN FREE CH	1	0	30	.1	.1
207 E.L.C.A.	12	5,373	7,135	20.1	24.4
220 FREE LUTHERAN	1	24	32	.1	.1
257 HUTTERIAN BR	3	NA	300	.8	1.0
283 LUTH—MO SYNOD	8	2,743	3,625	10.2	12.4
313 N AM BAPT CONF	1	251	316*	.9	1.1
355 PRESB CH (USA)	3	563	708*	2.0	2.4
373 REF CH IN U.S.	1	113	146	.4	.5
403 SALVATION ARMY	1	84	101	.3	.3
413 S.D.A.	1	86	108*	.3	.4
419 SO BAPT CONV	2	43	54*	.2	.2
443 UN C OF CHRIST	3	848	1,067*	3.0	3.6
449 UN METHODIST	9	2,088	2,627*	7.4	9.0
467 WESLEYAN	1	66	120	.3	.4
469 WELS	1	311	395	1.1	1.3
496 JEWISH EST[1]	1	NA	0	-	-
BRULE	**18**	**1,930**	**4,393***	**80.1**	**100.0**
053 ASSEMB OF GOD	1	32	70	1.3	1.6
057 BAPT GEN CONF	1	129	175*	3.2	4.0
081 CATHOLIC	3	NA	1,692	30.8	38.5
081d LATIN	3	NA	1,692	30.8	38.5
097 CHR CHS&CHS CR	1	75	102*	1.9	2.3
167 CHS OF CHRIST	1	20	35	.6	.8
193 EPISCOPAL	2	72	118	2.2	2.7
207 E.L.C.A.	2	369	507	9.2	11.5
220 FREE LUTHERAN	2	212	241	4.4	5.5
257 HUTTERIAN BR	1	NA	100	1.8	2.3
283 LUTH—MO SYNOD	1	426	547	10.0	12.5
355 PRESB CH (USA)	1	42	57*	1.0	1.3
443 UN C OF CHRIST	1	499	676*	12.3	15.4
449 UN METHODIST	1	54	73*	1.3	1.7
BUFFALO	**6**	**111**	**1,029***	**58.5**	**100.0**
081 CATHOLIC	2	NA	712	40.5	69.2
081d LATIN	2	NA	712	40.5	69.2
193 EPISCOPAL	1	27	75	4.3	7.3
339 PENT CH OF GOD	1	34	76	4.3	7.4
355 PRESB CH (USA)	1	48	76*	4.3	7.4
467 WESLEYAN	1	2	90	5.1	8.7
BUTTE	**17**	**1,593**	**3,246***	**41.0**	**100.0**
019 AMER BAPT USA	1	267	348*	4.4	10.7
053 ASSEMB OF GOD	1	30	56	.7	1.7
081 CATHOLIC	2	NA	824	10.4	25.4
081d LATIN	2	NA	824	10.4	25.4
151 L-D SAINTS	1	NA	220	2.8	6.8
193 EPISCOPAL	1	55	64	.8	2.0
207 E.L.C.A.	3	619	894	11.3	27.5
226 FRIENDS-USA	1	21	37*	.5	1.1
226b EFI	1	21	37*	.5	1.1
263 INT FOURSQ GOS	1	80	104*	1.3	3.2
329 OPEN BIBLE STD	2	NR	NR	-	-
419 SO BAPT CONV	1	9	12*	.2	.4
443 UN C OF CHRIST	1	264	344*	4.3	10.6
449 UN METHODIST	1	236	308*	3.9	9.5
467 WESLEYAN	1	12	35	.4	1.1
CAMPBELL	**12**	**1,059**	**1,714***	**87.2**	**100.0**
053 ASSEMB OF GOD	1	32	58	3.0	3.4
081 CATHOLIC	1	NA	344	17.5	20.1
081d LATIN	1	NA	344	17.5	20.1
127 CH GOD (CLEVE)	1	4	5*	.3	.3
207 E.L.C.A.	3	404	537	27.3	31.3
313 N AM BAPT CONF	1	165	208*	10.6	12.1
356 PRESB CH AMER	1	206	263	13.4	15.3
373 REF CH IN U.S.	2	138	171	8.7	10.0
443 UN C OF CHRIST	1	12	15*	.8	.9
469 WELS	1	98	113	5.8	6.6
CHARLES MIX	**37**	**2,630**	**6,540***	**71.6**	**100.0**
053 ASSEMB OF GOD	1	19	35	.4	.5
057 BAPT GEN CONF	1	48	64*	.7	1.0
081 CATHOLIC	6	NA	2,408	26.4	36.8
081d LATIN	6	NA	2,408	26.4	36.8
089 CHR & MISS AL	1	20	43	.5	.7
105 CHRISTIAN REF	1	337	490	5.4	7.5
151 L-D SAINTS	1	NA	36	.4	.6
163 CH OF LUTH BR	1	47	83	.9	1.3
193 EPISCOPAL	4	59	114	1.2	1.7
207 E.L.C.A.	3	411	575	6.3	8.8
257 HUTTERIAN BR	3	NA	300	3.3	4.6
283 LUTH—MO SYNOD	2	409	526	5.8	8.0
355 PRESB CH (USA)	6	550	733*	8.0	11.2
371 REF CH IN AM	1	187	363	4.0	5.6
413 S.D.A.	1	19	25*	.3	.4
443 UN C OF CHRIST	1	53	71*	.8	1.1
449 UN METHODIST	2	461	614*	6.7	9.4
467 WESLEYAN	1	2	50	.5	.8
469 WELS	1	8	10	.1	.2
CLARK	**28**	**2,299**	**4,009***	**91.1**	**100.0**
053 ASSEMB OF GOD	1	58	100	2.3	2.5
081 CATHOLIC	2	NA	538	12.2	13.4
081d LATIN	2	NA	538	12.2	13.4
207 E.L.C.A.	8	1,066	1,364	31.0	34.0
257 HUTTERIAN BR	4	NA	400	9.1	10.0
355 PRESB CH (USA)	2	123	157*	3.6	3.9
371 REF CH IN AM	1	69	194	4.4	4.8
419 SO BAPT CONV	1	0	0*	-	-
443 UN C OF CHRIST	2	200	256*	5.8	6.4
449 UN METHODIST	3	476	609*	13.8	15.2
469 WELS	4	307	391	8.9	9.8
CLAY	**27**	**3,560**	**8,089***	**61.3**	**100.0**
019 AMER BAPT USA	1	169	202*	1.5	2.5
053 ASSEMB OF GOD	1	29	60	.5	.7
081 CATHOLIC	3	NA	3,418	25.9	42.3
081d LATIN	3	NA	3,418	25.9	42.3
089 CHR & MISS AL	1	47	95	.7	1.2
105 CHRISTIAN REF	1	41	59	.4	.7
151 L-D SAINTS	1	NA	117	.9	1.4
167 CHS OF CHRIST	1	13	25	.2	.3
193 EPISCOPAL	1	51	70	.5	.9
207 E.L.C.A.	6	2,112	2,706	20.5	33.5
283 LUTH—MO SYNOD	1	226	298	2.3	3.7
329 OPEN BIBLE STD	1	NR	NR	-	-
419 SO BAPT CONV	1	57	68*	.5	.8
435 UNITARIAN-UNIV	1	15	15	.1	.2
443 UN C OF CHRIST	2	267	319*	2.4	3.9
449 UN METHODIST	5	533	637*	4.8	7.9
CODINGTON	**41**	**8,342**	**17,303***	**76.2**	**100.0**
019 AMER BAPT USA	1	240	311*	1.4	1.8
045 APOSTOLIC LUTH	1	45	70	.3	.4
053 ASSEMB OF GOD	1	101	177	.8	1.0
081 CATHOLIC	7	NA	5,760	25.4	33.3
081d LATIN	7	NA	5,760	25.4	33.3
089 CHR & MISS AL	1	43	87	.4	.5
097 CHR CHS&CHS CR	1	30	39*	.2	.2

NA–Not applicable   NR–Not reported   *Total adherents estimated from known number of communicant, confirmed, full members.   - Represents a percent less than 0.1.   Percentages may not total due to rounding.
[1]See Appendix E   [2]See Appendix F   [3]See Appendix G   Lines in *italic* represent a breakdown of Catholic rites or Friends affiliations. They are included in their respective denominational total.

Table 4. Churches and Church Membership by County and Denomination: 1990

County and Denomination	Number of churches	Communicant, confirmed, full members	Total adherents		
			Number	Percent of total population	Percent of total adherents
111 CH CR,SCIENTST	1	NR	NR	-	-
151 L-D SAINTS	1	NA	112	.5	.6
163 CH OF LUTH BR	1	34	83	.4	.5
164 CH LUTH CONF	1	106	140	.6	.8
165 CH OF NAZARENE	1	16	37	.2	.2
167 CHS OF CHRIST	1	42	68	.3	.4
193 EPISCOPAL	1	110	147	.6	.8
207 E.L.C.A.	5	3,138	4,365	19.2	25.2
220 FREE LUTHERAN	1	116	139	.6	.8
263 INT FOURSQ GOS	1	124	161*	.7	.9
283 LUTH—MO SYNOD	1	284	399	1.8	2.3
355 PRESB CH (USA)	1	59	76*	.3	.4
403 SALVATION ARMY	1	108	118	.5	.7
413 S.D.A.	1	55	71*	.3	.4
443 UN C OF CHRIST	2	434	563*	2.5	3.3
449 UN METHODIST	3	1,458	1,890*	8.3	10.9
467 WESLEYAN	1	94	260	1.1	1.5
469 WELS	5	1,705	2,230	9.8	12.9
CORSON	**30**	**1,515**	**3,993***	**95.2**	**100.0**
053 ASSEMB OF GOD	2	41	77	1.8	1.9
081 CATHOLIC	8	NA	1,229	29.3	30.8
081d LATIN	8	NA	1,229	29.3	30.8
127 CH GOD (CLEVE)	1	5	7*	.2	.2
151 L-D SAINTS	1	NA	148	3.5	3.7
193 EPISCOPAL	6	657	1,414	33.7	35.4
207 E.L.C.A.	3	296	397	9.5	9.9
313 N AM BAPT CONF	2	88	127*	3.0	3.2
355 PRESB CH (USA)	2	116	167*	4.0	4.2
443 UN C OF CHRIST	3	186	267*	6.4	6.7
469 WELS	2	126	160	3.8	4.0
CUSTER	**15**	**1,264**	**2,161***	**35.0**	**100.0**
063 BEREAN FUND CH	1	34	59	1.0	2.7
081 CATHOLIC	2	NA	420	6.8	19.4
081d LATIN	2	NA	420	6.8	19.4
167 CHS OF CHRIST	1	55	65	1.1	3.0
207 E.L.C.A.	2	418	571	9.2	26.4
283 LUTH—MO SYNOD	1	151	191	3.1	8.8
329 OPEN BIBLE STD	1	NR	NR	-	-
413 S.D.A.	1	49	63*	1.0	2.9
419 SO BAPT CONV	1	123	157*	2.5	7.3
443 UN C OF CHRIST	2	354	452*	7.3	20.9
449 UN METHODIST	1	33	42*	.7	1.9
467 WESLEYAN	1	23	103	1.7	4.8
469 WELS	1	24	38	.6	1.8
DAVISON	**33**	**5,816**	**14,226***	**81.3**	**100.0**
053 ASSEMB OF GOD	1	53	118	.7	.8
057 BAPT GEN CONF	1	141	181*	1.0	1.3
081 CATHOLIC	5	NA	5,593	32.0	39.3
081d LATIN	5	NA	5,593	32.0	39.3
097 CHR CHS&CHS CR	1	44	57*	.3	.4
151 L-D SAINTS	1	NA	71	.4	.5
165 CH OF NAZARENE	1	211	401	2.3	2.8
167 CHS OF CHRIST	1	13	26	.1	.2
193 EPISCOPAL	1	136	149	.9	1.0
207 E.L.C.A.	4	1,835	2,509	14.3	17.6
257 HUTTERIAN BR	3	NA	300	1.7	2.1
283 LUTH—MO SYNOD	1	640	814	4.7	5.7
355 PRESB CH (USA)	1	243	313*	1.8	2.2
371 REF CH IN AM	1	241	448	2.6	3.1
373 REF CH IN U.S.	1	72	94	.5	.7
403 SALVATION ARMY	1	77	84	.5	.6
413 S.D.A.	1	19	24*	.1	.2
419 SO BAPT CONV	1	23	30*	.2	.2
443 UN C OF CHRIST	2	368	473*	2.7	3.3
449 UN METHODIST	3	1,457	1,874*	10.7	13.2
467 WESLEYAN	1	142	512	2.9	3.6
469 WELS	1	101	155	.9	1.1
DAY	**35**	**3,346**	**6,438***	**92.3**	**100.0**
019 AMER BAPT USA	1	11	14*	.2	.2
053 ASSEMB OF GOD	1	38	50	.7	.8
081 CATHOLIC	6	NA	1,967	28.2	30.6
081d LATIN	6	NA	1,967	28.2	30.6
089 CHR & MISS AL	1	14	22	.3	.3
193 EPISCOPAL	2	187	381	5.5	5.9
207 E.L.C.A.	13	2,141	2,818	40.4	43.8
220 FREE LUTHERAN	2	66	81	1.2	1.3
283 LUTH—MO SYNOD	2	265	325	4.7	5.0
355 PRESB CH (USA)	1	22	28*	.4	.4
419 SO BAPT CONV	1	64	81*	1.2	1.3
443 UN C OF CHRIST	1	41	52*	.7	.8
449 UN METHODIST	3	392	499*	7.2	7.8
467 WESLEYAN	1	105	120	1.7	1.9
DEUEL	**20**	**2,718**	**3,977***	**87.9**	**100.0**
057 BAPT GEN CONF	1	48	60*	1.3	1.5
081 CATHOLIC	2	NA	505	11.2	12.7
081d LATIN	2	NA	505	11.2	12.7
105 CHRISTIAN REF	1	82	129	2.9	3.2
163 CH OF LUTH BR	1	33	65	1.4	1.6
167 CHS OF CHRIST	1	6	10	.2	.3
207 E.L.C.A.	7	1,408	1,772	39.2	44.6
355 PRESB CH (USA)	1	35	44*	1.0	1.1
443 UN C OF CHRIST	1	119	149*	3.3	3.7
449 UN METHODIST	2	410	514*	11.4	12.9
469 WELS	3	577	729	16.1	18.3
DEWEY	**35**	**1,588**	**4,742***	**85.9**	**100.0**
019 AMER BAPT USA	1	167	248*	4.5	5.2
081 CATHOLIC	10	NA	1,705	30.9	36.0
081d LATIN	10	NA	1,705	30.9	36.0
127 CH GOD (CLEVE)	1	30	44*	.8	.9
145 CH GOD PROPHCY	1	40	59*	1.1	1.2
151 L-D SAINTS	1	NA	249	4.5	5.3
176 CCC, NOT NAT'L	1	14	21*	.4	.4
193 EPISCOPAL	8	347	954	17.3	20.1
207 E.L.C.A.	1	70	104	1.9	2.2
220 FREE LUTHERAN	1	50	64	1.2	1.3
313 N AM BAPT CONF	1	67	99*	1.8	2.1
339 PENT CH OF GOD	1	35	77	1.4	1.6
419 SO BAPT CONV	1	221	328*	5.9	6.9
443 UN C OF CHRIST	4	351	520*	9.4	11.0
449 UN METHODIST	1	81	120*	2.2	2.5
469 WELS	2	115	150	2.7	3.2
DOUGLAS	**18**	**2,406**	**3,998***	**106.7**	**100.0**
081 CATHOLIC	1	NA	358	9.6	9.0
081d LATIN	1	NA	358	9.6	9.0
105 CHRISTIAN REF	3	592	868	23.2	21.7
207 E.L.C.A.	3	291	404	10.8	10.1
257 HUTTERIAN BR	1	NA	100	2.7	2.5
283 LUTH—MO SYNOD	3	612	798	21.3	20.0
307 NETH REF CONGR	1	81	171	4.6	4.3
371 REF CH IN AM	3	484	845	22.6	21.1
443 UN C OF CHRIST	2	310	407*	10.9	10.2
449 UN METHODIST	1	36	47*	1.3	1.2
EDMUNDS	**23**	**1,744**	**3,652***	**83.8**	**100.0**
019 AMER BAPT USA	1	132	166*	3.8	4.5
081 CATHOLIC	4	NA	1,215	27.9	33.3
081d LATIN	4	NA	1,215	27.9	33.3
127 CH GOD (CLEVE)	1	28	35*	.8	1.0
164 CH LUTH CONF	2	137	161	3.7	4.4
207 E.L.C.A.	2	492	609	14.0	16.7
257 HUTTERIAN BR	3	NA	300	6.9	8.2
283 LUTH—MO SYNOD	1	60	79	1.8	2.2
355 PRESB CH (USA)	1	33	41*	.9	1.1
373 REF CH IN U.S.	1	81	92	2.1	2.5
413 S.D.A.	1	65	82*	1.9	2.2
443 UN C OF CHRIST	3	204	256*	5.9	7.0
449 UN METHODIST	1	58	73*	1.7	2.0
469 WELS	2	454	543	12.5	14.9
FALL RIVER	**29**	**1,657**	**5,089***	**69.2**	**100.0**
019 AMER BAPT USA	1	52	64*	.9	1.3
053 ASSEMB OF GOD	2	85	170	2.3	3.3
081 CATHOLIC	4	NA	2,621	35.6	51.5
081d LATIN	4	NA	2,621	35.6	51.5
097 CHR CHS&CHS CR	1	50	61*	.8	1.2
151 L-D SAINTS	1	NA	161	2.2	3.2
167 CHS OF CHRIST	1	15	27	.4	.5
193 EPISCOPAL	1	57	68	.9	1.3
203 EVAN FREE CH	1	22	37	.5	.7
207 E.L.C.A.	2	225	320	4.4	6.3
283 LUTH—MO SYNOD	1	338	441	6.0	8.7
355 PRESB CH (USA)	1	97	119*	1.6	2.3
413 S.D.A.	1	64	78*	1.1	1.5
419 SO BAPT CONV	2	88	108*	1.5	2.1
443 UN C OF CHRIST	1	55	67*	.9	1.3
449 UN METHODIST	6	431	528*	7.2	10.4
467 WESLEYAN	2	36	161	2.2	3.2
469 WELS	1	42	58	.8	1.1
FAULK	**22**	**1,100**	**2,694***	**98.2**	**100.0**
081 CATHOLIC	4	NA	817	29.8	30.3
081d LATIN	4	NA	817	29.8	30.3
151 L-D SAINTS	1	NA	59	2.2	2.2
164 CH LUTH CONF	1	23	29	1.1	1.1

NA–Not applicable NR–Not reported *Total adherents estimated from known number of communicant, confirmed, full members. - Represents a percent less than 0.1. Percentages may not total due to rounding.

[1]See Appendix E [2]See Appendix F [3]See Appendix G Lines in *italic* represent a breakdown of Catholic rites or Friends affiliations. They are included in their respective denominational total.

Table 4. Churches and Church Membership by County and Denomination: 1990

County and Denomination	Number of churches	Communicant, confirmed, full members	Total adherents Number	Percent of total population	Percent of total adherents
207 E.L.C.A.	2	138	190	6.9	7.1
257 HUTTERIAN BR	4	NA	400	14.6	14.8
283 LUTH—MO SYNOD	3	214	273	9.9	10.1
443 UN C OF CHRIST	1	24	31*	1.1	1.2
449 UN METHODIST	6	701	895*	32.6	33.2
GRANT	**24**	**3,663**	**7,063***	**84.4**	**100.0**
053 ASSEMB OF GOD	1	86	135	1.6	1.9
057 BAPT GEN CONF	2	22	29*	.3	.4
081 CATHOLIC	3	NA	2,218	26.5	31.4
081d LATIN	3	NA	2,218	26.5	31.4
193 EPISCOPAL	1	26	26	.3	.4
207 E.L.C.A.	4	1,236	1,619	19.3	22.9
283 LUTH—MO SYNOD	3	1,033	1,388	16.6	19.7
313 N AM BAPT CONF	1	122	159*	1.9	2.3
355 PRESB CH (USA)	1	38	49*	.6	.7
443 UN C OF CHRIST	1	78	102*	1.2	1.4
449 UN METHODIST	5	919	1,197*	14.3	16.9
469 WELS	2	103	141	1.7	2.0
GREGORY	**29**	**2,211**	**4,106***	**76.6**	**100.0**
019 AMER BAPT USA	2	271	350*	6.5	8.5
053 ASSEMB OF GOD	2	49	69	1.3	1.7
063 BEREAN FUND CH	1	36	92	1.7	2.2
081 CATHOLIC	5	NA	1,149	21.4	28.0
081d LATIN	5	NA	1,149	21.4	28.0
151 L-D SAINTS	1	NA	39	.7	.9
193 EPISCOPAL	3	69	98	1.8	2.4
283 LUTH—MO SYNOD	2	518	673	12.6	16.4
355 PRESB CH (USA)	1	29	37*	.7	.9
419 SO BAPT CONV	1	42	54*	1.0	1.3
443 UN C OF CHRIST	3	290	374*	7.0	9.1
449 UN METHODIST	4	501	647*	12.1	15.8
469 WELS	4	406	524	9.8	12.8
HAAKON	**18**	**760**	**2,021***	**77.0**	**100.0**
019 AMER BAPT USA	1	26	36*	1.4	1.8
081 CATHOLIC	3	NA	762	29.0	37.7
081d LATIN	3	NA	762	29.0	37.7
151 L-D SAINTS	1	NA	104	4.0	5.1
203 EVAN FREE CH	2	48	83	3.2	4.1
207 E.L.C.A.	4	300	487	18.6	24.1
283 LUTH—MO SYNOD	2	181	263	10.0	13.0
329 OPEN BIBLE STD	1	NR	NR	-	-
355 PRESB CH (USA)	1	98	137*	5.2	6.8
443 UN C OF CHRIST	1	15	21*	.8	1.0
449 UN METHODIST	2	92	128*	4.9	6.3
HAMLIN	**22**	**2,386**	**3,996***	**80.3**	**100.0**
045 APOSTOLIC LUTH	1	50	90	1.8	2.3
057 BAPT GEN CONF	1	59	76*	1.5	1.9
081 CATHOLIC	3	NA	618	12.4	15.5
081d LATIN	3	NA	618	12.4	15.5
164 CH LUTH CONF	1	28	40	.8	1.0
207 E.L.C.A.	7	1,469	1,917	38.5	48.0
257 HUTTERIAN BR	2	NA	200	4.0	5.0
355 PRESB CH (USA)	1	251	325*	6.5	8.1
371 REF CH IN AM	1	118	215	4.3	5.4
443 UN C OF CHRIST	2	176	228*	4.6	5.7
469 WELS	3	235	287	5.8	7.2
HAND	**13**	**990**	**2,528***	**59.2**	**100.0**
053 ASSEMB OF GOD	1	24	34	.8	1.3
081 CATHOLIC	3	NA	1,105	25.9	43.7
081d LATIN	3	NA	1,105	25.9	43.7
151 L-D SAINTS	1	NA	19	.4	.8
165 CH OF NAZARENE	1	40	87	2.0	3.4
207 E.L.C.A.	1	311	405	9.5	16.0
257 HUTTERIAN BR	1	NA	100	2.3	4.0
355 PRESB CH (USA)	1	221	279*	6.5	11.0
419 SO BAPT CONV	1	36	46*	1.1	1.8
443 UN C OF CHRIST	1	41	52*	1.2	2.1
449 UN METHODIST	2	317	401*	9.4	15.9
HANSON	**13**	**868**	**2,629***	**87.8**	**100.0**
081 CATHOLIC	4	NA	1,313	43.9	49.9
081d LATIN	4	NA	1,313	43.9	49.9
257 HUTTERIAN BR	2	NA	200	6.7	7.6
283 LUTH—MO SYNOD	2	234	289	9.7	11.0
313 N AM BAPT CONF	2	407	531*	17.7	20.2
355 PRESB CH (USA)	1	58	76*	2.5	2.9
449 UN METHODIST	2	169	220*	7.3	8.4
HARDING	**12**	**368**	**822***	**49.3**	**100.0**
053 ASSEMB OF GOD	1	9	12	.7	1.5
081 CATHOLIC	4	NA	279	16.7	33.9
081d LATIN	4	NA	279	16.7	33.9
207 E.L.C.A.	4	237	367	22.0	44.6
220 FREE LUTHERAN	1	58	78	4.7	9.5
443 UN C OF CHRIST	1	46	62*	3.7	7.5
449 UN METHODIST	1	18	24*	1.4	2.9
HUGHES	**34**	**5,827**	**11,077***	**74.8**	**100.0**
019 AMER BAPT USA	1	200	262*	1.8	2.4
053 ASSEMB OF GOD	2	142	190	1.3	1.7
081 CATHOLIC	3	NA	2,853	19.3	25.8
081d LATIN	3	NA	2,853	19.3	25.8
097 CHR CHS&CHS CR	1	110	144*	1.0	1.3
151 L-D SAINTS	1	NA	162	1.1	1.5
164 CH LUTH CONF	1	5	6	-	.1
165 CH OF NAZARENE	1	35	117	.8	1.1
167 CHS OF CHRIST	2	73	90	.6	.8
193 EPISCOPAL	1	120	156	1.1	1.4
207 E.L.C.A.	2	1,676	2,330	15.7	21.0
263 INT FOURSQ GOS	1	33	43*	.3	.4
283 LUTH—MO SYNOD	3	1,043	1,430	9.7	12.9
329 OPEN BIBLE STD	1	NR	NR	-	-
355 PRESB CH (USA)	1	136	178*	1.2	1.6
373 REF CH IN U.S.	1	36	51	.3	.5
413 S.D.A.	2	289	379*	2.6	3.4
419 SO BAPT CONV	2	209	274*	1.8	2.5
443 UN C OF CHRIST	1	352	461*	3.1	4.2
449 UN METHODIST	4	1,238	1,623*	11.0	14.7
467 WESLEYAN	2	72	239	1.6	2.2
469 WELS	1	58	89	.6	.8
HUTCHINSON	**34**	**5,198**	**7,714***	**93.4**	**100.0**
053 ASSEMB OF GOD	1	9	25	.3	.3
081 CATHOLIC	2	NA	1,096	13.3	14.2
081d LATIN	2	NA	1,096	13.3	14.2
105 CHRISTIAN REF	3	320	407	4.9	5.3
207 E.L.C.A.	7	1,269	1,580	19.1	20.5
220 FREE LUTHERAN	1	81	112	1.4	1.5
237 GC MENN BR CHS	1	95	118*	1.4	1.5
257 HUTTERIAN BR	2	NA	200	2.4	2.6
283 LUTH—MO SYNOD	6	1,055	1,308	15.8	17.0
287 MENN GEN CONF	2	532	611	7.4	7.9
291 MISSIONARY CH	1	79	75	.9	1.0
313 N AM BAPT CONF	1	87	108*	1.3	1.4
373 REF CH IN U.S.	1	248	310	3.8	4.0
438 UN BRETH IN CR	1	21	24	.3	.3
443 UN C OF CHRIST	3	1,162	1,442*	17.5	18.7
449 UN METHODIST	2	240	298*	3.6	3.9
HYDE	**7**	**590**	**1,402***	**82.7**	**100.0**
081 CATHOLIC	3	NA	603	35.6	43.0
081d LATIN	3	NA	603	35.6	43.0
089 CHR & MISS AL	1	23	77	4.5	5.5
097 CHR CHS&CHS CR	1	42	53*	3.1	3.8
207 E.L.C.A.	1	351	448	26.4	32.0
449 UN METHODIST	1	174	221*	13.0	15.8
JACKSON	**11**	**395**	**1,192***	**42.4**	**100.0**
081 CATHOLIC	4	NA	387	13.8	32.5
081d LATIN	4	NA	387	13.8	32.5
151 L-D SAINTS	1	NA	151	5.4	12.7
193 EPISCOPAL	2	87	229	8.1	19.2
207 E.L.C.A.	2	219	304	10.8	25.5
283 LUTH—MO SYNOD	1	44	58	2.1	4.9
355 PRESB CH (USA)	1	45	63*	2.2	5.3
JERAULD	**11**	**1,189**	**1,781***	**73.4**	**100.0**
081 CATHOLIC	1	NA	270	11.1	15.2
081d LATIN	1	NA	270	11.1	15.2
207 E.L.C.A.	1	316	420	17.3	23.6
221 FREE METHODIST	1	28	36	1.5	2.0
283 LUTH—MO SYNOD	1	105	133	5.5	7.5
313 N AM BAPT CONF	1	95	118*	4.9	6.6
443 UN C OF CHRIST	3	318	396*	16.3	22.2
449 UN METHODIST	3	327	408*	16.8	22.9
JONES	**9**	**548**	**946***	**71.5**	**100.0**
053 ASSEMB OF GOD	1	13	35	2.6	3.7
081 CATHOLIC	2	NA	165	12.5	17.4
081d LATIN	2	NA	165	12.5	17.4
203 EVAN FREE CH	2	27	77	5.8	8.1
283 LUTH—MO SYNOD	2	254	341	25.8	36.0

NA–Not applicable   NR–Not reported   *Total adherents estimated from known number of communicant, confirmed, full members.   - Represents a percent less than 0.1.   Percentages may not total due to rounding.

[1]See Appendix E   [2]See Appendix F   [3]See Appendix G   Lines in *italic* represent a breakdown of Catholic rites or Friends affiliations. They are included in their respective denominational total.

Table 4. Churches and Church Membership by County and Denomination: 1990

County and Denomination	Number of churches	Communicant, confirmed, full members	Total adherents Number	Percent of total population	Percent of total adherents
449 UN METHODIST	2	254	328*	24.8	34.7
KINGSBURY	**30**	**3,528**	**5,749***	**97.0**	**100.0**
053 ASSEMB OF GOD	1	9	12	.2	.2
081 CATHOLIC	4	NA	883	14.9	15.4
081d LATIN	4	NA	883	14.9	15.4
089 CHR & MISS AL	1	44	143	2.4	2.5
097 CHR CHS&CHS CR	1	25	32*	.5	.6
143 CG IN CR(MENN)	1	97	123*	2.1	2.1
193 EPISCOPAL	1	10	23	.4	.4
207 E.L.C.A.	8	2,333	3,046	51.4	53.0
220 FREE LUTHERAN	1	92	120	2.0	2.1
257 HUTTERIAN BR	2	NA	200	3.4	3.5
283 LUTH—MO SYNOD	1	46	64	1.1	1.1
355 PRESB CH (USA)	1	55	70*	1.2	1.2
443 UN C OF CHRIST	3	319	403*	6.8	7.0
449 UN METHODIST	5	498	630*	10.6	11.0
LAKE	**24**	**4,165**	**7,665***	**72.7**	**100.0**
019 AMER BAPT USA	1	130	165*	1.6	2.2
053 ASSEMB OF GOD	1	59	102	1.0	1.3
081 CATHOLIC	2	NA	1,929	18.3	25.2
081d LATIN	2	NA	1,929	18.3	25.2
151 L-D SAINTS	1	NA	48	.5	.6
165 CH OF NAZARENE	1	52	111	1.1	1.4
193 EPISCOPAL	1	30	35	.3	.5
207 E.L.C.A.	4	1,735	2,366	22.4	30.9
257 HUTTERIAN BR	1	NA	100	.9	1.3
283 LUTH—MO SYNOD	3	608	839	8.0	10.9
284 LUTH CH-AM ASC	2	369	470	4.5	6.1
313 N AM BAPT CONF	1	267	339*	3.2	4.4
355 PRESB CH (USA)	2	207	263*	2.5	3.4
413 S.D.A.	1	38	48*	.5	.6
443 UN C OF CHRIST	1	120	152*	1.4	2.0
449 UN METHODIST	2	550	698*	6.6	9.1
LAWRENCE	**36**	**4,688**	**9,228***	**44.7**	**100.0**
019 AMER BAPT USA	1	122	155*	.8	1.7
045 APOSTOLIC LUTH	1	30	50	.2	.5
053 ASSEMB OF GOD	2	182	361	1.7	3.9
081 CATHOLIC	3	NA	2,585	12.5	28.0
081d LATIN	3	NA	2,585	12.5	28.0
111 CH CR,SCIENTST	1	NR	NR	-	-
151 L-D SAINTS	1	NA	181	.9	2.0
165 CH OF NAZARENE	1	71	85	.4	.9
167 CHS OF CHRIST	2	54	86	.4	.9
193 EPISCOPAL	3	275	389	1.9	4.2
207 E.L.C.A.	4	1,338	1,962	9.5	21.3
221 FREE METHODIST	1	7	21	.1	.2
223 FREE WILL BAPT	1	25	32*	.2	.3
263 INT FOURSQ GOS	1	124	158*	.8	1.7
283 LUTH—MO SYNOD	2	546	711	3.4	7.7
313 N AM BAPT CONF	1	143	182*	.9	2.0
355 PRESB CH (USA)	2	134	171*	.8	1.9
413 S.D.A.	1	98	125*	.6	1.4
419 SO BAPT CONV	2	71	90*	.4	1.0
443 UN C OF CHRIST	2	407	518*	2.5	5.6
449 UN METHODIST	3	1,006	1,280*	6.2	13.9
469 WELS	1	55	86	.4	.9
LINCOLN	**28**	**5,101**	**8,225***	**53.3**	**100.0**
053 ASSEMB OF GOD	1	25	35	.2	.4
081 CATHOLIC	4	NA	1,092	7.1	13.3
081d LATIN	4	NA	1,092	7.1	13.3
165 CH OF NAZARENE	1	44	61	.4	.7
207 E.L.C.A.	13	3,286	4,642	30.1	56.4
220 FREE LUTHERAN	1	77	102	.7	1.2
355 PRESB CH (USA)	1	124	165*	1.1	2.0
356 PRESB CH AMER	1	407	459	3.0	5.6
371 REF CH IN AM	3	483	799	5.2	9.7
443 UN C OF CHRIST	1	55	73*	.5	.9
449 UN METHODIST	2	600	797*	5.2	9.7
LYMAN	**16**	**867**	**2,080***	**57.2**	**100.0**
053 ASSEMB OF GOD	1	7	18	.5	.9
081 CATHOLIC	4	NA	808	22.2	38.8
081d LATIN	4	NA	808	22.2	38.8
151 L-D SAINTS	1	NA	56	1.5	2.7
193 EPISCOPAL	1	101	185	5.1	8.9
207 E.L.C.A.	3	255	324	8.9	15.6
283 LUTH—MO SYNOD	2	213	267	7.3	12.8
449 UN METHODIST	3	288	392*	10.8	18.8
467 WESLEYAN	1	3	30	.8	1.4

County and Denomination	Number of churches	Communicant, confirmed, full members	Total adherents Number	Percent of total population	Percent of total adherents
MC COOK	**26**	**2,572**	**5,400***	**94.9**	**100.0**
057 BAPT GEN CONF	2	341	436*	7.7	8.1
081 CATHOLIC	4	NA	2,038	35.8	37.7
081d LATIN	4	NA	2,038	35.8	37.7
097 CHR CHS&CHS CR	1	50	64*	1.1	1.2
165 CH OF NAZARENE	1	33	32	.6	.6
207 E.L.C.A.	5	764	980	17.2	18.1
237 GC MENN BR CHS	1	166	212*	3.7	3.9
257 HUTTERIAN BR	1	NA	100	1.8	1.9
283 LUTH—MO SYNOD	3	535	670	11.8	12.4
287 MENN GEN CONF	2	183	229	4.0	4.2
355 PRESB CH (USA)	3	238	304*	5.3	5.6
449 UN METHODIST	3	262	335*	5.9	6.2
MC PHERSON	**16**	**2,160**	**3,065***	**95.0**	**100.0**
081 CATHOLIC	2	NA	370	11.5	12.1
081d LATIN	2	NA	370	11.5	12.1
133 CH GOD(7TH)DEN	1	14	19	.6	.6
207 E.L.C.A.	3	1,043	1,253	38.8	40.9
257 HUTTERIAN BR	1	NA	100	3.1	3.3
283 LUTH—MO SYNOD	1	118	158	4.9	5.2
313 N AM BAPT CONF	2	185	223*	6.9	7.3
373 REF CH IN U.S.	2	314	355	11.0	11.6
413 S.D.A.	1	17	21*	.7	.7
443 UN C OF CHRIST	1	160	193*	6.0	6.3
449 UN METHODIST	2	309	373*	11.6	12.2
MARSHALL	**25**	**2,640**	**4,280***	**88.4**	**100.0**
053 ASSEMB OF GOD	1	9	31	.6	.7
081 CATHOLIC	4	NA	780	16.1	18.2
081d LATIN	4	NA	780	16.1	18.2
193 EPISCOPAL	1	24	26	.5	.6
203 EVAN FREE CH	1	30	46	.9	1.1
207 E.L.C.A.	7	1,512	1,912	39.5	44.7
220 FREE LUTHERAN	1	20	34	.7	.8
257 HUTTERIAN BR	1	NA	100	2.1	2.3
283 LUTH—MO SYNOD	1	244	327	6.8	7.6
355 PRESB CH (USA)	5	540	684*	14.1	16.0
371 REF CH IN AM	1	42	63	1.3	1.5
449 UN METHODIST	2	219	277*	5.7	6.5
MEADE	**41**	**3,326**	**8,019***	**36.7**	**100.0**
019 AMER BAPT USA	2	61	82*	.4	1.0
053 ASSEMB OF GOD	1	34	78	.4	1.0
081 CATHOLIC	7	NA	2,536	11.6	31.6
081d LATIN	7	NA	2,536	11.6	31.6
097 CHR CHS&CHS CR	2	129	174*	.8	2.2
127 CH GOD (CLEVE)	1	14	19*	.1	.2
145 CH GOD PROPHCY	1	40	54*	.2	.7
151 L-D SAINTS	2	NA	104	.5	1.3
165 CH OF NAZARENE	1	12	62	.3	.8
167 CHS OF CHRIST	2	111	158	.7	2.0
176 CCC, NOT NAT'L	1	30	40*	.2	.5
193 EPISCOPAL	2	75	102	.5	1.3
207 E.L.C.A.	2	720	996	4.6	12.4
220 FREE LUTHERAN	1	60	80	.4	1.0
283 LUTH—MO SYNOD	1	152	223	1.0	2.8
329 OPEN BIBLE STD	2	NR	NR	-	-
355 PRESB CH (USA)	2	371	501*	2.3	6.2
419 SO BAPT CONV	4	434	586*	2.7	7.3
449 UN METHODIST	3	687	927*	4.2	11.6
467 WESLEYAN	2	132	938	4.3	11.7
469 WELS	2	155	212	1.0	2.6
497 BLACK BAPT EST[2]	NA	109	147*	.7	1.8
MELLETTE	**14**	**460**	**971***	**45.4**	**100.0**
019 AMER BAPT USA	1	23	32*	1.5	3.3
053 ASSEMB OF GOD	1	7	8	.4	.8
081 CATHOLIC	4	NA	362	16.9	37.3
081d LATIN	4	NA	362	16.9	37.3
164 CH LUTH CONF	1	59	86	4.0	8.9
165 CH OF NAZARENE	1	25	29	1.4	3.0
193 EPISCOPAL	3	128	156	7.3	16.1
283 LUTH—MO SYNOD	1	72	94	4.4	9.7
443 UN C OF CHRIST	1	21	29*	1.4	3.0
449 UN METHODIST	1	125	175*	8.2	18.0
MINER	**15**	**1,204**	**2,564***	**78.4**	**100.0**
053 ASSEMB OF GOD	1	33	67	2.0	2.6
081 CATHOLIC	2	NA	889	27.2	34.7
081d LATIN	2	NA	889	27.2	34.7
165 CH OF NAZARENE	1	24	69	2.1	2.7
207 E.L.C.A.	3	462	571	17.5	22.3
257 HUTTERIAN BR	1	NA	100	3.1	3.9

NA–Not applicable NR–Not reported *Total adherents estimated from known number of communicant, confirmed, full members. - Represents a percent less than 0.1. Percentages may not total due to rounding.
[1]See Appendix E [2]See Appendix F [3]See Appendix G Lines in *italic* represent a breakdown of Catholic rites or Friends affiliations. They are included in their respective denominational total.

Table 4. Churches and Church Membership by County and Denomination: 1990

| County and Denomination | Number of churches | Communicant, confirmed, full members | Total adherents | | |
			Number	Percent of total population	Percent of total adherents
283 LUTH—MO SYNOD	1	275	344	10.5	13.4
355 PRESB CH (USA)	2	100	128*	3.9	5.0
443 UN C OF CHRIST	2	88	112*	3.4	4.4
449 UN METHODIST	2	222	284*	8.7	11.1
MINNEHAHA	**141**	**42,316**	**82,134***	**66.3**	**100.0**
019 AMER BAPT USA	5	2,296	2,938*	2.4	3.6
053 ASSEMB OF GOD	3	685	1,413	1.1	1.7
057 BAPT GEN CONF	2	1,207	1,544*	1.2	1.9
081 CATHOLIC	14	NA	23,364	18.9	28.4
081d LATIN	*14*	*NA*	*23,364*	*18.9*	*28.4*
089 CHR & MISS AL	1	27	82	.1	.1
093 CHR CH (DISC)	1	326	419	.3	.5
097 CHR CHS&CHS CR	1	75	96*	.1	.1
105 CHRISTIAN REF	3	860	1,360	1.1	1.7
111 CH CR,SCIENTST	1	NR	NR	-	-
123 CH GOD (ANDER)	1	90	90	.1	.1
151 L-D SAINTS	2	NA	566	.5	.7
164 CH LUTH CONF	1	21	34	-	-
167 CHS OF CHRIST	3	101	135	.1	.2
193 EPISCOPAL	3	744	921	.7	1.1
203 EVAN FREE CH	1	47	54	-	.1
207 E.L.C.A.	33	20,830	28,404	22.9	34.6
209 EVAN LUTH SYN	1	72	85	.1	.1
220 FREE LUTHERAN	1	51	68	.1	.1
221 FREE METHODIST	1	22	61	-	.1
226 FRIENDS-USA	1	1	9	-	-
226f INDEPENDNT	*1*	*1*	*9*	*-*	*-*
237 GC MENN BR CHS	1	17	22*	-	-
246 GREEK ORTHODOX	1	NR	NR	-	-
259 IFCA	1	NR	NR	-	-
274 LAT EVAN LUTH	1	24	24	-	-
283 LUTH—MO SYNOD	9	3,001	3,971	3.2	4.8
285 MENNONITE CH	1	31	34	-	-
287 MENN GEN CONF	2	96	124	.1	.2
291 MISSIONARY CH	1	13	28	-	-
307 NETH REF CONGR	1	37	85	.1	.1
313 N AM BAPT CONF	4	600	768*	.6	.9
329 OPEN BIBLE STD	1	NR	NR	-	-
355 PRESB CH (USA)	5	1,904	2,436*	2.0	3.0
371 REF CH IN AM	6	1,241	2,173	1.8	2.6
373 REF CH IN U.S.	1	20	31	-	-
403 SALVATION ARMY	1	180	197	.2	.2
413 S.D.A.	1	215	275*	.2	.3
419 SO BAPT CONV	3	270	345*	.3	.4
435 UNITARIAN-UNIV	1	39	57	-	.1
443 UN C OF CHRIST	5	1,293	1,654*	1.3	2.0
449 UN METHODIST	11	5,013	6,414*	5.2	7.8
467 WESLEYAN	1	203	800	.6	1.0
469 WELS	2	465	663	.5	.8
496 JEWISH EST[1]	2	NA	135	.1	.2
497 BLACK BAPT EST[2]	NA	199	255*	.2	.3
MOODY	**20**	**2,452**	**4,626***	**71.1**	**100.0**
019 AMER BAPT USA	1	121	160*	2.5	3.5
081 CATHOLIC	2	NA	1,149	17.7	24.8
081d LATIN	*2*	*NA*	*1,149*	*17.7*	*24.8*
151 L-D SAINTS	1	NA	55	.8	1.2
167 CHS OF CHRIST	1	9	13	.2	.3
193 EPISCOPAL	1	27	61	.9	1.3
207 E.L.C.A.	5	1,279	1,726	26.5	37.3
257 HUTTERIAN BR	1	NA	100	1.5	2.2
283 LUTH—MO SYNOD	1	96	144	2.2	3.1
355 PRESB CH (USA)	2	327	433*	6.7	9.4
449 UN METHODIST	4	544	720*	11.1	15.6
469 WELS	1	49	65	1.0	1.4
PENNINGTON	**90**	**19,917**	**43,485***	**53.5**	**100.0**
019 AMER BAPT USA	2	347	456*	.6	1.0
053 ASSEMB OF GOD	4	513	1,285	1.6	3.0
057 BAPT GEN CONF	1	10	13*	-	-
081 CATHOLIC	9	NA	13,673	16.8	31.4
081d LATIN	*9*	*NA*	*13,673*	*16.8*	*31.4*
089 CHR & MISS AL	1	24	61	.1	.1
097 CHR CHS&CHS CR	1	360	473*	.6	1.1
105 CHRISTIAN REF	2	76	185	.2	.4
111 CH CR,SCIENTST	1	NR	NR	-	-
123 CH GOD (ANDER)	1	79	95	.1	.2
127 CH GOD (CLEVE)	1	65	85*	.1	.2
145 CH GOD PROPHCY	1	41	54*	.1	.1
151 L-D SAINTS	2	NA	1,214	1.5	2.8
164 CH LUTH CONF	1	33	52	.1	.1
165 CH OF NAZARENE	1	76	118	.1	.3
167 CHS OF CHRIST	2	206	231	.3	.5
193 EPISCOPAL	3	878	1,227	1.5	2.8
203 EVAN FREE CH	3	432	999	1.2	2.3
207 E.L.C.A.	7	4,355	6,123	7.5	14.1
221 FREE METHODIST	1	27	46	.1	.1
237 GC MENN BR CHS	1	82	108*	.1	.2
283 LUTH—MO SYNOD	6	2,117	2,918	3.6	6.7
313 N AM BAPT CONF	1	283	372*	.5	.9
329 OPEN BIBLE STD	1	NR	NR	-	-
355 PRESB CH (USA)	4	1,413	1,857*	2.3	4.3
403 SALVATION ARMY	1	114	133	.2	.3
413 S.D.A.	1	436	573*	.7	1.3
415 S-D BAPTIST GC	1	30	39*	-	.1
419 SO BAPT CONV	9	3,178	4,177*	5.1	9.6
435 UNITARIAN-UNIV	1	20	21	-	-
443 UN C OF CHRIST	5	1,036	1,362*	1.7	3.1
449 UN METHODIST	9	2,561	3,366*	4.1	7.7
467 WESLEYAN	4	335	1,051	1.3	2.4
469 WELS	1	449	670	.8	1.5
496 JEWISH EST[1]	1	NA	0	-	-
497 BLACK BAPT EST[2]	NA	341	448*	.6	1.0
PERKINS	**26**	**1,752**	**3,012***	**76.6**	**100.0**
081 CATHOLIC	4	NA	713	18.1	23.7
081d LATIN	*4*	*NA*	*713*	*18.1*	*23.7*
105 CHRISTIAN REF	1	56	83	2.1	2.8
127 CH GOD (CLEVE)	2	203	256*	6.5	8.5
164 CH LUTH CONF	1	137	187	4.8	6.2
167 CHS OF CHRIST	1	18	28	.7	.9
193 EPISCOPAL	1	32	32	.8	1.1
207 E.L.C.A.	7	755	979	24.9	32.5
355 PRESB CH (USA)	3	316	398*	10.1	13.2
356 PRESB CH AMER	1	47	60	1.5	2.0
413 S.D.A.	2	47	59*	1.5	2.0
449 UN METHODIST	1	19	24*	.6	.8
467 WESLEYAN	1	44	84	2.1	2.8
469 WELS	1	78	109	2.8	3.6
POTTER	**13**	**969**	**3,357***	**105.2**	**100.0**
081 CATHOLIC	3	NA	2,147	67.3	64.0
081d LATIN	*3*	*NA*	*2,147*	*67.3*	*64.0*
127 CH GOD (CLEVE)	1	25	32*	1.0	1.0
193 EPISCOPAL	1	22	20	.6	.6
237 GC MENN BR CHS	1	70	89*	2.8	2.7
283 LUTH—MO SYNOD	2	402	494	15.5	14.7
419 SO BAPT CONV	1	13	16*	.5	.5
449 UN METHODIST	2	403	511*	16.0	15.2
467 WESLEYAN	1	17	26	.8	.8
469 WELS	1	17	22	.7	.7
ROBERTS	**41**	**4,451**	**7,788***	**78.6**	**100.0**
053 ASSEMB OF GOD	3	249	391	3.9	5.0
057 BAPT GEN CONF	1	28	36*	.4	.5
081 CATHOLIC	5	NA	1,633	16.5	21.0
081d LATIN	*5*	*NA*	*1,633*	*16.5*	*21.0*
089 CHR & MISS AL	3	89	134	1.4	1.7
193 EPISCOPAL	3	450	824	8.3	10.6
207 E.L.C.A.	10	2,190	2,804	28.3	36.0
220 FREE LUTHERAN	2	127	164	1.7	2.1
257 HUTTERIAN BR	1	NA	100	1.0	1.3
283 LUTH—MO SYNOD	4	619	788	7.9	10.1
355 PRESB CH (USA)	5	552	719*	7.3	9.2
413 S.D.A.	1	12	16*	.2	.2
419 SO BAPT CONV	1	84	109*	1.1	1.4
449 UN METHODIST	1	22	29*	.3	.4
469 WELS	1	29	41	.4	.5
SANBORN	**14**	**802**	**1,937***	**68.4**	**100.0**
081 CATHOLIC	3	NA	810	28.6	41.8
081d LATIN	*3*	*NA*	*810*	*28.6*	*41.8*
207 E.L.C.A.	4	372	461	16.3	23.8
257 HUTTERIAN BR	1	NA	100	3.5	5.2
283 LUTH—MO SYNOD	1	71	96	3.4	5.0
355 PRESB CH (USA)	1	25	33*	1.2	1.7
419 SO BAPT CONV	1	30	39*	1.4	2.0
443 UN C OF CHRIST	1	184	241*	8.5	12.4
449 UN METHODIST	2	120	157*	5.5	8.1
SHANNON	**41**	**1,279**	**4,818***	**48.7**	**100.0**
081 CATHOLIC	11	NA	2,244	22.7	46.6
081d LATIN	*11*	*NA*	*2,244*	*22.7*	*46.6*
123 CH GOD (ANDER)	1	6	16	.2	.3
151 L-D SAINTS	2	NA	359	3.6	7.5
193 EPISCOPAL	16	822	1,332	13.5	27.6
237 GC MENN BR CHS	2	25	39*	.4	.8
355 PRESB CH (USA)	3	157	246*	2.5	5.1
413 S.D.A.	1	45	71*	.7	1.5
419 SO BAPT CONV	1	114	179*	1.8	3.7

NA–Not applicable   NR–Not reported   *Total adherents estimated from known number of communicant, confirmed, full members.   - Represents a percent less than 0.1.   Percentages may not total due to rounding.
[1]See Appendix E   [2]See Appendix F   [3]See Appendix G   Lines in *italic* represent a breakdown of Catholic rites or Friends affiliations. They are included in their respective denominational total.

Table 4. Churches and Church Membership by County and Denomination: 1990

County and Denomination	Number of churches	Communicant, confirmed, full members	Total adherents Number	Percent of total population	Percent of total adherents
467 WESLEYAN	3	6	180	1.8	3.7
469 WELS	1	104	152	1.5	3.2
SPINK	**34**	**3,012**	**6,045***	**75.7**	**100.0**
053 ASSEMB OF GOD	1	43	80	1.0	1.3
081 CATHOLIC	7	NA	1,862	23.3	30.8
081d LATIN	*7*	*NA*	*1,862*	*23.3*	*30.8*
207 E.L.C.A.	2	529	683	8.6	11.3
237 GC MENN BR CHS	1	95	121*	1.5	2.0
257 HUTTERIAN BR	3	NA	300	3.8	5.0
283 LUTH—MO SYNOD	3	508	662	8.3	11.0
287 MENN GEN CONF	1	104	126	1.6	2.1
355 PRESB CH (USA)	1	29	37*	.5	.6
413 S.D.A.	1	52	66*	.8	1.1
419 SO BAPT CONV	1	47	60*	.8	1.0
443 UN C OF CHRIST	5	604	767*	9.6	12.7
449 UN METHODIST	7	923	1,173*	14.7	19.4
467 WESLEYAN	1	78	108	1.4	1.8
STANLEY	**4**	**189**	**615***	**25.1**	**100.0**
081 CATHOLIC	1	NA	364	14.8	59.2
081d LATIN	*1*	*NA*	*364*	*14.8*	*59.2*
193 EPISCOPAL	1	66	73	3.0	11.9
207 E.L.C.A.	1	36	63	2.6	10.2
443 UN C OF CHRIST	1	87	115*	4.7	18.7
SULLY	**7**	**617**	**1,073***	**67.5**	**100.0**
081 CATHOLIC	1	NA	283	17.8	26.4
081d LATIN	*1*	*NA*	*283*	*17.8*	*26.4*
237 GC MENN BR CHS	1	48	62*	3.9	5.8
283 LUTH—MO SYNOD	2	211	270	17.0	25.2
355 PRESB CH (USA)	1	126	161*	10.1	15.0
449 UN METHODIST	2	232	297*	18.7	27.7
TODD	**21**	**568**	**5,562***	**66.6**	**100.0**
053 ASSEMB OF GOD	1	12	54	.6	1.0
081 CATHOLIC	7	NA	4,351	52.1	78.2
081d LATIN	*7*	*NA*	*4,351*	*52.1*	*78.2*
151 L-D SAINTS	1	NA	254	3.0	4.6
164 CH LUTH CONF	1	29	37	.4	.7
193 EPISCOPAL	8	385	438	5.2	7.9
449 UN METHODIST	1	46	73*	.9	1.3
467 WESLEYAN	1	13	230	2.8	4.1
469 WELS	1	83	125	1.5	2.2
TRIPP	**26**	**1,933**	**4,127***	**59.6**	**100.0**
019 AMER BAPT USA	2	141	185*	2.7	4.5
053 ASSEMB OF GOD	1	48	71	1.0	1.7
081 CATHOLIC	5	NA	1,353	19.5	32.8
081d LATIN	*5*	*NA*	*1,353*	*19.5*	*32.8*
093 CHR CH (DISC)	1	52	125	1.8	3.0
165 CH OF NAZARENE	1	43	91	1.3	2.2
193 EPISCOPAL	2	119	153	2.2	3.7
257 HUTTERIAN BR	1	NA	100	1.4	2.4
283 LUTH—MO SYNOD	3	272	369	5.3	8.9
339 PENT CH OF GOD	2	69	154	2.2	3.7
355 PRESB CH (USA)	1	51	67*	1.0	1.6
443 UN C OF CHRIST	1	23	30*	.4	.7
449 UN METHODIST	2	485	635*	9.2	15.4
469 WELS	4	630	794	11.5	19.2
TURNER	**43**	**5,542**	**8,287***	**96.6**	**100.0**
019 AMER BAPT USA	3	317	400*	4.7	4.8
053 ASSEMB OF GOD	1	18	30	.3	.4
081 CATHOLIC	4	NA	1,114	13.0	13.4
081d LATIN	*4*	*NA*	*1,114*	*13.0*	*13.4*
105 CHRISTIAN REF	1	55	61	.7	.7
123 CH GOD (ANDER)	1	173	196	2.3	2.4
165 CH OF NAZARENE	1	31	72	.8	.9
207 E.L.C.A.	6	1,396	1,791	20.9	21.6
211 FEL EVG BIB CH	1	70	80	.9	1.0
220 FREE LUTHERAN	1	76	91	1.1	1.1
283 LUTH—MO SYNOD	4	429	549	6.4	6.6
287 MENN GEN CONF	4	1,057	1,309	15.3	15.8
313 N AM BAPT CONF	1	241	304*	3.5	3.7
355 PRESB CH (USA)	4	383	483*	5.6	5.8
356 PRESB CH AMER	1	215	292	3.4	3.5
371 REF CH IN AM	4	525	814	9.5	9.8
413 S.D.A.	1	61	77*	.9	.9
443 UN C OF CHRIST	1	138	174*	2.0	2.1
449 UN METHODIST	4	357	450*	5.2	5.4
UNION	**26**	**3,759**	**6,986***	**68.6**	**100.0**
053 ASSEMB OF GOD	1	17	24	.2	.3

County and Denomination	Number of churches	Communicant, confirmed, full members	Total adherents Number	Percent of total population	Percent of total adherents
057 BAPT GEN CONF	3	464	602*	5.9	8.6
081 CATHOLIC	4	NA	1,990	19.5	28.5
081d LATIN	*4*	*NA*	*1,990*	*19.5*	*28.5*
203 EVAN FREE CH	1	115	140	1.4	2.0
207 E.L.C.A.	7	2,068	2,759	27.1	39.5
283 LUTH—MO SYNOD	1	188	240	2.4	3.4
419 SO BAPT CONV	2	71	92*	.9	1.3
443 UN C OF CHRIST	3	356	462*	4.5	6.6
449 UN METHODIST	3	378	490*	4.8	7.0
467 WESLEYAN	1	102	187	1.8	2.7
WALWORTH	**24**	**3,060**	**5,243***	**86.1**	**100.0**
019 AMER BAPT USA	1	109	136*	2.2	2.6
053 ASSEMB OF GOD	1	75	100	1.6	1.9
081 CATHOLIC	2	NA	1,328	21.8	25.3
081d LATIN	*2*	*NA*	*1,328*	*21.8*	*25.3*
127 CH GOD (CLEVE)	1	44	55*	.9	1.0
151 L-D SAINTS	1	NA	75	1.2	1.4
193 EPISCOPAL	1	32	44	.7	.8
207 E.L.C.A.	4	1,296	1,616	26.5	30.8
413 S.D.A.	1	27	34*	.6	.6
419 SO BAPT CONV	1	164	205*	3.4	3.9
443 UN C OF CHRIST	5	624	781*	12.8	14.9
449 UN METHODIST	3	293	367*	6.0	7.0
469 WELS	3	396	502	8.2	9.6
YANKTON	**32**	**5,378**	**12,726***	**66.1**	**100.0**
019 AMER BAPT USA	1	29	37*	.2	.3
053 ASSEMB OF GOD	1	79	112	.6	.9
057 BAPT GEN CONF	1	226	287*	1.5	2.3
081 CATHOLIC	4	NA	5,432	28.2	42.7
081d LATIN	*4*	*NA*	*5,432*	*28.2*	*42.7*
111 CH CR,SCIENTST	1	NR	NR	-	-
165 CH OF NAZARENE	1	18	31	.2	.2
167 CHS OF CHRIST	1	22	28	.1	.2
193 EPISCOPAL	1	133	190	1.0	1.5
207 E.L.C.A.	9	2,511	3,325	17.3	26.1
221 FREE METHODIST	1	2	2	-	-
257 HUTTERIAN BR	1	NA	100	.5	.8
283 LUTH—MO SYNOD	2	835	1,127	5.9	8.9
371 REF CH IN AM	1	208	377	2.0	3.0
413 S.D.A.	1	44	56*	.3	.4
419 SO BAPT CONV	1	22	28*	.1	.2
443 UN C OF CHRIST	2	564	717*	3.7	5.6
449 UN METHODIST	2	641	815*	4.2	6.4
469 WELS	1	44	62	.3	.5
ZIEBACH	**15**	**327**	**1,206***	**54.3**	**100.0**
081 CATHOLIC	5	NA	370	16.7	30.7
081d LATIN	*5*	*NA*	*370*	*16.7*	*30.7*
151 L-D SAINTS	1	NA	143	6.4	11.9
193 EPISCOPAL	4	86	335	15.1	27.8
443 UN C OF CHRIST	4	202	308*	13.9	25.5
469 WELS	1	39	50	2.3	4.1

TENNESSEE

County and Denomination	Number of churches	Communicant, confirmed, full members	Total adherents Number	Percent of total population	Percent of total adherents
THE STATE.....	9,246	2,191,239	2,984,916*	61.2	100.0
ANDERSON	**124**	**38,785**	**51,876***	**76.0**	**100.0**
005 AME ZION	1	270	360	.5	.7
053 ASSEMB OF GOD	4	326	433	.6	.8
081 CATHOLIC	3	NA	3,300	4.8	6.4
081d LATIN	*3*	*NA*	*3,300*	*4.8*	*6.4*
089 CHR & MISS AL	1	73	128	.2	.2
093 CHR CH (DISC)	1	215	280	.4	.5
097 CHR CHS&CHS CR	2	341	418*	.6	.8
111 CH CR,SCIENTST	1	NR	NR	-	-
123 CH GOD (ANDER)	1	0	15	-	-
127 CH GOD (CLEVE)	4	709	870*	1.3	1.7
145 CH GOD PROPHCY	2	97	119*	.2	.2
146 CH GOD MTN ASM	3	59	72*	.1	.1
151 L-D SAINTS	1	NA	398	.6	.8
165 CH OF NAZARENE	1	206	241	.4	.5
167 CHS OF CHRIST	8	975	1,182	1.7	2.3
185 CUMBER PRESB	1	251	261	.4	.5
193 EPISCOPAL	2	705	919	1.3	1.8
207 E.L.C.A.	1	568	647	.9	1.2
223 FREE WILL BAPT	1	85	104*	.2	.2
226 FRIENDS-USA	1	0	11	-	-
226c FGC	*1*	*0*	*11*	-	-

NA–Not applicable   NR–Not reported   *Total adherents estimated from known number of communicant, confirmed, full members.   - Represents a percent less than 0.1.   Percentages may not total due to rounding.
[1]See Appendix E   [2]See Appendix F   [3]See Appendix G   Lines in *italic* represent a breakdown of Catholic rites or Friends affiliations. They are included in their respective denominational total.

355

Table 4. Churches and Church Membership by County and Denomination: 1990

County and Denomination	Number of churches	Communicant, confirmed, full members	Total adherents Number	Percent of total population	Percent of total adherents
283 LUTH—MO SYNOD	1	387	532	.8	1.0
355 PRESB CH (USA)	1	323	396*	.6	.8
356 PRESB CH AMER	1	287	370	.5	.7
361 PRIM BAPT ASCS	.1	28	34*	-	.1
413 S.D.A.	1	40	49*	.1	.1
419 SO BAPT CONV	57	26,172	32,116*	47.1	61.9
435 UNITARIAN-UNIV	1	217	282	.4	.5
449 UN METHODIST	17	5,541	6,799*	10.0	13.1
467 WESLEYAN	3	81	172	.3	.3
496 JEWISH EST[1]	2	NA	351	.5	.7
497 BLACK BAPT EST[2]	NA	829	1,017*	1.5	2.0
BEDFORD	**97**	**13,390**	**17,537***	**57.7**	**100.0**
053 ASSEM OF GOD	1	62	85	.3	.5
081 CATHOLIC	1	NA	264	.9	1.5
081d LATIN	*1*	*NA*	*264*	*.9*	*1.5*
093 CHR CH (DISC)	1	220	402	1.3	2.3
123 CH GOD (ANDER)	1	50	50	.2	.3
127 CH GOD (CLEVE)	2	95	118*	.4	.7
145 CH GOD PROPHCY	2	97	121*	.4	.7
157 CH OF BRETHREN	1	77	96*	.3	.5
165 CH OF NAZARENE	4	324	471	1.5	2.7
167 CHS OF CHRIST	22	1,982	2,383	7.8	13.6
185 CUMBER PRESB	4	65	67	.2	.4
189 DUCK RIVR BAPT	5	340	423*	1.4	2.4
193 EPISCOPAL	1	84	100	.3	.6
207 E.L.C.A.	2	166	205	.7	1.2
353 CHR BRETHREN	1	30	75	.2	.4
355 PRESB CH (USA)	3	365	454*	1.5	2.6
361 PRIM BAPT ASCS	1	12	15*	-	.1
419 SO BAPT CONV	19	6,084	7,561*	24.9	43.1
449 UN METHODIST	25	2,734	3,398*	11.2	19.4
497 BLACK BAPT EST[2]	NA	603	749*	2.5	4.3
499 INDEP.NON-CHAR[3]	1	NA	500	1.6	2.9
BENTON	**51**	**5,492**	**6,847***	**47.1**	**100.0**
053 ASSEM OF GOD	1	143	170	1.2	2.5
081 CATHOLIC	1	NA	188	1.3	2.7
081d LATIN	*1*	*NA*	*188*	*1.3*	*2.7*
127 CH GOD (CLEVE)	1	3	4*	-	.1
145 CH GOD PROPHCY	3	145	175*	1.2	2.6
157 CH OF BRETHREN	1	79	95*	.7	1.4
165 CH OF NAZARENE	1	76	101	.7	1.5
167 CHS OF CHRIST	8	604	754	5.2	11.0
185 CUMBER PRESB	1	105	122	.8	1.8
355 PRESB CH (USA)	1	6	7*	-	.1
361 PRIM BAPT ASCS	1	8	10*	.1	.1
419 SO BAPT CONV	12	2,752	3,324*	22.9	48.5
449 UN METHODIST	20	1,571	1,897*	13.1	27.7
BLEDSOE	**36**	**2,796**	**3,458***	**35.8**	**100.0**
081 CATHOLIC	0	NA	4	-	.1
081d LATIN	*0*	*NA*	*4*	*-*	*.1*
127 CH GOD (CLEVE)	7	425	520*	5.4	15.0
145 CH GOD PROPHCY	3	145	177*	1.8	5.1
167 CHS OF CHRIST	12	598	767	7.9	22.2
189 DUCK RIVR BAPT	3	181	221*	2.3	6.4
413 S.D.A.	2	103	126*	1.3	3.6
419 SO BAPT CONV	4	887	1,084*	11.2	31.3
449 UN METHODIST	5	457	559*	5.8	16.2
BLOUNT	**159**	**49,304**	**61,641***	**71.7**	**100.0**
005 AME ZION	4	1,775	2,130	2.5	3.5
053 ASSEM OF GOD	3	129	195	.2	.3
081 CATHOLIC	2	NA	930	1.1	1.5
081d LATIN	*2*	*NA*	*930*	*1.1*	*1.5*
097 CHR CHS&CHS CR	5	820	995*	1.2	1.6
123 CH GOD (ANDER)	1	0	81	.1	.1
127 CH GOD (CLEVE)	10	1,071	1,299*	1.5	2.1
151 L-D SAINTS	1	NA	278	.3	.5
165 CH OF NAZARENE	2	179	224	.3	.4
167 CHS OF CHRIST	4	504	655	.8	1.1
185 CUMBER PRESB	2	415	422	.5	.7
193 EPISCOPAL	1	342	366	.4	.6
207 E.L.C.A.	1	330	454	.5	.7
223 FREE WILL BAPT	1	300	364*	.4	.6
226 FRIENDS-USA	2	209	254*	.3	.4
226e FUM	*2*	*209*	*254*_	*.3*	*.4*
349 PENT HOLINESS	3	155	188*	.2	.3
355 PRESB CH (USA)	7	1,675	2,032*	2.4	3.3
356 PRESB CH AMER	2	112	140	.2	.2
361 PRIM BAPT ASCS	1	39	47*	.1	.1
413 S.D.A.	1	85	103*	.1	.2
419 SO BAPT CONV	83	33,527	40,679*	47.3	66.0
449 UN METHODIST	22	6,939	8,419*	9.8	13.7
496 JEWISH EST[1]	0	NA	189	.2	.3
497 BLACK BAPT EST[2]	NA	698	847*	1.0	1.4
499 INDEP.NON-CHAR[3]	1	NA	350	.4	.6
BRADLEY	**142**	**34,639**	**44,293***	**60.1**	**100.0**
053 ASSEM OF GOD	1	61	56	.1	.1
059 BAPT MISS ASSN	2	155	191*	.3	.4
081 CATHOLIC	1	NA	1,462	2.0	3.3
081d LATIN	*1*	*NA*	*1,462*	*2.0*	*3.3*
093 CHR CH (DISC)	1	132	186	.3	.4
097 CHR CHS&CHS CR	2	210	259*	.4	.6
123 CH GOD (ANDER)	1	5	5	-	-
127 CH GOD (CLEVE)	25	5,525	6,811*	9.2	15.4
145 CH GOD PROPHCY	10	500	616*	.8	1.4
151 L-D SAINTS	1	NA	163	.2	.4
165 CH OF NAZARENE	1	107	135	.2	.3
167 CHS OF CHRIST	4	956	1,087	1.5	2.5
185 CUMBER PRESB	5	529	577	.8	1.3
193 EPISCOPAL	1	434	615	.8	1.4
283 LUTH—MO SYNOD	1	243	311	.4	.7
339 PENT CH OF GOD	1	34	76	.1	.2
355 PRESB CH (USA)	2	357	440*	.6	1.0
356 PRESB CH AMER	1	0	0	-	-
403 SALVATION ARMY	1	35	43	.1	.1
413 S.D.A.	4	784	967*	1.3	2.2
419 SO BAPT CONV	56	19,667	24,246*	32.9	54.7
449 UN METHODIST	21	4,412	5,439*	7.4	12.3
497 BLACK BAPT EST[2]	NA	493	608*	.8	1.4
CAMPBELL	**80**	**14,383**	**18,873***	**53.8**	**100.0**
005 AME ZION	1	65	78	.2	.4
053 ASSEM OF GOD	1	34	53	.2	.3
081 CATHOLIC	1	NA	187	.5	1.0
081d LATIN	*1*	*NA*	*187*	*.5*	*1.0*
097 CHR CHS&CHS CR	1	20	25*	.1	.1
127 CH GOD (CLEVE)	6	1,115	1,379*	3.9	7.3
146 CH GOD MTN ASM	6	330	408*	1.2	2.2
151 L-D SAINTS	1	NA	107	.3	.6
167 CHS OF CHRIST	4	203	271	.8	1.4
355 PRESB CH (USA)	2	141	174*	.5	.9
413 S.D.A.	1	154	190*	.5	1.0
419 SO BAPT CONV	40	10,165	12,572*	35.8	66.6
436 UNITED BAPT	5	929	1,149*	3.3	6.1
449 UN METHODIST	7	1,217	1,505*	4.3	8.0
467 WESLEYAN	2	10	65	.2	.3
499 INDEP.NON-CHAR[3]	2	NA	710	2.0	3.8
CANNON	**50**	**4,799**	**6,162***	**58.9**	**100.0**
127 CH GOD (CLEVE)	2	125	155*	1.5	2.5
145 CH GOD PROPHCY	1	48	60*	.6	1.0
165 CH OF NAZARENE	1	29	32	.3	.5
167 CHS OF CHRIST	25	1,654	2,253	21.5	36.6
189 DUCK RIVR BAPT	2	275	342*	3.3	5.6
221 FREE METHODIST	1	45	59	.6	1.0
355 PRESB CH (USA)	1	22	27*	.3	.4
413 S.D.A.	1	95	118*	1.1	1.9
419 SO BAPT CONV	10	2,037	2,533*	24.2	41.1
449 UN METHODIST	6	469	583*	5.6	9.5
CARROLL	**86**	**12,765**	**15,760***	**57.3**	**100.0**
053 ASSEM OF GOD	2	69	98	.4	.6
145 CH GOD PROPHCY	1	48	59*	.2	.4
167 CHS OF CHRIST	18	1,825	2,331	8.5	14.8
185 CUMBER PRESB	9	603	607	2.2	3.9
323 OLD ORD AMISH	1	NA	150	.5	1.0
355 PRESB CH (USA)	4	157	192*	.7	1.2
361 PRIM BAPT ASCS	4	119	146*	.5	.9
413 S.D.A.	1	88	108*	.4	.7
419 SO BAPT CONV	24	6,772	8,293*	30.1	52.6
449 UN METHODIST	22	2,379	2,913*	10.6	18.5
497 BLACK BAPT EST[2]	NA	705	863*	3.1	5.5
CARTER	**107**	**25,233**	**30,775***	**59.8**	**100.0**
005 AME ZION	1	290	348	.7	1.1
053 ASSEM OF GOD	1	111	150	.3	.5
081 CATHOLIC	1	NA	440	.9	1.4
081d LATIN	*1*	*NA*	*440*	*.9*	*1.4*
089 CHR & MISS AL	1	47	89	.2	.3
097 CHR CHS&CHS CR	19	3,876	4,650*	9.0	15.1
123 CH GOD (ANDER)	2	66	102	.2	.3
127 CH GOD (CLEVE)	4	283	339*	.7	1.1
145 CH GOD PROPHCY	1	48	58*	.1	.2
165 CH OF NAZARENE	1	102	98	.2	.3
167 CHS OF CHRIST	4	430	525	1.0	1.7
193 EPISCOPAL	1	42	60	.1	.2
223 FREE WILL BAPT	14	2,748	3,297*	6.4	10.7

NA–Not applicable   NR–Not reported   *Total adherents estimated from known number of communicant, confirmed, full members.   - Represents a percent less than 0.1.   Percentages may not total due to rounding.

[1]See Appendix E   [2]See Appendix F   [3]See Appendix G   Lines in *italic* represent a breakdown of Catholic rites or Friends affiliations. They are included in their respective denominational total.

Table 4. Churches and Church Membership by County and Denomination: 1990

County and Denomination		Number of churches	Communicant, confirmed, full members	Total adherents		
				Number	Percent of total population	Percent of total adherents
283	LUTH—MO SYNOD	1	45	53	.1	.2
355	PRESB CH (USA)	4	333	399*	.8	1.3
356	PRESB CH AMER	1	212	222	.4	.7
361	PRIM BAPT ASCS	1	17	20*	-	.1
413	S.D.A.	1	58	70*	.1	.2
419	SO BAPT CONV	40	15,080	18,090*	35.1	58.8
449	UN METHODIST	9	1,445	1,733*	3.4	5.6
496	JEWISH EST[1]	0	NA	32	.1	.1
CHEATHAM		**51**	**7,620**	**10,205***	**37.6**	**100.0**
053	ASSEMB OF GOD	1	119	242	.9	2.4
081	CATHOLIC	1	NA	159	.6	1.6
081d	LATIN	1	NA	159	.6	1.6
145	CH GOD PROPHCY	1	48	62*	.2	.6
165	CH OF NAZARENE	2	87	132	.5	1.3
167	CHS OF CHRIST	19	1,689	2,182	8.0	21.4
223	FREE WILL BAPT	10	2,037	2,610*	9.6	25.6
413	S.D.A.	1	58	74*	.3	.7
419	SO BAPT CONV	5	1,768	2,265*	8.3	22.2
449	UN METHODIST	11	1,649	2,113*	7.8	20.7
496	JEWISH EST[1]	0	NA	155	.6	1.5
497	BLACK BAPT EST[2]	NA	165	211*	.8	2.1
CHESTER		**35**	**5,861**	**7,235***	**56.4**	**100.0**
053	ASSEMB OF GOD	1	64	130	1.0	1.8
081	CATHOLIC	1	NA	33	.3	.5
081d	LATIN	1	NA	33	.3	.5
097	CHR CHS&CHS CR	1	80	98*	.8	1.4
127	CH GOD (CLEVE)	1	41	50*	.4	.7
167	CHS OF CHRIST	8	1,103	1,362	10.6	18.8
185	CUMBER PRESB	1	238	256	2.0	3.5
361	PRIM BAPT ASCS	3	80	98*	.8	1.4
419	SO BAPT CONV	11	2,949	3,610*	28.2	49.9
449	UN METHODIST	8	1,011	1,237*	9.6	17.1
497	BLACK BAPT EST[2]	NA	295	361*	2.8	5.0
CLAIBORNE		**107**	**14,124**	**17,529***	**67.1**	**100.0**
053	ASSEMB OF GOD	1	20	30	.1	.2
081	CATHOLIC	1	NA	50	.2	.3
081d	LATIN	1	NA	50	.2	.3
097	CHR CHS&CHS CR	1	80	99*	.4	.6
127	CH GOD (CLEVE)	1	8	10*	-	.1
146	CH GOD MTN ASM	5	137	169*	.6	1.0
167	CHS OF CHRIST	4	115	163	.6	.9
283	LUTH—MO SYNOD	1	59	73	.3	.4
361	PRIM BAPT ASCS	1	34	42*	.2	.2
419	SO BAPT CONV	81	12,660	15,644*	59.9	89.2
449	UN METHODIST	11	1,011	1,249*	4.8	7.1
CLAY		**30**	**1,789**	**2,536***	**35.0**	**100.0**
081	CATHOLIC	1	NA	75	1.0	3.0
081d	LATIN	1	NA	75	1.0	3.0
123	CH GOD (ANDER)	1	50	60	.8	2.4
167	CHS OF CHRIST	23	1,250	1,772	24.5	69.9
419	SO BAPT CONV	2	288	348*	4.8	13.7
449	UN METHODIST	2	146	176*	2.4	6.9
467	WESLEYAN	1	55	105	1.5	4.1
COCKE		**93**	**12,733**	**15,771***	**54.1**	**100.0**
005	AME ZION	3	438	584	2.0	3.7
053	ASSEMB OF GOD	1	10	11	-	.1
081	CATHOLIC	1	NA	100	.3	.6
081d	LATIN	1	NA	100	.3	.6
089	CHR & MISS AL	1	51	73	.3	.5
097	CHR CHS&CHS CR	4	415	505*	1.7	3.2
123	CH GOD (ANDER)	2	35	101	.3	.6
127	CH GOD (CLEVE)	6	698	850*	2.9	5.4
165	CH OF NAZARENE	1	30	80	.3	.5
167	CHS OF CHRIST	3	214	271	.9	1.7
193	EPISCOPAL	1	63	85	.3	.5
207	E.L.C.A.	3	297	357	1.2	2.3
223	FREE WILL BAPT	8	836	1,018*	3.5	6.5
355	PRESB CH (USA)	1	79	96*	.3	.6
356	PRESB CH AMER	1	32	32	.1	.2
413	S.D.A.	1	61	74*	.3	.5
419	SO BAPT CONV	41	7,854	9,562*	32.8	60.6
449	UN METHODIST	15	1,414	1,721*	5.9	10.9
497	BLACK BAPT EST[2]	NA	206	251*	.9	1.6
COFFEE		**105**	**17,610**	**24,165***	**59.9**	**100.0**
053	ASSEMB OF GOD	2	75	105	.3	.4
081	CATHOLIC	1	NA	1,256	3.1	5.2
081d	LATIN	1	NA	1,256	3.1	5.2
093	CHR CH (DISC)	1	422	519	1.3	2.1
111	CH CR,SCIENTST	1	NR	NR	-	-

County and Denomination		Number of churches	Communicant, confirmed, full members	Total adherents		
				Number	Percent of total population	Percent of total adherents
123	CH GOD (ANDER)	1	46	46	.1	.2
127	CH GOD (CLEVE)	2	212	266*	.7	1.1
145	CH GOD PROPHCY	2	97	121*	.3	.5
151	L-D SAINTS	2	NA	453	1.1	1.9
165	CH OF NAZARENE	4	296	450	1.1	1.9
167	CHS OF CHRIST	29	2,885	3,908	9.7	16.2
185	CUMBER PRESB	3	207	223	.6	.9
189	DUCK RIVR BAPT	13	1,430	1,791*	4.4	7.4
193	EPISCOPAL	2	206	259	.6	1.1
207	E.L.C.A.	1	768	1,033	2.6	4.3
223	FREE WILL BAPT	2	157	197*	.5	.8
283	LUTH—MO SYNOD	1	134	175	.4	.7
320	"OLD" MB ASCS	1	32	40*	.1	.2
355	PRESB CH (USA)	2	357	447*	1.1	1.8
356	PRESB CH AMER	1	34	36	.1	.1
361	PRIM BAPT ASCS	1	14	18*	-	.1
413	S.D.A.	1	48	60*	.1	.2
419	SO BAPT CONV	14	6,387	7,999*	19.8	33.1
435	UNITARIAN-UNIV	1	22	28	.1	.1
449	UN METHODIST	17	3,496	4,378*	10.9	18.1
497	BLACK BAPT EST[2]	NA	285	357*	.9	1.5
CROCKETT		**49**	**8,432**	**10,368***	**77.5**	**100.0**
053	ASSEMB OF GOD	2	130	192	1.4	1.9
093	CHR CH (DISC)	2	195	226	1.7	2.2
097	CHR CHS&CHS CR	1	150	185*	1.4	1.8
127	CH GOD (CLEVE)	1	69	85*	.6	.8
146	CH GOD MTN ASM	1	83	102*	.8	1.0
167	CHS OF CHRIST	12	1,125	1,374	10.3	13.3
185	CUMBER PRESB	2	73	73	.5	.7
361	PRIM BAPT ASCS	1	24	30*	.2	.3
419	SO BAPT CONV	13	3,821	4,702*	35.1	45.4
449	UN METHODIST	14	1,854	2,282*	17.1	22.0
497	BLACK BAPT EST[2]	NA	908	1,117*	8.3	10.8
CUMBERLAND		**88**	**11,651**	**15,659***	**45.1**	**100.0**
053	ASSEMB OF GOD	2	216	315	.9	2.0
061	BEACHY AMISH	1	40	49*	.1	.3
081	CATHOLIC	2	NA	716	2.1	4.6
081d	LATIN	2	NA	716	2.1	4.6
093	CHR CH (DISC)	2	255	329	.9	2.1
127	CH GOD (CLEVE)	3	264	320*	.9	2.0
145	CH GOD PROPHCY	6	291	353*	1.0	2.3
151	L-D SAINTS	1	NA	248	.7	1.6
165	CH OF NAZARENE	2	163	247	.7	1.6
167	CHS OF CHRIST	12	1,061	1,381	4.0	8.8
175	CONGR CHR CHS	1	90	109*	.3	.7
189	DUCK RIVR BAPT	1	60	73*	.2	.5
193	EPISCOPAL	1	87	114	.3	.7
203	EVAN FREE CH	1	34	34	.1	.2
207	E.L.C.A.	1	69	70	.2	.4
223	FREE WILL BAPT	1	115	140*	.4	.9
226	FRIENDS-USA	1	30	35	.1	.2
226c	FGC	1	30	35	.1	.2
259	IFCA	1	NR	NR	-	-
283	LUTH—MO SYNOD	1	256	281	.8	1.8
339	PENT CH OF GOD	1	6	37	.1	.2
355	PRESB CH (USA)	2	305	370*	1.1	2.4
356	PRESB CH AMER	1	22	30	.1	.2
413	S.D.A.	1	176	214*	.6	1.4
419	SO BAPT CONV	28	5,682	6,896*	19.9	44.0
443	UN C OF CHRIST	3	476	578*	1.7	3.7
449	UN METHODIST	11	1,953	2,370*	6.8	15.1
499	INDEP.NON-CHAR[3]	1	NA	350	1.0	2.2
DAVIDSON		**512**	**232,161**	**322,655***	**63.2**	**100.0**
005	AME ZION	1	175	210	-	.1
019	AMER BAPT USA	2	1,517	1,855*	.4	.6
053	ASSEMB OF GOD	13	2,140	3,931	.8	1.2
081	CATHOLIC	16	NA	23,514	4.6	7.3
081d	LATIN	16	NA	23,514	4.6	7.3
093	CHR CH (DISC)	10	2,470	3,287	.6	1.0
097	CHR CHS&CHS CR	3	530	648*	.1	.2
105	CHRISTIAN REF	1	75	123	-	-
111	CH CR,SCIENTST	2	NR	NR	-	-
121	CH GOD (ABR)	1	10	12*	-	-
123	CH GOD (ANDER)	3	266	366	.1	.1
127	CH GOD (CLEVE)	7	959	1,172*	.2	.4
133	CH GOD(7TH)DEN	1	14	18	-	-
145	CH GOD PROPHCY	7	339	414*	.1	.1
151	L-D SAINTS	4	NA	1,466	.3	.5
157	CH OF BRETHREN	1	18	22*	-	-
165	CH OF NAZARENE	28	5,822	7,243	1.4	2.2
167	CHS OF CHRIST	116	32,204	41,607	8.1	12.9
185	CUMBER PRESB	12	4,165	4,469	.9	1.4
189	DUCK RIVR BAPT	1	131	160*		

NA–Not applicable NR–Not reported *Total adherents estimated from known number of communicant, confirmed, full members. - Represents a percent less than 0.1. Percentages may not total due to rounding.
[1]See Appendix E [2]See Appendix F [3]See Appendix G Lines in *italic* represent a breakdown of Catholic rites or Friends affiliations. They are included in their respective denominational total.

357

Table 4. Churches and Church Membership by County and Denomination: 1990

County and Denomination	Number of churches	Communicant, confirmed, full members	Total adherents Number	Percent of total population	Percent of total adherents
193 EPISCOPAL	13	5,526	7,079	1.4	2.2
207 E.L.C.A.	6	1,545	1,975	.4	.6
223 FREE WILL BAPT	18	2,117	2,588*	.5	.8
226 FRIENDS-USA	1	30	81	-	-
226c *FGC*	*1*	*30*	*81*	*-*	*-*
246 GREEK ORTHODOX	1	NR	NR	-	-
263 INT FOURSQ GOS	1	19	23*	-	-
283 LUTH—MO SYNOD	6	940	1,200	.2	.4
285 MENNONITE CH	1	25	45	-	-
320 "OLD" MB ASCS	11	2,234	2,731*	.5	.8
339 PENT CH OF GOD	1	34	76	-	-
349 PENT HOLINESS	1	35	43*	-	-
353 CHR BRETHREN	2	125	200	-	.1
355 PRESB CH (USA)	23	9,233	11,287*	2.2	3.5
356 PRESB CH AMER	3	1,374	1,909	.4	.6
403 SALVATION ARMY	2	223	236	-	.1
413 S.D.A.	9	4,154	5,078*	1.0	1.6
419 SO BAPT CONV	92	83,032	101,508*	19.9	31.5
435 UNITARIAN-UNIV	1	363	467	.1	.1
443 UN C OF CHRIST	3	413	505*	.1	.2
449 UN METHODIST	71	30,258	36,991*	7.2	11.5
467 WESLEYAN	3	82	242	-	.1
469 WELS	1	126	199	-	.1
496 JEWISH EST[1]	5	NA	2,887	.6	.9
497 BLACK BAPT EST[2]	NA	39,438	48,213*	9.4	14.9
498 INDEP.CHARIS.[3]	5	NA	4,325	.8	1.3
499 INDEP.NON-CHAR[3]	3	NA	2,250	.4	.7
DECATUR	**46**	**4,482**	**5,999***	**57.3**	**100.0**
053 ASSEMB OF GOD	1	242	500	4.8	8.3
081 CATHOLIC	1	NA	105	1.0	1.8
081d *LATIN*	*1*	*NA*	*105*	*1.0*	*1.8*
123 CH GOD (ANDER)	1	11	25	.2	.4
127 CH GOD (CLEVE)	1	63	76*	.7	1.3
151 L-D SAINTS	1	NA	256	2.4	4.3
157 CH OF BRETHREN	1	23	28*	.3	.5
167 CHS OF CHRIST	5	381	492	4.7	8.2
185 CUMBER PRESB	4	200	218	2.1	3.6
361 PRIM BAPT ASCS	1	7	8*	.1	.1
413 S.D.A.	1	63	76*	.7	1.3
419 SO BAPT CONV	17	2,445	2,951*	28.2	49.2
449 UN METHODIST	12	1,047	1,264*	12.1	21.1
DE KALB	**72**	**7,953**	**9,865***	**68.7**	**100.0**
053 ASSEMB OF GOD	1	33	44	.3	.4
075 BRETHREN IN CR	1	54	54	.4	.5
081 CATHOLIC	1	NA	82	.6	.8
081d *LATIN*	*1*	*NA*	*82*	*.6*	*.8*
127 CH GOD (CLEVE)	2	211	258*	1.8	2.6
165 CH OF NAZARENE	1	22	30	.2	.3
167 CHS OF CHRIST	9	569	789	5.5	8.0
185 CUMBER PRESB	2	228	243	1.7	2.5
189 DUCK RIVR BAPT	10	1,106	1,353*	9.4	13.7
193 EPISCOPAL	1	13	18	.1	.2
223 FREE WILL BAPT	1	100	122*	.8	1.2
355 PRESB CH (USA)	1	37	45*	.3	.5
413 S.D.A.	1	34	42*	.3	.4
419 SO BAPT CONV	22	4,240	5,187*	36.1	52.6
449 UN METHODIST	19	1,306	1,598*	11.1	16.2
DICKSON	**93**	**11,825**	**16,847***	**48.1**	**100.0**
053 ASSEMB OF GOD	1	89	121	.3	.7
081 CATHOLIC	1	NA	939	2.7	5.6
081d *LATIN*	*1*	*NA*	*939*	*2.7*	*5.6*
127 CH GOD (CLEVE)	1	50	64*	.2	.4
145 CH GOD PROPHCY	7	339	431*	1.2	2.6
151 L-D SAINTS	1	NA	233	.7	1.4
165 CH OF NAZARENE	2	208	374	1.1	2.2
167 CHS OF CHRIST	30	3,034	4,260	12.2	25.3
185 CUMBER PRESB	3	384	408	1.2	2.4
193 EPISCOPAL	1	60	76	.2	.5
223 FREE WILL BAPT	6	426	542*	1.5	3.2
349 PENT HOLINESS	1	65	83*	.2	.5
355 PRESB CH (USA)	2	166	211*	.6	1.3
413 S.D.A.	1	112	142*	.4	.8
419 SO BAPT CONV	14	3,584	4,558*	13.0	27.1
449 UN METHODIST	22	2,584	3,286*	9.4	19.5
496 JEWISH EST[1]	0	NA	198	.6	1.2
497 BLACK BAPT EST[2]	NA	724	921*	2.6	5.5
DYER	**100**	**18,316**	**23,750***	**68.1**	**100.0**
053 ASSEMB OF GOD	6	487	867	2.5	3.7
081 CATHOLIC	2	NA	632	1.8	2.7
081d *LATIN*	*2*	*NA*	*632*	*1.8*	*2.7*
097 CHR CHS&CHS CR	2	255	317*	.9	1.3
127 CH GOD (CLEVE)	2	401	499*	1.4	2.1
145 CH GOD PROPHCY	2	97	121*	.3	.5
151 L-D SAINTS	1	NA	114	.3	.5
165 CH OF NAZARENE	1	40	128	.4	.5
167 CHS OF CHRIST	21	1,855	2,301	6.6	9.7
185 CUMBER PRESB	7	1,018	1,134	3.3	4.8
193 EPISCOPAL	1	87	114	.3	.5
215 EVAN METH CH	1	49	61*	.2	.3
283 LUTH—MO SYNOD	1	63	90	.3	.4
355 PRESB CH (USA)	3	56	70*	.2	.3
356 PRESB CH AMER	1	119	135	.4	.6
413 S.D.A.	1	76	95*	.3	.4
419 SO BAPT CONV	29	9,532	11,867*	34.0	50.0
449 UN METHODIST	19	2,933	3,651*	10.5	15.4
497 BLACK BAPT EST[2]	NA	1,248	1,554*	4.5	6.5
FAYETTE	**57**	**7,547**	**10,020***	**39.2**	**100.0**
053 ASSEMB OF GOD	1	55	80	.3	.8
061 BEACHY AMISH	1	53	69*	.3	.7
081 CATHOLIC	1	NA	190	.7	1.9
081d *LATIN*	*1*	*NA*	*190*	*.7*	*1.9*
093 CHR CH (DISC)	2	50	155	.6	1.5
127 CH GOD (CLEVE)	1	54	70*	.3	.7
165 CH OF NAZARENE	1	30	48	.2	.5
167 CHS OF CHRIST	6	406	499	2.0	5.0
185 CUMBER PRESB	3	81	89	.3	.9
193 EPISCOPAL	2	22	25	.1	.2
355 PRESB CH (USA)	2	221	286*	1.1	2.9
356 PRESB CH AMER	1	95	110	.4	1.1
361 PRIM BAPT ASCS	1	14	18*	.1	.2
413 S.D.A.	1	68	88*	.3	.9
419 SO BAPT CONV	18	4,855	6,293*	24.6	62.8
449 UN METHODIST	16	1,343	1,741*	6.8	17.4
497 BLACK BAPT EST[2]	NA	200	259*	1.0	2.6
FENTRESS	**42**	**4,344**	**5,810***	**39.6**	**100.0**
081 CATHOLIC	1	NA	25	.2	.4
081d *LATIN*	*1*	*NA*	*25*	*.2*	*.4*
127 CH GOD (CLEVE)	1	133	165*	1.1	2.8
145 CH GOD PROPHCY	2	97	120*	.8	2.1
151 L-D SAINTS	1	NA	261	1.8	4.5
165 CH OF NAZARENE	2	129	268	1.8	4.6
167 CHS OF CHRIST	2	163	212	1.4	3.6
355 PRESB CH (USA)	1	115	143*	1.0	2.5
419 SO BAPT CONV	9	1,805	2,239*	15.3	38.5
436 UNITED BAPT	13	1,025	1,272*	8.7	21.9
449 UN METHODIST	9	868	1,077*	7.3	18.5
467 WESLEYAN	1	9	28	.2	.5
FRANKLIN	**103**	**15,279**	**19,979***	**57.5**	**100.0**
053 ASSEMB OF GOD	1	46	85	.2	.4
061 BEACHY AMISH	1	42	52*	.1	.3
081 CATHOLIC	2	NA	675	1.9	3.4
081d *LATIN*	*2*	*NA*	*675*	*1.9*	*3.4*
127 CH GOD (CLEVE)	6	398	490*	1.4	2.5
145 CH GOD PROPHCY	1	48	59*	.2	.3
151 L-D SAINTS	1	NA	226	.7	1.1
165 CH OF NAZARENE	8	578	914	2.6	4.6
167 CHS OF CHRIST	20	1,383	1,891	5.4	9.5
185 CUMBER PRESB	9	1,395	1,481	4.3	7.4
189 DUCK RIVR BAPT	7	628	772*	2.2	3.9
193 EPISCOPAL	6	644	885	2.5	4.4
226 FRIENDS-USA	1	0	4	-	-
226c *FGC*	*1*	*0*	*4*	*-*	*-*
355 PRESB CH (USA)	3	113	139*	.4	.7
361 PRIM BAPT ASCS	1	20	25*	.1	.1
413 S.D.A.	2	54	66*	.2	.3
419 SO BAPT CONV	22	6,483	7,975*	23.0	39.9
443 UN C OF CHRIST	1	125	154*	.4	.8
449 UN METHODIST	11	2,483	3,054*	8.8	15.3
497 BLACK BAPT EST[2]	NA	839	1,032*	3.0	5.2
GIBSON	**156**	**27,620**	**34,173***	**73.8**	**100.0**
053 ASSEMB OF GOD	5	562	819	1.8	2.4
081 CATHOLIC	2	NA	371	.8	1.1
081d *LATIN*	*2*	*NA*	*371*	*.8*	*1.1*
093 CHR CH (DISC)	1	165	371	.8	1.1
127 CH GOD (CLEVE)	2	167	205*	.4	.6
145 CH GOD PROPHCY	2	97	119*	.3	.3
165 CH OF NAZARENE	1	10	31	.1	.1
167 CHS OF CHRIST	30	2,536	3,040	6.6	8.9
185 CUMBER PRESB	17	1,857	1,937	4.2	5.7
193 EPISCOPAL	1	36	61	.1	.2
349 PENT HOLINESS	1	51	63*	.1	.2
355 PRESB CH (USA)	6	456	559*	1.2	1.6
361 PRIM BAPT ASCS	5	190	233*	.5	.7
413 S.D.A.	1	6	7*	-	-

NA–Not applicable   NR–Not reported   *Total adherents estimated from known number of communicant, confirmed, full members.   - Represents a percent less than 0.1.   Percentages may not total due to rounding.
[1]See Appendix E   [2]See Appendix F   [3]See Appendix G   Lines in italic represent a breakdown of Catholic rites or Friends affiliations. They are included in their respective denominational total.

Table 4. Churches and Church Membership by County and Denomination: 1990

County and Denomination		Number of churches	Communicant, confirmed, full members	Total adherents		
				Number	Percent of total population	Percent of total adherents
419	SO BAPT CONV	52	15,976	19,597*	42.3	57.3
449	UN METHODIST	30	4,037	4,952*	10.7	14.5
497	BLACK BAPT EST[2]	NA	1,474	1,808*	3.9	5.3
GILES		**96**	**11,876**	**15,123***	**58.8**	**100.0**
053	ASSEMB OF GOD	1	15	32	.1	.2
081	CATHOLIC	1	NA	160	.6	1.1
081d	*LATIN*	*1*	*NA*	*160*	*.6*	*1.1*
123	CH GOD (ANDER)	2	52	62	.2	.4
127	CH GOD (CLEVE)	1	164	203*	.8	1.3
145	CH GOD PROPHCY	2	97	120*	.5	.8
165	CH OF NAZARENE	1	14	32	.1	.2
167	CHS OF CHRIST	25	2,238	3,011	11.7	19.9
185	CUMBER PRESB	3	93	96	.4	.6
193	EPISCOPAL	1	97	131	.5	.9
355	PRESB CH (USA)	5	353	437*	1.7	2.9
361	PRIM BAPT ASCS	2	59	73*	.3	.5
413	S.D.A.	2	69	85*	.3	.6
419	SO BAPT CONV	23	5,468	6,771*	26.3	44.8
449	UN METHODIST	27	3,062	3,792*	14.7	25.1
497	BLACK BAPT EST[2]	NA	95	118*	.5	.8
GRAINGER		**66**	**11,065**	**13,607***	**79.6**	**100.0**
005	AME ZION	1	3	7	-	.1
081	CATHOLIC	0	NA	42	.2	.3
081d	*LATIN*	*0*	*NA*	*42*	*.2*	*.3*
127	CH GOD (CLEVE)	2	67	82*	.5	.6
157	CH OF BRETHREN	1	17	21*	.1	.2
167	CHS OF CHRIST	1	35	45	.3	.3
223	FREE WILL BAPT	3	203	248*	1.5	1.8
355	PRESB CH (USA)	1	8	10*	.1	.1
361	PRIM BAPT ASCS	1	61	75*	.4	.6
419	SO BAPT CONV	46	9,999	12,218*	71.5	89.8
449	UN METHODIST	10	672	821*	4.8	6.0
496	JEWISH EST[1]	0	NA	38	.2	.3
GREENE		**166**	**22,241**	**27,958***	**50.1**	**100.0**
005	AME ZION	2	408	544	1.0	1.9
053	ASSEMB OF GOD	1	64	85	.2	.3
081	CATHOLIC	1	NA	647	1.2	2.3
081d	*LATIN*	*1*	*NA*	*647*	*1.2*	*2.3*
082	CENTRAL BAPT	1	30	36*	.1	.1
123	CH GOD (ANDER)	6	555	1,072	1.9	3.8
127	CH GOD (CLEVE)	4	177	214*	.4	.8
145	CH GOD PROPHCY	1	48	58*	.1	.2
151	L-D SAINTS	1	NA	108	.2	.4
157	CH OF BRETHREN	1	79	95*	.2	.3
165	CH OF NAZARENE	1	61	188	.3	.7
167	CHS OF CHRIST	3	193	264	.5	.9
185	CUMBER PRESB	14	1,574	1,680	3.0	6.0
193	EPISCOPAL	1	154	156	.3	.6
207	E.L.C.A.	4	897	1,051	1.9	3.8
221	FREE METHODIST	1	2	26	-	.1
223	FREE WILL BAPT	24	2,381	2,875*	5.1	10.3
283	LUTH—MO SYNOD	1	32	41	.1	.1
349	PENT HOLINESS	3	170	205*	.4	.7
355	PRESB CH (USA)	10	826	997*	1.8	3.6
356	PRESB CH AMER	1	101	121	.2	.4
361	PRIM BAPT ASCS	1	80	97*	.2	.3
413	S.D.A.	3	540	652*	1.2	2.3
419	SO BAPT CONV	21	6,557	7,917*	14.2	28.3
449	UN METHODIST	60	6,922	8,358*	15.0	29.9
497	BLACK BAPT EST[2]	NA	390	471*	.8	1.7
GRUNDY		**46**	**3,349**	**4,240***	**31.7**	**100.0**
127	CH GOD (CLEVE)	4	219	277*	2.1	6.5
145	CH GOD PROPHCY	2	97	122*	.9	2.9
165	CH OF NAZARENE	2	153	202	1.5	4.8
167	CHS OF CHRIST	13	555	690	5.2	16.3
185	CUMBER PRESB	1	18	18	.1	.4
189	DUCK RIVR BAPT	1	140	177*	1.3	4.2
193	EPISCOPAL	3	159	181	1.4	4.3
353	CHR BRETHREN	1	30	75	.6	1.8
413	S.D.A.	3	201	254*	1.9	6.0
419	SO BAPT CONV	6	1,036	1,308*	9.8	30.8
449	UN METHODIST	10	741	936*	7.0	22.1
HAMBLEN		**89**	**26,750**	**33,211***	**65.8**	**100.0**
005	AME ZION	1	86	103	.2	.3
053	ASSEMB OF GOD	1	97	74	.1	.2
081	CATHOLIC	1	NA	542	1.1	1.6
081d	*LATIN*	*1*	*NA*	*542*	*1.1*	*1.6*
082	CENTRAL BAPT	2	88	107*	.2	.3
097	CHR CHS&CHS CR	2	220	268*	.5	.8
111	CH CR,SCIENTST	1	NR	NR		-

County and Denomination		Number of churches	Communicant, confirmed, full members	Total adherents		
				Number	Percent of total population	Percent of total adherents
123	CH GOD (ANDER)	1	50	55	.1	.2
127	CH GOD (CLEVE)	2	394	480*	1.0	1.4
145	CH GOD PROPHCY	1	48	59*	.1	.2
165	CH OF NAZARENE	1	61	98	.2	.3
167	CHS OF CHRIST	1	140	150	.3	.5
185	CUMBER PRESB	1	104	105	.2	.3
193	EPISCOPAL	1	231	390	.8	1.2
207	E.L.C.A.	1	215	267	.5	.8
223	FREE WILL BAPT	3	346	422*	.8	1.3
283	LUTH—MO SYNOD	1	100	109	.2	.3
355	PRESB CH (USA)	3	840	1,024*	2.0	3.1
361	PRIM BAPT ASCS	2	60	73*	.1	.2
413	S.D.A.	2	182	222*	.4	.7
419	SO BAPT CONV	44	19,356	23,599*	46.7	71.1
449	UN METHODIST	16	3,418	4,167*	8.3	12.5
467	WESLEYAN	1	11	40	-	.1
497	BLACK BAPT EST[2]	NA	703	857*	1.7	2.6
HAMILTON		**362**	**135,498**	**220,098***	**77.1**	**100.0**
001	ADVENT CHR CH	1	33	41*		-
005	AME ZION	5	1,201	1,802	.6	.8
053	ASSEMB OF GOD	4	402	750	.3	.3
081	CATHOLIC	5	NA	9,130	3.2	4.1
081d	*LATIN*	*5*	*NA*	*9,130*	*3.2*	*4.1*
089	CHR & MISS AL	1	193	278	.1	.1
093	CHR CH (DISC)	3	638	802	.3	.4
097	CHR CHS&CHS CR	4	716	881*	.3	.4
111	CH CR,SCIENTST	1	NR	NR	-	-
123	CH GOD (ANDER)	4	322	353	.1	.2
127	CH GOD (CLEVE)	44	6,637	8,167*	2.9	3.7
133	CH GOD(7TH)DEN	1	13	18	-	-
145	CH GOD PROPHCY	8	388	477*	.2	.2
146	CH GOD MTN ASM	1	10	12*	-	-
151	L-D SAINTS	4	NA	876	.3	.4
165	CH OF NAZARENE	9	1,514	1,643	.6	.7
167	CHS OF CHRIST	38	5,471	6,994	2.4	3.2
185	CUMBER PRESB	6	1,877	1,944	.7	.9
189	DUCK RIVR BAPT	1	93	114*	-	.1
193	EPISCOPAL	11	4,417	5,639	2.0	2.6
207	E.L.C.A.	3	1,130	1,471	.5	.7
215	EVAN METH CH	1	138	170*	.1	.1
216	EVAN PRESBY CH	1	556	566	.2	.3
223	FREE WILL BAPT	2	243	299*	.1	.1
226	FRIENDS-USA	1	23	36	-	-
226c	*FGC*	*1*	*23*	*36*	*-*	*-*
246	GREEK ORTHODOX	1	NR	NR	-	-
283	LUTH—MO SYNOD	5	1,388	1,830	.6	.8
355	PRESB CH (USA)	14	3,555	4,374*	1.5	2.0
356	PRESB CH AMER	11	5,174	5,704	2.0	2.6
361	PRIM BAPT ASCS	2	83	102*	-	-
403	SALVATION ARMY	2	260	274	.1	.1
413	S.D.A.	15	5,681	6,991*	2.4	3.2
419	SO BAPT CONV	93	53,845	66,257*	23.2	30.1
435	UNITARIAN-UNIV	1	171	220	.1	.1
443	UN C OF CHRIST	2	311	383*	.1	.2
449	UN METHODIST	46	20,198	24,854*	8.7	11.3
467	WESLEYAN	1	67	120	-	.1
496	JEWISH EST[1]	3	NA	1,124	.4	.5
497	BLACK BAPT EST[2]	NA	18,750	23,072*	8.1	10.5
498	INDEP.CHARIS.[3]	1	NA	350	.1	.2
499	INDEP.NON-CHAR[3]	6	NA	41,980	14.7	19.1
HANCOCK		**46**	**7,463**	**9,289***	**137.8**	**100.0**
081	CATHOLIC	1	NA	14	.2	.2
081d	*LATIN*	*1*	*NA*	*14*	*.2*	*.2*
145	CH GOD PROPHCY	1	48	60*	.9	.6
167	CHS OF CHRIST	1	10	13	.2	.1
361	PRIM BAPT ASCS	6	783	973*	14.4	10.5
419	SO BAPT CONV	36	6,502	8,080*	119.9	87.0
449	UN METHODIST	1	120	149*	2.2	1.6
HARDEMAN		**62**	**11,611**	**15,172***	**64.9**	**100.0**
053	ASSEMB OF GOD	1	15	30	.1	.2
081	CATHOLIC	1	NA	191	.8	1.3
081d	*LATIN*	*1*	*NA*	*191*	*.8*	*1.3*
167	CHS OF CHRIST	11	666	934	4.0	6.2
185	CUMBER PRESB	2	145	167	.7	1.1
193	EPISCOPAL	1	74	90	.4	.6
355	PRESB CH (USA)	1	24	31*	.1	.2
361	PRIM BAPT ASCS	3	94	121*	.5	.8
419	SO BAPT CONV	32	7,775	9,988*	42.7	65.8
449	UN METHODIST	10	1,128	1,449*	6.2	9.6
497	BLACK BAPT EST[2]	NA	1,690	2,171*	9.3	14.3
HARDIN		**70**	**9,327**	**11,950***	**52.8**	**100.0**
053	ASSEMB OF GOD	5	232	343	1.5	2.9

NA–Not applicable   NR–Not reported   *Total adherents estimated from known number of communicant, confirmed, full members.   - Represents a percent less than 0.1.   Percentages may not total due to rounding.
[1]See Appendix E   [2]See Appendix F   [3]See Appendix G   Lines in *italic* represent a breakdown of Catholic rites or Friends affiliations. They are included in their respective denominational total.

TENNESSEE

Table 4. Churches and Church Membership by County and Denomination: 1990

County and Denomination	Number of churches	Communicant, confirmed, full members	Total adherents Number	Percent of total population	Percent of total adherents
081 CATHOLIC	2	NA	385	1.7	3.2
081d LATIN	2	NA	385	1.7	3.2
097 CHR CHS&CHS CR	1	19	23*	.1	.2
123 CH GOD (ANDER)	1	16	31	.1	.3
127 CH GOD (CLEVE)	1	51	63*	.3	.5
145 CH GOD PROPHCY	2	97	120*	.5	1.0
165 CH OF NAZARENE	1	30	75	.3	.6
167 CHS OF CHRIST	9	881	1,133	5.0	9.5
185 CUMBER PRESB	4	642	662	2.9	5.5
263 INT FOURSQ GOS	3	318	392*	1.7	3.3
339 PENT CH OF GOD	1	34	77	.3	.6
355 PRESB CH (USA)	1	17	21*	.1	.2
413 S.D.A.	1	138	170*	.8	1.4
419 SO BAPT CONV	17	4,413	5,445*	24.1	45.6
449 UN METHODIST	21	2,133	2,632*	11.6	22.0
497 BLACK BAPT EST[2]	NA	306	378*	1.7	3.2
HAWKINS	**152**	**25,411**	**31,009***	**69.6**	**100.0**
005 AME ZION	2	387	421	.9	1.4
053 ASSEMB OF GOD	1	12	16	-	.1
081 CATHOLIC	1	NA	125	.3	.4
081d LATIN	1	NA	125	.3	.4
082 CENTRAL BAPT	3	614	747*	1.7	2.4
093 CHR CH (DISC)	1	65	88	.2	.3
097 CHR CHS&CHS CR	5	340	414*	.9	1.3
123 CH GOD (ANDER)	1	35	40	.1	.1
127 CH GOD (CLEVE)	4	189	230*	.5	.7
145 CH GOD PROPHCY	1	48	58*	.1	.2
157 CH OF BRETHREN	2	37	45*	.1	.1
165 CH OF NAZARENE	1	34	41	.1	.1
167 CHS OF CHRIST	2	156	179	.4	.6
223 FREE WILL BAPT	11	988	1,202*	2.7	3.9
355 PRESB CH (USA)	5	362	440*	1.0	1.4
361 PRIM BAPT ASCS	16	1,749	2,127*	4.8	6.9
413 S.D.A.	1	73	89*	.2	.3
419 SO BAPT CONV	67	17,691	21,519*	48.3	69.4
449 UN METHODIST	28	2,606	3,170*	7.1	10.2
496 JEWISH EST[1]	0	NA	28	.1	.1
497 BLACK BAPT EST[2]	NA	25	30*	.1	.1
HAYWOOD	**47**	**10,783**	**14,017***	**72.1**	**100.0**
053 ASSEMB OF GOD	3	246	325	1.7	2.3
081 CATHOLIC	1	NA	106	.5	.8
081d LATIN	1	NA	106	.5	.8
127 CH GOD (CLEVE)	1	47	61*	.3	.4
167 CHS OF CHRIST	6	406	505	2.6	3.6
193 EPISCOPAL	1	42	55	.3	.4
355 PRESB CH (USA)	3	144	186*	1.0	1.3
361 PRIM BAPT ASCS	1	1	1*	-	-
413 S.D.A.	1	20	26*	.1	.2
419 SO BAPT CONV	15	4,745	6,126*	31.5	43.7
449 UN METHODIST	14	1,827	2,359*	12.1	16.8
496 JEWISH EST[1]	1	NA	0	-	-
497 BLACK BAPT EST[2]	NA	3,305	4,267*	22.0	30.4
HENDERSON	**69**	**8,855**	**11,073***	**50.7**	**100.0**
053 ASSEMB OF GOD	1	26	39	.2	.4
081 CATHOLIC	2	NA	193	.9	1.7
081d LATIN	2	NA	193	.9	1.7
097 CHR CHS&CHS CR	1	0	0*	-	-
127 CH GOD (CLEVE)	1	89	110*	.5	1.0
167 CHS OF CHRIST	17	1,270	1,533	7.0	13.8
185 CUMBER PRESB	4	298	328	1.5	3.0
189 DUCK RIVR BAPT	4	262	324*	1.5	2.9
355 PRESB CH (USA)	1	11	14*	.1	.1
361 PRIM BAPT ASCS	4	50	62*	.3	.6
419 SO BAPT CONV	21	5,333	6,595*	30.2	59.6
449 UN METHODIST	13	1,422	1,759*	8.1	15.9
497 BLACK BAPT EST[2]	NA	94	116*	.5	1.0
HENRY	**89**	**15,353**	**19,782***	**70.9**	**100.0**
053 ASSEMB OF GOD	1	46	80	.3	.4
061 BEACHY AMISH	2	228	277*	1.0	1.4
081 CATHOLIC	1	NA	858	3.1	4.3
081d LATIN	1	NA	858	3.1	4.3
093 CHR CH (DISC)	1	130	175	.6	.9
145 CH GOD PROPHCY	1	48	58*	.2	.3
151 L-D SAINTS	1	NA	105	.4	.5
165 CH OF NAZARENE	1	80	87	.3	.4
167 CHS OF CHRIST	19	1,446	1,819	6.5	9.2
185 CUMBER PRESB	2	54	55	.2	.3
193 EPISCOPAL	1	89	153	.5	.8
283 LUTH—MO SYNOD	1	116	147	.5	.7
339 PENT CH OF GOD	1	22	65	.2	.3
355 PRESB CH (USA)	1	152	185*	.7	.9
361 PRIM BAPT ASCS	2	40	49*	.2	.2

County and Denomination	Number of churches	Communicant, confirmed, full members	Total adherents Number	Percent of total population	Percent of total adherents
413 S.D.A.	1	100	121*	.4	.6
419 SO BAPT CONV	31	9,418	11,438*	41.0	57.8
449 UN METHODIST	22	2,484	3,017*	10.8	15.3
497 BLACK BAPT EST[2]	NA	900	1,093*	3.9	5.5
HICKMAN	**71**	**5,930**	**7,706***	**46.0**	**100.0**
053 ASSEMB OF GOD	1	30	45	.3	.6
081 CATHOLIC	1	NA	106	.6	1.4
081d LATIN	1	NA	106	.6	1.4
145 CH GOD PROPHCY	2	97	119*	.7	1.5
157 CH OF BRETHREN	1	95	116*	.7	1.5
165 CH OF NAZARENE	1	47	81	.5	1.1
167 CHS OF CHRIST	39	2,776	3,564	21.3	46.2
185 CUMBER PRESB	2	34	34	.2	.4
323 OLD ORD AMISH	1	NA	150	.9	1.9
361 PRIM BAPT ASCS	1	11	13*	.1	.2
413 S.D.A.	1	21	26*	.2	.3
419 SO BAPT CONV	11	1,938	2,373*	14.2	30.8
449 UN METHODIST	10	841	1,030*	6.1	13.4
497 BLACK BAPT EST[2]	NA	40	49*	.3	.6
HOUSTON	**25**	**2,180**	**2,736***	**39.0**	**100.0**
053 ASSEMB OF GOD	1	26	50	.7	1.8
081 CATHOLIC	1	NA	80	1.1	2.9
081d LATIN	1	NA	80	1.1	2.9
145 CH GOD PROPHCY	2	97	118*	1.7	4.3
165 CH OF NAZARENE	2	370	413	5.9	15.1
167 CHS OF CHRIST	2	82	195	2.8	7.1
185 CUMBER PRESB	5	380	388	5.5	14.2
349 PENT HOLINESS	1	25	30*	.4	1.1
419 SO BAPT CONV	3	554	675*	9.6	24.7
449 UN METHODIST	8	646	787*	11.2	28.8
HUMPHREYS	**57**	**6,706**	**8,904***	**56.4**	**100.0**
053 ASSEMB OF GOD	2	65	104	.7	1.2
081 CATHOLIC	1	NA	300	1.9	3.4
081d LATIN	1	NA	300	1.9	3.4
145 CH GOD PROPHCY	2	97	120*	.8	1.3
151 L-D SAINTS	1	NA	126	.8	1.4
165 CH OF NAZARENE	2	137	294	1.9	3.3
167 CHS OF CHRIST	15	1,379	1,771	11.2	19.9
185 CUMBER PRESB	4	481	490	3.1	5.5
193 EPISCOPAL	1	72	93	.6	1.0
223 FREE WILL BAPT	5	358	443*	2.8	5.0
349 PENT HOLINESS	4	195	241*	1.5	2.7
355 PRESB CH (USA)	1	46	57*	.4	.6
419 SO BAPT CONV	7	2,119	2,622*	16.6	29.4
443 UN C OF CHRIST	1	49	61*	.4	.7
449 UN METHODIST	10	1,568	1,940*	12.3	21.8
467 WESLEYAN	1	25	100	.6	1.1
497 BLACK BAPT EST[2]	NA	115	142*	.9	1.6
JACKSON	**53**	**2,719**	**3,597***	**38.7**	**100.0**
053 ASSEMB OF GOD	1	38	65	.7	1.8
127 CH GOD (CLEVE)	1	49	59*	.6	1.6
167 CHS OF CHRIST	38	1,824	2,461	26.5	68.4
189 DUCK RIVR BAPT	1	40	48*	.5	1.3
221 FREE METHODIST	1	14	25	.3	.7
355 PRESB CH (USA)	1	3	4*	-	.1
419 SO BAPT CONV	3	341	410*	4.4	11.4
449 UN METHODIST	6	399	480*	5.2	13.3
467 WESLEYAN	1	11	45	.5	1.3
JEFFERSON	**102**	**17,578**	**21,865***	**66.2**	**100.0**
005 AME ZION	4	380	402	1.2	1.8
053 ASSEMB OF GOD	1	56	75	.2	.3
081 CATHOLIC	0	NA	262	.8	1.2
081d LATIN	0	NA	262	.8	1.2
097 CHR CHS&CHS CR	2	215	256*	.8	1.2
123 CH GOD (ANDER)	2	63	78	.2	.4
127 CH GOD (CLEVE)	7	572	681*	2.1	3.1
145 CH GOD PROPHCY	1	48	57*	.2	.3
151 L-D SAINTS	1	NA	317	1.0	1.4
167 CHS OF CHRIST	3	153	194	.6	.9
185 CUMBER PRESB	2	156	185	.6	.8
223 FREE WILL BAPT	2	165	197*	.6	.9
226 FRIENDS-USA	1	30	36*	.1	.2
226e FUM	1	30	36*	.1	.2
355 PRESB CH (USA)	8	563	671*	2.0	3.1
419 SO BAPT CONV	42	11,934	14,218*	43.1	65.0
449 UN METHODIST	25	3,183	3,792*	11.5	17.3
496 JEWISH EST[1]	0	NA	73	.2	.3
497 BLACK BAPT EST[2]	NA	60	71*	.2	.3
499 INDEP.NON-CHAR[3]	1	NA	300	.9	1.4

NA–Not applicable   NR–Not reported   *Total adherents estimated from known number of communicant, confirmed, full members.   - Represents a percent less than 0.1.   Percentages may not total due to rounding.
[1]See Appendix E   [2]See Appendix F   [3]See Appendix G   Lines in *italic* represent a breakdown of Catholic rites or Friends affiliations. They are included in their respective denominational total.

Table 4. Churches and Church Membership by County and Denomination: 1990

County and Denomination	Number of churches	Communicant, confirmed, full members	Total adherents		
			Number	Percent of total population	Percent of total adherents
JOHNSON	51	7,662	9,376*	68.1	100.0
053 ASSEMB OF GOD	1	42	52	.4	.6
081 CATHOLIC	0	NA	50	.4	.5
081d LATIN	*0*	*NA*	*50*	*.4*	*.5*
097 CHR CHS&CHS CR	9	780	940*	6.8	10.0
127 CH GOD (CLEVE)	1	32	39*	.3	.4
167 CHS OF CHRIST	6	385	520	3.8	5.5
223 FREE WILL BAPT	1	370	446*	3.2	4.8
285 MENNONITE CH	1	30	70	.5	.7
355 PRESB CH (USA)	3	122	147*	1.1	1.6
413 S.D.A.	1	30	36*	.3	.4
419 SO BAPT CONV	21	5,155	6,213*	45.1	66.3
449 UN METHODIST	7	716	863*	6.3	9.2
KNOX	448	176,242	236,075*	70.3	100.0
005 AME ZION	12	7,955	9,211	2.7	3.9
011 A.W.M.C.	3	0	0*	-	-
019 AMER BAPT USA	1	500	606*	.2	.3
053 ASSEMB OF GOD	10	901	1,250	.4	.5
059 BAPT MISS ASSN	4	481	583*	.2	.2
081 CATHOLIC	5	NA	10,356	3.1	4.4
081d LATIN	*5*	*NA*	*10,356*	*3.1*	*4.4*
093 CHR CH (DISC)	4	633	794	.2	.3
097 CHR CHS&CHS CR	9	1,399	1,696*	.5	.7
111 CH CR,SCIENTST	1	NR	NR	-	-
123 CH GOD (ANDER)	2	50	132	-	.1
127 CH GOD (CLEVE)	19	2,516	3,051*	.9	1.3
145 CH GOD PROPHCY	3	145	176*	.1	.1
151 L-D SAINTS	3	NA	1,296	.4	.5
165 CH OF NAZARENE	3	285	350	.1	.1
167 CHS OF CHRIST	16	2,179	2,869	.9	1.2
185 CUMBER PRESB	5	2,147	2,446	.7	1.0
193 EPISCOPAL	9	3,593	4,814	1.4	2.0
203 EVAN FREE CH	1	130	295	.1	.1
207 E.L.C.A.	5	2,035	2,563	.8	1.1
216 EVAN PRESBY CH	1	42	42	-	-
221 FREE METHODIST	1	0	18	-	-
223 FREE WILL BAPT	6	775	940*	.3	.4
226 FRIENDS-USA	3	117	157*	-	.1
226c FGC	*2*	*74*	*105*	*-*	*-*
226e FUM	*1*	*43*	*52*	*-*	*-*
246 GREEK ORTHODOX	1	NR	NR	-	-
263 INT FOURSQ GOS	1	19	23*	-	-
283 LUTH—MO SYNOD	3	757	969	.3	.4
285 MENNONITE CH	2	67	96	-	-
349 PENT HOLINESS	1	24	29*	-	-
355 PRESB CH (USA)	33	8,733	10,589*	3.2	4.5
356 PRESB CH AMER	3	2,359	3,124	.9	1.3
361 PRIM BAPT ASCS	2	102	124*	-	.1
403 SALVATION ARMY	1	169	173	.1	.1
413 S.D.A.	5	1,028	1,247*	.4	.5
419 SO BAPT CONV	180	103,347	125,315*	37.3	53.1
435 UNITARIAN-UNIV	2	480	675	.2	.3
443 UN C OF CHRIST	1	117	142*	-	.1
449 UN METHODIST	70	25,463	30,876*	9.2	13.1
469 WELS	1	76	98	-	-
496 JEWISH EST[1]	2	NA	748	.2	.3
497 BLACK BAPT EST[2]	NA	7,618	9,237*	2.8	3.9
498 INDEP.CHARIS.[3]	5	NA	2,800	.8	1.2
499 INDEP.NON-CHAR[3]	9	NA	6,165	1.8	2.6
LAKE	21	3,756	4,610*	64.7	100.0
081 CATHOLIC	1	NA	25	.4	.5
081d LATIN	*1*	*NA*	*25*	*.4*	*.5*
127 CH GOD (CLEVE)	1	47	56*	.8	1.2
145 CH GOD PROPHCY	1	48	57*	.8	1.2
167 CHS OF CHRIST	5	438	619	8.7	13.4
355 PRESB CH (USA)	1	32	38*	.5	.8
419 SO BAPT CONV	9	2,337	2,794*	39.2	60.6
449 UN METHODIST	3	498	595*	8.3	12.9
497 BLACK BAPT EST[2]	NA	356	426*	6.0	9.2
LAUDERDALE	65	11,577	14,955*	63.7	100.0
053 ASSEMB OF GOD	8	524	815	3.5	5.4
081 CATHOLIC	1	NA	70	.3	.5
081d LATIN	*1*	*NA*	*70*	*.3*	*.5*
093 CHR CH (DISC)	1	75	96	.4	.6
127 CH GOD (CLEVE)	4	242	308*	1.3	2.1
167 CHS OF CHRIST	8	346	443	1.9	3.0
185 CUMBER PRESB	2	59	67	.3	.4
193 EPISCOPAL	1	33	42	.2	.3
355 PRESB CH (USA)	1	71	90*	.4	.6
419 SO BAPT CONV	23	6,121	7,795*	33.2	52.1
449 UN METHODIST	16	2,160	2,751*	11.7	18.4
497 BLACK BAPT EST[2]	NA	1,946	2,478*	10.5	16.6
LAWRENCE	125	16,307	22,662*	64.2	100.0
053 ASSEMB OF GOD	1	73	150	.4	.7
081 CATHOLIC	3	NA	1,266	3.6	5.6
081d LATIN	*3*	*NA*	*1,266*	*3.6*	*5.6*
127 CH GOD (CLEVE)	6	438	550*	1.6	2.4
146 CH GOD MTN ASM	1	12	15*	-	.1
151 L-D SAINTS	1	NA	168	.5	.7
165 CH OF NAZARENE	4	256	319	.9	1.4
167 CHS OF CHRIST	34	3,163	4,121	11.7	18.2
185 CUMBER PRESB	2	245	256	.7	1.1
263 INT FOURSQ GOS	1	0	0*	-	-
323 OLD ORD AMISH	4	NA	600	1.7	2.6
355 PRESB CH (USA)	1	54	68*	.2	.3
361 PRIM BAPT ASCS	1	44	55*	.2	.2
413 S.D.A.	1	145	182*	.5	.8
419 SO BAPT CONV	34	8,891	11,163*	31.6	49.3
449 UN METHODIST	31	2,986	3,749*	10.6	16.5
LEWIS	33	2,913	3,770*	40.8	100.0
053 ASSEMB OF GOD	1	57	67	.7	1.8
081 CATHOLIC	1	NA	35	.4	.9
081d LATIN	*1*	*NA*	*35*	*.4*	*.9*
133 CH GOD(7TH)DEN	1	14	18	.2	.5
167 CHS OF CHRIST	17	1,267	1,693	18.3	44.9
185 CUMBER PRESB	1	114	118	1.3	3.1
419 SO BAPT CONV	6	959	1,207*	13.1	32.0
449 UN METHODIST	6	502	632*	6.8	16.8
LINCOLN	102	14,772	18,571*	66.0	100.0
053 ASSEMB OF GOD	1	83	110	.4	.6
055 AS REF PRES CH	3	529	575	2.0	3.1
081 CATHOLIC	1	NA	293	1.0	1.6
081d LATIN	*1*	*NA*	*293*	*1.0*	*1.6*
123 CH GOD (ANDER)	2	101	120	.4	.6
127 CH GOD (CLEVE)	1	51	63*	.2	.3
151 L-D SAINTS	1	NA	198	.7	1.1
165 CH OF NAZARENE	1	82	126	.4	.7
167 CHS OF CHRIST	33	2,544	3,157	11.2	17.0
185 CUMBER PRESB	9	988	1,032	3.7	5.6
193 EPISCOPAL	1	101	139	.5	.7
349 PENT HOLINESS	1	56	69*	.2	.4
355 PRESB CH (USA)	4	316	392*	1.4	2.1
413 S.D.A.	1	57	71*	.3	.4
419 SO BAPT CONV	29	8,280	10,263*	36.4	55.3
449 UN METHODIST	14	1,417	1,756*	6.2	9.5
497 BLACK BAPT EST[2]	NA	167	207*	.7	1.1
LOUDON	78	18,812	23,287*	74.5	100.0
005 AME ZION	3	474	632	2.0	2.7
081 CATHOLIC	1	NA	266	.9	1.1
081d LATIN	*1*	*NA*	*266*	*.9*	*1.1*
123 CH GOD (ANDER)	1	45	55	.2	.2
127 CH GOD (CLEVE)	6	1,394	1,695*	5.4	7.3
145 CH GOD PROPHCY	1	48	58*	.2	.2
165 CH OF NAZARENE	3	127	222	.7	1.0
167 CHS OF CHRIST	2	157	204	.7	.9
185 CUMBER PRESB	3	519	581	1.9	2.5
193 EPISCOPAL	1	131	222	.7	1.0
355 PRESB CH (USA)	4	300	365*	1.2	1.6
361 PRIM BAPT ASCS	1	9	11*	-	-
413 S.D.A.	1	57	69*	.2	.3
419 SO BAPT CONV	38	13,582	16,513*	52.8	70.9
449 UN METHODIST	13	1,969	2,394*	7.7	10.3
MC MINN	129	28,068	34,763*	82.0	100.0
005 AME ZION	9	970	1,070	2.5	3.1
053 ASSEMB OF GOD	1	30	71	.2	.2
081 CATHOLIC	1	NA	324	.8	.9
081d LATIN	*1*	*NA*	*324*	*.8*	*.9*
097 CHR CHS&CHS CR	2	187	230*	.5	.7
123 CH GOD (ANDER)	5	382	428	1.0	1.2
127 CH GOD (CLEVE)	4	591	726*	1.7	2.1
145 CH GOD PROPHCY	4	194	238*	.6	.7
165 CH OF NAZARENE	2	90	156	.4	.4
167 CHS OF CHRIST	10	490	665	1.6	1.9
193 EPISCOPAL	1	237	267	.6	.8
283 LUTH—MO SYNOD	1	143	190	.4	.5
355 PRESB CH (USA)	3	223	274*	.6	.8
413 S.D.A.	1	103	126*	.3	.4
419 SO BAPT CONV	64	20,262	24,882*	58.7	71.6
449 UN METHODIST	21	3,788	4,652*	11.0	13.4
497 BLACK BAPT EST[2]	NA	378	464*	1.1	1.3

NA–Not applicable   NR–Not reported   *Total adherents estimated from known number of communicant, confirmed, full members.   - Represents a percent less than 0.1.   Percentages may not total due to rounding.
[1]See Appendix E   [2]See Appendix F   [3]See Appendix G   Lines in *italic* represent a breakdown of Catholic rites or Friends affiliations. They are included in their respective denominational total.

Table 4. Churches and Church Membership by County and Denomination: 1990

County and Denomination		Number of churches	Communicant, confirmed, full members	Total adherents		
				Number	Percent of total population	Percent of total adherents
MC NAIRY		**87**	**10,900**	**13,750***	**61.3**	**100.0**
081	CATHOLIC	1	NA	141	.6	1.0
081d	*LATIN*	*1*	*NA*	*141*	*.6*	*1.0*
097	CHR CHS&CHS CR	3	280	344*	1.5	2.5
127	CH GOD (CLEVE)	3	120	148*	.7	1.1
145	CH GOD PROPHCY	4	194	239*	1.1	1.7
165	CH OF NAZARENE	1	12	47	.2	.3
167	CHS OF CHRIST	18	1,426	1,945	8.7	14.1
185	CUMBER PRESB	5	415	455	2.0	3.3
339	PENT CH OF GOD	1	34	77	.3	.6
355	PRESB CH (USA)	6	278	342*	1.5	2.5
361	PRIM BAPT ASCS	2	50	61*	.3	.4
419	SO BAPT CONV	27	6,285	7,730*	34.5	56.2
449	UN METHODIST	16	1,506	1,852*	8.3	13.5
497	BLACK BAPT EST[2]	NA	300	369*	1.6	2.7
MACON		**36**	**5,740**	**7,372***	**46.3**	**100.0**
053	ASSEMB OF GOD	1	39	117	.7	1.6
081	CATHOLIC	1	NA	75	.5	1.0
081d	*LATIN*	*1*	*NA*	*75*	*.5*	*1.0*
127	CH GOD (CLEVE)	1	74	92*	.6	1.2
167	CHS OF CHRIST	8	1,137	1,499	9.4	20.3
320	"OLD" MB ASCS	16	3,569	4,442*	27.9	60.3
419	SO BAPT CONV	3	575	716*	4.5	9.7
449	UN METHODIST	6	346	431*	2.7	5.8
MADISON		**112**	**44,172**	**57,193***	**73.3**	**100.0**
053	ASSEMB OF GOD	3	353	649	.8	1.1
081	CATHOLIC	1	NA	1,646	2.1	2.9
081d	*LATIN*	*1*	*NA*	*1,646*	*2.1*	*2.9*
093	CHR CH (DISC)	1	56	87	.1	.2
097	CHR CHS&CHS CR	1	550	692*	.9	1.2
111	CH CR,SCIENTST	1	NR	NR	-	-
123	CH GOD (ANDER)	1	25	28	-	-
127	CH GOD (CLEVE)	4	469	590*	.8	1.0
145	CH GOD PROPHCY	1	48	60*	.1	.1
151	L-D SAINTS	2	NA	399	.5	.7
165	CH OF NAZARENE	2	93	143	.2	.3
167	CHS OF CHRIST	11	2,749	2,831	3.6	4.9
185	CUMBER PRESB	4	621	674	.9	1.2
193	EPISCOPAL	1	365	414	.5	.7
207	E.L.C.A.	1	119	165	.2	.3
223	FREE WILL BAPT	1	36	45*	.1	.1
283	LUTH—MO SYNOD	1	212	284	.4	.5
355	PRESB CH (USA)	3	671	844*	1.1	1.5
356	PRESB CH AMER	1	96	96	.1	.2
361	PRIM BAPT ASCS	2	60	76*	.1	.1
403	SALVATION ARMY	1	82	90	.1	.2
413	S.D.A.	2	275	346*	.4	.6
419	SO BAPT CONV	41	21,899	27,561*	35.3	48.2
449	UN METHODIST	25	6,846	8,616*	11.0	15.1
496	JEWISH EST[1]	1	NA	100	.1	.2
497	BLACK BAPT EST[2]	NA	8,547	10,757*	13.8	18.8
MARION		**69**	**7,895**	**10,115***	**40.7**	**100.0**
081	CATHOLIC	1	NA	145	.6	1.4
081d	*LATIN*	*1*	*NA*	*145*	*.6*	*1.4*
127	CH GOD (CLEVE)	15	1,092	1,362*	5.5	13.5
145	CH GOD PROPHCY	1	48	60*	.2	.6
165	CH OF NAZARENE	2	93	166	.7	1.6
167	CHS OF CHRIST	11	687	945	3.8	9.3
185	CUMBER PRESB	6	457	477	1.9	4.7
193	EPISCOPAL	1	123	139	.6	1.4
413	S.D.A.	1	101	126*	.5	1.2
419	SO BAPT CONV	14	3,728	4,649*	18.7	46.0
449	UN METHODIST	17	1,309	1,632*	6.6	16.1
496	JEWISH EST[1]	0	NA	94	.4	.9
497	BLACK BAPT EST[2]	NA	257	320*	1.3	3.2
MARSHALL		**70**	**9,666**	**12,261***	**56.9**	**100.0**
053	ASSEMB OF GOD	2	88	185	.9	1.5
081	CATHOLIC	1	NA	200	.9	1.6
081d	*LATIN*	*1*	*NA*	*200*	*.9*	*1.6*
123	CH GOD (ANDER)	1	40	40	.2	.3
127	CH GOD (CLEVE)	3	137	170*	.8	1.4
145	CH GOD PROPHCY	2	97	121*	.6	1.0
165	CH OF NAZARENE	1	85	82	.4	.7
167	CHS OF CHRIST	23	2,833	3,628	16.8	29.6
185	CUMBER PRESB	4	417	417	1.9	3.4
223	FREE WILL BAPT	1	32	40*	.2	.3
355	PRESB CH (USA)	4	391	486*	2.3	4.0
361	PRIM BAPT ASCS	1	24	30*	.1	.2
419	SO BAPT CONV	10	3,501	4,351*	20.2	35.5
449	UN METHODIST	17	1,756	2,182*	10.1	17.8
497	BLACK BAPT EST[2]	NA	265	329*	1.5	2.7

County and Denomination		Number of churches	Communicant, confirmed, full members	Total adherents		
				Number	Percent of total population	Percent of total adherents
MAURY		**144**	**22,532**	**30,264***	**55.2**	**100.0**
053	ASSEMB OF GOD	1	173	480	.9	1.6
055	AS REF PRES CH	1	16	16	-	.1
081	CATHOLIC	1	NA	1,071	2.0	3.5
081d	*LATIN*	*1*	*NA*	*1,071*	*2.0*	*3.5*
097	CHR CHS&CHS CR	1	66	83*	.2	.3
127	CH GOD (CLEVE)	2	143	180*	.3	.6
145	CH GOD PROPHCY	3	145	183*	.3	.6
151	L-D SAINTS	1	NA	431	.8	1.4
165	CH OF NAZARENE	7	494	666	1.2	2.2
167	CHS OF CHRIST	51	5,884	7,411	13.5	24.5
185	CUMBER PRESB	10	1,017	1,061	1.9	3.5
193	EPISCOPAL	2	252	615	1.1	2.0
223	FREE WILL BAPT	3	334	421*	.8	1.4
283	LUTH—MO SYNOD	1	153	222	.4	.7
355	PRESB CH (USA)	6	839	1,057*	1.9	3.5
356	PRESB CH AMER	1	154	167	.3	.6
361	PRIM BAPT ASCS	1	0	0*	-	-
413	S.D.A.	2	89	112*	.2	.4
419	SO BAPT CONV	24	6,153	7,749*	14.1	25.6
449	UN METHODIST	25	4,100	5,163*	9.4	17.1
469	WELS	1	5	9	-	-
497	BLACK BAPT EST[2]	NA	2,515	3,167*	5.8	10.5
MEIGS		**31**	**3,628**	**4,469***	**55.6**	**100.0**
053	ASSEMB OF GOD	1	8	12	.1	.3
127	CH GOD (CLEVE)	4	273	336*	4.2	7.5
167	CHS OF CHRIST	1	30	38	.5	.9
413	S.D.A.	1	44	54*	.7	1.2
419	SO BAPT CONV	14	2,782	3,425*	42.6	76.6
449	UN METHODIST	10	491	604*	7.5	13.5
MONROE		**110**	**19,573**	**24,116***	**79.0**	**100.0**
005	AME ZION	1	150	225	.7	.9
053	ASSEMB OF GOD	1	326	307	1.0	1.3
097	CHR CHS&CHS CR	1	75	93*	.3	.4
123	CH GOD (ANDER)	1	40	53	.2	.2
127	CH GOD (CLEVE)	5	469	579*	1.9	2.4
145	CH GOD PROPHCY	1	48	59*	.2	.2
165	CH OF NAZARENE	1	23	38	.1	.2
167	CHS OF CHRIST	2	105	130	.4	.5
185	CUMBER PRESB	2	52	55	.2	.2
207	E.L.C.A.	1	66	77	.3	.3
223	FREE WILL BAPT	2	152	188*	.6	.8
226	FRIENDS-USA	3	109	135*	.4	.6
226e	*FUM*	*3*	*109*	*135***	*.4*	*.6*
355	PRESB CH (USA)	8	604	746*	2.4	3.1
356	PRESB CH AMER	2	64	74	.2	.3
419	SO BAPT CONV	64	14,732	18,197*	59.6	75.5
443	UN C OF CHRIST	1	69	85*	.3	.4
449	UN METHODIST	14	1,648	2,036*	6.7	8.4
497	BLACK BAPT EST[2]	NA	841	1,039*	3.4	4.3
MONTGOMERY		**126**	**35,215**	**48,698***	**48.5**	**100.0**
005	AME ZION	1	111	161	.2	.3
053	ASSEMB OF GOD	3	972	1,941	1.9	4.0
081	CATHOLIC	1	NA	2,446	2.4	5.0
081d	*LATIN*	*1*	*NA*	*2,446*	*2.4*	*5.0*
089	CHR & MISS AL	1	21	55	.1	.1
093	CHR CH (DISC)	1	220	303	.3	.6
097	CHR CHS&CHS CR	1	90	114*	.1	.2
123	CH GOD (ANDER)	3	124	204	.2	.4
127	CH GOD (CLEVE)	2	414	527*	.5	1.1
145	CH GOD PROPHCY	3	145	184*	.2	.4
151	L-D SAINTS	2	NA	641	.6	1.3
165	CH OF NAZARENE	5	940	1,178	1.2	2.4
167	CHS OF CHRIST	13	1,670	2,209	2.2	4.5
185	CUMBER PRESB	7	1,510	1,595	1.6	3.3
193	EPISCOPAL	2	329	354	.4	.7
207	E.L.C.A.	1	36	61	.1	.1
223	FREE WILL BAPT	8	379	482*	.5	1.0
259	IFCA	1	NR	NR	-	-
283	LUTH—MO SYNOD	1	188	246	.2	.5
355	PRESB CH (USA)	3	723	920*	.9	1.9
356	PRESB CH AMER	1	0	0	-	-
403	SALVATION ARMY	1	29	30	-	.1
413	S.D.A.	2	108	137*	.1	.3
419	SO BAPT CONV	30	15,844	20,156*	20.1	41.4
449	UN METHODIST	32	6,135	7,805*	7.8	16.0
497	BLACK BAPT EST[2]	NA	5,227	6,649*	6.6	13.7
498	INDEP.CHARIS.[3]	1	NA	300	.3	.6
MOORE		**22**	**2,377**	**2,975***	**63.0**	**100.0**
167	CHS OF CHRIST	6	516	677	14.3	22.8
189	DUCK RIVR BAPT	5	629	777*	16.5	26.1

NA–Not applicable   NR–Not reported   *Total adherents estimated from known number of communicant, confirmed, full members.   - Represents a percent less than 0.1.   Percentages may not total due to rounding.

[1]See Appendix E   [2]See Appendix F   [3]See Appendix G   Lines in *italic* represent a breakdown of Catholic rites or Friends affiliations. They are included in their respective denominational total.

Table 4. Churches and Church Membership by County and Denomination: 1990

County and Denomination		Number of churches	Communicant, confirmed, full members	Total adherents		
				Number	Percent of total population	Percent of total adherents
361	PRIM BAPT ASCS	1	167	206*	4.4	6.9
419	SO BAPT CONV	3	512	632*	13.4	21.2
449	UN METHODIST	7	553	683*	14.5	23.0
MORGAN		**38**	**6,126**	**7,692***	**44.5**	**100.0**
081	CATHOLIC	1	NA	61	.4	.8
081d	*LATIN*	*1*	*NA*	*61*	*.4*	*.8*
127	CH GOD (CLEVE)	1	15	19*	.1	.2
145	CH GOD PROPHCY	2	97	120*	.7	1.6
165	CH OF NAZARENE	2	60	128	.7	1.7
167	CHS OF CHRIST	2	80	104	.6	1.4
185	CUMBER PRESB	1	51	51	.3	.7
193	EPISCOPAL	1	10	12	.1	.2
283	LUTH—MO SYNOD	1	296	371	2.1	4.8
355	PRESB CH (USA)	2	45	56*	.3	.7
413	S.D.A.	2	204	252*	1.5	3.3
419	SO BAPT CONV	17	5,020	6,211*	35.9	80.7
443	UN C OF CHRIST	1	43	53*	.3	.7
449	UN METHODIST	5	205	254*	1.5	3.3
OBION		**118**	**18,427**	**22,824***	**72.0**	**100.0**
053	ASSEMB OF GOD	6	583	590	1.9	2.6
055	AS REF PRES CH	2	32	32	.1	.1
081	CATHOLIC	1	NA	365	1.2	1.6
081d	*LATIN*	*1*	*NA*	*365*	*1.2*	*1.6*
093	CHR CH (DISC)	1	130	261	.8	1.1
097	CHR CHS&CHS CR	2	186	228*	.7	1.0
123	CH GOD (ANDER)	1	94	125	.4	.5
127	CH GOD (CLEVE)	3	146	179*	.6	.8
145	CH GOD PROPHCY	2	97	119*	.4	.5
167	CHS OF CHRIST	27	2,056	2,639	8.3	11.6
185	CUMBER PRESB	14	1,184	1,234	3.9	5.4
193	EPISCOPAL	1	100	119	.4	.5
259	IFCA	1	NR	NR	-	-
283	LUTH—MO SYNOD	1	134	193	.6	.8
355	PRESB CH (USA)	1	25	31*	.1	.1
361	PRIM BAPT ASCS	1	18	22*	.1	.1
413	S.D.A.	1	6	7*	-	-
419	SO BAPT CONV	26	9,797	11,984*	37.8	52.5
449	UN METHODIST	27	3,059	3,742*	11.8	16.4
497	BLACK BAPT EST[2]	NA	780	954*	3.0	4.2
OVERTON		**60**	**7,555**	**9,392***	**53.3**	**100.0**
053	ASSEMB OF GOD	2	86	108	.6	1.1
093	CHR CH (DISC)	5	454	674	3.8	7.2
123	CH GOD (ANDER)	1	43	50	.3	.5
127	CH GOD (CLEVE)	1	34	41*	.2	.4
145	CH GOD PROPHCY	2	97	118*	.7	1.3
167	CHS OF CHRIST	14	1,284	1,645	9.3	17.5
185	CUMBER PRESB	2	68	69	.4	.7
223	FREE WILL BAPT	2	167	203*	1.2	2.2
355	PRESB CH (USA)	1	46	56*	.3	.6
419	SO BAPT CONV	14	3,573	4,353*	24.7	46.3
449	UN METHODIST	16	1,703	2,075*	11.8	22.1
PERRY		**26**	**2,250**	**2,822***	**42.7**	**100.0**
081	CATHOLIC	1	NA	15	.2	.5
081d	*LATIN*	*1*	*NA*	*15*	*.2*	*.5*
097	CHR CHS&CHS CR	1	200	247*	3.7	8.8
127	CH GOD (CLEVE)	1	43	53*	.8	1.9
143	CG IN CR(MENN)	1	19	23*	.3	.8
167	CHS OF CHRIST	8	675	863	13.1	30.6
413	S.D.A.	1	22	27*	.4	1.0
419	SO BAPT CONV	4	611	754*	11.4	26.7
449	UN METHODIST	9	680	840*	12.7	29.8
PICKETT		**13**	**1,552**	**1,926***	**42.3**	**100.0**
093	CHR CH (DISC)	1	38	58	1.3	3.0
097	CHR CHS&CHS CR	2	392	482*	10.6	25.0
145	CH GOD PROPHCY	1	48	59*	1.3	3.1
167	CHS OF CHRIST	1	70	91	2.0	4.7
259	IFCA	1	NR	NR	-	-
419	SO BAPT CONV	3	620	763*	16.8	39.6
436	UNITED BAPT	2	294	362*	8.0	18.8
449	UN METHODIST	2	90	111*	2.4	5.8
POLK		**63**	**9,267**	**11,433***	**83.8**	**100.0**
081	CATHOLIC	1	NA	67	.5	.6
081d	*LATIN*	*1*	*NA*	*67*	*.5*	*.6*
127	CH GOD (CLEVE)	5	430	521*	3.8	4.6
145	CH GOD PROPHCY	1	48	58*	.4	.5
151	L-D SAINTS	1	NA	143	1.0	1.3
167	CHS OF CHRIST	4	205	238	1.7	2.1
193	EPISCOPAL	1	32	41	.3	.4
355	PRESB CH (USA)	1	85	103*	.8	.9
419	SO BAPT CONV	44	7,990	9,684*	71.0	84.7
449	UN METHODIST	5	477	578*	4.2	5.1
PUTNAM		**125**	**23,023**	**29,270***	**57.0**	**100.0**
053	ASSEMB OF GOD	4	371	583	1.1	2.0
081	CATHOLIC	1	NA	814	1.6	2.8
081d	*LATIN*	*1*	*NA*	*814*	*1.6*	*2.8*
093	CHR CH (DISC)	1	33	56	.1	.2
097	CHR CHS&CHS CR	1	250	301*	.6	1.0
111	CH CR,SCIENTST	1	NR	NR	-	-
123	CH GOD (ANDER)	4	252	464	.9	1.6
127	CH GOD (CLEVE)	8	517	623*	1.2	2.1
143	CG IN CR(MENN)	1	35	42*	.1	.1
145	CH GOD PROPHCY	2	97	117*	.2	.4
165	CH OF NAZARENE	2	276	453	.9	1.5
167	CHS OF CHRIST	28	3,882	4,943	9.6	16.9
185	CUMBER PRESB	5	600	670	1.3	2.3
189	DUCK RIVR BAPT	1	58	70*	.1	.2
193	EPISCOPAL	1	304	392	.8	1.3
223	FREE WILL BAPT	10	1,795	2,164*	4.2	7.4
226	FRIENDS-USA	1	0	9	-	-
226c	*FGC*	*1*	*0*	*9*	*-*	*-*
283	LUTH—MO SYNOD	1	134	171	.3	.6
320	"OLD" MB ASCS	1	22	27*	.1	.1
355	PRESB CH (USA)	5	393	474*	.9	1.6
413	S.D.A.	1	125	151*	.3	.5
419	SO BAPT CONV	31	10,529	12,695*	24.7	43.4
449	UN METHODIST	14	3,116	3,757*	7.3	12.8
467	WESLEYAN	1	15	30	.1	.1
497	BLACK BAPT EST[2]	NA	219	264*	.5	.9
RHEA		**63**	**9,950**	**12,441***	**51.1**	**100.0**
053	ASSEMB OF GOD	1	38	50	.2	.4
081	CATHOLIC	1	NA	142	.6	1.1
081d	*LATIN*	*1*	*NA*	*142*	*.6*	*1.1*
127	CH GOD (CLEVE)	9	1,114	1,374*	5.6	11.0
133	CH GOD(7TH)DEN	1	13	18	.1	.1
145	CH GOD PROPHCY	1	48	59*	.2	.5
167	CHS OF CHRIST	4	259	339	1.4	2.7
193	EPISCOPAL	1	29	42	.2	.3
259	IFCA	1	NR	NR	-	-
263	INT FOURSQ GOS	3	495	610*	2.5	4.9
283	LUTH—MO SYNOD	1	53	64	.3	.5
355	PRESB CH (USA)	1	63	78*	.3	.6
356	PRESB CH AMER	1	0	0	-	-
413	S.D.A.	4	457	564*	2.3	4.5
419	SO BAPT CONV	21	5,487	6,766*	27.8	54.4
449	UN METHODIST	13	1,772	2,185*	9.0	17.6
497	BLACK BAPT EST[2]	NA	122	150*	.6	1.2
ROANE		**97**	**24,084**	**31,336***	**66.4**	**100.0**
081	CATHOLIC	1	NA	300	.6	1.0
081d	*LATIN*	*1*	*NA*	*300*	*.6*	*1.0*
093	CHR CH (DISC)	1	224	455	1.0	1.5
097	CHR CHS&CHS CR	7	627	761*	1.6	2.4
127	CH GOD (CLEVE)	3	247	300*	.6	1.0
145	CH GOD PROPHCY	2	97	118*	.2	.4
146	CH GOD MTN ASM	3	65	79*	.2	.3
151	L-D SAINTS	1	NA	170	.4	.5
165	CH OF NAZARENE	1	19	0	-	-
167	CHS OF CHRIST	6	932	1,193	2.5	3.8
185	CUMBER PRESB	2	177	184	.4	.6
193	EPISCOPAL	1	124	169	.4	.5
221	FREE METHODIST	1	7	23	-	.1
259	IFCA	1	NR	NR	-	-
263	INT FOURSQ GOS	1	234	284*	.6	.9
283	LUTH—MO SYNOD	1	181	220	.5	.7
355	PRESB CH (USA)	4	544	661*	1.4	2.1
356	PRESB CH AMER	1	78	93	.2	.3
361	PRIM BAPT ASCS	1	34	41*	.1	.1
413	S.D.A.	2	77	94*	.2	.3
419	SO BAPT CONV	38	17,277	20,983*	44.4	67.0
449	UN METHODIST	15	2,475	3,006*	6.4	9.6
467	WESLEYAN	1	22	21	-	.1
497	BLACK BAPT EST[2]	NA	643	781*	1.7	2.5
499	INDEP.NON-CHAR[3]	3	NA	1,400	3.0	4.5
ROBERTSON		**81**	**21,073**	**27,497***	**66.3**	**100.0**
053	ASSEMB OF GOD	2	201	291	.7	1.1
081	CATHOLIC	2	NA	413	1.0	1.5
081d	*LATIN*	*2*	*NA*	*413*	*1.0*	*1.5*
093	CHR CH (DISC)	1	92	114	.3	.4
165	CH OF NAZARENE	1	86	79	.2	.3
167	CHS OF CHRIST	12	1,781	2,307	5.6	8.4
185	CUMBER PRESB	2	359	387	.9	1.4
193	EPISCOPAL	1	18	20	-	.1

NA–Not applicable   NR–Not reported   *Total adherents estimated from known number of communicant, confirmed, full members.   - Represents a percent less than 0.1.   Percentages may not total due to rounding.
[1]See Appendix E   [2]See Appendix F   [3]See Appendix G   Lines in *italic* represent a breakdown of Catholic rites or Friends affiliations. They are included in their respective denominational total.

Table 4. Churches and Church Membership by County and Denomination: 1990

County and Denomination	Number of churches	Communicant, confirmed, full members	Total adherents Number	Total adherents Percent of total population	Total adherents Percent of total adherents
223 FREE WILL BAPT	3	474	605*	1.5	2.2
349 PENT HOLINESS	1	185	236*	.6	.9
355 PRESB CH (USA)	2	167	213*	.5	.8
413 S.D.A.	3	358	457*	1.1	1.7
419 SO BAPT CONV	27	11,805	15,064*	36.3	54.8
449 UN METHODIST	24	3,385	4,320*	10.4	15.7
496 JEWISH EST[1]	0	NA	232	.6	.8
497 BLACK BAPT EST[2]	NA	2,162	2,759*	6.6	10.0
RUTHERFORD	**172**	**38,375**	**54,334***	**45.8**	**100.0**
053 ASSEMB OF GOD	2	267	370	.3	.7
081 CATHOLIC	2	NA	3,343	2.8	6.2
081d *LATIN*	*2*	*NA*	*3,343*	*2.8*	*6.2*
093 CHR CH (DISC)	1	201	225	.2	.4
097 CHR CHS&CHS CR	2	50	63*	.1	.1
111 CH CR,SCIENTST	1	NR	NR	-	-
123 CH GOD (ANDER)	2	175	195	.2	.4
127 CH GOD (CLEVE)	1	215	273*	.2	.5
145 CH GOD PROPHCY	2	97	123*	.1	.2
151 L-D SAINTS	2	NA	677	.6	1.2
165 CH OF NAZARENE	2	188	206	.2	.4
167 CHS OF CHRIST	50	6,259	8,285	7.0	15.2
185 CUMBER PRESB	7	898	953	.8	1.8
189 DUCK RIVR BAPT	5	432	548*	.5	1.0
193 EPISCOPAL	1	379	508	.4	.9
207 E.L.C.A.	2	274	354	.3	.7
216 EVAN PRESBY CH	1	57	57	-	.1
221 FREE METHODIST	2	117	197	.2	.4
223 FREE WILL BAPT	1	107	136*	.1	.3
283 LUTH—MO SYNOD	1	308	430	.4	.8
353 CHR BRETHREN	1	125	190	.2	.3
355 PRESB CH (USA)	9	857	1,088*	.9	2.0
356 PRESB CH AMER	1	45	73	.1	.1
361 PRIM BAPT ASCS	2	14	18*	-	-
413 S.D.A.	2	184	234*	.2	.4
419 SO BAPT CONV	42	17,223	21,857*	18.4	40.2
435 UNITARIAN-UNIV	1	15	15	-	-
449 UN METHODIST	25	6,137	7,788*	6.6	14.3
496 JEWISH EST[1]	0	NA	668	.6	1.2
497 BLACK BAPT EST[2]	NA	3,751	4,760*	4.0	8.8
499 INDEP.NON-CHAR[3]	2	NA	700	.6	1.3
SCOTT	**51**	**8,858**	**11,555***	**62.9**	**100.0**
081 CATHOLIC	1	NA	158	.9	1.4
081d *LATIN*	*1*	*NA*	*158*	*.9*	*1.4*
127 CH GOD (CLEVE)	2	93	120*	.7	1.0
145 CH GOD PROPHCY	2	97	125*	.7	1.1
146 CH GOD MTN ASM	1	19	24*	.1	.2
167 CHS OF CHRIST	2	173	225	1.2	1.9
355 PRESB CH (USA)	1	165	212*	1.2	1.8
419 SO BAPT CONV	16	4,429	5,697*	31.0	49.3
436 UNITED BAPT	22	3,599	4,630*	25.2	40.1
443 UN C OF CHRIST	2	47	60*	.3	.5
449 UN METHODIST	2	236	304*	1.7	2.6
SEQUATCHIE	**26**	**3,215**	**4,036***	**45.5**	**100.0**
081 CATHOLIC	0	NA	7	.1	.2
081d *LATIN*	*0*	*NA*	*7*	*.1*	*.2*
127 CH GOD (CLEVE)	4	333	414*	4.7	10.3
167 CHS OF CHRIST	7	312	408	4.6	10.1
185 CUMBER PRESB	2	89	89	1.0	2.2
189 DUCK RIVR BAPT	1	0	0*	-	-
413 S.D.A.	1	143	178*	2.0	4.4
419 SO BAPT CONV	8	1,838	2,284*	25.8	56.6
449 UN METHODIST	3	500	621*	7.0	15.4
496 JEWISH EST[1]	0	NA	35	.4	.9
SEVIER	**114**	**22,866**	**29,299***	**57.4**	**100.0**
053 ASSEMB OF GOD	2	245	331	.6	1.1
081 CATHOLIC	2	NA	625	1.2	2.1
081d *LATIN*	*2*	*NA*	*625*	*1.2*	*2.1*
097 CHR CHS&CHS CR	2	425	520*	1.0	1.8
111 CH CR,SCIENTST	1	NR	NR	-	-
123 CH GOD (ANDER)	1	40	40	.1	.1
127 CH GOD (CLEVE)	5	1,088	1,330*	2.6	4.5
151 L-D SAINTS	1	NA	179	.4	.6
167 CHS OF CHRIST	5	195	259	.5	.9
193 EPISCOPAL	2	239	260	.5	.9
207 E.L.C.A.	1	154	177	.3	.6
283 LUTH—MO SYNOD	1	95	141	.3	.5
355 PRESB CH (USA)	3	267	326*	.6	1.1
356 PRESB CH AMER	1	116	121	.2	.4
361 PRIM BAPT ASCS	1	29	35*	.1	.1
413 S.D.A.	1	55	67*	.1	.2
419 SO BAPT CONV	61	16,822	20,565*	40.3	70.2
449 UN METHODIST	23	3,096	3,785*	7.4	12.9

County and Denomination	Number of churches	Communicant, confirmed, full members	Total adherents Number	Total adherents Percent of total population	Total adherents Percent of total adherents
496 JEWISH EST[1]	0	NA	113	.2	.4
499 INDEP.NON-CHAR[3]	1	NA	425	.8	1.5
SHELBY	**526**	**324,300**	**493,615***	**59.7**	**100.0**
001 ADVENT CHR CH	1	40	51*	-	-
005 AME ZION	6	1,076	1,176	.1	.2
019 AMER BAPT USA	6	2,575	3,290*	.4	.7
053 ASSEMB OF GOD	15	7,509	7,565	.9	1.5
055 AS REF PRES CH	4	461	499	.1	.1
059 BAPT MISS ASSN	4	802	1,025*	.1	.2
081 CATHOLIC	27	NA	50,000	6.1	10.1
081d *LATIN*	*27*	*NA*	*50,000*	*6.1*	*10.1*
089 CHR & MISS AL	1	48	83	-	-
093 CHR CH (DISC)	15	7,632	10,117	1.2	2.0
097 CHR CHS&CHS CR	5	952	1,216*	.1	.2
111 CH CR,SCIENTST	3	NR	NR	-	-
123 CH GOD (ANDER)	3	100	195	-	-
127 CH GOD (CLEVE)	10	1,288	1,645*	.2	.3
145 CH GOD PROPHCY	4	194	248*	-	.1
151 L-D SAINTS	6	NA	2,540	.3	.5
165 CH OF NAZARENE	10	1,170	1,805	.2	.4
167 CHS OF CHRIST	69	15,863	22,839	2.8	4.6
185 CUMBER PRESB	12	2,778	3,062	.4	.6
193 EPISCOPAL	20	7,820	10,439	1.3	2.1
203 EVAN FREE CH	1	0	60	-	-
207 E.L.C.A.	8	1,633	2,207	.3	.4
216 EVAN PRESBY CH	2	3,870	3,992	.5	.8
223 FREE WILL BAPT	5	381	487*	.1	.1
226 FRIENDS-USA	1	19	52	-	-
226c *FGC*	*1*	*19*	*52*	*-*	*-*
246 GREEK ORTHODOX	1	NR	NR	-	-
274 LAT EVAN LUTH	1	18	21	-	-
283 LUTH—MO SYNOD	10	3,438	4,781	.6	1.0
331 ORTH CH IN AM	1	NR	NR	-	-
349 PENT HOLINESS	6	569	727*	.1	.1
353 CHR BRETHREN	1	50	58	-	-
355 PRESB CH (USA)	30	9,132	11,667*	1.4	2.4
356 PRESB CH AMER	3	446	451	.1	.1
361 PRIM BAPT ASCS	2	111	142*	-	-
403 SALVATION ARMY	3	298	329	-	.1
413 S.D.A.	8	3,035	3,877*	.5	.8
415 S-D BAPTIST GC	1	12	15*	-	-
419 SO BAPT CONV	122	132,500	169,276*	20.5	34.3
435 UNITARIAN-UNIV	2	528	694	.1	.1
443 UN C OF CHRIST	2	187	239*	-	-
449 UN METHODIST	69	36,286	46,357*	5.6	9.4
467 WESLEYAN	1	31	10	-	-
469 WELS	1	108	148	-	-
496 JEWISH EST[1]	5	NA	8,417	1.0	1.7
497 BLACK BAPT EST[2]	NA	81,340	103,916*	12.6	21.1
498 INDEP.CHARIS.[3]	9	NA	5,150	.6	1.0
499 INDEP.NON-CHAR[3]	10	NA	12,747	1.5	2.6
SMITH	**46**	**5,010**	**6,344***	**44.9**	**100.0**
093 CHR CH (DISC)	1	17	23	.2	.4
127 CH GOD (CLEVE)	3	229	285*	2.0	4.5
145 CH GOD PROPHCY	2	97	121*	.9	1.9
165 CH OF NAZARENE	2	87	172	1.2	2.7
167 CHS OF CHRIST	7	472	658	4.7	10.4
185 CUMBER PRESB	2	78	78	.6	1.2
189 DUCK RIVR BAPT	1	155	193*	1.4	3.0
320 "OLD" MB ASCS	1	356	442*	3.1	7.0
419 SO BAPT CONV	11	2,215	2,752*	19.5	43.4
449 UN METHODIST	16	1,304	1,620*	11.5	25.5
STEWART	**61**	**4,984**	**6,331***	**66.8**	**100.0**
053 ASSEMB OF GOD	1	38	76	.8	1.2
081 CATHOLIC	1	NA	76	.8	1.2
081d *LATIN*	*1*	*NA*	*76*	*.8*	*1.2*
093 CHR CH (DISC)	1	91	139	1.5	2.2
123 CH GOD (ANDER)	4	230	270	2.8	4.3
165 CH OF NAZARENE	2	92	166	1.8	2.6
167 CHS OF CHRIST	10	358	496	5.2	7.8
185 CUMBER PRESB	1	64	65	.7	1.0
223 FREE WILL BAPT	5	426	511*	5.4	8.1
339 PENT CH OF GOD	1	34	77	.8	1.2
419 SO BAPT CONV	17	2,451	2,939*	31.0	46.4
449 UN METHODIST	17	1,181	1,416*	14.9	22.4
467 WESLEYAN	1	19	100	1.1	1.6
SULLIVAN	**232**	**62,557**	**78,026***	**54.3**	**100.0**
005 AME ZION	3	1,305	1,740	1.2	2.2
053 ASSEMB OF GOD	6	769	1,078	.8	1.4
081 CATHOLIC	1	NA	1,608	1.1	2.1
081d *LATIN*	*1*	*NA*	*1,608*	*1.1*	*2.1*

NA–Not applicable   NR–Not reported   *Total adherents estimated from known number of communicant, confirmed, full members.   - Represents a percent less than 0.1.   Percentages may not total due to rounding.
[1]See Appendix E   [2]See Appendix F   [3]See Appendix G   Lines in *italic* represent a breakdown of Catholic rites or Friends affiliations. They are included in their respective denominational total.

Table 4. Churches and Church Membership by County and Denomination: 1990

County and Denomination	Number of churches	Communicant, confirmed, full members	Total adherents		
			Number	Percent of total population	Percent of total adherents
082 CENTRAL BAPT	6	1,146	1,378*	1.0	1.8
093 CHR CH (DISC)	1	130	164	.1	.2
097 CHR CHS&CHS CR	16	4,623	5,559*	3.9	7.1
111 CH CR,SCIENTST	2	NR	NR	-	-
123 CH GOD (ANDER)	2	410	415	.3	.5
127 CH GOD (CLEVE)	5	584	702*	.5	.9
133 CH GOD(7TH)DEN	1	14	18	-	-
145 CH GOD PROPHCY	2	97	117*	.1	.1
151 L-D SAINTS	1	NA	521	.4	.7
157 CH OF BRETHREN	3	201	242*	.2	.3
165 CH OF NAZARENE	3	147	409	.3	.5
167 CHS OF CHRIST	6	390	542	.4	.7
193 EPISCOPAL	4	993	1,130	.8	1.4
207 E.L.C.A.	3	679	984	.7	1.3
216 EVAN PRESBY CH	1	60	61	-	.1
223 FREE WILL BAPT	24	2,415	2,904*	2.0	3.7
259 IFCA	1	NR	NR	-	-
283 LUTH—MO SYNOD	2	246	306	.2	.4
325 OLD REG BAPT	1	19	23*	-	-
355 PRESB CH (USA)	21	5,278	6,346*	4.4	8.1
356 PRESB CH AMER	8	903	1,008	.7	1.3
361 PRIM BAPT ASCS	5	273	328*	.2	.4
403 SALVATION ARMY	2	334	397	.3	.5
413 S.D.A.	3	256	308*	.2	.4
415 S-D BAPTIST GC	1	28	34*	-	-
419 SO BAPT CONV	48	25,556	30,729*	21.4	39.4
449 UN METHODIST	48	15,134	18,198*	12.7	23.3
496 JEWISH EST[1]	2	NA	95	.1	.1
497 BLACK BAPT EST[2]	NA	567	682*	.5	.9
SUMNER	**141**	**36,478**	**51,530***	**49.9**	**100.0**
053 ASSEM OF GOD	3	342	564	.5	1.1
081 CATHOLIC	2	NA	2,527	2.4	4.9
081d LATIN	*2*	*NA*	*2,527*	*2.4*	*4.9*
093 CHR CH (DISC)	1	136	191	.2	.4
097 CHR CHS&CHS CR	3	753	956*	.9	1.9
127 CH GOD (CLEVE)	1	126	160*	.2	.3
145 CH GOD PROPHCY	5	242	307*	.3	.6
151 L-D SAINTS	1	NA	311	.3	.6
165 CH OF NAZARENE	5	647	901	.9	1.7
167 CHS OF CHRIST	31	5,074	6,111	5.9	11.9
185 CUMBER PRESB	4	507	545	.5	1.1
193 EPISCOPAL	2	362	434	.4	.8
207 E.L.C.A.	2	432	583	.6	1.1
221 FREE METHODIST	2	57	102	.1	.2
223 FREE WILL BAPT	2	100	127*	.1	.2
283 LUTH—MO SYNOD	1	123	174	.2	.3
320 "OLD" MB ASCS	15	2,468	3,133*	3.0	6.1
355 PRESB CH (USA)	4	938	1,191*	1.2	2.3
413 S.D.A.	5	1,093	1,387*	1.3	2.7
419 SO BAPT CONV	30	16,860	21,400*	20.7	41.5
449 UN METHODIST	20	4,905	6,226*	6.0	12.1
496 JEWISH EST[1]	0	NA	583	.6	1.1
497 BLACK BAPT EST[2]	NA	1,313	1,667*	1.6	3.2
499 INDEP.NON-CHAR[3]	2	NA	1,950	1.9	3.8
TIPTON	**84**	**14,400**	**19,949***	**53.1**	**100.0**
053 ASSEM OF GOD	9	707	1,393	3.7	7.0
055 AS REF PRES CH	4	655	744	2.0	3.7
059 BAPT MISS ASSN	1	69	91*	.2	.5
081 CATHOLIC	1	NA	180	.5	.9
081d LATIN	*1*	*NA*	*180*	*.5*	*.9*
097 CHR CHS&CHS CR	2	230	303*	.8	1.5
127 CH GOD (CLEVE)	2	37	49*	.1	.2
165 CH OF NAZARENE	2	117	118	.3	.6
167 CHS OF CHRIST	8	535	939	2.5	4.7
185 CUMBER PRESB	4	556	585	1.6	2.9
193 EPISCOPAL	4	132	173	.5	.9
215 EVAN METH CH	1	39	51*	.1	.3
216 EVAN PRESBY CH	1	36	36	.1	.2
339 PENT CH OF GOD	1	35	77	.2	.4
355 PRESB CH (USA)	4	473	623*	1.7	3.1
356 PRESB CH AMER	1	15	21	.1	.1
413 S.D.A.	1	18	24*	.1	.1
419 SO BAPT CONV	18	7,161	9,435*	25.1	47.3
449 UN METHODIST	20	2,670	3,518*	9.4	17.6
496 JEWISH EST[1]	0	NA	383	1.0	1.9
497 BLACK BAPT EST[2]	NA	915	1,206*	3.2	6.0
TROUSDALE	**17**	**2,485**	**3,099***	**52.3**	**100.0**
145 CH GOD PROPHCY	1	48	59*	1.0	1.9
167 CHS OF CHRIST	4	260	377	6.4	12.2
185 CUMBER PRESB	1	62	62	1.0	2.0
320 "OLD" MB ASCS	4	1,010	1,242*	21.0	40.1
419 SO BAPT CONV	2	616	758*	12.8	24.5
449 UN METHODIST	5	314	386*	6.5	12.5
497 BLACK BAPT EST[2]	NA	175	215*	3.6	6.9
UNICOI	**43**	**8,240**	**9,928***	**60.0**	**100.0**
053 ASSEM OF GOD	1	19	45	.3	.5
097 CHR CHS&CHS CR	6	940	1,121*	6.8	11.3
123 CH GOD (ANDER)	1	25	90	.5	.9
127 CH GOD (CLEVE)	3	205	244*	1.5	2.5
157 CH OF BRETHREN	1	59	70*	.4	.7
165 CH OF NAZARENE	1	32	48	.3	.5
167 CHS OF CHRIST	2	165	210	1.3	2.1
223 FREE WILL BAPT	7	966	1,152*	7.0	11.6
355 PRESB CH (USA)	3	345	411*	2.5	4.1
419 SO BAPT CONV	14	4,475	5,334*	32.2	53.7
449 UN METHODIST	4	1,009	1,203*	7.3	12.1
UNION	**24**	**4,212**	**5,399***	**39.4**	**100.0**
053 ASSEM OF GOD	1	58	105	.8	1.9
167 CHS OF CHRIST	1	30	56	.4	1.0
361 PRIM BAPT ASCS	2	48	61*	.4	1.1
419 SO BAPT CONV	16	3,913	4,933*	36.0	91.4
449 UN METHODIST	4	163	205*	1.5	3.8
496 JEWISH EST[1]	0	NA	39	.3	.7
VAN BUREN	**21**	**1,286**	**1,720***	**35.5**	**100.0**
127 CH GOD (CLEVE)	4	214	270*	5.6	15.7
145 CH GOD PROPHCY	1	48	61*	1.3	3.5
167 CHS OF CHRIST	10	350	537	11.1	31.2
413 S.D.A.	1	44	56*	1.2	3.3
419 SO BAPT CONV	5	630	796*	16.4	46.3
WARREN	**116**	**14,492**	**18,904***	**57.3**	**100.0**
053 ASSEM OF GOD	4	231	471	1.4	2.5
075 BRETHREN IN CR	1	59	71	.2	.4
081 CATHOLIC	1	NA	271	.8	1.4
081d LATIN	*1*	*NA*	*271*	*.8*	*1.4*
097 CHR CHS&CHS CR	1	60	74*	.2	.4
123 CH GOD (ANDER)	1	200	200	.6	1.1
127 CH GOD (CLEVE)	4	465	576*	1.7	3.0
133 CH GOD(7TH)DEN	1	14	18	.1	.1
145 CH GOD PROPHCY	3	145	180*	.5	1.0
151 L-D SAINTS	1	NA	299	.9	1.6
165 CH OF NAZARENE	1	34	0		
167 CHS OF CHRIST	44	4,572	6,010	18.2	31.8
185 CUMBER PRESB	6	376	396	1.2	2.1
189 DUCK RIVR BAPT	6	545	676*	2.0	3.6
193 EPISCOPAL	1	45	60	.2	.3
221 FREE METHODIST	1	36	54	.2	.3
223 FREE WILL BAPT	3	270	335*	1.0	1.8
283 LUTH—MO SYNOD	1	72	80	.2	.4
355 PRESB CH (USA)	2	141	175*	.5	.9
413 S.D.A.	1	134	166*	.5	.9
419 SO BAPT CONV	17	5,310	6,582*	20.0	34.8
426 2SEED-SPRT BPT	1	8	10*	-	.1
449 UN METHODIST	15	1,491	1,848*	5.6	9.8
497 BLACK BAPT EST[2]	NA	284	352*	1.1	1.9
WASHINGTON	**189**	**42,126**	**54,933***	**59.5**	**100.0**
005 AME ZION	3	858	1,144	1.2	2.1
053 ASSEM OF GOD	3	200	361	.4	.7
081 CATHOLIC	1	NA	1,650	1.8	3.0
081d LATIN	*1*	*NA*	*1,650*	*1.8*	*3.0*
089 CHR & MISS AL	1	56	109	.1	.2
093 CHR CH (DISC)	1	112	134	.1	.2
097 CHR CHS&CHS CR	25	4,643	5,570*	6.0	10.1
111 CH CR,SCIENTST	1	NR	NR	-	-
123 CH GOD (ANDER)	5	344	402	.4	.7
127 CH GOD (CLEVE)	5	477	572*	.6	1.0
145 CH GOD PROPHCY	1	48	58*	.1	.1
151 L-D SAINTS	1	NA	495	.5	.9
157 CH OF BRETHREN	7	490	588*	.6	1.1
165 CH OF NAZARENE	2	131	102	.1	.2
167 CHS OF CHRIST	7	710	934	1.0	1.7
185 CUMBER PRESB	2	142	147	.2	.3
193 EPISCOPAL	1	691	768	.8	1.4
207 E.L.C.A.	1	479	620	.7	1.1
221 FREE METHODIST	1	7	8	-	-
223 FREE WILL BAPT	15	2,000	2,399*	2.6	4.4
226 FRIENDS-USA	1	3	22	-	-
226c FGC	*1*	*3*	*22*	*-*	*-*
259 IFCA	1	NR	NR	-	-
283 LUTH—MO SYNOD	1	253	297	.3	.5
355 PRESB CH (USA)	10	1,851	2,221*	2.4	4.0
356 PRESB CH AMER	6	644	914	1.0	1.7
361 PRIM BAPT ASCS	1	27	32*	-	.1
403 SALVATION ARMY	1	199	215	.2	.4

NA–Not applicable   NR–Not reported   *Total adherents estimated from known number of communicant, confirmed, full members.   - Represents a percent less than 0.1.   Percentages may not total due to rounding.
[1]See Appendix E   [2]See Appendix F   [3]See Appendix G   Lines in *italic* represent a breakdown of Catholic rites or Friends affiliations. They are included in their respective denominational total.

Table 4. Churches and Church Membership by County and Denomination: 1990

County and Denomination	Number of churches	Communicant, confirmed, full members	Total adherents		
			Number	Percent of total population	Percent of total adherents
413 S.D.A.	1	218	262*	.3	.5
419 SO BAPT CONV	50	17,838	21,399*	23.2	39.0
435 UNITARIAN-UNIV	1	111	146	.2	.3
449 UN METHODIST	32	8,886	10,660*	11.5	19.4
496 JEWISH EST[1]	0	NA	55	.1	.1
497 BLACK BAPT EST[2]	NA	708	849*	.9	1.5
499 INDEP.NON-CHAR[3]	1	NA	1,800	1.9	3.3
WAYNE	**58**	**5,228**	**6,507***	**46.7**	**100.0**
081 CATHOLIC	1	NA	27	.2	.4
081d LATIN	*1*	*NA*	*27*	*.2*	*.4*
093 CHR CH (DISC)	1	56	85	.6	1.3
127 CH GOD (CLEVE)	4	230	286*	2.1	4.4
145 CH GOD PROPHCY	2	97	121*	.9	1.9
165 CH OF NAZARENE	1	10	11	.1	.2
167 CHS OF CHRIST	12	741	885	6.4	13.6
185 CUMBER PRESB	1	40	44	.3	.7
349 PENT HOLINESS	1	51	64*	.5	1.0
355 PRESB CH (USA)	1	56	70*	.5	1.1
419 SO BAPT CONV	21	3,081	3,836*	27.5	59.0
449 UN METHODIST	13	866	1,078*	7.7	16.6
WEAKLEY	**117**	**17,849**	**22,038***	**68.9**	**100.0**
053 ASSEMB OF GOD	4	177	248	.8	1.1
081 CATHOLIC	1	NA	394	1.2	1.8
081d LATIN	*1*	*NA*	*394*	*1.2*	*1.8*
093 CHR CH (DISC)	1	40	54	.2	.2
097 CHR CHS&CHS CR	1	80	97*	.3	.4
145 CH GOD PROPHCY	1	48	58*	.2	.3
165 CH OF NAZARENE	1	16	36	.1	.2
167 CHS OF CHRIST	21	1,643	2,058	6.4	9.3
185 CUMBER PRESB	9	498	520	1.6	2.4
193 EPISCOPAL	1	17	18	.1	.1
339 PENT CH OF GOD	1	34	77	.2	.3
349 PENT HOLINESS	1	20	24*	.1	.1
355 PRESB CH (USA)	3	176	213*	.7	1.0
419 SO BAPT CONV	46	12,477	15,072*	47.1	68.4
449 UN METHODIST	26	2,498	3,018*	9.4	13.7
497 BLACK BAPT EST[2]	NA	125	151*	.5	.7
WHITE	**85**	**8,761**	**11,240***	**55.9**	**100.0**
053 ASSEMB OF GOD	1	56	110	.5	1.0
075 BRETHREN IN CR	1	68	68	.3	.6
081 CATHOLIC	1	NA	110	.5	1.0
081d LATIN	*1*	*NA*	*110*	*.5*	*1.0*
093 CHR CH (DISC)	1	100	136	.7	1.2
127 CH GOD (CLEVE)	9	816	999*	5.0	8.9
145 CH GOD PROPHCY	1	48	59*	.3	.5
151 L-D SAINTS	1	NA	459	2.3	4.1
165 CH OF NAZARENE	2	175	281	1.4	2.5
167 CHS OF CHRIST	26	1,860	2,120	10.6	18.9
185 CUMBER PRESB	2	42	48	.2	.4
189 DUCK RIVR BAPT	3	530	649*	3.2	5.8
223 FREE WILL BAPT	3	367	449*	2.2	4.0
355 PRESB CH (USA)	4	126	154*	.8	1.4
419 SO BAPT CONV	13	3,080	3,770*	18.8	33.5
449 UN METHODIST	17	1,493	1,828*	9.1	16.3
WILLIAMSON	**116**	**27,330**	**40,858***	**50.4**	**100.0**
081 CATHOLIC	3	NA	4,495	5.5	11.0
081d LATIN	*3*	*NA*	*4,495*	*5.5*	*11.0*
089 CHR & MISS AL	1	16	45	.1	.1
097 CHR CHS&CHS CR	1	108	140*	.2	.3
151 L-D SAINTS	2	NA	573	.7	1.4
165 CH OF NAZARENE	4	263	312	.4	.8
167 CHS OF CHRIST	35	4,361	5,679	7.0	13.9
185 CUMBER PRESB	8	747	761	.9	1.9
193 EPISCOPAL	2	680	927	1.1	2.3
203 EVAN FREE CH	1	0	60	.1	.1
207 E.L.C.A.	1	307	408	.5	1.0
223 FREE WILL BAPT	3	67	87*	.1	.2
283 LUTH—MO SYNOD	1	0	0	-	-
329 OPEN BIBLE STD	1	NR	NR	-	-
355 PRESB CH (USA)	6	1,283	1,661*	2.1	4.1
356 PRESB CH AMER	2	732	960	1.2	2.3
361 PRIM BAPT ASCS	3	377	488*	.6	1.2
413 S.D.A.	2	92	119*	.1	.3
419 SO BAPT CONV	18	8,759	11,338*	14.0	27.7
449 UN METHODIST	22	7,888	10,211*	12.6	25.0
496 JEWISH EST[1]	0	NA	458	.6	1.1
497 BLACK BAPT EST[2]	NA	1,650	2,136*	2.6	5.2
WILSON	**125**	**27,445**	**38,231***	**56.5**	**100.0**
053 ASSEMB OF GOD	2	138	260	.4	.7
081 CATHOLIC	2	NA	2,308	3.4	6.0

County and Denomination	Number of churches	Communicant, confirmed, full members	Total adherents		
			Number	Percent of total population	Percent of total adherents
081d LATIN	*2*	*NA*	*2,308*	*3.4*	*6.0*
097 CHR CHS&CHS CR	1	85	108*	.2	.3
123 CH GOD (ANDER)	1	130	140	.2	.4
127 CH GOD (CLEVE)	2	402	512*	.8	1.3
145 CH GOD PROPHCY	3	145	185*	.3	.5
151 L-D SAINTS	1	NA	400	.6	1.0
165 CH OF NAZARENE	3	215	271	.4	.7
167 CHS OF CHRIST	33	3,995	5,235	7.7	13.7
185 CUMBER PRESB	7	686	761	1.1	2.0
193 EPISCOPAL	2	105	169	.2	.4
207 E.L.C.A.	2	249	356	.5	.9
223 FREE WILL BAPT	2	29	37*	.1	.1
320 "OLD" MB ASCS	2	64	82*	.1	.2
355 PRESB CH (USA)	3	405	516*	.8	1.3
419 SO BAPT CONV	34	16,264	20,734*	30.6	54.2
449 UN METHODIST	25	3,589	4,575*	6.8	12.0
496 JEWISH EST[1]	0	NA	379	.6	1.0
497 BLACK BAPT EST[2]	NA	944	1,203*	1.8	3.1

TEXAS

THE STATE.....	16,961	5,282,341	10,896,401*	64.1	100.0
ANDERSON	**85**	**20,524**	**26,294***	**54.8**	**100.0**
053 ASSEMB OF GOD	8	541	772	1.6	2.9
059 BAPT MISS ASSN	5	1,028	1,260*	2.6	4.8
081 CATHOLIC	1	NA	949	2.0	3.6
081d LATIN	*1*	*NA*	*949*	*2.0*	*3.6*
093 CHR CH (DISC)	6	383	497	1.0	1.9
097 CHR CHS&CHS CR	1	100	123*	.3	.5
111 CH CR,SCIENTST	1	NR	NR	-	-
127 CH GOD (CLEVE)	1	28	34*	.1	.1
145 CH GOD PROPHCY	2	62	76*	.2	.3
165 CH OF NAZARENE	1	33	54	.1	.2
167 CHS OF CHRIST	13	1,266	1,562	3.3	5.9
193 EPISCOPAL	1	267	309	.6	1.2
283 LUTH—MO SYNOD	1	232	338	.7	1.3
355 PRESB CH (USA)	2	318	390*	.8	1.5
413 S.D.A.	1	78	96*	.2	.4
419 SO BAPT CONV	25	10,310	12,632*	26.3	48.0
449 UN METHODIST	16	2,915	3,572*	7.4	13.6
497 BLACK BAPT EST[2]	NA	2,963	3,630*	7.6	13.8
ANDREWS	**23**	**6,486**	**10,978***	**76.6**	**100.0**
053 ASSEMB OF GOD	4	315	528	3.7	4.8
081 CATHOLIC	1	NA	1,964	13.7	17.9
081d LATIN	*1*	*NA*	*1,964*	*13.7*	*17.9*
093 CHR CH (DISC)	1	20	20	.1	.2
097 CHR CHS&CHS CR	1	35	48*	.3	.4
127 CH GOD (CLEVE)	1	126	172*	1.2	1.6
151 L-D SAINTS	1	NA	102	.7	.9
165 CH OF NAZARENE	1	33	35	.2	.3
167 CHS OF CHRIST	2	403	523	3.6	4.8
193 EPISCOPAL	1	36	50	.3	.5
283 LUTH—MO SYNOD	1	56	59	.4	.5
355 PRESB CH (USA)	1	117	160*	1.1	1.5
419 SO BAPT CONV	6	4,578	6,267*	43.7	57.1
449 UN METHODIST	2	767	1,050*	7.3	9.6
ANGELINA	**117**	**33,224**	**47,756***	**68.3**	**100.0**
053 ASSEMB OF GOD	11	1,042	1,731	2.5	3.6
059 BAPT MISS ASSN	23	4,651	5,982*	8.6	12.5
081 CATHOLIC	2	NA	3,630	5.2	7.6
081d LATIN	*2*	*NA*	*3,630*	*5.2*	*7.6*
093 CHR CH (DISC)	1	600	872	1.2	1.8
111 CH CR,SCIENTST	1	NR	NR	-	-
127 CH GOD (CLEVE)	1	153	197*	.3	.4
151 L-D SAINTS	1	NA	297	.4	.6
165 CH OF NAZARENE	2	264	374	.5	.8
167 CHS OF CHRIST	17	2,158	2,721	3.9	5.7
193 EPISCOPAL	1	257	560	.8	1.2
283 LUTH—MO SYNOD	1	275	360	.5	.8
339 PENT CH OF GOD	3	89	183	.3	.4
355 PRESB CH (USA)	1	326	419*	.6	.9
403 SALVATION ARMY	1	96	98	.1	.2
413 S.D.A.	1	101	130*	.2	.3
419 SO BAPT CONV	37	17,235	22,169*	31.7	46.4
435 UNITARIAN-UNIV	1	19	19	-	-
449 UN METHODIST	11	3,104	3,993*	5.7	8.4
497 BLACK BAPT EST[2]	NA	2,854	3,671*	5.3	7.7
499 INDEP.NON-CHAR[3]	1	NA	350	.5	.7

NA–Not applicable   NR–Not reported   *Total adherents estimated from known number of communicant, confirmed, full members.   - Represents a percent less than 0.1.   Percentages may not total due to rounding.
[1]See Appendix E   [2]See Appendix F   [3]See Appendix G   Lines in *italic* represent a breakdown of Catholic rites or Friends affiliations. They are included in their respective denominational total.

Table 4. Churches and Church Membership by County and Denomination: 1990

County and Denomination		Number of churches	Communicant, confirmed, full members	Total adherents		
				Number	Percent of total population	Percent of total adherents
ARANSAS		**21**	**3,475**	**7,815***	**43.7**	**100.0**
053	ASSEMB OF GOD	1	143	127	.7	1.6
081	CATHOLIC	2	NA	3,340	18.7	42.7
081d	*LATIN*	2	*NA*	*3,340*	*18.7*	*42.7*
097	CHR CHS&CHS CR	1	74	93*	.5	1.2
123	CH GOD (ANDER)	1	64	64	.4	.8
151	L-D SAINTS	1	NA	144	.8	1.8
167	CHS OF CHRIST	2	223	290	1.6	3.7
193	EPISCOPAL	1	147	173	1.0	2.2
283	LUTH—MO SYNOD	1	159	214	1.2	2.7
339	PENT CH OF GOD	1	34	77	.4	1.0
349	PENT HOLINESS	1	28	35*	.2	.4
355	PRESB CH (USA)	1	331	414*	2.3	5.3
419	SO BAPT CONV	7	1,858	2,326*	13.0	29.8
449	UN METHODIST	1	414	518*	2.9	6.6
ARCHER		**20**	**3,536**	**6,221***	**78.0**	**100.0**
053	ASSEMB OF GOD	2	78	107	1.3	1.7
081	CATHOLIC	3	NA	1,693	21.2	27.2
081d	*LATIN*	3	*NA*	*1,693*	*21.2*	*27.2*
093	CHR CH (DISC)	1	37	50	.6	.8
167	CHS OF CHRIST	3	175	222	2.8	3.6
419	SO BAPT CONV	7	2,828	3,615*	45.3	58.1
449	UN METHODIST	4	418	534*	6.7	8.6
ARMSTRONG		**7**	**1,189**	**1,577***	**78.0**	**100.0**
081	CATHOLIC	0	NA	50	2.5	3.2
081d	*LATIN*	0	*NA*	*50*	*2.5*	*3.2*
093	CHR CH (DISC)	1	13	21	1.0	1.3
167	CHS OF CHRIST	1	93	121	6.0	7.7
419	SO BAPT CONV	3	756	967*	47.8	61.3
449	UN METHODIST	2	327	418*	20.7	26.5
ATASCOSA		**50**	**6,218**	**19,950***	**65.3**	**100.0**
053	ASSEMB OF GOD	5	255	543	1.8	2.7
081	CATHOLIC	11	NA	11,245	36.8	56.4
081d	*LATIN*	11	*NA*	*11,245*	*36.8*	*56.4*
127	CH GOD (CLEVE)	1	24	32*	.1	.2
151	L-D SAINTS	1	NA	141	.5	.7
167	CHS OF CHRIST	6	402	439	1.4	2.2
193	EPISCOPAL	1	44	107	.4	.5
203	EVAN FREE CH	1	89	89	.3	.4
207	E.L.C.A.	1	271	369	1.2	1.8
339	PENT CH OF GOD	1	24	87	.3	.4
355	PRESB CH (USA)	1	91	123*	.4	.6
413	S.D.A.	1	23	31*	.1	.2
419	SO BAPT CONV	13	4,049	5,467*	17.9	27.4
449	UN METHODIST	7	946	1,277*	4.2	6.4
AUSTIN		**40**	**7,306**	**14,236***	**71.8**	**100.0**
053	ASSEMB OF GOD	1	30	25	.1	.2
081	CATHOLIC	5	NA	5,025	25.3	35.3
081d	*LATIN*	5	*NA*	*5,025*	*25.3*	*35.3*
111	CH CR,SCIENTST	1	NR	NR	-	-
145	CH GOD PROPHCY	1	31	39*	.2	.3
151	L-D SAINTS	2	NA	138	.7	1.0
167	CHS OF CHRIST	3	133	163	.8	1.1
193	EPISCOPAL	2	290	358	1.8	2.5
207	E.L.C.A.	8	2,541	3,024	15.2	21.2
283	LUTH—MO SYNOD	2	535	678	3.4	4.8
339	PENT CH OF GOD	1	34	77	.4	.5
355	PRESB CH (USA)	1	104	132*	.7	.9
419	SO BAPT CONV	4	1,482	1,880*	9.5	13.2
449	UN METHODIST	9	1,447	1,836*	9.3	12.9
497	BLACK BAPT EST[2]	NA	679	861*	4.3	6.0
BAILEY		**18**	**3,331**	**5,279***	**74.7**	**100.0**
053	ASSEMB OF GOD	2	122	275	3.9	5.2
059	BAPT MISS ASSN	1	180	240*	3.4	4.5
081	CATHOLIC	1	NA	700	9.9	13.3
081d	*LATIN*	1	*NA*	*700*	*9.9*	*13.3*
165	CH OF NAZARENE	1	27	79	1.1	1.5
167	CHS OF CHRIST	3	302	393	5.6	7.4
361	PRIM BAPT ASCS	1	73	97*	1.4	1.8
419	SO BAPT CONV	7	2,018	2,685*	38.0	50.9
449	UN METHODIST	2	609	810*	11.5	15.3
BANDERA		**18**	**2,497**	**5,193***	**49.2**	**100.0**
053	ASSEMB OF GOD	1	24	30	.3	.6
081	CATHOLIC	2	NA	2,100	19.9	40.4
081d	*LATIN*	2	*NA*	*2,100*	*19.9*	*40.4*
097	CHR CHS&CHS CR	1	0	0*	-	-
167	CHS OF CHRIST	4	267	335	3.2	6.5
193	EPISCOPAL	1	94	108	1.0	2.1
207	E.L.C.A.	1	100	172	1.6	3.3
355	PRESB CH (USA)	1	74	90*	.9	1.7
419	SO BAPT CONV	4	1,333	1,622*	15.4	31.2
449	UN METHODIST	3	605	736*	7.0	14.2
BASTROP		**65**	**10,605**	**17,650***	**46.1**	**100.0**
053	ASSEMB OF GOD	7	235	351	.9	2.0
081	CATHOLIC	6	NA	3,626	9.5	20.5
081d	*LATIN*	6	*NA*	*3,626*	*9.5*	*20.5*
093	CHR CH (DISC)	3	143	181	.5	1.0
097	CHR CHS&CHS CR	1	56	73*	.2	.4
151	L-D SAINTS	1	NA	170	.4	1.0
165	CH OF NAZARENE	2	38	37	.1	.2
167	CHS OF CHRIST	7	460	609	1.6	3.5
193	EPISCOPAL	1	164	233	.6	1.3
203	EVAN FREE CH	2	100	100	.3	.6
207	E.L.C.A.	5	837	1,123	2.9	6.4
283	LUTH—MO SYNOD	2	585	772	2.0	4.4
339	PENT CH OF GOD	1	25	37	.1	.2
355	PRESB CH (USA)	3	271	352*	.9	2.0
413	S.D.A.	3	237	308*	.8	1.7
419	SO BAPT CONV	15	4,934	6,406*	16.7	36.3
449	UN METHODIST	6	1,320	1,714*	4.5	9.7
497	BLACK BAPT EST[2]	NA	1,200	1,558*	4.1	8.8
BAYLOR		**12**	**3,000**	**4,647***	**106.0**	**100.0**
053	ASSEMB OF GOD	2	96	104	2.4	2.2
081	CATHOLIC	1	NA	926	21.1	19.9
081d	*LATIN*	1	*NA*	*926*	*21.1*	*19.9*
093	CHR CH (DISC)	1	57	95	2.2	2.0
167	CHS OF CHRIST	1	152	200	4.6	4.3
283	LUTH—MO SYNOD	1	43	46	1.0	1.0
339	PENT CH OF GOD	1	34	77	1.8	1.7
355	PRESB CH (USA)	1	116	142*	3.2	3.1
419	SO BAPT CONV	3	2,051	2,506*	57.1	53.9
449	UN METHODIST	1	451	551*	12.6	11.9
BEE		**44**	**5,415**	**16,167***	**64.3**	**100.0**
053	ASSEMB OF GOD	2	85	160	.6	1.0
081	CATHOLIC	7	NA	8,540	34.0	52.8
081d	*LATIN*	7	*NA*	*8,540*	*34.0*	*52.8*
093	CHR CH (DISC)	2	117	173	.7	1.1
111	CH CR,SCIENTST	1	NR	NR	-	-
165	CH OF NAZARENE	1	29	31	.1	.2
167	CHS OF CHRIST	2	293	357	1.4	2.2
193	EPISCOPAL	1	179	218	.9	1.3
207	E.L.C.A.	2	340	459	1.8	2.8
339	PENT CH OF GOD	1	60	180	.7	1.1
355	PRESB CH (USA)	1	319	425*	1.7	2.6
413	S.D.A.	1	39	52*	.2	.3
419	SO BAPT CONV	16	2,931	3,908*	15.5	24.2
443	UN C OF CHRIST	1	47	63*	.3	.4
449	UN METHODIST	5	783	1,044*	4.2	6.5
497	BLACK BAPT EST[2]	NA	193	257*	1.0	1.6
498	INDEP.CHARIS.[3]	1	NA	300	1.2	1.9
BELL		**172**	**62,108**	**95,059***	**49.7**	**100.0**
053	ASSEMB OF GOD	12	1,050	1,723	.9	1.8
059	BAPT MISS ASSN	1	59	77*	-	.1
081	CATHOLIC	9	NA	11,178	5.8	11.8
081d	*LATIN*	9	*NA*	*11,178*	*5.8*	*11.8*
083	CHRIST CATH CH	1	3	3	-	-
093	CHR CH (DISC)	7	792	972	.5	1.0
097	CHR CHS&CHS CR	2	0	0*	-	-
111	CH CR,SCIENTST	1	NR	NR	-	-
127	CH GOD (CLEVE)	1	233	305*	.2	.3
145	CH GOD PROPHCY	1	31	41*	-	-
151	L-D SAINTS	6	NA	2,041	1.1	2.1
165	CH OF NAZARENE	5	514	622	.3	.7
167	CHS OF CHRIST	26	3,727	5,052	2.6	5.3
193	EPISCOPAL	4	1,209	1,670	.9	1.8
203	EVAN FREE CH	1	25	40	-	-
207	E.L.C.A.	4	1,470	1,864	1.0	2.0
223	FREE WILL BAPT	1	11	14*	-	-
283	LUTH—MO SYNOD	3	1,356	1,899	1.0	2.0
339	PENT CH OF GOD	5	323	434	.2	.5
353	CHR BRETHREN	1	25	50	-	.1
355	PRESB CH (USA)	4	1,010	1,321*	.7	1.4
361	PRIM BAPT ASCS	2	12	16*	-	-
413	S.D.A.	3	463	606*	.3	.6
419	SO BAPT CONV	48	29,420	38,488*	20.1	40.5
435	UNITARIAN-UNIV	1	27	36	-	-
449	UN METHODIST	22	8,432	11,031*	5.8	11.6
469	WELS	1	69	78	-	.1
497	BLACK BAPT EST[2]	NA	11,847	15,498*	8.1	16.3

NA–Not applicable NR–Not reported *Total adherents estimated from known number of communicant, confirmed, full members. - Represents a percent less than 0.1. Percentages may not total due to rounding.
[1]See Appendix E [2]See Appendix F [3]See Appendix G Lines in *italic* represent a breakdown of Catholic rites or Friends affiliations. They are included in their respective denominational total.

Table 4. Churches and Church Membership by County and Denomination: 1990

County and Denomination	Number of churches	Communicant, confirmed, full members	Total adherents Number	Percent of total population	Percent of total adherents
BEXAR	**628**	**216,265**	**769,565***	**64.9**	**100.0**
005 AME ZION	1	60	75	-	-
019 AMER BAPT USA	5	2,155	2,801*	.2	.4
053 ASSEMB OF GOD	48	6,982	8,897	.8	1.2
059 BAPT MISS ASSN	3	618	803*	.1	.1
081 CATHOLIC	96	NA	445,407	37.6	57.9
081b *BYZAN RUTH*	*1*	*NA*	*48*	-	-
081d *LATIN*	*94*	*NA*	*444,443*	*37.5*	*57.8*
081e *MARONITE*	*1*	*NA*	*916*	*.1*	*.1*
089 CHR & MISS AL	3	74	119	-	-
093 CHR CH (DISC)	8	1,492	1,848	.2	.2
097 CHR CHS&CHS CR	12	1,246	1,619*	.1	.2
111 CH CR,SCIENTST	4	NR	NR	-	-
123 CH GOD (ANDER)	5	250	300	-	-
127 CH GOD (CLEVE)	21	1,415	1,839*	.2	.2
133 CH GOD(7TH)DEN	4	156	220	-	-
145 CH GOD PROPHCY	1	31	40*	-	-
151 L-D SAINTS	17	NA	8,359	.7	1.1
165 CH OF NAZARENE	15	1,315	2,080	.2	.3
167 CHS OF CHRIST	42	6,669	9,020	.8	1.2
185 CUMBER PRESB	2	315	322	-	-
193 EPISCOPAL	20	9,580	12,972	1.1	1.7
203 EVAN FREE CH	4	1,113	2,900	.2	.4
207 E.L.C.A.	29	11,029	14,303	1.2	1.9
209 EVAN LUTH SYN	1	63	72	-	-
221 FREE METHODIST	1	36	48	-	-
226 FRIENDS-USA	1	51	94	-	-
226c *FGC*	*1*	*51*	*94*	-	-
246 GREEK ORTHODOX	1	NR	NR	-	-
263 INT FOURSQ GOS	1	62	81*	-	-
283 LUTH—MO SYNOD	13	6,722	8,944	.8	1.2
285 MENNONITE CH	2	73	176	-	-
287 MENN GEN CONF	1	21	36	-	-
331 ORTH CH IN AM	1	NR	NR	-	-
339 PENT CH OF GOD	1	12	25	-	-
349 PENT HOLINESS	7	207	269*	-	-
353 CHR BRETHREN	2	90	105	-	-
355 PRESB CH (USA)	33	9,315	12,106*	1.0	1.6
356 PRESB CH AMER	1	107	124	-	-
403 SALVATION ARMY	2	256	309	-	-
413 S.D.A.	11	1,670	2,170*	.2	.3
419 SO BAPT CONV	118	95,133	123,634*	10.4	16.1
435 UNITARIAN-UNIV	3	318	390	-	.1
443 UN C OF CHRIST	3	529	687*	.1	.1
449 UN METHODIST	61	29,087	37,801*	3.2	4.9
469 WELS	2	222	320	-	-
496 JEWISH EST[1]	5	NA	9,103	.8	1.2
497 BLACK BAPT EST[2]	NA	27,791	36,117*	3.0	4.7
498 INDEP.CHARIS.[3]	12	NA	20,680	1.7	2.7
499 INDEP.NON-CHAR[3]	5	NA	2,350	.2	.3
BLANCO	**17**	**2,255**	**3,533***	**59.2**	**100.0**
053 ASSEMB OF GOD	2	44	42	.7	1.2
081 CATHOLIC	3	NA	705	11.8	20.0
081d *LATIN*	*3*	*NA*	*705*	*11.8*	*20.0*
093 CHR CH (DISC)	1	25	35	.6	1.0
167 CHS OF CHRIST	2	125	173	2.9	4.9
193 EPISCOPAL	2	86	103	1.7	2.9
207 E.L.C.A.	1	298	354	5.9	10.0
339 PENT CH OF GOD	1	34	77	1.3	2.2
419 SO BAPT CONV	2	1,037	1,290*	21.6	36.5
449 UN METHODIST	3	606	754*	12.6	21.3
BORDEN	**2**	**167**	**215***	**26.9**	**100.0**
419 SO BAPT CONV	1	137	176*	22.0	81.9
449 UN METHODIST	1	30	39*	4.9	18.1
BOSQUE	**55**	**8,993**	**11,190***	**74.0**	**100.0**
053 ASSEMB OF GOD	1	19	25	.2	.2
081 CATHOLIC	2	NA	164	1.1	1.5
081d *LATIN*	*2*	*NA*	*164*	*1.1*	*1.5*
167 CHS OF CHRIST	9	523	665	4.4	5.9
193 EPISCOPAL	2	96	110	.7	1.0
207 E.L.C.A.	4	1,141	1,369	9.1	12.2
283 LUTH—MO SYNOD	1	185	243	1.6	2.2
339 PENT CH OF GOD	1	12	13	.1	.1
355 PRESB CH (USA)	1	102	125*	.8	1.1
419 SO BAPT CONV	22	5,179	6,348*	42.0	56.7
443 UN C OF CHRIST	1	168	206*	1.4	1.8
449 UN METHODIST	11	1,568	1,922*	12.7	17.2
BOWIE	**124**	**41,528**	**55,813***	**68.3**	**100.0**
053 ASSEMB OF GOD	9	802	1,419	1.7	2.5
059 BAPT MISS ASSN	3	799	1,013*	1.2	1.8
081 CATHOLIC	2	NA	903	1.1	1.6
081d *LATIN*	*2*	*NA*	*903*	*1.1*	*1.6*
093 CHR CH (DISC)	2	418	560	.7	1.0
097 CHR CHS&CHS CR	5	890	1,128*	1.4	2.0
127 CH GOD (CLEVE)	2	119	151*	.2	.3
145 CH GOD PROPHCY	2	62	79*	.1	.1
151 L-D SAINTS	1	NA	288	.4	.5
165 CH OF NAZARENE	2	481	410	.5	.7
167 CHS OF CHRIST	18	2,266	2,921	3.6	5.2
193 EPISCOPAL	3	585	810	1.0	1.5
207 E.L.C.A.	1	112	160	.2	.3
215 EVAN METH CH	1	28	35*	-	.1
263 INT FOURSQ GOS	1	37	47*	.1	.1
283 LUTH—MO SYNOD	1	343	453	.6	.8
355 PRESB CH (USA)	4	670	849*	1.0	1.5
403 SALVATION ARMY	1	121	125	.2	.2
413 S.D.A.	1	237	300*	.4	.5
419 SO BAPT CONV	42	21,611	27,390*	33.5	49.1
449 UN METHODIST	20	6,105	7,738*	9.5	13.9
496 JEWISH EST[1]	1	NA	0	-	-
497 BLACK BAPT EST[2]	NA	5,842	7,404*	9.1	13.3
498 INDEP.CHARIS.[3]	1	NA	1,200	1.5	2.2
499 INDEP.NON-CHAR[3]	1	NA	430	.5	.8
BRAZORIA	**175**	**63,564**	**118,935***	**62.0**	**100.0**
053 ASSEMB OF GOD	14	2,050	3,612	1.9	3.0
081 CATHOLIC	14	NA	31,299	16.3	26.3
081d *LATIN*	*14*	*NA*	*31,299*	*16.3*	*26.3*
093 CHR CH (DISC)	5	578	838	.4	.7
111 CH CR,SCIENTST	2	NR	NR	-	-
127 CH GOD (CLEVE)	1	102	133*	.1	.1
145 CH GOD PROPHCY	3	92	120*	.1	.1
151 L-D SAINTS	4	NA	1,420	.7	1.2
165 CH OF NAZARENE	4	402	499	.3	.4
167 CHS OF CHRIST	24	2,812	3,526	1.8	3.0
179 CONSRV BAPT	1	NR	NR	-	-
193 EPISCOPAL	6	1,583	2,131	1.1	1.8
203 EVAN FREE CH	1	140	185	.1	.2
207 E.L.C.A.	6	1,622	2,228	1.2	1.9
226 FRIENDS-USA	1	105	137*	.1	.1
226b *EFI*	*1*	*105*	*137***	*.1*	*.1*
283 LUTH—MO SYNOD	4	577	798	.4	.7
339 PENT CH OF GOD	1	25	35	-	-
349 PENT HOLINESS	1	150	196*	.1	.2
353 CHR BRETHREN	2	160	300	.2	.3
355 PRESB CH (USA)	9	2,194	2,863*	1.5	2.4
361 PRIM BAPT ASCS	1	23	30*	-	-
403 SALVATION ARMY	1	72	85	-	.1
419 SO BAPT CONV	47	35,249	45,998*	24.0	38.7
449 UN METHODIST	19	10,314	13,459*	7.0	11.3
467 WESLEYAN	1	50	61	-	.1
469 WELS	1	19	28	-	-
497 BLACK BAPT EST[2]	NA	5,245	6,844*	3.6	5.8
498 INDEP.CHARIS.[3]	1	NA	1,800	.9	1.5
499 INDEP.NON-CHAR[3]	1	NA	310	.2	.3
BRAZOS	**94**	**33,095**	**60,412***	**49.6**	**100.0**
053 ASSEMB OF GOD	6	706	953	.8	1.6
059 BAPT MISS ASSN	1	113	137*	.1	.2
081 CATHOLIC	6	NA	17,116	14.0	28.3
081d *LATIN*	*6*	*NA*	*17,116*	*14.0*	*28.3*
093 CHR CH (DISC)	1	261	370	.3	.6
097 CHR CHS&CHS CR	1	100	121*	.1	.2
111 CH CR,SCIENTST	1	NR	NR	-	-
123 CH GOD (ANDER)	1	80	117	.1	.2
145 CH GOD PROPHCY	1	31	38*	-	.1
151 L-D SAINTS	3	NA	1,020	.8	1.7
165 CH OF NAZARENE	1	110	178	.1	.3
167 CHS OF CHRIST	10	1,772	2,076	1.7	3.4
193 EPISCOPAL	3	746	1,191	1.0	2.0
203 EVAN FREE CH	1	68	72	.1	.1
207 E.L.C.A.	3	1,206	1,657	1.4	2.7
223 FREE WILL BAPT	5	414	502*	.4	.8
226 FRIENDS-USA	1	3	7	-	-
226c *FGC*	*1*	*3*	*7*	-	-
283 LUTH—MO SYNOD	3	555	776	.6	1.3
355 PRESB CH (USA)	2	1,317	1,598*	1.3	2.6
356 PRESB CH AMER	2	411	479	.4	.8
413 S.D.A.	1	68	83*	.1	.1
419 SO BAPT CONV	23	14,070	17,071*	14.0	28.3
435 UNITARIAN-UNIV	1	91	126	.1	.2
443 UN C OF CHRIST	3	549	666*	.5	1.1
449 UN METHODIST	11	5,863	7,113*	5.8	11.8
469 WELS	1	74	101	.1	.2
496 JEWISH EST[1]	1	NA	400	.3	.7
497 BLACK BAPT EST[2]	NA	4,487	5,444*	4.5	9.0
499 INDEP.NON-CHAR[3]	1	NA	1,000	.8	1.7

NA–Not applicable NR–Not reported *Total adherents estimated from known number of communicant, confirmed, full members. - Represents a percent less than 0.1. Percentages may not total due to rounding.
[1] See Appendix E [2] See Appendix F [3] See Appendix G

Lines in *italic* represent a breakdown of Catholic rites or Friends affiliations. They are included in their respective denominational total.

Table 4. Churches and Church Membership by County and Denomination: 1990

County and Denomination	Number of churches	Communicant, confirmed, full members	Total adherents Number	Percent of total population	Percent of total adherents
BREWSTER	**21**	**1,813**	**7,934***	**91.4**	**100.0**
053 ASSEMB OF GOD	1	60	100	1.2	1.3
081 CATHOLIC	3	NA	5,530	63.7	69.7
081d *LATIN*	*3*	*NA*	*5,530*	*63.7*	*69.7*
093 CHR CH (DISC)	1	65	98	1.1	1.2
151 L-D SAINTS	1	NA	95	1.1	1.2
165 CH OF NAZARENE	1	10	0	-	-
167 CHS OF CHRIST	2	38	59	.7	.7
193 EPISCOPAL	2	54	68	.8	.9
226 FRIENDS-USA	1	2	6	.1	.1
226c *FGC*	*1*	*2*	*6*	*.1*	*.1*
339 PENT CH OF GOD	1	34	77	.9	1.0
355 PRESB CH (USA)	1	131	161*	1.9	2.0
419 SO BAPT CONV	5	1,061	1,301*	15.0	16.4
449 UN METHODIST	2	358	439*	5.1	5.5
BRISCOE	**9**	**1,132**	**1,617***	**82.0**	**100.0**
053 ASSEMB OF GOD	1	7	8	.4	.5
081 CATHOLIC	1	NA	171	8.7	10.6
081d *LATIN*	*1*	*NA*	*171*	*8.7*	*10.6*
167 CHS OF CHRIST	3	144	188	9.5	11.6
419 SO BAPT CONV	2	782	996*	50.5	61.6
449 UN METHODIST	2	199	254*	12.9	15.7
BROOKS	**15**	**1,021**	**6,291***	**76.7**	**100.0**
053 ASSEMB OF GOD	2	63	90	1.1	1.4
081 CATHOLIC	3	NA	4,500	54.9	71.5
081d *LATIN*	*3*	*NA*	*4,500*	*54.9*	*71.5*
123 CH GOD (ANDER)	1	28	28	.3	.4
151 L-D SAINTS	1	NA	413	5.0	6.6
157 CH OF BRETHREN	1	35	47*	.6	.7
167 CHS OF CHRIST	1	30	45	.5	.7
355 PRESB CH (USA)	2	94	127*	1.5	2.0
413 S.D.A.	1	36	49*	.6	.8
419 SO BAPT CONV	1	571	771*	9.4	12.3
449 UN METHODIST	2	164	221*	2.7	3.5
BROWN	**68**	**17,937**	**25,107***	**73.0**	**100.0**
053 ASSEMB OF GOD	2	90	143	.4	.6
081 CATHOLIC	1	NA	1,809	5.3	7.2
081d *LATIN*	*1*	*NA*	*1,809*	*5.3*	*7.2*
093 CHR CH (DISC)	1	281	371	1.1	1.5
111 CH CR,SCIENTST	1	NR	NR	-	-
151 L-D SAINTS	1	NA	240	.7	1.0
165 CH OF NAZARENE	2	121	169	.5	.7
167 CHS OF CHRIST	13	1,357	1,832	5.3	7.3
193 EPISCOPAL	2	350	397	1.2	1.6
283 LUTH—MO SYNOD	1	177	245	.7	1.0
339 PENT CH OF GOD	2	155	195	.6	.8
355 PRESB CH (USA)	1	296	372*	1.1	1.5
413 S.D.A.	1	81	102*	.3	.4
419 SO BAPT CONV	30	12,093	15,193*	44.2	60.5
449 UN METHODIST	9	2,523	3,170*	9.2	12.6
497 BLACK BAPT EST[2]	NA	413	519*	1.5	2.1
498 INDEP.CHARIS.[3]	1	NA	350	1.0	1.4
BURLESON	**33**	**5,365**	**8,201***	**60.2**	**100.0**
053 ASSEMB OF GOD	2	250	233	1.7	2.8
081 CATHOLIC	3	NA	1,505	11.0	18.4
081d *LATIN*	*3*	*NA*	*1,505*	*11.0*	*18.4*
093 CHR CH (DISC)	1	51	65	.5	.8
123 CH GOD (ANDER)	1	50	50	.4	.6
167 CHS OF CHRIST	4	167	218	1.6	2.7
207 E.L.C.A.	3	484	588	4.3	7.2
283 LUTH—MO SYNOD	1	38	54	.4	.7
355 PRESB CH (USA)	2	66	84*	.6	1.0
419 SO BAPT CONV	10	2,728	3,462*	25.4	42.2
443 UN C OF CHRIST	1	165	209*	1.5	2.5
449 UN METHODIST	5	733	930*	6.8	11.3
497 BLACK BAPT EST[2]	NA	633	803*	5.9	9.8
BURNET	**49**	**9,141**	**12,972***	**57.2**	**100.0**
053 ASSEMB OF GOD	3	179	261	1.2	2.0
081 CATHOLIC	6	NA	1,673	7.4	12.9
081d *LATIN*	*6*	*NA*	*1,673*	*7.4*	*12.9*
093 CHR CH (DISC)	4	402	517	2.3	4.0
167 CHS OF CHRIST	12	1,078	1,283	5.7	9.9
185 CUMBER PRESB	1	170	196	.9	1.5
193 EPISCOPAL	2	251	309	1.4	2.4
207 E.L.C.A.	2	560	688	3.0	5.3
355 PRESB CH (USA)	2	262	324*	1.4	2.5
413 S.D.A.	1	39	48*	.2	.4
419 SO BAPT CONV	11	5,022	6,215*	27.4	47.9
449 UN METHODIST	5	1,178	1,458*	6.4	11.2
CALDWELL	**47**	**7,367**	**13,749***	**52.1**	**100.0**
053 ASSEMB OF GOD	3	154	221	.8	1.6
081 CATHOLIC	2	NA	4,140	15.7	30.1
081d *LATIN*	*2*	*NA*	*4,140*	*15.7*	*30.1*
093 CHR CH (DISC)	2	166	265	1.0	1.9
167 CHS OF CHRIST	4	292	380	1.4	2.8
193 EPISCOPAL	2	146	195	.7	1.4
207 E.L.C.A.	3	305	395	1.5	2.9
339 PENT CH OF GOD	2	80	137	.5	1.0
355 PRESB CH (USA)	3	206	265*	1.0	1.9
419 SO BAPT CONV	14	3,871	4,986*	18.9	36.3
443 UN C OF CHRIST	2	219	282*	1.1	2.1
449 UN METHODIST	10	1,177	1,516*	5.7	11.0
497 BLACK BAPT EST[2]	NA	751	967*	3.7	7.0
CALHOUN	**35**	**6,390**	**18,796***	**98.7**	**100.0**
053 ASSEMB OF GOD	7	471	695	3.6	3.7
081 CATHOLIC	4	NA	10,271	53.9	54.6
081d *LATIN*	*4*	*NA*	*10,271*	*53.9*	*54.6*
093 CHR CH (DISC)	1	37	52	.3	.3
133 CH GOD(7TH)DEN	1	39	55	.3	.3
145 CH GOD PROPHCY	1	31	40*	.2	.2
151 L-D SAINTS	1	NA	158	.8	.8
167 CHS OF CHRIST	5	353	453	2.4	2.4
193 EPISCOPAL	1	135	158	.8	.8
207 E.L.C.A.	2	498	626	3.3	3.3
355 PRESB CH (USA)	2	238	310*	1.6	1.6
419 SO BAPT CONV	7	3,496	4,555*	23.9	24.2
449 UN METHODIST	3	947	1,234*	6.5	6.6
497 BLACK BAPT EST[2]	NA	145	189*	1.0	1.0
CALLAHAN	**27**	**6,082**	**8,011***	**67.6**	**100.0**
053 ASSEMB OF GOD	1	34	36	.3	.4
059 BAPT MISS ASSN	1	200	256*	2.2	3.2
081 CATHOLIC	2	NA	228	1.9	2.8
081d *LATIN*	*2*	*NA*	*228*	*1.9*	*2.8*
127 CH GOD (CLEVE)	1	50	64*	.5	.8
167 CHS OF CHRIST	7	600	760	6.4	9.5
355 PRESB CH (USA)	2	96	123*	1.0	1.5
419 SO BAPT CONV	9	4,208	5,397*	45.5	67.4
449 UN METHODIST	4	894	1,147*	9.7	14.3
CAMERON	**195**	**26,234**	**248,470***	**95.5**	**100.0**
053 ASSEMB OF GOD	28	2,561	3,323	1.3	1.3
081 CATHOLIC	33	NA	210,697	81.0	84.8
081d *LATIN*	*33*	*NA*	*210,697*	*81.0*	*84.8*
089 CHR & MISS AL	3	61	158	.1	.1
093 CHR CH (DISC)	4	286	408	.2	.2
097 CHR CHS&CHS CR	2	265	362*	.1	.1
111 CH CR,SCIENTST	2	NR	NR	-	-
121 CH GOD (ABR)	1	25	34*	-	-
123 CH GOD (ANDER)	2	96	96	-	-
127 CH GOD (CLEVE)	3	123	168*	.1	.1
133 CH GOD(7TH)DEN	1	38	54	-	-
145 CH GOD PROPHCY	2	62	85*	-	-
151 L-D SAINTS	5	NA	1,901	.7	.8
165 CH OF NAZARENE	6	504	811	.3	.3
167 CHS OF CHRIST	20	1,351	1,766	.7	.7
193 EPISCOPAL	5	1,022	1,484	.6	.6
207 E.L.C.A.	1	211	229	.1	.1
259 IFCA	1	NR	NR	-	-
283 LUTH—MO SYNOD	5	1,078	1,309	.5	.5
285 MENNONITE CH	2	112	120	-	-
349 PENT HOLINESS	5	208	284*	.1	.1
355 PRESB CH (USA)	9	1,572	2,147*	.8	.9
356 PRESB CH AMER	1	85	100	-	-
403 SALVATION ARMY	1	75	82	-	-
413 S.D.A.	6	693	946*	.4	.4
419 SO BAPT CONV	32	12,085	16,503*	6.3	6.6
435 UNITARIAN-UNIV	1	9	9	-	-
449 UN METHODIST	12	3,441	4,699*	1.8	1.9
496 JEWISH EST[1]	2	NA	325	.1	.1
497 BLACK BAPT EST[2]	NA	271	370*	.1	.1
CAMP	**32**	**5,956**	**8,136***	**82.1**	**100.0**
053 ASSEMB OF GOD	1	83	140	1.4	1.7
059 BAPT MISS ASSN	8	1,030	1,295*	13.1	15.9
081 CATHOLIC	1	NA	325	3.3	4.0
081d *LATIN*	*1*	*NA*	*325*	*3.3*	*4.0*
127 CH GOD (CLEVE)	1	36	45*	.5	.6
145 CH GOD PROPHCY	1	31	39*	.4	.5
151 L-D SAINTS	1	NA	210	2.1	2.6
165 CH OF NAZARENE	1	43	101	1.0	1.2
167 CHS OF CHRIST	5	289	385	3.9	4.7
193 EPISCOPAL	1	109	145	1.5	1.8

NA–Not applicable NR–Not reported *Total adherents estimated from known number of communicant, confirmed, full members. - Represents a percent less than 0.1. Percentages may not total due to rounding.
[1]See Appendix E [2]See Appendix F [3]See Appendix G Lines in *italic* represent a breakdown of Catholic rites or Friends affiliations. They are included in their respective denominational total.

TEXAS

Table 4. Churches and Church Membership by County and Denomination: 1990

County and Denomination		Number of churches	Communicant, confirmed, full members	Total adherents		
				Number	Percent of total population	Percent of total adherents
355	PRESB CH (USA)	1	18	23*	.2	.3
419	SO BAPT CONV	8	3,143	3,952*	39.9	48.6
449	UN METHODIST	3	559	703*	7.1	8.6
497	BLACK BAPT EST[2]	NA	615	773*	7.8	9.5
CARSON		**19**	**4,006**	**6,170***	**93.8**	**100.0**
053	ASSEMB OF GOD	3	67	102	1.6	1.7
081	CATHOLIC	3	NA	949	14.4	15.4
081d	LATIN	3	NA	949	14.4	15.4
093	CHR CH (DISC)	1	170	202	3.1	3.3
167	CHS OF CHRIST	4	267	345	5.2	5.6
419	SO BAPT CONV	5	2,718	3,548*	54.0	57.5
449	UN METHODIST	3	784	1,024*	15.6	16.6
CASS		**75**	**16,398**	**21,301***	**71.0**	**100.0**
053	ASSEMB OF GOD	5	293	421	1.4	2.0
059	BAPT MISS ASSN	1	26	33*	.1	.2
081	CATHOLIC	1	NA	206	.7	1.0
081d	LATIN	1	NA	206	.7	1.0
097	CHR CHS&CHS CR	1	40	51*	.2	.2
123	CH GOD (ANDER)	2	40	49	.2	.2
151	L-D SAINTS	1	NA	319	1.1	1.5
165	CH OF NAZARENE	1	157	170	.6	.8
167	CHS OF CHRIST	4	548	670	2.2	3.1
193	EPISCOPAL	1	60	79	.3	.4
203	EVAN FREE CH	1	33	50	.2	.2
283	LUTH—MO SYNOD	1	29	36	.1	.2
355	PRESB CH (USA)	1	34	43*	.1	.2
361	PRIM BAPT ASCS	1	38	48*	.2	.2
413	S.D.A.	3	129	163*	.5	.8
419	SO BAPT CONV	37	11,018	13,956*	46.5	65.5
449	UN METHODIST	14	2,342	2,966*	9.9	13.9
497	BLACK BAPT EST[2]	NA	1,611	2,041*	6.8	9.6
CASTRO		**19**	**3,717**	**10,208***	**112.5**	**100.0**
053	ASSEMB OF GOD	1	60	150	1.7	1.5
081	CATHOLIC	3	NA	4,984	55.0	48.8
081d	LATIN	3	NA	4,984	55.0	48.8
097	CHR CHS&CHS CR	1	60	84*	.9	.8
167	CHS OF CHRIST	3	234	304	3.4	3.0
349	PENT HOLINESS	1	41	57*	.6	.6
355	PRESB CH (USA)	1	30	42*	.5	.4
419	SO BAPT CONV	7	2,627	3,660*	40.4	35.9
449	UN METHODIST	2	665	927*	10.2	9.1
CHAMBERS		**30**	**7,470**	**11,935***	**59.4**	**100.0**
053	ASSEMB OF GOD	3	213	282	1.4	2.4
081	CATHOLIC	2	NA	2,250	11.2	18.9
081d	LATIN	2	NA	2,250	11.2	18.9
167	CHS OF CHRIST	6	211	251	1.2	2.1
193	EPISCOPAL	1	71	86	.4	.7
283	LUTH—MO SYNOD	1	180	263	1.3	2.2
419	SO BAPT CONV	10	4,551	5,896*	29.4	49.4
449	UN METHODIST	7	1,580	2,047*	10.2	17.2
497	BLACK BAPT EST[2]	NA	664	860*	4.3	7.2
CHEROKEE		**98**	**19,230**	**26,560***	**64.7**	**100.0**
053	ASSEMB OF GOD	9	339	638	1.6	2.4
059	BAPT MISS ASSN	18	3,942	4,955*	12.1	18.7
081	CATHOLIC	1	NA	2,162	5.3	8.1
081d	LATIN	1	NA	2,162	5.3	8.1
093	CHR CH (DISC)	4	361	413	1.0	1.6
127	CH GOD (CLEVE)	1	64	80*	.2	.3
165	CH OF NAZARENE	3	245	438	1.1	1.6
167	CHS OF CHRIST	14	1,150	1,421	3.5	5.4
185	CUMBER PRESB	2	140	145	.4	.5
193	EPISCOPAL	1	97	107	.3	.4
283	LUTH—MO SYNOD	1	39	47	.1	.2
355	PRESB CH (USA)	2	291	366*	.9	1.4
356	PRESB CH AMER	1	25	29	.1	.1
413	S.D.A.	1	91	114*	.3	.4
419	SO BAPT CONV	18	7,859	9,879*	24.1	37.2
449	UN METHODIST	22	2,744	3,449*	8.4	13.0
497	BLACK BAPT EST[2]	NA	1,843	2,317*	5.6	8.7
CHILDRESS		**17**	**4,377**	**5,714***	**96.0**	**100.0**
053	ASSEMB OF GOD	1	117	80	1.3	1.4
081	CATHOLIC	1	NA	256	4.3	4.5
081d	LATIN	1	NA	256	4.3	4.5
093	CHR CH (DISC)	1	75	110	1.8	1.9
145	CH GOD PROPHCY	1	19	24*	.4	.4
165	CH OF NAZARENE	1	23	0	-	-
167	CHS OF CHRIST	3	439	610	10.2	10.7
193	EPISCOPAL	1	9	9	.2	.2
283	LUTH—MO SYNOD	1	12	15	.3	.3

County and Denomination		Number of churches	Communicant, confirmed, full members	Total adherents		
				Number	Percent of total population	Percent of total adherents
355	PRESB CH (USA)	1	83	104*	1.7	1.8
419	SO BAPT CONV	4	2,912	3,645*	61.2	63.8
449	UN METHODIST	2	688	861*	14.5	15.1
CLAY		**30**	**5,959**	**7,708***	**76.9**	**100.0**
053	ASSEMB OF GOD	1	50	72	.7	.9
081	CATHOLIC	1	NA	154	1.5	2.0
081d	LATIN	1	NA	154	1.5	2.0
093	CHR CH (DISC)	1	59	77	.8	1.0
127	CH GOD (CLEVE)	1	180	226*	2.3	2.9
165	CH OF NAZARENE	1	27	74	.7	1.0
167	CHS OF CHRIST	4	344	450	4.5	5.8
193	EPISCOPAL	1	34	52	.5	.7
223	FREE WILL BAPT	1	160	201*	2.0	2.6
419	SO BAPT CONV	13	4,403	5,522*	55.1	71.6
449	UN METHODIST	6	702	880*	8.8	11.4
COCHRAN		**14**	**2,761**	**4,801***	**109.7**	**100.0**
053	ASSEMB OF GOD	3	148	267	6.1	5.6
059	BAPT MISS ASSN	1	421	569*	13.0	11.9
081	CATHOLIC	1	NA	1,000	22.8	20.8
081d	LATIN	1	NA	1,000	22.8	20.8
167	CHS OF CHRIST	3	216	292	6.7	6.1
419	SO BAPT CONV	4	1,641	2,220*	50.7	46.2
449	UN METHODIST	2	335	453*	10.3	9.4
COKE		**15**	**2,297**	**2,875***	**84.0**	**100.0**
053	ASSEMB OF GOD	1	34	43	1.3	1.5
059	BAPT MISS ASSN	2	213	259*	7.6	9.0
081	CATHOLIC	2	NA	102	3.0	3.5
081d	LATIN	2	NA	102	3.0	3.5
167	CHS OF CHRIST	3	255	290	8.5	10.1
419	SO BAPT CONV	5	1,428	1,735*	50.7	60.3
449	UN METHODIST	2	367	446*	13.0	15.5
COLEMAN		**48**	**4,662**	**6,577***	**67.7**	**100.0**
053	ASSEMB OF GOD	2	54	84	.9	1.3
059	BAPT MISS ASSN	1	146	180*	1.9	2.7
081	CATHOLIC	1	NA	779	8.0	11.8
081d	LATIN	1	NA	779	8.0	11.8
093	CHR CH (DISC)	2	60	91	.9	1.4
165	CH OF NAZARENE	1	30	34	.4	.5
167	CHS OF CHRIST	7	315	409	4.2	6.2
185	CUMBER PRESB	1	4	4	-	.1
193	EPISCOPAL	1	47	61	.6	.9
339	PENT CH OF GOD	2	17	26	.3	.4
355	PRESB CH (USA)	2	170	209*	2.2	3.2
413	S.D.A.	2	68	84*	.9	1.3
419	SO BAPT CONV	17	2,827	3,479*	35.8	52.9
449	UN METHODIST	9	924	1,137*	11.7	17.3
COLLIN		**212**	**65,969**	**118,899***	**45.0**	**100.0**
053	ASSEMB OF GOD	12	1,213	1,657	.6	1.4
059	BAPT MISS ASSN	2	310	403*	.2	.3
081	CATHOLIC	6	NA	18,444	7.0	15.5
081d	LATIN	6	NA	18,444	7.0	15.5
089	CHR & MISS AL	2	42	122	-	.1
093	CHR CH (DISC)	14	2,483	3,257	1.2	2.7
097	CHR CHS&CHS CR	7	2,238	2,907*	1.1	2.4
111	CH CR,SCIENTST	1	NR	NR	-	-
127	CH GOD (CLEVE)	7	623	809*	.3	.7
151	L-D SAINTS	8	NA	3,307	1.3	2.8
165	CH OF NAZARENE	3	208	397	.2	.3
167	CHS OF CHRIST	27	3,471	4,381	1.7	3.7
193	EPISCOPAL	6	1,859	3,139	1.2	2.6
203	EVAN FREE CH	1	55	125	-	.1
207	E.L.C.A.	3	1,604	2,315	.9	1.9
221	FREE METHODIST	1	36	93	-	.1
263	INT FOURSQ GOS	1	0	0*	-	-
283	LUTH—MO SYNOD	4	1,141	1,572	.6	1.3
339	PENT CH OF GOD	2	94	157	.1	.1
353	CHR BRETHREN	2	493	863	.3	.7
355	PRESB CH (USA)	10	2,025	2,630*	1.0	2.2
356	PRESB CH AMER	1	131	194	.1	.2
371	REF CH IN AM	1	508	1,085	.4	.9
419	SO BAPT CONV	57	31,230	40,563*	15.4	34.1
435	UNITARIAN-UNIV	1	155	230	.1	.2
443	UN C OF CHRIST	1	56	73*	-	.1
449	UN METHODIST	23	12,259	15,923*	6.0	13.4
467	WESLEYAN	1	95	500	.2	.4
469	WELS	1	54	79	-	.1
496	JEWISH EST[1]	0	NA	3,516	1.3	3.0
497	BLACK BAPT EST[2]	NA	3,586	4,658*	1.8	3.9
498	INDEP.CHARIS.[3]	4	NA	1,850	.7	1.6
499	INDEP.NON-CHAR[3]	3	NA	3,650	1.4	3.1

NA–Not applicable   NR–Not reported   *Total adherents estimated from known number of communicant, confirmed, full members.   - Represents a percent less than 0.1.   Percentages may not total due to rounding.
[1]See Appendix E   [2]See Appendix F   [3]See Appendix G   Lines in *italic* represent a breakdown of Catholic rites or Friends affiliations. They are included in their respective denominational total.

Table 4. Churches and Church Membership by County and Denomination: 1990

County and Denomination	Number of churches	Communicant, confirmed, full members	Total adherents Number	Percent of total population	Percent of total adherents
COLLINGSWORTH	**11**	**2,144**	**2,907***	**81.4**	**100.0**
053 ASSEMB OF GOD	1	11	7	.2	.2
081 CATHOLIC	1	NA	97	2.7	3.3
081d *LATIN*	*1*	*NA*	*97*	*2.7*	*3.3*
097 CHR CHS&CHS CR	1	70	88*	2.5	3.0
151 L-D SAINTS	1	NA	72	2.0	2.5
165 CH OF NAZARENE	2	103	169	4.7	5.8
419 SO BAPT CONV	4	1,479	1,867*	52.3	64.2
449 UN METHODIST	1	481	607*	17.0	20.9
COLORADO	**44**	**5,890**	**19,069***	**103.7**	**100.0**
053 ASSEMB OF GOD	3	68	78	.4	.4
081 CATHOLIC	8	NA	11,632	63.3	61.0
081d *LATIN*	*8*	*NA*	*11,632*	*63.3*	*61.0*
123 CH GOD (ANDER)	1	7	7	-	-
145 CH GOD PROPHCY	1	31	39*	.2	.2
151 L-D SAINTS	1	NA	29	.2	.2
165 CH OF NAZARENE	1	61	88	.5	.5
167 CHS OF CHRIST	4	101	138	.8	.7
193 EPISCOPAL	2	146	160	.9	.8
207 E.L.C.A.	4	1,013	1,238	6.7	6.5
355 PRESB CH (USA)	1	72	91*	.5	.5
419 SO BAPT CONV	7	2,111	2,677*	14.6	14.0
443 UN C OF CHRIST	2	414	525*	2.9	2.8
449 UN METHODIST	9	1,054	1,337*	7.3	7.0
497 BLACK BAPT EST[2]	NA	812	1,030*	5.6	5.4
COMAL	**48**	**13,752**	**30,385***	**58.6**	**100.0**
053 ASSEMB OF GOD	2	144	211	.4	.7
081 CATHOLIC	7	NA	11,150	21.5	36.7
081d *LATIN*	*7*	*NA*	*11,150*	*21.5*	*36.7*
097 CHR CHS&CHS CR	1	250	312*	.6	1.0
111 CH CR,SCIENTST	1	NR	NR	-	-
151 L-D SAINTS	1	NA	415	.8	1.4
165 CH OF NAZARENE	1	98	144	.3	.5
167 CHS OF CHRIST	7	620	796	1.5	2.6
193 EPISCOPAL	2	508	664	1.3	2.2
207 E.L.C.A.	5	2,499	3,270	6.3	10.8
263 INT FOURSQ GOS	1	11	14*	-	-
283 LUTH—MO SYNOD	1	391	477	.9	1.6
355 PRESB CH (USA)	2	483	603*	1.2	2.0
356 PRESB CH AMER	1	0	0	-	-
413 S.D.A.	1	32	40*	.1	.1
419 SO BAPT CONV	9	4,838	6,045*	11.7	19.9
443 UN C OF CHRIST	2	1,853	2,315*	4.5	7.6
449 UN METHODIST	3	2,025	2,530*	4.9	8.3
496 JEWISH EST[1]	0	NA	399	.8	1.3
498 INDEP.CHARIS.[3]	1	NA	1,000	1.9	3.3
COMANCHE	**53**	**6,669**	**8,531***	**63.8**	**100.0**
053 ASSEMB OF GOD	2	101	146	1.1	1.7
081 CATHOLIC	3	NA	309	2.3	3.6
081d *LATIN*	*3*	*NA*	*309*	*2.3*	*3.6*
093 CHR CH (DISC)	1	30	43	.3	.5
097 CHR CHS&CHS CR	1	42	51*	.4	.6
167 CHS OF CHRIST	9	574	716	5.4	8.4
193 EPISCOPAL	1	40	51	.4	.6
207 E.L.C.A.	1	61	84	.6	1.0
223 FREE WILL BAPT	2	149	182*	1.4	2.1
339 PENT CH OF GOD	1	34	77	.6	.9
355 PRESB CH (USA)	1	25	30*	.2	.4
361 PRIM BAPT ASCS	3	40	49*	.4	.6
419 SO BAPT CONV	21	4,542	5,536*	41.4	64.9
449 UN METHODIST	7	1,031	1,257*	9.4	14.7
CONCHO	**19**	**1,176**	**1,782***	**58.5**	**100.0**
053 ASSEMB OF GOD	1	18	0	-	-
081 CATHOLIC	3	NA	357	11.7	20.0
081d *LATIN*	*3*	*NA*	*357*	*11.7*	*20.0*
093 CHR CH (DISC)	1	3	4	.1	.2
167 CHS OF CHRIST	4	161	204	6.7	11.4
193 EPISCOPAL	1	8	14	.5	.8
283 LUTH—MO SYNOD	2	144	183	6.0	10.3
419 SO BAPT CONV	4	684	829*	27.2	46.5
449 UN METHODIST	3	158	191*	6.3	10.7
COOKE	**58**	**11,714**	**20,946***	**68.1**	**100.0**
053 ASSEMB OF GOD	2	196	335	1.1	1.6
081 CATHOLIC	4	NA	5,710	18.6	27.3
081d *LATIN*	*4*	*NA*	*5,710*	*18.6*	*27.3*
093 CHR CH (DISC)	1	238	290	.9	1.4
111 CH CR,SCIENTST	1	NR	NR	-	-
165 CH OF NAZARENE	2	97	118	.4	.6
167 CHS OF CHRIST	9	1,196	1,503	4.9	7.2

County and Denomination	Number of churches	Communicant, confirmed, full members	Total adherents Number	Percent of total population	Percent of total adherents
193 EPISCOPAL	1	136	163	.5	.8
263 INT FOURSQ GOS	1	42	54*	.2	.3
283 LUTH—MO SYNOD	1	122	145	.5	.7
349 PENT HOLINESS	1	4	5*	-	-
355 PRESB CH (USA)	1	176	225*	.7	1.1
356 PRESB CH AMER	1	191	210	.7	1.0
413 S.D.A.	1	55	70*	.2	.3
419 SO BAPT CONV	23	7,604	9,703*	31.5	46.3
449 UN METHODIST	8	1,346	1,718*	5.6	8.2
497 BLACK BAPT EST[2]	NA	311	397*	1.3	1.9
499 INDEP.NON-CHAR[3]	1	NA	300	1.0	1.4
CORYELL	**71**	**21,604**	**30,135***	**46.9**	**100.0**
053 ASSEMB OF GOD	2	166	213	.3	.7
081 CATHOLIC	2	NA	2,343	3.6	7.8
081d *LATIN*	*2*	*NA*	*2,343*	*3.6*	*7.8*
093 CHR CH (DISC)	2	36	54	.1	.2
097 CHR CHS&CHS CR	1	71	91*	.1	.3
121 CH GOD (ABR)	1	31	40*	.1	.1
165 CH OF NAZARENE	2	111	164	.3	.5
167 CHS OF CHRIST	13	859	1,109	1.7	3.7
193 EPISCOPAL	2	36	115	.2	.4
207 E.L.C.A.	1	135	164	.3	.5
283 LUTH—MO SYNOD	4	659	848	1.3	2.8
339 PENT CH OF GOD	2	101	225	.4	.7
355 PRESB CH (USA)	2	251	320*	.5	1.1
419 SO BAPT CONV	26	12,191	15,566*	24.2	51.7
443 UN C OF CHRIST	1	75	96*	.1	.3
449 UN METHODIST	10	2,421	3,091*	4.8	10.3
497 BLACK BAPT EST[2]	NA	4,461	5,696*	8.9	18.9
COTTLE	**9**	**1,812**	**2,811***	**125.1**	**100.0**
053 ASSEMB OF GOD	1	17	24	1.1	.9
059 BAPT MISS ASSN	1	373	464*	20.6	16.5
081 CATHOLIC	1	NA	500	22.3	17.8
081d *LATIN*	*1*	*NA*	*500*	*22.3*	*17.8*
093 CHR CH (DISC)	1	91	155	6.9	5.5
167 CHS OF CHRIST	2	132	177	7.9	6.3
419 SO BAPT CONV	2	980	1,219*	54.3	43.4
449 UN METHODIST	1	219	272*	12.1	9.7
CRANE	**9**	**1,931**	**3,261***	**70.1**	**100.0**
053 ASSEMB OF GOD	2	66	123	2.6	3.8
081 CATHOLIC	1	NA	300	6.4	9.2
081d *LATIN*	*1*	*NA*	*300*	*6.4*	*9.2*
097 CHR CHS&CHS CR	1	300	409*	8.8	12.5
167 CHS OF CHRIST	2	215	287	6.2	8.8
419 SO BAPT CONV	1	1,098	1,498*	32.2	45.9
449 UN METHODIST	1	252	344*	7.4	10.5
499 INDEP.NON-CHAR[3]	1	NA	300	6.4	9.2
CROCKETT	**10**	**1,668**	**3,373***	**82.7**	**100.0**
053 ASSEMB OF GOD	1	41	52	1.3	1.5
081 CATHOLIC	1	NA	1,193	29.3	35.4
081d *LATIN*	*1*	*NA*	*1,193*	*29.3*	*35.4*
145 CH GOD PROPHCY	1	19	25*	.6	.7
167 CHS OF CHRIST	2	211	274	6.7	8.1
283 LUTH—MO SYNOD	1	15	19	.5	.6
419 SO BAPT CONV	3	979	1,282*	31.4	38.0
449 UN METHODIST	1	403	528*	12.9	15.7
CROSBY	**23**	**3,673**	**5,507***	**75.4**	**100.0**
053 ASSEMB OF GOD	3	94	182	2.5	3.3
081 CATHOLIC	2	NA	600	8.2	10.9
081d *LATIN*	*2*	*NA*	*600*	*8.2*	*10.9*
167 CHS OF CHRIST	6	332	433	5.9	7.9
349 PENT HOLINESS	2	70	93*	1.3	1.7
361 PRIM BAPT ASCS	1	31	41*	.6	.7
419 SO BAPT CONV	6	2,463	3,255*	44.6	59.1
449 UN METHODIST	3	683	903*	12.4	16.4
CULBERSON	**10**	**1,256**	**3,446***	**101.1**	**100.0**
081 CATHOLIC	1	NA	1,750	51.4	50.8
081d *LATIN*	*1*	*NA*	*1,750*	*51.4*	*50.8*
165 CH OF NAZARENE	2	3	0	-	-
167 CHS OF CHRIST	2	100	126	3.7	3.7
193 EPISCOPAL	1	14	11	.3	.3
413 S.D.A.	1	99	136*	4.0	4.0
419 SO BAPT CONV	2	931	1,274*	37.4	37.0
449 UN METHODIST	1	109	149*	4.4	4.3
DALLAM	**19**	**4,213**	**6,483***	**118.7**	**100.0**
053 ASSEMB OF GOD	1	46	60	1.1	.9
081 CATHOLIC	2	NA	818	15.0	12.6

NA–Not applicable   NR–Not reported   *Total adherents estimated from known number of communicant, confirmed, full members.   - Represents a percent less than 0.1.   Percentages may not total due to rounding.
[1]See Appendix E   [2]See Appendix F   [3]See Appendix G   Lines in *italic* represent a breakdown of Catholic rites or Friends affiliations. They are included in their respective denominational total.

TEXAS

Table 4. Churches and Church Membership by County and Denomination: 1990

County and Denomination	Number of churches	Communicant, confirmed, full members	Total adherents Number	Percent of total population	Percent of total adherents
081d LATIN	2	NA	818	15.0	12.6
097 CHR CHS&CHS CR	1	273	360*	6.6	5.6
143 CG IN CR(MENN)	2	158	208*	3.8	3.2
151 L-D SAINTS	1	NA	100	1.8	1.5
167 CHS OF CHRIST	3	298	387	7.1	6.0
193 EPISCOPAL	1	164	209	3.8	3.2
355 PRESB CH (USA)	1	131	173*	3.2	2.7
413 S.D.A.	1	29	38*	.7	.6
419 SO BAPT CONV	3	2,595	3,422*	62.7	52.8
449 UN METHODIST	2	504	665*	12.2	10.3
467 WESLEYAN	1	15	43	.8	.7
DALLAS	**1,071**	**636,501**	**1,116,423***	**60.3**	**100.0**
005 AME ZION	3	955	1,088	.1	.1
019 AMER BAPT USA	10	4,918	6,265*	.3	.6
053 ASSEMB OF GOD	91	21,783	27,900	1.5	2.5
059 BAPT MISS ASSN	36	13,441	17,124*	.9	1.5
075 BRETHREN IN CR	1	27	47	-	-
081 CATHOLIC	42	NA	207,535	11.2	18.6
081b BYZAN RUTH	1	NA	335	-	-
081d LATIN	41	NA	207,200	11.2	18.6
089 CHR & MISS AL	3	48	133	-	-
093 CHR CH (DISC)	38	12,179	19,042	1.0	1.7
097 CHR CHS&CHS CR	8	894	1,139*	.1	.1
105 CHRISTIAN REF	1	112	205	-	-
111 CH CR,SCIENTST	11	NR	NR	-	-
123 CH GOD (ANDER)	5	145	520	-	-
127 CH GOD (CLEVE)	28	3,105	3,956*	.2	.4
133 CH GOD(7TH)DEN	3	117	162	-	-
145 CH GOD PROPHCY	4	123	157*	-	-
151 L-D SAINTS	29	NA	11,080	.6	1.0
164 CH LUTH CONF	1	55	74	-	-
165 CH OF NAZARENE	25	3,649	5,235	.3	.5
167 CHS OF CHRIST	116	35,842	47,468	2.6	4.3
185 CUMBER PRESB	3	689	778	-	.1
193 EPISCOPAL	39	21,114	27,330	1.5	2.4
203 EVAN FREE CH	2	36	50	-	-
207 E.L.C.A.	27	8,140	10,622	.6	1.0
209 EVAN LUTH SYN	1	56	74	-	-
211 FEL EVG BIB CH	1	18	20	-	-
215 EVAN METH CH	2	273	348*	-	-
216 EVAN PRESBY CH	1	0	0	-	-
221 FREE METHODIST	4	174	241	-	-
223 FREE WILL BAPT	3	361	460*	-	-
226 FRIENDS-USA	1	89	129	-	-
226c FGC	1	89	129	-	-
246 GREEK ORTHODOX	1	NR	NR	-	-
249 AP CATH ASSYR	0	37	123	-	-
263 INT FOURSQ GOS	9	586	747*	-	.1
283 LUTH—MO SYNOD	19	7,427	9,713	.5	.9
285 MENNONITE CH	2	68	113	-	-
287 MENN GEN CONF	3	70	70	-	-
313 N AM BAPT CONF	3	290	369*	-	-
331 ORTH CH IN AM	1	NR	NR	-	-
339 PENT CH OF GOD	10	296	535	-	-
349 PENT HOLINESS	2	125	159*	-	-
353 CHR BRETHREN	11	2,420	3,575	.2	.3
355 PRESB CH (USA)	50	27,490	35,022*	1.9	3.1
356 PRESB CH AMER	8	1,006	1,305	.1	.1
361 PRIM BAPT ASCS	1	31	39*	-	-
371 REF CH IN AM	2	252	507	-	-
397 ROMANIAN ORTH	1	NR	NR	-	-
403 SALVATION ARMY	8	711	796	-	.1
413 S.D.A.	16	2,770	3,529*	.2	.3
419 SO BAPT CONV	209	252,234	321,341*	17.3	28.8
423 SYRIAN ANTIOCH	2	NA	900	-	.1
435 UNITARIAN-UNIV	4	930	1,263	.1	.1
443 UN C OF CHRIST	4	1,168	1,488*	.1	.1
449 UN METHODIST	99	88,519	112,771*	6.1	10.1
467 WESLEYAN	1	2	20	-	-
469 WELS	3	415	565	-	.1
496 JEWISH EST[1]	11	NA	24,672	1.3	2.2
497 BLACK BAPT EST[2]	NA	121,311	154,548*	8.3	13.8
498 INDEP.CHARIS.[3]	17	NA	18,725	1.0	1.7
499 INDEP.NON-CHAR[3]	35	NA	34,346	1.9	3.1
DAWSON	**39**	**8,489**	**14,391***	**100.3**	**100.0**
053 ASSEMB OF GOD	4	228	367	2.6	2.6
059 BAPT MISS ASSN	2	264	351*	2.4	2.4
081 CATHOLIC	2	NA	3,000	20.9	20.8
081d LATIN	2	NA	3,000	20.9	20.8
093 CHR CH (DISC)	1	45	67	.5	.5
165 CH OF NAZARENE	2	155	266	1.9	1.8
167 CHS OF CHRIST	6	594	753	5.2	5.2
193 EPISCOPAL	1	8	11	.1	.1
263 INT FOURSQ GOS	1	9	12*	.1	.1
283 LUTH—MO SYNOD	1	74	101	.7	.7

County and Denomination	Number of churches	Communicant, confirmed, full members	Total adherents Number	Percent of total population	Percent of total adherents
355 PRESB CH (USA)	1	172	229*	1.6	1.6
419 SO BAPT CONV	13	5,771	7,678*	53.5	53.4
449 UN METHODIST	5	1,007	1,340*	9.3	9.3
497 BLACK BAPT EST[2]	NA	162	216*	1.5	1.5
DEAF SMITH	**29**	**7,033**	**16,172***	**84.4**	**100.0**
053 ASSEMB OF GOD	4	222	337	1.8	2.1
081 CATHOLIC	2	NA	6,311	33.0	39.0
081d LATIN	2	NA	6,311	33.0	39.0
093 CHR CH (DISC)	1	131	223	1.2	1.4
127 CH GOD (CLEVE)	1	42	58*	.3	.4
151 L-D SAINTS	1	NA	180	.9	1.1
165 CH OF NAZARENE	1	504	580	3.0	3.6
167 CHS OF CHRIST	4	416	542	2.8	3.4
193 EPISCOPAL	1	67	82	.4	.5
283 LUTH—MO SYNOD	1	102	150	.8	.9
355 PRESB CH (USA)	1	232	322*	1.7	2.0
413 S.D.A.	1	36	50*	.3	.3
419 SO BAPT CONV	8	3,931	5,461*	28.5	33.8
449 UN METHODIST	3	1,350	1,876*	9.8	11.6
DELTA	**24**	**2,966**	**3,694***	**76.1**	**100.0**
053 ASSEMB OF GOD	1	30	45	.9	1.2
059 BAPT MISS ASSN	1	155	190*	3.9	5.1
165 CH OF NAZARENE	1	15	21	.4	.6
167 CHS OF CHRIST	3	182	235	4.8	6.4
339 PENT CH OF GOD	2	56	107	2.2	2.9
355 PRESB CH (USA)	1	7	9*	.2	.2
419 SO BAPT CONV	9	1,965	2,406*	49.5	65.1
449 UN METHODIST	6	556	681*	14.0	18.4
DENTON	**182**	**59,394**	**103,024***	**37.7**	**100.0**
019 AMER BAPT USA	1	300	384*	.1	.4
053 ASSEMB OF GOD	14	881	1,389	.5	1.3
059 BAPT MISS ASSN	3	310	397*	.1	.4
081 CATHOLIC	5	NA	15,160	5.5	14.7
081d LATIN	5	NA	15,160	5.5	14.7
093 CHR CH (DISC)	4	788	1,083	.4	1.1
097 CHR CHS&CHS CR	2	300	384*	.1	.4
111 CH CR,SCIENTST	1	NR	NR	-	-
127 CH GOD (CLEVE)	3	219	281*	.1	.3
151 L-D SAINTS	10	NA	3,707	1.4	3.6
165 CH OF NAZARENE	4	465	692	.3	.7
167 CHS OF CHRIST	21	3,506	4,547	1.7	4.4
175 CONGR CHR CHS	1	90	115*	-	.1
185 CUMBER PRESB	1	206	222	.1	.2
193 EPISCOPAL	5	1,023	1,366	.5	1.3
203 EVAN FREE CH	1	50	85	-	.1
207 E.L.C.A.	4	1,068	1,675	.6	1.6
215 EVAN METH CH	1	55	70*	-	.1
221 FREE METHODIST	1	19	43	-	-
283 LUTH—MO SYNOD	3	1,756	2,477	.9	2.4
331 ORTH CH IN AM	1	NR	NR	-	-
339 PENT CH OF GOD	3	182	320	.1	.3
355 PRESB CH (USA)	5	1,930	2,473*	.9	2.4
356 PRESB CH AMER	1	86	109	-	.1
413 S.D.A.	2	144	184*	.1	.2
419 SO BAPT CONV	54	30,233	38,735*	14.2	37.6
435 UNITARIAN-UNIV	1	80	100	-	.1
443 UN C OF CHRIST	1	189	242*	.1	.2
449 UN METHODIST	23	10,984	14,073*	5.1	13.7
469 WELS	1	76	112	-	.1
496 JEWISH EST[1]	0	NA	3,642	1.3	3.5
497 BLACK BAPT EST[2]	NA	4,454	5,707*	2.1	5.5
498 INDEP.CHARIS.[3]	1	NA	400	.1	.4
499 INDEP.NON-CHAR[3]	4	NA	2,850	1.0	2.8
DE WITT	**38**	**6,689**	**15,244***	**80.9**	**100.0**
053 ASSEMB OF GOD	2	63	68	.4	.4
081 CATHOLIC	8	NA	6,692	35.5	43.9
081d LATIN	8	NA	6,692	35.5	43.9
151 L-D SAINTS	1	NA	101	.5	.7
167 CHS OF CHRIST	2	128	154	.8	1.0
193 EPISCOPAL	1	119	141	.7	.9
207 E.L.C.A.	8	3,176	3,994	21.2	26.2
339 PENT CH OF GOD	1	35	77	.4	.5
355 PRESB CH (USA)	2	259	328*	1.7	2.2
419 SO BAPT CONV	9	1,873	2,375*	12.6	15.6
449 UN METHODIST	4	485	615*	3.3	4.0
497 BLACK BAPT EST[2]	NA	551	699*	3.7	4.6
DICKENS	**18**	**2,107**	**2,829***	**110.0**	**100.0**
053 ASSEMB OF GOD	2	52	107	4.2	3.8
059 BAPT MISS ASSN	1	47	57*	2.2	2.0
081 CATHOLIC	1	NA	200	7.8	7.1

Table 4. Churches and Church Membership by County and Denomination: 1990

County and Denomination	Number of churches	Communicant, confirmed, full members	Total adherents		
			Number	Percent of total population	Percent of total adherents
081d *LATIN*	*1*	*NA*	*200*	*7.8*	*7.1*
165 CH OF NAZARENE	1	10	33	1.3	1.2
167 CHS OF CHRIST	5	259	324	12.6	11.5
413 S.D.A.	0	6	7*	.3	.2
419 SO BAPT CONV	5	1,444	1,751*	68.1	61.9
449 UN METHODIST	3	289	350*	13.6	12.4
DIMMIT	**15**	**1,629**	**8,446***	**81.0**	**100.0**
053 ASSEMB OF GOD	2	50	66	.6	.8
081 CATHOLIC	4	NA	6,200	59.4	73.4
081d *LATIN*	*4*	*NA*	*6,200*	*59.4*	*73.4*
167 CHS OF CHRIST	1	40	50	.5	.6
193 EPISCOPAL	1	21	36	.3	.4
349 PENT HOLINESS	1	60	83*	.8	1.0
413 S.D.A.	1	29	40*	.4	.5
419 SO BAPT CONV	2	1,257	1,734*	16.6	20.5
449 UN METHODIST	3	172	237*	2.3	2.8
DONLEY	**14**	**2,315**	**2,847***	**77.0**	**100.0**
053 ASSEMB OF GOD	2	137	171	4.6	6.0
081 CATHOLIC	1	NA	52	1.4	1.8
081d *LATIN*	*1*	*NA*	*52*	*1.4*	*1.8*
165 CH OF NAZARENE	1	95	109	2.9	3.8
167 CHS OF CHRIST	2	213	277	7.5	9.7
193 EPISCOPAL	1	46	64	1.7	2.2
355 PRESB CH (USA)	1	51	61*	1.7	2.1
419 SO BAPT CONV	4	1,279	1,524*	41.2	53.5
449 UN METHODIST	2	494	589*	15.9	20.7
DUVAL	**15**	**1,396**	**9,723***	**75.3**	**100.0**
053 ASSEMB OF GOD	1	37	55	.4	.6
081 CATHOLIC	7	NA	7,860	60.8	80.8
081d *LATIN*	*7*	*NA*	*7,860*	*60.8*	*80.8*
167 CHS OF CHRIST	1	40	46	.4	.5
419 SO BAPT CONV	4	1,172	1,566*	12.1	16.1
449 UN METHODIST	2	147	196*	1.5	2.0
EASTLAND	**61**	**11,559**	**15,013***	**81.2**	**100.0**
053 ASSEMB OF GOD	2	60	87	.5	.6
081 CATHOLIC	3	NA	617	3.3	4.1
081d *LATIN*	*3*	*NA*	*617*	*3.3*	*4.1*
093 CHR CH (DISC)	2	222	314	1.7	2.1
123 CH GOD (ANDER)	1	45	45	.2	.3
127 CH GOD (CLEVE)	2	60	73*	.4	.5
145 CH GOD PROPHCY	1	19	23*	.1	.2
151 L-D SAINTS	1	NA	92	.5	.6
165 CH OF NAZARENE	1	78	138	.7	.9
167 CHS OF CHRIST	11	1,387	1,757	9.5	11.7
193 EPISCOPAL	1	23	31	.2	.2
215 EVAN METH CH	1	20	24*	.1	.2
283 LUTH—MO SYNOD	1	212	298	1.6	2.0
355 PRESB CH (USA)	2	96	117*	.6	.8
419 SO BAPT CONV	25	7,856	9,589*	51.9	63.9
449 UN METHODIST	7	1,481	1,808*	9.8	12.0
ECTOR	**107**	**40,713**	**76,309***	**64.2**	**100.0**
053 ASSEMB OF GOD	8	1,383	2,506	2.1	3.3
059 BAPT MISS ASSN	3	663	890*	.7	1.2
081 CATHOLIC	7	NA	15,478	13.0	20.3
081d *LATIN*	*7*	*NA*	*15,478*	*13.0*	*20.3*
093 CHR CH (DISC)	2	405	615	.5	.8
097 CHR CHS&CHS CR	3	850	1,141*	1.0	1.5
111 CH CR,SCIENTST	1	NR	NR	-	-
123 CH GOD (ANDER)	1	205	205	.2	.3
127 CH GOD (CLEVE)	3	254	341*	.3	.4
151 L-D SAINTS	2	NA	747	.6	1.0
165 CH OF NAZARENE	3	333	573	.5	.8
167 CHS OF CHRIST	18	2,669	3,649	3.1	4.8
185 CUMBER PRESB	1	694	795	.7	1.0
193 EPISCOPAL	1	578	759	.6	1.0
207 E.L.C.A.	2	642	864	.7	1.1
215 EVAN METH CH	1	130	175*	.1	.2
223 FREE WILL BAPT	1	107	144*	.1	.2
263 INT FOURSQ GOS	2	94	126*	.1	.2
283 LUTH—MO SYNOD	2	538	739	.6	1.0
349 PENT HOLINESS	1	32	43*	-	.1
355 PRESB CH (USA)	3	1,357	1,822*	1.5	2.4
361 PRIM BAPT ASCS	1	55	74*	.1	.1
413 S.D.A.	2	113	152*	.1	.2
419 SO BAPT CONV	27	23,423	31,442*	26.4	41.2
435 UNITARIAN-UNIV	1	27	34	-	-
449 UN METHODIST	8	4,337	5,822*	4.9	7.6
496 JEWISH EST[1]	0	NA	75	.1	.1
497 BLACK BAPT EST[2]	NA	1,824	2,448*	2.1	3.2
499 INDEP.NON-CHAR[3]	3	NA	4,650	3.9	6.1

County and Denomination	Number of churches	Communicant, confirmed, full members	Total adherents		
			Number	Percent of total population	Percent of total adherents
EDWARDS	**10**	**612**	**2,209***	**97.5**	**100.0**
081 CATHOLIC	2	NA	1,400	61.8	63.4
081d *LATIN*	*2*	*NA*	*1,400*	*61.8*	*63.4*
167 CHS OF CHRIST	2	100	127	5.6	5.7
355 PRESB CH (USA)	1	55	73*	3.2	3.3
419 SO BAPT CONV	2	331	441*	19.5	20.0
449 UN METHODIST	3	126	168*	7.4	7.6
ELLIS	**127**	**31,982**	**57,290***	**67.3**	**100.0**
053 ASSEMB OF GOD	16	1,430	2,321	2.7	4.1
059 BAPT MISS ASSN	16	5,763	7,624*	9.0	13.3
081 CATHOLIC	4	NA	11,368	13.3	19.8
081d *LATIN*	*4*	*NA*	*11,368*	*13.3*	*19.8*
093 CHR CH (DISC)	6	490	717	.8	1.3
127 CH GOD (CLEVE)	1	187	247*	.3	.4
151 L-D SAINTS	1	NA	435	.5	.8
165 CH OF NAZARENE	2	133	224	.3	.4
167 CHS OF CHRIST	19	2,155	3,005	3.5	5.2
185 CUMBER PRESB	1	141	156	.2	.3
193 EPISCOPAL	2	174	272	.3	.5
263 INT FOURSQ GOS	1	60	79*	.1	.1
283 LUTH—MO SYNOD	2	183	236	.3	.4
339 PENT CH OF GOD	2	43	95	.1	.2
349 PENT HOLINESS	1	24	32*	-	.1
355 PRESB CH (USA)	7	769	1,017*	1.2	1.8
413 S.D.A.	3	136	180*	.2	.3
419 SO BAPT CONV	17	12,058	15,952*	18.7	27.8
449 UN METHODIST	24	5,438	7,194*	8.4	12.6
496 JEWISH EST[1]	0	NA	1,134	1.3	2.0
497 BLACK BAPT EST[2]	NA	2,798	3,702*	4.3	6.5
499 INDEP.NON-CHAR[3]	2	NA	1,300	1.5	2.3
EL PASO	**278**	**58,213**	**486,969***	**82.3**	**100.0**
053 ASSEMB OF GOD	23	4,393	5,079	.9	1.0
081 CATHOLIC	49	NA	393,500	66.5	80.8
081d *LATIN*	*49*	*NA*	*393,500*	*66.5*	*80.8*
089 CHR & MISS AL	1	33	92	-	-
093 CHR CH (DISC)	5	923	1,367	.2	.3
097 CHR CHS&CHS CR	5	404	540*	.1	.1
105 CHRISTIAN REF	1	42	76	-	-
111 CH CR,SCIENTST	2	NR	NR	-	-
123 CH GOD (ANDER)	2	60	72	-	-
127 CH GOD (CLEVE)	2	56	75*	-	-
133 CH GOD(7TH)DEN	3	117	164	-	-
145 CH GOD PROPHCY	3	66	88*	-	-
151 L-D SAINTS	14	NA	5,978	1.0	1.2
165 CH OF NAZARENE	6	1,065	1,092	.2	.2
167 CHS OF CHRIST	11	1,705	2,162	.4	.4
175 CONGR CHR CHS	1	60	80*	-	-
185 CUMBER PRESB	2	131	183	-	-
193 EPISCOPAL	8	2,148	3,540	.6	.7
207 E.L.C.A.	6	1,192	1,635	.3	.3
215 EVAN METH CH	1	40	53*	-	-
226 FRIENDS-USA	1	15	20*	-	-
226f *INDEPENDNT*	*1*	*15*	*20**	-	-
246 GREEK ORTHODOX	1	NR	NR	-	-
263 INT FOURSQ GOS	3	199	266*	-	.1
283 LUTH—MO SYNOD	5	1,269	1,718	.3	.4
349 PENT HOLINESS	8	526	703*	.1	.1
353 CHR BRETHREN	1	52	100	-	-
355 PRESB CH (USA)	11	2,873	3,839*	.6	.8
403 SALVATION ARMY	2	196	255	-	.1
413 S.D.A.	7	1,008	1,347*	.2	.3
419 SO BAPT CONV	52	22,539	30,119*	5.1	6.2
435 UNITARIAN-UNIV	1	97	111	-	-
443 UN C OF CHRIST	3	352	470*	.1	.1
449 UN METHODIST	22	9,082	12,136*	2.1	2.5
469 WELS	4	313	462	.1	.1
496 JEWISH EST[1]	2	NA	4,900	.8	1.0
497 BLACK BAPT EST[2]	NA	7,257	9,697*	1.6	2.0
498 INDEP.CHARIS.[3]	6	NA	3,450	.6	.7
499 INDEP.NON-CHAR[3]	4	NA	1,600	.3	.3
ERATH	**61**	**12,785**	**19,037***	**68.0**	**100.0**
053 ASSEMB OF GOD	3	113	187	.7	1.0
081 CATHOLIC	2	NA	2,311	8.3	12.1
081d *LATIN*	*2*	*NA*	*2,311*	*8.3*	*12.1*
093 CHR CH (DISC)	2	153	314	1.1	1.6
105 CHRISTIAN REF	1	50	116	.4	.6
127 CH GOD (CLEVE)	1	70	86*	.3	.5
151 L-D SAINTS	1	NA	235	.8	1.2
165 CH OF NAZARENE	1	77	89	.3	.5
167 CHS OF CHRIST	11	1,437	1,764	6.3	9.3
193 EPISCOPAL	2	179	234	.8	1.2
283 LUTH—MO SYNOD	1	168	236	.8	1.2
323 OLD ORD AMISH	1	NA	150	.5	.8

NA–Not applicable   NR–Not reported   *Total adherents estimated from known number of communicant, confirmed, full members.   - Represents a percent less than 0.1.   Percentages may not total due to rounding.
[1]See Appendix E   [2]See Appendix F   [3]See Appendix G   Lines in *italic* represent a breakdown of Catholic rites or Friends affiliations. They are included in their respective denominational total.

TEXAS

Table 4. Churches and Church Membership by County and Denomination: 1990

County and Denomination	Number of churches	Communicant, confirmed, full members	Total adherents Number	Percent of total population	Percent of total adherents
355 PRESB CH (USA)	1	137	169*	.6	.9
413 S.D.A.	1	32	40*	.1	.2
419 SO BAPT CONV	22	8,233	10,168*	36.3	53.4
449 UN METHODIST	10	2,136	2,638*	9.4	13.9
499 INDEP.NON-CHAR[3]	1	NA	300	1.1	1.6
FALLS	**62**	**8,750**	**13,080***	**73.8**	**100.0**
053 ASSEMB OF GOD	2	84	127	.7	1.0
061 BEACHY AMISH	1	56	70*	.4	.5
081 CATHOLIC	6	NA	2,085	11.8	15.9
081d LATIN	6	NA	2,085	11.8	15.9
093 CHR CH (DISC)	1	40	65	.4	.5
167 CHS OF CHRIST	9	357	472	2.7	3.6
193 EPISCOPAL	1	83	107	.6	.8
207 E.L.C.A.	1	182	215	1.2	1.6
283 LUTH—MO SYNOD	3	565	713	4.0	5.5
355 PRESB CH (USA)	2	189	236*	1.3	1.8
361 PRIM BAPT ASCS	1	6	7*	-	.1
419 SO BAPT CONV	19	3,867	4,833*	27.3	36.9
443 UN C OF CHRIST	3	193	241*	1.4	1.8
449 UN METHODIST	13	1,342	1,677*	9.5	12.8
497 BLACK BAPT EST[2]	NA	1,786	2,232*	12.6	17.1
FANNIN	**101**	**14,819**	**18,768***	**75.7**	**100.0**
053 ASSEMB OF GOD	6	177	239	1.0	1.3
081 CATHOLIC	1	NA	424	1.7	2.3
081d LATIN	1	NA	424	1.7	2.3
093 CHR CH (DISC)	6	260	344	1.4	1.8
127 CH GOD (CLEVE)	2	278	342*	1.4	1.8
165 CH OF NAZARENE	1	161	199	.8	1.1
167 CHS OF CHRIST	20	1,144	1,447	5.8	7.7
193 EPISCOPAL	1	56	74	.3	.4
283 LUTH—MO SYNOD	2	80	93	.4	.5
339 PENT CH OF GOD	1	34	77	.3	.4
349 PENT HOLINESS	1	10	12*	-	.1
355 PRESB CH (USA)	4	280	344*	1.4	1.8
419 SO BAPT CONV	35	10,071	12,384*	49.9	66.0
449 UN METHODIST	21	1,843	2,266*	9.1	12.1
497 BLACK BAPT EST[2]	NA	425	523*	2.1	2.8
FAYETTE	**55**	**6,468**	**18,389***	**91.5**	**100.0**
053 ASSEMB OF GOD	1	38	53	.3	.3
081 CATHOLIC	15	NA	10,514	52.3	57.2
081d LATIN	15	NA	10,514	52.3	57.2
167 CHS OF CHRIST	3	188	242	1.2	1.3
193 EPISCOPAL	1	93	126	.6	.7
207 E.L.C.A.	10	2,195	2,590	12.9	14.1
283 LUTH—MO SYNOD	4	1,162	1,426	7.1	7.8
355 PRESB CH (USA)	1	205	252*	1.3	1.4
413 S.D.A.	1	17	21*	.1	.1
419 SO BAPT CONV	6	1,339	1,649*	8.2	9.0
443 UN C OF CHRIST	1	95	117*	.6	.6
449 UN METHODIST	11	697	858*	4.3	4.7
496 JEWISH EST[1]	1	NA	0	-	-
497 BLACK BAPT EST[2]	NA	439	541*	2.7	2.9
FISHER	**18**	**3,261**	**4,374***	**90.3**	**100.0**
081 CATHOLIC	2	NA	300	6.2	6.9
081d LATIN	2	NA	300	6.2	6.9
165 CH OF NAZARENE	1	13	14	.3	.3
167 CHS OF CHRIST	2	225	281	5.8	6.4
263 INT FOURSQ GOS	1	35	44*	.9	1.0
419 SO BAPT CONV	8	2,492	3,115*	64.3	71.2
449 UN METHODIST	4	496	620*	12.8	14.2
FLOYD	**27**	**5,033**	**10,562***	**124.3**	**100.0**
053 ASSEMB OF GOD	4	145	232	2.7	2.2
059 BAPT MISS ASSN	1	50	67*	.8	.6
081 CATHOLIC	3	NA	3,800	44.7	36.0
081d LATIN	3	NA	3,800	44.7	36.0
093 CHR CH (DISC)	1	46	56	.7	.5
167 CHS OF CHRIST	5	428	573	6.7	5.4
207 E.L.C.A.	1	71	94	1.1	.9
349 PENT HOLINESS	1	64	86*	1.0	.8
361 PRIM BAPT ASCS	1	80	107*	1.3	1.0
419 SO BAPT CONV	7	3,312	4,428*	52.1	41.9
449 UN METHODIST	3	837	1,119*	13.2	10.6
FOARD	**11**	**1,418**	**1,837***	**102.4**	**100.0**
053 ASSEMB OF GOD	1	47	65	3.6	3.5
081 CATHOLIC	1	NA	46	2.6	2.5
081d LATIN	1	NA	46	2.6	2.5
097 CHR CHS&CHS CR	1	125	154*	8.6	8.4
167 CHS OF CHRIST	1	50	60	3.3	3.3
223 FREE WILL BAPT	1	25	31*	1.7	1.7

County and Denomination	Number of churches	Communicant, confirmed, full members	Total adherents Number	Percent of total population	Percent of total adherents
339 PENT CH OF GOD	1	34	77	4.3	4.2
419 SO BAPT CONV	3	757	935*	52.1	50.9
449 UN METHODIST	2	380	469*	26.1	25.5
FORT BEND	**106**	**40,884**	**100,375***	**44.5**	**100.0**
053 ASSEMB OF GOD	8	663	761	.3	.8
081 CATHOLIC	10	NA	38,926	17.3	38.8
081d LATIN	10	NA	38,926	17.3	38.8
089 CHR & MISS AL	1	22	27	-	-
093 CHR CH (DISC)	1	66	84	-	.1
097 CHR CHS&CHS CR	3	710	968*	.4	1.0
111 CH CR,SCIENTST	2	NR	NR	-	-
123 CH GOD (ANDER)	3	109	143	.1	.1
127 CH GOD (CLEVE)	1	57	78*	-	.1
133 CH GOD(7TH)DEN	1	39	55	-	.1
145 CH GOD PROPHCY	1	31	42*	-	-
151 L-D SAINTS	4	NA	1,851	.8	1.8
165 CH OF NAZARENE	1	44	172	.1	.2
167 CHS OF CHRIST	8	1,650	2,711	1.2	2.7
193 EPISCOPAL	3	832	1,234	.5	1.2
207 E.L.C.A.	6	1,481	2,051	.9	2.0
221 FREE METHODIST	1	17	51	-	.1
263 INT FOURSQ GOS	1	14	19*	-	-
283 LUTH—MO SYNOD	3	596	837	.4	.8
355 PRESB CH (USA)	4	1,163	1,585*	.7	1.6
356 PRESB CH AMER	1	58	113	.1	.1
413 S.D.A.	3	101	138*	.1	.1
419 SO BAPT CONV	20	9,069	12,358*	5.5	12.3
443 UN C OF CHRIST	3	1,357	1,849*	.8	1.8
449 UN METHODIST	15	7,494	10,212*	4.5	10.2
469 WELS	1	18	32	-	-
496 JEWISH EST[1]	0	NA	2,908	1.3	2.9
497 BLACK BAPT EST[2]	NA	15,293	20,840*	9.2	20.8
499 INDEP.NON-CHAR[3]	1	NA	330	.1	.3
FRANKLIN	**24**	**4,556**	**6,097***	**78.1**	**100.0**
053 ASSEMB OF GOD	1	74	95	1.2	1.6
059 BAPT MISS ASSN	2	538	674*	8.6	11.1
081 CATHOLIC	2	NA	354	4.5	5.8
081d LATIN	2	NA	354	4.5	5.8
093 CHR CH (DISC)	1	8	12	.2	.2
145 CH GOD PROPHCY	1	31	39*	.5	.6
165 CH OF NAZARENE	1	16	13	.2	.2
167 CHS OF CHRIST	3	235	303	3.9	5.0
339 PENT CH OF GOD	1	35	76	1.0	1.2
419 SO BAPT CONV	11	3,136	3,926*	50.3	64.4
449 UN METHODIST	1	483	605*	7.8	9.9
FREESTONE	**43**	**8,053**	**10,765***	**68.1**	**100.0**
053 ASSEMB OF GOD	2	123	215	1.4	2.0
059 BAPT MISS ASSN	10	2,010	2,537*	16.0	23.6
081 CATHOLIC	1	NA	400	2.5	3.7
081d LATIN	1	NA	400	2.5	3.7
151 L-D SAINTS	1	NA	97	.6	.9
167 CHS OF CHRIST	5	287	383	2.4	3.6
283 LUTH—MO SYNOD	1	59	97	.6	.9
355 PRESB CH (USA)	4	174	220*	1.4	2.0
419 SO BAPT CONV	7	2,947	3,720*	23.5	34.6
449 UN METHODIST	12	1,668	2,105*	13.3	19.6
497 BLACK BAPT EST[2]	NA	785	991*	6.3	9.2
FRIO	**24**	**2,899**	**11,439***	**84.9**	**100.0**
053 ASSEMB OF GOD	3	184	209	1.6	1.8
081 CATHOLIC	5	NA	7,520	55.8	65.7
081d LATIN	5	NA	7,520	55.8	65.7
093 CHR CH (DISC)	1	8	11	.1	.1
167 CHS OF CHRIST	3	144	185	1.4	1.6
283 LUTH—MO SYNOD	1	74	106	.8	.9
355 PRESB CH (USA)	1	16	22*	.2	.2
419 SO BAPT CONV	5	1,607	2,200*	16.3	19.2
449 UN METHODIST	5	866	1,186*	8.8	10.4
GAINES	**27**	**6,409**	**12,321***	**87.2**	**100.0**
053 ASSEMB OF GOD	4	346	772	5.5	6.3
059 BAPT MISS ASSN	1	83	117*	.8	.9
081 CATHOLIC	2	NA	3,000	21.2	24.3
081d LATIN	2	NA	3,000	21.2	24.3
127 CH GOD (CLEVE)	1	11	15*	.1	.1
151 L-D SAINTS	1	NA	65	.5	.5
165 CH OF NAZARENE	1	23	45	.3	.4
167 CHS OF CHRIST	6	584	759	5.4	6.2
355 PRESB CH (USA)	1	121	170*	1.2	1.4
419 SO BAPT CONV	8	4,704	6,622*	46.9	53.7
449 UN METHODIST	2	537	756*	5.4	6.1

NA–Not applicable   NR–Not reported   *Total adherents estimated from known number of communicant, confirmed, full members.   - Represents a percent less than 0.1.   Percentages may not total due to rounding.
[1]See Appendix E   [2]See Appendix F   [3]See Appendix G   Lines in *italic* represent a breakdown of Catholic rites or Friends affiliations. They are included in their respective denominational total.

Table 4. Churches and Church Membership by County and Denomination: 1990

County and Denomination	Number of churches	Communicant, confirmed, full members	Total adherents Number	Percent of total population	Percent of total adherents
GALVESTON	**182**	**62,772**	**111,069***	**51.1**	**100.0**
053 ASSEMB OF GOD	16	1,272	1,831	.8	1.6
081 CATHOLIC	15	NA	27,124	12.5	24.4
081d LATIN	15	NA	27,124	12.5	24.4
093 CHR CH (DISC)	3	438	528	.2	.5
097 CHR CHS&CHS CR	2	860	1,101*	.5	1.0
111 CH CR,SCIENTST	1	NR	NR	-	-
123 CH GOD (ANDER)	2	54	67	-	.1
127 CH GOD (CLEVE)	1	54	69*	-	.1
145 CH GOD PROPHCY	2	62	79*	-	.1
151 L-D SAINTS	5	NA	1,774	.8	1.6
165 CH OF NAZARENE	2	213	298	.1	.3
167 CHS OF CHRIST	19	2,262	2,810	1.3	2.5
193 EPISCOPAL	10	2,761	3,722	1.7	3.4
203 EVAN FREE CH	1	50	80	-	.1
207 E.L.C.A.	9	2,346	3,183	1.5	2.9
223 FREE WILL BAPT	2	52	67*	-	.1
226 FRIENDS-USA	6	1,001	1,284*	.6	1.2
226b EFI	4	990	1,267*	.6	1.1
226c FGC	2	11	17	-	-
246 GREEK ORTHODOX	1	NR	NR	-	-
259 IFCA	1	NR	NR	-	-
263 INT FOURSQ GOS	1	0	0*	-	-
283 LUTH—MO SYNOD	3	1,231	1,726	.8	1.6
339 PENT CH OF GOD	1	34	77	-	.1
349 PENT HOLINESS	1	50	64*	-	.1
355 PRESB CH (USA)	7	1,301	1,665*	.8	1.5
361 PRIM BAPT ASCS	1	5	6*	-	-
403 SALVATION ARMY	2	143	149	.1	.1
413 S.D.A.	2	83	106*	-	.1
419 SO BAPT CONV	38	26,134	33,443*	15.4	30.1
435 UNITARIAN-UNIV	1	51	59	-	.1
449 UN METHODIST	24	9,792	12,531*	5.8	11.3
496 JEWISH EST[1]	2	NA	800	.4	.7
497 BLACK BAPT EST[2]	NA	12,523	16,026*	7.4	14.4
499 INDEP.NON-CHAR[3]	1	NA	400	.2	.4
GARZA	**19**	**2,303**	**3,380***	**65.7**	**100.0**
081 CATHOLIC	1	NA	335	6.5	9.9
081d LATIN	1	NA	335	6.5	9.9
093 CHR CH (DISC)	1	66	80	1.6	2.4
145 CH GOD PROPHCY	2	38	51*	1.0	1.5
165 CH OF NAZARENE	1	64	81	1.6	2.4
167 CHS OF CHRIST	4	195	248	4.8	7.3
355 PRESB CH (USA)	1	129	172*	3.3	5.1
419 SO BAPT CONV	7	1,511	2,013*	39.1	59.6
449 UN METHODIST	2	300	400*	7.8	11.8
GILLESPIE	**30**	**6,439**	**11,504***	**66.9**	**100.0**
053 ASSEMB OF GOD	1	56	100	.6	.9
081 CATHOLIC	4	NA	3,620	21.0	31.5
081d LATIN	4	NA	3,620	21.0	31.5
093 CHR CH (DISC)	1	19	25	.1	.2
167 CHS OF CHRIST	1	150	175	1.0	1.5
193 EPISCOPAL	1	229	265	1.5	2.3
203 EVAN FREE CH	1	59	80	.5	.7
207 E.L.C.A.	9	3,357	4,093	23.8	35.6
283 LUTH—MO SYNOD	1	0	0	-	-
349 PENT HOLINESS	2	217	266*	1.5	2.3
355 PRESB CH (USA)	2	219	268*	1.6	2.3
413 S.D.A.	1	46	56*	.3	.5
419 SO BAPT CONV	3	1,131	1,384*	8.0	12.0
449 UN METHODIST	2	901	1,103*	6.4	9.6
469 WELS	1	55	69	.4	.6
GLASSCOCK	**4**	**242**	**890***	**61.5**	**100.0**
081 CATHOLIC	1	NA	549	37.9	61.7
081d LATIN	1	NA	549	37.9	61.7
167 CHS OF CHRIST	1	29	43	3.0	4.8
419 SO BAPT CONV	1	160	224*	15.5	25.2
449 UN METHODIST	1	53	74*	5.1	8.3
GOLIAD	**18**	**1,756**	**4,315***	**72.2**	**100.0**
081 CATHOLIC	4	NA	2,090	34.9	48.4
081d LATIN	4	NA	2,090	34.9	48.4
111 CH CR,SCIENTST	1	NR	NR	-	-
167 CHS OF CHRIST	1	84	109	1.8	2.5
193 EPISCOPAL	1	33	46	.8	1.1
207 E.L.C.A.	4	726	911	15.2	21.1
355 PRESB CH (USA)	1	96	122*	2.0	2.8
419 SO BAPT CONV	2	537	682*	11.4	15.8
449 UN METHODIST	4	280	355*	5.9	8.2

County and Denomination	Number of churches	Communicant, confirmed, full members	Total adherents Number	Percent of total population	Percent of total adherents
GONZALES	**44**	**6,124**	**12,291***	**71.4**	**100.0**
053 ASSEMB OF GOD	2	63	99	.6	.8
081 CATHOLIC	5	NA	4,072	23.7	33.1
081d LATIN	5	NA	4,072	23.7	33.1
151 L-D SAINTS	1	NA	96	.6	.8
167 CHS OF CHRIST	3	100	123	.7	1.0
193 EPISCOPAL	1	101	164	1.0	1.3
207 E.L.C.A.	1	325	412	2.4	3.4
323 OLD ORD AMISH	1	NA	150	.9	1.2
355 PRESB CH (USA)	3	228	296*	1.7	2.4
419 SO BAPT CONV	13	3,352	4,345*	25.3	35.4
449 UN METHODIST	14	1,508	1,955*	11.4	15.9
497 BLACK BAPT EST[2]	NA	447	579*	3.4	4.7
GRAY	**78**	**19,003**	**26,088***	**108.8**	**100.0**
001 ADVENT CHR CH	1	0	0*	-	-
053 ASSEMB OF GOD	4	263	429	1.8	1.6
081 CATHOLIC	1	NA	1,288	5.4	4.9
081d LATIN	1	NA	1,288	5.4	4.9
093 CHR CH (DISC)	1	421	568	2.4	2.2
097 CHR CHS&CHS CR	1	165	209*	.9	.8
127 CH GOD (CLEVE)	1	159	201*	.8	.8
145 CH GOD PROPHCY	1	19	24*	.1	.1
151 L-D SAINTS	1	NA	245	1.0	.9
157 CH OF BRETHREN	1	60	76*	.3	.3
165 CH OF NAZARENE	1	87	115	.5	.4
167 CHS OF CHRIST	42	5,163	6,587	27.5	25.2
193 EPISCOPAL	1	255	366	1.5	1.4
223 FREE WILL BAPT	1	37	47*	.2	.2
283 LUTH—MO SYNOD	1	151	190	.8	.7
349 PENT HOLINESS	3	127	161*	.7	.6
355 PRESB CH (USA)	1	371	469*	2.0	1.8
403 SALVATION ARMY	1	55	55	.2	.2
413 S.D.A.	1	23	29*	.1	.1
419 SO BAPT CONV	9	9,450	11,951*	49.9	45.8
449 UN METHODIST	4	1,963	2,482*	10.4	9.5
497 BLACK BAPT EST[2]	NA	234	296*	1.2	1.1
499 INDEP.NON-CHAR[3]	1	NA	300	1.3	1.1
GRAYSON	**137**	**45,963**	**63,395***	**66.7**	**100.0**
053 ASSEMB OF GOD	12	2,400	2,716	2.9	4.3
059 BAPT MISS ASSN	1	85	106*	.1	.2
081 CATHOLIC	4	NA	4,350	4.6	6.9
081d LATIN	4	NA	4,350	4.6	6.9
093 CHR CH (DISC)	5	670	1,014	1.1	1.6
097 CHR CHS&CHS CR	1	25	31*	-	-
111 CH CR,SCIENTST	1	NR	NR	-	-
127 CH GOD (CLEVE)	2	294	367*	.4	.6
151 L-D SAINTS	1	NA	546	.6	.9
165 CH OF NAZARENE	3	486	709	.7	1.1
185 CUMBER PRESB	2	83	86	.1	.1
193 EPISCOPAL	3	806	837	.9	1.3
207 E.L.C.A.	1	134	183	.2	.3
223 FREE WILL BAPT	1	65	81*	.1	.1
283 LUTH—MO SYNOD	1	223	302	.3	.5
339 PENT CH OF GOD	3	124	192	.2	.3
349 PENT HOLINESS	1	36	45*	-	.1
355 PRESB CH (USA)	8	1,629	2,033*	2.1	3.2
356 PRESB CH AMER	1	69	69	.1	.1
361 PRIM BAPT ASCS	2	39	49*	.1	.1
403 SALVATION ARMY	1	97	98	.1	.2
413 S.D.A.	1	108	135*	.1	.2
419 SO BAPT CONV	53	30,748	38,382*	40.4	60.5
449 UN METHODIST	25	5,687	7,099*	7.5	11.2
496 JEWISH EST[1]	1	NA	125	.1	.2
497 BLACK BAPT EST[2]	NA	2,155	2,690*	2.8	4.2
499 INDEP.NON-CHAR[3]	3	NA	1,150	1.2	1.8
GREGG	**146**	**55,827**	**87,536***	**83.4**	**100.0**
053 ASSEMB OF GOD	14	1,138	1,956	1.9	2.2
059 BAPT MISS ASSN	7	1,149	1,470*	1.4	1.7
081 CATHOLIC	4	NA	3,473	3.3	4.0
081d LATIN	4	NA	3,473	3.3	4.0
089 CHR & MISS AL	3	181	402	.4	.5
093 CHR CH (DISC)	7	2,040	2,605	2.5	3.0
097 CHR CHS&CHS CR	1	100	128*	.1	.1
111 CH CR,SCIENTST	2	NR	NR	-	-
123 CH GOD (ANDER)	3	118	124	.1	.1
127 CH GOD (CLEVE)	5	611	781*	.7	.9
145 CH GOD PROPHCY	1	31	40*	-	-
151 L-D SAINTS	3	NA	1,012	1.0	1.2
165 CH OF NAZARENE	4	407	551	.5	.6
167 CHS OF CHRIST	25	3,863	5,050	4.8	5.8
185 CUMBER PRESB	3	983	1,055	1.0	1.2
193 EPISCOPAL	4	1,194	1,574	1.5	1.8
207 E.L.C.A.	1	410	570	.5	.7

Table 4. Churches and Church Membership by County and Denomination: 1990

County and Denomination	Number of churches	Communicant, confirmed, full members	Total adherents Number	Percent of total population	Percent of total adherents
263 INT FOURSQ GOS	1	62	79*	.1	.1
283 LUTH—MO SYNOD	2	352	515	.5	.6
331 ORTH CH IN AM	1	NR	NR	-	-
339 PENT CH OF GOD	1	34	77	.1	.1
353 CHR BRETHREN	1	70	105	.1	.1
355 PRESB CH (USA)	6	1,747	2,234*	2.1	2.6
361 PRIM BAPT ASCS	1	23	29*	-	-
403 SALVATION ARMY	1	128	132	.1	.2
413 S.D.A.	2	114	146*	.1	.2
419 SO BAPT CONV	24	25,863	33,078*	31.5	37.8
435 UNITARIAN-UNIV	1	27	33	-	-
443 UN C OF CHRIST	1	353	451*	.4	.5
449 UN METHODIST	12	8,285	10,596*	10.1	12.1
496 JEWISH EST[1]	1	NA	0	-	-
497 BLACK BAPT EST[2]	NA	6,544	8,370*	8.0	9.6
498 INDEP.CHARIS.[3]	2	NA	700	.7	.8
499 INDEP.NON-CHAR[3]	2	NA	10,200	9.7	11.7
GRIMES	**52**	**6,605**	**11,855***	**63.0**	**100.0**
005 AME ZION	1	25	33	.2	.3
053 ASSEMB OF GOD	2	65	123	.7	1.0
059 BAPT MISS ASSN	3	230	290*	1.5	2.4
081 CATHOLIC	5	NA	3,100	16.5	26.1
081d *LATIN*	*5*	*NA*	*3,100*	*16.5*	*26.1*
151 L-D SAINTS	1	NA	374	2.0	3.2
167 CHS OF CHRIST	6	116	157	.8	1.3
193 EPISCOPAL	1	99	130	.7	1.1
223 FREE WILL BAPT	1	150	189*	1.0	1.6
283 LUTH—MO SYNOD	3	697	864	4.6	7.3
355 PRESB CH (USA)	2	234	295*	1.6	2.5
413 S.D.A.	1	62	78*	.4	.7
419 SO BAPT CONV	13	2,820	3,561*	18.9	30.0
449 UN METHODIST	13	905	1,143*	6.1	9.6
497 BLACK BAPT EST[2]	NA	1,202	1,518*	8.1	12.8
GUADALUPE	**52**	**13,906**	**31,161***	**48.0**	**100.0**
053 ASSEMB OF GOD	4	268	438	.7	1.4
081 CATHOLIC	4	NA	12,400	19.1	39.8
081d *LATIN*	*4*	*NA*	*12,400*	*19.1*	*39.8*
097 CHR CHS&CHS CR	1	52	67*	.1	.2
151 L-D SAINTS	1	NA	264	.4	.8
167 CHS OF CHRIST	5	291	399	.6	1.3
193 EPISCOPAL	1	265	322	.5	1.0
207 E.L.C.A.	4	2,860	3,618	5.6	11.6
283 LUTH—MO SYNOD	2	345	469	.7	1.5
313 N AM BAPT CONF	1	16	21*	-	.1
355 PRESB CH (USA)	1	185	239*	.4	.8
413 S.D.A.	1	41	53*	.1	.2
419 SO BAPT CONV	17	4,442	5,736*	8.8	18.4
443 UN C OF CHRIST	4	1,763	2,276*	3.5	7.3
449 UN METHODIST	6	2,175	2,808*	4.3	9.0
496 JEWISH EST[1]	0	NA	498	.8	1.6
497 BLACK BAPT EST[2]	NA	1,203	1,553*	2.4	5.0
HALE	**71**	**19,566**	**32,728***	**94.4**	**100.0**
053 ASSEMB OF GOD	5	316	454	1.3	1.4
059 BAPT MISS ASSN	1	235	316*	.9	1.0
081 CATHOLIC	6	NA	6,150	17.7	18.8
081d *LATIN*	*6*	*NA*	*6,150*	*17.7*	*18.8*
093 CHR CH (DISC)	1	197	277	.8	.8
111 CH CR,SCIENTST	1	NR	NR	-	-
151 L-D SAINTS	1	NA	217	.6	.7
165 CH OF NAZARENE	6	399	511	1.5	1.6
167 CHS OF CHRIST	13	1,594	2,158	6.2	6.6
193 EPISCOPAL	1	67	114	.3	.3
263 INT FOURSQ GOS	1	27	36*	.1	.1
283 LUTH—MO SYNOD	1	198	244	.7	.7
339 PENT CH OF GOD	1	34	76	.2	.2
349 PENT HOLINESS	2	53	71*	.2	.2
355 PRESB CH (USA)	2	401	539*	1.6	1.6
361 PRIM BAPT ASCS	1	12	16*	-	-
403 SALVATION ARMY	1	59	62	.2	.2
413 S.D.A.	1	61	82*	.2	.3
419 SO BAPT CONV	19	13,178	17,726*	51.1	54.2
449 UN METHODIST	7	2,243	3,017*	8.7	9.2
497 BLACK BAPT EST[2]	NA	492	662*	1.9	2.0
HALL	**19**	**3,521**	**4,385***	**112.3**	**100.0**
053 ASSEMB OF GOD	2	69	79	2.0	1.8
081 CATHOLIC	2	NA	70	1.8	1.6
081d *LATIN*	*2*	*NA*	*70*	*1.8*	*1.6*
097 CHR CHS&CHS CR	1	50	61*	1.6	1.4
167 CHS OF CHRIST	4	316	406	10.4	9.3
355 PRESB CH (USA)	1	31	38*	1.0	.9
419 SO BAPT CONV	6	2,522	3,080*	78.9	70.2
449 UN METHODIST	3	533	651*	16.7	14.8

County and Denomination	Number of churches	Communicant, confirmed, full members	Total adherents Number	Percent of total population	Percent of total adherents
HAMILTON	**35**	**4,534**	**5,607***	**72.5**	**100.0**
053 ASSEMB OF GOD	1	11	25	.3	.4
081 CATHOLIC	2	NA	65	.8	1.2
081d *LATIN*	*2*	*NA*	*65*	*.8*	*1.2*
093 CHR CH (DISC)	1	10	14	.2	.2
167 CHS OF CHRIST	4	439	541	7.0	9.6
193 EPISCOPAL	1	34	54	.7	1.0
207 E.L.C.A.	2	201	234	3.0	4.2
283 LUTH—MO SYNOD	2	480	557	7.2	9.9
339 PENT CH OF GOD	1	35	76	1.0	1.4
355 PRESB CH (USA)	1	45	55*	.7	1.0
361 PRIM BAPT ASCS	1	17	21*	.3	.4
419 SO BAPT CONV	15	2,311	2,809*	36.3	50.1
449 UN METHODIST	4	951	1,156*	14.9	20.6
HANSFORD	**14**	**3,468**	**5,148***	**88.0**	**100.0**
053 ASSEMB OF GOD	1	40	56	1.0	1.1
081 CATHOLIC	1	NA	494	8.4	9.6
081d *LATIN*	*1*	*NA*	*494*	*8.4*	*9.6*
093 CHR CH (DISC)	2	206	310	5.3	6.0
167 CHS OF CHRIST	2	302	390	6.7	7.6
207 E.L.C.A.	2	135	187	3.2	3.6
355 PRESB CH (USA)	1	42	56*	1.0	1.1
419 SO BAPT CONV	3	1,688	2,249*	38.5	43.7
449 UN METHODIST	2	1,055	1,406*	24.0	27.3
HARDEMAN	**16**	**3,615**	**4,717***	**89.3**	**100.0**
053 ASSEMB OF GOD	1	82	115	2.2	2.4
081 CATHOLIC	1	NA	159	3.0	3.4
081d *LATIN*	*1*	*NA*	*159*	*3.0*	*3.4*
093 CHR CH (DISC)	1	175	200	3.8	4.2
165 CH OF NAZARENE	1	30	41	.8	.9
167 CHS OF CHRIST	4	417	533	10.1	11.3
193 EPISCOPAL	1	10	12	.2	.3
355 PRESB CH (USA)	1	40	50*	.9	1.1
419 SO BAPT CONV	4	2,311	2,914*	55.2	61.8
449 UN METHODIST	2	550	693*	13.1	14.7
HARDIN	**68**	**20,089**	**28,666***	**69.4**	**100.0**
053 ASSEMB OF GOD	13	959	1,196	2.9	4.2
081 CATHOLIC	4	NA	2,009	4.9	7.0
081d *LATIN*	*4*	*NA*	*2,009*	*4.9*	*7.0*
093 CHR CH (DISC)	1	25	35	.1	.1
097 CHR CHS&CHS CR	1	210	272*	.7	.9
127 CH GOD (CLEVE)	1	146	189*	.5	.7
145 CH GOD PROPHCY	1	31	40*	.1	.1
151 L-D SAINTS	2	NA	607	1.5	2.1
165 CH OF NAZARENE	1	15	0	-	-
167 CHS OF CHRIST	6	500	636	1.5	2.2
193 EPISCOPAL	1	83	111	.3	.4
339 PENT CH OF GOD	1	13	13	-	-
355 PRESB CH (USA)	1	96	124*	.3	.4
419 SO BAPT CONV	27	14,881	19,285*	46.7	67.3
449 UN METHODIST	8	1,986	2,574*	6.2	9.0
496 JEWISH EST[1]	0	NA	92	.2	.3
497 BLACK BAPT EST[2]	NA	1,144	1,483*	3.6	5.2
HARRIS	**1,361**	**785,161**	**1,643,405***	**58.3**	**100.0**
005 AME ZION	1	320	371	-	-
019 AMER BAPT USA	5	1,538	1,993*	.1	.1
053 ASSEMB OF GOD	97	18,544	25,892	.9	1.6
057 BAPT GEN CONF	2	123	159*	-	-
059 BAPT MISS ASSN	17	5,054	6,550*	.2	.4
081 CATHOLIC	108	NA	524,251	18.6	31.9
081b *BYZAN RUTH*	*1*	*NA*	*335*	*-*	*-*
081d *LATIN*	*105*	*NA*	*523,323*	*18.6*	*31.8*
081f *MELKITE-GK*	*1*	*NA*	*522*	*-*	*-*
081h *UKRAINIAN*	*1*	*NA*	*71*	*-*	*-*
089 CHR & MISS AL	9	461	861	-	.1
093 CHR CH (DISC)	23	5,568	7,511	.3	.5
097 CHR CHS&CHS CR	4	855	1,108*	-	.1
105 CHRISTIAN REF	4	187	273	-	-
111 CH CR,SCIENTST	13	NR	NR	-	-
123 CH GOD (ANDER)	15	1,044	1,582	.1	.1
127 CH GOD (CLEVE)	14	1,881	2,438*	.1	.1
133 CH GOD(7TH)DEN	6	234	324	-	-
145 CH GOD PROPHCY	6	176	228*	-	-
151 L-D SAINTS	39	NA	15,552	.6	.9
164 CH LUTH CONF	1	44	61	-	-
165 CH OF NAZARENE	26	3,155	5,359	.2	.3
167 CHS OF CHRIST	149	25,864	33,931	1.2	2.1
175 CONGR CHR CHS	1	406	526*	-	-
185 CUMBER PRESB	1	281	327	-	-
193 EPISCOPAL	43	27,593	35,705	1.3	2.2
203 EVAN FREE CH	1	18	30	-	-

NA–Not applicable   NR–Not reported   *Total adherents estimated from known number of communicant, confirmed, full members.   - Represents a percent less than 0.1.   Percentages may not total due to rounding.
[1]See Appendix E   [2]See Appendix F   [3]See Appendix G   Lines in *italic* represent a breakdown of Catholic rites or Friends affiliations. They are included in their respective denominational total.

Table 4. Churches and Church Membership by County and Denomination: 1990

County and Denomination	Number of churches	Communicant, confirmed, full members	Total adherents Number	Percent of total population	Percent of total adherents
207 E.L.C.A.	39	13,652	17,967	.6	1.1
215 EVAN METH CH	1	28	36*	-	-
216 EVAN PRESBY CH	2	154	161	-	-
221 FREE METHODIST	1	11	36	-	-
223 FREE WILL BAPT	2	410	531*	-	-
226 FRIENDS-USA	5	226	363*	-	-
226b EFI	*4*	*120*	*156**	*-*	*-*
226c FGC	*1*	*106*	*207*	*-*	*-*
246 GREEK ORTHODOX	1	NR	NR	-	-
249 AP CATH ASSYR	0	13	87	-	-
259 IFCA	1	NR	NR	-	-
263 INT FOURSQ GOS	4	104	135*	-	-
266 INTRSTAT & ASC	1	59	76*	-	-
283 LUTH—MO SYNOD	50	23,797	32,537	1.2	2.0
285 MENNONITE CH	1	64	91	-	-
287 MENN GEN CONF	2	55	73	-	-
313 N AM BAPT CONF	1	148	192*	-	-
329 OPEN BIBLE STD	1	NR	NR	-	-
331 ORTH CH IN AM	1	NR	NR	-	-
339 PENT CH OF GOD	19	1,316	2,113	.1	.1
349 PENT HOLINESS	5	214	277*	-	-
353 CHR BRETHREN	5	490	834	-	.1
355 PRESB CH (USA)	56	29,774	38,585*	1.4	2.3
356 PRESB CH AMER	9	1,145	1,551	.1	.1
361 PRIM BAPT ASCS	5	219	284*	-	-
403 SALVATION ARMY	2	360	391	-	-
413 S.D.A.	32	4,658	6,036*	.2	.4
415 S-D BAPTIST GC	2	75	97*	-	-
419 SO BAPT CONV	314	304,917	395,152*	14.0	24.0
423 SYRIAN ANTIOCH	2	NA	900	-	.1
435 UNITARIAN-UNIV	4	1,180	1,532	.1	.1
443 UN C OF CHRIST	11	3,015	3,907*	.1	.2
449 UN METHODIST	138	127,364	165,055*	5.9	10.0
467 WESLEYAN	2	30	43	-	-
469 WELS	5	709	1,076	-	.1
496 JEWISH EST[1]	14	NA	36,061	1.3	2.2
497 BLACK BAPT EST[2]	NA	177,628	230,194*	8.2	14.0
498 INDEP.CHARIS.[3]	22	NA	33,325	1.2	2.0
499 INDEP.NON-CHAR[3]	16	NA	8,675	.3	.5
HARRISON	**86**	**26,702**	**35,427***	**61.6**	**100.0**
053 ASSEMB OF GOD	5	320	534	.9	1.5
081 CATHOLIC	2	NA	713	1.2	2.0
081d LATIN	*2*	*NA*	*713*	*1.2*	*2.0*
093 CHR CH (DISC)	3	126	239	.4	.7
111 CH CR,SCIENTST	1	NR	NR	-	-
145 CH GOD PROPHCY	2	62	80*	.1	.2
151 L-D SAINTS	1	NA	214	.4	.6
165 CH OF NAZARENE	1	154	146	.3	.4
185 CUMBER PRESB	1	491	519	.9	1.5
193 EPISCOPAL	2	370	382	.7	1.1
216 EVAN PRESBY CH	1	172	178	.3	.5
339 PENT CH OF GOD	1	22	30	.1	.1
355 PRESB CH (USA)	3	263	339*	.6	1.0
413 S.D.A.	2	82	106*	.2	.3
419 SO BAPT CONV	38	17,323	22,320*	38.8	63.0
449 UN METHODIST	22	3,527	4,544*	7.9	12.8
496 JEWISH EST[1]	1	NA	200	.3	.6
497 BLACK BAPT EST[2]	NA	3,790	4,883*	8.5	13.8
HARTLEY	**9**	**1,086**	**1,620***	**44.6**	**100.0**
081 CATHOLIC	1	NA	219	6.0	13.5
081d LATIN	*1*	*NA*	*219*	*6.0*	*13.5*
165 CH OF NAZARENE	1	80	71	2.0	4.4
167 CHS OF CHRIST	1	30	38	1.0	2.3
283 LUTH—MO SYNOD	1	105	184	5.1	11.4
419 SO BAPT CONV	2	430	547*	15.1	33.8
449 UN METHODIST	3	441	561*	15.4	34.6
HASKELL	**26**	**5,534**	**7,467***	**109.5**	**100.0**
053 ASSEMB OF GOD	1	55	114	1.7	1.5
081 CATHOLIC	1	NA	600	8.8	8.0
081d LATIN	*1*	*NA*	*600*	*8.8*	*8.0*
097 CHR CHS&CHS CR	1	85	106*	1.6	1.4
167 CHS OF CHRIST	3	370	390	5.7	5.2
207 E.L.C.A.	2	318	386	5.7	5.2
263 INT FOURSQ GOS	2	50	62*	.9	.8
355 PRESB CH (USA)	1	63	79*	1.2	1.1
419 SO BAPT CONV	9	4,036	5,035*	73.8	67.4
449 UN METHODIST	6	557	695*	10.2	9.3
HAYS	**60**	**16,093**	**28,012***	**42.7**	**100.0**
053 ASSEMB OF GOD	4	117	174	.3	.6
081 CATHOLIC	8	NA	6,585	10.0	23.5
081d LATIN	*8*	*NA*	*6,585*	*10.0*	*23.5*
093 CHR CH (DISC)	2	997	1,622	2.5	5.8

County and Denomination	Number of churches	Communicant, confirmed, full members	Total adherents Number	Percent of total population	Percent of total adherents
111 CH CR,SCIENTST	1	NR	NR	-	-
151 L-D SAINTS	1	NA	387	.6	1.4
163 CH OF LUTH BR	1	36	71	.1	.3
165 CH OF NAZARENE	1	16	0	-	-
167 CHS OF CHRIST	6	551	721	1.1	2.6
193 EPISCOPAL	4	645	1,012	1.5	3.6
203 EVAN FREE CH	1	17	50	.1	.2
207 E.L.C.A.	2	565	690	1.1	2.5
283 LUTH—MO SYNOD	1	150	209	.3	.7
313 N AM BAPT CONF	1	111	137*	.2	.5
339 PENT CH OF GOD	1	45	50	.1	.2
355 PRESB CH (USA)	2	308	381*	.6	1.4
413 S.D.A.	1	126	156*	.2	.6
419 SO BAPT CONV	12	9,171	11,345*	17.3	40.5
435 UNITARIAN-UNIV	1	20	20	-	.1
443 UN C OF CHRIST	1	98	121*	.2	.4
449 UN METHODIST	9	2,391	2,958*	4.5	10.6
496 JEWISH EST[1]	0	NA	421	.6	1.5
497 BLACK BAPT EST[2]	NA	729	902*	1.4	3.2
HEMPHILL	**10**	**1,953**	**2,919***	**78.5**	**100.0**
053 ASSEMB OF GOD	2	106	176	4.7	6.0
081 CATHOLIC	1	NA	289	7.8	9.9
081d LATIN	*1*	*NA*	*289*	*7.8*	*9.9*
097 CHR CHS&CHS CR	1	250	331*	8.9	11.3
167 CHS OF CHRIST	1	186	242	6.5	8.3
193 EPISCOPAL	1	24	47	1.3	1.6
355 PRESB CH (USA)	1	96	127*	3.4	4.4
419 SO BAPT CONV	2	956	1,264*	34.0	43.3
449 UN METHODIST	1	335	443*	11.9	15.2
HENDERSON	**103**	**20,964**	**28,106***	**48.0**	**100.0**
053 ASSEMB OF GOD	11	1,065	1,416	2.4	5.0
059 BAPT MISS ASSN	15	2,792	3,436*	5.9	12.2
081 CATHOLIC	2	NA	1,190	2.0	4.2
081d LATIN	*2*	*NA*	*1,190*	*2.0*	*4.2*
093 CHR CH (DISC)	2	378	495	.8	1.8
111 CH CR,SCIENTST	1	NR	NR	-	-
123 CH GOD (ANDER)	1	25	45	.1	.2
127 CH GOD (CLEVE)	1	40	49*	.1	.2
151 L-D SAINTS	1	NA	303	.5	1.1
165 CH OF NAZARENE	2	86	113	.2	.4
167 CHS OF CHRIST	12	982	1,232	2.1	4.4
185 CUMBER PRESB	1	14	20	-	.1
193 EPISCOPAL	1	78	128	.2	.5
283 LUTH—MO SYNOD	2	326	428	.7	1.5
339 PENT CH OF GOD	2	69	154	.3	.5
355 PRESB CH (USA)	2	324	399*	.7	1.4
413 S.D.A.	2	109	134*	.2	.5
419 SO BAPT CONV	28	10,220	12,579*	21.5	44.8
449 UN METHODIST	16	3,192	3,929*	6.7	14.0
497 BLACK BAPT EST[2]	NA	1,264	1,556*	2.7	5.5
499 INDEP.NON-CHAR[3]	1	NA	500	.9	1.8
HIDALGO	**277**	**33,670**	**360,833***	**94.1**	**100.0**
053 ASSEMB OF GOD	24	2,155	3,085	.8	.9
059 BAPT MISS ASSN	1	202	280*	.1	.1
075 BRETHREN IN CR	1	26	26	-	-
081 CATHOLIC	51	NA	310,671	81.0	86.1
081d LATIN	*51*	*NA*	*310,671*	*81.0*	*86.1*
089 CHR & MISS AL	9	393	628	.2	.2
093 CHR CH (DISC)	7	944	1,417	.4	.4
097 CHR CHS&CHS CR	1	175	243*	.1	.1
111 CH CR,SCIENTST	3	NR	NR	-	-
123 CH GOD (ANDER)	1	21	40	-	-
127 CH GOD (CLEVE)	1	26	36*	-	-
133 CH GOD(7TH)DEN	2	78	109	-	-
151 L-D SAINTS	6	NA	2,846	.7	.8
165 CH OF NAZARENE	8	467	813	.2	.2
167 CHS OF CHRIST	21	1,223	1,703	.4	.5
193 EPISCOPAL	4	1,150	1,444	.4	.4
203 EVAN FREE CH	1	0	0	-	-
207 E.L.C.A.	5	921	1,220	.3	.3
220 FREE LUTHERAN	1	87	103	-	-
223 FREE WILL BAPT	2	230	319*	.1	.1
237 GC MENN BR CHS	5	159	221*	.1	.1
263 INT FOURSQ GOS	3	141	196*	.1	.1
283 LUTH—MO SYNOD	5	1,272	1,675	.4	.5
285 MENNONITE CH	2	70	108	-	-
313 N AM BAPT CONF	2	155	215*	.1	.1
331 ORTH CH IN AM	1	NR	NR	-	-
339 PENT CH OF GOD	1	14	40	-	-
349 PENT HOLINESS	12	288	400*	.1	.1
355 PRESB CH (USA)	10	1,492	2,071*	.5	.6
356 PRESB CH AMER	2	46	51	-	-
403 SALVATION ARMY	1	109	113	-	-

NA–Not applicable   NR–Not reported   *Total adherents estimated from known number of communicant, confirmed, full members.   - Represents a percent less than 0.1.   Percentages may not total due to rounding.
[1]See Appendix E   [2]See Appendix F   [3]See Appendix G   Lines in *italic* represent a breakdown of Catholic rites or Friends affiliations. They are included in their respective denominational total.

Table 4. Churches and Church Membership by County and Denomination: 1990

County and Denomination	Number of churches	Communicant, confirmed, full members	Total adherents Number	Total adherents Percent of total population	Total adherents Percent of total adherents
413 S.D.A.	17	2,052	2,849*	.7	.8
419 SO BAPT CONV	41	12,149	16,866*	4.4	4.7
435 UNITARIAN-UNIV	1	11	11	-	-
449 UN METHODIST	23	7,282	10,109*	2.6	2.8
469 WELS	1	67	82	-	-
496 JEWISH EST[1]	1	NA	475	.1	.1
497 BLACK BAPT EST[2]	NA	265	368*	.1	.1
HILL	**80**	**12,081**	**17,818***	**65.6**	**100.0**
053 ASSEMB OF GOD	2	126	200	.7	1.1
059 BAPT MISS ASSN	3	582	724*	2.7	4.1
081 CATHOLIC	3	NA	2,469	9.1	13.9
081d LATIN	*3*	*NA*	*2,469*	*9.1*	*13.9*
093 CHR CH (DISC)	1	104	145	.5	.8
123 CH GOD (ANDER)	1	10	11	-	.1
165 CH OF NAZARENE	2	145	288	1.1	1.6
167 CHS OF CHRIST	15	935	1,263	4.7	7.1
185 CUMBER PRESB	2	37	43	.2	.2
193 EPISCOPAL	2	56	63	.2	.4
207 E.L.C.A.	1	101	124	.5	.7
221 FREE METHODIST	1	21	29	.1	.2
263 INT FOURSQ GOS	1	19	24*	.1	.1
283 LUTH—MO SYNOD	3	505	652	2.4	3.7
339 PENT CH OF GOD	1	34	77	.3	.4
355 PRESB CH (USA)	3	486	605*	2.2	3.4
361 PRIM BAPT ASCS	1	42	52*	.2	.3
413 S.D.A.	2	60	75*	.3	.4
419 SO BAPT CONV	24	6,180	7,693*	28.3	43.2
449 UN METHODIST	11	1,952	2,430*	9.0	13.6
469 WELS	1	16	17	.1	.1
497 BLACK BAPT EST[2]	NA	670	834*	3.1	4.7
HOCKLEY	**47**	**12,249**	**18,285***	**75.6**	**100.0**
053 ASSEMB OF GOD	3	259	404	1.7	2.2
059 BAPT MISS ASSN	3	1,114	1,501*	6.2	8.2
081 CATHOLIC	3	NA	1,800	7.4	9.8
081d LATIN	*3*	*NA*	*1,800*	*7.4*	*9.8*
093 CHR CH (DISC)	1	50	77	.3	.4
165 CH OF NAZARENE	2	108	128	.5	.7
167 CHS OF CHRIST	14	1,391	1,806	7.5	9.9
193 EPISCOPAL	1	48	61	.3	.3
207 E.L.C.A.	1	145	197	.8	1.1
263 INT FOURSQ GOS	2	134	181*	.7	1.0
355 PRESB CH (USA)	1	156	210*	.9	1.1
361 PRIM BAPT ASCS	1	23	31*	.1	.2
419 SO BAPT CONV	10	7,369	9,932*	41.0	54.3
449 UN METHODIST	5	1,186	1,598*	6.6	8.7
497 BLACK BAPT EST[2]	NA	266	359*	1.5	2.0
HOOD	**39**	**10,793**	**14,646***	**50.5**	**100.0**
053 ASSEMB OF GOD	3	265	364	1.3	2.5
081 CATHOLIC	1	NA	463	1.6	3.2
081d LATIN	*1*	*NA*	*463*	*1.6*	*3.2*
093 CHR CH (DISC)	1	175	190	.7	1.3
111 CH CR,SCIENTST	1	NR	NR	-	-
127 CH GOD (CLEVE)	1	127	159*	.5	1.1
151 L-D SAINTS	1	NA	288	1.0	2.0
165 CH OF NAZARENE	1	48	86	.3	.6
167 CHS OF CHRIST	7	1,152	1,464	5.1	10.0
193 EPISCOPAL	1	220	263	.9	1.8
207 E.L.C.A.	1	101	142	.5	1.0
283 LUTH—MO SYNOD	1	190	240	.8	1.6
355 PRESB CH (USA)	1	135	169*	.6	1.2
413 S.D.A.	1	64	80*	.3	.5
419 SO BAPT CONV	13	6,059	7,605*	26.2	51.9
449 UN METHODIST	4	2,257	2,833*	9.8	19.3
499 INDEP.NON-CHAR[3]	1	NA	300	1.0	2.0
HOPKINS	**88**	**15,582**	**21,570***	**74.8**	**100.0**
053 ASSEMB OF GOD	5	265	373	1.3	1.7
059 BAPT MISS ASSN	13	2,364	2,987*	10.4	13.8
081 CATHOLIC	1	NA	716	2.5	3.3
081d LATIN	*1*	*NA*	*716*	*2.5*	*3.3*
093 CHR CH (DISC)	1	135	362	1.3	1.7
127 CH GOD (CLEVE)	1	272	344*	1.2	1.6
151 L-D SAINTS	1	NA	136	.5	.6
165 CH OF NAZARENE	1	118	191	.7	.9
167 CHS OF CHRIST	10	1,387	1,804	6.3	8.4
185 CUMBER PRESB	2	49	49	.2	.2
193 EPISCOPAL	1	84	113	.4	.5
283 LUTH—MO SYNOD	1	118	159	.6	.7
323 OLD ORD AMISH	1	NA	100	.3	.5
355 PRESB CH (USA)	3	147	186*	.6	.9
413 S.D.A.	1	16	20*	.1	.1
419 SO BAPT CONV	24	7,533	9,520*	33.0	44.1
449 UN METHODIST	21	2,436	3,078*	10.7	14.3

County and Denomination	Number of churches	Communicant, confirmed, full members	Total adherents Number	Total adherents Percent of total population	Total adherents Percent of total adherents
497 BLACK BAPT EST[2]	NA	658	832*	2.9	3.9
499 INDEP.NON-CHAR[3]	1	NA	600	2.1	2.8
HOUSTON	**63**	**11,469**	**14,738***	**68.9**	**100.0**
053 ASSEMB OF GOD	6	389	488	2.3	3.3
059 BAPT MISS ASSN	3	693	860*	4.0	5.8
081 CATHOLIC	1	NA	439	2.1	3.0
081d LATIN	*1*	*NA*	*439*	*2.1*	*3.0*
093 CHR CH (DISC)	3	155	207	1.0	1.4
127 CH GOD (CLEVE)	1	88	109*	.5	.7
165 CH OF NAZARENE	1	32	40	.2	.3
167 CHS OF CHRIST	9	585	776	3.6	5.3
193 EPISCOPAL	1	58	66	.3	.4
283 LUTH—MO SYNOD	1	71	97	.5	.7
355 PRESB CH (USA)	1	132	164*	.8	1.1
361 PRIM BAPT ASCS	1	13	16*	.1	.1
419 SO BAPT CONV	22	5,699	7,068*	33.1	48.0
449 UN METHODIST	13	1,205	1,495*	7.0	10.1
497 BLACK BAPT EST[2]	NA	2,349	2,913*	13.6	19.8
HOWARD	**61**	**14,337**	**26,607***	**82.3**	**100.0**
053 ASSEMB OF GOD	4	212	400	1.2	1.5
081 CATHOLIC	4	NA	6,724	20.8	25.3
081d LATIN	*4*	*NA*	*6,724*	*20.8*	*25.3*
093 CHR CH (DISC)	1	240	317	1.0	1.2
097 CHR CHS&CHS CR	1	70	89*	.3	.3
123 CH GOD (ANDER)	1	60	80	.2	.3
127 CH GOD (CLEVE)	1	281	357*	1.1	1.3
145 CH GOD PROPHCY	1	19	24*	.1	.1
151 L-D SAINTS	1	NA	204	.6	.8
165 CH OF NAZARENE	1	206	281	.9	1.1
167 CHS OF CHRIST	11	1,413	1,671	5.2	6.3
193 EPISCOPAL	1	135	176	.5	.7
283 LUTH—MO SYNOD	1	232	313	1.0	1.2
355 PRESB CH (USA)	2	521	663*	2.0	2.5
403 SALVATION ARMY	1	83	89	.3	.3
413 S.D.A.	1	37	47*	.1	.2
419 SO BAPT CONV	22	8,791	11,182*	34.6	42.0
449 UN METHODIST	5	1,711	2,176*	6.7	8.2
497 BLACK BAPT EST[2]	NA	326	415*	1.3	1.6
499 INDEP.NON-CHAR[3]	2	NA	1,399	4.3	5.3
HUDSPETH	**11**	**474**	**2,465***	**84.6**	**100.0**
053 ASSEMB OF GOD	2	56	74	2.5	3.0
081 CATHOLIC	3	NA	1,840	63.1	74.6
081d LATIN	*3*	*NA*	*1,840*	*63.1*	*74.6*
167 CHS OF CHRIST	1	20	24	.8	1.0
419 SO BAPT CONV	2	297	393*	13.5	15.9
449 UN METHODIST	3	101	134*	4.6	5.4
HUNT	**124**	**28,857**	**40,268***	**62.6**	**100.0**
053 ASSEMB OF GOD	7	562	827	1.3	2.1
059 BAPT MISS ASSN	3	373	471*	.7	1.2
081 CATHOLIC	3	NA	1,954	3.0	4.9
081d LATIN	*3*	*NA*	*1,954*	*3.0*	*4.9*
093 CHR CH (DISC)	7	558	927	1.4	2.3
097 CHR CHS&CHS CR	1	48	61*	.1	.2
111 CH CR,SCIENTST	1	NR	NR	-	-
151 L-D SAINTS	1	NA	453	.7	1.1
165 CH OF NAZARENE	2	204	234	.4	.6
167 CHS OF CHRIST	20	2,079	2,583	4.0	6.4
193 EPISCOPAL	2	188	226	.4	.6
207 E.L.C.A.	1	145	207	.3	.5
283 LUTH—MO SYNOD	1	58	70	.1	.2
339 PENT CH OF GOD	2	69	153	.2	.4
355 PRESB CH (USA)	3	655	827*	1.3	2.1
356 PRESB CH AMER	1	42	47	.1	.1
403 SALVATION ARMY	1	47	47	.1	.1
413 S.D.A.	2	74	93*	.1	.2
419 SO BAPT CONV	45	18,048	22,791*	35.4	56.6
435 UNITARIAN-UNIV	1	14	18	-	-
449 UN METHODIST	18	3,884	4,905*	7.6	12.2
497 BLACK BAPT EST[2]	NA	1,809	2,284*	3.5	5.7
499 INDEP.NON-CHAR[3]	2	NA	1,090	1.7	2.7
HUTCHINSON	**46**	**14,727**	**21,311***	**83.0**	**100.0**
053 ASSEMB OF GOD	3	192	325	1.3	1.5
081 CATHOLIC	2	NA	1,266	4.9	5.9
081d LATIN	*2*	*NA*	*1,266*	*4.9*	*5.9*
093 CHR CH (DISC)	3	359	497	1.9	2.3
097 CHR CHS&CHS CR	1	50	65*	.3	.3
111 CH CR,SCIENTST	1	NR	NR	-	-
127 CH GOD (CLEVE)	1	174	226*	.9	1.1
151 L-D SAINTS	1	NA	198	.8	.9
165 CH OF NAZARENE	4	242	368	1.4	1.7

NA–Not applicable NR–Not reported *Total adherents estimated from known number of communicant, confirmed, full members. - Represents a percent less than 0.1. Percentages may not total due to rounding.
[1]See Appendix E [2]See Appendix F [3]See Appendix G Lines in *italic* represent a breakdown of Catholic rites or Friends affiliations. They are included in their respective denominational total.

Table 4. Churches and Church Membership by County and Denomination: 1990

County and Denomination	Number of churches	Communicant, confirmed, full members	Total adherents Number	Percent of total population	Percent of total adherents
167 CHS OF CHRIST	7	1,269	1,782	6.9	8.4
193 EPISCOPAL	1	96	142	.6	.7
283 LUTH—MO SYNOD	1	160	212	.8	1.0
339 PENT CH OF GOD	1	34	77	.3	.4
349 PENT HOLINESS	1	84	109*	.4	.5
355 PRESB CH (USA)	1	150	195*	.8	.9
403 SALVATION ARMY	1	48	48	.2	.2
413 S.D.A.	1	14	18*	.1	.1
419 SO BAPT CONV	10	9,689	12,572*	48.9	59.0
449 UN METHODIST	5	1,986	2,577*	10.0	12.1
497 BLACK BAPT EST[2]	NA	180	234*	.9	1.1
499 INDEP.NON-CHAR[3]	1	NA	400	1.6	1.9
IRION	**6**	**725**	**1,212***	**74.4**	**100.0**
081 CATHOLIC	1	NA	286	17.6	23.6
081d *LATIN*	*1*	*NA*	*286*	*17.6*	*23.6*
093 CHR CH (DISC)	1	19	21	1.3	1.7
167 CHS OF CHRIST	1	45	57	3.5	4.7
419 SO BAPT CONV	1	442	567*	34.8	46.8
449 UN METHODIST	2	219	281*	17.2	23.2
JACK	**40**	**4,568**	**6,085***	**87.2**	**100.0**
001 ADVENT CHR CH	1	17	22*	.3	.4
053 ASSEMB OF GOD	4	133	245	3.5	4.0
059 BAPT MISS ASSN	1	135	171*	2.4	2.8
081 CATHOLIC	1	NA	163	2.3	2.7
081d *LATIN*	*1*	*NA*	*163*	*2.3*	*2.7*
093 CHR CH (DISC)	1	82	124	1.8	2.0
167 CHS OF CHRIST	12	713	917	13.1	15.1
193 EPISCOPAL	1	29	50	.7	.8
355 PRESB CH (USA)	1	44	56*	.8	.9
419 SO BAPT CONV	12	2,846	3,615*	51.8	59.4
426 2SEED-SPRT BPT	1	42	53*	.8	.9
449 UN METHODIST	5	527	669*	9.6	11.0
JACKSON	**27**	**4,797**	**9,397***	**72.1**	**100.0**
053 ASSEMB OF GOD	1	41	93	.7	1.0
081 CATHOLIC	4	NA	3,195	24.5	34.0
081d *LATIN*	*4*	*NA*	*3,195*	*24.5*	*34.0*
093 CHR CH (DISC)	1	21	23	.2	.2
193 EPISCOPAL	1	52	67	.5	.7
207 E.L.C.A.	1	263	317	2.4	3.4
283 LUTH—MO SYNOD	1	194	261	2.0	2.8
355 PRESB CH (USA)	2	192	246*	1.9	2.6
419 SO BAPT CONV	9	2,752	3,533*	27.1	37.6
449 UN METHODIST	6	860	1,104*	8.5	11.7
469 WELS	1	105	151	1.2	1.6
497 BLACK BAPT EST[2]	NA	317	407*	3.1	4.3
JASPER	**66**	**16,124**	**22,372***	**71.9**	**100.0**
053 ASSEMB OF GOD	5	345	518	1.7	2.3
059 BAPT MISS ASSN	14	1,387	1,775*	5.7	7.9
081 CATHOLIC	4	NA	1,072	3.4	4.8
081d *LATIN*	*4*	*NA*	*1,072*	*3.4*	*4.8*
151 L-D SAINTS	2	NA	452	1.5	2.0
165 CH OF NAZARENE	2	73	199	.6	.9
167 CHS OF CHRIST	7	814	1,067	3.4	4.8
193 EPISCOPAL	1	135	161	.5	.7
283 LUTH—MO SYNOD	1	90	104	.3	.5
339 PENT CH OF GOD	1	34	77	.2	.3
355 PRESB CH (USA)	1	74	95*	.3	.4
419 SO BAPT CONV	19	9,660	12,359*	39.7	55.2
449 UN METHODIST	9	1,952	2,497*	8.0	11.2
497 BLACK BAPT EST[2]	NA	1,560	1,996*	6.4	8.9
JEFF DAVIS	**8**	**500**	**2,121***	**109.0**	**100.0**
081 CATHOLIC	2	NA	1,510	77.6	71.2
081d *LATIN*	*2*	*NA*	*1,510*	*77.6*	*71.2*
097 CHR CHS&CHS CR	1	0	0*	-	-
167 CHS OF CHRIST	1	35	40	2.1	1.9
355 PRESB CH (USA)	1	124	152*	7.8	7.2
419 SO BAPT CONV	2	250	307*	15.8	14.5
449 UN METHODIST	1	91	112*	5.8	5.3
JEFFERSON	**212**	**94,803**	**187,882***	**78.5**	**100.0**
053 ASSEMB OF GOD	14	2,907	3,404	1.4	1.8
059 BAPT MISS ASSN	4	461	588*	.2	.3
081 CATHOLIC	27	NA	63,518	26.5	33.8
081d *LATIN*	*27*	*NA*	*63,518*	*26.5*	*33.8*
093 CHR CH (DISC)	5	1,164	1,354	.6	.7
097 CHR CHS&CHS CR	3	722	920*	.4	.5
111 CH CR,SCIENTST	1	NR	NR	-	-
123 CH GOD (ANDER)	2	169	196	.1	.1
151 L-D SAINTS	3	NA	1,114	.5	.6
165 CH OF NAZARENE	6	630	1,510	.6	.8
167 CHS OF CHRIST	28	3,691	4,742	2.0	2.5
193 EPISCOPAL	5	2,169	2,723	1.1	1.4
207 E.L.C.A.	2	727	952	.4	.5
246 GREEK ORTHODOX	1	NR	NR	-	-
263 INT FOURSQ GOS	1	10	13*	-	-
283 LUTH—MO SYNOD	6	2,004	2,576	1.1	1.4
353 CHR BRETHREN	1	20	30	-	-
355 PRESB CH (USA)	5	2,111	2,690*	1.1	1.4
356 PRESB CH AMER	1	21	27	-	-
361 PRIM BAPT ASCS	1	44	56*	-	-
403 SALVATION ARMY	2	211	223	.1	.1
413 S.D.A.	3	299	381*	.2	.2
419 SO BAPT CONV	56	44,758	57,044*	23.8	30.4
435 UNITARIAN-UNIV	1	94	104	-	.1
443 UN C OF CHRIST	1	96	122*	.1	.1
449 UN METHODIST	28	14,910	19,003*	7.9	10.1
496 JEWISH EST[1]	3	NA	630	.3	.3
497 BLACK BAPT EST[2]	NA	17,585	22,412*	9.4	11.9
498 INDEP.CHARIS.[3]	2	NA	1,550	.6	.8
JIM HOGG	**14**	**487**	**4,637***	**90.8**	**100.0**
053 ASSEMB OF GOD	1	35	40	.8	.9
081 CATHOLIC	6	NA	3,990	78.1	86.0
081d *LATIN*	*6*	*NA*	*3,990*	*78.1*	*86.0*
167 CHS OF CHRIST	3	26	35	.7	.8
193 EPISCOPAL	1	27	32	.6	.7
419 SO BAPT CONV	1	254	344*	6.7	7.4
449 UN METHODIST	2	145	196*	3.8	4.2
JIM WELLS	**42**	**6,260**	**31,857***	**84.5**	**100.0**
053 ASSEMB OF GOD	2	79	127	.3	.4
081 CATHOLIC	11	NA	23,580	62.6	74.0
081d *LATIN*	*11*	*NA*	*23,580*	*62.6*	*74.0*
093 CHR CH (DISC)	1	66	75	.2	.2
167 CHS OF CHRIST	5	276	341	.9	1.1
193 EPISCOPAL	1	142	182	.5	.6
207 E.L.C.A.	2	639	762	2.0	2.4
237 GC MENN BR CHS	1	20	27*	.1	.1
283 LUTH—MO SYNOD	2	82	114	.3	.4
285 MENNONITE CH	2	54	72	.2	.2
355 PRESB CH (USA)	2	208	279*	.7	.9
413 S.D.A.	2	56	75*	.2	.2
419 SO BAPT CONV	7	3,710	4,978*	13.2	15.6
443 UN C OF CHRIST	1	131	176*	.5	.6
449 UN METHODIST	3	797	1,069*	2.8	3.4
JOHNSON	**112**	**39,867**	**56,216***	**57.9**	**100.0**
053 ASSEMB OF GOD	8	1,045	1,494	1.5	2.7
059 BAPT MISS ASSN	1	47	61*	.1	.1
081 CATHOLIC	1	NA	772	.8	1.4
081d *LATIN*	*1*	*NA*	*772*	*.8*	*1.4*
093 CHR CH (DISC)	2	311	436	.4	.8
127 CH GOD (CLEVE)	3	99	128*	.1	.2
151 L-D SAINTS	2	NA	754	.8	1.3
165 CH OF NAZARENE	2	219	311	.3	.6
167 CHS OF CHRIST	15	2,395	3,170	3.3	5.6
185 CUMBER PRESB	1	326	419	.4	.7
193 EPISCOPAL	3	343	406	.4	.7
283 LUTH—MO SYNOD	2	335	468	.5	.8
339 PENT CH OF GOD	3	102	230	.2	.4
355 PRESB CH (USA)	2	355	460*	.5	.8
413 S.D.A.	10	4,792	6,211*	6.4	11.0
419 SO BAPT CONV	36	23,052	29,877*	30.7	53.1
449 UN METHODIST	17	5,619	7,283*	7.5	13.0
496 JEWISH EST[1]	0	NA	364	.4	.6
497 BLACK BAPT EST[2]	NA	827	1,072*	1.1	1.9
498 INDEP.CHARIS.[3]	1	NA	550	.6	1.0
499 INDEP.NON-CHAR[3]	3	NA	1,750	1.8	3.1
JONES	**51**	**9,446**	**13,008***	**78.9**	**100.0**
053 ASSEMB OF GOD	4	105	218	1.3	1.7
059 BAPT MISS ASSN	2	339	430*	2.6	3.3
081 CATHOLIC	2	NA	1,000	6.1	7.7
081d *LATIN*	*2*	*NA*	*1,000*	*6.1*	*7.7*
165 CH OF NAZARENE	1	96	125	.8	1.0
167 CHS OF CHRIST	13	1,098	1,355	8.2	10.4
207 E.L.C.A.	2	327	381	2.3	2.9
263 INT FOURSQ GOS	2	86	109*	.7	.8
355 PRESB CH (USA)	1	98	124*	.8	1.0
419 SO BAPT CONV	18	6,060	7,695*	46.7	59.2
449 UN METHODIST	6	1,064	1,351*	8.2	10.4
497 BLACK BAPT EST[2]	NA	173	220*	1.3	1.7
KARNES	**34**	**3,190**	**11,374***	**91.3**	**100.0**
053 ASSEMB OF GOD	2	80	112	.9	1.0

NA–Not applicable NR–Not reported *Total adherents estimated from known number of communicant, confirmed, full members. - Represents a percent less than 0.1. Percentages may not total due to rounding.
[1]See Appendix E [2]See Appendix F [3]See Appendix G Lines in *italic* represent a breakdown of Catholic rites or Friends affiliations. They are included in their respective denominational total.

Table 4. Churches and Church Membership by County and Denomination: 1990

County and Denomination	Number of churches	Communicant, confirmed, full members	Total adherents		
			Number	Percent of total population	Percent of total adherents
081 CATHOLIC	9	NA	7,223	58.0	63.5
081d LATIN	9	NA	7,223	58.0	63.5
167 CHS OF CHRIST	3	117	154	1.2	1.4
193 EPISCOPAL	1	8	8	.1	.1
207 E.L.C.A.	4	737	907	7.3	8.0
355 PRESB CH (USA)	1	58	77*	.6	.7
419 SO BAPT CONV	9	1,733	2,289*	18.4	20.1
449 UN METHODIST	5	457	604*	4.8	5.3
KAUFMAN	**85**	**22,600**	**33,110***	**63.4**	**100.0**
053 ASSEMB OF GOD	9	671	855	1.6	2.6
059 BAPT MISS ASSN	12	2,678	3,472*	6.6	10.5
081 CATHOLIC	3	NA	3,024	5.8	9.1
081d LATIN	3	NA	3,024	5.8	9.1
093 CHR CH (DISC)	2	485	636	1.2	1.9
111 CH CR,SCIENTST	1	NR	NR	-	-
145 CH GOD PROPHCY	1	31	40*	.1	.1
165 CH OF NAZARENE	1	63	123	.2	.4
167 CHS OF CHRIST	17	2,156	2,819	5.4	8.5
185 CUMBER PRESB	1	14	14	-	-
193 EPISCOPAL	2	234	342	.7	1.0
286 E.PA MENNONITE	1	30	39*	.1	.1
355 PRESB CH (USA)	4	429	556*	1.1	1.7
413 S.D.A.	1	41	53*	.1	.2
419 SO BAPT CONV	18	10,755	13,943*	26.7	42.1
449 UN METHODIST	12	2,619	3,395*	6.5	10.3
496 JEWISH EST[1]	0	NA	695	1.3	2.1
497 BLACK BAPT EST[2]	NA	2,394	3,104*	5.9	9.4
KENDALL	**19**	**4,364**	**9,573***	**65.6**	**100.0**
053 ASSEMB OF GOD	1	84	153	1.0	1.6
081 CATHOLIC	2	NA	3,540	24.3	37.0
081d LATIN	2	NA	3,540	24.3	37.0
151 L-D SAINTS	2	NA	398	2.7	4.2
167 CHS OF CHRIST	1	125	179	1.2	1.9
193 EPISCOPAL	2	381	539	3.7	5.6
203 EVAN FREE CH	1	45	95	.7	1.0
207 E.L.C.A.	2	867	1,075	7.4	11.2
355 PRESB CH (USA)	1	258	324*	2.2	3.4
419 SO BAPT CONV	5	1,763	2,214*	15.2	23.1
449 UN METHODIST	2	841	1,056*	7.2	11.0
KENEDY	**2**	**0**	**440***	**95.7**	**100.0**
081 CATHOLIC	2	NA	440	95.7	100.0
081d LATIN	2	NA	440	95.7	100.0
KENT	**6**	**689**	**967***	**95.7**	**100.0**
053 ASSEMB OF GOD	1	60	80	7.9	8.3
081 CATHOLIC	1	NA	100	9.9	10.3
081d LATIN	1	NA	100	9.9	10.3
167 CHS OF CHRIST	2	125	153	15.1	15.8
419 SO BAPT CONV	1	433	545*	54.0	56.4
449 UN METHODIST	1	71	89*	8.8	9.2
KERR	**43**	**11,985**	**17,916***	**49.3**	**100.0**
053 ASSEMB OF GOD	3	243	380	1.0	2.1
081 CATHOLIC	1	NA	3,000	8.3	16.7
081d LATIN	1	NA	3,000	8.3	16.7
089 CHR & MISS AL	1	24	29	.1	.2
093 CHR CH (DISC)	3	342	432	1.2	2.4
097 CHR CHS&CHS CR	1	18	22*	.1	.1
111 CH CR,SCIENTST	1	NR	NR	-	-
123 CH GOD (ANDER)	1	20	30	.1	.2
151 L-D SAINTS	1	NA	267	.7	1.5
165 CH OF NAZARENE	1	43	50	.1	.3
167 CHS OF CHRIST	3	602	735	2.0	4.1
193 EPISCOPAL	1	798	902	2.5	5.0
203 EVAN FREE CH	1	33	60	.2	.3
207 E.L.C.A.	1	687	790	2.2	4.4
226 FRIENDS-USA	1	15	18	-	.1
226c FGC	1	15	18	-	.1
263 INT FOURSQ GOS	1	43	53*	.1	.3
283 LUTH—MO SYNOD	2	393	497	1.4	2.8
355 PRESB CH (USA)	2	1,057	1,292*	3.6	7.2
403 SALVATION ARMY	1	69	81	.2	.5
413 S.D.A.	1	82	100*	.3	.6
419 SO BAPT CONV	10	5,118	6,256*	17.2	34.9
435 UNITARIAN-UNIV	1	52	54	.1	.3
449 UN METHODIST	5	2,132	2,606*	7.2	14.5
497 BLACK BAPT EST[2]	NA	214	262*	.7	1.5
KIMBLE	**11**	**1,909**	**2,700***	**65.5**	**100.0**
081 CATHOLIC	1	NA	300	7.3	11.1
081d LATIN	1	NA	300	7.3	11.1
167 CHS OF CHRIST	4	254	328	8.0	12.1
193 EPISCOPAL	1	62	92	2.2	3.4
355 PRESB CH (USA)	1	150	186*	4.5	6.9
419 SO BAPT CONV	2	1,194	1,484*	36.0	55.0
449 UN METHODIST	2	249	310*	7.5	11.5
KING	**2**	**188**	**242***	**68.4**	**100.0**
419 SO BAPT CONV	2	188	242*	68.4	100.0
KINNEY	**9**	**551**	**2,171***	**69.6**	**100.0**
053 ASSEMB OF GOD	1	23	20	.6	.9
081 CATHOLIC	2	NA	1,500	48.1	69.1
081d LATIN	2	NA	1,500	48.1	69.1
167 CHS OF CHRIST	1	77	101	3.2	4.7
193 EPISCOPAL	1	42	44	1.4	2.0
419 SO BAPT CONV	2	267	332*	10.6	15.3
435 UNITARIAN-UNIV	1	24	27	.9	1.2
449 UN METHODIST	1	118	147*	4.7	6.8
KLEBERG	**37**	**7,051**	**24,875***	**82.2**	**100.0**
053 ASSEMB OF GOD	2	323	564	1.9	2.3
081 CATHOLIC	8	NA	15,160	50.1	60.9
081d LATIN	8	NA	15,160	50.1	60.9
093 CHR CH (DISC)	1	147	190	.6	.8
123 CH GOD (ANDER)	1	20	25	.1	.1
145 CH GOD PROPHCY	1	31	40*	.1	.2
151 L-D SAINTS	1	NA	324	1.1	1.3
165 CH OF NAZARENE	2	61	125	.4	.5
167 CHS OF CHRIST	1	212	276	.9	1.1
193 EPISCOPAL	1	144	199	.7	.8
207 E.L.C.A.	2	421	556	1.8	2.2
283 LUTH—MO SYNOD	1	178	243	.8	1.0
355 PRESB CH (USA)	2	190	247*	.8	1.0
413 S.D.A.	1	28	36*	.1	.1
419 SO BAPT CONV	8	4,150	5,399*	17.8	21.7
449 UN METHODIST	5	881	1,146*	3.8	4.6
497 BLACK BAPT EST[2]	NA	265	345*	1.1	1.4
KNOX	**28**	**3,432**	**5,361***	**110.8**	**100.0**
053 ASSEMB OF GOD	1	32	40	.8	.7
081 CATHOLIC	2	NA	1,080	22.3	20.1
081d LATIN	2	NA	1,080	22.3	20.1
093 CHR CH (DISC)	2	46	53	1.1	1.0
097 CHR CHS&CHS CR	1	90	115*	2.4	2.1
167 CHS OF CHRIST	7	424	458	9.5	8.5
263 INT FOURSQ GOS	1	55	70*	1.4	1.3
419 SO BAPT CONV	8	2,207	2,809*	58.1	52.4
449 UN METHODIST	6	578	736*	15.2	13.7
LAMAR	**105**	**22,863**	**30,379***	**69.1**	**100.0**
053 ASSEMB OF GOD	5	591	695	1.6	2.3
059 BAPT MISS ASSN	1	0	0*	-	-
081 CATHOLIC	1	NA	867	2.0	2.9
081d LATIN	1	NA	867	2.0	2.9
093 CHR CH (DISC)	3	440	580	1.3	1.9
127 CH GOD (CLEVE)	5	886	1,113*	2.5	3.7
143 CG IN CR(MENN)	1	47	59*	.1	.2
145 CH GOD PROPHCY	1	31	39*	.1	.1
151 L-D SAINTS	1	NA	275	.6	.9
165 CH OF NAZARENE	2	187	284	.6	.9
167 CHS OF CHRIST	16	1,856	2,444	5.6	8.0
193 EPISCOPAL	1	215	256	.6	.8
203 EVAN FREE CH	1	35	50	.1	.2
259 IFCA	1	NR	NR	-	-
283 LUTH—MO SYNOD	1	97	114	.3	.4
285 MENNONITE CH	1	22	34	.1	.1
331 ORTH CH IN AM	1	NR	NR	-	-
339 PENT CH OF GOD	2	95	135	.3	.4
355 PRESB CH (USA)	4	422	530*	1.2	1.7
356 PRESB CH AMER	1	80	95	.2	.3
403 SALVATION ARMY	1	111	112	.3	.4
413 S.D.A.	1	26	33*	.1	.1
419 SO BAPT CONV	36	12,914	16,224*	36.9	53.4
449 UN METHODIST	17	3,107	3,903*	8.9	12.8
497 BLACK BAPT EST[2]	NA	1,701	2,137*	4.9	7.0
499 INDEP.NON-CHAR[3]	1	NA	400	.9	1.3
LAMB	**46**	**8,979**	**13,260***	**88.0**	**100.0**
053 ASSEMB OF GOD	3	79	116	.8	.9
059 BAPT MISS ASSN	1	121	159*	1.1	1.2
081 CATHOLIC	4	NA	1,500	10.0	11.3
081d LATIN	4	NA	1,500	10.0	11.3
093 CHR CH (DISC)	1	65	92	.6	.7
145 CH GOD PROPHCY	1	19	25*	.2	.2
151 L-D SAINTS	1	NA	33	.2	.2
165 CH OF NAZARENE	2	93	94	.6	.7

NA–Not applicable   NR–Not reported   *Total adherents estimated from known number of communicant, confirmed, full members.   - Represents a percent less than 0.1.   Percentages may not total due to rounding.
[1] See Appendix E   [2] See Appendix F   [3] See Appendix G   Lines in *italic* represent a breakdown of Catholic rites or Friends affiliations. They are included in their respective denominational total.

Table 4. Churches and Church Membership by County and Denomination: 1990

County and Denomination	Number of churches	Communicant, confirmed, full members	Total adherents Number	Total adherents Percent of total population	Total adherents Percent of total adherents
167 CHS OF CHRIST	10	950	1,190	7.9	9.0
207 E.L.C.A.	1	22	24	.2	.2
263 INT FOURSQ GOS	1	4	5*	-	-
283 LUTH—MO SYNOD	1	118	149	1.0	1.1
349 PENT HOLINESS	1	31	41*	.3	.3
355 PRESB CH (USA)	1	83	109*	.7	.8
361 PRIM BAPT ASCS	1	62	82*	.5	.6
413 S.D.A.	1	17	22*	.1	.2
419 SO BAPT CONV	10	5,553	7,302*	48.4	55.1
449 UN METHODIST	6	1,548	2,036*	13.5	15.4
497 BLACK BAPT EST[2]	NA	214	281*	1.9	2.1
LAMPASAS	**28**	**5,307**	**10,360***	**76.6**	**100.0**
053 ASSEM OF GOD	1	78	196	1.4	1.9
081 CATHOLIC	2	NA	3,425	25.3	33.1
081d LATIN	2	NA	3,425	25.3	33.1
093 CHR CH (DISC)	1	188	286	2.1	2.8
127 CH GOD (CLEVE)	1	14	18*	.1	.2
167 CHS OF CHRIST	5	600	790	5.8	7.6
193 EPISCOPAL	1	136	174	1.3	1.7
215 EVAN METH CH	1	138	176*	1.3	1.7
263 INT FOURSQ GOS	1	12	15*	.1	.1
283 LUTH—MO SYNOD	1	127	166	1.2	1.6
355 PRESB CH (USA)	2	236	301*	2.2	2.9
419 SO BAPT CONV	9	3,148	4,010*	29.7	38.7
449 UN METHODIST	3	630	803*	5.9	7.8
LA SALLE	**13**	**943**	**5,815***	**110.7**	**100.0**
081 CATHOLIC	2	NA	4,540	86.4	78.1
081d LATIN	2	NA	4,540	86.4	78.1
133 CH GOD(7TH)DEN	1	38	54	1.0	.9
167 CHS OF CHRIST	2	100	128	2.4	2.2
193 EPISCOPAL	1	14	18	.3	.3
355 PRESB CH (USA)	2	25	34*	.6	.6
419 SO BAPT CONV	3	619	841*	16.0	14.5
449 UN METHODIST	2	147	200*	3.8	3.4
LAVACA	**44**	**4,384**	**15,981***	**85.5**	**100.0**
053 ASSEM OF GOD	2	118	180	1.0	1.1
081 CATHOLIC	9	NA	10,507	56.2	65.7
081d LATIN	9	NA	10,507	56.2	65.7
111 CH CR,SCIENTST	1	NR	NR	-	-
123 CH GOD (ANDER)	1	19	19	.1	.1
167 CHS OF CHRIST	4	180	290	1.6	1.8
193 EPISCOPAL	2	58	78	.4	.5
207 E.L.C.A.	5	1,261	1,505	8.1	9.4
355 PRESB CH (USA)	1	35	43*	.2	.3
419 SO BAPT CONV	10	1,606	1,989*	10.6	12.4
449 UN METHODIST	8	757	937*	5.0	5.9
496 JEWISH EST[1]	1	NA	0	-	-
497 BLACK BAPT EST[2]	NA	350	433*	2.3	2.7
LEE	**28**	**6,551**	**8,908***	**69.3**	**100.0**
053 ASSEM OF GOD	1	51	98	.8	1.1
081 CATHOLIC	3	NA	555	4.3	6.2
081d LATIN	3	NA	555	4.3	6.2
093 CHR CH (DISC)	1	50	62	.5	.7
097 CHR CHS&CHS CR	1	110	141*	1.1	1.6
123 CH GOD (ANDER)	1	5	5	-	.1
167 CHS OF CHRIST	2	115	149	1.2	1.7
207 E.L.C.A.	2	810	996	7.7	11.2
283 LUTH—MO SYNOD	8	2,836	3,609	28.1	40.5
419 SO BAPT CONV	6	1,454	1,860*	14.5	20.9
449 UN METHODIST	3	656	839*	6.5	9.4
497 BLACK BAPT EST[2]	NA	464	594*	4.6	6.7
LEON	**60**	**6,683**	**8,903***	**70.3**	**100.0**
053 ASSEM OF GOD	5	138	183	1.4	2.1
059 BAPT MISS ASSN	15	1,333	1,678*	13.2	18.8
081 CATHOLIC	1	NA	300	2.4	3.4
081d LATIN	1	NA	300	2.4	3.4
093 CHR CH (DISC)	1	35	37	.3	.4
127 CH GOD (CLEVE)	1	46	58*	.5	.7
151 L-D SAINTS	1	NA	152	1.2	1.7
167 CHS OF CHRIST	8	412	546	4.3	6.1
283 LUTH—MO SYNOD	1	120	160	1.3	1.8
419 SO BAPT CONV	9	2,861	3,601*	28.4	40.4
449 UN METHODIST	18	1,317	1,658*	13.1	18.6
497 BLACK BAPT EST[2]	NA	421	530*	4.2	6.0
LIBERTY	**97**	**24,053**	**37,373***	**70.9**	**100.0**
053 ASSEM OF GOD	14	1,492	2,041	3.9	5.5
059 BAPT MISS ASSN	7	910	1,179*	2.2	3.2
081 CATHOLIC	6	NA	5,080	9.6	13.6
081d LATIN	6	NA	5,080	9.6	13.6

County and Denomination	Number of churches	Communicant, confirmed, full members	Total adherents Number	Total adherents Percent of total population	Total adherents Percent of total adherents
093 CHR CH (DISC)	2	13	20	-	.1
145 CH GOD PROPHCY	2	62	80*	.2	.2
151 L-D SAINTS	1	NA	270	.5	.7
167 CHS OF CHRIST	9	699	880	1.7	2.4
193 EPISCOPAL	2	98	136	.3	.4
207 E.L.C.A.	2	73	126	.2	.3
283 LUTH—MO SYNOD	1	104	145	.3	.4
339 PENT CH OF GOD	3	87	162	.3	.4
355 PRESB CH (USA)	2	86	111*	.2	.3
413 S.D.A.	1	48	62*	.1	.2
419 SO BAPT CONV	37	15,768	20,425*	38.7	54.7
449 UN METHODIST	8	2,345	3,038*	5.8	8.1
496 JEWISH EST[1]	0	NA	680	1.3	1.8
497 BLACK BAPT EST[2]	NA	2,268	2,938*	5.6	7.9
LIMESTONE	**49**	**9,820**	**13,010***	**62.1**	**100.0**
053 ASSEM OF GOD	4	150	219	1.0	1.7
059 BAPT MISS ASSN	3	429	541*	2.6	4.2
081 CATHOLIC	1	NA	600	2.9	4.6
081d LATIN	1	NA	600	2.9	4.6
093 CHR CH (DISC)	1	73	103	.5	.8
167 CHS OF CHRIST	12	879	1,076	5.1	8.3
193 EPISCOPAL	1	73	94	.4	.7
283 LUTH—MO SYNOD	1	26	45	.2	.3
339 PENT CH OF GOD	1	57	73	.3	.6
355 PRESB CH (USA)	1	227	286*	1.4	2.2
361 PRIM BAPT ASCS	2	25	32*	.2	.2
419 SO BAPT CONV	14	5,067	6,391*	30.5	49.1
449 UN METHODIST	8	1,732	2,185*	10.4	16.8
497 BLACK BAPT EST[2]	NA	1,082	1,365*	6.5	10.5
LIPSCOMB	**19**	**2,299**	**3,092***	**98.4**	**100.0**
081 CATHOLIC	1	NA	164	5.2	5.3
081d LATIN	1	NA	164	5.2	5.3
097 CHR CHS&CHS CR	1	120	154*	4.9	5.0
165 CH OF NAZARENE	1	44	48	1.5	1.6
167 CHS OF CHRIST	3	150	190	6.0	6.1
176 CCC, NOT NAT'L	1	18	23*	.7	.7
181 CONSRV CONGR	1	81	104*	3.3	3.4
207 E.L.C.A.	1	114	134	4.3	4.3
226 FRIENDS-USA	1	154	198*	6.3	6.4
226b EFI	1	154	198*	6.3	6.4
419 SO BAPT CONV	5	934	1,199*	38.1	38.8
449 UN METHODIST	4	684	878*	27.9	28.4
LIVE OAK	**26**	**3,137**	**7,824***	**81.9**	**100.0**
053 ASSEM OF GOD	1	63	85	.9	1.1
081 CATHOLIC	4	NA	3,840	40.2	49.1
081d LATIN	4	NA	3,840	40.2	49.1
133 CH GOD(7TH)DEN	1	39	55	.6	.7
167 CHS OF CHRIST	4	217	290	3.0	3.7
193 EPISCOPAL	2	140	152	1.6	1.9
207 E.L.C.A.	2	239	301	3.1	3.8
283 LUTH—MO SYNOD	1	23	21	.2	.3
339 PENT CH OF GOD	1	23	35	.4	.4
419 SO BAPT CONV	8	1,883	2,396*	25.1	30.6
449 UN METHODIST	2	510	649*	6.8	8.3
LLANO	**32**	**4,997**	**7,247***	**62.3**	**100.0**
053 ASSEM OF GOD	2	93	84	.7	1.2
081 CATHOLIC	3	NA	1,239	10.7	17.1
081d LATIN	3	NA	1,239	10.7	17.1
093 CHR CH (DISC)	1	75	123	1.1	1.7
151 L-D SAINTS	1	NA	159	1.4	2.2
167 CHS OF CHRIST	7	516	672	5.8	9.3
193 EPISCOPAL	1	105	131	1.1	1.8
207 E.L.C.A.	2	189	241	2.1	3.3
355 PRESB CH (USA)	1	50	57*	.5	.8
419 SO BAPT CONV	9	3,206	3,668*	31.5	50.6
449 UN METHODIST	5	763	873*	7.5	12.0
LOVING	**0**	**0**	**0**	**·**	**·**
LUBBOCK	**218**	**86,945**	**146,550***	**65.8**	**100.0**
053 ASSEM OF GOD	17	1,126	1,984	.9	1.4
059 BAPT MISS ASSN	7	2,016	2,557*	1.1	1.7
081 CATHOLIC	14	NA	20,700	9.3	14.1
081d LATIN	14	NA	20,700	9.3	14.1
093 CHR CH (DISC)	5	1,774	2,360	1.1	1.6
097 CHR CHS&CHS CR	1	255	323*	.1	.2
111 CH CR,SCIENTST	1	NR	NR	-	-
127 CH GOD (CLEVE)	3	322	408*	.2	.3
133 CH GOD(7TH)DEN	2	78	109	-	.1
145 CH GOD PROPHCY	2	33	42*	-	-
151 L-D SAINTS	4	NA	1,618	.7	1.1

NA–Not applicable   NR–Not reported   *Total adherents estimated from known number of communicant, confirmed, full members.   - Represents a percent less than 0.1.   Percentages may not total due to rounding.
[1]See Appendix E   [2]See Appendix F   [3]See Appendix G   Lines in *italic* represent a breakdown of Catholic rites or Friends affiliations. They are included in their respective denominational total.

Table 4. Churches and Church Membership by County and Denomination: 1990

County and Denomination		Number of churches	Communicant, confirmed, full members	Total adherents		
				Number	Percent of total population	Percent of total adherents
165	CH OF NAZARENE	5	659	835	.4	.6
167	CHS OF CHRIST	33	10,784	13,627	6.1	9.3
185	CUMBER PRESB	1	634	698	.3	.5
193	EPISCOPAL	3	1,455	2,115	.9	1.4
207	E.L.C.A.	4	589	732	.3	.5
215	EVAN METH CH	1	40	51*	-	-
223	FREE WILL BAPT	2	101	128*	.1	.1
226	FRIENDS-USA	1	7	9	-	-
226c	*FGC*	*1*	*7*	*9*	-	-
246	GREEK ORTHODOX	1	NR	NR	-	-
263	INT FOURSQ GOS	3	195	247*	.1	.2
283	LUTH—MO SYNOD	4	704	963	.4	.7
339	PENT CH OF GOD	1	34	77	-	.1
349	PENT HOLINESS	5	208	264*	.1	.2
353	CHR BRETHREN	1	20	40	-	-
355	PRESB CH (USA)	6	1,706	2,164*	1.0	1.5
361	PRIM BAPT ASCS	2	135	171*	.1	.1
403	SALVATION ARMY	1	112	113	.1	.1
413	S.D.A.	2	218	277*	.1	.2
415	S-D BAPTIST GC	1	30	38*	-	-
419	SO BAPT CONV	52	42,977	54,514*	24.5	37.2
435	UNITARIAN-UNIV	1	87	102	-	.1
443	UN C OF CHRIST	1	23	29*	-	-
449	UN METHODIST	21	14,886	18,882*	8.5	12.9
469	WELS	1	107	143	.1	.1
496	JEWISH EST[1]	1	NA	225	.1	.2
497	BLACK BAPT EST[2]	NA	5,630	7,141*	3.2	4.9
498	INDEP.CHARIS.[3]	4	NA	8,939	4.0	6.1
499	INDEP.NON-CHAR[3]	4	NA	3,925	1.8	2.7
LYNN		**30**	**4,079**	**6,306***	**93.3**	**100.0**
053	ASSEMB OF GOD	1	18	26	.4	.4
081	CATHOLIC	3	NA	800	11.8	12.7
081d	*LATIN*	*3*	*NA*	*800*	*11.8*	*12.7*
093	CHR CH (DISC)	1	8	11	.2	.2
151	L-D SAINTS	1	NA	101	1.5	1.6
165	CH OF NAZARENE	1	82	136	2.0	2.2
167	CHS OF CHRIST	6	217	276	4.1	4.4
207	E.L.C.A.	1	118	148	2.2	2.3
283	LUTH—MO SYNOD	1	128	174	2.6	2.8
419	SO BAPT CONV	10	2,808	3,709*	54.9	58.8
449	UN METHODIST	5	700	925*	13.7	14.7
MC CULLOCH		**33**	**3,365**	**6,145***	**70.0**	**100.0**
053	ASSEMB OF GOD	2	62	89	1.0	1.4
081	CATHOLIC	2	NA	1,640	18.7	26.7
081d	*LATIN*	*2*	*NA*	*1,640*	*18.7*	*26.7*
093	CHR CH (DISC)	2	217	267	3.0	4.3
127	CH GOD (CLEVE)	1	152	191*	2.2	3.1
167	CHS OF CHRIST	6	514	596	6.8	9.7
193	EPISCOPAL	1	97	110	1.3	1.8
203	EVAN FREE CH	1	10	10	.1	.2
283	LUTH—MO SYNOD	1	56	80	.9	1.3
355	PRESB CH (USA)	1	67	84*	1.0	1.4
403	SALVATION ARMY	1	111	115	1.3	1.9
419	SO BAPT CONV	9	1,506	1,893*	21.6	30.8
449	UN METHODIST	5	573	720*	8.2	11.7
499	INDEP.NON-CHAR[3]	1	NA	350	4.0	5.7
MC LENNAN		**237**	**92,357**	**139,264***	**73.6**	**100.0**
053	ASSEMB OF GOD	12	2,060	3,295	1.7	2.4
059	BAPT MISS ASSN	2	295	372*	.2	.3
081	CATHOLIC	11	NA	17,556	9.3	12.6
081d	*LATIN*	*11*	*NA*	*17,556*	*9.3*	*12.6*
089	CHR & MISS AL	1	32	79	-	.1
093	CHR CH (DISC)	5	1,168	1,461	.8	1.0
111	CH CR,SCIENTST	1	NR	NR	-	-
123	CH GOD (ANDER)	1	29	40	-	-
151	L-D SAINTS	3	NA	892	.5	.6
165	CH OF NAZARENE	4	487	576	.3	.4
167	CHS OF CHRIST	28	3,281	4,406	2.3	3.2
193	EPISCOPAL	3	1,602	2,553	1.3	1.8
203	EVAN FREE CH	1	175	425	.2	.3
207	E.L.C.A.	5	1,816	2,315	1.2	1.7
216	EVAN PRESBY CH	1	64	66	-	-
223	FREE WILL BAPT	1	60	76*	-	.1
246	GREEK ORTHODOX	1	NR	NR	-	-
283	LUTH—MO SYNOD	5	2,165	2,668	1.4	1.9
313	N AM BAPT CONF	2	216	272*	.1	.2
339	PENT CH OF GOD	5	113	296	.2	.2
349	PENT HOLINESS	1	72	91*	-	.1
353	CHR BRETHREN	1	25	50	-	-
355	PRESB CH (USA)	6	1,266	1,595*	.8	1.1
361	PRIM BAPT ASCS	1	42	53*	-	-
413	S.D.A.	3	294	370*	.2	.3
419	SO BAPT CONV	79	52,085	65,620*	34.7	47.1

County and Denomination		Number of churches	Communicant, confirmed, full members	Total adherents		
				Number	Percent of total population	Percent of total adherents
435	UNITARIAN-UNIV	1	50	66	-	-
443	UN C OF CHRIST	5	871	1,097*	.6	.8
449	UN METHODIST	42	14,400	18,142*	9.6	13.0
496	JEWISH EST[1]	2	NA	450	.2	.3
497	BLACK BAPT EST[2]	NA	9,689	12,207*	6.5	8.8
498	INDEP.CHARIS.[3]	1	NA	650	.3	.5
499	INDEP.NON-CHAR[3]	3	NA	1,525	.8	1.1
MC MULLEN		**3**	**162**	**384***	**47.0**	**100.0**
081	CATHOLIC	1	NA	180	22.0	46.9
081d	*LATIN*	*1*	*NA*	*180*	*22.0*	*46.9*
419	SO BAPT CONV	2	162	204*	25.0	53.1
MADISON		**29**	**5,423**	**6,836***	**62.5**	**100.0**
053	ASSEMB OF GOD	2	43	55	.5	.8
059	BAPT MISS ASSN	2	145	175*	1.6	2.6
081	CATHOLIC	1	NA	200	1.8	2.9
081d	*LATIN*	*1*	*NA*	*200*	*1.8*	*2.9*
167	CHS OF CHRIST	9	671	889	8.1	13.0
193	EPISCOPAL	1	33	39	.4	.6
223	FREE WILL BAPT	1	20	24*	.2	.4
283	LUTH—MO SYNOD	1	171	227	2.1	3.3
361	PRIM BAPT ASCS	1	36	43*	.4	.6
419	SO BAPT CONV	7	2,722	3,279*	30.0	48.0
449	UN METHODIST	4	911	1,097*	10.0	16.0
497	BLACK BAPT EST[2]	NA	671	808*	7.4	11.8
MARION		**38**	**4,899**	**6,121***	**61.3**	**100.0**
053	ASSEMB OF GOD	1	20	27	.3	.4
081	CATHOLIC	1	NA	118	1.2	1.9
081d	*LATIN*	*1*	*NA*	*118*	*1.2*	*1.9*
093	CHR CH (DISC)	1	5	7	.1	.1
165	CH OF NAZARENE	1	22	20	.2	.3
167	CHS OF CHRIST	3	185	219	2.2	3.6
185	CUMBER PRESB	1	46	53	.5	.9
193	EPISCOPAL	1	68	72	.7	1.2
413	S.D.A.	4	464	571*	5.7	9.3
419	SO BAPT CONV	12	2,172	2,674*	26.8	43.7
449	UN METHODIST	13	766	943*	9.4	15.4
497	BLACK BAPT EST[2]	NA	1,151	1,417*	14.2	23.1
MARTIN		**10**	**1,831**	**3,544***	**71.5**	**100.0**
053	ASSEMB OF GOD	1	45	51	1.0	1.4
081	CATHOLIC	2	NA	1,102	22.2	31.1
081d	*LATIN*	*2*	*NA*	*1,102*	*22.2*	*31.1*
167	CHS OF CHRIST	3	250	285	5.8	8.0
419	SO BAPT CONV	3	1,124	1,541*	31.1	43.5
449	UN METHODIST	1	412	565*	11.4	15.9
MASON		**11**	**1,693**	**2,424***	**70.8**	**100.0**
053	ASSEMB OF GOD	1	31	75	2.2	3.1
081	CATHOLIC	1	NA	305	8.9	12.6
081d	*LATIN*	*1*	*NA*	*305*	*8.9*	*12.6*
093	CHR CH (DISC)	1	18	50	1.5	2.1
167	CHS OF CHRIST	1	150	154	4.5	6.4
207	E.L.C.A.	1	397	496	14.5	20.5
419	SO BAPT CONV	1	488	598*	17.5	24.7
449	UN METHODIST	5	609	746*	21.8	30.8
MATAGORDA		**64**	**12,584**	**27,590***	**74.7**	**100.0**
053	ASSEMB OF GOD	2	182	242	.7	.9
081	CATHOLIC	6	NA	10,238	27.7	37.1
081d	*LATIN*	*6*	*NA*	*10,238*	*27.7*	*37.1*
093	CHR CH (DISC)	4	355	465	1.3	1.7
145	CH GOD PROPHCY	5	154	206*	.6	.7
151	L-D SAINTS	2	NA	397	1.1	1.4
165	CH OF NAZARENE	2	86	141	.4	.5
167	CHS OF CHRIST	5	462	607	1.6	2.2
193	EPISCOPAL	3	205	317	.9	1.1
207	E.L.C.A.	1	247	369	1.0	1.3
283	LUTH—MO SYNOD	2	116	167	.5	.6
349	PENT HOLINESS	1	30	40*	.1	.1
355	PRESB CH (USA)	5	595	797*	2.2	2.9
419	SO BAPT CONV	18	6,885	9,226*	25.0	33.4
449	UN METHODIST	8	1,909	2,558*	6.9	9.3
497	BLACK BAPT EST[2]	NA	1,358	1,820*	4.9	6.6
MAVERICK		**25**	**1,798**	**30,743***	**84.5**	**100.0**
053	ASSEMB OF GOD	3	257	286	.8	.9
081	CATHOLIC	6	NA	27,900	76.7	90.8
081d	*LATIN*	*6*	*NA*	*27,900*	*76.7*	*90.8*
097	CHR CHS&CHS CR	1	100	140*	.4	.5
123	CH GOD (ANDER)	1	170	190	.5	.6
145	CH GOD PROPHCY	1	19	27*	.1	.1

NA–Not applicable   NR–Not reported   *Total adherents estimated from known number of communicant, confirmed, full members.   - Represents a percent less than 0.1.   Percentages may not total due to rounding.
[1]See Appendix E   [2]See Appendix F   [3]See Appendix G   Lines in *italic* represent a breakdown of Catholic rites or Friends affiliations. They are included in their respective denominational total.

Table 4. Churches and Church Membership by County and Denomination: 1990

County and Denomination	Number of churches	Communicant, confirmed, full members	Total adherents Number	Percent of total population	Percent of total adherents
151 L-D SAINTS	1	NA	374	1.0	1.2
167 CHS OF CHRIST	2	98	128	.4	.4
193 EPISCOPAL	1	112	180	.5	.6
339 PENT CH OF GOD	2	69	154	.4	.5
413 S.D.A.	1	109	153*	.4	.5
419 SO BAPT CONV	3	652	914*	2.5	3.0
449 UN METHODIST	3	212	297*	.8	1.0
MEDINA	**40**	**5,594**	**20,550***	**75.2**	**100.0**
081 CATHOLIC	7	NA	12,800	46.9	62.3
081d LATIN	*7*	*NA*	*12,800*	*46.9*	*62.3*
093 CHR CH (DISC)	1	49	62	.2	.3
111 CH CR,SCIENTST	1	NR	NR	-	-
151 L-D SAINTS	1	NA	143	.5	.7
165 CH OF NAZARENE	1	32	105	.4	.5
167 CHS OF CHRIST	5	207	281	1.0	1.4
193 EPISCOPAL	1	62	99	.4	.5
207 E.L.C.A.	3	855	1,034	3.8	5.0
283 LUTH—MO SYNOD	1	46	62	.2	.3
339 PENT CH OF GOD	1	16	31	.1	.2
355 PRESB CH (USA)	1	20	26*	.1	.1
413 S.D.A.	1	48	62*	.2	.3
419 SO BAPT CONV	10	3,117	4,058*	14.9	19.7
449 UN METHODIST	5	1,142	1,487*	5.4	7.2
499 INDEP.NON-CHAR3	1	NA	300	1.1	1.5
MENARD	**14**	**1,418**	**2,123***	**94.3**	**100.0**
081 CATHOLIC	1	NA	300	13.3	14.1
081d LATIN	*1*	*NA*	*300*	*13.3*	*14.1*
093 CHR CH (DISC)	1	3	4	.2	.2
097 CHR CHS&CHS CR	1	406	505*	22.4	23.8
167 CHS OF CHRIST	5	224	280	12.4	13.2
193 EPISCOPAL	1	50	117	5.2	5.5
283 LUTH—MO SYNOD	1	33	45	2.0	2.1
355 PRESB CH (USA)	1	34	42*	1.9	2.0
413 S.D.A.	1	26	32*	1.4	1.5
419 SO BAPT CONV	1	474	589*	26.2	27.7
449 UN METHODIST	1	168	209*	9.3	9.8
MIDLAND	**100**	**39,790**	**74,586***	**70.0**	**100.0**
053 ASSEM OF GOD	3	554	859	.8	1.2
059 BAPT MISS ASSN	1	333	448*	.4	.6
081 CATHOLIC	4	NA	14,400	13.5	19.3
081d LATIN	*4*	*NA*	*14,400*	*13.5*	*19.3*
093 CHR CH (DISC)	2	871	1,236	1.2	1.7
097 CHR CHS&CHS CR	2	340	457*	.4	.6
111 CH CR,SCIENTST	1	NR	NR	-	-
127 CH GOD (CLEVE)	1	114	153*	.1	.2
133 CH GOD(7TH)DEN	2	78	110	.1	.1
145 CH GOD PROPHCY	1	19	26*	-	-
151 L-D SAINTS	4	NA	1,087	1.0	1.5
165 CH OF NAZARENE	2	199	266	.2	.4
167 CHS OF CHRIST	15	3,285	4,372	4.1	5.9
193 EPISCOPAL	2	1,198	1,826	1.7	2.4
207 E.L.C.A.	2	448	608	.6	.8
221 FREE METHODIST	2	37	58	.1	.1
223 FREE WILL BAPT	1	65	87*	.1	.1
226 FRIENDS-USA	1	8	11	-	-
226c FGC	*1*	*8*	*11*	*-*	*-*
249 AP CATH ASSYR	1	20	72	.1	.1
263 INT FOURSQ GOS	1	224	301*	.3	.4
283 LUTH—MO SYNOD	2	581	753	.7	1.0
331 ORTH CH IN AM	1	NR	NR	-	-
355 PRESB CH (USA)	3	2,536	3,412*	3.2	4.6
361 PRIM BAPT ASCS	1	116	156*	.1	.2
403 SALVATION ARMY	2	188	205	.2	.3
413 S.D.A.	3	121	163*	.2	.2
419 SO BAPT CONV	21	19,699	26,504*	24.9	35.5
435 UNITARIAN-UNIV	1	82	142	.1	.2
449 UN METHODIST	9	5,917	7,961*	7.5	10.7
469 WELS	1	39	56	.1	.1
496 JEWISH EST1	0	NA	75	.1	.1
497 BLACK BAPT EST2	NA	2,718	3,657*	3.4	4.9
498 INDEP.CHARIS.3	2	NA	1,200	1.1	1.6
499 INDEP.NON-CHAR3	6	NA	3,925	3.7	5.3
MILAM	**71**	**9,637**	**15,291***	**66.6**	**100.0**
053 ASSEM OF GOD	4	133	173	.8	1.1
081 CATHOLIC	5	NA	2,610	11.4	17.1
081d LATIN	*5*	*NA*	*2,610*	*11.4*	*17.1*
093 CHR CH (DISC)	4	296	531	2.3	3.5
097 CHR CHS&CHS CR	2	280	358*	1.6	2.3
151 L-D SAINTS	1	NA	87	.4	.6
165 CH OF NAZARENE	1	26	33	.1	.2
167 CHS OF CHRIST	13	639	860	3.7	5.6
193 EPISCOPAL	2	65	82	.4	.5

County and Denomination	Number of churches	Communicant, confirmed, full members	Total adherents Number	Percent of total population	Percent of total adherents
207 E.L.C.A.	4	860	1,047	4.6	6.8
283 LUTH—MO SYNOD	2	588	866	3.8	5.7
339 PENT CH OF GOD	1	10	18	.1	.1
355 PRESB CH (USA)	3	261	334*	1.5	2.2
361 PRIM BAPT ASCS	1	18	23*	.1	.2
419 SO BAPT CONV	17	4,484	5,739*	25.0	37.5
443 UN C OF CHRIST	1	89	114*	.5	.7
449 UN METHODIST	10	1,122	1,436*	6.3	9.4
497 BLACK BAPT EST2	NA	766	980*	4.3	6.4
MILLS	**18**	**2,981**	**3,748***	**82.7**	**100.0**
053 ASSEM OF GOD	1	137	105	2.3	2.8
081 CATHOLIC	1	NA	150	3.3	4.0
081d LATIN	*1*	*NA*	*150*	*3.3*	*4.0*
167 CHS OF CHRIST	6	362	460	10.2	12.3
207 E.L.C.A.	1	286	360	7.9	9.6
419 SO BAPT CONV	5	1,676	2,040*	45.0	54.4
449 UN METHODIST	4	520	633*	14.0	16.9
MITCHELL	**24**	**4,204**	**6,322***	**78.9**	**100.0**
053 ASSEM OF GOD	1	47	67	.8	1.1
081 CATHOLIC	2	NA	925	11.5	14.6
081d LATIN	*2*	*NA*	*925*	*11.5*	*14.6*
093 CHR CH (DISC)	1	38	78	1.0	1.2
097 CHR CHS&CHS CR	1	90	114*	1.4	1.8
167 CHS OF CHRIST	4	383	498	6.2	7.9
193 EPISCOPAL	1	45	64	.8	1.0
355 PRESB CH (USA)	1	40	51*	.6	.8
361 PRIM BAPT ASCS	1	34	43*	.5	.7
419 SO BAPT CONV	7	2,975	3,781*	47.2	59.8
449 UN METHODIST	5	552	701*	8.7	11.1
MONTAGUE	**60**	**8,596**	**11,545***	**66.8**	**100.0**
053 ASSEM OF GOD	6	205	313	1.8	2.7
059 BAPT MISS ASSN	3	137	169*	1.0	1.5
081 CATHOLIC	3	NA	309	1.8	2.7
081d LATIN	*3*	*NA*	*309*	*1.8*	*2.7*
093 CHR CH (DISC)	3	178	256	1.5	2.2
111 CH CR,SCIENTST	1	NR	NR	-	-
157 CH OF BRETHREN	1	80	99*	.6	.9
165 CH OF NAZARENE	2	119	109	.6	.9
167 CHS OF CHRIST	10	1,052	1,396	8.1	12.1
193 EPISCOPAL	1	29	34	.2	.3
223 FREE WILL BAPT	1	106	131*	.8	1.1
283 LUTH—MO SYNOD	1	130	179	1.0	1.6
339 PENT CH OF GOD	2	68	154	.9	1.3
355 PRESB CH (USA)	3	159	196*	1.1	1.7
419 SO BAPT CONV	15	5,182	6,382*	36.9	55.3
449 UN METHODIST	7	1,151	1,418*	8.2	12.3
499 INDEP.NON-CHAR3	1	NA	400	2.3	3.5
MONTGOMERY	**146**	**53,328**	**87,238***	**47.9**	**100.0**
005 AME ZION	1	82	138	.1	.2
053 ASSEM OF GOD	16	2,079	2,523	1.4	2.9
059 BAPT MISS ASSN	6	2,131	2,778*	1.5	3.2
081 CATHOLIC	4	NA	13,225	7.3	15.2
081d LATIN	*4*	*NA*	*13,225*	*7.3*	*15.2*
093 CHR CH (DISC)	2	513	594	.3	.7
097 CHR CHS&CHS CR	8	1,886	2,458*	1.3	2.8
111 CH CR,SCIENTST	2	NR	NR	-	-
123 CH GOD (ANDER)	1	33	33	-	-
127 CH GOD (CLEVE)	1	91	119*	.1	.1
133 CH GOD(7TH)DEN	2	77	109	.1	.1
151 L-D SAINTS	5	NA	1,495	.8	1.7
165 CH OF NAZARENE	2	249	419	.2	.5
167 CHS OF CHRIST	18	2,403	3,244	1.8	3.7
193 EPISCOPAL	2	1,187	1,605	.9	1.8
207 E.L.C.A.	3	843	1,232	.7	1.4
223 FREE WILL BAPT	1	67	87*	-	.1
283 LUTH—MO SYNOD	4	1,205	1,668	.9	1.9
339 PENT CH OF GOD	2	159	252	.1	.3
349 PENT HOLINESS	1	14	18*	-	-
355 PRESB CH (USA)	1	790	1,030*	.6	1.2
403 SALVATION ARMY	1	40	47	-	.1
413 S.D.A.	3	169	220*	.1	.3
419 SO BAPT CONV	40	29,474	38,417*	21.1	44.0
435 UNITARIAN-UNIV	1	114	152	.1	.2
443 UN C OF CHRIST	1	90	117*	.1	.1
449 UN METHODIST	15	6,939	9,044*	5.0	10.4
469 WELS	2	145	192	.1	.2
496 JEWISH EST1	0	NA	2,351	1.3	2.7
497 BLACK BAPT EST2	NA	2,548	3,321*	1.8	3.8
498 INDEP.CHARIS.3	1	NA	350	.2	.4

NA–Not applicable   NR–Not reported   *Total adherents estimated from known number of communicant, confirmed, full members.   - Represents a percent less than 0.1.   Percentages may not total due to rounding.
[1]See Appendix E   [2]See Appendix F   [3]See Appendix G   Lines in *italic* represent a breakdown of Catholic rites or Friends affiliations. They are included in their respective denominational total.

Table 4. Churches and Church Membership by County and Denomination: 1990

County and Denomination	Number of churches	Communicant, confirmed, full members	Total adherents Number	Percent of total population	Percent of total adherents
MOORE	36	7,177	11,677*	65.4	100.0
053 ASSEMB OF GOD	7	527	890	5.0	7.6
081 CATHOLIC	3	NA	1,122	6.3	9.6
081d LATIN	3	NA	1,122	6.3	9.6
093 CHR CH (DISC)	1	244	334	1.9	2.9
097 CHR CHS&CHS CR	1	135	183*	1.0	1.6
151 L-D SAINTS	1	NA	84	.5	.7
165 CH OF NAZARENE	1	159	160	.9	1.4
167 CHS OF CHRIST	7	617	931	5.2	8.0
193 EPISCOPAL	1	53	116	.6	1.0
283 LUTH—MO SYNOD	1	208	282	1.6	2.4
339 PENT CH OF GOD	2	70	153	.9	1.3
349 PENT HOLINESS	1	29	39*	.2	.3
355 PRESB CH (USA)	1	217	294*	1.6	2.5
419 SO BAPT CONV	4	3,948	5,350*	29.9	45.8
449 UN METHODIST	4	970	1,314*	7.4	11.3
499 INDEP.NON-CHAR[3]	1	NA	425	2.4	3.6
MORRIS	32	6,954	9,157*	69.4	100.0
053 ASSEMB OF GOD	3	381	357	2.7	3.9
059 BAPT MISS ASSN	1	30	38*	.3	.4
081 CATHOLIC	1	NA	350	2.7	3.8
081d LATIN	1	NA	350	2.7	3.8
093 CHR CH (DISC)	3	205	290	2.2	3.2
097 CHR CHS&CHS CR	1	55	70*	.5	.8
167 CHS OF CHRIST	6	704	965	7.3	10.5
185 CUMBER PRESB	1	25	25	.2	.3
207 E.L.C.A.	1	25	25	.2	.3
419 SO BAPT CONV	8	3,506	4,462*	33.8	48.7
449 UN METHODIST	7	1,183	1,506*	11.4	16.4
497 BLACK BAPT EST[2]	NA	840	1,069*	8.1	11.7
MOTLEY	12	1,054	1,445*	94.3	100.0
053 ASSEMB OF GOD	2	60	83	5.4	5.7
081 CATHOLIC	1	NA	150	9.8	10.4
081d LATIN	1	NA	150	9.8	10.4
167 CHS OF CHRIST	3	77	101	6.6	7.0
419 SO BAPT CONV	3	733	888*	58.0	61.5
449 UN METHODIST	3	184	223*	14.6	15.4
NACOGDOCHES	84	20,820	28,827*	52.6	100.0
053 ASSEMB OF GOD	2	407	550	1.0	1.9
059 BAPT MISS ASSN	18	2,218	2,715*	5.0	9.4
081 CATHOLIC	1	NA	2,775	5.1	9.6
081d LATIN	1	NA	2,775	5.1	9.6
093 CHR CH (DISC)	1	256	305	.6	1.1
123 CH GOD (ANDER)	1	50	65	.1	.2
127 CH GOD (CLEVE)	1	48	59*	.1	.2
151 L-D SAINTS	1	NA	266	.5	.9
165 CH OF NAZARENE	1	365	412	.8	1.4
167 CHS OF CHRIST	13	1,280	1,738	3.2	6.0
185 CUMBER PRESB	1	18	18	-	.1
193 EPISCOPAL	1	463	667	1.2	2.3
223 FREE WILL BAPT	2	81	99*	.2	.3
283 LUTH—MO SYNOD	1	190	251	.5	.9
355 PRESB CH (USA)	2	389	476*	.9	1.7
413 S.D.A.	2	59	72*	.1	.2
419 SO BAPT CONV	23	10,003	12,246*	22.4	42.5
449 UN METHODIST	13	2,594	3,176*	5.8	11.0
497 BLACK BAPT EST[2]	NA	2,399	2,937*	5.4	10.2
NAVARRO	82	20,101	27,357*	68.5	100.0
053 ASSEMB OF GOD	3	199	202	.5	.7
059 BAPT MISS ASSN	8	1,052	1,334*	3.3	4.9
081 CATHOLIC	1	NA	1,532	3.8	5.6
081d LATIN	1	NA	1,532	3.8	5.6
093 CHR CH (DISC)	2	289	405	1.0	1.5
127 CH GOD (CLEVE)	2	114	145*	.4	.5
151 L-D SAINTS	1	NA	205	.5	.7
165 CH OF NAZARENE	1	8	0	-	-
167 CHS OF CHRIST	8	1,370	1,782	4.5	6.5
185 CUMBER PRESB	1	7	7	-	-
193 EPISCOPAL	1	246	315	.8	1.2
283 LUTH—MO SYNOD	1	94	118	.3	.4
339 PENT CH OF GOD	2	170	340	.9	1.2
349 PENT HOLINESS	3	330	418*	1.0	1.5
355 PRESB CH (USA)	2	430	545*	1.4	2.0
361 PRIM BAPT ASCS	1	34	43*	.1	.2
403 SALVATION ARMY	1	65	68	.2	.2
413 S.D.A.	2	86	109*	.3	.4
419 SO BAPT CONV	21	9,843	12,480*	31.3	45.6
449 UN METHODIST	19	3,750	4,755*	11.9	17.4
496 JEWISH EST[1]	2	NA	0	-	-
497 BLACK BAPT EST[2]	NA	2,014	2,554*	6.4	9.3

County and Denomination	Number of churches	Communicant, confirmed, full members	Total adherents Number	Percent of total population	Percent of total adherents
NEWTON	26	5,003	6,500*	47.9	100.0
053 ASSEMB OF GOD	3	122	134	1.0	2.1
059 BAPT MISS ASSN	1	96	125*	.9	1.9
123 CH GOD (ANDER)	3	88	94	.7	1.4
167 CHS OF CHRIST	6	321	469	3.5	7.2
419 SO BAPT CONV	7	3,066	3,978*	29.3	61.2
449 UN METHODIST	6	518	672*	5.0	10.3
497 BLACK BAPT·EST[2]	NA	792	1,028*	7.6	15.8
NOLAN	42	9,507	14,927*	90.0	100.0
053 ASSEMB OF GOD	2	169	191	1.2	1.3
059 BAPT MISS ASSN	1	116	148*	.9	1.0
081 CATHOLIC	3	NA	2,230	13.4	14.9
081d LATIN	3	NA	2,230	13.4	14.9
093 CHR CH (DISC)	1	171	230	1.4	1.5
123 CH GOD (ANDER)	1	12	12	.1	.1
127 CH GOD (CLEVE)	1	102	131*	.8	.9
145 CH GOD PROPHCY	1	19	24*	.1	.2
165 CH OF NAZARENE	0	0	63	.4	.4
167 CHS OF CHRIST	8	899	1,079	6.5	7.2
193 EPISCOPAL	1	66	89	.5	.6
207 E.L.C.A.	1	93	110	.7	.7
215 EVAN METH CH	1	53	68*	.4	.5
283 LUTH—MO SYNOD	1	76	122	.7	.8
339 PENT CH OF GOD	1	34	77	.5	.5
355 PRESB CH (USA)	1	174	223*	1.3	1.5
419 SO BAPT CONV	12	6,079	7,781*	46.9	52.1
449 UN METHODIST	5	1,242	1,590*	9.6	10.7
497 BLACK BAPT EST[2]	NA	202	259*	1.6	1.7
499 INDEP.NON-CHAR[3]	1	NA	500	3.0	3.3
NUECES	224	67,436	217,181*	74.6	100.0
053 ASSEMB OF GOD	15	2,294	3,341	1.1	1.5
081 CATHOLIC	34	NA	122,500	42.1	56.4
081d LATIN	34	NA	122,500	42.1	56.4
093 CHR CH (DISC)	6	1,521	1,933	.7	.9
097 CHR CHS&CHS CR	1	60	79*	-	-
111 CHR CR,SCIENTST	1	NR	NR	-	-
123 CH GOD (ANDER)	4	271	335	.1	.2
127 CH GOD (CLEVE)	1	50	66*	-	-
133 CH GOD(7TH)DEN	1	38	54	-	-
145 CH GOD PROPHCY	1	31	41*	-	-
151 L-D SAINTS	5	NA	2,069	.7	1.0
165 CH OF NAZARENE	6	405	592	.2	.3
167 CHS OF CHRIST	23	2,841	3,701	1.3	1.7
193 EPISCOPAL	8	3,031	4,041	1.4	1.9
203 EVAN FREE CH	1	79	120	-	.1
207 E.L.C.A.	7	1,766	2,349	.8	1.1
221 FREE METHODIST	2	39	44	-	-
226 FRIENDS-USA	1	7	15	-	-
226c FGC	1	7	15	-	-
246 GREEK ORTHODOX	1	NR	NR	-	-
263 INT FOURSQ GOS	1	22	29*	-	-
283 LUTH—MO SYNOD	7	1,580	2,247	.8	1.0
285 MENNONITE CH	1	30	48	-	-
339 PENT CH OF GOD	1	20	40	-	-
349 PENT HOLINESS	3	175	230*	.1	.1
355 PRESB CH (USA)	9	2,297	3,022*	1.0	1.4
356 PRESB CH AMER	1	142	208	.1	.1
403 SALVATION ARMY	1	211	211	.1	.1
413 S.D.A.	4	339	446*	.2	.2
419 SO BAPT CONV	49	35,899	47,230*	16.2	21.7
435 UNITARIAN-UNIV	1	63	87	-	-
443 UN C OF CHRIST	2	157	207*	.1	.1
449 UN METHODIST	19	9,811	12,908*	4.4	5.9
469 WELS	1	92	143	-	.1
496 JEWISH EST[1]	2	NA	1,165	.4	.5
497 BLACK BAPT EST[2]	NA	4,165	5,480*	1.9	2.5
498 INDEP.CHARIS.[3]	2	NA	900	.3	.4
499 INDEP.NON-CHAR[3]	2	NA	1,300	.4	.6
OCHILTREE	22	4,075	6,309*	69.1	100.0
053 ASSEMB OF GOD	2	69	142	1.6	2.3
081 CATHOLIC	1	NA	458	5.0	7.3
081d LATIN	1	NA	458	5.0	7.3
093 CHR CH (DISC)	1	446	553	6.1	8.8
097 CHR CHS&CHS CR	1	95	127*	1.4	2.0
127 CH GOD (CLEVE)	1	74	99*	1.1	1.6
151 L-D SAINTS	1	NA	61	.7	1.0
157 CH OF BRETHREN	1	60	80*	.9	1.3
165 CH OF NAZARENE	1	52	82	.9	1.3
167 CHS OF CHRIST	2	200	265	2.9	4.2
193 EPISCOPAL	1	7	7	.1	.1
263 INT FOURSQ GOS	1	0	0*	-	-
283 LUTH—MO SYNOD	1	61	69	.8	1.1
285 MENNONITE CH	1	53	88	1.0	1.4

NA–Not applicable NR–Not reported *Total adherents estimated from known number of communicant, confirmed, full members. - Represents a percent less than 0.1. Percentages may not total due to rounding.
[1]See Appendix E [2]See Appendix F [3]See Appendix G Lines in *italic* represent a breakdown of Catholic rites or Friends affiliations. They are included in their respective denominational total.

Table 4. Churches and Church Membership by County and Denomination: 1990

County and Denomination	Number of churches	Communicant, confirmed, full members	Total adherents Number	Percent of total population	Percent of total adherents
339 PENT CH OF GOD	1	35	77	.8	1.2
355 PRESB CH (USA)	1	73	97*	1.1	1.5
419 SO BAPT CONV	3	1,955	2,609*	28.6	41.4
449 UN METHODIST	1	895	1,195*	13.1	18.9
498 INDEP.CHARIS.3	1	NA	300	3.3	4.8
OLDHAM	**9**	**1,043**	**1,630***	**71.6**	**100.0**
081 CATHOLIC	1	NA	242	10.6	14.8
081d *LATIN*	*1*	*NA*	*242*	*10.6*	*14.8*
167 CHS OF CHRIST	2	88	114	5.0	7.0
419 SO BAPT CONV	2	495	660*	29.0	40.5
449 UN METHODIST	4	460	614*	27.0	37.7
ORANGE	**95**	**36,888**	**60,578***	**75.2**	**100.0**
053 ASSEMB OF GOD	8	1,510	2,487	3.1	4.1
059 BAPT MISS ASSN	4	1,210	1,558*	1.9	2.6
081 CATHOLIC	7	NA	10,718	13.3	17.7
081d *LATIN*	*7*	*NA*	*10,718*	*13.3*	*17.7*
093 CHR CH (DISC)	3	345	519	.6	.9
097 CHR CHS&CHS CR	4	343	442*	.5	.7
123 CH GOD (ANDER)	1	35	45	.1	.1
127 CH GOD (CLEVE)	3	207	267*	.3	.4
145 CH GOD PROPHCY	2	62	80*	.1	.1
151 L-D SAINTS	4	NA	1,352	1.7	2.2
165 CH OF NAZARENE	2	288	455	.6	.8
167 CHS OF CHRIST	10	888	1,216	1.5	2.0
193 EPISCOPAL	1	267	354	.4	.6
207 E.L.C.A.	2	258	319	.4	.5
283 LUTH—MO SYNOD	1	184	311	.4	.5
355 PRESB CH (USA)	3	630	811*	1.0	1.3
361 PRIM BAPT ASCS	2	59	76*	.1	.1
403 SALVATION ARMY	1	91	104	.1	.2
413 S.D.A.	2	153	197*	.2	.3
419 SO BAPT CONV	27	24,233	31,202*	38.8	51.5
449 UN METHODIST	8	3,904	5,027*	6.2	8.3
496 JEWISH EST1	0	NA	178	.2	.3
497 BLACK BAPT EST2	NA	2,221	2,860*	3.6	4.7
PALO PINTO	**66**	**11,276**	**17,362***	**69.3**	**100.0**
053 ASSEMB OF GOD	3	96	98	.4	.6
059 BAPT MISS ASSN	2	318	401*	1.6	2.3
081 CATHOLIC	5	NA	3,086	12.3	17.8
081d *LATIN*	*5*	*NA*	*3,086*	*12.3*	*17.8*
093 CHR CH (DISC)	2	224	260	1.0	1.5
127 CH GOD (CLEVE)	1	197	249*	1.0	1.4
145 CH GOD PROPHCY	1	19	24*	.1	.1
151 L-D SAINTS	1	NA	116	.5	.7
165 CH OF NAZARENE	1	63	93	.4	.5
167 CHS OF CHRIST	11	954	1,134	4.5	6.5
193 EPISCOPAL	2	144	173	.7	1.0
283 LUTH—MO SYNOD	1	138	186	.7	1.1
339 PENT CH OF GOD	1	35	77	.3	.4
355 PRESB CH (USA)	1	121	153*	.6	.9
413 S.D.A.	1	73	92*	.4	.5
419 SO BAPT CONV	25	7,451	9,400*	37.5	54.1
449 UN METHODIST	8	1,232	1,554*	6.2	9.0
497 BLACK BAPT EST2	NA	211	266*	1.1	1.5
PANOLA	**53**	**9,564**	**12,427***	**56.4**	**100.0**
053 ASSEMB OF GOD	3	189	217	1.0	1.7
059 BAPT MISS ASSN	9	2,033	2,596*	11.8	20.9
081 CATHOLIC	1	NA	200	.9	1.6
081d *LATIN*	*1*	*NA*	*200*	*.9*	*1.6*
097 CHR CHS&CHS CR	1	140	179*	.8	1.4
165 CH OF NAZARENE	1	25	79	.4	.6
167 CHS OF CHRIST	5	237	316	1.4	2.5
193 EPISCOPAL	1	91	93	.4	.7
223 FREE WILL BAPT	4	205	262*	1.2	2.1
355 PRESB CH (USA)	1	56	72*	.3	.6
419 SO BAPT CONV	15	3,709	4,736*	21.5	38.1
449 UN METHODIST	12	1,822	2,327*	10.6	18.7
497 BLACK BAPT EST2	NA	1,057	1,350*	6.1	10.9
PARKER	**102**	**26,323**	**35,556***	**54.9**	**100.0**
053 ASSEMB OF GOD	6	596	670	1.0	1.9
059 BAPT MISS ASSN	4	474	607*	.9	1.7
081 CATHOLIC	1	NA	926	1.4	2.6
081d *LATIN*	*1*	*NA*	*926*	*1.4*	*2.6*
093 CHR CH (DISC)	1	331	474	.7	1.3
127 CH GOD (CLEVE)	2	411	527*	.8	1.5
151 L-D SAINTS	2	NA	555	.9	1.6
165 CH OF NAZARENE	1	45	119	.2	.3
167 CHS OF CHRIST	17	2,752	3,596	5.6	10.1
185 CUMBER PRESB	1	13	13	-	-
193 EPISCOPAL	2	444	576	.9	1.6

County and Denomination	Number of churches	Communicant, confirmed, full members	Total adherents Number	Percent of total population	Percent of total adherents
207 E.L.C.A.	1	62	80	.1	.2
223 FREE WILL BAPT	1	27	35*	.1	.1
263 INT FOURSQ GOS	1	85	109*	.2	.3
283 LUTH—MO SYNOD	1	184	242	.4	.7
349 PENT HOLINESS	1	11	14*	-	-
355 PRESB CH (USA)	1	427	547*	.8	1.5
413 S.D.A.	1	59	76*	.1	.2
419 SO BAPT CONV	44	16,731	21,442*	33.1	60.3
449 UN METHODIST	14	3,478	4,457*	6.9	12.5
496 JEWISH EST1	0	NA	244	.4	.7
497 BLACK BAPT EST2	NA	193	247*	.4	.7
PARMER	**24**	**4,183**	**6,472***	**65.6**	**100.0**
053 ASSEMB OF GOD	2	43	101	1.0	1.6
059 BAPT MISS ASSN	1	0	0*	-	-
081 CATHOLIC	2	NA	772	7.8	11.9
081d *LATIN*	*2*	*NA*	*772*	*7.8*	*11.9*
167 CHS OF CHRIST	6	401	522	5.3	8.1
283 LUTH—MO SYNOD	2	134	188	1.9	2.9
349 PENT HOLINESS	1	20	27*	.3	.4
419 SO BAPT CONV	4	2,392	3,244*	32.9	50.1
443 UN C OF CHRIST	1	71	96*	1.0	1.5
449 UN METHODIST	5	1,122	1,522*	15.4	23.5
PECOS	**31**	**3,998**	**8,081***	**55.1**	**100.0**
053 ASSEMB OF GOD	3	139	150	1.0	1.9
081 CATHOLIC	6	NA	2,555	17.4	31.6
081d *LATIN*	*6*	*NA*	*2,555*	*17.4*	*31.6*
093 CHR CH (DISC)	1	61	128	.9	1.6
097 CHR CHS&CHS CR	1	52	71*	.5	.9
151 L-D SAINTS	1	NA	65	.4	.8
167 CHS OF CHRIST	5	477	646	4.4	8.0
193 EPISCOPAL	1	26	29	.2	.4
283 LUTH—MO SYNOD	1	27	38	.3	.5
355 PRESB CH (USA)	1	241	330*	2.2	4.1
419 SO BAPT CONV	8	2,246	3,072*	20.9	38.0
449 UN METHODIST	3	729	997*	6.8	12.3
POLK	**68**	**13,351**	**18,631***	**60.7**	**100.0**
053 ASSEMB OF GOD	9	601	916	3.0	4.9
059 BAPT MISS ASSN	16	3,422	4,225*	13.8	22.7
081 CATHOLIC	2	NA	1,772	5.8	9.5
081d *LATIN*	*2*	*NA*	*1,772*	*5.8*	*9.5*
127 CH GOD (CLEVE)	1	93	115*	.4	.6
151 L-D SAINTS	1	NA	132	.4	.7
165 CH OF NAZARENE	1	48	113	.4	.6
167 CHS OF CHRIST	6	496	650	2.1	3.5
193 EPISCOPAL	1	77	98	.3	.5
207 E.L.C.A.	1	40	40	.1	.2
283 LUTH—MO SYNOD	1	144	162	.5	.9
355 PRESB CH (USA)	2	354	437*	1.4	2.3
419 SO BAPT CONV	17	5,500	6,791*	22.1	36.5
449 UN METHODIST	10	1,540	1,901*	6.2	10.2
497 BLACK BAPT EST2	NA	1,036	1,279*	4.2	6.9
POTTER	**127**	**62,074**	**98,507***	**100.6**	**100.0**
053 ASSEMB OF GOD	11	825	1,266	1.3	1.3
059 BAPT MISS ASSN	2	320	417*	.4	.4
081 CATHOLIC	11	NA	13,905	14.2	14.1
081d *LATIN*	*11*	*NA*	*13,905*	*14.2*	*14.1*
093 CHR CH (DISC)	4	1,146	1,663	1.7	1.7
097 CHR CHS&CHS CR	5	4,835	6,308*	6.4	6.4
111 CH CR,SCIENTST	1	NR	NR	-	-
123 CH GOD (ANDER)	1	28	48	-	-
145 CH GOD PROPHCY	1	19	25*	-	-
151 L-D SAINTS	4	NA	1,416	1.4	1.4
165 CH OF NAZARENE	3	470	520	.5	.5
167 CHS OF CHRIST	20	4,432	5,692	5.8	5.8
193 EPISCOPAL	2	1,052	1,358	1.4	1.4
223 FREE WILL BAPT	1	49	64*	.1	.1
246 GREEK ORTHODOX	1	NR	NR	-	-
263 INT FOURSQ GOS	2	55	72*	.1	.1
283 LUTH—MO SYNOD	2	873	1,013	1.0	1.0
339 PENT CH OF GOD	2	44	103	.1	.1
349 PENT HOLINESS	4	198	258*	.3	.3
353 CHR BRETHREN	1	100	300	.3	.3
355 PRESB CH (USA)	4	2,838	3,702*	3.8	3.8
361 PRIM BAPT ASCS	1	107	140*	.1	.1
403 SALVATION ARMY	1	168	168	.2	.2
413 S.D.A.	3	391	510*	.5	.5
419 SO BAPT CONV	26	35,175	45,889*	46.9	46.6
449 UN METHODIST	9	6,102	7,961*	8.1	8.1
496 JEWISH EST1	1	NA	95	.1	.1
497 BLACK BAPT EST2	NA	2,847	3,714*	3.8	3.8
498 INDEP.CHARIS.3	1	NA	650	.7	.7
499 INDEP.NON-CHAR3	3	NA	1,250	1.3	1.3

NA–Not applicable   NR–Not reported   *Total adherents estimated from known number of communicant, confirmed, full members.   - Represents a percent less than 0.1.   Percentages may not total due to rounding.
[1]See Appendix E   [2]See Appendix F   [3]See Appendix G   Lines in *italic* represent a breakdown of Catholic rites or Friends affiliations. They are included in their respective denominational total.

Table 4. Churches and Church Membership by County and Denomination: 1990

County and Denomination	Number of churches	Communicant, confirmed, full members	Total adherents Number	Total adherents Percent of total population	Total adherents Percent of total adherents
PRESIDIO	**14**	**494**	**5,309***	**80.0**	**100.0**
081 CATHOLIC	6	NA	4,670	70.4	88.0
081d *LATIN*	*6*	*NA*	*4,670*	*70.4*	*88.0*
093 CHR CH (DISC)	1	46	53	.8	1.0
167 CHS OF CHRIST	1	17	23	.3	.4
193 EPISCOPAL	1	48	56	.8	1.1
355 PRESB CH (USA)	1	58	77*	1.2	1.5
419 SO BAPT CONV	2	128	169*	2.5	3.2
449 UN METHODIST	2	197	261*	3.9	4.9
RAINS	**21**	**3,204**	**4,018***	**59.8**	**100.0**
053 ASSEMB OF GOD	3	117	170	2.5	4.2
059 BAPT MISS ASSN	2	215	268*	4.0	6.7
127 CH GOD (CLEVE)	2	178	222*	3.3	5.5
167 CHS OF CHRIST	3	189	239	3.6	5.9
419 SO BAPT CONV	9	2,200	2,739*	40.8	68.2
449 UN METHODIST	2	305	380*	5.7	9.5
RANDALL	**48**	**23,333**	**36,581***	**40.8**	**100.0**
053 ASSEMB OF GOD	3	549	773	.9	2.1
059 BAPT MISS ASSN	1	346	442*	.5	1.2
081 CATHOLIC	2	NA	1,313	1.5	3.6
081d *LATIN*	*2*	*NA*	*1,313*	*1.5*	*3.6*
093 CHR CH (DISC)	1	144	205	.2	.6
097 CHR CHS&CHS CR	1	70	89*	.1	.2
165 CH OF NAZARENE	3	429	493	.5	1.3
167 CHS OF CHRIST	6	1,775	2,279	2.5	6.2
193 EPISCOPAL	2	141	137	.2	.4
203 EVAN FREE CH	1	85	165	.2	.5
207 E.L.C.A.	1	335	450	.5	1.2
216 EVAN PRESBY CH	1	46	46	.1	.1
283 LUTH—MO SYNOD	2	294	429	.5	1.2
339 PENT CH OF GOD	1	34	77	.1	.2
355 PRESB CH (USA)	1	421	538*	.6	1.5
413 S.D.A.	1	184	235*	.3	.6
419 SO BAPT CONV	11	14,443	18,464*	20.6	50.5
435 UNITARIAN-UNIV	1	70	80	.1	.2
449 UN METHODIST	5	3,601	4,603*	5.1	12.6
496 JEWISH EST[1]	0	NA	95	.1	.3
497 BLACK BAPT EST[2]	NA	366	468*	.5	1.3
498 INDEP.CHARIS.[3]	1	NA	3,000	3.3	8.2
499 INDEP.NON-CHAR[3]	3	NA	2,200	2.5	6.0
REAGAN	**10**	**1,739**	**3,189***	**70.6**	**100.0**
053 ASSEMB OF GOD	3	162	224	5.0	7.0
081 CATHOLIC	1	NA	647	14.3	20.3
081d *LATIN*	*1*	*NA*	*647*	*14.3*	*20.3*
151 L-D SAINTS	1	NA	74	1.6	2.3
167 CHS OF CHRIST	1	150	191	4.2	6.0
419 SO BAPT CONV	3	1,184	1,703*	37.7	53.4
449 UN METHODIST	1	243	350*	7.8	11.0
REAL	**11**	**1,495**	**1,895***	**78.6**	**100.0**
053 ASSEMB OF GOD	1	25	33	1.4	1.7
081 CATHOLIC	1	NA	100	4.1	5.3
081d *LATIN*	*1*	*NA*	*100*	*4.1*	*5.3*
167 CHS OF CHRIST	3	227	251	10.4	13.2
419 SO BAPT CONV	4	1,087	1,321*	54.8	69.7
449 UN METHODIST	2	156	190*	7.9	10.0
RED RIVER	**48**	**6,605**	**8,213***	**57.4**	**100.0**
053 ASSEMB OF GOD	3	116	156	1.1	1.9
081 CATHOLIC	1	NA	118	.8	1.4
081d *LATIN*	*1*	*NA*	*118*	*.8*	*1.4*
093 CHR CH (DISC)	2	33	41	.3	.5
097 CHR CHS&CHS CR	1	50	61*	.4	.7
127 CH GOD (CLEVE)	1	25	31*	.2	.4
143 CG IN CR(MENN)	1	92	112*	.8	1.4
167 CHS OF CHRIST	9	437	537	3.8	6.5
185 CUMBER PRESB	1	40	42	.3	.5
283 LUTH—MO SYNOD	1	44	64	.4	.8
355 PRESB CH (USA)	3	212	259*	1.8	3.2
419 SO BAPT CONV	11	3,267	3,994*	27.9	48.6
449 UN METHODIST	14	1,541	1,884*	13.2	22.9
497 BLACK BAPT EST[2]	NA	748	914*	6.4	11.1
REEVES	**33**	**3,728**	**20,207***	**127.5**	**100.0**
053 ASSEMB OF GOD	1	16	27	.2	.1
059 BAPT MISS ASSN	1	0	0*	-	-
081 CATHOLIC	6	NA	15,000	94.6	74.2
081d *LATIN*	*6*	*NA*	*15,000*	*94.6*	*74.2*
093 CHR CH (DISC)	1	104	166	1.0	.8
127 CH GOD (CLEVE)	1	24	33*	.2	.2
151 L-D SAINTS	1	NA	129	.8	.6

County and Denomination	Number of churches	Communicant, confirmed, full members	Total adherents Number	Total adherents Percent of total population	Total adherents Percent of total adherents
165 CH OF NAZARENE	1	8	0	-	-
167 CHS OF CHRIST	5	207	296	1.9	1.5
193 EPISCOPAL	1	65	79	.5	.4
283 LUTH—MO SYNOD	1	48	62	.4	.3
355 PRESB CH (USA)	1	107	145*	.9	.7
413 S.D.A.	2	62	84*	.5	.4
419 SO BAPT CONV	7	2,732	3,705*	23.4	18.3
449 UN METHODIST	4	355	481*	3.0	2.4
REFUGIO	**32**	**3,157**	**7,993***	**100.2**	**100.0**
053 ASSEMB OF GOD	1	30	65	.8	.8
081 CATHOLIC	8	NA	3,960	49.6	49.5
081d *LATIN*	*8*	*NA*	*3,960*	*49.6*	*49.5*
123 CH GOD (ANDER)	1	5	7	.1	.1
167 CHS OF CHRIST	4	130	169	2.1	2.1
193 EPISCOPAL	1	31	51	.6	.6
207 E.L.C.A.	2	162	195	2.4	2.4
283 LUTH—MO SYNOD	1	21	21	.3	.3
355 PRESB CH (USA)	3	134	170*	2.1	2.1
419 SO BAPT CONV	7	2,054	2,607*	32.7	32.6
443 UN C OF CHRIST	1	57	72*	.9	.9
449 UN METHODIST	3	365	463*	5.8	5.8
497 BLACK BAPT EST[2]	NA	168	213*	2.7	2.7
ROBERTS	**8**	**1,045**	**1,451***	**141.6**	**100.0**
093 CHR CH (DISC)	1	75	117	11.4	8.1
167 CHS OF CHRIST	5	447	656	64.0	45.2
419 SO BAPT CONV	1	332	430*	42.0	29.6
449 UN METHODIST	1	191	248*	24.2	17.1
ROBERTSON	**35**	**6,349**	**10,643***	**68.6**	**100.0**
053 ASSEMB OF GOD	2	72	77	.5	.7
081 CATHOLIC	4	NA	2,254	14.5	21.2
081d *LATIN*	*4*	*NA*	*2,254*	*14.5*	*21.2*
151 L-D SAINTS	1	NA	188	1.2	1.8
193 EPISCOPAL	2	32	37	.2	.3
355 PRESB CH (USA)	1	12	16*	.1	.2
419 SO BAPT CONV	17	3,971	5,142*	33.2	48.3
449 UN METHODIST	8	681	882*	5.7	8.3
497 BLACK BAPT EST[2]	NA	1,581	2,047*	13.2	19.2
ROCKWALL	**22**	**6,588**	**17,336***	**67.7**	**100.0**
053 ASSEMB OF GOD	2	184	437	1.7	2.5
081 CATHOLIC	1	NA	2,172	8.5	12.5
081d *LATIN*	*1*	*NA*	*2,172*	*8.5*	*12.5*
093 CHR CH (DISC)	2	192	274	1.1	1.6
167 CHS OF CHRIST	3	380	494	1.9	2.8
193 EPISCOPAL	1	204	266	1.0	1.5
221 FREE METHODIST	1	27	32	.1	.2
283 LUTH—MO SYNOD	1	156	222	.9	1.3
355 PRESB CH (USA)	2	230	300*	1.2	1.7
419 SO BAPT CONV	4	3,142	4,096*	16.0	23.6
449 UN METHODIST	4	1,792	2,336*	9.1	13.5
496 JEWISH EST[1]	0	NA	341	1.3	2.0
497 BLACK BAPT EST[2]	NA	281	366*	1.4	2.1
498 INDEP.CHARIS.[3]	1	NA	6,000	23.4	34.6
RUNNELS	**46**	**5,891**	**9,723***	**86.1**	**100.0**
053 ASSEMB OF GOD	2	73	102	.9	1.0
081 CATHOLIC	5	NA	2,253	19.9	23.2
081d *LATIN*	*5*	*NA*	*2,253*	*19.9*	*23.2*
093 CHR CH (DISC)	1	119	138	1.2	1.4
123 CH GOD (ANDER)	1	21	34	.3	.3
165 CH OF NAZARENE	1	21	21	.2	.2
167 CHS OF CHRIST	10	652	821	7.3	8.4
207 E.L.C.A.	2	395	487	4.3	5.0
263 INT FOURSQ GOS	1	25	32*	.3	.3
283 LUTH—MO SYNOD	1	24	28	.2	.3
339 PENT CH OF GOD	1	35	77	.7	.8
353 CHR BRETHREN	1	50	53	.5	.5
355 PRESB CH (USA)	1	97	123*	1.1	1.3
419 SO BAPT CONV	13	3,295	4,179*	37.0	43.0
443 UN C OF CHRIST	1	45	57*	.5	.6
449 UN METHODIST	5	1,039	1,318*	11.7	13.6
RUSK	**94**	**20,283**	**26,682***	**61.0**	**100.0**
053 ASSEMB OF GOD	5	191	318	.7	1.2
059 BAPT MISS ASSN	6	632	805*	1.8	3.0
081 CATHOLIC	1	NA	275	.6	1.0
081d *LATIN*	*1*	*NA*	*275*	*.6*	*1.0*
093 CHR CH (DISC)	5	345	465	1.1	1.7
127 CH GOD (CLEVE)	1	45	57*	.1	.2
151 L-D SAINTS	1	NA	266	.6	1.0
165 CH OF NAZARENE	2	121	285	.7	1.1
167 CHS OF CHRIST	8	825	1,103	2.5	4.1

NA–Not applicable   NR–Not reported   *Total adherents estimated from known number of communicant, confirmed, full members.   - Represents a percent less than 0.1.   Percentages may not total due to rounding.
[1]See Appendix E   [2]See Appendix F   [3]See Appendix G   Lines in *italic* represent a breakdown of Catholic rites or Friends affiliations. They are included in their respective denominational total.

Table 4. Churches and Church Membership by County and Denomination: 1990

County and Denomination	Number of churches	Communicant, confirmed, full members	Total adherents		
			Number	Percent of total population	Percent of total adherents
185 CUMBER PRESB	1	31	31	.1	.1
193 EPISCOPAL	1	89	131	.3	.5
223 FREE WILL BAPT	4	310	395*	.9	1.5
263 INT FOURSQ GOS	1	0	0*	-	-
283 LUTH—MO SYNOD	1	56	78	.2	.3
355 PRESB CH (USA)	4	304	387*	.9	1.5
361 PRIM BAPT ASCS	2	20	25*	.1	.1
413 S.D.A.	1	19	24*	.1	.1
419 SO BAPT CONV	29	12,375	15,768*	36.1	59.1
449 UN METHODIST	21	2,531	3,225*	7.4	12.1
497 BLACK BAPT EST[2]	NA	2,389	3,044*	7.0	11.4
SABINE	**36**	**3,810**	**4,700***	**49.0**	**100.0**
053 ASSEMB OF GOD	2	51	60	.6	1.3
059 BAPT MISS ASSN	4	359	426*	4.4	9.1
081 CATHOLIC	1	NA	125	1.3	2.7
081d LATIN	1	NA	125	1.3	2.7
123 CH GOD (ANDER)	3	58	90	.9	1.9
165 CH OF NAZARENE	1	22	33	.3	.7
167 CHS OF CHRIST	5	180	225	2.3	4.8
221 FREE METHODIST	1	14	27	.3	.6
413 S.D.A.	1	27	32*	.3	.7
419 SO BAPT CONV	8	2,164	2,571*	26.8	54.7
449 UN METHODIST	10	644	765*	8.0	16.3
497 BLACK BAPT EST[2]	NA	291	346*	3.6	7.4
SAN AUGUSTINE	**24**	**3,713**	**4,686***	**58.6**	**100.0**
053 ASSEMB OF GOD	1	75	101	1.3	2.2
059 BAPT MISS ASSN	6	698	867*	10.8	18.5
081 CATHOLIC	1	NA	64	.8	1.4
081d LATIN	1	NA	64	.8	1.4
111 CH CR,SCIENTST	1	NR	NR	-	-
123 CH GOD (ANDER)	1	15	25	.3	.5
167 CHS OF CHRIST	3	201	239	3.0	5.1
193 EPISCOPAL	1	38	52	.7	1.1
355 PRESB CH (USA)	1	64	80*	1.0	1.7
419 SO BAPT CONV	7	1,488	1,849*	23.1	39.5
449 UN METHODIST	2	301	374*	4.7	8.0
497 BLACK BAPT EST[2]	NA	833	1,035*	12.9	22.1
SAN JACINTO	**27**	**4,089**	**5,187***	**31.7**	**100.0**
053 ASSEMB OF GOD	2	75	97	.6	1.9
059 BAPT MISS ASSN	4	425	532*	3.2	10.3
167 CHS OF CHRIST	2	125	159	1.0	3.1
339 PENT CH OF GOD	2	69	153	.9	2.9
419 SO BAPT CONV	11	2,218	2,774*	16.9	53.5
449 UN METHODIST	6	514	643*	3.9	12.4
497 BLACK BAPT EST[2]	NA	663	829*	5.1	16.0
SAN PATRICIO	**92**	**13,956**	**47,412***	**80.7**	**100.0**
053 ASSEMB OF GOD	7	293	553	.9	1.2
081 CATHOLIC	13	NA	28,160	47.9	59.4
081d LATIN	13	NA	28,160	47.9	59.4
093 CHR CH (DISC)	2	137	162	.3	.3
097 CHR CHS&CHS CR	1	100	134*	.2	.3
127 CH GOD (CLEVE)	1	88	118*	.2	.2
151 L-D SAINTS	3	NA	496	.8	1.0
165 CH OF NAZARENE	3	93	31	.1	.1
167 CHS OF CHRIST	13	1,022	1,189	2.0	2.5
193 EPISCOPAL	2	248	363	.6	.8
207 E.L.C.A.	4	569	716	1.2	1.5
283 LUTH—MO SYNOD	2	172	226	.4	.5
285 MENNONITE CH	2	62	66	.1	.1
339 PENT CH OF GOD	1	75	120	.2	.3
349 PENT HOLINESS	1	43	58*	.1	.1
355 PRESB CH (USA)	5	366	490*	.8	1.0
413 S.D.A.	1	11	15*	-	-
419 SO BAPT CONV	23	8,243	11,025*	18.8	23.3
449 UN METHODIST	8	2,116	2,830*	4.8	6.0
496 JEWISH EST[1]	0	NA	235	.4	.5
497 BLACK BAPT EST[2]	NA	318	425*	.7	.9
SAN SABA	**25**	**3,125**	**4,379***	**81.1**	**100.0**
053 ASSEMB OF GOD	1	19	26	.5	.6
081 CATHOLIC	1	NA	405	7.5	9.2
081d LATIN	1	NA	405	7.5	9.2
093 CHR CH (DISC)	1	30	42	.8	1.0
167 CHS OF CHRIST	7	430	578	10.7	13.2
193 EPISCOPAL	1	49	71	1.3	1.6
355 PRESB CH (USA)	2	153	192*	3.6	4.4
419 SO BAPT CONV	10	2,107	2,642*	48.9	60.3
449 UN METHODIST	2	337	423*	7.8	9.7
SCHLEICHER	**10**	**1,211**	**2,255***	**75.4**	**100.0**
053 ASSEMB OF GOD	1	48	109	3.6	4.8

County and Denomination	Number of churches	Communicant, confirmed, full members	Total adherents		
			Number	Percent of total population	Percent of total adherents
081 CATHOLIC	1	NA	600	20.1	26.6
081d LATIN	1	NA	600	20.1	26.6
167 CHS OF CHRIST	4	187	240	8.0	10.6
355 PRESB CH (USA)	1	106	142*	4.7	6.3
419 SO BAPT CONV	2	649	868*	29.0	38.5
449 UN METHODIST	1	221	296*	9.9	13.1
SCURRY	**40**	**9,170**	**13,702***	**73.5**	**100.0**
053 ASSEMB OF GOD	3	138	247	1.3	1.8
059 BAPT MISS ASSN	1	261	337*	1.8	2.5
081 CATHOLIC	1	NA	1,400	7.5	10.2
081d LATIN	1	NA	1,400	7.5	10.2
093 CHR CH (DISC)	1	193	235	1.3	1.7
123 CH GOD (ANDER)	1	50	63	.3	.5
127 CH GOD (CLEVE)	1	73	94*	.5	.7
145 CH GOD PROPHCY	1	19	25*	.1	.2
151 L-D SAINTS	1	NA	65	.3	.5
165 CH OF NAZARENE	1	25	45	.2	.3
167 CHS OF CHRIST	8	1,048	1,315	7.1	9.6
193 EPISCOPAL	1	15	16	.1	.1
207 E.L.C.A.	1	39	56	.3	.4
355 PRESB CH (USA)	1	156	201*	1.1	1.5
419 SO BAPT CONV	10	5,692	7,344*	39.4	53.6
449 UN METHODIST	7	1,232	1,589*	8.5	11.6
497 BLACK BAPT EST[2]	NA	229	295*	1.6	2.2
499 INDEP.NON-CHAR[3]	1	NA	375	2.0	2.7
SHACKELFORD	**12**	**2,243**	**2,820***	**85.0**	**100.0**
053 ASSEMB OF GOD	1	92	84	2.5	3.0
081 CATHOLIC	1	NA	17	.5	.6
081d LATIN	1	NA	17	.5	.6
093 CHR CH (DISC)	1	135	169	5.1	6.0
167 CHS OF CHRIST	2	157	202	6.1	7.2
193 EPISCOPAL	1	14	14	.4	.5
283 LUTH—MO SYNOD	1	111	148	4.5	5.2
355 PRESB CH (USA)	1	83	105*	3.2	3.7
419 SO BAPT CONV	2	1,328	1,674*	50.5	59.4
449 UN METHODIST	2	323	407*	12.3	14.4
SHELBY	**57**	**9,854**	**13,034***	**59.2**	**100.0**
053 ASSEMB OF GOD	3	237	393	1.8	3.0
059 BAPT MISS ASSN	10	1,856	2,324*	10.5	17.8
081 CATHOLIC	1	NA	185	.8	1.4
081d LATIN	1	NA	185	.8	1.4
093 CHR CH (DISC)	2	99	168	.8	1.3
097 CHR CHS&CHS CR	2	160	200*	.9	1.5
165 CH OF NAZARENE	1	37	30	.1	.2
167 CHS OF CHRIST	8	330	418	1.9	3.2
193 EPISCOPAL	1	52	88	.4	.7
355 PRESB CH (USA)	2	48	60*	.3	.5
419 SO BAPT CONV	13	4,467	5,593*	25.4	42.9
449 UN METHODIST	13	1,337	1,674*	7.6	12.8
497 BLACK BAPT EST[2]	NA	1,231	1,541*	7.0	11.8
499 INDEP.NON-CHAR[3]	1	NA	360	1.6	2.8
SHERMAN	**8**	**1,630**	**2,310***	**80.8**	**100.0**
053 ASSEMB OF GOD	1	46	82	2.9	3.5
081 CATHOLIC	1	NA	170	5.9	7.4
081d LATIN	1	NA	170	5.9	7.4
093 CHR CH (DISC)	1	174	206	7.2	8.9
167 CHS OF CHRIST	1	93	121	4.2	5.2
339 PENT CH OF GOD	1	34	77	2.7	3.3
419 SO BAPT CONV	1	784	1,011*	35.4	43.8
449 UN METHODIST	2	499	643*	22.5	27.8
SMITH	**186**	**75,779**	**106,144***	**70.2**	**100.0**
053 ASSEMB OF GOD	20	1,936	2,617	1.7	2.5
059 BAPT MISS ASSN	12	1,627	2,057*	1.4	1.9
081 CATHOLIC	1	NA	5,025	3.3	4.7
081d LATIN	1	NA	5,025	3.3	4.7
093 CHR CH (DISC)	3	1,114	1,506	1.0	1.4
097 CHR CHS&CHS CR	2	175	221*	.1	.2
111 CH CR,SCIENTST	1	NR	NR	-	-
123 CH GOD (ANDER)	1	58	58	-	.1
127 CH GOD (CLEVE)	4	1,070	1,353*	.9	1.3
145 CH GOD PROPHCY	1	31	39*	-	-
151 L-D SAINTS	2	NA	807	.5	.8
165 CH OF NAZARENE	4	477	481	.3	.5
167 CHS OF CHRIST	24	4,008	5,263	3.5	5.0
193 EPISCOPAL	3	1,477	1,652	1.1	1.6
207 E.L.C.A.	2	360	488	.3	.5
223 FREE WILL BAPT	2	55	70*	-	.1
226 FRIENDS-USA	1	4	4	-	-
226c FGC	1	4	4	-	-
263 INT FOURSQ GOS	1	0	0*	-	-

NA–Not applicable NR–Not reported *Total adherents estimated from known number of communicant, confirmed, full members. - Represents a percent less than 0.1. Percentages may not total due to rounding.
[1]See Appendix E [2]See Appendix F [3]See Appendix G Lines in *italic* represent a breakdown of Catholic rites or Friends affiliations. They are included in their respective denominational total.

Table 4. Churches and Church Membership by County and Denomination: 1990

County and Denomination	Number of churches	Communicant, confirmed, full members	Total adherents			County and Denomination	Number of churches	Communicant, confirmed, full members	Total adherents		
			Number	Percent of total population	Percent of total adherents				Number	Percent of total population	Percent of total adherents
283 LUTH—MO SYNOD	1	477	617	.4	.6	**SWISHER**	**27**	**5,033**	**8,106***	**99.7**	**100.0**
339 PENT CH OF GOD	1	35	76	.1	.1						
355 PRESB CH (USA)	4	1,540	1,947*	1.3	1.8	053 ASSEMB OF GOD	3	102	211	2.6	2.6
356 PRESB CH AMER	1	222	260	.2	.2	081 CATHOLIC	3	NA	1,402	17.2	17.3
361 PRIM BAPT ASCS	1	60	76*	.1	.1	081d LATIN	3	NA	1,402	17.2	17.3
375 REF EPISCOPAL	1	71	115	.1	.1	093 CHR CH (DISC)	1	29	30	.4	.4
403 SALVATION ARMY	1	97	101	.1	.1	127 CH GOD (CLEVE)	1	12	16*	.2	.2
413 S.D.A.	3	395	499*	.3	.5	167 CHS OF CHRIST	5	510	667	8.2	8.2
419 SO BAPT CONV	52	39,241	49,604*	32.8	46.7	355 PRESB CH (USA)	2	206	272*	3.3	3.4
435 UNITARIAN-UNIV	1	35	41	-	-	361 PRIM BAPT ASCS	1	25	33*	.4	.4
449 UN METHODIST	26	10,805	13,658*	9.0	12.9	419 SO BAPT CONV	6	3,289	4,340*	53.4	53.5
469 WELS	1	46	59	-	.1	449 UN METHODIST	5	860	1,135*	14.0	14.0
496 JEWISH EST[1]	2	NA	450	.3	.4						
497 BLACK BAPT EST[2]	NA	10,363	13,100*	8.7	12.3	**TARRANT**	**738**	**398,547**	**656,801***	**56.1**	**100.0**
498 INDEP.CHARIS.[3]	1	NA	500	.3	.5						
499 INDEP.NON-CHAR[3]	6	NA	3,400	2.2	3.2	001 ADVENT CHR CH	2	130	167*	-	-
						005 AME ZION	2	400	486	-	.1
SOMERVELL	**12**	**2,218**	**3,060***	**57.1**	**100.0**	019 AMER BAPT USA	2	975	1,250*	.1	.2
						053 ASSEMB OF GOD	64	15,150	19,748	1.7	3.0
053 ASSEMB OF GOD	1	41	73	1.4	2.4	057 BAPT GEN CONF	1	20	26*	-	-
081 CATHOLIC	1	NA	77	1.4	2.5	059 BAPT MISS ASSN	9	2,534	3,248*	.3	.5
081d LATIN	1	NA	77	1.4	2.5	081 CATHOLIC	28	NA	100,077	8.6	15.2
167 CHS OF CHRIST	2	150	191	3.6	6.2	081d LATIN	28	NA	100,077	8.6	15.2
361 PRIM BAPT ASCS	1	18	24*	.4	.8	089 CHR & MISS AL	5	162	255	-	-
419 SO BAPT CONV	6	1,616	2,168*	40.4	70.8	093 CHR CH (DISC)	23	9,073	14,431	1.2	2.2
449 UN METHODIST	1	393	527*	9.8	17.2	097 CHR CHS&CHS CR	4	1,221	1,565*	.1	.2
						105 CHRISTIAN REF	1	78	113	-	-
STARR	**27**	**1,129**	**34,669***	**85.6**	**100.0**	111 CH CR,SCIENTST	4	NR	NR	-	-
						121 CH GOD (ABR)	1	15	19*	-	-
053 ASSEMB OF GOD	2	86	92	.2	.3	123 CH GOD (ANDER)	2	170	310	-	-
081 CATHOLIC	15	NA	32,820	81.0	94.7	127 CH GOD (CLEVE)	10	2,095	2,685*	.2	.4
081d LATIN	15	NA	32,820	81.0	94.7	145 CH GOD PROPHCY	2	62	79*	-	-
151 L-D SAINTS	1	NA	268	.7	.8	151 L-D SAINTS	22	NA	8,110	.7	1.2
167 CHS OF CHRIST	1	40	60	.1	.2	165 CH OF NAZARENE	18	3,076	4,149	.4	.6
237 GC MENN BR CHS	1	50	71*	.2	.2	167 CHS OF CHRIST	94	24,148	30,636	2.6	4.7
313 N AM BAPT CONF	1	112	160*	.4	.5	185 CUMBER PRESB	6	1,903	2,218	.2	.3
349 PENT HOLINESS	1	21	30*	.1	.1	193 EPISCOPAL	23	10,381	13,292	1.1	2.0
419 SO BAPT CONV	4	598	852*	2.1	2.5	203 EVAN FREE CH	1	33	63	-	-
449 UN METHODIST	1	222	316*	.8	.9	207 E.L.C.A.	14	4,892	6,553	.6	1.0
						215 EVAN METH CH	2	278	356*	-	.1
STEPHENS	**26**	**4,320**	**6,969***	**77.3**	**100.0**	221 FREE METHODIST	1	33	40	-	-
						223 FREE WILL BAPT	3	186	238*	-	-
053 ASSEMB OF GOD	2	35	54	.6	.8	226 FRIENDS-USA	1	14	32	-	-
081 CATHOLIC	1	NA	1,080	12.0	15.5	226c FGC	1	14	32	-	-
081d LATIN	1	NA	1,080	12.0	15.5	246 GREEK ORTHODOX	2	NR	NR	-	-
093 CHR CH (DISC)	1	246	336	3.7	4.8	263 INT FOURSQ GOS	5	103	132*	-	-
111 CH CR,SCIENTST	1	NR	NR	-	-	283 LUTH—MO SYNOD	14	6,465	9,272	.8	1.4
127 CH GOD (CLEVE)	1	54	69*	.8	1.0	285 MENNONITE CH	1	26	47	-	-
165 CH OF NAZARENE	1	23	55	.6	.8	287 MENN GEN CONF	1	19	27	-	-
167 CHS OF CHRIST	2	467	541	6.0	7.8	313 N AM BAPT CONF	1	43	55*	-	-
193 EPISCOPAL	1	170	196	2.2	2.8	331 ORTH CH IN AM	1	NR	NR	-	-
355 PRESB CH (USA)	1	113	144*	1.6	2.1	339 PENT CH OF GOD	6	168	373	-	.1
361 PRIM BAPT ASCS	1	10	13*	.1	.2	349 PENT HOLINESS	2	275	352*	-	.1
413 S.D.A.	1	20	25*	.3	.4	353 CHR BRETHREN	3	173	286	-	-
419 SO BAPT CONV	7	2,502	3,189*	35.4	45.8	355 PRESB CH (USA)	27	10,071	12,909*	1.1	2.0
449 UN METHODIST	4	680	867*	9.6	12.4	356 PRESB CH AMER	4	220	312	-	-
496 JEWISH EST[1]	1	NA	0	-	-	361 PRIM BAPT ASCS	1	53	68*	-	-
499 INDEP.NON-CHAR[3]	1	NA	400	4.4	5.7	403 SALVATION ARMY	2	224	253	-	-
						413 S.D.A.	19	4,743	6,079*	.5	.9
STERLING	**7**	**680**	**1,163***	**80.9**	**100.0**	415 S-D BAPTIST GC	1	30	38*	-	-
						419 SO BAPT CONV	175	186,901	239,563*	20.5	36.5
053 ASSEMB OF GOD	1	20	18	1.3	1.5	435 UNITARIAN-UNIV	2	296	405	-	.1
081 CATHOLIC	1	NA	215	15.0	18.5	443 UN C OF CHRIST	2	396	508*	-	.1
081d LATIN	1	NA	215	15.0	18.5	449 UN METHODIST	74	64,860	83,135*	7.1	12.7
167 CHS OF CHRIST	1	64	110	7.6	9.5	469 WELS	3	258	382	-	.1
355 PRESB CH (USA)	1	40	55*	3.8	4.7	496 JEWISH EST[1]	4	NA	4,392	.4	.7
419 SO BAPT CONV	2	377	519*	36.1	44.6	497 BLACK BAPT EST[2]	NA	46,194	59,210*	5.1	9.0
449 UN METHODIST	1	179	246*	17.1	21.2	498 INDEP.CHARIS.[3]	14	NA	11,810	1.0	1.8
						499 INDEP.NON-CHAR[3]	29	NA	17,047	1.5	2.6
STONEWALL	**8**	**1,239**	**1,603***	**79.6**	**100.0**						
						TAYLOR	**151**	**58,942**	**86,791***	**72.5**	**100.0**
059 BAPT MISS ASSN	1	209	262*	13.0	16.3						
081 CATHOLIC	1	NA	50	2.5	3.1	053 ASSEMB OF GOD	9	786	933	.8	1.1
081d LATIN	1	NA	50	2.5	3.1	059 BAPT MISS ASSN	2	151	194*	.2	.2
167 CHS OF CHRIST	3	133	167	8.3	10.4	081 CATHOLIC	5	NA	7,152	6.0	8.2
419 SO BAPT CONV	2	716	897*	44.6	56.0	081d LATIN	5	NA	7,152	6.0	8.2
449 UN METHODIST	1	181	227*	11.3	14.2	089 CHR & MISS AL	1	18	46	-	.1
						093 CHR CH (DISC)	2	755	970	.8	1.1
SUTTON	**10**	**1,247**	**3,101***	**75.0**	**100.0**	097 CHR CHS&CHS CR	2	63	81*	.1	.1
						111 CH CR,SCIENTST	1	NR	NR	-	-
053 ASSEMB OF GOD	2	38	69	1.7	2.2	123 CH GOD (ANDER)	1	68	68	.1	.1
081 CATHOLIC	1	NA	1,480	35.8	47.7	127 CH GOD (CLEVE)	2	116	149*	.1	.2
081d LATIN	1	NA	1,480	35.8	47.7	145 CH GOD PROPHCY	1	19	24*	-	-
167 CHS OF CHRIST	1	140	182	4.4	5.9	151 L-D SAINTS	2	NA	792	.7	.9
193 EPISCOPAL	1	97	116	2.8	3.7	165 CH OF NAZARENE	3	376	503	.4	.6
283 LUTH—MO SYNOD	1	40	42	1.0	1.4	167 CHS OF CHRIST	38	8,279	11,574	9.7	13.3
355 PRESB CH (USA)	1	61	79*	1.9	2.5	193 EPISCOPAL	2	957	1,253	1.0	1.4
419 SO BAPT CONV	2	544	708*	17.1	22.8	207 E.L.C.A.	1	474	597	.5	.7
449 UN METHODIST	1	327	425*	10.3	13.7	215 EVAN METH CH	1	39	50*	-	.1

NA–Not applicable   NR–Not reported   *Total adherents estimated from known number of communicant, confirmed, full members.   - Represents a percent less than 0.1.   Percentages may not total due to rounding.
[1]See Appendix E   [2]See Appendix F   [3]See Appendix G   Lines in *italic* represent a breakdown of Catholic rites or Friends affiliations. They are included in their respective denominational total.

388

Table 4. Churches and Church Membership by County and Denomination: 1990

County and Denomination	Number of churches	Communicant, confirmed, full members	Total adherents		
			Number	Percent of total population	Percent of total adherents
221 FREE METHODIST	2	44	68	.1	.1
223 FREE WILL BAPT	1	24	31*	-	-
263 INT FOURSQ GOS	3	228	292*	.2	.3
283 LUTH—MO SYNOD	2	631	824	.7	.9
339 PENT CH OF GOD	1	34	77	.1	.1
355 PRESB CH (USA)	3	1,132	1,452*	1.2	1.7
403 SALVATION ARMY	1	226	250	.2	.3
413 S.D.A.	1	125	160*	.1	.2
419 SO BAPT CONV	40	33,866	43,439*	36.3	50.1
435 UNITARIAN-UNIV	1	10	10	-	-
449 UN METHODIST	18	8,022	10,290*	8.6	11.9
469 WELS	1	22	35	-	-
496 JEWISH EST[1]	1	NA	0	-	-
497 BLACK BAPT EST[2]	NA	2,477	3,177*	2.7	3.7
498 INDEP.CHARIS.[3]	1	NA	350	.3	.4
499 INDEP.NON-CHAR[3]	2	NA	1,950	1.6	2.2
TERRELL	**7**	**504**	**1,132***	**80.3**	**100.0**
053 ASSEMB OF GOD	1	13	0	-	-
081 CATHOLIC	1	NA	500	35.5	44.2
081d LATIN	*1*	*NA*	*500*	*35.5*	*44.2*
167 CHS OF CHRIST	1	37	48	3.4	4.2
355 PRESB CH (USA)	1	81	104*	7.4	9.2
419 SO BAPT CONV	1	213	274*	19.4	24.2
449 UN METHODIST	2	160	206*	14.6	18.2
TERRY	**34**	**6,130**	**9,294***	**70.3**	**100.0**
053 ASSEMB OF GOD	3	158	299	2.3	3.2
081 CATHOLIC	1	NA	1,000	7.6	10.8
081d LATIN	*1*	*NA*	*1,000*	*7.6*	*10.8*
093 CHR CH (DISC)	1	222	268	2.0	2.9
127 CH GOD (CLEVE)	2	147	199*	1.5	2.1
145 CH GOD PROPHCY	1	19	26*	.2	.3
165 CH OF NAZARENE	1	22	14	.1	.2
167 CHS OF CHRIST	6	886	1,135	8.6	12.2
193 EPISCOPAL	1	24	49	.4	.5
263 INT FOURSQ GOS	2	125	169*	1.3	1.8
355 PRESB CH (USA)	1	92	125*	.9	1.3
419 SO BAPT CONV	11	3,795	5,143*	38.9	55.3
449 UN METHODIST	4	640	867*	6.6	9.3
THROCKMORTON	**14**	**1,839**	**2,407***	**128.0**	**100.0**
053 ASSEMB OF GOD	1	21	28	1.5	1.2
081 CATHOLIC	1	NA	162	8.6	6.7
081d LATIN	*1*	*NA*	*162*	*8.6*	*6.7*
093 CHR CH (DISC)	1	40	56	3.0	2.3
167 CHS OF CHRIST	3	153	160	8.5	6.6
355 PRESB CH (USA)	1	11	14*	.7	.6
419 SO BAPT CONV	4	1,381	1,700*	90.4	70.6
449 UN METHODIST	3	233	287*	15.3	11.9
TITUS	**47**	**12,200**	**16,767***	**69.8**	**100.0**
053 ASSEMB OF GOD	5	747	1,107	4.6	6.6
059 BAPT MISS ASSN	3	1,106	1,427*	5.9	8.5
081 CATHOLIC	1	NA	1,000	4.2	6.0
081d LATIN	*1*	*NA*	*1,000*	*4.2*	*6.0*
093 CHR CH (DISC)	2	117	123	.5	.7
145 CH GOD PROPHCY	4	123	159*	.7	.9
165 CH OF NAZARENE	1	117	136	.6	.8
167 CHS OF CHRIST	10	1,049	1,298	5.4	7.7
193 EPISCOPAL	1	123	134	.6	.8
283 LUTH—MO SYNOD	1	74	100	.4	.6
355 PRESB CH (USA)	1	232	299*	1.2	1.8
413 S.D.A.	1	96	124*	.5	.7
419 SO BAPT CONV	12	6,155	7,943*	33.1	47.4
449 UN METHODIST	5	1,420	1,832*	7.6	10.9
497 BLACK BAPT EST[2]	NA	841	1,085*	4.5	6.5
TOM GREEN	**105**	**33,348**	**62,225***	**63.2**	**100.0**
053 ASSEMB OF GOD	11	1,248	1,575	1.6	2.5
059 BAPT MISS ASSN	1	231	295*	.3	.5
081 CATHOLIC	9	NA	15,717	16.0	25.3
081d LATIN	*9*	*NA*	*15,717*	*16.0*	*25.3*
093 CHR CH (DISC)	3	828	1,152	1.2	1.9
097 CHR CHS&CHS CR	1	170	217*	.2	.3
111 CH CR,SCIENTST	1	NR	NR	-	-
123 CH GOD (ANDER)	1	30	52	.1	.1
127 CH GOD (CLEVE)	2	121	155*	.2	.2
145 CH GOD PROPHCY	1	19	24*	-	-
151 L-D SAINTS	3	NA	804	.8	1.3
165 CH OF NAZARENE	2	204	275	.3	.4
167 CHS OF CHRIST	14	2,560	3,748	3.8	6.0
193 EPISCOPAL	2	610	792	.8	1.3
207 E.L.C.A.	2	541	713	.7	1.1
246 GREEK ORTHODOX	1	NR	NR	-	-
263 INT FOURSQ GOS	3	85	109*	.1	.2
283 LUTH—MO SYNOD	1	751	1,012	1.0	1.6
339 PENT CH OF GOD	3	67	122	.1	.2
355 PRESB CH (USA)	4	1,795	2,295*	2.3	3.7
403 SALVATION ARMY	1	221	226	.2	.4
413 S.D.A.	1	58	74*	.1	.1
419 SO BAPT CONV	23	18,963	24,243*	24.6	39.0
449 UN METHODIST	11	3,488	4,459*	4.5	7.2
496 JEWISH EST[1]	0	NA	100	.1	.2
497 BLACK BAPT EST[2]	NA	1,358	1,736*	1.8	2.8
498 INDEP.CHARIS.[3]	1	NA	500	.5	.8
499 INDEP.NON-CHAR[3]	3	NA	1,830	1.9	2.9
TRAVIS	**339**	**141,524**	**278,750***	**48.4**	**100.0**
053 ASSEMB OF GOD	23	3,388	4,244	.7	1.5
057 BAPT GEN CONF	1	75	93*	-	-
081 CATHOLIC	29	NA	84,424	14.6	30.3
081d LATIN	*28*	*NA*	*84,058*	*14.6*	*30.2*
081e MARONITE	*1*	*NA*	*366*	*.1*	*.1*
089 CHR & MISS AL	2	31	81	-	-
093 CHR CH (DISC)	10	1,960	2,636	.5	.9
097 CHR CHS&CHS CR	2	550	683*	.1	.2
105 CHRISTIAN REF	1	59	83	-	-
111 CH CR,SCIENTST	3	NR	NR	-	-
123 CH GOD (ANDER)	2	110	112	-	-
127 CH GOD (CLEVE)	2	120	149*	-	.1
133 CH GOD(7TH)DEN	1	38	54	-	-
145 CH GOD PROPHCY	1	31	38*	-	-
151 L-D SAINTS	6	NA	2,867	.5	1.0
164 CH LUTH CONF	1	8	9	-	-
165 CH OF NAZARENE	6	735	999	.2	.4
167 CHS OF CHRIST	39	5,369	7,228	1.3	2.6
185 CUMBER PRESB	5	1,469	1,676	.3	.6
193 EPISCOPAL	16	7,306	9,615	1.7	3.4
203 EVAN FREE CH	2	301	319	.1	.1
207 E.L.C.A.	18	8,643	11,412	2.0	4.1
216 EVAN PRESBY CH	1	37	39	-	-
221 FREE METHODIST	1	0	24	-	-
226 FRIENDS-USA	1	152	221	-	.1
226c FGC	*1*	*152*	*221*	*-*	*.1*
246 GREEK ORTHODOX	1	NR	NR	-	-
283 LUTH—MO SYNOD	12	6,267	8,470	1.5	3.0
285 MENNONITE CH	1	23	33	-	-
287 MENN GEN CONF	1	7	10	-	-
313 N AM BAPT CONF	1	39	48*	-	-
329 OPEN BIBLE STD	1	NR	NR	-	-
339 PENT CH OF GOD	4	212	432	.1	.2
349 PENT HOLINESS	1	52	65*	-	-
353 CHR BRETHREN	1	12	25	-	-
355 PRESB CH (USA)	17	7,236	8,985*	1.6	3.2
356 PRESB CH AMER	1	134	162	-	.1
403 SALVATION ARMY	1	157	157	-	.1
413 S.D.A.	4	835	1,037*	.2	.4
415 S-D BAPTIST GC	1	30	37*	-	-
419 SO BAPT CONV	62	58,230	72,367*	12.6	26.0
435 UNITARIAN-UNIV	2	386	558	.1	.2
443 UN C OF CHRIST	3	521	647*	.1	.2
449 UN METHODIST	33	15,966	19,825*	3.4	7.1
467 WESLEYAN	3	54	125	-	-
469 WELS	2	196	281	-	.1
496 JEWISH EST[1]	3	NA	3,687	.6	1.3
497 BLACK BAPT EST[2]	NA	20,735	25,747*	4.5	9.2
498 INDEP.CHARIS.[3]	7	NA	5,021	.9	1.8
499 INDEP.NON-CHAR[3]	4	NA	4,025	.7	1.4
TRINITY	**34**	**4,980**	**6,609***	**57.7**	**100.0**
053 ASSEMB OF GOD	3	157	160	1.4	2.4
081 CATHOLIC	1	NA	164	1.4	2.5
081d LATIN	*1*	*NA*	*164*	*1.4*	*2.5*
127 CH GOD (CLEVE)	1	206	253*	2.2	3.8
151 L-D SAINTS	1	NA	57	.5	.9
167 CHS OF CHRIST	8	350	444	3.9	6.7
355 PRESB CH (USA)	1	35	43*	.4	.7
419 SO BAPT CONV	14	3,219	3,946*	34.5	59.7
449 UN METHODIST	4	585	717*	6.3	10.8
497 BLACK BAPT EST[2]	NA	428	525*	4.6	7.9
499 INDEP.NON-CHAR[3]	1	NA	300	2.6	4.5
TYLER	**57**	**9,434**	**12,314***	**74.0**	**100.0**
053 ASSEMB OF GOD	7	409	446	2.7	3.6
059 BAPT MISS ASSN	2	60	74*	.4	.6
081 CATHOLIC	1	NA	500	3.0	4.1
081d LATIN	*1*	*NA*	*500*	*3.0*	*4.1*
093 CHR CH (DISC)	1	75	75	.5	.6
151 L-D SAINTS	2	NA	265	1.6	2.2
165 CH OF NAZARENE	1	6	0	-	-

NA–Not applicable   NR–Not reported   *Total adherents estimated from known number of communicant, confirmed, full members.   - Represents a percent less than 0.1.   Percentages may not total due to rounding.
[1]See Appendix E   [2]See Appendix F   [3]See Appendix G   Lines in *italic* represent a breakdown of Catholic rites or Friends affiliations. They are included in their respective denominational total.

TEXAS

Table 4. Churches and Church Membership by County and Denomination: 1990

County and Denomination		Number of churches	Communicant, confirmed, full members	Total adherents		
				Number	Percent of total population	Percent of total adherents
167	CHS OF CHRIST	7	287	362	2.2	2.9
193	EPISCOPAL	1	72	84	.5	.7
283	LUTH—MO SYNOD	1	83	94	.6	.8
361	PRIM BAPT ASCS	1	40	49*	.3	.4
413	S.D.A.	1	49	60*	.4	.5
419	SO BAPT CONV	28	7,166	8,841*	53.1	71.8
449	UN METHODIST	4	668	824*	5.0	6.7
497	BLACK BAPT EST2	NA	519	640*	3.8	5.2
UPSHUR		**89**	**14,570**	**20,308***	**64.7**	**100.0**
053	ASSEMB OF GOD	3	181	226	.7	1.1
059	BAPT MISS ASSN	19	3,260	4,166*	13.3	20.5
081	CATHOLIC	1	NA	510	1.6	2.5
081d	*LATIN*	*1*	*NA*	*510*	*1.6*	*2.5*
093	CHR CH (DISC)	1	45	63	.2	.3
127	CH GOD (CLEVE)	3	141	180*	.6	.9
151	L-D SAINTS	3	NA	1,128	3.6	5.6
165	CH OF NAZARENE	1	73	108	.3	.5
167	CHS OF CHRIST	18	1,177	1,539	4.9	7.6
361	PRIM BAPT ASCS	1	17	22*	.1	.1
419	SO BAPT CONV	28	7,259	9,277*	29.6	45.7
449	UN METHODIST	11	1,385	1,770*	5.6	8.7
497	BLACK BAPT EST2	NA	1,032	1,319*	4.2	6.5
UPTON		**18**	**2,746**	**4,844***	**108.9**	**100.0**
053	ASSEMB OF GOD	2	70	131	2.9	2.7
081	CATHOLIC	3	NA	1,025	23.0	21.2
081d	*LATIN*	*3*	*NA*	*1,025*	*23.0*	*21.2*
093	CHR CH (DISC)	1	59	69	1.6	1.4
167	CHS OF CHRIST	2	140	170	3.8	3.5
283	LUTH—MO SYNOD	1	15	27	.6	.6
355	PRESB CH (USA)	1	18	25*	.5	.5
419	SO BAPT CONV	5	2,129	2,959*	66.5	61.1
449	UN METHODIST	3	315	438*	9.8	9.0
UVALDE		**35**	**5,688**	**16,919***	**72.5**	**100.0**
053	ASSEMB OF GOD	2	193	250	1.1	1.5
081	CATHOLIC	4	NA	9,232	39.6	54.6
081d	*LATIN*	*4*	*NA*	*9,232*	*39.6*	*54.6*
089	CHR & MISS AL	1	23	50	.2	.3
093	CHR CH (DISC)	1	200	284	1.2	1.7
097	CHR CHS&CHS CR	1	110	146*	.6	.9
151	L-D SAINTS	1	NA	150	.6	.9
165	CH OF NAZARENE	1	38	48	.2	.3
167	CHS OF CHRIST	6	585	721	3.1	4.3
193	EPISCOPAL	2	262	340	1.5	2.0
207	E.L.C.A.	1	112	133	.6	.8
221	FREE METHODIST	1	3	8	-	-
283	LUTH—MO SYNOD	1	202	290	1.2	1.7
355	PRESB CH (USA)	1	151	201*	.9	1.2
413	S.D.A.	1	29	39*	.2	.2
419	SO BAPT CONV	7	2,731	3,632*	15.6	21.5
449	UN METHODIST	4	1,049	1,395*	6.0	8.2
VAL VERDE		**31**	**5,153**	**13,634***	**35.2**	**100.0**
053	ASSEMB OF GOD	4	466	573	1.5	4.2
081	CATHOLIC	4	NA	6,250	16.1	45.8
081d	*LATIN*	*4*	*NA*	*6,250*	*16.1*	*45.8*
093	CHR CH (DISC)	2	175	290	.7	2.1
111	CH CR,SCIENTST	1	NR	NR	-	-
151	L-D SAINTS	1	NA	475	1.2	3.5
165	CH OF NAZARENE	2	35	74	.2	.5
167	CHS OF CHRIST	3	163	206	.5	1.5
193	EPISCOPAL	1	228	252	.7	1.8
283	LUTH—MO SYNOD	2	172	268	.7	2.0
355	PRESB CH (USA)	1	175	235*	.6	1.7
413	S.D.A.	1	37	50*	.1	.4
419	SO BAPT CONV	6	2,796	3,747*	9.7	27.5
449	UN METHODIST	3	705	945*	2.4	6.9
497	BLACK BAPT EST2	NA	201	269*	.7	2.0
VAN ZANDT		**100**	**19,659**	**25,351***	**66.8**	**100.0**
053	ASSEMB OF GOD	7	765	1,045	2.8	4.1
059	BAPT MISS ASSN	21	3,938	4,897*	12.9	19.3
081	CATHOLIC	1	NA	245	.6	1.0
081d	*LATIN*	*1*	*NA*	*245*	*.6*	*1.0*
093	CHR CH (DISC)	1	23	28	.1	.1
127	CH GOD (CLEVE)	3	296	368*	1.0	1.5
151	L-D SAINTS	1	NA	327	.9	1.3
165	CH OF NAZARENE	3	147	245	.6	1.0
167	CHS OF CHRIST	17	1,342	1,860	4.9	7.3
207	E.L.C.A.	1	93	106	.3	.4
215	EVAN METH CH	1	32	40*	.1	.2
223	FREE WILL BAPT	1	20	25*	.1	.1
285	MENNONITE CH	1	16	16	-	.1
355	PRESB CH (USA)	3	88	109*	.3	.4
419	SO BAPT CONV	21	9,496	11,808*	31.1	46.6
449	UN METHODIST	18	3,017	3,752*	9.9	14.8
497	BLACK BAPT EST2	NA	386	480*	1.3	1.9
VICTORIA		**73**	**20,198**	**61,721***	**83.0**	**100.0**
053	ASSEMB OF GOD	3	339	453	.6	.7
081	CATHOLIC	13	NA	34,610	46.5	56.1
081d	*LATIN*	*13*	*NA*	*34,610*	*46.5*	*56.1*
093	CHR CH (DISC)	1	191	367	.5	.6
097	CHR CHS&CHS CR	1	22	29*	-	-
111	CH CR,SCIENTST	1	NR	NR	-	-
123	CH GOD (ANDER)	1	10	10	-	-
127	CH GOD (CLEVE)	2	122	161*	.2	.3
151	L-D SAINTS	2	NA	500	.7	.8
165	CH OF NAZARENE	1	55	77	.1	.1
167	CHS OF CHRIST	9	1,067	1,395	1.9	2.3
193	EPISCOPAL	2	570	765	1.0	1.2
207	E.L.C.A.	7	3,502	4,554	6.1	7.4
223	FREE WILL BAPT	1	35	46*	.1	.1
263	INT FOURSQ GOS	1	169	223*	.3	.4
283	LUTH—MO SYNOD	1	361	420	.6	.7
355	PRESB CH (USA)	3	872	1,149*	1.5	1.9
403	SALVATION ARMY	1	30	32	-	.1
413	S.D.A.	1	51	67*	.1	.1
419	SO BAPT CONV	12	8,912	11,742*	15.8	19.0
435	UNITARIAN-UNIV	1	21	24	-	-
449	UN METHODIST	8	2,259	2,976*	4.0	4.8
496	JEWISH EST1	1	NA	0	-	-
497	BLACK BAPT EST2	NA	1,610	2,121*	2.9	3.4
WALKER		**51**	**16,985**	**25,220***	**49.5**	**100.0**
053	ASSEMB OF GOD	2	1,017	780	1.5	3.1
059	BAPT MISS ASSN	1	70	82*	.2	.3
081	CATHOLIC	3	NA	4,890	9.6	19.4
081d	*LATIN*	*3*	*NA*	*4,890*	*9.6*	*19.4*
093	CHR CH (DISC)	1	350	657	1.3	2.6
123	CH GOD (ANDER)	1	13	26	.1	.1
151	L-D SAINTS	2	NA	351	.7	1.4
165	CH OF NAZARENE	1	20	63	.1	.2
167	CHS OF CHRIST	7	679	896	1.8	3.6
193	EPISCOPAL	1	148	196	.4	.8
207	E.L.C.A.	1	144	173	.3	.7
223	FREE WILL BAPT	2	120	141*	.3	.6
283	LUTH—MO SYNOD	1	296	379	.7	1.5
355	PRESB CH (USA)	2	383	450*	.9	1.8
413	S.D.A.	1	40	47*	.1	.2
419	SO BAPT CONV	14	8,140	9,556*	18.8	37.9
449	UN METHODIST	11	2,285	2,682*	5.3	10.6
497	BLACK BAPT EST2	NA	3,280	3,851*	7.6	15.3
WALLER		**38**	**7,000**	**11,965***	**51.2**	**100.0**
053	ASSEMB OF GOD	2	46	67	.3	.6
081	CATHOLIC	3	NA	2,702	11.6	22.6
081d	*LATIN*	*3*	*NA*	*2,702*	*11.6*	*22.6*
093	CHR CH (DISC)	1	30	53	.2	.4
151	L-D SAINTS	1	NA	144	.6	1.2
167	CHS OF CHRIST	3	145	220	.9	1.8
193	EPISCOPAL	2	159	208	.9	1.7
207	E.L.C.A.	1	144	187	.8	1.6
283	LUTH—MO SYNOD	1	140	150	.6	1.3
339	PENT CH OF GOD	1	8	18	.1	.2
413	S.D.A.	1	53	66*	.3	.6
419	SO BAPT CONV	10	2,968	3,713*	15.9	31.0
449	UN METHODIST	12	1,228	1,536*	6.6	12.8
496	JEWISH EST1	0	NA	300	1.3	2.5
497	BLACK BAPT EST2	NA	2,079	2,601*	11.1	21.7
WARD		**31**	**5,609**	**17,503***	**133.5**	**100.0**
053	ASSEMB OF GOD	2	76	123	.9	.7
081	CATHOLIC	2	NA	8,480	64.7	48.4
081d	*LATIN*	*2*	*NA*	*8,480*	*64.7*	*48.4*
093	CHR CH (DISC)	1	44	64	.5	.4
097	CHR CHS&CHS CR	1	50	67*	.5	.4
165	CH OF NAZARENE	1	12	0	-	-
167	CHS OF CHRIST	7	397	545	4.2	3.1
193	EPISCOPAL	1	40	62	.5	.4
283	LUTH—MO SYNOD	1	57	82	.6	.5
355	PRESB CH (USA)	2	116	155*	1.2	.9
419	SO BAPT CONV	7	4,027	5,371*	41.0	30.7
449	UN METHODIST	4	790	1,054*	8.0	6.0
498	INDEP.CHARIS.3	1	NA	800	6.1	4.6
499	INDEP.NON-CHAR3	1	NA	700	5.3	4.0

NA–Not applicable   NR–Not reported   *Total adherents estimated from known number of communicant, confirmed, full members.   - Represents a percent less than 0.1.   Percentages may not total due to rounding.

[1]See Appendix E   [2]See Appendix F   [3]See Appendix G

Lines in *italic* represent a breakdown of Catholic rites or Friends affiliations. They are included in their respective denominational total.

Table 4. Churches and Church Membership by County and Denomination: 1990

County and Denomination	Number of churches	Communicant, confirmed, full members	Total adherents Number	Percent of total population	Percent of total adherents
WASHINGTON	**44**	**11,514**	**17,964***	**68.7**	**100.0**
053 ASSEMB OF GOD	1	107	150	.6	.8
081 CATHOLIC	5	NA	3,010	11.5	16.8
081d LATIN	5	NA	3,010	11.5	16.8
093 CHR CH (DISC)	2	110	134	.5	.7
123 CH GOD (ANDER)	3	100	132	.5	.7
151 L-D SAINTS	2	NA	648	2.5	3.6
167 CHS OF CHRIST	2	145	188	.7	1.0
193 EPISCOPAL	1	265	351	1.3	2.0
207 E.L.C.A.	11	4,634	5,669	21.7	31.6
283 LUTH—MO SYNOD	2	1,124	1,386	5.3	7.7
313 N AM BAPT CONF	1	132	165*	.6	.9
355 PRESB CH (USA)	1	293	367*	1.4	2.0
419 SO BAPT CONV	6	1,535	1,922*	7.3	10.7
443 UN C OF CHRIST	3	765	958*	3.7	5.3
449 UN METHODIST	4	851	1,065*	4.1	5.9
497 BLACK BAPT EST[2]	NA	1,453	1,819*	7.0	10.1
WEBB	**60**	**4,591**	**107,333***	**80.6**	**100.0**
053 ASSEMB OF GOD	9	1,163	1,367	1.0	1.3
081 CATHOLIC	20	NA	100,110	75.1	93.3
081d LATIN	20	NA	100,110	75.1	93.3
093 CHR CH (DISC)	1	82	132	.1	.1
127 CH GOD (CLEVE)	1	23	32*	-	-
145 CH GOD PROPHCY	1	19	27*	-	-
151 L-D SAINTS	2	NA	771	.6	.7
165 CH OF NAZARENE	2	69	205	.2	.2
167 CHS OF CHRIST	2	136	176	.1	.2
193 EPISCOPAL	1	125	186	.1	.2
203 EVAN FREE CH	1	40	90	.1	.1
221 FREE METHODIST	1	38	44	-	-
237 GC MENN BR CHS	1	7	10*	-	-
283 LUTH—MO SYNOD	1	89	125	.1	.1
355 PRESB CH (USA)	2	133	186*	.1	.2
403 SALVATION ARMY	1	132	135	.1	.1
413 S.D.A.	2	235	328*	.2	.3
419 SO BAPT CONV	7	1,756	2,450*	1.8	2.3
449 UN METHODIST	3	544	759*	.6	.7
496 JEWISH EST[1]	2	NA	200	.2	.2
WHARTON	**60**	**11,110**	**31,673***	**79.3**	**100.0**
053 ASSEMB OF GOD	5	310	353	.9	1.1
081 CATHOLIC	9	NA	16,890	42.3	53.3
081d LATIN	9	NA	16,890	42.3	53.3
093 CHR CH (DISC)	2	86	121	.3	.4
111 CH CR,SCIENTST	1	NR	NR	-	-
123 CH GOD (ANDER)	3	20	50	.1	.2
127 CH GOD (CLEVE)	1	11	14*	-	-
143 CG IN CR(MENN)	1	109	143*	.4	.5
145 CH GOD PROPHCY	1	31	41*	.1	.1
151 L-D SAINTS	1	NA	95	.2	.3
167 CHS OF CHRIST	4	498	610	1.5	1.9
193 EPISCOPAL	1	123	220	.6	.7
207 E.L.C.A.	5	955	1,237	3.1	3.9
283 LUTH—MO SYNOD	1	293	370	.9	1.2
355 PRESB CH (USA)	2	370	486*	1.2	1.5
419 SO BAPT CONV	13	4,694	6,169*	15.4	19.5
449 UN METHODIST	9	1,933	2,540*	6.4	8.0
496 JEWISH EST[1]	1	NA	130	.3	.4
497 BLACK BAPT EST[2]	NA	1,677	2,204*	5.5	7.0
WHEELER	**26**	**3,981**	**5,307***	**90.3**	**100.0**
001 ADVENT CHR CH	1	25	32*	.5	.6
053 ASSEMB OF GOD	2	55	99	1.7	1.9
081 CATHOLIC	2	NA	186	3.2	3.5
081d LATIN	2	NA	186	3.2	3.5
127 CH GOD (CLEVE)	1	62	78*	1.3	1.5
165 CH OF NAZARENE	2	18	64	1.1	1.2
167 CHS OF CHRIST	3	352	467	7.9	8.8
193 EPISCOPAL	1	9	10	.2	.2
283 LUTH—MO SYNOD	1	67	86	1.5	1.6
419 SO BAPT CONV	7	2,511	3,171*	53.9	59.8
449 UN METHODIST	6	882	1,114*	18.9	21.0
WICHITA	**156**	**58,913**	**92,766***	**75.8**	**100.0**
053 ASSEMB OF GOD	14	1,848	3,151	2.6	3.4
081 CATHOLIC	6	NA	14,235	11.6	15.3
081d LATIN	6	NA	14,235	11.6	15.3
093 CHR CH (DISC)	6	1,639	2,064	1.7	2.2
097 CHR CHS&CHS CR	1	200	253*	.2	.3
111 CH CR,SCIENTST	1	NR	NR	-	-
123 CH GOD (ANDER)	1	0	0	-	-
127 CH GOD (CLEVE)	6	1,145	1,449*	1.2	1.6
145 CH GOD PROPHCY	1	19	24*	-	-
151 L-D SAINTS	2	NA	879	.7	.9
165 CH OF NAZARENE	3	361	478	.4	.5
167 CHS OF CHRIST	17	3,830	4,532	3.7	4.9
193 EPISCOPAL	4	772	1,092	.9	1.2
207 E.L.C.A.	2	444	575	.5	.6
220 FREE LUTHERAN	1	28	41	-	-
223 FREE WILL BAPT	2	155	196*	.2	.2
246 GREEK ORTHODOX	1	NR	NR	-	-
263 INT FOURSQ GOS	1	47	59*	-	.1
283 LUTH—MO SYNOD	5	972	1,310	1.1	1.4
339 PENT CH OF GOD	10	344	769	.6	.8
349 PENT HOLINESS	1	52	66*	.1	.1
355 PRESB CH (USA)	6	2,043	2,585*	2.1	2.8
361 PRIM BAPT ASCS	1	234	296*	.2	.3
403 SALVATION ARMY	1	137	141	.1	.2
413 S.D.A.	3	184	233*	.2	.3
415 S-D BAPTIST GC	1	25	32*	-	-
419 SO BAPT CONV	39	33,596	42,508*	34.7	45.8
449 UN METHODIST	15	7,155	9,053*	7.4	9.8
496 JEWISH EST[1]	2	NA	260	.2	.3
497 BLACK BAPT EST[2]	NA	3,683	4,660*	3.8	5.0
498 INDEP.CHARIS.[3]	1	NA	400	.3	.4
499 INDEP.NON-CHAR[3]	2	NA	1,425	1.2	1.5
WILBARGER	**32**	**9,667**	**13,241***	**87.6**	**100.0**
053 ASSEMB OF GOD	2	154	202	1.3	1.5
081 CATHOLIC	1	NA	1,080	7.1	8.2
081d LATIN	1	NA	1,080	7.1	8.2
093 CHR CH (DISC)	1	132	171	1.1	1.3
111 CH CR,SCIENTST	1	NR	NR	-	-
127 CH GOD (CLEVE)	1	111	139*	.9	1.0
145 CH GOD PROPHCY	1	19	24*	.2	.2
165 CH OF NAZARENE	1	52	86	.6	.6
167 CHS OF CHRIST	6	749	922	6.1	7.0
193 EPISCOPAL	1	29	44	.3	.3
207 E.L.C.A.	1	100	117	.8	.9
283 LUTH—MO SYNOD	3	732	924	6.1	7.0
355 PRESB CH (USA)	1	209	263*	1.7	2.0
413 S.D.A.	1	19	24*	.2	.2
419 SO BAPT CONV	8	5,934	7,453*	49.3	56.3
449 UN METHODIST	3	1,076	1,351*	8.9	10.2
497 BLACK BAPT EST[2]	NA	351	441*	2.9	3.3
WILLACY	**36**	**2,965**	**18,537***	**104.7**	**100.0**
053 ASSEMB OF GOD	4	249	301	1.7	1.6
081 CATHOLIC	8	NA	14,341	81.0	77.4
081d LATIN	8	NA	14,341	81.0	77.4
093 CHR CH (DISC)	1	43	50	.3	.3
145 CH GOD PROPHCY	1	31	43*	.2	.2
151 L-D SAINTS	1	NA	127	.7	.7
165 CH OF NAZARENE	1	31	62	.4	.3
167 CHS OF CHRIST	3	129	156	.9	.8
193 EPISCOPAL	1	14	15	.1	.1
207 E.L.C.A.	1	112	136	.8	.7
263 INT FOURSQ GOS	1	27	37*	.2	.2
283 LUTH—MO SYNOD	1	135	248	1.4	1.3
349 PENT HOLINESS	1	20	28*	.2	.2
355 PRESB CH (USA)	1	60	83*	.5	.4
413 S.D.A.	1	26	36*	.2	.2
419 SO BAPT CONV	5	1,517	2,099*	11.9	11.3
449 UN METHODIST	3	488	675*	3.8	3.6
467 WESLEYAN	2	83	100	.6	.5
WILLIAMSON	**128**	**34,472**	**65,499***	**46.9**	**100.0**
019 AMER BAPT USA	1	160	212*	.2	.3
053 ASSEMB OF GOD	7	280	432	.3	.7
081 CATHOLIC	6	NA	16,063	11.5	24.5
081d LATIN	6	NA	16,063	11.5	24.5
093 CHR CH (DISC)	3	205	241	.2	.4
097 CHR CHS&CHS CR	3	421	559*	.4	.9
127 CH GOD (CLEVE)	2	65	86*	.1	.1
151 L-D SAINTS	3	NA	1,515	1.1	2.3
165 CH OF NAZARENE	1	185	330	.2	.5
167 CHS OF CHRIST	16	1,998	2,560	1.8	3.9
185 CUMBER PRESB	1	61	61	-	.1
193 EPISCOPAL	4	531	821	.6	1.3
203 EVAN FREE CH	2	83	130	.1	.2
207 E.L.C.A.	10	3,336	4,300	3.1	6.6
283 LUTH—MO SYNOD	6	2,052	2,816	2.0	4.3
339 PENT CH OF GOD	2	40	62	-	.1
355 PRESB CH (USA)	6	737	979*	.7	1.5
413 S.D.A.	2	104	138*	.1	.2
419 SO BAPT CONV	29	14,620	19,413*	13.9	29.6
443 UN C OF CHRIST	2	351	466*	.3	.7
449 UN METHODIST	20	6,991	9,283*	6.7	14.2
496 JEWISH EST[1]	0	NA	892	.6	1.4
497 BLACK BAPT EST[2]	NA	2,252	2,990*	2.1	4.6

NA–Not applicable NR–Not reported *Total adherents estimated from known number of communicant, confirmed, full members. - Represents a percent less than 0.1. Percentages may not total due to rounding.
[1] See Appendix E [2] See Appendix F [3] See Appendix G Lines in *italic* represent a breakdown of Catholic rites or Friends affiliations. They are included in their respective denominational total.

Table 4. Churches and Church Membership by County and Denomination: 1990

County and Denomination	Number of churches	Communicant, confirmed, full members	Total adherents Number	Percent of total population	Percent of total adherents
499 INDEP.NON-CHAR[3]	2	NA	1,150	.8	1.8
WILSON	**30**	**4,035**	**13,887***	**61.3**	**100.0**
053 ASSEM OF GOD	2	162	179	.8	1.3
081 CATHOLIC	5	NA	8,531	37.7	61.4
081d *LATIN*	*5*	*NA*	*8,531*	*37.7*	*61.4*
133 CH GOD(7TH)DEN	1	39	55	.2	.4
167 CHS OF CHRIST	3	243	339	1.5	2.4
207 E.L.C.A.	4	1,013	1,348	6.0	9.7
339 PENT CH OF GOD	1	34	77	.3	.6
361 PRIM BAPT ASCS	1	6	8*	-	.1
419 SO BAPT CONV	8	1,701	2,245*	9.9	16.2
449 UN METHODIST	5	837	1,105*	4.9	8.0
WINKLER	**22**	**4,373**	**12,039***	**139.6**	**100.0**
053 ASSEM OF GOD	2	70	152	1.8	1.3
081 CATHOLIC	2	NA	5,970	69.2	49.6
081d *LATIN*	*2*	*NA*	*5,970*	*69.2*	*49.6*
093 CHR CH (DISC)	1	23	35	.4	.3
097 CHR CHS&CHS CR	1	60	81*	.9	.7
127 CH GOD (CLEVE)	1	58	78*	.9	.6
145 CH GOD PROPHCY	1	19	26*	.3	.2
151 L-D SAINTS	1	NA	129	1.5	1.1
165 CH OF NAZARENE	1	21	17	.2	.1
167 CHS OF CHRIST	3	221	298	3.5	2.5
193 EPISCOPAL	1	12	14	.2	.1
283 LUTH—MO SYNOD	1	54	67	.8	.6
419 SO BAPT CONV	5	3,309	4,463*	51.7	37.1
449 UN METHODIST	2	526	709*	8.2	5.9
WISE	**80**	**12,203**	**18,127***	**52.3**	**100.0**
053 ASSEM OF GOD	9	389	527	1.5	2.9
081 CATHOLIC	2	NA	617	1.8	3.4
081d *LATIN*	*2*	*NA*	*617*	*1.8*	*3.4*
093 CHR CH (DISC)	2	23	33	.1	.2
123 CH GOD (ANDER)	1	30	35	.1	.2
151 L-D SAINTS	1	NA	167	.5	.9
167 CHS OF CHRIST	14	942	1,182	3.4	6.5
185 CUMBER PRESB	1	58	72	.2	.4
193 EPISCOPAL	2	75	80	.2	.4
223 FREE WILL BAPT	1	26	33*	.1	.2
283 LUTH—MO SYNOD	1	63	88	.3	.5
349 PENT HOLINESS	1	22	28*	.1	.2
355 PRESB CH (USA)	1	83	106*	.3	.6
419 SO BAPT CONV	31	8,658	11,106*	32.0	61.3
449 UN METHODIST	10	1,834	2,353*	6.8	13.0
499 INDEP.NON-CHAR[3]	3	NA	1,700	4.9	9.4
WOOD	**91**	**16,333**	**21,559***	**73.4**	**100.0**
053 ASSEM OF GOD	6	320	503	1.7	2.3
059 BAPT MISS ASSN	25	4,039	4,958*	16.9	23.0
081 CATHOLIC	1	NA	390	1.3	1.8
081d *LATIN*	*1*	*NA*	*390*	*1.3*	*1.8*
093 CHR CH (DISC)	4	230	306	1.0	1.4
127 CH GOD (CLEVE)	1	34	42*	.1	.2
151 L-D SAINTS	1	NA	204	.7	.9
165 CH OF NAZARENE	2	85	135	.5	.6
167 CHS OF CHRIST	10	794	1,009	3.4	4.7
193 EPISCOPAL	1	125	145	.5	.7
263 INT FOURSQ GOS	1	0	0*	-	-
339 PENT CH OF GOD	3	102	231	.8	1.1
353 CHR BRETHREN	1	25	50	.2	.2
355 PRESB CH (USA)	1	86	106*	.4	.5
413 S.D.A.	1	66	81*	.3	.4
419 SO BAPT CONV	16	7,388	9,069*	30.9	42.1
449 UN METHODIST	16	2,400	2,946*	10.0	13.7
497 BLACK BAPT EST[2]	NA	639	784*	2.7	3.6
498 INDEP.CHARIS.[3]	1	NA	600	2.0	2.8
YOAKUM	**19**	**4,218**	**7,608***	**86.6**	**100.0**
053 ASSEM OF GOD	3	171	345	3.9	4.5
081 CATHOLIC	2	NA	1,400	15.9	18.4
081d *LATIN*	*2*	*NA*	*1,400*	*15.9*	*18.4*
097 CHR CHS&CHS CR	1	35	48*	.5	.6
127 CH GOD (CLEVE)	1	84	116*	1.3	1.5
165 CH OF NAZARENE	1	39	63	.7	.8
167 CHS OF CHRIST	3	367	476	5.4	6.3
419 SO BAPT CONV	5	2,945	4,064*	46.3	53.4
449 UN METHODIST	2	577	796*	9.1	10.5
499 INDEP.NON-CHAR[3]	1	NA	300	3.4	3.9
YOUNG	**53**	**11,559**	**15,411***	**85.0**	**100.0**
053 ASSEM OF GOD	4	335	483	2.7	3.1
081 CATHOLIC	2	NA	463	2.6	3.0

County and Denomination	Number of churches	Communicant, confirmed, full members	Total adherents Number	Percent of total population	Percent of total adherents
081d *LATIN*	*2*	*NA*	*463*	*2.6*	*3.0*
093 CHR CH (DISC)	2	119	206	1.1	1.3
127 CH GOD (CLEVE)	3	414	524*	2.9	3.4
151 L-D SAINTS	1	NA	102	.6	.7
165 CH OF NAZARENE	1	47	100	.6	.6
167 CHS OF CHRIST	10	970	1,189	6.6	7.7
185 CUMBER PRESB	1	104	126	.7	.8
193 EPISCOPAL	2	100	121	.7	.8
283 LUTH—MO SYNOD	2	258	328	1.8	2.1
339 PENT CH OF GOD	3	98	229	1.3	1.5
355 PRESB CH (USA)	1	416	527*	2.9	3.4
413 S.D.A.	1	29	37*	.2	.2
419 SO BAPT CONV	13	6,302	7,979*	44.0	51.8
449 UN METHODIST	7	2,367	2,997*	16.5	19.4
ZAPATA	**9**	**495**	**3,570***	**38.5**	**100.0**
040 AP CHR CH-AMER	1	8	13	.1	.4
081 CATHOLIC	4	NA	2,900	31.3	81.2
081d *LATIN*	*4*	*NA*	*2,900*	*31.3*	*81.2*
167 CHS OF CHRIST	1	50	62	.7	1.7
283 LUTH—MO SYNOD	1	48	63	.7	1.8
419 SO BAPT CONV	1	282	386*	4.2	10.8
449 UN METHODIST	1	107	146*	1.6	4.1
ZAVALA	**18**	**1,471**	**10,171***	**83.6**	**100.0**
053 ASSEM OF GOD	2	133	360	3.0	3.5
081 CATHOLIC	3	NA	8,000	65.8	78.7
081d *LATIN*	*3*	*NA*	*8,000*	*65.8*	*78.7*
097 CHR CHS&CHS CR	1	35	48*	.4	.5
167 CHS OF CHRIST	3	175	223	1.8	2.2
283 LUTH—MO SYNOD	1	13	15	.1	.1
355 PRESB CH (USA)	1	6	8*	.1	.1
419 SO BAPT CONV	4	862	1,179*	9.7	11.6
449 UN METHODIST	3	247	338*	2.8	3.3
# UTAH					
THE STATE.....	3,319	45,080	1,374,097*	79.8	100.0
BEAVER	**15**	**59**	**3,936***	**82.6**	**100.0**
081 CATHOLIC	3	NA	58	1.2	1.5
081d *LATIN*	*3*	*NA*	*58*	*1.2*	*1.5*
151 L-D SAINTS	9	NA	3,796	79.7	96.4
413 S.D.A.	1	15	21*	.4	.5
419 SO BAPT CONV	1	31	43*	.9	1.1
449 UN METHODIST	1	13	18*	.4	.5
BOX ELDER	**85**	**1,051**	**32,923***	**90.2**	**100.0**
053 ASSEM OF GOD	2	89	103	.3	.3
081 CATHOLIC	2	NA	630	1.7	1.9
081d *LATIN*	*2*	*NA*	*630*	*1.7*	*1.9*
105 CHRISTIAN REF	1	58	103	.3	.3
151 L-D SAINTS	73	NA	30,667	84.1	93.1
167 CHS OF CHRIST	1	19	34	.1	.1
193 EPISCOPAL	1	46	66	.2	.2
207 E.L.C.A.	1	129	262	.7	.8
259 IFCA	1	NR	NR	-	-
355 PRESB CH (USA)	1	165	246*	.7	.7
419 SO BAPT CONV	1	452	673*	1.8	2.0
449 UN METHODIST	1	93	139*	.4	.4
CACHE	**172**	**1,022**	**62,617***	**89.2**	**100.0**
053 ASSEM OF GOD	1	41	98	.1	.2
081 CATHOLIC	1	NA	1,200	1.7	1.9
081d *LATIN*	*1*	*NA*	*1,200*	*1.7*	*1.9*
151 L-D SAINTS	162	NA	59,974	85.5	95.8
167 CHS OF CHRIST	1	18	26	-	-
193 EPISCOPAL	1	214	243	.3	.4
226 FRIENDS-USA	1	29	41*	.1	.1
226f *INDEPENDNT*	*1*	*29*	*41**	*.1*	*.1*
259 IFCA	1	NR	NR	-	-
283 LUTH—MO SYNOD	1	86	132	.2	.2
355 PRESB CH (USA)	1	357	509*	.7	.8
413 S.D.A.	1	27	38*	.1	.1
419 SO BAPT CONV	1	250	356*	.5	.6
CARBON	**46**	**974**	**14,133***	**69.9**	**100.0**
053 ASSEM OF GOD	3	73	110	.5	.8
081 CATHOLIC	5	NA	2,525	12.5	17.9
081d *LATIN*	*5*	*NA*	*2,525*	*12.5*	*17.9*

NA–Not applicable   NR–Not reported   *Total adherents estimated from known number of communicant, confirmed, full members.   - Represents a percent less than 0.1.   Percentages may not total due to rounding.
[1]See Appendix E   [2]See Appendix F   [3]See Appendix G   Lines in *italic* represent a breakdown of Catholic rites or Friends affiliations. They are included in their respective denominational total.

Table 4. Churches and Church Membership by County and Denomination: 1990

County and Denomination		Number of churches	Communicant, confirmed, full members	Total adherents		
				Number	Percent of total population	Percent of total adherents
089	CHR & MISS AL	2	143	209	1.0	1.5
145	CH GOD PROPHECY	1	22	30*	.1	.2
151	L-D SAINTS	24	NA	10,194	50.4	72.1
167	CHS OF CHRIST	1	24	49	.2	.3
193	EPISCOPAL	2	21	33	.2	.2
207	E.L.C.A.	1	54	83	.4	.6
246	GREEK ORTHODOX	1	NR	NR	-	-
339	PENT CH OF GOD	1	35	76	.4	.5
413	S.D.A.	1	35	48*	.2	.3
419	SO BAPT CONV	3	413	565*	2.8	4.0
449	UN METHODIST	1	154	211*	1.0	1.5
DAGGETT		**3**	**0**	**530***	**76.8**	**100.0**
081	CATHOLIC	1	NA	20	2.9	3.8
081d	LATIN	1	NA	20	2.9	3.8
151	L-D SAINTS	2	NA	510	73.9	96.2
DAVIS		**332**	**4,291**	**151,455***	**80.6**	**100.0**
019	AMER BAPT USA	3	603	890*	.5	.6
053	ASSEMB OF GOD	2	326	1,094	.6	.7
081	CATHOLIC	2	NA	4,248	2.3	2.8
081d	LATIN	2	NA	4,248	2.3	2.8
097	CHR CHS&CHS CR	1	38	56*	-	-
151	L-D SAINTS	309	NA	139,375	74.2	92.0
165	CH OF NAZARENE	1	53	84	-	.1
167	CHS OF CHRIST	2	158	231	.1	.2
179	CONSRV BAPT	1	NR	NR	-	-
193	EPISCOPAL	2	314	454	.2	.3
283	LUTH—MO SYNOD	2	370	572	.3	.4
355	PRESB CH (USA)	1	107	158*	.1	.1
419	SO BAPT CONV	4	1,397	2,061*	1.1	1.4
443	UN C OF CHRIST	1	423	624*	.3	.4
496	JEWISH EST[1]	0	NA	517	.3	.3
497	BLACK BAPT EST[2]	NA	502	741*	.4	.5
499	INDEP.NON-CHAR[3]	1	NA	350	.2	.2
DUCHESNE		**35**	**294**	**10,469***	**82.8**	**100.0**
053	ASSEMB OF GOD	1	96	275	2.2	2.6
081	CATHOLIC	3	NA	250	2.0	2.4
081d	LATIN	3	NA	250	2.0	2.4
151	L-D SAINTS	26	NA	9,618	76.1	91.9
283	LUTH—MO SYNOD	1	17	26	.2	.2
339	PENT CH OF GOD	1	34	77	.6	.7
355	PRESB CH (USA)	1	42	64*	.5	.6
419	SO BAPT CONV	2	105	159*	1.3	1.5
EMERY		**23**	**26**	**8,473***	**82.0**	**100.0**
081	CATHOLIC	1	NA	30	.3	.4
081d	LATIN	1	NA	30	.3	.4
151	L-D SAINTS	21	NA	8,403	81.3	99.2
419	SO BAPT CONV	1	26	40*	.4	.5
GARFIELD		**15**	**69**	**3,520***	**88.4**	**100.0**
081	CATHOLIC	1	NA	20	.5	.6
081d	LATIN	1	NA	20	.5	.6
151	L-D SAINTS	12	NA	3,403	85.5	96.7
419	SO BAPT CONV	2	69	97*	2.4	2.8
GRAND		**18**	**863**	**3,615***	**54.6**	**100.0**
019	AMER BAPT USA	1	204	272*	4.1	7.5
053	ASSEMB OF GOD	1	43	69	1.0	1.9
081	CATHOLIC	2	NA	350	5.3	9.7
081d	LATIN	2	NA	350	5.3	9.7
145	CH GOD PROPHECY	1	22	29*	.4	.8
151	L-D SAINTS	6	NA	2,072	31.3	57.3
167	CHS OF CHRIST	1	10	12	.2	.3
193	EPISCOPAL	1	64	106	1.6	2.9
226	FRIENDS-USA	1	2	5	.1	.1
226f	INDEPENDNT	1	2	5	.1	.1
283	LUTH—MO SYNOD	1	24	40	.6	1.1
413	S.D.A.	2	69	92*	1.4	2.5
419	SO BAPT CONV	1	425	568*	8.6	15.7
IRON		**52**	**401**	**16,856***	**81.1**	**100.0**
053	ASSEMB OF GOD	1	11	30	.1	.2
081	CATHOLIC	3	NA	235	1.1	1.4
081d	LATIN	3	NA	235	1.1	1.4
151	L-D SAINTS	42	NA	16,058	77.2	95.3
167	CHS OF CHRIST	1	28	40	.2	.2
179	CONSRV BAPT	1	NR	NR	-	-
193	EPISCOPAL	1	31	32	.2	.2
283	LUTH—MO SYNOD	1	68	94	.5	.6
355	PRESB CH (USA)	1	73	102*	.5	.6
419	SO BAPT CONV	1	190	265*	1.3	1.6

County and Denomination		Number of churches	Communicant, confirmed, full members	Total adherents		
				Number	Percent of total population	Percent of total adherents
JUAB		**16**	**32**	**5,298***	**91.1**	**100.0**
081	CATHOLIC	3	NA	265	4.6	5.0
081d	LATIN	3	NA	265	4.6	5.0
151	L-D SAINTS	12	NA	4,987	85.7	94.1
449	UN METHODIST	1	32	46*	.8	.9
KANE		**18**	**248**	**3,959***	**76.6**	**100.0**
081	CATHOLIC	1	NA	95	1.8	2.4
081d	LATIN	1	NA	95	1.8	2.4
093	CHR CH (DISC)	1	55	62	1.2	1.6
151	L-D SAINTS	11	NA	3,531	68.3	89.2
179	CONSRV BAPT	1	NR	NR	-	-
355	PRESB CH (USA)	1	62	87*	1.7	2.2
419	SO BAPT CONV	1	49	69*	1.3	1.7
443	UN C OF CHRIST	1	62	87*	1.7	2.2
449	UN METHODIST	1	20	28*	.5	.7
MILLARD		**30**	**104**	**10,312***	**91.0**	**100.0**
081	CATHOLIC	1	NA	50	.4	.5
081d	LATIN	1	NA	50	.4	.5
151	L-D SAINTS	26	NA	10,104	89.2	98.0
167	CHS OF CHRIST	1	8	12	.1	.1
355	PRESB CH (USA)	1	43	65*	.6	.6
419	SO BAPT CONV	1	53	81*	.7	.8
MORGAN		**11**	**0**	**5,185***	**93.8**	**100.0**
081	CATHOLIC	0	NA	160	2.9	3.1
081d	LATIN	0	NA	160	2.9	3.1
151	L-D SAINTS	11	NA	5,025	90.9	96.9
PIUTE		**4**	**16**	**933***	**73.1**	**100.0**
089	CHR & MISS AL	1	16	28	2.2	3.0
151	L-D SAINTS	3	NA	905	70.9	97.0
RICH		**5**	**0**	**1,700***	**98.6**	**100.0**
151	L-D SAINTS	5	NA	1,700	98.6	100.0
SALT LAKE		**1,119**	**23,308**	**542,439***	**74.7**	**100.0**
019	AMER BAPT USA	4	804	1,118*	.2	.2
039	AP CHR CH(NAZ)	1	4	6*	-	-
053	ASSEMB OF GOD	6	1,485	3,096	.4	.6
081	CATHOLIC	22	NA	38,480	5.3	7.1
081b	BYZAN RUTH	1	NA	50	-	-
081d	LATIN	20	NA	38,164	5.3	7.0
081e	MARONITE	1	NA	266	-	-
083	CHRIST CATH CH	1	20	28	-	-
089	CHR & MISS AL	1	84	204	-	-
093	CHR CH (DISC)	2	251	402	.1	.1
097	CHR CHS&CHS CR	2	400	556*	.1	.1
105	CHRISTIAN REF	4	212	375	.1	.1
111	CH CR,SCIENTST	3	NR	NR	-	-
145	CH GOD PROPHECY	3	66	92*	-	-
151	L-D SAINTS	985	NA	466,551	64.3	86.0
165	CH OF NAZARENE	2	130	331	-	.1
167	CHS OF CHRIST	3	243	374	.1	.1
175	CONGR CHR CHS	1	290	403*	.1	.1
179	CONSRV BAPT	4	NR	NR	-	-
193	EPISCOPAL	5	2,555	3,075	.4	.6
203	EVAN FREE CH	2	200	350	-	.1
207	E.L.C.A.	5	2,294	3,299	.5	.6
226	FRIENDS-USA	1	49	68*	-	-
226f	INDEPENDNT	1	49	68*	-	-
246	GREEK ORTHODOX	2	NR	NR	-	-
259	IFCA	2	NR	NR	-	-
263	INT FOURSQ GOS	4	326	453*	.1	.1
283	LUTH—MO SYNOD	5	1,475	2,139	.3	.4
339	PENT CH OF GOD	1	34	77	-	-
355	PRESB CH (USA)	8	2,783	3,870*	.5	.7
403	SALVATION ARMY	2	15	19	-	-
413	S.D.A.	4	499	694*	.1	.1
419	SO BAPT CONV	16	3,779	5,255*	.7	1.0
435	UNITARIAN-UNIV	2	477	718	.1	.1
443	UN C OF CHRIST	2	550	765*	.1	.1
449	UN METHODIST	7	3,005	4,179*	.6	.8
469	WELS	1	70	135	-	-
496	JEWISH EST[1]	1	NA	1,997	.3	.4
497	BLACK BAPT EST[2]	NA	1,208	1,680*	.2	.3
498	INDEP.CHARIS.[3]	3	NA	950	.1	.2
499	INDEP.NON-CHAR[3]	2	NA	700	.1	.1
SAN JUAN		**33**	**548**	**6,114***	**48.4**	**100.0**
053	ASSEMB OF GOD	1	21	42	.3	.7
081	CATHOLIC	2	NA	160	1.3	2.6

NA–Not applicable   NR–Not reported   *Total adherents estimated from known number of communicant, confirmed, full members.   - Represents a percent less than 0.1.   Percentages may not total due to rounding.
[1]See Appendix E   [2]See Appendix F   [3]See Appendix G   Lines in *italic* represent a breakdown of Catholic rites or Friends affiliations. They are included in their respective denominational total.

Table 4. Churches and Church Membership by County and Denomination: 1990

County and Denomination	Number of churches	Communicant, confirmed, full members	Total adherents Number	Percent of total population	Percent of total adherents
081d LATIN	2	NA	160	1.3	2.6
151 L-D SAINTS	18	NA	4,992	39.6	81.6
167 CHS OF CHRIST	2	13	17	.1	.3
193 EPISCOPAL	4	110	213	1.7	3.5
203 EVAN FREE CH	1	19	40	.3	.7
221 FREE METHODIST	2	0	65	.5	1.1
413 S.D.A.	1	246	374*	3.0	6.1
419 SO BAPT CONV	2	139	211*	1.7	3.5
SANPETE	**44**	**137**	**15,121***	**93.0**	**100.0**
081 CATHOLIC	1	NA	40	.2	.3
081d LATIN	1	NA	40	.2	.3
151 L-D SAINTS	41	NA	14,886	91.6	98.4
355 PRESB CH (USA)	1	59	84*	.5	.6
419 SO BAPT CONV	1	78	111*	.7	.7
SEVIER	**42**	**284**	**14,318***	**92.8**	**100.0**
053 ASSEMB OF GOD	1	18	63	.4	.4
081 CATHOLIC	4	NA	400	2.6	2.8
081d LATIN	4	NA	400	2.6	2.8
151 L-D SAINTS	33	NA	13,475	87.3	94.1
226 FRIENDS-USA	1	1	6	-	-
226f INDEPENDNT	1	1	6	-	-
283 LUTH—MO SYNOD	1	36	42	.3	.3
355 PRESB CH (USA)	1	33	48*	.3	.3
419 SO BAPT CONV	1	196	284*	1.8	2.0
SUMMIT	**29**	**464**	**9,433***	**60.8**	**100.0**
081 CATHOLIC	2	NA	600	3.9	6.4
081d LATIN	2	NA	600	3.9	6.4
111 CH CR,SCIENTST	1	NR	NR	-	-
151 L-D SAINTS	22	NA	8,191	52.8	86.8
179 CONSRV BAPT	1	NR	NR	-	-
193 EPISCOPAL	1	84	115	.7	1.2
207 E.L.C.A.	1	111	158	1.0	1.7
449 UN METHODIST	1	269	369*	2.4	3.9
TOOELE	**47**	**571**	**19,988***	**75.1**	**100.0**
053 ASSEMB OF GOD	1	43	64	.2	.3
081 CATHOLIC	2	NA	2,635	9.9	13.2
081d LATIN	2	NA	2,635	9.9	13.2
151 L-D SAINTS	38	NA	16,582	62.3	83.0
167 CHS OF CHRIST	1	15	20	.1	.1
193 EPISCOPAL	1	87	82	.3	.4
283 LUTH—MO SYNOD	1	79	123	.5	.6
419 SO BAPT CONV	2	219	304*	1.1	1.5
449 UN METHODIST	1	128	178*	.7	.9
UINTAH	**48**	**1,471**	**16,689***	**75.1**	**100.0**
053 ASSEMB OF GOD	1	36	105	.5	.6
081 CATHOLIC	1	NA	550	2.5	3.3
081d LATIN	1	NA	550	2.5	3.3
097 CHR CHS&CHS CR	1	75	112*	.5	.7
151 L-D SAINTS	35	NA	13,780	62.0	82.6
165 CH OF NAZARENE	1	25	81	.4	.5
167 CHS OF CHRIST	1	24	39	.2	.2
193 EPISCOPAL	3	125	212	1.0	1.3
283 LUTH—MO SYNOD	1	115	183	.8	1.1
339 PENT CH OF GOD	1	35	77	.3	.5
419 SO BAPT CONV	2	976	1,460*	6.6	8.7
443 UN C OF CHRIST	1	60	90*	.4	.5
UTAH	**671**	**1,674**	**240,460***	**91.2**	**100.0**
053 ASSEMB OF GOD	3	182	341	.1	.1
081 CATHOLIC	4	NA	1,050	.4	.4
081d LATIN	4	NA	1,050	.4	.4
111 CH CR,SCIENTST	1	NR	NR	-	-
151 L-D SAINTS	649	NA	236,893	89.9	98.5
165 CH OF NAZARENE	1	21	43	-	-
167 CHS OF CHRIST	1	15	24	-	-
193 EPISCOPAL	1	124	137	.1	.1
203 EVAN FREE CH	1	60	125	-	.1
263 INT FOURSQ GOS	2	111	159*	.1	.1
283 LUTH—MO SYNOD	1	188	292	.1	.1
355 PRESB CH (USA)	2	161	231*	.1	.1
413 S.D.A.	1	112	161*	.1	.1
419 SO BAPT CONV	2	397	569*	.2	.2
443 UN C OF CHRIST	2	303	435*	.2	.2
WASATCH	**20**	**0**	**8,778***	**87.0**	**100.0**
081 CATHOLIC	1	NA	300	3.0	3.4
081d LATIN	1	NA	300	3.0	3.4
151 L-D SAINTS	19	NA	8,478	84.0	96.6
WASHINGTON	**108**	**586**	**39,657***	**81.7**	**100.0**
019 AMER BAPT USA	1	75	106*	.2	.3
053 ASSEMB OF GOD	1	27	75	.2	.2
081 CATHOLIC	1	NA	610	1.3	1.5
081d LATIN	1	NA	610	1.3	1.5
111 CH CR,SCIENTST	1	NR	NR		
151 L-D SAINTS	99	NA	38,097	78.5	96.1
193 EPISCOPAL	1	55	130	.3	.3
283 LUTH—MO SYNOD	1	107	185	.4	.5
355 PRESB CH (USA)	1	162	228*	.5	.6
413 S.D.A.	1	31	44*	.1	.1
419 SO BAPT CONV	1	129	182*	.4	.5
WAYNE	**8**	**15**	**1,900***	**87.3**	**100.0**
081 CATHOLIC	0	NA	5	.2	.3
081d LATIN	0	NA	5	.2	.3
151 L-D SAINTS	7	NA	1,874	86.1	98.6
419 SO BAPT CONV	1	15	21*	1.0	1.1
WEBER	**270**	**6,572**	**123,286***	**77.9**	**100.0**
019 AMER BAPT USA	1	285	389*	.2	.3
053 ASSEMB OF GOD	4	428	885	.6	.7
081 CATHOLIC	5	NA	11,350	7.2	9.2
081d LATIN	5	NA	11,350	7.2	9.2
093 CHR CH (DISC)	1	120	180	.1	.1
097 CHR CHS&CHS CR	1	165	225*	.1	.2
105 CHRISTIAN REF	1	87	124	.1	.1
111 CH CR,SCIENTST	1	NR	NR	-	-
127 CH GOD (CLEVE)	1	194	265*	.2	.2
145 CH GOD PROPHCY	1	22	30*	-	-
151 L-D SAINTS	224	NA	102,121	64.5	82.8
165 CH OF NAZARENE	1	37	44	-	-
167 CHS OF CHRIST	1	31	34	-	-
179 CONSRV BAPT	1	NR	NR	-	-
193 EPISCOPAL	1	482	538	.3	.4
203 EVAN FREE CH	1	36	85	.1	.1
207 E.L.C.A.	3	928	1,309	.8	1.1
246 GREEK ORTHODOX	1	NR	NR	-	-
263 INT FOURSQ GOS	2	93	127*	.1	.1
283 LUTH—MO SYNOD	1	463	719	.5	.6
339 PENT CH OF GOD	1	34	77	-	.1
355 PRESB CH (USA)	3	707	966*	.6	.8
403 SALVATION ARMY	1	23	52	-	-
413 S.D.A.	2	253	346*	.2	.3
419 SO BAPT CONV	5	624	853*	.5	.7
443 UN C OF CHRIST	2	154	210*	.1	.2
449 UN METHODIST	2	884	1,208*	.8	1.0
496 JEWISH EST[1]	0	NA	436	.3	.4
497 BLACK BAPT EST[2]	NA	522	713*	.5	.6

VERMONT

County and Denomination	Number of churches	Communicant, confirmed, full members	Total adherents Number	Percent of total population	Percent of total adherents
THE STATE.....	764	63,861	236,757*	42.1	100.0
ADDISON	**47**	**4,039**	**12,781***	**38.8**	**100.0**
019 AMER BAPT USA	5	546	687*	2.1	5.4
053 ASSEMB OF GOD	1	167	225	.7	1.8
081 CATHOLIC	7	NA	7,191	21.8	56.3
081d LATIN	7	NA	7,191	21.8	56.3
105 CHRISTIAN REF	1	203	369	1.1	2.9
111 CH CR,SCIENTST	1	NR	NR	-	-
151 L-D SAINTS	1	NA	159	.5	1.2
165 CH OF NAZARENE	1	73	147	.4	1.2
167 CHS OF CHRIST	1	20	28	.1	.2
176 CCC, NOT NAT'L	1	31	39*	.1	.3
181 CONSRV CONGR	1	124	156*	.5	1.2
193 EPISCOPAL	2	329	555	1.7	4.3
226 FRIENDS-USA	3	62	78*	.2	.6
226d FGC & FUM	3	62	78*	.2	.6
413 S.D.A.	1	36	45*	.1	.4
419 SO BAPT CONV	1	9	11*	-	.1
435 UNITARIAN-UNIV	1	37	67	.2	.5
443 UN C OF CHRIST	7	1,011	1,273*	3.9	10.0
449 UN METHODIST	12	1,391	1,751*	5.3	13.7
BENNINGTON	**47**	**4,819**	**15,807***	**44.1**	**100.0**
019 AMER BAPT USA	5	893	1,116*	3.1	7.1
053 ASSEMB OF GOD	1	75	147	.4	.9
081 CATHOLIC	7	NA	9,231	25.8	58.4
081d LATIN	7	NA	9,231	25.8	58.4

NA–Not applicable   NR–Not reported   *Total adherents estimated from known number of communicant, confirmed, full members.   - Represents a percent less than 0.1.   Percentages may not total due to rounding.
[1]See Appendix E   [2]See Appendix F   [3]See Appendix G   Lines in italic represent a breakdown of Catholic rites or Friends affiliations. They are included in their respective denominational total.

Table 4. Churches and Church Membership by County and Denomination: 1990

County and Denomination	Number of churches	Communicant, confirmed, full members	Total adherents Number	Percent of total population	Percent of total adherents
089 CHR & MISS AL	1	99	230	.6	1.5
097 CHR CHS&CHS CR	1	50	63*	.2	.4
111 CH CR,SCIENTST	1	NR	NR	-	-
123 CH GOD (ANDER)	1	15	21	.1	.1
151 L-D SAINTS	1	NA	179	.5	1.1
167 CHS OF CHRIST	1	30	40	.1	.3
175 CONGR CHR CHS	2	100	125*	.3	.8
176 CCC, NOT NAT'L	2	429	536*	1.5	3.4
179 CONSRV BAPT	1	NR	NR	-	-
193 EPISCOPAL	3	800	1,103	3.1	7.0
207 E.L.C.A.	1	71	92	.3	.6
226 FRIENDS-USA	1	33	41*	.1	.3
226d FGC & FUM	1	33	41*	.1	.3
413 S.D.A.	1	68	85*	.2	.5
419 SO BAPT CONV	1	14	18*	.1	.1
435 UNITARIAN-UNIV	1	32	42	.1	.3
443 UN C OF CHRIST	5	903	1,129*	3.1	7.1
449 UN METHODIST	9	1,207	1,509*	4.2	9.5
496 JEWISH EST[1]	1	NA	100	.3	.6
CALEDONIA	**50**	**4,084**	**10,482***	**37.6**	**100.0**
019 AMER BAPT USA	5	383	489*	1.8	4.7
053 ASSEMB OF GOD	1	73	170	.6	1.6
081 CATHOLIC	4	NA	4,797	17.2	45.8
081d LATIN	4	NA	4,797	17.2	45.8
111 CH CR,SCIENTST	1	NR	NR	-	-
151 L-D SAINTS	1	NA	232	.8	2.2
165 CH OF NAZARENE	1	16	50	.2	.5
176 CCC, NOT NAT'L	1	317	405*	1.5	3.9
193 EPISCOPAL	3	229	296	1.1	2.8
353 CHR BRETHREN	2	50	100	.4	1.0
355 PRESB CH (USA)	4	250	319*	1.1	3.0
413 S.D.A.	1	57	73*	.3	.7
419 SO BAPT CONV	1	27	34*	.1	.3
435 UNITARIAN-UNIV	2	36	39	.1	.4
443 UN C OF CHRIST	12	1,124	1,435*	5.2	13.7
449 UN METHODIST	10	1,522	1,943*	7.0	18.5
496 JEWISH EST[1]	1	NA	100	.4	1.0
CHITTENDEN	**83**	**11,149**	**62,495***	**47.4**	**100.0**
019 AMER BAPT USA	7	576	709*	.5	1.1
053 ASSEMB OF GOD	2	375	614	.5	1.0
081 CATHOLIC	19	NA	43,768	33.2	70.0
081d LATIN	19	NA	43,768	33.2	70.0
089 CHR & MISS AL	3	431	1,095	.8	1.8
111 CH CR,SCIENTST	1	NR	NR	-	-
151 L-D SAINTS	1	NA	543	.4	.9
165 CH OF NAZARENE	1	116	227	.2	.4
167 CHS OF CHRIST	2	99	166	.1	.3
193 EPISCOPAL	7	1,361	2,211	1.7	3.5
207 E.L.C.A.	2	345	478	.4	.8
221 FREE METHODIST	1	17	45	-	.1
226 FRIENDS-USA	1	87	107*	.1	.2
226d FGC & FUM	1	87	107*	.1	.2
246 GREEK ORTHODOX	1	NR	NR	-	-
263 INT FOURSQ GOS	1	9	11*	-	-
283 LUTH—MO SYNOD	1	301	454	.3	.7
355 PRESB CH (USA)	1	77	95*	.1	.2
403 SALVATION ARMY	1	60	64	-	.1
413 S.D.A.	1	53	65*	-	.1
419 SO BAPT CONV	2	73	90*	.1	.1
435 UNITARIAN-UNIV	1	524	694	.5	1.1
443 UN C OF CHRIST	12	3,466	4,266*	3.2	6.8
449 UN METHODIST	12	3,020	3,717*	2.8	5.9
496 JEWISH EST[1]	3	NA	2,880	2.2	4.6
497 BLACK BAPT EST[2]	NA	159	196*	.1	.3
ESSEX	**16**	**510**	**2,393***	**37.4**	**100.0**
081 CATHOLIC	3	NA	1,574	24.6	65.8
081d LATIN	3	NA	1,574	24.6	65.8
151 L-D SAINTS	1	NA	170	2.7	7.1
176 CCC, NOT NAT'L	1	13	16*	.2	.7
193 EPISCOPAL	3	82	111	1.7	4.6
443 UN C OF CHRIST	2	100	126*	2.0	5.3
449 UN METHODIST	6	315	396*	6.2	16.5
FRANKLIN	**55**	**4,439**	**22,528***	**56.3**	**100.0**
019 AMER BAPT USA	5	642	838*	2.1	3.7
053 ASSEMB OF GOD	2	234	419	1.0	1.9
081 CATHOLIC	13	NA	16,462	41.2	73.1
081d LATIN	13	NA	16,462	41.2	73.1
165 CH OF NAZARENE	1	56	68	.2	.3
176 CCC, NOT NAT'L	1	23	30*	.1	.1
193 EPISCOPAL	6	390	653	1.6	2.9
356 PRESB CH AMER	1	73	117	.3	.5
413 S.D.A.	1	31	40*	.1	.2

County and Denomination	Number of churches	Communicant, confirmed, full members	Total adherents Number	Percent of total population	Percent of total adherents
443 UN C OF CHRIST	7	532	694*	1.7	3.1
449 UN METHODIST	17	2,458	3,207*	8.0	14.2
496 JEWISH EST[1]	1	NA	0	-	-
GRAND ISLE	**11**	**538**	**2,695***	**50.7**	**100.0**
081 CATHOLIC	5	NA	1,888	35.5	70.1
081d LATIN	5	NA	1,888	35.5	70.1
193 EPISCOPAL	1	13	17	.3	.6
443 UN C OF CHRIST	1	228	291*	5.5	10.8
449 UN METHODIST	4	297	379*	7.1	14.1
496 JEWISH EST[1]	0	NA	120	2.3	4.5
LAMOILLE	**32**	**1,906**	**4,184***	**21.2**	**100.0**
001 ADVENT CHR CH	3	118	149*	.8	3.6
053 ASSEMB OF GOD	1	45	80	.4	1.9
081 CATHOLIC	6	NA	1,490	7.6	35.6
081d LATIN	6	NA	1,490	7.6	35.6
151 L-D SAINTS	1	NA	154	.8	3.7
165 CH OF NAZARENE	3	195	352	1.8	8.4
193 EPISCOPAL	1	109	148	.7	3.5
259 IFCA	1	NR	NR	-	-
263 INT FOURSQ GOS	1	33	42*	.2	1.0
286 E.PA MENNONITE	1	12	15*	.1	.4
413 S.D.A.	1	28	35*	.2	.8
443 UN C OF CHRIST	8	566	712*	3.6	17.0
449 UN METHODIST	5	800	1,007*	5.1	24.1
ORANGE	**54**	**3,224**	**7,212***	**27.6**	**100.0**
019 AMER BAPT USA	3	365	468*	1.8	6.5
081 CATHOLIC	8	NA	2,200	8.4	30.5
081d LATIN	8	NA	2,200	8.4	30.5
089 CHR & MISS AL	1	42	87	.3	1.2
111 CH CR,SCIENTST	1	NR	NR	-	-
151 L-D SAINTS	1	NA	261	1.0	3.6
176 CCC, NOT NAT'L	1	14	18*	.1	.2
179 CONSRV BAPT	1	NR	NR	-	-
193 EPISCOPAL	2	153	248	.9	3.4
203 EVAN FREE CH	1	52	95	.4	1.3
226 FRIENDS-USA	1	1	5	-	.1
226d FGC & FUM	1	1	5	-	.1
355 PRESB CH (USA)	1	47	60*	.2	.8
413 S.D.A.	2	68	87*	.3	1.2
419 SO BAPT CONV	2	216	277*	1.1	3.8
443 UN C OF CHRIST	17	1,604	2,057*	7.9	28.5
449 UN METHODIST	11	662	849*	3.2	11.8
498 INDEP.CHARIS.[3]	1	NA	500	1.9	6.9
ORLEANS	**53**	**2,697**	**10,548***	**43.9**	**100.0**
019 AMER BAPT USA	2	144	185*	.8	1.8
053 ASSEMB OF GOD	2	101	155	.6	1.5
081 CATHOLIC	11	NA	6,640	27.6	63.0
081d LATIN	11	NA	6,640	27.6	63.0
111 CH CR,SCIENTST	1	NR	NR	-	-
127 CH GOD (CLEVE)	1	40	51*	.2	.5
151 L-D SAINTS	1	NA	203	.8	1.9
165 CH OF NAZARENE	2	81	121	.5	1.1
167 CHS OF CHRIST	1	17	30	.1	.3
193 EPISCOPAL	1	130	307	1.3	2.9
203 EVAN FREE CH	1	21	40	.2	.4
226 FRIENDS-USA	1	1	35	.1	.3
226d FGC & FUM	1	1	35	.1	.3
259 IFCA	1	NR	NR	-	-
355 PRESB CH (USA)	1	72	92*	.4	.9
413 S.D.A.	1	27	35*	.1	.3
435 UNITARIAN-UNIV	1	51	71	.3	.7
443 UN C OF CHRIST	14	1,113	1,429*	5.9	13.5
449 UN METHODIST	11	899	1,154*	4.8	10.9
RUTLAND	**84**	**6,816**	**28,740***	**46.2**	**100.0**
019 AMER BAPT USA	7	1,071	1,326*	2.1	4.6
053 ASSEMB OF GOD	1	60	114	.2	.4
081 CATHOLIC	22	NA	19,188	30.9	66.8
081d LATIN	22	NA	19,188	30.9	66.8
089 CHR & MISS AL	1	33	73	.1	.3
097 CHR CHS&CHS CR	1	40	50*	.1	.2
111 CH CR,SCIENTST	2	NR	NR	-	-
151 L-D SAINTS	1	NA	181	.3	.6
167 CHS OF CHRIST	1	6	7	-	-
176 CCC, NOT NAT'L	4	229	284*	.5	1.0
193 EPISCOPAL	7	656	1,107	1.8	3.9
207 E.L.C.A.	2	420	518*	.8	1.8
226 FRIENDS-USA	1	22	27*	-	.1
226d FGC & FUM	1	22	27*	-	.1
246 GREEK ORTHODOX	1	NR	NR	-	-
259 IFCA	1	NR	NR	-	-

NA–Not applicable NR–Not reported *Total adherents estimated from known number of communicant, confirmed, full members. - Represents a percent less than 0.1. Percentages may not total due to rounding.
[1] See Appendix E [2] See Appendix F [3] See Appendix G Lines in *italic* represent a breakdown of Catholic rites or Friends affiliations. They are included in their respective denominational total.

Table 4. Churches and Church Membership by County and Denomination: 1990

County and Denomination	Number of churches	Communicant, confirmed, full members	Total adherents Number	Percent of total population	Percent of total adherents
283 LUTH—MO SYNOD	1	30	40	.1	.1
355 PRESB CH (USA)	1	42	52*	.1	.2
403 SALVATION ARMY	1	26	31	-	.1
413 S.D.A.	1	69	85*	.1	.3
419 SO BAPT CONV	1	36	45*	.1	.2
435 UNITARIAN-UNIV	1	56	76	.1	.3
443 UN C OF CHRIST	11	1,988	2,461*	4.0	8.6
449 UN METHODIST	12	1,980	2,451*	3.9	8.5
467 WESLEYAN	2	52	74	.1	.3
496 JEWISH EST[1]	1	NA	550	.9	1.9
WASHINGTON	**75**	**7,039**	**22,415***	**40.8**	**100.0**
019 AMER BAPT USA	4	348	436*	.8	1.9
053 ASSEMB OF GOD	1	82	150	.3	.7
081 CATHOLIC	11	NA	12,145	22.1	54.2
081d LATIN	11	NA	12,145	22.1	54.2
089 CHR & MISS AL	3	40	168	.3	.7
111 CH CR,SCIENTST	2	NR	NR	-	-
145 CH GOD PROPHCY	2	54	68*	.1	.3
151 L-D SAINTS	1	NA	343	.6	1.5
167 CHS OF CHRIST	2	70	97	.2	.4
176 CCC, NOT NAT'L	1	17	21*	-	.1
193 EPISCOPAL	3	514	886	1.6	4.0
203 EVAN FREE CH	2	40	122	.2	.5
207 E.L.C.A.	1	70	100	.2	.4
226 FRIENDS-USA	1	41	51*	.1	.2
226d FGC & FUM	1	41	51*	.1	.2
355 PRESB CH (USA)	2	330	413*	.8	1.8
403 SALVATION ARMY	1	44	48	.1	.2
413 S.D.A.	1	116	145*	.3	.6
419 SO BAPT CONV	2	135	169*	.3	.8
435 UNITARIAN-UNIV	5	368	537	1.0	2.4
443 UN C OF CHRIST	12	1,769	2,216*	4.0	9.9
449 UN METHODIST	17	2,925	3,664*	6.7	16.3
469 WELS	1	76	136	.2	.6
496 JEWISH EST[1]	0	NA	500	.9	2.2
WINDHAM	**67**	**5,459**	**13,289***	**32.0**	**100.0**
001 ADVENT CHR CH	1	141	178*	.4	1.3
019 AMER BAPT USA	15	1,274	1,604*	3.9	12.1
053 ASSEMB OF GOD	2	92	146	.4	1.1
081 CATHOLIC	10	NA	5,936	14.3	44.7
081d LATIN	10	NA	5,936	14.3	44.7
089 CHR & MISS AL	1	41	53	.1	.4
097 CHR CHS&CHS CR	1	20	25*	.1	.2
111 CH CR,SCIENTST	1	NR	NR	-	-
151 L-D SAINTS	1	NA	146	.4	1.1
167 CHS OF CHRIST	1	18	35	.1	.3
176 CCC, NOT NAT'L	1	48	60*	.1	.5
179 CONSRV BAPT	1	NR	NR	-	-
193 EPISCOPAL	3	526	793	1.9	6.0
207 E.L.C.A.	1	256	334	.8	2.5
226 FRIENDS-USA	1	54	68*	.2	.5
226d FGC & FUM	1	54	68*	.2	.5
413 S.D.A.	2	101	127*	.3	1.0
435 UNITARIAN-UNIV	1	91	113	.3	.9
443 UN C OF CHRIST	20	2,484	3,127*	7.5	23.5
449 UN METHODIST	4	313	394*	.9	3.0
496 JEWISH EST[1]	0	NA	150	.4	1.1
WINDSOR	**90**	**7,142**	**21,188***	**39.2**	**100.0**
001 ADVENT CHR CH	1	58	72*	.1	.3
019 AMER BAPT USA	5	745	928*	1.7	4.4
053 ASSEMB OF GOD	4	160	422	.8	2.0
081 CATHOLIC	13	NA	11,428	21.1	53.9
081d LATIN	13	NA	11,428	21.1	53.9
111 CH CR,SCIENTST	2	NR	NR	-	-
127 CH GOD (CLEVE)	1	44	55*	.1	.3
151 L-D SAINTS	1	NA	284	.5	1.3
167 CHS OF CHRIST	2	201	250	.5	1.2
176 CCC, NOT NAT'L	2	32	40*	.1	.2
193 EPISCOPAL	8	735	1,193	2.2	5.6
203 EVAN FREE CH	1	130	130	.2	.6
226 FRIENDS-USA	2	9	26	-	.1
226d FGC & FUM	2	9	26	-	.1
259 IFCA	1	NR	NR	-	-
263 INT FOURSQ GOS	1	31	39*	.1	.2
285 MENNONITE CH	3	173	280	.5	1.3
331 ORTH CH IN AM	1	NR	NR	-	-
349 PENT HOLINESS	1	5	6*	-	-
419 SO BAPT CONV	2	173	216*	.4	1.0
435 UNITARIAN-UNIV	6	311	417	.8	2.0
443 UN C OF CHRIST	20	2,604	3,245*	6.0	15.3
449 UN METHODIST	13	1,731	2,157*	4.0	10.2

County and Denomination	Number of churches	Communicant, confirmed, full members	Total adherents Number	Percent of total population	Percent of total adherents
VIRGINIA					
THE STATE.....	7,490	1,899,605	2,966,083*	47.9	100.0
ACCOMACK	**92**	**13,776**	**17,700***	**55.8**	**100.0**
053 ASSEMB OF GOD	1	42	68	.2	.4
081 CATHOLIC	3	NA	711	2.2	4.0
081d LATIN	3	NA	711	2.2	4.0
093 CHR CH (DISC)	1	46	74	.2	.4
127 CH GOD (CLEVE)	2	83	102*	.3	.6
167 CHS OF CHRIST	3	77	104	.3	.6
193 EPISCOPAL	4	370	397	1.3	2.2
283 LUTH—MO SYNOD	1	46	62	.2	.4
353 CHR BRETHREN	1	60	100	.3	.6
355 PRESB CH (USA)	5	270	331*	1.0	1.9
413 S.D.A.	1	41	50*	.2	.3
419 SO BAPT CONV	18	3,336	4,091*	12.9	23.1
449 UN METHODIST	49	6,686	8,200*	25.9	46.3
467 WESLEYAN	3	36	120	.4	.7
497 BLACK BAPT EST[2]	NA	2,683	3,290*	10.4	18.6
ALBEMARLE-CHARLOTTES	**115**	**34,675**	**50,015***	**46.1**	**100.0**
019 AMER BAPT USA	2	800	963*	.9	1.9
053 ASSEMB OF GOD	1	139	225	.2	.4
061 BEACHY AMISH	1	32	39*	-	.1
081 CATHOLIC	5	NA	5,301	4.9	10.6
081d LATIN	5	NA	5,301	4.9	10.6
089 CHR & MISS AL	1	47	88	.1	.2
093 CHR CH (DISC)	2	310	464	.4	.9
097 CHR CHS&CHS CR	3	1,350	1,625*	1.5	3.2
111 CH CR,SCIENTST	1	NR	NR	-	-
127 CH GOD (CLEVE)	3	372	448*	.4	.9
151 L-D SAINTS	2	NA	510	.5	1.0
157 CH OF BRETHREN	4	423	509*	.5	1.0
165 CH OF NAZARENE	1	112	134	.1	.3
167 CHS OF CHRIST	1	150	160	.1	.3
193 EPISCOPAL	13	3,014	4,467	4.1	8.9
207 E.L.C.A.	2	632	892	.8	1.8
216 EVAN PRESBY CH	1	51	52	-	.1
223 FREE WILL BAPT	1	110	132*	.1	.3
226 FRIENDS-USA	1	67	81*	.1	.2
226d FGC & FUM	1	67	81*	.1	.2
246 GREEK ORTHODOX	1	NR	NR	-	-
263 INT FOURSQ GOS	1	36	43*	-	.1
283 LUTH—MO SYNOD	1	266	346	.3	.7
285 MENNONITE CH	1	66	96	.1	.2
349 PENT HOLINESS	1	73	88*	.1	.2
355 PRESB CH (USA)	7	2,951	3,552*	3.3	7.1
356 PRESB CH AMER	1	979	1,505	1.4	3.0
403 SALVATION ARMY	1	158	165	.2	.3
413 S.D.A.	3	181	218*	.2	.4
419 SO BAPT CONV	31	11,366	13,682*	12.6	27.4
435 UNITARIAN-UNIV	1	287	441	.4	.9
449 UN METHODIST	19	5,945	7,157*	6.6	14.3
467 WESLEYAN	1	101	241	.2	.5
496 JEWISH EST[1]	1	NA	785	.7	1.6
497 BLACK BAPT EST[2]	NA	4,657	5,606*	5.2	11.2
ALLEGHANY-CLF FR-COV	**73**	**12,694**	**16,092***	**64.8**	**100.0**
001 ADVENT CHR CH	3	348	421*	1.7	2.6
019 AMER BAPT USA	3	794	961*	3.9	6.0
053 ASSEMB OF GOD	2	104	146	.6	.9
055 AS REF PRES CH	2	451	523	2.1	3.3
081 CATHOLIC	2	NA	407	1.6	2.5
081d LATIN	2	NA	407	1.6	2.5
093 CHR CH (DISC)	3	289	404	1.6	2.5
127 CH GOD (CLEVE)	1	51	62*	.2	.4
145 CH GOD PROPHCY	6	248	300*	1.2	1.9
151 L-D SAINTS	1	NA	173	.7	1.1
157 CH OF BRETHREN	1	29	35*	.1	.2
165 CH OF NAZARENE	1	85	97	.4	.6
167 CHS OF CHRIST	1	50	60	.2	.4
193 EPISCOPAL	2	161	200	.8	1.2
207 E.L.C.A.	1	30	43	.2	.3
259 IFCA	1	NR	NR	-	-
349 PENT HOLINESS	1	14	17*	.1	.1
355 PRESB CH (USA)	10	2,153	2,605*	10.5	16.2
403 SALVATION ARMY	1	79	80	.3	.5
419 SO BAPT CONV	10	2,781	3,365*	13.5	20.9
449 UN METHODIST	20	4,574	5,534*	22.3	34.4
467 WESLEYAN	1	53	175	.7	1.1
497 BLACK BAPT EST[2]	NA	400	484*	1.9	3.0
AMELIA	**25**	**3,117**	**3,920***	**44.6**	**100.0**
081 CATHOLIC	1	NA	48	.5	1.2

NA—Not applicable   NR—Not reported   *Total adherents estimated from known number of communicant, confirmed, full members.   - Represents a percent less than 0.1.   Percentages may not total due to rounding.
[1]See Appendix E   [2]See Appendix F   [3]See Appendix G   Lines in *italic* represent a breakdown of Catholic rites or Friends affiliations. They are included in their respective denominational total.

Table 4. Churches and Church Membership by County and Denomination: 1990

County and Denomination	Number of churches	Communicant, confirmed, full members	Total adherents Number	Percent of total population	Percent of total adherents
081d *LATIN*	*1*	*NA*	*48*	*.5*	*1.2*
093 CHR CH (DISC)	1	18	28	.3	.7
127 CH GOD (CLEVE)	1	62	78*	.9	2.0
145 CH GOD PROPHCY	1	41	51*	.6	1.3
193 EPISCOPAL	1	71	88	1.0	2.2
283 LUTH—MO SYNOD	1	34	40	.5	1.0
285 MENNONITE CH	1	120	120	1.4	3.1
355 PRESB CH (USA)	6	288	360*	4.1	9.2
419 SO BAPT CONV	6	976	1,221*	13.9	31.1
449 UN METHODIST	6	541	677*	7.7	17.3
497 BLACK BAPT EST[2]	NA	966	1,209*	13.8	30.8
AMHERST	**45**	**10,813**	**13,433***	**47.0**	**100.0**
093 CHR CH (DISC)	2	337	427	1.5	3.2
097 CHR CHS&CHS CR	1	447	544*	1.9	4.0
127 CH GOD (CLEVE)	1	67	82*	.3	.6
193 EPISCOPAL	4	221	420	1.5	3.1
349 PENT HOLINESS	1	22	27*	.1	.2
355 PRESB CH (USA)	4	622	757*	2.6	5.6
419 SO BAPT CONV	17	4,426	5,384*	18.8	40.1
449 UN METHODIST	15	2,928	3,562*	12.5	26.5
496 JEWISH EST[1]	0	NA	110	.4	.8
497 BLACK BAPT EST[2]	NA	1,743	2,120*	7.4	15.8
APPOMATTOX	**33**	**6,479**	**8,440***	**68.6**	**100.0**
053 ASSEMB OF GOD	1	34	58	.5	.7
081 CATHOLIC	1	NA	73	.6	.9
081d *LATIN*	*1*	*NA*	*73*	*.6*	*.9*
127 CH GOD (CLEVE)	1	70	86*	.7	1.0
145 CH GOD PROPHCY	1	41	51*	.4	.6
193 EPISCOPAL	1	104	140	1.1	1.7
349 PENT HOLINESS	2	64	79*	.6	.9
355 PRESB CH (USA)	3	271	334*	2.7	4.0
413 S.D.A.	1	73	90*	.7	1.1
419 SO BAPT CONV	13	3,635	4,482*	36.4	53.1
449 UN METHODIST	8	1,511	1,863*	15.1	22.1
497 BLACK BAPT EST[2]	NA	676	834*	6.8	9.9
499 INDEP.NON-CHAR[3]	1	NA	350	2.8	4.1
ARLINGTON-ALEXANDRIA	**164**	**61,088**	**117,898***	**41.8**	**100.0**
005 AME ZION	3	1,548	1,662	.6	1.4
019 AMER BAPT USA	2	700	800*	.3	.7
053 ASSEMB OF GOD	5	962	1,622	.6	1.4
081 CATHOLIC	11	NA	29,682	10.5	25.2
081d *LATIN*	*11*	*NA*	*29,682*	*10.5*	*25.2*
089 CHR & MISS AL	4	119	287	.1	.2
093 CHR CH (DISC)	2	348	439	.2	.4
097 CHR CHS&CHS CR	1	0	0*	-	-
111 CH CR,SCIENTST	3	NR	NR	-	-
123 CH GOD (ANDER)	2	45	45	-	-
127 CH GOD (CLEVE)	4	907	1,036*	.4	.9
145 CH GOD PROPHCY	1	41	47*	-	-
151 L-D SAINTS	7	NA	3,090	1.1	2.6
157 CH OF BRETHREN	1	124	142*	.1	.1
165 CH OF NAZARENE	3	140	254	.1	.2
167 CHS OF CHRIST	2	291	367	.1	.3
193 EPISCOPAL	19	9,051	11,725	4.2	9.9
207 E.L.C.A.	7	2,675	3,611	1.3	3.1
216 EVAN PRESBY CH	1	217	221	.1	.2
221 FREE METHODIST	1	46	54	-	-
223 FREE WILL BAPT	1	94	107*	-	.1
226 FRIENDS-USA	1	90	103*	-	.1
226c *FGC*	*1*	*90*	*103**	*-*	*.1*
283 LUTH—MO SYNOD	3	1,231	1,582	.6	1.3
331 ORTH CH IN AM	1	NR	NR	-	-
349 PENT HOLINESS	1	22	25*	-	-
353 CHR BRETHREN	1	29	58	-	-
355 PRESB CH (USA)	17	5,745	6,565*	2.3	5.6
356 PRESB CH AMER	5	136	142	.1	.1
397 ROMANIAN ORTH	1	NR	NR	-	-
403 SALVATION ARMY	2	359	421	.1	.4
413 S.D.A.	1	100	114*	-	.1
419 SO BAPT CONV	21	10,144	11,591*	4.1	9.8
435 UNITARIAN-UNIV	2	1,142	1,709	.6	1.4
443 UN C OF CHRIST	2	848	969*	.3	.8
449 UN METHODIST	21	10,991	12,559*	4.5	10.7
467 WESLEYAN	2	146	116	-	.1
496 JEWISH EST[1]	3	NA	12,130	4.3	10.3
497 BLACK BAPT EST[2]	NA	12,797	14,623*	5.2	12.4
AUGUSTA-STAUN-WAYNES	**197**	**41,864**	**55,595***	**56.9**	**100.0**
001 ADVENT CHR CH	2	69	84*	.1	.2
019 AMER BAPT USA	1	50	61*	.1	.1
053 ASSEMB OF GOD	2	107	294	.3	.5
055 AS REF PRES CH	2	429	490	.5	.9
061 BEACHY AMISH	2	169	206*	.2	.4

County and Denomination	Number of churches	Communicant, confirmed, full members	Total adherents Number	Percent of total population	Percent of total adherents
081 CATHOLIC	2	NA	2,073	2.1	3.7
081d *LATIN*	*2*	*NA*	*2,073*	*2.1*	*3.7*
089 CHR & MISS AL	1	151	384	.4	.7
097 CHR CHS&CHS CR	4	904	1,103*	1.1	2.0
111 CH CR,SCIENTST	1	NR	NR	-	-
123 CH GOD (ANDER)	1	120	120	.1	.2
127 CH GOD (CLEVE)	8	467	570*	.6	1.0
145 CH GOD PROPHCY	3	124	151*	.2	.3
151 L-D SAINTS	2	NA	570	.6	1.0
157 CH OF BRETHREN	16	2,926	3,571*	3.7	6.4
165 CH OF NAZARENE	4	350	685	.7	1.2
167 CHS OF CHRIST	2	278	361	.4	.6
193 EPISCOPAL	4	826	1,079	1.1	1.9
207 E.L.C.A.	13	2,436	3,028	3.1	5.4
221 FREE METHODIST	1	176	176	.2	.3
263 INT FOURSQ GOS	2	425	519*	.5	.9
283 LUTH—MO SYNOD	1	362	471	.5	.8
285 MENNONITE CH	8	825	1,139	1.2	2.0
339 PENT CH OF GOD	1	35	77	.1	.1
349 PENT HOLINESS	3	256	312*	.3	.6
353 CHR BRETHREN	1	50	55	.1	.1
355 PRESB CH (USA)	26	7,119	8,689*	8.9	15.6
356 PRESB CH AMER	1	52	72	.1	.1
403 SALVATION ARMY	2	316	339	.3	.6
413 S.D.A.	4	758	925*	.9	1.7
419 SO BAPT CONV	17	7,230	8,825*	9.0	15.9
435 UNITARIAN-UNIV	1	57	99	.1	.2
438 UN BRETH IN CR	3	476	476	.5	.9
443 UN C OF CHRIST	2	239	292*	.3	.5
449 UN METHODIST	50	12,300	15,013*	15.4	27.0
467 WESLEYAN	2	130	195	.2	.4
496 JEWISH EST[1]	1	NA	375	.4	.7
497 BLACK BAPT EST[2]	NA	1,652	2,016*	2.1	3.6
499 INDEP.NON-CHAR[3]	1	NA	700	.7	1.3
BATH	**22**	**2,253**	**2,757***	**57.4**	**100.0**
001 ADVENT CHR CH	2	26	31*	.6	1.1
081 CATHOLIC	1	NA	47	1.0	1.7
081d *LATIN*	*1*	*NA*	*47*	*1.0*	*1.7*
157 CH OF BRETHREN	1	129	154*	3.2	5.6
193 EPISCOPAL	1	68	100	2.1	3.6
349 PENT HOLINESS	1	170	203*	4.2	7.4
355 PRESB CH (USA)	5	458	547*	11.4	19.8
419 SO BAPT CONV	3	575	687*	14.3	24.9
449 UN METHODIST	8	827	988*	20.6	35.8
BEDFORD-BEDFORD CITY	**130**	**17,775**	**22,982***	**44.4**	**100.0**
019 AMER BAPT USA	1	35	43*	.1	.2
053 ASSEMB OF GOD	2	74	101	.2	.4
081 CATHOLIC	20	NA	764	1.5	3.3
081d *LATIN*	*20*	*NA*	*764*	*1.5*	*3.3*
089 CHR & MISS AL	1	63	74	.1	.3
093 CHR CH (DISC)	1	190	409	.8	1.8
097 CHR CHS&CHS CR	1	57	70*	.1	.3
123 CH GOD (ANDER)	2	18	53	.1	.2
127 CH GOD (CLEVE)	3	192	235*	.5	1.0
145 CH GOD PROPHCY	3	124	152*	.3	.7
151 L-D SAINTS	1	NA	78	.2	.3
157 CH OF BRETHREN	3	290	355*	.7	1.5
167 CHS OF CHRIST	1	38	48	.1	.2
193 EPISCOPAL	4	497	612	1.2	2.7
207 E.L.C.A.	1	0	0	-	-
223 FREE WILL BAPT	2	133	163*	.3	.7
339 PENT CH OF GOD	1	34	77	.1	.3
349 PENT HOLINESS	1	172	211*	.4	.9
355 PRESB CH (USA)	7	656	803*	1.6	3.5
361 PRIM BAPT ASCS	2	19	23*	-	.1
375 REF EPISCOPAL	1	12	19	-	.1
413 S.D.A.	1	49	60*	.1	.3
419 SO BAPT CONV	34	9,167	11,223*	21.7	48.8
449 UN METHODIST	35	4,514	5,526*	10.7	24.0
467 WESLEYAN	2	234	405	.8	1.8
497 BLACK BAPT EST[2]	NA	1,207	1,478*	2.9	6.4
BLAND	**46**	**2,465**	**3,053***	**46.9**	**100.0**
089 CHR & MISS AL	1	0	50	.8	1.6
093 CHR CH (DISC)	2	98	161	2.5	5.3
097 CHR CHS&CHS CR	2	78	94*	1.4	3.1
127 CH GOD (CLEVE)	3	270	324*	5.0	10.6
145 CH GOD PROPHCY	1	41	49*	.8	1.6
207 E.L.C.A.	3	48	59	.9	1.9
349 PENT HOLINESS	3	92	110*	1.7	3.6
355 PRESB CH (USA)	2	58	70*	1.1	2.3
419 SO BAPT CONV	5	376	451*	6.9	14.8
449 UN METHODIST	24	1,404	1,685*	25.9	55.2

NA–Not applicable   NR–Not reported   *Total adherents estimated from known number of communicant, confirmed, full members.   - Represents a percent less than 0.1.   Percentages may not total due to rounding.

[1]See Appendix E   [2]See Appendix F   [3]See Appendix G   Lines in *italic* represent a breakdown of Catholic rites or Friends affiliations. They are included in their respective denominational total.

Table 4. Churches and Church Membership by County and Denomination: 1990

County and Denomination	Number of churches	Communicant, confirmed, full members	Total adherents Number	Percent of total population	Percent of total adherents
BOTETOURT	**56**	**9,535**	**11,946***	**47.8**	**100.0**
053 ASSEMB OF GOD	1	16	26	.1	.2
097 CHR CHS&CHS CR	1	90	109*	.4	.9
145 CH GOD PROPHCY	2	83	101*	.4	.8
157 CH OF BRETHREN	9	1,009	1,222*	4.9	10.2
167 CHS OF CHRIST	1	16	19	.1	.2
193 EPISCOPAL	2	174	276	1.1	2.3
207 E.L.C.A.	3	432	566	2.3	4.7
355 PRESB CH (USA)	5	510	618*	2.5	5.2
356 PRESB CH AMER	1	35	62	.2	.5
419 SO BAPT CONV	18	5,526	6,692*	26.8	56.0
449 UN METHODIST	13	1,305	1,580*	6.3	13.2
496 JEWISH EST[1]	0	NA	264	1.1	2.2
497 BLACK BAPT EST[2]	NA	339	411*	1.6	3.4
BRUNSWICK	**42**	**7,932**	**10,098***	**63.2**	**100.0**
005 AME ZION	1	113	162	1.0	1.6
053 ASSEMB OF GOD	3	228	491	3.1	4.9
081 CATHOLIC	1	NA	9	.1	.1
081d LATIN	1	NA	9	.1	.1
093 CHR CH (DISC)	3	159	281	1.8	2.8
193 EPISCOPAL	6	401	545	3.4	5.4
355 PRESB CH (USA)	3	161	197*	1.2	2.0
419 SO BAPT CONV	8	1,411	1,728*	10.8	17.1
449 UN METHODIST	17	2,258	2,765*	17.3	27.4
497 BLACK BAPT EST[2]	NA	3,201	3,920*	24.5	38.8
BUCHANAN	**63**	**5,865**	**7,531***	**24.0**	**100.0**
081 CATHOLIC	1	NA	47	.2	.6
081d LATIN	1	NA	47	.2	.6
097 CHR CHS&CHS CR	7	1,240	1,550*	4.9	20.6
127 CH GOD (CLEVE)	2	177	221*	.7	2.9
151 L-D SAINTS	1	NA	109	.3	1.4
167 CHS OF CHRIST	4	100	128	.4	1.7
223 FREE WILL BAPT	1	20	25*	.1	.3
325 OLD REG BAPT	14	1,066	1,333*	4.3	17.7
355 PRESB CH (USA)	6	319	399*	1.3	5.3
361 PRIM BAPT ASCS	12	445	556*	1.8	7.4
419 SO BAPT CONV	8	1,915	2,394*	7.6	31.8
449 UN METHODIST	6	555	694*	2.2	9.2
467 WESLEYAN	1	28	75	.2	1.0
BUCKINGHAM	**43**	**6,065**	**7,494***	**58.2**	**100.0**
081 CATHOLIC	1	NA	74	.6	1.0
081d LATIN	1	NA	74	.6	1.0
097 CHR CHS&CHS CR	2	65	79*	.6	1.1
127 CH GOD (CLEVE)	1	9	11*	.1	.1
151 L-D SAINTS	1	NA	41	.3	.5
165 CH OF NAZARENE	1	35	24	.2	.3
193 EPISCOPAL	1	42	43	.3	.6
349 PENT HOLINESS	1	60	73*	.6	1.0
355 PRESB CH (USA)	4	206	252*	2.0	3.4
419 SO BAPT CONV	18	2,848	3,478*	27.0	46.4
449 UN METHODIST	13	999	1,220*	9.5	16.3
497 BLACK BAPT EST[2]	NA	1,801	2,199*	17.1	29.3
CAMPBELL-LYNCHBURG	**156**	**47,102**	**77,948***	**68.6**	**100.0**
019 AMER BAPT USA	1	348	425*	.4	.5
053 ASSEMB OF GOD	2	180	436	.4	.6
075 BRETHREN IN CR	1	27	27	-	-
081 CATHOLIC	3	NA	3,530	3.1	4.5
081d LATIN	3	NA	3,530	3.1	4.5
093 CHR CH (DISC)	7	1,996	2,844	2.5	3.6
097 CHR CHS&CHS CR	2	275	336*	.3	.4
111 CH CR,SCIENTST	1	NR	NR	-	-
123 CH GOD (ANDER)	2	109	109	.1	.1
127 CH GOD (CLEVE)	2	152	185*	.2	.2
145 CH GOD PROPHCY	4	166	203*	.2	.3
151 L-D SAINTS	2	NA	604	.5	.8
157 CH OF BRETHREN	1	101	123*	.1	.2
165 CH OF NAZARENE	1	153	195	.2	.3
167 CHS OF CHRIST	2	158	206	.2	.3
193 EPISCOPAL	6	1,809	2,377	2.1	3.0
203 EVAN FREE CH	1	71	90	.1	.1
207 E.L.C.A.	2	781	1,016	.9	1.3
246 GREEK ORTHODOX	1	NR	NR	-	-
263 INT FOURSQ GOS	2	117	143*	.1	.2
283 LUTH—MO SYNOD	2	78	86	.1	.1
285 MENNONITE CH	1	112	206	.2	.3
325 OLD REG BAPT	1	17	21*	-	-
349 PENT HOLINESS	5	336	410*	.4	.5
355 PRESB CH (USA)	14	4,441	5,419*	4.8	7.0
403 SALVATION ARMY	1	101	120	.1	.2
413 S.D.A.	1	153	187*	.2	.2
419 SO BAPT CONV	36	16,436	20,056*	17.7	25.7
435 UNITARIAN-UNIV	1	78	105	.1	.1
443 UN C OF CHRIST	1	12	15*	-	-
449 UN METHODIST	43	12,763	15,574*	13.7	20.0
467 WESLEYAN	4	249	556	.5	.7
496 JEWISH EST[1]	1	NA	165	.1	.2
497 BLACK BAPT EST[2]	NA	5,883	7,179*	6.3	9.2
499 INDEP.NON-CHAR[3]	2	NA	15,000	13.2	19.2
CAROLINE	**24**	**7,101**	**9,119***	**47.5**	**100.0**
081 CATHOLIC	1	NA	117	.6	1.3
081d LATIN	1	NA	117	.6	1.3
093 CHR CH (DISC)	1	17	40	.2	.4
193 EPISCOPAL	2	64	121	.6	1.3
223 FREE WILL BAPT	1	61	77*	.4	.8
419 SO BAPT CONV	11	3,591	4,522*	23.5	49.6
449 UN METHODIST	8	887	1,117*	5.8	12.2
497 BLACK BAPT EST[2]	NA	2,481	3,125*	16.3	34.3
CARROLL-GALAX CITY	**97**	**11,233**	**14,054***	**42.2**	**100.0**
053 ASSEMB OF GOD	1	19	32	.1	.2
075 BRETHREN IN CR	1	85	95	.3	.7
081 CATHOLIC	1	NA	110	.3	.8
081d LATIN	1	NA	110	.3	.8
093 CHR CH (DISC)	8	484	933	2.8	6.6
097 CHR CHS&CHS CR	5	491	588*	1.8	4.2
127 CH GOD (CLEVE)	4	670	802*	2.4	5.7
145 CH GOD PROPHCY	2	83	99*	.3	.7
157 CH OF BRETHREN	3	378	452*	1.4	3.2
167 CHS OF CHRIST	2	122	143	.4	1.0
207 E.L.C.A.	1	238	267	.8	1.9
226 FRIENDS-USA	2	29	35*	.1	.2
226e FUM	2	29	35*	.1	.2
295 MORAV CH-SOUTH	1	102	123	.4	.9
325 OLD REG BAPT	1	11	13*	-	.1
349 PENT HOLINESS	6	447	535*	1.6	3.8
355 PRESB CH (USA)	6	397	475*	1.4	3.4
361 PRIM BAPT ASCS	6	135	162*	.5	1.2
413 S.D.A.	1	143	171*	.5	1.2
419 SO BAPT CONV	23	4,037	4,831*	14.5	34.4
443 UN C OF CHRIST	2	118	141*	.4	1.0
449 UN METHODIST	19	3,135	3,751*	11.3	26.7
467 WESLEYAN	2	109	296	.9	2.1
CHARLES CITY	**7**	**3,044**	**3,975***	**63.3**	**100.0**
019 AMER BAPT USA	1	150	185*	2.9	4.7
193 EPISCOPAL	1	106	281	4.5	7.1
355 PRESB CH (USA)	1	21	26*	.4	.7
419 SO BAPT CONV	3	1,765	2,173*	34.6	54.7
449 UN METHODIST	1	137	169*	2.7	4.3
496 JEWISH EST[1]	0	NA	76	1.2	1.9
497 BLACK BAPT EST[2]	NA	865	1,065*	17.0	26.8
CHARLOTTE	**42**	**6,927**	**8,532***	**73.0**	**100.0**
093 CHR CH (DISC)	1	60	99	.8	1.2
097 CHR CHS&CHS CR	2	412	506*	4.3	5.9
193 EPISCOPAL	1	16	22	.2	.3
215 EVAN METH CH	1	64	79*	.7	.9
355 PRESB CH (USA)	13	660	810*	6.9	9.5
419 SO BAPT CONV	13	2,967	3,643*	31.2	42.7
449 UN METHODIST	11	1,288	1,581*	13.5	18.5
497 BLACK BAPT EST[2]	NA	1,460	1,792*	15.3	21.0
CHESTERFIELD	**142**	**64,462**	**99,163***	**47.4**	**100.0**
005 AME ZION	2	148	163	.1	.2
019 AMER BAPT USA	2	553	719*	.3	.7
053 ASSEMB OF GOD	5	625	1,003	.5	1.0
081 CATHOLIC	2	NA	7,289	3.5	7.4
081d LATIN	2	NA	7,289	3.5	7.4
089 CHR & MISS AL	2	37	62	-	.1
097 CHR CHS&CHS CR	1	140	182*	.1	.2
127 CH GOD (CLEVE)	2	71	92*	-	.1
145 CH GOD PROPHCY	1	41	53*	-	.1
151 L-D SAINTS	6	NA	2,337	1.1	2.4
157 CH OF BRETHREN	1	56	73*	-	.1
165 CH OF NAZARENE	3	795	1,609	.8	1.6
167 CHS OF CHRIST	6	356	440	.2	.4
193 EPISCOPAL	7	2,264	3,117	1.5	3.1
207 E.L.C.A.	2	566	803	.4	.8
216 EVAN PRESBY CH	1	64	65	-	.1
221 FREE METHODIST	2	0	33	-	-
223 FREE WILL BAPT	1	204	265*	.1	.3
226 FRIENDS-USA	2	25	109	.1	.1
226b EFI	1	16	40	-	-
226d FGC & FUM	1	9	69	-	.1
265 INT PENT C CHR	1	40	40	-	-

NA–Not applicable NR–Not reported *Total adherents estimated from known number of communicant, confirmed, full members. - Represents a percent less than 0.1. Percentages may not total due to rounding.
[1]See Appendix E [2]See Appendix F [3]See Appendix G Lines in *italic* represent a breakdown of Catholic rites or Friends affiliations. They are included in their respective denominational total.

398

Table 4. Churches and Church Membership by County and Denomination: 1990

County and Denomination	Number of churches	Communicant, confirmed, full members	Total adherents Number	Percent of total population	Percent of total adherents
283 LUTH—MO SYNOD	2	1,177	1,465	.7	1.5
295 MORAV CH-SOUTH	1	86	114	.1	.1
349 PENT HOLINESS	4	1,098	1,427*	.7	1.4
353 CHR BRETHREN	2	36	50	-	.1
355 PRESB CH (USA)	5	1,851	2,405*	1.1	2.4
356 PRESB CH AMER	2	424	545	.3	.5
419 SO BAPT CONV	50	32,905	42,761*	20.4	43.1
435 UNITARIAN-UNIV	1	30	30	-	-
443 UN C OF CHRIST	1	156	203*	.1	.2
449 UN METHODIST	20	12,482	16,221*	7.8	16.4
496 JEWISH EST[1]	0	NA	2,920	1.4	2.9
497 BLACK BAPT EST[2]	NA	8,232	10,698*	5.1	10.8
498 INDEP.CHARIS.[3]	1	NA	600	.3	.6
499 INDEP.NON-CHAR[3]	4	NA	1,270	.6	1.3
CLARKE	**23**	**3,124**	**4,304***	**35.6**	**100.0**
019 AMER BAPT USA	1	120	147*	1.2	3.4
053 ASSEMB OF GOD	1	19	21	.2	.5
081 CATHOLIC	1	NA	450	3.7	10.5
081d LATIN	1	NA	450	3.7	10.5
127 CH GOD (CLEVE)	1	39	48*	.4	1.1
193 EPISCOPAL	4	367	489	4.0	11.4
355 PRESB CH (USA)	2	159	194*	1.6	4.5
413 S.D.A.	1	38	46*	.4	1.1
419 SO BAPT CONV	4	867	1,059*	8.8	24.6
449 UN METHODIST	8	1,262	1,541*	12.7	35.8
497 BLACK BAPT EST[2]	NA	253	309*	2.6	7.2
CRAIG	**17**	**1,475**	**1,881***	**43.0**	**100.0**
053 ASSEMB OF GOD	1	11	9	.2	.5
093 CHR CH (DISC)	5	85	189	4.3	10.0
097 CHR CHS&CHS CR	4	530	647*	14.8	34.4
145 CH GOD PROPHCY	1	41	50*	1.1	2.7
419 SO BAPT CONV	1	163	199*	4.6	10.6
449 UN METHODIST	5	645	787*	18.0	41.8
CULPEPER	**41**	**8,501**	**12,706***	**45.7**	**100.0**
053 ASSEMB OF GOD	2	283	540	1.9	4.2
081 CATHOLIC	1	NA	1,300	4.7	10.2
081d LATIN	1	NA	1,300	4.7	10.2
089 CHR & MISS AL	1	0	0	-	-
127 CH GOD (CLEVE)	1	55	70*	.3	.6
151 L-D SAINTS	1	NA	342	1.2	2.7
167 CHS OF CHRIST	1	75	91	.3	.7
193 EPISCOPAL	4	446	657	2.4	5.2
207 E.L.C.A.	2	257	333	1.2	2.6
221 FREE METHODIST	1	35	37	.1	.3
353 CHR BRETHREN	1	100	120	.4	.9
355 PRESB CH (USA)	3	425	540*	1.9	4.2
356 PRESB CH AMER	1	29	35	.1	.3
413 S.D.A.	2	93	118*	.4	.9
419 SO BAPT CONV	13	3,721	4,731*	17.0	37.2
449 UN METHODIST	7	1,809	2,300*	8.3	18.1
497 BLACK BAPT EST[2]	NA	1,173	1,492*	5.4	11.7
CUMBERLAND	**17**	**2,728**	**3,450***	**44.1**	**100.0**
053 ASSEMB OF GOD	1	204	302	3.9	8.8
081 CATHOLIC	1	NA	1	-	-
081d LATIN	1	NA	1	-	-
193 EPISCOPAL	1	58	69	.9	2.0
285 MENNONITE CH	1	26	30	.4	.9
355 PRESB CH (USA)	2	232	290*	3.7	8.4
419 SO BAPT CONV	6	754	942*	12.0	27.3
449 UN METHODIST	5	417	521*	6.7	15.1
497 BLACK BAPT EST[2]	NA	1,037	1,295*	16.5	37.5
DICKENSON	**43**	**2,488**	**3,196***	**18.1**	**100.0**
005 AME ZION	1	28	43	.2	1.3
081 CATHOLIC	1	NA	77	.4	2.4
081d LATIN	1	NA	77	.4	2.4
097 CHR CHS&CHS CR	2	80	100*	.6	3.1
127 CH GOD (CLEVE)	1	33	41*	.2	1.3
145 CH GOD PROPHCY	2	83	104*	.6	3.3
157 CH OF BRETHREN	2	204	256*	1.5	8.0
167 CHS OF CHRIST	3	100	128	.7	4.0
325 OLD REG BAPT	18	508	637*	3.6	19.9
356 PRESB CH AMER	3	148	176	1.0	5.5
361 PRIM BAPT ASCS	6	352	441*	2.5	13.8
419 SO BAPT CONV	2	698	875*	5.0	27.4
449 UN METHODIST	2	254	318*	1.8	9.9
DINWIDDIE-COL HT-PET	**88**	**27,924**	**37,032***	**49.1**	**100.0**
005 AME ZION	2	523	637	.8	1.7
011 A.W.M.C.	1	11	13*	-	-
019 AMER BAPT USA	4	2,403	2,945*	3.9	8.0

County and Denomination	Number of churches	Communicant, confirmed, full members	Total adherents Number	Percent of total population	Percent of total adherents
053 ASSEMB OF GOD	1	141	330	.4	.9
081 CATHOLIC	3	NA	1,531	2.0	4.1
081d LATIN	3	NA	1,531	2.0	4.1
093 CHR CH (DISC)	4	313	542	.7	1.5
111 CH CR,SCIENTST	1	NR	NR	-	-
145 CH GOD PROPHCY	1	83	102*	.1	.3
151 L-D SAINTS	2	NA	417	.6	1.1
165 CH OF NAZARENE	1	30	35	-	.1
167 CHS OF CHRIST	3	400	509	.7	1.4
193 EPISCOPAL	7	1,304	1,873	2.5	5.1
207 E.L.C.A.	1	378	507	.7	1.4
223 FREE WILL BAPT	1	42	51*	.1	.1
349 PENT HOLINESS	1	27	33*	-	.1
353 CHR BRETHREN	1	25	25	-	.1
355 PRESB CH (USA)	7	1,195	1,465*	1.9	4.0
356 PRESB CH AMER	1	115	127	.2	.3
375 REF EPISCOPAL	1	25	38	.1	.1
403 SALVATION ARMY	1	86	111	.1	.3
413 S.D.A.	3	527	646*	.9	1.7
419 SO BAPT CONV	15	5,426	6,650*	8.8	18.0
449 UN METHODIST	24	7,208	8,834*	11.7	23.9
496 JEWISH EST[1]	1	NA	220	.3	.6
497 BLACK BAPT EST[2]	NA	7,662	9,391*	12.5	25.4
ESSEX	**19**	**4,094**	**5,579***	**64.2**	**100.0**
053 ASSEMB OF GOD	1	40	80	.9	1.4
081 CATHOLIC	1	NA	387	4.5	6.9
081d LATIN	1	NA	387	4.5	6.9
093 CHR CH (DISC)	1	130	180	2.1	3.2
127 CH GOD (CLEVE)	1	43	53*	.6	.9
193 EPISCOPAL	4	386	478	5.5	8.6
413 S.D.A.	1	204	250*	2.9	4.5
419 SO BAPT CONV	7	1,676	2,058*	23.7	36.9
449 UN METHODIST	2	465	571*	6.6	10.2
467 WESLEYAN	1	30	147	1.7	2.6
497 BLACK BAPT EST[2]	NA	1,120	1,375*	15.8	24.6
FAIRFAX-FAIRFX-FL CH	**363**	**143,935**	**363,037***	**42.8**	**100.0**
019 AMER BAPT USA	6	1,894	2,337*	.3	.6
053 ASSEMB OF GOD	9	2,955	3,851	.5	1.1
057 BAPT GEN CONF	1	72	89*	-	-
081 CATHOLIC	29	NA	149,354	17.6	41.1
081b BYZAN RUTH	2	NA	800	.1	.2
081d LATIN	25	NA	147,874	17.4	40.7
081f MELKITE-GK	1	NA	490	.1	.1
081h UKRAINIAN	1	NA	190	-	.1
089 CHR & MISS AL	3	106	165	-	-
093 CHR CH (DISC)	6	1,651	2,267	.3	.6
097 CHR CHS&CHS CR	8	1,280	1,580*	.2	.4
105 CHRISTIAN REF	1	97	146	-	-
111 CH CR,SCIENTST	5	NR	NR	-	-
121 CH GOD (ABR)	1	20	25*	-	-
123 CH GOD (ANDER)	3	188	245	-	.1
127 CH GOD (CLEVE)	2	67	83*	-	-
151 L-D SAINTS	25	NA	8,473	1.0	2.3
157 CH OF BRETHREN	2	392	484*	.1	.1
164 CH LUTH CONF	1	19	22	-	-
165 CH OF NAZARENE	3	558	532	.1	.1
167 CHS OF CHRIST	9	1,599	2,253	.3	.6
193 EPISCOPAL	28	14,907	24,166	2.9	6.7
203 EVAN FREE CH	1	134	194	-	.1
207 E.L.C.A.	16	9,034	11,817	1.4	3.3
216 EVAN PRESBY CH	1	71	78	-	-
223 FREE WILL BAPT	1	105	130*	-	-
226 FRIENDS-USA	2	305	376*	-	.1
226d FGC & FUM	2	305	376*	-	.1
246 GREEK ORTHODOX	1	NR	NR	-	-
283 LUTH—MO SYNOD	6	3,958	5,158	.6	1.4
285 MENNONITE CH	1	53	113	-	-
329 OPEN BIBLE STD	1	NR	NR	-	-
331 ORTH CH IN AM	2	NR	NR	-	-
349 PENT HOLINESS	1	15	19*	-	-
353 CHR BRETHREN	1	17	26	-	-
355 PRESB CH (USA)	19	10,510	12,969*	1.5	3.6
356 PRESB CH AMER	14	2,838	3,364	.4	.9
361 PRIM BAPT ASCS	2	36	44*	-	-
397 ROMANIAN ORTH	1	NR	NR	-	-
403 SALVATION ARMY	2	205	210	-	.1
413 S.D.A.	8	1,398	1,725*	.2	.5
419 SO BAPT CONV	49	27,462	33,888*	4.0	9.3
435 UNITARIAN-UNIV	3	1,063	1,548	.2	.4
443 UN C OF CHRIST	5	1,847	2,279*	.3	.6
449 UN METHODIST	54	37,936	46,813*	5.5	12.9
467 WESLEYAN	8	1,449	4,048	.5	1.1
469 WELS	1	234	278	-	.1
496 JEWISH EST[1]	6	NA	3,199	.4	.9
497 BLACK BAPT EST[2]	NA	19,460	24,014*	2.8	6.6

NA–Not applicable   NR–Not reported   *Total adherents estimated from known number of communicant, confirmed, full members.   - Represents a percent less than 0.1.   Percentages may not total due to rounding.

[1]See Appendix E   [2]See Appendix F   [3]See Appendix G   Lines in *italic* represent a breakdown of Catholic rites or Friends affiliations. They are included in their respective denominational total.

Table 4. Churches and Church Membership by County and Denomination: 1990

County and Denomination	Number of churches	Communicant, confirmed, full members	Total adherents Number	Total adherents Percent of total population	Total adherents Percent of total adherents
498 INDEP.CHARIS.[3]	3	NA	1,000	.1	.3
499 INDEP.NON-CHAR[3]	12	NA	13,675	1.6	3.8
FAUQUIER	**70**	**11,793**	**20,567***	**42.2**	**100.0**
053 ASSEMB OF GOD	4	256	422	.9	2.1
061 BEACHY AMISH	1	113	144*	.3	.7
081 CATHOLIC	1	NA	3,250	6.7	15.8
081d LATIN	1	NA	3,250	6.7	15.8
097 CHR CHS&CHS CR	1	0	0*	-	-
111 CH CR,SCIENTST	1	NR	NR	-	-
151 L-D SAINTS	2	NA	1,051	2.2	5.1
157 CH OF BRETHREN	1	167	213*	.4	1.0
165 CH OF NAZARENE	1	83	177	.4	.9
167 CHS OF CHRIST	1	140	182	.4	.9
193 EPISCOPAL	9	1,256	2,006	4.1	9.8
207 E.L.C.A.	1	290	426	.9	2.1
355 PRESB CH (USA)	3	483	616*	1.3	3.0
356 PRESB CH AMER	1	142	181	.4	.9
361 PRIM BAPT ASCS	4	71	91*	.2	.4
413 S.D.A.	1	65	83*	.2	.4
419 SO BAPT CONV	17	4,247	5,414*	11.1	26.3
449 UN METHODIST	20	3,141	4,004*	8.2	19.5
497 BLACK BAPT EST[2]	NA	1,339	1,707*	3.5	8.3
499 INDEP.NON-CHAR[3]	1	NA	600	1.2	2.9
FLOYD	**53**	**3,977**	**4,919***	**41.0**	**100.0**
075 BRETHREN IN CR	1	6	13	.1	.3
081 CATHOLIC	1	NA	23	.2	.5
081d LATIN	1	NA	23	.2	.5
093 CHR CH (DISC)	2	58	95	.8	1.9
127 CH GOD (CLEVE)	2	134	162*	1.3	3.3
145 CH GOD PROPHCY	1	41	50*	.4	1.0
157 CH OF BRETHREN	13	1,377	1,669*	13.9	33.9
165 CH OF NAZARENE	1	57	104	.9	2.1
167 CHS OF CHRIST	1	42	54	.4	1.1
207 E.L.C.A.	2	135	178	1.5	3.6
349 PENT HOLINESS	4	158	191*	1.6	3.9
355 PRESB CH (USA)	3	212	257*	2.1	5.2
356 PRESB CH AMER	1	54	60	.5	1.2
361 PRIM BAPT ASCS	7	143	173*	1.4	3.5
419 SO BAPT CONV	4	682	826*	6.9	16.8
449 UN METHODIST	10	878	1,064*	8.9	21.6
FLUVANNA	**26**	**5,065**	**6,956***	**56.0**	**100.0**
081 CATHOLIC	1	NA	128	1.0	1.8
081d LATIN	1	NA	128	1.0	1.8
127 CH GOD (CLEVE)	1	22	28*	.2	.4
151 L-D SAINTS	1	NA	392	3.2	5.6
193 EPISCOPAL	2	95	108	.9	1.6
355 PRESB CH (USA)	1	56	70*	.6	1.0
419 SO BAPT CONV	12	3,099	3,889*	31.3	55.9
449 UN METHODIST	8	932	1,170*	9.4	16.8
496 JEWISH EST[1]	0	NA	90	.7	1.3
497 BLACK BAPT EST[2]	NA	861	1,081*	8.7	15.5
FRANKLIN	**106**	**14,414**	**18,335***	**46.4**	**100.0**
005 AME ZION	1	62	82	.2	.4
019 AMER BAPT USA	3	271	329*	.8	1.8
053 ASSEMB OF GOD	4	215	370	.9	2.0
081 CATHOLIC	1	NA	153	.4	.8
081d LATIN	1	NA	153	.4	.8
093 CHR CH (DISC)	4	550	916	2.3	5.0
097 CHR CHS&CHS CR	3	184	223*	.6	1.2
123 CH GOD (ANDER)	1	40	50	.1	.3
127 CH GOD (CLEVE)	1	45	55*	.1	.3
145 CH GOD PROPHCY	1	41	50*	.1	.3
151 L-D SAINTS	2	NA	331	.8	1.8
157 CH OF BRETHREN	14	1,946	2,360*	6.0	12.9
165 CH OF NAZARENE	1	35	24	.1	.1
167 CHS OF CHRIST	1	21	35	.1	.2
193 EPISCOPAL	2	158	203	.5	1.1
349 PENT HOLINESS	4	315	382*	1.0	2.1
355 PRESB CH (USA)	2	186	226*	.6	1.2
361 PRIM BAPT ASCS	11	192	233*	.6	1.3
413 S.D.A.	1	31	38*	.1	.2
419 SO BAPT CONV	23	5,668	6,874*	17.4	37.5
449 UN METHODIST	25	3,385	4,105*	10.4	22.4
467 WESLEYAN	1	31	37	.1	.2
497 BLACK BAPT EST[2]	NA	1,038	1,259*	3.2	6.9
FREDERICK-WINCHESTER	**103**	**19,667**	**33,399***	**49.4**	**100.0**
019 AMER BAPT USA	1	231	289*	.4	.9
053 ASSEMB OF GOD	6	765	1,552	2.3	4.6
075 BRETHREN IN CR	1	17	17	-	.1
081 CATHOLIC	1	NA	4,750	7.0	14.2

County and Denomination	Number of churches	Communicant, confirmed, full members	Total adherents Number	Total adherents Percent of total population	Total adherents Percent of total adherents
081d LATIN	1	NA	4,750	7.0	14.2
089 CHR & MISS AL	1	8	73	.1	.2
093 CHR CH (DISC)	3	383	639	.9	1.9
097 CHR CHS&CHS CR	5	740	924*	1.4	2.8
111 CH CR,SCIENTST	1	NR	NR	-	-
127 CH GOD (CLEVE)	1	336	420*	.6	1.3
145 CH GOD PROPHCY	1	41	51*	.1	.2
151 L-D SAINTS	1	NA	547	.8	1.6
157 CH OF BRETHREN	2	416	520*	.8	1.6
165 CH OF NAZARENE	1	119	150	.2	.4
167 CHS OF CHRIST	1	94	122	.2	.4
193 EPISCOPAL	2	576	1,010	1.5	3.0
207 E.L.C.A.	7	1,591	2,220	3.3	6.6
223 FREE WILL BAPT	1	79	99*	.1	.3
226 FRIENDS-USA	2	101	126*	.2	.4
226d FGC & FUM	2	101	126*	.2	.4
246 GREEK ORTHODOX	1	NR	NR	-	-
283 LUTH—MO SYNOD	1	91	115	.2	.3
285 MENNONITE CH	1	88	106	.2	.3
339 PENT CH OF GOD	1	10	23	-	.1
355 PRESB CH (USA)	10	2,175	2,717*	4.0	8.1
361 PRIM BAPT ASCS	1	7	9*	-	-
403 SALVATION ARMY	1	85	91	.1	.3
413 S.D.A.	1	194	242*	.4	.7
419 SO BAPT CONV	3	2,249	2,809*	4.2	8.4
435 UNITARIAN-UNIV	1	82	104	.2	.3
443 UN C OF CHRIST	2	195	244*	.4	.7
449 UN METHODIST	39	8,262	10,321*	15.3	30.9
496 JEWISH EST[1]	1	NA	145	.2	.4
497 BLACK BAPT EST[2]	NA	732	914*	1.4	2.7
499 INDEP.NON-CHAR[3]	2	NA	2,050	3.0	6.1
GILES	**69**	**6,811**	**9,355***	**57.2**	**100.0**
053 ASSEMB OF GOD	2	38	69	.4	.7
081 CATHOLIC	1	NA	207	1.3	2.2
081d LATIN	1	NA	207	1.3	2.2
093 CHR CH (DISC)	9	596	1,060	6.5	11.3
097 CHR CHS&CHS CR	3	198	237*	1.4	2.5
123 CH GOD (ANDER)	1	30	30	.2	.3
127 CH GOD (CLEVE)	2	131	157*	1.0	1.7
145 CH GOD PROPHCY	2	83	100*	.6	1.1
151 L-D SAINTS	1	NA	610	3.7	6.5
157 CH OF BRETHREN	1	0	0*	-	-
167 CHS OF CHRIST	3	34	44	.3	.5
193 EPISCOPAL	1	36	46	.3	.5
207 E.L.C.A.	3	329	402	2.5	4.3
349 PENT HOLINESS	4	441	529*	3.2	5.7
355 PRESB CH (USA)	3	157	188*	1.1	2.0
356 PRESB CH AMER	1	79	89	.5	1.0
413 S.D.A.	2	45	54*	.3	.6
419 SO BAPT CONV	6	1,467	1,759*	10.7	18.8
449 UN METHODIST	24	3,147	3,774*	23.1	40.3
GLOUCESTER	**33**	**10,356**	**15,568***	**51.7**	**100.0**
053 ASSEMB OF GOD	1	771	1,625	5.4	10.4
081 CATHOLIC	1	NA	1,150	3.8	7.4
081d LATIN	1	NA	1,150	3.8	7.4
097 CHR CHS&CHS CR	1	56	71*	.2	.5
127 CH GOD (CLEVE)	1	67	85*	.3	.5
145 CH GOD PROPHCY	1	41	52*	.2	.3
151 L-D SAINTS	1	NA	245	.8	1.6
165 CH OF NAZARENE	1	44	107	.4	.7
167 CHS OF CHRIST	1	93	121	.4	.8
193 EPISCOPAL	2	683	978	3.2	6.3
207 E.L.C.A.	1	122	169	.6	1.1
226 FRIENDS-USA	1	28	42	.1	.3
226b EFI	1	28	42	.1	.3
355 PRESB CH (USA)	3	666	850*	2.8	5.5
413 S.D.A.	1	29	37*	.1	.2
419 SO BAPT CONV	8	4,173	5,325*	17.7	34.2
449 UN METHODIST	9	2,568	3,277*	10.9	21.0
496 JEWISH EST[1]	0	NA	139	.5	.9
497 BLACK BAPT EST[2]	NA	1,015	1,295*	4.3	8.3
GOOCHLAND	**21**	**5,218**	**6,838***	**48.3**	**100.0**
093 CHR CH (DISC)	3	284	566	4.0	8.3
165 CH OF NAZARENE	1	51	142	1.0	2.1
193 EPISCOPAL	2	712	967	6.8	14.1
349 PENT HOLINESS	1	51	61*	.4	.9
355 PRESB CH (USA)	2	142	170*	1.2	2.5
419 SO BAPT CONV	9	2,461	2,953*	20.9	43.2
449 UN METHODIST	3	599	719*	5.1	10.5
496 JEWISH EST[1]	0	NA	158	1.1	2.3
497 BLACK BAPT EST[2]	NA	918	1,102*	7.8	16.1

NA–Not applicable   NR–Not reported   *Total adherents estimated from known number of communicant, confirmed, full members.   - Represents a percent less than 0.1.   Percentages may not total due to rounding.
[1]See Appendix E   [2]See Appendix F   [3]See Appendix G   Lines in *italic* represent a breakdown of Catholic rites or Friends affiliations. They are included in their respective denominational total.

Table 4. Churches and Church Membership by County and Denomination: 1990

County and Denomination	Number of churches	Communicant, confirmed, full members	Total adherents Number	Percent of total population	Percent of total adherents
GRAYSON	**77**	**9,472**	**11,334***	**69.6**	**100.0**
097 CHR CHS&CHS CR	1	12	14*	.1	.1
127 CH GOD (CLEVE)	1	44	52*	.3	.5
145 CH GOD PROPHCY	2	83	99*	.6	.9
167 CHS OF CHRIST	5	227	307	1.9	2.7
193 EPISCOPAL	1	29	36	.2	.3
207 E.L.C.A.	1	49	62	.4	.5
349 PENT HOLINESS	2	203	242*	1.5	2.1
355 PRESB CH (USA)	1	159	190*	1.2	1.7
361 PRIM BAPT ASCS	3	68	81*	.5	.7
386 REGULAR BAPT	2	163	194*	1.2	1.7
419 SO BAPT CONV	25	5,798	6,913*	42.5	61.0
449 UN METHODIST	33	2,637	3,144*	19.3	27.7
GREENE	**20**	**2,340**	**3,219***	**31.3**	**100.0**
081 CATHOLIC	1	NA	120	1.2	3.7
081d LATIN	1	NA	120	1.2	3.7
127 CH GOD (CLEVE)	1	82	105*	1.0	3.3
157 CH OF BRETHREN	4	312	400*	3.9	12.4
193 EPISCOPAL	1	59	68	.7	2.1
285 MENNONITE CH	1	40	81	.8	2.5
419 SO BAPT CONV	5	858	1,101*	10.7	34.2
443 UN C OF CHRIST	1	51	65*	.6	2.0
449 UN METHODIST	6	737	946*	9.2	29.4
496 JEWISH EST[1]	0	NA	75	.7	2.3
497 BLACK BAPT EST[2]	NA	201	258*	2.5	8.0
GREENSVILLE-EMPORIA	**28**	**7,366**	**9,360***	**66.1**	**100.0**
053 ASSEMB OF GOD	1	67	104	.7	1.1
081 CATHOLIC	1	NA	101	.7	1.1
081d LATIN	1	NA	101	.7	1.1
093 CHR CH (DISC)	1	20	30	.2	.3
097 CHR CHS&CHS CR	1	68	85*	.6	.9
123 CH GOD (ANDER)	1	60	120	.8	1.3
145 CH GOD PROPHCY	1	41	51*	.4	.5
193 EPISCOPAL	3	196	246	1.7	2.6
283 LUTH—MO SYNOD	1	139	173	1.2	1.8
355 PRESB CH (USA)	2	214	267*	1.9	2.9
419 SO BAPT CONV	7	2,600	3,243*	22.9	34.6
449 UN METHODIST	9	1,449	1,807*	12.8	19.3
497 BLACK BAPT EST[2]	NA	2,512	3,133*	22.1	33.5
HALIFAX-SOUTH BOSTON	**85**	**19,171**	**24,014***	**66.7**	**100.0**
053 ASSEMB OF GOD	1	33	53	.1	.2
081 CATHOLIC	1	NA	161	.4	.7
081d LATIN	1	NA	161	.4	.7
127 CH GOD (CLEVE)	2	283	347*	1.0	1.4
145 CH GOD PROPHCY	3	124	152*	.4	.6
167 CHS OF CHRIST	1	25	33	.1	.1
193 EPISCOPAL	5	390	485	1.3	2.0
285 MENNONITE CH	2	54	88	.2	.4
349 PENT HOLINESS	1	45	55*	.2	.2
355 PRESB CH (USA)	9	640	784*	2.2	3.3
413 S.D.A.	3	141	173*	.5	.7
419 SO BAPT CONV	33	9,975	12,219*	33.9	50.9
443 UN C OF CHRIST	5	645	790*	2.2	3.3
449 UN METHODIST	18	3,141	3,847*	10.7	16.0
497 BLACK BAPT EST[2]	NA	3,675	4,502*	12.5	18.7
499 INDEP.NON-CHAR[3]	1	NA	325	.9	1.4
HAMPTON CITY	**82**	**41,628**	**61,318***	**45.8**	**100.0**
005 AME ZION	1	59	71	.1	.1
019 AMER BAPT USA	2	750	939*	.7	1.5
053 ASSEMB OF GOD	4	2,681	3,637	2.7	5.9
059 BAPT MISS ASSN	1	150	188*	.1	.3
081 CATHOLIC	4	NA	5,440	4.1	8.9
081d LATIN	4	NA	5,440	4.1	8.9
093 CHR CH (DISC)	2	315	533	.4	.9
097 CHR CHS&CHS CR	3	523	655*	.5	1.1
111 CH CR,SCIENTST	1	NR	NR	-	-
123 CH GOD (ANDER)	1	75	85	.1	.1
127 CH GOD (CLEVE)	3	435	544*	.4	.9
151 L-D SAINTS	2	NA	756	.6	1.2
165 CH OF NAZARENE	1	296	407	.3	.7
167 CHS OF CHRIST	1	126	156	.1	.3
193 EPISCOPAL	4	1,391	2,086	1.6	3.4
207 E.L.C.A.	2	764	1,107	.8	1.8
223 FREE WILL BAPT	1	272	340*	.3	.6
226 FRIENDS-USA	1	95	154	.1	.3
226b EFI	1	95	154	.1	.3
283 LUTH—MO SYNOD	1	210	266	.2	.4
284 LUTH CH-AM ASC	1	125	195	.1	.3
349 PENT HOLINESS	1	336	421*	.3	.7
355 PRESB CH (USA)	5	1,361	1,704*	1.3	2.8
356 PRESB CH AMER	1	137	190	.1	.3

County and Denomination	Number of churches	Communicant, confirmed, full members	Total adherents Number	Percent of total population	Percent of total adherents
403 SALVATION ARMY	1	161	164	.1	.3
413 S.D.A.	1	268	335*	.3	.5
419 SO BAPT CONV	16	13,100	16,397*	12.3	26.7
443 UN C OF CHRIST	2	644	806*	.6	1.3
449 UN METHODIST	13	5,997	7,506*	5.6	12.2
467 WESLEYAN	1	29	90	.1	.1
496 JEWISH EST[1]	2	NA	667	.5	1.1
497 BLACK BAPT EST[2]	NA	11,328	14,179*	10.6	23.1
498 INDEP.CHARIS.[3]	1	NA	500	.4	.8
499 INDEP.NON-CHAR[3]	2	NA	800	.6	1.3
HANOVER	**73**	**21,892**	**31,656***	**50.0**	**100.0**
001 ADVENT CHR CH	2	142	177*	.3	.6
053 ASSEMB OF GOD	1	386	510	.8	1.6
081 CATHOLIC	2	NA	1,920	3.0	6.1
081d LATIN	2	NA	1,920	3.0	6.1
093 CHR CH (DISC)	6	809	1,422	2.2	4.5
097 CHR CHS&CHS CR	5	1,182	1,469*	2.3	4.6
127 CH GOD (CLEVE)	1	181	225*	.4	.7
151 L-D SAINTS	1	NA	325	.5	1.0
165 CH OF NAZARENE	1	170	263	.4	.8
167 CHS OF CHRIST	1	70	70	.1	.2
193 EPISCOPAL	8	977	1,427	2.3	4.5
207 E.L.C.A.	1	186	288	.5	.9
226 FRIENDS-USA	2	209	242	.4	.8
226b EFI	1	208	222	.4	.7
226d FGC & FUM	1	1	20	-	.1
283 LUTH—MO SYNOD	1	133	195	.3	.6
355 PRESB CH (USA)	8	1,140	1,417*	2.2	4.5
413 S.D.A.	1	184	229*	.4	.7
419 SO BAPT CONV	16	9,583	11,913*	18.8	37.6
449 UN METHODIST	15	4,584	5,698*	9.0	18.0
467 WESLEYAN	1	17	80	.1	.3
496 JEWISH EST[1]	0	NA	1,376	2.2	4.3
497 BLACK BAPT EST[2]	NA	1,939	2,410*	3.8	7.6
HENRICO-RICHMOND CITY	**318**	**168,716**	**246,678***	**58.6**	**100.0**
005 AME ZION	16	1,785	2,633	.6	1.1
019 AMER BAPT USA	23	14,935	18,111*	4.3	7.3
039 AP CHR CH(NAZ)	1	21	25*	-	-
053 ASSEMB OF GOD	6	1,355	2,018	.5	.8
081 CATHOLIC	16	NA	29,445	7.0	11.9
081d LATIN	15	NA	28,223	6.7	11.4
081e MARONITE	1	NA	1,222	.3	.5
089 CHR & MISS AL	1	50	75	-	-
093 CHR CH (DISC)	11	2,289	3,291	.8	1.3
097 CHR CHS&CHS CR	8	1,664	2,018*	.5	.8
111 CH CR,SCIENTST	2	NR	NR	-	-
123 CH GOD (ANDER)	2	88	105	-	-
127 CH GOD (CLEVE)	5	817	991*	.2	.4
145 CH GOD PROPHCY	4	166	201*	-	.1
151 L-D SAINTS	3	NA	1,904	.5	.8
157 CH OF BRETHREN	1	188	228*	.1	.1
165 CH OF NAZARENE	4	399	586	.1	.2
167 CHS OF CHRIST	7	839	1,028	.2	.4
193 EPISCOPAL	22	11,083	15,769	3.7	6.4
203 EVAN FREE CH	1	13	35	-	-
207 E.L.C.A.	5	2,018	2,503	.6	1.0
226 FRIENDS-USA	2	190	235*	.1	.1
226b EFI	1	50	65	-	-
226d FGC & FUM	1	140	170*	-	.1
246 GREEK ORTHODOX	1	NR	NR	-	-
263 INT FOURSQ GOS	2	134	162*	-	.1
283 LUTH—MO SYNOD	4	1,358	1,744	.4	.7
285 MENNONITE CH	1	114	174	-	.1
331 ORTH CH IN AM	1	NR	NR	-	-
349 PENT HOLINESS	3	343	416*	.1	.2
353 CHR BRETHREN	2	70	90	-	-
355 PRESB CH (USA)	31	14,112	17,113*	4.1	6.9
356 PRESB CH AMER	3	429	620	.1	.3
403 SALVATION ARMY	1	161	187	-	.1
413 S.D.A.	3	1,202	1,458*	.3	.6
419 SO BAPT CONV	65	48,868	59,260*	14.1	24.0
435 UNITARIAN-UNIV	1	532	727	.2	.3
443 UN C OF CHRIST	1	500	606*	.1	.2
449 UN METHODIST	44	25,272	30,646*	7.3	12.4
469 WELS	1	20	30	-	-
496 JEWISH EST[1]	8	NA	3,001	.7	1.2
497 BLACK BAPT EST[2]	NA	37,701	45,718*	10.9	18.5
498 INDEP.CHARIS.[3]	4	NA	2,400	.6	1.0
499 INDEP.NON-CHAR[3]	2	NA	1,125	.3	.5
HENRY-MARTINSVILLE	**130**	**31,173**	**39,873***	**54.5**	**100.0**
053 ASSEMB OF GOD	3	412	445	.6	1.1
081 CATHOLIC	1	NA	585	.8	1.5
081d LATIN	1	NA	585	.8	1.5

NA–Not applicable NR–Not reported *Total adherents estimated from known number of communicant, confirmed, full members. - Represents a percent less than 0.1. Percentages may not total due to rounding.
[1]See Appendix E [2]See Appendix F [3]See Appendix G Lines in *italic* represent a breakdown of Catholic rites or Friends affiliations. They are included in their respective denominational total.

Table 4. Churches and Church Membership by County and Denomination: 1990

County and Denomination	Number of churches	Communicant, confirmed, full members	Total adherents		
			Number	Percent of total population	Percent of total adherents
093 CHR CH (DISC)	15	1,822	3,097	4.2	7.8
097 CHR CHS&CHS CR	11	2,834	3,447*	4.7	8.6
123 CH GOD (ANDER)	1	0	44	.1	.1
127 CH GOD (CLEVE)	4	627	763*	1.0	1.9
145 CH GOD PROPHCY	4	166	202*	.3	.5
151 L-D SAINTS	1	NA	257	.4	.6
157 CH OF BRETHREN	4	696	847*	1.2	2.1
165 CH OF NAZARENE	1	51	93	.1	.2
167 CHS OF CHRIST	7	361	478	.7	1.2
193 EPISCOPAL	2	485	518	.7	1.3
223 FREE WILL BAPT	1	158	192*	.3	.5
226 FRIENDS-USA	1	93	163	.2	.4
226b *EFI*	*1*	*93*	*163*	*.2*	*.4*
349 PENT HOLINESS	9	740	900*	1.2	2.3
355 PRESB CH (USA)	6	1,029	1,252*	1.7	3.1
361 PRIM BAPT ASCS	10	188	229*	.3	.6
403 SALVATION ARMY	1	43	52	.1	.1
413 S.D.A.	2	91	111*	.2	.3
419 SO BAPT CONV	28	12,437	15,127*	20.7	37.9
449 UN METHODIST	14	3,468	4,218*	5.8	10.6
467 WESLEYAN	3	207	319	.4	.8
496 JEWISH EST[1]	1	NA	130	.2	.3
497 BLACK BAPT EST[2]	NA	5,265	6,404*	8.8	16.1
HIGHLAND	**18**	**1,250**	**1,511***	**57.3**	**100.0**
001 ADVENT CHR CH	1	72	87*	3.3	5.8
145 CH GOD PROPHCY	1	41	50*	1.9	3.3
157 CH OF BRETHREN	1	40	48*	1.8	3.2
355 PRESB CH (USA)	5	241	291*	11.0	19.3
449 UN METHODIST	10	856	1,035*	39.3	68.5
ISLE OF WIGHT	**34**	**8,559**	**10,871***	**43.4**	**100.0**
053 ASSEMB OF GOD	2	241	386	1.5	3.6
097 CHR CHS&CHS CR	1	68	86*	.3	.8
127 CH GOD (CLEVE)	1	61	77*	.3	.7
145 CH GOD PROPHCY	1	41	52*	.2	.5
165 CH OF NAZARENE	1	55	94	.4	.9
167 CHS OF CHRIST	1	42	55	.2	.5
193 EPISCOPAL	1	158	193	.8	1.8
207 E.L.C.A.	1	23	23	.1	.2
223 FREE WILL BAPT	1	101	127*	.5	1.2
226 FRIENDS-USA	1	15	17	.1	.2
226b *EFI*	*1*	*15*	*17*	*.1*	*.2*
355 PRESB CH (USA)	1	171	215*	.9	2.0
419 SO BAPT CONV	9	3,258	4,102*	16.4	37.7
443 UN C OF CHRIST	6	642	808*	3.2	7.4
449 UN METHODIST	7	1,739	2,189*	8.7	20.1
497 BLACK BAPT EST[2]	NA	1,944	2,447*	9.8	22.5
JAMES CITY-WILLIAMS	**34**	**12,580**	**20,264***	**43.7**	**100.0**
053 ASSEMB OF GOD	1	78	133	.3	.7
081 CATHOLIC	1	NA	4,161	9.0	20.5
081d *LATIN*	*1*	*NA*	*4,161*	*9.0*	*20.5*
093 CHR CH (DISC)	1	240	433	.9	2.1
097 CHR CHS&CHS CR	2	211	252*	.5	1.2
111 CH CR,SCIENTST	1	NR	NR	-	-
151 L-D SAINTS	1	NA	348	.8	1.7
165 CH OF NAZARENE	1	81	33	.1	.2
167 CHS OF CHRIST	1	144	188	.4	.9
193 EPISCOPAL	3	1,643	2,139	4.6	10.6
207 E.L.C.A.	2	567	748	1.6	3.7
226 FRIENDS-USA	1	28	33*	.1	.2
226d *FGC & FUM*	*1*	*28*	*33***	*.1*	*.2*
283 LUTH—MO SYNOD	1	0	0	-	-
285 MENNONITE CH	1	68	143	.3	.7
331 ORTH CH IN AM	1	NR	NR	-	-
349 PENT HOLINESS	1	134	160*	.3	.8
355 PRESB CH (USA)	2	1,309	1,566*	3.4	7.7
356 PRESB CH AMER	1	54	86	.2	.4
413 S.D.A.	2	181	217*	.5	1.1
419 SO BAPT CONV	6	2,936	3,512*	7.6	17.3
435 UNITARIAN-UNIV	1	109	159	.3	.8
449 UN METHODIST	3	2,311	2,765*	6.0	13.6
496 JEWISH EST[1]	0	NA	214	.5	1.1
497 BLACK BAPT EST[2]	NA	2,486	2,974*	6.4	14.7
KING AND QUEEN	**17**	**3,050**	**3,866***	**61.5**	**100.0**
053 ASSEMB OF GOD	1	35	69	1.1	1.8
093 CHR CH (DISC)	1	115	140	2.2	3.6
193 EPISCOPAL	1	15	25	.4	.6
419 SO BAPT CONV	9	1,503	1,876*	29.8	48.5
449 UN METHODIST	4	431	538*	8.6	13.9
467 WESLEYAN	1	49	92	1.5	2.4
497 BLACK BAPT EST[2]	NA	902	1,126*	17.9	29.1

County and Denomination	Number of churches	Communicant, confirmed, full members	Total adherents		
			Number	Percent of total population	Percent of total adherents
KING GEORGE	**17**	**4,684**	**6,151***	**45.5**	**100.0**
053 ASSEMB OF GOD	1	27	35	.3	.6
151 L-D SAINTS	1	NA	74	.5	1.2
193 EPISCOPAL	3	272	351	2.6	5.7
283 LUTH—MO SYNOD	1	143	215	1.6	3.5
419 SO BAPT CONV	7	3,010	3,886*	28.7	63.2
449 UN METHODIST	4	575	742*	5.5	12.1
497 BLACK BAPT EST[2]	NA	657	848*	6.3	13.8
KING WILLIAM	**27**	**5,190**	**7,484***	**68.6**	**100.0**
011 A.W.M.C.	1	0	0*	-	-
019 AMER BAPT USA	1	100	127*	1.2	1.7
081 CATHOLIC	1	NA	567	5.2	7.6
081d *LATIN*	*1*	*NA*	*567*	*5.2*	*7.6*
093 CHR CH (DISC)	2	217	357	3.3	4.8
097 CHR CHS&CHS CR	2	280	355*	3.3	4.7
127 CH GOD (CLEVE)	1	39	49*	.4	.7
151 L-D SAINTS	1	NA	121	1.1	1.6
165 CH OF NAZARENE	1	38	86	.8	1.1
193 EPISCOPAL	3	179	325	3.0	4.3
355 PRESB CH (USA)	2	86	109*	1.0	1.5
419 SO BAPT CONV	9	2,404	3,047*	27.9	40.7
449 UN METHODIST	3	714	905*	8.3	12.1
497 BLACK BAPT EST[2]	NA	1,133	1,436*	13.2	19.2
LANCASTER	**26**	**5,820**	**7,676***	**70.4**	**100.0**
081 CATHOLIC	1	NA	600	5.5	7.8
081d *LATIN*	*1*	*NA*	*600*	*5.5*	*7.8*
111 CH CR,SCIENTST	1	NR	NR	-	-
193 EPISCOPAL	3	768	1,014	9.3	13.2
355 PRESB CH (USA)	3	473	564*	5.2	7.3
413 S.D.A.	1	66	79*	.7	1.0
419 SO BAPT CONV	9	1,973	2,351*	21.6	30.6
449 UN METHODIST	7	1,390	1,656*	15.2	21.6
467 WESLEYAN	1	24	70	.6	.9
497 BLACK BAPT EST[2]	NA	1,126	1,342*	12.3	17.5
LEE	**120**	**12,774**	**15,894***	**64.9**	**100.0**
005 AME ZION	1	85	124	.5	.8
053 ASSEMB OF GOD	1	15	21	.1	.1
081 CATHOLIC	1	NA	44	.2	.3
081d *LATIN*	*1*	*NA*	*44*	*.2*	*.3*
082 CENTRAL BAPT	2	54	67*	.3	.4
093 CHR CH (DISC)	1	20	33	.1	.2
097 CHR CHS&CHS CR	5	250	310*	1.3	2.0
127 CH GOD (CLEVE)	6	298	369*	1.5	2.3
145 CH GOD PROPHCY	3	124	154*	.6	1.0
146 CH GOD MTN ASM	1	26	32*	.1	.2
157 CH OF BRETHREN	2	123	152*	.6	1.0
165 CH OF NAZARENE	1	12	0	-	-
167 CHS OF CHRIST	2	26	36	.1	.2
193 EPISCOPAL	1	8	17	.1	.1
223 FREE WILL BAPT	7	302	374*	1.5	2.4
349 PENT HOLINESS	1	12	15*	.1	.1
355 PRESB CH (USA)	1	36	45*	.2	.3
361 PRIM BAPT ASCS	11	812	1,006*	4.1	6.3
419 SO BAPT CONV	45	8,378	10,378*	42.4	65.3
449 UN METHODIST	28	2,193	2,717*	11.1	17.1
LOUDOUN	**85**	**14,528**	**39,752***	**46.2**	**100.0**
053 ASSEMB OF GOD	4	175	251	.3	.6
081 CATHOLIC	4	NA	9,440	11.0	23.7
081d *LATIN*	*4*	*NA*	*9,440*	*11.0*	*23.7*
097 CHR CHS&CHS CR	1	112	143*	.2	.4
111 CH CR,SCIENTST	1	NR	NR	-	-
127 CH GOD (CLEVE)	2	32	41*	-	.1
151 L-D SAINTS	2	NA	710	.8	1.8
165 CH OF NAZARENE	2	189	389	.5	1.0
167 CHS OF CHRIST	1	84	109	.1	.3
193 EPISCOPAL	8	1,119	1,986	2.3	5.0
207 E.L.C.A.	3	1,082	1,650	1.9	4.2
221 FREE METHODIST	1	10	37	-	.1
226 FRIENDS-USA	1	164	210*	.2	.5
226d *FGC & FUM*	*1*	*164*	*210***	*.2*	*.5*
265 INT PENT C CHR	2	66	77	.1	.2
355 PRESB CH (USA)	6	1,107	1,416*	1.6	3.6
356 PRESB CH AMER	1	0	0	-	-
361 PRIM BAPT ASCS	1	8	10*	-	-
413 S.D.A.	1	48	61*	.1	.2
419 SO BAPT CONV	14	3,730	4,771*	5.5	12.0
443 UN C OF CHRIST	1	81	104*	.1	.3
449 UN METHODIST	27	4,614	5,902*	6.9	14.8
469 WELS	1	40	61	.1	.2
496 JEWISH EST[1]	0	NA	9,396	10.9	23.6
497 BLACK BAPT EST[2]	NA	1,867	2,388*	2.8	6.0

NA–Not applicable   NR–Not reported   *Total adherents estimated from known number of communicant, confirmed, full members.   - Represents a percent less than 0.1.   Percentages may not total due to rounding.
[1] See Appendix E   [2] See Appendix F   [3] See Appendix G   Lines in *italic* represent a breakdown of Catholic rites or Friends affiliations. They are included in their respective denominational total.

Table 4. Churches and Church Membership by County and Denomination: 1990

County and Denomination	Number of churches	Communicant, confirmed, full members	Total adherents Number	Percent of total population	Percent of total adherents
499 INDEP.NON-CHAR[3]	1	NA	600	.7	1.5
LOUISA	**47**	**7,451**	**9,882***	**48.6**	**100.0**
081 CATHOLIC	2	NA	283	1.4	2.9
081d LATIN	*2*	*NA*	*283*	*1.4*	*2.9*
093 CHR CH (DISC)	9	448	781	3.8	7.9
097 CHR CHS&CHS CR	2	136	170*	.8	1.7
165 CH OF NAZARENE	1	31	67	.3	.7
193 EPISCOPAL	2	153	213	1.0	2.2
223 FREE WILL BAPT	1	80	100*	.5	1.0
349 PENT HOLINESS	1	49	61*	.3	.6
355 PRESB CH (USA)	3	129	161*	.8	1.6
419 SO BAPT CONV	16	3,407	4,246*	20.9	43.0
435 UNITARIAN-UNIV	1	6	6	-	.1
449 UN METHODIST	8	1,201	1,497*	7.4	15.1
467 WESLEYAN	1	19	63	.3	.6
497 BLACK BAPT EST[2]	NA	1,792	2,234*	11.0	22.6
LUNENBERG	**35**	**5,727**	**7,839***	**68.6**	**100.0**
005 AME ZION	2	88	126	1.1	1.6
093 CHR CH (DISC)	7	800	1,474	12.9	18.8
097 CHR CHS&CHS CR	2	160	200*	1.8	2.6
127 CH GOD (CLEVE)	1	69	86*	.8	1.1
145 CH GOD PROPHCY	1	41	51*	.4	.7
165 CH OF NAZARENE	1	178	286	2.5	3.6
193 EPISCOPAL	3	95	124	1.1	1.6
283 LUTH—MO SYNOD	1	28	140	1.2	1.8
353 CHR BRETHREN	1	25	50	.4	.6
355 PRESB CH (USA)	2	74	92*	.8	1.2
419 SO BAPT CONV	7	1,687	2,108*	18.5	26.9
449 UN METHODIST	7	1,012	1,265*	11.1	16.1
497 BLACK BAPT EST[2]	NA	1,470	1,837*	16.1	23.4
MADISON	**30**	**3,859**	**5,248***	**43.9**	**100.0**
061 BEACHY AMISH	1	106	133*	1.1	2.5
081 CATHOLIC	1	NA	200	1.7	3.8
081d LATIN	*1*	*NA*	*200*	*1.7*	*3.8*
093 CHR CH (DISC)	2	175	308	2.6	5.9
157 CH OF BRETHREN	1	65	81*	.7	1.5
193 EPISCOPAL	2	109	161	1.3	3.1
207 E.L.C.A.	2	347	471	3.9	9.0
223 FREE WILL BAPT	1	71	89*	.7	1.7
259 IFCA	1	NR	NR	-	-
353 CHR BRETHREN	1	60	145	1.2	2.8
355 PRESB CH (USA)	1	123	154*	1.3	2.9
361 PRIM BAPT ASCS	1	52	65*	.5	1.2
419 SO BAPT CONV	6	1,133	1,417*	11.9	27.0
449 UN METHODIST	10	1,210	1,514*	12.7	28.8
497 BLACK BAPT EST[2]	NA	408	510*	4.3	9.7
MATHEWS	**23**	**3,830**	**4,980***	**59.7**	**100.0**
081 CATHOLIC	1	NA	174	2.1	3.5
081d LATIN	*1*	*NA*	*174*	*2.1*	*3.5*
093 CHR CH (DISC)	2	70	141	1.7	2.8
127 CH GOD (CLEVE)	1	57	67*	.8	1.3
165 CH OF NAZARENE	1	55	138	1.7	2.8
193 EPISCOPAL	1	220	434	5.2	8.7
226 FRIENDS-USA	2	84	85	1.0	1.7
226b EFI	*2*	*84*	*85*	*1.0*	*1.7*
419 SO BAPT CONV	5	1,176	1,386*	16.6	27.8
449 UN METHODIST	10	1,886	2,223*	26.6	44.6
497 BLACK BAPT EST[2]	NA	282	332*	4.0	6.7
MECKLENBURG	**78**	**13,624**	**17,164***	**58.7**	**100.0**
053 ASSEMB OF GOD	1	32	40	.1	.2
081 CATHOLIC	2	NA	280	1.0	1.6
081d LATIN	*2*	*NA*	*280*	*1.0*	*1.6*
093 CHR CH (DISC)	1	15	24	.1	.1
097 CHR CHS&CHS CR	1	100	122*	.4	.7
127 CH GOD (CLEVE)	2	105	128*	.4	.7
145 CH GOD PROPHCY	1	41	50*	.2	.3
151 L-D SAINTS	1	NA	231	.8	1.3
165 CH OF NAZARENE	1	13	29	.1	.2
167 CHS OF CHRIST	1	20	24	.1	.1
193 EPISCOPAL	10	381	483	1.7	2.8
263 INT FOURSQ GOS	1	56	68*	.2	.4
339 PENT CH OF GOD	1	16	39	.1	.2
349 PENT HOLINESS	1	11	13*	-	.1
355 PRESB CH (USA)	5	363	442*	1.5	2.6
413 S.D.A.	1	27	33*	.1	.2
419 SO BAPT CONV	24	6,088	7,416*	25.4	43.2
443 UN C OF CHRIST	3	355	432*	1.5	2.5
449 UN METHODIST	21	3,247	3,955*	13.5	23.0
497 BLACK BAPT EST[2]	NA	2,754	3,355*	11.5	19.5

County and Denomination	Number of churches	Communicant, confirmed, full members	Total adherents Number	Percent of total population	Percent of total adherents
MIDDLESEX	**17**	**3,980**	**5,102***	**59.0**	**100.0**
081 CATHOLIC	1	NA	197	2.3	3.9
081d LATIN	*1*	*NA*	*197*	*2.3*	*3.9*
093 CHR CH (DISC)	1	179	290	3.4	5.7
193 EPISCOPAL	1	209	263	3.0	5.2
349 PENT HOLINESS	1	23	27*	.3	.5
419 SO BAPT CONV	6	1,650	1,972*	22.8	38.7
449 UN METHODIST	6	1,357	1,622*	18.7	31.8
467 WESLEYAN	1	50	119	1.4	2.3
497 BLACK BAPT EST[2]	NA	512	612*	7.1	12.0
MONTGOMERY-RADFORD	**127**	**21,399**	**28,390***	**31.6**	**100.0**
053 ASSEMB OF GOD	1	48	65	.1	.2
081 CATHOLIC	2	NA	1,522	1.7	5.4
081d LATIN	*2*	*NA*	*1,522*	*1.7*	*5.4*
093 CHR CH (DISC)	5	702	1,044	1.2	3.7
097 CHR CHS&CHS CR	7	995	1,148*	1.3	4.0
111 CH CR,SCIENTST	1	NR	NR	-	-
123 CH GOD (ANDER)	4	227	263	.3	.9
127 CH GOD (CLEVE)	6	826	953*	1.1	3.4
145 CH GOD PROPHCY	3	124	143*	.2	.5
151 L-D SAINTS	3	NA	859	1.0	3.0
157 CH OF BRETHREN	3	497	573*	.6	2.0
167 CHS OF CHRIST	4	538	624	.7	2.2
193 EPISCOPAL	3	696	846	.9	3.0
207 E.L.C.A.	6	1,019	1,366	1.5	4.8
226 FRIENDS-USA	1	7	22	-	.1
226d FGC & FUM	*1*	*7*	*22*	*-*	*.1*
259 IFCA	1	NR	NR	-	-
263 INT FOURSQ GOS	1	18	21*	-	.1
285 MENNONITE CH	1	32	46	.1	.2
339 PENT CH OF GOD	1	15	25	-	.1
349 PENT HOLINESS	17	1,612	1,860*	2.1	6.6
353 CHR BRETHREN	1	350	550	.6	1.9
355 PRESB CH (USA)	6	1,788	2,063*	2.3	7.3
356 PRESB CH AMER	1	82	103	.1	.4
361 PRIM BAPT ASCS	2	6	7*	-	-
403 SALVATION ARMY	1	52	54	.1	.2
413 S.D.A.	1	98	113*	.1	.4
419 SO BAPT CONV	12	4,276	4,933*	5.5	17.4
435 UNITARIAN-UNIV	1	80	115	.1	.4
449 UN METHODIST	27	6,124	7,065*	7.9	24.9
467 WESLEYAN	5	260	637	.7	2.2
496 JEWISH EST[1]	0	NA	300	.3	1.1
497 BLACK BAPT EST[2]	NA	927	1,070*	1.2	3.8
NELSON	**43**	**6,407**	**8,197***	**64.1**	**100.0**
005 AME ZION	1	48	59	.5	.7
081 CATHOLIC	1	NA	41	.3	.5
081d LATIN	*1*	*NA*	*41*	*.3*	*.5*
093 CHR CH (DISC)	4	208	455	3.6	5.6
127 CH GOD (CLEVE)	1	64	79*	.6	1.0
157 CH OF BRETHREN	1	34	42*	.3	.5
167 CHS OF CHRIST	1	93	121	.9	1.5
193 EPISCOPAL	4	179	222	1.7	2.7
285 MENNONITE CH	1	19	63	.5	.8
349 PENT HOLINESS	3	91	112*	.9	1.4
355 PRESB CH (USA)	3	206	254*	2.0	3.1
419 SO BAPT CONV	18	3,975	4,909*	38.4	59.9
449 UN METHODIST	5	912	1,126*	8.8	13.7
497 BLACK BAPT EST[2]	NA	578	714*	5.6	8.7
NEW KENT	**12**	**3,202**	**4,126***	**39.5**	**100.0**
193 EPISCOPAL	1	129	191	1.8	4.6
349 PENT HOLINESS	1	75	93*	.9	2.3
355 PRESB CH (USA)	1	231	287*	2.7	7.0
419 SO BAPT CONV	6	1,483	1,839*	17.6	44.6
449 UN METHODIST	3	633	785*	7.5	19.0
496 JEWISH EST[1]	0	NA	124	1.2	3.0
497 BLACK BAPT EST[2]	NA	651	807*	7.7	19.6
NEWPORT NEWS CITY	**105**	**53,721**	**80,319***	**47.2**	**100.0**
005 AME ZION	3	2,244	2,454	1.4	3.1
019 AMER BAPT USA	3	2,140	2,764*	1.6	3.4
053 ASSEMB OF GOD	6	1,080	1,648	1.0	2.1
081 CATHOLIC	4	NA	8,498	5.0	10.6
081d LATIN	*4*	*NA*	*8,498*	*5.0*	*10.6*
093 CHR CH (DISC)	1	209	318	.2	.4
097 CHR CHS&CHS CR	4	1,700	2,196*	1.3	2.7
111 CH CR,SCIENTST	1	NR	NR	-	-
123 CH GOD (ANDER)	2	91	101	.1	.1
127 CH GOD (CLEVE)	2	668	863*	.5	1.1
145 CH GOD PROPHCY	2	83	107*	.1	.1
151 L-D SAINTS	3	NA	1,237	.7	1.5
157 CH OF BRETHREN	1	162	209*	.1	.3

NA–Not applicable   NR–Not reported   *Total adherents estimated from known number of communicant, confirmed, full members.   - Represents a percent less than 0.1.   Percentages may not total due to rounding.
[1]See Appendix E   [2]See Appendix F   [3]See Appendix G   Lines in *italic* represent a breakdown of Catholic rites or Friends affiliations. They are included in their respective denominational total.

403

Table 4. Churches and Church Membership by County and Denomination: 1990

County and Denomination	Number of churches	Communicant, confirmed, full members	Total adherents Number	Percent of total population	Percent of total adherents
165 CH OF NAZARENE	1	92	113	.1	.1
167 CHS OF CHRIST	3	376	489	.3	.6
193 EPISCOPAL	6	2,146	2,829	1.7	3.5
207 E.L.C.A.	2	710	945	.6	1.2
223 FREE WILL BAPT	1	432	558*	.3	.7
226 FRIENDS-USA	1	50	88	.1	.1
226b EFI	*1*	*50*	*88*	*.1*	*.1*
246 GREEK ORTHODOX	1	NR	NR	-	-
283 LUTH—MO SYNOD	1	279	423	.2	.5
285 MENNONITE CH	4	446	556	.3	.7
349 PENT HOLINESS	1	39	50*	-	.1
353 CHR BRETHREN	1	25	50	-	.1
355 PRESB CH (USA)	9	3,266	4,219*	2.5	5.3
413 S.D.A.	1	407	526*	.3	.7
419 SO BAPT CONV	21	17,057	22,034*	13.0	27.4
435 UNITARIAN-UNIV	1	73	88	.1	.1
443 UN C OF CHRIST	4	1,190	1,537*	.9	1.9
449 UN METHODIST	10	6,284	8,117*	4.8	10.1
467 WESLEYAN	1	33	150	.1	.2
496 JEWISH EST[1]	3	NA	784	.5	1.0
497 BLACK BAPT EST[2]	NA	12,439	16,068*	9.4	20.0
498 INDEP.CHARIS.[3]	1	NA	300	.2	.4
NORFOLK-CHESAP-PORTS	**357**	**169,562**	**246,353***	**47.6**	**100.0**
005 AME ZION	13	13,745	14,252	2.8	5.8
019 AMER BAPT USA	20	11,993	15,074*	2.9	6.1
053 ASSEMB OF GOD	11	1,827	2,779	.5	1.1
081 CATHOLIC	14	NA	19,532	3.8	7.9
081d LATIN	*14*	*NA*	*19,532*	*3.8*	*7.9*
089 CHR & MISS AL	2	384	1,659	.3	.7
093 CHR CH (DISC)	12	1,198	1,960	.4	.8
097 CHR CHS&CHS CR	15	2,101	2,653*	.5	1.1
105 CHRISTIAN REF	1	71	113	-	-
111 CH CR,SCIENTST	2	NR	NR	-	-
123 CH GOD (ANDER)	2	234	271	.1	.1
127 CH GOD (CLEVE)	9	1,118	1,412*	.3	.6
145 CH GOD PROPHCY	2	83	105*	-	-
151 L-D SAINTS	3	NA	1,311	.3	.5
165 CH OF NAZARENE	4	264	361	.1	.1
167 CHS OF CHRIST	7	859	1,179	.2	.5
179 CONSRV BAPT	1	NR	NR	-	-
193 EPISCOPAL	18	6,039	8,303	1.6	3.4
207 E.L.C.A.	8	2,807	3,979	.8	1.6
215 EVAN METH CH	1	45	57*	-	-
223 FREE WILL BAPT	5	998	1,260*	.2	.5
226 FRIENDS-USA	2	148	194	-	.1
226b EFI	*1*	*146*	*187*	*-*	*.1*
226d FGC & FUM	*1*	*2*	*7*	*-*	*-*
246 GREEK ORTHODOX	1	NR	NR	-	-
265 INT PENT C CHR	2	72	125	-	.1
283 LUTH—MO SYNOD	4	886	1,241	.2	.5
285 MENNONITE CH	5	379	541	.1	.2
331 ORTH CH IN AM	1	NR	NR	-	-
349 PENT HOLINESS	12	1,218	1,538*	.3	.6
353 CHR BRETHREN	1	10	50	-	-
355 PRESB CH (USA)	26	6,519	8,232*	1.6	3.3
356 PRESB CH AMER	2	285	338	.1	.1
403 SALVATION ARMY	2	925	941	.2	.4
413 S.D.A.	5	1,225	1,547*	.3	.6
419 SO BAPT CONV	68	47,606	60,115*	11.6	24.4
435 UNITARIAN-UNIV	1	211	261	.1	.1
443 UN C OF CHRIST	14	2,835	3,580*	.7	1.5
449 UN METHODIST	45	21,451	27,087*	5.2	11.0
467 WESLEYAN	1	25	30	-	-
469 WELS	1	27	34	-	-
496 JEWISH EST[1]	7	NA	7,805	1.5	3.2
497 BLACK BAPT EST[2]	NA	42,030	53,074*	10.3	21.5
499 INDEP.NON-CHAR[3]	7	NA	3,360	.6	1.4
NORTHAMPTON	**26**	**5,966**	**7,724***	**59.1**	**100.0**
005 AME ZION	1	126	158	1.2	2.0
053 ASSEMB OF GOD	1	18	25	.2	.3
081 CATHOLIC	1	NA	194	1.5	2.5
081d LATIN	*1*	*NA*	*194*	*1.5*	*2.5*
093 CHR CH (DISC)	1	21	51	.4	.7
123 CH GOD (ANDER)	1	19	24	.2	.3
193 EPISCOPAL	3	217	254	1.9	3.3
283 LUTH—MO SYNOD	1	31	40	.3	.5
355 PRESB CH (USA)	2	163	205*	1.6	2.7
419 SO BAPT CONV	6	1,432	1,797*	13.8	23.3
449 UN METHODIST	8	1,860	2,334*	17.9	30.2
467 WESLEYAN	1	12	48	.4	.6
497 BLACK BAPT EST[2]	NA	2,067	2,594*	19.9	33.6
NORTHUMBERLAND	**26**	**5,393**	**6,740***	**64.0**	**100.0**
081 CATHOLIC	0	NA	200	1.9	3.0

County and Denomination	Number of churches	Communicant, confirmed, full members	Total adherents Number	Percent of total population	Percent of total adherents
081d LATIN	*0*	*NA*	*200*	*1.9*	*3.0*
123 CH GOD (ANDER)	1	87	87	.8	1.3
151 L-D SAINTS	1	NA	89	.8	1.3
193 EPISCOPAL	3	270	363	3.4	5.4
419 SO BAPT CONV	9	1,925	2,294*	21.8	34.0
449 UN METHODIST	12	2,050	2,443*	23.2	36.2
497 BLACK BAPT EST[2]	NA	1,061	1,264*	12.0	18.8
NOTTOWAY	**33**	**6,375**	**8,116***	**54.1**	**100.0**
005 AME ZION	4	177	289	1.9	3.6
053 ASSEMB OF GOD	1	23	30	.2	.4
081 CATHOLIC	2	NA	95	.6	1.2
081d LATIN	*2*	*NA*	*95*	*.6*	*1.2*
093 CHR CH (DISC)	2	172	354	2.4	4.4
127 CH GOD (CLEVE)	1	48	58*	.4	.7
145 CH GOD PROPHCY	1	41	50*	.3	.6
165 CH OF NAZARENE	1	66	153	1.0	1.9
167 CHS OF CHRIST	2	30	38	.3	.5
193 EPISCOPAL	2	86	101	.7	1.2
355 PRESB CH (USA)	4	346	419*	2.8	5.2
413 S.D.A.	1	47	57*	.4	.7
419 SO BAPT CONV	3	1,515	1,835*	12.2	22.6
449 UN METHODIST	8	1,694	2,052*	13.7	25.3
467 WESLEYAN	1	22	32	.2	.4
497 BLACK BAPT EST[2]	NA	2,108	2,553*	17.0	31.5
ORANGE	**43**	**8,366**	**11,157***	**52.1**	**100.0**
053 ASSEMB OF GOD	1	92	125	.6	1.1
081 CATHOLIC	2	NA	658	3.1	5.9
081d LATIN	*2*	*NA*	*658*	*3.1*	*5.9*
093 CHR CH (DISC)	2	89	167	.8	1.5
097 CHR CHS&CHS CR	4	586	725*	3.4	6.5
127 CH GOD (CLEVE)	1	90	111*	.5	1.0
157 CH OF BRETHREN	1	52	64*	.3	.6
165 CH OF NAZARENE	1	37	48	.2	.4
167 CHS OF CHRIST	1	56	73	.3	.7
193 EPISCOPAL	2	336	482	2.3	4.3
207 E.L.C.A.	1	89	124	.6	1.1
349 PENT HOLINESS	2	104	129*	.6	1.2
355 PRESB CH (USA)	3	362	448*	2.1	4.0
413 S.D.A.	3	186	230*	1.1	2.1
419 SO BAPT CONV	13	4,366	5,398*	25.2	48.4
449 UN METHODIST	6	1,181	1,460*	6.8	13.1
497 BLACK BAPT EST[2]	NA	740	915*	4.3	8.2
PAGE	**57**	**6,977**	**9,625***	**44.4**	**100.0**
019 AMER BAPT USA	2	157	192*	.9	2.0
053 ASSEMB OF GOD	4	156	223	1.0	2.3
081 CATHOLIC	1	NA	274	1.3	2.8
081d LATIN	*1*	*NA*	*274*	*1.3*	*2.8*
093 CHR CH (DISC)	3	369	694	3.2	7.2
097 CHR CHS&CHS CR	1	150	184*	.8	1.9
157 CH OF BRETHREN	6	840	1,028*	4.7	10.7
167 CHS OF CHRIST	1	28	36	.2	.4
193 EPISCOPAL	3	193	256	1.2	2.7
207 E.L.C.A.	8	1,236	1,508	7.0	15.7
223 FREE WILL BAPT	1	65	80*	.4	.8
285 MENNONITE CH	2	58	92	.4	1.0
349 PENT HOLINESS	2	171	209*	1.0	2.2
361 PRIM BAPT ASCS	4	93	114*	.5	1.2
413 S.D.A.	2	330	404*	1.9	4.2
419 SO BAPT CONV	4	1,171	1,433*	6.6	14.9
443 UN C OF CHRIST	3	284	347*	1.6	3.6
449 UN METHODIST	9	1,676	2,051*	9.5	21.3
499 INDEP.NON-CHAR[3]	1	NA	500	2.3	5.2
PATRICK	**68**	**5,781**	**7,547***	**43.2**	**100.0**
081 CATHOLIC	1	NA	85	.5	1.1
081d LATIN	*1*	*NA*	*85*	*.5*	*1.1*
093 CHR CH (DISC)	4	214	348	2.0	4.6
097 CHR CHS&CHS CR	1	30	36*	.2	.5
127 CH GOD (CLEVE)	1	73	87*	.5	1.2
145 CH GOD PROPHCY	2	83	99*	.6	1.3
151 L-D SAINTS	1	NA	311	1.8	4.1
157 CH OF BRETHREN	2	268	321*	1.8	4.3
167 CHS OF CHRIST	2	77	99	.6	1.3
207 E.L.C.A.	1	90	105	.6	1.4
295 MORAV CH-SOUTH	2	86	119	.7	1.6
349 PENT HOLINESS	7	594	712*	4.1	9.4
355 PRESB CH (USA)	7	297	356*	2.0	4.7
361 PRIM BAPT ASCS	9	182	218*	1.2	2.9
413 S.D.A.	1	33	40*	.2	.5
419 SO BAPT CONV	13	2,197	2,632*	15.1	34.9
449 UN METHODIST	12	1,182	1,416*	8.1	18.8
467 WESLEYAN	2	72	200	1.1	2.7
497 BLACK BAPT EST[2]	NA	303	363*	2.1	4.8

NA–Not applicable   NR–Not reported   *Total adherents estimated from known number of communicant, confirmed, full members.   - Represents a percent less than 0.1.   Percentages may not total due to rounding.
[1]See Appendix E   [2]See Appendix F   [3]See Appendix G   Lines in *italic* represent a breakdown of Catholic rites or Friends affiliations. They are included in their respective denominational total.

Table 4. Churches and Church Membership by County and Denomination: 1990

County and Denomination	Number of churches	Communicant, confirmed, full members	Total adherents		
			Number	Percent of total population	Percent of total adherents
PITTSYLVANIA-DANVILL	**195**	**47,209**	**60,622***	**55.8**	**100.0**
005 AME ZION	1	195	258	.2	.4
053 ASSEMB OF GOD	3	192	347	.3	.6
081 CATHOLIC	2	NA	1,280	1.2	2.1
081d LATIN	2	NA	1,280	1.2	2.1
093 CHR CH (DISC)	7	557	835	.8	1.4
097 CHR CHS&CHS CR	11	2,092	2,555*	2.4	4.2
127 CH GOD (CLEVE)	4	1,085	1,325*	1.2	2.2
145 CH GOD PROPHCY	4	166	203*	.2	.3
151 L-D SAINTS	2	NA	503	.5	.8
157 CH OF BRETHREN	3	314	384*	.4	.6
165 CH OF NAZARENE	1	142	116	.1	.2
167 CHS OF CHRIST	1	70	118	.1	.2
176 CCC, NOT NAT'L	1	815	995*	.9	1.6
193 EPISCOPAL	6	610	772	.7	1.3
207 E.L.C.A.	1	347	488	.4	.8
215 EVAN METH CH	1	284	347*	.3	.6
226 FRIENDS-USA	2	71	97	.1	.2
226b EFI	2	71	97	.1	.2
246 GREEK ORTHODOX	1	NR	NR	-	-
283 LUTH—MO SYNOD	1	130	188	.2	.3
349 PENT HOLINESS	12	1,276	1,558*	1.4	2.6
353 CHR BRETHREN	1	90	125	.1	.2
355 PRESB CH (USA)	13	1,776	2,169*	2.0	3.6
361 PRIM BAPT ASCS	10	153	187*	.2	.3
403 SALVATION ARMY	1	66	80	.1	.1
413 S.D.A.	2	270	330*	.3	.5
419 SO BAPT CONV	60	20,310	24,806*	22.8	40.9
449 UN METHODIST	39	8,570	10,467*	9.6	17.3
467 WESLEYAN[1]	2	142	146	.1	.2
496 JEWISH EST[1]	2	NA	100	.1	.2
497 BLACK BAPT EST[2]	NA	7,486	9,143*	8.4	15.1
499 INDEP.NON-CHAR[3]	1	NA	700	.6	1.2
POWHATAN	**20**	**4,688**	**6,217***	**40.6**	**100.0**
053 ASSEMB OF GOD	1	30	36	.2	.6
081 CATHOLIC	1	NA	361	2.4	5.8
081d LATIN	1	NA	361	2.4	5.8
127 CH GOD (CLEVE)	1	103	124*	.8	2.0
167 CHS OF CHRIST	1	40	60	.4	1.0
193 EPISCOPAL	3	737	902	5.9	14.5
223 FREE WILL BAPT	1	42	51*	.3	.8
285 MENNONITE CH	1	106	174	1.1	2.8
355 PRESB CH (USA)	2	111	134*	.9	2.2
419 SO BAPT CONV	7	2,077	2,509*	16.4	40.4
449 UN METHODIST	2	446	539*	3.5	8.7
496 JEWISH EST[1]	0	NA	124	.8	2.0
497 BLACK BAPT EST[2]	NA	996	1,203*	7.8	19.4
PRINCE EDWARD	**43**	**7,599**	**9,785***	**56.5**	**100.0**
061 BEACHY AMISH	1	41	49*	.3	.5
081 CATHOLIC	2	NA	401	2.3	4.1
081d LATIN	2	NA	401	2.3	4.1
093 CHR CH (DISC)	2	318	484	2.8	4.9
097 CHR CHS&CHS CR	1	129	154*	.9	1.6
127 CH GOD (CLEVE)	1	23	27*	.2	.3
145 CH GOD PROPHCY	2	83	99*	.6	1.0
151 L-D SAINTS	1	NA	217	1.3	2.2
165 CH OF NAZARENE	1	23	0	-	-
167 CHS OF CHRIST	1	9	12	.1	.1
193 EPISCOPAL	1	210	277	1.6	2.8
226 FRIENDS-USA	1	0	16	.1	.2
226d FGC & FUM	1	0	16	.1	.2
283 LUTH—MO SYNOD	2	138	161	.9	1.6
355 PRESB CH (USA)	8	763	909*	5.2	9.3
413 S.D.A.	1	52	62*	.4	.6
419 SO BAPT CONV	10	2,373	2,827*	16.3	28.9
449 UN METHODIST	7	1,265	1,507*	8.7	15.4
467 WESLEYAN	1	27	27	.2	.3
497 BLACK BAPT EST[2]	NA	2,145	2,556*	14.8	26.1
PRINCE GEORGE-HOPEWE	**55**	**14,734**	**20,834***	**41.3**	**100.0**
005 AME ZION	2	606	713	1.4	3.4
053 ASSEMB OF GOD	1	21	25	-	.1
081 CATHOLIC	3	NA	1,806	3.6	8.7
081d LATIN	3	NA	1,806	3.6	8.7
093 CHR CH (DISC)	1	191	339	.7	1.6
097 CHR CHS&CHS CR	1	67	85*	.2	.4
127 CH GOD (CLEVE)	2	330	418*	.8	2.0
151 L-D SAINTS	1	NA	299	.6	1.4
157 CH OF BRETHREN	3	196	248*	.5	1.2
165 CH OF NAZARENE	1	119	173	.3	.8
167 CHS OF CHRIST	2	300	382	.8	1.8
181 CONSRV CONGR	1	102	129*	.3	.6
193 EPISCOPAL	3	381	587	1.2	2.8
246 GREEK ORTHODOX	1	NR	NR	-	-

County and Denomination	Number of churches	Communicant, confirmed, full members	Total adherents		
			Number	Percent of total population	Percent of total adherents
283 LUTH—MO SYNOD	1	374	476	.9	2.3
349 PENT HOLINESS	1	180	228*	.5	1.1
353 CHR BRETHREN	1	15	15	-	.1
355 PRESB CH (USA)	4	785	994*	2.0	4.8
356 PRESB CH AMER	3	875	986	2.0	4.7
403 SALVATION ARMY	1	200	213	.4	1.0
413 S.D.A.	1	36	46*	.1	.2
419 SO BAPT CONV	9	4,745	6,011*	11.9	28.9
443 UN C OF CHRIST	2	127	161*	.3	.8
449 UN METHODIST	8	2,039	2,583*	5.1	12.4
467 WESLEYAN	2	20	85	.2	.4
497 BLACK BAPT EST[2]	NA	3,025	3,832*	7.6	18.4
PRINCE WILLIAM-MANAS	**115**	**41,513**	**95,706***	**38.2**	**100.0**
019 AMER BAPT USA	3	662	876*	.3	.9
053 ASSEMB OF GOD	6	1,444	3,002	1.2	3.1
081 CATHOLIC	7	NA	28,046	11.2	29.3
081d LATIN	6	NA	27,791	11.1	29.0
081h UKRAINIAN	1	NA	255	.1	.3
089 CHR & MISS AL	2	34	78	-	.1
097 CHR CHS&CHS CR	2	461	610*	.2	.6
111 CHR CR,SCIENTST	1	NR	NR	-	-
127 CH GOD (CLEVE)	4	869	1,151*	.5	1.2
145 CH GOD PROPHCY	1	41	54*	-	.1
151 L-D SAINTS	7	NA	2,886	1.2	3.0
157 CH OF BRETHREN	3	714	945*	.4	1.0
165 CH OF NAZARENE	2	347	552	.2	.6
167 CHS OF CHRIST	4	505	655	.3	.7
193 EPISCOPAL	5	1,549	3,536	1.4	3.7
203 EVAN FREE CH	1	95	175	.1	.2
207 E.L.C.A.	6	2,218	3,457	1.4	3.6
223 FREE WILL BAPT	2	281	372*	.1	.4
283 LUTH—MO SYNOD	2	524	808	.3	.8
349 PENT HOLINESS	1	20	26*	-	-
353 CHR BRETHREN	1	40	75	-	.1
355 PRESB CH (USA)	5	1,827	2,419*	1.0	2.5
356 PRESB CH AMER	4	380	485	.2	.5
361 PRIM BAPT ASCS	1	5	7*	-	-
403 SALVATION ARMY	1	91	99	-	.1
413 S.D.A.	3	318	421*	.2	.4
419 SO BAPT CONV	19	11,106	14,705*	5.9	15.4
435 UNITARIAN-UNIV	1	61	104	-	.1
449 UN METHODIST	16	9,314	12,332*	4.9	12.9
469 WELS	1	142	208	.1	.2
496 JEWISH EST[1]	1	NA	3,689	1.5	3.9
497 BLACK BAPT EST[2]	NA	8,465	11,208*	4.5	11.7
498 INDEP.CHARIS.[3]	2	NA	1,900	.8	2.0
499 INDEP.NON-CHAR[3]	1	NA	825	.3	.9
PULASKI	**83**	**11,999**	**15,029***	**43.6**	**100.0**
053 ASSEMB OF GOD	1	141	200	.6	1.3
075 BRETHREN IN CR	1	142	142	.4	.9
081 CATHOLIC	1	NA	147	.4	1.0
081d LATIN	1	NA	147	.4	1.0
093 CHR CH (DISC)	6	443	751	2.2	5.0
097 CHR CHS&CHS CR	2	330	395*	1.1	2.6
127 CH GOD (CLEVE)	5	1,517	1,817*	5.3	12.1
145 CH GOD PROPHCY	4	166	199*	.6	1.3
157 CH OF BRETHREN	3	0	0*	-	-
165 CH OF NAZARENE	1	64	69	.2	.5
167 CHS OF CHRIST	1	95	105	.3	.7
193 EPISCOPAL	1	134	175	.5	1.2
207 E.L.C.A.	1	237	294	.9	2.0
265 INT PENT C CHR	1	9	15	-	.1
339 PENT CH OF GOD	1	53	127	.4	.8
349 PENT HOLINESS	10	759	909*	2.6	6.0
355 PRESB CH (USA)	6	1,108	1,327*	3.8	8.8
356 PRESB CH AMER	3	418	435	1.3	2.9
361 PRIM BAPT ASCS	2	38	46*	.1	.3
403 SALVATION ARMY	1	130	130	.4	.9
413 S.D.A.	1	59	71*	.2	.5
419 SO BAPT CONV	6	1,971	2,361*	6.8	15.7
449 UN METHODIST	23	3,694	4,426*	12.8	29.4
497 BLACK BAPT EST[2]	NA	491	588*	1.7	3.9
499 INDEP.NON-CHAR[3]	1	NA	300	.9	2.0
RAPPAHANNOCK	**19**	**2,232**	**3,111***	**47.0**	**100.0**
053 ASSEMB OF GOD	1	31	40	.6	1.3
081 CATHOLIC	1	NA	260	3.9	8.4
081d LATIN	1	NA	260	3.9	8.4
193 EPISCOPAL	1	154	312	4.7	10.0
361 PRIM BAPT ASCS	3	32	39*	.6	1.3
419 SO BAPT CONV	9	1,408	1,719*	26.0	55.3
449 UN METHODIST	4	607	741*	11.2	23.8

NA–Not applicable   NR–Not reported   *Total adherents estimated from known number of communicant, confirmed, full members.   - Represents a percent less than 0.1.   Percentages may not total due to rounding.
[1]See Appendix E   [2]See Appendix F   [3]See Appendix G   Lines in *italic* represent a breakdown of Catholic rites or Friends affiliations. They are included in their respective denominational total.

Table 4. Churches and Church Membership by County and Denomination: 1990

County and Denomination	Number of churches	Communicant, confirmed, full members	Total adherents Number	Percent of total population	Percent of total adherents
RICHMOND	**33**	**5,204**	**6,602***	**90.8**	**100.0**
005 AME ZION	3	744	869	11.9	13.2
081 CATHOLIC	0	NA	100	1.4	1.5
081d *LATIN*	*0*	*NA*	*100*	*1.4*	*1.5*
089 CHR & MISS AL	2	55	59	.8	.9
097 CHR CHS&CHS CR	2	118	145*	2.0	2.2
127 CH GOD (CLEVE)	1	41	50*	.7	.8
193 EPISCOPAL	2	181	223	3.1	3.4
223 FREE WILL BAPT	1	93	114*	1.6	1.7
283 LUTH—MO SYNOD	1	14	16	.2	.2
285 MENNONITE CH	3	0	20	.3	.3
349 PENT HOLINESS	1	30	37*	.5	.6
355 PRESB CH (USA)	2	273	334*	4.6	5.1
413 S.D.A.	1	56	69*	.9	1.0
419 SO BAPT CONV	8	2,003	2,454*	33.7	37.2
449 UN METHODIST	4	663	812*	11.2	12.3
467 WESLEYAN	2	182	380	5.2	5.8
497 BLACK BAPT EST[2]	NA	751	920*	12.6	13.9
ROANOKE-ROANOKE-SALM	**231**	**89,336**	**124,925***	**62.6**	**100.0**
001 ADVENT CHR CH	1	81	98*	-	.1
005 AME ZION	1	378	431	.2	.3
019 AMER BAPT USA	3	1,634	1,968*	1.0	1.6
053 ASSEMB OF GOD	5	519	719	.4	.6
055 AS REF PRES CH	1	44	48	-	-
075 BRETHREN IN CR	1	32	35	-	-
081 CATHOLIC	5	NA	8,574	4.3	6.9
081d *LATIN*	*4*	*NA*	*8,208*	*4.1*	*6.6*
081e *MARONITE*	*1*	*NA*	*366*	*.2*	*.3*
089 CHR & MISS AL	1	95	140	.1	.1
093 CHR CH (DISC)	9	2,017	3,504	1.8	2.8
097 CHR CHS&CHS CR	7	2,070	2,494*	1.3	2.0
111 CH CR,SCIENTST	1	NR	NR	-	-
123 CH GOD (ANDER)	5	454	509	.3	.4
127 CH GOD (CLEVE)	5	819	987*	.5	.8
145 CH GOD PROPHCY	7	291	351*	.2	.3
151 L-D SAINTS	5	NA	1,825	.9	1.5
157 CH OF BRETHREN	16	3,302	3,978*	2.0	3.2
165 CH OF NAZARENE	6	1,045	1,606	.8	1.3
167 CHS OF CHRIST	7	496	632	.3	.5
193 EPISCOPAL	6	2,791	4,042	2.0	3.2
207 E.L.C.A.	9	2,518	3,301	1.7	2.6
215 EVAN METH CH	1	134	161*	.1	.1
216 EVAN PRESBY CH	2	123	128	.1	.1
223 FREE WILL BAPT	1	77	93*	-	.1
226 FRIENDS-USA	1	18	22*	-	-
226d *FGC & FUM*	*1*	*18*	*22***	*-*	*-*
246 GREEK ORTHODOX	1	NR	NR	-	-
263 INT FOURSQ GOS	1	366	441*	.2	.4
283 LUTH—MO SYNOD	1	219	321	.2	.3
285 MENNONITE CH	1	2	2	-	-
331 ORTH CH IN AM	1	NR	NR	-	-
339 PENT CH OF GOD	1	50	190	.1	.2
349 PENT HOLINESS	3	930	1,120*	.6	.9
353 CHR BRETHREN	1	90	135	.1	.1
355 PRESB CH (USA)	13	5,732	6,905*	3.5	5.5
356 PRESB CH AMER	1	306	333	.2	.3
361 PRIM BAPT ASCS	3	45	54*	-	-
375 REF EPISCOPAL	1	19	23	-	-
403 SALVATION ARMY	1	220	226	.1	.2
413 S.D.A.	2	533	642*	.3	.5
419 SO BAPT CONV	50	37,450	45,116*	22.6	36.1
435 UNITARIAN-UNIV	1	210	379	.2	.3
449 UN METHODIST	29	14,867	17,910*	9.0	14.3
467 WESLEYAN	9	1,344	3,240	1.6	2.6
496 JEWISH EST[1]	2	NA	786	.4	.6
497 BLACK BAPT EST[2]	NA	8,015	9,656*	4.8	7.7
498 INDEP.CHARIS.[3]	1	NA	300	.2	.2
499 INDEP.NON-CHAR[3]	2	NA	1,500	.8	1.2
ROCKBRIDGE-BN VS-LEX	**78**	**11,355**	**14,581***	**46.0**	**100.0**
001 ADVENT CHR CH	2	34	40*	.1	.3
053 ASSEMB OF GOD	1	24	41	.1	.3
055 AS REF PRES CH	4	881	1,002	3.2	6.9
081 CATHOLIC	1	NA	537	1.7	3.7
081d *LATIN*	*1*	*NA*	*537*	*1.7*	*3.7*
127 CH GOD (CLEVE)	1	19	22*	.1	.2
145 CH GOD PROPHCY	4	166	196*	.6	1.3
151 L-D SAINTS	1	NA	496	1.6	3.4
157 CH OF BRETHREN	4	578	682*	2.2	4.7
167 CHS OF CHRIST	1	25	31	.1	.2
193 EPISCOPAL	3	462	657	2.1	4.5
207 E.L.C.A.	3	250	299	.9	2.1
215 EVAN METH CH	1	23	27*	.1	.2
226 FRIENDS-USA	1	0	33	.1	.2
226d *FGC & FUM*	*1*	*0*	*33*	*.1*	*.2*

County and Denomination	Number of churches	Communicant, confirmed, full members	Total adherents Number	Percent of total population	Percent of total adherents
263 INT FOURSQ GOS	1	31	37*	.1	.3
349 PENT HOLINESS	5	812	959*	3.0	6.6
355 PRESB CH (USA)	17	3,144	3,711*	11.7	25.5
356 PRESB CH AMER	1	63	95	.3	.7
413 S.D.A.	1	141	166*	.5	1.1
419 SO BAPT CONV	8	2,351	2,775*	8.7	19.0
449 UN METHODIST	18	2,018	2,382*	7.5	16.3
497 BLACK BAPT EST[2]	NA	333	393*	1.2	2.7
ROCKINGHAM-HARRISON	**187**	**31,793**	**41,979***	**47.6**	**100.0**
053 ASSEMB OF GOD	2	138	280	.3	.7
071 BRETHREN (ASH)	2	269	324*	.4	.8
075 BRETHREN IN CR	1	12	20	-	-
081 CATHOLIC	2	NA	1,603	1.8	3.8
081d *LATIN*	*2*	*NA*	*1,603*	*1.8*	*3.8*
097 CHR CHS&CHS CR	4	390	469*	.5	1.1
127 CH GOD (CLEVE)	5	580	698*	.8	1.7
145 CH GOD PROPHCY	2	83	100*	.1	.2
151 L-D SAINTS	2	NA	527	.6	1.3
157 CH OF BRETHREN	26	5,869	7,065*	8.0	16.8
165 CH OF NAZARENE	3	516	896	1.0	2.1
167 CHS OF CHRIST	2	141	185	.2	.4
193 EPISCOPAL	3	684	898	1.0	2.1
207 E.L.C.A.	8	1,426	1,744	2.0	4.2
216 EVAN PRESBY CH	1	79	80	.1	.2
223 FREE WILL BAPT	1	21	25*	-	.1
226 FRIENDS-USA	2	36	43*	-	.1
226a *CONSERV*	*1*	*9*	*11***	*-*	*-*
226d *FGC & FUM*	*1*	*27*	*32***	*-*	*.1*
263 INT FOURSQ GOS	1	0	0*	-	-
265 INT PENT C CHR	2	17	33	-	.1
285 MENNONITE CH	38	3,800	5,234	5.9	12.5
349 PENT HOLINESS	1	94	113*	.1	.3
355 PRESB CH (USA)	9	2,690	3,238*	3.7	7.7
356 PRESB CH AMER	1	82	156	.2	.4
403 SALVATION ARMY	1	141	152	.2	.4
413 S.D.A.	3	176	212*	.2	.5
419 SO BAPT CONV	7	2,053	2,471*	2.8	5.9
435 UNITARIAN-UNIV	1	62	62	.1	.1
438 UN BRETH IN CR	2	200	200	.2	.5
443 UN C OF CHRIST	14	1,290	1,553*	1.8	3.7
449 UN METHODIST	39	10,236	12,321*	14.0	29.4
496 JEWISH EST[1]	1	NA	0	-	-
497 BLACK BAPT EST[2]	NA	708	852*	1.0	2.0
498 INDEP.CHARIS.[3]	1	NA	425	.5	1.0
RUSSELL	**75**	**7,050**	**8,719***	**30.4**	**100.0**
005 AME ZION	2	483	541	1.9	6.2
053 ASSEMB OF GOD	2	56	107	.4	1.2
081 CATHOLIC	1	NA	50	.2	.6
081d *LATIN*	*1*	*NA*	*50*	*.2*	*.6*
093 CHR CH (DISC)	1	26	42	.1	.5
097 CHR CHS&CHS CR	2	150	184*	.6	2.1
127 CH GOD (CLEVE)	4	280	344*	1.2	3.9
145 CH GOD PROPHCY	3	124	152*	.5	1.7
167 CHS OF CHRIST	3	160	204	.7	2.3
223 FREE WILL BAPT	1	95	117*	.4	1.3
325 OLD REG BAPT	1	22	27*	.1	.3
355 PRESB CH (USA)	2	120	148*	.5	1.7
361 PRIM BAPT ASCS	7	135	166*	.6	1.9
419 SO BAPT CONV	27	3,632	4,465*	15.6	51.2
449 UN METHODIST	19	1,767	2,172*	7.6	24.9
SCOTT	**91**	**7,305**	**8,913***	**38.4**	**100.0**
053 ASSEMB OF GOD	1	39	55	.2	.6
081 CATHOLIC	2	NA	118	.5	1.3
081d *LATIN*	*2*	*NA*	*118*	*.5*	*1.3*
082 CENTRAL BAPT	11	467	557*	2.4	6.2
127 CH GOD (CLEVE)	1	44	53*	.2	.6
151 L-D SAINTS	1	NA	62	.3	.7
167 CHS OF CHRIST	1	50	65	.3	.7
223 FREE WILL BAPT	18	819	977*	4.2	11.0
355 PRESB CH (USA)	1	83	99*	.4	1.1
361 PRIM BAPT ASCS	11	783	935*	4.0	10.5
419 SO BAPT CONV	16	2,623	3,131*	13.5	35.1
449 UN METHODIST	28	2,397	2,861*	12.3	32.1
SHENANDOAH	**110**	**14,584**	**18,966***	**60.0**	**100.0**
053 ASSEMB OF GOD	3	109	206	.7	1.1
071 BRETHREN (ASH)	4	361	438*	1.4	2.3
081 CATHOLIC	1	NA	231	.7	1.2
081d *LATIN*	*1*	*NA*	*231*	*.7*	*1.2*
093 CHR CH (DISC)	8	960	1,727	5.5	9.1
121 CH GOD (ABR)	1	41	50*	.2	.3
127 CH GOD (CLEVE)	1	57	69*	.2	.4
145 CH GOD PROPHCY	1	41	50*	.2	.3

NA–Not applicable   NR–Not reported   *Total adherents estimated from known number of communicant, confirmed, full members.   - Represents a percent less than 0.1.   Percentages may not total due to rounding.
[1]See Appendix E   [2]See Appendix F   [3]See Appendix G   Lines in *italic* represent a breakdown of Catholic rites or Friends affiliations. They are included in their respective denominational total.

Table 4. Churches and Church Membership by County and Denomination: 1990

County and Denomination	Number of churches	Communicant, confirmed, full members	Total adherents Number	Percent of total population	Percent of total adherents
151 L-D SAINTS	1	NA	95	.3	.5
157 CH OF BRETHREN	15	1,783	2,162*	6.8	11.4
165 CH OF NAZARENE	1	22	87	.3	.5
167 CHS OF CHRIST	1	51	67	.2	.4
193 EPISCOPAL	3	181	257	.8	1.4
207 E.L.C.A.	25	4,461	5,577	17.6	29.4
223 FREE WILL BAPT	1	21	25*	.1	.1
285 MENNONITE CH	3	76	140	.4	.7
355 PRESB CH (USA)	3	448	543*	1.7	2.9
413 S.D.A.	2	584	708*	2.2	3.7
419 SO BAPT CONV	1	441	535*	1.7	2.8
443 UN C OF CHRIST	13	1,101	1,335*	4.2	7.0
449 UN METHODIST	22	3,846	4,664*	14.7	24.6
SMYTH	**97**	**12,371**	**15,224***	**47.0**	**100.0**
005 AME ZION	1	185	202	.6	1.3
053 ASSEMB OF GOD	1	19	26	.1	.2
081 CATHOLIC	2	NA	272	.8	1.8
081d *LATIN*	*2*	*NA*	*272*	*.8*	*1.8*
093 CHR CH (DISC)	1	100	165	.5	1.1
097 CHR CHS&CHS CR	4	265	319*	1.0	2.1
123 CH GOD (ANDER)	6	557	650	2.0	4.3
127 CH GOD (CLEVE)	4	425	512*	1.6	3.4
145 CH GOD PROPHCY	4	166	200*	.6	1.3
157 CH OF BRETHREN	2	89	107*	.3	.7
165 CH OF NAZARENE	3	123	243	.8	1.6
167 CHS OF CHRIST	2	52	67	.2	.4
193 EPISCOPAL	2	93	97	.3	.6
207 E.L.C.A.	5	739	834	2.6	5.5
223 FREE WILL BAPT	5	621	748*	2.3	4.9
349 PENT HOLINESS	1	40	48*	.1	.3
353 CHR BRETHREN	1	15	30	.1	.2
355 PRESB CH (USA)	5	488	588*	1.8	3.9
356 PRESB CH AMER	1	42	50	.2	.3
361 PRIM BAPT ASCS	2	47	57*	.2	.4
386 REGULAR BAPT	1	108	130*	.4	.9
413 S.D.A.	1	60	72*	.2	.5
419 SO BAPT CONV	16	4,473	5,391*	16.7	35.4
449 UN METHODIST	27	3,502	4,221*	13.0	27.7
497 BLACK BAPT EST[2]	NA	162	195*	.6	1.3
SOUTHAMPTON-FRANKLIN	**57**	**16,422**	**22,590***	**88.9**	**100.0**
005 AME ZION	7	1,611	4,018	15.8	17.8
081 CATHOLIC	1	NA	300	1.2	1.3
081d *LATIN*	*1*	*NA*	*300*	*1.2*	*1.3*
123 CH GOD (ANDER)	2	41	41	.2	.2
127 CH GOD (CLEVE)	1	143	176*	.7	.8
176 CCC, NOT NAT'L	1	189	233*	.9	1.0
193 EPISCOPAL	2	182	242	1.0	1.1
203 EVAN FREE CH	1	9	9	-	-
226 FRIENDS-USA	1	44	54*	.2	.2
226e *FUM*	*1*	*44*	*54**	*.2*	*.2*
355 PRESB CH (USA)	1	205	253*	1.0	1.1
413 S.D.A.	1	95	117*	.5	.5
419 SO BAPT CONV	18	5,886	7,259*	28.6	32.1
443 UN C OF CHRIST	6	1,345	1,659*	6.5	7.3
449 UN METHODIST	15	2,540	3,133*	12.3	13.9
497 BLACK BAPT EST[2]	NA	4,132	5,096*	20.1	22.6
SPOTSYLVANIA-FREDERI	**72**	**22,462**	**41,262***	**54.0**	**100.0**
019 AMER BAPT USA	1	110	141*	.2	.3
053 ASSEMB OF GOD	1	232	347	.5	.8
071 BRETHREN (ASH)	1	8	10*	-	-
081 CATHOLIC	2	NA	8,871	11.6	21.5
081d *LATIN*	*2*	*NA*	*8,871*	*11.6*	*21.5*
089 CHR & MISS AL	1	6	18	-	-
093 CHR CH (DISC)	2	375	467	.6	1.1
097 CHR CHS&CHS CR	1	36	46*	.1	.1
111 CH CR,SCIENTST	1	NR	NR	-	-
127 CH GOD (CLEVE)	1	273	350*	.5	.8
145 CH GOD PROPHCY	3	124	159*	.2	.4
151 L-D SAINTS	2	NA	926	1.2	2.2
165 CH OF NAZARENE	1	64	118	.2	.3
167 CHS OF CHRIST	2	159	206	.3	.5
193 EPISCOPAL	4	1,463	2,489	3.3	6.0
207 E.L.C.A.	2	592	877	1.1	2.1
223 FREE WILL BAPT	1	104	133*	.2	.3
246 GREEK ORTHODOX	1	NR	NR	-	-
283 LUTH—MO SYNOD	1	199	310	.4	.8
349 PENT HOLINESS	1	26	33*	-	.1
355 PRESB CH (USA)	3	1,024	1,312*	1.7	3.2
361 PRIM BAPT ASCS	1	13	17*	-	-
403 SALVATION ARMY	1	133	136	.2	.3
413 S.D.A.	1	345	442*	.6	1.1
419 SO BAPT CONV	24	11,381	14,577*	19.1	35.3
435 UNITARIAN-UNIV	1	92	132	.2	.3

County and Denomination	Number of churches	Communicant, confirmed, full members	Total adherents Number	Percent of total population	Percent of total adherents
449 UN METHODIST	8	3,200	4,099*	5.4	9.9
496 JEWISH EST[1]	1	NA	140	.2	.3
497 BLACK BAPT EST[2]	NA	2,503	3,206*	4.2	7.8
498 INDEP.CHARIS.[3]	1	NA	300	.4	.7
499 INDEP.NON-CHAR[3]	2	NA	1,400	1.8	3.4
STAFFORD	**43**	**11,672**	**25,745***	**42.0**	**100.0**
019 AMER BAPT USA	1	161	210*	.3	.8
053 ASSEMB OF GOD	2	254	608	1.0	2.4
081 CATHOLIC	1	NA	2,500	4.1	9.7
081d *LATIN*	*1*	*NA*	*2,500*	*4.1*	*9.7*
097 CHR CHS&CHS CR	1	30	39*	.1	.2
127 CH GOD (CLEVE)	1	194	254*	.4	1.0
145 CH GOD PROPHCY	1	41	54*	.1	.2
151 L-D SAINTS	1	NA	626	1.0	2.4
165 CH OF NAZARENE	1	26	47	.1	.2
167 CHS OF CHRIST	3	99	169	.3	.7
193 EPISCOPAL	1	281	286	.5	1.1
207 E.L.C.A.	1	370	567	.9	2.2
223 FREE WILL BAPT	1	125	163*	.3	.6
285 MENNONITE CH	1	12	12	-	-
355 PRESB CH (USA)	2	502	656*	1.1	2.5
419 SO BAPT CONV	16	6,497	8,492*	13.9	33.0
449 UN METHODIST	8	1,777	2,323*	3.8	9.0
496 JEWISH EST[1]	0	NA	6,686	10.9	26.0
497 BLACK BAPT EST[2]	NA	1,303	1,703*	2.8	6.6
499 INDEP.NON-CHAR[3]	1	NA	350	.6	1.4
SUFFOLK CITY	**63**	**21,038**	**27,993***	**53.7**	**100.0**
005 AME ZION	3	388	589	1.1	2.1
053 ASSEMB OF GOD	2	121	220	.4	.8
081 CATHOLIC	2	NA	519	1.0	1.9
081d *LATIN*	*2*	*NA*	*519*	*1.0*	*1.9*
093 CHR CH (DISC)	1	10	25	-	.1
123 CH GOD (ANDER)	1	28	42	.1	.2
127 CH GOD (CLEVE)	1	107	136*	.3	.5
145 CH GOD PROPHCY	2	83	106*	.2	.4
157 CH OF BRETHREN	1	49	62*	.1	.2
167 CHS OF CHRIST	1	79	103	.2	.4
193 EPISCOPAL	4	512	688	1.3	2.5
226 FRIENDS-USA	2	190	242*	.5	.9
226e *FUM*	*2*	*190*	*242**	*.5*	*.9*
349 PENT HOLINESS	1	116	148*	.3	.5
355 PRESB CH (USA)	2	374	476*	.9	1.7
356 PRESB CH AMER	2	207	253	.5	.9
403 SALVATION ARMY	1	77	93	.2	.3
413 S.D.A.	1	45	57*	.1	.2
419 SO BAPT CONV	11	6,011	7,649*	14.7	27.3
443 UN C OF CHRIST	15	4,618	5,876*	11.3	21.0
449 UN METHODIST	9	2,957	3,763*	7.2	13.4
497 BLACK BAPT EST[2]	NA	5,066	6,446*	12.4	23.0
499 INDEP.NON-CHAR[3]	1	NA	500	1.0	1.8
SURRY	**20**	**2,530**	**3,276***	**53.3**	**100.0**
053 ASSEMB OF GOD	1	15	18	.3	.5
081 CATHOLIC	1	NA	9	.1	.3
081d *LATIN*	*1*	*NA*	*9*	*.1*	*.3*
176 CCC, NOT NAT'L	2	42	53*	.9	1.6
193 EPISCOPAL	2	36	99	1.6	3.0
226 FRIENDS-USA	1	0	24	.4	.7
226b *EFI*	*1*	*0*	*24*	*.4*	*.7*
349 PENT HOLINESS	1	63	79*	1.3	2.4
419 SO BAPT CONV	5	714	901*	14.7	27.5
443 UN C OF CHRIST	1	21	26*	.4	.8
449 UN METHODIST	6	471	594*	9.7	18.1
497 BLACK BAPT EST[2]	NA	1,168	1,473*	24.0	45.0
SUSSEX	**25**	**6,121**	**7,685***	**75.0**	**100.0**
005 AME ZION	3	184	260	2.5	3.4
019 AMER BAPT USA	1	464	575*	5.6	7.5
081 CATHOLIC	1	NA	70	.7	.9
081d *LATIN*	*1*	*NA*	*70*	*.7*	*.9*
176 CCC, NOT NAT'L	1	184	228*	2.2	3.0
193 EPISCOPAL	1	48	60	.6	.8
413 S.D.A.	1	81	100*	1.0	1.3
419 SO BAPT CONV	8	1,675	2,075*	20.2	27.0
443 UN C OF CHRIST	2	138	171*	1.7	2.2
449 UN METHODIST	7	1,308	1,620*	15.8	21.1
497 BLACK BAPT EST[2]	NA	2,039	2,526*	24.6	32.9
TAZEWELL	**144**	**14,381**	**19,382°**	**42.2**	**100.0**
001 ADVENT CHR CH	2	75	92*	.2	.5
011 A.W.M.C.	1	16	20*	-	.1
053 ASSEMB OF GOD	12	891	1,501	3.3	7.7
081 CATHOLIC	2	NA	327	.7	1.7

NA–Not applicable   NR–Not reported   *Total adherents estimated from known number of communicant, confirmed, full members.   - Represents a percent less than 0.1.   Percentages may not total due to rounding.
[1]See Appendix E   [2]See Appendix F   [3]See Appendix G   Lines in *italic* represent a breakdown of Catholic rites or Friends affiliations. They are included in their respective denominational total.

VIRGINIA

Table 4. Churches and Church Membership by County and Denomination: 1990

County and Denomination	Number of churches	Communicant, confirmed, full members	Total adherents Number	Total adherents Percent of total population	Total adherents Percent of total adherents
081d *LATIN*	2	NA	327	.7	1.7
093 CHR CH (DISC)	9	764	1,346	2.9	6.9
097 CHR CHS&CHS CR	11	1,106	1,360*	3.0	7.0
123 CH GOD (ANDER)	4	194	215	.5	1.1
127 CH GOD (CLEVE)	11	990	1,218*	2.7	6.3
145 CH GOD PROPHCY	4	165	203*	.4	1.0
151 L-D SAINTS	1	NA	383	.8	2.0
167 CHS OF CHRIST	4	105	132	.3	.7
193 EPISCOPAL	4	210	247	.5	1.3
207 E.L.C.A.	1	25	31	.1	.2
223 FREE WILL BAPT	5	339	417*	.9	2.2
323 OLD ORD AMISH	1	NA	50	.1	.3
325 OLD REG BAPT	1	7	9*	-	-
349 PENT HOLINESS	3	208	256*	.6	1.3
355 PRESB CH (USA)	9	1,154	1,419*	3.1	7.3
356 PRESB CH AMER	2	157	222	.5	1.1
361 PRIM BAPT ASCS	4	122	150*	.3	.8
413 S.D.A.	2	66	81*	.2	.4
419 SO BAPT CONV	11	2,881	3,543*	7.7	18.3
449 UN METHODIST	38	4,507	5,543*	12.1	28.6
467 WESLEYAN	2	106	257	.6	1.3
497 BLACK BAPT EST²	NA	293	360*	.8	1.9
VIRGINIA BEACH CITY	**140**	**69,157**	**144,288***	**36.7**	**100.0**
053 ASSEMB OF GOD	5	762	1,284	.3	.9
061 BEACHY AMISH	1	45	58*	-	-
081 CATHOLIC	8	NA	25,043	6.4	17.4
081d *LATIN*	8	NA	25,043	6.4	17.4
089 CHR & MISS AL	1	76	146	-	.1
093 CHR CH (DISC)	3	409	739	.2	.5
097 CHR CHS&CHS CR	5	1,285	1,663*	.4	1.2
105 CHRISTIAN REF	1	58	70	-	-
111 CH CR,SCIENTST	1	NR	NR	-	-
123 CH GOD (ANDER)	1	60	60	-	-
127 CH GOD (CLEVE)	3	306	396*	.1	.3
145 CH GOD PROPHCY	1	41	53*	-	-
151 L-D SAINTS	6	NA	3,278	.8	2.3
157 CH OF BRETHREN	1	223	289*	.1	.2
165 CH OF NAZARENE	2	787	724	.2	.5
167 CHS OF CHRIST	2	257	334	.1	.2
179 CONSRV BAPT	1	NR	NR	-	-
193 EPISCOPAL	9	5,304	7,572	1.9	5.2
203 EVAN FREE CH	1	0	0	-	-
207 E.L.C.A.	5	1,767	2,520	.6	1.7
216 EVAN PRESBY CH	1	1,048	1,074	.3	.7
223 FREE WILL BAPT	2	1,512	1,957*	.5	1.4
226 FRIENDS-USA	2	105	270	.1	.2
226a *CONSERV*	1	41	164	-	.1
226b *EFI*	1	64	106	-	.1
246 GREEK ORTHODOX	1	NR	NR	-	-
265 INT PENT C CHR	1	61	183	-	.1
283 LUTH—MO SYNOD	2	1,066	1,371	.3	1.0
349 PENT HOLINESS	1	74	96*	-	.1
355 PRESB CH (USA)	10	4,151	5,373*	1.4	3.7
356 PRESB CH AMER	4	1,053	1,160	.3	.8
419 SO BAPT CONV	22	17,145	22,192*	5.6	15.4
435 UNITARIAN-UNIV	1	19	22	-	-
443 UN C OF CHRIST	4	981	1,270*	.3	.9
449 UN METHODIST	23	13,874	17,958*	4.6	12.4
469 WELS	1	140	218	.1	.2
496 JEWISH EST¹	3	NA	10,195	2.6	7.1
497 BLACK BAPT EST²	NA	16,548	21,420*	5.4	14.8
498 INDEP.CHARIS.³	2	NA	12,000	3.1	8.3
499 INDEP.NON-CHAR³	3	NA	3,300	.8	2.3
WARREN	**39**	**6,117**	**9,065***	**34.7**	**100.0**
053 ASSEMB OF GOD	3	379	635	2.4	7.0
081 CATHOLIC	1	NA	790	3.0	8.7
081d *LATIN*	1	NA	790	3.0	8.7
097 CHR CHS&CHS CR	1	0	0*	-	-
121 CH GOD (ABR)	2	81	101*	.4	1.1
123 CH GOD (ANDER)	1	5	5	-	.1
127 CH GOD (CLEVE)	1	68	85*	.3	.9
145 CH GOD PROPHCY	1	41	51*	.2	.6
151 L-D SAINTS	1	NA	362	1.4	4.0
157 CH OF BRETHREN	1	89	111*	.4	1.2
165 CH OF NAZARENE	1	61	48	.2	.5
167 CHS OF CHRIST	1	70	91	.3	1.0
193 EPISCOPAL	1	273	492	1.9	5.4
207 E.L.C.A.	1	170	218	.8	2.4
259 IFCA	1	NR	NR	-	-
355 PRESB CH (USA)	3	442	552*	2.1	6.1
361 PRIM BAPT ASCS	2	17	21*	.1	.2
403 SALVATION ARMY	1	105	111	.4	1.2
413 S.D.A.	1	45	56*	.2	.6
419 SO BAPT CONV	5	1,884	2,354*	9.0	26.0
449 UN METHODIST	10	2,070	2,586*	9.9	28.5
497 BLACK BAPT EST²	NA	317	396*	1.5	4.4
WASHINGTON-BRISTOL	**161**	**28,184**	**37,518***	**58.3**	**100.0**
005 AME ZION	3	495	590	.9	1.6
053 ASSEMB OF GOD	3	212	482	.7	1.3
081 CATHOLIC	2	NA	1,717	2.7	4.6
081d *LATIN*	2	NA	1,717	2.7	4.6
093 CHR CH (DISC)	1	28	46	.1	.1
097 CHR CHS&CHS CR	15	1,679	2,015*	3.1	5.4
123 CH GOD (ANDER)	4	133	313	.5	.8
127 CH GOD (CLEVE)	4	424	509*	.8	1.4
145 CH GOD PROPHCY	4	166	199*	.3	.5
151 L-D SAINTS	2	NA	521	.8	1.4
157 CH OF BRETHREN	1	53	64*	.1	.2
165 CH OF NAZARENE	2	92	107	.2	.3
167 CHS OF CHRIST	8	513	683	1.1	1.8
193 EPISCOPAL	2	548	715	1.1	1.9
207 E.L.C.A.	3	584	803	1.2	2.1
223 FREE WILL BAPT	3	715	858*	1.3	2.3
325 OLD REG BAPT	1	19	23*	-	.1
339 PENT CH OF GOD	2	62	117	.2	.3
349 PENT HOLINESS	2	124	149*	.2	.4
355 PRESB CH (USA)	15	2,108	2,530*	3.9	6.7
356 PRESB CH AMER	4	250	298	.5	.8
361 PRIM BAPT ASCS	4	212	254*	.4	.7
413 S.D.A.	1	102	122*	.2	.3
419 SO BAPT CONV	29	11,178	13,414*	20.9	35.8
435 UNITARIAN-UNIV	1	20	28	-	.1
449 UN METHODIST	43	7,939	9,527*	14.8	25.4
497 BLACK BAPT EST²	NA	528	634*	1.0	1.7
499 INDEP.NON-CHAR³	2	NA	800	1.2	2.1
WESTMORELAND	**24**	**6,225**	**8,240***	**53.2**	**100.0**
053 ASSEMB OF GOD	1	49	60	.4	.7
081 CATHOLIC	1	NA	353	2.3	4.3
081d *LATIN*	1	NA	353	2.3	4.3
093 CHR CH (DISC)	1	84	120	.8	1.5
193 EPISCOPAL	5	623	996	6.4	12.1
419 SO BAPT CONV	6	1,804	2,214*	14.3	26.9
449 UN METHODIST	10	1,917	2,352*	15.2	28.5
497 BLACK BAPT EST²	NA	1,748	2,145*	13.9	26.0
WISE-NORTON CITY	**121**	**12,570**	**16,514***	**37.7**	**100.0**
005 AME ZION	2	650	728	1.7	4.4
053 ASSEMB OF GOD	5	524	847	1.9	5.1
081 CATHOLIC	4	NA	389	.9	2.4
081d *LATIN*	4	NA	389	.9	2.4
082 CENTRAL BAPT	1	100	125*	.3	.8
093 CHR CH (DISC)	1	64	154	.4	.9
097 CHR CHS&CHS CR	3	385	480*	1.1	2.9
123 CH GOD (ANDER)	3	270	321	.7	1.9
127 CH GOD (CLEVE)	5	316	394*	.9	2.4
145 CH GOD PROPHCY	5	208	259*	.6	1.6
151 L-D SAINTS	1	NA	228	.5	1.4
167 CHS OF CHRIST	4	110	143	.3	.9
193 EPISCOPAL	3	189	264	.6	1.6
207 E.L.C.A.	1	43	59	.1	.4
223 FREE WILL BAPT	25	1,418	1,767*	4.0	10.7
259 IFCA	1	NR	NR	-	-
325 OLD REG BAPT	9	253	315*	.7	1.9
349 PENT HOLINESS	1	48	60*	.1	.4
355 PRESB CH (USA)	8	393	490*	1.1	3.0
356 PRESB CH AMER	1	35	67	.2	.4
361 PRIM BAPT ASCS	4	150	187*	.4	1.1
413 S.D.A.	1	168	209*	.5	1.3
419 SO BAPT CONV	15	4,329	5,394*	12.3	32.7
449 UN METHODIST	18	2,742	3,416*	7.8	20.7
497 BLACK BAPT EST²	NA	175	218*	.5	1.3
WYTHE	**96**	**9,722**	**12,725***	**50.0**	**100.0**
053 ASSEMB OF GOD	2	113	186	.7	1.5
081 CATHOLIC	1	NA	302	1.2	2.4
081d *LATIN*	1	NA	302	1.2	2.4
093 CHR CH (DISC)	3	184	295	1.2	2.3
123 CH GOD (ANDER)	2	49	92	.4	.7
127 CH GOD (CLEVE)	6	457	556*	2.2	4.4
145 CH GOD PROPHCY	6	249	303*	1.2	2.4
151 L-D SAINTS	2	NA	386	1.5	3.0
165 CH OF NAZARENE	1	19	39	.2	.3
167 CHS OF CHRIST	3	111	142	.6	1.1
193 EPISCOPAL	1	207	262	1.0	2.1
207 E.L.C.A.	9	1,065	1,317	5.2	10.3
339 PENT CH OF GOD	1	13	20	.1	.2
349 PENT HOLINESS	14	1,211	1,473*	5.8	11.6
355 PRESB CH (USA)	4	452	550*	2.2	4.3

NA—Not applicable   NR—Not reported   *Total adherents estimated from known number of communicant, confirmed, full members.   - Represents a percent less than 0.1.   Percentages may not total due to rounding.

¹See Appendix E   ²See Appendix F   ³See Appendix G   Lines in *italic* represent a breakdown of Catholic rites or Friends affiliations. They are included in their respective denominational total.

Table 4. Churches and Church Membership by County and Denomination: 1990

County and Denomination	Number of churches	Communicant, confirmed, full members	Total adherents Number	Percent of total population	Percent of total adherents
413 S.D.A.	1	146	178*	.7	1.4
419 SO BAPT CONV	3	884	1,075*	4.2	8.4
449 UN METHODIST	37	4,346	5,286*	20.8	41.5
497 BLACK BAPT EST[2]	NA	216	263*	1.0	2.1
YORK	**29**	**14,384**	**20,290***	**38.0**	**100.0**
011 A.W.M.C.	1	0	0*	-	-
053 ASSEMB OF GOD	2	276	502	.9	2.5
081 CATHOLIC	1	NA	1,449	2.7	7.1
081d *LATIN*	*1*	*NA*	*1,449*	*2.7*	*7.1*
093 CHR CH (DISC)	1	155	197	.4	1.0
097 CHR CHS&CHS CR	1	78	100*	.2	.5
193 EPISCOPAL	2	511	653	1.2	3.2
207 E.L.C.A.	1	607	735	1.4	3.6
223 FREE WILL BAPT	1	78	100*	.2	.5
349 PENT HOLINESS	1	3	4*	-	-
353 CHR BRETHREN	1	50	100	.2	.5
355 PRESB CH (USA)	2	1,084	1,394*	2.6	6.9
356 PRESB CH AMER	1	233	313	.6	1.5
419 SO BAPT CONV	7	3,930	5,054*	9.5	24.9
449 UN METHODIST	6	5,306	6,823*	12.8	33.6
469 WELS	1	71	96	.2	.5
496 JEWISH EST[1]	0	NA	196	.4	1.0
497 BLACK BAPT EST[2]	NA	2,002	2,574*	4.8	12.7

WASHINGTON

County and Denomination	Number of churches	Communicant, confirmed, full members	Total adherents Number	Percent of total population	Percent of total adherents
THE STATE.....	4,092	619,581	1,612,516*	33.1	100.0
ADAMS	**31**	**3,017**	**6,849***	**50.3**	**100.0**
053 ASSEMB OF GOD	4	385	749	5.5	10.9
081 CATHOLIC	4	NA	1,980	14.6	28.9
081d *LATIN*	*4*	*NA*	*1,980*	*14.6*	*28.9*
093 CHR CH (DISC)	1	78	191	1.4	2.8
151 L-D SAINTS	1	NA	94	.7	1.4
165 CH OF NAZARENE	2	178	677	5.0	9.9
167 CHS OF CHRIST	1	21	35	.3	.5
193 EPISCOPAL	1	12	21	.2	.3
207 E.L.C.A.	3	596	731	5.4	10.7
263 INT FOURSQ GOS	1	30	41*	.3	.6
283 LUTH—MO SYNOD	1	53	72	.5	1.1
287 MENN GEN CONF	1	165	200	1.5	2.9
355 PRESB CH (USA)	2	333	457*	3.4	6.7
413 S.D.A.	1	108	148*	1.1	2.2
419 SO BAPT CONV	2	121	166*	1.2	2.4
443 UN C OF CHRIST	3	391	537*	3.9	7.8
449 UN METHODIST	3	546	750*	5.5	11.0
ASOTIN	**21**	**2,274**	**5,673***	**32.2**	**100.0**
053 ASSEMB OF GOD	2	98	290	1.6	5.1
081 CATHOLIC	1	NA	1,800	10.2	31.7
081d *LATIN*	*1*	*NA*	*1,800*	*10.2*	*31.7*
093 CHR CH (DISC)	1	160	254	1.4	4.5
123 CH GOD (ANDER)	1	104	104	.6	1.8
151 L-D SAINTS	1	NA	627	3.6	11.1
164 CH LUTH CONF	1	70	98	.6	1.7
165 CH OF NAZARENE	1	0	0	-	-
167 CHS OF CHRIST	1	19	24	.1	.4
207 E.L.C.A.	1	317	414	2.4	7.3
221 FREE METHODIST	1	24	31	.2	.5
263 INT FOURSQ GOS	1	23	29*	.2	.5
339 PENT CH OF GOD	1	34	77	.4	1.4
355 PRESB CH (USA)	1	443	567*	3.2	10.0
413 S.D.A.	1	201	257*	1.5	4.5
419 SO BAPT CONV	2	286	366*	2.1	6.5
449 UN METHODIST	3	447	573*	3.3	10.1
467 WESLEYAN	1	48	162	.9	2.9
BENTON	**112**	**18,293**	**48,151***	**42.8**	**100.0**
019 AMER BAPT USA	3	536	704*	.6	1.5
039 AP CHR CH(NAZ)	1	33	43*	-	.1
053 ASSEMB OF GOD	7	768	1,421	1.3	3.0
059 BAPT MISS ASSN	1	21	28*	-	.1
081 CATHOLIC	5	NA	13,930	12.4	28.9
081d *LATIN*	*5*	*NA*	*13,930*	*12.4*	*28.9*
089 CHR & MISS AL	2	150	244	.2	.5
093 CHR CH (DISC)	4	638	1,131	1.0	2.3
097 CHR CHS&CHS CR	1	40	53*	-	.1
105 CHRISTIAN REF	1	210	326	.3	.7
111 CH CR,SCIENTST	1	NR	NR	-	-
123 CH GOD (ANDER)	1	0	196	.2	.4

County and Denomination	Number of churches	Communicant, confirmed, full members	Total adherents Number	Percent of total population	Percent of total adherents
127 CH GOD (CLEVE)	3	163	214*	.2	.4
145 CH GOD PROPHCY	1	27	35*	-	.1
151 L-D SAINTS	20	NA	8,554	7.6	17.8
165 CH OF NAZARENE	4	708	917	.8	1.9
167 CHS OF CHRIST	6	419	590	.5	1.2
179 CONSRV BAPT	3	NR	NR	-	-
193 EPISCOPAL	3	638	907	.8	1.9
203 EVAN FREE CH	1	35	70	.1	.1
207 E.L.C.A.	5	2,027	2,912	2.6	6.0
221 FREE METHODIST	1	17	22	-	-
223 FREE WILL BAPT	1	69	91*	.1	.2
226 FRIENDS-USA	1	2	4	-	-
226f *INDEPENDNT*	*1*	*2*	*4*	-	-
263 INT FOURSQ GOS	1	151	198*	.2	.4
283 LUTH—MO SYNOD	4	956	1,345	1.2	2.8
355 PRESB CH (USA)	8	1,878	2,468*	2.2	5.1
413 S.D.A.	3	588	773*	.7	1.6
419 SO BAPT CONV	7	3,318	4,360*	3.9	9.1
435 UNITARIAN-UNIV	1	78	133	.1	.3
443 UN C OF CHRIST	1	151	198*	.2	.4
449 UN METHODIST	9	4,276	5,619*	5.0	11.7
469 WELS	1	165	251	.2	.5
496 JEWISH EST[1]	1	NA	110	.1	.2
497 BLACK BAPT EST[2]	NA	231	304*	.3	.6
CHELAN	**72**	**11,728**	**24,032***	**46.0**	**100.0**
019 AMER BAPT USA	2	420	536*	1.0	2.2
053 ASSEMB OF GOD	8	809	1,732	3.3	7.2
081 CATHOLIC	4	NA	6,085	11.6	25.3
081d *LATIN*	*4*	*NA*	*6,085*	*11.6*	*25.3*
089 CHR & MISS AL	1	66	158	.3	.7
093 CHR CH (DISC)	3	247	430	.8	1.8
111 CH CR,SCIENTST	2	NR	NR	-	-
121 CH GOD (ABR)	2	190	243*	.5	1.0
127 CH GOD (CLEVE)	1	38	49*	.1	.2
151 L-D SAINTS	4	NA	1,381	2.6	5.7
157 CH OF BRETHREN	2	492	628*	1.2	2.6
165 CH OF NAZARENE	3	464	836	1.6	3.5
167 CHS OF CHRIST	3	486	563	1.1	2.3
193 EPISCOPAL	3	825	1,184	2.3	4.9
207 E.L.C.A.	5	1,160	1,503	2.9	6.3
221 FREE METHODIST	1	426	822	1.6	3.4
226 FRIENDS-USA	1	39	47	.1	.2
226b *EFI*	*1*	*39*	*47*	*.1*	*.2*
263 INT FOURSQ GOS	5	505	645*	1.2	2.7
283 LUTH—MO SYNOD	1	290	405	.8	1.7
339 PENT CH OF GOD	1	34	77	.1	.3
355 PRESB CH (USA)	3	749	956*	1.8	4.0
361 PRIM BAPT ASCS	1	16	20*	-	.1
413 S.D.A.	4	836	1,067*	2.0	4.4
419 SO BAPT CONV	3	1,216	1,552*	3.0	6.5
435 UNITARIAN-UNIV	1	59	99	.2	.4
443 UN C OF CHRIST	2	64	82*	.2	.3
449 UN METHODIST	6	2,297	2,932*	5.6	12.2
CLALLAM	**66**	**6,988**	**16,299***	**28.9**	**100.0**
005 AME ZION	1	288	355	.6	2.2
019 AMER BAPT USA	1	280	347*	.6	2.1
053 ASSEMB OF GOD	7	620	1,434	2.5	8.8
081 CATHOLIC	4	NA	4,892	8.7	30.0
081d *LATIN*	*4*	*NA*	*4,892*	*8.7*	*30.0*
089 CHR & MISS AL	2	82	234	.4	1.4
093 CHR CH (DISC)	1	56	113	.2	.7
111 CH CR,SCIENTST	2	NR	NR	-	-
123 CH GOD (ANDER)	2	55	69	.1	.4
127 CH GOD (CLEVE)	1	29	36*	.1	.2
145 CH GOD PROPHCY	1	27	33*	.1	.2
151 L-D SAINTS	4	NA	1,457	2.6	8.9
165 CH OF NAZARENE	3	91	214	.4	1.3
167 CHS OF CHRIST	2	91	115	.2	.7
193 EPISCOPAL	2	453	598	1.1	3.7
203 EVAN FREE CH	1	12	21	-	.1
207 E.L.C.A.	3	877	1,169	2.1	7.2
217 FIRE BAPTIZED	1	10	12*	-	.1
221 FREE METHODIST	1	23	42	.1	.3
226 FRIENDS-USA	1	29	69	.1	.4
226b *EFI*	*1*	*29*	*69*	*.1*	*.4*
259 IFCA	3	NR	NR	-	-
263 INT FOURSQ GOS	2	229	284*	.5	1.7
283 LUTH—MO SYNOD	3	681	916	1.6	5.6
329 OPEN BIBLE STD	1	NR	NR	-	-
355 PRESB CH (USA)	4	661	819*	1.5	5.0
403 SALVATION ARMY	1	75	75	.1	.5
413 S.D.A.	3	416	515*	.9	3.2
419 SO BAPT CONV	4	600	743*	1.3	4.6
435 UNITARIAN-UNIV	1	52	52	.1	.3
443 UN C OF CHRIST	1	98	121*	.2	.7

NA–Not applicable NR–Not reported *Total adherents estimated from known number of communicant, confirmed, full members. - Represents a percent less than 0.1. Percentages may not total due to rounding.
[1]See Appendix E [2]See Appendix F [3]See Appendix G Lines in *italic* represent a breakdown of Catholic rites or Friends affiliations. They are included in their respective denominational total.

Table 4. Churches and Church Membership by County and Denomination: 1990

County and Denomination	Number of churches	Communicant, confirmed, full members	Total adherents Number	Percent of total population	Percent of total adherents
449 UN METHODIST	2	1,147	1,421*	2.5	8.7
467 WESLEYAN	1	6	43	.1	.3
496 JEWISH EST¹	0	NA	100	.2	.6
CLARK	**179**	**28,366**	**72,068***	**30.3**	**100.0**
019 AMER BAPT USA	2	172	222*	.1	.3
045 APOSTOLIC LUTH	1	185	480	.2	.7
053 ASSEMB OF GOD	10	1,572	3,903	1.6	5.4
057 BAPT GEN CONF	1	510	658*	.3	.9
081 CATHOLIC	8	NA	17,670	7.4	24.5
081d LATIN	8	NA	17,670	7.4	24.5
089 CHR & MISS AL	1	23	64	-	.1
093 CHR CH (DISC)	2	315	495	.2	.7
097 CHR CHS&CHS CR	4	530	684*	.3	.9
105 CHRISTIAN REF	1	71	113	-	.2
111 CH CR,SCIENTST	2	NR	NR	-	-
123 CH GOD (ANDER)	3	81	1,158	.5	1.6
127 CH GOD (CLEVE)	2	180	232*	.1	.3
145 CH GOD PROPHCY	3	76	98*	-	.1
151 L-D SAINTS	23	NA	10,096	4.2	14.0
163 CH OF LUTH BR	1	16	41	-	.1
165 CH OF NAZARENE	11	2,265	2,760	1.2	3.8
167 CHS OF CHRIST	5	784	1,070	.4	1.5
179 CONSRV BAPT	8	NR	NR	-	-
193 EPISCOPAL	5	846	1,611	.7	2.2
203 EVAN FREE CH	6	490	790	.3	1.1
207 E.L.C.A.	11	4,303	5,706	2.4	7.9
215 EVAN METH CH	1	35	45*	-	.1
221 FREE METHODIST	1	44	86	-	.1
223 FREE WILL BAPT	1	49	63*	-	.1
226 FRIENDS-USA	5	371	541	.2	.8
226b EFI	5	371	541	.2	.8
249 AP CATH ASSYR	0	3	12	-	-
259 IFCA	1	NR	NR	-	-
263 INT FOURSQ GOS	4	493	636*	.3	.9
283 LUTH—MO SYNOD	5	2,079	2,956	1.2	4.1
291 MISSIONARY CH	1	15	15	-	-
313 N AM BAPT CONF	1	342	441*	.2	.6
329 OPEN BIBLE STD	3	NR	NR	-	-
339 PENT CH OF GOD	2	69	154	.1	.2
355 PRESB CH (USA)	5	2,391	3,084*	1.3	4.3
403 SALVATION ARMY	1	152	169	.1	.2
413 S.D.A.	10	2,798	3,609*	1.5	5.0
419 SO BAPT CONV	9	2,190	2,825*	1.2	3.9
435 UNITARIAN-UNIV	1	172	252	.1	.3
438 UN BRETH IN CR	1	21	29	-	-
443 UN C OF CHRIST	1	367	473*	.2	.7
449 UN METHODIST	10	3,496	4,510*	1.9	6.3
467 WESLEYAN	2	54	122	.1	.2
469 WELS	1	171	217	.1	.3
496 JEWISH EST¹	0	NA	1,509	.6	2.1
497 BLACK BAPT EST²	NA	635	819*	.3	1.1
498 INDEP.CHARIS.³	1	NA	1,000	.4	1.4
499 INDEP.NON-CHAR³	2	NA	650	.3	.9
COLUMBIA	**13**	**778**	**1,369***	**34.0**	**100.0**
053 ASSEMB OF GOD	1	75	101	2.5	7.4
081 CATHOLIC	1	NA	180	4.5	13.1
081d LATIN	1	NA	180	4.5	13.1
097 CHR CHS&CHS CR	1	160	196*	4.9	14.3
151 L-D SAINTS	1	NA	184	4.6	13.4
165 CH OF NAZARENE	1	28	52	1.3	3.8
179 CONSRV BAPT	1	NR	NR	-	-
193 EPISCOPAL	1	20	26	.6	1.9
263 INT FOURSQ GOS	1	18	22*	.5	1.6
283 LUTH—MO SYNOD	1	132	191	4.7	14.0
413 S.D.A.	1	50	61*	1.5	4.5
438 UN BRETH IN CR	1	37	39	1.0	2.8
443 UN C OF CHRIST	1	88	108*	2.7	7.9
449 UN METHODIST	1	170	209*	5.2	15.3
COWLITZ	**79**	**14,190**	**27,776***	**33.8**	**100.0**
019 AMER BAPT USA	3	951	1,212*	1.5	4.4
045 APOSTOLIC LUTH	1	39	80	.1	.3
053 ASSEMB OF GOD	8	1,347	1,958	2.4	7.0
081 CATHOLIC	5	NA	6,586	8.0	23.7
081d LATIN	5	NA	6,586	8.0	23.7
089 CHR & MISS AL	1	60	102	.1	.4
093 CHR CH (DISC)	1	140	190	.2	.7
097 CHR CHS&CHS CR	1	0	0*	-	-
111 CH CR,SCIENTST	1	NR	NR	-	-
123 CH GOD (ANDER)	1	57	69	.1	.2
127 CH GOD (CLEVE)	3	646	823*	1.0	3.0
145 CH GOD PROPHCY	1	27	34*	-	.1
151 L-D SAINTS	5	NA	2,101	2.6	7.6
163 CH OF LUTH BR	1	40	63	.1	.2
165 CH OF NAZARENE	5	768	1,295	1.6	4.7
167 CHS OF CHRIST	2	135	204	.2	.7
179 CONSRV BAPT	3	NR	NR	-	-
193 EPISCOPAL	1	429	620	.8	2.2
203 EVAN FREE CH	1	23	48	.1	.2
207 E.L.C.A.	6	2,689	3,673	4.5	13.2
221 FREE METHODIST	1	41	56	.1	.2
226 FRIENDS-USA	1	158	158	.2	.6
226b EFI	1	158	158	.2	.6
263 INT FOURSQ GOS	3	187	238*	.3	.9
274 LAT EVAN LUTH	1	21	21	-	.1
283 LUTH—MO SYNOD	1	263	346	.4	1.2
339 PENT CH OF GOD	1	34	77	.1	.3
353 CHR BRETHREN	1	30	65	.1	.2
355 PRESB CH (USA)	3	586	747*	.9	2.7
403 SALVATION ARMY	1	90	93	.1	.3
413 S.D.A.	3	700	892*	1.1	3.2
419 SO BAPT CONV	9	3,609	4,598*	5.6	16.6
449 UN METHODIST	4	1,120	1,427*	1.7	5.1
DOUGLAS	**39**	**2,936**	**7,966***	**30.4**	**100.0**
019 AMER BAPT USA	1	32	42*	.2	.5
053 ASSEMB OF GOD	4	126	236	.9	3.0
081 CATHOLIC	6	NA	3,150	12.0	39.5
081d LATIN	6	NA	3,150	12.0	39.5
093 CHR CH (DISC)	2	45	53	.2	.7
123 CH GOD (ANDER)	2	127	161	.6	2.0
127 CH GOD (CLEVE)	1	228	296*	1.1	3.7
151 L-D SAINTS	3	NA	874	3.3	11.0
165 CH OF NAZARENE	1	38	64	.2	.8
167 CHS OF CHRIST	1	15	21	.1	.3
179 CONSRV BAPT	1	NR	NR	-	-
207 E.L.C.A.	2	330	417	1.6	5.2
223 FREE WILL BAPT	1	122	159*	.6	2.0
259 IFCA	1	NR	NR	-	-
263 INT FOURSQ GOS	1	0	0*	-	-
283 LUTH—MO SYNOD	1	278	363	1.4	4.6
339 PENT CH OF GOD	1	34	77	.3	1.0
355 PRESB CH (USA)	3	235	306*	1.2	3.8
413 S.D.A.	1	163	212*	.8	2.7
419 SO BAPT CONV	1	738	959*	3.7	12.0
449 UN METHODIST	3	285	371*	1.4	4.7
469 WELS	2	140	205	.8	2.6
FERRY	**15**	**361**	**2,190***	**34.8**	**100.0**
053 ASSEMB OF GOD	2	37	97	1.5	4.4
081 CATHOLIC	5	NA	1,027	16.3	46.9
081d LATIN	5	NA	1,027	16.3	46.9
151 L-D SAINTS	2	NA	515	8.2	23.5
165 CH OF NAZARENE	1	40	126	2.0	5.8
193 EPISCOPAL	1	20	26	.4	1.2
283 LUTH—MO SYNOD	1	57	127	2.0	5.8
355 PRESB CH (USA)	2	89	117*	1.9	5.3
413 S.D.A.	1	118	155*	2.5	7.1
FRANKLIN	**62**	**5,977**	**19,467***	**51.9**	**100.0**
019 AMER BAPT USA	3	217	300*	.8	1.5
053 ASSEMB OF GOD	6	716	1,303	3.5	6.7
081 CATHOLIC	3	NA	5,680	15.2	29.2
081d LATIN	3	NA	5,680	15.2	29.2
097 CHR CHS&CHS CR	1	285	394*	1.1	2.0
111 CH CR,SCIENTST	1	NR	NR	-	-
127 CH GOD (CLEVE)	3	291	402*	1.1	2.1
143 CG IN CR(MENN)	1	44	61*	.2	.3
145 CH GOD PROPHCY	1	27	37*	.1	.2
151 L-D SAINTS	10	NA	3,159	8.4	16.2
165 CH OF NAZARENE	2	318	472	1.3	2.4
167 CHS OF CHRIST	3	181	251	.7	1.3
193 EPISCOPAL	1	92	153	.4	.8
207 E.L.C.A.	4	512	698	1.9	3.6
246 GREEK ORTHODOX	1	NR	NR	-	-
263 INT FOURSQ GOS	1	229	317*	.8	1.6
283 LUTH—MO SYNOD	1	137	185	.5	1.0
285 MENNONITE CH	1	64	64	.2	.3
349 PENT HOLINESS	3	100	138*	.4	.7
355 PRESB CH (USA)	1	67	93*	.2	.5
403 SALVATION ARMY	2	117	122	.3	.6
413 S.D.A.	3	504	697*	1.9	3.6
419 SO BAPT CONV	5	854	1,181*	3.2	6.1
443 UN C OF CHRIST	2	284	393*	1.0	2.0
449 UN METHODIST	4	659	911*	2.4	4.7
496 JEWISH EST¹	0	NA	70	.2	.4
497 BLACK BAPT EST²	NA	279	386*	1.0	2.0
499 INDEP.NON-CHAR³	1	NA	2,000	5.3	10.3

NA–Not applicable   NR–Not reported   *Total adherents estimated from known number of communicant, confirmed, full members.   - Represents a percent less than 0.1.   Percentages may not total due to rounding.

¹See Appendix E   ²See Appendix F   ³See Appendix G   Lines in *italic* represent a breakdown of Catholic rites or Friends affiliations. They are included in their respective denominational total.

Table 4. Churches and Church Membership by County and Denomination: 1990

County and Denomination	Number of churches	Communicant, confirmed, full members	Total adherents		
			Number	Percent of total population	Percent of total adherents
GARFIELD	**8**	**688**	**1,348***	**60.0**	**100.0**
053 ASSEMB OF GOD	1	23	30	1.3	2.2
081 CATHOLIC	1	NA	450	20.0	33.4
081d LATIN	1	NA	450	20.0	33.4
097 CHR CHS&CHS CR	1	170	212*	9.4	15.7
165 CH OF NAZARENE	1	98	165	7.3	12.2
193 EPISCOPAL	1	100	120	5.3	8.9
283 LUTH—MO SYNOD	1	20	26	1.2	1.9
413 S.D.A.	1	17	21*	.9	1.6
449 UN METHODIST	1	260	324*	14.4	24.0
GRANT	**111**	**7,780**	**24,934***	**45.5**	**100.0**
053 ASSEMB OF GOD	12	928	1,713	3.1	6.9
057 BAPT GEN CONF	1	279	372*	.7	1.5
081 CATHOLIC	9	NA	6,514	11.9	26.1
081d LATIN	9	NA	6,514	11.9	26.1
089 CHR & MISS AL	1	144	370	.7	1.5
093 CHR CH (DISC)	2	128	149	.3	.6
105 CHRISTIAN REF	1	86	146	.3	.6
111 CH CR,SCIENTST	2	NR	NR	-	-
145 CH GOD PROPHCY	1	27	36*	.1	.1
151 L-D SAINTS	19	NA	6,536	11.9	26.2
165 CH OF NAZARENE	4	221	444	.8	1.8
167 CHS OF CHRIST	4	154	208	.4	.8
179 CONSRV BAPT	2	NR	NR	-	-
193 EPISCOPAL	3	256	507	.9	2.0
203 EVAN FREE CH	1	51	77	.1	.3
207 E.L.C.A.	4	1,394	1,892	3.5	7.6
215 EVAN METH CH	2	32	43*	.1	.2
221 FREE METHODIST	2	122	322	.6	1.3
226 FRIENDS-USA	1	35	46	.1	.2
226b EFI	1	35	46	.1	.2
257 HUTTERIAN BR	2	NA	140	.3	.6
263 INT FOURSQ GOS	3	315	420*	.8	1.7
283 LUTH—MO SYNOD	6	675	998	1.8	4.0
287 MENN GEN CONF	1	56	74	.1	.3
291 MISSIONARY CH	1	42	82	.1	.3
339 PENT CH OF GOD	2	69	154	.3	.6
349 PENT HOLINESS	1	32	43*	.1	.2
355 PRESB CH (USA)	8	769	1,026*	1.9	4.1
413 S.D.A.	4	434	579*	1.1	2.3
419 SO BAPT CONV	5	413	551*	1.0	2.2
443 UN C OF CHRIST	2	213	284*	.5	1.1
449 UN METHODIST	5	801	1,069*	2.0	4.3
497 BLACK BAPT EST[2]	NA	104	139*	.3	.6
GRAYS HARBOR	**83**	**7,301**	**18,067***	**28.2**	**100.0**
019 AMER BAPT USA	3	426	542*	.8	3.0
053 ASSEMB OF GOD	12	896	1,745	2.7	9.7
057 BAPT GEN CONF	3	439	559*	.9	3.1
081 CATHOLIC	8	NA	6,321	9.8	35.0
081d LATIN	8	NA	6,321	9.8	35.0
089 CHR & MISS AL	3	85	152	.2	.8
093 CHR CH (DISC)	1	74	96	.1	.5
097 CHR CHS&CHS CR	1	69	88*	.1	.5
111 CH CR,SCIENTST	2	NR	NR	-	-
123 CH GOD (ANDER)	3	315	323	.5	1.8
145 CH GOD PROPHCY	1	27	34*	.1	.2
151 L-D SAINTS	4	NA	1,491	2.3	8.3
165 CH OF NAZARENE	1	71	92	.1	.5
167 CHS OF CHRIST	3	145	178	.3	1.0
179 CONSRV BAPT	1	NR	NR	-	-
193 EPISCOPAL	5	251	379	.6	2.1
207 E.L.C.A.	5	1,333	1,906	3.0	10.5
221 FREE METHODIST	1	29	29	-	.2
259 IFCA	1	NR	NR	-	-
283 LUTH—MO SYNOD	1	428	653	1.0	3.6
329 OPEN BIBLE STD	1	NR	NR	-	-
349 PENT HOLINESS	1	21	27*	-	.1
353 CHR BRETHREN	1	45	100	.2	.6
355 PRESB CH (USA)	5	598	761*	1.2	4.2
403 SALVATION ARMY	1	73	75	.1	.4
413 S.D.A.	2	289	368*	.6	2.0
419 SO BAPT CONV	3	512	652*	1.0	3.6
449 UN METHODIST	9	1,175	1,496*	2.3	8.3
496 JEWISH EST[1]	1	NA	0	-	-
ISLAND	**43**	**7,776**	**17,168***	**28.5**	**100.0**
019 AMER BAPT USA	1	300	381*	.6	2.2
053 ASSEMB OF GOD	3	172	300	.5	1.7
057 BAPT GEN CONF	1	51	65*	.1	.4
081 CATHOLIC	3	NA	4,308	7.2	25.1
081d LATIN	3	NA	4,308	7.2	25.1
089 CHR & MISS AL	1	181	741	1.2	4.3
105 CHRISTIAN REF	1	209	317	.5	1.8
111 CH CR,SCIENTST	2	NR	NR	-	-

County and Denomination	Number of churches	Communicant, confirmed, full members	Total adherents		
			Number	Percent of total population	Percent of total adherents
151 L-D SAINTS	4	NA	1,766	2.9	10.3
165 CH OF NAZARENE	1	227	358	.6	2.1
167 CHS OF CHRIST	2	137	211	.4	1.2
193 EPISCOPAL	3	457	715	1.2	4.2
203 EVAN FREE CH	1	32	55	.1	.3
207 E.L.C.A.	4	1,168	1,554	2.6	9.1
221 FREE METHODIST	1	20	47	.1	.3
249 AP CATH ASSYR	0	1	3	-	-
259 IFCA	1	NR	NR	-	-
263 INT FOURSQ GOS	2	340	432*	.7	2.5
283 LUTH—MO SYNOD	1	328	473	.8	2.8
339 PENT CH OF GOD	1	35	77	.1	.4
353 CHR BRETHREN	1	14	25	-	.1
355 PRESB CH (USA)	1	368	467*	.8	2.7
371 REF CH IN AM	1	486	745	1.2	4.3
413 S.D.A.	2	94	119*	.2	.7
419 SO BAPT CONV	2	1,533	1,947*	3.2	11.3
449 UN METHODIST	3	1,372	1,743*	2.9	10.2
497 BLACK BAPT EST[2]	NA	251	319*	.5	1.9
JEFFERSON	**22**	**2,124**	**4,655***	**23.1**	**100.0**
019 AMER BAPT USA	1	130	158*	.8	3.4
053 ASSEMB OF GOD	3	185	382	1.9	8.2
081 CATHOLIC	1	NA	1,190	5.9	25.6
081d LATIN	1	NA	1,190	5.9	25.6
111 CH CR,SCIENTST	1	NR	NR	-	-
151 L-D SAINTS	1	NA	481	2.4	10.3
165 CH OF NAZARENE	1	92	164	.8	3.5
167 CHS OF CHRIST	2	33	64	.3	1.4
193 EPISCOPAL	1	152	252	1.3	5.4
203 EVAN FREE CH	1	91	170	.8	3.7
207 E.L.C.A.	2	252	332	1.6	7.1
263 INT FOURSQ GOS	1	73	89*	.4	1.9
355 PRESB CH (USA)	2	304	370*	1.8	7.9
413 S.D.A.	1	126	154*	.8	3.3
419 SO BAPT CONV	1	178	217*	1.1	4.7
435 UNITARIAN-UNIV	1	57	82	.4	1.8
449 UN METHODIST	2	451	550*	2.7	11.8
KING	**920**	**187,146**	**539,726***	**35.8**	**100.0**
001 ADVENT CHR CH	1	177	216*	-	-
005 AME ZION	2	389	415	-	.1
019 AMER BAPT USA	42	10,790	13,198*	.9	2.4
045 APOSTOLIC LUTH	1	30	155	-	-
053 ASSEMB OF GOD	60	9,637	18,586	1.2	3.4
057 BAPT GEN CONF	15	2,972	3,635*	.2	.7
081 CATHOLIC	60	NA	211,528	14.0	39.2
081b BYZAN RUTH	1	NA	250	-	-
081d LATIN	59	NA	211,278	14.0	39.1
089 CHR & MISS AL	17	2,136	3,859	.3	.7
093 CHR CH (DISC)	13	2,474	3,690	.2	.7
097 CHR CHS&CHS CR	14	7,720	9,443*	.6	1.7
105 CHRISTIAN REF	3	607	989	.1	.2
111 CH CR,SCIENTST	26	NR	NR	-	-
121 CH GOD (ABR)	1	15	18*	-	-
123 CH GOD (ANDER)	5	367	840	.1	.2
127 CH GOD (CLEVE)	6	374	457*	-	.1
145 CH GOD PROPHCY	3	80	98*	-	-
151 L-D SAINTS	91	NA	38,195	2.5	7.1
157 CH OF BRETHREN	4	536	656*	-	.1
163 CH OF LUTH BR	4	266	504	-	.1
165 CH OF NAZARENE	24	4,093	5,267	.3	1.0
167 CHS OF CHRIST	28	3,456	4,719	.3	.9
175 CONGR CHR CHS	1	52	64*	-	-
179 CONSRV BAPT	9	NR	NR	-	-
193 EPISCOPAL	37	11,320	17,552	1.2	3.3
195 ESTONIAN ELC	1	71	87*	-	-
203 EVAN FREE CH	9	709	1,070	.1	.2
207 E.L.C.A.	70	28,350	38,704	2.6	7.2
215 EVAN METH CH	1	99	121*	-	-
216 EVAN PRESBY CH	2	597	612	-	.1
220 FREE LUTHERAN	1	193	246	-	-
221 FREE METHODIST	15	2,216	2,585	.2	.5
223 FREE WILL BAPT	1	60	73*	-	-
226 FRIENDS-USA	7	383	527*	-	.1
226b EFI	2	144	235	-	-
226f INDEPENDNT	5	239	292*	-	.1
246 GREEK ORTHODOX	2	NR	NR	-	-
249 AP CATH ASSYR	1	70	135	-	-
259 IFCA	3	NR	NR	-	-
263 INT FOURSQ GOS	20	6,169	7,546*	.5	1.4
274 LAT EVAN LUTH	1	427	517	-	.1
283 LUTH—MO SYNOD	31	8,331	11,022	.7	2.0
284 LUTH CH-AM ASC	1	0	68	-	-
285 MENNONITE CH	1	143	202	-	-
287 MENN GEN CONF	1	77	128	-	-
291 MISSIONARY CH	1	2	0	-	-

NA–Not applicable   NR–Not reported   *Total adherents estimated from known number of communicant, confirmed, full members.   - Represents a percent less than 0.1.   Percentages may not total due to rounding.
[1]See Appendix E   [2]See Appendix F   [3]See Appendix G   Lines in *italic* represent a breakdown of Catholic rites or Friends affiliations. They are included in their respective denominational total.

411

Table 4. Churches and Church Membership by County and Denomination: 1990

County and Denomination	Number of churches	Communicant, confirmed, full members	Total adherents Number	Percent of total population	Percent of total adherents
313 N AM BAPT CONF	2	172	210*	-	-
329 OPEN BIBLE STD	3	NR	NR	-	-
331 ORTH CH IN AM	2	NR	NR	-	-
339 PENT CH OF GOD	3	103	230	-	-
349 PENT HOLINESS	1	26	32*	-	-
353 CHR BRETHREN	9	753	1,100	.1	.2
355 PRESB CH (USA)	58	20,521	25,101*	1.7	4.7
356 PRESB CH AMER	7	920	1,158	.1	.2
371 REF CH IN AM	2	355	658	-	.1
375 REF EPISCOPAL	1	24	31	-	-
403 SALVATION ARMY	4	577	599	-	.1
413 S.D.A.	23	5,857	7,164*	.5	1.3
415 S-D BAPTIST GC	2	61	75*	-	-
419 SO BAPT CONV	36	9,266	11,334*	.8	2.1
435 UNITARIAN-UNIV	7	1,572	2,280	.2	.4
443 UN C OF CHRIST	33	6,954	8,506*	.6	1.6
449 UN METHODIST	48	17,630	21,564*	1.4	4.0
467 WESLEYAN	3	82	188	-	-
469 WELS	5	611	853	.1	.2
496 JEWISH EST[1]	13	NA	21,975	1.5	4.1
497 BLACK BAPT EST[2]	NA	16,274	19,906*	1.3	3.7
498 INDEP.CHARIS.[3]	16	NA	14,485	1.0	2.7
499 INDEP.NON-CHAR[3]	6	NA	4,550	.3	.8
KITSAP	**130**	**20,968**	**54,353***	**28.6**	**100.0**
019 AMER BAPT USA	6	1,143	1,475*	.8	2.7
053 ASSEMB OF GOD	13	1,900	4,060	2.1	7.5
057 BAPT GEN CONF	2	593	765*	.4	1.4
081 CATHOLIC	6	NA	16,629	8.8	30.6
081d *LATIN*	6	*NA*	*16,629*	*8.8*	*30.6*
089 CHR & MISS AL	6	473	1,317	.7	2.4
093 CHR CH (DISC)	2	239	250	.1	.5
097 CHR CHS&CHS CR	3	450	581*	.3	1.1
105 CHRISTIAN REF	1	38	78	-	.1
111 CH CR,SCIENTST	2	NR	NR	-	-
123 CH GOD (ANDER)	2	24	44	-	.1
145 CH GOD PROPHCY	1	27	35*	-	.1
151 L-D SAINTS	12	NA	6,524	3.4	12.0
165 CH OF NAZARENE	3	538	1,143	.6	2.1
167 CHS OF CHRIST	6	385	601	.3	1.1
179 CONSRV BAPT	1	NR	NR	-	-
193 EPISCOPAL	5	1,449	2,136	1.1	3.9
203 EVAN FREE CH	2	192	515	.3	.9
207 E.L.C.A.	10	4,333	5,812	3.1	10.7
209 EVAN LUTH SYN	1	303	451	.2	.8
221 FREE METHODIST	3	75	166	.1	.3
226 FRIENDS-USA	2	12	33	-	.1
226f *INDEPENDNT*	2	*12*	*33*	*-*	*.1*
237 GC MENN BR CHS	1	14	18*	-	-
259 IFCA	3	NR	NR	-	-
263 INT FOURSQ GOS	3	350	452*	.2	.8
283 LUTH—MO SYNOD	3	854	1,152	.6	2.1
313 N AM BAPT CONF	1	35	45*	-	.1
353 CHR BRETHREN	2	75	115	.1	.2
355 PRESB CH (USA)	4	1,447	1,868*	1.0	3.4
356 PRESB CH AMER	1	63	63	-	.1
403 SALVATION ARMY	1	108	112	.1	.2
413 S.D.A.	3	643	830*	.4	1.5
419 SO BAPT CONV	6	1,287	1,661*	.9	3.1
435 UNITARIAN-UNIV	2	140	216	.1	.4
443 UN C OF CHRIST	2	495	639*	.3	1.2
449 UN METHODIST	7	2,020	2,607*	1.4	4.8
469 WELS	1	174	254	.1	.5
497 BLACK BAPT EST[2]	NA	1,089	1,406*	.7	2.6
499 INDEP.NON-CHAR[3]	1	NA	300	.2	.6
KITTITAS	**38**	**3,053**	**9,396***	**35.2**	**100.0**
019 AMER BAPT USA	3	131	157*	.6	1.7
053 ASSEMB OF GOD	3	145	753	2.8	8.0
081 CATHOLIC	3	NA	3,175	11.9	33.8
081d *LATIN*	3	*NA*	*3,175*	*11.9*	*33.8*
089 CHR & MISS AL	2	299	872	3.3	9.3
097 CHR CHS&CHS CR	1	23	28*	.1	.3
111 CH CR,SCIENTST	1	NR	NR	-	-
123 CH GOD (ANDER)	1	30	30	.1	.3
151 L-D SAINTS	3	NA	984	3.7	10.5
165 CH OF NAZARENE	2	111	454	1.7	4.8
167 CHS OF CHRIST	1	51	67	.3	.7
179 CONSRV BAPT	1	NR	NR	-	-
193 EPISCOPAL	2	218	321	1.2	3.4
207 E.L.C.A.	1	483	648	2.4	6.9
226 FRIENDS-USA	2	2	20	.1	.2
226f *INDEPENDNT*	2	*2*	*20*	*.1*	*.2*
259 IFCA	1	NR	NR	-	-
263 INT FOURSQ GOS	1	171	205*	.8	2.2
329 OPEN BIBLE STD	1	NR	NR	-	-
355 PRESB CH (USA)	3	537	645*	2.4	6.9

County and Denomination	Number of churches	Communicant, confirmed, full members	Total adherents Number	Percent of total population	Percent of total adherents
413 S.D.A.	2	107	129*	.5	1.4
419 SO BAPT CONV	1	422	507*	1.9	5.4
449 UN METHODIST	1	258	310*	1.2	3.3
469 WELS	2	65	91	.3	1.0
KLICKITAT	**42**	**2,166**	**6,054***	**36.4**	**100.0**
045 APOSTOLIC LUTH	1	9	15	.1	.2
053 ASSEMB OF GOD	4	231	479	2.9	7.9
081 CATHOLIC	2	NA	2,003	12.1	33.1
081d *LATIN*	2	*NA*	*2,003*	*12.1*	*33.1*
097 CHR CHS&CHS CR	1	55	71*	.4	1.2
111 CH CR,SCIENTST	1	NR	NR	-	-
123 CH GOD (ANDER)	1	43	43	.3	.7
145 CH GOD PROPHCY	1	27	35*	.2	.6
151 L-D SAINTS	3	NA	970	5.8	16.0
165 CH OF NAZARENE	2	120	236	1.4	3.9
167 CHS OF CHRIST	4	111	148	.9	2.4
179 CONSRV BAPT	2	NR	NR	-	-
207 E.L.C.A.	1	135	197	1.2	3.3
263 INT FOURSQ GOS	2	41	53*	.3	.9
283 LUTH—MO SYNOD	2	138	171	1.0	2.8
355 PRESB CH (USA)	3	143	185*	1.1	3.1
413 S.D.A.	3	341	442*	2.7	7.3
419 SO BAPT CONV	4	228	296*	1.8	4.9
435 UNITARIAN-UNIV	1	19	29	.2	.5
443 UN C OF CHRIST	1	73	95*	.6	1.6
449 UN METHODIST	3	452	586*	3.5	9.7
LEWIS	**99**	**9,977**	**22,447***	**37.8**	**100.0**
019 AMER BAPT USA	3	440	565*	1.0	2.5
053 ASSEMB OF GOD	17	1,313	2,725	4.6	12.1
057 BAPT GEN CONF	1	46	59*	.1	.3
081 CATHOLIC	9	NA	5,633	9.5	25.1
081d *LATIN*	9	*NA*	*5,633*	*9.5*	*25.1*
089 CHR & MISS AL	1	29	62	.1	.3
093 CHR CH (DISC)	2	458	677	1.1	3.0
097 CHR CHS&CHS CR	2	783	1,006*	1.7	4.5
111 CH CR,SCIENTST	1	NR	NR	-	-
123 CH GOD (ANDER)	3	53	636	1.1	2.8
127 CH GOD (CLEVE)	1	31	40*	.1	.2
145 CH GOD PROPHCY	1	27	35*	.1	.2
151 L-D SAINTS	6	NA	2,014	3.4	9.0
157 CH OF BRETHREN	2	193	248*	.4	1.1
165 CH OF NAZARENE	2	437	543	.9	2.4
167 CHS OF CHRIST	2	109	161	.3	.7
179 CONSRV BAPT	3	NR	NR	-	-
193 EPISCOPAL	2	187	271	.5	1.2
203 EVAN FREE CH	1	44	44	.1	.2
207 E.L.C.A.	4	1,013	1,357	2.3	6.0
221 FREE METHODIST	1	91	119	.2	.5
263 INT FOURSQ GOS	3	518	665*	1.1	3.0
283 LUTH—MO SYNOD	1	143	217	.4	1.0
325 OLD REG BAPT	1	24	31*	.1	.1
329 OPEN BIBLE STD	1	NR	NR	-	-
339 PENT CH OF GOD	4	138	307	.5	1.4
353 CHR BRETHREN	1	54	100	.2	.4
355 PRESB CH (USA)	6	1,034	1,328*	2.2	5.9
403 SALVATION ARMY	1	52	58	.1	.3
413 S.D.A.	5	719	924*	1.6	4.1
415 S-D BAPTIST GC	1	18	23*	-	.1
419 SO BAPT CONV	4	770	989*	1.7	4.4
449 UN METHODIST	7	1,253	1,610*	2.7	7.2
LINCOLN	**33**	**3,292**	**6,439***	**72.6**	**100.0**
053 ASSEMB OF GOD	2	103	199	2.2	3.1
081 CATHOLIC	6	NA	1,920	21.7	29.8
081d *LATIN*	6	*NA*	*1,920*	*21.7*	*29.8*
093 CHR CH (DISC)	1	116	205	2.3	3.2
165 CH OF NAZARENE	2	98	134	1.5	2.1
207 E.L.C.A.	7	1,210	1,627	18.4	25.3
257 HUTTERIAN BR	2	NA	140	1.6	2.2
263 INT FOURSQ GOS	1	69	87*	1.0	1.4
283 LUTH—MO SYNOD	1	126	148	1.7	2.3
313 N AM BAPT CONF	1	42	53*	.6	.8
355 PRESB CH (USA)	4	641	808*	9.1	12.5
413 S.D.A.	0	22	28*	.3	.4
443 UN C OF CHRIST	2	511	644*	7.3	10.0
449 UN METHODIST	4	354	446*	5.0	6.9
MASON	**32**	**3,434**	**8,434***	**22.0**	**100.0**
019 AMER BAPT USA	1	252	314*	.8	3.7
053 ASSEMB OF GOD	5	425	762	2.0	9.0
081 CATHOLIC	2	NA	2,563	6.7	30.4
081d *LATIN*	2	*NA*	*2,563*	*6.7*	*30.4*
089 CHR & MISS AL	1	73	141	.4	1.7
097 CHR CHS&CHS CR	1	170	212*	.6	2.5

NA–Not applicable   NR–Not reported   *Total adherents estimated from known number of communicant, confirmed, full members.   - Represents a percent less than 0.1.   Percentages may not total due to rounding.

[1]See Appendix E   [2]See Appendix F   [3]See Appendix G   Lines in *italic* represent a breakdown of Catholic rites or Friends affiliations. They are included in their respective denominational total.

Table 4. Churches and Church Membership by County and Denomination: 1990

County and Denomination	Number of churches	Communicant, confirmed, full members	Total adherents Number	Percent of total population	Percent of total adherents
111 CH CR,SCIENTST	1	NR	NR	-	-
123 CH GOD (ANDER)	1	40	45	.1	.5
127 CH GOD (CLEVE)	1	117	146*	.4	1.7
151 L-D SAINTS	3	NA	1,220	3.2	14.5
165 CH OF NAZARENE	1	100	78	.2	.9
167 CHS OF CHRIST	1	35	65	.2	.8
179 CONSRV BAPT	2	NR	NR	-	-
193 EPISCOPAL	3	282	499	1.3	5.9
207 E.L.C.A.	2	571	698	1.8	8.3
263 INT FOURSQ GOS	1	113	141*	.4	1.7
283 LUTH—MO SYNOD	1	164	189	.5	2.2
413 S.D.A.	2	226	282*	.7	3.3
419 SO BAPT CONV	2	221	275*	.7	3.3
449 UN METHODIST	1	645	804*	2.1	9.5
OKANOGAN	**72**	**4,016**	**10,611***	**31.8**	**100.0**
019 AMER BAPT USA	1	95	123*	.4	1.2
053 ASSEMB OF GOD	7	455	730	2.2	6.9
057 BAPT GEN CONF	2	194	251*	.8	2.4
081 CATHOLIC	11	NA	4,368	13.1	41.2
081d LATIN	*11*	*NA*	*4,368*	*13.1*	*41.2*
111 CH CR,SCIENTST	1	NR	NR	-	-
151 L-D SAINTS	3	NA	629	1.9	5.9
157 CH OF BRETHREN	2	121	157*	.5	1.5
165 CH OF NAZARENE	1	38	121	.4	1.1
167 CHS OF CHRIST	4	82	119	.4	1.1
193 EPISCOPAL	3	163	209	.6	2.0
203 EVAN FREE CH	1	14	25	.1	.2
215 EVAN METH CH	1	82	106*	.3	1.0
221 FREE METHODIST	3	178	309	.9	2.9
263 INT FOURSQ GOS	3	253	328*	1.0	3.1
283 LUTH—MO SYNOD	5	351	417	1.3	3.9
339 PENT CH OF GOD	4	136	307	.9	2.9
353 CHR BRETHREN	1	13	25	.1	.2
355 PRESB CH (USA)	2	278	360*	1.1	3.4
413 S.D.A.	4	505	654*	2.0	6.2
419 SO BAPT CONV	2	229	297*	.9	2.8
443 UN C OF CHRIST	1	90	117*	.4	1.1
449 UN METHODIST	8	623	807*	2.4	7.6
469 WELS	2	116	152	.5	1.4
PACIFIC	**39**	**2,385**	**5,433***	**28.8**	**100.0**
019 AMER BAPT USA	1	300	368*	1.9	6.8
053 ASSEMB OF GOD	3	260	969	5.1	17.8
081 CATHOLIC	3	NA	1,095	5.8	20.2
081d LATIN	*3*	*NA*	*1,095*	*5.8*	*20.2*
111 CH CR,SCIENTST	2	NR	NR	-	-
151 L-D SAINTS	2	NA	463	2.5	8.5
165 CH OF NAZARENE	1	18	136	.7	2.5
179 CONSRV BAPT	3	NR	NR	-	-
193 EPISCOPAL	2	130	152	.8	2.8
207 E.L.C.A.	6	805	1,156	6.1	21.3
283 LUTH—MO SYNOD	1	37	41	.2	.8
325 OLD REG BAPT	1	50	61*	.3	1.1
339 PENT CH OF GOD	1	16	16	.1	.3
355 PRESB CH (USA)	2	193	236*	1.2	4.3
413 S.D.A.	2	56	69*	.4	1.3
419 SO BAPT CONV	1	40	49*	.3	.9
443 UN C OF CHRIST	1	53	65*	.3	1.2
449 UN METHODIST	5	409	501*	2.7	9.2
467 WESLEYAN	2	18	56	.3	1.0
PEND OREILLE	**28**	**1,476**	**3,525***	**39.5**	**100.0**
019 AMER BAPT USA	1	129	167*	1.9	4.7
053 ASSEMB OF GOD	4	148	305	3.4	8.7
081 CATHOLIC	4	NA	800	9.0	22.7
081d LATIN	*4*	*NA*	*800*	*9.0*	*22.7*
123 CH GOD (ANDER)	1	6	6	.1	.2
151 L-D SAINTS	2	NA	572	6.4	16.2
165 CH OF NAZARENE	1	2	0	-	-
167 CHS OF CHRIST	1	47	61	.7	1.7
181 CONSRV CONGR	1	24	31*	.3	.9
207 E.L.C.A.	1	215	358	4.0	10.2
220 FREE LUTHERAN	2	171	262	2.9	7.4
263 INT FOURSQ GOS	1	47	61*	.7	1.7
287 MENN GEN CONF	1	57	88	1.0	2.5
355 PRESB CH (USA)	1	18	23*	.3	.7
413 S.D.A.	3	227	293*	3.3	8.3
419 SO BAPT CONV	2	188	243*	2.7	6.9
443 UN C OF CHRIST	2	197	255*	2.9	7.2
PIERCE	**371**	**73,153**	**179,875***	**30.7**	**100.0**
019 AMER BAPT USA	18	4,436	5,698*	1.0	3.2
053 ASSEMB OF GOD	29	6,717	13,485	2.3	7.5
057 BAPT GEN CONF	6	1,607	2,064*	.4	1.1
059 BAPT MISS ASSN	1	61	78*	-	-

County and Denomination	Number of churches	Communicant, confirmed, full members	Total adherents Number	Percent of total population	Percent of total adherents
081 CATHOLIC	24	NA	53,259	9.1	29.6
081d LATIN	*24*	*NA*	*53,259*	*9.1*	*29.6*
089 CHR & MISS AL	4	255	692	.1	.4
093 CHR CH (DISC)	8	1,193	1,612	.3	.9
097 CHR CHS&CHS CR	10	1,762	2,263*	.4	1.3
105 CHRISTIAN REF	2	265	434	.1	.2
111 CH CR,SCIENTST	5	NR	NR	-	-
123 CH GOD (ANDER)	4	232	257	-	.1
127 CH GOD (CLEVE)	2	215	276*	-	.2
133 CH GOD(7TH)DEN	1	48	68	-	-
145 CH GOD PROPHCY	2	53	68*	-	-
151 L-D SAINTS	38	NA	16,534	2.8	9.2
157 CH OF BRETHREN	1	0	0*	-	-
165 CH OF NAZARENE	6	1,405	2,144	.4	1.2
167 CHS OF CHRIST	11	1,288	1,677	.3	.9
175 CONGR CHR CHS	1	281	361*	.1	.2
179 CONSRV BAPT	7	NR	NR	-	-
193 EPISCOPAL	10	2,647	3,648	.6	2.0
203 EVAN FREE CH	5	340	555	.1	.3
207 E.L.C.A.	30	11,151	15,804	2.7	8.8
209 EVAN LUTH SYN	2	461	638	.1	.4
221 FREE METHODIST	3	136	209	-	.1
226 FRIENDS-USA	3	193	212*	-	.1
226b EFI	*2*	*168*	*180*	*-*	*.1*
226f INDEPENDNT	*1*	*25*	*32***	*-*	*-*
246 GREEK ORTHODOX	1	NR	NR	-	-
249 AP CATH ASSYR	0	3	10	-	-
259 IFCA	2	NR	NR	-	-
263 INT FOURSQ GOS	8	677	870*	.1	.5
274 LAT EVAN LUTH	1	169	191	-	.1
283 LUTH—MO SYNOD	11	4,722	6,611	1.1	3.7
291 MISSIONARY CH	1	17	34	-	-
313 N AM BAPT CONF	4	729	936*	.2	.5
329 OPEN BIBLE STD	4	NR	NR	-	-
331 ORTH CH IN AM	1	NR	NR	-	-
339 PENT CH OF GOD	1	34	77	-	-
349 PENT HOLINESS	1	27	35*	-	-
353 CHR BRETHREN	1	12	24	-	-
355 PRESB CH (USA)	28	6,871	8,826*	1.5	4.9
356 PRESB CH AMER	1	149	310	.1	.2
403 SALVATION ARMY	2	293	312	.1	.2
413 S.D.A.	8	1,787	2,295*	.4	1.3
419 SO BAPT CONV	15	5,961	7,657*	1.3	4.3
435 UNITARIAN-UNIV	1	182	212	-	.1
443 UN C OF CHRIST	7	662	850*	.1	.5
449 UN METHODIST	27	6,812	8,750*	1.5	4.9
469 WELS	2	296	444	.1	.2
496 JEWISH EST[1]	1	NA	1,100	.2	.6
497 BLACK BAPT EST[2]	NA	9,004	11,565*	2.0	6.4
498 INDEP.CHARIS.[3]	8	NA	6,000	1.0	3.3
499 INDEP.NON-CHAR[3]	2	NA	730	.1	.4
SAN JUAN	**13**	**561**	**2,199***	**21.9**	**100.0**
053 ASSEMB OF GOD	1	14	19	.2	.9
081 CATHOLIC	1	NA	1,156	11.5	52.6
081d LATIN	*1*	*NA*	*1,156*	*11.5*	*52.6*
111 CH CR,SCIENTST	1	NR	NR	-	-
151 L-D SAINTS	1	NA	189	1.9	8.6
179 CONSRV BAPT	1	NR	NR	-	-
193 EPISCOPAL	3	180	376	3.7	17.1
207 E.L.C.A.	1	77	105	1.0	4.8
226 FRIENDS-USA	1	4	12	.1	.5
226f INDEPENDNT	*1*	*4*	*12*	*.1*	*.5*
355 PRESB CH (USA)	1	243	291*	2.9	13.2
413 S.D.A.	1	25	30*	.3	1.4
435 UNITARIAN-UNIV	1	18	21	.2	1.0
SKAGIT	**97**	**14,912**	**28,766***	**36.2**	**100.0**
019 AMER BAPT USA	4	1,027	1,299*	1.6	4.5
053 ASSEMB OF GOD	11	1,194	2,485	3.1	8.6
057 BAPT GEN CONF	1	516	653*	.8	2.3
081 CATHOLIC	7	NA	6,157	7.7	21.4
081d LATIN	*7*	*NA*	*6,157*	*7.7*	*21.4*
089 CHR & MISS AL	1	45	75	.1	.3
093 CHR CH (DISC)	1	100	110	.1	.4
097 CHR CHS&CHS CR	3	636	804*	1.0	2.8
105 CHRISTIAN REF	4	468	798	1.0	2.8
111 CH CR,SCIENTST	2	NR	NR	-	-
127 CH GOD (CLEVE)	1	52	66*	.1	.2
145 CH GOD PROPHCY	2	53	67*	.1	.2
151 L-D SAINTS	4	NA	1,850	2.3	6.4
163 CH OF LUTH BR	1	36	90	.1	.3
165 CH OF NAZARENE	3	240	396	.5	1.4
167 CHS OF CHRIST	4	253	301	.4	1.0
179 CONSRV BAPT	1	NR	NR	-	-
193 EPISCOPAL	3	333	522	.7	1.8
207 E.L.C.A.	10	4,019	5,442	6.8	18.9

NA–Not applicable NR–Not reported *Total adherents estimated from known number of communicant, confirmed, full members. - Represents a percent less than 0.1. Percentages may not total due to rounding.

[1]See Appendix E [2]See Appendix F [3]See Appendix G Lines in *italic* represent a breakdown of Catholic rites or Friends affiliations. They are included in their respective denominational total.

413

Table 4. Churches and Church Membership by County and Denomination: 1990

County and Denomination	Number of churches	Communicant, confirmed, full members	Total adherents Number	Percent of total population	Percent of total adherents
209 EVAN LUTH SYN	1	44	56	.1	.2
221 FREE METHODIST	3	114	196	.2	.7
223 FREE WILL BAPT	1	66	83*	.1	.3
226 FRIENDS-USA	1	0	35	-	.1
226b *EFI*	*1*	*0*	*35*	*-*	*.1*
263 INT FOURSQ GOS	3	520	658*	.8	2.3
283 LUTH—MO SYNOD	1	752	1,008	1.3	3.5
355 PRESB CH (USA)	4	682	862*	1.1	3.0
403 SALVATION ARMY	1	41	48	.1	.2
413 S.D.A.	3	578	731*	.9	2.5
419 SO BAPT CONV	5	1,046	1,323*	1.7	4.6
435 UNITARIAN-UNIV	1	31	38	-	.1
443 UN C OF CHRIST	2	94	119*	.1	.4
449 UN METHODIST	8	1,972	2,494*	3.1	8.7
SKAMANIA	**12**	**433**	**1,332***	**16.1**	**100.0**
081 CATHOLIC	1	NA	472	5.7	35.4
081d *LATIN*	*1*	*NA*	*472*	*5.7*	*35.4*
151 L-D SAINTS	1	NA	174	2.1	13.1
165 CH OF NAZARENE	2	132	292	3.5	21.9
167 CHS OF CHRIST	1	23	45	.5	3.4
179 CONSRV BAPT	1	NR	NR	-	-
207 E.L.C.A.	1	139	167	2.0	12.5
259 IFCA	2	NR	NR	-	-
329 OPEN BIBLE STD	1	NR	NR	-	-
413 S.D.A.	1	38	50*	.6	3.8
449 UN METHODIST	1	101	132*	1.6	9.9
SNOHOMISH	**296**	**45,479**	**120,661***	**25.9**	**100.0**
001 ADVENT CHR CH	1	46	60*	-	-
019 AMER BAPT USA	10	2,269	2,936*	.6	2.4
053 ASSEM OF GOD	26	2,552	5,032	1.1	4.2
057 BAPT GEN CONF	3	655	848*	.2	.7
081 CATHOLIC	15	NA	30,458	6.5	25.2
081d *LATIN*	*15*	*NA*	*30,458*	*6.5*	*25.2*
089 CHR & MISS AL	7	723	1,997	.4	1.7
093 CHR CH (DISC)	1	163	254	.1	.2
097 CHR CHS&CHS CR	7	669	866*	.2	.7
105 CHRISTIAN REF	13	2,885	4,648	1.0	3.9
111 CH CR,SCIENTST	4	NR	NR	-	-
123 CH GOD (ANDER)	3	265	280	.1	.2
127 CH GOD (CLEVE)	1	32	41*	-	-
145 CH GOD PROPHCY	3	80	104*	-	.1
151 L-D SAINTS	29	NA	12,596	2.7	10.4
163 CH OF LUTH BR	3	428	911	.2	.8
164 CH LUTH CONF	1	91	119	-	.1
165 CH OF NAZARENE	7	880	1,434	.3	1.2
167 CHS OF CHRIST	6	696	919	.2	.8
175 CONGR CHR CHS	1	71	92*	-	.1
179 CONSRV BAPT	5	NR	NR	-	-
193 EPISCOPAL	8	1,457	2,111	.5	1.7
203 EVAN FREE CH	3	171	262	.1	.2
207 E.L.C.A.	28	9,920	14,484	3.1	12.0
220 FREE LUTHERAN	3	244	323	.1	.3
221 FREE METHODIST	9	922	1,649	.4	1.4
226 FRIENDS-USA	1	2	8	-	-
226f *INDEPENDNT*	*1*	*2*	*8*	*-*	*-*
259 IFCA	4	NR	NR	-	-
263 INT FOURSQ GOS	6	3,410	4,412*	.9	3.7
283 LUTH—MO SYNOD	9	2,532	3,514	.8	2.9
313 N AM BAPT CONF	3	240	311*	.1	.3
329 OPEN BIBLE STD	6	NR	NR	-	-
339 PENT CH OF GOD	1	34	77	-	.1
353 CHR BRETHREN	3	440	545	.1	.5
355 PRESB CH (USA)	9	2,139	2,768*	.6	2.3
356 PRESB CH AMER	2	194	276	.1	.2
371 REF CH IN AM	2	185	384	.1	.3
403 SALVATION ARMY	1	132	138	-	.1
413 S.D.A.	10	1,755	2,271*	.5	1.9
419 SO BAPT CONV	13	1,814	2,347*	.5	1.9
435 UNITARIAN-UNIV	2	396	547	.1	.5
443 UN C OF CHRIST	4	454	587*	.1	.5
449 UN METHODIST	13	5,309	6,869*	1.5	5.7
469 WELS	3	207	337	.1	.3
496 JEWISH EST[1]	0	NA	7,325	1.6	6.1
497 BLACK BAPT EST[2]	NA	1,017	1,316*	.3	1.1
498 INDEP.CHARIS.[3]	4	NA	2,680	.6	2.2
499 INDEP.NON-CHAR[3]	3	NA	1,525	.3	1.3
SPOKANE	**289**	**47,389**	**123,194***	**34.1**	**100.0**
019 AMER BAPT USA	10	1,534	1,941*	.5	1.6
053 ASSEM OF GOD	15	2,102	4,089	1.1	3.3
057 BAPT GEN CONF	3	388	491*	.1	.4
081 CATHOLIC	25	NA	41,095	11.4	33.4
081b *BYZAN RUTH*	*1*	*NA*	*225*	*.1*	*.2*
081d *LATIN*	*24*	*NA*	*40,870*	*11.3*	*33.2*

County and Denomination	Number of churches	Communicant, confirmed, full members	Total adherents Number	Percent of total population	Percent of total adherents
089 CHR & MISS AL	3	385	889	.2	.7
093 CHR CH (DISC)	9	1,038	1,629	.5	1.3
097 CHR CHS&CHS CR	6	793	1,003*	.3	.8
105 CHRISTIAN REF	2	151	217	.1	.2
111 CH CR,SCIENTST	3	NR	NR	-	-
123 CH GOD (ANDER)	3	242	322	.1	.3
127 CH GOD (CLEVE)	1	74	94*	-	.1
133 CH GOD(7TH)DEN	1	49	68	-	.1
145 CH GOD PROPHCY	1	27	34*	-	-
151 L-D SAINTS	29	NA	11,976	3.3	9.7
164 CH LUTH CONF	2	398	552	.2	.4
165 CH OF NAZARENE	9	2,079	2,585	.7	2.1
167 CHS OF CHRIST	7	547	763	.2	.6
175 CONGR CHR CHS	2	715	904*	.3	.7
179 CONSRV BAPT	5	NR	NR	-	-
193 EPISCOPAL	9	3,625	4,673	1.3	3.8
203 EVAN FREE CH	4	68	120	-	.1
207 E.L.C.A.	22	7,478	10,781	3.0	8.8
220 FREE LUTHERAN	1	60	80	-	.1
221 FREE METHODIST	4	321	557	.2	.5
226 FRIENDS-USA	2	59	101	-	.1
226b *EFI*	*1*	*51*	*87*	*-*	*.1*
226f *INDEPENDNT*	*1*	*8*	*14*	*-*	*-*
246 GREEK ORTHODOX	1	NR	NR	-	-
249 AP CATH ASSYR	0	1	5	-	-
259 IFCA	1	NR	NR	-	-
263 INT FOURSQ GOS	5	660	835*	.2	.7
283 LUTH—MO SYNOD	9	2,806	3,995	1.1	3.2
287 MENN GEN CONF	1	0	0	-	-
313 N AM BAPT CONF	1	59	75*	-	.1
329 OPEN BIBLE STD	4	NR	NR	-	-
339 PENT CH OF GOD	2	69	153	-	.1
349 PENT HOLINESS	1	63	80*	-	.1
353 CHR BRETHREN	3	67	124	-	.1
355 PRESB CH (USA)	17	6,543	8,277*	2.3	6.7
356 PRESB CH AMER	1	0	0	-	-
403 SALVATION ARMY	1	237	265	.1	.2
413 S.D.A.	11	2,650	3,352*	.9	2.7
419 SO BAPT CONV	16	4,552	5,758*	1.6	4.7
435 UNITARIAN-UNIV	1	385	495	.1	.4
443 UN C OF CHRIST	7	1,049	1,327*	.4	1.1
449 UN METHODIST	18	4,824	6,102*	1.7	5.0
467 WESLEYAN	1	22	100	-	.1
469 WELS	2	180	234	.1	.2
496 JEWISH EST[1]	1	NA	800	.2	.6
497 BLACK BAPT EST[2]	NA	1,089	1,378*	.4	1.1
498 INDEP.CHARIS.[3]	4	NA	3,400	.9	2.8
499 INDEP.NON-CHAR[3]	3	NA	1,475	.4	1.2
STEVENS	**48**	**2,641**	**9,451***	**30.5**	**100.0**
053 ASSEM OF GOD	8	488	872	2.8	9.2
081 CATHOLIC	11	NA	4,206	13.6	44.5
081d *LATIN*	*11*	*NA*	*4,206*	*13.6*	*44.5*
093 CHR CH (DISC)	1	96	142	.5	1.5
111 CH CR,SCIENTST	1	NR	NR	-	-
123 CH GOD (ANDER)	1	0	52	.2	.6
151 L-D SAINTS	4	NA	1,138	3.7	12.0
165 CH OF NAZARENE	2	110	193	.6	2.0
167 CHS OF CHRIST	1	65	85	.3	.9
193 EPISCOPAL	1	57	87	.3	.9
203 EVAN FREE CH	1	77	170	.5	1.8
207 E.L.C.A.	2	278	405	1.3	4.3
221 FREE METHODIST	2	106	261	.8	2.8
339 PENT CH OF GOD	1	34	77	.2	.8
355 PRESB CH (USA)	3	37	49*	.2	.5
413 S.D.A.	3	407	539*	1.7	5.7
419 SO BAPT CONV	2	279	370*	1.2	3.9
443 UN C OF CHRIST	3	310	411*	1.3	4.3
449 UN METHODIST	1	297	394*	1.3	4.2
THURSTON	**118**	**17,774**	**43,838***	**27.2**	**100.0**
019 AMER BAPT USA	2	417	529*	.3	1.2
053 ASSEM OF GOD	10	1,634	3,466	2.1	7.9
057 BAPT GEN CONF	1	541	687*	.4	1.6
081 CATHOLIC	19	NA	13,009	8.1	29.7
081d *LATIN*	*19*	*NA*	*13,009*	*8.1*	*29.7*
089 CHR & MISS AL	3	207	442	.3	1.0
093 CHR CH (DISC)	2	507	672	.4	1.5
097 CHR CHS&CHS CR	2	255	324*	.2	.7
105 CHRISTIAN REF	1	79	117	.1	.3
111 CH CR,SCIENTST	2	NR	NR	-	-
123 CH GOD (ANDER)	2	165	348	.2	.8
127 CH GOD (CLEVE)	1	49	62*	-	.1
145 CH GOD PROPHCY	1	27	34*	-	.1
151 L-D SAINTS	10	NA	4,937	3.1	11.3
157 CH OF BRETHREN	1	136	173*	.1	.4
163 CH OF LUTH BR	1	66	102	.1	.2

NA–Not applicable   NR–Not reported   *Total adherents estimated from known number of communicant, confirmed, full members.   - Represents a percent less than 0.1.   Percentages may not total due to rounding.

[1]See Appendix E   [2]See Appendix F   [3]See Appendix G   Lines in *italic* represent a breakdown of Catholic rites or Friends affiliations. They are included in their respective denominational total.

414

Table 4. Churches and Church Membership by County and Denomination: 1990

County and Denomination	Number of churches	Communicant, confirmed, full members	Total adherents Number	Percent of total population	Percent of total adherents
165 CH OF NAZARENE	3	547	718	.4	1.6
167 CHS OF CHRIST	4	205	267	.2	.6
179 CONSRV BAPT	3	NR	NR	-	-
193 EPISCOPAL	3	1,092	1,465	.9	3.3
203 EVAN FREE CH	1	148	220	.1	.5
207 E.L.C.A.	7	2,469	3,447	2.1	7.9
209 EVAN LUTH SYN	1	102	143	.1	.3
221 FREE METHODIST	1	53	85	.1	.2
226 FRIENDS-USA	1	27	34*	-	.1
226f INDEPENDNT	1	27	34*	-	.1
249 AP CATH ASSYR	0	3	18	-	-
263 INT FOURSQ GOS	2	1,227	1,558*	1.0	3.6
283 LUTH—MO SYNOD	2	779	975	.6	2.2
313 N AM BAPT CONF	1	190	241*	.1	.5
329 OPEN BIBLE STD	1	NR	NR	-	-
339 PENT CH OF GOD	1	34	77	-	.2
355 PRESB CH (USA)	5	1,312	1,666*	1.0	3.8
403 SALVATION ARMY	1	97	114	.1	.3
413 S.D.A.	3	773	981*	.6	2.2
419 SO BAPT CONV	7	1,236	1,569*	1.0	3.6
435 UNITARIAN-UNIV	1	109	139	.1	.3
443 UN C OF CHRIST	2	302	383*	.2	.9
449 UN METHODIST	6	2,333	2,962*	1.8	6.8
469 WELS	1	42	48	-	.1
496 JEWISH EST[1]	1	NA	300	.2	.7
497 BLACK BAPT EST[2]	NA	611	776*	.5	1.8
498 INDEP.CHARIS.[3]	2	NA	750	.5	1.7
WAHKIAKUM	**11**	**398**	**685***	**20.6**	**100.0**
045 APOSTOLIC LUTH	1	16	23	.7	3.4
053 ASSEMB OF GOD	1	76	108	3.2	15.8
081 CATHOLIC	1	NA	45	1.4	6.6
081d LATIN	1	NA	45	1.4	6.6
151 L-D SAINTS	1	NA	111	3.3	16.2
207 E.L.C.A.	1	63	98	2.9	14.3
259 IFCA	1	NR	NR	-	-
349 PENT HOLINESS	1	40	49*	1.5	7.2
413 S.D.A.	1	32	40*	1.2	5.8
443 UN C OF CHRIST	1	69	85*	2.6	12.4
449 UN METHODIST	2	102	126*	3.8	18.4
WALLA WALLA	**51**	**10,742**	**24,370***	**50.3**	**100.0**
019 AMER BAPT USA	1	472	588*	1.2	2.4
053 ASSEMB OF GOD	4	458	841	1.7	3.5
059 BAPT MISS ASSN	1	90	112*	.2	.5
081 CATHOLIC	5	NA	8,569	17.7	35.2
081b BYZAN RUTH	1	NA	60	.1	.2
081d LATIN	4	NA	8,509	17.6	34.9
089 CHR & MISS AL	1	46	87	.2	.4
093 CHR CH (DISC)	2	348	465	1.0	1.9
111 CH CR,SCIENTST	1	NR	NR	-	-
123 CH GOD (ANDER)	1	0	470	1.0	1.9
133 CH GOD(7TH)DEN	1	48	67	.1	.3
151 L-D SAINTS	3	NA	1,198	2.5	4.9
165 CH OF NAZARENE	3	303	424	.9	1.7
167 CHS OF CHRIST	2	90	145	.3	.6
179 CONSRV BAPT	1	NR	NR	-	-
193 EPISCOPAL	1	402	595	1.2	2.4
207 E.L.C.A.	2	736	977	2.0	4.0
221 FREE METHODIST	1	30	95	.2	.4
226 FRIENDS-USA	1	4	12	-	-
226f INDEPENDNT	1	4	12	-	-
263 INT FOURSQ GOS	1	33	41*	.1	.2
283 LUTH—MO SYNOD	1	168	261	.5	1.1
339 PENT CH OF GOD	2	68	154	.3	.6
355 PRESB CH (USA)	4	868	1,081*	2.2	4.4
403 SALVATION ARMY	1	67	78	.2	.3
413 S.D.A.	6	4,549	5,667*	11.7	23.3
419 SO BAPT CONV	2	419	522*	1.1	2.1
443 UN C OF CHRIST	1	306	381*	.8	1.6
449 UN METHODIST	2	1,113	1,386*	2.9	5.7
497 BLACK BAPT EST[2]	NA	124	154*	.3	.6
WHATCOM	**120**	**15,728**	**36,414***	**28.5**	**100.0**
001 ADVENT CHR CH	3	297	371*	.3	1.0
019 AMER BAPT USA	4	476	595*	.5	1.6
053 ASSEMB OF GOD	12	1,849	3,506	2.7	9.6
057 BAPT GEN CONF	1	288	360*	.3	1.0
081 CATHOLIC	8	NA	10,250	8.0	28.1
081d LATIN	8	NA	10,250	8.0	28.1
089 CHR & MISS AL	3	252	494	.4	1.4
093 CHR CH (DISC)	1	398	442	.3	1.2
097 CHR CHS&CHS CR	1	24	30*	-	.1
105 CHRISTIAN REF	4	528	984	.8	2.7
111 CH CR,SCIENTST	1	NR	NR	-	-
123 CH GOD (ANDER)	1	200	220	.2	.6

County and Denomination	Number of churches	Communicant, confirmed, full members	Total adherents Number	Percent of total population	Percent of total adherents
127 CH GOD (CLEVE)	1	10	12*	-	.1
145 CH GOD PROPHCY	1	27	34*	-	.1
151 L-D SAINTS	6	NA	2,908	2.3	8.0
163 CH OF LUTH BR	2	62	126	.1	.3
165 CH OF NAZARENE	4	197	374	.3	1.0
167 CHS OF CHRIST	3	288	383	.3	1.1
193 EPISCOPAL	2	1,012	1,239	1.0	3.4
203 EVAN FREE CH	1	390	800	.6	2.2
207 E.L.C.A.	10	2,645	3,893	3.0	10.7
220 FREE LUTHERAN	1	70	103	.1	.3
221 FREE METHODIST	1	121	165	.1	.5
226 FRIENDS-USA	1	3	25	-	.1
226f INDEPENDNT	1	3	25	-	.1
237 GC MENN BR CHS	3	297	371*	.3	1.0
246 GREEK ORTHODOX	1	NR	NR	-	-
259 IFCA	3	NR	NR	-	-
263 INT FOURSQ GOS	3	111	139*	.1	.4
283 LUTH—MO SYNOD	2	606	762	.6	2.1
291 MISSIONARY CH	1	18	21	-	.1
307 NETH REF CONGR	1	77	164	.1	.5
339 PENT CH OF GOD	1	34	76	.1	.2
353 CHR BRETHREN	2	45	100	.1	.3
355 PRESB CH (USA)	6	851	1,063*	.8	2.9
371 REF CH IN AM	3	894	1,551	1.2	4.3
403 SALVATION ARMY	1	160	172	.1	.5
413 S.D.A.	3	524	655*	.5	1.8
419 SO BAPT CONV	4	324	405*	.3	1.1
435 UNITARIAN-UNIV	2	191	249	.2	.7
443 UN C OF CHRIST	4	792	989*	.8	2.7
449 UN METHODIST	7	1,528	1,909*	1.5	5.2
496 JEWISH EST[1]	1	NA	300	.2	.8
497 BLACK BAPT EST[2]	NA	139	174*	.1	.5
WHITMAN	**66**	**5,414**	**10,929***	**28.2**	**100.0**
019 AMER BAPT USA	5	617	719*	1.9	6.6
053 ASSEMB OF GOD	5	282	448	1.2	4.1
081 CATHOLIC	10	NA	2,950	7.6	27.0
081d LATIN	10	NA	2,950	7.6	27.0
089 CHR & MISS AL	1	9	22	.1	.2
093 CHR CH (DISC)	3	86	129	.3	1.2
097 CHR CHS&CHS CR	1	120	140*	.4	1.3
151 L-D SAINTS	4	NA	1,101	2.8	10.1
165 CH OF NAZARENE	4	236	292	.8	2.7
167 CHS OF CHRIST	1	47	61	.2	.6
181 CONSRV CONGR	1	48	56*	.1	.5
193 EPISCOPAL	3	207	291	.8	2.7
203 EVAN FREE CH	1	50	250	.6	2.3
207 E.L.C.A.	4	924	1,188	3.1	10.9
216 EVAN PRESBY CH	1	28	28	.1	.3
226 FRIENDS-USA	0	7	16	-	.1
226f INDEPENDNT	0	7	16	-	.1
259 IFCA	1	NR	NR	-	-
263 INT FOURSQ GOS	1	53	62*	.2	.6
283 LUTH—MO SYNOD	1	133	169	.4	1.5
313 N AM BAPT CONF	1	245	286*	.7	2.6
355 PRESB CH (USA)	1	125	146*	.4	1.3
413 S.D.A.	3	227	265*	.7	2.4
419 SO BAPT CONV	2	379	442*	1.1	4.0
443 UN C OF CHRIST	4	376	438*	1.1	4.0
449 UN METHODIST	7	1,180	1,376*	3.5	12.6
469 WELS	1	35	54	.1	.5
YAKIMA	**211**	**26,467**	**66,372***	**35.2**	**100.0**
019 AMER BAPT USA	5	845	1,114*	.6	1.7
053 ASSEMB OF GOD	21	1,942	3,452	1.8	5.2
059 BAPT MISS ASSN	1	55	73*	-	.1
081 CATHOLIC	16	NA	23,443	12.4	35.3
081d LATIN	16	NA	23,443	12.4	35.3
089 CHR & MISS AL	2	116	433	.2	.7
093 CHR CH (DISC)	8	877	1,408	.7	2.1
097 CHR CHS&CHS CR	4	130	171*	.1	.3
105 CHRISTIAN REF	3	596	943	.5	1.4
111 CH CR,SCIENTST	2	NR	NR	-	-
123 CH GOD (ANDER)	4	115	311	.2	.5
127 CH GOD (CLEVE)	5	627	827*	.4	1.2
145 CH GOD PROPHCY	2	53	70*	-	.1
151 L-D SAINTS	14	NA	5,035	2.7	7.6
157 CH OF BRETHREN	1	36	47*	-	.1
165 CH OF NAZARENE	11	1,832	2,564	1.4	3.9
167 CHS OF CHRIST	7	594	739	.4	1.1
179 CONSRV BAPT	3	NR	NR	-	-
193 EPISCOPAL	5	743	980	.5	1.5
207 E.L.C.A.	6	1,637	2,273	1.2	3.4
221 FREE METHODIST	3	141	141	.1	.2
223 FREE WILL BAPT	1	31	41*	-	.1
226 FRIENDS-USA	1	4	11	-	-
226f INDEPENDNT	1	4	11	-	-

NA—Not applicable NR—Not reported *Total adherents estimated from known number of communicant, confirmed, full members. - Represents a percent less than 0.1. Percentages may not total due to rounding.
[1]See Appendix E [2]See Appendix F [3]See Appendix G Lines in *italic* represent a breakdown of Catholic rites or Friends affiliations. They are included in their respective denominational total.

Table 4. Churches and Church Membership by County and Denomination: 1990

County and Denomination	Number of churches	Communicant, confirmed, full members	Total adherents Number	Percent of total population	Percent of total adherents
249 AP CATH ASSYR	0	1	1	-	-
259 IFCA	2	NR	NR	-	-
263 INT FOURSQ GOS	6	674	889*	.5	1.3
283 LUTH—MO SYNOD	5	1,550	2,208	1.2	3.3
291 MISSIONARY CH	3	141	162	.1	.2
307 NETH REF CONGR	1	57	126	.1	.2
339 PENT CH OF GOD	6	207	461	.2	.7
349 PENT HOLINESS	8	378	498*	.3	.8
353 CHR BRETHREN	3	310	430	.2	.6
355 PRESB CH (USA)	9	3,377	4,452*	2.4	6.7
371 REF CH IN AM	1	170	325	.2	.5
403 SALVATION ARMY	2	248	268	.1	.4
413 S.D.A.	9	1,782	2,349*	1.2	3.5
419 SO BAPT CONV	13	3,145	4,146*	2.2	6.2
435 UNITARIAN-UNIV	1	107	153	.1	.2
443 UN C OF CHRIST	2	71	94*	-	.1
449 UN METHODIST	11	2,927	3,859*	2.0	5.8
469 WELS	3	535	731	.4	1.1
496 JEWISH EST[1]	0	NA	100	.1	.2
497 BLACK BAPT EST[2]	NA	413	544*	.3	.8
499 INDEP.NON-CHAR[3]	1	NA	500	.3	.8

WEST VIRGINIA

County and Denomination	Number of churches	Communicant, confirmed, full members	Total adherents Number	Percent of total population	Percent of total adherents
THE STATE.....	4,443	482,485	741,998*	41.4	100.0
BARBOUR	**73**	**4,167**	**5,809***	**37.0**	**100.0**
019 AMER BAPT USA	7	918	1,134*	7.2	19.5
081 CATHOLIC	3	NA	463	2.9	8.0
081d LATIN	3	NA	463	2.9	8.0
127 CH GOD (CLEVE)	1	27	33*	.2	.6
151 L-D SAINTS	1	NA	130	.8	2.2
157 CH OF BRETHREN	3	80	99*	.6	1.7
165 CH OF NAZARENE	3	176	296	1.9	5.1
167 CHS OF CHRIST	7	379	459	2.9	7.9
193 EPISCOPAL	1	12	13	.1	.2
285 MENNONITE CH	1	29	35	.2	.6
339 PENT CH OF GOD	2	29	40	.3	.7
355 PRESB CH (USA)	2	70	86*	.5	1.5
419 SO BAPT CONV	3	179	221*	1.4	3.8
449 UN METHODIST	39	2,268	2,800*	17.8	48.2
BERKELEY	**82**	**15,277**	**23,493***	**39.6**	**100.0**
019 AMER BAPT USA	1	75	94*	.2	.4
053 ASSEMB OF GOD	5	811	1,317	2.2	5.6
081 CATHOLIC	3	NA	3,761	6.3	16.0
081d LATIN	3	NA	3,761	6.3	16.0
093 CHR CH (DISC)	1	274	516	.9	2.2
097 CHR CHS&CHS CR	5	972	1,224*	2.1	5.2
123 CH GOD (ANDER)	1	14	14	-	.1
127 CH GOD (CLEVE)	1	131	165*	.3	.7
145 CH GOD PROPHCY	1	29	37*	.1	.2
157 CH OF BRETHREN	4	380	479*	.8	2.0
165 CH OF NAZARENE	1	56	101	.2	.4
167 CHS OF CHRIST	1	105	130	.2	.6
193 EPISCOPAL	3	576	693	1.2	2.9
207 E.L.C.A.	2	994	1,313	2.2	5.6
223 FREE WILL BAPT	2	185	233*	.4	1.0
263 INT FOURSQ GOS	1	87	110*	.2	.5
265 INT PENT C CHR	1	70	70	.1	.3
339 PENT CH OF GOD	1	50	120	.2	.5
355 PRESB CH (USA)	9	1,012	1,274*	2.2	5.4
356 PRESB CH AMER	1	195	200	.3	.9
361 PRIM BAPT ASCS	1	5	6*	-	-
403 SALVATION ARMY	1	88	90	.2	.4
413 S.D.A.	1	252	317*	.5	1.3
419 SO BAPT CONV	5	1,412	1,778*	3.0	7.6
443 UN C OF CHRIST	1	385	485*	.8	2.1
449 UN METHODIST	28	6,577	8,283*	14.0	35.3
496 JEWISH EST[1]	1	NA	0	-	-
497 BLACK BAPT EST[1]	NA	542	683*	1.2	2.9
BOONE	**65**	**4,289**	**5,718***	**22.1**	**100.0**
001 ADVENT CHR CH	1	16	20*	.1	.3
019 AMER BAPT USA	7	1,364	1,696*	6.6	29.7
053 ASSEMB OF GOD	2	41	76	.3	1.3
081 CATHOLIC	2	NA	184	.7	3.2
081d LATIN	2	NA	184	.7	3.2
093 CHR CH (DISC)	1	38	61	.2	1.1
123 CH GOD (ANDER)	2	14	91	.4	1.6
127 CH GOD (CLEVE)	7	342	425*	1.6	7.4
145 CH GOD PROPHCY	1	29	36*	.1	.6

County and Denomination	Number of churches	Communicant, confirmed, full members	Total adherents Number	Percent of total population	Percent of total adherents
165 CH OF NAZARENE	3	149	212	.8	3.7
167 CHS OF CHRIST	18	1,035	1,354	5.2	23.7
223 FREE WILL BAPT	2	92	114*	.4	2.0
325 OLD REG BAPT	1	28	35*	.1	.6
355 PRESB CH (USA)	4	108	134*	.5	2.3
419 SO BAPT CONV	1	100	124*	.5	2.2
449 UN METHODIST	12	904	1,124*	4.3	19.7
467 WESLEYAN	1	29	32	.1	.6
BRAXTON	**61**	**3,937**	**5,169***	**39.8**	**100.0**
019 AMER BAPT USA	10	1,810	2,252*	17.3	43.6
053 ASSEMB OF GOD	1	25	34	.3	.7
081 CATHOLIC	1	NA	126	1.0	2.4
081d LATIN	1	NA	126	1.0	2.4
127 CH GOD (CLEVE)	1	20	25*	.2	.5
145 CH GOD PROPHCY	1	29	36*	.3	.7
151 L-D SAINTS	1	NA	128	1.0	2.5
167 CHS OF CHRIST	1	27	48	.4	.9
329 OPEN BIBLE STD	1	NR	NR	-	-
355 PRESB CH (USA)	1	49	61*	.5	1.2
413 S.D.A.	1	38	47*	.4	.9
419 SO BAPT CONV	1	218	271*	2.1	5.2
449 UN METHODIST	41	1,721	2,141*	16.5	41.4
BROOKE	**43**	**4,965**	**11,931***	**44.2**	**100.0**
019 AMER BAPT USA	1	101	121*	.4	1.0
053 ASSEMB OF GOD	1	40	106	.4	.9
081 CATHOLIC	5	NA	4,910	18.2	41.2
081d LATIN	5	NA	4,910	18.2	41.2
093 CHR CH (DISC)	3	375	742	2.7	6.2
097 CHR CHS&CHS CR	4	917	1,100*	4.1	9.2
123 CH GOD (ANDER)	3	138	191	.7	1.6
127 CH GOD (CLEVE)	1	61	73*	.3	.6
165 CH OF NAZARENE	6	864	1,682	6.2	14.1
167 CHS OF CHRIST	2	152	232	.9	1.9
193 EPISCOPAL	4	331	429	1.6	3.6
221 FREE METHODIST	1	156	158	.6	1.3
355 PRESB CH (USA)	3	561	673*	2.5	5.6
403 SALVATION ARMY	1	72	78	.3	.7
419 SO BAPT CONV	2	134	161*	.6	1.3
449 UN METHODIST	6	1,063	1,275*	4.7	10.7
CABELL	**148**	**32,335**	**46,969***	**48.5**	**100.0**
019 AMER BAPT USA	23	8,245	9,889*	10.2	21.1
053 ASSEMB OF GOD	1	138	191	.2	.4
081 CATHOLIC	6	NA	5,970	6.2	12.7
081d LATIN	6	NA	5,970	6.2	12.7
093 CHR CH (DISC)	2	717	976	1.0	2.1
097 CHR CHS&CHS CR	6	1,137	1,364*	1.4	2.9
111 CH CR,SCIENTST	1	NR	NR	-	-
123 CH GOD (ANDER)	3	290	305	.3	.6
127 CH GOD (CLEVE)	4	708	849*	.9	1.8
145 CH GOD PROPHCY	2	58	70*	.1	.1
151 L-D SAINTS	2	NA	605	.6	1.3
157 CH OF BRETHREN	1	13	16*	-	-
165 CH OF NAZARENE	3	708	1,009	1.0	2.1
167 CHS OF CHRIST	8	744	952	1.0	2.0
179 CONSRV BAPT	1	NR	NR	-	-
193 EPISCOPAL	4	1,199	1,493	1.5	3.2
203 EVAN FREE CH	1	35	60	.1	.1
207 E.L.C.A.	2	894	1,205	1.2	2.6
221 FREE METHODIST	3	102	102	.1	.2
223 FREE WILL BAPT	9	902	1,082*	1.1	2.3
246 GREEK ORTHODOX	1	NR	NR	-	-
259 IFCA	1	NR	NR	-	-
283 LUTH—MO SYNOD	1	98	137	.1	.3
353 CHR BRETHREN	1	40	60	.1	.1
355 PRESB CH (USA)	8	2,618	3,140*	3.2	6.7
356 PRESB CH AMER	1	56	90	.1	.2
361 PRIM BAPT ASCS	1	22	26*	-	.1
403 SALVATION ARMY	1	66	66	.1	.1
413 S.D.A.	1	35	42*	-	.1
419 SO BAPT CONV	4	3,544	4,251*	4.4	9.1
435 UNITARIAN-UNIV	1	10	10	-	-
436 UNITED BAPT	3	488	585*	.6	1.2
443 UN C OF CHRIST	1	90	108*	.1	.2
449 UN METHODIST	34	8,076	9,687*	10.0	20.6
467 WESLEYAN	3	102	257	.3	.5
496 JEWISH EST[1]	3	NA	183	.2	.4
497 BLACK BAPT EST[1]	NA	1,200	1,439*	1.5	3.1
499 INDEP.NON-CHAR[3]	1	NA	750	.8	1.6
CALHOUN	**30**	**2,013**	**2,614***	**33.2**	**100.0**
019 AMER BAPT USA	7	1,296	1,642*	20.8	62.8
081 CATHOLIC	1	NA	58	.7	2.2
081d LATIN	1	NA	58	.7	2.2

NA–Not applicable   NR–Not reported   *Total adherents estimated from known number of communicant, confirmed, full members.   - Represents a percent less than 0.1.   Percentages may not total due to rounding.

[1]See Appendix E   [2]See Appendix F   [3]See Appendix G   Lines in *italic* represent a breakdown of Catholic rites or Friends affiliations. They are included in their respective denominational total.

Table 4. Churches and Church Membership by County and Denomination: 1990

County and Denomination	Number of churches	Communicant, confirmed, full members	Total adherents Number	Percent of total population	Percent of total adherents
167 CHS OF CHRIST	2	41	57	.7	2.2
449 UN METHODIST	20	676	857*	10.9	32.8
CLAY	**35**	**2,144**	**2,825***	**28.3**	**100.0**
001 ADVENT CHR CH	4	93	120*	1.2	4.2
019 AMER BAPT USA	11	1,646	2,131*	21.3	75.4
081 CATHOLIC	1	NA	53	.5	1.9
081d LATIN	*1*	*NA*	*53*	*.5*	*1.9*
165 CH OF NAZARENE	3	90	114	1.1	4.0
223 FREE WILL BAPT	2	39	50*	.5	1.8
361 PRIM BAPT ASCS	2	18	23*	.2	.8
449 UN METHODIST	12	258	334*	3.3	11.8
DODDRIDGE	**35**	**2,349**	**3,066***	**43.8**	**100.0**
011 A.W.M.C.	1	29	36*	.5	1.2
019 AMER BAPT USA	9	895	1,125*	16.1	36.7
053 ASSEMB OF GOD	1	82	143	2.0	4.7
081 CATHOLIC	2	NA	85	1.2	2.8
081d LATIN	*2*	*NA*	*85*	*1.2*	*2.8*
097 CHR CHS&CHS CR	3	275	346*	4.9	11.3
127 CH GOD (CLEVE)	2	68	85*	1.2	2.8
167 CHS OF CHRIST	1	35	40	.6	1.3
207 E.L.C.A.	1	106	126	1.8	4.1
415 S-D BAPTIST GC	1	31	39*	.6	1.3
449 UN METHODIST	14	828	1,041*	14.9	34.0
FAYETTE	**149**	**14,058**	**20,166***	**42.1**	**100.0**
001 ADVENT CHR CH	2	20	25*	.1	.1
019 AMER BAPT USA	35	6,974	8,567*	17.9	42.5
053 ASSEMB OF GOD	4	161	256	.5	1.3
071 BRETHREN (ASH)	2	94	115*	.2	.6
081 CATHOLIC	6	NA	1,566	3.3	7.8
081d LATIN	*6*	*NA*	*1,566*	*3.3*	*7.8*
093 CHR CH (DISC)	1	88	94	.2	.5
097 CHR CHS&CHS CR	3	35	43*	.1	.2
123 CH GOD (ANDER)	11	439	802	1.7	4.0
127 CH GOD (CLEVE)	7	647	795*	1.7	3.9
145 CH GOD PROPHCY	3	88	108*	.2	.5
151 L-D SAINTS	1	NA	398	.8	2.0
157 CH OF BRETHREN	1	60	74*	.2	.4
165 CH OF NAZARENE	1	245	422	.9	2.1
167 CHS OF CHRIST	6	128	170	.4	.8
171 CH GOD-GEN CON	1	61	75*	.2	.4
193 EPISCOPAL	3	188	286	.6	1.4
223 FREE WILL BAPT	6	326	400*	.8	2.0
265 INT PENT C CHR	1	6	9	-	-
325 OLD REG BAPT	1	36	44*	.1	.2
349 PENT HOLINESS	2	186	228*	.5	1.1
355 PRESB CH (USA)	8	664	816*	1.7	4.0
419 SO BAPT CONV	4	505	620*	1.3	3.1
449 UN METHODIST	35	2,298	2,823*	5.9	14.0
467 WESLEYAN	4	69	221	.5	1.1
497 BLACK BAPT EST[1]	NA	740	909*	1.9	4.5
499 INDEP.NON-CHAR[3]	1	NA	300	.6	1.5
GILMER	**32**	**1,627**	**2,099***	**27.4**	**100.0**
019 AMER BAPT USA	5	804	982*	12.8	46.8
081 CATHOLIC	1	NA	96	1.3	4.6
081d LATIN	*1*	*NA*	*96*	*1.3*	*4.6*
127 CH GOD (CLEVE)	1	34	42*	.5	2.0
145 CH GOD PROPHCY	1	29	35*	.5	1.7
167 CHS OF CHRIST	3	99	123	1.6	5.9
193 EPISCOPAL	1	11	27	.4	1.3
355 PRESB CH (USA)	1	53	65*	.8	3.1
413 S.D.A.	1	26	32*	.4	1.5
419 SO BAPT CONV	1	15	18*	.2	.9
449 UN METHODIST	17	556	679*	8.9	32.3
GRANT	**45**	**3,947**	**5,139***	**49.3**	**100.0**
019 AMER BAPT USA	6	528	651*	6.2	12.7
053 ASSEMB OF GOD	4	306	509	4.9	9.9
081 CATHOLIC	1	NA	139	1.3	2.7
081d LATIN	*1*	*NA*	*139*	*1.3*	*2.7*
127 CH GOD (CLEVE)	2	245	302*	2.9	5.9
157 CH OF BRETHREN	9	1,014	1,251*	12.0	24.3
167 CHS OF CHRIST	1	28	36	.3	.7
207 E.L.C.A.	1	70	84	.8	1.6
355 PRESB CH (USA)	2	231	285*	2.7	5.5
419 SO BAPT CONV	1	50	62*	.6	1.2
449 UN METHODIST	18	1,475	1,820*	17.5	35.4
GREENBRIER	**131**	**12,630**	**16,532***	**47.7**	**100.0**
019 AMER BAPT USA	25	3,892	4,750*	13.7	28.7
053 ASSEMB OF GOD	1	26	34	.1	.2
055 AS REF PRES CH	1	153	165	.5	1.0

County and Denomination	Number of churches	Communicant, confirmed, full members	Total adherents Number	Percent of total population	Percent of total adherents
081 CATHOLIC	5	NA	665	1.9	4.0
081d LATIN	*5*	*NA*	*665*	*1.9*	*4.0*
097 CHR CHS&CHS CR	2	75	92*	.3	.6
123 CH GOD (ANDER)	4	258	317	.9	1.9
127 CH GOD (CLEVE)	9	563	687*	2.0	4.2
151 L-D SAINTS	2	NA	313	.9	1.9
165 CH OF NAZARENE	2	135	198	.6	1.2
167 CHS OF CHRIST	3	93	119	.3	.7
193 EPISCOPAL	4	258	374	1.1	2.3
215 EVAN METH CH	1	45	55*	.2	.3
223 FREE WILL BAPT	3	154	188*	.5	1.1
265 INT PENT C CHR	1	35	65	.2	.4
329 OPEN BIBLE STD	1	NR	NR	-	-
339 PENT CH OF GOD	1	34	77	.2	.5
349 PENT HOLINESS	6	339	414*	1.2	2.5
355 PRESB CH (USA)	12	1,461	1,783*	5.1	10.8
361 PRIM BAPT ASCS	2	29	35*	.1	.2
413 S.D.A.	2	75	92*	.3	.6
419 SO BAPT CONV	3	826	1,008*	2.9	6.1
449 UN METHODIST	41	3,866	4,719*	13.6	28.5
497 BLACK BAPT EST[1]	NA	313	382*	1.1	2.3
HAMPSHIRE	**67**	**4,890**	**7,094***	**43.0**	**100.0**
019 AMER BAPT USA	5	554	696*	4.2	9.8
053 ASSEMB OF GOD	7	393	886	5.4	12.5
081 CATHOLIC	1	NA	217	1.3	3.1
081d LATIN	*1*	*NA*	*217*	*1.3*	*3.1*
093 CHR CH (DISC)	3	190	268	1.6	3.8
097 CHR CHS&CHS CR	5	418	525*	3.2	7.4
127 CH GOD (CLEVE)	2	60	75*	.5	1.1
151 L-D SAINTS	1	NA	156	.9	2.2
157 CH OF BRETHREN	6	561	705*	4.3	9.9
165 CH OF NAZARENE	1	103	190	1.2	2.7
167 CHS OF CHRIST	1	35	45	.3	.6
193 EPISCOPAL	1	56	119	.7	1.7
207 E.L.C.A.	2	165	253	1.5	3.6
355 PRESB CH (USA)	4	399	501*	3.0	7.1
413 S.D.A.	1	57	72*	.4	1.0
419 SO BAPT CONV	1	63	79*	.5	1.1
443 UN C OF CHRIST	1	141	177*	1.1	2.5
449 UN METHODIST	25	1,695	2,130*	12.9	30.0
HANCOCK	**57**	**8,884**	**23,501***	**66.7**	**100.0**
019 AMER BAPT USA	2	974	1,170*	3.3	5.0
053 ASSEMB OF GOD	1	36	50	.1	.2
081 CATHOLIC	6	NA	11,335	32.2	48.2
081b BYZAN RUTH	*1*	*NA*	*1,434*	*4.1*	*6.1*
081d LATIN	*5*	*NA*	*9,901*	*28.1*	*42.1*
089 CHR & MISS AL	1	56	85	.2	.4
093 CHR CH (DISC)	1	320	492	1.4	2.1
097 CHR CHS&CHS CR	4	985	1,184*	3.4	5.0
127 CH GOD (CLEVE)	3	151	181*	.5	.8
165 CH OF NAZARENE	5	813	2,154	6.1	9.2
167 CHS OF CHRIST	4	895	1,151	3.3	4.9
171 CH GOD-GEN CON	1	37	44*	.1	.2
193 EPISCOPAL	1	23	47	.1	.2
207 E.L.C.A.	2	280	366	1.0	1.6
221 FREE METHODIST	3	113	179	.5	.8
246 GREEK ORTHODOX	1	NR	NR	-	-
331 ORTH CH IN AM	1	NR	NR	-	-
355 PRESB CH (USA)	7	1,396	1,677*	4.8	7.1
403 SALVATION ARMY	1	123	123	.3	.5
413 S.D.A.	1	46	55*	.2	.2
419 SO BAPT CONV	2	397	477*	1.4	2.0
449 UN METHODIST	8	1,921	2,308*	6.6	9.8
467 WESLEYAN	1	45	95	.3	.4
496 JEWISH EST[1]	1	NA	0	-	-
497 BLACK BAPT EST[1]	NA	273	328*	.9	1.4
HARDY	**50**	**4,789**	**6,106***	**55.6**	**100.0**
053 ASSEMB OF GOD	4	189	378	3.4	6.2
071 BRETHREN (ASH)	2	71	87*	.8	1.4
081 CATHOLIC	1	NA	77	.7	1.3
081d LATIN	*1*	*NA*	*77*	*.7*	*1.3*
097 CHR CHS&CHS CR	1	65	79*	.7	1.3
127 CH GOD (CLEVE)	1	47	57*	.5	.9
157 CH OF BRETHREN	10	1,744	2,132*	19.4	34.9
167 CHS OF CHRIST	1	80	89	.8	1.5
193 EPISCOPAL	1	39	56	.5	.9
207 E.L.C.A.	3	244	325	3.0	5.3
285 MENNONITE CH	4	151	186	1.7	3.0
355 PRESB CH (USA)	3	368	450*	4.1	7.4
419 SO BAPT CONV	2	120	147*	1.3	2.4
449 UN METHODIST	17	1,671	2,043*	18.6	33.5

NA–Not applicable   NR–Not reported   *Total adherents estimated from known number of communicant, confirmed, full members.   - Represents a percent less than 0.1.   Percentages may not total due to rounding.
[1]See Appendix E   [2]See Appendix F   [3]See Appendix G   Lines in *italic* represent a breakdown of Catholic rites or Friends affiliations. They are included in their respective denominational total.

Table 4. Churches and Church Membership by County and Denomination: 1990

County and Denomination	Number of churches	Communicant, confirmed, full members	Total adherents Number	Total adherents Percent of total population	Percent of total adherents
HARRISON	151	19,573	34,311*	49.5	100.0
011 A.W.M.C.	2	34	42*	.1	.1
019 AMER BAPT USA	30	6,181	7,582*	10.9	22.1
053 ASSEMB OF GOD	1	82	159	.2	.5
081 CATHOLIC	8	NA	8,663	12.5	25.2
081b *BYZAN RUTH*	*1*	*NA*	*72*	*.1*	*.2*
081d *LATIN*	*7*	*NA*	*8,591*	*12.4*	*25.0*
089 CHR & MISS AL	1	101	181	.3	.5
093 CHR CH (DISC)	3	163	248	.4	.7
111 CH CR,SCIENTST	1	NR	NR	-	-
123 CH GOD (ANDER)	4	198	259	.4	.8
127 CH GOD (CLEVE)	3	415	509*	.7	1.5
145 CH GOD PROPHCY	1	29	36*	.1	.1
151 L-D SAINTS	1	NA	172	.2	.5
157 CH OF BRETHREN	1	130	159*	.2	.5
165 CH OF NAZARENE	2	116	156	.2	.5
167 CHS OF CHRIST	7	577	780	1.1	2.3
193 EPISCOPAL	3	311	428	.6	1.2
207 E.L.C.A.	1	316	386	.6	1.1
221 FREE METHODIST	1	11	24	-	.1
223 FREE WILL BAPT	2	203	249*	.4	.7
246 GREEK ORTHODOX	1	NR	NR	-	-
339 PENT CH OF GOD	2	24	62	.1	.2
355 PRESB CH (USA)	4	909	1,115*	1.6	3.2
403 SALVATION ARMY	1	96	98	.1	.3
413 S.D.A.	1	147	180*	.3	.5
415 S-D BAPTIST GC	2	303	372*	.5	1.1
419 SO BAPT CONV	3	567	696*	1.0	2.0
438 UN BRETH IN CR	1	40	56	.1	.2
449 UN METHODIST	60	8,366	10,262*	14.8	29.9
467 WESLEYAN	1	15	79	.1	.2
496 JEWISH EST[1]	1	NA	115	.2	.3
497 BLACK BAPT EST[1]	NA	239	293*	.4	.9
498 INDEP.CHARIS.[3]	1	NA	600	.9	1.7
499 INDEP.NON-CHAR[3]	1	NA	350	.5	1.0
JACKSON	69	5,318	7,747*	29.9	100.0
019 AMER BAPT USA	11	1,290	1,612*	6.2	20.8
053 ASSEMB OF GOD	1	31	52	.2	.7
081 CATHOLIC	1	NA	339	1.3	4.4
081d *LATIN*	*1*	*NA*	*339*	*1.3*	*4.4*
093 CHR CH (DISC)	1	52	59	.2	.8
097 CHR CHS&CHS CR	1	122	152*	.6	2.0
123 CH GOD (ANDER)	1	16	24	.1	.3
127 CH GOD (CLEVE)	2	98	122*	.5	1.6
151 L-D SAINTS	1	NA	166	.6	2.1
165 CH OF NAZARENE	2	229	448	1.7	5.8
167 CHS OF CHRIST	5	259	350	1.3	4.5
179 CONSRV BAPT	1	NR	NR	-	-
193 EPISCOPAL	2	90	112	.4	1.4
207 E.L.C.A.	1	50	61	.2	.8
355 PRESB CH (USA)	2	207	259*	1.0	3.3
359 PRIM AD CHR CH	1	15	19*	.1	.2
413 S.D.A.	1	15	19*	.1	.2
419 SO BAPT CONV	1	246	307*	1.2	4.0
449 UN METHODIST	33	2,598	3,246*	12.5	41.9
499 INDEP.NON-CHAR[3]	1	NA	400	1.5	5.2
JEFFERSON	63	9,030	14,302*	39.8	100.0
019 AMER BAPT USA	2	170	212*	.6	1.5
053 ASSEMB OF GOD	5	421	820	2.3	5.7
081 CATHOLIC	3	NA	1,597	4.4	11.2
081d *LATIN*	*3*	*NA*	*1,597*	*4.4*	*11.2*
127 CH GOD (CLEVE)	1	102	127*	.4	.9
151 L-D SAINTS	1	NA	669	1.9	4.7
157 CH OF BRETHREN	2	223	279*	.8	2.0
171 CH GOD-GEN CON	1	13	16*	-	.1
193 EPISCOPAL	8	897	1,401	3.9	9.8
207 E.L.C.A.	4	822	1,131	3.1	7.9
265 INT PENT C CHR	2	58	150	.4	1.0
355 PRESB CH (USA)	5	709	886*	2.5	6.2
413 S.D.A.	1	103	129*	.4	.9
419 SO BAPT CONV	5	1,429	1,785*	5.0	12.5
443 UN C OF CHRIST	2	113	141*	.4	1.0
449 UN METHODIST	21	3,317	4,143*	11.5	29.0
497 BLACK BAPT EST[1]	NA	653	816*	2.3	5.7
KANAWHA	344	55,173	81,599*	39.3	100.0
001 ADVENT CHR CH	12	548	667*	.3	.8
005 AME ZION	2	54	106	.1	.1
019 AMER BAPT USA	38	13,666	16,627*	8.0	20.4
053 ASSEMB OF GOD	8	338	518	.2	.6
081 CATHOLIC	11	NA	8,902	4.3	10.9
081d *LATIN*	*11*	*NA*	*8,902*	*4.3*	*10.9*
089 CHR & MISS AL	1	42	65	-	.1
093 CHR CH (DISC)	4	433	895	.4	1.1
097 CHR CHS&CHS CR	6	977	1,189*	.6	1.5
111 CH CR,SCIENTST	2	NR	NR	-	-
123 CH GOD (ANDER)	17	1,093	1,780	.9	2.2
127 CH GOD (CLEVE)	11	755	919*	.4	1.1
145 CH GOD PROPHCY	5	148	180*	.1	.2
151 L-D SAINTS	2	NA	638	.3	.8
165 CH OF NAZARENE	35	4,529	7,091	3.4	8.7
167 CHS OF CHRIST	26	1,587	2,097	1.0	2.6
171 CH GOD-GEN CON	5	170	207*	.1	.3
193 EPISCOPAL	8	1,756	2,209	1.1	2.7
207 E.L.C.A.	4	1,026	1,282	.6	1.6
216 EVAN PRESBY CH	1	0	0	-	-
223 FREE WILL BAPT	15	906	1,102*	.5	1.4
226 FRIENDS-USA	1	13	25	-	-
226c *FGC*	*1*	*13*	*25*	*-*	*-*
246 GREEK ORTHODOX	1	NR	NR	-	-
283 LUTH—MO SYNOD	1	60	87	-	.1
339 PENT CH OF GOD	1	25	50	-	.1
349 PENT HOLINESS	2	112	136*	.1	.2
355 PRESB CH (USA)	26	6,363	7,742*	3.7	9.5
356 PRESB CH AMER	4	433	490	.2	.6
359 PRIM AD CHR CH	7	319	388*	.2	.5
361 PRIM BAPT ASCS	1	29	35*	-	-
403 SALVATION ARMY	2	116	132	.1	.2
413 S.D.A.	2	311	378*	.2	.5
419 SO BAPT CONV	11	2,731	3,323*	1.6	4.1
435 UNITARIAN-UNIV	1	90	112	.1	.1
449 UN METHODIST	62	12,245	14,898*	7.2	18.3
467 WESLEYAN	6	123	344	.2	.4
496 JEWISH EST[1]	1	NA	805	.4	1.0
497 BLACK BAPT EST[1]	NA	4,175	5,080*	2.4	6.2
499 INDEP.NON-CHAR[3]	2	NA	1,100	.5	1.3
LEWIS	57	4,343	6,875*	39.9	100.0
019 AMER BAPT USA	9	1,317	1,610*	9.3	23.4
053 ASSEMB OF GOD	1	123	185	1.1	2.7
081 CATHOLIC	2	NA	982	5.7	14.3
081d *LATIN*	*2*	*NA*	*982*	*5.7*	*14.3*
123 CH GOD (ANDER)	1	0	58	.3	.8
127 CH GOD (CLEVE)	1	79	97*	.6	1.4
151 L-D SAINTS	1	NA	303	1.8	4.4
165 CH OF NAZARENE	1	45	264	1.5	3.8
167 CHS OF CHRIST	1	65	77	.4	1.1
193 EPISCOPAL	1	214	243	1.4	3.5
355 PRESB CH (USA)	1	68	83*	.5	1.2
419 SO BAPT CONV	1	183	224*	1.3	3.3
449 UN METHODIST	37	2,249	2,749*	16.0	40.0
LINCOLN	56	4,031	5,167*	24.2	100.0
019 AMER BAPT USA	13	1,693	2,138*	10.0	41.4
053 ASSEMB OF GOD	1	37	46	.2	.9
081 CATHOLIC	1	NA	32	.1	.6
081d *LATIN*	*1*	*NA*	*32*	*.1*	*.6*
123 CH GOD (ANDER)	1	50	50	.2	1.0
127 CH GOD (CLEVE)	4	176	222*	1.0	4.3
165 CH OF NAZARENE	1	25	46	.2	.9
167 CHS OF CHRIST	9	536	721	3.4	14.0
171 CH GOD-GEN CON	1	3	4*	-	.1
223 FREE WILL BAPT	11	652	823*	3.8	15.9
325 OLD REG BAPT	1	18	23*	.1	.4
419 SO BAPT CONV	2	220	278*	1.3	5.4
436 UNITED BAPT	1	17	21*	.1	.4
449 UN METHODIST	10	604	763*	3.6	14.8
LOGAN	119	8,539	11,914*	27.7	100.0
019 AMER BAPT USA	10	894	1,118*	2.6	9.4
053 ASSEMB OF GOD	2	64	101	.2	.8
081 CATHOLIC	4	NA	798	1.9	6.7
081d *LATIN*	*4*	*NA*	*798*	*1.9*	*6.7*
093 CHR CH (DISC)	3	281	360	.8	3.0
097 CHR CHS&CHS CR	2	250	313*	.7	2.6
123 CH GOD (ANDER)	1	10	16	-	.1
127 CH GOD (CLEVE)	17	1,545	1,933*	4.5	16.2
145 CH GOD PROPHCY	2	58	73*	.2	.6
151 L-D SAINTS	1	NA	229	.5	1.9
165 CH OF NAZARENE	2	359	657	1.5	5.5
167 CHS OF CHRIST	7	343	417	1.0	3.5
193 EPISCOPAL	1	29	34	.1	.3
223 FREE WILL BAPT	44	2,731	3,416*	7.9	28.7
325 OLD REG BAPT	2	47	59*	.1	.5
355 PRESB CH (USA)	2	288	360*	.8	3.0
403 SALVATION ARMY	2	123	134	.3	1.1
413 S.D.A.	1	24	30*	.1	.3
419 SO BAPT CONV	1	93	116*	.3	1.0
436 UNITED BAPT	1	37	46*	.1	.4
449 UN METHODIST	12	1,018	1,273*	3.0	10.7

NA–Not applicable   NR–Not reported   *Total adherents estimated from known number of communicant, confirmed, full members.   - Represents a percent less than 0.1.   Percentages may not total due to rounding.
[1]See Appendix E   [2]See Appendix F   [3]See Appendix G   Lines in *italic* represent a breakdown of Catholic rites or Friends affiliations. They are included in their respective denominational total.

Table 4. Churches and Church Membership by County and Denomination: 1990

County and Denomination	Number of churches	Communicant, confirmed, full members	Total adherents Number	Percent of total population	Percent of total adherents
467 WESLEYAN	1	10	12	-	.1
496 JEWISH EST[1]	1	NA	0	-	-
497 BLACK BAPT EST[1]	NA	335	419*	1.0	3.5
MC DOWELL	**137**	**7,944**	**11,195***	**31.8**	**100.0**
001 ADVENT CHR CH	4	67	85*	.2	.8
005 AME ZION	5	816	931	2.6	8.3
011 A.W.M.C.	1	7	9*	-	.1
019 AMER BAPT USA	7	733	929*	2.6	8.3
022 EASTERN ORTH	1	38	38	.1	.3
053 ASSEMB OF GOD	5	118	205	.6	1.8
081 CATHOLIC	5	NA	782	2.2	7.0
081d LATIN	5	NA	782	2.2	7.0
089 CHR & MISS AL	1	2	7	-	.1
093 CHR CH (DISC)	1	29	47	.1	.4
097 CHR CHS&CHS CR	6	100	127*	.4	1.1
123 CH GOD (ANDER)	3	85	199	.6	1.8
127 CH GOD (CLEVE)	16	1,026	1,300*	3.7	11.6
151 L-D SAINTS	1	NA	158	.4	1.4
165 CH OF NAZARENE	1	83	164	.5	1.5
167 CHS OF CHRIST	2	50	65	.2	.6
193 EPISCOPAL	3	49	101	.3	.9
223 FREE WILL BAPT	3	171	217*	.6	1.9
265 INT PENT C CHR	1	15	15	-	.1
325 OLD REG BAPT	13	744	943*	2.7	8.4
339 PENT CH OF GOD	1	34	77	.2	.7
349 PENT HOLINESS	12	578	733*	2.1	6.5
355 PRESB CH (USA)	3	139	176*	.5	1.6
413 S.D.A.	2	67	85*	.2	.8
419 SO BAPT CONV	3	249	316*	.9	2.8
449 UN METHODIST	35	1,569	1,989*	5.6	17.8
467 WESLEYAN	1	9	19	.1	.2
496 JEWISH EST[1]	1	NA	0	-	-
497 BLACK BAPT EST[1]	NA	1,166	1,478*	4.2	13.2
MARION	**146**	**15,955**	**29,684***	**51.9**	**100.0**
011 A.W.M.C.	1	22	27*	-	.1
019 AMER BAPT USA	17	3,514	4,234*	7.4	14.3
022 EASTERN ORTH	1	35	35	.1	.1
053 ASSEMB OF GOD	4	712	3,342	5.8	11.3
081 CATHOLIC	12	NA	6,878	12.0	23.2
081d LATIN	12	NA	6,878	12.0	23.2
089 CHR & MISS AL	1	68	119	.2	.4
093 CHR CH (DISC)	3	295	556	1.0	1.9
123 CH GOD (ANDER)	1	8	10	-	-
127 CH GOD (CLEVE)	3	140	169*	.3	.6
145 CH GOD PROPHCY	4	117	141*	.2	.5
151 L-D SAINTS	1	NA	409	.7	1.4
157 CH OF BRETHREN	1	43	52*	.1	.2
165 CH OF NAZARENE	3	480	695	1.2	2.3
167 CHS OF CHRIST	15	1,598	2,074	3.6	7.0
193 EPISCOPAL	1	171	246	.4	.8
207 E.L.C.A.	1	352	488	.9	1.6
215 EVAN METH CH	1	45	54*	.1	.2
221 FREE METHODIST	4	145	189	.3	.6
329 OPEN BIBLE STD	1	NR	NR	-	-
355 PRESB CH (USA)	3	721	869*	1.5	2.9
356 PRESB CH AMER	1	70	87	.2	.3
403 SALVATION ARMY	1	47	50	.1	.2
413 S.D.A.	1	40	48*	.1	.2
419 SO BAPT CONV	2	272	328*	.6	1.1
449 UN METHODIST	61	6,592	7,942*	13.9	26.8
467 WESLEYAN	1	12	23	-	.1
496 JEWISH EST[1]	1	NA	70	.1	.2
497 BLACK BAPT EST[1]	NA	456	549*	1.0	1.8
MARSHALL	**67**	**9,014**	**16,649***	**44.6**	**100.0**
019 AMER BAPT USA	3	1,066	1,305*	3.5	7.8
053 ASSEMB OF GOD	1	44	60	.2	.4
071 BRETHREN (ASH)	1	42	51*	.1	.3
081 CATHOLIC	5	NA	4,249	11.4	25.5
081d LATIN	5	NA	4,249	11.4	25.5
093 CHR CH (DISC)	6	908	1,797	4.8	10.8
097 CHR CHS&CHS CR	1	71	87*	.2	.5
123 CH GOD (ANDER)	2	160	168	.4	1.0
127 CH GOD (CLEVE)	2	212	260*	.7	1.6
133 CH GOD(7TH)DEN	1	24	27	.1	.2
151 L-D SAINTS	1	NA	268	.7	1.6
165 CH OF NAZARENE	2	200	279	.7	1.7
167 CHS OF CHRIST	7	722	887	2.4	5.3
171 CH GOD-GEN CON	1	392	480*	1.3	2.9
193 EPISCOPAL	1	237	303	.8	1.8
207 E.L.C.A.	2	181	306	.8	1.8
331 ORTH CH IN AM	1	NR	NR	-	-
355 PRESB CH (USA)	6	544	666*	1.8	4.0
356 PRESB CH AMER	1	28	36	.1	.2

County and Denomination	Number of churches	Communicant, confirmed, full members	Total adherents Number	Percent of total population	Percent of total adherents
403 SALVATION ARMY	1	72	74	.2	.4
419 SO BAPT CONV	1	473	579*	1.5	3.5
435 UNITARIAN-UNIV	1	12	27	.1	.2
449 UN METHODIST	19	3,626	4,440*	11.9	26.7
499 INDEP.NON-CHAR[3]	1	NA	300	.8	1.8
MASON	**69**	**6,133**	**8,426***	**33.5**	**100.0**
001 ADVENT CHR CH	2	31	39*	.2	.5
011 A.W.M.C.	1	0	0*	-	-
019 AMER BAPT USA	9	1,407	1,751*	7.0	20.8
053 ASSEMB OF GOD	1	11	20	.1	.2
081 CATHOLIC	2	NA	414	1.6	4.9
081d LATIN	2	NA	414	1.6	4.9
123 CH GOD (ANDER)	2	158	305	1.2	3.6
145 CH GOD PROPHCY	1	29	36*	.1	.4
165 CH OF NAZARENE	1	253	420	1.7	5.0
167 CHS OF CHRIST	5	412	459	1.8	5.4
193 EPISCOPAL	1	114	152	.6	1.8
207 E.L.C.A.	4	212	270	1.1	3.2
325 OLD REG BAPT	1	11	14*	.1	.2
355 PRESB CH (USA)	1	255	317*	1.3	3.8
413 S.D.A.	1	47	58*	.2	.7
419 SO BAPT CONV	2	226	281*	1.1	3.3
449 UN METHODIST	34	2,949	3,670*	14.6	43.6
467 WESLEYAN	1	18	220	.9	2.6
MERCER	**154**	**23,343**	**31,889***	**49.1**	**100.0**
001 ADVENT CHR CH	1	99	121*	.2	.4
005 AME ZION	2	406	452	.7	1.4
011 A.W.M.C.	2	22	27*	-	.1
019 AMER BAPT USA	5	267	325*	.5	1.0
053 ASSEMB OF GOD	2	184	323	.5	1.0
081 CATHOLIC	2	NA	1,918	3.0	6.0
081d LATIN	2	NA	1,918	3.0	6.0
093 CHR CH (DISC)	7	967	1,575	2.4	4.9
097 CHR CHS&CHS CR	11	1,027	1,250*	1.9	3.9
111 CH CR,SCIENTST	1	NR	NR	-	-
123 CH GOD (ANDER)	5	343	478	.7	1.5
127 CH GOD (CLEVE)	9	1,315	1,601*	2.5	5.0
145 CH GOD PROPHCY	2	58	71*	.1	.2
157 CH OF BRETHREN	2	73	89*	.1	.3
165 CH OF NAZARENE	3	356	606	.9	1.9
167 CHS OF CHRIST	4	263	343	.5	1.1
193 EPISCOPAL	2	325	436	.7	1.4
207 E.L.C.A.	1	183	239	.4	.7
221 FREE METHODIST	1	49	68	.1	.2
223 FREE WILL BAPT	4	112	136*	.2	.4
325 OLD REG BAPT	1	40	49*	.1	.2
339 PENT CH OF GOD	1	34	76	.1	.2
349 PENT HOLINESS	9	1,071	1,304*	2.0	4.1
355 PRESB CH (USA)	7	1,440	1,753*	2.7	5.5
356 PRESB CH AMER	1	23	27	-	.1
361 PRIM BAPT ASCS	5	116	141*	.2	.4
403 SALVATION ARMY	2	147	158	.2	.5
413 S.D.A.	1	145	177*	.3	.6
419 SO BAPT CONV	23	7,198	8,764*	13.5	27.5
449 UN METHODIST	34	6,014	7,323*	11.3	23.0
467 WESLEYAN	2	52	74	.1	.2
496 JEWISH EST[1]	1	NA	250	.4	.8
497 BLACK BAPT EST[1]	NA	1,014	1,235*	1.9	3.9
499 INDEP.NON-CHAR[3]	1	NA	500	.8	1.6
MINERAL	**68**	**8,115**	**11,686***	**43.8**	**100.0**
011 A.W.M.C.	2	27	33*	.1	.3
053 ASSEMB OF GOD	7	405	873	3.3	7.5
081 CATHOLIC	3	NA	1,043	3.9	8.9
081d LATIN	3	NA	1,043	3.9	8.9
097 CHR CHS&CHS CR	1	35	43*	.2	.4
127 CH GOD (CLEVE)	4	396	489*	1.8	4.2
145 CH GOD PROPHCY	1	29	36*	.1	.3
151 L-D SAINTS	1	NA	233	.9	2.0
157 CH OF BRETHREN	6	832	1,027*	3.8	8.8
167 CHS OF CHRIST	1	14	20	.1	.2
193 EPISCOPAL	1	66	99	.4	.8
207 E.L.C.A.	1	278	379	1.4	3.2
349 PENT HOLINESS	2	197	243*	.9	2.1
355 PRESB CH (USA)	3	589	727*	2.7	6.2
419 SO BAPT CONV	5	780	963*	3.6	8.2
438 UN BRETH IN CR	1	153	153	.6	1.3
449 UN METHODIST	29	4,092	5,051*	18.9	43.2
497 BLACK BAPT EST[1]	NA	222	274*	1.0	2.3
MINGO	**86**	**8,144**	**11,028***	**32.7**	**100.0**
019 AMER BAPT USA	5	1,059	1,371*	4.1	12.4
053 ASSEMB OF GOD	5	357	481	1.4	4.4
081 CATHOLIC	1	NA	292	.9	2.6

NA–Not applicable NR–Not reported *Total adherents estimated from known number of communicant, confirmed, full members. - Represents a percent less than 0.1. Percentages may not total due to rounding.

[1]See Appendix E [2]See Appendix F [3]See Appendix G Lines in *italic* represent a breakdown of Catholic rites or Friends affiliations. They are included in their respective denominational total.

Table 4. Churches and Church Membership by County and Denomination: 1990

County and Denomination	Number of churches	Communicant, confirmed, full members	Total adherents Number	Percent of total population	Percent of total adherents
081d *LATIN*	*1*	*NA*	*292*	*.9*	*2.6*
093 CHR CH (DISC)	5	220	357	1.1	3.2
097 CHR CHS&CHS CR	4	371	480*	1.4	4.4
127 CH GOD (CLEVE)	13	1,207	1,563*	4.6	14.2
145 CH GOD PROPHCY	1	29	38*	.1	.3
167 CHS OF CHRIST	7	233	304	.9	2.8
193 EPISCOPAL	1	46	99	.3	.9
223 FREE WILL BAPT	13	766	992*	2.9	9.0
325 OLD REG BAPT	7	324	420*	1.2	3.8
355 PRESB CH (USA)	2	221	286*	.8	2.6
413 S.D.A.	1	35	45*	.1	.4
419 SO BAPT CONV	5	1,276	1,652*	4.9	15.0
436 UNITED BAPT	9	1,115	1,444*	4.3	13.1
449 UN METHODIST	5	658	852*	2.5	7.7
467 WESLEYAN	1	25	90	.3	.8
496 JEWISH EST[1]	1	NA	0	-	-
497 BLACK BAPT EST[1]	NA	202	262*	.8	2.4
MONONGALIA	**120**	**12,565**	**24,907***	**33.0**	**100.0**
019 AMER BAPT USA	9	1,687	1,996*	2.6	8.0
022 EASTERN ORTH	1	55	55	.1	.2
053 ASSEMB OF GOD	3	244	420	.6	1.7
081 CATHOLIC	7	NA	8,447	11.2	33.9
081b *BYZAN RUTH*	*1*	*NA*	*503*	*.7*	*2.0*
081d *LATIN*	*6*	*NA*	*7,944*	*10.5*	*31.9*
089 CHR & MISS AL	1	327	327	.4	1.3
093 CHR CH (DISC)	3	314	675	.9	2.7
111 CH CR,SCIENTST	1	NR	NR	-	-
123 CH GOD (ANDER)	1	28	34	-	.1
127 CH GOD (CLEVE)	2	110	130*	.2	.5
145 CH GOD PROPHCY	1	29	34*	-	.1
151 L-D SAINTS	2	NA	529	.7	2.1
157 CH OF BRETHREN	1	123	146*	.2	.6
165 CH OF NAZARENE	2	207	462	.6	1.9
167 CHS OF CHRIST	5	473	646	.9	2.6
193 EPISCOPAL	2	233	421	.6	1.7
207 E.L.C.A.	1	391	523	.7	2.1
215 EVAN METH CH	1	186	220*	.3	.9
221 FREE METHODIST	3	74	105	.1	.4
226 FRIENDS-USA	1	21	25*	-	.1
226c *FGC*	*1*	*21*	*25**	*-*	*.1*
246 GREEK ORTHODOX	1	NR	NR	-	-
263 INT FOURSQ GOS	1	35	41*	.1	.2
285 MENNONITE CH	1	119	147	.2	.6
329 OPEN BIBLE STD	1	NR	NR	-	-
353 CHR BRETHREN	1	25	50	.1	.2
355 PRESB CH (USA)	5	851	1,007*	1.3	4.0
403 SALVATION ARMY	1	87	90	.1	.4
413 S.D.A.	1	77	91*	.1	.4
419 SO BAPT CONV	4	624	738*	1.0	3.0
435 UNITARIAN-UNIV	1	25	34	-	.1
449 UN METHODIST	54	5,740	6,793*	9.0	27.3
467 WESLEYAN	1	30	38	.1	.2
496 JEWISH EST[1]	1	NA	150	.2	.6
497 BLACK BAPT EST[1]	NA	450	533*	.7	2.1
MONROE	**69**	**4,178**	**5,395***	**43.5**	**100.0**
019 AMER BAPT USA	11	1,049	1,285*	10.4	23.8
055 AS REF PRES CH	1	96	101	.8	1.9
061 BEACHY AMISH	1	31	38*	.3	.7
081 CATHOLIC	3	NA	198	1.6	3.7
081d *LATIN*	*3*	*NA*	*198*	*1.6*	*3.7*
093 CHR CH (DISC)	1	32	50	.4	.9
097 CHR CHS&CHS CR	4	490	600*	4.8	11.1
123 CH GOD (ANDER)	1	20	20	.2	.4
127 CH GOD (CLEVE)	2	135	165*	1.3	3.1
145 CH GOD PROPHCY	1	29	36*	.3	.7
157 CH OF BRETHREN	2	192	235*	1.9	4.4
165 CH OF NAZARENE	2	63	140	1.1	2.6
167 CHS OF CHRIST	1	6	10	.1	.2
193 EPISCOPAL	1	22	28	.2	.5
223 FREE WILL BAPT	2	82	100*	.8	1.9
265 INT PENT C CHR	2	32	62	.5	1.1
325 OLD REG BAPT	1	57	70*	.6	1.3
349 PENT HOLINESS	1	20	25*	.2	.5
355 PRESB CH (USA)	6	335	410*	3.3	7.6
361 PRIM BAPT ASCS	2	36	44*	.4	.8
449 UN METHODIST	24	1,451	1,778*	14.3	33.0
MORGAN	**30**	**2,769**	**4,212***	**34.7**	**100.0**
053 ASSEMB OF GOD	1	37	67	.6	1.6
081 CATHOLIC	2	NA	430	3.5	10.2
081d *LATIN*	*2*	*NA*	*430*	*3.5*	*10.2*
097 CHR CHS&CHS CR	1	100	121*	1.0	2.9
151 L-D SAINTS	1	NA	294	2.4	7.0
165 CH OF NAZARENE	1	24	94	.8	2.2

County and Denomination	Number of churches	Communicant, confirmed, full members	Total adherents Number	Percent of total population	Percent of total adherents
167 CHS OF CHRIST	2	155	177	1.5	4.2
193 EPISCOPAL	1	58	121	1.0	2.9
355 PRESB CH (USA)	1	230	279*	2.3	6.6
413 S.D.A.	1	145	176*	1.5	4.2
419 SO BAPT CONV	1	278	338*	2.8	8.0
449 UN METHODIST	18	1,742	2,115*	17.4	50.2
NICHOLAS	**93**	**9,299**	**12,463***	**46.5**	**100.0**
019 AMER BAPT USA	21	4,861	6,112*	22.8	49.0
053 ASSEMB OF GOD	1	178	250	.9	2.0
081 CATHOLIC	2	NA	538	2.0	4.3
081d *LATIN*	*2*	*NA*	*538*	*2.0*	*4.3*
097 CHR CHS&CHS CR	2	190	239*	.9	1.9
123 CH GOD (ANDER)	4	197	343	1.3	2.8
127 CH GOD (CLEVE)	2	140	176*	.7	1.4
145 CH GOD PROPHCY	1	29	36*	.1	.3
151 L-D SAINTS	1	NA	48	.2	.4
165 CH OF NAZARENE	4	191	298	1.1	2.4
167 CHS OF CHRIST	2	115	148	.6	1.2
193 EPISCOPAL	1	40	51	.2	.4
223 FREE WILL BAPT	7	239	301*	1.1	2.4
355 PRESB CH (USA)	2	197	248*	.9	2.0
413 S.D.A.	2	112	141*	.5	1.1
419 SO BAPT CONV	3	383	482*	1.8	3.9
449 UN METHODIST	38	2,427	3,052*	11.4	24.5
OHIO	**80**	**12,344**	**33,723***	**66.3**	**100.0**
019 AMER BAPT USA	2	465	560*	1.1	1.7
053 ASSEMB OF GOD	1	56	108	.2	.3
081 CATHOLIC	16	NA	17,561	34.5	52.1
081d *LATIN*	*14*	*NA*	*16,389*	*32.2*	*48.6*
081e *MARONITE*	*1*	*NA*	*916*	*1.8*	*2.7*
081h *UKRAINIAN*	*1*	*NA*	*256*	*.5*	*.8*
089 CHR & MISS AL	1	60	120	.2	.4
093 CHR CH (DISC)	2	490	843	1.7	2.5
097 CHR CHS&CHS CR	4	600	722*	1.4	2.1
111 CH CR,SCIENTST	1	NR	NR	-	-
123 CH GOD (ANDER)	3	150	170	.3	.5
127 CH GOD (CLEVE)	1	40	48*	.1	.1
167 CHS OF CHRIST	2	247	307	.6	.9
193 EPISCOPAL	5	900	1,246	2.4	3.7
207 E.L.C.A.	8	2,351	3,239	6.4	9.6
215 EVAN METH CH	1	28	34*	.1	.1
246 GREEK ORTHODOX	1	NR	NR	-	-
355 PRESB CH (USA)	8	2,027	2,441*	4.8	7.2
403 SALVATION ARMY	1	98	111	.2	.3
413 S.D.A.	1	96	116*	.2	.3
435 UNITARIAN-UNIV	1	39	45	.1	.1
443 UN C OF CHRIST	2	439	529*	1.0	1.6
449 UN METHODIST	16	3,748	4,513*	8.9	13.4
496 JEWISH EST[1]	2	NA	96	.2	.3
497 BLACK BAPT EST[1]	NA	510	614*	1.2	1.8
498 INDEP.CHARIS.[3]	1	NA	300	.6	.9
PENDLETON	**57**	**3,516**	**5,073***	**63.0**	**100.0**
053 ASSEMB OF GOD	1	20	30	.4	.6
081 CATHOLIC	1	NA	135	1.7	2.7
081d *LATIN*	*1*	*NA*	*135*	*1.7*	*2.7*
093 CHR CH (DISC)	1	34	55	.7	1.1
097 CHR CHS&CHS CR	1	82	101*	1.3	2.0
123 CH GOD (ANDER)	1	4	10	.1	.2
127 CH GOD (CLEVE)	1	54	67*	.8	1.3
151 L-D SAINTS	2	NA	565	7.0	11.1
157 CH OF BRETHREN	12	788	972*	12.1	19.2
167 CHS OF CHRIST	1	23	29	.4	.6
207 E.L.C.A.	5	452	560	7.0	11.0
223 FREE WILL BAPT	1	9	11*	.1	.2
285 MENNONITE CH	3	80	108	1.3	2.1
355 PRESB CH (USA)	5	348	429*	5.3	8.5
413 S.D.A.	1	25	31*	.4	.6
419 SO BAPT CONV	3	325	401*	5.0	7.9
449 UN METHODIST	18	1,272	1,569*	19.5	30.9
PLEASANTS	**25**	**2,553**	**3,815***	**50.6**	**100.0**
019 AMER BAPT USA	3	824	1,017*	13.5	26.7
081 CATHOLIC	1	NA	232	3.1	6.1
081d *LATIN*	*1*	*NA*	*232*	*3.1*	*6.1*
127 CH GOD (CLEVE)	1	55	68*	.9	1.8
165 CH OF NAZARENE	1	76	518	6.9	13.6
167 CHS OF CHRIST	7	439	561	7.4	14.7
193 EPISCOPAL	1	108	122	1.6	3.2
223 FREE WILL BAPT	1	50	62*	.8	1.6
320 "OLD" MB ASCS	1	13	16*	.2	.4
355 PRESB CH (USA)	1	138	170*	2.3	4.5
449 UN METHODIST	8	850	1,049*	13.9	27.5

NA–Not applicable   NR–Not reported   *Total adherents estimated from known number of communicant, confirmed, full members.   - Represents a percent less than 0.1.   Percentages may not total due to rounding.
[1]See Appendix E   [2]See Appendix F   [3]See Appendix G   Lines in *italic* represent a breakdown of Catholic rites or Friends affiliations. They are included in their respective denominational total.

Table 4. Churches and Church Membership by County and Denomination: 1990

County and Denomination	Number of churches	Communicant, confirmed, full members	Total adherents		
			Number	Percent of total population	Percent of total adherents
POCAHONTAS	**54**	**2,544**	**3,256***	**36.1**	**100.0**
081 CATHOLIC	2	NA	78	.9	2.4
081d *LATIN*	2	*NA*	*78*	*.9*	*2.4*
127 CH GOD (CLEVE)	1	57	70*	.8	2.1
157 CH OF BRETHREN	7	260	317*	3.5	9.7
165 CH OF NAZARENE	2	92	174	1.9	5.3
167 CHS OF CHRIST	3	43	62	.7	1.9
193 EPISCOPAL	1	22	26	.3	.8
207 E.L.C.A.	1	25	36	.4	1.1
285 MENNONITE CH	1	25	27	.3	.8
355 PRESB CH (USA)	6	454	554*	6.2	17.0
419 SO BAPT CONV	4	384	469*	5.2	14.4
449 UN METHODIST	26	1,182	1,443*	16.0	44.3
PRESTON	**111**	**6,800**	**10,849***	**37.4**	**100.0**
011 A.W.M.C.	1	8	10*	-	.1
019 AMER BAPT USA	7	683	861*	3.0	7.9
053 ASSEMB OF GOD	5	213	314	1.1	2.9
071 BRETHREN (ASH)	1	4	5*	-	-
081 CATHOLIC	6	NA	1,267	4.4	11.7
081d *LATIN*	6	*NA*	*1,267*	*4.4*	*11.7*
127 CH GOD (CLEVE)	1	8	10*	-	.1
151 L-D SAINTS	1	NA	244	.8	2.2
157 CH OF BRETHREN	10	659	830*	2.9	7.7
165 CH OF NAZARENE	4	338	918	3.2	8.5
167 CHS OF CHRIST	2	75	100	.3	.9
193 EPISCOPAL	1	41	51	.2	.5
207 E.L.C.A.	3	167	235	.8	2.2
221 FREE METHODIST	1	31	61	.2	.6
329 OPEN BIBLE STD	1	NR	NR	-	-
349 PENT HOLINESS	1	40	50*	.2	.5
353 CHR BRETHREN	1	50	150	.5	1.4
355 PRESB CH (USA)	3	275	346*	1.2	3.2
419 SO BAPT CONV	2	292	368*	1.3	3.4
438 UN BRETH IN CR	1	54	65	.2	.6
449 UN METHODIST	57	3,820	4,813*	16.6	44.4
467 WESLEYAN	2	42	151	.5	1.4
PUTNAM	**63**	**8,443**	**13,149***	**30.7**	**100.0**
019 AMER BAPT USA	10	3,875	4,880*	11.4	37.1
053 ASSEMB OF GOD	2	180	314	.7	2.4
081 CATHOLIC	2	NA	1,030	2.4	7.8
081d *LATIN*	2	*NA*	*1,030*	*2.4*	*7.8*
097 CHR CHS&CHS CR	1	127	160*	.4	1.2
123 CH GOD (ANDER)	5	313	485	1.1	3.7
127 CH GOD (CLEVE)	1	100	126*	.3	1.0
151 L-D SAINTS	1	NA	393	.9	3.0
165 CH OF NAZARENE	5	455	750	1.8	5.7
167 CHS OF CHRIST	6	527	689	1.6	5.2
171 CH GOD-GEN CON	1	33	42*	.1	.3
193 EPISCOPAL	1	78	129	.3	1.0
207 E.L.C.A.	1	118	184	.4	1.4
221 FREE METHODIST	1	0	6	-	-
223 FREE WILL BAPT	5	182	229*	.5	1.7
283 LUTH—MO SYNOD	1	24	29	.1	.2
339 PENT CH OF GOD	1	12	43	.1	.3
355 PRESB CH (USA)	5	553	696*	1.6	5.3
356 PRESB CH AMER	1	24	24	.1	.2
419 SO BAPT CONV	1	197	248*	.6	1.9
449 UN METHODIST	11	1,645	2,072*	4.8	15.8
496 JEWISH EST[1]	0	NA	120	.3	.9
499 INDEP.NON-CHAR[3]	1	NA	500	1.2	3.8
RALEIGH	**125**	**17,742**	**24,242***	**31.6**	**100.0**
001 ADVENT CHR CH	2	30	37*	-	.2
019 AMER BAPT USA	11	4,286	5,299*	6.9	21.9
053 ASSEMB OF GOD	4	303	523	.7	2.2
081 CATHOLIC	2	NA	1,948	2.5	8.0
081d *LATIN*	2	*NA*	*1,948*	*2.5*	*8.0*
089 CHR & MISS AL	1	0	27	-	.1
093 CHR CH (DISC)	2	700	828	1.1	3.4
097 CHR CHS&CHS CR	2	548	678*	.9	2.8
111 CH CR,SCIENTST	1	NR	NR	-	-
123 CH GOD (ANDER)	3	205	268	.3	1.1
127 CH GOD (CLEVE)	18	1,903	2,353*	3.1	9.7
145 CH GOD PROPHCY	3	88	109*	.1	.4
157 CH OF BRETHREN	1	108	134*	.2	.6
165 CH OF NAZARENE	1	131	152	.2	.6
167 CHS OF CHRIST	9	299	372	.5	1.5
193 EPISCOPAL	2	378	564	.7	2.3
207 E.L.C.A.	1	136	226	.3	.9
221 FREE METHODIST	2	41	67	.1	.3
223 FREE WILL BAPT	16	1,299	1,606*	2.1	6.6
259 IFCA	1	NR	NR	-	-
339 PENT CH OF GOD	2	44	102	.1	.4
349 PENT HOLINESS	4	116	143*	.2	.6

County and Denomination	Number of churches	Communicant, confirmed, full members	Total adherents		
			Number	Percent of total population	Percent of total adherents
355 PRESB CH (USA)	6	882	1,090*	1.4	4.5
361 PRIM BAPT ASCS	3	35	43*	.1	.2
403 SALVATION ARMY	1	61	69	.1	.3
413 S.D.A.	2	85	105*	.1	.4
419 SO BAPT CONV	3	2,173	2,687*	3.5	11.1
435 UNITARIAN-UNIV	1	18	23	-	.1
449 UN METHODIST	18	2,348	2,903*	3.8	12.0
467 WESLEYAN	1	57	66	.1	.3
469 WELS	1	25	36	-	.1
496 JEWISH EST[1]	1	NA	0	-	-
497 BLACK BAPT EST[1]	NA	1,443	1,784*	2.3	7.4
RANDOLPH	**74**	**6,156**	**9,636***	**34.7**	**100.0**
019 AMER BAPT USA	3	629	769*	2.8	8.0
053 ASSEMB OF GOD	3	212	315	1.1	3.3
081 CATHOLIC	4	NA	1,165	4.2	12.1
081d *LATIN*	4	*NA*	*1,165*	*4.2*	*12.1*
089 CHR & MISS AL	1	0	23	.1	.2
097 CHR CHS&CHS CR	3	301	368*	1.3	3.8
127 CH GOD (CLEVE)	3	348	426*	1.5	4.4
145 CH GOD PROPHCY	1	29	35*	.1	.4
151 L-D SAINTS	1	NA	439	1.6	4.6
157 CH OF BRETHREN	4	194	237*	.9	2.5
165 CH OF NAZARENE	2	275	585	2.1	6.1
167 CHS OF CHRIST	1	106	160	.6	1.7
193 EPISCOPAL	1	63	82	.3	.9
207 E.L.C.A.	1	128	188	.7	2.0
285 MENNONITE CH	3	79	98	.4	1.0
339 PENT CH OF GOD	1	35	150	.5	1.6
355 PRESB CH (USA)	11	715	875*	3.1	9.1
413 S.D.A.	1	41	50*	.2	.5
419 SO BAPT CONV	1	109	133*	.5	1.4
449 UN METHODIST	29	2,892	3,538*	12.7	36.7
RITCHIE	**57**	**3,447**	**4,362***	**42.6**	**100.0**
019 AMER BAPT USA	9	864	1,066*	10.4	24.4
081 CATHOLIC	2	NA	109	1.1	2.5
081d *LATIN*	2	*NA*	*109*	*1.1*	*2.5*
127 CH GOD (CLEVE)	1	77	95*	.9	2.2
165 CH OF NAZARENE	1	26	69	.7	1.6
167 CHS OF CHRIST	8	460	531	5.2	12.2
223 FREE WILL BAPT	2	173	213*	2.1	4.9
355 PRESB CH (USA)	1	25	31*	.3	.7
413 S.D.A.	1	84	104*	1.0	2.4
449 UN METHODIST	32	1,738	2,144*	21.0	49.2
ROANE	**69**	**4,013**	**5,472***	**36.2**	**100.0**
001 ADVENT CHR CH	7	157	197*	1.3	3.6
019 AMER BAPT USA	26	2,303	2,888*	19.1	52.8
053 ASSEMB OF GOD	1	65	75	.5	1.4
081 CATHOLIC	1	NA	192	1.3	3.5
081d *LATIN*	1	*NA*	*192*	*1.3*	*3.5*
151 L-D SAINTS	1	NA	56	.4	1.0
165 CH OF NAZARENE	2	192	441	2.9	8.1
167 CHS OF CHRIST	2	64	78	.5	1.4
349 PENT HOLINESS	1	15	19*	.1	.3
355 PRESB CH (USA)	1	28	35*	.2	.6
359 PRIM AD CHR CH	1	16	20*	.1	.4
413 S.D.A.	1	35	44*	.3	.8
419 SO BAPT CONV	1	162	203*	1.3	3.7
449 UN METHODIST	24	976	1,224*	8.1	22.4
SUMMERS	**44**	**4,735**	**6,014***	**42.3**	**100.0**
019 AMER BAPT USA	8	1,923	2,339*	16.5	38.9
081 CATHOLIC	1	NA	175	1.2	2.9
081d *LATIN*	1	*NA*	*175*	*1.2*	*2.9*
097 CHR CHS&CHS CR	2	130	158*	1.1	2.6
123 CH GOD (ANDER)	2	53	71	.5	1.2
127 CH GOD (CLEVE)	1	50	61*	.4	1.0
165 CH OF NAZARENE	1	49	89	.6	1.5
167 CHS OF CHRIST	3	115	155	1.1	2.6
193 EPISCOPAL	1	44	65	.5	1.1
353 CHR BRETHREN	1	60	90	.6	1.5
355 PRESB CH (USA)	2	100	122*	.9	2.0
361 PRIM BAPT ASCS	4	110	134*	.9	2.2
419 SO BAPT CONV	2	987	1,200*	8.4	20.0
449 UN METHODIST	16	939	1,142*	8.0	19.0
497 BLACK BAPT EST[1]	NA	175	213*	1.5	3.5
TAYLOR	**46**	**5,017**	**7,067***	**46.7**	**100.0**
011 A.W.M.C.	2	39	49*	.3	.7
019 AMER BAPT USA	8	1,675	2,086*	13.8	29.5
053 ASSEMB OF GOD	2	61	86	.6	1.2
081 CATHOLIC	1	NA	463	3.1	6.6
081d *LATIN*	1	*NA*	*463*	*3.1*	*6.6*

NA–Not applicable   NR–Not reported   *Total adherents estimated from known number of communicant, confirmed, full members.   - Represents a percent less than 0.1.   Percentages may not total due to rounding.

[1]See Appendix E   [2]See Appendix F   [3]See Appendix G   Lines in *italic* represent a breakdown of Catholic rites or Friends affiliations. They are included in their respective denominational total.

Table 4. Churches and Church Membership by County and Denomination: 1990

County and Denomination	Number of churches	Communicant, confirmed, full members	Total adherents Number	Percent of total population	Percent of total adherents
093 CHR CH (DISC)	1	79	135	.9	1.9
127 CH GOD (CLEVE)	1	70	87*	.6	1.2
157 CH OF BRETHREN	1	52	65*	.4	.9
165 CH OF NAZARENE	2	160	470	3.1	6.7
167 CHS OF CHRIST	2	110	137	.9	1.9
193 EPISCOPAL	1	30	35	.2	.5
207 E.L.C.A.	1	83	131	.9	1.9
223 FREE WILL BAPT	1	80	100*	.7	1.4
329 OPEN BIBLE STD	1	NR	NR	-	-
339 PENT CH OF GOD	1	34	77	.5	1.1
355 PRESB CH (USA)	1	58	72*	.5	1.0
403 SALVATION ARMY	1	99	101	.7	1.4
413 S.D.A.	1	39	49*	.3	.7
419 SO BAPT CONV	1	270	336*	2.2	4.8
449 UN METHODIST	17	2,078	2,588*	17.1	36.6
TUCKER	**40**	**2,024**	**2,994***	**38.7**	**100.0**
053 ASSEMB OF GOD	1	40	78	1.0	2.6
081 CATHOLIC	3	NA	423	5.5	14.1
081d LATIN	3	NA	423	5.5	14.1
127 CH GOD (CLEVE)	3	113	138*	1.8	4.6
145 CH GOD PROPHCY	1	29	35*	.5	1.2
157 CH OF BRETHREN	3	42	51*	.7	1.7
165 CH OF NAZARENE	1	103	140	1.8	4.7
167 CHS OF CHRIST	1	30	38	.5	1.3
207 E.L.C.A.	1	63	92	1.2	3.1
221 FREE METHODIST	1	24	60	.8	2.0
329 OPEN BIBLE STD	1	NR	NR	-	-
339 PENT CH OF GOD	2	75	102	1.3	3.4
355 PRESB CH (USA)	2	182	222*	2.9	7.4
413 S.D.A.	1	50	61*	.8	2.0
449 UN METHODIST	19	1,273	1,554*	20.1	51.9
TYLER	**42**	**2,238**	**3,300***	**33.7**	**100.0**
019 AMER BAPT USA	2	386	478*	4.9	14.5
081 CATHOLIC	2	NA	156	1.6	4.7
081d LATIN	2	NA	156	1.6	4.7
093 CHR CH (DISC)	1	50	81	.8	2.5
097 CHR CHS&CHS CR	2	100	124*	1.3	3.8
165 CH OF NAZARENE	1	79	360	3.7	10.9
167 CHS OF CHRIST	13	527	735	7.5	22.3
193 EPISCOPAL	1	34	60	.6	1.8
223 FREE WILL BAPT	1	35	43*	.4	1.3
339 PENT CH OF GOD	1	43	46	.5	1.4
355 PRESB CH (USA)	1	90	111*	1.1	3.4
449 UN METHODIST	17	894	1,106*	11.3	33.5
UPSHUR	**82**	**5,079**	**7,164***	**31.3**	**100.0**
011 A.W.M.C.	1	0	0*	-	-
019 AMER BAPT USA	7	822	1,020*	4.5	14.2
053 ASSEMB OF GOD	1	38	100	.4	1.4
081 CATHOLIC	1	NA	607	2.7	8.5
081d LATIN	1	NA	607	2.7	8.5
089 CHR & MISS AL	1	67	121	.5	1.7
127 CH GOD (CLEVE)	1	71	88*	.4	1.2
157 CH OF BRETHREN	1	27	34*	.1	.5
165 CH OF NAZARENE	1	68	259	1.1	3.6
167 CHS OF CHRIST	3	100	119	.5	1.7
193 EPISCOPAL	1	35	50	.2	.7
339 PENT CH OF GOD	1	36	30	.1	.4
355 PRESB CH (USA)	2	81	101*	.4	1.4
413 S.D.A.	1	96	119*	.5	1.7
419 SO BAPT CONV	2	406	504*	2.2	7.0
449 UN METHODIST	58	3,232	4,012*	17.5	56.0
WAYNE	**89**	**11,677**	**14,780***	**35.5**	**100.0**
019 AMER BAPT USA	16	3,035	3,755*	9.0	25.4
081 CATHOLIC	1	NA	83	.2	.6
081d LATIN	1	NA	83	.2	.6
093 CHR CH (DISC)	4	404	565	1.4	3.8
123 CH GOD (ANDER)	2	60	82	.2	.6
127 CH GOD (CLEVE)	8	416	515*	1.2	3.5
167 CHS OF CHRIST	11	826	1,061	2.5	7.2
175 CONGR CHR CHS	1	35	43*	.1	.3
223 FREE WILL BAPT	19	1,406	1,740*	4.2	11.8
265 INT PENT C CHR	1	30	81	.2	.5
355 PRESB CH (USA)	2	204	252*	.6	1.7
413 S.D.A.	1	79	98*	.2	.7
419 SO BAPT CONV	4	2,662	3,294*	7.9	22.3
436 UNITED BAPT	5	769	952*	2.3	6.4
449 UN METHODIST	14	1,751	2,167*	5.2	14.7
496 JEWISH EST[1]	0	NA	92	.2	.6
WEBSTER	**34**	**1,791**	**2,505***	**23.3**	**100.0**
019 AMER BAPT USA	6	760	956*	8.9	38.2
053 ASSEMB OF GOD	1	26	40	.4	1.6
081 CATHOLIC	1	NA	104	1.0	4.2
081d LATIN	1	NA	104	1.0	4.2
127 CH GOD (CLEVE)	1	35	44*	.4	1.8
151 L-D SAINTS	1	NA	120	1.1	4.8
167 CHS OF CHRIST	1	25	33	.3	1.3
339 PENT CH OF GOD	1	20	45	.4	1.8
355 PRESB CH (USA)	1	83	104*	1.0	4.2
419 SO BAPT CONV	2	271	341*	3.2	13.6
449 UN METHODIST	19	571	718*	6.7	28.7
WETZEL	**77**	**6,106**	**9,420***	**48.9**	**100.0**
011 A.W.M.C.	1	0	0*	-	-
019 AMER BAPT USA	3	359	444*	2.3	4.7
081 CATHOLIC	4	NA	1,490	7.7	15.8
081d LATIN	4	NA	1,490	7.7	15.8
093 CHR CH (DISC)	4	462	636	3.3	6.8
097 CHR CHS&CHS CR	3	510	631*	3.3	6.7
123 CH GOD (ANDER)	3	167	197	1.0	2.1
127 CH GOD (CLEVE)	3	133	165*	.9	1.8
165 CH OF NAZARENE	2	269	546	2.8	5.8
167 CHS OF CHRIST	26	1,324	1,713	8.9	18.2
171 CH GOD-GEN CON	1	35	43*	.2	.5
193 EPISCOPAL	1	87	125	.6	1.3
207 E.L.C.A.	1	117	144	.7	1.5
339 PENT CH OF GOD	1	34	77	.4	.8
355 PRESB CH (USA)	1	131	162*	.8	1.7
356 PRESB CH AMER	1	68	68	.4	.7
419 SO BAPT CONV	1	197	244*	1.3	2.6
449 UN METHODIST	20	2,195	2,718*	14.1	28.9
467 WESLEYAN	1	18	17	.1	.2
WIRT	**29**	**1,431**	**1,888***	**36.4**	**100.0**
019 AMER BAPT USA	9	673	844*	16.3	44.7
081 CATHOLIC	1	NA	88	1.7	4.7
081d LATIN	1	NA	88	1.7	4.7
165 CH OF NAZARENE	1	57	77	1.5	4.1
167 CHS OF CHRIST	1	23	30	.6	1.6
320 "OLD" MB ASCS	1	20	25*	.5	1.3
355 PRESB CH (USA)	1	37	46*	.9	2.4
449 UN METHODIST	15	621	778*	15.0	41.2
WOOD	**158**	**30,508**	**44,179***	**50.8**	**100.0**
019 AMER BAPT USA	24	8,957	11,020*	12.7	24.9
053 ASSEMB OF GOD	2	201	317	.4	.7
081 CATHOLIC	4	NA	4,842	5.6	11.0
081d LATIN	4	NA	4,842	5.6	11.0
093 CHR CH (DISC)	2	250	440	.5	1.0
097 CHR CHS&CHS CR	3	262	322*	.4	.7
111 CH CR,SCIENTST	1	NR	NR	-	-
123 CH GOD (ANDER)	1	71	92	.1	.2
127 CH GOD (CLEVE)	5	672	827*	1.0	1.9
133 CH GOD(7TH)DEN	1	25	28	-	.1
151 L-D SAINTS	1	NA	432	.5	1.0
165 CH OF NAZARENE	5	933	1,491	1.7	3.4
167 CHS OF CHRIST	21	2,808	3,568	4.1	8.1
193 EPISCOPAL	3	862	1,320	1.5	3.0
207 E.L.C.A.	2	873	1,073	1.2	2.4
215 EVAN METH CH	2	237	292*	.3	.7
223 FREE WILL BAPT	1	41	50*	.1	.1
226 FRIENDS-USA	0	6	14	-	-
226f INDEPENDNT	0	6	14	-	-
283 LUTH—MO SYNOD	1	273	375	.4	.8
329 OPEN BIBLE STD	1	NR	NR	-	-
349 PENT HOLINESS	1	100	123*	.1	.3
355 PRESB CH (USA)	6	1,140	1,403*	1.6	3.2
403 SALVATION ARMY	1	140	162	.2	.4
413 S.D.A.	3	329	405*	.5	.9
419 SO BAPT CONV	3	1,444	1,777*	2.0	4.0
449 UN METHODIST	58	10,545	12,974*	14.9	29.4
467 WESLEYAN	5	99	237	.3	.5
496 JEWISH EST[1]	1	NA	300	.3	.7
497 BLACK BAPT EST[1]	NA	240	295*	.3	.7
WYOMING	**86**	**8,554**	**11,430***	**39.4**	**100.0**
001 ADVENT CHR CH	1	40	50*	.2	.4
019 AMER BAPT USA	25	3,910	4,936*	17.0	43.2
081 CATHOLIC	2	NA	174	.6	1.5
081d LATIN	2	NA	174	.6	1.5
123 CH GOD (ANDER)	3	195	196	.7	1.7
127 CH GOD (CLEVE)	11	832	1,050*	3.6	9.2
145 CH GOD PROPHCY	1	29	37*	.1	.3
165 CH OF NAZARENE	2	313	574	2.0	5.0
167 CHS OF CHRIST	2	54	76	.3	.7
193 EPISCOPAL	1	24	30	.1	.3
223 FREE WILL BAPT	7	918	1,159*	4.0	10.1

NA–Not applicable   NR–Not reported   *Total adherents estimated from known number of communicant, confirmed, full members.   - Represents a percent less than 0.1.   Percentages may not total due to rounding.
[1] See Appendix E   [2] See Appendix F   [3] See Appendix G   Lines in italic represent a breakdown of Catholic rites or Friends affiliations. They are included in their respective denominational total.

Table 4. Churches and Church Membership by County and Denomination: 1990

County and Denomination	Number of churches	Communicant, confirmed, full members	Total adherents Number	Percent of total population	Percent of total adherents
325 OLD REG BAPT	6	445	562*	1.9	4.9
339 PENT CH OF GOD	4	80	158	.5	1.4
353 CHR BRETHREN	2	47	160	.6	1.4
355 PRESB CH (USA)	3	155	196*	.7	1.7
419 SO BAPT CONV	2	451	569*	2.0	5.0
449 UN METHODIST	13	1,032	1,303*	4.5	11.4
467 WESLEYAN	1	29	200	.7	1.7
WISCONSIN					
THE STATE.....	5,023	1,152,092	3,160,201*	64.6	100.0
ADAMS	**21**	**1,884**	**6,277***	**40.0**	**100.0**
053 ASSEMB OF GOD	1	150	200	1.3	3.2
081 CATHOLIC	2	NA	3,694	23.6	58.8
081d *LATIN*	2	*NA*	*3,694*	*23.6*	*58.8*
145 CH GOD PROPHCY	1	24	29*	.2	.5
151 L-D SAINTS	1	NA	112	.7	1.8
175 CONGR CHR CHS	2	111	133*	.8	2.1
207 E.L.C.A.	4	771	1,054	6.7	16.8
283 LUTH—MO SYNOD	3	510	674	4.3	10.7
413 S.D.A.	1	16	19*	.1	.3
419 SO BAPT CONV	2	100	120*	.8	1.9
443 UN C OF CHRIST	2	65	78*	.5	1.2
449 UN METHODIST	2	137	164*	1.0	2.6
ASHLAND	**32**	**4,206**	**11,404***	**69.9**	**100.0**
053 ASSEMB OF GOD	2	104	155	1.0	1.4
057 BAPT GEN CONF	1	272	348*	2.1	3.1
081 CATHOLIC	10	NA	5,832	35.8	51.1
081d *LATIN*	10	*NA*	*5,832*	*35.8*	*51.1*
167 CHS OF CHRIST	1	18	28	.2	.2
193 EPISCOPAL	1	74	80	.5	.7
207 E.L.C.A.	2	932	1,384	8.5	12.1
209 EVAN LUTH SYN	1	76	108	.7	.9
226 FRIENDS-USA	1	2	10	.1	.1
226c *FGC*	1	*2*	*10*	*.1*	*.1*
283 LUTH—MO SYNOD	5	1,728	2,180	13.4	19.1
355 PRESB CH (USA)	1	368	471*	2.9	4.1
413 S.D.A.	1	51	65*	.4	.6
443 UN C OF CHRIST	3	309	395*	2.4	3.5
449 UN METHODIST	3	272	348*	2.1	3.1
BARRON	**74**	**13,750**	**25,635***	**62.9**	**100.0**
001 ADVENT CHR CH	1	68	87*	.2	.3
053 ASSEMB OF GOD	2	213	398	1.0	1.6
057 BAPT GEN CONF	1	116	149*	.4	.6
081 CATHOLIC	9	NA	6,830	16.8	26.6
081d *LATIN*	9	*NA*	*6,830*	*16.8*	*26.6*
089 CHR & MISS AL	2	67	119	.3	.5
123 CH GOD (ANDER)	1	59	59	.1	.2
143 CG IN CR(MENN)	2	346	444*	1.1	1.7
151 L-D SAINTS	1	NA	222	.5	.9
157 CH OF BRETHREN	1	36	46*	.1	.2
193 EPISCOPAL	3	98	140	.3	.5
203 EVAN FREE CH	2	116	220	.5	.9
207 E.L.C.A.	17	6,588	8,783	21.6	34.3
220 FREE LUTHERAN	3	200	258	.6	1.0
221 FREE METHODIST	1	9	40	.1	.2
263 INT FOURSQ GOS	1	145	186*	.5	.7
283 LUTH—MO SYNOD	8	2,397	3,085	7.6	12.0
284 LUTH CH-AM ASC	1	65	83	.2	.3
323 OLD ORD AMISH	1	NA	150	.4	.6
355 PRESB CH (USA)	1	327	419*	1.0	1.6
413 S.D.A.	1	131	168*	.4	.7
419 SO BAPT CONV	1	17	22*	.1	.1
435 UNITARIAN-UNIV	1	17	39	.1	.2
449 UN METHODIST	8	2,056	2,636*	6.5	10.3
467 WESLEYAN	1	171	402	1.0	1.6
469 WELS	4	508	650	1.6	2.5
BAYFIELD	**35**	**1,985**	**4,264***	**30.4**	**100.0**
053 ASSEMB OF GOD	2	43	67	.5	1.6
057 BAPT GEN CONF	2	172	218*	1.6	5.1
081 CATHOLIC	12	NA	1,634	11.7	38.3
081d *LATIN*	12	*NA*	*1,634*	*11.7*	*38.3*
089 CHR & MISS AL	1	51	87	.6	2.0
193 EPISCOPAL	1	20	30	.2	.7
207 E.L.C.A.	7	893	1,216	8.7	28.5
220 FREE LUTHERAN	2	86	100	.7	2.3
283 LUTH—MO SYNOD	1	199	251	1.8	5.9

County and Denomination	Number of churches	Communicant, confirmed, full members	Total adherents Number	Percent of total population	Percent of total adherents
331 ORTH CH IN AM	1	NR	NR	-	-
355 PRESB CH (USA)	2	193	245*	1.7	5.7
443 UN C OF CHRIST	2	174	221*	1.6	5.2
449 UN METHODIST	2	154	195*	1.4	4.6
BROWN	**124**	**31,772**	**151,333***	**77.8**	**100.0**
019 AMER BAPT USA	1	327	417*	.2	.3
053 ASSEMB OF GOD	3	633	1,095	.6	.7
057 BAPT GEN CONF	1	634	808*	.4	.5
081 CATHOLIC	41	NA	105,905	54.4	70.0
081d *LATIN*	41	*NA*	*105,905*	*54.4*	*70.0*
089 CHR & MISS AL	3	507	610	.3	.4
097 CHR CHS&CHS CR	1	175	223*	.1	.1
111 CH CR,SCIENTST	1	NR	NR	-	-
127 CH GOD (CLEVE)	1	64	82*	-	.1
151 L-D SAINTS	1	NA	574	.3	.4
165 CH OF NAZARENE	1	41	139	.1	.1
167 CHS OF CHRIST	2	61	89	-	.1
175 CONGR CHR CHS	1	363	462*	.2	.3
193 EPISCOPAL	5	1,708	2,848	1.5	1.9
203 EVAN FREE CH	1	49	130	.1	.1
207 E.L.C.A.	13	9,771	13,302	6.8	8.8
226 FRIENDS-USA	1	12	28	-	-
226c *FGC*	1	*12*	*28*	*-*	*-*
283 LUTH—MO SYNOD	9	5,574	7,825	4.0	5.2
293 MORAV CH-NORTH	2	550	719	.4	.5
331 ORTH CH IN AM	1	NR	NR	-	-
355 PRESB CH (USA)	6	1,536	1,957*	1.0	1.3
367 PROT CONF (LU)	1	150	200	.1	.1
403 SALVATION ARMY	1	109	115	.1	.1
413 S.D.A.	1	382	487*	.3	.3
419 SO BAPT CONV	1	391	498*	.3	.3
443 UN C OF CHRIST	3	1,207	1,538*	.8	1.0
449 UN METHODIST	9	3,565	4,542*	2.3	3.0
469 WELS	11	3,695	4,939	2.5	3.3
496 JEWISH EST[1]	1	NA	260	.1	.2
497 BLACK BAPT EST[1]	NA	268	341*	.2	.2
498 INDEP.CHARIS.[3]	1	NA	1,200	.6	.8
BUFFALO	**30**	**5,232**	**9,774***	**72.0**	**100.0**
057 BAPT GEN CONF	1	8	10*	.1	.1
081 CATHOLIC	4	NA	3,060	22.5	31.3
081d *LATIN*	4	*NA*	*3,060*	*22.5*	*31.3*
167 CHS OF CHRIST	1	57	74	.5	.8
207 E.L.C.A.	8	2,282	2,922	21.5	29.9
283 LUTH—MO SYNOD	4	1,006	1,342	9.9	13.7
443 UN C OF CHRIST	3	424	540*	4.0	5.5
449 UN METHODIST	4	522	665*	4.9	6.8
469 WELS	5	933	1,161	8.5	11.9
BURNETT	**29**	**3,107**	**6,042***	**46.2**	**100.0**
053 ASSEMB OF GOD	1	56	90	.7	1.5
057 BAPT GEN CONF	2	265	328*	2.5	5.4
081 CATHOLIC	4	NA	1,814	13.9	30.0
081d *LATIN*	4	*NA*	*1,814*	*13.9*	*30.0*
089 CHR & MISS AL	2	42	87	.7	1.4
151 L-D SAINTS	1	NA	149	1.1	2.5
167 CHS OF CHRIST	1	32	42	.3	.7
203 EVAN FREE CH	2	64	126	1.0	2.1
207 E.L.C.A.	8	1,827	2,270	17.3	37.6
283 LUTH—MO SYNOD	2	246	327	2.5	5.4
449 UN METHODIST	5	532	659*	5.0	10.9
467 WESLEYAN	1	43	150	1.1	2.5
CALUMET	**37**	**5,308**	**20,861***	**60.8**	**100.0**
053 ASSEMB OF GOD	2	77	172	.5	.8
081 CATHOLIC	13	NA	13,513	39.4	64.8
081d *LATIN*	13	*NA*	*13,513*	*39.4*	*64.8*
089 CHR & MISS AL	1	96	156	.5	.7
151 L-D SAINTS	1	NA	203	.6	1.0
163 CH OF LUTH BR	1	71	156	.5	.7
193 EPISCOPAL	1	10	10	-	-
283 LUTH—MO SYNOD	6	1,927	2,497	7.3	12.0
355 PRESB CH (USA)	1	22	29*	.1	.1
443 UN C OF CHRIST	4	1,408	1,864*	5.4	8.9
449 UN METHODIST	4	648	858*	2.5	4.1
469 WELS	3	1,049	1,403	4.1	6.7
CHIPPEWA	**73**	**10,383**	**30,052***	**57.4**	**100.0**
053 ASSEMB OF GOD	3	236	384	.7	1.3
057 BAPT GEN CONF	1	53	68*	.1	.2
081 CATHOLIC	14	NA	15,966	30.5	53.1
081d *LATIN*	14	*NA*	*15,966*	*30.5*	*53.1*
089 CHR & MISS AL	1	26	64	.1	.2
097 CHR CHS&CHS CR	3	198	255*	.5	.8

NA–Not applicable NR–Not reported *Total adherents estimated from known number of communicant, confirmed, full members. - Represents a percent less than 0.1. Percentages may not total due to rounding.
[1]See Appendix E [2]See Appendix F [3]See Appendix G Lines in *italic* represent a breakdown of Catholic rites or Friends affiliations. They are included in their respective denominational total.

Table 4. Churches and Church Membership by County and Denomination: 1990

County and Denomination	Number of churches	Communicant, confirmed, full members	Total adherents Number	Percent of total population	Percent of total adherents
133 CH GOD(7TH)DEN	1	8	13	-	-
157 CH OF BRETHREN	2	97	125*	.2	.4
179 CONSRV BAPT	2	NR	NR	-	-
193 EPISCOPAL	2	107	135	.3	.4
203 EVAN FREE CH	1	70	178	.3	.6
207 E.L.C.A.	12	3,736	5,170	9.9	17.2
209 EVAN LUTH SYN	1	127	183	.3	.6
259 IFCA	1	NR	NR	-	-
283 LUTH—MO SYNOD	5	1,873	2,554	4.9	8.5
284 LUTH CH-AM ASC	1	430	550	1.1	1.8
329 OPEN BIBLE STD	1	NR	NR	-	-
331 ORTH CH IN AM	1	NR	NR	-	-
355 PRESB CH (USA)	3	423	545*	1.0	1.8
413 S.D.A.	1	35	45*	.1	.1
415 S-D BAPTIST GC	1	40	52*	.1	.2
443 UN C OF CHRIST	2	213	275*	.5	.9
449 UN METHODIST	9	1,706	2,199*	4.2	7.3
469 WELS	5	1,005	1,291	2.5	4.3
CLARK	**75**	**9,175**	**22,904***	**72.4**	**100.0**
053 ASSEMB OF GOD	2	85	167	.5	.7
081 CATHOLIC	11	NA	9,847	31.1	43.0
081d LATIN	11	NA	9,847	31.1	43.0
089 CHR & MISS AL	2	83	188	.6	.8
151 L-D SAINTS	1	NA	187	.6	.8
179 CONSRV BAPT	1	NR	NR	-	-
193 EPISCOPAL	1	59	75	.2	.3
203 EVAN FREE CH	2	44	159	.5	.7
207 E.L.C.A.	10	2,252	3,024	9.6	13.2
221 FREE METHODIST	1	21	45	.1	.2
259 IFCA	1	NR	NR	-	-
283 LUTH—MO SYNOD	11	2,909	3,909	12.4	17.1
285 MENNONITE CH	3	128	128	.4	.6
323 OLD ORD AMISH	4	NA	500	1.6	2.2
355 PRESB CH (USA)	1	181	238*	.8	1.0
413 S.D.A.	1	17	22*	.1	.1
443 UN C OF CHRIST	7	1,177	1,546*	4.9	6.7
449 UN METHODIST	13	1,307	1,717*	5.4	7.5
469 WELS	3	912	1,152	3.6	5.0
COLUMBIA	**78**	**16,696**	**34,369***	**76.2**	**100.0**
019 AMER BAPT USA	4	352	443*	1.0	1.3
053 ASSEMB OF GOD	3	278	528	1.2	1.5
081 CATHOLIC	9	NA	11,832	26.2	34.4
081d LATIN	9	NA	11,832	26.2	34.4
105 CHRISTIAN REF	2	467	736	1.6	2.1
111 CH CR,SCIENTST	1	NR	NR	-	-
165 CH OF NAZARENE	1	53	85	.2	.2
176 CCC, NOT NAT'L	1	131	165*	.4	.5
193 EPISCOPAL	1	44	69	.2	.2
203 EVAN FREE CH	2	83	145	.3	.4
207 E.L.C.A.	9	3,723	5,119	11.4	14.9
209 EVAN LUTH SYN	2	177	219	.5	.6
259 IFCA	2	NR	NR	-	-
283 LUTH—MO SYNOD	3	2,426	3,046	6.8	8.9
323 OLD ORD AMISH	3	NA	450	1.0	1.3
355 PRESB CH (USA)	10	1,677	2,112*	4.7	6.1
371 REF CH IN AM	1	338	564	1.3	1.6
413 S.D.A.	2	365	460*	1.0	1.3
443 UN C OF CHRIST	3	554	698*	1.5	2.0
449 UN METHODIST	10	2,628	3,310*	7.3	9.6
467 WESLEYAN	1	50	220	.5	.6
469 WELS	8	3,350	4,168	9.2	12.1
CRAWFORD	**37**	**3,143**	**9,898***	**62.1**	**100.0**
081 CATHOLIC	9	NA	5,639	35.4	57.0
081d LATIN	9	NA	5,639	35.4	57.0
097 CHR CHS&CHS CR	2	120	154*	1.0	1.6
127 CH GOD (CLEVE)	1	31	40*	.3	.4
175 CONGR CHR CHS	1	21	27*	.2	.3
193 EPISCOPAL	1	59	71	.4	.7
203 EVAN FREE CH	1	48	118	.7	1.2
207 E.L.C.A.	7	1,798	2,327	14.6	23.5
226 FRIENDS-USA	1	4	10	.1	.1
226c FGC	1	4	10	.1	.1
263 INT FOURSQ GOS	1	28	36*	.2	.4
353 CHR BRETHREN	1	25	50	.3	.5
413 S.D.A.	1	25	32*	.2	.3
443 UN C OF CHRIST	1	24	31*	.2	.3
449 UN METHODIST	8	780	1,003*	6.3	10.1
467 WESLEYAN	1	25	140	.9	1.4
469 WELS	1	155	220	1.4	2.2
DANE	**231**	**73,118**	**203,300***	**55.4**	**100.0**
001 ADVENT CHR CH	1	10	12*	-	-
019 AMER BAPT USA	2	938	1,150*	.3	.6

County and Denomination	Number of churches	Communicant, confirmed, full members	Total adherents Number	Percent of total population	Percent of total adherents
053 ASSEMB OF GOD	5	297	571	.2	.3
081 CATHOLIC	39	NA	102,227	27.8	50.3
081d LATIN	39	NA	102,227	27.8	50.3
089 CHR & MISS AL	2	156	195	.1	.1
105 CHRISTIAN REF	1	176	268	.1	.1
111 CH CR,SCIENTST	2	NR	NR	-	-
123 CH GOD (ANDER)	1	24	24	-	-
145 CH GOD PROPHCY	1	24	29*	-	-
151 L-D SAINTS	4	NA	1,373	.4	.7
164 CH LUTH CONF	2	62	99	-	-
165 CH OF NAZARENE	2	169	198	.1	.1
167 CHS OF CHRIST	2	121	139	-	.1
175 CONGR CHR CHS	1	235	288*	.1	.1
179 CONSRV BAPT	1	NR	NR	-	-
193 EPISCOPAL	6	1,615	2,146	.6	1.1
203 EVAN FREE CH	6	1,001	1,515	.4	.7
207 E.L.C.A.	51	36,791	47,758	13.0	23.5
209 EVAN LUTH SYN	5	1,869	2,437	.7	1.2
220 FREE LUTHERAN	1	82	112	-	.1
221 FREE METHODIST	1	35	58	-	-
226 FRIENDS-USA	1	166	418	.1	.2
226c FGC	1	166	418	.1	.2
246 GREEK ORTHODOX	1	NR	NR	-	-
259 IFCA	3	NR	NR	-	-
263 INT FOURSQ GOS	1	108	132*	-	.1
283 LUTH—MO SYNOD	10	3,699	4,714	1.3	2.3
285 MENNONITE CH	1	35	41	-	-
287 MENN GEN CONF	1	35	46	-	-
293 MORAV CH-NORTH	4	714	967	.3	.5
313 N AM BAPT CONF	1	84	103*	-	.1
353 CHR BRETHREN	2	43	67	-	-
355 PRESB CH (USA)	10	3,729	4,572*	1.2	2.2
403 SALVATION ARMY	1	123	133	-	.1
413 S.D.A.	3	593	727*	.2	.4
415 S-D BAPTIST GC	1	31	38*	-	-
419 SO BAPT CONV	3	501	614*	.2	.3
435 UNITARIAN-UNIV	2	861	1,350	.4	.7
443 UN C OF CHRIST	15	5,372	6,586*	1.8	3.2
449 UN METHODIST	22	7,641	9,368*	2.6	4.6
467 WESLEYAN	1	54	91	-	-
469 WELS	8	2,945	3,927	1.1	1.9
496 JEWISH EST[1]	3	NA	4,500	1.2	2.2
497 BLACK BAPT EST[1]	NA	2,779	3,407*	.9	1.7
498 INDEP.CHARIS.[3]	1	NA	900	.2	.4
DODGE	**99**	**24,843**	**49,081***	**64.1**	**100.0**
019 AMER BAPT USA	1	45	57*	.1	.1
053 ASSEMB OF GOD	2	218	330	.4	.7
057 BAPT GEN CONF	2	157	199*	.3	.4
081 CATHOLIC	18	NA	16,628	21.7	33.9
081d LATIN	18	NA	16,628	21.7	33.9
089 CHR & MISS AL	1	67	283	.4	.6
105 CHRISTIAN REF	1	144	263	.3	.5
167 CHS OF CHRIST	1	30	55	.1	.1
193 EPISCOPAL	3	208	307	.4	.6
203 EVAN FREE CH	1	129	200	.3	.4
207 E.L.C.A.	12	5,798	7,447	9.7	15.2
283 LUTH—MO SYNOD	13	5,391	7,073	9.2	14.4
355 PRESB CH (USA)	4	773	981*	1.3	2.0
371 REF CH IN AM	1	237	349	.5	.7
413 S.D.A.	1	26	33*	-	.1
443 UN C OF CHRIST	5	852	1,081*	1.4	2.2
449 UN METHODIST	8	2,010	2,550*	3.3	5.2
467 WESLEYAN	1	31	35	-	.1
469 WELS	24	8,482	10,899	14.2	22.2
497 BLACK BAPT EST[1]	NA	245	311*	.4	.6
DOOR	**51**	**7,687**	**19,352***	**75.3**	**100.0**
053 ASSEMB OF GOD	1	90	170	.7	.9
057 BAPT GEN CONF	3	494	621*	2.4	3.2
081 CATHOLIC	12	NA	9,133	35.6	47.2
081d LATIN	12	NA	9,133	35.6	47.2
111 CH CR,SCIENTST	1	NR	NR	-	-
151 L-D SAINTS	1	NA	55	.2	.3
193 EPISCOPAL	4	83	100	.4	.5
203 EVAN FREE CH	1	57	119	.5	.6
207 E.L.C.A.	8	2,018	2,589	10.1	13.4
226 FRIENDS-USA	2	44	57*	.2	.3
226c FGC	1	2	4	-	-
226e FUM	1	42	53*	.2	.3
283 LUTH—MO SYNOD	2	466	624	2.4	3.2
293 MORAV CH-NORTH	3	869	1,034	4.0	5.3
413 S.D.A.	2	55	69*	.3	.4
443 UN C OF CHRIST	1	356	448*	1.7	2.3
449 UN METHODIST	4	680	855*	3.3	4.4
469 WELS	6	2,475	3,478	13.5	18.0

NA–Not applicable   NR–Not reported   *Total adherents estimated from known number of communicant, confirmed, full members.   - Represents a percent less than 0.1.   Percentages may not total due to rounding.
[1]See Appendix E   [2]See Appendix F   [3]See Appendix G   Lines in *italic* represent a breakdown of Catholic rites or Friends affiliations. They are included in their respective denominational total.

Table 4. Churches and Church Membership by County and Denomination: 1990

County and Denomination	Number of churches	Communicant, confirmed, full members	Total adherents Number	Total adherents Percent of total population	Total adherents Percent of total adherents
DOUGLAS	**54**	**7,250**	**19,692***	**47.2**	**100.0**
053 ASSEMB OF GOD	2	210	648	1.6	3.3
057 BAPT GEN CONF	3	483	604*	1.4	3.1
081 CATHOLIC	11	NA	8,589	20.6	43.6
081d LATIN	11	NA	8,589	20.6	43.6
089 CHR & MISS AL	1	54	138	.3	.7
111 CH CR,SCIENTST	1	NR	NR	-	-
163 CH OF LUTH BR	1	30	45	.1	.2
165 CH OF NAZARENE	1	10	30	.1	.2
167 CHS OF CHRIST	1	3	8	-	-
181 CONSRV CONGR	1	76	95*	.2	.5
193 EPISCOPAL	1	134	186	.4	.9
203 EVAN FREE CH	1	47	75	.2	.4
207 E.L.C.A.	10	3,794	4,943	11.8	25.1
283 LUTH—MO SYNOD	2	547	754	1.8	3.8
355 PRESB CH (USA)	10	981	1,227*	2.9	6.2
403 SALVATION ARMY	1	120	130	.3	.7
413 S.D.A.	1	66	83*	.2	.4
449 UN METHODIST	3	535	669*	1.6	3.4
467 WESLEYAN	1	160	918	2.2	4.7
496 JEWISH EST[1]	1	NA	100	.2	.5
499 INDEP.NON-CHAR[3]	1	NA	450	1.1	2.3
DUNN	**63**	**11,728**	**22,470***	**62.6**	**100.0**
053 ASSEMB OF GOD	1	90	190	.5	.8
081 CATHOLIC	6	NA	6,830	19.0	30.4
081d LATIN	6	NA	6,830	19.0	30.4
089 CHR & MISS AL	2	158	461	1.3	2.1
111 CH CR,SCIENTST	1	NR	NR	-	-
123 CH GOD (ANDER)	1	20	20	.1	.1
145 CH GOD PROPHCY	1	24	30*	.1	.1
163 CH OF LUTH BR	2	56	133	.4	.6
165 CH OF NAZARENE	3	156	286	.8	1.3
193 EPISCOPAL	1	71	103	.3	.5
207 E.L.C.A.	17	6,422	8,358	23.3	37.2
220 FREE LUTHERAN	2	172	234	.7	1.0
226 FRIENDS-USA	1	18	49	.1	.2
226c FGC	1	18	49	.1	.2
259 IFCA	1	NR	NR	-	-
283 LUTH—MO SYNOD	4	596	828	2.3	3.7
413 S.D.A.	1	75	93*	.3	.4
419 SO BAPT CONV	1	50	62*	.2	.3
435 UNITARIAN-UNIV	1	34	52	.1	.2
443 UN C OF CHRIST	1	349	434*	1.2	1.9
449 UN METHODIST	12	1,982	2,464*	6.9	11.0
469 WELS	4	1,455	1,843	5.1	8.2
EAU CLAIRE	**89**	**27,394**	**52,697***	**61.9**	**100.0**
019 AMER BAPT USA	2	356	444*	.5	.8
053 ASSEMB OF GOD	4	435	936	1.1	1.8
057 BAPT GEN CONF	2	354	441*	.5	.8
081 CATHOLIC	12	NA	14,869	17.5	28.2
081d LATIN	12	NA	14,869	17.5	28.2
089 CHR & MISS AL	1	342	342	.4	.6
097 CHR CHS&CHS CR	1	145	181*	.2	.3
111 CH CR,SCIENTST	1	NR	NR	-	-
151 L-D SAINTS	2	NA	519	.6	1.0
163 CH OF LUTH BR	1	247	976	1.1	1.9
164 CH LUTH CONF	1	344	505	.6	1.0
165 CH OF NAZARENE	1	89	201	.2	.4
167 CHS OF CHRIST	2	69	110	.1	.2
179 CONSRV BAPT	1	NR	NR	-	-
193 EPISCOPAL	2	451	564	.7	1.1
203 EVAN FREE CH	2	32	110	.1	.2
207 E.L.C.A.	13	12,763	16,565	19.4	31.4
209 EVAN LUTH SYN	3	951	1,330	1.6	2.5
226 FRIENDS-USA	0	8	37	-	.1
226c FGC	0	8	37	-	.1
283 LUTH—MO SYNOD	14	5,760	7,544	8.9	14.3
285 MENNONITE CH	1	46	46	.1	.1
323 OLD ORD AMISH	4	NA	600	.7	1.1
355 PRESB CH (USA)	2	539	672*	.8	1.3
403 SALVATION ARMY	1	107	128	.2	.2
413 S.D.A.	1	93	116*	.1	.2
435 UNITARIAN-UNIV	1	103	141	.2	.3
443 UN C OF CHRIST	3	1,300	1,620*	1.9	3.1
449 UN METHODIST	8	2,342	2,918*	3.4	5.5
467 WESLEYAN	1	154	273	.3	.5
469 WELS	1	364	509	.6	1.0
496 JEWISH EST[1]	1	NA	0	-	-
FLORENCE	**9**	**315**	**1,721***	**37.5**	**100.0**
057 BAPT GEN CONF	1	36	46*	1.0	2.7
081 CATHOLIC	3	NA	1,284	28.0	74.6
081d LATIN	3	NA	1,284	28.0	74.6
207 E.L.C.A.	1	33	52	1.1	3.0

County and Denomination	Number of churches	Communicant, confirmed, full members	Total adherents Number	Total adherents Percent of total population	Total adherents Percent of total adherents
339 PENT CH OF GOD	1	35	77	1.7	4.5
355 PRESB CH (USA)	1	82	104*	2.3	6.0
469 WELS	2	129	158	3.4	9.2
FOND DU LAC	**107**	**24,642**	**66,721***	**74.1**	**100.0**
019 AMER BAPT USA	3	329	419*	.5	.6
053 ASSEMB OF GOD	3	288	601	.7	.9
057 BAPT GEN CONF	1	132	168*	.2	.3
081 CATHOLIC	28	NA	33,282	36.9	49.9
081d LATIN	28	NA	33,282	36.9	49.9
089 CHR & MISS AL	1	14	38	-	.1
105 CHRISTIAN REF	3	695	1,053	1.2	1.6
111 CH CR,SCIENTST	2	NR	NR	-	-
127 CH GOD (CLEVE)	1	46	59*	.1	.1
151 L-D SAINTS	1	NA	306	.3	.5
164 CH LUTH CONF	1	323	414	.5	.6
165 CH OF NAZARENE	1	11	12	-	-
167 CHS OF CHRIST	1	39	51	.1	.1
193 EPISCOPAL	3	741	1,074	1.2	1.6
203 EVAN FREE CH	1	65	130	.1	.2
207 E.L.C.A.	8	4,197	5,313	5.9	8.0
246 GREEK ORTHODOX	1	NR	NR	-	-
259 IFCA	1	NR	NR	-	-
274 LAT EVAN LUTH	1	60	63	.1	.1
283 LUTH—MO SYNOD	4	2,075	2,725	3.0	4.1
307 NETH REF CONGR	1	46	98	.1	.1
355 PRESB CH (USA)	1	742	944*	1.0	1.4
371 REF CH IN AM	6	2,449	3,813	4.2	5.7
403 SALVATION ARMY	1	74	89	.1	.1
435 UNITARIAN-UNIV	1	14	18	-	-
443 UN C OF CHRIST	8	3,793	4,827*	5.4	7.2
449 UN METHODIST	10	2,642	3,363*	3.7	5.0
469 WELS	13	5,867	7,861	8.7	11.8
496 JEWISH EST[1]	1	NA	0		
FOREST	**22**	**1,340**	**4,493***	**51.2**	**100.0**
081 CATHOLIC	6	NA	2,800	31.9	62.3
081d LATIN	6	NA	2,800	31.9	62.3
127 CH GOD (CLEVE)	1	88	111*	1.3	2.5
165 CH OF NAZARENE	1	31	50	.6	1.1
167 CHS OF CHRIST	1	14	18	.2	.4
181 CONSRV CONGR	1	60	76*	.9	1.7
283 LUTH—MO SYNOD	2	334	438	5.0	9.7
339 PENT CH OF GOD	1	14	24	.3	.5
355 PRESB CH (USA)	2	130	164*	1.9	3.7
413 S.D.A.	1	26	33*	.4	.7
436 UNITED BAPT	1	9	11*	.1	.2
449 UN METHODIST	2	222	280*	3.2	6.2
469 WELS	3	412	488	5.6	10.9
GRANT	**87**	**10,182**	**40,647***	**82.5**	**100.0**
053 ASSEMB OF GOD	2	71	125	.3	.3
081 CATHOLIC	19	NA	27,306	55.4	67.2
081d LATIN	19	NA	27,306	55.4	67.2
089 CHR & MISS AL	1	33	96	.2	.2
097 CHR CHS&CHS CR	1	25	32*	.1	.1
111 CH CR,SCIENTST	1	NR	NR	-	-
151 L-D SAINTS	1	NA	117	.2	.3
167 CHS OF CHRIST	1	17	22	-	.1
175 CONGR CHR CHS	1	43	54*	.1	.1
179 CONSRV BAPT	1	NR	NR	-	-
181 CONSRV CONGR	1	96	122*	.2	.3
193 EPISCOPAL	2	42	50	.1	.1
203 EVAN FREE CH	2	86	236	.5	.6
207 E.L.C.A.	10	3,187	4,106	8.3	10.1
220 FREE LUTHERAN	1	123	178	.4	.4
221 FREE METHODIST	2	117	121	.2	.3
259 IFCA	1	NR	NR	-	-
283 LUTH—MO SYNOD	3	223	300	.6	.7
285 MENNONITE CH	1	58	64	.1	.2
353 CHR BRETHREN	1	35	50	.1	.1
355 PRESB CH (USA)	3	347	439*	.9	1.1
363 PRIMITIVE METH	2	113	166	.3	.4
413 S.D.A.	1	86	109*	.2	.3
443 UN C OF CHRIST	8	1,244	1,575*	3.2	3.9
449 UN METHODIST	19	4,015	5,083*	10.3	12.5
469 WELS	2	221	296	.6	.7
GREEN	**42**	**10,043**	**18,393***	**60.6**	**100.0**
019 AMER BAPT USA	1	113	144*	.5	.8
053 ASSEMB OF GOD	1	100	266	.9	1.4
081 CATHOLIC	4	NA	4,938	16.3	26.8
081d LATIN	4	NA	4,938	16.3	26.8
111 CH CR,SCIENTST	1	NR	NR	-	-
165 CH OF NAZARENE	2	59	98	.3	.5
167 CHS OF CHRIST	1	45	60	.2	.3

NA–Not applicable   NR–Not reported   *Total adherents estimated from known number of communicant, confirmed, full members.   - Represents a percent less than 0.1.   Percentages may not total due to rounding.
[1]See Appendix E   [2]See Appendix F   [3]See Appendix G   Lines in *italic* represent a breakdown of Catholic rites or Friends affiliations. They are included in their respective denominational total.

Table 4. Churches and Church Membership by County and Denomination: 1990

County and Denomination	Number of churches	Communicant, confirmed, full members	Total adherents Number	Percent of total population	Percent of total adherents
193 EPISCOPAL	1	39	39	.1	.2
203 EVAN FREE CH	1	39	55	.2	.3
207 E.L.C.A.	8	2,694	3,732	12.3	20.3
220 FREE LUTHERAN	1	71	95	.3	.5
283 LUTH—MO SYNOD	1	81	108	.4	.6
323 OLD ORD AMISH	1	NA	150	.5	.8
329 OPEN BIBLE STD	1	NR	NR	-	-
353 CHR BRETHREN	1	25	50	.2	.3
355 PRESB CH (USA)	1	227	289*	1.0	1.6
419 SO BAPT CONV	1	20	25*	.1	.1
443 UN C OF CHRIST	6	4,069	5,181*	17.1	28.2
449 UN METHODIST	7	2,184	2,781*	9.2	15.1
469 WELS	2	277	382	1.3	2.1
GREEN LAKE	**34**	**5,841**	**16,701***	**89.5**	**100.0**
019 AMER BAPT USA	2	101	127*	.7	.8
053 ASSEMB OF GOD	1	42	116	.6	.7
081 CATHOLIC	7	NA	8,902	47.7	53.3
081d LATIN	7	NA	8,902	47.7	53.3
164 CH LUTH CONF	1	257	376	2.0	2.3
175 CONGR CHR CHS	1	45	57*	.3	.3
203 EVAN FREE CH	1	60	103	.6	.6
207 E.L.C.A.	1	624	801	4.3	4.8
259 IFCA	2	NR	NR	-	-
283 LUTH—MO SYNOD	2	903	1,226	6.6	7.3
443 UN C OF CHRIST	2	239	300*	1.6	1.8
449 UN METHODIST	5	996	1,251*	6.7	7.5
469 WELS	9	2,574	3,442	18.5	20.6
IOWA	**46**	**4,103**	**12,681***	**62.9**	**100.0**
019 AMER BAPT USA	1	59	77*	.4	.6
081 CATHOLIC	10	NA	7,299	36.2	57.6
081d LATIN	10	NA	7,299	36.2	57.6
181 CONSRV CONGR	1	132	171*	.8	1.3
193 EPISCOPAL	1	64	89	.4	.7
203 EVAN FREE CH	1	19	60	.3	.5
207 E.L.C.A.	8	1,656	2,118	10.5	16.7
226 FRIENDS-USA	1	3	3	-	-
226c FGC	1	3	3	-	-
259 IFCA	3	NR	NR	-	-
283 LUTH—MO SYNOD	1	109	140	.7	1.1
355 PRESB CH (USA)	2	134	174*	.9	1.4
363 PRIMITIVE METH	2	37	37	.2	.3
443 UN C OF CHRIST	3	550	713*	3.5	5.6
449 UN METHODIST	11	1,340	1,738*	8.6	13.7
467 WESLEYAN	1	0	62	.3	.5
IRON	**14**	**856**	**2,741***	**44.5**	**100.0**
081 CATHOLIC	5	NA	1,646	26.8	60.1
081d LATIN	5	NA	1,646	26.8	60.1
089 CHR & MISS AL	1	32	37	.6	1.3
165 CH OF NAZARENE	1	30	88	1.4	3.2
283 LUTH—MO SYNOD	2	328	428	7.0	15.6
355 PRESB CH (USA)	2	157	187*	3.0	6.8
449 UN METHODIST	1	117	140*	2.3	5.1
469 WELS	2	192	215	3.5	7.8
JACKSON	**41**	**5,882**	**9,625***	**58.0**	**100.0**
053 ASSEMB OF GOD	2	203	372	2.2	3.9
057 BAPT GEN CONF	1	54	69*	.4	.7
081 CATHOLIC	5	NA	1,881	11.3	19.5
081d LATIN	5	NA	1,881	11.3	19.5
089 CHR & MISS AL	1	21	46	.3	.5
097 CHR CHS&CHS CR	1	47	60*	.4	.6
164 CH LUTH CONF	1	80	130	.8	1.4
167 CHS OF CHRIST	1	72	96	.6	1.0
203 EVAN FREE CH	1	24	65	.4	.7
207 E.L.C.A.	12	3,072	3,926	23.7	40.8
283 LUTH—MO SYNOD	3	512	700	4.2	7.3
284 LUTH CH-AM ASC	1	75	98	.6	1.0
355 PRESB CH (USA)	1	153	194*	1.2	2.0
367 PROT CONF (LU)	1	200	250	1.5	2.6
413 S.D.A.	1	24	30*	.2	.3
443 UN C OF CHRIST	1	117	149*	.9	1.5
449 UN METHODIST	7	1,185	1,504*	9.1	15.6
469 WELS	1	43	55	.3	.6
JEFFERSON	**79**	**26,337**	**53,371***	**78.7**	**100.0**
001 ADVENT CHR CH	1	15	19*	-	-
053 ASSEMB OF GOD	2	173	360	.5	.7
081 CATHOLIC	10	NA	19,037	28.1	35.7
081d LATIN	10	NA	19,037	28.1	35.7
089 CHR & MISS AL	1	92	199	.3	.4
111 CH CR,SCIENTST	1	NR	NR	-	-
151 L-D SAINTS	1	NA	124	.2	.2
165 CH OF NAZARENE	1	0	0	-	-
167 CHS OF CHRIST	1	9	12	-	-
193 EPISCOPAL	2	236	343	.5	.6
207 E.L.C.A.	10	5,844	7,713	11.4	14.5
283 LUTH—MO SYNOD	6	1,550	1,978	2.9	3.7
293 MORAV CH-NORTH	4	1,419	1,800	2.7	3.4
313 N AM BAPT CONF	1	122	153*	.2	.3
355 PRESB CH (USA)	1	41	51*	.1	.1
413 S.D.A.	3	112	140*	.2	.3
443 UN C OF CHRIST	4	1,596	2,001*	3.0	3.7
449 UN METHODIST	13	2,777	3,482*	5.1	6.5
469 WELS	17	12,351	15,959	23.5	29.9
JUNEAU	**38**	**5,551**	**12,688***	**58.6**	**100.0**
019 AMER BAPT USA	1	89	113*	.5	.9
053 ASSEMB OF GOD	1	44	66	.3	.5
057 BAPT GEN CONF	1	41	52*	.2	.4
081 CATHOLIC	9	NA	5,244	24.2	41.3
081d LATIN	9	NA	5,244	24.2	41.3
145 CH GOD PROPHCY	1	24	31*	.1	.2
165 CH OF NAZARENE	1	68	165	.8	1.3
193 EPISCOPAL	1	18	43	.2	.3
207 E.L.C.A.	8	2,033	2,866	13.2	22.6
283 LUTH—MO SYNOD	3	391	532	2.5	4.2
355 PRESB CH (USA)	1	71	90*	.4	.7
449 UN METHODIST	6	1,171	1,491*	6.9	11.8
469 WELS	5	1,601	1,995	9.2	15.7
KENOSHA	**88**	**18,565**	**63,940***	**49.9**	**100.0**
019 AMER BAPT USA	3	287	365*	.3	.6
053 ASSEMB OF GOD	2	894	2,330	1.8	3.6
057 BAPT GEN CONF	1	98	125*	.1	.2
081 CATHOLIC	16	NA	37,054	28.9	58.0
081b BYZAN RUTH	1	NA	80	.1	.1
081d LATIN	15	NA	36,974	28.8	57.8
097 CHR CHS&CHS CR	1	365	464*	.4	.7
105 CHRISTIAN REF	1	182	282	.2	.4
123 CH GOD (ANDER)	1	34	34	-	.1
127 CH GOD (CLEVE)	1	98	125*	.1	.2
145 CH GOD PROPHCY	1	24	31*	-	-
151 L-D SAINTS	1	NA	544	.4	.9
165 CH OF NAZARENE	1	70	76	.1	.1
167 CHS OF CHRIST	3	128	170	.1	.3
175 CONGR CHR CHS	2	350	445*	.3	.7
193 EPISCOPAL	2	452	717	.6	1.1
203 EVAN FREE CH	1	257	465	.4	.7
207 E.L.C.A.	9	5,459	7,303	5.7	11.4
221 FREE METHODIST	1	10	27	-	-
263 INT FOURSQ GOS	1	38	48*	-	.1
283 LUTH—MO SYNOD	2	550	731	.6	1.1
313 N AM BAPT CONF	1	288	366*	.3	.6
331 ORTH CH IN AM	1	NR	NR	-	-
339 PENT CH OF GOD	1	34	77	.1	.1
355 PRESB CH (USA)	1	360	458*	.4	.7
403 SALVATION ARMY	1	95	127	.1	.2
413 S.D.A.	2	117	149*	.1	.2
419 SO BAPT CONV	6	1,130	1,437*	1.1	2.2
435 UNITARIAN-UNIV	1	74	106	.1	.2
443 UN C OF CHRIST	2	352	448*	.3	.7
449 UN METHODIST	10	2,350	2,988*	2.3	4.7
469 WELS	9	3,069	4,018	3.1	6.3
496 JEWISH EST[1]	2	NA	200	.2	.3
497 BLACK BAPT EST[1]	NA	1,400	1,780*	1.4	2.8
499 INDEP.NON-CHAR[3]	1	NA	450	.4	.7
KEWAUNEE	**30**	**3,361**	**18,022***	**95.5**	**100.0**
053 ASSEMB OF GOD	1	66	90	.5	.5
081 CATHOLIC	16	NA	13,664	72.4	75.8
081d LATIN	16	NA	13,664	72.4	75.8
167 CHS OF CHRIST	1	7	8	-	-
175 CONGR CHR CHS	1	168	215*	1.1	1.2
193 EPISCOPAL	1	21	23	.1	.1
207 E.L.C.A.	1	133	193	1.0	1.1
283 LUTH—MO SYNOD	3	961	1,301	6.9	7.2
353 CHR BRETHREN	1	39	59	.3	.3
449 UN METHODIST	2	161	206*	1.1	1.1
469 WELS	3	1,805	2,263	12.0	12.6
LA CROSSE	**86**	**25,689**	**57,216***	**58.4**	**100.0**
019 AMER BAPT USA	2	176	219*	.2	.4
053 ASSEMB OF GOD	2	139	210	.2	.4
081 CATHOLIC	13	NA	22,351	22.8	39.1
081d LATIN	13	NA	22,351	22.8	39.1
089 CHR & MISS AL	1	230	265	.3	.5
097 CHR CHS&CHS CR	3	286	357*	.4	.6
105 CHRISTIAN REF	1	78	116	.1	.2

NA–Not applicable   NR–Not reported   *Total adherents estimated from known number of communicant, confirmed, full members.   - Represents a percent less than 0.1.   Percentages may not total due to rounding.
[1]See Appendix E   [2]See Appendix F   [3]See Appendix G   Lines in *italic* represent a breakdown of Catholic rites or Friends affiliations. They are included in their respective denominational total.

Table 4. Churches and Church Membership by County and Denomination: 1990

County and Denomination		Number of churches	Communicant, confirmed, full members	Total adherents		
				Number	Percent of total population	Percent of total adherents
111	CH CR,SCIENTST	1	NR	NR	-	-
151	L-D SAINTS	2	NA	460	.5	.8
164	CH LUTH CONF	1	52	65	.1	.1
165	CH OF NAZARENE	2	72	100	.1	.2
167	CHS OF CHRIST	1	49	69	.1	.1
193	EPISCOPAL	1	408	623	.6	1.1
203	EVAN FREE CH	2	380	735	.8	1.3
207	E.L.C.A.	16	11,225	15,052	15.4	26.3
220	FREE LUTHERAN	1	74	105	.1	.2
226	FRIENDS-USA	1	3	14	-	-
226c	*FGC*	*1*	*3*	*14*	*-*	*-*
283	LUTH—MO SYNOD	2	713	976	1.0	1.7
313	N AM BAPT CONF	1	88	110*	.1	.2
353	CHR BRETHREN	1	38	90	.1	.2
355	PRESB CH (USA)	6	1,419	1,769*	1.8	3.1
356	PRESB CH AMER	1	48	60	.1	.1
367	PROT CONF (LU)	1	275	325	.3	.6
403	SALVATION ARMY	1	129	140	.1	.2
413	S.D.A.	1	74	92*	.1	.2
419	SO BAPT CONV	2	57	71*	.1	.1
435	UNITARIAN-UNIV	1	26	36	-	.1
443	UN C OF CHRIST	3	1,173	1,462*	1.5	2.6
449	UN METHODIST	5	2,298	2,865*	2.9	5.0
467	WESLEYAN	1	49	172	.2	.3
469	WELS	9	6,130	8,157	8.3	14.3
496	JEWISH EST[1]	1	NA	150	.2	.3
LAFAYETTE		**42**	**4,587**	**12,365***	**76.9**	**100.0**
019	AMER BAPT USA	1	169	221*	1.4	1.8
081	CATHOLIC	13	NA	6,462	40.2	52.3
081d	*LATIN*	*13*	*NA*	*6,462*	*40.2*	*52.3*
193	EPISCOPAL	1	4	8	-	.1
203	EVAN FREE CH	1	22	50	.3	.4
207	E.L.C.A.	9	2,420	3,061	19.0	24.8
363	PRIMITIVE METH	5	163	197	1.2	1.6
443	UN C OF CHRIST	2	394	515*	3.2	4.2
449	UN METHODIST	10	1,415	1,851*	11.5	15.0
LANGLADE		**35**	**4,113**	**14,474***	**74.2**	**100.0**
019	AMER BAPT USA	1	132	166*	.9	1.1
053	ASSEMB OF GOD	2	104	235	1.2	1.6
081	CATHOLIC	9	NA	8,824	45.2	61.0
081d	*LATIN*	*9*	*NA*	*8,824*	*45.2*	*61.0*
127	CH GOD (CLEVE)	1	72	91*	.5	.6
151	L-D SAINTS	1	NA	82	.4	.6
165	CH OF NAZARENE	1	37	95	.5	.7
167	CHS OF CHRIST	2	33	42	.2	.3
193	EPISCOPAL	1	41	61	.3	.4
207	E.L.C.A.	3	607	795	4.1	5.5
259	IFCA	1	NR	NR	-	-
283	LUTH—MO SYNOD	6	2,237	2,977	15.3	20.6
355	PRESB CH (USA)	1	37	47*	.2	.3
413	S.D.A.	1	40	50*	.3	.3
443	UN C OF CHRIST	3	425	535*	2.7	3.7
449	UN METHODIST	1	248	312*	1.6	2.2
469	WELS	1	100	162	.8	1.1
LINCOLN		**39**	**10,343**	**19,264***	**71.4**	**100.0**
053	ASSEMB OF GOD	2	141	268	1.0	1.4
057	BAPT GEN CONF	2	67	84*	.3	.4
081	CATHOLIC	5	NA	5,790	21.5	30.1
081d	*LATIN*	*5*	*NA*	*5,790*	*21.5*	*30.1*
111	CH CR,SCIENTST	2	NR	NR	-	-
193	EPISCOPAL	2	35	60	.2	.3
207	E.L.C.A.	4	2,177	3,046	11.3	15.8
259	IFCA	1	NR	NR	-	-
283	LUTH—MO SYNOD	8	5,288	6,660	24.7	34.6
355	PRESB CH (USA)	2	201	253*	.9	1.3
356	PRESB CH AMER	1	91	138	.5	.7
413	S.D.A.	2	91	114*	.4	.6
443	UN C OF CHRIST	2	1,414	1,777*	6.6	9.2
449	UN METHODIST	3	522	656*	2.4	3.4
469	WELS	3	316	418	1.5	2.2
MANITOWOC		**85**	**18,532**	**66,420***	**82.6**	**100.0**
019	AMER BAPT USA	1	75	95*	.1	.1
053	ASSEMB OF GOD	2	94	174	.2	.3
081	CATHOLIC	27	NA	41,981	52.2	63.2
081d	*LATIN*	*27*	*NA*	*41,981*	*52.2*	*63.2*
089	CHR & MISS AL	1	288	292	.4	.4
111	CH CR,SCIENTST	1	NR	NR	-	-
151	L-D SAINTS	1	NA	101	.1	.2
167	CHS OF CHRIST	1	66	105	.1	.2
193	EPISCOPAL	1	120	170	.2	.3
203	EVAN FREE CH	1	174	400	.5	.6
207	E.L.C.A.	5	3,120	4,251	5.3	6.4

County and Denomination		Number of churches	Communicant, confirmed, full members	Total adherents		
				Number	Percent of total population	Percent of total adherents
226	FRIENDS-USA	1	10	16	-	-
226c	*FGC*	*1*	*10*	*16*	*-*	*-*
283	LUTH—MO SYNOD	2	1,062	1,426	1.8	2.1
313	N AM BAPT CONF	1	75	95*	.1	.1
355	PRESB CH (USA)	3	737	932*	1.2	1.4
367	PROT CONF (LU)	1	35	50	.1	.1
373	REF CH IN U.S.	1	297	395	.5	.6
403	SALVATION ARMY	1	124	132	.2	.2
413	S.D.A.	1	9	11*	-	-
419	SO BAPT CONV	1	41	52*	.1	.1
443	UN C OF CHRIST	7	2,287	2,893*	3.6	4.4
449	UN METHODIST	6	1,094	1,384*	1.7	2.1
469	WELS	18	8,824	11,365	14.1	17.1
496	JEWISH EST[1]	1	NA	100	.1	.2
MARATHON		**126**	**31,608**	**83,084***	**72.0**	**100.0**
053	ASSEMB OF GOD	3	372	972	.8	1.2
057	BAPT GEN CONF	2	198	254*	.2	.3
081	CATHOLIC	26	NA	39,761	34.5	47.9
081d	*LATIN*	*26*	*NA*	*39,761*	*34.5*	*47.9*
089	CHR & MISS AL	2	220	520	.5	.6
111	CH CR,SCIENTST	1	NR	NR	-	-
127	CH GOD (CLEVE)	1	113	145*	.1	.2
151	L-D SAINTS	1	NA	194	.2	.2
165	CH OF NAZARENE	1	63	115	.1	.1
167	CHS OF CHRIST	1	45	65	.1	.1
193	EPISCOPAL	2	362	490	.4	.6
203	EVAN FREE CH	2	110	215	.2	.3
207	E.L.C.A.	20	10,176	13,682	11.9	16.5
209	EVAN LUTH SYN	1	118	161	.1	.2
226	FRIENDS-USA	1	9	18	-	-
226c	*FGC*	*1*	*9*	*18*	*-*	*-*
259	IFCA	2	NR	NR	-	-
263	INT FOURSQ GOS	1	190	244*	.2	.3
283	LUTH—MO SYNOD	16	8,320	11,061	9.6	13.3
285	MENNONITE CH	2	69	78	.1	.1
313	N AM BAPT CONF	1	401	515*	.4	.6
323	OLD ORD AMISH	3	NA	350	.3	.4
355	PRESB CH (USA)	2	1,118	1,437*	1.2	1.7
371	REF CH IN AM	1	285	500	.4	.6
403	SALVATION ARMY	1	88	108	.1	.1
413	S.D.A.	2	122	157*	.1	.2
419	SO BAPT CONV	2	104	134*	.1	.2
435	UNITARIAN-UNIV	1	255	326	.3	.4
443	UN C OF CHRIST	5	2,691	3,458*	3.0	4.2
449	UN METHODIST	5	1,808	2,324*	2.0	2.8
469	WELS	17	4,371	5,560	4.8	6.7
496	JEWISH EST[1]	1	NA	240	.2	.3
MARINETTE		**58**	**9,235**	**26,203***	**64.6**	**100.0**
053	ASSEMB OF GOD	5	396	890	2.2	3.4
057	BAPT GEN CONF	2	176	223*	.5	.9
081	CATHOLIC	11	NA	13,837	34.1	52.8
081d	*LATIN*	*11*	*NA*	*13,837*	*34.1*	*52.8*
097	CHR CHS&CHS CR	4	389	494*	1.2	1.9
111	CH CR,SCIENTST	1	NR	NR	-	-
167	CHS OF CHRIST	1	5	5	-	-
193	EPISCOPAL	1	105	160	.4	.6
207	E.L.C.A.	7	2,377	3,078	7.6	11.7
209	EVAN LUTH SYN	1	251	313	.8	1.2
263	INT FOURSQ GOS	1	29	37*	.1	.1
283	LUTH—MO SYNOD	1	185	296	.7	1.1
284	LUTH CH-AM ASC	1	267	355	.9	1.4
313	N AM BAPT CONF	1	128	162*	.4	.6
355	PRESB CH (USA)	6	693	880*	2.2	3.4
403	SALVATION ARMY	1	68	79	.2	.3
413	S.D.A.	1	72	91*	.2	.3
443	UN C OF CHRIST	1	130	165*	.4	.6
449	UN METHODIST	5	1,094	1,389*	3.4	5.3
469	WELS	6	2,870	3,749	9.2	14.3
496	JEWISH EST[1]	1	NA	0	-	-
MARQUETTE		**29**	**3,607**	**7,577***	**61.5**	**100.0**
081	CATHOLIC	5	NA	3,072	24.9	40.5
081d	*LATIN*	*5*	*NA*	*3,072*	*24.9*	*40.5*
207	E.L.C.A.	3	421	518	4.2	6.8
259	IFCA	2	NR	NR	-	-
283	LUTH—MO SYNOD	7	1,404	1,792	14.5	23.7
355	PRESB CH (USA)	3	287	356*	2.9	4.7
413	S.D.A.	1	52	64*	.5	.8
443	UN C OF CHRIST	1	80	99*	.8	1.3
449	UN METHODIST	5	703	871*	7.1	11.5
469	WELS	2	660	805	6.5	10.6
MENOMINEE		**4**	**10**	**2,775***	**71.3**	**100.0**
053	ASSEMB OF GOD	1	10	18	.5	.6

NA–Not applicable   NR–Not reported   *Total adherents estimated from known number of communicant, confirmed, full members.   - Represents a percent less than 0.1.   Percentages may not total due to rounding.
[1]See Appendix E   [2]See Appendix F   [3]See Appendix G   Lines in *italic* represent a breakdown of Catholic rites or Friends affiliations. They are included in their respective denominational total.

Table 4. Churches and Church Membership by County and Denomination: 1990

County and Denomination	Number of churches	Communicant, confirmed, full members	Total adherents Number	Percent of total population	Percent of total adherents
081 CATHOLIC	3	NA	2,757	70.9	99.4
081d LATIN	*3*	*NA*	*2,757*	*70.9*	*99.4*
MILWAUKEE	**499**	**182,353**	**569,737***	**59.4**	**100.0**
005 AME ZION	1	65	82	-	-
019 AMER BAPT USA	17	5,686	7,172*	.7	1.3
053 ASSEMB OF GOD	20	3,451	6,982	.7	1.2
057 BAPT GEN CONF	3	220	278*	-	-
081 CATHOLIC	109	NA	304,275	31.7	53.4
081d LATIN	*107*	*NA*	*303,692*	*31.7*	*53.3*
081f MELKITE-GK	*1*	*NA*	*400*	*-*	*.1*
081h UKRAINIAN	*1*	*NA*	*183*	*-*	*-*
089 CHR & MISS AL	3	1,126	1,359	.1	.2
093 CHR CH (DISC)	1	110	136	-	-
097 CHR CHS&CHS CR	2	157	198*	-	-
111 CH CR,SCIENTST	9	NR	NR	-	-
123 CH GOD (ANDER)	4	467	475	-	.1
127 CH GOD (CLEVE)	3	173	218*	-	-
145 CH GOD PROPHCY	2	52	66*	-	-
151 L-D SAINTS	2	NA	1,085	.1	.2
164 CH LUTH CONF	1	50	71	-	-
165 CH OF NAZARENE	2	37	93	-	-
167 CHS OF CHRIST	11	1,192	1,765	.2	.3
175 CONGR CHR CHS	5	3,142	3,963*	.4	.7
176 CCC, NOT NAT'L	1	295	372*	-	.1
181 CONSRV CONGR	1	25	32*	-	-
193 EPISCOPAL	17	4,233	6,082	.6	1.1
203 EVAN FREE CH	2	302	607	.1	.1
207 E.L.C.A.	53	27,916	36,981	3.9	6.5
226 FRIENDS-USA	1	42	224	-	-
226c FGC	*1*	*42*	*224*	*-*	*-*
246 GREEK ORTHODOX	2	NR	NR	-	-
263 INT FOURSQ GOS	2	53	67*	-	-
274 LAT EVAN LUTH	1	605	655	.1	.1
283 LUTH—MO SYNOD	48	30,115	39,731	4.1	7.0
313 N AM BAPT CONF	1	112	141*	-	-
331 ORTH CH IN AM	1	NR	NR	-	-
353 CHR BRETHREN	3	255	400	-	.1
355 PRESB CH (USA)	19	5,108	6,443*	.7	1.1
356 PRESB CH AMER	1	52	78	-	-
371 REF CH IN AM	3	572	973	.1	.2
403 SALVATION ARMY	3	452	483	.1	.1
413 S.D.A.	8	1,778	2,243*	.2	.4
415 S-D BAPTIST GC	1	30	38*	-	-
419 SO BAPT CONV	21	4,460	5,626*	.6	1.0
435 UNITARIAN-UNIV	2	431	553	.1	.1
443 UN C OF CHRIST	16	5,278	6,657*	.7	1.2
449 UN METHODIST	26	9,003	11,356*	1.2	2.0
467 WESLEYAN	3	145	358	-	.1
469 WELS	48	23,483	31,002	3.2	5.4
496 JEWISH EST[1]	15	NA	18,755	2.0	3.3
497 BLACK BAPT EST[1]	NA	51,680	65,187*	6.8	11.4
498 INDEP.CHARIS.[3]	3	NA	5,650	.6	1.0
499 INDEP.NON-CHAR[3]	2	NA	825	.1	.1
MONROE	**63**	**9,763**	**24,022***	**65.6**	**100.0**
019 AMER BAPT USA	1	239	311*	.8	1.3
053 ASSEMB OF GOD	3	225	632	1.7	2.6
081 CATHOLIC	10	NA	9,447	25.8	39.3
081d LATIN	*10*	*NA*	*9,447*	*25.8*	*39.3*
097 CHR CHS&CHS CR	1	31	40*	.1	.2
123 CH GOD (ANDER)	1	24	24	.1	.1
151 L-D SAINTS	1	NA	163	.4	.7
165 CH OF NAZARENE	2	65	297	.8	1.2
167 CHS OF CHRIST	1	40	73	.2	.3
181 CONSRV CONGR	2	145	189*	.5	.8
193 EPISCOPAL	2	160	231	.6	1.0
203 EVAN FREE CH	3	147	318	.9	1.3
207 E.L.C.A.	7	2,778	3,856	10.5	16.1
323 OLD ORD AMISH	4	NA	600	1.6	2.5
349 PENT HOLINESS	1	42	55*	.2	.2
413 S.D.A.	3	167	217*	.6	.9
419 SO BAPT CONV	1	48	62*	.2	.3
443 UN C OF CHRIST	2	555	722*	2.0	3.0
449 UN METHODIST	6	1,406	1,829*	5.0	7.6
467 WESLEYAN	1	21	125	.3	.5
469 WELS	11	3,670	4,831	13.2	20.1
OCONTO	**56**	**7,333**	**20,920***	**69.2**	**100.0**
053 ASSEMB OF GOD	2	96	248	.8	1.2
081 CATHOLIC	14	NA	10,607	35.1	50.7
081d LATIN	*14*	*NA*	*10,607*	*35.1*	*50.7*
089 CHR & MISS AL	3	166	561	1.9	2.7
097 CHR CHS&CHS CR	2	105	133*	.4	.6
111 CH CR,SCIENTST	1	NR	NR	-	-
193 EPISCOPAL	1	33	60	.2	.3

County and Denomination	Number of churches	Communicant, confirmed, full members	Total adherents Number	Percent of total population	Percent of total adherents
207 E.L.C.A.	6	2,656	3,690	12.2	17.6
283 LUTH—MO SYNOD	10	2,352	3,079	10.2	14.7
323 OLD ORD AMISH	1	NA	50	.2	.2
355 PRESB CH (USA)	2	264	336*	1.1	1.6
413 S.D.A.	3	167	212*	.7	1.0
449 UN METHODIST	7	967	1,229*	4.1	5.9
469 WELS	4	527	715	2.4	3.4
ONEIDA	**42**	**7,912**	**16,042***	**50.6**	**100.0**
019 AMER BAPT USA	1	51	63*	.2	.4
053 ASSEMB OF GOD	1	72	139	.4	.9
057 BAPT GEN CONF	1	119	146*	.5	.9
081 CATHOLIC	8	NA	5,649	17.8	35.2
081d LATIN	*8*	*NA*	*5,649*	*17.8*	*35.2*
111 CH CR,SCIENTST	2	NR	NR	-	-
167 CHS OF CHRIST	2	79	103	.3	.6
193 EPISCOPAL	3	298	429	1.4	2.7
203 EVAN FREE CH	2	118	320	1.0	2.0
207 E.L.C.A.	5	2,047	2,800	8.8	17.5
263 INT FOURSQ GOS	1	365	449*	1.4	2.8
283 LUTH—MO SYNOD	4	768	992	3.1	6.2
339 PENT CH OF GOD	1	34	77	.2	.5
413 S.D.A.	1	119	146*	.5	.9
435 UNITARIAN-UNIV	1	28	38	.1	.2
443 UN C OF CHRIST	3	981	1,207*	3.8	7.5
449 UN METHODIST	2	957	1,177*	3.7	7.3
469 WELS	4	1,876	2,307	7.3	14.4
OUTAGAMIE	**107**	**34,485**	**127,647***	**90.8**	**100.0**
019 AMER BAPT USA	2	117	151*	.1	.1
053 ASSEMB OF GOD	4	870	2,265	1.6	1.8
057 BAPT GEN CONF	2	100	129*	.1	.1
081 CATHOLIC	26	NA	78,419	55.8	61.4
081d LATIN	*26*	*NA*	*78,419*	*55.8*	*61.4*
089 CHR & MISS AL	2	569	1,369	1.0	1.1
105 CHRISTIAN REF	1	75	135	.1	.1
111 CH CR,SCIENTST	1	NR	NR	-	-
151 L-D SAINTS	1	NA	568	.4	.4
165 CH OF NAZARENE	1	50	62	-	-
167 CHS OF CHRIST	2	142	176	.1	.1
181 CONSRV CONGR	1	125	162*	.1	.1
193 EPISCOPAL	1	596	789	.6	.6
203 EVAN FREE CH	1	92	210	.1	.2
207 E.L.C.A.	9	8,921	12,228	8.7	9.6
226 FRIENDS-USA	0	4	8	-	-
226c FGC	*0*	*4*	*8*	*-*	*-*
246 GREEK ORTHODOX	1	NR	NR	-	-
263 INT FOURSQ GOS	1	29	38*	-	-
283 LUTH—MO SYNOD	5	4,572	6,147	4.4	4.8
293 MORAV CH-NORTH	1	150	196	.1	.2
355 PRESB CH (USA)	2	731	946*	.7	.7
367 PROT CONF (LU)	1	110	130	.1	.1
403 SALVATION ARMY	1	91	95	.1	.1
413 S.D.A.	2	167	216*	.2	.2
419 SO BAPT CONV	1	259	335*	.2	.3
435 UNITARIAN-UNIV	1	144	229	.2	.2
443 UN C OF CHRIST	6	2,971	3,846*	2.7	3.0
449 UN METHODIST	10	3,162	4,093*	2.9	3.2
469 WELS	17	10,438	13,605	9.7	10.7
496 JEWISH EST[1]	2	NA	250	.2	.2
498 INDEP.CHARIS.[3]	2	NA	850	.6	.7
OZAUKEE	**59**	**17,629**	**50,700***	**69.6**	**100.0**
005 AME ZION	1	164	221	.3	.4
019 AMER BAPT USA	2	113	144*	.2	.3
053 ASSEMB OF GOD	2	239	412	.6	.8
081 CATHOLIC	12	NA	25,539	35.1	50.4
081d LATIN	*12*	*NA*	*25,539*	*35.1*	*50.4*
089 CHR & MISS AL	1	114	439	.6	.9
111 CH CR,SCIENTST	1	NR	NR	-	-
151 L-D SAINTS	1	NA	434	.6	.9
175 CONGR CHR CHS	1	300	381*	.5	.8
193 EPISCOPAL	1	83	105	.1	.2
207 E.L.C.A.	11	4,578	5,984	8.2	11.8
259 IFCA	1	NR	NR	-	-
283 LUTH—MO SYNOD	8	6,218	8,097	11.1	16.0
355 PRESB CH (USA)	1	1,361	1,731*	2.4	3.4
435 UNITARIAN-UNIV	1	198	307	.4	.6
443 UN C OF CHRIST	5	1,188	1,511*	2.1	3.0
449 UN METHODIST	3	1,176	1,495*	2.1	2.9
469 WELS	7	1,897	2,476	3.4	4.9
496 JEWISH EST[1]	0	NA	1,424	2.0	2.8
PEPIN	**16**	**1,642**	**6,183***	**87.0**	**100.0**
081 CATHOLIC	3	NA	3,942	55.5	63.8
081d LATIN	*3*	*NA*	*3,942*	*55.5*	*63.8*

NA–Not applicable NR–Not reported *Total adherents estimated from known number of communicant, confirmed, full members. - Represents a percent less than 0.1. Percentages may not total due to rounding.
[1]See Appendix E [2]See Appendix F [3]See Appendix G Lines in *italic* represent a breakdown of Catholic rites or Friends affiliations. They are included in their respective denominational total.

Table 4. Churches and Church Membership by County and Denomination: 1990

County and Denomination	Number of churches	Communicant, confirmed, full members	Total adherents Number	Percent of total population	Percent of total adherents
175 CONGR CHR CHS	1	25	32*	.5	.5
203 EVAN FREE CH	1	21	40	.6	.6
207 E.L.C.A.	5	897	1,268	17.8	20.5
283 LUTH—MO SYNOD	1	164	213	3.0	3.4
293 MORAV CH-NORTH	1	24	25	.4	.4
413 S.D.A.	1	47	61*	.9	1.0
449 UN METHODIST	3	464	602*	8.5	9.7
PIERCE	**47**	**8,540**	**17,000***	**51.9**	**100.0**
053 ASSEMB OF GOD	1	88	208	.6	1.2
081 CATHOLIC	6	NA	5,662	17.3	33.3
081d LATIN	*6*	*NA*	*5,662*	*17.3*	*33.3*
167 CHS OF CHRIST	1	23	43	.1	.3
181 CONSRV CONGR	1	85	108*	.3	.6
193 EPISCOPAL	1	94	104	.3	.6
203 EVAN FREE CH	1	32	55	.2	.3
207 E.L.C.A.	13	4,345	5,832	17.8	34.3
226 FRIENDS-USA	0	3	6	-	-
226c FGC	*0*	*3*	*6*	*-*	*-*
259 IFCA	1	NR	NR	-	-
283 LUTH—MO SYNOD	2	393	544	1.7	3.2
355 PRESB CH (USA)	2	167	212*	.6	1.2
435 UNITARIAN-UNIV	1	40	40	.1	.2
443 UN C OF CHRIST	4	1,222	1,553*	4.7	9.1
449 UN METHODIST	11	1,656	2,105*	6.4	12.4
469 WELS	2	392	528	1.6	3.1
POLK	**87**	**13,076**	**20,810***	**59.8**	**100.0**
053 ASSEMB OF GOD	2	89	172	.5	.8
057 BAPT GEN CONF	4	389	501*	1.4	2.4
081 CATHOLIC	9	NA	2,793	8.0	13.4
081d LATIN	*9*	*NA*	*2,793*	*8.0*	*13.4*
089 CHR & MISS AL	2	195	535	1.5	2.6
165 CH OF NAZARENE	1	70	189	.5	.9
167 CHS OF CHRIST	1	14	23	.1	.1
179 CONSRV BAPT	3	NR	NR	-	-
193 EPISCOPAL	1	29	29	.1	.1
203 EVAN FREE CH	3	200	337	1.0	1.6
207 E.L.C.A.	29	7,573	10,400	29.9	50.0
220 FREE LUTHERAN	2	195	270	.8	1.3
263 INT FOURSQ GOS	1	64	82*	.2	.4
283 LUTH—MO SYNOD	4	640	843	2.4	4.1
284 LUTH CH-AM ASC	2	213	260	.7	1.2
331 ORTH CH IN AM	1	NR	NR	-	-
355 PRESB CH (USA)	1	107	138*	.4	.7
413 S.D.A.	2	145	187*	.5	.9
443 UN C OF CHRIST	1	255	329*	.9	1.6
449 UN METHODIST	12	1,182	1,523*	4.4	7.3
469 WELS	6	1,716	2,199	6.3	10.6
PORTAGE	**62**	**8,255**	**44,614***	**72.7**	**100.0**
019 AMER BAPT USA	3	308	387*	.6	.9
053 ASSEMB OF GOD	1	270	534	.9	1.2
057 BAPT GEN CONF	1	21	26*	-	.1
081 CATHOLIC	19	NA	32,839	53.5	73.6
081d LATIN	*19*	*NA*	*32,839*	*53.5*	*73.6*
089 CHR & MISS AL	1	0	5	-	-
111 CH CR,SCIENTST	1	NR	NR	-	-
165 CH OF NAZARENE	1	26	0	-	-
167 CHS OF CHRIST	2	109	149	.2	.3
193 EPISCOPAL	2	182	244	.4	.5
203 EVAN FREE CH	2	130	210	.3	.5
207 E.L.C.A.	6	2,643	3,752	6.1	8.4
209 EVAN LUTH SYN	1	20	24	-	.1
226 FRIENDS-USA	1	8	24	-	.1
226c FGC	*1*	*8*	*24*	*-*	*.1*
283 LUTH—MO SYNOD	6	2,366	3,150	5.1	7.1
323 OLD ORD AMISH	3	NA	450	.7	1.0
339 PENT CH OF GOD	1	34	76	.1	.2
355 PRESB CH (USA)	1	330	415*	.7	.9
413 S.D.A.	2	120	151*	.2	.3
435 UNITARIAN-UNIV	1	18	39	.1	.1
443 UN C OF CHRIST	1	107	134*	.2	.3
449 UN METHODIST	5	1,287	1,617*	2.6	3.6
469 WELS	1	276	388	.6	.9
PRICE	**32**	**3,872**	**9,596***	**61.5**	**100.0**
053 ASSEMB OF GOD	1	53	77	.5	.8
057 BAPT GEN CONF	4	481	606*	3.9	6.3
081 CATHOLIC	6	NA	4,532	29.1	47.2
081d LATIN	*6*	*NA*	*4,532*	*29.1*	*47.2*
167 CHS OF CHRIST	1	8	16	.1	.2
193 EPISCOPAL	2	37	55	.4	.6
207 E.L.C.A.	6	1,219	1,567	10.0	16.3
283 LUTH—MO SYNOD	4	1,338	1,809	11.6	18.9
355 PRESB CH (USA)	1	200	252*	1.6	2.6

County and Denomination	Number of churches	Communicant, confirmed, full members	Total adherents Number	Percent of total population	Percent of total adherents
413 S.D.A.	1	13	16*	.1	.2
443 UN C OF CHRIST	2	261	329*	2.1	3.4
449 UN METHODIST	3	207	261*	1.7	2.7
469 WELS	1	55	76	.5	.8
RACINE	**129**	**36,347**	**101,904***	**58.2**	**100.0**
019 AMER BAPT USA	1	414	532*	.3	.5
049 ARMEN AP CH AM	1	250	1,000	.6	1.0
053 ASSEMB OF GOD	5	622	1,024	.6	1.0
081 CATHOLIC	25	NA	50,459	28.8	49.5
081d LATIN	*25*	*NA*	*50,459*	*28.8*	*49.5*
105 CHRISTIAN REF	1	261	429	.2	.4
111 CH CR,SCIENTST	2	NR	NR	-	-
123 CH GOD (ANDER)	2	184	213	.1	.2
127 CH GOD (CLEVE)	2	48	62*	-	.1
145 CH GOD PROPHCY	1	24	31*	-	-
165 CH OF NAZARENE	3	399	998	.6	1.0
167 CHS OF CHRIST	3	106	159	.1	.2
175 CONGR CHR CHS	1	243	312*	.2	.3
193 EPISCOPAL	5	827	1,008	.6	1.0
203 EVAN FREE CH	1	92	122	.1	.1
207 E.L.C.A.	19	12,859	17,750	10.1	17.4
246 GREEK ORTHODOX	1	NR	NR	-	-
259 IFCA	1	NR	NR	-	-
283 LUTH—MO SYNOD	15	5,546	7,908	4.5	7.8
313 N AM BAPT CONF	1	464	596*	.3	.6
355 PRESB CH (USA)	3	1,111	1,427*	.8	1.4
371 REF CH IN AM	1	129	215	.1	.2
403 SALVATION ARMY	1	96	112	.1	.1
413 S.D.A.	3	266	342*	.2	.3
419 SO BAPT CONV	4	491	631*	.4	.6
435 UNITARIAN-UNIV	1	190	310	.2	.3
443 UN C OF CHRIST	4	644	827*	.5	.8
449 UN METHODIST	14	3,966	5,093*	2.9	5.0
469 WELS	6	2,621	3,498	2.0	3.4
496 JEWISH EST[1]	1	NA	375	.2	.4
497 BLACK BAPT EST[1]	NA	4,494	5,771*	3.3	5.7
499 INDEP.NON-CHAR[3]	1	NA	700	.4	.7
RICHLAND	**32**	**3,460**	**7,408***	**42.3**	**100.0**
019 AMER BAPT USA	2	190	242*	1.4	3.3
053 ASSEMB OF GOD	1	49	116	.7	1.6
081 CATHOLIC	6	NA	2,672	15.3	36.1
081d LATIN	*6*	*NA*	*2,672*	*15.3*	*36.1*
097 CHR CHS&CHS CR	1	230	293*	1.7	4.0
165 CH OF NAZARENE	1	125	240	1.4	3.2
175 CONGR CHR CHS	1	135	172*	1.0	2.3
193 EPISCOPAL	1	30	44	.3	.6
207 E.L.C.A.	3	819	1,118	6.4	15.1
221 FREE METHODIST	1	105	147	.8	2.0
283 LUTH—MO SYNOD	2	181	225	1.3	3.0
285 MENNONITE CH	1	39	41	.2	.6
355 PRESB CH (USA)	1	203	259*	1.5	3.5
413 S.D.A.	1	90	115*	.7	1.6
449 UN METHODIST	9	1,219	1,554*	8.9	21.0
467 WESLEYAN	1	45	170	1.0	2.3
ROCK	**138**	**40,119**	**85,803***	**61.5**	**100.0**
001 ADVENT CHR CH	1	54	69*	-	.1
019 AMER BAPT USA	7	1,759	2,240*	1.6	2.6
053 ASSEMB OF GOD	4	511	1,003	.7	1.2
057 BAPT GEN CONF	1	140	178*	.1	.2
081 CATHOLIC	12	NA	32,193	23.1	37.5
081d LATIN	*12*	*NA*	*32,193*	*23.1*	*37.5*
089 CHR & MISS AL	1	117	292	.2	.3
093 CHR CH (DISC)	1	147	235	.2	.3
097 CHR CHS&CHS CR	4	1,198	1,526*	1.1	1.8
111 CH CR,SCIENTST	3	NR	NR	-	-
127 CH GOD (CLEVE)	1	50	64*	-	.1
145 CH GOD PROPHCY	2	49	62*	-	.1
151 L-D SAINTS	1	NA	339	.2	.4
165 CH OF NAZARENE	1	109	109	.1	.1
167 CHS OF CHRIST	1	20	40	-	-
175 CONGR CHR CHS	5	1,280	1,630*	1.2	1.9
193 EPISCOPAL	2	423	583	.4	.7
203 EVAN FREE CH	1	30	30	-	-
207 E.L.C.A.	18	13,718	18,518	13.3	21.6
209 EVAN LUTH SYN	1	26	34	-	-
220 FREE LUTHERAN	1	64	88	.1	.1
221 FREE METHODIST	3	237	354	.3	.4
226 FRIENDS-USA	1	9	22	-	-
226c FGC	*1*	*9*	*22*	*-*	*-*
263 INT FOURSQ GOS	1	68	87*	.1	.1
283 LUTH—MO SYNOD	11	5,961	7,640	5.5	8.9
284 LUTH CH-AM ASC	1	80	94	.1	.1
323 OLD ORD AMISH	1	NA	150	.1	.2

NA–Not applicable   NR–Not reported   *Total adherents estimated from known number of communicant, confirmed, full members.   - Represents a percent less than 0.1.   Percentages may not total due to rounding.
[1]See Appendix E   [2]See Appendix F   [3]See Appendix G   Lines in *italic* represent a breakdown of Catholic rites or Friends affiliations. They are included in their respective denominational total.

Table 4. Churches and Church Membership by County and Denomination: 1990

County and Denomination	Number of churches	Communicant, confirmed, full members	Total adherents Number	Percent of total population	Percent of total adherents
329 OPEN BIBLE STD	1	NR	NR	-	-
353 CHR BRETHREN	2	27	61	-	.1
355 PRESB CH (USA)	6	1,802	2,295*	1.6	2.7
363 PRIMITIVE METH	1	85	115	.1	.1
371 REF CH IN AM	1	156	286	.2	.3
403 SALVATION ARMY	2	354	396	.3	.5
413 S.D.A.	4	306	390*	.3	.5
415 S-D BAPTIST GC	2	478	609*	.4	.7
419 SO BAPT CONV	4	338	430*	.3	.5
443 UN C OF CHRIST	5	1,199	1,527*	1.1	1.8
449 UN METHODIST	18	6,198	7,893*	5.7	9.2
467 WESLEYAN	1	59	92	.1	.1
469 WELS	4	1,312	1,774	1.3	2.1
496 JEWISH EST[1]	1	NA	120	.1	.1
497 BLACK BAPT EST[1]	NA	1,755	2,235*	1.6	2.6
RUSK	**41**	**3,437**	**7,761***	**51.5**	**100.0**
053 ASSEMB OF GOD	2	84	120	.8	1.5
057 BAPT GEN CONF	1	54	69*	.5	.9
081 CATHOLIC	12	NA	3,210	21.3	41.4
081d *LATIN*	*12*	*NA*	*3,210*	*21.3*	*41.4*
097 CHR CHS&CHS CR	2	425	540*	3.6	7.0
193 EPISCOPAL	1	14	16	.1	.2
207 E.L.C.A.	4	1,260	1,662	11.0	21.4
259 IFCA	1	NR	NR	-	-
283 LUTH—MO SYNOD	2	746	991	6.6	12.8
285 MENNONITE CH	5	167	278	1.8	3.6
413 S.D.A.	1	35	44*	.3	.6
415 S-D BAPTIST GC	1	30	38*	.3	.5
443 UN C OF CHRIST	3	198	252*	1.7	3.2
449 UN METHODIST	5	403	512*	3.4	6.6
469 WELS	1	21	29	.2	.4
ST CROIX	**55**	**13,907**	**33,122***	**65.9**	**100.0**
019 AMER BAPT USA	1	274	361*	.7	1.1
053 ASSEMB OF GOD	3	170	212	.4	.6
057 BAPT GEN CONF	2	144	190*	.4	.6
081 CATHOLIC	8	NA	14,079	28.0	42.5
081d *LATIN*	*8*	*NA*	*14,079*	*28.0*	*42.5*
105 CHRISTIAN REF	1	141	201	.4	.6
151 L-D SAINTS	1	NA	237	.5	.7
179 CONSRV BAPT	1	NR	NR	-	-
193 EPISCOPAL	2	106	144	.3	.4
207 E.L.C.A.	14	7,312	9,828	19.6	29.7
283 LUTH—MO SYNOD	4	1,984	2,820	5.6	8.5
355 PRESB CH (USA)	2	623	820*	1.6	2.5
371 REF CH IN AM	1	358	555	1.1	1.7
443 UN C OF CHRIST	2	374	492*	1.0	1.5
449 UN METHODIST	8	1,760	2,316*	4.6	7.0
469 WELS	5	661	867	1.7	2.6
SAUK	**79**	**14,292**	**34,309***	**73.0**	**100.0**
001 ADVENT CHR CH	2	206	263*	.6	.8
019 AMER BAPT USA	1	64	82*	.2	.2
053 ASSEMB OF GOD	2	150	266	.6	.8
081 CATHOLIC	9	NA	15,329	32.6	44.7
081d *LATIN*	*9*	*NA*	*15,329*	*32.6*	*44.7*
097 CHR CHS&CHS CR	1	16	20*	-	.1
111 CH CR,SCIENTST	1	NR	NR	-	-
123 CH GOD (ANDER)	2	75	75	.2	.2
151 L-D SAINTS	1	NA	170	.4	.5
165 CH OF NAZARENE	2	85	250	.5	.7
167 CHS OF CHRIST	1	25	28	.1	.1
175 CONGR CHR CHS	1	86	110*	.2	.3
193 EPISCOPAL	2	210	283	.6	.8
203 EVAN FREE CH	2	116	189	.4	.6
207 E.L.C.A.	8	3,743	4,908	10.4	14.3
226 FRIENDS-USA	1	113	144*	.3	.4
226e *FUM*	*1*	*113*	*144***	*.3*	*.4*
259 IFCA	1	NR	NR	-	-
283 LUTH—MO SYNOD	6	1,846	2,398	5.1	7.0
313 N AM BAPT CONF	1	95	121*	.3	.4
323 OLD ORD AMISH	2	NA	200	.4	.6
355 PRESB CH (USA)	3	576	735*	1.6	2.1
413 S.D.A.	2	79	101*	.2	.3
419 SO BAPT CONV	1	97	124*	.3	.4
435 UNITARIAN-UNIV	1	35	45	.1	.1
443 UN C OF CHRIST	2	549	700*	1.5	2.0
449 UN METHODIST	14	3,250	4,145*	8.8	12.1
467 WESLEYAN	2	70	174	.4	.5
469 WELS	8	2,806	3,449	7.3	10.1
SAWYER	**33**	**2,300**	**5,591***	**39.4**	**100.0**
053 ASSEMB OF GOD	2	76	84	.6	1.5
057 BAPT GEN CONF	1	54	68*	.5	1.2
081 CATHOLIC	9	NA	2,388	16.8	42.7

County and Denomination	Number of churches	Communicant, confirmed, full members	Total adherents Number	Percent of total population	Percent of total adherents
081d *LATIN*	*9*	*NA*	*2,388*	*16.8*	*42.7*
127 CH GOD (CLEVE)	1	13	16*	.1	.3
175 CONGR CHR CHS	1	138	174*	1.2	3.1
193 EPISCOPAL	1	46	70	.5	1.3
203 EVAN FREE CH	2	63	135	1.0	2.4
207 E.L.C.A.	4	1,166	1,508	10.6	27.0
283 LUTH—MO SYNOD	1	267	333	2.3	6.0
285 MENNONITE CH	2	65	103	.7	1.8
355 PRESB CH (USA)	3	95	120*	.8	2.1
413 S.D.A.	1	26	33*	.2	.6
443 UN C OF CHRIST	1	33	42*	.3	.8
449 UN METHODIST	2	103	130*	.9	2.3
467 WESLEYAN	1	49	225	1.6	4.0
469 WELS	1	106	162	1.1	2.9
SHAWANO	**83**	**15,249**	**29,846***	**80.3**	**100.0**
053 ASSEMB OF GOD	2	157	295	.8	1.0
057 BAPT GEN CONF	1	74	93*	.3	.3
081 CATHOLIC	13	NA	9,858	26.5	33.0
081d *LATIN*	*13*	*NA*	*9,858*	*26.5*	*33.0*
151 L-D SAINTS	2	NA	389	1.0	1.3
165 CH OF NAZARENE	1	160	215	.6	.7
193 EPISCOPAL	1	38	38	.1	.1
207 E.L.C.A.	18	3,710	4,848	13.0	16.2
209 EVAN LUTH SYN	1	146	187	.5	.6
226 FRIENDS-USA	1	5	10	-	-
226c *FGC*	*1*	*5*	*10*	*-*	*-*
259 IFCA	1	NR	NR	-	-
283 LUTH—MO SYNOD	24	8,208	10,327	27.8	34.6
323 OLD ORD AMISH	1	NA	100	.3	.3
339 PENT CH OF GOD	1	34	76	.2	.3
355 PRESB CH (USA)	2	330	416*	1.1	1.4
413 S.D.A.	1	32	40*	.1	.1
419 SO BAPT CONV	1	66	83*	.2	.3
443 UN C OF CHRIST	2	823	1,038*	2.8	3.5
449 UN METHODIST	7	733	925*	2.5	3.1
469 WELS	3	733	908	2.4	3.0
SHEBOYGAN	**125**	**37,284**	**81,297***	**78.3**	**100.0**
019 AMER BAPT USA	1	96	122*	.1	.2
053 ASSEMB OF GOD	2	372	1,083	1.0	1.3
075 BRETHREN IN CR	1	34	37	-	-
081 CATHOLIC	18	NA	31,346	30.2	38.6
081d *LATIN*	*18*	*NA*	*31,346*	*30.2*	*38.6*
089 CHR & MISS AL	3	358	731	.7	.9
105 CHRISTIAN REF	4	1,132	1,598	1.5	2.0
111 CH CR,SCIENTST	1	NR	NR	-	-
127 CH GOD (CLEVE)	1	28	35*	-	-
165 CH OF NAZARENE	1	12	0	-	-
167 CHS OF CHRIST	2	88	118	.1	.1
193 EPISCOPAL	3	557	908	.9	1.1
203 EVAN FREE CH	2	322	595	.6	.7
207 E.L.C.A.	6	3,191	4,212	4.1	5.2
246 GREEK ORTHODOX	1	NR	NR	-	-
259 IFCA	2	NR	NR	-	-
283 LUTH—MO SYNOD	25	15,558	19,763	19.0	24.3
307 NETH REF CONGR	1	93	176	.2	.2
313 N AM BAPT CONF	1	99	125*	.1	.2
349 PENT HOLINESS	1	3	4*	-	-
353 CHR BRETHREN	2	69	120	.1	.1
355 PRESB CH (USA)	3	676	856*	.8	1.1
371 REF CH IN AM	8	3,144	4,681	4.5	5.8
403 SALVATION ARMY	1	133	164	.2	.2
413 S.D.A.	1	75	95*	.1	.1
419 SO BAPT CONV	1	93	118*	.1	.1
435 UNITARIAN-UNIV	1	18	25	-	-
443 UN C OF CHRIST	21	7,649	9,687*	9.3	11.9
449 UN METHODIST	7	2,509	3,177*	3.1	3.9
469 WELS	3	975	1,361	1.3	1.7
496 JEWISH EST[1]	1	NA	160	.2	.2
TAYLOR	**32**	**4,096**	**12,922***	**68.4**	**100.0**
053 ASSEMB OF GOD	1	17	30	.2	.2
057 BAPT GEN CONF	1	153	201*	1.1	1.6
081 CATHOLIC	10	NA	6,987	37.0	54.1
081d *LATIN*	*10*	*NA*	*6,987*	*37.0*	*54.1*
111 CH CR,SCIENTST	1	NR	NR	-	-
207 E.L.C.A.	3	683	912	4.8	7.1
283 LUTH—MO SYNOD	3	572	778	4.1	6.0
323 OLD ORD AMISH	3	NA	450	2.4	3.5
331 ORTH CH IN AM	1	NR	NR	-	-
355 PRESB CH (USA)	1	60	79*	.4	.6
443 UN C OF CHRIST	1	234	308*	1.6	2.4
449 UN METHODIST	2	290	381*	2.0	2.9
469 WELS	5	2,087	2,796	14.8	21.6

NA–Not applicable   NR–Not reported   *Total adherents estimated from known number of communicant, confirmed, full members.   - Represents a percent less than 0.1.   Percentages may not total due to rounding.

[1]See Appendix E   [2]See Appendix F   [3]See Appendix G   Lines in *italic* represent a breakdown of Catholic rites or Friends affiliations. They are included in their respective denominational total.

Table 4. Churches and Church Membership by County and Denomination: 1990

County and Denomination	Number of churches	Communicant, confirmed, full members	Total adherents Number	Percent of total population	Percent of total adherents
TREMPEALEAU	**45**	**8,805**	**20,207***	**80.0**	**100.0**
053 ASSEMB OF GOD	1	36	61	.2	.3
081 CATHOLIC	10	NA	8,671	34.3	42.9
081d LATIN	10	NA	8,671	34.3	42.9
165 CH OF NAZARENE	1	10	53	.2	.3
179 CONSRV BAPT	2	NR	NR	-	-
207 E.L.C.A.	22	7,718	9,809	38.8	48.5
283 LUTH—MO SYNOD	1	140	161	.6	.8
323 OLD ORD AMISH	2	NA	300	1.2	1.5
355 PRESB CH (USA)	1	340	427*	1.7	2.1
413 S.D.A.	0	10	13*	.1	.1
443 UN C OF CHRIST	1	230	289*	1.1	1.4
449 UN METHODIST	3	255	320*	1.3	1.6
469 WELS	1	66	103	.4	.5
VERNON	**71**	**10,719**	**18,103***	**70.7**	**100.0**
019 AMER BAPT USA	1	99	126*	.5	.7
053 ASSEMB OF GOD	1	35	70	.3	.4
057 BAPT GEN CONF	1	98	125*	.5	.7
081 CATHOLIC	5	NA	2,635	10.3	14.6
081d LATIN	5	NA	2,635	10.3	14.6
089 CHR & MISS AL	1	17	29	.1	.2
097 CHR CHS&CHS CR	3	485	619*	2.4	3.4
151 L-D SAINTS	1	NA	80	.3	.4
163 CH OF LUTH BR	2	122	208	.8	1.1
164 CH LUTH CONF	1	30	32	.1	.2
165 CH OF NAZARENE	1	38	56	.2	.3
181 CONSRV CONGR	1	469	599*	2.3	3.3
207 E.L.C.A.	22	6,406	8,117	31.7	44.8
221 FREE METHODIST	1	51	51	.2	.3
323 OLD ORD AMISH	10	NA	1,400	5.5	7.7
353 CHR BRETHREN	1	38	65	.3	.4
449 UN METHODIST	10	1,374	1,755*	6.9	9.7
467 WESLEYAN	3	142	447	1.7	2.5
469 WELS	6	1,315	1,689	6.6	9.3
VILAS	**31**	**2,947**	**13,149***	**74.3**	**100.0**
053 ASSEMB OF GOD	1	48	84	.5	.6
081 CATHOLIC	8	NA	9,207	52.0	70.0
081d LATIN	8	NA	9,207	52.0	70.0
111 CH CR,SCIENTST	1	NR	NR	-	-
151 L-D SAINTS	1	NA	227	1.3	1.7
165 CH OF NAZARENE	2	20	31	.2	.2
203 EVAN FREE CH	2	150	245	1.4	1.9
207 E.L.C.A.	3	454	554	3.1	4.2
259 IFCA	1	NR	NR	-	-
283 LUTH—MO SYNOD	3	734	887	5.0	6.7
355 PRESB CH (USA)	2	224	271*	1.5	2.1
413 S.D.A.	1	96	116*	.7	.9
443 UN C OF CHRIST	4	722	875*	4.9	6.7
469 WELS	2	499	652	3.7	5.0
WALWORTH	**84**	**14,922**	**34,933***	**46.6**	**100.0**
019 AMER BAPT USA	7	1,198	1,480*	2.0	4.2
053 ASSEMB OF GOD	3	137	335	.4	1.0
057 BAPT GEN CONF	2	101	125*	.2	.4
081 CATHOLIC	10	NA	15,099	20.1	43.2
081d LATIN	10	NA	15,099	20.1	43.2
105 CHRISTIAN REF	1	280	462	.6	1.3
111 CH CR,SCIENTST	2	NR	NR	-	-
151 L-D SAINTS	1	NA	224	.3	.6
167 CHS OF CHRIST	2	63	83	.1	.2
193 EPISCOPAL	4	404	565	.8	1.6
203 EVAN FREE CH	3	124	253	.3	.7
207 E.L.C.A.	9	3,370	4,410	5.9	12.6
259 IFCA	2	NR	NR	-	-
283 LUTH—MO SYNOD	4	1,904	2,571	3.4	7.4
353 CHR BRETHREN	1	25	50	.1	.1
355 PRESB CH (USA)	1	222	274*	.4	.8
371 REF CH IN AM	1	118	240	.3	.7
413 S.D.A.	1	52	64*	.1	.2
415 S-D BAPTIST GC	1	5	6*	-	-
435 UNITARIAN-UNIV	1	21	21	-	.1
443 UN C OF CHRIST	9	2,367	2,924*	3.9	8.4
449 UN METHODIST	14	2,652	3,276*	4.4	9.4
469 WELS	5	1,879	2,471	3.3	7.1
WASHBURN	**33**	**3,126**	**6,685***	**48.5**	**100.0**
053 ASSEMB OF GOD	1	34	80	.6	1.2
081 CATHOLIC	7	NA	2,404	17.5	36.0
081d LATIN	7	NA	2,404	17.5	36.0
089 CHR & MISS AL	1	32	57	.4	.9
151 L-D SAINTS	1	NA	68	.5	1.0
165 CH OF NAZARENE	2	95	238	1.7	3.6
193 EPISCOPAL	3	124	152	1.1	2.3

County and Denomination	Number of churches	Communicant, confirmed, full members	Total adherents Number	Percent of total population	Percent of total adherents
207 E.L.C.A.	5	1,379	1,800	13.1	26.9
283 LUTH—MO SYNOD	2	420	553	4.0	8.3
355 PRESB CH (USA)	1	20	25*	.2	.4
413 S.D.A.	1	11	14*	.1	.2
419 SO BAPT CONV	1	19	24*	.2	.4
443 UN C OF CHRIST	1	54	68*	.5	1.0
449 UN METHODIST	4	710	895*	6.5	13.4
467 WESLEYAN	3	228	307	2.2	4.6
WASHINGTON	**76**	**19,788**	**61,749***	**64.8**	**100.0**
053 ASSEMB OF GOD	2	358	754	.8	1.2
057 BAPT GEN CONF	1	32	41*	-	.1
081 CATHOLIC	20	NA	32,872	34.5	53.2
081d LATIN	20	NA	32,872	34.5	53.2
089 CHR & MISS AL	1	143	264	.3	.4
111 CH CR,SCIENTST	2	NR	NR	-	-
151 L-D SAINTS	1	NA	444	.5	.7
165 CH OF NAZARENE	1	21	36	-	.1
167 CHS OF CHRIST	1	23	30	-	-
175 CONGR CHR CHS	1	124	160*	.2	.3
193 EPISCOPAL	2	277	393	.4	.6
207 E.L.C.A.	8	4,407	5,849	6.1	9.5
209 EVAN LUTH SYN	1	271	369	.4	.6
259 IFCA	1	NR	NR	-	-
283 LUTH—MO SYNOD	4	3,409	4,531	4.8	7.3
355 PRESB CH (USA)	2	139	179*	.2	.3
371 REF CH IN AM	1	38	74	.1	.1
443 UN C OF CHRIST	14	3,015	3,885*	4.1	6.3
449 UN METHODIST	3	1,840	2,371*	2.5	3.8
469 WELS	10	5,691	7,633	8.0	12.4
496 JEWISH EST[1]	0	NA	1,864	2.0	3.0
WAUKESHA	**190**	**59,925**	**194,696***	**63.9**	**100.0**
019 AMER BAPT USA	5	720	913*	.3	.5
053 ASSEMB OF GOD	2	1,401	2,450	.8	1.3
081 CATHOLIC	31	NA	98,501	32.3	50.6
081d LATIN	31	NA	98,501	32.3	50.6
089 CHR & MISS AL	3	238	594	.2	.3
093 CHR CH (DISC)	1	59	65	-	-
105 CHRISTIAN REF	1	230	374	.1	.2
111 CH CR,SCIENTST	4	NR	NR	-	-
127 CH GOD (CLEVE)	1	36	46*	-	-
151 L-D SAINTS	3	NA	1,432	.5	.7
165 CH OF NAZARENE	3	241	357	.1	.2
167 CHS OF CHRIST	2	64	109	-	.1
175 CONGR CHR CHS	2	448	568*	.2	.3
193 EPISCOPAL	11	1,581	2,229	.7	1.1
203 EVAN FREE CH	3	297	527	.2	.3
207 E.L.C.A.	30	17,622	24,588	8.1	12.6
209 EVAN LUTH SYN	1	405	518	.2	.3
221 FREE METHODIST	1	111	111	-	.1
259 IFCA	2	NR	NR	-	-
283 LUTH—MO SYNOD	15	11,044	14,160	4.6	7.3
285 MENNONITE CH	1	37	67	-	-
313 N AM BAPT CONF	2	601	762*	.3	.4
355 PRESB CH (USA)	12	2,813	3,568*	1.2	1.8
371 REF CH IN AM	1	147	242	.1	.1
403 SALVATION ARMY	1	54	56	-	-
413 S.D.A.	1	117	148*	-	.1
419 SO BAPT CONV	2	225	285*	.1	.1
435 UNITARIAN-UNIV	2	413	635	.2	.3
443 UN C OF CHRIST	12	4,582	5,812*	1.9	3.0
449 UN METHODIST	14	5,511	6,991*	2.3	3.6
467 WESLEYAN	1	108	182	.1	.1
469 WELS	16	10,530	13,981	4.6	7.2
496 JEWISH EST[1]	1	NA	5,957	2.0	3.1
497 BLACK BAPT EST[1]	NA	290	368*	.1	.2
499 INDEP.NON-CHAR[3]	3	NA	8,100	2.7	4.2
WAUPACA	**70**	**20,911**	**36,997***	**80.2**	**100.0**
053 ASSEMB OF GOD	3	307	599	1.3	1.6
081 CATHOLIC	8	NA	9,263	20.1	25.0
081d LATIN	8	NA	9,263	20.1	25.0
097 CHR CHS&CHS CR	1	40	51*	.1	.1
111 CH CR,SCIENTST	1	NR	NR	-	-
123 CH GOD (ANDER)	1	14	14	-	-
127 CH GOD (CLEVE)	1	19	24*	.1	.1
165 CH OF NAZARENE	1	32	111	.2	.3
167 CHS OF CHRIST	4	182	236	.5	.6
193 EPISCOPAL	2	102	141	.3	.4
203 EVAN FREE CH	2	187	424	.9	1.1
207 E.L.C.A.	15	7,638	10,175	22.1	27.5
209 EVAN LUTH SYN	2	167	254	.6	.7
283 LUTH—MO SYNOD	10	4,453	5,658	12.3	15.3
355 PRESB CH (USA)	1	216	274*	.6	.7
413 S.D.A.	1	3	4*	-	-

NA–Not applicable   NR–Not reported   *Total adherents estimated from known number of communicant, confirmed, full members.   - Represents a percent less than 0.1.   Percentages may not total due to rounding.
[1]See Appendix E   [2]See Appendix F   [3]See Appendix G   Lines in *italic* represent a breakdown of Catholic rites or Friends affiliations. They are included in their respective denominational total.

Table 4. Churches and Church Membership by County and Denomination: 1990

County and Denomination	Number of churches	Communicant, confirmed, full members	Total adherents Number	Percent of total population	Percent of total adherents
419 SO BAPT CONV	1	23	29*	.1	.1
443 UN C OF CHRIST	3	539	683*	1.5	1.8
449 UN METHODIST	8	1,883	2,386*	5.2	6.4
469 WELS	5	5,106	6,671	14.5	18.0
WAUSHARA	**43**	**6,194**	**11,959***	**61.7**	**100.0**
019 AMER BAPT USA	2	115	143*	.7	1.2
053 ASSEMB OF GOD	2	176	295	1.5	2.5
081 CATHOLIC	4	NA	3,235	16.7	27.1
081d LATIN	4	NA	3,235	16.7	27.1
175 CONGR CHR CHS	1	75	93*	.5	.8
203 EVAN FREE CH	1	15	45	.2	.4
207 E.L.C.A.	7	2,051	2,746	14.2	23.0
283 LUTH—MO SYNOD	8	1,504	1,907	9.8	15.9
323 OLD ORD AMISH	2	NA	300	1.5	2.5
355 PRESB CH (USA)	1	89	111*	.6	.9
413 S.D.A.	2	49	61*	.3	.5
443 UN C OF CHRIST	2	161	200*	1.0	1.7
449 UN METHODIST	7	1,255	1,560*	8.0	13.0
467 WESLEYAN	2	205	645	3.3	5.4
469 WELS	2	499	618	3.2	5.2
WINNEBAGO	**102**	**36,524**	**89,787***	**64.0**	**100.0**
019 AMER BAPT USA	3	235	291*	.2	.3
053 ASSEMB OF GOD	2	301	675	.5	.8
057 BAPT GEN CONF	1	97	120*	.1	.1
081 CATHOLIC	14	NA	39,842	28.4	44.4
081d LATIN	14	NA	39,842	28.4	44.4
089 CHR & MISS AL	1	88	88	.1	.1
097 CHR CHS&CHS CR	1	79	98*	.1	.1
111 CH CR,SCIENTST	1	NR	NR	-	-
127 CH GOD (CLEVE)	2	76	94*	.1	.1
165 CH OF NAZARENE	1	0	43	-	-
167 CHS OF CHRIST	2	103	131	.1	.1
175 CONGR CHR CHS	1	509	631*	.4	.7
181 CONSRV CONGR	1	356	441*	.3	.5
193 EPISCOPAL	2	1,175	1,577	1.1	1.8
207 E.L.C.A.	18	13,975	18,983	13.5	21.1
226 FRIENDS-USA	1	12	25	-	-
226c FGC	1	12	25	-	-
263 INT FOURSQ GOS	1	0	0*	-	-
283 LUTH—MO SYNOD	7	3,595	4,675	3.3	5.2
339 PENT CH OF GOD	3	103	231	.2	.3
355 PRESB CH (USA)	5	1,888	2,340*	1.7	2.6
403 SALVATION ARMY	1	81	87	.1	.1
413 S.D.A.	1	37	46*	-	.1
443 UN C OF CHRIST	7	2,388	2,960*	2.1	3.3
449 UN METHODIST	8	3,419	4,237*	3.0	4.7
469 WELS	15	7,823	10,194	7.3	11.4
496 JEWISH EST[1]	1	NA	150	.1	.2
497 BLACK BAPT EST[1]	NA	184	228*	.2	.3
499 INDEP.NON-CHAR[3]	2	NA	1,600	1.1	1.8
WOOD	**88**	**19,477**	**54,175***	**73.6**	**100.0**
019 AMER BAPT USA	1	160	206*	.3	.4
053 ASSEMB OF GOD	3	456	1,028	1.4	1.9
057 BAPT GEN CONF	1	47	60*	.1	.1
081 CATHOLIC	21	NA	27,310	37.1	50.4
081d LATIN	21	NA	27,310	37.1	50.4
089 CHR & MISS AL	1	72	242	.3	.4
105 CHRISTIAN REF	1	85	129	.2	.2
111 CH CR,SCIENTST	2	NR	NR	-	-
145 CH GOD PROPHCY	1	24	31*	-	.1
151 L-D SAINTS	2	NA	348	.5	.6
165 CH OF NAZARENE	1	34	41	.1	.1
167 CHS OF CHRIST	3	93	145	.2	.3
193 EPISCOPAL	2	367	468	.6	.9
203 EVAN FREE CH	2	229	395	.5	.7
207 E.L.C.A.	6	2,711	3,678	5.0	6.8
259 IFCA	1	NR	NR	-	-
283 LUTH—MO SYNOD	13	8,423	10,963	14.9	20.2
293 MORAV CH-NORTH	5	868	1,105	1.5	2.0
339 PENT CH OF GOD	1	35	77	.1	.1
355 PRESB CH (USA)	2	675	867*	1.2	1.6
371 REF CH IN AM	1	213	379	.5	.7
413 S.D.A.	3	312	401*	.5	.7
435 UNITARIAN-UNIV	1	13	29	-	.1
443 UN C OF CHRIST	6	1,323	1,700*	2.3	3.1
449 UN METHODIST	4	1,668	2,143*	2.9	4.0
467 WESLEYAN	1	52	250	.3	.5
469 WELS	3	1,617	2,180	3.0	4.0

WYOMING

County and Denomination	Number of churches	Communicant, confirmed, full members	Total adherents Number	Percent of total population	Percent of total adherents
THE STATE.....	766	74,414	216,375*	47.7	100.0
ALBANY	**34**	**4,000**	**9,843***	**32.0**	**100.0**
019 AMER BAPT USA	1	359	434*	1.4	4.4
053 ASSEMB OF GOD	3	127	255	.8	2.6
081 CATHOLIC	3	NA	2,987	9.7	30.3
081d LATIN	3	NA	2,987	9.7	30.3
093 CHR CH (DISC)	1	271	316	1.0	3.2
151 L-D SAINTS	4	NA	1,639	5.3	16.7
165 CH OF NAZARENE	1	77	136	.4	1.4
167 CHS OF CHRIST	1	129	167	.5	1.7
179 CONSRV BAPT	1	NR	NR	-	-
193 EPISCOPAL	2	230	420	1.4	4.3
203 EVAN FREE CH	1	28	28	.1	.3
207 E.L.C.A.	1	402	521	1.7	5.3
226 FRIENDS-USA	1	12	14*	-	.1
226f INDEPENDNT	1	12	14*	-	.1
263 INT FOURSQ GOS	1	97	117*	.4	1.2
283 LUTH—MO SYNOD	2	251	316	1.0	3.2
353 CHR BRETHREN	1	25	25	.1	.3
355 PRESB CH (USA)	2	592	715*	2.3	7.3
413 S.D.A.	1	114	138*	.4	1.4
419 SO BAPT CONV	3	629	760*	2.5	7.7
435 UNITARIAN-UNIV	1	58	67	.2	.7
443 UN C OF CHRIST	1	149	180*	.6	1.8
449 UN METHODIST	1	437	528*	1.7	5.4
467 WESLEYAN	1	13	80	.3	.8
BIG HORN	**34**	**1,371**	**6,180***	**58.7**	**100.0**
019 AMER BAPT USA	2	88	115*	1.1	1.9
053 ASSEMB OF GOD	2	62	141	1.3	2.3
081 CATHOLIC	3	NA	893	8.5	14.4
081d LATIN	3	NA	893	8.5	14.4
089 CHR & MISS AL	2	47	144	1.4	2.3
111 CH CR,SCIENTST	1	NR	NR	-	-
145 CH GOD PROPHCY	1	18	24*	.2	.4
151 L-D SAINTS	10	NA	3,276	31.1	53.0
165 CH OF NAZARENE	1	6	21	.2	.3
193 EPISCOPAL	1	62	110	1.0	1.8
283 LUTH—MO SYNOD	3	585	799	7.6	12.9
355 PRESB CH (USA)	2	88	115*	1.1	1.9
413 S.D.A.	1	51	67*	.6	1.1
419 SO BAPT CONV	1	158	206*	2.0	3.3
449 UN METHODIST	4	206	269*	2.6	4.4
CAMPBELL	**32**	**4,914**	**17,698***	**60.3**	**100.0**
019 AMER BAPT USA	1	208	292*	1.0	1.6
053 ASSEMB OF GOD	3	223	427	1.5	2.4
081 CATHOLIC	2	NA	5,058	17.2	28.6
081d LATIN	2	NA	5,058	17.2	28.6
089 CHR & MISS AL	1	42	162	.6	.9
097 CHR CHS&CHS CR	1	250	350*	1.2	2.0
145 CH GOD PROPHCY	1	18	25*	.1	.1
151 L-D SAINTS	3	NA	1,129	3.8	6.4
165 CH OF NAZARENE	1	52	149	.5	.8
167 CHS OF CHRIST	2	118	189	.6	1.1
193 EPISCOPAL	2	249	309	1.1	1.7
207 E.L.C.A.	1	386	686	2.3	3.9
226 FRIENDS-USA	1	1	4	-	-
226f INDEPENDNT	1	1	4	-	-
263 INT FOURSQ GOS	1	177	248*	.8	1.4
283 LUTH—MO SYNOD	2	716	1,108	3.8	6.3
313 N AM BAPT CONF	1	71	100*	.3	.6
329 OPEN BIBLE STD	1	NR	NR	-	-
355 PRESB CH (USA)	1	676	948*	3.2	5.4
413 S.D.A.	1	41	57*	.2	.3
419 SO BAPT CONV	3	1,231	1,726*	5.9	9.8
449 UN METHODIST	1	221	310*	1.1	1.8
467 WESLEYAN	1	151	4,284	14.6	24.2
469 WELS	1	83	137	.5	.8
CARBON	**44**	**2,451**	**7,216***	**43.3**	**100.0**
019 AMER BAPT USA	1	194	253*	1.5	3.5
053 ASSEMB OF GOD	4	146	299	1.8	4.1
081 CATHOLIC	5	NA	2,459	14.8	34.1
081d LATIN	5	NA	2,459	14.8	34.1
089 CHR & MISS AL	1	11	27	.2	.4
151 L-D SAINTS	6	NA	1,065	6.4	14.8
165 CH OF NAZARENE	1	38	174	1.0	2.4
167 CHS OF CHRIST	3	65	79	.5	1.1
193 EPISCOPAL	6	241	524	3.1	7.3
283 LUTH—MO SYNOD	3	232	353	2.1	4.9
355 PRESB CH (USA)	3	397	517*	3.1	7.2

NA–Not applicable   NR–Not reported   *Total adherents estimated from known number of communicant, confirmed, full members.   - Represents a percent less than 0.1.   Percentages may not total due to rounding.
[1]See Appendix E   [2]See Appendix F   [3]See Appendix G   Lines in *italic* represent a breakdown of Catholic rites or Friends affiliations. They are included in their respective denominational total.

Table 4. Churches and Church Membership by County and Denomination: 1990

County and Denomination	Number of churches	Communicant, confirmed, full members	Total adherents		
			Number	Percent of total population	Percent of total adherents
413 S.D.A.	1	47	61*	.4	.8
419 SO BAPT CONV	7	691	899*	5.4	12.5
449 UN METHODIST	3	389	506*	3.0	7.0
CONVERSE	**25**	**1,593**	**4,017***	**36.1**	**100.0**
019 AMER BAPT USA	2	305	409*	3.7	10.2
053 ASSEMB OF GOD	2	94	188	1.7	4.7
081 CATHOLIC	4	NA	1,250	11.2	31.1
081d LATIN	*4*	*NA*	*1,250*	*11.2*	*31.1*
097 CHR CHS&CHS CR	1	35	47*	.4	1.2
151 L-D SAINTS	2	NA	383	3.4	9.5
167 CHS OF CHRIST	2	56	72	.6	1.8
179 CONSRV BAPT	1	NR	NR	-	-
193 EPISCOPAL	3	166	243	2.2	6.0
283 LUTH—MO SYNOD	2	262	352	3.2	8.8
413 S.D.A.	1	32	43*	.4	1.1
419 SO BAPT CONV	2	172	231*	2.1	5.8
443 UN C OF CHRIST	1	222	298*	2.7	7.4
449 UN METHODIST	1	224	301*	2.7	7.5
467 WESLEYAN	1	25	200	1.8	5.0
CROOK	**15**	**986**	**1,748***	**33.0**	**100.0**
019 AMER BAPT USA	1	161	216*	4.1	12.4
053 ASSEMB OF GOD	1	70	116	2.2	6.6
081 CATHOLIC	1	NA	194	3.7	11.1
081d LATIN	*1*	*NA*	*194*	*3.7*	*11.1*
151 L-D SAINTS	2	NA	178	3.4	10.2
167 CHS OF CHRIST	1	51	67	1.3	3.8
193 EPISCOPAL	1	47	79	1.5	4.5
283 LUTH—MO SYNOD	2	167	245	4.6	14.0
355 PRESB CH (USA)	1	108	145*	2.7	8.3
413 S.D.A.	1	29	39*	.7	2.2
419 SO BAPT CONV	2	192	258*	4.9	14.8
449 UN METHODIST	1	157	211*	4.0	12.1
467 WESLEYAN	1	4	0	-	-
FREMONT	**71**	**5,258**	**15,405***	**45.8**	**100.0**
019 AMER BAPT USA	1	230	306*	.9	2.0
053 ASSEMB OF GOD	4	125	226	.7	1.5
081 CATHOLIC	10	NA	3,925	11.7	25.5
081d LATIN	*10*	*NA*	*3,925*	*11.7*	*25.5*
089 CHR & MISS AL	1	53	93	.3	.6
097 CHR CHS&CHS CR	2	145	193*	.6	1.3
111 CH CR,SCIENTST	1	NR	NR	-	-
123 CH GOD (ANDER)	1	9	25	.1	.2
151 L-D SAINTS	7	NA	2,521	7.5	16.4
165 CH OF NAZARENE	3	284	466	1.4	3.0
167 CHS OF CHRIST	3	153	199	.6	1.3
179 CONSRV BAPT	2	NR	NR	-	-
193 EPISCOPAL	8	767	2,616	7.8	17.0
203 EVAN FREE CH	1	50	50	.1	.3
207 E.L.C.A.	2	353	575	1.7	3.7
221 FREE METHODIST	2	0	55	.2	.4
226 FRIENDS-USA	1	3	7	-	-
226f INDEPENDNT	*1*	*3*	*7*	*-*	*-*
283 LUTH—MO SYNOD	5	816	1,132	3.4	7.3
329 OPEN BIBLE STD	1	NR	NR	-	-
355 PRESB CH (USA)	2	192	256*	.8	1.7
356 PRESB CH AMER	1	64	77	.2	.5
413 S.D.A.	2	106	141*	.4	.9
419 SO BAPT CONV	8	1,006	1,340*	4.0	8.7
449 UN METHODIST	3	902	1,202*	3.6	7.8
GOSHEN	**23**	**2,899**	**5,407***	**43.7**	**100.0**
019 AMER BAPT USA	1	279	356*	2.9	6.6
053 ASSEMB OF GOD	3	88	125	1.0	2.3
057 BAPT GEN CONF	2	312	398*	3.2	7.4
063 BEREAN FUND CH	1	48	65	.5	1.2
081 CATHOLIC	1	NA	1,376	11.1	25.4
081d LATIN	*1*	*NA*	*1,376*	*11.1*	*25.4*
097 CHR CHS&CHS CR	3	143	183*	1.5	3.4
151 L-D SAINTS	1	NA	190	1.5	3.5
165 CH OF NAZARENE	1	20	60	.5	1.1
193 EPISCOPAL	1	156	282	2.3	5.2
223 FREE WILL BAPT	1	23	29*	.2	.5
283 LUTH—MO SYNOD	1	384	497	4.0	9.2
355 PRESB CH (USA)	3	615	785*	6.3	14.5
413 S.D.A.	1	72	92*	.7	1.7
419 SO BAPT CONV	1	55	70*	.6	1.3
443 UN C OF CHRIST	1	248	317*	2.6	5.9
449 UN METHODIST	1	456	582*	4.7	10.8
HOT SPRINGS	**12**	**666**	**1,572***	**32.7**	**100.0**
053 ASSEMB OF GOD	1	43	91	1.9	5.8
081 CATHOLIC	1	NA	331	6.9	21.1

County and Denomination	Number of churches	Communicant, confirmed, full members	Total adherents		
			Number	Percent of total population	Percent of total adherents
081d LATIN	*1*	*NA*	*331*	*6.9*	*21.1*
145 CH GOD PROPHCY	1	18	22*	.5	1.4
151 L-D SAINTS	1	NA	327	6.8	20.8
167 CHS OF CHRIST	1	20	26	.5	1.7
193 EPISCOPAL	1	102	150	3.1	9.5
263 INT FOURSQ GOS	1	41	51*	1.1	3.2
283 LUTH—MO SYNOD	1	89	137	2.8	8.7
355 PRESB CH (USA)	1	88	109*	2.3	6.9
413 S.D.A.	1	9	11*	.2	.7
419 SO BAPT CONV	1	126	156*	3.2	9.9
449 UN METHODIST	1	130	161*	3.3	10.2
JOHNSON	**17**	**1,201**	**2,893***	**47.1**	**100.0**
053 ASSEMB OF GOD	1	28	31	.5	1.1
081 CATHOLIC	3	NA	1,007	16.4	34.8
081d LATIN	*3*	*NA*	*1,007*	*16.4*	*34.8*
145 CH GOD PROPHCY	1	18	23*	.4	.8
151 L-D SAINTS	1	NA	195	3.2	6.7
167 CHS OF CHRIST	1	28	38	.6	1.3
193 EPISCOPAL	1	207	304	4.9	10.5
207 E.L.C.A.	1	222	311	5.1	10.8
263 INT FOURSQ GOS	1	43	54*	.9	1.9
283 LUTH—MO SYNOD	1	90	120	2.0	4.1
413 S.D.A.	1	37	47*	.8	1.6
419 SO BAPT CONV	1	158	199*	3.2	6.9
443 UN C OF CHRIST	1	123	155*	2.5	5.4
449 UN METHODIST	2	138	174*	2.8	6.0
467 WESLEYAN	1	109	235	3.8	8.1
LARAMIE	**79**	**14,494**	**35,849***	**49.0**	**100.0**
019 AMER BAPT USA	3	2,096	2,693*	3.7	7.5
053 ASSEMB OF GOD	5	343	541	.7	1.5
057 BAPT GEN CONF	2	267	343*	.5	1.0
063 BEREAN FUND CH	1	90	250	.3	.7
071 BRETHREN (ASH)	1	73	94*	.1	.3
081 CATHOLIC	5	NA	12,692	17.4	35.4
081d LATIN	*5*	*NA*	*12,692*	*17.4*	*35.4*
089 CHR & MISS AL	1	96	296	.4	.8
093 CHR CH (DISC)	1	593	800	1.1	2.2
097 CHR CHS&CHS CR	1	300	385*	.5	1.1
111 CH CR,SCIENTST	1	NR	NR	-	-
127 CH GOD (CLEVE)	1	55	71*	.1	.2
145 CH GOD PROPHCY	1	18	23*	-	.1
151 L-D SAINTS	7	NA	2,648	3.6	7.4
164 CH LUTH CONF	1	73	105	.1	.3
165 CH OF NAZARENE	2	129	285	.4	.8
167 CHS OF CHRIST	1	112	200	.3	.6
175 CONGR CHR CHS	1	850	1,092*	1.5	3.0
179 CONSRV BAPT	1	NR	NR	-	-
193 EPISCOPAL	2	432	502	.7	1.4
203 EVAN FREE CH	1	44	124	.2	.3
207 E.L.C.A.	3	1,378	1,850	2.5	5.2
221 FREE METHODIST	1	4	6	-	-
223 FREE WILL BAPT	1	44	57*	.1	.2
226 FRIENDS-USA	1	3	4*	-	-
226f INDEPENDNT	*1*	*3*	*4**	*-*	*-*
246 GREEK ORTHODOX	2	NR	NR	-	-
263 INT FOURSQ GOS	1	74	95*	.1	.3
283 LUTH—MO SYNOD	5	1,326	1,839	2.5	5.1
329 OPEN BIBLE STD	1	NR	NR	-	-
355 PRESB CH (USA)	3	959	1,232*	1.7	3.4
403 SALVATION ARMY	2	47	50	.1	.1
413 S.D.A.	1	203	261*	.4	.7
419 SO BAPT CONV	5	2,148	2,760*	3.8	7.7
435 UNITARIAN-UNIV	1	44	60	.1	.2
443 UN C OF CHRIST	1	139	179*	.2	.5
449 UN METHODIST	7	1,993	2,561*	3.5	7.1
467 WESLEYAN	1	0	0	-	-
469 WELS	1	88	138	.2	.4
496 JEWISH EST[1]	1	NA	230	.3	.6
497 BLACK BAPT EST[1]	NA	473	608*	.8	1.7
499 INDEP.NON-CHAR[3]	2	NA	775	1.1	2.2
LINCOLN	**33**	**513**	**10,534***	**83.4**	**100.0**
053 ASSEMB OF GOD	1	28	37	.3	.4
081 CATHOLIC	3	NA	1,706	13.5	16.2
081d LATIN	*3*	*NA*	*1,706*	*13.5*	*16.2*
151 L-D SAINTS	20	NA	8,035	63.6	76.3
193 EPISCOPAL	2	52	134	1.1	1.3
203 EVAN FREE CH	1	19	25	.2	.2
263 INT FOURSQ GOS	1	28	40*	.3	.4
283 LUTH—MO SYNOD	1	128	188	1.5	1.8
413 S.D.A.	1	11	16*	.1	.2
419 SO BAPT CONV	2	152	217*	1.7	2.1
449 UN METHODIST	1	95	136*	1.1	1.3

NA–Not applicable   NR–Not reported   *Total adherents estimated from known number of communicant, confirmed, full members.   - Represents a percent less than 0.1.   Percentages may not total due to rounding.
[1]See Appendix E   [2]See Appendix F   [3]See Appendix G   Lines in *italic* represent a breakdown of Catholic rites or Friends affiliations. They are included in their respective denominational total.

Table 4. Churches and Church Membership by County and Denomination: 1990

County and Denomination	Number of churches	Communicant, confirmed, full members	Total adherents Number	Percent of total population	Percent of total adherents
NATRONA	**66**	**12,420**	**27,941***	**45.6**	**100.0**
019 AMER BAPT USA	2	367	478*	.8	1.7
053 ASSEMB OF GOD	3	337	629	1.0	2.3
081 CATHOLIC	5	NA	8,280	13.5	29.6
081d LATIN	5	NA	8,280	13.5	29.6
089 CHR & MISS AL	1	16	45	.1	.2
093 CHR CH (DISC)	1	493	526	.9	1.9
097 CHR CHS&CHS CR	4	475	619*	1.0	2.2
111 CH CR,SCIENTST	1	NR	NR	-	-
123 CH GOD (ANDER)	1	600	600	1.0	2.1
145 CH GOD PROPHCY	1	18	23*	-	.1
151 L-D SAINTS	6	NA	2,967	4.8	10.6
165 CH OF NAZARENE	1	174	368	.6	1.3
167 CHS OF CHRIST	3	256	349	.6	1.2
179 CONSRV BAPT	1	NR	NR	-	-
193 EPISCOPAL	3	636	913	1.5	3.3
203 EVAN FREE CH	1	59	129	.2	.5
207 E.L.C.A.	4	1,442	2,104	3.4	7.5
226 FRIENDS-USA	1	2	3*	-	-
226f INDEPENDNT	1	2	3*	-	-
246 GREEK ORTHODOX	1	NR	NR	-	-
263 INT FOURSQ GOS	1	44	57*	.1	.2
283 LUTH—MO SYNOD	2	809	1,101	1.8	3.9
329 OPEN BIBLE STD	2	NR	NR	-	-
355 PRESB CH (USA)	3	990	1,290*	2.1	4.6
403 SALVATION ARMY	1	38	39	.1	.1
413 S.D.A.	1	208	271*	.4	1.0
419 SO BAPT CONV	8	3,312	4,316*	7.0	15.4
435 UNITARIAN-UNIV	1	12	12	-	-
443 UN C OF CHRIST	1	103	134*	.2	.5
449 UN METHODIST	3	1,926	2,510*	4.1	9.0
467 WESLEYAN	1	54	0	-	-
469 WELS	1	49	78	.1	.3
496 JEWISH EST[1]	1	NA	100	.2	.4
NIOBRARA	**11**	**722**	**1,323***	**52.9**	**100.0**
019 AMER BAPT USA	1	251	307*	12.3	23.2
081 CATHOLIC	1	NA	262	10.5	19.8
081d LATIN	1	NA	262	10.5	19.8
089 CHR & MISS AL	2	30	113	4.5	8.5
097 CHR CHS&CHS CR	1	30	37*	1.5	2.8
145 CH GOD PROPHCY	1	18	22*	.9	1.7
151 L-D SAINTS	1	NA	61	2.4	4.6
193 EPISCOPAL	1	36	60	2.4	4.5
283 LUTH—MO SYNOD	1	135	190	7.6	14.4
419 SO BAPT CONV	1	23	28*	1.1	2.1
443 UN C OF CHRIST	1	199	243*	9.7	18.4
PARK	**45**	**4,372**	**9,878***	**42.6**	**100.0**
053 ASSEMB OF GOD	3	153	283	1.2	2.9
081 CATHOLIC	4	NA	1,091	4.7	11.0
081d LATIN	4	NA	1,091	4.7	11.0
089 CHR & MISS AL	1	23	91	.4	.9
097 CHR CHS&CHS CR	1	76	98*	.4	1.0
111 CH CR,SCIENTST	1	NR	NR	-	-
123 CH GOD (ANDER)	2	21	134	.6	1.4
145 CH GOD PROPHCY	2	28	36*	.2	.4
151 L-D SAINTS	7	NA	2,727	11.8	27.6
165 CH OF NAZARENE	2	71	102	.4	1.0
167 CHS OF CHRIST	2	157	207	.9	2.1
179 CONSRV BAPT	2	NR	NR	-	-
193 EPISCOPAL	3	303	496	2.1	5.0
207 E.L.C.A.	2	505	691	3.0	7.0
263 INT FOURSQ GOS	2	25	32*	.1	.3
283 LUTH—MO SYNOD	2	414	551	2.4	5.6
329 OPEN BIBLE STD	1	NR	NR	-	-
355 PRESB CH (USA)	2	1,090	1,402*	6.0	14.2
413 S.D.A.	1	49	63*	.3	.6
419 SO BAPT CONV	3	607	781*	3.4	7.9
449 UN METHODIST	2	850	1,093*	4.7	11.1
PLATTE	**24**	**1,980**	**3,723***	**45.7**	**100.0**
053 ASSEMB OF GOD	3	234	350	4.3	9.4
057 BAPT GEN CONF	1	71	91*	1.1	2.4
081 CATHOLIC	3	NA	828	10.2	22.2
081d LATIN	3	NA	828	10.2	22.2
097 CHR CHS&CHS CR	1	360	464*	5.7	12.5
111 CH CR,SCIENTST	1	NR	NR	-	-
145 CH GOD PROPHCY	1	18	23*	.3	.6
151 L-D SAINTS	1	NA	107	1.3	2.9
165 CH OF NAZARENE	1	42	121	1.5	3.3
179 CONSRV BAPT	1	NR	NR	-	-
193 EPISCOPAL	3	136	237	2.9	6.4
207 E.L.C.A.	1	206	310	3.8	8.3
283 LUTH—MO SYNOD	2	163	227	2.8	6.1
355 PRESB CH (USA)	1	98	126*	1.5	3.4

County and Denomination	Number of churches	Communicant, confirmed, full members	Total adherents Number	Percent of total population	Percent of total adherents
419 SO BAPT CONV	1	239	308*	3.8	8.3
443 UN C OF CHRIST	1	165	212*	2.6	5.7
449 UN METHODIST	2	248	319*	3.9	8.6
SHERIDAN	**31**	**3,750**	**9,278***	**39.4**	**100.0**
053 ASSEMB OF GOD	1	51	66	.3	.7
081 CATHOLIC	3	NA	2,994	12.7	32.3
081d LATIN	3	NA	2,994	12.7	32.3
089 CHR & MISS AL	1	6	13	.1	.1
093 CHR CH (DISC)	1	211	265	1.1	2.9
111 CH CR,SCIENTST	1	NR	NR	-	-
123 CH GOD (ANDER)	1	47	65	.3	.7
145 CH GOD PROPHCY	1	18	23*	.1	.2
151 L-D SAINTS	3	NA	842	3.6	9.1
165 CH OF NAZARENE	1	52	106	.4	1.1
167 CHS OF CHRIST	2	68	85	.4	.9
179 CONSRV BAPT	1	NR	NR	-	-
193 EPISCOPAL	1	655	1,043	4.4	11.2
207 E.L.C.A.	1	684	1,076	4.6	11.6
226 FRIENDS-USA	1	1	10	-	.1
226f INDEPENDNT	1	1	10	-	.1
263 INT FOURSQ GOS	1	41	52*	.2	.6
283 LUTH—MO SYNOD	1	475	642	2.7	6.9
329 OPEN BIBLE STD	1	NR	NR	-	-
355 PRESB CH (USA)	1	445	560*	2.4	6.0
403 SALVATION ARMY	1	19	20	.1	.2
413 S.D.A.	1	102	128*	.5	1.4
419 SO BAPT CONV	3	251	316*	1.3	3.4
443 UN C OF CHRIST	1	139	175*	.7	1.9
449 UN METHODIST	1	427	537*	2.3	5.8
467 WESLEYAN	1	58	260	1.1	2.8
SUBLETTE	**14**	**502**	**1,896***	**39.1**	**100.0**
053 ASSEMB OF GOD	1	23	30	.6	1.6
081 CATHOLIC	3	NA	562	11.6	29.6
081d LATIN	3	NA	562	11.6	29.6
151 L-D SAINTS	2	NA	579	12.0	30.5
167 CHS OF CHRIST	1	19	24	.5	1.3
175 CONGR CHR CHS	1	80	103*	2.1	5.4
193 EPISCOPAL	2	95	189	3.9	10.0
283 LUTH—MO SYNOD	2	119	196	4.0	10.3
419 SO BAPT CONV	1	70	90*	1.9	4.7
443 UN C OF CHRIST	1	96	123*	2.5	6.5
SWEETWATER	**59**	**4,410**	**21,410***	**55.1**	**100.0**
019 AMER BAPT USA	2	151	207*	.5	1.0
053 ASSEMB OF GOD	3	213	596	1.5	2.8
081 CATHOLIC	5	NA	8,307	21.4	38.8
081d LATIN	5	NA	8,307	21.4	38.8
089 CHR & MISS AL	2	46	157	.4	.7
097 CHR CHS&CHS CR	1	60	82*	.2	.4
111 CH CR,SCIENTST	1	NR	NR	-	-
127 CH GOD (CLEVE)	1	14	19*	-	.1
151 L-D SAINTS	17	NA	6,339	16.3	29.6
165 CH OF NAZARENE	2	72	175	.5	.8
167 CHS OF CHRIST	4	172	222	.6	1.0
179 CONSRV BAPT	1	NR	NR	-	-
193 EPISCOPAL	2	311	607	1.6	2.8
203 EVAN FREE CH	1	100	140	.4	.7
207 E.L.C.A.	1	249	373	1.0	1.7
246 GREEK ORTHODOX	1	NR	NR	-	-
283 LUTH—MO SYNOD	2	410	604	1.6	2.8
355 PRESB CH (USA)	1	74	101*	.3	.5
373 REF CH IN U.S.	1	20	35	.1	.2
413 S.D.A.	1	79	108*	.3	.5
419 SO BAPT CONV	7	1,576	2,157*	5.6	10.1
443 UN C OF CHRIST	2	606	829*	2.1	3.9
449 UN METHODIST	1	257	352*	.9	1.6
TETON	**14**	**769**	**2,847***	**25.5**	**100.0**
019 AMER BAPT USA	1	349	435*	3.9	15.3
053 ASSEMB OF GOD	1	25	45	.4	1.6
081 CATHOLIC	3	NA	581	5.2	20.4
081d LATIN	3	NA	581	5.2	20.4
151 L-D SAINTS	3	NA	1,235	11.1	43.4
167 CHS OF CHRIST	1	33	42	.4	1.5
193 EPISCOPAL	1	138	211	1.9	7.4
226 FRIENDS-USA	1	3	20	.2	.7
226f INDEPENDNT	1	3	20	.2	.7
283 LUTH—MO SYNOD	1	87	111	1.0	3.9
419 SO BAPT CONV	2	134	167*	1.5	5.9
UINTA	**42**	**1,603**	**11,958***	**63.9**	**100.0**
019 AMER BAPT USA	1	100	146*	.8	1.2
053 ASSEMB OF GOD	2	60	145	.8	1.2

NA–Not applicable   NR–Not reported   *Total adherents estimated from known number of communicant, confirmed, full members.   - Represents a percent less than 0.1.   Percentages may not total due to rounding.
[1] See Appendix E   [2] See Appendix F   [3] See Appendix G   Lines in italic represent a breakdown of Catholic rites or Friends affiliations. They are included in their respective denominational total.

Table 4. Churches and Church Membership by County and Denomination: 1990

County and Denomination	Number of churches	Communicant, confirmed, full members	Total adherents		
			Number	Percent of total population	Percent of total adherents
081 CATHOLIC	2	NA	1,026	5.5	8.6
081d LATIN	*2*	*NA*	*1,026*	*5.5*	*8.6*
089 CHR & MISS AL	2	80	295	1.6	2.5
151 L-D SAINTS	20	NA	8,301	44.4	69.4
165 CH OF NAZARENE	1	38	107	.6	.9
167 CHS OF CHRIST	2	28	36	.2	.3
193 EPISCOPAL	2	126	152	.8	1.3
207 E.L.C.A.	1	0	0	-	-
263 INT FOURSQ GOS	1	22	32*	.2	.3
283 LUTH—MO SYNOD	2	154	266	1.4	2.2
355 PRESB CH (USA)	2	205	299*	1.6	2.5
413 S.D.A.	1	30	44*	.2	.4
419 SO BAPT CONV	3	760	1,109*	5.9	9.3
WASHAKIE	**22**	**2,027**	**4,776***	**56.9**	**100.0**
019 AMER BAPT USA	1	255	330*	3.9	6.9
053 ASSEMB OF GOD	1	134	300	3.6	6.3
081 CATHOLIC	1	NA	992	11.8	20.8
081d LATIN	*1*	*NA*	*992*	*11.8*	*20.8*
111 CH CR,SCIENTST	1	NR	NR	-	-
123 CH GOD (ANDER)	1	99	136	1.6	2.8
145 CH GOD PROPHCY	1	18	23*	.3	.5
151 L-D SAINTS	3	NA	878	10.5	18.4
165 CH OF NAZARENE	1	20	14	.2	.3
167 CHS OF CHRIST	1	77	115	1.4	2.4
193 EPISCOPAL	1	131	240	2.9	5.0
207 E.L.C.A.	1	184	273	3.3	5.7
246 GREEK ORTHODOX	1	NR	NR	-	-
283 LUTH—MO SYNOD	1	170	254	3.0	5.3
287 MENN GEN CONF	1	17	27	.3	.6
355 PRESB CH (USA)	1	115	149*	1.8	3.1
413 S.D.A.	2	82	106*	1.3	2.2
419 SO BAPT CONV	1	288	373*	4.4	7.8
449 UN METHODIST	2	437	566*	6.7	11.9
WESTON	**19**	**1,513**	**2,983***	**45.8**	**100.0**
053 ASSEMB OF GOD	4	183	291	4.5	9.8
057 BAPT GEN CONF	1	79	103*	1.6	3.5
081 CATHOLIC	3	NA	764	11.7	25.6
081d LATIN	*3*	*NA*	*764*	*11.7*	*25.6*
097 CHR CHS&CHS CR	1	36	47*	.7	1.6
151 L-D SAINTS	1	NA	171	2.6	5.7
167 CHS OF CHRIST	1	33	42	.6	1.4
193 EPISCOPAL	1	39	73	1.1	2.4
207 E.L.C.A.	1	246	318	4.9	10.7
263 INT FOURSQ GOS	1	44	58*	.9	1.9
413 S.D.A.	2	98	128*	2.0	4.3
419 SO BAPT CONV	1	158	207*	3.2	6.9
449 UN METHODIST	2	597	781*	12.0	26.2

NA–Not applicable   NR–Not reported   *Total adherents estimated from known number of communicant, confirmed, full members.   - Represents a percent less than 0.1.   Percentages may not total due to rounding.
[1]See Appendix E   [2]See Appendix F   [3]See Appendix G   Lines in *italic* represent a breakdown of Catholic rites or Friends affiliations. They are included in their respective denominational total.

Table 5. Churches and Church Membership by Metropolitan Status and Denomination: 1990

Denomination		Total Adherents	Percent Adherents in Metro Size of:				Percent Adherents Outside Metro Area	Percent Churches Outside Metro Area
			1,000,000 or More	250,000 to 999,999	100,000 to 249,999	Less Than 100,000		
TOTAL U.S. POPULATION		**248,709,873**	**49.5**	**19.8**	**7.6**	**.7**	**22.4**	**NA**
TOTAL CHURCH ADHERENTS		**137,064,509** *	**49.3**	**19.5**	**7.4**	**.8**	**23.0**	**45.8**
001	ADVENT CHR CH	23,794 *	19.4	17.1	10.4	.3	52.8	56.5
005	AME ZION	1,142,016	48.5	19.2	4.0	.2	28.2	46.4
007	ALBAN ORTH ARC	NR	NR	NR	NR	NR	NR	.0
009	ALBAN ORTH DIO	NR	NR	NR	NR	NR	NR	.0
011	A.W.M.C.	2,526 *	13.8	15.7	10.5	.0	59.9	53.3
019	AMER BAPT USA	1,873,731 *	51.1	16.5	6.5	.5	25.3	36.5
022	EASTERN ORTH	14,610	49.6	27.9	13.1	.0	9.5	18.8
039	AP CHR CH(NAZ)	3,516 *	64.4	15.6	20.0	.0	49.2	45.6
040	AP CHR CH-AMER	19,809	12.6	32.3	5.7	.2	49.2	45.6
045	APOSTOLIC LUTH	7,812	24.9	20.3	1.6	.0	53.2	69.8
049	ARMEN AP CH AM	73,300	81.0	19.0	.0	.0	.0	.0
053	ASSEMB OF GOD	2,161,610	39.1	21.6	11.4	.9	27.0	43.7
055	AS REF PRES CH	37,988	32.1	26.3	3.8	.0	37.8	47.6
057	BAPT GEN CONF	167,874 *	56.9	11.8	10.4	.3	20.6	31.8
059	BAPT MISS ASSN	289,969 *	18.5	12.4	7.2	.7	61.1	68.2
060	BRN RVR MB ASC	1,408 *	.0	.0	.0	.0	100.0	100.0
061	BEACHY AMISH	8,243 *	7.2	16.3	12.7	2.9	60.9	69.2
063	BEREAN FUND CH	5,457	3.8	5.2	22.2	4.6	64.2	80.9
066	BIBLE CH OF CR	8,156 *	91.0	.0	.0	.0	9.0	50.0
071	BRETHREN (ASH)	16,331 *	16.2	13.5	29.7	.8	39.8	46.8
075	BRETHREN IN CR	19,769	18.4	49.7	4.6	.0	27.3	31.9
080	BYELORSSN ORTH	NR	NR	NR	NR	NR	NR	25.0
081	CATHOLIC	53,385,998	63.9	17.5	5.2	.6	12.7	38.6
081A	*ARMENIAN*	*26,520*	*100.0*	*.0*	*.0*	*.0*	*.0*	*.0*
081B	*BYZAN RUTH*	*215,753*	*59.1*	*22.3*	*10.6*	*.0*	*8.0*	*11.8*
081C	*CHALDEAN*	*49,800*	*94.0*	*6.0*	*.0*	*.0*	*.0*	*.0*
081D	*LATIN*	*52,900,126*	*63.9*	*17.5*	*5.2*	*.6*	*12.8*	*39.3*
081E	*MARONITE*	*53,795*	*53.9*	*35.5*	*2.4*	*.0*	*8.2*	*7.3*
081F	*MELKITE-GK*	*27,613*	*78.9*	*19.3*	*.9*	*.0*	*.9*	*2.4*
081G	*ROMANIAN*	*5,152*	*68.8*	*25.0*	*6.2*	*.0*	*.0*	*.0*
081H	*UKRAINIAN*	*107,239*	*70.3*	*19.2*	*1.4*	*.3*	*8.8*	*13.6*
082	CENTRAL BAPT	4,031 *	5.0	71.9	.0	.0	23.1	31.4
083	CHRIST CATH CH	235	13.6	21.3	47.2	3.0	14.9	8.3
089	CHR & MISS AL	271,865	41.0	24.5	11.3	.6	22.7	29.4
093	CHR CH (DISC)	1,037,757	28.1	19.8	11.0	1.6	39.5	51.3
097	CHR CHS&CHS CR	1,213,188 *	28.6	18.3	10.1	1.0	42.0	52.4
105	CHRISTIAN REF	226,163	28.6	35.6	8.1	.3	27.3	31.1
111	CH CR,SCIENTST	NR	NR	NR	NR	NR	NR	28.4
121	CH GOD (ABR)	5,370 *	18.9	26.7	10.9	1.0	42.5	47.7
123	CH GOD (ANDER)	232,876	30.6	23.1	11.4	.6	34.4	43.5
127	CH GOD (CLEVE)	695,074 *	30.2	22.6	8.7	.9	37.6	47.5
133	CH GOD(7TH)DEN	7,511	43.8	24.1	7.5	1.1	23.6	28.1
143	CG IN CR(MENN)	12,535 *	1.1	8.2	7.9	.0	82.8	86.7
145	CH GOD PROPHCY	91,861 *	19.9	21.7	7.9	.7	49.8	49.7
146	CH GOD MTN ASM	6,231 *	31.9	9.8	1.5	3.1	53.8	54.4
151	L-D SAINTS	3,540,820	47.4	17.7	5.5	.5	29.0	34.0
157	CH OF BRETHREN	186,588 *	14.0	22.8	18.7	.3	44.1	51.4
163	CH OF LUTH BR	17,793	36.1	5.0	15.6	3.8	39.5	45.9
164	CH LUTH CONF	8,753	16.2	15.9	9.8	2.8	55.2	52.2
165	CH OF NAZARENE	888,123	31.4	22.4	10.4	1.2	34.7	43.3

NA–Not applicable   NR–Not reported   *Total adherents estimated from known number of communicant, confirmed, full members.   Percentages may not total due to rounding.

[1]See Appendix E   [2]See Appendix F   [3]See Appendix G   Lines in *italic* represent a breakdown of Catholic rites or Friends affiliations. They are included in their respective denominational total.

Table 5. Churches and Church Membership by Metropolitan Status and Denomination: 1990

	Denomination	Total Adherents	Percent Adherents in Metro Size of:				Percent Adherents Outside Metro Area	Percent Churches Outside Metro Area
			1,000,000 or More	250,000 to 999,999	100,000 to 249,999	Less Than 100,000		
167	CHS OF CHRIST	1,681,013	26.2	23.2	11.9	.9	37.8	54.1
171	CH GOD-GEN CON	41,499 *	10.8	41.8	11.9	.1	35.4	44.6
175	CONGR CHR CHS	99,110 *	51.6	17.1	8.3	1.1	21.9	36.8
176	CCC, NOT NAT'L	36,679 *	32.1	18.3	10.1	.0	39.5	65.1
179	CONSRV BAPT	NR	NR	NR	NR	NR	NR	31.4
181	CONSRV CONGR	35,600 *	47.5	15.2	9.8	.2	27.2	38.4
185	CUMBER PRESB	91,040	8.5	30.8	10.0	2.4	48.4	68.8
189	DUCK RIVR BAPT	13,215 *	.3	7.0	.0	1.2	91.4	89.2
191	ENTRPR BPT ASC	6,001 *	16.0	12.9	.0	.0	71.1	64.3
193	EPISCOPAL	2,445,286	53.0	22.7	7.5	.6	16.2	34.2
195	ESTONIAN ELC	4,942 *	98.0	2.0	.0	.0	.0	.0
199	EVAN CONGR CH	33,166	7.7	70.9	1.9	.0	19.5	22.6
203	EVAN FREE CH	181,692	48.1	15.8	8.9	2.2	25.0	37.9
207	E.L.C.A.	5,226,798	37.2	18.8	9.9	1.5	32.5	42.4
209	EVAN LUTH SYN	21,523	18.7	17.1	17.0	.0	47.1	58.7
211	FEL EVG BIB CH	2,089	1.0	51.5	3.2	.0	44.4	56.2
213	EVAN MENN INC	5,122 *	1.8	69.0	1.5	.0	27.8	30.8
215	EVAN METH CH	11,105 *	28.6	18.7	18.3	.0	34.3	38.3
216	EVAN PRESBY CH	45,464	65.8	18.4	8.0	.2	7.6	18.1
217	FIRE BAPTIZED	889 *	6.6	6.7	7.4	.0	79.2	59.2
220	FREE LUTHERAN	27,316	23.1	2.5	4.2	2.3	67.9	73.4
221	FREE METHODIST	82,766	40.1	14.5	10.7	.9	33.7	40.9
223	FREE WILL BAPT	293,448 *	12.5	23.1	9.7	.4	54.4	56.8
226	FRIENDS-USA	130,484 *	40.3	20.4	5.7	1.8	31.7	39.2
226A	CONSERV	1,873 *	13.1	14.6	23.2	1.8	47.3	44.0
226B	EFI	29,701 *	30.7	18.8	9.3	.8	40.4	48.2
226C	FGC	23,573 *	74.0	14.0	5.2	.3	6.5	21.4
226D	FGC & FUM	17,053 *	56.6	20.8	5.2	.3	17.1	32.1
226E	FUM	49,844 *	25.9	26.3	3.1	3.9	40.9	49.6
226F	INDEPENDNT	5,345 *	59.6	15.6	8.6	.3	16.0	38.2
226G	INDEP EVAN	3,095 *	2.2	.0	6.1	.8	90.9	80.0
230	FUND METHODIST	1,037	.0	.0	23.4	.0	76.6	61.5
237	GC MENN BR CHS	22,097 *	9.4	47.3	3.1	3.0	37.3	38.1
241	GEN SIX PR BPT	172 *	.0	85.5	.0	.0	14.5	50.0
246	GREEK ORTHODOX	NR	NR	NR	NR	NR	NR	9.1
249	AP CATH ASSYR	34,646	86.7	11.4	.5	.0	1.4	5.9
257	HUTTERIAN BR	11,037	4.1	2.0	.9	3.2	89.8	92.8
259	IFCA	NR	NR	NR	NR	NR	NR	36.7
263	INT FOURSQ GOS	255,092 *	58.7	15.0	7.6	1.0	17.7	29.7
265	INT PENT C CHR	4,102	25.7	25.8	.6	.0	47.9	60.3
266	INTRSTAT & ASC	18,293 *	4.4	10.5	4.5	.0	80.6	80.6
269	JASPER&PVB ASC	9,209 *	41.3	.0	.0	.0	58.7	55.0
274	LAT EVAN LUTH	14,299	82.2	10.1	6.3	.0	1.4	5.4
283	LUTH—MO SYNOD	2,603,725	42.8	14.2	9.7	1.1	32.1	43.2
284	LUTH CH-AM ASC	14,545	31.9	9.0	13.7	1.4	44.0	50.6
285	MENNONITE CH	154,259	19.2	30.9	11.6	1.2	37.2	42.3
286	E.PA MENNONITE	3,881 *	11.4	56.6	.0	.0	32.1	40.4
287	MENN GEN CONF	40,951	15.4	22.0	7.8	.5	54.3	41.6
289	NEW HOPE B ASC	3,150 *	61.5	.0	.0	.0	38.5	54.5
291	MISSIONARY CH	39,948	31.6	23.4	19.7	.0	25.3	32.0
292	MORAV CH-AK	5,338	.0	.0	2.6	.0	97.4	100.0
293	MORAV CH-NORTH	31,250	28.1	41.6	4.1	.0	26.2	27.6

NA–Not applicable   NR–Not reported   *Total adherents estimated from known number of communicant, confirmed, full members.   Percentages may not total due to rounding.

[1]See Appendix E   [2]See Appendix F   [3]See Appendix G   Lines in *italic* represent a breakdown of Catholic rites or Friends affiliations. They are included in their respective denominational total.

Table 5. Churches and Church Membership by Metropolitan Status and Denomination: 1990

	Denomination	Total Adherents	Percent Adherents in Metro Size of:				Percent Adherents Outside Metro Area	Percent Churches Outside Metro Area
			1,000,000 or More	250,000 to 999,999	100,000 to 249,999	Less Than 100,000		
295	MORAV CH-SOUTH	21,269	8.6	83.7	1.5	.0	6.2	10.9
296	MIDW CONGR FEL	1,880 *	.0	1.6	12.7	.0	85.7	83.3
307	NETH REF CONGR	5,169	19.5	28.2	17.6	.0	34.7	26.7
313	N AM BAPT CONF	54,010 *	45.6	11.5	8.0	5.0	30.0	38.2
320	"OLD" MB ASCS	16,289 *	1.6	39.8	.0	.0	58.7	54.8
323	OLD ORD AMISH	121,750	8.1	15.5	6.2	1.1	69.1	69.3
324	OLD ORD RVR BR	514	.0	46.7	.0	.0	53.3	57.1
325	OLD REG BAPT	19,257 *	7.3	4.5	1.1	.0	87.1	84.4
329	OPEN BIBLE STD	NR	NR	NR	NR	NR	NR	33.5
331	ORTH CH IN AM	NR	NR	NR	NR	NR	NR	30.3
339	PENT CH OF GOD	91,072	21.9	21.0	11.1	1.1	44.8	47.7
349	PENT HOLINESS	157,728 *	12.7	27.7	11.7	.2	47.6	55.4
353	CHR BRETHREN	85,600	57.5	18.2	8.0	.8	15.4	21.3
355	PRESB CH (USA)	3,553,335 *	45.5	20.5	9.0	.9	24.1	41.8
356	PRESB CH AMER	221,392	38.3	35.3	8.2	.5	17.7	31.0
359	PRIM AD CHR CH	427 *	.0	90.9	.0	.0	9.1	22.2
361	PRIM BAPT ASCS	49,294 *	7.1	20.0	7.7	.5	64.8	70.6
363	PRIMITIVE METH	7,937	29.0	48.0	1.4	.0	21.6	30.9
367	PROT CONF (LU)	1,095	6.8	17.8	18.3	29.7	27.4	28.6
371	REF CH IN AM	362,932	41.3	23.4	8.3	.4	26.5	28.1
373	REF CH IN U.S.	3,722	7.4	9.7	7.2	.0	75.7	62.9
375	REF EPISCOPAL	6,559	48.4	48.3	2.6	.0	.7	2.5
386	REGULAR BAPT	4,722 *	7.5	2.4	.0	.0	90.1	87.8
397	ROMANIAN ORTH	NR	NR	NR	NR	NR	NR	7.0
403	SALVATION ARMY	127,577	37.6	21.4	13.7	2.0	25.3	32.1
405	SCHWENKFELDER	3,031 *	100.0	.0	.0	.0	.0	.0
413	S.D.A.	903,062 *	52.5	18.2	8.8	.6	19.8	40.6
415	S-D BAPTIST GC	6,439 *	30.4	20.7	18.1	.6	30.1	28.9
419	SO BAPT CONV	18,940,682 *	21.9	25.1	11.2	1.3	40.4	56.5
423	SYRIAN ANTIOCH	30,000	93.7	6.3	.0	.0	.0	.0
426	2SEED-SPRT BPT	87 *	.0	.0	.0	.0	100.0	100.0
430	TRUEVINE B ASC	561 *	.0	.0	.0	.0	100.0	100.0
431	UKRANIAN AMER	NR	NR	NR	NR	NR	NR	8.7
435	UNITARIAN-UNIV	190,193	58.9	22.3	8.7	.5	9.6	23.2
436	UNITED BAPT	68,187 *	3.2	11.0	1.9	.2	83.7	84.2
438	UN BRETH IN CR	25,749	12.9	19.6	5.9	1.7	59.9	58.8
441	UN CHRISTIAN	770	.0	100.0	.0	.0	.0	.0
443	UN C OF CHRIST	1,993,459 *	40.8	25.8	7.7	.7	25.0	36.9
449	UN METHODIST	11,091,032 *	29.4	22.3	10.3	1.0	36.9	55.9
466	WAYN TR MB ASC	2,467 *	.0	24.0	57.0	.0	19.0	36.4
467	WESLEYAN	259,740	24.3	21.0	12.5	1.7	40.4	47.8
469	WELS	419,928	32.5	14.0	7.4	2.4	43.6	46.8
496	JEWISH EST[1]	5,982,529	89.4	8.6	1.1	.1	.8	5.6
497	BLACK BAPT EST[2]	8,737,667 *	53.0	20.2	7.1	.5	19.2	NA
498	INDEP.CHARIS.[3]	794,254	69.0	20.6	6.7	.5	3.2	6.9
499	INDEP.NON-CHAR[3]	1,207,173	52.7	27.2	11.4	.6	8.1	14.1

NA–Not applicable   NR–Not reported   *Total adherents estimated from known number of communicant, confirmed, full members.   Percentages may not total due to rounding.
[1]See Appendix E   [2]See Appendix F   [3]See Appendix G   Lines in *italic* represent a breakdown of Catholic rites or Friends affiliations. They are included in their respective denominational total.

Appendices

Appendix A

DESCRIPTIVE DEFINITIONS OF CHURCHES AND CHURCH MEMBERSHIP

[The word "communicants" in the table below refers to "communicant, confirmed, full members."]

001 Advent Christian Church
Churches: A group which holds regularly scheduled meetings and is formally recognized by the Advent Christian General Conference and is affiliated with an Advent Christian Conference organization.
Communicants: Full members - attend regularly.

005 African Methodist Episcopal Zion Church
Churches: Individual congregations.
Communicants: Regular members with full membership status.
Adherents: Probationary, baptized children and full members.

011 Allegheny Wesleyan Methodist Connection
Churches: "Any number of believers in Jesus Christ, united as a religious society, for the maintenance of Christian fellowship and worship, constitutes a Christian church" (Allegheny Wesleyan Methodist Discipline, 1986 edition, Paragraph 96).
Communicants: Full members are persons who meet the following conditions: regeneration and seeking for sanctification if not already attained; Christian baptism; adherence to the Discipline of the Allegheny Wesleyan Methodist Connection; covenant to support the church as described in the Discipline; approving vote of a majority of the members of the receiving church who are present and voting (condensed from the Allegheny Wesleyan Methodist Discipline, 1986 edition, Paragraph 56).

019 American Baptist Churches U.S.A.
Churches: Congregations which have applied for membership in the ABC/USA and have been approved by one of our regions, plus mission congregations which have begun worshiping but have not yet chartered.
Communicants: The total membership reported by each congregation (using Baptist definition of members as baptized believers), plus an estimate of membership for non-reporting churches provided by our regional offices.

022 American Carpatho-Russian Orthodox Greek Catholic Diocese of the U.S.A.
Churches: A parish community of Orthodox Christian believers administered by a canonically ordained priest appointed by the Ruling Bishop of the Diocese.
Communicants: He (or she) who is baptized and chrismated into the Church and receives the Holy Eucharist.
Adherents: Total adherents are total communicants. Those who are not communicants are not considered an adherent of the parish church in any way.

040 Apostolic Christian Churches of America
Churches: Organized churches with regular services.
Communicants: Baptized members in good standing in the church.

053 Assemblies of God
Churches: Congregations who have officially affiliated with us.
Communicants: This is a composite number derived from the number of enrolled members (which may or may not be voting members only, depending on local church policies) and persons attending Sunday A.M. worship.
Adherents: The number of people who consider an A/G church to be their church home, whether or not they are enrolled as members.

055 Associate Reformed Presbyterian Church (General Synod)
Churches: Affiliated congregations of the denomination.
Communicants: One who has been baptized, who has made public his profession of faith in Jesus Christ and who has submitted his life to His Lordship and the ministry of the church.
Adherents: Communicant members plus the children of believers bond into covenant relationship.

060 Barren River Missionary Baptist
Churches: The number of churches in each county.
Communicants: The number of members in each county.

061 Beachy Amish Mennonite Churches
Churches: Each separate congregation.
Communicants: Number of attendants furnished by direct contact with each congregation.

063 Berean Fundamental Church Fellowship
Churches: Churches
Communicants: Members
Adherents: Morning worship attendance (except for a few cases in which membership was used because that figure was larger).

071 The Brethren Church, Inc. (Ashland, Ohio)
Churches: Recognized congregations of The Brethren Church including mission congregations and classes (beginning churches).
Communicants: Generally, this is the active, baptized membership of each local church. In some cases, churches also include inactive, baptized members.
Adherents: We do not record this statistic nationally or locally.

081 The Catholic Church
Churches: The number of churches in each county.
Adherents: The number of members in each county.

Appendix A/Definitions

082   Central Baptist
Churches: The number of churches in each county
Communicants: The number of members in each county.

089   The Christian and Missionary Alliance
Churches: Alliance Churches: churches that have adopted the regular constitution for Christian and Missionary Alliance churches. Affiliated Churches: churches outside the C&MA but desiring to cooperate in various degrees of fellowship with the Alliance.
Communicants: Full members are adults who have completed a membership class, confessed Jesus Christ as Savior, and have full sympathy with the principles and objectives of The Christian and Missionary Alliance and cooperate by systematic support of its work.
Adherents: Total inclusive membership: full members and adherents (nonmembers regularly attending and financially contributing to the work of the Alliance).

093   Christian Church (Disciples of Christ)
Churches: Congregations are included if they (1) seek recognition and (2) are endorsed by their region.
Communicants: Members who during the year showed continuing interest in the church. We call this category "Participating." Each congregation decides its own specific definition.
Adherents: All members regardless of residence or participation. Most congregations would not include children under 12-14.

105   Christian Reformed Church in North America
Churches: All worshiping centers, whether emerging or established.
Communicants: Those members who were baptized and made a public profession of faith.
Adherents: Members by infant baptism but not yet having made a public profession of faith, plus members by baptism and profession of faith.

121   Church of God General Conference
Churches: Group that meets weekly for worship services.
Communicants: Active, baptized members who attend at least 13 times per year.

123   Church of God (Anderson, Indiana)
Communicants: Members.
Adherents: The largest figure listed from members, Sunday School enrollment, Sunday School attendance, and A.M. worship attendance.

143   Church of God in Christ, Mennonite
Churches: Organized churches.
Communicants: Baptized members.

146   Church of God of the Mountain Assembly, Inc.
Communicants: Full members.

151   The Church of Jesus Christ of Latter-day Saints
Churches: Each ward (congregation) is counted as a "church."
Adherents: Those counted are members for which a membership record exists and the membership record is assigned to a ward (congregation) in the U.S. at the end of 1990. Records for members in transit, where the new address is not yet known, were not included in county data.

157   Church of the Brethren
Churches: Congregations of members.
Communicants: We count only baptized and confirmed members.
Adherents: We have no records of these.

163   Church of the Lutheran Brethren of America
Churches: Any organized congregation that is a member of our synod plus a few independent congregations who are served by Lutheran Brethren pastors and support our ministries.
Communicants: Members includes those of voting age and above.
Adherents: Parishioners includes baptized children under voting age (18) and also those who though not members consider this congregation their church home.

164   Church of the Lutheran Confession
Churches: Congregations.
Communicants: Communicants.
Adherents: Total souls. Includes children and those baptized, but not confirmed.

165   Church of the Nazarene
Churches: Local groups organized according to the Nazarene bylaws.
Communicants: Full members.
Adherents: Total Sunday School enrollment plus outreach.

167   Churches of Christ
Churches: Free-standing congregations.
Communicants: Baptized.
Adherents: Baptized plus other regular attenders.

171   Churches of God, General Conference
Churches: Churches reported include all congregations across the denomination which are formally organized and have received members into the fellowship.
Communicants: The Churches of God, General Conference recognizes adult membership. Individuals are received into church membership through a formal process.

175   Congregational Christian Churches, National Association of
Churches: "A body of Christians complete under God in spiritual authority and ecclesiastical power, regularly meeting and worshiping in one place, united by a mutually owned covenant, in fellowship with sister Congregational Christian Churches and recognized by the laws of the place of location as a duly constituted church" (Articles of Association, III,1,a).
Communicants: Total active members.

176   Additional Congregational Christian Churches (not part of any national CCC body)
Churches: A "local continuing body of believers which is a congregation of the universal Church of Christ." Report of the Commission on the Study of the Constitutional Problem, General Council of the Congregational Christian Churches, 1956.
Communicants: Total membership (believers).

181   Conservative Congregational Christian Conference
Churches: Member congregations.

Communicants: Figures reported by the congregations–is unspecified as to communicants, confirmed or full members.

185 Cumberland Presbyterian Church
Churches: Organized congregations and fellowships.
Communicants: Communicant members.
Adherents: Communicant members plus children.

189 Duck River (and Kindred) Associations of Baptists
Churches: The number of churches in each county.
Communicants: The number of members in each county.

203 Evangelical Free Church of America
Churches: Congregations who have been formally incorporated as part of the denomination (does not include "Church Plants").
Communicants: Those who have gone through the church's procedure and been formally accepted as "members."
Adherents: "Attenders"—people who attend may or may not be members—adults and children included.

209 Evangelical Lutheran Synod
Churches: Any location where a group assembles and there is worship.
Communicants: Those who have been confirmed into full membership.
Adherents: This includes also those who are of pre-confirmation age.

211 Fellowship of Evangelical Bible Churches
Communicants: Resident members.
Adherents: Morning worship.

216 Evangelical Presbyterian Church
Communicants: Active members.
Adherents: Active members plus baptized members (usually children).

217 Fire Baptized Holiness Church
Churches: Groups meeting a minimum of once a week and registered as subordinate organizations with IRS.
Communicants: Members who are eligible to vote at annual local church business meeting.

220 The Association of Free Lutheran Congregations
Communicants: Confirmed members.
Adherents: Baptized members.

221 Free Methodist Church of North America
Churches: Fully organized churches and churches in the process of becoming fully organized.
Communicants: Full members (adults 16 and over) in good standing with membership status in an organized church or fellowship.
Adherents: Average Sunday morning worship attendance. Although this figure may underestimate total adherents, it represents the number of adherents the best of any of our figures. This is a different method than was used in the 1980 study. The formula used in 1980 produced too large a figure.

226 Friends
Churches: Monthly meetings (local congregations), preparative meetings and worship groups.

Adherents: Members plus non-member attenders, where reported. Some meetings do not report attender figures and are estimated by the CMS staff.

237 General Conference of Mennonite Brethren Churches
Churches: Churches.
Communicants: Full members.

249 Holy Apostolic Catholic Assyrian Church of the East
Churches: Church buildings only; rented space is not counted, but congregations are established.
Communicants: Head of household and/or working, supporting family member.
Adherents: Total adherents are only baptized communicants and confirmed.

263 International Church of the Foursquare Gospel
Churches: Chartered Church. A Foursquare Gospel Church which has been granted a charter by the Board of Directors pursuant to these Bylaws.
Communicants: 13.5.01 Requirements. In order to be entitled to membership in a Foursquare Gospel Church, a person shall satisfy the following requirements:
A. Show evidence of a born-again experience and a Christian life;
B. Have been baptized in water by immersion;
C. Be nine years of age or over;
D. Subscribe and adhere to the "Declaration of Faith," compiled by Aimee Semple McPherson; and
E. Agree to comply with the Articles and these Bylaws.

265 International Pentecostal Church of Christ
Churches: Full member churches, cooperating with the denomination.
Communicants: Full members active on the roll with voting rights in their respective churches.
Adherents: The largest number from each church from the categories of Sunday School enrollment or attendance.

274 Latvian Evangelical Lutheran Church in America
Churches: Churches.
Communicants: Confirmed.
Adherents: Confirmed and baptized.

283 Lutheran Church—Missouri Synod
Churches: Established (organized formally) congregations. Does not include informal preaching stations.
Communicants: Those who have been confirmed.
Adherents: Baptized members.

284 The American Association of Lutheran Churches
Communicants: Comfirmed.
Adherents: Baptized.

285 Mennonite Church
Churches: Local organized body of believers.
Communicants: Baptized members.
Adherents: Baptized members and non-baptized children, youth and adults who take part in congregational life.

287 General Conference Mennonite Church
Churches: Congregations or fellowships which meet regularly and are either official members or associate members of the General Conference Mennonite Church.

Appendix A/Definitions

Communicants: Those who have their official membership in General Conference congregations.
Adherents: Official members plus children not yet members.

291 The Missionary Church
Churches: Organized, affiliate and unorganized churches.
Communicants: Baptized, full members.
Adherents: Average weekly worship attendance. (The estimated number of people who are a part of our churches to some degree of regularity is about 60,000-61,000 different people).

292 Moravian Church in America, Alaska Province
Churches: Organized congregations.
Communicants: Communicant members.
Adherents: Includes baptized children and others associated with the congregation.

293 Moravian Church in America, Northern Province
Churches: Organized congregations.
Communicants: Communicant membership.
Adherents: Includes baptized children and others associated with the congregation.

295 Moravian Church in America, Southern Province
Churches: Churches.
Communicants: Communing adults—includes all those received into membership by adult baptism, confirmation, letter of transfer, reaffirmation of faith, and readmission.
Adherents: Includes communing adults (see above); communing children—all baptized as children who have been admitted to Holy Communion by the Board of Elders or Church Board of the congregation; non-communicants—all baptized children under age 21 of communicant members except those who are communing children; and children—include all unbaptized children of members and children under the care of the church who have not reached the age of 16.

296 Midwest Congregational Christian Fellowship
Churches: A "local continuing body of believers which is a congregation of the universal Church of Christ." Report of the Commission on the Study of the Constitutional Problem, General Council of Congregational Christian Churches, 1956.
Communicants: Total members.

307 Netherlands Reformed Congregations
Churches: Organized congregations.
Communicants: Professing members.
Adherents: Professing and baptized members.

324 Old Order River Brethren
Churches: Church districts.
Communicants: Full members.
Adherents: Full members plus dependent children living in the homes of members.

329 Open Bible Standard Churches, Inc.
Churches: Chartered or fellowshipping.

339 Pentecostal Church of God
Churches: A body of believers set in order and/or chartered with PC/G.
Communicants: Voting members of local church.

Adherents: Includes members as well as others who call the PC/G their home church.

349 Pentecostal Holiness Church, International
Churches: Only those churches that have been "set in order" are included. Mission churches are not included in the stats.
Communicants: Those who have met criteria set by the local church and have requested their name be added to the membership roll.

355 Presbyterian Church (USA)
Churches: The congregation consists of those persons in a particular place who, representing the universal church, gather together for the service of God, professing their faith in Jesus Christ and subject to a particular form of church government.
Communicants: Persons who have undergone baptism and who have made a public confession of faith.

356 Presbyterian Church in America
Communicants: Adult members.
Adherents: Communicant (adults) and non-communicant (children). Ministers are not included as they are members of Presbytery.

361 Primitive Baptists
Churches: The number of churches in each county.
Communicants: The number of members in each county.

363 Primitive Methodist Church in the U.S.A.
Communicants: Adult members. Not listed would be adult attenders.
Adherents: Adult, junior, inactive members.

367 Prostestant Conference (Lutheran)
Communicants: Members.
Adherents: Communicants and baptized.

371 Reformed Church in America
Communicants: Members who have received Christian baptism and have been received by the Board of Elders through public confession of faith, reaffirmation of faith, or presentation of a satisfactory certificate of transfer of membership from an evangelical church, and who continue confessing their faith by word and deed (this figure will be used as the basis for assessment).
Adherents: Total baptized members plus all who participate in the life, work, and worship of the church, but are not members.

373 Reformed Church in the United States
Churches: "In its earthly manifestation (the Church of God) is a covenant society consisting of professing believers and their children organized into particular congregations..." "The membership of a Reformed Church consists of believers and their children." The Reformed Church in the U.S. p. 5.
Communicants: Communicant members.
Adherents: Baptized members (includes unconfirmed).

375 Reformed Episcopal Church
Churches: Full parishes in union with a synod or jurisdiction of the Reformed Episcopal Church.
Communicants: Those accepted into regular membership by

profession of faith or letter of transfer.

Adherents: Regular attenders not accepted into full membership, or inactive members.

386 Regular Baptists

Churches: The number of churches in each county.
Communicants: The number of members in each county.

403 Salvation Army, The

Adherents: Those who call the Salvation Army their church home.

419 Southern Baptist Convention

Churches: Churches cooperating with the SBC.
Communicants: Membership totals reported by churches.

413 Seventh Day Adventist Church

Churches: Our denomination has companies that are not recognized as fully organized churches. In these instances the report will show no church in the column "Number of Churches," but will show members in the column "Communicant, Confirmed, Full Members."
Communicants: Baptized members only.
Adherents: We have no tabulation of total adherents.

430 Truevine Baptists

Churches: The number of churches in each county.
Communicants: The number of members in each county.

435 Unitarian Universalist Association

Churches: Societies belonging to the Unitarian Universalist Association; includes both fellowships and churches.
Communicants: Members.
Adherents: Members and children.

436 United Baptists

Churches: The number of churches in each county.
Communicants: The number of members in each county.

438 United Brethren in Christ

Churches: Churches.
Communicants: Full members.
Adherents: Sunday morning worship attendants.

443 United Church of Christ

Churches: "A local Church is composed of persons who, believing in God as Heavenly Father, and accepting Jesus Christ as Lord and Saviour, and depending on the guidance of the Holy Spirit, are organized for Christian worship, for the furtherance of Christian Fellowship, and for the ongoing work of Christian witness." (Constitution Par 8)
Communicants: "In accordance with the custom and usage of a local Church, persons become members by (a) baptism and either confirmation or profession of faith in Jesus Christ as Lord and Saviour; (b) reaffirmation or reprofession of faith; or (c) letter of transfer or certification from other Christian churches. All persons who are or shall become members of a local Church of the United Church of Christ are thereby members of the United Church of Christ." (Constitution Par. 9 & 10)

449 The United Methodist Church

Churches: "The local church is a connectional society of persons who have professed their faith in Christ, have been baptized, have assumed the vows of membership in The United Methodist Church, and are associated in fellowship as a local United Methodist church in order that they may hear the Word of God, receive the Sacraments, and carry forward the work which Christ has committed to his Church. Such a society of believers, being within The United Methodist Church and subject to its Discipline, is also an inherent part of the Church Universal, which is composed of all who accept Jesus Christ as Lord and Savior, and which in the Apostles' Creed we declare to be the Holy Catholic Church." Book of Discipline 1980, par 203.
Communicants: "The membership of a local United Methodist church shall include all baptized persons who have come into membership by confession of faith or transfer and whose names have not been removed from the membership rolls by reason of death, transfer, withdrawal, or removal for cause." Book of Discipline 1980, par.209

466 Wayne Trail Missionary Baptists

Churches: The number of churches in each county.
Communicants: The number of members in each county.

469 Wisconsin Evangelical Lutheran Synod

Churches: Congregations.
Communicants: communicants.
Adherents: Baptized.

Appendix B

DENOMINATIONAL COMMENTS ON THE CMS FORMULA FOR ESTIMATING TOTAL ADHERENTS

001 Advent Christian Church

This is as reasonable as anything we can think of.

011 Allegheny Wesleyan Methodist Connection

Children are not included in our full membership figures; therefore, I presume an estimation is necessary.

019 American Baptist Churches U.S.A.

Your procedure has been followed in previous editions and thus provides the best continuity factor in regard to our data.

059 Baptist Missionary Association of America

This is not reported and therefore we are unable to give an answer.

060 Barren River Missionary Baptist

Your formula would likely be low for this group, as members probably join later in life after attending for many years. I cannot, however, think of a better procedure.

061 Beachy Amish Mennonite Churches

We are satisfied with your formula.

071 The Brethren Church, Inc. (Ashland, Ohio)

This would probably be reasonably accurate, no suggestions.

Appendix B/Adherents Formula

082 Central Baptist
Your formula is likely low for this group, as members probably join later in life after attending for many years. I cannot, however, think of a better procedure.

097 Christian Churches/Churches of Christ
Please use the formula you have devised for all the other denominations.

127 Church of God (Cleveland, TN)
The procedure described to estimate adherents is acceptable.

143 Church of God in Christ, Mennonite
Baptized membership statistics are as accurate as possible; number of adherents or attenders not known.

171 Churches of God, General Conference
It is difficult for us to estimate total adherents. We would, however, accept your formula.

189 Duck River (and Kindred) Associations of Baptists
Likely low for this group, as members probably join later in life after attending for many years. I cannot, however, think of a better procedure.

191 Enterprise Baptists Association
Likely low for this group, as members probably join later in life after attending for many years. I cannot, however, think of a better procedure.

217 Fire Baptized Holiness Church
Your estimation formula will be close.

223 National Association of Free Will Baptist, Inc.
The procedure described in the instruction sheet in acceptable.

237 General Conference of Mennonite Brethren Churches
Yes—acceptable.

263 International Church of the Foursquare Gospel
We have no way of being able to judge the accuracy; however, the method is acceptable to us.

266 Interstate & Foreign Landmark Missionary Baptists Association
Likely low for this group, as members probably join later in life after attending for many years. I cannot, however, think of a better procedure.

269 Jasper and Pleasant Valley Baptists Associations
Likely low for this group, as members probably join later in life after attending for many years. I cannot, however, think of a better procedure.

289 New Hope Baptist Association
Likely low for this group, as members probably join later in life after attending for many years. I cannot, however, think of a better procedure.

320 "Old" Missionary Baptists Associations
Likely low for this group, as members probably join later in life after attending for many years. I cannot, however, think of a better procedure.

325 Old Regular Baptists
Likely low for this group, as members probably join later in life after attending for many years. I cannot, however, think of a better procedure.

349 Pentecostal Holiness Church, International
We do not have a way to calculate total adherents. Since your formula is used consistently for all denominations that have no way to estimate adherents, it seems appropriate to use it for us as well.

355 Presbyterian Church (USA)
OK

361 Primitive Baptists
Your formula is likely low for this group, as members probably join later in life after attending for many years. I cannot, however, think of a better procedure.

386 Regular Baptists
Your formula is likely low for this group, as members probably join later in life after attending for many years. I cannot, however, think of a better procedure.

413 Seventh Day Adventist Church
Procedure is acceptable.

419 Southern Baptist Convention
Acceptable.

430 Truevine Baptists
Your formula is likely low for this group, as members probably join later in life after attending for many years. I cannot, however, think of a better procedure.

436 United Baptists
Your formula is likely low for this group, as members probably join later in life after attending for many years. I cannot, however, think of a better procedure.

443 United Church of Christ
83.47% of all United Church congregations submitted reports this year. Most other figures represent relatively recent reports within the last few years. A few minor corrections have been made from the numbers shown in our *1991 Yearbook*, including the insertion of five members each for three churches with blank membership reports. Sixty-five congregations in Puerto Rico and 2 in Canada are also part of the Church, though not reported here.

449 The United Methodist Church
1) Appears to assume that children under 13 will be "adherents" in the same proportion as adults—a questionable assumption.

2) Affords no way of estimating adult "adherents."

466 Wayne Trail Missionary Baptists
Your formula is likely low for this group, as members probably join later in life after attending for many years. I cannot, however, think of a better procedure.

Appendix C

SELF-ASSESSMENT OF THE ACCURACY OF REPORTING PROCEDURES

[An asterisk indicates that the group also supplied forms that were used in gathering the data. Those groups that supplied forms but did not comment on the accuracy of their reporting procedures are listed at the end.]

001   Advent Christian Church

We have annual reports that are supposed to be sent in by each church, but some fail to report. We have done some estimating.

005*   African Methodist Episcopal Zion Church

Report is dependent upon yearly Statistical Report Blanks submitted to each Annual Conference by pastors. Impossible to determine degree of accuracy.

011*   Allegheny Wesleyan Methodist Connection

We feel that the pastor's monthly reports, as well as a yearly statistical report, result in a fair and accurate evalutation of our churches' data.

019   American Baptist Churches U.S.A.

Over 70% of the churches have reported their data. Regional executives have been polled for updating membership of nonreporting churches.

We believe these figures to be reasonably accurate, though likely overstated in some cases due to two factors: 1) some congregations maintain very inflated figures for total membership so that a significant proportion would not be residents of the county in which that church building is located; and 2) some racial/ethnic minority churches claim exceptionally large memberships compared with their stated worship attendance.

022*   American Carpatho-Russian Orthodox Greek Catholic Diocese of the U.S.A.

The figures are accurate according to statistics provided the Diocese through December 31, 1988, as forwarded to the Diocesan Chancery early in 1989. There are no more recent figures. A census will not be taken again until the spring of 1992.

040   Apostolic Christian Churches of America

Surveys of all churches are carried out every 2-3 years and responsible pastors provide data. Adherents are determined by estimates of regular attenders plus members.

053*   Assemblies of God

If a current (i.e. 1990) report is not available from a church, we use its most recent report. In the few cases where no data is available, we assign the county average size of membership and adherents to those churches.

059*   Baptist Missionary Association of America

The statistics reported are obtained either from questionnaires directly from the member churches or from local associational yearbooks. For those counties that have a zero in the membership listing, this is because these churches did not report their membership.

060   Barren River Missionary Baptist

Accuracy probably complete.

071*   The Brethren Church, Inc. (Ashland, Ohio)

We believe the reports are fairly accurate. We follow up by phoning churches who do not report in writing. We have a verbal or written report from every congregation for 1990.

075   Brethren in Christ Church

These statistics are gathered from pastors and reported annually.

081   The Catholic Church

Overall count includes Eastern Rite dioceses in the United States. The overall count is probably an undercount.

082   Central Baptist

Several counties warrant special mention:

Perry, Kentucky: The church there did not report a membership total; its average Sunday School attendance is used to estimate its membership.

Cherokee, South Carolina: The church there reported neither membership nor Sunday School attendance, hence no reliable estimate of membership for it is available.

Hamblen, Tennessee: One church reported neither membership nor Sunday School attendance, hence no reliable estimate of membership is available.

Lee, Virginia: One church did not report membership; its Sunday School attendance figure is used to estimate membership.

Scott, Virginia: one church reported neither membership nor Sunday School estimate, hence no reliable estimate of membership for it is available. Two other churches also failed to report membership, but their Sunday School figures were used.

089*   The Christian and Missionary Alliance

Each church is responsible for completing an annual report form and sending it to its district office. The district office is responsible for checking the report for accuracy, making any necessary corrections, and then submitting the report to the National Office. At the National Office, final editing is done for each church report form before the statistics are entered into the data base. Because of bi-lingual, multi-ethnic churches in our denomiantion there is not 100% accurate reporting, usually due to not understanding all of the questions asked on the form. Inaccurate reporting can also occur when the pastors do not read the instruction booklet accompanying the report form, and answer the report questions according to their own interpretation.

093*   Christian Church (Disciples of Christ)

Each congregation develops its own definition of membership. In addition, nearly 700 congregations send no report. Membership figures for these congregations are estimated—based on the last report received.

105*   Christian Reformed Church in North America

We believe the reporting to be accurate within 5%.

121   Church of God General Conference

Each June, local church secretaries review a computer print-out which we provide to them. They note additions, subtractions, and revisions.

123 Church of God (Anderson, Indiana)

Fifty-three churches did not report membership or adherent figures.

133 The Church of God (Seventh Day)

Membership and children figures are from census cards and reported by state. These figures were equally distributed among the number of churches within the state.

143 Church of God in Christ, Mennonite

Accurate as possible as of 12/31/1990.

145 Church of God of Prophecy

Membership figures were not available for each church, only for states. State totals were divided among the churches in that state as evenly as possible.

151 The Church of Jesus Christ of Latter-day Saints

Counts are based on automated membership records. The number of members should be very accurate. However, our method of determining county could create some discrepancies. Wards (congregations) are defined geographically. For this data, all members are allocated to the county in which the congregation leader (Bishop) lives. If a ward covers parts of multiple counties, the members will be allocated to the county where the bishop lives. Bishops are lay members and new ones are called every 3 to 6 years. In cases where the number of members shows a significant decrease for a county between 1980 and 1990, the ward (congregation) is probably still there. But, as explained earlier, the members have probably been allocated to another county.

163 Church of the Lutheran Brethren of America

We believe this is a reasonably accurate report, less than ten percent of the churches in our fellowship failed to respond so we estimated their numbers on the basis of parochial reports which are current.

164 Church of the Lutheran Confession

All of our congregations respond each year to our call for statistics in various categories. Unanswered requests are followed up until a report is received. Accuracy in all categories is verified each year. This includes comparison with the previous year's reports.

165* Church of the Nazarene

Our procedures have been well established and our polity assures 100 percent of local churches participating.

167 Churches of Christ

Year long survey by mail, phone and informants. Fairly accurate assessment.

171* Churches of God, General Conference

We trust that our reporting procedure is accurate. Each local conference has a statistical secretary who reviews statistical data. That data is then compiled in our General Conference Administrative Office.

175 Congregational Christian Churches, National Association of

Reports are for full member Churches in the U.S.A. Of the 399 Churches, 333 (83.5%) are current reports. 48 congregations (12.0%) have relatively recent reports repeated in the Yearbook. For 17 congregations (4.3%) with membership blank in the Yearbook, we have inserted the last reported membership, a total of 2,903 members. These are older reports. One congregation (0.2%) has never submitted a membership report and has been left blank.

The Association also includes 2 full member churches in Canada, 2 Honorary Churches (both in the Unitarian Universalist Association, one in the District of Columbia, one in Massachusetts), 21 Affiliated Churches (12 in Georgia, 9 in North Carolina), and 12 Associate Churches (all outside the U.S.A.), none of which are reported here.

176 Additional Congregational Christian Churches (not part of any national CCC body)

These churches are affiliated with the United Church of Christ Associations and Conferences but are not part of any national Congregational Christian body. Therefore, statistics are collected by the United Church of Christ.

Only 66 congregations (28.4%) are current reports for this year. Another 55 congregations (23.7%) are relatively recent reports (within the last decade) that have been repeated. However, 111 congregations (47.8%) are old statistics. This latter group is concentrated in certain areas including North Carolina (24 churches), New York (13), Maine (9) and all the congregations in Indiana, Pennsylvania, Louisiana, Colorado, Oregon, and Texas (29).

185* Cumberland Presbyterian Church

The figures are fairly accurate, except for churches not reporting for a period of two years. For the first missed reporting year, prior year figures for membership are used. For the second missed reporting year the stats are left out. If a church is in litigation (wishing to leave denomination) old membership figures are used if available, otherwise a note is typed in that column stating "property in litigation" or appropriate notes.

191 Enterprise Baptists Association

Lawrence County, Ohio bears a special mention. One of the two churchs there did not report a membership total. Otherwise data are probably highly accurate. Statistics are from the 1990 minutes of the Enterprise Association of Regular Baptists.

189 Duck River (and Kindred) Associations of Baptists

Statistics are taken from the following minutes of associations comprising the grouping: Duck River-1990, East Union-1989, Mount Pleasant #1-1987, Mount Pleasant #2-1989, Mount Zion-1988, New Liberty-1990, Union-1990.

One Church in Sequatchie County, Tennessee did not report a membership total. Otherwise, this represents a complete count of Duck River and Kindred Baptists.

199* Evangelical Congregational Church

Each year we receive from the pastor of each church a statistical form with asked for information. Thus the information is pretty accurate.

203 Evangelical Free Church of America

These statistics are based on the response from churches—not all churches respond to our request for information.

209 Evangelical Lutheran Synod

Each congregation reports at the end of each calendar year on a form sent out from the secretary's office.

216*   Evangelical Presbyterian Church

Very accurate.

217   Fire Baptized Holiness Church

Accuracy is fairly good.

221*   Free Methodist Church of North America

All figures are fairly accurate. Each church is required to report annually. Specific instructions are given for reporting active members, but a small minority of the churches do include inactive members in membership figures.

223   National Association of Free Will Baptist, Inc.

The procedure used to collect data was Form C of the Church Membership Study. Copies of these forms were sent to the clerks in each state. The statistics were then compiled.

226   Friends

Used yearly meeting minutes. Comparability of Friends 1980 and 1990 data in Idaho, Oregon, and Washington is obscured by a difference in definition of reported figures by Evangelical Friends (over 90% of total). In 1980 Evangelical Friends reported total members, including children. In 1990 "active" (adult) members were reported. In 1980, "adherents" were total members increased by a formula. In 1990 they are total members of all ages. For comparative purposes, total members for Evangelical Friends are given below. These include children from birth.

State	1980	1990	Change	%
Idaho	1,863	2,180	+ 317	+ 17%
Oregon	4,718	3,833	- 885	- 19%
Washington	1,859	1,655	- 204	- 11%
Totals	*8,440*	*7,668*	*- 772*	*- 9%*

These figures are based on Yearly Meeting Minutes for the two years.

237*   General Conference of Mennonite Brethren Churches

We receive a reporting form from our churches each year. This year we received a very high percentage of them (approx. 95%) back from the churches, reporting current statistics. Therefore we believe our report to be highly accurate.

249   Holy Apostolic Catholic Assyrian Church of the East

From books of Registry in the church; from membership printouts; and from firsthand knowledge of family members.

263   International Church of the Foursquare Gospel

The districts reporting to us on the method used to determine the counties of their churches and membership took computer printouts from their year-end reports and used maps and an atlas to divide these into counties. The total churches and membership appear to be very accurate, as they line up very closely with the year-end figures which we previously received.

265*   International Pentecostal Church of Christ

The vast majority of our churches have reported their own figures. The remainder of the figures are projected on the basis of previous reports.

266   Interstate & Foreign Landmark Missionary Baptists Association

Probably complete. Statistics are from the 1990 minutes of the Interstate & Foreign Landmark Missionary Baptist Association.

269   Jasper and Pleasant Valley Baptists Associations

Probably complete. Statistics are from the 1988 minutes of the Jasper Baptist Association, and the 1989 Pleasant Valley Association.

274   Latvian Evangelical Lutheran Church in America

Numbers are quite accurate.

283   Lutheran Church—Missouri Synod

Those counties which have stations but list no members are recently formed and had not reported statistics as of date needed.

285   Mennonite Church

Totals are based on reports from congregations.

287*   General Conference Mennonite Church

We believe that these figures are reasonably accurate. Even where January 1, 1990 figures are used, our experience is that membership figures for General Conference congregations do not fluctuate sharply from one year to the next.

289   New Hope Baptist Association

Complete.

291   The Missionary Church

With the exception of 3-4 churches all figures are very reliable. Of the exceptions, estimates were conservative and fairly reliable. Such estimates were made in worship due to records being destroyed by fire, lost, etc. Membership records were carried over from previous years.

293*   Moravian Church in America, Northern Province

Statistics are accurate as of December 31, 1990. Where there is no report, 1989 statistics were used (only two congregations).

295*   Moravian Church in America, Southern Province

We sometimes pick up on errors in reports from our congregations when doing our year-end report. Inaccuracies may be due to lack of understanding of how the report form relates to a congregation's method of record keeping, the failure to keep records up-to-date, or simply mistakes in addition and subtraction. In such cases, we contact the pastor and work with them to get the records as nearly accurate as possible.

296   Midwest Congregational Christian Fellowship

100% current reports.

307   Netherlands Reformed Congregations

Annual updates; very accurate.

320   "Old" Missionary Baptists Associations

Associations in this grouping include (1) Enon, 1990, (2) Siloam, 1989, and (3) Wiseman, 1990. Accuracy is complete for the associations presented in this grouping. These three associations form the core of "Old" Missionary Baptists. There are other associations, however, which correspond with at least one of these three, which also might be included with "Old" Missionary Baptists, but whose cooperation was not gained in time for inclusion with this work.

323   Old Order Amish Church

There is no accurate way to determine Old Order Amish *membership*. Adherents were estimated at 150 per congregation

Appendix C/Accuracy of Reporting

for settlements established before 1987. Settlements established in 1987 and 1988 were estimated to have 100 adherents per congregation. Settlements established in 1989 and 1990 were estimated to have 50 adherents per congregation.

324 Old Order River Brethren

I think the statistics should be quite accurate.

325 Old Regular Baptists

Statistics are taken from the following minutes of associations: Bethel, 1988; Cumberland, 1990; Friendship, 1990; Old Friendship, 1987; Indian Bottom, 1989; Old Indian Bottom, 1990; Little Dove, 1990; Mountain (Feltner faction), 1990; Mountain (Gross faction), 1990; Original Mountain Liberty, 1990; Mud River, 1990; New Salem, 1989; Northern New Salem, 1989; Philadelphia, 1990; Sardis, 1990; Thornton Union, 1990; Union, 1989.

These statistics may not represent all Old Regular Baptists churches and associations, though they do represent all associations known to the compiler.

349* Pentecostal Holiness Church, International

Annual forms listing each church are sent to all conference offices. Conference superintendents are responsible for collecting data from all local churches in the conference. Completed forms are returned and keyed into database. All totals/summaries are built from local church data.

355* Presbyterian Church (USA)

We are correct on membership figures, we believe. We are accurate on number of churches.

361 Primitive Baptists

Statistics for this group come from the following minutes: Eastern District Association of Primitive Baptists-1990, Abbott's Creek-1989, Black Creek-1987, Buttahatchie-1989, Contentnea-1989, Eastern Kehukee-1989, Hopewell-1989, Kehukee-1989, Laurel Springs-1990, Little River-1990, Lower Country Line-1990, Lower Mayo-1987, Mates Creek-1987, New River-1990, Pigg River District-1989, Salem-1987, Smith River-1990, South Quachita-1989, Staunton River-1990, White Oak-1990, Yellow River-1990, Bethel-1987, Brushy Creek-1987, Duffau-1987, Echeconnee-1987, Elk River-1987, Fellowship-1987, Lower Canoochee-1987, Primitive Western-1987, Providence-1987, Sequatchie Valley-1987, Towaliga-1987, Upper Canoochee-1987, Bethel Church (TN)-1987, Bethlehem Church (GA)-1987, Concord Church (IL)-1987, Grace Church (TN)-1987, Hardwick Church (GA)-1987, Haven Church (FL)-1987, Northside Church (GA)-1987, Palma Ceia (FL)-1987, Southside (FL)-1987, Waycross Church (FL)-1987, Woodcrest Church (MO)-1987, Wills Creek Association of United Baptists of the Primitive Faith and Order-1990, Alabaha-1989, Amite (Myers faction)-1989, Amite (Poe faction)-1989, Antioch-1990, Original Bear Creek-1989, Bethany-1989, Original Bethany-1987, Beulah-1990, Big Sandy-1990, Bithynia-1989, Bosque River—Little Flock-1989, Burning Spring-1989, Center Creek-1989, Choctawhatchee-1990, Cumberland-1990, Ebenezer-1989, Echeconnee-1900, Euharlee-1989, First (of OK)-1990, Fishers River-1989, Fishing River (Key faction)-1990, Fishing River (Surbaugh faction)-1990, Flint River of Alabama-1989, Flint River of Georgia-1989, Original Old Line Flint River-1989, Fork Deer-1989, Friendship-1990, Good Hope-1989, Harmony (AL and GA)-1989, Harmony (AR and MO)-1989, Old

Harmony-1989, Highland-1989, Hillabee-1989, Hopewell-1989, Indian Creek District-1989, Ketocton-1990, Lebanon-1990, Little Hope (AL)-1989, Little Hope (TX)-1990, Little River of Georgia-1989, Original Little River-1989, Little Vine-1989, Little Wabash-1990, Little Yadkin River-1989, Little Zion-1990, Lott's Creek-1989, Louisiana-1990, Lower Wetumpka-1989, Marietta-1989, Original Mates Creek-1989, Original Mayo-1990, Mississippi River-1989, Mount Enon-1989, Original Mount Enon (Dixie faction)-1989, Original Mount Enon (Williams faction)-1989, Mount Salem-1990, Mount Zion (AL)-1990, Mount Zion (WV)-1990, Mountain District-1989, Mountain Springs-1989, Mud Creek-1990, Muskingum-1990, New Hope-1989, New Liberty-1990, New River District-1990, North Florida-1990, Original Mayo-1990, Obion-1989, Ocholcknee-1989, Ocmulgee-1989, Original Oconee-1990, Old Line of the West Coast-1990, Owl Creek Harmony-1990, Ozark-1989, Pacific-1989, Patsaliga-1989, Pilgrim Rest-1989, Pilot Grove-1988, Pitney Grove-1989, Pleasant Valley-1986, Original Powell's Valley-1989, Predestinarian-1989, Primitive-1989, Primitive of Texas-1989, Primitive Ebenezer-1990, Prince William-1989, Pulaski-1990, Rich Mountain-1989, Rock Springs-1989, Saint Clair's Bottom District-1989, Salem (AR and OK)-1990, Salem (IL)-1990, Salem (OK)-1989, San Pedro-1989, Sand Mountain-1989, Sandlick District-1989, Sandusky-1990, Scioto-1989, Second Creek-1989, Senter District-1989, Original Sequatchie Valley and Blue Ridge-1990, Reorganized Silver Creek-1989, Skillet Fork-1990, South Arkansas-1990, Suwannee River-1989, Tallahatchie-1989, Tennessee and Nolachucky-1990, Original Tombigbee-1989, Original Towaliga-1989, Union-1989, Upatoi-1990, Original Upper Canoochee-1987, Washington District (Colley moderator)-1990, Washington District (Fields moderator)-1989, West Providence-1989, West Texas-1989, Wetumpka-1990, White River-1990, Whitewater-1989, Yellow Creek-1989.

In addition, there was one church in each of the following counties which did not provide statistics through their associations: Imperial, CA; Baker, FL; Duval, FL; Lee, FL; Wilkinson, GA; Jackson, MI; Yalobusha, MS; Cabarrus, NC; and Montgomery, VA.

In Anson County, NC, two churches did not provide statistics through their associations.

367 Prostestant Conference (Lutheran)

At best, our reporting procedures are educated guesses. We keep no forms for gathering exact data.

375 Reformed Episcopal Church

Individual churches report to Committee on State of the Church. Yearly membership roll revision is required.

373 Reformed Church in the United States

100% current report.

386 Regular Baptists

All these associations refer to themselves as "Regular Baptist" in their title. While several other associations also call themselves Regular, many of these in fact are Primitive, and some of my Regular associations have also called themselves " Union" Baptists, Howard Dorgan has advised me there are no substantial differences between these associations and "mainstream" Regular Baptist beliefs and practices. These statistics may not represent all Regular Baptist churches and associations, though they do represent all associations known to the compiler. Statistics are taken

from the following minutes: Little River-1990, Mountain Union-1990, Original Mountain Union-1989, & Primitive-1989.

403 Salvation Army, The

This is an ecclesiastical count. The 1980 study included numbers from non-church groups which have not been included this time.

413 Seventh Day Adventist Church

A. Membership records in local churches are almost universally compared on a regular basis with statistical records in the regional headquarters office.

B. The figures we are reporting here correspond exactly with the national statistical reports for December 31, 1990.

430 Truevine Baptists

Complete.

436 United Baptists

These statistics may not represent all United Baptist churches and associations, though they do represent all associations legitimately in the tradition known to the compiler. A few other comments should also be made:

1. See comment on Cumberland River Association and Pulaski County under dual affiliation.

2. Two churches of the Cumberland River Association in Pulaski County did not submit membership totals. Their Sunday School attendance figures are used as a proxy for membership, though this is probably a low estimate—nearly every other church in that association reported far greater membership than Sunday School attendance.

3. One church in Clinton County, Kentucky did not report a membership total.

4. Three churches in McCreary County, Kentucky did not report memberships.

5. Two churches in Fentress County, Tennessee did not report memberships.

Statistics are taken from the following minutes: Ancient Christian-1990, Bethel-1989, Bethlehem-1989, Centerpoint-1990, Cumberland River-1990, Green River-1990, Iron Hill-1990, Laurel River-1986, Little Friendship-1990, Mount Zion-1990, Old Mount Zion-1989, New Bethel-1989, New Hope-1990, Paint Union-1990, Old Paint Union-1990, Second North Concord-1986, South Concord-1986, South Fork-1988, Stockton Valley-1986, Tri-State-1990, Tri-State Zion-1990, Union-1989, West Union-1987, Zion-1989.

443 United Church of Christ

83.47% of all United Church congregations submitted reports this year. Most other figures represent relatively recent reports within the last few years. A few minor corrections have been made from the numbers shown in our 1991 Yearbook including the insertion of five members each for three churches with blank membership reports. Sixty-five congregations in Puerto Rico and 2 in Canada are also part of the Church, though not reported here.

466 Wayne Trail Missionary Baptists

Association's church in Seneca County, Ohio did not report membership. Accuracy otherwise probably complete.

467* Wesleyan Church

We believe reports are verifiable.

469* Wisconsin Evangelical Lutheran Synod

98.4% response from congregations.

Groups who supplied forms used to collect the data, but which did not comment on the accuracy of their reporting procedures: 045 Apostolic Lutheran Church of America; 055 Associate Reformed Presbyterian Church (General Synod); 127 Church of God (Cleveland, TN); 339 Pentecostal Church of God; 359 Primitive Advent Christian Church; 363 Primitive Methodist Church in the U.S.A.; 438 United Brethren in Christ.

Appendix D

COMMENTS ON DUAL AFFILIATION OF CONGREGATIONS.

019 American Baptist Churches U.S.A.

Some congregations affiliate with as many as 4 other denominations. The most extensive relationships are with the following denominations (in descending order by number of congregations having that affiliation):

National Baptist Convention USA, Inc (489)
Progressive National Baptist Convention (212)
Southern Baptist Convention (112, of which 71 are in DC and MD)
United Church of Christ (57)
National Baptist Convention of America (49)
United Methodist Church (21)
Presbyterian Church, USA (21)
Christian Church (Disciples of Christ) (20)
North American Baptist Conference (11)
Church of the Brethren (8)

An additional 16 congregations are affiliated among 9 other denominations, none of which has more than 4 in number.

071 The Brethren Church, Inc. (Ashland, Ohio)

One church with Church of the Brethren. We are reporting only the 4 persons who align with our church.

075 Brethren in Christ Church

One Mennonite/Brethren in Christ.

093 Christian Church (Disciples of Christ)

Fifty-one congregations relate to one (or more) other denominations. The most common additional affiliations are: United Church of Christ, Presbyterian, Methodist, Baptist.

171 Churches of God, General Conference

One of our congregations is the merger of two congregations in the same community. One, a Churches of God, General Conference congregation; the other, a Church of God, Anderson congregation.

175 Congregational Christian Churches, National Association of

Yes. Dual affiliation: 10 with United Church of Christ; 6 with Conservative Congregational Christian Conference; 2 with Christian Church (Disciples of Christ); 1 with American Baptist Churches; and 1 with Unitarian Universalist Association; Total: 20 congregations. In addition 6

congregations are Federated to congregations in the American Baptist Churches, Christian Church (Disciples of Christ), Unitarian Universalist Association, and Society of Friends.

176   Additional Congregational Christian Churches (not part of any national CCC body)

Yes. These churches are affiliated with the United Church of Christ Associations and Conferences but are not part of any national Congregational Christian body.

The Constitution of the United Church of Christ provides that local Conferences and Associations of that Church may remain in fellowship with Congregational Christian Churches not part of the United Church of Christ. Their statistics are to be kept separately. These are the Churches reported here. They are generally reported as Schedule I Churches (Churches "which have not voted" on whether to join the United Church of Christ, "or which have voted to abstain from voting" [177 congregations]), and Schedule II Churches (Churches "which have voted not to be part of the United Church of Christ" [127 congregations]). Total: 304 congregations.

Of these congregations, 65 belong to the Congregational Christian Churches, National Association; 5 to the Conservative Congregational Christian Conference; and 2 to both of these groups. Since those are primary relationships, the statistics for these 72 congregations have been removed from this report.

Of the 232 congregations reported, 7 have dual affiliation: 3 to the American Baptist Churches, 2 to the Evangelical Covenant Church, and 2 to the Unitarian Universalist Association. In addition 11 congregations are Federated to congregations of the United Methodist Church, the American Baptist Churches, and the Unitarian Universalist Association.

181   Conservative Congregational Christian Conference

Yes. A couple of our churches have dual membership with the Congregational Christian Churches in National Association. Ashford, CT (Westford); Canterbury, CT (Westminster); Lihue, HI (First); Boston, MA (Park St.); Memphis, MI (First); Plymouth, PA (Pilgrim). Total 6. Also the following appear in the United Church of Christ: East Rochester, MA (Cong.); Middletown, NY (First); Total 2.

185   Cumberland Presbyterian Church

Yes. Union churches—Cumberland Presbyterian/Presbyterian Church (USA). Our membership totals reflect 1/2 of full totals. We have a total of 8 churches who share in Union work.

203   Evangelical Free Church of America

Yes. Only one of our churches has dual affiliation. (It is also affiliated with the Covenant Church.)

237   General Conference of Mennonite Brethren Churches

Yes. Only two churches are a combined Mennonite and Mennonite Brethren church. (Manhattan Mennonite Fellowship, KS; United Mennonite, Premont TX.)

249   Holy Apostolic Catholic Assyrian Church of the East

Yes. Where the Church of the East exists, no one goes to other Christian sects. However, in states to the contrary they will attend Roman churches, Greek or Russian Orthodox; or Episcopal.

274   Latvian Evangelical Lutheran Church in America

Yes. Two churches; 1 in Yonkers, NY and 1 in Minneapolis, MN - both ELCA.

285   Mennonite Church

Yes. Eighty-six U.S. Mennonite Church congregations hold affiliations with another church body. Seventy-six of these relate to another Mennonite body; ten to the Church of the Brethren, This report includes only the Mennonite Church segment in a dual or multi-affiliated congregation.

287   General Conference Mennonite Church

Yes. About 70 of these congregations are also members of the Mennonite Church. In counting the full members and total adherents, we used only half of the actual figures from those congregations. Mennonite church is using half in their reporting.

293   Moravian Church in America, Northern Province

Yes. Only in terms of sharing pastoral leadership.

355   Presbyterian Church (USA)

Yes. About 100 churches out of the total are so-called Union churches. These are relationships with various denominations. Most frequently, however, the other denominations will be United Methodist or United Church of Christ.

371   Reformed Church in America

Yes. Four Presbyterian Church USA, one Baptist, five United Methodist, one Advent Lutheran, one Quaker, and five United Church of Christ.

419   Southern Baptist Convention

Yes. Many of our churches in the District of Columbia state convention are affiliated with the American Baptists and National (Black) Baptists Conventions. These churches are located both in DC and Maryland.

436   United Baptists

None known. Churches of Cumberland River Association (mostly in Pulaski County, KY), however, may have become affiliated with the American Baptist Association (though if they have, they were apparently not included in the ABA's 1980 count)

443   United Church of Christ

Yes. We are currently studying this phenomena in our churches. We would estimate that there are between 165 and 190 congregations affiliated with us and one or more other denominations. The denominations most commonly represented in these groupings are United Methodist Church; Christian Church (Disciples of Christ); American Baptist Churches; Presbyterian Church, USA. Others are also found with the Congregational Christian Churches (National Association); Church of the Brethren; Church of God in Christ; National Baptist Convention USA; Unitarian Universalist Association; Council of Community Churches; Reformed Church in America; Evangelical Covenant Church; Conservative Congregational Christian Conferences; Pan-African Orthodox Church; Schwenkfelder Church. There are also between 215 and 240 Federated congregations.

449   The United Methodist Church

Yes. "Federated churches", but they are instructed to report only their United Methodist membership to this office.

Appendix E

JEWISH ESTIMATE METHODOLOGY

Unlike the data for Christian denominations, which are estimates of institutional adherence, these data are estimates of client populations made by some 200 Jewish Federations, which are fund raising agencies in local communities. These statistics for places reporting 100 or more Jewish residents, as published in the *American Jewish Yearbook*, have been allocated to counties by William M. Newman and Peter L. Halvorson. When place names are reported as general population areas ("Greater Hartford," "Metropolitan Detroit," etc.) Jewish population has been allocated to counties in a manner consistent with the distribution of population in metropolitan area counties as reported by the United States Census. This procedure no doubt has given some preference to suburban rather than urban counties in such areas, and also results in some counties reporting less than 100 Jewish residents.

The Church Membership Study staff located synagogues by county using *The 1987-88 Jewish Almanac—Yellow Pages* provided by Barry Kosmin. These have been included along with the adherent estimates. The differing reporting procedures result in some counties with adherents but no synagogues (areas were the Jewish estimate has been allocated according to the general population distribution), and some counties with synagogues but no adherents (mainly rural areas where the Jewish population is less than 100).

Appendix F

BLACK BAPTISTS ESTIMATE METHODOLOGY

The Estimation of Membership in Black Baptist Churches in the United States by County—1990

I. PURPOSE

To develop formulas to estimate the number of church members in Black Baptist churches for each county in the United States.

II. THE INITIAL VISION

After looking in each county at the proportion of population who were Blacks, it was clear that we lacked sufficient resources to conduct a full survey of all U.S. counties. The distribution of Blacks revealed large concentrations in metropolitan central cities and coastal plains of the South.

III. SELECTION OF A SAMPLE

Efforts turned to selecting representative counties based on region, metropolitan and nonmetropolitan classification, and size of Black population.

Enlistment efforts were made to secure organizers/supervisors for selected cities: San Diego, Chicago, Philadelphia, Atlanta and Nashville. Due to time constraints and lack of willing workers, Portland, OR; Memphis, TN; Nashville, TN; Knoxville, TN; Chattanooga, TN; Tri-Cities, TN; Atlanta, GA; and Savannah,GA, were studied.

The distribution of Blacks by counties revealed that the major

concentrations outside metropolitan areas were in the South. Primary study efforts were made within Tennessee and Georgia.

IV. DATA COLLECTION METHODS

Under the leadership of Albert W. Wardin of Belmont University, Nashville, collection of data for known Black Baptist groups in Tennessee was completed. The Georgia project, headed by Lorna D. Clark, graduate student at Columbia Theological Seminary, Decatur, Georgia benefited from Dr. Wardin's experience.

The political environment among Baptist bodies differs between the two states. Contacts with statewide and regional Black Baptist leaders went very well in Tennessee, but rather poorly in several regions of Georgia. This situation greatly impacted the progress of the survey. Atlanta judicatory officials offered no access to information of names of churches affiliated with their respective bodies. Therefore, Ms. Clark and her workers started with the Yellow Pages and used informants and field trips to discover congregations not listed in the telephone directory.

Work on the Atlanta Metro began with DeKalb County, an eastern suburb. The first three months of telephone calls and on-site visits were very slow. Data on only 45 churches was secured, at an average cost of $40 per church. The decision was made to develop a stratified sample of the 159 counties of Georgia based on a 3 x 2 grid: metropolitan, nonmetro urban, and rural, divided between those with 25 percent or more Blacks, and those with fewer than 25 percent Blacks. Thirty-three counties composed the Georgia sample.

Dr. Wardin helped expand the data collection by securing Black Baptist membership data for Portland, Oregon, and two nearby counties in the summer of 1991. The three Oregon counties encompassed the known constituency of Black Baptists in that state.

V. THE RESULTS FROM THE DATA GATHERING

The two-year project netted data on 1,489 Black Baptist churches. These churches account for approximately 403,000 members. The population in the 131 counties covered in the data gathering phase numbered 2,248,500 according to 1990 Census figures. The sample membership is distributed in the six cells denoting location and percentage of black population for counties as shown below.

Location/population	Percentage of county population Black	
	25% or more	Less than 25%
Metropolitan county	232,137	90,055
Nonmetro county with 25,000 total population	21,070	27,749
Nonmetro county with fewer than 25,000 population	25,076	4,866

VI. DEVELOPMENT OF ESTIMATES

Compatible data was available for 32 counties in Georgia, 46 in Tennessee, and 3 in Oregon. Three different steps in estimating the number of Black Baptists geographically evolved, progressing from simple to more complicated/inclusive.

Step 1. The 68 study counties in Georgia and Tennessee were grouped according to the density of the Black population in 1990 (at least 25% Black, or less than 25% Black) and the

county type (within a Metropolitan Statistical Area [MSA], within a non-MSA county of 25,000 or more population, and within a non-MSA county of less than 25,000 population). This classification resulted in an analysis grid with six cells. Cell sums were calculated for the Black population from the 1990 census and the number of Black Baptist members from the field testing.

The ratio of Black Baptists to Black population was then calculated for each cell using the appropriate cell sums. Since these 68 counties were all in the South, a regional adjustment was developed using the EXCEL Religious Identification Survey. The EXCEL Study[1] identified proportions of Blacks that were Baptists as follows—.364 for the Northeast, .497 for the Midwest, .569 for the South, and .401 for the West. EXCEL ratios were also available for individual states with the largest Black populations.

Each county in the nation was identified by its analysis cell. The number of Black Baptists for each county was computed by adjusting the proportion calculated above for the South to the state EXCEL ratio and multiplying by the number of Blacks from the 1990 census. For example, the EXCEL ratio for New York was .309. The number of Black Baptists for a New York county in a given cell was calculated as .309/.569 times the cell proportion estimated for the South times the 1990 Black population for the county. Appropriate regional EXCEL ratios were substituted for states without individual EXCEL scores.

Step 2. The second estimation method used the given EXCEL ratio of .610 for the state of Georgia. The regional EXCEL ratio of .569 for the South was used for Tennessee, since no state ratio was provided. The incidence of Black Baptists in Georgia exceeded the portion for the South as a whole. The total number of Black Baptists in each cell of the grid was thus calculated as .569/.610 times the number of Black Baptists in the Georgia counties plus the number of Black Baptists in the Tennessee counties. The resulting adjusted number of Black Baptists in each cell was then divided by the total Black population, yielding an estimated proportion of Blacks who are Baptists for each cell.

These new cell estimates were for the South region. The number of Black Baptists for each county in the nation was computed as described in Step 1, using the new cell estimates and appropriate EXCEL ratios to adjust for regional differences.

Step 3. A third estimation procedure was developed in order to incorporate the field information from the three counties in Oregon. Rather than calculating an estimate for the South and then adjusting to the other regions, the first action of this step yields an estimate for the nation. The national EXCEL ratio of .500 was utilized in making these adjustments.

The three state totals (Georgia, Tennessee, Oregon) for Black Baptists in each cell were adjusted for regional differences. The total number of Black Baptists in each cell of the grid was calculated as .500/.610 times the Georgia cell total plus .500/.569 times the Tennessee cell total plus .500/.401 times the Oregon cell total. The resulting adjusted number of Black Baptists in each cell was then divided by the total Black population in all the cell counties, yielding an estimated

proportion of Blacks who are Baptist. The resulting regional estimates for each cell in the grid are given in Table A.

TABLE A

Estimated Percentage of Black Population that are Members of Black Baptist Churches in Counties by Region, Location and Percentage of Population Black; 1990

Location	Percentage of Population Black			
	25% or higher	Less than 25%	25% or higher	Less than 25%
	NORTHEAST		*MIDWEST*	
Within a Metropolitan Statistical Area (MSA)	.139	.194	.190	.264
Within a non-MSA county of 25.000 or more population	.157	.157	.214	.214
Within a non-MSA county of less than 25,000 population	.219	.154	.299	.210
	SOUTH		*WEST*	
Within a Metropolitan Statistical Area (MSA)	.218	.303	.154	.213
Within a non-MSA county of 25,000 or more population	.245	.245	.173	.173
Within a non-MSA county of less than 25,000 population	.342	.240	.241	.169

The number of Black Baptists for each county in the nation was computed by adjusting the national proportion calculated above to the state EXCEL ratio and multiplying by the number of Blacks from the 1990 census. For example, the EXCEL ratio for New York was .309. The number of Black Baptists for a New York county in a given cell was calculated as .309/.500 times the national cell proportion estimate times the 1990 Black population for the county. As in the previous steps, appropriate regional EXCEL ratios were used for states without individual ratios.

VII. ESTIMATES USED

Authors of the current report document, Churches and Church Membership in the United States, 1990, made the decision to prepare and include estimates (see VI above) only for counties having a black population of 500 or more in 1990. This avoidance of estimates with a likelihood of higher estimate error leads to a possible omission of approxomately 32,948 Black Baptists from the published estimates.

VIII. BLACK POPULATION DISTRIBUTION

Sorting of the 3,141 counties in the United States reveals that

---

[1] The study was sponsored by the Center for Jewish Studies, CUNY Graduate Center, New York. Data was collected by telephone from 113,000 households in the U.S. during the period April 1989 - April 1990. The survey agency was ICR Survey Research Group, Media PA. Self-identification of persons as Baptists occurred in response to the question, "What is your religion?"

only 9 Metro counties outside the South have 25 percent or more Blacks. Further, there are no urban counties outside the South with 25 percent or more Blacks, and only 3 rural counties. Table B shows the distribution of counties by location and Black population density for each region.

TABLE B

DISTRIBUTION OF U.S. COUNTIES BY URBANIZATION AND PROPORTION BLACK; 1990

Region	Metro Co 25% or More Blk.	Metro Co less than 25% Blk.	Urban Co. 25% or More Blk.	Urban Co less than 25% Blk.	Rural Co 25% or More Blk.	Rural Co less than 25% Blk.	Total
Northeast	4	114	0	83	0	16	217
Midwest	5	192	0	233	3	662	1055
South	65	286	108	244	220	502	1425
West	0	80	0	102	0	262	444
Total	74	672	108	662	223	1402	3141

Prepared 12/91 Orrin D. Morris, Richie Stanley
Home Mission Board, Southern Baptist Convention

Revised 1/92

Appendix G

INDEPENDENT CHURCHES METHODOLOGY

Scope: Congregations included in this census have a minimum adherent base of 300 people or more. While information for churches below 300 is available, the ability to have a comprehensive representation of churches that size becomes increasingly difficult as size decreases. Churches below 300 adherents tend to have a high percentage of bi-vocational pastors, part-time or no secretary, and more disconnected telephones, making it increasingly difficult to get data.

Definition: All churches called were asked initially if they considered themselves as an independent church or a denominational church. Once identified as one or the other, each church was then asked to classify itself as either charismatic or non-charismatic. "Charismatic" was defined to include the practice of "speaking in tongues."

Included in the questions asked of each church (i.e. Sunday School attendance, worship attendance, home group attendance, and total membership) was the final question relating to "adherents."

"Adherent" was defined for the church representative (usually the pastor, his secretary, or staff person one of them designated) through the question: "How many people, both members and non-members, attend with some regularity and definitely consider your church as their PRIMARY church home?"

Satellite missions, chapels, and churches owned and operated in the same metro area by the sponsoring church were included. Extension ministries such as nursing homes, prisons, radio and television audience, and general mailing list totals were excluded.

"Adherent" is the official statistic used for this census. Total membership or worship attendance was used when the congregation was unable to provide an "adherent" figure. When very large churches declined or were unable to share the requested information—approximately a dozen churches—the latest available data (i.e. membership or average worship attendance) in the census director's records were substituted when more than 1,000 people were involved in their known total.

The Census Team: Approximately 50 students (three served as project supervisors) scheduled the use of 10 telephone watts lines from January 2, 1990, through April 1, 1990. Calls were made from 7:30 a.m. until 7:00 p.m.

City Size for the Study: The target city size for the census was a community population of 20,000 and larger. In some instances churches were located in communities with a population base smaller than 20,000 people.

Sources of Data: Telephones were the primary tools used to gather the data. Earlier plans to use direct mail were changed to insure maximum response. A few churches requested that a letter be sent as a means of making formal request for the information. In several instances information was exchanged by FAX.

Designation of Independent Churches: As indicated below, the total sample of churches (excluding Churches of Christ and Independent Christian Churches) is classified into one of two categories for the census: (1) Independent, Non-Charismatic, or (2) Independent, Charismatic.

Statistical Summary
(Churches with 300 or More Adherents)

Category	No. of Churches	Adherents
Independent Non-Charismatic	1,363	1,207,173
Independent Charismatic	829	794,254
Total	*2,192*	*2,001,427*

Appendix H

INSTRUMENTS FOR GATHERING THE DATA

Initial Invitation:

Dear Friend,

We are writing to you at the suggestion of Constant Jacquet, editor of the *Yearbook of American Churches*. This is a cordial invitation to your denomination to participate in the 1990 update of the Church Membership Study. This study is a unique gathering of information which has the potential of meeting various needs of the institutional Church, the religious community at large, and religious and academic researchers. As a compilation of statistics from many religious bodies, it is an important analytical tool. From its data we learn about our own and other communions in geographical, historical and comparative perspective. It is an important resource for documenting our challenge to evangelize the unchurched. Finally, it is the statistical foundation upon which much research is constructed, beneficial to religious and academic communities.

Denominations are asked to furnish 1990 county data on number of churches and members, by JUNE, 1991. Details are on the enclosed green sheet.

We will, of course, furnish complimentary copies of the study's printed publications to all participating communions.

A flyer about the study is enclosed. If you need more information, please let me know. In the meantime, PLEASE INDICATE YOUR WILLINGNESS TO PARTICIPATE IN THE STUDY BY RETURNING THE BLUE MEMORANDUM in the self-addressed envelope. We hope to hear from you soon.

Sincerely,

Dale E. Jones
Vice Chairman &
Liaison for Data Collection

Memorandum of Participation—Form F

1. DENOMINATION:

2. CONTACT PERSON FOR DATA:
   Name:
   Address:
   Title:
   Phone:

3. EXPECTED DATE OF TRANSMITTAL:

The Operations Committee is asking that statistics be sent to us by June, 1991. We hope to receive data for your statistical year that ends during 1990; earlier data may be reported only if that is all that is available by June, 1991.

Please indicate the approximate date on which we might expect to receive the statistics in our office:_____.
_____We do not believe we can participate at this time.

4. FORM OF TRANSMITTAL. Please check one:

_____We plan to furnish the data by magnetic media.
_____We plan to furnish the data by means of our own printout, etc.

_____Please send us Form C, containing a list of counties by state.

5. DATA AVAILABLE. Please check one:

_____We are able to furnish county data (or church list) on (1) number of churches (or city/state location of church), (2) number of communicant-confirmed-full members, and (3) number of total adherents.
_____We are able to furnish county data (or church list) on (1) and (2) only.

SIGNED:_____Date:_____
Please mail to: Church Membership Study, Research Center, 6401 The Paseo, Kansas City, Missouri 64131.

Instructions for Reporting Denominational Data—Form A

DATA REQUESTED
For each state and county of the United States, we are requesting three items of information:
   1. The number of CHURCHES or SYNAGOGUES: local parishes or congregations;
   2. The number of COMMUNICANT, CONFIRMED, FULL MEMBERS: regular members with full membership status;
   3. (If available), the number of TOTAL ADHERENTS: all members, including full members, their children, and the estimated number of other regular participants who are not considered as communicant, confirmed, or full members, for example, the "baptized," "those not confirmed," "those not eligible for communion," and the like.
Procedure: Data may be reported on the State-County List (Form C) furnished by us upon request, or, if more convenient, on your own computer printout or list of comparable format. Data may be sent on magnetic media, also. **Please complete the Transmittal Sheet** (Form B), which will be useful for determining the comparability of statistics reported by the various religious bodies.

DATE OF STATISTICS
We are asking that statistics be reported to us by the month of June, 1991. We hope to receive data for your statistical year that ends during 1990; report earlier data only if that is all that is available by June, 1991. Enter the date of your statistics on the Transmittal Sheet, Item 2.

SPECIAL PROBLEMS:
DATA ON TOTAL ADHERENTS NOT AVAILABLE
It is our hope that denominations reporting full members will also be able to furnish data on total adherents. If they are unable to do so, the total adherents will be estimated by the staff of the Church Membership Study as follows: the total county population will be divided by the total county population less children 13 years of age and under, and the resulting figure will be multiplied by the communicant, confirmed, or full members. In the published report, an asterisk will indicate that total adherents were estimated through use of this procedure.

If you will not be furnishing data on total adherents, please complete Item 5 on the Transmittal Sheet.

DUAL AFFILIATION OF LOCAL CHURCHES
Some local churches maintain affiliation with two denominations. If this is true of local churches in your denomination, please complete Item 6 on the Transmittal Sheet.

ALASKA
The data of the U.S. Census for Alaska has been classified by "census divisions." Since Alaska has no counties, the census divisions serve as county equivalents for statistical reporting purposes. A list of census divisions follows: (See *Appendix I*).

VIRGINIA
In Virginia there are 41 "Independent Cities" which are legally separate from the counties of that state. Most denominations probably still record churches by location within the counties from which the cities have separated. For this reason we request that the data of your denomination be so organized as to record the data of the following Independent Cities with the counties indicated: (See *Appendix J*).

Transmittal Sheet for Denominational Data—Form B

1. DENOMINATION
   Name:
   Code: Abbreviation:

   Denominational Contact Person: (Name, title, address, phone)

2. DATE OF STATISTICS REPORTED:

3. UNITED STATES TOTALS:
   Churches or Synagogues:
   Communicant, Confirmed or Full Members
   Total Adherents (if available):

4. DEFINITIONS ACTUALLY EMPLOYED IN REPORTING DATA:
   Churches or Synagogues:
   Communicant, Confirmed or Full Members:
   Total Adherents:

5. IF TOTAL ADHERENTS ARE NOT REPORTED:
   Please comment on the procedure described in the Instruction Sheet whereby we propose to estimate the total adherents. Is the procedure acceptable as reasonably accurate for your group or denomination? Would you offer any suggestions?

6. DUAL AFFILIATION OF LOCAL CHURCHES:
   Do any local congregations of your denomination maintain affiliation with another denomination as well?_____ If "yes," please indicate the general extent of this practice and the denomination(s) involved.

7. COMMENTS ON ACCURACY OF YOUR GROUPS REPORTING PROCEDURES (Attach additional sheets if needed.):

NOTE: It would be greatly appreciated if you could attach to this Transmittal Sheet sample copies of forms used for gathering local data.

SIGNED:
DATE:
PLEASE SEND TO: Church Membership Study
                Research Center
                6401 The Paseo
                Kansas City, MO 64131

State-County Form for Reporting Statistics—Form C

Church Membership Study, 1990   Page 1
Group   **Alabama**

County Code and Name	Number of Churches or Synagogues (1)	Communicant, Confirmed, Full Members (2)	Total Adherents (3)
01 001 Autauga	_____	_____	_____
01 003 Baldwin	_____	_____	_____
01 005 Barbour	_____	_____	_____
01 007 Bibb	_____	_____	_____
01 009 Blount	_____	_____	_____
01 011 Bullock	_____	_____	_____
01 013 Butler	_____	_____	_____
01 015 Calhoun	_____	_____	_____
01 017 Chambers	_____	_____	_____
01 019 Cherokee	_____	_____	_____
01 021 Chilton	_____	_____	_____
01 023 Choctaw	_____	_____	_____
01 025 Clarke	_____	_____	_____
01 027 Clay	_____	_____	_____
01 029 Cleburne	_____	_____	_____
01 031 Coffee	_____	_____	_____
01 033 Colbert	_____	_____	_____
01 035 Conecuh	_____	_____	_____
01 037 Coosa	_____	_____	_____
01 039 Covington	_____	_____	_____
01 041 Crenshaw	_____	_____	_____
01 043 Cullman	_____	_____	_____
01 045 Dale	_____	_____	_____
01 047 Dallas	_____	_____	_____
01 049 DeKalb	_____	_____	_____

Appendix I

ALASKA COUNTY-EQUIVALENTS

1990	1980
Aleutians East	from part of Aleutian Islands
Aleutians West	from part of Aleutian Islands
Anchorage	no change
Bethel	no change
Bristol Bay	no change
Dillingham	part of Dillingham
Fairbanks North Star	no change
Haines	no change
Juneau	no change
Kenai Peninsula	no change
Ketchikan Gateway	no change
Kodiak Island	no change
Lake & Peninsula	from part of Dillingham
Matanuska-Susitna	no change
Nome	no change
North Slope	part of North Slope
Northwest Arctic	from Kobuk and part of North Slope
Prince of Wales-Outer Ketchikan	no change
Sitka	no change
Skagway-Yakutat-Angoon	no change
Southeast Fairbanks	no change
Valdez-Cordova	no change
Wade Hampton	no change
Wrangell-Petersburg	no change
Yukon-Koyukuk.	no change

86095

Appendix J

VIRGINIA INDEPENDENT CITY/COUNTY COMBINATIONS

Independent City	County	Abbreviation
Alexandria city *with*	Arlington	Arlington-Alexandria
Bedford city *with*	Bedford	Bedford-Bedford City
Bristol city *with*	Washington	Washington-Bristol
Buena Vista city *with*	Rockbridge	Rockbridge-Bn Vs-Lex
Charlottesville city *with*	Albemarle	Albemarle-Charlottes
Clifton Forge city *with*	Alleghany	Alleghany-Clf Fr-Cov
Colonial Heights city *with*	Dinwiddie	Dinwiddie-Col Ht-Pet
Covington city *with*	Alleghany	Alleghany-Clf Fr-Cov
Danville city *with*	Pittsylvania	Pittsylvania-Danvill
Emporia city *with*	Greensville	Greensville-Emporia
Fairfax city *with*	Fairfax	Fairfax-Fairfx-Fl Ch
Falls Church city *with*	Fairfax	Fairfax-Fairfx-Fl Ch
Franklin city *with*	Southampton	Southampton-Franklin
Fredericksburg city *with*	Spotsylvania	Spotsylvania-Frederi
Galax city *with*	Carroll	Carroll-Galax City
Harrisonburg city *with*	Rockingham	Rockingham-Harrison
Hopewell city *with*	Prince George	Prince George-Hopewe
Lexington city *with*	Rockbridge	Rockbridge-Bn Vs-Lex
Lynchburg city *with*	Campbell	Campbell-Lynchburg
Manassas city *with*	Prince William	Prince William-Manassas
Manassas Park city *with*	Prince William	Prince William-Manassas
Martinsville city *with*	Henry	Henry-Martinsville
Norton city *with*	Wise	Wise-Norton City
Petersburg city *with*	Dinwiddie	Dinwiddie-Col Ht-Pet
Poquoson city *with*	York	York-Poquoson City
Radford city *with*	Montgomery	Montgomery-Radford
Richmond city *with*	Henrico	Henrico-Richmond City
Roanoke city *with*	Roanoke	Roanoke-Roanoke-Salm
Salem city *with*	Roanoke	Roanoke-Roanoke-Salm
South Boston city *with*	Halifax	Halifax-South Boston
Staunton city *with*	Augusta	Augusta-Staun-Waynes
Waynesboro city *with*	Augusta	Augusta-Staun-Waynes
Williamsburg city *with*	James City	James City-Williams
Winchester city *with*	Frederick	Frederick-Winchester

The only exceptions to the above pattern occur in the case of Independent Cities which have annexed their parent counties. These are usually treated as separate "city-county" combinations and will be treated as such in the membership study.

Independent City	Name
Hampton city	Hampton City
Newport News city	Newport News City
Norfolk city	Norfolk-Chesap-Ports
Chesapeake city	
Portsmouth city	
Suffolk city	Suffolk City
Virginia Beach city	Virginia Beach City